20/1

Get **more** out of libraries

Please return or renew this item by the last date shown.

You can renew online at www.hants.gov.uk/library

Or by phoning 0300 555 1387

Hampshire
County Council

2/16

Footprint Handbook

Ind

DAVID ST
& VICTOR

C016176621

This is
India

Colour maps at back of book

India strikes its visitor with a sensory, intellectual, spiritual and philosophical assault that's unmatched by any other place on earth, all set in an awesome physical environment teeming with a resilient, indefatigable 1.2 billion-strong population. Every expectation – be it of beauty, mysticism, poverty, bigotry or bureaucracy – will be outdone by what hits you on the ground. When VS Naipaul wrote "there is little subtlety to India", it was itself an understatement: whether measured in passion for cricket, film, faith or politics, India revels in the extreme, and rejects all apathy, minimalism and restraint.

The subcontinent's sheer diversity is staggering: India ranges from tropical beach paradises to primary forests of teak and jackfruit trees where elephants roam and macaques leap; desert tundras broken by fairytale forts ruled by haughty princes with Rajput moustaches; chilly foothills clad in tea plantations and dotted with British clubhouses opening onto vistas of the world's highest mountain peaks, through outsized metropoles whose infrastructure buckles under the weight of the unceasing movement of their vast human populations, right down to atavistic village life of tapping toddy, ploughing seed and tilling soil.

And despite the fact that India is embracing modernity with open arms, it has shunned secularism. Most of Indian society remains fiercely religious, a religiosity which remains a source of both social harmony and sporadic tension. The north holds hushed Tibetan Buddhist monasteries of frugal understatement, their air thick with incense, lit with ghee lamps, hewn into jagged Himalaya cliff faces, where prayer wheels chime and flags flutter in the high-altitude granite desert. The south answers with riotous candypop Hindu confections, crammed with gaudy gods, flanked by painted festival elephants and bugle-playing Brahmins. In between lie Muslim mausoleums, mosques of vast proportions, sprawling Sikh temple complexes plated with gold and the tombs of Sufi mystics peopled by pilgrims of every denomination.

Victoria McCulloch

David Stott

Vanessa Betts

Best of
India

❶ Delhi

India's capital city is dynamic, chaotic and a perfect introduction to the country. From the labyrinthine streets of Chandni Chowk to the serene Lotus Temple and the colonnades of Connaught Place – it is a city of magical variety. See page 54.

❷ Taj Mahal

The romance of the world's most famous building still astonishes in its power and beauty. Come early in the morning while the marble is cool. There are some good vantage points around Agra, especially the arches of Agra's Red Fort. See page 114.

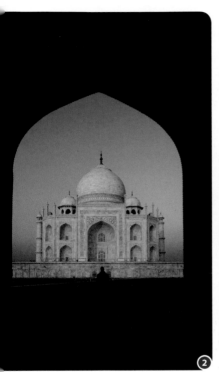

❸ Varanasi

The holiest of cities defies easy description. This is India in the raw: utterly fascinating, deeply spiritual and often uncomfortable. Take a sunset boat trip along the Ganga to see the evening *aarti* ceremonies on the riverside. See page 135.

❹ Rishikesh

Gateway to the Himalaya and setting for the International Yoga Festival, Rishikesh has always been a home to gurus, sadhus and teachers; now it also draws people for the powerful whitewater rafting on the Ganga. See page 171.

❺ Trekking

With a range of climbs from easy valley walks to high-altitude plateaux and epic Himalayan treks, India gets you closer to nature. You can trek to the source of the Ganges, walk in the beautiful Valley of the Flowers or visit Buddhist gompas in Spiti. See pages 178, 184 and 432.

❻ Corbett National Park

India's first national park and one of its finest, Corbett's forests and riverine plains are home to wild tiger and hundreds of elephant. You can explore the park from the top of an elephant or in a jeep. There are also opportunities to stay inside the park. See page 196.

❼ Jaisalmer

This magical medieval city shimmers like a mirage in the desert and has an incredible atmosphere, with narrow streets inside the fort walls, beautiful mansion houses and Jain temples. See page 343.

❽ Camel safari from Bikaner

Desert camp fires with live music and endless starry nights are your treats at the end of a day's camel riding. Get insight into village life and try typical Rajasthani dishes, such as desert beans – *kej sangri*. See page 383.

❾ Kolkata

The country's intellectual hub also retains many of its most striking colonial buildings. The spiritual highlight of the year is Durga Puja, celebrating the Goddess Durga. See page 534.

❿ Sikkim

Bordering Nepal, Bhutan and Tibet, Sikkim offers an insight into Buddhist culture and provides dramatic Himalayan views and alpine meadows. Almost a quarter of the state is covered by the Khangchendzonga National Park. See page 596.

⓫ Madurai

This noisy, dusty and overcrowded Tamil centre is a heady cocktail of temple elephants, crumbling buildings, flower sellers, cycle-rickshaws and musicians. See page 862.

⓬ Backwater Kerala

This is the ultimate way to find serenity in India. Converted rice barges ply the waterways of Kerala granting access to a huge variety of birdlife, small riverside villages and some exceptional Keralan dishes from your on-board chef. It's truly magical. See page 903.

⓭ Nagarhole

Experience wild India at Karnataka's Nagarhole National Park. It is the richest tiger habitat in India, with herds of wild elephants and a wide variety of birds. It is part of the Nilgiri Biosphere Reserve and you can do safaris by boat and jeep. See page 995.

⑭ Hampi

The former capital of the Vijayanagar Empire is a place of hugely impressive ruins and a hypnotic, chilled-out vibe. Many people come here to try rock climbing as there are stunning boulders and you can climb up to the Hanuman Temple for a bird's-eye view. See page 1012.

⑮ Mumbai

Maximum City is the home of Bollywood; you can even be an extra in a movie. Take tea at the Taj Mahal Hotel, eat delicious fish dishes at numerous restaurants or try the local *bhel puri*. See page 1088.

⑯ Ellora Caves

Hewn from the vertical face of the Charanandri hills, these magnificent cave temples represent Buddhist, Jain and Hindu mythology. Cave 10 is the most significant of the Buddhist rock cut caves with a massive Buddha at its heart, while the awe-inspiring Hindu Mount Kailash (Kailasa) temple is the abode of Lord Shiva; absolutely stunning. See page 1122.

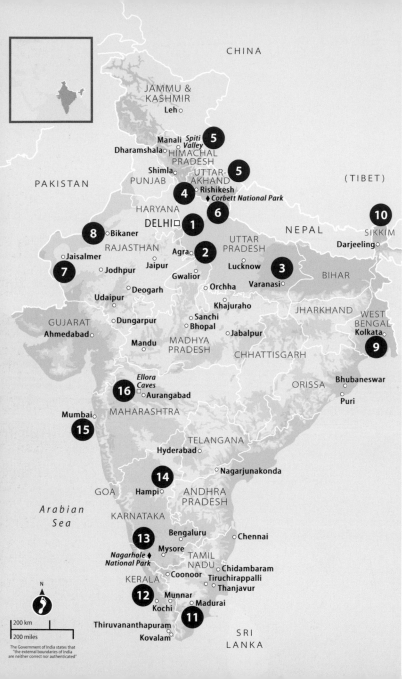

CHINA

JAMMU &
KASHMIR
Leh○

○Manali *Spiti* **5**
          Valley
Dharamshala○ HIMACHAL
              PRADESH
Shimla○ UTTAR-
         AKHAND **5**
4 ○Rishikesh
     ◆*Corbett National Park*
DELHI□ **1** **6**

PUNJAB

PAKISTAN

(TIBET)

10
SIKKIM

8 ○Bikaner   NEPAL
                         Darjeeling○
HARYANA

RAJASTHAN   Agra○ **2**   UTTAR
                             PRADESH
○Jaisalmer   Lucknow○   **3**
7   Jaipur○   Varanasi○   BIHAR
    ○Jodhpur
              Gwalior○
Udaipur○ ○Deogarh   Orchha○
                          Khajuraho○   JHARKHAND   WEST
                      Sanchi○   BENGAL
GUJARAT   ○Dungarpur   Bhopal○   Kolkata○
Ahmedabad○   Jabalpur○   **9**
         Mandu○   MADHYA
                   PRADESH   CHHATTISGARH
                                              Bhubaneswar○
                                         ORISSA
         Ellora   Puri○
         Caves
16 ○Aurangabad
    □
Mumbai○ MAHARASHTRA
15
         TELANGANA
         Hyderabad○
                          ○Nagarjunakonda
              14
Arabian   Hampi○ ANDHRA
Sea   PRADESH
         KARNATAKA
              13
GOA   Bengaluru○
         Mysore○   Chennai○
Nagarhole ◆ TAMIL
National Park NADU
         ○Coonoor   ○Chidambaram
KERALA   Tiruchirappalli○
    12 Munnar○   Thanjavur○
    Kochi○ **11** Madurai○
Thiruvananthapuram○   SRI
    Kovalam○   LANKA

N

200 km
200 miles

The Government of India states that
"the external boundaries of India
are neither correct nor authenticated"

BHUTAN

ASSAM

BANGLADESH

MYANMAR
(BURMA)

Bay of
Bengal

Andaman
Islands

Nicobar
Islands

This page: Desert life
Opposite page: Confluence of the Indus and Zanskar rivers

Route
planner

The heart of India beats in the densely populated plains of the River Ganga, settled and cultivated for millennia and the home of great civilizations which shape the lives of more than 1.2 billion people today. To the south lies the peninsula, politically always more fragmented than the plains and agriculturally less fertile, but with mineral resources that have supplied empires from the Indus Valley Civilization over 4000 years ago to the present. Beyond lies one of India's great natural frontiers, the palm-fringed Indian Ocean, stretching from the Arabian Sea in the west to the Bay of Bengal in the east, and offering nothing but scattered island chains between Kanniyakumari and Antarctica.

North India

from snowfields to deserts

To the north of the plains stand the Himalaya, what a 19th-century Surveyor General of India described as "the finest natural combination of boundary and barrier that exists in the world. It stands alone. For the greater part of its length only the

Himalayan eagle can trace it. It lies amidst the eternal silence of vast snowfield and icebound peaks". In the eastern foothills of the Himalaya, for example, are some of the wettest regions in the world, still covered in dense rainforest, while in their western ranges are the high-altitude deserts of Ladakh. Similarly the Gangetic plains stretch from the fertile and wet delta of Bengal to the deserts of northern Rajasthan. Even the peninsula ranges from the tropical humid climate of the western coast across the beautiful hills of the Western Ghats to the dry plateau inland.

Central India

land of sacred rivers

India's most holy river, the Ganga, runs across the vital heartland of the country and through the mythology of Hinduism. Joined by other holy rivers along its route, its waters are a vital source of irrigation. Its path is dotted with towns and settlements of great sanctity, and it is a vital economic asset as well as the focus of devotion for hundreds of millions of people. To the south the great rivers of the peninsula – the Narmada, Krishna, Tungabhadra and Kaveri to name only the largest – also have a spiritual significance to match their providers of water and power.

South India

Goa's palm-fringed golden beaches on the sun-drenched tropical west coast have long provided a magical getaway for travellers from around the world. But there are still many less well-known hideaways up and down the often sandy coastline. Lushly vegetated and densely populated, Kerala in the far southwest adds idyllic backwaters to its coastal fringe, while offshore the almost unvisited Lakshadweep Islands offer a coral paradise for divers equalling that of the better-known Maldives to the south. Far to the east in the Bay of Bengal the Andamans add another dimension to the exotic character of India's coast, its scattered islands being home to some of the world's most primitive aboriginal tribes.

Opposite page: Western Ghats
Above: Aarti at Haridwar
Below: Goan beach

Itineraries

First-time visitors are often at a loss when faced with the vast possibilities for travel in India. We have made a few suggestions for two- to three-week trips on the basis that some journeys will be flown and that tickets have been booked in advance. Two or three of these itineraries could be combined to make a longer trip. However, since travelling times are often quite long compared to Western standards, it is advisable to stick to a particular region rather than trying to cover too much ground in a short time. Listed throughout the book are reliable travel agencies who can make arrangements for a relatively small fee, saving you time and bother. Air tickets can be difficult to get at short notice for some trips, eg Leh–Delhi and Varanasi–Delhi. Railway tickets can be just as elusive, especially during school holidays. Indian railways are divided into regions and, despite computerized booking and the growing number of booking offices where All India reservations can be made, there are still places where it is impossible to book tickets for travel to regions outside the one you are in. Allow more time if you are planning to travel entirely by road and rail. On the plus side, however, if you use overnight trains for longer journeys you can cover almost as much ground in the same time as flying.

Figures in brackets are the number of nights we suggest you spend.

Himalayan foothills

two to three weeks

Delhi (2) has both the British-built New Delhi and Shah Jahan's 17th-century capital. The city also provides access to some of the most beautiful sights in the Himalayan foothills and awe-inspiring mountain peaks. You can fly to **Shimla** (2), the British summer capital, then continue by road to **Dharamshala** (3) associated with the Dalai Lama and the Tibetan settlement. Spend a night in **Mandi** (1) en route to **Naggar** (2) and **Manali** (4) for some trekking. Fly back to Delhi from Kullu and take the fast Shatabdi Express to **Agra** (1) for the Taj Mahal and splendid fort.

Above: Hemis Monastery, Ladakh
Left: Jaisalmer, Rajasthan
Opposite page left: Ellora Caves, Aurangabad
Opposite page top right: Gwalior, Madhya Pradesh
Opposite page bottom right: Satukunda paintings

Between late June and September the tour could be altered to take in the Tibetan Buddhist area of **Ladakh** (3) (instead of Dharamshala) by travelling to **Leh** (5) along the stunning road from **Manali** (2).

Northwest India

three weeks

This route taking in Mughal and Rajput India starts in **Delhi** (2) and moves to **Agra** (2) and **Jaipur** (2). Relax at the sleepy village of **Samode** (2) before flying across the desert to **Jaisalmer** (3) and then head for **Jodhpur** (2). On the way to lakeside **Udaipur** (3) you can visit the exquisite Jain temples at Ranakpur and the impressive fort at Kumbhalgarh from restful **Deogarh** (2). As a bonus, you can sample the charming hospitality at heritage hotels in former palaces and forts in both Rajasthan and Gujarat. Stop at **Poshina Fort** (2) or Balaram Palace en route to **Ahmadabad** (2) with its architectural heritage and Calico Museum, before flying back.

Central North India

two to three weeks

Across the heart of central North India you can see some of the best examples of Buddhist, Hindu and Muslim art and architecture. Travelling partly by road or rail, you also experience the varied scenery and agriculture, going first across the Deccan plateau, with its rich black lava soils, then over Rajasthan and Khajuraho on the northern edge of the peninsula. Travel from **Mumbai** (2) to **Aurangabad** (3) for Ajanta, Ellora and Daulatabad Fort, then to **Udaipur** (3) and **Deogarh** (2), visiting Ranakpur Jain temples and Kumbhalgarh Fort. Onwards to **Jaipur** (2), **Agra** (2), **Khajuraho** (2) and **Varanasi** (3) before returning to **Delhi** (2).

Central India

two weeks

This tour of India is characterized by prehistoric interest and palaces. It starts in the centre of Muslim influence in **Delhi** (2) and **Agra** (1), and passes through some of the great Rajput palaces and forts in **Gwalior** (3), visiting Datia and idyllic **Orchha** (2) via Jhansi en route to **Bhopal** (3). Around Bhopal are impressive prehistoric rock art at Bhimbetka, and early Hindu and Buddhist remains at Bhojpur and Sanchi. On the way to **Mumbai** (2) a brief diversion from Indore takes you to the quaint fortified site at **Mandu** (2) with its picturesque past.

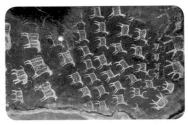

East India

two weeks

This tour, characterized by mountains and temples, starts in **Kolkata** (2), a vibrant city that was once the capital of the Raj, and then takes you to the foothills of the Himalaya starting with **Darjeeling** (3), famous for its tea estates and magnificent views of Khangchendzonga. Distant **Sikkim** (3) with its distinctive Buddhist influence is a fascinating side trip. Magnificent Orissan

Top left: Kolkata
Top right: Ravangla, Sikkim
Above: Varkala, Kerala
Opposite page: Brahminy starling, Bharatpur

temples can be seen at **Bhubaneswar** (3) and Konark, with a possible beach diversion near the pilgrimage centre of **Puri** (3), and on to the holy city of **Varanasi** (2) to see India laid bare for the first-time visitor. The tour winds up with a visit to see the fabulous carvings at **Khajuraho** (2) and concludes in **Delhi** (2) with a stop en route at **Agra** (1) to see the finest of the Mughal buildings, the Taj Mahal.

South India

three weeks

The historical South India circuit starts at **Mumbai** (2) where you can first visit the rockcut caves rich in frescoes and carvings at Ajanta and Ellora and the rugged Daulatabad fort near **Aurangabad** (3). Then on to **Hyderabad** (3), with the former capital of the Muslim Nizam and the Golconda fort and the tombs nearby. You then visit centres of ancient Tamil culture at Chidambaram, Gangaikondacholapuram and **Thanjavur** (3) after **Chennai** (1), fitting in a visit to **Mahabalipuram's shore temple** (2). The tour returns through southern Karnataka via **Mysore** (3), visiting the exquisite carvings in the Hindu and Jain temples at Belur and Halebid from Hassan or **Chikmagalur** (2), and finally to **Bengaluru** (Bangalore) (2).

Far South

From **Chennai** (2) drive to **Swamimalai** (2) known for traditional bronze casting and continue south to the ancient Tamil temples at **Thanjavur** (2) and **Madurai** (2). A morning start allows a stop at Padmanabhapuram Palace on the way across to Kerala on the west coast to relax on the beach at **Kovalam** (3) near Thiruvananthapuram. Take a boat along the backwaters as you move to **Kochi** (3), a fascinating meeting point of Eastern and European cultures. Then drive across to the tea estates of **Munnar** (2), high in the Western Ghats before dropping to the Tamil plains to visit the ancient fort and temples at **Trichy** (2) and Srirangam. Before returning home from Chennai, stop by the sea for the rock-cut cave temples at Mahabalipuram (3).

Wildlife

Northern tour This starts in **Delhi** (2) and goes via **Bhopal** (2) and **Jabalpur** (1) to **Kanha** (3), one of the most outstanding reserves in Central India, with a very rich habitat and still little visited. It continues to **Khajuraho** (2), where there is a chance to see magnificent 10th-century temples, en route to **Agra**'s (2) magnificent Taj Mahal and the abandoned city of Fatehpur Sikri before arriving at the peaceful bird sanctuary at **Bharatpur** (2), excellent for waterside birds.

Southern tour This starts in **Chennai** (2) to visit the bird sanctuary of Vedanthangal and **Mahabalipuram** (2), by the sea, with its ancient temples. Then travel down to **Trichy** (2) to climb up the rock fort and see the great temple of Srirangam on the banks of the Kaveri. From there the route continues to the hill station of **Coonoor** (1) going up to Udhagamandalam (Ooty) (1) on the Blue Mountain Railway (if it is running), then on to the rich wildlife sanctuary of **Mudumalai Bandipur** (3). Travelling north into Karnataka, you can visit the beautiful national park of **Nagarhole** (3).

Best
temples, forts & palaces

Golden Temple, Amritsar
The spiritual nerve centre of the Sikh faith, every Sikh tries to make a visit to the temple and bathe in the holy water. It is an immensely powerful and spiritual experience, with an all-pervasive air of strength and self sufficiency. Visitors of all faiths are welcome. Page 404.

Jaisalmer Fort
On the roughly triangular-shaped Trikuta Hill, the fort stands 76 m above the town, enclosed by a 9-km wall with 99 bastions. Often called the Golden Fort because

of the colour of its sandstone walls, it dominates the town. You enter the fort from the east from Gopa Chowk. The inner, higher fort wall and the old gates up the ramp (Suraj Pol, Ganesh Pol, Hawa Pol and Rang Pol) provided further defences. The Suraj Pol, once an outer gate, is flanked by heavy bastions and has bands of decoration which imitate local textile designs. Page 344.

Red Fort, Delhi
Between the new city and the River Yamun, Shah Jahan built a fort. Most of it was built out of red *lal* (sandstone), hence the name Lal Qila (Red Fort), the same as that at Agra on which the Delhi fort is modelled. Begun in 1639 and completed in 1648, it is said to have cost Rs 10 million, much of which was spent on the opulent marble palaces within. Page 58.

Taj Mahal, Agra
Of all the world's great monuments, the Taj Mahal is one of the most photographed, televised, written and talked about. To India's Nobel poet laureate, Tagore, the Taj was a "tear drop on the face of humanity", a building to echo the cry "I have not forgotten, I have not forgotten, O beloved" and its mesmerizing power is such that despite the hype, no one comes away disappointed. Page 114.

Hawa Mahal, Jaipur
The 'Palace of the Winds' (circa 1799) forms part of the east wall of the City Palace complex and is best seen from the street outside. Possibly Jaipur's most famous building, this pink sandstone façade of the palace was built for the ladies of the harem by Sawai Pratap Singh. The five storeys stand on a high podium with an entrance from the west.

The elaborate façade contains 953 small casements in a huge curve, each with a balcony and crowning arch. The windows enabled *hawa* (cool air) to circulate and allowed the women who were secluded in the *zenana* to watch processions below without being seen. Page 274.

Hampi Vijayanagar
Hampi, in Karnataka, is the site of the capital city of the Vijayanagar Hindu Empire that rose to conquer the entire south of India in the 14th century. It is an extraordinary site of desolate temples, compounds, stables and pleasure baths, surrounded by a stunning boulder-strewn landscape. Little of the kingdom's riches remains; now the mud huts of gypsies squat under the boulders where noblemen once stood, and the double-decker shopfronts of the bazaar where diamonds were once traded by the kilo is now geared solely towards profiting from Western tourists and domestic pilgrims. Away from the bazaar, there is a unique romantic desolation. You'll need at least a full day to do it justice. Page 1021.

Best festivals

Makar Sankranti

One date that remains constant is Makar Sankranti (14 January), marking the start of the northern journey of the sun. In West and North India this is the time of the Kite Festival. The clear blue winter sky comes alive with delicate tissue paper squares of every hue as children and adults skilfully manipulate the ends of their glassen-crusted threads to 'cut' and down their rivals' kites.

Pongal

In the south, the winter festival is Pongal, the Tamil Harvest Thanksgiving, when cows and bulls are specially honoured in recognition of their invaluable contribution to village life. They are allowed to share the first rice which is ritually offered to the Sun God. Swathed in garlands, their long horns painted in vivid colours, the cattle are taken around neighbouring villages accompanied by bands of musicians and cheering children.

Rath Yatra of Orissa

Under the blazing summer sun in June, the Raja of Puri, dressed as a humble servant of the gods, ceremonially sweeps the path before the massive wooden *raths*, or temple chariots, in the great Rath Yatra of Orissa in Eastern India. The chariot, drawn by hundreds of heaving men and watched by thousands of pilgrims, carries Jagannath and his brother and sister on their slow annual journey from the temple. This was the ceremony that led early English observers to borrow the name of the god for any apparently unstoppable vehicle, or 'juggernaut'.

Holi

Spring brings new hope and the promise of plenty. Holi, which coincides with the March/April full moon, is marked by the

lighting of great bonfires to symbolize the triumph of good over evil in the burning of the insatiable demoness Holika, who demanded a diet of children. If you venture out you may find it hard to escape the coloured powder and water thrown in remembrance of the romantic Lord Krishna who engaged in similar playful games with his favourite milkmaids. Take great care though, as the revelry can get out of hand.

Navratri

The nine autumnal nights of Navratri in October culminate in the great Dasara celebration commemorating the victory of Rama over the supposedly invincible 10-headed King Ravana who had stolen his beautiful wife Sita. The Ramlila, drawing on Ramayana stories, is enacted for nine nights leading up to the 10th (*dasara*) when gigantic bamboo and paper effigies of the evil giant and his aides are set alight amidst great jubilation. Bengalis celebrate the festival by communal worship or Puja of the triumphant mother goddess Durga riding a lion who defeats the buffalo demon after a great battle. On the 10th night, her splendid image, together with those of her four children, is taken in procession by cheering crowds to be immersed in the waters of the holy river, returning clay to clay.

Diwali

Perhaps the most striking of all festivals is Diwali which follows soon after Navratri, on the dark night of the new moon in October-November, when row upon row of little clay oil lamps (now often enhanced by strings of electric bulbs) are lined up on window ledges and balconies, in remembrance of the lights which greeted Rama's return after 14 years in exile. The night sky bursts out with spectacular displays of fireworks while deafening firecrackers take passersby by surprise.

Best
treks

Valley of Flowers (Uttarakhand)
As the rains start, this high-altitude valley bursts into colour with a stunning array of flowers. It's best to visit in August, starting this gentle trek from Govindghat. It was discovered in 1931 when a group of British mountaineers got lost. You will find rare flowers and valuable medicinal plants (Ayurvedic). There is also an option to spend a night at a guesthouse in Ghangaria and do another stunning ascent up to Hemkund Sahib, a Sikh pilgrimage, where there is a simple temple and a lake surrounded by 4500-m-high mountains. Page 184.

Pin-Bhaba (Himachal Pradesh)
The fantastic Spiti Ecosphere collective create interesting volunteer programmes, spiritual sojourns and off-the-beaten-track treks. You can experience a wide range of treks around the epic Spiti Valley taking in awe-inspiring mountain scenery, Buddhist gompas and simple villages. Venture out on their Pin-Bhaba (Tarikhango) Pass trek taking in mountain views and wildlife and staying in traditional homestays getting an insight into high-altitude life as well as camping. Page 435.

Tosh Valley (Himachal Pradesh)
The trek begins from the village of Tosh, which is 25 km ahead of Manikaran. The Tosh is a feeder valley of the popular Parvati Valley which leads to the Pin Parvati Pass. The trek follows the raging River Tosh from the village to the snout of the Tosh Glacier. Along the way you cross several beautiful meadows and run into

Gaddis (the shepherd tribe of Himachal); there is an amazing variety of birdlife and you might even catch a rare glimpse of the Himalayan black or brown bear. Page 442.

Markha Valley (Jammu and Kashmir)
Ladakh's most famous trek is relatively close to Leh and boasts some of the best contrasting views of lush river valleys against stark mountain peaks. The route enters Hemis National Park, home to rare species of wildlife, including snow leopards, and crosses two high-altitude passes – Gandha La and Kongmaru La – at around 5000 m. Tiny Buddhist villages, remote monasteries and impressive ruined forts along the way add to the rich mix of culture and landscape. Page 525.

Gocha La (Sikkim)
Many travellers go to Sikkim purely to make the trek to Gocha La. Taking eight or nine days there and back, the staggering mountain scenery culminates in a close-up view of the sheer eastern face of Khangchendzonga. The trail runs through semi-tropical forests, giant magnolia and rhododendron, before entering wilder rocky terrain interspersed with meadows and glacial lakes. It's not just Khangchendzonga views that draw hikers, the numerous other peaks in sight make this trek comparable with those in Nepal. Page 612.

Nandi Bull statue, Varanasi

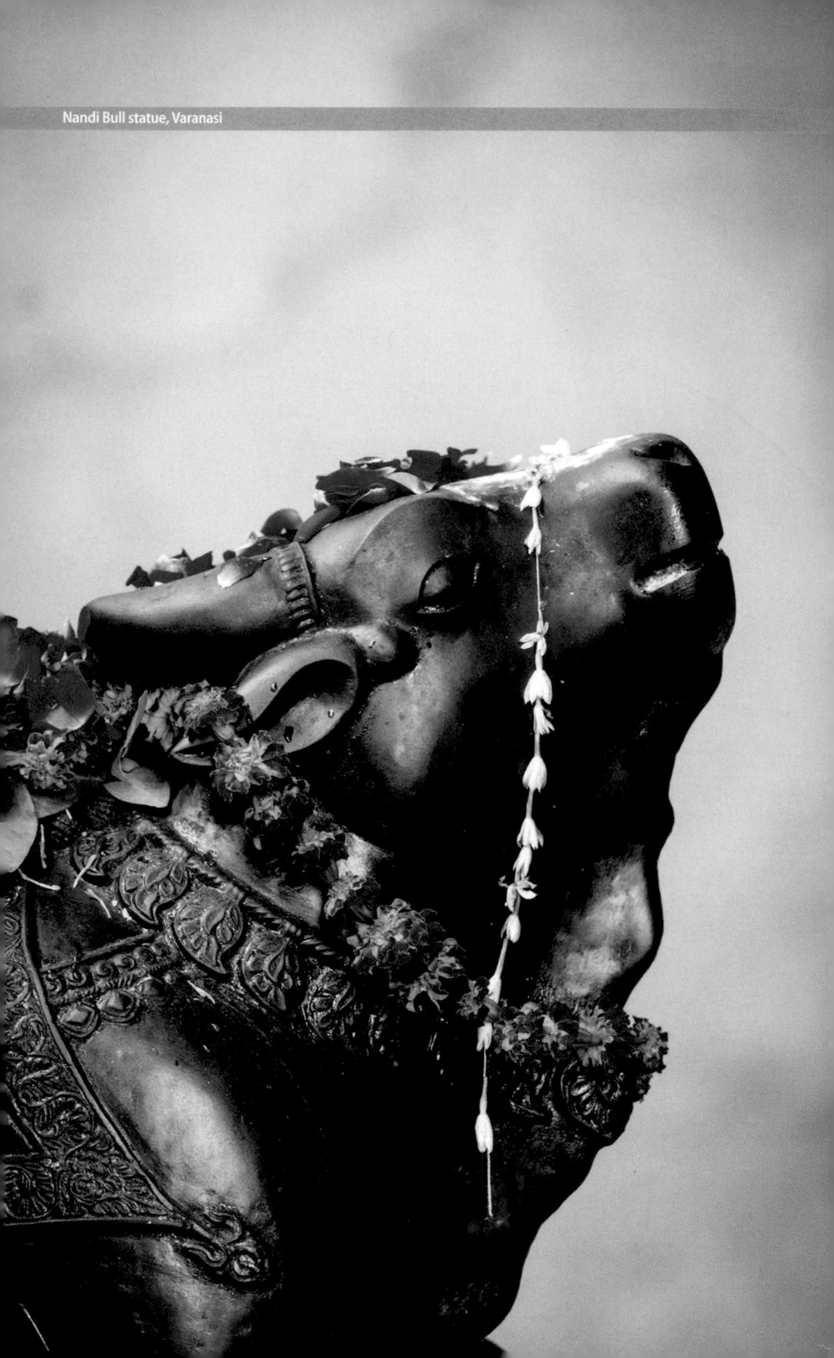

When to go

...and when not to

Climate

India is divided almost exactly in half by the Tropic of Cancer, stretching from the near-equatorial Kanniyakumari to the Mediterranean latitudes of Kashmir – roughly the same span as from the Amazon to San Francisco, or from Melbourne to Darwin. Not surprisingly, climate varies considerably and high altitudes further modify local climates.

In most of India, by far the best time to visit is from the end of the monsoon in October to the end of March. However, there are important exceptions. The hill stations in the Himalaya and the Western Ghats are beautiful in the hot months of April to early June. Parts of the western Himalaya can be excellent until September though it can be very cold and sometimes wet in spring.

The monsoon season lasts from between three and five months depending on the region. If you are travelling in the wetter parts of India during the monsoon you need to be prepared for extended periods of torrential rain and disruption to travel. However, many parts of India receive a total of under 1000 mm a year, mainly in the form of heavy isolated showers. Rainfall generally decreases towards the northwest, Rajasthan and northern Gujarat merging imperceptibly into genuine desert. Tamil Nadu in the southeast has an exceptional rainfall pattern, receiving most of its rain in the period of the retreating monsoon, October to December.

Trekking seasons

If you are planning to do some trekking, the optimum season will vary depending on which area you visit. Autumn is best in most parts of the Himalaya though March to May can be pleasant. The monsoons (mid-June to end-September) can obviously be very wet and localized thunderstorms can occur at any time, particularly in the spring and summer. Start your trek early in the morning as the monsoon approaches. It often continues to rain heavily up to mid-October in the eastern Himalaya. The Kullu Valley is unsuitable for trekking during the monsoons but areas beyond the central Himalayan range, eg Ladakh, Zanskar, Lahul and Spiti, are largely unaffected. Be prepared for extremes in temperatures in all seasons and come prepared with light clothing as well as enough waterproof protection. Winters can be exceptionally cold; high passes can be closed and you will need more equipment. Winter treks on all but a few low-altitude ones (up to 3200 m) are only recommended for the experienced trekker accompanied by a knowledgeable local guide.

Festivals

India has a wealth of festivals with many celebrated nationwide, while others are specific to a particular state or community or even a particular temple. Many fall on different dates each year depending on the Hindu lunar calendar so check with the tourist office.

Some of the country's great festivals such as **Dasara** and **Diwali** (celebrated across India) and **Pongal** (celebrated in Tamil Nadu) take place in the autumn and winter. In Rajasthan, local camel and cattle fairs and the **Desert Festival** among the dunes are added attractions during these seasons.

The Hindu calendar

Hindus follow two distinct eras: The *Vikrama Samvat* which began in 57 BC and the *Salivahan Saka* which dates from AD 78 and has been the official Indian calendar since 1957. The *Saka* new year starts on 22 March and has the same length as the Gregorian calendar. The 29½ day lunar month with its 'dark' and 'bright' halves based on the new and full moons, are named after 12 constellations, and total a 354-day year. The calendar cleverly has an extra month (*adhik maas*) every 2½ to three years, to bring it in line with the solar year of 365 days coinciding with the Gregorian calendar of the West.

Some major national and regional festivals are listed below; details of these and others appear under the particular state or town. A few count as national holidays: **26 January**: Republic Day; **15 August**: Independence Day; **2 October**: Mahatma Gandhi's Birthday; **25 December**: Christmas Day.

For dates of upcoming national and local festivals check www.drikpanchang.com.

Purnima (Full Moon)

Many religious festivals depend on the phases of the moon. Full moon days are particularly significant and can mean extra crowding and merrymaking in temple towns throughout India, and are sometimes public holidays.

Major festivals and fairs

1 January New Year's Day is accepted officially when following the Gregorian calendar but there are regional variations which fall on different dates, often coinciding with spring/harvest time in March and April: **Losar** in Ladakh, **Naba Barsha** in Bengal (14 April), **Goru** in Assam, **Ugadi** in Andhra, **Vishu** in Kerala and **Jamshed Navroj** for the Parsi community.

14 January **Makar Sankranti** marks the end of winter and is celebrated with kite flying, especially in Gujarat. **Pongal** is Tamil Nadu's harvest festival.

26 January **Republic Day Parade** in New Delhi. Communist-style display of military strength.

February **Vasant Panchami**, the spring festival when people wear bright yellow clothes to mark the advent of the season with singing, dancing and feasting. In Bengal it is also **Saraswati Puja** when the goddess of learning is worshipped. **Desert Festival** – Jaisalmer, Rajasthan. **Nagaur Camel Fair** in Rajasthan. **Surajkund Crafts Mela** in Haryana. **International Yoga Festival** in Rishikesh, Uttarakhand. **Elephanta Festival** in Maharashtra. **Konark Festival** in Odisha.

February/March **Maha Sivaratri** marks the night when Siva danced his celestial dance of destruction (*Tandava*), which is celebrated with feasting and fairs at Siva temples, but preceded by a night of devotional readings and hymn singing. **Carnival** in Goa. Spectacular costumes, music and dance, float processions and feasting mark the three-day event.

March **Ellora Festival of Classical Dance and Music** in Maharashtra. **Khajuraho**

Dance Festival in Madhya Pradesh. **Gangaur Mela** in Rajasthan. **Holi**, the festival of colours, marks the climax of spring. The previous night bonfires are lit in parts of North India symbolizing the end of winter (and conquering of evil). People have fun throwing coloured powder and water at each other and in the evening some gamble with friends. If you don't mind getting covered in colours, you can risk going out but celebrations can sometimes get very rowdy (and unpleasant). Some worship Krishna who defeated the demon Putana.

April **Mahavir Jayanti**. **Baisakhi** in North India.

April/May **Buddha Jayanti**, the first full moon night in April/May marks the birth of the Buddha. **Pooram** in Thrissur, Kerala; a grand spectacle staged by rival temples with elaborately ornamented elephants.

June/July **Rath Yatra** in Puri, Odisha. **Hemis Festival** in Leh, Ladakh. **Teej** in Jaipur, Rajasthan.

July/August **Raksha (or Rakhi) Bandhan** symbolizes the bond between brother and sister, celebrated mainly in North India at full moon. A sister says special prayers for her brother and ties coloured threads around his wrist to remind him of the special bond. He in turn gives a gift and promises to protect and care for her. Sometimes *rakshas* are exchanged as a mark of friendship. **Narial Purnima** on the same full moon. Hindus, particularly in coastal areas of West and South India, make offerings of *narial* (coconuts) to the Vedic god Varuna (Lord of the waters) by throwing them into the sea. **15 August** is **Independence Day**, a national secular holiday is marked by special events, and in Delhi there is an impressive flag-hoisting ceremony at the Red Fort. **Ganesh Chaturthi** was established just over 100 years ago by the Indian nationalist leader Tilak. The elephant-headed God of good omen is shown special reverence. On the last of the five-day festival after harvest, clay images of Ganesh are taken in procession with dancers and musicians, and are immersed in the sea, river or pond.

August/September **Janmashtami**, the birth of Krishna is celebrated at midnight at Krishna temples. Special festivities are held in Mathura his birth place and nearby at Vrindavan where *Rasalilas* (dance dramas) are performed all night.

September/October **Dasara** has many local variations. In North India, celebrations for the nine nights *(navaratri)* are marked with **Ramlila**, various episodes of the *Ramayana* story (see page 872) are enacted with particular reference to the battle between the forces of good and evil. In some parts of India it celebrates Rama's victory over the Demon king Ravana of Lanka with the help of loyal Hanuman (Monkey). Huge effigies of Ravana made of bamboo and paper are burnt on the 10th day *(Vijaya dasami)* of **Dasara** in public open spaces. other regions the focus is on Durga's victory over the demon Mahishasura. Bengal celebrates **Durga puja**. **Onam** in Kerala.

October/November **Gandhi Jayanti** (2 October), Mahatma Gandhi's birthday, is remembered with prayer meetings and devotional singing.

Diwali/Deepavali, the festival of lights, is celebrated particularly in North India.

Some Hindus celebrate Krishna's victory over the demon Narakasura, some Rama's return after his 14 years' exile in the forest when citizens lit his way with oil lamps. The festival falls on the dark *chaturdasi* (14th) night (the one preceding the new moon), when rows of lamps or candles are lit in remembrance, and *rangolis* are painted on the floor as a sign of welcome. Fireworks have become an integral part of the celebration which are often set off days before Diwali. Equally, Lakshmi, the Goddess of Wealth (as well as Ganesh) is worshipped by merchants and the business community who open the new financial year's account on the day. Most people wear new clothes; some play games of chance.

In Bengal **Kali Puja** is celebrated the day before Diwali but is a distinct festival. **Pushkar Fair** in Rajasthan. **Guru Nanak Jayanti** commemorates the birth of Guru Nanak. **Akhand Path** (unbroken reading of the holy book) takes place and the book itself (*Guru Granth Sahib*) is taken out in procession. **Sonepur Fair** in Bihar.

December **Christmas Day** (25 December) sees Indian Christians celebrate the birth of Christ in much the same way as in the West; many churches hold services/mass at midnight. There is an air of festivity in city markets which are specially decorated and illuminated. Over **New Year's Eve** (31 December) hotel prices peak and large supplements are added for meals and entertainment in the upper category hotels. Some churches mark the night with a Midnight Mass. **Shekhavati Festival** in Rajasthan. **Hampi-Vijaynagar Festival** in Karnataka.

Muslim holy days

These are fixed according to the lunar calendar, see page 34. According to the Gregorian calendar, they tend to fall 11 days earlier each year, dependent on the sighting of the new moon.

Ramadan is the start of the month of fasting when all Muslims (except young children, the very elderly, the sick, pregnant women and travellers) must abstain from food and drink, from sunrise to sunset.

Id ul Fitr is the three-day festival that marks the end of Ramadan.

Id-ul-Zuha/Bakr-Id is when Muslims commemorate Ibrahim's sacrifice of his son according to God's commandment; the main time of pilgrimage to Mecca (the Hajj).

It is marked by the sacrifice of a goat, feasting and alms giving.

Muharram is when the killing of the Prophet's grandson, Hussain, is commemorated by Shi'a Muslims. Decorated *tazias* (replicas of the martyr's tomb) are carried in procession by devout wailing followers who beat their chests to express their grief. Hyderabad and Lucknow are famous for their grand *tazias*. The Shi'as fast for the 10 days.

What to do

India has a wealth of opportunities for adventure sports. Such thrills can be combined with more conventional sightseeing. Apart from the activities listed here, you can also try ballooning, heli-skiing, hang-gliding, mountain or rock climbing and even motor rallying. There are even ski resorts in Himachal Pradesh (namely Manali and Narkanda) but don't expect them to compare to Western resorts.

Birdwatching

The country's diverse and rich natural habitats harbour over 1200 species of bird of which around 150 are endemic. Visitors to all parts of the country can enjoy spotting oriental species whether it is in towns and cities, in the countryside or more abundantly in the national parks and sanctuaries. On the plains, the cooler months (November-March) are the most comfortable for a chance to see migratory birds from the hills, but the highlands themselves are ideal between May and June and again after the monsoons when visibility improves in October and November. Water bodies large and small draw visiting waterfowl from other continents during the winter.

Birds of the Indian Subcontinent, by Grimmett, Inskipp & Inskipp (published by Helm, 2014), is the best field guide.

Some prime spots include: Chilika Lake in Odisha; Keoladeo Ghana National Park in Rajasthan; Nalsarovar Bird Sanctuary in Gujarat; Pulicat Lake in Andhra Pradesh; Ranganathittu Bird Sanctuary in Karnataka; Saharanpur Bird Sanctuary in Delhi; Tadoba National Park in Maharashtra; and Vedanthangal Bird Sanctuary in Tamil Nadu.

For more information, try local websites such as www.delhibird.net, www.kolkata birds.com or www.orientalbirdclub.org, and www.cloudbirders.com for recent trip reports.

Camel safaris

Today's camel safaris try to recreate something of the atmosphere of the early camel trains. The guides are expert navigators and the villages that are passed through along the way add colour to an unforgettable experience, if you are prepared to sit out the somewhat uncomfortable ride.

For information, see the Thar Desert National Park in Rajasthan, page 350.

Cycling

Cycling offers a peaceful and healthy alternative to cars, buses or trains. Touring on locally hired bicycles is possible along country roads – ideal if you want to see village life in India and the lesser-known wildlife parks. Consult a good Indian agent for advice. For example, a week's cycling trip could cover about 250 km in the Garhwal foothills, starting in Rishikesh, passing through the Corbett and Rajaji national parks over easy gradients, to finish in Ramnagar. Expert guides, cycles and support vehicle, accommodation in simple rest houses or tents, are included.

For local operators, see the listings section of the relevant town.

Horse safaris

Gaining in popularity, the conditions are similar to camel safaris with grooms (and often the horse owner) accompanying. The best months are November to March when it is cooler in the day (and often cold at night). The trails chosen usually enable you to visit small villages, old forts and temples, and take you through a variety of terrain and vegetation from scrub-covered arid plains to forested hills. The charges can be a lot higher than for a camel safari but the night stays are often in comfortable palaces, forts or *havelis*.

For information see Kumbhalgarh Wildlife Sanctuary (page 309) and Shekhawati (page 386).

Trekking

The Himalaya offers unlimited opportunities to view the natural beauty of mountains, unique flora and fauna and the diverse groups of people who live in the ranges and valleys, many of whom have retained cultural identities because of their isolation. The treks described in this book try to give a flavour of an area or a destination but are only for guidance. See also When to go, page 33, and Best treks, page 30. For further information on trekking in India, see Footprint's *Indian Himalaya* guide.

Trekking permits Independent trekking is permitted in all areas other than those described as Restricted or Protected and within the 'Inner Line' (running parallel and 40 km inside the international boundary). Destinations falling within these 'sensitive' zones are either off limits or require permits; some treks must be organized by a recognized Indian travel agent and accompanied by a representative/liaison officer. In some areas, a pre-arranged itinerary must be followed.

On arrival in India, government-approved agencies can obtain permits relatively easily, usually within three or four days

Trekking in India

There are some outstandingly beautiful treks, though they are often not through the icy wilderness that 'trekking in the Himalaya' conjures up. Nevertheless, trekking alone is not recommended as you may not be able to communicate with the local people and if injured help may not be at hand. Independent trekkers should get a specialist publication with detailed up-to-date route descriptions and a good map. Seek advice from someone who knows the area well and has recently been trekking to the places you intend to visit.

Backpacking/camping Hundreds of people arrive each year with a pack and some personal equipment, buy some food and set off trekking, carrying their own gear and choosing their own campsites or places to stay. Supplies of fuel wood are scarce and flat ground suitable for camping rare. It is not always easy to find isolated and 'private' campsites.

Trekking without a tent Although common in Nepal, only a few trails in India offer the ease and comfort of this option. Examples are the Singalila Ridge trail in the Darjeeling area, the Sikkim Khangchendzonga trek, the Markha Valley trek in Ladakh and some lower-elevation trails around Shimla, Almora and Manali. On these, it is often possible to stay in trekking huts or in simple village homes. Food is simple, usually vegetable curry, rice and dhal. This approach brings you into closer contact with the local population, the limiting factor being the routes where accommodation is available.

Locally organized treks Porters can usually be hired through an agent in the town or village at the start of a trek. They will help carry your baggage, sometimes cook for you, and communicate with the local people. Make sure they are experienced in carrying loads over distances at high altitude. Some porters speak a little English but you may still have misunderstandings. Remember, you may be expected to

though note that it can be tricky to get a permit as a solo traveller; some offices demand a minimum group of four people. It can be much slower applying for trekking permits from abroad. Permits are issued at the Foreigners' Regional Registration Offices in Delhi, Mumbai, Kolkata and Chennai (and sometimes at a local FRRO), from immigration officers at some points of entry, and sometimes at the district magistrate's office in towns such as Shimla. There are also entrance fees for the various national parks and conservation areas which can be as much as Rs 350 for foreigners.

Affected areas include the Spiti Valley (Himachal Pradesh), which is now open to group trekkers with an Inner Line Permit (available from the Deputy Collector's Offices in Shimla or Recong Peo). Other restricted areas now open to tourists include Kalindi Khal (Garhwal), Milam Glacier (Kumaon), Khardung La, Tso Moriri and Pangong (Ladakh), Tsangu Lake, Lachung and Yumthang (Sikkim) and Kameng Valley (Arunachal Pradesh). See page 1392.

Code of conduct Deforestation Do not make open fires and discourage others from making one for you. Limit use of firewood

provide your porter's warm clothing and protective wear including shoes, gloves and goggles on high-altitude treks.

In remote areas, tracks may be indistinct and a *sardar* (mountain guide) is recommended. This is more expensive but worthwhile since they will speak some English, take care of engaging porters and cooks, arrange for provisions and sort out all logistical problems. Make sure your *sardar* is experienced in the area you will be travelling in and can provide references which are their own and not borrowed.

Using a trekking agent Trekking agents based in Delhi or at hill stations (eg Dehradun, Shimla, Manali, Dharamshala, Leh, Darjeeling, Gangtok) will organize treks for a fee and provide a *sardar*, porters, cooks, food and equipment. This method takes some effort and negotiation but can be excellent and is recommended for a group, preferably with some experience, that wants to follow a specific itinerary. You can organize this in advance or wait until you get to India, but allow at least a week to make arrangements.

Fully organized and escorted treks This is where a company or individual with local knowledge and expertise organizes a trip and sells it. Some or all camping equipment, food, cooking, liaison with porters, guides, etc, are taken care of. The agency may even take care of foreign travel arrangements, ticketing, visas and permits. This option offers a good, safe introduction to the country. You will be able to travel with limited knowledge of the region and its culture and get to places you may not have reached alone.

An escorted trek will involve going with a group; you will camp together but not necessarily walk together. If you are willing to trade some of your independence, the experience can be very rewarding. Ideally there should be no around 12 trekkers per group. Before booking, check the itinerary – is it too demanding, or not adventurous enough? Is the leader qualified and familiar with the route? Also make sure both you and the trekking company understand exactly who is to provide what equipment.

and heated water and use only permitted dead wood. Choose accommodation where kerosene or fuel-efficient wood-burning stoves are used.

Litter Remove it. Burn or bury paper and carry away non-degradable litter. If you find other people's litter, remove it too. Pack food in biodegradable containers.

Plants Do not take cuttings, seeds and roots – it is illegal in all parts of the Himalaya.

Water Keep local water clean. Do not use detergents and pollutants in streams and springs. Where there are no toilets be sure you are at least 30 m away from a water source and bury or cover. Do not allow cooks or porters to throw rubbish in streams and rivers.

Watersports

Snorkelling, surfing, parasailing, windsurfing and waterskiing are popular along the touristy stretches of India's coast. Scuba-diving centres include Bogmalo beach in Goa (though visibility is typically poor), Malvan in Maharashtra, Netrani Island off Murudeshwar in Karnataka and, above all, Havelock Island and the Marine National Park in the Andamans. Coastal resorts in Kerala and Goa also offer fishing trips and dolphin viewing.

Shopping tips

India excels in producing fine crafts at affordable prices through the tradition of passing down of ancestral skills. You can get handicrafts of different states from the government emporia in the major cities which guarantee quality at fixed prices (no bargaining), but many are poorly displayed, a fact not helped by reluctant and unenthusiastic staff. Private upmarket shops and top hotel arcades offer better quality, choice and service but at a price. Vibrant and colourful local bazars are often a great experience but you must be prepared to bargain.

Bargaining can be fun and quite satisfying but it is important to get an idea of prices being asked by different stalls for items you are interested in, before taking the plunge. Some shopkeepers will happily quote twice the actual price to a foreigner showing interest, so you might well start by halving the asking price. On the other hand it would be inappropriate to do the same in an established shop with price tags, though a plea for the 'best price' or a 'special discount' might reap results even here. Remain good humoured throughout. Walking away slowly might be the test to ascertain whether your custom is sought and you are called back.

Warning The country is a vast market place but there are regional specializations. If you are planning to travel widely, wait to find the best places to buy specific items. Export of certain items is controlled or banned (see page 1376).

Taxi/rickshaw drivers and tour guides get a commission when they deliver tourists to certain shops, but prices are invariably inflated. Small private shops can't always be trusted to pack and post your purchases: unless you have a specific recommendation from a person you know, only make such arrangements in government emporia or a large store. Don't enter into any arrangement to help 'export' marble items, jewellery, etc, no matter how lucrative your 'cut' of the profits may sound. Many's the traveller that's been cheated through misuse of credit card account, and left with unwanted goods. Make sure, too, that credit cards are run off just once when making a purchase.

Carpets and dhurries

The superb hand-knotted carpets of Kashmir, using old Persian designs woven in wool or silk or both, are hard to beat for their beauty and quality. Kashmiri traders can now be found throughout India, wherever there is a hint of foreign tourism. Agra too has a long tradition of producing wool carpets and welcomes visitors to their factories. Tibetan refugees in Karnataka, Darjeeling and Gangtok produce excellent carpets which are less expensive but of very high quality. They will make carpets to order and parcel post them safely. Flat woven cotton dhurries in subtle colours are best seen in Rajasthan.

Jewellery

Whether it is chunky tribal necklaces from the Himalaya, heavy 'silver' bangles from Rajasthan, fine Odishan filigree, legendary pearls from Hyderabad, Jaipuri uncut gems set in gold or semi-precious stones in silver, or glass bangles from Varanasi, you will be drawn to the arcade shop window as much as the wayside stall. It's best to buy from reputable shops as street stalls often pass off fake ivory, silver, gems and stones as real. Gold and silver should have a hallmark, but antique pieces often do not.

Metal work

The choice is vast, from brass, copper and white-metal plates and bowls from the North, with ornate patterns or plain polished surfaces, exquisite Jaipuri enamelled silver pill boxes, tribal lost-wax *dhokra* toys from Odisha, Bihar and Bengal, Nawabi silver-on-gunmetal Bidri pieces from around Hyderabad, to copies of Chola bronzes cast near Thanjavur.

Paintings

Contemporary Indian art is exhibited in modern galleries in the state capitals often at a fraction of London or New York prices. Traditional 'Mughal' miniatures, sometimes using natural pigments on old paper (don't be fooled) and new silk, are reaching mass production levels in Rajasthan's back alleys. Fine examples can still be found in good craft shops.

Stoneware

Artisans inspired by the Taj Mahal continue the tradition of inlaying tiny pieces of gem stones on fine white marble, to produce something for every pocket, from a small coaster to a large table top. Softer soapstone is cheaper. Stone temple carvings are produced for sale in Tamil Nadu (try Mahabalipuram), Odisha (Puri, Konark) and Uttar Pradesh (near Hamirpur).

Textiles

Handlooms produce rich shot silk from Kanchipuram, skilful *ikat* from Gujarat, Odisha and Andhra, brocades from Varanasi, golden *muga* from Assam, printed silks and batiks from Bengal or opulent *Himroo* shawls from Aurangabad. Sober handspun *khadi*, colourful Rajasthani block-printed cottons using vegetable dyes, tribal weaving from remote Himalayan villages and tie-dyed Gujarati *bandhni* are easier on the pocket. Unique pieces also from Kashmiri embroidery on wool, Lucknowi *chickan* shadow-work on fine voil or *zari* (gold/silver thread) work on silk. The *pashmina* shawl and scarf from Kashmir have travelled to every continent and are available in dozens of colours at less inflated prices. They come in various widths and quality (often mixed with silk). See page 496. All trade in tush (toosh) wool is banned.

Wood craft

Each region of India has its special wood – walnut in Kashmir, sandalwood in Mysore, rosewood in the South, sheesham in the North. Carving, inlay and lacquerwork are particular specialities. The southern states produce fine carved wooden panels and images which are sold through the state emporia (they offer a posting service).

Whitewater rafting

The snow-fed rivers that flow through regions such as Sikkim and Arunachal Pradesh offer excellent whitewater rafting. The popular waters range from Grades II-III for amateurs (Zanskar, Indus) to the greater challenges of Grades IV-VI for the experienced (eg Chenab, Beas, Sutlej, Rangit, Tons). Trips range from a half day to several days and allow a chance to see scenery, places and people off the beaten track. The trips are organized and managed by professional teams who have trained abroad. The rivers can sometimes be dangerous in August and September when the water levels are high.

For local operators, see the listings section of the relevant town.

Where to stay

from heritage hotels to homestays

India has an enormous range of accommodation, and you can stay safely and very cheaply by Western standards right across the country.

The mainstay of the budget traveller is the ubiquitous Indian 'business hotel': within walking distance to train and bus stations, anonymous but generally decent value, with en suite rooms of hugely variable cleanliness and a TV showing 110 channels of cricket and Bollywood MTV. At the top end, alongside international chains like **ITC** (ostentatious) and **Radisson Blu** (dependable), India boasts several home-grown hotel chains, best of which are the exceptional heritage and palace hotels operated by the **Taj** and **Oberoi** group. Four-star boutique hotels abound in cities like Delhi and Bengaluru, some offering truly excellent value in the US$100-150 price bracket; elsewhere, especially in tourist magnets like Agra, hotels in this category tend to be massive, mediocre and full of tour groups, and you're better off either splashing out or settling for something cheaper and more basic.

Head up to the mountains and you'll find find restored castles, tea planters' bungalows and judges' houses to stay in. In Rajasthan and many of the major cities in the north, you will find a huge number of lovingly restored palaces and *havelis* in which to hang your hat. Meanwhile, Kerala and Tamil Nadu offer abundant opportunities to stay in fine style in converted mansions, tea bungalows and farmhouses – a great way to help preserve architectural heritage while keeping your money in the local economy. And while the coastal holiday belts of Goa and Kerala have their share of big and bland resorts, you'll also find a huge variety of individual lodgings, from porous coconut-fibre beach shacks that don't even come

Price codes

Where to stay	Restaurants
$$$$ over US$150	$$$ over US$12
$$$ US$66-150	$$ US$6-12
$$ US$30-65	$ under US$6
$ under US$30	

For a double room in high season, excluding taxes.

For a two-course meal for one person, excluding drinks or service charge.

with a lock to luxurious restored forts overlooking the Arabian Sea and minimalist Zen retreats hidden in paddy fields.

There are a good number of 'eco' properties dotted around the country.

If you're really trying to stretch your rupee, you'll find genuinely cheap accommodation easier to come by in North India than South. Delhi's notorious backpacker enclave of Paharganj is the classic Indian baptism of fire; elsewhere you can find perfectly clean and acceptable rooms in family houses in Rajasthan for well under US$10 a night. In other large cities such as Mumbai and Bengaluru it's more of a challenge to find really cheap accommodation; budget on a minimum of Rs 700 a night.

In the high season (October to April, peaking at Christmas/New Year and again at Easter) bookings can be extremely heavy in popular destinations. Be aware that prices rise around Diwali (October/November) when domestic tourists head off on holiday. Similarly, as the temperatures start to rise in May and June, hill stations become extremely busy and pricey in Kerala and in Himachal Pradesh. It is generally possible to book in advance by phone or email, sometimes on payment of a deposit, but double check your reservation a day or two beforehand and always try to arrive as early as possible in the day to iron out problems.

Hotels

Price categories The category codes used in this book are based on prices of double rooms excluding taxes (see previous page). They are not star ratings and individual facilities vary considerably. Modest hotels may not have their own restaurant but will often offer 'room service', bringing in food from outside. In temple towns, restaurants may only serve vegetarian food. Expect to pay more in Mumbai, Delhi and Jaipur, to a lesser extent, Chennai for all categories. Prices away from large cities tend to be lower for comparable hotels.

Online booking agencies Often you can score large discounts on a hotel's official rack rate by booking through online hotel booking agencies such as Booking.com, expedia.com and the useful Indian-only www.goibibo.com. Note that these do not always offer the best rate – it still pays to call the hotel and check the best price they can offer.

Off-season rates Large reductions are made by hotels in all categories out-of-season in many resorts. Always ask if any is available. You may also request the 10-15% agent's commission to be deducted from your bill if you book direct. Clarify whether the agreed figure includes all taxes.

Taxes In general most hotel rooms rated at Rs 3000 or above are subject to a tax of 10%. Many states levy an additional luxury tax of 10-25%, and some hotels add a service charge of 10% on top of this. Taxes are not necessarily payable on meals, so it is worth settling your meals bill separately. Most hotels in the **$$** category and above accept payment by credit card. Check your final bill carefully. Visitors have complained of incorrect bills, even in the most expensive hotels. The problem particularly afflicts groups, when last-minute extras appear mysteriously on some guests' bills. Check the evening before departure, and keep all receipts.

Facilities   You have to be prepared for difficulties which are uncommon in the West. It is best to inspect the room and check that all equipment (air conditioning, TV, water heater, flush) works before checking in at a modest hotel. Many hotels try to wring too many years' service out of their linen, and it's quite common to find sheets that are stained, frayed or riddled with holes. Don't expect any but the most expensive or tourist-savvy hotels to fit a top sheet to the bed.

In some states power cuts are common, or hot water may be restricted to certain times of day. The largest hotels have their own generators but it is best to carry a good torch. Don't be too surprised by intermittent Wi-Fi connection.

In some regions water supply is rationed periodically. Keep a bucket filled to use for flushing the toilet during water cuts. Occasionally, tap water may be discoloured due to rusty tanks. During the cold weather and in hill stations, hot water will be available at certain times of the day, sometimes in buckets, but is usually very restricted in quantity. Electric water heaters may provide enough for a shower but not enough to fill a bath tub. For details on drinking water, see below.

Hotels close to temples can be very noisy, especially during festivals. Music blares from loudspeakers late at night and from very early in the morning, often making sleep impossible. Mosques call the faithful to prayers at dawn. Some find ear plugs helpful.

Some hotels offer 24-hour checkout, meaning you can keep the room a full 24 hours from the time you arrive – a great option if you arrive in the afternoon and want to spend the morning sightseeing.

Homestays
At the upmarket end, increasing numbers of travellers are keen to stay in private homes and guesthouses, opting not to book large hotel chains that keep you at arm's length from a culture. Instead, travellers get home-cooked meals in heritage houses and learn about a country through conversation with often fascinating hosts. Kerala in particular has embraced the homestay model – though the term is increasingly abused as a marketing term by small hotels – while Delhi and Chennai have a number of smart family-run B&Bs. Tourist offices have lists of families with more modest homestays. Companies specializing in homestays include **Home & Hospitality** ① *www.homeandhospitality.co.uk*, **MAHout** ① *www.mahoutuk.com*, and **Sundale Vacations** ① *www.sundale.com*.

Food
& drink

tandoori dishes and traditional *thalis*

Food

You find just as much variety in dishes crossing India as you would on an equivalent journey across Europe. Combinations of spices give each region its distinctive flavour.

North Indian food offers tandoori dishes, kebabs and the richer flavoursome cuisine of Lucknow and well-known dishes from the Punjab. In Bengal, there is an emphasis on fish and seafood, especially river fish, the most popular being *hilsa* and *bekti*. In Gujarat, you will find many dishes sweetened with jaggery (palm sugar), while in Himachal Pradesh familiar dishes are flavoured with buttermilk.

The South has given rise to a particularly wide variety of cuisine. Most ubiquitous are the humble snacks that appear on the menu in South Indian cafés the length and breadth of India: *masala dosa*, a crispy rice pancake folded over and stuffed with a lightly spiced potato filling; *uttapam*, a cross between a pancake and a pizza, topped with tomato and onion or slices of banana; and *iddli*, soft steamed rice cakes served with a spicy stew called *sambar* and coconut chutney. Every town in the south has a slew of places serving these staples, and for less than US$1 you can fuel yourself up for a full morning's sightseeing.

Vegetarian food is prevalent throughout India. Along the Kerala coast, with its largely Christian and Muslim population, you'll find excellent seafood and fish dishes, which might be served grilled or stewed in a potent coconut-laden curry with tapioca. Goa, meanwhile, is the birthplace of the vindaloo – a more subtle, sweet-sour ancestor to the highly flammable offerings found in your local curry house – and also does a nice line in Portuguese pastries. And if you find yourself in Hyderabad, don't miss the opportunity to try India's most famous biryani, a succulent mound of rice and spices piled high with chunks of lamb or goat.

Throughout India the best value food comes in the shape of the traditional *thali*, known as 'meals' in the South, a complete meal served on a large stainless steel plate, or on a banana leaf in traditional Brahmin restaurants. Several preparations, placed in small bowls, surround the central serving of wholewheat chapati and rice. A typical vegetarian *thali* will include *dhal* (lentils), two or three curries (which can be quite hot) and crisp poppadums. A variety of pickles are offered – mango and lime are two of the most popular. These can be exceptionally hot, and are designed to be taken in minute quantities alongside the main dishes. Plain *dahi* (yoghurt), or *raita*, usually acts as a bland 'cooler', and there's usually a bowl of sweet *kheer* (rice pudding) to finish off.

If you're unused to spicy food, go slow. Food is often spicier when you eat with families or at local places, and certain cuisines (notably those of Andhra Pradesh, the Chettinad region of Tamil Nadu and traditional Goan) are notorious for going heavy on the chilli. Most restaurants are used to toning things down for foreign palates, so if you're worried about being overpowered, feel free to ask for the food to be made less spicy.

Food hygiene has improved immensely in recent years. However, you still need to take extra care, as flies abound and refrigeration in the hot weather may be inadequate and intermittent because of power cuts. It is safest to eat only freshly prepared food by ordering from the menu (especially meat and fish dishes). Be suspicious of salads and cut fruit, which may have been lying around for hours or washed in unpurified tap water – though salads served in top-end hotel restaurants and places primarily catering to foreigners (eg in Goa and Puducherry) can offer a blissful break from heavily spiced curries.

Choosing a good restaurant can be tricky if you're new to India. Many local eateries sport a grimy look that can be off-putting, yet serve brilliant and safe food, while swish four-star hotel restaurants that attract large numbers of tourists can dish up buffet food that leaves you crawling to the bathroom at midnight. A large crowd of locals is always a good sign that the food is freshly cooked and good. Even fly-blown *dhabas* on the roadside can be safe, as long as you stick to freshly cooked meals and avoid timebombs like deep-fried samosas left in the sun for hours.

Sunday brunch buffets are becoming increasingly popular in big cities and from Delhi to Goa you can find restaurants run by celebrity chefs.

Many city restaurants and backpacker eateries offer a choice of so-called European options such as toasted sandwiches, stuffed pancakes, apple pies, fruit crumbles and cheesecakes. Italian favourites (pizzas, pastas) can be very different from what you are used to. Ice creams, on the other hand, can be exceptionally good; there are excellent Indian ones as well as some international brands.

India has many delicious tropical fruits. Some are seasonal (eg mangoes, pineapples and lychees), while others (eg bananas, grapes and oranges) are available throughout the year. It is safe to eat the ones you can wash and peel. Up in the mountains, plums and apricots are in abundance.

Don't leave India without trying its superb range of indigenous sweets. *Srikhand* is a popular dessert in Maharashtra, and is a thick yoghurt laden with sugar, while a piece or two of milk-based *peda* or Mysore *pak* make a perfect sweet postscript to a cheap dinner. *Kheer* (rice pudding) and *kulfi* (Indian ice cream) are popular across the country.

Drink

Drinking water used to be regarded as one of India's biggest hazards. It is still true that water from the tap or a well should never be considered safe to drink since public water supplies are often polluted. Bottled water is now widely available although not all bottled water is mineral water; most are simply purified water from an urban supply. Buy from a shop or stall, check the seal carefully and avoid street hawkers; when disposing bottles puncture the neck which prevents misuse but allows recycling.

There is growing concern over the mountains of plastic bottles that are collecting and the waste of resources needed to produce them, so travellers are being encouraged to carry their own bottles and take a portable water filter. It is important to use pure water for cleaning teeth.

Tea and coffee are safe and widely available. Both are normally served sweet, and with milk. If you wish, say 'no sugar' (*chini nahin*), 'no milk' (*dudh nahin*) when ordering. Alternatively, ask for a pot of tea and milk and sugar to be brought separately. Freshly brewed coffee is a common drink in South India, but in the North, ordinary city restaurants will usually serve the instant variety. Even in aspiring smart cafés, espresso or cappuccino may not turn out quite as you'd expect in the West.

Bottled soft drinks such as Coke, Pepsi, Teem, Limca and Thums Up are universally available but always check the seal when you buy from a street stall. There are also several brands of fruit juice sold in cartons, including mango, pineapple and apple – Indian brands are very sweet. Don't add ice cubes as the water source may be contaminated. Take care with fresh fruit juices or *lassis* as ice is often added. It's well worth trying *lassis*; especially famous are saffron *lassis* in Rajasthan.

Two masala dosai and a pot of tea

One traveller to Ooty reported that a hotel bar had closed, apparently permanently. He found, however, that it was still possible to obtain alcoholic drinks from the restaurant. Having ordered and been served a beer, he was intrigued that when the bill came it was made out for "two masala dosai". The price was, of course, correct for the beer.

Another traveller found that a well-known hotel in the heart of New Delhi also appeared to have been forced to adapt its attitude to serving alcohol to the prevailing laws. Asked in the early evening for a double whisky the barman was very happy to comply until he was asked to serve it in the garden. On being told that he could only drink it in the bar the visitor expressed great disappointment, on which the barman relented, whispering that if the visitor really wanted to drink it outside he would serve it to him in a tea pot.

If you are thirsting for alcohol in a prohibitionist area perhaps you need to order two masala dosai and a pot of tea.

Keeping hydrated in the heat is important, coconut water is widely available, especially in the southern states. Another good option for rehydration is a sweet/salted lime soda.

Indians rarely drink alcohol with a meal. In the past wines and spirits were generally either imported and extremely expensive, or local and of poor quality. Now, the best Indian whisky, rum and brandy (IMFL or 'Indian Made Foreign Liquor') are widely accepted, as are good Champenoise and other wines from Maharashtra. If you hanker after a bottle of imported wine, you will only find it in the top restaurants or specialist liquor stores for at least Rs 1000.

For the urban elite, refreshing Indian beers are popular when eating out and so are widely available. Pubs have sprung up in the major cities, with Bengaluru in particular nurturing a growing number of craft brewpubs. Elsewhere, seedy, all-male drinking dens in the larger cities are best avoided for women travellers, but can make quite an experience otherwise – you will sometimes be locked into cubicles for clandestine drinking. If that sounds unsavoury then head for the better hotel bars instead; prices aren't that steep. In rural India, local rice, palm, cashew or date juice *toddy* and *arak* is deceptively potent.

Most states have alcohol-free dry days or enforce degrees of Prohibition, while in Gujarat you have to obtain a permit in order to drink alcohol. Some upmarket restaurants may serve beer even if it's not listed, so it's worth asking. You might be served beer in a tea pot. In some states there are government approved wine shops where you buy your alcohol through a metal grille. For information on liquor permits, see page 1392.

Menu reader

Meat and fish
chicken *murgh*
fish *macchli*
meat *gosht, mas*
prawns *jhinga*

Vegetables (sabzi)
aubergine *baingan*
cabbage *band gobi*
carrots *gajar*
cauliflower *phool gobi*
mushroom *khumbhi*
onion *piaz*
okra, ladies' fingers *bhindi*
peas *matar*
potato *aloo*
spinach *sag*

Styles of cooking
bhoona in a thick, fairly spicy sauce
chops minced meat, fish or vegetables, covered with mashed potato, crumbed and fried
cutlet minced meat, fish, vegetables formed into flat rounds or ovals, crumbed and fried (eg prawn cutlet, flattened king prawn)
dopiaza with onions (added twice during cooking)
dum pukht steam baked
jhal frazi spicy, hot sauce with tomatoes and chillies
jhol thin gravy (Bengali)
Kashmiri cooked with mild spices, ground almonds and yoghurt, often with fruit
kebab skewered (or minced and shaped) meat or fish; a dry spicy dish cooked on a fire
kima minced meat (usually 'mutton')
kofta minced meat or vegetable balls
korma in fairly mild rich sauce using cream/yoghurt
masala marinated in spices (fairly hot)
Madras hot
makhani in butter rich sauce

moli South Indian dishes cooked in coconut milk and green chilli sauce
Mughlai rich North Indian style
Nargisi dish using boiled eggs
navratan curry ('9 jewels') colourful mixed vegetables and fruit in mild sauce
Peshwari rich with dried fruit and nuts (northwest Indian)
tandoori baked in a tandoor (special clay oven) or one imitating it
tikka marinated meat pieces, baked quite dry
vindaloo hot and sour Goan meat dish using vinegar

Typical dishes
aloo gosht potato and mutton stew
aloo gobi dry potato and cauliflower with cumin
aloo, matar, kumbhi potato, peas, mushrooms in a dryish mildly spicy sauce
bhindi bhaji okra fried with onions and mild spices
boti kebab marinated pieces of meat, skewered and cooked over a fire
dhal makhani lentils cooked with butter
dum aloo potato curry with a spicy yoghurt, tomato and onion sauce
matar panir curd cheese cubes with peas and spices (and often tomatoes)
murgh massallam chicken in creamy marinade of yoghurt, spices and herbs with nuts
nargisi kofta boiled eggs covered in minced lamb, cooked in a thick sauce
rogan josh rich, mutton/beef pieces in creamy, red sauce
sag panir drained curd (*panir*) sautéed with chopped spinach in mild spices
sarson-ke-sag and makkai-ki-roti mustard leaf cooked dry with spices served with maize flour roti from Punjab
shabdeg a special Mughlai mutton dish with vegetables
yakhni lamb stew

Rice

bhat/sada chawal plain boiled rice
biriyani partially cooked rice layered over meat and baked with saffron
khichari rice and lentils cooked with turmeric and other spices
pulao/pilau fried rice cooked with spices (cloves, cardamom, cinnamon) with dried fruit, nuts or vegetables. Sometimes cooked with meat, like a biriyani

Roti – breads

chapati (roti) thin, plain, wholemeal unleavened bread cooked on a *tawa* (griddle), usually made from *ata* (wheat flour). Makkaikiroti is with maize flour.
nan oven baked (traditionally in a tandoor) white flour leavened bread often large and triangular; sometimes stuffed with almonds and dried fruit
paratha fried bread layered with *ghi* (sometimes cooked with egg or with potatoes)
poori thin deep-fried, puffed rounds of flour

Sweets

These are often made with reduced/thickened milk, drained curd cheese or powdered lentils and nuts. They are sometimes covered with a flimsy sheet of decorative, edible silver leaf.

barfi fudge-like rectangles/diamonds
gulab jamun dark fried spongy balls, soaked in syrup
halwa rich sweet made from cereal, fruit, vegetable, nuts and sugar
khir, payasam, paesh thickened milk rice/vermicelli pudding

kulfi cone-shaped Indian ice cream with pistachios/almonds, uneven in texture
jalebi spirals of fried batter soaked in syrup
laddoo lentil-based batter 'grains' shaped into rounds
rasgulla (roshgulla) balls of curd in clear syrup
sandesh dry sweet made of curd cheese

Snacks

bhaji, pakora vegetable fritters (onions, potatoes, cauliflower, etc) deep-fried in batter
chat sweet and sour fruit and vegetables flavoured with tamarind paste and chillies
chana choor, chioora ('Bombay mix') lentil and flattened rice snacks mixed with nuts and dried fruit
dosai South Indian pancake made with rice and lentil flour; served with a mild potato and onion filling (*masala dosai*) or without (*ravai* or plain *dosai*)
iddli steamed South Indian rice cakes, a bland breakfast given flavour by spiced accompaniments
kachori fried pastry rounds stuffed with spiced lentil/peas/potato filling
samosa cooked vegetable or meat wrapped in pastry triangles and deep fried
utthappam thick South Indian rice and lentil flour pancake cooked with spices/onions/ tomatoes
vadai deep fried, small savoury lentil 'doughnut' rings. *Dahi vada* are similar rounds in yoghurt

Delhi

Delhi can take you aback with its vibrancy and growth. Less than 70 years ago the spacious, quiet and planned New Delhi was still the pride of late colonial British India, while the lanes of Old Delhi resonated with the sounds of a bustling medieval market.

Old and new, simple and sophisticated, traditional and modern, East and West are juxtaposed in Old and New Delhi. Close to New Delhi Railway Station, the cheap hotels and guesthouses of Paharganj squeeze between cloth merchants and wholesalers. Old Delhi, further north, with the Red Fort and Jama Masjid, is still a dense network of narrow alleys, tightly packed markets, noise, smells and apparent chaos. Another area comprises the remorselessly growing squatter settlements (*jhuggies*), which provide shelter for more than a third of Delhi's population. To the south is a newer, chrome-and-glass city of the modern suburbs, where the rural areas of Gurgaon have become the preserve of the prosperous, with shopping malls, banks and private housing estates.

Whatever India you are looking for, the capital has it all: getting lost in warrens of crowded streets and spice markets, eating kebabs by the beautiful Jama Masjid, lazing among Mogul ruins, listening to Sufi musicians by a shrine at dusk or shopping in giant shining malls, drinking cocktails in glitzy bars and travelling on the gleaming Metro.

Best for
Architecture ■ Markets ■ Museums

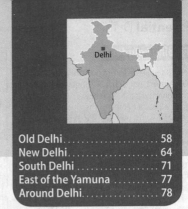

Footprint
picks

★ **Chandni Chowk and the bazars**, page 63

Take a bicycle rickshaw along the atmospheric Chandni Chowk to visit the narrow alleys, mosques and food stalls.

★ **Jama Masjid**, page 63

Don't miss the superb views from the minaret at Jama Masjid, the biggest mosque in India.

★ **Gurudwara Bangla Sahib**, page 70

Come for sunset prayers at this beautiful Sikh temple with a large water tank; it's magical.

★ **Lodi Gardens**, page 71

Escape the mid-city madness at this cool oasis and then go for lunch at Khan Market.

★ **Hauz Khaz village**, page 73

Visit the ruins of Delhi's oldest university and the deer park, and sample tastes from around the world at the many restaurants in Hauz Khas village.

★ **Qutb Minar Complex**, page 73

Close to the roots of Delhi's first city, this complex has stunning architecture and the Victory Tower.

Essential Delhi

Finding your feet

Delhi is served by **Indira Gandhi International (IGI) Airport**, which handles both international and domestic traffic. The new T3 (International Terminal) is connected to the city centre by Metro, taking 20 minutes. It is about 23 km from the centre, taking 30-45 minutes from the Domestic Terminal and 45-60 minutes from the International Terminal by road in the day. A free shuttle runs between the terminals. Alternatively, take a pre-paid taxi (see Transport, page 92), an airport coach, or ask your hotel to collect you.

The **Inter State Bus Terminus (ISBT)** is at Kashmere Gate, near the Red Fort, about 30 minutes by bus from Connaught Place.

There are three main railway stations. The busy **New Delhi Station**, a 10-minute walk north of Connaught Place, can be maddeningly chaotic; you need to have all your wits about you. The quieter **Hazrat Nizamuddin** is 5 km southeast of Connaught Place. The overpoweringly crowded **Old Delhi Station** (2 km north of Connaught Place) has a few important train connections.

Orientation

The sights are grouped in three main areas. In the centre is the British-built capital of New Delhi, with its government buildings, wide avenues and Connaught Place: New Delhi's centre and a hub of colonial England with restaurants and shops. New Delhi Railway Station and the main backpackers' area, Paharganj, are also here. Running due south of Connaught Place is Janpath, with hotels and small craft shops, and intersected by Rajpath with major state buildings at its western end. Immediately south is the diplomatic enclave, Chanakyapuri. Most upmarket hotels are scattered across the wide area between Connaught Place and the airport.

About 2 km north of Connaught Circus, the heart of Shahjahanabad (Old Delhi) has the Red Fort and Jama Masjid. Chandni Chowk, the main commercial area, heads west from the fort. Around this area are narrow lanes packed with all different types of wares for sale.

As Delhi's centre of gravity has shifted southwards, new markets have emerged for the South Extension, Greater Kailash and Safdarjang Enclave housing colonies. This development has brought a major historic site, the Qutb Minar complex, within the city limits, about 15 km south of Connaught Place. The old fortress city of Tughluqabad is 8 km east of Qutb Minar.

East of the centre across Yamuna River is the remarkable new Akshardham Temple.

Footprint picks

1 **Chandni Chowk and the bazars**, page 63
2 **Jama Masjid**, page 63
3 **Gurudwara Bangla Sahib**, page 70
4 **Lodi Gardens**, page 71
5 **Hauz Khaz village**, page 73
6 **Qutb Minar Complex**, page 73

Best places to eat

High Tea at the Taj Mahal Hotel, page 82
Jalebi Wala in Chandni Chowk, page 83
Indian Accent at The Manor, page 84

Getting around

Delhi is a vast city but the wide roads and new Metro has made it feel smaller. You can travel by Metro, taxi and bus (the latter only off peak). Hiring a car and driver saves much haggling with rickshaw drivers. The Metro has made the sprawling city very navigable: it's now possible to get from Connaught Place to Old Delhi in a cool five minutes; while Connaught Place to Qutb Minar takes 30 minutes, and all the way to the final stop in Gurgaon takes an hour. Auto-rickshaws and taxis are widely available. City buses are usually packed and have long queues. Fleets of radio taxis are the newest additions to Delhi's transport options.

When to go

October to March are the best months to visit, but December and January can get quite cold and foggy at night. Pollution can affect asthma sufferers and a lot of people develop respiratory problems and sore throats if they spend more than a few days in Delhi; echinacea can help. Monsoon lasts from the end of June to mid-September. May and June are very hot and dry and, with the whole city switching on its air-conditioning units, power cuts occur more frequently at this time.

Time required

At least three days to explore Old Delhi and the key museums and archaeological sites.

Best urban oases

Lodi Gardens, page 71
Deer Park at Hauz Khas Village, page 73
The Spa at the Imperial, page 80

Weather New Delhi

January	February	March	April	May	June
20°C 8°C 20mm	24°C 11°C 24mm	30°C 16°C 25mm	37°C 21°C 10mm	40°C 26°C 41mm	38°C 28°C 97mm

July	August	September	October	November	December
35°C 27°C 190mm	34°C 27°C 201mm	34°C 25°C 134mm	33°C 19°C 12mm	28°C 13°C 4mm	23°C 8°C 10mm

narrow alleys, teeming bazars and impressive Mughal monuments

Shah Jahan (ruled 1628-1658) decided to move back from Agra to Delhi in 1638. Within 10 years the huge city of Shahjahanabad, now known as Old Delhi, was built. The plan of Shah Jahan's new city symbolized the link between religious authority enshrined in the Jama Masjid and political authority represented by the Diwan-i-Am in the Fort.

Shahjahanabad was laid out in blocks with wide roads, residential quarters, bazars and mosques. Its principal street, Chandni Chowk, had a tree-lined canal flowing down its centre which became renowned throughout Asia. The canal is long gone, but there is a jumble of shops, alleys crammed with craftsmen's workshops, food stalls, mosques and temples.

The city was protected by rubble-built walls, some of which still survive. These walls were pierced by 14 main gates. The Ajmeri Gate, Turkman Gate (often referred to by auto-rickshaw wallahs as 'Truckman Gate'), Kashmere Gate and Delhi Gate still survive.

Red Fort (Lal Qila) *See plan, page 62.*
Tue-Sun sunrise to sunset, Rs 250 foreigners, Rs 15 Indians, allow 1 hr. The entrance is through the Lahore Gate (nearest the car park) with the admission kiosk opposite; keep your ticket as you will need to show it at the Drum House. There are new toilets inside, best to avoid the ones in Chatta Chowk. You must remove shoes and cover all exposed flesh from your shoulders to your legs.

Between the new city and the River Yamuna, Shah Jahan built a fort. Most of it was built out of red *lal* (sandstone), hence the name **Lal Qila** (Red Fort), the same as that at Agra on which the Delhi Fort is modelled. Begun in 1639 and completed in 1648, it is said to have cost Rs 10 million, much of which was spent on the opulent marble palaces within. In recent years much effort has been put into improving the fort and gardens, but visitors may be saddened by the neglected state of some of the buildings, and the gun-wielding soldiers lolling around do nothing to improve the ambience. However, despite the modern development of roads and shops and the never-ending traffic, it's an impressive site.

The approach The entrance is by the Lahore Gate. The defensive barbican that juts out in front of it was built by Aurangzeb. A common story suggests that Aurangzeb built the curtain wall to save his nobles and visiting dignitaries from having to walk – and bow – the whole length of Chandni Chowk, for no one was allowed to ride in the presence of the emperor. When the emperor sat in the Diwan-i-Am he could see all the way down the chowk, so the addition must have been greatly welcomed by his courtiers. The new entrance arrangement also made an attacking army more vulnerable to the defenders on the walls.

Chatta Chowk and the Naubat Khana Inside is the **Covered Bazar**, which was quite exceptional in the 17th century. In Shah Jahan's time there were shops on both upper and lower levels. Originally they catered for the Imperial household and carried stocks of silks, brocades, velvets, gold and silverware, jewellery and gems. There were coffee shops too for nobles and courtiers.

The **Naqqar Khana** or **Naubat Khana** (Drum House or music gallery) marked the entrance to the inner apartments of the fort. Here everyone except the princes of the royal family had to dismount and leave their horses or *hathi* (elephants), hence its other name of **Hathi Pol** (Elephant Gate). Five times a day ceremonial music was played on the kettle drum, *shahnais* (a kind of oboe) and cymbals, glorifying the emperor. In 1754 Emperor Ahmad Shah was murdered here. The gateway with four floors is decorated with floral designs. You can still see traces of the original panels painted in gold or other colours on the interior of the gateway.

Diwan-i-Am Between the first inner court and the royal palaces at the heart of the fort, stood the **Diwan-i-Am** (Hall of Public Audience), the furthest point a normal visitor would reach. It has seen many dramatic events, including the destructive whirlwind of the Persian Nadir Shah in 1739 and of Ahmad Shah the Afghan in 1756, and the trial of the last 'King of Delhi', **Bahadur Shah II** in 1858.

ON THE ROAD

A gift from Florence?

There are 318 Florentine pietra dura plaques in the niche behind the throne in the Diwan-i-Am (see page 58), showing flowers, birds and lions as well as the central figure of Orpheus, playing to the beasts. In between these Italian panels are Mughal pietra dura works with flowery arabesques and birds. Ebba Koch argues that the techniques employed by the Mughal artisans are exactly the same as the Italian ones, so there must have been a direct connection.

This is not to say that there was no independent development of Mughal inlay craftsmanship. Such a view has been described by Tillotson as the result of wishful thinking by Europeans, eager to claim a stake in the superb work. In fact the Mughals had an equally fine tradition of stone carving and of inlay work on which to draw as the Florentine princes, as can be seen from the work in the Jama Masjid in Ahmedabad, built in 1414.

The well-proportioned hall was both a functional building and a showpiece intended to hint at the opulence of the palace itself. In Shah Jahan's time the sandstone was hidden behind a very thin layer of white polished plaster, *chunam*. This was decorated with floral motifs in many colours, especially gilt. Silk carpets and heavy curtains hung from the canopy rings outside the building; such interiors were reminders of the Mughals' nomadic origins in Central Asia, where royal durbars were held in tents.

At the back of the hall is a platform for the emperor's throne. Around this was a gold railing, within which stood the princes and great nobles separated from the lesser nobles inside the hall. Behind the throne canopy are 12 marble panels inlaid with motifs of fruiting trees, parrots and cuckoos. Figurative workmanship is very unusual in Islamic buildings, and these panels are the only example in the Red Fort.

Shah Jahan spent two hours a day in the Diwan-i-Am. According to Bernie, the French traveller, the emperor would enter to a fanfare and mount the throne by a flight of movable steps. As well as matters of official administration, Shah Jahan would listen to accounts of illness, dream interpretations and anecdotes from his ministers and nobles. Wednesday was the day of judgement. Sentences were often swift and brutal and sometimes the punishment of dismemberment, beating or death was carried out on the spot. The executioners were close at hand with axes and whips. On Friday, the Muslim holy day, there would be no business.

Inner palace buildings Behind the Diwan-i-Am is the private enclosure of the fort. Along the east wall, overlooking the River Yamuna, Shah Jahan set six small palaces (five survive). Also within this compound are the Harem, the Life-Bestowing Garden and the Nahr-i-Bihisht (Stream of Paradise).

Life-Bestowing Gardens (Hayat Baksh Bagh) The original gardens were landscaped according to the Islamic principles of the Persian *char bagh*, with pavilions, fountains and water courses dividing the garden into various but regular beds. The two pavilions **Sawan** and **Bhadon**, named after the first two months of the rainy season (July-August), reveal something of the character of the garden. The garden used to create the effect of the monsoon and contemporary accounts tell us that in the pavilions – some of which were especially erected for the **Teej** festival, which marks the arrival of the monsoon – the royal ladies would sit in silver swings and watch the rains. Water flowed from the back wall of the pavilion through a slit above the marble shelf and over the niches in the wall. Gold and silver pots of flowers were placed in these alcoves during the day whilst at night candles were lit to create a glistening and colourful effect.

Shahi Burj From the pavilion next to the Shahi Burj (**Royal Tower**) the canal known as the **Nahr-i-Bihisht** (Stream of Paradise) began its journey along the Royal Terrace. The three-storey octagonal tower was seriously damaged in 1857 and is still unsafe. In Shah Jahan's time the Yamuna lapped the walls. Shah Jahan used the tower as his most private office and only his sons and a few senior ministers were allowed with him.

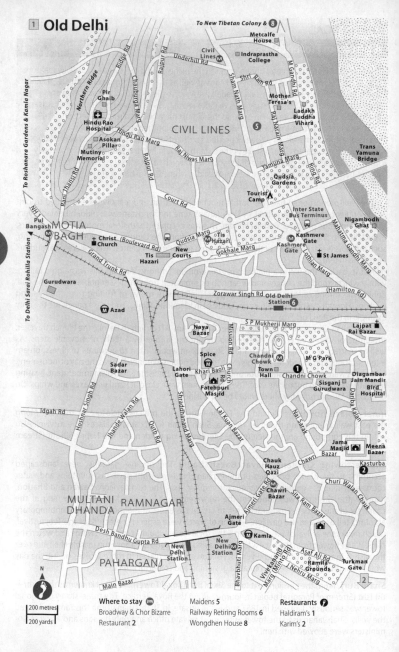

To New Tibetan Colony & 8

Metcalfe
House

Civil
Lines Ⓜ

Underhill Rd

Indraprastha
College

Sham Nath Marg

Shri Ram Rd

M Gandhi Rd

Ridge Rd

Chauburja Marg

Raipur Rd

Pir
Ghaib

Northern Ridge

Mother
Teresa's

Ladakh
Buddha
Vihara

Raj Narain Marg

5

Hindu Rao
Hospital

Hindu Rao Marg

CIVIL LINES

Asokan
Pillar

Rai Niwas Marg

Mutiny
Memorial

Raipur Rd

Trans
Yamuna
Bridge

Rani Jhansi Rd

Yamuna Marg

Court Rd

Qudsia
Gardens

Ring Rd

Tourist
Camp

Inter State
Bus Terminus

Nigambodh
Ghat

NH 1

Pul
Bangash Ⓜ

MOTIA
BAGH

To Roshanara Gardens & Kamla Nagar

To Delhi Sarai Rohilla Station

Christ
Church

Qudsia Marg

(Boulevard Rd)

Tis
Hazari

Kashmere
Gate

Kashmere
Gate

St James

Lothian Marg

Mahatma Gandhi Marg

Grand Trunk Rd

Tis
Hazari

New
Courts

Gokhale Marg

Gurudwara

Ⓜ Azad

Zorawar Singh Rd

Old Delhi
Station 6

(Hamilton Rd)

Lajpat
Rai Bazar

S P Mukherji Marg

Naya
Bazar

Mission Rd

Spice

Sadar
Bazar

Lahori
Gate

Khari Baoli

Church Rd

Chandni
Chowk Ⓜ

Town
Hall 1

Chandni Chowk

M G Park

Digambar
Jain Mandir
Bird
Hospital

Hoshiar Singh Rd

Fatehpuri
Masjid

Sisganj
Gurudwara

Daribe Kalan

Idgah Rd

Jhande Walan Rd

Qutb Rd

Shradhanand Marg

Lal Kuan Bazar

Nai Sarak

Jama
Masjid

Meena
Bazar

Chawri
Bazar

Kasturba

Chauk
Hauz
Qazi

Chawri
Bazar

Sita Ram Bazar

Churi Walan Chauk

MULTANI
DHANDA

RAMNAGAR

Ajmeri Gate Rd

Ajmeri
Gate

Desh Bandhu Gupta Rd

New
Delhi
Station

New
Delhi Ⓜ
Station

Ⓜ Kamla

Bhavbhuti Marg

Asaf Ali Rd

Turkman
Gate

Vivekanand Marg (Minto Rd)

Ramlila
Grounds

J Nehru Marg

2

PAHARGANJ

Main Bazar

N

200 metres
200 yards

Where to stay 🛏
Broadway & Chor Bizarre
Restaurant 2

Maidens 5
Railway Retiring Rooms 6
Wongdhen House 8

Restaurants 🍴
Haldiram's 1
Karim's 2

➡ **Delhi maps**
1 Old Delhi, page 60
2 New Delhi, page 66
3 Connaught Place, page 70

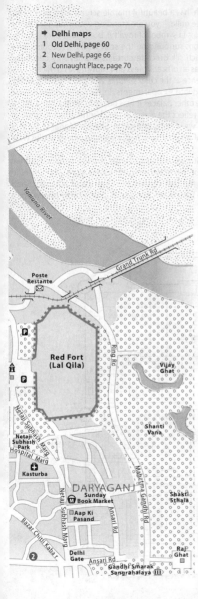

Moti Masjid To the right are the three marble domes of Aurangzeb's 'Pearl Mosque' (shoes must be removed). Bar the cupolas, it is completely hidden behind a wall of red sandstone, now painted white. Built in 1662 of polished white marble, it has some exquisite decoration. All the surfaces are highly decorated in a fashion similar to rococo, which developed at the same time as in Europe. Unusually the prayer hall is on a raised platform with inlaid outlines of individual *musallas* ('prayer mats') in black marble. While the outer walls were aligned to the cardinal points like all the other fort buildings, the inner walls were positioned so that the mosque would correctly face Mecca.

Hammam The **Royal Baths** have three apartments separated by corridors with canals to carry water to each room. The two flanking the entrance, for the royal children, had hot and cold baths. The room furthest away from the door has three basins for rose water fountains.

Diwan-i-Khas Beyond is the single-storeyed **Hall of Private Audience**, topped by four Hindu-style *chhattris* and built completely of white marble. The *dado* (lower part of the wall) on the interior was richly decorated with inlaid precious and semi-precious stones. The ceiling was silver but was removed by the Marathas in 1760. Outside, the hall used to have a marble pavement and an arcaded court. Both have gone.

This was the Mughal office of state. Shah Jahan spent two hours here before retiring for a meal, siesta and prayers. In the evening he would return to the hall for more work before going to the harem. The hall's splendour moved the 14th-century poet Amir Khusrau to write the lines inscribed above the corner arches of the north and south walls: *"Agar Firdaus bar rue Zamin-ast/Hamin ast o Hamin ast o Hamin ast"* (If there be a paradise on earth, it is here, it is here, it is here).

Royal palaces Next to the Diwan-i-Khas is the three-roomed **Khas Mahal** (Private Palace). Nearest the Diwan-i-Khas is the **Tasbih Khana** (Chamber for the Telling of Rosaries) where the emperor would worship privately with his rosary of 99 beads, one for each of the mystical names of Allah. In the centre is the **Khwabgah** (Palace of Dreams) which gives on to the octagonal **Mussaman Burj** tower. Here Shah Jahan would be seen each morning. A balcony was added to the tower in 1809 and here George V and Queen Mary appeared in their Coronation Durbar of

1911. The **Tosh Khana** (Robe Room), to the south, has a beautiful marble screen at its north end, carved with the scales of justice above the filigree grille. If you are standing with your back to the Diwan-i-Khas you will see a host of circulating suns (a symbol of royalty), but if your back is to the next building (the Rang Mahal), you will see moons surrounding the scales. All these rooms were sumptuously decorated with fine silk carpets, rich silk brocade curtains and lavishly decorated walls. After 1857 the British used the Khas Mahal as an officer's mess and sadly it was defaced.

The **Rang Mahal** (Palace of Colours), the residence of the chief *sultana*, was also the place where the emperor ate most of his meals. It was divided into six apartments. Privacy and coolness were ensured by the use of marble *jali* screens. Like the other palaces it was beautifully decorated with a silver ceiling ornamented with golden flowers to reflect the water in the channel running through the building. The north and south apartments were both known as **Sheesh Mahal** (Palace of Mirrors) since into the ceiling were set hundreds of small mirrors. In the evening when candles were lit a starlight effect would be produced.

Through the palace ran the **Life-bestowing Stream** and at its centre is a lotus-shaped marble basin which had an ivory fountain. As might be expected in such a cloistered and cosseted environment, the ladies sometimes got bored. In the 18th century the **Empress of Jahandar Shah** sat gazing out at the river and remarked that she had never seen a boat sink. Shortly afterwards a

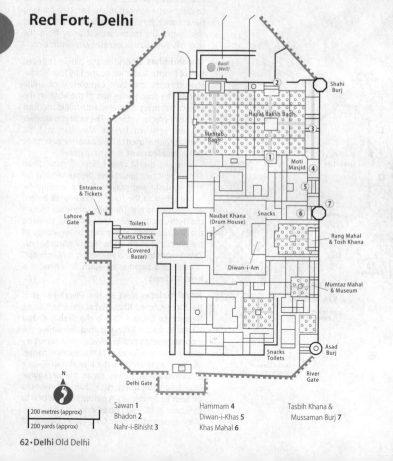

Red Fort, Delhi

Baoli (Well)

Shahi Burj

Hayat Baksh Bagh

Mehtab Bagh

Moti Masjid

Entrance & Tickets

Lahore Gate

Toilets

Chatta Chowk

(Covered Bazar)

Naubat Khana (Drum House)

Snacks

Rang Mahal & Tosh Khana

Diwan-i-Am

Mumtaz Mahal & Museum

Snacks Toilets

Asad Burj

Delhi Gate

River Gate

N

| 200 metres (approx) |
| 200 yards (approx) |

Sawan 1
Bhadon 2
Nahr-i-Bihisht 3

Hammam 4
Diwan-i-Khas 5
Khas Mahal 6

Tasbih Khana &
Mussaman Burj 7

boat was deliberately capsized so that she could be entertained by the sight of people bobbing up and down in the water crying for help.

The southernmost of the palaces, the **Mumtaz Mahal** (Palace of Jewels) ① *Tue-Sun 1000-1700*, was also used by the harem. The lower half of its walls are of marble and it contains six apartments. After the Mutiny of 1857 it was used as a guardroom and since 1912 it has been a museum with exhibits of textiles, weapons, carpets, jade and metalwork as well as works depicting life in the court. It should not be missed.

★ Chandni Chowk and the bazars

The impressive red sandstone façade of the **Digambar Jain Mandir** (temple) standing at the eastern end of Chandni Chowk, faces the Red Fort. Built in 1656, it contains an image of Adinath. The charity bird hospital (www.charitybirdshospital.org) within this compound releases the birds on recovery instead of returning them to their owners; many remain within the temple precincts. Outside the Red Fort, cycle rickshaws offer a trip to the spice market, Jama Masjid and back through the bazar. You travel slowly westwards down Chandni Chowk passing the town hall. Dismount at Church Road and follow your guide into the heart of the market on Khari Baoli where wholesalers sell every conceivable spice. Ask to go to the roof for an excellent view over the market and back towards the Red Fort. The ride back through the bazar is equally fascinating – look up at the amazing electricity system. The final excitement is getting back across Netaji Subhash Marg. Panic not, the rickshaw wallahs know what they are doing. Expect to pay about Rs 100 for a one-hour ride. The spice laden air may irritate your throat. Also ask a cycle rickshaw to take you to Naughara Street, just off Kinari Bazar; it's one of the most atmospheric streets in Delhi, full of brightly painted and slowly crumbling havelis.

★ Jama Masjid (Friday Mosque)

Visitors welcome from 30 mins after sunrise until 1215; and from 1345 until 30 mins before sunset, free, still or video cameras Rs 150, tower entry Rs 20.

The magnificent Jama Masjid is the largest mosque in India and the last great architectural work of Shah Jahan, intended to dwarf all mosques that had gone before it. With the fort, it dominates Old Delhi. The mosque is much simpler in its ornamentation than Shah Jahan's secular buildings: a judicious blend of red sandstone and white marble, which are interspersed in the domes, minarets and cusped arches.

The gateways symbolize the separation of the sacred and the secular, the threshold is a place of great importance where the worshipper steps to a higher plane. There are three huge gateways, the largest being to the east. This was reserved for the royal family who gathered in a private gallery in its upper storey. Today, the faithful enter through the east gate on Fridays and for **Id-ul-Fitr** and **Id-ul-Adha**. The latter commemorates Abraham's (Ibrahim's) sacrificial offering of his son Ishmael (Ismail). Islam (unlike the Jewish and Christian tradition) believes that Abraham offered to sacrifice Ishmael, Isaac's brother.

The courtyard The façade has the main *iwan* (arch), five smaller arches on each side with two flanking minarets and three bulbous domes behind, all perfectly proportioned. The *iwan* draws the worshippers' attention into the building. The minarets have great views from the top; well worth the climb for Rs 10 (women may not be allowed to climb alone). The **hauz**, in the centre of the courtyard, is an ablution tank placed as usual between the inner and outer parts of the building to remind the worshipper that it is through the ritual of baptism that one first enters the community of believers. The **Dikka**, in front of the ablution tank, is a raised platform. Muslim communities grew so rapidly that by the eighth century it sometimes became necessary to introduce a second *muballigh* (prayer leader) who stood on this platform and copied the postures and chants of the *imam* inside to relay them to a much larger congregation. With the introduction of the loudspeaker and amplification, the *dikka* and the *muballigh* became redundant. In the northwest corner of the mosque there is a small shed. For a small fee, the faithful are shown a hair from the beard of the prophet, as well as his sandal and his footprint in rock.

Civil Lines and Northern Ridge

Beyond Shahjahanabad to the north lies Kashmere Gate, Civil Lines and the Northern Ridge. The siting of the railway line which effectively cut Delhi into two unequal parts was done deliberately. The line brought prosperity, yet it destroyed the unity of the walled city forever. The Northern Ridge was the British cantonment and Civil Lines housed the civilians. In this area the temporary capital of the British existed from 1911-1931 until New Delhi came. The Northern Ridge is a paradise for birds and trees. Follow the **Mutiny Trail** by visiting Flagstaff Tower, Pir Ghaib, Chauburj, Mutiny Memorial. Around Kashmire Gate and Civil Lines, you can discover the Old Residency, St James Church, Nicholson's Cemetery and Qudsia Bagh.

New Delhi

tree-lined boulevards, landscaped gardens and Delhi's top museums

Delhi's present position as capital was only confirmed on 12 December 1911, when George V announced at the Delhi Durbar that the capital of India was to move from Calcutta to Delhi. The new city, New Delhi, planned under the leadership of British architect Edwin Lutyens with the assistance of his friend Herbert Baker, was inaugurated on 9 February 1931.

The city was to accommodate 70,000 people and have boundless possibilities for future expansion. The king favoured something in form and flavour similar to the Mughal masterpieces but fretted over the horrendous expense that this would incur. A petition signed by eminent public figures such as Bernard Shaw and Thomas Hardy advocated an Indian style and an Indian master builder. Herbert Baker had made known his own views even before his appointment when he wrote "first and foremost it is the spirit of British sovereignty which must be imprisoned in its stone and bronze". Lutyens himself despised Indian architecture. "Even before he had seen any examples of it", writes architectural historian Giles Tillotson, "he pronounced Mughal architecture to be 'piffle', and seeing it did not disturb that conviction". Yet in the end, Lutyens was forced to compromise.

India Gate and around

A tour of New Delhi will usually start with a visit to this war memorial, situated at the eastern end of **Rajpath**. Designed by Lutyens, it commemorates more than 70,000 Indian soldiers who died in the First World War. Some 13,516 names of British and Indian soldiers killed on the Northwest Frontier and in the Afghan War of 1919 are engraved on the arch and foundations. Under the arch is the Amar Jawan Jyoti, commemorating Indian armed forces' losses in the Indo-Pakistan War of 1971. The arch (43 m high) stands on a base of Bharatpur stone and rises in stages. Similar to the Hindu *chhattri* signifying regality, it is decorated with nautilus shells symbolizing British maritime power. Come at dusk to join the picnicking crowds enjoying the evening. You may even be able to have a pedalo ride if there's water in the canal.

National Gallery of Modern Art

Jaipur House, near India Gate, T011-2338 4640, www.ngmaindia.gov.in, Tue-Sun 1000-1700, Rs 150 foreigners, Rs 40 Indians.

There is now a new air-conditioned wing of this excellent gallery and select exhibits in the old building are housed in a former residence of the Maharaja of Jaipur. The *'In the Seeds of Time...'* exhibition traces the trajectory of modern Indian art. Artists include: Amrita Shergil, with over 100 exhibits, synthesizing the flat treatment of Indian painting with a realistic tone; Rabindranath Tagore (ground floor) with examples from a brief but intense spell in the 1930s; and The Bombay School or Company School (first floor) which includes Western painters who documented their visits to India. Realism is reflected in Indian painting of the early 19th century represented by the schools of Avadh, Patna, Sikkim and Thanjavur; The Bengal School (the late 19th-century Revivalist Movement) showcases artists such as Abanindranath Tagore and Nandalal Bose have their works exhibited here. Western influence was discarded in response to the nationalist movement.

ON THE ROAD

A Master Plan for Delhi?

A tale of two cities – anyone arriving in Delhi in the few months building up to the 2010 Commonwealth Games who got stuck in endless detours, had to dodge falling masonry in Connaught Place and negotiate piles of rubble while staring into the open fronts of buildings sliced off in Paharganj's Main Bazar would have to pinch themselves now as they arrive in the sparkly new T3 at Indira Gandhi Airport and jump on the metro into downtown Delhi.

The going did not look good at the start of the Commonwealth Games with the media reporting on the shoddy workmanship, collapsing flyovers and the words "filthy and unhygenic" imprinted in the memories of incoming travellers from all over the world. Chief Minister Sheila Dikshit announced plans to clear Delhi of 60,000 beggars in a move reminiscent of the 'beautification' dreamt up by Indira Gandhi during the state of emergency back in 1975. In the aftermath, there have been investigations into every backhander, kickback and dodgy dealing.

"When the world came visiting, we could've showcased how we manage poverty, instead of pretending it doesn't exist", says Shoma Chaudhury, managing editor of *Tehelka* magazine. "We could have showcased how we live in a proud, integrated city, instead of pretending it was a doll's house. Those who wish to turn Delhi into Dubai and Mumbai into Shanghai must remember: a great and unsustainable ugliness underpins their artificial beauty."

Thing is, the average guy on the street in India knows that their politicians are corrupt, and as they secured an unprecedented medal tally and the games closed without incident, President Pratibha Patil and Delhiites at large saw the whole shenanigans as a great success.

And beyond that Delhi is a new city post CWG. The games were a catalyst for improving the city's infrastructure. As well as T3 and the metro taking the pressure off the streets, three million new trees were planted, 1100 new low floorboard buses have taken to the avenues and the road network of Delhi has been widened and lengthened by about 25%. Surekha Narain who conducts walking tours in Delhi feels "Delhi is a much more polished city than it was".

Delhi's population is expected to exceed 23 million by 2021. In a city that averages six power cuts a day during summer, where almost half the population lacks access to an organized sewerage system, and which may have already outgrown its capacity to supply water, the recent wave of hectic growth is unlikely to prove sustainable.

The Delhi Development Authority (DDA) has released a marvellously quixotic Master Plan, which prescribes solutions to the problems of housing, land acquisition for industry and commercial developments, provision of green space, air and noise pollution, waste disposal and parking. But with 75% of Delhi already violating previous Master Plans, it is difficult to see how enforcing such a plan in the face of endemic corruption and vested interests will ever be possible.

Delhi 2050 is a think tank led by Dutch architect Anne Feenstra – they have created an exhibition of architectural models and scenarios showcasing Delhi in 35 years' time. One future scenario is a Delhi which is 'copy-paste Dubai, more inequality, less healthy, more aggression', but this is counterbalanced by four positive scenarios including 'heritage city', 'profit city' and 'self-sustained city'. Feenstra does not want to create another Master Plan, but they do want to create debate, ultimately they want to get people thinking about the future of their city.

Inspiration derived from Indian folk art is evident in the works of Jamini Roy and YD Shukla. Prints from the gallery shop are incredibly good value – up to Rs 80 for poster-size prints of famous works.

National Museum

Janpath, T011-2301 9272, www.nationalmuseumindia.gov.in, Tue-Sun 1000-1700, foreigners Rs 300 (including audio tour), Indians Rs 10, camera Rs 300; free guided tours 1030, 1130, 1200, 1400, films are screened every day (1430), marble squat toilets, but dirty.

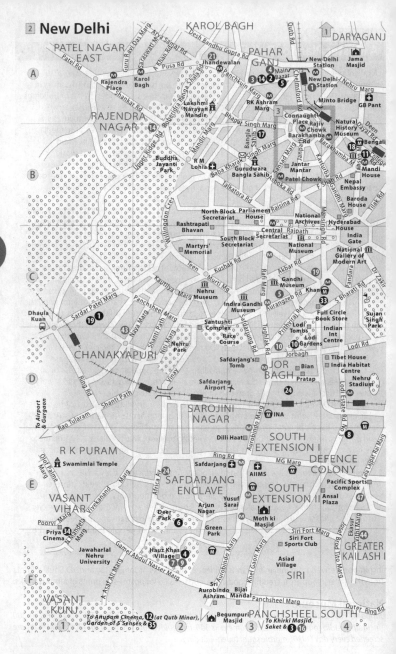

KAROL BAGH

DARYAGANJ

PATEL NAGAR
EAST

PAHAR
GANJ

Desh Bandhu Gupta Rd

Qutb Rd

New Delhi
Station

Jama
Masjid

Patel Rd

Guru Ravi Das Marg

Saraswati Rd

Arya Samaj Rd

K Bhan Rd

Pusa Rd

Jhandewalan

Panchkuin Marg

Main
Bazar

New Delhi/ Nehru Marg

New Delhi
Station

Rajendra
Place

Karol
Bagh

Shankar Rd

Lakshmi
Narayan
Mandir

RK Ashram
Marg

Minto Bridge

GB Pant

RAJENDRA
NAGAR

Bouerda Range Shala Rd

Boulevard Rd

Chelmsford Rd

Connaught
Place

Natural
History
Museum

Bengali

Bhagat Singh Marg

Rajiv
Chowk

Barakhamba
Rd

Upper Ridge Rd

Buddha
Jayanti
Park

R M
Lohia

Mandir Marg

Baba Kharak Singh Marg

Ashoka Rd

Bangla
Sahib

Gurudwara
Bangla Sahib

Jantar
Mantar

Patel Chowk

Barakhamba Rd

College

Mandi
House

Nepal
Embassy

Baroda
House

Willingdon Cres

Talkatora Rd

Raisina Rd

Sansad Marg

K G Shah Rd

K Gandhi Marg

North Block
Secretariat

Parliament
House

National
Archives

Hyderabad
House

Rashtrapati
Bhavan

South Block
Secretariat

Central
Secretariat

Rajpath

National
Museum

India
Gate

Martyrs'
Memorial

Kushak Rd

National
Gallery of
Modern Art

Teen Murti Mg

Kautilya Marg

Akbar Rd

Nehru
Museum

Raj Marg

Gandhi
Museum

Khan

Dhaula
Kuan

Sardar Patel Marg

Panchsheel Marg

Aurangzeb Rd

Full Circle
Book Store

Sujan
Singh
Park

Indira Gandhi
Museum

Prithviraj Rd

Indian
Int
Centre

CHANAKYAPURI

Nava Marg

Shanti Path

Niti Marg

Santushti
Complex

Race
Course

Nehru
Park

Safdarjung Rd

Tughlak Rd

Lodi
Tombs

Lodi
Gardens

Jorbagh

Tibet House

India Habitat
Centre

Nehru
Stadium

Safdarjang's
Tomb

JOR
BAGH

Bian

Pratap

Lodi Rd

Shanti Path

Vinay

Safdarjung
Airport

Lodi Estate Rd No 3

Rao Tularam

Ring Rd

SAROJINI
NAGAR

INA

SOUTH
EXTENSION I

R K PURAM

Olof Palme Marg

Swamimlai Temple

Dilli Haat

Aurobindo Marg

Ring Rd

MG Marg

Safdarjang

DEFENCE
COLONY

Lala Lajpat Rai Marg

Africa Av

SAFDARJANG
ENCLAVE

AIIMS

SOUTH
EXTENSION II

Pacific Sports
Complex

VASANT
VIHAR

Vivekanand Marg

Arjun
Nagar

Yusuf
Sarai

Ansal
Plaza

Poorvi Marg

Priya
Cinema

Mandela Marg

Deer
Park

Green
Park

Moth ki
Masjid

Siri Fort Marg

Siri Fort
Sports Club

GREATER
KAILASH I

Ekasur Vethi Marg

Deer Bird Tilto Marg

Jawaharlal
Nehru
University

Gamel Abdul Nasser Marg

Hauz Khas
Village

Aurobindo Marg

Asiad
Village

SIRI

VASANT
KUNJ

A Asaf Ali Marg

To Anupam Cinema, (at Qutb Minar),
Garden of 5 Senses &

Sri
Aurobindo
Ashram

Begumpuri
Masjid

Bijai
Mandal

Panchsheel Marg

Khel Gaon Marg

To Khirki Masjid,
Saket &

PANCHSHEEL SOUTH

Outer Ring Rd

➡ **Delhi maps**
1 Old Delhi, page 60
2 New Delhi, page 66
3 Connaught, page 70

N

700 metres

700 yards

Where to stay 🛏
Amarya Villa **24** E2
Claridges &
  Sevilla restaurant **5** C3
Joyti Mahal **1** A3
K One One **28** D4
Life Tree **12** E4
Lutyens Bungalow **10** D3
Manor **13** E5
Master Guest House **14** B2
Oberoi **15** C4
Prince Polonia **3** A3
Rak International **4** A3
Taj Mahal & Rick's Bar **19** C3
Tree of Life **16** F3
Yatri Paying Guest House **21** A2

Restaurants 🍽
Baci **21** C4
Bukhara **1** C1
Café Sim Tok **2** A3
Desi Roots **3** F3
Diva **15** F4
Dum Pukht **19** C1
Everest Bakery Café **5** A3
Indian Accent **13** E5
Kainoosh **34** E1
Khan Cha Cha **33** C4
Lodi **10** D3
Magique **35** F2
Naivedyam **4** F2
Nathu's & Bengali Sweet
  House **18** B4
Oh! Calcutta **16** F5

Olive at the Qutb **12** F2
Park Baluchi **6** E2
Ploof **24** D3
Sagar Ratna **8** E4
Sakura **17** B3
Tadka **14** A3
Triveni Tea Terrace **11** B4

Bars & clubs 🍸
Living Room **7** F2
Out of the Box **9** F2
Pegs-n-Pints **43** D1
Shalom **44** F4
Urban Pind **47** E4

Metro Stops (Yellow Line) Ⓜ
Metro Stops (Violet Line) Ⓜ

The collection was formed from the nucleus of the Exhibition of Indian Art, London (1947). Now merged with the Asian Antiquities Museum it displays a rich collection of the artistic treasure of Central Asia and India including ethnological objects from prehistoric archaeological finds to the late Medieval period. Replicas of exhibits and books on Indian culture and art are on sale. There is also a research library.

Ground floor Prehistoric: seals, figurines, toy animals and jewellery from the Harappan civilization (2400-1500 BC). **Maurya Period**: terracottas and stone heads from around the third century BC include the *chaturmukha* (four-faced) *lingam*. **Gandhara School**: stucco heads showing the Graeco Roman influence. **Gupta terracottas** (circa AD 400): including two life-size images of the river goddesses Ganga and Yamuna and the four-armed bust of Vishnu from a temple near Lal Kot. **South Indian sculpture**: from Pallava and early Chola temples and relief panels from Mysore. Bronzes from the Buddhist monastery at Nalanda. Some of Buddha's relics were placed in the Thai pavilion in 1997.

First floor Illustrated manuscripts: include the *Babur-i-nama* in the emperor's own handwriting and an autographed copy of Jahangir's memoirs. **Miniature paintings**: include the 16th-century Jain School, the 18th-century Rajasthani School and the Pahari schools of Garhwal, Basoli and Kangra. **Aurel Stein Collection** consists of antiquities recovered by him during his explorations of Central Asia and the western borders of China at the turn of the 20th century.

Second floor Pre-Columbian and Mayan artefacts: anthropological section devoted to tribal artefacts and folk arts. **Sharad Rani Bakkiwal Gallery of Musical Instruments**: displays over 300 instruments collected by the famous *sarod* player.

Rashtrapati Bhavan and Nehru Memorial Museum

Once the Viceroy's House, Rashtrapati Bhavan is the official residence of the President of India. The Viceroy's House, New Delhi's centrepiece of imperial proportions, was 1 km around the foundations, bigger than Louis XIV's palace at Versailles. It had a colossal dome surmounting a long colonnade and 340 rooms in all. It took nearly 20 years to complete, similar to the time it took to build the Taj Mahal. In the busiest year, 29,000 people were working on the site and buildings began to take shape. The project was surrounded by controversy from beginning to end. Opting for a fundamentally classical structure, both Baker and Lutyens sought to incorporate Indian motifs, many entirely superficial. While some claim that Lutyens achieved a unique synthesis of the two traditions, Tillotson asks whether "the sprinkling of a few simplified and classicized Indian details (especially *chhattris*) over a classical palace" could be called a synthesis. The Durbar Hall, 23 m in diameter, has coloured marble from all parts of India.

To the south is **Flagstaff House**, formerly the residence of the commander-in-chief. Renamed Teen Murti Bhawan it now houses the **Nehru Memorial Museum** ① *T011-2301 4504, Tue-Sun 1000-1500, planetarium Mon-Sat 1130-1500, library Mon-Sat 0900-1900, free*. Designed by Robert Tor Russell, in 1948 it became the official residence of India's first prime minister, Jawaharlal Nehru. Converted after his death (1964) into a national memorial, the reception, study and bedroom are intact. A *Jyoti Jawahar* (torch) symbolizes the eternal values he inspired and a granite rock is carved with extracts from his historic speech at midnight on 14 August 1947; an informative and vivid history of the Independence Movement.

The **Martyr's Memorial**, at the junction of Sardar Patel Marg and Willingdon Crescent, is a magnificent 26-m-long, 3-m-high bronze sculpture by DP Roy Chowdhury. The 11 statues of national heroes are headed by Mahatma Gandhi.

Eternal Gandhi Multimedia Museum

Birla House, 5 Tees Jan Marg (near Claridges Hotel), T011-3095 7269, www.eternalgandhi.org, closed Mon and 2nd Sat, 1000-1700, free, film at 1500.

Gandhi's last place of residence and the site of his assassination, Birla House has been converted into a whizz-bang display of 'interactive' modern technology. Over-attended by young guides eager to demonstrate the next gadget, the museum seems aimed mainly at those with a critically short attention span, and is too rushed to properly convey the story of Gandhi's life. However, a monument in the garden marking where he fell is definitely worth a visit. Other museums in the city related to Gandhi include: **National Gandhi Museum** ① *opposite Raj Ghat, T011-2331 1793, www. gandhimuseum.org, Tue-Sat 0930-1730*, with five pavilions – sculpture, photographs and paintings of Gandhi and the history of the *Satyagraha* movement (the philosophy of non-violence); **Gandhi Smarak Sangrahalaya** ① *Raj Ghat, T011-2301 1480, Fri-Wed 0930-1730*, displays some of Gandhi's personal belongings and a small library includes recordings of speeches; and the **Indira Gandhi Museum** ① *1 Safdarjang Rd, T011-2301 1358, Tue-Sun 0930-1700, free*, charting the phases of her life from childhood to the moment of her death. Exhibits are fascinating, if rather gory – you can see the blood-stained, bullet-ridden sari she was wearing when assassinated.

Parliament House and around

Northeast of the Viceroy's House is the **Council House**, now **Sansad Bhavan**. Baker designed this based on Lutyens' suggestion that it be circular (173 m diameter). Inside are the library and chambers for the Council of State, Chamber of Princes and Legislative Assembly – the **Lok Sabha**. Just opposite the Council House is the **Rakabganj Gurudwara** in Pandit Pant Marg. This 20th-century white marble shrine, which integrates the late Mughal and Rajasthani styles, marks the spot where the headless body of Guru Tegh Bahadur, the ninth Sikh Guru, was cremated in 1657. West of the Council House is the **Cathedral Church of the Redemption** (1927-1935) and to its north the Italianate Roman Catholic **Church of the Sacred Heart** (1930-1934), both conceived by Henry Medd.

Connaught Place and Connaught Circus *See map, page 70.*

Connaught Place and its outer ring, Connaught Circus (now officially named **Rajiv Chowk** and **Indira Chowk**, but still commonly referred to by their old names), comprise two-storey arcaded buildings, arranged radially around a circular garden that was completed after the Metro line was installed. Designed by Robert Tor Russell, they have become the main commercial and tourist centre of New Delhi. Sadly, the area also attracts bands of insistent touts.

Paharganj

Delhi's backpacker ghetto occupies a warren of lanes and dingy alleys immediately to the west of New Delhi Railway Station, a few hundred metres north of Connaught Circus. The crowded Main Bazar offers an instant immersion into the chaos of which India is capable, as stray cows and cycle rickshaws tangle with a throng of pedestrians, hotel touts, and salesmen hawking knock-off handbags, books and cheap clothing. Though there's little other than shopping to hold your interest, the hundreds of guesthouses here offer the greatest concentration of genuinely cheap accommodation in the city.

Northwest of Paharganj, the grid of streets comprising **Karol Bagh** contains what is, by some definitions, the biggest market in Asia. Conveniently linked to the city by Metro, the area is full of mid-range hotels, but mainly populated by Indians.

Lakshmi Narayan Mandir

To the west of Connaught Circus is the Lakshmi Narayan **Birla Temple** in Mandir Marg. Financed by the prominent industrialist Raja Baldeo Birla in 1938, this is one of the most popular Hindu shrines in the city and one of Delhi's few striking examples of Hindu architecture. Dedicated to Lakshmi, the goddess of well-being, it is commonly referred to as **Birla Mandir**. The design is in the Orissan style with tall curved *sikharas* (towers) capped by large *amalakas*. The exterior is faced with red and ochre stone and white marble. Built around a central courtyard, the main shrine has images of Narayan and his consort Lakshmi while two separate cells have icons of Siva (the Destroyer) and Durga (the 10-armed destroyer of demons). The temple is flanked by a *dharamshala* (rest house) and a Buddhist *vihara* (monastery).

★ Gurudwara Bangla Sahib
Baba Kharak Singh Rd, free.

This is a fine example of Sikh temple architecture, featuring a large pool reminiscent of Amritsar's Golden Temple. The 24-hour reciting of the Guru Granth Sahib – the Sikh holy book – adds to the atmosphere. There's free food on offer from their community kitchen, although don't be surprised if you're asked to help out with the washing up! You must remove your shoes and cover your head to enter; suitable scarves are provided if you arrive without. It is very special to come here during sunset for evening prayers.

Further northeast on Baba Kharak Singh Marg is **Hanuman Mandir**. This small temple was built by Maharaja Jai Singh II of Jaipur. **Mangal haat (Tuesday Fair)** is a popular market.

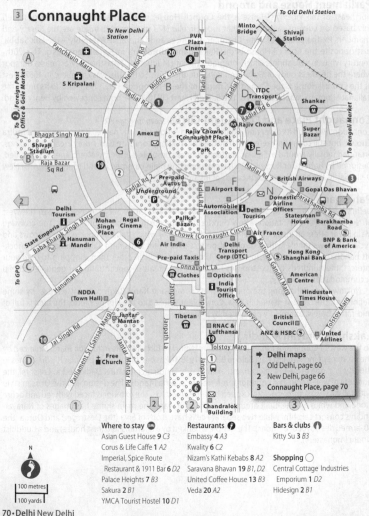

3 Connaught Place

➡ Delhi maps
1 Old Delhi, page 60
2 New Delhi, page 66
3 Connaught Place, page 70

Where to stay 🛏
Asian Guest House **9** *C3*
Corus & Life Caffe **1** *A2*
Imperial, Spice Route
Restaurant & 1911 Bar **6** *D2*
Palace Heights **7** *B3*
Sakura **2** *B1*
YMCA Tourist Hostel **10** *D1*

Restaurants 🍴
Embassy **4** *A3*
Kwality **6** *C2*
Nizam's Kathi Kebabs **8** *A2*
Saravana Bhavan **19** *B1, D2*
United Coffee House **13** *B3*
Veda **20** *A2*

Bars & clubs 🍸
Kitty Su **3** *B3*

Shopping ⚪
Central Cottage Industries
Emporium **1** *D2*
Hidesign **2** *B1*

Jantar Mantar

Just to the east of the Hanuman Mandir in Sansad Marg (Parliament Street) is Jai Singh's **observatory** (Jantar Mantar) ① *sunrise to sunset, Rs 100 foreigners, Rs 5 Indians*. The Mughal Emperor Mohammad Shah (ruled 1719-1748) entrusted the renowned astronomer Maharaja Jai Singh II with the task of revising the calendar and correcting the astronomical tables used by contemporary priests. Daily astral observations were made for years before construction began and plastered brick structures were favoured for the site instead of brass instruments. Built in 1725 it is slightly smaller than the later observatory at Jaipur.

Memorial Ghats

Beyond Delhi Gate lies the **Yamuna River**, marked by a series of memorials to India's leaders. The river itself, a kilometre away, is invisible from the road, protected by a low rise and banks of trees. The most prominent memorial, immediately opposite the end of Jawaharlal Nehru Road, is that of Mahatma Gandhi at **Raj Ghat**. To its north is **Shanti Vana** (Forest of Peace), landscaped gardens where Prime Minister Jawaharlal Nehru was cremated in 1964, as were his grandson Sanjay Gandhi in 1980, daughter Indira Gandhi in 1984 and elder grandson, Rajiv, in 1991. To the north again is **Vijay Ghat** (Victory Bank) where Prime Minister Lal Bahadur Shastri was cremated.

South Delhi

modern commercial area with some of Delhi's best historic sights

South Delhi is often overlooked by travellers. This is a real pity as it houses some of the city's most stunning sights, best accommodation, bars, clubs and restaurants, as well as some of its most tranquil parks. However be warned, South Delhi can be hell during rush hour when the traffic on the endless flyovers comes to a virtual standstill. But with the Metro, you can explore all the way down to Gurgaon with relative ease.

★ Lodi Gardens

These beautiful gardens, with mellow stone tombs of the 15th- and 16th-century Lodi rulers, are popular for gentle strolls and jogging. In the middle of the garden facing the east entrance from Max Mueller Road is **Bara Gumbad** (Big Dome), a mosque built in 1494. The raised courtyard is provided with an imposing gateway and *mehman khana* (guest rooms). The platform in the centre appears to have had a tank for ritual ablutions.

The **Sheesh Bumbad** (Glass Dome, late 15th century) is built on a raised incline north of the Bara Gumbad and was once decorated with glazed blue tiles, painted floral designs and Koranic inscriptions. The façade gives the impression of a two-storey building, typical of Lodi architecture. **Mohammad Shah's Tomb** (1450) is that of the third Sayyid ruler. It has sloping buttresses, an octagonal plan, projecting eaves and lotus patterns on the ceiling. **Sikander Lodi's Tomb**, built by his son in 1517, is also an octagonal structure decorated with Hindu motifs. A structural innovation is the double dome which was later refined under the Mughals. The 16th-century **Athpula** (Bridge of Eight Piers), near the northeastern entrance, is attributed to Nawab Bahadur, a nobleman at Akbar's court.

Safdarjang's Tomb

Sunrise to sunset, Rs 100 foreigners, Rs 5 Indians.

Safdarjang's Tomb, seldom visited, was built by Nawab Shuja-ud-Daulah for his father Mirza Mukhim Abdul Khan, entitled Safdarjang, who was Governor of Oudh (1719-1748), and Wazir of his successor (1748-1754). Safdarjang died in 1754. With its high enclosure walls, *char bagh* layout of gardens, fountain and central domed mausoleum, it follows the tradition of Humayun's tomb. Typically, the real tomb is just below ground level. Flanking the mausoleum are pavilions used by Shuja-ud-Daulah as his family residence. Immediately to its south is the battlefield where Timur and his Mongol horde crushed Mahmud Shah Tughluq on 12 December 1398.

Hazrat Nizamuddin

Dress ultra-modestly if you don't want to feel uncomfortable or cause offence.

At the east end of the Lodi Road, Hazrat Nizamuddin Dargah (Nizamuddin 'village') now tucked away behind the residential suburb of Nizamuddin West, off Mathura Road, grew up around the shrine of Sheikh Nizamuddin Aulia (1236-1325), a Chishti saint. This is a wonderfully atmospheric place. *Qawwalis* are sung at sunset after *namaaz* (prayers), and are particularly impressive on Thursdays – be prepared for crowds. Highly recommended.

West of the central shrine is the **Jama-at-khana Mosque** (1325). Its decorated arches are typical of the Khalji design also seen at the Ala'i Darwaza at the Qutb Minar. South of the main tomb and behind finely crafted screens is the grave of princess Jahanara, Shah Jahan's eldest and favourite daughter. She shared the emperor's last years when he was imprisoned at Agra Fort. The grave, open to the sky, is in accordance with the epitaph written by her: "Let naught cover my grave save the green grass, for grass suffices as the covering of the lowly". Pilgrims congregate at the shrine twice a year for the Urs (fair) held to mark the anniversaries of Hazrat Nizamuddin Aulia and his disciple Amir Khusrau, whose tomb is nearby.

Humayun's Tomb

Sunrise to sunset, Rs 250 foreigners, Rs 10 Indians, video cameras Rs 25, located in Nizamuddin, 15-20 mins by taxi from Connaught Circus, allow 45 mins.

Eclipsed later by the Taj Mahal and the Jama Masjid, this tomb is the best example in Delhi of the early Mughal style of tomb. Superbly maintained, it is well worth a visit, preferably before visiting the Taj Mahal. Humayun, the second Mughal emperor, was forced into exile in Persia after being heavily defeated by the Afghan Sher Shah in 1540. He returned to India in 1545, finally recapturing Delhi in 1555. The tomb was designed and built by his senior widow and mother of his son Akbar, Hamida Begum. A Persian from Khurasan, after her pilgrimage to Mecca she was known as Haji Begum. She supervised the entire construction of the tomb (1564-1573), camping on the site.

The plan The tomb has an octagonal plan, lofty arches, pillared kiosks and the double dome of Central Asian origin, which appears here for the first time in India. Outside Gujarat, Hindu temples make no use of the dome, but the Indian Muslim dome had until now, been of a flatter shape as opposed to the tall Persian dome rising on a more slender neck. Here also is the first standard example of the garden tomb concept: the **char bagh** (garden divided into quadrants), water channels and fountains. This form culminated in the gardens of the Taj Mahal. However, the tomb also shows a number of distinctively Hindu motifs. Tillotson has pointed out that in Humayun's tomb, Hindu *chhattris* (small domed kiosks), complete with temple columns and *chajjas* (broad eaves), surround the central dome. The bulbous finial on top of the dome and the star motif in the spandrels of the main arches are also Hindu, the latter being a solar symbol.

The approach The tomb enclosure has two high double-storeyed gateways: the entrance to the west and the other to the south. A *baradari* occupies the centre of the east wall, and a bath chamber that the north wall. Several Moghul princes, princesses and Haji Begum herself lie buried here. During the 1857 Mutiny Bahadur Shah II, the last Moghul emperor of Delhi, took shelter with his three sons. Over 80, he was seen as a figurehead by Muslims opposing the British. When captured he was transported to Yangon (Rangoon) for the remaining four years of his life. The tomb to the right of the approach is that of Isa Khan, Humayun's barber.

The dome Some 38 m high, the dome does not have the swell of the Taj Mahal and the decoration of the whole edifice is much simpler. It is of red sandstone with some white marble to highlight the lines of the building. There is some attractive inlay work, and some *jalis* in the balcony fence and on some of the recessed keel arch windows. The interior is austere and consists of three storeys of arches rising up to the dome. The emperor's tomb is of white marble and quite plain without any inscription. The overall impression is that of a much bulkier, more squat building than the Taj Mahal. The cavernous space under the main tombs is home to great colonies of bats.

★ Hauz Khas village

South of Safdarjang's Tomb, and entered off either Aurobindo Marg on the east side or Africa Avenue on the west side, is Hauz Khas. This is a great area to explore at leisure. Here you will find the heritage buildings of the **madrasa** (Delhi's oldest university), a green oasis with the **Deer Park** and the small but lovely **Delhi Art Gallery**. Labyrinthine alleys lead to numerous design studios, boutiques and restaurants. Wandering the streets of Hauz Khas village, with its boho vibe, you can almost forget that you are in India.

Ala-ud-din Khalji (ruled 1296-1313) created a large tank at Hauz Khas for the use of the inhabitants of Siri, the second capital city of Delhi founded by him. Fifty years later Firoz Shah Tughluq cleaned up the silted tank and raised several buildings on its east and south banks which are known as Hauz Khas or Royal Tank.

Firoz Shah's austere **tomb** is found here. The multi-storeyed wings, on the north and west of the tomb, were built by him in 1354 as a *madrasa* (college). The octagonal and square *chhattris* were built as tombs, possibly to the teachers at the college. Hauz Khas is now widely used as a park for early-morning recreation – walking, running and yoga *asanas*. Classical music concerts, dance performances and a *son et lumière* show are held in the evenings when monuments are illuminated by thousands of earthen lamps and torches.

★ Qutb Minar Complex See plan, page 74.

Sunrise to sunset, Rs 250 foreigners, Rs 10 Indians. The Metro goes to Qutb Minar. Bus 505 from New Delhi Railway Station (Ajmeri Gate), Super Bazar (east of Connaught Circus) and Cottage Industries Emporium, Janpath. Auto Rs 110, though drivers may be reluctant to take you. This area is also opening up as a hub for new chic restaurants and bars.

Muhammad Ghuri conquered northwest India at the very end of the 12th century. The conquest of the Gangetic plain down to Benares (Varanasi) was undertaken by Muhammad's Turkish slave and chief general, Qutb-ud-din-Aibak, whilst another general took Bihar and Bengal. In the process, temples were reduced to rubble, the remaining Buddhist centres were dealt their death blow and their monks slaughtered. When Muhammad was assassinated in 1206, his gains passed to the loyal Qutb-ud-din-Aibak. Thus the first sultans or Muslim kings of Delhi became known as the **Slave Dynasty** (1026-1290). For the next three centuries the Slave Dynasty and the succeeding Khalji (1290-1320), Tughluq (1320-1414), Sayyid (1414-1445) and Lodi (1451-1526) dynasties provided Delhi with fluctuating authority. The legacy of their ambitions survives in the tombs, forts and palaces that litter Delhi Ridge and the surrounding plain. Qutb-ud-din-Aibak died after only four years in power, but he left his mark with the **Qutb Minar** and his **citadel**. Qutb Minar, built to proclaim the victory of Islam over the infidel, dominates the countryside for miles around. Visit the *minar* first.

Qutb Minar In 1199 work began on what was intended to be the most glorious tower of victory in the world and was to be the prototype of all *minars* (towers) in India. Qutb-ud-din-Aibak had probably seen and been influenced by the brick victory pillars in Ghazni in Afghanistan, but this one was also intended to serve as the minaret attached to the Might of Islam Mosque. From here the muezzin could call the faithful to prayer. Later every mosque would incorporate its minaret.

As a mighty reminder of the importance of the ruler as Allah's representative on earth, the Qutb Minar (literally 'axis minaret') stood at the centre of the community. A pivot of Faith, Justice and Righteousness, its name also carried the message of Qutb-ud-din's (Axis of the Faith) own achievements. The inscriptions carved in Kufi script tell that "the tower was erected to cast the shadow of God over both east and west". For Qutb-ud-din-Aibak it marked the eastern limit of the empire of the One God. Its western counterpart was the Giralda Tower built by Yusuf in Seville.

The Qutb Minar is 73 m high and consists of five storeys. The diameter of the base is 14.4 m and 2.7 m at the top. Qutb-ud-din built the first three and his son-in-law Iltutmish embellished these and added a fourth. This is indicated in some of the Persian and Nagari (North Indian) inscriptions which also record that it was twice damaged by lightning in 1326 and 1368. While repairing the damage caused by the second, Firoz Shah Tughluq added a fifth storey and used marble to face the red and buff sandstone. This was the first time contrasting colours were used decoratively, later to become such a feature of Mughal buildings. Firoz's fifth storey was topped by a graceful cupola but this fell down during an earthquake in 1803. A new one was added by a Major Robert Smith in 1829 but was so out of keeping that it was removed in 1848 and now stands in the gardens.

The original storeys are heavily indented with different styles of fluting, alternately round and angular on the bottom, round on the second and angular on the third. The beautifully carved honeycomb detail beneath the balconies is reminiscent of the Alhambra Palace in Spain. The calligraphy bands are verses from the Koran and praises to its patron builder.

Quwwat-ul-Islam Mosque The Quwwat-ul-Islam Mosque (The Might of Islam Mosque), the earliest surviving mosque in India, is to the northwest of the Qutb Minar. It was begun in 1192, immediately after Qutb-ud-din's conquest of Delhi and completed in 1198, using the remains of no fewer than 27 local Hindu and Jain temples.

The architectural style contained elements that Muslims brought from Arabia, including buildings made of mud and brick and decorated with glazed tiles, *squinches* (arches set diagonally across the corners of a square chamber to facilitate the raising of a dome and to effect a transition from a square to a round structure), the pointed arch and the true dome. Finally, Muslim buildings came alive through ornamental calligraphy and geometric patterning. This was in marked contrast to indigenous Indian styles of architecture. Hindu, Buddhist and Jain buildings relied on the post-and-beam system in which spaces were traversed by corbelling, ie shaping flat-laid stones to create an arch. The arched screen that runs along the western end of the courtyard beautifully illustrates the fact that it was Hindu methods that still prevailed at this stage, for the 16-m-high arch uses Indian corbelling, the corners being smoothed off to form the curved line.

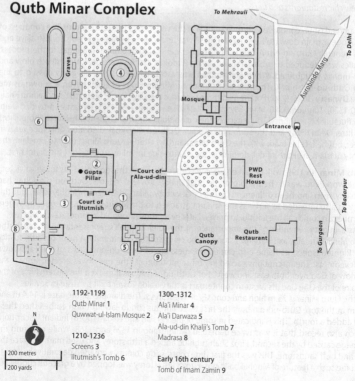

Qutb Minar Complex

1192-1199	1300-1312
Qutb Minar 1	Ala'i Minar 4
Quwwat-ul-Islam Mosque 2	Ala'i Darwaza 5
	Ala-ud-din Khalji's Tomb 7
	Madrasa 8
1210-1236	
Screens 3	Early 16th century
Iltutmish's Tomb 6	Tomb of Imam Zamin 9

200 metres
200 yards

Screens Qutb-ud-din's screen formed the façade of the mosque and, facing in the direction of Mecca, became the focal point. The sandstone screen is carved in the Indo-Islamic style, lotuses mingling with Koranic calligraphy. The later screenwork and other extensions (1230) are fundamentally Islamic in style, the flowers and leaves having been replaced by more arabesque patterns. Indian builders mainly used stone, which from the fourth century AD had been intricately carved with representations of the gods. In their first buildings in India the Muslim architects designed the buildings and local Indian craftsmen built them and decorated them with typical motifs such as the vase and foliage, tasselled ropes, bells and cows.

Iltutmish's extension The mosque was enlarged twice. In 1230 Qutb-ud-din's son-in-law and successor, Shamsuddin Iltutmish, doubled its size by extending the colonnades and prayer hall – 'Iltutmish's extension'. This accommodated a larger congregation, and in the more stable conditions of Iltutmish's reign, Islam was obviously gaining ground. The arches of the extension are nearer to the true arch and are similar to the Gothic arch that appeared in Europe at this time. The decoration is Islamic. Almost 100 years after Iltutmish's death, the mosque was enlarged again, by Ala-ud-din Khalji. The conductor of tireless and bloody military campaigns, Ala-ud-din proclaimed himself 'God's representative on earth'. His architectural ambitions, however, were not fully realized, because on his death in 1316 only part of the north and east extensions were completed.

Ala'i Minar and the Ala'i Darwaza To the north of the Qutb complex is the 26-m **Ala'i Minar**, intended to surpass the tower of the Qutb, but not completed beyond the first storey. Ala-ud-din did complete the south gateway to the building, the **Ala'i Darwaza**; inscriptions testify that it was built in 1311 (Muslim 710 AH). He benefited from events in Central Asia: since the early 13th century, Mongol hordes from Central Asia fanned out east and west, destroying the civilization of the Seljuk Turks in West Asia, and refugee artists, architects, craftsmen and poets fled east. They brought to India features and techniques that had developed in Byzantine Turkey, some of which can be seen in the Ala'i Darwaza.

The gatehouse is a large sandstone cuboid, into which are set small cusped arches with carved *jali* screens. The lavish ornamentation of geometric and floral designs in red sandstone and white marble produced a dramatic effect when viewed against the surrounding buildings.

The inner chamber (11 sq m) has doorways and, for the first time in India, true arches. Above each doorway is an Arabic inscription with its creator's name and one of his self-assumed titles – 'The Second Alexander'. The north doorway, which is the main entrance, is the most elaborately carved. The dome, raised on squinched arches, is flat and shallow. Of the effects employed, the arches with their 'lotus-bud' fringes are Seljuk, as is the dome with the rounded finial and the façade. These now became trademarks of the Khalji style, remaining virtually unchanged until their further development in Humayun's Tomb.

Iltutmish's Tomb Built in 1235, Iltutmish's Tomb lies in the northwest of the compound, midway along the west wall of the mosque. It is the first surviving tomb of a Muslim ruler in India. Two other tombs also stand within the extended Might of Islam Mosque. The idea of a tomb was quite alien to Hindus, who had been practising cremation since around 400 BC. Blending Hindu and Muslim styles, the outside is relatively plain with three arched and decorated doorways. The interior carries reminders of the nomadic origins of the first Muslim rulers. Like a Central Asian *yurt* (tent) in its decoration, it combines the familiar Indian motifs of the wheel, bell, chain and lotus with the equally familiar geometric arabesque patterning. The west wall is inset with three *mihrabs* that indicate the direction of Mecca.

The tomb originally supported a dome resting on *squinches* which you can still see. The dome collapsed (witness the slabs of stone lying around) suggesting that the technique was as yet unrefined. From the corbelled squinches it may be assumed that the dome was corbelled too, as found in contemporary Gujarat and Rajput temples. The blocks of masonry were fixed together using the Indian technology of iron dowels. In later Indo-Islamic buildings lime plaster was used for bonding.

Tughluqabad

Sunrise to sunset, foreigners Rs100, Indians Rs 5, video camera Rs 25, allow 1 hr for return rickshaws, turn right at entrance and walk 200 m. The site is often deserted so don't go alone. Take plenty of water.

Tughluqabad's ruins, 7.5 km east from Qutb Minar, still convey a sense of the power and energy of the newly arrived Muslims in India. From the walls you get a magnificent impression of the strategic advantages of the site. **Ghiyas'ud-Din Tughluq** (ruled 1321-1325), after ascending the throne of Delhi, selected this site for his capital. He built a massive fort around his capital city which stands high on a rocky outcrop of the Delhi Ridge. The fort is roughly octagonal in plan with a circumference of 6.5 km. The vast size, strength and obvious solidity of the whole give it an air of massive grandeur. It was not until Babur (ruled 1526-1530) that dynamite was used in warfare, so this is a very defensible site.

East of the main entrance is the rectangular **citadel**. A wider area immediately to the west and bounded by walls contained the **palaces**. Beyond this to the north lay the **city**. Now marked by the ruins of houses, the streets were laid out in a grid fashion. Inside the citadel enclosure is the **Vijay Mandal tower** and the remains of several halls including a long underground passage. The fort also contained seven tanks.

A causeway connects the fort with the tomb of Ghiyas'ud-Din Tughluq, while a wide embankment near its southeast corner gave access to the fortresses of **Adilabad** about 1 km away, built a little later by Ghiyas'ud-Din's son Muhammad. The tomb is very well preserved and has red sandstone walls with a pronounced slope (the first Muslim building in India to have sloping walls), crowned with a white marble dome. This dome, like that of the Ala'i Darwaza at the Qutb, is crowned by an *amalaka*, a feature of Hindu architecture. Also Hindu is the trabeate arch at the tomb's fortress wall entrance. Inside are three cenotaphs belonging to Ghiyas'ud-Din, his wife and son Muhammad.

Ghiyas'ud-Din Tughluq quickly found that military victories were no guarantee of lengthy rule. When he returned home after a victorious campaign the welcoming pavilion erected by his son and successor, Muhammad-bin Tughluq, was deliberately collapsed over him. Tughluqabad was abandoned shortly afterwards and was thus only inhabited for five years. The Tughluq dynasty continued to hold Delhi until Timur sacked it and slaughtered its inhabitants. For a brief period Tughluq power shifted to Jaunpur near Varanasi, where the Tughluq architectural traditions were carried forward in some superb mosques.

Baha'i Temple (Lotus Temple)

1 Apr-30 Sep 0900-1900, 1 Oct-31 Mar Tue-Sun 0930-1730, free entry and parking, visitors welcome to attend services, at other times the temple is open for silent meditation and prayer. Audio-visual presentations in English are at 1100, 1200, 1400 and 1530, remove shoes before entering. Bus 433 from the centre (Jantar Mantar) goes to Nehru Place, within walking distance (1.5 km) of the temple at Kalkaji, or take a taxi or auto-rickshaw.

Architecturally the Baha'i Temple is a remarkably striking building. Constructed in 1980-1981, it is built out of white marble and in the characteristic Baha'i temple shape of a lotus flower – 45 lotus petals form the walls – which internally creates a feeling of light and space (34 m high, 70 m in diameter). It is a simple design, brilliantly executed and very elegant in form. All Baha'i temples are nine-sided, symbolizing 'comprehensiveness, oneness and unity'. The Delhi Temple, which seats 1300, is surrounded by nine pools, an attractive feature also helping to keep the building cool. It is particularly attractive when flood-lit. Baha'i temples are "dedicated to the worship of God, for peoples of all races, religions or castes. Only the Holy Scriptures of the Baha'i Faith and earlier revelations are read or recited".

Fact...

The Baha'i faith was founded by a Persian, Baha'u'llah (meaning 'glory of God'; 1817-1892), who is believed to be the manifestation of God for this age. His teachings were directed towards the unification of the human race and the establishment of a permanent universal peace.

Designated as the site of the athletes' village for the 2010 Commonwealth Games, East Delhi has just one attraction to draw visitors across the Yamuna.

Swaminarayan Akshardham

www.akshardham.com, Apr-Sep Tue-Sun 1000-1900, Oct-Mar Tue-Sun 0900-1800, temple free, Rs 170 for 'attractions', musical fountain Rs 20, no backpacks, cameras or other electronic items (bag and body searches at entry gate). Packed on Sun; visit early to avoid crowds.

Opened in November 2005 on the east bank of the Yamuna, the gleaming Akshardham complex represents perhaps the most ambitious construction project in India since the foundation of New Delhi itself. At the centre of a surreal 40-ha 'cultural complex' complete with landscaped gardens, cafés and theme park rides, the temple-monument is dedicated to the 18th-century saint Bhagwan Swaminarayan, who abandoned his home at the age of 11 to embark on a lifelong quest for the spiritual and cultural uplift of Western India. It took 11,000 craftsmen, all volunteers, no less than 300 million hours to complete the temple using traditional building and carving techniques.

If this is the first religious site you visit in India, the security guards and swarms of mooching Indian tourists will hardly prepare you for the typical temple experience. Yet despite this, and the boat rides and animatronic shows which have prompted inevitable comparisons to a 'spiritual Disneyland', most visitors find the Akshardham an inspiring, indeed uplifting, experience, if for no other reason than that the will and ability to build something of its scale and complexity still exist.

The temple You enter the temple complex through a series of intricately carved gates. The Bhakti Dwar (Gate of Devotion), adorned with 208 pairs of gods and their consorts, leads into a hall introducing the life of Swaminarayan and the activities of BAPS (Bochasanwasi Shri Akshar Purushottam Swaminarayan Sanstha), the global Hindu sect-cum-charity which runs Akshardham. The main courtyard is reached through the Mayur Dwar (Peacock Gate), a conglomeration of 869 carved peacocks echoed by an equally florid replica directly facing it.

From here you get your first look at the central monument. Perfectly symmetrical in pink sandstone and white marble, it rests on a plinth encircled by 148 elephants, each sculpted from a 20-tonne stone block, in situations ranging from the literal to the mythological: mortal versions grapple with lions or lug tree trunks, while Airavatha, the eight-trunked mount of Lord Indra, surfs majestically to shore after the churning of the oceans at the dawn of Hindu creation. Above them, carvings of deities, saints and *sadhus* cover every inch of the walls and columns framing the inner sanctum, where a gold-plated *murti* (idol) of Bhagwan Swaminarayan sits attended by avatars of his spiritual successors, beneath a staggeringly intricate marble dome. Around the main dome are eight smaller domes, each carved in hypnotic fractal patterns, while paintings depicting Swaminarayan's life of austerity and service line the walls (explanations in English and Hindi).

Surrounding the temple is a moat of holy water supposedly taken from 151 sacred lakes and rivers visited by Swaminarayan on his seven-year barefoot pilgrimage. 108 bronze *gaumukhs* (cow heads) representing the 108 names of God spout water into the tank, which is itself hemmed in by a 1-km-long *parikrama* (colonnade) of red Rajasthani sandstone.

Going south

Surajkund Meaning 'sun pool', Surajkund is a perennial lake surrounded by rock-cut steps, built by the Rajput king Surajpal Tomar. According to tradition this is where the Rajputs first settled near Delhi in the 11th century AD. At the head of the reservoir, to the east, are the ruins of what is believed to have been a sun temple. A little south is Siddha Kund, a pool of freshwater trickling from a rock crevice which is said to have healing properties.

The annual **Craft Mela**, held in February, draws potters, weavers, metal and stone workers, painters, printers, wood carvers and embroiderers from all over India.

Gurgaon and Saharanpur Bird Sanctuary Eight kilometres southwest of Indira Gandhi Airport, **Gurgaon** is as good a place as any to witness the rising of the 'New India'. A succession of multinational corporations have set up call centres, offices and factories, taking advantage of cheap land and labour prices and proximity to Delhi, and this one-time rural backwater is now a mushrooming city with closer links to the USA than to the rest of India. Shopping malls, fast-food chains, hotels and nightclubs have sprouted, the yellow line of the metro extends down to three stations in Gurgaon MG Road, IFFCO terminating at Huda City. For the new extravaganza of Kingdom of Dreams, you need IFFCO station. If you feel the need to explore, it's best to visit by car or taxi.

Beyond Gurgaon, 46 km from Delhi, is the small **Saharanpur Bird Sanctuary** with a *jheel* (shallow lake) surrounded by reeds. The large and handsome Sarus, the only indigenous Indian crane, breeds here. The migratory demoiselle, the smallest member of the crane family, flock to the lakeside in winter. White (rosy) pelicans, flamingos and waders can be seen, as can indigenous birds including grey pelican, cormorant, painted stork, grey and pond heron and egret. Take a blue Haryana bus to Gurgaon from Delhi (every 10 minutes from Dhaula Khan). At Gurgaon take a Chandu bus (three to four daily) and get off at Sultanpur.

Leaving Delhi

The Delhi–Jaipur Road The NH8 is the main route between Delhi and Jaipur. Although it is very busy there are some attractive stops en route, notably **Neemrana**. Another rural escape is **Tikli**, 8 km off the Sonah road (turn off at Badshapur), about an hour's drive from Delhi towards the Aravalli Hills. Lovingly conceived by an English couple, the exclusive 'farmhouse' stands in a flower- and bird-filled garden, has an inviting pool and is a place to spoil yourself. Ask for Manender Farm, Gairatpur Bass village.

Rewari, 83 km from Delhi, was founded in AD 1000 by Raja Rawat but there are the ruins of a still older town east of the 'modern' walls. It has been a prosperous centre for the manufacture of iron and brass vessels, and now serves as a rail hub for much of Rajasthan; many trains that once ran to Delhi now start and finish here.

On a rocky outcrop just above a village is the beautiful **Neemrana Fort** ① *T01494-246006, www. neemranahotels.com*, built in 1464 by Prithvi Raj Chauhan III and converted into an exceptional hotel. It is quiet and peaceful (occasional chanting from village below), full of character and beautifully furnished with collectors' pieces. Particularly recommended are Baag, Dakshin, Jharoka, Surya Mahals, though some (eg Moonga) are a testing climb up to the seventh level. Superb Rajasthani and French cuisine is served (non-residents Rs 350, which allows looking around or you can opt for the Rs 100 tour). It has a magical atmosphere and is highly recommended; reservations essential. The village and the fort ruins above are worth exploring.

Going north *Colour map 1, C4.*

Meerut Known to this day as the place where the Indian Mutiny broke out in 1857, Meerut (phone code: 0121, population: 850,000), is a busy marketing, commercial and administrative town. It reputedly produces 80% of the world's cricket equipment. Although the old city is compact, the cantonment to the north is typically spaced out with some attractive broad tree-lined streets, including a particularly fine mall.

On 10 May 1857 the first revolt that was to end the East India Company's rule and usher in the era of the British Indian Empire rocked the streets of Meerut. However, the town's history goes back as early as Asoka's time: the modern town contains various Hindu and Muslim buildings from the 11th century onwards. The cemetery of **St John's**, the old garrison church (1821) contains interesting memorials. The **Baleshwar Nath Temple** and several old Hindu shrines surround the **Suraj Kund** tank (1714) which is fed by a canal from the Ganga. The mausolea and mosques indicate strong Mughal influence. The **Jama Masjid** (1019, later restored by Humayun), is one of the oldest in India. The red sandstone **Shah Pir Maqbara** (1628) on Hapur Road was built by the Empress Nur Jahan and further west on Delhi Road is the **Abu Maqbara**, with a large tank. Qutb-ud-din Aibak is believed to have built the maqbara of **Salar Masa-ud Ghazi** (1194). The **Nauchandi Mela** is held in March. The train takes 1½ hours from Delhi, the bus takes two hours. The railway stations are to the west and the City Bus Stand nearly 2 km to the southeast.

Saharanpur Seventy kilometres north of Meerut, is famous for carved wood furniture. It was founded in 1340 as a summer retreat for the Mughals. The Eastern Yamuna Canal, one of the first great 19th-century canals to irrigate the Ganga-Yamuna doab, transformed the landscape of what had been a heavily overpopulated region. It has become a particularly important source of fruit trees. The Mango Festival is held in June/July when hundreds of varieties are displayed. Woodcarvers can be seen at work in Lakdi Bazar and the old market place.

Going to Nepal

The road east from Delhi to the Nepal border gives access to some popular hill stations of the Uttarakhand Himalaya and to the Corbett National Park.

Ghaziabad is a modern satellite town for Delhi, with a population of 520,000 but little of aesthetic appeal. Beyond Ghaziabad is countryside, an area where two crops are cultivated each year, mostly rice in the monsoon and wheat in winter, but also sugarcane. Countless bullock carts trundle along the highway and line up outside the refineries.

The small town of **Garmukhteswar**, with some typical North Indian temples, stands on the west bank of the Ganga, with riverside ghats. According to the Mahabharata, this is where King Santanu met the Goddess Ganga in human form. Each year at the full moon in October and November, thousands of pilgrims converge to bathe in the holy waters. From the road bridge you may see turtles swimming around in the waters below.

Rampur was founded in 1623 by two Afghan Rohillas who served under the Mughals. Subsequently, the Rohillas united and expanded their empire, but in 1772 the region was invaded by the Marathas. The Nawab of Rampur remained loyal to the British during the Mutiny and supported them in the second A ghan War. There is an extensive palace and fort here. The State Library has an excellent collection of 16th- to 18th-century portraits, plus a small book of Turkish verse with notes by both Babur and Shah Jahan.

Banbassa is a small town on the India–Nepal border with a large Nepali population and a friendly feel. See Border crossing box, page 1362.

Tourist information

Most tourist offices are open Mon-Fri 1000-1800.

Delhi Tourism
N-36 Connaught Pl, T011-2331 5322 (touts pester you to use one of many imposters; the correct office is directly opposite 'Competent House'), www.delhitourism.gov.in.
Other branches at: **Coffee Home Annexe** (Baba Kharak Singh Marg, T011-336 5358); at the airport terminals; the Inter-State Bus Terminal; and New Delhi Railway Station (T011-2373 2374). The branch at **Coffee Home Annexe** is close to Connaught Pl and offers hotel, transport and tour bookings (T011-2462 3782, open 0700-2100).

Government of India Tourist Office
88 Janpath, T011-332 0005. Mon-Sat 0900-1800; also at the international airport.
Helpful and issues permits for visits to Rashtrapati Bhavan and gardens.

Where to stay

Avoid hotel touts. Airport taxis may pretend not to know the location of your chosen hotel so give full details and insist on being taken there. Around Paharganj particularly, you might be followed around by your driver trying to eek a commission out of the guesthouse once you have checked in.

It really saves a lot of hassle if you make reservations. Even if you change hotel the next day, it is good to arrive with somewhere booked especially if you are flying in late at night.

Hotel prices in Delhi are significantly higher than in most other parts of the country. Smaller **$$** guesthouses away from the centre in **South Delhi** (eg Kailash, Safdarjang) or in **Sunder Nagar**, are quieter and often good value but may not provide food. **$** accommodation is concentrated around **Janpath** and **Paharganj** (New Delhi), and **Chandni Chowk** (Old Delhi); well patronized but basic and usually cramped yet good for meeting other backpackers.

Signs in some hotels warn against taking drugs as this is becoming a serious cause for concern. Police raids are frequent.

Old Delhi and beyond

$$$$ Maidens Hotel
7 Sham Nath Marg, T011-2397 5464, www.maidenshotel.com.
Opened in 1903, this is one of Delhi's oldest hotels packed full of colonial charm. 54 large well-appointed rooms, restaurant (barbecue nights are excellent), characterful bar, spacious gardens with excellent pool, friendly welcome, personal attention. Recommended.

$$$ Broadway
4/15A Asaf Ali Rd, T011-4366 3600, www.hotelbroadwaydelhi.com.
Charming hotel with 36 rooms, some wonderfully quirky. Interior designer Catherine Levy has decorated some of the rooms in a quirky kitsch style, brightly coloured with psychedelic bathroom tiles. The other rooms are classic design. **Chor Bizarre** restaurant and 'Thugs' pub are highly regarded. Great walking tours of Old Delhi. Easily one of the best options.

$$-$ Wongdhen House
15A New Tibetan Colony, Manju-ka-Tilla, T011-2381 6689, wongdhenhouse@hotmail.com.
Very clean rooms, some with a/c and TV, safe, cosy, convivial, good breakfast and great Tibetan meals, an insight into Tibetan culture, peacefully located by Yamuna River yet 15 mins by auto-rickshaw north of Old Delhi Station. Recommended.

Connaught Place

$$$$ Imperial
Janpath, T011-2334 1234, www.theimperialindia.com.
Quintessential Delhi. 230 rooms and beautiful 'deco suites' in supremely elegant Lutyens-designed 1933 hotel. Unparalleled location, great bar, antiques and art everywhere, beautiful gardens with spa and secluded pool, amazing **Spice Route** restaurant. Highly recommended.

$$$ Hotel Corus
B-49 Connaught Pl, T011-4365 2222, www.hotelcorus.com.
Comfortable hotel right at the heart of things. Good-value rooms. You get 15% discount in their onsite **Life Caffe**.

$$$ Palace Heights
D26-28 Connaught Pl, T011-4358 2610,
www.hotelpalaceheights.com.
Bright, modern rooms with good attention to
detail, best choice in Connaught Pl in this price
bracket. There's also an attractive glass-walled
restaurant, **Zaffran**, overlooking the street.

$$$-$ YMCA Tourist Hostel
Jai Singh Rd, T011-2336 1915,
www.newdelhiymca.org.
120 rooms, for both sexes, common areas have
been recently refurbished. Prices are creeping
up here. Good location. Good pool, luggage
storage, pay in advance but check bill, reserve
ahead, very professional.

$ Asian Guest House
14 Scindia House, off Kasturba Gandhi Marg,
the sign is hidden behind petrol pump, T011-
2331 0229, www.asianguesthouse.com.
Great central location. Friendly faces greet you
here, although it's a bit tricky to find – call ahead
for directions. Clean basic rooms, some with a/c,
some with TV.

Paharganj
Paharganj is where backpackers congregate.
Sandwiched between the main sights and near
the main railway station, it's noisy, dirty and a
lot of hassle. Its chief virtues are economy and
convenience, with plenty of shops, travel agents,
budget hotels and cafés catering for Western
tastes. Avoid **Hotel Bright**.

$$$$-$$$ Jyoti Mahal
2488 Nalwa St, behind Imperial Cinema,
T011-2358 0524, www.jyotimahal.net.
An oasis in Paharganj with large and
atmospheric rooms in a beautiful converted
haveli and new deluxe rooms in a stylish new
wing. Cool and quiet with antique pieces dotted
around and bowls of floating rose petals lining
the staircases. Top-notch rooftop restaurant
serving Continental and Indian dishes. It's a very
atmospheric place to dine. Nice boutique, **Pink
Safari**, too. Highly recommended.

$$ Prince Polonia
2325-26 Tilak Gali (behind Imperial Cinema),
T011-4762 6600, www.hotelprincepolonia.com.
Very unusual for Paharganj in that it has a rooftop
pool (small, but good for a cool down). Breezy
rooftop café. Attracts a slightly more mature
crowd. Safe, clean. Recently refurbished.

$ Rak International
820 Main Bazar, Chowk Bowli, T011-2358 6508,
www.hotelrakinternational.com.
27 basic but clean rooms. Professionally run.
Quiet, friendly hotel with a rooftop restaurant.

Karol Bagh and Rajendra Nagar
West of Paharganj on the Metro line, **Karol
Bagh** is full of identikit modern hotels, albeit a
degree more upmarket than Paharganj. There
are plentiful good eating places, and the area is
handy for Sarai Rohilla station. Nearby **Rajendra
Nagar**, a residential suburb, this has one of Delhi's
best homestays.

$$$ Yatri Paying Guest House
Corner of Panchkuin and Mandir margs,
T011-2362 5563, www.yatrihouse.com.
A quiet, peaceful oasis with beautiful gardens.
6 large, attractive rooms all with 42-inch
televisions, nice bathrooms, Wi-Fi, fridge and a/c.
Free airport pick-up or drop off. Breakfast, tea/
coffee and afternoon snack included.

$$$-$$ Master Guest House
*R-500 New Rajendra Nagar (Shankar Rd and
GR Hospital Rd crossing), T011-2874 1089,*
www.master-guesthouse.com.
3 beautiful rooms, a/c, Wi-Fi, rooftop for
breakfast, *thalis*, warm welcome that makes you
feel like Delhi is home. Each room has a different
vibrant colour scheme and named after a god.
Very knowledgeable, caring owners run excellent
tours of 'hidden Delhi'. Recommended.

South Delhi
Most of the city's smartest hotels are located
south of Rajpath, in a broad rectangle between
Chanakyapuri and Humayun's Tomb. The southern
residential suburbs are also peppered with
homestays; a list is available from **Delhi Tourism**,
BK Singh Marg (see Tourist information), or arrange
with the reliable **Metropole** (see Car hire, page 91).

$$$$ Claridges
12 Aurangzeb Rd, T011-3955 5000,
www.claridges.com.
138 chic rooms, art deco-style interiors, colonial
atmosphere, attractive restaurants (**Jade Garden**
and **Sevilla**), beautiful **Aura** bar, impeccable
service, charming atmosphere. Recommended.

$$$$ Manor
77 Friends Colony, T011-2692 5151,
www.themanordelhi.com.
Contemporary boutique hotel with 10 stylish
rooms, heavenly beds, relaxing garden, a haven.

Beautiful artwork and relaxed vibe. Award-winning restaurant **Indian Accent**. Charming service.

$$$$ Oberoi
Dr Zakir Hussain Marg, T011-2436 3030, www.oberoihotels.com.
300 rooms and extremely luxurious suites overlooking golf club, immaculate, quietly efficient, beautiful touches, carved Tree of Life in the lobby. 5-star facilities including 2 pools and a spa, superb business centre and good restaurants – **360°** gets rave reviews for its Sun brunch.

$$$$ Taj Mahal
1 Mansingh Rd, T011-2302 6162, www.tajhotels.com.
1 of 3 **Taj** hotels in Delhi. 300 attractive rooms, comfortable, new club levels outstanding, excellent restaurants and service (**Haveli** offers a wide choice and explanations for the newcomer; **Ming House's** spicing varies; **Machan** overlooks palm trees and has a wildlife library), good Khazana shop, lavishly finished with 'lived-in' feel, friendly 1920s-style bar. There is also a **Vivanta by Taj** hotel close to khan with a more business mood.

$$$$-$$$ Amarya Villa
A2-20 Safdarjung Enclave, T011-4103 6184, www.amaryagroup.com.
Truly hip boutique guesthouse, run by 2 Frenchmen. Unique, bright, en suite rooms with TV and Wi-Fi. The decor is inspired by *Navratna* (nine gems). Fantastic roof garden. Great home-cooked food. Effortlessly chic. Highly recommended.

$$$ K One One
K11, Jangpura Extn, 2nd floor, T011-4359 2583, www.parigold.com.
Homely guesthouse in a quiet, central residential area. Run by wonderful ex-TV chef, who also gives cooking lessons. All rooms en suite with a/c, minibar, Wi-Fi, some with balconies. Wonderful roof terrace with views of Humayan's Tomb. Rooftop room is lovely. Book ahead.

$$$ Lutyens Bungalow
39 Prithviraj Rd, T011-2469 4523, www.lutyensbungalow.co.in.
Private guesthouse in a bungalow that has been running for more than 35 years – it's looking a little faded around the edges. Eccentric, rambling property with 15 a/c rooms, a wonderful pool and beautiful gardens with a garden accessory shop on-site. Free airport pickup/drop off, full services, used for long-stays by NGOs and foreign consultants.

$$$-$$ Tree of Life B&B
D-193, Saket, T(0)9810-277699, www.tree-of-life.in.
Stylish B&B with beautifully decorated rooms, simple but chic. Kitchen access, excellent on-site reflexology and yoga – really good atmosphere. The owner also runs **Metropole Tourist Service** (see page 91). Close to Saket Metro station and to **PVR** cinema and malls.

$$ Life Tree
G 14 Lajpat Nagar Part II (near Central Market), T(0)9910-460898, lifetreebnb@gmail.com.
A more simple but charming B&B from the **Tree of Life** family – well located for Khan Market and the centre.

Airport
Unless you can afford a 5-star, hotels around the airport are overpriced and best avoided.

$$$-$$ Sam's Snooze at My Space
T3 IGI Airport, opposite Gate 17, T(0)8800-230013, www.newdelhiairport.in.
You can book a snooze pod for US$12 per hr – only if you are flying out of T3. There's Wi-Fi, TV and DVD, work stations.

$$-$ Hotel Eurostar International
A 27/1 Street No 1, near MTNL office, Mahipalpur Extension, T011-4606 2300, www.hoteleurostar.in.
Good-value option near the airport.

Restaurants

The larger hotel restaurants are often the best for cuisine, decor and ambience. Sun buffets are very popular costing around Rs 3000 or more. Some hotels may only open around 1930 for dinner; some close on Sun. Alcohol is served in most top hotels, but only in some non-hotel restaurants.

The old-fashioned 'tea on the lawn' is still served at **The Imperial**, **Claridges** and **Taj Mahal** hotels (see Where to stay, pages 80, 81 and above). **Aapki Pasand**, at 15 Netaji Subhash Marg, offers unusual tea-tasting in classy and extremely professional surroundings; it's quite an experience. Hauz Khas in South Delhi is a great area where there are many restaurants and bars in walking distance of each other – there is a fast turnover of what is hip in this area however so walk around and see what you fancy.

Old Delhi

In **Paranthewali Gali**, a side street off Chandni Chowk, stalls sell a variety of *paranthas* including *kaju badam* (stuffed with dry fruits and nuts). Other good places to try local foods like *bedmi aloo puri* with spiced potato are **Mahalaxmi Misthan Bhandhar**, 659 Church Mission St, and **Natraj Chowk**, 1396 Chandni Chowk, for *dahi balli* and *aloo tikki*. For sweets you have to seek out **Old Famous Jalebi Wala**, 1797 Dariba Corner, Chandni Chowk – as they are old and famous!

$$$-$$ Chor Bizarre
Broadway Hotel (see Where to stay, page 80), T011-4366 3600.
Tandoori and Kashmiri cuisine (Wazwan, Rs 500). Fantastic food, quirky decor, including salad bar that was a vintage car. Well worth a visit.

$ Haldiram's
1454/2 Chandni Chowk.
Stand-up counter for excellent snacks and sweets on the run (try *dokhla* with coriander chutney from seller just outside), and more elaborate sit-down restaurant upstairs.

$ Karim's
Gali Kababiyan (south of Jama Masjid), Mughlai.
Authentic, busy, plenty of local colour. The experience, as much as the food, makes this a must. Not a lot to tempt vegetarians though.

Connaught Place

$$$ Sakura
Hotel Metropolitan (see New Delhi map, page 66), Bangla Sahib Rd, T011-2334 0200.
Top Japanese royal cuisine in classic, uncluttered surroundings. One of the best in the city, priced accordingly.

$$$ Spice Route
Imperial Hotel (see Where to stay, page 80).
Award-winning restaurant charting the journey of spices around the world. Extraordinary temple-like surroundings (took 7 years to build), Kerala, Thai, Vietnamese cuisines, magical atmosphere.

$$$ Veda
27-H, T011-4151 3535, www.vedarestaurants.com.
Owned by fashion designer Rohit Bal with appropriately beautiful bordello-style decor, done out like a Rajasthani palace with high-backed leather chairs and candles reflecting from mirror work on ceilings. Food is contemporary Indian. Great atmosphere at night. There is another branch at DLF Vasant Kunj.

$$ Embassy
D-11, T(0)93110 85132.
International food. Popular with an artistic/intellectual/political crowd, good food, longstanding local favourite.

$$ Kwality
7 Regal Building, near Park Hotel, T011-2374 2310.
International. Spicy Punjabi dishes with various breads. Try *chhole bhature*.

$$ Life Caffe
Hotel Corus (see Where to stay, page 80), B49 Connaught Pl, T(0)99589 66357.
Tranquil garden, imaginative, good-value food. Perfect for when you want to escape the noise of CP.

$$ United Coffee House
E-15 Connaught Pl, T011-2341 1697.
Recommended more for the colonial-era cake-icing decor than for the fairly average food. Often someone waxing lyrical over a Casio keyboard. Always attracts a mixed crowd, well worth a visit.

$ Nathu's and Bengali Sweet House
Both in Bengali Market (east of Connaught Pl, see New Delhi map).
Sweet shops also serving vegetarian food. Good *dosa, iddli, utthapam* and North Indian *chana bathura, thalis*, clean, functional. Try *kulfi* (hard blocks of ice cream) with *falooda* (sweet vermicelli noodles).

$ Nizam's Kathi Kebabs
H-5 Plaza, T011-2332 1953.
Very good, tasty filled *parathas*, good value, clean. There's another branch in Defence Colony.

$ Saravana Bhavan
P-15/90, near McDonalds, T011-2334 7755; also at 46 Janpath.
Chennai-based chain, light and wonderful South Indian, superb chutneys, unmissable *kaju anjeer* ice cream with figs and nuts. No reservations so can take ages to get a table at night or at weekends. Highly recommended.

$ Street stalls
At entrance to Shankar Market.
Stalls dish out *rajma chawal* (bean stew and rice) to an appreciative crowd on weekdays.

$ Triveni Tea Terrace
Triveni Kala Sangam, 205 Tansen Marg, near Mandi House Metro station (not Sun).
Art galleries, an amphitheatre and this little café in quite an unusual building close to CP – the tea terrace is a bit of an institution.

Paharganj

The rooftop restaurants at **Jyoti Mahal** and **Shelton** are great locations for a bite to eat.

$$-$ Café Sim Tok
Tooti Chowk, above Hotel Navrang, near Hotel Rak, T(0)9810-386717.
Tucked away little gem of a Korean restaurant. No signage, ask for **Hotel Navrang** and keep going up stairs to find delicious *kimbab* (Korean sushi), *kimchi* and all sorts of soups, in a sweet little café. You can always calm the spice with cold beer too.

$ Everest Bakery Café
Dal Mandi, near Star Palace Hotel.
Fantastic *momos*, cakes and pies, green teas, sociable. Recommended.

$ Tadka
Off Main Bazar (near veg market).
Good option for tasty food in this area. Great range of all the usual Indian favourites, with nice decor, friendly staff and good hygiene levels.

South Delhi

$$$ Baci
23 Sunder Nagar Market, near HDFC Bank, T011-4150 7445.
Classy, top-quality Italian food, run by gregarious Italian-Indian owners. There are also branches of her cheaper café **Amici** springing up in Khan Market and Hauz Khas.

$$$ Bukhara
ITC Maurya Sheraton, Sardar Patel Marg, T011-2611 2233, www.itcwelcomgroup.com.
Stylish Northwest Frontier cuisine amidst rugged walls draped with rich rugs (but uncomfortable seating). Outstanding meat dishes and dhal. Also tasty vegetable and *paneer* dishes, but vegetarians will miss out on the best dishes.

$$$ Desi Roots
G-16/17, Salcon Rasvilas Mall, Near Saket City Walk, T011-4161 4008.
Expect the unexpected at this concept restaurant, where your mutton curry will be served in a toy truck and your chipotle chicken tikka in an old iron. Try the avocado raita or a kichdi made from quinoa. Fun and delicious.

$$$ Diva
M8, M-Block Market, Greater Kailash II, T011-2921 5673.
Superb Italian in minimalist space popular with celebrity crowd. Great fish dishes, inventive starters, dedicated vegetarian section, extensive wine list. Owner Ritu Dalmia has also opened **Latitude 28,** a delightful café in Khan Market.

$$$ Dum Pukht
ITC Maurya Sheraton, Sardar Patel Marg, T011-2611 2233, www.itcwelcomgroup.com. Open evenings; lunch only on Sun.
Voted one of the best restaurants in the world, it marries exquisite tastes and opulent surroundings.

$$$ Indian Accent
At The Manor, 77 Friends Colony West, T011-4323 5151.
With a menu designed by Manish Mehotra, who runs restaurants in Delhi and London, this acclaimed restaurant offers Indian food with a modern twist: *dosas* will reveal masala morel mushrooms; and rather than the traditional Goan prawns *balchao,* here you will find it with roasted scallops. Or how about toffee *chyawanprash* cheesecake with badam milk (*chyawanprash* is a health elixir from the amla fruit)? The menu reflects the changing of the seasons and there is live fusion music on Sat. Highly recommended.

$$$ Kainoosh
122-124 DLF Promenade Mall, Vasant Kunj, T(0)9560-715533.
Under the watchful eye of celebrity chef Marut Sikka, delicious *thalis* marry the traditional and modern faces of Indian food. This is *thali* with a difference – bespoke with giant morel mushrooms, sea bass mousse and chicken cooked in orange juice and saffron in a terracotta pot.

$$$ Lodi
Lodi Gardens, T(0)98187 43232.
Excellent location; come here for fusion foods taking in tastes from around the globe. Mediterranean-style surroundings, nice terrace and garden.

$$$ Magique
Gate No 3, Garden of 5 Senses, Mehrauli Badarpur Rd, T(0)9717-535533.
Delicious fusion food, in a magical setting. Sit outside among the candles and fairy lights. One of Delhi's most romantic restaurants.

$$$ Olive at the Qutb
T011-2957 4444, www.olivebarandkitchen.com.
Branch of the ever popular Mumbai restaurant and some people say the Delhi version wins hands down. Serving up delicious platters of Mediterranean food and good strong cocktails.

$$$ Park Baluchi
Inside Deer Park, Hauz Khas Village, T011-2685 9369.
Atmospheric dining in Hauz Khas Deer Park. The
lamb wrapped in chicken served on a flaming
sword comes highly recommended. Can get
crowded, book ahead.

$$$ Ploof
13 Main Market, Lodhi Colony, T(0)99580 27772.
Billed as a Gourmet Kitchen, this is the place
to come for seafood. Very popular. Bright,
comfortable restaurant.

$$$ Sevilla
Claridges Hotel (see Where to stay, page 81).
Beautiful restaurant with lots of outdoor seating
serving up specialities like tapas and paella as
well as wood-fired pizza and the dangerous
house special sangria.

$$ Naivedyam
Hauz Khas village, T011-2696 0426.
Very good South Indian, great service and
very good value in a very beautiful restaurant.
Highly recommended.

$$ Oh! Calcutta
*E-Block, ground floor, International Trade
Towers, Nehru Pl, T011-3040 2415.*
Authentic Bengali cuisine, with excellent
vegetarian and fish options in a somewhat odd
location but not far from the Baha'i temple.

$ Khan Cha Cha
Khan Market, 75 Middle Lane.
This no-frills joint serves some of the best kebabs
in the city from a window in the middle lane of
Khan Market. Fantastic value. You can recognize
the place from the crowd clamouring at the
counter. There is another branch in CP.

$ Sagar Ratna
18 Defence Colony Market, T011-2433 3440.
Other branches in Vasant Kunj, Malviya Nagar
and NOIDA. Excellent South Indian. Cheap and
"amazing" *thalis* and coffee, very hectic (frequent
queues). One of the best breakfasts in Delhi.

Bars and clubs

Many national holidays are 'dry' days. Delhi's
bar/club scene has exploded over the last few
years. Expect to pay a lot for your drinks and,
when in doubt, dress up; some clubs have strict
dress codes. Delhi's 'in' crowd is notoriously
fickle. For more insight into Delhi check out
the website www.bringhomestories.com and
www.timeout.com/delhi.

Connaught Place

1911
Imperial Hotel (see page 80).
Elegantly styled colonial bar, good snacks.

Kitty Su
Lalit Hotel, Barakhamba Av.
Boasting molecular mixology with their cocktails
and regular turns by prominent DJs and more
alternative acts.

South Delhi

Out of the Box
9 Hauz Khaz, T011-4608 0533.
Party place with themed nights and live music.
Café and bar.

Pegs-n-Pints
*Chanakya Lane, Chanakyapuri (tucked away
behind Akbar Bhawan), T011-2687 8320.*
On Tue evenings it hosts Delhi's only gay club.
Western and Indian pop. It gets packed. A lot
of fun.

Rick's
*Taj Mahal Hotel, 1 Mansingh Rd, T011-2302 6162,
www.tajhotels.com.*
Suave Casablanca-themed bar with long martini
list, a long-time fixture on Delhi's social scene.

Shalom
*'N' Block Market, Greater Kailash 1,
T011-4163 2280.*
Comfortable, stylish lounge bar serving Lebanese
cuisine; the resident DJ plays ambient music. Sufi
and soul on Thu, House on Fri.

Urban Pind
N4, N-block market, GK1, T011-3951 5656.
Multi-level bar, with large roof terrace, popular –
recently refurbished. Hosts a controversial expat/
journalist night on Thu with an 'all-you-can-drink'
entry fee, unsurprisingly this normally features a
lot of drunk foreigners.

Entertainment

For advance notice of upcoming events see
www.delhievents.com. Current listings and
reviews can be found on *www.timeout.com* and
www.brownpaperbag.in/delhi. For programmes
see cinema listings in the daily *Delhi Times*.

Cinema

PVR is a multiplex chain with branches
everywhere, mostly screening Hindi movies,
including **PVR Plaza** in Connaught Pl. Now with

the Metro, it's pretty easy to get to PVR Saket, for example, whereas previously it was extremely unlikely you would bother.

Music, dance and culture
Goethe Institute, *3 Kasturba Gandhi Marg, T011-2347 1100*. Recommended for arts, film festivals, open-air cinema, plays and events.
India Habitat Centre, *Lodi Rd, T011-2468 2022*. Good programme of lectures, films, exhibitions, concerts, excellent restaurant.
Indian International Centre, *40 Lodhi Estate, Max Mueller Marg, T011-2461 9431, www.iicdelhi.nic.in*. Some fantastic debates and performances, well worth checking the 'forth-coming programmes' section of their website.
Kingdom of Dreams, *Great Indian Nautanki Company Ltd. Auditorium Complex, Sector 29, Gurgaon, Metro IFFCO, T0124-452 8000, www.kingdomofdreams.in*. Ticket prices Rs 750-3000 depending on where you sit and more pricey at the weekend. The highlight is a much acclaimed all-singing, all-dancing Bollywood-style performance. A little like an Indian Disneyland showcasing Indian tastes, foods, culture, dress and dance all in one a/c capsule, but done impeccably.
Triveni Kala Sangam, *205 Tansen Marg (near Mandi House Metro station), T011-2371 8833*. Strong programme of photography and art exhibitions, plus an excellent North Indian café.

Son et lumière
Red Fort *(see page 58), Apr-Nov 1800-1900 (Hindi), 1930-2030 (English). Entry Rs 50. Tickets available after 1700*. Take anti-mosquito cream.

Festivals

For exact dates consult the weekly *Delhi Diary* available at hotels and many shops and offices around town. Muslim festivals of **Ramadan**, **Id-ul-Fitr**, **Id-ul-Zuha** and **Muharram** are celebrated according to the lunar calendar.

Jan
26 Jan Republic Day Parade, Rajpath. A spectacular fly-past and military march-past, with colourful pageants and tableaux from every state, dances and music. Tickets through travel agents and most hotels, Rs 100. You can see the full dress preview free, usually 2 days before; week-long celebrations during which government buildings are illuminated.

29 Jan Beating the Retreat, Vijay Chowk, a stirring display by the armed forces' bands marks the end of the Republic Day celebrations.
30 Jan Martyr's Day, Marks the anniversary of Mahatma Gandhi's death; devotional *bhajans* and Guard of Honour at Raj Ghat.
Kite Flying Festival, Makar Sankranti above Palika Bazar, Connaught Pl.

Feb
2 Feb Vasant Panchami, celebrates the 1st day of spring. The Mughal Gardens are opened to the public for a month.
Thyagaraja Festival, South Indian music and dance, Vaikunthnath Temple.

Apr
Amir Khusrau's Birth Anniversary, a fair in Nizamuddin celebrates this with prayers and *qawwali* singing.

Aug
Janmashtami, celebrates the birth of the Hindu god Krishna. Special *puja*, Lakshmi Narayan Mandir.
15 Aug Independence Day, Impressive flag-hoisting ceremony and prime ministerial address at the Red Fort.

Oct-Nov
2 Oct Gandhi Jayanti, Mahatma Gandhi's birthday; devotional singing at Raj Ghat.
Dasara, with over 200 Ramlila performances all over the city recounting the *Ramayana* story.
Ramlila Ballet, the ballet, which takes place at Delhi Gate (south of Red Fort) and Ramlila Ground, is performed for a month and is most spectacular. Huge effigies of Ravana are burnt on the 9th night; noisy and flamboyant.
Diwali, the festival of lights; lighting of earthen lamps, candles and firework displays.
National Drama Festival, Rabindra Bhavan.
Oct/Nov Dastkar Nature Bazar, working with over 25,000 crafts people from across India, **Dastkar's** main objective is to empower rural artisans and keep alive the traditional crafts of India. They hold many events each year, but this is the pinnacle. Knowing that shopping here will bring a difference to the lives of rural people.

Dec
25 Dec Christmas, Special Christmas Eve entertainments at major hotels and restaurants; Midnight Mass and services at all churches.

Shopping

There are several state emporia around Delhi including the **Cottage Industries Emporium** (CIE), a huge department store of Indian handicrafts, and those along Baba Kharak Singh Marg (representing crafts from most states of India). In this stretch, there are several places selling products from women's collectives or rural artisans, like **Mother Earth** and **Hansiba**). Shops generally open 1000-1930 (winter 1000-1900). Food stores and chemists stay open later. Most shopping areas are closed on Sun.

Art galleries

Galleries exhibiting contemporary art are listed on www.timeout.com.

Delhi Art Gallery, *Hauz Khas Village, www. delhiartgallery.com.* A newly expanded gallery with a good range of moderately priced contemporary art.

Nature Morte, *A-1 Neethi Bagh, near Kamla Nehru College, www.naturemorte.com.* With a twin gallery in Berlin, you can expect the most profound and inspiring of contemporary art here.

Photo Ink, *Hyundai MGF building, 1 Jhandewalan Faiz Rd, www.photoink.net.* Close to Paharganj, this gallery offers up top notch contemporary photography.

Books and music

Serious bibliophiles should head to the Sunday book market in Daryaganj (Kabaadi Bazar), Old Delhi, when 2 km of pavement are piled high with books – some fantastic bargains to be had.

Bahri & Sons, *opposite Main Gate, Khan Market.* One among many in the booklovers' heaven of Khan Market. Wide choice.

Central News Agency, *P 23/90, Connaught Pl.* Carries national and foreign newspapers and journals.

Full Circle, *5 B, Khan Market, T011-2465 5641.* Helpful knowledgeable staff. Sweet café upstairs for a quick drink – food is hit and miss though.

Manohar, *4753/23 Ansar Rd, Daryaganj, Old Delhi.* A real treasure trove for books on South Asia and India especially, most helpful, knowledgeable staff. Highly recommended.

Rikhi Ram, *G Block Connaught Circus, T011-2332 7685.* This is the place to come if you've wondered about how easy it is to learn to play and travel with a sitar. Has a range of guitars and other stringed instruments too.

Carpets

Carpets can be found in shops in most top hotels and a number round Connaught Pl, not necessarily fixed price. If you are visiting Agra, check out the prices here first.

Clothing

For designer wear, try **Ogaan** and for more contemporary, less budget blowing try **Grey Garden** both in **Hauz Khas Village**, **Sunder Nagar Market** near the Oberoi hotel, or the Crescent arcade near the Qutab Minar. The new market of choice is Meherchand in South Delhi.

For inexpensive (Western and Indian) clothes, try shops along Janpath and between Sansad Marg and Janpath; you can bargain down 50%.

Fab India, *14N-Gt Kailash I (also in B-Block Connaught Pl, Khan Market and Vasant Kunj).* Excellent shirts, Nehru jackets, *salwar kameez*, linen, furnishing fabrics and furniture. The most comprehensive collection is in N block.

Earthenware

Unglazed earthenware *khumba matkas* (water pots) are sold round New Delhi Railway Station (workshops behind main road).

Emporia

Most open 1000-1800 (close 1330-1400).

Central Cottage Industries Emporium, *corner of Janpath and Tolstoy Marg.* Offers hassle-free shopping, gift wrapping, will pack and post overseas; best if you are short of time.

Dilli Haat, *opposite INA Market. Rs 15, open 1100-2200.* Well-designed open-air complex with rows of brick alcoves for craft stalls from different states; local craftsmen's outlets (bargaining obligatory), occasional fairs (tribal art, textiles, etc). Also good regional food – hygienic, safe, weighted towards non-vegetarian. Pleasant, quiet, clean (no smoking) and uncrowded, not too much hassle.

Khazana, *Taj Mahal and Taj Palace hotels (daily 0900-2000).* High class.

Jewellery

Traditional silver and goldsmiths in Dariba Kalan, off Chandni Chowk (north of Jama Masjid). Cheap bangles and accessories along Janpath; also at Hanuman Mandir, Gt Kailash I, N-Block. Also Sunder Nagar market. Bank St in Karol Bagh is recommended for gold.

Amrapali, Khan Market has an exceptional collection from affordable to mind-blowing.

Ashish Nahar, *1999 Naughara St, Kinari Bazar, Chandni Chowk, T011-2327 2801.* On quite possibly the prettiest street in Delhi, full of brightly painted and slowly crumbling *havelis*, you will find a little gem of a jewellery shop.

Leather

Cheap sandals from stalls on Janpath (Rs 150). **Yashwant Place Market** next to Chanakya Cinema Hall, Chanakyapuri. **Khan Market** (see below) sells leather goods and shoes. **Hidesign**, *G49, Connaught Pl*. Beautifully made leatherware.

Markets and malls

Beware of pickpockets in markets and malls. **Hauz Khas village**, *South Delhi*. Authentic, old village houses converted into designer shops selling handicrafts, ceramics, antiques and furniture in addition to luxury wear. Many are expensive, but some are good value. A good place to pick up old Hindi film posters with many art galleries and restaurants. **Khan Market**, *South Delhi*. Great bookshops, cafés, restaurants and boutiques. Full of expats so expect expat prices. **Sarojini Nagar**, *South Delhi*. Daily necessities as well as cheap fabric and clothing. Come for incredible bargains. This is where a lot of the Western brands dump their export surplus or end-of-line clothes. Haggle hard. **Select City Walk**, *Saket*. An enormous, glitzy mall for the ultimate in upmarket shopping. Lots of chains, cinemas, etc. **Shahpur Jat**, is a new up and coming shopping area, south of **South Extension**. **Tibetan Market**, *North Delhi*. Stalls along Janpath have plenty of curios – most are new but rapidly aged to look authentic.

Unique souvenirs

Aap ki Pasand, *opposite Golcha cinema, Netaji Subhash Marg, Old Delhi*. Excellent place to taste and buy Indian teas. **Dastkari Haat**, *39 Khan Market, www.indiancrafts journey.in*. Charming selection of conscious crafts from around India working with rural artisans and women's collectives. **Gulabsingh Johrimal Perfumers**, *467 Chandni Chowk, T011-2326 3743*. Authentic *attars* (sandalwood based perfumes), perfumes and incense. High-quality oils are used. **Haldiram's**, *Chandni Chowk near Metro*. Wide selection of sweet and salty snack foods. **Khazana India**, *50A Hauz Khas village*. Little treasure trove of Bollywood posters, old photographs and all sorts of interesting bric-a-brac. **People Tree**, *8 Regal Building, Connaught Pl*. Handmade clothing, mostly T-shirts with arty and people conscious slogans. Great posters made up of all those weird signs that you see around India and wide-range of ecological books. A real find. **Playclan**, *17 Meherchand Market, www.the playclan.com*. Fantastic shop selling all manner of clothes, notebooks, lighters and pictures with great colourful cartoon designs created by a collective of animators and designers – giving a more animated view of India's gods, goddesses, gurus, Kathakali dancers and the faces of India. **Purple Jungle**, *16 Hauz Khas Village, T(0)9650-973039, www.purple-jungle.com*. Offering up kitsch India with bollywood pictures and curious road signs refashioned onto bags, clothes, cushions, etc.

What to do

Body and soul

Integral Yoga, *Sri Aurobindo Ashram, Aurobindo Marg, T011-2656 7863*. Regular yoga classes (Tue-Thu and Sat 0645-0745 and 1700-1800) in *asana* (postures), *pranayama* (breathing techniques) and relaxation.
Laughter Club of Delhi, *various locations, T011-2721 7164*. Simple yogic breathing techniques combined with uproarious laughter. Clubs meet early morning in parks throughout the city.
Sari School, *Jangpura Extension, near Lajpat Nagar, T011-4182 3297*. Author of *Saris in India*, Rta Christi Kapur holds classes every Sat in different styles of sporting a sari.
Tree of Life Reflexology, *T(0)9810-356677*. Reflexology with acclaimed teacher Suruchi. She also does private and group yoga classes on the roof and in the park.
The Yoga Studio, *Hauz Khas, www.theyoga studio.in*. Regular yoga classes with Seema Sondhi, author of several yoga books, and her team. Sometimes they run outside classes.

Sport

Members only clubs, but maybe you can find a willing member to take you.
Delhi Gymkhana Club, *2 Safdarjang Rd, T011-2301 5533*. Mostly for government and defence personnel, squash, tennis, swimming, bar and restaurant.
Pacific Sports Complex, *next to Central School, Andrews Ganj, T(0)98999 91333*. Can be hard to find – it's near Lady Sri Ram College.
Siri Fort Club, *August Kranti Marg, New Delhi, near Siri Fort Auditorium, T011-2649 7482*. You can get temporary membership – wonderful outdoor swimming pool (summer only), tennis, squash, basketball, reiki, taekwondo, etc.

Tours and tour operators

Delhi Tourism tours

Departs from **Delhi Tourism** (Baba Kharak Singh Mg near State Govt Emporia, T011-2336 3607, www.delhitourism.gov.in). Book a day in advance. Check time. Offers morning, afternoon and evening tours taking in various sites (Rs258) – see website. **Evening Tour** (Tue-Sun 1830-2200): Rajpath, India Gate, Kotla Firoz Shah, Purana Qila, *son et lumière* (Red Fort), Rs 207.

Taj Mahal tours

Many companies offer coach tours to Agra (eg **Delhi Tourism**, see above), from L1 Connaught Circus, Sat-Thu 0630-2200, Rs 1340, a/c coach). However, travelling by road is slow and uncomfortable; by car, allow at least 4 hrs each way. Train is a better option: either *Shatabdi* or *Taj Express*, but book early.

Walking tours

Walking tours are a fantastic way to get an insight into the city.

Chor Bizarre, *Hotel Broadway, T011-2327 3821*. Special walking and cycle rickshaw tours of Old Delhi, with good lunch, 0930-1330, 1300-1630, Rs 350 each, Rs 400 for both.

Delhi Metro Walks, *T(0)9811-330098, www. delhimetrowalks.com*. With the charismatic Surekha Narain guiding your every step, informative heritage walks around Delhi. She offers group walks but can also do private tours. Highly recommended.

Master Guest House *(see Where to stay, page 81)*. Highly recommended walking tours for a more intimate experience.

Salaam Baalak Trust, *T(0)9873-130383, www. salaambaalaktrust.com*. NGO-run tours of New Delhi station and the streets around it, guided by former street children. Your Rs 200 goes to support the charity's work with street children. Excellent.

Tour operators

There are many operators offering tours, ticketing, reservations, etc, for travel across India. Many are around Connaught Circus, Parharganj, Rajendra Pl and Nehru Pl. Most belong to special associations (IATA, PATA) for complaints.

Ibex Expeditions, *30 Community Centre East of Kailash, New Delhi, T011-2646 0244, www.ibex expeditions.com*. Offers a wide range of tours and ticketing, all with an eco pledge. Recommended.

Kunzum Travel Café, *T-49 Hauz Khas village, T011-2651 3949*. Unusual travel centre and meeting place for travellers. Free Wi-Fi, walls lined with photos, magazines, and buzzing with people. Also hosts photography workshops and travel writing courses.

Namaste Voyages, *I-Block 28G/F South City, 2 Gurgaon, 122001, T0124-221 9330, www. namastevoyages.com*. Specializes in tailor-made tours, tribal, treks, theme voyages.

Royal Expeditions, *26 Community Center (2nd floor), East of Kailash, New Delhi 110065, T011-2623 8545, www.royalexpeditions.com*. Specialist staff for customized trips, knowledgeable about options for senior travellers. Owns luxury 4WD vehicles for escorted self-drive adventures in Himalaya, offers sightseeing in classic cars in Jaipur.

Shanti Travel, *F-189/1A Main Rd Savitri Nagar, T011-4607 7800, www.shantitravel.com*. Tailor-made tours throughout India.

Wild Frontiers India, *D-131 (2nd floor), Mohammadpur, Bhakaji Cama Place, New Delhi, T011-2619 5950, www.wildfrontiersindia.com*. Great local outfit that are a subsidiary of **Wild Frontiers UK**. Responsible tours offering an excellent insight into India.

Transport

For up-to-date transport contact numbers check out www.delhitourism.gov.in.

Air

Indira Gandhi International Airport (IGI), 20 km southwest of Connaught Pl, T0124-377 6000, www.newdelhiairport.in, has one of the longest runways in Asia. All international and some domestic flights arrive at the shiny new Terminal 3; Terminal 1 is now used mostly by low-cost domestic carriers. A free shuttle runs between the 2 terminals every 30 mins during the day (show your boarding pass and onward ticket), every 20 mins, but can take more than an hour so allow plenty of time. At check-in, be sure to tag your hand luggage, and make sure it is stamped after security check, otherwise you will be sent back at the gate to get it stamped.

The domestic air industry is in a period of massive growth, so check a 3rd-party site such as www.cleartrip.com or www.makemytrip.com for the latest flight schedules and prices.

The most extensive networks are with **Air India**, T140/T011-2562 2220, www.airindia. com; and **Jet Airways**, T011-3989 3333, www. jetairways.com. **Indigo**, T(0)9910-383838, www.goindigo.in, has the best record for being on time etc, and **Spicejet**, T(0)9871-803333, www.spicejet.com.

Transport to and from the airport

The **Metro** is up and running and it is now possible to travel between New Delhi Railway Station and the airport in just 20 mins (orange line).

By road, it can take 30-45 mins from the Domestic Terminal and 45-60 mins from the International Terminal to travel to the centre. There is a booth just outside 'Arrivals' at the International and Domestic terminals for the **bus** services. It is a safe, economical option. Some hotel buses leave from the Domestic terminal. **Bus 780** runs between the airport and New Delhi Railway Station.

Both terminals have **pre-paid taxi** counters outside the baggage hall (3 price categories) which ensure that you pay the right amount (give your name, exact destination and number of items of luggage). Most expensive are white '**DLZ**' **limousines** and then white '**DLY**' **luxury taxis**. Cheapest are '**DLT**' **ordinary Delhi taxis** (black with yellow top Ambassador/Fiat cars and vans, often very old). 'DLY' taxis charge 3 times the DLT price. A 'Welcome' desk by the baggage reclamation offers expensive taxis only. Take your receipt to the ticket counter outside to find your taxi and give it to the driver when you reach the destination; you don't need to tip, although they will ask. From the International terminal DLT taxis charge about Rs 240 for the town centre (Connaught Pl area); night charges double 2300-0500.

Bus

Be on your guard from thieves around New Delhi Station. Also watch your change or cash interactions even at the pre-paid booths – sometimes they do a switch of a Rs 100 note for a Rs 10 for example.

Local

The city bus service run by the **Delhi Transport Corporation** (**DTC**) connects all important points in the city and has more than 300 routes. Information is available at www.dtc.nic.in, at DTC assistance booths and at all major bus stops. Don't be afraid to ask conductors or fellow passengers. Buses are often hopelessly overcrowded so only use off-peak.

State Entry Rd runs from the southern end of Platform 1 to Connaught Pl. This is a hassle-free alternative to the main Chelmsford Rd during the day (gate closed at night).

Long distance

The main **Inter-State Bus Terminal** (**ISBT**) is at Kashmere Gate (see below), from where buses run to most major towns in North India. Services are provided by **Delhi Transport Corporation** (**DTC**) and State Roadways of neighbouring states. Local buses connect it to the other ISBTs. Allow at least 30 mins to buy your ticket and find the right bus.

Kashmere Gate, north of Old Delhi near the Red Fort, T011-440 0400 (general enquiries), is accessible by Metro (yellow line; 15 mins from Connaught Pl) or bus. Facilities include a restaurant, left luggage, bank (Mon-Fri 1000-1400; Sat 1000-1200), post office (Mon-Sat 0800-1700) and telephones (includes international calls). The following operators run services to neighbouring states from here: **Delhi Transport Corp**, T011-2386 5181; **Haryana Roadways**, T011-2296 1262; daily to **Agra** (5-6 hrs, quicker by rail), **Chandigarh** (5 hrs), **Jaipur** (6½ hrs, again quicker by rail), **Mathura**, etc, **Himachal Roadways**, T011-2296 6725; twice daily to **Dharamshala** (12 hrs), **Manali** (15 hrs), **Shimla** (10 hrs), etc. **J&K Roadways**, T011-2332 4511; **Punjab Roadways**, T011-2296 7892, to **Amritsar**, **Chandigarh**, **Jammu**, **Pathankot**. **UP Roadways**, T011-2296 8709, city office at Ajmeri Gate, T011-2323 5367; to **Almora** (5 hrs), **Dehradun**, **Haridwar**, **Mussoorie**, **Gorakhpur**, **Kanpur**, **Jhansi**, **Lucknow**, **Nainital**, **Varanasi**.

Sarai Kale Khan Ring Rd, smaller terminal near Nizamuddin Railway Station, T011-2469 8343 (general enquiries), for buses to Haryana, Rajasthan and UP: **Haryana Roadways**, T011-2296 1262. **Rajasthan Roadways**, T011-2291 9537. For **Agra**, **Mathura** and **Vrindavan**; **Ajmer**; **Alwar**; **Bharatpur** (5 hrs); **Bikaner** (11 hrs); **Gwalior**; **Jaipur**; **Jodhpur**; **Pushkar**; **Udaipur**, etc.

Anand Vihar, east side of Yamuna River, T011-2215 2431, for buses to Uttar Pradesh, Uttarakhand and Himachal Pradesh.

Bikaner House, Pandara Rd (south of India Gate), T011-2338 1884; for several 'Deluxe' a/c buses to **Jaipur** (6 hrs, Rs 300); ask for 'direct' bus (some buses stop at Amber for a tour of the fort). Also to **Udaipur** via **Ajmer**, and to **Jodhpur**.

HPTDC, Chandralok Bldg, 36 Janpath, T011-2332 5320, hptdcdelhi@hub.nic.in, runs a/c Volvo and Sleeper buses to **Manali** and **Dharamshala**. Of the myriad private bus operators, **Raj National Express** has by far the best buses, and highest prices.

Car hire

Hiring a car is an excellent way of getting about town either for sightseeing or if you have several journeys to make. However, the main roads out of Delhi are very heavily congested; the best time to leave is in the very early morning.

Full-day local use with driver (non a/c) Rs 900 and for (a/c) is about Rs 13-1600, 80 km/8 hrs, driver overnight *bata* Rs 150 per day; to Jaipur, about Rs 6 to 8000 depending on size of car. The **Government of India** tourist office (see page 80), 88 Janpath, has a list of approved agents. We highly recommend **Metropole**, see below.

Cozy Travels, N1 BMC House, Middle Circle, Connaught Pl, T011-4359 4359, cozytravels@ vsnl.net.com. **Metropole Tourist Service**, 224 Defence Colony Flyover Market (Jangpura side), New Delhi, T011-2431 2212, T(0)9810-277699, www.metrovista.co.in. Car/jeep (US$45-70 per day), safe, reliable and recommended, also hotel bookings and can help arrange homestays around Delhi. Highly recommended.

Metro

The sparkling new Metro system (T011-2436 5202, www.delhimetrorail.com) has revolutionized transport within Delhi. For travellers, the yellow line is the most useful as it stops Chandni Chowk, Connaught Pl, Qutb Minar and the Kashmere Gate ISBT. The blue line connects to Parhaganj; the violet line runs to Khan Market; and the orange line links the airport with New Delhi Railway Station.

Line 1 (Red) Running northwest to east, of limited use to visitors; from Rithala to Dilshad Garden.

Line 2 (Yellow) Running north–south through the centre from Jahangipuri to Huda City via Kashmere Gate, Chandni Chowk, New Delhi Station, Connaught Pl (Rajiv Chowk), Hauz Khas, Qutb Minar and Saket – probably the most useful line for visitors.

Line 3 (Blue) From Dwarka 21 to Valshall or City Centre (splits after Yamuna Bank) Intersecting with Line 2 at Rajiv Chowk and running west through Paharganj (RK Ashram station) and Karol Bagh.

Line 4 (Orange) Just 4 stations for now including IGI Airport to New Delhi Railway Station.

Line 5 (Green) From Mundka to Inderlok.

Line 6 (Violet) From Central Secretariat to Badarpur, including Khan Market and Lajpat Nagar. Useful.

Trains run 0600-2200; rush hour is best avoided. Fares are charged by distance: tokens for individual journeys cost Rs6-19. **Smart Cards**, Rs 100, Rs 200 and Rs 500, save queuing and money. **Tourist Cards** valid for 1 or 3 days (Rs 70/200) are useful if you plan to make many journeys. Luggage is limited to 15 kg; guards may not allow big backpacks on board. At each Metro station you have to go through airport-like security and have your bag x-rayed.

Look out for the women-only carriages at the front of each train, clearly marked in pink; these are much less crowded. For an insight into the construction of the Metro, there is a Metro museum at **Patel Chowk** on the yellow line.

Motorcycle hire

Chawla Motorcycles, 1770, Shri Kissan Dass Marg, Naiwali Gali, T(0)98118 88913. Very reliable, trustworthy, highly recommended for restoring classic bikes. **Ess Aar Motors**, Jhandewalan Extn, west of Paharganj, T011-2353 4426, www. essaarmotors.com. Recommended for buying Enfields, very helpful. For scooter rentals try **U Ride**, T(0)9711-701932, www.uridescooters.com.

Rickshaw

Auto-rickshaws These are widely available at about half the cost of taxis. Normal capacity for foreigners is 2 people (3rd person extra); the new fare system is encouraging rickshaw wallahs to use the meter, even with foreigners. Expect to pay Rs 30 for the shortest journeys. Allow Rs 150 for 2 hrs' sightseeing/shopping. It is best to walk away from hotels and tourist centres to look for an auto. Try to use pre-paid stands at stations, airport terminals and at the junction of Radial Road 1 and Connaught Place if possible.

Cycle-rickshaws Available in the Old City. Be prepared to bargain. They are not allowed into Connaught Pl. When looking for a cycle-rickshaw, follow the advice under auto-rickshaws above.

Taxi

Yellow-top taxis, which run on compressed natural gas, are readily available at taxi stands or you can hail one on the road. Meters should start at Rs 13; ask for the conversion card. Add 25% at night (2300-0500) plus Rs 5 for each piece of luggage over 20 kg.

Easy Cabs, T011-4343 4343. Runs clean a/c cars and claim to pick up anywhere within 15 mins; Rs 20 per km (night Rs 25 per km). Waiting charges Rs 50/30 mins.

ON THE ROAD

Taxi tips

First-time visitors can be vulnerable to exploitation by taxi drivers at the airport. If arriving at night, you are very strongly advised to have a destination in mind and get a pre-paid taxi. Be firm about being dropped at the hotel of your choice and insist that you have a reservation; you can always change hotels the next day if you are unhappy. Don't admit to being a first-time visitor.

If you don't take a pre-paid taxi, the driver will demand an inflated fare. He may insist that the hotel you want to go to has closed or is full and will suggest one where he will get a commission (and you will be overcharged).

Some travellers have been told that the city was unsafe with street fighting, police barricades and curfews and have then been taken to Agra or Jaipur. In the event of taxi trouble, be seen to note down the licence plate number and threaten to report the driver to the police; if you need to do this, the number is T011-2331 9334.

Also recommended are: **Mega Cabs**, T011-4141 4141; and **Quick Cab**, T011-4533 3333.

Avoid app-based companies like **Uber** and **Ola** which are not licensed by the government.

Train

The busy **New Delhi Station**, a 10-min walk north of Connaught Place, connects with most destinations; you need to have all your wits about you. The quieter **Hazrat Nizamuddin** is 5 km southeast of Connaught Place and has some southbound trains. The overpoweringly crowded **Old Delhi Station** (2 km north of Connaught Place) has a few important train connections. The smaller **Delhi Sarai Rohilla**, northeast of Connaught Place, serves Rajasthan. Trains that originate from Delhi stations have codes: **OD** – Old Delhi, **ND** – New Delhi, **HN** – Hazrat Nizamuddin, **DSR** – Delhi Sarai Rohilla.

New Delhi and Hazrat Nizamuddin stations have pre-paid taxi and rickshaw counters with official rates per km posted; expect to pay around Rs 25 for 1st km, Rs 8 each km after. Authorized *coolies* (porters), wear red shirts and white *dhotis;* agree the charge, there is an official rate, before engaging one. For left luggage, you need a secure lock and chain.

Buying tickets

The publication *Trains at a Glance* (Rs 30) lists important trains across India, available at some stations, book shops and newsagents. Each station has a computerized reservation counter where you can book any Mail or Express train in India. Train enquiries T131. Reservations T1330.

International Tourist Bureau (ITB), 1st floor, Main Building, New Delhi Station, T011-2340 5156, Mon-Fri 0930-1630, Sat 0930-1430, provides assistance with planning and booking journeys, for foreigners only; efficient and helpful if slow. You need your passport; pay in US$, or rupees (with an encashment certificate/ATM receipt). Those with **Indrail** passes should confirm bookings here. Be wary of rickshaw drivers/travel agents who tell you the ITB has closed or moved elsewhere. (There are also counters for foreigners and NRIs at **Delhi Tourism**, N-36 Connaught Pl, 1000-1700, Mon-Sat, and at the airport; quick and efficient.)

Services

There are a couple of trains which get you to Agra at a good time to view the Taj Mahal – **Agra**: *Shatabdi Exp 12002*, ND, usually leaving 0600, 2 hrs; *Taj Exp 12280*, HN, around 0700, 2¾ hrs. The *Shatabdi Express* will also give you a breakfast. **Ahmedabad**: *Rajdhani Exp 12958, ND,* 14½ hrs. **Amritsar**: *Shatabdi Exp 12013*, ND, 6 hrs; *Shan-e-Punjab Exp 12497*, ND (early morning) 7½ hrs. **Bengaluru (Bangalore)**: *Ktk Smprk K Exp 12650*, Mon, Tue, Sat, Sun, HN, 36 hrs; **Chandigarh**: *Shatabdi Exp 12011*, ND, 3½ hrs. **Chennai**: *Tamil Nadu Exp 12622*, ND, 33½ hrs. **Dehradun**: *Shatabdi Exp 12017*, ND, early morning 5¾ hrs; same train stops at **Haridwar** for **Rishikesh**. **Jaipur**: *Shatabdi Exp 12015*, ND, 4½ hrs goes on to **Ajmer. Jhansi** for **Orchha** and **Khujarho**: *Shatabdi Exp 12002*, ND, 4½ hrs. **Jodhpur**: *Mandore Exp 12461*, OD, 2115, 11 hrs. **Kolkata**: *Rajdhani Exp 12314*, ND, 17½ hrs. **Madgaon (Goa)**: *Mngla Lksdp Exp 12618*, HN, 35 hrs, goes on to **Ernakulum (Kochi)**. **Mumbai (Central)**: *Rajdhani Exp 12954*, ND, 17½ hrs; *Golden Temple Mail 12904*, ND, 22 hrs. **Udaipur**: *Mewar Exp 12963*, HN, 12 hrs; *Chetak Exp 12981*, DSR,12 hrs. **Varanasi**: *Swatantrta S Ex 12562*, ND, 12 hrs.

For the special diesel *Palace on Wheels* and other tours, see page 1365.

Background Delhi

History

In the modern period, Delhi has only been India's capital since 1911. It is a city of yo yo-ing fortunes and has been repeatedly reduced to rubble. There have been at least eight cities founded on the site of modern Delhi.

According to Hindu mythology, Delhi's first avatar was as the site of a dazzlingly wealthy city, Indraprastha, mentioned in the Mahabharata and founded around 2500 BC. The next five cities were to the south of today's Delhi. First was Lalkot, which, from 1206, became the capital of the Delhi Sultanate under the Slave Dynasty. The story of the first Sultan of Delhi, Qutb-ud-din Aybak, is a classic rags-to-riches story. A former slave, he rose through the ranks to become a general, a governor and then Sultan of Delhi. He is responsible for building Qutb Minar, but died before its completion.

The 1300s were a tumultuous time for Delhi, with five cities built during the century. Siri, the first of these, has gruesome roots. Legend has it that the city's founder, Ala-ud-din, buried the heads of infidels in the foundation of the fort. Siri derives its name from the Hindi word for 'head'. After Siri came Tughlaqabad, whose existence came to a sudden end when the Sultan of Delhi, Muhammad Tughlaq, got so angry about a perceived insult from residents, he destroyed the city. The cities of Jahanpanah and Ferozebad followed in quick succession. Delhi's centre of gravity began to move northwards. In the 1500s Dinpanah was constructed by Humayun, whose wonderful tomb (1564-1573) graces Hazrat Nizamuddin. Shahjahanabad, known today as Old Delhi, followed, becoming one of the richest and most populous cities in the world. The Persian emperor Nadir Shah invaded, killing as many as 120,000 residents in a single bloody night and stealing the Kohinoor Diamond (now part of the British royal family's crown jewels).

The next destroyers of Delhi were the British, who ransacked the city in the wake of the Great Uprising/Mutiny of 1857. The resulting bloodbath left bodies piled so high that the victors' horses had to tread on them. For the next 50 years, while the port cities of Calcutta and Bombay thrived under the British, Delhi languished. Then, in 1911, King George, on a visit to India, announced that a new city should be built next to what remained of Delhi, and that this would be the new capital of India. The British architect Edwin Lutyens was brought in to design the city. You could argue that the building hasn't stopped since.

The central part of New Delhi is an example of Britain's imperial pretensions. The government may have been rather more reticent about moving India's capital, if it had known that in less than 36 years' time, the British would no longer be ruling India. Delhi's population swelled after the violence of partition, with refugees flooding to the city. In 10 years the population of Delhi doubled, and many well-known housing colonies were built during this period.

Modern Delhi

The economic boom that began in the 1990s has led to an explosion of construction and soaring real estate prices. Delhi is voraciously eating into the surrounding countryside. It is a city changing at such breakneck speed that shops, homes and even airports seem to appear and disappear almost overnight.

Uttar Pradesh

Hinduism and Islam meet on the plains of the Ganges

Uttar Pradesh holds what are arguably the most famous cultural landmarks of both Indian Islam (the Taj Mahal at Agra) and Hinduism (the bathing ghats of Varanasi).

While the former is the world's greatest architectural gesture to a single instance of inconsolable grief, the latter is a riverbank that has for centuries born witness to a constant stream of death at its funeral pyres. Many – from the most seasoned Indophile to the first-time traveller – count these shrines as the high-water marks of any trip to the subcontinent.

UP's modern history and domestic reputation is less enviable, with widespread and high-scale corruption under the former leadership of the Congress Party. What's more, the state's position as the heartland of both Hinduism (bisected as it is by the holy River Ganga) and Indian Islam means it is one of the most febrile frontlines in the contemporary conflict between India's two largest religions.

Best for
Heritage ■ River Ganga ■ Temples

Footprint
picks

★ **Lucknow**, page 98

Find historic monuments and beautiful crafts in the state capital.

★ **Taj Mahal**, page 114

Wonder at India's eternal love monument.

★ **Sikandra**, page 122

Soak up the serenity at Akbar's beautiful mausoleum.

★ **Mathura**, page 126

Listen to Krishna mantras at Dwarkadhesh Temple.

★ **Varanasi**, page 135

Don't miss a sunrise boat trip along the Ganga.

★ **Sarnath**, page 147

Gain an insight into Buddhist architecture.

Essential Uttar Pradesh

Finding your feet

Uttar Pradesh (Northern Province) covers an area of 238,155 sq km. The landscape is dominated by the flat alluvial plains of the Ganga and its tributaries. The north of the state runs along the southern margins of the Shiwalik Hills, which parallel the Himalaya. These are succeeded on their south by the often marshy tropical Terai, which, until they were cleared for cultivation in the 1950s, formed a belt of jungle 65 km wide from the Ganga gorge at Haridwar to Bihar. The Gangetic Plain occupies most of the state; flat and almost featureless, it is stiflingly hot, dry and dusty in summer. Further south are the northern margins of the peninsula, including the outer slopes of the Vindhyan

Mountains in the southeast, which in places rise to more than 600 m.

Getting around

Trains are best for getting between major cities, although there are also domestic flights to Lucknow and Varanasi. Agra is a standard stop on tours of the 'Golden Triangle'.

When to go

Although winter nights are cold everywhere in Uttar Pradesh, daytime temperatures can reach 25°C on the plains even in December and January. Between April and June temperatures soar and a desiccating hot wind known as the Loo

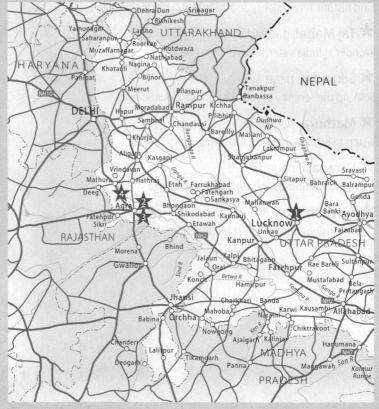

January		February		March		April		May		June	
	23°C		26°C		32°C		38°C		40°C		37°C
	8°C		10°C		16°C		21°C		25°C		27°C
	10mm		10mm		0mm		0mm		10mm		110mm

July		August		September		October		November		December	
	33°C		32°C		33°C		32°C		28°C		24°C
	26°C		26°C		25°C		19°C		12°C		8°C
	300mm		290mm		180mm		30mm		0mm		0mm

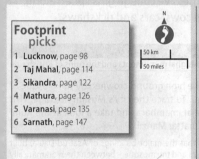

Footprint picks

50 km
50 miles

N

often blows from the west. Humidity and rainfall increase between June and September, making it a very uncomfortable season for travelling.

Time required

You will need two days for Agra's main sights, two days each for Lucknow and Dudhwa National Park and a week for Varanasi and nearby sights.

Modern Uttar Pradesh

Uttar Pradesh today is a vast, socially conservative and deeply agricultural state.

The majority of the 200 million-strong population is Hindu but nearly one fifth is Muslim, concentrated between Aligarh and Faizabad in what is called the 'Muslim Belt'. Today, adherents of Buddhism, Jainism, Christianity and Sikhism together constitute less than 3% of the state's population. Ethnically, the great majority of people on the plains are of Indo-Aryan stock. Most people speak Hindi, but Urdu is still quite widely used among Muslims. There are numerous local dialects.

Uttar Pradesh has produced eight of India's 15 prime ministers since Independence, including Jawaharlal Nehru, his daughter Indira Gandhi and grandson Rajiv Gandhi; Rajiv's widow, Sonia Gandhi, was also President until 2014. However, after three decades of Congress dominance, Narendra Modi, leader of the BJP (Bharatiya Janata Party) was elected as Prime Minister of India on 26th May 2014. He is also the MP for Varanasi.

Lucknow

★ In Kipling's *Kim* "no city – except Bombay, the queen of all – was more beautiful in her garish style than Lucknow". The capital of the state sprawls along the banks of the Gomti River in the heart of Uttar Pradesh. The ordered Cantonment area contrasts with the cream-washed buildings of the congested city centre, dotted with an incredible variety of decaying mansions and historic monuments, the best of which are breathtaking. In the heart of the old city traditional craftsmen continue to produce the rich gold zari work, delicate chikan embroidery and strong attar perfume. The arts still flourish and the bookshops do a brisk trade in serious reading. Veils have largely disappeared; now progressive college girls speed along on their scooters, weaving between cows, cars and rickshaws.

Sights   *Colour map 3, A2.*

Mughal monuments and the ruins of British rule

The original city centre is believed to be the high ground crowned by the Mosque of Aurangzeb on the right bank of the Gomti. To trace the city's Muslim heritage, visit the Bara and Chhota Imambaras, Shah Najaf Imambara and take a look at the Rumi Darwaza (Turkish Gate), Clock Tower and Chattar Manzil.

The architectural historian G Tillotson suggests that the major buildings of Asaf-ud-Daula, built after 1775 – the Bara Imambara, the Rumi Darwaza and the mosque – between them dramatically illustrate the 'debased Mughal' style of 'Indo-European' architecture in decline. Among the colonial monuments, the Residency and Constantia are the most rewarding. The monuments have been divided into three main groups. They are usually open between 0600 and 1700.

Northwest and Hussainabad
Allow 2-3 hrs for the Hussainabad tour.

Just south of the Hardinge Bridge was the **Machhi Bhavan** (Fish House) enclosure. Safdarjang, Governor of Oudh (1719-1748), was permitted to use the fish insignia (a royal/imperial symbol/crest) by the Mughal Emperor Akbar. The Machhi Bhavan itself, once a fort, was blown up by the British in 1857, the only surviving part being the *baoli* which escaped because it was sunk into the hillside.

The **Bara Imambara** ① *foreigners Rs 350, ticket also allows access to the Chhota Imambara and the Baradari, guide fees are posted outside, foreigners not permitted in the Asifi Mosque,* is a huge vaulted hall which, like all *imambaras*, serves as the starting point for the Muharram procession (see page 37). The vast hall (50 m long and 15 m high), built by Asaf-ud-Daula to provide employment during a famine (see box, page 103, is one of the largest in the world unsupported by pillars. Look out for the notice: "Spiting (sic), smoking and call of nature strictly prohibited"! The remarkable *bhul-bhulaya*, a maze of interconnecting passages above, is reached by stairs; a delightful diversion. One visitor spent over an hour trying to find his way out. The five-storeyed *baoli* is connected directly with the River Gomti. Legends suggest that secret tunnels connect the lower steps, which are always under water, with a treasure stored beneath the *imambara* itself.

At the end of the avenue leading up to the *imambara* from the river is the **Rumi Darwaza** (1784), a spectacular gate that resembles a conch-shell, built in the Byzantine style. Further along is the 19th-century Gothic 67-m-high Hussainabad **clock tower** (1880s) designed by Roskell Payne, which contains the largest clock in India though three of the four faces have been smashed. Next to it is the attractive octagonal Hussainabad Tank (1837-1842), around which is the Taluqdar's Hall and the incomplete Satkhanda (1840) seven-storeyed watchtower. There are excellent views of Lucknow from the top. Also worth a look is the restored **Baradari** ① *Tue-Sun 0800-1800, entrance included in the Bara Imambara ticket,* housing a picture gallery with portraits of the Nawabs of Oudh.

Hussainabad Imambara (Chhota Imambara) ① *sunrise-sunset, entrance included in the Bara Imambara ticket,* with its golden dome and elaborate calligraphy and containing beautiful chandeliers, gilt-edged mirrors and a silver throne (1837), is illuminated during Muharram. Further west is the extensively renovated **Jami Masjid** begun by Muhammad Shah and finished by his wife in the mid-1840s. **Victoria Park** (1890) with several British tombs is nearby. South of the park is the Chowk, the Old City bazar, where there are some interesting old buildings including the **Dargah of Hazrat Abbas** which contains a relic, a metal crest from the battle at Kerbala. Nearby is **Nadan Mahal** (c 1600), with the tomb of Shaikh Abdur Rahim, Akbar's Governor of Oudh, and son of Ibrahim Chishti. This is a fine building, built in the Mughal style and faced with red sandstone.

Essential Lucknow

Finding your feet

The modern airport is 14 km south of the city. There are direct flights to Delhi, Kolkata, Mumbai and Patna. Lucknow is also well connected by train and road to other major cities of the north. Lucknow is on the Northern and Northeastern railway lines with two main stations, **Charbagh** and **Lucknow Junction**, located next to each other about 3 km southwest of the city centre. The Kaiserbagh Bus Stand near the centre is for long-distance services, while most interstate buses terminate at the Charbagh Station Bus stand near the train stations.

Getting around

The main sights and the bus and train stations are close enough to the centre to visit by cycle-rickshaw, or by hopping on a cheap shared *tempo*, which run on fixed routes (Rs 3 minimum) and are easy to use. However, the city is quite spread out, so for extended sightseeing or to reach the airport it is worth hiring a taxi. See Transport, page 105.

Best Lucknow experiences

Live ghazal performances at Clarks Avadh, page 103
A walking tour with Tornos, page 104
Qawali singing on Thursdays at Sufi shrine Dewa Sharif, page 104

Residency and around

The Residency's 3000 mostly European occupants, hastily brought there by **Sir Henry Lawrence**, came under siege on 30 June 1857. Two days later Lawrence was fatally injured. After 90 days, General Sir Henry Havelock and General Sir James Outram appeared through the battered walls with a column of Highlanders. However, the siege was intensified and sepoy engineers began tunnelling to lay mines to blow the place up. From quite early on, there was a shortage of food and eventually smallpox, cholera and scurvy set in. Havelock was slowly dying of dysentery. Heroic Irishman Henry Kavanagh sat in the tunnels and shot mutineers as they wriggled forward to lay more mines. He then volunteered to run the gauntlet through the enemy lines to find Sir Colin Campbell's relieving force, which he did by swimming the Gomti. When the relieving force finally broke through on 17 November, the once splendid Residency was a blackened ruin, its walls pockmarked and gaping with cannonball holes. Today it is a mute witness to a desperate struggle. Of the 2994 men, women and children who had taken refuge in the Residency, only 1000 marched out.

The **Residency Compound** is now a historic monument. You enter through the Bailey Guard gate. The **Treasury** on your right served as an arsenal, while the grand Banquet Hall next door housed the wounded during the 'Uprising'. On the lawn of **Doctor Fayrer's House**, to your left, stands a marble cross to Sir Henry Lawrence. **Begum Kothi**, which belonged to Mrs Walters who married the Nawab of Oudh, can be reached through the long grass, but the old officers' mess has made way for flats and apartments.

The **Residency** (1800) ① *foreigners Rs 100, cameras Rs 25*, to the northeast, built by Saadat Ali Khan, has *tykhanas* (cool underground rooms) where there is a museum, the highlight of which is an 1873 model of the complex, which gives you a good idea of how extensive and self-sufficient the original settlement was. At the time of the 'Uprising' the Residency was overlooked by high houses, now all destroyed, which gave cover to snipers firing into the compound. There are many etchings and records including Tennyson's *Relief of Lucknow*. Suggestions of a wooden staircase for officers, an underground passage to the palace, a secret room hidden in the wall behind false doors, all conjure up images of the past. The graves of Lawrence, Neill and others are in the church **cemetery**. Women visitors should not visit the cemetery alone. Just outside the Residency on the banks of the Gomti is a white obelisk commemorating the 'Nationalist Insurgents' who lost their lives in 1857.

Southeast of the Residency, near the Hanuman Setu, is the **Chattar Manzil** (Umbrella Palace) now the Central Drug Research Institute, where the submerged basement provided natural air conditioning. There are also the sad remains of the **Kaisarbagh Palace** (1850) conceived as a grand chateau. Better preserved are the almost twin **tombs** of Saadat Ali Khan (1814) and Khurshid Begum. To its east again are **Nur Bakhsh Kothi** and Tarawali Kothi (circa 1832), the observatory of the royal astronomer Colonel Wilcox, which is now the **State Bank of India**.

1 Lucknow

➡ **Lucknow maps**
1 Lucknow, page 100
2 Lucknow centre, page 102

Where to stay 😴
Lucknow Homestay **4**
Vishwanath **1**

Vivanta by Taj & Oudhyana
Restaurant 🍴
3

BACKGROUND

Lucknow

Today Lucknow is a major administrative centre and market city with a population of over four and half million. It has grown rapidly on both sides of the Gomti River, expanding out from its historic core along the river's right bank. Although the discovery of Painted Grey Ware and Northern Black pottery demonstrates the long period over which the site has been occupied, its main claim to fame is as the capital of the cultured Nawabs of Oudh (*Avadh*), and later as the scene of one of the most remarkable episodes in the 'Uprising' of 1857.

Lucknow developed rapidly under the Mughal Emperor Akbar's patronage in the 16th century. In the early 18th century, Nawab Saadat Khan Burhan-ul-Mulk, a Persian courtier, founded the Oudh Dynasty. The city's growing reputation as a cultural centre attracted many others from Persia, leaving an indelible Shi'a imprint on the city's life. Under the Nawabs, Lucknow evolved specialized styles of dance, poetry, music and calligraphy. The builder of 'modern' Lucknow was Nawab Asaf-ud-Daula who shifted his capital here from Faizabad in 1775. In the attempt to build a wonderful city he emptied the regal coffers.

In the mid-1850s under Lord Dalhousie, the British annexed a number of Indian states. Dalhousie evolved a policy of lapse whereby the states of Indian princes without direct heirs could be taken over on the ruler's death. Chronic mismanagement was also deemed just cause for takeover; this was the justification given for the annexation of Oudh. The novelist Premchand in *The Chess Players* attributes the fall of Oudh to the fact that "small and big, rich and poor, were dedicated alike to sensual joys ... song, dance and opium". History suggests that Nawab Wajid Ali Shah continued with his game of chess even as British soldiers occupied his capital. A strong British presence was established in the city as it became a key administrative and military centre. Satyajit Ray's film *'Satranj Ki Khilari (The Chess Players)'* is an excellent portrayal of these times.

When the 'Uprising' (previously referred to as the Mutiny) broke in 1857, Sir Henry Lawrence gathered the British community into the Residency (see page 99), which rapidly became a fortress. The ensuing siege lasted for 87 days, leaving hundreds dead and the Residency in ruins.

Parivartan Chowk and the black Mayawati monument, which faces Clarks Avadh Hotel, symbolize *parivartan* (the spirit of 'change') which the 1997-1998 government of the fiery Chief Minister Mayawati hoped to encourage by giving increasing power to the scheduled castes. Recently Lucknow has been through periods of violent communal tension which is partly explained by the important BJP presence here. The city remains the region's cultural capital, however, and the Lucknowi *gharana* (house) of music and exquisite crafts are reminders of its splendid past. Today, of the vintage modes of travel, only the *ekka* (one-horse carriage) has survived. See Books, page 1355, for further reading.

Eastern group

Shah Najaf Imambara (1814-1827) ① *free entry*, near the Gomti, has the tombs of Nawab Ghazi-ud-Din Haidar and his three wives, with its white dome and elaborate interior decorations, including a huge array of chandeliers, mirrors and paintings. It was used by sepoy mutineers as a stronghold in 1857. Wajid Ali Shah's (ruled 1847-1856) pleasure garden **Sikander Bagh**, created for his favourite wife, retains the original gateway and mosque.

To the south of these are **Wingfield Park**, laid out in the 1860s, which contains a marble pavilion and some statues. Within the **Zoo** ① *Tue-Sun 0830-1730, foreigners Rs 100*, off Park Rd, is the **State Museum** ① *Banarsi Bagh, T0522-220 6158, Tue-Sun 1000-1700 (last entrance at 1600), foreigners Rs 50*, the oldest in Uttar Pradesh and one of the richest in India. It exhibits Hindu, Buddhist and Jain works including stone sculptures from Mathura, and busts and friezes from Allahabad and Garhwal, dating from the first to 11th centuries, plus marble sculptures, paintings, natural history and anthropology. Marvellous relics of the British Raj, removed at the time of Independence, languish in the backyard. **Christchurch** (1860), a memorial to the British killed during the

'Uprising' is nearby, along with the imposing Legislative Council Chamber (1928) and **Raj Bhawan** (Government House), enlarged in 1907.

To the east is Constantia, now **La Martinière College**, planned as the country residence of Major-General Claude Martin (1735-1800), a French soldier of fortune who is buried in the crypt. He ran highly successful indigo and money-lending businesses. The curious wedding cake of a building was completed after Martin's death from the endowment set aside by him for a school here and at Kolkata for 'Anglo-Indians' (Kipling's *Kim* being one of them). For the students' bravery during the siege of the Residency, the school was unique in being awarded Battle Honours. The chapel, historical photos and the crypt are interesting. You may ask to look around both outside and within. The office is at the east end.

Further south is **Dilkusha** (Heart's Delight), once a royal shooting lodge in what was a large deer park. There are graves of soldiers who died here during the 'Uprising', including that of General Havelock; his grave obelisk is in Alam Bagh, 100 m northeast of the garden's main gateway.

2 Lucknow centre

Lucknow maps
1 Lucknow, page 100
2 Lucknow centre, page 102

N

500 metres
500 yards

Where to stay
Arif Castles **1**
Clarks Avadh & Falaknuma
Restaurant **4**
Gomti & UP Tours **5**

Tekarees Inn & Koolbreak **9**

Restaurants
Moti Mahal **1**
Royal Inn/Royal Café **2**

BACKGROUND
Food for work

In 1784 Lucknow and its region suffered an appalling famine, and thousands of starving people flocked into the city. In a spectacular example of 'food for work' (pre-Keynes Keynesian economics) Asaf-ud-Daula decided to build the Great Imambara. He offered work night and day, reputedly employing 22,000 men, women and children. However, in order to ensure that the task was not finished too quickly, he divided it into two parts. During the day, normal building proceeded. At night the workmen destroyed one quarter of what had been built the previous day. Nobles were allowed to work at night to spare them the embarrassment of being seen as having to labour to survive. To the labourers this was a life-saving act of charity, even if the building itself is widely reported as something of a monstrosity.

Listings Lucknow *maps p100 and p102*

Tourist information

Tourist office
Charbagh Railway Station, Main Hall.
Daily 0600-2200.
Brochures and enthusiastic staff; also at the airport. Information is also available from **UP Tours** at **Gomti Hotel** (see below), Mon-Sat 0900-1800.

Where to stay

$$$$ Clarks Avadh
8 MG Marg, T0522-262 0131,
www.hotelclarks.com.
98 rooms, modern, clean, comfortable, efficient, attentive service, good restaurants. Well known for its live music. Recommended.

$$$$ Vivanta by Taj
Vipin Khand, Gomti Nagar, 5 km east of railway station, T0522-671 1000, www.vivantabytaj.com.
110 rooms in elegant colonial-style modern building, excellent restaurants, good pool, attractive gardens (transplanted mature palms). The city's most luxurious hotel and the only really quiet one.

$$$ Arif Castles
4 Rana Pratap Marg, Hazratganj,
T0522-409 8777, www.arifcastles.com.
The exterior is uninspiring, but inside is since it re-opened in 2010 as a boutique hotel, 42 rooms and suites with full amenities and chic furnishings. 2 good restaurants, specializing in Nawabi and Italian food. Great location.

$$ Tekarees Inn
17/3 Ashok Marg, T0522-228 8928,
www.tekareesinn.com.
Tiled floors, TV, fridge, rooms feel bright but layout varies so look at a few. Disappointing shower rooms for the price. Recommended restaurant.

$$-$ Gomti (UP Tourism)
6 Sapru Marg, T0522-262 0624,
www.up-tourism.com.
65 rooms covering a range of categories, all with TV, some a/c, but getting shabby and fusty at the lower end of the spectrum. However, the location is good, as is the restaurant and bright attractive bar (open 1100-2400, beer Rs 120), plus service is attentive.

$$ Carlton
Rana Pratap Marg, T0522-262 2445.
Charming ex-British residency, large rooms and huge lawn. A little bit of heritage in the heart of Lucknow.

$ Lucknow Homestay
10 Mall Av, T0522-223 5460, www.
lucknowhomestay.wordpress.com.
7 modest rooms a couple of kilometres southeast of the city centre (expect train noise), but homely and clean. Use of fridge/kettle, free Wi-Fi, breakfast included, delicious dinners available, good library. Contact them for potential volunteer work and internships. Recommended.

$ Vishwanath
Subhash Marg, Charbagh, T0522-245 0879,
vishwanath_04@yahoo.com.
Good-value rooms in convenient location. Decent restaurant on site and friendly welcome.

Restaurants

The better hotels serve good Lucknowi food: rich *biryanis*, *roomali roti*, *kebabs* and *kulfis* to end the meal. Special *cum pukht* (steam-cooked) dishes are worth trying. 1st and 7th of month and public holidays are 'dry' days.

$$$ Falaknuma
Rooftop of Clarks Avadh (see Where to stay).
Serves tasty, spicy Nawabi cuisine by candle light, good views, beer available, attentive service and live *ghazals* of exceptionally high quality. Recommended.

$$$ Oudhyana
At Vivanta by Taj (see Where to stay).
Special Avadhi food, lovely surroundings, the finest fine dining in town. Book in advance.

$$ Royal Inn/Royal Café
9/7 Shahnajaf Rd, T0522-409 5555.
Open 1100-2300.
Excellent and huge menu of mainly Indian and Chinese dishes, veg or non-veg. Large modern surrounds, attracts families, deservedly popular. It's not cheap but expect quality.

$ Moti Mahal
75 Hazratgang, T0522-404 8101.
Open 0800-2330.
Huge menu, mainly North Indian but some Chinese and South Indian, good ice creams, family-friendly split-level restaurant.

$ Tunde Kababi
Branches in the main Chowk and Aminabad Chowk.
Kebabs (named after a one-armed ancestor) are sought after locally and famed throughout the city. Recommended.

Entertainment

Dewa Sharif, *35 km northeast of Lucknow, free entry*. The atmospheric shrine of *Haji Waris Ali Shah* has beautiful Sufi Qawali singing every Thu evening (before sunset).

Festivals

Feb **Lucknow Literary Festival** with literature and music events.
Oct-Nov **National Kite Flying Competition** at the Patang Park, MG Marg the day after **Diwali**.
25 Nov-5 Dec **Mahotsav Festival** with emphasis on Indian classical music: song, drama and dance, processions, boating and *ekka* races, crafts and cuisine.

Shopping

Lucknow is famous for fine floral *chikan* or 'shadow' embroidery in pastel colours, produced around the chowk. You will also find gold *zari* and sequin work and prized *attar* (perfumes). Shops are usually open 1000-1930, markets until 2000. **Janpath market**, Hazratganj, is closed on Sun; **Aminabad**, Chowk, Sadar, Super Bazar closed on Thu. The following are in Hazratganj:

Asghar Ali, *near Chowk*. Heady scents of spices and flowers – a sensual experience with *attar* perfumes.
Gangotri, *31/29*. Handloom and crafts, and other government emporia.
Lal Behari Tandon, *17 Ashok Marg*. Good-quality *chikan*.
Ram Advani, *Mayfair Cinema Building, Hazratganj, T0522-262 3511. Mon-Sat 1000-1930*. Lucknow's best bookshop since 1951. A booklover's oasis.

What to do

Golf
Golf course at **La Martinière Boys College**, open to public. One of the hazards is the tomb of Augustus Nayne, a British officer who fell in the 'Uprising' and was reputedly buried with his monocle still in place.

Horse racing
Race course at Cantonment.

Tour operators
Tornos, *Tornos House, C-2016 Indira Nagar, T(0)9935-538105, toll free T1800-1022882, www. tornosindia.com*. Offering exceptional insight into Lucknow from culinary tours to Thursday Sufi Qawali music tours. Very reliable. Whole host of special interest walking tours, as well as trips to local villages, mango orchards and possibly tea with a Nawab. Highly recommended.
UP Tours, *Hotel Gomti, T0522-261 2659*. Good for air/rail tickets and car hire. They run *tonga* sightseeing tours (4 people, Rs 400, 4 hrs, 2 hrs advance notice required) and **Heritage Walks** which start near the Hardinge Bridge and take in lesser-known sights in the Chowk (daily starting 0800, 3 hrs; contact directly on T(0)9415-013047). Interesting and very good value.

Transport

Air

Amausi Airport (recently renamed Chaudhry Charan Singh International Airport) is 14 km south of the city, about 30 mins by taxi (pre-paid Rs 310) or auto (available outside for about Rs 150). Flights to most Indian cities, daily to **Delhi** with **Air India** and **IndiGo**, also to **Mumbai**, **Kolkata** and **Patna**. Thrice weekly flights to **Kathmandu** with **Buddha Air**, www.buddhaair.com.

Bus

Long-distance UP Roadways, Charbagh Bus Stand, T0522-245 0988 (left luggage, 0600-2200, Rs 5-10 per piece). Frequent services to **Allahabad** (4½ hrs), **Faizabad** (3 hrs), **Gorakhpur** (9 hrs), **Kanpur** (2½ hrs) and **Varanasi** (9 hrs). From **Kaisarbagh Bus Stand**, T0522-222 2503, to **Delhi** (12-13 hrs), also services to **Gorakhpur** for Nepal.

Train

Lucknow is on the Northern and Northeastern railway lines with 2 main railway stations, **Charbagh** and **Lucknow Junction**. Take special care of belongings at the railway stations. Theft is common. To get from the stations to the centre, catch a *tempo*-rickshaw from across the road and ask for a landmark nearby, eg GPO. **Northern Railway** trains leave from both stations: enquiries T131, Arrivals T1331, Departures T1332; reservations Charbagh T0522-263 5841. **Northeastern Railway** trains leave from Junction station: enquiries T0522-263 5877. Key trains for **Agra Fort**: *Marudhar Exp 14853/14863/14865*, 5½ hrs. **Allahabad**: *Nauchandi Exp 14512*, 4½ hrs; *Ganga-Gomti Exp 14216*, 4¼ hrs; *Intercity Exp 14210*, 0730, 4¼ hrs. **Bhopal**: *GKP Exp 12589/12591*, 9½ hrs; *Pushpak Exp 12533*, 10¼ hrs. **Gorakhpur** (for Nepal): several, best are *Kathgodam Howrah Bagh Exp 13020*, leaving early morning, 6 hrs; *Krishak Exp 15008*, 7¼ hrs. **Jabalpur** (for Kanha): *Chitrakoot Exp 15009*, 14¼ hrs. **Jhansi** (for **Orchha**) *Kushinagar Exp 11016*, 6¼ hrs; *Pushpak Exp 12533*, 6 hrs. **Kanpur**: *Gomti Exp 12419*, 1½ hrs; *Shatabdi Exp 12003*, 1¼ hrs. **Kolkata** (H): *Amritsar-Howrah Mail 13006*, 20½ hrs; *Doon Exp 13010*, 22½ hrs. **Kathgodam** (for **Nainital**): *Bagh Exp 13019*, 9 hrs. **New Delhi**: *Gomti Exp 12419*, 0525, 8½ hrs; or the fastest option is *Shatabdi Exp 12003*, 6½ hrs; **Varanasi**: *Kashi Vishwanath Exp 14258*, 7 hrs; *Varuna Exp 14228/24228*, 5½ hrs.

Beyond
Lucknow

Uttar Pradesh has been involved in some of the most turbulent events in modern Indian history, from the 1857 Uprising in Kanpur, now the state's largest industrial city, to the clashes in 2002 between Hindus and Muslims over the holy site of Ayodhya. East of Ayodhya, Gorakhpur makes a convenient base for exploring a number of key Buddhist sites, as well as being a popular jumping-off point for the crossing to Nepal, while north of Lucknow in the Himalayan foothills, the rarely visited Dudhwa National Park protects a handful of tigers and a reintroduced population of Indian one-horned rhino.

North of Lucknow *Colour map 3, A2.*

go wildlife-spotting on an elephant

Dudhwa National Park

Reception Centre, Dudhwa National Park, Lakhimpur Kheri, near Dist Magistrate's house, 220 km north of Lucknow, T(0)9559758965, www.dudhwanationalpark.in. Open mid-Nov to mid-Jun. Foreigners Rs 300 per day; Indians and students pay reduced rates; camera free, video Rs 500; road fees for light vehicles Rs 150 per day, jeep hire Rs 20-30 per km; elephant ride for up to 4 people, 2½ hrs, minimum charge Rs 200. Night driving is not allowed in the park so arrive before sunset.

A reserve since 1879, Dudhwa was designated a national park in 1977 and became a Project Tiger Reserve in 1988 by adding 200 sq km of the Kishanpur Sanctuary, 30 km away. Bordering the Sarda River in the Terai, it is very similar to the Corbett National Park. It has sal forest (in addition to sheesham, asna, khair and sagaun), tall savannah grasslands and large marshy areas watered by the Neora and Sohel rivers.

The swamps are the ideal habitat of the barasingha (swamp deer with 12 tined antlers, *Cervus duvanceli*), now numbering about 2000, which are best seen in the Sathiana and Kakraha blocks. The tiger population is believed to be about 140 though they are rarely spotted. Dudhwa also has sambar, nilgai, some sloth bears (*Melursus ursinus*), the endangered hispid hare, fishing cats and a few leopards. The one-horned rhino was reintroduced from northeast India in 1985 but visitors are not allowed into the enclosure. The 400 species of avifauna includes *Bengal floricans*, pied and great Indian hornbills, owls and king vultures. It also attracts a wide variety of water birds (swamp partridge, eastern white stork) in addition to birds of prey (osprey, hawks, fishing eagles). Banke Tal is good for birdwatching.

To view the wildlife you can hire a jeep or minibus from the park office at Dudhwa, or book an elephant ride on arrival at the park, recommended. The best time to visit is February to April; from April to June it becomes very hot, dry and dusty, but it is good for viewing big game. In summer the maximum temperature is 35°C, minimum 10°C. In winter the maximum is 30°C, minimum 4°C. Annual rainfall is 1500 mm; the wettest months are June to September. The nearby town of Palia has a bank, a basic health centre and a post office; Dudhwa itself has a dispensary.

Where to stay

Dudhwa National Park

$$$ Jambolana Safari Camp
Dudhwa, T(0)98100 17372,
www.jambolanasafaricamp.com.
Atmospheric safari camp with 9 tents (3 luxury)
with lovely outdoor bathrooms. You can opt
for jungle jeep trips, guided walks and birding.
Recommended.

$$-$ Forest Rest Houses

There are rest houses at both Dudhwa, Sathiana
and Bankatti. There is air con at Dudhwa. There
are also log huts and 25 dorm beds at Dudhwa.
In some of the rest houses you need to bring your
own food and utensils – call ahead. For bookings
look at www.dudhwanationalpark.in.

Transport

Dudhwa National Park

Air The nearest airports are Lucknow (219 km);
and Bareilly (160 km) in India, and Dhangari
(35 km) in Nepal.

Bus UP Roadways and private buses connect
Palia (10 km from the park) with the Reception
Centre at **Lakhimpur Kheri** and **Lucknow**
(219 km), **Shahjahanpur** (107 km), **Bareilly**
(160 km; extensive connections with all major
cities on the plains) and **Delhi** (420 km).

Train Dudhwa is on the **Northeast Railway**,
metre gauge line, and is connected with Bareilly
via **Mailani** (45 km from the park). Mailani to
Bareilly: *Rohilkand Exp 15309*, 3½ hrs. From Bareilly:
Rohilkand Exp 15310, 3½ hrs. A branch line from
Mailani links places in the park. Transport is not
always available at **Dudhwa Station**; best to get
off at **Palia** (10 km) and take the hourly bus or taxi.

a hotbed of religious fervour and dispute

Faizabad

Faizabad, 124 km east of Lucknow, is handy for visiting Ayodhya and was once the capital of Oudh.
Shuja-ud-Daula (1754-1775), the third Nawab of Oudh, built Fort Calcutta here after his defeat
by the British at Buxar in 1764. The 42-m-high white marble **Mausoleum of Bahu Begum** (circa
1816), his widow, is particularly fine. Gulab Bari (Mausoleum of Shuja-ud-Daula, circa 1775) nearby,
contains the tombs of his mother and father.

Ayodhya

Ayodhya ('a place where battles cannot take place'), 9 km from Faizabad on the banks of the **Saryu
River**, is one of the seven holy Hindu cities (the others are Mathura, Haridwar, Varanasi, Ujjain,
Dwarka and Kanchipuram). It is regarded by many Hindus as the birthplace of Rama (see box,
page 108) and where he once reigned, though the historian Romila Thapar stresses that there is no
evidence for such a belief. Jains regard it as the birthplace of the first and fourth Tirthankars, and the
Buddha is also thought to have stayed here.

The **Archaeological Survey of India** (ASI) and the **Indian Institute of Advanced Study** began
excavation at Ayodhya in 1978. According to Professor BB Lal, the site was occupied from at least the
seventh century BC if not earlier, when both iron and copper were in use. Later finds include a Jain
figure from the fourth to third century BC, possibly the earliest Jain figure found in India. Houses
during this period were built in kiln-baked brick, and various coins have been found from periods
up to the fourth century AD, some indicating extensive trade with East India. Under the Mughals,
in accordance with Muslim practice elsewhere, a number of temples were razed and mosques were
built on the site, often using the same building material. However, as BB Lal points out: "many of the
now standing temples [were] erected during the past two centuries only".

In recent decades Ayodhya has become the focus of intense political activity by the Vishwa
Hindu Parishad, an organization asserting a form of militant Hinduism, and the BJP, its leading
political ally. They claim that Ayodhya was '**Ramajanambhumi**' (Rama's birthplace) and that this

holy site lay beneath the remains of the 15th-century **Babri Mosque**, built by Babur. On 6 December 1992, the mosque was destroyed by militant Hindus. This was followed by widespread disturbances resulting in over 2500 deaths across the country. The massacre of young Hindu activists returning from Ayodhya to Gujarat in February 2002 resulted in over 1000 deaths in the following months. The site of the razed mosque continues to be a focus of contention to this day and is the subject of long-standing legal battles between Hindus and Muslims. Ayodhya remains a potential flashpoint, so check conditions first if you plan to visit.

Other sites include **Lakshmana Ghat**, 3 km from the station, where Rama's brother committed suicide. **Hanumangarh** takes its name from the Hanuman and Sita temple and the massive walls surrounding it.

Gorakhpur
Gorakhpur, at the confluence of the Rapti and Rohini rivers, is the last major Indian town before the Nepali border (see box, page 1362). The British and the Gurkha armies clashed nearby in the early 18th century. Later it became the recruitment centre for Gurkha soldiers enlisting into the British and Indian armies. The Gorakhnath Temple attracts Hindu pilgrims, particularly *Kanfata sadhus* who have part of their ears cut. Unusual terracotta pottery figures and animals are made here.

Kushinagar
Kushinagar, 50 km east of Gorakhpur, is celebrated as the place where the Buddha died and was cremated and passed into parinirvana; the actual site is unknown. Originally called Kushinara, it is one of four major Buddhist pilgrimage sites (see page 1339). Monasteries established after the Buddha's death flourished here until the 13th century.

In the main site, the core of the Main Stupa possibly dates from Asoka's time with the **Parinirvana Temple**. The restored 6-m recumbent sandstone figure of the dying Buddha in a shrine in front may have been brought from Mathura by the monk Haribala during King Kumargupta's reign (AD 413-455). The *stupas*, *chaityas* and *viharas*, however, were 'lost' for centuries. The Chinese pilgrims Fa Hien, Hiuen Tsang, and I Tsing, all recorded the decay and ruins of Kushinagar between 900 and 1000 years after the Buddha's death. The *stupa* and the temple were rediscovered only in the 1880s. The **Mathakuar shrine** to the southwest has a large Buddha in the *bhumisparsha mudra* and marks the place where the Buddha last drank water. **Rambahar stupa** (Mukutabandhana), 1 km east, was built by the Malla Dynasty to house the Buddha's relics after the cremation. Some of the bricks (which have holes for easier firing) were carved to form figures.

Excavations were begun by the Archaeological Survey of India in 1904-1905, following clues left by the Chinese travellers. A shaft was driven through the centre of the Nirvana *stupa* "which brought to light a copper plate placed on the mouth of a relic casket in the form of a copper vessel with charcoal, cowries, precious stones and a gold coin of Kumaragupta I." In all there are eight groups of monasteries, *stupas* and images, indicating that Kushinagar was a substantial community.

Listings East of Lucknow

Tourist information

Gorakhpur

Tourist office
Park Rd, Civil Lines, T0551-233 5450; also a counter on Platform 1 at the railway station.

Where to stay

Faizabad
For visits to Ayodhya, it is best to stay in Faizabad where there are better hotels.

$$-$ Shan-e-Avadh
Near Civil Lines Bus Stand, T05278-223586.
Clean hotel, 52 rooms with bath, hot water, good restaurant, clean.

$$-$ Tirupati
Main Rd, T05278-223231, next door to Shan-e-Avadh.
35 rooms with bath (bucket hot water), some a/c, best upstairs at rear, good restaurant, modern.

Ayodhya

$ Rahi Tourist Bungalow (UPTDC)
Turn right from railway station, T05278-232435, www.up-tourism.com.
Very clean, basic rooms, 1 a/c, simple restaurant, tourist information, friendly. They have another property Rahi Yatra.

Gorakhpur
Budget hotels opposite the railway station can be noisy.

$$$ Clarks Grand
6 Park Rd, Civil Lines, T0551-220 5016, www.clarksinngrand.in.
Upmarket hotel with all the mod cons, bit faceless. Good family restaurant on-site.

$$-$ Avantika
Airport Rd (NH28), beyond crossroads 3 km from railway station, T0551-220 0765.
Modern, good rooms and restaurant in good location.

$$-$ Ganges
Tarang Crossing, T0551-605 9099.
Some a/c rooms, good restaurant and ice cream parlour, well managed. Recommended.

$ Upvan
Nepal Rd, T0551-233 8003.
Ask rickshaw for **Bobina** next door. Some a/c or good air-cooled rooms, Indian restaurant, clean, efficient room service. Recommended.

Kushinagar

$$-$ Pathik Niwas
UPTDC, near ASI office, T05564-273045, www.up-tourism.com.
8 rooms, tourist office, good restaurant.

$ Dharamshalas
T05564-273093.
The Chinese temple's new block is recommended.

Restaurants

Gorakhpur
$$-$ Recommended hotel restaurants include **Avantika**, **Ganges** and **Clarks Grand** (see Where to stay), also fast-food outlets near Indira Children's Park.

$ Ganesh
Park Rd.
South Indian vegetarian.

Festivals

Kushinagar
Apr/May Buddha Jayanti (1st full moon) marks the Buddha's birth. A huge fair is held when his relics (on public display at this time only) are taken out in procession.

Transport

Faizabad
Bus Bus stand, T05278-222964, bus to **Lucknow**, 3 hrs; **Varanasi**, 0630, 6 hrs.

Train Railway station, T05278-244119.

Ayodhya

Train T05278-232023. **Jodhpur**, via **Agra** and **Jaipur**: *Marudhar Exp 14853* (Mon, Wed, Sat), 10 hrs (Agra), 15½ hrs (Jaipur), 21¼ hrs (Jodhpur). **Varanasi**: *Marudhar Exp 14854* (Tue, Fri, Sun), 4 hrs.

Gorakhpur

Bus The **main bus stand** is a 3-min walk from the railway station, with services to **Lucknow** (6-7 hrs), **Faizabad** (4 hrs), **Kushinagar** (on the hr, 2 hrs), and **Patna** (10 hrs). Buses for **Varanasi** (205 km, 6 hrs) leave from Katchari Stand.

To Nepal (See border box, page 1362.) UP Government buses (green and yellow) are 'Express' and depart the main bus stand from 0500, for **Nautanwa** (95 km; 2½ hrs) or **Sonauli**, just beyond, on the border (102 km; Rs 40; 3 hrs). Private buses leave from opposite the railway station; touts will try to sell you tickets all the way to Kathmandu or Pokhara, but there's no guarantee of bus quality across border. Buses to **Kathmandu** (12 hrs), **Pokhara** (10 hrs), **Nepalganj** or **Narayanghat** (for national park). Most depart at 0700. Beware of ticket touts in Gorakhpur (private buses opposite railway station) and Nepal border. Some overcharge and others demand excessive 'luggage charge'. When buying a ticket, make absolutely sure which bus to catch by getting the number or registration; check what is included in ticket (meals, overnight accommodation) and find out when and from where it departs (may be 2 hrs' delay). Avoid **International Tourism Agency** opposite railway station; its buses are very poorly maintained.

Train **Gorakhpur Junction**, NE Railway HQ station, has tourist information, left luggage (only with padlocks, Rs 15 per piece) and computerized reservations; good waiting rooms. **Old Delhi**: *Barauni-Katihar Amritsar Exp 15707*, 15½ hrs. **New Delhi**: *Vaishali Exp 12553*, 13½ hrs (often longer, up to 20 hrs); several others. **Kolkata (H)**: *Howrah Bagh Exp 13020*, 22½ hrs. **Lucknow**: *Lucknow Exp 15007*, 7 hrs. **Varanasi**: *Krishak Exp 15008* (early morning), 6¼ hrs; *Manduadih Exp 15103* (evening), 5½ hrs. For access to Nepal, you can take trains to **Nautanwa** and then onward bus: the most convenient are 2 *Fast Passenger trains 95*, 0615, 2½ hrs (return *96* departs Nautanwa 0910); *93*, 3¼ hrs (return *94*). No need to book ahead (1st class, Rs 100; 2nd class, Rs 35). See above for bus services to Kathmandu and Pokhara from Nautanwa.

Kushinagar
Bus and taxi From **Gorakhpur** (30 mins).

Kanpur and around *Colour map 3, B2.*

this teeming industrial centre is not for the faint-hearted

Kanpur was one of the most important British garrisons on the Ganga and was besieged during the 'Uprising' (see box, opposite). Some of the first cotton mills in India were established here in 1869. It is now the most important industrial centre in the state, with aviation, woollen and leather industries, cotton, flour and vegetable oil mills, sugar refineries and chemical works. As a result of this high level of industry, the city is extremely polluted and has become one sprawling, congested market, with seemingly every street constantly choked with traffic. As an example of industry run riot it somehow has a perverse attraction and perhaps needs to be experienced once in a lifetime.

Sights
The principal British monuments are in the southeast of the city in the old cantonment area. Stone posts mark the lines of the siege trenches near **All Souls' Memorial Church** (1862-1875), a handsome Gothic-style building designed by Walter Granville. A tiled pavement outside marks the graves of those executed on 1 July 1857, soon after the Satichaura Ghat massacre. To the east, the **Memorial Garden** has a statue by Marochetti and a screen designed by Sir Henry Yule, which were

Essential Kanpur

Getting around

City Bus Service has an extensive network for getting around the city. Tempos, auto-rickshaws, cycle-rickshaws and horse *tongas* are also available. Private taxis can be hired from Canal Road taxi stand, hotels and agencies.

BACKGROUND
The uprising in Kanpur

Kanpur was one of the most important British garrisons on the Ganga. During the 'Uprising' the insurgents rallied under Nana Sahib, who bore a grievance against the British because he had received only a small pension. They laid siege to the British community of around 400 men, women and children who had been gathered together under General Sir Hugh Wheeler. Inadequately protected and without enough food, after 18 days the defenders were severely reduced through gunshot wounds, starvation and disease. Nana Sahib then offered a truce and arranged for boats to take the survivors downstream to Allahabad. When they were boarding at Satichaura Ghat, they were raked with fire and hacked down by horsemen. One boat escaped. The survivors were either butchered and thrown down a well or died of cholera and dysentery. The reprisals were as horrible. General Sir James Neill "was seized with an Old Testamental vision of revenge" (Moorhouse). To break a man's religion and caste, pork and beef were stuffed down his throat, thus condemning him to eternal damnation. More often than not, suspected mutineers were bayoneted on sight. Nana Sahib escaped after pretending to commit suicide in the Ganga and is believed to have died in Nepal in 1859. For further reading, see Books, page 1355.

brought here after Independence. The infamous **Satichaura Ghat**, 1 km northeast of the church by the Ganga, has a small Siva temple. You can walk along the river from the Lucknow Road bridge (about 200 m, but dirty) which leads to the site of the boat massacre just upstream of the temple, where cannons were stationed on the high banks. The temple is altered but the landing ghats are still used by fishermen's boats and for washing clothes.

At the siege site, remains of the walls are still visible – as is the privy drain system and the well. The Massacre House was north of the canal about 250 m from the Ganga, and north of the Arms Factory, now marked by a statue of Nana Sahib. In the city centre there is the King Edward VII **Memorial (KEM) Hall** and **Christ Church** (1848). The higher-grade hotels are along the Mall, some within reach of Meston Road with its interesting, faded, colonial architecture and cheap leather goods shops.

Bithur

Nana Sahib's home town, 20 km north of Kanpur, has pleasant ghats by the Ganga. His opulent palace was destroyed by the British in 1857 and is now marked by a memorial bust. Ruins of a few large well heads survive in a park west of the main road into town from Kanpur. 'Enthusiasts' should allow two hours.

Listings Kanpur and around

Tourist information

UPTDC
26/51 Birhana Rd, opposite the post office, T(0)91962 13079.

Where to stay

Some budget hotels are reluctant to take foreigners as it means filling out forms.

$$$ Landmark
Som Datta Plaza, 10 The Mall, T0512-230 5305, www.thehotellandmark.com.
131 plain but comfortable rooms, smart restaurants, casual coffee lounge, station/ airport pick-up, large pool (open to non-residents) and a huge games room including a 4-lane bowling alley.

$$ Attic
15/198 V Singh Rd, Civil Lines, T0512-230 6691, www.theattickanpur.com.
Charming colonial house with 13 a/c rooms in a modern block behind. There is a beautifully kept garden. Probably the most peaceful place in town. Recommended.

$ Geet
18/174-5 The Mall, T0512-231 1042, www.geethotel.com.
40 a/c rooms, restaurant good, exchange. Slightly cheaper than **Gaurav**.

$ Meera Madhuvan
37/19 The Mall, T0512-231 9972.
Clean, modern and friendly, 50 rooms, some a/c, restaurant (Indian snacks, drinks), good value, recommended.

Restaurants

$$$ Cwanpore 1857
The Landmark (see Where to stay).
Delicious and stylish 5-star experience. Good for tandoor and biryani – lovely ambience and great service.

$$ Kwality
16/97 The Mall.
International, bar. Deservedly popular chain restaurant.

$$ Shanghai
The Mall.
Chinese.

$ Shalaka
In shopping arcade opposite Landmark.
Pizzas and South Indian snacks.

Shopping

The main shopping areas are **The Mall**, Birhana Rd, and **Navin Market**. Kanpur is famous for cotton and leather products, which can be found along **Meston Rd**.

What to do

Tour operators
Sita, *18/53 The Mall, T0512-235 2980, www.sita india.com.* Package tours and local information. **UPTDC**, *Birhama Rd, T(0)91962 13059.* Local tours.

Transport

Bus UP Roadways Bus Stand, Fazalganj, T0512-232 5381, for **Lucknow, Allahabad**, etc; **Chunniganj**, T0512-253 0646, for **Delhi, Agra**.

Train Kanpur is on the main broad gauge Delhi–Kolkata line and also has lines from Lucknow, Agra and Central India. **Central Station**, T139, T0512-2032 8170; **Anwarganj**, T0512-254 5488. **Agra**: *Toofan Exp 13007,* 7 hrs (Agra Cantt); *Jodhpur/Bikaner Exp 12307,* 4 hrs (Agra Fort). **Kolkata (H)**: *Rajdhani Exp* (via Gaya) *12302/12306,* 12½ hrs. **Lucknow**: *Shatabdi Exp 12004,* 1¼ hrs. **New Delhi**: *Shatabdi Exp 12003* (late afternoon), 5 hrs; *Rajdhani Exp 12301/12305* (early morning), 5 hrs. **Patna**: *Rajdhani Exp 12302/12306,* 8 hrs. **Varanasi**: *Lichhavi Exp 15206,* 6 hrs.

Agra

The romance of what is arguably the world's most famous building still astonishes in its power. In addition to the Taj Mahal, Agra also houses the great monuments of the Red Fort and the I'timad-ud-Daulah, but to experience their beauty you have to endure the less attractive sides of one of India's least prepossessing industrial cities. The monuments are often covered in a haze of polluted air, and visitors may be subjected to a barrage of high-power selling. Despite it all, the experience is unmissable. The city is also a convenient gateway to the wonderful, abandoned capital of Fatehpur Sikri, the beautifully serene Akbar's Mausoleum and some of Hinduism's holiest sites.

Essential Agra

Finding your feet

By far the best way to arrive is on the *Shatabdi Express* train from Delhi, which is much faster than travelling by car and infinitely more comfortable than the frequent 'express' buses, which can take five tiring hours. Agra airport only receives charter flights.

Getting around

Buses run a regular service between the station, bus stands and the main sites. Cycle-rickshaws,

Best Taj views

From the arches of the Red Fort, page 118.
From a balcony at the Oberoi Amarvilas, page 123.
From the rooftop restaurant of the Hotel Kamal, page 123.

autos and taxis can be hired to venture further afield, or you can hire a bike if it's not too hot. The area around the Taj Mahal itself is only accessible by cycle rickshaw. See Transport, page 125.

Useful information

Note that there is an Agra Development Authority Tax of Rs 500 levied on each day you visit the Taj Mahal, which includes the Red Fort, Fatehpur Sikri and other attractions. This is in addition to the individual entry fees to the monuments. The Taj Mahal is closed every Friday.

When to go

The best time to visit is between November and March. Avoid the city on Indian public holidays. See also Essential Taj Mahal, page 115.

BACKGROUND

Agra

With minor interruptions, Agra alternated with Delhi as the capital of the Mughal Empire. Sikander Lodi seized it from a rebellious governor and made it his capital in 1501. He died in Agra but is buried in Delhi (see page 71). Agra was Babur's capital. He is believed to have laid out a pleasure garden on the east bank of the River Yamuna and his son Humayun built a mosque here in 1530. Akbar lived in Agra in the early years of his reign. Ralph Fitch, the English Elizabethan traveller, described a "magnificent city, with broad streets and tall buildings". He also saw Akbar's new capital at Fatehpur Sikri, 40 km west, describing a route lined all the way with stalls and markets. Akbar moved his capital again to Lahore, before returning to Agra in 1599, where he spent the last six years of his life. Jahangir left Agra for Kashmir in 1618 and never returned. Despite modifying the Red Fort and building the Taj Mahal, Shah Jahan also moved away in 1638 to his new city Shah Jahanabad in Delhi, though he returned in 1650, taken prisoner by his son Aurangzeb and left to spend his last days in the Red Fort. It was Aurangzeb, the last of the Great Mughals, who moved the seat of government permanently to Delhi. In the 18th century Agra suffered at the hands of the Jats was taken, lost and retaken by the Marathas who, in turn, were ousted by the British in 1803. It was the centre of much fighting in the 'Uprising' and was the administrative centre of the Northwest Provinces and Oudh until that too was transferred to Allahabad in 1877.

★ Taj Mahal

the pearl of India

Of all the world's great monuments, the Taj Mahal is one of the most written about, photographed, filmed and talked about. To India's Nobel Laureate poet, Tagore, the Taj was a "tear drop on the face of humanity", a building to echo the cry "I have not forgotten, I have not forgotten, O beloved," and its mesmerizing power is such that despite the hype, no one comes away disappointed.

Shah Jahan, the fifth of the Great Mughals, was so devoted to his favourite wife, Mumtaz Mahal (Jewel of the Palace) that he could not bear to be parted from her and insisted that she always travel with him, in all states of health. While accompanying him on a military campaign, she died at the age of 39 giving birth to their 14th child. On her deathbed, it is said, she asked the emperor to show the world how much they loved one another.

The grief-stricken emperor went into mourning for two years. He turned away from the business of running the empire and dedicated himself to architecture, resolving to build his wife the most magnificent memorial on earth. On the right bank of the River Yamuna in full view of his fortress palace, it was to be known as the Taj-i-Mahal (Crown of the Palace).

According to the French traveller Tavnier, work on the Taj commenced in 1632 and took 22 years to complete, employing a workforce of 20,000. The red sandstone was available locally but the white marble was quarried at Makrana in Rajasthan and transported 300 km by a fleet of 1000 elephants. Semi-precious stones for the inlay came from far and wide: red carnelian from Baghdad; red, yellow and brown jasper from the Punjab; green jade and crystal from China; blue lapis lazuli from Ceylon and Afghanistan; turquoise from Tibet; chrysolite from Egypt; amethyst from Persia; agates from the Yemen; dark green malachite from Russia; diamonds from Central India and mother-of-pearl from the Indian Ocean. A 3-km ramp was used to lift material up to the dome

Fact...

The white marble of the Taj is extraordinarily luminescent and even on dull days seems bright. To reduce damage to the marble by the polluted atmosphere, local industries now have to comply with strict rules, and vehicles emitting noxious fumes are not allowed within 2 km of the monument.

and, because of the sheer weight of the building; boreholes were filled with metal coins and fragments to provide suitable foundations. The resemblance of the exquisite double dome to a huge pearl is not coincidental; a saying of the Prophet describes the throne of God as a dome of white pearl supported by white pillars.

Myths and controversy surround the Taj Mahal. On its completion it is said that the emperor ordered the chief mason's right hand to be cut off to prevent him from repeating his masterpiece. Another legend suggests that Shah Jahan intended to build a replica for himself in black marble on the other side of the river, connected to the Taj Mahal by a bridge built with alternate blocks of black and white marble. Some have asserted that architects responsible for designing this mausoleum must have come from Turkey, Persia or even Europe (because of the pietra dura work on the tomb). In fact, no one knows who drew the plans. What is certain is that in the Taj Mahal, the traditions of Indian Hindu and Persian Muslim architecture were fused together into a completely distinct and perfect art form.

Visiting the Taj

Approach and entrance In the unique beauty of the Taj, subtlety is blended with grandeur and a massive overall design is matched with immaculately intricate execution. You will already have seen the dome of the tomb in the distance, looking almost like a miniature, but as you go into the open square, the Taj itself is so well hidden that you almost wonder where it can be. The glorious surprise is kept until the last moment, for wholly concealing it is the massive red sandstone gateway of the entrance, symbolizing the divide between the secular world and paradise.

The gateway was completed in 1648, though the huge brass door is recent. The original doors (plundered by the Jats) were solid silver and decorated with 1100 nails whose heads were contemporary silver coins. Although the gateway is remarkable in itself, one of its functions is to prevent you getting any glimpse of the tomb inside until you are right in the doorway itself. From here only the tomb is visible, stunning in its nearness, but as you move forward the minarets come into view.

Garden The Taj garden, though well kept, is nothing compared with its former glory (see box, page 118). The guiding principle is one of

Essential Taj Mahal

Arrival

Since polluting vehicles are not allowed near the site, visitors are increasingly using horse-drawn carriages or walking to reach the Taj. You can approach from three directions. The western entrance is usually used by those arriving from the fort and is an easy 10-minute walk along a pleasant garden road. At the eastern entrance, rickshaws and camel drivers offer to take visitors to the gate for up to Rs 100 each; however, an official battery bus also ferries visitors from the car park to the gate for a small fee.

Admission

Admission is Rs 750 for foreigners (including Development Tax), Rs 20 for Indians, payable in cash only, and includes use of a still camera. Video cameras, tripods, mobile phones and other electronic items are not allowed and should be left in the lockers at the East and West Gates (Rs 1). No photos may be taken inside the tomb (instant fines). The Archaeological Survey of India explicitly asks visitors not to make 'donations' to anyone including custodians in the tomb.

When to go

The site is open Saturday to Thursday from sunrise to sunset (last entry 1700). The whole building appears to change its hue according to the light in the sky, so consider carefully what time to arrive. In winter (December to February), it is worth being there at sunrise when the site is less busy. The mists that often lie over the River Yamuna lift as the sun rises and casts its golden rays over the pearl-white tomb; beautifully lit in the soft light, the Taj appears to float on air. At sunset, the view from across the river is equally wonderful. Another magical experience is a Full Moon trip to the Taj. These take place 2030-0030 on two nights either side of the full moon (see www.stardate. org/nightsky/moon for dates) and cost Rs 750 for foreigners, Rs 510 for Indians. Tickets should be booked the day before at **Architectural Survey of India**, 22 The Mall, T0562-222 7261.

Agra

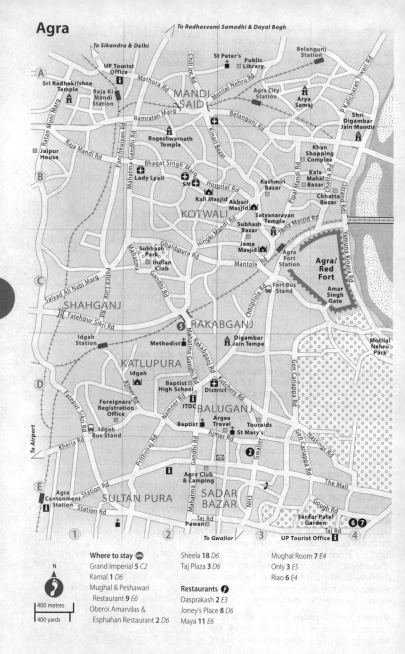

N

400 metres

400 yards

Where to stay 🛏
Grand Imperial **5** *C2*
Kamal **1** *D6*
Mughal & Peshawari
  Restaurant **9** *E6*
Oberoi Amarvilas &
  Esphahan Restaurant **2** *D6*

Sheela **18** *D6*
Taj Plaza **3** *D6*

Restaurants 🍴
Dasprakash **2** *E3*
Joney's Place **8** *D6*
Maya **11** *E6*

Mughal Room **7** *E4*
Only **3** *E5*
Riao **6** *E4*

symmetry. The *char bagh*, separated by the watercourses (rivers of heaven) originating from the central, raised pool, were divided into 16 flower beds, making a total of 64. The trees, all carefully planted to maintain the symmetry, were either cypress (signifying death) or fruit trees (life). The channels were stocked with colourful fish and the gardens with beautiful birds. It is well worth wandering along the side avenues for not only is it much more peaceful but also good for framing photos of the tomb with foliage. You may see bullocks pulling the lawnmowers around.

Mosque and jawab On the east and west sides of the tomb are identical red sandstone buildings. On the west (left-hand side) is a mosque. It is common in Islam to build one next to a tomb. It sanctifies the area and provides a place for worship. The replica on the other side is known as the **Jawab** (answer). This can't be used for prayer as it faces away from Mecca.

Tomb There is only one point of access to the **plinth** and tomb, where shoes must be removed (socks can be kept on; remember the white marble gets very hot) or cloth overshoes worn (Rs 2, though strictly free).

The **tomb** is square with bevelled corners. At each corner smaller domes rise while in the centre is the main dome topped by a brass finial. The dome is actually a double dome and this device, Central Asian in origin, was used to gain height. The exterior ornamentation is calligraphy (verses of the Koran), beautifully carved panels in bas relief and superb inlay work.

The **interior** of the mausoleum comprises a lofty central chamber, a *maqbara* (crypt) immediately below this, and four octagonal corner rooms. The central chamber contains replica tombs, the real ones being in the crypt. The public tomb was originally surrounded by a jewel-encrusted silver screen. Aurangzeb removed this, fearing it might be stolen, and replaced it with an octagonal screen of marble carved from one block of marble and inlaid with precious stones. It is an incredible piece of workmanship. This chamber is open at sunrise, but may close during the day.

Above the tombs is a **Cairene lamp** whose flame is supposed never to go out. This one was given by Lord Curzon, Governor General of India (1899-1905), to replace the original which was stolen by Jats. The tomb of Mumtaz with the 'female' slate, rests immediately beneath the dome. If you look from behind it, you can

BACKGROUND
Char bagh: the Mughal garden

In the Koran, the garden is repeatedly seen as a symbol for paradise. Islam was born in the deserts of Arabia. Muslims venerate water, without which plants will not grow – the old Persian word *pairidaeza* means 'garden'. It is no coincidence then that green is the colour of Islam.

Four main rivers of paradise are also specified: water, milk, wine and purified honey. This is the origin of the quartered garden (*char bagh*). The watercourses divided the garden into quadrats and all was enclosed behind a private wall. To the Muslim the beauty of creation and of the garden was held to be a reflection of God. The great Sufi poet **Rumi** used much garden imagery: "The trees are engaged in ritual prayer and the birds in singing the litany". Thus, the garden becomes as important as the tomb.

see how it lines up centrally with the main entrance. Shah Jahan's tomb is larger and to the side, marked by a 'male' pen-box, the sign of a cultured or noble person. Not originally intended to be placed there but squeezed in by Aurangzeb, this flaws the otherwise perfect symmetry of the whole complex. Finally, the acoustics of the building are superb, the domed ceiling being designed to echo chants from the Koran and musicians' melodies.

The **museum** ① *Sat-Thu 1000-1700*, has a small collection of Mughal memorabilia, photographs and miniatures of the Taj through the ages but has no textual information. Sadly, the lights do not always work.

Agra Fort (Red Fort) *See map, page 120.*

a mighty Mughal monument

On the west bank of the River Yamuna, Akbar's magnificent fort dominates the centre of the city. Akbar erected the walls and gates and the first buildings inside. Shah Jahan built the impressive imperial quarters and mosque, while Aurangzeb added the outer ramparts. Although it served as a model for Shah Jahan's Red Fort in Delhi, its own model was the Rajput Fort built by Raja Man Singh Tomar of Gwalior in 1500.

The fort is crescent-shaped with a long, nearly straight wall facing the river, punctuated at regular intervals by bastions. The main entrance, the Delhi Gate, used to be in the centre of the west wall, facing the bazar. It led to the Jami Masjid in the city but is now permanently closed. Only the southern third of the fort is open to the public, but this portion includes nearly all the buildings of interest.

Fortifications and entrance

The fortifications tower above the 9-m-wide, 10-m-deep moat, formerly filled with water from the Yamuna River; it's still evident but now contains stagnant water. There is an outer wall on the riverside, faced with red sandstone, and an imposing 22-m-high inner main wall, giving a feeling of great defensive power. The entrance to the fort is through the southern Amar Singh gate. If an aggressor managed to get through the outer gate they would have to make a right-hand turn and thereby expose their flank to the defenders on the inner wall. The inner gate is solidly powerful but has been attractively decorated with tiles. The tilework's similarities with Islamic patterns are obvious, though the Persian blue was also used in the Gwalior Fort and may well have been imitated from that example. The incline up to this point and beyond was suitable for elephants; as you walk past the last gate and up the broad brick-lined ramp with ridged slabs, it is easy to imagine arriving on elephant back. At the top of this 100-m ramp is a gate with a map and description board on your left.

Akbar's palace buildings

Jahangiri Mahal Despite its name, this was built by Akbar (circa 1570) as women's quarters. It is all that survives of his original palace buildings. In front is a large stone bowl, with steps both inside and outside, which was probably filled with fragrant rose water for bathing. The palace has a simple stone exterior and is almost 75 m sq. Tillotson has pointed out that the blind arcade of pointed arches inlaid with white marble which decorate the façade is copied from 14th-century monuments of the Khaljis and Tughluqs in Delhi. He notes that they are complemented by some features derived from Hindu architecture, including the *jarokhas* (balconies) protruding from the central section, the sloping dripstone in place of *chajja* (eaves) along the top of the façade, and the domed *chhattris* at its ends. The presence of distinctively Hindu features does not, however, indicate a synthesis of architectural styles at this early stage of Mughal architecture. Most of the features inside the Jahangiri Mahal are straightforwardly Hindu; square-headed arches and extraordinarily carved capitals and brackets illustrate the

Essential Agra Fort

Admission

You can only enter the fort through the Amar Singh Gate in the south. The fort is open daily 0600-1800; allow a minimum of 1½ hours for a visit. Admission is Rs 300 for foreigners (or Rs 250 if you've been to the Taj on the same day), and Rs 15 for Indians; video cameras are charged at Rs 25. The best route around the site is to start with the sandstone Jahangiri palace, which is on your right as you ascend the ramp from the entrance.

Tip...

At the gate you will have to contend with vendors of cheap soapstone boxes and knick-knacks; if you want to buy something, bargain hard. Guides will also offer their services – most are not particularly good.

vivid work of local Hindu craftsmen employed by Akbar without any attempt either to curb their enthusiasm for florid decoration and mythical animals nor to produce a fusion of Hindu and Islamic ideas. Tillotson argues that the central courtyard is essentially Hindu, in significant contrast with most earlier Indo-Islamic buildings. In these, an Islamic scheme was modified by Hindu touches. He suggests, therefore, that the Jahangiri Mahal marks the start of a more fundamental kind of Hinduization, typical of several projects during Akbar's middle period of rule, including the palace complex in Fatehpur Sikri. However, it did not represent a real fusion of ideas – this developed later under Shah Jahan – simply a juxtaposition of sharply contrasting styles.

Jodh Bai's Palace On the south side, this is named after one of Jahangir's wives. On the east the hall court leads onto a more open yard by the inner wall of the fort. In contrast to other palaces in the fort, this is quite simple. Through the slits in the wall you can see the Taj.

Shah Jahan's palace buildings

Turn left from the Jahangiri Mahal to reach Shah Jahan's Khas Mahal (1636). The open tower allows you to view the walls and see to your left the decorated Mussaman Burj tower. The defensive qualities of the site and the fortifications are obvious. In the area between the outer rampart and the inner wall gladiatorial battles were staged, pitting man against tiger, or elephant against elephant. The tower was the emperor's grandstand seat. The use of white marble transforms the atmosphere, contributing to a sense of grace and light.

Khas Mahal This was the model for the Diwan-i-Khas at the Red Fort in Delhi. Some of the original interior decoration has been restored (1895) and gives an impression of how splendid the painted ceiling must have been. The metal rings were probably used for *punkhas*. Underneath are cool rooms used to escape the summer heat. The Khas Mahal illustrates Shah's original architectural contribution. The buildings retain distinctively Islamic Persian features – the geometrical planning of the pavilions and the formal layout of the gardens, for example. Tillotson points out that here "Hindu motifs are treated in a new manner, which is less directly imitative of the Hindu antecedents. The temple columns and corbel capitals have been stripped of their rich carving and turned into simpler, smoother forms ... the *chhattris* have Islamic domes. Through these subtle changes the indigenous motifs have lost their specifically Hindu identity; they therefore contrast less strongly with the Islamic components, and are bound with them into a new style. The unity is assisted by the use of the cusped arch and the *Bangladar* roof." Seen in this light, the Khas Mahal achieves a true synthesis which eluded Akbar's designs.

Anguri Bagh (Vine Garden) The formal, 85-m-sq, geometric gardens are on the left. In Shah Jahan's time the geometric patterns were enhanced by decorative flower beds. In the middle of the white marble platform wall in front is a decorative water slide. From the pool with its bays for seating and its fountains, water would drain off along channels decorated to mimic a stream. The

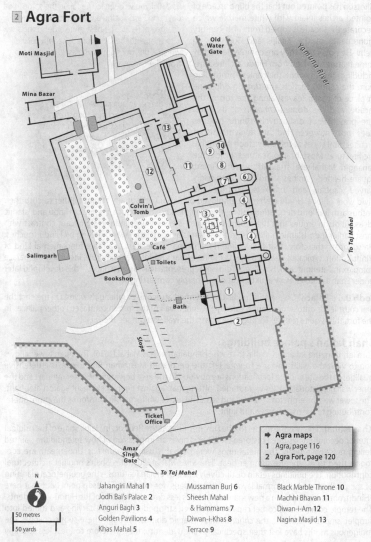

② Agra Fort

Jahangiri Mahal	1	Mussaman Burj	6	Black Marble Throne	10
Jodh Bai's Palace	2	Sheesh Mahal		Machhi Bhavan	11
Anguri Bagh	3	& Hammams	7	Diwan-i-Am	12
Golden Pavilions	4	Diwan-i-Khas	8	Nagina Masjid	13
Khas Mahal	5	Terrace	9		

➡ **Agra maps**
1 Agra, page 116
2 Agra Fort, page 120

surface was scalloped to produce a rippling waterfall, or inlaid to create a shimmering stream bed. Behind vertical water drops, there are little cusped arch niches into which flowers would be placed during the day and lamps at night. The effect was magical.

Golden Pavilions The curved *chala* roofs of the small pavilions by the Khas Mahal are based on the roof shape of Bengali village huts constructed out of curved bamboo, designed to keep off heavy rain. The shape was first expressed in stone by the Sultans of Bengal. Originally gilded, these were probably ladies' bedrooms, with hiding places for jewellery in the walls. These pavilions are traditionally associated with Shah Jahan's daughters, Roshanara and Jahanara.

Mussaman Burj On the left of the Khas Mahal is the Mussaman Burj (Octagonal Tower, though sometimes corrupted into Saman Burj, then translated as Jasmine Tower). It is a beautiful octagonal tower with an open pavilion. With its openness, elevation and the benefit of cooling evening breezes blowing in off the Yamuna River, this could well have been used as the emperor's bedroom. It has been suggested that this is where Shah Jahan lay on his deathbed, gazing at the Taj. Access to this tower is through a magnificently decorated and intimate apartment with a scalloped fountain in the centre. The inlay work here is exquisite, especially above the pillars. In front of the fountain is a sunken courtyard which could be filled by water carriers, to work the fountains in the pool.

Sheesh Mahal (Mirror Palace) Here are further examples of decorative water engineering in the *hammams*; the water here may have been warmed by lamps. The mirrors, which were more precious than marble, were set into the walls, often specially chiselled to accommodate their crooked shape.

Diwan-i-Khas (Hall of Private Audience, 1637) This is next to the Mussaman Burj, approached on this route by a staircase which brings you out at the side. The interior of the Diwan-i-Khas, a three-sided pavilion with a terrace of fine proportions, would have been richly decorated with tapestries and carpets. The double columns in marble have finely carved capitals and are inlaid with semi-precious stones in delightful floral patterns in pietra dura. At the centre is the white marble throne platform where the emperor would wait to meet visiting dignitaries. Gascoigne recounts how Shah Jahan tried to trick a haughty Persian ambassador into bowing low as he approached the throne by erecting a fence with a small wicket gate so that his visitor would have to enter on hands and knees. The ambassador did so, but entered backwards, thus presenting his bottom first to the Emperor. Above the marble platform was the famous Peacock Throne: "the canopy was carved in enamel work and studded with individual gems, its interior was thickly encrusted with rubies, garnets and diamonds, and it was supported on 12 emerald covered columns" writes Tillotson. When Shah Jahan moved his capital to Delhi he took the throne with him to the Red Fort, only for it to be taken back to Persia as loot by Nadir Shah in 1739. The earlier **black marble throne** platform at the rear of the terrace was used by Jahangir when claiming to be Emperor at Allahabad. Facing the Diwan-i-Khas is the **Machhi Bhavan** (Fish Enclosure), which once contained pools and fountains,

Diwan-i-Am (Hall of Public Audience) Go down an internal staircase and you enter the Diwan-i-Am from the side. The clever positioning of the pillars gives the visitor arriving through the gates in the right- and left-hand walls of the courtyard an uninterrupted view of the throne. On the back wall of the pavilion are *jali* screens to enable the women of the court to watch without being seen. The open-sided, cusped arched hall built of plaster on red stone, is very impressive. The throne alcove of richly decorated white marble was completed in 1634 after seven years' work.

Nagina Masjid From the corner opposite the Diwan-i-Khas two doorways lead to a view over the small courtyards of the *zenana* (harem). Further round in the next corner is the Nagina Masjid. Shoes must be removed at the doorway. Built by Shah Jahan, this was the private mosque of the ladies of the court. Beneath it was a *mina* bazar for the ladies to make purchases from the marble balcony above.

Other fort buildings

Looking out of the Diwan-i-Am you can see the domes of the **Moti Masjid** (Pearl Mosque, 1646-1653), an extremely fine building closed to visitors because of structural problems. Opposite the Diwan-i-Am are the barracks and **Mina Bazar**, also closed to the public. In the paved area in front of the Diwan-i-Am is a large well and the **tomb of Mr John Russell Colvin**, the Lieutenant Governor of the Northwest Provinces who died here during the 1857 'Uprising'. Stylistically it is sadly out of place. The yellow buildings date from the British period.

Jama Masjid The mosque, located near the fort railway, was built in 1648 and is attributed to Shah Jahan's dutiful elder daughter Jahanara. It is no longer connected to the fort and is not comparable to the other fort buildings. Its symmetry has suffered since a small minaret fell in the 1980s. The fine marble steps and bold geometric patterns on the domes are quite striking, however.

Other sights in Agra
beautiful mausoleums steeped in history

I'timad-ud-Daulah
Sunrise-sunset, foreigners Rs 100 plus Rs 10 tax, Indians Rs 10, video Rs 25.

Located northeast of the Red Fort on the east bank of the Yamuna River, the tomb of I'timad-ud-Daulah (Pillar of Government), known as the 'Baby Taj', set a startling precedent as the first Mughal building to be faced with white marble inlaid with contrasting stones. Unlike the Taj it is small, intimate and has a gentle serenity, but it is just as ornate.

The tomb was built for **Ghiyas Beg**, a Persian who had obtained service in Akbar's court. On Jahangir's succession in 1605, Beg became *Wazir* (chief minister). Jahangir fell in love with his daughter, **Mehrunissa**, who at the time was married to a Persian. When her husband died in 1607, she entered Jahangir's court as a lady-in-waiting. Four years later Jahangir married her. Thereafter she was known first as **Nur Mahal** (Light of the Palace), later being promoted to **Nur Jahan** (Light of the World). Her niece Mumtaz married Shah Jahan.

Nur Jahan built the tomb for her father in the *char bagh* that he himself had laid out. It is beautifully conceived in white marble, mosaic and lattice. There is a good view from the roof of the entrance. Marble screens of geometric lattice work permit soft lighting of the inner chamber. The yellow marble caskets appear to have been carved out of wood. On the engraved walls of the chamber is the recurring theme of a wine flask with snakes as handles – perhaps a reference by Nur Jahan, the tomb's creator, to her husband Jahangir's excessive drinking. Stylistically, the tomb marks a change from the sturdy and masculine buildings of Akbar's reign to softer, more feminine lines. The main chamber, richly decorated in pietra dura with mosaics and semi-precious stones inlaid in the white marble, contains the tomb of I'timad-ud-Daulah and his wife. Some have argued that the concept and technique of pietra dura must have come from 16th-century Florence to India. However, Florentine pietra dura is figurative whereas the Indian version is essentially decorative and can be seen as a refinement of its Indian predecessor, the patterned mosaic.

★ Sikandra (Akbar's Mausoleum)
10 km northwest of the city centre. Sunrise-sunset. Foreigners Rs 100, Indians Rs 10, includes camera, video Rs 25. Morning is the quietest time to visit.

Following the Timurid tradition, Akbar (ruled 1556-1605) had started to build his own tomb at Sikandra. He died during its construction and his son **Jahangir** completed it in 1613. The result is an impressive, large but architecturally confused tomb. A huge gateway, the **Buland Darwaza**, leads to the great garden enclosure, where spotted deer run free on the immaculate lawns. The decoration on the gateway is strikingly bold, with its large mosaic patterns, a forerunner of the pietra dura technique. The white minarets atop the entrance were an innovation which reappear, almost unchanged, at the Taj Mahal. The walled garden enclosure is laid out in the *char bagh* style, with the mausoleum at the centre.

A broad paved path leads to the 22.5-m-high tomb with four storeys. The lowest storey, nearly 100 m sq and 9 m high, contains massive cloisters. The entrance on the south side leads to the tomb chamber. Shoes must be removed or cloth overshoes worn (hire Rs 2). In a niche opposite the entrance is an alabaster tablet inscribed with the 99 divine names of Allah. The sepulchre is in the centre of the room, whose velvety darkness is pierced by a single slanting shaft of light from a high window. The custodian, in expectation of a donation, makes "Akbaaarrrr" echo around the chamber – quite amazing though.

Some 4 km south of Sikandra, near the high gateway of the ancient **Kach ki Sarai** building, is a sculptured horse, believed to mark the spot where Akbar's favourite horse died. There are also *kos minars* (marking a *kos*, about 4 km) and several other tombs on the way.

Listings Agra map p116

Tourist information

Government of India tourist office
191 The Mall, T0562-222 6377.
Guides available (Rs 100), helpful and friendly.

UPTDC
64 Taj Rd, T0562-222 6431, also at Agra Cantt, T0562-242 1204, and Tourist Bungalow Raja-ki-Mandi, T0562-285 0120.

Where to stay

It's a mixed bag in Agra. Some of the cheap hotels have great rooftop views in Taj Ganj but little else going for them. The only upscale place with a view is the Amar Vilas. Most of the upscale hotels are along Fatehabad Rd, a rather charmless strip of pricey restaurants, international fast-food outlets and handicrafts emporia. Many hotels are over-priced and only have their proximity to the Taj Mahal as their selling point.

$$$$ Grand Imperial
Mahatma Gandhi Rd, T0562-225 1190,
www.hotelgrandimperial.com.
Agra's first bid at a genuine heritage hotel, with 30 opulent rooms, some still displaying their original red brickwork, arcaded around a pleasant lawn in a 100-year-old neoclassical mansion, all modern facilities, smart international restaurant with live classical Indian music at dinner. Swimming pool and small spa. Charming staff. The only drawback is the distance from the Taj and the proximity to a loud main road. Recommended.

$$$$ The Oberoi Amarvilas
Near Taj East Gate, T0562-223 1515,
www.amarvilas.com.
102 beautiful rooms, all Taj-facing – the only place in Agra with such superlative views – designed in strict adherence to the Mughal style. Stunning swimming pool, lovely gardens, extraordinary ambience. Guests are entertained at sunset with traditional dancing and musicians.

If you can splash out on your trip, this is the place to do it. A magical experience.

$$$$ The Mughal
Fatehabad Rd, T0562-233 1700,
www.itchotels.in.
Stunning suites, beautiful gardens, lovely pool. The new wing is particularly good. They have the award-winning **Kaya Kalp** spa. Low-rise construction means only rooftop observatory offers good views of the Taj. Excellent restaurant.

$$$-$$ Hotel Taj Plaza
Taj East Gate, near Oberoi Amarvilas, T0562-223 1010.
Great views from the rooftop and a short walk to the Taj Mahal itself. Spacious rooms with a/c and a friendly welcome.

$$-$ Hotel Kamal
South Gate, near Taj Ganj police station, T(0)94121 80575, www.hotelkamal.com.
Good option in this area – variety of rooms, some with more mod cons and a/c. Great view from the rooftop restaurant although the food is fairly mediocre; enjoy a sundowner instead.

$ Sheela
East Gate, 2 mins' walk from the Taj, T0562-329 3437, www.hotelsheela agra.com.
Popular although fairly basic rooms. Friendly place – good for meeting other travellers. Pleasant garden, good restaurant. Very helpful manager. Good location in low pollution area.

Restaurants

$$$ Esphahan
The Oberoi Amarvilas (see Where to stay).
Outstanding, rich Avadhi food in high-class setting – there are 2 sittings 1830 and 2100, but non-residents will find it hard to get a table.

$$$ Mughal Room
Hotel Clarks Shiraz, 54 Taj Rd.
Standard 5-star fare, rich and meaty, mainly distinguished by glassed-in rooftop setting with great views over the city.

$$$ Peshawari
The Mughal (see Where to stay).
Regarded as the city's best, refined North Indian cuisine, smart surroundings, vegetarian offerings less inspired.

$$ Only
45 Taj Rd, T0562-236 4333.
Interesting menu, attractive outside seating, popular with tour groups, live entertainment.

$$ Riao
Next to Clarks Shiraz, 44 Taj Rd, T(0)9412-154311.
Good North Indian food, puppet shows and live music, great garden and atmosphere.

$ Dasprakash
Shamshabad Rd, Vibhav Nagar,
T(0)81713 90066.
Excellent South Indian food – extensive *thalis*, great doas and uttapam.

$ Joney's Place
Near South Gate, Taj Ganj.
The original and, despite numerous similarly named imitators, still the best. Tiny place but the food is consistently good. Can produce Israeli and Korean specialities. Recommended.

$ Maya
18 Purani Mandi Circle, Fatehabad Rd,
T0562-405 2665.
Varied menu, good Punjabi *thalis*, pasta, 'special tea', friendly, prompt service, hygienic, tasty, Moroccan-style decor. Also have good colourful rooms. Recommended.

Festivals

18-27 Feb **Taj Mahotsav**, a celebration of the region's arts, crafts, culture and cuisine.
Aug/Sep A **fair** at Kailash (14 km away). A temple marks the spot where Siva is believed to have appeared in the form of a stone lingam.

Shopping

Agra specializes in jewellery, inlaid and carved marble, carpets and clothes. The main shopping areas are Sadar Bazar (closed Tue), Kinari Bazar, Gwalior Rd, Mahatma Gandhi Rd and Pratap Pura. Many rickshaws, taxi drivers and guides earn up to 40% commission by taking tourists to shops. Insist on not being rushed away from sights and shop independently. To get a good price you have to bargain hard anyway.

Tip...
Beware, if you order a carpet or an inlaid marble piece and have it sent later it may not be what you ordered. Never agree to any export 'deals' and take great care with credit card slips (scams reported).

Carpets
Silk/cotton/wool mix hand-knotted carpets and woven *dhurries* are all made in Agra. High quality and cheaper than in Delhi.
Kanu Carpet Factory, *Purani Mandi, Fetehabad Rd, T0562-233 1307.* A reliable source.

Marble
Delicately inlaid marble work is a speciality. Sometimes cheaper alabaster and soapstone is used and quality varies.
Akbar International, *289 Fatehabad Rd.* Good selection, inlay demonstration, fair prices.
Handicrafts Inn, *3 Garg Niketan, Fatehabad Rd, Taj Ganj.*
Krafts Palace, *506 The Mall.* Watch craftsmen working here.
UP Handicrafts Palace, *49 Bansal Nagar.* Wide selection from table tops to coasters, high quality and good value.

What to do

Tour operators
City Tours, *www.tajmahal.gov.in, T0562-222 6431.* Organize good walking tours and coach tours: Fatehpur Sikri–Taj Mahal–Agra Fort (full day), 1030-1830, Rs 2000 (Indian Rs 500) including guide and entry fees; half-day Fatehpur Sikri tour ends at 1300 which only gives 45 mins at the site, not worthwhile, better take a taxi or rickshaw. Tours start and finish at Agra Cantt Railway Station and tie in with arrival/departure of *Taj Express* (see Transport); check times. Pick-up also possible from **India Tourism** office on The Mall.
Mercury, *Hotel Clarks Shiraz, 54 Taj Rd, T0562-222 6531.* Helpful and reliable.
Travel Bureau, *near Taj View Hotel, T0562-233 0245, www.travelbureauagra.com.* Long-established local company, highly experienced (handle ground arrangements for most foreign travel agents), helpful, can arrange anything. Recommended.

Walking tours
Agra Walks, *T(0)90277 11144, www.agrawalks.com.* Fun walking tours that give an insight into the city, from the spice market and small hidden temples

to Agra Fort. You can try local tastes and sweets along the way. Tours start at 1600 and take 3 hrs.

Transport

Air Kheria Airport is 7 km from city centre. It's only served by charter flights. Rail transport tends to be the faster option.

Bus Local City Bus Service covers most areas and main sights. Plenty leave from the Taj Mahal area and the **Fort Bus Stand**.

Long-distance Most long-distance services leave from the **Idgah Bus Stand**, T0562-242 0324, including to: **Delhi** (4-5 hrs) via **Mathura** (1 hr); **Fatehpur Sikri** (40 km, 1 hr); **Bharatpur** (2 hrs); **Khajuraho** (10 hrs). **Agra Fort Stand**, T0562-216 6588, has additional buses to **Delhi**. Deluxe buses for **Jaipur** arrive and depart from a stop near **Hotel Sakura**: closer to most hotels and where there is less hassle from touts. **Delhi** from tourist office, 0700, 1445, deluxe, 4 hrs.

Rickshaw Auto rickshaw Pre-paid stand at Agra Cantt Station has prices clearly listed for point-to-point rates and sightseeing. Expect to pay Rs 80-100 to Fatehabad Rd or Taj Ganj.

Cycle rickshaw Negotiate (pay more to avoid visiting shops); Taj Ganj to Fort Rs 5; Rs 80-200 for visiting sights.

Taxi/car hire Tourist taxis from travel agents, remarkably good value for visiting nearby sights. Full day Rs 1500 (100 km), half day Rs 950 (45 km); a/c rates and more luxury cars are pricier; to **Fatehpur Sikri**, Rs 2300 but can be pricier depending on car. **Travel Bureau**, T0562-233 0245; **UP Tours**, T0562-222 6431.

Train To/from **Delhi** train is the quickest and most reliable way. Most trains use **Agra Cantonment Railway Station**, 5 km west of Taj Mahal, enquiries T131, reservations T0562-242 1039, open 0800-2000. Foreigners' queue at Window 1. Pre-paid taxi/auto-rickshaw kiosk outside the station. Some trains to Rajasthan from quieter **Agra Fort Station**, T132, T0562-236 9590. The following arrive and depart from **Agra Cantt** unless specified. To **Delhi** there are 2 evening trains: *Shatabdi Exp 12001* (**ND**), 2½ hrs; *Taj Exp 12279* (**HN**), 3¼ hrs (CC/II); and a good early morning train *Intercity Exp 11103* (**HN**), 3½ hrs (2nd class only). To **Jaipur**: *Intercity Exp 12307*, 6 hrs (from Agra Fort); *Marudhar Exp 14853/63*, 6¾ hrs. **Jhansi** (via **Gwalior**): *Taj Express 12280*, 3 hrs (Gwalior 1¾ hrs). There are 3 convenient trains for **Sawai Madhopur** (for **Ranthambore**) at 0600, 0900, 1800.

Around Agra

the holiest sites of Vaishnavite Hinduism

Located 50 km from Agra on the west bank of the Yamuna, the city of Mathura and its surroundings are among the most sacred sites of Hinduism, dating back to 600 BC. For Vaishnavites, Mathura is perhaps the supremely sacred city of India, being the reputed birthplace of Krishna, the most human aspect of Vishnu. Krishna is widely seen as the embodiment of the ideal lover, soldier, statesman, as well as the adorable baby, or wayward child. Many places around Mathura are associated with episodes in his life.

Mathura's ancient structures were mostly destroyed by Muslims but its religious association draws thousands of pilgrims. Today, it is also an important industrial city with much evidence of modernizing on the approach from the highway and a large oil refinery on the outskirts.

Sights

There are no pre-Muslim monuments of any significance, and some of the finest buildings have been badly scarred by decay, neglect and misuse. You enter Mathura by the finely carved **Holi Gate**. In the centre of the bustling old city is the **Jami Masjid** (1660-1661) with four minarets, which was built by Abd-un-Nadi, Aurangzeb's governor. It has a raised courtyard and a façade once covered with brightly coloured enamel tiles; above are the 99 names of Allah.

The Katra/Sri Krishna Janmabhumi To the west, the **Katra** contains a mosque built by Aurangzeb. This stands over the ruins of one of Mathura's most famous temples, the **Kesava Deo Mandir** which in turn had been built on the ruins of a Buddhist monastery of the Kushan period. This is considered to be **Sri Krishna Janmabhumi** (Krishna's birthplace). The main statues are particularly serene and attractive, but it is sometimes difficult to gain entry due to extra security since there is a mosque next to it. At the rear of the enclosure is a newer **Temple of Kesava**, built by Bir Singh of Orchha, see box, page 245. Nearby is the impressive **Potara Kund**, a stepped tank in which Krishna's baby clothes were washed. It is faced in the familiar local red sandstone with access for cattle and horses.

Yamunua River and its ghats The river and its ghats are the focal point for Hindu pilgrims. A paved street runs their length, but recent developments have made the area very congested, and the two industrial-looking bridges which cross the river close to the ghats have taken away some of the charm. **Vishram Ghat** (rebuilt in 1814) is where Krishna rested after killing Kamsa. Cows, monkeys and turtles are fed when the *Arati* ceremony is performed in the morning and evening; best seen from a boat.

Built in 1814 close to the Yamuna, **Dwarkadhesh Temple** is incredibly atmospheric. Evening prayers here are accompanied by music. The **Sati Burj** (late 16th century), on the river, is a square, four-storey red sandstone tower with a plastered dome said to commemorate the *sati* by the wife of Rajbihari Mal of Amber. The **Kans Qila** fort was built by Raja Man Singh of Amber and was rebuilt by Akbar but only the foundations remain.

Archaeological Museum ① *Dampier Nagar, T0565-250 0847, Tue-Sun 1030-1630, foreigners Rs 25, Indians Rs 5, camera Rs 20.* The museum has an extensive and impressive collection of sculptures, terracottas, bronzes and coins housed in an octagonal red sandstone building. Also exhibited is the fifth-century 'Standing Buddha', numerous Gupta figures, a first-century headless Buddha, Kushana sculptures and Gandhara pieces.

Around Mathura

Gokul This site 2 km away is approached by a long flight of steps from the river. It is associated with very early Hindu legends, where Vishnu first appeared as Krishna. It is the headquarters of the Vallabhacharya Sect who built some large temples.

Mahaban Located 9 km southeast of Mathura on the east bank of the Yamuna, Mahaban means 'a great forest'. There is no forest now but in 1634 Shah Jahan is recorded as having killed four tigers in a hunt here. The town was sacked by Mahmud of Ghazni in the 11th century. Each year in August Vaishnavite pilgrims come to the **Nanda Krishna Palace** where Krishna was believed to have been secretly raised. His cradle stands in the hall, the hole in the wall is where the *gopis* hid his flute, and the place where his mother stood churning butter is marked by a polished pillar.

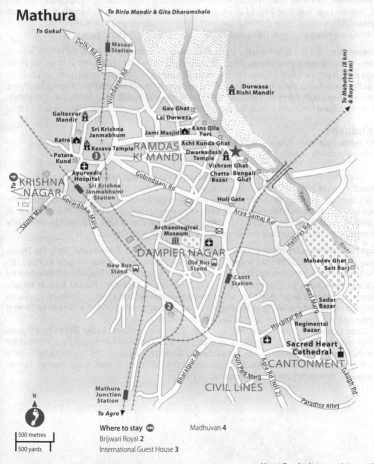

Mathura

Where to stay
Brijwari Royal 2
International Guest House 3
Madhuvan 4

Mathura

Ptolemy mentioned the town and it assumed the importance of a capital city during the first to second century **Kushan Empire**. When the Chinese traveller Hiuen Tsang visited it in AD 634 it was an important Buddhist centre with several monasteries. However, **Mahmud of Ghazni** sacked the city and desecrated its temples in 1017, followed by **Sikander Lodi** in 1500, whilst the Mughal **Emperor Aurangzeb** used a local revolt in which his governor was killed as an excuse to destroy the main temples. Jats and Marathas fought over the city as the Mughal Empire declined, but at the beginning of the 19th century it came under British control. They laid out a cantonment in the south and left a cemetery and the Roman Catholic Sacred Heart Cathedral (1870).

Baraderi of Sikander Lodi Twenty-eight kilometres south of Mathura is the 12 pillared pavilion of Sikander Lodi, one time King of Delhi, built in 1495. Also here is the 1611 **tomb of Mariam uz Zamani**, Akbar's Hindu Rajput wife who is said to have been converted to Christianity, though there is little supporting evidence. There are beautiful carvings on the red sandstone structure.

Govardhan This site 26 km west of Mathura lies in the narrow range of the Girraj Hills. In legend, when Indra caused a tremendous flood, Krishna raised these hills up above the flood for seven days so that people could escape. The **Harideva Temple**, by the Manasi Ganga River, was built by Raja Bhagwan Das in the reign of Akbar. On the opposite bank are the *chhattris* of Ranjit Singh and Balwant Singh, both rulers of Bharatpur. There are stone ghats on all sides, built in 1817. Krishna is believed to have ritually bathed at the temple to purify himself after killing the demon bull Arishta.

Vrinduvan
The temples are open morning and evening usually 0900-1200 and 1800-2100 when visitors are welcome to attend worship.

Vrindavan (Forest of Tulsi Plants) is the most famous of the holy sites around Mathura and the most sacred region of India for Vaishnavite Hindus, where many of the stories surrounding Krishna are set (see page 126). In Vrindavan Krishna played with the *gopis* (cowgirls), stealing their clothes while they bathed. The town retains a tranquil, welcoming atmosphere, and offers an interesting mix of stunning temples, narrow medieval alleyways and beautiful river scenes, observed by an equally interesting mix of local Sadhus and international devotees of Hare Krishna.

Sights At the entrance to the town is the 16th-century **temple of Gobind Dev** (1590), the 'Divine Cowherd', Krishna. Built by Man Singh of Jaipur during Akbar's reign, it was severely damaged by the less tolerant Aurangzeb. Nearby there is a Dravidian-style temple dedicated to **Sri Ranganathji** (Vishnu), with three *gopura*, each nearly 30 m high. The 16th-century **Madan Mohan temple** stands above a ghat on an arm of the river; there is a pavilion decorated with cobra carvings. Siva is believed to have struck Devi here and made it a place for curing snake bites. The octagonal tower is similar to the one on the 16th-century **Jagat Krishna temple**.

Other temples include **Jugal Kishor** (reputedly 1027) near Kesi Ghat, **Banke Behari** near Purana Bazar where great excitement builds up each time the curtain before the deity is opened for *darshan*, and **Radha Ballabh**, partly demolished by Aurangzeb, close by. The **International Society for Krishna Consciousness (ISKCON)** at the Shri Krishna Balaram Temple has a modern marble memorial. The centre runs yoga and meditation courses.

Tourist information

UPTDC
Near Old Bus Stand, T0565-250 5351.

Where to stay

Mathura

Hotels serve vegetarian food only. No alcohol.

$$$ Brijwasi Royal
Station Rd, T(0)88998 81881,
www.brijwasiroyal.com.
40 comfortable, well-appointed rooms in this
busy, friendly hotel in the heart of the city.
Professionally run, a very popular pure veg
restaurant serves delicious north Indian food.
A new sister hotel, Brijwasi Lands End, has the
same contact details.

$$ Madhuvan
Krishna Nagar, T0565-242 0064,
madhuvanhotel@indiatimes.com.
28 clean, fragrant rooms, some a/c with bath.
Restaurant, exchange, travel, pool, a little gloomy
but friendly.

$ International Guest House
Katra Keshav Deo, T0565-242 3888.
Some air-cooled rooms, interesting place to stay.

$ Tourist Reception Centre
(UPTDC), State Bank Crossing, near
Railway Station Rd, T(0)94156 09454,
www.up-tourism.com.
All you expect from a government-run place –
clean but uninspiring. Restaurant on site.

Vrindavan

$$ Ananda Krishna Van
Parikrama Marg, near ISKCON, T0565-329 8855,
www.ananda krishnavan.com.

Vrindavan

Where to stay 🛏
Ananda Krishna Van **1**
MVT Guest House **3**

Shree Shree Radha Shyam
Palace **4**

Sprawling new construction complete with waterfall, bathing pool, temple and restaurants. Many rooms taken on timeshare basis, but some 4 bed a/c rooms available to visitors, remarkable undertaking.

$ MVT Guest House
Next to ISKCON, T(0)99977 38666, www.mvtindia.com.
Atmospheric place to stay with lovely gardens. Comfortable rooms, some a/c, set around pleasant gardens. Highly rated restaurant.

$ Shree Shree Radha Shyam Palace
Signposted behind ISKCON, T0565-254 0729.
22 clean rooms in friendly, well-located hotel.

Festivals

Mathura
Mar **Rang Gulal**, the colourful Holi festival. Similar festivities at **Janmashtami**.
Aug/Sep **Banjatra** (Forest Pilgrimage). During the monsoon, episodes from Krishna's life are enacted.

Vrindavan
Mar/Apr Annual 10-day **Rath** (car) **festival**.

Transport

Mathura
Bus Frequent service to **Delhi**, **Jaipur** and neighbouring towns from the **New Bus Stand** opposite Hotel Nepal. Buses to **Govardhan** and **Agra** from **Old Bus Stand** near the railway station, T0565-240 6468.

Taxi From opposite District Hospital. Also, buses, auto and cycle rickshaws.

Train **Mathura Junction** is the main station, T0565-240 6463. **Cantt Station** is at Bahadurganj (metre gauge). **Sri Krishna Janmabhumi** is at Bhuteshwar. For Delhi and Agra, the best is to **Agra Cantt**: *Taj Exp 12280*, 0900, 47 mins. **New Delhi (HN)**: *Taj Exp 12279*, 2¼ hrs. **Sawai Madhopur (for Ranthambhore)**: *Golden Temple Mail 12904*, 3 hrs; *Bandra Exp 19020*, 3½ hrs.

Vrindavan
There are buses, *tempos* and rickshaws to and from **Mathura** and regular train services from Mathura Junction.

Fatehpur Sikri

a manifestation of Mughal might

The red sandstone capital of Emperor Akbar, one of his great architectural achievements, spreads along a ridge 40 km from Agra. The great mosque and palace buildings, deserted after only 14 years, are still a vivid reminder of his power and vision, conjuring up the lifestyle of the Mughals at the height of their glory. Fatehpur Sikri is over 400 years old and yet perfectly preserved, thanks to careful conservation work carried out by the Archaeological Survey of India at the turn of the century. There are three sections to the city: the 'Royal Palace', 'Outside the Royal Palace' and the 'Jami Masjid'.

Agra Gate and around
Entry to Fatehpur Sikri is through the **Agra Gate**. The straight road from Agra was laid out in Akbar's time. If approaching from Bharatpur you will pass the site of a large lake, which provided one defensive barrier. On the other side was a massive defensive wall with nine gates (clockwise): Delhi, Lal, Agra, Bir or Suraj (Sun), Chandar (Moon), Gwaliori, Tehra (Crooked), Chor (Thief's) and Ajmeri.

From the Agra Gate you pass the sandstone **Tansen's Baradari** on your right and go through the triple-arched **Chahar Suq** with a gallery with two *chhattris* above which may have been a **Nakkar khana** (Drum House). The road inside the main city wall leading to the entrance would have been lined with bazars. Next, on your right is the square, shallow-domed **Mint,** with artisans' workshops or animal shelters around a courtyard. Workmen still chip away at blocks of stone in the dimly lit interior.

Essential Fatehpur Sikri

Admission

The site is open sunrise to sunset. Admission is Rs 260 for foreigners, Rs 5 for Indians. Avoid the main entrance, where there are lots of hawkers; instead, take the right-hand fork after passing through Agra Gate to the hassle-free second entrance. It is best to visit early, before the crowds. Allow three hours and carry plenty of drinking water. Official guides are good (Rs 100; Rs 30 off season) but avoid others.

Tip...

Sadly there are men with 'performing' bears along the road from Agra; they should be discouraged: do not stop to look, photograph or tip.

Royal Palace

Diwan-i-Am The Hall of Public Audience was also used for celebrations and public prayers. It backed onto the private palace. It has cloisters on three sides of a rectangular courtyard and to the west, a pavilion with the emperor's throne, with *jali* screens on either side separating the court ladies. Some scholars suggest that the west orientation may have suggested Akbar's vision of himself playing a semi-divine role.

In the centre of the courtyard behind the throne is the **Pachisi Board** or Chaupar. It is said that Akbar had slave girls dressed in yellow, blue and red, moved around as 'pieces'!

Diwan-i-Khas The Hall of Private Audience, to your right, is a two-storey building with corner kiosks. It is a single room with a unique circular throne platform. Here Akbar would spend long hours in discussion with Christians, Jains, Buddhists, Hindus and Parsis. They would sit along the walls of the balcony connected to the **Throne Pillar** by screened 'bridges', while courtiers could listen to the discussions from the ground floor. Decorative techniques and metaphysical labels are incorporated here – the pillar is lotus shaped (a Hindu and Buddhist motif), the Royal Umbrella (*chhattri*) is Hindu, and the Tree of Life, Islamic. The bottom of the pillar is carved in four tiers: Muslim, Hindu, Christian and Buddhist designs. The Throne Pillar can be approached by steps from the outside although there is no access to the upper floor. The design of the hall deliberately followed the archaic universal pattern of establishing a hallowed spot from which spiritual influence could radiate. In his later years, Akbar developed a mystical cult around himself that saw him as being semi-divine.

An Archaeological Survey of India team recently discovered an 'air-conditioned palace' built for Akbar, while digging up steps leading down to a water tank set in the middle of the main palace complex. The subterranean chambers were found under the small quadrangle in sandstone, set in the middle of a water tank and connected on all four sides by narrow corridors. It's not yet open to the public.

Treasury In the Treasury, in the northwest corner of the courtyard, is the **Ankh Michauli** (Blind Man's Buff), possibly used for playing the game, comprising three rooms each protected by a narrow corridor with guards. The *makaras* on brackets are mythical sea creatures who guard the treasures under the sea. Just in front of the Treasury is the **Astrologer's Seat**, a small kiosk with elaborate carvings on the Gujarati 'caterpillar' struts which may have been used by the court astrologer or treasurer.

Anup Talao Pavilion The **Turkish Sultana's House** or Anup Talao Pavilion is directly opposite, beyond the Pachisi Board. Sultana Ruqayya Begum was Akbar's favourite, and her 'house', with a balcony on each side, is exquisitely carved with Islamic decorations. Scholars suggest this may have been a pleasure pavilion. The geometrical pattern on the ceiling is reminiscent of Central Asian carvings in wood while the walls may have been set originally with reflecting glass to create a Sheesh Mahal (Mirror Palace). In the centre of this smaller south courtyard is the **Anup Talao** where the Emperor may have sat on the platform, surrounded by perfumed water. The *Akbarnama* mentions the emperor's show of charity when he filled the Talao with copper, silver and gold coins and distributed them over three years.

Dawlatkhana-i-Khas The emperor's private chambers are next to the rose-water fountain in the corner of the courtyard. There are two main rooms on the ground floor. One housed his library – the recesses in the walls were for manuscripts. Although unable to read or write himself, Akbar enjoyed having books read to him. Wherever he went, his library of 50,000 manuscripts accompanied him.

Fatehpur Sikri

The first two Great Mughals, Babur (ruled 1526-1530) and his son Humayun (ruled 1530-1540, 1555-1556) both won (in Humayun's case, won back) Hindustan at the end of their lives, and they left an essentially alien rule. Akbar, the third and greatest of the Mughals, changed that. By marrying a Hindu princess, forging alliances with the Rajput leaders and making the administration of India a partnership with Hindu nobles and princes rather than armed foreign minority rule, Akbar consolidated his ancestors' gains, and won widespread loyalty and respect. Akbar had enormous magnetism. Though illiterate, he had great wisdom and learning as well as undoubted administrative and military skills. Fatehpur Sikri is testimony to this remarkable character.

Although he had many wives, the 26-year-old Akbar had no living heir; the children born to him had all died in infancy. He visited holy men to enlist their prayers for a son and heir. Sheikh Salim Chishti, living at Sikri, a village 37 km southwest of Agra, told the emperor that he would have three sons. Soon after, one of his wives, the daughter of the Raja of Amber, became pregnant, so Akbar sent her to live near the sage. A son Salim was born, later to be known as Jahangir. The prophecy was fulfilled when, in 1570, another wife gave birth to Murad and, in 1572, to Daniyal.

Akbar, so impressed by this sequence of events, resolved to build an entirely new capital at Sikri in honour of the saint, whose tomb is here. The holy man had set up his hermitage on a low hill of hard reddish sandstone, an ideal building material, easy to work and yet very durable. The building techniques used imitated carvings in wood, as well as canvas from the Mughal camp (eg awnings). During the next 14 years a new city appeared on this hill: 'Fatehpur' (town of victory) added to the name of the old village, 'Sikri'. Later additions and alterations were made and debate continues over the function and dates of the various buildings.

When Akbar left, the city was slowly abandoned to become ruined and deserted by the early 1600s. Some believe the emperor's decision was precipitated by the failure of the water supply, whilst local folklore claims the decision was due to the loss of the court singer Tansen, one of the 'nine gems' of Akbar's court. However, there may well have been political and strategic motives. Akbar's change in attitude towards orthodox Islam and the new imperial ideology which supplanted his earlier veneration of the Chishti saints may have influenced his decision. In 1585 he moved his court to Lahore, and when he returned south again, it was to Agra. But it was at Fatehpur Sikri that Akbar spent the richest and most productive years of his 49-year reign.

The larger room behind was his resting area. On the first floor is the **Khwabgah** (Palace of Dreams) which would have had rich carpets, hangings and cushions. This too was decorated with gold and ultramarine paintings. The southern window (Jharokha Darshan) was where the emperor showed himself to his people every morning.

Ladies' Garden Leaving the Dawlatkhana-i-Khas you enter another courtyard which contained the Ladies' Garden for the *zenana*, and the **Sunahra Makan** or the Christian wife **Maryam's** House, a two-storeyed affair for the emperor's mother, which was embellished with golden murals in the Persian style. The inscriptions on the beams are verses by **Fazl**, Akbar's poet laureate, one of the '*Navaratna*' (Nine Jewels) of the Court. Toilets in the corner of the garden are quite clean.

Panch Mahal The Panch Mahal is an elegant, airy five-storeyed pavilion just north of the garden, each floor smaller than the one below, rising to a single domed kiosk on top. The horizontal line of this terraced building is emphasized by wide overhanging eaves (for providing shade), parapets broken by the supporting pillars of which there are 84 on the ground floor (the magic number of seven planets multiplied by 12 signs of the zodiac). The 56 carved columns on the second floor are all different and show Hindu influence. Originally, dampened and scented *khuss* (grass screens) were hung in the open spaces to provide protection from the heat and sun, as well as privacy for the women who used the pavilion.

Jodh Bai's Palace Jodh Bai, the daughter of the Maharaja of Amber, lived in the spacious palace in the centre, assured of privacy and security by high walls and a 9-m-high guarded gate to the east. Outside the north wall is the 'hanging' **Hawa Mahal** (Palace of Winds) with beautiful *jali* screens facing the *zenana* garden which was once enclosed; the bridge (a later addition) led to the Hathipol. Through the arch is the small **Nagina Masjid**, the mosque for the ladies of the court. The *hammams* (baths) are to the south of the palace. The centre of the building is a quadrangle around which were the harem quarters, each section self-contained with roof terraces. The style, a blend of Hindu and Muslim (the lotus, chain and bell designs being Hindu, the black domes Muslim), is strongly reminiscent of Gujarati temples, possibly owing to the identity of the craftsmen: look out for the *jarokha* windows, niches, pillars and brackets. The upper pavilions north and south have interesting ceiling structure (imitating the bamboo and thatch roof of huts), here covered with blue glazed tiles, adding colour to the buildings of red sandstone favoured by Akbar. Jodh Bai's vegetarian kitchen opposite the palace has attractive chevron patterns.

Raja Birbal's Palace The highly ornamented house to the northwest of Jodh Bai's Palace has two storeys – four rooms and two porches with pyramidal roofs below, and two rooms with cupolas and screened terraces above. Birbal, Akbar's Hindu prime minister, was the brightest of Akbar's 'Nine Jewels'. Again, the building combines Hindu and Islamic elements (note the brackets, eaves, *jarokhas*). Of particular interest is the insulating effect of the double-domed structure of the roofs and cupolas which kept the rooms cool, and the diagonal positioning of the upper rooms which ensured a shady terrace. Some scholars believe that this building, Mahal-i-Ilahi, was not for Birbal, but for Akbar's senior queens.

South of the Raja's house are the **stables**, a long courtyard surrounded by cells which probably housed zenana servants rather than the emperor's camels and horses, though the rings suggest animals may have been tied there.

Jami Masjid

Leaving the Royal Palace you proceed across a car park to the Jami Masjid and the sacred section of Fatehpur Sikri. The oldest place of worship here was the **Stone Cutters' Mosque** (circa 1565) to the west of the Jami Masjid. It was built near Sheikh Salim Chishti's cell by stonecutters who settled on the ridge when quarrying for the Agra Fort began. It has carved monolithic 'S' brackets to support the wide sloping eaves.

Built in 1571-1572, the Jama Masjid is one of the largest mosques in India. The **Badshahi Darwaza** (King's Gate) is the entrance Akbar used. Shoes must be left at the gate, but there are strips of carpet cross the courtyard to save burning your feet. The porch is packed with aggressive salesmen. The two other gates on the south and north walls were altered by subsequent additions (see below). Inside is the congregational courtyard (132 m by 111 m). To your right in the corner is the **Jamaat Khana Hall** and next to this the **Tomb of the Royal Ladies** on the north wall. The square nave carries the principal dome painted in the Persian style, with pillared aisles leading to side chapels carrying subsidiary domes. The **mihrab** in the centre of the west wall orientates worshippers towards Mecca. The sanctuary is adorned with carving, inlay work and painting.

Tomb of Sheikh Salim Chishti This masterpiece in brilliant white marble dominates the northern half of the courtyard. The Gujarati-style serpentine 'S' struts, infilled with *jali*, are highly decorative while the carved pillar bases and lattice screens are stunning pieces of craftsmanship. The canopy over the tomb is inlaid with mother of pearl. On the cenotaph is the date of the saint's death (1571) and the date of the building's completion (1580); the superb marble screens enclosing the veranda were added by Jahangir's foster brother in 1606. Around the entrance are inscribed the names of God, the Prophet and the four Caliphs of Islam. The shrine inside, on the spot of the saint's hermitage, originally had a red sandstone dome, which was marble veneered around 1806. Both Hindu and Muslim women pray at the shrine, tying cotton threads, hoping for the miracle of parenthood that Akbar was blessed with.

Next to it, in the courtyard, is the larger, red, sandstone tomb of **Nawab Islam Khan**, Sheikh Salim's grandson, and other members of the family.

Buland Darwaza The Triumphal Gate dominates the south wall but it is a bit out of place. Built to celebrate Akbar's brilliant conquest of Gujarat (circa 1576), it sets the style for later gateways. The high gate is approached from the outside by a flight of steps which adds to its grandeur. The decoration shows Hindu influence, but is severe and restrained, emphasizing the lines of its arches with plain surfaces. You see an inscription on the right of a verse from the Qur'an:

> Said Jesus Son of Mary (on whom be peace):
> The world is but a bridge; pass over it but build no houses on it.
> He who hopes for an hour, hopes for Eternity.
> The world is an hour. Spend it in prayer, for the rest is unseen.

Outside the Royal Palace

Between the Royal Palace and the Jami Masjid, a paved pathway to the northwest leads to the **Hathipol** (Elephant Gate). This was the ceremonial entrance to the palace quarters, guarded by stone elephants, with its *nakkar khana* and bazar alongside. Nearby are the **waterworks**, with a deep well which had an ingenious mechanism for raising water to the aqueducts above ridge height. The **caravanserai** around a large courtyard fits on the ridge side, and was probably one of a series built to accommodate travellers, tradesmen and guards. Down a ramp immediately beyond is the **Hiran Minar**, an unusual tower studded with stone tusks, thought to commemorate Akbar's favourite elephant, Hiran. However, it was probably an *akash diya* (lamp to light the sky) or the 'zero point' for marking road distances in *kos*. You can climb up the spiral staircase inside it but take care as the top has no rail. This part of Fatehpur Sikri is off the main tourist track, and though less well preserved it is worth the detour to get the 'lost city' feeling, away from the crowds.

Listings Fatehpur Sikri

Where to stay

It is worth spending a night here to make an early start.

$$-$ Govardhan
Buland Darwaza Rd Crossing, T05613-882643,
www.hotelfatehpursikriviews.com.
Clean shared bathrooms, air-cooled suites with fridge, camping (Rs 20), 20% student discount, garden restaurant, pool, badminton, well maintained, lively and conscientious owner. Recommended.

$ Hotel Vrinduvan
Bulund Gate Crossing, T05613-282 318,
www.hotelvrindavanfts.com.
Hospitable place with good-value rooms. There's internet on site, campfires in the winter, music and tours can also be provided.

Transport

Frequent buses from **Agra Idgah Bus Stand** (1 hr) Rs 17. Taxis from Agra include the trip in a day's sightseeing (expect to pay around Rs 2300 return depending on car).

Varanasi
& around

★ Perhaps the holiest of India's cities, Varanasi defies easy description. Highly congested narrow alleys wind in a maze behind waterfront ghats that are at once highly sacred yet physically often far from clean. As an image, an idea and a symbol of Hinduism's central realities, the city draws pilgrims from around the world to worship, to meditate and, above all, to bathe. In the cold mists of a winter's dawn, you can see life and death laid bare. For an outside observer it can be an uncomfortable, albeit unmissable experience, juxtaposing the inner philosophical mysteries of Hinduism with the practical complications of living literally and metaphorically on the edge.

At dawn the riverbank's stone steps begin to hum with activity. Early risers immerse themselves in the water as they face the rising sun; boatmen wait expectantly on the waterside; pilgrims flock to the temples; flower sellers do brisk business; astrologers prepare to read palms and horoscopes, while families carry the dead to their last rites by the holy river. A few steps away from the ghats, motorbikers negotiate the laneways past wandering *sadhus*, hopeful beggars, curious visitors and wandering cows, while packs of stray dogs scavenge among the piles of rubbish.

More holy places surround Varanasi: Sarnath, one of Buddhism's major centres; Jaunpur, a city with a strong Islamic history, and Allahabad, a sacred place for Hindus due to its position at the confluence of the Ganga and Yamuna rivers.

Essential Varanasi

Finding your feet

Several airlines link Varanasi's Babatpur airport with Delhi, Kolkata, Mumbai and other cities; during the high season there are also direct flights to Khajuraho. The airport is 22 km from the city, best reached by pre-paid taxi. Varanasi is quite spread out: the university to the south is nearly 7 km from the spacious Cantonment area and Junction Station to the north, where most trains stop. The station is about 5 km northwest of the Old City and the budget hotels. Some trains (eg Delhi–Kolkata *Rajdhani* and *Expresses* to New Jalpaiguri and Guwahati) do not pass through Varanasi itself but stop at Mughal Sarai, 17 km away; shared jeeps and private taxis run between the two stations. Most long-distance buses arrive at stands near Junction Station. The riverside city, and the focus for most tourists and pilgrims, extends from Raj Ghat in the north to Assi Ghat in the south.

On arrival at Junction Station, you will be accosted by rickshaw-wallahs desperate to get you to a hotel which pays them commission. It can be stressful; don't believe touts who say your chosen hotel is closed or full. Several budget hotels offer free pick-up from the station (call on arrival), or try to get at least 50 m outside of the station area before bargaining for an auto (Rs 80) or cycle-rickshaw (Rs 50). Shared autos leave from the far side of the main road outside the station to Godoulia, near Main Ghat. Note that autos are not permitted into the congested streets near the ghats.

Getting around

Boats are the best way to explore Varanasi (see below). Around town, cycle-rickshaws and autos are plentiful. However, these cannot go down the narrow lanes of the Old City, which are a confusing maze on first arrival. The only way to see this area is on foot. Shared autos run along main routes, though it is difficult (as a tourist) to avoid being pressured into private hire. Unmetered taxis are best for longer sightseeing trips and for getting to/from the airport. The city has some of the disadvantages of pilgrimage centres, notably rickshaw drivers who seem determined to extort as much as possible from unsuspecting visitors. See also Transport, page 146.

River trips

No visit is complete without an early-morning boat trip along the ghats. Start a river trip at Dasasvamedha Ghat where you can hire a boat quite cheaply especially if you can share (bargain to about Rs 200-300 per hour for two to eight people, at dawn). You may go either upstream (south) towards Harishchandra Ghat or downstream to Manikarnika Ghat. You may prefer to have a boat on the river at sunset and watch the leaf-boat lamps floated on the river, or go in the afternoon at half the price quoted at dawn.

Best Varanasi restaurants

Brown Bread Bakery
Lotus Lounge
Megu Café
Poonam
Sheena
See page 144

Sights Colour map 3, B4.

colourful bathing ghats and chaotic streets in India's spiritual capital

Old Centre and back lanes

The maze of narrow lanes, or *galis*, through the old quarter exude the smells and sounds of this holy city. They are fascinating to stroll through though easy to get lost in. Ask for directions as you make your way around the temples.

Visvanath Mandir has been the main Siva temple in Varanasi for over 1000 years. Tourists have to enter by Gate 2 (but can exit from any gate) and there is stiff security by the entrances. The original temple, destroyed in the 12th century, was replaced by a mosque. It was rebuilt in the 16th and again destroyed within a century. The present **'Golden' temple** was built in 1777 by Ahilya Bai of Indore. The gold plating on the roof was provided by Maharaja Ranjit Singh in 1835. Its pointed spires are typically North Indian in style and the exterior is finely carved. The **Gyan Kup**

(Well of Knowledge) next door is said to contain the Siva lingam from the original temple – the well is protected by a stone screen and canopy. The nearby **Gyanvapi Mosque** (Great Mosque of Aurangzeb), with 71-m-high minarets, shows evidence of the original Hindu temple in the foundations, the columns and at the rear.

The 18th-century **Annapurna Temple** (*anna* food; *purna* filled) to the south, built by Baji Rao I, has shrines dedicated to Siva, Ganesh, Hanuman and Surya.

Further north, near the Town Hall (1845) built by the Maharaja of Vizianagram, is the **Kotwali** (Police Station) with the Temple of **Bhaironath**, built by Baji Rao II in 1825. The image inside is believed to be of the Kotwal (Superintendent) who rides on a ghostly dog. Stalls sell sugar dogs to be offered to the image. In the temple garden of **Gopal Mandir** near the Kotwali is a small hut in which Tulsi Das is said to have composed the *Binaya Patrika* poem.

South of the central area, the **Bhelupura Temple** with a museum marks the birthplace of the 23rd Jain Tirthankar **Parsvanath** who preached non-violence. The **Durga Temple** (18th-century) to the south along Durga Kund Road, was built in the Nagara style. It is painted red with ochre and has the typical five spires (symbolizing the elements) merging into one (Brahma). Non-Hindus may view from the rooftop nearby. Next door in a peaceful garden, the **Tulsi Manas Temple** (1964) in white marble commemorates the medieval poet Tulsi Das. It has walls engraved with verses and scenes from the *Ramcharitmanas*, composed in a Hindi dialect, instead of the conventional Sanskrit, and is open to all (closed 1130-1530) with good views from the second floor.

Riverfront

The hundred and more **ghats** on the river are the main attraction for visitors to Varanasi. At dusk synchronized *pujas* are performed, usually from 1800 (later in summer). Large crowds gather at Dasasvamedha (Main) Ghat and Mir Ghat every night, or there's a more low-key affair at Assi Ghat. **Kite flying** is a popular pastime, as elsewhere in India. The serious competitors endeavour to bring down other flyers' kites and so fortify their twine by coating it with a mix of crushed light bulbs and flour paste to make it razor sharp. The quieter ghats, eg Panchganga, are good for watching the fun: boys in their boats on the river scramble to retrieve downed kites as trophies that can be re-used even though the kites themselves are very cheap. Cricket is also played on the ghats, particularly those to the north which are more spacious and less crowded.

Dasasvamedha Ghat Commonly called 'Main Ghat', Dasasvamedha means the 'Place of Ten Horse Sacrifices' performed here by Brahma, God of Creation. Some believe that in the age of the gods when the world was in chaos, Divodasa was appointed King of Kashi by Brahma. He accepted, on condition that all the gods would leave Varanasi. Even Siva was forced to leave but Brahma set the test for Divodasa, confident that he would get the complex ceremony wrong,

Tip...

For photographs, visit the riverside at first light (0430 in summer, 0600 in winter), when Hindu pilgrims come to bathe in the sacred Ganga, facing the rising sun. The foggy sunshine early in the morning often clears to produce a beautiful light.

allowing the gods back into the city. However, the ritual was performed flawlessly, and the ghat has thus become one of the holiest, especially at eclipses. Bathing here is regarded as being almost as meritorious as making the sacrifice. This is the place to hire boats for trips up- or downriver (see Essential Varanasi, opposite).

Upstream (south) You will pass **Munshi Ghat**, where some of the city's sizeable Muslim population (25%) come to bathe, although the river has no religious significance for them. Close by is **Darbhanga Ghat** where the mansion had a hand-operated cable lift. Professional washermen work at the **Dhobi Ghat**; there is religious merit in having your clothes washed in the Ganga. Brahmins have their own washermen to avoid caste pollution. The municipality has built separate washing facilities away from the ghat.

Narad Ghat and **Chauki Ghat** are held sacred since the Buddha received enlightenment here under a *peepul* tree. Those who bathe together at Narad supposedly go home and quarrel! The pink water tower here is for storing Ganga water.

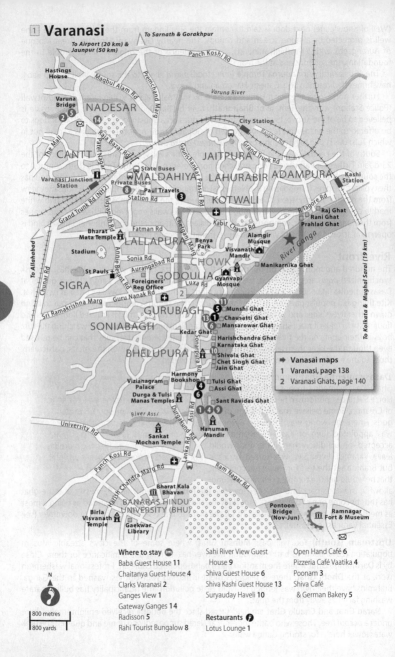

1 Varanasi

To Sarnath & Gorakhpur

To Airport (20 km) & Jaunpur (50 km)

Hastings House

Panch Koshi Rd

Macbul Alam Rd

Premchand Marg

Varuna River

Varuna Bridge

NADESAR

The Mall

City Station

Raighat Rd

CANTT

Raja Bazar Rd

Patel Nagar

Gaurishankar Prasad Rd

Grand Trunk Rd

JAITPURA

LAHURABIR

ADAMPURA

Kashi Station

State Buses

Private Buses

MALDAHIYA

Varanasi Junction Station

Station Rd

Paul Travels

KOTWALI

Grand Trunk Rd (NH2)

Vidyapith Rd

Chetganj Marg

Kabir Chaura Rd

Raj Ghat
Rani Ghat
Prahlad Ghat

R Tagore Rd

Bharat Mata Temple

Fatman Rd

Benya Park

Alamgir Mosque

LALLAPURA

Stadium

Sonia Rd

CHOWK

Visvanath Mandir

River Ganga

To Kolkata & Mughal Sarai (19 km)

St Pauls

Annie Besant Rd

Aurangabad Rd

GODOULIA

Manikarnika Ghat

SIGRA

Chunar Rd

To Allahabad

Foreigners' Reg Office

Luxa Rd

Gyanvapi Mosque

Guru Nanak Rd

Sri Ramakrishna Marg

GURUBAGH

Munshi Ghat

Chausatti Ghat

SONIABAGH

Mansarowar Ghat

Kedar Ghat

Harishchandra Ghat

BHELUPURA

Karnataka Ghat

Shivala Ghat

Chet Singh Ghat

Jain Ghat

Harmony Bookshop

Tulsi Ghat

Vizianagram Palace

Assi Ghat

Durga & Tulsi Manas Temples

Sant Ravidas Ghat

River Assi

University Rd

Durgakund Rd

Assi Rd

Tanka Rd

Hanuman Mandir

Sankat Mochan Temple

Panch Kosi Rd

Ram Nagar Rd

Hatch Chandra Marg Rd

Bharat Kala Bhavan

BANARAS HINDU UNIVERSITY (BHU)

Birla Visvanath Temple

Gaekwar Library

Pontoon Bridge (Nov-Jun)

Ramnagar Fort & Museum

➡ Vanasai maps
1 Varanasi, page 138
2 Varanasi Ghats, page 140

N

800 metres
800 yards

Where to stay 🛏
Baba Guest House 11
Chaitanya Guest House 4
Clarks Varanasi 2
Ganges View 1
Gateway Ganges 14
Radisson 5
Rahi Tourist Bungalow 8

Sahi River View Guest House 9
Shiva Guest House 6
Shiva Kashi Guest House 13
Suryauday Haveli 10

Restaurants 🍴
Lotus Lounge 1

Open Hand Café 6
Pizzeria Café Vaatika 4
Poonam 3
Shiva Café
 & German Bakery 5

BACKGROUND
Varanasi

Varanasi derives its name from two streams, the Varuna to the north and the Assi, a small trickle, on the south. Banaras is a corruption of Varanasi but it is also called Kashi (Siva's 'City of Light') by Hindus. As one of the seven sacred cities of Hinduism (see page 1324), it attracts well over one million pilgrims each year, while about 50,000 Brahmins are permanent residents. The Jains too consider it holy because three *tirthankars* (seventh Suarsvanath, 11th Shyeyanshnath, 23rd Parsvanath) were born here.

Varanasi is said to combine the virtues of all other places of pilgrimage, and anyone dying within the area marked by the Panch Kosi Road is transported straight to heaven. Some devout Hindus move to Varanasi to end their days and have their ashes scattered in the holy Ganga. Every pilgrim, in addition to visiting the holy sites, must make a circuit of the Panch Kosi Road which runs outside and round the sacred territory of Varanasi. This starts at Manikarnika Ghat, runs along the waterfront to Assi Ghat, then round the outskirts in a large semi-circle to Barna Ghat. The 58-km route is lined with trees and shrines and the pilgrimage is supposed to take six days, each day's walk finishing in a small village, equipped with temples and *dharamshalas*.

Varanasi was probably an important town by the seventh century BC when Babylon and Nineveh were at the peak of their power. The Buddha visited in 500 BC and it was mentioned in both the *Mahabharata* and the *Ramayana*. It became a centre of culture, education, commerce and craftsmanship, but was raided by Mahmud of Ghazni's army in 1033 and by Qutb-ud-din Ghuri in 1194. Ala-ud-din Khalji, the King of Delhi (1294-1316), destroyed temples and built mosques in their place. The Muslim influence was so strong that in the 18th century the city was known briefly as Mohammadabad. Despite its early foundation hardly any building here dates before the 17th century, and few are more than 200 years old.

Mansarovar Ghat leads to ruins of several temples around a lake. **Kedar Ghat** is named after Kedarnath, a pilgrimage site in the Uttarakhand, with a Bengali temple nearby.

The **Harishchandra Ghat** is particularly holy and is dedicated to King Harishchandra. It is now the most sacred *smashan* or cremation ghat although Manikarnika is busier. Behind the ghat is a *gopuram* of a Dravidian-style temple. The **Karnataka Ghat** is one of many regional ghats which are attended by priests who know the local languages, castes, customs and festivals.

The **Hanuman Ghat** is where Vallabha, the leader of a revivalist Krishna bhakti cult was born in the late 15th century. **Shivala Ghat** (Kali Ghat) is privately owned by the ex-ruler of Varanasi. **Chet Singh's Fort**, Shivala, stands behind the ghat. The fort, the old palace of the Maharajas, is where the British imprisoned him, but he escaped by climbing down to the river and swimming away. **Anandamayi Ghat** is named after the Bengali saint Anandamayi Ma (died 1982) who received 'enlightenment' at 17 and spent her life teaching and in charitable work. **Jain Ghat** is near the birthplace of Tirthankar Shyeyanshnath.

Tulsi Ghat commemorates the great saint-poet Tulsi Das who lived here (see Tulsi Manas Temple, page 137). Furthest upstream is the **Assi Ghat**, where the River Assi meets the Ganga, one of the five ghats where pilgrims should bathe in a day; the order is Assi, Dasasvamedha, Barnasangam, Panchganga and Manikarnika. Further upstream on the east bank is the Ramnagar Fort, the Maharaja of Varanasi's residence (see page 141).

Downstream (north) Heading downstream from Dasasvamedha Ghat, you come to **Man Mandir Ghat** dominated by a Rajput palace ① *dawn-dusk, Rs100 foreigners, Rs 5 Indians*, built by Maharajah Man Singh of Amber in 1600 and one of the oldest in Varanasi. The palace was restored in the last century with brick and plaster. The beautiful stone balcony on the northeast corner gives an indication of how the original looked. Maharaja Jai Singh of Jaipur converted the palace into an **observatory** in 1710 (see also Jaipur, page 278). Like its counterparts in Delhi, Jaipur and Ujjain, the rooftop observatory comprises a collection of instruments built of brick, cement and stone. At the entrance is the Bhittiyantra, or wall quadrant, over 3 m high and in the same plane as the line of longitude. Similarly placed is the Samratyantra which is designed to slope upwards pointing at the

Pole Star. From the top of the Chakra Yantra there is a superb view of the ghats and the town. Near the entrance to the palace is a small **Siva Temple** whose shrine is a lingam immersed in water. During droughts, water is added to the cistern to make it overflow for good luck.

The **Dom Raja's House** is next door, flanked by painted tigers. The *doms* are the 'Untouchables' of Varanasi and are integral to the cremation ceremony. As Untouchables they can handle the corpse, a ritually polluting act for Hindus. They also supply the flame from the temple for the funeral pyre. Their presence is essential and also lucrative since there are fees for the various services they provide. The Dom Raja is the hereditary title of the leader of these Untouchables.

Tip...
Photography is not permitted at the burning ghats, though travellers might be told that it is allowed and then be presented with a large fine. Other scams involve conmen collecting 'donations' to provide wood for burning the poor. Beware of pestering individuals declaring they are "not a guide, just talking"; they have the potential to ruin your experience.

Mir Ghat leads to a sacred well; widows who dedicate themselves to prayer, are fed and clothed here. Then comes **Lalita Ghat** ① *entrance Rs 10*, with its distinctive Nepalese-style temple with a golden roof above and wood carvings decorating the exterior.

Above **Manikarnika Ghat** is a well into which Siva's dead wife Sati's earring is supposed to have fallen when Siva was carrying her after she committed suicide (see page 1329). The Brahmins managed to find the jewel from the earring (*manikarnika*) and returned it to Siva who blessed the place. Offerings of *bilva* flowers, milk, sandalwood and sweetmeats are thrown into the tank where pilgrims come to bathe. Between the well and the ghat is *Charanpaduka*, a stone slab with Vishnu's footprint. Boatmen may try to persuade you to leave a 'private' offering to perform a *puja* (a ploy to increasing their earnings).

2 Varanasi Ghats

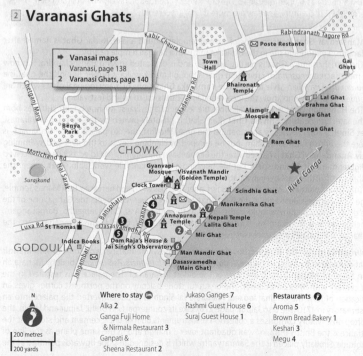

⮕ **Vanasai maps**
1 Varanasi, page 138
2 Varanasi Ghats, page 140

Where to stay
Alka 2
Ganga Fuji Home & Nirmala Restaurant 3
Ganpati & Sheena Restaurant 2
Jukaso Ganges 7
Rashmi Guest House 6
Suraj Guest House 1

Restaurants
Aroma 5
Brown Bread Bakery 1
Keshari 3
Megu 4

The adjoining **Jalasayin Ghat** is the principal burning ghat of the city. The expensive scented sandalwood which the rich alone can afford is used sparingly; usually not more than 2 kg. You may see floating bundles covered in white cloth. Children and those dying of 'high fever' (or smallpox in the past) are not cremated but put into the river to avoid injuring Sitala the goddess of smallpox.

Tourists are few and far between after the burning ghat. **Scindia Ghat**, originally built in 1830, was so large that it collapsed. **Ram Ghat** was built by the Maharaja of Jaipur.

Five rivers are supposed to meet at the magnificent **Panchganga Ghat** – the Ganga, Sarasvati, Gyana, Kirana and Dhutpapa. The stone column can hold around 1000 lamps at festivals. The impressive flights of stone steps run up to the impressively situated 17th-century Alamgir Mosque (Beni Madhav ka Darera). This was Aurangzeb's smaller mosque and was built on the original Vishnu temple of the Marathas, parts of which were used in its construction. Two minarets are missing – one fell and killed some people and the other was taken down by the government as a precaution. You can climb to the top of the mosque for fantastic views (donation expected); again, bags are prohibited and you may be searched.

At **Gai Ghat** there is a statue of a Nandi bull, whilst at **Trilochana Ghat** there is a temple to Siva in his form as the 'Three-eyed' (*Trilochana*); two turrets stand out of the water. A beautiful little palace is found at **Rani Ghat**, then **Raj Ghat** is the last ghat you can reach before the path peters out. Excavations have revealed the site of a city from the eighth century BC on a grassy mound nearby. Raj Ghat was where the river was forded until bridges were built. High water levels are recorded here, though the flood levels are difficult to imagine when the river is at its lowest in January and February.

> **Tip...**
> You can watch weavers at work in Piti Kothi, the Muslim area inland from Raj Ghat.

South of the centre

Banaras Hindu University (BHU) This is one of the largest campus universities in India and enjoys a pleasant, relaxed atmosphere. Founded at the turn of the 19th century, it was originally intended for the study of Sanskrit, Indian art, music and culture. The **New Visvanath Temple** (1966), one of the tallest in India, is in the university semicircle and was financed by the Birla family. It was planned by Madan Mohan Malaviya (1862-1942), chancellor of the university, who believed in Hinduism without caste distinctions. The marble Siva temple, modelled on the old Visvanath Temple, is open to all.

Bharat Kala Bhavan ① *BHU, Mon-Sat 1030-1630 (Jul-Apr), 0730-1300 (May-Jun) closed holidays, foreigners Rs 100, camera Rs 50 (lockers at entrance)*, is a peaceful museum containing a wealth of sculptures from Mathura and Sarnath, and an excellent gallery of miniature paintings including Mughal and Company works. Don't miss the Nidhi Gallery (limited hours, 1200-1300 and 1500-1600) containing treasures such as Jahangir's opium cup and priceless pieces of jewellery. Upstairs is an interesting exhibition on Benares containing old prints and photos, and also the Alice Boner gallery showing the life and work of this Swiss painter/sculptor who immigrated to India in 1935.

Ramnagar Fort Across the river in a dramatic setting on the edge of narrow crowded streets is the run-down 17th-century **Ramnagar Fort**, the former home of the Maharaja of Varanasi. The ferry costs Rs 10 return, or there are rickshaws from the main gate of BHU which cross a bone-jarring pontoon bridge to the fort (underwater June to October), Rs 10 each way, or walk over the pontoon bridge. The **museum** ① *T0542-233 9322, 1000-1700, Rs 16*, has palanquins, elephant *howdahs* and headdresses, costumes, arms and furniture gathering dust. Look out for the amazing locally made astrological clock and peer inside the impressive Durbar Hall, cunning designed to remain cool in the summer heat, with lifesize portraits lining one wall. Nearby Ramnagar village has *Ramlila* performances during Dasara (October to November) and has some quieter backalleys which make for a relaxing hour's wandering.

Chunar

35 km southwest of Varanasi. Buses from Varanasi's City Station take 1½ hrs.

Chunar is famous for Chunar sandstone, the material of the Asoka pillars, highly polished in a technique said to be Persian. The town is also noted for its **fort** built on a spur of the Kaimur Hills, 53 m above the surrounding plain. It was of obvious strategic importance and changed hands a number of times. The army occupies the fort today, but you can look around. There is an impressive well with steps leading down to a water gate; watch out for snakes. The **British cemetery** below the fort overlooks the Ganga. The **Islamic tombs** of Shah Kasim Suleiman and his son here feature in paintings by the Daniells and others.

Listings Varanasi *maps p138 and p140*

Tourist information

Government of India Tourist Office
The Mall, Cantonment, T0542-250 1784.
Mon-Sat 0900-1630.
Well run, with helpful manager and staff; guides available at set rates. Also at Babatpur Airport.

Tourist Information Counter
Junction Railway Station, near 'Enquiry',
T0542-250 6670. Daily 0600-2000.
Provides helpful maps and information.

Where to stay

Off-season discounts are available May-Aug, when rates (especially in higher-end hotels) drop very significantly. Rooms with river views are worth the extra cost, but note that autos are not permitted in the congested streets behind the central ghats, so on arrival you will have to walk the last stretch (10-20 mins) to reach a riverside hotel. These hotels can be difficult to locate, particularly at night, when walking along the minor ghats is not advisable. Be prepared for power-cuts and carry a torch at night. Look for hotel signs (with arrows) painted on walls to find your way, or ask shopkeepers. As an alternative, there are hotels in the area around Assi Ghat to the south, which can be reached by auto and 2-min walk. Staying in the Cantonment area may be more comfortable, but it means missing out on the atmosphere of the city.

$$$$ Jukaso Ganges
Guleria Ghat, between Bosie and Ram ghats,
near Manikarnika Ghat, T0542-240 6666,
www.welcomeheritagehotels.in.
Beautiful renovated old palace with 15 comfortable rooms (mostly river-facing, some with delightful private balconies), great

bathrooms, around an elegant inner courtyard. Roof terrace for dining, lovely seating out the front on the ghats. Breakfast included. Located on the northern ghats among stunning ancient buildings – a less touristed area.

$$$$ Suryauday Haveli
Shivala Ghat, Nepali Kothi, T0542-654 0390,
www.suryaudayhaveli.com.
Directly on the Ganga in a renovated century-old stone edifice built by the Nepali kings. Some rooms river-facing. There's a roof deck and lovely courtyard, candlelit dinner accompanied by live Indian music in evenings, vegetarian menu only. Rooms are spacious with traditional elements of decor. An excellent location and a characterful place to stay. Breakfast included and free sunset boat ride.

$$$ Clarks Varanasi
The Mall, T0542-250 1011-20,
www.clarkshotels.com.
In the quieter Cantonment area, not as plush as other high-end options as rooms are a bit dated, but the facilities are good and it has some character. The pool has pleasing surroundings of established trees and plants (charge for non-residents), restaurant and nice bar. Discounts available online.

$$$ Ganges View
Assi Ghat, T0542-231 3218,
www.hotelgangesview.com.
Old patrician home converted into a welcoming guesthouse with a tastefully decorated range of small rooms, more expensive on the upper level with the better views, very pleasant atmosphere, interesting clientele, lovely riverside verandas, beautiful artwork adorns public spaces, vegetarian restaurant (guests only). Deservedly popular so book ahead.

$$$ Gateway Ganges
Nadesar Palace Ground, T0542-666 0001, www.thegatewayhotels.com.
130 rooms (plus suites), those on the 3rd floor have walk-in showers, 2 good restaurants serve alcohol, pool is the nicest in town, busy but formal efficient service.

$$$ Radisson
The Mall, Cantonment, T0542-250 1566, www.radisson.com/varanasi.in.
The grandest rooms in town, large with quality furnishings, wide white beds, sofas and good bathrooms. Good health facilities, disappointing pool (small with few loungers), excellent restaurant and modern bar.

$$$-$$ Rashmi Guest House
Manmandir Ghat, T0542-240 2778, www.palaceonriver.com.
This modernized tower has an excellent location close to Main Ghat, rooms are clean with a/c, hot water and TV, those at the front have excellent river views. The rooftop restaurant is reliable and hygienic.

$$$-$$ Shiva Ganges View
Mansarovar Ghat, T0542-245 0063, www.varanasiguesthouse.com.
In a British-built old family house, 8 large spotless rooms have high ceilings, multiple windows, mosquito nets – but strange furniture and clashing decor. Great views from the front upstairs rooms, which share a balcony and have a/c; lower rooms have air-coolers and are cheaper. Very chatty owner.

$$$-$ Alka
Mir Ghat, T0542-240 1681, www.hotelalkavns.com.
Wide variety of clean rooms in a modern building, though some are in need of a lick of paint. Expect towels, a/c and TV in the more expensive rooms, cheaper end share bathrooms. The prime riverside location means it is often full, book ahead. Handy access down to the ghats from the courtyard.

$$$-$ Ganpati
Next to Alka on Mir Ghat, T0542-239 0059, www.ganpatiguesthouse.com.
Atmospheric old building, rooms range from colourful cubby holes to spacious a/c rooms with river views, all have private baths. Great views from rooftop restaurant (see below). Ganpati's ever-increasing popularity means it's pretty pricey; they have a cheaper overspill guesthouse close by.

$$-$ Rahi Tourist Bungalow (UP Tourism)
Off Parade Kothi, opposite railway station, T0542-220 8545, www.up-tourism.com.
A/c, air-cooled or fan rooms (try to see a few) and dorm in barrack-style 2-storey building, restaurant, bar, shady veranda, pleasant garden, simple, clean and efficient, popular – wise to phone ahead. Can arrange cars for the day (at government-fixed prices), has parking space and is very close to railway station.

$ Baba Guest House
D20/15 Munshi Ghat, T0542-245 5452, www.babaguesthouse.com.
Basic, freshly painted rooms, some recently renovated, some with bath, dorm has views, huge Korean menu, food served in downstairs café when it's too hot to use rooftop restaurant. Wi-Fi good. Typical old-school Varanasi backpackers.

$ Chaitanya Guest House
B1/158-A, Assi Ghat, T0542-231 3686, knpsahi@yahoo.com.
A cosy place with only 4 rooms, attached bathrooms, in an old building with moulded ceilings, coloured glass windows and tiny terrace at the front. Sadly views are over a car park to the Ganga. Rooms with a/c cost more; air coolers are provided in summer. Pleasant family will leave you to your own devices.

$ Ganga Fuji Home
Shakarkand Gali, near Golden Temple, T0542-239 7333, www.gangafujihomevaranasi.com.
An excellent choice with a wide range of price categories, from very cheap with shared bath up to comfortable deluxe rooms with a/c and TV. Free Wi-Fi, hot water, decent pillows and mattresses, competent management, **Nirmala** restaurant on rooftop (see below). They can pick up from the train station – call on arrival.

$ Sahi River View Guest House
Assi Ghat, T0542-236 6730, sahi_rvgh@sify.com.
12 rooms of all standards, great views from balcony and rooftops, food from spotless kitchen, owner eager to please, no commission given to touts.

$ Shiva Guest House
D20/14 Munshi Ghat, T0542-245 2108, shiva_guest_house@hotmail.com.
17 simple rooms in an old building, some with tiny private bathrooms, hot water, great views from the rooftop, family-run, friendly, popular with Japanese and Korean backpackers.

$ Shiva Kashi Guesthouse
Chausatti Ghat, T0542-245 0166,
http://shivakashiguesthouse.in.
Very respectable rooms, range of a/c or fan, modern decor but in an old medieval building, some with balcony, not on the river but very close, free Wi-Fi, peaceful, comfortable and well-managed. Good choice with some rooms at the upper end of this price bracket.

$ Suraj Guest House
Lalita Ghat near Nepali Temple, T0542-239 8560,
http://surajguesthouse.hpage.co.in/index.html.
Tucked away behind a tiny temple, 5 quaint simple clean rooms with attached bath, owned by eccentric kindly family, extremely cheap, nice vibe, free Wi-Fi and good rooftop. It's hard to find – they can arrange pick-up.

Restaurants

Restaurants outside high-end hotels tend to be vegetarian and are not allowed to serve alcohol (although a couple do). Dry days are on the 1st and 7th of each month, and on some public holidays. Many tourist-oriented eateries are on Bengali Tola (the large alley running from Main Ghat to Assi Ghat), and there are some excellent and cheap South Indian places at its southern end.

$$ Lotus Lounge
Mansarovar Ghat, T(0)9838-567717.
Top spot for Ganga views from a high-up chilled-out terrace, away from the bustle on the ghats. Prices are reasonable for inventive Asian and Western dishes (excellent satay, or pumpkin ravioli), interesting salads and great breakfasts. Some low tables at the front with cushion seating.

$$ Pizzeria Café Vaatika
Assi Ghat.
A shady plant-filled terrace on the Ganga, friendly staff, Italian (OK pizza) and Indian food, excellent cold coffee. Perfect place to relax.

$$ Poonam
Pradeep Hotel, Jagatganj,
T0542-220 4963/220 4994.
Good variety of fabulous Indian dishes, served by professional staff in classy surroundings. **Eden** restaurant on the roof is equally good – and has a garden.

$$-$ Brown Bread Bakery
Tripura Bhairavi (near Golden Temple),
http://bakerybreadbrown.blogspot.co.uk.
Excellent salads, huge array of different cheeses and bread, diverse menu in an attractive setting with cushions for lounging and live sitar music every evening, plus rooftop seating. Organic ingredients used where possible and profits to charity.

$$-$ Nirmala
Ganga Fuji Home (see Where to stay).
Hygienic kitchen, food tempered down for Western palate, live classical music every evening at 1930. Recommended for the exceptional city views, ambiance and hospitality, serves beer.

$$-$ Open Hand Café
Dumraun Bagh Colony, near Assi Ghat,
www.openhand.in.
Excellent fair-trade coffee, great pastries and snacks, and a relaxing cosy place to hang out with free Wi-Fi. The shop is worth checking out (see below).

$$-$ Sheena
Ganpati (see Where to stay).
Rooftop restaurant with sublime river views and lower balcony with Mediterranean feel, serving quality food, especially good *shakshuka*. Great place for hanging out, plus there's clandestine beer.

$ Aroma
Dasasvamedha Rd, Godoulia, T0542-326 4564.
Bland pastel decor and low ceilings but a clean a/c environment off the tourist circuit, best for south Indian meals. Free delivery 0800-2200 on orders over Rs 220.

$ Keshari
Teri Neem, Godoulia (off Dasasvamedha Rd),
T0542-240 1472.
Excellent vegetarian *thalis* plus north and south Indian dishes, and some Chinese, "the longest menu in town" although not every item is available, efficient service, generous portions.

$ Megu
Kalika Lane near Golden Temple. Lunchtimes only, 1000-1600, closed Sun.
This tiny restaurant specializes in Japanese food, and is owned by a Japanese-Indian couple. Very popular, fantastic ginger chicken, miso soup, and the Korean *bibimbap* is a winner.

$ Shiva Café and German Bakery
Bengali Tola near Naraol Ghat. Open from 0800.
Very popular, especially for breakfasts which are excellent (proper porridge). Spartan decor on the ground floor but the 2nd storey is a bit jazzier with low seating and a Nepalese theme. Staff are delightful.

Festivals

Feb **Ganga Water Rally** is an international and national kayak get-together from Allahabad to Mirzapur then Chunar Fort. A 40-km race from Chunar to Rajghat in Varanasi takes place on the final day. Also **International Yoga Week**.
Late Feb/early Mar 3 days at Sivaratri, **festival of Dhrupad music** attracts performers from near and far, beginners and stars, in a very congenial atmosphere, a wonderful experience, many *naga babas* (naked *sadhus*) set up camp on ghats.
Mar/Apr **Holi** is celebrated with great fervour.
Apr Pilgrims walk around 'Kashi', as laid down in the scriptures. Jain **Mahavir Jayanti**.
Apr/May **Sankat Mochan Music Festival**, Sankat Mochan Mandir. Non-stop temple music, open to all.
May **Ganga Dasara** celebrates the day the waters of the Ganga reached Haridwar.
Jul/Aug Month-long **carnival** with funfair opposite Monkey Temple, monsoon fever makes it particularly crazy.
Oct/Nov Dasara Ramlila at Ramnagar. **Ganga Festival** is organized by UP Tourism alongside a 10-day craft fair. **Nagnathaiya** draws up to 50,000 worshippers to Tulsi Ghat, re-enacting the story of Krishna jumping into the Yamuna to overcome Kalija, the King of the Serpents.
Nakkataiya A fair at Chetganj recalling Rama's brother, Lakshmana, cutting off Ravana's sister's nose when she attempted to force him into a marriage. At Nati Imli, **Bharat Milap**, the meeting of Rama and Bharat after 14 years' separation is celebrated – the Maharaja of Varanasi attends in full regalia on elephant back.
Dec-Feb Music festivals.

Shopping

Varanasi is famous for silks including brocades (Temple Bazar, Visvanath Gali), ornamental brassware, gold jewellery, glass beads, sitar-making and hand-block printed goods. The main shopping areas are Chowk, Godoulia, Visvanath Gali, Gyanvapi and Thatheri Bazar.

Books

Harmony, *B1/158 Assi Ghat*. Best selection in town (some say in all India), excellent fiction, coffee-table books and travel guides.
Indica Books, *D 40/18 Godoulia, near crossing*. Specialist Indological bookshop.

Handloom and handicrafts

Benares Art Culture, *2/114 Badhaini Assi*. Aims to promote local artists, interesting selection of sculpture, paintings and silks at fixed prices.
Ganga Handlooms, *D10/18 Kohli Katra, off Viswanath Gali, near Golden Temple (ask locally). Open 1100-2000.* Large selection of beautiful cotton fabrics, *ikats*, vegetable dyes, good tailors, great patterns (Western).
Open Hand Café & Shop, *see Restaurants, opposite*. Home furnishings, textiles, crafts, jewellery, and a good place to buy silk. Fair-trade credentials.

What to do

Body and soul

Panch Mandir, *Assi Ghat*. Drop-in yoga classes each morning 0600-0930, reasonably priced.
Satya Foundation, *B-37/54B Rukma Bhawan, Birdopur, T(0)9336-877455, www.satyafoundation. com.* Music, meditation and yoga, highly authentic teachings. Recommended.
Siddhartha Yoga Centre, *below Lotus Lounge, Mansarowar Ghat, T(0)9236-830966. 2-hr classes at 0800 and 1530.* You can 'drop-in' but better to call ahead as there is only room for 4-5 people.
Yoga Institute, *BHU, T0542-230 7208.* 1-month courses.

Language courses

'Tourist Hindi' courses are advertised in several hotels and restaurants.

Swimming

Pools at **Radisson**, **Gateway Ganges**, and **Clarks Varanasi** hotels.

Tour operators

Many small travel agents in laneways of Old City, usually charging Rs 100 commission on railway tickets.
TCI, *Sri Das Foundation, S20/51-5 and S20/52-4, The Mall, T0542-250 0866, www.tcindia.com.* Long-established operator. Tours cover all interests from wildlife to luxury train trips.
Tiwari Tours and Travel, *Assi Ghat, T0542-2130 805, www.tiwaritravel.com.* Good service, bus tickets, yoga tours, and budget to high-end tours.

Transport

Air Babatpur airport, 22 km from the city, has flights to **Delhi**, **Mumbai** and other cities daily; 2 or 3 per week to **Khajuraho** in the high season. There is also 1 direct flight per week on Thu from Varanasi to **Kathmandu**, with **Air India**. An unreliable airport bus runs to the Indian Airlines office in the Cantonment area but it's better to take a taxi from the pre-paid booth.

Bus UP Roadways Bus Stand, Sher Shah Suri Marg, is opposite Junction Station, open 24 hrs, T(0)9415-049623. Buses to **Sarnath**, 10 km. To **Allahabad**, every 15 mins 0330-2300 (3 hrs), better than train; to **Gorakhpur**, hourly 0400-0030 (7 hrs, see Transport to Nepal, below, for information on private bus to Nepal). For **Delhi** go via **Kanpur**, frequent service from 0700 (8 hrs); **Lucknow**, every 30 mins (8 hrs), also an a/c sleeper bus at 2300. **Agra**, at 1230, 1700 and 2000 (14 hrs). **Gaya**: better by rail. Private buses from opposite the railway station go frequently to **Allahabad** and **Jaunpur** (1½ hrs).

Rickshaw and taxi *Tempos* and auto-rickshaws run on fixed routes; those near hotel gates overcharge (fix the fare before hiring). They are not allowed in the narrow streets of the old city but can go to **Godoulia** in the centre near Dasasvamedha Ghat, Rs 80 from station. Private taxis can be hired from agents and hotels; **Uttar Pradesh Tourist Bungalow**, Parade Kothi, T0542-220 6638, is a good place to start. There is a pre-paid taxi and rickshaw booth near the station reservations office.

Train The official Reservations office is outside the station on the left as you exit. Be extra careful with your possessions on trains bound for Varanasi as theft is common.

Most trains stop at the **Junction** (or **Cantonment**) **Station**, with 24-hr left luggage; to reach a Cantonment hotel on foot, use the back exit. Tickets (preferably a day in advance) from the **Foreign Tourist Assistance** inside the main hall which is helpful and efficient, passport required (0800-2200, Sun 0800-1400). When it is closed use the computerized railway reservations (0800-1400, 1430-2000). **Agra Fort**: several daily 8-12 hrs; or go to Tundla from Mughal Sarai Station (see below). **Allahabad**: many options 2½-3½ hrs, but bus is easier. **Chennai**: at least 1 per day, 37 hrs, reserve early. **Dehra Dun**: 3 per day, 14-22 hrs. **Gaya**: frequent service, 3-4 hrs. **Jaunpur**: several daily, around 1¼ hrs, but easier by bus. **Kolkata** (**H** or **S**): several daily, often running late, around 12-16 hrs; quicker/more reliable from Mughal Serai. **Lucknow**: frequent trains, 5-7 hrs. **Mahoba** (for **Khajuraho**): *Bundelkhand Exp 11108*, 1745 but often late, 10 hrs (take onward bus). **Satna** (for **Khajuraho**): frequent service, 6-7 hrs (from Satna, bumpy bus, 4 hrs). **Mumbai** (**CST**): *Varanasi Lokmanya Tilak Exp 11066*, 2320, Tue, Thu, Sat, 28½ hrs. **New Delhi**: *Shramjeevi Exp 12401*, 2220, 13½ hrs.

Mughal Sarai Station (with retiring rooms and left luggage) is 16 km away. Take a connecting train from Varanasi (45 mins), or allow plenty of time as you need to cross the Ganga and there are huge jams. Easiest to take a taxi from Varanasi, although shared autos leave from the railway station. Mughal Sarai has several trains to Gaya; a good one is *Purushottam Exp 12802*, 1040, 3 hrs. Also to: **Kolkata**: (**H**) *Rajdhani Exp 12302/12306*, 0155, 8-11 hrs; (**S**) *Rajdhani Exp 12314*, 0140, 9 hrs; (**H**) *Kalka Mail 12312*, 2025, 10¾ hrs. **New Delhi**: several daily, best is *Rajdhani* at around 0100, 9 hrs. **New Jalpaiguri** (for **Darjeeling**): 4 per day, best is *Rajdhani* at 2250, 12 hrs, and on to **Guwahati**, 18¼ hrs and **Dibrugarh**, 30 hrs.

Transport to Nepal There is 1 direct flight per week on Thu from Varanasi to **Kathmandu,** with Air India. As of Mar 2015, a direct a/c 'friendship' bus runs from Varanasi to **Kathmandu**, taking around 12-13 hrs, on Mon, Wed, Fri and Sun. Departs Varanasi at 0000, and goes via the border crossing at **Sonauli**. Tickets can be booked at the UP Roadways office or online at https://www.upsrtconline.co.in. Using local buses or a train/bus combination is long (around 20 hrs), tiring and may require an overnight stay near the border. UP Roadways buses go via **Gorakhpur** to **Sonauli**, every 1-2 hrs, check at bus stand for timings, 7-9 hrs; from Sonauli, 0600. Private buses (agents near **UP Tourist Bungalow**, around Bengali Tola/Assi Ghat and opposite railway station), often demand inclusive fares for hotel stay; you may prefer to opt for their deluxe buses to the border. There are about 6 trains per day to **Gorakhpur**, the best is the *Chauri Chura Exp, 15003*, leaving at 0040 arriving around 0700, so you should have time to catch an onward bus/jeep to Kathmandu (which leave in morning. See box, page 1362 for detailed information on the border crossing with Nepal.

monasteries, stupas and temples mark where the Buddha first preached

Sarnath, 10 km northeast of Varanasi, is one of Buddhism's major centres in India. The museum houses some superb pieces, including the famed four-lion capital that is the symbol of the Indian Union. The *stupas*, monasteries and Buddha statues make an interesting contrast to nearby Hindu Varanasi. The Enclosure containing the main sacred buildings is open from sunrise to sunset; admission is Rs 100 for foreigners; videos are charged at Rs 25.

Sights

Archaeological Museum ① *Sat-Thu 0900-1700, entrance Rs 5, cameras and bags must be left outside.* The museum has a well-displayed collection of pieces from the site, including the famous lion capital from the Asokan Column. The four lions sitting back to back are of highly polished sandstone and show Mauryan sculpture at its best. Also on display are a Sunga period (first

Sarnath

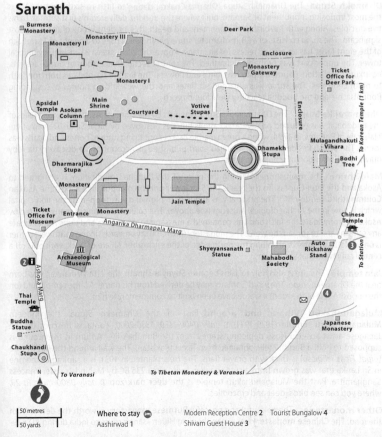

50 metres
50 yards

Where to stay 🛏
Aashirwad 1
Shivam Guest House 3

Modern Reception Centre 2   Tourist Bungalow 4

Sarnath

When he had gained enlightenment at Bodhgaya, the Buddha came to the deer park at Sarnath and delivered his first sermon (circa 528 BC), usually referred to as *Dharmachakra* (The Wheel of Law). Since then, the site has been revered. The Chinese traveller Hiuen Tsang described the *sangharama* (monastery) in AD 640 as having 1500 monks, a 65-m-high *vihara*, a figure of the Buddha represented by a wheel, a 22-m-high stone *stupa* built by Asoka, a larger 90-m-high *stupa* and three lakes. The remains here and the sculptures now at the Indian Museum, Kolkata and the National Museum, Delhi, reveal that Sarnath was a centre of religious activity, learning and art, continuously from the fourth century BC until its abandonment in the ninth century AD and ultimate destruction by Muslim armies in 1197.

century BC) stone railing, Kushana period (second century AD) Boddhisattvas and Gupta period (fifth century AD) figures, including a magnificent seated Buddha.

Dhamekh Stupa The Dhamekh Stupa (Dharma Chakra) dating to fifth to sixth century AD, is the most imposing monument at Sarnath, built where the Buddha delivered his first sermon to his five disciples. Along with his birth, enlightenment and death, this incident is one of the four most significant. The *stupa* consists of a 28-m-diameter stone plinth which rises to a height of 13 m. Each of the eight faces has an arched recess for an image. Above this base rises a 31-m-high cylindrical tower. The upper part was probably unfinished. The central section has elaborate Gupta designs, eg luxuriant foliation, geometric patterns, birds and flowers. The Brahmi script dates from the sixth to ninth centuries. The *stupa* was enlarged six times and the well-known figures of a standing Boddhisattva and the Buddha teaching were found nearby.

Dharmarajika Stupa The Dharmarajika Stupa was built by the Emperor Asoka to contain relics of the Buddha. It was enlarged on several occasions but was destroyed by Jagat Singh, Dewan of the Maharaja of Benares, in 1794, when a green marble casket containing human bones and pearls was found. The British Resident at the maharaja's court published an account of the discovery thereby drawing the attention of scholars to the site.

Main shrine The main shrine, marking the place of the Buddha's meditation, is attributed to Asoka and the later Guptas. To the rear is the 5-m lower portion of a polished sandstone **Asokan Column** (third century BC). The original was about 15 m high and was topped by the lion capital which is now in the Archaeological Museum (see above). The column was one of many erected by Asoka to promulgate the faith and this contained a message to the monks and nuns not to create any schisms and to spread the word. The monastery (fifth century onwards) in the southwest corner is one of four (the others are along the north edge of the enclosure). All are of brick, with cells off a central courtyard that are in ruins.

Jain temple The site is also holy to Jains because **Shyeyanshnath**, the 11th Tirthankar, was born near the Dhamekh *stupa*. The word 'Sarnath' may be derived from his name. A large temple and (on the opposite side of the road) a statue have been built to commemorate him.

Mulagandhakuti Vihara and around East of the Dhamekh Stupa, the modern **Mulagandhakuti temple** (1929-1931) ① *daily 0400-1130, 1330-2000*, contains frescoes by the Japanese artist Kosetsu Nosu depicting scenes from the Buddha's life. An urn in the ground is supposed to hold a Buddha relic obtained from Taxila (Pakistan). The wall around the **Bodhi tree** (*pipal, Ficus religiosa*) is thick with prayer flags. The tree, planted in 1931, is a sapling of the one in Sri Lanka that was grown from a cutting taken there circa 236 BC by Mahinda's sister Princess Sanghamitta. Past the Mulagandhakuti temple is the **deer park/zoo** ① *daily 0800-dusk, Rs 20*, where you can see birds, deer and crocodiles.

Other monasteries The colourful and peaceful **Burmese monastery** is worth the detour from the road. The **Chinese monastery** has a map showing Hiuen Tsang's route to India during AD 629-

644, as well as old photos on display. Tibetan, Japanese, Cambodian, Korean and Thai monasteries have also been built around the old complex. A 24-m-high **standing statue** of Lord Buddha, next to the Thai monastery, was completed in March 2011.

Chaukhandi Chaukhandi, south of the enclosure, has a fifth-century *stupa*. On top of this is an octagonal brick tower built by Akbar in 1588 to commemorate the visit his father Humayun made to the site. The inscription above the doorway reads, "As Humayun, king of the Seven Climes, now residing in paradise, deigned to come and sit here one day, thereby increasing the splendour of the sun, so Akbar, his son and humble servant, resolved to build on this spot a lofty tower reaching to the blue sky."

Listings Sarnath *map p147*

Tourist information

Modern Reception Centre
T0542-259 5965, Mon-Sat 1000-1700.
Provides a map and information.

Where to stay

As Varanasi is only 10 km away, most people visit Sarnath for the day. Should you wish to overnight there are several options. The Chinese monastery also has plenty of beds.

$$-$ Shivam Guest House
Opposite Chinese Temple, T0542-259 5450, shivamguesthouse.pandey38@gmail.com.
Smart new place, clean and tiled, TV, pay more for larger rooms with balconies. Good choice.

$ Aashirwad
On the road south of the Chinese temple, T0542-259 5475.
The best of the paying guesthouses along this road.

$ Modern Reception Centre
T(0)9580-574420, http://uptourism.gov.in.
Clean rooms with attached bath and TV, even those without a/c are cool. Nothing special, but furniture and fittings haven't had time to deteriorate yet. Restaurant.

$ Rahi Tourist Bungalow (UP Tourism)
T0542-259 5965-7, http://www.up-tourism.com/online1/index.asp.
Old but clean rooms, some with a/c, dorm (awful bathrooms), antique Indian restaurant.

Festivals

May On 1st full-moon, **Buddha Jayanti** marks the Buddha's birthday. A fair is held and relics which are not on public display at any other time are taken out in procession.

Transport

There is an infrequent bus service from the Roadways bus stand in **Varanasi**; Sarnath is also included in coach tours. Alternatively, autos from opposite the railway station charge Rs 150. A shared *tempo* is another option, although you might have to change to another *tempo* halfway. Taxis take 30 mins

Jaunpur *Colour map 3, B4.*
magnificent Islamic ruins in little-visited capital of the Sharqi kings

Jaunpur, 58 km from Varanasi, is a uniquely important centre of 14th- and 15th-century regional Islamic architecture. Though it was once the short-lived capital of the Sharqi Dynasty, today only the ruins of some magnificent mosques, the fort and the famous Akbari Bridge distinguish Jaunpur from dozens of other dusty and congested Uttar Pradesh cities. The buildings that remain remind us of its brief period as one of India's main centres of political, architectural and artistic development, and it is well worth a visit if you can spare the time. Allow three hours on foot for the main sights.

Jaunpur

Located at a strategic crossing point of the Gomti River, Jaunpur was established by Feroz Shah Tughluq in 1360 as part of his drive to the East. Earlier Hindu and Jain structures were destroyed to provide material for the mosques with which the Sharqi Dynasty rapidly embellished their capital. The Sharqi kings (named 'Kings of the East' by Feroz Shah) established effective independence from the Tughluqs who had been crushed in Timur's sack of Delhi in 1398. Under the great king Shams-ud-din-Ibrahim (1402-1436) Jaunpur became a centre of the arts and university education. It maintained its status until 1479, when Husain Shah, the last Sharqi king, was violently deposed by Ibrahim Lodi. Although all the secular buildings, including palaces and courts, were razed to the ground, Ibrahim Lodi spared at least some of the mosques. Some of the city's destruction visible today can be put down to much later events – floods in 1773 and 1871 and an earthquake in 1934.

Sights

Akbari Bridge According to Rushbrook Williams, the catastrophic earthquake in 1934 destroyed seven of the 15 arches in the great 200-m-long Akbari Bridge. The impressive bridge was designed by the Afghan architect Afzal Ali and built between 1564 and 1568. The stone lion above an elephant at the end of the bridge marks the point from which distances from the city were measured. The **bridge** emphasized Jaunpur's role as the centre of a pre-Mughal trading network. In the 17th century ships up to 18 tonnes could navigate the Gomti River for over 200 km upstream.

Shahi Fort ① *Rs 100*. The old Shahi Fort, just north of the Akbari Bridge, is an irregular grassy quadrangle enclosed by ruined stone walls. It shelters the oldest **mosque** in Jaunpur (1377), a narrow arcade (40 m by 7 m) supported by carved pillars, named after its builder, Ibrahim Naib Barbak, Feroz Shah Tughluq's brother. In the mid-19th century Fergusson described some distinctive yellow and blue enamelled bricks on the fine 15-m-high stone gateway and an inscribed monolith (1766) at the entrance, still visible today. Of particular interest is the almost perfect model of a **hammam** (Turkish bath) which you can wander around.

Atala Mosque Perhaps the most striking of the surviving mosques, the Atala, stands less than 400 m north of the fort. Built in 1408 on the site of the Hindu Atala Devi temple, it marks the triumphant beginning of Shams-ud-din-Ibrahim's reign and introduces unique features of Jaunpuri style. An arched gateway or 'pylon' fronts the sanctuary on the west side of the 50-m-sq court; the remaining three sides are spacious cloisters, two-storeyed and five aisles deep. The pylon has sloping sides, as in other Tughluq building, and its central arch is over 22 m high – along with the arch of the great Jami Masjid nearby, the highest in India. Other features borrowed from the Tughluq style are a recessed arch with its ornamented fringe, and tapering turrets on the west wall. Although artisans were brought in from Delhi, Jaunpur builders soon articulated their Tughluq traditions in a highly distinctive way. Note the beautiful sanctuary interior with its decorated nave and transepts, and the perforated stone screens. At the far end, the transepts are two-storeyed, with the upper section screened off for the zenana.

Jami Masjid The 'most ambitious' of Jaunpur's mosques, the Jami Masjid, is about 1 km north of the fort. Begun by Shah Ibrahim in 1438 it was completed by Husain Shah, the last Sharqi king, in 1470. The worshipper is forced to climb a steep flight of steps to enter the 60-m-sq courtyard, which is raised about 6 m on an artificial platform. Built on an even grander scale than the Atala Mosque, the 25-m-high central pylon dominates the sanctuary. Note the unsupported transept halls which create a remarkable covered open space. Despite the lack of pillars, they have survived earthquakes as well as normal ageing.

Where to stay

$ JP Centenarian
Olandganj, T05452-268056.
Cleanish rooms in central location, helpful staff,
cheap non-a/c singles and doubles, or some
with a/c.

Transport

Bus Frequent service along NH56 to/from
Varanasi and **Lucknow** including *Express* (under
2 hrs). Ask to be dropped at the Akbari Bridge
(crossroads north of the bus stand).

Train Several trains per day to **Varanasi** (1¾ hrs),
although the bus is just as quick and is easier.

Allahabad   *Colour map 3, B3.*
the greatest human gathering on earth at the confluence of three holy rivers

The narrow spit of land at the confluence of the Ganga and Yamuna rivers, normally
an almost-deserted river beach of fine sand, becomes home for two weeks once
every 12 years to the Kumbh Mela, when tens of millions of Hindu pilgrims converge
to bathe in the holy waters. Allahabad has grown around this spot and is today a
rapidly expanding commercial and administrative city with a permanent population
of nearly six million. It is particularly sacred for Hindus because it is at the confluence
of three rivers, the Ganga, Yamuna and the mythological underground Saraswati. The
Muslims first conquered the city in 1194 and renamed it Allahabad in 1584. For the
Muslims and, later, the British, it became a strategically vital centre. Both have left
their imprint on the landmarks of the city, making it an interesting place to explore,
particularly the Civil Lines area to the north.

Prayag (The confluence) Boats leave from
nearby ghats, the nearest being the one by
the fort, to reach the confluence of the Ganga
and Yamuna rivers. Bathing here is auspicious
at all times of the year, more so at **Magh Mela**,
which occurs annually for 15 days in January/
February, and especially at the **Kumbh Mela**
every 12th year, when pilgrims bathe at *prayag*
to wash away a lifetime's sins. There are still
rows of tents at the *prayag*, which give a good
indication of the sheer size of the Kumbh Mela,
when the area becomes a canvas city, home to
millions of people.

The basis for the festival is the Hindu legend
in which the gods and demons vied for the
kumbha (pot) that held the *amrit* (nectar
of immortality). During the 12-day fight for
possession, Vishnu spilt four drops of *amrit*,
which fell to earth making four sacred places:
Allahabad, Haridwar (Uttarakhand), Ujjain (MP)
and Nasik (Maharashtra). The festival takes
place at one of these sites every three years
in rotation, with an Ardh (half) Kumbh Mela
at Haridwar or Allahabad every sixth year;
the next Ardh Kumbh Mela in Allahabad is in
2019. Allahabad is the holiest of all the sites

Essential Allahabad

Finding your feet

Bamrauli airport is 12 km west of town. Many
of the city's hotels are in the Civil Lines area,
within easy reach of the Junction station
(rear exit) and the bus stands. The Civil Lines
(MG Marg) Bus Stand is used by buses arriving
from the north and west, while Zero Road Bus
Stand, halfway between the Junction and City
railway stations, serves local and southern
routes, including Khajuraho. Allahabad
Junction Station is the main stop for Delhi and
Kolkata trains. There are also direct trains from
Mumbai and key cities of South India.

Getting around

Although the centre is quite compact, you
need an auto-rickshaw to get to some of
the main sights, including the Fort and the
Sangam. Taxis and cycle-rickshaws are also
widely available. See Transport, page 155.

as the purifying power of a sacred river is strongest at a confluence. In addition, the mythical underground **Sarasvati River** is also said to surface here. Allahabad hosts the Maha (great) Kumbh Mela every 144 years; the last was in 2013 and was the largest peaceful human gathering ever recorded, attracting 80 million pilgrims.

Allahabad Fort The fort, begun in 1583, was the largest of Akbar's forts. It has three massive gateways and 7-m-high walls, seen to advantage from across the river. The Marathas held it from 1739 to 1750, then the Pathans, and finally the British from 1801. Most of the fort is closed to visitors, including the third-century BC Asoka pillar, moved there from Kaushambi under Akbar's orders. Under the fort's east wall is the **Undying Banyan Tree** (*Akshaivata*), an underground temple from which pilgrims threw themselves to achieve salvation in death. To see it, ask for a permit at the tourist office.

Khusrau Bagh This typical Mughal garden enclosure makes a peaceful retreat from the city and houses the handsome tomb of Prince Khusrau. After staging an unsuccessful rebellion against his father Jahangir in 1607, Khusrau spent the next year in chains. When freed, he encouraged a plot to assassinate his father but was discovered. Partially blinded and kept a captive, he was murdered in 1615 by his own brother, who became the Emperor Shah Jahan (ruled 1627-1658). Of the three impressive mausoleums, Khusrau's is the furthest east with decorative plasterwork, stone lattice windows and his burial chamber underground. The central tomb is thought to be his sister's and is beautifully painted inside. Furthest west is the tomb of his Rajput mother, whose cenotaph of

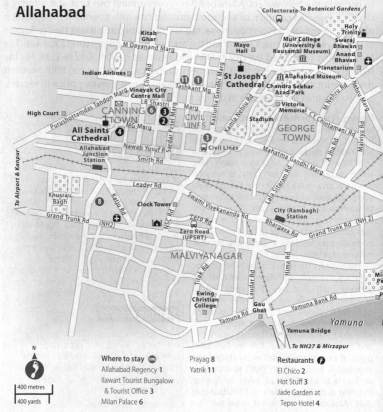

Allahabad

Where to stay
Allahabad Regency 1
Ilawart Tourist Bungalow
& Tourist Office 3
Milan Palace 6

Prayag 8
Yatrik 11

Restaurants
El Chico 2
Hot Stuff 3
Jade Garden at
Tepso Hotel 4

white marble is located at the top of the building; she committed suicide in 1603 by overdosing on opium. On arrival someone will appear with the keys to the mausoleums and expect a bit of baksheesh. The southern gate to the gardens remains impressively intact, the large wood door covered with horseshoes.

British Allahabad Allahabad became the headquarters of the British government of the Northwest Provinces and Oudh. The transfer of government from the East India Company to the crown was announced by Lord Canning here in 1858. Canning Town, opposite Junction Railway Station, was laid out on a grid in the 1860s. Within it are classical-style buildings from the late 19th century including the Old High Court and Public Offices, and the Gothic-style **All Saint's Cathedral**. At the east end of the Civil Lines is Alfred Park (now Chandra Sekhar Azad Park), north of which stands **Muir College**, a fine example of 'Indo-Saracenic' architecture. It was later established as the University of Allahabad. West of this is the extraordinary **Mayo Hall** with **St Joseph's Roman Catholic Cathedral** (1879) to its south. **Holy Trinity Church** (early 19th century) on J Nehru Marg contains memorials from the Gwalior Campaign (1843) and the 'Uprising' (1857).

Allahabad Museum ① Chandra Sekhar Azad Park, Kamla Nehru Rd, T0532-260 1200, Tue-Sun 1000-1700 (closed 2nd Sun of month), foreigners Rs 100. The museum has 18 galleries and contains a wide range of artefacts, including second-century BC pieces from Bharhut and Kaushambi (see below); first-century AD Kushana from Mathura; fourth- to sixth-century Gupta, and 11th-century carvings from Khajuraho. It also has a fine collection of Rajasthani miniatures, terracotta figurines, coins and paintings by Nicholas Roerich.

Anand Bhavan ① T0532-246 7071, Tue-Sun 1000-1700, Rs 50. The former Nehru family home contains many interesting items relating to: Motilal Nehru (1861-1931), active in the Independence Movement; Jawaharlal Nehru (1889-1964), independent India's first prime minister; Indira Gandhi (1917-1984; prime minister 1966-1977, 1980-1984); and her sons Sanjay Gandhi, who died in 1980, and Rajiv Gandhi (prime minister 1984-1989), who was assassinated in 1991. The **garden** is free to enter and pleasant to relax in. Next to it stands **Swaraj Bhawan** ① Tue-Sun 1000-1700, Rs 50, where Indira Gandhi was born; it is interesting to wander through.

Kaushambi Colour map 3, B3.
Kaushambi is 60 km southwest of Allahabad. According to the epics, Kausam was founded by a descendant of the Pandavas who left Hastinapur when it was destroyed by floods from the Ganga. It is one of the earliest historical cities of the region. According to Hiuen Tsang

ON THE ROAD

Ganga

The magnificent River Ganges is the spiritual heart of Hinduism and the blood that flows through its veins. Running from a high mountain glacier in Uttarakhand and flowing out at the Bay of Bengal, the river, worshipped as the goddess Ganga, attracts people from all over the world to pray and make purification *pujas*.

The story goes that when the goddess Ganga came to earth she fell upon the head of Lord Shiva, the first man of yoga, was caught in his hair and let out in small streams to spread across the earth. Lord Shiva sat and received her at Gangotri in Uttarakhand, which is considered to be the source of the Ganges and is now one of the most sacred places to dip in the holy waters.

Over time, the actual source has receded a further 18 km to the Gaumukh glacier; you can find *sadhus* (holy men) and pilgrims along the route to the glacier.

Other auspicious places to dip are at Rishikesh and Haridwar in Uttarkhand, and then further downstream at Allahabad and Varanasi. They are seen as *tirthas* – places where the veil between the physical and spiritual world is at its thinnest. People come to pray, to leave offerings of flowers and to bring the ashes of their dead. Haridwar and Allahabad (see pages 152 and 169) both play host to the Kumbh Mela, the largest spiritual gathering on earth. Spectacular Ganga Arti fire *pujas* are performed by Brahmin priests every evening in Rishikesh, Haridwar and Varanasi.

The Ganges river basin – the most heavily populated in the world – is inhabited by 37% of India's mighty 1.2 billion population and this has evidently impacted on the river itself. This is a place where people bathe, perform *pujas*, do their laundry and bring the ashes of the dead. On top of that are the contamination of municipal and industrial waste and the impact of dams. Indeed, the pollution is shocking, with coliform bacteria levels reaching 5500, a level too high to be safe for agricultural use, let alone drinking and bathing. While the Ganga as a celestial being enjoys immortality, the river itself is struggling. An action plan is in place targeting industry, but progress is slow.

the Buddha preached here and two *viharas* (monasteries) were built to commemorate the event. The enormous ruins are spread through several villages.

The ramparts of a fort form an approximate rectangle over 6 km in perimeter with bastions that tower up to nearly 23 m. Originally made of mud they were later surfaced with bricks. The town was occupied continuously from the eighth century BC to sixth century AD. In the southwest corner are possibly the remains of a palace. The main *stupa* (fifth century BC) measured 25 m in diameter and 25 m in height. There is also the damaged and defaced shaft of a sandstone column, probably erected during the rule of the Mauryan Emperor Asoka. Many of the coins and terracottas discovered here are now on display in the Allahabad City Museum (see above) and in the Ancient History Department Museum at the University of Allahabad, T0532-246 1694.

Listings Allahabad and around *map p152*

Tourist information

Ilawart Tourist Bungalow
35 MG Marg, T0532-2440 8873. Mon-Sat 1000-1700 (closed 2nd Sat in month); also at the railway station, daily 0800-1800.
Competent staff can provide city maps and numerous leaflets. Car hire can be arranged here (government-fixed prices).

Where to stay

$$$ Allahabad Regency
16 Tashkent Marg, Civil Lines, T0532-240 7835, www.hotelallahabadregency.com.
A red-and-white heritage bungalow with arched portico dating from 1866, modernized rooms capture a period atmosphere with cream walls and dark furniture, probably worth paying bit extra for the pleasing duplexes, excellent shower rooms. Delightful manicured gardens, wood-

panelled reception hall, salubrious bar, small pool and gym.

$$$ Milan Palace
4/2 Strachy Rd, Civil Lines, T0532-242 1505, www.hotelmilanpalace.com.
Modern, lively hotel in good central location, 40 spotless rooms but bathrooms in need of renovation, contemporary-styled restaurant and bar, professional staff, charge for Wi-Fi.

$$ Yatrik
33 Sardar Patel Marg, Civil Lines, T0532-226 0921-6, www.hotelyatrik.com.
The stark modernist façade hides a lovely back garden with sizable pool (closed in winter), 38 a/c rooms are smart and homely, if not fashionably decorated; deluxe ones are fresher and larger than standard doubles, but all have good shower rooms. Public areas are pleasant with airy terraces, good service, restaurant but no bar. Well-priced for what you get.

$$-$ Ilawart Tourist Bungalow (UP Tourism)
35 MG Marg, T0532-240 7440, rahiilawart@ up-tourism.com.
Rooms are clean and of a good size, a/c with bath and hot water, but standard ones are costly for shabby furnishings and dirty corridors. 8-bed dorm. Restaurant, bar, pleasant garden but can be noisy, helpful staff. Next to main bus station.

$ Hotel Prayag
73 Noorullah Rd, T0532-265 6416, www.prayaggroupofhotels.com.
Vast range of rooms, from bargain-basic with shared bath (clean sheets on request) to super-deluxe (**$$**). Most have TV, many have a/c, or pay a bit extra for air-cooler. Very handy if travelling by train, efficient staff who are used to foreigners, 24-hr checkout. A reliable choice.

Restaurants

$$ El Chico
24 MG Marg.
Good quality Indian and Chinese food, with bakery next door, over 40 years of service.

$$ Jade Garden
Tepso Hotel, MG Marg, T0532-256 1408.
For upmarket Chinese and Indian, recommended.

$ Hot Stuff
21C LB Shastri Mg.
Smart. Serves fast food, also good ices.

Entertainment

Prayag Sangeet Samiti, *near Hanuman temple, Civil Lines*. Music and dance programmes in the evenings.

Festivals

Jan/Feb Annual Marg Mela; next Ardh (half) Kumbh Mela in 2019. Also **International Yoga Week**.

Transport

Air Bamrauli Airport is 12 km from the city with daily **Air India** flights to **Delhi** and 4 per week to **Mumbai**.

Bus UP Roadways buses leave from the bus station in Civil Lines and link Allahabad with **Delhi** at 1230 (643 km), **Jaunpur, Jhansi, Kanpur, Lucknow** every 45 mins 0630-2100 (4½ hrs), and **Varanasi** every 15 mins from 0600-2000 (3½ hrs). Zero Rd bus stand has buses to **Rewa**. There are also private bus stands at Ram Bagh and Civil Lines for frequent luxury coaches to **Lucknow** and **Varanasi**.

Train Allahabad is on the major broad-gauge route from Delhi to Kolkata. **Allahabad Junction** is the main station, T0532-260 0179; **Allahabad City** is mostly for Varanasi. **Jhansi**: At least 2 per day, 9-12 hrs. **Lucknow**: about 5 per day, 4-7 hrs. **Kolkata**: several per day, best is *Rajdhani Exp 12302/12306*, 2345, 10¼/13 hrs. **Mumbai (CST)**: at least 8 per day, around 24 hrs. **New Delhi**: frequent trains, including *Rajdhani Exp*, 9 hrs. **Patna**: around 10 per day, taking 6-9 hrs. **Varanasi**: many options 2½-3½ hrs, but bus is easier.

Uttarakhand

With Himachal Pradesh to the west, Tibet to the north and Nepal to the east, it's small wonder that the Himalayan hill state of Uttarakhand holds some of India's most magnificent mountain scenery.

Garhwal and Kumaon's thickly wooded hillsides break softly towards a stunning range of snow-capped Himalayan peaks, including India's second highest mountain Nanda Devi, forming one of the world's most awesome natural borders.

Many of Uttarakhand's most stunning treks are in fact age-old pilgrimage routes (or 'yatra' routes). As the source of the Ganga and Yamuna rivers, the state looms large in India's mythological history – it is the setting for much of the *Mahabharata* – and contains some of India's holiest shrines.

On the banks of the Ganga, the holy cities of Haridwar and Rishikesh have served as spiritual magnets for millennia, and receive a continuous stream of pilgrims from all over India, and foreign visitors who come to study yoga or the vedas.

Further east, Almora and Nainital have long served as charming, cool holiday resorts in the hills, while the great tiger reserve of Corbett National Park stands as a beacon of successful wildlife management. With India's whitewater rafting capital just north of Rishikesh at Shivpuri, and the development of skiing facilities at Auli, Uttarakhand is now establishing a reputation for adventure sports, too.

Best for
Adventure ▪ Pilgrimage ▪ Trekking

Footprint
picks

★ **Haridwar**, page 167

Experience the sunset fire puja at one of Hinduism's seven holy cities.

★ **Rishikesh**, page 171

Perfect your downward dog in the temple town of Rishikesh.

★ **Char Dham**, page 176

Visit the atmospheric temples of the Char Dham: Kedarnath, Yamunotri, Gangotri and Badrinath.

★ **Valley of Flowers**, page 184

Go trekking in beautiful, varied landscape, with panoramic views and alpine flowers.

★ **Corbett National Park**, page 196

Try and spot a tiger in one of India's best wildlife parks.

Essential Uttarakhand

Finding your feet

Uttarakhand (population 8.5 million) is a land of hills and mountains that rise from the banks of the Ganga. The outer ranges of the Shiwaliks, generally less than 2500 m high, are a jumble of deeply dissected sediments. In places these are separated from the Lesser Himalayan ranges by great longitudinal valleys, or duns, such as Dehra Dun. The Lesser Himalayan towns immediately to the north of the Shiwaliks, such as Mussoorie, Almora and Nainital, offer coolness from the overpowering summer heat of the plains. Forming a massive barrier to their north are the permanent snows of Nanda Devi (7816 m), Shivling (6543 m) and other peaks over 6000 m.

Best epic views

A room at The Amber, page 163
Surkhanda Devi Temple, page 163
Ziplining in Mussoorie, page 165
Rest House at Chianhuala, page 170

Getting around

Trains reach the foot of the Himalaya; use buses, share jeeps or car hire on mountain routes to travel around Uttarakhand.

When to go

The climate of Uttarakhand is dominated by the monsoon, with over three quarters of the rainfall coming between June and September, but temperature is controlled both by height and by season. It's warm to steamy in the lowlands, cool and fresh to snowy in the mountains. In the lower valleys, such as Dehra Dun, summers are hot and sticky. Towns on the ridges up to 2000 m, such as Almora and Ranikhet, are hot in summer, while in winter they experience snow, and temperatures even in the outer valleys fall to a few degrees above freezing. June and September are uncomfortably humid in the foothills, despite lower temperatures. The high peaks are under permanent snow and in the higher hills the air can be very cold.

Late April to early June and September to October tend to be the best times for trekking. During the rambunctious Siva festival in August the towns by the Ganges become crowded beyond belief.

Weather Dehra Dun

Month	Temp (high)	Temp (low)	Rainfall
January	19°C	16°C	55mm
February	22°C	8°C	59mm
March	26°C	12°C	49mm
April	32°C	17°C	23mm
May	36°C	21°C	42mm
June	35°C	23°C	202mm
July	31°C	23°C	673mm
August	29°C	22°C	728mm
September	30°C	21°C	297mm
October	29°C	16°C	50mm
November	25°C	10°C	9mm
December	21°C	7°C	24mm

Time required

One to two weeks for the eastern hill stations and a retreat around Rishikesh; 12 days for a Char Dham pilgrimage; three to four days for Corbett National Park and a week for the Kumaon hill stations.

Best for yoga and meditation
Parmath Niketan ashram, page 171
Ananda-in-the-Himalayas, page 172
Sanskriti Vedic Retreat, page 173

Eastern
hill stations

The quickest cool escape from Delhi's sweltering summer, the old Raj hill stations of Mussoorie and Landour still make a popular getaway, with their crumbling bungalows, pine-scented pathways and grand Himalayan panoramas. The state capital, Dehra Dun, sprawls across the valley below and is home to some of India's most important educational, research and military facilities.

Dehra Dun *Colour map 1, B4.*

doorway to Shiva's mountains

Dehra Dun (population 578,000, altitude 640 m) lies in a wooded valley in the Shiwalik Hills and makes a pleasant and relaxing stop on the way to the hills. Its mild climate has made it a popular retirement town. The cantonment, across the seasonal Bindal Rao River, is spacious and well wooded, while the Mussoorie road is lined with very attractive houses.

Essential Dehra Dun

Finding your feet

The railway station, off Haridwar Road to the south of town, has trains from Delhi, Varanasi, Rajasthan and Kolkata. Buses and shared taxis heading for the Mussoorie and the Garhwal hills use the Mussoorie Bus Stand, just outside the station, while those bound for the plains and the Kumaon hills use the new inter-state bus terminal (ISBT, often referred to as the 'New' Delhi Bus Stand) 5 km southwest of the centre. Shared *tempos* and rickshaws (Rs 50-60) can take you into town.

Getting around

The City Bus Stand, also used by private buses, is just north of the clock tower in the busy town centre, about 10 minutes on foot from the railway station. Although the town centre is compact it is best to get a taxi or auto-rickshaw for visiting the various sights, which are between 4 km and 8 km away. See Transport, page 162.

Its name comes from *dera* – camp and *dun* – valley, pronounced 'doon'. In Hindu legend the Dun Valley was part of Siva's stamping ground. Rama and his brother are said to have done penance for killing Ravana, and the five Pandavas stopped here on their way to the mountains.

There is not much to recommend the town other than a place to stay if you are caught late at night on your way to a hill station. It is busy, with some international chain stores and coffee shops recently opened on the Rajpur road up to Mussoorie. If you happen to be caught in traffic on your way through, keep your eyes open for the unique miniature suits of armour displayed in the iron shops along the main roads.

Sights

The **Survey of India** (founded 1767), has its headquarters on Rajpur Road, 4 km north of the clock tower. **Robber's Cave** (8 km), **Lakshman Sidh** (12 km), the snows at **Chakrata** (9 km) and sulphur springs at **Shahasradhara** (14 km) are also within easy reach. The springs were threatened by limestone quarrying until the High Court forced the closure of the quarries. Replanting of the deforested hills has been allowing the water table to recover.

BACKGROUND

Dehra Dun

A third-century BC Asoka rock inscription found near Kalsi suggests that this area was ruled by the emperor. During the 17th and 18th centuries Dehra Dun changed hands several times. The Gurkhas overran it on their westward expansion from Kumaon to Kangra, finally ceding it in 1815 to the British, who developed it as a centre of education and research. It is still a major centre for government institutions like the Survey of India and the Royal Indian Military College, and in November 2000 it became the provisional state capital of Uttaranchal (renamed in 2007 as Uttarakhand), but there is still no sign of agreement of an alternative state capital.

In the west of town, off Kaulagarh Road, the **Doon School**, India's first public school, is still one of its most prestigious. Further along, the highly regarded **Forest Research Institute** (1914), an impressive red-brick building which was designed by Lutyens, is surrounded by the fine lawns of the **Botanical Gardens** and forests. It has excellent **museums** ① *Mon-Fri 0900-1730*. The **Tapkesvar Cave Temple** ① *5 km northwest of town, open sunrise to sunset*, is in a pleasant setting with cool sulphur springs for bathing. There is a simple Indian café nearby. Buses stop 500 m from the temple.

Six kilometres south of town, close to the ISBT, the Tibetan enclave of Clement Town is home to **Mintokling Monastery**, with a striking new 60-m-high *stupa*. The nearby **Dhe Chen Chokhor Kagyupa Monastery** has a similarly tall statue of the Buddha.

Listings Dehra Dun

Tourist information

GMVN
74/1 Rajpur Rd, T0135-274 8478.

Uttarakhand Tourism
45 Gandhi Rd, next to Drona Hotel,
T0135-265 3217. Mon-Sat 1000-1700.

Where to stay

There are good discounts out of season (Aug-Feb). The cheaper hotels are near the station and the clock tower; the upmarket ones are north, along **Rajpur Rd**. A good option is the Tibetan Colony.

$$$$ Vishranti
Lower Kandoli Village, Doon Valley, T0135-3987750, www.vishrantiresorts.com.
A beautiful resort and spa and a good getaway, although it's popular with weddings; Indian cricket legend MS Dhoni got married here.

$$$$-$$$ Shaheen Bagh
Upper Dehradun, T0135-210 8199, T(0)9897-046353, www.shaheenbagh.in.
Price includes breakfast and dinner. Beautiful guesthouse on a 3-ha property by the river, with lovely interior spaces in grand country-house style, large canopied beds, pretty

gardens (370 bird species recorded) with mountain views in the Ton River valley, fruit trees and pool. Distant from town; a refuge. The service has gone downhill in recent years but it's still recommended.

$$$-$$ Saffron Leaf
GMS Rd, T0135-252 1400, www.saffronleaf.com.
New popular hotel in a good location with smart rooms and decent restaurant.

$$-$ Deepshikha
57/1 Rajpur Rd, T()99999-89548.
22 basic rooms (some a/c) that overlook a busy road. There's a good restaurant.

$ Private guesthouses
Clement Town (Tibetan Colony), 6 km south of centre near ISBT.
Spacious, clean rooms (Rs 250). Quiet and peaceful atmosphere close to the world's largest Tibetan stupa; there's no phone for bookings, so it's best to show up and ask at the monasteries.

Restaurants

$$ Kabila
447 Rajpur Rd, T(0)135-65999.
Come up the stairs and find a Rajasthani village – excellent, but pricey Rajasthani *thali*.

$$ Orchard
3-D, Dak Patti, near MDDA Park, Rajpur Rd.
Great location with good valley views. They
serve Chinese, Tibetan and Thai food here.
Great chicken *momos*.

$ Sheetal Restaurant
West of town on canal bank.
Attractive setting.

Bakeries
Ellora and **Grand**, *both on Rajpur Rd, Paltan Bazar*.
Fresh bread, biscuits and sticky toffees.

What to do

Tour operators
GMVN, *Old Survey Chowk, 74/1 Rajpur Rd, T0135-274 8478, www.gmvnl.com*. They run daily city
tours and trips to Mussoorie and Kempty Falls,
and further afield to Haridwar and Rishikesh.
President Travel, *T0135-265 5111,
prestrav@sancharnet.in*. Ticketing
and general travel arrangements.

Yoga
Yog Ganga Centre, *101 Old Rajpur, near
Shahenshah Ashram, Dehra Dun, T0135-273 3653,
www.yog-ganga.com*. Highly regarded Iyengar
yoga school established by a couple who have
advised the Indian government on the yogic
syllabus for India's education system.

Transport

Air Jolly Grant air strip (24 km), enquiry
T0135-241 2412; limited flights to/from **Delhi**
with **Jet Airways**.

Bus Local buses leave from Rajpur Rd, near
clock tower. Long-distance buses leave from
Dehradun Bus Stand (ISBT), Clement Town,
T0135-213 1309, for most hill destinations and
the plains, including **Chandigarh** (5 hrs), **Delhi**
(7-8 hrs), **Dharamshala** (14 hrs), **Haridwar**
(1 hr) **Kullu/Manali** (14 hrs), **Nainital** (12 hrs);
Ramnagar for **Corbett** (7 hrs), **Rishikesh** (1 hr;
board inside terminal as buses fill to bursting at
the main gate), **Shimla** (8-9 hrs). **Mussoorie Bus
Stand**, outside the railway station, T0135-263
2258. Half hourly to **Mussoorie**, 0600-2000,
tickets from counter No 1. Private buses from **City
Bus Stand**, Parade Ground. Regular services to
Mussoorie (1 hr), with **Drona Travels** (GMVN),
45 Gandhi Rd, T0135-265 3309.

Taxi/rickshaw Auto-rickshaw Rs 50 from
station to centre. Cheaper but crowded *vikrams*
easily available.

Train Railway Station, T(0)97192 73933.
Reservations opposite, 0800-2000, Sun 0800-
1400; book early for Haridwar. **New Delhi**:
Shatabdi Exp 12018, 6 hrs. *Jan Shatabdi 12056*
(early morning) 6 hrs. **Kolkata**: *Doon Exp 13010*,
34 hrs (via **Varanasi**, 19 hrs).

Mussoorie and Landour *Colour map 1, B4.*

old world charm at high altitude

Mussoorie (population 30,000, altitude 1970 m), named after the Himalayan shrub
mansoor, has commanding views over the Doon Valley to the south and towards the
High Himalaya to the north. It is spread out over 16 km along a horseshoe-shaped
ridge up to which run a series of buttress-like subsidiaries. Being the nearest hill
station to Delhi, it is very popular with Indian tourists though no longer as clean as it
was once, and it has nothing over other hill stations. Landour, 300 m higher and away
from the crowds, by contrast has fresh, pine-scented air.

Sights
Captain Young 'discovered' Mussoorie in 1826 and it developed as an escape from the heat of the
plains for the British troops. To the east, **Landour**, at 2270 m, has the old barracks area. The first
British residence was built here, followed by The Mall, Club, Christ Church (1837) and the library.
It's a very pleasant walk up through the woods and away from the crowds of The Mall. There
are good views, though the weather can change quickly. 'Char Dukan' is a small junction in the
cantonment area with two snack bars/shops and a post office; the road to the right leads to the
International Language School and the one to the left to **Lal Tibba** – a worthwhile viewpoint (take
binoculars). The Woodstock School and the Language School are in a magnificent location, and
some of the guesthouses have stunning views. To the west are **Convent Hill**, **Happy Valley** (where

Tibetan refugees have settled; the school may welcome volunteers to teach English), and the pleasant **Municipal Garden**.

Walks

From the tourist office, it is 5 km to **Lal Tibba** and nearby **Childe's Lodge** on the highest hill. **Gun Hill**, where before Independence a midday gun fire enabled residents to set their watches, has a stunning view of snow-capped peaks, best at sunrise. It can be reached in around half an hour on foot or horseback by a bridle path leaving from the Kutchery on The Mall, or by a 400-m **ropeway** ① 0900-1900, Rs 75 return. However, the mess of souvenir stalls, cafés and photographers later in the day may not appeal to all. The **Camel's Back Road**, from Kulri to the library, is a pleasant 3-km walk.

Trips from Mussoorie

Kempty Falls, 15 km away on the Chakrata Road, is a rather dispiriting 'beauty spot', with fabulous ribbon-like falls spoiled by mounds of rubbish and a pair of resorts gaudily advertising soft drink brands. A taxi is about Rs 300 with a one-hour stop. Heading to **Dhanolti**, 25 km away, you can go on a further 3 km to find the **Surkhanda Devi Temple** at 3030 m. There are superb views of several high peaks over 6500 m. A taxi is Rs 800 with a two-to-three-hour stop. Buses between Mussoorie and Chamba take you within 2 km of the hill top.

Essential Mussoorie

Finding your feet

Other than a 7-km trek, the 30-km road from Dehra Dun (just under 1¾ hours by bus) is the only way to the town. Buses arrive at the library (west end of the long Mall) or the Masonic Lodge Bus Stand (east end). Buses from Delhi take six to seven hours.

Getting around

Taxis are available for longer journeys, including the steep climb to Landour. For local trips cycle rickshaws are available or you can hire a bike. See Transport, page 165.

Listings Mussoorie and Landour *map p164*

Tourist information

GMVN
Library Bus Stand, Mussoorie, T0135-263 1281.

Uttarakhand Tourism
The Mall, Mussoorie, T(0)93123 18417.

Where to stay

Lots of atmospheric heritage properties. The Mall is closed to cars and buses. You may have to walk to your hotel; porters are available at the bus stands.

$$$$ The Amber
Near Company Bagh, Hathi Paon Rd, T0135-2630202, www.theamber.in.
Epic views from this resort. A beautiful deck overhangs the valley and all rooms and the restaurant share the view of the rolling hills.

$$$$-$$$ Nabha Residence (Claridges)
Airfield, Barlow Ganj Rd, 2 km from town centre, T0135-263 1426, www.claridges.com.
22 rooms with veranda arranged around attractive garden in converted hill palace, superb

views, Raj-style but with all mod cons. Very good family rooms with lofts. Includes half-board. Delightful old-world charm.

$$$ Kasmanda Palace Hotel
Near The Mall, T0135-263 2424, www.kasmandapalace.com.
14 comfortable rooms, once Basset Hall of the Christ Church complex (built 1836), a British sanatorium, then royal guesthouse from 1915, interesting furnishings (hunting trophies, amazing photo history on walls), peaceful, spacious grounds. Steep climb from Mall Rd so call for jeep transfer. Highly recommended.

$$$-$$ Cloud End Forest Resort
7 km from town, in the forest, T(0)96340-96861, www.cloudend.com.
Rustic, fabulous views, 7 rooms with bath in colonial-period lodge, there are some tents on-site too. Home-cooked meals.

$$$-$$ Padmini Nivas
Library, The Mall, T0135-263 1093.
27 rooms in former palace with character, some with good views, also ($$$) cottages, not grand but pleasant ambience, good restaurant (pure

vegetarian Gujarati). Car parking and access before the gated mall area. Highly recommended.

$$ Broadway
3 km from main mall, Camels Back Rd, next to rink, T0135-263 2243, www. hotelbroadwaymussoorie.com.
Renovated 19th-century hotel, 10 rooms with bath, best with views and geyser, some with bucket hot water, Indian meals, cheap and atmospheric.

$$-$ Valley View
The Mall (Kulri) near Ropeway, T0135-263 2324.
Friendly, with 14 clean rooms (some with kitchenette). Great open-air terrace and all the rooms have a shared balcony, restaurant, bakery, garden, good service.

$ Hotel Dev Dar Woods
Fair View, Sisters Bazar, Landour Cant, T0135-263 2544.
A great trekkers' hotel, clean rooms in a period house, budget hotel in woods, secluded but next to a well-stocked shop with local honey, jam and cheese. Surprisingly good pizza is the only thing on the menu.

Restaurants

$$$ Emily's
Landour (Rokeby Manor).
Excellent breakfast buffet and good range of kebabs and international tastes like houmus and pitta.

$$ Hotel Dev Dar Woods
See Where to stay, above.
A lovely stop for a fantastic pizza, which is the only thing on the menu but worth it for the mountain views and pine-scented air.

$$ Tavern
Kulri.
Respectable Thai and roasts, live music and dancing some nights.

$$ Whispering Windows
Library Bazar, Gandhi Chowk.
International food served. Also has a popular bar.

Mussoorie

To Kempty Falls (13 km)

Where to stay		Nabha Residence 6		Restaurants	
The Amber 2		Padmini Nivas 4		Emily's 8	
Broadway 10		Valley View 14		Kalsang-Tibetan 1	
Dev Dar Woods 8				Tavern 2	
Kasmanda Palace 3				Whispering Windows 3	

$ Kalsang-Tibetan Restaurant
Near bank on main mall.
Tasty Tibetan food, lively ambience.
Recommended.

Shopping

The main areas are Library, Kulri and Landour
Bazars and Shawfield Rd near Padmini Niwas.
Several shops on The Mall sell handcrafted
walking sticks. For woollen goods try **Garhwal
Wool House**, near GPO; **Natraj**, Picture Palace;
or the **Tibetan market**, near Padmini Nivas.
Banaras House on The Mall sells silks. **Baru
Mal Janki Dass** has tribal silver jewellery.

What to do

Fishing
Fishing is popular in the Aglar and Yamuna rivers
for mahseer and hill trout. A permit is required;
available from Division Forest Officer, Yamuna
Division.

Horse riding
A 1-hr ride (7 km) around Camels Back Rd, Rs 250.
Off-season, Rs 100. Lots of opportunities along
Camels Back Rd.

Language classes
Landour Language School, *41/2 Landour Cantt,
Mussoorie, T0135-263 1487, www.landourlanguage
school.com.* One of the best schools in India,
including Urdu, Garhwali and Sanskrit as well as
Hindi. Courses for all levels and timescales – look
at website for range of courses and fees.

Paragliding and ziplining
Zip Lines India, *T(0)94129 73448, www.zip
linesindia.com.* Enjoy a bird's eye view with
paragliding and ziplining with professional outfit.

Tours and tour operators
GMVN, *see under Tourist information, above.*
Tours to Kempty Falls, Dhanolti, the beautiful
Surkhanda Devi Temple and Mussoorie Lake.

Transport

Bus Long-distance stands: **Library** (Gandhi
Chowk), T0135-263 2258; **Picture Palace** (Kulri),
T0135-263 2259. Frequent service to **Chamba**,
scenic trip via **Dhanolti**, 3 hrs; **Dehra Dun**
through Ghat roads, 1 hr. Private buses **to Delhi**,
are Rs 200-250 depending on a/c facility. Also
buses from **Saharanpur Railway** and **Tehri**.

Taxi/rickshaw Cycle rickshaws for The Mall,
fixed-fare chart from tourist office. Taxi stand
at Library, T0135-263 2115; stand at Masonic
Lodge, T0135-2613 1407.

Haridwar,
Rishikesh & around

The sacred cities of Haridwar and Rishikesh abound in Hindu religious history and seethe with modern-day pilgrims. Yet, although only a few kilometres apart, they share little in tempo or atmosphere. One of the oldest cities in the world, dilapidated, heady Haridwar, fabled for holding Vishnu's footprint and the site of numerous scenes from the *Mahabharata*, is one of Hinduism's seven holiest cities and correspondingly overrun with Indian pilgrims.

Meanwhile, ashram and swami-filled Rishikesh, upriver, is much more geared towards Western spiritual seekers: a place one writer summed up as a hybrid of Blackpool and Lourdes. Along with an array of sound hatha yoga and vedanta classes come all the accoutrements of international budget travel: internet cafés and shops selling self-help books, clothes and mantra CDs. Further upstream, the sacred Ganga has a new following, hungry for adventure not enlightenment: they are drawn to Shivpuri in its role as India's unofficial whitewater rafting capital.

The Char Dham pilgrimage route begins at Rishikesh, and the town makes a good base from which to arrange treks in the Garhwal Himalaya or elephant-spotting trips into the nearby Rajaji National Park.

★ Haridwar *Colour map 1, C4.*
connecting to the Goddess Ganga

Haridwar (population 175,000) lies at the base of the Shiwalik Hills where the River Ganga begins a 2000-km journey across the plains. In setting foot on the western bank here (Hari-Ki-Pairi), Vishnu made it one of Hinduism's seven holy cities (see Hindu Holy places, page 1326), a place where pilgrims bathe to cleanse themselves of sins, where *swamies* sermonize, Brahmin priests preside over spectacular sunset ceremonies, *sadhus* sit at makeshift shelters under trees and beggars huddle and urchins dart between the crowds.

Essential Haridwar

Finding your feet

The nearest airport is at Jolly Grant, 30 km away on the Dehra Dun road. Haridwar is connected by rail to all major cities. It is 214 km from Delhi by road on NH 45, but the train is much faster.

Getting around

Locally there are private buses, *tempos*, autos, *tongas*, cycle rickshaws and taxis. Haridwar is also the stepping off point for Rishikesh. See Transport, page 169.

Fact...
Hari-ki-Pairi, where Vishnu trod, is now where some of the Ganga is drawn off as irrigation water for the Upper Ganga Canal system and for a hydroelectric power station.

Haridwar

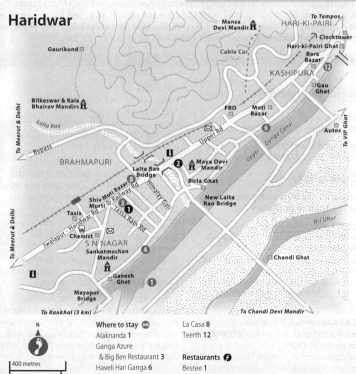

N
400 metres
400 yards

Where to stay 🛏
Alaknanda **1**
Ganga Azure
  & Big Ben Restaurant **3**
Haveli Hari Ganga **6**
Inder Kutir **4**

La Casa **8**
Teerth **12**

Restaurants 🍽
Bestee **1**
Chotiwalas **2**

Sights

Near the steps at Hari-ki-Pairi is a modern clock tower and some temples, none particularly old. Further down, foodstalls and shrines line alleyways leading off into the bazar. There are six bridges to take you across the river, where it is quieter. A new footbridge leads directly to Hari-ki-Pairi. Foreign visitors are likely to be approached for donations for its construction and upkeep. There are many *ashrams* here, including Shatikunj, Ananda Mayee Ma, said by some to have the most authentic Ganga arti, and Premnagar. Many have herb gardens producing Ayurvedic medicines.

Moti (Lower) Bazar, parallel to the Jawalapur–Haridwar road, is interesting, colourful, invariably crowded and surprisingly clean and tidy. Stalls sell coloured powder piled high in carefully made cones (for *tikas*). Others sell saris, jewellery, brass and aluminium pots, sweets and snacks. **Mansa Devi Temple** is worth visiting for the view. Set on the southernmost hill of the Shiwaliks, it is accessible on foot or by the crowded cable car (0630-2030, Rs 80 return; or take the package ticket to include Chanda Devi temple, 4 km away on the other side of the Ganga). Towards Rishikesh, 5 km from Haridwar, are the newer temples: **Pawan Dham** with a Hanuman temple, its spectacular glittering glass interior and the seven-storey **Bharat Mata Mandir** to Mother India.

Kankhal, 3 km downstream, with the **Temple of Dakseshwara**, is where legend holds that Siva's wife, Sati, burned herself to death, irked at her father Daksa's failure to invite her husband Siva to a grand sacrifice. Siva temporarily destroyed the sacrifice, and gave Daksa (himself a son of Brahma) the head of a goat. Professor Wendy Doniger says that when Siva learned that of Sati's suicide, "he took up her body and danced in grief, troubling the world with his dance and his tears until the gods cut the corpse into pieces. When the *yoni* fell, Siva took the form of a *linga*, and peace was re-established in the universe".

> ### Fact...
> Seventh-century Chinese traveller Hiuen Tsang mentioned the city in his writing, and Timur (Tamburlaine) sacked it in AD 1399, see page 1303.

Listings Haridwar map p167

Tourist information

UP Tourism
Lalta Rao Bridge, T0133-422 8686.

Uttarakhand tourist office
Motel Rahi, T0133-422 6430. Mon-Sat 1000-1700.

Where to stay

Many places offer off-season discounts outside Jun and Jul, and up to 50% Nov-Feb.

$$$$-$$$ Haveli Hari Ganga
Pilibhit House, 21 Ramghat, T01334-226443, www.havelihariganga.com.
Attractively restored *haveli* with exclusive bathing ghat on the Ganga, rooms decorated along mythological themes, old-world charm and modern luxury, Ayurvedic treatments and yoga. Recommended.

$$$-$$ Alaknanda (UP Tourism)
Belwala (east bank), By-pass Rd, T01334-226379, www.up-tourism.com.
Good option from UP Tourism. 32 rooms, best a/c with bath, restaurant (simple vegetarian), small garden, on riverbank, quiet.

$$ La Casa
Bilkeshwar Rd, close to Hari-ki-Pairi Rd, T01334-221197.
Great value rooms at this stylish hotel where they have put some imagination into the decor with jewelled colour walls and stenciling.

$$ Teerth
Subhash Ghat, Hari-ki-Pairi, T01334-225 221.
Excellent central location, great views over ghats, 32 reasonable rooms, some air-cooled, but not the value it once was.

$$-$ Ganga Azure
Railway Rd, T01334-227101, www.hotelgangaazure.com.
32 adequate rooms, TV, hot water, some a/c, decent restaurant. They have also opened the **Ganga Heritage** which has lovely decor.

$ Inder Kutir
Niranjani Akhara Rd, SN Nagar, T01334-226336.
A good new budget option, with bright and airy rooms opening on to a terrace. One room has a balcony from which you can peep through to the river. It's in a family home and friendly.

ON THE ROAD

Guru TV

In today's India, where even renounced *Swamis* communicate with their devotees via smartphones, some of the more pro-active yogis have adopted television as a means to spread their message. Far and away the most successful has been a young guru named Baba Ramdev, whose yoga camps, aired live on several national TV channels every day, attract the devoted and the curious in their thousands.

Guru TV offers an illuminating contrast to morning TV elsewhere in the world. The photogenic Ramdev sits in *padmasana* (cross-legged pose) on a stage, microphones rigged up before him, and with vivid demonstrations expounds upon the virtues of stomach rolling exercises that strengthen the digestive system and *anuloma viloma pranayama*, a breathing technique in which one breathes through each nostril in turn, focusing the mind.

Baba Ramdev's fame has, inevitably, earned him the scorn of some *swamis*, not to mention unwanted media attention, particularly after his ill-advised acceptance of an offer from the Madhya Pradesh government to build a college campus on tribal land. Yet despite making some high-profile enemies, including the makers of certain carbonated soft drinks whose products he publicly compares to toilet cleaning fluid, Ramdev has had a significant impact on the popularity of yoga, particularly among housewives and young children – the core viewers of morning TV. His new 'five-star' ashram and Yogic hospital, Patanjali Yogpeeth, on the Haridwar–Delhi highway (www.divyayoga.com), is one of the most visited in India.

Alternatively you can catch him on tour, live at a stadium near you.

Restaurants

Only vegetarian food is available in town and there is no alcohol.

$$ Big Ben
Ganga Azure (see Where to stay, above).
Decent, large range of Indian, Chinese and continental dishes.

$ Bestee
Railway Rd.
Mughlai and South Indian. Stuffed *parathas* are recommended.

Festivals

Thousands of pilgrims visit the city when the birth of the river (*Dikhanti*) is celebrated in spring. **Kumbh Mela**, held here every 12th year (next in Mar-Apr 2021), and **Ardha Kumbh** also every 12 years (next in 2016), attract millions of devotees who come to bathe in the confined area near Hari-ki-Pairi. In 2013 over 55 days nearly 100 million devotees arrived as the city played host to the epic Kumbh Mela festival.

What to do

Body and soul
Patanjali Yogpeeth, *near Bahadarabad, Delhi–Haridwar National Highway, T01334-240008,*

www.divyayoga.com. Simple rooms. Enormous and exceptionally well-equipped ashram/yogic hospital, offering yoga camps and treatments for diseases from diabetes to impotence. However, daily yoga classes are taught in Hindi only.

Tours and tour operators
GMVN, *www.gmvnl.com.* Daily tours of Haridwar-Rishikesh, and further afield to Dehra Dun and Mussoorie.
Mohan's Adventure, *next to Chitra Cinema, Railway Rd, T01334-265543, www.mohans adventure.in.* Very reliable trips run by Sanjeev Mehta. Trekking, jeep safaris, rafting. Jungle trips into Rajaji National Park, with night stay in tribal village. Highly recommended.

Transport

Bus The long-distance bus stand is opposite the railway station. Frequent buses to/from **Delhi** (5-7 hrs) and **Dehra Dun** (1¾ hrs). Buses for **Rishikesh** leave irregularly and only when enough passengers turn up; better to take a *tempo* or taxi.

Rickshaw, jeep and taxi The taxi stand is outside railway station, rates negotiable. To **Rishikesh** costs Rs 600-800. *Tempos* shuttle around town and to nearby destinations; to **Rishikesh**, Rs 25 (more for Lakshman Jhula). Catch them outside the railway station where the chance of getting a seat is highest. **Taxi Union**, outside bus stand, has share jeeps to **Joshimath** (Rs 320 a seat) via **Deoprayag**, **Rudraprayag** (Rs 180) and **Karanprayag** (Rs 220). There is also a private Haridwar Taxi Hire T(0)73511 76688 (www.haridwartaxi.com) offering taxis, day tours and packages.

Train Railway Station, T131. Reservation office 0800-2000. There are 3 trains per day to **Rishikesh**, but better to take road transport; **Delhi** (ND) *Shatabdi Exp 12018*, 4½ hrs is the fastest option. **Dehra Dun**: *Shatabdi Exp 12017*, 1¼ hrs, among several others. **Varanasi**: *Dehra Dun Varanasi Exp 14266*, 20 hrs. For **Nainital (Kathgodam)**: *Dehradun-Kathgodam Exp 14120*, 7 hrs.

Rajaji National Park *Colour map 1, B4.*

Uttarakhand's largest protected area

Rajaji National Park (altitude 302-1000 m) covers 820 sq km and is named after C Rajagopalachari, the only Indian to hold the post of governor general. Spread across the rugged and dangerously steep slopes of the Shiwaliks, the park's vegetation ranges from rich *sal*, *bhabbar* tracts, broad-leaf mixed forest to *chir* pine forests interspersed with areas of scrub and pasture which provide a home for a wide variety of wildlife including over 23 mammal and 438 species of bird. On foot, however, you are likely to see very little. Even by car or jeep many are disappointed as few animals are spotted.

A large number of **elephants**, together with the rarely seen **tiger**, are found, here at the northwest limit of their range in India. The elephants move up into the hills when the water holes are dry. A census taken in 2001 recorded 453 elephants, 30 tigers and 236 **leopards** in the park. Other animals include spotted deer, sambar, muntjac, nilgai and ghoral. Along the tracks, you may spot wild boar, langur and macaque; the Himalayan yellow-throated marten and civet are rare. Peacocks, jungle fowl and kaleej pheasants can be spotted in the drier areas, while waterbirds attracted by the Ganga and the Song rivers include many kinds of geese, ducks, cormorant, teal and spoonbill, among others.

You can stay at the lovely **Wild Brook Retreat** (details in Where to stay, below).

Essential Rajaji National Park

Finding your feet

The park can be reached from Haridwar, Rishikesh and Dehra Dun (see Transport, opposite).

Permits

Permits are available from the Director, 5/1 Ansari Road, Dehra Dun, T0135-262 1669; Mohan's Adventure, T01334-26554; or at the Chilla park office, T01382-266757.

Opening times

Open from 15 November to 15 June between sunrise and sunset.

Entry fees

Entry for the first three days: foreigners Rs 500, Indians Rs 150; camera Rs 50; video, Rs 5000. Car permit Rs 2500-500. Jeep hire from Haridwar, Rishikesh or Dehradun. See also www.rajajinationalpark.co.in.

Listings Rajaji National Park

Where to stay

For reservation of a guesthouse, contact Rajaji National Park (5/1 Ansari Marg, Dehra Dun, T0135-262 1669). To stay in a tribal village, contact Mohan's Adventure (T01334-265543), see page 169.

$$$ Wild Brook Retreat
T(0)93148 80887, www.wildbrookretreat.com.
Lovely stone cottages and spacious tents both with lovely sit outs. Environmentally aware with use of resources and opportunities for volunteer work. Recommended.

$$ Tourist Bungalow
Chilla, T1334 951382.
With rooms, dorm (Rs 150) and tents.

$ Forest Rest Houses
Near all the gates.
All have at least 2 suites. Those at Chilla (apparently best spot for wildlife) and Motichur cost Rs 1000. Others at Asarodi, Beribara, Kansrao,

Kunnao, Phandowala, Ranipur and Satyanarain are Rs 600. All have electricity and water supply except Beribara and Kansrao which are very basic.

Transport

The park has 8 entry gates. From **Dehra Dun**: Mohan (25 km on Delhi–Dehra Dun highway, 5-hr drive from Delhi), **Ramgarh** (14 km, Delhi–Dehra Dun highway, via Clement Town) and **Lachhiwala** (18 km, Dehra Dun–Haridwar route, right turn before Doiwala). From **Haridwar**: Chilla (7 km, via private bus route to Rishikesh), **Motichur** (9 km, Haridwar–Rishikesh or Dehra Dun–Haridwar highways) and **Ranipur** (9 km, Haridwar–BHEL–Mohand Rd). From **Rishikesh**: Kunnao (6 km, via private bus route on Rishikesh–Pashulok route). From **Kotdwara**: Laldhang (25 km, via private bus route Kotdwara to Chilla).

★ Rishikesh   *Colour map 1, B4.*

Rishikesh (population 72,000) stands on the banks of the Ganga where it runs swiftly through a forested gorge in the southernmost foothills of the Shiwaliks. The quiet of these hills has drawn sages for centuries, including many of the greatest luminaries of 20th-century yoga, such as Swami Sivananda, founder of the Divine Life Society, Swami Satyananda of the Bihar school, and perhaps most famously Maharishi Mahesh Yogi, whose Western-tinged spiritual patter captured the imagination of the Beatles and paid for a then space age, now abandoned, ashram.

Today it's a mixed bag of ashrams, sadhus, Ayurveda clinics and globetrotting teachers, yet, Rishikesh still has a certain magic. In the evening, chants of *Om Namoh Shivaya* drift on the air, as the last whitewater rafters of the day paddle in to shore, in what must be one of the most surreal endings to a rafting trip anywhere in the world. Some find it disappointing and lacking in atmosphere; others stay for weeks.

Clean Himalaya ⓘ *www.cleanhimalaya.org*, is an award-winning environmental group, established by members of the **Divine Life Society** (contact Swami Susan T(0)9897-946696) running local rubbish collections and campaigning for greater public awareness of green issues. Volunteer, donate, and encourage local businesses to sign up.

Sights

Many travel to Rishikesh (Hair of Sages) to study in one of its numerous ashrams, seats of spiritual learning often housed in bizarrely colourful architectural curiosities. As a result, the town has become something of a yoga supermarket. Evening *aarti* is popular at Parmath Niketan, but the Triveni ghat (which has striking statues of Siva) is where local pilgrims perform the ritual. The trees along the east bank between Lakshman and Ram Jhula shade scores of bungalows, the homes to the ubiquitous saffron-robed sadhus you'll find sitting at every pathside, swinging tiffins and sparking up chillums. Follow the track northeast, beyond Lakshman Jhula, to reach beautiful, secluded swimming beaches.

Essential Rishikesh

Finding your feet

From Haridwar, buses are both quicker and far more frequent than trains. Buses from Delhi and Dehra Dun arrive at the main bus stand in the town centre.

Getting around

The compact town centre, with the bus stands and bus station, is 1 km from the river. But it is the ashrams further north, concentrated around Ram Jhula and Lakshman Jhula (the two pedestrian suspension bridges), that are where most foreigners consider Rishikesh proper to be. Frequent shared taxis (Rs 5-10) go between the Bazar and the bridges, or you can cross by boat near Ram Jhula (Rs 10). Shared jeeps link the quarters on the east bank (Rs 5-10). See Transport, page 175.

Fact...

Rishikesh is a vegetarian temple town, meat and alcohol are prohibited; eggs are only eaten in private.

Rishikesh is the base for several pilgrimages and treks, including the **Char Dham Pilgrimage** (see page 176), or going to the Garhwal hills and Hemkund Sahib.

Listings Rishikesh *map p173*

Tourist information

Garhwal Mandal Vikas Nigam (GMVN)
Shail Vihar, Haridwar Bypass Rd, T0135-243 1793, also at Yatra Office, Kailash Gate, Bypass Rd, T0135-243 1793, yatra@gmvnl.com.
Organizes trekking, mountaineering, rafting and the Char Dham tour (4-12 days).

Uttarakhand Tourism
Kailash Gate, T0135-243 0799.
Helpful.

Where to stay

The noisy and congested town around the bazar and Triveni ghats couldn't be further from the spiritual calm for which many travel to Rishikesh, but it does hold some good accommodation. There is a huge swathe of ashram options (see under Body and Soul in What to do, below), which often have curfews and some moderate constraints on behaviour. For a quieter stay, head across the river to the Swiss Cottage area.

$$$$ Ananda-in-the-Himalayas
The Palace, Narendra Nagar, T01378-451 6650, www.ananda spa.com.
Exclusive destination spa with 75 rooms (including a literally palatial suite in the Viceregal Palace, which has its own open-air hot tub and 3 cottages with their own infinity pools and saunas), in a superb location 30 mins above Rishikesh with panoramic views across the valley. Winner of many international awards.

$$$$ Atali Ganga
Atali Dogi, Milestone 30, Badrinath Rd, T(0)9756-611114, www.ataliganga.com.
Pioneering responsible tourism in the area, Atali Ganga is run by the excellent **Aquaterra Adventures** who organize exceptional treks and rafting expeditions. This beautiful property is 30 km up river of Rishikesh and as well as stunning rooms, there is a great pool, climbing wall and fantastic food. Highly recommended.

$$$$ Glasshouse on the Ganges
23rd Milestone Rishikesh–Badrinath Rd, Gular Dogi District, 23 km from Rishikesh towards

Badrinath, T(0)99171-91115, www.neemranahotels.com.
A lovely riverside retreat in lychee and mango tree garden once used by the Rajas of Garwhal. Rooms either in main block or cottages. The property has its own beach and yoga is complimentary.

$$$ Camp Silver Sands
Beach No 12 Rishikesh, Badrinath Rd, T011-29212760 (Delhi), www.aquaterra.in.
The best tent option along the banks of the Ganga. With a close eye on the environment and conscious tourism, they run exceptional rafting expeditions. The tents are simple but comfortable and the food is great – dinner under the stars by the rushing river. Meals included. Exceptional.

$$$ Ganga Banks
Shivpuri, contact Wanderlust in Delhi, T011-4163 6757, www.wanderlust india.com.
A 'green' resort with 28 comfortable, eco-friendly cottages with bath, built using local raw materials, restaurant, pool, health spa, in natural surroundings employing recycling techniques (no plastics), solar heating, well placed for trekking, rafting, etc.

$$$ Rainforest House
Below Neer Gaddu forest chowkie, Badrinath Rd, 3 km from Tapovan, T(0)80067 79298, www.rainforest-house.com.
Charming, isolated guesthouse upstream from Rishikesh on the Ganga with 9 rustic but beautifully designed double rooms set around a central court. Very peaceful forested retreat without phones or TVs, run by English chap and his lovely Indian wife and team. Lovely relaxed restaurant serving delicious Indian and Italian food, delicious salads and great pizzas. There is a beautiful yoga space as well. Whole-heartedly recommended.

$$ Divine Ganga Cottage
Tapovan village, T0135-2442175, www.divinegangacottage.com.
Quiet location away from Laxman Jhula with newly renovated rooms and a friendly atmosphere. In the winter months, you can enjoy good food at **Ramana's Garden**, see Restaurants, below. Recommended.

$$ Sanskriti Vedic Retreat
Swarg Ashram, T0135-244 2444,
www.sanskritivedicretreat.com.
Newly reopened and renovated after a fire,
this great yoga and ayurvedic centre has lovely
accommodation and good views of the Ganga.
There's healthy food and excellent teachers.

$$-$ Rishilok (GMVN)
Badrinath Rd, Muni-ki-Reti, T0135-243 0373.
Within walking distance of Ram Jhula, set far
enough from the main road and taxi stand to
be quiet, is this charming 1970s government
guesthouse. Although its fading upholstery is as
old as the building, it holds 46 clean rooms, some
with bath, in blocks set around a beautifully kept

garden of bamboo, bougainvillea and butterflies.
Excellent service.

$ Bhandari Swiss Cottage
High Bank, off Lakshman Jhula Rd,
T0135-243 2939.
Most rooms here are gifted with a heavenly
view over the Ganga and to the hills beyond.
Big rooms, clean and basic and a tranquil
setting. Internet café and little restaurant.

$ Ishan
West end of Lakshman Jhula, T0135-243 1534,
www.ishanhotel.com.
Clean and pleasant rooms, some with balconies
overlooking the river, internet downstairs and an
excellent restaurant.

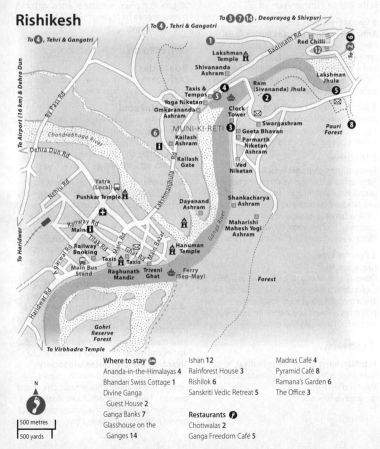

Rishikesh

Where to stay
Ananda-in-the-Himalayas 4
Bhandari Swiss Cottage 1
Divine Ganga
  Guest House 2
Ganga Banks 7
Glasshouse on the
  Ganges 14

Ishan 12
Rainforest House 3
Rishilok 6
Sanskriti Vedic Retreat 5

Madras Café 4
Pyramid Café 8
Ramana's Garden 6
The Office 3

Restaurants
Chotiwalas 2
Ganga Freedom Café 5

Restaurants

Madras Café, on the West Bank, and **Chotiwalas**, on the East Bank, are Ram Jhula's 2 long-running, cheap fast-food joints.

$$ Ramana's Garden
Uphill from Lakshman Jhula then right at Tapovan Resort, 5 mins' walk, www. friendsoframanasgarden.org. Daily 1100-1530 and Sat 1830-2100 (closed May-Oct).
If the organic home-grown salad plates and scrumptious cakes weren't enough in themselves, this pleasant garden restaurant funds a school for local orphan children, who spill out across its grounds during breaks and help Ramana's multinational team of volunteers in the kitchen. Film nights on Sat.

$ Ganga Freedom Café
Behind Dr Kothari clinic, Lakshman Jhula.
Easily the tastiest scran on the East Bank – serving the likes of rosemary roast tatties and ratatouille, a little pricier than some local *dabhas* but food comes in big portions. Lovely atmosphere and views along the river.

$ Mount Valley Mama Cottage
Next to Bhandari Swiss Cottage.
All-you-can-eat *thalis* are much famed among travellers. Delicious and highly recommended.

$ The Office
Swargashram ghats near clock tower.
Although tiny, this is so much more than a chai joint: it has excellent specials, such as fresh chick pea salad or houmous and apple and chocolate banana samosas. Minimalist bulletin board for upcoming courses, yoga, cookery and Ayurveda. Plus a teeny balcony on the Ganges. Lovely.

$ Pyramid Café
Lakshman Jhula.
Offers all sorts of veggie and vegan health food, such as tofu brown rice *kombucha* and spirulina. The atmosphere and soundtrack in the mellow tipi garden make it well worth the short walk up the hill. There's Wi-Fi too.

Festivals

Feb-Mar International Yoga Festival, hosted by the Parmarth Niketan ashram. An opportunity to meet and learn from some of the leading lights in the yoga community.

Shopping

Rishikesh has several excellent bookshops specializing in yoga and the spiritual life, especially the one by Laxman Jhula bridge and German Bakery; good places to rummage for reading material are on the east bank of the Ganga near Ram Jhula and the west bank at Lakshman Jhula. The central market area around Dehra Dun, Haridwar, Ghat and Railway roads has markets and curio shops.

Gecko, *under Hotel Ishan, Lakshman Jhula.*
Intriguing and colourful range of Nepali-made dresses and winter jackets.
Pundir General Store, *Badrinath Rd, Tapovan Sarai.* Whether you are hankering for Korean *miso*, V8 juice, European chocolate or a new yoga mat – this place has a bit of everything. There's a little café upstairs too.

What to do

Boat rides
On the Ganga from from Lakshman Jhula. Fix rates with local boatmen.

Body and soul
Yoga classes, meditation courses and instruction in Ayurveda and Vedanta are Rishikesh's stock-in-trade. As well as **Sanskriti Retreat** (see Where to stay, above) here are some of the most reputable ashrams.

Dayananda, *Purani Jhadi near Chandrabhaga River, T0135-243 0769, www.dayananda.org.* They run regular yoga and meditation intensives and have daily lectures on Vedanta, and rooms with marble floors and tiled bathrooms.
Omkarananda Ashram (Durga Mandir), *above Yoga Niketan, Ram Jhula, T0135-243 0713.* Good Iyengar yoga courses, also offers music and classical dance.
Parmarth Niketan, *Swargashram, T0135-243 4301, www.parmarth.com/home.* Large scale ashram, with well attended sunset *aarti* on the Ganga. Atmospheric ashram with many courses in yoga, meditation and philosophy. Tidy rooms in blocks set around pleasant leafy gardens full of stucco deities and friezes of passages from the *Gita*.
Sivananda Ashram (Divine Life Society), *T0135-243 0040.* Short to 3-month courses (apply 1 month ahead); holds music classes and produces herbal medicines. Forest Academy open to male students; non-Indians can attend classes informally, but are not given certificates.

Swami Rama Sadhaka Grama, *south of town centre on Virbhadra Rd, T0135-245 0093, www. sadhakagrama.org.* Yoga training with a strong focus on meditation, based on the Himalayan tradition laid out by Sankaracharya. There's a rigorous 600-hr yoga teacher training program, or you can simply use the cottages for a few days' retreat. There is an exceptional ayurvedic hospital too.

Ved Niketan, *south end of Swargashram ghats, T0135-2430279.* Has a flexible programme of yoga; also Hindi, Sanskrit, music and dance classes and basic rooms.

Music
Sivananda Ramesh, *towards Muni-ki-Reti Taxi Stand, T(0)98871 05154.* Lessons in tabla, sitar, santoor, singing, etc.

Rafting and trekking
There are more than 60 whitewater rafting outfits in town, and Shivpuri, 17 km north, has become an adventure sports playground. You can book onto daily trips on the Grade III waters the day before, or go for more adventurous, longer-haul expeditions with meals and overnights at camps. Below are 3 companies known for their sound environmental records and exceptional safety record.

Aquaterra, *T011-29212641, www.aquaterra.in.* Based in Delhi with an outpost 30 km north of Rishikesh, Aquaterra is the only Indian company to be included in the National Geographic's *Best Adventure Travel Companies on Earth.* With impeccable safety standards and fantastic guides, they offer many rafting and trekking opportunities in the area. Highly recommended.
De-N-Ascent Expeditions, *Tapovan Sarai T0135-244 2354, www.kayakhimalaya.com.* Excellent equipment and stringent safety, with a background in kayaking. Runs day trips and more adventurous routes through less charted waters.
Red Chilli, *Tapovan, above Lakshman Jhula, T0135-243 4021, www.redchilliadventure.com.* Enthusiastic local outfit with good environmental standards. Recommended.

Tour operators
Garhwal Himalayan Exploration, *Muni Ki Reti, T0135-244 2267, www.thegarhwalhimalayas.com.* Wide range of trekking and rafting trips.
GMVN, *Yatra Office, T0135-243 1793, www.gmvnl. com.* Char Dham pilgrimage tours, plus 4-to 5-day adventure tours.

Transport

Rishikesh is the main staging post for visiting the Himalayan pilgrim centres of **Badrinath** (301 km); **Gangotri** (258 km); **Kedarnath** (228 km); **Uttarkashi** (154 km); **Yamunotri** (288 km).

Bus Long-distance buses use **main bus stand**, Haridwar Rd, T0135-243 0066. Various State Government bus services (**DTC**, **Haryana Roadways**, **Himachal RTC**, **UP Roadways** serve destinations including: **Chandigarh** (252 km), **Dehra Dun** (42 km, every 30 mins), **Delhi** (238 km, 6 hrs), **Haridwar** (24 km, every 30 mins), **Mussoorie** (77 km). For **Shimla**, stay overnight in Dehra Dun and catch 0600 bus. Share taxis for Dehra Dun and Haridwar leave from outside the bus stand.

The **Yatra Bus Stand**, Dehra Dun Rd, has buses for local destinations and the mountain pilgrimage sites. Reserve tickets the day before (especially during *yatra* season, May-Nov); open 0400-1900, 0400-1400 out of season. To **Char Dhams**: buses leave early for the very long routes to Hanuman Chatti (for Yamunotri), **Badrinath**, **Gangotri**, **Gaurikund** (for Kedarnath); best to take a luxury bus, and break your journey. For **Badrinath** and **Hemkund** stop overnight at Joshimath (after 1630 road to Govindghat is southbound only). Although the *yatra* season ends in late Oct (Yamunotri, Gangotri, Kedarnath) to mid-Nov (Badrinath), bus frequency drops drastically during Oct. Even light rains can cause severe road blocks, mainly due to landslides. Bus for Badrinath departs from **Tehri Bus Stand** (100 m right from station), 1600, Rs 180, but noisy, crowded and uncomfortable. **Garhwal Motor Owners Union**, T0135-243 0076.

Ferry Ferry boat from near Ram Jhula for river crossing, Rs 10, return Rs 15.

Motorbike Motorbike mechanic at **Bila**, opposite **Ganga View Hotel**, Lakshman Jhula.

Rickshaw Auto-rickshaw rates are negotiable; allow around Rs 30 to **Ram Jhula**, Rs 35-40 for **Lakshman Jhula**.

Taxi Fixed rates from from taxi stands south of **Ram Jhula** and in the market near **Lakshman Jhula**.

Tempo Mostly fixed routes. From Ram Jhula shared, to Rishikesh Bazar Rs 5; from Lakshman Jhula Rs 10; to **Haridwar** Rs 25, 50 mins. Foreigners may be asked for more.

Train There is a branch line from **Haridwar** to **Rishikesh**, but the bus is quicker.

Garhwal &
the Pilgrimage (Yatra)

★ The shrines of Kedarnath, Yamunotri, Gangotri and Badrinath, collectively known as the Char Dham, are visited by hundreds of thousands of Hindu pilgrims each summer. They come from all corners of the subcontinent to engage in what William Dalrymple calls "a modern-day Indian Canterbury Tales".

Garhwal's fragmented political history gives no clue as to the region's religious significance. The sources of the Yamuna and the Ganga, and some of Hinduism's holiest mountains, lie in the heart of the region. Since the seventh-century Tamil saint Sankaracharya travelled north on his mission to reinvigorate Hinduism's northern heartland, some have been watched over permanently by South Indian priests. The most famous is the Rawal – head priest – at the Badrinath temple, who to this day comes from Kerala. Badrinath is one of the four *dhams*, 'holiest abodes' of the gods. Along with Dwarka, Puri and Ramesvaram, they mark the cardinal points of Hinduism's cultural geography.

After a ritual purificatory bathe in the Ganga at Haridwar and, preferably, Rishikesh, the pilgrim begins the 301-km journey to Badrinath. The purpose is to worship, purify and acquire merit. Roads go all the way to Gangotri and Badrinath, and to within 5 km of Yamunotri and 14 km of Kedarnath. The correct order for pilgrims is to visit the holy places from west to east: Yamunotri, Gangotri, Kedarnath and Badrinath. The journey is long and bumpy, but the views, the heady atmosphere of the temples and the humbling spirit of the pilgrims is a rich reward. The floods of June 2013 where over 10,000 people were killed badly affected Kedarnath and the roads leading up to these pilgrimage places. The routes are all reopened but as Vaibhav Kala, who has been leading treks and expeditions in the Himalayas for many years, says: "The lives that have changed will take years to get back to normal."

Essential Garhwal and the Pilgrimage (Yatra)

Finding your feet

Yatra tourists on public buses are required to register with the Yatra Office at the Yatra (Local) Bus Stand, Rishikesh (0600-2200). A certificate of immunization against cholera and typhoid is needed. In practice, 'Registration' is often waived, but the immunization certificate is checked. See Transport in Rishikesh, page 175, for all travel details.

When to go

The best time to visit is May and mid-September to mid-October. Temples and trekking routes open from the end of April to mid-November

Tip...
Take bottled water or a filter and take a good torch as electricity is extremely dodgy.

Best Himalayan moments
Trek to the source of the Ganges at Gaumukh, page 178
Learn to cook Himalayan food at Saur Project, page 179
Darshan at Badrinath Temple, page 183

(October for Badrinath). June is very crowded; heavy rains from July to mid-September may trigger landslips.

Tours and trekking

GMVN (www.gmvnl.com) organizes 12-day pilgrimage tours from Delhi and Rishikesh during season. See also page 30 for trekking in the Valley of Flowers. For more specific information on trekking routes, see Footprint's *Indian Himalaya Handbook*.

Yamunotri and Gangotri
look into the eyes of God at these Himalayan holy temples

Yamunotri can be reached from Rishikesh or from Dehra Dun via Yamuna Bridge and Barkot. The former is the more popular. From Rishikesh it is 83 km to Tehri, or 165 km via Deoprayag. Tehri, northeast of Rishikesh, the capital of the former princely state, will eventually be submerged by the waters behind the controversial and still unfinished Tehri Dam. New Tehri, 24 km from the original town, is a 'planned' town and the new district headquarters.

Yamunotri *Colour map 1, B4.*
Dominated by **Banderpunch** (6316 m), Yamunotri (altitude 3291 m), the source of the Yamuna, is believed to be the daughter of Surya (the sun) and the twin sister of Yama (the 'Lord of Death'). Anyone who bathes in her waters will be spared an agonizing death.

To begin the trek to reach the temple take a jeep from **Hanuman Chatti** (large vehicles also stop here and pick up) to **Janki Chatti**, 8 km further up, which is more pleasant and where you can leave luggage. The trek along the riverbank is exhilarating with the mountains rising up on each side, the last 5 km somewhat steeper. The source itself is a difficult 1-km climb from the 19th-century **Yamunotri Temple** ① *0600-1200, 1400-2100*, with a black marble deity. The modern temple was rebuilt this century after floods and snow destroyed it.

There are **hot springs** nearby (the most sacred being Surya Kund) in which pilgrims cook potatoes and rice tied in a piece of cloth. The meal, which takes only a few minutes to cook, is first offered to the deity and then distributed as *prasad*. On the return to Hanuman Chatti, you can visit the **Someshwar Temple** at Kharsali, 3 km across the river from Janki Chatti. The temple is one of the oldest and finest in the region.

Uttarkashi and around *Colour map 1, B4.*
The busy town of Uttarkashi (altitude 3140m), en route to Gangotri, 155 km from Rishikesh, has several places to staybut all are full during the season. There are also many new places on the way

Uttarakhand dams

Development of the new state's massive hydroelectric potential is highly controversial. The Tehri Dam, at over 250 m high the eighth tallest dam in the world, was the focus of intense opposition from environmental campaigners for more than 30 years. The lower tunnels were closed in 2001 and the upper tunnel in October 2005, allowing the first electricity to be generated in 2006. The stored water provides little benefit to the state, being primarily used to enhance irrigation and supply urgent water needs of Delhi and other rapidly growing cities on the plains.

In 2009, a 77-year-old retired academic, GD Agrawal, staged a month-long hunger strike in his fight to halt work on the Lohari Nag Pala hydroelectric project, a series of six dams and numerous tunnels, which environmentalists argued would dry up 125 km of the Bhagirathi River, the source stream of the Ganges, between Gangotri and Uttarkashi.

The central government has now established a Ganga River Basin Authority to manage the basin's development, and Environment Minister Jairam Ramesh has declared that "India is a civilization of rivers, and it should not become a land of tunnels", yet work is nearly complete on a huge new dam on the Alaknanda, the second of the Ganges' two key tributaries, with plans in place for up to 30 more dams in the Ganga basin, which if completed would see several of the sacred confluences inundated under metres of water. The protests and investigations have magnified since the devastating flash floods in Uttarakhand in June 2013 where over 10,000 people lost their lives, which many blamed on the increasing number of dams in the area.

out of Uttarkashi towards Rishikesh. There's a **tourist office**① *T01374-222290*, the **Nehru Institute of Mountaineering**① *T01374-222 123*, offers courses and you can trek to **Dodital**; porters can be hired. You can buy provisions from the bazar near the bus stand. If you are in town on 14 January you will see the **Makar Sankranti Garhwal festival** of music and dance. Uttarkashi was badly affected by the floods and landslides in June 2013.

If you can, make a detour at Saur, a small village between Rishikesh and Uttarkashi. Abandoned when the residents moved to nearby towns four decades ago, it has since become a responsible tourism project set up by DueNorth. You can stay in beautifully restored cottages (see Where to stay, opposite) with stunning scenery.

Gangotri and around *Colour map 1, B5.*

Gangotri (altitude 3140 m), 240 km from Rishikesh, is the second of the major shrines in the Garhwal Himalaya. A high bridge now takes the road across the Jad Ganga River, joining the Bhagirathi which rushes through narrow gorges, so buses travel all the way. The 18th-century granite **temple** is dedicated to the goddess Ganga, where she is believed to have descended to earth. It was built by a Gurkha commander, Amar Singh Thapa, in the early 18th century and later rebuilt by the Maharaja of Jaipur. Hindus believe that Ganga (here Bhagirathi) came down from heaven after **King Bhagirath**'s centuries-long penance. He wanted to ensure his dead relatives' ascent to heaven by having their ashes washed by the sacred waters of the Ganga. When the tempestuous river arrived on earth, the force of her flow had to be checked by Siva who received her in the coils of his hair, lest she sweep all away. A submerged lingam is visible in the winter months.

Rishikund, 55 km from Uttarkashi, has hot sulphur springs near **Gangnani** suitable for bathing, and a 15th-century temple. The **Gaurikund waterfall** here is one of the most beautiful in the Himalaya. Below Gangotri are **Bhojbasa** and **Gaumukh**, which are on a gradual but scenically stunning trek. You can continue to trek another 6 km to Nandanvan (4400 m), base camp for Bhagirathi peak, and continue 4 km to Tapovan (4463 m), known for its meadows that encircle the base of Shivling peak.

> **Tip...**
> Note that it is an offence to photograph sensitive installations, troop movements and bridges on most routes. Offenders can be treated very severely.

Purification and piety

Bad karma (see page 1324), the impurity caused by bad actions in previous births, and death itself, is the focus of some of Hinduism's most important rituals. Rivers are believed to have great purifying power, stronger at the source, at their confluence, and at the mouth. There are five *prayags* (confluences) in the Himalayan section of the Ganga – Deoprayag, Rudraprayag, Karnaprayag, Nandaprayag and Vishnuprayag, called Trayayagraj (King of Prayags). On the plains, Allahabad is the most important confluence of all, where the Yamuna, the Ganga and the mythical underground river, the Sarasvati, all meet.

Hardship enhances the rewards of the *yatra* pilgrims. The really devout prostrate themselves either for the whole distance or around the temple, lying face down, stretching the arms forwards, standing up, moving up to where their fingertips reached and then repeating the exercise, each one accompanied by a chant. Most pilgrims today make the journey by bus or by car.

Listings Yamunotri and Gangotri

Where to stay

Prices are higher than average. During yatra season prices double from one day to the next as the season starts, and advance reservations are essential; **GMVN** (T0135-243 1793, www.gmvnl.com) places may only be available if you book their organized tour. Contact GMVN for reservations in their **$$-$** rest houses along the routes. Some have 'deluxe' rooms which are still basic, with toilet and hot water, and most have dorms (Rs 200). There are also simple guesthouses in places. **Himalayan Eco Lodges** (www.himalayanecolodges.com) offer several camps and lodges in beautifully remote spots. Recommended.

Yamunotri

There are several GMVN rest houses (the one by the river is the best), lodges and *dharamshalas* and also places to eat.

$ Rest House
Janki Chatti, GMVN, T01375-235639.
Closed Dec-Mar.

Uttarkashi and around

$$$ Saur Project
South of Tehri, between Uttarkashi and Rishikesh, T(0)9899-061383, www.duenorth.in.
Amazing restoration project of local cottages in the 'ghost' village of Saur which was abandoned 40 years ago. With stunning views, terraced fields, this is a place to connect to nature and conscious farming. Food is included in price and you can learn to cook local foods; delicious. More village cottages are being restored using local traditions. Highly recommended.

$$$ Shikhar Nature Resort
5 km out of town, by the Bhagirathi River, T01374-223762, www.naturecampsindia.com.
Luxury tents with pretty furnishings with mod cons in scenic setting.

$$-$ Sahaj Villa
Gangotri Highway, Gyansu, Uttarkashi, T(0)95574 20698.
Basic, clean rooms. Restaurant on site.

Gangotri

Expect very basic accommodation here with erratic electricity.

$$ Tourist Rest House (GMVN)
Across the footbridge, T01377-222221.
20 rooms and dorm, meals.

$ Ganga Niketan
Across the road bridge.
Good rooms and a simple terrace restaurant.

$ Gangotri Guest House
Near bus stand, T(0)75790-57689.
Simple rooms.

What to do

Uttarkashi and around

Mount Support, *Gangotri Rd, near bus stand, T01374-222419.* Foreign exchange at monopoly rates. Hire guides and porters.

From Rishikesh the road follows the west bank of the Ganga and enters forest. At the 23rd milestone, at Gular-dogi village, is the orchard and garden of the Maharaja of Tehri Garhwal, close to a white-sand and rock beach, which is now home to a luxury hotel.

The section up to **Deoprayag** (68 km) is spectacular. The folding and erosion of the hills can be clearly seen on the mainly uninhabited steep scarps on the opposite bank. Luxuriant forest runs down to the water's edge which in many places is fringed with silver sand beaches. In places the river rushes over gentle rapids. A few kilometres before Byasi is **Vashisht Gufa** (the cave where the saint meditated) which has an ashram. About 5 km after **Byasi** the road makes a gradual ascent to round an important bluff. At the top, there are fine views down to the river. The way tiny fields have been created by terracing is marvellous. Jeeps can be hired from here to Badrinath or Rishikesh.

Deoprayag This is the most important of the hill *prayags* because it is here, where the frothing Bhagirathi from Gangotri joins the calm Alaknanda flowing down from Badrinath, that the Ganga herself is born. The town tumbles down the precipitous hillside in the deeply cut 'V' between the rivers, with houses almost on top of one another. Where the rivers meet is a pilgrims' bathing ghat, artificially made into the shape of India. From Deoprayag, the road is flat as far as Srinagar (35 km) and the land is cultivated. The Siva and Raghunath temples here attract pilgrims.

Srinagar The old capital of Tehri Garhwal, Srinagar was devastated when the Gohna Lake dam was destroyed by an earthquake in the mid-19th century. The most attractive part of Srinagar, which is a university town, runs from the square down towards the river. There are some typical hill houses with elaborately carved door jambs.

Srinagar to Rudraprayag The 35-km route from Srinagar to Rudraprayag, at the confluence of the Mandakini and Alaknanda, passes through cultivated areas, wild ravines, and the vast construction works for a new dam. Halfway, an enormous landslip indicates the fragility of the mountains. Some 5 km before reaching Rudrapayag, in a grove of trees by a village, is a tablet marking the spot where the 'man-eating leopard of Rudraprayag' was killed by Jim Corbett. Rudraprayag with its temples is strung out along a narrow part of the Alaknanda Valley.

The route to Kedarnath For Kedarnath, 77 km from Rudraparyag, leave the Pilgrim road at Rudraprayag, cross the Alaknanda River, and go through a tunnel before following the Mandakini Valley through terraced cultivation and green fields. The road goes past **Tilwara**, 9 km, then **Kund**, to **Guptakashi** where Siva

> ### Fact...
> Many of Uttarakhand's most stunning treks are in fact age-old pilgrimage routes (or 'yatra' routes).

proposed to Parvati. If time permits and you have hired a jeep from Guptakashi, stop at **Sonprayag**, 26 km, a small village at the confluence of the Mandakini and Son Ganga rivers, to visit the **Triyuginarayan Temple** where the gods were married. Enjoy the viewpoint here before continuing to **Gaurikund**, 4 km away, where the motorable road ends. Hundreds of pilgrims bathe in the hot sulphur springs in season. From here you either trek (start early) or ride a mule to **Kedarnath**, 14 km away. The ascent, which is steep at first, is through forests and green valleys to **Jungle Ghatti** and **Rambara** (over 1500 m); the latter part goes through dense vegetation, ravines and passes beautiful waterfalls. Beyond Rambara the path is steep again. At intervals tea stalls sell refreshments.

Where to stay

$$-$ New Tourist Bungalow
On a hill 1 km south of the village centre, Rudraprayag, T01364-233347, www.gmvnl.com.
25 rooms with bath, all with excellent views of prayag, plus dorm.

$$-$ Tourist Rest House
Near bus stop in central square, Srinagar, T01346-252199, www.gmvnl.com.
90 rooms, deluxe en suite, cabins and dorm, restaurant, tourist office, clean and quiet.

$ Chandrapuri Camp
North Rudraprayag, T01364-283207.
By the river. 10 safari-type tents for 4.

$ Tourist Bungalow
Gaurikund, T01364-269202, www.gmvnl.com. May-Nov.
10 rooms.

$ Tourist Bungalow
Guptakashi, T01364-267221, www.gmvnl.com.
6 basic, clean rooms.

$ Tourist Bungalow
On a hillside, 1.5 km from the main bazar and bus stand, Deoprayag, T01378-266013, www.gmvnl.com.
16 rooms, some with bath, meals.

Kedarnath Temple and around *Colour map 1, B5.*
an older and more impressive temple than Badrinath

The area around Kedarnath is known as Kedarkhand (the Abode of Siva). Kedarnath has one of the 12 *jyotirlingas* (luminous energy of Siva manifested at 12 holy places, miraculously formed lingams). In the *Mahabharata*, the Pandavas built the temple to atone for their sins after the battle at Kurukshetra.

Kedarnath Temple
Pujas at 0600 and 1800.

Some claim the Kedarnath Temple (altitude 3584 m) is more than 800 years old. Built of stone, unpainted but carved outside, it comprises a simple, squat, curved tower and a wooden-roofed *mandapa*. Set against an impressive backdrop of snow-capped peaks, the principal one being the Kedarnath peak (6970 m), the view from the forecourt is ruined by ugly 'tube' lights. At the entrance to the temple is a large Nandi statue. Near the temple is **$ Tourist Rest House** (Kedarnath, T01364-2632280), 16 rooms, some with bath, and dorm.

Vasuki Tal
A guide is necessary to visit Vasuki Tal (altitude 4235 m), about 6 km away. The source of Son Ganga, it's to the west up along a goat track. It has superb views of the Chaukhamba Peak (7164 m). A short distance northwest is the beautiful Painya Tal where through the clear water you can see the rectangular rocks which form the lake bottom.

Kedarnath Musk Deer Sanctuary
Permits to visit from DFO, Kedarnath Wildlife Division in Gopeshwar, T01372-252149, dfokedarnath@rediffmail.com; Rs 100, Indians Rs 40.

The area bounded by the Mandal–Ukhimath road and the high peaks to the north (the Kedarnath Temple is just outside) was set aside in 1972 principally to protect the endangered Himalayan musk deer – the male carries the prized musk pod. There is a **breeding centre** at Khanchula Kharak about 10 km from Chopta.

The diversity of the park's flora and fauna are particular attractions. Dense forested hills of chir pine, oak, birch and rhododendron and alpine meadows with the presence of numerous Himalayan flowering plants, reflect the diverse climate and topography of the area while 40% of the rocky heights remain under permanent snow. Wildlife includes jackal, black bear, leopard, snow leopard, sambar, *bharal* and Himalayan tahr, as well as 146 species of bird. A 2-km trek from Sari village near Chopta leads to Deoriatal, at 2438 m, overlooking Chaukhamba Peak.

Rudraprayag to Badrinath

steep-sided valleys and gorges with a cable car and ski resort

The road to Joshimath *Colour map 1, B5.*

Along the Pilgrim road, about midway between Rudraprayag and Karnaprayag, you pass **Gauchar**, famous locally for its annual cattle fair. The valley is wider here providing the local population with very good agricultural land. The beautiful Pindar River joins the Alaknanda at **Karnaprayag**, 17 km, while **Nandaprayag** is the confluence with the Nandakini River. All these places have GMVN accommodation.

Chamoli, 40 km further on, is the principal market for the Chamoli district though the administrative headquarters is at Gopeshwar on the hillside opposite. By this point, the valley walls have become much higher and steeper and the road twists and turns more. Troop movements up to the border with Tibet/China are common and military establishments are a frequent sight on the Pilgrim road. From Chamoli onwards the road is an impressive feat of engineering.

Joshimath *Colour map 1, B5.*

Joshimath (altitude 1875 m) is at the junction of two formerly important trans-Himalayan trading routes. Travellers to Govindghat and beyond may be forced to spend a night here as the road closes to northbound traffic at 1630. Joshimath is now the base for India's longest and highest **cable car route** ① *generally begins 0800 or 0900, Rs 200 one way to Auli Ski Resort*, with beautiful views of Nanda Devi, Kamet, Mana Parvat and Dunagiri peaks, all above 7000 m. There is a restaurant in the meadow. The **tourist office** ① *in the annexe above Neelkanth Motel, T01389-222181*, is helpful.

Vishnuprayag

Vishnuprayag is at the bottom of the gorge at the confluence of the Alaknanda and Dhauliganga rivers. Some 12 km and a steep downhill stretch brings the road from Joshimath to the winter headquarters of the Rawal of Badrinath. Buses for Badrinath, along the narrow hair-raising route start around 0600, the one-way flow regulated by police. You travel through precipitous gorges, past another Hanuman Chatti with a temple and climb above the tree-line to reach the most colourful of the *Char Dhams*, in the valley.

The **Bhotias** (Bhutias), a border people with Mongoloid features and strong ties with Tibet, live along these passes (see page 617). The women wear a distinctive Arab-like headdress. Like their counterparts in the eastern Himalaya, they used to combine high-altitude cultivation with animal husbandry and trading, taking manufactured goods from India to Tibet and returning with salt and borax. When the border closed following the 1962 Indo-Chinese War, they were forced to seek alternative income and some were resettled.

Auli *Colour map 1, B5.*

By road it is 16 km from Joshimath, or a 5-km trek; there is also a cable car.

The extensive meadows at Auli (altitude 2159 m), on the way to the Kauri Pass, had been used for cattle grazing by the local herders. After the Indo-Chinese War (1962), a road was built from Joshimath to Auli and a Winter Craft Centre set up for the border police in the 1970s. With panoramic views of mountains, particularly Nanda Devi and others in the sanctuary, and Mana and Kamet on the Indo-Tibet border, along with good slopes, Auli has been developed as a **ski** resort by GMVN and Uttarakhand Tourism operating from mid-December to early March. Though not a spectacularly equipped resort by world standards, Auli offers a 500-m ski lift (Rs 30) and 800-m chair lift (Rs 200), and has cheap lessons and gear hire.

Where to stay

The road to Joshimath

$ Tourist Bungalow
Gauchar, T01363-240611, www.gmvnl.com.
Open all year.

$ Tourist Bungalow
Nandaprayag, T01372-261215, www.gmvnl.com.
Open all year.
Small but clean rooms.

$ Tourist Bungalow
Karnaprayag, T01363-244210, www.gmvnl.com.
Open all year.
Attractive setting.

Joshimath

Hotel prices rise in high season.

$$$-$$ Himalayan Abode
Upper Mall, by bus stand, T(0)9412-082247.
Attractive homestay with wall-to-wall views and great home-cooked food.

$$ Dronagiri Hotel
T01389-222622.
Comfortable hotel with restaurant.

$$ Nanda Inn
Auli Rd, 3 km from Joshimath, T(0)98379-37948.
Away from the bustle of the bazar, this homestay is on the way to Auli. Friendly family.

$ Tourist Rest House (New)
T01389-222226.
OK rooms in ugly block, adequate for stopovers.

Auli

$$ Devi Darshan Lodge
Near Helipad T(0)9719-316777.
Simple rooms, but epic views. Good restaurant.

$$-$ Tourist Bungalow
T01389-223208, www.gmvni.com.
Wide range, including huts and a dorm (Rs 150), large restaurant.

What to do

Joshimath

Eskimo Adventures, *next to GMVN, T01389-221177.* Recommended for trekking, climbing and skiing.
Mountain Shepherds, *Lata village, T(0)971-931 6777, www.mountainshepherds.com.* Unique community tourism venture, with treks around the Nanda Devi region led by properly trained guides, plus unusual options including the chance to accompany local shepherds on their daily rounds. Recommended.

Badrinath and around *Colour map 1, B5.*

one of the four holiest places in India

According to Hindu Shastras, no pilgrimage is complete without a visit to Badrinath (altitude 3150 m), the abode of Vishnu. Guarding it are the Nar and Narayan ranges and in the distance towers the magnificent pyramid-shaped peak of Neelkanth, at 6558 m; a hike to its base takes two hours.

Badri is derived from a wild fruit that Vishnu was said to have lived on when he did penance at Badrivan, the area which covers all five important temples including Kedarnath. Shankaracharya, the monist philosopher from South India, is credited with establishing the four great pilgrimage centres in the early ninth century AD, see page 1325.

Badrinath Temple

The main Badrinath Temple is small and brightly painted in green, blue, pink, yellow, white, silver and red. The shrine is usually crowded with worshippers. The *Rawal* (Head Priest) always comes from a Namboodri village in Kerala, the birthplace of Shankaracharya. Badrinath is snowbound over winter, when the images are transferred to Pandukeshwar, and is open late April to October.

Along with worshipping in the temple and dispensing alms to the official (sometimes wealthy) temple beggars outside, it is customary to bathe in **Tapt Kund**, a hot pool nearby below the temple. This is fed by a hot sulphurous spring in which Agni (the god of fire) resides by kind permission of Vishnu. The temperature is around 45°C. **Badrinath Festival** takes place 3-10 June.

★ Hemkund and the Valley of Flowers *Colour map 1, B5.*

Permits to enter the park are issued at the police post at the road head of Govindghat and the Forest Check Post at Ghangharia, Rs 600 (Indians Rs150) for a 3-day permit. Camping overnight in the valley or taking back plants or flowers is prohibited.

Govindghat, 20 km from Joshimath, is on the road to Badrinath. A bridle track leads to Ghangharia, for the Valley of Flowers, 19 km further on, and Hemkund Sahib. This trail-head is very crowded in peak season (May-June). You can trek or hire mules for the two-day journey; there are several tea-stalls along the route.

Ghangharia, at 3048 m, is a 14-km walk from Govindghat. May to June are very busy. Those arriving late without a reservation may only find floor space in the Sikh Gurudwara.

To reach **Hemkund** (6 km further on, 4329 m) after 1 km from Ghangharia leave the main Valley of Flowers track, up a path to the right. **Guru Gobind Singh** is believed to have sat here in meditation during a previous incarnation, see page 1342. It is an important Sikh pilgrimage site. On the shore of the lake where pilgrims bathe in the icy cold waters is a modern *gurudwara*; well worth the long trek though some may suffer from the high altitude. Hemkund is also a Hindu pilgrimage site, referred to as **Lokpal**. Lakshman, the younger brother of Rama, meditated by the lake and regained his health after being severely wounded by Ravana's son, Meghnath. A small Lakshman temple stands near the *gurudwara*. Despite its ancient connections, Hemkund/Lokpal was 'discovered' by a Sikh *Havildar*, Solan Singh, and only became a major pilgrimage centre after 1930.

The 14-km trail from Govindghat to Ghangharia runs along a narrow forested valley past the villages of **Pulna** and **Bhiyundar**. The **Valley of Flowers** (3000-3600 m; best time to visit July-August), is a further 5 km. **Hathi Parbat** (Elephant Peak), at 6700 m, rises dramatically at the head of the narrow side valley. Close views of mountains can be seen from Bhiyundar. The trek has beautifully varied scenery. After crossing the Alaknanda River by suspension bridge the winding path follows the Laxman Ganga as its constant companion, passing dense forests and commanding panoramic views of the lovely Kak Bhusundi Valley on its way to the hamlet of **Ghangaria** (Govind Dham), the base for the Valley of Flowers, nestling amidst giant deodars. As the path from Ghangaria gradually climbs to the Valley of Flowers, glaciers, snow bridges, alpine flowers and wildlife appear at intervals.

The 6-km-long and 2-km-wide U-shaped valley is laced by waterfalls. The River Pushpati and many other small streams wind across it, and its floor, carpeted with alpine flowers during the monsoons, are particularly beautiful. It is especially popular because of its accessibility.

The valley was popularized by **Frank Smythe**, the well-known mountaineer, in 1931. Local people had always kept clear of the valley because of the belief that it was haunted, and any who entered it would be spirited away. A memorial stone to Margaret Legge, an Edinburgh botanist, who slipped and fell to her death in 1939 reads, "I will lift up mine eyes unto the hills from whence cometh my strength".

Satopanth

Satopanth, a glacial lake, takes a day to reach from Badrinath, 25 km away, via the track along the Alaknanda Valley (take a guide); it's a gentle climb up to **Mana** village (6 km north) near the border, inhabited by Bhotias. Foreigners need to register here and deposit their cameras since they are not permitted to take photographs. Nearby is the cave where Vyasa is said to have written the epic *Mahabharata*.

The track disappears and you cross a snowbridge, trek across flower-filled meadows before catching sight of the impressive 144-m **Vasudhara Falls**. The ascent becomes more difficult as you approach the source of the

Tip...

Continue your walk from Govinghharia up to Hemkund Sahib – a lake high in the Himalayas and a stunning Sikh pilgrimage site.

Alaknanda near where the Satopanth and Bhagirathi Kharak glaciers meet. The remaining trek takes you across the **Chakra Tirth** meadow and over the steep ridge of the glacier till you see the striking green Satopanth Lake. According to legend its three corners mark the seats of Brahma, Vishnu and Siva. The peaks of **Satopanth** (7084 m) from which the glacier flows, **Neelkanth** (6558 m) and **Chaukhamba** (7164 m) make a spectacular sight.

Listings Badrinath and around

Where to stay

Badrinath
For pilgrims there are *dharamshalas* and *chattis* (rest houses), T01381-225204.

$$ Devlok (GMVN)
Near bus stand, T01381-222212.
The best option in the trekking area with 30 large rooms and a restaurant.

Hemkund and Valley of Flowers
Ghangaria was badly affected by the floods in 2013, although the Hemkund Yatra did start again in Oct 2013.

$$$ Himalayan Eco Lodges
Ghangharia, T01244-081500 (Gurgaon), www.himalayanecolodges.com.
Good tents with attached bathrooms, price includes meals and tea. Check out their other locations.

$$-$ Hotel Bhagat
At the far end of Govindghat, T(0)94129-36360, www.hotelbhagat.com.
Good clean rooms – a cut above the rest.

$ Krishna
Ghangharia.
Rooms with bath.

Forest Rest House and Govind Singh Gurudwara
Govindghat.
Free beds and food to all (donations accepted) and reliable cloakroom service for trekkers.

Nainital
& around

Kumaon's hill stations offer access to some relatively unexplored sections of the Himalaya. Nainital itself is a congested Indian holiday town set around a steadily diminishing lake, albeit in the midst of some excellent birdwatching territory. Further northeast, the lush hillsides around Almora have inspired some of India's greatest mystics, and now provide a venue for some interesting projects in sustainable tourism.

Nainital *Colour map 1, C5.*

escape the heat at this hill station

Much of the historic appeal of Nainital (population 50,000, altitude 1938 m) has waned with the influx of mass tourism. Its villas, bungalows and fine houses are popular with Indian holidaymakers in the summer season. There are some attractive walks close to the town but many now prefer to break the journey to Almora from Corbett or Rishikesh at Ranikhet instead.

Essential Nainital

Finding your feet

The nearest railway station is 1¾ hours away at Kathgodam, linked to Nainital by frequent buses. The climb from Kathgodam to Nainital is dramatic, rising 1300 m over 30 km. The road follows the valley of the Balaya stream then winds up the hillsides through forests and small villages. After the long drive the town around the *tal* (lake) appears suddenly; the land south and on the plains side falls away quite steeply so you only see the lake when you are at its edge.

Buses from Delhi and the surrounding hill stations use the Tallital Bus Stand at the southern end of the lake, while some buses from Ramnagar (for Corbett National Park) use the Mallital Bus Stand at the northern end.

Getting around

The Mall, pedestrianized at peak times, is the hub of Nainital's life. You can hire a cycle-rickshaw if the walk feels too much, or take a taxi for travelling further afield. See Transport, page 190.

Congestion and pollution are taking their toll, particularly on the fragile ecosystem of the lake. It can be very cold in winter, and depressions sometimes bring cloud and rain, obscuring the views of the mountains.

Sights

There is little of architectural interest other than the colonial-style villas overlooking the lake (walking is the major attraction of this town). The **Church of St John in the Wilderness** (1846), one of the earliest buildings, is beyond Mallital, below the Nainital Club. The most distinctive building is **Government House** (1899, now the Secretariat) which was designed in stone by FW Stephens who was also responsible for VT (now CST) and Churchgate Stations in Mumbai. Early in the season it is pleasant to walk round (the Lower Mall is pedestrianized) or take a boat across the lake; remember it can still be very cold in March.

Naina (Cheena) Peak (2610 m) is a 5-km walk from the lake. From the top, there are stunning views of the Himalaya including Nanda Devi (7816 m) and the mountains on the Tibetan border. In season there is a **'cable car'** (ropeway) ⓘ *0900-1700, winter 1000-1600, Rs 15 return,*

BACKGROUND

Nainital

In 1839 the small hamlet of Nainital was 'discovered' by a Mr P Barron, a sugar manufacturer from Saharanpur. He was so impressed by the 1500-m-long and 500-m-wide lake that he returned with a sailing boat a year later, carried up in sections from the plains. In due course Nainital became the summer capital of the then United Provinces.

An old legend of Siva and Sati, see page 1329, associates the place as where Sati's eyes fell (hence *naini*). The *tal* (lake) is surrounded by seven hills, the Sapta-Shring.

On 18 September 1880 disaster struck the town. At the north end of the lake, known now as Mallital (the southern part is Tallital) stood the **Victoria Hotel**. In two days nearly 1000 mm of rain fell leading to a landslip which crushed some outhouses, burying several people. The cliff overhanging the hotel collapsed, burying the soldiers and civilians engaged in rescue work and making it impossible to save the 150 buried. Later the area was levelled, became known as The Flats, and was used for public meetings and impromptu games of football and cricket. Today it is more a bus park in the tourist season, though sports tournaments are held here in June, August and December.

which runs from the Mallital end of the lake to Snow View (2270 m), another good vantage point for viewing the snow-capped peaks. It is also possible to make the 2-km steep climb up to the viewpoint from the north end of the lake, passing the small Tibetan *gompa* which has fluttering prayer flags marking it.

Hanumangarh with a small temple off Haldwani Road, and the **Observatory** ① *3 km from the lake, Mon-Sat 1400-1600 and 1930-2100*, further along the path, have lookouts for watching the sun set over the plains. The opposite side has only a few cottages and much higher up near the ridge are two private boys' schools – Sherwood College and St Joseph's. The atmospheric **British Cemetery** with its crumbling graves is about 3 km southeast of town. Take the minor road at the south end of the lake (not the Rampur Road); on the right side, the remains of the entrance gate are just visible behind some trees.

Trips from Nainital

Sat Tal, 24 km away, has seven lakes including the jade green Garud Tal, the olive green Rama Tal and Sita Tal. **Naukuchiyatal**, 26 km away, is a lake with nine corners, hence the name. It is beautifully unspoilt and quiet paddling round the lake allows you to see lots of birds; boats for hire. Tour buses stop around 1630.

Pangot, 15 km from Nainital via Kilbury, is in ideal birding territory where over 580 species have been recorded. **Jeolikote**, a small hamlet on the main road up from Ranpur, 18 km south of Nainital, is known for its health centre and butterflies, honey and mushrooms. It offers a peaceful weekend retreat.

Listings Nainital *map p188*

Tourist information

KMVN Information Centre Head Office
Oak Park House, T05942-236356.

KMVN Information
T05942-231436.

Where to stay

Peak rates (given here) can be high. Off-season discounts of up to 60% are usual but may mean inadequate heating.

$$$$ Shervani Hilltop Inn
Waverly Rd, T05942-233800,
www.shervanihotels.com.
21 rooms in an old royal home, some in cottages and some in a new block but

in keeping with heritage style of hotel. It's peaceful, and there's a lovely garden and a free jeep to the centre.

$$$$-$$$ Abbotsford
Prasada Bhawan, T05942-236188,
www.abbotsford.in.
There are just 4 rooms in this stunning former summer mansion for the Agra and Oudh's ruler.

Nainital

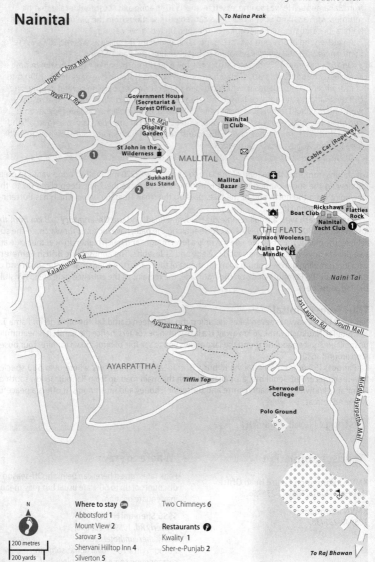

To Naina Peak

Upper China Mall

Waverly Rd ❹

Government House (Secretariat & Forest Office)

Nainital Club

The Mall Display Garden

St John in the Wilderness ❶

MALLITAL

Cable Car (Ropeway)

Sukhatal Bus Stand ❷

Mallital Bazar

Rickshaws Flatties Rock

Boat Club

THE FLATS

Nainital Yacht Club ❶

Kumaon Woolens

Naina Devi Mandir

Kaladhungi Rd

Naini Tai

East Laggan Rd

South Mall

Ayarpattha Rd

AYARPATTHA

Tiffin Top

Middle Ayarpatha Mall

Sherwood College

Polo Ground

To Raj Bhawan

N

200 metres
200 yards

Where to stay 🛏
Abbotsford **1**
Mount View **2**
Sarovar **3**
Shervani Hilltop Inn **4**
Silverton **5**

Two Chimneys **6**

Restaurants 🍴
Kwality **1**
Sher-e-Punjab **2**

A classic mountain house with tinned roof and pinewood flooring and art deco interiors. Library with antiquarian books.

$$$ Two Chimneys
House No 1, Chinkuwa, Village Gethia, T05942-224541, www.twochimneysgethia.com.
With 1 careful British lady owner back in the 1890s, this thoughtfully renovated property has bags of history and myth. Simple but beautiful rooms, lovely pool, you can even stay in the goat shed. Perfect place to read Tarun J Tejpal's *Alchemy of Desire* which was inspired by this house and its stories. Also lovely for birdwatching. Recommended.

$$$-$$ Rewa Retreat
Ramgarh Rd, Bhowali, T(0)9411-199490, www.rewaretreat.com.
Friendly place with spacious airy rooms. There is an art gallery with local Kumaon *aiparn* folk art.

$$ Silverton
Sher-ka-Danda, 2.5 km to centre, T05942-235549, www.hotelsilverton.com.
27 rooms in 'chalets', some with good views, peaceful, vegetarian restaurant.

$$-$ Sarovar
Near Tallital Bus Stand, T05942-235570.
Good value, with 30 rooms, 8-bed dorms, hot water.

$ Mount View (KMVN)
Near Sukhatal Bus Stand, T05942-235400, www.kmvn.org.
Good value, 42 small, grubby rooms with bath, some with TV. There's also a restaurant and gardens.

Restaurants

There are a few decent restaurants in town. The good chain restaurant Kwality, on the lake, and Kumaon Farm Products, towards Ropeway, are great for vegetarian snacks.

$ Sher-e-Punjab
Mallital Bazar.
Tasty, North Indian. Halfway to Tallital, serving very good local Kumaon dishes.

What to do

Boating
Boat Club, *Mallital, T05942-235153.* Sail on the lake or try out a pedal boat.

Fishing
Permits for the lake from Executive Officer, Nagar Palika. For other lakes, contact the Fisheries Officer in Bhimtal.

Horse riding

There is a horse stand in Bara Pathar. Various treks: Snow View; Tiffin Top; Naina (Chinna) Peak (2½-3 hrs; can leave at 0500 to see sunrise from the top, but dress warmly); Naina Devi; horses are generally fit and well cared for. You can no longer ride through the town itself. You can phone Nainital Tourism for more info T05942-237476.

Mountaineering and trekking

Equipment can be hired from **Nainital Mountaineering Club** (T05942-222051), and **KMVN** (Tourist Office, Mallital, T05942-236356). The club organizes rock climbing at Barapathar, 3 km away.

Tour operators

Parvat Tours & Information (KMVN), *Dandi House, Tallital, near rickshaw stand, T05942-235656, among others on the Mall*. Day tours: Sat tal; Ranikhet; Mukteshwar (with the Veterinary Research Centre); Kaladhungi. 2-day trips: Kausani; Ranikhet/Almora; Corbett.
Shakti Experience, *T01244-563899, www.shakti himalaya.com*. Educated guides steer you through the pristine mountain terrain between villages in the Kumaon. Food is immaculate and cooked by local villagers. Accommodation is with local families, in rooms that are adapted to an elegantly understated high standard. A highly recommended way to immerse yourself in rural India.

Transport

Wherever possible, avoid night driving. The hill roads can be dangerous. Flat, straight stretches are rare, road lighting does not exist and villagers frequently drive their animals along them or graze them at the curbside. During the monsoon (Jun-Sep) landslides are fairly common. Usually these are cleared promptly but in the case of severe slips requiring days to clear, bus passengers are transferred.

On the Mall Rd there is an **access toll** of Rs 50. Access is barred, May, Jun, Oct: heavy vehicles, 0800-1130, 1430-2230; light vehicles, 1800-2200; Nov-Apr: all vehicles, 1800-2000.

Air The nearest airport is Pantnagar (71 km) on the plains; No flights at time of writing.

Bus **Roadways**, Tallital, for major inter-city services, T05942-235518, 0930-1200, 1230-1700; **DTC**, Hotel Ashok, Tallital, T35180. **Kumaon Motor Owners' Union (KMOU)**, bus stand near tourist office, Sukhatal, Mallital, T05942-235451; used by private operators. Regular services to **Almora** (66 km, 3 hrs); **Dehra Dun** (390 km); **Delhi** (322 km), a/c night coach, 2100 (8-9 hrs), or via Haldwani. **Haridwar** (390 km, 8 hrs); **Kausani** (120 km, 5 hrs); **Ranikhet** (60 km, 3 hrs) and **Ramnagar** for **Corbett** (66 km, 3½ hrs plus 3½ hrs).

Rickshaw Cycle-rickshaw and *dandi* Rs 5-10 along The Mall.

Ropeway Cable car/gondola, from 'Poplars', Mallital (near GB Pant Statue) to Snow View, summer 0800-1730 in theory, but usually opens at 1000, winter 1000-1630, return fare Rs 150, advance booking recommended in season, tickets valid for a 1-hr halt at the top. Some claim its anchorage is weak.

Taxi From **Parvat Tours** (see Tour operators, above).

Train All India computerized reservation office, Tallital Bus Stand, T05942-235518. Mon-Fri, 0900-1200, 1400-1700, Sat, 0900-1200. The nearest railhead is **Kathgodam** (35 km), taxi, Rs 850 (peak season), bus Rs 30. **Delhi (OD)**: *Ranikhet Exp 15014*, 7 hrs. Towards **Dehradun** and **Haridwar (OD)**: *Dehradun-Kathgodam Exp 14321*, 9 hrs. **Kolkata (H)** via **Lucknow** and **Gorakhpur**, *Howrah Bagh Exp 13020*, 40 hrs (Lucknow 8 hrs, Gorakhpur 15 hrs).

Almora and around *Colour map 1, C5.*

Almora (population 32,500, altitude 1646 m) is a charming bustling hill town occupying a picturesque horseshoe-shaped ridge, 66 km northeast of Nainital. It's an important market town and administrative centre, and is also regarded as the cultural capital of the area. It richly rewards exploring. The Mall runs about 100 m below the ridge line, while the pedestrianized historic bazar above is jostling and colourful.

The town was founded in 1560 by the Chand Dynasty who ruled over most of Kumaon, which comprises the present districts of Nainital, Almora and Pithoragarh. Overrun by the Gurkhas in 1798, it was heavily bombed by the British as they tried to expel them in the Gurkha Wars of 1814-1815. Traces of an old Chand fort, stone-paved roads, wooden houses with beautifully carved façades and homes decorated with traditional murals, reflect its heritage.

Swami Vivekenanda came to Almora and gained enlightenment in a small cave at **Kasar Devi** on Kalimatiya Hill, 7 km northeast of town. This is a tranquil mountain hamlet with stunning views, visited by everyone from Cat Stevens to DH Lawrence, and was dubbed '**Crank's Ridge**' after Timothy Leary streaked here in the 1960s. Another vantage point for sunrise and sunset is **Bright End Corner**, 2.5 km southwest of Mall Road, near All India Radio. The stone **Udyotchandesvar Temple**, above Mall Road, houses Kumaon's presiding deity, Nanda Devi, whose festival is in August/September.

Almora's Tamta artisans still use traditional methods to work with copper. Copper metallurgy was used here as early as the second century BC and is associated with the Kuninda Dynasty who traded in copper articles. The hand-beaten copper pots are 'silver plated' in the traditional way, *kalhai*.

Jageswar, 34 km northeast, lies beside a brook in a dappled clearing in the nape of a serene cedar wooded gorge. It is famous for the 164 ornamented temples built by the Chand rajas and also holds one of the 12 *jyotirlingas*. The scores of temples here, shaded by the trees' canopy, and in nearby Gandeswar are very fine examples of early medieval hill temple architecture but are rarely visited by outsiders. Some elegant examples of vernacular architecture lie in the village.

The temple dedicated to Jogeswar with finely carved pillars has a small museum; 6 km before Jageswar, a roadside sign points to stone-age **cave paintings**, about 50 m off the road. Though several paintings were damaged by storage of cement bags during bridge-building work nearby, many can be seen and are worth the short stop.

Once the capital of the Chand rajas, **Binsar** has a bird sanctuary sited at 2410 m with panoramic mountain views. It is 28 km away.

Kausani *Colour map 1, C5.*

Around 50 km north of Almora, Kausani (altitude 1892 m) sits on a narrow ridge among pine forests with wonderfully wide views of the **Nanda Devi** group of mountains stretching over 300 km along the horizon; the view is particularly stunning at sunrise. Modern Kausani has a strong military presence, so be careful with your camera. You may trek from here to Bageswar, Gwaldam and the Pindari Glacier. In 1929 **Mahatma Gandhi** spent 12 days at what is now Anashakti Ashram.

Baijnath and Garur *Colour map 1, C5.*

From Kausani, the road descends to Garur and Baijnath. The small town of **Baijnath** on the banks of the Gomti River, 17 km northwest of Kausani, has distinctively carved 12th-and 13th-century Katyuri temples. They are now mostly ruined, but its houses have intricately carved wooden doors and windows. The main 10th-century temple houses a beautiful image of Parvati. Siva and Parvati are believed to have married at the confluence of the Gomti and Garur Ganga. The Katyur Dynasty, which ruled the valley for 500 years, took their name from Siva and Parvati's mythical son, Karttikeya. **Garur** has plenty of buses and taxis northwards. Just north of Garur a road runs to Gwaldam and another east to Bageshwar.

Dunagiri

Dunagiri (altitude 2400 m) is a small village 65 km north of Almora en route to the pilgrimage sites of the Char Dham. It is steeped in spiritual legend and has been the home of many yogis and sages including Mahavatar Babaji (there is an account of a meeting between Babaji and Lahiri Mahashaya in a cave at Dunagiri in *Autobiography of a Yogi*) and Neemkaroli Baba who was the guide for US teacher Ram Dass (formerly Harvard professor Dr Richard Alpert and co-conspirator of Timothy Leary) in the 1960s. There is a powerful Shakti temple here – Dunagiri Devi. See box, above, for more on the myths of the area.

Bageshwar and the Saryu Valley

Bageshwar (altitude 960 m), meaning Siva as 'Lord of Eloquent Speech', stands at the confluence of the Gomti and Saryu rivers, 90 km north of Almora and 23 km east of Baijnath. It is Kumaon's most important pilgrimage centre and has several temples, the most important of which is the 17th-century Bhagnath temple, overlooking the confluence.

From Bageshwar a jeep road runs northwards along the Saryu, through beautiful wooded gorges where lammergeiers and griffon vultures soar overhead, to Talai. This is an alternative trailhead for treks to the **Pindari Glacier**, and also gives access to a string of beautiful villages perched on mountainsides among terraced fields and rhododendron forests: Supi, Basham and Khal Jhuni. This area has virtually no tourist infrastructure, but is being developed by the communities in association with **Village Ways** (see Where to stay, opposite).

Munsiari

Munsiari (altitude 2300 m) is a quiet hill town, 207 km from Almora, overlooked by the majestic five peaks of **Panchchuli** which, in legend, served as the five *chulis* (stoves) used to cook the last meal of the five Pandava brothers before they ascended to heaven. Munsiari is a base for treks into the Milam, Ralam and Namik glaciers, and towards Panchchuli. It is also the start of an easy trek (three to four days) via Namik to Dwali in the Pindar Valley.

Pithoragarh *Colour map 1, C5.*

Sitting in a small valley with some fine temples built by the Chands, it is overlooked by a hill fort, 7 km away, dating from times when the town was at the crossroads of trade routes. The district, separated from Almora in 1962, borders Nepal and Tibet and has a number of high peaks such as Nanda Devi East (7434 m) and West (7816 m), and offers trekking to many glaciers including **Milam**, **Namik**, **Ralam** and **Panchchuli**. See page 39 (no permit needed). There are good views from **Chandak Hill** (1890 m), 7 km away. It is on the Pilgrim road to **Mount Kailash** and **Mansarovar Lake**. The Mount Kailash trek (Indian nationals only) starts from Askot (The only way to go to Mount Kailash if you are a foreigner is from the Chinese side). The place is known for its fine gold and silver jewellery and bowls carved out of *sal* wood.

Tourist information

Almora

Almora Tourism
Opposite GPO, T05962-230180. Open 1000-1700.

KMVN
Holiday Home, 2 km west of the bus stop.
T05942-231436, www.kmvn.gov.in.
Regional tourist office. Contact for details
of rest houses and budget treks to Pindari,
Panchachuli, Adi Kailash (from Rs 3000 for
1 week).

Where to stay

KMVN (see above), has rest houses throughout
the state, including: Bhimtal; Ramnagar;
Almora; Ranikhet; Jageshwar; Binsar, Munsyari;
Dharchula; Kausani; Pindari Glacier route; and
Kashipur.

$$$$ The Cottage
Nestled on the hillside, Jeolikot, T05942-224013,
www.thecottagejeolikot.com.
Swiss-chalet style, with 6 beautiful spacious rooms
with good valley views, great walks to be had,
delicious meals included. Highly recommended.

$$$ Jungle Lore Birding Lodge
Pangot, T0120-422 2797 (book through Asian
Adventures Delhi), www.pangot.com.
Comfortable cottages and huts with baths,
2 tents with shared facilities, meals included
(from home-grown produce), library, naturalist
guides. Over 200 species of bird on property.
Recommended.

$$ Lake Side
Naukuchiyatal, T05942-247138, www.kmvn.org.
Well-maintained and attractive 12 rooms and
dorm (Rs 100).

Almora
Most hotels give off-season discounts of 50%.

$$-$ Holiday Home (KMVN)
2 km southwest of the bus stand, T05962-
230250, www.kmvn.gov.in.
14 simple cottages and 18 rooms with hot
bath, dorm (Rs 60), restaurant, garden, good
mountain views.

$$-$ Savoy
Uphill opposite the GPO, near Uttarakhand
Tourism, T(0)9411-327415.
17 good-sized but basic rooms, some with
hot bath, restaurant, pleasant terrace and
quiet garden.

$ Shyam
East and uphill from bus stand on LR Shah Rd,
T05962-235467, www.hotelshyam.com.
18 small but clean rooms, good terrace views.

Around Almora

$$$ Kalmatia Sangam
Kalimat Estate, T05962-251176,
www.kalmatia-sangam.com.
10 cottages with stunning mountain views
spread across the hillside on the approach to
Kesar Devi. Some beds are on a mezzanine from
where you can see Nanda Devi. Cottages are
named after local birds, such as the Himalaya
magpie and the cuckoo. The construction
and day-to-day running of the cottages is
environmentally friendly.

$$$ Village Ways
T05946-260 379, www.villageways.com.
This excellent community-based enterprise can
arrange stays in lovely guesthouses managed by
locals with fantastic tours and treks around Binsar
Wildlife Sanctuary and Supi Village. (See What to
do, below).

$$$-$$ Mohan's Binsar Retreat
Kasar Devi Binsar Rd, T05962-251215,
www.mohansbinsarretreat.com.
Characterful place with amazing views,
close to the bird sanctuary.

$$-$ Nanda Devi (KMVN)
In the heart of the sanctuary, Binsar,
T05962-251110.
Only filtered rainwater, electricity from solar
batteries for few hours each evening.

$$-$ Tourist Rest House (KMVN)
Binsar, T(0)86500 02537.
On a thickly wooded spur near Nanda Devi,
1920s with antique cutlery and table linen lists
still hanging on the walls. The furniture and
decor are evocative of the Raj, and the caretaker
may occasionally be persuaded to open the
house for a viewing.

Jageshwar

$ Jageshwar Jungle Lodge
Near Jataganga, T(0)9818-069440,
www.jageshwarjunglelodge.com.
Airy rooms with pretty balconies, nice
grounds, with a pleasant 25-min walk
to the Jageshwar temples.

$ Tara
T05962-263068, www.jageshwar.co.uk.
A cottage set in a garden with 6 simple rooms
on the hillside above the tourist office bungalow,
overlooking the beautiful temple.

Kausani

$$$-$$ Kausani Best Inn
View Point Kausani Estate, T05962-258310,
www.kausanibestinn.com.
Great views and long verandas at this small hotel
with 8 rooms. Good Kumaoni home-cooked
food. No lie-ins though; the staff insist that you
see the spectacular sunrise!

$$-$ Uttarakhand
5-min walk from bus stand, T05962-258012,
www.uttarakhandkausani.com.
Clean and spacious rooms in a freshly
upgraded hotel.

$ Trishul (KMVN)
2 km from town, T05962-258006,
www.kmvn.gov.in.
12 deluxe rooms plus 12 separate cottages, food
available with a few hours' notice. Superb views
and compass on the lawn to spot the peaks.

Dunagiri

$$$ Dunagiri Nature Retreat
Dunagiri Village, 2 hrs from Kausani,
T(0)9810-267719, www.dunagiri.com.
With 360-degree views and at 2400 m, you can
literally feel on top of the world at this beautiful
retreat space. You can walk to the Sukhdevi
temple from here; Sukhdev Muni was the son
of Ved-Vyasa, a great Rishi (seer) and author of
the *Mahabharata*. This whole area is steeped in
the legends of the Vedas. Simple rooms, friendly
atmosphere and organic vegetables available.
Recommended.

Bageshwar and the Saryu Valley

$$$$ 360 Leti
In the village of Leti, near Sharma village,
2 hrs north of Bageshwar, T0124-456 3899,
www.shaktihimalaya.com. Oct to Apr.
4 understated but exquisitely deluxe cottages
on a 2700-m plateau at the very brink of
the Himalaya in the Ramganga Valley. Solar
electricity, en suites, private sit outs, Indian,
Tibetan and continental food, guided tours, yoga
and meditation by appointment, but the main
prize are the glorious views of sky and mountains.
Absolutely unique.

$$ Wayfarer Retreat
Vijaypur, 13 km before Chaukori, T011-4106
2463, book via www.campsindia.com.
Cottages surrounded by forest, nighttime
campfires and good home-cooked food.
Camps of India have a whole host of tented
accommodation through Uttarkhand (and India
at large).

$ Gomati
Pindari Rd, Bageshwar, a 2-min walk from bus
stand, T05963-220071.
Smart, newly refurbished rooms, some with
views over mango orchards and river. Good
room service meals and obliging staff.

Munsiyari

$$$ Wayfarer Munsiyari
1 km beyond town, T011-4760 3625,
www.wayfareradventures.com.
Comfortable Swiss tents, toilets, electricity,
phone, forest walks, treks, trout fishing, jeeps,
professionally run.

$ Tourist Rest House
Main road just before the town, T05961-222339.
Comfortable, welcome hot showers, good value;
also 2 other cheap lodges.

Pithoragarh

$ Ulka Devi (KMVN)
T05964-225434.
Has a restaurant. Others near the bus station are
very basic.

Restaurants

Almora
There is plenty of choice along the busy Mall Rd including **Glory** for North Indian.

$ Dolma's Place
Papersallie village near Kasar Devi.
Fluffy pancakes, good Tibetan dishes, as well as lemon ginger tea and spring rolls.

$ Mohan's
Binsar Rd, Kasar Devi, T05962-251215, mohan_rayal72@hotmail.com.
Popular backpacker hangout with excellent pizza, internet and confectionery and travel services. Also has 4 rooms down the hillside with kitchenettes.

Festivals

Almora
Sep-Oct **Dasara** is celebrated with colourful Ramlila pageants. There is also **Kumaon Festival of Arts.**

Shopping

Almora
Almora Kithab Ghar, *The Mall*. Has a good selection of books.
Anokhe Lal Hari Kishan Karkhana, *Bazar Almora, T05962-230158*. Traditional copper ware manufacturer.
Ashok Traders. Also sells local copper articles.
Panchachuli Women Weavers Cooperative, *www.panchachuli.co.uk*. 10-year-old self-sufficient artisan cooperative turning high-quality raw materials into beautiful pashmina, lambswool, merino and sheepswool stoles, fabrics, scarves and tweeds. Expensive but stunning.

What to do

Almora
High Adventure, *Mall Rd, opposite the Post Office, T(0)9012-354501*. Organizes treks, cave tours, bus tickets.
Village Ways, *Khali Estate, Ayapani, Almora, T05946-260 379, www.villageways.com*. This award-winning community-based enterprise runs walking tours of 9-12 days through the Binsar Wildlife Sanctuary, staying in specially constructed guesthouses managed by locals.

The tours take in beautiful scenery and provide an interesting insight into village life, while bolstering economic opportunities for the villagers.

Bageshwar and the Saryu Valley
Village Ways, *see above for contact details*. In a similar vein to the company's tours in Binsar, but here the walking is through wilder country around Supi village, with the high Himalaya almost at your fingertips. Nights in cosy village guesthouses are combined with a campout on alpine meadows at 3000 m, with exhilarating sunrise views of the Nanda Devi range. Guiding, accommodation and food are all of a high standard.

Munsiari
Nanda Devi Mountaineering Institution, in the SBI Building. In the main bazar is **Panchuli Trekking** and **Nanda Devi Trekking**, the former run by an elderly Milam tribal villager who has vast and accurate knowledge of the area.

Transport

Almora
Bus Connect Almora with **Kathgodam** (90 km, 3 hrs) for rail links, and with **Nainital** (3 hrs) and **Ranikhet** (2½ hrs). Hourly buses to **Kausani** (3 hrs). For the **Nepal border**, take a bus from the Dhara Naula bus stand (4 km from town centre) to Champawat, and change there for Banbassa.

Jeep Share jeeps to **Ranikhet**, Rs 70; **Kathgodam**, Rs 120. For **Nainital**, take **Haldwani** jeep as far as **Bhowali**, then bus or jeep to Nainital.

Kausani
Bus From **Almora** and **Ranikhet** (2½-3½ hrs). **Joshimath** is a tough but spectacular 10-hr journey.

Bageshwar and the Saryu Valley
Buses and share jeeps to **Almora**. To reach the far end of the Saryu Valley, take jeeps bound for Kapkot, and change there for Song or Munar.

Munsiari
Bus From **Almora**, change at Thal; from **Haldwani** or **Nainital**, take a bus to Pithoragarh and change. To **Almora** (11 hrs) and **Pithoragarh** (8 hrs), 0500 and another for Pithoragarh in the afternoon.

Corbett
National Park

★ The journey from Delhi to one of the finest wildlife parks in
India offers excellent views of the almost flat, fertile and densely
populated Ganga-Yamuna doab, one of the most prosperous agricultural
regions of North India. Corbett is India's first national park and one of its
few successfully managed tiger reserves. As well as superb wildlife it is also
extremely picturesque with magnificent sub-montane and riverain views.

Visiting the park   Colour map 1, C5.

rich and varied wildlife and birdlife

Wildlife
Corbett National Park (altitude 400-1200 m) has always been noted for its tigers; there are now
over 150 but they are not easily spotted. About 10% of visitors see one, usually entering at the
Bijrani Gate. There are leopards too but they are seldom seen. Sambar, chital, para (hog deer) and
muntjac (barking deer) are the main prey of the big cats and their population fluctuates around
20,000. Some, like the chital, are highly gregarious whilst the large sambar, visually very impressive
with its antlers, is usually solitary. The two commonly seen monkeys of North India are the rhesus
(a macaque – reddish face and brownish body) and the common langur (black face and silvery
coat). Elephants are now permanent inhabitants since the Ramganga Dam has flooded their old
trekking routes. There are a few hundred of them and they are seen quite often. Other animals
include porcupine and wild boar (often seen around Dhikala – some can be quite dangerous,
attacking unsuspecting visitors who have food with them). In total there are more than 50 species
of mammal alone, though the dam appears to have caused significant losses. The last swamp deer
was seen in March 1978, and the loss of habitat has been keenly felt by the cheetal, hog deer and
porcupine, all of which appear to be declining.

There are 26 species of reptile and seven of amphibian. In certain stretches of the river and in the
Ramganga Lake are the common mugger crocodile: notices prohibiting swimming warn "Survivors
will be prosecuted"! The fish-eating gharial can also be found, as can soft-shelled tortoises, otters
and river fish. The python is quite common.

The birdlife is especially impressive with over 600 species including a wide range of water birds,
birds of prey such as the crested serpent eagle, harriers, Pallas' fishing eagle, osprey, buzzards and
vultures. Woodland birds include: Indian and great pied hornbills, parakeets, laughing thrushes,
babblers and cuckoos. Doves, bee-eaters, rollers, bulbuls, warblers, finches, robins and chats are to
be seen in the open scrub from the viewing towers. The rarer ibisbill is one of the main attractions for
serious twitchers.

Vegetation
There are 110 species of trees, 51 species of shrubs, three species of bamboos and 27 species of
climbers. The valley floor is covered with tall elephant grass (Nal in the local terminology), lantana
bushes and patches of sal and sheesham (Dalbergia sissoo) forest, whilst the enclosing hills on both
sides are completely forest covered, with sal, bakli, khair, jhingan, tendu, pula and sain. Charas grows
wild in the fields. Nullahs and ravines running deep into the forests are dry for much of the year, but
there are swift torrents during the monsoon. These hold brakes of bamboo and thick scrub growth.

Essential Corbett National Park

Finding your feet

The main gate at Dhangarhi (for Dhikala) is approximately 16 km north of Ramnagar on the Ranikhet road. Only visitors who are staying overnight may enter Dhikala. Day visits are allowed at the Amdanda and Laldhang gates for Bijrani and Jhirna respectively. There are also entry gates for the Sonanadi Wildlife Sanctuary, which borders Corbett to the north and forms part of the larger tiger reserve, at Sonanadi and Doumunda.

Getting around

A limit of 30 vehicles per day at each entrance is applied, half of which can be booked in advance – try to reserve at the time of booking your accommodation, with several months' notice.

Prior reservation to enter is recommended for day visits, although not always necessary at dawn, when half the entry is determined on a first-come first-served basis. This can mean queuing for hours in the dark in Ramnagar, being shuffled from one office to another, and still not getting in – you may be refused entry when the quota is filled. Travel agents cannot help as they are not allowed to apply for permits. A reservation at the Bijrani or Dhela **Forest Rest Houses** does not entitle visitors to enter by the Dhangari Gate.

From 1 March until the monsoon all roads around Dhikala, except the main approach road, are closed between 1100 and 1500 when visitors are not allowed to move about the forest. Most of the park is closed 30 June to 15 October; the Dhikala section is closed 15 June to 15 November.

Entry fees

For information, contact the **Corbett Tiger Reserve Reception Centre**, T05947-251489. Current fees and opening hours are also available from the website: www.corbett nationalpark.in. At **Dhikala Gate**: foreigners Rs 1000, Indians Rs 200, valid for three days (two nights); each additional day, Rs 450, Indians Rs 100. At **Bijrani**, **Sonanadi**, **Jhirna** and **Doumunda** gates: Rs 450, Indians Rs 100 per visit (four hours). Entrance permits are not transferable between gates (eg a morning visit to Bijrani and a night halt at Dhikala will require separate payment). **Vehicle fees**: Dhikala Rs 1500 per car/jeep, Indians Rs 500 (covers overnight stay). Bijrani, Sonanadi, Jhirna and Doumunda: Rs 500 per car/jeep, Indians Rs 250.

Viewing

Elephant rides are available from Dhikala, Khinanauli, Bijrani, Gairal and Jhirna. Each elephant can carry four people. This is the best way to see the jungle and the wildlife. Morning and evening, two hours, Rs 1000, Indians Rs 300 from government, more with private operators; book at Dhikala or Bijrani reception (whichever is relevant). Book as early as possible on arrival since these rides are very popular. **Cars** and **jeeps** may drive round part of the park. A seat in a **cantor** (large open-topped truck) costs Rs 1500 for foreigners, Rs 620 Indians for a full-day tour (0800-1800). Apart from the immediate area within the complex at Dhikala, **don't go walking in the park**. Tiger and elephant attacks are not unknown. The two watch towers are good vantage points for spotting wildlife. Night driving is not allowed in the park.

When to go

Rainfall is heavier in the higher hills; on average the valley receives 1550 mm, the bulk from July to mid-September. Summer days are hot but the nights quite pleasant. Winter nights can get very cold and there is often a frost and freezing fog in the low-lying tracts. Birdwatching is best between December and February. Summer is the best time for seeing the larger mammals, which become bolder in leaving the forest cover to come to the river and water holes; early summer is best for scenic charm and floral interest.

ON THE ROAD
Tiger, tiger, burning bright?

Jim Corbett was born in 1875 into the large family of the postmaster of Nainital. Fascinated as a child by the jungles surrounding his home, he developed a considerable knowledge of the eco-system's workings, while at the same time honing his rifle skills on the local population of tigers and leopards; he killed his first big cat at the age of eight, and continued to hunt throughout his career in the Bengal Northeast Railway.

But from the 1920s Corbett turned from hunting to photography, only picking up his gun to kill the man-eating cats that from time to time terrorized the Kumaon hills. Later in life he recounted his exploits in a series of books: *The Man-Eating Leopard of Rudraprayag*, *The Man-eaters of Kumaon* and *Jungle Lore*. These classic adventure stories were a major source of inspiration to Indian conservationists, who in 1973 instituted **Project Tiger** to protect the country's dwindling population of tigers.

The elder Corbett would rightfully be proud of the park that today bears his name. With a committed Field Director and motivated staff, the tiger population has, according to the latest census, climbed steadily over the last few years to reach 160 in early 2008.

Unfortunately, Corbett National Park seems to be one of Project Tiger's few success stories. As each park depends on its director's will and ability to use funds earmarked for conservation, poaching in many areas goes ignored, unchecked, and often denied.

Worldwide, tigers are vanishing at an alarming rate. Of a global population of around 3500 wild tigers, India currently holds roughly 1400 – a decline of 60% in the last 10 years. Many tigers live in parks. Many live in parks surrounded by human settlements, from which poaching gangs can easily gain access to the animals. A male tiger fetches up to Rs 60,000, and a tigress Rs 45,000, on the illegal international market, which is most heavily concentrated in China. If China goes through with its threat to contravene the CITES Treaty (Convention on the International Trade in Endangered Species) by lifting a ban on the use of tiger parts in medicine, pressure on the tiger is likely to become critical within the next decade.

If travellers can have any impact on this situation, it is by paying the ever-increasing entry fees to visit one or two national parks, and where possible staying in lodges that spread wealth to the local community. The UK-based organization **Travel Operators for Tigers** (T01285-643333, www.toftiger.org) offers a number of useful pointers to encourage pro-tiger tourism.

Beyond the park

Ramnagar Ramnagar, with a railway station, 134 km from Moradabad, is 18 km from the park boundary and 50 km from **Dhikala**. It is a noisy town with the Project Tiger Office for Corbett reservations, and provides a night halt. They will receive faxes and hold them.

Kaladhungi At Kaladhungi visit **Jim Corbett's house** ① *Rs 10*, now a small museum. The area is an extension of the Tiger Reserve with equally good wildlife but minus the restrictions, and is also excellent for birdwatching. If you turn up the road opposite and continue up into the hills, travelling along a delightful, metalled road that winds its way up the hillsides through *chir* pine forest and the occasional village, you'll see impressive views of the plains. You enter Nainital at the north end of the lake.

Ranikhet Rani Padmadevi, the queen of Raja Sudhardev is believed to have chosen the site of this scenic place, hence Ranikhet (Queen's Field). In 1869 the land was bought from local villagers and the British established a summer rest and recreation settlement for their troops, made it a cantonment town and developed it as a quiet hill station. Set along a 1800-m-high ridge, Ranikhet sprawls out through the surrounding forest without having a proper centre. This is one of its attractions and there are many enjoyable walks. The views from the ridge are magnificent and the twin peaks of Nanda Devi (at a height of 7816 m and 7434 m) can be clearly seen. **Uttarakhand Tourist Office** ① *The Mall, T05966-220127, 1000-1700*. At **Upat**, 6 km away, there is Kali temple.

Where to stay

Corbett National Park

Corbett is hugely popular, and it's essential to book your accommodation as far ahead as possible – up to 2 months in high season. If you are travelling to the park without reserved accommodation, you must go to Ramnagar first to make a booking. Dhikala is the park centre and has accommodation. Remember to get a clearance card from Dhikala from the office here before leaving in the morning.

Within the park

Reservations for all accommodation, except the Annexe at Dhikala, can be booked at the **Corbett Tiger Reserve Reception Centre** in Ramnagar, T05947-251489 or online at www.corbettonline. uk.gov.in. Office open daily 0830-1300, 1500-1700. Foreigners pay 2-3 times the price of Indians, and prices are raised frequently. Entry permits and vehicle charges are payable at the respective gate.

For information on the various rest houses, see www.corbettnationalpark.in as well and follow links to 'Permits and Reservations'. Rates range from Rs 400 per night for a dorm bed in Dhikala's Log Hut to Rs 5000 for a room in the **Old Forest Rest House**.

Outside the park

$$$$ Infinity Resorts
8 km north of Ramnagar, T(0)9650-193662, www.infinityresorts.com.
Established by the **Corbett Foundation**, who have done pioneering work in compensating farmers for lost livestock to prevent revenge killings of big cats. 24 rooms, pool, lawns, mango orchards, good food, old world feel, charming staff. Don't miss the Jim Corbett documentary. Elephant safaris and excellent birdlife. Highly recommended.

$$$$ Riverview Retreat
On the periphery of the park, T05947-284135, www.corbetthideaway.com.
1.2 ha of luxury tented accommodation actually inside the tiger sanctuary. The jungle cacophony is incredibly atmospheric, and staying a number of nights overlooking the stunning Ramganga river plain gets you a ringside seat to the park's wildlife. They also have the lovely **Corbett Hideaway** with lovely cottages.

$$$$-$$$ Corbett Ramganga Resort (WelcomHeritage)
Jhamaria, 17 km from Dhangarhi, T(0)9310-510582, www.ramganga.com.
10 well-appointed rooms in cottages, 8 Swiss cottage tents, safe spring water, river rafting, riding, climbing, gliding, fishing, excellent pool and picturesque position on river edge.

$$$ Tiger Camp
Dhikuli, T0120-422 2797. Book through Asian Adventures, www.tiger-camp.com.
20 cottages in Kumaoni Village style but modern interiors, rooms with fan and bath electricity (plus generator), good food, beautiful garden, jeep, hiking, friendly owner, lovely atmosphere. Recommended.

$$$-$$ Serenity
Close to Infinity Resorts, T05974-244415, www.serenitycorbett.com.
A good option with nice airy rooms and restaurant on-site.

$$-$ Sunbird Guest House
Dhikuli, T05947-284226, www.corbettsunbirdguesthouse.com.
Best of the budget options, clean and friendly place with a/c and non a/c options.

$ Homestay
Nature Shop, Dhikuli, close to Infinity.
Look for the **Nature Shop** sign (there are a few) and behind the shop are 2 lovely rooms. Basic but full of charm. Friendly family and home-cooked food.

Kaladhungi

$$$ Camp Corbett
25 km east of Corbett, T05942-242126, www.campcorbett.net.
Cottages and tents, wonderful meals, an outstanding resort run by the hospitable Anand family, relaxing and totally hassle free, pick-up from Haldwani station arranged. They also have **Mountain Quail Lodge** in Pangot, 1½ hrs from Corbett surrounded by oak and rhododendron forests.

Ranikhet

There are good Tourist Rest Houses (**$**) at **Kalika** (T05966-220893) and **Chilianaula** (T86500-02534), www.kmvn.gov.in. Chilianaula has stunning mountain views.

Good choice from 32 large rooms, restaurant, friendly staff, credit cards accepted, best in the town itself. You can choose from Himalaya or garden view.

What to do

Corbett National Park

KMVN runs 3-day tours from Delhi departing every Fri in season, around Rs 11000 for foreigners, Rs 9000 Indians, taxes extra.
Reservations: 1st floor, Indraprastha Building, Barakhamba Rd, New Delhi, T011-2371 2246, www.kmvn.gov.in, or from **Uttar Pradesh**

Tourist Office, Chandralok Building, 36 Janpath, New Delhi, T011-2335 0048.
Reception Centre in Ramnagar runs day tours to Dhikala – the only access to this part of the park without reserved accommodation.
Tigerland Safaris, *T05947-284173, www. tigerlandsafaris.com*. Well-organized safaris, professional service. Recommended.

Transport

Corbett National Park

Air Air India fly from Delhi into Phoolbagh airport at Pantnagar (130 km).

Bus The Delhi–Dhikala road (260 km) passes through Moradabad (turn left after Moradabad,

Corbett National Park

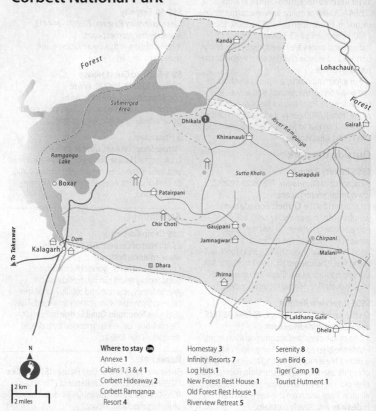

N

2 km
2 miles

Where to stay 🏠
Annexe **1**
Cabins 1, 3 & 4 **1**
Corbett Hideaway **2**
Corbett Ramganga
Resort **4**

Homestay **3**
Infinity Resorts **7**
Log Huts **1**
New Forest Rest House **1**
Old Forest Rest House **1**
Riverview Retreat **5**

Serenity **8**
Sun Bird **6**
Tiger Camp **10**
Tourist Hutment **1**

towards Kashipur and Ramnagar), 5½-6 hrs –
strewn with bus/lorry/car crashes. Frequent
buses from Ramnagar **Delhi**, **Dehra Dun**,
Moradabad, **Nainital** and **Ranikhet** (if coming
from Dhikala wait outside Dhangarhi gate, no
need to return to Ramnagar). Bus to **Dhikala**,
1530, not reliable; return leaves 1000 from
Dhikala after elephant ride.

Jeep These are becoming very expensive.
Expect to pay Rs 1800-2500 for a day. Hire from
near Ramnagar park office. Petrol vehicles are
cheaper (up to Rs 2000 per day) and quieter.
You also pay Rs 50 admission for the driver.

Train Nearest station is at Ramnagar (50 km),
for **Moradabad** and Delhi. To **Delhi (OD)**:
Ramnagar Delhi Link Exp 25036, 5½ hrs;
Corbett Park Link Exp 25014, 6 hrs.

🏠 Forest Rest House

🏠 Watch Tower

Background Uttarakhand

Geography

The extraordinarily contorted geology of the Garhwal and Kumaon Himalaya reflects the fierce uplifting and the complex movements that have happened since the great mountain range first started to form. The high peaks of Nanda Devi (7816 m) and Shivling (6543 m) are surrounded by deep valleys, with some of the world's largest glaciers at their heads. Some meteorologists predict that the Himalaya will be glacier-free within 30 years or so. Although partly attributed to a 10,000-year retreat of the last northern hemisphere Ice Age, the speed of glacial melt has accelerated since the 1970s. The Gangotri Glacier, one of the 'water towers' of the River Ganga, is receding at a rate of 23 m per year, a pattern repeated across all of the great Himalayan ice sheets. The resultant loss of river flow threatens irrigation and drinking water supplies to 500 million people in the Gangetic Basin.

Culture

Ethnically, the people of the plains are largely of Indo-Aryan origin, with stronger Mongoloid influences closer to the border with Tibet. Hindi and Urdu are widely spoken, but there are numerous local dialects such as Garhwali and Kumaoni (hill) dialects.

History

The 14th century ruler Ajai Pal (1358-1370) consolidated a number of petty principalities that made up Garhwal (Land of the Forts) to become the region's raja. The area was a popular plundering ground for Sikh brigands. The Gurkhas overran it in 1803, taking women and children into slavery and conscripting men into their army. Gurkha encroachments on the land around Gorakhpur prompted the British to expel them from Garhwal and Kumaon in 1814. They took the eastern part of Garhwal as British Garhwal and returned the western part, Tehri Garhwal, to the deposed raja. The hillsmen here have long resented their political domination by the plainsmen of Uttar Pradesh, so the creation of Uttarakhand (Sanskrit for 'northern section', but initially called Uttaranchal) on 9 November 2000 was the fulfilment of a long cherished dream. In the first state elections, held in February 2002, the Congress swept the BJP from power, and the veteran Congress leader ND Tiwari became chief minister. The question of the capital is still contentious. Dehra Dun has initially been given the status of 'interim capital', but there are still demands that it should be transferred to Gairsain, a hill town in the heart of the new state.

Agriculture

Scattered farming villages among picturesque terraces show the skill with which Uttarakhand's mountain people have adapted to their environment. Agriculture is still by far the most important economic activity for people in the hills, often carried out with considerable sophistication, both of engineering and of crop selection. On many of the hillsides terracing is wonderfully intricate, and a wide variety of crops are grown: paddy, wheat, barley, hemp and lentils on the low-lying irrigated terraces; sugar cane, chilli, buckwheat and millet higher up. The terraces themselves, sometimes as high as 6 m, may have as many as 500 flights, and some villages have up to 6000 individual terraces. Given that it takes someone a day to build a wall 1 m high and 2 m long, it is easy to see the vast amount of labour that has gone into their construction, and how much care is lavished on their maintenance.

Madhya Pradesh & Chhattisgarh

stunning monuments meet tiger-rich jungle

Madhya Pradesh and Chhattisgarh are at the heart of India. They contain many of the tribal groups least touched by modernization and most of India's remaining genuine forest.

The magnificent paintings made in rock shelters at Bhimbetka illustrate the continuity of settlement for over half a million years, while Buddhism left a still-visible mark in the glories of Sanchi's 2000-year-old stupas. The magnificent palaces of Orchha and temples of Khajuraho testify to the power of Rajput dynasties for over a thousand years.

Flowing westwards along the southern edge of the great Vindhyan ranges runs the Narmada, subject of one of the largest – and most controversial – dam development programmes in the world. Yet Madhya Pradesh remains largely unindustrialized and little visited, allowing the dense forests and grasslands of the east to house two of India's best national parks at Kanha and Bandhavgarh.

To the southeast, Chhattisgarh is a largely tribal state, and one of the least accessible areas of peninsular India. Rich in mineral resources, it is in the throes of a modern-day peasant rebellion.

Best for
Monuments ▪ Palaces ▪ Walking ▪ Wildlife

Footprint
picks

★ **Mandu**, page 228

A high fortified plateau, dotted with romantically crumbling ruins.

★ **Gwalior**, page 234

The mighty fortress towers over spectacular Jai Vilas palace and museum.

★ **Orchha**, page 243

Explore fascinating bat-filled palaces, visit vibrant temples and watch the sunset over the River Betwa.

★ **Khajuraho**, page 248

India's most vividly erotic sculptures pulsate from the walls of Khajuraho's 10th-century temples.

★ **Kanha National Park**, page 264

The landscape that inspired Kipling's *Jungle Book* is still rich in tigers, leopards, sloth bear and elephant.

★ **Kawardha**, page 266

Little-visited Chhattisgarh is home to fascinating tribal cultures and a handful of opulent palaces.

Essential Madhya Pradesh and Chhattisgarh

Finding your feet

Madhya Pradesh (population 73.34 million, area 308,00 sq km) has some magnificent scenery. The dominating Vindhyan mountains run diagonally across the heart of Madhya Pradesh while the Kaimur range runs to the north and east, overlooking the Gangetic plain around Varanasi and Allahabad. Both rise to 600 m but are frequently cut by deep forest-clad ravines. Behind the Kaimur range is the Baghelkhand plateau while the Hazaribagh range juts into the state in the east. The Narmada rising in the east, flows west to the Arabian Sea, along with the Tapti to its south. Black volcanic soils are often visible across the state, but in some places the land is stony and inhospitable. Between Gwalior and Jhansi the Chambal River has dug deep gorges, creating a badlands area which dacoits have enjoyed as hideouts.

The hilly and forested region of Chhattisgarh ("36 forts"), is one of the least densely populated and urbanized regions of peninsular India with a population of under 21 million spread across an area of 135,000 sq km. It retains a strongly rural character. The ancient granites, gneisses and sedimentaries which comprise the major geological formations of the state contain an abundance of minerals, from gold and diamonds to coal and iron ore, dolomite and bauxite. Chhattisgarh is estimated to have reserves of nearly 27 billion tonnes of coal and nearly 200 million tonnes of top quality iron ore. Yet there is also fertile agricultural land, and where the brown forest soils have been converted to agricultural land they yield good rice harvests, lending the state the reputation of being India's 'rice bowl'. Forest cover extends up to 40% of the state's area, with 70% of India's *tendu* leaf production, used for making *bidis*.

Getting around

Bhopal, Indore and Jabalpur are the transport hubs of Madhya Pradesh and Chhattisgarh, with buses and trains to all points. Car hire/taxis are advisable on long road journeys eg Satna–Khajuraho–Orchha. There has been a major overhaul of the road network going on in the state in recent years.

When to go

The weather is best in October and November and spring. Winters are dry and pleasant, although mornings are chilly. Most rain falls between June and September. March to May is hot and dry. During the monsoon the landscape turns green and places like Mandu are particularly attractive. Avoid Christmas and Holi, when the tiger parks are packed with tourists, and 1 July to 30 September, when they're closed altogether.

Time required

Allow seven to 10 days for a western circuit of the region and five days for Northern Madhya Pradesh. You'll need a minimum of two to three days for each of the tiger parks, and four days for a trek through tribal Chhattisgarh.

Safari fees

A uniform fee structure applies to Kanha, Bandhavgarh and every other tiger reserve in Madhya Pradesh, but the fees change frequently and unpredictably.

The latest version does away with individual entry fees and instead charges a levy on each vehicle that enters the gates, with a strict quota system limiting the number of cars allowed into each zone of each park on a given day.

Weather Bhopal

January	February	March	April	May	June
25°C 11°C 13mm	28°C 12°C 9mm	34°C 17°C 8mm	38°C 22°C 4mm	41°C 26°C 12mm	37°C 25°C 120mm

July	August	September	October	November	December
31°C 23°C 354mm	29°C 22°C 363mm	31°C 22°C 185mm	32°C 19°C 31mm	29°C 14°C 12mm	26°C 11°C 11mm

(Diesel vehicles older than five years are banned altogether.) A car or jeep carrying up to eight passengers, including the driver, costs Rs 2400 per 'round', or visit, with two rounds being available per day – one beginning just before sunrise, the other ending half an hour after sunset. In addition, each vehicle has to carry a qualified guide, who will charge between Rs 300 and Rs 1000 per round depending on their level of experience and wildlife knowledge.

Further fees apply to elephant rides and 'tiger shows' (Rs 1500 for an hour), in which you ride on elephant back to see a tiger that has been tracked by forest guards; though touristy, and probably on their way out for good, these are a uniquely organic way to get close to the quarry. Where watchtowers and hides have been constructed, as in Bandhavgarh, access to them costs Rs 500-1000 for up to four hours.

The greatest innovation to be introduced in recent times is the ability to book and pay for your slot weeks in advance on the internet:

follow the 'National Parks' link from www.mponline.gov.in.

One thing that remains firmly entrenched, however, is the dual pricing system, with Indian visitors paying half the price paid by foreigners for most fees. Note that the presence of a single foreign face in a jeep will invoke the higher charge. Nevertheless, the potential benefits of this scheme are clear: more people in your jeep means a less costly safari, and fewer cars churning up dust in tiger country ought to create a better experience for everyone – not least of all the tigers themselves.

Footprint picks

1 **Mandu**, page 228
2 **Gwalior**, page 234
3 **Orchha**, page 243
4 **Khajuraho**, page 248
5 **Kanha National Park**, page 262
6 **Kawardha**, page 266

Central
Madhya Pradesh

Rarely visited by travellers, this section of the Indian interior features a number of hidden jewels, including the Palaeolithic cave paintings of Bhimbetka, the silent Buddhist ruins of Sanchi, and Pachmarhi, one of India's most unassuming hill stations. The hub of the region is state capital Bhopal, an enjoyable and relatively prosperous city of lakes and atmospheric warren-like bazars.

Bhopal and around   Colour map 2, C6.

a surprisingly pleasant city of lakes, mosques and museums

Perhaps most unfortunately well known for the tragic Union Carbide disaster, see box, opposite, Bhopal (population 2,795,000) today has its own quite unusual and interesting character

Situated around two huge artificial lakes and on gently rolling hills, parts of Bhopal have a spacious feel, with pleasant parks, ambitious royal palaces and modern public buildings. To the north lies the busier and crowded Old City, filled with mosques and bazars, as well as the crowded commercial centre in the New Market area of TT Nagar beyond the lakes to the southwest.

Sights

In 1878 Shah Jahan Begum (ruled 1868-1901), began work on the pink **Taj-ul Masjid**, one of the largest mosques in India, but it was left unfinished for over a century. It is a striking sight, with three white domes, two massive minarets and an impressive hall with attractive pillars. Today it is used as a *madrassa* (religious school). The main Chote Talao entrance, which has steps, is closed, so enter by the Lall Market gate. The smaller **Jama Masjid** (1837) in the bazar, with its minarets topped by gold spikes, was built by Qudsia Begum, and the **Moti Masjid** (1860, based on the Jama Masjid in Delhi), was built by her daughter, Sikander Begum. At the entrance to the Chowk in the old city area is **Shaukat Mahal**, designed by a Frenchman, combining post-Renaissance and Gothic styles. Nearby is the **SadarManzil**, the Hall of Public Audience of the former rulers of Bhopal. South of the Lower Lake is the modern **Lakshmi Narayan** (Birla) **Temple** (Vaishnavite), Arera Hills. There are good views from here and in the evening from Shamla Hills. There are pedalo and sailing boats for hire on the Upper Lake.

The State Archaeological Museum ① *Shamla Hills, TT Nagar, Tue-Sun 1030-1730,*

Essential Bhopal

Finding your feet

The airport is about 20 minutes by bus from the town centre. There are direct flights from Delhi, Gwalior and Mumbai. Bhopal is on the main train line to South India and is just seven hours by the *Shatabdi Express* from Delhi. There is an extensive bus network; the bus stand is on Hamidia Road. See Transport, page 212.

Getting around

The town is quite spread out: it takes about 15 minutes to walk through the Old City centre from the railway station to the bus station. Local buses go to all parts of town but your best bet is an auto-rickshaw. You will have to pay a surcharge to go to the Shamla Hills or other points on the edge of town.

foreigners Rs 50, Indians Rs 10, camera Rs 10, houses sculptures, antiquities and tribal handicrafts, stone sculptures in gallery grounds and an interesting collection of 87 small Jain bronzes of the Paramar period (12th century) from a single site in Dhar District. **Birla Museum** ① *Tue-Sun 1000-1700, foreigners Rs 50, Indians Rs 10*, by the Lakshmi Narayan Temple, has a small collection of well-displayed rare sculptures (seventh to 12th centuries) in Siva, Vishnu and Devi galleries. **Bharat Bhawan** ① *Shamla Hills, Tue-Sun 1000-1700, foreigners Rs 20, Indians Rs 10*, designed by Charles Correa, houses an impressive collection of rural and tribal arts, a modern art gallery, crafts gallery and print maker's studio, as well as a library and theatre for performing arts, and a café. **Indira Gandhi Rashtriya Manav Sangrahalaya (Museum of Man)** ① *www.igrms.com, Tue-Sun, Mar-Aug 1100-1830, Sep-Feb 1000-1730, Rs 10*, south of Shamla Hills, is the largest open-air anthropological

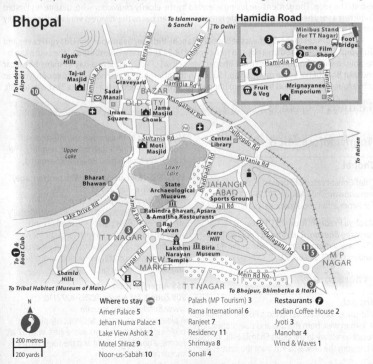

Where to stay 🛏
Amer Palace **5**
Jehan Numa Palace **1**
Lake View Ashok **2**
Motel Shiraz **9**
Noor-us-Sabah **10**
Palash (MP Tourism) **3**
Rama International **6**
Ranjeet **7**
Residency **11**
Shrimaya **8**
Sonali **4**

Restaurants 🍴
Indian Coffee House **2**
Jyoti **3**
Manohar **4**
Wind & Waves **1**

Bhopal

Legend suggests that Bhopal stands on an 11th-century site created by Raja Bhoja, who is believed to have built a *pal* (dam) which created the lakes. The modern city was developed by Dost Mohammad Khan, one of Aurangzeb's Afghan governors, who planned to set out wide roads, adorn it with monuments and replant the gardens. After his death Bhopal remained almost an island state in Malwa. Loyal to the British throughout the 18th century, from 1857 until 1926, Bhopal was ruled by two Muslim women, Sultan Shahjahan Begum and her mother Sikander Begum. It still retains a strong Muslim character. In 1984, the city hit international news headlines with the Union Carbide disaster (see box, page 209).

museum in India with a permanent exhibition of tribal huts in typical village settings from across India, from the desert to the Himalayas, coastal belt to the plains, with details of interiors. A shop sells good tribal crafts. There are also a whole host of music and drama programmes here too. Check their website for details.

Around Bhopal

Islamnagar, 11 km from the town centre on a drive north past the former Union Carbide factory, is an attractive little oasis of calm in a tiny village. The palace at the heart of the gardens was built by Dost Mohammad Khan, the early Afghan ruler of Bhopal. The pavilion pillars are decorated with floral patterns. The two-storeyed Rani Mahal and the *hammam* (baths) of the Chaman Mahal can also still be seen. The gardens are lovingly tended by the elderly *chowkidar* who, despite his limited English, is a very helpful guide. The gate is normally locked but as the village is very small it is usually easy to find him.

A cluster of sites to the northeast of Bhopal – **Sanchi**, **Vidisha**, **Gyaraspur**, the **Udaygiri caves** and **Udaypur** – can be visited on a day trip (see pages 218-222). Equally, **Bhimbetka** to the south can be combined with Bhojpur, 28 km from Bhopal (see below). If you just have a day to spare, hire a car and visit Bhimbetka in the morning and Sanchi in the afternoon. If you have an afternoon, you can fit in a four-hour excursion by taxi from Bhopal to Bhojpur and Bhimbetka – it's the best way to visit.

Listings Bhopal and around *map p209*

Tourist information

Bhopal

Chief Conservator of Forests
Van Bhawan, Tulsi Nagar, T0755-267 4318.
For information about national parks.

Madhya Pradesh Tourism Offices
Paryatan Bhavan, Bhadbhada Rd, T1800-233 7777, www.mptourism.com. Also at the Railway Station (T0755-274 6827).

Where to stay

Bhopal

Mid-price hotels are in Hamidia Rd and Berasia Rd (a 15-min walk from the bus and train stations). Better hotels are in the quiet Shamla Hills, 5 km from the railway, 2 km from the centre.

Most budget hotels are dire and infested with mosquitoes. Some refuse to take foreigners. The cheap hotels on Station Rd are best avoided.

$$$$-$$$ Noor-us-Sabah (WelcomHeritage)
VIP Rd, Koh-e-Fiza, T0755-422 3333,
www.noorussabahpalace.com.
39 beautifully decorated rooms in a wonderfully atmospheric 1920s palace perched up and away on the top of a hill with fantastic views of Bhopal lake. 3 restaurants, one of which is outside, fitness centre, swimming pool, Wi-Fi and currency exchange.

$$$ Amer Palace
209 Zone 1, MP Nagar, T0755-4272110,
www.hotelamerpalace.com.
A pleasant and far more aesthetically pleasing business hotel than others in the area, with 57 a/c rooms, a good restaurant and the "best pastry shop in town".

$$$ Jehan Numa Palace
157 Shamla Hill, T0755-266 1100,
www.jehannuma.com.
Pristinely converted 19th-century palace with
100 luxurious rooms set around 2 courtyards
of immaculately kept gardens. A newish area
has rooms with balconies overlooking a large
swimming pool and spa/fitness centre. There are
3 superb restaurants, coffee shop/bakery and 2 bars,
all with a thriving and international atmosphere.
Outstanding service and a complimentary breakfast
buffet fit for kings. Internet, currency exchange
and very helpful travel desk. Trips to **Reni Pani**
jungle lodge in Satpura National Park can also be
booked from here. Highly recommended.

$$$ Lake View Ashok (ITDC)
Shamla Hills, opposite TV Tower, T0755-
266 0090, www.lake viewashok.com.
Modern business style hotel now somewhat
in need of a refurb. 45 comfortable but
slightly shabby rooms (with erratic hot water),
good restaurant, theoretical Wi-Fi, car hire, pool
and health club. Its redeeming feature is the quiet
location with great views of Upper Lake.

$$$ Palash
Near '45 Bungalows', TT Nagar, T0755-255 3006,
www.mptourism.com.
60 pleasant rooms in a refurbished business hotel,
with very helpful staff and a restaurant. It's handily
located for the tourist office and MPTDC buses.

$$$ Residency
208 MP Nagar, T0755-255 6001,
www.hotel-residency.com.
58 a/c rooms in a modern, business-style hotel,
with an excellent restaurant. Hopefully the
shockingly dirty swimming pool will be given
a clean soon.

$$ Motel Shiraz
No 7 Service Rd, T0755-255 2513,
www.motelshiraz.com.
A good lower budget option for the area in this
basic motel, with 20 rooms. The best ones are
on the 2nd floor at the back overlooking the
garden. Curiously much more expensive are the
a/c cottages that are not much larger and pretty
dark, dismal and mouldy. There's 24-hr checkout.

$ Hotel Ranjeet
Hamidia Rd, T0755-274 0500,
www.ranjeethotels.com.
28 clean, simple, but good-sized rooms,
attached bath, TV, good restaurant and bar
and complimentary breakfast.

$ Rama International
Hamidia Rd, T0755-274 0542.
Peaceful place nicely tucked back from the
busy main road. 12 large, clean, simple, rooms,
some a/c.

$ Shrimaya
No 3 Hamidia Rd (in a side street off the main
road, near No 6 platform of the railway station),
T0755-274 7401, shrimaya@sancharnet.in.
27 modern rooms, some a/c, in a bright and friendly
hotel, 1 min from the station. Recommended

$ Sonali
Near Radha Talkies, Hamidia Rd, T0755-
274 0880, www.hotelsonaliregency.com.
Decent, clean rooms (best a/c), good food
(room service) and professional, courteous staff.
Recommended.

Restaurants

Bhopal

$$$ Jehan Numa Palace
See Where to stay, above.
3 superb restaurants, one under a giant mango
tree, serving excellent Indian and international
dishes in a vibrant, modern atmosphere. Garden
barbecues, 24-hr coffee shop with Western
snacks and an impressive coffee selection.

$$$ Lake View Ashok
See Where to stay, above.
Some excellent international dishes, served in
a pleasant ambience but service can be slow.

$$ Kwality
Hamidia Rd and New Market. T0755-4224744
www.kwality.emsindia.com.
Indian, Chinese and continental cuisine in dark
but cool and comfortable surroundings.

$$ Wind and Waves
Boat Club, Lake Drive Rd, T0755-266 1523.
Their unrivalled location delivers everything the
name promises. Food is predictable Madhya
Pradesh Tourism multi-cuisine fare. It's well
known for its bar.

$ Indian Coffee House
Hamidia Rd, Sivaji Nagar and New Market.
Indian dishes, including good *thalis* but
uninspired greasy *dosas*.

$ Jyoti
53 Hamidia Rd. T0755-2747858,
www.jyotihotel.com.
Spartan but excellent cheap vegetarian *thalis*.

$ Manohar

6 Hamidia Rd, MP Nagar and New Market,
www.manohardairy.com.
An Indian café *offering very reasonable dosas*
and snacks (fantastic *pakoras*), excellent sweets
and delicious fresh fruit juices.

Festivals

Bhopal

26-30 Jan Lok Rang features local crafts and
cultural performances.
Feb Bhopal Mahotsav is similar.
Summer Festival, Bharat Bhawan centre stages
art exhibitions, theatre and music.

Shopping

Bhopal

Most shops open 0930-2000 and close on Sun
(some on Mon). **Chowk** and **New Market** are the
main shopping centres.

Books

Landmark, *Arera Colony*. Also near water tower
in the Old City.
Variety Bookhouse, *GTB Complex, New Market*.
Has an extensive choice of books in English.

Handicrafts

Handicrafts Emporium, *Hamidia Rd*. Souvenirs
and local handicrafts.
MP State Emporium, *GTB Complex, TT Nagar*.
Specializes in local *chanderi* (cotton/silk mix, so sheer
that Aurangzeb insisted that his daughter wear
7 layers of it) as well as *tussar* and other raw silks.
Mrignayanee Emporium, *23 New Shopping
Centre*. Stock souvenirs and local handicrafts.

What to do

Bhopal
Tour operators

MP Tourism, *Paryatan Bhavan, Bhadbhada Rd,
Bhopal.* T0755-277 4340, www.mptourism.com.
Runs bus tours of main city sights for Rs 100.

Watersports

Boat Club, *Lake Drive Rd. Wed-Mon 1100-2200, Tue
1700-2200*. Boat and canoe hire, and windsurfing.

Transport

Bhopal

Air The airport is 11 km from centre.
Transport to town by taxi, about Rs 200
(non a/c). Flights to **Mumbai** via **Indore**;
and **Delhi** (some via Gwalior).

Bus Hamidia Rd Bus Stand, T0755-254 0841.
Daily services include: **Agra** 541 km; **Gwalior**
422 km, 0600, 1900; **Indore** 187 km, frequent,
good a/c coach 0700, 1330, 4 hrs; **Jaipur**
572 km; **Khajuraho** better to take train;
Nagpur 345 km; **Pachmarhi** 0230-1615, a/c
0800; **Sanchi** 45 km, 1½ hrs, hourly; **Shivpuri**,
1130-1500. For **Ujjain** take bus to Devas (about
3 hrs) then jeep or bus to Ujjain. MP Tourism
buses to **Indore** and **Pachmarhi** can be more
comfortable, T0755-329 5040.

Car Local companies including **Dwarka Travels**
(T0755-427-0032, www.dwarkatravels.in) offer
sightseeing packages: 4 hrs/40 km, Rs 650;
8 hrs/80 km, Rs 1000.

Taxi **Bhojpur** and **Bhimbetka** cost about
Rs 1200 by taxi, 4 hrs round trip. Unmetered.

Train City Booking T0755-255 3599. Railway
Station, enquiry T131, reservation T1335. Booking
office and tourist information outside Platform 1.
Agra Cantt: at least 20 per day, 4-5 hrs; most
via Gwalior, 6½ hrs. **Bengaluru**: 3 daily, 26 hrs.
Chennai: at least 3 daily, 23 hrs. **Delhi (ND)**:
frequent trains day and night, 8-10 hrs. Indore:
at least 8 daily, 3½-6 hrs; all go via Ujjain, 2½-4 hrs.
Jabalpur: 8 daily, 6-8 hrs; **Jalgaon** (for **Ajanta/
Ellora**): at least 12 daily, 6½ hrs. **Lucknow**: at least
3 daily, 11½ hrs. **Mumbai (CST)**: 3 daily, 15 hrs;
several others terminate at Mumbai LTT.

Bhojpur *Colour map 2, C6.*

famous for its Siva temple and its dams

Accessed from Bhopal by taxi, Bhojpur is well known for its temple and its dams, a
testimony to the crucial importance of irrigation in this region. Both the religious
and civil functions implicit in these buildings owed their origin to the 11th-century
Paramar king of Dhar, Raja Bhoj (1010-1053), who was noted not only as a great
builder but also as a scholar.

The huge lake that once lay to the west behind two massive stone and earth dams has now disappeared. Built between two hills, the Cyclopean dams were up to 100 m wide at the base and retained a lake of over 700 sq km, but in 1430 Hoshang Shah of Malwa demolished the dams. The Gonds believe that it took three years to drain, and that the local climate underwent a major change as a result of its drying out.

Bhojeshwar Temple

Bhojeshwar Temple, sometimes referred to as the 'Somnath of the North', is a simple square with sides of just over 20 m. Surmounted by a corbelled dome, the lower doorposts are plain while the columns and upper sections inside are richly carved. Two ornamental figures guard the entrance. On a striking three-tiered sandstone platform over 6 m sq is a polished stone lingam 2.35 m high and nearly 6 m in circumference, the largest in India. The temple was never completed but the traditional medieval means of building the towering structures of great Hindu temples are still visible in the earth ramp, built as a temporary expedient to enable large stones to be raised to the height of the wall, yet in this case never cleared away. The gigantic patterns engraved on surrounding rocks, which are now protected by rails, suggest that the temple was part of a grand plan (note one depicting a Siva temple with pilgrims' footprints). Equally interesting are over 1300 masons' marks that appear on and around the temple which would have been erased on completion. Stone masons can be seen working on site.

Jain shrine

There is a whitewashed Jain shrine nearby, behind a modern community centre, which encloses a 6-m-high black statue of a Tirthankara flanked by two smaller ones. The inscription on the pedestal uses 11th-century script. A caretaker holds the keys.

Bhimbetka Caves *Colour map 2, C6.*

extraordinary prehistoric paintings

Set in the middle of dense deciduous forest, the caves of Bhimbetka Hill hold a wealth of archaeological treasures. More than 1000 shelters have been discovered, with evidence of occupation from the early Stone Age to as recent as 1000 BC.

Essential Bhimbetka Caves

Finding your feet

A taxi from Bhopal is the easiest way to visit the caves. Alternatively, from Bhopal, take the Hoshangabad bus and ask to be dropped at the Bhimbetka turning (the caves are a 3-km walk). You may get a lift from a truck on the main road to Bhojpur, or from Bhopal take a bus to Obaidullaganj, 7 km north of the Bhimbetka turning, and hire a bicycle there. There is no obvious signpost to Bhimbetka on the main road. At a Hindi sign (on the left), a lane turns right with a railway crossing just after the turn. The caves are to the right, off this lane.

Access

The site has been enclosed to allow visitors to be taken around nine representative caves by Archaeological Survey guides during daylight hours. The tour, along a well-made path linking the major shelters, takes about 45 minutes; allow longer if you wish to explore independently (there are about 130 caves along 4 km). The caretaker will expect a small tip. The area is often virtually deserted and it is not easy to find specific caves with worthwhile paintings outside the enclosure.

What to take

Take drinking water with you; there are no facilities. There are plans to build a picnic area and water supply.

BACKGROUND
Bhimbetka Caves

The site was discovered by VS Wakanker of the Vikram University, Ujjain, in 1957, but dating of the site's occupation is far from complete. In the bottom layers of the settlement sequence were a few pebble tools. There was a thin layer of bare material above this, followed by a thick layer of **Acheulian deposits**. Over 2.5 m of accumulated material were excavated in Cave III F-23, bringing to light successive floors paved with stone and large quantities of stone implements that were clearly being made in the cave. This period is dominated by flake tools – blades, scrapers, cleavers and hand axes. Some of the core tools, often beautifully executed, were found to weigh up to 40 kg.

This level is followed in many caves by **Middle Palaeolithic** materials (c 40,000-12,000 BC), suggesting that this culture developed on the same site out of the preceding Acheulian culture. The same raw materials are used, although the tools are generally smaller. During the **Upper Palaeolithic** period (c 12,000-5500 BC) short thin blades made their appearance for the first time. It was in the **Mesolithic** period (5500-1000 BC), immediately following the Upper Palaeolithic, that the largest number of caves were occupied. A Ghosh suggests that during this period there was a huge increase in population, possibly related to a change in the climate, and some of the cave paintings can be correlated with this period. A brand new technology appeared too, in the shape of tiny stone tools – microliths – such as knives, arrow heads, spearheads and sickles. Hard, fine-grained rocks like chert and chalcedony were brought in – the nearest source is near Barkhera, 7 km to the southeast. The dead were buried in caves still occupied by the living, usually, though not always, in a crouched position with the head to the east. Antlers and stone tools were buried alongside them. In the middle level of the deposits are copper tools and pottery. The site seems to have been largely deserted by the end of the first millennium BC. Several circular structures on the hills around have been interpreted as Buddhist *stupas* of a much later era, a view supported by Asokan inscription, found 20 km west of Bhimbetka.

Watered by perennial springs, Bhimbetka's forests remain a vital food source for tribal people even today, providing edible fruits, flower seeds and tubers. You may notice teak and *tendu*, the latter harvested in May and June to make *bidis* for smoking. The area is also rich in wildlife including several species of deer, wild boar, sloth bear, antelope, leopard, jackal, pangolin and many birds. Some enthusiasts and visitors, however, have found the site disappointing.

The caves

By far the most striking remains at Bhimbetka are the paintings: animal figures and hunting scenes daubed in red, white, green and yellow across the walls and ceilings of over 500 shelters and rocky hollows. Some are quite small, while others are up to 10 m long.

The **paintings** belong to three periods. The Upper Palaeolithic paintings, usually in white, dark red and green lines (the colours are derived from manganese, haematite, soft red stone and charcoal, sometimes combined with animal fat and leaf extract), depict large animals, eg bison, rhinoceros and tiger. The Mesolithic figures and animals, usually in red, are smaller but they lose their proportions and naturalism. Hunting is a common theme, with 'stick men' shown grazing, riding and hunting animals, dancing in groups. Women are sometimes seen with a child or appear pregnant. The later period, probably dating from the early centuries AD when green and yellow colours are also used, is quite different, showing battle scenes with men riding on elephants and horses, holding spears, shields, bows and arrows. Religious symbols, Ganesh and Siva, trees and flowers also appear.

Some shelters were used over several periods and you can spot interesting details: **Auditorium 3** has deer, peacock, leopard, old men and dancers; **Rock Shelter 1** shows two elephants and a nilgai; **No 8** has a garlanded king on horseback with hunters and a cheetah; **No 9** has a flower pot, elephant and an old man; **No 10** shows Ganesh, a Siva lingam and a tree; **No 7**, stylized hunters on horseback based on simple crosses; **No 6**, drummer, group dancers, tree roots and branches and bison.

one of the most beautiful and friendliest hill stations in Central India

Pachmarhi (population 12,100, altitude 1100 m) rarely sees Western visitors and, except at the height of summer, the air remains pleasantly fresh and cool. The massive iron-rich sandstones, which rise steeply from the trough of the Narmada Valley floor to form the Satpura Range, offer plenty of scope for quiet, wooded walks, with several viewpoints, waterfalls, rock pools and hills to climb within easy reach. The Gondwana series, known locally as Pachmarhi sandstones, are rich in plant fossils, notably of ferns. The area is also known for its ancient cave paintings.

Sights

The **Panch Pandav** 'caves', south of the town centre beyond the Cantonment, are believed to have sheltered Buddhist monks in the first century BC, a fact confirmed by the relatively recent discovery at the caves of the remains of a *stupa* from this period (6 m in circumference). There are several delightful spots nearby. The small natural bathing pool **Apsara Vihar** is along a path to the left. The pool has a broad shallow edge, suitable for children to paddle. There is a short scramble from there to the top of **Rajat Pratap** (the 'big fall'), over 110 m high.

There are other falls in the area, some of which fall within the bounds of the **Satpura National Park** (see below). Attractive outings include **Jalwataran** (Duchess Fall), 3 km along the path from Belle Vue. It is a strenuous 4-km walk to the base of the first cascade, perhaps the most attractive in Pachmarhi. Wildlife safaris into the park can be arranged by some Pachmarhi hotels.

Short one-day treks are possible to Mahadeo and Dhupgarh peaks, and the spectacular hilltop temple of Chauragarh. The square-topped hill at **Chauragarh**, on the southern edge of the Pachmarhi plateau, is 10 km away. The ridge-top temple draws crowds of tribals and pilgrims for **Sivaratri** in February and March. It owes its sanctity to a legend in which Siva and Vishnu defeated the demon Bhasmasur by tricking him into turning himself to stone. A remarkable spring flows out of the **Cave of Mahadeo**, nearly 100 m inside the hillside. The temple itself is reached by a 3-km walk through beautiful forest culminating in a climb up 1300 steps, and there are superb views from the top. Take a jeep to the start of the walk as the road is too steep for bikes. **Priyadarshini Point**, on the way, from which Captain Forsyth is said to have first set eyes on the Pachmarhi region, still gives a commanding view over the town and the region. You can look back at the **Handi Khoh** ravine from this vantage point.

To the north of the bazar, a 3-km hike past some ancient rock shelters leads to the **Jatashankar Cave** where the Siva lingam bears the likeness of the god's coiled matted hair.

Satpura National Park

Nov-May sunrise-sunset, foreigners Rs 200 per person on foot (Indians Rs 20), foreigners Rs 1500 per car (Indians Rs 400).

Joined with Pachmarhi and Bori National Parks, the tiger and leopard reserve of Satpura is close to Pachmarhi town and around 200 km from Bhopal and is still a relatively unknown wildlife sanctuary of over 524 sq km of dry, deciduous forest landscape, rugged sandstone peaks, deep gorges and ravines. A wide range of animals, birds and plant life inhabit the terrain, including leopards, sloth bears, gaur, deer, flying squirrels, crocodiles and the increasingly elusive tiger.

If you want a much more off the beaten track national park experience, then this is definitely the place. Set up in 1981 and still with only a few

Essential Pachmarhi

Finding your feet

Pachmarhi can easily be reached by bus from Bhopal in about six hours. It is similarly accessible from Nagpur. Pipariya (see Where to stay, below), between Jabalpur and Itarsi on the Mumbai–Kolkata line, is the nearest railway station. See Transport, page 218.

Getting around

Most hotels are either near the bus stand or in the bazar. You can share a jeep to the more far-flung hotels and major points of interest.

BACKGROUND

Pachmarhi

In 1857 Captain Forsyth of the Bengal Lancers 'discovered' the spot on which Pachmarhi came to be built. He was said to have headed a column of troops but in fact was accompanied by just two others. The beautiful landscape of the plateau of the Satpura range impressed him with its tranquil forests of wild bamboo, *sal, yamun, amla* and *gular* trees, interspersed with deep pools fed by the streams that ran across the iron-stained sandstone hills. Later, the British developed Pachmarhi as a military sanatorium and hot weather resort.

lodges in the surrounding areas, you can cruise around the park by jeep, on elephant, by boat or even on foot, knowing that you won't be seeing hordes of other enthusiasts desperately on the lookout for now-elusive 'stripes'.

Listings Pachmarhi and around *map p217*

Tourist information

Pachmarhi

Tourist office
Amaltas Complex, T07578-252100.

Where to stay

Pachmarhi

Prices increase tenfold during Diwali, Christmas and other holidays. Most hotels have wood boilers which provide hot water for a few hours morning and evening.

$$$ Rock End Manor Heritage Hotel
Pachmarhi, 2 km from the market area,
T07578-252079, www.mp tourism.com.
6 deluxe a/c rooms, some with 6-m-high ceilings in restored colonial building, and 6 more in the slightly cheaper annexe, with lovely views of the old golf course and polo fields. Recommended.

$$ Misty Meadows
Patel Marg, T07578-252136,
www.hotelmistymeadows.com.
Pleasant, spacious rooms (some renovated), 2 with access to the terrace, set in a peaceful garden. Home-cooked food available. Mr Bhakshi is a friendly and knowledgeable host.

$$ Nandan Van (SADA)
T07578-252018.
12 old-fashioned but well-kept cottages in spacious, peaceful gardens. Friendly, though little English is spoken.

$$ Panchvati Cottages
Near Tehsil, T07578-252096,
www.mptourism.com.
Quiet and well-maintained, with 5 a/c huts and 2 air-cooled cottages, all with TV and hot water. There's also a good-value restaurant and a bar.

$$ Satpura Retreat
Mahadeo Rd, 2 km from centre, T07578-252097,
www.mptourism.com.
6 a/c rooms in an attractive old bungalow with a veranda, in a pleasant if rather far-flung setting. Also has a restaurant (see Restaurants, below).

$$-$ Kachnar
Arvind Marg, T07578-252323
11 spacious, clean, comfortable rooms with bath and good views from upper-floor terraces. Staff are very friendly and helpful. Wildlife safaris can be arranged in Satpura from the travel desk downstairs and they also have a restaurant; see Restaurants, below.

$ Abhilasha
T07578-252203. www.hotelabhilasha.in
Hotel with 24 rooms, bucket hot water and a 24-hr check-out.

$ Abhimanyu
Arvind Rd, T07578-252126,
abhimanyuhotel@gmail.com.
Spacious and clean enough rooms, enthusiastic owner, a lively atmosphere, and a simple rooftop restaurant with good hill views. Willing local guides hang out in lobby.

$ Nilambar

T07578-252030 www.pachmarhisada.com
Good views from 6 attractive twin-bed cottages, which have hot water.

Pipariya

$ Alka

Across footbridge from station, T07576-224222. www.alkahotelpipariya.com.
Range of simple rooms, some a/c, some amazingly cheap, handy for trains and buses, very popular restaurant (although there's little competition).

Satpura National Park

$$$$ Reni Pani Lodge

Village Reni Pani, Tehsil Sohagpur, District Hoshangabad. 135 km from Bhopal and 45 km from Hoshangabad (nearest railway station is at Pipariya, 35 km away), T0755-266 1100, www.renipanijunglelodge.com.
In a refreshingly remote location a few kilometres outside the park, brothers Faiz and Ali are impeccable hosts at this luxuriously rustic, yet newish lodge. There are 12 immaculately designed ethnic-style cottages which even come with your very own locally employed butler. Swimming pool, library, souvenir shop selling local handicrafts, fantastic cuisine and evening fireside candlelit drinks where you can discuss the various animal, bird and local tribal village sightings of the day. All activities in the park are arranged and enthusiastically guided by either one of the brothers or the highly knowledgeable local naturalist. Visits can be arranged directly or through **Jehan Numa Palace Hotel** in Bhopal. Highly recommended.

Pachmarhi

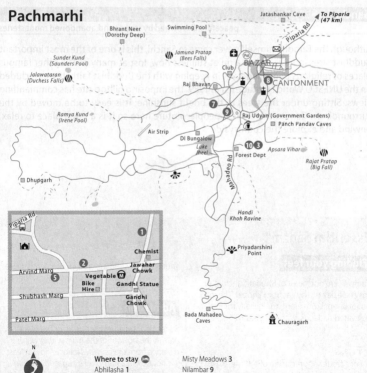

Where to stay 🛏

Abhilasha 1
Abhimanyu 5
Kachnar & Maheshwari Restaurant 2
Misty Meadows 3
Nilambar 9
Panchvati Cottages 8
Rock End Manor 7
Satpura Retreat 10

Restaurants

Pachmarhi
MP Tourism hotels have bland restaurants serving Indian and a few Chinese dishes.

$ Satpura Retreat
See Where to stay, above.
Very pleasant restaurant.

$ Maheshwari
Kachnar Hotel, see Where to stay, above.
Excellent vegetarian dishes, including *thalis*, served in this clean and bright restaurant, the best in the bazar area.

Transport

Pachmarhi
4WD Most hotels can arrange 4WD Gypsys. You can usually get seat in a shared jeep for a cheaper price.

Bus Bus stand, T07578-252058. Daily services to **Bhopal** 0730, 1530, 5-6 hrs; **Indore** 0630; **Khargon** 1830; **Nagpur** 0700 (returns 1000), 12 hrs; **Pipariya** every 30 mins until 2000, 1½ hrs. Also share jeeps, frequent but crowded.

Train The nearest station is Pipariya, 47 km, with daily trains east to **Kolkata** (25 hrs) via **Jabalpur** (2½ hrs), **Satna** (5 hrs) and **Allahabad** (10½ hrs), and west to **Mumbai** (15 hrs) via **Jalgaon** (7½ hrs). Computerized reservations in Pachmarhi at DI Bungalow near lake, 0800-1400 (closed Tue).

Sanchi *Colour map 2, C6.*

peaceful hill crowned by stupas and abandoned monasteries

Although the Buddha himself never came to Sanchi, this is one of the most important Buddhist sites in India. It has a quiet stillness now, lost at many of the other famous places of religious pilgrimage, yet in keeping with the Buddhist faith. It was included on the UNESCO World Heritage list in 1989. The imposing hilltop site has commanding views. Sitting under the trees in the bright sunshine, it is easy to be moved by the surroundings. Comparatively few people venture here so it is a good place to relax, unwind and explore the countryside.

Essential Sanchi

Finding your feet

Some 47 km northeast of Bhopal, Sanchi is an easy half-day trip by car from Bhopal. The road out of Bhopal runs along the railway through cultivated flatlands, with the Vindhya Hills to

your right, covered in scrub jungle. Regular local buses run from both Bhopal and nearby Vidisha. See Transport, page 221.

Admission

Sunrise-sunset, foreigners Rs 250. The main gate at the bottom of the hill is within walking distance from the railway station. Allow at least 1½ hours. If in a hurry, visit Stupas 1, 2 and 3, Gupta Temple (17), Temple 18, and Monasteries 45 and 51.

Tip...
For a better appreciation of the site, make the short pilgrimage up the hill and if possible visit at the most spectacular times of either sunrise or sunset.

BACKGROUND

Sanchi

The first *stupa* was built during Asoka's reign in the third century BC, using bricks and mud mortar. Just over a century later it was doubled in size; a balcony/walkway and a railing were added. The gateways were built 75 years later. Finally in AD 450 four images of the Buddha (belonging to the later period), were placed facing each of the gateways. The entrances are staggered because it was commonly believed that evil spirits could only travel in a straight line. The wall was built for the same purpose. The Great Stupa, one of the largest in India (37 m in diameter, 16 m high), does not compare with the one at Anuradhapura in Sri Lanka.

Indian *stupas* evolved to be taller in proportion to their bases with the great *stupas* surrounded by lesser ones, often containing the ashes of monks famous for their piety and learning, plus an attendant complex of monasteries, dining rooms, shrine-rooms, preaching halls and rest houses for pilgrims. These can all be seen at Sanchi.

From the 14th century Sanchi lay half buried, virtually forgotten and deserted until 'rediscovered' by General Taylor in 1818, the year before the Ajanta caves were found. Amateur archaeologists and treasure hunters caused considerable damage. Some say Taylor used the Asoka Pillar to build a sugarcane press, breaking it up in the process; others blame a local landholder. Sir John Marshall, Director General of Archaeology from 1912-1919, ordered the jungle to be cut back and extensive restoration to be effected, restoring it to its present condition.

Originally, the brick and mortar domes were plastered and shone brilliant white in the tropical sun. The earliest decorative carving was done on wood and ivory but the craftsmen at Sanchi readily transferred their skills to the yellow sandstone here, which lends itself to intricate carving. The carvings illustrate scenes from the life of Buddha, events in the history of Buddhism and the *Jataka* stories (legends about the Buddha's previous lives). See also Books, page 1355.

The site

The Gateways The basic model consists of two pillars joined by three architraves (cross beams), sculpted as if they actually passed through the upright posts. They are regarded as the finest of all Buddhist *toranas*. The **East Gate** shows the young prince Siddhartha Gautama, leaving his father's palace and setting off on his journey towards enlightenment, and the dream his mother had before Gautama's birth. The **West Gate** portrays the seven incarnations of the Buddha. The **North Gate**, crowned by a wheel of law, illustrates the miracles associated with the Buddha as told in the *Jatakas*. The **South Gate** reveals the birth of Gautama in a series of dramatically rich carvings. Just to the right of the south gate is the stump of the pillar erected by Asoka in the third century BC. The capital, with its four lion heads, is in the local museum. It recalls the one in the Sarnath Museum, of superior workmanship, that was adopted as the national symbol of Independent India.

Monastery 51 This is reached by steps opposite the west gateway of the Great Stupa. It is well preserved with thick stone walls faced with flat bricks and is typical in plan. A raised, pillared veranda with 22 monastic cells behind, surrounds a brick-paved courtyard. The discovery of charred wood suggested that roofs and pillars may have been constructed with wood. There was possibly a chapel at the centre of the west side; the massive 'bowl' beyond the west gate was caused by removal of a large boulder which you can see on your way to Stupa 2.

Stupa 2 This *stupa* stands on a terrace down the slope. The original balustrade has been dated to the second century BC with later additions. The decoration, though interesting, is much simpler than on Stupa 1, especially when dealing with the human form. The relic chamber of the *stupa* contained valuable relics of 10 saints belonging to three generations after the Buddha's immediate disciples, which may explain the choice of this site, below the main terrace.

The Gupta Temple Constructed in the fifth century, this is one of the early structural temples of India, built of stone slabs with a flat roof. It has a square sanctuary and a pillared portico and shows the sombre decoration and symmetry typical of Gupta style.

Temple 18 Built in the seventh century on the site of an earlier apsidal temple, this has only nine of its 12 pillars still standing. They resemble those found in the Buddhist cave temples of Western India.

Monastery and Temple 45 On the eastern edge, built in seventh-11th centuries, this shows a more developed style of a North Indian temple. The monastery is built around a courtyard with a ruined temple of which only the core of the carved spire remains. The ornamental doorway and the Buddha image in the sanctuary, with a decorative oval halo, are still visible.

The **Archaeological Museum** ① *Sat-Thu 1000-1700, Rs 5*, is near the entrance to monument. Exhibits include finds from the site (caskets, pottery, parts of gateway, images), dating from the Asokan period. Archaeological Survey guide books to the site and museum are available.

Listings Sanchi *map below*

Where to stay

$$ Gateway Retreat
*Vidisha Bhopal Rd, T07482-266723,
www.mptourism.com.*

The smartest place in town although quite overpriced. 18 rooms and 6 suites (some a/c) are set around attractive gardens, plus there's a bar and restaurant (see Restaurants, below). Breakfast is included.

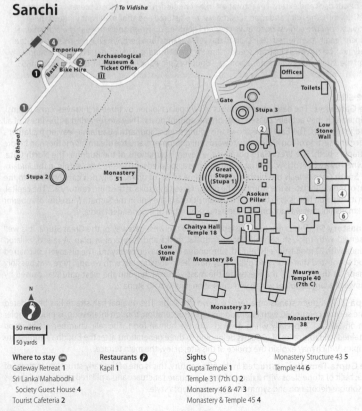

Sanchi

Where to stay 🛏	Restaurants 🍴	Sights ○	Monastery Structure 43 **5**
Gateway Retreat **1**	Kapil **1**	Gupta Temple **1**	Temple 44 **6**
Sri Lanka Mahabodhi		Temple 31 (7th C) **2**	
Society Guest House **4**		Monastery 46 & 47 **3**	
Tourist Cafeteria **2**		Monastery & Temple 45 **4**	

$$ Tourist Cafeteria
By the museum, T07482-266743.
Café with 2 basic but clean rooms.

$$-$ Sri Lanka Mahabodhi Society Guest House
Near the railway station, T07482-266739. Rooms are available Apr-May and Nov-Dec only.
When it's not full with large groups of Sri Lankan Buddhist pilgrims, this place offers 2 options: a relatively new, quite overpriced hotel with clean, spacious but spartan rooms with bath and a/c, or a more humble place next door with smaller, simpler and cheaper rooms and a dorm set around a couple of courtyards and gardens.

Restaurants

$ Kapil
New Bus Stand.
Good, cheap vegetarian food.

$ Tourist Cafeteria
By the museum, T07482-266743.
Clean, pricey average meals, can be a bit oily. Small tidy garden.

Gateway Retreat
See Where to stay, above.
Indian and Chinese dishes. Non-residents welcome with advance notice.

Transport

Bus Frequent buses from **Bhopal**, Hamidia Rd, 0630-1930, 1½ hrs direct or over 2 hrs via **Raisen**; the latter more attractive. Buses also go to **Vidisha**.

Taxi Hire in Bhopal; allow Rs 2500 for a visit and 1½ hrs each way.

Train Some trains on the Jhansi–Itarsi section of the Central Railway stop in Sanchi. Slow local passenger trains run to and from **Bhopal** a couple of times a day, 1 hr, and to **Vidisha**, 20 mins.

Gupta sites near Sanchi

fascinating temples and caves

Vidisha

In the fifth to sixth centuries BC Vidisha (known as Besnagar in Pali), located at the junction of the Betwa and Bes rivers, was an important trade centre of the Sunga Dynasty, of which Asoka was governor in the third century BC. The use of lime mortar in the construction of a shrine dedicated to Vishnu, dating from the second century BC, suggests this was one of the first structures in India to use 'cement'. Deserted after the sixth century AD, it came into prominence again as Bhilsa between the ninth and 12th centuries. It later passed on to the Malwa Sultans, the Mughals and the Scindias. The ruins of the Bijamandal Mosque and Gumbaz-ka Makbara both date from the Muslim period with remains of votive pillars nearby. The small museum contains some of Vidisha's earliest antiquities.

Heliodorus Pillar, the 'Khambha Baba', is a free-standing monolithic column, similar to Asokan pillars but much smaller, dated to 140 BC. It is 3 km after crossing the Betwa River. The inscription demonstrates that relations existed between the Greeks in the Punjab and the kings of this area and that Heliodorus had become a follower of Vishnu.

Udaygiri Caves

From Vidisha take a tonga or auto-rickshaw, or cycle from Bhopal and visit Vidisha and Udaygiri (an enjoyable 20 km each way).

The group of rock-cut sanctuaries, 4 km north of Vidisha, are carved into the sandstone hillside, an inscription in one indicating that they were produced during the reign of **Chandragupta II** (AD 382-401). The caves possess all the distinctive features that gave Gupta art its unique vitality, vigour and richness of expression: the beautifully moulded capitals, the design of the entrance, and the system of continuing the architrave as a string-course around the structure. The caves have been numbered, probably in the sequence in which they were excavated.

Cave 1 has a frontage created out of a natural ledge of rock. The row of four pillars bear the 'vase and foliage' pattern about which Percy Brown wrote: "the Gupta capital typifies a renewal of faith, the water nourishing the plant trailing from its brim, an allegory which has produced the vase and flower motif". The shrines become progressively more ornate. **Cave 5** depicts Vishnu in a massive carving in his Varaha (Boar) incarnation holding the earth goddess Prithvi aloft on one tusk. Another large sculpture is of the reclining Vishnu. Both reflect the grand vision and aspirations of the carvers. **Cave 19** is notable for its high pillars, its long portico and pillared hall.

Udaypur

At Udaypur, 60 km north from Udaygiri, is the colossal **Neelkantheswara Temple**. Built of red sandstone and set on a high platform, it has a delicately carved, beautifully proportioned spire, and is an outstanding example of 11th-century Paramara architecture. **Basoda** is 24 km away and has accommodation.

Gyaraspur

Some 64 km northeast of Bhopal, Gyaraspur is an attractive and important site of medieval Jain and Hindu activity. The partly rock-cut late ninth-century **Maladevi Temple**, on the hill above the village, is the most striking of the remains with the ruins of a *stupa* to its west.

Eran

Eran, north of Gyaraspur, has the only extant standing Gupta column (AD 485). The large (5-m-long) late fifth-century Vishnu Varaha here (represented wholly as a boar) is carved with tiny figures of *sadhus* who are believed to have sheltered in its bristles during the Flood.

Listings Gupta sites near Sanchi

Transport

Regular buses run to **Vidisha** from Bhopal and Raisen, and local trains to Sanchi. For **Udaypur**,

take a train from Bhopal to Basoda (the station is Ganjbasoda), then bus or *tonga* to Udaypur.

Western
Madhya Pradesh

The pearl of western Madhya Pradesh is Mandu, an abandoned citadel littered with empty palaces, gazing out over the Narmada River plains from the top of a craggy plateau. Temple ghats line the Narmada banks in the holy towns of Omkareshwar and Maheshwar, while Ujjain, further north on the river Shipra, is one of Hinduism's seven holiest cities, and a venue of the Maha Kumbh Mela.

Indore   *Colour map 2, C5.*

a rapidly growing industrial city with useful transport links but few sights

Indore (population two million), on the banks of the rivers Sarasvati and Khan, is a major centre for cotton textiles and the car industry, and notable for Hindustani classical music. Most travellers pass straight through on their way to Mandu, Maheshwar or Ujjain, but the city offers a few museums and temples and an interesting bazaar if you're in the mood to explore between trains.

Sights

The **Rajwada** (Old Palace) with its seven-storeyed gateway, faces the main square. A fire in 1984 destroyed most of it; now only the façade remains. On the north side is the **New Palace** and garden. In the streets are some good timber houses with deep recessed verandas and carved pillars.

Kanch Mandir ① *allow 30 mins, shoes to be left at door*, is on Jawahar Marg next to **Hotel Sheesh Mahal**. Inside this Jain temple thousands of mirrors adorn the walls, floor and ceilings, supplemented by brightly patterned ceramic tiles, Chinese lantern-type glass lamps and cut-glass chandeliers, all exquisitely crafted. There are about 50 murals depicting scenes of conversion to Jainism and 19th-century courtly life. The use of glass beads and raised figures produces a pleasing 3D effect. The image of Mahavir is in plain black onyx. This mirrored palace is at variance with the austerity and simplicity of the Mahavir's supposed existence and teachings.

Lal Bagh (Nehru Centre) ① *Tue-Sun 1100-1800, small entry fee*, southwest of town, once the residence of the maharaja, built and decorated in a confusion of styles, is now a museum and cultural centre. The rooms have been restored and furnished to pleasing effect. Queen Victoria looks on to the main 'entrance portico' (you leave through this and enter through a side entrance). There are a number of sporting trophies including stuffed tigers. The maharaja, a keen sportsman, is seen in photographs rowing on a lake, and flying in an early aeroplane. Both these are in fact 'backdrop paintings' with a hole for him to stand in to be

Essential Indore

Finding your feet

Indore has direct flights to Delhi, Mumbai and Pune. It is under five hours by the fastest train from Bhopal. The railway station and the Sarwate Bus Stand are near the town centre, but buses to Mandu go from the Gangwal Bus Stand, a 10-minute auto ride away. See Transport, page 226.

Getting around

Indore is quite spread out and very congested so it is best to take an auto to visit the sights away from the centre.

BACKGROUND

Indore

The land on which Indore was built was given to **Malhar Rao Holkar** in 1733 by the Maratha Peshwas, see page 1309, in appreciation of his help in many of their battles. Malhar Rao left much of the statecraft in the highly gifted hands of his widowed daughter-in-law who succeeded him on the throne. The city was destroyed in 1801 but recovered and was the British headquarters of their Central India Agency. The ruling family of Indore, the **Holkars**, took the British side during the Mutiny in 1857. Indore was one of the first states to open temples and schools to *Harijans*, in support of Gandhi's campaign against untouchability.

photographed! There are also good prints of the Old Palace. The entrance hall is in marble and gilt rococo with a display of prehistoric artefacts. Two attractive rooms are predominantly 'Indian' and include Mughal exhibits. On the first floor is the coin collection which dates mostly from the Muslim period. Exhibits include miniatures, contemporary Indian sculptures and paintings, Italian sculptures and intricately inlaid boxes. If your time is limited, visit this riotously varied and fascinating museum rather than the Cental Museum.

Indore

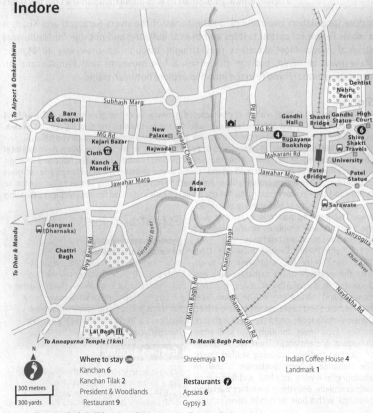

Where to stay 🛌
Kanchan **6**
Kanchan Tilak **2**
President & Woodlands
Restaurant **9**

Shreemaya **10**

Restaurants 🍴
Apsara **6**
Gypsy **3**

Indian Coffee House **4**
Landmark **1**

Central Museum ① *Agra–Mumbai Rd, near GPO, Tue-Sun 0900-2000, free, guides available, allow 30 mins*, has two main galleries: **Gallery I** with artefacts from circa 50,000-4000 BC, some from west Malwa including stone tools, quartz sickles, ornaments. There's also a model of the first Hindu temple at Bharhut. **Gallery II** contains Hindu mythological carvings. Sculptures stand in the grounds, which were possibly a battlefield during the Mutiny.

Listings Indore *map below*

Tourist information

Madhya Pradesh Tourism
42 Residency Area, T0731-249 9566.

Where to stay

$$$-$$ President
163 RN Tagore Marg, T0731-252 8866,
www.hotelpresidentindore.com.

Modern, friendly hotel with 49 comfortable a/c rooms, a great South Indian restaurant (see Restaurants, below) and a good travel desk.

$$ Kanchan Tilak
585/2 Mahatma Gandhi Rd, Palasia, T0731-253 8606, hotelkanchantilak@gmail.com.
Clean, modern hotel with 39 a/c rooms, a good restaurant, pleasant lobby, garden and a family atmosphere. Good service and value but noisy.

$$ Shreemaya
12 RNT Marg (near railway), T0731-251 5555, www.shreemaya.com.
Indian-style hotel offering 52 a/c rooms with bath, a good popular South Indian café and exchange. There's a 1000 check-out.

$$-$ Kanchan
Kanchan Bagh, T0731-251 8501, hotelkanchan@yahoo.co.in.
28 comfortable rooms, all a/c with bath, restaurant, bar, good value. Recommended.

Restaurants

There are several places near the bus stand and train station.

$$ Gypsy
17 Mahatma Gandhi Rd.
Fast food and good Western snacks, cakes and ice cream.

$$ Landmark
RN Tagore Marg, by President hotel, see Where to stay, above.
Indian and continental. Good ambience, with unusual offerings.

$$ Woodlands
At the President hotel (see Where to stay, above).
Good South Indian vegetarian dishes served in an a/c restaurant with a bar.

$ Apsara
RN Tagore Marg.
Indian vegetarian. A/c and outdoors (evening).

$ Indian Coffee House
Off Mahatma Gandhi Rd.
Light Indian snacks, dated decor.

$ Sarafa Bazar and **Chhappan Bazar**
These streets come alive at night with stalls selling delicious authentic local Malwa specialities: try *bafla* (wheat flour balls soaked in dhal) and the charmingly named *bhutta kis* (fried grated corn tossed with coconut and coriander).

What to do

MP Tourism, *T1800-233 7777*. They can design bespoke itineraries.

Transport

Air The airport is 9 km west of town; taxis charge Rs 150-300. Flights to **Ahmedabad**, **Delhi**, **Hyderabad**, **Mumbai** and **Pune**.

Bus **Sarwate Bus Stand** (south of railway station, through Exit 1), timetables in Hindi only but helpful enquiry desk, T0731-246 5688, has buses to **Bhopal** (187 km) 0800-2300, **Gwalior** 0500-1830; **Ujjain** (2 hrs) and Omkareshwar Rd (hourly, 3 hrs); change at the last for **Jhansi**, **Khajuraho** and **Omkareshwar**.

Gangwal Bus Stand (3 km west of town), T0731-238 0688, serves **Ahmedabad**, **Aurangabad** (for Ajanta and Ellora), **Amrawati** and **Dhar** (hourly). 1 bus a day goes direct to **Mandu** (99 km, 4-5 hrs); otherwise change at Dhar.

Private bus companies serving Rajasthan operate from east of the railway station. Most are overnight services.

Train **Bhopal**: 8 daily, **Delhi**: 2 daily, 14-17 hrs. **Mumbai Central** 1-3 daily. **Ujjain**: at least 12 daily.

Around Indore

holy cities and the ghost of EM Forster

Dewas *Colour map 2, C5.*
EM Forster served in the court of the Raja of Dewas in 1921, ploughing his experiences in the dusty town into *A Passage to India* and the autobiographical *The Hill of Devi. He* came to regard his stay here as the 'great opportunity' of his life. It's worth going up the 'Hill of Devi' overlooking the town for the views; you can drive all the way to the temple at the top. Dewas today is an important industrial centre.

Ujjain *Colour map 2, C5.*
Ujjain (population 430,000), one of the best-known cities of ancient India and one of Hinduism's seven sacred cities, see page 1324, is one of the four centres of the **Kumbh Mela**, see page 228, attracting about three million pilgrims every 12 years. At other times, a constant stream of people comes to bathe in the River Shipra and worship at the temples. Despite its sanctity and its age, it has few remarkable buildings. In its heyday, Ujjain was on a flourishing trade route to Mesopotamia and Egypt. Nowadays, it is little more than a provincial town.

Many dynasties ruled over this prosperous city and it is said to have been the seat of the viceroyalty of Asoka in 275 BC. His sons were born here, and it was from here that they set out to preach Buddhism. The poet **Kalidasa**, one of the *Nava Ratna* (Nine Gems) of Hindu literature, wrote some of his works here. Ujjain stands on the first meridian of longitude for Hindu astronomers, who believed that the **Tropic of Cancer** also passed through the site. This explains the presence of the **Vedha Shala** observatory, southwest of town, built by Raja Jai Singh II of Jaipur around 1730 when he was the Governor of Malwa under the Mughals. Small, compared to the Jantar Mantars, it has only five instruments. Even today the *Ephemeris* tables (predicted positions of the planets), are published here.

Mahakaleshwar Temple, dedicated to Siva, was rebuilt by Marathas in the 18th century. The temple lingam is one of the 12 *jyotirlingas* (in India, believed to be *swayambhu*, born of itself). The myths surrounding the 'linga of light' go back to the second century BC and were developed to explain and justify linga worship, see page 1329. The **Chaubis Khambha Darwaza** (circa 11th century) has 24 carved pillars which probably belonged to the medieval temple.

Close to the tank near Mahakaleshwar is a large sculpted image of Ganesh in the **Bade Ganeshji-ka Mandir**. A rock covered with turmeric is worshipped as the head of a legendary king Vikramaditya in the centre of the **Harsiddhi Mandir**. **Gopal Mandir** in the bazar contains a silver image of Krishna and an ornamental silver door. The **Bina-Niv-ki-Masjid** in Anantpeth, originally a Jain temple (see entrance porch), was converted to a mosque (circa 1400), by the first independent Sultan of Malwa. The **Chintamani Ganesh Temple** across the river is believed to have ancient medieval origins. There are other temples and shrines along the river where the atmosphere is generally very relaxed.

Listings Around Indore *map below*

Where to stay

Ujjain

$$$-$$ Shipra (MP Tourism)
University Rd, T0734-255 1495,
www.mptourism.com.
This is a quiet but run-down place with 30 rooms (10 all a/c), a restaurant, beer bar and garden. Mosquitos are a major nuisance.

$$-$ Surana Palace
23 GDC Rd, southeast of Madhav Chowk, T0734-253 0045, palacehotel surana@yahoo.co.in.
22 comfortable rooms, 6 non-a/c. Also serves good food.

$ Ajay
Opposite the railway station, T0734-255 0856.
Some rooms are air-cooled with bath.

$ Ramakrishna
Subhash Marg, opposite the railway station,
T0734-255 7012, www.hotelramakrishna.co.in.
Basic rooms, some with bath, and a vegetarian restaurant. They also have another property in a different location.

Restaurants

Ujjain

$$ Ashnol
University Rd.
Indian vegetarian in pleasant a/c surroundings.

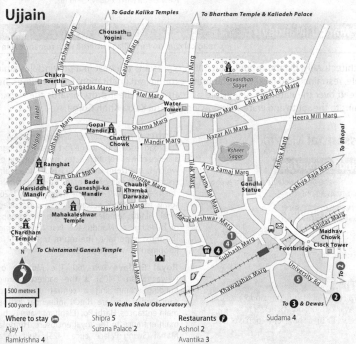

Ujjain

Where to stay 😴	Shipra **5**	Restaurants 🍴	Sudama **4**
Ajay **1**	Surana Palace **2**	Ashnol **2**	
Ramkrishna **4**		Avantika **3**	

$$ Surana Palace
See Where to stay, above.
Indian and Chinese dishes. Pleasant outdoor
seating option, the best in town.

$$-$ Avantika (MP Tourism)
*LB Shastri Marg, 2.5 km south of the station,
T0734-251 1398, www.mptourism.com.*
Clean canteen serving excellent food.
Recommended.

$ Sudama
Next to Ramkrishna, Subhash Marg.
Good Indian meals.

$ Zarokha
Near the Clock tower.
Delicious Chinese, Kashmiri and Punjabi food.

Festivals

Ujjain
Kumbh Mela takes place here every 12 years,
see page 226. The next one is in 2016.
Feb/Mar Mahasivaratri Fair is held at the
Mahakaleshwar Temple.

Nov Kartik Mela, the month-long fair, draws
large crowds from surrounding villages.

What to do

Ujjain
MP Tourism, *T0734-255 1495, www.mptourism.
com/sightseeting-tour.html.* **Ujjain Darshan** bus
covers 13 temples and sights, Rs 60, 6 hrs, 0730-
1330 and 1400 1900.

Transport

Ujjain
Bus Direct to **Bhopal**; regular to: **Dhar, Indore**
(53 km, 1½ hrs), **Gwalior, Mandu** (149 km, 6 hrs),
Omkareshwar.

Taxi and rickshaw Sights by taxi (Rs 1200-
1500), auto-rickshaw (Rs 600-800), *tempos* and
cycle-rickshaws.

Train Ahmedabad: 2-3 daily, 8½ hrs. **Bhopal**:
at least 10 daily, 3-4 hrs. **Indore**: at least 12 daily,
1¾ hrs. **Mumbai (Central)**: 2-3 daily, 12-13¼ hrs.
New Delhi (HN): 2 daily, 12-15 hrs.

★ Mandu (Mandav) *Colour map 2, C5.*
magical clifftop fort-village littered with romantic ruins

Architecturally, Mandu (population 5000) represents the best in a provincial Islamic
style, restrained and lacking in elaborate external ornamentation. Fine buildings are
spread over the naturally defensible plateau with a sheer drop towards the Namar
plains to the south and waterfalls flowing into the Kakra Khoh Gorge.

Essential Mandu

Finding your feet
Indore is the nearest centre for air, bus and
train connections.

Getting around
Everything worth visiting can be reached on
foot or bike. Cars can be hired informally for
day trips. See Transport, page 231.

Tip...
You can visit Mandu from Indore on a long
day excursion, but it's better to have a
peaceful break here for a couple of days.

Sights *Numbers in brackets below refer to map.*
The road leading up to the fort passes through
a series of well-fortified gates, most notable of
which is the **Delhi Gate** (1405-1407), the main
entrance to the city. Most of the buildings within
the 45-km parapet wall date from 1401 to 1526;
some have stones salvaged from desecrated
local Hindu temples. There are six groups
of buildings at Mandu, the first three being
the most important. The return trip taking in
Roopmati's Pavilion is about 14 km.

Royal Enclave ① *Rs 100.* The **Mosque of
Dilwar Khan** (1405) is the earliest Islamic
building, comprising a central colonnaded
courtyard. There are Hindu influences in the
main entrances. **Hathi Pol** (Elephant Gate) is the
main entrance to the royal enclosure. **Hindola
Mahal** (Swing Palace, circa 1425), built on a

'T' plan, was the audience hall, acquiring its name from its inward sloping walls which give the impression of swaying. Behind and to the west of the Hindola Mahal is a jumble of ruins which was once the palace of the Malwa sultans.

Here is the 6.5-m-deep **Champa Baoli**, an underground well (its water is said to have smelt like the *champak* flower), cool vaulted *tyhkhanas* (rooms for summer use), a *hammam* (hot bath) and a water pavilion.

The late 15th-century **Jahaz Mahal** (Ship Palace), reflects the spirit of romantic beauty characteristic of the palace life of the Muslim rulers of India. Built between two artificial lakes, Munj and Kapur Talaos, it is 122 m long and only 15 m wide. Its shape and kiosks give it the impression of a stately ship. Built to house Ghiyas'ud-Din's increasing *harem*, it was 'crewed' entirely by women, some from as far afield as Turkey and Abyssinia, and consists of three great halls with a beautiful bath.

Other places of interest in this enclave are **Taveli Mahal (1)** (stables and guardhouse), which has a wonderful panorama of the Mandu ruins; it has a small **museum** ① *Sat-Thu 0900-1700*. Nearby are two deep, bat-filled wells – the *Ujala* (bright) and *Andheri* (dark) **baolis** – and **Gada Shah's Shop (2)**. The last, in ruins, retains a romantic second name, the Kesar Kasturi Mahal. Gada Shah taking pity on a group of gypsies trying to sell their perfumed *kesar* and *kasturi* which had been ruined by a downpour, bought their wares and then had to use it all in his palace since it was unsaleable.

Central Group Hoshang Shah's Tomb **(3)** (circa 1440) ① *Mandu Bazar, Rs 100*, is India's first marble monument, a refined example of Afghan architecture. It has a well-proportioned dome, delicate marble latticework and porticoed courts and towers. The square base of the interior changes to an octagon through being raised by arches to the next level, and then becomes 16-sided further up. Shah Jahan sent four of his architects, including Ustad Ahmed, who is associated with the Taj

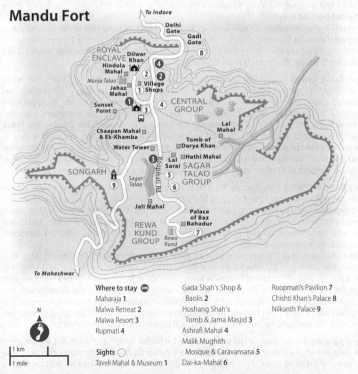

Mandu Fort

To Indore

Delhi Gate
Gadi Gate **8**

ROYAL ENCLAVE
Dilwar Khan.
Hindola Mahal
Munja Talao
Jahaz Mahal
Sunset Point
Village Shops **1**
2 **4**
2
1
3

CENTRAL GROUP **4**

Lal Mahal

Chaapan Mahal & Ek-Khamba
Water Tower
Tomb of Darya Khan
Lal Sarai **3**
Hathi Mahal
SAGAR TALAO GROUP
Roopmati Rd
5
6

SONGARH **9**
Sagar Talao

Jali Mahal
Palace of Baz Bahadur

REWA KUND GROUP
Rewa Kund
7

To Maheshwar

N

1 km
1 mile

BACKGROUND

Mandu

Perched along the Vindhya ranges, Mandu was fortified as early as the sixth century. By 1261, King Jayavaram transferred the Paramara capital from Dhar to Mandu itself. The whole area fell to the Muslims in 1293, though Mandu remained under Hindu rule until 1305, when it came under the Khaljis in Delhi. The first of these Pathan sultans re-named Mandu **Shadiabad** (City of Joy). Hoshang Shah (1405-1435) made it his capital and as Mandu's strategic importance grew he embellished it with its most important civic buildings. Under his successor, the liberal Mahmud Khalji, a resurgence of art and literature followed, fostering Hindu, Jain as well as Muslim development. Mandu remained a prosperous centre of peace and stability under his son Ghiyasuddin until 1500. Several early Mughal rulers enjoyed visiting Mandu, but by the end of the Mughal period it had effectively been abandoned, and in 1732 it passed into Maratha hands.

Mahal, to study it for inspiration. The adjoining **Jama Masjid (3)** (1454), which took three generations to complete, was inspired by the great mosque at Damascus. Conceived by Hoshang Shah on a grand scale, it is on a high plinth (4.6 m), with a large domed porch ornamented with jali screens and bands of blue enamel tiles set as stars. The courtyard is flanked by colonnades. The western one is the Prayer Hall, the most imposing of all with numerous rows of arches and pillars which support the ceilings of the three great domes and 58 smaller ones. The central *mihrab* (niche) is beautifully designed and ornamented along its sides with a scroll of interwoven Arabic letters containing quotations from the Koran.

Ashrafi Mahal (4) (Palace of Gold Coins, circa 1436-1440) was conceived as the first *madrassa* of Persian studies. Its builder Mahmud Shah Khilji (1436-1469) constructed the seven-storey tower to celebrate his victory over Rana Khumba of Mewar. Only one storey survives. Also in ruins is the tomb, intended to be the largest building in Mandu.

Sagar Talao Group To the east of the road between the village and Sagar Talao is the **Hathi Mahal** (Elephant Palace). It takes its names from its stumpy pillars supporting the dome and was probably a *baradari* (pleasure pavilion), turned into a tomb with a mosque by it. The **Tomb of Darya Khan** (circa 1526), a red masonry mausoleum once embellished with rich enamel patterns, is nearby.

In the large group of monuments around the picturesque **Sagar Talao** (lake) is the **Malik Mughith Mosque (5)** built in 1432. Its west wall retains blue tile decoration in carved niches. In front is the **caravanserai** (also 1432), an open courtyard with two halls with rooms at both ends. The **Dai-ka-Mahal (6)** (Gumbad) to the south is the tomb belonging to the wet nurse of a Mandu prince. Alongside, the ruins of a pretty mosque include a fine octagonal base decorated with small kiosks.

Rewa Kund Group ① *Foreigners Rs 100.* This is a sacred tank, 3.2 km south of the village, whose waters were lifted to supply the **Palace of Baz Bahadur** (1508-1509), the musician prince, on the rising ground above. The palace was built before Baz Bahadur, the last Sultan of Malwa (1555), came to occupy it. The main portion of the palace consists of a spacious open court with halls and rooms on all sides and a beautiful cistern in its centre. On the terrace above are two *baradaris* (pavilions) from which there are lovely views.

On higher ground at the southern edge of the plateau is **Roopmati's Pavilion (7)**, built as a military observation post but later modified and added to as a palace, so that Baz Bahadur's mistress could have her view of the sacred **Narmada River**, seen 305 m below winding like a white serpent across the plains. The shepherdess **Roopmati**, the story goes, so impressed Baz Bahadur with her singing that he captured her. She agreed to go to Mandu only when he promised that she would live in a palace within sight of her beloved river. He built the Rewa Kund so that she could practise her Hindu rites. The pavilions, square with hemispherical domes, are the latest additions.

Other palaces On the edge of the plateau is the **Lal Mahal** (Red/Ruby Palace) or Lal Bungalow, once used as a royal summer retreat. **Chishti Khan's Palace (8)**, used during the monsoon, is now in ruins but offers good views. West of Sagar Talao the Islamic **Nilkanth Palace (9)**, built for Akbar's

Hindu wife, contains the Nilkanth (Siva) shrine. On the scarp of one of the great ravines, reached by steps and commanding a magnificent view of the valleys below, it was used by the Mughals as a water palace. On one of the outer room walls is an inscription recording Akbar's expeditions into the Deccan and the futility of temporal riches.

The **Lohani Caves** and temple ruins are near Hoshang Shah's Tomb. Approached by steep rock-cut steps, they are a maze of dark and damp caverns in the hillside. Panoramic views of the surroundings from **Sunset Point** in front of the caves.

Listings Mandu map p229

Where to stay

Severe water shortage is likely before the monsoon; buckets are provided.

$$$-$$ Malwa Resort (MP Tourism)
Roopmati Rd, a 20-min walk from the bus stand, T07292-263235, www.mptourism.com.
In a peaceful setting by Sagar Talao Lake, Malwa Resort has 20 rooms (all a/c), plus suites and 'Swiss' cottages, a good restaurant and gardens.

$$-$ Malwa Retreat (MP Tourism)
Next to Rupmati, T07292-263221, www.mptourism.com.
A bright, cheerful and very pleasant place, with 8 a/c rooms plus 3 tents and 30-bed dorm (Rs 200), a restaurant (order ahead) and an excellent view of the plateau. It's worth negotiating if it's quiet.

$$-$ Rupmati
500 m beyond entrance, T07292-263270, hotelrupmatimandu@gmail.com.
19 clean rooms and cottages with attached bath, mostly a/c, with balcony and set around spacious garden. There are stunning gorge views, a very pleasant outdoor garden restaurant and beer.

$ Maharaja
Opposite police post, T07292-263288.
Run-down and grimy cheapie set around a grassy courtyard. The prime location makes it a worthwhile option though.

Transport

Bus Regular bus services to **Dhar** (35 km, 1½ hrs), 1st departure 0530; change there for **Indore** (99 km, 4-5 hrs) and **Ujjain**. The direct morning bus to Indore is very slow. From Dhar buses also go to **Bhopal** (286 km), **Ratlam** (124 km) and **Ujjain** (152 km).

Bicycle and rickshaw Cycle-rickshaws and bicycles are available for local sightseeing.

Car A private car from Indore should charge around Rs 900-1000 one way. Some local car owners offer day trips from Mandu to Maheshwar and Omkareshwar.

Train The most convenient railheads are **Ratlam** (124 km) on the Mumbai–Delhi line, and **Indore** (99 km) on the branch route. Ratlam has connections from **Vadodara**, **Bhopal** and **Kanpur**.

Maheshwar Colour map 2, C5.

fascinating riverside temple town

On the north bank of the Narmada, Maheshwar has been identified as Mahishmati, the ancient capital of King Kartivirarjun, mentioned in the *Ramayana* and *Mahabharata* epics.

The Holkar queen **Maharani Ahilyabai of Indore** who died in 1795 was responsible for revitalizing the city by building temples and a fort complex. She is also famous for restoring and building many other Hindu temples all around India. According to Scottish statesman Sir John Malcolm, the queen was widely revered. She had "an almost sacred respect for native rights ... she heard every complaint in person". Her reign has become almost legendary as a time when peace, order and good government prevailed and the people prospered. After her death she was made a saint. The palace inside the fort contains exhibits of the Holkar family treasures and memorabilia including the small shrine on a palanquin which is carried down from the fort during the annual Dasara ceremony. Most Indians who come to Maheshwar always visit and pay their respects at this shrine. There is also a statue of the Rani seated on her throne.

Essential Maheshwar

Finding your feet

Buses run regularly from Indore with a change at either Dhamnod or Omkareshwar. The nearest railway link is at Barwah. Some of the roads running from Mandu and Indore bear little resemblance to anything you may know as a road, so be prepared for very slow travel if you are coming by car. See Transport, below.

Fact...

In the middle of the river on a small island is Baneshwar temple, which, legend has it, is located at the centre of the Universe.

The small town is renowned for its *Maheshwari* saris woven in a unique way for over 200 years. At one time almost lost, the tradition has been revived by the Holkar family, and today the **Rehwa Society** ① *www.rehwasociety.org*, is a thriving cottage industry, the profits of which go to fund both the housing of the local female weavers, their families and a thriving school for local children from poorer families.

The **ghats** on the riverbank are perhaps some of the cleanest and least touristy in India. Local women wash clothes along the ghats and sadhus quietly go about their day. Lining the banks are many small temples, lingams and stone memorials to the *satis* (recently widowed women who would commit suicide by throwing themselves onto their husband's funeral pyre, a practice outlawed since 1829).

The temples to see are **Kaleshwara**, **Rajarajeshwara**, **Vithaleshwara** and **Ahileshwar**.

Listings Maheshwar

Where to stay

$$$$ Ahilya Fort
At the top of the walled city, T07283-273329, www.ahilyafort.com.
One of the most atmospheric heritage hotels in central India, the 18th-century home of Queen Ahilyabhai. It is in fact still the home of Prince Richard Holkar, the 22nd generation descendant of Ahilyabhai, who will even cook meals for the guests when he is home! Each room has its own style, tastefully decorated with antique furniture and beautifully retaining its original character. Many rooms have stunning views out over the Ghats of the Narmada river. There are rambling antique-filled courtyards, tranquil seating areas with fountains and flower-filled urns, a family temple, large pool, and organic veg gardens whose produce is used for the delicious communal dinner. Sunset boat ride with optional dip in the river and evening drinks at the candlelit fort ramparts all make for a very special and highly memorable experience. 11 rooms and a Maharaja tent. Highly recommended.

$$-$ Narmada Retreat
T07283-273455, www.mptourism.com.
Set a few kilometres away from the centre, bungalows and family tents are set in well-tended gardens with good views of the river. There's also a restaurant.

$ Hotel Sanginee
Sahasradhara Rd, T07283-273862, www.hotelsanginee.com.
Clean rooms with attached bath.

Transport

Regular bus services from **Barwaha**, **Khandwa**, **Dhar** and **Dhamnod**. The nearest railhead is **Barwaha** (39 km) on the Western Railway.

a magnet for pilgrims for centuries

Omkareshwar is a sacred island shaped like the holy Hindu symbol 'Om' at the confluence of the Narmada and the Kaveri. Over 2 km long and 1 km wide the island is divided north to south by a deep gully. The ground slopes gently along the north edge but in the south and east there are cliffs over 150 m high forming a gorge. The village spreads to the south bank from the island, now linked by a bridge. The river is reputedly very deep and has crocodiles.

Sri Omkareshwar Mahadeo Temple has one of the 12 *jyotirlingas* in India, natural rock features that are believed to be representations of Siva. The oldest temple is at the east end of the island. **Siddhnath Temple** on the hill is a fine example of early medieval temple architecture, its main feature being a frieze of elephants over 1.5 m high carved on a stone slab at its outer perimeter. Craftsmen have carved elaborate figures on the upper portion of the temple and its roof. Encircling the shrine are verandas with columns carved in circles, polygons and squares. A gigantic Nandi bull is carved in the hillside opposite the temple to **Gauri Somnath** at the west end of the island.

The temples were severely damaged after the Muslim invasions of **Mahmud of Ghazni**. Every dome was overturned and the sculptured figures mutilated. They became completely overgrown, and *Murray's Guide* records that when the Peshwa Baji Rao II wanted to repair the temple it could not be found, so he built a new one.

Listings Omkareshwar (Mandhata)

Transport

Bus and train Omkareshwar is connected to Indore, Ujjain, Khandhwa and Omkareshwar Rd railway station (12 km) by regular bus services. The railhead is on the Ratlam–Khandwa section of the Western Railway.

Northern
Madhya Pradesh

The boulder-strewn, thinly wooded Vindhya hills stretch across the north of the state, connecting some of the most fascinating historic monuments in central India. Foremost among them are the mesmerizing Tantric temples of Khajuraho, whose walls explode with intricate carvings that suggest 11th-century Madhya Pradesh must have been a swinging place indeed. Further west, the riverside village of Orchha has all the ingredients for a relaxing break from the road, with bat-strewn palaces and ruined mausoleums to explore, while Gwalior, a couple of hours by train from Agra, boasts one of the most awesome palace forts in the state.

★ Gwalior *Colour map 3, B1.*

towering fort with magnificent views

Surrounded by attractive open plateau country immediately to the north of the Vindhyas, Gwalior (population 827,000) is set in one of the state's driest regions. The majestic hill fort, formerly the key to control of the Central Provinces, dominates a ridge overlooking the town spread out below. It contains awe-inspiring Jain sculptures, Jain and Hindu temples and the charming sandstone palace. The Jai Vilas Palace, within its walls, bears testimony to the idiosyncratic tastes of the Scindia Maharajas. Much of the town, which sees few tourists, is very busy, noisy and crowded.

The fort

Sunrise-sunset, Foreigners Rs 100, Indians Rs 5 allow at least 2-3 hrs. Palaces open 0930-1700. English-speaking guides here expect Rs 200 (hotel guides charge more).

The fort stands on a sandstone precipice 91 m above the surrounding plain, 2.8 km long and 200-850 m wide. In places the cliff overhangs, elsewhere it has been steepened to make it unscaleable. The main entrance to the north comprised a twisting, easily defended approach. On the west is the **Urwahi Gorge** and another well-guarded entrance. The fort's size is impressive but the eye cannot capture all of it at once. Apart from its natural defences, Gwalior had the advantage of an unlimited water supply with many tanks on the plateau.

Essential Gwalior

Finding your feet

There are daily flights from Delhi and Indore, but the *Shatabdi Express* gives Gwalior excellent train connections with Agra and Delhi to the north and Jhansi and Bhopal to the south. The railway station and Madhya Pradesh State Bus Stand are southeast of the fort. From there, it is 6 km along the dusty MLB Road to the Jayaji Chowk area of Lashkar, the New Town. See Transport, page 239.

Getting around

In addition to a *tempo* stand near the station, there are unmetered autos and taxis. Gwalior is quite spread out and the fort is a stiff climb.

Approach The fort is a long walk from the town. You may enter from the northeast by the Gwalior or Alamgiri Gate but it is quite a steep climb. Mineral water is sold at the ticket counter; decline the booklet. Alternatively, take a taxi or an auto-rickshaw and enter from the west by the Urwahi Gate, where there are interesting Jain sculptures. After visiting the temples and palaces, you can descend to the Gujari Mahal in the northeast and pick up an auto from the Gwalior Gate. Visitors to the fort, particularly young women, should be prepared and aware that they may receive some unwanted attention from bored local teenage boys who often hang around inside the fort. Dressing modestly is definitely recommended.

Western entrance Above the **Urwahi Gate** there are 21 Jain sculptures dating from the seventh to 15th centuries, some up to 20 m tall. An offended Babur ordered their faces and genitalia to be destroyed. Modern restorers have only repaired the faces. There is a paved terrace along one side (ask to be dropped near the steps to view the sculptures since vehicles may not park along the road).

Northeast entrance A 1-km steep, rough ramp, with good views, leads to the main palace buildings. You pass through the **Gwalior Gate** (1660), the first of several gates, mostly built between 1486 and 1516. Next is the Badalgarh or **Hindola Gate**, named because of the swing which was once here. It is (unusually) a true structural arch, flanked by two circular towers. Note the use of material from older buildings.

At the base of the ramp the **Gujari Mahal Palace** (circa 1510) containing the **Gujari Mahal Archaeological Museum** ① *Tue-Sun 1000-1700, Rs 30*. The pretty palace has an interesting collection including sculptures and archaeological pieces (second and first century BC), terracottas (Vidisha, Ujjain), coins and paintings and copies of frescoes from the Bagh caves. Ask the curator to show you the beautiful 10th-century Shalbhanjika (Tree Goddess) miniature. Some museums and palaces are closed on Monday. Some distance from the fort above, this palace was built by Raja Man Singh for his Gujar queen Mrignayani. The exterior is well preserved. The 'Bhairon' Gate no longer exists and the fourth is the simple **Ganesh Gate** with a *kabutar khana* (pigeon house) and a small tank nearby. The mosque beyond stands on the site of an old shrine to the hermit

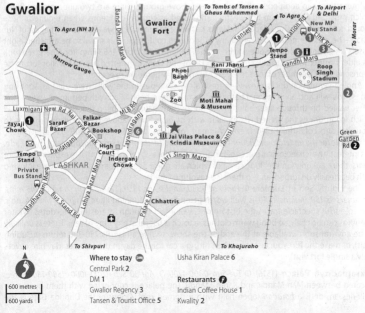

Gwalior

To Agra (NH 3)
To Tombs of Tansen & Ghaus Muhammad
To Agra
To Airport & Delhi
To Morar
To Shivpuri
To Khajuraho

Gwalior Fort

Banda Dhura Marg

Narrow Gauge

Rani Jhansi Memorial

Phool Bagh

Zoo

Moti Mahal & Museum

Luxmiganj New Rd Nai

Jayaji Chowk

Sarafa Bazar

Falkar Bazar

Bookshop

High Court

Indergani Chowk

LASHKAR

Daulatganj

Tempo Stand

Private Bus Stand

Jai Vilas Palace & Scindia Museum

Hari Singh Marg

Chhattris

Palace Rd

Tansen Rd

Station Rd

Link Rd

New MP Bus Stand

Tempo Stand

Gandhi Marg

Roop Singh Stadium

Green Garden Rd

Where to stay
Central Park **2**
DM **1**
Gwalior Regency **3**
Tansen & Tourist Office **5**

Usha Kiran Palace **6**

Restaurants
Indian Coffee House **1**
Kwality **2**

600 metres
600 yards

Gwalipa, the present temple having been built later with some of the original material. Before the **Lakshman Gate** (circa 14th century) is the ninth-century Vishnu **Chaturbhuja Temple**, with later additions, in a deep gap. A Muslim tomb and the northeast group of Jain sculptures are nearby. **Hathia Paur** (Elephant Gate, 1516), the last, is the entrance to the main Man Mandir palace which also had a Hawa gate, now demolished.

Man Mandir Palace (1486-1516) Built by Raja Man Singh, this is the most impressive building in the fort. The 30-m-high eastern retaining wall is a vast rock face on the cliff-side interrupted by large rounded bastions. The palace had ornamental parapets and cupolas, once brightly gilded, while blue, green and yellow tile-work with patterns of elephants, human figures, ducks, parrots, banana plants and flowers covered the exterior walls. The remarkable tiles, and the style of their inlay, are probably derived from Chanderi (200 km south) or Mandu. The beautifully decorated little rooms arranged round two inner courts have small entrances, suggesting they were built for the royal ladies. The iron rings here were used for swings and decorative wall hangings.

Interestingly, in addition to the two storeys above ground there are two underground floors which provided refuge from hot weather and acted as circular dungeons when required; these should not be missed. Guru Har Gobind who was once detained here was freed at the behest of Nur Jahan – he was permitted to take out any others who could touch his shawl so he attached eight tassels which enabled 56 prisoners to be freed with him. On 24 June 1658 Emperor Aurangzeb took his elder brother Murad captive en route to Delhi and then transferred him to Gwalior fort to be imprisoned. In December of the same year Aurangzeb ordered his execution.

Angled ventilation ducts allowed in fresh air while pipes in the walls were used as 'speaking tubes'. You will find an octagonal bath which would have been filled with perfumed water – the water welled up through inlet holes in the floor which have now been blocked. The south wall which incorporates the arched Hathia Paur with its guardroom above is particularly ornate with moulded and colourfully tiled friezes. A small **museum** ① *Sat-Sun 0800-1800, guides available, worthwhile for the underground floors if you don't have a torch; give a small tip,* opposite the façade, has interesting archaeological pieces of Hindu deities. **Note** A torch is essential to explore the lower floors: there are holes in the floor, some of which are quite deep. Underground levels are infested with bats (easily disturbed) and so there is a revolting smell.

The nightly **Son et Lumière** ① *Hindi at 1830, English at 1930 (1 hr later in summer), 45 mins, foreigners Rs 150, Indians Rs 40,* is well worth attending for stunning illumination of Man Mandir. The colourful spectacle traces the history of Gwalior fort through interesting anecdotes. Winter evenings can be chilly, so bring warm clothes; a torch is useful at any time of year. There is unlikely to be any transport available at the end of the show, so hire a taxi (Rs 250-300 return including wait), or make the fort your last stop when hiring a car for the day in the summer (day hire covers only a single fort visit).

Vikramaditya Palace (1516) ① *Tue-Sun 0800-1700 (1 Apr-30 Sep, 0700-1000, 1500-1800), free.* Located between Man Mandir and Karan Mandir, the palace is connected with them by narrow galleries. Inside is a *baradari* (open hall) with a domed roof. Opposite the Dhonda Gate is the

Karan Mandir (1454-1479), more properly called the Kirtti Mandir after its builder Raja Kirtti Singh. It is a long, two-storeyed building with a large, pillared hall and fine plaster moulding on ceilings of adjacent rooms. Just northwest is the **Jauhar Tank** where the Rajput women performed *jauhar* (mass suicide) just before the fort was taken by Iltutmish in 1232 (see page 1302), and also at Chittaurgarh (see page 319). The two unremarkable Muslim palaces, Jahangiri and Shah Jahan Mahals are further north. Moving south from Hathia Paur, towards the east wall, are the **Sas Bahu Mandirs**. Dedicated to Vishnu, the 11th-century 'Mother and Daughter-in-law' pair of temples built by Mahipala Kachhawaha (1093) still preserves fine carvings in places. The larger 12-sided temple is more interesting although only the *Mahamandapa* (Assembly Hall) remains. The smaller temple has an ornately carved base with a frieze of elephants, and a vaulted ceiling under the pyramidal roof. The wide ridged stone 'awning' is well preserved. An impressive marble **gurudwara** (1970) in memory of Sikh Guru Har Gobind (1595-1644), who had been imprisoned in the fort, is to its south, providing a haven of cool respite for visitors; the Guru Granth Sahib is read throughout the day. West of the *gurudwara* is **Suraj Kund**, a large tank, first referred to in the fifth century, where Suraj Sen's leprosy was cured. The water is now green and stagnant.

Teli-ka Mandir Teli-ka Mandir probably means 'oil man's temple'. It is the earliest temple in Gwalior, and architecturally has more in common with some early Orissan temples than those in the south (though sometimes guides suggest a link with Telangana in modern Andhra Pradesh indicating the fusion of Dravidian and North Indian architectural styles). This unique 25-m-high Pratihara (mid-eighth century) Vishnu Temple is essentially a sanctuary with a *Garuda* at the entrance. The oblong vaulted roof rather resembles a Buddhist *chaitya* and the Vaital Deul (Bhubaneswar). Tillotson records how after the 'Mutiny' "this great medieval temple, for example, was put to service as a soda-water factory and coffee shop. By such acts of desecration the British showed Indian rulers how the ancient Hindu heritage was then regarded by those who laid claim to power and authority". It was reconstructed in 1881-1883. The Katora Tal behind was excavated when the fort was built, like many others here. The Ek-khamba Tal has a single stone column standing in it.

Rani Tal, further south, was supposedly intended for the royal ladies; it is connected underground to the neighbouring **Chedi Tal**. Jain sculptures in the southeast corner can be seen from a path below the wall.

The town

After Daulat Rao Scindia acquired Gwalior in 1809 he pitched camp to the south of the fort. The new city that arose was **Lashkar** (The Camp) with palaces, King George Park (now Gandhi Park) and the *chhattris* of the Maharajas. **Jayaji Chowk**, once an elegant square, dominated by late 19th- and early 20th-century buildings, notably the Regal Cinema, and the Chowk Bazar is still a pleasant place to watch people going about their business from one of the good little restaurants.

Jai Vilas Palace (1872-1874) ① *Tue-Sun 0930-1700, tickets at gate: foreigners Rs 100, Indians Rs 25, camera Rs 25, video Rs 75, guided tours (1 hr) sometimes compulsory*, designed by Lieutenant-Colonel Sir Michael Filose, resembles an Italian palazzo in places, using painted sandstone to imitate marble. Part of the palace is the present maharaja's residence but 35 rooms house the **Scindia Museum**, an idiosyncratic collection of royal possessions, curiosities (eg 3-D mirror portraits), carpets (note the Persian rug with royal portraits) and interesting memorabilia.

In a separate building opposite (show your ticket) is the extraordinary **Durbar Hall**. It is approached by a crystal staircase, gilded in 56 kg of gold, and in it hang two of the world's largest chandeliers each weighing 3.5 tonnes; before they were hung the ceiling was tested by getting 10 elephants to climb on to it via a 2-km ramp. Underneath is the dining room. The battery-operated silver train set transported cigars, dry fruit and drinks round the table, after dinner. The lifting of a container or bottle would automatically reduce pressure on the track, and so stop the train. Southeast of the fort is the spot where **Rani Lakshmi Bai** of Jhansi was cremated, marked by a stirring statue.

The **Royal Chhattris**, south of town, are each dedicated to a Gwalior Maharaja. These ghostly pavilions are in various stages of neglect. The lighted images are still clothed and 'fed' daily. Be there at 1600 when they are shown again by the guardians after their afternoon nap.

In the crowded Hazira in the **Old Town**, northeast of the fort, is the **Tomb of Ghaus Muhammad**, a 16th-century Afghan prince who helped Babur to win the fort. It is in an early Mughal style with finely carved *jali* screens. Hindus and Muslims both make pilgrimage to the tomb. Nearby, in an attractive garden setting, is the **Tomb of Tansen**, the most famous musician of Akbar's court. It is the venue for the annual music festival (November/December). The present tamarind tree replaces the old one which was believed to have magical properties. Tansen was an exponent of the *dhrupad* style, and laid the foundations for what in the 19th century became the Gwalior *ghurana* style, noted for its stress on composition and forceful performance. One of the best-known contemporary exponents is Amjad Ali Khan, a renowned sarod player. A recently built **Sun Temple** similar in style to Konark is at Morar, a few kilometres east of the tombs.

Listings Gwalior *map p235*

Tourist information

Tourist office
Platform 1, railway station, T0751-504 0777.

Where to stay

$$$ Central Park
Madhav Rao Scindia Marg, city centre, T0751-404 2440, www.thecentral park.net.
Modern a/c rooms in Gwalior's top business hotel. Pool, health club, coffee shop, good restaurant and bar, currency exchange and breakfast included. Recommended.

$$$ Usha Kiran Palace
Jayendraganj Lashkar, T0751-244 4000, www.tajhotels.com.
In a 120-year-old maharaja's palace are these 30 unique and very atmospheric a/c rooms, 6 suites and some villas. Beautiful spa and gardens, swimming pool, good restaurant, billiards and bar. It retains character of charming royal guesthouse, with all the trimmings and attention to detail you would expect from somewhere where members of various royal families do actually come and stay sometimes. Recommended.

$$$-$$ Gwalior Regency
Near New Bus Stand, T0751-234 0670, www.hotel regencygroup.com.
Smallish but well-maintained hotel with 51 modern rooms, a restaurant, coffee shop and pool.

$$$-$$ Tansen
6A Gandhi Rd, T0751-405 6789, www.mptourism.com.
In a quiet location and handy for bus and train, Tansen has 36 rooms, all a/c, a good restaurant, bar, garden, car hire and tourist information.

$$-$ DM
Link Rd, near New Bus Stand, T0751-234 1049.
Small and pretty shabby rooms with attached bath (hot water) and small garden at the back. Reasonably quiet and handy for the bus stand.

Restaurants

$$$ Usha Kiran Palace
See Where to stay, above.
Good rich Mughlai meals and snacks, live classical music, bar, and attentive service, all in a pleasant ambience in ornate surroundings looking out over attractive gardens.

$$ Kwality
Green Garden road behind SP Office, T0751-242 3243, www.kwalitygwalior.com.
Pretty decent and tasty mainly Indian and snacks in a clean but rather dark restaurant. Helpful staff.

$ Indian Coffee House
India Hotel, just off Jayaji Chowk.
Great for South Indian breakfasts, snacks and *thalis*.

Shopping

Ganpatlal Krishna Lal, *Sarafa Bazar. Closed Tue.* Jewellery and antiques.
Kothari, *Sarafa Bazar.* Brocade, *chanderi* (light and flimsy cotton and silk material) and silk saris.
Loyal, *near High Court, Nai Sarak.* Books.
MD Fine Arts, *Subhash Market.* Paintings and objets d'art.
MP Emporium, *Sarafa Bazar.* Handlooms.
MP Khadi Sangh, *Sarafa Bazar.* Handlooms.

What to do

Tours
MP Tourism, *T0751-4040777, www.mptourism. com/sightseeting-tour.html.* Gwalior Darshan 1100-1430, Rs 200, about 7 places in Gwalior are visited.

Transport

Air The airport is 9 km from town. Flights to **Delhi** and **Indore**.

Bus Bus stand, Link Rd. Frequent buses to **Agra**, **Bhopal**, **Indore** and **Shivpuri**. Daily to **Khajuraho**.

Rickshaw Prepaid auto-rickshaw stand at the railway station. Cycle-rickshaw charge around Rs 25 for rides within town. *Tempos* on fixed routes, Rs 3-8.

Train Gwalior is on the main Delhi–Mumbai and Delhi–Chennai lines. Enquiries T131, reservations T135. Tickets for the *Shatabdi Express* are usually sold in the separate, 'non-computerized' queue. For **Bhopal**: more than 20 a day 5-8 hrs, via **Jhansi**, 1-1½ hrs. **Delhi**: dozens of trains daily, 4-6 hrs, all via **Agra**, 1¾ hrs. **Khajuraho**: 1 daily, 7 hrs. **Mumbai** (**CST**): 2 daily, 23-25 hrs. **Varanasi**: 1 overnight train, 14½ hrs, via **Allahabad**, 11 hrs.

a useful base for visiting nearby Orchha

Jhansi (population 405,000) is best known for its fort and the involvement in the 1857 Mutiny of its queen Rani Lakshmi Bai. Today, it is a useful stop on the train from Delhi en route to visiting Khajuraho by road. Although it's technically across the border in Uttar Pradesh, we've included it here as you're most likely to stay here while visiting peaceful Orchha, just a few minutes down the road.

Jhansi

Jhansi was a small village until taken in 1742 by the Marathas, who extended the old Fort. In 1853 it 'lapsed' to the British, when the raja died without leaving a male heir. The fort was seized in 1857 by

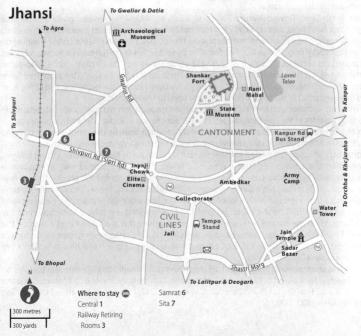

Jhansi

To Gwalior & Datia

To Agra

To Shivpuri

🏛 Archaeological Museum

Gwalior Rd

Shankar Fort

Laxmi Talao

🔲 Rani Mahal

🏛 State Museum

CANTONMENT

To Kanpur

Kanpur Rd 🚍 Bus Stand

Shivpuri Rd (Sipri Rd)

Jayaji Chowk

Elite 🔲 Cinema

Pol

Ambedkar

Army Camp

To Orchha & Khejuraho

Collectorate

CIVIL LINES

Jail

🚍 Tempo Stand

Water 🔲 Tower

Jain Temple 🛕

Sadar Bazar

Pol

✉

Shastri Marg

To Bhopal

N

To Lalitpur & Deogarh

300 metres
300 yards

Where to stay 🛏
Central **1**
Railway Retiring Rooms **3**

Samrat **6**
Sita **7**

mutineers and most of the occupants were slaughtered. The young Rani, who had been denied rule by the British, joined the rebels but had to retire to Gwalior. She continued her attempts to return after the British regained control of Jhansi. She was killed in action on 18 June 1858 at Kotah-ki-Saraï "dressed like a man ... holding her sword two-handed and the reins of her horse in her teeth ..." (Hibbert). The British ceded the fort to the Maharaja of Scindia and exchanged it for Gwalior in 1866.

Shankar Fort ① *sunrise-sunset*, was built by Bir Singh Deo in 1613. The nucleus of the fort, which has concentric walls up to 9 m high with 10 gates, was breached by the British in 1858. There are good views from the walls. Rani Mahal, once Lakshmi Bai's home, is an **archaeological museum** (ninth to 12th century). **Retribution Hill** ① *Tue-Sun 1030-1630 (6 Apr-30 Jun 0730-1230), closed 2nd Sun each month, foreigners US$2*, marks the last stand of the Mutineers in 1858. The **State Museum** ① *Tue-Sun 1000-1700*, near the fort in a vast modern building, has a good collection of stone sculptures in addition to weapons and ethnography.

Barua Sagar
Some 24 km east along the Khajuraho road are the ruins of a historic fort where the Maratha Peshwas fought the Bundelas. The deserted sandstone fort has excellent views over the *sagar* (lake) created by a dam across the Betwa River. The ninth-century early **Pratihara Temple** (Jarai-ka-Math), dedicated to Siva and Parvati, is built in red sandstone and highly ornamented. Yet the place is rarely visited and is wonderfully peaceful; you can swim in the lake. Buses from Jhansi travelling to Khajuraho will stop here on request (about one hour from Jhansi). It is then a five-minute walk along a narrow tree-lined canal to the fort; ask locally for keys. To return, wave down any bus to Jhansi (frequent service).

Datia and Sonagiri *75 km south of Gwalior, 34 km from Jhansi.*
Datia itself is not nearly as attractive as Orchha but is interesting to visit nevertheless, particularly as there is hardly a tourist in sight. The forgotten palace lies on the edge of the lively town with a significant Muslim population.

Bir Singh Deo's **Govind Mandir Palace** (c 1620) ① *0800-1700, caretaker 'guide' (speaks little English but holds keys), expects Rs 50 for a tour*, unlike other Bundelkhand palaces, was conceived as an integrated whole, its form and decoration blending Mughal and Rajput styles. Standing on an uneven rocky ridge, the palace has five storeys visible, while several cool underground floors excavated out of the rock remain hidden. The lower floors are very dark – carry a torch. Dilapidated and deserted, it is still imposing and atmospheric. The Bundela chief Bir Singh Deo supported Salim (later Jahangir) against his father Akbar, and may have been responsible for robbing and killing Abul Fazl in an ambush. His successors, however, were loyal to the Mughals.

The main entrance is on the east side, approached through very narrow crowded streets, while the south overlooks the lake Karna Sagar. There is a profusion of arches, *chhattris*, ornamental *jali* screens, coloured tiling, balconies and oriel windows which open up delightful views. Within the square plan which surrounds the central courtyard, a separate five-storey 'tower' houses the royal apartments which are connected with the surrounding palace by four colonnaded flying bridges, completing this unusual architectural marvel. Strangely it was occupied only intermittently (possibly never by the royal family). The paintings – in deep red, orange and green – though few, are lovely. The first floor has a Dancing Room with stucco figures, the second floor the Queen's Room and a Dancing Room with beautiful wall and ceiling paintings of peacocks, elephants and kings, while the third floor has bridges and the Diwan-i-khas, for private audience (note the Mughal tomb in the corner). Keys are needed to go above this level. The King's Room on the fourth floor with its shallow dome has a beautifully sculpted ceiling with geometric designs of flower petals and stars while the roof parapet has remains of green and blue tiles. There are excellent views all round.

A few kilometres north of Datia, just off the main road, **Sonagiri** has 77 white Jain temples on a hill reached by a paved path. Some date from the 17th century: the one to Chatranatha is the best. It is a pilgrim site for *Digambara* Jains, see page 1342, many of whom attend the evening *arati* between 1800-2100.

Shivpuri National Park *Colour map 3, B1.*

The dense forests of the Shivpuri or Madhav National Park, 114 km southwest of Gwalior, were the hunting grounds of the Mughal emperors when great herds of elephants were captured for Emperor Akbar. Now mainly a deer park in forested hill territory, this was also where Maharajas of Gwalior once hunted.

The park is a 156-sq-km dry deciduous forest, with Sakhya Sagar, a large perennial lake, attracting a large number of migratory birds in the winter. Stop where the forest track crosses the stream from the Waste Wier. **George Castle** on high ground, once the Scindias' hunting lodge, and **Burah Koh** watchtower have good views over the lake at sunset. Animals include nilgai, chinkara, chowsingha, sambar, cheetal and wild pig. **Chandpata Lake** attracts numerous waterbirds including migratory pochard, pintail, teal, mallard, demoiselle crane and bar-headed geese which remain until May. The best time to visit is from January to March.

Near the **Tourist Village**, the pink **Madhav Vilas summer palace** ① *evening prayers (arati) and concert of quality classical singing around 1900*, is now a government building. The impressive marble *chhattris* of the Scindia rulers, with fine pietra dura inlay and *jali* work, are set in formal Mughal gardens with flowering trees. They synthesize Hindu and Islamic styles with their *sikharas* and Mughal pavilions. Curiously, meals are still prepared for the past rulers. **Bhadaiya Kund** nearby has a spring rich in minerals.

From Jhansi to Khajuraho

This route, across the mainly agricultural hill region of Bundelkhand, runs along the northern edge of the peninsula, crossing a number of significant rivers such as the Betwa and Dhasan as they flow off the plateau. Before Independence this was a land of small Rajput and Muslim states, struggling to maintain and expand their power against the greater forces from the plains to the north. Much is now open farmland pimpled with rock outcrops and forested hills, making for very attractive scenery – best appreciated from a car, or from the roof of one of the notoriously overcrowded buses that ply this busy road. For a stop-off, **Nowgong** has a pleasant breezy restaurant in a pretty garden, on the Jhansi side of town.

Listings Jhansi and around *map p239*

Tourist information

Jhansi

Madhya Pradesh Tourism
Railway station, T0510-244 2620.

Where to stay

Jhansi

Unless you arrive on a desperately late train it's far better to stay at Orchha. Power cuts are frequent, and standards of cleanliness are poor across the board.

$ Central
701 Civil Lines (500 m from railway station), T0510-244 0509.
39 rooms (some 4-bed), some air-cooled, with bath, Indian meals.

$ Railway Retiring Rooms
6-bed dorm. Other hotels near the station are dirty.

$ Samrat
Chitra Chauraha near railway station, T0510-244 4943.
Rooms with fan, some with a/c; check rooms before you commit, as some are fine but some are hideous so that extra Rs 100 could make a big difference on what you get. Mosquitos are a real problem.

$ Sita
Shivpuri Rd, T0510-244 2956, www.hotelsitamanor.com.
29 smart, clean a/c rooms with bath, a good restaurant, car hire and exchange.

Datia

$$ Tourist Motel (MP Tourism)
2 km from town on Gwalior Rd, T07522-238125, www.mptourism.com.
Overlooks the palace and lake with 8 spotless, airy rooms and a restaurant.

$ Shri Raghunath Ganga Hotel
Station Rd, opposite Pitambra Peeth Temple,
T07522-236754.
The owners are helpful and very welcoming at
this clean, secure hotel, offering 9 air-cooled
rooms, with baths.

Shivpuri National Park

$$ Tourist Village (MP Tourism)
Jhansi Rd, 5 km east of town, Bhadaiya Kund,
T07492-223760, www.mptourism.com.
Set in an attractive location overlooking the lake
and close to the park, this place has 17 rooms and
4 suites, all a/c, with a pleasant restaurant, and
jeep hire.

$ Delhi Hotel
Madhav Chowk, A-B Rd, T07492-233093.
Hotel with 12 simple rooms, some a/c, with bath,
and a vegetarian restaurant.

Restaurants

Jhansi
Hotels Sita and Samrat are recommended.

$$ Holiday
Shastri Marg.
Reasonably priced Indian and Western dishes
served in a clean a/c restaurant.

$ Nav Bharat
Shastri Marg.
Indian snacks.

What to do

Jhansi
Tour operators
Touraids, *Jai Complex, Civil Lines, T0510-233 1760,*
www.touraidsi.com. Helpful and reliable manager
with a fleet of cars for hire.

Transport

Jhansi
Bus From **Kanpur Rd Bus Stand**, 3 km east
of railway station: **Gwalior** 0645-1800 via
Datia; **Khajuraho**, bumpy and crowded, 0530,

1100, 1145, 1330, 1545 (tickets from booth on
Platform 1, claim your seat early; Rs 100, plus
luggage Rs 5, 5-6 hrs); **Lalitpur** 0730, 1025, 2100,
2300. **Shivpuri** 0500-1800. **Orchha** half-hourly
during daylight, about 30 mins, Rs 8. *Tempos*
leave when full, 30 mins, Rs 15.

Car To **Khajuraho**, Travel Bureau or **Touraids**
charge around Rs 2400, reliable drivers.

Rickshaw and taxi Rickshaws can be found at
the station; use the prepaid counter or it's Rs 20-
30 to the bus stand; drivers visiting **MP Tourism**
office at station quote overpriced 'friends' rate.
Tempo to bus stand Rs 8 each. To Orchha from
station, allow Rs 250; return after sightseeing,
Rs 450-500. Taxis are equally overpriced, about
Rs 300-450; to **Khajuraho**, around Rs 1800-2400.

Train Bhopal: at least 20 a day, 4-5 hrs. **Delhi**:
25-30 trains a day, 5-8 hrs. Most stop at **Gwalior,**
1-1½ hrs, and **Agra** 3-3½ hrs. **Jabalpur** (for
Kanha): 3 a day, 9-12 hrs. **Jalgaon** (for **Ajanta/**
Ellora): more than 10 a day, 12-15 hrs. **Lucknow**:
at least 6 a day, 6-9 hrs. **Khajuraho**: 3 daily,
4-5 hrs **Mumbai**: 5 daily, 18-20 hrs. **Varanasi**:
1 daily, 13 hrs.

Datia and Sonagiri
Bus Frequent from **Jhansi** (1 hr, Rs 10), and
Gwalior (Rs 30).

Rickshaw *Tempos* and cycle-rickshaws run the
2 km between Datia station and the fort/palace
(Rs 40), and the 5 km between Sonagiri station
and the temples.

Train Datia and Sonagiri are on the Delhi–
Mumbai main line, with frequent trains to both
Gwalior and **Jhansi**.

Shivpuri National Park
Air The nearest airport is at **Gwalior** (112 km).

Bus Regular bus services from **Bhopal,**
Chanderi, **Indore**, **Jhansi** (101 km, 3 hrs
by car) and **Ujjain**. Auto-rickshaws available
at bus stand.

Train The nearest stations are **Jhansi**
and **Gwalior**.

a largely untouched island of peace and calm

Highly picturesque, in the middle of nowhere, abandoned and somewhat neglected, Orchha (population 8500) is an ideal stop between Gwalior and Khajuraho. Set on an island on a bend in the Betwa River, the fort palace from a bygone era is raised on a rocky promontory above the surrounding wooded countryside. Orchha is approached from the congested, increasingly touristy village centre by a remarkable early 17th-century granite bridge built by Bir Singh Deo, while all around, the forest encroaches on the tombs and monuments.

The site *Numbers in bracket refer to the map, page 244.*

Orchha is a wonderful example of a medieval fort palace. Within the turreted walls are gardens, gateways, pavilions and temples, near the Betwa and Jamni rivers. On a moonlit night, the view across the palaces with their *chhattris* and ornamented battlements is enchanting. A suggested route is to visit the Raj Mahal with its Hall of Private Audience then go through the doorway to the Hall of Public Audience. From here go down the ramp and follow the path to the Rai Praveen Mahal. Continue along the path to the Jahangir Mahal, arriving back at the courtyard of the Sheesh Mahal.

The **Raj Mahal (1)**, to the right of the quadrangle, exemplifies Bundela Rajput architecture. There are two rectangular courtyards around which the floors rise in tiers (inspired by the Koshak Mahal in Chanderi, which was built a century earlier); typically there are cool chambers below ground and a fountain. Some of the original blue tile decoration remains on the upper outer walls. To the left of the first courtyard is the Hall of Private Audience which would have been covered with rich carpets and cushions (note the floor-level windows). The Hall of the Public Audience has two quarter-size plaster elephants. Despite the neglected appearance of the royal chambers off the second courtyard, some have beautiful murals on the ceilings and walls. Representing both religious and secular themes, one series is devoted to the *Ramayana*, another to Vishnu's incarnations, others to scenes of court life: musicians, hunters, river excursions and a fairground. Normally locked, but the caretaker will unlock some ground floor rooms. Don't miss Rooms 5 and 6 which have the best paintings but you will need a torch. There is a Sheesh Mahal upstairs as well as good views of other palaces and temples from the very top; watch your step though, especially in strong winds.

The **Rai Praveen Mahal (2)** was probably named after the musician-courtesan who was a favourite at the princely court of Indrajit, brother of Ram Shah (1592-1604). The low two-storey brick palace with cool underground chambers and beautifully carved stone niches is built to

Essential Orchha

Finding your feet

Orchha is easily reached by road from Jhansi. After travelling 9 km southeast along the Khajuraho Road, a minor road turns south for the remaining 7 km to Orchha. There are taxis, *tempos* or buses from Jhansi station, but it is best to travel during daylight hours, and book and enquire about onward buses well ahead.

Admission prices

Foreigners Rs 250, Indians Rs 5, camera (no flash) Rs 20, video Rs 50; ticket office at palace, 0800-1800. Allow two hours. An audio tour is available from Sheesh Mahal hotel, Rs 50, and is highly recommended.

Getting around

The fort palace complex and the village are all easily seen on foot. The riverside is a 10-minute stroll away. If you are laden with luggage you can get a rickshaw from the village centre to your hotel. Women are advised not to wander around the site alone.

Tip...

The buildings are in a bad state of repair. If you go to the top take extra care and carry a torch.

scale with surrounding trees and the Anand Mandal gardens. To get to the underground rooms, turn left down steps on exiting the main rooms.

The octagonal flowerbeds are ingeniously watered from two wells. A new path takes you via the **hamaam (3)**, bypassing the **Royal Gate (4)**, and past the **Camel Stables (5)** to the most impressive of the three palaces.

Jahangir Mahal (6), built in the 17th century by Raja Bir Singh Deo to commemorate the Emperor's visit, synthesizes Hindu and Muslim styles as a tribute to his benefactor. The

Orchha

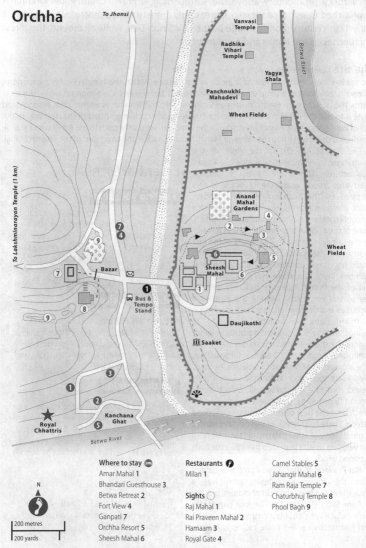

Where to stay

Amar Mahal 1
Bhandari Guesthouse 3
Betwa Retreat 2
Fort View 4
Ganpati 7
Orchha Resort 5
Sheesh Mahal 6

Restaurants

Milan 1

Sights

Raj Mahal 1
Rai Praveen Mahal 2
Hamaam 3
Royal Gate 4

Camel Stables 5
Jahangir Mahal 6
Ram Raja Temple 7
Chaturbhuj Temple 8
Phool Bagh 9

Orchha

The Bundela chief Raja Rudra Pratap (1501-1531) chose an easily defended and beautiful site for his capital. In the 11th century, a Rajput prince is said to have offered himself as a sacrifice to the mountain goddess Vrindavasini; she prevented his death and named him *'Bundela'* (one who offered blood). The dynasty ruled over the area between the Yamuna and Narmada rivers, having stepped into the vacuum left by the Tughlaqs and extended their power, moving their base to Orchha (meaning hidden). Raja Rudra Pratap threw a wall around the existing settlement and began work on the palace building (circa 1525-1531) and an arched bridge to it. This was completed by his successor Bharti Chand (1531-1554) who was installed in the Raj Mahal with great ceremony.

The continuing fortunes of the dynasty may have stemmed from the rulers' diplomatic skills. Though the third ruler, the religious Madhukar Shah, was defeated in battle by Akbar and was exiled in 1578 (died 1592), he nevertheless won the Mughal emperor's friendship. Later Bir Singh Deo (1605-1627, see Datia, page 240), while opposing Akbar, aligned himself with Prince Salim (Jahangir), who later rewarded him with the throne of Orchha, thus ensuring its ongoing prosperity. The Jahangir Mahal was built to commemorate the emperor's visit to Orchha. However, Bir Singh's first son, Jhujan, ran foul of Shah Jahan and, ignoring orders, treacherously killed the neighbouring chief of Chauragarh. The imperial army routed Jhujan and Orchha was pillaged. In 1783 the Bundela capital was moved to Tikamgarh, leaving Orchha to the *dhak* forests, the Betwa River and its guardian eagles.

70-m-sq palace, which is best entered from the east, the original main entrance flanked by elephants, can also be entered from the south. It has a large square interior courtyard, around which are the apartments in three storeys. The guided tour goes to the top of these up narrow and dark stairways. Each corner bastion and the projection in the middle of each side is topped by a dome. These contain apartments with intervening terraces – hanging balconies with balustrades and wide eaves create strong lines set off by attractive arches and brackets, decorative cobalt and turquoise blue tiles, *chhattris* and *jali* screens giving this huge palace a delicate and airy feel. There is a small **museum**① *Sat-Thu 1000-1700*, with a run-down assortment of photos, sculptures and *sati* stones; labels are in Hindi.

A few minutes' walk south of the main palace complex is **Saaket** ① *1000-1700, Rs 40*, an excellent newish museum displaying Ramayana paintings in traditional folk styles from Orissa, Bihar, Maharashtra, Andhra Pradesh and Bengal. The paintings, on palm leaves, silk and organically dyed cotton, are of the highest quality, and the stories behind them fascinating.

The village

Just south of the crossroads is the **Ram Raja Temple (7)** ① *0800-1230, 1900 2130 (1 hr later on summer evenings), cameras and leather articles must be left outside*, which forms a focus for village life. The temple courtyard and the narrow lane leading to it have stalls selling souvenirs and the area occasionally swells with pilgrims and *sanyasis*. The pink and cream paint is not in keeping with the other temples. It is interesting to visit during *arati*; otherwise there is little to see inside. Following the appearance of Rama in a dream, the pious Madhukar Shah brought an image of the god from Ayodhya and placed it in this palace prior to its installation in a temple. However, when the temple was ready it proved impossible to shift the image and the king remembered, only too late, the divine instruction that the deity must remain in the place where it was first installed. It is the only palace-turned-temple in the country where Rama is worshipped as king.

Chaturbhuj Temple (8) ① *usually open 0800-1700*, up the steps from the Ram Raja Temple courtyard, was built by King Madhukar Shah for his Queen Kunwari to house the image of Rama brought from Ayodhya. Laid out in the form of a cross, a symbolic representation of the four-armed god Krishna, there is a triple-arched gate with attractive *jharokas* on the exterior. The tallest *sikhara* is over the Garbagriha shrine, to the left of which you will see a Ganesh and a set of kettle drums.

The high arches and ceilings with vaulting and lotus domes painted in a rich red in places, are particularly striking. You can climb up any of the corner staircases, which lead up, by stages, to the very top of the temple. The second level gives access to tiny decorated balconies which provided privileged seating. There are good

Tip...
The riverside is ideal for lazing under a shady tree. Cross the bridge and head upstream for better spots for swimming (watch out for currents).

views of the nine palaces from the top, reached by the mini labyrinth of narrow corridors and steps. On the roof are langurs, wild bee hives and vultures nesting in corner towers.

A 1-km paved path links the Ram Raja with Bir Singh Deo's early 17th-century **Lakshminarayan Temple** ① *0900-1700, 15-min walk*, on a low hill, which incorporates elements of fort architecture. The ticket attendant gives a 'tour', naming the characters illustrated; go up the tower, the steps are steep but there are very good views of the entire area. The typical village houses along the path are freshly whitewashed for Diwali. The diagonal plan enclosing the central square temple structure is most unusual. The excellent murals (religious and secular), on the interior walls and ceilings of the four cool galleries around the temple here, are well-preserved examples of the Bundela school. The paintings in red, black, yellow, grey and turquoise portray Hindu deities, scenes from the epics, historical events including the early British period (note the interesting details of Lakshmi Bai's battle against the British), as well as giving an insight into the domestic pleasures of royalty.

Phool Bagh (9) is a formal garden and an eight-pillared pavilion which has a cool underground apartment. It's well worth a visit.

Of the 15 **Royal Chhattris** to former rulers grouped by the Kanchana Ghat by the river, about half are neglected and overgrown but pleasant for walking around in the late afternoon. A few are well preserved; ask the watchman if you want to look inside. He will take you to the upper levels by some very narrow, dark stairs: it's good fun but take a torch and be careful. He will expect a small tip. The chhattris are best photographed from the opposite bank: take a stick as dogs can be a problem.

The small but busy **village bazar**, with some interesting temples nearby, is about 10 minutes' walk from the riverside where a series of royal *chhattris* still stand as sentinels.

Listings Orchha *map p244*

Where to stay

Hotels are best on the idyllic riverside.

$$$ Amar Mahal
T07680-252102, www.amarmahal.com.
Decorated in traditional Bundelkhand architectural style, this modern-day palace has luxurious, attractive and extremely spacious rooms with 4-poster beds arranged around 2 courtyards, one with a pool. The well-maintained and tranquil gardens are where local musicians play during the evening, perfect for relaxing after a day walking around the sites. The excellent buffet-style restaurant has a 24-carat gold-painted ceiling, and there's Ayurvedic massage, a gym and a doctor on call. Recommended.

$$$-$$ Betwa Retreat (MP Tourism)
A 10-min walk from the bus stand, T07680-252618, www.mptourism.com.
Overlooking the river are these 14 clean and bright, but typically dated government-style

cottages, some a/c. The best (**$$$**) are in the beautiful high-ceilinged Maharaja Villa, plus there are 15 'luxury' tents, in serious need of mould fumigation. Spacious well-kept gardens, scattered ruins, nightly folk music and dance, but an average restaurant.

$$$-$$ Orchha Resort
Kanchanghat, T07680-252222, www.orchharesort.com.
On the riverside, these 32 immaculate but characterless a/c rooms and 12 musty tents are arranged around a parched tennis court with the redeeming feature of an extraordinary backdrop of the royal *chhatris*. There's a reasonable pool and an excellent veg restaurant (see Restaurants, below).

$$$-$$ Sheesh Mahal (MP Tourism)
T07680-252624.
In a stunning location inside the fort are these 5 beautiful ornate rooms and 2 majestic suites (**$$$**) with terrace, antique fittings and furniture, huge marble tub, and a panoramic view from the toilet. They are full of character and atmospheric

charm. The restaurant (see below) has great views, and the staff are friendly. Book in advance. Recommended.

$$-$ Fort View
Next to Ganpati, T07680-252701.
A retired school teacher's clean and friendly guesthouse, offering hot water, a dorm, and good views. Negotiate prices for longer stays.

$$-$ Ganpati
Just north of the main crossroads, Main Rd, Main Bazar, T07680-252765.
A wide range of clean rooms with hot showers. The best ones are the large 'sweet rooms' with a/c, murals and great views of the fort. There's a small courtyard and gardens, great views of palace and a very friendly owner. Recommended.

$ Bhandari Guesthouse
5 mins' walk south near the river bridge, T07680-252745, T(0)9425-342559.
Spotless, good-value rooms with attached bathrooms set around a small courtyard.

Restaurants

$$$ Orchha Resort
See Where to stay, above.
Vegetarian restaurant with pleasant decor and a choice of à la carte or buffet options (breakfast Rs 200, lunch/dinner Rs 400).

$$ Sheesh Mahal
See Where to stay, above.
International non-vegetarian meals are served in a large foyer in the fantastic and atmospheric palace. Great North Indian dishes, chilled beer and good service.

$ Milan restaurant
Just before the fort bridge.
Small, clean and well cared for place serving a range of cuisine and living up to its name serving 'real' expresso coffee, not so easy to find in these parts. Great breakfast too. Recommended.

Festivals

Nov/Dec Ram Vivah (Rama's marriage). Colourful processions draw crowds particularly as superbly trained horses perform extraordinary feats where one removes a horseman's eye make-up with a hoof.

What to do

River rafting
River rafting trips (Oct-Feb) can be organized by **MP Tourism** (www.mptourism.com), or contact the manager of **Betwa Retreat** or **Sheesh Mahal** (see Where to stay, above). Scenic 90-min and 3-hr trips on the Betwa with a few fairly gentle rapids (around Rs 1200-2000). The Jamuni River has more adventurous runs (Rs 3000).

Deogarh and Chanderi *Colour map 3, B1.*
hiking and wildlife watching in the forest, and numerous ruined temples

Deogarh
On the Uttar Pradesh side of the Betwa River, the small village of Deogarh (Fort of the Gods), offers the chance to rest and enjoy cliff-top views of the Betwa River. Impressive cliffs overlook the river with shrines and reliefs carved into the cliff walls. On the southern fringes of the great Gupta Empire (fourth to sixth century AD), its relative isolation has meant that some fine temples survive.

The temples were built of local stone (and occasionally granite), rather than the more easily destroyed brick. The sixth-century red sandstone, ruined in parts but otherwise well-preserved **Dasavatara Temple** is the finest here. The central sanctum had four flat-roofed entrance porticoes in place of the normal one, and the first northern pyramidal temple *sikhara*, though little of it remains. There are fine sculptures on the three walls, of Vishnu legends and a doorway with carvings of Ganga and Yamuna. The remarkable Anantashayi Vishnu, in Harle's phrase, lies "dreaming another aeon into existence". While Lakshmi gently holds Vishnu, the sacred lotus with Brahma rises from his navel.

The dramatic **hilltop fort** encloses 31 Jain temples dating from the ninth to 10th centuries with sculpted panels, images and 'thousand image pillars'; the best examples are in temples 11 and 12. Nearby, the Sahu Jain Sangrahalaya has some fine 10th- to 11th-century carvings. A well-marked path from the car park here leads to the river and the shrines; it is a fairly long walk.

Chanderi
The road climbs steeply to approach Chanderi, 37 km west of Lalitpur, an important town under the Mandu sultans, which was dominated by a hill fort. It is attractively placed in an embayment in

the hills overlooking the Betwa River and contains the 15th-century Koshak Mahal and other ruined palaces, market places, mosques and tombs. The old town, 8 km north and buried in jungle, has Jain temples dating from the 10th century. Chanderi is famous for very fine saris and brocades. Visitors can stay in the Dak Bungalow.

Listings Deogarh and Chanderi

Where to stay

Deogarh

$ Rahi Tourist Bungalow
Opposite Dasavatara Temple, T09359-865501.
Just 1 clean double room and a 4-bed dorm. The caretaker will prepare meals and escort you on hikes to temples in the woods, 5-10 km away.

Transport

Deogarh
Bus/train Jakhlaun (13 km) is the nearest station, with buses to **Deogarh** and **Lalitpur**. Lalitpur (30 km away) has auto-rickshaws for transfer to Deogarh (1 hr). It also has trains to **Jhansi**, 1½ hrs. **Bina–Etawa**, south of Deogarh, is an important railway junction.

★ Khajuraho and around *Colour map 3, B2.*

home to India's most famous temples

Khajuraho (population 6500) lies in a rich, well-watered plain. Set miles from the nearest town in an open forested and cultivated landscape with the striking Vindhyan ranges as a backdrop, it is listed as a World Heritage Site.

Be warned, though: Khajuraho's drastically defined rich and lean seasons breed a particular culture, and you may find yourself subjected to a barrage of sleazy salesmen, touts and junior con artists capable of sweet-talking you in three different languages. Nevertheless, the village away from the tourist areas maintains a pleasant laid-back feel, and early mornings even at the main temples can be wonderfully calm and peaceful.

The temples

The temples, built mostly of a fine sandstone from Panna and Ajaigarh – although granite was used in a few – can be conveniently divided into three groups: the **Western** (opposite bazar), **Eastern** (30 minutes away on foot) and **Southern**. The Western Group, which dominates the village, is the most impressive and the gardens the best kept, although the temples in the other two groups are remarkable and pleasing in their own right. Allow a day (minimum five hours) for sightseeing.

The temples here are compact and tall, raised on a high platform with an ambulatory path around, but with no enclosure wall. Each follows an east–west axis and has the essential *garbha-griha* (sanctum) containing the chief image, joined to the hall for *mandapa* (worshippers) by a *antarala* (vestibule). The hall is approached through an *ardha mandapa* (porch); both have pyramidal towers. Larger temples have lateral transepts and balconied windows, an internal ambulatory and subsidiary shrines. The sanctuary is surmounted by a tall *sikhara* (tower), while smaller towers rise from other parts of the temple, imitating mountain peaks culminating in the highest. The sanctum is usually *sapta-ratha* (seven projections in plan and elevation), while the cubical section below the *sikhara* repeats the number, having seven bands, *sapta-bada*. The whole, studded with sculptured statues with clear lines of projections and recesses, makes most effective use of light and shade. The sculptures themselves are in the round or in high or medium relief depicting cult images, deities, celestial nymphs, secular figures and animals or mythical beasts.

In India's medieval period of temple building, simple stonework techniques

Tip...
Early morning offers the best light; grab a chai in the square opposite the entrance and get in the temples before the crowds.

replaced previous wooden and brick work. Temples were heavily and ornately decorated. Heavy cornices, strong, broad pillars and the wide base of the *sikhara* (tower) give them the feeling of strength and solidity, only partly counteracted by the ornate friezes.

Western Group The temples are in a peaceful setting of a beautiful park. The area covered by the Western Group was originally a sacred lake, perhaps a reason for the high plinths. **Varaha Temple** (circa AD 900-925), a shrine dedicated to Vishnu in his third incarnation as Varaha, the boar. Vishnu, the preserver, is usually depicted resting on a bed of serpents, until summoned to save the world from disaster. The rat-demon Hiranyaksha stole the earth and dragged it down to his underwater home. The gods begged for Vishnu's help. The demon created 1000 replicas of himself to confuse any pursuer, but Vishnu incarnated himself as a boar and was able to dig deep and seek out the real demon. Thus, Hiranyaksha was destroyed and the world saved. The 2.6-m-long Varaha is of highly polished sandstone covered with 674 deities. He is the Lord of the Three Worlds – water, earth and heaven – and under him is the serpent *Sesha* and the feet of the broken figure of *Prithvi*, the earth goddess. The lotus ceiling shows superb relief carving.

Lakshmana Temple (c AD 950) best preserves the architectural features that typify the larger temples here. The **platform** has friezes of hunting and battle scenes with soldiers, elephants and horses as well as scenes from daily life including the erotic. The **basement** again has bands of carvings – processional friezes showing animals, soldiers, acrobats, musicians, dancers, domestic scenes, festivities, ceremonies, loving couples and deities. The details differentiate between an officer (beard), **general** (beard and belly) and **priest** (beard, belly and stick). An ordinary soldier has none of these. You might spot the occasional error – a camel with legs jointed like a horse, for example. Note the beautifully carved elephants at shoulder height, each one different. On the **walls** are the major sculptures of gods and goddesses in two rows, with *sura-sundaris* or *apsaras* in attendance on the raised sections and loving couples discreetly placed in the recesses. All the figures are relaxed, resting their weight on one leg, thus accentuating their curves. The bands are broken by ornate balconied windows with carved pillars and overhanging eaves. The

Essential Khajuraho

Finding your feet

Daily flights connect Khajuraho with Delhi and Varanasi. The airport is only 5 km from most hotels, with cycle-rickshaws and taxis available for transfer. Buses travel to Jhansi and Satna, both with good railway connections, but they become horrifically packed: if you can afford only one taxi ride in India, let it be here. We hope that **MP Tourism** and the local governments get around to doing something about the roads. There is a railway station around 7 km north of town, on the line to Mahoba and Varanasi with daily trains between Jhansi and Khajuraho. See Transport, page 256.

Getting around

Khajuraho is still a small village though the temples are scattered over 8 sq km. Although some are within walking distance, hiring a bike is a good alternative to getting a cycle-rickshaw to visit the temples to the east and south.

Tip...

If you feel that temple fatigue is likely to set in, then the Western Group is the one to see, especially the Lakshmana Temple.

When to go

The best time to visit is between October and March. From April to June it becomes very hot, dry and dusty.

Opening hours

Sunrise to sunset.

Admission fees and tours

Foreigners Rs 250, camera Rs 25. Guides charge around Rs 400 for a small group (enquire at the India Tourism Office). Choose carefully as some push the new Cultural Centre, souvenir shop and puppet show (overpriced at Rs 250) and others can be a little leary around the sculptures. Audio tours Rs 50 plus Rs 500 deposit. Avoid the toilets. Son et lumière every evening at the Western group of temples, in English at 1900, Hindi at 2000, foreigners Rs 250, Indians Rs 50.

nymphs shown attending to their toilet, bearing offerings, dancing, playing musical instruments or as sensual lovers, are executed with great skill. They are graceful and fluid (note the taut muscle or creased skin), with expressive faces and gestures. The best examples are seen in the recesses below the main tower. The **façades** are covered in superb sculpture. On the south façade are a couple of minstrels, their faces expressing devotional ecstasy, a dancing Ganesh, ladies attending to their toilet, and groups of lovers. Moving to the southwest, a *sura-sundari* applies vermilion while another plays with a ball. In the northwest corner is a nymph after her bath in her wet clothes. The south face of the northwest shrine has a fine Ganesh panel. On the north face, returning towards the porch, there is a group of *apsaras* accomplished in art and music (one plays the flute, another paints, yet another writes a letter). The east face of the subsidiary shrine in the southeast corner has a master architect with his apprentices.

Leave shoes at the entrance and enter the **interior** through a simple *makara-torana* flanked by gladiators. The circular ceiling of the porch (*ardha mandapa*) is a superbly carved open lotus blossom. In the hall (*mandapa*) is a raised platform possibly used for dancing and tantric rituals.

Khajuraho

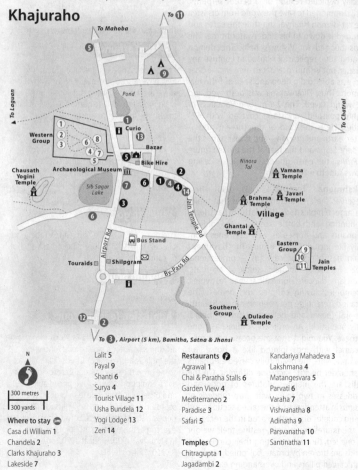

BACKGROUND

Khajuraho

Khajuraho was formerly the capital of the old kingdom of Jajhauti, the region now known as Bundelkhand. The name Khajuraho may be derived from *khajura* (date palm), which grows freely in the area and perhaps because there were two golden *khajura* trees on a carved gate here. The old name was Kharjuravahaka (scorpion bearer), the scorpion symbolizing poisonous lust.

Khajuraho's temples were built under later Chandela kings between AD 950 and 1050 in a truly inspired burst of creativity, but were 'lost' for centuries until they were accidentally 'discovered' by a British army engineer in 1839. Of the original 85 temples, the 20 surviving are among the finest in India.

Basham suggested that India's art came from secular craftsmen who, although they worked to instructions, loved the world they knew, their inspiration not so much a ceaseless quest for the absolute as a delight in the world as they saw it.

The gods and demi-gods in temples all over India are young and handsome, their bodies rounded, often richly jewelled. They are often smiling and sorrow is rarely portrayed. Temple sculpture makes full use of the female form as a decorative motif. Goddesses and female attendants are often shown naked from the waist up, with tiny waists and large, rounded breasts, posing languidly – a picture of well-being and relaxation. See Books, page 1355.

Shakti worship and erotic sculptures Although each temple here is dedicated to a different deity, each expresses its own nature through the creative energy of Shakti. Tantric beliefs within Hinduism led to the development of Shakti cults which stressed that the male could be activated only by being united with the female in which sexual expression and spiritual desire were intermingled. Since this could not be suppressed it was given a priestly blessing and incorporated into the regular ritual. Romila Thapar traces its origin to the persisting worship of the Mother Goddess (from the Indus Valley civilization, third millennium BC), which has remained a feature of religion in India. Until last century, many temples kept *devadasis* (literally, servants of God), women whose duty included being the female partner in these rituals.

The presence of erotic temple sculptures, even though they account for less than 10% of the total carvings, has sometimes been viewed as the work of a degenerate society obsessed with sex. Some believe they illustrate the Kama Sutra, the sensuality outside the temple contrasting with the serenity within. Yet others argue that they illustrate ritual symbolism of sexual intercourse in Tantric belief, see page 1332. The Chandelas were followers of the Tantric cult which believes that gratification of earthly desires is a step towards attaining the ultimate liberation or *moksha*.

Whatever the explanation, the sculptures are remarkable and show great sensitivity and warmth, reflecting society in an age free from inhibitions. They express the celebration of all human activity, displaying one aspect of the nature of Hinduism itself, a genuine love of life.

Chandela Rajputs The Chandela Rajputs claimed descent from the moon. Hemwati, the lovely young daughter of a Brahmin priest, was seduced by the Moon God while bathing in a forest pool. The child born of this union was Chandravarman, the founder of the dynasty. Brought up in the forests by his mother who sought refuge from a censorious society, Chandravarman, when established as ruler of the local area, had a dream visitation from his mother. She implored him to build temples that would reveal human passions and in doing so bring about a realization of the emptiness of desire.

The Chandelas, whose symbol recalls the 16-year-old king who slayed a lion bare-handed, developed into a strong regional power in the early 10th century. Under their patronage Jajhauti became prosperous, and the rulers decorated their kingdom with forts, palaces, tanks and temples, mainly concentrated in their strongholds of Mahoba, Kalinjar, Ajaigarh and also Dudhai, Chandpur, Madanpur and Deogarh (Jhansi District).

With the fading of Chandela fortunes, the importance of Khajuraho waned but temple building continued, at a much reduced pace, until the 12th century. Far removed from the political centres of the kingdom, the location of Khajuraho minimized the danger of external attack and symbolized its role as a celestial refuge.

At each corner of the platform are pillars with carved brackets with *apsaras* which are among the finest sculptures at Khajuraho. There are eight figures on each column, representing the eight sects of Tantra. The sanctum (*garba-griha*) doorway has a panel showing incarnations of Vishnu while the lintel has Lakshmi with Brahma and Siva on either side. A frieze above depicts the nine planets including *Rahu*, while Krishna legends and innumerable carvings of animals, birds and humans, appear on the wall. The *pancha-ratha* sanctum has a three-headed Vishnu as Vaikuntha, and around it are 10 incarnations and 14 forms of Vishnu.

Kandariya Mahadeva Temple (circa 1025-1050) is the most developed, the largest and tallest of the Khajuraho temples. Dedicated to Siva, the elaborately carved *makara torana* doorway leads to a porch with an ornate ceiling and a dark inner sanctum with a marble linga. The temple roof rises in a series of seven bands of peaks to the summit of the central, 31-m-high *sikhara*. There are 84 smaller, subsidiary towers which are replicas. The architectural and sculptural genius of Khajuraho reaches its peak in this temple where every element is richly endowed. The platform is unique in the way it projects to the sides and rear, reflecting the plan of the transepts. It also has the highest and most ornamental basement with intricately carved processional friezes. Leaving the temple, walk to the rear of the delightful gardens to the other two temples.

Along the same platform, to Kandariya's north is the **Jagadambi Temple** (early 11th century), which is similar in layout and predates the next temple, the Chitragupta. It has a standing Parvati image in the sanctum but was originally dedicated to Vishnu. The outer walls have no projecting balconies but the lavish decorations include some of the best carvings of deities – several of Vishnu, a particularly fine *Yama*, numerous nymphs and amorous couples. In between is the ruined **Mahadeva Shrine** (11th century). Little remains except a porch, under which Sardula, a mythical lion, towers over a half-kneeling woman.

Chitragupta Temple (early 11th century) is the only one here dedicated to Surya, the Sun God. Longer and lower than its companions, it has been much restored (platform, steps, entrance porch, northeast façade). Unlike the simple basement mouldings of the Jagadambi, here there are processional friezes; the *maha-mandapa* ceiling too has progressed from the simple square in the former to an ornate octagonal ceiling. The *garbha griha* has Surya driving his chariot of seven horses, while on the south façade is a statue of Vishnu with 11 heads signifying his 10 incarnations, see page 1327.

Vishvanatha Temple (1002) is dedicated to Siva. According to the longer inscription on the wall, it originally had an emerald linga in addition to the stone one present today. Built before the Kandariya Mahadeva, they are similar in design and plan. The high, moulded basement has fine scrollwork and carvings of processions of men and animals as well as loving couples. On the nine principal basement niches of both are the *Sapta-matrikas* (seven 'Mothers') with Ganesha and Virabhadra. The excellent carvings include a fine musician with a flute and amorous couples inside the temple, and divinities attended by enchanting nymphs in innumerable poses (one removing a thorn from her foot), on the south façade. Only two subsidiary shrines of the original four remain. Sharing the same raised platform and facing the temple is the **Nandi Pavilion** with a fine elephant frieze on the basement. It houses a 2.2-m polished sandstone Nandi bull (Siva's vehicle). Before coming down the steps note the sleeping *mahout* on an elephant!

Outside this garden complex of temples and next to the Lakshmana temple is the **Matangesvara Temple** (AD 900-925), simpler in form and decoration than its neighbour and unlike all the others, still in everyday use. It has an interesting circular interior which contains a large Siva linga dating back 1000 years. You do not need to pay to get into this temple and morning or evening *puja* is very beautiful and very welcoming.

Chausath Yogini (late ninth century) is a ruined Jain temple in coarse granite on a platform. It stands apart from the rest of the Western Group beyond the tank. Only 35 of the original *chausath* (64) shrines to the *yoginis* (attendants of Kali) for the 'open-air' temple, remain.

Eastern Group South of the village is the ruined '**Ghantai**' Temple (late 10th century). The fine carvings of *ghanta* (chains-and-bells) on the pillars, the richly ornamented doorway and ceiling of the entrance porch can only be seen from the road. Walk through Khajuraho village to the small **Javari Temple** (late 11th century), with its tall, slender *sikhara*. It has a highly decorative doorway and finely sculpted figures on the walls. About 200 m north is the **Vamana Temple** (late 11th century), with a four-armed Vamana incarnation of Vishnu in the sanctum. This is in the fully developed Chandela style and has a single tower and no ambulatory. The walls are adorned with sensuous *sura-sundaris*. Returning to the modern part of Khajuraho, you pass the early 10th-century so-called **Brahma Temple** on the bank of Ninora-tal. A Vishnu temple, wrongly attributed to Brahma, it has a sandstone *sikhara* on a granite structure.

Three Jain temples stand within an enclosure about 500 m southeast of the Ghantai Temple; others are scattered around the village. The **Parsvanatha Temple** (mid-10th century), is the largest and one of the finest. The curvilinear tower dominates the structure and is beautifully carved. There are no balconies but light enters through fretted windows. Although a Jain temple, there are numerous Vaishnav deities, many of them excellently carved on the three wall panels. Some of the best known non-erotic sculptures too are found here, particularly the graceful *sura-sundaris* (one applying kohl and another removing a thorn, on the south façade; one tying ankle-bells on the north façade), as well as the fine *Dikpalas* in the corners. The interior is richly carved with elephants, lions, sea goddesses and Jain figures. The temple was originally dedicated to Adinatha, but the modern black marble image of Parsvanatha was placed in the sanctum in 1860. Next, is the smaller and simpler **Adinatha Temple** (late 11th century), where only the sanctum (containing a modern image) and vestibule have survived – the porch is modern. The sculptures on three bands again depict attractive *sura-sundaris*, the niches have *yakshis*, the corners, *Dikpalas*. **Santinatha Temple** with its 4.5-m statue of Adinatha is the main place of Jain worship. An inscription dating it at AD 1027-1028 is covered with plaster – the thoroughly renovated temple retains its ancient heart and medieval sculptures. The small sand-coloured structures around the temples are reconstructions around remains of old shrines. There is also a small Jain museum and picture gallery here.

Southern Group The two temples stand on open land. The setting, attractive at sunset, lacks the overall ambience of the Western Group but the backdrop of the Vindhyas is impressive. **Duladeo Temple**, 800 m southwest of the Jain temples down a path off the road, is the last the Chandelas built here, when temple building was already in decline. There are 20 *apsara* brackets but the figures are often repetitive and appear to lack the quality of carving found in earlier temples. The shrine door and *mandapa* ceiling have some fine carving while the linga has 11 rows of 100 lingas. **Chaturbhuja Temple** (c1100), 3 km south of the village, anticipates the Duladeo but lacks erotic sculptures. The sanctum contains an exceptional 2.7-m four-armed *Dakshina-murti* Vishnu image while outside there are some fine *Dikpalas*, nymphs and mythical beasts in niches.

Trips from Khajuraho

At **Rajgarh**, 5 km south, is the imposing ruined 19th-century hilltop fort-palace of the Maharaja which the Oberoi Group will convert to a heritage hotel. It is particularly interesting when villagers congregate for the Tuesday Market. Get there by auto-rickshaw or car.

Panna National Park ① *Nov-May, for fees, page 206,* is accessed along the Satna Road with attractive waterfalls (Rs 100) on the way. Ken River, parts of which have been declared a sanctuary for fish eating gharials, flows across the Panna National Park, which is a Project Tiger Reserve. The park, rich in biodiversity, covers dense forest, open meadows, plateaus and gorge with waterfalls, and supports chinkara, sambar, nilgai and the big cats. Although tiger sightings are rare, it is pleasant to visit in winter. There is little wildlife to be seen in the dry season (when the gharials are removed for their own protection). Access is easiest from Madla, 27 km from Khajuraho. Jeep or motorbike hire is available from Khajuraho, or take a bus; tour of park can be arranged in Madla.

Listings Khajuraho and around *map p250*

Tourist information

Khajuraho

Government of India Tourist Office
Opposite W Group, T07686-242347.
Mon-Fri 0930-1800.

Madhya Pradesh Tourism
At the bus stand, T07686-274163.

Where to stay

Khajuraho

Most hotels are within 1 km of the Western
Temples, notably along Jain Temples Rd.
They have frequent power cuts but top
hotels have generators.

$$$$ The Lalit
Opposite Circuit House, T07686-272111,
www.thelalit.com.
Slightly soulless top-notch hotel with all the
trimmings including sparkling rooms and
extravagant suites. Here you can comfortably
forget the outside world watching 42-inch
plasma TV screens, enjoying the luxury spa,
eating at the 24-hr multi-cuisine restaurant,
shopping at the overpriced gift store or lounging
by the pool.

$$$ Chandela (Taj)
Airport Rd, T07686-272355, www.tajhotels.com.
A bustling but slightly dated complex with
94 comfortable rooms, 2 restaurants, good
pool and fitness centre, the best bookshop
in town (though pricey), currency exchange
and pleasant gardens.

$$$ Clarks Khajuraho
Khajuraho Village, T07686-274038,
www.hotelclarks.com.
With a deceptively plain exterior, inside are
104 tastefully decorated, modern rooms with
views of the pool and extensive well-kept
grounds, badminton and tennis courts, a large
restaurant, massage rooms and a gym.

$$ Payal
10-min walk from the centre, T07686-274076,
www.mptourism.com.
25 reasonable rooms with bath, some a/c,
restaurant (good breakfast and tea), bar, quiet
garden, small pool and helpful staff.

$$ Tourist Village
T07686-274062, www.mptourism.com.
Veering away from the norm, 11 well-equipped
attractive 2-room 'ethnic' huts, with bath and a/c,
and a outdoor restaurant. It's useful to have
a bike. Campsite nearby.

$$ Usha Bundela
Temple Rd, T07686-272386,
www.ushalexushotels.com.
Full of character, although in need of some
maintenance. Well-managed hotel with comfy
rooms, a restaurant, bar and good pool.

$$-$ Lakeside
Opposite Shivsagar Lake, T07686-274120,
avinashkhr@gmail.com.
There are beautiful evening views at this clean
but noisy place with 18 functional rooms and
a dorm. It's often full.

$ Casa di William
Opposite the Western Group of temples,
T07686-274244.
Very conveniently located, 15 pleasant and clean
rooms with bath, some a/c. Views of the temples
at sunset are absolutely stunning sunset from
the rooftop restaurant. They also have massage,
internet and bike rental. Very friendly and helpful
staff; Italian management. Good value.

$ Hotel Shanti
Opposite Shiv Sagar Lake, T07686-274560,
shanti.hotelkhajuraho@ yahoo.com.
Great location by the lake, offering spacious,
clean and light rooms with bath, temple views
and TV. There's also a restaurant. Good value.

$ Sunset View
South of bazar, alongside Chandela Emporium,
T07686-274077.
Well-located near the lake and bus stand, with an
unimposing entrance. The 12 simple rooms (6 air-
cooled with tubs) are fairly clean, and there's a
pleasant terrace and garden. Good value.

$ Surya
Jain Temple Rd, T(0)94251-46203,
www.hotelsuryakhajuraho.com.
Set around a lovely garden are 45 comfortable
and pleasant rooms, the best ones in the
newer block, with attached bath, balconies
and a/c. Excellent vegetarian restaurant, bike
hire, extremely helpful travel desk and staff.
Excellent value. Highly recommended.

$ Yogi Lodge
Western Temples, T07686-274158.
Excellent budget option, with 25 spartan but clean rooms, a rooftop café, internet, bike hire and yoga classes. Well run. They have links to a nearby ashram if you'd like a quiet retreat.

$ Zen
Jain Temple Rd, T07686-274228, www.hotelzenkhajuraho.co.in.
Large, bright ramshackle rooms with clean attached bath. It's a good place to stay but has a strange atmosphere; beware attempts to charge a spurious 'luxury tax' on cheap rooms. The attractive garden has water features, and a spectacularly overpriced Italian restaurant although the owner promises a 10% discount for all Footprint readers.

Trips from Khajuraho

$$$$ Pashan Ghar
12 km from Panna National Park entrance, T1800-111 825, www.tajsafaris.com.
This is at the supremely luxurious end of the spectrum. Beautifully decorated stone cottages with a nod to traditional style and a watchtower overlooking the water hole. This is a perfect place for a romantic getaway with candlelit suppers in a palanquin or dinners delivered through the 'butler hatch' to your own private veranda.

$$$$-$$$ Ken River Lodge
Village Madla, T07732-275235, www.kenriverlodge.com.
In a beautiful location with cottages and 'Swiss' tents, a tree-top restaurant, fishing, boating and swimming.

$ Rest Houses
Ask at gate or park office, Panna National Park.
Take provisions.

Restaurants

Khajuraho
Chai and *parathas* cooked fresh at stalls in the market square on Jain Temples Rd make a good, quick breakfast before the temples.

$$ Blue Sky Restaurant
Main Rd, overlooking the Western Temples.
Pop in here for a good sundowner over the temples, but the food is pretty ropey. They will be always busy because of their location and they know this. There's a surcharge to sit in the treehouse.

$$ Garden View Restaurant
Inside Hotel Surya, see Where to stay, above.
Fantastic Indian and local dishes served in attractive garden surroundings.

$$ Mediterraneo
Opposite Hotel Surya, see Where to stay, above.
Good bruschetta, fresh pasta dishes, tasty pizza and good desserts, cooked by Indian chefs. Beware of imitators; a 'branch' has opened in Orchha but has nothing to do with this great place.

$$ Paradise
Main Rd, opposite Shiv Sagar Lake, T09179-386484.
Good Western and Indian meals are reasonably priced at this friendly and inviting family-run restaurant. Excellent biryanis and banana pancakes, served on a pleasant rooftop with lake views.

$$ Raja's Café
Main Rd, near the Western Temples entrance, T07686-272307, www.rajacafe.com.
Probably the best food in Khajuraho, and great coffee, all with the backdrop of the temples. There's a well-designed a/c room downstairs or head up the spiral staircase for great views. Highly recommended.

$ Agrawal
Near Hotel Surya, see Where to stay, above.
The only local-feeling place in town, serving good *thalis* (vegetarian only), not too oily.

$ Safari
Opposite Western Group.
Bizarre array of menus, good food but specify if you want vegetarian dishes (may be made with meat gravy), large helpings, good *lassis*, supreme *thalis*, and amazing Indian muesli but very slow service.

Entertainment

Khajuraho
Shilpgram, *Airport Rd.* Interesting programme of cultural performances in season, 1900-2100, often free. A more rustic, less commercial experience than the similarly named cultural centre across the street, which attracts tour buses.

Festivals

Khajuraho
Feb-Mar Dance Festival. Many of the country's most accomplished dancers perform in the spectacular setting of the Western Group. Ask at the tourist office for details.

Shopping

Khajuraho
Gift shops sell cheap stone and bronze sculptures, handicrafts and gems in the bazar near the Western Group (**Panna diamond mines**, the largest in the country, are nearby).
Chandela Emporium, *near Sibsagar*. Large selection of gifts, crafts and jewellery.
Ganesh Garments, *Jain Temples Rd*. Reasonable Western clothes and speedy alterations.
Karan Jewellers. Good for diamonds.
MP Emporium. For fixed prices; small craft shops on the way to Javeri temple are cheaper than the bazar.

What to do

Khajuraho
Tour operators
Touraids, *Bamitha Rd, near Shilpgram, T07686-274125*. Reliable cars with drivers.
Travel Bureau, *Holiday Inn, Hotel Ramada, T07686-274037, www.travelbureauindia.com*. Car hire with drivers.

Transport

Khajuraho
Air The airport, 5 km south of the village centre, T07686-740415, has daily flights to **Delhi** and **Varanasi**. Flights are heavily booked in season. Transport to town: taxi Rs 200-300, auto-rickshaw Rs 100 (overpriced; difficult to bargain).

Bicycle Cycle hire in Gole Market behind museum and along Jain Temples Rd; Rs 50 per day, the recommended mode though not allowed in the temple complex.

Bus Long-distance buses arrive at a newish bus stand 1.5 km south of the main bazar on Airport Rd, with a computerized counter for reservations on buses and trains elsewhere. Daily buses to **Agra** 391 km, 0700, 0800, 0900, 1800 (an exhausting 10-12 hrs via Jhansi and Gwalior); **Bhopal** 350 km, 0600, 0700; **Indore** 480 km, 0600; **Jhansi** 176 km, several 0500-1800 (4½-5 hrs), semi-deluxe via Orchha 1115; **Mahoba** (stops 3 km from the railway station), several 0600-1700 (3 hrs); **Satna** (for rail connections to Jabalpur, **Allahabad** and **Kolkata**), 0745, 0830, 0930, 1400, 1500, 4 hrs (very uncomfortable).

Car Car hire with driver to **Jhansi**, Rs 2900-3800, arranged through hotels or by **Touraids** and Travel Bureau (see What to do, above), 4 hrs. **Satna**, Rs 1900-2600. **Agra** or **Varanasi**, Rs 6500-8000, 8-9 hrs.

Rickshaw and taxi Cycle-rickshaws try to charge Rs 30 for shortest journey; approximate locals' price from bazar to bus stand, Rs 15, Rs 75-100 per half day. Taxis are from **MP Tourism** or **Touraids** near Usha Hotel, but overpriced. To Satna, cheaper fares are available from returning drivers who have dropped off passengers in Khajuraho.

Train Khajuraho station is 8 km south of the temples; auto-rickshaws charge around Rs 150 to town, shared *tempos* Rs 10. A handful of useful trains call here. To **Delhi**: 1 train each way per day, 11 hrs, via Jhansi (5 hrs). **Udaipur**: 1 a day, 22 hrs, via Jhansi, Gwalior (6½ hrs), Agra (7½ hrs) and Jaipur (13 hrs). **Varanasi**: 3 a week, 12 hrs, via Allahabad, 7 hrs. There's also a slow train to **Jhansi** that calls at **Orchha** (4½ hrs). The station doesn't sell advance tickets, but there's a counter at the bus stand, T07686-274416.

Trips from Khajuraho
Bus **Satna** is a useful railhead for Khajuraho if you're coming from Kolkata or Jabalpur. Buses to **Khajuraho** depart from the railway bridge, 2 km north of the station (*tempo* Rs 5, rickshaw Rs 40). There are several uncomfortable buses daily with MPSRTC, 0630-1530, 4-5 hrs; after 1530 catch bus to **Bamitha** (hourly until 1800) then taxi (Rs 100) or share jeep to **Khajuraho**. Buses also leave Satna for **Amarkantak** 0750; **Chitrakoot** 0500, 1200, 1530; **Tala** for Bandhavgarh, daily, 0800, 4 hrs, but it's better to take a train to Katni then a bus to the place.

Train Reservations from office on right outside main entrance; enquiries T131. The 0745 bus from Khajuraho connects with several useful trains. To **Kolkata**, 1 daily, 20-24 hrs. **Mumbai** (**CST**): at least 8 a day, 20 hrs, all via Katni (1-2 hrs) and Jabalpur (3 hrs). **Varanasi**: 15-20 a day, 7 hrs, though many leave at awkward times.

The Chandela kings' main defensive bases were Mahoba and Kalinjar, but as the kingdom expanded these were complemented by other forts at Ajaigarh, Orchha, Datia, Deogarh and Chanderi. Like other kings, they donated villages to maintain the families of soldiers who had died in war. Heroic virtues were instilled into a child from birth and women admired men who fought well; *sati* became common practice throughout the region. After the mid-10th century the independent Chandelas joined a Hindu confederacy to repel Afghan invasions. Mahmud of Ghazni, the 'Idol Breaker', made at least 17 of his plunder raids into India between 1000-1027, ultimately taking the title, albeit briefly, Lord of Kalinjar. The forts suffered varied fortunes until the British took them over in the early 19th century.

Now the area is being invaded by forests of teak and ebony. Ajaigarh and Kalinjar are quite primitive but a visit, particularly to the former, is worthwhile. Take water with you.

Tip...
Enlist a local guide to show you the best spots.

Ajaigarh
Ajaigarh, 36 km north of Panna, surrounded by dense forest, stands on a granite outcrop crowned by a 15-m perpendicular scarp. Ajaigarh was a self-contained hill fort, intended to withstand long sieges and to house the entire population of the region, which accounts for its great size. Despite its inaccessibility and the difficult 250-m climb involved (allow about 40 minutes on the way up), the fort is worth visiting for its peaceful atmosphere and wonderful views. Two of the original five gates are accessible; the large stone steps here once helped elephants in their steep ascent. Encircling the hill, the fort wall encloses part-ruined temples; only four of the original 22 temples remain. Rock carvings, pillars and sculptures from Hindu and Jain temples, some later used by Muslims to reinforce the fortifications, today lie scattered amongst woodland. The old stone quarry now filled by a lake is said to have provided stone for Khajuraho.

Some believe it is auspicious to eat here, hence the remains of bonfires and presence of picnickers; but the town is dirty with few facilities; it's best to bring your own food and water.

Kalinjar
Some 20 km from Ajaigarh this fort stands on the last spur of the Vindhya hills overlooking the Gangetic plains, a plateau with a steep scarp on all sides. One of the most ancient sites in Bundelkhand (Ptolemy's Kanagora), it combines the sanctity of remote hilltops with natural defensive strength. One legend names Kalinjar after Siva, the Lord of Destruction (*kal* = death, *jar* = decay). The ancient hill has long been a place of pilgrimage and worship for Hindu *sadhus*, *rishis* and pilgrims. It is rarely visited by other travellers.

The design of the fort has a mystical significance. The only approach is from the north and entry is through **seven gates** with barbicans corresponding to the seven known planets and stations through which the soul must pass before being absorbed into Brahma. At the crest, crumbling Hindu and Muslim monuments stand side by side on the 1.5-km-long plateau. Beyond the last gate, a drop of about 3.6 m leads to **Sita Sej**, a stone couch set in a rock-cut chamber (fourth century). Beyond, a passage leads to Patalganga (underground Ganga), believed to run through Kalinjar.

Mahoba
Some 63 km north of Khajuraho. There is a Tourist Bungalow here with a restaurant and bar. The station is 3 km from the bus stand. To Jhansi (4 hrs); to Varanasi via Allahabad (11 hrs).

Mahoba was reputedly founded by Raja Chandravarman, in AD 800. Today, it is a small town with a fort on a low hill, several ancient tanks and a thriving 'Dariba' or betel market. The vines are grown under traditional shelters to produce high quality *paan* (betel leaf) for which the area is famous.

After winning Bundelkhand, the Chandela kings dedicated themselves not only to building temples for their gods, but also to bringing water to the land. They created large tanks by damming shallow valleys. Mahoba's oldest tank, **Rahila Sagar** (circa AD 900) has impressive ruins of a ninth-century granite Sun Temple. The 12th-century **Madan Sagar** has a granite Siva temple nearby and a ruined Vishnu temple on one of its rocky islets. Along its embankment is the old fort, **Qila Mismar**, with ruins of palaces, Hindu temples and a tomb. In the fields, remains of Buddhist and Jain sculptures lie abandoned. **Gokhar Hill**, near Madan Sagar, with 24 Jain Tirthankaras figures carved out of sheer rock, is worth exploring.

Chitrakoot   *Colour map 3, B2.*

forests and peaceful rivers, dotted with ghats and temples

On the north flank of the Vindhyas where they dip gently beneath the Ganges Plains, 175 km from Khajuraho, Chitrakoot was home to Rama and Sita in 11 of their 14 years of exile.

Ramghat, the principal bathing ghat on the banks of the beautiful Mandakini River, is widely revered in India and the site of countless pilgrimages, though scarcely known to foreigners. Like the much more famous waters of the Yamuna at Allahabad or the Ganga at Varanasi, the River Mandakini is lined with temples. A good way to see the ghats is to hire a boat. Upstream from Ramghat the Mandakini passes through a beautiful stretch of wooded valley.

Listings Chitrakoot

Where to stay

$$-$ Tourist Bungalow
Near the bus stand, T07670-265326,
www.mptourism.com.
13 a/c, 8 air-cooled rooms, 26 dorm beds and a restaurant (pre-ordering required).

$ Jaipuria Bhavan
Ramghat, Hathi Darwaza, T09415-134685,
www.jaipuriabhawan.com.
Pleasant place, with 16 basic rooms, some a/c with fairly clean bath. Friendly manager. Vegetarian options; no alcohol.

Restaurants

$ Annapurna
Ramghat, T05198-224415.
Excellent *thalis*.

$ Kamad Giri Bhavan
Ramghat.
Famous for North Indian food.

Transport

Bus Regular services to **Jhansi**, **Mahoba**, **Satna** and **Chhattarpur**.

Train The nearest station is Karwi (Chitrakoot Dham) with services to **Delhi** (14 hrs), **Jabalpur** (4-5 hrs), **Lucknow** (7 hrs) and **Varanasi** (7 hrs). A *tempo* to **Chitrakoot** takes 30 mins, Rs 10-20.

Eastern
Madhya Pradesh

The modern city of Jabalpur makes a convenient jumping-off point for some of India's quintessential wildernesses. Kanha and Bandhavgarh national parks protect the landscapes that inspired Kipling's *Jungle Book* and, despite the continued predations of poachers, Bandhavgarh at least still offers the possibility of tracking a tiger from the back of an elephant. Facilities for wildlife viewing in the parks are improving and a number of new safari resorts have opened: some massively luxurious, others working to involve local communities in the conservation effort.

Jabalpur and around *Colour map 3, C2.*
gateway to two of India's finest wildlife reserves: Kanha and Bandhavgarh

On the upper reaches of the River Narmada in the heart of India's forested tribal belt, Jabalpur (population 952,000) receives remarkably few visitors. Jabalpur town was the capital and pleasure resort of the Gond kings during the 12th century. It was later the seat of the Kalchuri Dynasty until it fell to the Marathas. The British took it in 1817 and left their mark with the cantonment residences and barracks.

Sights

Madan Mahal Fort (1116) ① *Tue-Sun 1000-1700, closed holidays, free,* built by the Gond ruler Madan Shah on a hill just to the west of the city, has superb views. To get there take a *tempo* from the stand near the Krishna Hotel to Sharda Chowk (Rs 5), then walk up the left-hand hill. **Rani Durgavati Museum and Memorial** houses a collection of sculptures and prehistoric relics, and the **Tilwara Ghat** where **Mahatma Gandhi's** ashes were immersed in the Narmada, are all places of interest. There are also Jain temples.

Around Jabalpur

The **Marble Rocks** are 22 km west of Jabalpur. Captain J Forsyth wrote of them: "The eye never wearies of the effect produced by the broken and reflected sunlight, glancing from a pinnacle of snow-white marble reared against the deep blue of the sky and again losing itself in the soft bluish greys of their recesses". These white rocks, with views of black/dark green volcanic seams, rise to 30 m on either side of the Narmada River and in moonlight produce a magical effect;

Essential Jabalpur

Finding your feet

Although there are long-distance buses to Jabalpur from the surrounding large cities, it is most comfortable to travel here by train. Taking less than eight hours from Bhopal or Allahabad, there are also good connections to Nagpur and South India. The main station is on the edge of the Civil Lines, less than 2 km from the town centre. The cheaper hotels are easily reached from the main bus stand. **Warning** Hotel touts are very active round the station and bus stand so it is best to have a hotel in mind. Rickshaws offer cheap fares to hotel and then charge a commission. See Transport, page 261.

Getting around

The town is too spread out to cover on foot easily but there are plenty of taxis, unmetered autos and cheap shared *tempos* for sights further afield.

BACKGROUND

Tribal culture

Even though the majority of the former state of Madhya Pradesh's tribal people now have their own state of Chhattisgarh, Madhya Pradesh remains the home of many tribal groups, including Bhils, Gonds and Baigas. Many have been painfully absorbed into the mainstream of Indian life. Hindi is the most widely spoken language. On each of the borders the languages of neighbouring states – particularly Marathi and Gujarati in the west – are quite commonly used. The Bhils speak Bhili and the Gonds, Gondi, independent in origin to the Indo-European and Dravidian language groups.

Textiles are important but Madhya Pradesh also has a strong traditional village handicraft industry. Handloom Chanderi and Maheshwar silks are especially sought after.

floodlights have been added, though boating may not be possible. Stalls sell cheap soap-stone carvings. There's lodging nearby in Bhedaghat, if needed. To get to the rocks take a *tempo* from the stand near Krishna Hotel to Bhedaghat, Rs 8, which takes you right to the Marble Rocks car park. Walk up to see the waterfalls, or go past the Mandir to the town and follow steps down for boat trips (30 minutes, Rs 10, recommended, though if you're alone and hire the whole boat it costs Rs 200).

Other sights nearby are the **Dhuandhar Falls** (smoke cascade), where the Narmada plunges through a narrow chasm, **Hathi-ka-paon** (Elephant's Foot Rock) and **Monkey's Leap** ledge. Nearby is the **Chausath Yogini Mandir**, a 10th-century temple with stone carvings. Legend suggests that it is connected to the Gond queen Durgavati's palace by an **underground passage**. Approached by a long flight of steps, there is an excellent view of the Narmada from the top.

The British era **Pariyat tank**, 12 km from Jabalpur, is a popular picnic and fishing spot for locals.

Mandla

Ninety-five kilometres southeast of Jabalpur, Mandla was the capital of the ancient Gond Kingdom of Garha-Mandla early in the Christian era, and is of great historical significance to the Gond tribal peoples. The Gond Queen Rani Durgavati took her life here when her army was cornered by Mughal forces under Asaf Khan in 1564. The **fort** was built in the 17th century and is surrounded on three sides by the Narmada River. It passed to the Marathas and then to the British in 1818. The jungle has since taken over the ruins (only a few towers remain), though there are some temples and ghats in the town. The Gond Raja Hirde Shah built a large **palace** in a commanding site nearby in Ramnagar (15 km), of which little remains. Rail fans head for Mandla to ride the lovely narrow gauge railway to Nainpur, a unique line on which trains wait before and after each level crossing while an attendant jumps down to close and open the road gates.

Listings Jabalpur and around *map p261*

Tourist information

Jabalpur

Madhya Pradesh Tourism
Railway station, T0761-267 7690.
Car hire, and runs a daily bus to Kanha, departs at 0800, return 1900.

Where to stay

Jabalpur

$$$-$$ Kalchuri Residency (MP Tourism)
20 km from the airport, and 2.5 km from the railway, T0761-267 8491, www.mptourism.com.

30 clean rooms (all a/c), decent restaurant and bar. Good value but close to noisy temple.

$$ Samdariya
Off Russell Chowk, T0761-400 4132, www.hotelsamdareeya.com.
Modern, quiet hotel, with 62 a/c rooms and suites (some cheaper) and a good **Woodlands** South Indian restaurant.

$$ Satya Ashoka
Wright Town, T0761-241 5111, www.hotelsatyaashoka.com.
50 rooms, central a/c, restaurant, bar, garden and tours. Recommended.

$$-$ Krishna
Opposite Rani Durgavati Museum,
T0761-400 4023.
www.krishnahotels.com. 25 rooms, some a/c,
restaurant, garden and a pool.

$$-$ Rishi Regency
Opposite State Bank of India, T0761-404 6001,
www.hotelrishiregency.com.
40 rooms, a/c, with a restaurant, bar, exchange
and free internet.

$ Anand
Near Naudra Bridge, T0761-500 7174.
32 clean though noisy rooms with bath.
Helpful staff.

Restaurants

Jabalpur

$$ Samdariya
International meals or snacks, smart decor.

$ Indian Coffee House
Near the clock tower.
South Indian cuisine, including good breakfasts,
snacks and coffee.

$ Satyam Shivam Sundaram
1st floor, near Krishna Hotel.
Air-cooled restaurant offering excellent value
Indian vegetarian dishes, including tasty *thalis*.

Shopping

Jabalpur
Universal Book Service, *opposite India Coffee
House.* Interesting stock. Recommended.

Transport

Jabalpur
Air Jabalpur airport is 25 km east of the city,
with flights to **Bengaluru**, **Bhopal**, **Delhi**,
Hyderabad and **Mumbai**.

Bus Services for **Kanha** via Mandla; MP Tourism
bus from their railway station office at 0800
(6 hrs, Rs 100), is much faster than the 1100
service, Rs 50 (see Kanha transport, page 264).
Khajuraho, 0900. Also to **Allahabad**, **Bhopal**,
Nagpur, **Varanasi** and other main centres by
private coach.

Train Jabalpur is on the Mumbai–Allahabad–
Kolkata railway line. **Allahabad**: around 15 trains
a day, 6½ hrs. **Bhopal**: 7 a day, 8 hrs. **Delhi** (**HN**):
3 a day, 15-18 hrs, all via **Agra** 9-12 hrs. **Lucknow**:
1 daily, 14 hrs. **Kolkata**: at least 5 daily, 22 hrs.

Mandla
Train For rail enthusiasts, a wonderful narrow
gauge runs between **Mandla** and **Nainpur**.

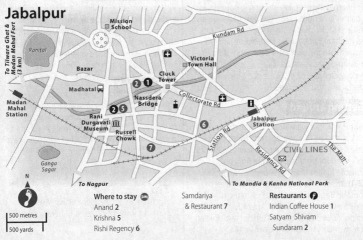

Madhya Pradesh & Chhattisgarh Eastern Madhya Pradesh•261

The area was famed as a hunter's paradise but now the valley has been well developed as a national park. It is worth spending a couple of days here. Lying in the Maikal hills in the eastern part of the Satpura Range, 40 km from Mandla, the park has deciduous hardwoods, rolling grasslands and meandering streams of the Banjar River. The park forms the core of the Kanha Tiger Reserve. It was created in 1974 and also protects the rare hardground-adapted barasingha (swamp deer). George Schaller, the zoologist, conducted the first ever scientific study of the tiger here and research is also being done on deer and langur habitat.

Wildlife

Kanha has 22 species of mammal, the most easily spotted of which are the three-striped palm squirrel, common langur monkey, jackal, wild boar, cheetal, sambar, Branden barasingha and blackbuck. Less commonly seen are Indian hare, *dhole* (Indian wild dog) and gaur. Rarely seen are Indian fox, sloth bear, striped hyena, tiger (estimated at about 100), leopard, *nilgai* (blue bull), Indian porcupine, wolf (outside park proper) and the Indian pangolin (sometimes called a scaly anteater).

As for birds, Kanha has 230 species recorded. Good vantage points are in the hills where the mixed and bamboo forest harbours many species. Commonly seen species are: leaf warblers, minivets, black ibis, common peafowl, racket-tailed drongo, hawk eagle, red-wattled lapwing, various species of flycatcher, woodpecker, pigeon, dove, parakeet, babbler, mynah, Indian roller, white-breasted kingfisher and grey hornbill.

Essential Kanha National Park

Finding your feet

The journey by car takes about five hours from Jabalpur on a poor road. The main gates are at Kisli and Mukki. If arriving in the evening, stop overnight at Khatia or Kisli as vehicles are not allowed into the park after dark. From Nagpur or Raipur enter via Mukki Gate. Diesel vehicles, motorcycles and bicycles are not allowed in the park. See Transport, page 264.

Getting around

Visitors may not walk around inside the park, but you can walk in the peaceful forest between the gate at Kanha and the park itself. Elephants, once used for tiger tracking, are now only available for 'joy rides' outside the park at Kisli. **MP Tourism** hires out Gypsy 4WDs and jeeps from the **Baghira Log Huts**, Kisli in the park (for a maximum of six people, Rs 9 per kilometre. Book the previous day. Petrol is often not available at Kisli; the nearest pumps are at Mandla.

Park information

Visitor centres are at Khatia and Mukki gates and at Kanha (the largest), open 0700-1030 and 1600-1800. There are informative displays, short films, audio-visual shows and books for sale. Recommended minimum stay is two nights. See also page 206.

When to go

The best time to visit is January to June. It can get very cold on winter nights, down to just a few degrees above freezing, while in summer temperatures can hit 43°C. The monsoon season is July to September. The park is closed 1 July-31 October.

Tip...
Ask for boiled water specifically. Water served at private lodges is generally filtered.

Viewing

Forest Department guides accompany visitors around the park on mapped-out circuits to see a cross-section of wildlife from an open jeep (or Gypsy) (see Essential box, opposite); there are two viewing sessions a day, the first beginning 30 minutes before sunrise and the second ending 30 minutes after sunset; confirm locally for the exact times. However, one traveller comments that "vehicles chase each other round, their paths crossing and re-crossing and their noisy engines presumably driving the more timid wildlife way back from the tracks". It is better to stop the vehicle on the forest track and in front of the grasslands.

The *sal* forests do not normally allow good viewing. The best areas are the meadows around Kanha. **Bamni Dadar** (Sunset Point) has a view of the dense jungle and animals typical of the mixed forest zone: sambar, barking deer and chausingha (four-horned antelope). Early morning and late afternoon are ideal times and binoculars are invaluable. *Machans* (viewing platforms/observation towers), are available for use during daylight; those above waterholes (eg **Sravantal**), are recommended.

Listings Kanha National Park

Where to stay

Some hotels offer pick-up from Jabalpur. Most offer the option of a 'Jungle Plan', including all meals, 2 safaris a day, entry fees and a naturalist guide. Reserve rooms in advance; most are open 1 Nov-30 Jun. Private lodges are outside the park and usually offer good discounts in May-Jun when visitors are few.

$$$$ The Baagh Forest Retreat
Village Gudma, Mukki Gate, T08802-352349, www.thebaagh.com.
A sister property to the beautiful **Bagh** in Bharatpur, Rajasthan, this certainly does not disappoint, with 16 deluxe cottages and 8 suites. There's an attractive swimming pool, multi-cuisine restaurant and barbecue (dinners can also be arranged in special outdoor nooks), guided walks, tribal dancing and bonfires. And giving back to the community, rainwater harvesting at the resort has created new arable land for the local farmers.

$$$$ Kanha Jungle Lodge
Balaghat–Raipur Rd, Just south of Mukki, 12 km from Baihar and the main road, T07637-216015, www.kanhajunglelodge.com.
Beautifully decorated and comfortably furnished cottages with private patios overlooking the forest. Modern facilities, attached bathroom and hot water. There's even a hot water bottle to keep you warm at night.

$$$$ Kipling Camp
Near Khatia, T07649-277218, bookings T011-6519 6377, www.kiplingcamp.com.
Well-run place with 18 chalets and a pleasant ambience. All-inclusive package. Rates keep changing so for up-to-date prices contact the resort.

$$$$ Shergarh
Bahmni Village, T(0)9098-187346, www.shergarh.com. Nov-May.
Beautiful camp run by an Anglo-Indian couple, with 6 tents surrounding a picturesque lake. Included in the price are 2 safaris and all meals. It's possible to go birdwatching, visit local markets and even paint elephants. Highly recommended.

$$$ Wild Chalet Resort
Mocha Village, T07649-277203, reservations via Indian Adventures, T022-264 08742, www.indianadventures.com/WildChalet.htm.
Cottages with shower overlooking the river. Good food and park tours, and a helpful and efficient manager. Recommended.

Inside the park

Arrive by sunset as no entry is allowed after dark. Reservations can be made via www.mptourism.com.

$$$ Baghira Log Huts
Kisli, T07649-277227, www.mptourism.com.
16 rooms, restaurant and a cheaper canteen.

$ Tourist Hostel
Kisli, opposite the bus stand, T07649-277310.
Reasonably well kept 6-8 bed dorms (Rs 1300 per person). Uninspiring vegetarian meals in a grim canteen nearby.

Restaurants

Most lodges include meals. Cold drinks are usually available but fresh fruit is not.

Baghira Log Huts
See Where to stay, above.
Restaurant and bar.

Bus Kanha is connected with **Jabalpur**, **Nagpur** and **Bilaspur** by motorable but often poor roads. From Jabalpur there are daily buses to **Kisli** (via Mandla and Chiraidongri, 0800, 1100) and **Mukki** (0900).

Jeep Private hire to **Jabalpur** around Rs 3500-4000.

Train **Jabalpur** (173 km) is the most convenient mainline station.

Bandhavgarh National Park Colour map 3, C2.
compact park with elusive tigers and other wildlife spotting

The park (altitude 800 m) is set in extremely rugged terrain with many hills. The marshes which used to be perennial now support a vast grassland savannah. Though it involves quite a journey you may be rewarded with sighting one of the few tigers; a three-day stay gives you a 90% chance of seeing one. There are also interesting cave shrines scattered around the park, with Brahmi inscriptions dating from the first century BC. You can visit the remains of a fort believed to be 2000 years old where you may spot crag martins and brown rock thrush.

Bandhavgarh (pronounced Bandogarh) is not very far from Rewa, famous as the original home of the white tiger, now only found in zoos. Before becoming a national park in 1968, it was the game reserve of the Maharajas of Rewa. The conservation programme helps to protect wildlife from disease, fire, grazing and poaching.

Essential Bandhavgarh National Park

Getting around

Jeeps are available from dawn to 1000 and from 1500 until dusk when the animals are most active. The short way round is 18 km, the long way is 37 km. The fort, 18 km away, requires a 4WD vehicle; ask at the **White Tiger Forest Lodge** about **MP Tourism Canter Safari** (Rs 2400, Indians Rs 1200 per person). **Jeep tours** (with up to six passengers) cost around Rs 3800-5000, depending on the forest zone, and include entry ticket and guide fees.

Park information

This park is in the Vindhya hills with a core area of 105 sq km and a buffer zone of 437 sq km. The main entrance and park office is at Tala to the north of the park. The park is open 1 October-30 June. Rainfall: 1500 mm. For admission fees, see page 206; for Transport, see opposite page.

Useful contacts

For more information, contact the **Field Director**, Bandhavgarh Tiger Reserve, Umaria, T07653-222214.

Wildlife

The park has a wide variety of game and has a longer 'season' than Kanha. Its main wild beasts are tiger, leopard, sloth bear, gaur, sambar, chital, muntjac, nilgai, chinkara and wild pigs. There are over 60 tigers, but they remain very hard to spot. The flowering and fruit trees attract woodland birds which include green pigeon, Jerdon's leaf bird, crested serpent eagle and variable hawk eagle.

Viewing

Bandhavgarh is divided into three safari zones – Tala, Maghdi and Khitauli – each with a separate entry gate. Within each zone are a number of set safari routes, each 35-40 km in length. **Tala** is the 'premium' zone, richest in scenery, history and wildlife sightings. A game drive here comes at double the cost of the less popular zones, but it's a false economy to try to save money by avoiding Tala; if you give yourself the recommended three days in Bandhavgarh, taking all six safaris here represents your best chance of seeing a tiger. If it's open, the 10th-century fort on top of Bandhavgarh hill (park rules change frequently), is littered with poignant ruins and silent shrines, and offers phenomenal views.

Maghdi, to the south of Tala, has no shortage of tigers, but sightings are less common. The Rajbehra meadow here is always busy with chital and wild boar, and the occasional jackal. Maghdi's waterholes are also the best place in the park to look for gaur, reintroduced to the park in recent years. **Khitauli**, somewhat unfairly cast as the ugly sister, offers few tigers, but is one of the best parts of the park to look for sloth bear, nilgai and dhole.

Listings Bandhavgarh National Park

Where to stay

Rates for the **$$$$** places below include all meals and 2 jungle safaris.

$$$$ Bandhavgarh Jungle Lodge
Within walking distance of the park gates, T07627-265317, www.bandhavgarhjunglelodge.com.
8 rooms in 2 separate villas with typical Indian village theme, modern facilities with attached bathroom, hot water. Also offers 13 spacious, comfortable cottages.

$$$$ Samode Safari Lodge
T07653-280579, www.samode.com.
This stunning addition to the **Samode** chain in Rajasthan is the ultimate in luxury, while still leaving a light footprint. Designed to blend with the surroundings, no trees were cut down in this new build and there is a good nod to eco-tourism with rainwater harvesting, solar energy and villas made from local materials by local craftsmen. Recommended.

$$$$ Treehouse Hideaway
T(0)8800-637711, www.treehousehideaway.com.
Worlds apart from any treehouse you might have had as a kid, these are boutique treehouses made of dark wood with beautiful decor and stunning views. They also have a hide overlooking the water hole and a 2-tier restaurant in a large *mahua* tree. Very special.

$$$-$$ White Tiger Forest Lodge (MP Tourism)
Tala, overlooking the river, T07627-265366, www.mptourism.com.
Modest place but good value, 26 rooms (8 a/c), restaurant (expensive, tiny portions, but good), bar and jeep hire (for residents). The best rooms are in the detached cottages by the river, but are "in need of a good sweep". Also have **Forest Rest House**.

$$ Bagh Sarai
Parasi village, 6 km from Ghori Gate, T09818-680958, www.baghsarai.com.
Stylish luxury tented bungalows, run by Neeraj Pathania, who has worked on wildlife films for

National Geographic among others. Excellent levels of comfort and service and a good wildlife knowledge. Recommended.

$$ Skay's Camp
Tala, T09425331209, www.skayscamp.in.
Owned by a pair of passionate naturalists, Skays (pronounced Ess-kay's) offers simple comforts in a home environment, with 7 a/c en suite rooms set in a garden of flowers, and mango and papaya trees. Satyendra and Kay are seasoned campaigners for conservation and experts on everything from tiger hideouts to butterfly biology. They accompany guests on safari at every opportunity. Superb value and highly recommended.

$ Kum-kum
Opposite White Tiger, see above, T07627-265324.
Very basic but well-run place offering 4 large, clean rooms with fan, hot water, excellent vegetarian food. Friendly and helpful staff. The jeep driver Saleem is an expert tiger spotter. Recommended.

Transport

Air Jabalpur is the nearest airport.

Bus From Tala buses go to **Umaria**, **Rewa**, **Satna** and **Katni**, all with rail connections.

Jeep From Tala it's possible to get a jeep seat (Rs 100) to **Satna** (insist on your full seat); poor road, bumpy and dusty 3-hr ride. From **Umaria**: jeep to Tala for park, Rs 500, good for sharing. From **Jabalpur** drive to Shajpura (144 km) then take a country road (fairly hilly) to Umaria. From **Khajuraho** (237 km) 6-7 hrs.

Taxi Available from **Satna** (129 km) 3 hrs, **Katni** and **Umaria**.

Train Umaria (35 km) is the nearest station, on the Katni-Bilaspur sector (1 hr by road). Rickshaw to bus stand (Rs 40-50), from where you can get a bus to Tala. Direct trains run from Umaria to: **Delhi** (18 hrs), **Bhubaneswar** (28 hrs). **Jabalpur** (2 daily, 3-5 hrs), **Varanasi** (9 hrs) and **Satna** (early morning, 5 hrs).

Chhattisgarh

A mixture of heavy industrial belts and untouched forest, Chhattisgarh remains terra incognita for most travellers, and the relative lack of infrastructure makes travelling here a genuine adventure. Though potentially hugely rewarding for anyone interested in tribal culture, parts of the state have in recent years been consumed by violent struggle between Maoist Naxalites and state-sponsored militias. It is imperative to check local conditions and wise to seek advice from your government before travelling beyond the main towns.

Exploring Chhattisgarh
tribal cultures, palace hotels and adventures off the beaten track

Raipur *Colour map 6, A3.*
Raipur (population 605,000) is the rapidly growing state capital of Chhattisgarh, and also the regional transport centre. Water tanks and a temple date from the 17th and 18th centuries. **Jai Stambh Chowk** (Chhattisgarh Circle) is generally regarded to be the centre of town with the Head Post Office, State Bank and several hotels close by.

★ Kawardha *Colour map 6, A2.*
Kawardha is a small town in the Rajnandgaon region of Chhattisgarh. In this remote area Maharaja Vishwaraj Singh welcomes visitors to his late 1930s palace. It provides a delightfully quiet unspoiled contrast with India's big cities and with the much busier tourist route of Rajasthan's 'palace circuit'. The Radha Krishna family temple with underground rooms is nearby. You can visit the 11th-century Chandela-style temples at Bhoramdev with beautiful carvings, step wells, enjoy excellent birdwatching or explore the area's natural beauty on foot with the Yuvraj. The Gonds and the gentle Baiga tribe continue to follow a primitive lifestyle in the surrounding forests; ecologically sensitive visits are arranged.

Kanker *Colour map 6, A3.*
Some 140 km south of Raipur, Kanker is a district headquarters town, with some fine century-old colonial buildings. It nestles by a tributary of the Mahanadi River, amidst unspoilt forests and hills, the home of several tribal groups who continue to practise age-old crafts and traditions. Kanker's royal family, who trace their ancestors back to the 12th century, welcomes guests to their palace to share their region's culture and history.

Bastar District
Lying in the southern tip of Chhattisgarh, Bastar district is home to several indigenous tribal groups in one of the state's more densely forested areas. There are two national parks within driving distance of Jagdalpur, the district headquarters, which also serves as a useful base for visiting the region's tribal areas. To visit the area, car hire costs around Rs 3000 per day from Kanker Palace.

Jagdalpur, 160 km south of Kanker, is the centre of the tribal heartland of Bastar where you can see the Gond, Halba, Muriya, Madia, Dhurwa and Bhattra people. *Mrignayani* emporium collects and sells their arts and crafts. There is a small **tribal museum** maintained by the Anthropological Society of India and a **tourist office** ⓘ *near Sahid Park, T099938-54165*.

Situated 35 km south west of Jagdalpur, in the transition zone marking the natural southern limit of *sal* and the northern limit of teak, **Kanger Valley National Park** is a narrow stretch of mixed virgin forest, with tiger, panther, sambhar, wild pig, flying squirrel as well as a wide range of reptiles and birds. Within the park the **Kailash** and **Kutumsar Gupha** are attractive limestone caves which are popular with visitors. Forest guides are available. The 30-m-high **Tirathgarh Falls**, 39 km southwest of Jagdalpur, sees the Kanger River descend the valley in a series of steps. Overnight stays are possible in basic forest rest houses at Kutumsar, Netanar and Teerathgarh. Contact Director Kangerghati NP, Jagdalpur, T07782-228640.

Indravati National Park

This park along the Indravati River was designated a Project Tiger reserve in 1982. The dense monsoon forest interspersed with grassy glades is known as ancient Dandakaranya, cited in the *Ramayana* as the place where Rama was exiled. Apart from increasing tiger protection, the park is seen as the best reserve for the wild buffalo (*Bubalus amee*) and an ideal alternative home for the endangered Branden barasingha (hardground swamp deer), which is only found in Kanha further north. For more information on fees, see page 206.

The NH43 is a good, scenic road, ideal for seeing the Bastar tribal area. Following the Indravati west from Jagdalpur, the popular waterfalls at **Chitrakote** (38 km) drop some 30 m in a horseshoe curve and provide an attractive diversion.

Barnawapara Sanctuary

Permission to enter from DFO, Wildlife Division, in front of the bus stand T07727-223526.

Occupying 245 sq km in the northern part of Mahasamund District, near Sirpur, this sanctuary offers the chance to see several species of deer in the hilly *sal* forest as well as sloth bear and bison; tigers and panthers are present though rarely seen. Migratory birds are attracted by artificial waterholes in the winter. **Dev Travels** (see What to do, below) organizes tours. The best time to visit is from November to April.

You can stay in forest rest houses on the outskirts of the sanctuary or inside at Barnawapara which has two basic rooms.

Listings Chhattisgarh

Tourist information

Rajpur

Paryatan Bhavan
GE Rd, T0771-422 4600,
www.chhattisgarhtourism.net.
Provides minimal information. You might do better with the head office information line, T0771-422 4999, T1800-102 6415.

Where to stay

Raipur

There are several **$** hotels near the railway station, although earplugs may be needed for a good night's sleep.

$$$-$$ Hotel Grand International
Behind Gurudwara, Station Rd, T0771-403 9401,
www.hotelgrandinternational.com.
Top-notch hotel with all mod cons and some nice decorative features. There's a multi-cuisine restaurant and a bar.

$$$-$$ Mayura
GE Rd, near Raj Talkies, 2 km from the stations,
T0771-420 0500, www.themayurahotels.com.
50 good rooms, central a/c, TV, excellent **Kapri** restaurant, and airport pickup.

$$ Piccadilly
Mohaba Bazar, 5 km from town towards Durg,
T0771-4060124, www.piccadilyraipur.in.
Well-run place with 54 comfortable rooms, a/c, attached bath with tubs, TV, airport/station pickup, pool (roadside) and friendly staff. The out-of-town location is the only drawback.

$$-$ Aditya
KK Rd, Jaistambh Chowk, T0771-403 2941,
www.hoteladityaraipur.com.
34 decent rooms, central a/c, and TV.

$$-$ Hotel Chhattisgarh (Hotel Johar)
Tehbanda, 4 km from the centre towards airport,
T0771-244 2769, www.chhattisgarhtourism.net
22 rooms, 4 suites, some a/c, hot bath, TV and a restaurant.

$ Radhika
Jai Stambh Chowk, T0771-223 3806.
26 rather scruffy rooms with TV and bath, some
a/c, and a good restaurant. Rooms at the front
suffer from road noise.

Kawardha

$$$ Palace Kawardha
T07741-232085, www.kawardhapalace.com.
5 large suites with pleasant verandas, Western
baths, imposing Durbar Hall, attractive gardens,
a unique experience visiting tribal settlements,
temples, jeep excursions, short treks into
surrounding hills (5-8 km, 2½-5 hrs), longer treks
into the jungle with advance notice, very warm
hospitality. Reservations essential.

Kanker

$$$$-$$$ Royal Palace
in a garden setting, T07868-222005,
www.kankerpalace.com.
Once residency of British Agent, has 3 modern
suites but aims to retain 'earthy flavour' with
cottages on site too. Maharajkumar Surya Pratap
Deo arranges interesting excursions to explore
both the natural surroundings as well as the
area's rich tribal heritage. Reserve well ahead.

Bastar District

$$$$ Royal Bastar Farm
In a village near Jagdalpur, T09406-358172,
www.royalbastarfarm.com.
Owned by the Kanker royal family, it has
3 comfortable cottages for visitors who wish
to experience rural living with a difference.
Advance notice needed.

$ Hotel Akansha Deluxe
Motitalab Para, Jagdalpur, T07782-225335,
www.hotelakanksha.com.
Rooms all have a/c, and there's a restaurant.

What to do

Raipur
Dev Travels, *behind Netaji Subhash Stadium,
Ahmedji Colony, T0771-405100, www.
devtravelindia.com.* Professional agency, can
arrange cars for visiting tribal areas, wildlife
sanctuaries, etc.
Oberoi Tours & Travels, *KK Rd, opposite Punjab
and Sindh Bank, T0771-4266666, oberoitours@
hotmail.com.* Efficient air ticketing office.

Transport

Raipur
Air Mana Airport, 15 km southeast of town.
Taxis take around 30 mins to the centre; the better
hotels provide free pickup with advance notice.
Daily flights to **Delhi** via **Jabalpur** or **Nagpur**, and
to **Mumbai** via **Bhubaneswar**.

Bus New Bus Stand, 3 km from the railway
station, has services to all towns in **Chhattisgarh**
and Madhya Pradesh.

Train Enquiry, T0771-252 8130/131. Trains to
Kolkata, 14 hrs; **Mumbai**, 21½ hrs; **New Delhi**
(20 hrs) via **Bhopal** (16 hrs). **Varanasi** (20 hrs)
via Allahabad (16 hrs).

Kawardha
Bus and car Express buses run from **Raipur**,
where cars can also be hired, or ask Palace
Kawardha (see Where to stay, above) to arrange
a pick-up; they will also fetch guests from **Kanha
National Park** (5½ hrs).

Jeep Ask at **Palace Kawardha**, **Raipur** US$40,
Kanha US$50.

Train From **Raipur** (140 km) and **Bilaspur**
(124 km).

Background Madhya Pradesh and Chhattisgarh

Rock paintings and stone artefacts prove the existence of Stone Age cultures. Although the region was incorporated into successive states from the empire of Asoka to that of the Mughals, it was rarely the centre of a major power. In the 10th century a number of dynasties controlled different parts of the region, most notably the Chandelas at Khajuraho. Gwalior was conquered in the 11th century by the Muslims, whose influence spread southeast under the Khaljis into Malwa during the 13th century. Akbar annexed this into his empire in the mid-16th century. The Scindia and Holkar dynasties of Marathas ruled independently at Gwalior and Indore respectively during the 18th century. Under the British the region became known as the Central Provinces; it wasn't until the state re-organization that followed Independence that the modern state of Madhya Pradesh was created.

Chhattisgarh, comprising the largely tribal districts of the southeast corner of Madhya Pradesh, became an independent state on 1 November 2000, though the first demand for the state's creation can be traced back to 1925. Some suggested that the long-standing tribal demand for a separate state was finally ceded by Madhya Pradesh because of the difficulty of controlling the violent Naxalites, groups of revolutionary guerrillas. The political and economic challenge facing Chhattisgarh's government is huge, but its policy of arming a counter militia, the Salwa Judum (Peace March), and granting it the powers of an emergency police force, has achieved little but to entirely polarize rural tribal communities between the Naxalites and those who violently oppose them. Parts of the state have effectively become consumed by a civil war in which the rule of law has dissolved. Many villages have been depopulated, their inhabitants forced to move to refugee camps in fear of being seen by either side to be supporters of the other. The challenge to Chhattisgarh is equally obvious in terms of social and economic development. Literacy rates are among the lowest in India, with 43% literate across the state as a whole, 58% of men but only 28% of women, and Bastar District having over 80% still illiterate. Half the households have no drinking water, only one third has any electricity connection, over 40% of girls are married before they are 20 and infant mortality is 46%.

Madhya Pradesh, meanwhile, along with Gujarat, has been at the centre of protests around the Narmada River project. The extensive damming of the Narmada river over the last 25 years has displaced thousands of villagers with little or no consideration, let alone compensation. Arundhati Roy's essay *The Greater Common Good* shines a light on the Narmada project's geographical and cultural impact on Madhya Pradesh.

Rajasthan

palaces, forts, tigers and camel safaris

Rajasthan exceeds the most far-fetched fantasies of what India might be: women dazzle in bright fabrics; mustachioed men drive camels over dunes; tigers prowl through ancient forests; and princely palaces loom up from the Thar Desert.

Over the centuries Rajasthan's rulers have built scores of evocative forts and palaces in places like Samode, Deogarh and Udaipur. In Jodhpur, the majestic Mehrangarh sits high above iridescent blue houses, while the far-flung wonder of Jaisalmer rises proudly from the surrounding sands. But much of Rajasthan's more recent architectural bounty is due to British imperial policy towards the state's then maharajas. The colonial regime allowed them great wealth but little power, creating a civilization of great extravagance. This surfeit of opulence is everywhere, so sadly but atmospherically crumbling into decay.

Rajasthan's people are as theatrical as their architectural backdrop, and you'll encounter an eye-popping cast of characters: from suave polo-playing Rajputs to tall, peasant camel-drivers in incandescent turbans, and tribal women who are a shock of colour against the sands.

Although synonymous with desert dunes, Rajasthan has other landscape: some of the world's oldest mountains; green, rolling hills; and dense jungle with Rathambhore's famous tigers.

Best for
Deserts ■ Heritage ■ Wildlife

Footprint picks

★ **Nahargarh Fort, Jaipur**,
page 280
Don't miss the stunning sunset at
this fort.

★ **Jodhpur**, page 331
Marvel at Meherangarh, the
'Majestic Fort', and its views over the
remarkable blue Old City below.

★ **Khuldara**, page 350
Visit this abandoned ghost village in the Thar Desert close to Jaisalmer.

★ **Ranthambhore National Park**, page 363
Take a jungle jeep ride for tiger and leopard spotting.

★ **Desert life**, page 384
Experience the desert close up with a ride on a camel in Kakoo.

Essential Rajasthan

Finding your feet

Running like a spine through Rajasthan (population 56.47 million), the Aravalli Hills are some of the oldest mountains in the world. A series of jagged, heavily folded ranges, they stretch from Mount Abu in the southwest (1720 m) to Kota and Bundi in the east. In the northwest is the forbidding Thar Desert, with its shifting sand dunes and crushingly high summer temperatures. In the south the average elevation is higher (330-1150 m). In the northeast the landscape forms part of the nearly flat Yamuna drainage basin.

Getting around

Trains, buses and 'sleeper' buses cover all major towns. A car is worthwhile to explore more obscure areas.

When to go

One of the driest regions in India, Rajasthan has a desert climate, with hot days and cool nights most of the year. By far the best time to visit is from October to April. Summer is stiflingly hot; May and June can be draining and then the humidity builds up as the monsoon approaches. The monsoon season lasts from July to September. The European summer holidays of July and August bring many visitors to Rajasthan despite the temperatures. In Jaipur and the desert temperatures can plummet to near freezing in January. Some of the region's great festivals, such as Diwali and the Pushkar Camel Fair, take place in the autumn and winter.

Time required

You could spend an infinite amount of time exploring Rajasthan, but try and aim for a minimum of two to three days each for Jaipur, Jodhpur, Jaisalmer, Udaipur, Moundt Abu, Bundi and Ranthambhore.

Language

The principal language is Rajasthani, a close relative of Hindi.

Festivals

There are several music and literary festivals in the region which draw large crowds of both international and domestic travellers to see artists and writers from around the globe. Hosted by William Dalrymple, the **Jaipur Literary Festival** happens every January in Jaipur and speakers have included Kiran Desai, Vikram Seth, Orhan Pamuk, Richard Ford and Simon Shama (www.jaipurliteraturefestival.org). In October, at the magnificent Mehrangarh Fort in Jodhpur there is the **Rajasthan Folk Festival** with musicians from around the world exploring eastern folk traditions like *qawwali* and baul singing (www.jodhpurriff.org); and split between Mehrangarh Fort and the beautiful Nagaur Fort you will find the **World Sufi Spirit Festival** every February (www.worldsufispiritfestival.org).

On 14 January **Makar Sankranti** marks the end of winter and is celebrated with kite flying; it's very popular in Jaipur. In February, it's the

Weather	Jaipur				
January	**February**	**March**	**April**	**May**	**June**
23°C 9°C 6mm	26°C 17°C 13mm	32°C 17°C 7mm	38°C 23°C 13mm	41°C 27°C 15mm	40°C 28°C 63mm
July	**August**	**September**	**October**	**November**	**December**
35°C 26°C 156mm	33°C 25°C 199mm	35°C 24°C 72mm	34°C 20°C 36mm	30°C 15°C 7mm	25°C 10°C 10mm

Nagaur Camel Fair and Desert Festival in Jaisalmer. **Ganesh Chaturthi** was established in August just over 100 years ago by the Indian nationalist leader Tilak. The elephant-headed God of good omen is shown special reverence. On the last of the five-day festival after harvest, clay images of Ganesh are taken in procession with dancers and musicians, and are immersed in the sea, river or pond. It's gaining popularity in Udaipur and Pushkar.

Food and drink

In cities and larger towns, you will see all types of Indian food on the menus, with some restaurants specializing in regional cuisine. North Indian kebabs and the richer flavoursome cuisine of the Northwest Frontier are popular. Good Rajasthani dishes to try are *kadhi pakoka* (small veggie dumplings in a yoghurt curry) and *kej sangri* (lightly spiced desert beans). For snacks try the crispy, spicy and delicious *kachori* rather than the usual samosa. There are also amazing *kulfis* in Rajasthan, often served in hand-thrown clay pots, or try the delicious saffron *lassis*. Freshly brewed coffee is rare in North India; ordinary city restaurants will usually serve the instant variety.

Footprint picks

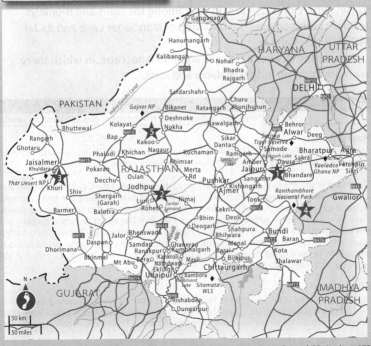

Jaipur

The sandstone 'pink city' of Jaipur, Rajasthan's capital, is the heady gateway to the state. The city is on the popular 'Golden Triangle' route (Delhi–Agra–Jaipur–Delhi) which for many short-haul visitors is their only experience of Rajasthan. The steady stream of tourists means the city has to make little effort to attract visitors; as a result its pastel-hued buildings are not what they used to be, but it is effortlessly charming nonetheless.

The old city, with its bazars, palaces and *havelis*, along with a couple of forts and the ancient city of Amber nearby, are well worth a wander. Knotted, narrow streets hold cupboard-sized workshops where elderly women dash out clothes on rusty Singers; men energetically stuff mattresses with piles of rags; boys mend bicycles next to old men rolling pellets of paste into sweets; and whole families carve table legs or hammer bed headboards out of sheet metal.

Escape the bustle and head up to the Tiger Fort (Nahargarh) for sunset, where proud peacocks pick among the ruins and monkeys scamper about against the backdrop of Man Sagar Lake and its Jal Mahal (Water Palace).

Outside the city lies a tranquil agrarian landscape, in which there are many hunting lodges, palaces and forts.

Sights
splendid fortresses, majestic palaces, tranquil temples and beautiful havelis

Hawa Mahal
Enter from Tripolia Bazar, Sat-Thu 0900-1630, foreigners Rs 50, Indians Rs 10 – audio tours possible; for the best views accept invitations from shop owners on upper floors across the street.

The 'Palace of the Winds' (circa 1799) forms part of the east wall of the City Palace complex and is best seen from the street outside. Possibly Jaipur's most famous building, this pink sandstone façade of the palace was built for the ladies of the harem by Sawai Pratap Singh. The five storeys stand on a high podium with an entrance from the west. The elaborate façade contains 953 small casements in a huge curve, each with a balcony and crowning arch. The windows enabled *hawa* (cool air) to circulate and allowed the women who were secluded in the *zenana* to watch processions below without being seen. The museum has second-century BC utensils and old sculpture. It's a magical place.

City Palace
0930-1700 (last entry 1630). Foreigners Rs 300 (includes still camera and a good audio guide), Indians Rs 75 (camera Rs 50 extra); includes Sawai Man Singh II Museum and Jaigarh Fort, valid for 1 week. Video (unnecessary) Rs 200; doorkeepers expect tips when photographed. Photography in galleries prohibited.

The City Palace (1728-1732) occupies the centre of Jaipur, covers one seventh of its area and is surrounded by a high wall – the Sarahad. Its style differs from conventional Rajput fort palaces in its separation of the palace from its fortifications, which in other Rajput buildings are integrated in one massive interconnected structure. In contrast the Jaipur Palace has much more in common with Mughal models, with its main buildings scattered in a fortified campus. In Jai Singh's day, the buildings were painted in a variety of colours, including grey with white borders. Pink, a traditional colour of welcome, was used in 1853 in honour of the visit by Prince Albert, and the colour is still used.

To find the main entrance, from the Hawa Mahal go north about 250 m along the Sireh Deori Bazar past the Vidhan Sabha (Town Hall) and turn left through an arch – the Sireh Deori (Boundary Gate). Pass under a second arch – the Naqqar Darwaza (Drum Gate) – into Jaleb Chowk, the courtyard which formerly housed the palace guard. Today it is where coaches park. This is surrounded by residential quarters which were modified in the 19th century under Sawai Ram Singh II. A gateway to the south leads to the Jantar Mantar, the main palace buildings and museum and the Hawa Mahal.

Mubarak Mahal The main entrance leads into a large courtyard at the centre of which is the Mubarak Mahal, faced in white marble. Built in 1890, originally as a guesthouse for the Maharaja, the Mubarak Mahal is a small but immaculately conceived two-storeyed building, designed on the same cosmological plan in miniature as the city itself – a square divided into a three by three square grid.

The **Textile and Costume Museum** on the first floor has fine examples of fabrics and costumes from all over India, including some spectacular wedding outfits, as well as musical instruments and toys from the royal nursery. In the northwest corner of the courtyard is the **Armoury Museum** containing an impressive array of weaponry – pistols, blunderbusses, flintlocks, swords, rifles and daggers, as well as some fascinating paintings on the way in. This was originally the common room of the harem. From the north-facing first-floor windows you can get a view of the Chandra Mahal (see below). Just outside the Armoury Museum is **Rajendra Pol**, a gate flanked by two elephants, each carved from a single block of marble, which leads to the

Essential Jaipur

Finding your feet

The airport is 15 km south of town while Jaipur Railway Station is on Station Road, southwest of the Old City; the Central Bus Stand at Sindhi Camp is nearby. Buses from Delhi use the dramatically improved NH8; the journey now takes under four hours by car. The alternative Gurgaon–Alwar–Jaipur route is more interesting but much slower.

Best views

The rooftop restaurant at Pearl Palace, page 282
Hot-air ballooning at Amber Fort, page 286
Sunset at Nawalgarh (Tiger Fort), page 388

Getting around

The best way to get to the Old City is to take a rickshaw, then explore on foot. Excellent heritage walking tours through the labyrinthine streets are offered by Virasat Experiences (see page 286). The few attractions of the new town are spread out so explore by rickshaw, bus or taxi. There is also a new metro which takes you direct to Chandpole at the start of the Old City. See Transport, page 286.

Orientation

The heart of Jaipur is the old walled 'pink city', northeast of the centre. Most of the main sights are here including the City Palace, the Jantar Mantar Observatory, the Hawa Mahal and the intricate streets of the bazars. South of the pink city is a quieter, leafier area containing the Ram Niwas Gardens and Central Museum, while on the outskirts of town are the Naharqarh (Tiger) Fort and the Surya Mandir Temple.

Nearly all accommodation and even restaurants are outside of the Old City. The hotels and restaurants of Bani Park are to the west; C-Scheme is to the southwest.

Best hidden treasures

Exquisite dining room at Samode Haveli Gangapole, page 282
Delicious lassiwalla, page 284
Havelis and Temples Walk with Virasat Experiences, page 286
Shila Mata Temple (Kali Temple) at Amber Fort, page 288

Jaipur

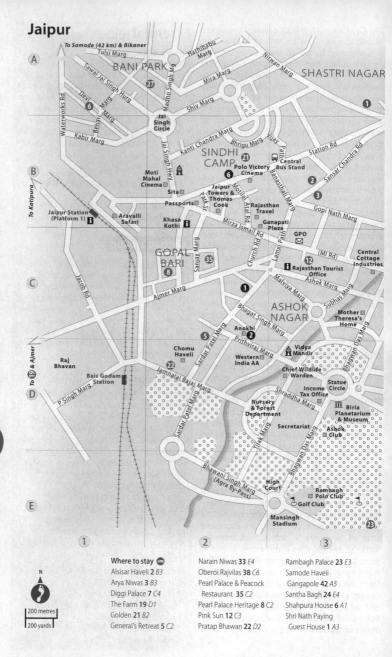

Tulsi Marg

BANI PARK

Hathibabu Marg

Mira Marg

Nirwan Marg

SHASTRI NAGAR

Sawai Jai Singh Hurg

Madho Singh Mg

Shiv Marg

Devi Marg

Bahan Marg

Waterworks Rd

Kabir Marg

Jai Singh Circle

Kanti Chandra Marg

Bhrigu Marg

Vijay Path

Station Rd

Sansar Chandra Rd

Moti Mahal Cinema

SINDHI CAMP

Polo Victory Cinema

Central Bus Stand

To Katipura

Jaipur Station (Platform 1)

Sita

Passports

Jai Singh Hwy

Jaipur Towers & Thomas Cook

Park St.

Rajasthan Travel

Gopi Nath Marg

Aravalli Safari

Khasa Kothi

Mirza Ismail Rd

Motilal Atal Rd

Ganapati Plaza

GPO

(MI Rd)

Central Cottage Industries

To Katipura

GOPAL BARI

Stanley Marg

Church Rd

Laxmi Path

Rajasthan Tourist Office

Malviya Marg

Ashok Marg

Subhas Marg

Ajmer Marg

Bhagat Singh Marg

ASHOK NAGAR

Mother Theresa's Home

Jacob Rd

Anokhi

Prithviraj Marg

Vidya Mandir

Chomu Haveli

Sardar Patel Marg

Western India AA

Chief Wildlife Warden

Bhagwan Das Marg

Raj Bhavan

To ID & Ajmer

Bais Godam Station

Jamnalal Bajai Marg

Sardar Patel Marg

Nursery & Forest Department

Income Tax Office

Shraddha Marg

Statue Circle

Birla Planetarium & Museum

P Singh Marg

Tilak Marg

Secretariat

Ashok Club

Bhawani Singh Marg (Agra By-Pass)

High Court

Rambagh Polo Club

Golf Club

Mansingh Stadium

N

200 metres
200 yards

Umaid Bhawan **27** *A2*

Lassiwala **4** *C4*
LMB **1** *B5*
Niros & Book Corner **7** *C4*
Palladio **8** *E4*

Restaurants 🍴
Anokhi Café **2** *C2*
Chokhi Dhani **5** *E4*
Jaipur Modern **1** *C2*
Kanji **6** *B2*

inner courtyard. There are beautifully carved alcoves with delicate arches and *jali* screens and a fine pair of patterned brass doors.

Diwan-i-Khas (Sarbato Bhadra) The gateway leads to the courtyard known variously as the Diwan-i-Am, the Sarbato Bhadra or the Diwan-i-Khas Chowk. Today, the building in its centre is known as the Diwan-i-Khas (circa 1730). Originally the Diwan-i-Am, it was reduced to the hall of private audience (Diwan-i-Khas) when the new Diwan-i-Am was built to its southeast at the end of the 18th century. The courtyard itself reflects the overwhelming influence of Mughal style, despite the presence of some Hindu designs, a result of the movement of Mughal-trained craftsmen from further north in search of opportunities to practise their skills. In the Diwan-i-Khas (now known by the Sanskrit name Sarbato Bhadra) are two huge silver urns – ratified by Guinness as being the largest pieces of silver in the world – used by Sawai Madho Singh for carrying Ganga water to England.

Diwan-i-Am (Diwan Khana) Art Gallery With its entrance in the southeast corner of the Diwan-i-Am courtyard, the 'new' Hall of Public Audience built by Maharaja Sawai Pratap Singh (1778-1803) today houses a fine collection of Persian and Indian miniatures, some of the carpets the maharajas had made for them and an equally fine collection of manuscripts. To its north is the **Carriage Museum**, housed in a modern building. In the middle of the west wall of the Diwan-i-Am courtyard, opposite the art gallery, is the **Ganesh Pol**, which leads via a narrow passage and the Peacock Gate into **Pritam Niwas Chowk**. This courtyard has the original palace building 'Chandra Mahal' to its north, the *zenana* on its northwest, and the Anand Mahal to its south. Several extremely attractive doors, rich and vivid in their peacock blue, aquamarine and amber colours, have small marble Hindu gods watching over them.

Chandra Mahal Built between 1727 and 1734 the Moon Palace is the earliest building of the palace complex. Externally it appears to have seven storeys, though inside the first and second floors are actually one high-ceilinged hall. The top two floors give superb views of the city and Tiger Fort. On the ground floor (north) a wide veranda – the **Pritam Niwas** (House of the Beloved) – with Italian wall paintings, faces the formal Jai Niwas garden. The main section of the ground floor is an Audience Hall. The palace is not always open to visitors.

The hall on the first and second floors, the **Sukh Niwas** (House of Pleasure), underwent a Victorian reconstruction. Above it are the **Rang Mandir** and the **Sobha Niwas**, built to the same plan. The two top storeys are much smaller, with the mirror palace of the **Chavi Niwas** succeeded by the small open marble pavilion which crowns the structure, the **Mukat Niwas**.

In the northeast corner of the Pritam Niwas Chowk, leading into the *zenana*, is the **Krishna door**, its surface embossed with scenes of the deity's life. The door is sealed in the traditional way with a rope sealed with wax over the lock.

Jantar Mantar (Observatory)
0900-1630, foreigners Rs 200, Indians Rs 40.

Literally 'Instruments for measuring the harmony of the heavens', the Jantar Mantar was built between 1728 and 1734. Jai Singh wanted things on a grand scale and chose stone with a marble facing on the important planes. Each instrument serves a particular function and each gives an accurate reading. Hindus believe that their fated souls move to the rhythms of the universe, and the matching of horoscopes is still an essential part in the selection of partners for marriage. Astrologers occupy an important place in daily life and are consulted for all important occasions and decision-making. The observatory is fascinating. It is best to hire a guide who will explain the functions of the instruments. There is little shade so avoid the middle of the day. Moving clockwise the *yantras* (instruments) are as follows:

Small 'Samrat' is a large sundial (the triangular structure) with flanking quadrants marked off in hours and minutes. The arc on your left shows the time from sunrise to midday, the one on the right midday to sundown. Read the time where the shadow is sharpest. The dial gives solar time, so to adjust it to Indian Standard Time (measured from Allahabad) between one minute 15 seconds and 32 minutes must be added according to the time of year and solar position as shown on the board. **'Dhruva'** locates the position of the Pole Star at night and those of the 12 zodiac signs. The

BACKGROUND

Jaipur

Jaipur origins

Jaipur ('City of Victory') was founded in 1727 by Maharaja Jai Singh II, a Kachhawaha Rajput, who ruled from 1699 to 1744. He had inherited a kingdom under threat not only from the last great Mughal Emperor Aurangzeb, but also from the Maratha armies of Gujarat and Maharashtra. Victories over the Marathas and diplomacy with Aurangzeb won back the favour of the ageing Mughal, so that the political stability that Maharaja Jai Singh was instrumental in creating was protected, allowing him to pursue his scientific and cultural interests. Jaipur is very much a product of his intellect and talent. A story relates an encounter between the Emperor Aurangzeb and the 10-year-old Rajput prince. When asked what punishment he deserved for his family's hostility and resistance to the Mughals, the boy answered "Your Majesty, when the groom takes the bride's hand, he confers lifelong protection. Now that the Emperor has taken my hand, what have I to fear?" Impressed by his tact and intelligence, Aurangzeb bestowed the title of Sawai (one and a quarter) on him, signifying that he would be a leader.

City planning

Jai Singh loved mathematics and science, and was a keen student of astronomy, via Sanskrit translations of Ptolemy and Euclid. A brilliant Brahmin scholar from Bengal, Vidyadhar Bhattacharya, helped him to design the city. Work began in 1727 and it took four years to build the main palaces, central square and principal roads. The layout of streets was based on a mathematical grid of nine squares representing the ancient Hindu map of the universe, with the sacred Mount Meru, home of Siva, occupying the central square. In Jaipur the royal palace is at the centre. The three-by-three square grid was modified by relocating the northwest square in the southeast, allowing the hill fort of Nahargarh (Tiger Fort) to overlook and protect the capital. At the southeast and southwest corners of the city were squares with pavilions and ornamental fountains. Water for these was provided by an underground aqueduct with outlets for public use along the streets. The main streets are 33 yds wide (33 is auspicious in Hinduism). The pavements were deliberately wide to promote the free flow of pedestrian traffic and the shops were also a standard size. Built with ancient Hindu rules of town planning in mind, Jaipur was advanced for its time. Yet many of its buildings suggest a decline in architectural power and originality.

Late 19th-century buildings

In addition to its original buildings, Jaipur has a number of examples of late 19th-century buildings which marked an attempt to revive Indian architectural skills. A key figure in this movement was Sir Samuel Swinton Jacob. A school of art was founded in 1866 by a group of English officers employed by Maharaja Sawai Madho Singh II to encourage an interest in Indian tradition and its development. In February 1876 the Prince of Wales visited Jaipur, and work on the Albert Hall, now the Central Museum, was begun to a design of Jacob. It was the first of a number of construction projects in which Indian craftsmen and designers were employed in both building and design. This ensured that the Albert Hall was an extremely striking building in its own right. The opportunities for training provided under Jacob's auspices encouraged a new school of Indian architects and builders. One of the best examples of their work is the Mubarak Mahal (1900), now Palace Museum, designed by Lala Chiman Lal.

graduation and lettering in Hindi follows the traditional unit of measurement based on the human breath, calculated to last six seconds. Thus: four breaths = one *pala* (24 seconds), 60 *palas* = one *gati* (24 minutes), 60 *gatis* = one day (24 hours).
'**Narivalya**' has two dials: south facing for when the sun is in the southern hemisphere (21 September-21 March) and north facing for the rest of the year. At noon the sun falls on the north–south line.

The Observer's Seat was intended for Jai Singh. Small 'Kranti' is used to measure the longitude and latitude of celestial bodies.
'Raj' (King of Instruments) is used once a year to calculate the Hindu calendar, which is based on the Jaipur Standard as it has been for 270 years. A telescope is attached over the central hole. The bar at the back is used for sighting, while the plain disk is used as a blackboard to record observations.

'**Unnathamsa**' is used for finding the altitudes of the celestial bodies. Round-the-clock observations can be made and the sunken steps allow any part of the dial to be read.

'**Disha**' points to the north.

'**Dakshina**', a wall aligned north–south, is used for observing the position and movement of heavenly bodies when passing over the meridian.

Large 'Samrat' is similar to the small one (see above) but 10 times larger and thus accurate to two seconds instead of 20 seconds. The sundial is 27.4 m high. It is used on a particularly holy full moon in July/August, to predict the length and heaviness of the monsoon for the local area.

'**Rashivalayas**' has 12 sundials for the signs of the zodiac and is similar to the Samrat yantras. The five at the back (north to south), are Gemini, Taurus, Cancer, Virgo and Leo. In front of them are Aries and Libra, and then in the front, again (north to south), Aquarius, Pisces, Capricorn, Scorpio and Sagittarius. The instruments enable readings to be made at the instant each zodiacal sign crosses the meridian.

'**Jai Prakash**' acts as a double check on all the other instruments. It measures the rotation of the sun, and the two hemispheres together form a map of the heavens. The small iron plate strung between crosswires shows the sun's longitude and latitude and which zodiacal sign it is passing through.

Small 'Ram' is a smaller version of the Jai Prakash Yantra (see above).

Large 'Ram Yantra' Similarly, this finds the altitude and the azimuth (arc of the celestial circle from Zenith to horizon).

'**Diganta**' also measures the azimuth of any celestial body.

Large 'Kranti' is similar to the smaller Kranti (see above).

★ Nahargarh (Tiger Fort)

1000-1630, foreigners Rs 50, Indians Rs 5, camera Rs 30, video Rs 70. Rickshaw for sunset Rs 5000-6500 return. Snacks and drinks are available at the Durg Café.

The small fort with its immense walls and bastions stands on a sheer rock face. The city at its foot was designed to give access to the fort in case of attack. To get there on foot you have to first walk through some quiet and attractive streets at the base of the hill, then 2 km up a steep, rough winding path to reach the top. Alternatively, it can also be reached by road via Jaigarh Fort. Beautifully floodlit at night, when it is incredibly atmospheric, Tiger Fort dominates the skyline by day. Much of the original fort (1734) is in ruins but the walls and 19th-century additions survive, including rooms furnished for maharajas. This is a 'real fort', quiet and unrushed, and well worth visiting for the breathtaking views, to look inside the buildings and to walk around the battlements. However, it is an active fort used as a training ground for soldiers; women alone may feel quite vulnerable here.

You can combine this visit with Jaigarh Fort (see page 289), 7 km away along the flat-topped hill, which is part of the same defensive network.

Albert Hall Museum and Modern Art Gallery

Ram Niwas Gardens, www.alberthalljaipur.gov.in, museum daily (closed public holidays) 0900-1630, foreigners Rs 150, Indians Rs 20.

Within the Ram Niwas Gardens you can visit the museum, gallery and a zoological garden. Housed in the beautiful Albert Hall is the **Central Museum**, displaying mainly excellent decorative metalware, miniature portraits and other art pieces. It also features Rajasthani village life – including some gruesome torture techniques – displayed through costumes, pottery, woodwork, brassware, etc. The first floor displays are covered in dust and poorly labelled. The **Modern Art Gallery**, Ravindra Rang Manch, has an interesting collection of contemporary Rajasthani art. Finally, outside is the **Zoological Garden** containing lions, tigers, panthers, bears, crocodiles and deer, plus a bird park opposite.

SRC Museum of Indology
24 Gangwal Park, 0800-1600, foreigners Rs 100, Indians Rs 40.

Further south, along J Nehru Marg, is the extraordinarily eclectic, and not a little quirky, SRC Museum of Indology. It houses a collection of folk and tantric art including all manner of manuscripts, textiles, paintings, Hindi written on a grain of rice, Sanskrit on a rabbit hair, fossils, medals, weapons and so on.

Surya Mandir
Galta Pol can be reached by taking a bus or by walking 2 km east from the Hawa Mahal; from there it is about 600 m uphill and then downhill.

From Galta Pol take a walk to the 'Valley of the Monkeys' to get a view of the city from the Surya Mandir (Sun Temple), which is especially impressive at sunset. It is not on the tourist circuit and so you are less likely to get hassled here. There are plenty of monkeys on the way up to the temple and you can buy bags of nuts to feed them. Walk down the steps from the top of the ridge to the five old temples, with impressive wall paintings, dedicated to Rama-Sita and Radha-Krishna. Hundreds of monkeys can be seen playing in the water tank below.

Listings Jaipur *map p276*

Tourist information

Jaipur for Aliens, a free miniature guidebook created by the owner of the Hotel Pearl Palace, has regularly updated information on transport and attractions; available at the hotel (see Where to stay, below). There is now also an excellent website too: www.jaipurforaliens.com.

Government of India Tourism
Tourist Reception Center, MI Rd, T0141-237 5466; also has counters at the Railway Station, T0141-231 5714; and Central Bus Stand, T0141-220 6720.
Guides for 4-8 hrs cost Rs 250-400 (Rs 100 extra for French, German, Japanese or Spanish).

Where to stay

Jaipur has an amazing range of hotels and guesthouses with the opportunity to stay in palaces and live like a maharajah for a night or 2. The city's popularity has meant that foreigners are targeted by hotel and shop touts, many of whom drive rickshaws, so be on your guard. Under renovation at the time of writing was the stunning floating Jal Mahal, www.jalmahal.com.

$$$$ The Farm
Prithvisinghpura, Dhankiya Rd, 30 km outside of Jaipur, off Ajmer Rd, T(0)9828-023030, www. thefarmjaipur.com.
This is a place to escape to. Although named The Farm, this place is urban and quirky. The rooms are large and the furniture is antique and recycled and put together with effortless chic. There is a beautiful large communal lounge and a stunning swimming pool surrounded by gazebos.

$$$$ The Oberoi Rajvilas
8 km from town on Goner Rd, T0141-268 0101, www.oberoi hotels.com.
This award-winning hotel is housed in a low-lying recreated fort-palace within large, exquisitely landscaped gardens with orchards, pools and fountains. There are 71 rooms including 13 'tents' and 3 private villas with their own pools. Room interiors are not especially imaginative, but the safari-style 'tents' in a desert garden area are delightful. There is also an Ayurvedic spa in a restored *haveli*.

$$$$ Rambagh Palace (Taj)
Bhawani Singh Rd, T0141-238 5700, www.tajhotels.com.
90 luxuriously appointed rooms and extraordinary suites arranged around a courtyard in the

former maharaja's palace, still feels like the real thing. Set in 19 ha of beautifully maintained garden, larger groups are invited to participate in elephant polo on the back lawn! Stunning indoor pool and a tented spa, but the real pièce de résistance is the spectacular dining hall, reminiscent of Buckingham Palace. Pleasant, relaxed atmosphere, good food and friendly staff. Extremely pricey but unforgettable.

$$$$ Samode Haveli Gangapole
T0141-263 2407, www.samode.com.
150-year-old beautifully restored *haveli* with a leafy courtyard and gardens. 30 rooms and 2 suites (the spectacular Maharaja and Maharani suites have original mirrored mosaics, faded wall paintings, pillars, lamp-lit alcoves, cushions and carved wooden beds). Evening meals are served in the peaceful, atmospheric courtyard or in the magnificent, somewhat over-the-top dining room. Large pool with bar. Excellent food. Highly recommended.

$$$$-$$$ Diggi Palace
SMS Hospital Rd, T0141-237 3091, www.hoteldiggipalace.com.
43 attractive rooms in a charming 125-year-old building. Not as glitzy as some but wonderfully chic. Lovely open restaurant, great home-grown food, peaceful garden, enthusiastic, helpful owners who host the **Jaipur Literature and Heritage Festival**. Craft and cookery workshops available, as well as trips to their organic farm. Highly recommended.

$$$$-$$$ Narain Niwas
Kanota Bagh, Narain Singh Rd, T0141-256 1291, www.hotelnarainniwas.com.
The well-presented rooms pale in comparison to the suites in this characterful old mansion. There's a great dining room and lounge area, and clean pool in beautiful gardens with roaming peacocks, lots of room to sit around the pool (which is rare). You can also pay to use the pool as a non-resident. The beautiful boutique **Hot Pink** is in the grounds and offers designer names.

$$$ Alsisar Haveli
Sansar Chandra Rd, T0141-236 8290, www.alsisarhaveli.com.
36 intricately painted a/c rooms, modern frescoes, excellent conversion of 1890s house, heaps of character, attractive courtyards, beautiful pool, but average food and below par service can be frustrating, village safaris available.

$$$ Shahpura House
Devi Marg, Bani Park, T0141-220 2293, www.shahpurahouse.com.
The only genuine 'heritage' option in the area, this 1950s maharaja's residence is still run by the family and has with many original features including mirrored *thekri* ceilings, comfortable individually decorated suites, old-fashioned bathrooms, lovely canopied rooftop restaurant (pricey meals), and a pool. Recommended.

$$$-$$ Pratap Bhawan Bed & Breakfast
A-4 Jamnalal Bajaj Marg, C-Scheme, T(0)9829-074354, www.pratapbhawan.com.
Run by delightful couple, this is a lovely homestay with delicious food. Rooms are decorated with wildlife photography. Excellent cookery lessons available. Highly recommended.

$$ Arya Niwas
Sansar Chandra Rd (behind Amber Tower), T0141-407 3400, www.aryaniwas.com.
95 very clean, simple rooms but not always quiet, modernized and smart, good very cheap vegetarian food, pleasant lounge, travel desk, tranquil lawn, friendly, helpful, impressive management, book ahead (arrive by 1800), great value.

$$ General's Retreat
9 Sardar Patel Marg, C-Scheme, T0141-237 7134, www.generalsreterat.com.
Friendly welcome at this comfortable hotel with large rooms, expansive verandas and beautiful gardens. Great for families – a little oasis in the heart of town.

$$ Pearl Palace Heritage
54 Gopal Bari Lane 2, T0141-237 5242, www.pearlpalaceheritage.com.
An amazing new heritage-style property from the charming owner of the extremely popular **Hotel Pearl Palace**. Beautiful stone carvings line the walls, while each room is themed: the desert room has golden stone from Jaisalmer; there is a mirrored Udaipur room; and a Victoriana room. The rooms are large here with big sitting areas, TVs and beautifully tiled bathrooms. Exceptionally good value. There is a swimming pool and beautiful restaurant on the way. Whole-heartedly recommended.

$$ Santha Bagh
Kalyan Path, Narain Singh Rd, T0141-256 6790.
12 simple, comfortable rooms (a/c or air-cooled), very friendly, helpful and charming staff, excellent meals, lawn, quiet location. Recommended.

$$ Umaid Bhawan
D1-2A Bani Park, T0141-231 6184,
www.umaidbhawan.com.
28 beautifully decorated and ornately furnished
rooms, many with balconies, one of the most
charming *haveli*-style guesthouses with a lovely
pool and friendly, knowledgeable owners.
Recommended.

$ Hotel Pearl Palace
Hari Kishan Somani Marg, Hathroi Fort, Ajmer
Rd, T0141-237 3700, www.hotelpearlpalace.com.
A real gem. Rooms are quirky and decorated with
art pieces collected by the charming owner; some
have a/c and Wi-Fi but all are modern, comfortable
and have lots of character. The **Peacock** restaurant
on the roof (see below) has great views and serves
excellent food. Great value. Advance booking
essential. Whole-heartedly recommended.

$ Hotel Pink Sun
Chameliwala market, off Mirza Ismail Rd,
T0141-237 6753.
Clean, simple rooms in busy location, right at
the heart of things. Good rooftop restaurant.

$ Shri Sai Nath Paying Guest House
1233 Mali Colony, outside Chandpol Gate,
T0141-230 4975.
10 clean, quiet rooms, meals on request,
very hospitable, helpful and warm.

Restaurants

$$$ Palladio
Narain Niwas (see Where to stay, opposite),
T0141-256 5556.
Stunning decor in shades of blue with antiques.
On your plate you will find delicious Italian tastes
and a great range of speciality juices.

$$$-$$ Chokhi Dhani
19 km south on Tonk Rd, T(0)93145 12033,
www.chokhidhani.com.
Enjoyable 'village' theme park with camel and
elephant rides, traditional dancing and puppet
shows popular with families from Delhi. If
you are only coming to Jaipur, this gives you
a Disney view of the rest of Rajasthan, but it is
done very well.

$$ Anokhi Café
KK Square Shopping Complex, Prithviraj Rd,
C-Scheme, T0141-400 7244.
Great café offering up international tastes like
Thai green bean salad, quiches and sandwiches.

Try the pomegranate and pineapple juice, great
filter coffee and an array of cakes and biscuits. A
little oasis and right next door to the beautiful
Anokhi shop with handblock prints galore.

$$ Diggi Palace
See Where to stay, opposite.
Many of the ex-pats who call Jaipur home head
to Diggi Palace for food. Some produce comes
from their organic farm near Ramgarh and they
offer up all types of Indian fare. They even have
their own cookbook – *Tastes of Diggi*.

$$ Jaipur Modern
51 Sardar Patel Marg, C-Scheme,
T0141-411 3000.
Beautiful café with modern decor based on
traditional design motifs. Great selection of
salads, sandwiches and delicious carrot cake
among other diet-threatening cakes.

$$ LMB
Johari Bazar, T0141 256 5844.
Rajasthani vegetarian in slightly confused
contemporary interior matched by upbeat
dance tunes. Tasty (if a little overpriced) *thalis*;
(*panchmela saag* particularly good). Popular
sweet shop and egg-free bakery attached.
During **Diwali**, this is a feast for the senses.

$$ Niros
Mirza Ismail Rd, T0141-237 4493.
International. This is a characterful restaurant
serving up good Indian and the obligatory
Chinese and Continental dishes.

$$-$ Peacock
On roof of Hotel Pearl Palace (see Where to stay).
Excellent Indian and Continental dishes, with
vegetarian and non-vegetarian food prepared in
separate kitchens. Superb views by day and night
from this 2-tiered restaurant, eclectic collection
of quirky furniture designed by the owner.
Advisable to book in advance. Very atmospheric –
highly recommended. Beware of imitators! They
have created a restaurant website to combat
this – www.thepeacockrooftoprestaurant.com.

$ Kanji
Opposite Polo Victory Cinema, Station Rd.
Clean and extremely popular sweets-and-snacks
joint, a good place to experiment with exotica
such as *Raj kachori* or *aloo tikki*, both of which
come smothered in yoghurt and mild sweet
chutney. Stand-up counters downstairs, a/c
seating upstairs.

Jaipur Literary Festival

Started in 2006, the Jaipur Literary Festival is an exciting gathering of writers and musicians with readings, workshops and performances.

The creative directors are William Dalrymple and Namita Gokhale and speakers have included Vikram Seth, Pico Iyer, Hanif Kureshi, Simon Shama, Nobel laureate Orhan Pamuk, Booker winner Kiran Desai and founder of *Tehelka* magazine Tarun Tejpal.

At the last event in 2015, the local news estimated that the event, held in the beautiful and relaxed atmosphere of Hotel Diggi Palace, attracted in excess of 50,000 people.

There are music events in the evening including performances by musicians from all over India and the world, such as Susheela Raman and Natacha Atlas. The 2016 the event will run 12-25 January. In 2015, the JLF also hosted events in London and Boulder, Colorado. For more information on this fantastic annual event check out http://jaipurliteraturefestival.org.

$ Lassiwala
Mirza Ismail Rd, opposite Niro's.
The unrivalled best *lassis* in the city, served in rough clay cups and topped off with a crispy portion of milk skin. Of the 3 'original' *lassiwalas* parked next to each other, the genuine one is on the left, next to the alley. Come early; they run out by afternoon.

Entertainment

Raj Mandir Cinema, *off Mirza Ismail Rd.* 'Experience' a Hindi film in shell pink interior. Recommended.
Ravindra Rang Manch, *Ram Niwas Garden.* Hosts cultural programmes and music shows.

Festivals

Jan Jaipur Literary Festival, see box, above.
14 Jan Makar Sankranti The kite-flying festival is spectacular. Everything closes down in the afternoon and kites are flown from every rooftop, street and even from bicycles. The object is to bring down other kites to the deafening cheers of huge crowds.
Feb/Mar Elephant Festival at Chaugan Stadium, stunning procession and elephant polo.
Mar/Apr Gangaur Fair (about a fortnight after **Holi**), when a colourful procession of women starts from the City Palace with the idol of Goddess Gauri. They travel from the Tripolia Gate to Talkatora, and these areas of the city are closed to traffic during the festival.
Jul/Aug Teej The special celebrations in Jaipur have elephants, camels and dancers joining in the processions.

Shopping

Jaipur specializes in printed cotton, handicrafts, razia (fine quilts) carpets and *durries* (thick handloomed rugs); also embroidered leather footwear and blue pottery. You may find better bargains in other cities in Rajasthan.

Antiques and art
Art Palace, *Chomu Haveli.* Specializes in 'ageing' newly crafted items – alternatives to antiques. Also found around Hawa Mahal.
Mohan Yadav, *9 Khandela House, behind Amber Gauer, SC Rd, T0141-378 009.* Visit the workshop to see high-quality miniatures produced by the family.

Bazars
Traditional bazars and small shops in the Old City are well worth a visit; cheaper than Mirza Ismail Rd shops but may not accept credit cards. Most open Mon-Sat 1030-1930.
Bapu Bazar specializes in printed cloth.
Chaupar and **Nehru Bazars** for textiles.
Johari Bazar for jewellery.
Khajanewalon-ka-Rasta, *off Chandpol Bazar.* For marble and stoneware.
Maniharon-ka-Rasta for lac bangles which the city is famous for.
Ramganj Bazar has leather footwear while opposite Hawa Mahal you will find the famous featherweight Jaipuri *rezais* (quilts).
Tripolia Bazar (3 gates), inexpensive jewellery.

Blue pottery
Blue Pottery Art Centre, *Amer Rd, near Jain Mandir, T)141-263 5375.* For unusual pots.
Kripal Kumbha, *B-18, Shiv Marg, Bani Park, T0141-220 0127.* Gives lessons by appointment. Recommended.

Carpets

Channi Carpets and Textiles, *Mount Rd opposite Ramgarh Rd*. Factory shop, watch carpets being hand-knotted, then washed, cut and quality checked with a blow lamp.

Maharaja, *Chandpol (near Samode Haveli)*. Watch carpet weavers and craftsmen, good value carpets and printed cotton.

The Reject Shop, *Bhawani Singh Rd*. For 'Shyam Ahuja' durrie collections.

Clothing and lifestyle

Hot Pink, *Narain Niwas (see Where to stay, page 282), Kanota Bagh, Narain Singh Rd, T0141-510 8932, www.hotpinkindia.com*. Beautiful boutique in the grounds of Narain Niwas Palace in the south of city with pieces from Indian designers including Manish Arora (the master of Kitsch chic), Abraham & Thakore (for true elegance) and Tarun Tahliani (for Bollywood style). Homeware also available. There is also a lovely small branch in Amber Fort.

Handicrafts

Anokhi, *KK Shopping Complex, Prithviraj Rd, C-Scheme, T0141-400 7244*. Beautifully crafted clothes, great designs. Some mens and childrens clothes, attractive block-printed homeware and bags. Recommended.

Rajasthali, *Government Handicrafts, Mirza Ismail Rd, 500 m west of Ajmeri Gate*.

Ratan Textiles, *Papriwal Cottage, Ajmer Rd, T0141-408 0438, www.ratantextiles.com*. Great array of textiles, homeware, clothing and unique souvenirs. Well crafted.

Jewellery

Jaipur is famous for gold, jewellery and gem stones (particularly emeralds, rubies, sapphires and diamonds; the latter require special certification for export). Semi-precious stones set in silver are more affordable (but check for loose settings, catches and cracked stones); sterling silver items are rare in India and the content varies widely. **Johari Bazar** is the scene of many surreptitious gem deals, and has backstreet factories where you may be able to see craftsmen at work. Bargaining is easier on your own so avoid being taken by a 'guide'. For about Rs 40 you can have gems authenticated and valued at the **Gem Testing Laboratory** (off Mirza Ismail Rd, near New Gate, T0141-256 8221), reputable jewellers should not object.

Do not use credit cards to buy these goods and never agree to 'help to export' jewellery. There have been reports of misuse of credit card accounts at **Apache Indian Jewellers** (also operating as **Krishna Gems** or **Ashirwad Gems & Art**, opposite Samodia Complex, Loha Mandi, SC Rd); and **Monopoli Gems** (opposite Sarga Sooli, Kishore Niwas (1st floor) Tripolia Bazar).

Reputable places include **Beg Gems** (Mehdi-ka-Chowk, near Hawa Mahal).

Bhuramal Rajmal Surana, *1st floor, between Nos 264 and 268, Haldiyon-ka-Rasta*. Highly recommended.

Dwarka's, *H2O Bhagat Singh Marg*. Crafts high-quality gemstones in silver, gold and platinum in modern and traditional designs.

Gem Palace, *Mirza Ismail Rd, opposite Natraj and Niros, T0141-237 4175, www.gempalacejaipur.com*. Exceptional range of jewellery in diverse styles, from traditional Indian bridal to chic modern pieces. It's a great place to see the unique styles of Indian jewellery from tribal regions to high society. Recommended.

Pearl Palace Silver Shop, *at Hotel Pearl Palace (see Where to stay, page 282)*. Great-value jewellery and bits and pieces of traditional crafts from Jaipur from a trusted source.

What to do

Some hotels (such as the **Rambagh Palace**, see Where to stay, above) will arrange golf, tennis, squash, or elephant polo.

Body and soul

Kerala Ayurveda Kendra, *T(0)93146-435574, www.keralaayurvedakendra.com*. Great place to reinvigorate after a long day looking at the sites. There are a whole range of massages available and if you are interested in more long-term treatment, a great doctor on-site offering consultations and panchakarma. Phone for free pick-up.

Vipassana Centre, *Dhammathali, Galta, 3 km east of centre, T0141-268 0220, www.thali.dhamma.org*. Meditation courses for new and experienced students.

City tours

RTDC City Sightseeing Half day: 0800-1300, Rs 300; Central Museum, City Palace, Amber Fort and Palace, Gaitore, Laxmi Narayan Temple, Jantar Mantar, Jal Mahal, Hawa Mahal. **Full day**: 0900-1800, Rs 350; including places above, plus Jaigarh Fort, Nahargarh Fort, Birla Planetarium, Birla Temple and Kanak Vrindavan. **Pink City by Night**: 1830-2230, Rs 450. Includes views of Jai Mahal, Amber Fort, etc, plus dinner at Nahargarh Fort. For full details check rtdc.tourism.gov.in or call T0141-220 6720 or book at railway station or RTDC **Gangaur Hotel.**

Virasat Experiences Heritage Walks, *T(0)94140 66260), www.virasatexperiences.com*. This company offers a fantastic range of walks and tours designed to show you the 'real' Jaipur. Walks include 'Bazars, Crafts & Cuisines', where you can watch local artisans at work and try the best samosas in town; and 'Havelis & Temples' which visits hidden temples. You will hear fascinating stories about the buildings and families that populate the labyrinthine lanes of the old town. Cookery lessons available. Highly recommended.

General tours

Aravalli Safari, *opposite Rajputana Palace Hotel, Palace Rd, T(0)98872 41181, aravalli2@ datainfosys.net*. Very professional.

Forts & Palaces Tours Ltd, *S-1, Prabhakar Apartment, Vaishali Nagar, T0141-235 4508, www.palaces-tours.com*. A very friendly, knowledgeable outfit offering camel safaris, sightseeing tours, hotel reservations, etc.

Hot-air ballooning

SkyWaltz, *Sharma Farm House, Sun City Project Rd, Kukas, T992-999 3115, www.skywaltz.com*. Offer ballooning in Jaipur, Udaipur, Pushkar or Pune. Flights in Jaipur are operated in the area surrounding the Amber Fort and around traditional villages on the outskirts of Jaipur. Morning and evening flights possible.

Transport

Air **Sanganer Airport**, 15 km south of town, T0141-272 1333, has good facilities. Taxis (Rs 250-300) and auto-rickshaws (Rs 150) take 30 mins to the centre.

Air India, T0141-272 5197, flies to **Delhi**, **Mumbai**, **Udaipur**, **Ahmedabad**. Jet Airways, T0141-3989 333; flies to **Delhi**, **Mumbai** and **Udaipur**. Air Costa flies to **Chennai**.

Auto-rickshaw Avoid hotel touts and use the pre-paid auto-rickshaw counter to get to your hotel. Persistent auto-rickshaw drivers at railway station may quote Rs 10 to anywhere in town, then overcharge for a city tour. Station to city centre hotel, about Rs 50; sightseeing 3-4 hrs, Rs 300; 6-7 hrs, Rs 500 (Rs 75 an hour). From railway and bus stations, drivers (who expect to take you to shops for commission) offer whole-day hire including Amber for Rs 150; have your list of sights planned and refuse to go to shops.

Local bus Unless you have plenty of time and a very limited budget, the best way to get around the city is by auto-rickshaw. To **Amber**, buses originate from Ajmeri Gate, junction with Mirza Ismail Rd, so get on there if you want a seat.

Long-distance bus Central Bus Stand, Sindhi Camp, Station Rd, is used by state and private buses. Enquiries: *Deluxe*, Platform 3,

T0141-220 7912, *Express*, T0141-511 6044 (24 hrs). Left luggage, Rs 10 per item per day. When arriving, particularly from Agra, you may be told to get off at Narain Singh Chowk, a bus stand some distance south of the centre; to avoid paying an inflated auto-rickshaw fare, insist on staying on until you reach the bus stand. Private buses will drop you on Station Rd but are not allowed inside the terminal. State and private Deluxe buses are very popular so book 2 days in advance.

To **Agra**, 12 buses a day 0600-2400, 6½ hrs with 1 hr stop; **Ajmer** (131 km), regular service 0400-2330, 3 hrs; **Bharatpur** 5 buses a day, but all deluxe and a/c buses to Agra go through Bharatpur but you have to pay Agra fare; **Delhi** (261 km), half hourly, 5½ hrs, almost hourly service with deluxe, Pink Line and Volvo buses running Rs 400/700 for a/c; **Jaisalmer** (654 km), 2145, 13 hrs via Jodhpur. **Jodhpur** (332 km), frequent, 7 hrs around Rs 400; **Udaipur** (374 km), 12 hrs; **Kota** via **Bundi** (7 daily), 4-5 hrs.

Cycle rickshaw These are often pretty rickety. From the station to the central hotels costs Rs 30.

Taxi Unmetered taxis; 4 hrs costs Rs 450 (40 km), 8 hrs costs Rs 750 (city and Amber). Extra hill charge for Amber, Raigarh, Nahargarh. Out of city Rs 5-8 per km; Pink City Cabs, T(0)98282 86040, excellent radio cab service.

Train Jaipur Railway Station, Station Rd, has links with most major cities. Enquiry, T131, T0141-220 4536, reservation T135. Computerized booking office in separate building to front and left of station; separate queue for foreigners. Use pre-paid rickshaw counter. Best train for Delhi is the Shatabdi taking about 4½ hrs. **Abu Rd** (for **Mount Abu**): *Aravali Exp 19708* (goes on to Mumbai), 8 hrs; **Agra Cantt**: *Marudhar Exp 14854/14864*, 7 hrs. **Ajmer**: *Aravali Exp 19708*, 0845, 2½ hrs; **Bikaner**: *Bikaner Exp 14710*, 7 hrs. **Chittaurgarh**: *Jp Udz Exp 12992*, 5 hrs. **Delhi**: *Shatabdi 12016*, 1745, 4 hrs 25 mins, *Dee Double Dcke 12985*, DSR (for early morning option), 4½ hrs. **Jodhpur**: *Ranthambhore Exp 12465*, 5½ hrs; **Mumbai (C)**: *Jaipur BCT Superfast 12956*, 17½ hrs; **Udaipur** *Jp Udz Sf Spl 09721*, 7 hrs.

Around
Jaipur

Amber Fort is one of Jaipur's biggest draws, with an elephant ride to the top a priority on many people's 'to do' list. It's still an impressive building but has been poorly maintained in recent years. In the backstreets of Amber, you will also find the Anokhi Museum of Handprinting in a beautifully converted *haveli*. Bagru offers good opportunities to see handicrafts in production, while Samode is perhaps the last word in elegant living.

Amber (Amer)
majestic fort city in the hills; one of Rajasthan's major draws

Today there is no town to speak of in Amber, just the palace clinging to the side of the rocky hill, overlooked by the small fort above, with a small village at its base. In the high season this is one of India's most popular tourist sites, with a continuous train of colourfully decorated elephants walking up and down the ramp to the palace. One penalty of its popularity is the persistence of the vendors.

The approach
Rs 900 per elephant carrying 2 people, no need to tip, though the driver will probably ask, takes 10 mins. Jeeps Rs 200 each way. It can be quite a long wait in a small garden with little shade and you will be at the mercy of the hawkers. If you do want to buy, wait until you reach the steps when the price will drop dramatically.

From the start of the ramp you can either walk or ride by elephant; the walk is quite easy and mainly on a separate path. Elephants carry up to four people on a padded seat. The ride can be somewhat unnerving when the elephant comes close to the edge of the road, but it is quite safe. You have to buy a 'return ticket' even if you wish to walk down later. The elephants get bad tempered as the day wears on. If you are interested in finding out more about the welfare of Amber's elephants, or indeed any of Jaipur's street animals, contact Help in Suffering ① T0141-276 0803, www.his-india. org.au. Or for an alternative elephant experience, check out Amber's elephant farm (see below).

The palace
11 km north of Jaipur, 0900-1630 (it's worth arriving at 0900), foreigners Rs 200, Indians Rs 25 (tickets in the chowk, below the steps up to Shila Mata). Take the green bus from the Hawa Mahal. Auto-rickshaw Rs 100 (Rs 250 for return, including the wait). Guides are worth hiring, Rs 400 for a half day (group of 4), find one with a government guide licence.

After passing through a series of five defensive gates, you reach the first courtyard of the **Raj Mahal** built by Man Singh I in 1600, entered through the **Suraj Pol** (Sun Gate). Here you can get a short ride around the courtyard on an elephant, but bargain very hard. There are some toilets near the dismounting platform. On the south side of this Jaleb Chowk with the flower beds, is a flight of steps leading up to the **Singh Pol** (Lion Gate) entrance to the upper courtyard of the palace.

Amber, which takes its name from Ambarisha, a king of the once-famous royal city of Ayodhya, was the site of a Hindu temple built by the Mina tribes as early as the 10th century. Two centuries later the Kachhawaha Rajputs made it their capital, which it remained until Sawai Jai Singh II moved to his newly planned city of Jaipur in 1727. Its location made Amber strategically crucial for the Mughal emperors as they moved south, and the Maharajahs of Amber took care to establish close relations with successive Mughal rulers. The building of the fort palace was begun in 1600 by Raja Man Singh, a noted Rajput general in Akbar's army, and Mughal influence was strong in much of the subsequent building.

Do not miss the green marble-pillared **Shila Mata Temple** (to Kali as Goddess of War). It's accessed by a separate staircase to the right. It opens at certain times of the day and then only allows a limited number of visitors at a time (so ask before joining the queue). The temple contains a black marble image of the goddess that Man Singh I brought back from Jessore (now in Bangladesh; the chief priest has always been Bengali). The silver doors with images of Durga and Saraswati were added by his successor.

In the left-hand corner of the courtyard, the **Diwan-i-Am** (Hall of Public Audience) was built by Raja Jai Singh I in 1639. Originally, it was an open pavilion with cream marble pillars supporting an unusual striped canopy-shaped ceiling, with a portico with double red sandstone columns. The room on the east was added by Sawai Ram Singh II. **Ganesh Pol** (circa 1700-1725), south of the chowk, colourfully painted and with mosaic decoration, takes its name from the prominent figure of Ganesh above the door. It separates the private from the public areas.

This leads onto the **Jai Singh I** court with a formal garden. To the east is the two-storeyed cream-coloured marble pavilion **Jai Mandir** (Diwan-i-Khas or Hall of Private Audience), below, and **Jas Mandir** (1635-1640) with a curved Bengali roof, on the terrace above. The former, with its marble columns and painted ceiling, has lovely views across the lake. The latter has colourful mosaics, mirrors and marble *jali* screens which let in cooling breezes. Both have **Shish Mahals** (Mirror Palaces) faced with mirrors, seen to full effect when lit by a match. To the west of the chowk is the **Sukh Niwas**, a pleasure palace with a marble water course to cool the air, and doors inlaid with ivory and sandalwood. The Mughal influence is quite apparent in this chowk.

Above the Ganesh Pol is the **Sohag Mandir**, a rectangular chamber with beautiful latticed windows and octagonal rooms to each side. From the rooftop there are stunning views over the palace across the town of Amber, the long curtain wall surrounding the town and further north, through the 'V' shaped entrance in the hills, to the plains beyond. Beyond this courtyard is the **Palace of Man Singh I**. A high wall separates it from the Jai Singh Palace. In the centre of the chowk which was once open is a *baradari* (12-arched pavilion), combining Mughal and Hindu influences. The surrounding palace, a complex warren of passages and staircases, was turned into *zenana* quarters when the newer palaces were built by Jai Singh. Children find it great fun to explore this part.

Jaigarh Fort
20- to 40-min walk from Amber Fort, free with ticket for Jaipur City Palace.

A stone path (currently being restored) from the Chand Pol in the first courtyard of Amber Palace leads up to the ruins of the Old Palace (1216) at the base of the Jaigarh Fort. Though there is little interest today, nearby are several worthwhile temples. These include the **Jagatsiromani Temple**, dedicated to Krishna, with carvings and paintings; it is associated with Mira Bai.

Anokhi Museum of Hand Printing
Anokhi Farm, 10-min walk from the fort, T0141-398 7100, www.anokhi.com.

Set in a magnificently restored haveli, this fantastic museum is well worth a visit. With a great textile collection, you can even try your hand at handblock printing. It offers an insight into the rich textile and handicrafts heritage of northern India. Recommended.

Elephant Farm
Chandra Mahal Colony, Delhi Rd, www.elefantastic.in.

Amber has India's first elephant farm. You can come here to feed and bathe the elephants in the afternoons and learn stories from the mahouts (elephant trainers). Conservation and respect is high on the list here as the founders come from a long line of mahouts.

Listings Amber

Where to stay

$$ Mosaics Guesthouse
Sirayam Ki Doongri, Amber, T0141-253 0031, www.mosaicsgueshouse.com.

With lovely views of Amber Fort, this place has just 4 rooms packed full of art and curiosities. A welcome change to staying in Jaipur.

North of Jaipur
rugged hills with a spectacular palace, now a luxury hotel

Ramgarh Lake and Jamwa Sanctuary
28 km north of Jaipur, a 45-min drive. Contact the tourist office in Jaipur (see page 281) for details of public buses.

The 15-sq-km lake of Jamwa Ramgarh attracts large flocks of waterfowl in winter, and lies within a game sanctuary with good boating and birdwatching. Built to supply Jaipur with water, it now provides less than 1% of the city's needs and in years of severe drought may dry up completely. The 300-sq-km Jamwa Sanctuary, which once provided the Jaipur royal family with game, still has some panthers, nilgai and small game.

Samode
40 km north of Jaipur, a 1-hr drive. Buses from Chandpol Gate go to Chomu where you can pick up a local bus to Samode.

At the head of the enclosed valley in the dry rugged hills of the northern Aravallis, Samode stands on a former caravan route. The sleepy village, with its local artisans producing printed cloth and glass bangles, nestles within a ring of old walls. The painted *havelis* are still full of character. Samode is well worth the visit from Jaipur, and makes a good stop en route to the painted towns of Shekhawati (see page 386). Both the palace and the *bagh* are wonderful, peaceful places to spend a night.

The **palace** ① *now a heritage hotel, Rs 500 for non-residents includes tea/coffee*, which dominates the village, is fabulously decorated with 300-year-old wall paintings (hunting scenes, floral motifs, etc) which still look almost new. Around the first floor of the Darbar Hall are magnificent alcoves, decorated with mirrors like *shish mahal* and *jali* screens through which the royal ladies would have looked down into the grand jewel-like Darbar Hall.

Towering immediately above the palace is **Samode Fort**, the maharajah's former residence, reached in times of trouble by an underground passage. The old stone zigzag path has been replaced by 300 steps. Though dilapidated, there are excellent views from the ramparts; a caretaker has the keys. The main fort gate is the starting point of some enticing walks into the Aravallis. A paved path leads to a shrine about 3 km away. There are two other powerful forts you can walk to, forming a circular walk ending back in Samode. Allow three hours, wear good shoes and a hat, and carry water.

Samode Bagh, a large 400-year-old Mughal-style formal garden with fountains and pavilions, has been beautifully restored. It is 3 km southeast of Samode, towards the main Jaipur–Agra road. Within the grounds are modest-sized but elaborately decorated tents.

Listings North of Jaipur

Where to stay

Ramgarh Lake and Jamwa Sanctuary

$$$$ Ramgarh Lodge (Taj)
Overlooking the lake, T01426-252217, www.tajhotels.com.
18 elegant a/c rooms (3 enormous suites) in a former royal hunting lodge. There's a museum and library, furnished appropriately with various hunting trophies on display. The restaurant is limited but there are delightful walks, fishing and boating, plus the ruins of old Kachhawaha Fort are nearby. **$$$** in summer.

$ Jheel Tourist Village (RTDC)
Mandawa Choraha, T01426-214 084.
Pleasant surroundings for 10 not especially well-maintained village-style rustic huts.

Samode

$$$$ Samode Bagh
3 km from the palace, T01423-240235, www.samode.com.
44 luxury a/c tents decorated in the Mughal style, each with a beautiful modern bathroom and its own veranda. *Darbar* tent, al fresco meals, pool with slide, tennis, volleyball, badminton, lovely setting in peaceful walled Mughal gardens, plenty of birdwatching, safaris to sand dunes, amazing. Reservations essential.

$$$$ Samode Palace
T01423-240014, www.samode.com.
Reservations essential. Half price 1 May-30 Sep. Contact **Samode Haveli**, T0141-263 2407, to

reserve and arrange taxi from Jaipur. Magical place to indulge your fantasies of being a maharajah or maharani for a night. 42 a/c rooms, tastefully modernized without losing any of the charm. The setting is magnificent, with 2 pools, beautiful gardens traditional buffet and an International boutique-style restaurant. You can take a camel ride around the village. Great atmosphere and romantic setting. Well worth a visit even if not staying. Highly recommended.

$$$$ The Treehouse Resort
35th Km stone on NH-8, 35 km out of Jaipur, T(0)9001-797422, www.treehouseresort.in.
Unique property inspired by naturalist Jim Corbett's treehouses, Sunil Mehta has built what they call 'deluxe nests' in the trees. If you like nature and creature comforts, such as a/c, then these are the treehouses for you. It has great eco credentials and a back-to-nature vibe. There is a good restaurant and stunning **Peacock Bar** reconstructed from a 400-year-old heritage building. Recommended.

$ Prem Devi Artist's Homestay
CB Mugal Art Galary, Shilp Colony, Samode T(0)9828-643924, sureshmdw1983@yahoo.com.
Simple, friendly homestay run by a lovely family of artists – the ever cheerful Prem Devi, her husband and 2 grown-up children. 5 sparse but very clean rooms with attached bathrooms. The exterior and lobby of the house are beautifully decorated with traditional art and miniature paintings. 3 home-cooked vegetarian meals per day available for an extra Rs 250 (no restaurants in Samode); free art classes.

Udaipur

Enchanting Udaipur, set in southern Rajasthan, must be one of the most romantic cities in India, with marble palaces, placid blue lakes, attractive gardens and green hills that are a world away from the surrounding desert. High above the lake towers the massive palace of the Maharanas. From its rooftop gardens and balconies, you can look over Lake Pichola, the Lake Palace "adrift like a snowflake" in its centre.

The monsoons that deserted the city earlier in the decade have returned – though water shortage remains a threat – to replenish the lakes and ghats, where women thrash wet heaps of washing with wooden clubs, helped by splashing children.

The houses and temples of the old city stretch out in a pale honeycomb, making Udaipur an oasis of colour in a stark and arid region. Sunset only intensifies the city's beauty, turning the city palace's pale walls to gold, setting the lake to shimmer in silvery swathes against it, while mynah birds break out into a noisy twilight chorus. Ochre skies line the rim of the hills while roof terraces light up and the lake's islands appear to float on waters turning purple in the fading light.

Sights

'Venice of the East'; Rajput-era palaces in a romantic setting

Old City

Udaipur is a traditionally planned fortified city. Its bastioned rampart walls are pierced by massive gates, each studded with iron spikes as protection against enemy war elephants. The five remaining gates are: Hathi Pol (Elephant Gate – north), Chand Pol (Moon Gate – west), Kishan Pol (south), the main entrance Suraj Pol (Sun Gate – east) and Delhi Gate (northeast). On the west side, the city is bounded by the beautiful Pichola Lake and to the east and north, by moats. To the south is the fortified hill of Eklingigarh. The main street leads from the Hathi Pol to the massive City Palace on the lakeside.

The walled city is a maze of narrow winding lanes flanked by tall whitewashed houses with doorways decorated with Mewar folk art, windows with stained glass or *jali* screens, majestic *havelis* with spacious inner courtyards and shops. Many of the houses here were given by the Maharana to retainers – barbers, priests, traders and artisans – while many rural landholders (titled jagirdars) had a *haveli* conveniently located near the palace.

The **Jagdish Mandir** ① *150 m north of the palace, 0500-1400, 1600-2200*, was built by Maharana Jagat Singh in 1651. The temple is a fine example of the Nagari style, and contrasts with the serenity of Udaipur's predominantly whitewashed buildings, surrounded as it often is by chanting Sadhus, gambolling monkeys and the smell of incense. A shrine with a brass Garuda stands outside and stone elephants flank the entrance steps; within is a black stone image of Vishnu as Jagannath, the Lord of the Universe.

A quiet, slightly eccentric museum, including what they claim is the world's largest turban, now lies in the lovely 18th-century **Bagore ki Haveli** ① *1000-1900, Rs 25, camera Rs 10.* The *haveli* has 130 rooms and was built as a miniature of the City Palace. There are cool shady courtyards containing some peacock mosaics and fretwork, and carved pillars made from granite, marble and the local blueish-grey stone. A slightly forlorn but funny puppet show plays several times a day on the ground floor.

City Palace
0930-1730, last entry 1630. From Ganesh Deori Gate: Rs 250 (more from near Lake Palace Ghat). Camera Rs 100, video Rs 300. From 'Maharajah's gallery', you can get a pass for Fateh Prakash Palace, Shiv Niwas and Shambu Niwas, Rs 75. Guided tour, 1 hr, Rs 100 each. Guides hang around the entrance; standards vary wildly and they can cause a scene if you have already hired a guide. Ask at the ticket office. Rs 30 gets you access to the complex and a nice walk down to the jetty.

This impressive complex of several palaces is a blend of Rajput and Mughal influences. Half of it, with a great plaster façade, is still occupied by the royal family. Between the **Bari Pol** (Great Gate, 1608, men traditionally had to cover their heads with a turban from this point on) to the north, and the **Tripolia Gate** (1713), are eight *toranas* (arches), under which the rulers were weighed against gold and silver on their birthdays, which was then distributed to the poor. One of the two domes on top of the Tripolia originally housed a water clock; a glass sphere with a small hole at the base was filled with water and would take exactly one hour to empty, at which point a gong would be struck and the process repeated. The gate has three arches to allow the royal family their private entrance, through the middle, and then a public entry and exit gate to either side. Note the elephant to the far left (eastern) end of the gate structure; they were seen as bringers of good fortune and appear all over the palace complex. The Tripolia leads in to the **Manak Chowk**, originally a large courtyard which was converted in to a garden only in 1992. The row of lumps in the surface to the left are original, and demarcate elephant parking bays! Claiming descent from Rama, and therefore the sun, the Mewars always insured that there was an image of the sun available for worship even on a cloudy day, thus the beautiful example set in to the exterior wall of the palace. The large step in front of the main entrance was for mounting horses, while those to the left were for elephants. The family crest above the door depicts a Rajput warrior and one of the Bhil tribesmen from the local area whose renowned archery skills were much used in

Finding your feet

The airport, about 30-45 minutes by taxi or city bus, is well connected to the rest of the country. The main bus stand is east of Udai Pol, 2-3 km from most hotels, while Udaipur City Railway Station is another 1 km south. Both have auto-rickshaw stands outside as well as pushy hotel touts.

Tip...
A boat trip on the lake is a great way to see the city.

Getting around

It is unlikely you would need to use a bus, explore on foot or jump into shared *tempos*, auto-rickshaws and taxis for sights like the Monsoon Palace or Shillipgram. The brave at heart can hire a scooter or bike. See Transport, page 302.

Best lake views
Boat trip to Jag Mandir Island, page 297
Candlelight at Ambrai, page 300
Sunset at Monsoon Palace, page 303

Orientation

The touristy area around the Jagdish Temple and the City Palace are the main focus of interest and where a lot of the hotels are clustered. It is easy to explore this area on foot.

Best day trips
Delicate frescoes at Juna Mahal, Dungarpur, page 304
Siva Temples at Eklingji, page 305
Fort life at Deogarh, page 306

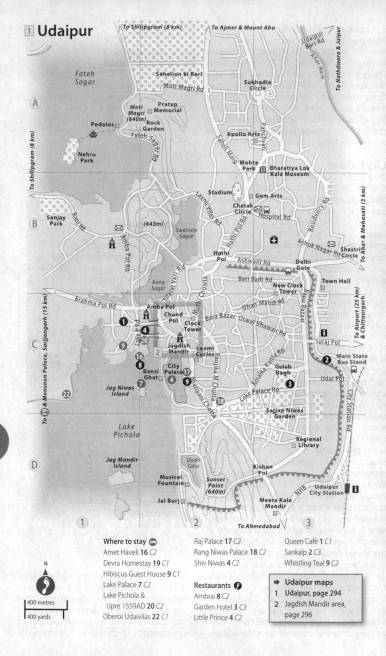

To Shilpigram (8 km)

To Ajmer & Mount Abu

Udaipur Bari Rd

To Nathdwara & Jaipur

Ahar Nadi

Fateh
Sagar

Sahelion ki Bari

Moti Magri Rd

Sukhadia
Circle

A

Panchvati

Moti
Magri
(640m)
Rock
Garden

Pratap
Memorial

Pedalos

Nehru
Park

Fateh Sagar Rd

Apollo Arts

Saheli Marg

Mohta
Park

Bharatiya Lok
Kala Museum

Amba Pol Rd

Bari Rd

Sanjay
Park

(643m)

Swaroop
Sagar

Stadium

Gem Arts

Laxmi Vilas Rd

Chetak
Circle

Hospital Rd

Hathi Pol

B

Residency Rd

To Ahar & Mahasati (3 km)

Ashok Nagar Rd

Shastri
Circle

Hathi
Pol

Ashwani Rd

Delhi
Gate

Town Hall

Rang
Sagar

Shivrati Rd

Bari Badi Rd

New Clock
Tower

Moti Chowta

Bapu Bazaar

To Airport (25 km)
& Chittaurgarh

Brahma Pol Rd

Amba Pol
Chand Pol

Dhan Mandi Rd

Bara Bazaar

Oswal Bhawan Rd

Suraj Pol

C

Lake Rd

Clock
Tower

1

4

9

Jagdish
Mandir

Laxmi
Cycles

Rajika M Chotta

Main State
Bus Stand

2

16

2

Bansi
Ghat

8

City
Palace

Gulab
Bagh

Udai Pol

7

4

9

17

3

Jag Niwas
Island

Lake Palace Rd

To Monsoon Palace, Sarjjangarh (15 km)

22

18

Sajjan Niwas
Garden

City Station Rd

Lake
Pichola

Bhattiyani Chotta

D

Regional
Library

Jag Mandir
Island

Dudh
Talai

Kishan
Pol

Musical
Fountain

Sunset
Point
(640m)

NH8

Udaipur
City Station

Jal Burj

Meera Kala
Mandir

1

2

To Ahmedabad

3

N

400 metres
400 yards

Where to stay
Amet Haveli **16** *C2*
Devra Homestay **19** *C1*
Hibiscus Guest House **9** *C1*
Lake Palace **7** *C2*
Lake Pichola &
  Upre 1559AD **20** *C2*
Oberoi Udaivilas **22** *C1*

Raj Palace **17** *C2*
Rang Niwas Palace **18** *C2*
Shiv Niwas **4** *C2*

Restaurants
Ambrai **8** *C2*
Garden Hotel **3** *C3*
Little Prince **4** *C2*

Queen Café **1** *C1*
Sankalp **2** *C3*
Whistling Teal **9** *C2*

➡ **Udaipur maps**
1 Udaipur, page 294
2 Jagdish Mandir area,
  page 296

The legendary Ranas of Mewar who traced their ancestry back to the Sun, first ruled the region from their seventh-century stronghold Chittaurgarh. The title 'Rana', peculiar to the rulers of Mewar, was supposedly first used by Hammir who reoccupied Mewar in 1326. In 1568, Maharana Udai Singh founded a new capital on the shores of Lake Pichola and named it Udaipur (the city of sunrise) having selected the spot in 1559. On the advice of an ascetic who interrupted his rabbit hunt, Udai Singh had a temple built above the lake and then constructed his palace around it.

In contrast to the house of Jaipur, the rulers of Udaipur prided themselves on being independent from other more powerful regional neighbours, particularly the Mughals. In a piece of local princely one-upmanship, Maharana Pratap Singh, heir apparent to the throne of Udaipur, invited Raja Man Singh of Jaipur to a lakeside picnic. Afterwards he had the ground on which his guest had trodden washed with sacred Ganga water and insisted that his generals take purificatory baths. Man Singh reaped appropriate revenge by preventing Pratap Singh from acceding to his throne. Udaipur, for all its individuality, remained one of the poorer princely states in Rajasthan, a consequence of being almost constantly at war. In 1818, Mewar, the Kingdom of the Udaipur Maharanas, came under British political control but still managed to avoid almost all British cultural influence.

the defence of the Mewar household. The motto translates as 'God protects those who stand firm in upholding righteousness'.

As you enter the main door, a set of stairs to the right leads down to an armoury which includes an impressive selection of swords, some of which incorporate pistols into their handles. Most people then enter the main museum to the right, although it is possible to access the government museum from here (see below). The entrance is known as **Ganesh Dori**, meaning 'Ganesh's turn'; the image of the elephant god in the wall as the steps start to turn has been there since 1620. Note the tiles underneath which were imported from Japan in the 1930s and give even the Hindu deities an oriental look to their eyes. The second image is of Laxmi, bringer of good fortune and wealth. The stairs lead in to **Rai Angan**, the 'Royal Court' (1559). The temple to the left is to the sage who first advised that the royal palace be built on this side. Opposite is a display of some of Maharana Pratap Singh's weapons, used in some of his many battles with the Mughals, as well as his legendary horse, Chetak. The Mughals fought on elephants, the Mewars on horses; the elephant trunk fitted to Chetak's nose was to fool the Mughal elephants in to thinking that the Mewar horses were baby elephants, and so not to be attacked. A fuller version of this nosepiece can be seen in one of the paintings on the walls, as indeed can an elephant wielding a sword in its trunk during battle.

The stairs to the left of the temple lead up to **Chandra Mahal**, featuring a large bowl where gold and silver coins were kept for distribution to the needy. Note that the intricately carved walls are made not from marble but a combination of limestone powder, gum Arabic, sugar cane juice and white lentils.

From here steps lead up in to **Bari Mahal** (1699-1711), situated on top the hill chosen as the palace site; the design has incorporated the original trees. The cloisters' cusped arches have wide eaves and are raised above the ground to protect the covered spaces from heavy monsoon rain. This was an intimate 'playground' where the royal family amused themselves and were entertained. The painting opposite the entrance is an aerial view of the palace; the effect from the wall facing it is impressive. The chair on display was meant for Maharana Fateh Singh's use at the Delhi Darbar, an event which he famously refused to attend. The chair was sent on and has still never been used.

The picture on the wall of two elephants fighting shows the area that can be seen through the window to the left; there is a low wall running from the Tripolia Gate to the main palace building. An elephant was placed either side of the wall, and then each had to try to pull the other until their opponent's legs touched the wall, making them the victor. The next room is known as **Dil Kushal Mahal** ('love entertainment room'), a kind of mirrored love nest. This leads on to a series of incredibly intricate paintings depicting the story of life in the palace, painted 1782-1828. The **Shiv Vilas Chini ki Chatar Sali** incorporates a large number of Chinese and Dutch tiles in to its decoration, as well as an early petrol-powered fan. Next is the Moti Mahal, the ladies' portion of the men's palace, featuring a changing room lined with mirrors and two game boards incorporated into the design of the floor.

Pritam Niwas was last lived in by Maharana Gopal Singh, who died in 1955 having been disabled by polio at a young age. His wheel armchair and even his commode are on display here. This leads on to **Surya Chopar**, which features a beautiful gold-leaf image of the sun; note the 3D relief painting below. The attractive **Mor Chowk** court, intended for ceremonial darbars, was added in the mid-17th century, and features beautiful late 19th-century peacock mosaics. The throne room is to its south, the **Surya Chopar**, from which the Rana (who claimed descent from the Sun) paid homage to his divine ancestor. The **Manak Mahal** (Ruby Palace) was filled with figures of porcelain and glass in the mid-19th century. To the north, the **Bari Mahal** or Amar Vilas (1699-1711) was added on top of a low hill. It has a pleasant garden with full grown trees around a square water tank in the central court.

A plain, narrow corridor leads in to the **Queen's Palace**, featuring a series of paintings, lithographs and photographs, and leading out in to **Laxmi Chowk**, featuring two cages meant for trapping tigers and leopards. The entrance to the **Government Museum** ① *Sat-Thu 1000-1600, Rs 3*, is from this courtyard. The rather uncared for display includes second-century BC inscriptions, fifth- to eighth-century sculptures and 9000 miniature paintings of 17th- and 19th-century Mewar schools of art but also a stuffed kangaroo and Siamese twin deer.

2 Jagdish Mandir area

➡ **Udaipur maps**
1 Udaipur, page 294
2 Jagdish Mandir area, page 296

Chand Pol 2
Gangaur Ghat 9
Ganesh Chowk
5
7 4
Shreeji Sari Centre
Jagdish Mandir 1
Mewar International 11
Motorbike Hire
Gangaur Ghat
Bagore ki-Haveli 12 17
8
Lal Ghat
16
Lake Pichola
Lal Ghat 15
Sai Books
Moti Chotta
Bara Bazar
Clock Tower
Moti Chowk
Kailash Marg
Bhatiyani Chotta
To City Palace
To City Palace

N
100 metres
100 yards

Nayee Haveli 4
Nukkad Guest House 9
Poonam Haveli 12
The Tiger 11
Udai Garh 15

Where to stay
Jheel Guest House 7
Kankarwa Haveli 16
Lake Ghat 8
Lal Ghat Haveli 17

Restaurants
Café Edelweiss 1
Papu's Juice Bar 5
Savage Garden 2

On the west side of the Tripolia are the **Karan Vilas** (1620-1628) and **Khush Mahal**, a rather grotesque pleasure palace for European guests, whilst to the south lies the **Shambhu Niwas Palace** the present residence of the Maharana.

Maharana Fateh Singh added to this the opulent **Shiv Niwas** (see page 298) with a beautiful courtyard and public rooms, and the **Fateh Prakash Palace**. Here the Darbar Hall's royal portrait gallery displays swords still oiled and sharp. The Bohemian chandeliers (1880s) are reflected by Venetian mirrors, the larger ones made in India of lead crystal. Both, now exclusive hotels, are worth visiting.

On the first floor is the **Crystal Gallery** ① *0900-2000, Rs 500 for a guided tour with a talk on the history of Mewar, followed by a cup of tea (overpriced with a cold reception according to some; avoid the cream tea as the scones are so hard they will crack your teeth)*. The gallery has an extensive collection of cut-crystal furniture, vases, etc, made in Birmingham (England) in the 1870s, supplemented by velvet, rich 'zardozi' brocade, objects in gold and silver and a precious stone-studded throne.

'The Legacy of honour', outlining the history of the Mewar dynasty, is a good **Son et Lumière** show, the first privately funded one in India. There are two shows daily at 1930 and 2030, Rs 100 for ground seating, Rs 300 on terrace; book at the City Palace ticket office.

Eco-Udaipur

"Save Lakes, Save Water, Save Udaipur", reads a sign painted on the wall on Gangaur Ghat. Increased environmental awareness in the city in the past few years has centred around Udaipur's glorious lakes, both as a water supply and tourist draw. **Udaipur Lake Conservation Society** (Jheel Sanrakshan Samiti, see http://green ingindia.net/content/view/23/43) was formed in 1992 by a group of volunteers in order to protect the city's six large lakes and more than 100 smaller ones.

Waste from residential areas and hotels located on the sloping land around the lake, can easily drain into it, threatening the quality of drinking water and spreading waterborne disease. For the city's population, the lake is a convenient means of rubbish disposal, religious rituals, bathing, ablutions, washing clothing, and even washing vehicles, but the resulting pollution, water shortage and eutrophication endanger not only the lakes' ecosystems but threaten their existence altogether.

As a result of the campaign, the JSS has become a leading NGO on water conservation in India. Working alongside the **Global Water Partnership**, regular rallies, seminars and street demonstrations bring its message to city residents. Government-backed plans include the transferal of water from other nearby lakes and basins.

Lake Pichola

Fringed with hills, gardens, *havelis*, ghats and temples, Lake Pichola is the scenic focus of Udaipur though parts get covered periodically with vegetation, and the water level drops considerably during the summer. Set in it are the Jag Niwas (Lake Palace) and the Jag Mandir palaces.

Jag Mandir, built on an island in the south of the lake, is notable for the Gul Mahal, a domed pavilion started by Karan Singh (1620-1628) and completed by Jagat Singh (1628-1652). It is built of yellow sandstone inlaid with marble around an attractive courtyard. Maharajah Karan Singh gave the young Prince Khurram (later Shah Jahan), refuge here when he was in revolt against his father Jahangir in 1623, cementing a friendly relationship between the Mewar Maharaja and the future Mughal emperor. Refugee European ladies and children were also given sanctuary here by Maharana Sarap Singh during the Mutiny. There is a lovely pavilion with four stone elephants on each side (some of the broken trunks have been replaced with polystyrene!). You get superb views from the balconies. It's possible to take an enjoyable **boat trip** ① *Apr-Sep 0800-1100, 1500-1800, Oct-Mar 1000-1700, on the hour, Rs 400 for 1-hr landing on Jag Mandirm*, from Rameshwar Ghat, south of the City Palace complex. It's especially attractive in the late afternoon light. Rates from the boat stand at Lal Ghat may be slightly cheaper. There is a pricey bar/restaurant on the island but it's worth stopping for the stunning views.

Jag Niwas Island (**Lake Palace**) ① *it is no longer possible to go to the Lake Palace for lunch or dinner unless you are a resident at Lake Palace, Leela or Oberoi*, is entirely covered by the Dilaram and Bari Mahal palaces, which were built by **Maharana Jagat Singh II** in 1746. Once the royal summer residences and now converted into a hotel, they seem to float like a dream ship on the blue waters of the lake.

On the hill immediately to the east of Dudh Talai, a pleasant two-hour walk to the south of the city, is **Sunset Point** which has excellent free views over the city. The path past the café (good for breakfast) leads to the gardens on the wall, which are a pleasant place to relax. Although it looks steep it is only a 30-minute climb from the café.

Fateh Sagar and around

This lake, north of Lake Pichola, was constructed in 1678 during the reign of Maharana Jai Singh and modified by Maharana Fateh Singh. There is a pleasant lakeside drive along the east bank but, overall, it lacks the charm of the Pichola. **Nehru Park** on an island (accessible by ferry) has a restaurant.

Overlooking the Fateh Sagar is the **Moti Magri** (**Pearl Hill**) ① *0900-1800, Rs 20, camera free*. There are several statues of local heroes in the attractive rock gardens including one of Maharana Pratap on his horse Chetak, to which he owed his life. Local guides claim that Chetak jumped an abyss of extraordinary width in the heat of the battle of Haldighati (1576) even after losing one leg. For more information, read *Hero of Haldighati* by Kesri Singh.

Sahelion ki Bari (Garden of the Maids of Honour) ① *0900-1800, Rs 10, plus Rs 2 for 'fountain show'*, a little north from Moti Magri, is an ornamental pleasure garden; a great spot, both attractive and restful. There are many fountains including trick ones along the edge of the path which are operated by the guide clapping his hands! In a pavilion in the first courtyard, opposite the entrance, a children's museum has curious exhibits including a pickled scorpion, a human skeleton and busts of Einstein and Archimedes.

Listings Udaipur *maps p294 and p296*

Tourist information

Be prepared for crowds, dirt and pollution and persistent hotel touts who descend on new arrivals. It is best to reserve a hotel in advance or ask for a particular street or area of town. Travellers risk being befriended by someone claiming to show you the city for free. If you accept, you run the risk of visiting one shop after another with your 'friend'.

Rajasthan Tourism Development Corporation (RTDC)
Tourist Reception Centre, Fateh Memorial, Suraj Pol, T0294-241 1535. Open 1000-1700.
Guides 4-8 hrs, Rs 250-400.

Where to stay

Frenzied building work continues to provide more hotels, while restaurants compete to offer the best views from the highest rooftop. The area around the lake is undeniably the most romantic place to stay, but also the most congested. Many hotels have views of the lake, some are blessed with stunning vistas.

$$$$ Lake Palace (Taj)
Lake Pichola, T0294-252 8800, www.tajhotels.com.
84 rooms, most with lake view, in one of the world's most spectacularly located hotels; quite an experience. Standard rooms are tasteful but unremarkable, suites are outstanding and priced to match. It was the location for the 1980s Bond film *Octopussy*. Be aware that unless you are staying here or at **Fateh Prakash**, **Shiv Niwas** or the **Leela** you cannot come over to Lake Palace to eat.

$$$$ Shiv Niwas (HRH)
City Palace (turn right after entrance), T0294-252 8016, www.hrhindia.com.
19 tasteful rooms, 17 luxurious suites including those stayed in by Queen Elizabeth II and Roger Moore, some with superb lake views, very comfortable, good restaurant, very pleasant outdoor seating for all meals around a lovely marble pool tennis, squash, excellent service, beautiful surroundings, reserve ahead in high season. This place will have you feeling like a Maharani. Recommended. You can also stay at its equally luxurious neighbour **Fateh Prakash**, see the website for details.

$$$$ The Oberoi Udaivilas
Lake Pichola, T0294-243 3300, www.oberoihotels.com.
The elegant but monochrome exterior of this latter-day palace does nothing to prepare you for the opulence within; the stunning entry courtyard sets the scene for staggeringly beautiful interiors. The 87 rooms are the last word in indulgence; some have one of the hotel's 9 swimming pools running alongside their private balcony. The setting on the lake, overlooking both the Lake and City palaces, is superb, as are the food and service. This is probably one of the most perfect hotels in India. Outstanding.

$$$ Amet Haveli
Outside Chandpole, T0294-243 1085, www.amethaveliudaipur.com.
Enviable location on the lakefront. Beautiful rooms – some with unparalleled views across the lake. The highly recommended **Ambrai** restaurant is on site.

$$$ Devra Homestay
Sisarma–Bujra Rd, Kalarohi, T0294-2431049,
www.devraudaipur.com.
Head inland for this lovely guest house near the
small village of Kalarohi. It has beautiful views
of the rolling hills around Udaipur. There are
9 rooms. It's peaceful and quiet, with abundant
birdlife. Activities include yoga, village walks
and birdwatching.

$$$ The Tiger
33 Gangaur Ghat, T0294-242 0430,
www.thetigerudaipur.com.
Stylish rooms and funky decor (lots of animal print
unsurprisingly). Fantastic in-house spa with steam
room, sauna, jacuzzi and traditional massage.
Great sunset view from the rooftop restaurant.

$$$-$$ Kankarwa Haveli
26 Lal Ghat, T0294-241 1457,
www.kankarwahaveli.com.
Wide range of rooms in a renovated 250-year-
old *haveli* on the lakeshore, some rooms have
views and beautiful original artwork. Each
room is unique. 2 new stunning suites have
been built – modern glass-fronted design but
fitting in seamlessly with this classic building –
1 suite has possibly the best view of the lake
in this area. Lovely roof terrace where you
can sample some great home cooking. Lots
of cosy nooks to sit in. You will be welcomed
warmly by Janardan Singh and his family. Very
atmospheric. Highly recommended.

$$$-$$ Udai Garh
21 Lal Ghat, behind Jagdish Temple,
T0294-242 1239, www.udaigarhudaipur.in.
Beautiful rooms with classic furniture, but the
crowning glory here is the rooftop swimming
pool with great views across the lake. Seductive
rooftop restaurant too.

$$ Hibiscus Guest House
*190 Naga Nagri, Chandpol, follow signs
to Leela Palace Hotel, T(0)94147 57985,*
www.hibiscusudaipur.in.
Tucked away on the Chandpol side of the
lake, this lovely guesthouse has a relaxed vibe.
Beautifully decorated rooms, lovely dining room,
pretty garden, and a massive dog!

$$ Lake Pichola
Hanuman Ghat, overlooking the lake,
T0294-243 1197, www.lakepicholahotel.com.
32 rooms, some a/c, fantastic views with lots of
beautiful window seats overlooking the lake,

boat rides, friendly. Home to the rather lovely
Upre restaurant and chic rooftop bar. The
swimming pool is ill thought-out though.

$$ Rang Niwas Palace
Lake Palace Rd, T0294-252 3890,
www.rangniwaspalace.com.
20 beautifully renovated a/c rooms in a 200-year-
old building, some with charming balconies
facing the garden, some with beautiful window
seats. There's a restaurant, pool, pretty gardens,
helpful staff. Plenty of old-world charm. Good
location, but some road noise.

$$-$ Jheel Guest House
*56 Gangaur Ghat (behind temple), T0294-
242 1352, www.jheelguesthouse.com.*
Friendly owner and fantastic views. Don't be
deceived by the unremarkable entrance, one
room in particular practically hangs over the
ghats with a spectacular view towards the **Lake
Palace** hotel. The new extension has 6 pleasant
rooms with bath and hot water; 8 rooms in the
older part, good rooftop restaurant. There is the
Ginger Café downstairs, too. Recommended.

$$-$ Raj Palace
103 Bhatiyani Chotta, T0294-241 0364,
www.hotelrajpalaceudaipur.com.
26 beautiful rooms arranged around a pleasant
courtyard garden, lovely rooftop restaurant,
excellent service with views of the City Palace.

$ Krishna Ranch
Badi Village, 8 km northwest of Udaipur,
T(0)9828-059506, www.krishnaranch.com.
Run by a Dutch-Indian couple, there are a few
cottages here as well as an organic vegetable
garden and lots of opportunities to be close to
nature. The focus of this retreat is horse safaris –
they have 14 Marwari horses and a whole host of
other animals. They also own the **Kumbha Palace
Guest House** in the centre of Udaipur – www.
hotelkumbhapalace.com. Recommended.

$ Lake Ghat Guest House
4/13 Lalghat, 150 m behind Jagdish Mandir,
T0294-252 1636.
13 atmospheric, well-decorated rooms, friendly,
lots of greenery cascading down the inner
staircase, light and airy, great views from the
terraces, good food. Try not to get it muddled
with **Lalghat Guest House** – all the names are
pretty similar in this area.

$ Lal Ghat Haveli
4 Lal Ghat, T0294-241 3666.
8 well-maintained rooms, particularly charming lower down, cheap but with character. Disappointing restaurant.

$ Nayee Haveli
55 Gangaur Marg, T(0)9829-511573, www.nayeehaveli.com.
This is a really sweet little place – very welcoming. 5 clean, basic rooms in a friendly family home with home-cooked food. Great value. Recommended.

$ Nukkad Guest House
56 Ganesh Chowk (signposted from Jagdish Temple), T0294-241 1403, nukkad_raju@ yahoo.com.
10 small, simple rooms, some with bath, in a typical family house, home-cooked meals, rooftop, very friendly and helpful, clean. There is morning yoga and highly recommended afternoon cookery classes.

$ Poonam Haveli
39 Lal Ghat, T0294-241 0303, www.hotelpoonamhaveli.com.
16 modern, attractive, clean rooms all with nice touches of Rajasthani decor, plus there's a large roof terrace. The restaurant serves good food from around the globe. Recommended.

Restaurants

Note it is no longer possible to go for lunch or dinner at the Lake Palace Hotel unless you are a guest at the hotel itself or staying at the Leela or the Oberoi.

$$$ Ambrai
Amet Haveli, Lake Pichola Rd, T0294-243 1085.
Magical garden restaurant with tables under trees by lake shore, superb views of the City Palace, good at sunset. Recommended by everyone you speak to in Udaipur. Book in advance.

$$$ Savage Garden
Up an alley near the east end of Chandpol bridge, well signposted, T0294-242 5440.
Striking blue interior and excellent food including Indian-style pasta dishes, fish dishes, risottos and great mezze. Recommended.

$$$ Upre by 1559AD
Lake Pichola Hotel, Hanuman Ghat, T0294-243 1197, www.1559AD.com.
Run by Arwan Shaktawat, this is a stunning chic rooftop restaurant and lounge with great Udaipur

views – best at night. There's an interesting menu of Indian classics and European treats.

$$ Sankalp
Outside Suraj Pol, City Station Rd, T0294-510 2686.
Upmarket South Indian, modern, great range of chutneys.

$$ Whistling Teal
Jhadol Haveli, 103 Bhattiyana Chohatta, T0294-242 2067.
Delicious traditional Rajasthani food as well as a bit of everything from around the globe in this lovely garden restaurant.

$ Café Edelweiss
73 Gangaur Ghat, opposite The Tiger.
Great coffee. Small patisserie – sometimes you just have to sit on the side of the road – but the coffee is that good. Recommended.

$ Garden Hotel
Opposite Gulab Bagh.
Excellent Gujarati/Rajasthani vegetarian *thalis*, Rs 50, served in the former royal garage of the Maharanas of Mewar, an interesting circular building. The original fuel pumps can still be seen in the forecourt where 19 cars from the ancestral fleet have been displayed. Packed at lunch, less so for dinner, elderly Laurel-and-Hardyesque waiters shout at each other and forget things! Recommended.

$ The Little Prince
Hanuman Ghat, near the footbridge.
At this charming little café you can sit right at water's edge and get big portions of the usual travellers fare from around the globe. Very popular.

$ Papu's Juice Stand
By the footbridge.
Extremely popular hole-in-the-wall juice stand serving up great juice combos and fantastic fruit salads.

$ Queen Café
14 Bajrang Marg.
Fantastic menu of unusual curries (mango, pumpkin) and irresistible chocolate balls. Also offers cooking lessons. Highly recommended.

Entertainment

Bagore-ki-Haveli, *T0294-242 3610 (after 1700). Daily cultural shows 1900-2000. Foreigners Rs 100, Indians Rs 60 (museum Rs 30).* Enjoyable music and dance performances, including traditional dances with women balancing pots of fire on their heads. Recommended. No need to book.

Bharatiya Lok Kala Museum, *T0294-252 5077.* The 20-min puppet demonstrations during the day are good fun. Evening puppet show and folk dancing Sep-Mar 1800-1900, Rs 30, camera Rs 50. Recommended.

Festivals

Mar/Apr Mewar Festival. Colourful festival celebrating coming of spring.

Shopping

The local handicrafts are wooden toys, colourful portable temples (*kavad*), Bandhani tie-dye fabrics, embroidery and Pichchwai paintings. Paintings are of 3 types: miniatures in the classical style of courtly Mewar; *phads* or folk art; and *pichchwais* or religious art (see Nathdwara, page 305). The more expensive ones are 'old' (20-30 years) and are in beautiful dusky colours; the cheaper ones are brighter.

The main shopping centres are: Chetak Circle, Bapu Bazar, Hathipol, Palace Rd, clock tower, Nehru Bazar, Shastri Circle, Delhi Gate, Sindhi Bazar, Bada Bazar.

Indiabeat, *www.indiabeat.com*. Offers a vibrant shopping tour whizzing through the streets and bazars of Udaipur by rickshaw.

Books
BA Photo and Books, *708 Palace Rd*. Very good selection in several languages, also has internet access.
Mewar International, *35 Lalghat*. A wide selection of English books, exchange, films.

Handicrafts and paintings
Ganesh Handicraft Emporium, *City Palace Rd*, T0294-252 3647, *ganeshemporium@yahoo.com*. Through the dull entrance of Ganesh on the main road, you disappear down an alley and come out at a huge old *haveli* spilling with traditional Udaipur and Gujarati embroideries, wooden horses and all manner of textiles. Maybe not the cheapest place, but great selection and ask for a tour of the exceptionally beautiful building.
Honest Art Gallery, *inside Chandpol 18*. Honest Art supports Indian artists who receive 60% for each piece – find unique artworks.
Modern Art Gallery, *outside Chandpol, near the footbridge*. Beautiful collection of artwork by local artists, including Sharmila Rathore, who runs the shop.

Sadhna Women's Collective, *Jagdish Temple Rd*, *www.sadhna.org*. Sadhna started in 1988 with 15 women and has grown to include the work of 600 women today as artisans and co-owners. On offer is a beautiful variety of clothes, *kurtas* and scarves as well as a homeware range with traditional appliqué, tanka and patchwork. The patterns incorporated in the pieces reflect rural life in Rajasthan. Recommended.

What to do

Art, cooking and Hindi classes
Ashoka Arts, *339 'Ashoka Haveli' Gangaur Ghat*. In the courtyard of Gangaur Palace, art classes are available.
Hare Krishna Arts, *City Palace Rd*, T0294-242 0304. Rs 450 per 2-hr art lesson, miniature techniques a speciality. Cooking classes, too.
Queen Café, *14 Bajrang Marg*, T0294-243 0875. Rs 2000 for 5-hr introductory class in the basics of Indian cooking: tiny kitchen but a very good class. Also Hindi lessons. Both are highly recommended.

Body and soul
Bharti Guesthouse, *Lake Pichola Rd*, T0294-243 3469. Therapeutic, Swedish-style massage.
The Tiger, *33 Gangaur Ghat*, T0294-242 0430. Great spa, with real sauna and steam rooms, jacuzzi and a range of traditional massages on offer. Recommended.

Cycling tours
Rajasthan Cycle Tours, *www.rajasthancycling tours.com*. If you would prefer a more mechanical mode of transport than the ubiquitous camel and the local horse safaris of Rajasthan, how about a cycle tour? Head into the Aravali Hills for long and short cycle trips.

Elephant, camel and horse riding
Travel agencies (eg **Namaskar, Parul** in Lalghat) arrange elephant and camel rides, but need sufficient notice. Horse riding through **Krishna Ranch** (see Where to Stay), or **Princess Trails** (T(0)9829-042012, www.princesstrails.com), a German-Indian company that has Marwari horses for everything from half-day treks to 9-day horse safaris. Experience a totally different side of Rajasthan from horseback – see village life and be a part of nature. Highly recommended.

Heritage walks
Virasat Experiences, *www.virasatexperiences. com*. The great team at Virasat offer interesting heritage walks and city tours, but also an outback

walk into the villages around Udaipur meeting the Bhil tribe.

Sightseeing tours

In addition to sightseeing tours, some of the following tour operators offer accommodation bookings and travel tickets.

Parul, *Jagat Niwas Hotel, Lalghat, T0294-242 1697, parul_tour@rediffmail.com.* Air/train, palace hotels, car hire, exchange. Highly recommended.

RTDC Fateh Memorial, *Suraj Pol, ww.rajasthantourism.com.* Half- and full-day sightseeing, as well as excursions including trips to the temples at Eklingji.

Shree Ji Tours, *Hotel Minerva, Ghangor Ghat, T(0)93144 50111, www.shreejitoursudaipur.com.* Reliable and friendly company for all travel and sightseeing options.

Swimming

Some hotel pools are open to non-residents: **Rang Niwas** (Rs 100); **Shiv Niwas** (Rs 300) and Udai Garh. Also at Shilipgram Craft Village, Rs 100.

Transport

Air Maharana Pratap (Dabok) Airport is 25 km east, T0294-265 950. Security check is thorough; no batteries allowed in hand luggage. Transport to town: taxis, Rs 190. **Air India**, Delhi Gate, T0294-241 0999, open 1000-1315, 1400-1700; airport, T0294-265 5453, enquiry T142. Reserve well ahead.

Indian Airlines flights to **Delhi**, via **Jodhpur** and **Jaipur**; **Mumbai**. Jet Airways, T0294-3989 3333: **Delhi** via **Jaipur**, **Mumbai**.

Auto-rickshaw Agree rates: about Rs 40 from bus stand to Jagdish Mandir.

Bicycle Laxmi Bicycles, halfway down Bhatiyani Chotta, charges Rs 30 per day for hire, well maintained and comfortable. Also shops near **Kajri Hotel**, Lalghat and Hanuman Ghat area, which also have scooters (Rs 250 per day).

Long-distance bus Main State Bus Stand, near railway line opposite Udai Pol, T0294-248 4179; reservations 0700-2100. State RTC buses to **Agra**, 15 hrs; **Ahmedabad**, 252 km, 6 hrs; **Ajmer**, 274 km, 7 hrs; **Bikaner**, 500 km, 13 hrs; **Chittaurgarh**, 2½ hrs; **Delhi**, 635 km, 17 hrs; **Jaipur**, 405 km, 9 hrs; **Jaisalmer**, 14 hrs; **Jodhpur**, 8 hrs (uncomfortable, poorly maintained but scenic road); **Mount Abu**, 270 km, 0500-1030, 6 hrs; **Mumbai**, 802 km, very tiring, 16 hrs; **Pushkar**, tourist bus, 7 hrs; **Ujjain**, 7 hrs. Private buses and luxury coaches run mostly at night; ticket offices offices on City Station Rd, from where most buses depart. Try **Shrinath**, T0294-645 0503, www.shrinath.biz, or a reliable firm for booking bus tickets in the city is **Shree Ji Tours**, Hotel Minerva, Ghangor Ghat, T0294-242 7052, www.shreejitoursudaipur.com.

Motorbike Scooters and bikes can be hired from **Heera Tours & Travels** in a small courtyard behind Badi Haveli (Jagdish Temple area), Rs 250-500 per day depending on size of machine.

Taxi RTDC taxis from Fateh Memorial, Suraj Pol. Private taxis from airport, railway station, bus stands and major hotels; negotiate rates. **Taxi Stand**, Chetak Circle, T0294-252 5112. **Tourist Taxi Service**, Lake Palace Rd, T0294-252 4169.

Train Udaipur City Station, 4 km southeast of the centre, T0294-252 7390, T131, reservations T135. **Ahmedabad**: *Ahmedabad Exp 19943*, 10½ hrs. **Chittaurgarh**: 5 local trains daily. **Delhi** (HN): *Mewar Exp 12964*, 12 hrs, via Chittaurgarh, Kota and Bharatpur. **Jaipur**: *Udz Kurj Express 19666*, 7½ hrs, and on to **Agra** (12 hrs) and **Gwalior** (14 hrs) and **Khajuraho**; **Mumbai Bandra**: *Udz Bdts Sf Exp 12966*, 16½ hrs.

Around
Udaipur

The area around Udaipur is dotted with a wide range of attractions, from some of the grandest of Rajasthan's heritage hotels to some of its cosiest castles, from secluded forest lakes, surrounded by wildlife, to one of the largest reservoirs in Asia. It's also home to some ancient temples and perhaps the most evocative of Rajasthan's plentiful palaces, the Juna Mahal near Dungarpur.

Sights
off-the-beaten track sights and some stunning fort paintings

Most sights in this area are a little isolated and not well connected by train. However, the quality of the region's roads has greatly improved recently, making travel either by bus or taxi both quick and convenient.

Monsoon Palace
15 km west. In order to reach the Monsoon Palace, you enter into Sajjangarh: foreigners Rs 160, Indians Rs 20, car Rs 130. Allow about 3 hrs for the round trip. Rickshaws cannot make it up the steep hill to the palace, so expect a good hike up or get a taxi.

There are good views from this deserted palace on a hilltop. The unfinished building on **Sajjangarh**, at an altitude of 335 m, which looks picturesque from the west-facing battlements, was named after Sajjan Singh (1874-1884) and was planned to be high enough to see his ancestral home, Chittaurgarh. Normally, you need a permit from the police in town to enter, though many find a tip to the gateman suffices. It offers panoramic views of Udaipur (though the highest roof is spoilt by radio antennas); the windows of the Lake Palace can be seen reflecting the setting sun. The palace itself is very run down but the views from the hill top are just as good. The views to the other sides of the rolling hills are equally as sublime. A visit in the late afternoon is recommended – sunset is spectacular. Take binoculars.

Jaisamand Lake
Before the building of huge modern dams in India, Jaisamand was the second largest artificial lake in Asia, measuring 15 km by 10 km. Dating from the late 17th century, it is surrounded by the summer palaces of the Ranis of Udaipur. The two highest surrounding hills are topped by the **Hawa Mahal** and **Ruti Rani palaces**, now empty but worth visiting for the architecture and views. A small sanctuary nearby has deer, antelope and panther. Tribals still inhabit some islands on the lake while crocodiles, keelback water snakes and turtles bask on others.

Bambora
The imposing 18th-century hilltop fortress of Bambora has been converted to a heritage hotel by the royal family of Sodawas, at an enormous restoration cost, and has retained its ancient character. The impressive fort is in Mewari style with domes, turrets and arches. To get here from Udaipur, go 12 km east along the airport road and take the right turn towards Jaisamand Lake passing the 11th-century Jagat Temple (38 km) before reaching Bambora.

ON THE ROAD

Tribals

Today tribals constitute 12% of the state population, nearly double the national average. The Bhils and Minas are the largest groups, but Sahariyas, Damariyas, Garasias and Gaduliya Lohars are all important. The tribes share many common traits but differ in their costumes and jewellery; their gods, fairs and festivals also set them apart from one another. The Bhils comprise nearly 40% of Rajasthan's tribal population with their stronghold in Baneshwar.

Bhil (meaning 'bow') describes their original skill at hunting. Physically short, stocky and dark with broad noses and thick lips, the Bhils once lived off roots, leaves and fruits of the forest and the increasingly scarce game. Most now farm land and keep cattle, goats and sheep, or work as day labourers. Thousands congregate near the confluence of the Mahi and Som rivers for the Baneshwar fair in January and February. The Minas are Rajasthan's largest and most widely spread tribal group. Tall, with an athletic build, light brown complexion and sharp features, men wear a loincloth round the waist, a waistcoat and a brightly coloured turban while the women wear an *aghaghra* (a long gathered skirt), an *akurti-kanchali* (a small blouse) and a large scarf. Most Minas are cultivators who measure their wealth in cattle and other livestock. Like other tribal groups they have a tradition of giving grain, clothes, animals and jewellery to the needy.

Sitamata Wildlife Sanctuary

The reserve of dense deciduous forests covers over 400 sq km and has extensive birdlife (woodpeckers, tree pies, blue jays, jungle fowl). It is one of the few sanctuaries between the Himalaya and the Nilgiris where giant brown flying squirrels have been reported. Visitors have seen hordes of langur monkey, nilgai in groups of six or seven, four-horned antelope, jackal and even panther and hyena, but the thick forests make sightings difficult. There are crocodiles in the reservoirs.

Rishabdeo

Rishabdeo, off the highway, has a remarkable 14th-century Jain temple with intricate white marble carving and black marble statuary, though these are not as fine as at Dilwara or Ranakpur. Dedicated to the first Jain Tirthankar, Adinath or Rishabdev, Hindus, Bhils as well as Jains worship there. An attractive bazar street leads to the temple, which is rarely visited by tourists. Special worship is conducted several times daily when Adinath, regarded as the principal focus of worship, is bathed with saffron water or milk. The priests are friendly; a small donation (Rs 10-20) is appreciated.

Dungarpur

Dungarpur (City of Hills) dates from the 13th century. The district is the main home of the Bhil tribal people; see box, above. It is also renowned for its stone masons, who in recent years have been employed to build Hindu temples as far afield as London.

The attractive and friendly village has one of the most richly decorated and best-preserved palaces in Rajasthan, the Juna Mahal. Surrounded on three sides by Lake Gaibsagar and backed by picturesque hills, the more recent **Udai Bilas Palace** (now a heritage hotel, see page 306) was built by Maharawal Udai Singhji in the 19th century and extended in 1943. The huge courtyard surrounds a 'pleasure pool' from the centre of which rises a four-storeyed pavilion with a beautifully carved wooden chamber.

The **Juna Mahal** ① *open to guests staying at Udai Bilas and by ticket (Rs 150) for non-residents, obtainable at the hotel*, above the village, dates from the 13th century when members of the Mewar clan at Chittaur moved south to found a new kingdom after a family split. The seven-storeyed fortress-like structure with turrets, narrow entrances and tiny windows has colourful and vibrant rooms profusely decorated over several centuries with miniature wall paintings (among the best in Rajasthan), and glass and mirror inlay work. There are some fine *jarokha* balconies and sculpted panels illustrating musicians and dancers in the local green-grey parava stone which are strikingly set against the plain white walls of the palace to great effect. The steep narrow staircases lead to a series of seven floors giving access to public halls, supported on decorated columns, and to intimate private chambers.

There is a jewel of a Sheesh Mahal and a cupboard in the Maharawal's bedroom on the top floor covered in miniatures illustrating some 50 scenes from the *Kama Sutra*. Windows and balconies open to the breeze command lovely views over the town below.

Perhaps nowhere else in Rajasthan gives as good an impression of how these palaces must have been hundreds of years ago; it is completely unspoilt and hugely impressive. It is amazing, but not very accessible to people with limited mobility. There is no actual path.

Some interesting temples nearby include the 12th-century Siva temple at **Deo Somnath**, 12 km away, and the splendid complex of temple ruins profusely decorated with stone sculptures.

Khempur

This small, attractive village is conveniently located midway between Udaipur and Chittaurgarh. To find it turn off the highway, 9 km south of Mavli and about 50 km from Udaipur. The main reason for visiting is to eat or stay in the charming heritage hotel (see Where to stay, below).

Eklingji and Nagda

0400-0700, 1000-1300 and 1700-1900. No photography. RTDC (see page 298) runs tours from Udaipur, 1400-1900.

The white marble Eklingji Temple has a two-storey mandapa to Siva, the family deity of the Mewars. It dates from AD 734 but was rebuilt in the 15th century. There is a silver door and screen and a silver Nandi facing the black marble Siva. The evenings draw crowds of worshippers and few tourists. Many smaller temples surround the main one and are also worth seeing. Nearby is the large but simple **Lakulisa Temple** (AD 972), and other ruined semi-submerged temples. The back-street shops sell miniature paintings. It is a peaceful spot attracting many waterbirds. Occasional buses go from Udaipur to Eklingji and Nagda which are set in a deep ravine containing the Eklingji Lake.

At Nagda, are three temples: the ruined 11th-century Jain temple of **Adbhutji** and the **Vaishnavite Sas-Bahu** (Mother-in-law/Daughter-in-law) temples. The complex, though comparatively small, has some very intricate carving on pillars, ceiling and mandapa walls. You can hire bicycles in Eklingji to visit them. There are four 14th-century Jain temples at **Delwara**, about 5 km from Eklingji, which also boast the **Devi Garh**, one of India's most luxurious hotels.

Nathdwara

Shrinathji Temple is one of the richest Hindu temples in India and is a centre of the Krishna worshipping community of Gujarati merchants who are followers of Vallabhacharya (15th century).

Non-Hindus are not allowed inside the temple, which contains a black marble Krishna image, but the outside has interesting paintings. At one time only high caste Hindus (Brahmins, Kshatriyas) were allowed inside, and the *pichhwais* (temple hangings) were placed outside, for those castes and communities who were not allowed into the sanctum sanctorum, to experience the events in the temple courtyard and learn about the life of lord Krishna.

You can watch the 400-year-old tradition of *pichhwai* painting which originated here. The artists had accompanied the Maharana of Mewar, one of the few Rajput princes who still resisted the Mughals, who settled here when seeking refuge from Aurangzeb's attacks. Their carriage carrying the idol of Shrinathji was stuck at Nathdwara in Mewar, 60 km short of the capital Udaipur. Taking this as a sign that this was where God willed to have his home, they developed this into a pilgrim centre for the worship of lord Krishna's manifestation, Shrinathji. Their paintings, *pichhwais*, depict Lord Krishna as Shrinathji in different moods according to the season. The figures of lord Krishna and the *gopis* (milkmaids) are frozen on a backdrop of lush trees and deep skies. The bazar sells *pichhwais* painted on homespun cloth with mineral and organic colour often fixed with starch.

Rajsamand Lake

At **Kankroli** is the Rajsamand Lake. The **Nauchoki Bund**, the embankment which contains it, is over 335 m long and 13 m high, with ornamental pavilions and *toranas*, all of marble and exquisitely carved. Behind the masonry bund is an 11-m-wide earthen embankment, erected in 1660 by Rana Raj Singh who had defeated Aurangzeb on several occasions. He also commissioned the longest inscription in the world, "Raj Prashasthi Maha Kavyam", which tells the story of Mewar on 24 granite slabs in Sanskrit. Kankroli and its beautiful temple are on the southeast side of the lake.

Deogarh

Deogarh (Devgarh) is an excellent place to break the journey between Udaipur and Jaipur or Pushkar. It is a very pleasant, little frequented town with a dusty but interesting bazar (if you are interested in textiles, visit **Vastra Bhandar** ① *T02904-252187*, for reasonably priced and good-quality textiles). Its elevation makes it relatively cool and the countryside and surrounding hills are good for gentle treks. There is an old fort on a hill as well as a magnificent palace on a hillock in the centre with murals illustrating the fine local school of miniature painting. **Raghosagar Lake**, which is very pleasant to walk around, has an island with a romantic ruined temple and centotaphs (poor monsoons leave the lake dry). It attracts numerous migratory birds and is an attractive setting.

Perched at the top of the hill town is the lovingly restored 17th-century **Deogarh Mahal Palace** (see Where to stay, opposite), run by the charismatic family of Rawat Saheb Nahar Singhji. Sadly, the Rawat recently passed, but you can still get insight into his private collection of art (advance notice required). You can also still hear his voice in conversation with William Dalrymple on a fascinating audio tour of the palace. The shop at the hotel has good modern examples to buy. There is plenty to do here including an excellent 45-minute train journey from Deogarh to Phulud which winds down through the Aravalli hills to the plain below through tunnels and bridges.

Listings Around Udaipur

Where to stay

Bambora

$$$$-$$$ Karni Fort
Bambora, T0291-251 2101, www.karnihotels.com.
Heritage hotel with 30 beautifully decorated rooms (circular beds) in a large, imposing fort, with marble bathrooms, modern facilities, impressive interiors and an enthusiastic and friendly manager. There's an exceptional marble pool, folk concerts, great beer bar and delicious food. All are hugely enjoyable. They also have a 10-room colonial manor, **Karni Kot**, with art deco-style rooms. Recommended.

Sitamata Wildlife Sanctuary

$$$-$$ Fort Dhariyawad
At the sanctuary, T(0)9829-820516, www.fortdhariyawad.com.
14 rooms and 4 suites in a converted mid-16th-century fort, and some rooms in a contemporary cottage cluster. Period decor and a medieval flavour. Great location by the sanctuary (flying squirrels, langur monkeys in garden, crocodiles in reservoir), tribal village tours, jeeps to park, horse safaris, treks.

$$ Forest Lodge
At the sanctuary, Dhariyawad, contact District Forest Officer, Chittorgarh, T01472-244915.
Rather expensive considering the lack of amenities, but it has a fantastic location and views, and it's a paradise for birders.

Dungarpur

$$$$-$$$ Udai Bilas Palace
2 km from Dungarpur, T02964-230808, www.udaibilaspalace.com.
22 individually designed a/c rooms (including 16 suites of which 6 are vast 'grand suites') mirror mosaics, some dated with art deco furniture, marble bathrooms. Charming host Harshvardhan Singh has built quite possibly the most beautiful restaurant in India, set around a central water feature. He has also created a very eccentric bar to appeal to every car fanatic which complements his vintage car collection. There is a lovely relaxing pool area too. Highly recommended.

$ Vaibhav
Saghwara Rd, T02964-230244.
Simple rooms, tea stall/restaurant, owner very friendly and helpful.

Khempur

$$$-$$ Ravla Khempur
T02955-237154, www.ravlakhempur.com.
The former home of the village chieftain, this is a charming, small-scale heritage property. The rooms have been sensitively renovated with modern bathrooms, pleasant lawns, horse rides a speciality. With a UK management team, this is a slick operation.

Eklingji and Nagda

$$$$ Devi Garh
Delwara, 5 km from Eklingji, T02953-289211, www.lebua.com/devigarh.
Devi Garh is spectacular and the ultimate in luxury. This is not a typical palace renovation; it is chic and super-stylish with amazing attention to detail. The rooms are themed, so you might find yourself in the Lapis Lazuli room or the Marigold room. The original paintings in the restaurant are exquisite. Recently taken over by the **Lebua** group so there might be changes afoot. Stunning.

Nathdwara

$$-$ Gokul (RTDC)
Near Lalbagh, 2 km from the bus stand, Nathdwara, T02953-230917, www.rtdc.in.
6 rooms and dorm, restaurant.

Deogarh

$$$$-$$$ Deogarh Mahal
T(0)9928-834777, www.deogarhmahal.com.
This labyrinthine fort dates back to 1617 and boasts 50 beautifully restored rooms, including atmospheric suites furnished in traditional style with good views, the best have balconies with private jacuzzis. Fabulous lotus flower-shaped pool, Keralan massage, Mewari meals, home-grown produce, bar, great gift shop, log fires, folk entertainment, boating, birdwatching, jeep safaris, audio tour by William Dalrymple, talks on art history, hospitable and delightful hosts. They can organize romantic dinners in private courtyards around the mahal or out in abandoned forts in the surrounding countryside or gala dinners with camel cart rides and fireworks. Stunning.

$$$ Deogarh Khayyam
4 km from Deogarh, T02904-252 777, www.deogarhmahal.com.
These wonderfully luxurious tents are spread out across a jungle plateau and utterly surrounded by nature. Log fires and starry skies in the evening, and the same amazing food as **Deogarh Mahal**. Camping has never been so exciting.

Festivals

Dungarpur
Feb **Baneshwar Fair** (19-24 Feb 2016, 7-10 2017). The tribal festival at the Baneshwar Temple, 70 km from Dungarpur, is one of Rajasthan's largest tribal fairs when Bhils gather at the temple in large numbers for ritual bathing at the confluence of rivers. There are direct buses to Baneshwar during the fair. The temporary camp during the fair is best avoided.
Vagad Festival in Dungarpur offers an insight into local tribal culture. Both are uncommercialized and authentic. Details from **Udai Bilas Palace**, see Where to stay, opposite.

Transport

Bus For **Nathdwara**, several buses from Udaipur from early morning. Buses also go to **Nagda**, **Eklingji** and **Rajsamand**. Private transport only for Khempur and Deogarh.
From Dungarpur buses travel to/from **Udaipur** (110 km), 2 hrs, **Ahmedabad** (170 km), 4 hrs. You will need to hire a taxi to get to the other destinations.

Kumbhalgarh,
Ranakpur & around

Little-known Kumbhalgarh is one of the finest examples of defensive fortification in Rajasthan. You can wander around the palace, the many temples and along the walls – 36 km in all – to savour the great panoramic views. It is two hours north (63 km) of Udaipur through the attractive Rajasthani countryside. The small fields are well kept and Persian wheels and 'tanks' are dotted across the landscape. In winter, wheat and mustard grow in the fields, and the journey itself is as magical as the fort.

The temples of Ranakpur are incredibly ornate and amazingly unspoilt by tourism, having preserved a dignified air which is enhanced by the thick green forests that surround them. There are a number of interesting villages and palaces in the nearby area; if time allows this is a great region to explore at leisure, soaking in the unrushed, rural way of life.

Kumbhalgarh

a sleepy town of forts and wildlife

Kumbhalgarh Fort
Foreigners Rs 100, Indians Rs 5.

Kumbhalgarh Fort, off the beaten tourist track, was the second most important fort of the Mewar Kingdom after Chittaurgarh. Built mostly by Maharana Kumbha (circa 1485), it is situated on a west-facing ridge of the Aravalli hills, commanding a great strategic position on the border between the Rajput kingdoms of Udaipur (Mewar) and Jodhpur (Marwar). It is accessible enough to make a visit practicable and getting there is half the fun. There are superb views over the lower land to the northwest, standing over 200 m above the pass leading via Ghanerao towards Udaipur.

The approach Passing though charming villages and hilly terrain, the route to the fort is very picturesque. The final dramatic approach is across deep ravines and through thick scrub jungle. Seven gates guarded the approaches while seven ramparts were reinforced by

Essential Kumbhalgarh, Ranakpur and around

Getting around

While most of the places in this section do have bus links, a private car is indispensable and makes the most of the scenic drives on offer. A round trip from Udaipur could also take in Eklingji, Nagda and Nathdwara.

Best special hotels

Under canvas at Dera, Kumbhalgarh, page 310
Boulder climbing at Rawla Narlai, page 311
Modern glass at the Mana Hotel, page 312

Wildlife

The natural jungle in Rajasthan is ideal territory for tigers, leopards, sloth bear, sambhar (large deer) and chital (smaller spotted deer), now normally restricted to game reserves. Nilgai (blue bulls), blackbuck and ravine deer are fairly numerous on the plains and there's a great variety of birds. Bharatpur and other low-lying swampy areas in the southeast are popular winter grounds for migratory birds from Siberia and Northern Europe.

semicircular bastions and towers. The 36-km-long black walls with curious bulbous towers exude a feeling of power as they snake their way up and down impossibly steep terrain. They were built to defy scaling and their width enabled rapid deployment of forces – six horses could walk along them side by side. The walls enclose a large plateau containing the smaller Katargarh Fort with the decaying palace of Fateh Singh, a garrison, 365 temples and shrines, and a village. The occupants (reputedly 30,000) could be self-sufficient in food and water, with enough storage to last a year. The fort's dominant location enabled defenders to see aggressors approaching from a great distance. Kumbhalgarh is believed to have been taken only once and that was because the water in the ponds was poisoned by enemy Mughals during the reign of Rana Pratap.

The gates The first gate **Arait Pol** is some distance from the main fort; the area was once thick jungle harbouring tigers and wild boar. Signals would be flashed by mirror in times of emergency. **Hulla Pol** (Gate of Disturbance) is named after the point reached by invading Mughal armies in 1567. **Hanuman Pol** contains a shrine and temple. **Bhairava Pol**, records the 19th-century chief minister who was exiled. The fifth gate, **Paghra** (Stirrup) **Pol**, is where the cavalry assembled; the star tower nearby has walls 8 m thick. The **Top-Khana** (Cannon Gate) is alleged to have a secret escape tunnel. The last, **Nimbu** (Lemon) **Pol** has the Chamundi temple beside it.

The palace It is a 30-minute walk (fairly steep in parts) from the car park to the roof of the Maharana's darbar hall. Tiers of inner ramparts rise to the summit like a fairytale castle, up to the appropriately named Badal Mahal (19th century) or 'palace in the clouds', with the interior painted in pastel colours. Most of the empty palace is usually unlocked (a *chaukidar* holds the keys). The views over the walls to the jungle-covered hillsides (now a wildlife reserve) and across the deserts of Marwar towards Jodhpur, are stunning. The palace rooms are decorated in a 19th-century style and some have attractive coloured friezes, but are unfurnished. After the maze-like palace at Udaipur, this is very compact. The Maharana's palace has a remarkable blue darbar hall with floral motifs on the ceiling. Polished *chunar* (lime) is used on walls and window sills, but the steel ceiling girders give away its late 19th-century age. A gap separated the *mardana* (men's) palace from the *zenana* (women's) palace. Some of the rooms in the *zenana* have an attractive painted frieze with elephants, crocodiles and camels. A circular Ganesh temple is in the corner of the *zenana* courtyard. A striking feature of the toilets was the ventilation system which allowed fresh air into the room while the toilet was in use.

Kumbhalgarh Wildlife Sanctuary
Foreigners Rs 100, Indians Rs 10, car Rs 65, open sunrise to sunset.

The sanctuary to the west of the fort covering about 600 sq km has a sizeable wildlife population but you have to be extremely lucky to spot any big game in the thick undergrowth. Some visitors have seen bear, panther, wolf and hyena but most have to be contented with seeing nilgai, sambhar deer, wild boar, jackal, jungle cat and birds. Crocodiles and water fowl can be seen at **Thandi Beri Lake**. Jeep and horse safaris can be organized from hotels in the vicinity including **Aodhi**, **Ranakpur**, **Ghanerao** and **Narlai**. The rides can be quite demanding as the tracks are very rough. There is a 4WD jeep track and a trekking trail through the safari area can be arranged through **Shivika Lake Hotel**, www.shivikalakehotel.com, in Ranakpur.

The tribal Bhils and Garasias – the latter found only in this belt – can be seen here, living in their traditional huts. The Forest Department may permit an overnight stay in their Rest House in **Kelwara**, the closest town, 6 km from sanctuary. With steep, narrow streets devoid of cars it is an attractive little place.

Listings Kumbhalgarh

Where to stay

$$$$ Aodhi (HRH)
2 km from the fort gate, T02954-242341, www.hrhhotels.com.
The closest place to the fort, great location set into the rock face. 27 rooms in modern stone 'cottages' decorated in colonial style to good effect with attached modern bathrooms. Beautiful restaurant, pool, relaxing atmosphere, very helpful staff, fabulous views, very quiet, superb horse safaris (US$200 per night), trekking, tribal village tours. Highly recommended.

$$ Dera
Kelwara, T(0)97839 07100, www.derakumbhalgarh.com.
Great array of tents, some of which are semi-permanent so are beautifully furnished and have a/c, others are a fabulous purple inside rather than the standard white. Great views. Recommended.

$$-$ Ratnadeep
Kelwara, in the middle of a bustling village, T02954-242217, hotelratnadeep@yahoo.co.in.

14 basic rooms, some deluxe with cooler and marble floors, Western toilets, small lawn, restaurant, camel, horse and jeep safaris, friendly, well run.

$ Forest Department Guest House
Near the Parsram Temple, about 3 km from Aodhi by road then 3 km by 4WD jeep or on foot.
Basic facilities but fantastic views over the Kumbalgarh sanctuary towards the drylands of Marwar.

Transport

Bus and taxi For the fort: buses (irregular times) from Chetak Circle, Udaipur go to **Kelwara**, Rs 20, 3 hrs (cars take 2 hrs); from there a local bus (Rs 6) can take you a further 4 km up to a car park; the final 2-km climb is on foot; the return is a pleasant downhill walk of 1 hr. Jeep taxis charge Rs 50-100 from Kelwara to the fort (and say there are no buses). Return buses to Udaipur from Kelwara until 1730. Buses to **Saira** leave in the afternoon.

From Udaipur, a taxi for 4 costs about Rs 2600-3500, depending on the car. An 11-hr trip will cover the fort and Ranakpur; very worthwhile.

Ghanerao and Rawla Narlai

palaces, havelis and temples

Ghanerao was founded in 1606 by Gopal Das Rathore of the Mertia clan, and has a number of red sandstone *havelis* as well as several old temples, *baolis* and marble *chhatris*, 5 km beyond the reserve. The village lay at the entrance to one of the few passes through the Aravallis between the territories held by the Rajput princes of Jodhpur and Udaipur. The beautiful 1606 royal castle has marble pavilions, courtyards, paintings, wells, elephant stables and walls marked with cannon balls. The present Thakur Sajjan Singh has opened his castle to guests (see Where to stay, opposite), and organizes two- to three-day treks to Kumbhalgarh Fort, 50 km by road (4WD only), and Ranakpur.

The **Mahavir Jain Temple**, 5 km away, is a beautiful little 10th-century temple. It is a delightful place to experience an unspoiled rural environment.

Rawla Narlai, 25 km from Kumbhalgarh Fort, and an hour's drive from Ranakpur, is a Hindu and Jain religious centre. It has a 17th-century fort with interesting architecture, right in the heart of the village, which is ideal for a stopover.

Where to stay

$$$$ Fort Rawla Narlai
Rawla Narlai, T02934-260 443,
www.rawlanarlai.com.
Overlooked by a huge granite boulder, this
place is rather special. The energy of the
boulder and the temples and caves that are
dotted around it, plus the beautifully renovated
fort create a very serene place to hideaway.
20 rooms (11 a/c) individually decorated with
antiques, new showers, plus 5 luxurious, well-
appointed 'tents', good simple meals under the
stars, helpful, friendly staff, attractive garden
setting, good riding. You can wander up to the
Shiva temple on top of the boulder by scaling

700 steps. Check out the special dinner they
host at a candlelit stepwell – so romantic.
Highly recommended.

$$$ Ghanerao Jungle Lodge
Ghanerao, T02934-284035,
www.ghaneraoroyalcastle.com.
Formerly **Bagha-ka-Bagh** (Tiger's Den). Spartan
hunting lodge among tall grass jungle near
the wildlife sanctuary gate. 8 basic rooms,
but atmospheric location. Great for birdlife
and wildlife. There is an organic farm under
the guidance of Vandana Shiva's Navdanya –
her project involves tribal participation and
conserving local seeds to create an Organic Seed
Bank. Guests can volunteer. Recommended.
Also runs the nostalgic **Ghanerao Royal Castle**.

Ranakpur

important pilgrimage site and an insight into the Jain religion

One of five holy Jain sites and a popular pilgrimage centre, Ranakpur has one of
the best-known Jain temple complexes in the country. Though not comparable
in grandeur to the Dilwara temples in Mount Abu (see page 313), it has very fine
ornamentation and is in a wonderful setting with peacocks, langurs and numerous
birds. The semi-enclosed deer park with spotted deer, nilgai and good birdlife next
to the temple, attracts the occasional panther! You can approach Ranakpur from
Kumbhalgarh through the wildlife reserve in 1½ hours although you will need to
arrange transport from the Sanctuary entrance. A visit is highly recommended.

The **Adinatha** (1439), the most noteworthy of the three main temples here, is dedicated to the
first Tirthankar. Of the 1444 engraved pillars, in Jain tradition, no two are the same and each
is individually carved. The sanctuary is symmetrically planned around the central shrine and is
within a 100-sq-m raised terrace enclosed in a
high wall with 66 subsidiary shrines lining it,
each with a spire; the gateways consist of triple-
storey porches. The sanctuary, with a clustered
centre tower, contains a *chaumukha* (four-fold)
marble image of Adinatha. The whole complex,
including the extraordinary array of engraved
pillars, carved ceilings and arches are intricately
decorated, often with images of Jain saints,
friezes of scenes from their lives and holy sites.
The lace-like interiors of the corbelled domes
are a superb example of western Indian temple
style. The **Parsvanatha** and **Neminath** are two
smaller Jain temples facing this, the former
with a black image of Parsvanatha in the
sanctuary and erotic carvings outside. The star-
shaped **Surya Narayana Temple** (mid-15th
century) is nearby.

Essential Ranakpur

Opening hours

Open daily. Non-Jains are only allowed to visit
the Adinatha 1200-1700.

Entry information

Free. Photos with permission from Kalyanji
Anandji Trust office next to the temple, camera
Rs 50, video Rs 150, photography of the principal
Adinatha image is prohibited. No tips, though
unofficial 'guides' may ask for baksheesh. Shoes
and socks must be removed at the entrance.
Black clothing and shorts are not permitted.

There is a beautiful 3.7-km trek around the wildlife sanctuary, best attempted from November to March; contact the sanctuary office next to the temples for information.

Listings Ranakpur

Where to stay

$$$$-$$$ Mana Hotel
Ranakpur–Sadri Rd, Ranakpur Rd, T011-4808 0000 (Delhi), www.manahotels.in.
Innovative contemporary design in rural Rajasthan – quite unexpected and pulled off successfully. Lovely common areas, large glass and steel villas and a variety of rooms.

$$$ Maharani Bagh (WelcomHeritage)
Ranakpur Rd, T02934-285105,
www.welcomheritagehotels.in.
18 well-furnished modern bungalows with baths in a lovely 19th-century walled orchard of the Jodhpur royal family, full of bougainvillea and mangos, outdoor Rajasthani restaurant (traditional Marwari meals Rs 400), pool, jeep safaris, horse riding. Your wake-up call is care of the peacocks or langur monkeys tap dancing on the roof.

$$$-$$ Ranakpur Hill Resort
Ranakpur Rd, T(0)98291 57303,
www.ranakpurhillresort.com.
16 good-sized, well-appointed rooms, 5 a/c, in a new construction, pleasant dining room, there are some royal tents as well, clean pool.

$ Roopam
Ranakpur Rd, T(0)88758 50531.
12 well-maintained rooms, some a/c, pleasant restaurant, attractive lawns.

Transport

Bus From **Udaipur**, there are 6 buses daily (0530-1600), slow, 3 hrs. Also buses from **Jodhpur** and **Mount Abu**. To get to **Kumbhalgarh**, take Udaipur bus as far as **Saira** (20 km, 45 mins), then catch a bus or minibus to the Kumbhalgarh turn-off (32 km, 1 hr).

Train The nearest railway line is Falna Junction on the Ajmer–Mount Abu line, 39 km away.

Mount Abu
& around

Mount Abu, Rajasthan's only hill resort, stretches along a 20-km plateau. Away from the congestion and traffic of the tourist centres on the plains, Mount Abu is surrounded by well-wooded countryside filled with flowering trees, numerous orchids during the monsoon and a good variety of bird and animal life.

Many rulers from surrounding princely states had summer houses built here and today it draws visitors from Rajasthan and neighbouring Gujarat who come to escape the searing heat of summer (and Gujarat's alcohol prohibition) and also to see the exquisite Dilwara Jain temples. In the hot months between April and June, and around Diwali, it's a good place to see Indian holidaymakers at play: softy ice creams, portrait sketchers and pedaloes on Nakki Lake abound. There are some fabulous heritage hotels in the area, well off the beaten track and worthwhile experiences in themselves.

Mount Abu
popular with local holidaymakers seeking a respite from the heat

Mount Abu was the home of the legendary sage Vasishtha. One day Nandini, his precious wish-fulfilling cow, fell into a great lake. Vasishtha requested the gods in the Himalaya to save her so they sent Arbuda, a cobra, who carried a rock on his head and dropped it into the lake, displacing the water, and so saved Nandini. The place became known as Arbudachala, the 'Hill of Arbuda'. Vasishtha also created the four powerful 'fire-born' Rajput tribes, including the houses of Jaipur and Udaipur at a ritual fire ceremony on the mount. Nakki Talao (Lake), sacred to Hindus, was, in legend, scooped out by the *nakki* (fingernails) of gods attempting to escape the wrath of a demon. Abu was leased by the British government from the Maharao of Sirohi and was used as the headquarters for the Resident of Rajputana until 1947, and as a sanatorium for troops.

Dilwara Jain Temples
Free (no photography), shoes and cameras, mobile phones, leather items and backpacks (Rs 1 per item) are left outside, tip expected; 1200-1800 for non-Jains; some guides are excellent, it's a 1-hr uphill walk from town, or share a jeep, Rs 5 each.

Set in beautiful surroundings of mango trees and wooded hills, 5 km from the town centre, the temples have superb marble carvings. The complex of five principal temples is surrounded by a high wall, dazzling white in the sunlight. There is a rest house for pilgrims on the approach road, which is also lined with stalls selling a collection of tourist kitsch lending a carnival atmosphere to

Essential Mount Abu and around

Finding your feet

The nearest airport is at Udaipur, and the nearest railway station is Abu Road, 27 km away. It is usually quicker to take a bus directly to Mount Abu, instead of going to Abu Road by train and then taking a bus up the hill. Note that there is a toll on entering the town, Rs 10 per head. Frequent rockfalls during the monsoon makes the road from Mount Abu hazardous; avoid night journeys. See Transport, page 317.

Getting around

The compact area by Nakki Lake, with hotels, restaurants and shops, is pedestrianized. Taxis are available at a stand nearby. A form of transport unique to Mount Abu is the baba gari, a small trolley generally used to pull small children up the steepest of Mount Abu's hills.

> **Tip...**
>
> During peak season (April-June) and during major festivals (see page 317), room rates shoot up in price and it's best to book accommodation in advance.

the sanctity of the temples. It would be beautiful and serene here, but noisy guides and visitors break the sanctity of the magnificent temples.

Chaumukha Temple The grey sandstone building is approached through the entrance on your left. Combining 13th- and 15th-century styles, it is generally regarded as inferior to the two main temples. The colonnaded hall (ground floor) contains four-faced images of the Tirthankar Parsvanatha (hence *chaumukha*), and figures of *dikpalas* and *yakshis*.

Adinatha Temple (Vimala Shah Temple) This temple lies directly ahead; the oldest and most famous of the Dilwara group. Immediately outside the entrance to the temple is a small portico known as the Hastishala (elephant hall), built by Prithvipal in 1147-1159 which contains a figure of the patron, Vimala Shah, the chief minister of the Solanki king, on horseback. Vimala Shah commissioned the temple, dedicated to Adinatha, in 1031-1032. The riders on the 10 beautifully carved elephants that surround him were removed during Alauddin Khilji's reign. Dilwara belonged to Saivite Hindus who were unwilling to part with it until Vimala Shah could prove that it had once belonged to a Jain community. In a dream, the goddess Ambika (Ambadevi or Durga) instructed him to dig under a champak tree where he found a huge image of Adinatha and so won the land. To the southwest, behind the hall, is a small shrine to Ambika, once the premier deity. In

common with many Jain temples the plain exterior conceals a wonderful ornately carved interior, remarkably well preserved given its age. It is an early example of the Jain style in West India, set within a rectangular court lined with small shrines and a double colonnade. The white marble of which the entire temple is built was brought not from Makrana, as some suggest, but from the relatively nearby marble quarries of Ambaji in Gujarat, 25 km south of Abu Road. Hardly a surface is left unadorned. Makaras guard the entrance, and below them are conches. The cusped arches and ornate capitals are beautifully designed and superbly made.

Lining the walls of the main hall are 57 shrines. Architecturally, it is suggested that these are related to the cells which surround the walls of Buddhist monasteries, but in the Jain temple are reduced in size to house simple images of a seated Jain saint. Although the carving of the images themselves is simple, the ceiling panels in front of the saints' cells are astonishingly ornate. Going clockwise round the cells, some of the more important ceiling sculptures illustrate: cell 1, lions, dancers and musicians; cells 2-7, people bringing offerings, birds, music-making; cell 8, Jain teacher preaching; cell 9, the major auspicious events in the life of the Tirthankars; and cell 10, Neminath's life, including his marriage, and playing with Krishna and the *gopis*. In the southeast corner of the temple between cells 22 and 23 is a large black idol of Adinath, reputedly installed by Vimal Shah in 1031.

Cell 32 shows Krishna subduing Kaliya Nag, half human and half snake, and other Krishna scenes; cell 38, the 16-armed goddess Vidyadevi (goddess of knowledge); cells 46-48, 16-armed goddesses, including the goddess of smallpox, Shitala Mata; and cell 49, Narasimha, the 'man-lion' tearing open the stomach of the demon Hiranya-Kashyapa, surrounded by an opening lotus.

As in Gujarati Hindu temples, the main hall focuses on the sanctum which contains the 2.5-m image of Adinatha, the first Tirthankar. The sanctum with a pyramidal roof has a vestibule with entrances on three sides. To its east is the Mandapa, a form of octagonal nave nearly 8 m in diameter. Its 6-m-wide dome is supported by eight slender columns; the exquisite lotus ceiling carved from a single block of marble, rises in 11 concentric circles, carved with elaborately repeated figures. Superimposed across the lower rings are 16 brackets carved in the form of the goddesses of knowledge.

Risah Deo Temple Opposite the Vimala Visahi, this temple is unfinished. It encloses a huge brass Tirthankar image weighing 4.3 tonnes and made of *panchadhatu* (five metals) – gold, silver, copper, brass and zinc. The temple was commenced in the late 13th century by Brahma Shah, the Mewari Maharana Pratap's chief minister. Building activity was curtailed by war with Gujarat and never completed.

Luna Vasihi or Neminatha Temple (1231) To the north of the Adinatha Temple, this one was erected by two wealthy merchants Vastupala and Tejapala, and dedicated to the 22nd Tirthankar;

Mount Abu

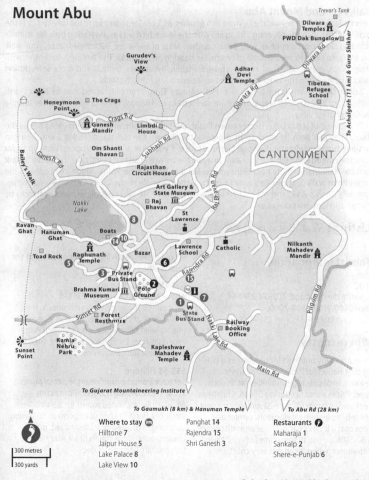

N

300 metres
300 yards

Where to stay 🛏
Hilltone **7**
Jaipur House **5**
Lake Palace **8**
Lake View **10**

Panghat **14**
Rajendra **15**
Shri Ganesh **3**

Restaurants 🍴
Maharaja **1**
Sankalp **2**
Shere-e-Punjab **6**

they also built a similar temple at Girnar. The attractive niches on either side of the sanctum's entrance were for their wives. The craftsmanship in this temple is comparable to the Vimala Vasahi; the decorative carving and *jali* work are excellent. The small domes in front of the shrine containing the bejewelled Neminatha figure, the exquisitely carved lotus on the sabhamandapa ceiling and the sculptures on the colonnades are especially noteworthy.

There is a fifth temple for the Digambar ('Sky-Clad') Jains which is far more austere.

Spiritual University, Art Gallery and State Museum and Spiritual Museum

The headquarters of the Spiritual University movement of the Brahma Kumaris is **Om Shanti Bhavan** ① *T02974-238268*, with its ostentatious entrance on Subhash Road. You may notice many residents dressed in white taking a walk around the lake in the evening. It is possible to stay in simple but comfortable rooms with attached baths and attend discourses, meditation sessions, yoga lessons, and so on. The charitable trust runs several worthy institutions including a really good hospital.

Walks around Mount Abu

Trevor's Tank ① *50 m beyond the Dilwara Jain temples, Rs 5, car/jeep taken up to the lake Rs 125*, is the small wildlife sanctuary covering 289 sq km with the lake which acts as a watering hole for animals including sloth bear, sambhar, wild boar, panther. Most of these are nocturnal but on your walk you are quite likely to see a couple of crocodiles basking on the rocks. The birdlife is extensive with eagles, kites, grey jungle fowl, red spurfowl, francolin, flycatchers, bulbuls and more seen during walks on the trails in the sanctuary. There are superb views from the trails.

Adhar Devi, 3 km from town, is a 15th-century Durga temple carved out of a rock and approached by 220 steep steps. There are steep treks to Anandra point or to a Mahadev temple nearby for great views.

To the west of Nakki Lake, **Honeymoon Point** and **Sunset Point** afford superb views across the plains. They can both be reached by a pleasant walk from the bus stand (about 2 km). You can continue from Honeymoon Point to **Limbdi House**. If you have another 1½ hours, walk up to **Jai Gurudev's meditation eyrie**. If you want to avoid the crowds at Sunset Point, take the **Bailey's Walk** from the Hanuman Temple near Honeymoon Point to **Valley View Point**, which joins up with the Sunset Point walk. You can also walk from the Ganesh temple to the Crags for some great views. Note only do this walk, and others in the area, when there are other people around as attacks by animals and robberies do occur.

Listings Mount Abu *map p315*

Tourist information

RTDC
Opposite the bus stand, T02974-238944.
Open 0800-1100, 1600-2000.
Guides available, 4-8 hrs, Rs 250-400.

Where to stay

There are many hotels in Mount Abu as it is a big destination for Indian tourists. Touts can be a nuisance to budget travellers at the bus stand. Prices shoot up during Diwali, Christmas week and summer (20 Apr-20 Jun) when many $ hotels triple their rates; meals, ponies and jeeps cost a lot more too. Off-season discounts of 30-50% are usual, sometimes up to 70% in mid-winter (when it can get very cold). For a

list of families receiving paying guests visit the tourist office.

$$$ The Jaipur House
Above Nakki Lake, T02974-235176.
9 elegant rooms and 14 new cottages in the Maharaja of Jaipur's former summer palace, unparalleled hilltop location, fantastic views, especially from the terrace restaurant, friendly, professional staff. Recommended.

$$$-$$ Hilltone
Set back from the road near the petrol pump, T02974-238391, www.hotelhilltone.com.
66 tastefully decorated rooms (most a/c), attractive Handi (a style of cooking using baking/steaming in covered pots) restaurant, pool, garden, quiet, most stylish of Mt Abu's hotels, helpful staff. Recommended.

\$\$\$-\$\$ Sunrise Palace
Bharatpur Kothi, T02974-235573.
20 large, sparsely furnished rooms, great
bathrooms, in a grand, slightly unloved
converted mansion, good small restaurant,
open-air BBQ, elevated with excellent views
from the restaurant.

\$\$ Lake Palace
Facing lake, T02974-237154,
www.savshantihotels.com.
13 rooms (some a/c), garden restaurant,
beautifully situated with great lake views from
terrace, rear access to hill road for Dilwara, well
run and maintained. Recommended.

\$ Lake View
On a slope facing the lake, T02974-238659.
Beautiful location, 15 basic rooms, Indian WC,
helpful staff.

\$ Shri Ganesh
West of the polo ground, uphill behind Brahma
Kumari, T02974-237292.
Basic, clean rooms, plenty of solar-heated hot
water, very quiet, cookery classes, wildlife walks
in morning and afternoon, one of the few places
catering specifically for foreigners.

Restaurants

Small roadside stalls sell tasty local vegetarian
food. You can also get good *thalis* (Rs 30-40) at
simple restaurants.

\$\$ Sankalp
Opposite Samrat International.
Excellent South Indian chain restaurant with
amazing chutneys.

\$\$ Shere-e-Punjab
Near the taxi stand.
One of the best in town for vegetarian/non-
vegetarian Indian (some Chinese/Western).

\$ Maharaja
Near the bus stand.
Gujarati. Simple, clean, produces excellent
value *thalis*.

Festivals

Diwali is especially colourful here.

May Summer Festival (20-21 May 2016,
9-10 May 2017) featuring folk music, dancing,
fireworks, etc.
29-31 Dec Winter Festival.

What to do

Mountain sports
For rock climbing and rapelling, contact
the **Mountaineering Institute**, near Gujarat
Bhawan Hostel. Equipment and guide/
instructors are available.

Polo
Occasional matches and tournaments have
begun to take place at the long-abandoned polo
ground in the town centre. Entry is free, with local
investors keen to generate income from 'polo
tourism'. Ask the tourist office for information on
upcoming matches.

Transport

Bus Local buses go to **Dilwara** and **Achalgarh**
at 1100 and 1500, go early if doing a day-trip.
State Bus Stand, Main Rd (opposite tourist
office, T02974-235434); **Private Bus Stand**,
south of Govt Bus Stand on Petrol Pump road.
Many 'direct' long-distance buses involve a
change at Abu Rd bus stand, T02974-222323.
To **Abu Rd**: every 30 mins (45 mins-1 hr), Rs 20.
Ahmedabad: several (7 hrs) via Palanpur (3 hrs,
change here for Bhuj, Gujarat); **Delhi**: overnight.
Jaipur (overnight, 9 hrs), **Jodhpur** morning and
afternoon (7 hrs). **Mumbai**, **Pune**: early morning
(18 hrs). **Udaipur**: 0830, 1500, 2200 (5-6 hrs).
Vadodara: 0930, 1930 (5 hrs). **Gujarat Travels**,
T02974-235564, www.gujarattravels.co.in, runs
private buses.

Taxi and jeep Posted fares for sightseeing
in a jeep; about Rs 800 per day, but open to
negotiation; anywhere in town Rs 40; to Sunset
Point Rs 70. Taxi (for sharing) Abu Rd Rs 300;
shared taxis for Jain Temples from Dilwara
stand near the bazar opposite Chacha Museum
(from Rs 5).

Train Abu Rd, T02974-222222, is the railhead
with frequent buses to Mt Abu. **Western Railway
Out Agency**, Tourist Reception Centre, has a
small reservation quota, Mon-Sat 0900-1600, Sun
0900-1230. Book well in advance; you may have
to wait 2-3 days even in the off-season.
    To **Ahmedabad**: *Aravalli Exp 19708*, 5 hrs
(continues to **Mumbai**, further 8½ hrs).
Jaipur: *Aravalli Exp 19707*, 9 hrs, via **Ajmer**,
6 hrs; **Jodhpur**: *Adi Jat Express 19223*, 4½ hrs.
Delhi: *Ashram Exp 12915*, 12 hrs.

Bera

The large panther population in the surrounding hills of Bera and the Jawai River area draws wildlife photographers. Antelopes and jackals also inhabit the area. Visit the **Jawai Dam**, 150 km from Mount Abu towards Jodhpur, to see historic embankments, numerous birds and basking marsh crocodiles. A bed for the night is provided by **Leopard's Lair** in a colourful Raika village near the lake and jungle (see Where to stay, below).

Jalor

Jalor is a historic citadel. In the early 14th century, during court intrigues, the Afghani Diwan of Marwar, Alauddin Khilji, took over the town and set up his own kingdom. Later, the Mughal emperor Akbar captured it and returned the principality to his allies, the Rathores of Marwar by means of a peaceful message to the Jalori Nawabs, who moved south to Palanpur in Gujarat. The **medieval fort** straddles a hill near the main bazar and encloses Muslim, Hindu and Jain shrines. It is a steep climb up but the views from the fort are rewarding. The old **Topkhana** at the bottom of the fortified hill has a mosque built by Alauddin Khilji using sculptures from a Hindu temple. Of particular interest are the scores of domes in different shapes and sizes, the symmetry of the columns and the delicate arches. **Jalor bazar** is good for handicrafts, silver jewellery and textiles, and is still relatively unaffected by tourist pricing.

Bhenswara

Bhenswara is a small, colourful village on the Jawai River. It has another Rajput country estate whose 'castle' has been converted into an attractive hotel. The jungles and the impressive granite Esrana hills nearby have leopard, nilgai, chinkara, blackbuck, jungle cat, porcupines, jackals and spiny-tailed lizards. It's a good place to stay for a couple of nights.

Bhinmal

Bhinmal has some important archaeological ruins, notably one of the few shrines in the country to Varaha Vishnu. It is also noted for the quality of its leather embroidered *mojdis*. Nearby, at **Vandhara**, is one of the few marble *baolis* (step wells) in India, while the historic **Soondha Mata Temple** is at a picturesque site where the green hills and barren sand dunes meet at a freshwater spring fed by a cascading stream.

Daspan

Daspan is a small village where the restored 19th-century castle built on the ruins of an old fort provides a break between Mount Abu and Jaisalmer.

Listings Around Mount Abu

Where to stay

$$$ Leopard's Lair
Bera, T(0)82393 65771,
www.leopardslairresort.com.
Set in a colourful Raika village are these well-designed stone cottages, 6 a/c rooms and lovely Rajasthani tents. Delicious meals included (fresh fish from the lake), bar, pool, garden, riding, bird-watching, panther-viewing 'safaris' with the owner.

$$$ Ravla Bhenswara
Bhenswara, T02978-282187,
www.hotelravlabhenswara.com.

40 rooms, inspired decor ('Badal Mahal' with cloud patterns, 'Hawa Mahal' with breezy terrace, etc), delicious Marwari meals. Courtyard lawns with a lovely swimming pool. Walk to parakeet-filled orchards and a pool at the nearby Madho Bagh. The hospitable family are very knowledgeable and enterprising. Visits to Rabari herdsmen, Bhil tribal hamlets, night safaris for leopards, camping safaris including the Tilwara cattle fair or even treks to Mount Abu. Recommended.

Festivals

Sep The **Navratri Festival** is held in Bhinmal. Despan also holds special Navratri celebrations.

Chittaurgarh
& around

This is a relatively undiscovered corner of Rajasthan but it's home to some of the state's oldest and most interesting treasures. Chittaurgarh's 'Tower of Victory' has become well known in recent years, but the whole of this ancient, historically important city is worth exploring. Kota and the area around Jhalawar contain some of the oldest and most impressive temples and cave paintings in India, while nowhere takes you back in time as far as Bundi, which has been seemingly untouched for centuries. There are limited rail connections in this area, but a new highway has been constructed pretty much across the whole of southern Rajasthan. Limited transport links mean that a visit to this region does require a little more time and effort than to other areas in Rajasthan, but also that the region has remained uncrowded, unspoilt and hugely hospitable.

Essential Chittaurgarh and around

Finding your feet

All of the region's major towns are served by the railway, but often by branch lines some way off the main routes. Buses starting from all the major cities surrounding the area give quick access to the main towns; from Udaipur to Chittaurgarh takes 2½ hours. See Transport, page 323.

Getting around

Most of the principal sights are fairly close together, making travel by road a convenient option. Frequent buses criss-cross the area, but a private taxi might be worth considering as some of the sights and most interesting places to stay are somewhat off the beaten track.

Best hidden gems

Padmini Haveli in Chittaurgarh Fort, page 322
Bundi's Raniji-ki-baori step well, page 327
Miniature paintings at Bundi Palace, page 327

BACKGROUND

One of the oldest cities in Rajasthan, Chittaurgarh was founded formally in AD 728 by Bappu Rawal, who according to legend was reared by the Bhil tribe. However, two sites near the River Berach have shown stone tools dating from half a million years ago and Buddhist relics from a few centuries BC. From the 12th century it became the centre of Mewar. Excavations in the Mahasati area of the fort have shown four shrines with ashes and charred bones, the earliest dating from about the 11th century AD. This is where the young Udai Singh was saved by his nurse Panna Dai; she sacrificed her own son by substituting him for the baby prince when, as heir to the throne, Udai Singh's life was threatened.

Chittaurgarh

stunning fort for late afternoon rambles

The hugely imposing Chittaurgarh Fort stands on a 152-m-high rocky hill, rising abruptly above the surrounding plain. The walls, 5 km long, enclose the fascinating ruins of an ancient civilization, while the slopes are covered with scrub jungle. The modern town lies at the foot of the hill with access across a limestone bridge of 10 arches over the Gambheri River.

Chittaurgarh Fort
0600-1800, entry Rs 100. Visiting the fort on foot means a circuit of 7 km; allow 4 hrs. The views from the battlements and towers are worth the effort.

The fort dominates the city. Until 1568 the town was situated within the walls. Today the lower town sprawls to the west of the fort. The winding 1.5-km ascent is defended by seven impressive gates: the **Padal Pol** is where Rawat Bagh Singh, the Rajput leader, fell during the second siege; the Bhairon or **Tuta Pol** (broken gate) where Jaimal, one of the heroes of the third siege, was killed by Akbar in 1567 (*chhatris* to Jaimal and Patta); the **Hanuman Pol** and **Ganesh Pol**; the **Jorla** (or Joined) **Pol** whose upper arch is connected to the **Lakshman Pol**; finally the **Ram Pol** (1459) which is the main gate. Inside the walls is a village and ruined palaces, towers and temples, most of which are out in the open and so easy to explore.

Rana Kumbha's Palace, on the right immediately inside the fort, are the ruins of this palace (1433-1468), originally built of dressed stone with a stucco covering. It is approached by two gateways, the large Badi Pol and the three-bay deep Tripolia. Once there were elephant and horse stables, *zenanas* (recognized by the *jali* screen), and a Siva temple. The *jauhar* committed by Padmini and her followers is believed to have taken place beneath the courtyard. The north frontage of the palace contains an attractive combination of canopied balconies. Across from the palace is the Nau Lakha Bhandar (The Treasury). The temple to Rana Kumbha's wife **Mira Bai** who was a renowned poetess is visible from the palace and stands close to the Kumbha Shyama Temple (both circa 1440). The older 11th-century Jain **Sat Bis Deori** with its 27 shrines, is nearby. The **Shringara Chauri Temple** (circa 1456), near the fort entrance, has sculptured panels of musicians, warriors and Jain deities.

Rana Ratan Singh's Palace is to the north by the Ratneshwar Lake. Built in stone around 1530 it too had stucco covering. Originally rectangular in plan and enclosed within a high wall, it was subsequently much altered. The main gate to the south still stands as an example of the style employed.

The early 20th-century **Fateh Prakash Palace** built by Maharana Fateh Singh (died 1930) houses an interesting **museum** ① *Sat-Thu 0800-1630, Rs 10.* To the south is the **Vijay Stambha** (1458-1468), one of the most interesting buildings in the fort, built by Rana Kumbha to celebrate his victory over Mahmud Khilji of Malwa in 1440. Visible for miles around, it stands on a base 14 sq m and

3 m high, and rises 37 m. The nine-storeyed sandstone tower has been restored; the upper section retains some of the original sculpture. For no extra charge you can climb to the top. Nearby is the Mahasati terrace where the *ranas* were cremated when Chittaurgarh was the capital of Mewar. There are also numerous *sati* stones. Just to the south is the **Samdhishvara Temple** to Siva (11th and 15th centuries), which still attracts many worshippers and has some good sculptured friezes. Steps down lead to the deep Gomukh Kund, where the sacred spring water enters through a stone carved as a cow's mouth (hence its name).

Of the two palaces of **Jaimal** and **Patta**, renowned for their actions during the siege of 1567, the latter, based on the *zenana* building of Rana Kumbha's palace, is more interesting. You then pass the Bhimtal before seeing the **Kalika Mata Temple** (originally an eighth-century Surya temple, rebuilt mid-16th century) with exterior carvings and the ruins of Chonda's House with its three-storey domed tower. Chonda did not claim the title when his father, Rana Lakha, died in 1421.

Chittaurgarh

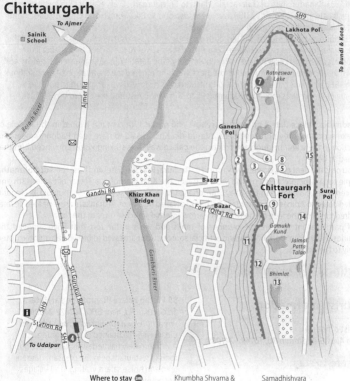

Where to stay 🛏

Meera **4**
Pratap Palace
& Padmini Haveli **7**

Sights ○
Padal Pol **1**
Tuta Pol **2**
Rana Kumbha's Palace,
Nau Lakha Bandar &
Archaeological Office **3**

Khumbha Shyama &
Mira Bai Temples **4**
Sat Bis Deori Temple **5**
Shringara Chauri
Temple **6**
Rana Ratan Singh's
Palace **7**
Fateh Prakash Palace
& Museum **8**
Vijay Stambha &
Mahasati **9**

Samadhishvara
Temple **10**
Palaces of Jaimal &
Patta **11**
Kalika Mata Temple &
Chonda's House **12**
Padmini's Palace **13**
Adbhutanatha Temple **14**
Kirti Stambha **15**

The jauhar – Rajput chivalry

On three occasions during Chittaurgarh's history its inhabitants preferred death to surrender, the women marching en masse into the flames of a funeral pyre in a form of ritual suicide known as *jauhar* before the men threw open the gates and charged towards an overwhelming enemy and annihilation.

The first was in 1303 when Ala-ud-din Khalji, the King of Delhi, laid claim to the beautiful Padmini, wife of the Rana's uncle. When she refused, he laid siege to the fort. The women committed *jauhar*, Padmini entering last, and over 50,000 men were killed. The fort was retaken in 1313.

In 1535 Bahadur Shah of Gujarat laid claim to Chittaurgarh. Every Rajput clan lost its leader in the battle in which over 32,000 lives were lost, and 13,000 women and children died in the sacred *jauhar* which preceded the final charge.

The third and final sack of Chittaurgarh occurred only 32 years later when Akbar stormed the fort. Again, the women and children committed themselves to the flames, and again all the clans lost their chiefs as 8000 defenders burst out of the gates. When Akbar entered the city and saw that it had been transformed into a mass grave, he ordered the destruction of the buildings.

In 1567 after this bloody episode in Chittaurgarh's history, it was abandoned and the capital of Mewar was moved to Udaipur. In 1615 Jahangir restored the city to the Rajputs.

Padmini's Palace (late 13th century, rebuilt end of the 19th century) is sited in the middle of the lake surrounded by pretty gardens. Ala-ud-din Khilji is said to have seen Padmini's beautiful reflection in the water through a mirror on the palace wall. This striking vision convinced him that she had to be his.

You pass the deer park on your way round to the **Suraj Pol** (Sun Gate) and pass the **Adbhutanatha Temple** to Siva before reaching the second tower, the **Kirti Stambha**, a Tower of Fame (13th and 15th centuries). Smaller than the Vijay Stambha (23 m) with only seven storeys, but just as elegant, it is dedicated to Adinath, the first Jain Tirthankar. Naked figures of Tirthankars are repeated several hundred times on the face of the tower. A narrow internal staircase goes to the top.

Of particular interest are the number of tanks and wells in the fort that have survived the centuries. Water, from both natural and artificial sources, was harnessed to provide an uninterrupted supply to the people.

Listings Chittaurgarh *map p321*

Tourist information

Tourist office
Janta Avas Grih, Station Rd, T01472-241089.

Where to stay

$$$ Padmini Haveli
Anna Poorna Temple Rd, Shah Chowk, T01472-241 251, www.thepadminihaveli.com.
This newly restored *haveli* within the fort walls provides a rare opportunity to stay within Chittaurgarh Fort. 9 beautifully furnished rooms built around a central courtyard. Home-cooked meals available.

$$ Pratap Palace (Rajput Special Hotels)
Sri Gurukul Rd, near GPO, T01472-240099, www.hotelpratappalacechittaugarh.com.
Clean, well-maintained rooms, some a/c, 2 with ornately painted walls, good fun, good food in restaurant or in the pleasant garden, jeep and horse safaris visiting local villages. Recommended.

$ Meera
Near railway station, Neemuch Rd, T01472-240466.
Modern, 24 a/c and non-a/c rooms with TV and phone, Gujarati/Punjabi restaurant, bar, laundry, car rental, travel assistance, internet, characterless but efficient.

Festivals

Oct/Nov **Mira Utsav**, 2 days of cultural evening programmes and religious songs in the fort's Mira temple.

Transport

Bicycle hire By the railway station, Rs 5 per hr.

Bus Enquiries, T01472-241177. Daily buses to **Bundi** (4 hrs), **Kota** (5 hrs), **Ajmer** (5 hrs) and frequent buses to **Udaipur**.

Train Enquiries, T01472-240131. A 117-km branch line runs from Chittaurgarh to **Udaipur**. At **Mavli Junction** (72 km) another branch runs down the Aravalli scarp to **Marwar Junction** (150 km). The views along this line are very picturesque, though trains are slow, with hard seats. By taking this route you can visit **Udaipur**, **Ajmer** and **Jodhpur** in a circular journey. Call for times as services have been scaled back in recent years. **Jaipur**: *Udz Jp Exp 1299*, 5 hrs.

Chittaurgarh to Kota

low-key sights and a transport hub

Bassi, Bijaipur and Menal

Bassi, 28 km from Chittaurgarh, is famous for handicrafts and miniature wooden temples painted with scenes from the epics. The palace, a massive 16th-century fort, has been opened as a hotel (see Where to stay, page 324).

Bijaipur is a feudal village with a 16th-century **castle**, set among the Vindhya hills and also now open as a hotel (see Where to stay, page 324). It has a splendid location near the **Bassi-Bijaipur Wildlife Sanctuary**, which is home to panther, antelope and other wildlife. The forests are interspersed with lakes, reservoirs, streams and waterfalls with good birdlife in the winter months. The ruined **Pannagarh Fort** facing a lily covered lake is believed to be one of the oldest in Rajasthan.

Menal, further east, has a cluster of Siva temples believed to date from the time of the Guptas. They are associated with the Chauhans and other Rajput dynasties. Though neglected the temples have some fine carvings and a panel of erotic sculptures somewhat similar to those at Khajuraho in Madhya Pradesh. Behind is a deep, wooded ravine with a seasonal waterfall.

Kota

Kota's attractive riverside location and decent hotels make it a comfortable place to stay, with good transport connections. The town itself is of no special appeal, but can be used as a base from which to visit nearby Bundi if you're short on time. There's a **tourist office** ① *Hotel Chambal, T0744-232 6257*, for information.

At the south end of the town, near the barrage, is the vast, strongly fortified **City Palace** (1625) which you enter by the south gate having driven through the bustling but quite charming old city. There are some striking buildings with delicate ornamental stonework on the balconies and façade, though parts are decaying. The best-preserved murals and carved marble panels are in the chambers upstairs and in the Arjun Mahal. These murals feature motifs characteristic of the Kota School of Art, including portraiture (especially profiles), hunting scenes, festivals and the Krishna Lila.

The 15th-century **Kishore Sagar** tank between the station and the palace occasionally has boats for hire. **Jag Mandir Island Palace**, closed to visitors, is in the centre of the lake. The **Chambal Gardens** by Amar Niwas, south of the fort, is a pleasant place for a view of the river, although the rare fish-eating gharial crocodiles with which the pond was stocked are rarely seen these days. A variety of birds, occasionally including flamingos, can be seen at the river and in nearby ponds.

The **Umed Bhawan** (1904), 1 km north of town, was built for the Maharao Umaid Singh II and designed by Sir Samuel Swinton Jacob in collaboration with Indian designers. The buff-coloured stone exterior with a stucco finish has typical Rajput detail. The interior, however, is Edwardian with a fine drawing-room, banquet hall and garden. It has now been converted into a heritage hotel (see Where to stay, page 324).

ON THE ROAD

Flower power

Crossing the high plateau between Bundi and Chittaurgarh the landscape is suddenly dotted with tiny patches of papery white flowers. These two Rajasthani districts, along with the neighbouring districts of Madhya Pradesh, are India's opium poppy growing belt, accounting for over 90% of production. As early as the 15th century this region produced opium for trade with China. Today the whole process is tightly monitored by the government. Licences to grow are hard won and easily lost. No farmer can grow more than half a *bigha* of opium poppy (less than one-twentieth of a hectare), and each must produce at least 6 kg of opium for sale to the government. Failure to reach this tough target results in the loss of the licence to grow. Laying out the field, actual cultivation and sale are all government controlled. Between late February and early April the farmers harvest the crop by incising fine lines in one quarter of each poppy head in the evening, and collecting the sap first thing in the morning. The harvesting has to be so precise that each evening a different quarter of the seed head will be cut on a different face – north, south, east or west. Finally the government announces the collection point for the harvested opium just two or three days in advance, and farmers have to travel miles to the centre selected for weighing and final payment.

Listings Chittaurgarh to Kota

Where to stay

Bassi, Bijaipur and Menal

$$$-$$ Castle Bijaipur (Rajput Special Hotels)
Bijaipur, T01472-276 351,
www.castlebijaipur.com.
25 simple rooms in traditional style with comfortable furniture and modern bathrooms in castle and a new wing. Lawns and gardens, hill views from breezy terrace, superb pool, delicious Rajasthani meals, also tea on the medieval bastion, jeep/horse safaris with camping and jungle trekking. Popular with yoga groups.

$$ Bassi Fort Palace
Bassi, T01472-225321, www.bassifortpalace.com.
16 unpretentious rooms in a family-run 16th-century fort. The same family runs an abandoned fort on the top of the nearby hill (where dinner can be arranged) and a hunting lodge 6 km away accessible by boat or horse. Safaris to this lodge and local tribal villages can be arranged. Refreshingly informal. Recommended.

Kota

$$$ Umed Bhawan (WelcomHeritage)
Palace Rd, T0744-232 5262,
www.welcomheritagehotels.in.
32 large, comfortable rooms, impressive building and interesting memorabilia and billiards rooms with more stuffed animals than you can shake a stick at, it's not such a great surprise that there are so few tigers left in the wild when you come to some of these Raj-era establishments. Elegant dining room, great beer bar, sunny terraces, behind woods (langurs, deer, parakeets, peacocks), tennis, attentive staff.

$$ Palkiya Haveli
Mokha Para (in walled city), near Suraj Pol,
T0744-238 7497, www.palkiyahaveli.com.
A beautifully restored *haveli*, with a nice family vibe. 6 traditionally furnished a/c rooms with bath (tubs), carved wood furniture, exquisite murals, very good fixed meals, peaceful courtyard garden (full of birds). Recommended.

$$ Sukhdham Kothi
Civil Lines, T0744-232 0081,
www.sukhdhamkothi.com.
15 elegant rooms (size varies), 10 a/c, in a 19th-century British residence with sandstone balconies and screens, good home-made Rajasthani food, large, private garden well set back from the road, family-run, friendly. Peacocks in the garden. Recommended.

Kota

$ Jodhpur Sweets
Shumanpura Market.
Saffron *lassis* and flavoured milks.

$ Palace View
Outdoor meals/snacks.
Handy for visitors to the City Palace.

Festivals

Kota

Mar/Apr Colourful **Gangaur Goddess festival.**
Jul/Aug **Teej.** Renowned for its
elephant processions.
Sep/Oct **Dasara Mela.** Great atmosphere,
with shows in lit up palace grounds.

Transport

Kota
Kota is a transport hub for this area.

Bus At least hourly to **Bundi** (45 mins)
and several daily to **Ajmer**, **Chittaurgarh**,
Jhalarapatan (2½ hrs) and Udaipur; also to
Gwalior, **Sawai Madhopur** and **Ujjain**.

Train From **Kota Junction: Bharatpur**: *Golden
Temple Mail 12903*, 4 hrs (continues to **Mathura**,
5 hrs). **Mumbai** (**Central**): *Jp Bct Supfast 12956*,
14 hrs; **New Delhi**: *Rajdhani Exp 12951*, (early
hours), 5½ hrs so the mid-morning *Golden Temple
Mail 12903*, 7½ hrs, is better option potentially, all
via **Sawai Madhopur**, 1½ hrs.

South of Kota

some charming sights that you may have all to yourself

Jhalawar

Jhalawar, 85 km southeast of Kota, was the capital of the princely state of the Jhalas, which was
separated from Kota by the British in 1838. It lies in a thickly forested area on the edge of the
Malwa plateau with some interesting local forts, temples and ancient cave sites nearby. The Garh
Palace in the town centre, now housing government offices, has some fine wall paintings which
can be seen with permission. The **museum** ① *Sat-Thu 1000-1630, Rs 3*, established in 1915, has a
worthwhile collection of sculptures, paintings and manuscripts. The **Bhawani Natyashala** theatre
(1921) was known for its performances ranging from Shakespearean plays to Shakuntala dramas.
The stage with a subterranean driveway allowed horses and chariots to be brought on stage during
performances. The **tourist office** ① *T07432-230081*, is at the **Hotel Chandravati**.

Jhalarapatan

The small walled town of Jhalarapatan, 7 km south of Jhalawar, has several fine 11th-century Hindu
temples, the **Padmanath Sun Temple** on the main road being the best. The **Shantinath Jain
Temple** has an entrance flanked by marble elephants. There are some fine carvings on the rear
façade and silver polished idols inside the shrines.

Chandrawati

About 7 km away, Chandrawati, on the banks of the Chandrabhaga River, has the ruins of some
seventh-century Hindu temples with fragments of fine sculpture.

Bundi lies in a beautiful narrow valley with Taragarh Fort towering above. The drive into the town is lovely as the road runs along the hillside overlooking the valley opposite the fort. You might feel 'forted out' by the time you reach Bundi, but this beautiful old town nestles under the palace and fort and offers spectacular views and a unique charm.

Much less developed than the other fort towns, Bundi is starting to blossom – now more classic *havelis* are being 'boutiqued', and there are plenty of more down-home family guesthouses springing up too. Popular with backpackers and now increasingly tour buses, Bundi is relaxed and friendly and still a long way off the bazar bustle of Pushkar and the speed and hustle of the more

Bundi

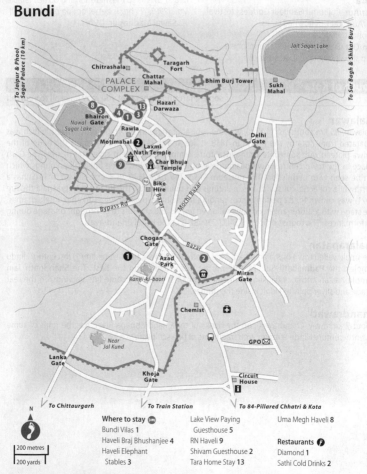

Where to stay
Bundi Vilas 1
Haveli Braj Bhushanjee 4
Haveli Elephant
  Stables 3

Lake View Paying
  Guesthouse 5
RN Haveli 9
Shivam Guesthouse 2
Tara Home Stay 13

Uma Megh Haveli 8

Restaurants
Diamond 1
Sathi Cold Drinks 2

BACKGROUND
Bundi

Formerly a small state founded in 1342, Bundi's fortunes varied inversely with those of its more powerful neighbours. Neither wealthy nor powerful, it nevertheless ranked high in the Rajput hierarchy since the founding family belonged to the specially blessed Hada Chauhan clan. After Prithviraj Chauhan was defeated by Muhammad Ghuri in 1193, the rulers sought refuge in Mewar. However, adventurous clan members overran the Bhils and Minas in the Chambal valley and established the kingdom of Hadavati or Hadoti which covers the area around Bundi, Kota and Jhalawar in southeastern Rajasthan. It prospered under the guidance of the able 19th-century ruler Zalim Singh, but then declined on his death. The British reunited the territory in 1894.

developed fort towns of Jodhpur and Jaisalmer, but good cafés serving cappuccinos cannot be too far along the line. It is well worth spending a day or two here to soak in the atmosphere. Bundi is especially colourful and interesting during the many festivals (see Festivals, page 329).

Sights

Taragarh Fort (1342) ① *0600-1800, foreigners Rs 100, Indians Rs 20, camera Rs 50, video Rs 100,* stands in sombre contrast to the beauty of the town and the lakes below. There are excellent views but it is a difficult 20-minute climb beset in places by aggressive monkeys; wear good shoes and wield a big stick. The eastern wall is crenellated with high ramparts while the main gate to the west is flanked by octagonal towers. The **Bhim Burj** tower dominates the fort and provided the platform for the Garbh Ganjam ('Thunder from the Womb'), a huge cannon. A pit to the side once provided shelter for the artillery men, and there are several stepped water tanks inside. Cars can go as far as the TV tower then it is 600 m along a rough track. The **Palace Complex** ① *below Taragarh, 0900-1700, foreigners Rs 100, Indians Rs 20,* which was begun around 1600, is at the northern end of the bazar, and was described by Kipling as "such a palace as men build for themselves in uneasy dreams – the work of goblins rather than of men". The buildings, on various levels, follow the shape of the hill. A steep, rough stone ramp leads up through the **Hazari Darwaza** (Gate of the Thousand) where the garrison lived; you may need to enter through a small door within the *darwaza*. The palace entrance is through the **Hathi Pol** (Elephant Gate, 1607-1631), which has two carved elephants with a water clock. Steps lead up to **Ratan Daulat** above the stables, the unusually small Diwan-i-Am which was intended to accommodate a select few at public audience. A delicate marble balcony overhangs the courtyard giving a view of the throne to the less privileged, who stood below.

The **Chattar Mahal** (1660), the newer palace of green serpentine rock, is pure Rajput in style and contains private apartments decorated with wall paintings, glass and mirrors. The **Badal Mahal** bedroom has finely decorated ceilings.

The **Chitrashala** ① *0900-1700, Rs 20,* a cloistered courtyard with a gallery running around a garden of fountains, has a splendid collection of miniatures showing scenes from the Radha Krishna story. Turquoise, blues and greens dominate (other pigments may have faded with exposure to sunlight) though the elephant panels on the dado are in a contrasting red. The murals (circa 1800) are some of the finest examples of Rajput art but are not properly maintained.

There is supposedly a labyrinth of catacombs in which the state treasures are believed to have been stored. Each ruler was allowed one visit but when the last guide died in the 1940s the secret of its location was lost. At night, the palace is lit up and thousands of bats pour out of its innards.

There are several 16th- to 17th-century step wells and 'tanks' (*kunds*) in town. The 46-m-deep **Raniji-ki-baori** ① *Mon-Sat 1000-1700, closed 2nd Sat each month, free, caretaker unlocks the gate,*(80rs) with beautiful pillars and bas relief sculpture panels of Vishnu's 10 *avatars*, is the most impressive. No longer in use, the water is stagnant.

Sukh Mahal, a summer pleasure palace, faces the **Jait Sagar** lake; Kipling spent a night in the original pavilion. Further out are the 66 royal memorials at the rarely visited **Sar Bagh**, some of which have beautiful carvings. The caretaker expects Rs 10 tip. The square artificial **Nawal Sagar** lake has in its centre a half-submerged temple to Varuna, the god of water. The lake surface beautifully reflects the entire town and palace, but tends to dry up in the summer months. A dramatic tongue-slitting ceremony takes place here during Dussehra.

West of the Nawal Sagar, 10 km away, is **Phool Sagar Palace**, which was started in 1945 but was left unfinished. Prior permission is needed to view.

West of Bundi

The small town of **Shahpura**, 95 km west of Bundi, is a beautiful stopover on your way west to Deogarh or Jodhpur or north to Ajmer. It's an average bustling market town close to the beautiful Ram Dwara Temple and the crumbling Dhikhola Fort.

There is a delightful heritage hotel here, perfect for a rural retreat (see Where to stay, below), which focuses on its responsibility to the local environment, putting money into restoring water tables and reservoirs. It's well worth a visit.

Listings Bundi map p326

Tourist information

Bundi

Tourist office
Circuit House, near Raniji ki Baori, T0747-244 3697.

Where to stay

Bundi

$$$-$$ Bundi Vilas
Below the palace, behind Haveli Braj Bhushanjee, T0747-244 4614, www.bundivilas.com.
Wander up a beautiful atmospheric alleyway and you find yourself at a super-stylish, newly restored *haveli* with good views from the rooftop. Great attention to detail, rose petals everywhere scenting the way, Wi-Fi, stylishly furnished. Delicious food – brown bread is brought daily from Delhi, jams from the Himalaya and the lady of the house makes a great sesame dessert. Recommended.

$$$-$ Haveli Braj Bhushanjee
Below the fort, opposite the Ayurvedic Hospital, T0747-244 2322, www.kiplingsbundi.com.
16 quaint rooms with clean bath (hot showers), in a 19th-century 4-storey *haveli* covered in frescos, plenty of atmosphere and memorabilia but a bit stuffy and overpriced, although some of the cheaper rooms are good value. Home-cooked vegetarian meals (no alcohol), pleasant terrace, good fort views, pick-up from station on request, good craft shop below, mixed reports on service. Also offers modern rooms in attached, newly restored 17th-century **Badi Haveli**.

$ Haveli Elephant Stables
At the base of the palace near gate, T(0)9928-154064, elephantstable_guesthouse@hotmail.com.
Formerly used to house royal elephants, the 4 simple but huge rooms have mosquito nets and basic Indian toilets, beneath a huge peepal tree in a dusty courtyard. Good home cooking, relaxed.

$ Lake View Paying Guest House
Bohra Meghwan Ji Ki Haveli, Balchand Para, below the palace, by Nawal Sagar, T0747-244 2326, lakeviewbundi@yahoo.com.
7 simple clean rooms (3 in a separate, basic garden annexe with shared bath) in a 150-year-old *haveli* with wall paintings, private terrace shared with monkeys and peacocks, lovely views from the rooftop, warm welcome, popular, very friendly hosts.

$ R N Haveli
Behind Laxmi Nath Temple, T0747-244 3287, rnhavelibundi@yahoo.co.in.
5 rooms in a friendly family home – home cooking is good. Recommended.

$ Shivam Guesthouse
Outside the walls near the Nawal Sagar, T0747-244 7892, www.shivam-bundi.co.in.
Simple, comfortable rooms around a shaded blue courtyard, exceptionally friendly, come for food even if you're not staying. Recommended.

$ Tara Home Stay
Near Elephant Stables, T(0)9829-718554, tarahomestay@gmail.com.
Only a couple of rooms, but exceptional views of the palace.

$ Uma Megh Haveli
Balchand Para, T0747-244 2191.
Very atmospheric, 11 unrestored rooms, 7 with
basic attached bathrooms, plus a pleasant garden
and restaurant.

West of Bundi

$$$-$$ Shahpura Bagh
Shahpura, T(0)99822 26606,
www.shahpurabagh.com.
An elegant retreat close to nature. Beautiful,
spacious rooms and stunning swimming pool
make this a great getaway. If you can tear yourself
away from the pool, there are lovely walks, bike
rides and an amazing dawn chorus, great for
bird-lovers. Recommended.

Restaurants

Bundi
Several of the hotels have pleasant rooftop
restaurants, namely Bundi Vilas, see Where to
stay, above.

$ Diamond
Suryamahal Chowk.
Very popular locally for cheap vegetarian meals,
handy when visiting step wells.

$ Sathi Cold Drinks
Palace Rd.
Excellent *lassis* (saffron, spices, pistachio and fruit).

Festivals

Aug **Kajli Teej** and **Bundi Utsav** takes place
3 days after the Pushkar fair has finished (see box,
page 377).
Nov Jhalawar sees the **Chandrabhaga
Fair**. A cattle and camel fair with all the
colour and authenticity of Pushkar but less
commercialization. Animals are traded in large
numbers, pilgrims come to bathe in the river
as the temples become the centre of religious
activity and the town is abuzz with all manner
of vendors.

Transport

Bus Enquiries: T0747-244 5422. To **Ajmer**
(165 km), 5 hrs; **Jaipur**, several daily, 4 deluxe,
4-5 hrs; **Kota** (37 km), 45 mins; **Chittaurgarh**
(157 km), 5 hrs; **Udaipur** (120 km), 3 hrs. For
Jhalarapatan catch a bus from **Kota** to
Jhalawar; then auto-rickshaw or local bus for
sights. The Ujjain–Jhalawar road is appalling.

Train Enquiries: T0747-244 3582. The station
south of town has a train each way between
Kota and **Neemuch** via **Chittaurgarh**. A direct
Delhi service may be running, but involves hours
waiting in Kota; better to take the bus to Kota and
board trains there.

Jodhpur
& around

Rajasthan's second largest city, Jodhpur is entirely dominated by its spectacular Mehrangarh fort, towering over proceedings below with absolute authority. You could spend most of a day wandering this grand stone edifice on its plinth of red rock, pausing in the warm shafts of sunlight in its honey-coloured courtyards and strolling its chunky, cannon-lined ramparts high above the moat of blue buildings which make up the Old City. Up there, birds of prey circle on the thermals, close to eye level, while the city hums below, its rickshaw horns and occasional calls to prayer still audible.

Jodhpur's fascinating Old City is a hive of activity, the vibrant bazars, narrow lanes, and bustling Sardar Market frequented by equally colourful tribal people from the surrounding areas.

South of the railway line, things are altogether more serene, and nowhere more so than the impressive Umaid Bhawan Palace, its classic exterior belying the art deco extravaganza within.

There are also some remarkable sights around Jodhpur: the temples of Osian and Nagaur are well worth a visit and there are some great heritage hotels set in quiet nearby villages.

'Blue city' with a spectacular fort, on the edge of the desert

Old City

The Old City is surrounded by a huge 9.5-km-long wall which has 101 bastions and seven gates, above which are inscribed the names of the places to which the roads underneath them lead. It comprises a labyrinthine maze of narrow streets and lively markets, a great place to wander round and get lost. Some of the houses and temples are of richly carved stone, in particular the red sandstone buildings of the **Siré (Sardar) Bazar**. Here the **Taleti Mahal** (early 17th century), one of three concubines' palaces in Jodhpur, has the unusual feature of *jarokhas* decorated with temple columns.

Mehrangarh

T0291-254 8790, 0900-1700, foreigners Rs 500, students Rs 400, Indians Rs 60, includes excellent MP3 audio guide and camera fee, video Rs 200, allow at least 2 hrs, there is a pleasant restaurant on the terrace near the ticket office. For a novel way of viewing the fort, try ziplining with Flying Fox, www.flyingfox.asia.

The 'Majestic Fort' sprawls along the top of a steep escarpment with a sheer drop to the south. Originally started by Rao Jodha in 1459, it has walls up to 36 m high and 21 m wide, towering above the plains. Most of what stands today is from the period of Maharajah Jaswant Singh (1638-1678). On his death in 1678, Aurangzeb occupied the fort. However, after Aurangzeb's death Mehrangarh returned to Jaswant Singh's son Ajit Singh and remained the royal residence until the Umaid Bhavan was completed in 1943. It is now perhaps the best preserved and presented palace in Rajasthan, an excellent example which the others will hopefully follow.

The summit has three areas: the palace (northwest), a wide terrace to the east of the palace, and the strongly fortified area to the south. There are extensive views from the top. One approach is by a winding path up the west side, possible by rickshaw, but the main approach and car park is from the east. The climb is quite stiff; those with walking difficulties may use the elevator (Rs 15 each way).

The gateways There were originally seven gateways. The first, the **Fateh Gate**, is heavily fortified with spikes and a barbican that forces a 45° turn. The smaller **Gopal Gate** is followed

Essential Jodhpur and around

Finding your feet

Jodhpur has good air, rail and road links with the other major cities of Rajasthan as well as Delhi and Mumbai. Many visitors stop here either on the way to or from Jaisalmer, or on their way down to Udaipur. See Transport, page 338.

Fact...

The fort is used for film shoots and adverts and hosts the Rajasthan Folk Music Festival which is patronized by Mick Jagger.

Getting around

The train and bus stations are conveniently located close to the old city, with most hotels a Rs 20-30 rickshaw ride away, while the airport is 5 km south of town. The Old City is small enough to walk around, although many people find a rented bicycle the best way to get about.

Best hidden gems

Ziplining at Mehrangarh Fort, see left column
Saffron *lassis* at Mishrilal, by Jodhpur clocktower, page 337
Ancient eco-technology at Ahhichatragarh Fort in Nagaur, page 339

Orientation

The town itself is pretty spread out, but the Old City is easy to walk around although narrow streets sometimes make it confusing. Many of the hotels are located in this old city hub, while others are on the airport road.

Best village experiences

Majestic Marwar Village Tour, page 338
Chhatra Sagar nature and village safari, pages 341 and 342
Chhotaram Prajapat's Village Homestay, page 342

by the **Bhairon Gate**, with large guardrooms. The fourth, **Toati Gate**, is now missing but the fifth **Dodhkangra Gate**, marked with cannon shots, stands over a turn in the path and has loopholed battlements for easy defence. Next is the **Marti Gate**, a long passage flanked by guardrooms. The last, **Loha (Iron) Gate**, controls the final turn into the fort and has handprints (31 on one side and five on the other) of royal *satis*, the wives of maharajas. It is said that six queens and 58 concubines became *satis* on Ajit Singh's funeral pyre in 1724. *Satis* carried the Bhagavad Gita with them into the flames and legend has it that the holy book would never perish. The main entrance is through the Jay (Victory) Pol.

Jodhpur

Where to stay 🛏

Ajit Bhawan **2** *B2*
Bal Samand Palace **1** *A3*
Devi Bhavan **6** *C2*
Durag Niwas Guest House **7** *B2*
Hare Krishna Guest House **9** *A1*
Haveli Inn Pal **16** *A1*
Juna Mahal **19** *B1*

Pal Haveli &
 Indique restaurant **29** *A1*
Raas **13** *A1*
Singhvi's Haveli **25** *B1*
Umaid Bhawan Palace **20** *B3*
Yogi's Guest House **14** *A1*

Restaurants 🍴
Café Sheesh Mahal **12** *A1*
Chokelao **1** *A1*

Hotel Priya **5** *B1*
Jhankar **13** *A1*
Jodhpur Coffee House **10** *B1*
Mishrilal **4** *B1*
On the Rocks **11** *B2*
Sankalp **7** *C1*
Softy & Softy **14** *B2*

ON THE ROAD
True blue

As you approach the fort you will notice the predominance of blue houses which are often inaccurately referred to as 'Brahmin houses' – the colour being associated with the high caste. In fact they are blue due to termites (white ants). It appears that the white limewash used originally did not deter the pests which have caused havoc, making unsightly cavities in local homes. The addition of chemicals (eg copper sulphate), which resulted in turning the white lime to a blue wash, was found to be effective in limiting the pest damage and so was widely used in the area around the fort. This also happens to be a part of town where large numbers of the Brahmin community live.

The palaces From the Loha Gate the ramp leads up to the Suraj (Sun) Pol, which opens onto the Singar Choki Chowk, the main entrance to the museum, see below. Used for royal ceremonies such as the anointing of rajas, the north, west and southwest sides of the Singar Choki Chowk date from the period immediately before the Mughal occupation in 1678. The upper storeys of the chowk were part of the *zenana*, and from the **Jhanki Mahal** (glimpse palace) on the upper floor of the north wing the women could look down on the activities of the courtyard. Thus the chowk below has the features characteristic of much of the rest of the *zenana*, *jarokhas* surmounted by the distinctive Bengali-style eaves and beautifully ornate *jali* screens. These allowed cooling breezes to ventilate rooms and corridors in the often stiflingly hot desert summers.

Also typical of Mughal buildings was the use of material hung from rings below the eaves to provide roof covering, as in the columned halls of the **Daulat Khana** and the **Sileh Khana** (armoury), which date from Ajit Singh's reign. The collection of Indian weapons in the armoury is unequalled, with remarkable swords and daggers, often beautifully decorated with calligraphy. Shah Jahan's red silk and velvet tent, lavishly embroidered with gold thread and used in the Imperial Mughal campaign, is in the **Tent Room**. The **Jewel House** has a wonderful collection of jewellery, including diamond eyebrows held by hooks over the ears. There are also palanquins, howdahs and ornate royal cradles, all marvellously well preserved.

The **Phool Mahal** (Flower Palace), above the Sileh Khana, was built by Abhai Singh (1724-1749) as a hall of private audience. The stone *jali* screens are original and there are striking portraits of former rulers, a lavishly gilded ceiling and the Jodhpur coat of arms displayed above the royal couch; the murals of the 36 musical modes are a late 19th-century addition.

The **Umaid Vilas**, which houses Rajput miniatures, is linked to the **Sheesh Mahal** (Mirror Palace), built by Ajit Singh between 1707 and 1724. The room has characteristic large and regularly sized mirror work, unlike Mughal 'mirror palaces'. Immediately to its south, and above the Sardar Vilas, is the **Takhat Vilas**. Added by Maharajah Takhat Singh (1843-1873), it has wall murals of dancing girls, love legends and Krishna Lila, while its ceiling has two unusual features: massive wooden beams to provide support and the curious use of colourful Belgian Christmas tree balls.

The **Ajit Vilas** has a fascinating collection of musical instruments and costumes. On the ground floor of the Takhat Vilas is **Sardar Vilas**, and to its south the **Khabka** and **Chandan Mahals** (sleeping quarters). The **Moti Vilas** wings to the north, east and south of the Moti Mahal Chowk, date from Jaswant Singh's reign. The women could watch proceedings in the courtyard below through the *jali* screens of the surrounding wings. Tillotson suggests that the **Moti Mahal** (Pearl Palace) ① *Rs 150 for 15 mins*, to the west, although placed in the *zenana* of the fort, was such a magnificent building that it could only have served the purpose of a Diwan-i-Am (Hall of Public Audience). The Moti Mahal is fronted by excellently carved 19th-century woodwork, while inside waist-level niches housed oil lamps whose light would have shimmered from the mirrored ceiling. A palmist reads your fortune at Moti Mahal Chowk (museum area).

Mehrangarh Fort Palace Museum is in a series of palaces with beautifully designed and decorated windows and walls. It has a magnificent collection of the maharajas' memorabilia – superbly maintained and presented. The fort now hosts several music festivals including a flamenco

The **Rathore** Rajputs had moved to Marwar – the 'region of death' – in 1211, after their defeat at Kanauj by Muhammad Ghori. In 1459, Rao Jodha – forced to leave the Rathore capital at Mandore, 8 km to the north – chose this place as his capital because of its strategic location on the edge of the Thar Desert. The Rathores subsequently controlled wide areas of Rajasthan.

Rao Udai Singh of Jodhpur (died 1581) received the title of Raja from Akbar, and his son, Sawai Raja Sur Singh (died 1595), conquered Gujarat and part of the Deccan for the emperor. Maharaja Jaswant Singh (died 1678), having supported Shah Jahan in the Mughal struggle for succession in 1658, had a problematic relationship with the subsequent Mughal rule of Aurangzeb, and his son Ajit Singh was only able to succeed him after Aurangzeb's own death in 1707. In addition to driving the Mughals out of Ajmer he added substantially to the Mehrangarh Fort in Jodhpur. His successor, Maharaja Abhai Singh (died 1749) captured Ahmedabad, and the state came into treaty relations with the British in 1818.

Jodhpur lies on the once strategic Delhi–Gujarat trading route and the Marwaris managed and benefitted from the traffic of opium, copper, silk, sandalwood, dates, coffee and much more besides.

festival, the World Sufi Festival and the acclaimed RIFF Rajasthani International Folk Festival (www.mehrangarh.org).

Jaswant Thada ① *off the road leading up to the fort, 0900-1700, Rs 30*, is the cremation ground of the former rulers with distinctive memorials in white marble which commemorate Jaswant SinghII (1899) and successive rulers of Marwar. It is situated in pleasant and well-maintained gardens and is definitely worth visiting on the way back from the fort.

New city

The new city beyond the walls is also of interest. Overlooking the Umaid Sagar is the **Umaid Bhawan Palace** on Chittar Hill. Building started in 1929 as a famine relief exercise when the monsoon failed for the third year running. Over 3000 people worked for 14 years, building this vast 347-room palace of sandstone and marble. The hand-hewn blocks are interlocked into position, and use no mortar. It was designed by HV Lanchester, with the most modern furnishing and facilities in mind, and completed in 1943. The interior decoration was left to the artist JS Norblin, a refugee from Poland; he painted the frescoes in the Throne Room (East Wing). For the architectural historian, Tillotson, it is "the finest example of Indo-Deco. The forms are crisp and precise, and the bland monochrome of the stone makes the eye concentrate on their carved shapes". The royal family still occupies part of the palace.

The **Umaid Bhawan Palace Museum** ① *T0291-251 0101, 0900-1700, Rs 100*, includes the Darbar Hall with its elegantly flaking murals plus a good collection of miniatures, armour and quirky old clocks as well as a bizarre range of household paraphernalia; if it was fashionable in the 1930s, expensive and not available in India, it's in here. Many visitors find the tour and the museum in general disappointing with not much to see (most of the china and glassware you could see in your grandma's cabinets). The palace hotel which occupies the majority of the building has been beautifully restored, but is officially inaccessible to non-residents; try sneaking in for a cold drink and a look at the magnificent domed interior, a remarkable separation from the Indian environment in which it is set (see Where to stay, opposite). In 1886, before steam engines were acquired, the Jodhpur Railway introduced camel-drawn trains. The maharaja's luxurious personal saloons (1926) are beautifully finished with inlaid wood and silver fittings and are on display near the Umaid Bhawan Palace.

The **Government Museum** ① *Umaid Park, Sat-Thu 1000-1630, Rs 50*, is a time-capsule from the British Raj, little added to since Independence, with some moth-eaten stuffed animals and featherless birds, images of Jain Tirthankars, miniature portraits and antiquities. A small zoo in the gardens has a few rare exotic species.

Just southeast of Raikabagh Station are the **Raikabagh Palace** and the **Jubilee Buildings**, public offices designed by Sir Samuel Swinton Jacob in the Indo-Saracenic style. On the Mandore Road, 2 km to the north, is the large **Mahamandir Temple**.

Trips from Jodhpur

Taking a 'safari' to visit a **Bishnoi village** is recommended, although these trips have naturally become more touristy over the years. Most tours include the hamlets of **Guda**, famous for wildlife, **Khejarali**, a well-known Bishnoi village, **Raika** cameleers' settlement and **Salawas**. Interesting and alternative trips are run by Virasat Experiences. See What to do, page 338.

The small, semi-rural village of **Jhalamand**, 12 km south of Jodhpur, is a good alternative to staying in the city, particularly if you have your own transport. It works especially well as a base from which to explore the Bishnoi and Raika communities.

Marwar, 8 km north of Jodhpur, is the old 14th-century capital of Mandore, situated on a plateau. Set around the old cremation ground with the red sandstone *chhatris* of the Rathore rulers, the gardens are usually crowded with Indian tourists at weekends. The **Shrine of the 33 Crore Gods** is a hall containing huge painted rock-cut figures of heroes and gods, although some of the workmanship is a little crude. The largest deval, a combination of temple and cenotaph, is Ajit Singh's (died 1724), though it is rather unkempt. The remains of an eighth-century Hindu temple is on a hilltop nearby.

Bal Samand Lake is the oldest artificial lake in Rajasthan, 5 km north. Dating from 1159, it is surrounded by parkland laid out in 1936 where the 19th-century **Hawa Mahal** was turned into a royal summer palace. Although the interior is European in style, it has entirely traditional red sandstone filigree windows and beautifully carved balconies. The peaceful and well-maintained grounds exude calm and tranquillity, while the views over the lake are simply majestic.

Listings Jodhpur *map p332*

Tourist information

Government of Rajasthan tourist office
On the grounds of the RTDC Hotel Ghoomar, High Court Rd, T0291-254 4010.
As well as the usual supply of maps and pamphlets, it organizes half-day city tours and village safaris. Also, the **Tourist Assistance Force** has a presence at the railway station bus stand and clock tower.

Where to stay

Certain budget hotels, including some of those listed below, may quote low room prices that depend on you booking a tour or camel safari with them; some have been known to raise the price dramatically or even evict guests who refuse. Confirm any conditions before checking in.

$$$$ Raas
Tunvarji Ka Jhalra, Makrana Mohalla, www.raasjodhpur.com, T0291-263 6455.
Raas is a gem at the heart of the city. Built from the same warm rose-red sandstone as the fort that towers above it; stunning balconies with carved stone shutters discreetly open up to reveal

exceptional fort views. There is a contemporary vibe inspired by the essence of Rajasthan, rather than the traditional 'heritage' style' and yet it blends into the old city – it looks chic and stylish without looking out of place. As well as all the mod cons, you will find sumptuous fabrics and evocative photographs in every room. There are 2 restaurants, one open for non-residents as well as a very inviting pool. Simply stunning.

$$$$ Umaid Bhawan Palace
T0291-251 0101, www.tajhotels.com.
Stylish art deco hotel, with 36 rooms and 40 beautifully appointed suites, best with garden-view balconies and unforgettable marble bathrooms, rather cool and masculine, far removed from the typical Rajasthani colour-fest, soaring domed lobbies, formal gardens and an extraordinary underground swimming pool. Famous for celebrity weddings.

$$$$-$$$ Ajit Bhawan
Circuit House Rd, T0291-251 3333, www.ajitbhawan.com.
With a rather imposing palace façade, it is hard to imagine the variety of rooms, cottages and tents at this fantastic property. All luxuriously kitted out, the cottages are particularly beautiful.

There is a very ornate swimming pool, several restaurants on-site, an opulent bar and heaps of character. This is India's first heritage hotel, started in 1927, and still leads the way.

$$$$-$$$ Pal Haveli
Behind the clock tower in the middle of town, T0291-329 3328, www.palhaveli.com.
20 chic and atmospheric rooms in an authentic 200-year-old *haveli* with stylishly decorated drawing room/mini-museum and beautiful rooftop restaurant Indique. Massage available, friendly staff and chilled vibe. They also have a newly renovated fort property, **Pal Garh**, in a neighbouring village. Recommended.

$$ Devi Bhawan
1 Ratanada Circle, T0291-251 2215, www.devibhawan.com.
Beautiful rooms around delightful shady garden with lovely swimming pool in a peaceful area. There is an excellent Indian dinner (set timings) and a warm welcome at this traditional Rajput family home. Charming.

$$ Haveli Inn Pal
T0291-261 2519, www.haveliinnpal.com.
Quirkily designed rooms, some with huge windows overlooking the fort, some with lake views and unusual marble shower troughs, others with beds you need a ladder to get into, fantastic furniture, rooftop restaurant with commanding views and a rare patch of lawn. Recommended.

$$ Juna Mahal
Ada Bazar, Daga St, T0291-244 5511, www.junamahal.com.
Special little place, recently renovated 472-year-old *haveli* with bags of charm and stylish decor. The Lord Krishna room is particularly lovely.

$$-$ Singhvi's Haveli
Navchokiya, Ramdevjika Chowk, T0291-262 4293, www.singhvihaveli.com.
11 rooms in a charming, 500-year-old *haveli* (one of the oldest), tastefully decorated, friendly family. Beautiful suite with mirror-work ceiling reminiscent of the fort that towers above. Nice chill-out area. Recommended.

$ Durag Niwas Guest House
Old Public Park Lane, near Circuit House, T0291-251 2385, www.durag-niwas.com.
Cheaper and more character than **Durag Vilas** next door. Runs a women's craft collective 'Sambhali' on-site.

$ Hare Krishna Guest House
Killi Khana, Mehron Ka Chowk, T0291-263 5307, www.harekrishnaguesthouse.net.
Run by the president of the **Jodhpur Guest House Association**, you are definitely well looked after here. Variety of rooms, lots of character and great views from the restaurant and chill-out space on the roof. They also run excellent Bishnoi village safaris and have a sister guesthouse **Kesar** nearby. Great place to meet other travellers.

$ Yogi's Guest House
Raj Purohit Ji Ki Haveli, Manak Chowk, old town, T0291-264 3436, yogiguesthouse@hotmail.com.
12 rooms, most in the 500-year-old *haveli*, clean, modern bathrooms, camel/jeep safaris, experienced management. Very popular – book ahead. Lovely atmosphere.

Trips from Jodhpur

$$$ Bal Samand Palace (WelcomHeritage)
Bal Samand Lake, T011-460 3550 (Delhi), www.welcomheritagehotels.com.
Essentially this is 2 properties together, the **Palace** and the **Garden Retreat**. In extensive grounds on the lake, there are 10 attractively furnished suites in an atmospheric palace and 26 'garden retreat' rooms in the imaginatively renovated stables, restaurant (mainly buffet), lovely pool, boating on the lovely lake, pleasant orchards which attract nilgai, jackals and peacocks. Calming, tranquil atmosphere.

Restaurants

The best restaurants are in hotels; reserve ahead. Rooftop restaurants in most budget and mid-range hotels welcome non-residents. For *daal-bhatti*, *lassi* and *kachoris* head for Jalori and Sojati gates. Great food at Panorama Haveli Inn Pal and Hotel Haveli.

$$$ Ajit Bhawan
See Where to stay, page 335.
Evening buffet, excellent meals in the garden on a warm evening with entertainment, but lacking atmosphere if eating indoors in winter.

$$$ Bijolai
Water Habitat Retreat, Air Force Radar Rd, Kailana Lake, 8 km from the city, T(0)8104-000909, www.1559AD.com.
This is another serving by the team behind **1559 AD** in Udaipur. There are mixed reports on the food and service; however, the location and

ambience is unbeatable. There is indoor dining as well as lakeside gazebos.

$$$ Chokelao
Mehrangarh Fort, T0291-254 9790.
What a backdrop. Great Rajasthani food as you sit perched over the city of Jodhpur at the majestic Mehrengarh Fort. Breathtaking.

$$ Indique
Haveli Inn Pal (see Where stay, opposite).
Beautiful rooftop restaurant by the clocktower. They describe their food as "good, wholesome, spicy and traditional" with recipes passed down through the generations. Great views.

$$ On the Rocks
Near Ajit Bhawan, T0291-510 2701.
Good mix of Indian and Continental, plus a relaxing bar, patisserie, ice cream parlour and lovely gardens.

$$ Sankalp
12th Rd (west of the city centre). Open 1030-2300.
Upmarket a/c South Indian, *dosas* come with a fantastic range of chutneys, good service. Recommended.

$ Café Sheesh Mahal
Behind the clocktower and next to Pal Haveli.
Great cappuccino and macchiato in a stylish coffee lounge. You can get sandwiches and hot chocolate brownie too.

$ Hotel Priya
181 Nai Sarak.
Fantastic special *thalis* for Rs 55 and extra quick service. Always busy.

$ Jhankar
Follow signs to Ganesh Guest House or ask at Blue Guest House.
This little courtyard café has great character – very pretty and a menu of all the usual traveller favourites to boot.

$ Jodhpur Coffee House
Sojati Gate.
Good South Indian snacks and *thalis*.

$ Mishrilal
Clocktower.
The best *lassis* in town, if not the world. The saffron *lassi* is the way to go. Quintessential Jodhpur experience.

$ Softy and Softy
High Court Rd.
Excellent sweets and *namkeen*, thick shakes, fun for people-watching.

Festivals

Jul/Aug Nag Panchami, when Naga (*naag*), the cobra, is worshipped. The day is dedicated to Sesha, the 1000-headed god or *Anant* (infinite) Vishnu, who is often depicted reclining on a bed of serpents. In Jodhpur, snake charmers gather for a colourful fair in Mandore.
Oct Marwar Festival is held at full moon, includes music, puppet shows, turban-tying competitions, camel polo and ends with a fire dance on the dunes at Osian.
Rajasthan International Folk Festival (RIFF), www.jodhpurfolkfestival.org. Coinciding with **Kartik Purnima**, the brightest full moon of the year, Jodhpur's annual RIFF is an eclectic mix of master musicians from local Rajasthan communities, acts from around the world and cutting-edge global dance music at **Club Mehran**. There are workshops and interactive daytime sessions for visitors. Some performances are around the city, while the main stage and club are in the stunning Mehrangahr Fort itself.

Shopping

Jodhpur is famous for its once-popular riding breeches (although it is pricey to get a pair made these days), tie-dye fabrics, lacquer work and leather shoes. Export of items over 100 years old is prohibited. The main areas are: **Sojati Gate** for gifts; **Station Rd** and Sarafa Bazar for jewellery; **Tripolia Bazar** for handicrafts; **Khanda Falsa** and Kapra Bazar for tie-dye; **Lakhara Bazar** for lac bangles. **Raj Rani** has a nice selection of more unusual designed clothes (probably from Pushkar) at Makrana Mohalla, near the clocktower. Shoes are made in **Mochi Bazar**, **Sardarpura** and **Clock Tower**, *bandhanas* in Bambamola, and around **Siwanchi** and **Jalori Gates**. *Durries* are woven at **Salawas**, 18 km away. In most places you'll need to bargain.

Antiques
Shops on the road between Umaid and Ajit Bhawans do a flourishing trade, though are pricey.
Kirti Art Collection, *T(0)98280 33136*. Has a good selection. Recommended.

Clothing and lifestyle
There's a parade of shops next to Ajit Bhawan (Circuit House Road) including beautiful designer jewellery shop **Amrapali**, clothes and prints from **Anokhi** and **Pahnava**.

Handloom and handicrafts

Krishna Arts and Crafts, *by Tija Mata temple on main road running west from the clocktower.* There's an interesting shop by the temple, with fixed prices.

Jewellery

Gems & Art Plaza, *Circuit House Rd.* As patronized by Angelina Jolie. Some nice pieces in Kundan and Minakari styles, gaudy rings.

Spices

Mohanlal Verhomal Spices, *209-B, Kirana Merchant Vegetable Market (inside the market to the left of clocktower),* T0291-261 5846, *www.mvspices.com.* Sought after for hand-mixed spices, but quality assured and is simply the best spice outlet in the city. Usha, along with her 6 sisters and mother, runs the shop. Insist your guide takes you here as many shops have tried to pass themselves off as the original.

What to do

Adventure sports

Flying Fox, *www.flyingfox.asia.* Offers ziplining around Mehrengarh Fort. Boris Johnson hailed it the best thing in Jodhpur: "the zipwire sends you like Batman around the moats and crenellations; it's stunning".

Art school

Umaid Heritage Art School, *www.umaid heritageartschool.com.* Great insight into the world of miniature painiting with short courses.

Tour operators

Many of the hotels organize village safaris, as does the tourist office, which charges Rs 1100 for 4 people including car, guide and tips given to villagers. City sightseeing, starts from tourist office at **Ghoomar Hotel** (T0291-254 5083, half day, 0830-1300, 1400-1800). Fort and palaces, Jaswant Thada, Mandore Gardens, Government Museum, bazar around Old City Clock Tower.

Aravali Safari, *4 Kuchaman House Area, Airport Rd,* T0291-643 649.

Forts & Palaces, *15 Old Public Park,* T0291-251 1207, *www.palaces-tours.com.* Knowledgeable outfit that spans Rajasthan.

Virasat Experiences, *www.virasatexperiences.com.* Fantastic walking tours to see behind the usual tourist sites, which provides a more intimate experience of Jodhpur. Also runs the very interesting and non-touristy **Majestic Marwar – Rural Villages Tour**, visiting the villages around Jodhpur. The tour costs Rs 2500, but Rs 500

of that goes to the villages to create rainwater harvesting projects and improve hygiene. You are really giving something back here, unlike some of the other 'tribal tours' touted locally, which can be exploitative. Also organizes private dinners and cookery classes with local families. Highly recommended.

Transport

Air Jodhpur Airport is 5 km south of the centre. Transport to town: by taxi, Rs 400; auto-rickshaw, Rs 200. **Air India**, near Bhati crossroads, T0291-251 0758, 1000-1300, 1400-1700; airport enquiries T0291-251 2617, flies to **Delhi, Jaipur, Mumbai, Udaipur.** Jet Airways, T0291-3989 3333, to **Delhi** and **Mumbai.**

Local bus Minibuses cover most of the city except the Mehrangarh Fort and Umaid Bhavan Palace. For **Mandore**, frequent buses leave from **Paota Bus Stand.** Also several daily buses to **Salawas, Luni** (40 km), **Rohet** (450 km) and **Osian** (65 km).

Long-distance bus RST Bus Stand, near Raikabagh Railway Station, T0291-254 4989. 1000-1700; bookings also at tourist office. A convenient bus route links Jodhpur with **Ghanerao** and **Ranakpur, Kumbhalgarh** and **Udaipur.** Other daily services include: **Abu Rd,** 6 hrs; **Ahmedabad,** 10 hrs; **Ajmer,** 5 hrs; **Jaipur,** frequent, 8 hrs; **Jaisalmer,** 0530 (depart Jaisalmer, 1400), 5-6 hrs; faster than train but scenically tedious; **Pali,** 1 hr; **Udaipur,** 7 hrs by rough road, best to book a good seat a day ahead.

Private operators arrive at Barakuttulah Stadium west of town, in a scrum of rickshaw drivers: pay around Rs 30 to the old city. Some companies have offices opposite railway station, eg **HR Travels, Sun City Tours**, and **Sethi Yatra**, or book at **Govind Hotel.**

Car and taxi Car hire from tourist office, **Ghoomar Hotel**, or with private firm whole day about Rs 1700; half day Rs 1200.

Rickshaw Railway station to fort should be about Rs 25 (may demand Rs 50; try walking away).

Train Raikabagh Railway Station enquiries: T131. Open 0800-2400. Reservations: T0291-263 6407. Open 0900-1300, 1330-1600. Advance reservations, next to GPO. Tourist Bureau, T0291-254 5083 (0500-2300). **International tourist waiting room** for passengers in transit (ground floor), with big sofas and showers; clean Indian toilets in 2nd-class waiting room on the 1st floor of the station Foyer. To **Agra**: *Jodhpur-Howrah Superfast 12308*, 9½ hrs, continues to **Kolkata. Ahmedabad** via **Abu Rd (Mount Abu)**: *Ranakpur Exp 14707*, 5½ hrs; both continue to **Mumbai** (19 hrs). **Delhi**: *Mandore Exp 12462*, 11 hrs (OD).**Jaipur**: *Inter-City Exp 12466*, 0610, 4½ hrs; *Marudhar Exp 14864*, 5½ hrs. **Jaisalmer** (via **Osian**): *Dli Jaisalmer Exp 14059*, 6 hrs; *Jaisalmer Exp 14810*, 6 hrs.

Around Jodhpur
from the desert temples of Osian to the Mallinathji Cattle Fair

The temples of Osian are remarkable as much for their location in the middle of the desert as for their architecture, while Nagaur is one of Rajasthan's busiest but most unaffected cities. The area south of Jodhpur is refreshingly green and fertile compared to the desert landscapes of most of Western Rajasthan (although it can be very dry from March until the monsoon). Leaving the city, the landscape soon becomes agricultural, punctuated by small, friendly villages, in some of which are stunning heritage hotels.

Osian
Surrounded by sand dunes, this ancient town north of Jodhpur in the Thar Desert contains the largest group of eighth- to 10th-century Hindu and Jain temples in Rajasthan. The typical Pratihara Dynasty **temple complex** is set on a terrace whose walls are finely decorated with mouldings and miniatures. The sanctuary walls have central projections with carved panels and curved towers rising above them. The doorways are usually decorated with river goddesses, serpents and scrollwork. The 23 temples are grouped in several sites to the north, west and south of the town. The western group contains a mixture of Hindu temples, including the **Surya Temple** (early eighth century) with beautifully carved pillars. The Jain **Mahavira Temple** (eighth to 10th centuries), the best preserved, 200 m further on a hillock, rises above the town, and boasts a fantastically gaudy interior. The 11th- to 12th-century **Sachiya Mata Temple** is a living temple of the Golden Durga. Osian is well worth visiting.

Khimsar
On the edge of the desert, 80 km northeast of Jodhpur, Khimsar was founded by the Jain saint Mahavir 2500 years ago. The isolated, battle-scarred 16th-century moated castle of which a section remains, had a *zenana* added in the mid-18th century and a regal wing added in the 1940s.

Nagaur
Foreigners Rs 50, Indians Rs 10, camera Rs 25, video Rs 50.

One of the finest forts with amazing restoration project, amazing hotel and often overlooked – a real gem. Nagaur, 137 km north of Jodhpur, was a centre of Chishti Sufis. It attracts interest as it preserves some fine examples of pre-Mughal and Mughal architecture.

The dull stretch of desert is enlivened by Nagaur's fort palace, temples and *havelis*. The city walls are said to date from the 11th- to 12th-century Chauhan period. Akbar built the mosque here and there is a shrine of the disciple of Mu'inuddin Chishti of Ajmer (see page 370). **Ahhichatragarh Fort**, which dominates the city, is absolutely vast and contains palaces of the Mughal emperors and of the Marwars. It was restored with help from the Paul Getty Foundation and under the watchful eye of Maharah Gaj Singh of Jodhpur. It is quite an exceptional renovation; the Akbar Mahal is stunningly elegant and perfectly proportioned. The fort also has excellent wall paintings and interesting ancient systems of rainwater conservation and storage, ably explained by a very knowledgeable curator. It was awarded a UNESCO Heritage Award in 2000. One of the most spectacular forts in Rajasthan, it now hosts the **World Sufi Spirit Festival** every February; see page 342.

Khichan

Four kilometres from Phalodi, southwest of Bikaner just off the NH15, is a lovely, picturesque village with superb red sandstone *havelis* of the Oswal Jains. Beyond the village are sand dunes and mustard fields, and a lake which attracts ducks and other waterfowl. The once quiet village has grown into a bustling agricultural centre and a prominent bird-feeding station. Jain villagers put out grain behind the village for winter visitors; up to 8000 demoiselle cranes and occasionally common eastern cranes can be seen in December and January on the feeding grounds. At present you can go along and watch without charge.

Pokaran

Pokaran, between Jaisalmer and Jodhpur, stands on the edge of the great desert with dunes stretching 100 km west to the Pakistan border. It provides tourists with a midway stopover between Bikaner/Jodhpur and Jaisalmer as it did for royal and merchant caravans in the past. The impressive 16th-century yellow sandstone **Pokaran Fort** ① *foreigners Rs 50, Indians Rs 10, camera Rs 50*, overlooking a confusion of streets in the town below, has a small museum with an interesting collection of medieval weapons, costumes and paintings. There are good views from the ramparts. Pokaran is also well known for its potters who make red-and-white pottery and terracotta horses/elephants. **Ramdeora**, the Hindu and Jain pilgrim centre nearby, has Bishnoi hamlets and is a preserve for blackbuck antelope, Indian gazelle, bustards and sand grouse. Ramdeora Fair (September) is an important religious event with cattle trading.

Khetolai, about 25 km northwest of Pokaran, is the site of India's first nuclear test explosion held underground on 18 March 1974, and of further tests in May 1998.

Balotra and around

The small textile town, 100 km southwest of Jodhpur, is known for its traditional weaving using pit looms and block prints, although many are now mechanized causing pollution of the Luni River. Nearby is the beautiful Jain temple with elephant murals at **Nakoda**. **Kanana**, near Balotra, celebrates **Holi** with stage shows and other entertainment. There is a *dharamshala* at Nakoda and guesthouses at Balotra.

At **Tilwara**, 127 km from Jodhpur, the annual **Mallinathji Cattle Fair** is a major event, which takes place just after **Holi** on the dry Luni riverbed. Over 50,000 animals are brought (although this has declined in recent years due to the drought), including Kapila (Krishna's) cows and Kathiawari horses, making it Rajasthan's largest animal fair. Few tourists make it this far so it is much less commercial than Pushkar. Try and go with a Rajasthani-speaking guide as the farmers and traders are very happy to allow you in on the negotiations as well as describing the key things to look for when buying a camel (the front legs should not rub against its belly, for instance). There are some interesting trade stalls including sword makers.

Salawas

Salawas, about 30 minutes' drive south from Jodhpur, is well known for its pit loom weaving. The village produces *durries*, carpets, rugs, bed covers and tents using camel hair, goat hair, wool and cotton in colourful and interesting patterns. You can visit the weavers' co-operatives such as **Roopraj** and **Salawas Durry Udhyog** (anyone on a Bishnoi village tour is normally frogmarched into one of them), where you can buy authentic village crafts, but watch out for high prices and pushy salesmen.

Luni

The tiny bustling village of Luni, 40 km from Jodhpur, sits in the shadow of the 19th-century red sandstone **Fort Chanwa** which has been converted to a hotel (see Where to stay, opposite). With its complex of courtyards, water wheels, and intricately carved façades, the fort and its village offer an attractive and peaceful alternative to the crowds of Jodhpur. The village of **Sanchean**, which you will pass through on the way, is worth exploring.

Rohet and Sardar Samand

Rohet, 50 km north of Jodhpur, was once a picturesque hamlet settled by the Bishnoi community. It is now a busy highway village although it has a busy bazar and is pleasant to wander around. At the end of the village a lake attracts numerous winter migrants in addition to resident birds. Here also are the family cenotaphs. **Rohetgarh**, a small 'castle' beside the lake, which has been converted in to a hotel (see Where to stay, page 342), has a collection of antique hunting weapons. The hotel will organize trips to the local Bishnoi villages. It is quite usual to see blue bull, black buck and other antelopes in the fields. Village life can be very hard in this arid environment but the Bishnoi are a dignified people who delight in explaining their customs. You can take part in the opium tea ceremony which is quite fun and somewhat akin to having a pint with the locals down at the pub.

The lake nearby is a beautiful setting for the royal 1933 art deco hunting lodge, **Sardar Samand Palace**. The lake attracts pelicans, flamingos, cranes, egrets and kingfishers, and the wildlife sanctuary has blackbuck, gazelle and nilgai. The water level drops substantially during summer; the lake has actually dried up from April to June in recent years. Sardar Samand is 60 km southeast of Jodhpur.

Nimaj and Chhatra Sagar

Chhatra Sagar is a reservoir close to the small feudal town of Nimaj, 110 km east of Jodhpur on the way to the Jaipur–Udaipur highway. The ex-ruling family has recreated a 1920s-style tented hunting lodge on the lake's dam, which offers amazing views over the water and a genuine family welcome (see Where to stay, below). The lake attracts an amazing array of birdlife.

Listings Around Jodhpur

Where to stay

Osian
There are some **$** guesthouses in town.

$$$$ Camel Camp
On the highest sand dunes, T0291-243 7023, www.camelcamposian.com.
A beautiful complex of 50 double-bedded luxury tents with modern conveniences (attached baths, hot showers), superb restaurant and bar plus an amazing pool – quite a sight at the top of a sand dune. Tariff inclusive of meals and camel safaris, ask in advance for jeep/camel transfers to avoid a steep climb up the dunes. Recommended.

Nagaur

$$$$ Ranvas (Jodhana Heritage)
T0291-257 2321, www.ranvasnagaur.com.
Stunningly restored *havelis* within the magical fort of Nagaur. This venture is extremely stylish and yet comfortable. With beautiful furnishings, sumptuous fabrics, rare artefacts, charming courtyards and secluded spots, Ranvas is effortlessly chic. The rooms are converted from the *havelis* of the 16 wives of the Royal Court. There is an amazing pool and delicious restaurant. Opt for a spectacular private tour of the fort – magical. Highly recommended.

$$$$ Royal Camp
T011-460 3550, www.jodhanaheritagehotels. com. Operates Oct-Mar and during the camel fair (when prices rise).
20 delightful deluxe 2-bed furnished tents (hot water bottles, heaters, etc), flush toilets, hot water in buckets, stunning dining area, all inside the fort walls. Although you seem very secluded, Nagaur fort is right in the middle of the city and not elevated, so you do get traffic and mosque noise. An experience.

$ Mahaveer International
Vijay Vallabh Chowk, near the bus stand, T01582-243158, www.minagaur.com.
Excellent cheaper option so that you can access this magical fort with less tourist traffic. 15 reasonable rooms, 7 a/c, huge dining hall, friendly knowledgeable manager.

Luni

$$$ Fort Chanwa
T02931-284216, www.fortchanwa.com.
47 good rooms in 200-year-old fort, not large but well furnished, individually designed, excellent Rajasthani meals in an impressive dining room, pleasant lawn for drinks, excellent pool and well managed.

$ Chhotaram Prajapat's Home Stay
Village Salawas, 20 km from Jodhpur on the way to Luni, T(0)94147 20724, www.salawashomestay.com.
Atmospheric taste of village life, in fact they call themselves "an initiative in reality" rather than a hotel! Simple mud hut rooms, local food, village walks and friendly atmosphere. Head here for a true Rajasthani experience.

Rohet and Sardar Samand

$$$$ Mihirgarh
1 hr from Rohet, T0291-243 1161, www.mihirgarh.com.
The 'sun fortress' is a new venture from the team at **Rohetgarh** (see below) offering stunning suites with private courtyards and plunge pools. There is also an infinity pool, spa, beautiful restaurant and barbeque area, and 360-degree views of the desert landscape. Breathtaking.

$$$ Rohetgarh
Rohet, T02936-268231, www.rohetgarh.com.
Come here to write a book. Both William Dalrymple and Bruce Chatwin have used the inspiring Rohetgarh to put pen to paper. Dating to 1622, there are a range of rooms (avoid rooms near the outdoor restaurant). Fine Rajasthani food, ordinary architecture but in a beautiful environment, pleasant lake view terraces, lovely pool, health club, riding and safaris to Bishnoi, Raika and artisans' villages, boating on the lake, a relaxing getaway. They have also set up a **Wilderness Camp** 17 km away in the desert.

Nimaj

There are a few hotels in Nimaj itself, but the most atmospheric place to stay is by the reservoir.

$$$$ Chhatra Sagar
4 km from Nimaj, Pali, T02939-230118, www.chhatrasagar.com. 1 Oct-31 Mar.
11 beautiful colonial-style tents on the banks of the very picturesque reservoir. The ex-rulers of Nimaj have recreated the hunting lodge of their forefathers to great effect, and still live on the lake themselves, so there's a very convivial family atmosphere. You might see a peacock fly across the lake. Safaris arranged – great village safari and bird walks, all meals included in the tariff (and the food is delicious). Really captures the magic of Rajasthani nature and village life. Highly recommended.

$$$$ Lakshman Sagar
Near Raipur village, Pali, T011-2649 4531, www.sewara.com.
Lakeside cottages in stunning desert locale. Although super stylish, the decor borrows from classic Rajasthan village life so it has a rustic chic vibe. There are plenty of outdoor spaces to sit and gaze out into the desert and a beautiful swimming pool to lounge by. Great for romantic getaways.

Festivals

Nagaur
Jan/Feb Cattle and Camel Fair. This popular is held just outside the town. There are camel races, cock fights, folk dancing and music. The fields become full of encampments of pastoral communities, tribal people and livestock dealers with their cattle, camels, sheep, goats and other animals.
Feb World Sufi Spirit Festival, www.worldsufi spiritfestival.org. Held in late Feb, this festival is hosted between the stunning Nagaur and Jodhpur's Mehrengarh forts. Bringing together Sufi musicians from around the world – the 2015 event had artists from Iran, Kazakhstan, Israel, the Atlas Mountains and *qawwalli* singers from Gujarat and Rajasthan, as well as whirling dervishes from Turkey and India's acclaimed Midival Punditz doing a dance set check their website for videos. Exceptional event. Book early to stay on site.

Shopping

Pokaran
Kashida, *just outside town, Jaisalmer–Bikaner Rd, T02994-222511*. Excellent handwoven crafts from the desert region, clean, well laid out, reasonably priced, profits help local self-help projects, part of the **URMUL** trust.

Jaisalmer
& around

The approach to Jaisalmer is magical as the city rises out of the vast barren desert like an approaching ship. With its crenellated sandstone walls and narrow streets lined with exquisitely carved buildings, through which camel carts trundle leisurely, it has an extraordinarily medieval feel and an incredible atmosphere. The fort inside, perched on its hilltop, contains some gems of Jain temple building, while beautifully decorated merchants' *havelis* are scattered through the town.

Unlike the other forts you visit in Rajasthan, Jaisalmer's is fully alive with shops, restaurants and guesthouses inside its walls and labyrinthine alleyways.

The town's charm has not failed to attract the attention of mass tourism and at times Jaisalmer can feel overrun with package tourists. Over the years, increased development has put pressure on the sewage, drainage and foundations of the fort. Several bastions crumbled a few years ago and several people were killed. These bastions have now been replaced, but you can see signs of water discolouration (see box, page 346).

If you find Jaisalmer's magic diminished there's always the romantic desolation of the Thar Desert, easily accessible beyond the edge of the city. Highlights include the remarkable ghost city of Kuldhara and, of course, camel rides.

The fort

On the roughly triangular-shaped Trikuta Hill, the fort stands 76 m above the town, enclosed by a 9-km wall with 99 bastions (mostly 1633-1647). Often called the Golden Fort because of the colour of its sandstone walls, it dominates the town. You enter the fort from the east from Gopa Chowk. The inner, higher fort wall and the old gates up the ramp (Suraj Pol, Ganesh Pol, Hawa Pol and Rang Pol) provided further defences. The Suraj Pol (1594), once an outer gate, is flanked by heavy bastions and has bands of decoration which imitate local textile designs. Take a walk through the narrow streets within the fort, often blocked by the odd goat or cow, and see how even today about 1000 of the town's people live in tiny houses inside the fort often with beautiful carvings on doors and balconies. It is not difficult to get lost.

As with many other Rajput forts, within the massive defences are a series of palaces, the product of successive generations of rulers' flights of fancy. The local stone is relatively easy to carve and the dry climate has meant that the fineness of detail has been preserved through the centuries. The *jali* work and delicately ornamented balconies and windows with wide eaves break the solidity of the thick walls, giving protection from the heat, while the high plinths of the buildings keep out the sand. '**Sunset Point**', just north of the fort, is popular at sundown for views over Jaisalmer.

The entire **Fort Palace Museum and Heritage Centre** ① *0800-1800 summer, 0900-1800 winter, foreigners Rs 250 includes an excellent audio guide and camera, Indians Rs 10, video Rs 150*, has been renovated and an interesting series of displays established, including sculpture, weapons, paintings and well-presented cultural information. The view from the roof, the highest point

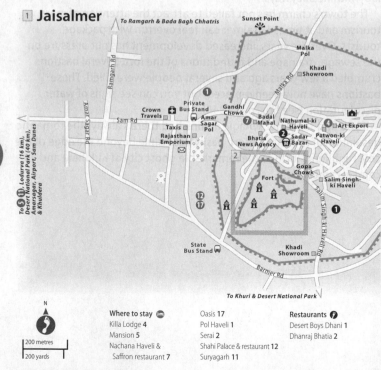

1 Jaisalmer

To Ramgarh & Bada Bagh Chhatris

Sunset Point

To Khuri & Desert National Park

Where to stay 🛏
Killa Lodge **4**
Mansion **5**
Nachana Haveli &
Saffron restaurant **7**

Oasis **17**
Pol Haveli **1**
Serai **2**
Shahi Palace & restaurant **12**
Suryagarh **11**

Restaurants 🍴
Desert Boys Dhani **1**
Dhanraj Bhatia **2**

Essential Jaisalmer

Finding your feet

Jaisalmer is on NH15 (Pathankot–Samakhiali). The nearest airport is at Jodhpur, 275 km away, which is connected to Jaisalmer by buses and several daily trains. Most long-distance buses arrive at the bus stand, a 15-minute walk from the fort, or take an auto-rickshaw or jeep. Your hotel may offer a pick-up so call ahead. If not, have a place in mind and prepare for a barrage of competing touts. Touts may board buses outside town to press you to take their jeep; it is better to walk 10-15 minutes from Amar Sagar Pol and choose a hotel. The presence of police is easing the situation. See Transport, page 349.

Best sand dune experiences

Sandboarding at Damodra
A night under the stars with
 the Shahi Palace team
Camel adventures with Trotters
See page 349 and box, page 351

Getting around

Unmetered jeeps and auto-rickshaws can be hired at the station but they are no help inside the fort so you may have to carry your luggage some distance uphill if you choose a fort hotel. Rickshaws are allowed into the fort at certain times. You can hire a bike from Gopa Chowk (Rs 30) though the town is best explored on foot. Most hotels and restaurants are clustered around the two chowks and inside the fort.

---

inside the fort, is second to none. The **Juna Mahal** (circa 1500) of the seven-storey palace with its *jali* screens is one of the oldest Rajasthani palaces. The rather plain *zenana* block to its west, facing the *chauhata* (square) is decorated with false *jalis*. Next to it is the *mardana* (men's quarters)

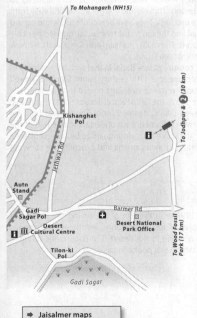

To Mohangarh (NH15)

Kishanghat
Pol

Jethwal Rd

Auto
Stand

Gadi
Sagar Pol

Barmer Rd

Desert
Cultural Centre

Desert National
Park Office

Tilon-ki
Pol

Gadi Sagar

To Jodhpur & ❷ (30 km)

To Wood Fossil
Park (17 km)

including the Rang Mahal above the Hawa Pol, built during the reign of Mulraj II (1762-1820), which has highly detailed murals and mirror decoration. **Sarvotam Vilas** built by Akhai Singh (1722-1762) is ornamented with blue tiles and glass mosaics. The adjacent **Gaj Vilas** (1884) stands on a high plinth. Mulraj II's **Moti Mahal** has floral decoration and carved doors.

The open square beyond the gates has a platform reached by climbing some steps; this is where court was held or royal visitors entertained. There are also fascinating **Jain temples** (12th-16th centuries) ① *0700-1200, Rs 10, camera Rs 50, video Rs 100, leather shoes not permitted,* within the fort. Whilst the Rajputs were devout Hindus they permitted the practice of Jainism. The **Parsvanatha** (1417) has a fine gateway, an ornate porch and 52 subsidiary shrines surrounding the main structure. The brackets are elaborately carved as maidens and dancers. The exterior of the **Rishbhanatha** (1479) has more than 600 images as decoration whilst clusters of towers form the roof of the **Shantinatha** built at the same time. **Ashtapadi** (16th century) incorporates the Hindu deities of Vishnu, Kali and Lakshmi into its decoration. The **Mahavir Temple** ① *view 1000-1100,* has an emerald statue. The **Sambhavanatha** (1431) ① *1000-1100,* has vaults beneath it that were used for document storage. The **Gyan Bhandar** here is famous for its ancient manuscripts.

ON THE ROAD
Jaisalmer in Jeopardy

Jaisalmer in Jeopardy is a UK-based charity fighting to preserve the unique historical architecture of the city. Through raising awareness and funds, it has achieved the restoration of buildings such as the Rajput Palace and Rani-ka Mahal (Maharani's Palace) and helped ensure that Jaisalmer Fort is listed on the World Monuments Fund '100 Most Endangered Sites in the World'.

Some visitors feel that it is unethical to stay in the fort guesthouses and add to the problems of water consumption and waste disposal. As far back as the late 1990s guesthouses inside the fort were offered incentives to start their businesses in new locations outside the walls, although only one, Shahi Palace Guest House, took up the offer. Nowadays, thanks to greater awareness, there are many beautiful guesthouses both within the walls of the fort and outside gazing up at the fairy tale. Jaisalmer in Jeopardy want to ensure that the Jaisalmer Fort can be enjoyed for another 400 years. Check out www.jaisalmer-injeopardy. org and www.intach.org (Indian National Trust for Art and Cultural Heritage) for further information.

Havelis

There are many exceptional *havelis* in the fort and in the walled town. Many have beautifully carved façades, *jali* screens and oriel windows overhanging the streets below. The ground floor is raised above the dusty streets and each has an inner courtyard surrounded by richly decorated apartments. Further east, **Patwon-ki Haveli** (1805) ① *1030-1700, foreigners Rs 150, Indians Rs 50 (audio tour Rs 250/camera Rs 50)*, is the best of the restored *havelis* and you get a beautiful view from the rooftop. It's a cluster of five *havelis* built for five brothers. They have beautiful murals and carved pillars. A profusion of balconies cover the front wall and the inner courtyard is surrounded by richly decorated apartments; parts have been well restored. The main courtyard and some roofs are now used as shops. The views from the decorative windows are stunning.

Inside Amar Sagar Pol, the former ruler's 20th-century palace **Badal Mahal** with a five-storeyed tower, are some fine carvings. Near the fort entrance, the 17th-century **Salim Singh-ki Haveli** ① *0800-1800, Rs 10, good carvings but is being poorly restored, over-long guided tour*, is especially attractive with peacock brackets; it is often referred to as the 'Ship Palace' because of its distinctive and decorative upper portion. **Nathumal-ki Haveli** (1885), nearer Gandhi Chowk, was built for the prime minister. Partly carved out of rock by two craftsmen, each undertaking one half of the house, it has a highly decorative façade with an attractive front door guarded by two elephants. Inside is a wealth of decoration; notice the tiny horse-drawn carriage and a locomotive showing European influence.

Desert Cultural Centre
Gadisar Circle, T02992-252 188, 1000-1700, Rs 10.

The Desert Cultural Centre was established in 1997 with the aim of preserving the culture of the desert. The museum contains a varied display of fossils, paintings, instruments, costumes and textiles which give an interesting glimpse in to life in the desert. The charismatic founder, Mr Sharma, is a fount of information and has written several books on Jaisalmer.

BACKGROUND

Jaisalmer

Founded by Prince Jaisal in 1156, Jaisalmer grew to be a major staging post on the trade route across the forbidding Thar Desert from India to the West. The merchants prospered and invested part of their wealth in building beautiful houses and temples with the local sandstone. The growth of maritime trade between India and the West caused a decline in trade across the desert which ceased altogether in 1947. However, the wars with Pakistan (1965 and 1971) resulted in the Indian government developing the transport facilities to the border to improve troop movement. This has also helped visitors to gain access. Today, the army and tourism are mainstays of the local economy; hotel touts and pushy shopkeepers have become a problem in recent years.

Listings Jaisalmer *maps p344 and below*

Tourist information

RTDC
Near TRC, Station Rd, Gadi Sagar Pol, T02992-252406. Open 0800-1200, 1500-1800.
Also has a counter at railway station.

Where to stay

$$$$ The Serai
Near Chandan village, 30 km outside Jaisalmer, T02997-200014, www.sujanluxury.com.

2 Jaisalmer Fort

➡ Jaisalmer maps
1 Jaisalmer, page 344
2 Jaisalmer Fort, page 347

Where to stay 🛏
Desert Haveli 9
Jaisal Castle 3
Killa Bhawan 2
Suraj 10
Temple View 7

Restaurants 🍴
Jaisal Italy 1
Kanchan Shree 5

N
100 metres
100 yards

Already guest starring on the front cover of *Condé Nast Traveller* magazine, this luxurious resort is inspired by the colours of the desert, with warm sandstone and beautiful natural textiles. The beautiful swimming pool is based on an Indian step-well and 6 of the luxury tents have their own plunge pools. Sit by a desert fire for delicious supper with your feet in the sand. This is the most stylish way to experience desert life. It's a place for landmark moments, like honeymoons. Breathtaking.

$$$$ Suryagarh
Kahala Phata, Sam Rd, T02992-269269, www.suryagarh.com.
Stunning heritage-style project and the outer façade of the hotel mirrors the famous Jaisalmer fort. Beautiful suites, vibey bar area and lovely indoor pool. The spa is exceptional. Attention to detail everywhere you turn.

$$$$-$$$ The Mansion
Sam Rd, Mool Sagar, T(0)96160 22760, themansion11@ymail.com.
Don't be fooled by the name: this is a stunning luxury tented camp out in the desert, beautifully created by Riyaz Ahmed. You could spend all your time here just gazing out into the desert from the beautiful pool.

$$$ Killa Bhawan
Kotri Para, T02992-251204, www.killabhawan.com.
7 rooms, 2 a/c, in characterful old building, beautiful interiors but teeny tiny rooms, the classiest place in the fort by some margin. They also run a lovely boutique hotel **Killa Lodge ($$)**, opposite the picturesque Patwon-ki below the fort.

$$ Nachana Haveli
Gandhi Chowk, T02992-252110,
www.nachanahaveli.com.
Converted 18th-century Rajput *haveli* with
carved balconies and period artefacts. Rooms are
stylishly done with great bathrooms, particularly
upstairs suites. Rooftop restaurant in the season,
has very authentic feel overall. Friendly family.
Highly recommended.

$$-$ Hotel Pol Haveli
Near Geeta Ashram, Dedansar Rd,
T02992-250131.
New *haveli*-style building with stylish decor and
chilled-out vibe. Beautiful furnishings, especially
the beds. Slightly odd area as it feels you are
staying in a dusty village, but it is just a short
walk from Gandhi Chowk and the heart of things.
Good views of sunset point and the fort in the
distance from their attractive rooftop café.

$$-$ Jaisal Castle
In the fort, T02992-252362,
www.jaisalcastle.com.
11 quirky rooms in rambling, characterful old
haveli. Room 101 is particularly lovely, ironically.
Beautiful communal areas.

$$-$ Oasis
Near Shahi Palace, Shiv St, T02992-255 920.
Another offering from the brothers at **Shahi
Palace** (see below), Oasis boasts bigger rooms
than its older sibling and some of the 7 rooms
have a/c. It's beautifully decorated with
sumptuous fabrics with lovely loungy diwans in
the rooms. The same team have opened a larger
25 room hotel in Gandhi Chowk – Heera Court.

$$-$ Shahi Palace
Shiv St, near SBBJ bank, outside the fort,
T02992-255920, www.shahipalacehotel.com.
16 super-stylish rooms in a beautiful sandstone
building with outstanding bathrooms. The team
of 4 brothers here work hard to make everyone
feel at home. Beautiful chic rooftop restaurant
with lots or archways and even a wooden boat
from Karnataka masquerading as a flowerpot. The
view of the fort is outstanding as is their food.
They provide free station pick-up and all manner
of travel support. Excellent reports on their camel
safaris. Wholeheartedly recommended.

$$-$ Suraj
Behind Jain Temple, T02992-251623,
www.hotelsurajjaisalmer.webs.com.
Suraj boasts beautiful rooms in this 530-year-
old *haveli* overlooking the Jain temple. It may
have seen better days and can get quite chilly in
winter, but it's very atmospheric.

$ Temple View
Next to Jain Temple, T02992-252832,
luna_raju@yahoo.com.
7 well-decorated rooms, 3 with attached bath,
attention to detail, great view of the temples
from the roof, entertaining owner.

$ The Desert Haveli
Near Jain Temple, T(0)7568-455656,
www.deserthaveli-hostel.com.
7 characterful rooms in a charming, 400-year-old
haveli, honest, friendly owner. Very atmospheric.
Recommended.

Restaurants

$$-$ Desert Boy's Dhani
Near Nagar Palika, Dhibba, T(0)94622 50149.
Lovely garden restaurant with good range of
Indian classics and traditional Rajasthani food.
Folk dance and music.

$ Dhanraj Bhatia
Scrumptious Indian sweets including Jaisalmeri
delights (try *godwa*).

$ Jaisal Italy
In the main fort gate.
Charming, cool interiors with windows looking
up the pathway to the fort: excellent bruschetta
and a great meeting point before or after-fort
walks. Recommended.

$ Kanchan Shree
Gopa Chowk, 250 m from Salim Singh-ki Haveli.
Lassis (19 varieties) and ice cream floats, as well
as cheap, tasty *thalis*. Many recommendations
for this place.

$ Saffron
Nachana Haveli (see Where to stay, above).
Another hotel with great views of the fort at
night. Beautiful decor, lovely food and a relaxed
vibe. Often with live music and dance.

$ Shahi Palace
See Where to stay, left.
Great food from this beautiful rooftop restaurant
with amazing views of the fort. Try traditional
Rajasthani meals like *kej sangari* (desert beans)
and *kadi pakoda* (yoghurt turmeric curry) and,
if they're not busy, you can go in the kitchen
and watch how they make it. And if you need a
little oomph, they have a cappuccino machine.
Recommended.

Entertainment

The more expensive hotels have bars.
Desert Cultural Centre, *Gadisar Circle*.
2 puppet shows every evening, at 1830
and 1930, Rs 30 entry.

Festivals

Feb/Mar Holi is especially colourful but
gets riotous.

Shopping

Shops open 1000-1330 and 1500-1900. Jaisalmer
is famous for its handicrafts – stone-carved
statues, leather ware, brass enamel engraving,
shawls, tie-dye work, embroidered and block
printed fabrics, but garments are often poorly
finished. Look in **Siré Bazar**, **Sonaron-ka-Bas**
and shops in the narrow lanes of the old city
including **Kamal Handicrafts**, **Ganpati Art
Home**, and **Damodar** in the fort. In Gandhi
Chowk: **Rajasthali**, closed Tue; the good, fairly
priced selection at **Khadi Emporium** at the end
of the courtyard just above Narayan Niwas Hotel.
Jaisalmer Art Export, behind Patwon-ki Haveli
has high-quality textiles. For textiles try **Amrit
Handprint Factory**, just inside Sagar Gate on the
left. **Geeta Jewellers** on Aasni Rd near Fort Gate
is recommended, good value and no hard sell.

What to do

Camel safaris
Camel safaris are big business in Jaisalmer (see
box, page 351). Many guesthouses offer their
own trips. **Hotel Shahi Palace** (see Where to stay)
offer recommended camel safaris and camps
which respect the desert and offer a wonderful
insight into desert life.
Damodra Desert Camp, *T(0)9783-207819, www.
damodra.com*. For a luxury desert experience,
Damodra offer camel safaris, sandboarding and
what they dub 'a spiritual winddown' in the
desert south west of Jaisalmer. Beautiful tents,
pristine sand and delicious campfire suppers.
Real Desert Man Safari, *near Madrasa Rd,
T(0)9649-865500, www.realdesertmansafari
jaisalmer.com*. Recommended outfit heading
into the desert for short day trips, over night
camps and longer treks. Magical.
Trotters' Independent Travels, *Gopa Chowk,
near Bhang Shop, T(0)9414-469292, www.trotters
jaisalmer.net*. Warm smiles from those who return
from a camel safari with Trotters – you are well

looked after and well fed on all desert excursions,
long or short.

Cooking
Karuna, *Ishar Palace, in the fort near
the Laxminath Temple, T02992-253062,
karunaacharya@yahoo.com*. Learn Indian
cookery with Karuna. Courses of any length
can be arranged. Highly recommended.

Swimming
Gorbandh Palace (non-residents Rs 350);
also **Heritage Inn** (meal plus swim deals)
and **Fort Rajwada**.

Tour operators
Rajasthan Tourism, *T02992-252406*.
City sightseeing: half day, 0900-1200.
Fort, *havelis*, Gadisagar Lake. Sam sand dunes:
half day, 1500-1900.
Sunny Tours, *Shahi Palace, T(0)9414-365495,
www.sunnytourntravels.com*. One of the oldest
tour operators in Jaisalmer they offer top notch
travel support and camel and jeep safaris.
Professional. Recommended.
Thar Safari, *Gandhi Chowk, near Trio, T02992-
252722*. Reliable tours and desert safaris.

Transport

Bus State Roadways buses, from near the
station just to the southwest of the old city walls,
T02992-251541, and at SBBJ Bank Government
Bus Stop. There is now a new Volvo bus running
daily Jaisalmer to **Delhi**, via **Jodhpur** and **Jaipur**,
but takes a whopping 18 hrs – leaves 1730 from
Jaisalmer (from Delhi to Jaisalmer starts at 1730
too). Services to **Ajmer**, **Barmer**, **Bikaner** (330 km
on good road, 8 hrs, Rs 160), **Jaipur** (638 km);
Abu Rd for **Mount Abu**. **Jodhpur** (285 km, 0500,
0600, 0630, 0730 and 2230, 5 hrs). **Udaipur**
(663 km, a tiring 14 hrs). **Bikaner** 0600 and 2130
from Hanuman Chowk. Private deluxe coaches
from outside Amar Sagar Pol or Airforce Circle,
to a similar range of destinations. Most hotels
can reserve bus tickets. Operators: **Marudhara
Travels**, Station Rd, T02992-252351; **National
Tours**, Hanuman Choraha, T02992-252348.

Train Jaisalmer Railway Station is on the eastern
side of the city walls. The military presence can
make getting tickets slow; book in advance if
possible. Foreign Tourist Bureau with waiting
room, T02992-252354, booking office T02992-
251301. *Jsm Hwh Sf Exp 12372*, to **Bikaner** (5½ hrs)
and **Delhi** (15 hrs). Can get very cold (and dusty)
try and book 3AC where bedding is provided.

Amar Sagar and Lodurva

The pleasant **Amar Sagar**① *5 km northwest of Jaisalmer, foreigners Rs 30, Indians free, camera Rs 50, video Rs 100,* was once a formal garden with a pleasure palace of Amar Singh (1661-1703) on the bank of a lake which dries up during the hot season. The Jain temple there has been restored.

A further 10 km away is **Lodurva**① *0630-1930, foreigners Rs 20, Indians free, camera Rs 50, video Rs 100,* which contains a number of Jain temples that are the only remains of a once-flourishing Marwar capital. Rising honey-coloured out of the desert, they are beautifully carved with *jali* outside and are well maintained and worth visiting. The road beyond Lodurva is unsealed.

★ Khuldara

This is a fascinating ghost town, and well worth stopping at on the way to Sam. The story goes that 400 or so years ago, Salim Singh, the then prime minister of Jaisalmer, took a distinct shine to a Paliwal girl from this village. The rest of the Paliwal people did not want this beautiful girl taken away from them, and so after intense pressure from the prime minister decided to abandon the village one night, with everyone dispersing in different directions, never to return. It is remarkably well preserved, and best visited with a guide who can point out the most interesting buildings from the many still standing. **Khabha**, just south of here, is also recommended.

Sam Dunes (Sain)

Rs 10, car Rs 20 (camera fees may be introduced), camel rates start at Rs 100 per hr.

Sam Dunes, 40 km west of Jaisalmer, is popular for sunset camel rides. It's not a remote spot in the middle of the desert but the only real large stretch of sand near town; the dunes only cover a small area, yet they are quite impressive. Right in the middle of the dunes, **Sunset View** is like a fairground, slightly tacky with lots of day-trippers – as many as 500 in the high season; the only escape from this and the camel men is to walk quite a way away.

Khuri

Rs 10, buses from Jaisalmer take 1½ hrs, jeep for 4 people Rs 450 for a sunset tour.

Khuri, 40 km southwest of Jaisalmer, is a small picturesque desert village of decorated mud-thatched buildings which was ruled by the Sodha clan for four centuries. Visitors are attracted by shifting sand dunes, some 80 m high, but the peace of the village has been spoilt by the growing number of huts, tents and guesthouses which have opened along the road and near the dunes. Persistent hotel and camel agents board all buses bound for Khuri. The best months to visit are from November to February.

Thar Desert National Park

Rs 150 per person; car permits Rs 500; permits are required, apply 2 days in advance to Forest Department, T02992-252489, or through travel agents.

The Thar Desert National Park is near Khuri, the core being about 60 km from Jaisalmer (the road between Sam and Khuri is passable with a high-clearance vehicle). The park was created to protect 3000 sq km of the Thar Desert, the habitat for drought resistant, endangered and rare species which have adjusted to the unique and inhospitable conditions of extreme temperatures. The desert has undulating dunes and vast expanses of flat land where the trees are leafless, thorny and have long roots. Fascinating for birdwatching, it is one of the few places in India where the great Indian bustard is proliferating (it can weigh up to 14 kg and reach a height of 40 cm). In winter it also attracts the migratory houbara bustard. You can see imperial black-bellied and common Indian sand grouse, five species of vulture, six of eagle, falcons, and flocks of larks at Sudasari, in the core of the park, 60 km from Jaisalmer. Chinkaras are a common sight, as are desert and Indian foxes. Blackbuck and desert cat can be seen at times. Close to sunset, you can spot desert hare in the bushes.

ON THE ROAD

On a camel's back

Camel safaris draw many visitors to Rajasthan. They allow an insight into otherwise inaccessible desert interiors and a chance to see rural life, desert flora and wildlife. The 'safari' is not a major expedition into the middle of nowhere. Instead, it is often along tracks, stopping off for sightseeing at temples and villages along the way. The camel driver/owner usually drives the camel or rides alongside (avoid one sharing your camel), usually for two hours in the morning and three hours in the afternoon, with a long lunch stop in between. There is usually jeep or camel cart backup with tents and 'kitchen' close by, though thankfully out of sight. It can be fun, especially if you are with companions and have a knowledgeable camel driver.

Camel safaris vary greatly in quality with prices ranging from around Rs 500 per night for the simplest (sleeping in the open, vegetarian meals) to those costing Rs 4500 (deluxe double-bedded tents with attached Western baths). Bear in mind that it is practically impossible for any safari organizer to cover his costs at anything less than Rs 500 – if you're offered cheaper tours, assume they'll be planning to get their money back by other means, ie shopping/drug selling along the way. Safaris charging Rs 500-1000 can be adequate (tents, mattresses, linen, cook, jeep support, but no toilets). It's important to ascertain what is included in the price and what are extras.

The popular 'Around Jaisalmer' route includes **Bada Bagh**, **Ramkunda**, **Moolsagar**, **Sam dunes**, **Lodurva** and **Amar Sagar** with three nights in the desert. Some routes now include **Kuldhara**'s medieval ruins and the colourful **Kahla** village, as well as **Deda**, **Jaseri lake** (good birdlife) and **Khaba** ruins with a permit. Most visitors prefer to take a two days/one night or three days/two nights camel safari, with jeep transfer back to Jaisalmer.

Camel safaris are also popular around Bikaner, where there is a Camel Research Centre – even if you don't fancy a camel ride, maybe you want to try camel milk ice cream.

A more comfortable alternative is to be jeeped to a tented/hut camp in the desert as a base for a night and enjoy a camel trek during the day without losing out on the evening's entertainment under the stars. Pre-paid camel rides have now been introduced – Rs 80 for a 30-minute ride. For some, "half an hour is enough on a tick-ridden animal". For tour operators offering camel safaris, see below and page 349.

Sunny Tours from Shahi Palace, T(0)9414-365495, www.sunnytourntravels.com, is one of the oldest tour operators in Jaisalmer. They are a professional team offering fantastic camel and jeep safaris. They provide tents in the winter as well as delicious food, fruit and cookies and your very own camel. Their camel safari can last anything from half a day and their route takes in the usual peaceful dunes and tribal villages.

In Bikaner, you can head out into the desert with **Camel Man Safaris** (www.camelman.com) or delve deeper into the dunes at the lesser-known Kaku with great safaris arranged by **Kaku Castle** (www.kakusafaris.com).

If you fancy a more regal and upmarket affair try **Damodra Desert Camp**, www.damodra.com, in Jaisalmer, or **Ossian Camp** near Jodhpur, www.camelcampossian.com, who both have luxurious Rajasthani tents with attached toilets near the dunes.

No matter who you go with, make sure you cover up all exposed skin and use sunscreen to avoid getting burnt.

While most hotels will try to sell you a tour by 4WD vehicle, this is no longer necessary. You can hire any jeep or high-clearance car (Ambassador, *Sumo*) for the trip to the park. Off-the-road journeys are by camel or camel cart (park tour Rs 50 and Rs 150 respectively).

Barmer

This dusty desert town, 153 km south of Jaisalmer, is surrounded by sand dunes and scrublands. It is a major centre for wood carving, *durrie* rug weaving, embroidery and block printing (you can watch printers in Khatriyon ki galli). The 10th- to 11th-century Kiradu temples, though badly damaged, are interesting. **Someshvara** (1020), the most intact, has some intricate carving but the dome and the tower have collapsed. The town itself is surprisingly industrial and not especially charming; those interested in seeking out handicrafts are well advised to locate **Gulla**, the town's only guide. He can normally be contacted at the **KK Hotel** (see Where to stay, page 352), or emailed in advance on gulla_guide@yahoo.com. The small number of visitors to Barmer means that he doesn't get too many opportunities to practise his profession; be sure to explain exactly what you would like to see, and try to fix a price before starting the tour.

Dhorimana

The area further south of Barmer has some of the most colourful and traditional Bishnoi villages and a large population of *chinkaras* and desert fauna. The village women wear a lot of attractive jewellery but may be reluctant to be photographed so it is best to ask first. **PWD Rest House** has clean and comfortable rooms.

Listings Around Jaisalmer

Where to stay

For other desert getaway options, see Camel safaris, pages 349 and 351.

Khuldara

$$ Dreamtime Bungalow
18 km west of Jaisalmer, behind the abandoned Khuldara heritage village, T(0)9413-865745, www.dreamtimebungalow.com.
Beautifully desert-ed, these attractive bungalows are definitely off the beaten track – a perfect place to connect with the desert. Comfortable bungalows and delicious food on top. Great for families.

Sam Dunes

$ Sam Dhani (RTDC)
T02992-252392.
8 huts facing the dunes, very busy in the late afternoon and sunset but very pleasant at night and in the early morning. Includes all meals.

Khuri

$$$ The Mama's Resort and Camp
Khuri, T03014-274042, www. themamasjaisalmer.com.
Stay in the desert in style with luxury tents and 4-poster beds. There are also nice rooms, but the tents win. You can book packages which include a camel safari.

$ Registhan Guest House
Village Dhoba, Khuri, T(0)9784-840053, www.registhanguesthouse.com.
Colourful place to stay close to the dunes – campfires and dancing. Attractive mud huts.

Barmer

$$ New KK Hotel
Station Rd, T02982-221087.
Close to the original cheaper **KK Hotel**, this has more of a modern vibe. The original **KK** is quite reasonable too.

Festivals

Sam Dunes
Feb Desert Festival, 3-day festival with *son et lumière* amid the sand dunes at Sam, folk dancing, puppet shows and camel races, camel polo and camel acrobatics, Mr Desert competition. You can also watch craftsmen at work. Rail and hotel reservations can be difficult.

Barmer
Mar Thar Festival highlights desert culture and handicrafts.

Transport

Barmer
From Barmer, the hot and dusty bus journey to **Jaisalmer** takes 4 hrs; **Mt Abu**, 6 hrs.

Alwar,
Sariska & around

Alwar, in northeastern Rajasthan, has fascinating monuments including the Bala Quilla fort, overlooking the town, and the Moti Doongri fort, in a garden. The former, which was never taken by direct assault, has relics of the early Rajput rulers, the founders of the fort, who had their capital near Alwar. Over the centuries it was home to the Khanzadas, Mughals, Pathans, Jats and finally the Rajputs. There are also palaces and colonial period parks and gardens. The town itself is very untouristy and spread over a large area, making navigation difficult at times, but is generally very welcoming.

The 480-sq-km Sariska reserve is a dry deciduous forest set in a valley surrounded by the barren Aravalli hills. The princely shooting reserve of the Maharajah of Alwar was declared a sanctuary in 1955. Exactly 50 years later it acquired the dubious honour of being the first Project Tiger reserve to be declared free of tigers, the last ones presumably having been poached. Nevertheless, the park still holds some wildlife, and a certain rugged appeal.

Alwar

fortified hilltop town, a good base for visiting Sariska

Alwar is protected by the hilltop Bala Quilla, which has the remains of palaces, temples and 10 tanks built by the first rulers of Alwar. It stands 308 m above the town, to the northwest, and is reached by a steep 4WD track (permission must be obtained from the police station). There are splendid views.

The city palace, **Vinai Vilas Mahal** (1840) ① *closed Mon, 1000-1700, free, museum Rs 50 foreigners, Rs 5 for Indians*, with intricate *jali* work, ornate *jarokha* balconies and courtyards, houses government offices on the ground floor, and a fine museum upstairs. The palace is impressive but is poorly maintained, with dusty galleries (you may find children playing cricket in the courtyard). The Darbar Room is closed, and the throne, miniatures and gilt-edged mirrors can only be viewed through the glass doors and windows or by prior permission of the royal family (not easily obtained). The museum is interesting, housing local miniature paintings, as well as some of the Mughal, Bundi and other schools, an array of swords, shields, daggers, guns and armour, sandalwood carvings, ivory objects, jade art,

Essential Alwar, Sariska and around

Finding your feet

Alwar is well connected to both Delhi and Jaipur by bus and train, and is only a three-hour drive from Delhi, or 1½ hours from Jaipur. Sariska is an easy 35-km drive from Alwar. See Transport, page 355.

Alwar

As Mughal power crumbled, Rao Pratap Singhji of Macheri founded Alwar as his capital in 1771. He shook off Jat power over the region and rebelled against Jaipur suzerainty making Alwar an independent state. His successors lent military assistance to the British in their battles against the Marathas in AD 1803, and in consequence gained the support of the colonial power. The Alwar royals were flamboyant and kept a fleet of custom-made cars (including a throne car and a golden limousine), and collected solid silver furniture and attractive walking sticks.

musical instruments and princely relics. Next to the city palace are the lake and royal cenotaphs. On the south side of the tank is the Cenotaph of Maharaja Bakhtawar Singh (1781-1815) which is made of marble on a red sandstone base. The gardens are alive with peacocks and other birds. To the right of the main entrance to the palace is a two-storey processional elephant carriage designed to carry 50 people and be pulled by four elephants.

The **Yeshwant Niwas**, built by Maharaja Jai Singh in the Italianate style, is also worth seeing. Apparently on its completion he disliked it and never lived in it. Instead he built the **Vijay Mandir** in 1918, a 105-room palace beside Vijay Sagar, 10 km from Alwar. Part of it is open with prior permission from the royal family or their secretary, but even without it is worth seeing from the road, with its façade resembling an anchored ship. When not in Delhi, the royal family now lives in Phool Bagh, a small 1960s mansion opposite the new stadium.

Alwar to Sariska

Kesroli, 10 km northeast, has a seven-turreted 16th-century fort atop a rocky hillock, now sympathetically (though more modestly) restored. It is a three-hour drive from Delhi and convenient for an overnight halt. Turn left off the NH8 at Dharuhera for Alwar Road and you will find it. **Kushalgarh Fort** is en route to Sariska. Near Kushalgarh is the temple complex of **Talbraksha** (or Talvriksh) with a large population of rhesus macaque monkeys. Guides report panthers having been seen near the **Cafeteria Taal** here, probably on the prowl for monkeys near the canteen.

Listings Alwar, Sariska and around

Tourist information

Alwar

Rajasthan Tourist Reception Centre
Nehru Marg, opposite railway station, T0144-234 7348. Closed weekends.

Where to stay

Alwar

$$$$-$$$ Hill Fort Kesroli (Heritage Hotel)
Alwar Rd, Kesroli, T01468-289352, www.neemranahotels.com.
Comfortable, if eccentric, airy rooms and plush suites, set around a courtyard, delicious lunch and dinner buffet included, some of the best food in Rajasthan, relaxing, and in a lovely isolated rural location. Often overrun by groups though.

$$$$-$$$ Neemrana Fort Palace
65 km north of Alwar, Delhi–Jaipur Highway, T01494-246 007, www.neemranahotels.com.
The pinnacle of the Neemrana properties, this palace looks like it has come straight out of a fairy-tale, with many tiers and turreted rooms. There are many rooms with their own private rooftop terraces. Ziplining available. Good for a taste of Rajasthan if you are on a short trip as it's relatively close to Delhi.

$$$-$$ Hotel Hill View
Moti Doongri, T0144-329 8111, www.hillviewalwar.com.
Excellent value for money, mid-range hotel run by an enthusiastic and helpful manager. Clean and comfortable – most rooms have views across to Moti Doongri. The hotel will happily arrange a tiger safari and guide.

$ Hotel Yuvraj Kothi Rao
31 Moti Dungri, T0144-270 0741,
www.hotelkothirao.com.
Dubbed a 'House Hotel' by the very charming
family who offer up home cooked meals and take
great pride in their home-style hospitality. It's a
bit shabby around the edges for the price.

Alwar to Sariska

$$ Burja Haveli
*Burja, 7th Mile Stone Rajgarh Rd, T(0)0144-
288 390, www.burja-haveli.com.*
Atmospheric little place outside of Alwar. It's a
240-year-old *haveli* with a homely atmosphere.

Transport

Alwar
Bus Regular buses to/from **Delhi** (4½-5 hrs) and
Jaipur. Frequent service to **Bharatpur** (2½ hrs),
Deeg (1½ hrs) and **Sariska** (1 hr).

Train Alwar is the nearest station to Sariska.
New Delhi: *Shatabdi Exp 12016*, not Sun, 2½ hrs.
Delhi: *Jodhpur Delhi Exp 14860*, 3 hrs; *Jaipur-JAT
Exp 12413*, 3 hrs.

Sariska Tiger Reserve

lush green wildlife sanctuary but don't expect to see a tiger

Despite the lack of tigers, Sariska provides plenty of opportunities to see wildlife. The
main rhesus monkey population lives at Talvriksh near Kushalgarh, while at Bhartri-
Hari you will see many langurs. The chowsingha, or four-horned antelope, is found
here, as are other deer including chital and sambar. You may see nilgai, wild boar,
jackals, hyenas, hares and porcupines; leopards are present but rarely seen since
the reserve is closed at night to visitors. During the monsoons many animals move
to higher ground, but the place is alive with birds. There are ground birds such as
peafowl, jungle fowl, spur fowl and grey partridge. Babblers, bulbuls and treepies are
common round the lodges. Since 2008, a number of tigers have been relocated from
Ranthambhore National Park further south, in the hope of repopulating Sariska, but
only time will tell if this has been a success.

The organization **Save Our Tigers** ① *www.save
ourtigers.com*, sponsored by the communications
company Aircel, has launched a big TV and
billboard campaign to raise awareness. In the
2011 Tiger Census, numbers were up across the
country to 1706, but only by four in Rajasthan.

During the monsoon travel through the
forest may be difficult. The best season to visit is
between November and April. In the dry season,
when the streams disappear, the animals
become dependent on man-made water holes
at Kalighatti, Salopka and Pandhupol.

Outside the reserve

Sariska, the gateway to the national park, is a
pleasant, quiet place to stay and relax. Trips by
jeep are possible to forts and temples nearby.
The **Kankwari Fort** (2 km) – where Emperor
Aurangzeb is believed to have imprisoned
his brother **Dara Shikoh**, the rightful heir to
the Mughal throne – is within the park. The
old **Bhartrihari** temple (6 km) holds a fair and

Essential Sariska Tiger Reserve

Entry information

Rs 470 including still camera, Indians Rs 60,
video Rs 200; vehicle Rs 250 per trip. Early
morning jeep trips from Sariska Palace Hotel
or Tiger Den (see Where to stay, below)
venture into the park as far as the Monkey
Temple, where you can get a cup of tea and
watch monkeys and peacocks. Jeep hire for
non-standard trips in the reserve Rs 2500 for
three hours, excluding entry fees. Compulsory
guide Rs 150. Closed July-September. For
online booking and more infomation, see
www.rajasthanwildlife.rajasthan.gov.in.

Permits

You need to get permit from the Forest
Registry Office for early morning and late
afternoon safaris (0600-1000 and 1500-1800).

six-hour dance-drama in September and October. **Neelkanth** (33 km) has a complex of sixth- to 10th-century carved temples. **Bhangarh** (55 km), on the outskirts of the reserve, is a deserted city of some 10,000 dwellings established in 1631. It was abandoned 300 years ago, supposedly after it was cursed by a magician.

Listings Sariska Tiger Reserve

Where to stay

$$$ Alwar Bagh
T(0)9799-398610, next door to Sariska Tiger Camp (see below).
Extremely well-run hotel in a peaceful location. 32 deluxe rooms and suites in 2 separate villas and a traditional *'haveli* style' building. Suites offer such delights as hanging beds and private rooftop terraces, most rooms overlook pretty orchard gardens and a beautiful pool, very child friendly, great food, solar panels and an opportunity to become involved in village social projects for a day. Recommended.

$$$ Sariska Tiger Camp
19 km towards Alwar on the main road, T(0)9314-017210.
Eccentric design with 20 simply furnished 'mud concept' rooms in traditional 'village style with wall paintings'; well-tended garden and swimming pool, the restaurant has a lovely terrace. Often caters for groups and feels a bit 'empty' without them.

$$ Tiger Den (RTDC)
In the sanctuary, T(0)9928-369139.
Superbly located tourist bungalow with views of hill and park, 30 rooms with attached baths (hot showers) but shabby, dirty public areas, vegetarian restaurant, bar and shop sells cards and souvenirs, nice garden, friendly management.

$ Forest Rest House
Main Rd, opposite turning to Kushalgarh, T0144-284 1333.
6 simple rooms, only open during winter.

Deeg, Bharatpur
& around

For a typical dusty and hot North Indian market town, Deeg gained the somewhat surprising reputation as the summer resort of the Raja of Bharatpur. Located on the plains just northwest of Agra, the raja decided to develop his palace to take full advantage of the monsoon rains. The fort and the 'monsoon' pleasure palace have ingenious fountains and are of major architectural importance, their serenity in stark contrast to the barely controlled chaos of the rest of the town.

One of the most popular stopping places on the 'Golden Triangle', Bharatpur is best known for its Keoladeo Ghana Bird Sanctuary. Once the hunting estate of the Maharajas of Bharatpur, with daily shoots recorded of up to 4000 birds, the 29-sq-km piece of marshland, with over 360 species, is potentially one of the finest bird sanctuaries in the world, but has suffered badly in recent years from water deprivation.

Lesser visited are the sights off the road which connects Agra to Jaipur, NH11, which sees huge volumes of tourist traffic. The Balaji temple is particularly remarkable.

Essential Deeg, Bharatpur and around

Finding your feet

The nearest airport is Jaipur. There are regular bus services from both Mathura and Bharatpur to Deeg, with the road from Bharatpur being by far the smoother of the two. Bharatpur, 40 km south of Deeg, has good bus and train connections with Agra, Jaipur and Delhi. Keoladeo Ghana National Park is 4 km south of Bharatpur town.

Tip...
If Agra is too busy for you, stay in Bharatpur and drive to Agra for a day trip.

The rubble and mud walls of the square fort are strengthened by 12 bastions and a wide, shallow moat. It has a run-down *haveli* within, but is otherwise abandoned. The entrance is over a narrow bridge across the moat, through a gate studded with anti-elephant spikes. Negotiating the undergrowth, you can climb the ramparts which rise 20 m above the moat; some cannons are still in place on their rusty carriages. You can walk right around along the wide path on top of the walls and climb the stairs to the roof of the citadel for good views.

The **palaces** ① *opposite the fort, Sat-Thu 0930-1730, Rs 200*, are flanked by two reservoirs, Gopal (west) and Rup Sagar (east), and set around a beautifully proportioned central formal garden in the style of a Mughal *char bagh*. The main entrance is from the north, through the ornamental, though unfinished, Singh (Lion) Pol; the other gates are Suraj (Sun) Pol (southwest) and Nanga Pol (northeast).

The impressive main palace **Gopal Bhavan** (1763), bordering Gopal Sagar, is flanked by Sawon and Bhadon pavilions (1760), named after the monsoon months (mid-July to mid-September). Water was directed over the roof lines to create the effect of sheets of monsoon rain. The palace still retains many of the original furnishings, including scent and cigarette cases made from elephant's feet and even a dartboard. There are vegetarian and non-vegetarian dining rooms, the former particularly elegant, with floor seating around a low-slung horseshoe-shaped marble table.

Outside, overlooking the formal garden, is a beautiful white marble *hindola* (swing) which was brought as booty with two marble thrones (black and white) after Suraj Mal attacked Delhi. To the south, bordering the central garden, is the single-storey marble **Suraj Bhavan** (circa 1760), a temple, and **Kishan Bhavan** with its decorated façade, five arches and fountains.

Tip...
If you have to spend a night in Deeg there are a couple of very basic options near the bus stand.

Bhandarej, 62 km from Jaipur, south of NH11 after Dausa, is a relaxing place to stop for the night. From here the NH11 goes through a series of small towns and villages to Sakrai (77 km) which has a good roadside RTDC restaurant.

Some 15 km after Sakrai is the turning for Balaji, home to the truly extraordinary **Balaji Temple**. People who believe themselves to have been possessed by demons come here, to have the evil spirits exorcized. The scenes on the first floor in particular are not for the faint-hearted; methods of restraining the worst afflicted include chaining them to the walls and placing them under large rocks. Most exorcisms take place on Tuesdays and Saturdays, when there are long queues to get in. From **Mahuwa** a road south leads through Hindaun to Karauli (64 km).

Noted for its pale red sandstone, **Karauli** (1348) was the seat of a small princely state which played a prominent part in support of the Mughal emperors. The impressive **City Palace** has some fine wall paintings, stone carvings and a fine Darbar Hall. Fairs are held at nearby temples lasting a week to a fortnight. Mahavirji, associated with the 24th Tirthankar Mahavir, is an important Jain pilgrimage centre.

Where to stay

$$$-$$ Bhanwar Vilas Palace (Heritage Hotel)
Karauli, T07464-220024, www.karauli.com.
29 comfortable rooms, including 4 a/c suites in
a converted palace, most air-cooled, cheaper
in cottage, Rajasthani restaurant, pool, tours,
camping, amazingly ornate lounge and dining
halls, real air of authenticity. Recommended.

$$$-$$ Chandra Mahal
*Peharsar, Jaipur–Agra Rd, Nadbai, Peharsar,
T(0)86969 19085, www.amritara.co.in.*
23 rooms in simply furnished, 19th-century Shia
Muslim *haveli* with character, quality set meals
(from Rs 250), jeep hire and good service.

Festivals

Feb/Mar **Sivaratri**. In Karauli, this is a colourful
festival celebrating Lord Siva.
Mar/Apr **Kaila Devi**. Festival celebrates Kaila
Devi, an in carnation of Goddess Lakshmi and
her abundance. Held in Karauli.

Transport

Train Nearly all trains on the main Delhi–
Mumbai line stop at Gangapur City, 30 km
from Karauli.

Bharatpur

gateway to the wonderful Keoladeo Ghana National Park

Just 2 km north of Keoladeo Ghana National Park, Bharatpur is a noisy and dusty
place, though it does have a couple of historic sights, including Lohagarh Fort.

Built by Suraj Mal, the Lohagarh Fort, which occupies the island at the centre of Bharatpur village,
appears impregnable, but the British, initially repulsed in 1803, finally took it in 1825. There are
double ramparts, a 46-m-wide moat and an inner moat around the palace. Much of the wall has
been demolished but there are the remains of some of the gateways. Inside the fort are three
palaces (circa 1730) and Jewel House and Court to their north. The **museum** ① *1000-1630, closed Fri,
Rs 3*, in the Kachhari Kalan, exhibits archaeological finds from villages nearby, dating from the first
to 19th centuries as well as paintings and artefacts; the armoury is upstairs.

    Peharsar ① *23 km away, Rs 30 to 'headman' secures a tour*, with a carpet-weaving community,
makes a very interesting trip from Bharatpur.

Where to stay

Most of Bharatpur's accommodation is out of
town, close to the bird sanctuary. Also if you
want to avoid the busy-ness of Agra and have
your own transport, it is a good option to stay
around the bird sanctuary and drive.

Festivals

2-4 Feb **Brij Festival**. Honours lord Krishna with
folk dances and drama relating the love story of
Radha-Krishna.

Transport

Air The nearest airport is at Jaipur (175 km).

Bus The main stand is at Anah Gate just off
NH11 (east of town). Buses from Bharatpur tend to
get very crowded but give an insight into Indian
rural life. To **Agra** (55 km, 1½ hrs), **Deeg**; **Delhi**,
185 km, 6 hrs; and **Jaipur** 175 km, 5 hrs.

Train An auto-rickshaw from train station
(6 km) to park Rs 80; from bus stand (4 km), Rs 50.
Delhi (**ND**): *Golden Temple Mail 12904*, 3 hrs; this
train also leaves Bharatpur at 1030 for **Sawai
Madhopur** (2½ hrs) and **Kota**. Also to **Delhi**
Golden Temple Mail 12903, 3½ hrs.

Keoladeo Ghana National Park has been designated a World Heritage Site, and can only be entered by bicycle or cycle rickshaw, thus maintaining the peaceful calm of the park's interior.

The late Maharaja Brajendra Singh converted his hunting estate into a bird sanctuary in 1956 and devoted many of his retired years to establishing it. He had inherited both his title and an interest in wildlife from his deposed father, Kishan Singh, who grossly overspent his budget – 30 Rolls Royces, a private jazz band and some extremely costly wild animals including "dozens of lions, elephants, leopards and tigers" – for Bharatpur's jungles.

Tragically, in 2004 the state government bowed to pressure from local farmers and diverted 97% of the park's water supply for irrigation projects. The catastrophic damage to its wetlands has resulted in the loss of many of the migratory birds on which Bharatpur's reputation depends and potentially they will lose their UNESCO status. The battle goes on and in recent years the Chief Minister Ashok Gehlot has released water from the nearby Panchna Dam to help restore the park's natural habitat. It's an ongoing story but certainly the nature of the park is changing.

Wildlife

The handful of rare Siberian cranes that used to visit Bharatpur each year have been missing since 2003. The ancient migratory system, some 1500 years old, may have been lost completely, since young cranes must learn the route from older birds (it is not instinctive). These cranes are disappearing worldwide – eaten by Afghans and sometimes employed as fashionable 'guards' to protect Pakistani homes (they call out when strangers approach). The Sarus crane can still be seen in decent numbers.

Other birds that can be spotted include Asian openbills, Ferruginous ducks, spoonbills, storks, kingfishers, a variety of egrets, ducks and coots, as well as birds of prey including Laggar falcon, greater-spotted eagle, marsh harrier, Scops owl and Pallas' eagle. There are also chital deer, sambar, nilgai, feral cattle, wild cats, hyenas, wild boar and monitor lizards, whilst near Python Point, there are usually some very large rock pythons.

Essential Keoladeo Ghana National Park

Finding your feet

Official cycle-rickshaws at the entrance are numbered and work in rotation, Rs 50 per hour for two people (drivers may be reluctant to take more than one). This is well worthwhile as some rickshaw-wallahs are very knowledgeable and can help identify birds (and know their location): a small tip is appropriate. The narrower paths are not recommended as the rough surface makes rickshaws too noisy. It is equally feasible to just walk or hire a bike, particularly once you're familiar with the park. If there's any water, a boat ride is highly recommended for viewing.

Park information

Entry costs Rs 400, video Rs 200, professional video Rs 1500, payable each time you enter. Information and guides are available from **RTDC**, Hotel Saras, T05644-222542, and **Wildlife Office**, Forest Rest House, T05644-222488. Good naturalist guides (costing Rs 70-100 per hour, depending on group size) are also available at the gate. There are cafés inside the park, or ask your hotel to provide a packed lunch.

When to go

The park is closed May and June. Winters can be very cold and foggy, especially in the early morning. It is traditionally best November to February when it is frequented by northern hemisphere migratory birds. To check in advance whether there is any water, try contacting the tourist information numbers above, or use the contact form on www.rajasthanwildlife.rajasthan.gov.in.

Tip...

It is worth buying the well-illustrated *Collins Handguide to the Birds of the Indian Sub-continent* (available at the reserve and in bookshops in Delhi, Agra, Jaipur, etc). *Bharatpur: Bird Paradise* by Martin Evans (Lustre Press, Delhi) is also extremely good.

Birds, accustomed to visitors, can be watched at close range from the road between the boat jetty and Keoladeo temple, especially at Sapan Mori crossing. Dawn (which can be very cold) and dusk are the best times; trees around Keoladeo temple are favoured by birds for roosting, so are particularly rewarding. Midday may prove too hot so take a book and find a shady spot. Carry a sun hat, binoculars and plenty of water.

Keoladeo Ghana National Park

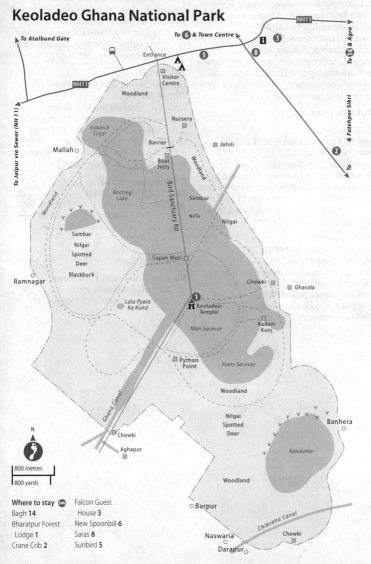

Where to stay

Bagh **14**
Bharatpur Forest
 Lodge **1**
Crane Crib **2**
Falcon Guest
 House **3**
New Spoonbill **6**
Saras **8**
Sunbird **5**

Where to stay

Inside the park

$$ Bharatpur Forest Lodge (Ashok)
2.5 km from the gate, 8 km from railway and bus stand, T05644-222760,
www.bharatpurforestlodge.com.
Book in advance. 17 comfortable a/c rooms with balconies, pricey restaurant and bar, very friendly staff, peaceful, boats for birdwatching, animals (eg wild boar) wander into the compound. Entry fee each time you enter park.

Outside the park

$$$$ The Bagh
Agra Rd, 4 km from town, T05644-228 333,
www.thebagh.com.
Set in a beautiful orchard, space is everything here. There are 14 elegant, well decorated, centrally a/c rooms with outstanding bathrooms. Attractive dining room, lovely pool, beautiful 200-year-old gardens, some may find facilities rather spread out. Recommended.

$$$-$$ Sunbird
Near the park gate, T05644-225701,
www.hotelsunbird.com.
Attractive red-brick building with clean rooms with hot shower, better on the 1st floor. Now also 4 deluxe cottages, pleasant restaurant, friendly staff, bike hire, good value, well maintained. Highly recommended.

$$-$ New Spoonbill
Near Saras, T05644-223 571,
www.hotelspoonbill.com.
4 good-size rooms, nice decor and a family friendly vibe. There is also the original **Spoonbill** down the road with cheaper rooms but still a good standard with shared bathroom, run by a charming ex-army officer, courteous and friendly service, good food, bike hire.

$ Crane Crib
Fatehpur Sikri Rd, 3 km from the park,
T05644-222224.
Attractive sandstone building, 25 rooms of wide-ranging standards and tariffs, all reasonable value. Small cinema where wildlife films are shown nightly, bonfires on the lawn during winter and welcoming staff. Run by the honorary warden of the park. Recommended.

$ Falcon Guest House
Near Saras, T05644-223815.
10 clean, well-kept rooms, some a/c with bath, owned by a naturalist, good information, bike hire, quiet, very helpful, warm welcome, off-season discount.

Transport

Bicycles There are bikes for hire near Saras or ask at your hotel; Rs 40 per day; hire on the previous evening for an early start next day.

Ranthambhore
National Park

⭐ This is one of the finest tiger reserves in the country, although even here their numbers have dwindled due to poachers. Most visitors spending a couple of nights here are likely to spot one of these wonderful animals, although many leave disappointed.

Set in dry deciduous forest covering 410 sq km between the Aravalli and Vindhya hills, some trees trailing matted vines, the park's rocky hills and open valleys are dotted with small pools and fruit trees. Scrubby hillsides surrounding Ranthambhore village are pleasantly peaceful, their miniature temples and shrines glowing pink in the evening sun before they become silhouetted nodules against the night sky.

Once the private tiger reserve of the Maharajah of Jaipur, in 1972 the sanctuary came under the Project Tiger scheme following the government Wildlife Protection Act. By 1979, 12 villages inside the park had been 'resettled' into the surrounding area, leaving only a scattering of people living within the park.

Should the tigers evade you, you may well spot leopard, hyena, jackal, marsh crocodile, wild boar, langur monkey, bear, and many species of deer and birdlife. The park's 10th-century fort, proudly flanked by two impressive gateways, makes a good afternoon trip after a morning drive.

Essential Ranthambhore National Park

Finding your feet

The park is 10 km east of Sawai Madhopur, with the approach along a narrow valley; the main gate is 4 km from the boundary.

Getting around

The park has good roads and tracks. Entry is by park jeep (gypsy) or open bus (canter) on four-hour tours; 16 jeeps and 20 canters are allowed in at any one time. Some lodges organize trips or there are a few jeeps and canters reserved for same-day bookings, which involves queuing and you may get gazumped by hotels. Jeeps are better but must be booked in advance so request one when booking your lodge (passport number required) or try online. Visitors are picked up from their hotels.

Park information

You can book online at www.rajasthanwildlife.rajasthan.gov.in. The park is open 1 October-30 June for two sessions a day: winter 0630-1030, 1400-1800; summer 0600-1000, 1430-1830, but check as times change. Jeep hire: Rs 800-1200 per person for up to five passengers; jeep entry Rs 125; guide Rs 150. A seat in a canter, Rs 500-550, can often be arranged on arrival, bookings start at 0600 and 1330 for same-day tours; advance bookings from 1000-1330. Individual entry fees are extra: foreigners Rs 475-530 (canter/jeep), Indians Rs 75, camera free, video Rs 200. Regulations on park entry in India keep changing, so double check with your hotel beforehand.

When to go

The park is best from November to April, though the vegetation dies down in April. Maximum temperatures are 28-49°C. It can be very cold at dawn in winter.

> **Best** wildlife conservation
> **Tiger Nation Campaign**, see Wildlife in the park, right column
> **Travel Operators for Tigers**, see Wildlife for the future, opposite page
> **Khem Villas Hotel Conservation Project**, page 366

Wildlife in the park

Tiger sightings are recorded almost daily, usually in the early morning, especially from November to April. Travellers report the tigers seem "totally unconcerned, ambling past only 10 m away". Sadly, poaching is prevalent: between 2003 and 2005, 22 tigers were taken out of the park by poachers operating from surrounding villages – a wildlife scandal that spotlighted official negligence in Ranthambhore. Since then the population has recovered somewhat, with about six cubs being born each year. Across the country, the Tiger Census of 2010 revealed that tiger numbers are up by 295 making a total of 1706 tigers. The current estimate is that there are 61 including newborns in the park. As well as Save the Tiger campaigns from Aircel, there is a Travel Operators for Tigers group which many of the hotels in Ranthambhore are a part of. It is also worth checking out the conservation efforts of Tiger Nation – www.tigernation.org.

The lakeside woods and grassland provide an ideal habitat for herds of chital and sambar deer and sounders of wild boar. Nilgai antelope and chinkara gazelles prefer the drier areas of the park. Langur monkeys, mongoose and hare are prolific. There are also sloth bear, a few leopards, and the occasional rare caracal. Crocodiles bask by the lakes, and some rocky ponds have freshwater turtles. Extensive birdlife includes spurfowl, jungle fowl, partridges, quails, crested serpent eagle, woodpeckers, flycatchers, etc. There are also water birds like storks, ducks and geese at the lakes and waterholes. Padam Talao by the Jogi Mahal is a favourite water source; there are also water holes at Raj Bagh and Milak.

Ranthambhore Fort

The entrance to the fort is before the gate to the park. Open from dawn to dusk, though the Park Interpretation Centre near the small car park may not be open. Free entry.

There is believed to have been a settlement here in the eighth century. The earliest historic record is of it being wrested by the Chauhans in the 10th century. In the 11th century, after Ajmer was lost to Ghori, the Chauhans made it their capital. Hamir Chauhan, the ruler of Ranthambhore in the 14th century, gave shelter to enemies of the Delhi sultanate, resulting in a massive siege and the Afghan conquest of the fort. The fort was later surrendered to Emperor Akbar in the 16th century when Ranthambhore's commander saw resistance was useless, finally

Wildlife for the future

Travel Operators for Tigers (TOFT), www.toftigers.org, was established in 2002 to promote responsible wildlife tourism across India. In partnership with **Global Tiger Patrol**, www.globaltigerpatrol.org, TOFT counts accommodation providers and international and domestic tour operators among its members, and works across Rajasthan, Madhya Pradesh and Uttarakhand. Funded through a small levy imposed by participating operators, TOFT aims to reverse the decline in tiger numbers, to support the park's efforts against poaching, to assist local community employment, as well as to cover the costs of running park tours. To ensure such tourism is sustainable, there are 'best practice' guidelines for tour operators, service providers and visitors. Visitors are urged to book lodges and tours with TOFT members and to abide by a code of conduct when visiting conservation areas. TOFT also seeks to empower and inspire local communities to become involved in wildlife tourism projects to benefit themselves and to help park conservation. Also among the organization's initiatives are waste and water management, trade cooperatives and fair wage plans. They hold an annual TOFT Wildlife Tourism Awards in Delhi. In the 2010 Tiger Census, tiger population was on the up – a rise of 295 to 1706. So initiatives like TOFT are hopefully raising awareness amongst the travel industry and individuals.

Ranthambhore National Park

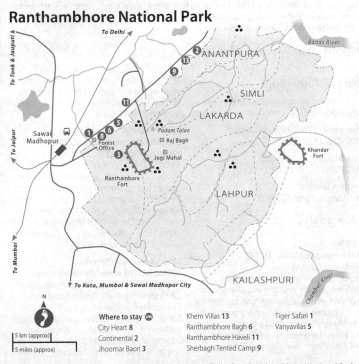

Where to stay	Khem Villas **13**	Tiger Safari **1**
City Heart **8**	Ranthambhore Bagh **6**	Vanyavilas **5**
Continental **2**	Ranthambhore Haveli **11**	
Jhoomar Baori **3**	Sherbagh Tented Camp **9**	

Ranthambhore National Park

Much of the credit for Ranthambhore's present position as one of the world's leading wildlife resorts goes to India's most famous 'tiger man', Mr Fateh Singh Rathore. His enthusiasm for all things wild has been passed on to his son, Dr Goverdhan Singh Rathore, who set up the Prakratik Society in 1994. This charitable foundation was formed in response to the increasing human encroachment on the tiger's natural forest habitat; in 1973 there were 70,000 people living around Ranthambhore Park, a figure which has now increased to 200,000.

The human population's rapidly increasing firewood requirements were leading to ever-more damaging deforestation, and the founders of the Prakratik Society soon realized that something needed to be done. Their solution was as brilliant as it was simple; enter the 'biogas digester'. This intriguingly named device, of which 225 have so far been installed, uses cow dung as a raw material, and produces both gas for cooking, negating the need for firewood, and organic fertilizer, which has seen crop yields increase by 25%. The overwhelming success of this venture was recognized in 2004, when the Prakratik Society was presented with the prestigious Ashden Award for Sustainable Energy in London.

passing to the rulers of Jaipur. The forests of Ranthambhore historically guarded the fort from invasions but with peace under the Raj they became a hunting preserve of the Jaipur royal family. The fort wall runs round the summit and has a number of semi-circular bastions, some with sheer drops of over 65 m and stunning views. Inside the fort you can see a Siva temple – where Rana Hamir beheaded himself rather than face being humiliated by the conquering Delhi army – ruined palaces, pavilions and tanks. Mineral water, tea and soft drinks are sold at the foot of the climb to the fort and next to the Ganesh temple near the tanks.

Listings Ranthambhore National Park *map p365*

Tourist information

For background information on the park and photography tips, see www.ranthambhore.com.

Conservator of Forests/Field Director
T07462-220223.

Forest Officer
T07462-221142.

Rajasthan Tourism
Hotel Vinayak, T07462-220808.

Where to stay

$$$$ Khem Villas
Sherpur-Khiljipur, T07462-252347,
www.khemvilas.com.
Super-stylish accommodation beautifully complementing the environment. Over 25 years ago this was essentially barren land, but over the years it has been replanted with indigenous flora. The family here is pioneering tiger conservation and there are incredibly knowledgeable in-house naturalists. There are beautiful rooms, and tents and cottages; the latter have stunning open-air bathrooms. Great for romantics, families and nature-lovers alike. Whole-heartedly recommended.

$$$$ Sherbagh Tented Camp
Sherpur-Khiljipur, T011-4617 2700,
www.sujanluxury.com. 1 Oct-30 Mar.
Award-winning eco-camp with luxury tents and hot showers, bar, dinner around fire, lake trips for birders, stunning grounds and seated areas for quiet contemplation, jungle ambience, well organized. All meals included. Beautiful shop on site. Owner Jaisal Singh has put together a new book *Ranthambhore – The Tiger's Realm*. Highly recommended.

$$$$ Vanyavilas (Oberoi)
T07462-223999, www.oberoihotels.com.
Very upmarket 8-ha garden resort set around a recreated *haveli* with fantastic frescoes. 25 unbelievably luxurious a/c tents (wooden floors, marble baths). There are, elephant rides, wildlife lectures, dance shows in open-air auditorium, and a beautiful spa. Elephants greet you at the door for the full maharajah expreience.

$$$ Jhoomar Baori (RTDC)
Ranthambore Rd, T07462-220495.
Set high on a hillside, this former hunting lodge is an interesting building and offers fantastic views of the area. 12 quirky rooms, varying in size, plus a small bar, reasonable restaurant and beautifully decorated communal lounges on each floor.

$$$-$$ Ranthambore Bagh
Ranthambhore Rd, T(0)8239-166777, www.ranthambhore.com.
12 tents and 12 simple but attractive rooms in this pleasantly laid-back property owned by a professional photographer and his lovely family. Pride has been taken in every detail. Fantastic food including traditional Rajasthani and atmospheric suppers around the campfire. Highly recommended for insider tiger knowledge.

$$ Tiger Safari
Ranthambore Rd, T07462-221137, www.tiger safariresort.com.
14 cosy rooms, 4 attractive a/c cottages, very clean, hot shower, quiet, jeep/bus to the park, very helpful, good value, ordinary food but few other options. Recommended.

$$-$ Ranthambhore Haveli
Opposite FCI, Ranthambore Rd, T(0)77259 36603, www.ranthambhorehaveli.com.
Basic large rooms behind a pretty façade, in a convenient location for the park.

$ City Heart
Ranthambhore Rd, 100 m from Ranthambhore Bagh, T07462-233 402.
Good, spacious rooms, some with TV – convenient location for park and amenities.

Shopping

Dastkar, www.dastkar.org, the original women's collective shop is near Sherbagh. Many locals have jumped on the 'Women's Collective Crafts' bandwagon but Dastkar is the only genuine one. The collective empowers women by making them self sufficient. They started with just 6 women, but now employ 360 women to do quilting, patchwork, block printing and sequin embroidery based on traditional local skills that were dying out. Beautiful fabrics, clothes, toys and collectibles are sold at extremely fair prices. Highly recommended.

Transport

Bus The bus stand is 500 m from Sawai Madhopur Railway Station. Buses go to **Kota** and **Jaipur**, but trains are quicker and more pleasant.

Train The railway station at Sawai Madhopur, T07462-220222, is on the main Delhi–Mumbai line. To **Jaipur**: *Ranthambore Exp 12465*, 2¼ hrs. **Mumbai**: *Ag Kranti Rjdhn 12954*, 13½ hrs. **Jodhpur**: *Ranthambore Exp 12465*, **Mumbai**: *Ag Kranti Rjdhn 12954*, 13½ hrs. **New Delhi** (via Bharatpur and Mathura) *Golden Temple Mail 12903*, 6 hrs; *Kota Jan Shtbdi 12059*, 5½ hrs.

Ajmer
& Pushkar

Although geographically close, these towns could hardly be more different. Ajmer is a rather crowded and traffic-choked city. Most travellers choose to stay in laidback Pushkar, 13 km away, and visit Ajmer on a day trip.

Situated in a basin at the foot of Taragarh Hill (870 m), Ajmer is surrounded by a stone wall with five gateways. Renowned throughout the Muslim world as the burial place of Mu'inuddin Chishti, who claimed descent from the son-in-law of Mohammad, seven pilgrimages to Ajmer are believed to equal one to Mecca. Every year, especially during the annual Islamic festivals of Id and Muharram, thousands of pilgrims converge on this ancient town on the banks of Ana Sagar Lake. Many visitors are discouraged by the frantic hustle of Ajmer on first arrival, but it's worth taking time to explore this underrated city.

Separated from Ajmer by Nag Pahar (Snake Mountain), Pushkar lies in a narrow valley overshadowed by rocky hills, which offer spectacular views of the desert at sunset. The lake at its heart is one of India's most sacred, and is almost magically beautiful at dawn and dusk. The village is transformed during the celebrated camel fair into a colourful week of heightened activity.

Sambhar Lake

The salt lake, one of the largest of its kind in India, until recently attracted thousands of flamingos and an abundance of cranes, pelicans, ducks and other waterfowl; some 120 species of bird have been recorded. However, the poor monsoons of recent years have caused the lake to dry up leaving only a few marshy patches. Check the situation before visiting. Nilgai, fox and hare are spotted around the lake. The saline marshes are used for the production of salt. **Sakambari Temple**, nearby, dedicated to the ancestral deity of the Chauhans, is believed to date from the sixth century.

Kuchaman

Kuchaman is a large village with temples and relics. Many visitors stop here for tea and snacks between Shekhawati and Ajmer. If you do stop, make time for a visit to the fort; it is a unique experience.

Before the eighth century, Kuchaman lay on the highly profitable Central Asian caravan route. Here Gurjar Pratiharas built the massive **cliff-top fort** with 10 gates leading up from the Meena bazar in the village to the royal living quarters. The Chauhans drove the Pratiharas out of the area and for some time it was ruled by the Gaurs. From 1400, it has been in the hands of the Rathores who embellished it with mirrors, mural and gold work in superb palaces and pavilions such as the golden Sunheri Burj and the mirrored Sheesh Mahal, both in sharp contrast to the fort's exterior austerity. The Sariska Palace Group have restored and renovated the fort at enormous cost.

You can also visit the **Krishna temple** with a 2000-year-old image, and the **Kalimata ka Mandir** which has an eighth-century black stone deity and you can shop in the **Meena Bazar** or watch local village crafts people.

Kishangarh

Enormous blocks of marble in raw, polished and sculpted forms line the road into Kishangarh, the former capital of a small princely state founded by Kishan Singh in 1603, with a fort facing Lake Gundalao. Local artists – known for their depiction of the Krishna legend and other Hindu themes – were given refuge here by the royal family during the reign of the Mughal emperor, Aurangzeb, who, turning his back on the liberal views of earlier emperors, pursued an increasingly zealous Islamic purity. Under their patronage the artists reached a high standard of excellence and they continue the tradition of painting Kishangarh miniatures which are noted for sharp facial features and elongated almond-shaped eyes. Most of those available are cheap copies on old paper using water colours instead of the mineral pigments of the originals. The town has a bustling charm, and is an interesting place to wander around.

The fort palace stands on the shores of Lake Gundalao. Its **Hathi Pol** (Elephant Gate) has walls decorated with fine murals and, though partly in ruins, you can see battlements, courtyards with gardens, shady balconies, brass doors and windows with coloured panes of glass. The temple has a fine collection of miniatures.

Essential Ajmer and Pushkar

Finding your feet

Pushkar has relatively few direct buses, but Ajmer is well connected by bus and train to the main towns and cities. The station is in the centre, while the main bus stand is 2 km east. Buses to Pushkar leave from the State Bus Stand, and also from a general area 1 km northwest of the station, near the Jain temple. In Pushkar, most buses arrive at the Central (Marwar) Bus Stand, to the usual gauntlet of touts; others pull in at a separate stand 10 minutes' walk east of the lake.

Getting around

The main sights and congested bazars of Ajmer, which can be seen in a day at a pinch, are within 15 to 20 minutes' walk of the railway station but you'll need a rickshaw to get to Ana Sagar. Pushkar is small enough to explore on foot. Hire a bike to venture further. See Transport, pages 373 and 378.

Best sacred places

Dargah of Khwaja Mu'inuddin Chishti, page 370
Nasiyan Jain Temple, page 371
Climbing up to Savitri Temple, page 374

Roopangarh

About 20 km from Kishangarh, Roopangarh was an important fort of the Kishangarh rulers founded in AD 1649 on the old caravan route along the Sambhar Lake. The fort stands above the village which is a centre for craft industries – leather embroidery, block printing, pottery and handloom weaving can all be seen. The Sunday market features at least 100 cobblers making and repairing *mojdi* footwear.

Listings Jaipur to Ajmer

Where to stay

$$$$ Kuchaman Fort (Heritage Hotel)
Kuchaman, T(0)9811-143684.
35 distinctive a/c rooms in a part of the fort, attractively furnished, restaurant, bar, jacuzzi, gym, luxurious pools (including a 200-year-old cavernous one underground), camel/horse riding, royal hospitality, superb views and interesting tour around the largely unrestored fort.

$$$ Phool Mahal Palace
Old City, Kishangarh, T01463-247405,
www.royalkishangarh.com.
Superbly located at the base of Kishangarh Fort and perched on the banks of Gundalao Lake

(dries up in summer), this 1870 garden palace has 21 well-maintained a/c rooms, as well as an elegant lounge and dining room, all with period furnishings and marble floors. Some of the rooms are beautifully adorned with frescoes – the bathing pictures are particularly lovely. See the website for their other stunning property Kishangarh Fort Palace.

Transport

Train and jeep For **Sambhar Lake** take the train to **Phulera**, 7 km from Sambhar village, 9 km from the lake. Jeeps charge Rs 50 for the transfer.

Kishangarh is an important railway junction between Jaipur and Ajmer, with regular trains from both places.

Ajmer

mystical Sufi inspiration with a beautiful mosque

Set around the Ana Sagar lake, Ajmer is surrounded by the Aravalli Hills. In the heart of the old town is the shrine of Khwaja Mu'inuddin Chishti, founder of the Chistiya Sufi order and considered the second holiest Muslim site after Mecca.

Dargah of Khwaja Mu'inuddin Chishti (1143-1235)
The main gate is reached on foot or by tonga or auto-rickshaw through the bazar.

The tomb of the Sufi saint (also called 'The Sun of the Realm') was begun by Iltutmish and completed by Humayun. The Emperor Akbar first made a pilgrimage to the shrine to give thanks for conquering Chittor in 1567, and the second for the birth of his son Prince Salim. From 1570 to 1580 Akbar made almost annual pilgrimages to Ajmer on foot from Agra, and the *kos minars* (brick marking pillars at about two-mile intervals) along the road from Agra are witness of the popularity of the pilgrimage route.

On their first visit, rich Muslims pay for a feast of rice, ghee, sugar, almonds, raisins and spices to be cooked in one of the huge pots in the courtyard inside the high gateway. These are still in regular use. On the right is the **Akbar Masjid** (circa 1570); to the left, an assembly hall for the poor. In the inner courtyard is the white marble **Shah Jahan Masjid** (circa 1650), 33 m long with 11 arches and a carved balustrade on three sides. In the inner court is the square *dargah* (tomb), also white marble, with a domed roof and two entrances. The ceiling is gold-embossed velvet, and silver rails and gates enclose the tomb. At festival times the tomb is packed with pilgrims, many coming from abroad, and the crush of people can be overpowering.

The whole complex has a unique atmosphere. The areas around the tomb have a real feeling of community; there is a hospital and a school on the grounds, as well as numerous shops. As you approach the tomb the feeling of religious fervour increases – as does the barrage of demands for

A saint of the people

Khwaja Mu'inuddin Chishti probably came to India before the Turkish conquests which brought Islam sweeping across Northern India. A sufi, unlike the Muslim invaders, he came in peace. He devoted his life to the poor people of Ajmer and its region. He was strongly influenced by the Upanishads; some reports claim that he married the daughter of a Hindu raja.

His influence during his lifetime was enormous, but continued through the establishment of the Chishti school or *silsila*, which flourished "because it produced respected spiritualists and propounded catholic doctrines". Hindus were attracted to the movement but did not have to renounce their faith, and Sufi khanqah (a form of hospice) were accessible to all.

Almost immediately after his death Khwaja Mu'innuddin Chishti's followers carried on his mission. The present structure was built by Ghiyasuddin Khalji of Malwa, but the embellishment of the shrine to its present ornate character is still seen as far less important than the spiritual nature of the saint it commemorates.

'donations' – often heightened by the music being played outside the tomb's ornate entrance. For many visitors, stepping into the tomb itself is the culmination of a lifetime's ambition, reflected in the ardour of their offerings.

Other sites

Nearby is the **Mazar** (tomb) of Bibi Hafiz Jamal, daughter of the saint, a small enclosure with marble latticework. Close by is that of Chimni Begum, daughter of Shah Jahan. She never married, refusing to leave her father during the seven years he was held captive by Aurangzeb in Agra Fort. She spent her last days in Ajmer, as did another daughter who probably died of tuberculosis. At the south end of the Dargah is the **Jhalra** (tank).

The **Arhai-din-ka Jhonpra Mosque** ('Hut of Two and a Half Days') lies beyond the Dargah in a narrow valley. Originally a Jain college built in 1153, it was partially destroyed by Muhammad of Ghori in 1192, and in 1210 turned into a mosque by **Qutb-ud-din-Aibak** who built a massive screen of seven arches in front of the pillared halls, allegedly in 2½ days (hence its name). The temple pillars which were incorporated in the building are all different. The mosque measures 79 m by 17 m with 10 domes supported by 124 columns and incorporates Hindu and Jain masonry. Much of it is in ruins though restoration work was undertaken at the turn of the century; only part of the 67-m screen and the prayer hall remain.

Akbar's Palace, built in 1570 and restored in 1905, is in the city centre near the east wall. It is a large rectangular building with a fine gate. Today it houses the **Government Museum** ① *Sat-Thu 1000-1630, Rs 50, no photography*, which has a dimly presented collection of fine sculpture from sixth to 17th centuries, paintings and old Rajput and Mughal armour and coins.

The ornate **Nasiyan Jain Temple (Red Temple)** ① *Prithviraj Marg, 0800-1700, Rs 25*, has a remarkable museum alongside the Jain shrine, which itself is open only to Jains. It is well worth visiting. Ajmer has a large Jain population (about 25% of the city's total). The Shri Siddhkut Chaityalaya was founded in 1864 in honour of the first Jain Tirthankar, Rishabdeo, by a Jain diamond merchant, Raj Bahadur Seth Moolchand Nemichand Soni (hence its alternative name, the Soni temple). The opening was celebrated in 1895. Behind a wholly unimposing exterior, on its first floor the Svarna Nagari Hall houses an astonishing reconstruction of the Jain conception of the universe, with gold-plated replicas of every Jain shrine in India. Over 1000 kg of gold is estimated to have been used, and at one end of the gallery diamonds have been placed behind decorative coloured glass to give an appearance of backlighting. It took 20 people 30 years to build. The holy mountain, Sumeru, is at the centre of the continent, and around it are holy sites as Ayodhya, the birthplace of the Tirthankar, recreated in gold plate, and a remarkable collection of model temples. Suspended from the ceiling are *vimanas* (airships

Tip...

From Station Road, a walk through the bazars, either to Dargah/Masjid area or to Akbar's Palace/Nasiyan Temple area, is worth doing.

of the gods) and silver balls. On the ground floor, beneath the model, are the various items taken on procession around the town on the Jain festival day of 23 November each year. The trustees of the temple are continuing to maintain and embellish it.

Trips from Ajmer

Mayo College (1873), only 4 km from the centre, was founded to provide young Indian princes with a liberal education, one of two genuinely Indo-Saracenic buildings designed by De Fabeck in Ajmer, the other being the **Mayo Hospital** (1870). The college was known as the 'Eton of Rajputana' and was run along the lines of an English public school. Access is no longer restricted to Rajput princes.

Ana Sagar, an artificial lake (circa 1150), was further enhanced by emperors Jahangir and Shah Jahan who added the baradari and pavilions. The **Foy Sagar**, 5 km away, another artificial lake, was a famine relief project.

Taragarh (**Star Fort**), built by Ajaipal Chauhan in 1100 with massive 4.5-m-thick walls, stands on the hilltop overlooking the town. There are great views of the city but the walk up the winding bridle path is tiring. A road accessible by road has reduced the climb on foot and made access easier. Jeeps charge Rs 500 for the trip. Along the way is a graveyard of Muslim 'martyrs' who died storming the fort.

Listings Ajmer

Tourist information

There are offices at the railway station and next to **Khadim Hotel** (T0145-262 7426, tourismajmer@rediffmail.com, Mon-Sat 0800-1800, closed 2nd Sat of the month). Both are very helpful.

Where to stay

Prices rise sharply, as much as tenfold, during the week of the festival (see Festivals, below). Many hotels are booked well in advance. The tourist office has a list of Paying Guest accommodation.

$$-$ Haveli Heritage Inn
Kutchery Rd, T0145-262 1607.
12 good-sized, clean, comfortable rooms in a homely 125-year-old building, no hot water in cheaper rooms. Rooms are quite expensive for what you get. Family-run, good home cooking, located on a busy main road but set back with a pleasant courtyard, very charming owner.

$$-$ Hotel Embassy
*Jaipur Rd, T0145-262 3859,
www.hotelembassyajmer.com.*
31 smart a/c rooms in a building newly renovated to 3-star standard. Enthusiastic, professional staff, elegant restaurant.

$ Hotel Jannat
*Very close to Durgah, T0145-243 2494,
www.ajmerhoteljannat.com.*
36 clean, modern rooms in a great location, within the labyrinthine alleys of the Old City,

friendly staff, a/c restaurant, all mod cons. Good location in the heart of things, but tricky to find.

Restaurants

Son halwa, a local sweet speciality, is sold near the Dargah and at the market. Delicious street snacks can be found in the back lanes between Delhi and Agra gates.

$ Jai Hind
In an alley by the clocktower, opposite railway station.
Best for Indian vegetarian. Delicious, cheap meals.

$ Mango Masala
Sandar Patel Marg, T0145-242 2100.
American diner-styled place with wide-ranging menu including pizzas, sizzlers, Indian and sundaes. The standard is high, portions are large and service is outstanding.

Festivals

Urs Festival, commemorating Khwaja Mu'inuddin Chishti's death in 1235, is celebrated with 6 days of almost continuous music, and devotees from all over India and the Middle East make the pilgrimage. Qawwalis and other Urdu music developed in the courts of rulers can be heard. Roses cover the tomb. The festival starts on sighting the new moon in Rajab, the 7th month of the Islamic year. The peak is reached on the night between the 5th and 6th days when tens of thousands of pilgrims pack the shrine. At 1100 on the last morning, pilgrims and visitors are banned from the *dargah*, as the khadims, who are responsible through the year for the maintenance of worship at the shrine, dressed in their best clothes, approach the shrine with flowers and sweets. On the final day, women wash the tomb with their hair, then squeeze the rose water into bottles as medicine for the sick.

Shopping

Fine local silver jewellery, tie-dye textiles and camel hide articles are best buys. The shopping areas are Madar Gate, Station Rd, Purani Mandi, Naya Bazar and Kaisarganj. Some alleys in the old town have good shopping.

Transport

Bus The State Bus Stand is 2 km east of centre, enquiries T0145-242 9398. Buses to **Agra**, 9 hrs; **Delhi**, 9 hrs; **Jaipur**, 2½ hrs; **Jodhpur**, 5 hrs; **Bikaner**, 7 hrs; **Chittaurgarh**, 5 hrs; **Udaipur**, 7 hrs via Chittaurgarh; **Kota** via Bundi; **Pushkar**, 45 mins, frequent. Private buses for **Pushkar** leave from near the Jain Temple.

Train Ajmer Station is seemingly overrun with rats and is not a great place to wait for a night train. Reservations, T0145-243 2535, 0830-1330, 1400-1630, enquiries, T131/132. Taxis outside the station charge Rs 200-250 to **Pushkar**. **Delhi** via **Jaipur**: *Shatabdi Exp 12016*, 7 hrs.

★ Pushkar

temple bells, holy men and rose petals

Surrounded by bathing ghats and whitewashed temples, Pushkar Lake is one of India's most sacred sites and an important Hindu pilgrimage town. The town is famous for its annual Pushkar Camel Fair held in October/November (see box, page 377), when it can be particularly busy, but a visit outside this annual extravaganza is also worthwhile.

Dozens of hotels, restaurants, cafés and shops cater to Western tastes and many travellers find it hard to drag themselves away from such creature comforts. The village's main bazar, though busy, has banned rickshaws so is relieved of revving engines and touting drivers. The village has been markedly changed in recent years by the year-round presence of large numbers of foreigners, originally drawn by the Pushkar Fair, and there is a high hassle factor from cash-seeking Brahmin 'priests' requesting a donation for the 'Pushkar Passport' (a red string tied around the wrist as part of a *puja*/blessing). However, there are still plenty of chances for an unhurried stroll around the lake (now healthy and thriving after a two-year cleaning project), or to take the short trek up to the Savitri Temple where you can swap village activity for open swathes of valley and fringes of desert beyond. From on high, the houses crowd the lake's edges as if it's a plug-hole down which all of Pushkar is slowly being drawn.

Sights

Pushkar Lake is believed to mark the spot where a lotus thrown by Brahma landed. Fa Hien, the Chinese traveller who visited Pushkar in the fifth century AD, commented on the number of pilgrims, and although several of the older temples were subsequently destroyed by Aurangzeb, many remain. Ghats lead down to the water to enable pilgrims to bathe, cows to drink, and the town's young fools to wash off after the riotous **Holi** celebrations. They also provide a hunting ground for Brahmin 'priests', who press a flower into the hand of any passing foreigner and offer – even demand – to perform *puja* (worship) in return for a sum of money. If this hard-sell version of spirituality appeals, agree your price in advance – Rs 50 should be quite sufficient – and be aware that a proportion of so-called priests are no such thing.

There are dozens of temples in Pushkar, most of which are open 0500-1200, 1600-2200. The **Brahma Temple**① *0600-1330, 1500-2100 (changes seasonally)*, beyond the western end of the lake, is a particularly holy shrine and draws pilgrims throughout the year. Although it isn't the only Brahma temple in India, as people claim, it is the only major pilgrim place for followers of the Hindu God of Creation. It is said that when Brahma needed a marital partner for a ritual, and his consort Saraswati (Savitri) took a long time to come, he married a cow-girl, Gayatri, after giving her the powers of a goddess (Gayatri because she was purified by the mouth of a cow or *gau*). His wife learnt of this and put a curse on him – that he would only be worshipped in Pushkar.

There are 52 ghats around the lake, of which the Brahma Ghat, Gan Ghat and Varah Ghat are the most sacred. The medieval **Varah Temple** is dedicated to the boar incarnation of Vishnu. It is said the idol was broken by Emperor Jahangir as it resembled a pig. The **Mahadev Temple** is said to date from 12th century while the **Julelal Temple** is modern and jazzy. Interestingly enough the two wives of Brahma have hilltop temples on either side of the lake, with the Brahma temple in the valley.

A steep 3-km climb up the hill which leads to the **Savitri Temple** (dedicated to Brahma's first wife), offers excellent views of the town and surrounding desert. It's a magical place in the evening when groups of women promenade the bazars, the clashing colours of their saris all flowing together; while men dry their turbans in the evening sun after washing them in the lake, wafting the metres of filmy fabric in the breeze or draping it on nearby trees.

The **Main (Sadar) Bazar** is full of shops selling typical tourist, as well as pilgrim knick-knacks and is usually very busy. At full moon, noisy religious celebrations last all night so you may need your ear plugs here.

Pushkar

Where to stay
Bharatpur Palace 3 *B1*
Colonel's Camp 10 *A1*
Dia 28 *C3*
Greenhouse Resort 1 *A1*
Inn Seventh Heaven
  & Sixth Sense 4 *B2*
Paramount Palace 5 *B1*
Pushkar Bagh Resort 2 *C1*

Pushkar Palace 9 *C2*
Sai Baba Haveli 17 *B2*
Sarovar 12 *C2*
Shannu's Ranch &
  Horse Rides 27 *C3*
Sunset 8 *C2*
U-Turn 14 *B2*
White House 20 *B2*

Restaurants
Halwai Ki Gali 6 *B2*
Honey & Spice 7 *B2*
Karmima 1 *C1*
Little Italy Pizzeria 4 *C3*
Neem Tree Farm 2 *C2*
Sunset Café 3 *C2*

Ghat ≈

Tourist information

Ask at the **Sarovar Hotel** (T0145-277 2040).

Where to stay

The town suffers from early morning temple bells. During the fair, hotel charges can be 10 times the normal rate. Booking in advance is essential for the better places. To escape the noise of the Main Bazar, choose one in a back street of Bari Basti or Panch Kund Rd.

$$$$-$$$ Greenhouse Resort
Tilora village, 8 km from Pushkar, T0145-230 0079, www.thegreenhouseresort.com.
This is a truly unique place with luxurious tents mixed with giant greenhouses growing roses and strawberries and lots of organic vegetables for the kitchen. With a nod to the environment, they are experimenting with water conservation, innovative irrigation and solar panels and the resort is staffed mainly with local people. The beds are stunning and there are all mod cons in the tents. This is a serene place, relaxing and inspiring. Recommended.

$$$$-$$$ Pushkar Palace
On lakeside, T0145-277 3001, www.hotelpushkarpalace.com.
52 overpriced rooms including 25 suites overlooking the lake, in a beautifully renovated old palace, with attractive gardens. It looks good but is rather uncomfortable and lakeside rooms have very small windows. Alas, too the terrace restaurant is now closed, so the restaurant is in the courtyard with no lake view.

$$$ Pushkar Bagh Resort
Motisar Link Rd, Village Ghanehera, T(0)9414-030669, www.pushkarbaghresort.com.
Out of town this is a heritage-style property with lots of charm. The rooms are decorated with lovely wooden furniture and there are nice communal sitting areas, themed dinners and gala nights.

$$$-$$ Dia
Panch Kund Rd, T0145-510 5455, www.inn-seventh-heaven.com/dia.
Fantastic big rooms in a new chic building. Offering just 4 stylish a/c rooms and plenty of open spaces to curl up with a book or look out at Pushkar and the surrounding hills, this is in a quiet part of town away from the bustle. Highly recommended.

$$-$ Inn Seventh Heaven
Next to Mali ka Mandir, T0145-510 5455, www.inn-seventh-heaven.com.
Beautiful rooms spiral out from the inner courtyard in this fantastically well-restored 100-year-old *haveli*, plus a handful of ascetic but much cheaper rooms in neighbouring building. Lots of seating areas dotted throughout the 3-storey building, including some lovely swinging diwans. Very friendly, informal, excellent rooftop restaurant (baked potatoes from open coal fire in winter), the restaurant goes from strength to strength. Charming owner and a sociable atmosphere. Exceptionally good value. Whole-heartedly recommended.

$$-$ Sarovar (RTDC)
On lakeside, T0145-277 2040.
38 clean rooms (the best are in the old part with amazing lake views), some a/c with bath, new rooms good but no atmosphere, cheap 6-bed dorm, set around the courtyard in a former lakeside palace, attractive gardens.

$$-$ U-Turn
Lake Vahara Ghat Choti Basti, T(0)9928-737798, www.hoteluturn.com.
A chic little number right on the lake. The rooms are small due to the age of the building, but with bags of charm. Formerly the **Bhola Guest House**, the 2nd oldest guesthouse in Pushkar. Of the 6 beautifully decorated rooms, you can choose from the 'Princess Villa' or the 'Kama Sutra Villa'. The rooftop café is also a cut above the rest, with nice fabrics and comfy chairs and serves up the usual global fare.

$ Bharatpur Palace
Lakeside, T0145-277 2320.
Exceptional views of the ghats, 1 very simple room practically hangs over the ghat, 18 unusually decorated rooms, clean bathrooms.

$ Paramount Palace
Bari Basti, T0145-277 2428, hotelparamountpalace@hotmail.com.
16 clean, basic rooms, some with bath, best with balcony, elevated site with splendid views from the rooftop, the highest in Pushkar. Very friendly host.

$ Sai Baba Haveli
Near the market post office, T0145-510 5161, www.saibabahavelipushkar.com.
Nice big rooms around a central courtyard, lots of greenery and hanging plants. It is well loved by its patrons.

$ Shannu's Ranch
Panch Kund Rd, T0145-277 2043.
On the edge of town, with basic quirky, 'rustique' cottages in a garden, owned by a French/Canadian riding instructor, some will find it charming, some will find it too basic – certainly unique.

$ Sunset
On the lake, T0145-277 2382, hotelsunset@hotmail.com.
20 plain, clean rooms, 3 a/c, around a lovely garden, lots of flowers and papaya trees. Well located close to the lake, plus access to the **Sunset Café**.

$ White House
In a narrow alley near Marwar Bus Stand, T0145-277 2147, hotelwhitehouse@hotmail.com.
Very clean, well-maintained building overlooking the nursery gardens. Good views from the pleasant rooftop restaurant with excellent food. Also good cheaper rooms available at their sister guesthouse, **Kohinoor**. Recommended.

During the fair
It is best to visit early in the week when toilets are still reasonably clean.

Tourist village Erected by **RTDC**, this is a remarkable feat, accommodating 100,000 people. Conveniently placed with deluxe/super-deluxe tents (Rs 6000-6500 with meals), ordinary/dorm tents (Rs 300 per bed), 30 'cottages', some deluxe (Rs 4000-5000). Beds and blankets, some running water, Indian toilets are standard. Meals are served in a separate tent (or eat cheap, delicious local food at the tribal tented villages near the show ground). Reservation with payment, essential (open 12 months ahead); contact **RTDC** in Jaipur, T0141-510 598, www.rajasthantourism.gov.in.

Private camps Privately run camps charge over US$150-250 including meals for Regular and 'Swiss' double tent. They might be some distance from the fair ground and may lack security.

Colonel's Camp
Motisar Rd, Ghanera, T0141-220 2034, www.meghniwas.com.
120 deluxe tents with toilet and shower in attractive gardens.

Pushkar Palace
See page 375.
Sets up 351 plush 'tent cottages', well equipped with bathroom, furniture, carpet and and heating.

Also check out tent accommodation set up by **Jodhana Heritage**, www.jodhanaheritage.com; **Camp Bliss**, www.pushkarcamelfair.com and **Royal Safari Camp**, www.royalsafaricamp.com. Many of these camps also set up during the Nagaur fair too.

Restaurants

No meat, fish or eggs are served in this temple town, and alcohol is banned, as are 'narcotics' – in theory. Take special care during the fair: eat only freshly cooked food and drink bottled water. Long-stay budget travellers have resulted in an increase of Western and Israeli favourites like falafel, granola and apple pie. Hotels on the city limit sell all of the contraband items.

$$-$ Little Italy Pizzeria
Panch Kund Rd.
High-quality Italian dishes plus Israeli and Indian specialities, pleasant garden setting. They have opened another restaurant, **La Pizzeria**, near Varah Temple, Chhoti Basti.

$$-$ Sixth Sense
Perched at the top of Inn Seventh Heaven (see Where to stay, page 375).
By far the most stylish dining experience in Pushkar. Serving up the usual Indian fare and beyond, with baked potatoes, pastas and fantastic home-baked desserts. Highly recommended.

$ Halwai Ki Gali (alley off Main Bazar)
Sweet shops sell *malpura* (syrupy pancake) as well as other Rajasthani/Bengali sweets.

$ Honey and Spice
Laxmi Market.
Only open during the day, this little café offers up great coffees like aniseed and cinnamon, renowned banana bread and steaming plates of brown rice and veggies.

ON THE ROAD
The pull of the cattle and camels

The huge Mela is Pushkar's biggest draw. Over 200,000 visitors and pilgrims and hordes of cattle and camels with their semi-nomadic tribal drivers, crowd into the town. Farmers, breeders and camel traders buy and sell. Sales in leather whips, shoes, embroidered animal covers soar while women bargain over clay pots, bangles, necklaces and printed cloth.

Events begin four to five days before the full moon in November. There are horse and camel races and betting is heavy. In the Ladhu Umt race teams of up to 10 men cling to camels, and one another, in a hilarious and often chaotic spectacle. The Tug-of-War between Rajasthanis and foreigners is usually won by the local favourites. There are also sideshows with jugglers, acrobats, magicians and folk dancers. At nightfall there is music and dancing outside the tents, around friendly fires – an unforgettable experience despite its increasingly touristy nature, even including a laser show. The cattle trading itself actually takes place during the week before the fair; some travellers have reported arriving during the fair and there being no animals left.

$ Karmima
Opposite Ashish-Manish Riding.
One of several small places here offering home-cooked *thalis* (Rs 15/20) and excellent fresh, orange/sweet lime juice.

$ Neem Tree Farm
Outside Pushkar, T(0)7737-777903, www.neemtreefarm.weebly.com.
This place specializes in permaculture, natural farming and solar architecture. You can head out during the day for a 'permaculture' picnic or have a dinner in the desert. Great experience.

$ Sunset Café
Next to Pushkar Palace.
Particularly atmospheric in the evening when crowds gather to listen to music and watch sunset. Lacklustre food. Recommended for ambience.

Festivals

Oct/Nov Kartik Purnima Is marked by a vast cattle and camel fair, see box, above. Pilgrims bathe in the lake – the night of the full moon being the most auspicious time – and float 'boats' of marigold and rose petals in the moonlight. Camel traders often arrive a few days early to engage in the serious business of buying and selling and most of the animals disappear before the official starting date. Arrive 3 days ahead if you don't want to miss this part of the fair. The all-night drumming and singing in the Mela Ground can get tiring, but the fair is a unique spectacle. Travellers warn of pickpockets.

Shopping

There is plenty to attract the Western eye; check quality and bargain hard. Miniatures on silk and old paper are everywhere. Cheap clothes, baba pants and bags are ubiquitous:
Essar, *shop 6, Sadar Bazar, opposite Narad Kunj.* Excellent tailoring (jacket Rs 250-300 including fabric).
Galaxy, *main bazar, near Varah Ghat.* Their card says they deal in books, fireworks and ice, which is a strange combination. Certainly they have a great selection of books, from trashy novels to all things yogic.
Manu Maloo Antiques and Collectibles, *Badi Basti* (sweet street). Take the street opposite Gau Ghat past the array of bubbling sweet stalls and you will discover a little hole-in-the-wall shop with a great range of framed pictures and all manner of wooden and bronze objects. Bargain hard, they are interesting but not hugely valuable.

What to do

Horse and camel safaris
Ambay Camel Safari, *Master Paying Guest House, Panch Kund Road, T(0)94146 67148, www.ambaycamelsafaripushkar.com.* Day trips with camels, horses, jeeps or bikes. Also offers sunset and overnight desert trips.
Pushkar Camel Safari, *Vinayak-C, near Petrol Pump, T(0)98281 78603, www.pushkarcamelsafari. com.* Head into the sunset on a camel's back. Well recommended for camel and horse safaris, there are also camel carts and even jeeps if you prefer less sweaty transport.

Shannu's Riding School, *Panch Kund Rd, T0145-277 2043.* Run by a French Canadian riding instructor – there are horses for hire and riding lessons.

Body and soul

Pushkar Yoga Garden, *Vamdev Rd, near Gurudwara, www.pushkaryoga.org.* Regular hatha classes with Yogesh Yogi and also longer courses.
Shakti School of Dance, *Old Rangi Temple Complex, near Honey and Spice, www.colleena shakti.com.* You can learn traditional Odissi style dance, tribal fusion belly dance and local Khalbelia Rajasthani gypsy dance. Also hosts yoga and dance retreats. Recommended.

Swimming

Sarovar Oasis, **Navratan** hotels, non-residents pay Rs 80.

Tour operators

Ekta Travels, *opposite Marwar Bus Stand, T0145-277 2131, www.ektatravelspushkar.com.* Tours, excellent service, good buses, reliable.

Transport

Bicycle/car/motorbike hire Rs 10 entry 'tax' per vehicle. **Michael Cycle SL Cycles**, Ajmer Bus Stand Rd, very helpful, Rs 30 per day; also from the market. **Hotel Oasis** has Vespa scooters, Rs 300 per day. **Enfield Ashram**, near Hotel Oasis, Rs 400 per day for an Enfield.

Bus Frequent service to/from **Ajmer**, Rs 10. Long-distance buses are more frequent from Ajmer, and tickets bought in Pushkar may involve a change. Direct buses to **Jaipur**, **Jodhpur** via Merta (8 hrs), **Bikaner**, and **Haridwar**. Sleeper bus to **Delhi**, Rs 250, 1930 (11 hrs); **Agra**, Rs 250, 1930 (11 hrs); **Jaisalmer**, Rs 450, 2200 (11 hrs), **Udaipur**, Rs 250, 2200 (8 hrs) and 2300 (8 hrs). Many agents in Pushkar have times displayed. **Pushkar Travels**, T0145-277 2437, reliable for bookings.

Bikaner
& around

Bikaner is something of a dusty oasis town among the scrub and sand dunes of northwest Rajasthan. Its rocky outcrops in a barren landscape provide a dramatic setting for the Junagarh Fort, one of the finest in western Rajasthan. The old walled city retains a medieval air, and is home to over 300 *havelis*, while outside the walls some stunning palaces survive. Well off the usual tourist trail, Bikaner is en route to Jaisalmer from Jaipur or Shekhawati, and is well worth a visit.

Bikaner

dusty outpost town with an impressive fort and camel safaris

Junagarh Fort

1000-1630 (last entry), Rs 100 foreigners, Rs 10 Indians; camera Rs 30, video Rs 100 (limited permission), guided tours in Hindi and English, private guides near the gate offer better 'in-depth' tours; Rs 100 for 4 people, 2 hrs.

This is one of the finest examples in Rajasthan of the paradox between medieval military architecture and beautiful interior decoration. Started in 1588 by Raja Rai Singh (1571-1611), a strong ally of the Mughal Empire, who led Akbar's army in numerous battles, it had palaces added for the next three centuries.

You enter the superbly preserved fort via the yellow sandstone **Suraj Prole** (Sun Gate, 1593) to the east. The pale red sandstone perimeter wall is surrounded by a moat (the lake no longer exists) while the chowks have beautifully designed palaces with balconies, kiosks and fine *jali* screens. The interiors are beautifully decorated with shell-work, lime plaster, mirror-and-glass inlays, gold leaf, carving, carpets and lacquer work. The ramparts offer good views of the elephant and horse stables and temples, the old city with the desert beyond, and the relatively more recent city areas around the medieval walls. The walls of the **Lal Niwas**, which are the oldest, are elaborately decorated in red and gold.

Karan Singh commemorated a victory over Aurangzeb by building the **Karan Mahal** (1631-

Essential Bikaner and around

Finding your feet

Bikaner is a full day's drive from Jaipur so it may be worth stopping a night in the Shekhawati region (see pages 388 and 390). The railway station is central and has services from Delhi (Sarai Rohilla), Jaipur and Jodhpur. The New Bus Stand is 3 km to the north, so if arriving from the south you can ask to be dropped in town. There are regular bus services to Desnok, but to get to Gajner, Kakoo or Tal Chappar you'll need to hire private transport. See Transport, page 383.

Getting around

The fort and the Old City are within easy walking distance from the station. Auto- and cycle-rickshaws transfer passengers between the station and the New Bus Stand. Taxis can be difficult to get from the Lallgarh Palace area at night.

Best places to stay

Old-world charm at Bhairon Vilas, page 382
In the desert with Vinayak Desert Safaris, page 383
Kaku Castle for desert sunsets, page 385

1639) across the chowk. Successive rulers added the **Gaj Mandir** (1745-1787) with its mirrored Shish Mahal, and the **Chattra Niwas** (1872-1887) with its pitched roof and English 'field sport' plates decorating the walls. The magnificent **Coronation Hall**, adorned with plaster work, lacquer, mirror and glass, is in Maharaja Surat Singh's **Anup Mahal** (1788-1828). The decorative façades around the Anup Mahal Chowk, though painted white, are in fact of stone.

The fort also includes the **Chetar Mahal** and **Chini Burj** of Dungar Singh (1872-1887) and **Ganga Niwas** of Ganga Singh (1898-1943), who did much to modernize his state and also built the Lallgarh Palace to the north.

Mirror work, carving and marble decorate the ornate **Chandra Mahal** (Moon Palace) and the **Phul Mahal** (Flower Palace), built by Maharaja Gaj Singh. These last two, the best rooms, are shown to foreigners at the end as a 'special tour' when the guide expects an extra tip. The royal chamber in the Chandra Mahal has strategically placed mirrors so that any intruder entering could be seen by the maharaja from his bed.

The fort **museum** has Sanskrit and Persian manuscripts, miniature paintings, jewels, enamelware, silver, weapons, palanquins, howdahs and war drums. **Har Mandir**, the royal temple where birth and wedding ceremonies were celebrated, is still used for Gangaur and other festivities. The well nearby is reputedly over 130 m deep.

Prachina Museum ① *1000-1700, foreigners Rs 50 (guided tour), Indians Rs10, camera Rs 20, small clean café outside is open-air but shady*, in the grounds, exhibits beautifully crafted costumes, carpets and ornamental objects.

Bikaner

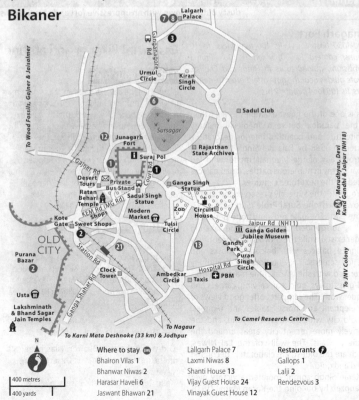

Where to stay
Bhairon Vilas 1
Bhanwar Niwas 2
Harasar Haveli 6
Jaswant Bhawan 21

Lallgarh Palace 7
Laxmi Niwas 8
Shanti House 13
Vijay Guest House 24
Vinayak Guest House 12

Restaurants
Gallops 1
Lalji 2
Rendezvous 3

ON THE ROAD
Life after the drought

When in Bikaner, drop in at URMUL's showroom, Abhiviyakyi, opposite the New Bus Stand. A fair trade NGO, URMUL works with the marginalized tribespeople of the Thar Desert. The droughts of the 1980s made farming, the traditional source of livelihood for the majority of these people, no longer a viable option. URMUL was formed in 1991 with the aim to teach people new skills which could bring them the income that the absent rains had taken away. As the range of products on offer testifies, the project has been a huge success. All the items on sale, including clothing, tablecloths, bed linen, shoes and bags, have been made by the project's participants, and are of a quality previously unseen in the often all-too amateur 'craft' sector. Visit the shop before agreeing to go with rickshaw drivers or touts to a 'URMUL' village; scams are not unknown.

Lallgarh Palace
Palace Thu-Tue, museum Mon-Sat 1000-1700, Rs 40 (museum extra Rs 20).

The red sandstone palace stands in huge grounds to the north of the city, surrounded by rocks and sand dunes. Designed by Sir Swinton Jacob in 1902, the palace complex, with extensions over the next few decades, has attractive courtyards overlooked by intricate *zenana* screen windows and *jarokha* balconies, columned corridors and period furnishings. The banquet hall is full of hunting trophies and photographs. His Highness Doctor Karni Singh of Bikaner was well known for his shooting expertise – both with a camera and with a gun. The bougainvillea, parakeets and peacocks add to the attraction of the gardens in which the Bikaner State Railway Carriage is preserved. The Lallgarh complex has several hotels (see Where to stay, page 382).

Rampuria Street and the Purana Bazar
There are some exquisite *havelis* in Bikaner belonging to the Rampuria, Kothari, Vaid and Daga merchant families. The sandstone carvings combine traditional Rajasthani *haveli* architecture with colonial influence. Around Rampuria Street and the Purana Bazar you can wander through lanes lined with fine façades. Among them is **Bhanwar Niwas** which has been converted into a heritage hotel.

Ganga Golden Jubilee Museum
Public Park, 1000-1630, Rs 3.

This museum has a fine small collection of pottery, massive paintings, stuffed tigers, carpets, costumes and weapons. There are also some excellent examples of Bikaner miniature paintings which are specially prized because of their very fine quality.

Listings Bikaner *map p380*

Tourist information

Dhola-Maru Tourist Bungalow
Poonam Singh Circle, T0151-222 6701.
Oct-Mar 0800-1800.
As well as information, car hire is available.

Where to stay

$$$$ Laxmi Niwas
Lallgarh Palace Complex, T0151-2252 1188,
www.laxminiwaspalace.com.
60 large rooms and suites which once formed Maharaja Ganga Singh's personal residence, with fabulous carvings and beautifully painted ceilings, all arranged around the stunningly ornate courtyard. Superb bar, restaurant and

lounge, discreet but attentive service, absolutely one-off. Recommended. You can also pay Rs 100 to have a tour if you are not staying here.

$$$$-$$$ Bhanwar Niwas
Rampuria St, Old City (500 m from Kote Gate), ask for Rampuria Haveli, T0151-252 9323, www.bhanwarniwas.com.
26 beautifully decorated rooms (all different) around a fantastic courtyard in an exquisite early 20th-century *haveli*. Original decor has been painstakingly restored to stunning effect, takes you back to another era, great service. Recommended.

$$$$-$$$ Lallgarh Palace
3 km from the railway, T0151-254 0201, www.lallgarhpalace.com.
Large a/c rooms in beautiful and authentic surroundings, after some much needed renovation the indoor pool is beautiful, there's an atmospheric dining hall, but mixed reports on food and service unfortunately. Run by the royal family.

$$ Bhairon Vilas
Near fort, T0151-254 4751, www.hotelbhaironvilas.com.
Restored 1800s aristocratic *haveli*, great atmosphere, 18 eclectic rooms decorated with flair – you can spend hours simply exploring the antiquities in your own room, huge amount of character, lovely indoor restaurant, and great great views across the city and fort from top rooms and rooftop. There's also an atmospheric bar and funky boutique shop. This place sums up the whole Rajasthan experience. Kitsch chic, whole-heartedly recommended.

$$-$ Harasar Haveli
Opposite Karni Singh Stadium, T0151-220 9891, www.harasar.com.
Friendly place, ornate building with nicely decorated rooms, some with verandas and good views, TVs, dining room with period memorabilia, plus great atmospheric rooftop restaurant – you might end up dancing.

$ Jaswant Bhawan
Alakh Sagar Rd, near railway station, T0151-2548848.
15 rooms in a charming old building, quiet location, excellent home cooking, lawn, good value. Very popular. Recommended.

$ Shanti House
New Well (City Kotwali), behind Jain Paathshala, T(0)94611 59796, www.shantihousebikaner.com.
One of the few places you can stay in the old city. It's a new building though, basic and clean with 4 rooms (5 with a/c) and a dorm. They offer tours of the old city and free cookery lessons. Great value and great location.

$ Vijay Guest House
Opposite Sophia School, Jaipur Rd, T0151-223 1244, www.camelman.com.
6 clean rooms with attached bathrooms, plus 2 with shared bath. Slightly distant location compensated for by free use of bicycles or scooter, free pick-ups from bus/train, Rs 5 in shared rickshaw to town. Delicious home-cooked meals, pleasant garden, quiet, very hospitable (free tea and rum plus evening parties on the lawn), knowledgeable host, great value. Good camel safaris. Recommended.

$ Vinayak Guest House
Near Junagarh Fort, Hanuman Temple, Old Ginani, T(0)94144 30948, www.vinayakdesertsafari.com.
Friendly homestay run by the manager of URMUL shop and his wildlife expert son who cannot do enough for you, excellent home cooking and cooking lessons, also runs camel safaris, photography classes, village and wildlife tours. Highly recommended.

Restaurants

You can dine in style at several of the hotels. Try the local specialities of *Bikaneri bhujia/sev/namkeen* – savoury snacks made from dough. Purana Bazar sells ice-cold *lassis* by day, hot milk, sugar and cream at night.

$$ Bhanwar Niwas
See Where to stay, above.
Amazingly ornate dining hall, good way of having a look around.

$$ Gallops
Court Rd.
Excellent views of the fort, but overpriced and disappointing food but good for a rest after exploring the fort.

$$ Rendezvous
Lallgarh Palace Complex.
With traditional artwork and Rajasthani decor, this is an atmospheric place serving up a good range of Rajasthani dishes as well as a few other tastes from around the globe. Recommended.

$ Lalji
Station Rd near Evergreen Hotel.
Popular local joint serving good *dosas* and sweets.

Festivals

Oct/Nov Bikaner is a great place for **Diwali**.
Dec/Jan **Camel Fair** A popular, colourful fair.
The Camel Fair is especially spectacular in
Junagarh Fort in the Old City near Kote Gate
and some smaller palaces.

What to do

Camel safaris
Camel Man, *Vijay Guest House, Jaipur Rd, T0151-
223 1244, www.camelman.com.* Good-value,
reliable, friendly and professional safaris, jeep
tours, cycling. Lightweight 'igloo' tents, clean
mattresses, sheets, good food and guidance.
Safaris to see antelopes, colourful villages
and potters at work; from 1- to 2-hr rides to
5-day trips; Rs 800-1000 per person per day.
Deservedly popular.
Vinayak Desert Safari, *T(0)9414-430948,
www.vinayakdesertsafari.com.* Eco-friendly

camel trekking with Jitu Solanki who has a
Masters degree in wildlife and specializes in the
study of reptiles. Camel, jeep and wildlife safaris
and village homestays on offer. Highly informed
and friendly guide.

Transport

Bus The New Bus Stand is 3 km north of town.
Private buses leave from south of the fort.
Rajasthan Roadways, enquiries, T0151-252
3800; daily deluxe buses to **Ajmer**, **Jodhpur**,
Jaisalmer (8 hrs), **Udaipur**. 2 daily to **Delhi** via
Hissar (12 hrs).

Rickshaw/taxi Autos between station and
bus stand or Lallgarh Palace, Rs 25. Taxis are
unmetered. Shared *tempos* run on set routes, Rs 5.

Train Enquiries, T0151-220 0131, reservations,
Mon-Sat 0800-1400, 1415-2000, Sun 0800-1400.
For tourist quota (when trains are full) apply to
Manager's Office by Radio Tower near **Jaswant
Bhawan Hotel**. **Delhi**: *Dee Intercity 22471,*
8 hrs arrives DSR; *Bkn Dee S F Exp 12458,* 8 hrs.
Jaisalmer: *Bkn Jsm Express 14702,* 6 hrs.

Around Bikaner

an interesting camel-breeding farm and a fascinating rat temple

Bhand Sagar
Free but caretakers may charge Rs 10 for cameras.
....

Some 5 km southwest of Bikaner, Bhand Sagar has a group of Hindu and Jain temples which are
believed to be the oldest extant structures of Bikaner, dating from the days when it was just a desert
trading outpost of Jodhpur. The white-painted sandstone **Bandeshwar Temple** with a towering
shikhara roof and painted sculptures, murals and mirrorwork inside, is the most interesting. The
Sandeshwar Temple, dedicated to Neminath, has gold-leaf painting, *meenakari* work and marble
sculptures. They are hard to find and difficult to approach by car but rickshaw wallahs know the way.
There are numerous steps but wonderful views.

Camel Research Centre
10 km from Bikaner in Jorbeer, 1400-1630, foreigners Rs 50, Indians Rs 5, camera Rs 20.
....

This 800-ha facility is dedicated to scientific research into various aspects of the camel, with the
aim of producing disease-resistant animals that can walk further and carry more while consuming
less water. As well as genetically increasing the camel's tolerances, researchers are investigating the
nutritional benefits of drinking camel milk; camel ice cream is for sale if you want to test for yourself,
and coming soon are camel milk moisturizers. It's particularly worth being here between 1530 and
1600, when the camels return to the centre for the evening: the spectacle of 100 or more camels
ambling out of the desert towards you is quite unforgettable.

Gajner National Park
Now part of a palace hotel, this park, 30 km west of Bikaner, used to be a private preserve which
provided the royal family of Bikaner with game. It is a birder's paradise surrounded by 13,000 ha of

scrub forest which also harbours large colonies of nilgai, chinkara, blackbuck, wild boar and desert reptiles. Throughout the day, a train of antelope, gazelle and pigs can be seen arriving to drink at the lake. Winter migratory birds include the Imperial black-bellied sand grouse, cranes and migratory ducks. Some visitors have spotted great Indian bustard at the water's edge. It is worth stopping for an hour's mini-safari if you are in the vicinity.

Kolayat

Some 50 km southwest via Gajner Road, Kolayat is regarded as one of the 58 most important Hindu pilgrimage centres. It is situated around a sacred lake with 52 ghats and a group of five temples built by Ganga Singhji (none of which is architecturally significant). The oasis village comes alive at the November full moon when a three-day festival draws thousands of pilgrims who take part in ritual bathing.

Karni Mata Mandir

Deshnoke, closed 1200-1600, free, camera Rs 40.

This 17th-century temple, 33 km south of Bikaner at Deshnoke, has massive silver gates and beautiful white marble carvings on the façade. These were added by Ganga Singh (1898-1943), who dedicated the temple to a 15th-century female mystic Karniji, worshipped as an incarnation of Durga. A gallery describes her life. Mice and rats, revered and fed with sweets and milk in the belief that they are reincarnated saints, swarm over the temple around your feet; spotting the white rat is supposed to bring good luck. Take socks as the floor is dirty, but note that the rats are far less widespread than they are made out to be. Sensationalized accounts give the impression of a sea of rats through which the visitor is obliged to walk barefoot, whereas in reality, while there are a good number of rats, they generally scurry around the outskirts of the temple courtyard – you're very unlikely to tread on one. The temple itself is beautiful, and would be well worth visiting even without the novelty of the rats.

★ Kakoo (Kaku)

This picturesque village, 75 km south of Bikaner, with attractive huts and surrounded by sand dunes, is the starting point for desert camel safaris costing Rs 1500 per day with tented facilities. Staying here makes a fantastic introduction to the practicalities of life in the desert; this is probably the most authentic desert settlement in this area that can be easily reached by road. Good trips to Kakoo are organized by Mr Bhagwan Singh (T(0)9829-254 2237, www.kakusafari.com). You can travel to Kakoo by bus changing at Nokhamandi (62 km) from Bikaner.

Kalibangan and Harappa sites

One of North India's most important early settlement regions stretches from the Shimla hills down past the important Harappan sites of **Hanumangarh** and **Kalibangan**, north of Bikaner. Late Harappan sites have been explored by archaeologists, notably A Ghosh, since 1962. They were identified in the upper part of the valley, the easternmost region of the Indus Valley civilization. Across the border in Pakistan are the premier sites of Harappa (200 km) and Mohenjo Daro (450 km). Here, the most impressive of the sites today is that of Kalibangan (west off the NH15 at Suratgarh). On the south bank of the Ghaggar River it was a heavily fortified citadel mound, rising about 10 m above the level of the plain. There were several pre-Harappan phases. Allchin and Allchin record that the bricks of the early phase were already standardized, though not to the same size as later Harappan bricks. The ramparts were made of mud brick and a range of pottery and ornaments have been found. The early pottery is especially interesting, predominantly red or pink with black painting.

Where to stay

$$$ Gajner Palace
Gajner National Park, T01534-275061,
www.hrhindia.com. Visitors are welcome
0800-1730, Rs 100.
44 a/c rooms in the elegant palace and its
wings, set by a beautiful lake. Rooms in the main
building are full of character (Edwardian Raj
nostalgia), those in the wings are well maintained
but very middle England. Sumptuous lounge bar
and restaurant overlooking the lake, magnificent
gardens, boating, good walking, pleasantly
unfrequented and atmospheric, friendly manager
and staff, no pool.

$ Kaku Castle
Kaku, T01532-254 2237, www.kakusafari.com.
Dr Karni Singh has been running a well-loved
desert getaway for many years. Now his 'castle'
has 4 rooms and 4 lovely domed huts with
attached baths, hot water in buckets, a great
experience. Good camel safaris arranged, with
the advantage of getting straight in to the desert
rather than having to get out of town first as in
Jaisalmer/Bikaner.

Festivals

Oct/Nov Cattle and Camel Fair. In Kolayat
(Kartik Purnima – brightest full moon of the
year), is very colourful and authentic but it can
get quite riotous after dark. Since facilities are
minimal, it is best to arrive before the festival to
find a local family with space to spare, or ask a
travel agent in Bikaner.

Transport

Bus For **Karni Mata Mandir**, buses leave from
Bikaner New Bus Stand, or on Ganga Shahar Rd
and at Ambedkar Circle. Taxis charge around
Rs 500 return. For **Kalibangan** catch a bus to
Suratgarh then change; this junction town
also has connections to Hanumangarh, Sirsa
(Haryana) or Mandi Dabwali (Punjab).

Train The broad-gauge train line from
Suratgarh to **Anupgarh**, about 15 km from the
Pakistan border, calls at Raghunathgarh, the
closest station to Kalibangan; travel from there
to Kalibangan is difficult (check at Suratgarh).
Trains from Suratgarh: **Anupgarh**: *Passenger
10755*, 2¼ hrs. **Bikaner** (Lallgarh Junction):
Chandigarh Exp 14887, 3¼ hrs. **Bhatinda**:
Chandigarh Exp 14888, 3¼ hrs.

Shekhawati

Covering an area of about 300 sq km on the often arid and rock-studded plains to the northwest of the Aravalli mountain range, Shekhawati is the homeland of the Marwari community. The area is particularly rich in painted *havelis*; Sikar district in the southwest and Jhunjhunun in the northeast form an 'open-air art gallery' of paintings dating from the mid-19th century. It's worth spending a few nights in Shekhawati to see the temples, frescoed forts, *chhatris* and step wells at leisure. Other attractions include horse or camel safaris and treks into the hills.

Shekhawati sees far fewer visitors than the better-known areas of Rajasthan, and retains something of a 'one pen/rupee' attitude to tourists. This is quite innocent and should not be a deterrent to visitors.

Ramgarh has the highest concentration of painted *havelis*, though they are not as well maintained as those of Nawalgarh which has the second largest selection. It is easier to visit *havelis* in towns that have hotels, such as Nawalgarh, Mandawa, Dundlod, Mukundgarh, Mahansar, Fatehpur, Baggar and Jhunjunun, and where the caretakers are used to visitors, though towns like Bissau, Alsisar, Malsisar and Churu have attractive *havelis* as well.

Sikar

The late 17th-century fort was built when Sikar was an important trading centre and the wealthiest *thikana* (feudatory) under Jaipur. It now has a population of 148,000. You can visit the old quarter and see the Wedgwood blue 'Biyani' (1920) and 'Mahal' (1845), Murarka and Somani *havelis* and murals and carvings in Gopinath, Raghunath and Madan Mohan temples. From Jaipur take the NH11 to Ringas (63 km) and Sikar (48 km).

Pachar

This is a little town west of Jaipur in the middle of the sand dunes with a golden sandstone castle scenically situated on a lakeshore. A road north from Bagru on the NH8 also gives access.

Ramgarh

Ramgarh was settled by the Poddars in the late 18th century. In addition to their many *havelis* and that of the Ruias, visit the *chhatris* with painted entrances near the bus stand, as well as the temples to Shani (with mirror decoration) and to Ganga. Ramgarh has the highest concentration of painted *havelis*, though they are not as well maintained as those of Nawalgarh which has the second largest assemblage. The town has a pleasantly laid-back feel. Look for handicrafts here.

Fatehpur

Fatehpur has a whole array of *havelis*, many are rather dishevelled. Fatehpur is worth a visit simply for the **Nadine Le Prince Haveli Cultural Centre** ① *near Chauhan Well, T0157-123 1479, www.cultural-centre.com.* Following a visit to the area, Nadine Le Prince took it upon herself to safeguard the cultural heritage of Fatehpur and the restoration of this *haveli* is exceptional. The frescoes here are exquisite and have served as an inspiration to Nadine's own artwork. As well as the restored *haveli*, there is a fine art gallery, sculpture garden and tribal art gallery and she hopes to create an artistic exchange between local and international artists. The centre also organizes walking tours of Fatehpur. There will soon be a few rooms at the *haveli* and there are a couple of lacklustre accommodation options in Fatehpur, it's better to visit from Mandawa.

Essential Shekhawati

Finding your feet

You can get to the principal Shekhawati towns by train but road access is easier. A car comes in handy, though there are crowded buses from Delhi, Jaipur and Bikaner to some towns. Buses leave every 30 minutes from 0500-2000 from Jaipur's Main Bus Station and take three hours. See Transport, page 392.

Tip...

A recommended read is *The Painted Towns of Shekhawati*, by Ilay Cooper, a great Shekhawati enthusiast, with photos and maps.

Getting around

You can get from one Shekhawati town to another by local bus, which run every 15 to 20 minutes. Within each town it is best to enlist the help of a local person (possibly from the hotels listed below) to direct you to the best *havelis*, as it can be very difficult to find your way around. Bicycle tours of Shekhawati can be arranged by **Apani Dhani** in Nawalgarh.

The *havelis* are often occupied by the family or retainers who will happily show you around, either for free or for a fee of about Rs 20. Many *havelis* are in a poor state of repair with fading paintings which may appear monotonously alike to some.

Best haveli restoration
Fatehpur's Nadine Le Prince Haveli Art Gallery, see left column
Malji Ka Kamra in delightful Churu, page 390
The charming Mandawa Haveli, page 390

Where to stay

$$$-$$ Castle Pachar
Pachar, T011-2568 6868 (Delhi office),
www.heritagehotelsofindia.com.
16 well-decorated rooms in a fascinating
old property with portraits, paintings and
weaponry, delicious if very rich food, charming
hosts, swimming pool under construction.
Recommended.

Restaurants

$ Natraj Restaurant
Main Rd, Sikar.
Good meals and snacks, clean, reasonable.

Jhunjhunun District

rolling hills dotted with lavishly painted *havelis*

Jhunjhunun

A stronghold of the Kayamkhani Nawabs, Jhunjhunun was defeated by the Hindu Sardul Singh
in 1730. The Mohanlal **Iswardas Modi** (1896), **Tibriwala** (1883) and the Muslim **Nuruddin Farooqi
Haveli** (which is devoid of figures) and the *maqbara* are all worth seeing. The Chhe Haveli complex,
Khetri Mahal (1760) and the Biharilal temple (1776), which has attractive frescoes (closed during
lunch time), are also interesting. The **Rani Sati** temple commemorates Narayana Devi who is
believed to have become a *sati*; her stone is venerated by many of the wealthy *bania* community
and an annual Marwari fair is held (protesting women's groups feel it glorifies the practice of *sati*).
Since 1947, 29 cases of *sati* have been recorded in Jhunjhunun and its two neighbouring districts.
Jhunjhunun is the most bustling town in Shekhawati and serves as the district's headquarters – it is
preferable to stay in Nawalgarh or Mandawa.

Nawalgarh

Some 25 km southeast of Mandawa, Nawalgarh was founded in 1737 by Thakur Nawal Singh.
There are numerous fine *havelis* worth visiting here. The town has a colourful bazar – though lone
tourists have been harassed here – and two forts (circa 1730). **Nawalgarh Fort** has fine examples
of maps and plans of Shekhawati and Jaipur. The **Bala Kila**, which has a kiosk with beautiful ceiling
paintings, is approached via the fruit market in the town centre and entered through the **Hotel
Radha**. It also has the Roop Niwas Palace (now a hotel) and some 18th-century temples with 19th-
and early 20th-century paintings. There are other interesting temples in town including Ganga Mai
near Nansa Gate.

The **Anandilal Poddar Haveli**, now converted to the **Poddar Haveli Museum** ① *foreigners Rs 100,
includes camera and guide*, is perhaps the best restored *haveli* of Shekhawati. The 1920s *haveli* has
around 700 frescoes including a Gangaur procession, scenes from the Mahabharata, trains, cars, the
avatars of Vishnu, bathing scenes and British characters. Exceptionally well restored throughout,
some of the best paintings frame the doors leading from the courtyard to the rooms. The upper
storey of the *haveli* is now a school but the ground floor has been opened as a museum. The photo
gallery records the life of congressman and freedom fighter Anandilal Poddar, and the merchant-
turned-industrialist Poddar family. There is a diorama of costumes of various Rajasthani tribes and
communities, special bridal attires and a gallery of musical instruments.

Other remarkable Murarka *havelis* include the 19th-century **Kesardev Murarka**, which has
a finely painted façade, and the early 20th-century **Radheshyam Murarka**. The latter portrays
processions, scenes from folk tales and various Hindu and Christian religious themes, sometimes
interspersed with mirror-work. Other fine *havelis* are those of the Bhagat, Chokhani, Goenka,
Patodia, Kedwal, Sangerneria, Saraogi, Jhunjhunwala, Saha and Chhauchuria families. The paintings
here depict anything from European women having a bath to Hindu religious themes and Jesus

Christ. Some of the *havelis* are complexes of several buildings which include a temple, dharamshala, cenotaph and a well. Most charge Rs 15-20 for a viewing.

Mandawa
Similar to Nawalgarh, Mandawa has a high density of *havelis* in its pleasant streets and is one of the preferred places to stay in the area with plenty of characterful accommodation. Even the State Bank of Bikaner and Jaipur is an old *haveli*.

Parasarampura
About 12 km southeast of Nawalgarh, Parasarampura has a decorated *chhatri* to Sardul Singh (1750) and the adjacent **Gopinath Temple** (1742); these are the earliest examples of Shekhawati frescoes painted with natural pigments (the caretaker has the keys, and will point things out with a peacock feather).

Baggar
The grand *haveli* of the **Makharias**, 10 km north east of Jhunjhunun, has rooms along open corridors around grassy courtyards; worth seeing if only for the wall paintings of gods and angels being transported in motor cars.

Churu
Set in semi-desert countryside, Churu, northwest of Baggar, was believed to have been a Jat stronghold in the 16th century. In the 18th century it was an important town of Bikaner state and its fort dates from this period. The town thrived during the days of overland desert trade. The town has some interesting 1870s Oswal Jain *havelis* like those of the Kotharis and the Suranas. Also worth a look are the **Banthia** (early 20th century), **Bagla** (1880), **Khemka** (1800s), **Poddar** and **Bajranglal Mantri** *havelis* – some are well looked after but most are crumbling façades. A few *havelis* have even been destroyed. The main attraction, however, is the extraordinary '**Malji-ka-Kamra**', which has been lovingly restored in recent years. It's a stunning colonnaded *haveli* which houses some amazing interior scenes and is now a heritage hotel (www.maljikakamra.com). The hotel organizes fantastic walking tours of Churu taking in the *havelis* and temples of the area (the Jain temple is particularly special). Churu is a special place which should not be missed.

Tal Chappar Wildlife Sanctuary
A possible day excursion from one of the castle hotels is a visit to Tal Chappar Wildlife Sanctuary near Sujjangarh covering 71 sq km of desert scrubland with ponds and salt flats. It has some of the largest herds of Blackbuck antelope in India (easily seen at the watering point near the park gate itself during the dry season), besides chinkara gazelle, desert cat, desert fox and other dryland wildlife. Huge flocks of demoiselle and common cranes can be seen at nearby lakes and wetlands during the winter months (September to March) where they feed on tubers and ground vegetation.

Some 175 different species of bird visit the park over the course of a year, including sandgrouse, quails, bar-headed geese and cream-coloured desert courser.

Visiting Tal Chappar The best time to visit is just after the rainy season, generally August and September. The enthusiastic and charming forest guard, Brij Dansamor, is a good guide to the area. A local NGO, **Krishna Mirg**, is active in tree plantation and in fundraising for the eco-development of Tal Chappar, providing support fodder during dry months to blackbuck and cranes. **Forest Department Rest House** has five basic but adequate rooms. To book ahead call the head office in Churu on T01562-250938. Try **Hanuman** tea stall for delicious *chai* and the local sweet, *malai laddoo*. The drive to Tal Chappar can be long and tiring but if you are travelling between Bikaner and Shekhawati in a jeep, it is worth making a detour.

Listings Jhunjhunun District

Tourist information

RTDC
Mandawa Circle, Jhunjhunun, T01592-232909.

Where to stay

$$$$ Malji Ka Kamra
Behind Jain Market, Churu, T01562-254 514,
www.maljikakamra.com.
Lovingly restored *haveli* – it's incredible to see the before and after pictures. Good-size rooms some with expansive balconies, lovely restaurant but also with possibility to eat outside. As well as informative heritage walks of Churu, they offer village tours and trips into the surrounding desert for breakfast or supper – quite magical. Highly recommended.

$$$$-$$$ Castle Mandawa
Mandawa, T0141-237 4112 (Jaipur office),
www.mandawahotels.com.
Huge castle with lots of character, 68 a/c rooms, some in the tower, complete with swing, most with 4-posters and period trappings but rooms vary and beds can be hard so select with care, excellent views, atmospheric, lovely swimming pool, interesting miniature shop with on-site artist, mixed reports, some disappointed with meals (Rs 450-500).

$$$$-$$$ Desert Resort
1 km south of Mandawa, T0141-237 4112,
www.mandawahotels.com.
Palatial mud-huts with serene swimming pool and inspiring views. This unique resort puts a new spin on traditional mud huts with interiors ornamented with mirrorwork and glass beads and all the mod cons. Very beautiful, highly recommended.

$$$-$$ Jamuna Resort
Baggar Rd, Jhunjhunun, T01592-232871,
www.hoteljamunaresort.com.
14 a/c cottage rooms with attractive mirror work and murals, the 'Golden Room' has a painted ceiling "like a jewel box", frescos, open-air Rajasthani vegetarian/non-vegetarian restaurant serving delicious food, gardens, pool (open to hotel/restaurant guests only), local guided tours. Recommended.

$$$-$$ Roop Niwas Kothi
1 km north of Nawalgarh, T01594-222008,
www.roopniwaskothi.com.
25 rooms in sunny colonial-style buildings. Beautiful grounds with peacocks, pool, and good food. This is the place to come for excellent horse safaris of the region.

$$ Mandawa Haveli
Near Sonthaliya Gate, Mandawa, T01592-223088, www.hotelmandawa.com.
18 stunning rooms with modernized baths in a 3-storeyed, characterful *haveli* with original 19th-century frescoes in the courtyard, every aspect is beautiful inside and out, great Rajasthani meals, museum and library. Friendly staff, authentic feel. A real gem. The inner courtyard is stunning and there are charming rooftop meals. Recommended.

$$ Piramal Haveli
Baggar, T0159-221220,
www.neemranahotels.com.
Stunning 100-year-old home, restored sensitively with a few roaming peacocks, excellent vegetarian meals and attentive service, quirky original frescoes.

$$-$ Narayan Niwas Castle
Near bus stand, Mehansar, T01595-264322,
www.mehansarcastle.com.
Rooms in the fort, converted by Thakur Tejpal
Singh. Only 16 rooms are open (out of a total
of 500); Nos 1 and 5 are really exceptional.
Attractive wall paintings, pleasingly unspoilt.
This is a well-loved place. Delicious meals (cooked
by Mrs Singh), home-made liqueurs, charming
owners, a *Fawlty Towers* experience.

$ Apani Dhani
Jhunjhunu Rd, 1 km from railway station,
500 m north of bus stand, Nawalgarh,
T01594-222239, www.apanidhani.com.
8 environmentally friendly huts and 3 beautiful
tents on an ecological farm run by the charming
and knowledgeable Ramesh Jangid. Attractive,
comfortable, solar-lit thatched cottages
traditionally built using mud and straw, modern
bathrooms (some with 'footprint' toilets), home-
grown vegetarian, immaculately presented,
relaxing atmosphere. Accommodation and
education in one enticing package. Cooking
lessons also possible. Very special place. No
alcohol permitted and modest respectful dress
requested. Recommended.

$ Shekawati Guest House
Near Roop Niwas, Nawalgarh, T01594-224 658,
www.shekawatiguesthouse.com.
6 clean, well-presented rooms and also now a
circle of simple, yet beautiful thatched cottages,
as well as an attractive thatched restaurant run
by the friendly qualified cook Kalpana Singh.
The food is exceptional and cooking classes can
be arranged, as can local tours. Check out their
organic garden. Recommended.

$ Tourist Pension
Behind Maur Hospital, Nawalgarh, T01594-
224060, www.touristpension.com.
8 rooms, some family-sized, in a modern
house run by Rajesh, the son of the owner of
Apani Dhani (see above), and his wife Sarla, an
excellent cook. Some nice big rooms, beautiful
old furniture made by Rajesh's grandfather, very
welcoming. Another guesthouse has opened up
calling itself **Tourist Pension** near Roop Niwas;
make sure you come to the right one.

Restaurants

$$ Roop Niwas Kothi
Nawalgarh.
For heritage experience (and unreliable service).

$ Shekawati Guest House
Nawalgarh.
For delicious, hygienically prepared fare.

What to do

Camel safaris
A typical 5-day safari might include Nawalgarh–
Mukundgarh–Mandawa–Mahansar–Churu
(crossing some of the finest sand dunes in
Shekawati); 3-day safaris might include
Nawalgarh–Fatehpur. Also 1-week country
safaris to Tal Chappar Wildlife Sanctuary. The
cost depends on the number in the group and
the facilities provided ranging from Rs 800-1500
per day. 1-day safaris arranged by the heritage
hotels cost about Rs 800 with packed lunch and
mineral water. **Mandawa** (see Where to stay,
opposite) offers trips.

Horse safaris
Roop Niwas at Nawalgarh (see Where to stay,
above) offers 1-week safaris staying overnight
in royal tents (occasionally in castles or heritage
hotels) to cover the attractions of the region. The
most popular take in the Pushkar or Tilwara fairs.
You can expect folk music concerts, campfires,
guest speakers, masseurs, and sometimes even a
barber, all with jeep support. You ride 3 hrs in the
morning and 2 hrs in the afternoon, and spend
time visiting eco-farms, rural communities and
havelis en route.

Trekking
There are some interesting treks in the Aravalli
hills near Nawalgarh starting from Lohargal
(34 km), a temple with sacred pools. Local
people claim that this is the place recorded in the
Mahabharata where Bhim's mace is said to have
been crafted. A 4- to 5-day trek would take in the
Bankhandi Peak (1052 m), Krishna temple in Kirori
Valley, Kot Reservoir, Shakambari mata temple,
Nag Kund (a natural spring) and Raghunathgarh
Fort. The cost depends on the size of the group
and the facilities. **Apani Dhani**, see Where to stay,
above, arranges highly recommended treks with
stays at the temple guesthouses and villages for
US$50 per person per day (minimum 2 people).

Transport

Bus All major towns in the region including Sikar, Nawalgarh and Jhunjhunun are linked by bus with **Jaipur** (3-6 hrs) and **Bikaner**, and some have a daily service to **Delhi** (7-10 hrs); it's best to book a day ahead for these as buses fill up.

Jeep For hire in Nawalgarh, Mandawa and Dundlod, about Rs 1500 per day.

Taxi From **Jaipur**, a diesel Ambassador costs around Rs 3000 for a day tour of parts of Shekhawati; with detours (eg Samode) and a/c cars coming in around Rs 5000.

Local hire is possible in Mandawa, Mukundgarh and Nawalgarh. Also see Car hire in Delhi, page 91, as Shekhawati lies on a sensible if slightly elongated route between there and Jaipur.

Train Most trains through Shekhawati are slow passenger services, which tend to run to their own schedule. Most begin their journeys at **Rewari** (see Bikaner, page 78), and connect with **Bikaner** and **Jaipur**. Check locally for current schedules.

Background Rajasthan

History

Early origins

Humans lived along the Banas River 100,000 years ago. Harappan and post Harappan (third to second millennium BC) cultures have been discovered, as at Kalibangan where pottery has been dated to 2700 BC. The Mauryan Emperor Asoka controlled this part of the state in the third century BC, to be succeeded by the Bactrian Greeks (second century BC), the Sakas (Scythians, second to fourth centuries AD), the Guptas (fourth to sixth centuries) and the Huns (sixth century). Rajput dynasties rose from the seventh to the 11th centuries and until the end of the 12th century they controlled much of North India.

Rajputs

Rajputs claimed to be the original *Kshatriyas* (warriors) of the ancient *varna* system, born out of the fire offering of the Gods on Mount Abu. They were probably descended from the Huns and Scythians who had entered India in the sixth century, and they modelled themselves on Rama (the hero of the *Ramayana* epic), seeing themselves as protectors of the Hindu *dharma* against invaders. The Brahmins made considerable efforts to give them royal lineages and accorded them *kshatriya* status. The Rajputs went to great lengths to insist on their *Kshatriya* status – a means of demonstrating to their subjects that not only was it foolhardy, but also sacrilegious to oppose their authority. Associated with this was promotion of those qualities ascribed to the martial castes: chivalry, bravery and unquestioning loyalty.

The Mughals and the Rajputs

Rather than engage in costly campaigns to crush the Rajputs, the Mughal Emperor Akbar (ruled 1556-1605) sought conciliation. Many Rajput princes were given high office in return for loyalty and Akbar sealed this important strategic alliance by marrying a Rajput princess, Jodha Bai, the daughter of the Maharaja of Amber. The relationship between the Rajput princes and the Mughals did not always remain so close, and in the later Mughal period several Rajput princes sought to secure their autonomy from Mughal rule. Such autonomy was brought to an end by the spread of British colonial power. After the quelling of the Mutiny in 1858 and establishment of the British Indian Empire, the Rajput Princely States gained in show of power, with 21-gun salutes, royal polo matches and durbars, just as they lost its reality.

Modern Rajasthan

After Independence the region's 18 princely states were ultimately absorbed into the new state of Rajasthan on 1 November 1956. The successors of royal families have lost power but retain considerable political influence. The palaces, many of them converted to hotels with varying degrees of success, maintain the memory of princely India.

Rajasthan is one of the least densely populated and poorest states in India. Primarily an agricultural and pastoral economy, it does have good mineral resources. Tourism makes a large contribution to the regional economy. Two of the main industries are textiles and the manufacture of rugs and woollen goods, while traditional handicrafts such as pottery, jewellery, marble work, embossed brass, block printing, embroidery and decorative painting are now very good foreign exchange earners.

Haryana
& Punjab

serene temples and bustling cities

The flat, open and richly cultivated plains of Haryana and Punjab witnessed some of ancient India's most significant battles. Kurukshetra, Krishna's battlefield in the Mahabharata, and Panipat, where Muslim power was established, lie in Haryana just north of Delhi.

Today, however, it is the Punjab, peopled by the gregarious and industrious Sikhs, which is the foremost of the two states. Although only 2% of the Indian population, the Sikh contribution to the life and character, not to mention cuisine, of Northern India, greatly outweighs their relatively meagre numbers.

Amritsar's Golden Temple, one of the great treasures of North India and compared by many to the Taj Mahal, is the holiest centre of worship for the Sikhs, whose roots lie in the soil of the Punjab. Le Corbusier's specially designed capital, Chandigarh, modernist in conception and secular in spirit, could scarcely stand in greater contrast.

Haryana has a less distinct identity, culturally subsumed by the capital city which it surrounds, and for most visitors will simply serve as a transit state on their way elsewhere.

Best for
Countryside ▪ Heritage ▪ Temples

Footprint
picks

★ **Chandigarh**, page 398

Don't miss Chand's remarkable Rock Garden.

★ **Khalsa Heritage Complex**, page 402

Marvel at the stunning architecture at Anandapur Sahib's Sikh museum.

★ **Golden Temple**, page 404

Get up early to see the sunrise glinting on Amritsar's Golden Temple.

★ **Guru Ram Das Langar**, page 406

Have lunch in the temple's impressive community kitchen.

★ **Wagah**, page 409

Catch the ceremonial changing of the guard at the India–Pakistan border.

Essential Haryana and Punjab

Finding your feet

Haryana (population 21.1 million) and Punjab (population 24.9 million) occupy the strategic borderlands between the Indus and Yamuna-Ganga river systems. Well over 1000 km from the sea, their gently sloping plains are less than 275 m above sea level. In the southwest, on the arid borders of Rajasthan, sand dunes form gentle undulations in the plain.

Most major towns and cities of the region are close to the Grand Trunk Road, the great highway from Peshawar to Kolkata which Rudyard Kipling described as "the backbone of all Hind". Today, the Grand Trunk Road is a multi-lane highway, lined not only with Punjabi *dhabas* but also drive-thru fast-food joints and coffee chains. And you can spy Audi dealerships as well as Maruti.

Fact...

The Punjab consumes more than twice as much butter and chicken than any other state, perhaps one reason for the average Sikh being heavier than the average Indian. Such is the esteem in which butter, in particular, is held that car stickers bearing nothing but the word 'butter' can be bought in Amritsar.

Best hidden treasures

Chandigarh's Museum of Evolution, page 399
Stunning temples at Anandapur Sahib, page 402
Mythical power of Kurukshetra, page 403

Getting around

Chandigarh and Amritsar have frequent train connections with Delhi and buses to Himachal Pradesh.

Fact...

Two-thirds of the 21 million people in Punjab speak Punjabi, closely related to Hindi, while the remainder speak Hindi.

When to go

It's dry, dusty and hot most of the year, with numbingly cold winter mornings. Avoid the middle of summer when it's the monsoon, from July to September.

Time required

One day in Chandigarh is enough for most people. Allow at least a day for the Golden Temple.

Weather Chandigarh

January	February	March	April	May	June
20°C 6°C 30mm	22°C 8°C 40mm	28°C 13°C 20mm	35°C 18°C 10mm	40°C 24°C 10mm	40°C 27°C 70mm

July	August	September	October	November	December
35°C 26°C 240mm	33°C 25°C 200mm	34°C 23°C 120mm	33°C 16°C 20mm	27°C 10°C 0mm	22 6°C 10mm

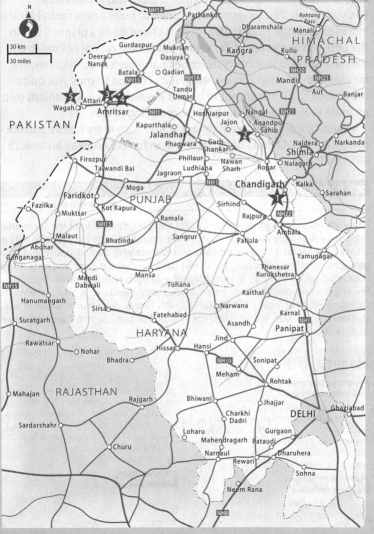

Footprint
picks
1 **Chandigarh**, page 398
2 **Khalsa Heritage Complex**, page 402
3 **Golden Temple, Amritsar**, page 404
4 **Guru Ram Das Langar**, page 406
5 **Wagah**, page 409

Chandigarh
& around

In 1947 when Lahore, Punjab's former capital, was allocated to Pakistan, the Indian government decided to build a new capital for the Indian state of the Punjab. The result is Chandigarh, a planned city in the post-war modernist style, acting as the dual capital of Punjab and Haryana states. Some critics describe Chandigarh as soulless; anyone familiar with England may be reminded of Milton Keynes. Not quite the garden city it was meant to be, it is nevertheless a convenient stop en route to Himachal Pradesh, or before flying to Leh.

Ironically, many now seem to visit Chandigarh more for the quixotic delights of Nek Chand's Rock Garden than for its European architect's alien buildings.

★ Chandigarh

an example of urban planning

Chandigarh's major centres are the Capitol Complex, consisting of the Secretariat, Legislative Assembly and High Court in the northeast with the Shiwalik Hills as a backdrop; Sector 17, the central business district with administrative and state government offices, shopping areas and banks; a Cultural Zone in Sector 14 for education, which includes a museum and a campus university with institutions for engineering, architecture, Asian studies and medicine. A vast colonnaded shopping mall has opened in Sector 35, with hotels, restaurants, banks, a well-stocked supermarket and internet/international phones. Sector 7 also has a high density of shops.

Essential Chandigarh

Finding your feet

The airport and railway stations are some distance from the centre with pre-paid auto rickshaws to town. From the large **Inter-State Bus Terminus (ISBT)** in the busy Sector 17, you can walk to several budget hotels and restaurants. See Transport, page 401.

Getting around

Buses serve the different sectors but if you are only here for a few hours, it is best to hire transport as there are long distances to cover in this widely spread out city and it is not always easy to find a taxi or auto-rickshaw for single journeys. Half-day tours 'Fun on Wheels' offer a hop-on hop-off service around the attractions; contact **CITCO** for information (see under Tourist information in Listings, below).

When to go

The best time to visit is November to March; monsoon season is June to August. See also the weather chart on page 396.

Sights

The multi-pillared **High Court** stands nearby with a reflective pool in front. Primary colour panels break up the vast expanses of grey concrete but this classic work of modernist architecture looks stark and bleak. The **Legislative Assembly** has a removable dome and a mural by Le Corbusier that symbolizes evolution. In the same sector is the **Open Hand Monument**. The insignia of the Chandigarh Administration, it symbolizes "the hand to give and the hand to take; peace and prosperity, and the unity of humankind". The metal monument, 14 m high and weighing 50 tonnes, rotates in the wind and sometimes resembles a bird in flight. The geometrical hill nearby, known as the **Tower of Shadows** ① *tours 1030-1230 and 1420-1630, ask at Secretariat reception desk (you may need special permission to enter)*, was designed to beautify the complex, breaking its symmetrical lines.

The **Government Museum and Art Gallery** ① *Sector 10, Tue-Sun 1000-1630*, has a collection of stone sculptures dating back to the Gandhara period, as well as miniature paintings, modern art, prehistoric fossils and artefacts. The **Museum of Evolution of Life** ① *Sector 10, Tue-Sun 1000-1630*, has exhibits covering 5000 years from the Indus Valley Civilization to the present day. The **Fine Arts Museum** ① *Punjab University, Sector 14 (all the faculties of the university are in Gandhi Bhavan, Sector 14), Mon-Fri 1000-1700 (closed between 1300-1400)*, specializes in Gandhi studies. The **Chandigarh Architecture Museum** ① *Sector 10-C, Tue-Sun 1000-1645* charts the planning and creation of Chandigarh.

The **Rock Garden** or **Garden of Nek Chand** ① *Apr-Sep 0900-1900, Oct-Mar closes1800, Rs 15, allow 3 hrs*, an unusual place, is the creation of Nek Chand, a road inspector in the Capitol City project. The 'garden' comprises an extraordinary collection of stones from the nearby Shiwaliks (carried on his bike) and domestic rubbish transformed into sculptures. Nek Chand dreamed of "creating a temple to Gods and Goddesses" out of discarded items of everyday use, for example bottle tops, fluorescent

1 Chandigarh

Chandigarh maps
1 Chandigarh, page 399
2 Chandigarh – Sectors 17 & 22, page 401

Where to stay 🛏
Classic 1
Divyadeep &
  Bhoj Restaurant 4
Kaptain's Retreat 5
Jullunder 3
Maya 2

Restaurants 🍴
Mehfil 4
Sagar Ratna 2

lights, mud guards, tin cans, and by highly imaginative re-assembling made models of people and animals. These have been set out along a maze of paths, creating an amusing and enjoyable park. First opened in 1976 the park is still being extended. The low archways make visitors bow to the gods who have blessed the park. It definitely challenges the uniformity of the rest of Chandigarh.

Just below the rock garden is the man-made **Sukhna Lake**, the venue of the Asian rowing championships which is circled by a walk. It gets crowded on holidays and Sunday. There are cafés, boating and fishing (permits needed).

The **Rose Gardens** ① *Sector 16, until sunset,* are one of the largest in Asia (25 ha), contains over 1500 varieties of rose; well worth visiting in spring. There's a rose show in early March.

The **Zoological Park** ① *Chaat Bir, a few kilometres out of the city centre, Rs 30 per person,* has a lion and deer safari park.

Listings Chandigarh *maps p399 and p401*

Tourist information

Chandigarh Tourism
*ISBT, Sector 17, T0172-270 3839,
www.chandigarhtourism.gov.in.*

Himachal Tourism
1st floor, ISBT, T0172-270 8569.

Uttarakhand and Uttar Pradesh Tourism
ISBT, T0172-271 3988.

Where to stay

$$$$-$$$ Maya
SCO 325-28, S35-B, T0172-260 0547.
After quite the nip and tuck, Maya is a stylish, boutique hotel with comfortable rooms and chic restaurant. Definitely worth checking out.

$$$ Deep Roots Retreat
Village Ranjitpur, 25 km from Chandigarh, T(0)98784 30085, www.deeprootsretreat.com.
Out in the countryside beyond Chandigarh, you get insight into the life of a Punjabi farm. Stylish rooms, great home-cooked food and good for dipping into Chandigarh for sightseeing. Picnics, tractor rides and bonfires can all be arranged. They have another fort property close to Anandapur Sahib.

$$$ Kaptain's Retreat
303 S35-B, T0172-500 5599, kaptainsretreat@hotmail.com.
Owned by the legendary cricketer, Kapil Dev, this is Chandigarh's first boutique hotel. Each room is named after one of the great man's achievements, eg 'nine wickets', although the interiors are more than cricket chic with attractive decor and excellent attention to detail. There's also an appealing bar and restaurant. Good value. Recommended.

$$$-$$ Classic
S35-C, T0172-260 6092, www.hotelclassicchandigarh.com.
Comfortable modern hotel (buffet breakfast included), with a bar, lively bar and disco. Reasonable value.

$$$-$$ Jullunder
S22, opposite ISBT, T0172-461 1121,
www.jullunderhotel.com.
17 average a/c rooms with restaurant on site.

$$-$ Divyadeep
S22-B, Himalaya Marg, T0172-270 5191.
15 rooms, some a/c, neat and clean, great value,
good **Bhoj** restaurant. Recommended.

Restaurants

$$$ Elevens
Kaptain's Retreat (see Where to stay, above).
Unusual combination of Pakistani, Indian and
Thai cuisines in Mediterranean-style interior.
Recommended.

$$$ Mehfil
183, S17-C, T0172-502 5599.
International. Upmarket, a/c, comfortable seating,
spicy meals.

$$ Bhoj
S22-B, Divyadeep (see Where to stay, above).
Indian Vegetarian. Good set *thalis* only, pleasant,
clean, busy at lunch, good value.

$$ Pashtun
S35-B.
Excellent frontier-style cuisine in pleasant
ground-floor restaurant plus 'Wild West' bar
in basement, complete with cowboy waiters.
Formerly called **Khyber**. Recommended.

$$ Sagar Ratna
S35-C.
High-quality South Indian. Well-presented,
nationwide chain, very professional.

Festivals

Apr All the Hindu festivals are celebrated
especially **Baisakhi**, celebrated by both Hindus
and Sikhs as **New Year's Day** (13-14 Apr).
Bhangra dancers perform, celebrating harvest.

What to do

Tour operators
Chandigarh Tourism, *T0172-505 5462, www.
chandigarhtourism.gov.in, or book at ISBT (see
Finding your feet, page 398).* Local tours including
good-value open-top bus and further afield
to Pinjore Gardens, Bhakra Dam, Amritsar,
Shimla, Kullu and Manali. They do half-day
tours of the city in their double decker fun bus.

Transport

Air Airport, 11 km. Taxis charge Rs 300 to
centre. **Air India**: reservations, S17, T0172-265
4941, airport, T0172-622 6029, 1000-1630. Daily
to **Mumbai** and **Delhi**. Jet Airways, 14 S 9D
Madhya Marg, T0172-3939 3333, daily to **Delhi**.

Bicycle hire Free to **CITCO** hotel guests.

2 Chandigarh – Sectors 17 & 22

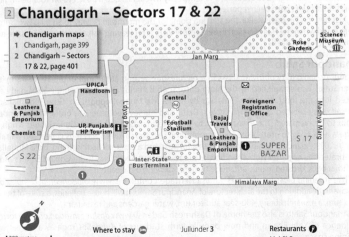

➡ **Chandigarh maps**
1 Chandigarh, page 399
2 Chandigarh – Sectors
  17 & 22, page 401

300 metres
300 yards

Where to stay 🛏
Divyadeep & Bhoj
Restaurant **2**

Jullunder **3**

Restaurants 🍴
Mehfil **5**

Bus It is easier to get a seat on the **Shimla** bus from Chandigarh than from Kalka. Many buses daily from **ISBT**, S17. A 2nd terminal in S43 has some buses to **Himachal Pradesh**, **Jammu** and **Srinagar**; city buses connect the 2. Transport offices: ISBT, S17, 0900-1300, 1400-1600; Chandigarh, T0172-270 0006; Haryana, T0172-272 2980; Himachal, T0172-266 8943; Punjab, T0172-270 4023, you can also check out www.punbusonline.com. Buy bus tickets from the designated booths next to platforms before boarding. Seat numbers (written on the back of tickets) are often assigned. **Shimla** buses (via Kalka) leave from platform 10. To **Amritsar**, 6 hrs (from Aroma Hotel, T0172-270 0045); **Pathankot**, 7 hrs; **Dharamshala**, 10 hrs; **Kalka** (from Platform 10), Rs 11-28. Buses to **Shimla** also stop at **Kalka**; **Kullu** 12 hrs. Also **Himachal Tourism** coaches during the season, to **Delhi**, 5 hrs; **Manali**, 0800, 10 hrs; **Shimla**, 5 hrs.

Rickshaw Auto-rickshaws are metered with a minimum fare, but you can bargain. Stands at bus station, railway station and the Rock Garden. Cycle rickshaws are unmetered.

Taxi Private taxi stands in S22, S17, S35. **Mega Cabs**, T0172-414 1414. To **Kalka**, up to Rs 400.

Train The station (8 km) has a clean waiting room but a poor bus service to the city. Pre-paid auto-rickshaws, Rs 45 to S22; to bus stand Rs 34; to Kalka (for the brave) Rs 200. Enquiries/reservations, T1333, T0172-264 1651, 1000-1700; City Booking Office, 1st floor, Inter-State Bus Terminal (ISBT), S17, T0172-270 8573, Mon-Sat 0800-1345, 1445-2000, Sun 0800-1400. Tourist office, 0600-2030. **New Delhi**: *Shatabdi Exp 12006* (early morning), 3¾ hrs; *Shatabdi Exp 12012* (evening), 3½ hrs; **Shimla** (via Kalka): *Himalayan Queen 14095*, 1 hr to Kalka, then 40 mins' wait for *Himalayan Queen 52455* to **Shimla** (1210, 6 hrs, book ahead). See also Kalka, page 423.

Chandigarh to Himachal Pradesh

cities dotted with Sikh temples

Pinjore (Pinjaur)

The **Yadavindra Gardens**, at Pinjore, 20 km on the Kalka road, were laid out by Aurangzeb's foster brother Fidai Khan, who also designed the Badshahi Mosque in Lahore. Within the Mughal *char bagh* gardens are a number of palaces in a Mughal-Rajasthani style: **Shish Mahal**, which has mirror-encased ceiling and is cooled by water flowing underneath (remove a slab to see!); **Rang Mahal**, a highly decorated pavilion; and **Jal Mahal**, set among fountains, cool and delightful. There are also camel rides and fairground attractions to tempt city dwellers. Keep a close eye on your belongings at all times; thefts have been reported.

Just beyond Pinjore is **Kalka**, the starting point for the mountain railway to Shimla. Two Britons were killed when the train derailed in September 2015 after leaving Kalka station. Services are now running at lower speeds.

Anandpur Sahib

Anandpur Sahib (City of Divine Bliss), in a picturesque setting at the foot of the Shiwaliks by the River Sutlej, was established by the ninth guru, Tegh Bahadur, in 1664, when the Sikhs had been forced into the foothills of the Himalaya by increasing Mughal opposition. Guru Tegh Bahadur himself was executed in Chandni Chowk, Delhi, and his severed head was brought to Anandpur Sahib to be cremated. The event added to the determination of his son, Guru Gobind Singh, to forge a new body to protect the Sikh community. The Khalsa Panth was thus created on Baisakhi Day in 1699. Anandpur Sahib became both a fortress and a centre of Sikh learning. **Hola Mohalla** is celebrated the day after Holi when battles are re-enacted by *nihangs* (Guru Gobind Singh's army) on horseback, dressed in blue and huge turbans, carrying old weapons.

The stunning blossom of the ★ Khalsa Heritage Complex ⊕ *www.khalsaheritagecomplex.org*, is a dramatic addition to the architecture of Anandpur Sahib. It will house galleries, a state of the art museum, a research library, 400-seat auditorium, water gardens and restaurant.

Anandpur Sahib is also the home of **Dashmesh Sadan** ⊕ *www.dashmeshsadan.org*, the former residence of Yogi Bhajan and now popular with students of Kundalini Yoga as a retreat and training space.

Where to stay

Anandpur Sahib

It is possible to stay in one of the many *gurudwaras* in town.

$$-$ Kissan Haveli
Dashmesh Academy Rd, T01887-232 650.
10 rooms in this characterful heritage-style property.

$ Holy City
Dashmesh Academy Rd, T01887-232 330,
www.hotelholycity.com.
Clean basic rooms and good value restaurant.

Transport

Anandpur Sahib

Bus From **Chandigarh** and **Ropar**.

historical and mythical battlefields

Kurukshetra

The battlefield where Arjuna learned the meaning of *dharma* has left no trace. The plain around Kurukshetra is described in Sanskrit literature as "Brahmavarta" (Land of Brahma). Like many other sacred sites it becomes the special focus of pilgrimage at the time of exceptional astronomical events. In Kurukshetra, eclipses of the sun are marked by special pilgrimages, when over one million people come to the tank. It is believed that the waters of all India's sacred tanks meet together at the moment of eclipse, giving extra merit to anyone who can bathe in it at that moment.

Panipat

Panipat is the site of three great battles which mark the rise and fall of the Mughal Empire. It stands on the higher ground made up of the debris of earlier settlements near the old bank of the River Yamuna. Today it is an important textile town with over 30,000 looms. A high proportion of the products – carpets, curtains and tablewear are exported.

In the first battle of Panipat on 21 April 1526 Babur, the first Mughal emperor, fought Ibrahim Lodi, the Sultan of Delhi, which reputedly resulted in the death of 20,000 of the sultan's army, including Ibrahim Lodi.

The second battle, on 5 November 1556, changed the course of India's history, as it secured Mughal power. Akbar, who had just succeeded his father Humayun and his general, defeated Hemu, the nephew of the Afghan Sher Shah. There was a mass slaughter of the captives, and in the gruesome tradition of Genghis Khan, a victory pillar was built with their heads plastered in.

The third battle took place on 13 January 1761. The once great Mughal Empire was threatened from the west by the resurgent Rajputs and from the northwest by the Afghans. The distracted Mughal minister called in the Marathas. Despite their numbers, the Marathas lost and their soldiers fled. However, the Afghan leader Ahmad Shah Durrani was unable to take advantage of his victory as his followers mutinied for the two years' arrears of pay he owed them. North India was thus left in a political vacuum which adventurers tried to fill during the next 40 years.

The main old building in Panipat is a **shrine** to the Muslim saint Abu Ali Kalandar.

Where to stay

Kurukshetra

$ Neelkanthi Yatri Niwas
Well signposted, T01744-291 1615.

Haryana Tourism offers over-priced simple rooms, but there are dorm beds at Rs 300 a pop, as well as a restaurant.

Amritsar
& around

Amritsar ('Pool of the Nectar of Immortality') is named after the sacred pool in the Golden Temple, the holiest of Sikh sites. The temple itself, the city's singular attraction, is a haven of peace amidst an essentially congested city. The atmosphere is particularly powerful during *amritvela* (dawn to early light), when the surrounding glistening white-marble pavement is still cold under foot and the gold begins to shimmer on the lightening water. Sunset and evening prayers are also a special time to visit.

You cannot help but be touched by the sanctity and radiance of the place, the friendly welcome of the people and the community spirit. Music constantly plays from within the inner sanctum of the Hari Mandir.

Essential Amritsar

Finding your feet

Sri Guru Ram Das Jee International Airport is 11 km away with taxi or auto-rickshaw transfers. The railway is central, the bus station 2 km east; both are a 15-minute auto-rickshaw ride from the Golden Temple to the south. If you have a couple of hours to spare between connections, you can fit in a visit. See Transport, page 410.

Getting around

The city is quite spread out. Cycle-rickshaws squeeze through the crowded lanes. Auto-rickshaws are handy for longer journeys unless you get a bike. The old city is south of the railway station encircled by a ring road, which traces the line of the city walls built during the reign of Ranjit Singh.

Best Punjabi tastes

Guru Ram Das Langar community food, page 406
Free chai outside the Golden Temple at 0600, page 410
Food with a view from Le Golden, page 410

★ Golden Temple
the spiritual nerve centre of the Sikh faith

Every Sikh tries to make a visit and bathe in the holy water at the Golden Temple. It is immensely powerful, spiritual and welcoming to all, with an all-pervasive air of strength and self-sufficiency.

Visiting the temple
Shoes, socks, sticks and umbrellas can be left outside the cloakroom free of charge. Visitors should wash their feet outside the entrance. It is best to go early as for much of the year the marble gets too hot by noon. Dress appropriately and cover your head in the temple precincts. Head scarves are available during the day but not at night; a handkerchief suffices. Avoid sitting with your back towards the temple or with your legs stretched out. Tobacco, narcotics and intoxicants are not permitted. The community kitchen provides food all day, for a donation. The information office① *near the main entrance, T0183-255 3954*, is very helpful.

Worship
Singing is central to Sikh worship, and the 24-hour chanting at the Golden Temple adds greatly to the reverential atmosphere. After

building the temple, Guru Arjan Dev compiled a collection of hymns of the great medieval saints and this became the *Adi Granth* (Original Holy book). It was installed in the temple as the focus of devotion and teaching. Guru Gobind Singh, the 10th and last Guru (1675-1708) revised the book and also refused to name a successor saying that the book itself would be the Sikh Guru. It thus became known as the *Guru Granth Sahib* (The Holy Book as Guru).

The temple compound

Entering the temple compound through the main entrance or clock tower you see the **Harmandir** (the Golden Temple itself, also spelt Harimandir, and known by Hindus as the Durbar Sahib) beautifully reflected in the stunning expanse of water that surrounds it. Each morning (0400 summer, 0500 winter) the *Guru Granth Sahib* is brought in a vivid procession from the **Akal Takht** at the west end to the Harmandir, to be returned at night (2200 summer, 2100 winter). The former represents temporal power, the latter spiritual – and so they do not quite face each other. Some like to attend **Palki Sahib** (night ceremony).

All pilgrims walk clockwise round the tank, stopping at shrines and bathing in the tank on the way round to the Harmandir itself. The tank is surrounded by an 8-m-wide white marble pavement, banded with black and brown Jaipur marble.

1 Amritsar

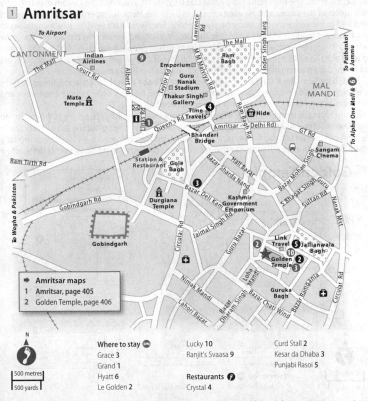

Amritsar maps
1 Amritsar, page 405
2 Golden Temple, page 406

N
500 metres
500 yards

Where to stay
Grace 3
Grand 1
Hyatt 6
Le Golden 2
Lucky 10
Ranjit's Svaasa 9

Restaurants
Crystal 4

Curd Stall 2
Kesar da Dhaba 3
Punjabi Rasoi 5

East end

To the left of the entrance steps are the bathing ghats and an area screened off from public view for women to dip. Also on this side are the **68 Holy Places** representing 68 Hindu pilgrimage sites as referenced in Guru Nanak's Japji Sahib. When the tank was built, Guru Arjan Dev told his followers that rather than visit all the orthodox Hindu places of pilgrimage, they should just bathe here, thus acquiring equivalent merit.

Tip...
Morning prayers at sunrise are beautiful.

A shrine contains a copy of the **Guru Granth Sahib**. Here and at other booths round the tank the Holy Book is read for devotees. Sikhs can arrange with the temple authorities to have the book read in their name in exchange for a donation. The *granthi* (reader) is a temple employee and a standard reading lasts for three hours, while a complete reading takes 48 hours. The tree in the centre at the east end of the tank is popularly associated with a healing miracle.

Dining Hall, Kitchen, Assembly Hall and Guesthouses

The surrounding *bunghas* (white arcade of buildings), are hostels for visitors. Through the archway a path leads to the ★ **Guru Ram Das Langar** (kitchen and dining hall) immediately on the left, while two tall octagonal minarets, the 18th-century **Ramgarhia Minars**, provide a vantage point over the temple and inner city. At the far end of the path are a series of guesthouses including **Guru Ram Das Sarai**, where pilgrims can stay free for up to three nights.

Sikhs have a community kitchen where all temple visitors, regardless of their religious belief, can eat together. The third Guru, Guru Amar Das (1552-1574), abolished the custom of eating only with others of the same caste. He even refused to bless the Mughal Emperor Akbar unless he was prepared to eat with everyone else who was present. *Seva* (voluntary service), which continues to be a feature of modern Sikhism, extends to the kitchen staff and workers; visitors are also welcome to lend a hand. The Amritsar kitchen may feed up to 10,000 people a day, with 3000 at a sitting and up to 1 Lakh (100,000) visitors at the weekends. It is free of charge and vegetarian, though Sikhs are not banned from eating meat. Lunch is 1100-1500 and dinner 1900 onwards.

Next to the Guru Amar Das Langar is the **residence of Baba Kharak Singh** who is hailed by Sikhs as a saint. His followers are distinguished by their orange turbans while temple employees and members of the militant Akali sect wear blue or black turbans.

Returning to the temple tank, the **shrine** on the south side is to Baba Deep Singh. When Ahmad Shah Durrani attacked Amritsar in 1758, Baba Deep Singh was copying out the *Guru Granth Sahib*. He went out to fight with his followers, vowing to defend the temple with his life. He was mortally wounded, 6 km from town; some say that his head was hacked from his body. Grimly determined

② Golden Temple

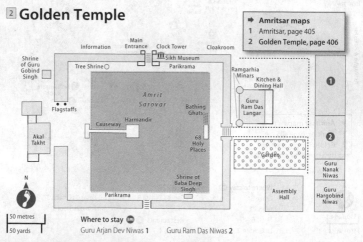

→ Amritsar maps
1 Amritsar, page 405
2 **Golden Temple, page 406**

Where to stay 🛏
Guru Arjan Dev Niwas **1**   Guru Ram Das Niwas **2**

Amritsar

The original site for the city was granted by the Mughal Emperor Akbar (ruled 1556-1605) who visited the temple, and it has been sacred to the Sikhs since the time of the fourth guru, Guru Ram Das (1574-1581). He insisted on paying its value to the local Jats who owned it, thereby eliminating the possibility of future disputes on ownership. Guru Ram Das then invited local merchants to live and trade in the immediate vicinity. In 1577 he heard that a cripple had been miraculously cured while bathing in the pool here. The pool was enlarged and named Amrit Sarovar (Immortality).

Guru Arjan Dev (1581-1601), Guru Ram Das' son and successor, enlarged the tank further and built the original temple at its centre from 1589-1601. The Afghan Ahmad Shah Durrani, desecrated the Golden Temple in 1757. The Sikhs united and drove him out, but four years later he defeated the Sikh armies, sacking the town and blowing up the temple. Later, the Sikhs reconquered the Punjab and restored the temple and tank. Under their greatest secular leader, Maharaja Ranjit Singh, the temple was rebuilt in 1764. In 1830 he donated 100 kg (220 lbs) of gold which was applied to the copper sheets on the roof and much of the exterior of the building, giving rise to the name the 'Golden Temple'.

Now Punjab's second largest town, Amritsar was a traditional junction of trade routes. The different peoples, Yarkandis, Turkomans, Kashmiris, Tibetans and Iranians indicate its connections with the Old Silk Road.

and holding his head on with one hand he fought on. On his way back to the temple he died on this spot. The story is recounted in the picture behind glass.

West end

The complex to the west has the Akal Takht, the flagstaffs, and the Shrine of Guru Gobind Singh. The **flagstaffs** symbolize religion and politics, in the Sikh case intertwined. They are joined in the middle by the emblem of the Sikh nation, the two swords of Hargobind, representing spiritual and temporal authority. The circle is inscribed with the Sikh rallying call *Ek Onkar* (God is One).

Started when Arjan Dev was Guru (1581-1605), and completed by Guru Hargobind in 1609, the **Akal Takht** is the seat of the Sikhs' religious committee. It is largely a mixture of 18th- and early 19th-century building, the upper storeys being the work of Ranjit Singh. It has a first-floor room with a low balcony which houses a gilt-covered ark, central to the initiation of new members of the Khalsa brotherhood.

To the side of the flagstaffs is a **shrine** dedicated to the 10th and last guru, Gobind Singh (Guru 1675-1708). In front of the entrance to the temple causeway is a square, a gathering place for visitors.

Sometimes you may see Nihang (meaning 'crocodile') Sikhs, followers of the militant Guru Gobind Singh, dressed in blue and armed with swords, lances and curved daggers.

At the centre of the tank stands the most holy of all Sikh shrines, the **Harmandir** (The Golden Temple). Worshippers obtain the sweet *prasad* before crossing the causeway to the temple where they make their offering. The 60-m-long bridge, usually crowded with jostling worshippers, is built out of white marble like the lower floor of the temple. The rest of the temple is covered in copper gilt. On the doorways verses from the *Guru Granth Sahib* are inscribed in Gurumukhi script while rich floral paintings decorate the walls and excellent silver work marks the doors. The roof has the modified onion-shaped dome, characteristic of Sikh temples, but in this case it is covered in the gold that Ranjit Singh added for embellishment.

The ground floor of the three-storey temple contains the Holy Book placed on a platform under a jewel-encrusted canopy. *Guru Granth Sahib* contains approximately 3500 hymns. Professional singers and musicians sing verses from the book continuously from 0400-2200 in the summer and 0500-2130 in winter. An excited crowd of worshippers attempts to touch the serpent horn. Each evening the holy book is taken ceremoniously to the Akal Takht and brought back the next morning; visitors are welcome. The palanquin used for this, set with emeralds, rubies and diamonds with

Relations with the British had soured in 1919. *Hartals* (general strikes) became a common form of demonstration. The Punjab, which had supplied 60% of Indian troops committed to the First World War, was one of the hardest hit economically in 1918 and tension was high. The lieutenant governor of the province decided on a 'fist force' to repulse the essentially non-violent but vigorous demonstrations. Some looting occurred in Amritsar and the British called in reinforcements. These arrived under the command of General Dyer.

Dyer banned all meetings but people were reported to be gathering on Sunday 13 April 1919 as pilgrims poured into Amritsar to celebrate Baisakhi, the Sikh New Year and the anniversary of the founding of the *khalsa* in 1699. That afternoon thousands were crammed into Jallianwala Bagh, a piece of waste ground popular with travellers, surrounded on all sides by high walls with only a narrow alley for access. Dyer personally led some troops to the place, gave the crowd no warning and ordered his men to open fire leaving 379 dead and 1200 wounded. Other brutal acts followed.

The massacre was hushed up and the British government in London was only aware of it six months later at which time the Hunter Committee was set up to investigate the incident. It did not accept Dyer's excuse that he acted as he did in order to prevent another insurrection on the scale of the Mutiny of 1857. He was asked to resign and returned to England where he died in 1927. However, he was not universally condemned. A debate in the House of Lords produced a majority of 126 to 86 in his favour and the *Morning Post* newspaper launched a fund for 'The Man who Saved India'. More than £26,000 was raised to comfort the dying general.

India was outraged by Dyer's massacre. Gandhi, who had called the nationwide *hartal* in March, started the Non Co-operation Movement, which was to be a vital feature of the struggle for Independence. This was not the end of the affair. O'Dwyer, the governor of the province, was shot dead at a meeting in Caxton Hall, London, by a survivor of Jallianwala Bagh who was hanged for the offence. For a modern take on the whole story, check out the Bollywood movie *Rang de Basanti*.

silver poles and a golden canopy, can be seen in the treasury on the first floor of the entrance to the temple. Throughout the day, pilgrims place offerings of flowers or money around the book. There is no ritual in the worship or pressure from temple officials to donate money. The marble walls are decorated with mirror-work, gold leaf and designs of birds, animals and flowers in semi-precious stones in the Mughal style.

On the first floor is a balcony on which three respected Sikhs always perform the **Akhand Path** (Unbroken Reading). In order to preserve unity and maintain continuity, there must always be someone practising devotions. The top floor is where the gurus used to sit and here again someone performs the *Akhand Path*; this is the quietest part of the building and affords a good view over the rest of the complex.

On the edge of the tank just west of the entrance is the **Tree Shrine**, a gnarled, 450-year-old *jubi* tree, reputed to have been the favourite resting place of the first chief priest of the temple. Women tie strings to the ingeniously supported branches, hoping to be blessed with a son by the primaeval fertility spirits that choose such places as their home. It is also a favourite spot to arrange and sanctify marriages, despite the protests of the temple authorities. The **Sikh Museum** ① *at the main entrance to the temple (just before steps leading down to the parikrama)*, 0700-1830, free, is somewhat martial, reflecting the struggles against the Mughals, the British and the Indian Army. The **Sikh Library** ① *in the Guru Nanak Building, Mon-Sat 0930-1630*, has a good selection of books in English as well as current national newspapers.

Amritsar town

Jallianwala Bagh, noted for the most notorious massacre under British rule (see box, opposite), is 400 m north of the Golden Temple. Today the gardens are a pleasant enclosed park. They are entered by a narrow path between the houses, opening out over lawns. A **memorial plaque** recounts the history at the entrance, and a large memorial dominates the east end of the garden. There is an interesting museum. On the north side is a well in which many who tried to escape the bullets were drowned, and remnants of walls have been preserved to show the bullet holes.

The old town has a number of mosques and Hindu temples – the **Durgiana Temple** (16th century), and the new **Mata Lal Devi Temple**, which imitates the difficult access to the famous Himalayan Mata Vaishno Devi Cave Temple of Katra by requiring the worshipper to wade awkwardly through water and crawl through womb-like tunnels is well worth a visit. The whole temple area is Disneyesque with plastic grottoes and statues. Women who wish to have children come here to pray, there is community food and a charity hospital run from the temple's trust. It's a very popular and lively temple, and definitely worth a visit. Northeast of the railway station are the **Ram Bagh gardens**, the Mall and Lawrence Road shopping areas.

Trips from Amritsar

★ **Wagah** The changing of the guards and the ceremonial lowering of the flags ceremony at sundown on the border with Pakistan, carried out with great pomp and rivalry, are quite a spectacle. There is much synchronized foot stamping, gate slamming and displays of scorn by colourful soldiers! It is the ministry of funny walks. New viewing galleries have been built but crowds still clamour to get the best view. Women are allowed to get to the front, and there is a VIP section (open to foreign visitors) next to the gate. It is best to get there near closing time though photography is difficult with the setting sun.

Goindwal and Tarn Taran On the way from Amritsar to Jalandar, there are important *gurudwaras* where Sikhs on pilgrimage traditionally stop. There are separate bathing places for men and women at Goindwal, with a small market place outside the temple. The *gurudwara* at Taran Tarn is surrounded by a busy bazar. The *gurudwara* itself is very beautiful, with a very large water tank and cloisters providing welcome shade.

Listings Amritsar *maps p405 and p406*

Tourist information

Tourist office
Opposite the railway station, T07837-613 500.
There is another branch outside the Golden Temple (T07837-613200).

Where to stay

More chain hotels are opening up in Amritsar.

$$$$ Hyatt
Next to Alpha One Mall, GT Rd, T0183-287 1234, www.hyatt.com.
Formerly Ista hotel, this is a beautiful boutique hotel. There is a stunning spa with all the usual ayurvedic fare, but also rose quartz and amethyst facials.

$$$$-$$$ Ranjit's Svaasa
47-A The Mall Rd, T0183-256 6618, www.welcomheritage hotels.in.
Ramada hotel. Tastefully restored rooms with huge windows in a 250-year-old red-brick manor surrounded by palms and lawns, elegant service, great food, beautiful Spa Pavilion offering Ayurvedic and international treatments. Recommended.

$$$-$$ Hotel Le Golden
Clock tower extension, outside Golden Temple complex, T0183-255 6949, www.hotellegolden.com.
Modern rooms close to the temple, with views of Akal Takht. The rooftop restaurant **The Glass** has views of Siri Harmandir Sahib.

$$ Grand
Queens Rd, opposite the train station,
T0183-256 2424, www.hotelgrand.in.
32 modern but characterful rooms, some a/c,
set around an attractive garden. There's a
popular restaurant and appealing bar with
Kingfisher on draught and good food. Very
friendly management.

$ Grace
35 Braham Buta Market, close to Golden Temple,
T0183-255 9355.
Good range of rooms, friendly management.

$ Lucky
Mahna Singh Rd, near Golden Temple and
Jallianwala Bagh, T0183-254 2175.
Basic rooms, some with a/c. Good value.

$ Rest Houses
In/near the Golden Temple, eg Guru Ram Das
Niwas and for foreigners especially Guru Gobind
Singh Niwas.
Some free (up to 3 nights), very simple food;
please leave a donation. Tobacco, alcohol
and drugs are prohibited. They can be noisy
sometimes because people stay in the courtyard,
but it's an eye-opening experience.

Restaurants

Eating with pilgrims in the *langar* (Golden
Temple community kitchen) can be a great
experience. Remember to hold out both hands
(palms upwards) when receiving food. The
corner of the Mall and Malaviya Rd comes
alive with ice cream and fast-food stalls in the
evening. *Dhabas* near the station and temple
sell local *daal*, *saag paneer* and mouthwatering
stuffed *parathas*.

$$$ The Glass
At Le Golden Hotel close to Golden Temple.
Glass rooftop restaurant serves up range of
foods and great views of the temple.

$$ Crystal
Queens Rd, T0183-222 5555.
Good international food, excellent service,
pleasant ambience, huge portions. There is
Crystal on the ground floor proclaiming that
there is only 1 branch. And there is Crystal on
the 2nd floor proclaiming the same thing – the
2 brothers have fallen out and both refuse to
change the name.

$$ Punjabi Rasoi
Near Jallianwala Bagh.
The best option near the Golden Temple. Very
good *thalis*, South Indian food and traditional
Punjabi fare. Internet café upstairs too.
Recommended.

$ Kesar da Dhaba
Passian Darwaza, near Durgiana Temple.
Serves extremely popular sweet *phirni* in small
earthenware bowls. Also Punjabi *thalis*.

Festivals

The birth anniversaries of the 10 gurus are
observed as holy days and those of Guru Gobind
Singh (Dec/Jan) and Guru Nanak in Nov, which is
also a National Holiday, are celebrated as festivals
with *Akhand Path* and processions.
Apr Baisakhi, for Sikhs, the Hindu New Year
marks the day in 1699 Guru Gobind Singh
organized the Sikhs into the Khalsa, see page 402.
The vigorous *bhangra* dance is a common sight
in the villages and falls on 13 or 14 Apr.
Oct/Nov Diwali Illumination of the Golden
Temple, fireworks.

What to do

Time Travels, *14 Kapoor Plaza, Crystal Sq, T0183-
240 0131, www.travelamritsar.com.* Organizes
homestays, tours to Dharamshala, Manali,
Shimla, etc, local villages, as well as to important
Gurudwaras in the state. Very efficient, helpful.
Recommended.

Transport

Air Raja Sansi Airport – taxi (Rs 550)
or auto-rickshaw (Rs 200) to town.
   Domestic flights Daily flights to
New Delhi with Air India,T0183-220 4012,
Jet Airways T0183-3939 3333.
   International flights Weekly flights to/
from **London** and **Birmingham** on Air India.
Jet Airways, both via Delhi.

Bicycle hire A bicycle is worthwhile here;
available for hire from Hide Market.

Bus Daily services to **Delhi** (tiring 10 hrs);
Dharamshala (7 hrs); **Dalhousie** (8 hrs), **Jammu**
(5 hrs); **Pathankot** (3 hrs); **Chandigarh** (5 hrs);
Shimla 0530 and 0730, 10 hrs. **Link Travels** and
other private operators leave for Delhi from
outside railway station, 2200; for **Jammu** and
Chandigarh from Hall Gate. Cross-border bus
service to **Lahore** (Tue, Wed, Fri and Sat). Contact

International Bus Terminal, T0183-255 1734. Advance booking is necessary.

Rickshaw Auto-rickshaw/*tonga*: full day, Rs 600, half day Rs 400.

Taxi Non-a/c car from **Time Travels** near Crystal restaurant, Queens Rd, T0183-240 0131/4, www.travelamritsar.com, and **Link Travels**, outside Golden Temple Clock Tower Car Park: full day, Rs 1200, half day Rs 800, Wagah Rs 900. To **Delhi** from Rs 7500, **Dharamshala** Rs 4000.

Train Enquiries T131. There is a free shuttle bus from the station to the Golden Temple.

Computerized reservations in the Golden Temple Complex (far right of the office), open until 2000 on weekdays. **New Delhi**: *Amritsar Shatabdi Exp 12014* (early morning), 6¼ hrs; *Shan-e-Punjab Exp 12498*, 8 hrs (HN). **Pathankot** (for **Kangra** and **Dharamsala**); *Jammu Tawi Exp 18101/18601*, 2¾ hrs, continues to Jammu, 6 hrs.

From Pathankot, you can continue onto Kangra for Dharamsala on the spectacular narrow-gauge Kangra Valley Railway, built in 1928, which runs to **Jogindernagar**, 56 km northwest of Mandi in HP or you can get a taxi direct to Dharamsala and Mcleod Ganj.

Background Haryana and Punjab

History

Before Independence

The Ghaggar Valley, running from the Shiwalik Hills down to the Rajasthan desert, was the home of fortified urban settlements before 3000 BC and the rise of the Harappan civilization. The rising tide of Aryan influence steadily became the dominant force. It was here that the Vedas took shape. The region became vital for the Muslim kings of the Delhi sultanate; 1500 years later it was part of the Mughals' core region of power.

Sikhism became an increasingly powerful force after Guru Nanak, who lived in the Punjab from 1469 to 1539, first established his community of 'seekers'. See page 1342. Aurangzeb tried to put down Sikhism by force, encouraging the Sikhs to become militant. In 1799 **Ranjit Singh** set up a Sikh confederacy, which governed until the late 1830s. Two wars with the British ended in 1849, after which the Sikh community played an important role in British India, see page 1308. In 1857 they took the British side in the Mutiny, and were given prominent positions in the Indian armed services throughout the later period of British rule. However, many Sikhs also joined the struggle for Independence, and suffered grievously at the **Jallianwala Bagh massacre** in 1919, see box, page 408.

In 1947 Punjab was torn apart by the massacres that accompanied **Partition**. In the atmosphere of increasing communal violence, the Punjab was divided in two, leaving over five million Sikhs and Hindus in Muslim West Pakistan and 40 million Muslims in predominantly Hindu India. Many people, terrified by the prospect of losing all that they had worked for, turned on each other. Amritsar, 24 km from the border and the main railway station between Delhi and Lahore, witnessed some of the worst carnage. In six terrible weeks from August to mid-September at least half a million people died, and more than 13 million people crossed the new borders of India and Pakistan.

After Independence

Sikh political opinion in Punjab continued to stress the need for a measure of autonomy within India's federal constitution. The creation of linguistic states in 1956 encouraged the Sikh Akali Dal to press for the further division of Punjab. Religious identity in itself was inadmissible under the Indian Constitution as a basis for separate statehood, and the Akalis therefore argued the distinctiveness of Punjabi from Hindi. Punjabi agitation in 1966 succeeded in achieving the further subdivision of the Punjab into the present states of Punjab (predominantly Sikh), Haryana (predominantly Hindu) and Himachal Pradesh (a purely mountain state, 96% Hindu). After the decade of political turmoil in the 1980s, marked by widespread violence surrounding the emergence of an Independence movement in Punjab, normality has returned.

In 1947, the Indian government built Chandigarh as the modern administrative capital for the Punjab. When Haryana was created in 1966 Chandigarh became the capital for both states. Arbitration was promised to decide its ultimate allocation, but its future remains undecided.

Through extensive irrigation Haryana and Punjab have become the most productive states of India. These two states also hold the key to Delhi's water supply, giving them powerful political leverage

Culture

Despite the strong influence of Hinduism and to a much lesser extent Islam, Sikhism displays a distinctive character of its own. Its literature has strong connections with Sufism. Guru Nanak travelled the region with two musicians and delivered his sermons to music as poetry through the sacred language *gurmukhi*. Typically Hindu celebrations and festivals such as **Dasara** and **Diwali** are enthusiastically observed, as are the birth and death anniversaries of the gurus and saints. Sikh music, much of it like the Mughal *ghazal* and *qawwali*, is immensely popular.

The long *kurta* (shirt) and baggy trousers drawn in at the ankle are traditional and popular forms of dress with Punjabi men. Women usually wear a similar *salwar kamiz* with a *dupatta* (long scarf). Sikh men are distinctive for their turbans and beards. The Sikhs are often thought of as enterprising and practical people and are often found driving buses, taxis and hire cars. They were the drivers in the Indian army and have maintained this role ever since.

Sikhs are officially exempt from wearing motorcycle helmets, although strictly speaking the length of cloth used to form the turban should be not less than 5 m as anything less is not deemed to give adequate protection.

Himachal Pradesh

epic mountain views and valleys

Himachal Pradesh is defined more than anything by the mighty Himalaya, towering over its northern periphery with implacable dominance, both feared and revered by the state's sparse population.

The mountains have long attracted nature lovers and trekkers, but in recent years adrenalin-inducing sports have also come to prominence, with Manali becoming a centre for adventurous activities.

The arrival of the Tibetans after the Chinese invasion of Tibet in 1959 has added attractions of an altogether more mellow manner. McLeodganj (Dharamshala), home to His Holiness the Dalai Lama, attracts those into Buddhism meditation, yoga, or the Tibetan cause.

Some of the state's finest mountain views can be seen from Dalhousie, a popular hill station during the Raj and today a quaint if anachronistic town. Himachal's other Raj relic, the city of Shimla, is part picturesque English village, part state capital full of traffic, touts and mayhem.

Although most come to see the mountains, the plains also have much to offer. Kangra Valley is especially pretty, with charming villages. Kinnaur, Spiti and Lahaul offer more rugged adventure in a barren but spectacular landscape. This area also forms the start of the spectacular Manali–Leh highway from Himachal to Ladakh.

Best for
Momos ■ Mountains ■ Views

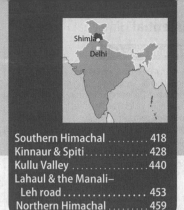

Footprint picks

★ Bhimakali Temple, page 427

Go to evening *pujas* and then climb behind the Bhimakali Temple for a great view across Sarahan.

★ Chos Khor Gompa, page 432

See the colourful murals at the beautiful Chos Khor Gompa in Tabo.

★ Naggar, page 444

Explore the stunning Roerich Gallery set in attractive gardens.

★ Manali to Leh road, page 453

Travel along the incomparable route from Manali to Leh, one of the world's best road trips, with glaciers, gorges and waterfalls.

★ Walking the Kora, page 461

Walk the Kora around His Holiness the Dalai Lama's residence.

Essential Himachal Pradesh

Finding your feet

Himachal Pradesh (Himalayan Province) is wholly mountainous, with peaks rising to over 6700 m. The Dhaula Dhar range runs from the northwest to the Kullu Valley. The Pir Panjal is further north and parallel to it. High, remote, arid and starkly beautiful, Lahaul and Spiti are sparsely populated. They contrast strongly with the well-wooded lushness of those areas to the south of the Himalayan axis.

Since 1966 Shimla has been the state capital. Dharamshala (McLeodganj) has been the home of His Holiness the Dalai Lama and the Tibetan government in exile since 1959, following the Chinese takeover of Tibet. With the long-term closure of routes through Kashmir, Himachal Pradesh has seen a sharp rise in tourism, and is the main land route to Ladakh. The new strategically important tunnel under the Rohtang Pass is scheduled for completion in 2016.

Getting around

Buses or cars are the only way to get around most of this mountainous state. There is also the Kalka–Shimla narrow-gauge train (see page 473) and the Kangra Valley Railway.

Best days out

Chadwick Falls, page 419
Bhimakali Temple, Sarahan, page 427
Nicholas Roerich Museum, Naggar, page 445
Traditional Tibetan craftmaking,
Norbulingka, page 461

Best scenic walks

Stroll through pink fields in Baspa Valley, page 428
Hike to Buddhist Gompa close to Dankar in Spiti, page 432
Trek with Spiti Ecosphere, page 435
See the beautiful flowers in Tosh Valley, page 442
Walk the Kora around the Dalai Lama's residence, McLeodganj, page 461

When to go

The hills are a mercifully cool retreat in April and May. At lower altitudes the summers can be very hot and humid whereas the higher mountains are permanently under snow. Monsoon rains can bring landslides and closed roads. In Shimla, the Kangra Valley, Chamba and the Kullu Valley, the monsoon arrives in mid-June and lasts until mid-September, giving periods of very heavy rain; in the Kullu Valley there can be sudden downpours in March and early April. To the north, Lahaul and Spiti are beyond the influence of the monsoon, and consequently share the high-altitude desert climatic characteristics of Ladakh.

Time required

Two or three days each for Shimla and Manali; many people spend weeks in Dharamshala.

Weather Shimla

January	February	March	April	May	June
9°C 2°C 58mm	10°C 3°C 64mm	14°C 7°C 62mm	19°C 11°C 46mm	23°C 14°C 63mm	24°C 16°C 161mm

July	August	September	October	November	December
21°C 15°C 419mm	20°C 15°C 386mm	20°C 14°C 207mm	18°C 11°C 39mm	14°C 7°C 12mm	11°C 4°C 24mm

Southern Himachal offers an intriguing mix of experiences. While it almost vies with its rival tour destination Spiti and Lahaul, it also seems to be reluctant for unveiling itself the mountains to the degree expected. Give the area a glance. Southern Himachal, one of the foothills of the Himalaya and some of their

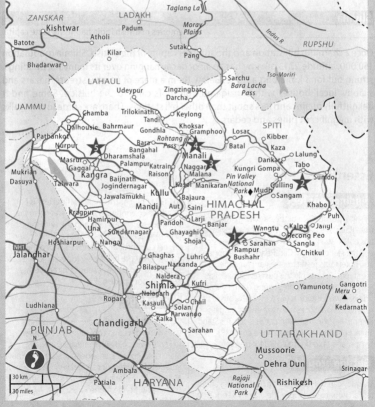

Southern
Himachal

Southern Himachal offers an intriguing mix of experiences. Shimla's colonial past, with its Little England architecture and anachronistic air, seems to be fighting for survival amidst the modern-day bustle of Himachal's capital city. The area around Shimla offers stunning views of the foothills of the Himalaya and plenty of attractive places to stay nestled amongst the cool pine forests. This area is also the gateway to the altogether more rugged landscapes of Kinnaur, a world far less affected by the advance of time.

Shimla *Colour map 1, B3.*

memories of British India haunt the state capital

Once a charming hill station and the summer capital of the British, Shimla (population 150,000, altitude 2213 m) now has an air of decay hanging over its many Raj buildings, strung out for 3 km along a ridge. Below them a maze of narrow streets, bazars and shabby 'local' houses with corrugated-iron roofs cling to the hillside. Some find it delightfully quaint and less spoilt than other hill stations. There are some lovely walks with magnificent pines and cedars.

Essential Shimla

Finding your feet

Despite the romance of the narrow-gauge railway from Kalka, see page 422, most arrive in Shimla by bus or taxi as it is so much quicker. The bus stand and the station are on Cart Road, where porters and hotel touts jostle to take your luggage up the steep hill; possibly the best few rupees you will ever spend. If you are staying on the western side of town it is worth getting off the bus at the railway station. Buses from the east, including Rampur and Kinnaur, stop at the Rivoli Bus Stand. Shimla (Jabbarhatti) airport has a coach (Rs 50) in season, and taxis (Rs 400-500) for transfer.

Getting around

The Mall can only be seen on foot; it takes about half an hour to walk from the Viceroy's Lodge to Christ Church. The main traffic artery is Cart Road, which continues past the station to the main bus stand, taxi rank and the two-stage lift which goes to The Mall above. The Victory Tunnel cuts through from Cart Road to the north side of the hill. A new ropeway (cable car system) to avoid congestion is in the works. See Transport, page 422.

When to go

October and November are very pleasant, with warm days and cool nights. December to February is cold and there are snowfalls. March and April are changeable; storms are not infrequent and the air can feel very chilly. Avoid May and June, the height of the Indian tourist season prior to the monsoon.

BACKGROUND
The British in Shimla

For the British, the only way of beating the hot weather on the plains in May and June was to move to hill stations, which they endowed with mock-Tudor houses, churches, clubs, parks with bandstands of English county towns, and a main street invariably called The Mall.

So beneficial were the effects of the cooler mountain air that Shimla, 'discovered' by the British in 1819, became the summer seat of government from 1865 to 1939. The capital was shifted there from Calcutta and later from Delhi (1912 onwards) and all business was transacted from this cool mountain retreat.

Huge baggage trains were needed to transport the mountains of files and the whole operation cost thousands of rupees. At the end of the season back they would all go.

Women heavily outnumbered men, as wives of many British men who ran the empire escaped to the hills for long periods. Army officers spent their leave there. Social life in hill stations became a round of parties, balls, formal promenades along The Mall and brief flirtations.

Sights

Shimla is strung out on a long crescent-shaped ridge that connects a number of hilltops from which there are good views of the snow-capped peaks to the north: Jakhu (2453 m), Prospect Hill (2176 m), Observatory Hill (2148 m), Elysium Hill (2255 m) and Summer Hill (2103 m).

Christ Church (1844), on the open area of The Ridge, dominates the eastern end of town. Consecrated in 1857, a clock and porch were added later. The original chancel window, designed by Lockwood Kipling, Rudyard's father, is no longer there. The mock Tudor **library** building (circa 1910) is next door. The Mall joins The Ridge at Kipling's **'Scandal Point'**, where today groups gather to exchange gossip. Originally the name referred to the stir caused by the supposed 'elopement' of a lady from the Viceregal Lodge and a dashing Patiala prince after they arranged a rendezvous here.

The **Gaiety Theatre** (1887) and the **Town Hall** (circa 1910) are reminiscent of the arts and crafts style, as well as the timbered **General Post Office** (1886). Beyond, to the west, is the **Grand Hotel**. Further down you pass the sinister-looking **Gorton Castle**, designed by Sir Samuel Swinton Jacob, which was once the Civil Secretariat. A road to the left leads to the railway station, while one to the right goes to Annandale, the racecourse and cricket ground. The Mall leads to the rebuilt **Cecil Hotel**.

On Observatory Hill, the **Viceregal Lodge** (1888) is the most splendid of Shimla's surviving Raj-era buildings, built for Lord Dufferin in the Elizabethan style. Now the **Rashtrapati Niwas**① *1000-1630, Rs 10 including a brief tour*, it stands in large grounds with good views of the mountains. Reminders of its British origins include a gatehouse, a chapel and the meticulously polished brass fire hydrants imported from Manchester. Inside, you can visit the main reception rooms and the library which are lined from floor to ceiling with impressive teak panelling. It is a long up the hill walk from the gate. It is now the Indian Institute of Advanced Study and there is a café on-site.

Himachal State Museum① *near Chaura Maidan, www.himachalstatemuseum.in, Tue-Sun 1000-1330, 1400-1700, Rs 100*, is a 30-minute walk west from the GPO along The Mall; then it's a short climb from the Harsha Hotel. Small, with a good sculpture collection and miniatures from the Kangra School, it also houses contemporary art including work by Nicholas Roerich, costumes, jewellery, bronzes and textiles (everything is well labelled).

Walks

Jakhu Temple on a hill with excellent views (2455 m), dedicated to Hanuman the monkey god, is 2 km from Christ Church. Walking sticks (handy for warding off monkeys, which can be vicious – keep all food out of sight) are available at *chai* shops at the start of the ascent. **The Glen** (1830 m), to the northwest, is a 4-km walk from the centre past the Cecil Hotel. **Summer Hill** (1983 m), a pleasant 'suburb' 5 km from town, is a stop on the Shimla–Kalka railway. **Chadwick Falls** (1586 m), 3 km further, drops 67 m during the monsoon season.

Prospect Hill (2175 m) is 5 km from The Ridge and a 20-minute walk from Boileauganj to the west. **Tara Devi** (1851 m), with a hilltop temple, 11 km southwest from the railway station, can also be reached by car or train.

Listings Shimla maps below and p422

Tourist information

Himachal Pradesh Tourism Development Corportation (HPTDC)
The Mall, T0177-265 2561, www.hptdc.nic.in. Open 0900-1800, in season 0900-1900; also at Cart Rd, near Victory Tunnel, T0177-265 4589, open 1000-1700.
Very informative and helpful. For details of their tours, see What to do, below.

Where to stay

Prices soar May-Jun when modest rooms can be difficult to find especially after midday, so book ahead. Some places close off-season; those that remain open may offer discounts of 30-50%. From the railway or bus station it is a stiff climb up to hotels on or near the Ridge. Porters are available (Rs 20 per heavy bag).

$$$$ The Oberoi Cecil
Chaura Maidan (quiet end of The Mall), T0177-280 4848, www.oberoihotels.com.
A beautifully renovated hotel, with 79 sumptuous rooms, stylishly furnished, and superb views. Colonial grandeur on the edge of town. There's a good restaurant and a special ultra-modern pool. Rates are full board. Recommended.

$$$$-$$$ Woodville Palace (Heritage)
Raj Bhavan Rd, The Mall, T0177-262 3919, www.woodvillepalacehotel.com.
A spacious hotel, one of the quietest in town, set in large grounds. It has 30 rooms of variable quality, including some good suites with period furniture (freezing in winter). The dining hall is worth visiting for its eclectic mixture of portraits, weapons and hunting trophies (non-residents need to give advance notice), owned by the Raja of Jubbal's family and featured in *Jewel in the Crown*.

1 Shimla

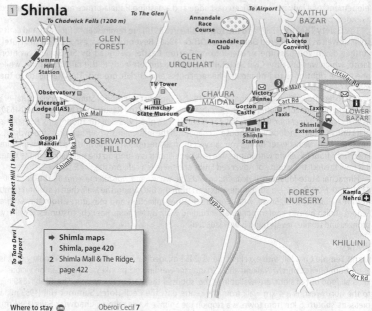

➡ **Shimla maps**
1 Shimla, page 420
2 Shimla Mall & The Ridge, page 422

Where to stay 🛌   Oberoi Cecil **7**
Dalziel **3**   Woodville Palace **10**

$$$ Combermere
2 entrances, next to the lift at top and bottom,
T0177-265 1246, www.hotelcombermere.com.
In a good central location, this place has
40 decent rooms (including penthouses) on
5 levels (partly served by lift). Staff are friendly,
efficient and very helpful. There's a pleasant
terrace café and bar, games room and central
heating/a/c; the super deluxe rooms worth
spending a little extra on.

$$ Aapo Aap Homestay
Panthaghati Bazar, Sargheen Chowk,
10 km outside Shimla, T(0)8091-208353,
www.aapoaapshimla.com.
In a beautiful location outside of Shimla with
stunning views, this homestay has 3 lovely guest
rooms. There is also Wi-Fi and a meditation room.
Recommended.

$$ Dalziel
The Mall, above station, T0177-280 6725,
www.dalzielhotel.com.
30 clean enough, comfy, creaky valley-facing
rooms with bath (hot water) in a heritage
building. Indian meals are served; prices depend
on the size of TV.

$$-$ Mayur
Above Christ Church, T0177-265 2393,
www.hotelmayur.com.
This modern, clean hotel is in a great central
location. It has 30 rooms in 1970s style, some with
mountain views, some with tub. Good restaurant,
but check the bill.

$$-$ Woodland
Daisy Bank, The Ridge, T(0)94180-21100,
www.hotelwoodlandshimla.com.
An off-season bargain, this hotel has 21 rooms,
some wood-panelled, some with great views, all
with bath, although cleanliness varies. Avoid the
noisy downstairs rooms near reception. Friendly
staff, room service and safe luggage storage.

Restaurants

$$ Alfa's
The Mall.
Modern interior, range of continental dishes in
addition to good *thalis*, courteous service.

$$ Café Sol
Hotel Combermere, see Where to stay, above.
Set in an airy glass building, this café serves
decent Western and Indian foods.

$$ Wake & Bake
The Mall.
Up some rickety stairs, you will find good coffee,
baked goods and international food; a cute place.
There is an internet café below.

$ Guptajee's Vaishnav Bhojanalaya
62 Middle Bazar.
First-class Indian vegetarian fare including tasty
stuffed tomatoes and great *thali*. Recommended.

$ Sagar Ratna
6/1 The Mall, upstairs, T0177-280 0526.
Good vegetarian South Indian food, including
dosas and *idlis*; all good value.

Festivals

May-Jun Summer Festival includes cultural
programmes from Himachal and neighbouring
states, and art and handicrafts exhibitions.
25 Dec An **ice skating carnival** is held on
Christmas Day.

What to do

Ice skating
Skating rink: below Rivoli, winter only, Rs 50 to
skate all day to loud Indian film hits.

Tour operators

HPTDC, *see under Tourist information, above.*
HPTDC organize well-run tours during the season, usually 1000-1700. All start from Rivoli, enquire when booking for other pick-up points. Return drop at Lift or Victory Tunnel. 2 tours visit Kufri, Chini Bungalow and Nature Park; 1 returns to Shimla via Fagu, Naldehra and Mashobra, the other by Chail and Kairighat. A further tour visits Fagu, Theog, Matiana and Narkanda. Book in advance at the HPTDC office on The Mall, where staff are very friendly and helpful.

Transport

Air Shimla (Jabbarhatti) airport (23 km from town) had flights with Kingfisher until their demise, and at the time of writing no other airline was operating flights.

Local bus From Cart Rd. Lift: 2-stage lift from the Taxi Stand on Cart Rd and near **Hotel Samrat** on The Mall, takes passengers to and from The Mall, 0800-2200. Porters at bus stand and upper lift station will ask anything from Rs 10 to Rs 50 per bag; lower prices mean hotel commission.

Long distance bus From the main bus stand, Cart Rd, T01772-265 8765. Buy tickets from counter before boarding bus (signs are in Hindi so ask for help) some long-distance buses can be reserved in advance: HPTDC coaches during the season are good value and reliable. **Kalka**, 3 hrs quicker than the train but requires a strong stomach; **Chandigarh**, 4 hrs **Dehra Dun**, 9 hrs; **Delhi**, 10-12 hrs; overnight to **Dharamshala**, 10 hrs. **Manali**, departs outside the 'Tunnel', 8-10 hrs, tickets from main bus stand. HPTDC deluxe buses between Shimla and **Delhi** in the summer, 9 hrs.

From **Rivoli Bus Stand** (Lakkar Bazar): frequent buses to **Kufri**, **Rampur**, 8 hrs, and **Chitkul**, 2 daily; **Jeori** for **Sarahan** (8 hrs).

Car hire HPTDC (see under Tourist information, above), has a/c cars. Shimla Taxis, T(0)9418-082385, www.shimlataxis.in, have a wide range of cars.

Taxi Local taxis have fixed fares and run from near the lift on Cart Rd, T01772-657645. Long-distance taxis run from Union Stands near the lift, T01772-805164, and by the main bus stand on Cart Rd. **Chandigarh**, Rs 2500; **Kalka** (90 km), Rs 1600; **Mussoorie**, Rs 5500, 8 hrs, including stops; **Rekong-Peo**, around Rs 7000 (11 hrs).

Train Enquiry T131. Computerized reservations at main station (T01772-652915), 1000-1330, 1400-1700, Sun 1000-1400, and by tourist office on The Mall. The newer extension station, where some trains start and terminate, is just below the main bus stand. Travel to/from Shimla involves a change of gauge to the slow and

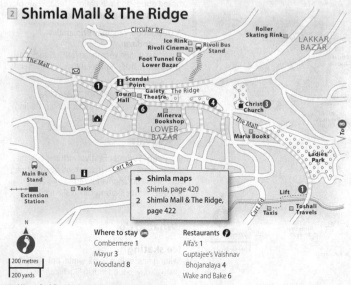

☑ Shimla Mall & The Ridge

Circular Rd

Roller Skating Rink

LAKKAR BAZAR

Ice Rink
Rivoli Cinema Rivoli Bus Stand

The Mall

Foot Tunnel to Lower Bazar

Scandal Point

Gaiety The Ridge
Town Hall Theatre

❶

Minerva Bookshop

❻

LOWER BAZAR

Christ Church ❸

The Mall

Maria Books

To ❽

Ladies Park

Cart Rd

Main Bus Stand

ℹ️

Taxis

➡ Shimla maps
1 Shimla, page 420
2 Shimla Mall & The Ridge, page 422

Extension Station

Lift ❶

Cart Rd

Taxis Toshali Travels

N

200 metres
200 yards

Where to stay 🛏
Combermere 1
Mayur 3
Woodland 8

Restaurants 🍴
Alfa's 1
Guptajee's Vaishnav Bhojanalaya 4
Wake and Bake 6

cramped but extremely picturesque 'toy train' at **Kalka**. To reach Shimla from **Delhi** in a day by train, catch the *Himalayan Queen* or *Shatabdi Exp 12011* leaving New Delhi station at 0740 to arrive in Kalka by 1200 (see below). In the reverse direction, the 1030 train from Shimla gets you to Kalka at 1600 in time to board the Delhi-bound *Himalayan Queen 14096*. Book tickets for the toy train in advance; the 'Ticket Extension Booth' on Kalka station sells out by 1200 when the *Shatabdi* arrives, and the train often arrives on the Kalka platform already full of locals who board it while it waits in the siding. It's worth paying Rs 150-170 plus a reservation fee of Rs 20 to guarantee a seat on 1st class. **Kalka to Shimla**: *Kalka Shimla Passenger 52457*, 0400, 5½ hrs; *Shivalik Exp Deluxe 52451*, 4¾ hrs (has bigger windows and comfy seats); *Kalka Shimla Express 52453*, 5 hrs; *Himalayan Queen 52455*, 5 hrs. Extra trains in season (1 May-15 Jul; 15 Sep-30 Oct; 15 Dec-1 Jan): You can book a special train carriage which can be attached to regular trains with elegant furnishings and big windows which accommodates 8 people through IRCTC Chandigarh. **Shimla to Kalka**: *Himalayan Queen*, 5½ hrs; *Shivalik Exp Deluxe 52452*, 4¾ hrs.

beautiful forests and hill outposts

Kufri

About 16 km from Shimla, at 2500 m, Kufri hosts a winter sports festival in January which includes the National Snow Statue Competition. Don't expect European or American resort standards though. There are some attractions around and about the town. At **Danes Folly** (2550 m), 5 km away, is a government-run orchard. A 10-minute walk uphill takes you to a mini zoo of Himalayan wildlife. **Mahasu Peak** (bus, Rs 15) 20 minutes from a path behind the Kufri Resort cottages, offers fabulous mountain views on a clear day and there is a small but interesting temple at the start of the walk. The best time to visit is in January and February.

Chharabra

Chharabra is an enjoyable 3-km forest walk down from Kufri. The Wildflower Hall which once stood here was the residence of **Lord Kitchener**, commander-in-chief of the Indian Army. The original building was replaced; its successor was converted into a hotel which burnt down in 1993. **Oberoi** has opened a new luxury hotel (see Where to stay, below).

Naldera

Off the Hindusthan–Tibet road, 26 km north of Shimla, Naldera has a nine-hole golf course, possibly the oldest in India and one of the highest in the world, and the beautiful Mahung temple. The colourful **Sipi Fair** in June attracts handicraft sellers from surrounding villages.

Chail

In a superb forest setting with fine snow views, 45 km southeast of Shimla (2½ hours by bus), off the NH22, Chail was once the Maharaja of Patiala's summer capital. Built across three hills, it claims to have the country's highest cricket ground at 2444 m, a 2-km walk from the bus stand. The old palace on Rajgarh Hill has been converted to a hotel while the old residency, Snow View, and a Sikh temple stand on the other hills. The **Chail Sanctuary**, once a private hunting reserve, is popular with birders and has a Cheer pheasant-breeding programme. It is an idyllic spot until the weekend when day-trippers descend on the tiny resort.

Kalka

Kalka is the terminus for the narrow-gauge railway from Shimla. The Kalka–Shimla line (0.76 m), completed in 1903, runs 97 km from Kalka in the foothills to Shimla at over 2000 m. The magnificent journey takes just over five hours. The steepest gradient is 1:33; there are 107 tunnels covering 8 km and 969 bridges over 3 km. See also Transport, above.

Tragically, there was a derailment in September 2015 where several Britons were killed or injured. Investigations were continuing at the time of writing.

Nalagarh

The area around Nalagarh was once ruled by the Chandela Rajputs. The fort has wonderful views above an estate of forests and orchards and is built on five levels around manicured grassy courts. Originally built in the 15th century; the **Diwan-i-Khas** (1618) is now the Banquet Hall. The present raja has opened his home to guests. You can request the **Nalagarh Fort** hotel pickup from Ropar (20 km) or Kalka (40 km).

Listings Around Shimla

Where to stay

Kufri

$$$$ Kufri Holiday Resort
T0177-264 8341, www.kufriholidayresort.com.
30 rooms and 8 modern cottages (2-3 bedrooms), limited hot water, cold in winter, but attractive design and setting with flower-filled gardens, outstanding views from cottages above and good walks.

Chharabra

$$$$ Wildflower Hall
T0177-264 8585, www.oberoihotels.com.
Standing on the grounds of the former residence of Lord Kitchener, this place retains period exterior but has been completely refurbished inside. 87 sumptuous rooms, beautifully decorated, mountain views, good restaurants and lovely gardens surrounded by deodar forest with beautifully peaceful walks, plus extensive spa, yoga classes under pine trees, Ayurvedic treatments.

Naldera

$$$$ The Chalets Naldehra
Durgapur Village, T0177-274 7715, www.chaletsnaldehra.com.
14 alpine-style pine chalets plus restaurant and a wide range of outdoor activities including world's highest golf course.

$$$ Koti Resort
T0177-274 0177, www.kotiresort.net.
A beautifully located hotel surrounded by deodar forest with 40 modern, if slightly spartan, rooms in. Friendly manager, very relaxing.

$$-$ Mitwa Cottage
Near Koti Resort, T0177-201 2279.
Sweet little homestay with kitchens and balconies. Lovely food as well and plenty of nature walks around. Recommended.

Chail

$$$$-$$$ Toshali Royal View Resort
Shilon Bagh (5 km outside Chail), T0177-200 6470, www.toshaliroyalview.com.
There are 77 modern rooms in this huge alpine-style lodge, with great views from dining terrace and friendly staff.

$ Himneel
T01792-248141, www.hptdc.nic.in.
The 16 rooms here are modest but full of character. The **Kailash** restaurant serves good-value breakfasts and lunches.

Kalka

If using your own transport, there are many hotels, guesthouses and *dhabas* along the Kalka–Shimla road. **Kasauli** is an attractive hill resort with a distinctly English feel, 16 km off the main road with a few hotels, notably:

$$$$ Baikunth
Village Chabbal, near Kasauli, T(0)98571 66230, www.baikunth.com.
Red brick building in the hills. Lovely airy, sunny rooms with all mod cons. Recommended for its spa.

$$$-$$ Alasia
T01792-272008.
Hugely atmospheric Raj-era hotel with 13 rooms, remarkably authentic English cuisine and impeccable staff.

Nalagarh

$$$ Nalagarh Fort
T01795-223179, www.nalagarh.com.
Set in rural surroundings, this hotel has plenty of atmosphere and 15 comfortable rooms (some suites), with modern baths and traditional furniture. There's good food (buffets only), a small pool and tennis. Book ahead. Recommended.

Naldera

Golf

There is a 9-hole course in Naldera. Casual members: green fee and equipment, about Rs 100, see page 423.

Kalka

Bus or taxi Easily reached from **Shimla**, by bus or taxi (Rs 1600), and from **Chandigarh** by taxi (Rs 500).

Train To Delhi: *Shatabdi Exp 12006*, 4 hrs; *Shatabdi Exp 12012*, 4 hrs. All via Chandigarh, 45 mins. For information on the Kalka–Shimla train, see page 422.

Old Hindustan Tibet Road   *Colour map 1, B3/4.*

lush valleys, snow-clad peaks and precipitous gorges

The Old Hindustan Tibet road runs east from Shimla to the Tibetan border, connecting a string of prosperous-looking farms, villages and towns. It passes through terraced slopes covered with orchards before entering the high-altitude deserts of Spiti. As the narrow road winds even deeper towards the Tibetan border its unprotected sides plunge hundreds of metres to the roaring monsoon-swollen River Sutlej below, grasping at huge boulders brought down by thundering landslides into the gloomy gorges. By bus or jeep, this road is not for the faint-hearted. The road may be severely damaged in the rains.

Narkanda

The small market town of Narkanda (altitude 2700 m) occupies a superb position. The town offers a base from which to ski but the skiing does not compare with that found in Western resorts. Enquire at the Marketing Office in Shimla for skiing in winter and the seven-day beginners' course.

Nirath

The road drops sharply through woodland interspersed with apple orchards from Narkanda, down to Kingel from where it zig-zags down to Sainj. The seasonal route is best by 4WD though buses cover this route very carefully. Some 5 km beyond Sainj there are superb views both across the valley, and of a wall of eroded outwash deposits at least 50 m thick. The main road passes through Nirath where there is a **Surya Temple** believed to date from the eighth century which still has some fine carving preserved on the outer walls and has carved wooden panels within. At an altitude of 800-900 m the Sutlej Valley towards Rampur has a subtropical summer climate, with mango trees and bananas replacing apples.

Rampur Bushahr

This is one of Himachal's most important market towns. **Padam Palace** (1920s), opposite the bus stand, once the residence of the raja, has interesting carved wooden panels and wall murals, but is difficult to enter. **Sat Narain Temple** in the main bazar (1926) has a beautiful but decaying façade. **Lavi Fair** (November) draws large crowds of colourful hill people who bring their produce – handicrafts, carpets, rugs, fruit and nuts and animals – to the special market. There are sporting competitions in the day, and dancing and making music around bonfires after dark.

Rampur to Sarahan

From Rampur the highway enters one of the most exciting (and geologically active) stretches of road in the region. During the rains, the Sutlej River is a surging torrent of muddy water, dropping over 450 m in under 30 km and passing through gorges and deeply incised valleys. Although an ancient trade route, the road is comparatively recent and is constantly being upgraded particularly in connection with the Nathpa-Jhakhri HEP scheme, with a 28-km-long tunnel from **Nathpa**, near

Wangtu, to **Jhakhri**, about 10 km beyond Rampur. When completed this will be one of the largest Hydel schemes in the world. The blasting both for the shafts and for road widening has further destabilized the already landslide-prone hillsides and during the rains the road may be blocked. Blockages are usually cleared within hours, though travelling times are wholly unpredictable. You also need a strong stomach, both for the main road and for diversions, especially up the Baspa Valley to Sangla.

Essential Old Hindustan Tibet Road

Permits

Inner Line Permits, which are needed for travel close to the Tibetan border (essentially the area between Kaza and Jangi), are easy enough to get. Permits are issued free to individuals for seven days from the date of issue (easily renewable for three days at Kaza or Recong Peo). Take your passport, two copies of the details and Indian visa pages, and three passport photos and complete the form from the **Sub-Divisional Magistrate's office (SDM)** in **Shimla**, T0177-265 5988; **Recong Peo**, T01786-222252; or **Kaza**, T01906-222202, where you need the additional 'No Objection' certificate from the chief of police (a mere formality of a stamp and signature). In Recong Peo, the whole process takes about an hour, which may include *chai* or breakfast with the SDM.

Permits are also available (in theory) from the **Resident Commissioner of Himachal Pradesh**, Himachal Bhavan, 27 Sikandra Road, New Delhi, T011-2371 6574, and other magistrates offices. In Shimla, travel agents charge Rs 150.

Permits are checked at Jangi if coming from Shimla and at Sumdo coming from Spiti. Carry about 10 photocopies as some checkpoints demand to keep one.

Where to stay

Rules regarding overnight stays have been relaxed considerably; it is now possible to sleep in Puh and Nako. Accommodation is limited to simple rest houses, lodges or tents. In some places enterprising local families are opening their modest homes to paying guests. Local village shops often stock canned food and bottled water.

> **Tip...**
> It is virtually impossible to get foreign exchange in this area.

Some 9 km west of Jeori the river passes through a dramatic gorge. On the north side of the river isolated tiny pockets of cultivated land cling to the hillside. **Jeori** is the junction for Sarahan, 21 km south, an hour away. There are several provisions stores to pick up the basics here since Sarahan has very limited supplies.

Listings Old Hindustan Tibet Road

Where to stay

Narkanda

$$$$ Banjara Orchard Retreat
Thanedar Village, 15 km from Narkanda (80 km from Shimla), T(0)98167 47451, www.banjaracamps.com.
6 double rooms, 2 suites and 2 lovely log cabins, set in apple orchards with stunning views down the Sutlej Valley. Evenings are spent round the fire under the stars. There's also trekking and excellent food available. Recommended.

$$$$ Tethy's Narkanda Resort
T01782-242641.
Comfortable rooms and some swiss cottage tents with stunning views. They organize snow skiing, hiking, mountain biking, river rafting and horse riding. Meals are included.

$$$-$$ The Hatu (HPTDC)
T01782-242430.
Typical government fare, but with great views.

Rampur Bushahr

$$ Bushehar Regency
2 km short of Rampur on NH22, T01782-234103.
20 well-positioned rooms, some with a/c. There's also a restaurant, a huge lawn and a bar nearby.

What to do

Skiing

Early Jan to mid-Mar. Ski courses at Narkanda organized by **HPTDC**, 7- and 15-day courses, Jan-Mar, Rs 1700-3000; see page 425.

Transport

Bus Buses are often late and overcrowded. To **Chandigarh**, **Delhi**; **Mandi** (9 hrs); **Recong Peo** (5 hrs) and **Puh**; **Sarahan** (2-3 hrs), better to change at Jeori; **Shimla**, several (5-6 hrs); **Tapri** (and Kalpa) 0545 (3¼ hrs), change at Karchham for Sangla and Chitkul.

Sarahan *Colour map 1, B4.*

stunning Kali temple and high mountain peaks

An important market for traders of neighbouring regions, Sarahan (population 1200, altitude 2165 m) is an attractive town, surrounded by high peaks. The bazar is interesting: friendly villagers greet travellers, and shops sell flowers, bright red and gold scarves and other offerings for worshippers among local produce, fancy goods, clothes and jewellery. It is also a stop on the trekkers' route.

★ Bhimakali Temple

Sarahan was the old capital of the local Rampur Bushahr rulers and has a palace complex containing the strikingly carved wood-bonded Bhimakali Temple (rebuilt circa 1927), in a mixture of Hindu and Buddhist styles. The two temples stand on a slope among apple and apricot orchards behind the bazar. The Bhimakali is dedicated to Durga as the destroyer of the *asuras*

> **Tip...**
>
> A pilgrimage route encircles Shrikhand Mahadev peak (5227 m), which takes pilgrims seven days to go round. On a clear day you get fantastic panoramic views of the snow-covered peaks.

(demons) and has a Brahmin priest in attendance. Plan for an early morning visit to the temple to see morning prayers; evening prayers are around 1900. Leave shoes and leather objects with the attendant and wear the saffron cap offered to you before entering. You may only photograph the outside of the temples. It is worth climbing around the back of the complex for a picturesque view.

According to some sources the ancient temple on the right (closed for safety reasons) is many centuries old. Built in traditional timber-bonded style it has whitewashed dry stone and rubble masonry alternating with horizontal deodar or spruce beams to withstand earthquakes. The upper floors have balconies and windows with superb ornamental woodcarving; the silver repoussée-work doors are also impressive. The first floor has a 200-year-old gold image of goddess Bhimkali which is actively worshipped only during the **Dasara festival** when animals and birds are sacrificed in the courtyard, while on the second floor daily early-morning *puja* is carried out to a second image. The sacrificial altar and the old well are in the courtyard with three other shrines. The palace of the Rampur rajas behind the temple has a drawing room with ornate furniture and a painted ceiling; the caretaker may let you in.

Listings Sarahan

Where to stay

$$-$ Srikhand (HPTDC)
T01782-274234, www.hptdc.nic.in.
Superb hilltop site, overlooking the Sutlej Valley, Srikhand peak and beyond. The 19 rooms have bath and hot water (3 are large with a balcony, 8 are smaller with views, and the 4 in the annexe are cheaper), dorm (Rs 75), 2-bedroom royal cottage, restaurant but limited menu. It's also very close to the stunning temple.

$ Bhimakali Temple
You can stay in the temple itself. Rooms are very basic with clean bathrooms and shared balconies; it's highly atmospheric.

Transport

Bus Daily buses between **Shimla** (Rivoli Bus Stand) and **Jeori** on the Highway (6 hrs), quicker by car. Local buses between Jeori and the army cantonment below Sarahan.

Kinnaur
& Spiti

The regions of Kinnaur and Spiti lie in the rain shadow of the outer Himalayan ranges. The climate in Spiti is much drier than in the Kullu Valley and is similar to that of Ladakh. The temperatures are more extreme both in summer and winter and most of the landscape is barren and bleak. The wind can be bitingly cold even when the sun is hot. The annual rainfall is very low so cultivation is restricted to the ribbons of land that fringe rivers with irrigation potential. The crops include potatoes, wheat, barley and millet. The people are of Mongol origin and almost everyone follows a Tibetan form of Buddhism.

Kinnaur and Spiti are accessible only in the summer when the snow melts on the higher passes, meaning they can be crossed by road. They can be seen by following a circular route, first along the Old Hindustan Tibet Road by the Sutlej River, then crossing into the wild Spiti Valley, which has the evocative Tibetan Buddhist sites of Tabo and Kaza set against the backdrop of a rugged mountain landscape. The road continues round to the Rohtang Pass and Manali, or on up to Ladakh. It's also worth making a side trip up the Baspa Valley via Sangla to Chitkul for its views and landscapes, villages, pagodas and culture.

Kinnaur   *Colour map 1, B3. For general trekking information, see page 39.*

stunning peaks and Buddhist prayer wheels

Along the Sutlej

An exciting mountain road runs through cliffside cuttings along the south bank of the Sutlej, which is frequently blocked by rockfalls and landslides during the monsoons. At **Choling** the Sutlej roars through a narrow gorge, and at **Wangtu** the road re-crosses the river where vehicle details are checked. Immediately after crossing the Wangtu bridge a narrow side road goes to **Kafnoo village** (2427 m), in the Bhabha Valley (a camping site and the start for an attractive 10-day trek to the Pin Valley). From Wangtu the road route runs to **Tapri** (1870 m) and **Karchham** (1899 m) both of which have hot springs. Here the Baspa River joins the Sutlej from the south.

Baspa Valley

A hair-raising excursion by a precipitous winding rough road leads 16 km up the Baspa Valley to Sangla; buses take approximately 1½ hours. The valley carries the marks of a succession of glacial events which have shaped it, although the glaciers which formed the valley have now retreated to the high slopes above Chitkul at over 4500 m. Recently the valley has been terribly scarred by the Baspa Hydroelectric Project, with blasting, dust and truck logjams commonplace, but persevere and carry on up the valley and the rewards are worth it.

All villages in Baspa are characterized by exaggerated steeply sloping slate roofs, rich wood carving and elaborate pagoda temples. Although Kinner Kailash (sacred to Hindus and Buddhists) is not visible from here, the valley is on the circumambulating **Parikrama/Kora** route which encircles the massif. Fields of the pink coloured *ogla*, a small flower seed grown specifically in the Baspa Valley for grinding into grain, add a beautiful colouring in the season.

Sangla At 2680 m, is built on the massive buttress of a terminal moraine which marks a major glacial advance of about 50,000 years ago. The Baspa River has cut a deep trench on its south flank. Immediately above is the flat valley floor, formed on the dry bed of a lake which was once dammed behind the moraine. The village has excellent carving and is full of character. No foreign exchange is available but there are telephone facilities. Sangla is famous for its apples, while a saffron farm just north of the village is claimed to be better than that at Pampore in Kashmir.

The old seven-storey **Killa** (Fort) ① *0800-0900, 1800-1900*, where the Kinnaur rajas were once crowned, is 1 km north of new Sangla just before the road enters the village. It was occupied by the local rulers for centuries. It now has a temple to Kamakshi where the idol is from Guwahati, Assam, see page 622.

Kinnaur & Spiti

ON THE ROAD

The stuff of epics

The *bhoj patra*, found distinctively in the Sangla Valley, is a revered product. The extraordinarily fine waterproof layers just beneath the bark of the *bhoj patra* tree were used for writing centuries ago, particularly where palm leaves were not available. Renowned for its suppleness, strength and apparent indestructibility, bark from this valley was used for some of Hinduism's most ancient writings, including the epics, and it is still highly valued for copying sacred texts. Genealogies which trace the descent of some families in the Sangla Valley to the legendary Pandavas are still widely accepted, and connections between the residents of the valley and the early roots of Hinduism are treasured.

Barseri Eight kilometres from Sangla, is situated on an outwash cone which has engulfed part of the Baspa's valley floor. This well-kept 'green village' is happy to show visitors its solar heaters, *chakkis* (water mills) and water-driven prayer wheels. The Buddha Mandir, with *Shakyamuni* and other images and a large prayer wheel, is beautiful inside. Villagers weave shawls and do woodcarving.

The beautifully carved pagoda-style Rakcham temple is dedicated to Shamshir Debta, Devi and Naga, combining Buddhist and Hindu deities. The ibex horns on the roof are ancient male fertility symbols. There is also a pre-Buddhist, animist Bon cho shrine and a Siva temple.

Chitkul Some 18 km from Barseri, at an altitude of 3450 m, is the furthest point foreigners can travel without special permits. With its typical houses, Buddhist temple and a small tower, it is worth the trip. The Kagyupa (Oral Transmission School) has a highly valued, old image of the Shakyamuni Buddha. There are four directional kings on either side of the door as well as a Wheel of Life. You can walk along the Baspa River which has paths on both sides. The rough path along the tributary starting at the bridge across the river, below the bus stand, is very steep in places with loose stones. Do not attempt it alone. A shop sells a few provisions.

Recong Peo and around

Recong Peo, also called 'Peo', at 2290 m, is the District HQ and a busy little market town. The Sub-Divisional Magistrate's office in a three-storey building below the bus stand deals with Inner Line Permits. Inner Line Permits are checked at **Jangi** and travellers without them may not be allowed any further. Contact SDM in Recong Peo a day ahead (see Permits, page 426).

A short walk above the town takes you to the Kalachakra Temple with a large Buddha statue outside and good views of Kinner Kailash. A shop here sells provisions, medicines and has a telephone, but there's nowhere to change money. **Kothi village**, reached by a path from the Kalachakra Temple, has ancient Hindu temples associated with the Pandavas. One has a tank of sacred fish, 30 minutes' walk from the bazar.

Kalpa (Chini), 12 km from Recong Peo at 2960 m, is reached after a stiff climb. It has an interesting temple complex and Budh mandir and is surrounded by apple, *bemi* (wild apricot) and plum orchards and chilgoza pine forests, with striking views across to Kinner Kailash (6050 m).

A high road from Kalpa/Recong Peo with little traffic passes through Chilgoza pine forests, north to the hamlet of **Pangi**, 10 km away. Pangi is surrounded by apple orchards. The colourful Sheshri Nag temple at the top of the village has an inscription in a strange script above the entrance and standing stones in the courtyard. Apart from two Buddhist temples, the carved pagoda temple to Sheshri's mother encloses a huge boulder representing the Devi. The road then goes over bare and rugged hills beyond to **Morang** which has impressive monasteries with wood carvings and sculptures.

Tip...

Most Kinnauri Buddhist temples only accept visitors at around 0700 and 1900. You must wear a hat and a special belt available locally.

Where to stay

Baspa Valley

$$$$ Banjara Camps
Barseri, 8 km beyond Sangla, T(0)98168 81936,
www.banjaracamps.com.
Superb riverside site with impressive mountains
looming above you. 18 twin-bed rooms and
some 4-bed deluxe tents, delicious meals
included, hot water bottles in the bed. Friendly
staff, mountain biking, trekking and Lahaul,
Spiti and Ladakh tours. Buses stop 2 km from
the site, where the road drops down to the right.
The car park at the foot of the hill is a 500-m
walk from camp (a horn will summon porters).
Highly recommended.

$$ Hotel River Rupin View
Rakcham Village, 12 km from Sangla,
T(0)98166 86789.
Pretty little place well off the beaten track, set in
a garden with basic rooms.

$$ Kinner Camp
Barseri, T(0)9769-375993,
www.kinnerkamps.com.
Small tents with beds/sleeping bags and shared
baths in a superb location. There's birdwatching,
trekking and jeep safaris. Meals are available in
the cafeteria.

$ Hotel Apple Pie
Sangla, T07186-226304.
Run by a veteran mountaineer.

$ Negi Cottage
Sangla, T(0)9418-904161.
The 3 rooms, all with bath, are brightly coloured
inside and out so they have more character
than most.

$ Shruti Guest House
Sangla, near market,
www.shrutiguesthouse.com.
Comfortable, clean rooms with TV and attached
bath. You get a friendly welcome, and there
is good home-cooked food as well as mighty
Himalaya views.

Recong Peo and around

$$$-$$ Inner Tukpa
Between Kalpa and Recong Peo, T01786-223077,
www.innertukpahotel.com.

Nestled in the woods between Kalpa and Recong
Peo, there are spacious rooms here and even
more spacious views.

$$ Monk Resort Roshi Rd
1.5 km from Kalpa, T(0)9816-737004,
www.kinnaurgeotourism.com.
Set in pretty surroundings are these 4 spacious
swiss cottage tents, huts and airy rooms.
Recommended.

$$-$ Aucktong Guest House ('Aunties')
Near Circuit House, 1 km north on Pangi road,
Kalpa, T(0)98161 79457.
Pleasant place offering 6 clean spacious rooms
with large windows. There's also a restaurant.
It's very friendly: "arrived for one night and stayed
a week!".

$$-$ Kinner Kailash Cottage (HPTDC)
Kalpa, T01786-226159, www.hptdc.nic.in.
May-Nov.
In a commanding position, this place has
5 rooms (bath tub Rs 1100) and camping.
There's a limited menu.

$ Forest Rest House
Chini, 2 km from Kalpa.
In a modern building, camping is also available
overnight (with permission) in the school
grounds 1600-1000. The caretaker here can
prepare meals.

Transport

Baspa Valley
Bus Twice daily between Karchham (0930) and
Chitkul via **Sangla** (1100) and **Rakcham**. 4WD is
recommended between Karchham and Chitkul
in bad weather. Sangla to **Chitkul** (often 2-3 hrs
late). Sangla to **Shimla** via **Tapri** (9 hrs). Sangla to
Recong Peo, 0630. Tapri to **Chitkul**, 0930; Recong
Peo to **Chitkul**, 0600 (prompt).

Recong Peo and around
Bus Reserve tickets from the booth shortly
before departure. Bus to **Chandigarh**; **Delhi**
1030; **Kalpa**, occasional; **Kaza** (9 hrs), gets very
crowded so reserve seat before 0700; **Puh**;
Rampur, frequent (5 hrs); **Sangla/Chitkul** (4 hrs);
Shimla; **Tabo**, via Kaza (9-10 hrs). There are buses
from Kalpa to **Shimla**, 0730, and **Chitkul**, 1300.
To get to Peo for the Kaza bus at 0730, walk down
(40 mins) or arrange taxi from Peo.

From the checkpoint at Jangi the road goes to Puh, a steep climb with hairpin bends. The bridge at Khab, 11 km beyond Puh, marks the confluence of the Sutlej and Spiti rivers. The entry into the Spiti Valley at Khab is a rare example of crossing from the Himalaya to the Trans-Himalaya without going over a major pass. The Sutlej now disappears east towards the Tibet border, while the road follows the Spiti. Major deforestation of the mountain slopes has resulted in sections of the road being washed away. The new road, a remarkable feat of engineering, hairpins up to the village of Nako, with some basic guesthouses, and rejoins the river at Chango.

Sumdo, the last village of Kinnaur, has a border police checkpost and a tea shop, and is the starting point of State Highway 30, which passes through an arid valley with small patches of cultivation of peas and barley near the snow melt streams. It is 31 km from Sumdo to Tabo. For details of trekking in the Spiti Valley, see page 30. See also Trekking, page 39.

Tabo *Colour map 1, B4.*
At the crossroads of two ancient trade routes, Tabo (altitude 3050 m) was one of the great centres of Buddhist learning and culture. Founded in 996, the **Chos Khor Gompa** (see below) is the oldest living Buddhist establishment in this part of the world. Today, the small town is rapidly being modernized with paved streets and electric lights. Government offices have appeared alongside traditional mud homes and the local shops stock basic provisions for trekkers. There is a post office.

★ **Chos Khor Gompa** Founded in AD 996 as a scholastic institution, the monastery's original layout was planned as a *mandala* centred around a **Du khang** (Assembly Hall). The deodar wood used was imported from Kullu, Kinnaur, Chamba and Kashmir while the lack of quality structural stone resulted in the extensive use of earth, strengthened with gypsum for the high walls. Today the *gompa* is recognized as a historic Buddhist site. It comprises nine temples, four stupas and some cave shrines. The monastery houses 60 *lamas* and has a good collection of scriptures, *thangkas* and art pieces, including murals and frescos covering the walls. Carry a torch. No photography is allowed.

At the centre of the 'mandala' is the **Dri Tsang khang** (Inner Sanctum) and **Kora** (Circumambulatory Path). The five *Dhyani* Buddhas, escorted here by four Bodhisattvas, emerge from the darkness lit by a shaft of sunlight. The **Tsuglhakhang** (academy) features a 'resplendent' central *Mahavairochana*, a composite of four figures, each facing a cardinal direction, which represents the unity of all Buddhas. On the walls inside are stucco figures of different Buddhas and Bodhisattvas. The floral ceiling decorations are in the Ajanta style. Masks, weapons and ritual costumes are stored in the **Gon Khang,** which is closed to visitors. The **Zhalma** (Picture Hall) has a 17th-century entrance temple where the murals are recent and in pure Tibetan style. **Dromton Lhakhang Chenpo** (17th century) is dominated by Medicine Buddhas. The ceiling in high Tibetan style is exceptional, depicting *nagas*, titans, peacocks and parrots amongst rainbows. The walls of the **Ser Khang** (Golden Temple) were believed to have been coated with a layer of gold dust as thick as a yak's skin for painting the numerous larger-than-life figures. They were renewed in the 16th and 17th centuries. Dedicated to the Maitreya (Future) Buddha, **Chamba Chenpo La Khang** has a 6-m-high seated statue. The murals of the eight Buddhas here may be some of the earliest in Tabo.

To the north, the small natural caves above the road were an integral part of the monastic complex. **Pho Gompa**, the only surviving, with early murals showing pure Indian influence, has been restored. These post-Ajantan paintings, however, are already fading. On open ground to the east, on both sides of a dyke, there are pre-Buddhist rock carvings on metamorphosed igneous rocks showing ibex, swastikas, *yonis*, horses, panthers and human figures.

Dankar
Once the capital of Spiti, Dankar is a tiny village. The early 16th-century fort/monastery **Dankar Gompa** (3890 m), which once served as a jail, stands on an impressive overhang, perched on

The art of Chos Khor Gompa

Many of the colourful murals come close to the pure Indian style identified with Ajanta. The technique required the surface to be coated with several thin layers of lime and yak-skin glue and burnished vigorously to provide the 'ground' which was then smoothed and freshened with animal fat and butter. Natural vegetable dyes and powdered stone colours were mixed with *dzo* milk and yak urine for painting. The early Indian style murals used a profusion of reds and yellows with little stress on landscaping, the area around the principal figures being filled with small divinities. These images wear seraphic smiles and have half-shut dreamy eyes denoting introspective meditation. The later 17th-century paintings illustrate the Central Tibetan/Chinese art form where ultramarine takes over from the earlier dominance of reds and yellows, and landscapes become lively and vivid with the appearance of cliffs, swirling clouds, stylized flames, flora and fauna. Here the twists and turns of the limbs and the flowing elaborate drapery show great fluency. This is one of the few *gompas* in the Tibetan Buddhist-influenced areas of Ladakh, Lahaul and Spiti where the highly structured art of painting the complex Tibetan religious iconography is taught. What appears outwardly as a free art form is taught on lined paper where each shape and form is closely measured.

crumbling towers. Today it has more than 160 *lamas* in residence. The 'highest temple' has a collection of Bhotia Buddhist scriptures, a four-in-one *Dhyani Buddha* and interesting murals of Medicine Buddhas and protector deities. A large Mala (sacrificial wood) tree at the northwest corner of the monastery, the only one of four to survive, is held sacred by the villagers.

The *gompa* is a very steep two-hour climb from a point 2 km away, beyond Shichling on the main road. The 4WD road from the SH30, about 1 km west of Shichling, winds up 8 km to Dankar (a two-hour walk) and is easier. A beautiful large pond at just under 4100 m is reached by a 2.5-km track.

Lalung Gompa
Lalung Gompa, known for its carved wood panelling, is off the SH30, 22 km from Kaza, reached by 8-km narrow, drivable track. From Dankar Gompa this is a two-hour trek. Carry plenty of water as there are no streams and it can get very hot.

Pin Valley
About 5 km from Dankar is a sign for the Pin Valley National Park which is on the other side of the river. The Pin River joins the Spiti at Attargo. Above Attargo, 10 km along the Pin Valley, is the **Kungri Gompa** (circa 1330), which though not old is in an established monastic site with old carved wooden sculptures and is commonly understood to be a Bon monastery still practising elements of the pre-Buddhist Bon religion. The trek from the Bhabha Valley ends at the road head at Kungri, see page 30. See also Trekking, page 39. One bus a day departs from Kaza at 1200, goes along the Pin Valley as far as Mikkim and turns straight back at 1400, not allowing enough time to visit the *gompa*. You therefore face a long walk unless you can hitch a lift on a passing tractor, truck or yak.

At the confluence of the Pin River and one of its tributaries, 1 km from Mikkim, **Sangam** can be reached by car over a new iron bridge, or more adventurously by a pulley system with a person-sized bucket, 750 m west of the bus stop along the river. It requires a reasonable degree of fitness to negotiate, especially if crossing alone. The local greeting is *joolay, joolay*!

Pin Valley National Park is described as the "land of ibex and snow leopard" and was created to conserve the flora and fauna of the cold desert. It adjoins the Great Himalayan National Park (southwest), and Rupi Bhabha Sanctuary (south) with the Bara Shigri Glacier forming its north boundary. The park covers 675 sq km with a buffer zone of 1150 sq km mainly to its east where there are villages, and varies in altitude from 3600 m to 6630 m. The wildlife includes Siberian ibex, snow leopard, red fox, pika,

Fact...
Although rugged, the summer brings more rain here than the rest of Spiti resulting in a profusion of wild flowers.

weasels, lammergeier, Himalayan griffon, golden eagle, Chakor partridge, Himalayan snow cock and a variety of rose finches. The Siberian ibex can be sighted at high altitudes, beyond Hikim and Thango village. From July to September the young ibex kids need protection and so the females move up to the higher pastures near cliffs while the adult males concentrate on feeding lower down. The 60-km-long Lingti Valley is famous for its fossils.

Kaza

Kaza, at 3600 m, is 13 km from Lingti village and is the main town of the Spiti Valley. Old Kaza has village homes while New Kaza sports government offices. It is a busy bus terminus with plenty of hotels and homestays, a small market, a basic health centre and jeeps for hire. Inner Line Permits are issued by the SDM's office ① *T01906-222202, open 1030-1700, closed 2nd Sat of each month.* Tourist facilities are open May to October. For an exceptional insight into the area, check out www.spitiecosphere.com with a focus on conservation.

There is an attractive one-day circular trek from here to **Hikim** and **Komik** villages visiting the monastery midway. **Hikim Gompa** (early 14th century), modelled on a Chinese castle, was built under Mongol patronage. For more treks in Himachal Pradesh, see page 30. See also Trekking, page 39.

Kibber-Gete Wildlife Sanctuary

One of the world's highest wildlife sanctuaries, covering an area of 98 sq km, Kibber-Gete has **Mount Gya** (6754 m) to the north and **Kamelong** (5867 m) to the south. On the drive from Kibber to Tashigang, you may spot musk deer and bharal sheep but to see larger mammals (bear, wolf and the rare snow leopard) you would need to trek. Also to be seen are Himalayan birds of prey as well as snowcock and other high-altitude birds. Buses from Kaza take about an hour.

Tashigang

Tashigang, 18 km away, is one of the highest villages in the world connected by road. **Ki Monastery** on the way is the largest in Spiti and houses 300 *lamas*. Although it has suffered from wars, fires and earthquakes it still has a good collection of *thangkas* and *kangyurs* (scriptures). Although no permit is needed, the monks have instituted their private 'entrance fee' system which, by all accounts, appears quite flexible and linked to the visitor's perceived ability to pay. There are a few cheap guesthouses and camping is possible. If you cannot stay take a bus up and walk down via the Ki Monastery, 11 km from Kaza.

To Lahaul

Losar, at 4079 m, is the last village in Spiti, reached after driving through fields growing peas and cabbage among poplars, willows and apple orchards. There is a rest house and guesthouse and a couple of cafés serving Tibetan/Spitian food.

The road continues up for 18 km to the **Kunzum La** (Pass) at 4551 m. It means 'meeting place for ibex' and gives access to Lahaul and good views of some of the highest peaks of the Chandrabhaga group that lies immediately opposite the Kunzum La to the west. To the southeast is the Karcha Peak (6271 m). The pass has an ancient *chorten* marker. The temple to **Gyephang**, the presiding deity, is circumambulated by those crossing the pass; the giver of any offering in cash which sticks to the stone image receives special blessing.

The road descends through 19 hairpin curves to reach the rock strewn valley of the River Chandra at **Batal**, where a tea shop serves noodles and sells biscuits and bottled water. It continues to **Chhota Dhara** and **Chhatru**, with rest houses and eateries, and then **Gramphoo** joining the Manali–Keylong–Leh highway around three hours after leaving the pass. From Gramphoo to Manali is 62 km.

Where to stay

Tabo

Guesthouses in the village allow camping.
There is a good list of homestays throughout
Tabo and Spiti on www.spitiecosphere.com
and www.himachaltourism.gov.in.

$$$ Dewachen Retreat
Tabo T(0)9459-566689,
www.dewachenretreats.com.
Large comfortable cosy rooms with hot water
and great views. They have another property in
Rangrik, Kaza.

$$-$ Millennium Monastery Guest House
Run by monks in monastery complex.
13 colourful rooms, shared dirty toilets,
hot water on request and meals available.

Dankar

$ The *gompa* has 2 rooms; only 1 has a bed.

$ Dolma Guest House
8 perfectly fine rooms.

Pin Valley

There is a **PWD** Rest House.

$ Norzang Guest House
Rooms for Rs 100.

Kaza

Kaza is ideal for camping and there are great
opportunities for homestays in this area; for
more information contact the fantastic **Spiti
Ecosphere**, see What to do, below.

$$$ Kaza Retreat
T(0)9418-718123, www.banjaracamps.com.
11 clean, modern rooms with attached
bathrooms. You can expect high standards
here, good food and relaxing atmosphere,
with stunning views a bonus. Recommended.

$$ Monk Resorts
Shego, 6 km from Kaza, T(0)9816-737004,
www.kinaurgeotourism.com.
Set in a pretty location surrounded by flowers
are these 8 spacious Swiss cottage tents. They
have other camps in Nako and Kalpa and can
arrange homestays.

$$-$ Sakya's Abode
T(0)94182 08987, www.sakyaabode.com.
10 rooms in a fine-looking building with a wide
range of rooms and a cheap dorm (Rs 80). It
offers a friendly welcome and delicious home-
cooked food. You can now book for 2 other local
guesthouses through their website. Snow Lion
has 8 large rooms and majestic views, while the
cheaper **Kumphen Guest House** has simple
rooms and delicious Tibetan food right inside the
monastery compound.

Restaurants

Kaza

The fantastic **Spiti Ecospheres** (see What to
do, below) have opened 2 exceptional cafés in
Kaza. Check out www.spitiecosphere for more
information on their work.

$$-$ Sol Café
Underneath the Spiti Ecosphere office,
see What to do, below.
Sol Café focuses on great coffees, speciality teas,
homemade chocolates and crêpes under the
guidance of a French baker. The decor is influenced
by Spitian and Tibetan culture. It's a travellers' café
so a great place to meet people; there are movie
nights, a book exchange and free water refills.

$$-$ Taste of Spiti
With stunning views and fantastic fusion food,
Taste of Spiti serves up a healthy local grain
pasta keu, black pea veggie burgers and
hummus, as well as drinks with local crop
seabuckthorn. They specialize in healthy heart-
warming food and their proceeds go to fund
various eco initiatives and work with local Spitian
families. Highly recommended.

What to do

Kaza
Tour operators
Spiti Ecospheres, *www.spitiecospheres.com.*
This is an exceptional project with a nod
towards conservation, environmental and
livelihoods; also volunteering projects, unique
treks and promoting organic agriculture. They
have an interesting range of tours including
Spiritual Sojourns where you spend time with
the Bhuchens, a rare sect of Tibetan Buddhist
theatrical artists, and **Rustic Revelations** and

Spiti Kaleidoscope where you get real insight into the lives and culture of these Himalayan peoples. There are also several **Carbon Neutral** volunteering projects. Ecosphere also put in 6 solar installations in 2013 as part of its initiative to provide reliable, green and decentralized energy to the Spiti valley. Highly recommended.

Transport

Tabo
Bus To Chandigarh via Kinnaur, 0900; **Kaza**, 1000.

Kaza
Bus Reserve a seat at least 1 hr ahead or night before. The road via Kunzum-La and Rohtang Pass can be blocked well into Jul. New bus stand, bottom end of village. In summer: from **Manali** (201 km), 12 hrs via Rohtang Pass and Kunzum La; **Shimla** (412 km) on the route described, 2 days. Approximate times shown: daily to **Chango**, 1400; **Kibber** 0900, **Losar** 0900; **Mikkim** (19 km from Attargo), in the Pin Valley, 1200 (2 hrs).

North of Shimla

high mountain passes and sacred lakes

Bilaspur and Bhakra-Nangal Dam *Colour map 1, B3.*
Bilaspur used to be the centre of a district in which the tribal Daora peoples panned in the silts of the Beas and Sutlej for gold. Their main source, the Seer Khud, has now been flooded by the Bhakra Nangal Lake and they have shifted their area of search upstream. For a bite to eat visit the Lake View Café.

The dam on the River Sutlej is one of the highest dams in the world at 225 m and was built as part of the Indus Waters Treaty between India and Pakistan (1960). The Treaty allocated the water of the rivers Sutlej, Beas and Ravi to India. The dam provides electricity for Punjab, Haryana and Delhi. It is also the source for the Rajasthan Canal project, which takes water over 1500 km south to the Thar Desert. There is accommodation should you wish to stay.

Una to Mandi
Having passed through Una, along the main bus route, **Ghanahatti**, 18 km further on, has the adequate **Monal Restaurant**. There are some magnificent views, sometimes across intensively cultivated land, sometimes through plantations of chilgoza, khir and other species. In **Shalaghat**, further on, accommodation is available. The road descends into a deep valley before climbing again to the small market town of **Bhararighat**. A jeep can take over two hours for this part of the journey. In **Brahmpukar** the road to Beri and Mandi is a very attractive country lane. The more heavily used though still quiet road to the main Bilaspur–Manali road joins it at **Ghaghas**. During the monsoons landslides on the NH21 may cause long delays. Carry plenty of water and some food. The tree-lined and attractive approach to **Sundernagar** from the south gives some indication of the town's rapid growth and prosperity.

Mandi (Sahor) *Colour map 1, B3.*
Founded by a Rajput prince in circa 1520, Mandi (population 26,900, altitude 760 m) is held sacred by both Hindus and Buddhists. The old town with the main (Indira) bazar is huddled on the left bank of the Beas at the southern end of the Kullu Valley, just below its junction with the River Uhl. The Beas bridge – claimed to be the world's longest non-pillar bridge – is across Sukheti Khad at the east end of town. The main bus station is across the river, just above the open sports ground. It is worth stopping a night in this quaint town with 81 temples, a 17th-century palace and a colourful bazar. For tourist information ⓘ *T01905-225036.*

Triloknath Temple (1520), on the riverbank, built in the Nagari style with a tiled roof, has a life-size three-faced Siva image (Lord of Three Worlds), riding a bull with Parvati on his lap. It is at the centre of a group of 13th- to 16th-century sculpted stone shrines. The Kali Devi statue which emphasizes the natural shape of the stone, illustrates the ancient Himalayan practice of stone worship.

Panchavaktra Temple, at the confluence of the Beas and a tributary with views of the Triloknath, has a five-faced image (*Panchanana*) of Siva. The image is unusually conceived like a temple *shikhara* on an altar plinth. Note the interesting frieze of yogis on a small temple alongside.

Bhutnath Temple (circa 1520) by the river in the town centre is the focus at Sivaratri Fair (see page 439). The modern shrines nearby are brightly painted.

In lower Sumkhetar, west of the main bazar, is the 16th-century **Ardhanarishvara Temple** where the Siva image is a composite male/female form combining the passive Siva (right) and the activating energy of Parvati (left). Although the *mandapa* is ruined, the carvings on the *shikhara* tower and above the inner sanctum door are particularly fine.

From the old suspension bridge on the Dharamshala road, if you follow a narrow lane up into the main market you will see the slate roof over a deep spring which is the **Mata Kuan Rani Temple**, dedicated to the 'Princess of the Well'. The story of this Princess of Sahor (Mandi) and her consort **Padmasambhava**, who introduced Mahayana Buddhism in Tibet, describes how the angry king condemned the two to die in a fire which raged for seven days and when the smoke cleared a lake appeared with a lotus – Rewalsar or *Tso Pema* (Tibetan 'Lotus Lake').

Around Mandi

The small dark **Rewalsar Lake**, 24 km southeast, with its floating reed islands, is a popular pilgrimage centre. The colourful Tibetan Buddhist monastery was founded in the 14th century, though the pagoda-like structure is late 19th century. The Gurudwara commemorates Guru Gobind Singh's stay here. Start early for the hilltop temples by the transmission tower as it is a steep and hot climb. The **Sisu fair** is held in February/March. There are many buses to the lake from Mandi Bus Stand, one hour; you can also board them below the palace in Indira Bazar.

At **Prashar**, a three-tiered pagoda Rishi temple sits beside a sacred lake in a basin surrounded by high mountains with fantastic views of the Pir Panjal range. The rich woodcarvings here suggest a date earlier than the Manali Dhungri Temple (1553), which is not as fine. No smoking, alcohol or leather items are allowed near the temple or lake. There are basic pilgrim rest houses. A forest rest house is 1 km west of temple. To reach the temple, follow a steep trail from Kandi, 10 km north of Mandi, through the forest of rhododendron, oak, deodar and kail (three hours). After arriving at a group of large shepherd huts the trail to the left goes to the temple, the right to the forest rest house.

You can walk to **Aut**, see below, from Prashar in six to seven hours. A level trail east crosses a col in under a kilometre. Take the good path down to the right side of the *nullah* (valley) and cross the stream on a clear path. Climb a little and then follow a broad path on the left bank to the road. Turn right and down to **Peon village** in the *Chir nullah* and continue to Aut.

Tirthan Valley and Jalori Pass *For trekking information sees pages 30 and 39.*

From Mandi the NH21 runs east then south along the left bank of the Beas, much diminished in size by the dam at **Pandoh**, 19 km from Mandi, from which water is channelled to the Sutlej. The dam site is on a spectacular meander of the Beas (photography strictly prohibited). The NH21 crosses over the dam to the right bank of the Beas then follows the superb **Larji Gorge**, in which the Beas now forms a lake for a large part of the way upstream to Aut. A large hydroelectric project is being constructed along this stretch. At **Aut** (pronounced 'out') there is trout fishing (season March to October, best in March and April); permits are issued by the Fishery Office in Largi, Rs 100 per day. The main bazar road has a few cheap hotels and eating places. It is also a good place to stop and stock up with trekking supplies such as dried apricots and nuts.

From Aut, a road branches off across the Beas into the **Tirthan Valley** climbing through beautiful wooded scenery up to the Jalori Pass. Allow at least 1½ hours by jeep to **Sojha**, 42 km from Mandi, and another 30 minutes to Jalori. Contact the tourist office in Kullu for trekking routes. One suggested trek is Banjar–Laisa–Paldi–Dhaugi/Banogi–Sainj, total 30 km, two days.

Banjar, with attractive wood-fronted shops lining the narrow street, has the best examples in the area of timber-bonded Himalayan architecture in the fort-like rectangular temple of **Murlidhar** (Krishna). Halfway to **Chaini**, 3 km away, the large **Shring Rishi Temple** to the deified local sage is very colourful with beautiful wooden balconies and an impressive 45-m-tall tower which was damaged in the last earthquake. The entrance, 7 m above ground, is reached by climbing a notched tree trunk. Such free-standing temple towers found in eastern Tibet were sometimes used for defence and incorporated into Thakur's castles in the western Himalaya. The fortified villages here even have farmhouses like towers.

From Banjar the road climbs increasingly steeply to **Jibhi**, 9 km away, where there are sleeping options and trekking. Two kilometres beyond is **Ghayaghi**, also with accommodation. A few kilometres on is **Sojha**, a Rajput village in the heart of the forest, which offers a base for treks in the Great Himalayan National Park.

Finally you reach the **Jalori Pass** (altitude 3350 m), open only in good weather from mid-April, which links Inner and Outer Seraj and is 76 km from Kullu. You may wish to take the bus up to the pass and walk down, or even camp a night at the pass. Check road conditions before travelling. A ruined fort, **Raghupur Garh**, sits high to the west of the pass and from the meadows there are fantastic views, especially of the Pir Panjal range. Take the path straight from the first hairpin after the pass and head upwards for 30-40 minutes. The road is suitable for 4WD vehicles. There is a very pleasant, gradual walk, 5 km east, through woodland (one hour), starting at the path to the right of the temple. It is easy to follow. **Sereuil Sar** (Pure Water) is where local women worship Burhi Nagini Devi, the snake goddess, and walk around the lake pouring a line of *ghee*. It is claimed that the lake is kept perpetually clear of leaves by a pair of resident birds. *Dhabas* provide simple refreshments and one has two very basic cheap rooms at the pass.

The Great Himalayan National Park and Tirthan Sanctuary
www.greathimalayannationalpark.com, foreigners Rs 200 per day, Indians Rs 50, students half price, video Rs 300/150.

The Great Himalayan National Park and Tirthan Sanctuary lies southeast of Kullu town in the Seraj Forest Division, an area bounded by mountain ridges (except to the west) and watered by the upper reaches of the rivers Jiwa, Sainj and Tirthan. The hills are covered in part by dense forest of blue pine, deciduous broadleaved and fir trees and also shrubs and grassland; thickets of bamboo make it impenetrable in places. Attractive species of iris, frittilaria, gagea and primula are found in the high-altitude meadows. Wildlife include the panther, Himalayan black bear, brown bear, tahr, musk deer, red fox, goral and bharal. The rich birdlife includes six species of pheasant. The park is 60,561 ha with an altitude of 1500-5800 m and the sanctuary covers 6825 ha; its headquarters are in Shamshi. Access is easiest from April to June and September to October.

Goshiani is the base for treks into the park. The first 3 km along the river are fairly gentle before the track rises to harder rocky terrain; there are plenty of opportunity to see birds and butterflies. The trout farm here sells fresh fish at Rs 150 per kg. Fishing permits, Rs 100, are obtainable from the Fisheries Department.

Listings North of Shimla

Where to stay

Mandi

$$$-$$ Raj Mahal
Lane to the right of the palace, Indira Bazar, T01905-222401, www.rajmahalpalace.com.
This former palace has character but is in need of attention. There are 14 rooms, including atmospheric deluxe rooms with bath (the sharpened sword in one might be mistaken for a towel rail). Rooms in the palace are charming whereas in the other block they are quite dull but cheap. There's a restaurant, bar and garden temple. You have to be persistent to book as they don't always answer the phone. Recommended.

$$$-$$ Visco Resorts
2 km south of Mandi, T01905-225057, www.viscoresorts.com.

In a modern resort by the river are 18 large rooms (some for 4). There's a good cheap vegetarian restaurant, and it's extremely well run.

$$ Hotel Regent Palms
Near Kargil Park, close to Raj Mahal, T01905-222777.
This bright newish hotel is centrally located and has all mod cons and attractive decor.

$ Evening Plaza
Indira Bazar, T01905-223318.
14 reasonable rooms, some a/c, TV, changes cash at a good rate.

$ Hotel Lotus Lake
Rewalsar, above the lake, T01905-240239.
Run by the folks at Ziggar Monastery, this place has had a fresh lick of paint. If going to Rewalsar you can also stay by donation at the Sikh *gurudwara* (temple).

$ Rewalsar Inn (HPTDC)
Above the lake, T01905-240252, www.hptdc.nic.in.
There are good lake views from this hotel offering
12 reasonable rooms with bath, some with a TV
and balcony. Dorm Rs 75.

Tirthan Valley and Jalori Pass

$$$$-$$$ Himalayan Trout House
Below Banjar, T01903-225112,
www.mountainhighs.com.
All-weather eco-cabins, mud hut suites and stone
cottage suites in a stunning location. Fine food
is served, and there's great hospitality. Also here
is an artist's studio, gazebo with fire and library.
Trekking and fishing can be arranged. A little
shop sells organic wares. Highly recommended.

$$$ Banjara Sojha Retreat
Sojha, T01903-200070, www.banjaracamps.com.
There are 5 basic double rooms and 4 lovely
suites in this wooden lodge with fantastic views,
good food and trekking information. You can see
all the way to the mountains above Manali from
here. Stunning.

$ Dev Ganga
9 km from Banjar in Jibhi, T(0)94181 54754.
8 comfortable double rooms, with exceptional
views. Friendly staff.

$ Doli Guest house
Jhibi village, T01903-227034, www.kshatra.com.
Good little rooms in a traditional building. There's
also a sweet little café by the river in very pretty
little village. Also ask about the cottages above
the village with sitting rooms and woodburning
stove. In tune with the local area and a growing
number of backpackers, they are offering healthy
retreats. Recommended.

$ Forest Rest House
Near Sojha.
Spectacular and isolated just below the Jalori Pass.

$ Fort View Home Stay
Sojha, just by entrance to Banjara Camp,
T(0)9418-626634.
An atmospheric traditional building with 4 rooms
inside and shared bathroom.

$ Raju's Place
Goshaini.
A family-run river-facing guesthouse, offering
3 rooms with bath. They provide great home-
cooked food, treks and safaris. Access is by zip
wire over the river.

Restaurants

Mandi
You can eat at **Raj Mahal Palace**; see Where to
stay, above.

$$ Mayfair
Efficient and tasty North Indian food some
continental and Chinese.

$ Gomush Tibetan Restaurant
Near gompa at Rewalsar Lake.
Excellent *momos*.

Festivals

Mandi
Feb/Mar Sivaratri Fair, a week of dance,
music and drama as temple deities from
surrounding hills are taken in procession
with chariots and palanquins to visit the
Madho Rai and Bhutnath temples.

Transport

Mandi
Bus Bus information T01905-235538.
Chandigarh 1100 (203 km, 5 hrs). **Dharamshala**
1215, 6 hrs; **Kullu/Manali** every 30 mins, 3 hrs
(Kullu), 4 hrs (Manali); **Shimla** (5½ hrs). Book
private buses in town or opposite the bus stand
at least 1 day in advance; they do not originate in
Mandi. **Dharamshala**, 5 hrs; **Kullu/Manali**, 2 hrs
(Kullu), 3½ hrs (Manali).

Taxi Rs 1500 to Kullu; Rs 2200 to **Manali**;
Rs 2200 to **Dharamshala**.

Train Jogindernagar (55 km), easier to travel
by road.

Tirthan Valley and Jalori Pass
Bus From **Jibli** the bus to **Jalori** can take 1 hr.
Some go via **Ghayaghi** (approximate times):
If heading for Shimla or Kinnaur, change buses
at Sainj on NH22.
   Bus from **Ani** and **Khanag** to the south, runs
to **Jalori Pass** and back. 4 buses daily traverse the
pass in each direction when it is open (8-9 months).
Bus to **Sainj**, 3½ hrs, and on to **Shimla**, 5 hrs.

Taxi From **Banjar** to Jalori Pass costs Rs 800
(Rs 1200 return), to **Jibhi/Ghayaghi**, Rs 300,
to **Kullu**, Rs 600, to **Manali**, Rs 1200, to **Mandi**
Rs 700, to **Shimla**, Rs 3000. Buses are rare.

Kullu
Valley

The Kullu Valley was the gateway to Lahaul for the Central Asian trade in wool and borax. It is enclosed to the north by the Pir Panjal range, to the west by the Bara Bangahal and to the east by the Parvati range, with the Beas River running through its centre. The approach is through a narrow funnel or gorge but in the upper part it extends outwards. The name Kullu is derived from Kulantapith 'the end of the habitable world'. It is steeped in Hindu religious tradition; every stream, rock and blade of grass seemingly imbued with some religious significance. Today, the main tourist centre is Manali, a hive of adventurous activity in the summer months, a quiet and peaceful place to relax in the winter snow.

Essential Kullu Valley

Finding your feet

Kullu-Manali (Bhuntar) airport, 10 km south of Kullu, has flights from Delhi, Shimla and Ludhiana; transfer by bus or taxi to Manali (Rs 750), Manikaran (Rs 650). If travelling on buses from the south, alight at Dhalpur Bus Stand in Kullu. Most buses to Kullu continue to Manali. See Transport, page 442.

When to go

Mid-September to mid-November is the best time to visit. May and June are hot but offer good trekking. March to mid-April can be cold with occasional heavy rain.

Where to stay

The choice of hotels is widening, with some good hotels in all ranges, though these are very full during Dasara. There are large off-season discounts (30-50%). Manali has a vast number of hotels catering mainly for Indian tourists and honeymooners.

Safety

Cases of Western travellers going missing in the Kullu Valley in recent years continue to be reported. They seem to have occurred mostly when trekking alone or camping. Some suggest that there have been genuine accidents in the mountains or that some drug users have 'opted out' and chosen to sever their ties and remain with *sadhus* in remote caves. However, the threat to personal safety is very real so if you're trekking beyond Manikaran, or from Naggar across the Chandrakhani Pass to the Malana Valley, you should not walk alone. Only use registered guides through local trekking agents.

Sprawling along the grassy west bank of the Beas, Kullu (population 18,300, altitude 1219 m), the district headquarters, hosts the dramatically colourful Dasara festival. Less commercialized than its neighbour Manali, it is known across India as the home of apple-growing and for the locally woven woollen shawls. There is little to occupy you here as a tourist.

The central area, including the main bus stand and Dhalpur (with ample hotels and restaurants) are close enough to cover on foot. Buses and taxis go to nearby sights.

Sights

Kullu's bulky curvilinear temples seem to have been inspired by the huge boulders that litter the riverbeds and hillsides outside town. A peculiar feature of the Nagari temples is the umbrella-shaped covering made of wood or zinc sheets placed over and around the *amalaka* stone at the top of the spire.

The **Raghunathji Temple** is the temple of the principal god of the **Dasara** festival. The shrine houses an image of Shri Raghunath (brought here from Ayodhya circa 1657) in his chariot. **Bhekhli**, a 3-km climb, has excellent views from the **Jagannathi Temple**. The copper 16th- to 17th-century mask of the Devi inside has local Gaddi tribal features. The wall painting of Durga is in traditional folk style. There are also superb views on the steep but poorly marked climb to the tiny **Vaishno Devi Temple**, 4 km north, on Kullu-Manali road.

Around Kullu

Bijli Mahadev, 11 km from Kullu at 2435 m, is connected by road most of the way with a 2-km walk up steps from the road head. The temple on a steep hill has a 20-m rod on top which is reputedly struck by *bijli* (lightning) regularly, shattering the stone *lingam* inside. The priests put the *lingam* together each time with *ghee* (clarified butter) and a grain mixture until the next strike breaks it apart again. Several buses until late afternoon from Left Bank Bus Stand, the road to Bijli is rough and the buses are in a poor state.

Bajaura Temple, on the banks of the Beas River, about 200 m off the NH21 at **Hat** (Hatta), is one of the oldest in the valley. The massive pyramidal structure is magnificently decorated with stone images of Vishnu, Ganesh and Mahishasuramardini (Durga as the Slayer of the Buffalo Demon, see page 695 in the outer shrines. The slender bodies, elongated faces and limbs suggest East Indian Pala influence. Floriated scrollwork decorate the exterior walls.

Listings Kullu

Tourist information

Himachal Pradesh Tourism Development Corporation (HPTDC)
T01902-222349, near Maidan. Open 1000-1700.
Provides maps and advice on trekking.

Where to stay

$$$-$$ Airport Inn
Next to Bhuntar airport, T01902-268286,
airportinncomplex@gmail.com.
A convenient place to stay before travelling the 50 km to Manali.

$$$-$$ Shobla
Dhalpur, T01902-222800,
www.shoblainternational.com.
25 rooms, flashy exterior, clean, pleasant atmosphere, airy restaurant, overlooking river.

$$-$ Sarwari (HPTDC)
10-min walk south of Dhalpur Bus Stand,
T01902-222471.
Peaceful hotel with 16 simple but comfortable rooms (10 in more spacious new wing), 8-bed dorm (Rs 75), good-value restaurant, beer, pleasant gardens, elevated with good views.

Trekking the Tosh Valley

One of my favourite treks begins from Tosh, which is 25 km ahead of Manikaran. The Tosh is a feeder valley of the popular Parvati Valley which leads to the Pin Parvati Pass. The route follows the raging river all the way to the snout of the Tosh Glacier. You trek across beautiful meadows full of flowers, run into Gaddis (the shepherd tribe of Himachal) and maybe catch a rare glimpse of the Himalayan black or brown bear. On a recent trip, I also spotted the rare golden eagle.

Kaushal Desai, tour guide with **Above 14000 ft**

$ Silver Moon (HPTDC)
Perched on a hill, 2 km south of centre,
T01902-222488, www.hptdc.nic.in.
6 rooms with bath and heaters, each with small sitting room in traditional style, very clean, good food, has character (enhanced because Mahatma Gandhi stayed here).

Festivals

End Apr The colourful 3-day **Cattle Fair** attracts villagers from the surrounding area. Numerous cultural events accompany it.
Oct-Nov **Dasara** is sacred to the Goddess Durga which, elsewhere in India, tends to be overshadowed by **Diwali** which follows a few weeks later. In this part of the Himalaya it is a big social event and a get-together of the gods.

Shopping

Best buys are shawls, caps, *gadmas*; see also box, page 471. The state weaving cooperative, **Bhutti Weavers Colony**, 6 km south, has retail outlets; **Bhuttico**, is 1 store 2 km south of Apple Valley Resorts.

Akhara Bazar has a **Government Handicrafts Emporium**, **Himachal Khadi Emporium** and

Khadi Gramudyog. Charm Shilp is good for sandals.

What to do

Tour operators
Look East, *c/o Bajaj Autos, Manikaran Chowk, Shamshi, T01902-065771.* Recommended for river rafting and bike hire.

Transport

Air Bhuntar Airport, T01902-265727. **Air India**, T1-800-180 1407, www.airindia.in.

Bus Most buses coming to Kullu continue to Manali. Most long-distance buses use the main bus stand, **Sarvari Khad**, with a booking office. For long distance and to **Manali**, left bank bus stand across the bridge: buses for **Naggar** (every 30 mins in summer) and **Bijli Mahadev**, and several to **Manali**; HPTDC deluxe bus to **Chandigarh** (270 km), 0800, 8 hrs; **Delhi**, 512 km, 15 hrs, extra buses during season, often better than private buses, you will pay more for a/c, the Volvo service is pricier; **Dharamshala**, 0800-0900, 8 hrs; **Shimla** (235 km), 0900, 8 hrs, Tickets from the tourist office; see under Tourist information, page 441.

Parvati Valley *Colour map 1, B3.*

orchards, hot springs and high peaks

The Parvati (Parbati) Valley runs northeast from Bhuntar. Attractive orchards and the fresh green of terraced rice cultivation line the route. Known for its hot springs at Manikaran, more recently the valley has become infamous for the droves of chillum-smoking Israelis and Europeans who decamp here in the summer months attracted by the intensive cultivation of narcotics.

Several local buses (and jeep taxis) travel daily to the valley from Kullu via Bhuntar, taking about two hours to Manikaran, which also has buses from Manali. The area is prone to landslides and flash floods; take special care. See Transport, page 444. For more on trekking in the area, see page 30, and for general information on trekking, see page 39.

Jari

Jari is the point where the deep Malana Nala joins the Parvati River. It is a popular resting place for trekkers but also for drug users. The guesthouses vary; a few away from the village centre have better views.

Kasol

Kasol is the next village en route to Manikaran. The rapidly expanding village has spread on both sides of the road bridge which crosses a tributary that flows into the Parvati, not far from the village itself. About 500 m beyond the village, a narrow side road leads to the river and the location of a fine hot spring on the riverbank. Kasol is the main destination for long-stay visitors, many of whom sit in a haze of *charas* smoke by day and night.

Chhalal is a 20-minute walk from Kasol. It is a quiet village where families take in guests. A couple of guesthouses have also sprung up here.

Manikaran

Manikaran, 45 km from Kullu, is at the bottom of a dark gorge with **hot sulphur springs** emerging from the rock-strewn banks of the Parvati. A local legend describes how while Parvati bathed in the river, Naga, the serpent god stole her *manikaran* (earrings). At Siva's command Naga angrily blew them back from underground causing a spring to flow. Hindu and Sikh pilgrims come to the Rama temple and the *gurdwara* and gather to cook their food by the springs, purportedly the hottest in the world. There are separate baths for men and women.

Manikaran, though not attractive in itself, provides a brief halt for trekkers. Short treks go to Pulga and Khirganga beyond while a footpath (affected by landslips in places), leads to the Pin Valley in Spiti. If trekking this route, always go with a registered guide; do not attempt it alone. A road continues for 15 km to **Barseni**, which has become a popular place with long-term travellers.

Pulga and Khirganga

Pulga is in a beautiful location with some cheap guesthouses. It is a good four-hour walk east of Manikaran. Some long-stay travellers prefer the basic airy guesthouses outside the village which offer meals.

Khirganga is along the trek which winds through the lush Parvati Valley, east of Pulga. It is known for its sacred ancient hot springs marking the place where Siva is thought to have meditated for 2000 years. There is an open bathing pool for men and an enclosed pool for women, next to the humble shrine at the source. A few tents may be hired. *Dhabas* sell vegetarian food. This is the last village in this valley.

Listings Parvati Valley

Where to stay

Jari

$$$ The Himalayan Village
Doonkhara, between Jari and Kasol, T01902-276266, www.thehimalayanvillage.in.
Inspiring new construction based on traditional principles, in fact builders had to be trained in how to build this old-style property with layered wood and stone. Planning to expand with more rooms and tented area but seamlessly blending into the forest. Good restaurant and spa. Recommended.

$ Village Guest House
10-min walk beyond the village, follow signs, T(0)98051 90051.
One of several budget options that are springing up along the main road. This one is in the most peaceful setting and has 5 simple rooms with clean, shared hot bath and a restaurant. An excellent location on the edge of a traditional farming village, very friendly, good value.

Kasol

$ Alpine
T01902-273710, www.alpine guesthouse.net.
By far the best place in town right next to the
river and deservedly popular. Friendly and
welcoming with good clean rooms.

$ Panchali Holiday Home
T(0)98163 55095.
Good range of spacious rooms, many
with balconies.

Manikaran

There are a large number of budget guesthouses
but it is better to stay in Jari or Kasol and do a
day trip.

$ Padha Family Guest House
*Manikaran bazar, near Gurudwara,
T(0)9817-044874.*
Cheap rooms, super basic but clean with hot
shower. Downstairs separate hot bathing room.
Moon Guest House nearby offers much the same.

$ Parvati
Near the temple, T01902-273735.
10 simple rooms, sulphur baths, restaurant.

Restaurants

Manikaran

$ Gurudwara
Near the temple.
Excellent meals, steam-cooked at the springs
(donation only).

Pulga

$ Paradise Restaurant
In the village.
Great vegetarian dishes. Also has information on
guides and equipment for treks up the valley and
over the Pin-Parvati Pass (5300 m). If you are lucky,
you may be able to persuade the watchman of the
old **Forest Rest House** to let you in. The 'visitors'
registration book' contains entries that date back
to the 1930s and include several well-known
mountaineers who have passed by.

Transport

Parvati Valley
Bus There are frequent buses from **Bhuntar Bus
Stand**, outside the airport, with many connections
to/from **Kullu** and **Manali**. To **Manikaran**, 2½ hrs.

Kullu to Manali *Colour map 1, B3.*

magnificent views and Himachali castles

The NH21 continues north along the west side of the Beas. The older road to the
east of the river goes through terraced rice fields and endless apple orchards, and
is rougher and more circuitous but more interesting. Sections of both roads can be
washed away during the monsoon.

Kullu to Katrain
As you wind out the centre of Kullu along the right bank you'll pass the **Sitaramata Temple**
embedded in the conglomerate cliff and **Raison**, a grassy meadow favoured by trekkers. **Katrain**, in
the widest part of the Kullu Valley, mid-way between Kullu and Manali, is overlooked by **Baragarh
Peak** (3325 m). There are plenty of options for an overnight stay. Across the bridge at **Patli Kuhl**, the
road climbs through apple orchards to Naggar.

★ Naggar *Colour map 1, B3.*
Naggar's (Nagar) interesting castle sits high above Katrain. Built in the early 16th century, it
withstood the earthquake of 1905 and is a fine example of the timber-bonded building of West
Himalaya. It was built around a courtyard with verandas, from where there are enchanting views
over the valley. With a pleasant, unhurried atmosphere, it is a good place to stop a while. It is also an
entry for treks to Malana, see page 446.

The **castle**, probably built by Raja Sidh Singh, was used as a royal residence and state headquarters
until the 17th century when the capital was transferred to Sultanpur (see Kullu, above). It continued
as a summer palace until the British arrived in 1846, when it was sold to Major Hay, the first assistant
commissioner, who Europeanized part of it, fitting staircases, fireplaces and so on. Extensive

renovations have produced fine results, especially in the intricately carved woodwork. In the first courtyard are several black *barselas* (sati stones) with primitive carvings. Beyond the courtyard and overlooking the valley the **Jagti Pat Temple** houses a cracked stone slab measuring 2.5 m by 1.5 m by 2 m believed to be a piece of Deo Tibba, which represents the deity in 'the celestial seat of all the gods'. A priest visits the slab every day.

The small **museum** ① *Rs 10*, has some interesting exhibits, including examples of local *pattu* and *thippu* (women's dress and headdress) and *chola* (folk dance costumes). There are also local implements for butter and tea making, and musical instruments like the *karnal* (broad bell horn) and *singa* (long curled horn).

Roerich Art Gallery ① *Tue-Sun 0900-1300 (winter from 1000), 1400-1700, Rs 50*, a 2-km climb from the castle, is Nicholas Roerich's old home in a peaceful garden with excellent views. The small museum downstairs has a collection of photos and his distinctive stylized paintings of the Himalaya using striking colours. It's a beautiful collection from an inspiring family. Nicholas Roerich created the Roerich Pact in the 1930s in order to preserve culture and the arts in the wake of WWI. It was originally signed by 21 countries.

Uruswati Institute ① *uphill from the main house, Rs 15*, was set up in 1993. The **Himalayan Folk and Tribal Art Museum** is well presented, with contemporary art upstairs. One room upstairs is devoted to a charming collection of Russian traditional costumes, dolls and musical instruments.

There are a number of **temples** around the castle including the 11th-century Gauri Shankar Siva near the bazar, with some fine stone carving. Facing the castle is the Chaturbhuj to Vishnu. Higher up, the wooden Tripura Sundari with a multi-level pagoda roof in the Himachal style celebrates its fair around mid-May. Above that is the Murlidhar Krishna at Thawa, claimed as the oldest in the area which has a beautifully carved stone base. Damaged in the 1905 earthquake, it is now well restored. There are fine mountain views from here.

Listings Kullu to Manali

Where to stay

Katrain and Raison

$$$$ Neeralaya
Raison, T0 1902-245725, www.neeralaya.com.
Beautiful riverside cottages and villas made of stone and wood in the local *kathkuni* style with private kitchens and large verandas. Great local food. It's a sedate place here by the river with walks through the orchards, trout fishing possibilities and campfire suppers. Recommended.

$$$-$$ Ramgarh Heritage Villa
Near Raison between Kullu and Manali, T(0)9816-248514, www. ramgarhheritagevillamanali.com.
A farm since 1928, well-furnished rooms with TV and Wi-Fi, but beyond the front door there are orchards of pear, pomegranate and walnut trees and great views of the mountains. You can do trips to their kiwi plantation and they can organize paragliding, river rafting, yoga and picnics. Recommended.

$ Orchard Resorts
Dobhi, 2 km south of Katrain, T01902-240160.
Good off-season discount. 16 attractive wood-panelled 'cottages', with hot water, TV and heaters.

Naggar

Naggar is an atmospheric place to stay.

$$$-$ Castle
T01902-248316, www.hptdc.nic.in.
An absolutely beautiful property with an amazing temple. Castle was built in 1460 and has been a hotel since 1978. It has 13 rooms, which are stylish with traditional decor and furniture, comfortable beds, fireplaces and modernized baths. The best rooms (**$$**) overlook the valley, some share bath, and there's a very basic dorm (Rs 75). The restaurant, open May-Jun, has good service; add Rs 150 for vegetarian meals.

$ Alliance
200 m above the castle, T01902-248263, www.allianceguesthouse.com.
Run by French expat, this homely place has 6 very good value, clean, simple rooms, with hot water and meals available. Good for families.

$ Poonam Mountain Lodge
Close to Castle, T01902-248248,
www.poonammountain.in.
6 spotless rooms, very good food, run by a
friendly family. They also organize treks and jeep
safaris and have a traditional cottage to rent.

$ Ragini
T01902-248185, raginihotel@hotmail.com.
16 smart rooms with modernized baths (hot
water), large windows, good views from rooftop
restaurant, excellent breakfasts, Ayurvedic
massage and yoga, good value, friendly.

$ Sheetal
T01902-248250.
Overlooking valley, this clean and spacious place
has 14 very pleasant rooms with bath, hot water
(some tubs), TV and use of a kitchen.

$ Snow View
Down steps past Tripura Sundari Temple,
T(0)98160 77132, snowviewhomestay@gmail.com.
Weaving co-op outlet, with 7 rooms and a
restaurant. Small and charming.

Restaurants

Naggar
There is also a *dhaba* up at the Jana waterfall
recommended for trying real Himachal food –
dhal made with sour milk, and cornflour *rotis*.

$$ Nightingale
200 m above bus stand.
Serves trout and Italian dishes.

$ German Bakery
Next to Ragini.
Sweet little café offering up the usual German
bakery fare, and yak cheese sandwiches. Also
beautiful photography on walls.

What to do

Naggar

Trekking
For trekking to **Malana**, it is best to employ a
local guide. Pawan, from the old *chai* shop in
the main village, is recommended.

Transport

Naggar
Bus The bus stop is in the bazar, below the
castle. Several buses operate daily between
Kullu and **Manali** via the scenic east bank route
(1½ hrs). From Manali, more frequent buses to
Patli Kuhl (6 km from Naggar, 45 mins), where
you can get a local bus (half hourly in summer)
or rickshaw.

Manali and around   *Colour map 1, B3.*

mountain vistas and honeymooners

Set amidst picturesque apple orchards, Manali (population 30,000, altitude 1926 m)
is a major tourist destination for Indian holidaymakers and adventure-seeking
foreigners, attracted by the culturally different hill people and the scenic treks this
part of the Himalaya offers. In summer months Manali is the start of an exciting two-
day road route to Leh.

The town occupies the valley of the Beas, now much depleted by hydroelectric projects, with the
once-unspoilt Old Village to the north and Vashisht up on the opposite hillside across the river. The
town is packed with Pahari-speaking Kullus, Lahaulis, Nepali labourers and enterprising Tibetan
refugees who have opened guesthouses, restaurants and craft shops. It's become increasingly
built-up with dozens of new hotel blocks.

Sights
The **Tibetan Monastery**, built by refugees, is not old but is attractive and is the centre of a small
carpet-making industry. Rugs and other handicrafts are for sale. The colourful **bazar** sells Kullu
shawls, caps and Tibetan souvenirs.

   Old Manali is 3 km away, across Manalsu Nala. Once a charming village of attractive old
farmsteads with wooden balconies and thick stone-tiled roofs, Old Manali is rapidly acquiring the
trappings of a tourist economy: building work continues unchecked in the lower reaches of the

village, as ever more guesthouses come up to thwart those seeking an escape from the crowds of modern Manali, while the arrival of the drugs and rave scene in summer extinguishes most of Old Manali's remaining charm. The main road continues through some unspoilt villages to the modern **Manu Mandir**, dedicated to Manu, the Law Giver from whom Manali took its name and who, legend tells, arrived here by boat when fleeing from a great flood centuries ago. Aged rickshaws may not make it up the hill, so visitors might have to get off and walk.

Around Manali

Vashisht is a small hillside village that can be reached by road or a footpath, a 30- to 40-minute walk from the tourist office. Note the carvings on the houses of the wealthy farmers. Vashist Temple is very atmospheric and there are hot spring baths for men and women. The village, with its messy jumble of old village houses and newer buildings, has cheap places to stay which attract young travellers. A two-hour walk past the village up the hillside leads to a **waterfall**.

Essential Manali

Finding your feet

Kullu–Manali (Bhuntar) airport is 50 km away with bus and taxi transfers. The bus and taxi stands are right in the centre (though many private buses stop short of the centre) within easy reach of some budget hotels; the upmarket ones are a taxi ride away. See Transport, page 452.

Getting around

Manali, though hilly, is ideal for walking. For journeys outside the town taxi rates are high, so it is worth hiring a motorcycle to explore.

Best places to eat river trout

Smoked, baked or curried trout at Johnson Café
Trout cooked with almonds at La Plage
Korean trout sashimi at Café Yun
See page 450

Hadimba Devi Temple

The Dhungri temple (1553), in a clearing among ancient deodars, is an enjoyable 2-km walk from the tourist office. Built by Maharaja Bahadur Singh, the 27-m-high pagoda temple has a three-tier roof and some fine naturalistic wood carving of animals and plants, especially around the doorway. The structure itself is relatively crude, and the pagoda is far from perfectly perpendicular. Massive deodar planks form the roof but in contrast to the scale of the structure the brass image of the goddess Hadimba inside, is tiny. A legend tells how the God Bhima fell in love with Hadimba, the sister of the demon Tandi. Bhima killed Tandi in battle and married Hadimba, whose spirituality, coupled with her marriage to a god, led to her being worshipped as a goddess. Today, she is seen as an incarnation of Kali.

The small doorway, less than 1 m high, is surrounded by wood-carved panels of animals, mythical beasts, scrolls, a row of foot soldiers and deities, while inside against a natural rock is the small black image of the Devi. To the left is a natural rock shelter where legend has it that Hadimba took refuge and prayed before she was deified. The greatly enlarged footprints imprinted on a black rock are believed to be hers. Hadimba Devi plays a central part in the annual festival in May, at both Kullu and Manali. To prevent the master craftsman producing another temple to equal this elsewhere, the king ordered his right hand to be cut off. The artist is believed to have mastered the technique with his left hand and reproduced a similar work of excellence at Trilokinath (see page 456) in the Pattan Valley. Unfortunately, his new master became equally jealous and had his head cut off. It's a stunning temple, incredibly atmospheric.

A **feast and sacrifice** is held in mid-July when the image from the new temple in Old Manali is carried to the Hadimba Temple where 18 ritual blood sacrifices are performed. Sacrifices include a fish and a vegetable, and culminate with the beheading of an ox in front of a frenzied crowd. This ceremony is not for the faint-hearted. Pickpockets are known to take advantage of awestruck tourists, so take care.

Walks

Manali is the trail-head for a number of interesting and popular treks (see below). Beyond Old Manali, the **shepherd trail**, which winds its way up and down the hillside, allows you to capture a picture of Himalayan life as well as see some superb birdlife. The path starts at some concrete steps (after The Lazy Dog lounge/bar) on the first hairpin bend along the paved road to Old Manali (or you can pick it up where the road ends and taxis turn around at the top of the hill) and continues along the cemented path, which turns into a dirt trail. Return the same way, four to five hours.

Walk 1 This walk takes you towards Solang. In Old Manali Village take the right fork and then turn left in front of the new temple. This trail is a classic, following the right bank of the Beas River up

Manali

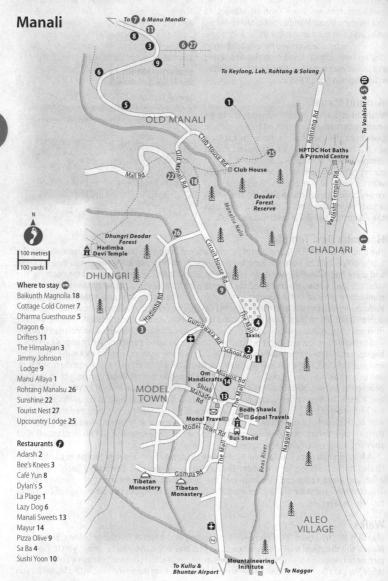

Where to stay 🏠
Baikunth Magnolia **18**
Cottage Cold Corner **7**
Dharma Guesthouse **5**
Dragon **6**
Drifters **11**
The Himalayan **3**
Jimmy Johnson
  Lodge **9**
Manu Allaya **1**
Rohtang Manalsu **26**
Sunshine **22**
Tourist Nest **27**
Upcountry Lodge **25**

Restaurants 🍴
Adarsh **2**
Bee's Knees **3**
Café Yun **8**
Dylan's **5**
La Plage **1**
Lazy Dog **6**
Manali Sweets **13**
Mayur **14**
Pizza Olive **9**
Sa Ba **4**
Sushi Yoon **10**

towards the Solang Valley passing the villages of **Goshal**, **Shanag**, **Buruwa** to **Solang** (2480 m), a small ski resort with 2.5 km of runs. Solang is 14 km (five hours). You can get tea, biscuits, nuts and plates of steaming spicy noodles along the walk, and there are also places to stay (see Where to stay, below). To return to Manali it is a steady walk down the valley side to the main Rohtang Pass-Manali Highway where you can pick up a bus (Rs 5) or shared jeep (Rs 10).

Walk 2 This is an enjoyable three- to four-hour walk. Go prepared for cold for this walk as it takes you through woodland shading you from the sun. Keeping the **Hadimba Temple** on your right follow the contour of the hill and bear right to pick up a clear pack-horse trail which heads up the steep valley. This is a steady uphill climb through woodland giving superb views of the river below, abundant Himalayan birdlife and a chance to see all manner of activity in the woods, chopping, cutting and burning.

Walk 3 This walk takes you to the village of **Sethan** (12 km). Take a local bus to the Holiday Inn on the Naggar road. With the hotel behind you, cross the road and pass through the orchard and fields which have low mud walls all round which can be walked on. Bear east till you come to a disused track and then bear right and follow it to the once-untouched village of **Prini** which now has several five-star hotels. If you are lucky the *chai* shop will be open. Further east, the trail to Sethan village becomes somewhat indistinct, though local people are at hand to point you in the right direction. It is a superb three-hour hike up a wooded valley to Sethan (3000 m), which is well off the tourist trail.

Listings Manali and around *map p448*

Tourist information

HPTDC
Next to Kunzam Hotel, The Mall, T01902-253 351.
Helpful staff.

Where to stay

Hotels are often full in May and Jun so it's better to visit off-season when most places offer discounts. Winter heating is a definite bonus.

In **Old Manali**, generally the further you walk, the greater the reward. Those above the Club House are almost out of Old Manali and are in a great location overlooking the valley but still close enough to town.

  Vashisht village is another popular choice.

$$$$ The Himalayan
Hadimba Rd, T01902-250999,
www.thehimalayan.com.
One Manali resident described this place as a bit like Hogwarts, it's a new build echoing a Gothic castle with turrets to boot. You can expect rooms with 4-posters and fireplaces and there is a magnificent view from the Crow's Nest.

$$$$ Manu Allaya
Sunny Side, Chadiari, overlooking Old Manali,
T01902-252235, www.manuallaya.com.
53 smart, imaginative rooms, most done in a contemporary design using wood and marble,

stunning views and good facilities, a definite cut above the rest, ie an architect has been involved. Recommended.

$$$ Baikunth Magnolia
Circuit House Rd, The Mall, T(0)9816-792888,
www.baikunth.com.
Definitely the most stylish place to stay in Manali with beautiful decor, heavy wooden doors and floors, and chic 4-posters. Come in Apr to catch the magnolia tree in bloom. A great place for a romantic getaway. Highly recommended.

$$$ Jimmy Johnson Lodge
The Mall, T01902-253023, www.johnsonhotel.in.
12 very elegant rooms (cottages also available), great bathrooms, pretty gardens, great views and an outstanding restaurant. Recommended.

$$$ Strawberry Garden Cottages
Below Sersai village on the Manali–
Nagar road, T(0)9218-924435, www.
strawberrygardenmanali.com.
Set in a stunning location, these 4 self-contained, cute 2-floor cottages are in a beautiful garden with great views. Friendly, helpful English owner. Recommended.

$$ Himalayan Country House
Near Manu Temple, T01902-252294.
Popular place offering 15 smart double rooms, with plenty of marble and pine, and great views over Old Manali. Specializes in trekking and motorbike safaris. Getting a bit pricey though.

$$-$ Dharma Guest House
Above Vashist, T01902-252354,
www.hoteldharmamanali.com.
Perched high on the hill above Vashist, this
place has great views. Rooms are clean and
comfortable. Buns of steel guaranteed climbing
up there.

$$-$ Dragon
Old Manali, T01902-252290,
www.dragontreks.com.
This hardy perennial of the Old Manali scene has
had a chic facelift and offers a smarter alternative
in this part of town. Attractive decor, lovely
outdoor sitting areas and a great vibe. There's
also a good family suite. Recommended.

$$-$ Drifters' Inn
Old Manali, T(0)9805-033127,
www.driftersinn.in.
In the heart of Old Manali, comfortable rooms
with TV, free Wi-Fi and a popular café downstairs.

$$-$ Rohtang Manalsu (HPTDC)
Near Circuit House, The Mall, T01902-252332,
www.hptdc.nic.in.
27 large rooms, good restaurant, a garden and
superb views.

$ Cottage Cold Corner
Old Manali, T(0)98050 43677.
Strange name and certainly not the vibe, with a
very warm and friendly welcome indeed. There
are basic rooms, and a little outdoor seating area.

$ Didi Guest House
Vashisht, T(0)78319 20896.
Through the village and above the school, on
the way to the waterfall. 10 wood-panelled
bedrooms. Cheap, chilled and cheerful, with yoga
and excellent views up and down the valley.

$ Sunshine
The Mall, next to Leela Huts, T01902-252320.
There's lots of character at this friendly, peaceful
place, with 9 rooms in an old traditional
house, and others in a newer cottage. Log
fires, restaurant, lovely garden, and a family
atmosphere. It's such good value you might need
them to repeat the price! Highly recommended.

$ Tourist Nest Guest House
Near Dragon, Old Manali, T(09816-266571.
Bright clean rooms with balconies; the top
floors still have views, whereas building in front
obscures views from lower floors. There are now
family rooms on the top floor. Recommended.

$ Upcountry Lodge
Above Club House, Old Manali, T01902-252257.
In a quiet location in orchards, with 9 clean rooms
and attached hot bath, set in a pleasant garden.

Restaurants

There are some great fine dining options. In
Old Manali there are plenty of Israeli dishes and
music which can range from techno to Tibetan.

$$$ Johnson Café
Circuit House Rd, T01902-253023.
Elegant restaurant in a large garden, specializing
in trout – you can have it oven-baked, curried,
in masala or smoked. There are also Western
dishes, including excellent home-made pasta,
good filter coffee and delicious ice creams. The
beautiful lighting makes it quite magical at night.
Highly recommended.

$$$ La Plage
T(0)98053 40977, Old Manali.
Sister of the renowned La Plage from Goa,
this is a beautiful restaurant with divine food.
You can expect delicious trout cooked with
almonds, chicken in soy and sesame with wasabi
mash and amazing deserts. It's a stunning
location with amazing views, attractive interiors
and garden/terrace dining and great service.
Highly recommended.

$$$ The Lazy Dog
Old Manali, on left past shops going uphill
(before road swings to right).
Funky interior as well as excellent food, good
music, filter coffee, free Wi-Fi and a lovely terrace
overlooking the river.

$$ Adarsh
The Mall (opposite Kunzam).
One of many Punjabi places, but this one has
more style and a better menu than others.

$$ Café Yun
Opposite Drifters Inn, Old Manali.
Korean café with lovely vibe serving up trout
sushi and *sashimi*, as well as other Korean delights
and plenty of veggie options. There is an amazing
whole-cooked trout on the menu too.

$$ Mayur
Mission Rd.
There's subdued decor and a great ambience at
this pleasant restaurant, with linen tablecloths
and candles on tables, Indian classical music,
a cosy wood-burning stove, and a generator.

Excellent food from a vast international menu, served by smart and efficient staff.

$$ Sa Ba
Nehru Park.
Excellent Indian dishes, snacks, pizzas and cakes, with some outdoor seating for people-watching. Recommended.

$$ Sushi Yoon
Vashist.
Chic little hole-in-the-wall café with just 12 seats serving up tasty sushi, delicious teas and coffees and the ultimate green tea ice cream. Highly recommended.

$$ Vibhuti's
The Mall, corner of Model Town Rd, up a short flight of steps.
South Indian vegetarian. Delicious *masala dosas*.

$ Bee's Knees
Old Manali.
Under the watchful eye of Avi, the man with the greatest smile, you can get big plentiful plates of Mexican food and all the usual Indian fare. Recommended.

$ Dylan's Toasted and Roasted
Old Manali, www.dylanscoffee.com.
The best coffee this side of Delhi, if not one of the best in India, served up by the affable Raj. The cookies are legendary as is his 'Hello to the Queen'; great atmosphere. Highly recommended.

$ Manali Sweets
Shiali Mahadev Rd.
Excellent Indian sweets (superb *gulab jamuns*); also good *thalis*.

$ Pizza Olive
Old Manali.
Very tasty wood-oven pizzas, a great range of pastas and even tiramisu. Recommended.

Festivals

Mid-Feb Week-long **Winter Sports Carnival**.
May 3-day colourful **Dhungri Forest festival** at Hadimba Devi Temple, celebrated by hill women.

Shopping

Crafts and local curios
Bhutico Bodh, *by the Hindu temple*. A good range of shawls.
Great Hadimba Weaver's, *near Manu Temple, Old Manali*. Excellent value, hand-woven, co-op produced shawls/scarves and there is a little

workroom to the side where you can watch them at work. Recommended.
Manushi, *in the market*. Women's co-op producing good quality shawls, hats, socks.
Shree-la Crafts, *near the main taxi stand*. Friendly owner, good value silver jewellery. Tibetan Bazar and Tibetan Carpet Centre.

Tailors
Gulati Traders, *Gulati Complex*. Sikh tailors, quick, good quality, copies and originals.

Trekking equipment
Ram Lal and Sons, *E9 Manu Market, behind bus stand*. Good range of well-made products, friendly, highly recommended.

What to do

From heli-skiing to rafting, mountain biking to paragliding and horse riding, there's a huge range of activities on offer in Manali.

Body and soul
Spa Magnolia, *at Johnson's Lodge Circuit House Rd, T(0)9816-100023*. Stylish spa with pricey treatments, but it's a bit of a treat. Ayurvedic and Western treatments available.
Yogena Matha Ashram, *Kanchani Koot, below Vashist, T(0)9418-240369, www.yogainmanali.com.* Swami Yogananda has a great following and offers down-to-earth spirituality with your downward dog. Recommended.

Skiing and mountaineering
Mountaineering and Allied Sports Institute, *1.5 km out of town, T01902-252342*. Organizes courses in mountaineering, skiing, watersports, high-altitude trekking and mountain rescue courses, as well as 5- and 7-day ski courses, Jan-Mar. There is a hostel, an exhibition of equipment and an auditorium.

Tour operators
Himalayan Adventurers, *opposite the tourist office, T01902-252750, www.himalayan adventurers.com*. Wide range of itineraries and activities from trekking and motorbiking to ski-touring and birdwatching.
HPTDC, *T01902-253531/252116*. Daily, in season by luxury coach (or car for 5): to Nehru Kund, Rahla Falls, Marhi, Rohtang Pass, 1000-1700, Rs 200 (car Rs 1200); to Solang, Jagatsukh and Naggar; 1000-1600, Rs 190 (car Rs 1200); to Manikaran, 0900-1800, Rs 250 (car Rs 1100).
Swagatam, *opposite Kunzam, The Mall, T01902-251073*. Long-distance buses, trekking, rafting; very efficient.

Trekking

Clarify details and the number of trekkers involved; shop around before making any decisions. For general trekking information, see page 39.

Above 14000ft, *log huts area, T(0)9816-632281, www.above14000ft.com.* Expert, environmentally conscious adventure organizers, specializing in treks, mountain biking, climbing expeditions and mountaineering courses throughout the region. Paperless office. Highly recommended.

Magic Mountain, *no office as such, but call Raju on T(0)9816-056934, www.magicmountain adventures.com.* Manali's most experienced cycling guide, Raju also offers trekking and jeep safaris, and is honest, friendly and reliable. Highly recommended.

Transport

Air Flights connect **Bhuntar Airport** near Kullu T01902-265037, with **Delhi**. Transport to town: taxi to Manali, Rs 1000 **Himachal Transport** (green) bus, every 15 mins (allow 2½ hrs travel time from Manali).

Bus Local bus stand, T01902-252323. Various state RTCs offer direct services to major towns. HRTC Bus Stand, the Mall, T01902-252116, reservations 1000-1200, 1400-1600. HPTDC coaches in season (fewer in winter); deluxe have 2 seats on either side: **Swagatam** (see Tour operators, above), run their own buses. **Chandigarh** 0700, 10 hrs, Rs 415; **Delhi** a/c 15 hrs, Rs 825; a/c sleeper Rs 1100; non a/c, Rs 425.

Dharamshala, Rs 210, **Keylong**, 6 hrs, Rs 145. **Kullu** via **Naggar**: 2 daily, Rs 30, 1 hr; most Kullu buses go via the national highway and stop at **Patli Kuhl** (see Naggar, page 446). **Mandi**, Rs 112. **Rohtang Pass**, day trip with photo stops, striking scenery (take sweater/jacket), 1½ hrs at pass, Rs 120. **Shimla** (280 km), 0830, 1900, 9 hrs, Rs 415.

For details of transport to **Leh**, via the Rohtang Pass, Keylong and Sarchu, see Essential box, page 454.

Motorbike The uncrowded Kullu–Manali road via Naggar is an ideal place for a test ride. **Anu Auto Works**, halfway up the hill to Vashisht. Excellent selection; insurance and helmets provided. Mechanical support and bike safaris organized throughout the region. **Bike Point**, Old Manali. Limited choice of bikes in good condition, mechanical support and competitive rates. **Enfield Club**, Vashisht Rd, T(0)9418-778899. Enfields and Hondas for hire; reasonable charges, friendly, honest service.

Local taxi The local union is very strong, office near tourist office, T01902-265 8225. Fares tend to be high; from bus stand: Rs 50 for hotels (2-3 km). To Vashisht or top of Old Manali Rd, Rs 90; auto-rickshaws Rs 50.

Long distance taxi Manali Taxi Services T(0)94181 83993. **Dharamshala**, Rs 3500; **Kaza**, Rs 6000; **Keylong**, Rs 4200; **Kullu**, Rs 700; **Mandi**, Rs 1500; **Naggar**, Rs 650; **Rohtang Pass**, Rs 1900.

Train Reservations at HPTDC office, T01902-251925.

Lahaul & the
Manali–Leh road

★ The stunningly beautiful road from Manali to Leh is one of the highest in the world and is currently the main route for foreigners into the regions of Lahaul and Ladakh.

Lying between the green alpine slopes of the Kullu and Chamba valleys to the south and the dry, arid plateau of Ladakh, the mountainous arid landscapes of Lahaul manage to get enough rain during the monsoon months to allow extensive cultivation, particularly on terraces, of potatoes, green peas and hops (for beer making). Lahaul potatoes are some of the best in the country and are used as seed for propagation. These and rare herbs have brought wealth to the area. Most people follow a curious blend of both Hindu and Buddhist customs though there are a few who belong wholly to one or the other religion.

Manali to Tandi *Colour map 1, B3–A3.*

feel on top of the world

The first 52 km of this route runs up the Kullu Valley from Manali, then climbs through the Rohtang Pass.

Leaving Manali
From Manali the NH21 goes through the village of Palchan and then begins a sharp climb to **Kothi**, at 2530 m, set below towering cliffs. Beautiful views of coniferous hillsides and meadows unwind as the road climbs through 2800 m, conifers giving way to poplars and then banks of flowers. The 70-m-high **Rohalla Falls**, 19 km from Manali at an altitude of 3500 m, are a spectacular sight.

The landscape, covered in snow for up to eight months of the year, becomes totally devoid of trees above Marrhi, a seasonal settlement and restaurant stop, as the road climbs through a series of tight hairpins to the Rohtang Pass.

Rohtang Pass *Colour map 1, B3.*
From the pass you get spectacular views of precipitous cliffs, deep ravines, large glaciers and moraines. Buses stop for photos. From June until mid-October, when **Himachal Tourism** (HPTDC) runs a daily bus tour from Manali, the pass becomes the temporary home to a dozen or more noisy roadside 'cafés'.

The descent to **Gramphoo** (Gramphu), which is no more than a couple of houses at the junction of the road from Tabo and Kaza, offers superb views of the glaciated valley of the Chandra River, source of the Chenab. To the north and east rise the peaks of Lahaul, averaging around 6000 m and with the highest, Mulkila, reaching 6520 m. As the road descends towards Khoksar there is an excellent view of the Lumphu Nala coming down from the Tempo La glacier. An earlier glacial maximum is indicated by the huge terminal moraine visible halfway up the valley.

There is a police check post in **Khoksar**, at 3140 m, where you may be required to show your passport and sign a register. This can take some time if more than one bus arrives at the same time.

Essential Lahaul and the Manali–Leh road

Finding your feet

Lahaul can be approached by road from three directions: from Shimla via the Spiti Valley; from Manali over the Rohtang Pass (3985 m) into Upper Lahaul; from Zanskar (see page 501) over the Shingo La Pass, and from Ladakh over the Baralacha La Pass (4880 m). A much-delayed tunnel on the Manali–Leh road into Lahaul is currently scheduled to open in 2016. There is also a trekking route from Manali to Zanskar. No permits are necessary.

Best breathtaking moments

Spectacular view from Rohtang Pass, page 453

Stunning Buddhist Khardong Monastery, page 457

High-altitude desert camp at Jispa, page 458

Getting around

The journey from Manali to Leh takes about 24-28 hours by bus, so if you leave at 0600, you'll arrive in Leh the next afternoon. HPTDC and private coaches run ordinary and luxury buses from Manali during the season, but these are usually based on demand and are not always daily. Seats should be reserved ahead. Front seats are best, though the cab gets filled by locals wanting a 'lift'. Those joining the bus in Keylong must reserve from Manali to be certain of a seat. Tickets cost Rs 1600 for the whole journey (including tent and meals); the usual overnight stop is at Sarchu where other cheaper tents may be available (some choose to sleep on the bus). There are reports of some bus drivers getting drunk or taking 'medicines' to keep them awake. For tips on travelling the road by motorbike, see box, page 456. Note that streams cross the Manali–Leh road at several places and may make the road impassable during heavy rain. Rockfalls are also a common hazard. See Transport, page 458.

When to go

The 530-km highway is usually open from July to September, depending on snowfall; most buses stop in mid-September. The Rohtang Pass itself normally opens at the end of May. Streams fed by snow-melt swell significantly during the day, making travel in the late afternoon more difficult than in the early morning when the flow is at its lowest.

BACKGROUND

Lahaul

Historically there are similarities between this region and Ladakh since in the 10th century Lahaul, Spiti and Zanskar were part of the Ladakh Kingdom. The Hindu rajas in Kullu paid tribute to Ladakh. In the 17th century Ladakh was defeated by a combined Mongol-Tibetan force. Later Lahaul was separated into Upper Lahaul which fell under the control of Kullu, and Lower Lahaul which came under the Chamba rajas. The whole region came under the Sikhs as their empire expanded, whilst under the British Lahaul and Kullu were part of the administrative area centred on Kangra.

About 8 km west of Khoksar work is in progress on the Rohtang tunnel, which will link the Solang Valley with the Chandra Valley. If you cross the bridge here you find an attractive waterfall.

Gondhla to Tandi

It is worth stopping here to see the 'castle' belonging to the local *thakur* (ruler), built around 1700. The seven-storey house with staircases made of wooden logs has a veranda running around the top and numerous apartments on the various floors. The fourth floor was for private prayer, while the Thakur held court from the veranda. There is much to see in this neglected, ramshackle house, particularly old weapons, statues, costumes and furniture. The 'sword of wisdom', believed to be a gift from the His Holiness the Dalai Lama, is of special interest. On close inspection you will notice thin wires have been hammered together to form the blade, a technique from Toledo, Spain. The huge rock near the Government School, which some claim to be of ancient origin, has larger-than-life figures of *Bodhisattvas* carved on it.

As the road turns north approaching **Tandi**, the Chandra rushes through a gorge, giving a superb view of the massively contorted, folded and faulted rocks of the Himalaya. Tandi itself is at the confluence of the Chandra and Bhaga rivers, forming the Chandrabhaga or Chenab. **Keylong** is 8 km from here, see page 457. At Tandi you can take a left turn and visit the Pattan Valley before heading to Keylong to continue on the journey.

Pattan Valley *Colour map 1, A3/B3.*
Hindu temples and fluttering Buddhist prayer flags

The Pattan Valley has a highly distinctive agricultural system which despite its isolated situation is closely tied in to the Indian market. Pollarded willows are crowded together all around the villages, offering roofing material for the flat-roofed houses and fodder for the cattle during the six-month winter. Introduced by a British missionary in the 19th century to try and help stabilize the deeply eroded slopes, willows have become a vital part of the valley's village life, with the additional benefit of offering shade from the hot summer sun.

Equally important are the three commercial crops which dominate farming: hops, potatoes and peas, all exported, while wheat and barley are the most common subsistence grain crops.

Tandi to Trilokinath

Just out of **Tandi** after crossing the Bhaga River on the Keylong road, the Udeypur road doubles back along the right bank of the Chenab running close to but high above the river. The road passes through **Ruding**, **Shansha**, 15 km from Tandi, **Jahlma**, 6 km and **Thirot**, another 11 km on (rest house here). A bridge at **Jhooling** crosses the Chenab. Some 6 km further on, the road enters a striking gorge where a bridge crosses the river before taking the road up to **Trilokinath**, 6 km away.

ON THE ROAD

Motorcycling from Manali to Leh

Allow four days on the way up to help acclimatize, as the 500-km road will take you from 2000 m to 5420 m and down to 3500 m (Leh). The last petrol station is in Tandi, 7 km before Keylong. A full tank plus five to 10 litres of spare petrol will take you to Leh. Above 3500 m, you should open the air intake on your carb to compensate for the loss of power.

Apart from Keylong, there are no hotels, only a few tented camps, providing basic food and shelter from mid-June to mid-September. Some will be noisy and drafty. The lack of toilet facilities leads to pollution near the camps (don't forget your lighter for waste paper). A tent and mini-stove plus pot, soups, tea, biscuits, muesli, will add extra comfort, allowing you to camp in the wild expanses of the Moray Plains (4700 m).

Unless you plan to sleep in the camp there, you must reach Pang before 1300 on the way up, 1500 on the way down, as the police will not allow you to proceed beyond the checkpoint after these times. The army camp in Pang has helpful officers and some medical facilities.

Trilokinath

Trilokinath, at 2760 m, is approached by a very attractive road which climbs up the left bank of the Chenab. The glitteringly white-painted Trilokinath temple stands at the end of the village street on top of a cliff. The **Siva temple** has been restored by Tibetan Buddhists, whose influence is far stronger than the Hindu. Tibetan prayer flags decorate the entrance to the temple which is in the ancient wooden-pagoda style. In the courtyard is a tiny stone Nandi and a granite lingam, Saivite symbols which are dwarfed in significance by the Buddhist symbols of the sanctuary, typical prayer-wheels constantly being turned by pilgrims, and a 12th-century six-armed white marble Avalokiteshwara image (Bodhisatva) in the shrine, along with other Buddhist images. The original columns date from Lalitaditya's reign in the eighth century, but there has been considerable modernization as well as restoration, with the installation of bright electric lights including a strikingly garish and flickering *chakra* on the ceiling. Hindus and Buddhists celebrate the three-day **Pauri Festival** in August.

Udeypur

Some 10 km from the junction with the Trilokinath road is Udeypur (Udaipur). Visited in the summer it is difficult to imagine that the area is completely isolated by sometimes over 2 m of snow during the six winter months. It is supplied by weekly helicopter flights (weather permitting). The helipad is at the entrance to the village. Trekking routes cross the valley here and further west.

The unique **Mrikula** (Markula) **Devi temple** (AD 1028-1063) is above the bazar. The temple dedicated to Kali looks wholly unimposing from the outside with a battered-looking wood-tiled 'conical' roof and crude outside walls. However, inside are some beautiful, intricate deodar-wood carvings belonging to two periods. The façade of the shrine, the *mandapa* (hall) ceiling and the pillars supporting it are earlier than those beside the window, the architraves and two western pillars. Scenes from the *Mahabharata* and the *Ramayana* epics decorate the architraves, while the two *dvarapalas* (door guardians), which are relatively crude, are stained with the blood of sacrificed goats and rams. The wood carvings here closely resemble those of the Hadimba Temple at Manali and some believe it was the work of the same 16th-century craftsman (see page 447). The silver image of Kali (*Mahisha-shurmardini*) 1570, inside, is a strange mixture of Rajasthani and Tibetan styles (note the *lama*-like head covering), with an oddly proportioned body.

Where to stay

Udeypur

Camping is possible in an attractive site about 4 km beyond the town (with permission from the Forest Officer) but since there is no water supply, water has to be carried in from a spring about 300 m further up the road. You'll need to carry provisions too as there is little in the bazar.

$ Amandeep Guest House
T01909-222256.
7 semi-deluxe rooms with limited hot water. A decent *dhaba* opposite serves good Indian food.

$ Forest Rest House
Off the road in a pleasant raised position, T01900-222235.
2 rooms with bath, very basic; bring your own sleeping bag.

Keylong to Leh *Colour map 1, B3.*

high passes, tented camps and superlative views

The principal town of the district of Lahaul, Keylong (altitude 3350 m) is an increasingly widely used stopping point for people en route to Leh or for those trekking in the Lahaul/Spiti area. Beyond Keylong, the road passes through very high-altitude desert with extraordinary mountain vistas.

Keylong and around

Set amidst fields of barley and buckwheat surrounded by brown hills and snowy peaks, Keylong was once the home of Moravian missionaries. Only traders and trekkers can negotiate the pass out of season. Landslides on the Leh–Manali road can cause quite long delays and the town can be an unintended rest halt for a couple of days. There is a State Bank of India but no foreign exchange.

There is a pleasant circuit of the town by road which can be done comfortably in less than two hours. Tracks run down into the town centre. The **local deity** 'Kelang Wazir' is kept in Shri Nawang Dorje's home which you are welcome to visit. There is a **Tibetan Centre for Performing Arts**. A statue in the centre of Keylong commemorates the Indian nationalist **Rash Behari Bose**, born 15 May 1886 near Kolkata.

Khardong Monastery, 3 km away across the Chandra River up a steep tree-shaded path, is the most important in the area. It is believed to have been founded 900 years ago and was renovated in 1912. Nuns and monks enjoy equality; married *lamas* spend the summer months at home cultivating their fields and return to the monastery in winter. The monastery contains a huge barrel drum, a valuable library and collections of *thangkas*, Buddha statues, musical instruments, costumes and ancient weapons.

Sha-Shur Monastery, a kilometre away, was in legend reputedly founded as early as AD 17 by a Buddhist missionary from Zanskar, Lama Deva Tyatsho who was sent by the Bhutanese king. It has ancient connections with Bhutan and contains numerous wall paintings and a 4.5-m *thangka*. The annual festival is held in June/July.

Tayul Monastery, above Satingri village, has a 4-m-high statue of Padma Sambhava, wall paintings and a library containing valuable scriptures and *thangkas*. The *mani* wheel here is supposed to turn on its own marking specially auspicious occasions, the last time having been in 1986.

The road beyond Keylong

Jispa, 21 km on from Keylong at an altitude of 3200 m, has a hotel, a campsite, a few tea stalls and a mountaineering institute. About 2 km beyond Jispa is **Teh** which has accommodation. There is a 300-year-old palace, built in the Tibetan style, comprising 108 rooms over four storeys; apparently the largest traditional structure in Lahaul. It is 3.5 km off the main highway (turn off at Ghemur, between Keylong and Jispa) in a village called **Kolong**, and has recently been converted in to a heritage hotel. A museum has also been opened there, with some interesting exhibits depicting the traditional and ceremonial life of the local rulers, who still own the property.

All vehicles must stop for passport checks at **Darcha** checkpost where the Bhaga River is bridged. Tents appear on the grassy riverbank in the summer to provide a halt for trekkers to Zanskar. The road climbs to **Patseo** where you can get a view back of Darcha. A little further is **Zingzingbar**. Icy streams flow across the road while grey and red-brown scree reach down from the bare mountainside to the road edge.

The road then goes over the **Baralacha La** (54 km; 4880 m), 107 km from Keylong, at the crossroads of Lahaul, Zanskar, Spiti and Ladakh regions before dropping to **Sarchu** (on the state border). There are a dozen or so tented camps in Sarchu, some run by **Himachal Tourism** (HPTDC), mostly with two-bed tents (sometimes reported dirty), communal toilet tents, late-night Indian meal and breakfast; private bus passengers without reservations are accommodated whenever possible (Rs 150 per person); open mid-June to mid-September.

The road runs beyond **Brandy Nala** by the Tsarap River before negotiating 22 spectacular hairpin bends, known as the 'Gata Loops', to climb up to the **Nakli La** (4950 m) and **Lachalung La** (5065 m). It then descends past tall earth and rock pillars to **Pang**, a summer settlement in a narrow valley where you can stop for an expensive 'breakfast' (usually roti, vegetables and omelettes to order). The camp remains open beyond 15 September; an overnight stop is possible in communal tents.

The 40-km-wide Moray plains (4400 m) provide a change from the slower mountain road. The road then climbs to **Taglang La** (5370 m), the highest motorable pass along this route and the second highest in the world; the altitude is likely to affect many travellers at this point.

You descend slowly towards the Indus valley, passing small villages, before entering a narrow gorge with purple coloured cliffs. The road turns left to continue along the Indus basin passing **Upshi** with a sheep farm and a checkpost, and then **Thikse**, before reaching **Leh**.

Listings Keylong to Leh

Where to stay

Keylong

$$-$ Chandrabhaga (HPTDC)
T01900-222247. Mid-Jun to mid-Oct.
3 rooms with bath, 2-bed tents, dorm (Rs 150), meals to order, and a solar-heated pool. Rates include vegetarian meals. Advance reservation is needed.

$ Dekyid
Below the police station, T01900-222217.
Quiet, friendly 3-storey hotel, with a helpful reception, decent-sized rooms with bath, excellent views over fields and a good restaurant, but service is very slow.

$ Gyespa
On main road, T01900-222207.
11 basic but adequate rooms plus a good restaurant.

$ Snowland
Above Circuit House, T01900-222219.
Modest but adequate 15 rooms with bath, and a friendly reception. Recommended.

$ Tashi Deleg
On main road through town, T01900-222450.
This place does well from being the first one you come to from Tandi, but it's slightly overpriced

as a result. Rooms are comfortable though, and the restaurant is one of the best in town. It's also has a car park.

The road beyond Keylong

There are summer tented camps at Jipsa, Darcha, Sarchu and Pang. Other accommodation is more limited. **Himachal Tourism** has a concrete 'lodge' in Jipsa with 3 basic rooms and toilets, and cheap camping in the yard.

$$ Ibex Hotel
Jispa, T01900-233204, www.ibexhoteljispa.com.
In an impressive location is this glass and cement block housing 27 comfortable rooms and a dorm. Reserve ahead.

Transport

Keylong

Bus State and private luxury buses are the most comfortable but charge more than double the 'B'-class fare. To **Manali** (6-8 hrs); to **Leh** (18 hrs). To board deluxe buses to Leh in Keylong, reserve ahead and pay full fare from Manali (Rs 1300, plus Rs 300 for tent and meals in Sarchu).

Jeep To **Manali** by jeep, 4 hrs, weather permitting; **Sarchu** 6 hrs, **Leh** 14 hrs.

Northern
Himachal

Dominated by Dharamshala, this is a region replete with some of the most breathtaking mountain views imaginable. From Dalhousie eastwards there are tantalizing glimpses of snow-capped peaks, while McLeodganj has been attracting Western travellers for decades, coming in search of peace, tranquillity, the Dalai Lama and sometimes even themselves. The Kangra Valley sees far fewer visitors, but has an unhurried charm all of its own, epitomized by Pragpur, India's first heritage village.

Dharamshala *Colour map 1, B3.*

magical atmosphere with the Dalai Lama presiding

Dharamshala (population 30,774) has a spectacular setting along a spur of the Dhauladhar range, from 1250 m at the 'Lower Town' bazar to 1768 m at McLeodganj. It is this 'Upper' and more attractive part of town that draws the vast majority of visitors.

Although the centre of McLeodganj itself has now become somewhat overdeveloped, it is surrounded by forests, set against a backdrop of high peaks on three sides, with superb views over the Kangra Valley and Shiwaliks, and of the great granite mountains that almost overhang the town.

Essential Dharamshala

Finding your feet

Flights to Gaggal Airport (13 km). Lower Dharamshala is well connected by bus with towns near and far. You can travel from Shimla to the southeast or from Hoshiarpur to the southwest along the fastest route from Delhi. The nearest station on the scenic mountain railway is at Kangra, while Pathankot to the west is on the broad gauge and is a three-hour drive away.

Best Tibetan experiences
Watch the Tibetan Monks debate at
Namgyal Monastery, page 460
See handicraft traditions kept alive at
Norbulingka, page 461
Watch Tibetan dance and culture at TIPA,
page 467

Tip...
A visitor's attempt to use a few phrases in Tibetan is always warmly responded to: *tashi delek* (hello, good luck), *thukje-chey* (thank you), *thukje-sik* (please), *gong-thag* (sorry), and *shoo-den-jaa-go* (goodbye).

Getting around

From Dharamshala, it is almost 10 km by the bus route to McLeodganj but a shorter, steeper path (3 km) takes about 45 minutes on foot. Local jeeps use this bumpy, potholed shortcut. Compact McLeodganj itself, and its surroundings, are ideal for walking. A ropeway (cable car) is being built between Lower Dharamshala and McLeodganj.

Tsuglagkhang complex

This has been the home of the Dalai Lama and the religious focal point for exiled Tibetans in India since 1959. The *Tsuglagkhang* (main temple) opposite the Dalai Lama's residence resembles the sacred temple in Lhasa and is five minutes' walk from the main bazar. It contains large gilded bronzes of the Buddha, Avalokitesvara and Padmasambhava. The **Namgyal Monastery** ① *0500-2100*, within the complex has a Buddhist School of Dialectics, mostly attended by small groups of animated 'debating' monks, and is known as 'Little Lhasa'.

To the left of the Tsuglagkhang is the **Kalachakra Temple** with very good modern murals of *mandalas*, protectors of the Dharma, and Buddhist masters of different lineages of Tibetan Buddhism, with the central image of Shakyamuni. Sand *mandalas* (which can be viewed on completion), are constructed throughout the year, accompanied by ceremonies. The temple is very important as the practice of Kalachakra Tantra is instrumental in bringing about world peace and harmony.

Also within the complex is the **Tibetan Museum** ① *T0189-222 2510, Tue-Sun 0900-1700, Rs 10*, with an interesting collection of documents and photographs detailing Tibetan history, the Chinese occupation of Tibet and visions of the future for the country. It is an essential visit for those interested in the Tibetan cause.

☐ Dharamshala

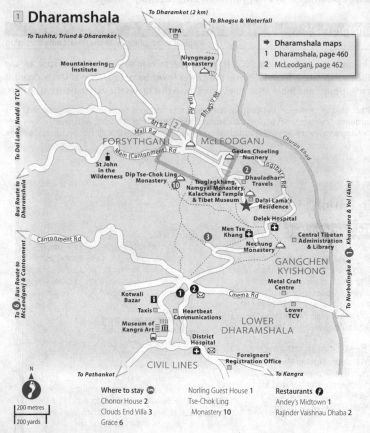

To Dharamkot (2 km)
To Bhagsu & Waterfall
TIPA
To Tushita, Triund & Dharamkot

→ Dharamshala maps
1 Dharamshala, page 460
2 McLeodganj, page 462

Nyingmapa Monastery
Mountaineering Institute
To Dal Lake, Naddi & TCV
Mall Rd
Mr Rd
Tipa Rd
Bhagsu Rd
FORSYTHGANJ   McLEODGANJ
Churan Khod
Main (Cantonment) Rd
Geden Choeling Nunnery
St John in the Wilderness
Dip Tse-Chok Ling Monastery
Jogibara Rd
Dhauladhar Travels
Tsuglagkhang, Namgyal Monastery, Kalachakra Temple & Tibet Museum
Dalai Lama's Residence
Delek Hospital
Men Tse Khang
Nechung Monastery
Central Tibetan Administration & Library
Cantonment Rd
GANGCHEN KYISHONG
Bus Route to Dharamshala
Bus Route to McLeodganj & Cantonment
Metal Craft Centre
Kotwali Bazar
Taxis
Heartbeat Communications
Cinema Rd
Lower TCV
Museum of Kangra Art
LOWER DHARAMSHALA
District Hospital
To McLeodganj & Cantonment
Foreigners' Registration Office
CIVIL LINES
To Pathankot
To Kangra
To Norbolingka & Khanyiara & Yol (4km)

N
200 metres
200 yards

Where to stay 🛏
Chonor House 2
Clouds End Villa 3
Grace 6

Norling Guest House 1
Tse-Chok Ling
  Monastery 10

Restaurants 🍴
Andey's Midtown 1
Rajinder Vaishnau Dhaba 2

Dharamshala

The hill station was established by the British between 1815 and 1847, but remained a minor town until His Holiness the **Dalai Lama** settled here after Chinese invasion of Tibet in October 1959. There is an obvious Tibetan influence in McLeodganj. The Tibetan community has tended to take over the hospitality business, sometimes a cause of friction with the local population. Now many Westerners come here because they are particularly interested in Buddhism, meditation or the Tibetan cause.

It is traditional to walk the ★ **Kora** in Mcleodganj, which is a ritual circuit of the temple complex and the Dalai Lama's residence. The Kora in Mcleodganj replicates the ancient Lingkhor path around the Potala Palace in Lhasa. The beautiful walk is done clockwise, with stunning views of the mountains and numerous prayer wheels and prayer flags along the way; it finishes by the Namgyal Temple entrance.

The **Dalai Lama** ① *www.dalailama.com*, usually leads the prayers on special occasions – 10 days for **Monlam Chenmo** following **Losar**, **Saga Dawa** (May) and his own birthday (6 July). If you wish to have an audience with him, you need to sign up in advance at the Security Office (go upstairs) by **Hotel Tibet**. On the day, arrive early with your passport. Cameras, bags and rucksacks are not permitted. His Holiness is a Head of State and the incarnation of Avalokitesvara, the Bodhisattva of Love and Great Compassion; show respect by dressing appropriately (no shorts, sleeveless tops, dirty or torn clothes); monks may 'monitor' visitors.

Other sights in Dharamshala

Church of St John-in-the-Wilderness ① *open for Sun morning service*. Dating from 1860, this church with attractive stained-glass windows, is a short distance below McLeodganj. Along with other buildings in the area, it was destroyed by the earthquake of 1905 but has been rebuilt. In April 1998 thieves tried to steal the old bell, cast in London, which was installed in 1915, but could only move it 300 m. The eighth Lord Elgin, one of the few viceroys to die in office, is buried here according to his wish as it reminded him of his native Scotland.

Tsechokling Monastery In a wooded valley 300 m below McLeodganj (down rather slippery steps), this little golden-roofed monastery can be seen from above. Built between 1984 and 1986, the monks here are known for their skill in crafting *tormas* (butter sculptures) and sand *mandalas*, which decorate the prayer hall (see Where to stay, below). Further down the 3-km steep but motorable road to Dharamshala is the Nechung Monastery in **Gangchen Kyishong** with the **Central Tibetan Administration** (CTA), which began work in 1988.

Norbulingka Institute ① *T01892-246405, www.norbulingka.org*. This institute is becoming a major centre for Buddhist teaching and the preservation of traditional crafts and techniques like sculpture and tangka painting. Named after the summer residence of the Seventh Dalai Lama built in 1754, it was set up to ensure the survival of Tibetan Buddhism's cultural heritage. Up to 100 students and 300 Tibetan employees are engaged in a variety of crafts in wood, metal, silk and metal, *thangka* painting (some excellent) and Tibetan language. The temple has a 4.5-m-high gilded statue of the Buddha and over 1000 painted images. There is a small **museum** of traditional 'dolls' made by monks and a **Tibetan Library** with a good range of books and magazines. You can attend lectures and classes on Tibetan culture and language and Buddhism or attend two **meditation** classes, free but a donation is appreciated.

Tip...

Lhamo Tso who runs **Lhamo's Croissant**, recommends tuning into the heart of Mcleodganj and the Tibetan people by walking the Kora (see above) and buying the *Essence of the Heart Sutra* at **The Namgyal Bookshop** by the temple. It is a commentary by His Holiness the Dalai Lama on one of the Buddha's main teachings. She says "It is a book that can transform your life".

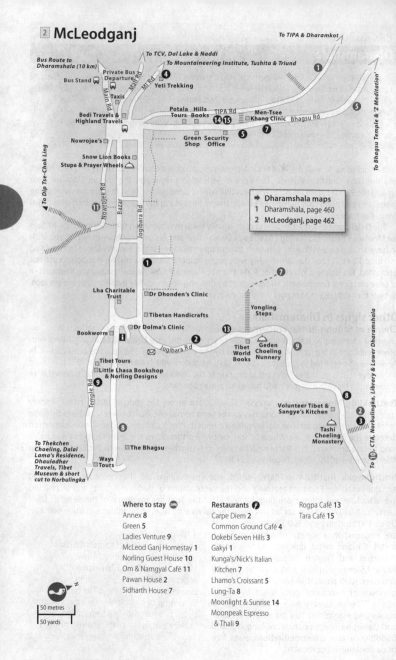

To TIPA & Dharamkot

To TCV, Dal Lake & Naddi
To Mountaineering Institute, Tushita & Triund

Bus Route to
Dharamshala (10 km)

Private Bus
Departure

Bus Stand

Taxis

Yeti Trekking

Bedi Travels &
Highland Travels

Potala
Tours

Hills
Books

TIPA Rd

Men-Tsee
Khang Clinic

Bhagsu Rd

To Bhagsu Temple & 'Z Meditation'

Nowrojee's

Snow Lion Books

Stupa & Prayer Wheels

Green
Shop

Security
Office

To Dip Tse-Chok Ling

Nowrojee Rd

Bazar

Jogibara Rd

→ Dharamshala maps
1 Dharamshala, page 460
2 McLeodganj, page 462

Lha Charitable
Trust

Dr Dhonden's Clinic

Tibetan Handicrafts

Dr Dolma's Clinic

Bookworm

Jogibara Rd

Yongling
Steps

Tibet
World
Books

Geden
Choeling
Nunnery

Tibet Tours

Little Lhasa Bookshop
& Norling Designs

Temple Rd

Volunteer Tibet &
Sangye's Kitchen

Tashi
Choeling
Monastery

To ⑩ - CTA, Norbulingka, Library & Lower Dharamshala

To Thekchen
Choeling, Dalai
Lama's Residence,
Dhauladhar
Travels, Tibet
Museum & short
cut to Norbulingka

Ways
Tours

The Bhagsu

50 metres

50 yards

Where to stay 🛏
Annex 8
Green 5
Ladies Venture 9
McLeod Ganj Homestay 1
Norling Guest House 10
Om & Namgyal Café 11
Pawan House 2
Sidharth House 7

Restaurants 🍴
Carpe Diem 2
Common Ground Café 4
Dokebi Seven Hills 3
Gakyi 1
Kunga's/Nick's Italian
  Kitchen 7
Lhamo's Croissant 5
Lung-Ta 8
Moonlight & Sunrise 14
Moonpeak Espresso
  & Thali 9

Rogpa Café 13
Tara Café 15

Open your heart: volunteering in Mcleodganj

There are many opportunities for volunteer work in and around Dharamshala, from English conversation to work at the hospital. Many offer a great insight into Tibetan culture and are key in empowering refugees.

Lha Charitable Trust (Temple Rd, T01892-220992, www.lhasocialwork.org, office open Monday-Saturday 0900-1700, lunch 1200-1300) needs volunteers for language classes, IT and web design, healthcare, fundraising, etc. Short-term or long-term placements are possible, or you can just drop in. They also offer Tibetan cooking classes, language, meditation, homestay, etc. Lha means 'innate goodness'.

Also look in at or check the free monthly magazine *Contact*, T(0)98161-55523, www.contact magazine.net (also a useful resource for restaurant information and events in McLeodganj, Buddhist-related and otherwise). English-language teachers are in high demand to teach newly arrived refugees, for short- or long-term stints. There are a couple of places for teaching and volunteering near Dokebi restaurant including Learning and Ideas for Tibet (www.learningandideasfortibet.org) who have conversation classes, movie parties and talks from ex-political prisoners. You can also volunteer with Rogpa (www.tibetrogpa.org) who provide free childcare for Tibetan people trying to juggle jobs and education – they run a lovely café on the Jogibara road too.

Museum of Kangra Art ① *Main Rd, Tue-Sun 1000-1330, 1400-1700, free, allow 30 mins.* Near the bus stand in Lower Dharamshala, this museum includes regional jewellery, paintings and carvings; a reminder of the rich local heritage contrasted with the celebrated Tibetan presence. Copies of Roerich paintings will be of interest to those not planning to visit Naggar.

Around McLeodganj

Bhagsu, an easy 2-km stroll east, or Rs 40 auto-rickshaw ride, has a temple to Bhagsunath (Siva). The mountain stream here feeds a small pool for pilgrims, while there is an attractive waterfall 1 km beyond. Unfortunately this has resulted in it becoming very touristy, with increasing building activity and an influx of noisy day-trippers. The hill leading up the valley towards Dharamkot is known as Upper Bhagsu, and is lined with little shops, restaurants and guesthouses. It is a relaxing place with great views, and so attracts many backpackers for long stays here. Outside the rainy season lovely walks abound.

Dharamkot, 3 km away (from McLeodganj by auto Rs 80, or on foot from Bhagsu), has very fine views and you can continue on towards the snowline. Villagers' homes and guesthouses are dotted up the hillside, accessible via pathways, and there is even a Chabbad House for the numerous Israeli tourists. In September, a fair is held at Dal Lake (1837 m), 3 km from McLeodganj Bus Stand; it is a pleasant walk but the 'lake', no more than a small pond, is disappointing.

Naddi Gaon, 1.5 km further uphill from the bridge by Dal Lake (buses from Dharamshala, 0800-1900), has really superb views of the Dhauladhar Range. **Kareri Lake** is further on. The TCV (Tibetan Childrens' Village) nearby educates and trains children in traditional handicrafts. Big hotels are rapidly appearing next to the traditional Naddi village. Most enjoy excellent views.

It is an 8-km trek to **Triund**, 2827 m, at the foot of the Dhauladhar where there is a **Forest Lodge** on a hill top. Some trekkers pitch tents, whilst others make use of caves or shepherds' huts. Take provisions and warm sleeping gear if planning to stay overnight. It's well worth the effort. A further 5 km, one-hour walk, brings you to **Ilaka**.

Tourist information

HPTDC
*Behind post office, McLeodganj, T01892-221205.
Mon-Sat 1000-1700.*
There are many opportunities for foreign
volunteers (see box, page 463).

Where to stay

Most visitors stay in McLeodganj (see below).

$$$$-$$$ White Haven Tea Estate
*Below Dharamshala, T(0)86790 26162,
www.hotelwhitehaven.in.*
Charming working colonial tea estate set in
2.8 ha of beautiful gardens. 8 sumptuous rooms
with creaking floorboards, log fires, lots of wood
panelling and period antiques, exceptional
service and tons of history. Recommended.

$$$ Clouds End Villa
*North of Dharamshala, steep approach
off Naoroji Rd, T01892-222109,
www.cloudsendvilla.com.*
7 rooms and 1 bungalow in Raja of Lambagraon's
bungalow (Raj period), not luxurious but
very clean, annexe has excellent valley views,
authentic local cuisine (everything home-made),
tours, peaceful, very friendly, excellent service.

$$$ Grace Hotel
*558 Old Chari Rd, Kotwali Bazar, T01892-223265,
www.welcomheritagegracehotel.com.*
14 comfortable suites in a 200-year-old wooden
manor, formerly the residence of India's first Chief
Justice. Pleasantly situated slightly out of town, a
good place to relax and admire the views. This is
a stunning place with beautiful artefacts. There
is a meditation room and do try the delicious
Himachali food, it's exquisite with subtle spicing
and yoghurt (sour milk). Highly recommended.

$$$-$$ Blossoms Village
*Sidhpur, near Dharamshala, T01892-246 880,
www.blossomsvillage.com.*
19 lovely rooms including cottages and suites.
Stylishly decorated using local timber. New
spa in 2013, with treatments and wellbeing
therapies. Lovely rooftop bar and restaurant.

$$$-$$ Norling Guest House
*Norbulingka Institute, Gangchen Kyishong,
T01892-246406, normail@norbulingka.org.*

Clean, comfortable rooms, in modern facilities in
a Tibetan-style house. Café accepts Master/Visa
cards. Beautiful setting inside the Norbulingka
Institute, so surrounded by art and meditative
peace. Highly recommended.

$ Tsechokling Monastery
*Camel Track Rd, 300 m below McLeodganj,
down 300 steps, T01892-221726.*
20 clean rooms, 3 attached, some singles, hot
showers, breakfast and dinner at set times.
'Wonderfully peaceful'.

McLeodganj

$$$-$$ Chonor House
*Thekchen Choeling Rd, T01892-221006,
www.norbulingka.org.*
11 very comfortable, stylish rooms furnished
in Tibetan style (murals of lost monasteries
and mythical beasts), good restaurant, clean,
well-managed, popular with foreign diplomats,
beautiful garden, a quiet and lovely place. Book
ahead. Accepts credit cards. Highly recommended.

$$ Annex Hotel
*Hotel Surya Rd, T01892-221002, 0941-8020814,
www.annexhotel.in.*
A short walk from the bus stand, all the rooms
in this clean hotel have a balcony and are
reached by the free Wi-Fi. Lounge and library,
plus rooftop restaurant is excellent and has
majestic sunset views.

$$ Pema Thang
*Opposite Hotel Bhagsu, T01892-221871,
www.pemathang.net.*
15 rooms with a bit more character than the
average, good views from private balconies
(better from upper floors), wooden floors, quiet,
friendly, hot water and Wi-Fi works in rooms, nice
rooftop restaurant with good pizza and pasta.
Yoga hall at the rear (see What to do, below).

$$-$ McLeod Ganj Homestay
*Flourishing Flora, close to TIPA Gate,
Dharamkot Rd, T(0)9736-083878,
www.mcleodganjhomestay.net.*
With 3 lovely rooms and 1 hillside hut, this is a
short walk up the TIPA road towards Dharmkot
and has a lovely family vibe. All the rooms have
a little touch of Tibet, there's great Indian home-
cooked food with as much organic as possible
and cookery lessons with Nisha. Sometimes there
is roast chicken on an open fire. Recommended.

$ Green Hotel
Bhagsu Rd, T01892-221200, www.greenhotel.in.
Popular with backpackers, 30 variable rooms
(avoid ground floor ones near the noisy courtyard),
restaurant with comfy sofas. Good internet.

$ Ladies Venture
Jogibara Rd, T01892-221559,
www.ipcardesign.com/ladies venture.
Peaceful hotel with dorm and 13 clean rooms,
cheapest with shared bath, standard rooms have
bath and TV, while top category are huge with
seating areas. Very popular (partly due to the
helpful staff) and a good place to meet people.
As they say, it's "just a name" and every body and
soul is welcome. Small restaurant (good Chinese
and Western food) and a terrace. Often full so
book ahead.

$ Om
Western edge of bazar, T01892-221322,
(0)9857-632037.
Friendly hotel with 18 clean rooms, the en suite
ones are excellent value, freshly painted and
have consistent hot water, while cheap room
share baths, great views at sunset from patio
terrace and rooftop. Free Wi-Fi. The excellent
Namgyal restaurant which used to be at the
Temple has moved here, so expect the best
pizza in northern India.

$ Pawan House
Next to Dokebi, Jogibara Rd, T01892-220069,
www.pawanhouse.com.
Good views across the valley. Attractive spacious
clean rooms with balconies; a good vibe.
Recommended.

$ Sidharth House
Bottom of Yongling School Steps off Jogibara
Rd, T(0)8679-591907.
Great guesthouse with conscious eco-vibe
who established the 'Clean McLeodganj
Project' and they have bins for compost as
well as encouraging recycling. Much needed.
Highly recommended.

Around McLeodganj

$$$ Eagles Nest
Upper Dharamkot, T(0)9218-402822,
www.hoteleaglesnest.com.
8 lovely themed rooms and suites in a beautiful
old colonial house set in 20 ha of forest. Perched
on top of the hill with spectacular views over
Kangra and Kullu valleys. All inclusive, with

excellent food and plenty of activities. Price
includes all meals, horse riding and guides for
trekking. Recommended.

$$-$ Udechee Huts
Naddi Gaon, T01892-221781,
www.udecheehuts.com.
Blending in with local style, 10 pleasantly
furnished circular huts with bath (hot water),
restaurant plus dining terrace, well kept,
friendly hosts.

$ 9 Chimes
Upper Bhagsu, T(0)9736-130284,
www.9chimes.com.
8 spacious rooms with balconies and good
views and 1 apartment. Recommended.

$ DK House
Upper Bhagsu, T(0)94187 97494.
14 comfortable, spacious and clean rooms with
big terrace and **Evergreen Restaurant** attached.
Run by a friendly family.

$ Om Tara
Lower Dharamkot, T(0)981-687949,
www.houseomtara.com.
Keeping their eye on the environment and with
friendly service, this is a popular little guesthouse
among fruit trees. There are big verandas to enjoy
the views. Recommended.

$ Pink House
Between Dharamkot and Bhagsu,
T(0)9805-642060.
Excellent value place with great views. It's really
peaceful and run by president of local women's
group; she is quite right-on.

$ Shiv Shakti Guest House
Off Dharamkot Rd, T(0)9418-247776.
Run by friendly father and son, there are 18 basic
rooms here with attached bath, plus a well-
equipped cottage.

$ Trimurti Garden Café
Above Unity Pizza, Bhagsu, T(0)9816-869144,
www.trimurtigarden.in.
A favourite haunt with simple rooms, café
and numerous workshops, yoga classes and
a music school.

$ ZKL Guesthouse
Above Bhagsu Rd, 500 m before Bhagsu itself,
T01892-221581, www.zkl-monastery.com.
12 very basic but clean rooms in this charming
monastery, with Buddhist teachings and a café
in the summer. Outstanding value.

Restaurants

Most memorable food is in McLeodganj, as well as excellent Tibetan, there is also amazing Korean and Japanese food to be had.

$$-$ Andey's Midtown
Kotwali Bazar.
Indian and Chinese, some continental; the best in town.

$ Rajinder Vaishnau Dhaba
Kotwali Bazar.
Very simple sit-down *dhaba* serving Punjabi basics and *thalis*, tasty and busy.

McLeodganj

Enterprising Tibetans in the upper town offer good traveller favourites for those tired of curries; some serve beer. Try *thukpa* (Tibetan soups), noodle dishes, steamed or fried *momos* and *shabakleb*. Save plastic waste (and money) by refilling your bottles with safe filtered, boiled water at the eco-friendly **Green shop** on Bhagsu Rd, Rs 5 per litre; they also recycle used batteries.

$$ Café Illiterati Books and Coffee
LHS Jogiwara Rd, near Usho Institute.
This trendy mellow café has slate floors and wonderful views, full bookshelves on Buddhism, society or literature and coffee-table tomes, and an exciting menu (eg chilli ginger red-bean burger), including good salads.

$$ Carpe Diem
Past the Post Office, Jogibara Rd.
A Nepali-run joint with excellent Indian, Thai and continental flavours. Good vibe, appealing rooftop, beer under the table and open mic nights. Recommended.

$$ Dokebi Seven Hills
Near Lung Ta, Jogibara Rd.
Wonderful cosy restaurant with a delicious range of food including spicy hotpot-style soups, spicy kimchi and kimbap (Korean sushi); mainly vegetarian with some spicy chicken too. Upstairs there is lovely airy room with floor seating. Great fresh juices and smoky green tea. Highly recommended.

$$ Kunga's/Nick's Italian Kitchen
Bhagsu Rd.
Good vegetarian food, Italian including excellent pumpkin ravioli, plus quiches, pies, cakes and very good Tibetan food too. With a huge terrace and great valley views, deservedly popular. Recommended.

$$ Namgyal
At Om Hotel, western end of bazar.
Open 1000-2200.
Cosy and welcoming venue with amazing pizzas like roquefort and walnut or smoked cheese and spinach; possibly best pizza in India! Good salads and Tibetan dishes too. Highly recommended.

$ Common Ground Café
Tushita Rd, above bus stand, behind Asian Plaza, www.commongroundsproject.org.
Serving up a Chinese-Tibetan food fusion, their menu underpins their ethos to foster shared understanding and respect between Chinese and Tibetans. It's a lovely place with great teas and desserts too.

$ Gakyi
Jogibara Rd.
Great range of Tibetan dishes, also excellent porridge and fruit muesli. Lovely lady owner.

$ Hotel Tibet
Bhagsu Rd behind the old bus stand.
Good Tibetan/Japanese restaurant and takeaway bakery. Very popular.

$ Lhamo's Croissant
Bhagsu Rd.
Beautiful café with furniture from **Norbulingka** offering tip-top cappuccino, healthy salads, monumental club sandwiches, home-made soups and outrageously good cakes and tarts, all served up by the eponymous Lhamo. They show films about the Tibetan cause every evening. Free Wi-Fi. Highly recommended.

$ Lung-Ta
Jogibara Rd. Mon-Sat 1200-2030.
Classy Japanese vegetarian restaurant, not for profit, daily set menu or à la carte, good breads and cakes, sushi on Tue and Fri. Try the *okononiyak* (Japanese veg omelette). Great value and very popular. There's a little shop on-site too. Highly recommended.

$ Snow Lion
Near the prayer wheels, T01892-221289.
Renowned for their Tibetan specialities, they also have Western meals and excellent cakes.

Cafés and snacks

Moonlight and Sunrise
Opposite Tibetan Welfare Office, Bhagsu Rd.
Small *chai* shops adjacent to each other with basic food. It's an excellent spot for meeting other travellers, especially in the evenings when overspill occupies benches opposite.

Moonpeak
Temple Rd, www.moonpeak.org.
Very atmospheric café where people spill out
onto outside tables to enjoy great cappuccinos,
sandwiches and fantastic cakes. The first of the
many coffee shops. Holds photography and art
exhibitions. Free Wi-Fi.

Moonpeak Thali
Next door to Moonpeak.
Has some Himachali dishes.

Rogpa
Jogibara Rd.
Tiny little café serving up lovely cakes and tasty
coffee, all for charity. There's a little shop and
second-hand stuff too. Recommended.

Tara Café
Bhagsu Rd.
Super-friendly place serving up huge pancakes.

Tenyang
Temple Rd.
Delicious coffee and cakes in a small cafe.
Recommended.

Around McLeodganj

$$ Unity
Upper Bhagsu, on path to Dharamkot.
English owner creates amazing food, well
presented and now a larger restaurant so more
opportunity for wood oven pizzas.

$ Family Pizzeria
Between Upper Bhagsu and Dharamkot.
Excellent pizzas, French pastries, quiches
and desserts, friendly staff and cider.

$ Sansu's
Upper Bhagsu.
Renowned for its epic 'fruit-muesli-curd',
the best on the hillside.

$ Singh Corner
Bhagsu.
Ah Bhagsu cake straight from the fridge; the
original and best chocolate, caramel, biscuit
combo. Beware of imitators!

$ Wa Blu
Upper Bhagsu.
Climb the steps for tempting Japanese food,
miso soups and juices.

Entertainment

See *Contact*, a free monthly publication. With
everyone travelling with laptops now, there
is only 1 film club on the strip remaining on
Jogibara Rd with a programme of Western films
at a rather pricey Rs 150. **Lhamos Croissant**
shows documentaries on Tibet. There are open
mics at **Carpe Diem**. Indian classical music and
Tibetan traditional music often at Yongling
School and TIPA.

One Nest, *Lower Dharamkot*. Regular live music
in the evenings (Indian Classical and Western
nomads), contact dance and free dance sessions.
Tibetan Institute of Performing Arts (TIPA),
McLeodganj, www.tibetanarts.org. Stages
occasional music and dance performances;
details at the tourist office (see under Tourist
information, above).

Shopping

It is pleasantly relaxed to shop here, although
competition and prices have increased in
recent years. Many items on sale have been
imported from the Tibetan market in New
Delhi. McLeodganj Bazar is good for Tibetan
handicrafts (carpets, metalware, jewellery,
jackets, handknitted cardigans, gloves) and lots
of Kashmiri items too; there's a special market
on Sun.

Bookworm, *near Surya Resort*. Has a good
selection of paperbacks, some second-hand.
Recommended.
Dolls 4 Tibet is an initiative bringing together
Tibetan refugees and local Indian women,
making beautiful dolls together. 'We see our
Doll Makers grow in confidence and their sense
of self worth. Their eyes and smiles say it all
when a doll they've finished is admired. The skills
they learn are empowering, the money they
take home spells a new-found independence
and their social interactions across our diverse
community benefits not only our team but the
wider society.' You can buy them at **The Green
Shop** and **Common Ground Café**.
Doritsang Tibetan Culture Centre, *Temple Rd,
near SBBI.* Great range of books, CDs, clothes and
Tibetan bits and pieces.
Green Shop, *Bhagsu Rd.* Sells recycled and
handmade goods including cards and paper.
Also sells filtered drinking water for half the
price of bottled water.
Jewel of Tibet, *opposite prayer wheels.* Best
selection of singing bowls, jewellery and Tibetan

arts. Maybe not the cheapest, but certainly the best value.

Norbulingka Shop, *Temple Rd, close to Moonpeak*. Well-crafted bags, cushion covers and clothes from **Norbulingka** – preserving Tibetan cultural arts.

Rogpa, *Jogibara Rd*. Charity based shop selling great gifts, notebooks, cards, bags and wallets. And second hand clothes.

Tibet Book World, *Jogibara Rd, near Yongling School steps*. Best bookshop in town – great range of Buddhist and yogic titles as well as bestsellers.

Tibetan Children's Villages (**TCVs**), *main office on Temple Rd and workshops at various locations around town*. Fabrics and jewellery at fixed prices.

Tibetan Handicrafts Centre, *Jogibara Rd, near the tourist office*. Ask at the office for permission to watch artisans working on carpets, *thangkas*, etc. Reasonable prices.

What to do

Body and soul

McLeodganj and Dharmkot are a haven for all sorts of healing pursuits; check out One Nest and Body Temple in Dharmkot for yoga, massage trainings and courses. There are also several meditation intensive courses in the area.

Buddha Hall, *Main Rd, Bhagsu*, T01892-221749. Yoga, meditation and healing courses.

Himachal Vipassana Centre, *Dhamma Sikhara, next to Tushita*, T(0)9218-414051, www.sikhara. dhamma.org. *Donations only, reserve in advance, information and registration Mon-Sat 1600-1700*. 10-day retreat, meditation in silence.

Himalayan Iyengar Yoga Centre, *Dharamkot*, www.hiyogacentre.com. *Starting every Thu at 0830. Information and registration Mon 1330*. Offers 5-day course in Hatha yoga. Now has retreat centre too.

Tushita Meditation Centre, *Dharamkot village 2 km north of McLeodganj*, www.tushita.info. *Enquiries Mon-Sat 0930-1130, 1230-1600*. Quiet location, offers individual and group meditation; 10-day 'Introduction to Buddhism' including lectures and meditation (residential courses get fully subscribed, also drop-in guided meditation Mon-Sat 0915-1015 throughout the year, movies relevant to Buddhist interests Mon and Fri 1400, simple accommodation on site.

Z Meditation, *Kandi village*, T(0)9418-036956, www.zmeditation.com. Interesting course including yoga and meditation. Retreats offered in silence with separate discussion sessions,

5 days (Mon 1600-Sat 1100), includes a 'humble' breakfast; highly recommended for beginners, run by friendly couple in a peaceful location with beautiful views.

Tibetan cookery

Lhamo's Kitchen, *next to Green Shop, Bhagsu Rd* T(0)9816-468719. Runs 3 courses (soups, bread, *momos*), 1100-1300, 1700-1900, Rs 200 each. Friendly, fun, eat what you cook.

Tour operators

Dhauladhar Travels, *Temple Rd, McLeodganj*, T01892-221158, dhauladhar@hotmail.com. Agents for **Indian Airlines**.

HPTDC, *tickets from HPTDC Marketing Office, near SBI, Kotwali Bazar in Dharamshala*, T018920-224928. Luxury coach in season: Dharamshala to McLeodganj, Kangra Temple and Fort, Jawalamukhi, 1000-1900, Rs 200; Dharamshala to McLeodganj, Bhagsunath, Dal Lake, Talnu, Tapovan, Chamunda, 1000-1700, Rs 200.

Skyways Travels, *just off main square, Temple Rd*, T(0)9857-400001. Reliable travel agent who is a mine of knowledge and even has Paypal. Can make travelling in India a whole lot easier. Also for tours to Jammu and Kashmir, Rajasthan; trekking, camping and paragliding locally.

Summit Adventures, *main square, Bhagsu Nag, McLeodganj*, T01892-221679, www.summit-adventures.net. Specialist in trekking and climbing, also cultural trips and a yoga trekking tour.

Ways Tours & Travels, *Temple Rd*, T01892-221775, waystour@vsnl.net. Most reliable, Mr Gupta is very experienced, and provides professional service.

Trekking

The best seasons are Apr-Jun and Sep-Oct. Rates are upwards of Rs 1400 per person per day. See also Summit Adventures above. For general trekking information, see page 39.

Highpoint Adventures, *Kareri Lodge*, T01892-220931, www.trek.123himachal.com. Organize treks for smaller groups and a range of tours.

Mountaineering Institute, *Mirza Ismail Rd*, T01892-221787. *Mon-Sat 1000-1700*. Invaluable advice on routes, equipment, accommodation, campsites, etc. Equipment and porters can be hired for groups of 8 or more, with reasonable charges. The deputy director (SR Saini) has described many routes in *Treks and Passes of Dhauladhar and Pir Pinjal* (Rs 150) although the scale of maps can be misleading. Consult the author for detailed guidance.

Transport

It is dangerous to drive at night in the hills.

Air Nearest airport is at Gaggal, T01892-232374, 13 km away (taxi Rs 650). To/from **Delhi** with **Air India** and **Spicejet**, www.spicejet.com.

Local bus Buses and share jeeps between Dharamshala and McLeodganj, 10 km, 30 mins, Rs 10/Rs 25.

Long-distance bus Most originate in Dharamshala, T01892-224903, but some super and semi-deluxe buses leave from below the taxi stand in McLeodganj. HRTC enquiries, T01892-221750. HPTDC run luxury coaches in season). **Delhi** (Kashmir Gate, 521 km), semi-deluxe coach departs McLeodganj 1700, 14 hrs; deluxe coach 1830, 1945; super deluxe coach, 1900 (Volvo). Prices vary – deluxe coach is around Rs 880 and some of the private companies charge Rs 1200. Avoid **Bedi Travels** with bad suspension. From Delhi at same times. 1930 arrives Lower Dharamshala 1000, recommended for best morning views of the foothills (stops en route). **Dalhousie** and **Chamba**, 8 hrs; **Manali**, 1700, Rs 400, 8 hrs; luxury coaches, Rs 650, **Pathankot**, from Mcleod, Rs150. HRTC buses to **Baijnath**, 2½ hrs; **Chandigarh** (248 km), 9 hrs,
via Una (overnight stop possible); also deluxe buses to **Dehra Dun**, Rs 410 and **Shimla** (from Dharamshala). **Kangra**, 50 mins, Rs 14; **Kullu** (214 km) 10 hrs; **Manali** (253 km) 11 hrs; best to travel by day (0800), fabulous views but bus gets overcrowded; avoid sitting by door where people start to sit on your lap! Always keep baggage with you; **Pathankot** (90 km), several 1000-1600, 4 hrs, connection for **Amritsar**, 3 hrs; **Shimla** (317 km, via Hamirpur/Bilaspur), 10 hrs.

There are also a range of **private bus services** to Dalhousie, **Delhi** (Connaught Pl), **Dehra Dun**, **Kullu Manali** and **Rishikesh** Several private agents, see **Skyway Travels**.

Local taxi Shared by 4, pick up shuttle taxi at Kotwali Bazar on its way down before it turns around at the bus stand, as it is usually full when it passes the taxi stand.

Long-distance taxi Can be hired from near the bus stands, T01892-221205. Between Dharamshala and McLeodganj, Rs 150; to Pathankot around Rs 1500-2000 depending on size of vehicle.

Train The nearest broad-gauge railhead is at Pathankot. Booking office at the bus stand, below the tourist office, 1000-1100. For narrow-gauge railway, see page 473.

Kangra Valley *Colour map 1, B3.*

pretty valleys and paragliding opportunities

The Kangra Valley, between the Dhauladhar and the Shiwalik foothills, starts near Mandi and runs northwest to Pathankot. It is named after the town of Kangra but now the largest and main centre is Dharamshala. Chamba State, to its north, occupies part of the Ravi River Valley and some of the Chenab Valley.

Kangra

Kangra (altitude 615 m), 18 km south of Dharamshala, was once the second most important kingdom in the West Himalaya after Kashmir. Kangra town, the capital, was also known as Bhawan or Nagarkot. It overlooks the Banganga River and claims to have existed since the Vedic period with historical reference in Alexander's war records.

Kangra Fort ① *foreigners Rs 300, Indians Rs 150 (all admissions include audio guide), auto-rickshaw Rs 150 return, taxi Rs 250,* stands on a steep rock dominating the valley. A narrow path leads from the ticket office up steps to the fort, which was once protected by several gates (now reconstructed) and had the palace of the Katoch kings at the top. Just inside the complex is a small museum displaying Hindu and Jain stone statues, while further up the hill is an old Jain temple (still in use) and the ruins of a temple with exquisite carvings on its rear outer wall. At the very top, the remains of Sansar Chand's palace offer commanding views. The fort is worth the effort for these views alone. At its foot is a large modern Jain temple which has pilgrim accommodation (worth considering if you get stuck). There is also an overgrown British cemetery just next to the fort entrance.

Brajesvari Devi Temple, in Kangra Town, achieved a reputation for gold, pearls and diamonds and attracted many Muslim invaders from the 11th century, including Mahmud of Ghazni, the

Tughlaqs and the Lodis, who periodically plundered its treasures and destroyed the idols. In the intervening years the temple was rebuilt and refurbished several times but in the great earthquake of 1905 both the temple and the fort were badly damaged. The Devi received unusual offerings from devotees. According to Abul Fazal, the pilgrims "cut out their tongues which grew again in the course of two or three days and sometimes in a few hours"! The present temple in which the deity sits under a silver dome with silver *chhatras* (umbrellas) was built in 1920 and stands behind the crowded, colourful bazar. The State Government maintains the temple; the priests are expected to receive gifts in kind only. The area is busy, atmospheric and rather dirty, with mostly pilgrim-oriented stalls. Above these is **St Paul's Church** and a Christian community.

Along the river between Old Kangra (where the main road meets the turning to the fort) and Kangra Mandir is a pleasant trail, mostly following long-disused roads past ruined houses and temples which evidence a once sizeable town. Kangra's bus stand is 1.5 km north of the temple.

Masrur
A sandstone ridge to the northeast of the village of Masrur (altitude 800 m), 34 km southwest of Dharamshala, has 15 ninth- to 10th-century *sikhara* temples excavated out of solid rock. They are badly eroded and partly ruined. Even in this state they have been compared with the larger rock-cut temples at Ellora in Maharashtra and at Mamallapuram south of Chennai. Their ridge-top position commands a superb view over the surrounding fertile countryside, but few of the original *shikharas* stand, and some of the most beautifully carved panels are now in the State Museum, Shimla. There are buses from Kangra.

Jawalamukhi
This is one of the most popular Hindu pilgrimage sites in Himachal and is recognized as one of 51 *Shakti pitha*. The **Devi temple**, tended by the followers of Gorakhnath, is set against a cliff and from a fissure comes a natural inflammable gas which accounts for the blue 'Eternal Flame'. Natural springs feed the two small pools of water; one appears to boil, the other with the flame flaring above the surface contains surprisingly cold water. Emperor Akbar's gift of gold leaf covers the dome. In March/April there are colourful celebrations during the **Shakti Festival**; another in mid-October. There is accommodation here, and buses to/from Kangra.

Handicrafts

Handicrafts in Himachal Pradesh include woodcarving, spinning wool, leather tanning, pottery and bamboo crafts. Wool products are the most abundant and it is a common sight in the hills to see men spinning wool by hand as they watch over their flocks or as they are walking along. Good-quality shawls made from the fine hair from pashmina goats, particularly in Kullu, are highly sought after. *Namdas* (rugs) and rich pile carpets in Tibetan designs are also produced. Buddhist *thangkas*, silverware and chunky tribal silver jewellery are popular with tourists and are sold in bazars.

Pragpur

Pragpur, across the River Beas, 20 km southwest of Jawalamukhi, is a medieval 'heritage village' with cobbled streets and slate-roofed houses. The fine 'Judges Court' (1918) nearby has been carefully restored using traditional techniques. A three- to four-day stay is recommended here and it is advisable to reserve ahead.

Stops along the Kangra Valley Railway See also box, page 473.

Jogindernagar is the terminus of the beautiful journey by narrow-gauge rail (enquiries Kangra, T01892-252079) from Pathankot via Kangra. The hydro-power scheme here and at nearby Bassi channels water from the River Uhl. Paragliding and hang-gliding is possible at Billing (33 km), reached via Bir (19 km, see below).

Baijnath's temples are old by hill standards, dating from at least 1204. Note the Lakshmi/Vishnu figure and the graceful balcony window on the north wall. The **Vaidyanatha Temple** (originally circa 800), which contains one of 12 *jyotirlingas*, stands by the roadside on the Mandi-Palampur road, within a vast rectangular enclosure. Originally known as **Kirangama**, its name was changed after the temple was dedicated to **Siva** in his form as the Lord of Physicians. It is a good example of the Nagari style; the walls have the characteristic niches enshrining images of Chamunda, Surya and Karttikeya and the *sikhara* tower is topped with an *amalaka* and pot. A life-size stone Nandi stands at the entrance. There is a bus to and from Mandi taking 3½ hours.

Palampur, 16 km from Baijnath, 40 km from Dharamshala (via Yol), is a pleasant little town for walking, with beautiful snow views, surrounded by old British tea plantations, thriving on horticulture. It is a popular stop with trekkers. The Neugal Khad, a 300-m-wide chasm through which the Bandla flows is very impressive when the river swells during the monsoons. It holds a record for rainfall in the area.

Bir, 30 km east of Palampur, has a fast-growing reputation as one of the best paragliding locations in the world. Bordered by tea gardens and low hills, it also has four Buddhist monasteries worth visiting. Most prominent among these are Choling. You can also pick up fine Tibetan handicrafts from Bir, which has a large Tibetan colony. The village of Billing is 14 km up sharp, hair-raising hairpins and has the hilltop from where paragliders launch; see What to do, below. **Andretta** is an attractive village 13 km from Palampur. It is associated with **Norah Richards**, a follower of Mahatma Gandhi, who popularized rural theatre, and with the artist **Sardar Sobha Singh** who revived the Kangra School of painting. His paintings are big, brightly coloured, ultra-realistic and often devotional, incorporating Sikh, Christian and Hindu images. There is an art gallery dedicated to his work and memory; prints, books and soft drinks are sold in the shop. The **Andretta Pottery** (signposted from the main road), is charming. It is run by an artist couple (Indian/English), who combine village pottery with 'slipware'. The Sikh partner is the son of Gurcharan Singh (of Delhi Blue Pottery fame) and is furthering the tradition of studio pottery; works are for sale.

Where to stay

Kangra

Most hotels on the busy main road are noisy, even at night.

$$$$ Raas Kangra
20 km from Kangra aiport, www.raashimalaya. com. Opening in late 2015 from the team behind the stunning Raas in Jodhpur.
Boutique hotel with 41 suites all featuring balconies for panoramic views. It will bring innovative design together with natural beauty.

$ Jannat
Chamunda Rd, T01892-265479.
5 rooms with TV and hot water; there's also a restaurant. The closest to Kangra Mandir railway station.

Pragpur

$$$ Judge's Court (Heritage)
Set in a large orchard, T01970-245035, www.judgescourt.com.
10 tastefully decorated rooms in a fine mansion, 1 in an annexe, 1 large private modernized suite with veranda. Family hospitality, home-grown vegetables and fruit, fresh river fish and authentic Himachali meals. Tours are available of Kangra Fort and other sights in this pretty village. Lovely atmosphere. Recommended.

Stops along the Kangra Valley Railway

$$$ Taragarh Palace
Al-hilal, 11 km southeast of Palampur, T01894-242034, www.taragarh.com.
26 rooms in 1930s summer resort, period furniture and tasteful decor in public spaces, tennis, pool, lovely meandering gardens and mango orchards, and luxury Swiss tents in summer.

$$ Colonel's Resort
1 km out of Bir on the Billing road, T(0)9805-534220, www.colonelsresort.com.
8 doubles, 2 singles (simple, comfortable rooms) and 2 cottages, tents in garden (seasonal). Set in pear orchards and a working tea plantation, with sublime views down the valley and behind into Dhauladhar mountains. Its proximity to Bir makes it popular with paragliders, plus there's good hiking in the area.

$$ Darang Tea Estate
10 km from Palampur, T(0)9418-012565, www.darangteaestate.com.
2 cottages and 1 room in the main house. A family-run homestay in a beautiful working tea estate. Exceptional food and warm hospitality. Recommended.

$$ The Tea-Bud (HPTDC)
2 km from bus stand, Palampur, T01894-231298, www.hptdc.nic.in.
A clean and quiet place in a beautiful setting, with 31 rooms. The deluxe category are in a newer block, while the older rooms are totally acceptable. There's hot water, restaurant, pleasant lawn, good service and ayurvedic treatments available.

$ Uhl (HPTDC)
Near Power House, on the hill outside Jogindernagar, T01908-222002, www.hptdc.nic.in.
Unpretentious, clean and peaceful hotel offering 16 rooms with bath; the best are upstairs with a balcony. Restaurant.

Restaurants

Kangra

$ Chicken Corner
Dharamshala Rd, near the main bazar.
An eccentric though fairly clean little hut does chicken dinners.

What to do

Bir
Paragliding
Although unsuitable for beginners, there are courses available for intermediate fliers and a few residential pilots with tandem rigs.
Touching Cloud Base, *www.touchingcloudbase. com.* An excellent company offering great instruction and tandem flights.

Transport

Kangra
Air Gaggal Airport, see Dharamshala, page 469.

Bus To Dharamshala, Rs 20, under 1 hr.

Taxi A taxi to Dharamshala costs Rs 400.

The little-known 'mountain' railway

A superb narrow-gauge railway links Pathankot in the west with Jogindernagar 'ia Kangra (near Dharamshala) and Baijnath. The views of the Kangra Valley are quite spectacular. This is very much a working service and not a 'relic' (this train can be packed with ordinary users). Sadly, it is often very late as it is incredibly slow, and very uncomfortable because of the hard seats. 'Tourists' would do better to sample short sections of the line, and allow for delays – any purposeful journey is better done by bus. See Train, below, for an optimistic timetable.

Train Narrow-gauge **Kangra Valley Railway**, enquiries T01892-265026. From **Pathankot** to **Jogindernagar** (10 hrs) or **Baijnath**, reaching Kangra after 4½ hrs. **Jogindernagar to Pathankot**: reaches Kangra in 5-6 hrs; **Baijnath to Pathankot** arrives in Kangra in 3-4 hrs.

Chamba Valley *Colour map 1, B2.*

pretty temples and picturesque villages

Dalhousie

The spectacular mountain views in the hill station of Dalhousie (population 7400, altitude 2030 m) make it a popular bolt hole for tourists from the plains, but the main reason for its importance today is due to the number of good schools and the presence of the army.

The town was named after its governor-general (1848-1856) and was developed on land purchased by the British in 1853 from the Raja of Chamba. It sprawls out over five hills just east of the Ravi River. By 1867 it was a sanatorium and reached its zenith in the 1920s and 1930s as a cheaper alternative to Shimla, and the most convenient hill station for residents of Lahore. Rabindranath Tagore wrote his first poem in Dalhousie as a boy and Subhash Chandra Bose came secretly to plan his strategies during the Second World War. Its popularity declined after 1947 and it became a quiet hill station with old colonial bungalows, now almost hidden among thick pine forests interspersed with oak, deodar and rhododendron.

The three Malls laid out for level walks are around Moti Tibba, Potreyn Hill and Upper Bakrota. The last, the finest, is about 330 m above **Gandhi Chowk** around which the town centres. From there two rounds of the Mall lead to Subhash Chowk. The sizeable Tibetan community makes and sells handicrafts, woollens, jackets, cardigans and rugs. Their paintings and rock carvings in low relief can be seen along Garam Sarak Mall.

Echoes of the colonial past include five functioning churches: diminutive **St John's** (1863) on Gandhi Chowk is open for Sunday service (0930 summer, 1000 winter) and the large Catholic church of St Francis (1894) on Subhash Chowk is often open to visitors. The nostalgic **Dalhousie Club** (1895) displays old Raj-era photos and has preserved the original billiards table. The library contains bizarre English fiction and biographies, but sadly beer is not available in the bar.

Just over 2 km from Gandhi Chowk is the **Martyr's Memorial** at Panchpulla (five bridges), which commemorates Ajit Singh, a supporter of Subhash Bose and the Indian National Army during the Second World War. There are several small waterfalls in the vicinity, and on the way you can see the **Satdhara** (seven springs), said to contain mica and medicinal properties. **Subhash Baoli** (1.5 km from Gandhi Square), is another spring. It is an easy climb and offers good views of the snows. Half a kilometre away **Jhandri Ghat**, the old palace of Chamba rulers, is set among tall pine trees. For a longer walk try the Bakrota Round (5 km), which gives good views of the mountains and takes you through the Tibetan settlement.

Kalatope and Khajjiar

Kalatope Wildlife Sanctuary, 9 km from Dalhousie, with good mountain views, is a level walk through a forest sanctuary with accommodation in a pretty forest rest house bungalow (permission required from the DFO, Wildlife, Chamba, dfocha-hp@nic.in). There are good walking routes in the area, and wildlife includes black bears, leopards and serows. **Khajjiar**, 22 km further along the motorable road, is a long, wide glade ringed by cedars with a small lake and a floating island. Locals call it 'Mini Switzerland'. You can explore both areas in a pleasant three-day walk, alternatively a 30-km path through dense deodar forest leads from Khajjiar to Chamba. Buses to Khajjiar from Dalhousie take one hour.

Chamba *Colour map 1, B2.*

Picturesque Chamba (population 20,000, altitude 996 m) is on the south bank of the Iravati (Ravi), its stone houses clinging to the hillside. Some see the medieval town as having an almost Italian feel, surrounded by lush forests and with its Chaugan (or grassy meadow) in the centre. Although that's stretching it a little and recent developments have somewhat diminished its appeal, the warmer climes, unusual temples and mellow ambiance remain most attractive. Most hotels, temples and palaces are within walking distance of the bus stand.

Founded in the 10th century, Chamba State was on an important trade route from Lahaul to Kashmir and was known as the 'Middle Kingdom'. Though Mughal suzerainty was accepted by the local rajas, the kingdom remained autonomous but it came under Sikh rule from 1810-1846. Its relative isolation led to the nurturing of the arts – painting, temple sculpture, handicrafts and unique 'rumal'. These pieces of silk/cotton with fine embroidery imitate miniature paintings; the reverse is as good as the front.

The **Chaugan**, once almost a kilometre long, is the central hub of the town but sadly, over the last three decades, shops have encroached into the open space. There are several ancient Pahari temples in the town with attractive curvilinear stone towers. Follow the steep and winding road through the market to the **Lakshmi Narayana Temple Complex** (ninth to 11th centuries) containing six *sikhara* temples with deep wooden eaves, several smaller shrines and a tank. Three are dedicated to Vishnu and three to Siva, with some of the brass images inlaid with copper and silver. The **Hari Rai Temple**, next to the Chaugan (14th century), contains a fine 11th-century life-sized bronze Chaturmurti (four-armed Vishnu), rarely visible as it is usually 'dressed'; carved on the outer wall are Tantric couples. Close to the Aroma Hotel is the **Champavati Temple**, with carved wooden pillars, named after the daughter of Raja Sahil Varma who moved the capital here from Bharmour in 920 AD at her request. Others of note in the town centre are the Bansigopal, Sita Ram and Radha Krishna temples.

The 10th-century wooden **Chamunda Devi Temple**, 500 m uphill via steep steps from the bus stand, has some interesting wood carvings on its eaves and a square sanctum decked with bells. A further 500 m along the road to Saho is the elegantly slender **Bajreshwari Temple** with an octagonal roof, adjoined by a small, square unadorned temple.

The eye-catching **Akhand Chandi**, the Chamba Maharajas' palace, beyond the Lakshmi Narayan complex, is now a college. The old **Rang Mahal** (Painted Palace) in the Surara Mohalla was built by Raja Umed Singh in the mid-18th century. A prisoner of the Mughals for 16 years, he was influenced by their architectural style. The wall paintings in one room are splendid. The theme is usually religious, Krishna stories being particularly popular. Some of these were removed, together with carvings and manuscripts, to the Bhuri Singh Museum after a fire. The building now houses a sub-post office and a handicrafts workshop.

Bhuri Singh Museum ① *Museum Rd, Mon-Sat 1000-1700, Rs 100*, is a three-storey building (top floor currently closed) housing a heritage collection including some excellent *rumals*, carvings and fine examples of Chamba, Kangra and Basholi schools of miniature paintings. Archaeological finds include the remarkable 'fountain slabs' that adorned the spouts of village water sources. Dating from the 10th-18th centuries and hewn from local stone, these were memorials erected to the deceased; they are unique in Indian art. There are also many old photographs showing Chamba in its heyday. Opposite the museum is the finely built **St Andrew's Church**, belonging to the Church of Scotland and completed in 1905.

Bharmour *Colour map 1, B2.*

Capital of the princely state of Chamba for over 400 years, the tiny town of Bharmour (altitude 2130 m) is surrounded by high ranges and is snow-covered for six months of the year. It's 65 km from Chamba along a gruelling but incredibly scenic road, beset by landslides. Bharmour's ancient temples and its proximity to Manimahesh Lake and Manimahesh Kailash peak (5656 m) make it hallowed place, while alpine pastures in the region are home to Gaddi tribespeople (see below). The stone-built villages with slate-roofed houses adjoining Bharmour, and the snowy peaks all round, make it a beautiful spot.

The famous **Chaurasi** temple square has 84 shrines within, of varying architectural styles, built between the seventh and 10th centuries. The towering *sikhara* of **Manimahesh (Shiv) Temple** dominates the complex. Giant deodars flank the entrance, which is guarded by a life-size Nandi bull in polished brass; devotees whisper a wish in his ear and crawl under him for good health (a tight squeeze for some). The sanctum of the delicate **Lakshna Devi temple** (c 700 AD) houses a metre-high idol of the goddess cast in bronze. The wooden exterior, particularly the door jambs, is beautifully carved; a marvellous pair of un-eroded lions flank the door to the inner shrine.

Manimahesh, 34 km distant, has a lake in which pilgrims bathe during the Yatra (August-September) and worship at the lakeside temple. Shiva resides on the holy mountain of the same name. Helicopter flights go from the helipad above the Chaurasi complex in Bharmour to Gaurikund during the Yatra, return journey Rs 7000 (www.simmsammairways.com).

Bharmour is the centre of the **Gaddis**, shepherds who move their flocks of sheep and goats, numbering from a couple of hundred to a thousand, from lower pastures at around 1500 m during winter to higher slopes at over 3500 m, after snow-melt. They are usually found in the Dhauladhar range which separates Kangra from Chamba. Some believe that these herdsmen first arrived in this part of Himachal in the 10th century though some moved from the area around Lahore (Pakistan) in the 18th century, during the Mughal period. Their religious belief combines animism with the worship of Siva; Bharmour's distinctive Manimahesh Temple is their principal centre of worship. In the winter the Gaddis can be seen round Kangra, Mandi and Bilaspur and in the small villages between Baijnath and Palampur. The men traditionally wear a *chola* (a loose white woollen garment), tied at the waist with a black wool rope and a white embroidered cap.

Listings Chamba Valley

Tourist information

Dalhousie

Himachal Tourism
Near the bus stand, T01899-242 136.
Open 1000-1700.
Helpful for transport information, but opening hours can be irregular out of season.

Chamba

Tourist Office
Hotel Iravati complex, see Where to stay, below, T01899-222 671. Mon-Sat 1000-1630.

Where to stay

Dalhousie

Some hotels look neglected and run-down, because the cost of maintaining the Raj-built structures is prohibitive. Most have good mountain views and massive discounts out of season.

$$$ Grand View
Near bus stand, T(0)86288 10659,
www.grandviewdalhousie.in.

53 spacious, well-equipped rooms (5 price categories) in the best-preserved of Dalhousie's many Raj-era hotels. The views from the terrace are stunning, while the restaurant and lounge bar (awaiting license at the time of research!) are quintessentially British. Gym and sauna and off-season package deals are worth checking out. Recommended.

$$$-$$ Silverton Estate Guest House
Near Circuit House, the Mall, T01899-240674,
www.heritagehotels.com/silverton. Closed off season.
Old colonial building in large grounds, 5 rooms with dressing rooms, TV.

$$ Manimahesh (HPTDC)
Near the bus stand, T01899-242793,
www.hptdc.nic.in.
The 18 carpeted rooms are rather faded in this typical tourist department hotel, which has a cheap restaurant, bar with sofas and good mountain views.

$ Crags
Off the Mall, T(0)89881 74574.
The 100 steps separating this place from the Mall are the only disadvantage to this excellent budget choice. The rooms are dated but very

clean with attached bath (hot water) and a bell to ring for service. Cheap and delicious meals are served, there are good views east down the valley from the huge (if not particularly attractive) a terrace. Staff are very friendly, and the elderly owner is pretty stylish and used to catering to foreign travellers. A separate cottage is a more recent addition for a slightly higher price.

$ Geetanjali (HPTDC)
Thandi Sarak, steep 5-min climb from the bus stand, T01899-242155.
10 huge rooms with bath (reliable hot water), towels and clean sheets provided – but expect mildew-scented air as it's a very run-down colonial building.

$ Youth Hostel
Behind Manimahesh, T01899-242189, www.youthhosteldalhousie.org.
Well-maintained modern building with double rooms (Rs 300) and single sex dorms (Rs 150). Internet, free Wi-Fi and dining hall. Gets busy with groups so book ahead.

Kalatope and Khajjiar

$$$-$$ Mini Swiss
Khajjiar, T01189-923 6364, www.miniswiss.in.
Comfortable, very clean rooms in a 5-storey building with great views, good restaurant and bar, pool table and ping-pong.

$$ Devdar (HPTDC)
Khajjiar, T01899-236333, www.hptdc.nic.in.
Clean rooms (doubles and suites), dorm (Rs 150) and a nice cottage (Rs 3000), simple restaurant, horse riding, beautiful setting. Free Wi-Fi.

Chamba
During Manimahesh Yatra in Sep hotels are often full.

$$ Iravati (HPTDC)
Court Rd, near bus stand, T01899-222671.
Friendly management, 19 variable rooms with bath and hot water. Regular rooms start at Rs 1500; they're spacious, nicely tiled, clean and overlook the Chaugan. The higher up the building, the better the views and the higher the prices. Decent restaurant.

$$-$ Aroma Palace
Near Rang Palace, Court Lane, T01899-225677, www.hotelaromapalacechamba.com.
Rooms range from economy to sumptuous

honeymoon suite, which are all spotless, plus there's a restaurant and airy terrace. Breakfast is included and discounts are possible.

$$-$ Himalayan Orchard Huts
10 km out of town, T(0)94180 20401, www.himalayanlap.com.
Idyllic location, 20 mins' walk from nearest road, rooms in the guesthouse are set in a delightful garden with a spring-water pool, beautiful views from large terraces with hammocks, clean shared shower and toilets. Or you can pitch a tent in the garden. There's superb home cooking (a great all-inclusive deal), and it's run by a very friendly family. Recommended. They also own **Ridgemore Cottage**, a trekkers' hut atop a ridge, 4 hrs' walk from Orchard Hut. Highly recommended.

$ Akhand Chandi
College Rd, Dogra Bazar, 1 km from bus stand, T01899-222371.
Attractive stone building with 10 rooms, attached bath and TV, restaurant.

$ Chamba Guesthouse
Gopal Nivas, near Gandhi Gate, by the Chaugan, T01899-222564.
Simple lodgings with wooden floors and charm, this budget hotel almost hangs over the Ravi River with amazing views from the balcony. A popular choice, try to book ahead.

Bharmour

$ Him Kailash Homestay
Near the bus stop, T01895-225100.
Simple, friendly place with clean freshly painted rooms that have good valley views. The cheapest rooms (Rs 500) don't have a TV or geyser, or even curtains; much larger rooms with proper amenities cost Rs1000. There's not much English spoken.

Restaurants

Dalhousie

$$ Napoli
Near Gandhi Chowk.
Serving pizza, Indian and Chinese, meat and veg dishes in large portions. Very friendly and comfortable.

$ Friend's Dhaba
Subhash Chowk.
Good, unpretentious Punjabi, including *paneer burji* to die for.

Chamba

There are a number of atmospheric little *dhabas* in the alleys through Dogra Market.

$$-$ Copper Chimney
5th floor, White House Hotel.

Great tandoor over offerings and veg/non-veg Indian and Chinese food. Comfy a/c indoor section or 4 intimate tables on the roof terrace. It's a long slog up the stairs, however.

$ Jagaan
1st floor, Museum Rd.

Good selection served in a relatively calm atmosphere. *Chamba madhra* (Rs 90), a rich stew of kidney beans, ghee and curd, is a local speciality.

$ Ravi View Café
Next to Chaugan.

Reasonable snacks and Indian veg food plus beer. This HPTDC-run circular hut even has outside tables with killer views overlooking the river.

Festivals

Chamba

Apr Suhi Mela, lasts 3 days, commemorates a Rani who consented to be buried alive in a dry stream bed in order that it could flow and provide the town with water. Women and children in traditional dress carry images of her to a temple on the hill, accompanied by songs sung in her praise. Men are strictly prohibited from participating.
Jul-Aug Gaddis and Gujjars take part in many cultural events to mark the start of harvesting. **Minjar** is a 7-day harvest festival when people offer thanks to Varuna the rain god. Decorated horses and banners are taken out in procession through the streets to mark its start. Sri Raghuvira is followed by other images of gods in palanquins and the festival ends at the River Irawati where people float *minjars* (tassels of corn and coconut).

Shopping

Dalhousie

Bhuttico, *The Mall (Garam Sarak), www.bhuttico shawls.com. Mon-Sat 0900-1930.* Fixed price shop, with branches nationwide, selling top quality Kullu shawls, socks and pullas (slippers with grass soles) that incorporate traditional designs.

Chamba

Handicrafts Centre, *Rang Mahal.* Rumal embroidery and leather goods.

Transport

Dalhousie

Air The nearest airport is at Gaggal; see Dharamshala, page 469.

Bus Dalhousie is on the NH1A. **Amritsar**, 7 hrs; **Delhi**, 12 hrs; To **Chamba** 4 buses daily, 2 go via Khajjiar, 2½ hrs; **Dharamshala**, 7 hrs; **Jammu**, 7 hrs. There's a regular service to **Pathankot** (change in Pathankot for frequent services to main towns/cities); **Shimla**, 1245, 14 hrs. Note that Banikhet village, 10 mins from Dalhousie, has many more bus options.

Jeep/Taxi From bus stand up to **Gandhi Chowk**, Rs 100, **Bakrota**, Rs 200.

Train Nearest station is at Pathankot, 2 hrs by taxi. There is a helpful Railway Out Agency close to the bus stand.

Chamba

Bus The hectic bus stand is at the south end of the Chaugan. To **Bharmour** (3 hrs, Rs 70); **Dalhousie** (2½ hrs, Rs 50); and to **Shimla** once per day.

Jeep hire is relatively expensive. Special service during **Manimahesh Yatra**.

Train Nearest station is at Pathankot, 120 km away.

Background Himachal Pradesh

History

Originally the region was inhabited by a tribe called the Dasas who were later assimilated by the Aryans. From the 10th-century parts were occupied by the Muslims. Kangra, for example, submitted to Mahmud of Ghazni and later became a Mughal province. The Gurkhas of Nepal invaded Himachal in the early 19th century and incorporated it into their kingdom as did the Sikhs some years later. The British finally took over the princely states in the middle of the 19th century.

Culture

Although the statistics suggest that Himachal is one of the most Hindu states in India, its culture reflects the strong influence of Buddhism, notably in the border regions with Tibet and in the hill stations where many Tibetan refugees have made their homes. In the villages many of the festivals are shared by Hindus and Buddhists alike. There are also small minorities of Sikhs, Muslims and Christians.

Hill tribes such as the Gaddis, Gujars, Kinnaurs, Lahaulis and Pangwalas have all been assimilated into the dominant Hindu culture though the caste system is simpler and less rigid than elsewhere. The tribal peoples in Lahaul and Spiti follow a form of Buddhism while Kinnauris mix Buddhism with Hinduism in their rituals. Their folklore has the common theme of heroism and legends of love. Natti, the attractive folk dance of the high hills, is widely performed.

The dominant local language is Pahari, a Hindi dialect derived from Sanskrit and Prakrit but largely unintelligible to plains dwellers. Hindi is the medium for instruction in schools and is widely spoken.

Jammu & Kashmir

epic treks through dramatic landscapes

The shimmering lakes, fertile valleys and remote, snow-covered peaks of Kashmir have had a magnetic appeal to rulers, pilgrims and humble travellers, from the Mughals onwards.

With levels of political violence going down in recent years, and the prominent marketing of houseboats, golf courses and ski resorts, Indian tourists are returning to Srinagar in large numbers. However, there remains an obvious military presence, and be aware that curfews or demonstrations might still occur. Trekking in the Vale of Kashmir should be undertaken only after careful research and with a reliable guide. Yet foreigners will find themselves warmly welcomed by the Kashmiris, and in Srinagar and the surrounding area there is plenty to see and do, not to mention to buy and to eat.

The state is equally famed for the magnificent realm of Ladakh and its capital, Leh, set in some of the world's most beautiful scenery. Here you can trek to your heart's content among some of the highest-altitude passes in the world, in one of India's remotest regions. The spectacular high-altitude deserts of Ladakh and Zanskar provide the setting for a hardy Buddhist culture whose villages and monasteries retain strong links with Tibet. Alchi, Hemis and Thiksey are just three of many striking monasteries clinging to mountainsides.

Best for
Monasteries ▪ Mountains ▪ Scenery ▪ Shopping ▪ Trekking

Footprint picks

★ **Srinagar**, page 488

Sleep on a houseboat, try Kashmiri cooking and shop for shawls.

★ **Alchi**, page 519

View the ancient murals of Alchi Monastery and explore the scenic surroundings of the village.

★ **Lamayuru**, page 520

Don't miss the picture-perfect monastery and weird moonscapes in Lamayuru.

★ **Nubra-Shyok valleys**, page 523

Travel north through wild, arid landscapes to Nubra Valley's remote and friendly hamlets.

★ **Pangong-Tso**, page 523

Experience true natural beauty, where the lake's turquoise waters are framed by snowy summits.

★ **Trekking in Ladakh**, page 525

Challenge your body and mind on a high-altitude trek.

Essential Jammu and Kashmir

Finding your feet

The largest of India's Himalayan states, Jammu and Kashmir (population 10.1 million) comprises three regions of stark geographical and cultural diversity. Jammu, in the southwest, is a predominantly Hindu region bordering the Punjab, its foothills forming the transitional zone between the plains and the mountains. To the north the Shiwalik mountains give way to the Pir Panjal (5000 m). Between the Pir Panjal and the High Himalaya, around 1580 m, lies the largely Islamic Vale of Kashmir, where snow-capped peaks form a backdrop to the capital, Srinagar, and the Nagin and Dal lakes. Rising behind the Vale are the Great Himalaya which culminate in the west with Nanga Parbat (Naked Mount) at 8125 m.

To the west and north are the Buddhist mountain provinces of Ladakh and Zanskar, crossed by four mountain ranges – Great Himalaya, Zanskar, Ladakh and Karakoram – as well as by the River Indus and its tributaries the Zanskar, Shingo and Shyok. The Zanskar cuts an impressive course of 120 km before slicing through the Zanskar range in a series of impressive gorges to join the Indus at Nimmu near Leh, the capital of Ladakh. During the winter months, the frozen Zanskar River provides the only access for Zanskaris into Ladakh. Combined with its two subsidiary valleys, the Stod (Doda Chu) and the Lung-Nak (Tsarap Chu or 'Valley of Darkness'), which converge below Padum, the main 300-km-long valley is ringed by mountains, so access to it is over one of the high passes. The most important are the Pensi La connecting Zanskar with the Suru Valley in the west, the Umasi La with the Chenab Valley in the south and the Shingo La with Lahul in the east. Ladakh also has the world's largest glaciers outside

the polar regions, and the large and beautiful lake Pangong Tso, 150 km long and 4 km wide, at a height of over 4000 m. This makes for spectacular trekking country.

Getting around

Trains run as far as Jammu. Buses and jeeps go to Srinagar and on to Leh, which also has a spectacular road connection to Manali in Himachal Pradesh. There are domestic flights to Jammu, Srinagar and Leh.

When to go

Kashmir and Ladakh are best visited from May to October, unless you like freezing temperatures and harsh winter. The snow season in Gulmarg runs from December to April. Avoid the Vale of Kashmir on contentious dates such as Republic Day (26 January). Even in the Vale, the air in summer is fresh and at night can be quite brisk. The highest daytime temperatures in July rarely exceed 35°C but may fall as low as -11°C in winter. A short climb quickly reduces these temperatures. In Ladakh the sun cuts through the thin atmosphere, and daily and seasonal temperature variations are even wider. The rain-bearing clouds drifting in from the Arabian Sea never reach Ladakh, while Srinagar receives over 650 mm per annum, Leh has only 85 mm, much as snow. Over half Srinagar's rain comes with westerly depressions in the winter.

Time required

At least a week for the Vale of Kashmir and a houseboat stay; eight days in Ladakh to acclimatize and visit sights, more if you want to add in a trek or the Nupra Valley.

Weather Srinagar

January	February	March	April	May	June
5°C -2°C 62mm	8°C -1°C 71mm	14°C 3°C 101mm	19°C 7°C 91mm	24°C 11°C 68mm	29°C 15°C 36mm

July	August	September	October	November	December
30°C 18°C 54mm	28°C 18°C 65mm	28°C 13°C 35mm	22°C 6°C 31mm	15°C 0°C 18mm	9°C -2°C 41mm

Safety warning for the Kashmir Valley

Many governments still advise against travel to the Kashmir Valley, with the exceptions of: the cities of Jammu and Srinagar; travel between these two cities on the Jammu-Srinagar highway; and the region of Ladakh. Take advice from your consulate, and be aware that travelling against their advice can render your travel insurance void. Most travellers report no problems, but it is essential to be careful and keep informed about the current political situation. For an on-the-ground perspective, check www.greaterkashmir.com and www.kashmirtimes.com.

Grenade attacks on army bunkers in the city used to be common and in the past, splinter groups took hostages as a means of putting pressure on the Indian government. Given the tensions between Kashmir and the government, Indian tourists are more likely to be directly targeted than foreigners. However, in recent years there has been a decline in violence overall and increasing numbers of Indian and Western tourists are visiting the valley.

If you are in town and see the shop shutters coming down before closing time, this is generally a sign that a protest is approaching. Either beat a hasty retreat in an auto-rickshaw, or take shelter in a shop until the demonstrators and police have passed. Always ask how the situation is before heading to the old city (Downtown) and don't go there on Fridays, when spontaneous demonstrations following afternoon prayers are more likely to occur. The Dal and Nagin lake areas are hardly affected on such occasions; at worst, you might not be able to get transport during a bandh (general shutdown). For background information on the political situation in Kashmir, see pages 486 and 529.

Kashmir
Valley

The beauty of the Vale of Kashmir, with its snow-dusted mountains looming in shades of purple above serene lakes and wildflower meadows, still has the power to reduce grown poets to tears. Nonetheless, the reality of military occupation pervades many aspects of daily life, with army camps, bunkers and checkposts positioned every few hundred metres along the highways and throughout the countryside. Travellers can expect to encounter extremes of beauty and friendliness, not to mention hard salesmanship in an economy that was starved of tourist income for over 20 years.

Jammu and around *Colour map 1, A2.*

low-key winter capital with a strongly Hindu flavour

Jammu (population 951,373), the second largest city in the state, is the winter capital of government and main entry point for Kashmir by train. While it doesn't possess the charm of Srinagar, it is a pleasant enough city to spend a day. Built in 1730 by the Dogra rulers as their capital, Jammu marks the transition between the Punjab plains and the Himalaya hills.

Sights

Raghunath Temple ① *0600-2130, inner sanctum closes 1130-1800, museum 0600-1000, cloakroom for bags/cameras.* Raghunath Temple, in the old centre, is one of the largest temple complexes in North India, and dates from 1857. The temple, dedicated to Lord Rama, has a series of glittering gilded spires and seven shrines. The main shrine's interior is gold-plated, while surrounding shrines contain millions of 'saligrams' (mini-lingams fixed onto slabs of stone), most of which are fossils.

Essential Jammu

Finding your feet

The airport is within the city with prepaid taxis available to the centre (Ragunath Bazar). There are daily flights from Delhi, Mumbai and Srinagar, and twice-weekly flights to Leh (in high season). The railway station is in the New Town, across the Tawi River, a few kilometres from the old hilltop town where most of the budget hotels are located. The general bus stand, where inter-state buses arrive, is at the foot of the steps off the Srinagar Road in the old town. See Transport, page 488.

Getting around

The frequent, cheap city bus service or an auto-rickshaw come in handy, as the two parts of town and some sights are far apart.

When to go

The best time to visit is from November to March.

Safety

For safety information see page 483.

The people of Kashmir and Ladakh

Culturally, the people of Jammu, Kashmir and Ladakh could scarcely be more different from each other. The 12.5 million population is unevenly scattered. The Vale of Kashmir has more than half the population, whilst Ladakh is the most sparsely populated region. Jammu was traditionally the seat of Dogra power and serves a largely Hindu population whose affinities lie more with the Punjab than the Vale. Kashmir marks the northernmost advance of Islam in the Himalaya.

Ladakh is aptly named 'Little Tibet'. Ethnically the Ladakhis are of Tibetan stock. Indeed, it was once a province of Tibet and was governed in secular matters by an independent prince and in spiritual affairs by the Dalai Lama. Tibetan Changpas form the bulk of the population in central and eastern Ladakh. These nomadic herdsmen can be seen living in black yak-hair tents on the mountains with their yaks, goats and sheep. They still provide the fine *pashm* goat wool. The Mons, nomads of Aryan stock, introduced Buddhism and established settlements in the valleys. The Droks or Dards from the Gilgit area settled along the Indus Valley and introduced irrigation; many converted to Islam 300 years ago. Most are cultivators speaking a language based on Sanskrit.

The Baltis with Central Asian origins mostly live in the Kargil region. The Zanskaris are of the same stock as the Ladakhis and because of the sheer isolation of their homeland were able to preserve their Buddhist culture against the onslaughts of Mughal India. The majority of Zanskaris are Buddhist, though there are Muslim families in Padum, the capital, dating from the Dogra invasion.

Kashmiri is influenced by Sanskrit and belongs to the Dardic branch of the Indo-Aryan languages. Linguistically and physically Kashmiris are similar to the tribes around Gilgit in Pakistan. The Ladakhis physically reveal Tibetan-Mongolian and Indo-Aryan origins while their language belongs to the Tibetan-Burmese group.

In the Vale of Kashmir, 97% of the people are Muslim, the majority being Sunnis, while in Jammu about 65% are Hindu. In Ladakh, just under half the population are Lamaistic Buddhists.

Rambiresvar Temple Centrally located on the Shalimar Road, **Rambiresvar Temple** (1883) is the largest Siva temple in North India. It is dedicated to Siva and named after its founder Maharaja Ranbir Singh. The 75-m orange tower is rather unattractive, but the central 2.3-m sphatik shivling is an extraordinary crystal lingam. A fine bronze Nandi bull watches the entrance to the shrine.

Mubarak Mandi About 700 m from the Rambiresvar Temple are the palace buildings of Mubarak Mandi. Dating from 1824, they blend Rajasthani, Mughal and baroque architectural elements. Within the dilapidated complex is the **Dogra Art Gallery** ⓘ *Tue-Sun 1030-1630, foreigners Rs 5*, displaying royal memorabilia in the Pink Hall.

Amar Mahal Museum ⓘ *Apr-Sep 0900-1300, 1400-1800, Oct-Mar 0900-1300, 1400-1700, foreigners Rs100, Rs 150 by auto-rickshaw from the centre of town, or take a minibus.* The Amar Mahal Museum is superbly sited on the bend of the Tawi, just off Srinagar Road, and has great views of the river. There is a maharajas' portrait gallery and 18th-century Pahari miniature paintings of *Mahabharata* scenes. The early 20th-century palace is a curiosity`; its French designer gave it château-like roofs and turrets. Look through a rear window to see Hari Singh's 100 kg golden canopied throne. Other rooms show modern art; admission to the library (with a fine collection of antique books) is only for researchers. The Hari Niwas Hotel is adjacent; the lawns are a welcome spot for refreshments when it's not too hot.

Bahu Fort Across the Tawi River lies the impressive **Bahu Fort**, thought to have a 3000-year history. The ramparts have been renovated and are now surrounded by a lush terraced garden, the Bagh-e-Bahu.

Vaishno Devi *Colour map 1, A2.*

The Vaishno Devi cave, 61 km north of Jammu, is one of the region's most important pilgrimage sites. As the temple draws near you hear cries of 'Jai Matadi' (Victory to the Mother Goddess). Then at the shrine entrance, pilgrims walk in batches through cold ankle-deep water to the low and narrow cave entrance to get a glimpse of the deity. Visitors joining the *yatra* find it a very moving experience. The main pilgrimage season is March to July.

The arduous climb along the 13-km track to the cave temple has been re-laid, widened and tiled, and railings provided. Another road from Lower Sanjichat to the Darbar brings you 2 km closer with 300 m less to climb. Ponies, *dandies* (a kind of local palanquin for carrying tourists) and porters are available from Katra at fixed rates. Auto-rickshaws and taxis can go as far as the Banganga.

Yatra slips are issued free of charge by the **Yatra Registration Counter (YRC)** in the bus stand in Katra. The slip must be presented at the Banganga checkpoint within six hours (or you face disciplinary action if caught). One slip can be used for up to nine people. If you are on your own or in a small group, you can usually avoid having to wait for a group if you present yourself at Gates 1 or 2, and smile.

Visitors should leave all leather items in a cloakroom at Vaishno Devi before entering the cave; take bottled water and waterproofs. Tea, drinks and snacks are available on the route.

The Jammu–Srinagar road

It's a stunning journey through the mountains as the bus winds its way up to the Jawahar tunnel that burrows through the Pir Panjal, with the jade-green Chenab river flowing hundreds of feet below. Emerging from the tunnel on the other side, high in the hills of south Kashmir, travellers are treated to a breathtaking view of the valley spread before out before them. Two new tunnels are being constructed, due to open in 2016/2017, which will cut the journey time to five hours, so now is the time to enjoy this road.

Tourist information

Jammu

Jammu and Kashmir Tourist Reception Centre
Vir Marg, T0191-254 8172, www.jktourism.org.
Has brochures.

JKTDC
T0191-257 9554, http://jktdc.co.in.

Where to stay

Jammu

$$$ Asia Jammu-Tawi
Nehru Market, north of town, T0191-243 5757,
www.asiahotelsjammu.com.
The 44 rooms are beginning to show their
age, but this Jammu stalwart has an excellent
Chinese restaurant, bar, and a clean pool.
Close to the airport.

$$$ Hari Niwas Palace
Palace Rd, T0191-254 3303,
www.hariniwaspalace.in.
40 a/c rooms and suites in a heritage property
with an elegant bar and classy restaurant.
Meals and drinks are also served on the
immaculate lawns, with a sweeping view. The
cliff-top location next to Amar Mahal is the chief
attraction. The Royal Deluxe rooms and Suites
(**$$$$**) are huge, with wonderful views from
either front or back. Heated pool and health club.

$$$ KC Residency
Vir Marg, T0191-252 0770,
www.kcresidency.com.
Rising from the heart of Jammu, the KC tower
has 61 good-quality a/c rooms, and a health club
specializing in Ayurvedic massage, all crowned by
a superb, multi-cuisine revolving restaurant.

$$ Jewel's
Jewel Chowk, T0191-252 0801-3,
www.jewelshotel.com.
Located in a busy, congested area, but the 18 a/c
rooms are good value in an increasingly expensive
city. There's a good fast-food restaurant and bar.

$$-$ Tourist Reception Centre
AKA Hotel Jammu Residency, Vir Marg,
T0191-257 9554.
Set back from the main road, the TRC has
173 rooms with bath, arranged around well-kept

gardens; price is dictated by size, quality and
views. The restaurant has a good reputation, in
particular for its Kashmiri food, and there's a bar.

$ Kranti Hotel
Near the railway station, T0191-247 0525.
One of the better budget hotels in the railway
area with 45 clean rooms with attached bath
and a restaurant.

Vaishno Devi
Katra is an attractive town at the foot of the
Trikuta Hills where visitors to the Vaishno Devi
cave can stay.

$$ Ambica
Katra, T01991-232062, www.hotelambika.com.
58 rooms, a/c, *puja* shop and health centre,
spacious lawns.

$$ Asia Vaishnodevi
Katra, T01991-232061, www.asiavaishnodevi.in.
37 a/c rooms, restaurant, transport to Banganga.

$ Dormitories
At the halfway point to Vaishno Devi.
Simple rooms, provides sheets.

$ Prem
Main Bazar, Katra, T01991-232014.
Adequate rooms with hot water and a fire.

Restaurants

Jammu
The best eateries tend to be found in the upmarket
hotels. However, there are some good snack places
dotted around town, which can be fun to check out.

$$-$ Sagar Ratna
Hotel Premier, opposite KC Plaza, Residency Rd.
Vegetarian delights, both South and North Indian
plus Chinese, at reasonable prices for smart-casual
surrounds (a/c), and generous portions. Loud TV.

$$-$ Smokin' Joes Pizza
Bahu Plaza, near the railway station.
Very acceptable veg and non-veg pizza and
pasta, but strictly no pork. Takeaway and home
delivery are also available.

$ Barista
KC Cineplex and City Square Mall.
Popular Indian café chain, also sells sandwiches
and cakes.

Vaishno Devi

Excellent vegetarian food is available; curd and *paneer* dishes are especially good. For non-*dhaba* food try the 2 vegetarian fast food places on the main street. Both are clean and good.

Shopping

Jammu

J&K Arts Emporium, *next to J&K Tourism, Residency Rd. Mon-Sat 1000-2000.* Good selection of cheap items.

Transport

Jammu

Air Rambagh Airport, 6 km. Transport to town: prepaid taxis and auto-rickshaws. Daily flights to **Delhi**. **Mumbai** and **Srinagar**; to **Leh** in high season on Mon and Fri (Air India, book well in advance).

Bus J&KSRTC, TRC, Vir Marg, T0191-257 9554 (1000-1700), general bus stand, T0191-257 7475 (0400-2000). To **Amritsar** (6 hrs) at least hourly via **Pathankot** (3 hrs); direct buses to **Srinagar** (9 hrs), **Katra** (for Vaishno Devi), and **Kishtwar**. To **Delhi** (12 hrs), hourly. **Srinagar** buses also leave from the railway station, usually 0600-0700.

Jeep *Sumos* to **Srinagar** leaving early morning (8-9 hrs).

Train 5 km from centre; allow at least 30 mins by auto. Enquiries T0191-245 3027. To **Delhi**: around 8 trains daily, taking 9-14 hrs. To **Amritsar**: 3 per day, taking 4½ hrs.

★ Srinagar *Colour map 1, A2.*

houseboats and Mughal gardens, against a backdrop of the Himalaya

Founded by Raja Pravarasen in the sixth century, ringed by mountains and alluringly wrapped around the Dal and Nagin lakes, Srinagar, meaning 'beautiful city', is divided in two by the River Jhelum.

Srinagar is the largest city in the state, with a population of 1,269,751, and the summer seat of government. Sadly the troubles of the past 25 years have scarred the town, leading to the desertion and neglect of many of its fine houses, buildings and Hindu temples. Older Srinagaris lament the passing of the formerly spruce city, yet Srinagar remains a charming place with a strong character, unique in India for its Central Asian flavour.

Devastating floods in 2014 saw the Jhelum burst its banks, causing much of the city to be submerged under water; many of the worst hit businesses, hotels and restaurants are yet to recover.

Dal Lake

Of all the city's sights, Dal Lake must be its trademark. Over 6.5 km long and 4 km wide, it is divided into three parts by manmade causeways. The small islands are willow covered, while round the lake are groves of *chinar*, poplar and willow. The Mihrbahri people have lived around the lakes for centuries and are market gardeners, tending the floating beds of vegetables and flowers that they have made and cleverly shielded with weeds to make them unobtrusive. Shikaras, the gondola-like pleasure boats that ply the lake, can be hired for trips around the Dal (the official rate Rs 300 per hour, but it's possible to bargain). The morning vegetable market is well worth seeing by boat: it starts around 0600 and a one-hour tour is adequate; it is in a Shi'ite area adorned with corresponding flags. At the end of the Boulevard in Nehru Park the tiny **Post Office Museum** ① *daily 1100-2000*, is unique in that it floats. You can also send your mail from here.

Hazratbal Mosque (Majestic Place) is on the western shore of Dal Lake, and commands excellent lake views. The modern mosque stands out for its white marble dome and has a special sanctity as a hair of the prophet Mohammad is preserved here. Just beyond is little **Nazim Bagh** (Garden of the Morning Breeze), one of the earliest Mughal gardens and attributed to Akbar.

Mughal Gardens

Set in front of a triangle of the lake created by intersecting causeways (now demolished), with a slender bridge at the centre, lies the famous **Nishat Bagh** (Garden of Gladness) ① *Sat-Thu*

Essential Srinagar

Finding your feet

The airport is 14 km south of town; a taxi to the main tourist areas takes 30-45 minutes. Srinagar has daily direct flights from Delhi, and weekly flights from Leh during the summer months. Direct buses from New Delhi take 24 hours, but this is an arduous trip. If you want to travel overland, it's more comfortable to take the train as far as Jammu (12 hours), stop for the night and then travel to the valley by jeep or bus the next day (eight to nine hours, including stops for lunch and tea). Srinagar is on NH1A linked to Jammu (293 km) by narrow 'all-weather' mountain road, through superb scenery. Often full of lorries and military convoys, the journey takes nine to 10 hours; few stops for food. Tourist buses from Jammu and Delhi arrive and leave from the Tourist Reception Centre, see page 492.

Tip...
Qayaam Chowk street, close to Dalgate, is known as 'the barbecue'. It's lined with small restaurants and stalls serving *sheesh* and *seekh* kebabs, accompanied by an array of delicious, home-made Kashmiri chutneys.

Best views
Sunset from **Pari Mahal**, page 489
From the top of **Shankaracharya Temple**, page 490
From the veranda of a **houseboat**, page 494

Getting around

There are government taxi stands with fixed rates at the Tourist Reception Centre (Residency Road), Dal Gate and Nehru Park, and an abundance of auto-rickshaws. Local buses are cheap, but can be crowded and slow. The days of dusk-to-dawn curfews are over, but even so, the city shuts down relatively early; by 2100 the streets are deserted and it can be tricky to find transport. See Transport, page 497.

Orientation

Once known as the city of seven *kadals* (bridges), there are now 12 that connect the two sides, the older ones giving their names to their adjoining neighbourhoods.

The city falls into three parts; the commercial area (**Uptown**), the old city (**Downtown**) and the area around the lakes (**Dalgate**, the **Boulevard**, **Nehru Park**). Uptown is the place for shopping, particularly Polo View and the Bund, which is a footpath that runs along the Jhelum, and Lal Chowk on the western side.

0900-sunset, Rs 10. Sandwiched between the hills and the lake, the steep terraces and central channel with fountains were laid out by Asaf Khan, Nur Jahan's brother, in 1632.

The **Shalimar Bagh** ① *Apr-Oct 0900-sunset, Nov-Mar 1000-sunset, Rs 10*, gardens are about 4 km away and set back from the lake. Built by Jahangir for his wife, Nur Jahan, the gardens are distinguished by a series of terraces linked by a water channel with central pavilions. These are surrounded by decorative pools, which can be crossed by stones. The uppermost pavilion has elegant black marble pillars and niches in the walls for flowers during the day and candles or lamps at night. The chinar (plane trees) have become so huge that some are falling down.

Chashma Shahi (Royal Spring, 1632) ① *0900-sunset, Rs 10*, is a much smaller garden built around the course of a renowned spring, issuing from a miniature stone dome at the garden's summit. It is attributed to Shah Jahan though it has been altered over the centuries. Nearby are the **Botanical Gardens** ① *Sat-Thu 0800-sunset, Rs 10*. Rather wilder than the other gardens, its tucked-away location makes it popular with runners.

West (2.5 km) of Chashmi Shahi, nestling in the hills, is the smallest and sweetest of the Mughal gardens, the charmingly named **Pari Mahal** (Fairy Palace) ① *sunrise-sunset, Rs 10*. Built in the 17th century by the ill-fated prince Dara Shikoh, who was later beheaded by his brother Aurangzeb, the garden has six terraces and the best sunset views of Srinagar. The terraced gardens, backed by arched ruins, are being restored and are illuminated at night.

Shankaracharya Temple

Set up on a hill, behind the Boulevard (known as Takht-i-Sulaiman or 'Throne of Soloman'), is the Shankaracharya Temple, with great views; it's a good place to orientate yourself. The temple was constructed during Jahangir's reign but is said to be on the same site as a second-century BC temple built by Asoka's son. The inelegant exterior houses a large lingum, while beneath is a cave where Shankaracharya is said to have performed a *puja*. The temple is 5.5 km up a steep road from the Boulevard; walking up the road is not permitted, although hitching a ride from the security check (open 0900-1700) at the bottom is possible. There is an alternative rough path starting from next to the gate of the City Forest Hotel on Durganag Road (one hour up, 30 minutes down).

Sri Pratap Singh Museum

Lal Mandi, Tue-Sun 1030-1630, foreigners Rs 50.

South of the old city and the river is the dark and dusty Sri Pratap Singh Museum (1898). Kashmir's Hindu and Buddhist past stares you in the face as 1000-year-old statues of Siva, Vishnu and the Buddha, excavated from all over the valley, casually line the walls. One room houses an eclectic mix of stuffed animals, bottled snakes and birds' eggs, topped off by the dissembled skeleton of

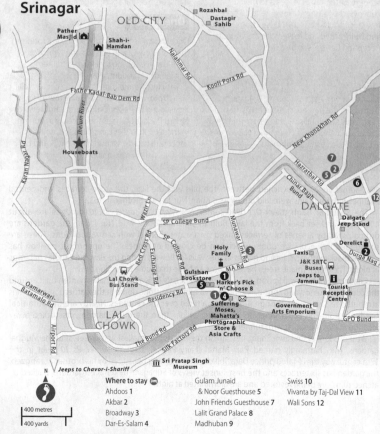

Srinagar

Where to stay

Ahdoos **1**	Gulam Junaid
Akbar **2**	& Noor Guesthouse **5**
Broadway **3**	John Friends Guesthouse **7**
Dar-Es-Salam **4**	Lalit Grand Palace **8**
	Madhuban **9**

Swiss **10**
Vivanta by Taj-Dal View **11**
Wali Sons **12**

a woolly mammoth and looked down on by a collection of stags' heads, mounted on the papier-mâché walls. There are also miniature paintings, a selection of ancient manuscripts and coins, as well as weapons, musical instruments and an anthropology section. Look out for the extraordinary Amli shawl in the textiles room: an embroidered map of Srinagar, showing the Jamia mosque and the Jhelum dotted with houseboats (it took 37 years to complete). The museum suffered damage in the 2014 floods, and the collection will be reorganized when the museum extends into a larger building being constructed next door.

Old City

Srinagar's old city (known locally as Downtown) is a fascinating area to wander around with rather a Central Asian feel. Once the manufacturing and trade hub of Kashmir, each *mohalla* (neighbourhood) had its own speciality, such as carpet weaving, goldsmithery and woodcarving. It was said that you could find even the milk of a pigeon in the thriving bazars and its traders grew rich, building themselves impressive brick and wood houses, in a style that is a charming fusion of Mughal and English Tudor.

In the north of the Old City is the distinctive mound of **Hari Parbat Hill**, on which stands a fort built by Shujah Shah Durrani in 1808. You need permission from the TRC to visit the fort, which opened to the public in 2014. On the southern side of Hari Parbat, the **Makhdoom Sahib shrine** is dedicated to Hazrat Sultan and has wonderful views of the city. The actual shrine is off-limits to women and non-Muslims, but you can peek through the ornate, carved screen from outside and marvel at the fabulous array of chandeliers. The Makhdoom Ropeway, a **cable car** ① *tourists Rs 100*, goes up to the shrine giving fabulous views, although it often seems to close for maintenance. Alternatively, you can access the steps up the hill from near the Sikh Gurdwara **Chhatti Padshahi**, by the imposing **Kathi Darwaza** (gate) in the Old City walls. This arched gateway was the principle entrance to the fort; a Persian inscription states that it was built by Akbar in 1597-8. In the city wall on the opposite side of fort is the Sangeen Darwaza, which is more ornate.

From Makhdoom Sahib take an auto-rickshaw (or walk 15 minutes) to the **Jama Masjid** (1674). The mosque is notable for the 370 wooden pillars supporting the roof, each made from a single *deodar* tree. The building forms a square around an inner courtyard, with a beautiful fountain and pool at its centre. Its four entrance archways are topped by the striking, pagoda-like roofs that are an important architectural characteristic of the valley's mosques and shrines. The mosque was where the sacred hair of the Prophet Mohammed was kept before being moved to the Hazratbal Mosque.

About 10 minutes' walk to the southeast lies the 17th-century **tomb of Naqash Band Sahib**, a sufi saint. The interior of the shrine is covered with (modern) colourful papier-mâché flower designs; there is a women's section. The ornate mosque adjacent to the shrine is meticulously

Restaurants 🍴
Café Robusta **1**
Krishna Dha ba **2**
Lhasa **3**
Mughal Darbar **4**

Shakti Sweets
& Modern Sweets **5**
Shamyana **6**

Mosque etiquette

Before entering a shrine or mosque, remove your shoes. Most places have a cloakroom where you can leave them for a few rupees. Women should put a scarf over their head and both sexes must cover arms and legs. You can put a donation for the shrine's upkeep in the green *tameer* (building) fund box, usually at the entrance.

maintained, and is constructed of brick and wood alternate layers. Next to the shrine lie the graves of the 'martyrs' who died in the 1931 uprising against the Dogras. They are claimed as heroes by both the state government and the separatists – one of the few things both sides agree on.

Continue further in the same direction and you will reach the **Dastagir Sahib shrine**, which houses the tomb of Abdul Qazi Geelani. A fire in 2012 almost entirely destroyed the main structure, including antique chandeliers, exquisite papier mâché and carved wood decoration. The 300-year-old giant handwritten Qu'ran and the holy relic of the saint were saved, as they were in a fireproof vault. The shrine is to be rebuilt according to its original structural character, and many devotees still come to pray here. A minute's walk away is little **Rozahbal shrine**, which claims to contain the 'tomb of Jesus' (Holger Kersten's *Jesus Lived in India* recounts the legend; also see www.tombofjesus.com). The community here is sensitive about inquiring visitors: do not produce a camera, and don't be surprised if locals warn you away.

Head west towards the river for the beautiful **Shah-i-Hamdan Masjid**, the site of Srinagar's first mosque, built in 1395 by Mir Sayed Ali Hamadni. The original building was destroyed by fire and the current wooden structure dates back to the 1730s. The entrance is worth seeing for its exquisite papier-mâché work and woodcarving, but non-Muslims are not allowed inside the actual shrine. However, there is a women's section at the rear which female non-Muslims can enter and you can linger by the doorway with devotees, peeping inside to see the richly painted walls and chandeliers. Facing Shah-i-Hamdan, across the river is the limestone **Pathar Masjid** (1623), built for the Empress Nur Jahan and renamed Shahi Mosque.

Further up the river, on the same side as Shah-i-Hamdan, lies the 15th-century bulbous brick **Badshah Tomb of Zain-ul-Abidin's mother** ① *daily 0900-1700*, which is embellished with glazed turquoise tiles. The tomb adjoins a graveyard, containing the sultan Zain-ul-Abidin's grave and those of his wives and children, enclosed by an old stone wall that has been reused from an earlier Hindu temple. The area, Zaina Kadal, is interesting to walk around; carved copperwork is still produced here and you can see the craftsmen at work. It's the best place to buy your souvenir samovar.

Dachigam National Park

22 km east, past the Shalimar gardens.

This national park is home to the endangered Hangul deer as well as black and brown bears, leopards, musk deer and various migratory birds. Permits and further information about the best time to see the wildlife can be obtained from the TRC in Srinagar.

Listings Srinagar *map p490*

Tourist information

Tourist Reception Centre (TRC)
Residency Rd, T0194-245 2691,
www.jktourism.org. Open 24/7.
Houses the state department of tourism, the **Jammu and Kashmir Tourism Development**
Corporation (JKTDC) (T0194-2457927, http://jktdc.co.in), and **Adventure Tourism** for booking accommodation and tours. Also within the complex is the **J&K State Transport Corporation** (T0194-245 5107) for bus tickets. You can pick up an excellent map showing both the city and the whole state at the TRC.

Where to stay

Hotels on the Boulevard are popular – particularly with Indian tourists – but tend to be huge, impersonal and overpriced. The Uptown area is good to stay in if you are interested in exploring the city and prefer to be away from the tourist rush. There are also some houseboats on the Jhelum River, with walk-on/walk-off access. You can hear the noise of the traffic from these boats, but there are no hawkers.

Hotels around Dalgate tend to offer more budget options and can be very enjoyable. Those on the lakeshore just opposite the Boulevard (eg **Akbar**) are a good choice, as the area is interesting and there is less hassle from Shikara-men. The room costs quoted reflect peak-season prices (Mar-Aug); if you go in the winter, you can expect to get a hefty discount. Be prepared to haggle.

$$$$ Broadway
Maulana Azad Rd, T0194-245 9001, www.hotelbroadway.com.
One of Srinagar's best-known hotels, the Broadway's original 1970s interior has been well maintained. With lots of wood panelling, rooms can be a little dark. Staff are professional and polite, while the comfortable, centrally heated rooms and city location make it popular with business travellers and journalists. It houses one of the city's few drinking spots, has an outdoor pool and is attached to the city's first coffee shop, **Café Arabica**. Book online for discounts.

$$$$ The Lalit Grand Palace
Gupkar Rd, T0194-250 1001, www.thelalit.com.
This former palace was the residence of Kashmir's last maharajah, Hari Singh. Situated on a hillside overlooking Dal Lake, it has been tastefully kitted out with antiques befitting its history, including India's largest handmade carpet. One wing houses enormous, classically styled suites, while the other has 70 modern rooms. The restaurant, bar and health club are open to non-guests. It's a good place to go on a summer evening for the alfresco buffet.

$$$$ Vivanta by Taj – Dal View
Kralsangri Hill, Brein, T0194-246 1111, www.vivantabytaj.com.
All-out luxury in this sprawling elegant resort, atop a peak with sublime Dal Lake views. Rooms are chic without being over-the-top, with Kashmiri details and warm colours. 24-hr fitness suite, fantastic restaurants and spa. A gorgeous place, worth going for a meal if you can't afford a stay.

$$$ Ahdoo's
Residency Rd, T0194-247 2593, www.ahdooshotel.com.
A Srinagar institution, Ahdoo's backs onto the Jhelum river and is close to the city's classiest handicraft and shawl shops around Polo View. Deluxe rooms are huge with new TVs, while standard rooms are not much smaller, and all have marble bathtubs. Back rooms have river views. It's a good place to get a feel of the city, rather than the more touristy area around the lake. The restaurant is renowned for its Kashmiri (Wazwan) food, chicken patties, and their tea.

$$$ Dar-Es-Salam
Rainawari, T0194-242 7803, www.hoteldaressalam.com.
This white art deco ex-stately home is the only hotel on Nagin Lake, with an established garden and a sweep of lawn overlooking houseboats. Mounted heads over the entrance set the colonial tone, while period furnishings in the 2 lounges include brass antique pots and a Raj-era tiger's head. An enclosed balcony surveys the lake. There are modernized rooms (and **$$$$** suites), central heating, white duvets, and meals available in the (formal) dining room.

$$$-$$ Hotel Akbar
Dalgate, Gate No 1, T0194-250 0507, www.hotelakbar.com.
36 spacious rooms, some with balcony, arranged around a pretty lawn with rose arbours. Attractive lobby and restaurant and it's a great location on the lakeside; however, rooms are a little dated. Souvenir shop and travel desk.

$$ Hotel Madhuban
Gagribal Rd, T0194-245 3800, www.hotelmadhuban-kashmir.net.
The Madhuban has bags of character, with a lot of wood going on in its homely rooms. The restaurant has an attractive veranda where guests can sit out in the summer and there is a small but well-kept garden.

$$ Hotel Wali Sons
Boulevard Lane No 1, T0194-250 0345, http://www.walisonshotelsandresorts.com/boulevard.
A smart red-brick building, complemented by white window frames and green roof. The 17 spacious rooms have white duvets, flatscreen TV, fan, clean carpets and huge bathrooms with modern fixtures and decor. Central location, and some public balconies overlook Shankaracharya Hill. There's 24-hr electricity and respectful staff.

Houseboats are peculiar to Srinagar and can be seen moored along the busy shores of Dal Lake, the quieter and distant Nagin Lake and along the Jhelum River. They were originally thought up by the British as a ruse to get around the law that foreigners could not buy land in the state: being in the water, the boats didn't technically count as property. In the valley's heyday the boats were well kept and delightfully cosy; today, some are still lavishly decorated with antiques and traditional Kashmiri handicrafts, but others have become distinctly shabby.

Still mostly family-run, they usually include all meals and come in 5 categories: deluxe, A, B, C and D. The tariff for each category is given by the Houseboat Owners Association, www.houseboatowners.org, through whom you can also make bookings.

Most tourists enjoy their houseboat holidays; however, a significant number complain of being ripped off in various ways. It's better to spend extra on a boat with a good reputation than go for a bargain. If the deal sounds too good to be true, then it probably is and you will end up paying in other ways (ie by being coerced into shopping trips, from which your hosts will take a hefty commission). Try and find a boat with good references from other travellers, and look at sites such as www.tripadvisor.com. Also be aware that many boats in the Dal and Nagin lakes can only be accessed by *shikara*. While boat owners will always insist that a *shikara* will always be at your disposal, some tourists have found that this has not been the case and have found themselves marooned on boats with hosts they don't particularly like.

$$-$ Swiss Hotel
Old Gagribal Rd, T0194-2500115, www.swisshotelkashmir.com.
The Swiss has 35 clean rooms with attached bath and hot water (morning and evening) with greatly discounted rates for foreign tourists. The attractive red-painted old house has the best-value budget rooms in town. In the annex, prices increase as you go up to the 3rd floor, where rooms with coffee-table, sofa and numerous lamps are immaculate. There's a big garden. One of the few hotels with a stated environmental policy.

$ John Friends Guesthouse
Pedestrian Mall Rd (opposite Ghat No 1), Dalgate, T0194-245 8342.
Set back from Dal Lake, along walkways and gangplanks, is this family guesthouse with 9 rooms in 2 buildings. Flowery garden with seating, surrounded by poplars and willows, with fairy lights at night. Decent budget rooms, some with attached bath and TV, 24-hr hot water. A fascinating snapshot into life on the lake.

$ There's a backpacker-conscious enclave on the lake at Dalgate, where small and simple guesthouses include **Gulam Junaid** and **Noor Guesthouse**.

Houseboats
The following all quote **$$$$-$$**, but prices are generally negotiable if you go in person. See also box, above.

Athena Houseboats
Opposite Hotel Duke, Dal Lake, T(0)941 9063866, www.athenahouseboats.com.
One of the larger houseboat operators with voluminous boats that can comfortably sleep larger groups. Excellent service, with real integrity: discourages hawkers and tries to support only legitimate retail and onward tourism.

Butt's Clermont Houseboats
West side of Dal Lake, T0194-241 5325, www.buttsclermonthouseboat.com.
Moored by Naseem Bagh, 'Garden of Breezes', shaded by chinar trees, by a wall built by Emperor Akbar. Far from the densely packed south side of Dal Lake, 4 cream-painted boats feature crewelwork on fabrics, carved cedar panels, rosewood tables and a view of Hazratbal mosque. In operation since 1940, former guests include Lord Mountbatten, George Harrison, PG Wodehouse, Ravi Shankar and Michael Palin.

Gurkha Houseboats
Nagin Lake, http://welcomeheritagehotels.in.
The Gurkha group are renowned for their comfortable rooms and stylish boats on peaceful Nagin Lake. Good service and food.

Mantana
Dal Lake, Gate 2, T0194-250 1488, www.mantanatours.com.
A good choice to experience the old-style opulence of a traditional Kashmiri

houseboat. As well as the carefully preserved, sumptuous interiors, there is an ingeniously constructed floating garden. Owned and run by a reliable family.

Marguerite
The Bund, T0194-247 6699.
A charming boat with some lovely woodcarving. The trustworthy Thulla family are great fun and as the boat is moored to the river bank, guests can come and go as they please with no need to take a *shikara*.

Zaffer Houseboats
On Nagin Lake, T01954-250 0507, www.zafferhouseboats.com.
Deluxe boats with a long history, panelled walls, single-piece walnut tables, old writing desks, backed onto the lake which means the front terrace is delightful place to sit. Peaceful and quiet despite the *sikhara* salesmen. Excellent food, courteous staff and interesting owners.

Restaurants

While Kashmiris generally prefer to eat at home, being a tourist town, Srinagar has its fair share of good restaurants catering for all tastes. For a special treat, do the buffet at the Lalit Grand or a meal at the Taj Vivanta (with killer views). There are 3 wine shops on the left side of the ground floor of the Hotel Heemal building on the Boulevard.

Traditional Kashmiri food is centred around meat, with mutton generally being the favoured flesh. The traditional 36-course banquet served at weddings is known as a *wazwan* and you will find several of its signature dishes on the menu in restaurants. *Yakhnee* is a delicious mutton stew cooked in a spiced curd sauce. *Goshtabas* and *rishtas* are meatballs made from pounded (not ground) meat, which makes a big difference in consistency. *Goshtabas* come in a curd sauce; *rishtas* in red sauce. *Roganjosh* is made with chicken or mutton and is curd based, owing its colour to red Kashmiri chilies. *Hakh* is the Kashmiri version of spinach and *nadroo* are lotuses, usually served in a *yakhnee* sauce.

$$ Char Chinar
Boulevard Rd, near Brein village.
You'll need to take a *shikara* to get to this houseboat restaurant, moored on a tiny island in Dal Lake. Named after the 4 giant *chinar* trees

that grow there, the food is average, but it's a perfect place to sit in peace with a good book on a sunny day.

$$ Lhasa
Boulevard Lane No 2. Daily 1200-2230.
Enjoy the lovely back garden with rose bushes and well-spaced tables, each with its own awning; the central fountain is defunct, but old houses surround. The low-ceilinged indoor area has fish-tanks and is cosy on a cold night. They serve a varied menu of excellent Chinese, Tibetan, and Indian non-veg and veg food.

$$ Mughal Darbar
Residency Rd.
Popular with middle-class locals, the cosy Mughal Darbar offers multi-cuisine fare, specializing in Kashmiri *wazwan*. It's located on the 1st floor, up the stairs.

$$ Shamyana
Boulevard Rd, www.shamyana.net. Daily 1230-2230.
Consistently highly rated by locals and popular with middle-class customers, this restaurant serves high-quality Chinese and Indian food (meat and veg, good tikka). The calm front section is separated from a funkier back room by wooden lattices. Professional service.

$$-$ Café Robusta
Maulana Azad Rd, near Polo View.
Competes with nearby **Café Arabica** (in the Broadway Hotel) to attract Srinagar's latte lovers. Aside from pizza, kebabs and cake, you can also sample a *shisha* (Middle Eastern water pipe) with a range of flavoured tobaccos on offer. Bring your laptop and make use of the Wi-Fi.

$ Krishna Dhaba
Durga Nag Rd. Closed 1600-1900.
A haven for vegetarians in a city of meat-eaters, the Krishna's canteen environment gets the thumbs-up from fastidious Indian tourists for its cleanliness and delicious pure veg fare, the best in town.

$ Shakti Sweets and Modern Sweets
Residency Rd.
If you are invited to a Kashmiri home, a box of *burfi* will go down well as a gift. Both serve great snack food at rock-bottom prices, such as *channa bhatura* and *masala dosa*, as well as very popular chow mein.

ON THE ROAD

Kashmir handicrafts

Kashmir is deservedly famous for its distinctive and fine handicrafts. Many of these developed when Srinagar was a trading post on the ancient trans-Himalayan trade route. High-quality craftsmanship in India initially owed much to the patronage of the court and Kashmir was no exception. From the 15th century onwards, carpet making, shawl weaving and embroidery and decorative techniques were actively encouraged and the tradition grew to demands made at home and abroad. Since tourism has been severely affected in the Vale since 1989, Kashmiri tradesmen have sought markets in other parts of India.

Kashmir shawls are world renowned for their softness and warmth. The best are pashmina and shahtush, the latter being the warmest, the rarest and, consequently, the most expensive. Prized by Moghuls and maharajas they found their way to Europe and, through Napoleon's Egyptian campaign, became an item of fashion in France. The craft was possibly introduced from Persia in the 15th century. Originally a fine shawl would take months to complete especially if up to 100 colours were used. The soft fleece of the pashmina goat or the fine under hairs of the Tibetan antelope were used, the former for pashmina (cashmere) shawls, the latter for shahtush. The very best were soft and warm and yet so fine that they could be drawn through a finger ring. The designs changed over the years from floral patterns in the 17th century to Paisley in the 19th century. The Mughals, especially Akbar, used them as gifts. However, with the introduction of the Jacquard loom, cheap imitations were mass produced at a fraction of the price of hand woven shawls. Kashmiri shawls thus became luxury items, their manufacture remaining an important source of employment in the Vale, but they ceased to be the major export.

Hand-knotted carpets were traditionally made in either pure wool or mixed with cotton or silk. However, nowadays pure wool carpets are hardly produced in the valley, the preference being for silk. The patterns tend to the traditional, the Persian and Bukhara styles being common, though figurative designs such as The Tree of Life are becoming increasingly popular. A large carpet will take months to complete, the price depending on the density of knots and the material used, silk being by far the most expensive. The salesmen usually claim that only vegetable dyes are used and whilst this is true in some instances, more readily available and cheaper chemical dyes are commonplace. After knotting, the pile is trimmed with scissors, loose threads burnt off and the carpet washed and dried. Young boys work with a master and it is common to hear them calling out the colour changes in a chant. Child labour in carpet making across North India is increasingly widely criticized, but government attempts to insist on limiting hours of work and the provision of schooling are often ignored. Look for the rug mark awarded when no child labour is used.

Papier mâché boxes, trays, coasters make ideal gifts. Paper is soaked, dried in a mould, then painted and lacquered. Traditionally, natural colouring was used (lapis lazuli for blue, gold leaf for gold, charcoal for black) but this is unlikely today. The patterns can be highly intricate and the finish exquisite.

Other crafts include crewel work (chain stitching) on fabric, Kashmiri silver jewellery, silk and fine woodcarving, particularly on walnut wood.

Festivals

Apr Tulip Festival, Indira Gandhi Memorial Tulip Garden. 1st 2 weeks of Apr, with over 1 million blooms.

Shopping

If you arrived in Srinagar without your thermals or you're craving a bar of chocolate, a bowl of cornflakes, Marmite on toast or just about any other Western goods, then look no further than **Harker's Pick 'n' Choose Supermarket** on Residency Rd, for all your expat needs.

Books

Gulshan Bookstore, *a few mins' walk from Residency Rd, towards Lal Chowk*. Here you will find all manner of books about Kashmir, some of them extremely rare. It's an excellent place for books on Kashmir's history and the political situation.

Handicrafts

There are plenty of handicraft shops, particularly around Dal Lake and Dalgate, but beware of touts who are on commission. Much of what is sold is not even Kashmiri: inferior quality papier-mâché products from Bihar and shawls from Amritsar have flooded the market and are bought merrily by tourists who don't know the difference. As a result, along with the troubles of the past 25 years, the valley's handicraft industry has been tragically eroded. For a real understanding of Kashmiri craftwork and to support the local industry, call into any of the quality shops on **Polo View** or the **Bund**. The prices may seem high, but the quality and authenticity are guaranteed. Shopkeepers here are rather more restrained than the average Kashmiri salesman making it a pleasant place to wander around. See also box, opposite.

Asia Crafts, *next to Suffering Moses (see below)*. Very fine embroidery and genuine Kashmiri carpets, but much of its stock is now sold in New Delhi.

Habib Asian Carpets, *Zaldagar Chowk, Downtown, T0194-247 8640*. If you are serious about buying a genuine Kashmiri carpet, this is one of the few companies that has its workshop in the city.

Heritage Woodcrafts, *on the way to Shalimar gardens*. It's worth making the trip here for the carved walnut wood. Stuffed with fine pieces including some antiques, the authenticity of the work is guaranteed by the on-site workshop.

Kashmir Government Arts Emporium, *the Bund. Mon-Sat 1000-1800, closed for noon prayers*. In the old British Residency, a beautifully restored building with heritage gardens (and moth-eaten tigers lurking among the wares). Large showroom of fixed-price Kashmiri goods: rugs, papier mâché, crewel-work, furniture and more.

Suffering Moses, *next to Mughal Darbar restaurant*. Famous for its exquisite papier-mâché goods; really beautiful top-quality stock, and they ship overseas. The curious name was apparently awarded to the owner's father by the British, who were impressed by the amount of suffering that went into each work. **Sadiq's Handicrafts**

is owned by the same family and is almost as much a museum as a shop; many of the antique treasures are not for sale and Mr Sadiq, a man passionate about art, will happily explain their history to you. Prices in both shops are fixed and there is no pressure to buy.

Photography

Mahatta's Photographic Store, *next to Suffering Moses (see above). Mon-Sat 1030-1830*. Worth a visit for its old-world charm, history and above all the priceless visual memory of old Srinagar it houses. Founded in 1918, this was once the place to have your portrait taken and was patronized by the elite of the day. The walls are lined with large prints of the city, taken up in the 1930s and 1940s. They are not for sale, but they have produced a booklet, Srinagar Views 1934-1965, and sell black and white postcards, and books.

Transport

Air Srinagar Airport, 14 km south. Taxi to town: Rs 500-600. Stringent security checks on roads plus 2 hrs' check-in at airport. Tight on hand luggage but you can generally get away with a laptop. Daily flights to **Delhi** and **Mumbai**; 1 direct flight per week to **Leh** with Air India.

Bus J&KSRTC, TRC, Srinagar, T0194-245 5107. Summer 0600-1800, winter 0700-1700. To **Kargil** (alternate days in summer), **Leh** (434 km). **Gulmarg**, daily bus at 0800 in ski season from TRC, returning in the evening. Taxis charge around Rs 3000 for same-day return. Or take **J&KSRTC** bus to **Tangmarg**, 8 km before Gulmarg and a *sumo* from there. To **Pahalgam** at 0830 (2-3 hrs).

Jeep Jeeps are faster than the bus and leave when full from various locations near Dalgate. To **Jammu**, 8-9 hrs. To **Yusmarg**, 2 hrs, at 1400. Shared jeeps to **Charar-i-Sharief**, 1 hr, leave when full from Iqbal Park, in west Srinagar.

Train The nearest railhead is **Jammu Tawi**.

Gulmarg

Some 56 km west of Srinagar, Gulmarg (altitude 2650 m) attracts a colourful mix of characters, from the off-piste powder-addict adventurers who stay for months to the coachloads of Indian tourists. Three times host of the country's annual Winter Games and India's premier winter sports resort, it is one of the cheapest places in the world to learn to ski, although there are only a few beginners' runs.

The season runs from December to April (best in January-February), and equipment is available for hire for around Rs 500 a day. Check with **Gulmarg J&K Tourism** ① *T01954-254 439*, about opportunities for heli-skiing. Outside the winter season, Gulmarg is a popular day trip from Srinagar, with pony rides, walks and the world's highest green golf course being the main attractions.

The resort is served by three ski lifts and boasts the world's second highest **gondola** ① *daily 1000-1800, Rs 600/800 return*, which stops at the Kangdori mid-station before rising up to Apharwat Top (4000 m), from where you can ski the 5.2 km back to Gulmarg. Or in summertime, it's fun to take the cable car up to the top, then get off halfway back, to walk down the remaining distance (take a picnic). Be prepared for pushy touts and pony-men when trying to buy your ticket; unfortunately, the gondola system is chronically mismanaged.

Charar-i-Sharief

From Srinagar it's a scenic one-hour drive to Charar-i-Sharief (27 km), the last 10 km of road climbing through orchards and vales of willow. Spread over a series of ridges, the colourful roofs of modern houses date from a fire in 1995, when most of the town was burnt down – including the famed 700-year-old wooden **shrine and mosque** – during a battle between militants and Indian troops. The complex is now rebuilt as a grand tiered pagoda with carved walnut-wood screens. Entombed here is Sheikh Noor-u-Din Noorani, one of many names given to the great Sufi poet, seer, philosopher and saint who died in 1438. He preached peace, tolerance and non-violence, and his shrine attracts thousands of visitors both Muslim and Hindu. It's possible to combine a visit to the shrine and a day-trip to **Yusmarg** (45 minutes away); or there's a nice J&K bungalow on the edge of town, should you get stranded.

Yusmarg

A rolling meadowland 47 km southwest of Srinagar, surrounded by conifer forests and snowy peaks, Yusmarg (altitude 2400 m) is an up-and-coming tourist spot for Indian day-trippers. Pony rides are popular, and you will probably be inundated by horsemen on arrival (a board shows official rates). Views over **Nilnag Lake** are a pleasant one-hour walk (or pony ride) through undulating forest. The walk to **Doodh Ganga** river takes 30 minutes through the meadows; you can link Doodh Ganga and Nilnag for a longer day-trek. There's a tourist reception centre and JKTDC have huts and cottages (or locals will offer you cheaper accommodation); there are a couple of very simple eateries near the jeep stop.

Pahalgam

Ninety kilometres southeast of Srinagar, Pahalgam (altitude 2133 m), meaning 'village of shepherds', is the main base for the yearly **Amarnath Yatra** pilgrimage, which sees thousands of Hindu pilgrims climbing to a cave housing an 'ice lingam'. During the Yatra season, which runs from June to August, it gets very busy. Situated at the convergence of two dramatic river valleys, the town is surrounded by conifer forests and pastures.

Central Pahalgam is packed with shawl shops, eateries and hotels; there's a striking mosque and some pleasant parks (one of which surrounds the Pahalgam Club). The pointy-roofed **Mamleshwar Temple**, across Kolahoi stream, is devoted to Shiva.

There are many short walks you can take from Pahalgam and it is also a good base for longer treks to the **Suru Valley** and **Kishtwar**. A good day walk is the 12 km up the beautiful Lidder Valley to Aru; from there you can continue on to to **Lidderwat** (22 km) and **Kolahoi Glacier** (35 km). A wide selection of accommodation caters for all budgets; some of the best options are a couple of kilometres up the valley from the town centre.

Sonamarg

Literally meaning the 'golden valley', Sonamarg – 84 km northeast of Srinagar – gets its name from the yellow crocus blooms that carpet the valley each spring. At an altitude of 2740 m, it's the last major town in Kashmir before the Zoji La Pass – the gateway to Ladakh. Mountains and blankets of pine trees surround the village, and Indian tourists make pony trips to nearby **Thajiwas glacier**. It's also a start/end point for the **Amarnath Yatra** ⓘ *www.amarnathyatra.org*. The area is highly regarded for its trekking and fishing; trout were introduced here by the British in the 19th century.

Treks to high-altitude Himalayan alpine lakes, including Vishnasar (4084 m), Krishnasar (3810 m), Satsar, Gadsar, and Gangabal (3658 m), take eight days; the trekking season runs from July to October. Accommodation is available through JKTDC (see below) in the summer months and there are several hotels.

Listings Around Srinagar

Where to stay

Gulmarg

As with Srinagar, prices can be negotiated in the winter months, particularly for longer stays.

$$$$ Khyber Himalayan Resort & Spa
T01954-254666, khyberhotels.com.
Absolute luxury in a new resort with an Ayurvedic spa, gym, heated pool and amazing restaurants. Rooms are beautifully furnished with teak floors, silk carpets, walnut carving and rich Kashmiri fabrics. There are state-of-the-art bathrooms, while huge windows make the most of views. Also 4 cottages, some with own pool.

$$$ Hotel Highlands Park
T01954-254430, www.hotelhighlandspark.com.
Oozing with old-world charm, rooms and suites are decorated with Kashmiri woodcraft and rugs. Renowned for its atmosphere – the best bar in Gulmarg is here, a large yet cosy lounge, straight out of the 1930s – it's a wonderful place to unwind after a hard day on the slopes. Rooms have *bukharis* (wood stoves) to keep you warm and electric blankets are available on request. Also recommended for the food.

$$$ Nedou's Hotel
T01954-254428, http://nedoushotelgulmarg.com.
The oldest hotel in Gulmarg, the **Nedou's** has the same cosy colonial charm as **Highlands Park**. Its rooms and suites are comfortingly old-fashioned, with spotless bathrooms. The food isn't flash, but it's home-cooked, wholesome and delicious.

$$ Hotel Yemberzal
T01954-254523, www.yemberzalhotel.com.
Rooms are on the small side, but at least this means they heat up quickly. Each has its own gas heater and the bathrooms have 24-hr running hot water. If you ask for the corner room, you can enjoy a panoramic view of the mountains. The restaurant is excellent and the management are extremely helpful. It's a 10-min walk to the lifts, but there's a taxi stand next door if you feel lazy.

$$-$ Green Heights
T01954-254404.
This wood-built hotel is slightly shabby, but the quirky staff more than compensate, making this a budget choice with character. The decent-sized rooms come with wood stoves and if you ask nicely, you might get a hot-water bottle. Close to the gondola.

$$-$ JK Tourism Huts
T(0)9419-488181, http://jktdc.co.in.
These comfortable huts come with 1-2 bedrooms, a living room and kitchen. Very good value and close to the drag-lift.

$ Raja's
T(0)9797-008107.
Buried in the woods, **Raja's** colourful shack consists of 3 rooms with shared bath and can accommodate up to 9 people. Popular with long-stayers.

Yusmarg

$$-$ J&KTDC Huts
T(0)9797-292001, http://jktdc.co.in.
Dotted around the centre of Yusmarg's meadow, connected by flagged paths, these comfortable huts are well-maintained and fresh, if simple. There are various configurations, some with pine walls, others whitewashed with pretty bedspreads, so check them all out. Basic doubles Rs 750; 30% discounts low-season.

Pahalgam

$$$$ Pahalgam Hotel
T01936-243252, www.pahalgamhotel.com.
Upper-end Raj-era hotel dating back to 1931,
4 buildings, with 36 of the 40 rooms enjoying
splendid views of forested peaks across the
River Lidder. Rooms are tasteful, centrally heated
and very spacious. Some have been recently
renovated but all are pleasing (18 suites). The
pool is open in summer. Prices include all meals.
There's an excellent shop (see Shopping, below).

$$-$ Brown Palace
T01936-243255, www.brownpalace.in.
A decent option with a range of rooms; all have
attached bath with hot water. Wood panelling
abounds, the lounge has bark walls and a fire,
and there are 2 newer bungalows with living
rooms at the rear.

$$-$ Himalaya House
*3 km from the bus stand, 1 km from Laripora
village, T01936 243072, http://himalayahouse.in.*
A cosy hotel on the river with an enchanting
island garden and a restaurant of repute. All
rooms have attached bath and hot water, some
with tubs and balcony, attractive crewelwork
curtains and bedspreads. The comfortable lobby
has a fireplace and is a good place to make
friends. Free Wi-Fi. Cheaper older rooms are in a
house across laneway. They can organize good
tours and treks.

Sonamarg

$$ Snow Land Resorts
Mammar, www.snowlandresorts.com.
This is a good choice, well managed with cosy
wood-panelled rooms. Those at the back are
quieter and have great mountain views, but
the vegetarian restaurant is merely average.

Restaurants

Gulmarg
Most hotels serve their own food but some close
their kitchens in low season. In the bazar there is
a row of *dhabas* serving a wide variety

of Indian vegetarian food including *thalis*, *dosas*
and *Punjabi*, with outside seating.

$$ Sahara Hotel
Next to Yemberzal Hotel.
Well worth venturing out in the cold for. The
owner spent 15 years working as a chef in
Saudi Arabia, Japan and China, so has a wide
repertoire. If you need a break from Indian food,
the continental choice here is good, especially
the chicken champion.

$ Lala's
*Close to the JK Tourism Huts
(see Where to stay, above).*
Good, honest home-cooked food.

Pahalgam
$$$-$ Trout Beat restaurant and the welcoming
Café Log Inn, both at the Pahalgam Hotel. Serve
the same menu of vegetarian meals and snacks
and, of course, fish.

$ Nathu's Rasoi
Open 0800-2230.
You can't miss this self-service fast-food
vegetarian restaurant near the bus stand,
which serves excellent Indian and Chinese
dishes – most famed for its South Indian,
the best in Kashmir.

Shopping

Pahalgam
Almirah Books etc, *at Pahalgam Hotel.* An
average book selection and some tasteful
souvenirs. Also sell 'Shepherd's Craft' goods:
brightly decorated bags/purses, embellished
with the traditional designs of the Bakkarwala
nomadic shepherds (who embroider saddlebags
and hats with colourful threads).

Transport

Yusmarg
Jeep To Batmulla bus stand, **Srinagar**, at 0800
(2 hrs). Or go via Charar-i-Sharief (last *sumo* from
Yusmarg 1630).

Kargil

On the bank of the River Suru and with a largely Shi'ite population, Kargil (population 119,307, altitude 2704 m) has a very different vibe to both Srinagar and Leh. The town is considered grim by most visitors; however, it is the main overnight stop on the Srinagar–Leh highway and provides road access to the Zanskar Valley.

Kargil was an important trading post on two routes, from Srinagar to Leh, and to Gilgit and the lower Indus Valley. In 1999 the Pakistan army took control briefly of the heights surrounding the town before being forced to retreat.

Centred around the busy main bazar are cheap internet cafés (unreliable), ATMs and plenty of hotels (see page 502). There is a **tourist office** ① *behind the bus station, T01985-232721, Mon-Sat 1000-1600*. Walking up the valley slope, perpendicular to the main bazar, takes you past old village houses to finish at Goma Kargil (4 km) for excellent views.

Suru Valley

The motorable road extends from Kargil south to Padum through the picturesque and relatively green Suru Valley, where willow trees dot a wide valley floor flanked by mountain ridges. The valley's population has been Muslim since the 16th century, but some ancient Buddhist monuments remain.

The first (and largest) settlement is **Sankoo**, 42 km from Kargil, which has a 7-m rock-carved relief of the Maitreay Buddha and the ruins of Kartse Khar (a fort) 3 km distant. It's also a bus rest-spot and place to pick up last-minute supplies. The road continues 15 km to **Purtikchay**, a lonely spot with just a scattering of houses but with stunning views down to the **Nun-Kun** peaks. A further 10 km on is **Panikhar**, set in an attractive agricultural bowl of the valley and where a glacier and Nun-Kun frame the horizon.

From Panikar you can trek (a hard day) over the Lago La to Parkachik, or take pleasant strolls around the hamlet and the neighbouring village of Te-Suru. It is also possible to cross the mountains to Pahalgam in Kashmir from here, and you should be able to find local guides and ponies to make the one-week trek. The regular bus from Kargil terminates at **Parkachik**, after which is Rangdum and the Zanskar Valley (see below). There are J&K tourist bungalows at settlements along the Suru Valley (see page 502 for details).

Rangdum

Making a convenient night's stop between Kargil and the Zanskar Valley, 130 km from Kargil, halfway to Padum, Rangum (altitude 3657 m) sits on a plateau of wild and incredible beauty. The isolated **Rangdum Monastery** perched on a hillock is particularly striking, and two Buddhist villages surrounded by *chortens* lie nearby.

Zanskar *Colour map 1, A2/3.*

Zanskar is a remote area of Ladakh contained by the Zanskar range to the north and the Himalaya to the south. It can be cut off by snow for as much as seven months each year when access is solely along the frozen Zanskar River. This isolation has helped Zanskar to preserve its cultural identity, though this is now being steadily eroded; a road is being currently being constructed to link Padum with Nimmu, on the Kargil–Leh highway.

Traditional values include a strong belief in Buddhism, frugal use of resources and population control: values which for centuries have enabled Zanskaris to live in harmony with their hostile yet fragile environment. The long Zanskar Valley was 'opened' up for tourism even later than the rest of Ladakh and quickly became popular with trekkers. There is river rafting on the Zanskar River, with trips up to 11 days. For trekking, see pages 39 and 517.

Padum ① *No permit needed.* About 40% of Padum (population 1300), the capital of Zanskar, are Sunni Muslim. The present king of the Zanskar Valley, Punchok Dawa, who lives in his modest home in Padum, is held in high regard. The ruined old town, palace and fort are 700 m from the rather uninspiring new town, which has transport, guesthouses and internet. Access is by the jeep road over the **Pensi La** (4401 m), generally open from mid-June to mid-October with a twice weekly bus service from Leh via Kargil (highly unreliable and crammed); the alternative method is to trek in. There is accommodation available (see Where to stay, below).

Listings Kargil to the Zanskar Valley

Where to stay

Kargil

Hotels are quite expensive, but bargaining is expected. On Hospital Rd, running uphill just off the Main Bazar, there's a further cluster of budget hotels (not listed here). Restaurants all serve meat; for vegetarian food look for signs advertising Punjabi meals. There's a little dairy outlet selling superb *lassi* near the J&K ATM off the Main Bazar (it's locally famous, ask around).

$$ Green Land
Signed down an alley off Main Bazar, T01985-232324, www.hotelgreenlandkargil.com. Open all year round.
A popular and well-kept place, it's not cheap but prices reflect the standard of the rooms. Old block doubles are much cheaper, but the new block is much preferable with a range of rooms.

$$ PC Palace
Off Main Bazar, T(0)9906356533, http://hotelpcpalacekargil.com.
Smart building with well-appointed rooms with flatscreen TV, fawn carpets, blankets and curtains, fancy lights and good bathrooms. Slightly smaller, darker rooms are at the rear, but they are also cheaper and quieter.

$ Tourist Marjina
Off Main Bazar, T09419-831517.
An ageing pink- and blue-painted building that is being encircled by high new hotels, making dark rooms even darker. It's a bearable budget option though, with reliable hot showers.

Suru Valley

J&K tourist bungalows, costing around Rs 200 per person, are found in villages along the Suru Valley. Sankoo also has plenty of shops and several *dhabas*, while the **Tourist Bungalow** in Panikhar enjoys remarkable views of Nun and Kun, but is isolated (take supplies). In Panikhar, the **Dak Bungalow** has 3 gloomy rooms and a better choice is **$ Khayoul Hotel** (T(0)9469-293976), with 2 sunny rooms in a family house, decked with cheerful fabrics and plants, meals are cheap.

Padum
Places to stay are limited, but there is a choice of 4 simple lodges. There is also a **tourist complex** with basic rooms and meals; you can camp there.

$ Ibex
Has the best rooms in town, a decent restaurant and a courtyard garden.

What to do

Most agents in Leh can arrange trekking expeditions to the Zanskar Valley.
Aquaterra Adventures, *www.aquaterra.in.* Have 12-day rafting trips down the Zanskar River every Aug.

Transport

Kargil
Bus To **Leh** at 0430 (7 hrs); to **Srinagar** at 2230-2300, some are deluxe (9 hrs). Buses to the Suru Valley leave from the crossroads of Main Bazar and Lal Chowk, to **Panikhar** daily at 0700 (4 hrs; return bus at 0600, 0800 and 1100) and to **Parkachik** at 1130 on alternate days (5 hrs, returning at 0700).

Jeep Shared jeeps to **Srinagar** leave from taxi stand on Lal Chowk, connected to the bus station by an alleyway, at 0400-0600 and 1300-1500 (6 hrs). Shared jeeps to **Leh** (7 hrs).

one of the most fascinating journeys in the world

The road to Leh from Srinagar negotiates high passes and fragile mountainsides. There are dramatic scenic and cultural changes as you go from verdant Muslim Kashmir to ascetic Buddhist Ladakh.

When there is political unrest in Kashmir, the route, which runs very close to the Line of Control, may be closed to travellers. For more on the political situation, see box, page 486. For details about the monasteries and villages along the way, see page 517. The alternative route to Leh from Manali is equally fascinating, see page 453.

The route

After passing through **Sonamarg**, you reach the pass of **Zoji La** (3528 m). The pass is slippery after rains and usually closed by snow during winter months (November to April). From Zoji La the road descends to **Minamarg meadow** and **Dras** (3230 m). The winter temperatures have been known to go down to -50°C, and heavy snow and strong winds cut off the town. **Dras** has a spectacular setting and a scruffy centre with restaurants and shops; there's a TIC and decent enough J&K bungalows. The broad Kargil basin and its wide terraces are separated from the Mulbekh Valley by the 12-km-long **Wakha Gorge**.

From **Kargil** (see page 501) the road continues 30 km to **Shargol** – the cultural boundary between Muslim and Buddhist areas, with a very atmospheric and very tiny monastery located down a side-road – and then after another 10 km reaches **Mulbek**, a pretty village with a large (9 m) ancient Maitreya Buddha relief fronted by a *gompa* on the roadside. The ruins of **Mulbek Khar** (fort) sit atop a stalk of cliff next to two small *gompas*, a steep climb with fabulous views. Shortly after Mulbek is its larger sister village of **Wahka**, then the road crosses **Namika La**, at 3720 m (known as the 'Pillar in the Sky'). There is a tourist bungalow in tiny **Haniskut**, set in a pretty river valley marred by roads and pylons, where a very ruined fort lies on the northern side of the valley. The road then climbs to **Fotu La** at 4093 m, the highest pass on the route. From here you can catch sight of the monastery at Lamayuru. The road does a series of loops to descend to the ramshackle village of **Khaltse** with a couple of garden-restaurants, shops and lodges, where it meets the milky green Indus River.

Lamayuru, 10 km from Khaltse, with a famous monastery and spectacular landscapes, is worth a long lunch break or overnight stop (see Where to stay, below). There is a comfortable eco-camp in **Uletokpo**, just by the highway (see page 521). From Uletokpo village a 6-km track leads to dramatic **Rizong**, with a monastery and nunnery, which sometimes accommodate visitors. **Saspol** village marks the wide valley from which you can reach **Alchi** by taking a branch road across the Indus after passing some caves. **Lekir** is off the main road, 8 km after Saspol.

Further along the road you catch sight of the ruins of **Basgo** before it crosses the Chargyal Thang plain with *chortens* and *mani* walls and enters **Nimmu**. The road rejoins the Indus Valley and rises to a bare plateau to give you the first glimpse of Leh, 30 km away. **Phyang** is down a side valley, and finally **Spituk** is reached.

Listings Srinagar to Leh road

Where to stay

Mulbek

$ Karzoo Guesthouse
T(0)9419-880463.
In an impressive old Ladakhi building, with restaurant and camping space, conveniently located for walking to the monastery; all rooms share clean bathrooms, and the family are very hospitable. There are also a couple of other simple guesthouses and a J&K Tourist Bungalow. In Wahka, the sister village 3 km on the road towards Leh, there are a few *dhabas* and shops.

Ladakh

The mountains of Ladakh – literally 'many passes' – are not typical of the high Himalaya: the summits are often only 3000 m higher than the valleys, which themselves lie at an altitude of 3500 m. Because it is desert, there is little snow on the peaks, and they look like big brown hills, dry and dusty, with clusters of willows and desert roses along the streams. Bright blue skies are an almost constant feature, as the monsoon rains do not reach here, and the contrast with the dramatic landscape creates a beautiful and heavenly effect. For thousands of visitors Ladakh is a completely magical place, remote and relatively unspoilt, with delightful, gentle, ungrasping people.

Essential Ladakh

Finding your feet

Ladakh (population 280,000) is entirely mountainous. The mountains range from 2500 m to 4500 m, with passes from 4000 m to 6000 m, and peaks up to 7500 m. The main road routes to the capital, Leh, are from Srinagar in the west and Manali in the south, although for much of the year, the only access is by air.

Protected Area Permits (PAPs)

Foreign tourists require a **PAP** to visit the Nubra Valley, Dha-Hanu villages, Tso-moriri and Pangong Tso, for a maximum of seven days in

Tip...

Carry your passport with you because Ladakh is a sensitive border region. It's also worth carrying multiple photocopies of your passport and permits, as some checkpoints demand a copy.

each place. Permits are available from the District Commissioner's office in Leh (T01982-252010); you'll need to take your passport, and photocopy your visa and personal details pages, along with two photos. But all trekking/travel agents can also arrange them for you, which is a much easier option. Allow at least half a day for an agent to obtain a permit, officially given only for groups of two or more (although solo travellers rarely experience problems). Permits are not extendable, but can be post-dated. Many people opt for permits covering all restricted areas.

When to go

The temperature can drop to -30°C in Leh and Kargil and -50°C in Dras, remaining sub-zero from December to February. Yet on clear sunny days in the summer, it can be scorching hot and you can easily get sunburnt; take plenty of sun cream. Ladakh lies beyond the monsoon line so rainfall is only 50 mm annually and there are even occasional dust storms.

BACKGROUND

Ladakh

Until recently Ladakhi society has generally been very introverted and the economy surprisingly self-sufficient. An almost total lack of precipitation has meant that cultivation must rely on irrigation. The rivers have been harnessed but with difficulty as the deep gorges presented a problem. Altitude and topography determine the choice of crop and farming is restricted to the areas immediately around streams and rivers. Barley forms the staple food. Apricots are one of the most popular fruits and are dried for winter sustenance, while the kernel yields oil for burning in prayer lamps.

Livestock is precious, especially the yak which provides meat, milk for butter, hair and hide for tents, boots, ropes and dung for fuel. Goats, especially in the eastern region, produce fine *pashm* for export. Animal transport is provided by yaks, ponies, Bactrian camels and the broad-backed *hunia* sheep. The Zanskar pony is fast and strong and used for transport and for the special game of Ladakhi polo. Travellers venturing out of Leh are likely to see villagers using traditional methods of cultivation with the help of *dzos* and donkeys and using implements that have not changed for centuries.

Cut off from the outside world for six months a year, Ladakh also developed a very distinct culture. Polyandry (where a woman has more than one husband) was common but many men became *lamas* (monks) and a few women *chomos* (nuns).

Most people depended on subsistence agriculture but the harsh climate contributed to very high death rates and a stable population. That is rapidly changing. Imported goods are now widely available and more and more people are taking part in the monetary economy. Ladakh and its capital Leh have been open to tourists since 1974, and some feel there are now far too many; the pitfalls of modern society are all too evident in the mounds of plastic rubbish strewn along the roadsides.

The population of Leh has increased by more than five times in the last decade, and during the summer months tourists descend in numbers that equal the local population. In winter, those who can, leave for the plains, so this is when a more traditional Leh experience can be had, if you can bear the cold and the inconvenience.

Leh *Colour map 1, A3.*

magical kingdom surrounded by mountains, palaces and stupas

Mysterious dust-covered Leh (population 147,104, altitude 3500 m) sits in a fertile side valley of the Indus, about 10 km from the river. Encircled by stark awe-inspiring mountains with the cold desert beyond, it is the nearest experience to Tibet in India. The old Palace sits precariously on the hill to the north and looms over Leh.

The city developed as a trading post and market, attracting a wide variety of merchants from Yarkand, Kashgar, Kashmir, Tibet and North India. Tea, salt, household articles, wool and semi-precious stones were traded in the market. Buddhism travelled along the Silk Road and the Kashmir and Ladakh feeder, which has also seen the passage of soldiers, explorers and pilgrims, forerunners of the tourists who today contribute most to the urban economy.

Sights

The wide Main Bazar Street dating from the 1840s, which once accommodated caravans, has a colourful vegetable market where unpushy Ladakhi women sell local produce on the streetside while they knit or chat. Makeshift craft and jewellery stalls are dotted around, along with plenty of shops run by Kashmiri shopkeepers. The Old Town, mainly to the east of the Main Street, with its maze of narrow lanes, sits on the hillside below the palace and is worth exploring.

ON THE ROAD

Religion in Ladakh

In Ladakh, just under half the population are Lamaistic Buddhists. Most follow Mahayana Buddhism of the Vajrayana sect with a mixture of Bon animism and Tantric practices. The Red Hat Drukpa (or Kagyupa) sect of Tibetan monastic Buddhists enjoy royal patronage. The reformist Yellow Hat sect are Gelugpa Buddhists and, like the Dalai Lama, wear a yellow headdress with their maroon robes. The more ancient Nyingmapa Buddhists have their seat in Takthok.

Ladakhi *lamas* may also be physicians, teachers and astrologers; they also work in the fields, as do the *chomos* (nuns). Nearly every family has a member who chooses to become a *lama* (often the third son) or a *chomo*. The most important in the Tibetan tradition are recognized reincarnate *lamas* (Trulku), who are born to the position.

The Buddhist *gompas* (monasteries) are places of worship, meditation and religious instruction and the structures, often sited on spectacular mountain ridges, add to the attraction of the landscape while remaining a central part of Ladakhi life.

Ladakh also has a large number of Shi'a Muslims, mainly in Kargil District, many being immigrant Kashmiris and Dards. Their mosques and *imambaras*, influenced by Persian architecture, can be found in Leh proper and villages nearby.

The foundation of Sani in the 11th century is recognized as the first monastery in Zanskar. Phugtal and Karsha date from the same period. The sects developed alongside those in Ladakh. The Gelugpa (Yellow Hat) order was established in the 15th century and monasteries at Karsha, Lingshet and Mune belong to this. The Drukpa sect set up monasteries at Bardan and Zangla and 'occupied' that at Sani. These have links with Stakna near Leh and the Gelugpa is associated with the Lekir monastery. Traditional Ladakhi and Zanskari life, even today, comes close to Gandhi's idealized vision of life in ancient India.

Leh Palace ① *Sunrise to sunset, Rs 100.* Dun-coloured Leh Palace has been described as a miniature version of Lhasa's Potala Palace. Built in the mid-16th century, the palace was partly in ruins by the 19th century. It has nine storeys, sloping buttresses and projecting wooden balconies. From the town below it is dazzling in the morning sun and ghostly at night. Built by King Singe Namgyal and still owned by the royal family, it is now unoccupied – they live in the palace at Stok. Visible damage was caused during Zorawar Singh's invasion from Kashmir in the 1830s.

The palace is under restoration, with new window and door frames fitted, and structural improvements being made, but still be wary of hazardous holes in the floor. After a steep climb some find the palace disappointing, but the views from the roof are exceptional. Like the Lhasa Potala Palace it has numerous rooms, steps and narrow passages (take a torch). The central prayer room has religious texts lining the walls, and contains dusty deities and time-worn masks. The upper levels have some painted carved wooden lintels and old murals that give a hint of past splendours.

Central Asian Museum The new Central Asian Museum is housed in a beautifully constructed building in the Tsa Soma gardens, where camel caravans used to camp. The museum explores the history of the caravan trade that for centuries linked Ladakh, until its mid-20th century isolation, with Tibet, Afghanistan, Samarkand, Kashmir and other city states. The museum is shaped like a Ladakhi fortress tower, with four floors inspired by the architecture of Ladakh, Kashmir, Tibet and Baltistan. Exhibits, including metalware, coins and masks, reveal the cultural exchange throughout the region; a garden café and museum shop are planned.

A walking tour that includes the museum and visits restored buildings of the Old Town leaves from Lala's Art Café (see page 512) daily, 1000-1300.

Tsemo Gompa and Fort The 15th-century Tsemo Gompa ('Red' Temple) is a strenuous walk north of the city and has a colossal two-storey-high image of Maitreya, flanked by figures of Avalokitesvara (right) and Manjusri (left). It was founded in 1430 by King Graspa Bum-Lde of the Namgyal rulers and a portrait of Tashi Namgyal hangs on the left at the entrance.

Just above the *gompa* is **Tsemo Fort** ① *dawn-dusk, Rs 20*, the classic landmark above Leh which can be seen from miles around.

Leh Mosque ① *The inner section is not open to women visitors*. The striking Leh Mosque in the main bazar is worth visiting. The Sunni Muslim mosque is believed to stand on land granted by King Deldan Namgyal in the 1660s; his grandmother was the Muslim Queen of Ladakh.

Chokhang Gompa The Chokhang Gompa (New Monastery, 1957), off Main Bazar, was built to commemorate the 2500th anniversary of the birth of Buddha. The remains of the **Leh Gompa** houses a large golden Buddha.

Mani walls From the radio station there are two long *mani* walls. **Rongo Tajng** is in the centre of the open plain and was built as a memorial to Queen Skalzang Dolma by her son Dalden Namgyal. It is about 500 m long and was built in 1635. The stones have been meticulously carved. The other, a 350-m wall down the hill, is believed to have been built by Tsetan Namgyal in 1785 as a memorial to his father the king.

Sankar Gompa ① *3 km north of the centre, 0700-1000, 1700-1900, prayers at 1830 with chanting, drums and cymbals*. Sankar Gompa (17th-18th centuries) of the Yellow Hat Sect, is one of the few *gompas* built in the valley bottom; it's an enjoyable walk through fields from town. It houses the chief *lama* of Spituk and 20 others. The newer monks' quarters are on three sides of the courtyard with steps leading up to the *dukhang* (Assembly Hall). There are a number of gold statues, numerous wall paintings and sculptures including a large one of the 11-headed, 1000-armed *Avalokitesvara*. It's an atmospheric and beautiful enclave in the increasingly busy valley.

Shanti Stupa On Changspa Lane, across the stream from Sankar Gompa, you reach the start of the stiff climb up to the white Japanese **Shanti Stupa** (1989). This is one of a series of 'Peace Pagodas' built by the Japanese around the world. There are good views from the top where a café offers a welcome sight after the climb. There Is also a road which is accessible by jeep. Below the *stupa*, the **New Ecology Centre**, has displays on appropriate technology, as well as a handicrafts centre, a technical workshop and an organic vegetable garden.

Donkey Sanctuary ① *Korean Temple Rd, www.donkeysanctuary.in*. One kilometre past Shanti Stupa, the Donkey Sanctuary, opened in 2008. This charity looks after around 40 donkeys at any one time and is well worth a visit.

Ladakh Ecological Development Group ① *T01982-253221, www.ledeg.org, Mon-Fri 100-1800*. The Ecological Centre of LEDeG and the **craft shop** opened in 1984 to spread awareness of Ladakhi environmental issues, encourage self-

Essential Leh

Finding your feet

For seven to eight months in the year Leh is cut off by snow and the sole link with the outside world is by air. Tickets are in high demand so it is essential to book well ahead. From mid-June to the end of September (weather permitting) the Manali–Leh highway opens to traffic, bringing travellers to the New Bus Stand south of town. Taxis wait at both the airport and bus stand to take you to town.

Tip...
Given the darkness of many buildings in Leh, even at midday, it is worth taking a torch wherever you go. At night it is essential.

Getting around

Many hotels are within a few minutes' walk of the Main Bazar Street around which Leh's activities are concentrated. Most visitors prefer to stay on the outskirts of town, a short walk away, in guesthouses that have a more rural setting. All the places of interest in Leh itself can also be tackled on foot, though those arriving by air or from Manali are urged to acclimatize for 48 hours before exerting themselves. For visiting monasteries and spots out of town arrange a jeep or taxi, although there are some buses and hitchhiking is possible. See Transport, page 513.

Tip...
Use your own bags for shopping in Leh. Plastic bags are not allowed in the bazar, as they were finding their way into streams.

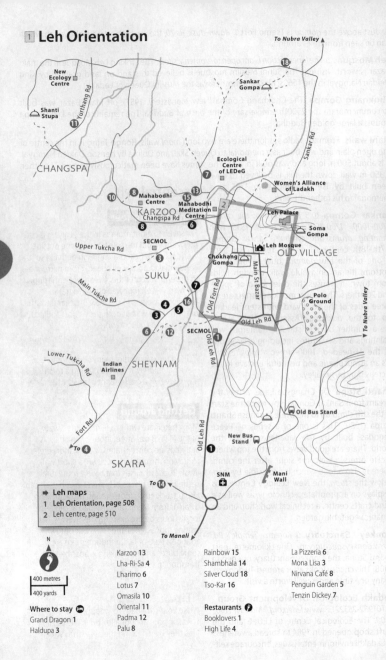

1 Leh Orientation

To Nubra Valley

New Ecology Centre

Shanti Stupa 11

Yurthang Rd

CHANGSPA

Sankar Gompa 18

Sankar Rd

Ecological Centre of LEDeG 7

Women's Alliance of Ladakh

10   8   Mahabodhi Centre
Mahabodhi Meditation Centre
15 13

KARZOO
Changspa Rd
8   6

Leh Palace

Soma Gompa

Leh Mosque

2

Upper Tuckha Rd   SECMOL
3

Chokhang Gompa

OLD VILLAGE

SUKU

Main Tuckha Rd
4   5   16
3
7

Old Fort Rd

Main St Bazar

Polo Ground

To Nubra Valley

6   12
SECMOL   1
Old Leh Rd

Old Leh Rd

Lower Tuckha Rd

Indian Airlines

SHEYNAM

Fort Rd
To 4

Old Leh Rd

Old Bus Stand

New Bus Stand

SKARA

Mani Wall

SNM

⮕ **Leh maps**
1 Leh Orientation, page 508
2 Leh centre, page 510

To 14

To Manali

N

400 metres
400 yards

Where to stay 🛏
Grand Dragon 1
Haldupa 3

Karzoo 13
Lha-Ri-Sa 4
Lharimo 6
Lotus 7
Omasila 10
Oriental 11
Padma 12
Palu 8

Rainbow 15
Shambhala 14
Silver Cloud 18
Tso-Kar 16

La Pizzeria 6
Mona Lisa 3
Nirvana Café 8
Penguin Garden 5
Tenzin Dickey 7

Restaurants 🍴
Booklovers 1
High Life 4

ON THE ROAD

Prepare for a different lifestyle in Leh

The whitewashed sun-dried brick walls of a typical two-storey, flat-roofed Ladakhi house, often with decorative woodwork around doors and windows and a carefully nurtured garden, look inviting to a traveller after a long hard journey. Many local families have opened up their homes to provide for the increasing demand for accommodation over a very short peak season, and new hotels are springing up everywhere.

On the whole, rooms are kept clean and the standard of budget hotels is better that you would expect elsewhere in India. There is usually a space for sitting out: a 'garden' with a tree or two, some flower beds and perhaps a vegetable patch.

Electricity is limited, so expect power cuts, which are random and unpredictable. Some hotels have generators. Those without may run out of tap water but buckets are always at hand. Hot water is a luxury, available only during mornings and evenings. Plumbing allows for flush WCs in most hotels, although compost toilets are the more ecological method. Guests are encouraged to economize on water and electricity; you will notice the low-power bulbs and scarcity of lights in rooms and public areas, so put away your reading material until sunrise.

help and the use of alternative technology. It has a library of books on Ladakhi culture, Buddhism and the environment. Handicrafts are sold, and you can refill water.

Women's Alliance of Ladakh (WAL) ① *Sankar Rd, Chubi, T01982-250293, www.womenalliance ladakh.org, video shown Mon-Sat 1500 (minimum 10 people)*. The Women's Alliance of Ladakh is an alliance of 5000 Ladakhi women, concerned with raising the status of traditional agriculture, preserving the traditionally high status of women and creating an alternative development model based on self-reliance for Ladakh. The centre has a café selling local and organic foods (see Restaurants, below), and a craft shop. They hold festivals, cultural shows, dances, etc, which are advertised around Leh; it's mainly aimed at local people, but all visitors are welcome.

Listings Leh *maps p508 and p510*

Tourist information

J&K Tourism
2 km south on Airport Rd, T01982-252297, www.jktourism.org, or a more convenient office on Fort Rd, T01982-253462, 1000-1600.

Where to stay

There are now scores of guesthouses, often in traditional Ladakhi homes. Outside the peak period expect discounts (as much as 25-50%). Those in Karzoo and Changspa (some way from the bus stand) are quieter and more rural. Many hotels and guesthouses close during the winter months. There is lots of budget accommodation along Fort Rd and in the Changspa area; some are very basic and you might want to use your own sleeping bag. But generally you can find a clean simple room without needing to book in advance. For eco-conscious homestays in Ladakh, see www.himalayan-homestays.com.

$$$$-$$$ Grand Dragon
Old Leh Rd, Sheynam, T01982-257786, www.thegranddragonladakh.com.
Big hotel with all mod cons, Wi-Fi and great views. Stunning dining room and a nod to eco-tourism with double glazing, underfloor heating and solar panels.

$$$ Lharimo
Fort Rd, T01982-252101, www.lharimo.com.
An attractive central hotel with scarlet window frames and a whitewashed exterior. The large comfortable rooms have traditional bamboo ceilings and inoffensive ageing wooden furniture, TV and clean tiled bathrooms. The big grassy lawn is perfect for relaxing.

$$$ Lha-Ri-Sa
Skara, T01982-252000, www.ladakh-lharisa.com.
With a boutique vibe, they offer stylish rooms and the outside of the building is simply beautiful. The restaurant serves up flavours from

all over India as well as traditional Ladakhi food. On the outskirts of town.

$$$ Lotus
Upper Karzoo, T01982-257265, www.lotushotel.in.
High-spec rooms with quality furniture, modern amenities, and a nod to traditional Ladakhi decor. 24-hr hot water, central heating and good multicuisine restaurant. The views from the flowery garden look straight onto the palace.

$$$ Shambhala
Skara, T01982-251100, www.hotelshambhala.com.
Large airy rooms, an excellent restaurant (often catering for German packages), breakfast included, very pleasant, friendly staff and lovely owners. Peaceful and away from crowds, with an

$$$ Tso-Kar
Fort Rd, T01982-253071, www.lehladakhhotel.com.
Very reasonably priced and well-maintained rooms. The bathrooms are a little old but clean, and there's TV and comfortable beds. Astroturf, flowers, and cane chairs and tables are in the courtyard.

$$$ Yak-Tail
Fort Rd, T01982-252118, www.hotelyaktail.com. May-Oct.
One of Leh's oldest hotels, comfortable and cosy (with decent heating). Some of the 30 rooms are 'houseboat style', others have balconies, some have lots of patterns. The restaurant is well-decorated with murals and serves good Indian food. The courtyard has been astro-turfed but swinging vines create a pleasing greenhouse effect.

$$ Omasila
Changspa, T01982-252119, www.hotelomasila.com.
A series of annexes around a pleasant back lawn, plus a huge terrace and ornate restaurant (serving their vegetables from the garden). Rooms have TV and wooden floors; it's worth paying a bit extra for the deluxe rooms with seating areas. All have decent tiled bathrooms and heating. Attracts a more mature clientele. Free Wi-Fi.

$$ Oriental
Below Shanti Stupa, T01982-253153, www.orientalguesthouse.com.
35 very clean rooms in a traditional friendly family home, with good home cooking served in the dining hall, great views across the valley, and reliable treks and travel arrangements.

$$ Shanti Guest House
Below Shanti Stupa, Changspa, T01982-253084, http://shantihome.co.in.
A guesthouse with well-heated rooms, most with great views. Excellent food, summer/winter treks arranged with guide and free Wi-Fi. Run by a friendly Ladakhi family.

$$ Tsomo-Ri
Fort Rd, T019822-252271, www.ladakhtsomori.com.
15 rooms arranged around a central whitewashed courtyard with trellises of runner beans running up the stairs. Surprisingly quiet, rooms have TV,

---

2 Leh centre

➤ **Leh maps**
1 Leh Orientation, page 508
2 Leh centre, page 510

N
Not to scale

Where to stay 🛏
Atisha **7**
Malpak **6**
Old Ladakh **4**
Tsomo-Ri **8**
Yak Tail **5**

Restaurants 🍴
Chansa Traditional
  Ladakhi Kitchen **6**
Chopsticks **2**
Lala's Art Café **9**
Mentokling Apple
  Garden **13**
Open Hand Espresso Bar **7**
Pumpernickel **10**
Shubh Panjabi Dhaba **14**
Tibetan Friend's Corner **12**

carpets, plain wood furniture, clean walls and plenty of good bedding. There are wicker chairs for relaxing in the courtyard.

$$-$ Padma Guesthouse & Hotel
Off Fort Rd down an alley, T01982-252630, www.padmaladakh.net.
Clean, charming rooms with common bath in a guesthouse in the old family home. Upstairs, including a rooftop restaurant, has mountain views, plus there are hotel-style rooms in the newer block. There's a beautiful and peaceful garden, a Buddhist chapel/meditation room, solar panels and a good library, but they are mostly known for their outstanding hospitality.

$$-$ Silver Cloud
By Sankar Gompa, 15 mins' walk from centre, T01982-253128, http://silvercloudguesthouse. blogspot.co.uk. Open during the winter months.
Ladakhi guesthouse with a rural homestay atmosphere offering a wide range of spotless rooms and dorm, run by a friendly helpful family. Free Wi-Fi, excellent food and a large garden.

$ Atisha
Malpak, off Fort Rd, T09906-992187, atisha_leh@rediffmail.com.
This place is not much to look at on arrival, but simple rooms are spotless with bright paint and shiny tiled bathrooms. Prices increase as you go up from ground to 3rd floor. The rooftop terrace is lovely, and although there's not much of an aspect it feels rural and a burbling brook surrounds. Very pleasant low-key family.

$ Haldupa
Upper Tukcha Rd, Malpak, T01982-251374.
Cheapest rooms in the old building share (smelly) bathrooms, hot buckets available, and a memorable shrine is in the same building. The new 2-level wing is swish and there's a delightful garden with plenty of seating. Organic food is available.

$ Karzoo
Karzoo Lane, T01982-252324.
The usual flowery garden; very cheap rooms with shared bath in an old Ladakhi house and modern clean rooms in the new annex (still waiting for the upper storey to be built), but very relaxed and helpful staff. Omelettes are served for breakfast. Recommended.

$ Malpak
Upper Tukcha Rd, Malpak, T01982-257380, dollayleh@yahoo.co.in.
Quaint 6-room guesthouse in an old building, all rooms with attached bath. Shady outdoor tables

next to a luxuriant flower and vegetable garden, and a convenient yet peaceful location. A recommended budget choice.

$ Old Ladakh
In the Old Town, T01982-252951.
8 rooms around an inner courtyard (varying in comfort), has bags of character with red lacquered windows and door frames, the odd cracked window and great views from top floor. Pleasant atmosphere (old-school vibes).

$ Palu Guest House
Changspa, T(0)9419-218674.
This sweet family home is secluded and set back from Changspa Rd. The spacious rooms have clean sheets, carpets and big windows; some have private bath and TV, others share a bathroom, all have working geysers. There's a particularly attractive flowery garden and veg patch, with shady seating.

$ Rainbow
Karzoo, T01982-252332, http://rainbowghleh.com.
Big clean rooms, some with wonderful views of mountains and Shanti Stupa, hot water in the morning, great hospitality, and lovely garden with restaurant. Rooms in the old house share baths, or the new wing has en suite ones.

Restaurants

$$ Chopsticks Noodle Bar
Fort Rd.
Great East Asian, Tibetan and regional food in a clean and attractive restaurant. Deservedly popular and worth at least one visit when in Leh.

$$ Penguin Garden
Just off Fort Rd.
Good garden café with a pleasant atmosphere, care of Nepali owners.

$$-$ Booklovers' Retreat
Changspa.
A perennial favourite as a cosy place for food and hanging out. There's a roof terrace.

$$-$ La Pizzeria
Changspa Rd, Changspa.
Pretty authentic pizza, very pleasant ambiance, some mattress seating, and soft lantern light at night.

$$-$ Mona Lisa
Fort Rd.
International food covers all bases (pizzas, *momos*, garlic cheese bread), and is particularly

recommended for the tandori selection. Lovely atmosphere under lamps on the terrace.

$$-$ Nirvana Café
Live music after 2100. Indoor and outdoor seating under lanterns and fairy lights, some Sinai-style slouching areas. Laid-back vibe and varied menu of South Asian, Asian and lots of Italian, prices slightly higher than average. No alcohol.

$$-$ Open Hand Espresso Bar & Bistro
Off Fort Rd, www.openhand.in.
A chic retreat, with loungers and seating on decking by a vegetable garden, chunky wood furniture inside, great cakes, cappuccinos and home-cooked meals, healthy smoothies and more. Ethical shopping – clothes, silks, cushions, gifts etc – plus Wi-Fi.

$ Chansa Traditional Ladakhi Kitchen
Next to Chokhang Vihara, off Main Bazar.
A chance to try traditional Ladakhi cuisine (vegetarian); simple indoor seating, or outside under the shade of a parachute. Whiteboard shows the day's dishes, such as *sku* – a delicious chunky wholewheat pasta and veg broth, plus limited offerings of Chinese, Indian (great mushroom masala) and Western food. Cheap and tasty.

$ High Life Tibetan Restaurant
Fort Rd.
Exceptional range of high quality Tibetan food, plus good salads and Western dishes, inviting indoor seating with gingham tablecloths or big outdoor area.

$ Lala's Art Café
Off Main Bazar, Old Town.
Quaint restored Ladakhi house in the Old Town with a roof terrace, and a shrine on the ground floor. Coffee and cakes are the order of the day.

$ Local Food Café
Mon-Sat 1100-1630.
Serves good Ladakhi snacks, while promoting traditional farming methods threatened by the modern cash economy, run by the Women's Alliance.

$ Mentokling Apple Garden
Changspa Rd, Zangsti.
Great *paratha* breakfasts, good menu generally, with Indian and Thai dishes. Lovely garden.

$ Shubh Panjabi Dhaba
Main Bazar.
Typical Sikh-style *thalis* and cheap dishes in a basic restaurant; half-plates available, great *lassis* and good *paratha* breakfasts.

$ Tenzin Dickey
Fort Rd.
Delicious *kothay* (fried *momos*), soups, and other Tibetan/Chinese dishes, some western food, all veg, and the Tibetan herbal tea is good. Simple and neat little place with checked tablecloths.

$ Tibetan Friend's Corner
Main St, Bazar.
Clean and cheerful, *kothay* and a wide menu of Tibetan/Chinese veg and non-veg, thick pancakes and great hot drinks, locally popular.

$ Also recommended are the kebab stalls near the mosque.

Bakeries
Several German bakeries sell good bread (trekking bread keeps for a week) and excellent cakes and muesli.
Pumpernickel, *Zangsti Rd.* The original German bakery is the best and friendliest, with indoor/outdoor seating, excellent apricot and apple crumble/pie and a message board for trekkers. There are also traditional ovens turning out delicious local bread in the lane next to the museum, behind the mosque.

Entertainment

Dancing and singing
Ladakhi dancing and singing, below entrance to the palace, by Soma Gompa, 1730 (1 hr), Rs 200.

Festivals

Dates vary depending on the lunar calendar.
Apr-May Buddha Purnima marks the Buddha's birth, at full moon.
Sep Ladakh Festival. The main events are held in the Leh polo grounds with smaller events in other districts. Usually during the first 2 weeks in Sep, there are dances, displays of traditional costumes, handicrafts, Ladakhi plays, archery and polo matches.
Dec Celebration of Losar which originated in the 15th century to protect people before going to battle.

Shopping

In **Dzomsa** you can get water bottles refilled, dispose of batteries, get laundry done and there are organic goods available. At the **Ecological Shop for Organic Products** you can stock up on local produce including apricot jam, fruit and nuts in season, and bottled juice.

Leh Bazar is full of shops and market stalls selling curios, clothes and knick-knacks. Tea and *chang* (local barley brew) vessels, cups, butter churns, knitted carpets with Tibetan designs, Tibetan jewellery, prayer flags, musical bowls and pashminas are all available. Prices are high especially in Kashmiri shops so bargain vigorously. There are tight restrictions on the export of anything over 100 years old. However, even though most items are antique-looking, they are, in fact, fresh from the backstreet workshops. If you walk down the narrow lanes, you will probably find an artisan at work from whom you can buy direct.

Books
Book Worm. Second-hand books, coffee table books and fiction.
Leh-Ling Bookshop, *near the Post Office, Main Bazar.* Good selection, especially on trekking in the region.

Tailors
There are many tailors lining Nowshara Gali.

What to do

Archery
The **Archery Stadium** is nearby where winter competitions attract large crowds; the target is a hanging white clay tablet.

Meditation
Mahabodhi Meditation Centre, *Changspa Lane, off Changspa Rd,* www.mahabodhi-ladakh.org. *Closed in winter.* Enquire about short courses and yoga classes. Also a centre in Chogsalmar, open all year.

Polo
Polo, the 'national' sport, is popular in the summer and is played in the polo ground east of the city. The local version which is fast and rough appears to follow no rules! The **Polo Club** is the highest in the world.

Tour operators
There are dozens of trekking agents in Leh town, and it's no problem to turn up in high season and get organized in a day or 2.

K2, *Hill Top Building, Main Bazar, T01982-253980,* www.k2adventureleh.com. Good rates for treks (Markha Valley); very friendly, environment conscious.
Rimo Expeditions, *Kang-lha Chen Hotel, T01982-253348,* www.rimoexpeditions.com. Insightful and informative about the local area, running a whole host of treks, as well as mountain biking, mountaineering, river rafting, cultural tours and family holidays.
Shakti Experiences, *Gurgaon, Delhi,* www.shaktihimalaya.com. Sensitively run sustainable tours and personalized treks to remote villages in the rugged high mountains. Luxurious but understated.
Yama Treks, *Leh, T01982-250833* www.yamatreks. com. Efficient, run by the very personable Mr Rinchen Namgial; cultural tours as well as treks.

Whitewater rafting and kayaking
Possible on the Tsarap Chu, Indus and Zanskar rivers from mid-Jun; the upper reaches of the former (Grade IV rapids) are suitable for experienced rafters only, though the remaining stretch can be enjoyed by all. Along the Indus: Hemis to Choglamsar (easy, very scenic); Phey-Nimmu (Grade III); Nimmu-Khaltse (professional). Ensure that life jackets and wet suits are provided. Half- to full-day trips possible, including transport and lunch.

Transport

Air The small airport is 5 km away on Srinagar Rd. It is surrounded by hills on 3 sides and the flight over the mountain ranges is spectacular. Transport to town by taxi is around Rs 200.

Allow 2 hrs for check in. Weather conditions may deteriorate rapidly even in the summer resulting in flight cancellations (especially outside Jul and Aug) so always be prepared for a delay or to take alternative road transport out of Ladakh. Furthermore, the airlines fly quite full planes into Leh but can take fewer passengers out because of the high-altitude take-off. This adds to the difficulty of getting a flight out. Book your tickets well in advance.

To Delhi daily, throughout the year (weather permitting). **Srinagar**, direct on Wed with **Air India**. For **Jammu**, connections via Delhi, or direct with **Air India** on Mon and Fri.

Bus Local buses leave from the **stand** near the cemetery. The vehicles are ramshackle but the fares are low. See under relevant monasteries for details of timings. Enquiries **J&KSRTC**, T01982-252285.

Long distance Leh is connected to Manali via Keylong and to Srinagar, via Kargil, by state highways. Both roads can be seriously affected by landslides, causing long delays. The Leh–Srinagar road is also often blocked by army convoys.

Himachal Tourism runs regular deluxe buses between Leh and Manali, 530 km, usually mid-Jun to end Sep. Book at HPTDC Office, 1st floor, Fort Rd, T(0)9622-374300, a/c Volvo, leaves alternate days at 0500 from opposite the J&K Bank, Fort Rd, overnight in Keylong. **J&K SRTC** run cheaper ordinary/deluxe buses, a gruelling journey departing at 0430, booked at bus stand, stop overnight at Keylong.

J&K SRTC bus to **Kargil**, 230 km, 0430, 10 hrs, bus to **Srinagar** 434 km, 0800 (and 1400 if passengers), overnight stop in Kargil.

Shared jeeps or **minibuses** Make the journey to **Manali** in 1 day, leaving at between 2400-0200 taking 22-24 hrs, costing about Rs 1800 per seat. Jeeps leave from the Old Bus Station, to **Srinagar** at 1700, 15 hrs; to **Kargil** at 0700, 8-9 hrs. Book seats a day in advance; it's worth paying extra for front seats.

The road to Manali This route crosses some very high passes and is open mid-Jun/Jul until late Sep (depending on the weather), taking 2 days by bus. Road conditions may be poor in places. Departure from Leh can be early (0400) with overnight stop in Keylong; next day to Manali. Alternatively, camp in Sarchu (10 hrs from Leh), or Jespa; next day 14 hrs to Manali. Roadside tents provide food en route during the tourist season; carry snacks, water and a good sleeping bag when planning to camp. Many travellers find the mountain roads extremely frightening and they are comparatively dangerous. Some are cut out of extremely unstable hillsides, usually with nothing between the road's edge and the near-vertical drop below; parts remain rough and pot-holed and during the monsoons, landslides and rivers can make it impassable for 2-3 days. It is also a long and uncomfortable journey, but there is some spectacular scenery. See also page 453.

Taxi Tourist taxi and jeep Ladakh Taxi Operators' Union, 1st floor at bus stand, T01982-252723, 0700-1900 daily, with fixed-rate fares. A day's taxi hire to visit nearby *gompas* can also be arranged through travel agents. Private 4WD between Leh and Manali is expensive, but recommended if you want to stop en route to visit monasteries on a 2-day trip.

Southeast of Leh *Colour map 1, A3.*

vast monastery complexes and tiny gompas within easy reach of Leh

South and east of Leh is an amazing stretch of road with some fascinating monasteries strung along it. Many of these make good day trips from Leh, and are possible excursions by bus and hitching. If you hire a car or jeep (which is good value when shared by four), you can see several places in a single day.

Choglamsar

The road between Leh and Choglamsar is now quite built up and at times clogged with traffic. On the east bank of the Indus, 7 km south of Leh, Choglamsar is a green oasis with poplars and willows where there are golf links and a polo ground as well as horticultural nurseries. The Central Institute of Buddhist Studies is here with a specialist library. Past the Tibetan refugee camps, children's village and the arts and crafts centre, the Choglamsar Bridge crosses the Indus. The **Chochot Yugma Imambara**① *a few minutes' walk from the bridge*, is worth a visit. Buses depart Leh hourly from 0800-1800.

Stok

Across Choglamsar Bridge, 16 km south of Leh, is **Stok Palace**, dating from the 1840s when the King of Ladakh was deposed by the invading Dogra forces. The royal line continues till today, and the present king lives in a private wing of the palace with his wife and son. The palace is a rambling building and the family use only a dozen of the 80 rooms. The small **Palace Museum** ① *May-Oct 0900-1300 and 1400-1900, Rs 50*, with three rooms, is a showpiece for the royal *thangkas*, many 400 years old, crown jewels, dresses, coins, *peraks* (headdresses) encrusted with turquoise and lapis lazuli as well as religious objects. There's also a rather lovely café, which has superb views.

The **gompa**, a short distance away, has some ritual dance masks. Tsechu is held for two days in February and there is an **archery contest** in July. A three-hour walk up the valley behind Stok takes you to some extraordinary mountain scenery dominated by the 6121-m-high Stok Kangri. There are at least three simple guesthouses in town, of which the Yarsta is most comfortable. Buses to Stok leave Leh at 0730 and 1700, or taxis from the Leh central taxi stand are available at fixed rates.

Shey
Palace open all day; try to be there 0700-0900, 1700-1800 when prayers are chanted, Rs 20.

Until the 16th century, Shey was the royal residence, located at an important vantage point in the Indus Valley. Kings of Leh were supposed to be born in the monastery. The royal family moved to Stok in order to escape advancing Dogra forces from Kashmir who came to exploit the trade in pashmina wool. Shey, along with Thiksey, is also regarded as an auspicious place for cremation.

Most of the fort walls have fallen into disrepair but the palace and its wall paintings have now been restored. The **palace gompa** with its 17.5-m-high blue-haired Maitreya Buddha, imitating the one at Tsemo Gompa, is attended by Drukpa monks from Hemis. It is made of copper and brass but splendidly gilded and studded with precious gem stones. Paintings in the main shrine have been chemically cleaned by the Archaeological Society of India. The large victory **stupa** is topped with gold. Extensive grounds covering the former lake bed to the east contain a large number of *chortens* in which cremated ashes of important monks, members of the royal family and the devout were buried. A newer temple houses another old giant Buddha statue. There are several **rock carvings**; particularly noteworthy is that of five *dhyani* Buddhas (circa eighth century) at the bottom of the hill. The small hotel below the *gompa* has spartan but clean rooms. It is 15 km southeast of Leh on the Indus River or can be reached along a stone path from Thiksey. Hourly buses depart Leh 0800-1800.

> **Tip...**
> Camera flash is usually not allowed in monasteries to reduce damage to wall paintings and *thangkas*, carry a torch.

Thiksey
Rs 30, hourly buses from Leh 0800-1800.

Situated 25 km south of Leh on a crag overlooking the flood plain on the east bank of the Indus, Thiksey Monastery is one of the most imposing monasteries in Ladakh and was part of the original Gelugpa order in the 15th century. The 12-storey monastery, with typical tapering walls painted deep red, ochre and white, has 10 temples, a nunnery and 80 *lamas* in residence whose houses cling to the hillside below. The complex contains numerous *stupas*, statues, *thangkas*, wall paintings (note the fresco of the 84 Mahasiddhas, high above) swords and a large pillar engraved with the Buddha's teachings.

The new temple interior is dominated by a giant 13-m-high Buddha figure near the entrance. The principal **Dukhang** (assembly hall) at the top of the building has holes in the wall for storing religious texts and contains the guardian deities. At the very top, the Old Library has old wooden bookcases with ancient texts and statues; adjacent is the tiny **Chamsing Lhakhang**. Views from the roof are staggeringly good. The slightly creepy **Gonkhang** has Tibetan-style wall paintings. The **museum** ① *0600-1800, closed 1300-1330*, is near the entrance, and also sells souvenirs. There's a restaurant and guestrooms, below the museum.

Thiksey is a popular place to watch religious ceremonies, usually at 0630 or 1200. An early start by taxi makes even the first possible, or it's possible to stay overnight (see page 517). They are preceded by the playing of large standing drums and long horns similar to *alpenstock*. Masked dances are performed during special festivals.

Stakna

Across the valley on a hill, Stakna is the earliest Drukpa monastery, built before Hemis though its decorations are not as ancient. It is also called 'Tiger's nose' because of the shape of the hill site. This small but well-kept monastery has a beautiful silver-gilt *chorten* in the assembly hall, installed around 1955, and some interesting paintings in the dark temple at the back. No need for a local guide as the *lamas* are always willing to open the doors. There are excellent views of the Indus Valley and the Zanskar range.

Hemis Monastery
0800-1300, 1400-1800.

On the west bank of the Indus, 45 km southeast of Leh, Hemis Monastery, built on a green hillside surrounded by spectacular mountain scenery, is tucked into a gorge. The **Drukpa monastery** was founded by Stagsang Raspa during the reign of Senge Namgyal (circa 1630). It is the biggest (350 lamas) and wealthiest in Ladakh and it's a 'must', thus is busy with tourists.

Pass by *chortens* and sections of *mani* walls to enter the complex through the east gate which leads into a large 40 m by 20 m courtyard. Colourful flags flutter in the breeze from posts, and the balconied walls of the buildings have colourfully painted door and window frames. On the north side are two assembly halls approached by steps. The large three-tiered *Dukhang* to the right used for ceremonies is old and atmospheric; the smaller *Tshogskhang* (main temple) contains three silver gilt *chortens* and is covered in murals. The murals in the verandas depict guardian deities, the *kalachakra* (wheel of life) and 'Lords of the four quarters' are well preserved.

A staircase alongside the *Tshogskhang* leads to a roof terrace where there are a number of shrines including a bust of the founder. The *Tsom Lakhang* (chapel) has ancient Kashmiri bronzes, a golden Buddha and a silver *chorten*. The largest of the monastery's prized possession is a heavy silk *thangka*, beautifully embroidered in bright coloured threads and pearls, which is displayed every 12 years (next time in 2016). The museum contains an important library of Tibetan-style books and an impressive collection of *thangkas*.

Not many people make the walk to the new golden Buddha on a nearby cliff, and there is also a pleasant 3-km walk uphill to another *gompa*. A stay in Hemis overnight enables you to attend early morning prayers, a moving experience and recommended. Bus services make a day trip possible.

Chemrey

Picture-perfect Chemrey is a short way off the main road, walkable from where the bus drops passengers. Perched on a little peak above encircling barley fields is **Thekchok Gompa**, home to 70 monks. A road winds to the top, but it's nicer to walk up the steep steps through traditional homesteads. The wonky prayer hall has countless murals of the Buddha, and there are three further *lhakhang* (image halls) to visit; a museum on the roof contains *thangkas* and statues. The beautiful setting and relative lack of visitors makes Chemrey a very worthwhile stop.

Sakti and Takthok

The road continues through a sloping valley to Takthok, first passing Sakti village with the dramatic ruins of a fortress by the roadside. At ancient **Takthok Gompa** ① *Rs 30*, there is a holy cave-shrine in which the sage Padmasambhava meditated in the eighth century. The walls and ceiling are papered with rupee notes and coins, numerous statues are swathed in prayer scarves, and centuries of butter lamps have left their grime. A highly colourful *dukhang* hall contains three beautiful statues. It is the only monastery in Ladakh belonging to the Nyingma sect of Buddhism; about 60 lamas reside here, and at the new *gompa* constructed nearby in 1980. It's possible to take a morning bus from Leh to Takthok and walk the 5 km back down the valley to Chemrey. Should you get stranded in Takthok, a Tourist Bungalow ① *opposite the Gompa, T(0)9622-959513*, has four jaded but sunny rooms, some with squat toilets.

Where to stay

Thiksey

$ Chamba
T01982-267385.
Basic chalet rooms with Indian toilets lie next to a scruffy yard, or the main building has more comfortable rooms. The garden restaurant makes for a good lunch break after exploring the monastery.

Festivals

Hemis

Jun **Hemis Tsechu** is perhaps the biggest cultural festival in Ladakh. It commemorates the birth of **Guru Padmasambhava** who is believed to have fought local demons to protect the people. Young and old of both sexes join *lamas* in masked dance-dramas, while stalls sell handicrafts A colourful display of Ladakhi Buddhist culture, lasting 3 days, it attracts large numbers of foreign visitors.

Along the Srinagar road *Colour map 1, A3.*

staggeringly located monasteries, fascinating overnight stops

The Srinagar road out of Leh passes through a flat dusty basin mostly occupied by army encampments with mile after mile of wire fencing. The scenery is stunning and, as with the Leh–Manali Road, is punctuated with monasteries. A bus leaves Leh each afternoon for Alchi (see below), allowing access to most of the sites described in this section. A few places make for interesting and peaceful overnight stops.

Spituk

Standing on a conical hill, some 8 km from Leh, **Spituk Monastery** was founded in the 11th century. The buildings themselves, including three chapels, date from the 15th century and are set in a series of tiers with courtyards and steps. The Yellow-Hat Gelugpa monks created the precedent in Ladakh for building on mountain tops rather than valley floors. You can get good views of the countryside around.

The long 16th- to 17th-century **dukhang** (assembly hall) is the largest building and has two rows of seats along the length of the walls to a throne at the far end. Sculptures and miniature *chortens* are displayed on the altar. Spituk has a collection of ancient Jelbagh masks, icons and arms including some rescued from the Potala Palace in Lhasa.

Also 16th- to 17th-century, the **Mahakal Temple**, higher up the hill, contains a shrine of Vajrabhairava, often mistaken for the Goddess Kali. The terrifying face is only unveiled in January, during the Gustor festival.

Phyang

Phyang Gompa, 16 km from Leh, dominates a beautiful side valley dotted with poplars, homesteads and *chortens* with a village close by. It belongs to the Red-Hat Kagyupa sect, with its 16th-century Gouon monastery built by the founder of the Namgyal Dynasty which is marked by a flagstaff at the entrance. It houses 60 lamas and hundreds of statues including some Kashmiri bronzes (c14th century), *thangkas* and manuscript copies of the Kangyur and Tengyur.

The temple walls have colourful paintings centred on the eight emblems of happiness. The walls in the main prayer hall are covered with ancient smoke-blackened murals, and a giant rolled-up *thangka* hangs from the ceiling. The faces of the statues in the Protector's Hall have been covered. A grand new wing has been constructed, with rather gawdy paintings by the artists (many of whom came from Bhutan). Morning prayers take place 0600-0730. Phyang is the setting for a spectacular July Tseruk festival with masked dancing.

There are three buses daily (0900, 1400 and 1630, 45 minutes; return to Leh at 0800, 1000, 1300 from the monastery, 1600 and 1730); the morning bus allows you to explore the valley and walk back to Leh. However, it is worth overnighting in Phyang as there is a pleasing guesthouse (see page 520), good walks around the traditional village and dramatic valley up to the fort, as well as stunning views to the pyramid-peak of Stok Kangri.

Phyang to Nimmu

About 2 km before Nimmu the Indus enters an impressive canyon before the Zanskar joins it, a good photo opportunity. As the road bends, a lush green oasis with lines of poplars comes into view. The mud brick houses of Nimmu have grass drying on the flat rooftops to provide fodder for the winter. A dry stone *mani* wall runs along the road; beyond Nimmu the walls become 2 m wide in places with innumerable *chortens* alongside. The rocky outcrops on the hills to the right appear like a natural fortress. Nimmu serves mainly as a bus rest-stop, but there are a couple of small hotels (Nilza Guesthouse is most acceptable) and a collection of *dhabas* and shops.

Basgo

The road, lined by *mani* walls and *chortens*, passes through Basgo Village with the ruins of a Buddhist citadel impressively sited on a spur overlooking the Indus Valley. It served as a royal residence for several periods between the 15th and 17th centuries. The **fort palace** was once considered almost impregnable having survived a three-year siege by Tibetan and Mongol armies in the 17th century.

Among the ruins two temples have survived. The higher **Maitreya Temple** (mid-16th century) built by Tashi Namgyal's son contains a very fine Maitreya statue at the rear of the hall, flanked by *bodhisattvas*. Some murals from the early period illustrating the Tibetan Buddhist style have also survived on the walls and ceiling; among the Buddhas and *bodhisattvas* filled with details of animals, birds and mermaids, appear images of Hindu divinities.

The 17th-century **Serzang Temple** (gold and copper), with a carved doorway, contains another large Maitreya image whose head rises through the ceiling into a windowed box-like structure. The murals look faded and have been damaged by water. The fort is very photogenic, particularly so in the late afternoon light. The Chamba View guesthouse and restaurant is by the road, as you exit the village.

Lekir (Likir)

Some 5.5 km from Basgo, a road on the right leads up to **Lekir Monastery** via a scenic route. Lower Lekir, a scattering of houses where most accommodation is found, is about 1 km off NH1 accessed by confusing unpaved tracks. You can walk from Lower Likir up to the monastery, about 5 km on the road, or via short-cuts crossing the river. The picturesque whitewashed monastery buildings rise in different levels on the hillside across the Lekir River. A huge gold-coloured Maitreya Buddha flanks the complex.

Lekir was built during the reign of Lachen Gyalpo who installed 600 monks here, headed by Lhawang Chosje (circa 1088). The *gompa* was invested with a collection of fine images, *thangkas* and murals to vie with those at Alchi. The present buildings date mainly from the 18th century since the original were destroyed by fire. A path up leads to the courtyard where a board explains the origin of the name: Klu-Khyil (snake coil) refers to the *nagas* here, reflected in the shape of the hill. Lekir was converted to the Gelugpa sect in the 15th century. The head *lama*, the younger brother of the Dalai Lama, has his apartments here, which were extended in the mid-1990s.

The **Dukhang** (assembly hall) contains large clay images of the Buddhas (past, present and future), *thangkas*, and Kangyur and Tengyur manuscripts, the Kangyur having been first compiled in Ladakh during Lachen Gyalpo's reign. The **Nyenes-Khang** contains beautiful murals of the 35 confessional Buddhas and 16 arahats. Wooden steps lead up to the **Gon-Khang** housing a statue of the guardian deity here, as well as *thangkas* and murals. Further steps lead to a small but very interesting **museum** ① Rs 20, opened on request (climb to a hall above, up steep wooden stairs), displays *thangkas*, old religious and domestic implements, costumes, etc, which are labelled in English.

Village craftsmen produce *thangkas*, carved wooden folding seats and clay pottery. If you wish to stay overnight, the monastery has guestrooms which share bathrooms (by donation); for further accommodation options in the villages, see page 520. A bus goes to Leh at 0730 from the monastery.

The road enters Saspol, 8 km after the Lekir turn-off. About 2 km beyond the village, a link road with a suspension bridge over the river leads to Alchi, which is hidden from view as you approach. As the road enters the village, impressive old houses in various states of repair can be seen. It's possible to climb up the small rocky peak behind these, to a square white turret with graves around, for good views up the Indus valley and of the village. A patchwork of cultivated fields surrounds the monastery complex.

A narrow path from the car park winds past village houses, donkeys and apricot trees to lead to the **Dharma Chakra monastery**. You will be expected to buy a ticket from one of the three *lamas* on duty. The whole complex, about 100 m long and 60 m wide, is enclosed by a whitewashed mud and straw wall. Alchi's large temple complex is regarded as one of the most important Buddhist centres in Ladakh and a jewel of monastic skill. Founded in the 11th century by Rinchen Zangpo, the 'Great Translator', it was richly decorated by artists from Kashmir and Tibet. Paintings of the *mandalas*, which have deep Tantric significance, are particularly fine; some decorations are reminiscent of Byzantine art. The monastery is maintained by monks from Lekir and is no longer a place for active worship.

A path on the right past two large prayer wheels and a row of smaller ones leads to the river which attracts deer down to the opposite bank in the evenings. At the rear, small *chortens* with inscribed stones strewn around them, line the wall. It is worth walking around the exterior of the complex, and you'll get a beautiful view of the Indus River with mountains as a backdrop. For accommodation options, see Where to stay, below.

The temple complex The entrance *chortens* are worth looking in to. Each has vividly coloured paintings within, both along the interior walls as well as in the small *chorten*-like openings on the ceilings. The first and largest of these has a portrait of the founder Rinchen Zangpo (closed at the time of research).

The first temple you come to is the **Sum-stek**, the three-tier temple with a carved wooden gallery on the façade and triple arches. Inside are three giant four-armed, garlanded stucco figures of *Bodhisattvas*: the white *Avalokitesvara* on the left, the principal terracotta-red *Maitreya* in the centre at the back, and the ochre-yellow *Manjusri* on the right; their heads project to the upper storey which is reached by a rustic ladder (inaccessible). The remarkable features here are the brightly painted and gilded decorations on the clothing of the figures which include historical incidents, musicians, palaces and places of pilgrimage. Quite incongruous court scenes and Persian features appear on *Avalokitesvara* while the figures on *Maitreya* have Tantric connotations illustrating the very different styles of ornamentation on the three sculptures. The walls have numerous *mandalas* and inscriptions, as well as thousands of tiny Buddhas.

The oldest temple is the **Dukhang**, which has a covered courtyard (originally open to the sky) with wooden pillars and painted walls; the left wall shows two rowing boats with fluttering flags, a reminder perhaps of the presence in ancient times of lakes in this desert. The brightly painted door to the *dukhang*, about 1.5 m high, and the entrance archway has some fine woodcarving. The subsidiary shrines on either side of the doorway contain *Avalokitesvaras* and *Bodhisattvas* including a giant four-armed Maitreya figure to the extreme right. This main assembly hall, which was the principal place of worship, suffers from having very little light so visitors need a good torch. The 'shrine' holds the principal gilded *Vairocana* (Resplendent) Buddha (traditionally white, accompanied by the lion) with ornate decorations behind, flanked by four important Buddha postures among others. The walls on either side of the main hall are devoted to damaged *Mandala* paintings illustrating the four principal manifestations of the *Sarvavid* (Omniscient) Buddha – *Vairocana*, *Sakyamuni* (the Preacher), *Manjusri* (Lord of Wisdom) and as *Prajna Paramita* (Perfection of Wisdom). There are interesting subsidiary panels, friezes and inscriptions. On exiting, note the terrifying figure of *Mahakala* the guardian deity above the door with miniature panels of royal and military scenes. The one portraying a drinking scene shows the royal pair sanctified with haloes with wine-cups in hand, accompanied by the prince and attendants – the detail of the clothing clearly shows Persian influence.

The **Lotsawa** (Translator's) and **Jampang** (Manjusri) *lhakhangs* were built later and probably neglected for some time. The former contains a statue of Rinchen Zangpo along with a seated

Buddha, while the latter has a finely carved doorway and exterior lintels. Ask for the lights to be switched on.

Lhakhang Soma (New Temple) is a square hall used as a meditation centre with a *chorten* within; its walls are totally covered with *mandalas* and paintings portraying incidents from the Buddha's life and historic figures; the main figure here is the preaching Buddha. There is an interesting panel of warriors on horseback near the door. Ask for the temple to be opened if it is locked. **Kanjyur Lhakhang** in front of the Lhakhang Soma houses the scriptures.

★ Lamayuru

In Lamayuru, 10 km before Khaltse, the famous **Yungdrung Gompa** is perched on a crag overlooking the Indus in a striking lunar landscape between a drained lake and high mountains. Little medieval houses nestle on the steep slope beneath the monastery, and the effect is dramatically photogenic.

The monastery complex, which includes a library thought to be the oldest in the region, was founded in the 11th century and belongs to the Tibetan Kagyupa sect. The present monastery dating from the 16th century was partly destroyed in the 19th. You can still see some of the murals, along with the redecorated **Dukhang** (assembly hall). A small glass panel in the right hand wall of the *dukhang* protects a tiny holy cave, and there are many beautiful bronzes displayed. In a small temple, below the monastery, is an 11-headed and 1000-armed Avalokiteshvara image; the walls here are coated with murals – you will need to ask someone to get the key. Some of the upper rooms are richly furnished with carpets, Tibetan tables, statues, silver *stupas* and butter lamps.

In June/July the monastery holds the famous **Yuru Kabgyat** festival, with colourful masked dancing, special prayers, and burning of sacrificial offerings. There are several guesthouses strung along the road and up the hillside (see Where to stay, below); it's also possible to camp near the stream in a willow grove. There are daily buses from Leh at 0800; buses to Leh and Kargil leave Lamayuru at around 0930, and to Chitkan at 1000.

Wanla

Shortly after Lamayuru, a jeep road leaves the highway heading south down the Yapola Valley to **Wanla** which has a beautiful *gompa*, from the same era as Alchi and decorated by same artists. It has been recently restored, see www.achiassociation.org, and is adjoined on a dramatic ridge by a ruined fort. In Wanla village there are guesthouses. The next village is **Phanjila**, and further along there is a homestay in the delightful village of **Hinju**, from where the track peters out into a fantastic trekking route.

Drokhpa area

Dha and **Biama** (Bema) are two Drokhpa (aka Brokpa) villages where the so-called pure Aryan tribe speak a distinct dialect and live in a fair degree of isolation; Buddhism here is mixed with animist practices. You may reach these Indus Valley villages from **Khaltse** on the Leh–Srinagar road via the scenic villages of Dumkhar, Tirit, Skurbuchan and Hanu. There are homestays and a campsite at Biama, but Dha (3 km further) is the more popular option for overnight stays.

Listings Along the Srinagar road

Where to stay

Phyang

$ Hidden North Guesthouse
T(0)9906-999950, http://ladakhtrek.com/
accommodation-in-ladakh/.
This attractive guesthouse, set on a hillside, has marvellous views. There are 7 unfussy clean rooms, one with private terrace, some with private bath; run by a nice Ladakhi-German

couple. There's a huge shared terrace and garden and meals are available. It's perched at the top end of the village, a 5-min uphill walk from the last bus stop. Treks can also be arranged by their responsible outfit.

Lekir

The bus directly to the monastery facilitates staying in one of four options near the monastery. Or, if you are dropped off on NH1, there are half a dozen choices in Lower Likir, about 1 km walk on dirt tracks from NH1. Hotels all provide dinner and breakfast. Just below the monastery gate is the **Gonpa Restaurant** (0630-2030) for breakfast and reasonably priced Tibetan and Chinese food.

$$ Lhukhil
T01982-253588, www.ladakhpackages.com.
Grand gateway and luxuriant garden, although outdoor seating is on patchy grass next to scary statues and dragon-wrapped pillars. 24 rooms are well-fitted out and comfortable, with towels, toiletries, and some views. Meals are included.

$ Lotos Guesthouse
T01982-227171, (0)9469-297990, opposite Hotel Lhukhil, Lower Likir.
3 clean modern rooms with mats over the floor and plenty of warm bedding, sharing a bathroom, attractive front garden and fruit trees, food costs extra. Cheap and cheerful.

$ Norboo Lagams Chow Guesthouse and Camp
Lower Likir.
A bit of a building site, set at the back of a long scruffy orchard (camping possible) with small uncurtained rooms, one with (unfinished) bath, others using the traditional Ladakhi toilet in the house behind. It's cheap and dinner is served in the traditional kitchen-cum-dining room, surrounded by pots of all shapes and sizes.

$ Norboo Spon Guesthouse and Camping
Lower Likir.
Signposted off the road to the monastery, or a 300-m walk from Lower Likir on the way to the monastery. In a large Ladakhi house, roof decked with prayer flags, bright white paint and red trims, set among trees in a large garden with plenty of seating. Dining seating area of little tables, rugs and cushions with the odd decorative mask is homely; there's a shared balcony. Rooms upstairs have good views, wicker chairs and a decent shared bathroom. Charming and kind family.

$ Old Likir Guesthouse
A 10-min walk downhill through the fields from the monastery (signposted).
Only 3 very simple rooms (the 2 upstairs one are best) in a farming family's home. There are mattresses on the floor and little else, but fabulous views either of the valley below or the Buddha's back and monastery above. Very cheap rates include breakfast and dinner.

$ A short walk up from the monastery are **Dolker Tongol** and **Chhuma** guesthouses; both are basic, but have views.

Alchi
Alchi has a several guesthouses, some are not great value, but the ones listed here are well-priced for what they offer. It is a pleasant little village with some shops, *dhabas*, hotel restaurants and souvenir stalls, none of which are a long walk from the bus stop or the monastery.

$$ Alchi Resort
T(0)9419-218636, http://alchiresort.com.
Cross a little bridge after the unattractive main building (restaurant downstairs) to a flowery fruit-filled garden edged by whitewashed cottages in adjoining pairs; those at the end, around a central gazebo, enjoy more privacy. Well-appointed motel-layout rooms differ slightly in configuration, all have flatscreens, laminate wood floors or carpets, and plain tiled bathrooms.

$$ Ule Ethnic Resort
Uletokpo, next to the highway, 10 km past Saspol, T01982-253640, www.uleresort.com.
15 cottages and 31 posh canvas tents in a well set up eco-resort. It caters mainly to groups, but is an alternative night's stop to Alchi village.

$$-$ Zimskhang Holiday Home
On the lane to the monastery, T01982-227086, www.zimskhang.com.
Some pricier rooms in a large building that is more attractive outside than in, with an appealing public balcony upstairs, spacious rooms with flatscreen TVs, bathrooms with marble basin-tops and floors, but by no means swanky. Cheaper clean rooms in an older building share bathrooms and are good value, overlooking the open-air restaurant.

$ Choskor
15-min walk back along the road towards Leh, T01982-227084.
Set in a lovely garden, this colourful guesthouse has rooms ranging from simple doubles with shared baths, to great-value upstairs rooms with attached bath. A roof terrace with rural views; eat in the garden or inside the restaurant with painted motifs on the wall. Cheap for pitching your own tent. Taxi and laundry services are available, and they pride themselves on their clean sheets.

$ Heritage Home
Right next to the monastery entrance, T(0)9419811535.
A very pleasant and convenient choice. Rooms are large, carpeted, freshly painted, en suite (hot water in the evening), with soap and clean

towels. Upstairs is more expensive, and there's a decent restaurant out front with apricot trees.

Lamayuru

Most guesthouses are on the NH1 in the lower village, with a couple of homestays on the hill towards the monastery. They all provide food, and little **Zambala Restaurant**, on the highway opposite the Dragon Hotel, does surprisingly good chai and *aloo paratha*.

$$ Fotola
T(0)9469-048470, http://hotelfotola.com.
12 plain rooms, slightly set back from the road facing the rocky valley wall, with attached bath, towels provided. There's no garden as such, but a bonus is the upstairs restaurant serving a variety of Indian and Italian food.

$ Dragon
Lower Rd, T01982-224501, dragon_skyabu@ yahoo.com.
A range of spacious carpeted rooms, 4 with en suite by the garden restaurant, 8 with shared bath in the building to the rear. Most are south-facing, and room 10 has attractively painted walls. There are clean sheets and it's very reasonably priced. The restaurant serves up excellent Indian meals. Internet available (during the 3 hrs of power in the evenings), as is hot water.

$ Lion's Den
300 m from the village centre, T01982-224542, liondenhouse@gmail.com.
Ignore the unfinished concrete ground floor, as the upstairs rooms are given warmth by colourful walls, rugs and bedding (shared bath). Good views of the weird rock formations in the valley from the 2 corner rooms with attached bath. The little outdoor restaurant with checked cloths has shade or there's a Ladakhi dining room.

$ Niranjana Hotel
T01982-224555.
Next to the monastery, this institutional-looking hotel has 20 rooms on 3 levels with excellent valley views. Rooms are plain but comfortable, they take the time to turn down the sheets. All share modern, clean communal bathrooms, with hot showers available in the evenings. Downstairs restaurant is good.

$ Tharpaling
100 m past the village centre on main road, T01982-224516.
The warm family atmosphere is what appeals most to visitors to this simple guesthouse.

Restaurants

Alchi
$$-$ Zimskhang and **Heritage** both have good drop-in restaurants, other hotels provide meals when there are guests.

$ Golden Oriole German Bakery
Good cake selection but they don't always have bread. They serve Chinese and Indian dishes and pizza, and are a good place for breakfast. Same menu as Zimskhang but at lower prices. The terrace is a nice place to sit and watch folks pass on their way to the monastery.

There are a couple of *dhabas* near the bus stop; **Dil Dil Restaurant** is kept clean and does cheap dal, veg and rice. Most shops near bus stop also serve omelettes, dal and chai, and sell strong beer.

Transport

Alchi
Bus 1 daily direct bus from **Leh** in summer, 1500, 3 hrs, returns around 0700. **Srinagar**-bound buses stop at **Saspol**, from there it is a 2.5-km walk across the bridge.

These once-restricted areas are open to foreign visitors with a PAP (see box, page 504). Travel to the valleys and lakes is far easier by jeep, although twice-weekly buses go to Panamik and Pangong-Tso in summertime, and hitching is not impossible in the Nubra valley. There are guesthouses in villages throughout the Nubra-Shyok valleys, and temporary tented camps are occasionally set up by tour companies during the season, but it's still a good idea to take a sleeping bag.

★ Nubra Valley

For an exhilarating high-altitude experience over possibly the highest motorable pass in the world, travel across the Ladakh range over the 5600-m **Khardung La**. This is along the old Silk Route to the lush green Nubra Valley up to **Panamik**, 140 km north of Leh. Camel caravans once transported Chinese goods along this route for exchanging with Indian produce. The relatively gentle climate here allows crops, fruit and nuts to grow, so some call it 'Ldumra' (orchard).

It is possible to visit the Nubra-Shyok valleys over two days, but it's much preferable (and much the same cost) to make the journey over three. After crossing the Khardung La, the first village is **Khardung**, 42 km later, in a majestic setting. The road continues down the Shyok Valley to **Deskit**, which has an old and a new (less appealing) town centre and several places to stay. On a hill above the old village is a Gelugpa sect **monastery** (the largest in Nubra) built by the Ladakhi king Sohrab Zangpo in the early 1700s. There is large statue of Tsongkhapa, and the Rimpoche of Thiksey monastery south of Leh oversees this monastery also. A further 10 km past Diskit is the village of **Hunder**, probably the most popular place to stay overnight, with several garden-guesthouses to choose from. Highly prized double-humped camels can occasionally be seen on the sand dunes near Hunder, allegedly descendants of the caravan-camels that used to ply the Silk Route, and it is possible to take a 15- to 30-minute camel ride (on a tame beast). Past Hunder the road continues to **Turtuk**, opened to tourists in 2010. The scenery is impressive and the tiny settlements here are culturally Balti and practice Islam.

The second biggest monastery in Nubra is near **Tiger** village along the road to Panamik in the Nubra Valley. Called the **Samtanling** *gompa*, it was founded in 1842 and belongs to the Gelugpa sect. **Panamik** has several guesthouses and reddish, sulphurous hot springs nearby. The ILP allows travel only up **Ensa Gompa**, included on some itineraries, and approached by foot for the last 30 minutes.

Traffic into and out of the Nubra Valley is controlled by the army at Pulu. From Leh there are two buses per week from June to September; a few have tried by bike, which can be put on the roof of the bus for the outward journey.

★ Pangong-Tso

A popular excursion from Leh is to the narrow 130-km-long Pangong-Tso, a lake at 4250 m, the greater part of which lies in Tibet. The road, which is only suitable for 4WD in places, is via **Karu** on the Manali–Leh Highway, where the road east goes through **Zingral** and over the Chang La pass. Beyond are **Durbuk**, a small village with low-roofed houses, and **Tangste**, the 'abode of Chishul warriors' with a Lotswa Temple, which is also an army base with a small bank. The rough jeep track takes you through an impressive rocky gorge which opens out to a valley which has camping by a fresh water stream in the hamlet of **Mugleb** and then on to **Lukung** and finally **Spangmik**, 153 km from Leh. On the way you will be able to see some Himalayan birds including *chikhor* (quail) which may end up in the cooking pot.

An overnight stop on the lake shore allows you to see the blue-green lake in different lights. You can walk between Lukung and Spangmik, 7 km, on the second day, passing small settlements growing barley and peas along the lake shore. You return to Leh on the

Tip...

Always carry multiple photocopies of your passport and PAP with you, to facilitate the crossing of checkpoints.

third day. There are tented camps at Durbuk, Tangtse and Lukung. At Spangmik there is a wider choice of accommodation, in the form of homestays (mats on floor) or in the rather pricey Pangong Tso Resort (rooms have attached bath). Buses go from Leh at 0630 on Saturdays and Sundays, but almost everyone makes the journey by private jeep.

Tso-Moriri

The Rupshu area, a dry, high-altitude plateau to the east of the Leh–Manali Highway, is where the nomadic Changpas live (see box, page 485), in the bleak and windswept Chamathang highlands bordering Tibet. The route to the beautiful Tso-Moriri (*tso* – lake), the only nesting place of the bar-headed geese on the Indus, is open to visitors. It is 220 km from Leh; jeeps make the journey. To the south of the 27-km-long lake is the land of the Tibetan wild ass.

You can travel either via **Chhumathang**, 140 km, visiting the hot spring there or by crossing the high pass at Taglang La, leaving the Manali–Leh Highway at Debring. The route takes you past the **Tsokar** basin, 154 km, where salt cakes the edges. A campsite along the lake with access to fresh water is opposite **Thukje** village which has a *gompa* and a 'worm-catching trap'. The road then reaches the hot sulphur springs at **Puga** before arriving at the beautiful Tso-Moriri, about four hours' drive from Tsokar. You can follow the lake bank and visit the solitary village of **Karzog**, at 4500 m, north of the lake, which also has a *gompa*. There are some rest houses and guesthouses at Chhumathang and Karzog and camping at Tsokar and Karzog as well as a tent camp at Chhumathang.

Listings North and east of Leh

Where to stay

Nubra valley
There are lots of little guesthouses springing up in the Nubra Valley, mainly located around the village of Hunder.

$$ Yarab Tso
Tiger, T(0)9622-820661, www.hotelyarabtso.com.
Carpeted rooms with private baths and attractive furnishings; in an idyllic setting with large garden, plus very good food.

$ Olgok
Hunder, T01980-221092.
Large simple rooms are very clean and neat in this homely guesthouse where the owners go out of their way to be helpful. Fresh food from the quaint garden; located in the centre of Hunder and close to the sand dunes.

★ Trekking in Ladakh *Colour map 1, A3.*

some of the best trekking in the world, with camping and homestays

Make sure your trekking guide is experienced and competent. A detailed book, although dated, is the Trailblazer guide *Trekking in Ladakh*, which can be bought in bookshops in Leh. Some treks, eg Spituk to Hemis and Hemis High Altitude National Park, charge a fee of Rs 25 per person per day or Rs 10 for Indians. For trekking, July and August are pleasant months. Go earlier and you will be trudging through snow much of the time. September and October are also good months, though colder at night.

Markha Valley Trek, Spituk to Hemis

Both places are in the Indus Valley, just 30 km apart. A very satisfying nine to 10 days can be undertaken by traversing the Stok range to the Markha Valley, walking up the valley and then back over the Zanskar range to Hemis. The daily walking time on this trek is five to six hours so you must be fit. Places to camp are highlighted below, but there are also basic homestays or guesthouses in the villages if you don't want to carry equipment.

There is an interesting monastery at **Spituk**, a short drive from Leh (see page 517). From Spituk proceed southwest of the Indus along a trail passing through barren countryside. After about 7 km you reach the **Zingchen Valley** and in a further five hours, the beautiful village of **Rumbak**. Camp below the settlement. You can also trek here from Stok which takes one-two days and a steep ascent of the **Namlung La** (4570 m).

From Rumbak it is a five-hour walk to **Utse** village. The camp is two hours further on at the base of the bleak **Gandha La** (4700 m), open, bare and windswept. To go over the pass takes about three hours, then the same time again to negotiate the wooded ravine to **Skiu**. Here the path

Ladakh & Zanskar

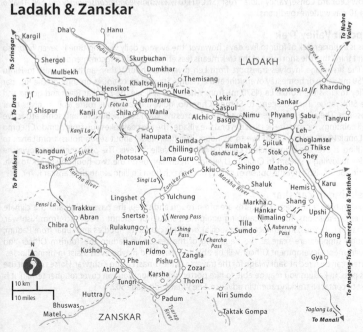

meets the Markha Valley. You can make a half-day round trip from Skiu to see the impressive gorges on the Zanskar River. The stage to **Markha**, where there is an impressive fort, is a six-hour walk. The monastery, while not particularly impressive from the outside, has some superb wall paintings and *thangkas*, some dating from the 13th century. You need to take a torch.

The next destination is **Hankar** village, whose ruined fort forms an astonishing extension of the natural rock face, an extremely impressive ruin. From here the path climbs quite steeply to a plateau. There are good views of Nimaling Peak (6000 m) and a number of *mani* walls en route. From **Nimaling** it is a two-hour climb to **Gongmaru La** (5030 m) with views of the Stok range and the Indus Valley. The descent is arduous and involves stream crossings. There is a lovely campsite at **Shogdu** and another at **Sumda** village, 3 km further on. The final stage is down the valley to **Martselang** from where you can walk down 5 km to **Karu** village on the Leh–Manali road or take a 2-km diversion to visit **Hemis** monastery.

Hemis High Altitude National Park

Set up in 1981, the park adjoining the monastery comprising the catchments of Markha, Rumbak and Sumda *nalas*. The reserve area has been expanded a couple of times, and now covers 4400 sq km making it the largest national park in South Asia. The rugged terrain with valleys often littered with rocks and rimmed by high peaks (some over 6000 m), supports limited alpine vegetation but contains some rare species of flora and fauna, including the ibex, Pallas' cat, *bharal* and *shapu*. It is the habitat of the endangered and elusive snow leopard, now numbering around 200 (mainly in the Rumbak area, best spotted in winter). It is hoped that the activities of local villagers, who graze livestock within the park, can be restricted to a buffer zone so that their animals can be kept safe from attack by wolves and snow leopards. Villages used to trap the leopard, but now they are reimbursed for any livestock lost to snow leopard attacks.

There are camping sites within the park, which can be reserved through the Wildlife Warden in Leh. There are also homestays, see www.himalayan-homestays.com, run in conjunction with the Snow Leopard Conservancy India Trust (SNC-IT) ① *www.snowleopardconservancy.org*. SNC-IT also run 10-day winter expeditions.

Ripchar Valley Trek

This is a shorter trek of four to five days; however, the average daily walking time is seven hours so don't think that the shortness of the trek means less effort. A guide is recommended.

The first stage involves transport from Leh (five to six hours), then an hour's walk to **Hinju** (3750 m); camp or homestay overnight at the village. Stage two continues up through the Ripchar Valley to cross the **Konze La** (4570 m), from where you will see the Zanskar River and gorge and the Stok range. Then descend to **Sumdo Chenmo**, quite a treacherous route as it involves river crossings. There is a monastery here with an impressive statue of the Buddha and some attractive wall paintings. A campsite lies just beyond the village. The next day takes you from Sumdo Chenmo to **Lanak** (4000 m), a walk of five to six hours. The final stage, about seven hours, from Lanak to **Chilling**, is over the **Dungduchan La** (4700 m) with excellent views. The path continues down the valley following a stream to Chilling. Overnight in Chilling or do the two-hour drive back to Leh. Some agents also offer the option of rafting back to Leh from Chilling along the Zanskar River.

Trekking in Zanskar

Trekking here is not easy. The paths are often rough and steep, the passes high and the climate extreme. Provisions, fuel and camping equipment should be bought in advance from Kishtwar, Manali or Leh. You can get necessities such as dried milk, biscuits, noodles and sugar from Padum, though supplies are scarce at the beginning of the season. In Padum the Tourism Officer and Government Development Officer will be able to advise and maybe even assist in hiring horses. Porters can be hired at **Sani** village for the traverse of the **Umasi La** into Kishtwar. Horses cannot use this pass. In Padum you may be able to hire porters with whom you can cover rougher terrain. It is best to contact a trekking agent in advance. See What to do, page 502.

ON THE ROAD
Taking a walk on the wild side

The Himalayan range is the longest and the highest mountain range in the world. The sheer diversity of the topography makes it one of the best places to spot some of the rarest wildlife and birds. The forested regions offer a large variety of birds. You might see Himalayan griffons, crested serpent eagles, lamagiers, forest owlets, common flamebacks, golden orioles, scarlet minivets, rose finches, chukors, snow cocks, pigeons, Himalayan blue magpies, monals, khaleej pheasants, the critically endangered western tragopans, or black-necked cranes around Tso Kar. In fact, the flatlands around Tso Kar in Ladakh is one of my favourite places to see birds. Another great place to venture to in order to see birds and wildlife is the Great Himalayan National Park, in Himachal Pradesh. The park is a habitat to 375 fauna species, which includes 31 mammals, 181 birds and 127 insects.

In my 18 odd years of trekking in the Western Himalayas the sighting that has had me the most excited is seeing a snow leopard for the first time in Rumbak valley of Ladakh in 1995. Watching a snow leopard was awe-inspiring. Once I was even offered a chanko cub, which is a Tibetan wolf. I was camped in the village of Rumtse where I met a villager from the Khanag valley who had a three-month-old cub that he had found and was not sure what to do with.

My work as a trekking and climbing guide takes me to some remote parts and over the years I have seen dramatic changes in not just glaciers receding due to global warming but also extensive deforestation because of many hydroelectric projects. This has affected carnivores like the snow leopard and the chanko due to the loss of prey caused by habitat destruction. A positive development is the increase in snow leopard tourism in Ladakh which has prompted the locals to stop viewing the big cat as an enemy and has opened doors to alternative income generation.

Kaushal Desai, tour guide at Above 14000ft, www.above14000ft.com.

Pensi La to Padum You can trek this three-day route before the road opens (June-October) when it is free of vehicles.

Karsha to Lamayaru This is a demanding nine-day trek which includes seven passes, five of which are over 4500 m. The highest is the Singi La (5060 m). It is essential to be very fit before starting the trek. Each day's walking should take under six hours, but with time for rests and lunch this adds up to a full day. An extra day allows for flexibility.

The 16th-century monastery of the Tibetan Gelugpa (Yellow Hat) sect at **Karsha** is the largest and wealthiest in the Zanskar Valley and is occupied by nearly 200 monks. Karsha has an inn with dormitory beds and a vegetarian canteen.

Padum to Leh This is another demanding trek which also takes about 10 days. Some are through the spectacular gorges between Markha and Zangla. A local guide is recommended as this is truly a wilderness area. The trek involves walking along stream beds and in July there is still too much snow melt to allow safe crossings. Recommended only for August/September.

It is seven hours' walking from Padum to Zangla and this includes crossing the Zanskar River by a string and twig bridge that spans over 40 m. Ponies are not allowed on it and if it is windy sensible humans don't cross. You can now start your trek at Zangla as there is a motorbike route from Padum to Zangla. At **Zangla** you can see the King's Palace, which has a collection of *thangkas* painted by the king's son (who was once a monk). The third stage takes you over the **Cha Cha La** (5200 m). On the next stage river crossings are again necessary. This is time consuming and if you are travelling in mid-summer, an extra day may be called for.

You then follow the **Khurna River** to a narrow gorge that marks the ancient border between Zanskar and Ladakh, and end up below the **Rubarung La**. When you cross this you get good views of the Stok range. You then descend into the Markha Valley and from here you can reach Leh in six stages by heading west into the heart of the valley and then crossing the Ganda La to Spituk, or in three stages by crossing the Gongmaru La and descending to Martselang and nearby Hemis.

Padum to Darcha This is a week-long trek and starts with a walk along the Tsarap Chu to **Bardan**, which has *stupas* and interesting idols, and **Reru**. There is a now a motorable road till Mune from where the trek starts towards Darcha.

After two stages you reach **Purni** (with a couple of shops and a popular campsite), where you can stay two nights and make a side trip to the impressive 11th-century **Phugtal monastery** (a two-hour walk). On a spectacular site, it has been carved out of the mountainside round a limestone cave. Usually there are about 50 monks in attendance. From Purni you continue on to Kargiakh, the last village before the **Shingo La**. It's another day's walk to the camp below this high pass (5200 m).

The mountain scenery is stunning with 6000-m-plus peaks all around. Once over the pass you can stop at **Rumjack** where there is a campsite used by shepherds or you can continue to the confluence of the **Shingo** and the **Barai** rivers where there is now a bridge. From here the trail passes through grazing land and it is about 15 km to **Darcha**, the end of the trek. Keen trekkers can combine this with a trek from Darcha to **Manali**. The average daily walking time of the Padum-Darcha trek is six hours so you have to be very fit. There is now a motorable road from Darcha all the way to Zanskar Sumdo which is after the Shingo La Pass.

Trekking in the Nubra and Shyok valleys

The easing of controls to visit the Nubra-Shyok valleys has made possible treks that start from points in the Indus Valley not far from Leh, cross the Ladakh Range to enter the Shyok River valley and then re-cross the Ladakh range further to the west to re-enter the Indus Valley near Phyang monastery. Ask a good local trekking agent for advice on how to get the required 'Restricted Area Permits'.

Day 1 Drive from Leh south along the Manali road to Karu, near Hemis, where you turn left and drive about 10 km to the roadhead at the village of Sakti, just past **Takthak monastery**. Trek about 90 minutes to **Chumchar** and camp.

Day 2 Cross the Ladakh range at the **Wari La** (4400 m) and descend to Junlez on the northern flank.

Day 3 Walk downhill to **Tangyar** (3700 m) with a nice *gompa*.

Days 4, 5, 6 A level walk along the **Shyok River** valley takes you to **Khalsar** from where you follow the military road west to the confluence of the Shyok and Nubra rivers at **Diskit** (see Nubra Valley, above).

Days 7, 8, 9 Three days to gradually ascend the northern flanks of the Ladakh Range passing the hamlets of **Hunder**, **Wachan** and **Hunder Dok** to the high pastures of **Thanglasgo** (4700 m).

Days 10, 11 Trek back over the Ladakh Range via the Lasermo La pass (5150 m) to a campsite on the southern base of the pass.

Day 12 Camp at Phyang village about 1 km above Phyang monastery before driving back to Leh.

Background Jammu and Kashmir

Ruled for many years by Scythian and then Tartar princes, Kashmir was captured in 1341 by Shams ud Din who spread Islam across the Vale. In 1588 the Mughal Emperor Akbar conquered Kashmir and his son Jahangir (1605-1627), captivated by the beauty of the Vale of Kashmir, planted chinar trees and constructed pleasure gardens. Later, the area fell under Sikh rule and when they were defeated by the British at the end of the first Sikh War in 1846, Jammu, the Vale of Kashmir, Ladakh, Baltistan and Gilgit were assigned to the Maharaja Gulab Singh of Jammu, who had aided the British victory. He founded a dynasty of Dogra Rajputs, and thus began a period of Hindu rule over the mainly Muslim population of the Vale of Kashmir.

Rock carvings in Ladakh indicate that it has been used for thousands of years by nomadic tribesmen, including the Mons of North India, the Dards, the Mongols and Changpa shepherds from Tibet. By the late 10th century, Ladakh was controlled by the Thi Dynasty which founded a capital at Shey and built many forts. Tibetan Lamaistic Buddhism grew at the same time and over 100 *gompas* were built.

In 1533 Soyang Namgyal made his capital at Leh. The Namgyals extended Ladakhi power but the expansion ended when the fifth Dalai Lama of Tibet, Nawang Lobsang Gyatso (1617-1682) persuaded the Mongols, whom he had converted to Buddhism, to fight West Tibet and Ladakh. The Ladakhis turned to Kashmir for help. The Mughal Governor of Kashmir sent troops but in return they had to build a mosque. From then on Ladakh became part of the Mughal Empire. In 1834 Zorwar Singh, an army general, conquered Ladakh. The dethroned royal family received the Stok Palace where they still live today.

Zanskar became an administrative part of Ladakh under Senge Namgyal whose three sons became the rulers of Ladakh, Guge and Zanskar/Spiti. This arrangement collapsed after Ladakh's war with Tibet and the Zanskar royal house divided, one administering Padum, the other Zangla. Under the Dogras, the marauding army wreaked havoc on the villages, monasteries and people.

When India gained Independence from Britain, rulers of 'princely states' such as Kashmir were given the choice of whether to stay with India or join Pakistan. But they remained undecided. In October 1947, Kashmir was invaded by tribesmen from Pakistan's North West Frontier Province, supported by the Pakistani army. Nehru sent in the Indian army and 18 months of fighting followed until 1949, when the state was split by a UN-monitored ceasefire line, much of which remains the de facto border between India and Pakistan today (see box, page 486).

Following India's Independence and partition in 1947, Ladakh, like Kashmir, was divided. Indian and Chinese troops have been stationed on the eastern border since the Chinese invasion of Tibet in 1950-1951. From the early 1950s Chinese troops were stationed in the Aksai Chin, which India also claimed, and without Indian knowledge built a road linking Tibet with Xinjiang. Since the 1962 war the Indian army has maintained a strong presence in Ladakh.

West Bengal

No visit to India is complete without some time spent in West Bengal; this cultured corner of the subcontinent has added immeasurably to India's overall identity.

Kolkata is considered to be the country's cultural hub. Many visitors have preconceived ideas of this oft-maligned city, but a little time spent here is enough for those to be rapidly dispelled and gives a fascinating glimpse into the way more than 15 million people manage to rub along. Travelling north takes you through a fertile land containing such treasures as the terracotta temples at Bishnupur and Murshidabad, the delightful old capital of the Nawabs of Bengal.

Darjeeling is synonymous with tea the world over. Made popular by the British, the hill station has always been a holiday destination, particularly during the summer months, when the cool mountain air provides relief from the heat of the plains. With large Tibetan and Nepali populations, Darjeeling and the region around it have a very different feel from the India of the plains. The monasteries and prayer flags give a taste of the land and peoples that lie deeper within the Himalaya.

If the mountains are too cold, head south from Kolkata to the Sunderbans. A World Heritage Site, these mangrove forests are home to a large Bengal tiger population.

Best for
Culture ■ Festivals ■ History ■ Landscapes

Footprint
picks

★ **Kolkata**, page 534

Get lost in colonial-era streets and jam-packed markets, and try some
Bengali specialities at street stalls.

★ **Sunderbans Tiger Reserve**, page 563

Take a scenic boat-safari through the mangroves.

★ **Murshidabad**, page 570

Spend a peaceful weekend by the river in this charming historic town.

★ **Gaur and Pandua**, pages 572 and 573

Explore atmospheric Islamic ruins and see rural Bengali village life.

★ **Darjeeling**, page 577

Visit a tea estate and trek in the autumn or spring.

★ **Kalimpong**, page 591

Enjoy scenic walks, quiet monasteries, heritage hotels and local cheese.

Essential West Bengal

Finding your feet

Most of West Bengal lies on the western delta of the Ganga. The flat landscape of the Bengali plains is given variety by the contrasting greens of the rice paddies; higher ground is limited to the Rajmahal Hills just west of Murshidabad. In the north, however, are the southern slopes of the Himalaya which provide far greater scenic contrasts, including remains of the dense forests that once covered the state. In the far south are the mangrove swamps of the Sunderbans. Kolkata is the region's economic, political and cultural hub and is located at the eastern end of the Grand Trunk Rd (NH2).

Getting around

Kolkata's Subhas Chandra Bose Airport at Dum Dum receives international and domestic flights. An extensive hub-and-spoke bus operation from Kolkata allows cheap travel within West Bengal and beyond, but long bus journeys in this region are gruelling as roads are generally terrible; use buses only as a last resort when trains are full.

Trains link Kolkata with Siliguri in the north of the state, which is the transport hub for the West Bengal Hills, served by Bagdogra airport and two railway stations (Siliguri Junction and New Jalpaiguri). It is also on NH31, well connected by buses from West Bengal, Assam, Bihar, Sikkim and Bhutan. Darjeeling, Gangtok and Kalimpong are easily reached from Siliguri.

Shared jeeps are the best way to get to and around the hills, as they are faster and more frequent than buses and only a little more expensive. Note, however, that roads in the hills can get washed away during the monsoon and may remain in poor condition till October.

When to go

It is extremely hot and oppressively humid in the lowlands from April until the monsoon arrives in early June. Inhabitants of steamy Kolkata evacuate en masse to the hills at this time. The monsoon hits between June and September, when large parts of Kolkata are knee-deep in water for hours at a time. It is best to visit Kolkata from October to February, when the weather is much cooler and clearer. October and March to May are also good times to go trekking in the hills. However, heavy storms occur in late March and April, marked by massive cloud formations, strong winds and heavy rain. Occasionally tropical cyclones also strike coastal areas at this time of year, though they are far more common between October and December.

Time required

You'll need three to four days to get to grips with Kolkata, two to three days for a Sunderbans visit, and a week for a trek in the hills around Darjeeling.

Weather Kolkata

January	February	March	April	May	June
26°C 14°C 13mm	29°C 17°C 27mm	33°C 22°C 38mm	36°C 25°C 53mm	36°C 27°C 92mm	34°C 27°C 257mm

July	August	September	October	November	December
32°C 26°C 308mm	32°C 26°C 356mm	32°C 26°C 283mm	31°C 24°C 136mm	29°C 17°C 17mm	26°C 15°C 7mm

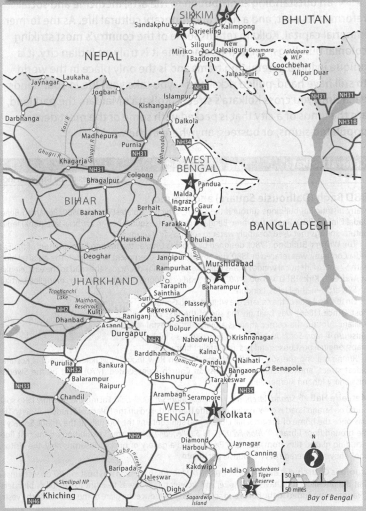

1 Kolkata, page 534

2 Sunderbans Tiger Reserve, page 563

3 Murshidabad, page 570

4 Gaur and Pandua, pages 572 and 573

5 Darjeeling, page 577

6 Kalimpong, page 591

Essential West Bengal • 533

Kolkata
(Calcutta)

★ To Bengalis Kolkata is the proud intellectual capital of India, with an outstanding contribution to the arts, medicine and social reform in its past, and a rich contemporary cultural life. As the former imperial capital, Kolkata retains some of the country's most striking colonial buildings, yet at the same time it is truly an Indian city. It is unique in India in retaining trams and is the only place in the world to still have hand-pulled rickshaws – you take your life in your hands each time you cross Kolkata's streets. Kolkata's Maidan, the parkland, are the lungs of a city that is packed with some of the most densely populated slums, or bustees, anywhere in the world.

Central Kolkata

memories of the British in India

BBD Bagh (Dalhousie Square) and around

Many historic Raj buildings surround the square, which is quietest before 0900. Renamed Benoy Badal Dinesh (BBD) Bagh after three Bengali martyrs, the square has an artificial lake (tank) fed by natural springs that used to supply water to Kolkata's first residents.

The **Writers' Building** (1780), designed by Thomas Lyon as the trading headquarters of the East India Company, was refaced in 1880. It is now the state Government Secretariat. The classical block with 57 sets of identical windows was built like barracks inside. Across the road to the east, elegant **St Andrew's Kirk** (1814) ① *0900-1400*, like the earlier St John's Church (1787), was modelled partially on St Martin-in-the-Fields, London.

On the west side of the square, the white domed **General Post Office** (1866) was built on the site of the first Fort William. Around the corner, there is a quaint little **Postal Museum** ① *Mon-Sat 1100-1600, free*, which displays shabby maps, original post boxes and has a philatelic library.

> **Tip...**
> Asthma sufferers will find the traffic pollution in Kolkata very trying.

Running along the south of the square, **Mission Row** (now RN Mukherjee Road) is Kolkata's oldest street, and contains the **Old Mission Church** (consecrated 1770), built by the Swedish missionary Johann Kiernander.

Metcalfe Hall ① *Strand Rd, entrance from rear. Mon-Sat 1000-1700.* Facing the Hooghly (also spelt Hugli) on Strand Road is colonnaded **Metcalfe Hall** modelled on the Palace of Winds in Athens. This was once the home of the Imperial Library, and still contains the journals of the Asiatic Society in the ground floor **library** ① *Mon-Fri 0945-1815 (allegedly)*, plus a small exhibition on the first floor including glazed tiles from Gaur and Pandua, and a gallery of bricks. Unsurprisingly, the visitors' book shows an average of two tourists per month.

St John's Church ① *Council House St, 0800-1700, Rs 10.* The church was built in 1787 on soft subsoil that did not allow it to have a tall spire, and architecturally it was thought to be 'full of blunders'. Verandas were added to the north and south in 1811 to reduce the glare of the sun. Inside the vestry are Warren Hastings's table and chair, plus Raj-era paintings and prints. *The Last Supper*, by Johann Zoffany was restored in 2010 and shows the city's residents dressed as the apostles. Job Charnock is buried in the grounds. His octagonal mausoleum, the oldest piece of masonry in the city, is of Pallavaram granite (from Madras Presidency), which is named charnockite after him. The memorial built by Lord Curzon to the **Black Hole of Calcutta** was brought here from Dalhousie Square (BBD Bagh) in 1940.

Raj Bhavan Directly south of BBD Bagh is the imposing Raj Bhavan (1799-1802), the residence of the Governor of West Bengal, formerly Government House. It was modelled on Kedleston Hall in Derbyshire, England (later Lord Curzon's home), and designed by Charles Wyatt, one of many Bengal engineers who based their designs on famous British buildings (entrance not permitted). Nearby, the **Great Eastern Hotel** (1841) was in Mark Twain's day "the best hotel East of the Suez", but from the 1970s it steadily declined. However, it recently underwent major restoration by the Lalit group of hotels and reopened in 2014.

Kolkata Museum ① *Mon-Sat 1100-1800, last entry 1700, foreigners Rs 10 (Rs 15 on Sat), bag deposit.* The beautiful old **Town Hall** (1813) has been converted into the Kolkata Museum, telling the story of the independence movement in Bengal through a panoramic, cinematic display, starring an animatronic Rabindranath Tagore. Visitors are sped through in grouped tours, however, and some of the videos drag on rather. There's a good life-size diorama of a Bengali street and some great film posters.

High Court The bright-red gothic High Court (1872) was modelled on the medieval cloth merchants' hall at Ypres in Flanders. It is possible to enter through Gate F: a fascinating glimpse into Bar Rooms crammed floor-to-ceiling with books, and bustling with black-robed lawyers (no cameras allowed).

State Bank Archives and Museum ① *11th Fl, SBI, 1 Strand Rd, open Tue-Fri 1430-1700, free.* In a recent building designed to look period is a grand marble-floored repository of information; it also contains paintings of Raj India, furniture and memorabilia related to the early days of banking. The nearby **Floatel** bar (see page 557), on the Hooghly, is a good place to relax after wanderings.

Essential Kolkata

Finding your feet

Subhas Chandra Bose Airport at Dum Dum has an 'integrated terminal' for domestic and international flights, which opened in 2013. Transport to the city centre is by prepaid taxi or private bus; public buses are not recommended. Arrival at Howrah Train Station, on the west bank of the Hooghly, can be daunting and the taxi rank outside is often chaotic; use the prepaid taxi booth to the right as you exit – check the price chart and note that Sudder Street is less than 5 km. Trains to/from the north use the slightly less chaotic Sealdah Terminal east of the centre, which also has prepaid taxis. Long-distance buses arrive at Esplanade, 15 minutes' walk from most budget hotels. For further details, see Transport, page 561.

Getting around

You can cover much of Central Kolkata on foot. You may not fancy using hand-pulled rickshaws, but they become indispensable (and more costly) when the streets are flooded during monsoons. Buses and minibuses are often jam-packed, but routes comprehensively cover the city – conductors and bystanders will help you find the correct bus. The electric trams are slow but they are incredibly cheap and cover some interesting routes. The Metro, though limited to one line and very crowded, is the easiest way of getting from north to south. Taxis are relatively cheap (note that the meter reading is not the true fare; expect to pay double the meter fare, based on the driver's conversion chart), but you should allow plenty of time to get through very congested traffic. Many city centre roads become one-way or change direction from 1400 to 2100, so expect tortuous detours. Despite the footpath, it is not permitted to walk across the Vidyasagar Bridge (taxi drivers expect passengers to pay the Rs 10 toll). For further details, see Transport, page 561.

Best Kolkata watering holes

Indian Coffee House, page 553
Flury's, page 554
Blue & Beyond, page 557
Broadway Bar, page 557
Fairlawn Hotel, page 557
Oly Pub, page 557

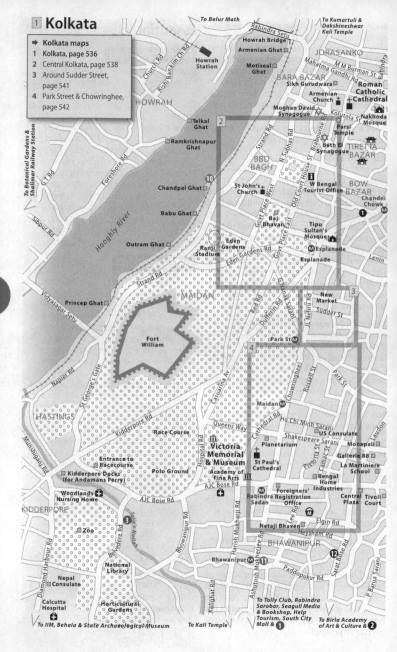

Kolkata

➡ **Kolkata maps**
1 Kolkata, page 536
2 Central Kolkata, page 538
3 Around Sudder Street, page 541
4 Park Street & Chowringhee, page 542

To Belur Math

To Kumartuli & Dakshineshwar Kali Temple

Rabindra Setu

Howrah Bridge
Armenian Ghat

JORASANKO

Howrah Station

Motiseal Ghat

Mahatma Gandhi Rd

M M Burman St

BARA BAZAR

Sikh Gurudwara

Armenian Church

Roman Catholic Cathedral

Moghan David Synagogue

Kolutola St

Nakhoda Mosque

Parsi Temple

HOWRAH

Telkal Ghat

2

Ramkrishnapur Ghat

Strand Rd

N Subhas Rd

Brabourne Rd

Beth El Synagogue

TIRETTA BAZAR

BBD BAGH

Old Court House St

Court House St

W Bengal Tourist Office

BOW BAZAR

Chandpal Ghat

St John's Church

Chandni Chowk

Babu Ghat

Raj Bhavan

Tipu Sultan's Mosque

Ranji Stadium

Eden Gardens

Esplanade

Esplanade

Lenin

To Botanical Gardens & Shalimar Railway Station

Foreshore Rd

Hooghly River

GT Rd

Sibpur Rd

Outram Ghat

Govt Place West

Govt Place East

Eden Gardens Rd

Strand Rd

Princep Ghat

Vidyasagar Setu

MAIDAN

Red Rd

Dufferin Rd

Cathedral Rd

JL Nehru Rd

New Market

3

Sudder St

Fort William

Park St

M

4

HASTINGS

Napier Rd

St George's Gate

Kidderpore Rd

Casuarina Av

Queens Way

Maidan

M

Chowringhee

Russell St

Park St

Laudon

Ho Chi Minh Sarani

US Consulate

Shakespeare Sarani

Monapali

Race Course

Hospital Rd

Victoria Memorial & Museum

Planetarium

St Paul's Cathedral

Camac St

Gallerie 88

La Martiniere School

Entrance to Racecourse

Kidderpore Docks (for Andamans Ferry)

Polo Ground

Academy of Fine Arts

AJC Bose Rd

Bengal Home Industries

Pretoria St

Foreigners' Registration Office

Central Plaza

Tivoli Court

Woodlands Nursing Home

AJC Bose Rd

Rabindra Sadan

M

Netaji Bhaven

M

Elgin Rd

Heysham Rd

KIDDERPORE

Munshiganj Rd

Diamond Harbour Rd

Zoo

Tolly's Nullah

Belvedere Rd

National Library

BHAWANIPUR

Bhawanipur Rd

Harish Mukharji Rd

Ashutosh Mukherjee Rd

Bhawanipur

M

11

12

Sarat Bose Rd

Nepal Consulate

Calcutta Hospital

Horticultural Gardens

Kalighat Rd

Paddopukur Rd

P Banua Sarani

To IIM, Behala & State Archaeological Museum

To Kali Temple

To Tolly Club, Rabindra Sarobar, Seagull Media & Bookshop, Help Tourism, South City Mall & 1

To Birla Academy of Art & Culture & 2

Esplanade Esplanade Mansions is a stunning Art Nouveau building on Esplanade Row East, built in 1910 by Jewish millionaire David Ezra. At the other end of the street, the minarets and domes of **Tipu Sultan's Mosque**, built by Tipu's son in 1842, poke above market stalls selling stationery and little kebab restaurants. The **Ochterlony Monument** (1828), renamed Shahid Minar (Martyrs' Memorial) in 1969, was built as a memorial to Sir David Ochterlony, who led East India Company troops against the Nepalese in 1814-1816. The 46-m-tall Greek Doric column has an Egyptian base and is topped by a Turkish cupola.

Eden Gardens ① *Daily 1200-1700.* Situated in the northwest corner of the Maidan (see below), the gardens were laid out in 1834 and named after Lord Auckland's sisters Emily and Fanny Eden. There are pleasant walks, a lake and a small Burmese pagoda (typical of this type of Pyatthat). Also here is the **Ranji Stadium** ① *usually open for matches only, a small tip at Gate 14 gains entry on other days*, where the first cricket match was played in 1864. Revamped in 2011 for the Cricket World Cup, it attracts massive crowds for IPL and Test matches.

The Maidan and around

Two hundred years ago this area was covered in dense jungle. Often called the 'lungs of the city', it is a unique green space, covering over 400 ha along Chowringhee (JL Nehru Road). Larger than New York's Central Park, it is perhaps the largest urban park in the world. In it stands Fort William and several clubhouses providing tennis, football, rugby, cricket and even crown green bowls. Thousands each day pursue a hundred different interests here: early morning yogis, model plane enthusiasts, weekend cricketers and performers earning their living, to vast political gatherings.

Fort William The massive Fort William was built by the British after their defeat in 1756, on the site of the village of Govindapur. Designed to be impregnable, it was roughly octagonal and large enough to house all the Europeans in the city in case of an attack. Water from the Hooghly was channelled to fill the wide moat and the surrounding jungle was cleared to give a clear field of fire; this later became the Maidan. The barracks, stables, arsenal, prison and St Peter's Church are still there, but the fort now forms the Eastern Region's Military Headquarters and entry is forbidden.

Where to stay 📍
66/2B The
  Guest House **7**
Bodhi Tree & Art Café **1**
Park Palace **6**
Residency
  Guest House **8**
Sharani Lodge **9**
Taj Bengal &
  Chinoiserie
  Restaurant **3**
Vedic Village **5**

Restaurants 🍴
6 Ballygunge Place **12**
Anand **1**
Banana Leaf **2**
Bhojohori Manna **4**
Dolly's the Tea Shop **8**
Indian Coffee House **3**
Krystal Chopsticks **6**
Mainland China **5**
Mirch Masala **9**
Rehmania & Shiraz **7**

Bars & clubs 🍷
Floatel **10**
Tripti's **11**

Victoria Memorial (1906-1921) ① T033-2223 1889-91, www.victoriamemorial-cal.org; gardens 0530-1815 (last entry 1745), Rs 4; museum Tue-Sun 1000-1700 (last entry 1630, very crowded on Sun), foreigners Rs 150, cameras not permitted inside; son et lumière show summer 1945, winter 1915, 45 mins, Rs 20 front seats, Rs 10 elsewhere. Located in the far southeast corner of the Maidan, the white marble monument to Queen Victoria and the Raj was the brain-child of Lord Curzon. Designed in Italian Renaissance/Indo-Saracenic style, it stands in large, well-kept grounds with ornamental pools.

2 Central Kolkata

➡ **Kolkata maps**
1 Kolkata, page 536
2 Central Kolkata, page 538
3 Around Sudder Street,
  page 541
4 Park Street & Chowringhee,
  page 542

Where to stay 🛏
Broadway & Bar 1
Buddha Dharmankur
  Sabha 6
Cosmos Guest House 5
Oberoi Grand &

Baan Thai Restaurant 2

Restaurants 🍴
Aaheli at Peerless Inn 3
Amber 1
Anand 2

Bhojohori Manna 5
Chung Wah 4
Madras 6

Bars & clubs 🍸
Floatel 8
Local Bars 9

Tram Line - - - - -

Kolkata

Calcutta, as it came to be named, was founded by the remarkable English merchant trader Job Charnock in 1690. He was in charge of the East India Company factory (ie warehouse) in Hooghly, then the centre of British trade from eastern India. Attacks from the local Muslim ruler forced him to flee – first downriver to Sutanuti and then 1500 km south to Chennai. However, in 1690 he selected three villages – Kalikata, Sutanuti and Govindpur – where Armenian and Portuguese traders had already settled, leased them from Emperor Aurangzeb and returned to what became the capital of British India.

The first fort here, named after King William III (completed 1707), was on the site of the present BBD Bagh. A deep defensive moat was dug in 1742 to strengthen the fort – the Maratha ditch. The Maratha threat never materialized but the city was captured easily by the 20-year-old Siraj-ud-Daula, the new Nawab of Bengal, in 1756. The 146 British residents who failed to escape by the fort's river gate were imprisoned for a night in a small guard room about 6 m by 5 m with only one window – the infamous 'Black Hole of Calcutta'. Some records suggest 64 people were imprisoned and only 23 survived.

The following year Robert Clive re-took the city. The new Fort William was built, and in 1772 Calcutta became the capital of British administration in India, with Warren Hastings as the first Governor of Bengal. Some of Calcutta's most impressive colonial buildings were built in the years that followed when it became the first city of British India. It was also a time of Hindu and Muslim resurgence.

Colonial Calcutta grew as new traders, soldiers and administrators arrived, establishing their exclusive social and sports clubs. Trade in cloth, silk, lac, indigo, rice, areca nut and tobacco had originally attracted the Portuguese and British to Bengal. Later Calcutta's hinterland producing jute, iron ore, tea and coal led to large British firms setting up headquarters in the city. Calcutta prospered as the commercial and political capital of British India until 1911, when the capital was transferred to Delhi.

Calcutta had to absorb huge numbers of migrants immediately after Partition in 1947. And, when Pakistan ceased trading with India in 1949, Calcutta's economy suffered a massive blow: it lost its supplies of raw jute, and its failure to attract new investment created critical economic problems. In the late 1960s the Communist Party of India Marxist, the CPI(M), was elected; their dominance was to last over 30 years. From 2000 the CPI(M) was committed to a mixed economy and sought foreign private investment, and the city's economy experienced a much needed upturn. In the 2011 state assembly election the communist government was defeated after 34 years in power by the Trinamool Congress. Controversial politician Mamata Bannerjee, known as "Didi", remains the current Chief Minister and the first woman to hold this position. The city officially changed its name to Kolkata in 2001.

A seated bronze Queen Victoria dominates the approach from the north, while a marble statue stands in the main hall where visitors sometimes leave flowers at her feet. The building is illuminated in the evening, when the musical fountain is a special draw. The statues over the entrance porches (including Motherhood, Prudence and Learning), and around the central dome (of Art, Architecture, Justice, Charity) came from Italy. The impressive weather vane, a 5-m-tall bronze winged Angel of Victory weighing three tonnes, looks tiny from below.

The principal gallery, covering the history of the city, is well presented and makes interesting reading. It includes some fascinating lithographs and illustrations of the city during the Raj period. The painting gallery has magnificent works by European artists in India from 1770-1835, including Zoffany, the two Daniells and Samuel Davis. Recently, the upper gallery of the Queen's Hall was reopened after more than a decade, and visitors can now walk around the inside of the rotunda again.

St Paul's Cathedral ① *Cathedral Rd, 0900-1200, 1500-1800, 5 services on Sun.* East of the memorial, this is the original metropolitan church of British India. Completed in 1847, its Gothic tower (dedicated in 1938) was designed to replace the earlier steeples which were destroyed by earthquakes. The cathedral has a fine altar piece, three 'Gothic' stained-glass windows, two Florentine frescoes and the great West window by Burne-Jones. The original stained-glass East window, intended for St George's Windsor, was destroyed by a cyclone in 1964 and was replaced by the present one four years later.

Academy of Fine Arts ① *2 Cathedral Rd, Tue-Sun 1500-2000 (ground floor galleries), 1200-1900 (museum), free.* The Academy was founded in 1933. The first floor museum has a newly restored gallery showing 33 pictures by Rabindranath Tagore, plus his writings and some personal effects. The textiles gallery and other sections have been closed for years, but may reopen soon. The ground floor galleries show changing exhibitions contemporary paintings and sculptures by Indian artists.

Park Street and Chowringhee

Along Chowringhee, you can still see some of the old imposing structures with pillared verandas (designed by Italian architects as residences of prominent Englishmen), though modern high-rise buildings and a flyover have transformed the skyline of what was the ancient pilgrim route to Kalighat. Conveniently close to Chowringhee and Esplanade, **Sudder Street** is the focus for Kolkata's backpackers and attracts touts, beggars and the odd drug pusher.

> **Tip...**
> Beggars on Chowringhee and Park Street often belong to organized syndicates to whom they have to pay a large percentage of their earnings for the 'privilege' of working the area. Women asking for milk or rice for their baby are commonly deployed on Sudder Street.

New Market Just north of Sudder Street is the vast and archaic shopping hub of New Market, opened in 1874 as Sir Stuart Hogg Market, largely rebuilt following a fire in 1985 and recently revamped. The clock tower outside, which strikes every 15 minutes, was imported from England. It used to be said that you could buy anything from a needle to an elephant (on order) in one of its stalls. Today it's still worth a visit; arrive early in the morning to watch it come alive (many shops closed on Sundays).

Indian Museum ① *27 Chowringhee (JL Nehru Rd), T033-2286 1679, www.indianmuseumkolkata.org, Mar-Nov Tue-Sun 1000-1700, Dec-Feb 1000-1630, foreigners Rs 150, cameras Rs 50/100 with tripod; no bags allowed (there is a cloakroom).* Around the corner from Sudder Street is the Indian Museum possibly Asia's largest. The Jadu Ghar (House of Magic) was founded in 1814 and has an enormous collection. The colonnaded Italianate building around a central courtyard has 36 galleries (though sections are often closed for restoration). Parts are poorly lit and gathering dust so it is best to be selective. Highlights include: the stone statutory with outstanding exhibits from the Harappa and Mohenjo Daro periods; the Cultural Anthropology room with information on India's tribes; and the excellent new Mask Gallery (hidden on the fourth floor, up the stairs past the ground floor coin collection and library). There are some lovely miniature paintings, the Egyptian room has a popular mummy and the Plant Gallery is curiously beautiful, with jars, prints and samples filling every inch of space. The animals in the Natural History Gallery have been there since 1878, while the birds are so dirty they are all uniformly black in colour. The geological collection with Siwalik fossils is mind-bogglingly huge. Allow at least couple of hours.

Asiatic Society ① *1 Park St, T033-2229 0779, www.asiaticsocietycal.com. Mon-Fri 1000-1800, free. Bring a passport, and note that signing in is (at least) a triplicate process.* This is the oldest institution of Oriental studies in the world and was founded in 1784 by the great Orientalist, Sir William Jones. It is a treasure house of 150,000 books and 60,000 ancient manuscripts in most Asian languages, although permission is required to see specific pieces. The museum includes an Ashokan edict, rare coins and paintings. The library is worth a visit for its dusty travelogues and titles on the history of Kolkata. The original 1804 building is to the rear; you can ask to view the impressive staircase adorned with statues and paintings. Here also is the manuscript restoration department, where staff are pleased to explain the work they undertake.

Park Street Cemetery ① *Daily 0800-1630, free, information booklet Rs 100, security guard opens gate and will expect you to sign the visitors' book.* The cemetery was opened in 1767 to accommodate

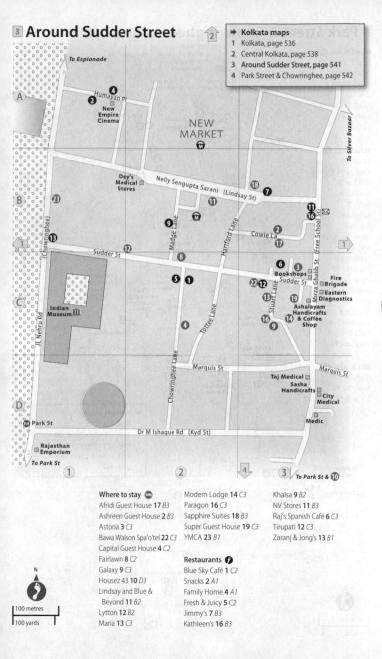

3 Around Sudder Street

To Esplanade

→ Kolkata maps
1 Kolkata, page 536
2 Central Kolkata, page 538
3 **Around Sudder Street, page 541**
4 Park Street & Chowringhee, page 542

To Silver Bazaar

NEW MARKET

Humayan Pl
New Empire Cinema

To Esplanade

Dey's Medical Stores
Nelly Sengupta Sarani (Lindsay St)

Madge Lane
Hartford Lane
Cowie La

Sudder St

Tottee Lane

Chowringhee Lane

Marquis St
Marquis St

Chowringhee
JL Nehru Rd

Indian Museum

Bookshops
Sudder St
Stuart Lane
Mirza Ghalib St (Free School St)

Fire Brigade
Eastern Diagnostics
Ashalayam Handicrafts & Coffee Shop

Taj Medical
Sasha Handicrafts
City Medical
Medic

Park St
Rajasthan Emporium
To Park St

Dr M Ishaque Rd (Kyd St)

To Park St & 10

N
100 metres
100 yards

Where to stay
Afridi Guest House **17** B3
Ashreen Guest House **2** B3
Astoria **3** C3
Bawa Walson Spa'o'tel **22** C3
Capital Guest House **4** C2
Fairlawn **8** C2
Galaxy **9** C3
Housez 43 **10** D3
Lindsay and Blue & Beyond **11** B2
Lytton **12** B2
Maria **13** C3

Modern Lodge **14** C3
Paragon **16** C3
Sapphire Suites **18** B3
Super Guest House **19** C3
YMCA **23** B1

Restaurants
Blue Sky Café **1** C2
Snacks **2** A1
Family Home **4** A1
Fresh & Juicy **5** C2
Jimmy's **7** B3
Kathleen's **16** B3

Khalsa **9** B2
NV Stores **11** B3
Raj's Spanish Café **6** C3
Tirupati **12** C3
Zaranj & Jong's **13** B1

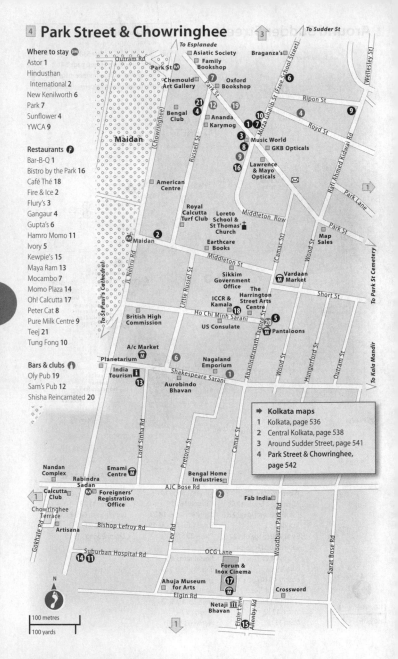

④ Park Street & Chowringhee

To Sudder St

To Esplanade

Where to stay
Astor **1**
Hindusthan
 International **2**
New Kenilworth **6**
Park **7**
Sunflower **4**
YWCA **9**

Restaurants
Bar-B-Q **1**
Bistro by the Park **16**
Café Thé **18**
Fire & Ice **2**
Flury's **3**
Gangaur **4**
Gupta's **6**
Hamro Momo **11**
Ivory **5**
Kewpie's **15**
Maya Ram **13**
Mocambo **7**
Momo Plaza **14**
Oh! Calcutta **17**
Peter Cat **8**
Pure Milk Centre **9**
Teej **21**
Tung Fong **10**

Bars & clubs
Oly Pub **19**
Sam's Pub **12**
Shisha Reincarnated **20**

Asiatic Society
Braganza's
Family Bookshop
Park St
Chemould Art Gallery
Oxford Bookshop
Ripon St
Bengal Club
Ananda
Karymog
Music World
GKB Optics
Lawrence & Mayo Opticals
Royd St

Maidan

Russell St

Outram Rd

(Chowringhee)

American Centre

Royal Calcutta Turf Club

Loreto School & St Thomas' Church

Middleton Row

Park Lane

Park St

Earthcare Books

Middleton St

Map Sales

Maidan

JL Nehru Rd

Little Russel St

To St Paul's Cathedral

Sikkim Government Office

The Harrington Street Arts Centre

ICCR & Kamala

Ho Chi Minh Sarani

US Consulate

Pantaloons

Vardaan Market

Camac St

Wood St

Short St

To Park St Cemetery

British High Commission

A/c Market

Planetarium

India Tourism

Aurobindo Bhavan

Nagaland Emporium

Shakespeare Sarani

Abanindranath Tagore St

Wood St

Hungerford St

Outram St

To Kala Mandir

Nandan Complex

Rabindra Sadan

Emami Centre

Calcutta Club

Chowringhee Terrace

Artisana

Foreigners' Registration Office

AJC Bose Rd

Bishop Lefroy Rd

Lord Sinha Rd

Pretoria St

Lee Rd

Camac St

Bengal Home Industries

Fab India

Woodburn Park Rd

Sarat Bose Rd

Gokhale Rd

Suburban Hospital Rd

OCG Lane

Forum & Inox Cinema

Ahuja Museum for Arts

Crossword

Elgin Rd

Netaji Bhavan

Elgin Lane

Allenby Rd

> **Kolkata maps**
> 1 Kolkata, page 536
> 2 Central Kolkata, page 538
> 3 Around Sudder Street, page 541
> 4 Park Street & Chowringhee,
>   page 542

N

100 metres
100 yards

the large number of British who died 'serving' their country. It is a peaceful paradise and a step into history, located on the south side of one of Kolkata's busiest streets, with a maze of soaring obelisks shaded by tropical trees. The heavily inscribed decaying headstones, rotundas, pyramids and urns have been restored, and gardeners are actively trying to beautify the grounds.

Several of the inscriptions make interesting reading. Death, often untimely, came from tropical diseases or other hazards such as battles, childbirth and even melancholia. More uncommonly, it was an excess of alcohol, or as for Sir Thomas D'Oyly, through "an inordinate use of the hokkah". Rose Aylmer died after eating too many pineapples! Tombs include those of Colonel Kyd, founder of the Botanical Gardens, the great oriental scholar Sir William Jones, and the fanciful mausoleum of the Irish Major-General 'Hindoo' Stuart.

Scottish Cemetery ① *Karaya Rd, daily 0700-1730, free, pamphlet by donation to the caretaker.* Across AJC Bose Road is the smaller and far more derelict Scottish Cemetery, established in 1820. The Kolkata Scottish Heritage Trust began work in 2008 to restore some of the 1600 tumbledown graves but the undergrowth is rampant and jungle prevails. It is also known as the 'dissenters' graveyard', as this was where non-Anglicans were buried. Also nearby, on AJC Bose Road, is the enormous **Lower Circular Road Cemetery** created in 1840 when Park Street Cemetery became full.

North Kolkata

potters, intellectuals and some interesting museums

College Street
This is the heart of intellectual Kolkata with the **university** and several academic institutions, including the old **Sanskrit College** and the elite **Presidency College**. Europeans and Indian benefactors established the Hindu College (1817) to provide a liberal education. In 1855, this became the Presidency College. A centre for 19th-century Bengali writers, artists and reformers, it spawned the early 20th-century Swadeshi Movement. The famous **Indian Coffee House** (opened in 1944), cavernous haunt of the city's intelligentsia, has tonnes of atmosphere and is always packed despite the average coffee and food. Along the pavements are interesting second-hand book stalls.

Ashutosh Museum of Indian Art ① *University Centenary Building, College Street, Mon-Fri 1100-1630, closed university holidays, Rs 10, camera Rs 200.* This is well maintained and worth a visit. The ground floor is packed with eastern Indian sculptures and terracotta tiles depicting figures. The first floor has colourful Bengali and Orissan folk art, faded textiles, and a hoard of paintings including 14th- to 19th-century miniatures, Kalighat paintings, Nepalese art and Tibetan *thankas*. Also look out for the model of the Senate Hall (1873-1960), which was pulled down to make way for the concrete monster of the present Centenary block in the days before heritage buildings were accorded any value.

Howrah Bridge area
Howrah Bridge (Haora), or Rabindra Setu, was opened in 1943. This single-span cantilever bridge, a quintessential image of Kolkata, replaced the old pontoon (floating) bridge that first joined the city of Kolkata with Howrah and the railway station. To avoid affecting river currents and silting, the two 80-m-high piers rise from road level; the 450-m span expands by a metre on a hot day. It is the busiest bridge in the world in terms of foot passengers (many with improbable loads on their heads). Wrestlers can be seen underneath and there is a daily **flower market** beneath the eastern end at Mullik Ghat, with piles of marigolds glowing against the mud. The pedestrian-free **Vidyasagar Setu Bridge**, further south, has eased the traffic burden slightly.

> **Tip...**
> At night Howrah bridge is illuminated, which makes a fine sight. If waiting for a night train at Howrah station, go to the first floor waiting rooms for a good view.

Armenian Kolkata Southeast of Howrah Bridge, the gorgeously well-kept **Armenian Church** of **Holy Nazareth** (1724) is a reminder of the important trading role the small Armenian community, who mostly came from Iran, played from the 17th century. The church is open 0600-1200 on weekdays or you can ask someone to open up in order to view the beautifully maintained interior.

A gravestone in the compound is inscribed with the date 1630. The 150 or so Armenians in the city still hold a service in Armenian in one of their two churches in the city every Sunday. Their college on Mirza Ghalib Street (also the birthplace of William Makepeace Thackery in 1811) has boarding pupils from Armenia who are usually orphans. To the east of the Church of Holy Nazareth is the **Roman Catholic Cathedral** (1797), built by the Portuguese.

Jewish Kolkata The Jewish community, mostly Sephardic and of Baghdadi origin, was once very prominent in commerce in the city and numbered about 6000 before the Second World War. Their two synagogues are well maintained with stained-glass windows. The grander of the two is the church-like and cavernous **Moghan David Synagogue** (1884) ① *Canning St, daily 0900-1700*, while the nearby **Beth El Synagogue** ① *26/1 Pollock St, Sun-Fri 1000-1700*, is smaller. Just around the corner from the Moghan David Synagogue, on Brabourne Road hidden behind market stalls, is the older and derelict **Neveh Shalome Synagogue** (now inaccessible). To view the interior of the synagogues, it is necessary to get signed permission either from **Nahoum & Son's Bakery** ① *Shop F20, New Market, T033-6526 9936 (easiest)*, or from the office at 1 Hartford Lane. There are only around 30-40 elderly Jews left in the city, but they continue to congregate at Nahoum & Son's Bakery. The Jewish Girls School in Park Street no longer has Jewish pupils; in fact the vast majority of the girls are Muslims from a nearby neighbourhood.

Chinese Kolkata A few reminders that there was once a Chinatown in Kolkata remain in the form of Chinese 'churches'. Seek out the **Sea Ip Church** (1905), which has an intricately carved wooden altar and the **Nam Soon Church**, with a school at the rear. The latter is gorgeously maintained with bright paint, a huge bell and drum, and a little courtyard with trees. Both are willingly opened by the custodians. At the top of Bentinck Street, where it meets BB Ganguly Street, are several tiny old-fashioned shoe shops run by aging members of the Chinese community.

Rabindra Sarani and around
Trams run along Rabindra Sarani, previously known as the Chitpur Road and one of the oldest streets in the city. Rising above the street-level are the three green domes, 27 minarets and multiple archways of **Nakhoda Mosque** (1926), Kolkata's principal mosque holding 10,000 worshippers.

Rabindra Bharati Museum ① *6/4 Dwarakanath Tagore Lane (red walls visible down lane opposite 263 Rabindra Sarani), Mon-Fri 1000-1700, Sat 1000-1330, Sun and holidays 1100-1400, www.museum. rbu.ac.in/about_rb*. A large brick gateway leads to the family home of Rabindranath Tagore, who won the Nobel Prize for Literature in 1913. It's a peaceful enclave away from the teeming chaos of Rabindra Sarani and showcases Tagore's life and works, as well as the 19th-century Renaissance movement in Bengal. Be sure to explore along all the corridors, as it's easy to miss the galleries of Indian and European art, and the Japanese exhibition rooms.

Marble Palace ① *46 Muktaram Babu St, Tue, Wed, Fri-Sun 1000-1600. Free pass from WBTDC (see page 550) 24 hrs ahead, or baksheesh (Rs 20 per visitor) to the security man at the gate and a further tip to the attendant who will accompany you around. Shoes must be removed, no photography allowed.* Located in Chor Bagan ('Thieves' Garden'), the one-man collection of Raja Rajendra Mullick is housed in his ornate home (1835) with an Italianate courtyard, classical columns and Egyptian sphinxes. Family members still inhabit a portion of the house while servants' descendants live in the huts that encircle the grounds. Six sleeping marble lions and statuary grace the lawns and there is a veritable menagerie at the back of the garden. The galleries, disorganized and gathering dust, are crammed with statues, porcelain, clocks, mirrors, chandeliers and English (Reynolds), Dutch (Reubens) and Italian paintings. The pink, grey and white Italian marble floors are remarkable, as is the solid rosewood statue of Queen Victoria. Allow one hour to look round, or take a book and relax in the garden. The rambling two-floor museum has more than just curiosity appeal – it is one of Kolkata's gems.

Northeast of the city centre
Northeast of the city centre, accessed from Belgachia Metro station, is a cluster of three Digambar Jain temples, one of the most tranquil spots in the city. The meticulously maintained and ornate **Paresnath Temple** ① *0700-1200, 1500-2000, no leather*, is dedicated to the 10th Tirthankara. Consecrated around 1867, it is richly decorated with mirrors, Victorian tiles and Venetian glass mosaics.

ON THE ROAD

Worship of the clay goddess

Durga Puja, the 17th-century festival in honour of the clay goddess, precedes the full moon in late September/early October, when all offices and institutions close down and the metro only operates from the late afternoon.

Images of the 10-armed, three-eyed goddess, a form of Shakti or Kali astride her 'vehicle' the lion, portray Durga slaying Mahisasura, the evil buffalo demon. Durga, shown with her four children Lakshmi, Sarasvati, Ganesh and Kartik, is worshipped in thousands of brightly illuminated and beautifully decorated *pandals* (marquees). Traditionally these are made of bamboo and coloured cloth, but often modern *pandals* are veritable works of art constructed to complex designs and tapping into current themes or re-creating popular Indian landmarks. The priests perform prayers at appointed times in the morning and evening. On the fourth and last day of festivities, huge and often emotionally-charged processions follow devotees who carry the clay figures to be immersed in the river at many points along the banks. The potters return to collect clay from the river bank once again for the following year.

You can see the image makers in Kumartuli (see below) a few days earlier and visit the *pandals* early in the day, before they become intensely crowded. Local communities are immensely proud of their *pandals* and no effort is spared to put on the most impressive display. The images are decorated with intricate silver, golden or *shola* (white pith) ornaments; there are moving electric light displays, and huge structures are built (sometimes resembling a temple) in order to win competitions.

Clive's House ① *Off Jessore Rd in Nagarbajar, Dum Dum.* Difficult to find (and perhaps not worth the effort unless you are a true aficionado of Raj history) is the country home of the first governor general of the East India Company. It is the oldest colonial monument in Kolkata. For years, Bangladeshi immigrants lived in and around the derelict property until it was restored in 2008. The brick walls are being re-consumed by plant life and it requires some imagination to envisage its former glory.

North along the Hooghly

Kumartuli Off Chitpur Road, the *kumars* or potters work all year, preparing clay images around cores of bamboo and straw. For generations they have been making life-size idols for the *pujas* or festivals, particularly of goddess Durga on a lion, slaying the demon. The images are usually unbaked since they are immersed in the holy river at the end of the festival. As the time of the *pujas* approaches, you will see thousands of images, often very brightly painted and gaudily dressed, awaiting the final finishing touch by the master painter. There are also *shola* artists who make decorations for festivals and weddings. The potters' area of Kumartuli Is being slowly rebuilt, and concrete structures are replacing the towering bamboo workshops that were so very photogenic.

Belur Math ① *Some 16 km north of the city, daily 0600-1200, 1600-1900.* Belur Math is the international headquarters of the **Ramakrishna Mission**, founded in 1899 by Swami Vivekananda, a disciple of the 19th-century Hindu saint Ramakrishna. He preached the unity of all religions, as symbolized in the architecture of the *Math* ('monastery'), which synthesizes Hindu, Christian and Islamic styles in a peaceful and meditative atmosphere.

Tip...
Ride the ferry boat (Rs 15) across the Hooghly between Belur Math and Dakshineshwar Temple for a lovely 20-minute journey at any time of day.

Dakshineshwar Kali Temple ① *0600-1200, 1500-1800, 1830-2100, no photography allowed inside. Buses from BBD Bagh go to Dunlop Intersection, from where it's a short auto ride to the temple; or trains run from Sealdah to Dakshineshwar.* On the opposite side of the river from Belur Math is the Dakshineshwar Temple, a huge Kali temple was built in 1847 by Rani Rashmoni. The 12 smaller temples in the courtyard are dedicated to Siva and there are also temples to Radha and Krishna. Because of the Rani's low caste, no priest would serve there until Ramakrishna's elder brother agreed and was succeeded by Ramakrishna himself. Here, Ramakrishna achieved his spiritual vision of the unity of all religions. The temple is crowded with colourfully clad devotees, particularly on Sundays when there are lengthy queues, and is open to all faiths.

South Kolkata

temples, markets, gardens and museums

Netaji Museum
Netaji Bhavan, 38/1 Elgin Rd, Tue-Sun 1100-1430 (last entry 1615), Rs 5, no photography.

This museum remembers the mission of Subas Chandra Bose, the leader of the INA (Indian National Army), and is in the house where he lived before he had to flee the British oppressors. On the first floor, you can view his bedroom and study (where walls are painted with the tricolours of the Congress flag), although panes of glass prevent close inspection of his possessions. A detailed video is played in the second floor rooms showing old footage and giving a detailed explanation of his life's work. Interesting is the German Room, with a photo of Netaji meeting Hitler and information on Azad Hind and the Indo-German Friendship Society.

Kalighat Kali Temple and around
Off Ashok Mukherjee Rd, 0500-1500, 1700-2200.

This is the temple to Kali (1809), the patron goddess of Kolkata, usually seen in her bloodthirsty form garlanded with skulls. There was an older temple here, where the goddess's little toe is said to have fallen when Siva carried her charred corpse in a frenzied dance of mourning, and she was cut into pieces by Vishnu's *chakra*. Where once human sacrifices were made (up until 1835, a boy was beheaded every Friday), the lives of goats are offered daily on two wooden blocks to the south of the temple.

When visiting the temple, priests will attempt to snare foreigners for the obligatory *puja*. A barrage may start as far away as 500 m from the temple. Don't be fooled in to handing over your shoes and succumbing to any priests until you are clearly inside the temple, despite being shown 'priest ID' cards. An acceptable minimum donation is Rs 50, books showing previous donations of Rs 3000 are doubtless faked. Having done the *puja*, you'll probably be left alone to soak up the atmosphere.

Nirmal Hriday Mother Teresa, an Albanian by birth, came to India to teach as a Loreto nun in 1931. She started her Order of the Missionaries of Charity in Kalighat to serve the destitute and dying 19 years later. Nirmal Hriday ('Pure Heart'), near the Kali Temple, the first home for the dying was opened in 1952. Mother Teresa died on 5 September 1997 but her work continues. You may see nuns in their white cotton saris with blue borders busy working in the many homes, clinics and orphanages in the city.

Gariahat
The neighbourhoods around Gariahat are more middle class and greener than Central Kolkata, but no less interesting, with plenty of good restaurants and small hotels.

Birla Mandir ① *0600-1100 and 1630-2030.* On Gariahat Road, the shiny white edifice pulls in a lot of devotees and is particularly impressive when lit up at night. Taking 22 years to complete, another gift of the Birla family, it is modelled on the Lingaraj Temple at Bhubaneshwar and is covered with carvings both inside and out. No photos are permitted inside. Just north of the temple is the **CIMA Gallery** (see page 558) which is worth a look.

Gariahat Market South of the Birla Mandir, beyond the southeast corner of Gariahat Crossing, is Gariahat Market which specializes in fish and is a fascinating hive of activity, especially in the early morning. Take a walk west from the crossing along 2-km Rash Behari Avenue, one of the city's veliest streets, lined with sari stalls, *mehdi* (henna) artists, momo vendors and vegetable sellers; it's especially atmospheric at dusk.

Birla Academy of Art and Culture ① *108/109 Southern Av, T033-2466 2843, Tue-Sun 1600-2000.* A couple of blocks south in a modern high-rise, the Academy concentrates on medieval and contemporary paintings and sculpture. The ground floor sculpture gallery has been recently remodelled, and displays some beautiful pieces including Buddhist and Hindu statues. It is well lit and worth visiting. The upper levels host changing art exhibitions.

Rabindra Sarobar

The large and pleasant lake of Rabindra Sarobar is shaded by ancient trees and surrounded by a pathway perfect for joggers and walkers. There are several rowing clubs (the oldest dates from 1858), and Laughing Clubs meet in the mornings (around 0600) to mix yoga and group laughing.

> **Tip...**
> It's possible to walk from the Buddhist Temple, via Dhakuria Bridge, to the **Dakshinapan** shopping complex (see page 559) and refresh at **Dolly's The Tea Shop** (see page 556).

A road from the southwest corner of the lake leads to the trim little **Japanese Buddhist Temple** (1935), the oldest temple of the Nichiren sect in India. Visitors are welcomed, and can join in the hypnotic prayers by beating handheld drums (at dawn and dusk). A slim congregation of ex-Ghurkhas, Nepali ladies and bemused Bengalis are drawn in. The interior is restful with an elaborate golden shrine, gaudy flowers, ornamental lanterns and origami birds which somehow come together to pleasing effect.

Alipore

South of the Maidan, the elite address of Alipore is home to a couple of sights.

National Library ① *Belvedere Rd.* The National Library was once the winter residence of the Lieutenant Governors of Bengal. Built in the Renaissance Italian style, with a double row of classical columns, it is approached through a triple arched gateway and a drive between mahogany and mango trees. The library itself, the largest in the country with over eight million books, is now mainly housed in an adjacent newer building; sadly, the old building can no longer be entered.

Kolkata Zoo ① *Opposite the library. Fri-Wed 0900-1700, Rs 10.* Opened in 1876, the zoo houses a wide variety of animal and bird life. The white tigers from Rewa and the tigon – a cross between a tiger and a lion – are the rarest animals. A reptile house and aquarium are across the road. There are restaurants and picnics are permitted, but it's often terrifyingly busy (particularly at the weekend).

Agri-Horticultural Gardens ① *Alipore Rd, 0600-1300 and 1400-1830, Rs 10.* The expansive gardens are the most peaceful green space in the city. The Horticultural Society was started in 1820 by the Baptist missionary William Carey. Bring a book; you'll be the only visitor during the week.

State Archaeological Museum

Next to Behala tram depot, 1 Satyen Roy Rd, off Diamond Harbour Rd, Behala, Wed-Sun 1000-1630 (last entry 1600), Rs 5. Shared autos run from Kalighat metro to Behala, finishing close to the museum entrance.

This little-visited yet well-presented museum has seven galleries over two floors, housed in a modern structure adjacent to the original colonial building. Galleries are devoted to West Bengal sites, such as the Buddhist remains of Nandadirghi Vihara near Malda, and the terracotta Hindu temples in Purulia. There's a meagre selection of local stone sculpture, intricate metal work, and a selection of Bengali paintings including Kalighat Pat (mostly religious in nature, but the famous *Two Women and a Rose* is a notable secular exception), and Murshidabad-style painting.

Botanical Gardens

20 km south from BBD Bagh, 0700-1700, Rs 50, avoid Sun and public holidays when it is very crowded, catch a bus from Esplanade; minibuses and CTC buses (No C-12) ply the route.

Kolkata's Botanical Gardens, on the west bank of the Hooghly, were founded in 1787 by the East India Company. The flourishing 250-year-old banyan tree, with a circumference of almost 400 m, is perhaps the largest in the world. The original trunk was destroyed by lightning in 1919 but over 2800 offshoots form an impressive sight. The avenues of Royal Cuban palms and mahogany trees are impressive and there are interesting and exotic specimens in the herbarium and collection of ferns and cactii. The gardens are peaceful and deserted during the week and make a welcome change from the city.

Around Kolkata

take the train uprive

There are several interesting places for a day's outing north of Kolkata in Hooghly District. When the Mughals lost power, several of the ancient seats of earlier rulers of Bengal became centres of foreign trade. Many European nations had outposts along the river. The Portuguese and British settled at Hooghly; the Dutch chose Chinsura, the French, Chandernagore; the Danes, Serampore; the Greeks had an outpost at Rishra, and the Germans and Austrians had one at Bhadreswar.

These old colonial towns straggle up the west bank of the Hooghly, providing insight into contemporary small-town life in Bengal as well as preserving some beautiful old colonial and Muslim buildings. It's best to take a train (buses are slow); avoid peak hours, and keep an eye on your possessions.

Barrackpur

In Barrackpur, on the eastern side of the Hooghly (25 km north of Kolkata), the riverside **Gandhi Ghat** is a picturesque spot. There is **Gandhi Memorial Museum** and a pleasant garden in memory of Jawaharlal Nehru. The bronze Raj statues, removed from their pedestals in Central Kolkata after Independence, have found their way to the gardens of the bungalow of the former governor (Flagstaff House). The tower was part of the river signalling system. The town is accessed by train from Sealdah station.

Shrirampur (Serampore)

Founded by the Danes in 1616 as Fredricnagore, Serampore, became a Danish colony in 1755. From the early 19th century it was the centre of missionary activity, until sold to the East India Company in 1845. The Government House, two churches (one of which is closed and unsafe to enter), the Old Court House (which is being renovated) and a Danish cemetery remain. There is a **College of Textile Technology** ① *12 Carey Rd, 1000-1630 (Sat 1000-1300)*. The Baptist missionaries, Carey, Marshman and Ward came to Serampore since they were not welcomed by the English administrators in Calcutta. They set up the Baptist Mission Press, which by 1805 was printing in seven Indian languages. **Serampore College** (1818) ① *T033-2662 2322, Mon-Fri 1000-1600, Sat 1000-1300, with permission from the principal*, India's first Christian theological college and still operating as such, was allowed to award degrees by the Danish king in 1829. The library has rare Sanskrit, Pali and Tibetan manuscripts and the Bible in more than 40 Asian languages. Serampore is half an hour on a local train from Howrah station.

Chandernagore

The former French colony, which dates back to 1673, was one of the tiny pockets of non-British India that did not gain Independence in 1947, but was handed over to India after a referendum in 1950. The churches, convents and cemeteries of the French are still there, although the old French street names have been replaced by Bengali ones. The former **Quai du Dupleix**, with its riverfront benches, still has a somewhat Gallic air. The Bhubanesvari and Nandadulal temples are worth visiting, especially during **Jagaddhatri Puja**. The **Institute Chandernagore** ① *at the Residency, Mon-Sat except Thu 1600-1830, Sun 1100-1700*, has interesting documents and relics of the French in India. The orange-painted Italian missionary church (1726) also stands witness to Chandernagore's European past.

Chinsura

The Dutch acquired Chinsura from the Nawab of Murshidabad in 1628 and built the **Fort Gustavus**, but it was exchanged with Sumatra (Indonesia) and became British in 1825. The octagonal Dutch church (1678) with its cemetery nearby, a 17th-century Armenian church and three East India Company barracks remain. The Dutch are still remembered at the **Shandesvar Siva Temple** on special occasions, when the lingam is bizarrely decked in Western clothes and a Dutch sword!

Hooghly

The Portuguese set up a factory in Hooghly in 1537 but Emperor Shah Jahan took the important trading post in 1632. The East India Company built their factory in 1651, destroyed in skirmishes marking the following six years, but Clive regained Hooghly for the company in 1757. The **Shi'a Imambara of Hazi Mohammed Mohasin** (1836-1876) has fine marble inlay decoration, a silver pulpit and elaborate lanterns. In **Chota Pandua**, nearby, interesting Muslim buildings include the ruins of the 14th-century Bari Masjid which has elements of Buddhist sculpture. In Rajbalhat, the **Amulya Pratnasala Museum** ① *Thu-Tue 1400-2100, closed 2nd and 4th Tue of the month*, exhibits sculpture, coins, terracottas and manuscripts.

Bandel

Bandel (Portuguese *bandar* or wharf) is now a railway junction town. The Portuguese built **Bandel Church** to Our Lady of the Rosary around 1660, on the site of an older Augustinian monastery. The keystone of the original church (1599), perhaps the earliest in Bengal, is on the riverside gate. Destroyed in 1640 by Shah Jahan, the church was reinstated 20 years later. The seafaring Portuguese believed that the statue of Our Lady of Happy Voyages in the bell tower could work miracles. Lost in the river, while being carried to save it from Shah Jahan's soldiers, it miraculously reappeared two centuries later. The 18th-century stone and terracotta **Hanseswari Temple** is 4 km away.

Tribeni and Pandua (Hooghly District)

Originally *Saptagram* (seven villages), **Tribeni** (three rivers) is particularly holy, being at the confluence of the Ganga, Saraswati and Kunti. It has many Hindu temples and 11th- to 12th-century Vaishnavite and Buddhist structures. The remains of the **Mazar of Zafarkhan Ghazi** (1313), the earliest mausoleum in eastern India, shows how black basalt sculpture and columns of earlier Hindu temples and palaces were incorporated into Muslim buildings. To the west, **Pandua** (not to be confused with the site further north; see page 573) has several remains of the Pala and Sena periods. Shah Sufi-ud-din is thought to have built the 39-m **Victory Tower** after defeating the local Hindu ruler in 1340. Its circular base had a court house. Outside, a staircase spirals up the fluted surface, while inside there is enamelled decoration. Hoards of Kushana and Gupta Dynasty gold coins have been found in nearby **Mahanad**.

Kalna

The town north of Pandua, centred on the **Maharaja of Burdwan's Palace**, has several fine 18th-century terracotta temples. Look for the *Ramayana* scenes on the large Lalji (1739), Krishna panels on the Krishnachandra (1752), assorted friezes on the Ananta Vasudeva (1754) and the later Pratapesvara (1849). Across the way is the unusual circular **Siva Temple** (1809) with 108 small double-vaulted shrines. Kalna has trains from Kolkata, and there are rickshaws at the station, 3 km from the temples.

Nabadwip

The birthplace of Sri Chaitanya – the 14th-century Bengali religious reformer – is a pilgrimage centre for his followers, and the river ghats are lined with temples where devotees worship by singing *keertans* and *bhajans*. **International Society for Krishna Consciousness** (ISKCON) has a **Chandrodaya Mandir** ① *Mayapu, across the river, until 1300*, and a guesthouse (inexpensive dorms, air-conditioned rooms and cheap meals). Nabadwip has trains from Sealdah and Howrah, and ferries across to Mayapur.

Tourist information

British Council
L&T Chambers, 16 Camac St,
www.britishcouncil.org/indea.htm.
Mon-Sat 1100-1900.
Good for UK newspapers, reference books.

India Tourism
4 Shakespeare Sarani, T033-2282 5813.
Mon-Fri 0930-1800, Sat 0900-1300.
Can provide a city map and also information
for all India.

West Bengal Tourism Development
Corporation (WBTDC)
BBD Bagh, T033-2248 8271, www.wbtourism.
gov.in. Mon-Fri 1030-1630, Sat 1030-1300;
also a counter at the station in Howrah.
More useful.

Where to stay

Watch out for the 10% luxury tax and
10% service charge in the higher price
brackets. Medium-price and budget
hotels attracting foreigners are
concentrated in the Sudder St area.

Central Kolkata

$ Broadway
27A Ganesh Chandra Av, T033-2236 3930,
www.broadwayhotel.in.
Amazingly good-value hotel in a characterful
building that hasn't changed much since it
opened in 1937. Very clean rooms are non-a/c
but airy with powerful fans, antique furniture
and Bengali-red floors, towels, some with
common bath, plus 24-hr checkout. Noisy
on the lower levels at the front. The bar is
very appealing (see Bars and clubs, page 557).

$ Buddha Dharmankur Sabha
1 Buddhist Temple St, Bow Bazar, T033-2211
7138, www.bengalbuddhist.com.
Run by the Bengal Buddhist Association and
with plenty of monks wandering around, cheap
clean rooms with twin beds, fans, decent shared
bathrooms. A/c options with bath attached are
a bit larger, with a few sticks of furniture. The
compound gates are locked at 2230; call ahead
to reserve.

$ Cosmos Guest House
Ground floor, 9 Chittaranjan Av, T033-2236 1383.
Decent simple rooms aren't huge but have fresh
paint, clean bedding, TV and good bathrooms.
At the rear of the building, so surprisingly quiet.
A good cheap choice for single travellers, also
a/c rooms. There are 2 other hotels in the same
building should Cosmos be full (which they
often are).

Park Street, Chowringhee and
Sudder Street

Kyd St has changed its name to Dr Md Ishaque Rd
and Free School St is also called Mirza Ghalib St.

$$$$ Oberoi Grand
15 Chowringhee (JL Nehru), T033-2249 2323,
www.oberoihotels.com.
Atmospheric Victorian building opposite the
Maidan, exquisitely restored, suites with giant
4-posters, all rooms are spacious, those with
balconies overlook the garden and pool are
charming, bathrooms a tad old-fashioned but
in keeping with the colonial style, excellent
Thai restaurant and 24-hr **Le Terrasse** with
international cuisine, billiards in the bar, lovely
pool for guests, wonderful spa. Reasonable
prices available online for a standard room.

$$$$ Park
17 Park St, T033-2249 9000,
www.theparkhotels.com.
Trendy designer hotel, one of Kolkata's most
reputable, good restaurants, nightclubs, health
club, 24-hr café, service can be disappointing,
entrance themed on underground car park.
Go online for the best discounts.

$$$$-$$$ Astor
15 Shakespeare Sarani, T033-2282 9957-9,
www.astorkolkata.com.
In a red-brick colonial building, comfortable a/c
rooms with bath tubs, inferior annexe, have not
retained original features, although public areas
have fared better. The tiny blue-lit bar is decent,
and **Plush** lounge-bar is fun. Breakfast included,
mini-bar, off-season discounts, free Wi-Fi.

$$$ Lindsay
8-A Lindsay St, T033-3021 8666,
http://thelindsay.in.
Refurbished hotel towering over New Market,
mainly for business travellers, good breakfast,

gym. Smart **Blue & Beyond** rooftop restaurant/bar has panoramic city views and great food.

$$$ Lytton
14 Sudder St, T033-2249 1875-9,
www.lyttonhotelindia.com.
Comfortable, tastefully furnished rooms with flatscreen TVs, a/c bar, efficient and attracts a business clientele, breakfast included.

$$$ New Kenilworth
1 & 2 Little Russell St, T033-2282 3939,
www.kenilworthhotels.com.
A very comfortable and attractive hotel, though overpriced at rack rates (excellent deals online). Foyer is all marble and chandeliers, but modern rooms are neutrally furnished with soft lighting, minibar, and nice bathrooms. The older period building contains suites and the appealing **Big Ben** English-style pub, with a pool table and sports TV, plus there's a spa.

$$$ Sapphire Suites
15 Lindsay St, T033-2252 3052-4,
www.sapphiresuites.in.
29 a/c rooms in a new hotel in an attractive period building, right next to New Market. Rooms have sleek black and white furnishings, flatscreen TVs, bathrobes, tea/coffee facilities. Breakfast included, good multicuisine restaurant and fitness centre. Deals online.

$$$-$$ Bawa Walson Spa'o'tel
5A Sudder St, T033-2252 1512,
http://m-walson.bawahotels.com.
An unlikely situation for a Spa'o'tel, but the **Walson** is immaculate with Thai accents throughout. Rooms are wood and white, swish shower rooms, free Wi-Fi, open-air Arabic restaurant. Big discounts possible.

$$$-$$ Housez 43
43 Mirza Ghalib St, T033-2227 6020,
https://thesparkhotels.com.
A 'value boutique' hotel with contemporary, well-presented rooms, nice public areas with leather beanbags and seats, restaurant, elevator, breakfast included in the colourful café, pleasant staff.

$$ Astoria Hotel
6 Sudder St, near fire station, T033-2252 2241,
www.astoria.in.
Offers 41 rooms of a good standard, after being recently renovated. All have a/c, hot water, and free Wi-Fi, it's a good standard for the price. Great top-floor room with a terrace.

$$ Fairlawn
13A Sudder St, T033-2252 1510/8766,
www.fairlawnhotel.com.
A Calcutta institution, the old-fashioned but characterful rooms have a/c, TV, hot water, and are comfortable. Semi-formal meals at set times aren't the best, but breakfast and afternoon tea are included. The hotel provides a throwback to the Raj, bric-a-brac everywhere, photos cover all the communal spaces, quite a place and the garden terrace is great for a beer.

$ Afridi Guest House
Opposite Ashreen Guest House (see below),
calcutta_guest house@yahoo.com.
Most rooms share bathrooms, some have a/c, most have TV, but many rooms are windowless. Sheets are clean and standards better than many Sudder St options. Try and book ahead, though that's easier said than done.

$ Ashreen Guest House
2 Cowie Lane, T033-2252 0889,
ashreen_guesthouse@yahoo.com.
Modern rooms with above-average facilities (for Sudder St) with TV and hot water, a suitable place to break yourself into Kolkata gently, however prices are ever escalating while standards slip. Pick-up for late night flights.

$ Capital Guest House
11B Chowringhee Lane, T033-2252 0598.
Tucked away from the road in a freshly painted old building, Capital is relatively quiet and all rooms have TV and private bath, though ones with windows are more expensive. Good value compared to nearby options but not a place to meet other travellers.

$ Galaxy
3 Stuart Lane, T033-2252 4565,
hotelgalaxy@vsnl.net.
12 good tiled rooms with attached bath and TV, some with a/c, a decent choice but often full with long-stayers. Try at around 1030 just after checkout.

$ Maria
5/1 Sudder St, T033-2252 0860.
24 clean, basic rooms (hard beds), some with bath, dorm, internet, TV in the 'lobby', hot water, water filter for guests' use. Popular budget place with a good atmosphere.

$ Modern Lodge
1 Stuart Lane, T033-2252 4960.
Very popular, 14 rooms, attached or shared bath, cheapest at ground level, prices rise as you go up

to the breezy rooftop, pleasant lobby with plants but sinister 'lounge', quirky staff, no reservations so try at 1000.

$ Paragon
2 Stuart Lane, T033-2252 2445.
Textbook backpacker haunt with 45 rooms, some tiny and prison-like but it's clean just about (some doubles have attached bath) and mixed sex dorms (with shared/private bath), rooftop rooms are better. Water heater to fill buckets. Open communal spaces, indifferent management.

$ Sunflower Guest House
7 Royd St, T033-2229 9401,
www.sunflowerguesthouse.com.
An airy 1950s building with very clean well-maintained rooms, TV, hot water, more costly with a/c and newer bathrooms. Spacious lounge area, the numerous staff are kindly. Good location, near Sudder St but out of the backpacker scene. No single room rates.

$ Super Guest House
30A Mirza Ghalib St, T033-2252 0995,
super_guesthouse@hotmail.com.
This guesthouse has some of the cleanest rooms in the area for the price, all a/c with hot bath, tiled and simple box rooms. Be sure to ask for a room that does not suffer noise from the daily live music in **Super Pub Bar**. No single rates.

$ YMCA
25 Jl Nehru Rd, T033-2249 2192.
17 rooms, some a/c, all with bath, geyser and TV, in large, rambling colonial building, clean linen, recently renovated but check room first as some are nicer than others. Helpful staff, rates include bed tea and breakfast. The oldest YMCA in Asia.

$ YWCA
1 Middleton Row, T033-2265 2494,
www.ywcacalcutta.org.
Old colonial building with good atmosphere, airy verandas and tennis courts. Some rooms with bath, but doubles with shared bath have windows, dorm, all spotless, very friendly staff. Rates include breakfast, alcohol forbidden, a pleasant if shabby oasis in the city. A recommended alternative to Sudder St, especially for female travellers.

South Kolkata

South Kolkata is a more salubrious area, where quiet residential streets hide some good (mainly mid-range) guesthouses. Excellent little restaurants and vibrant markets are in plentiful supply.

$$$$ Hindusthan International
235/1 AJC Bose Rd, T033-2283 0505,
www.hhihotels.com.
Comfortable quiet rooms on 8 floors are priced right, but staff are distracting with their demands for tips. The food is nothing special although there are a couple of quite cool bars/coffee shop and **Underground** nightclub is popular, pool and spa. Big discounts possible.

$$$$ Taj Bengal
34B Belvedere Rd, Alipore, T033-2223 3939,
www.tajhotels.com.
Opulent and characterful, several restaurants are plush, imaginative, intimate, with good food, leisurely service, unusual Bengali breakfast, **Khazana** shop is excellent.

$$ 66/2B The Guest House
66/2B Purna Das Rd, T033-2464 6422/1,
www.662btheguesthouse.com.
On a tree-lined street with some great restaurants a 2-min walk away, this cheerful place is well furnished, with decent baths, all rooms have a/c, geysers and flatscreens. A more relaxing area to stay in. Breakfast included, as is Wi-Fi. Recently refurbished.

$$ The Bodhi Tree
48/44 Swiss Park (near Rabindra Sarovar metro), T033-2424 6534, www.bodhitreekolkata.com.
Simply beautiful little boutique hotel with just 6 rooms, each uniquely furnished in a different regional style (eg rural Bengal, with mud-plastered walls), and 1 **$$$** penthouse. The in-house art-café is a delight (see Coffee shops, page 556), dinner is available, business centre, free Wi-Fi, small library, serves alcohol. Prices are very reasonable for a special experience.

$$ Park Palace
Singhi Villa, 49/2 Gariahat Rd, T033-2461 9108-11, www.parkpalacehotel.co.in.
The main draws are the peaceful residential area, **Mirch Masala** restaurant/bar next door, and the roof terrace with excellent views. Rooms have fitted furniture and are large yet cosy, if twee. Ask for the 20% discount. Staff delightful. Behind **Pantaloons**, just off Gariahat Rd.

$$ The Residency Guest House
50/1C Purna Das Rd, T033-2466 9382,
www.theresidency.co.in.
A very appealing mid-range hotel, with clean tiled rooms, quality furnishings, a/c, TV, good bathrooms and comfortable beds. Close to Gariahat markets, but on a quiet street.

$$ Tollygunge Club
120 Deshapran Sasmal Rd, T033-2473 4539,
www.tollygungeclub.org.
On the south side of the city in 100 acres of
grounds with an 18-hole golf course, swimming
pool, tennis and other activities. Good bar and
restaurants, one of which is open air. The place
has charm and atmosphere which helps you
overlook worn-out towels and casual service.
Ask for a renovated room, and enjoy the colonial
feel. An interesting mid-range choice.

$ Sharani Lodge
71/K Hindustan Park, T033-2463 5717,
gautam_sharani@rediffmail.com.
In a quiet street, yet very close to hectic Rash
Behari Av, this well-maintained and well-run
lodge has an old-fashioned Indian ambiance. The
a/c rooms are not worth really worth the extra
money, but non-a/c are a great deal, those with
common bath also share balconies at the front,
all have TV, towels and plenty of space. There's a
second building, across Rash Behari, with lovely
little outdoor terrace (again, non-a/c rooms are
more spacious and attractive than a/c ones).

Other areas

$$$$ Vedic Village
T(0)9830025900, www.thevedicvillage.com.
In Rajarhat, 20 mins from the airport on the
eastern edge of the city, but a world away from
the rest of Kolkata. The appeal is the clean air and
rural surrounds as much as the luxurious rooms,
fabulous pool and of course the spa. Top-end
villas and suites are stunning while studio rooms
are not unreasonably priced when compared to
other options in the city.

Restaurants

Licensed restaurants serve alcohol (some are
unpleasant places to eat in since the emphasis is
on drink). Be prepared for a large surcharge for
live (or even recorded) music. This, plus taxes,
can double the price on the menu.

Central Kolkata

$$$ Aaheli and Oceanic
At the Peerless Inn, 12 JL Nehru Rd,
www.peerlesshotels.com/Kolkata.
Aaheli has an excellent menu of Bengali
specialities, carefully selected from around the
state by the chef, open from 1900. **Oceanic** has
interesting seafood and is more pricey, open

> **Tip...**
> Special Bengali sweets are made fresh every
> afternoon at thousands of sweet shops (1600-
> 1730): try *shingaras*, *kochuris* and *nimkis*.

lunch and dinner. Both are comfortable with a/c
and serve alcohol.

$$$-$$ Amber
11 Waterloo St. Open 1100-2330.
2 floors of North Indian and continental delights
(best for meat tandoori), generous helpings,
fast service. **Essence** on 2nd floor fancies itself
as a cocktail bar, but alcohol is served in both.
Functional bar on the ground floor is strictly
no women. Also has a smaller restaurant on
Middleton Row, open 1200-1600 and 1900-2300.

$$-$ Anand
*19 Chittaranjan Ave. Open 0900-2130, Sun from
0700, closed Wed.*
Great South Indian food. Mammoth *dosas*, stuffed
iddli, all-vegetarian, family atmosphere and
warmly decorated. Barefoot waiters are efficient.
Big queues at weekends.

$$-$ Bhojohori Manna
*Esplanade. Open 1130-2130 (closed for cleaning
1630-1800).*
Branch of the Bengali chain, with budget prices
for veg dishes and pricier fish items. Ticks on the
whiteboard indicate availability, choice can be
limited in the evenings as they sell out.

$$-$ Chung Wah
13A Chittaranjan Av. Open 1100-2300.
This hectic restaurant is functional and basic, with
curtained-off booths along the sides. Hugely
popular and with a large menu, it attracts a mostly
male clientele, alcohol served. Recommended for
the old-style atmosphere rather than the spicy
Chinese food. Lone women are not encouraged.

$ Madras Restaurant
25/B Chittaranjan Av.
A simpler setting than nearby **Anand** and
slightly cheaper, but still has a/c. The list of *dosa*
and *uttampams* is endless, plus there are a few
Chinese dishes. Go between 1130-1530 for the
South Indian *thalis*.

Coffee shops, sweets and snacks

Indian Coffee House
Albert Hall, just off College St.
A must for its history and atmosphere
(see page 543).

Park Street, Chowringhee and Sudder Street

Visitors craving Western fast food will find plenty of familiar names around Park St.

$$$ Baan Thai
Oberoi Grand (see Where to stay, page 550).
Excellent selection, imaginative decor, Thai-style seating on floor, or chairs and tables.

$$$ Bar-B-Q
43 Park St, T033-2229 9916.
Always popular, always delicious. 3 sections serving Indian and Chinese food, bar.

$$$ Bistro by the Park
2A Middleton Row.
It's near the park rather than 'by' it, but this attractive contemporary place serves world cuisine (including Southeast Asian, Middle Eastern) with the main focus on Italian fare (salads, pockets, pizzas, etc). Serves alcohol.

$$$ Ivory
Block D, 5th floor, 22 Camac St, www. ivorykitchen.com. Daily 1230-1500, 1900-2230.
Slightly formal and functional, yet pleasingly decorated in ivory tones, dishes encompass a wide selection of Oriental and international dishes, with an Indian twist. Top-class dining.

$$$ Zaranj and Jong's
26 JL Nehru Rd.
Adjacent restaurants, both stylish, subdued decor, excellent food. Try *pudina paratha, murgh makhani*, tandoori fish in Zaranj, or delectable Burmese fare in Jong's.

$$ Fire and Ice
Kanak Building, Middleton St, www. fireandicepizzeria.com. Open 1100-2330.
Pizzas here are the real deal, service is excellent, and the ambience relaxing. Decor is very much what you would expect from a pizza place at home.

$$ Flury's
18 Park St.
Classic Kolkata venue with hit-and-miss Western menu, but pastries and afternoon tea are winners and the bakery has brown bread. It's an institution.

$$ Gangaur
2 Russell St.
A wide menu of Indian delights, if you can resist the superb *thali* (1130-1530). Afterwards head next door for Bengali sweets.

$$ Jimmy's
14D Lindsay St.
Chinese. Small, a/c, good *momos*, Szechuan dishes, ice cream. Alcohol served.

$$ Mocambo
25B Park St.
International. A/c, pleasant lighting, highly descriptive menu. Long-standing reliable favourite.

$$ Peter Cat
18A Park St (entrance on Middleton Row).
Chiefly Indian, with some international dishes. Good kebabs and sizzlers, hilarious menu of cheap cocktails, pleasant ambience but can rush you on busy weekend nights. No booking system, expect to queue outside.

$$ Teej
2 Russell St.
Pure vegetarian Rajasthani delights washed down with cold beer, in a colourful *haveli*-esque setting.

$$ Tung Fong
Mirzah Ghalib St.
Quality Chinese food for a reasonable price, the setting spacious and subtly Asian, white linens and Ming vases. Great Manchurian dishes, good fish and chilli garlic paneer, excellent desserts. Super-swift service.

$$-$ Gupta's
53C Mirza Ghalib St. Open 1100-2300.
Excellent Indian and Chinese. More intimate and softly lit upstairs, low ceilings (beware of the fans), try fish *tikka peshwari* and *bekti tikka*, alcohol reasonably priced.

$ Blue Sky Café
3 Sudder St.
Chiefly Western. Very popular travellers' meeting place, a/c, always full and cramped, opinions on food vary, however.

$ Family Home
Humayan Place, near New Market.
Excellent Indian vegetarian meals, particularly recommended for South Indian, good *lassis*, cheap and busy.

$ Fresh and Juicy
Chowringhee Ln, T033-2286 1638.
Recently renovated with a/c and 1st floor seating, good place for a sociable breakfast or reasonably authentic Indian meals and Western favourites, attracts a loyal following. Phone ahead for parcel-order.

$ Khalsa
4C Madge Ln, T033-2249 0075.
Excellent *lassis*, Western breakfasts, Indian mains, all super-cheap, and with excellent service from the utterly charming Sikh owners.

$ Maya Ram
1 Lord Sinha Rd. Open 1100-2300.
A good place to try 'snacks' such as *paw bhaji*.

$ Momo Plaza
2A Suburban Hospital Rd. Open 1200-2200.
With black half-tiling and pastel pink walls accentuated by kitsch ornaments, which could be intentionally bohemian. Recommended for plentiful and delicious Tibetan and Chinese meals. Try the soups, chilli chicken, huge *momos* and *thukpa*. Nearby **$ Hamro Momo** is also good, cheaper and more crowded.

$ NV Stores and Maa Kali
12/2 Lindsay St. Closed Sun.
Stand-up street eateries making surprisingly good sandwiches (toasted are best) from any possible combination of ingredients; great *lassis* too.

$ Raj's Spanish Café
7 Sudder St. Daily 0800-2200.
Spanish nibbles, real coffee from a real machine, salads, pastries, pasta and sandwiches also good. Wi-Fi. A sociable spot.

$ Tirupati
Street stall next to Hotel Maria.
A Sudder St institution; find a spot on the busy benches and enjoy enormous helpings of food from every continent.

Coffee shops, sweets and snacks

Ashalayam
44 Mirza Ghalib St.
Peaceful oasis run by an NGO, sells handicrafts made by street children as well as coffee and snacks.

Brothers Snacks
1 Humayun Pl, Newmarket.
Safe, tasty bet with outdoor seats. Kati rolls (tender kebabs wrapped in *parathas*) are hard to beat. Try mutton/chicken egg roll (if you don't want raw onions and green chillis, order *'no piaaz e mirchi'*) There are also plenty of great vegetarian options.

Café Thé
Tagore Centre, 9A Ho Chi Min Sarani. Daily 0900-2100.
Modern, clean cafe serving Western/Indian/Chinese snacks and meals, with an interesting menu of hot/cold teas.

Kathleen's
Several branches, including 12 Mirza Ghalib St, corner of Lord Sinha Rd.

Nahoum's
Shop F20, New Market.
Good pastries, cakes, savouries and brown bread. The original 1930s till and some fixtures still in situ.

Pure Milk Centre
Near Rafi Ahmed Kidwai St/Ripon St corner.
Good sweet 'curd' (*mishti doi*), usually sold out by lunchtime. Excellent hot *roshogollas*.

Rehmania and Shiraz Golden Restaurant
On opposite corners of Park St/ AJC Bose Rd crossing.
Muslim joints famed for their mutton rolls and kebabs.

South Kolkata

$$$ Chinoiserie
Taj Bengal (see Where to stay, page 552), T033-2223 3939.
Good for a splurge on excellent Chinese.

$$$ Mainland China
3A Gurusaday Rd, T033-2283 7964; also at South City Mall, 3rd floor.
Sublime Chinese. Unusual offerings, especially fish and seafood, tastefully decorated with burnished ceiling and evocative wall mural, pleasant ambience, courteous. Book ahead.

$$$ Oh! Calcutta
In the Forum Mall, 10/3 Elgin Rd, T033-2283 7161.
Fantastic fish and seafood, plus many vegetarian options, this award-winning restaurant (branches across India, another in Kolkata on EM Bypass) re-creates Bengali specialties. It's an attractive venue, although located inside a mall.

$$$-$$ 6 Ballygunge Place
Ballygunge, T033-2460 3922.
In a charming Raj-era bungalow, the intricate Bengali menu is as delightful as the ambiance. For more than a decade, this has been the perfect place for a special night out. Again, the fish dishes are a highlight.

Bengali cuisine

Bengalis are said to be obsessed about what they eat. The men often take a keen interest in buying the most important elements of the day's meal, namely fresh fish. Typically, it is river fish, the most popular being *hilsa* and *bekti* or the widely available shellfish, especially king prawns. *Bekti* is grilled or fried and is tastier than the fried fish of the west as it has often been marinated in mild spices first. The prized smoked *hilsa*, although delicious, has thousands of fine bones. Maachh (fish) comes in many forms as *jhol* (in a thin gravy), *jhal* (spicy and hot), *malai curry* (in coconut milk, mildly spiced), *chop* (in a covering of mashed potato and crumbs) or *chingri maachher* cutlet (flattened king prawn 'fillets', crumbed and fried).

Bengali cooking uses mustard oil and mustard which grows in abundance, and a subtle mixture of spices. *Mishti* (sweetmeats) are another distinctive feature. Many are milk based and the famous *sandesh*, *roshogolla*, *roshomalai*, *pantua* and *ledikeni* (named after Lady Canning, the wife of the first Viceroy of India) are prepared with a kind of cottage cheese, in dozens of different textures, shapes, colours and tastes.

Pale pinkish brown *mishti doi* is an excellent sweet yoghurt eaten as a dessert, typically sold in hand-thrown clay pots. You will only find the true flavour of Bengali cooking in someone's home or at a few special Bengali restaurants.

$$ Kewpie's
2 Elgin Lane (just off Elgin Rd), T033-2486 1600/9929. Tue-Sun 1200-1500, 1700-2245.
Authentic Bengali home cooking at its best, add on special dishes to basic *thali*, unusual fish and vegetarian. Just a few tables in rooms inside the owners' residence, a/c, sells recipe book.

$$ Krystal Chopsticks
71H Hindustan Park. Open 1200-2230.
Attractive East Asian decor and an excellent menu (chiefly Chinese) attracts well-heeled Bengalis. It's not outrageously priced, plenty of interesting vegetarian as well as chicken, fish and meat dishes.

$$ Mirch Masala
49/2 Gariahat Rd, Gariahat, T033-2461 8900. Lunch 1200-1500, dinner 1900-2230.
This popular restaurant-bar has walls decorated with *pukkah* murals depicting Bollywood stars. Food can be a bit heavy (mainly Indian, non-veg), but the atmosphere is lively and staff competent.

$$-$ Bhojohori Manna
13 PC Sorcar Sarani (aka Ekdalia Rd); also at JD Park.
Budget prices and a perfect little place to sample pure Bengali cuisine, veg and non-veg. Ticks on the wall menu indicate availability, try *echor dalna* (jackfruit curry) and *bhekti paturi* (mustard-drenched fish steamed in banana leaves). 2 people should order 4-5 different dishes to share. Much better than the newer **Bhojohori 6** outlet on Hindustan Rd nearby. Decent toilet.

$ Banana Leaf
73-75 Rash Behari Av. Open 0730-2200.
Vegetarian South Indian, top-notch *dosas* and *thalis* plus superb *mini-iddli* and decent southern-style coffee.

$ Bliss
53 Hindustan Park.
For Chinese in a fast-food environment, Bliss is ideal. Portions are generous, the soups delicious. It's tiny but there's seating.

$ South India Club
Off Rash Behari Av. Daily 0700-2130.
An authentic taste of the South in a canteen environment, full meals for under Rs 50, and a good place to experiment with less commonly seen dishes such as *pongal* or *upma*.

Coffee shops, sweets and snacks

Art Café
At The Bodhi Tree (see Where to stay, page 552). Tue-Sat, 1400-1830.
Half-inside/half-outside, this beautiful slate-floored café is lit by green lights and decorated with Buddhas, palm trees and original works of art (exhibitions are occasionally held). There's a tempting drinks menu (plus beer) in addition to light meals. Something quite out of the ordinary for Kolkata.

Dolly's The Tea Shop
Dakshinapan market (just after Dhakuria Bridge).
The quaintest place in the city for a variety of teas, refreshing iced-teas (try watermelon) and decent

oasties. Tea-chest tables, low basket chairs, indoor and outdoor seating, even the walls are lined with old tea-crates. Dolly is a formidable lady.

Nepal Sweets
16B Sarat Bose Rd.
Chandrakala, almond *pista barfi*, mango *roshogolla*, *kheer mohan* (also savouries). Recommended.

Other areas

Chinese food fans also go to South Tangra Rd off EM bypass, east of the city centre. The approach is none too picturesque, past tanneries and open drains, but among the maze of lanes (in places lit by lanterns) many eateries are quite swanky.

$$ Beijing
77/1A Christopher Rd, T033-2328 1001.
Try garlic chicken, sweet and sour fish, chop suey, steamed fish, generous portions.

$$ Golden Joy, **Kafulok** and **Sin Fa**, to name but a few, offer excellent soups, jumbo prawns and honey chicken, best to go early (1200 for lunch, 2000 for dinner).

Bars and clubs

The larger hotels have pleasant bars and upmarket restaurants serve alcohol. The top hotels are well stocked, luxurious but pricey. 'Local' bars are usually open 1100-2230, often lack atmosphere or have deafening live singing; some are for men only; there is a seedy choice down Dacres Lane, just north of Esplanade.

Central Kolkata

Broadway Bar
At the Broadway Hotel (last orders 2230), see Where to stay.
Has marble floors, polished Art Deco seating, soft lighting, whirring fans and windows open to the street, making it probably the best choice in the city. Lone women will feel comfortable as it's a busy and respectable place. For a sunset drink on the water, try the **Floatel**, a floating hotel on the Hooghly moored close to Babu Ghat. The simple bar is usually quiet, and has a small outdoor area, good for watching the river life.

Park Street, Chowringhee and Sudder Street

Fairlawn's pleasant garden terrace is popular at dusk attracting anyone seeking a chilled beer. The clientele is mixed, fairy lights set the greenery glowing and it's perfect for a 1st night drink to acclimatize – but beware the below-average food and stiff charges for snacks. **Super Pub Bar** (Sudder St), is always busy and sociable, but expect gruff service and check your change. **Blue & Beyond** (at the **Lindsay Hotel**) is a rooftop bar/restaurant with great views over Kolkata from the 9th-floor (quite pricey), plus an indoor a/c section. The bar at the **New Empire Cinema** (between New Market and Chowringhee), is pleasant, blue-lit and efficiently staffed. **Sam's Pub** (off Park St, is open later than most, last orders at 2330 on weekend nights) and still permits smoking in a curious indoor gazebo; football and cricket matches are shown on the flatscreen. **Oly Pub** (21 Park St), is an institution: very noisy, serves steak and eggs, more airy downstairs. At **Someplace Else** (**Park Hotel**), live bands play loud music to the same crowd each week. **Tantra** (also in **Park Hotel**) has taped dancefloor, young crowd, no shorts or flip-flops, cover charge. Next door, **Roxy** is less popular, but has free entry and is more relaxed, with slouchy sofas upstairs. **Shisha Reincarnated** (Block D, 6th floor, 22 Camac St, www.shishareincarnated.com, open 1800-2400, Wed, Fri and Sat 1800-0200) is dark and stylish, with a chilled atmosphere, low red lights, a huge bar lined with spirits, DJs every night (varying music styles) and a decent sized dancefloor. Hookahs available. The roof-deck is the best place to hang out.

South Kolkata

Tripti's (SP Mukerjee Rd (next to Netaji Bhavan metro), Mon-Sat 1100-2300, Sun 1100-2200), is a classic. Established in 1935 and styled like a canteen, it's been tackily refurnished, but the 1950s flooring and shuttered windows remain. Expect rowdiness and cheap booze. On the 1st floor up hidden steps; look for the sign. Take a wander round sprawling and atmospheric **Jadu Babu Bazar** to the rear while in the area. Also here is pub/club **The Basement** (**Samilton Hotel**, 35A Sarat Bose Rd), where you can hear a variety of live music (Wed-Fri); there's also a shisha place on the rooftop. **Underground** (at the **Hindusthan International**) has good music and a young crowd; it's a long-stayer on the scene. The noisy dance-bar beneath **Ginger** restaurant (106 SP Mukerjee Rd, T033-2486 3052/3, near JD Park metro) accommodates same-sex couples, open 1130-2330.

Entertainment

The English-language dailies (*Telegraph*, *Times of India*, etc) carry a comprehensive list.

Art galleries

Academy of Fine Arts, *Cathedral Rd (see page 540)*.

Ahuja Museum for Arts, *26 Lee Rd (Elgin Rd crossing with AJC Bose)*, www.ahujaptm.com/museum. The private collection of Mr SD Ahuja contains over 1200 works of art, which are displayed in rotation.

Bengal Gallery, *Rabindranath Tagore Centre, 9A Ho Chi Min Sarani*. The Indian Council for Cultural Relations has a large space showing established artists.

Chemould Art Gallery, *12F Park St*. One of the big names in contemporary art, and worth keeping an eye on.

CIMA, *2nd floor, Sunny Towers, 43 Ashutosh Chowdhury Av*, www.cimaartindia.com. Tue-Sat 1100-1900, closed Sun, Mon 1500-1900. The best exhibition space in the city and the shop has a good stock in wall-hangings, metalwork, clothes, stoles, ornaments, etc.

Experimenter, *2/1 Hindustan Rd, Gariahat*. A trendy contemporary space with great exhibitions by Indian and international artists.

Harrington Street Arts Centre, *2nd Floor, 8 Ho Chi Minh Sarani*, http://hstreetartscentre.com. Cool white space in an old apartment, hosting quality photography and art exhibitions.

Seagull Arts and Media Centre, *36C SP Mukherjee Rd (just off Mukherjee on a sidestreet)*, www.seagullindia.com. Holds regular photography exhibitions from 1400-2000. Also has a bookshop on the opposite side of SP Mukherjee.

Studio 21, *17/L Dover Terrace (off Ballygunge Phari)*, www.studio21kolkata.com. A minimalist new space for emerging artists from all disciplines, art/photography exhibitions change regularly.

Cinema

A/c and comfortable cinemas showing English-language films are a good escape from the heat, and many are still very cheap. Check the newspapers for timings; programmes change every Fri. **Elite** (SN Banerjee Rd), and **New Empire Cinema** (New Market St) are conveniently close to Sudder St. **Nandan Complex** (AJC Bose Rd) shows classics and art house movies; the **Kolkata International Film Festival** is held here in Nov, an excellent event. Swish **Inox** multiplexes

Tip...
Jatra is community theatre, highly colourful and exaggerated both in delivery and make-up, drawing for its subject romantic favourites from mythology or more up to date social, political and religious themes.

(www.inoxmovies.com) are scattered around town (Forum, City Centre); tickets for these can be booked by credit card over the phone. **Fame cinema** (www.famecinemas.com) in South City Mall, is open 1000-0100.

Performing arts

There are regular performances at **Rabindra Sadan** (Cathedral Rd); the adjacent **Sisir Mancha** has Bengali theatre. **Kala Mandir** (48 Shakespeare Sarani), has regular cultural performances, Rabindranath Tagore Centre (9A Ho Chi Min Sarani, www.tagorecentreiccr.org) has a lovely new concert hall. You can also see Bengali theatre of a high standard at **Biswaroopa** (2A Raja Raj Kissen St) and **Star Theatre** (79/34 Bidhan Sarani). English-language productions are staged by the British Council and theatre clubs. **Sangeet Research Academy** (www.itcsra.org), near Mahanayak Uttam (Tollygunge) Metro station, is a national centre for training in Indian classical music and stages a free concert on Wed evenings. **Rabindra Bharati University** (6/4 Dwarakanath Tagore Ln) holds performances, particularly during the winter, including singing, dancing and *jatras*.

Festivals

Jan Ganga Sagar Mela at Sagardwip, 105 km south of Kolkata, where the River Hooghly joins the sea, draws thousands of Hindu pilgrims. See page 563.

Apr Bengali New Year (Poila Baiskh) is celebrated around 15 Apr.

Jun-Jul Ratha Yatra at Mahesh, near Serampur, Hooghly District. Week-long chariot festival.

Sep-Oct Durga Puja, Bengal's celebration of the goddess during **Dasara**. See box, page 545.

Oct-Nov *Kali Puja* is the 1-day festival of lights.

Dec Christmas. Many churches hold special services, including Midnight Mass, and the New Market takes on a new look in Dec as **Barra Din** (Big Day) approaches with stalls selling trees and baubles. Other religious festivals are observed as elsewhere in India.

ON THE ROAD
Bengali crafts

Silk has been woven in India for more than 3500 years and continues today with the weaving of natural-coloured wild silk called *tassar*. Bengal silk has had a revival in the exquisite brocade weaving of *baluchari* saris, produced in the past under royal patronage and now carried out in Bankura. The saris are woven in traditional style with untwisted silk and have beautiful borders and *pallu* decorations, depicting peacocks, flowers and human figures. Fine cotton is also woven.

The Bankura horse has become a symbol of West Bengali pottery, which is still produced in the districts of Bankura, Midnapore and Birbhum. Soft soap stone is used for carving copies of temple images, while shell bangles are considered auspicious. Ivory carvers once produced superb decorative items, a skill developed in the Mughal period; today, bone and plastic have largely replaced ivory in inlay work. Metal workers produce brass- and bell metalware, while the tribal *dhokra* casters still follow the ancient *cire perdue* method. Kalighat *pat* paintings are in a primitive style using bold colours.

Shopping

Most shops open Mon-Sat 1000-1730 or later (some break for lunch). New Market stalls, and most shops, close on Sun.

Books
College St, a thicket of second-hand pavement bookstalls along this street. They're mainly for students, but may reveal an interesting 1st edition for a keen collector (see page 543).
Crossword, *Elgin Rd*. Deservedly popular chain store, with 2 floors of books, films, good selection of magazines and films and a busy coffee shop.
Earthcare Books, *10 Middleton St (by Drive Inn), T033-2229 6551, www.earthcarebooks.com*. Excellent selection of children's books, Indian-focussed titles, socially conscious books, plenty of fiction, has small photo exhibitions.
Family Book Shop, *1A Park St*. Good selection of guidebooks. 10-15% discounts possible.
Kolkata Book Fair, *Milan Mela Prangan, EM Bypass, www.kolkatabookfair.net*. End of Jan for a fortnight, stalls sell paperback fiction to antiquarian books.
Mirza Ghalib St. Has a string of small shops selling new, used and photocopied versions of current favourites. Bargaining required.
Oxford Book Shop, *Park St*. Huge selection of English titles, postcards and films, café upstairs where you can browse through titles. Excellent for books on Kolkata, and a children's bookshop next door.
Seagull, *31A SP Mukherjee Rd, www.seagullindia. com*. Large and unusual stock of art-related books, coffee-table tomes, etc.

Starmark, *top floor, Emami Centre, 3 Lord Sinha Rd; also City Centre and South City Mall*. The best selection of fiction in Kolkata, plus imported magazines, films.

Clothes and accessories
Anokhi, *Shop 209, Forum Shopping Mall, 10/3 Lala Lajpat Rai Sarani, near AJC Bose Rd*. Beautiful block-print bed-linens, floaty bed-wear, scarves, accessories, clothes and more. Made in Jaipur, mid-range prices.
Biba, *South City Mall, Prince Anwar Shar Rd, www.bibaindia.com*; also has franchises in **Pantaloons** department stores. Chic cotton print dresses, tasteful *salwar*.
Fabindia, *16 Hindustan Park (also branches at Woodburn Park Rd, near AJC Bose Rd, and City Centre Mall in Salt Lake)*. Clothes, textiles, toiletries, rugs and home furnishings from fair-trade company. Hugely successful due to their tasteful and high-quality selection. Well worth a visit.
Gomukh, *next to Raj's Spanish Café, 7 Sudder St*. Traveller wear, plus a range of scarves and wall-hangings, cheap and well stocked.
Khazana, *Taj Bengal (see Where to stay, page 552)*. For pricey textiles, Baluchari saris, *kantha* embroidery, etc, and souvenirs.

Government emporia
Government emporia are mainly in the town centre and are fixed-price shops. All the Indian states are represented at **Dakshinapan** (near Dhakuria Bridge, Mon-Fri 1030-1930, Sat 1030-1400), which has an excellent selection of handloom and handicrafts. **Central Cottage Industries** (7 JL Nehru Rd), is convenient as is **Kashmir Art** (12 JL Nehru Rd). **Phulkari** (Punjab

Emporium, 26B Camac St). **Rajasthali** (30E JL Nehru Rd). **Tripura** (58 JL Nehru Rd). **UP** (12B Lindsay St).

Handicrafts and handloom
There are many handicraft shops around Newmarket St, selling batik prints, handloom, blockprints and embroidery, but starting prices are usually excessive so bargain hard. Shops listed below are all either fair trade-based or associated with self-help groups.

Artisana, *13 Chowringhee Pl (off Gokhale Rd), T033-2223 9422*. Handloom and handicrafts, traditional hand-block textiles, designer jewellery, metalware and more.

Ashalayam Handicrafts, *1st floor, 44 Mirza Ghalib St*. Products made by street children who have been trained and given shelter by the **Don Bosco Ashalayam Project**. Proceeds are split between the artisans and the trust.

Bengal Home Industries Association, *11 Camac St*. Good selection of printed cotton (bedspreads, saris) and assorted knick-knacks. Relaxed, fixed price.

Calcutta Rescue Handicrafts, *Fairlawn Hotel. Thu 1830*. Medical NGO sells great selection of cards, bags and trinkets made and embroidered by former patients.

Kamala, *1st floor, Tagore Centre, 9A Ho Chi Min Sarani*. Outlet shop for the Crafts Council of West Bengal; great selection of textiles, jewellery, gifts and trinkets at very reasonable prices (sourced directly from the artisans).

Karmyog, *12B Russell St*. Gorgeous handcrafted paper products.

Sasha, *27 Mirza Ghalib St, www.sashaworld.com*. Attractive range of good-quality, fair-trade textiles, furnishings, ceramics, metalwork, etc, but not cheap, welcome a/c.

Jewellery
Bepin Behari Ganguly St (Bow Bazar) is lined with mirrored jewellers' shops; **PC Chandra, BB Dutt, B Sirkar** are well known. Also many on Rash Behari Av. The **silver market** (*rupa bajar*) is off Mirza Ghalib St opposite Newmarket. Gold and silver prices are listed daily in the newspapers.

Markets
The **New Market**, Lindsay St, has more than 2500 shops (many closed Sun). You will find mundane everyday necessities and exotic luxuries, from fragrant florists to gory meat stalls. Be prepared to deal with pestering basket-wallahs.

Kolkata has a number of bazars, each with a character of its own. In **Bentinck St** are

Muslim tailors, Chinese shoemakers plus Indian sweetmeat shops and tea stalls. **Gariahat market** early in the morning attracts a diverse clientele (businessmen, academics, cooks) who come to select choice fresh fish. In **Shyambazar** the coconut market lasts from 0500 to 0700. **Burra Bazar** is a hectic wholesale fruit market held daily. The colourful **flower market** is on Jagannath Ghat on the river bank. The old **China Bazar** no longer exists although **Tiretta Bazar** area still retains its ethnic flavour; try an exceptional Chinese breakfast from a street stall.

Musical instruments
Braganza's, *56C Free School (Mirza Ghalib) St*. An institution; with an extensive collection. Also head to the southern end of Rabindra Sarani for musical instruments (sitars, tablas, etc).

Tailors
Garments can be skillfully copied around New Market and on Madge Lane. Tailors will try to overcharge foreigners as a matter of course.

What to do

Body and soul
Look out for adverts around Sudder St for yoga classes held on hotel rooftops.

Aurobindo Bhavan, *8 Shakespeare Sarani, www.sriaurobindobhavankolkata.org*. Very informal yoga classes, women on Mon/Wed/Fri 1530-1930, men on Tue/Thu/Sat 1530-1930 (Rs 200). Bring a copy of your passport and visa.

Mystic Yoga, *20/A Camac St, www.mysticyoga.in*. Drop-in classes Rs 300, or monthly memberships, healthy café on site.

Cricket
Occasional Test matches and One-Day Internationals and regular IPL fixtures at Eden Gardens, see page 537, 100,000 capacity.

Golf
Royal Calcutta Golf Club, *18 Golf Club Rd, www.rcgc.in*. Founded in 1829, the oldest golf club in the world outside the UK.

The Tollygunge Club, *120 Despran Sasmal Rd, www.tollygungeclub.org*. The course is on land that was once an indigo plantation.

Horse racing
At the southern end of the Maidan is **Kolkata Race Course**, run by the Royal Calcutta Turf Club, www.rctconline.com. The history of racing goes back to the time of Warren Hastings, and the 1820s grandstand is especially impressive. Racing takes place in the cool season (Nov to

early Apr) and monsoon season (Jul-Oct). The Derby is in the 1st week of Jan. It's a fun, cheap day out in the public stands, better still if you can access the members' enclosure to get up close to the racehorses and enjoy a drink in the bar with antlers mounted on the wall.

Sightseeing tours
WBTDC, *departure point is Tourism Centre, 3/2 BBD Bagh E, 1st floor, T033-2248 8271. Daily tours, 0830-1730.* Tour stops at: Eden Gardens, High Court, Writers' Building, Belur Math, Dakshineswar Kali Temple, Jain Temple, Netaji Bhavan, Kolkata Panorama and Esplanade, Victoria Memorial, St Paul's Cathedral and Kali Ghat. Entry fees not included. Approved guides from **Govt of India Tourist Office**, T033-2582 5813.

Swimming
Wet 'O' Wild, *at Nicco Park, HM Block, Salt Lake City, http://niccoparks.com/wet-o-wild.* Kolkata's best waterpark with a truly enormous pool and wave machine. The **Hindusthan International Hotel** pool is open to non-residents for a fee.

Tour operators
Deals in air tickets to/from the East (through Bangkok) are offered by agents in the Sudder St area, or book online.
Help Tourism, *Sadananda Kothi (1st floor), 67A Kali Temple Rd, Kalighat, www.helptourism. com.* Wide variety of wildlife and adventure tours in Assam, Arunachal and North Bengal, with strong eco credentials and involvement of local communities.

Volunteer work
Many people come to Kolkata to work with one of the many NGOs. The following organizations accept volunteers, though it's wise to contact them in advance (except for the **Missionaries of Charity**, where you only need to attend one of the registration days).
Don Bosco Ashalayam Project, *www.dbasha.org.* Rehabilitates young homeless people by teaching skills.
Hope Kolkata Foundation, *39 Panditya Pl, www.hopechild.org.* An Irish charity focussing on the needs of disadvantaged children.
Missionaries of Charity (Mother Teresa), *The Mother House, 54A AJC Bose Rd, T033-2249 7115.* The majority of volunteers work at one of the Mother Teresa homes. Induction/ registration sessions are at 1500 on Mon, Wed and Fri in various languages.

Air The large terminals of Nataji Subhas Chandra Bose airport are well organized and have been recently renovated. A reservation counter for rail (same-day travel only) is found in the Arrivals hall. There are money changers by the exit of the terminal and a prepaid taxi booth.

Transport to the city Taxis take 45-60 mins and cost about Rs 400 (deluxe cars Rs 600-800); you can get a discount on the journey from the city centre to the airport if you bargain hard. A/c buses are available from outside Terminal 1 Arrivals; some go to Howrah (via the city centre) and Esplanade (from where it is a 15-min walk to Sudder St), taking at least 1 hr and costing about Rs 50. They also go to Tollygunge. The public bus is not recommended for new arrivals as it requires a 400-m walk across the car park to the main road, and then changing to the nearest Metro station at Dum Dum; auto-rickshaws to the Metro cost about Rs 100.

Bicycle Bike hire is not easy; ask at your hotel if a staff bike is free. Spares are sold along Bentinck St, north of Chowringhee.

Bus Local State transport services run throughout the city and suburbs from 0500-2030; usually overcrowded after 0830, but very cheap (the big blue-yellow buses are noteworthy for their artwork) and a good way to get around. Maroon minibuses (little more expensive) also cover major routes. Newer a/c buses are becoming commonplace.

Long distance Long-distance buses use the Esplanade depot, 15 mins' walk from Sudder St. Advance bookings are made at the computerized office of **Calcutta State Transport Corp (CSTC)**, Esplanade, T033-2248 1916. To **Digha** 0530-1600; **Malda**; **Siliguri** (12 hrs); **Bishnupur** and other towns in West Bengal. More comfortable private a/c buses with push-back seats to Siliguri also depart from Esplanade; good are **Royal Cruisers**, T(0)9903-400926. **Odisha & Bihar STC**, Babu Ghat: to **Ranchi**; **Dhaka**, **Gaya**, **Puri** (11 hrs). **Bhutan Govt**, to **Phuntsholing** via **Siliguri**, 1900, 16 hrs.

To Bangladesh Private buses to **Dhaka** can be booked from numerous agencies on Marquis St, from where they also depart.

Ferry Local To cross the Hooghly, between Howrah station and Babu Ghat, Rs 5, except Sun. During festivals a ferry goes from Babu Ghat to Belur Math, 1 hr.

Long distance Shipping Corp of India, 1st floor, 13 Strand Rd (enter from Hare St),

T033-2248 4921, 1000-1300 (for tickets), 1400-1745 (information only), see schedules at www.andamantourism.in/shipschedule.html, operates a steamer to **Port Blair** in the Andamans. Some 2 or 3 sailings a month (66 hrs), Rs 1961-7631 one way. For tickets go 4 days in advance, and be there by 0830; huge queue for 'bunk class'.

Metro The recently extended Metro line runs for 25 km from Dum Dum in the north to Kavi Subhash in the south, every 7-12 mins Mon-Sat 0700-2145, Sun 1400-2145; fare Rs 5-25. Note that Tollygunge has been renamed 'Mahanayak Uttam Kumar' on station signs, but is still commonly referred to as Tollygunge. There are women-only sections interspersed throughout the train. A further 5 metro lines are planned for the future.

Rickshaw Hand-pulled rickshaws are used by locals along the narrow congested lanes. Auto-rickshaws operate outside the city centre, especially as shuttle service to/from Metro stations along set routes. Auto-rickshaws from Sealdah station to Sudder St cost about Rs 80.

Taxi Tourist taxis are available from **India Tourism** and **WBTDC** offices. Local taxis are yellow Ambassadors: insist on the meter, then use conversion chart to calculate correct fare.

Train Kolkata is served by 2 main railway stations, **Howrah** (enquiries, T033-2638 7412/3542) and **Sealdah** (T033-2350 3535). Howrah station has a separate complex for platforms 18-21 (T033-2660 2217). Foreign tourist quota tickets are sold at both stations until 1400,

at which point tickets go on general sale. Railway reservations can be made at Fairlie Place, BBD Bagh, Mon-Sat 1000-1300, 1330-1700, Sun 1000-1400 (best to go early). Tourists are automatically told to go to the Foreign Tourist Counter to get Foreign Tourist Quota; it takes 10-30 mins; you will need to show your passport and complete a reservation form; payment in rupees is accepted.

Trains listed depart from Howrah (**H**), unless marked '(**S**)' for Sealdah. **Agra Fort**: at least 6 per day, around 20 hrs. **Bhubaneswar** and on to **Puri**: over 10 per day, 6-7 hrs. **Chennai**: at least 2 per day, 28 hrs. **Mumbai**: at least 4 per day, 27-38 hrs, via **Nagpur** (18 hrs) or **Gaya** (7½ hrs); at least 5 per day to **New Delhi** via **Gaya** and **Allahabad**, or **Patna**, between 17-27 hrs. **New Jalpaiguri** (NJP): at least 10 per day, by far the best is the *Darjeeling Mail 12343*, leaving from Sealdah at 2205, 10 hrs. **Ranchi**: best is *Howrah Shatabdi Exp 12019*, 0605 (except Sun), 7 hrs.

To Bangladesh It is possible to travel direct to **Dhaka** on the *Maitree Express* from **Chitpur Terminal**, twice weekly, 0710, 11 hrs.

Tram Kolkata is the only Indian city to run a tram network. Many trams originate at **Esplanade depot** and it's a great way to see the city: ride route 1 to Belgachia through the heart of North Kolkata's heritage, or route 36 to Kidderpore through the Maidan. Route 26 goes from the **Gariahat depot** in the south all the way to Howrah, via Sealdah and College St. Services run 0430-2230, with a restricted service at the weekends.

South
of Kolkata

To the south of Kolkata are the tidal estuary of the Hooghly and the mangrove forests of the Sundarbans, which reach into Bangladesh and are famous for their population of Bengal tigers. It's possible to take a day trip down to the mouth of the Hooghly or a boat trip into the Sundarbans themselves: a magical experience through gorgeous scenery, although tiger sightings are rare.

Sagardwip Island
The Ganga Sagar Mela festival is held in mid-January, attracting over 500,000 pilgrims each year who come to bathe and then visit the **Kapil Muni Temple**. The island has been devastated many times by cyclones. To get there catch a bus from Esplanade or take a taxi to Kakdwip and then take a ferry across to Kochuberia Ghat (Sagardwip). From there it is a 30-minute bus ride across the island to where the Ganga meets the sea by the temple.

Digha
Digha was described by Warren Hastings visiting in 1780 as the 'Brighton of the East', though there is not a pebble for at least 2000 km. The casuarina-lined, firm wide beach is popular with Bengalis and hotels are clustered around one main road. The small **Chandaneswar Temple**, 9 km away, actually in Odisha, is an important Siva temple which can be reached by bus.

★ Sunderbans Tiger Reserve
search for Bengali tigers among the mangroves

Sunderbans (pronounced Shunder-bon) is named after the Sunderi trees and literally means 'a beautiful forest'. The mangrove swamps are said to be the largest estuarine forests in the world.

The reserve, a World Heritage Site, preserves the habitat of about 300 Bengal tigers (*Panthera tigris*). They are bigger and richer in colour than elsewhere in South Asia and are thought to be able to survive on salt water (rainwater is the only fresh water in the park). Tigers here are strong swimmers and known to attack fishermen.

Most villagers depend on fishing and forestry, although local honey gatherers are active in April and May. (They are said to wear masks on the backs of their heads to frighten away tigers, which they believe only attack from the rear!) You will notice large areas of *bheries* for aquaculture. Prawn fisheries are the most lucrative, and co-operative efforts are being encouraged by the government. Improved management is battling to halt the loss of mangrove cover, which is exploited for fuel, and to provide permanent sources of fresh water for the tigers by digging deep, monsoon-fed ponds and installing solar-powered lighting to scare them away from villages.

Although you are unlikely to see a tiger, there are spotted deer, wild boar, monkeys, snakes, fishing cats, water monitors, olive ridley sea turtles and a few large estuarine crocodiles here, particularly on Lothian Island and Chamta block.

Essential Sunderbans Tiger Reserve

Permits

A permit is required to visit the reserve for a maximum of five days. If you're travelling independently, permits are available from the WBTDC in Kolkata (see page 550); take your passport. Alternatively, contact the Secretary, Department of Forests, G Block (top floor), Writers Building, T033-2221 5999. It is much easier to visit on a tour, when all permits will be organized for you.

Getting around

Motor launches can be hired from Canning and Sonakhali (Basanti), but it is better to go down the narrow creeks in human-powered boats. You may be able to go ashore on bamboo jetties to walk in the fenced-in areas of the forest which

have watchtowers (dawn to dusk only). You must be accompanied by armed forest rangers. Since these are tidal waterways, boats are not always able to moor near the ghats, and during monsoons or bad weather they will not sail.

When to go

The best season is October to March. Heavy rains and occasional cyclones in April/May and November/December can make visiting difficult at these times. Avoid visiting the Sunderbans at weekends, when the reserve is very busy with domestic tourists.

What to bring

Take drinking water, a torch and mosquito repellent, and be prepared for cool nights.

Listings South of Kolkata

Where to stay

Sagardwip
WBTDC runs expensive 2-day boat trips with lodging on board during **Ganga Sagar Mela**, including a/c coach. You can also stay at the *dharamshala* for a donation.

$ Youth Hostel
Book via the Youth Services office in Kolkata, T033-2248 0626, ext 27.

Digha
There is plenty of choice close to the beach to suit all budgets.

$$ Sea Coast
T032-2026 6305, www.hotelseacoast.com.
With some a/c rooms, this is the best 3-star option.

$$-$ Tourist Lodge
T032-2026 6255.
Rooms on 3 floors, some a/c, dorm, bar, restaurant.

Sunderbans Tiger Reserve
A few basic lodges are found in Gosaba. There is also one in Pakhirala, the last village before Sajnekhali.

$$$$ Vivada Cruises
T1-800 345 0088, www.sunderbancruises.com.
The first luxury cruise boat to be launched on this route, eco-friendly with 32 rooms, internet, open-air gym, sauna, sunbathing deck and multicuisine restaurants. Package for 3 days/4 nights, or 7 days/8 nights including meals and excursions.

$$$-$$ Sunderbans Jungle Camp
Bali village; book through Help Tourism in Kolkata, www.helptourism.com.
Indigenous-style bungalows with modern bathrooms, in a community tourism venture set up by a group of ex-poachers. Local fishermen supply fish and offer trips into mangrove forests; it's also a chance to interact with villagers and experience authentic folk performances. Book as a package, all meals included (open-air restaurant), prices go down the more members in your group.

$$$-$$ Sunderban Tiger Camp
Dayapur Island, T033-3293 5749, www.sunderbantigercamp.com.
'Tents' with thatched roofs, huts, mud cottages and a/c cottages, in a peaceful location with nice gardens. Village walks and fishing trips, as well as tours on comfortable boats. Restaurant serves range of cuisines and seafood, there's a bar and a library. Price includes transport from Kolkata.

$ Tourist Lodge
Sajnekhali, contact through WBTDC,
T03218-214960, www.wbtdc.gov.in.
Raised on pillars and fenced from wildlife, solar
power, small basic rooms with mosquito nets,
hot water in buckets, 20-bed dorm, simple meals
(price includes breakfast and 1 meal). Book
ahead; carry your permit.

What to do

Sunderbans Tiger Reserve
Help Tourism, *Kolkata (see page 561)*. Excellent
community-based tours and has a camp near
the reserve (see Where to Stay, above).
WBTDC Tours: 2-day and 3-day trips (infrequent
during monsoon, Jul-Sep), by coach from
Kolkata then 'luxury' launch with onboard
accommodation. Prices vary between vessels and
with standard of lodging. The launch is the only
way to visit the Sunderbans during monsoon.

Transport

Digha
Bus A/c luxury buses leave from **Kolkata's
Esplanade**, taking 4 hrs. Public buses leave from
Esplanade and Howrah and take 4½-5 hrs.

Train Direct train from Kolkata (H), 5 per day,
taking 3-5 hrs.

Sunderbans Tiger Reserve
It is best to visit the reserve on a tour, but
independent travel is possible.

Bus and boat From **Kolkata**: CSTC bus
from Babu Ghat, Strand Rd, to **Sonakhali**
(1st departure 0630 then hourly, 3½ hrs), then
hire a boat to **Sajnekhali** (3 hrs). Alternatively,
from **Basanti**, take public ferry to **Gosaba**
(1½ hrs), then travel across the island by flat-bed
van rickshaw (5 km, 45 mins) which enables you
to see interesting village life, and finally get
a boat to **Sajnekhali**; recommended at least
one way. Motor boat hire with park guide can be
arranged at Sajnekhali for about Rs 1200 for 4 hrs,
Rs 2000 for 8 hrs; boats can take 6-8 people.

Train and boat Kolkata (S) to **Canning**
(105 km) and then boat to **Docghat** where you
can get a shared auto or bus to **Sonakhali**, where
you get another boat. From Canning you can get
a private boat direct to **Sajnekhali Lodge**, but the
journey is long and dependent on the tide.

North
of Kolkata

Intensely populated and cultivated, the area north of Kolkata has been left wonderfully fertile by both the ever-shifting course of the great Ganga and run-off from the Himalaya. The plains encompass the peaceful university town of Santiniketan, home of Tagore, and the 300-year-old terracotta temples of Bishnupur. The legacy of the Muslim Nawabs lives on in the impressive ruins of Gaur and Pandua, while atmospheric Murshidabad provides an accessible blend of Bengali history and relaxation

Bishnupur

terracotta temples and locally made handicrafts

The warrior Malla Kings of Bengal ruled this area from Bishnupur for nearly two centuries, until the East India Company sold it to the Maharajah of Burdwan in 1805, for arrears of land revenue. The Mallas were great patrons of the arts and built uniquely ornamental terracotta temples. It is also where the Dhrupad style of classical Indian singing originated, as testified by continued existence of the legendary Bishnupur Gharana (School of Music). Local handicrafts include silk, tassar, conch-shell and bell-metalware and the famous terracotta Bankura horse, Dokhra, and also slate statues and artefacts. Bengali sweetmeats and flavoured tobacco are local specialities.

Essential Bishnupur

Finding your feet

The town is haphazardly clustered around the Pokabandh Lake; most visitors stay on College Road. Buses from Kolkata and Durgapur drop passengers on the edge of town. The train station is 3 km out of town, from where a cycle-rickshaw to the Tourist Lodge (see Where to stay) costs Rs 30. See Transport, opposite.

Getting around

It is possible to see all the temples listed on foot (and much more besides), but it's very easy to get lost in the intricate network of streets. Cycle-rickshaws can be hired for Rs 150-200 for two hours.

Sights

There are more than two dozen temples in Bishnupur, mostly dedicated to Krishna and Radha. They are usually built of brick, but sometimes of laterite, and on a square plan with a gently curved roof imitating the Bengali thatched *chala* (hut). The terracotta tiles depict episodes from the *Ramayana* and *Mahabharata*, and also scenes from daily life. Inside, there is a *thakurbari* (sanctuary) and a *vedi* (platform) for the image, on one side. The upper storey has a gallery topped by one, five or even nine towers.

Most of the temples are concentrated within the fort, which was built later by Muslim rulers. Distances given are from the **Tourist Lodge** (see Where to stay). The **Rasmancha** (500 m) is a unique Vishnu shrine with a pyramidal roof, built by Bir Hambir in 1600. It is illuminated at night by coloured floodlights. The well-preserved cannons, in particular the 4-m-long **Dalmadal** to the south of the Rasmancha, date back to the Mallas. Further south is **Jor Mandir** (1 km), a pair of hut-shaped temples with a single *sikhara* flanking a smaller diminutive temple with attractively ornamented panels, built in 1726 by Gopala Singha. The **Shyam Rai Temple** (1 km), perhaps the earliest example of the *pancharatna* (five towers), has a fine *sikhara* and dates from 1643. Each façade is triple arched and the terracotta panels show scenes from the *Ramayana*, the *Mahabharata* and Krishna's life. The large **Madan Mohan Temple** (3 km), with a white façade, was built of brick with terracotta panels in 1694 by King Durjan, while the 17th-century **Lalji** and **Madan Gopal** are built of laterite. The **Mrinmoyee Mandir** (3 km) has a clay idol of Durga dating from AD 997, and in the courtyard a curiosity of nine trees growing together. Little remains of the Malla kings' **Fort** (2.5 km). You can see the gate of laterite, with firing holes drilled in different directions and a 13th-century stone chariot. The water reservoirs are still there though the moat, once served by seven lakes, is partly dry.

Listings Bishnupur

Where to stay

$$-$ Tourist Lodge
End of College Rd, T03244-252013.
Lovely clean and spacious rooms, more expensive with a/c, Western toilets, balconies with view over garden, restaurant and bar, breakfast included. Run by WBTDC, it's the best option in town.

Restaurants

$ Sree Hotel
College Rd, beside Tagore statue.
Open 0930-1500, 1800-2000.
Bengali and South Indian food, excellent *dosas*, great value.

Festivals

Aug Jhapan This regional harvest festival in honour of the serpent goddess Manasa dates from the 17th century. It is linked with the fertility

cult and is unique. Venomous snakes (cobras, pythons, vipers, kraits, flying snakes) are brought in baskets by snake-charmers who display amazing tricks.

Shopping

Cottage industries flourish in the different *paras* (quarters) each devoted to a specialized craft: pottery in Kamarpara, *sankha* (conchshell) cutting in Sankharipara, and weaving, particularly Baluchari silk saris, in Tantipara. **Silk Khadi Seva Mandal**, Buttala, and **Terracotta Crafts**, 500 m from the Tourist Lodge, are recommended.

Transport

Bus WBSTC buses to **Kolkata**, 5½ hrs on local roads.

Train Trains from **Kolkata** (**H**) to **Bankura**: 5 per day, often running late, 3½-5 hrs.

Santiniketan, the 'Abode of Peace', is a welcome change from the hectic traffic, noise and dirt of Kolkata. Even a brief visit to the shady university campus, with its artistic heritage and its quiet, rural charm, makes a profound impression, and is a must for aficionados of Bengal's greatest poet.

Vishva Bharati University

Sightseeing permitted only after university hours: summer 1430-1700, winter 1415-1630 and during holidays 0700-1200; closed Wed and Tue afternoon. No photography. All compounds are subdivided by wire fences.

The university has an interesting history. The Maharishi Debendranath Tagore, father of Nobel laureate Rabindranath Tagore, started an *ashram* here. In 1901 Rabindranath founded an experimental place of learning with a classroom under the trees, and a group of five pupils. It went on to become the Vishva Bharati University in 1921. It now attracts students from all over the world and aspires to be a spiritual meeting ground in a serene, culturally rich and artistic environment. Open-air classes are still a feature of this unique university.

Among the many *Bhavans* are those concentrating on fine art (Kala Bhavan) and music and dance (Sangit Bhavan). The **Uttarayan Complex**, where the poet lived, consists of several buildings in distinctive architectural styles. **Sadhana Prayer Hall**, where Brahmo prayers are held on Wednesday, was founded in 1863. The unusual hall enclosed by stained-glass panels has a polished marble floor which is usually decorated with fresh *alpana* designs. **Chhatimtala**, where Maharishi Debendranath sat and meditated, is the site of special prayers at Convocation time. In keeping with its simplicity, graduates are presented with a twig with five leaves from the locally widespread *Saptaparni* trees.

Rabindra Bhavan ① *Uttarayan complex, Thu-Mon 1030-1330 and 1400-1630, Tue 1030-1330; no photography, bags may not be permitted, shoes must be removed before entering each building.* This museum and research centre contains photographs, manuscripts and Tagore's personal belongings; the peripheral buildings also contain photos. The museum is well documented and very informative so allow at least an hour. The garden is delightful, particularly when the roses are blooming.

Kala Bhavan and Nandan Museum ① *Thu-Mon 1500-1700*. Kala Bhavan has a rich collection of 20th-century Indian art, particularly sculptures, murals and paintings by famous Bengali artists. **Nandan Museum** ① *Thu-Mon 1000-1330 and 1400-1700, Tue 1000-1330*, has a collection of terracotta, paintings and original tracings of Ajanta murals.

Around Santiniketan

Surul (4 km), with its evocative village atmosphere and small terracotta temples with interesting panels on their façades, makes a pleasant trip. The *zamindari* 'Rajbari' with its durga shrine gives an impression of times past. **Ballavpur Deer Park** (3 km) ① *Thu-Tue 1000-1600*, is a reclaimed wooded area of rapidly eroding laterite *khowai* frequented by spotted deer and winter migratory birds.

Essential Santiniketan

Finding your feet

The nearest railway station is Bolpur, which has trains from Kolkata's Haora and Sealdah stations. Cycle-rickshaws charge Rs 30 to Santiniketan, 3 km away. Local buses use a stand near the station. The road journey from Kolkata on the congested NH2 (213 km) can be very slow.

Getting around

The Vishva Bharati campus and Santiniketan's residential area are ideal for exploring on foot. See Transport, page 570.

Tourist information

For general information contact the campus
Public Relations Office (PRO) (Vishva Bharati
Office, T03463-252751, Thu-Tue 1000-1700).

Where to stay

There are a couple of cheap guesthouses
within the campus; to arrange a stay
(maximum 3 days) contact the Public
Relations Office (PRO; see above).

$$ Mark and Meadows
*Sriniketan Rd, Birbhum, T03463-264871,
www.markandmeadows.com.*
32 cottages in lovely grounds, pool and other
activities, and a good multicuisine restaurant.
Lively with Bengali families.

$$-$ Chhuti Holiday Resort
*241 Charupalli, Jamboni, T03463-252692,
www.chhutiresort.com.*
Comfortable thatched rooms with bath,
some a/c, good restaurant, innovative.

$$-$ Santiniketan Tourist Lodge (WBTDC)
Off main road, Bolpur, T03463-252398.

Slightly faded standard rooms, some quite small,
plusher with a/c, pleasant garden, breakfast
included (but poor meals).

$ Manasi Lodge
Santiniketan Rd, Bolpur, T03463-254200.
Clean rooms, attached bath, lovely staff,
popular courtyard restaurant.

$ Rangamati
*Prabhat Sarani, Bhubandanga, Bolpur,
T03463-252305.*
22 decent rooms, some with balcony, dorm,
restaurant (Indian and Chinese).

$ Royal Bengal
Bhubandanga, Bolpur, T03463-257148.
Clean and modern, all rooms with balcony and
attached bath, dorm, soulless restaurant.

Restaurants

$ Kalor Dokan
Open all hours.
An institution since the time of Tagore.

$ Maduram
Santiniketan Rd, Bolpur.
Highly recommended sweet shop.

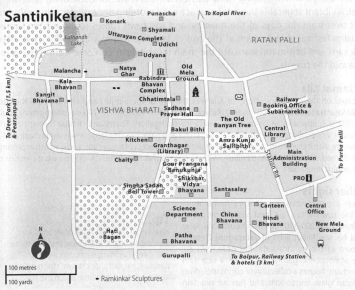

Santiniketan

Festivals

Programmes of dance, music and singing are held throughout the year, but are particularly good during festivals.

End Jan/early Feb Magh Mela, an agricultural and rural crafts fair at Sriniketan marks the anniversary of the founding of Brahmo Samaj.
Vasanta Utsav coincides with **Holi**.
Late Dec (check with Bengal TIC) **Poush Mela**, an important fair, coinciding with the village's **Foundation Day**. Folk performances include Santals dances and Baul songs.

Shopping

The local embossed leather work is distinctive.
Smaranika Handicraft Centre, *opposite Bolpur Station*. Sells interesting embroidery, jewellery and saris at fixed prices.
Subarnarekha, *next to railway booking office in Santiniketan*. Sells rare books.
Suprabhat Women Handicrafts, *Prabhat Sarani, Bhuban Nagar, opposite Tourist Lodge, Bolpur, open 0930-1300, 1700-1900*. Excellent, creative embroidery (including *kantha*), ready made or to order, crafted by local women.

Transport

Train Many trains from **Kolkata** (**H**) to Bolpur, near Santiniketan, taking 2½-3½ hrs. Also trains to NJP (for **Darjeeling**) via **Malda**.

★ Murshidabad

historic mosques, palaces and ruins set on a beautiful stretch of river

Named after Nawab Murshid Kuli Khan, a Diwan under Emperor Aurangzeb, Murshidabad became the capital of Bengal in 1705 and remained so until the battle of Plassey. The town lies on the east bank of the Bhagirathi, a picturesque tributary of the Ganga, with imposing ruins scattered around and an enchanting time-warp feel. A vibrant vegetable bazar takes place each morning beneath decaying columns left over from the days of the *nawabs*, and the town comes to life for the famed Muslim festival of Muhurram at the end of January. Woven and handblock-printed silk saris and bell-metal ware are the main local industries. Come during the week to avoid the crowds.

Nizamat Kila

Located on the river bank, Nizamat Kila was the site of the old fort and encloses the Nawabs' Italianate **Hazarduari** ('1000 doors') **Palace** ① *Sat-Thu 1000-1500, Rs 100, no photography*, built in 1837. It is now a splendid museum with a portrait gallery, library and circular durbar hall and contains a rare collection of old arms, curios, china and paintings. The large newer **Imambara** (1847) opposite, also Italianate in style, is under a continuous process of renovation and is worth exploring. The domed, square **Madina** (pavillion) with a veranda that stands nearby may be what remains of the original Imambara.

Other sights

There are numerous 18th-century monuments in the town which are best visited by cycle-rickshaw (Rs 200-300 for three hours). Mir Jafar and his son Miran lived at **Jafaragunj Deorhi**, known as the traitor's gate. **Kat-gola** ① *Rs 50*, the atmospheric garden palace of a rich Jain merchant, houses a collection of curios including Belgian glass mirror-balls and has an old Jain temple and boating 'lake' in the grounds. The **Palace of Jagat Sett**, one of the richest financiers of the 18th century, is 2 km from the Jafargunj cemetery to the north of the palace. The brick ruins of **Katra Masjid** (1723), modelled on the great mosque at Mecca and an important centre of learning, are outside the city to the east. It was built by Murshid Kuli Khan who lies buried under the staircase. **Moti Jheel** (Pearl Lake) and the ruins of **Begum Ghaseti's Palace** are 2 km south of the city; only a mosque and a room remain. **Khosbagh** (Garden of Delight), across the river and easily accessible by bamboo ferries (Rs1), has three walled enclosures.

Listings Murshidabad

Where to stay

$ Ashoke Mahal
Omrahaganj, T03482-320855.
Clean and pleasant, rear room 202 is the best with a balcony overlooking the river.

$ Indrajit
Near railway station, T03482-271858.
Wide choice of rooms of all standards, some a/c, friendly staff. Truly excellent multi-cuisine restaurant; the Indian dishes are especially recommended, serves strong beer.

$ Manjusha
By Hazarduari Palace, T03482-270321.
The best location in town, with serene riverside setting for spotting dolphins, lush garden of flowers and fruit trees, charming manager can help with bike, rickshaw and boat hire. Rooms are simple with fans. Food isn't recommended.

$ Sagnik
77 Omrahaganj, T03482-271492,
www.hotelsagnik.com.

Newer hotel with some a/c rooms, check a few, some allow glimpses of the river. Tiny tiled bathrooms, TVs and keen staff.

Festivals

Late Dec (check with Bengal TIC) **Muharram**, a fair lasting a few days, which culminates in a 6-hr procession through the village.

Transport

Bus Buses between Berhampur and Kolkata are painful.

Train Many trains daily to **Berhampur** (for Murshidabad) direct *Lalgola Passenger 53181* from **Kolkata** (**S**) leaves 2345, 5 hrs, daily; also *Sealdah Lalgola Pass 53173* at 0800. From Murshidabad, the *Bagirathi Mail 13104*, 0615, taking 4 hrs back to Sealdah is best. Arriving from northern destinations, trains stop at New Farakka from where it's a 2-bus to **Berhampur**. Jeeps/shared autos run from Berhampur local bus stand to **Lalbagh** near Murshidabad, 30-40 mins. Then catch a cycle-rickshaw to Hazarduari gate, Rs 30.

Gaur, Pandua and Malda

ruins of medieval Islamic capitals, off the beaten path

Gaur's situation on the banks of the River Ganga, yet within easy reach of the Rajmahal Hills with their fine black basalt, made it possible for gifted stonemasons to construct beautiful religious and secular buildings. Muslim monuments of the sultanate period are strewn around the quiet, deserted city. Pandua alternated with Gaur as a capital of Bengal between 1338 and 1500, when it was abandoned. Some of the ruins here show clearly how the Muslims made free use of material from Hindu temples near Malda.

Malda

Malda is a convenient and comfortable base from which to visit the atmospheric ruins of Gaur and Pandua, with plenty of banks and other amenities in the town centre. Now famous mainly for its large juicy Fajli mangoes, Malda was established around 1680 by the English, who bought an entire village from a local landlord and expanded it into a market town.

Malda has some worthy sights of its own, including the **Malda Museum** (1937), which has a collection of stone images, coins and inscriptions from Gaur and Pandua. The **market** behind the

Tourist Lodge is fascinating. Old Malda, which lies at a confluence of rivers 4 km away, is the site of the **Jami Masjid**, built in 1596 out of decorated brick and stone with some good carving on the entrance pillars. The 17-m **Nimasarai Tower** across the river dates from the same period, and has strange stones embedded on the outer surface, which may once have been used to display beheaded criminals.

★ Gaur

Most visitors arrange a half-day taxi tour of the sites, through the tourist office in Malda. But getting to the sites on local transport has its own rewards: take a bus for Mohodipur from near the Tourist Lodge in Malda, and ask to be dropped at Pyasbari (tea and snacks available). Stay on the narrow tarmac road and you won't get lost. Turn right from the NH34 for the site, which you can wander around for free. To return to Malda, stop a bus or share a taxi.

On the ancient site of Lakshanavati, Gaur was the capital of King Sasanka in the seventh century, followed by the Buddhist Pala kings. The city became famous as a centre of education and culture during the reign of the Hindu Sena kings in the 12th century. In the early 13th century it was invaded by Bhaktiar Khalji and then captured by the Afghan Fakhr-ud-din Dynasty in the 14th century. They plundered the temples to construct their own mosques and tombs. During the 15th century, a number of mosques and mausoleums were built in the new architectural style. Gaur was sacked by Sher Shah Suri in 1537 and the city's population was wiped out by plague in 1575.

The great golden mosque, **Bari Sona Masjid** or Baroduari (12-door), was built in 1526 and is an enormous rectangular stone-faced brick structure with a large open square in front. Fine marble carving is still visible on the remains of the minarets. Note the small Kali temple at the entrance.

Ramkeli, not far from the Bari Sona Masjid, has the Madan Mohan Jiu Mandir and is of religious significance for followers of **Sri Chaitanya**, the 14th-century Bengali religious reformer. **Tamaltola** marks where he meditated under a tree. Pilgrims come to see a footprint in stone.

The remains of the embankments of Gaur fort are to the south on the bank of the Bhagirati. Bangladesh can be seen from the **Dakhil Darwaza** (early 15th century), the main fort gateway with its five-storeyed towers. It was built of small red bricks embossed with terracotta decorations. The turrets and circular bastions produce a striking contrast of light and shade with decorative motifs of suns, rosettes, lamps and fretted borders. The **Firuz Minar** (Victory Tower), built by Sultan Firuz Shah in 1486, has a spiral staircase. The lower storeys are 12 sided while the upper are circular, with striking blue and white glazed tiles, used in addition to the terracotta and brick.

The builders of the **Chika Mosque** ('Bat Mosque', early 15th century), near the Kadam Rasul, made free use of Hindu idols in its construction. The **Chamkati Mosque** (circa 1475) shows the vaulted ceiling of the veranda. Inside the southeast corner of the fort is the massive **Baisgazi Wall**, which enclosed the old palace with its *darbar*, harem, etc.

Kadam Rasul (1513) is a domed building with a Bengali *chala* roof, which housed the relic of the Prophet, a footprint in stone. The two-storeyed **Lukochuri Darwaza** (Hide-and-Seek Gate, circa 1655) is in the later Mughal style.

The **Tantipara Mosque** (circa 1475; *tanti*, weaver) has superbly decorated red brick with octagonal turrets and five entrance arches. The elegant **Lattan** (Painted) **Mosque** (1475), attributed to Yusuf Shah, was decorated with bands of blue, green, yellow and white glazed tiles. Some 2 km south, close to the Bangladeshi border, the ruined **Chhoti Sona Masjid** has a carved gate.

★ Pandua

To get to the site by public transport, take a Siliguri or Raiganj bus from the Tourist Lodge in Malda and ask to be dropped at Pandua bus stand. The old brick-paved road, nearly 4 m wide and about 10 km long, passes through the village giving a fascinating behind-the-scenes view of Bengali life, and most of the monuments lie close to it. Buses from Adina return to Malda.

The **Adina Masjid** (1364-1374) exemplifies Muslim architecture in medieval Bengal. Built by Sultan Sikander Shah and once comparable to the great eighth-century mosque at Damascus, it is sadly in a poor state of repair. The vast space enclosed by pillared aisles has an 88-arch screen around a quadrangle with the mosque. Influence of 12th-century Sena architecture is evident in the tall, ornate, tiered *sikhara* and trefoil arches and the remarkable absence of a large entrance gateway. Most of the substructure and some pillars were of basalt plundered from existing Hindu temples and palaces. A small doorway in the western back wall of the mosque, clearly taken from an earlier Vishnu temple, exhibits the stonemasons' skill and the exceptional metalwork of the time.

The **Eklakhi Mausoleum**, built of brick (circa 1412), has a Hindu idol carved on its front lintel. The **Qutb Shahi Mosque** (also *Sona* or Golden Mosque) was built in 1582. Further along are the ruins of the 17th-century **Chhoti** and **Bari Dargahs**.

Listings Gaur, Pandua and Malda

Where to stay

Malda

$ Continental Lodge
22 KJ Sanyal Rd, by State Bus Stand, T03512-252388, www.continentallodge.com.
Reasonable range of rooms, restaurant, friendly, views over town from public balcony.

$ Tourist Lodge
NH34, T03512-220911.
13 rooms around courtyard, some a/c, bar, restaurant.

Transport

Malda

Road Buses, taxis and *tongas* are available for trips to **Gaur** and **Pandua**, Bus to **Murshidabad**, 3-4 hrs. **Siliguri**, WBSTC Rocket buses 1700-2400, 6½ hrs. Bus to Kolkata not recommended.

Train To NJP: for Darjeeling, several trains daily, around 4½ hrs. **Kolkata** (**S**): *Kanchenjunga Exp 15658*, 1235, 7 hrs.

West
Bengal Hills

The Himalayan foothills of northern West Bengal contain a wealth of trekking opportunities and hill stations in stunning locations, including the region's prime tourist destination, Darjeeling. The old colonial summer retreat is surrounded by spectacular views and still draws plenty of visitors to enjoy cooler climes and a good cuppa. The smaller, less touristed hill stations of Kalimpong, Kurseong and Mirik also offer wonderful walking and a relaxed vibe. The area also holds one of the Indian one-horned rhino's last safe havens in the Jaldapara Wildlife Sanctuary.

Siliguri and around
gateway to the hills and wildlife parks

Siliguri
Surrounded by tea plantations, Siliguri is a largely unattractive transport hub with busy main roads lined with shops, a couple of good markets and one of the largest stupas in India (30 m) at **Salugara Monastery**, 5 km away. The town is a stopping-off point for travel into the hills and to some national parks in the vicinity. Visitors spend a night here if they wish to ride the Darjeeling Himalayan Railway (DHR), which has UNESCO World Heritage listing (see box, page 580).

Jaldapara Wildlife Sanctuary
T0353-2511974, www.jaldapara.in. Public access 16 Sep-14 Jun only, Rs 150, still camera Rs 50. Elephant safari daily 0600-0800, Rs 750 per person for 1 hr. Guide fees Rs 1600 for 6 people.

The River Torsa flows through Jaldapara Wildlife Sanctuary, which covers an area of 216 sq km (only 30 sq km is open to tourists) and is situated close to Phuntsholing in Bhutan. The riverine forests of sal, khair and sheeshu harbour the one-horned rhino, elephants, leopards, gaur (Indian bison), wild boar, several species of deer and sloth bears. Ornithologists come to see crested and fishing eagles, and the rare Bengal florican. Elephant and jeep safaris are available to take visitors around, and there is good accommodation in the form of tourist lodges which are bookable in Siliguri. The best time to visit is from October to April, when forest cover is thinner and animals are easier to spot.

About a 1000-strong population of the Toto tribe still maintain their traditions and customs in the village of **Totopara**, 30 km to the north of the sanctuary.

Gorumara National Park
90 km east of Siliguri, www.dooarstourism.com. Public access 16 Sep-14 Jun only; closed Thu. Rs 70-120 (depending which watchtower you visit), still camera free, video Rs 200, jeep Rs 700-1200 for up to 6 persons, guide Rs 150.

Located in the Dooars (meaning 'door' in Bengali and Assamese) region, the Gorumara National Park is an interesting diversion little visited by foreign tourists. Covering 85 sq km, the riverine grasslands and forests hide rhinos, gaur, leopard, elephants, deer and more than 200 species of bird. A few watchtowers give great views and the chance to spot elephants as they come to water.

Tourist information

Darjeeling Gorkha Hill Council (DGHC)
*Opposite WBTDC, Hill Cart Rd, T0353-251 1974/9.
Mon-Fri 0900-1700, Sat-Sun 0900-1300.*
This tourism office has little information, but
takes bookings for its lodges in North Bengal.

WBTDC
*1st floor, 4 Hill Cart Rd, T0353-251 7561. Mon-Fri
1000-1730, also at NJP Station and airport.*
Provides useful information. The Forest
Development Corporation in the main office
books the lodges in Jaldapara Wildlife Sanctuary.

Where to stay

Siliguri
Hill Cart Rd is officially Tenzing Norgay Rd.

$$$ Cindrella
*Sevoke Rd, '3rd mile' (out of town), T0353-254
7136, www.cindrellahotels.com.*
Comfortable a/c rooms, pool, competent
vegetarian restaurant, internet, car hire, pick-up
from airport, breakfast included. Drinks in the bar
or on the rather lovely roof terrace are a drawcard.

$$-$ Conclave
Hill Cart Rd, T0353-251 6144.
A newish hotel with good-quality rooms, a/c,
satellite TV, licensed bar, **Eminent** restaurant
serving Indian/European food, internet, parking.

$$-$ Vinayak
*Hill Cart Rd, T0353-243 1130,
www.vinayakonline.com.*
Clean rooms with bath, some a/c, good
restaurant, look at a few rooms, some of the
budget options are better than others.

$ Anjali Lodge
*Nabin Sen Rd (next to the Gurudwara),
off Sevoke Rd, T0353-252 2964.*
Institutional building, bright white paint
throughout, large rooms with concrete floors have
clean sheets, towels, soap, TV, cheaper without
a/c, some have balcony or there is spacious public
balcony. Suspicious staff soon warm up.

$ Mainak Tourist Lodge (WBTDC)
*Hill Cart Rd (opposite main bus stand),
T0353-251 2859, www.wbtdc.gov.in.*
Large and open 1970s-style hotel, comfortable
rooms (check a few, they vary), 14 a/c, and some

$$ suites. Set back from the road in dusty gardens,
with restaurant and bar, helpful staff. Be sure not
to overlap with a wedding party; call ahead.

$ Siliguri Lodge
Hill Cart Rd (near SNT bus stand), T0353-251 5290.
A rock-bottom basic option, grotty exterior but
clean sheets and relatively quiet, being set back
from the road. Kind staff.

Jaldapara Wildlife Sanctuary

$$ Hollong Forest Tourist Lodge
*Hollong, 6 km from Madarihat, T03563-262228,
book well in advance (4 months) either directly,
online at www.wbtdc.gov.in, or via the Tourist
Bureau, Siliguri, T0353-251 1974.*
Built of timber, on stilts, deep inside the sanctuary.
6 rooms, excellent meals, the lodge is very popular.

Gorumara National Park

$$$ Riverwood Forest Retreat
www.waxpolhotels.com.
This eco-friendly resort has lush surrounds, and
some balconies have views of mountain peaks.
Comfortable well-appointed rooms, fitness
centre, library, pool, and plenty of other activities.
Guided excursions into Gorumara, plus day treks,
village visits and tea tourism.

Restaurants

Siliguri

$$ Havelli
*SS Market Complex, Hill Cart Rd,
T(0)9800803395. Open 1100-2230.*
Subtly lit, beige walls and wood sculptures
prevail, more intimate than most. Multicuisine
is high standard and the choices endless.
Family atmosphere.

$$-$ Khana Khazana
Hill Cart Rd. Open 0700-2230.
Pleasant outdoor terrace plus indoor seating
(fans), generous portions, South Indian is decent
or there's a choice of tandoori, rolls, Chinese,
veg/non-veg, but *lassis* and shakes are average.
Clean family atmosphere.

$$-$ Rasoi
*Ganeshayan Building (2nd floor), beside Sky
Star Building, Sevoke Rd, T(0)99758-802071.
Open 1030-2230.*

Pure veg food in a modern spacious environment, great for kebabs and South Indian (40 kinds of *dosa*), interesting *dhals*, plus some Chinese options.

$ Amit's Amardeep
7 Sevoke Rd. Open 0830-2230.
Upstairs a/c, cheap youthful place with North Indian and Chinese, good biryani, friendly able staff.

$ Jain Jaika Bhojnalaya
Shikha Deep Building (3rd floor), Sevoke Rd.
Opens 0800-1530, 1830-2130.
Look for their red-and-white sign down a tiny alley (there's a lift). Sunny orange walls and a chequered floor, pure veg food, best as a breakfast option (excellent *paratha* and veg – other items on menu generally unavailable).

What to do

Siliguri
Tour operators
Help Tourism (Association of Conservation & Tourism), *143 Hill Cart Rd, 1st floor, T0353-253 5893, www.helptourism.com*. Recommended for eastern Himalaya and arranging homestays in villages around the tea gardens.

Transport

Siliguri
Air Bagdogra Airport, 13 km away, has daily flights to **Kolkata**, **Guwahati**, **Delhi** and **Chennai**. Pawan Hans helicopter goes twice daily in fine weather to/from **Gangtok**, T03592-203960, 35 mins, Rs 3500, maximum luggage weight strictly 10 kg. Taxis from airport to Darjeeling, Gangtok, Kalimpong, Siliguri and NJP charge set rates.

Bus Tenzing Norgay Central Bus Terminus (CBT) is on Hill Cart Rd, next to Siliguri Junction Railway Station. There are also many private operators just outside the CBT offering similar services. To **Madarihat** (for Jaldapara) leaves from the CBT at 0700, 3 hrs; to **Malda**, frequent buses from 0430-2300, 6 hrs. The WBSTC's overnight Rocket bus to **Kolkata** departs 1800, 1900 and 2000 from Hill Cart Rd, 12 hrs, but it's a tortuous journey on terrible roads. For greater comfort on a Volvo bus try **Gupta Tour & Travels**, T0353-645 4077, departing at 2000. Ticket counter 13 in the CBT for buses to Assam: **Guwahati** at 1700, 12 hrs; **Tezpur** at 1400, 16 hrs. SNT Bus Station, is opposite CBT: **Gangtok**, buses leave regularly between 0730-1330, 5 hrs; deluxe private buses from CBT (separate ticket window).

To Bhutan Bhutan Government buses, tickets from Counter 14 at CBT, 0700-1200. To **Phuntsholing**: buses at 0720, 1200, 1400, 1500, 3-4 hrs. NBSTC buses run at 0700 and 1200.

To Nepal To **Kathmandu** buses (or more conveniently taxi or jeep, every 15 mins or so from opposite CBT) to **Panitanki** on the border (35 km, 1 hr); transfer to **Kakarbhitta** by cycle-rickshaw. Through tickets are available from private bus companies.

Jeep **Kalimpong** (54 km), from Sevoke Rd stand, 2½ hrs; **Gangtok** (114 km), Sevoke Rd or outside CBT on Hill Cart Rd, 3½-4 hrs; **Darjeeling** (80 km), from Hill Cart Rd, 3 hrs; **Kurseong**, from Hill Cart Rd (near Conclave Hotel), 1½ hrs; **Mirik**, from Hill Cart Rd, opposite CBT, 2 hrs; and from the same place to **Jorethang**, 3½ hrs (you need to have an ILP in advance to cross this border). Jeeps also leave from outside NJP direct for Darjeeling, Kalimpong and Gangtok, at a slightly higher price and with some waiting while drivers tout for customers.

Train Siliguri is served by 2 railway stations: **Siliguri Junction** and **NJP**, 5 km away; both have tourist information. There are buses, *tempos* (Rs 15), cycle-rickshaws (Rs 60) and taxis (Rs 150) between the 2. Note that rickshaw drivers can be quite aggressive at NJP. NJP has good connections to other major destinations in India. Several daily from NJP to **Kolkata**, best is the *Darjeeling Mail 12344*, 2000, 10 hrs, finishing at Sealdah. To **Delhi**: at least 5 trains per day, best is the *Rajdhani Exp 12423*, 1315, 21 hrs. Try to arrive at Siliguri or NJP in daylight (before 1900).

To **Darjeeling** (via **Kurseong**) the *Toy Train* leaves from NJP, calling at Siliguri Junction on its way. The daily diesel service leaves at 0900, 7½ hrs, though in reality the journey is usually 9 hrs, and services are often disrupted by landslides during the monsoon. In high season, a *Toy Train Jungle Safari* runs at 1000 to Tindharia village, a 6-hr round journey, Rs 595, going through Mahanada Wildlife Sanctuary. These trips are bookable at Siliguri Junction or on the **IRCTC** website www.irctc.co.in.

Jaldapara
Bus Buses from **Siliguri** to **Madarihat**, then change for Jaldapara Park. There is Forest Department transport to Hollong inside the sanctuary.

Train Hasimara station (18 km from park) has several trains daily to **Siliguri Junction** including: *Mahananda Exp 14083*, 0752, 2½ hrs.

mountain views, tea gardens and a holiday vibe

For tens of thousands of visitors from Kolkata and the steamy plains, Darjeeling is a place to escape the summer heat. Built on a crescent-shaped ridge, the town is surrounded by hills that are thickly covered with coniferous forests and terraced tea gardens. The idyllic setting, the exhilarating air outside town, and stunning views of the Kangchenjunga range (when you can see through the clouds) attract plenty of trekkers too. However, modern reality means that Darjeeling's lower market area resembles any other crowded, noisy, polluted Indian town.

Sights

The **Mahakal Mandir** atop **Observatory Hill**, sacred to Siva, is a pleasant walk, but the views of the mountains are obscured by tall trees. Sacred to both Hindus and Buddhists, the temple is active and colourful, with prayer flags tied to every tree and pole in the vicinity. Beware of the monkeys as they bite. Further along Jawahar Road West is **Shrubbery (Nightingale) Park**, a pleasant detour if it's still too early to visit the zoo. Views to the north are excellent from the renovated park, and evening cultural shows take place here (information from the **DGHC** tourist office).

Padmaja Naidu Himalayan Zoological Park ⓘ *www.pnhzp.gov.in. Daily 0830-1630 (summer), 0830-1600 (winter) except Thu, Rs 100.* The zoo houses high-altitude wildlife including Himalayan black bears, Siberian tigers, Tibetan wolves and plenty of red pandas, as well as deer, a multitude of birds and the gorgeously marked rare clouded leopard. There are large enclosures over a section of the hillside, though at feeding time and during wet weather the animals retreat into their small cement enclosures giving the impression that they are restricted to their cells. The zoo has a reasonably successful snow leopard breeding programme, with over 40 births since 1983, and is the only Asian zoo to have successfully introduced red pandas into the wild.

Essential Darjeeling

Finding your feet

Bagdogra, near Siliguri, is Darjeeling's nearest airport. The narrow-gauge diesel 'toy train' runs from Siliguri/NJP at 0900 in season and is picturesque but very slow, supposedly taking seven hours, but in reality taking much longer (see box, page 580). Most people reach Darjeeling by jeep and arrive at the motor stand in the lower town, though some go to **Clubside** on The Mall, which is more convenient for most accommodation. In the pedestrianized centre of town, on the ridge, **Chowrasta** is the natural heart of Darjeeling and particularly atmospheric at dawn and dusk.

Getting around

Most of Darjeeling's roads slope quite gently so it is easy to walk around the town. The lower and upper roads are linked by a series of connecting roads and steep steps. For sights away from the centre you need to hire a taxi; these are readily available in the lower part of town.

When to go

Between June and September the monsoons bring heavy downpours, sometimes causing landslides, but the air clears after mid-September. Winter evenings are cold enough to demand log fires and lots of warm clothing. Be prepared for seasonal water shortages and frequent power cuts. After dark a torch is essential.

Tip...

Tensions sometimes flare in the region over demands for a separate Gorkha (ethnic Nepali) state to be carved out of West Bengal. Protests result in strikes (*bandhs*), road closures and occasional violence, although this is never directed at foreigners.

Himalayan Mountaineering Institute ① *Entrance through the zoo on Jawahar Rd West, T0354-227 0158, no photography, entrance fee included in zoo ticket.* Previously headed by Tenzing Norgay, who shared the first successful climb of Everest in 1953, the Institute runs training courses during dry months of the year (see page 584). Within the complex, the **Everest Museum** traces the history of attempted climbs from 1857, and the **Mountaineering Museum** displays old equipment including that used on the historic Tenzing-Hillary climb.

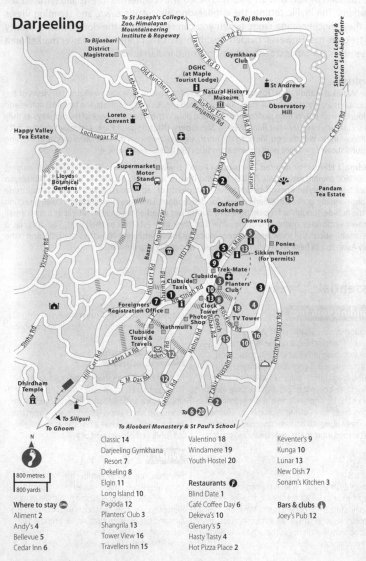

Darjeeling

BACKGROUND

Darjeeling

Darjeeling means region of the *dorje* (thunderbolt) and its official but rarely used spelling is Darjiling. The surrounding area once belonged to Sikkim, although parts were annexed from time to time by the Bhutanese and Nepalese. The East India Company returned the territory's sovereignty to the Rajas of Sikkim, which led to the British obtaining permission to gain the site of the hill station called Darjeeling in 1835, in return for an annual payment. It was practically uninhabited and thickly forested but soon grew into a popular health resort after a road and several houses were built and tea growing was introduced. The Bengal government escaped from the Kolkata heat to take up its official summer residence here. The upper reaches were originally occupied by the Europeans, who built houses with commanding views. Down the hillside on terraces sprawled the humbler huts and bazars of the Indian town.

Darjeeling Ropeway ① *Lebong Cart Rd, Singamari, open daily, summer 1000-1400, winter 1000-1600, Rs 150.* Starting from Singamari, the cable car offers magnificent views over the Rangeet Valley during the 15-minute ride down to Tukva. Note that in high season, there can be queues for over an hour to board.

Natural History Museum ① *Bishop Eric Benjamin Rd, daily 0900-1630, Rs 10.* The decaying Natural History Museum was set up in 1903 and has a large collection of fauna of the region and a certain charm; the basement has a curious diorama and specimen jars.

Tibetan Refugee Self-help Centre ① *North of town (from Chowrasta, take the lane to the right towards the viewpoint, and then walk down for about 30 mins and ask), www.tibetancentre darjeeling.com. Mon-Sat 0800-1700, closes for lunch.* After the Chinese invasion, thousands of Tibetan refugees settled in Darjeeling (many having accompanied the Dalai Lama) and the rehabilitation centre, with its temple, school and hospital, was set up in 1959 to enable them to continue to practise their skills and provide a sales outlet. You can watch carpet weaving, spinning, dyeing, woodwork, etc, during the season, when the centre is well worth a visit. The shop sells fabulous woollen carpets (orders taken and posted), textiles, curios and jewellery, though these are not cheap to buy.

On the way to the refugee centre is the lovely **Bhutia Bustee Monastery**, which was built on Observatory Hill in 1765 but was moved to its present position in 1861. Someone will show you around and point out gold-flecked murals that have been gorgeously restored.

Lloyd Botanical Gardens ① *Near the market, Mon-Sat 0600-1700.* These were laid out in 1878 on land given by Mr W Lloyd, owner of the Lloyd's Bank. They have a modest collection of Himalayan and Alpine flora, including banks of azaleas and rhododendrons, magnolias, a good hothouse (with over 50 species of orchid) and a herbarium. It is a pleasant and quiet spot. **Victoria Falls**, which is only impressive in the monsoons, provides added interest to a three-hour nature trail.

Aloobari Monastery South of town, the Aloobari Monastery, on Tenzing Norgay Road, is open to visitors. Tibetan and Sikkimese handicrafts made by the monks are for sale.

Lebong Race Course The disused Lebong Race Course, 8 km from Darjeeling, was once the smallest and highest in the world and makes a pleasant walk, heading down from Chowrasta. It was started as a parade ground in 1885, and there is now talk of it becoming a race course once more.

Darjeeling to Ghoom (Ghum)

It is highly recommended to make the 11-km (45-minute) journey to Ghoom from Darjeeling by steam train, ending up at the highest railway station in India (also see box, page 580). All trains pass through **Batasia Loop**, 5 km from Darjeeling, where the narrow-gauge rail does a figure-of-eight loop. There's a war memorial here in a pleasant park with good mountain views. A few spruced-up carriages offer a tourist-only ride in summer with a photo stop at **Batasia**; bookings must be made 90 days in advance, although it is possible to buy spare seats on the day from agents who have private counters set up at Darjeeling station. Three steam trains make the return journey

Darjeeling Himalayan Railway – a mini miracle

Travelling on the somewhat erratic narrow-gauge 'Toy Train' between New Jalpaiguri (NJP) and Darjeeling, which used to be hauled by sparkling tank engines, is a rewarding experience. The brainchild of East Bengal Railway agent Franklyn Prestage, the railway line improved access to the hills from the sweltering humidity of the Kolkata plains in the summer and was completed in 1881. It is a stunning achievement, winding its way up the hillside, often with brilliant views over the plains, covering the 82 km with gradients of up to 1:19. At Ghoom it reaches 2438 m and then descends 305 m to Darjeeling. The service was suspended for five years recently, due to a landslide, but reopened in June 2015. (For details of the tourist steam service between Darjeeling and Ghoom, see page 579).

at 1040, 1310 and 1605, Rs 1090; a diesel train runs at 0800, Rs 625 (all seats are first class). A much more economical option is to take the passenger steam train at 1015, which goes to Kurseong (first class Rs 210; second class Rs 60) via Ghoom (Rs 140/30). From Ghoom, you can also return to Darjeeling on foot or by jeep.

Sights in Ghoom (Ghum) The little **Railway Museum** ⓘ *daily 1000-1300 and 1400-1600, Rs 20, buy your ticket from the station and staff will unlock the gate*, outlines the history of the Darjeeling Himalayan Railway and has some interesting old photos. Also at **Ghoom** is the important **Yiga Choeling Gompa**, a Yellow Hat Buddhist Monastery, built in 1875 by a Mongolian monk. It houses famous Buddhist scriptures (beautifully displayed) in an interior the colour of the surrounding forests. The austere monastery is a nice walk, at the end of Ghoom's main market street. Also worth visiting is the **Sakyaguru Monastery**, closer to the Darjeeling road, which has 95 monks.

Tiger Hill
Shared jeep departs 0430 from Clubside motor stand in Darjeeling Rs 80-100 return.

If the weather is clear, it is worth rising at 0400 to make the hour's journey to **Tiger Hill** for a breathtaking view of the sunrise on Kangchenjunga. Mount Everest (8846 m), 225 km away, is visible on a good day. The mass of jeeps and the crowds at sunrise disappear by mid-morning. It's a nice walk back from Tiger Hill (about two hours, 11 km) via Ghoom and the **Japanese Peace Pagoda**, where drumming 1630-1900 is worth seeing.

Listings Darjeeling *map p578*

Tourist information

DGHC
Maple Tourist Lodge, Old Kutchery Rd (below Natural History Museum), T0354-225 5351. Mon-Sat 1030-1600 (closed 2nd and 4th Sat in month).
There's also a DGHC kiosk at Clubside.

WBTDC
Bellevue Hotel, 1st floor, 1 Nehru Rd, T0354-225 4102. Open 1000-1700, off-season 1030-1600.
Not much information available.

Where to stay

Most hotels are within 2 km of the station and motor stand, a stiff walk uphill. Some top-end hotels include all meals and most offer discounts off season (Jul-Sep, Dec-Feb). Some charge extra for Christmas and New Year. Prices listed are for high season. There is a chronic water shortage, and you may find budget hotels ration their water supply.

$$$$ Glenburn Tea Estate
T(0)9830-070213, www.glenburnteaestate.com.
Located over an hour from Darjeeling, in a beautiful tea garden. Lots of activities and good walking nearby; gorgeously restored main bungalow and equally attractive newer

bungalow, each with 4 unique suites. Dinners are candlelit, public lounges charming, and the hospitality warm yet refined.

$$$$ Windamere
Observatory Hill, T0354-225 4041/2,
www.windamerehotel.com.
Enviable location, good views when clear, a true relic of the Raj. Spacious rooms and cottages (no phone or TV in some), beware those with dated bathrooms, terraces, chintzy and cluttered with memorabilia, coal fires (can be smoky), hotties in bed, pre-war piano favourites accompany tea. Lounge/bar is a characterful place for a drink, outside guests welcome for high tea (disappointing) or beer. Full-board only.

$$$$-$$$ Cedar Inn
Dr Zakir Hussain Rd, T0354-225 4446,
www.cedarinndarjeeling.com.
Slightly out of town, but great views and free shuttle service throughout the day. Family-friendly, health club, sauna, lovely garden with wrought iron furniture. Wood-panelled rooms are stylish and thoughtfully laid out (bathrooms a bit 1980s), fireplaces in some, public areas with enormous plants, bar and restaurant are welcoming and informal. Extension in same style as the original building. Essential to book in advance.

$$$ Darjeeling Gymkhana Resort
Next to Gymkhana Club, T0354-225 4391,
www.darjeelinggymkhanaresort.in.
Wood-panelled rooms (with fireplaces) are large and modern yet warm and welcoming. Nice location on Observatory Hill, club on doorstep for sports/activities. Many rooms suited to families and groups. Indian restaurant good, but its position in the central foyer means chatter can be irritating when you're in your room.

$$$ The Elgin
HD Lama Rd, T0354-225 7226,
www.elginhotels.com.
Beautifully renovated 125-year-old colonial hotel, rooms full of atmosphere with polished floors, fireplaces, nooks and crannies, yet plush with marble bathrooms. Photos, brass fittings and carpets give warmth to lounge and bar area, like a country sitting room. Tiered garden is flower-filled but looks onto a high fence. All meals included. High tea grossly overpriced for outside guests.

$$ Bellevue
Chowrasta, T0354-225 4075, www.
bellevuehotel-darjeeling.com.
Wide range of rooms with bath and geysers, some large, bright and airy (eg rooms 35, 49), some with fireplaces or stoves, all have loads of character with old wooden fittings. Genuinely friendly management. Central located, and the small rooftop has unparalleled K'junga view.

$$ Classic Guesthouse
CR Das Rd (below Chowrasta), T0354-225 7025,
www.classicguesthouse.in.
A small quiet guesthouse with a cute lawn, stunning views from the private balcony of each of the 4 large rooms. Plenty of furniture, heaters in winter, carpets, TV, decent big bathrooms. Rooms aren't stylish but they're very comfortable and the manager is nice.

$$ Planters' Club
The Mall, T0354-225 4348.
Aka the 'Darjeeling Club', this wooden building dates from 1868 and oozes history from the curved veranda and creaking balconies. New decor in VIP rooms is unattractive, a better choice are the 'super' doubles which are dated but have a Raj ambience; huge fireplaces, white-painted furniture, bathrooms feel Victorian. Nice staff and a good place for an evening tipple among moth-eaten animal trophies inside, or out on the terrace (residents only).

$$ Shangrila
5 Nehru Rd, T0354-225 4149, www.
hotelshangriladarjeeling.com.
A small and characterful hotel in a good spot near Chowrasta. Large rooms, tastefully renovated, subtly lit, TVs, some with good views from the window seating. new bathrooms, all double beds (no twins, discount for single), 3 rooms have Victorian fireplaces. Excellent restaurant (see page 582).

$$ Travellers Inn
Dr Zakir Hussein Rd, T0354-225 8497,
www.travellersinndarjeeling.in.
Very respectable rooms in a modern hotel, hot water, good views from the restaurant with booths, and a sweet indoor 'garden room' that catches any rays of sun.

$$-$ Dekeling
51 Gandhi Rd (The Mall), T0354-225 4159,
www.dekeling.com.
Homely rooms are noticeably warm, most have private bath (24-hr hot water), delightful lounge areas with stoves. Range of room tariffs, some attic front rooms with views, 2 doubles with shared bath are a bargain (No 11 is best). Good

restaurant, brilliant hosts, reserve ahead (1 month in advance in high season). Noisy when jeeps depart at 0400 for Tiger Hill with lots of hooting.

$ Aliment
40 Zakir Hussain Rd, T0354-225 5068, alimentweb98@gmail.com.
Clean rooms vary in size and cheerfulness, pay more for TV and 24-hr hot shower (otherwise hot water for 2 hrs each evening), cheap singles and triples (hot buckets) average food in social restaurant (cheap beer), internet, packed with travellers, good atmosphere, excellent library.

$ Andy's
102 Zakir Hussain Rd, T0354-225 3125, T(0)9434-166968.
Airy twin-bed rooms are notable for their cleanliness, some have hot shower or hot buckets provided. Storage for trekkers, friendly and very honest atmosphere if slightly institutional. Discount for single travellers. Often full, ring ahead. No food.

$ Long Island
Rockville Dham, Dr Zakir Hussein Rd, near TV tower, T0354-225 2043, pritaya19@yahoo.com.
Attractive exterior, clean basic rooms, some with private shower (hot water 0800-2000) or share communal bathroom. Appealingly quaint restaurant, quiet location, internet, great views from rooftop and upper rooms. Run by friendly Nepali family. Single room rates.

$ Pagoda
1 Upper Beechwood Rd, T0354-225 3498.
Clean but basic rooms with period furniture in a characterful building, some with bath (limited free bucket hot water), peaceful, good value. Rooms at front better, though not much view from shared balcony. Away from the main backpacker scene and an easier walk from transport links. Very friendly, small library.

$ Tower View
Rockville Dham, down the back of TV Tower, T0354-225 4452.
Pleasant, clean rooms, some with toilet but sharing bathrooms (hot bucket), more expensive with 24-hr hot water, wood stove and dusty book collection in the homely restaurant (a popular place to eat, with a nice back terrace if the weather permits).

$ Valentino
6 Rockville Rd, T0354-225 2228, tashiphuntsok30@yahoo.com.

Clean rooms with a green theme with good mountain views (especially from upper storeys), central heating and 24-hr hot water, good Chinese restaurant, bar, excellent sundeck.

$ Youth Hostel
Dr Zakir Hussain Rd, T0354-225 2290.
Mainly cheap dorm beds, superb position on top of the ridge, no restaurant, trekking information available.

Restaurants

Hotels with restaurants will usually serve non-residents. Several have bars.

$$ Glenary's
Nehru Rd (The Mall), T0354-225 8408.
Tearoom with excellent confectionery and pastries, friendly, 1st-class breakfast, Kalimpong cheese and wholemeal bread sold. Licensed restaurant upstairs is pricier but lively and with a good atmosphere, bar downstairs has local band on Sat (supposedly 1900-2200 but often finishes early). A Darjeeling 'must'.

$$ Shangrila
See Where to stay, page 581.
Darjeeling's most chic dining experience, contemporary decor mixed with tasteful Tibetan artefacts, and a wide menu of delicious multicuisine food plus bar. Gracious service, open later than most.

$$-$ Café Coffee Day
Chowrasta.
A good spot to watch the world go by with a decent coffee, plus great views from the terrace.

$$-$ Lunar
51 Gandhi Rd, T0354-225 4194. Open from 0730.
Thoroughly delicious pure veg Indian dishes, and some decent sandwiches, pizzas and Chinese. Modern and informal, family environment, big windows for the view. *Lassis* are fragrant and creamy, service competent and kindly.

$ Blind Date
Top floor, Fancy Market, NB Singh Rd, T0354-225 5404. Open 0930-1900.
Warm and friendly place always packed with locals, cheap Tibetan and Chinese mains, divine soups and clean kitchen in open view, more limited choice for vegetarians.

$ Dekeva's
Dekling Hotel, 52 Gandhi Rd, Clubside.
Nice little place with Tibetan specialities, plus Chinese and Continental, cosy, very popular.

ON THE ROAD
Tea in Darjeeling

An ancient Chinese legend suggests that 'tay', or tea, originated in India, although tea was known to have been grown in China around 2700 BC. It is a species of Camellia (*Camellia thea*). After 1833, when its monopoly on importing tea from China was abolished, the East India Company made attempts to grow tea in Assam using wild chai plants found growing there. Tea plants were later introduced to Darjeeling and the Nilgiri hills in the south. Today India is the largest producer of tea in the world. Assam grows over half and Darjeeling about a quarter of the nation's output. Once drunk only by the tribal people, it has now become India's national drink.

The orthodox method of tea processing produces the aromatic lighter coloured liquor of the Golden Flowery Orange Pekoe in its most superior grade. The fresh leaves are dried by fans on withering troughs to reduce the moisture content and then rolled and pressed to express the juices which coat the leaves. These are left to ferment in a controlled environment to produce the desired aroma. Finally the leaves are dried by passing them through a heated drying chamber and then graded – the unbroken being the best quality, down to the fannings and dust. The more common crushing, tearing, curling (CTC) method produces tea which gives a much darker liquor.

Most of Darjeeling's tea is sold through auction houses, the largest centre being in Kolkata. Tea tasting and blending are skills that have developed over a long period of time and are highly prized. The industry provides vital employment in the hill areas and is an assured foreign exchange earner.

There are several tea gardens close to Darjeeling, but not all welcome visitors. Two that do are the **Pattabong Estate** on the road towards Sikkim, and **Happy Valley Tea Estate**, signed 1 km northeast of town off Hill Cart Road.

$ Hasty Tasty
Nehru Rd.
Good pure vegetarian fast food, Indian, Chinese, pizzas and sandwiches, popular *thalis* aren't very spicy. Canteen-style service, cheap.

$ Hot Pizza Place
HD Lama Rd.
Genuinely great pizza plus other Western-friendly meals and snacks, one big table holds all-comers. Folks rave about it.

$ Keventer's
Nehru Rd, Clubside.
This Darjeeling classic has a rooftop, serving snacks, with fabulous views.

$ Kunga
Gandhi Rd. Open 0830-2030.
Cheerful unpretentious Tibetan joint, with great *momos*, also pizzas and huge backpacker-friendly breakfasts. But it's the range of fantastic soups that are most memorable.

$ New Dish
JP Sharma Rd. Open 0800-1930.
Chinese. Adventurous menu, mainly Chinese (cheap), excellent chicken entrées, friendly staff. Scruffy aquamarine mirrored walls, serves beer.

$ Sonam's Kitchen
Dr Zakir Hussein Rd.
Open for breakfast, lunch and dinner (but not in between), Sonam has built up a loyal following for her home-cooking. Menu is limited, service can take a while, but the French toast is a must. Coffee will blow your head off.

Bars

There are some great options for a *chota peg* in Raj-era surroundings.

Try the **Windamere** (see Where to stay, page 581) with a cosy lounge-feel among knick-knacks, or the **Gymkhana Club** for billiards, worn leather seats and bags of atmosphere. **Joey's Pub**, though housed in an unlikely looking heritage cottage, gathers a rowdy crowd every night for drinks in a true pub ambiance. Surprisingly good typical British bar snacks, very social, open 0930-2300. English-language films show at the **Inox** cinema in Rink Mall.

Festivals

Apr/May Buddha Purnima/Jayanti celebrates the birth of the Buddha in the monasteries.

Shopping

The markets by the motor stand are colourful and worth visiting.

Books

Oxford Bookshop, *Chowrasta*. Good stock especially local interest: one of West Bengal's best bookshops.

Handicrafts

Local handicrafts sold widely include Buddhist *tankhas* (hand-painted scrolls surrounded by Chinese brocade), good woodcarving, carpets, hand-woven cloth, jewellery, copper, brass and white metal religious curios such as prayer wheels, bowls and statues. Chowrasta shops are closed on Sun, Chowk Bazar and Middle Bazar on Thu.

Dorjee (Laden La Rd). **Eastern Arts** (Chowrasta). **H Mullick**, curios from Chowrasta, a cut above the rest. **Nepal Curios** (Laden La Rd). **Tibetan Refugee Self-help Centre** (see page 579), hand-woven carpets in bold designs and colours, from US$360 including packaging, at least 6-month waiting list.

Tea

Nathmull's, *Laden La Rd (above GPO) and at Rink Mall*. An institution, vast selection (Rs 150-10,000 per kg), avoid fancy packs, knowledgeable owner.

What to do

Clubs

Gymkhana Club, *T0354-2254342, http://darjeelinggymkhanaclub.com. Open 0700-2200*. For a whole host of activities and sports, indoor and out, a day at the club is excellent fun. Enquire about temporary membership.
Planters' Club, *The Mall, T0354-225 4348*. The old Darjeeling Club, a relic of the Raj, membership (Rs 50 per day for hotel residents only) allows use of pleasant colonial restaurant (buffet meals cost extra), faded but charming bar, billiards, a bit run down but log fires, warm and friendly.

Mountaineering

Himalayan Mountaineering Institute, *T0354-225 4087, www.hmi-darjeeling.com. Office open Mon-Sat 1000-1300*. Mountaineering training courses.

Riding

Pony rides are popular starting at Chowrasta; also possible to do a scenic half-day ride to Ghoom – agree price in writing.

River rafting

On the Tista, a range of trips from 1½ hrs to 2-day camps with fishing, contact **DGHC** (see below).

Trekking and tours

Clubside Tours & Travels, *JP Sharma Rd, T0354-225 5123, www.clubside.in*. Hotel booking, tours, treks, good jeep hire, air tickets for all domestic carriers.
DGHC, *see page 580*. Runs a variety of tours leaving from the tourist office, including to Mirik, Tiger Hill, Darjeeling town and surrounding areas. Price lists are available at the office.
Darjeeling Transport Corp, *30 Laden La Rd*. Maruti vans, jeeps, Land Rovers and a few *sumos* are available. Prices vary according to the season so negotiate rates.
Himalayan Travels, *18 Gandhi Rd, T0354-225 2254, kkgurung@cal.vsnl.net.in*. Long established, good for Sikkim and Singalila treks, tours to Bhutan (need 3-5 days' notice).
Samsara Travel, *7 Laden-La Rd, T0354-225 2874, www.samsaratourstravelsandtreks.com*. Treks, homestays, village tours, rafting, etc.
Trek-Mate, *Singalila Arcade, Nehru Rd, T0354-225 6611, trekmatedarj@gmail.com*. Well-equipped trekking agents, English-speaking guides.

Transport

Air Taxi transfer from Bagdogra airport (90 km) takes 3 hrs.

Bus Minibuses go from the main transport stand to nearby villages, including **Mirik** at 0825, 0900 and 0925, via **Sukhia** and **Pashupati Fatak** (on the Nepalese border).

Jeep Jeeps leave regularly to local destinations. The journeys to Kalimpong and Mirik are particularly stunning, along narrow ridges planted with tea bushes and past wooden villages teetering on precipices. To **Siliguri** from 0600-1630 (2-2½ hrs); to **Gangtok** from 0700-1500 (4-5 hrs); to **Mirik** (2 hrs); to **Kalimpong** from 0700-1600 (2½ hrs); to **Jorethang** from 0800-1500 (Sikkim permit not available at this border, 2 hrs), change at Jorethang for **Pelling**.

Tip...

Pick a jeep that is already over half full, so that you don't have to wait long before setting off. During the high season book a day in advance (particularly to reserve seat No 1).

Motorbike Enfields and other models can be rented from **Adventures Unlimited**, based in the internet café, opposite Cyber Planet on Zakir Hussein Rd, daily 0830-2000. Around Rs 350 per day.

Train Diesel service to **NJP** at 0915, 7½ hrs, 88 km away. A passenger train runs to **Kurseong** (Rs 60/210) via **Ghoom** (Rs 30/140) daily at 1015, taking 3 hrs and returning at 1500. For the tourist-only service to Ghoom, see page 579. The ticket office at the station is open Mon-Sat 0800-1700, Sun 0800-1400, with a break for lunch 1200-1230.

Trekking around Darjeeling

challenging trekking on well-used tracks with stunning views

The trekking routes around Darjeeling are well established, having been popular for over 100 years. Walks lead in stages along safe tracks and through wooded hills up to altitudes of 3600 m. Trails pass through small villages, forests and meadows filled with rhododendrons, magnolias, orchids and wild flowers. A stunning backdrop of mountains stretches from Mount Everest to the Bhutan hills, including the third highest mountain in the world, Kanchenjunga. The entire area is a birdwatcher's paradise with more than 600 species, including orioles, minivets, flycatchers, finches, sunbirds, thrushes, piculets, falconets and Hoodson's Imperial pigeons. The mixed rhododendron, oak and conifer forests are particularly well preserved.

There is an extensive network of varied trails that link the hillside towns and villages. Agents in Darjeeling can organize four- to seven-day treks, providing guide, equipment and accommodation (see Trekking and tours, opposite), though it is perfectly possible to go it alone.

Darjeeling treks

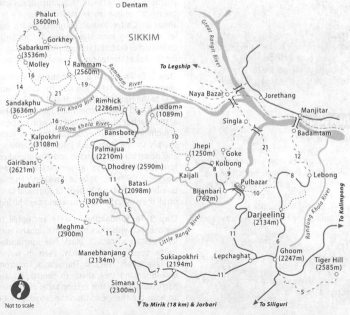

Singalila trek

The 160-km Singalila trek passes through the **Singalila National Park** and takes in the highest peak in West Bengal, **Sandakphu** (3636 m). The trek starts from the small border town of **Manebhanjang**, 26 km from Darjeeling. The journey to and from Darjeeling can be done by shared or private jeep in one hour. Walking north to Sandakphu (rather than starting in Sandakphu and heading south) means you are always walking towards the most stunning views. Other possible starting points are: **Dhotrey** (a further hour by jeep, north of Manebhanjang), which cuts out a large chunk of the steep ascent to Tonglu; or **Rimbick**, which means going via Gurdum to Sandakphu. If you have not arranged for transport to meet you at a particular point then it is entirely possible to travel back to Darjeeling from any roadhead by jeep, with services at least once daily, often three to four times daily.

Essential Singalila trek

Fees

Entry fees for Singalila National Park are paid at the checkpoint in Manebhanjang (foreigners Rs 200, camera Rs 100, video camera Rs 400). In a bid to provide employment for local youth, the West Bengal Forest and Wildlife Department is strongly encouraging visitors to take a guide/porter when entering the Singalila National Park. If you haven't arranged a trek through an agent in Darjeeling, local guides can be hired in Manebhanjang for upwards of Rs 400 per day (although paying more secures someone who speaks good English and has a better knowledge of local flora and fauna); porters are Rs 250-300.

Tip...
Singalila is not an easy trek: several parts are very steep and tough. Even up to May, temperatures at night are freezing and it is essential to take plenty of warm clothes.

When to go

The best trekking seasons are April to May, when the magnolias and rhododendrons are in full bloom, and October to November when air clarity is best. In spring there may be the occasional shower. In autumn the air is dry and the visibility excellent. In winter the lower altitude trails that link Rimbick with Jhepi (18 km) can be very attractive for birdwatchers.

Tip...
If you're staying at a private lodge, be sure to sample hot *chhang*, the local millet brew, served in a wooden keg and sipped through a bamboo straw.

Day 1 To Tonglu (or Tumling) 1 km beyond Manebhanjang town you reach a rough stone paved track leading sharply up to the left. Tonglu (3030 m) is 11 km from this point if you follow the jeep track, slightly less if you take the frequent but very steep short cuts. Alternatively, head for Tumling, just the other side of the peak of the hill from Tonglu (you take the alternative road from Meghma and rejoin the main route 1 km after Tumling). There is a Trekkers' Hut at **Tonglu** with 24 beds and a fine view of the Kanchenjunga range. From here you can also see the plains of North Bengal and some valleys of Nepal in the distance. Closer to hand are the snow-fed rivers, the Teesta in the east and Koshi in the west. You can also sleep in **Tumling** where Shikhar Lodge has simple basic and clean rooms, run by a local teacher's friendly family, "fabulous supper and breakfast" plus a lovely garden. There are tea shops at **Chitre** and at **Meghma**, which has an interesting monastery noted for its large collection of Buddhist statues; (108, according to locals). Ask at the tea house opposite to get in.

Day 2 To Jaubari and Gairibans A level walk along the ridge takes you past the long 'mani' wall to the Nepalese village of Jaubari; no visa is needed and good accommodation is available at the Teacher's Lodge should you wish to spend a night in Nepal. After Jaubari the trail turns sharply to the right back into Indian territory and down through bamboo and rhododendron forests to the village of Gairibans in a forest clearing. There is a large Trekkers' Hut at Gairibans with about 20 beds, or you could carry on all the way to Sandakphu, a long day's hiking.

Day 3 To Sandakphu It is 14 km uphill to Sandakphu, with a lunch break in Kalpokhri with its attractive attractive 'black' lake surrounded by fir trees, about midway. Even in winter the lake never freezes. The last 3 km from Bhikebhanjang (tea shop) to Sandakphu are particularly steep; this section takes more than an hour but the views from the Singalila Ridge make it all worthwhile. **Sandakphu**, a small collection of lodges and government buildings, is the the finest viewpoint on the trek and the prime destination for most visitors. Located 57 km from Darjeeling, it is accessible by jeep (the same narrow bumpy track used by trekkers), which is how many Indian tourists make the journey during the season. Sandakphu offers fantastic views, including the eastern face of

Tip...
Although Gorkhey, Phalut, Rammam and Rimbick lie just south of the border with Sikkim, entering Sikkim is not permitted on this route, though agents say this may change in future; ask in Darjeeling about the current situation.

Everest (8846 m, 140 km away as the crow flies), Kanchenjunga (8586 m), Chomolhari (the highest peak in Bhutan), Lluhe and Makchu (the fourth and fifth highest peaks in the world, respectively) and numerous peaks such as Pandim that lie in Sikkim. A five-minute walk past the towering Sherpa lodge brings you to three hillocks on the left side of the path; the middle one of these is the very highest point at 3636 m.

There is a Trekkers' Hut and several lodges, each with a dining area, toilets and cookhouse. The drive back to Manebhanjang by pre-arranged 4WD can take four hours along the very rough track, if you finish the trek here.

Day 4 Sandakphu to Phalut Phalut, 22 km from Sandakphu along an undulating jeepable track, is at the junction of Nepal, Sikkim and West Bengal. It offers even closer views of Kanchenjunga. It is best to avoid trekking here in May and June and mid-September to 25 October when large numbers of college trekking teams from West Bengal descend on the area. From Phalut it's possible to get a jeep back the way you came, via Sandakphu. Alternatively you can walk through the fine forests of the Singalila National Park down to **Rimbick**.

Day 5 Phalut to Rimbick From Phalut, walk south for 4 km towards **Bhikebhanjang** and then take the trail towards Rimbick. It takes around four hours to reach **Gorkhey**, which has accommodation, and it's a further 3 km to the village of **Samanden**, hidden in a hanging valley. From Samanden, it is a 6-km walk to **Rammam** where there is a clean, comfortable Sherpa Lodge in a tiny garden, recommended for friendly service and good food. Alternatively, the Trekkers' Hut is a 100-m climb (in the direction of Molley) before Rammam village. From Rammam it is a 1½-hour walk down to a couple of private lodges and a Trekkers' Hut at **Siri Khola** and a further 1½ hours to Rimbick. Again, this area has a wealth of birdlife. From Rimbick there are around three jeeps a day to Darjeeling (four hours), or you can return to Manebhanjang via Palmajua and Batasi (80 km).

Days 4/5 alternative route Sabarkum to Ramman via Molley An alternative quieter trail links Sabarkum (7 km before Phalut on the main Sandakphu–Phalut trail) with Rammam, with a possible overnight stay at the Trekkers' Hut in **Molley**. (Note: the manager of Molley Trekkers' Hut is often to be found at the Forest Office in Sabarkum; look for him on the way through in order to secure a room). From Rammam you could make detour, crossing by a suspension bridge over the Siri Khola River and following the path up the valley to Dentam in Sikkim. This less well-trodden valley has rich birdlife (particularly kingfishers) and excellent views of undisturbed forest.

Days 6-10 extension Those with five days to spare can return to Darjeeling by the **Rammam–Rimbick–Jhepi–Bijanbari** route (153 km). From **Bijanbari** (762 m) it is possible to return to Darjeeling, 36 km away by jeep, or climb a further 2 km to Pulbazar and then return to Darjeeling, 16 km away.

Where to stay

There are plenty of government trekkers' huts and private lodges of varying standards and prices (on an organized trek these will have been booked for you) at Tonglu, Sandakphu, Phalut, Gorkhey, Molley, Rammam, Rimbick, Siri Khola and other villages. Those at Sandakphu vary widely in standards and price, some costing up to Rs 500 per person with attached bathroom, so it's worth seeing a few. Although room is usually available, it's wise to book in advance during May/Jun and Oct when trails can be very busy. Any trekking agent in

Darjeeling can arrange bookings for a small fee. Private lodges, such as Sherpa Lodge in Rimbick and Rammam, and other trailside lodges in Meghma, Jaubari and Kalpokhri, are generally friendly, flexible and provide reasonable basic accommodation. Some places can prepare yak curry on request.

$$ Karmi Farm
North of Bijanbari (access via Kaijali, 4WDs stop 20 mins walk away, or it's 2-3 hrs by pony from Pulbazar), www.karmifarm.com.
A haven of rural peace at Kolbong, which you may choose to use as a base. 4 doubles with bath, simple but spotless, superb food.

Mirik
low-key alternative to Darjeeling for walking and resting

The small low-key hill station of Mirik, at an altitude of 1600 m, has forests of japonica, orange orchards and tea gardens all within easy walking distance. Its restful ambience, dramatic views and homely accommodation make it an appealing stop for a couple of days' relaxation or for good day-trekking.

The focal point is Sumendu Lake encircled by a 3.5-km cobbled promenade that makes a pleasant stroll, and which offers boating and pony rides. Krishnannagar, south of the lake, is the main tourist centre while older Mirik Bazar, north of the lake, has a more local vibe. To orientate yourself and plan treks, pick up an excellent map from the Ratnagiri Hotel in Krishnanagar.

Sights and walks around Mirik
Towering **Bokar Gompa**, a 15-minute uphill walk from the main road in Krishnanagar, is definitely worth visiting (daily chanting at 0530 and 1500). If you continue walking from the monastery, past old Mirik Church and some pretty houses, you reach **Rametay Dara** (Mirik's highest point at 1695 m) with a series of viewpoints across the hills to the plains. Equally impressive are the views to Nepal from the look-out tower at **Kawlay Dara** (east of Mirik), considered best at sunrise but worthwhile at any time. Near here, the tea gardens of the **Thurbo Tea Estate** roll over perfect hillocks and encompass the little **Mahadev Tar Temple** where the mark of Siva's footprint and trident imprint the rocks. Visits to the Thurbo factory can be arranged, ask your hotel for help.

Another excellent walk (four to five hours) goes from the Don Bosco Church (open 0900-1000, 1400-1600) down a new road and stone paths to the *bustee* (village) and tea gardens of **Marma Tea Estate**. From here forest trails and tracks can be followed up and down past orange orchards, squash canes and colourful houses to Mirik Bustee and on to Mirik Bazar. Jeeps ply this route should you become weary; from Marma to Mirik Bazar costs Rs 25. You can even trek to Kurseong (five to six hours) from Marma, going down to the Balasan River to cross a large bridge, and up the winding road on the other side. Or, less ambitiously, take a jeep 6 km up the Darjeeling road and walk back past the rolling Thurbo Tea Estate and little villages of flower-laden cottages.

Where to stay

The vast majority of accommodation is found in Krishnanagar on the south side of the lake, although there are also 3 hotels in bustling Mirik Bazar on the north side, with a local village atmosphere.

$$-$ Ratnagiri
Krishnanagar, T(0)9832010013,
www.hotelratnagiri.com.
A range of bright spotless rooms, all with bath, some with great views, and a cute garden for breakfast. Discounts for single travellers. The 2 split-level wooden cabins with working fireplaces are lovely. Excellent choice.

$ Boudi
Main Rd, Mirik Bazar, T(0)9932-483476
(ask for Nitai).
The back rooms have stupendous balcony views to Kanchenjunga and are a bargain. Bright paint, laminate floors, TV, hot water in the morning only, restaurant downstairs. Ask for clean sheets if it's low season – chances are dust will have collected.

$ Hotel Payal-cum-bar
Main Rd, Mirik Bazar, T(0)9734-977541.
Should the **Boudi** be full, the Payal has cheap singles with hot bucket, and more spacious rooms with geyser, all have TV. The restaurant-cum-bar is well stocked and staff sweet.

$ Lodge Ashirvad
Krishnanagar, T0354-224 3272.
The best budget option with clean bright rooms, new paint and half-panelling, pay more for geyser, or cheap hot buckets. Rooftop with monastery views and run by a lovely family. Food available during high season.

$ Tourist Lodge
5 mins uphill from the lake, T0354-224 3371.
Huge wood-panelled rooms, slightly more expensive for suites with balconies (excellent views), standard rooms have carpets (No 102 is best), newly tiled bathrooms, no single room rates, ignore the faded exterior.

Restaurants

There are extremely cheap *dhabas* near the bus stand offering passable noodle and other dishes. Meals in Mirik Bazar are half the price of Krishnanagar (Boudi Hotel has great veg *momos*).

$ Blue Lagoon
Behind PWD Rest House, near the lake,
Krishnanagar. Open 0600-2130.
Good Indian and Chinese veg and non-veg, served in a pleasant 'hut' with checked tablecloths and windows all around.

$ Hills Restaurant
Near the jeep stand, Main Rd, Krishnanagar.
Open from 0700 but closes early.
Popular little place, with some Indian dishes alongside Tibetan and Chinese, delicious *thukpa*.

$ Lakeside Restaurant
Near the boat shed.
Pure vegetarian food in a simple little eatery, with a couple of tables outside on the edge of the lake.

$ Samden
Next to Jagjeet Hotel, Main Rd, Krishnanagar.
Open 0700-2030 (later than most).
Great Tibetan food, spicy chai, monks for dining companions.

Transport

Jeep From Krishnanagar, jeeps to **Darjeeling** 0900-1430 (2 hrs); to **Siliguri** every 30 mins 0700-1530 (2 hrs); to **Kurseong** at 1500 (2 hrs); to **Kalimpong** at 0600 (4-5 hrs). Also jeeps to the above destinations from Mirik Bazar, departing 0600-1000. You can reach **Sandakphu** from Mirik; change jeep at **Sukhia**.

Train Mirik Out Agency, Main Rd, Krishnanagar, can book train tickets to/from NJP.

Kurseong (1450 m) or 'Place of the White Orchid' is a small town worthy of a couple of nights' pause on the way between Siliguri and Darjeeling. (The steam train to Darjeeling leaves every afternoon, supposedly at 1500.) It is famed for its plethora of boarding schools and is surrounded by tea gardens and orange orchards through which there are pleasant walking routes. Locals will sincerely tell you that they call Kurseong "paradise".

Sights and walks around Kurseong

There are no grand sights in the town, but it is an interesting hike up to the ridge, via St Mary's hamlet (north of the market along Hill Cart Road). Shortcuts past quaint houses and the eerie Forestry College lead up to **St Mary's Well** and **Grotto**, which has fine views and a shrine with candles. Tracks through a young forest reach imposing Dow Hill School, established 1904, and either continue up and over the ridge to tiny Chetri Bustee, or bear right to the little **Forest Museum** at Dow Hill. Head back down via scenically located **Ani Gompa**, housing a small community of nuns belonging to the Red Hat sect, and past pretty cottages. It's around a five-hour walk with stops; ask locals for directions, but double any time frame they give to destinations. Useful sketch maps can be provided by **Cochrane Place** (see Where to stay, below), where it is also possible to arrange guided hikes tailored to match walkers' interests and stamina.

In the town itself there's the narrow and crowded *chowk* market to explore, while a half-hour walk from the railway station brings you to **Eagle's Crag** (shadowed by the TV tower), an awesome vantage point in clear weather.

Tea estates

The **Makaibari Tea Estate**, 4 km from town, makes an interesting excursion. Dating from 1859 it is India's oldest tea garden, responsibly managed by charismatic Rajah Banerjee who has done much to support the community and initiate environmental and organic development on the estate. The highest price ever fetched at a tea auction was for Makaibari leaves when Rs 18,000 was paid for a kilogram in 2003. Nearby **Ambootia Tea Estate** also conducts factory visits, and from here there's a walk to an ancient Siva temple amid massive Rudraksh and Banyan trees.

Listings Kurseong

Where to stay

$$ Cochrane Place
132 Pankhabari Rd, Fatak (2 km from Kurseong on the road to Mirik), T0354-233 0703, www.imperialchai.com.
Rebuilt and recreated colonial home with rooms crammed with antiques and atmosphere, the personal touch of owner in evidence throughout. Passion fruit grows by balconies, delightful tiered garden, very reasonably priced spa/yoga/and massage, superlative meals and tea menu (see Restaurants, opposite). Views of Kanchenjunga from some rooms. Newer annex is cheaper and simpler, with a chalet air. Dorm beds (**$**) for backpackers. Lovely walking through tea gardens and villages nearby. Management informative and interesting. Wheelchair access.

$$-$ Tourist Lodge
Hill Cart Rd (1 km from station), T0354-234 4409.
Gloomy corridors but some lovely wooden rooms (check a couple), good views, 24-hr hot water, heaters in winter, snack bar, decent bar and restaurant. Car hire.

$ Kurseong Palace
11 Hill Cart Rd, T0354-234 5409, kurseong_palace@yahoo.com.
Acceptable rooms with TV and carpets, hot water, nice staff.

$ Makaibari Homestays
Makaibari, T033-2287 8560, www.makaibari.com.
Villagers from the tea community provide all meals and a unique experience in their family homes, Western toilets.

Restaurants

$$ Chai Country
At Cochrane Place (see Where to stay, above).
A meal at Cochrane is not to be missed when in Kurseong. Food is gourmet and inventive, best are the Anglo-Indian dishes with a twist (*dhal* with mint, oyster mushrooms smoked with tea) otherwise African curry, veggie shepherd's pie and more; puddings are exquisite (baked mango).

$ Abhinandan Fast Food Corner
Naya Bazar (on way to Eagle's Crag).
Open 0900-2030.
Cubby hole, with character, good veg rolls, *thukpa, momos*.

$ Gorkha Bhancha Ghar
At the railway, opposite the platform.
Open 0700-1900.
This specialist *bhancha ghar* (kitchen) serves up cheap and excellent Nepali food in clean surroundings.

$ Hill Top
11 TN Rd, T(0)9933-129177.

Good for Chinese and Tibetan in a cosy restaurant-cum-bar that makes a nod to Chinese decor. Cheap beer.

What to do

Voluntary work
St Alphonsus Social and Agricultural Centre, *Tung, near Kurseong, T0354-234 2059, sasac@ satyam.net.in*. Run by a Canadian Jesuit, the centre works with the local community through education, housing, agricultural, forestry and marketing projects. They welcome volunteers.

Transport

Bus and jeep Buses and jeeps to **Siliguri**, 1½ hrs and **Darjeeling**, 1 hr, leave from near the railway station; for **Mirik** jeeps leave from Pankhabari Rd.

Train The daily diesel service from **NJP** to **Darjeeling** departs at 0900 and reaches Kurseong after 3½ hrs (in theory). From Darjeeling, the train to Kurseong departs at 1015 (1st class Rs 210; 2nd class Rs 60).

★ Kalimpong

relaxed mountain town with an atmospheric market and beautiful walks

Set in beautiful wooded mountain scenery with an unhurried air about it, Kalimpong was a meeting point of the once 'Three Closed Lands' on the trade route to Tibet, Bhutan and Nepal. Away from the crowded and scruffy centre near the motor stand, the town becomes more spacious as mountain roads wind up the hillsides leading to monasteries, mission schools and orchid nurseries. The centre is compact enough to be seen comfortably on foot and the surroundings are ideal for walking, though transport is available to visit nearby sights.

From Darjeeling, the 51-km journey (2½ hours) to Kalimpong is through beautiful scenery. The road winds down through tea estates and then descends to 250 m at Tista where it crosses the river on a concrete bridge. 'Lovers' Meet' and 'View Point' give superb views of the Rangit and Tista rivers.

Fact...
Some say that the name 'Kalimpong' is derived from *pong* (stronghold) of *kalon* (king's minister), or from *kalibong*, a plant fibre.

Sights

Market The traditional *haat* at 10th Mile has a great atmosphere. Held every Wednesday and Saturday, it draws villagers who come to sell fruit, unfamiliar vegetables, traditional medicines, woollen cloth, yarn and much more. It is remarkably clean and laid back, a delight to explore. Unusual merchandise includes: curly young fern tops, bamboo shoots, dried mushrooms, fragrant spices, musk, *chaang* paraphernalia, large chunks of brown soap, and tiny chickens in baskets alongside gaudy posters.

Monasteries There a number of monasteries in and around Kalimpong, the oldest of which, **Thongsa Gompa Bhutanese Monastery** (1692), 10th Mile, has been renovated. The colourful **Tharpa Cheoling Monastery** (1922) has a library of Tibetan manuscripts and *thangkas*. Further nort, is the **Tibetan Monastery** (Yellow Hat) at Tirpai. The **Pedong Bhutanese Monastery** (1837) near the old Bhutanese Damsang Fort at Algara (15 km away) holds ceremonial dances every February.

Churches As well as monasteries, there are a couple of old churches worth visiting. The **Macfarlane Church** is close to the town centre, visible from the main street, and built in the Scottish style. **St Theresa's** was built by the Jesuits and resembles a Buddhist *gompa*; it is 2.5 km from the centre in Ninth Mile. Another Scottish church is found at **Dr Graham's Home** on Deolo Hill, www. drgrahamshomes.org. The school was started by the missionary Doctor John Anderson Graham in 1900 when he admitted six Anglo-Indian children. Now there are about 1000 pupils; visitors are welcome to the school as well as the dairy, poultry and bakery projects.

Paper making There are two handmade **paper factories** in town, both are small-scale enterprises employing around four people. You can buy their products and watch the paper-making process. **Gangjong Paper Factory** is a short walk from the centre of town, while **Himalayan Handmade Paper Industry** is a good place to stop if walking from Tharpa Chelong Monastery back to Kalimpong; both are open Monday to Saturday 1000-1600.

Kalimpong

Where to stay [bed]		Restaurants [fork]
Crown Lodge 1	Kalimpong Park 7	3 C's 1
Deki Lodge 2	Morgan House 8	Balaji Chowrasta 4
Himalayan 4	Orchid Retreat 9	Gompus 3
Holumba Haven 3	Silver Oaks 11	King Thai 5
JP Lodge 5		Vegetarian Snacketeria 6

Plant nurseries Kalimpong excels in producing orchids, amaryllis, roses, cacti, dahlias and gladioli. **Nurseries** include **Ganesh Mani Pradhan** on 12th Mile; **Universal** on Eighth Mile; **Shanti Kunj** on BL Dikshit Road; and **Himalayan** on East Main Road.

Around Kalimpong

There are pleasant hikes along the Tista Road through rice fields to **Chitray Falls** (9 km), a three-hour walk to **Bhalu Khop**, and a 1½-hour downhill walk from the motor stand to the Relli River. You can picnic on the river beaches at Tista Bazar and Kalijhora.

Further afield, scenic two- to three-hour treks are possible from **Lava**, 32 km east, and **Kaffer** (**Lolaygaon**), 56 km southeast by road via Lava, which has spectacular views of Kangchenjunga. Lava especially is a popular destination for Bengali tourists in the school holidays, with a monastery and weekly market on Tuesday. Both villages are accessible by public jeep/bus from Kalimpong and have reasonably priced private and government accommodation (bookable at the Forest Dept at WBTDC office in Siliguri; see www.wbtdc.com). Walking between the two is a lovely trek of about 10 km. There are other pleasant trails in the vicinity, and generally the walking is fairly level without too many ups and downs. Rhododendrons flower in April around this region.

Listings Kalimpong *map p592*

Tourist information

DGHC
DB Giri Rd. Mon-Sat 0930-1700, Sun-1230.
The tourist office can advise on walking routes and rafting. Also see www.kalimpong.org.

Where to stay

Discounts offered during winter and monsoon.

$$$ Silver Oaks
Main Rd, T03552-255296, www.elginhotels.com.
Beautiful rooms of a high standard have a Raj feel, some with fabulous views, buffet restaurant and rather formal bar, gorgeous terraced garden with views from the numerous seating areas.

$$ Himalayan Hotel
Upper Cart Rd, 10-min walk from town centre, T03552-255248, www.himalayanhotel.biz.
The original stone-built characterful family home of the McDonalds has 8 rooms with traditional furnishings, wooden floors, working fireplaces, no TV, lovely common verandas. 2 well-designed cottages to the rear both have 4 rooms with TV, more modern, trellises and flowers in abundance. Mountain views from the attractive lawn, the restaurant has atmosphere (set menu), comfortable bar with TV, helpful management. One of the oldest hotels in the area (since 1924). Charming.

$$ Kalimpong Park
Ringkingpong Rd, T03552-255304, www.kalimpongparkhotel.com.
Raj atmosphere aplenty in the 4 good-sized, airy rooms in the Maharaja of Dinajpur's old 2-storeyed house, plus 20 rooms in newer building at rear. Both have new bathrooms and wooden floors; request a front room as back ones are decidedly gloomy. The **$$$** suites are not significantly better, soulless multi-cuisine restaurant but the pleasing bar (see Bars, page 594), large lawn and peaceful location are a big plus. It's a stiff walk from town. Car rental available, Wi-Fi.

$$ Orchid Retreat
Ganesh Villa, long walk from town (4 km from the market), T03552-274517, www.theorchidretreat.com.
In an interesting orchid nursery, 6 rooms in traditional thatched cottages (built with local materials) and 4 in a duplex building, hot water (no TV or phone), home-cooked meals, lovely terrace garden with special palm collection, personal attention, peaceful. No walk-ins, must book in advance. Bring your own alcohol.

$$-$ Holumba Haven
1 km before the motor stand, 9th Mile, T03552-256936, www.holumba.com.
This charming place has 8 cottages (you will struggle to choose between them) spread through a nursery garden, amongst trees and with spacious lawns. Rooms are delightfully decorated, spotless and comfortable (no TVs), with piping hot water and real character. The owners have created a homestay atmosphere and are really friendly and informative. Singles, doubles and triple rooms.

$ Crown Lodge
Off Bag Dhara Rd, near Motor Stand, T03552-255846.

21 clean well-maintained rooms with hot water (Indian toilets), TV, generator, friendly and helpful, old-style kind of place. Doubles at the back with much light are spacious.

$ Deki Lodge
Tirpai Rd, 10 mins uphill from Motor Stand, T03552-255095, www.kalimpong.org/ dekilodge/index.html.
Very well-maintained rooms aimed at various budgets, nice terrace restaurant and outdoor seating area, kind and knowledgeable staff, a place with character.

$ JP Lodge
RC Mintry Rd, T03552-257457, www.jplodge.com.
Clean and simple rooms, charming staff, designated meditation space in a wood-panelled garret (also just a good place to hang out). Rates have increased too much though, and there are no single rates. See the website for details of their homestay, 20 km away in Munsong village.

$ Morgan House (Kalimpong Tourist Lodge)
Singamari, Durpin Dara Hill, T03552-255384, www.wbtdc.gov.in.
Beautiful location 3 km from centre and a Raj-era building, 7 rooms with bath (good views from upstairs) but run-down and ill-managed, restaurant, bar, gardens.

Restaurants

Most restaurants shut at 2000. Little restaurants behind the jeep stand dish out delicious *momos* and noodle soups at rock-bottom prices.

$$ Gompus
Open 1000-2100.
Largely meat-based menu, good for Tibetan and Chinese, very popular and a nice environment, alcohol served.

$$ King Thai
3rd floor, Maa Supermarket. Open from 0900-2130 (but sometimes till 0200 at weekends).
Excellent food (more Chinese than Thai, despite the name) attracting a real mix of people. Warmly decorated and professional staff, alcohol served. Live music every night.

$$-$ 3C's (formerly Glenary's)
Main Rd.
Hangout for local youth, with mainly Western food, breakfast items, great pastries and average coffee. Best for the buzzy vibe rather than the food.

$ Balaji Chowrasta
Great choice of vegetarian South/North Indian and Chinese dishes, cheap and good but definitely not glamorous.

$ Vegetarian Snacketeria
Main Rd, opposite Main Bazar.
Tasty South and North Indian plus a wide choice of drinks.

Bars

The nicest place for a drink is the bar at the **Kalimpong Park Hotel**, which has a cosy lounge attached and green cane furniture on the small terrace, open until 2100 (beer Rs 130). Also pleasant, though not very pub-like, is the **Himalayan Hotel**.

Shopping

Handicrafts
Tibetan and Nepalese handicrafts and woven fabrics are particularly good. There is an abundance of shops on RC Mintry Rd.
Gangjong, *Primtam Rd (ask at Silver Oaks Hotel for directions).* Interesting paper factory.
Soni Emporium, *near Motor Stand, Mani Link Rd.* Specializes in Himalayan handicrafts.

What to do

Gurudongma Tours & Travels, *T03552-225204.* High-quality, personalized treks, priced accordingly.

Transport

Air Nearest airport is at Bagdogra (see page 576), 80 km, 2½-3 hrs by taxi. Returning to the airport, you could get a seat in a shared jeep to Bagdogra, then an auto for the last couple of kilometres to the airport.

Bus and jeep Buses use the Bazar Motor Stand. Frequent to **Siliguri/NJP**, 0530-1700 (2½ hrs); **Lava** (2 hrs) and **Kaffer** (3 hrs) at 0800; to **Karkabitta** at 0530 and 1345 (3 hrs); to **Gangtok** at 0730 (3½ hrs). Shared jeeps depart 0630-1500, depending on demand, and are significantly quicker than buses.

Train The nearest mainline railhead is New Jalpaiguri (NJP), 67 km. Tickets are available from **Rly Out Agency**, next to Soni Emporium, Motor Stand, which has computerized bookings and a small tourist quota for trains departing to NJP.

Background West Bengal

History

In prehistoric times Bengal was home to Dravidian hunter-gatherers. In the first millennium BC, the Aryans from Central Asia, who had learned agricultural techniques and the art of weaving and pottery, arrived in Bengal, bringing with them the Sanskrit language. From about the fifth century BC trade in cotton, silk and coral from Ganga Nagar flourished. In the third century BC, Bengal was part of the Mauryan Empire.

The Guptas conquered Bengal in the fourth century AD and trade with the Mediterranean expanded for the next 200 years, particularly with Rome. The fall of the Roman Empire in the fifth century led to a decline in Bengal's fortunes. Only with the founding of the Pala Dynasty in AD 750 was the region united once again. Bengal became a centre of Buddhism, and art and learning flourished. The Senas followed. They were great patrons of the arts and ruled for 50 years until deposed by the invading Turks, who began a century of Muslim rule under the Khaljis of the Delhi Sultanate. The most notable of the Pathan kings who followed the Khaljis was Sher Shah, who extended his territory from Bihar into Bengal. The land was taken back by the Mughal emperor Akbar in 1574-1576, who wanted the rich resources of rice, silk and saltpetre.

The increasing power of the Muslims lured the Portuguese towards the subcontinent, and they began trading with Bengal in the mid-16th century. Before long they faced competition from the Dutch and the British, and in 1632 an attack on their port near Kolkata by Emperor Shah Jahan reduced their merchant power.

In 1690 the purchase of the three villages which grew into Calcutta enabled the British to build a fort and consolidate their power. In 1700, Bengal became an independent presidency and Calcutta prospered. The *firmans* (permits) granted were for trading from the ports but the British gained a monopoly over internal trade as well. After the death of Emperor Aurangzeb, the authority of Delhi slowly crumbled. In 1756, Siraj-ud-Daula, the then Nawab of Bengal, noticed Kolkata's growing wealth. He attacked Fort William and captured the city. Within a year, however, Clive took the city back and then defeated the Nawab at Plassey; a turning point for the British in India.

During the 19th century West Bengal became the economic and political centre of British India, and Calcutta developed as the principal centre of cultural and political activity. Bengali literature, drama, art and music flourished. Religious reform movements such as the Brahmo Samaj, under the leadership of Raja Ram Mohan Roy in the 1830s, developed from the juxtaposition of traditional Hinduism with Christian missionary activity at the beginning of the 19th century. Later, one of India's greatest poets, Nobel Prize winner Rabindranath Tagore (1861-1941), dominated India's cultural world, breathing moral and spiritual life into the political movement for independence.

Until 1905 Bengal had included much of modern Bihar and Orissa, as well as the whole of Bengal. Lord Curzon's short-lived Partition of Bengal in 1905 roused fierce opposition and also encouraged the split between Muslims and Hindus which finally resulted in Bengali Muslim support for the creation of Pakistan in 1947. The division into the two new states was accompanied by the migration of over five million people and appalling massacres as Hindus and Muslims fled. West Bengal was again directly affected by the struggle to create Bangladesh, when about 10 million refugees arrived from East Pakistan after 25 March 1971. Most returned after Bangladesh gained its Independence in December 1971.

Culture

Today the majority of the people in the state are Bengalis. Tribal groups include Santals, Oraons and Mundas in the plains and the borders of Chota Nagpur, and Lepchas and Bhotias in the Himalaya. The gently rising slopes which lead from the delta to Bihar and Odisha are the home of some of India's most isolated tribal peoples, though their forest habitat has been severely degraded. Over 85% of the population speak Bengali. Hindi, Urdu and tribal languages account for most of the remainder.

Essential Sikkim

Finding your feet

Sikkim nestles between the peaks of the eastern Himalaya, stretching only 112 km from south to north and 64 km from east to west. This small area (7298 sq km) is home to around 600,000 people and contains a vast range of landscapes and habitats, from subtropical river valleys to snow-covered peaks. On the border with Nepal is Khangchendzonga (known as Kanchenjunga in West Bengal, or the 'Five Treasures of the Great Snows'), the third highest peak in the world at 8586 m. The Sikkimese believe it to be the repository of minerals, grains, salt, weapons and holy scriptures. On its west is the massive 31-km-long Zemu Glacier. The state encompasses the upper valley of the Tista River, a tributary of the Brahmaputra, the watershed of which forms the borders with Tibet and Nepal. In the east lies the Chumbi Valley, a tongue of Tibetan land separating Sikkim from Bhutan that gives the state its strategic and political sensitivity.

Fact...
Despite comprising just 0.2% of India's landmass, Sikkim accounts for an astounding 26% of its biodiversity.

Permits

Foreign tourists need a permit in order to enter Sikkim. Free Inner Line Permits (ILPs) are issued for up to 30 days. The main checkpoint for entry to Sikkim is at Rangpo, which issues a permit on arrival; processing time is 10 minutes. Jeeps will wait for foreigners while the permits are processed, before travelling on to Gangtok. If you wish to enter via Jorethang (for quicker access to West Sikkim) you need to arrange your ILP in advance. This can be done in Darjeeling at the Sikkim Tourist Office (Main Old Bellevue Hotel, Nehru Road, Monday-Saturday 1000-1600), where the processing time is 10 minutes; take one copy of your passport and visa, and one passport photo. You can also apply online at www.sikkimilp.in, but this involves choosing a tour operator. ILPs are extendable for a further 30 days at the FRO in Gangtok (Yangthang Building, Kazi Road, Gangtok, T03592-203041, daily 1000-1600) or by the Superintendent of Police in Namchi (south) and Geyzing (west). Once you exit Sikkim, you are not permitted to return for three months.

Certain areas in North and West Sikkim (Yumthang, Tsopta, Chhangu Lake, Dzongri) are open to groups of two or more travellers, on condition that travel is with a registered travel agency. The required Protected Area Permit (PAP) can be arranged by local agents; apply with photocopies of your passport (Indian visa and personal details pages), ILP and two photos.

Getting around

The nearest airport is Bagdogra in West Bengal. Most visitors from the south arrive in Sikkim by the attractive road following the Tista (NH31A), which is accessible all year except in very wet weather (mid-June to September) when there may be landslips. Permits and passports are checked at Rangpo where 30-day permits are available (see above).

Road journeys within Sikkim are very scenic, but numerous hairpin bends and unsealed sections can also make them extremely slow, so expect to travel at 10-40 kph. Conditions deteriorate considerably during the monsoon, which can sometimes make travel impossible. Shared jeeps are cheap, fast and much more frequent than buses. They run to/from Gangtok and between all main settlements in the west, often leaving early morning; check locally for current times. If no jeep is going directly to your destination, it may be best to go to Gezing, Jorethang or Namchi, which have more frequent services in all directions (including to Darjeeling and Siliguri). It's also possible to trek from town to town, if you're prepared to do some road walking and ask villagers to show you short cuts.

When to go

The best time to visit is in September and October. In the lower valleys Sikkim's climate is subtropical. Above 1000 m, it is temperate, while the higher mountain tops are permanently under snow. Sikkim is one of the Himalaya's wettest regions, with most rain falling between mid-May and September. Road transport can be very unreliable at this time, but May to July is the best time to see primula and other alpine flowers in bloom in

Fact...

Lepchas call the region Nye-mae-el, meaning 'Paradise'. To Bhutias it is Beymul Denjong, or the 'Hidden Valley of Rice'. The Tsong word Su-khim means 'New' or 'Happy House'.

the high-altitude meadows. The weather tends to be clear and warm in September, chilly from October to February and warm and dry but often foggy from March until the start of the monsoon in late May/June.

Time required

Allow two days in and around Gangtok, three days for the Yumthang Valley and a minimum of four to five days for West Sikkim.

Footprint picks

1 **Gangtok**, page 600
2 **Rumtek Monastery**, page 605
3 **Pemayangtse Monastery**, page 608
4 **Yuksom**, page 609
5 **Kangchendzonga National Park trek**, page 612
6 **Yumthang and Tsopta valleys**, page 615

homegrown organic food served in cosy dining room, a unique choice.

$$ Mintokling Guest House
Secretariat Rd, Bhanu Path, T03592-204226, www.mintokling.com.
12 prettily decorated rooms with bath, timber-floored on 2nd storey or carpets on ground/1st,

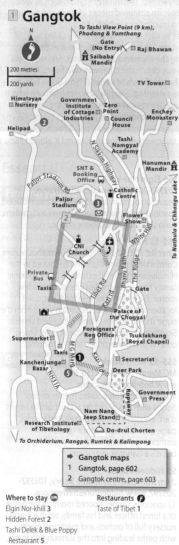

Gangtok

N

To Tashi View Point (9 km), Phodong & Yumthang

Gate (No Entry) — Raj Bhawan

Saibaba Mandir

200 metres
200 yards

Himalayan Nursery

Government Institute of Cottage Industries

Zero Point

Council House

Enchey Monastery

TV Tower

Helipad

N Sikkim Highway

Tashi Namgyal Academy

Hanuman Mandir

SNT & Booking Office

Catholic Centre

Paljor Stadium Rd

Paljor Stadium

Flower Show

White Hall

To Nathula & Chhangu Lake

CNI Church

The Ridge

Private Bus

Taxis

Tibet Rd

Kazi Rd

Bhanu Path

Gate

Palace of the Chogyal

Supermarket

Foreigners' Reg Office

Tsuklakhang (Royal Chapel)

Kanchenjunga Bazar

M G Marg

Taxis

NH31A

Secretariat

Deer Park

Government Press

Ropeway

Nam Nang Jeep Stand

Research Institute of Tibetology

Do-drul Chorten

To Orchidarium, Rangpo, Rumtek & Kalimpong

→ **Gangtok maps**
1 Gangtok, page 602
2 Gangtok centre, page 603

Where to stay 🛏
Elgin Nor-khill **3**
Hidden Forest **2**
Tashi Delek & Blue Poppy Restaurant **5**

Restaurants 🍴
Taste of Tibet **1**

602 • Sikkim Gangtok

---

among working veg gardens, flowers, lawns and prayer flags, good restaurant, charming Sikkimese owner. Book in advance through website, as often full.

$$-$ Mount Jopuno (Sikkim Tourism)
PS Rd, T03592-203502.
Out of 12 rooms, 4 de luxe, good restaurant and service, eager young staff (at Institute of Hotel Management).

$$-$ Sonam Delek
Tibet Rd, T03592-202566, www.hotelsonamdelek.com.
Balconied rooms with bath, best choice for views of the mountains, pleasant restaurant (great local food), terrace garden, some $$$ suites.

$$-$ Tibet (Dalai Lama Trust)
PS Rd, T03592-203468, www.hoteltibetgangtok.com.
30 rooms, good views from those at rear, restaurant, bar, exchange, Tibetan books and crafts for sale, very pleasant and peaceful, some pricier suites.

$ Lhakpa
Tibet Rd, T03592-223002.
Cheap rooms, some with bath, even cheaper dorm, restaurant (excellent Chinese), views.

$ Modern Central Lodge
MG Marg, T03592-204670, www.modern-hospitality.com.
Simple, clean and colourful rooms with bath, best in front on upper floors, a bit noisy, great lounge packed with books on Sikkim, basic but good restaurant, jeep tours (long-established, using high standard accommodation), very friendly and helpful.

$ Sunny Guest House
By jeep stand on NH31A, T(0)8533-287109.
Pleasant old-school rooms with bath, TV, carpets, super K'dzonga views from top floor, forgettable room service. Handy location means no walking up hills with luggage.

$ Travel Lodge
Tibet Rd, T03592-203858, travellodge.gangtok@gmail.com.
Decent modern hotel, with rooms at the front that are spacious and light. Can get a good deal on smaller side rooms, a good step up from backpacker places but at budget prices. All have reliable geysers and TV; affable staff.

Restaurants

Lightly spiced Sikkimese meat and vegetable dishes are usually eaten with noodles or rice. *Churpi* is a local yak milk curd cheese.

$$ Blue Poppy
Tashi Delek (see Where to stay).
International, but Sikkimese recommended (order in advance), the restaurant itself is a bit soulless; also a wonderful roof terrace and **Yak Bar**.

$$ Snow Lion
In Hotel Tibet (see Where to stay).
Good Tibetan and Sikkimese in elaborately decorated room, but service can be glacial.

$$ Tangerine
Chumbi Residency (see Where to stay).
Down in the bowels of the hotel, this appealing split-level restaurant has a mix of Thai cushions and standard seating, and a nice little terrace for drinks. Sikkim dishes are good (seasonal availability) and there is a diverse menu of Indian, Chinese, and continental plus some Thai mains.

$$-$ Masala
MG Marg under Karma Hotel. Open 0800-2230.
Funkily decorated and fastidiously clean, serving pure vegetarian Indian (paneer is their strength) and Chinese. Intimate and cosy, serves alcohol.

$ Baker's Café
Branches dotted around town (including MG Marg).
Reliable for pastries and authentic brown bread.

$ China Palate
Star Cinema Building, MG Rd. Open 1030-2030.
Excellent value Chinese in a laid-back place with a bar.

$ Famous Roll Corner
New Market, Lal Bazar Bridge.
Delicious, fast and famous rolls are spicy or not, depending on your choice of sauce.

$ Marwari & Gujarati Thali (Jain Restaurant)
Tibet Rd. Open 0700-2100.
Utterly delicious *thalis*, endlessly refilled, and very cheap. Plus surprisingly good *momos* and competent staff.

$ Rasoi (aka Blue Sheep)
MG Marg (by the Tourist Office). Opens at 0830.
Wonderful South Indian breakfast items and a broad spectrum of multicuisine, served in an airy, clean, smart family restaurant. Creamy thick *lassis* and juices are particularly notable, gets very busy at night.

$ Taste of Tibet
MG Marg.
The better of 2 similarly named places, serving excellent Tibetan soups and noodles to an accompaniment of whatever internet radio channel happens to be tuned in.

Bars and clubs

Bars in most restaurants serve local spirits distilled at Rangpo: brandy, rum, whiskey and liqueurs. *Chhang* is the unofficial national drink. A bamboo mug (*thungba*) is filled with fermented millet through which boiled water is allowed to percolate; the drink is sipped through a bamboo straw. You can enjoy this mildly intoxicating pleasant drink for over an hour simply by adding hot water. More conventional alcoholic drinks are available at Gangtok's numerous wine shops.

Gangtok centre

→ **Gangtok maps**
1 Gangtok, page 602
2 Gangtok centre, page 603

Thakurbari Temple & Dharamsala 2

100 metres
100 yards

Until 1962 the Nathula highway was the main route for mule trains trading between Gangtok and Lhasa in Tibet. The sanctuary extends from the '15th Mile' check post to the ridges bordering Rongchu and Chhangu Lake at an altitude of 3200 to 4100 m. The best time to visit is April to August and October to November. Among the junipers and silver firs the sanctuary harbours some rare ground orchids and rhododendrons and numerous medicinal plants including the *Panax pseudo-ginseng*. The Himalayan marmot has been reintroduced here. Other mammals include goral, serow, red panda, Himalayan black bear, Tibetan fox and yellow-throated martens, together with very colourful pheasants.

Two easy treks lead to the Shiv Gufa (1 km from the road), where you can crawl into a tiny cave on your hands and knees to see a small Siva image and several tridents embedded in the soft floor, and to Kheding (4 km). There are also longer and more difficult treks to Simulakha, Namnang Lakha and Nakcho, which are very scenic. Trekkers with permits for Chhangu may return from Nakcho via the lake (see below).

Chhangu (Tsomgo) Lake

36 km from Gangtok. Permits required (apply with photo and passport a day ahead). Allow 6 hrs for the return trip from Gangtok by jeep/minivan (Rs 800-1000), or there are organized tours.

The holy Chhangu Lake lies at 3774 m, 5 km further along the precipitous Nathula road. Completely frozen in mid-winter, it is best visited from March to May and September to mid-December. There are superb sunsets and excellent views of Khangchendzonga from the nearby ridge, but the lake area is overcrowded and spoilt by snack kiosks and loud Hindi music. You can walk around the lake in about an hour.

Listings Around Gangtok

Where to stay

Rumtek Monastery

$$$-$$ Bamboo Retreat
Sajong Village, T03592-252516,
www.bambooretreat.in.
Gorgeous views of the mountains, set on the edge of paddy fields, with 10 large comfortable bedrooms in different colour themes. The Swiss owner has created a wonderful retreat, with meditation, massage, creative workshops and a library to relax guests. Organic food is delicious, panoramic views from the restaurant, plus a bar.

$$$-$$ Martam Village Resort
Gangkha, Upper Martam, 14 km from the monastery, T03592-203314, www.sikkim-martam-resort.com.
Overlooking the valley and a short day-trek from Phamnongla Wildlife Sanctuary, 14 traditional-style thatched cottages with large picture windows, excellent Sikkimese meals included in the price.

$ Sungay
Near monastery gate.
Basic rooms in old guest house, hot water, friendly.

Kyongnosla Alpine Sanctuary

$ Log Huts
2 rooms in each at Kyongnosla and Lamnang Lakha.

Festivals

Rumtek Monastery
Feb Special colourful **Losar** dances are held 2 days before the Tibetan New Year. Arrive 3 days earlier to see rehearsals without masks. *Pujas* and ceremonies are held during this period.
Jun The important **Rumtekchaam** is performed on the 10th day of the 5th month of the Tibetan calendar; masked dancers present 8 manifestations of the Guru Rimpoche.

Transport

Rumtek Monastery
Bus From **Gangtok** about 1600 (1½ hrs) along a steep narrow road, returns about 0800.

Jeep Shared jeep from Gangtok, Rs 50 each; last return 1500. Rumtek to **Pemayangtse**, 4 hrs.

Taxi From Gangtok, Rs 1000 one way or Rs 1500 return including 1½-hr wait.

This enchanting region contains plunging rice terraces, thundering rivers, Buddhist monasteries etched against the sky and the ever-brooding presence of Mount Khangchendzonga. The administrative headquarters of West Sikkim, Gezing (Gayzing, Gyalshing), 105 km west of Gangtok, is useful as a transport hub and has a busy market with food stalls, shops, a few hotels, but little else to detain visitors.

Jorethang

For travellers, the market town of Jorethang on the Sikkimese border is chiefly a transport hub for destinations in South and West Sikkim and northern West Bengal. Darjeeling is just 30 km away, but to enter Sikkim via Jorethang (bypassing Gangtok altogether) it is necessary to obtain permission in advance as the border post does not issue permits (see Essential Sikkim, page 598). There is not much to see in the grid-pattern town itself; a stroll east along the riverbed from the suspension bridge brings you to a colourful hybrid temple with shady pagodas, and the market is a good place to stock up on food supplies. Near the bridge is the SNT bus station, opposite which is a tourist information centre ① *daily 0830-2000*, where keen staff proffer a couple of brochures. The three jeep stands, plus hotels and bars, are in the street behind and beyond the tourist office.

Ravangla and Maenam Sanctuary

Ravangla (Rabongla), 65 km southwest of Gangtok, is a small village whose timber-fronted main street retains a strong frontier flavour and serves as the gateway to one of Sikkim's best day hikes. The 12-km trek through the sanctuary to **Maenam Peak** (3260 m), which dominates the town, takes about three hours. The sanctuary harbours red panda, civet, blood pheasant and black eagle, and is most beautiful when the magnolia and rhododendron are in bloom in April-May. **Bhaledunga**, another 30-minute hike along the ridge, on the steep cliff edge above the Tista, juts out in the shape of a cockerel's head.

Towering above it on the 'wish-fulfilling hill' of Samdruptse is a 45-m statue of **Guru Padmasambhava** ① *0700-1700, free*, the patron saint of Sikkim who spread Buddhism to Tibet in the ninth century. Resplendent in copper and a coat of bronze paint, the statue can be seen from Darjeeling, around 40 km away. Not to be outdone, a 33-m statue of Siva on another hill at Solophok outside Namchi was completed in 2011.

Tashiding

Some 40 km north of Gezing is the gold-topped **Tashiding monastery**, built in 1716, which stands on a conical hill between the Rathong and Rangit rivers on a spot consecrated by Guru Rimpoche. The most sacred *chorten* in Sikkim is here; even the sight of it brings blessing and washes away sins. It

> **Tip...**
> Tashiding is a day's trek from Pemayangtse or Yukşom (see pages 608 and 609); allow seven hours.

contains relics of the Buddha and stands in a field of many *stupas* surrounded by *mani* walls. You will see numerous stones with high-class carvings of *mantras* around the monastery, made on site by a prolific artisan. Following the track beyond the *stupa* field brings you to a small cemetery where cremations are performed, and continuing down (beware of leeches) is an area designated for 'burial of dissenters' who are left in wooden boxes while their clothes and possessions are thrown down the hillside.

The main *gompa* has been refurbished and all the frescos repainted; these particularly fine murals are intricate and expansive, with Tantric motifs. Pilgrims attend the **Bumchu Festival** in February/March to drink water from the sacred pot which has never run dry for over 300 years. Below the monastery is the small **Tshchu Phur Cave** where Guru Rinpoche meditated; follow the trail on the left of the main steps to the monastery until you see a small building, opposite which is a painting on the rocks. Carry a torch if you plan to crawl into the cave.

Pelling

2 km from Pemayangtse monastery and 9 km by road from Gezing.

Pelling sits on a ridge with good views of the mountains. The rather bleak little town has three areas linked by a winding road, Upper and Middle with views and hotels, and Lower Pelling with banks and other services. Upper Pelling is expanding rapidly, with new hotels springing up to accommodate honeymooners from Kolkata, and makes the most convenient base for visits to Pemayangtse Monastery. You can also visit the **Sanga Choelling Monastery** (circa 1697), possibly the oldest in Sikkim, which has some colourful mural paintings. The hilltop monastery is about 3 km along a fairly steep track through thick woods (about 30 minutes). The area is excellent for walking. One of the best circuits, for up to seven days but also enjoyable in smaller sections, begins from Pelling or Pemayangtse, descending through terraced fields to the Rimbi Khola river, then climbing up to Khecheopalri Lake. From here you can easily reach Yuksom in a day, then continue on to Tashiding, and either return to Pemayangtse or climb eastwards towards Kewzing and Ravangla.

★ Pemayangtse

112 km west of Gangtok. Daily 0700-1600, Rs 10, good guided tours, 0700-1000 and 1400-1600 (if closed, ask for key), no photography inside.

A full-day trip by car from Gangtok, along a very scenic road, Pemayangtse (Perfect Sublime Lotus) was built during the reign of the third Chogyal Chador Namgyal in 1705. It is located about 7 km from Gezing, above the main road to Pelling at 2085 m.

> **Tip...**
> Take an early morning walk to the rear of the monastery to see a breathtaking sunrise in perfect peace.

The awe-inspiring **monastery** is Sikkim's second oldest and, for many visitors, is the highlight of their trip to Sikkim; it certainly has an aura about it. The walls and ceiling of the large *Dukhang* (prayer hall) have numerous *thangkas* and wall paintings, and there is an exceptional collection of religious artworks including an exquisite wooden sculpture on the top floor depicting the heavenly palace of Guru Rimpoche, the *Santhokpalri*, which was believed to have been revealed in a dream. The old stone and wood buildings to the side are the monks' quarters. According to tradition the monks have been recruited from Sikkim's leading families as this is the headquarters of the Nyingmapa sect. Annual *chaam* dances are held in late February and in September.

Rabdantse, the ruined palace of the 17th- to 18th-century capital of Sikkim, is along the Gezing-bound track from the monastery, 3 km from Pelling. From the main road, turn left just before the white sign 'Gezing 6 km', cross the archery field and turn right behind the hill (road branches off just below Pemanyangtse). Follow the narrow rocky track for 500 m to reach the palace.

Khecheopalri Lake

Last bus from Pelling at 1400, jeep share 1½ hrs, or you can walk there in 5 hrs (parts are very steep).

A road west of the Pelling–Yuksom road leads to this tranquil lake where the clear waters reflect the surrounding densely wooded slopes of the hills with a monastery above; Lepchas believe that birds remove any leaf that floats down. Prayer flags flutter around the lake, and it is particularly atmospheric when leaf lamps are floated with special prayers at dusk. The sanctity of the lake may be attributed to its foot-like shape (symbolizing the Buddha's footprint), which can be seen from the surrounding hills.

> **Tip...**
> A couple of simple homestays/guesthouses are located in the tiny village on the ridge; an idyllic spot for those who don't mind basic facilities.

The lake itself is not visually astonishing, but walks in the surrounding hills are rewarding and a night or two can easily be spent here. There are staggering views from the tiny hamlet by the *gompa* on the ridge (accessed by the footpath in the car park, just ask for the *gompa*). You can trek from Pelling to Yuksom via the lake (without a permit) in two days, a beautiful journey. Or, after spending a night near the lake, put your bags on a public jeep to either Yuksom or Pelling (to be dropped off at a hotel) and make a one-day trek to catch them up; locals will advise you on the way.

★ Yuksom

Delightfully scenic little Yuksom (Yuksam), 42 km north from Pelling by jeepable road, is where the first Chogyal was crowned in 1641, thus establishing the kingdom of Sikkim. The wooden altar and stone throne stand beside Nabrugang *chorten*, with lovely wall paintings and an enormous prayer wheel, in a beautifully peaceful pine forest. During **Buddha Purnima** (the Buddha's birthday) in late April and May, women from the local community gather mid-morning to sing and pray in a low-key yet moving ceremony. Below Nabrugang, past pretty houses, **Kathok Lake** is a small green pool. The reflection of the prayer flags that surround it are photogenic, and the nearby monastery of the same name is worth the short uphill walk.

Although most people are in Yuksom because it is the starting point for the Gocha La trek (see page 612), the village makes a quiet and relaxing base for a few days' stay, with several day walks leading out from the centre. It's a 45-minute climb to the attractive **hermit's retreat** at **Dhubdi** (circa 1700) above the village. A rewarding three-hour hike leads to **Hongri Monastery**, about halfway to Tashiding, mainly following a stone trail. Descending the path between the Yangri Gang and Panathang hotels, it is 45 minutes to a wooden bridge over the Phamrong Khola which has deliciously icy pools (accessed from the other side). The trail continues to Tsong village, with a sweet homestay in the first cottage in Lower Tsong (three beds) and onwards up the steep hill to the plain stone-slab monastery. It's a perfect picnic spot, with stone tables among the mossy *chortens* and glorious views. From here, it is another three to four hours' walk to Tashiding.

Listings South and West Sikkim

Tourist information

Pelling

Sikkim Tourist Centre
Upper Pelling, near Garuda, T03595-25085.
Helpful.

Where to stay

Jorethang

$ Hotel Janta
Near tourist information, T03595-276104.
Basic place but fills up fast, only 7 rooms, dorm beds and single-person discounts. Restaurant is cosy, with good *thukpa* and *momos*, well-stocked bar.

$ Hotel Namgyal
Near SNT bus station, T03595-276852.
Best choice in town with simple rooms (doubles only), typically slab-floored with walls painted split colours. Fans, TVs, hot water in garish bathrooms. Best at the back, where they have windows as well as balconies. Decent restaurant and cheap beer.

Ravangla

$$ Bon Farmhouse
Kewzing village, 8 km towards Legship, T09547-667799, www.sikkimbonfarmhouse.com.
Beautiful setting in a quiet Bhutia village, practising responsible tourism, 5 rooms and cottages have Sikkimese decor and modern amenities. Set in a tea garden, with a small organic farm, birdwatching, trekking to the Maenam and Tendong hills, and tours available, as well as herbal stone baths.

$$-$ Mt Narsing Village Resort
15th Mile, www.mtnarsingresorts.com.
2 rooms in a cottage and 3 in bungalow situated in a delightfully flower-filled garden, with incredible views over the terraced valley slopes to a monastery. Also cottages in an isolated annex, 1 km from the main road, which are more luxurious and enjoy even better views. Quaint homely rooms, with simple bamboo furniture and modern bathrooms. Good meals are served in restaurants at both locations.

$ Melody
Ralang Rd, T03595-260817.
Basic but charming rooms with wooden floors, clean, friendly.

Tashiding

$$-$ Yatri Niwas
B monastery gate (250 m south of jeep stand), T(0)9832-623654.
Tasteful and comfortable rooms (pay more for wood walls and parquet floors), plus dorm beds. Pleasant gardens and good restaurant.

$ Blue Bird
Main market, 50 m uphill from jeep stand, T03595-243248.
Very basic old-school rooms, single/double/dorm, all share a bath (hot water if there is electricity), run by a kind Bengali family. Restaurant below is by far the best place to eat.

$ Dhakkar Tashiding Lodge
200 m down from jeep stand, T03595-243249.
Large concrete rooms with great views from the back, 3 or 4 beds, best of the shared bathrooms in town.

Pelling
Power and water cuts can last 4 hrs or more and dogs often bark all night. Several $ in Upper Pelling, with excellent views if you can overlook their dubious cleanliness. With over 70 places to choose from, and hotel building going on unchecked, the following are recommended.

$$$-$$ Norbu Ghang Resort
Main Rd, Upper Pelling, T03595-250566.
Cottage rooms in a pretty sloped garden, better views from those away from road, views from the terrace are superb. Restaurant and bar. The **Norbu Ghang Retreat and Spa** is adjacent (meals included).

$$-$ Sikkim Tourist Centre
Upper Pelling, near Jeep Stand, T03595-258556.
Simple rooms, some with views, cheaper on roadside, rooftop restaurant (cooking excellent but service limited; only snacks after 1400), tours.

$ Garuda
Upper Pelling, near bus stop, T03595-258319, www.hotelgarudapelling.com.
Variety of rooms with bath (including $$ suites) in a popular lodge, hot water, dorm, restaurant (breakfast on rooftop, mountain views), internet, backpackers' favourite.

$ Kabur
Upper Pelling, T03595-258504.
With a charming terrace restaurant, sun deck and internet, clean doubles have hot running water and heaters.

$ Sisters Family Guest House
Near Garuda, T03595-250569.
8 simple clean rooms, shared bath (bucket hot water). Friendly, great food.

Pemayangtse

$$$$ Elgin Mount Pandim
15-min walk below monastery, T03593-250756, www.elginhotels.com.
Sparkling bright rooms, some with beautiful mountain views, in freshly renovated and upmarket building that once belonged to the Sikkimese royal family. Large grounds, breakfast included.

Khecheopalri Lake
A couple of families take in guests at homestays in the small village on the ridge (25 mins' walk up the hill, left up the path by the car park near the lake). Highly recommended for a relaxing interlude with stunning mountain views.

$ Pilgrims' Lodge
On the edge of the lake.
Enterprising Mr Tenang provides Sikkimese porridge and millet bread (and much more), and leads short circular hikes.

$ Trekkers Hut
400 m before the lake on the left.
Simple rooms and friendly staff provide food, information and a bonfire at night.

Yuksom

$$$ Yuksum Residency
Main Rd, T03595-241277, www.yuksumresidency.com.
Huge construction, white marble predominates, with terrace lit-up at night. Rooms are massive and well appointed (especially the suite with parquet flooring), furnishings high quality rather than rustic, flatscreen TVs, lots of light and some good views. Giftshop has nice jewellery, restaurant a bit stiff.

$$ Tashigang
T03595-241202, hoteltashigang@gmail.com.
Intimate rooms with lovely views (some with balcony), wooden floors, striped bedspreads and simple tasteful furnishings. Ageing but in a good way. Marble and tile bathrooms, some suites, everything clean and polished. Own vegetable patch and restaurant (see below), peaceful garden.

$ Dragon
Main Rd, T03595-241290.
Friendly and sociable guesthouse with clean
small rooms (shared bath, hot water unreliable).
Nice outdoor area, and good for a snug beer/
meal in the family kitchen.

$ Hotel Yangrigang
Main Rd, T03595-241217.
A backpacker hub, with an acceptable restaurant
and internet access, good standard rooms mostly
have twin beds, bigger and better views upstairs,
geysers and comfy beds. Manager is informative
and pleasant. Treks easily arranged.

$ Pemalingpa Cottage
Just below Tashigang Hotel.
Lovely little homestay, basic, only 2 rooms one
of which is delightfully rustic and sunny. Outside
toilet, hot buckets provided, family make every
effort to make guests welcome.

Restaurants

Pelling

$$-$ Alpine
*Khecheopalri Rd (below Garuda,
see Where to stay).*
Chinese, Kashmiri especially good. Yellow,
wooden cottage run by friendly Ladakhi lady.

$ Mock-Too
*Upper Pelling opposite Sikkim Tourist Centre
(see What to do, below).*
Excellent fresh snacks including *momos*, paratha
and samosas.

Yuksom
A 2000 curfew is imposed by the police in
Yuksom, when all activities move indoors –
get your food order in early.

$$-$ Tashigang
See Where to stay.
Cheery hotel restaurant is unpretentious,
with delicious Sikkimese specialities (seasonal)
such as nettle soup and wild fern curry. Other
more typically Indian dishes also available.
Ingredients come from their vegetable garden
or surrounding countryside.

$ Gupta's
On the main street.
Attracts travellers to its social outdoor seating
area, and does surprisingly good quesadillas and
pizza, as well as *thali* (no refills) and yak's cheese

momos. Next door, **$ Yak** is of a similar ilk and
with friendlier owners.

Festivals

Tashiding
Jan/Feb Bumchu meaning 'sacred pot' is a
1-day festival. The sacred pot is opened once
a year and the water level within forecasts the
prosperity of Sikkim in the coming year.
Feb/Mar Losar (Tibetan New Year) is celebrated
for about a week at Tashiding. It is preceded by
Lama dances in Rumtek.

Pemayangtse
Aug/Sep Pang Lhabsol commemorates the
consecration of Khangchendzonga as Sikkim's
guardian deity; the Lepchas believe that the
mountain is their birthplace. The masked warrior
dance is especially spectacular; warriors wear
traditional armour of helmets, swords and shields.

What to do

Pemayangtse
The **Denjong Padma Choeling Academy**
(DPCA), set up to educate needy children, runs
several projects, such as crafts and dairy, and
welcomes volunteers, who can also learn about
Buddhism and local culture. The meditation
centre offers courses and can accommodate
visitors for a small charge and volunteers for free:
a rewarding experience. Volunteer teachers can
stay for up to 6 wks Mar-Dec.

Transport

Jorethang
Bus The SNT bus stand has services to: **Siliguri**,
0930; **Gangtok**, 1230; **Rangpo**, 1230; **Namchi**,
0830, 1200 and 1600; **Soreng**, 1400; **Pelling**,
1500; **Ravangla**, 1200; **Teesta**, 0930.

Jeep There are 3 jeep stands in Jorethang, close
together on the south side of town near the
Tourism Office. The main stand serves: **Siliguri**,
departures 0700-1600, 2½ hrs; **Gangtok**, 0700-
1600, 3 hrs; **Karkabita** (for Nepal), 0730, 0830,
0930 and 1330, 4 hrs; **Kalimpong**, 0900-1430,
1½ hrs, and **Gezing**, regular service, 2 hrs. The
block slightly uphill behind the main stand has
jeeps for: **Tashiding**, 1½ hrs, and **Yuksom**, 3 hrs,
1200-1500. Jeeps for **Darjeeling**, 0800-1530,
2 hrs, and **Namchi**, 0600-1100, 45 mins, depart
from closer to the Tourism Office.

Tashiding

Several jeeps arrive in Tashiding from **Gezing** via **Legship**, and from **Yuksom** (early morning). To **Jorethang**, 0700 and 0800, 1½ hrs; to **Gangtok**, 0630 and 0700, 3½ hrs, via **Ravangla**, 1½ hrs; to **Yuksom**, 1100 and 1300, 1 hr; to **Gezing**, 1½ hrs, 0730.

Pemayangtse

From **Gezing**: bus or shared jeep to monastery, 1000-1430. From **Pelling**, taxi Rs 100 one way; easy walk back.

Pelling

To **Gezing** reasonably frequent jeeps, or walk along steep downhill track, 1-2 hrs. To **Khecheopalri Lake**: last bus at 1400, or you can walk. Buses and shared jeeps to **Yuksom** (until 1500, 3 hrs), **Damthang**, **Gangtok** (4 hrs), **Darjeeling** via Jorethang, tickets from stand opposite **Hotel Garuda**. **Siliguri**: SNT bus 0700; tickets sold at provision store next to **Hotel Pelling** where bus starts, and stops uphill at jeep stand near **Garuda** hotel.

Khecheopalri Lake

From **Pelling**: jeep share, 1½ hrs; to **Tashiding** (3 options): **1)** 0700 bus to Gezing, then jeep. **2)** Bus to Yuksom 1500 (irregular) from 'junction', 10 km from lake, overnight in Yuksom, then bus at 0700 (or jeep) to Tashiding, 1 hr. **3)** Hitch a lift on the Pelling to Tashiding jeep, which passes the 'junction'at about 1400 (try sitting on top of jeep to enjoy the beautiful scenery).

Yuksom

Shared jeeps leave from near Gupta's restaurant, buy ticket a day ahead in season. To **Pelling**, 0630, 2½ hrs; **Gezing**, 0630, 3 hrs; **Jorethang**, 0630, 3½ hrs, via **Tashiding**, 1 hr; **Gangtok**, 0630 and 1300, 5 hrs; **Pelling**, 0630, 2½ hrs. To reach **Khecheopalri Lake**, private hire only.

Khangchendzonga National Park
a classic trekking route in the shadow of the mighty mountain

The park offers trekking routes through picturesque terraced fields of barley, past fruit orchards to lush green forests of pines, oak, chestnut, rhododendrons, giant magnolias, then to high passes crossing fast mountain streams and rugged terrain. Animals in the park include Himalayan brown bear, black bear, the endangered musk deer, flying squirrel, Tibetan antelope, wild ass and Himalayan wild goat. The red panda lives mostly on treetops at 3000-4000 m. There are about 600 species of bird.

The Khangchendzonga trek falls within the national park, from which all forms of industry and agriculture have been officially banished. The park office in Yuksom, about 100 m below the trekkers' huts, has interesting exhibits and helpful staff. See also page 609.

★ Kangchendzonga trek
8-9 days from Yuksom to Gocha La. Most people arrange their trek in Gangtok/Darjeeling; US$40-60 per person per day, depending on service. Trekkers' huts ($), in picturesque places at Yuksom, Tsokha and Dzongri, are fairly clean with basic toilets; bring sleeping bags; meals are cooked by a caretaker.

The classic trekking route goes from **Yuksom to Gocha La** (variously spelt Goecha La and Gochela, see page 31) and includes some magnificent scenery around Khangchendzonga. There are excellent views as you travel up the Ratong Chu River to the amphitheatre of peaks at the head of the valley. These include Kokthang (6150 m), Ratong (6683 m), Kabru Dome (6604 m), Forked Peak (6116 m) and the pyramid of Pandim (6720 m) past which the trail runs.

> ### Tip...
> For walks around Gangtok and descriptions of treks throughout the state, with trekking profiles, get *Sikkim: A Guide and Handbook*, by Rajesh Verma, which is regularly updated.

Day 1 Yuksom to Tsokha An eight-hour climb to the growing village of Tsokha, settled by Tibetan refugees. The first half of the climb passes through dense semi-tropical forests and across the Prek Chu on a suspension bridge. A steep climb of two hours leads first to **Bakhim** (2740 m), which has a tea stall, a forest bungalow and good views. The track goes through silver fir and magnolia to Tsokha (2950 m), the last village on the trek. Trekkers' hut and campsite at Tsokha.

Day 2 Tsokha to Dzongri Mixed temperate forests give way to rhododendron. **Phedang** is less than three hours up the track. Pandim, Narsingh and Joponu peaks are clearly visible, and a further hour's climb takes the track above the rhododendrons to a ridge. A gentle descent

Tip...
There's a growing trend for tour agents to tag on extra group members (picked up in Yuksom) who get a greatly discounted price. This can seem unfair to those members of the trekking group who are funding the majority of the trip.

leads to Dzongri (4030 m, 8 km from Bakhim). There is a trekkers' hut and campsite. Dzongri attracts pilgrims to its *chortens* holding Buddhist relics. From exposed and windswept hillsides nearby are good panoramic views of the surrounding mountains and of spectacular sunrises or sunsets on Khangchendzonga.

Day 3 Dzongri to Thangshing A trail through dwarf rhododendron and juniper climbs the ridge for 5 km. Pandim is immediately ahead. A steep drop descends to the Prek Chu again, crossed by a bridge, followed by a gentle climb to Thangshing (3900 m). The southern ridge of Khangchendzonga is ahead. There is a trekkers' hut and campsite.

Day 4 Thangshing to Samity Lake The track leads through juniper scrub to a steeper section up a lateral moraine, followed by the drop down to the glacial and holy Samity Lake. The surrounding moraines give superb views of Khangchendzonga and other major peaks. You can't camp at the lake; a new campsite is 1 km away at Lammuney.

Day 5 To Zemathang and Gocha La and return The climb up to Zemathang (4800 m) and Gocha La (4900 m) gives views up to the sheer face of the eastern wall of Khangchendzonga. It is a vigorous

Sikkim treks

Trekking in Sikkim

Trekking is Sikkim's biggest draw for many foreign tourists, and no previous experience is necessary as most treks are at 2000-3800 m. The trail to Dzongri (three to four days) or on to Gocha La (eight to nine days) is the most popular and climbs to nearly 5000 m (see page 613), but there are plenty of day trails on clear paths that are less physically taxing. An added attraction is that dzos (a cross between a cow and a yak) can carry your gear instead of porters, though they are slower. The trekking routes also pass through villages that give an insight into the tribal people's lifestyle. This area is under threat from pollution by rubbish left by trekkers, so be sure to choose a trekking agency that enforces good environmental practices; ECOSS in Gangtok (see page 601) can point you in the right direction. March to late May and October to early December are the best months although April is best for flowers. Leeches can be a problem in the wet season below 2000 m. Foreigners must be in a group of at least two before applying for a trekking permit. Approved trekking agents assist with applications, which last for 15 days, and can be arranged in a morning in Gangtok or Yuksom. The U 502 map sheets for Sikkim are *NG 45-3* (East) and *NG 45 -4 (*West).

walk to reach the pass, but equally impressive views can be gained from nearby slopes. Sometimes guides stop before the official 'Gocha La' viewpoint, be wary of this and ask the advice of other trekkers that you meet on the way. Much of the walk is on rough moraine.

Day 6 Samity Lake to Thangshing Return to Thangshing. This is only a two-hour walk, so it is possible to take it gently and make a diversion to the former yak grazing grounds of Lam Pokhari Lake (3900 m) above Thangshing. The area is rich in medicinal plants, and you may see some rare high-altitude birds and blue sheep.

Days 7 and 8 Thangshing to Tsokha The return route can be made by a lower track, avoiding Dzongri. Dense rhododendrons flank the right bank of the Prek Chu, rich in birdlife. Day 7 ends in Tsokha village. The next morning you retrace your steps to Yuksom.

North Sikkim

high alpine valleys, surrounded by peaks and covered in flowers

You'll need to join an organized tour to explore the outposts of the Yumthang and Tsopta valleys, where traditional Lepcha and Bhotia villages huddle beneath mountains that rear steeply towards Tibet. The scenery is spectacular, though the road is well travelled – particularly by Indian tourists. Expect to be restricted in your movements and to spend long days in a jeep.

Phodong Colour map 4, A2.

The renovated early 18th-century monastery of Phodong is 1.5 km above the north Sikkim Highway, about 2 km before Phodong village. The track is accessible by jeep, and tours of North Sikkim usually include a visit to the monastery on the way back down to Gangtok. Otherwise, it is a pleasant walk up to the *gompa* where friendly monks show you around; there are especially beautiful frescoes and wall paintings. A further hike of 2 km takes you to picturesque **Labrang** monastery of the Nyingmapa sect, unique in that it retains its original structure undamaged by time or fire. Below the track nearby is the ruined palace of **Tumlong**, the capital of Sikkim for most of the 19th century.

Phodong to Chumthang

In addition to several police checkpoints, the road beyond Phodong passes through some mildly attractive villages, along forested slopes and past dramatic waterfalls on the way to bustling **Mangan**, the district headquarters, and then **Singhik**. In both places there are perfectly acceptable lodges with good views and a friendly welcome to the rare independent traveller who stops here (though Mangan has more opportunities for decent eating and transport connections). Beyond

Singhik, permits are required for foreign tourists; travel agents in Gangtok arrange these, along with vehicle, driver and accommodation, as part of a tour. The road and the Tista River part ways at Chumthang, which is dominated by a hydroelectric project, with one track leading northeast to the Yumthang Valley and the other northwest to Tsopta Valley.

★ Yumthang Valley Colour map 4, A2.

Lachung sits among spectacular mountain scenery at 2400 m, 135 km north of Gangtok, and acts as a gateway to the increasingly popular Yumthang Valley. Still run on the traditional democratic Dzomsa system, the village is a stronghold of Bhotia culture, though the daily influx of tourists from Gangtok and the rapid construction of lodges to accommodate them has begun to take its toll. Hotels, most over three storeys high, have started to dominate the series of small villages which make up Lachung. The central point is Faka Bazar by the suspension bridge, worth crossing to visit pretty **Lachung Monastery** (open mornings/evenings only) up the opposite hillside in Sharchog village; shortcuts past patches of cultivation and neat pastel-hued homes reach the monastery in about 30 minutes. The paintings of demons and the Wheel of Life in the porch are particularly dramatic, and a path behind the *gompa* climbs up for gorgeous views back down the valley.

The road north to Yumthang passes through the **Shingba Rhododendron Sanctuary**, which has 24 of the 40 rhododendron species found in Sikkim, along with attractive aconites, gentians, poppies, saxifrages, potentillas and primulas.

The valley slopes of **Yumthang**, the 'Valley of the Flowers', are surrounded by imposing snow-clad mountains. May to July is the best time to see high-altitude alpine flowers growing in the wild. Glaciers flow down slopes forested with fir towards the milky turquoise water of Lachung River and, in summertime, the valley floor is indeed carpeted with purple primulas. This is the official end-point for foreigners, and a place where all jeep tours stop for a photo opportunity. A few minutes' walk from the refreshments stalls on the main road are unappealing sulphur hot springs; from here a stone path leads to a lovely hour's walk through the rhododendron forests. It is (unofficially) possible, and usually offered (for an additional charge), to continue for a further hour along the rough road to Samdong (Tibetan, meaning 'bridge'). This is a dramatic drive, with views above the pink rocky riverbed and pale khaki-coloured valley walls, to a closer encounter with snowy peaks. Indians tourists can carry on further to Zero Point, but the final halting point for foreigners is signalled by impromptu noodle and liquor stands.

★ Tsopta Valley

The Bhotia village of **Lachen**, 122 km from Gangtok, is the chief overnight stop when visiting the stark landscape of the Tsopta (Chopta) Valley. Lachen straggles along one edge of the road in the steep river valley, surrounded by thick alpine forests. The 2000-strong population are known as Lachenpas and were traditionally ere yak-herders.

An unmetalled road follows the river from Lachen up the mountainside, past ponies, yaks and rhododendron cover to the more interesting village of Thangu (altitude 4260 m), 30 km north, where accommodation is also available. On the edge of Thangu, potato, cabbage and spinach are cultivated from the arid land, men and women sharing the workload in the fields. Traditional sturdy wooden dwellings and dry stone walls demarcate the land, and the scent of smouldering pine prevails. The wide river valley beyond the village has spectacular views towards the mountains and Tibet. It is a seasonal grazing ground for yaks; here grow Jatamasi plants which are used to make incense. Foreign tourists spend a couple of hours wandering the valley floor, covered in wild flowers in summer, while Indian tourists can continue up to Gurudongmar Lake, to which foreigners are not permitted.

Thangu is the starting point for the gruelling trek to **Green Lake** (altitude 5120 m) which takes around 14 days in total. Special permits are necessary that require at least six weeks to arrange – they are expensive, as is the entire venture, as all supplies and equipment have been carried. The high cost means that tourist numbers are few. Much of the trek goes through thick spruce and fir forests, as well as the huge variety of rhododendron species for which the region is famed.

Where to stay

Phodong

$ Yak and Yeti
T03595-260884.
Quiet and clean. Some rooms with toilet, hot water in buckets, but meals a bit pricey.

Yumthang Valley
Lachung

The tour agents usually determine where you stay in North Sikkim. Try to specify a certain hotel if you don't wish to leave it up to chance; the cost will be built into the tour accordingly. Particularly nice options are listed below, in descending order of price and comfort.

Taagsing Retreat (aka Modern Residency)
Singring, www.modernresidency.com.
Lachung's most comfortable accommodation is a striking bottle-green pagoda on the southern edge of the village. The 22 Sikkimese-styled rooms are arranged on several levels, with balconies and great views. Pure veg restaurant serves buffet meals, plus there's a meditation hall, bar, library and little museum.

Golden Fish
Main Rd, Singring, T(0)76020 28800, www.hotelsinlachung.in.
This very clean and warm option has friendly, relaxed and efficient staff. Excellent food is

prepared and high standards maintained. Some suites with TVs. Can book a package through the website.

Sela Inn
Faka Bazar, T03592-214808.
Older and shabbier, this well-established welcoming place has an atmospheric restaurant and is closer to any 'action' in town.

Season House
Up the hill, Singring, T(0)9434-449042.
Quaint rooms in the old log cabin or newer in the chalet, excellent bathrooms. Quietly efficient staff and good food. At the highest point on the road, save for the Rimpoche's residence next door, so fabulous views from the terrace.

Sonam In Lodge
Main Rd, Singring, T03592-214830.
Run by a charming family who speak little English, cosy simple rooms in an old-style wooden building, hot buckets provided.

Transport

Phodong

From Gangtok, take a bus to the start of the jeep track, 0800 (2 hrs), Rs 35; return bus, 1500. Jeeps travel up to **Labrang** monastery. Jeeps to **Mangan** leave in the early morning and it is advisable to book at least 2 days in advance.

Background Sikkim

History

From the 13th century Tibetans, like the Namgyal clan, immigrated to Sikkim. In 1642 Phuntsog Namgyal (1604-1670) became the Chogyal (king). With a social system based on Tibetan Lamaistic Buddhism, the land was split into 12 *dzongs* (fortified districts).

In the 18th century Sikkim lost land to Nepal, Bhutan and the British. When the Gurkhas of Nepal launched a campaign into Tibet and were defeated by the Chinese in 1791-1792, Sikkim won back its northern territories. The narrow Chumbi Valley, which separates Sikkim from Bhutan, remained with Tibet. When the British defeated Nepal in 1815, the southern part of the country was given back to Sikkim. However, in the next conflict with Nepal, Darjeeling was handed over to the British in return for their assistance. In 1848 the Terai region at the foot of the mountains was annexed by the British.

Nepalis migrated into Sikkim from the beginning of the 19th century, eventually becoming more numerous than the local inhabitants. This led to internal conflict also involving the British and the Tibetans. The British won the ensuing battles and declared Sikkim a Protectorate in 1890. The state was controlled by a British Political Officer who effectively stripped the *Gyalpos* of executive power. It was many years before the Sikkimese regained control.

In 1950, Sikkim became a Protectorate of India. In 1973 there were growing demands for accession to India by the local population, consisting mainly of Nepalis, and Sikkim was formally made an associate state. The Gyalpos lost their power as a result of the new democratic constitution and Sikkim became the 22nd state in the Union in 1975.

Although there is no separatist movement, India's takeover and the abolition of the monarchy, supported by many of Nepali origin, is still resented by many Sikkimese who don't regard themselves as Indians. The state enjoys special tax and other privileges, partly because of its highly sensitive geopolitical location on the disputed border with China. In the 2014 election the Sikkim Democratic Front (SDF), a party confined to Sikkim, won all 32 seats in the State Assembly.

Culture

The Naong, Chang and Mon are believed to have inhabited Sikkim in prehistoric times. Each ethnic group has an impressive repertoire of folk songs and dances. The Lepchas, who call themselves Rongpas and claim to be the original inhabitants of Sikkim, may have come from Tibet well before the eighth century and brought Lamaistic Buddhism, which is still practised. They are now regarded as the indigenous peoples. They are deeply religious, peace loving and typically shy but cheerful. The government has reserved the Dzongu area in North and Central Sikkim for Lepchas, who now make up less than 10% of the population. For a long time, the Lepchas' main contact with the outside world was the market-place at Mangan, where they bartered oranges and cardamom. Their alphabet was only devised in the 18th century by the king.

The Bhotias (meaning 'of Bhot/Tibet') or Bhutias entered Sikkim in the 13th century from Kham in Tibet. Many adapted to sedentary farming from pastoral nomadism and displaced the Lepchas. Some, however, retained their older lifestyle, and combined animal husbandry with trading over the Trans-Himalayan passes: Nathula (4392 m), Jelepla (4388 m), Donkiala (5520 m) and Kongrala (4809 m). Over the years the Bhutias have come into increased contact with the Lepcha and intermarried with them. Nearly every Bhutia family has one member who becomes a monk. Monasteries remain the repositories of Bhutia culture and festivals here are the principal social events. The Bhutias are famous for their weaving and are also skilled woodcarvers.

The Newars entered Sikkim in large numbers from Nepal in the 19th century. Skilled in metal and woodwork, they were granted the right by the Chogyal to mine copper and mint the Sikkimese coinage. Other Nepali groups followed. With high-altitude farming skills, they settled new lands and built houses directly on the ground unlike the Lepcha custom of building on stilts. The Newars were followed by the Chettris and other Nepali clans who introduced Hinduism, which became more popular as their numbers swelled.

Northeast States

remote, diverse and distinctive

The Northeast is a true frontier region. Its border with Bhutan, Myanmar (Burma) and Bangladesh stretches for more than 2000 km, and it is connected to the rest of India by a narrow 20-km-wide corridor of land – aptly coined the 'chicken neck' by locals.

Each of the Northeast States has its distinct culture and tradition; combined they form one of the most ethnically and linguistically diverse regions in Asia.

Arunachal Pradesh, which opened to tourists in the late 1990s, is home to fascinating tribal cultures and the Buddhist enclave of the majestic Tawang Valley – more like Tibet than India. To its south, Assam occupies the scenic lowlands of the Brahmaputra Valley and attracts visitors to some of India's best national parks. Meghalaya's beautiful hills have the dubious distinction of being the wettest region in the world, as well as one of the friendliest. The little-visited states of Nagaland, Manipur, Mizoram and Tripura make up a fascinating area, hilly and remote, where the cultures of Asia intertwine.

Best for
Rain ■ Tea ■ Tribal culture ■ Wildlife

Footprint picks

★ **Kaziranga National Park**,
page 629

See the greater one-horned rhinocerous on a jeep or elephant safari.

★ **Nameri National Park**, page 632

Go rafting, walking and fishing in the forest, and spend a night in a great eco-camp.

★ **Shillong**, page 642

Place a bet on the Archery Stakes in Meghalaya's small capital.

★ **Cherrapunji**, page 647

Cross living root-bridges between jungle villages in the wettest place on earth.

★ **Tawang Monastery**, page 653

Make the spectacular four-day journey to a remote and magical monastery.

★ **Nagaland**, page 661

Visit tribal settlements deep in the Naga Hills, including pretty Khonoma 'green' village.

★ **Tripura's palaces**, pages 681 and 684

Explore Ujjayanta Palace and Neermahal water-palace in this tiny princely state.

Essential Northeast States

Permits

Since 1 January 2011, foreigners have not needed a permit to visit Nagaland, Manipur and Mizoram. Foreigners visiting these states now only need register themselves at the local Foreigners Regional Registration Office (FRRO) within 24 hours of arrival (see below). Foreigners can now enter these states freely as well as Assam and Tripura. However, a **Protected Area Permit** (**PAP**) is still required for Arunachal Pradesh, as it is a sensitive border region. Local travel agents can obtain PAPs for individual travellers within a few days and supply them by email, at a cost of around US$100 plus commission, valid for up to 30 days. See pages 651 and 655 for tour agents who can help. In Kolkata PAPs are issued at the **Foreigners Regional Registration Office** (**FRRO**), 237A AJC Bose Road, T033-2283 7034, Monday-Friday 1100-1630; arrive between 1100 and 1400 and ask for the Officer in Charge. Bring one photo and a copy of your passport and visa. It takes a minimum of 24 hours for permits to be issued, which essentially means coming in the morning and returning the following afternoon to collect. The cost is at the discretion of the FRRO.

Getting around

Guwahati in Assam is the gateway to the Northeast; its Lokpriya Gopinath Bordoloi International Airport has flights to/from Kolkata, Delhi, Bagdogra and airports throughout the region, plus flights from Bangkok and Bhutan. There are helicopter services from Guwahati to Shillong and Tura in Meghalaya. There are also direct flights from Kolkata to Salonibari,

Jorhat, Dibrugarh and Lilabari (Assam), Dimapur (Nagaland), Imphal (Manipur), Aizawl (Mizoram) and Agartala (Tripura). Public buses run between towns and across state borders, but jeeps and *sumos* (local SUVs) are usually faster and more convenient, especially on poor roads. The rail network is neither as extensive nor as efficient as in other parts of India; in most cases, travel by road or air is preferable.

Best wildlife lodgings

Bansbari Lodge, Manas, page 629
Wild Grass, Kaziranga, page 631
Eco Camp, Nameri, page 633

When to go

This region is wet and humid most of the year. Unless you really want to see rain, avoid the monsoon season between May and September, especially July when extraordinary downpours occur. Meghalaya in the west is the wettest region on earth; parts of Tripura receive more than 4000 mm of annual rainfall, and even the central Brahmaputra Valley, protected by the rain shadow of the Shillong Plateau, has over 1600 mm of annual rainfall. Summer temperatures are high, but from December to February it can be cold, especially at night, and in the mountains of Arunachal Pradesh temperatures can drop far below freezing. However, clear skies are most likely October to December, and it is also when many alpine flowers are in bloom. Many tribal areas celebrate memorable festivals; try to time your visit to coincide with one.

Weather Guwahati					
January	**February**	**March**	**April**	**May**	**June**
24°C 10°C 12mm	26°C 12°C 17mm	30°C 16°C 55mm	31°C 20°C 147mm	31°C 23°C 249mm	32°C 25°C 317mm
July	**August**	**September**	**October**	**November**	**December**
32°C 26°C 351mm	32°C 26°C 269mm	32°C 25°C 187mm	30°C 22°C 91mm	28°C 17°C 19mm	25°C 12°C 7mm

Time required

To do this region justice, you'll need one to two days for Kaziranga, three days for Shillong and Cherrapunji, a week each for central and western Arunachal, and a week or more to explore tribal Nagaland.

Safety

The Northeast has been a politically sensitive region since Independence, and insurgency still occasionally surfaces making travel in some areas unsafe. Advice should be sought before travel (particularly to Nagaland and Manipur), and it's wise to keep an eye on local news when there.

Footprint picks

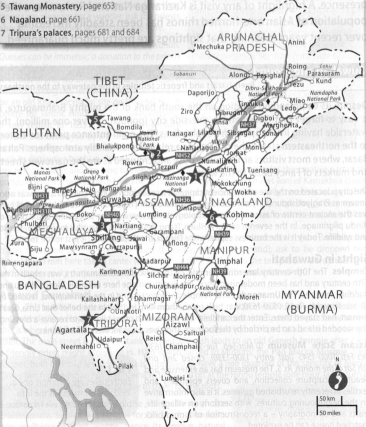

Assam

The Ahoms, a Shan ruling tribe, arrived in the area in the early 13th century, deposed the ruler and established the kingdom of Assam with its capital in Sibsagar. They later inter-mixed with Aryan stock and also with existing indigenous peoples (Morans, Chutiyas) and most converted to Hinduism. The Mughals made several attempts to invade without success, but the Burmese finally invaded Assam at the end of the 18th century and held it almost continuously until it was ceded to the East India Company in 1826. The British administered it in name until 1947 though many areas were beyond their effective control.

Nearly 90% of Assam's 31.1 million-strong population continues to live in rural areas. The ethnic origin of the Assamese varies from Mongoloid tribes to those of directly Indian stock. There has been a steady flow of Muslim settlers from Bengal since the late 19th century. The predominant language is Assamese, similar to Bengali although harder to pronounce.

The Assam Valley is in a strategically sensitive corridor for India, lying close to the Chinese frontier. Its sensitivity has been increased by the tension between local Assamese and immigrant groups. The state has suffered a long-running low-intensity conflict and in late 2006 and early 2007 a number of bombings occurred in the capital Guwahati. The most troubled area recently has been the very west of Assam, with violent clashes between indigenous Bodo people and Bengali-speaking Muslims in 2012.

colour. Every household is involved with weaving of *muga*, *endi* or *pat* silk; prices are 30% cheaper than in Guwahati. Take the ferry from Guwahati or a bus from Hajo (20 minutes).

Pobitora Wildlife Sanctuary Pobitora is a small wildlife sanctuary (38 sq km) a one-hour drive from Guwahati (40 km), on the border of Nagaon and Kamrup districts; nearly 100 one-horned rhinos can be found here, and you can take an elephant safari. Entrance for foreigners is Rs 500.

Madan Kamdev The temples of Madan Kamdev, 45 km north of Guwahati, have been called Assam's Khajuraho due to the dozen or so erotic sculptures that adorn the walls. The temples, which may date from the 11th to 12th centuries, possibly reconstructed in the 18th, are believed to be associated with tantric practices. The principal shrine to Uma-Mahesvara (Siva-Parvati) is still in use and the setting, surrounded by fields and nature, is picturesque. Buses from Guwahati go to Baihata on NH31, 4 km from the site; rickshaws transfer visitors from there.

Listings Guwahati *map p625*

Tourist information

Information booths for Assam, Nagaland and Meghalaya are at the airport, with useful maps; there's also a counter for Assam at the railway station.

Assam Tourism
Tourist Lodge, Station Rd, T0361-254 7102, http://assamtourism.gov.in. Daily 1000-1630.

Assam Tourism Development Corporation (ASTDC)
AK Azad Rd, Paryatan Bhawan, T0361-263 3654.

Where to stay

There are some budget hotels at Sadullah and M Nehru Rd crossing; those in Paltan Bazar are often full by the afternoon. Most medium-priced hotels have some a/c rooms and a restaurant.

$$$ Brahmaputra Ashok
MG Rd, T0361-260 2281, www. hotelbrahmaputraashok.com.
Standard rooms are old style but with wooden floors and decent shower rooms (riverside ones with nice views), central a/c, TV, bamboo and cane furniture, restaurant, travel agency, Wi-Fi. The **Kaziranga** bar, with its zebra print furniture, is fun and there's Silver Streak disco on Sat nights.

$$$ Dynasty
SS Rd, T0361-251 6021, www.dynastyhotel.in.
76 comfortable rooms and suites, this is
Guwahati's top hotel and even has a spa. Rooms
are tastefully designed and modern, public
areas quiet and refined, excellent restaurants
serve Indian and Chinese food (see Restaurants,
page 626). Gym, breakfast included, staff efficient.

$$$-$$ Nandan
*GS Rd, Paltan Bazar, T0361- 254 0855,
www.hotelnandan.com.*
The 55 clean rooms don't quite match up to the
stylish frontage and feel a bit 1970s, some a/c,
expensive suites, restaurants (including Thai,
Mexican and Italian food), decent bar.

$$ Baruah Bhavan
*40 MC Rd, Uzanbazar, T0361-254 9316,
www.heritagehomeassam.com.*
An Assamese mansion over 100 years old with
6 luxurious rooms, modern amenities and a
charming roof terrace. Home-cooking (Assamese,
Indian, Chinese, reasonably priced), breakfast
included, internet, transport can be arranged.
A short walk from the riverside.

$$ Nova
*SS Rd, Fancy Bazar, T0361-251 1464,
www.novahotel.in.*
Standard rooms are a bit fusty with dated
bathrooms and no a/c (double a/c, much
brighter), but the vibe and public areas are nice.

Guwahati

Where to stay 🛏
Baruah Bhavan **1**
Brahmaputra Ashok **3**
Broadview Lodge **14**
Centre Point **13**
City Palace **4**
Dynasty & Tandoor **5**
Nandan **6**
Nova **12**
Orchid & Magnolia
    Restaurant **7**
Tourist Lodge **10**

Restaurants 🍴
4 Seasons **8**
Beatrix **1**
Breeze & Sun Flower **7**
New Zealand Natural **3**
Woodlands **5**

300 metres
300 yards
N

Orang National Park
66 km northwest of Tezpur. Foreigners Rs 250.

The 79-sq-km Orang National Park is often called a miniature Kaziranga. It has similar flora and fauna, though viewing is not as rewarding and rhinos appear only occasionally. This is compensated by the peaceful and intimate atmosphere, especially if you're staying inside the park. Elephants safaris are available. Arriving by car is best from Tezpur, though buses between Guwahati and Tezpur go via Orang village, from where it is a 15-km dusty track to the park.

★ Nameri National Park
35 km north of Tezpur on the Arunachal border. Foreigners Rs 250, camera Rs 500, plus boat Rs 550.

The park is on the river Jia Bhoroli and covers 210 sq km. It is home to tigers (26 in 2006), elephants, Indian bison, barking and hog deer, Himalayan black bears as well as 300 bird species, including the shy and endangered white-winged wood ducks. Flora includes evergreens, bamboo and some open grassland. Buses/*sumos* travelling between Tezpur and Tawang can drop travellers off at Hatigate on the main road. From here, it is 2.5 km down a track to the Eco Camp (see Where to stay, opposite), a recommended overnight stop and good place to arrange visits to the park. There are no roads in the park but you can trek with a forest guide after taking a boat across the river. The Eco-Camp can also organize catch-and-release angling and low-level rafting excursions. The best time (climatically) to visit is October to April, and the best chance of animal sightings is December to March.

Bhalukpong
Bhalukpong, 20 km west of Nameri, is on the Assam-Arunachal border. This nondescript village is surrounded by the forests of **Pakhui Game Sanctuary**, a mass of ferns, moss and orchids, with a hot spring, orchid garden and good fishing. You can camp (take your own tent) on the picturesque bank of the River Jia Bhoreli or stay in the government tourist cottages overlooking the river. Jeeps and buses from Tezpur all pass through Bhalukpong en route to Tawang (see page 653).

Listings Tezpur and around

Tourist information

Tezpur

Tourist Lodge
Jenkins Rd, T03712-221016, Mon-Sat 1000-1615; closed every 2nd and 4th Sat of the month.
Staff provide a brochure and can sketch out a map of town.

Where to stay

Tezpur

$$ Wild Mahseer
Addabarie Tea Estate, near Balipara, T(0)9833-631377, www.wildmahseer.com.
In a world of its own, this pristine heritage bungalow sits among 9 ha of gardens and trees on the edge of a working tea garden. Rooms are luxurious yet homely with huge beds and

bathrooms in modern colonial style. Absorbing library, tea-tasting café and 3 (cheaper) bungalows in the grounds. Delicious Anglo-Indian food, warm and entertaining hosts.

$$-$ Luit
Ranu Singh Rd, 200 m from bus stand, T03712-222083.
Set back from the main road, this retro hotel has large but average rooms in new wing, some a/c (and some bargain rooms in the old wing), restaurant, bar.

$ Aditya's Hotel CentrePoint
Main Rd (opposite the police station), Tezpur, www.adityashotelcenterpoint.com.
Modern hotel with fresh linen and plumped up pillows, plain but pleasing decor and TVs. Cheaper rooms have hot water by the bucket, some suites (**$$**) staff are eager to please and **Tiffin Restaurant** is good.

$ Tourist Lodge

Jenkins Rd (opposite Chitralekha Udyan), Tezpur, T03712-221016.

Budget non-a/c rooms or refurbed with a/c. All twin bed with attached bath. Book ahead, there are only 10 rooms. Cheap simple restaurant.

Orang National Park

$ Forest Bungalows

Reservations: District Forest Officer, Mangaldoi, T03713-230708, or Chief Conservator of Forests, Reharbari, Guwahati, T0361-251 7064.

There's a newer lodge at the entrance to the park at Silbari and another 1 km inside the park at Satsimulu, overlooking swampy grasslands where animal spotting is possible. Both are basic: bring your own sleeping bags and provisions; the cook/guide will prepare your food.

Nameri National Park

$$ Eco Camp

Sonitpur, T(0)9854-019932, or contact Network Travels, see page 627.

Thatched-cottage tents with twin bamboo beds, bathrooms with hot water, brightly furnished with local fabrics, set among jungle trees around a grassy lawn. 6 bunk beds in the bamboo dorm, wash block, sunny little restaurant. A friendly and special place, worth spending a couple of nights.

Bhalukpong

$ Tourist Lodge

T03782-234037.

10 raised cottages with octagonal bedrooms, or 4 airy rooms sharing a terrace (good value) look out across the Jia Bhoroli River to Nameri and Pakhuya parks. Work is underway to turn the watch-tower into a restaurant. Can arrange local transport to visit Nameri. (The private **Kunki Resort** next door is not nearly as appealing, but it's there if the lodge is full.)

Restaurants

Tezpur

$ Chinese Villa

NC Rd, T03712-232726.

Magnificent *momos* and a whole host of other delicacies in a high-rise block that also incorporates an Indian restaurant on the upper level and excellent south Indian snacks and *lassis* on the ground floor.

$ Madras Hotel

Off Main Rd.

Decent *dosas*, *iddli* and other south Indian delights provide welcome spice after the relative blandness of Assamese cooking. Basic, busy but under-staffed, and smoky from the kitchen fires.

What to do

Nameri National Park

Eco Camp, *Potasali, T03714-244246.* Organizes whitewater rafting, nature watching and mahseer fishing on the Bhoreli River. Reasonable rates.

Transport

Tezpur

Air Salonibari Airport is 15 km north of Tezpur, with 3 flights per week to **Kolkata**.

Bus Frequent buses to/from **Guwahati** 0500-1330 (4½-5 hrs); **Kaziranga** 0600-1400 (2 hrs). Daily to **Dibrugarh**, 0615-1230, luxury at 0800 (7 hrs) via **Jorhat**; to **Itanagar** at 1000 and 1215 (4½ hrs); to **North Lakhimpur**, 0545-1300 (5-6 hrs); **Tawang** (14 hrs). To **Nameri**, take a Bomdila-bound bus/*sumo* and get off at Hatigate, from where it is 2.5 km to the Eco-camp.

Sumos ASTC and several private companies with offices near the bus stand run *sumos* to **Tawang** and destinations in between, leaving at 0530, 14-16 hrs, pickup from hotel.

Train The train station is 1 km past the main bus stand at Jhaj Ghat. Irregular services to **Guwahati** take 10 hrs; much better to take a bus. Trains also run from Rangapara to North Lakhimpur, via Tezpur.

Dibru-Saikhowa National Park

Contact DFO, Rangagora Rd, Tinsukia, T0374-233 1472, for day visits. Foreigners, Rs 250.

Located on the southern flood plain of the Brahmaputra near Tinsukia, this semi-wet evergreen forest has been a national park since March 1999. The 340-sq-km core area is within a large biosphere reserve and provides a refuge for endangered species such as tiger, leopard, leopard cat, clouded leopard and elephant, though sightings are rare. The real draw is the rich birdlife, which includes the very rare white-winged wood duck (the state bird), best spotted during a dawn boat ride. Other attractions for ornithologists include the marsh babbler, the black-breasted parrotbill and the Jerdon's bushchat. Silky brown dolphins are more commonly seen at sunset, while wild horses congregate on the western edges of the park (allegedly the ancestors of these horses escaped from the World War II army camps). The best time to visit is November-March. Average annual rainfall is 2300-3600 mm.

Entry points are at **Guijan** on the southern edge of the park, and **Dhola** (near Saikhowa Ghat) in the north, both accessible by auto-rickshaw/jeep from Tinsukia. Arrival from Guijan is easier as a boat across the river takes you to the Range Office at the park entrance. If you cross from Dhola, the Range Office is 5 km into the park at Narbarmora; in either case it is best to notify the rangers of your arrival beforehand. If you're staying overnight, the only options are two simple eco-camps on the riverbank at Guijan.

Margherita and around *Colour map 4, A6.*

Margherita, the constituency of the present chief minister, is on the Dihing River at the foot of the Patkoi Range and was named by Italian railway engineers in the late 19th century after the Queen of Italy. The town is surrounded by tea estates and is the headquarters of Coal India Ltd.

The small coal mining town of Ledo, 6 km northwest of Margherita, was the headquarters of Northern Combat Area Command during the Second World War and is the start of the 470-km **Stilwell Road**. Named after General Joseph Stilwell, the road was the most ambitious and costly engineering project of the war, US$137 million at the time. The two-lane bitumen highway once linked Ledo with Myitkyina in North Burma, via the Pangso Pass, and with Kunming in China; it is now closed beyond Nampong in Arunachal Pradesh. A sign, 6 km west of Ledo, commemorates the 'Road to Mandalay' but there is little else remaining.

Listings Northeast Assam

Where to stay

Jorhat

A few hotels and the Tourist Lodge are on MG Rd; more salubrious options (all pretty similar) cluster on Solicitor Rd (off AT Rd) near the ASTC bus station. Some old planter's bungalows lie in splendid isolation on the tea estates on the outskirts of town.

$$$ Banyan Grove and Kaziranga Golf Resort
www.heritagetourismindia.com.
The joy of these 2 properties is in their location deep in the heart of tea country, in sweeping time-warp gardens, the air heavy with nostalgia. There's a range of modern cottages and period bungalows. You can enjoy wide verandas and strolls through the plantations. Guests can use the golf course nearby, and there are swimming pools.

$$ MD's Continental
MD House, Marwari Patty (off AT Rd), T0376-230 0430, www.hotelmdscontinental.com.
Tastefully furnished Asian-style rooms, with wooden floors, contemporary art and luxury bathrooms. Restaurant is slick and very reasonably priced, lounge-bar is more of a bistro (imported liquor), MD's sweets on the ground floor is the best in town. Staff extremely professional.

$$-$ Paradise
Solicitor Rd, T0376-332 1521.
Spacious 1970s rooms are clean with TV, most with balcony, some (overpriced) with a/c and heater, laundry, free internet. If you're lucky, your room might have alpine scenes or banana groves painted on the wall. Soulless restaurant and gloomy (but cheap) bar.

$ Dilip
Solicitor Rd, T0376-232 1610 www.hoteldilip.com.
Modern rooms are good value (especially non-
a/c) with clean towels and sheets, TV, decent
bathrooms with reliable hot water. Very dark
almost-funky bar opens 0900-2200.

$ Janata Paradise
Solicitor Rd, T0376-232 0610, T(0)943 5659461.
Basic rooms are more cheerful than most with
colourful walls, fans, free hot buckets, but no
mossie nets and ask for a top sheet, pay extra for
TV. Atmosphere is friendly, there's a decent cheap
restaurant with Assamese *thalis* (open 1100-1600,
2000-2130) and the handy location makes this a
good budget choice.

$ Prashaanti Tourist Lodge
MG Rd, T0376- 232 1579.
Spotless twin-bed rooms with essential mosquito
nets have been recently refurbished (room 101
has best balcony), deluxe rooms cost not much
extra and have a/c. 24-hr hot water and TVs in all
rooms. Men-only dorm and nice new restaurant-
cum-bar out the back is an unthreatening place
for a quiet drink. Assam Tourism in the same
building with helpful staff.

Majuli Island

$ Circuit House
Garamur, T0375-274439.
Twin-bed rooms, very basic but have mosquito
nets and attached bath, decent food and bed
tea. Foreigners should phone ahead, or write a
letter of application on arrival at the SDO's office
next door.

$ La Maison de Ananda and Do:ni Po:lo
*Garamur, T03775-274768, T09425-205539,
danny002in@yahoo.com.*
A Mishing-style stilt house designed by a
French architect who fell in love with Majuli,
La Maison is quaint, made entirely of bamboo
and yet comfortable (sleeps 3 people). Do:ni
Po:lo next door has a dorm with 2 doubles and
2 single beds, clean linen, blankets and nets,
lit by pinpricks of light through the woven
walls. A further 2 rooms have twin beds. Clean
Indian-style toilet out the back and hot bucket on
request. Bicycles/motorbikes for rent. Both places
have relaxing verandas and are managed by local
fixer Danny Gam. Family atmosphere.

$ You could also stay at one of the *satras*, but bring
a sleeping bag. Garamur and Uttar Kamalabari
both have very simple rooms for guests.

Sibsagar

$$ Brahmaputra
BG Rd, T03772-222200.
Endless corridors lead to deluxe double/single
rooms with a/c, TV, hot water, and new furniture.
Also some cheaper singles with fans and lots
of space. Kaveri restaurant serves good food,
the elevator works, staff are helpful. Gentle
bargaining can achieve a significant reduction
in price. An annoying 2 km from the centre of
town, however.

$$ Shiva Palace
*AT Rd, T03772-225204,
hotel_shiva_palace@rediffmail.com.*
Best in town, with an excellent restaurant and
'trendy' bar, rooms are Western-style with mod
cons. Cheaper rooms getting scuffed, however.
Less than 1 km from Shivadol.

$$-$ Siddhartha
BG Rd, T03772-222276, e7safari@rediffmail.com.
29 rooms, those with a/c are homely and new,
while non-a/c are getting faded, but both have
TV and hot running water. Smart public areas and
modern restaurant (open from 0630), bar. Nearly
2 km out of town centre.

$ Tourist Lodge
By Siva Dol, T03772-222394.
On the southwest corner of the tank, clean and
newly tiled/painted rooms with attached bath
are a real bargain (some with a/c and geyser, or
non-a/c with fan and hot bucket). Front garden,
restaurant, quiet location. Only 9 rooms so
often full, call in advance. Tourist office in same
building (Mon-Sat 1000-1600, closed 2nd and
4th Sat in month).

Dibrugarh and Borajan Reserve Forest

$$$-$$ Chowkidinghee Chang Bungalow
(aka Jalannagar South Bungalow)
*Off Mancotta Rd, 1.5 km from Dibrugarh,
www.assamteatourism.com.*
A truly charming indulgence in colonial history,
this managers' bungalow on the edge of a tea
estate has gloriously period rooms opening out
onto enormous screened verandas with white
cane furniture. It's built on stilts to avoid floods
and wild animals. There are shiny wood floors
throughout and a Victorian fireplace in the
sitting-cum-dining room. Both bedrooms are
en suite and have dressing rooms. An additional
room downstairs is not nearly as attractive. The

Bars and clubs

Shillong is known for its retro music scene and weekend nights sometimes see rock bands performing in town, look for flyers.

Cloud 9 at Centre Point Hotel is a nice watering hole with great night-time views over the city, attracts a younger crowd, with DJs on Fri/Sat nights (2000-2300), open till 2130 weekends. Hotel Polo Towers has popular **Platinum** bar with Happy Hours 1300-1600, DJ on Sat, weekends open till 0100, sporting events shown; also **Piccadilly** British-style pub. The bars at the **Pinewood** and **Shillong Club** have some atmosphere. *Kiad*, the local rice wine, is popular in roadside bars.

Festivals

Feb/Mar Jammin' is a Bob Marley festival that attracts a few thousand, usually held at the Orchid Lake Resort.
Apr Shad Suk Mynsiem is a 3-day Khasi dance festival during which fantastic costumes and jewellery are worn.
Late May Annual **Bob Dylan Festival** to celebrate his birthday.
Oct/Nov The 5-day Khasi **Nongkrem dance festival** is held in Smit, 11 km from Shillong.
Nov Wangala dance festival celebrates the harvest in the Garo Hills.

Shopping

You can get handwoven shawls, canework, Khasi jewellery, handicrafts, orange flower honey.

Govt Emporia are on Jail Rd and GS Rd. Look out in **Bara Bazar** for women selling attractive Khasi silver, gold and amber jewellery.

What to do

Tour operators
Green Routes, *T(0)986-349 5777, greenrouteshg@gmail.com*. Eco-conscious motorbike tours and treks in Meghalaya and other Northeast states, reasonable rates; Ashley Lyngdoh is an experienced and helpful guy.

Meghalaya Tourism Development Corporation, *see Tourist information, above*. Cheap tours around Shillong, stopping at sights, daily 0800-1430. Also to Cherrapunji, Nartiang and Mawsynram. Tours only occur when there are sufficient numbers, so Sun is the safest bet. Good value for solo travellers.

Transport

Air **Meghalaya Helicopter Service**, MTC Bus Stand, Jail Rd, T0364-222 3129, http://megtransport.gov.in/helicopter_service.html, flies to/from **Guwahati** (127 km; see above) Mon-Sat (maximum 10 kg baggage).

Bus Meghalaya TC, Jail Rd, booking office open 0600-1600. To **Guwahati** hourly 0700-1600 (3½ hrs); **Silchar** 1 per day at 1900 (10 hrs, recommended to book in the morning); to **Tura** at 0715 and 1600 (9-10 hrs). Also from stands near Anjali Cinema, Bara Bazar to towns in Meghalaya, including **Cherrapunji** from Mawlong Hat bus stand at 1330 (1½ hrs), carrying on to **Laitkynsew** (for the Cherrapunji Resort). Private bus companies (such as Network Travels) have offices/booths around Police Bazar for long-distance connections in the Northeast: **Agartala** at 1830 (18 hrs); **Aizawl** at 1900 (17 hrs) via **Silchar**; **Imphal** at 1500 (18 hrs); **Kohima** at 1500 (12 hrs) via **Dimapur**; **Siliguri** at 1600 (14-15 hrs).

Sumo For **Guwahati** (3½ hrs) *sumos* leave from Police Bazar until 0800, after that from the Polo Grounds or move conveniently (but slower to fill up) from GS Rd. For **Cherrapunji (Sohra)** jeeps leave when full from Mowlang Hat bus stand (upper level), near Anjali Cinema in Bara Bazar (1½ hrs). Jeeps to **Jowai** leave from the Jowai stand, also near Anjali Cinema.

Taxi Yellow-top taxis pick up passengers to share rides; flag one down and hop in if it is going your way, around Rs 10. **Tourist Taxi Association**, Kacheri Rd, Police Bazar, T0364-222 3895, offers shared/private taxi to **Guwahati** and **Cherrapunji**.

Train Guwahati (103 km; see page 628) is the nearest railhead. Tickets are available from MTC Bus Stand, daily 0600-1100, 1300-1600.

★ Cherrapunji and around *Colour map 4, B4.*

The old administrative headquarters of the Khasis, picturesque Cherrapunji (also known as Shora, the official government name) is a pleasant, quiet town spread out along a ridge with gravestones dotting the surrounding hillocks. The best time to visit for spectacular views is during the drier months of November to February; the heat and humidity can be oppressive in the summer, and by mid-March it is hazy most days and you should expect the odd torrential downpour.

> **Fact...**
> Cherrapunji holds the record as the wettest place on earth, with an average of 11,900 mm rainfall annually.

Cherra Bazar market If possible, time your visit to Cherrapunji to coincide with a market day (see www.cherrapunji.com for dates). The colourful **Ka Iewbah Sohrarim** (market) is held every eight days in Cherra Bazar and attracts hordes of Khasi tribespeople. If the market is due to fall on a Sunday, the date is moved to the preceding Saturday as most people observe the Christian day of rest. There is also a smaller *Iewrit* (market) every fourth day. Khasi women all wear a checked apron tied over one shoulder, and both sexes wrap up in Welsh plaid blankets against the cold. The local orange flower honey is sold during the winter season, along with sacks of betel nuts (*kwai*), gruesome chunks of meat, and anything else you care to imagine. Little food stalls are a good place to sample Khasi food.

Waterfalls and caves Nohkalikai Falls, reputedly the world's fourth highest, are 5 km west of Cherrapunji, near Sohrarim. There is always a significant flow of water, while multiple torrents are seen during the rainy season. Limestone caves nearby include Krem Mawmluh (4503 m) with a five-river passage and Krem Phyllut (1003 m) at **Mawsmai**, with a large fossil passage and two stream ways. Mawsmai also has high waterfalls in the wet season. Between Shillong and Cherrapunji at **Mawsynram** ① *55 km from Shillong; take a bus from Bara Bazar at 1400 (3 hrs),* **Mawjymbuin cave** has water dripping from a breast-shaped stone on to what looks like a Siva lingam, and plenty of stalactites and stalagmites. **Meghalaya Tourism** in Shillong runs tours to some of these locations.

Living root-bridges The most astonishing sight around Cherrapunji and a must-see of the Northeast are a series of living root-bridges found near Mawshamok. Here, Khasi tribespeople have trained the roots of the *ficus elastica* rubber tree into robust bridges, spanning streams that become raging torrents in the monsoon. It takes 15 to 20 years for the bridges to become strong enough to support the crossing of people and goods between the villages, but they last for several centuries (possibly up to 800 years) – getting sturdier as they age. There is an excellent eco-friendly resort (see Where to stay, page 648) that can provide sketch maps for the challenging treks to the bridges. From the resort, a short trek entails a very steep 45-minute descent to the tangled mass of Ummunoi 'single' root-bridge, well worth the effort and pain of the ascent back up. Or it is possible to make a day trek to the extraordinary **Umshiang 'double-decker' model** ① *camera Rs 10, video Rs 50,* in Nongriat village, from where it is a short walk to icy turquoise pools. This trek involves descending 3000 steps through the dense jungle, past pretty hamlets and several other root-bridges, with plenty of ups as well as downs. It is possible and highly recommended to stay overnight at **Nongriat** (see Where to stay, page 649).

> **Tip...**
> If you are heading straight to the Cherrapunji Resort, there is one bus a day from Shillong to Laitkynsew village close by (see Shillong Transport, opposite).

Jainta Hills

The once beautiful scenery of the Jainta Hills has been spoilt somewhat in the last few decades by the coal mines that sustain the economy of the area. Jowai, 64 km southeast of Shillong on NH44, is the headquarters of the Jaintia Hills, circled by the Myntdu River. The market, full of tribal women, is especially colourful. From Shillong cars take 2½ hours, buses a little longer. **Nartiang**, 12 km from Jowai, is a scenic spot famed for its monoliths, which were raised in

0500 and again at 0715 for worship (observers welcome), after which the young trainees go to the monastic school next door. It generally takes 15-20 years for the *lamas* to complete their doctorates in Buddhist philosophy, though the current Dalai Lama was just 25 when he finished. The **museum** ① *opened on request, Rs 20, cameras Rs 20*, contains a wealth of treasures, including

Tip...
Get up before dawn to visit the monastery for first morning prayers. It's a mystical experience, and you may even be served a salt tea and cabbage curry breakfast.

700-year-old sculptures, numerous *thangkas* and priceless manuscripts. These, and other precious objects left in storage, are soon to be properly displayed in a new two-storey building.

Exiting via the south gate of the monastery complex takes you down a grassy ridge, strung with small *chortens* and *mani* walls, for some excellent views. Visible on a ridge northeast from the monastery is the **Gyangong Ani Gompa**, home to some three dozen nuns who are studying there; it's a 1½-hour (5 km) walk down and up a steep ravine (only advisable in dry weather).

Lake District
Just above Tawang beyond the monastery is the Lake District, an exceptionally beautiful area with many high-altitude lakes, including the tranquil Sangeshar Lake where a dance sequence from the film *Koyla* was shot. After a fork and an army outpost, the road continues towards **Klemta**, just a few kilometres from the border. There are a few scattered monasteries and a shrine to all faiths at the spot where Guru Nanak rested as he trekked into Tibet, 500 years ago. **Ptso**, 25 km from Tawang, has a small cabin by a lake which is used by the military. To explore this area you'll have to hire a jeep and guide, carry snacks and drinks, and be prepared for steep, treacherous mountain roads. It is all worth it for the breathtaking mountain scenery.

Gorsam Chorten
This immense 12th-century *chorten* (*stupa*) is 100 km from Tawang, near Jimithang, where there are some simple places to stay. The setting is amazing, and the road little travelled by foreigners. A few public *sumos* run to the village each week, taking two to three hours; book ahead with an agent in Tawang, or hire a private vehicle.

Listings Western Arunachal Pradesh

Where to stay

Dirang

$$-$ Awoo Dirang Resort
Bushthang, T03780-242036,
www.awooresort.com.
Standard rooms are simple, clean and bright others have faux-wood-panelled rooms giving a more cosy feel. Multicuisine restaurant and generator back-up for the inevitable power cuts, and garden terrace has amazing views.

$$-$ Heritage Pemaling
1.5 km out of the village, T03780-242615,
www.hotelpemaling.com.
Standard/deluxe rooms are frumpy but clean with new tiled bathrooms, the only real difference being the valley views from the deluxe. Suites are much more attractive in a chintz-and-wicker way, with large bathroom and balcony. Restaurant for residents only.

$ Dirang Tourist Lodge
Next to Heritage Pemaling, T03780-242175,
www.himalayan-holidays.com.
Spacious clean rooms, attached bath with geyser, and great views down over the river and Dirang. Only 4 rooms so booking necessary, same price single or double. Meals provided, but give advance warning.

$ Dreamland
Main Rd, T03780-242296.
3 simple twin rooms in a family home (sharing their basic clean bathroom), potted plants aplenty, plenty of bedding provided although beds are hard. Appealing little restaurant serves beer, but avoid the food. Hot buckets for a small fee.

$ Moon
Main Rd, T03780-242438.
Upstairs 4-bed room has a decent bathroom with geyser, but others share a smelly common bath

(hot bucket available). Rooms have clean sheets and paintwork, hard beds, and nothing more.

Tawang

Apart from dormitory beds (men only), single travellers to Tawang will have to pay the price of a double room. There are plenty of lodges clustered around the Old Market area, where sumos terminate.

$$ Dolma Khangsar Guesthouse
Gompa Rd, near the monastery, a 20- to 30-min walk from the town centre.
A homestay atmosphere and excellent food. Rooms are a good size, have a cosy feel, amazing views from upper levels, and there's easy access to the monastery and good hikes.

$$ Tawang Inn
Nehru Market, T03794-224096.
The highest-spec rooms in town, particularly in terms of bathrooms. Carpets, attractive furnishings, thick pillows, TV, heaters, lots of wood and cane. 6 suites. Ask for a room with a view.

$$-$ Tourist Hut
Nehru Market, T03794-222739, T(0)9436-051291.
The best value in Tawang, 7 rooms with heaters, towels, laminate floors, and plenty of colourfully clashing patterns and blankets – preferable on the 1st floor. A range of prices, pay more for TV or front-facing view, kind management willing to negotiate.

$ Tenzin Guest House
6 km from Tawang village by road, or a 45-min hike up footpaths (as is the monastery directly above), T03794-200095.
A modern concrete house with 4 spotless rooms upstairs, very comfortable, and a peaceful and attractive setting.

$ Tourist Lodge
200 m (signed) from jeep stand in the Old Market, T03794-222359.
A lodge with 20 well-furnished but poorly maintained rooms, but they do have heaters and hot water. The Tourist Office is in the same complex.

Restaurants

Dirang

$ Dipak Sweets & Snacks
Main Rd. Open 0600-1900.
Excelllent *chola* with samosa or *puris* in the morning. One of few places open on Thu afternoon.

$ Hotel Raj
Main Rd. Open 0600-1800.
Good *dal baht* and *thukpa*.

$ Hotel Samaroh
Main Rd.
Cheap and busy, rice meals/chowmein/greasy rolls are tasty. Veg and non-veg.

Tawang

In Nehru Market, a small bakery sells substantial muffins and pastries.

$$-$ Hotel Tawang View
Nehru Market, T03794-223009. Open 0830-2100.
Probably the best restaurant in town, with a huge vegetarian and non-vegetarian menu, most of which is actually available (unlike other places). Indian dishes particularly recommended. Red walls, coloured bulbs, plastic flowers, and the occasional drunk local.

$ Dragon Restaurant
Old Market, T03794-224475. Open 0700-2030.
Delicious Chinese and Tibetan staples take a while to prepare, meat is rarely available, quite cosy surrounds with fairy lights. Look for the Chinese lanterns outside.

Festivals

Feb/Mar Losar is celebrated for 8-15 days in western Arunachal.
Oct/Nov Buddha Mahatsova has cultural programmes, monastic and tribal dances, over 3 days in Tawang.

What to do

Bomdila

Dawa Tsering, *based between Bomdila and Dirang, T(0)9436-676225, dawaap@yahoo.com.*
Trustworthy and informative Dawa arranges treks and tours with a cultural slant, visiting villages, camping and homestays, and can swiftly arrange permits for Arunachal.
Himalayan Holidays, *ABC Buildings, Main Market, T03782-222017.* Useful for booking *sumo* tickets.

Tawang

Himalayan Holidays, *Old Market, T03794- 223151, T(0)94362-48216. Open 0500-1930.* Organizes tours and jeep hire, good for booking advance *sumo* tickets back to Tezpur.
Tribal Discovery (same office as **Himalayan**), *Old Market, T03794-223151, T(0)9436-045075, davidsongtom@yahoo.com.* Reasonable prices on

$$-$ Ziro Valley Resort

Biiri village, 3 km from Old Ziro, T(0)985-691 0173, tagetabin@gmail.com.

Very pleasing chalet rooms with modern if simple amenities, brand new and spacious, duvets, TV, best on the 1st floor with terraces. Also cheaper, simpler rooms next to the restaurant, less stylish but also have geysers. A great choice if you don't have to depend on public transport (1 km off the main road, before Hari village, sign-posted) and the villages around Ziro are an easy walk away. Worth going for a meal even if you aren't staying (see Restaurants, opposite).

$ Blue Pine

Pai Gate, Hapoli, T03788-224812.

Most people's first choice for good reason, although other places are closer to town. Cosy rooms have wood panelling, TV, hot water, but dirty floors. Standard doubles (which they will be reluctant to tell you about), larger deluxe rooms with more character. No single room rates, but room 304 is a 'dorm' with 2 beds, sharing common bathroom. Pleasant restaurant area though food is merely OK; laundry service.

$ Circuit House

Hapoli, reservations through Deputy Commissioner's Office, T03788-224255.

Excellent value, on a hill with views, worth the effort of contacting the DC. 6 rooms in the new block have tiled floors, TV, fresh paint, heaters, hot water (request the VIP room, it is the same price as standard rooms). 3 rooms in the original bungalow. Food available.

$ Government Guesthouse

Old Ziro, T(0)8575-202663.

Perched on top of a hill, with amazing views of the valley and the villages enclosed within it; 6 double rooms with bath are a steal, nets, cheerful patterns but musty smells. Essential to phone ahead for permission to stay.

$ Hibu Tan homestay

Near Siiro village, 6 km from Hapoli, T03788-225808.

To stay even deeper in the valley, next to paddies and streams, friendly Hibu Tatu has 2 chalets in his market garden of apple trees and veggies, simple concrete affairs with a front veranda, hot buckets, very clean, rooms have 2 big beds, B&B, all meals can be provided.

$ Hotel Valley View

Hapoli, T03788-225398.

Institutional corridors lead to acceptable rooms with heaters and TV. Good choice for single travellers (Rs 400, attached bath, Rm 213 is best), also has doubles with shared bath for those on a budget (Rs 400), pay more for rooms with hot water. Extensive menu in the not unattractive restaurant.

$ Ngunu Ziro homestay

Siiro village, about 5 km from Hapoli, T03788-225809, punyochada@gmail.com.

3 cheerful rooms (2 share a bathroom) surrounded by a bamboo grove. Nicest on the upper floor among the eaves, hot water, meals available. Camping trips and treks to the Wildlife Sanctuary can be arranged.

$ Pine Ridge

MG Rd, Hapoli, T03788-224725.

You could get lost in this maze of a place, particularly as the lights never seem to be switched on in the corridors. It's good central location, but rooms are musty at the cheaper end. They come with TV and hot water. Restaurant is gloomy and deserted.

Daporijo

$ Circuit House

On hill above town, T03792- 223250.

It's a steal for clean sheets, mossie nets, fans, plenty of space and excellent views. Food is good and bed-tea available, as are hot buckets. But it is a 10-min uphill slog from town and permission is required from the DC's office in order to stay; however, on our visit, a telephone call made by staff to the EAC sufficed.

$ Hotel Sanatu

T03792-223531.

7 grim rooms with TV, fan, water by hot bucket in the scary bathrooms, dirty sheets. However, the very pleasant manager also has some decent rooms in the **KK Palace Hotel**, but it's across the river.

Daporijio to Pasighat

$$ Hotel Aane

MG Rd, Pasighat, T0368-222 7777/3333.

The best hotel in Pasighat, all rooms are newly and bluely painted, with fans, shiny floors, balcony, geyser and clean furnishings. A couple can easily fit in the single rooms with double beds, 2 suites are not worth the extra money. Restaurant pleasant, and roof terrace opens in the season.

$ Aagaam
Yubo Complex, Nehru Chowk, on the main road in Along/Aalo, T03783-223640/(0)940-2471774.
More expensive than the Holiday Cottage for rooms with less appeal, but they do have geysers. Deluxe and suite rooms also available, newly renovated. There is a musty 3-bed dorm.

$ Circuit House
Opposite SBI, Main Rd, Along/Alao, T03783- 222232.
An absolute bargain at Rs 300, 13 clean simple rooms, new block at the rear. On a small hill with views from the grounds. Often full, but try your luck.

$ Holiday Cottage
Near General Hospital, Along/Aalo, T03783-222463.
On a quiet street, rooms with a bit of character and it's good value. Standard rooms with nets and fans, 2 deluxe rooms have more light, space and sofas. Hot buckets, restaurant is good.

$ Hotel Oman
Oman Complex, Main Market, Pasighat, T0368-222 4464.
Absolutely the best budget choice, rooms have attached bath, decent furniture, clean sheets, new mossie nets, towels, TV. Deluxe doubles are good value (but couples can squeeze into the single rooms with 'family bed'). Food available.

The Hotel Siang close to the *sumo* counters is fine, should the Oman be full, though it is more costly for less appealing rooms.

Restaurants

Ziro Valley
The restaurant at the Hotel Valley View has a varied menu, better for vegetarians than others. There are also several cheap eateries on MG Rd.

$ Tribal Food Plaza
MG Rd, Hapoli, T03788-225322.
Mon-Sat 0800-1830.
Indigenous cuisine is meat-oriented, also some Chinese, Indian, soups, fish and Nagaland dishes. Colourful lighting and lighting, view over the street as it is the 1st floor.

$ Ziro Valley Resort
Biiri village, T(0)985-691 0173. Open 0630-2130.
A popular place with locals, excellent Indian/Chinese dishes, dining is either in the main restaurant or 3 little huts in the grounds. Alcohol

available. It's well placed for taking a break when walking around the valley villages.

Daporijo to Pasighat
The food at the Circuit House in Daporijo is good for residents; nothing in town is outstanding though the **$ Sanatu** hotel is a safe bet. In Along/Aalo, the restaurants at the **$ Aagaam** (T03783-222838), and **Holiday Cottage** hotels do good meals and are the best places in town to dine; both have a few tribal dishes in the menu. **$ CT Restaurant** (below the Aagaam), does tasty Chinese/Tibetan fare (no menu). In Pasighat, the **$ Shangrila** (opposite Main Market), is excellent and always busy: *thukpa*, chowmein, meat momos, all come with delicious soup. Half-plates are very generous and very cheap. Open 0730-1930.

Transport

Ziro Valley
Bus APST bus to **Daporijo** on Mon, **Guwahati** on Sun and Thu at 1200. Ticket counter opens at 0600.

Sumo Getting from Ziro to **Daporijo** by *sumo* is tricky, as you have to join a *sumo* coming from Itanagar, at around 1100, and take any free seats available (usually the rear seats); be warned, the road is particularly windy and bumpy on this stretch. To **Itanagar**, at 0530.

Daporijo
Bus APST bus (T03792-223107) to **Itanagar**, to **Ziro** on Tue at 0700, to **Along** except Mon (9 hrs).

Sumo *Sumo* counters/departures are in the bazar area, about 200 m from the **Sanatu** hotel. To **Ziro** at 0600 (5 hrs), to **Itanagar** at 0500 (12 hrs). For reservations try **Arunachal Yatayat**, T03792-223679. **Note** There are no public *sumos* to Along, so it is the bus or a privately hired *sumo*.

Along/Aalo
Bus APST (T03783-222475) bus to **Itanagar** at 0600 and 1600 (except Mon, 12 hrs), to **Guwahati** at 1000 (Mon/Thu only, 14 hrs), to **Daporijo** at 0700 (except Mon, 9 hrs). To **Mechukha** at 0615 (except Fri, 12 hrs).

Sumo It is necessary to report to the *sumo* counter 30 mins before departure. To **Pasighat** at 1100 (4½-5 hrs); to **Itanagar** at 0530 (9 hrs). There are no public *sumos* along the route to **Daporijo**, so either take the bus or hire a private *sumo*.

Naga culture

Tribal groups Nagaland is almost entirely inhabited by 16 groups of the Tibeto-Burmese tribes – among them are the Angamis, Aos, Konyaks, Kukis, Lothas, Semas and Wanchus, collectively known as the Nagas. There are many tribal languages spoken: Angami, Ao, Chang are a few. The Nagas were once head hunters and were known for their fierceness and the regular raids they made on Assam and Burma. The warring tribes believed that since the enemy's animated soul (*yaha* in Wanchu dialect) was to be found at the nape of the neck, it could only be set free once beheaded. However, since the spiritual soul, *mio*, resided in the head and brought good fortune, enemy heads (and those of dead comrades) were prized as they could add to a community's own store of dead ancestors. The hilltop villages are protected by stone walls. The *morung*, a meeting house, acts as a boys' dormitory, and is used for storing weapons and once displayed the prizes of war (enemy heads). The huge sacred drum stands by each *morung* is a hollowed-out tree trunk resembling a buffalo head. Some believe that the Nagas' ancestors came from the seafaring nation of Sumatra and retain this link in legends, village drums and ceremonial jewellery, which uses shells.

Festivals When it comes to festivals Nagaland leads the party, with all 16 tribes enjoying their own ceremonies, feasts and dancing throughout the year. However, the big event is the five-day Hornbill Festival in the first week of December. Originally orchestrated by the government as a cultural *mêlée* to attract tourists from India and abroad, the festival has taken on a life of its own and many people plan a trip to Nagaland around it. Tribes rival with each other to put on the most memorable display, clad in fabulous traditional dress, and as well as the prevalent tribal music recent years have also seen a rock festival take place. Handicrafts and food stalls, distinctive to each tribe, give both locals and tourists a chance to sample different styles of home-cooking and local brews. The festival is held in Kisama village, 16 km from Kohima.

Religion Today 98% of the Nagas are Baptist Christians. Originally, although they revered natural spirits, the Nagas believed in a single overseeing superforce, and hence incorporated the Christian Gospel into their cosmology quite readily. The Bible was translated into many of the Naga dialects (written in a Roman script devised by missionaries, as the languages were previously unwritten), yet many old customs have been retained.

Crafts The ancient craft of weaving on portable looms is still practised by the women. The strips of colourful cloth are stitched together to produce shawls in different patterns which distinguish each tribe. Ao warriors wear the red and black striped shawl with a central white band embroidered with symbols.

$$-$ Kent
Golaghat Rd, T03862-234077.
The executive rooms are a good deal – clean, new, tiled, reliable hot water, TV and plenty of lights and plug sockets. Conveniently near the train station and private bus stand, without suffering too much road noise. Pleasant staff, restaurant, can arrange transport. There is a handy map of town on the back of their flyer.

$ de Oriental Dream
Bank Colony, opposite Naga Shopping Arcade, T03862-231211, deorientaldream@yahoo.com.
More attractive than other budget options, with stone floors and decent decor. All rooms

have a/c, TV, hot water; a couple are cheaper as they are unrenovated. One of few hotels to offer a single room rate, some **$$** deluxe rooms, multicusine restaurant. No lift, which is a killer for the 4th floor.

Restaurants

There are numerous basic 'rice hotels' near the private bus stand; most serve meat *thalis* (look for a Hindu sign if you are veg), otherwise try a multicuisine restaurant in one of the better hotels; *lassis* in town are excellent.

Transport

Air Airport is 3 km from town. Flights to **Kolkata** and **Guwahati** daily.

Bus Private buses from Golaghat Rd to **Guwahati** (11-12 hrs), **Imphal** (9 hrs); from NST Bus Stand to **Kohima** hourly, 3 hrs.

Shared taxis To **Kohima** (2½ hrs) from the taxi park next to the NST stand.

Train To **Delhi**: 3 per day, best is *Rajdhani Exp 12423*, 0205 32½ hrs, via **Guwahati** around 5 hrs. **Dibrugarh**: at least 8 per day, 6-8 hrs.

The town of Kohima (population 270,063) is spread over a series of ridges at 1495 m, surrounded by higher peaks, with the original Angami Kohima village set on a hill overlooking the Main Bazar. Kohima attracted global attention during the Second World War because it was here that the Japanese advance was halted by the British and Indian Naga forces. The local bazar attracts colourful tribal women who come to buy and sell their produce, which includes snails, bags of frogs and the occasional dog. Most businesses and shops shut up as soon as it gets dark, and there may be a strong military presence in town. The Heritage Village of Kisama, which hosts the Hornbill Festival, is 12 km from the capital.

Sights

Second World War Cemetery ① *Mon-Sat 0830-1530 in winter, until 1630 in summer.* The cemetery is in a beautiful setting, with well-maintained lawns where rose bushes bloom. Two tall crosses stand out at the lowest and highest points. The stone markers each have a polished bronze plaque with epitaphs commemorating the men who fell here to halt "the invasion of India by the forces of Japan in April 1944" by the British 14th Army under General William Slim. The cherry tree, which was used by Japanese soldiers as a snipers' post, was destroyed; what grew from the old stump marks the limit of the enemy advance. At the base of the Second Division lower cross, near the main entrance, are the lines: "When you go home/Tell them of us and say/For your tomorrow/ We gave our today." The markings of the DC's tennis court still remain Three kilometres away by road, the striking red-roofed **Cathedral of Reconciliation** (1995) overlooks the cemetery from a hill.

State Museum ① *Bayavu Hill Colony, 3 km north of the main centre (shared taxis can drop you nearby). Tue-Sun 0930-1530 winter, 1000-1600 in summer, Rs 5.* The excellent State Museum has a collection of anthropological exhibits including textiles, figurines, weaponry, skulls and carved totems. Dioramas effectively show the clothing and lifestyle of the different Naga tribes. The lower gallery displays some colourful jewellery including girdles, as well as the chunky armlets worn by men and, of course, their extraordinary headgear. Look out for the elaborate matchboxes and a chair made of elephant bones.

Kohima village The sprawling and appealing Kohima village (aka T-Khel or Bara Basti, signed off the main road north of the centre) has a ceremonial gateway with two doors carved with motifs of guns, warriors and symbols of prosperity. Steps lead up, passing megaliths on the way, to the pinnacle of the village where a traditional Naga house remains. Though made of corrugated iron, there are crossed horns on the gables; the wooden doors are painted with tigers and *mithun* heads to signify the status of the family, and huge grain baskets stand in front.

Manipur culture

The majority of the population are Vaishnavite Hindus. They belong to the *Meitei* tribe and are related to the *Shans* of Burma, and live in the valleys. Twenty-nine hill tribes (mainly Naga and Kuki) constitute about a third of the population, most of whom are Christian. Like the Nagas, the Manipuris have a reputation for being great warriors, still practising their skills of wrestling, sword fighting and martial arts. They are also keen on sport; polo, which is said to have originated in Manipur, is the principal sport.

The ancient musical forms of the valley dwellers are closely connected to the worship of Vishnu, expressed in Manipuri dancing. The *Ras Leela* dances performed at every ceremony are characterized by graceful and restrained movements and delicate hand gestures. The ornate costumes worn by the veiled women are glittering and colourful; the stiff, tubular skirts barely move. The *Sankirtana* dance is vigorous, rhythmic and athletic. It is usually performed by men, who play on the *pung* (drums) and cymbals while they dance. The tribal ritual dances, some of which are performed by priests and priestesses before deities, may end in a trance. Others can last several days, observing a strict form and accompanied by the drone of a bowed instrument, *pena*. *Thang-ta* is a skilful martial art performed to beating drums, and is practised by both sexes dressed in black.

maintained and serenely peaceful sites, open during daylight hours (someone will materialise with the key).

Around Imphal

Zoological Gardens ① *7 km west of Imphal in a rural setting, Tue-Sun 1000-1530, zoo Rs 10, Biological Museum Rs 5, camera Rs 25.* The gardens are well maintained and allow close-up viewing of sambar, hog and muntjac deer. The enclosures for the primates, birds, jackals and bears are less appealing. There's also a bizarre and dilapidated Biological Museum. To reach the zoo, take a shared rickshaw (Rs 10) from Ima Market to the Agricultural University in Iroisemba, from where it's a pleasant 10-min walk.

Palace of Langthabal Access via the university main gate, 8 km along the Indo-Burma road, Rs 10 in a shared auto. Overlooking the university, the historic Palace of Langthabal stands on a hill within an Assam Rifles compound (permission will be given for you to view the remains). Despite recent renovation, there is not much to detain you and a visit to the palace/temple is a short one.

Konghampat Orchidarium ① *12 km along the NH39, best time to visit Apr-May.* Set up by the Forest Department, this has over 120 of the 500 species of orchid found in Manipur, including some rare ones.

Andro Cultural Complex ① *26 km from Imphal (less than 1 hr on public transport from Andro Parking, daily 0830-1630.* The centre seeks to preserve Manipuri and Northeastern culture. Run by the charming Mr Mutua, the Complex has replicas of various tribal dwellings and displays artefacts such as rare manuscripts, textiles, basketry, carving and jewellery.

Tourist information

India Tourism
Old Lambulane, Jail Rd, T0385-245 1131. Mon-Fri 0930-1630 in winter, 0930-1730 in summer.
Helpful staff can advise on transport and other matters. Information desk at airport opens for flights and has a map of Imphal that is worth picking up.

Manipur Tourism
Next to Hotel Imphal, T0385-245 1916, http://manipurtourism.gov.in. Mon-Sat 0930-1600, closed 2nd Sat of the month.

Where to stay

Hotels in Imphal add 20% tax to the price of a room (the price codes below include this). Check-out is usually 1200.

Imphal

To Dimapur & Konghampat Orchidarium
To Ukhrul
Stadium
Commonwealth War Cemetery
NH 39
Dimapur Rd
Imphal River
Manipur Tourism **3**
Thangal Bazar
Exit Gate
Kangla Pat
Nagampal Rd
Khwairambahd Bazar
Kangchup Rd
Laxmi Bazar
KANGLA
Entrance Gate
Manipur State Museum
CHECKON
Entrance Gate
Palace Rd
India Tourism Office
To Airport & Zoo
Tidim Rd
Nambu River
Jail Rd
Solbam Leikai Rd
Indian War Cemetery
Old Palace
Shri Govindaji Temple
Kongba Rd
To Langthabal, Manipur University & Moreh

N
Not to scale

Where to stay
Classic & Classic Café **2**
Imphal & Emoinu Restaurant **3**
New Airlines **4**
Nimala & Chamu Restaurant **5**
White Palace **6**

Restaurants
Sagar Pure Veg **1**

$$-$ The Classic Hotel
North AOC, T0385-244 3967/9, www.theclassichotel.in.
This 3-star hotel is by far the best in town, with spotless paintwork, shiny floors, flatscreens and quality furnishings. The cheapest room come without a/c, other categories all include breakfast, and there are **$$$** suites. The **Classic Café** restaurant is stylish and has Indian/Chinese food and a chance to eat a Manipuri *thali*. Wi-Fi, fitness centre, souvenir shop.

$$-$ Nimala
MG Av, T0385-245 9014.
Popular choice, large rooms have flatscreens, geysers and clean furniture/paint. Central location close to Ima Market. Chamu restaurant has very good Indian/Chinese. Advisable to book ahead.

$ Imphal
Dimapur Rd, North AOC, T0385-242 3372, hotelimphal@yahoo.in.
Run by Manipur Tourism, this imposing white edifice has some renovated rooms, they are large, with modern tiling, comfy beds, TV, fridge and reliable hot water. Some **$$** suites have a/c and new bathrooms. Pleasant gardens, restaurant is good (see Restaurants). Definitely the best value budget choice in town.

$ New Airlines
MG Av, T0986-234 2968, hotelnewairlines@ymail.com.
Clean and spacious rooms, with TV and colourful homely furnishings, the price is upper-end budget, but the hotel is well maintained. Rooms at the back are pretty quiet. Xanadu Restaurant is open 0600-2100.

$ White Palace
113 MG Av, T0385-245 2322.
Rooms are weathered and could be cleaner, but they are a decent size, with plenty of furniture, TV and free hot buckets. Pleasant staff, food available in the room, hot buckets given. Cheap singles, doubles and triples, suites are not worth the extra money.

Restaurants

Manipur is a 'dry' state, though booze is available if you ask around. If you get a chance, try *iromba*, the Manipuri savoury dish of fish, vegetables and bamboo shoots and the sweet *kabok* made with molasses and rice. In the markets, women mix up snacks such as *kelichana* and *shingju*, a tasty mix of sprouts, raw veg, seasoning and split peas. The restaurants in the hotels are the safest bet for a decent meal; all serve veg and non-veg Indian and Chinese dishes.

$$ Classic Café
At the Classic Hotel. Open 0600-2200.
Does a Manipuri *thali* in addition of several other types of cuisine and is the smartest in town.

$$-$ Emoinu
At the Hotel Imphal. Open 0630-2130.
Serves up very tasty Indian food, as well as Chinese/some Western food, and interesting Manipuri feasts (slower to prepare).

$ Chamu
At the Nimala Hotel
Has good mains, the *muttar paneer* is excellent. It's popular with locals, the gloomy lighting is brightened by pink walls and wood veneers.

$ Sagar Pure Veg
Hotel Airlines, MG Av (look for the sign, go up the stairs). Open 1030-2100.
The usual Chinese and Indian dishes are OK and at a slightly cheaper price, but the main attraction here is alcohol, expect Formica tables dimly lit by yellow lamps and the odd rat. Free delivery. Not to be confused with the **Hotel New Airlines**, nearby.

Entertainment

Cultural shows with Manipuri dancing can be seen at Rupmahal Theatre, BT Rd, near Kangla Gate, and at **Kala Academy**.

Festivals

Jan Gang Ngai celebrated by Kabui Nagas with dancing in ceremonial costumes in Imphal.
Feb/Mar Yaosang a Hindu festival on full moon night, boys and girls dance the Thabal Chongba and sing in a circle in the moonlight.
Apr-May Lai Haraoba is celebrated across the state with traditional dances and music.
Sep Heikru Hitongba is mainly non-religious, when there are boat races along a 16-m-wide moat in narrow boats with large numbers of rowers.
Nov Sangai Festival runs for 7 days and showcases the culture, dance, food, sports and music of Manipur.

Shopping

Silk thread embroidery in dark colours decorates the borders of the traditional phaneks worn by women.
The best shopping experience is at the Khwairamband (see page 669). For woven wicker, handloom and souvenir items try **Eastern Handlooms Handicrafts**, Paona Bazar, open Mon-Sat 0900-1730.

What to do

Manipur Tourism. Tours to Sri Govindaji Temple, Bishnupur, INA Memorial, Moirang, KL National Park and the Loktak Lake, depart from **Hotel Imphal**, Sun 0800.

Transport

Air Flights to **Kolkata**, daily (some via **Aizwal**); also to **Delhi**, **Guwahati**, **Jorhat**, 2-3 times weekly

Bus/sumo From North AOC, near Hotel Imphal, private buses connect with **Dimapur** (215 km) in Nagaland, the nearest railhead (8-9 hrs) via **Kohima** (6-7 hrs). Daily private buses (some a/c) for **Guwahati** (579 km, 24 hrs) via Silchar (198 km) and to **Shillong**. To **Moirang** (for Loktak Lake) transport leaves from Wahengban Leikai Parking. To **Moreh**, *sumos* from Moreh Parking near Kangla Gate leave when full 0600-1100 (best to go early), 3-4 hrs. Fare is more expensive returning from Moreh.

floating islands, dancing deer and mountain lilies

Loktak Lake

Loktak Lake is the largest freshwater lake in the Northeast, where fishermen live in huts on islands of floating weeds, using nets to farm fish and *singhara* (water chestnut). Perfectly circular floating pens made of weeds stretch as far as the eye can see, with enough room between each for the narrow wooden canoes to pass.

Tip...
The light across Loktak Lake is best for photographs in the afternoon.

Moirang On the south side of the lake, 45 km from Imphal, Moirang is noted for its early Manipuri folk culture and traditional folk dance form. The temple to the forest god, known as Lord Thankjing, has robes of the 12th-century Moirang kings and holds the Lai Haraoba ritual dance festival each year. During the Second World War Moirang was the headquarters of the Indian National Army (INA) for a while; their flag was raised as a symbol of national independence for the first time on 12 April 1944. There is an INA memorial and a **War Museum** ① *Tue-Sun 1000-1600, entrance Rs 2,* displaying photos, letters and dusty war memorabilia relating to Subhas Chandra Bose. It also has a gallery devoted to Manipur freedom fighters.

You can walk to **Sendra Island**, about 1 km from Moirang Bazar, where there is a tourist lodge; there are good views from the top. Better is to continue on a shared auto/van for 20 minutes or so to the villages further along the lake. Tin-roofed huts are strung out along a series of hilly promontories which afford excellent views.

Keibul Lamjao National Park The park, covering 40 sq km, is the only floating sanctuary of its kind and protects a small population of thamin (Sangai), the endangered brow-antlered deer. The sanctuary was set up in 1977 when the swamps, the natural habitat of the Sangai, had been reclaimed for cultivation resulting in the near extinction of this 'dancing deer'. The Sangai feed on mats of floating humus covered with grass and *phumdi* reeds until the rainy season when they move to the hills. You can walk 20 minutes to a viewing tower on Babet Ching hillock and travel through the creeks on small wooden boats (when you are more likely to spot a Sangai). Other wildlife includes hog deer, wild boar, panther, fishing cat and water birds. There is a forest rest house in which you can stay with permission (see Where to stay, page 674).

Moreh and the Myanmar boder

Moreh 110 km southeast of Imphal on the Indo-Myanmar border, Moreh has an interesting mix of cultures and is basically a giant market. A friendly police escort will accompany you during trips across the border (no phones or cameras allowed, but no visa/paperwork for Myanmar is necessary) where trading begins in earnest. After about 200 m, there are autos going to the larger market at **Tamu**, 5 km further into Myanmar. Both market areas are a good place to sample local cuisines,

Tip...
Be aware that, due to its location, Moreh has become a principal export route for heroin out of the Golden Triangle (as well as a main smuggling route for shoes, electronics, toys, and all else).

as well as shop for Chinese-made goods. There is transport back to Imphal in the afternoon, or plenty of basic hotels and restaurants should you wish to stay overnight (recommended, as the journey is tiring). Alcohol is plentiful in shops on both sides of the border. It is a good idea to carry copies of your passport and visa to facilitate movement through several police and army check-posts along the road to Moreh.

Ukhrul

Located 83 km northeast of Imphal, Ukhrul is the domain of the Tanghul Nagas and the home of the siroi lily which grows on the Shirui-Kashong range at a height of 2591 m. The lily blooms in mid-May when trekking is possible from Shirui village, about 14 km from Ukhrul. The trek is not long (about 5 km, with a possible 10 km extension up Phungrei peak) through a mix of grassland and forest with rhododendrons. Volunteer guides are available from Shirui village and there are basic hotels in Ukhrul.

above while the lake attracts migrating birds. Elephant rides are offered too. It may be possible to visit a rubber plantation and watch the processing on a trip. A couple of tourist lodges have cottages bookable through the Wildlife Warden.

Udaipur *Colour map 4, C4.*
57 km south from Agartala; buses and jeeps take about 1 hr.

The Tripura Sundari Temple, near the ancient capital Udaipur, was built on Dhanisagar Hill in the mid-16th century. The Matabari is believed to be one of the 51 holy *pithasthans* mentioned in the *Tantras*, where the Mother Goddess is served by red-robed priests. The pond behind has huge turtles which are delighted to be fed. A large fair is held during Diwali in October/November. Other temples of interest, in various states of atmospheric decrepitude, are the Jagannath Mandir and the Bhubaneswari Mandir. There is a good lodge.

★ Neermahal
53 km southeast of Agartala.

This water-palace in the middle of Rudrasagar Lake was built in 1930 by the late maharaja. The striking white and red fairytale castle with towers, kiosks, pavilions and bridges is fun to explore although the interiors are empty. Boats take passengers from the litter-strewn shore (cheap, set prices for shared or private boat) throughout the day. It is particularly beautiful illuminated at night, and at weekends there is a **son et lumière show** ① *Sat and Sun 1745-1845, Rs 50 includes boat ride and entrance, commentary in Bengali,* the highlight of which is witnessing the palace become floodlit, perfectly reflected in the still waters, as you journey across. The lake itself attracts migratory birds. Sunset across the water is marred somewhat by the chimney of a brick factory.

Pilak
The eighth- to ninth-century archaeological remains of Buddhist and Hindu statutory at Pilak are distinctly underwhelming. That said, the nearby village of **Jolaibari** has a pleasant tourist lodge and active nightmarket, and the walk through the paddies and villages to the sites is rewarding in itself. About 1.5 km beyond the village (signed off the main road) is the **Shyamsundar** *stupa*; the cross-shaped brick base is all that remains, lined with terracotta tiles of frolicking people and animals. Another 2 km brings you to weathered stone images of Avolokiteshwar and Narasimha, where further excavations are still unearthing intricate metal and stone artefacts.

Kailashahar and Unakoti *Colour map 4, B4.*
Ten kilometres from the friendly town of Kailashahar, Unakoti is the site of the largest bas-relief sculpture in India. The seventh-century rock carvings are cut vertically into the hillside, the largest being an impressive 10-m-high depiction of Siva. The style is unusual, reminiscent of statues in South America more than representations of the Hindu pantheon. It is a quiet and peaceful place, unless you come during the *mela* (March/April). Kailashahar has a good market. Buses from Kailashahar drop off on the main road 1 km from the site but finding transport back can be difficult; auto-rickshaws will do a round trip.

Jampui Hills
Some 220 km from Agartala, the Jampui Hills are a serene and forested area good for walking and tasting tribal culture. Between October and December the orange groves are heavy with fruit, while the famed orchids bloom between March and May. Very much off the foreign tourist trail, it's a worthy excursion if travelling into Tripura from the north.

Listings Tripura

Where to stay

Sepahijala Wildlife Sanctuary

$ Forest Bungalow
Contact Chief Conservator of Forests, Agartala, T0381-222 3779.
In well-kept gardens above the lake, meals provided.

Udaipur

All of Udaipur's accommodation is found in the centre of town, 1 km from the bus/jeep stand.

$ Gomati Yatriniwas
T03821-223478, http://tripuratourism.gov.in/govtaccomodation.
Government lodge with passable range of rooms, some with a/c, and a restaurant.

Neermahal

$ Sagarmahal Tourist Lodge
On the lake, 1 km from Melagarh village, T0381-252 4418, http://tripuratourism.gov.in/govtaccomodation.
The majority of the comfortable rooms (a/c or non a/c) overlook the lake, as does the dorm. Rooms in the newer block have no views, but are modern and superior. The restaurant serves generous and cheap meals (though salt-heavy), and staff are lovely.

Pilak

$ Pilak Tourist Lodge
Jolaibari, T03823-263863, http://tripuratourism.gov.in/govtaccomodation.
Large rooms (and bathrooms) with wooden furniture, curtains, balconies, mosquito nets and old-style concrete floors. All non a/c, great value, but directly on the road. Last room on the 1st floor is best, with lots of light coming through the many windows. Meals possible, or food available in the small village.

Kailashahar

$ Unakoti Tourist Lodge
T03824-223635, http://tripuratourism.gov.in/govtaccomodation

Literally a stone's throw from the Bangladeshi border (fence-views from your window), this friendly and decent place has double rooms only (non-a/c or a/c).

Jampui Hills

$ Eden Tourist Lodge
Vanghmun, T03824-238252, http://tripuratourism.gov.in/govtaccomodation.
A simple place that's good value and clean, as is typical of Tripura's government accommodation; all rooms non-a/c.

Restaurants

Neermahal

Superb Bengali snacks and sweets are sold along the road, and simple clean restaurants serve good meals.

Transport

Udaipur

The bus and jeep stand are adjacent to each other, about 1 km from the town centre. Jeeps run more frequently to **Neermahal** and all nearby towns and villages. Autos are readily available to take you to the sights of **Udaipur**. If you need to leave luggage while you go sightseeing, the bus ticketing men have a safe room where they will store bags (till 1800).

Neermahal

Jeeps and buses drop off in the village of Melagarh. It's a short rickshaw ride or 15-min walk to cover the 1.5 km to the lake.

Pilak

Between 0600-0800 5 buses leave Jolaibari (just north of the Tourist Lodge) for **Agartala**, others at 1200, 1300 and 1500, stopping at **Udaipur** (2 hrs). Jeeps leave when full from the same place.

Kailashahar

The train to **Agartala**, when running, leaves from Kumarghat; shared rickshaws cover the 20 km between Kailashahar and Kumarghat. Bus is more reliable.

Khandagiri The Jain temple at the top affords excellent views. There are lovely carvings of Digambara Jains on the back wall of the shrine with a corrugated iron roof halfway up.

Caves 1 and 2 Known as **Tatowa Gumpha** from the parrots carved above their door arches. Two sentries in *dhotis* guard Cave 1 which bears the name **Kusuma**. Modern steps lead up to the more elaborately carved Cave 2 on the left. On the back of the cell are Brahmi inscriptions in red pigment (first century BC to first century AD), obscured by modern Odishan graffiti.

Cave 3 Ananta Gumpha, at the top of the flight of steps, named after the two serpents on the door arches, has some very interesting reliefs using unique motifs, though the protective glass makes them hard to see. On the back wall of the cell, among the various symbols is the *svastika*, auspicious to the Jains. There are tigers, elephants including white ones, lion and wheel.

Cave 7 Navamuni Gumpha, named after the nine Tirthakaras (*munis*) carved on the back and right walls, was originally a residential cell. On the back wall of the original right hand cell are seven Tirthankaras in high relief including Parsvanatha under a seven-hooded canopy, and Risabanatha with a halo, seated on a bull.

Udayagiri & Khandagiri Caves

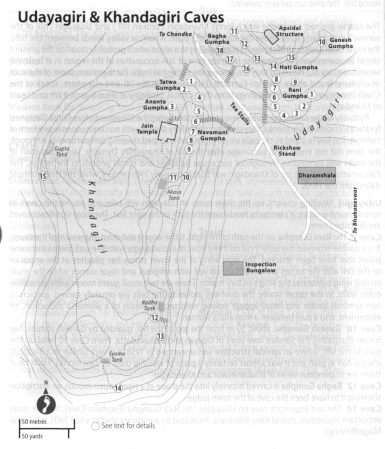

50 metres

50 yards

○ See text for details

Dhauli Hill

The horrors of the Kalinga war at Dhauli, south of Bhubaneswar, in 262 BC led Emperor Asoka to acknowledge the value of Buddhist teachings, which he codified in a series of inscriptions ('edicts') across his empire. His two 'Kalinga Edicts' differ from others which expound Buddhist principles. The rock edicts at the bottom of Dhauli Hill give detailed instructions to Asoka's administrators to rule his subjects with gentleness and fairness.

"...You are in charge of many thousand living beings. You should gain the affection of men. All men are my children, and as I desire for my children that they obtain welfare and happiness both in this world and next, the same do I desire for all men..."

Above the inscription you can see the front of an elephant carved out of an enormous rock. Unfortunately, the edict is difficult to see clearly behind its protective cage and is almost ignored by the bus loads of tourists who are taken on up the hill to the Buddhist **Peace Pagoda**. Known as the **Shanti Stupa**, the pagoda was built in the early 1970s by the Japan Buddha Sangha and Kalinga Nippon Buddha Sangha. The old Hindu temple of Lord Dhavaleswar which was reconstructed in 1972 is also on the hilltop here.

Pipli

Pipli, a small town about 20 km south of Bhubaneswar on the road to Puri, is well known for its appliqué work using brightly coloured embroidered cloth, probably originally designed for use in the Jagannath temple. The roadside stalls sell items for the house and garden – parasols, cushion covers, wall hangings – using striking animal, bird and flower patterns on a backcloth. Unfortunately, mass production has resulted in the loss of attention to detail of the original fine Pipli work, which picked out the motifs by cleverly stuffing sections of the pattern. Today, the best pieces of work are usually sent away to be sold in the government emporia in Bhubaneswar, Delhi and Kolkata.

$ Honey Bee Bakery and Pizzeria
CT Rd, T06752-320479.
Best for fresh bread, muffins and great coffee in a clean and chilled environment, no hint of staff resting on their laurels.

Entertainment

Top hotels and resorts have bars. Classical *Odissi* dance, folk dances and drama, which are always performed for festivals, are also staged from time to time and worth seeking out.

Festivals

Mid-Apr 21-day **Chandan Yatra** coincides with the **Hindu New Year** when images of Jagannath, his brother and sister are taken out in boats on the Narendra Tank. **Snana Yatra**, which follows, marks the ritual bathing of the deities on a special barge. Every few years new images of the deities are carved from specially selected trees and the old ones are secretly buried by the temple priests.
Jun Rath Yatra, see box, page 704. Rath Yatra is due to fall on 6 Jul 2016, 25 Jun 2017 and 14 Jul 2018.
Nov Beach Festival, a week of cultural shows, crafts and food stalls.

Shopping

Visit the vast **bazar** around the Jagannath Temple, along Bada Danda and Swargadwara; you have to bargain. Stone carvings, papier-mâché masks, painted wood figures, paintings, appliqué and hornwork all make good buys.
Pathuria Sahi is the stone carvers' quarter and **Raghurajpur** (12 km away) produces *pattachitras* and etchings on palm leaf.

Odissi, *Dolamandap Sahi.* Handlooms.
Sudarshan, *Station Rd.* Stone carving, where you can also watch masons at work carving out images of deities.
Sun Crafts, *Tinikonia Bagicha.*
Utkalika and **Crafts Complex**, *Mochi Sahi Sq.*
Weavers' Co-op Society, *Grand Rd.*
For handlooms.

What to do

The tourist office has a list of government-approved tour companies. Almost every hotel on CT Rd has a travel office, but for 'tribal tours' it's worth paying more to go with a conscientious agency.

Grass Routes, *CT Rd, T(0)9437-029698/T(0)9437-022663, www.grassroutesjourneys.com.* Offers a fascinating selection of outings in and around Puri, Claire and her husband are keenly promoting responsible tourism. Cooking classes go via the market to learn local dishes, rural bike tours, or excursions further afield visit tribal areas. Trips to Chilika Lake need 24 hrs' notice so the camping spot can be set up. Not cheap, but highly recommended.
Heritage Tours, *Mayfair Heritage Hotel, T(0)9437023656, www.heritagetoursorissa.com.* Expensive yet moral enterprise, offering a variety of tours. A good benchmark for comparing prices but, more importantly, 'tribal tourism' is taken seriously. Well-established and friendly.
OTDC, *T06752-223526.* Inexpensive full-day tours (except Mon, entry fees extra) to Konark, Dhauli, Bhubaneswar, Khandagiri, Udayagiri and Nandankanan Zoo. It is a long day, 0630-1830. Chilika Lake (Satapada), 0730-1730. Half-day tours also available.

Transport

Air Bhubaneswar, 60 km, is the nearest airport (see page 698). Prepaid taxi to Puri from the airport, 1-1½ hrs.

Bus The huge, open bus stand on Grand Rd runs regular buses to **Bhubaneswar** and **Konark**. Minibuses are faster. There are also services to **Cuttack**, **Visakhapatnam** and **Kolkata**.

Rickshaw Cycle-rickshaws available all over town. From the bus stand to CT Rd costs Rs 50; from the railway station Rs 40.

Train Kolkata (H):about 10 daily, 8-9 hrs.
New Delhi: 3 per day, best is *Purushottam Exp 12801*, 2145, 31 hrs. To **Chennai:** 2 per day, best is *Coromandel Exp 12841*, 2215, 19 hrs.

Konark (Konarak) is one of the most vivid architectural treasures of Hindu India and is a World Heritage Site. The Sun Temple was built by King Langula Narasimha Deva in the 13th century, although there may have been an older ninth-century temple on the same site. Built of *khondalite*, it is said to have taken 1200 masons 16 years to complete. It was only in 1901 that the first tentative steps were taken to reclaim the ruins of the temple from the encroaching sand. By that stage not only had the sanctuary or *deul* collapsed but a number of the statues had been removed, many in the 1830s by the Hindu Raja of Khurda, who wanted them to decorate temples he was building in his own fort, 100 km away, and at Puri. The temple no longer stands as a landmark on the seashore, since the land has risen and the sea is now 2 km away. Much of it now lies in ruins, but the porch is still magnificent, and there has been substantial renovation, some of it protective and some replacing fallen stonework and sculptures.

The site

Daily 0600-1800. Foreigners, Rs 250.

The **Surya Temple** is set back 180 m from the road and is reached by a wide laterite path. The sanctuary has no deity for worship, so shoes may be worn. The exception is the small structure in the northeast corner of the site which houses the old *Navagraha* (nine planets) doorway arch, removed from the temple. The path to the temple is lined with beggars, as in major centres of Hindu pilgrimage.

Temple compound The temple presents its most imposing aspect from the steps of the *bhoga mandira* (refectory) at the eastern end of the complex, an isolated hall with pillars raised on a richly decorated platform guarded by a pair of stone lions; some believe this may have been a *nata mandira* (dancing hall). To its west is an open space leading to the porch (*jagamohana*) which rises magnificently to its original height of 39 m. The massive lower section of the original *deul* (sanctuary) was once over 60 m tall.

From the south wall you can see that the temple was built in the form of a war chariot. Twelve pairs of great wheels were sculpted on either side of the temple platform. In front of the eastern entrance a team of seven horses were shown straining to pull the chariot towards the dawn. In Hindu mythology the Sun god traverses the sky in a chariot drawn by seven horses, each representing a day of the week. The 12 pairs of wheels may have symbolized the 12 months of the year, and the eight spokes in each wheel, the divisions of the day into eight *prahars*. Each wheel also functions as a working sundial.

The sculptures The walls of the *bhoga mandir* are covered by carvings, but as Debala Mitra writes, they are of "mediocre quality". The platform gives an excellent view of the whole east front of the main temple with its porch doorway, and the large, remarkably vivid carvings on the terraces of its pyramidal roof, unique in Odishan architecture.

Essential Kornak

Finding your feet

The 35-km drive from Puri to Konark goes through attractive scenery and passes villages with beautifully decorated houses including Chaitan, a stone-carving hamlet. The energetic can cycle to Konark and bring the bike back on the bus.

Site information

Be forewarned that the high volume of tourist traffic at the site inevitably means that levels of 'hassle' increase proportionally. The site itself is very compact and can only be seen on foot. Archaeological Survey and government-approved guides conduct tours of less than an hour. Unofficial guides will press their services, but they are best avoided.

Rayagada

Travelling west from Ganjam, Rayagada is a good stopping place en route to Koraput district, with a number of sleeping options. The **Saoras**, a major tribe, live in the hills around Gunupur in Rayagada district.

Koraput

Koraput, 375 km west of Ganjam, is an attractive town and a useful base for visiting the district's tribal areas. Each Sunday there is a large all-day market which brings Adavasis, as well as townspeople, to trade and sell. The elevated **Jagannath Temple** admits non-Hindus (unlike the temple in Puri) and is an interesting place to lunch (see Restaurants, page 724). Note the painting ceilings inside the main building. Further up the hill, there is a worthwhile **Tribal Museum** ① *daily 1000-2130, donation*, where you can purchase the *Tribes of Koraput* booklet, which is a valuable introduction to the region. Displays include tribal jewellery, weaving, cultivation methods and some illuminating maps of the area. The **Odisha Coffee Planters' Association**, around 20 km from Koraput, is happy to show visitors around the plantation which has fruits and spices as well as coffee.

Jeypore

Jeypore in Koraput District is relatively unspoiled by tourism and surrounded by incredibly beautiful scenery. There is a derelict fort and palace, to which entrance is sadly forbidden, and an interesting market that is bustling until 2200. A good range of accommodation and friendly locals make it an excellent base for a few days. It is possible to organize a tour or private transport from Jeypore, and it's reportedly easier to get permits here to visit Koraput's tribal areas than it is in Bhubaneswar. Most people stay in Jeypore on Wednesdays in order to visit Ankadeli market the next morning (see below); it's a glorious 75-km drive through the rolling hills, past brown rivers and glassy reservoirs. One of the world's oldest terracing systems creeps up the shallow valleys between hills wooded with cashew and mango trees, the undergrowth thick with coffee and black pepper plants. Women working in the paddies add splashes of colour to a landscape already made vibrant by emerald and gold crops against the tangerine earth.

★ Koraput's tribal markets

Ramgiri, 70 km southwest of Jeypore, has a picturesque Tuesday market where Kondh people come to sell fresh vegetables and baskets and to buy salt. **Chatikona** brings Kondh women to the colourful Wednesday market where they sell beedi leaves and large almond-flavoured seeds. **Ankadeli**, 70 km southwest of Jeypore, has a tourist-heavy Thursday market where Bondo women, clad entirely in beads, sell handloom fabric, lengths of coloured beads, metal jewellery (don't be tempted to purchase one of their antique neck-rings) and exquisite woven grass bracelets. The later you stay, the busier it gets. **Nandapur**, 44 km south of Koraput, has a huge Thursday *haat* where trading in livestock, saris, vegetables and the local alcohol takes place on either side of the National Highway.

Kotapad

46 km northwest of Jeypore on N43.
....

The clean area of weavers' houses in Kotapad has large pots of cotton and tussore silk soaking in natural dyes, while skeins hang drying. Weavers are happy to show you work in progress. The Co-op ensures even pricing. As the word gets around that there are visitors in town, weavers will find you to show you their pieces but there is no pressure to buy.

Tourist information

Berhampur

Tourist office
New Bus Stand, 1st floor, T0680-228 0226.

Koraput

Odisha Tourism
Raipur-Visakhapatnam Rd, T06852-250318.
Mon-Sat 1000-1700.
Can help arrange car hire.

Where to stay

Jeypore in particular has some good accommodation. Sleeping and eating options are also available at Laxmipur, Rayagada and Baliguda.

Berhampur

Few visitors stay overnight. However, if arriving late, there are several basic hotels in town.

$ Hotel Radha
Near the railway station, T0680-222 2341.
45 rooms, a mix of a/c and non-a/c, cheap and adequate.

Taptapani

$$-$ Tourist Lodge
Padamari, T06816-255031, http://otdc.in/taptapani.html.
For breaking the journey in a place where there's literally nothing to do but relax, this is ideal. Variety of simple accommodation – 12 rooms, 5 tents, log cabins and a treehouse furnished entirely from woven reeds. The 2 de luxe suites in the main cottage have gigantic wet rooms and, although the Roman baths aren't that appealing, the low-lit barn-like rooms are tastefully so. **Hillview Restaurant** is OK, breakfast included. Irritating 0800 checkout.

Rayagada

$ Hotel Sai International
JK Rd, Rayagada, T06856-225554/5.
A bit out on a limb on the edge of town. Multi-cuisine restaurant is decent, and there's a bar and travel desk that can help with car rental. Non-a/c rooms are clean with hot water by the bucket,

or pay extra for a geyser and a/c. Staff are well meaning but a little confused.

$ Jyoti Mahal
Convent Rd, T06856-223015.
Decent and friendly, 25 reasonably sized rooms with bath, good restaurant, non-a/c rooms are great value.

$ Swagath
New Colony, T06856-222208.
44 clean rooms, good local-style restaurant.

Koraput

$ Athithi Bhavan
Gundicha Chowk, T06852-250610.
At the base of the temple and managed by the Jagannath Temple Trust, non-a/c and a/c rooms with bath have TV and are clean and attractively painted with faux chalk designs on terracotta. The whole building is light and airy and characterful. Temple *thalis* available in the restaurant.

Jeypore

$ Hello Jeypore
East Octroi Check Post, NH43, 2 km from centre, T06854-231127, www.hellojeypore.com.
Comfortable, renovated, well-furnished a/c rooms (and great value $$ suites) some overlooking garden (roadside is noisy). Hot shower, TV, efficient service, restaurant or dinner in the garden, plus a pool. Smoky blue-lit bar gets busy or drinks on the lawn at reasonable prices. It has the best atmosphere in Jeypore, though it's out of the town centre.

$ Madhumati
NKT Rd, T06854-241377, hotelmadhumati@yahoo.com.
30 large rooms, some renovated with a/c, older non-a/c are a bargain, TV, mosquitoes, hot water sporadic, restaurant, noisy bar only has strong beer. Attractive location next to the palace. The best choice in town for backpackers on a budget.

$ Mani Krishna
MG Rd, T06854-231139.
Modern a/c rooms are spacious and nicely fitted-out, fan rooms also available, decent baths, all with balconies some of which see the sunset over the ramshackle roofs of Jeypore. Good management, but lacking any character or space to relax. Restaurant and alcohol via room service.

ON THE ROAD

Monastic university for the Buddhist world

It is assumed that the Gupta emperors were responsible for Nalanda's first monasteries. In the seventh century Hiuen-Tsang spent 12 years, both as a student and a teacher, at Nalanda which once had over 3000 teachers and philosophers. The monks were supported by 200 villages, and a library of nine million manuscripts attracted men from countries as far flung as Java, Sumatra, Korea, Japan and China. Great honour was attached to a Nalanda student and admission was restricted with seven or eight out of 10 applicants failing to gain a place.

I-Tsing, another Chinese scholar, arrived in AD 673 and also kept detailed records, describing the severe lifestyle of the monks. The divisions of the day were measured by a water clock, and the syllabus involved the study of Buddhist and Brahmanical scriptures, logic, meta-physics, medicine and Sanskrit grammar.

The university flourished until 1199 when the Afghan Bhaktiar Khalji sacked it, burning, pillaging and driving the surviving residents into hiding. It was the end of living Buddhism in India until the modern revival.

a special attraction for local tourists. The Kund Market nearby, where buses stop, has shops, stalls and basic rooms.

Gridhrakuta Hill About 5 km south of the *kund* (take a *tonga*, Rs 100 one way) the Gridhrakuta ('Hill of Vultures') was one of the Buddha's favourite places where he delivered many important sermons. He is believed to have converted the Magadhan King Bimbisara here, who had built the old stone road up the hill. The road was used by Hiuen Tsang in the seventh century and still provides good access. Alternatively, you can take the 600-m **cable car** ① *usually 0900-1300, 1500-1700, Rs 40 (good for the views),* to the **Visva Santi Stupa** built by the Japanese and dedicated to world peace. From here it is an easy walk to Gridhrakuta.

Saptaparni Cave The first Buddhist Council was held in the Saptaparni Cave on Vaibhara Hill, six months after the Buddha's death, and his teachings were written down for the first time. On the way to the cave is the large, 7-m-high **tone house**, an extraordinary 'watchtower' built of blocks of stone. On all sides there are small cells for guards which were later used by monks. Allow plenty of time for this walk, it takes about 40 minutes to reach Saptaparni Cave from the drop-off point.

Fort and city walls You can still see parts of the 40-km cyclopean dry stone wall that once enclosed the ancient city and fort. Little survives of the fifth century BC **Ajatasatru Fort**. The outer wall was built with blocks of stone up to 1.5 m long, with smaller boulders in its core. In places it was 4 m high and over 5 m wide. Of the 32 large gates (and 64 small ones) mentioned in ancient texts, only one to the north has survived. Of the inner city wall, which was about 5 km long and roughly pentagonal, only a section to the south remains, with three gaps through which the old roads ran.

Venuvana and the valley Excavations at Venuvana, the bamboo grove where the Buddha spent some time, have revealed a room, some *stupas* and the Karanda Tank. The area is now a deer park with a small zoo. To the south are Jain and Hindu temples. Elsewhere in the valley is the old Jain shrine of **Maniyar Math** (a 6-m-high circular brick structure decorated with stucco figures) and the ruins of Buddha's favourite retreat, called the **Jivakamarvana Monastery** (fourth to third century BC). The large white Nipponzan Myohoji *stupa* has four golden statues of the Buddha representing his birth, enlightenment, preaching and death.

Tip...

For an idea of the layout of sites around Rajgir, visit the Gautam Vihar Tourist Bungalow (a five-minute walk from the bus stand), which has a map outside and a tourist information office.

Where to stay

Nalanda

Nalanda is small, and although accommodation is available in the Chinese monastery, it is recommended to stay in Rajgir.

Rajgir

There are several Jain *dharamshalas* near the bazar, plus a host of unpleasant cheapies by the bus stand (many will not accept foreigners).

$$ Indo Hokke (Royal Residency)
1 km from Kund Market, T06112-255245, www.theroyalresidency.co.in.

The best hotel in town, 44 attractive rooms in an austere brick edifice, with lots of space, wide beds and East Asian influences, primarily catering to Japanese pilgrims, excellent restaurant with Indian, Thai and Japanese food, reserve well ahead in high season, or get significant discounts in low season. Free Wi-Fi. Located 3 km from the centre of town.

$ Siddharth
Near Kund Market, T06112-255616.

Good rooms with bath (Western toilets), TV, Wi-Fi and decent food, about 2 km out of the centre.

$ Tathagat Vihar
Near Viragtan, T06112-225176.

32 rooms that are a standard government offering in that they are simple but clean, with TV, tiled floors and bathrooms. Slightly smaller rooms with Indian toilets are a bit cheaper, pay more for a/c, plus some $$ suites, Indian restaurant. Nice location at the foot of the hills, with a garden.

$ Mahalaxmi
Kund Market, T(0)9431-487646.

Of the cheap options near the bus stand, this is the best choice with clean sheets provided and airy terraces. Not much English spoken.

Restaurants

Rajgir

Thalis in the *dhabas* near the bus stop are not great; for a decent meal you will have to try one of the higher-end hotels.

Transport

Nalanda

Regular buses run from **Patna** to **Bihar Sharif** where you change to **Nalanda**. Cycle-rickshaws and *tongas* run between the bus stop and the site.

Rajgir

Buses run to **Bihar Sharif** (15 km) then change for **Patna**, 3½ hrs total journey time; to **Gaya** 2 hrs.

Port Blair has a handful of sights, but most travellers head straight for the islands, spending just one night here before catching their flight back to the mainland. It has changed in the last 40 years from a small town that received a ship once a month, if the weather permitted, to a quickly developing capital with a population of over one hundred thousand, connected by daily flights. However, it is still very small, and you can easily see the sights in a couple of days. There is a hospital and a few museums, in addition to hotels and a busy bazar. The centre around Aberdeen Bazar is easily walkable though hilly.

Around Aberdeen Bazar

The **Cellular Jail** ① *Tue-Sun 0900-1230, 1330-1615, Rs 10, camera Rs 25, video camera Rs 100, allow 1 hr*, was originally built (1886-1906) by the British to house dangerous criminals and could hold 698 solitary prisoners in small narrow cells. Subsequently, until 1938, it was used to incarcerate Indian freedom fighters. The Japanese used it to hold their prisoners of war during their occupation from 1942 to 1945. Three of the original seven wings, which extended from the central guard tower in a star-shape, survive. The jail is well maintained and the gardens filled with flowers. The **galleries** display photographs and lists of 'convicts' held. There is a 'death house' with gallows and implements used in torture. Entering the cells gives an impression of the conditions within the prison in the early 1900s. There is a **son et lumière show** ① *Mon, Wed and Fri at 1845, Rs 20, 45 mins, in English*, (more sound than light) on prison life under the British.

Near the Watersports Complex and Aberdeen Jetty is an **Aquarium** ① *Tue-Sun (closed on 2nd Sat in the month) 0900-1300 and 1400-1645, Rs 5.*

South of the centre is the **Zonal Anthropological Museum** ① *Fri-Wed 0900-1300, 1330-1630, Rs 10*, which is worth a visit. It has a small but interesting collection of photographs of 'exploratory expeditions' to visit the islanders and their dwellings. Woven baskets, pottery, bows and arrows, and other beautifully crafted artefacts are on display.

West of the centre

The **Marine Museum** ① *opposite Andaman Teal House, Tue-Sun 0830-1200, 1400-1700, Rs 10, camera Rs 20, video camera Rs 40*, has a collection of corals and shells and a display of 350 species of marine life. To the north, the **Mini Zoo** ① *Tue-Sun 0800-1700*, has a small, uninspiring collection in some very old wooden cages with a few specimens of unusual island fauna including a sea crocodile farm. The saltwater crocodile that killed a tourist on Havelock in 2010 has been re-homed here.

On **Chatham Island** is **Chatham Saw Mill** ① *Mon-Sat 0830-1430, entrance Rs 10, allow 1½ hrs, no photography*, the oldest and largest saw mill in Asia, established in 1883. Tours take you through the different processes of turning logs into 'seasoned' planks. For tours, report to the Security Office just outside the main gate. The **Forest Museum** ① *0800-1200, 1430-1700*, near here has unusual local woods including red paduk, satin and marble woods. It shows how different wood is used in the timber industry and methods of lumbering/finishing.

Near Haddo Wharf in the bay, Viper Island is where convicts were interned before the Cellular Jail was built. Boat trips go at 1500 or you can visit as part of a three-island tour (including Ross and Northbay) from Aberdeen jetty daily.

★ Ross Island

Boats leave Thu-Mon 0830, 1030, 1230 and 1400 from Aberdeen jetty, returning 2 hrs later; buy tickets (Rs 75) at the Watersports Centre before the jetty. Entrance to the island is Rs 20.

This extraordinary place was originally developed under the British as the Residence of the Chief Commissioner and administrative headquarters. The **Farzand Ali store** near the jetty has a few interesting old photos of the island as it looked under the British. During the Second World War, it was occupied by the Japanese whose legacy is a complex of concrete bunkers, mostly still intact. Almost all the other buildings on the island are ruins with spotted deer living peacefully among them. In many cases the walls are only still standing because of the climbing trees – the best example being the AC's house at the summit. The remains of the Anglican church (the spire of which has turned into a tree) and the Subalterns' club are evocative, and when wandering off down any path you will find yourself spookily alone. The tiny Ross Restaurant near the jetty is pricey but surprisingly good.

Wandoor and Mahatma Gandhi Marine National Park

An easy bus ride away from Port Blair, about 30 km away, the attractive beach at Wandoor is made more interesting by the vast hulks of skeleton trees that were deposited by the tsunami. The beach gets very busy at weekends, particularly Sundays. The jetty at Wandoor is the starting point for boat trips to **Jolly Buoy** or **Red Skin islands,** which have spectacular snorkelling, in the **Mahatma Gandhi Marine National Park** ① *boats run in high season only and should cost Rs 450 per person (plus Rs 500 permit).* Visit the Directorate of Tourism in Port Blair to buy tickets and get boat schedules.

The park protects some exceptional coral beds and underwater life. Covering an area of 280 sq km, it comprises 15 uninhabited tropical islands dense with forest and with mangrove shores interrupting the aquamarine waters. Several species of exotic birds and plants thrive on the land while underwater lurk turtles, sharks and barracuda. The rich marine life includes angelfish, green parrot, yellow butterfly, black surgeon, blue damsel fish, silver jacks, squirrel, clown fish and sweetlips as well as sea cucumbers, sea anemones, starfish and a variety of shells – cowries, turbots, conches and the rarer giant clam, up to a 1 m wide. There are many beautiful corals – brain, finger, mushroom and antler – their colours derived from the algae that thrive in the living coral. Coral- and shell-collecting is strictly forbidden.

Chiriya Tapu

At the southern tip of South Andaman, Chiriya Tapu is 28 km from Port Blair (an hour by road). Popular for birdwatching, it has excellent beaches with good snorkelling. From the bus stop, which has some tea shops, a track past the **Forest Guest House** leads to the first beach. Continue along the trail through the forest for 20 minutes (several smaller trails are ideal for birdwatching), until you reach a second beach with corals 50 m out; at low tide you can walk a long way. The corals are not so spectacular along the coastline, but there is a large range of fish.

Mount Harriet

Mount Harriet can be visited in a morning or as a whole day trip, but make an early start to avoid the heat. A path through the forest starts by the derelict water viaduct in Hope Town, which joins the surfaced road near the top. Allow 1½ hours to the top. Alternatively, the bus from the jetty stops in Hope Town near the viaduct, or will drop you at the start of the road up the hill with a 4-km walk from here. Near the top of the road lie the ruins of the chief commissioner's bungalow, abandoned in 1942. Taking the forest path on foot avoids the check post and fees. From Mount Harriet, a signpost marks the 2-km **nature trail**, which is easy to follow to **Black Rocks**, the spot where prisoners were pushed to their death.

Listings Port Blair and South Andaman *map p758*

Tourist information

Directorate of Tourism
Opposite Air India office, T03192-232694, www.andamans.gov.in. Mon-Fri 0830-1300, 1400-1430, Sat 0830-1300.
Books boat tours, and has up-to-date ferry schedules. An essential stop if you want to book accommodation in the government hotels around the islands (T03192-232747, bookings taken Mon-Sat 0845-1130 and 1415-1515, 25% deposit required).

Government of India Tourism
2nd floor, 189 Junglighat, Main Rd (VIP Rd), T03192-233006.

Towards Kalipur

A small settlement on a creek where ferries once called, **Kalighat** is now a sleepy village that can be visited as a day trip between Mayabunder and Diglipur. You have to sign in at the police station on arrival; there is no accommodation but shops in the market will look after luggage. You can cross the river by the mangrove footbridge and follow a path up into the forest (good for birdwatching) that leads 3 km to Nischintapur village; it's a lovely jungle path, although the village itself is not especially pretty. A new road has been built to the village, but avoid this, and stick to the jungle route. You can (with some effort; little English is spoken) take a bus or hire a rickshaw to a beautiful beach near Ramnagar Bazar (11 km), from where you will have to walk the last 2 km to **Ramnagar beach**.

North Andaman

Further along the trunk road, **Diglipur** (previously known as Port Cornwallis) has a good market and shops. A Mela is held January/February, which attracts many traders.

Buses between Diglipur and Kalipur stop at **Ariel Bay**, a small fishing village that is handy for getting supplies if you are staying in Kalipur (as almost everyone does). It's the departure point for the line ferry back to Port Blair.

Kalipur and around

Kalipur, a few kilometres south of Aerial Bay, has appealing accommodation and is where most travellers are heading. There is a beach with good snorkelling off its northern side; Saddle Peak gives an impressive backdrop, and two small islands in the bay have even better snorkelling. The sand is volcanic, however, and sandflies are a problem.

Lamiya Bay, 3.5 km south of Kalipur, has a pebble beach which you can walk to (from the bus stop, the road leads straight on for 30 minutes). To the north, there are small bays strewn with large eroded boulders along which it is possible to clamber your way back to Kalipur beach (not recommended for lone women), while the beaches to the south stretch towards Saddle Peak.

Theoretically, permits (Rs 500) for **Saddle Peak National Park** are required; however, the path is clearly signed from Lamiya Bay on to Saddle Peak (8.5 km). Despite the relatively short ascent to the peak (730 m), the initial walk on flat ground for 4.5 km, followed by the steep climb, the thick forest and the heat, mean that you need a whole day for the trek, starting very early in the morning. It is essential to take at least four litres of water per person, plus food, and expect the excursion to take around seven to eight hours.

Smith and Ross islands

From Aerial Bay, you can visit Smith and Ross islands to the north, connected to one another by a white sandbar. You need permission (Rs 500 per person for foreigners) from the Range Officer, opposite the jetty entrance. This permit plus hire of a *dunghy* (Rs 1000-2000 depending on number

Tip...
The easiest way to arrange a trip to idyllic Smith and Ross islands is through Pristine Beach Resort, where you can team up with others and share the costs.

of passengers, 40-minute crossing) make it an expensive day trip, but it is well worth doing. Smith Island, the larger of the two, has sun-loungers and wicker huts providing a bit of shade. Seventeen families live on the island. There is good snorkelling. Take your own food and water.

Narcondam Island

East of North Andaman, this is the most remote island in the group. An extinct craterless volcano, it is covered in luxuriant forest (home to the Narcondam hornbill) and was declared a sanctuary in 1977. It is a birdwatchers' paradise, but permission to visit is very hard to get and only 24-hour stops are allowed.

Listings North Andaman

Where to stay

Towards Kalipur
Most travellers are heading straight to Kalipur, but should you get stuck in Diglipur or want to take the early bus, try:

$ Drua
Diglipur, T03192-272313, T(0)9933-257995.
The 15 rooms are about the best in town, some with private bathrooms, respectable families keep it busy, unhelpful manager.

$ MV Lodge
Diglipur, T03192-320197, T(0)9434-297998.
Surprisingly (judging from the outside) the best of the ultra-cheap options, front rooms (with clean common bath) are bright if basic, and the manager speaks some Eng. Back rooms have private bath. Very close to the bus stop.

$ Aerial Bay
There is a nameless lodge in the bazar in Aerial Bay, with bare rooms sharing a primitive bathroom, Rs 100 per bed, handy if you are catching the early morning bus to Port Blair and don't mind meeting rats in the passageways. Pleasant manager.

Kalipur
$$$-$$ Pristine Beach Resort
Kalipur, T03192-271793, www. andamanpristineresorts.com.
Nestled in the jungle, a short walk from the beach, 21 rooms include stylish chalets and split-level huts with bamboo balconies. Rather posh

multicuisine restaurant, beer usually available. Can provide snorkelling equipment and arrange interesting trips. Most travellers love it here, and end up spending longer than they intended.

$$-$ Turtle Resort
Kalipur, book through Directorate of Tourism in Port Blair T03192-232747/232369.
Newly refurbished rooms, some a/c, cheap dorm, food available only for guests. Very peaceful, on a hillock directly opposite Pristine Beach Resort, the views are magnificent. Essential to book ahead in Port Blair, however.

Restaurants

Towards Kalipur
There are a couple of cheap and very basic *dhabas* in Kalighat, and shops with cold drinks. Diglipur has plenty of little restaurants, plus fresh fruit for sale in the market. A few shops in Aerial Bay sell provisions and there is a small veg market, plus some little *dhabas* near the bus stop.

$ Mohan
On the edge of Aerial Bay towards the jetty (no sign).
The owner speaks English and is helpful, good *thalis*, *dosas*, etc. There's a dodgy bar next door.

Transport

Towards Kalipur
Bus Local From Kalighat: to **Diglipur** regular local service 0500-2000 (45 mins) and faster jeeps; for **Mayabunder** and **Rangat** change at

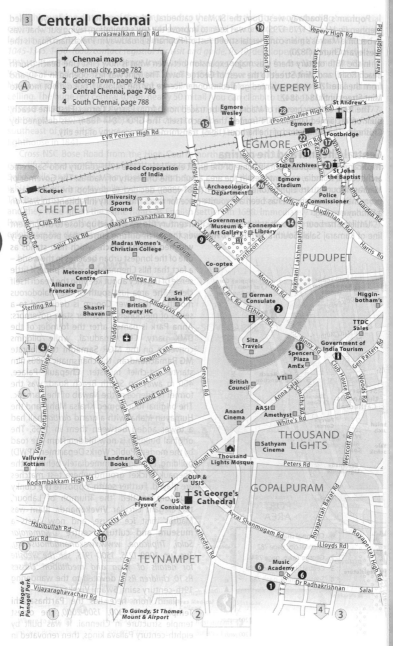

③ Central Chennai

→ **Chennai maps**
1 Chennai city, page 782
2 George Town, page 784
3 Central Chennai, page 786
4 South Chennai, page 788

Purasawalkam High Rd

Vepery High Rd
Ritherdon Rd

Naval Hospital Rd

VEPERY

St Andrew's

Egmore Wesley

Poonamallee High Rd

Egmore

Footbridge

EVR Periyar High Rd

LEGMORE

Police Commissioner's Office Rd

State Archives

Gandhi Irwin Rd

Kennet Lane

Whannels Rd

St John the Baptist

Food Corporation of India

Chetpet

Gengu Reddy Rd

Egmore Stadium

Archaeological Department

Police Commissioner

CHETPET

University Sports Ground

Halls Rd

Casa Major Rd

Government Museum & Art Gallery

Pantheon Rd

Connemara Library

PUDUPET

(Audithanar Rd)

Rukmani Lakshmipathi Rd

Harris Rd

Club Rd

(Mayor Ramanathan Rd)

River Cooum

Co-optex

Monteith Rd

Spur Tank Rd

Madras Women's Christian College

Meteorological Centre

Alliance Francaise

College Rd

C in C Rd (Ethiraj Rd)

German Consulate

Higginbotham's

Sterling Rd

Sri Lanka HC

Anderson Rd

McNichols Rd

Haddows Rd

Shastri Bhavan

British Deputy HC

TTDC Sales

Government of India Tourism

Greams Lane

Sita Travels

Binny Rd

Village Rd

MG Rd

Greams Rd

Spencers Plaza

AmEx

Club House Rd

Gen Patters Rd

Woods Rd

Nungambakkam High Rd

K Nawaz Khan Rd

Rutland Gate

British Council

VTI

Valluvar Kottam High Rd

Anna Salai

AASI

Smiths Rd

Anand Cinema

Amethyst

White's Rd

THOUSAND LIGHTS

Valluvar Kottam

Landmark Books

Mahatma Gandhi Rd

Mount Rd

Sathyam Cinema

Thousand Lights Mosque

Peters Rd

Westcott Rd

Kodambakkam High Rd

OUP & USIS

GOPALPURAM

Habibullah Rd

GN Chetty Rd

Anna Flyover

US Consulate

St George's Cathedral

Avvai Shanmugam Rd

Royapettah Bazar Rd

Royapettah High Rd

Giri Rd

Cathedral Rd

(Lloyds Rd)

TEYNAMPET

Music Academy

Dr Radhakrishnan Salai

Vijayaraghavachari Rd

To T Nagar & Panagal Park

To Guindy, St Thomas Mount & Airport

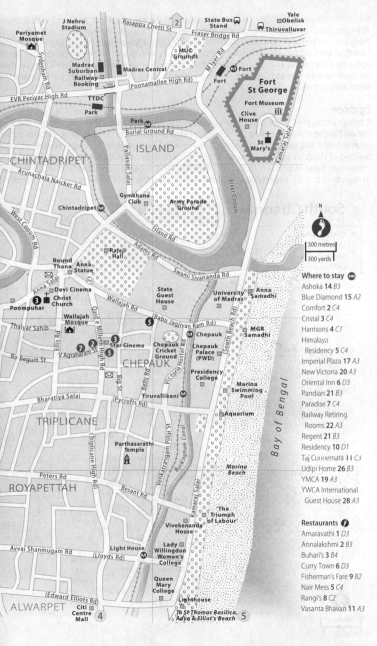

Where to stay 🛏

Ashoka 14 *B3*
Blue Diamond 15 *A2*
Comfort 2 *C4*
Cristal 3 *C4*
Harrisons 4 *C1*
Himalaya
  Residency 5 *C4*
Imperial Plaza 17 *A3*
New Victoria 20 *A3*
Oriental Inn 6 *D3*
Pandian 21 *B3*
Paradise 7 *C4*
Railway Retiring
  Rooms 22 *A3*
Regent 21 *B3*
Residency 10 *D1*
Taj Connemara 11 *C3*
Udipi Home 26 *B3*
YMCA 19 *A3*
YWCA International
  Guest House 28 *A3*

Restaurants 🍴

Amaravathi 1 *D3*
Annalakshmi 2 *B3*
Buhari's 3 *B4*
Curry Town 6 *D3*
Fisherman's Fare 9 *B2*
Nair Mess 5 *C4*
Rangi's 8 *C2*
Vasanta Bhavan 11 *A3*

the 16th by Vijayanagara rulers. Dedicated to Krishna as the royal charioteer, it shows five of Vishnu's 10 incarnations, and is the only temple dedicated to Parthasarathi. Further north in the heart of Triplicane, the **Wallajah Mosque** ① *0600-1200, 1600-2200*, or 'Big Mosque', was built in 1795 by the Nawab of the Carnatic. There are two slender minarets with golden domes on either side. North again, near the Round Thana which marks the beginning of Anna Salai, is the Greek temple-style banqueting hall of the old Government House, now known as **Rajaji Hall** (1802), built to mark the British victory over Tipu Sultan.

Egmore

A bridge across the Cooum at Egmore was opened in 1700, and by the late 18th century, the area around Pantheon Road became the fulcrum of Madras's social and cultural life, a 'place of public entertainment and balls'. Egmore's development, which continued for a century, started with the building of Horden's garden house in 1715. The original pantheon (public assembly rooms) was completely replaced by one of India's National Libraries. The **Connemara Library** (built 1896) traces its roots back to 1662, when residents exchanged a bale of Madras calico for books from London.

4 **South Chennai**

➡ **Chennai maps**
1 Chennai city, page 782
2 George Town, page 784
3 Central Chennai, page 786
4 South Chennai, page 788

Where to stay	Restaurants	Buses
Footprint 2	Benjarong & Teppan 1	Adyar 1
Karpagam International 4	Dakshin 4	Anakaputhur 2
Leela Palace 8	Mylai Karpagambal Mess 2	Dr Ambedkar Bridge 3
Park Hyatt 9	Saravana Bhavan 3	Foreshore Estate 4
Rain Tree 6		Guindy Industrial Estate 5
Shelter 7		Indira Nagar 6

500 metres
500 yards

At the southwest corner of the site stands Irwin's Victoria Memorial Hall, now the **Government Museum and Art Gallery** ① *486 Pantheon Rd, T044-2819 3238, Sat-Thu 0930-1630, closed Fri, foreigners Rs 250, Indians Rs 15, camera Rs 500.* The red-brick rotunda surrounded by an Italianate arcade was described by Tillotson as one of "the proudest expressions of the Indo-Saracenic movement". There are locally excavated Stone and Iron Age implements and striking bronzes including a 11th-century Nataraja from Tiruvengadu, seated images of Siva and Parvati from Kilaiyur, and large figures of Rama, Lakshmana and Sita from Vadak-kuppanaiyur. Buddhist bronzes from Nagapattinam have been assigned to Chola and later periods. The beautiful Ardhanariswara statue here is one of the most prized of all Chola bronzes: Siva in his rare incarnation as a hermaphrodite. There are also good old paintings including Tanjore glass paintings, Rajput and Mughal miniatures and 17th-century Deccan paintings. Contemporary art is displayed at the **Gallery of Modern Art** ① *Government Museum, T044-2819 3035.*

Egmore has other reminders of the Indo-Saracenic period of the 19th and early 20th centuries, the station itself being one of the last to be built, in the 1930s. Northeast of the station is the splendid **St Andrew's Church** ① *Poonamalle High Rd, T044-2561 2608.* With a façade like that of London's St Martin-in-the-Fields, it has a magnificent shallow-domed ceiling. Consecrated in 1821, it has an active congregation.

Mylapore and South Chennai

Mylapore, which is technically older than Chennai and is the seat of city's urban elite, is more charming than the city centre.

The present **Basilica of San Thomas** (1898) ① *24 San Thome High Rd, T044-2498 5455,* surrounded now by the tenement rehousing scheme of a fishermen's colony, is claimed as one of the very few churches to be built over an apostle's tomb. St Thomas Didymus (Doubting Thomas) is believed to have come to India in AD 52. According to one legend, he crossed the peninsula from his landing on the west coast to reach Mylapore (the 'town of peacocks') where he proceeded to live and preach, taking shelter from persecution in Little Mount (see page 790). An alternative story argues King Gondopherenes invited him to Taxila, where he converted the king and his court before moving to South India. Some claim that his body was ultimately buried in the Italian town of Ortona. Marco Polo in his travels in 1293 recorded the chapel on the seashore and a Nestorian monastery on a hill to the west where the apostle was put to death. In 1523, when the Portuguese started to rebuild the church they discovered the tomb containing the relics consisting of a few bones, a lance head and an earthenware pot containing bloodstained earth. The church was replaced by the neo-Gothic structure which has two spires and was granted the status of a basilica in 1956. The relics are kept in the sacristy and can be seen on request. There are 13th-century wall plaques, a modern stained glass window, a 450-year-old Madonna brought from Portugal and a 16th-century stone sundial. The basilica is now

Tamil stats in words

Tamil Nadu's state's wealth and literacy rates are far lower here than in neighbouring Kerala: Tamil Nadu's infant mortality rate is more than double Kerala's and its literacy levels is 20% less. Tamil is deeply agricultural: Keralites, whose higher level of education have made them tire of tending fields, import most of their vegetables from here. The bullock cart continues to square up against the goods truck on the state's roads and housing is often basic: mud thatch with woven banana roofs. Migrant workers in the steel industry, cotton, or road building cross the countryside for jobs, while for those at the higher end of society, the metro lifestyles of Chennai and preferably Bengaluru (Bangalore) beckon.

subject to an ambitious US$164,400 restoration project. To stop the Mangalore tile roof leaking, concrete reparations are being peeled back and replaced with original lime mortar.

Kapaleeswarar Temple ① *0600-1300, 1600-2200*, to the west, is a 16th-century Siva temple with a 40-m *gopuram* (gateway), built after the original was destroyed by the Portuguese in 1566. Sacred to Tamil Shaivites, non-Hindus are only allowed in the outer courtyard, but a visit here still makes for an unmissable prologue or coda to a journey on the Tamil temple trail.

> **Tip...**
> Visit Kapaleeswarar Temple at sunset when it's especially atmospheric, with worshippers gathering for the evening *puja*, conducted amidst ropes of incense smoke and swirling pipe music.

The nearby **Sri Ramakrishna Math** ① *31 Ramakrishna Mutt Rd, www.sriramakrishnamath.org, 0500-1145, 1500-2100*, is one of the city's more appealing quiet corners, with a spectacular multi-faith temple, a quieter memorial to Ramakrishna in a prettily tiled Chettinad-style house, and a bookshop packed with writings by Ramamkrishna and notable devotees, including Swami Vivekananda.

The diminutive Portuguese **Luz Church**, 1547-1582 (the 1516 date in the inscription is probably wrong), is possibly the oldest church in Chennai. Its Tamil name, *Kattu Kovil*, means 'jungle temple'. Legend has it that Portuguese sailors lost at sea in a storm followed a light to the shore, where it disappeared. In gratitude they built the church. There are a number of 19th-century marble plaques to wives of the Madras civil service in the church and an ornate crypt.

To the south of Elphinstone Bridge, the **Theosophical Society** ① *Mon-Fri 0830-1000, 1400-1600, Sat 0830-1000, bus 5 from Central Chennai, ask taxi for Ayappa Temple on San Thome High Rd*, is set in large and beautifully quiet gardens. There are several shrines of different faiths and a Serene Garden of Remembrance for Madame Blavatsky and Colonel Olcott who founded the society in New York in 1875 and moved its headquarters to Madras in 1882. There's a huge 400-year-old banyan past the kitchen garden, a library and a meditation hall. The brackish river attracts waders and seabirds.

Tucked away near Saidapet is the **Little Mount** area. The older of the two churches (1551) with its small vaulted chapel, was built by the Portuguese. The modern circular church was built in 1971. St Thomas is believed to have been martyred and bled to death in AD 52 on the **Great Mount**, though others believe he was accidentally killed by a hunter's arrow. On top of the 90-m-high 'mount' is the **Church of Our Lady of Expectation**. The altar marks the spot where, according to legend, Thomas fell. Some legends suggest that after St Thomas had been martyred on the Little Mount, near Saidapet Bridge, his body was brought back to the beach which had been his home and was buried there.

Tourist information

For city information see also
www.chennaionline.com.

Government of India Tourism
*154 Anna Salai, T044-2846 0285. Mon-Fri 0915-
1745, Sat until 1300.*
Possibly the best organized office.

India Tourism Development Corporation (ITDC)
*29 Ethiraj Salai, T044-2821 1782. Mon-Sat 1000-
1800, Sun closed.*

Tamil Nadu Tourism (TN)
T044-2536 8358, www.tamilnadutourism.org.
Apart from its office in the Tourism Complex (see
below), TN also has offices opposite Central station
(T044-2535 3351), in Egmore (T044-2819 2165),
and at the Domestic and International airports.

Tamil Tourist Development Corporation (TTDC)
T044-2538 9857, www.ttdconline.com.

Tourism Complex
2 Wallajah Rd, near Kalaivanar Arangam.
Most tourist offices are located in this
new complex.

Where to stay

Chennai has seen a major increase of luxury
accommodation options in the last few years,
all pitched at the city's ever-growing business
sector. These include the ITC Grand Chola,
Leela Palace, Hyatt Regency, Park Hyatt, Hilton
and the Westin. There continue to be excellent
mid-range options, including a slew of service
apartments and 1 solitary but wonderful B&B.
Cheap hotels congregate around Central and
Egmore stations and on hectic Triplicane High
Rd, but even here you'll tramp a long way to
find an acceptably clean room for under Rs 400.
For more atmosphere, up your budget a little
and stay near the temple in Mylapore.

Chennai airport

These hotels offer free airport transfers.
Other hotels are 12-15 km from the airport.

$$$$-$$$ Hilton
*JN Salai, near the Kathipara Grade Separator,
T044-2225 5555, www.chennaiguindy.hilton.com.*
Flashy design, great restaurants, popular rooftop
bar, and just 15 mins from the airport.

$$$ Radisson Blu
*531 GST Rd, St Thomas Mount, T044-2231 0101,
www.radissonblu.com.*
Excellent value if rather anonymous rooms just
2 km from the airport. With amenable staff and
a good variety of restaurants and bars, plus free
airport pick-up, this is a good choice if you just
want to flop for a night off the plane.

$$ Mount Manor
*14, GST Rd, St Thomas Mount, T044-2231 1625,
www.mountmanor.com.*
Decent business-style hotel with modern
facilities and free airport transfers, but guests
warn drivers may try to take you to inferior nearby
hotels (eg Mount Heera) for commission.

George Town

Good location for Central Station and State bus
stands. Many cheap hotels are along VOC (Walltax)
Rd, while slightly more salubrious places jostle for
space with cheap restaurants and travel agencies
along EVR Periyar (Poonamallee) High Rd.

$ Railway Retiring Rooms
*Central Station, bookings with confirmed ticket
via www.irctctourism.com.*
Some a/c rooms, dorms.

$ Sonata Park
41 Sydenhams Rd, T044-4215 2272.
Simple but well-looked-after rooms and
excellent-value suites, within walking distance
of the station, but away from the usual budget
hotel belt.

$ Sornam International
*11 Stringer St, T044-2535 3060,
www.hotelsornam.com.*
Pleasant, 50 rooms with TV, balcony and hot
water, and there's a rooftop vegetarian restaurant.

Central Chennai

Many accommodation options are within 1 km
of Anna Salai (Mount Rd). **$$$-$** hotels charge an
extra 19.42% tax.

$$$$-$$$ Taj Connemara
*2 Binny Rd (off Anna Salai), T044-6600 0000,
www.tajhotels.com.*
Supremely comfortable hotel with 148 renovated
rooms that retain splendid art deco features.
Excellent restaurants, bar and good **Giggles**
bookshop – so heavily stocked you can't get
in the door. Heavily booked Dec-Mar.

$$$ Raintree

Taj Connemara (see Where to stay, above).
Romantic outdoor restaurant with good food, atmosphere and ethnic entertainment but cavalier service. Excellent buffet dinner on Sat night.

$$ Annalakshmi

18/3 Rukmani Lakshmipathy Rd, Egmore, T044-2852 5109, www.annalakshmichennai.co.in. Closed Mon.
Wholesome, health-restoring offerings, Southeast Asian specialities (profits to charity, run by volunteers). Recommended.

$$ Buhari's

83 Anna Salai, and EVR Periyar Rd, opposite Central Station.
Good Indian. Dimly lit a/c restaurant, with terrace and unusual decor. Try crab curry, egg *rotis* and Muslim dishes; also in Park Town near Central Station.

$$ Rangi's

Continental Chambers, 142 Nungambakkam High Rd, T044-6519 2344.
Tiny but excellent hole-in-the-wall Chinese bistro.

$$ Southern Spice

Taj Coromandel, 37, MG Rd, Nungambakkam, T044-6600 2827.
Very good South Indian, along with evening dance recitals and freezing a/c.

$ Amaravathi

Corner of TTK Rd and Cathedral (Dr Radhakrishan) Rd, T044-2811 3505, www.shyamshospitality.com.
Great value for spicy Andhra food, but relatively little joy for vegetarians.

$ Nair Mess

22 Mohammed Abdullah 2nd St, Chepauk. Open until 2100.
Fast and furious Kerala 'meals' joint, dishing out rice and *sambhar* in mountain-sized portions.

$ Saravana Bhavan

Branches all over the city including Cathedral Rd opposite Savera Hotel, both railway stations, Spencer Plaza Mall and Pondy Bazar.
Spotlessly clean Chennai-based chain restaurant, serving excellent snacks and 'mini tiffin', fruit juices (try pomegranate) and sweetmeats; all freshly made.

Egmore

$$ Jewel Box

Blue Diamond (see Where to stay, above).
Cool a/c, good for breakfasts, snacks and main courses.

$ Fisherman's Fare

21 Spur Tank Rd.
Outstanding value fish and seafood cooked in Indian, Chinese and Western styles.

$ Mathsya

Udipi Home (see Where to stay, above).
Chennai's night-owl haunt par excellence has been burning the midnight oil (the kitchen stays open until 0200) by government order since the 1960s. It also happens to serve some of the city's best pure veg food; their Mathsya *thali* comes with tamarind and sweetened coconut *dosas* and will keep you going all day. Recommended.

$ Vasanta Bhavan

1st floor, 10 Gandhi Irwin Rd, opposite Egmore station (and branches all over the city).
Very clean and super cheap, excellent food, friendly staff, downstairs bakery does delicious sweets.

South Chennai

$$$ Dakshin

Sheraton Park Hotel, 132 TTK Rd, T044-2499 4101.
High on the list of the best South Indian restaurants in the city, with Kanchipuram silk draped everywhere and a huge range of veg and non-veg choices. Book ahead.

$$ Benjarong & Teppan

146 TTK Rd, Alwarpet, T044-2432 2640.
2 great restaurants in the same building: one an upscale Thai affair, doing very passable renditions of *tom kha* and *pad thai* (and plenty of vegetarian options) amid a collection of Buddhas in glass cases; the other a smart new teppanyaki restaurant with live cooking.

$ Mylai Karpagambal Mess

20 East Mada St, Mylapore.
If you can handle the all-round dinginess, this place serves superb, simple food – *vada, dosas* and a sweet *pongal* to die for – to an avid Tamil Brahmin crowd.

$ Saravana Bhavan

North of the temple tank, Mylapore.
Similarly excellent food in a more salubrious, less interesting environment.

Bars and clubs

Central Chennai

Alcohol can be purchased only through government-run TASMAC shops, which are generally unsavoury locations with a street-bar on the side and not recommended for women travellers. Instead go to TASMAC a/c shops located at Alsa Mall in Egmore or at Parsn Complex near Park Hotel Chennai.

10 Downing
Kences Inn, BN Rd, T Nagar, T044-4354 6565.
Noisy and popular bolthole, with live jazz and classic rock bands, but not a place for a quiet conversation.

365 AS
Hyatt Regency, 365 Anna Salai, Teynampet, T044-6100 1234.
Want to meet the city's expats? Head out to this popular centrally located lounge bar on the weekend. Lots of intimate seating options and excellent, well-priced drinks and snacks.

Bike and Barrel
Residency Towers, Sri Thyagaraya Rd, T044-2815 6363.
Split-level restaurant and bar, playing rock, trance and house.

Distil Bar
Taj Connemara (see Where to stay, above).
A large, bright bar, offering huge tankards of beer, great snacks and a massive TV.

Dublin
Sheraton Park Hotel & Towers, T044-24994101.
A notionally Irish pub by day, at night Dublin turns into a pulsating nightclub, pumping out the tunes until the early hours.

Flying Elephant
Park Hyatt, see Where to stay, above.
Chennai's hottest restaurant, built on 3 floors with central sunken bar. Converts into a nightclub from Thu-Sat after 2300. Move over Leather Bar (Park Hotel), Chennai's young and hip congregate at this watering hole now. Reservations needed.

Havana
Rain Tree (see Where to stay, above).
Lounge bar with dance floor, hosts various theme nights.

Leather Bar
The Park Hotel, 601 Nungambakkam High Rd, T044-4267 6000.
Not as kinky as the name suggests, but this dark womb of a bar, with black leather floors and olive suede walls, is still one of the city's sexiest.

Pasha
The Park Hotel (see Leather Bar, above).
The city's sleekest dance club.

The Tapas Bar
Oriental Inn (see Where to stay, above).
Cocktails and Indian-style Spanish classics are the order of the day at this buzzing tapas bar, where you can lounge on leather banquettes with the trendies of Chennai.

Entertainment

Although Chennai is revered for its strong cultural roots, much of it is difficult for tourists to access. Events are often publicized only after they have passed. Check the free *Cityinfo* guide, published fortnightly, and www.explocity.com, for upcoming events.

Cinemas
Cinemas showing foreign (usually English-language) films are mostly in the centre of town on Anna Salai.
Escape, *Express Avenue Mall, Whites Rd.* Sathyam's swanky new multiplex located on the top-floor of Chennai's new city-centre mall. 30 mins from both Central and Egmore stations, the food-court and restaurants make this a great place to while away an afternoon with food and a movie before your train.
Sathyam, *8 Thiru-vi-ka Rd, Royapettah, T044-4392 0200.* Chennai's first multiplex is also India's highest grossing cinema, with 6 screens and a mix of new-release Hollywood, Bollywood and Tamil films. Worth visiting if only to overload on chocolate and caffeine at Michael Besse's **Ecstasy** bakery.

Music, dance and art galleries
Sabhas are membership societies that offer cultural programmes 4 times a month to their members, but occasionally tickets are available at the door.
Chennai Music Academy, *TTK Rd, T044-2811 2231, www.musicacademymadras.in.* The scene of many performances of Indian music, dance and theatre, not only during the prestigious 3-week music festival from mid-Dec but right through the year.

Sports clubs and associations

Most clubs are members-only domains, though temporary membership may be available for sports facilities. The **Chennai Cricket Club** in Chepauk and the **Gymkhana Club** at the racecourse on Anna Salai both offer tennis, swimming, cricket, billiards, library and a bar; definitely worth experiencing if you can make friends with a member.

Chennai Riders' Club, *Race View, Race Course, 136 Velachery Rd, T080224-54645, www. madrasridingschool.com*. Riding (including lessons) throughout the year except Jun.

Tamil Nadu Sailing Association, *57 Arathoon Rd, Royapuram, T044-2538 2253*. Open to the public.

Wildertrails Adventure Club, *T044-2644 2729*. Camping and hiking trips.

Swimming

Pools open to the public are at Marina Beach and the YMCA pool at Saidapet. Sea bathing is safe at Elliot's Beach, though no longer attractive.

Tennis

Clubs allowing members' guests and temporary members to use courts are: **Chennai Club, Gymkhana Club, Cricket Club, Cosmopolitan Club, Presidency Club** and **Lady Willingdon Club**. YMCA at Saidapet also has courts.

Tours and tour operators

Cox & Kings, *10 Karuna Corner, Spur Tank Rd, T044-2820 9500, www.coxandkings.com*.

Milesworth Holidays, *RM Towers, 108 Chamiers Rd, T044-2433 8664, www.milesworth.com*. Tamil Nadu specialists, but cover all of India. The favourite among Chennai's expats.

Surya, *1st floor, Spencer's Plaza, Anna Salai, T044-2849 3934, www.suryatravels.com*. Very efficient, friendly, personal service.

Tamil Nadu Tourism, *T1800-4253 1111*, has sales counters at: Tourism Complex, 2 Wallajah Rd, *T044-2536 8358*; 4 EVR Periyar High Rd (opposite Central Station), and Express Bus Stand near High Ct compound (open 0600-2100). You can book the some tours online, www.ttdconline.com. The following tours are on deluxe a/c coaches and accompanied by a guide.

City sightseeing half-day, daily 1330-1830. Fort St George, Government Museum (closed Fri), Valluvar Kottam, Snake Park, Kapaleeswarar Temple, Elliot's Beach, Marina Beach. Rs 375 a/c.

Mahabalipuram and Kanchipuram, open 0630-1900, Rs 1025. Tirupati, 0500-2100, Rs 1375-1525.

Walking tours

Detours, *T(0)9000-850505, www.detoursindia.com*. Off-beat walking and car-based thematic city experiences covering British history, religions and spirituality, food and bazars. Exclusive and guided by local experts.

Story Trails, *T(0)9940-040215, www.storytrails.in*. Themed walking tours that allow the city to unfold through its stories, including Spice Trail, Mystic Trail and Bazar Trail.

Transport

Air

The **Arignar Anna International Airport**, T044-2234 6013, and the **Kamaraj Domestic Airport**, T044-2256 0501, are on one site at Trisulam in Meenambakkam, 12 km south of the centre. A new Metro line linking the airport to central Chennai is scheduled to open in late 2015, with a station connected by walkway directly to the airport. Until it opens, the easiest way into town is by taxi. Both terminals have booths selling tickets for prepaid taxis, a good way to avoid taxi overcharging. Look for the longest queue – this will be for the cheaper yellow taxis. To **Chennai Central** or **Egmore** costs Rs 600-800, 45-60 mins; to **Mahabalipuram**, Rs 1800-2400. Buses to centre Rs 75 (day), Rs 100 (night). Auto-rickshaws to Chennai Central charge around Rs 200, but it's a long trip through choking fumes and you have to walk to the main road to catch one. **Suburban railway is** the cheapest way into town, from Trisulam suburban line station to Egmore and Fort, but trains are often packed

Domestic Flights to **Bengaluru (Bangalore), Bhubaneswar, Coimbatore, Delhi, Goa, Hyderabad, Kochi, Kolkata, Madurai**, via **Tiruchirappalli; Mumbai, Port Blair** and **Pune, Puttaparthy, Thiruvananthapuram, Visakhapatnam**.

International Connections with: **Abu Dhabi, Bangkok, Colombo, Doha, Dubai, Frankfurt, Hong Kong, Kuala Lumpur, Kuwait, London, Male, Mauritius, Muscat, Paris, Reunion** and **Singapore**.

Bus

Local The cheap and convenient local bus service is not overcrowded and offers a realistic alternative to auto-rickshaws and taxis outside the rush hour (0800-1000, 1700-1900). Make sure you know route numbers as most bus signs are in Tamil (timetables from major bookshops).

Metropolitan Transport Corp (MTC), www.mtcbus.org, runs an excellent network of buses from 0500-2300 and a skeleton service through the night. 'M' service on minibuses is good for the route between Central and Egmore stations and journeys to the suburban railway stations. The 'V' service operates fast buses with fewer stops and has a yellow board with the route number and LSS (Limited Stop Service).

Long-distance The fast new highways leading north and south of Chennai and the East Coast Rd (ECR) to Puducherry have helped to cut journey times. Fast long-distance a/c buses run on main routes.

Chennai's long distance bus station, officially titled the **Chennai Mofussil Bus Terminus (CMBT)** but known to rickshaw drivers as Koyambedu, is a particular source of civic pride: claimed to be Asia's biggest, it boasts 30 arrival and 150 departure terminals. Almost all long-distance services start and terminate here. Enquiries, T044-2479 4705.

Tamil Nadu Govt Express, T044-2534 1835, offers good connections within the whole region and the service is efficient and inexpensive. Best to take a/c coaches or super deluxe a/c. Bookings 0700-2100. Other state and private companies cover the region but you may wish to avoid their video coaches which make listening, if not viewing, compulsory as there are no headphones.

Beware of children who 'help' you to find your bus in the expectation of a tip; they may not have a clue. There have also been reports of men in company uniforms selling tickets, which turn out to be invalid; it is best to buy on the bus. The listings given are for route number, distance. **Coimbatore** *No 460*, 500 km; **Chidambaram** and **Nagapattinam** *326*; **Kanchipuram** *76B*; **Kanniyakumari** *282 and 284*, 700 km; **Kumbakonam** *303H*, 289 km, 6½ hrs; **Madurai** *137*, 447 km, 10 hrs; **Mahabalipuram** *109*, Rs 19, 1½ hrs (*108B* goes via Meenambakkam airport, 2½ hrs) can be very crowded; **Nagercoil** *198*, 682 km, 14 hrs; **Ooty** *468*, 565 km, 13 hrs; **Puducherry** *803*, 106 km, 3 hrs; **Thanjavur** *323*, 320 km, 8 hrs; Tiruchirappalli *123*, 320 km and Route *124*, 7 hrs; **Tiruvannamalai** 180 km, 5 hrs; **Yercaud** *434*, 360 km, 8 hrs; **Bengaluru (Bangalore)** via **Vellore** and **Krishnagiri** *831*, 360 km, 8 hrs; **Bengaluru** (via **Kolar**) 350 km, 7½ hrs; **Tirupati** via **Kalahasti** *802*, 150 km, 3½ hrs.

Car
A/c or ordinary cars with drivers are good value and convenient for sightseeing, especially for short journeys out of the city when shared between 3 and 5 people.

Ganesh Travels, 35/1 Police Commissioner Office Rd, T044 2319 0202, www.ganeshtravels.net. **Milesworth**, 108 Chamiers Rd, Alwarpet, T044-2433 8664, vacations@milesworth.com. Efficient and friendly company, good touring cars and English speaking drivers; **TTDC**, T044-2538 3333.

Ferry
Passenger ships leave every 7-10 days to the **Andaman** and **Nicobar Islands**, taking 3 days, and as visas are now issued on arrival at Port Blair the process of getting a ticket is slightly less complicated than it used to be. Ships are operated by the **Shipping Corporation of India**, Jawahar Building, Rajaji Salai, T044-2522 0841, www.shipindia.com. Check sailing schedules at www.and.nic.in, then take 4-5 passport photos, your passport plus 3 copies of the photo and visa pages, and queue up for a ticket, 1000-1300. Women have an advantage when queuing.

Metro
Chennai's new Metro began operating in Jun 2015, with trains running on a stretch from Alandur (north of the airport) to Koyambedu via the CMBT bus terminal. A 2nd line, connecting the airport to Washermanpet (near George Town), was scheduled to open by late 2015.

Motorbike hire or purchase
Southern Motors, 995A Koleth Court, 11th Main Rd, 2nd Av, Anna Nagar, T044-2616 4666, T044-2499 0784, is a good modern garage with efficient service. The **YWCA**, EVR Periyar Rd, is a good hotel for bikers and has a big shaded garden to park bikes securely.

MRTS
The **Mass Rapid Transit System** (the old raised, above-ground railway) runs from Chennai Beach south to Velacheri in the IT belt, passing through Chepauk, Triplicane (Thiruvallikeni) and Mylapore on the way. Station facilities are minimal, and there's little information about when the next train might depart.

Rickshaws
Auto-rickshaws are the most common form of transport around the city. A recent court ruling has forced rickshaw drivers, in defiance of the age-old Chennai tradition of radical price gouging, to charge by the meter. Look out for the **Namma Auto-rickshaw** fleet (reliable and safe), or check out **Autoraja.com** for pre-booked rickshaws. Minimum charge is Rs 25 for up to

1.8 km, additional km Rs 12; waiting charges Rs 3.5 per 5 mins; travel between 2300-0500 costs 50% extra. As elsewhere, drivers get kickbacks from emporium owners to deliver you to their shops, so be suspicious of unsolicited offers to take you anywhere for a few rupees.

Taxi

Taxis are better than rickshaws for extended trips and sightseeing. Many companies offer 'packages' of fixed times and distances – Rs 700 for 40 km and 4 hrs, Rs 1200 for 80 km and 8 hrs, plus Rs 100 for each extra hour. Expect to pay more for a/c. There are a number of companies, all charging similar rates. **Bharati Call Taxi**, T044-3000 2000. **Chennai Call Taxi**, T044-3000 3000. **Fast Track**, T044-6000 6000, is reliable.

Train

Suburban railway Inexpensive and handy, but very crowded at peak times. Stops between Beach Railway Station and Tambaram (every 5 mins in rush hour) include Fort, Park, Egmore, Chetpet, Nungambakkam, Kodambakkam, Mambalam, Saidapet, Guindy, St Thomas Mt. Also serves suburbs of Perambur and Villivakkam. Convenient stop at Trisulam for the airports, 500-m walk from the terminals.

Long distance Chennai has 2 main stations **Chennai Central (MC)** for broad-gauge trains to all parts of India and **Egmore (ME)** for trains to the south; a few significant trains also start from Tambaram, in the southern suburbs. Egmore and Central are linked by minibus; taxis take 5 mins. There is a reservations counter at the domestic airport, as well as at the stations. **Chennai Central** enquiries, T131, reservations, T132, arrivals and departures, T133, then dial train no. Advance Reservations Centre, Mon-Sat 0800-1400, 1415-2000, Sun 0800-1400, is in a separate building in front of the suburban station, to the left of the main station. Indrail Passes and booking facilities for foreigners and NRIs on the 1st floor. From Chennai Central to **Coimbatore** *Kovai Exp 12675*, 0615, 7¾ hrs; *West Coast Exp 16627*, 1100, 8¾ hrs; *Cheran Exp 12673*, 2145, 8½ hrs. **Kochi (Cochin)** *Chennai-Alleppey Exp 16041*, 1945, 13¾ hrs; *Guwahati Cochin Exp 15624*, 1210, Fri, 14¾ hrs. **Mettupalayam** *Nilgiri Exp 16605*, 2015, 10 hrs.

Egmore enquiry, T135, arrivals and departures, T134. No counter for foreign tourist quota bookings. To **Kanniyakumari** *Chennai-Kanniyakumari Exp 16121*, 1900, 15 hrs. **Madurai** *Chennai-Kanniyakumari Exp 16121*, 1815, 10 hrs; *Vaigai Exp 12635*, 1225, 8 hrs; *Pandyan Exp 16717*, 2100, 9½ hrs via Kodai Rd (this connects with the bus service at **Kodaikanal** arriving at midday). **Tiruchirappalli** *Vaigai Exp 12635*, 1225, 5½ hrs; *Pallavan Exp 12606*, 1530, 5½ hrs.

Around Chennai

South of the capital, easily reached in a day but worthy of at least a weekend, lies Mahabalipuram, an intriguing little beachside town given over entirely to sculpture, both ancient and modern. Part open-air museum and part contemporary workshop, its seventh-century bas-reliefs are some of the world's largest and most intricate, telling the Indian flood myth, the *Descent of the Ganga*. Within earshot of the old shore temples you can find modern-day masons industriously piling their shacks and yards high with freshly and beautifully chiselled deities.

Inland from Chennai, the former Pallava capital of Kanchipuram is one of India's seven sacred cities, chock-full of temples and overflowing with silks spun straight from the loom.

Chennai to Mahabalipuram   *Colour map 7, A5/B6.*
an artist community, cultural village and crocodile breeding centre

If you're travelling from Chennai, there are three good stop-off points before Mahabalipuram.

Cholamandal Artists' Village   *Colour map 7, B6.*
East Coast Rd, Enjumpakkam, T044-2449 0092, 0900-1900, free.

The first of three good stop offs, travelling from Chennai to Mahabalipuram, is 19 km from Chennai. The artists' community, started in 1969, gives living, working and exhibition space for artists creating sculptures, pottery and batik. They sometimes hold dance performances in a small open-air theatre, and there are some simple cottages for hire if you want to stick around for a workshop or residency.

Dakshinchitra
East Coast Rd, T044-2747 2603, www.dakshinachitra.net, Wed-Mon 1000-1830, Rs 200, Indians Rs 75.

The second stop is the **Madras Craft Foundation**'s model village, which showcases the rich cultural heritage of the four southern states against a backdrop of 17 authentic buildings, each relocated piece by piece from their original homes around South India. There's a regular programme of folk performances, including puppet shows, plus a newly opened art gallery with an excellent collection of tribal art from across India, a small textile museum, a restaurant and a fortune-telling parrot.

Madras Crocodile Bank
Tue-Sun 0830-1730, Rs 35, camera Rs 20, video Rs 100.

Finally, 14 km before Mahabalipuram, is Romulus Whitaker's captive breeding centre for Indian crocodiles. Established by the Americanborn herpetologist (known as the Snake Man of India), you can now see several rare species from India and beyond, including Siamese and African dwarf crocodiles, basking around the open pools. There's a small extra charge to visit the snake venom bank, where snakes donate small quantities of poison for use in antivenins before being released back to the wild.

an ancient Hindu city full of temples and silk shops

What Darjeeling is to tea, and Cheddar is to cheese, so Kanchipuram (population 153,000) is to silk. One of Hinduism's seven most sacred cities, 'the Golden City of a Thousand Temples' dates from the early Cholas in the second century. The main temple complexes are very spacious and only a few of the scattered 70 or so can be seen in a day's visit. The town itself is relatively quiet except for crowds of pilgrims.

Kanchipuram

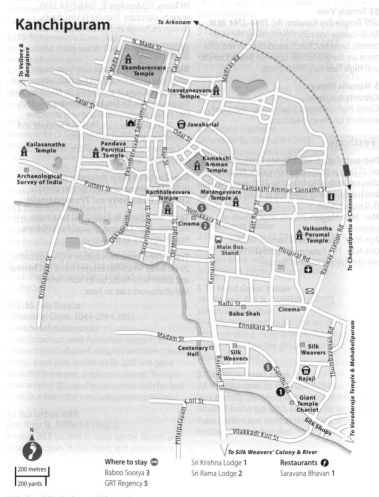

To Arkonam

To Vellore & Bangalore

N. Mada St

W. Mada St

Car St

Madras Rd

Ekambaresvara Temple

Iravatanesvara Temple

Salai St

Jawaharlal

Odai St

Kailasanatha Temple

Pandava Perumal Temple

Ekambaresvara Sannathi St

Raja St

Kamakshi Amman Temple

Archaeological Survey of India

Putteri St

Kachhaleesvara Temple

Matangesvara Temple

Kamakshi Amman Sannathi St

Kamaraj St

Nellukkara St

Cinema 2

Krishnamurti St

Olakapiranthar St

Nalasingarayar St

Main Bus Stand

East Raja St

Vaikuntha Perumal Temple

To Chengalpattu & Chennai

Hospital Rd

Railway Station Rd

Nadu St

Babu Shah

Cinema

Ennakara St

Madam St

Centenary Hall

Silk Weavers

Rajampet St

Gandhi Rd

Silk Weavers

Rajaji

Thumbavanan Rd

To Varadaraja Temple & Mahabalipuram

Koll St

Giant Temple Chariot

Silk Shops

Pillaipalayam

Vilakkadi Koll St

To Silk Weavers' Colony & River

N

200 metres
200 yards

Where to stay 🛏
Baboo Soorya 3
GRT Regency 5

Sri Krishna Lodge 1
Sri Rama Lodge 2

Restaurants 🍴
Saravana Bhavan 1

BACKGROUND

Kanchipuram

The Pallavas of Kanchi came to power in the fourth century AD and were dominant from AD 550 to 869. Possibly of northern origin, under their control Mahabalipuram became an important port in the seventh century. Buddhism is believed to have reached the Kanchipuram area in the third century BC. Successive dynasties made it their capital and built over 100 temples, the first as early as the fourth century. As well as being a pilgrimage site, it was a centre of learning, culture and philosophy. Sankaracharya and the Buddhist monk Bodhidharma lived and worked here.

Sights

Ekambaresvara Temple ① *Small entry fee, only Hindus are allowed into the inner sanctuary.* The temple has five enclosures and a 'Thousand-pillared Hall' (if you're pedantically inclined, the number is actually 540). Dedicated to Siva in his ascetic form it was begun by the Pallavas and developed by the Cholas. In the early 16th century the Vijayanagara king Krishna Deva Raya built the high stone wall which surrounds the temple and the 59-m-tall *rajagopuram* (main tower) on which are sculpted several figures of him and his consort.

The main sanctuary has a *lingam* made of earth (Siva as one of the elements) and the story of its origin is told on a carved panel. The teasing Parvati is believed to have unthinkingly covered her husband Siva's eyes for a moment with her hands which resulted in the earth being enveloped in darkness for years. The enraged Siva ordered Parvati to do severe penance during which time she worshipped her husband in the form of an earth *lingam* which she created. When Siva sent a flood to test her, she clung to the *lingam* with her hands until the waters subsided. Some believe they can see her fingerprints on the *lingam* here. On 18 April each year the sun's rays enter the sanctum through a small square hole.

Kailasanatha Built in the early seventh century, this is considered to be the most beautiful of the town's temples. It was built of sandstone by the Pallava king Narasimha Varman II with the front completed by his son Mahendra III. The outer structure has a dividing wall with a shrine and doorways, separating a large courtyard from a smaller one. The unusual enclosure wall has 58 small raised shrines with a *Nandi* in most pavilions and some frescoes have survived. The seven shrines in the temple complex have images of different Siva forms. The intricately carved panels on the walls depict legends about Siva with accompanying text in ancient Grantha script. It has been extensively restored. The festival **Mahashivaratri** is held here in February.

Vaikuntha Perumal Eighth century and dedicated to Vishnu, this temple was built by the Pallava king Nandivarman just after the Kailasanatha and illustrates the progress of Dravidian temple architecture. The sanctuary is separated from the *mandapa* by an open space. The cloisters are built from rows of lion pillars. Panels of bas relief accompanied by lines in old Tamil trace the history of the wars between the Pallavas and Chalukyas. There is an unusual *vimana* (tower) with shrines in three tiers with figures of Vishnu in each.

Varadaraja (Devarajasvami) ① *0630-1200, 1530-2000, Rs 5, camera Rs 5, video Rs 100.* Built by the Vijayanagara kings in the 16th century, 3 km southeast of town, it has superb sculpture in its marriage hall (with 96 pillars). Figures on horseback wear half North Indian/half South Indian costumes. Note the rings at each corner and the massive flexible chain supposedly carved out of one piece of granite, although it is no longer in one piece. The main shrine is on an elephant-shaped rock, Hastagiri. The **Float Festival** is in February and November, **Brahmotsavam** in May and **Garuda Sevai** in June.

Chengalpattu (Chingleput) The fort here was built by the Vijayanagar king Thimmu Raya after his defeat at the Battle of Talikotta in 1565.

> **Tip...**
> Temples are usually open from 0600 and closed 1200-1600, but very few allow non-Hindus into the inner sanctum. Have change ready for 'donations' to each temple you visit.

Puducherry
& Auroville

Pretty little Puducherry (still widely known by its old name of Pondicherry) has all the lazy charm of a former French colony: its stately whitewashed 18th-century homes froth with bright pink bougainvillea and its kitchens still smack gloriously of Gaul – excellent French breads, hard cheese and ratatouilles that run with olive oil, accompanied by real French wines. The primly residential French quarter contrasts wonderfully with the dog-eared heritage houses of the Tamil districts, whose streets were built to tilt towards Mecca, while the scores of pristine grey mansions indicate the offices of the Sri Aurobindo Ashram, headquarters of one of India's liveliest spiritual schools of thought.

Up the road is the 1960s Westernized branch of Sri Aurobindo's legacy, Auroville, the 'City of Dawn', which was conceived as "a place where human beings could live freely as citizens obeying one single authority, that of the supreme Truth". This is the industrious fulcrum of people seeking an alternative lifestyle – a place of spirulina, incense and white cotton weeds – and while many tourists visit Auroville on a rushed day trip from Puducherry, if you're of a meditative mindset and can forgo your fix of Gallic good cheer, it can be far more interesting to do it the other way round.

a tiny pocket of colonial France on the Tamil coast

Puducherry (244,400) is the archetypal ambling town: cleaved in two with the French quarter along the beach, with pretty high-ceilinged wood-slatted residential houses that have walled gardens and bougainvillea, and with the markets, mess, businesses and 'talking streets' of the Tamil ('black') town to its west.

While the French area, with 300 heritage buildings, is well maintained (the majority owned by the ashram), the Tamil area, despite its 1000 homes now classified as heritage, is in places dangerously dilapidated. The European Commission has funded the restoration of Calve Subraya Chettiar (Vysial) street (between Mission and Gandhi streets), while Muslim domestic architecture is clearly visible in the streets of Kazy, Mulla and Tippu Sultan, in the southern part of the Tamil quarter.

Many people come to Puducherry to visit the campus-like ashram of **Sri Aurobindo Ghosh** and his chief disciple Mirra Alfassa ('The Mother'). Ghosh was an early 20th-century Bengali nationalist and philosopher who struggled for freedom from British colonial power and wrote prodigiously on a huge variety of subjects, particularly Integral Yoga and education. In his aim to create an ashram utopia he found a lifelong *compadre* in the charismatic Frenchwoman Alfassa, who continued as his spiritual successor after his death in 1950. It was Alfassa who pushed into practice Sri Aurobindo's ideas on integral schooling, the aim of which is to develop all aspects of the student's being – "mind, life, body, soul and spirit". In the ashram school, class sizes are limited to eight students, and both pupils and teachers enjoy an extraordinary freedom to alter classes according to individual needs. Alfassa died in 1973 at the age of 93. Both Sri Aurobindo and Alfassa live on as icons, their images gazing down from the walls of almost every building in Puducherry.

Sights

The **French Quarter**, which extends from the seafront promenade inland to the canal, contains most of Puducherry's sights, and wandering the quiet streets, stopping into antique shops and colonial mansions, is a pleasure in itself.

The **Sri Aurobindo Ashram** ① *rue de la Marine, 0800-1200, 1400-1800, free, meditation Mon-Wed, Fri 1925-1950,* has its main centre in rue la Marine. Painted in neat grey and white like most of the ashram's buildings, it contains the flower-bedecked marble Samadhi (resting place and memorial) of both Sri Aurobindo and the Mother.

The **French Institute** ① *rue St Louis,* was set up in 1955 for the study of Indian culture and the 'Scientific and Technical Section' for ecological studies. There's a French and English library looking over the sea, and the colonial building is an architectural treat in its own right.

Puducherry Museum ① *next to the library, rue St Louis, Tue-Sun 0940-1300 and 1400-1720, closed public holidays, free,* has a good sculpture gallery and an archaeological section with finds discovered at the Roman settlement at Arikamedu. The French gallery charts the history of the colony and includes Dupleix's four-poster bed.

Essential Puducherry

Finding your feet

Buses take under four hours from Chennai on the East Coast Road. The well-organized bus stand is just west of the town, within walking distance, or a short auto-ride from the centre (expect the usual hassle from rickshaw-wallahs). The train station, on a branch line from Villupuram which has trains to major destinations, is a few minutes' walk south of the centre.

Getting around

Puducherry is lovely to explore on foot, but hiring a bike or moped will give you the freedom to venture further along the coast. See Transport, page 819.

Useful contacts

Foreigners' Regional Registration Office, Goubert Salai.

Puducherry

To 19, Serenity Beach,
Auroville & Chennai

Cinema

Sangara Dass St

Thiyagaraja St
Sri Sakthi
Sri Varadaraja Temple Travels
Bharatidasan Museum
Sri Vedapuriswarar Temple Aroma Clinic
Muttu Mariamman

Eswaran Dharmaraja Koil St

Kamatchi Amman Koil St

Sri Aurobindo St (Arvindar)

Calve Supraya Chettiar St

Caltisvaran Koil St

Vysial St

Amballattadayar Madam St

Bike Hire

Jail Chemist Bazar
Poompuhar Jawaharlal Nehru St
Raju Moped Thiaga St Chemist 5

Ananda Rangapillai St Grand Bazar

Vellaja St Maison Ananda Rangapillai

Nidarajapayer St (Big Brahmin St)

Focus Books

St Theresa St Cathedral

Chinna Vaikal St Saint Theresa St

Savarirayalu St (Small Brahmin St) Chinna Vaikal St

La Porte St

Rue Montorsier

(Anna Salai)

Candappa St Coffee.com

Kamban Kalaiarargam Lal Bahadur Shastri St

Kailash French Bookshop Ignas Mestry St (Rue Bussy)

City Bus Stand Yanam Vangadasala Pillar St 8

Botanical Gardens Thillai Mestry St

Jeevandam St 7 Kuthpa Mosque

VOC St 12

Badar Sahib St

Eglise de Sacre Coeur de Jesus Rajasingh St

Ramaraja St Water Tower

Subbaiyah Salai

SV Patel Salai
Bharati St
Mahatma Gandhi Rd
Anna Salai (West Boulevard)
To Tindivanam & Chennai
To Botanical Gardens & Main Bus Stand
Chinna Subraya Billai St
Cathedral St Mission St
Mahatma Gandhi Rd
Ellaman Koil St
Mulla St
Chanda Sahib St
Carivar St

Where to stay
Aurodhan 5 A5
De l'Orient 3 E4
De Pondicherry
and Le Club 4 F4
Executive Inn 6 B4
Family Guest House 7 E2
International Guest
House 9 C4
Maison Perumal 1 A3
Mother Guest
House 10 C4
Mother Sea View
Residency 15 F5
Palais de Mahe 2 E5
Park Guest House 11 F5
Ram Guest House 12 E2
Sea Side Guest
House 13 C5
Villa Helena 16 E4
Youth Hostel 19 A2

Restaurants
Ananda Bhavan 7 C4
Ashram Dining Hall 1 C4
Baker Street 8 E3
Café des Arts 16 D5
Hot Breads 4 C4
Indian Coffee House 5 C3
La Terrasse 6 F4
Le Café 9 D5
Le Club 7 F4
Lighthouse 10 D5
Rendezvous 13 E4
Satsanga 14 F4

Bars & clubs
Asian House 11 F4
Le Space 12 E4
Seagulls 15 F5

N

100 metres
100 yards

$$ Rendezvous
30 Suffren St.
Attractive, modern, reasonable French and continental food but overpriced wine. Attractive roof terrace and a pleasant atmosphere. The owner worked for a wealthy American family for 20 years and so his continental grub is first rate.

$$ Satsanga
32 rue Mahe de Labourdonnais, T0413-222 5867. Closed Thu.
Friendly restaurant offering continental dishes (with quite expensive wine) in a French atmosphere with art 'gallery'. The garden setting and staff make up for mediocre food.

$ Ananda Bhavan
15 Nehru St.
Big, buzzy and modern pure veg place, excellent for sweets and *thalis*, and good fun if you don't mind elbowing your way to the front of the queue.

$ Ashram Dining Hall
North of Government Place.
Simple, filling, Indian vegetarian meals (Rs 30 per day) in an unusual setting. Seating is on cushions at low tables, and the dishes are made with farm-grown produce, and are non-spicy and non-greasy. Buy a ticket (from ashram guesthouses or Central Bureau), then turn up at 0640, 1115, 1745 or 2000. Recommended, though non-ashramites can expect a grilling before being sold a ticket.

$ Baker Street
123 rue Bussy. Closed Mon.
Excellent newish French sandwich shop and patisserie, with good but pricey coffee and handmade chocolates.

$ Hot Breads
Ambur Salai. Open 0700-2100.
Good burgers, chicken puffs, pizzas, pastries, sandwiches and shakes.

$ Indian Coffee House
41 Nehru St.
Real local vegetarian fare from 0700.

$ Le Café
Goubert Salai, by Gandhi statue.
Cute beachside pavilion in a grassy garden, great for hanging out with a milkshake or ice cream, though service is stretched and you'll be in for a long wait if it's busy.

Futuristic Auroville (population 2400), 'City of Dawn', was founded in 1968 by 'The Mother' (Mirra Alfassa) as a tribute to Sri Aurobindo, and remains a fascinating experiment in communal living and spiritual evolution.

The founding charter reads: "To live in Auroville one must be a willing servitor of the Divine Consciousness," and describes it as belonging "to humanity as a whole ... the place of an unending education, of constant progress ... a bridge between the past and the future ... a site of material and spiritual researches for a living embodiment of actual human unity".

A baked and desolate plateau when the first residents moved here, Auroville has been transformed into a lush forest, among which are scattered 100 distinct hamlets, housing a permanent population of 2200 people plus a regular through flow of international eco-warriors, holistic therapists and spiritually inclined intellectuals. It's a place where concepts that would be deemed too flakey to fly in the outside world are given free rein: the town plan is based on the shape of a spiralling galaxy, with the Matrimandir – an extraordinary 30-m-high globe-shaped meditation chamber clad in shimmering discs of gold leaf, with a lotus bud shaped foundation urn and a centrepiece crystal said to be the largest in the world – at its spiritual and geographic fulcrum. The main buildings are based on principles espoused in Sri Aurobindo's philosophical tracts. And a town that can't provide enough housing to accommodate all its would-be residents has found the money to build a gleaming pavilion dedicated to study of Aurobindo's epic poem Savitri. Yet there's a great deal of serious and innovative work going on here, in the fields of sustainable architecture, reforestation, community development, education, organic agriculture, renewable energy and self-development.

Residents are quick to point out that Auroville is not a tourist attraction, and a casual day trip here can be as much an exercise in frustration as inspiration. Tours from Puducherry visit the Matrimandir gardens for a view of the dome, but to experience the unforgettable womb-like interior and spend 10 minutes in silent 'concentration' you have to request permission in person at the Matrimandir office, at least 24 hours in advance.

On the other hand, the community welcomes visitors who have a genuine interest in its philosophy – all the more so if you can find a project you'd like to work on – and an extended stay here makes a very pleasant retreat. An ideal way to get to know the place is to take the three-day orientation tour, which guides you around many of Auroville's 'villages' by bike and provides a good opportunity to interact with Aurovilians.

Essential Auroville

Visitor centre

The visitor centre is in the **International Zone**, T0413-262 2239, www.auroville.org, and is open Monday-Saturday 0900-1300 and 1400-1730, Sunday 1000-1200 and 1400-1730. All visitors are expected to report here first.

Passes for visits to Matrimandir gardens and Amphitheatre are issued here (Monday-Saturday 0930-1230 and 1400-1600, Sunday 0930-1230; gardens open daily 1000-1250 and 1400-1630). A five-minute video about the Matrimandir is shown according to demand.

Visitors may enter the Inner Chamber for 10 minutes' silent 'concentration' with at least one day's notice; apply in person at the **Visitor Centre** 1000-1100 or 1400-1500 any day except Tuesday.

Information booklet

A useful information booklet, *The Auroville Handbook*, is available here and at La Boutique d'Auroville, 38 JL Nehru Street, Puducherry.

Listings Auroville

Where to stay

For details of the dozens of guesthouses scattered around Auroville, see www.aurovilleguesthouses.com. Accommodation ranges from basic thatched huts with shared toilets to self-contained studios, with rooms available in 4 distinct zones: Centre (close to the Matrimandir, theatres and cafés), Residential, Forest and Beach. The Auroville Guest Service (T0413-262 2704), can also help with finding a room. Costs vary from **$$-$**, though some operate a kibbutz-type arrangement.

$ Centre Guest House
T0413-262 2155.
Most short-stay visitors are accommodated here ("welcomes those who wish to see and be in Auroville, but not to work there"). It's in a lovely setting under a huge banyan tree. Bikes and scooters for rent, famous weekly pizza.

Shopping

Shops at the visitor centre sell products made in the hive of industry that is Auroville, including handmade paper, bamboo lamps, incense, wind chimes and the like. **La Boutique d'Auroville** has excellent clothes and accessories, cut to suit Western tastes. If you're interested in music, don't miss a visit to **Svaram** (in Kottakarai, www.svaram.org), where inventor-genius Aurelio and his team create and sell items that are part musical instrument, part sculpture.

What to do

Body and soul
With a guest pass to Auroville you can participate in retreat activities from Indian dance to ashtanga yoga. There's also a Quiet Healing Centre on the nearby beach, well known for its underwater body treatments. The hydrotherapy treatment tank is a little public so it may be best to stick to the good Ayurvedic massages.

Tours
Available 0830-1100 from **Ashram** (Puducherry, autocare@auroville.org.in); 1430-1745 from **Cottage Complex** (Ambur Salai), includes Auroville Visitor Centre and Matrimandir. A 5-day residential introduction to Auroville is available through the **Guest Service** (T0413-262 2704, www.aurovilleguestservice.org).

Transport

Bicycle hire Rent a bicycle (Rs 25 per day, though at some guesthouses they are free) and take advantage of the many cycle paths. **Centre Guest House** is one of several places renting bikes/mopeds.

Rickshaw/taxi Either of the 2 roads north from Puducherry towards Chennai leads to Auroville. A rickshaw from **Puducherry** will cost around Rs 200, a taxi costs around Rs 500 return.

$ Babarchee
Babu Rao St.
Good fast food and pizzas.

$ Best
Ida Scudder Rd.
Some meals very spicy, nice parathas, opens at 0600 for excellent breakfast.

$ Chinatown
Gandhi Rd.
Small, friendly, a/c. Good food and service.

$ Dawn Bakery
Gandhi Rd.
Fresh bread and biscuits, cakes, also sardines and fruit juices.

$ Geetha and $ Susil
Ida Scudder Rd.
Rooftop or inside, good service and food.

$ Shimla
Ida Scudder Rd.
Tandoori and excellent naan.

Shopping

Most shops are along Main Bazar Rd and Long Bazar St. Vellore specializes in making 'Karigari' glazed pottery in a range of traditional and modern designs. Vases, water jugs, ashtrays and dishes are usually coloured blue, green and yellow.

Beauty, *Ameer Complex, Gandhi Rd.* Cheapest good-quality tailoring.
Mr Kanappan, *Gandhi Rd.* Very friendly, good-quality tailors, bit pricier.

Transport

Bus The new long-distance bus stand is 2 km north of the town centre, which can be reached by local buses No 1 and No 2 or auto-rickshaw. Buses to **Tiruchirappalli**, **Tiruvannamalai**, **Bengaluru (Bangalore)**, **Chennai**, **Ooty**, **Thanjavur** and **Tirupathi**. The regional state bus company **PATC** runs frequent services to **Kanchipuram** and **Bengaluru** from 0500 (2½ hrs) and **Chennai**. From the **Town Bus Stand**, off Long Bazar Rd near the fort, buses 8 and 8A go to the Sripuram temple.

Train Vellore Town station has daily passenger trains to **Tirupati** at 1015 and 1800. The main station, **Katpadi Junction**, 8 km north of town, is on the broad gauge line between **Chennai** and **Bengaluru**, with dozens of trains a day in each direction. It is also on the metre gauge line to **Villupuram** to the south, with 1 or 2 trains per week to **Puducherry** mostly at inconvenient hours of the night.

Gingee *Colour map 7, B5.*

remote boulder-strewn fort

Gingee (pronounced *Senjee*), just off the NH45, situated between Chennai and Tiruvannamalai, has a remarkable 15th-century Vijayanagar fort with much to explore. It is well off the beaten track, very peaceful and in beautiful surroundings. Spend the night here if you can. Lovers come here at the weekends; it's on the domestic tourist map because it is often used as a film location. The landscape is made up of man-sized boulders, like Hampi, piled on top of each other to make mounds the texture of cottage cheese.

The fort ⓘ *0900-1700, allow 2½ hrs for Rajagiri, and 2 hrs for Krishnagiri (if you have time), foreigners Rs 100, Indians Rs 20, camera Rs 50, video Rs 250, includes both forts,* was intensely contested by successive powers before being captured by an East India Company force in 1762, by the end of the century, however, it had lost its importance. Although it had Chola foundations, the 'most famous fort in the Carnatic' was almost entirely rebuilt in 1442. It is set on three strongly fortified Charnockite hills: Krishnagiri, Chakklidrug and Rajagiri. In places the hills on which the fort stands are sheer cliffs over 150 m high. The highest, Rajagiri ('King's Hill'), has a south-facing overhanging cliff face, on top of which is the citadel. The inner fort contains two temples and the Kalyana Mahal, a square court with a 27-m breezy tower topped by pyramidal roof, surrounded by apartments for the women of the governor's household. On

Tip...
Climb up to the fort in the morning when it's cooler and the views are less hazy.

top of the citadel is a huge cannon and a smooth granite slab known as the Raja's bathing stone. An extraordinary stone about 7 m high and balanced precariously on a rock, surrounded by a low circular brick wall, it is referred to as the Prisoner's Well. There are fine Vijaynagara temples, granary, barracks and stables and an 'elephant tank'. A caretaker may unlock a temple and then expect a tip.

The Archaeological Survey of India Office is just off the main road towards the fort. They may have guides to accompany you to the fort. Carry provisions, especially plenty of drinks; a few refreshments are sold, but only at the bottom of the hill. The climb is only for the fit and healthy.

Listings Gingee

Where to stay

Avoid Aruna Lodge, near the bus stand.

$ Shivan
M Gandhi Rd, opposite the bus stand,
T04145-222218, www.hotelshivan.com.
Good views of the fort from the roof, this hotel offers 21 clean rooms with bath, some a/c, a veg restaurant, a/c bar and helpful manager.

Transport

Bicycles There are bicycles for hire next to the bus station.

Bus Direct buses to/from **Puducherry** are infrequent (2 hrs); it's better to go via Tindivanam (45 mins). To/from **Tiruvannamalai**, 39 km: several buses a day (1 hr); Express buses will not stop at the fort.

Rickshaw To visit the fort take a cycle-rickshaw from the bus stand to the hills; Rs 30 for the round trip, including a 2-hr wait. There are bicycles for hire next to the bus station.

Tiruvannamalai *Colour map 7, B5.*

sacred hills and pilgrimage centre

At the foot of rocky Arunachala Hill, revered by Hindus across South India as the physical manifestation of Siva, Tiruvannamalai (population 145,300) is one of Tamil Nadu's holiest towns. It is a major pilgrimage centre, focused around the enormous and fascinating Arunachaleshwar Temple whose tall *gopurams* stand dazzling white against the blue sky, and for the first half of the 20th century was home to one of India's most beloved saints, Sri Ramana Maharishi.

One of the largest temples in South India, the 16th- and 17th-century **Arunachala Temple** was built mainly under the patronage of the Vijayanagar kings and is dedicated to Siva as God incarnate of Fire. Its massive bright white *gopurams*, the tallest of which is 66 m high, dominate the centre of the town. The temple has three sets of walls forming nested rectangles. Built at different periods they illustrate the way in which many Dravidian temples grew by accretion. The east end of each is extended to make a court, and the main entrance is at the east end of the temple. The lower parts of the *gopurams*, built of granite, date from the late Vijayanagar period but have been added to subsequently. The upper 10 storeys and the decoration are of brick and plaster. There are some remarkable carvings on the *gopurams*. On the outer wall of the east *gopuram*, for example, Siva is shown in the south corner dancing, with an elephant's skin. Inside the east doorway of the first courtyard is the 1000-pillared *mandapa* (hall, portico) built in the late Vijayanagar period. To the south of the court is a small shrine dedicated to Subrahmanya. To the south again is a large tank. The pillars in the *mandapa* are typically carved vigorous horses, riders and lion-like *yalis*. The middle court has four much earlier *gopurams* (mid-14th century), a large columned *mandapa* and a tank. The innermost court may date from as early as the 11th century and the main sanctuary with carvings of deities is certainly of Chola origin. In the south is Dakshinamurti, the west shows Siva appearing out of a lingam and the north has Brahma. The outer porch has small shrines to Ganesh and Subrahmanya. In front of the main shrine are a brass column lamp and the *Nandi* bull.

Chola Heartland
& the Kaveri Delta

Chidambaram, Trichy and Tanjore together represent the apotheosis of Tamilian temple architecture: the great temples here act as *thirthas*, or gateways, linking the profane to the sacred. This pilgrim's road boasts the bare granite Big Temple in the charming agricultural town of Tanjore, which was for 300 years the capital of the Cholas; Trichy's 21-*gopuram*, seven-walled island city of Srirangam, a patchwork quilt of a temple built by successive dynastic waves of Cholas, Cheras, Pandyas, Hoysalas, Vijayanagars and Madurai Nayaks; and the beautiful Nataraja Temple at Chidambaram, with its two towers given over to bas reliefs of the 108 *mudras*, or gestures, of classical dance.

★ Chidambaram   *Colour map 7, B5.*

flyblown little town with a hugely atmospheric temple

The capital of the Cholas from AD 907 to 1310, the temple town of Chidambaram is one of Tamil Nadu's most important holy towns. The town (population 59,000) has lots of character and is rarely visited by foreigners. Its main attraction is the temple, one of the only ones to have Siva in the cosmic dance position. It is an enormously holy temple with a feeling all its own.

The **Nataraja Temple** ① *0400-1200, 1630-2200, visitors may be asked for donations, entrance into the inner sanctum Rs 50, men must remove their shirts*, was the subject of a Supreme Court battle that ended in Delhi, where it was decided that it should remain as a private enterprise. All others fall under the state, with the Archeological Survey of India's sometimes questionable mandate to restore and maintain them. The unique Brahmin community, with their right forehead shaved to indicate Siva, the left grown long and tied in a front top knot to denote his wife Parvati, will no doubt bear this out to you.

As a private temple, it is unique in allowing non-Hindus to enter the sanctum (for a fee); however, the Brahmins at other shrines will ask you to sign a book with other foreign names in it, supposedly having donated Rs 400. The lack of state support does make this temple poorer than its neighbours, but if you want to give a token rupee coinage instead then do so. The atmosphere of this temple more than compensates for any money-grabbing tactics, however. Temple lamps still hang from the hallways, the temple music is rousing and the *puja* has the statues coming alive in sudden illumination. The Brahmins themselves have a unique, stately presence too. The evening *puja* at 1800 is particularly interesting. At each shrine the visitor will be daubed with *vibhuti* (sacred ash) and paste.

It is not easy to see some of the sculptures in the interior gloom. You may need patience and persuasive powers if you want to take your own time but it is worth the effort.

There are records of the temple's existence before the 10th century and inscriptions from the 11th century. One legend surrounding its construction suggests that it was built by 'the golden-coloured emperor', Hiranya Varna Chakravarti, who suffered from leprosy. He came to Chidambaram on a pilgrimage from Kashmir in about AD 500. After bathing in the temple tank he was reputed to have recovered from the disease and in gratitude offered to rebuild and enlarge the temple.

On each side are four enormous *gopurams*, those on the north and south being about 45 m high. The east *gopuram* (AD 1250), through which you enter the temple, is the oldest. The north *gopuram* was built by the great Vijayanagar king **Krishna Deva Raya** (1509-1530). Immediately on entering the East Gate is the large **Sivaganga Tank**, and the **Raja Sabha**, a 1000-columned *mandapa* (1595-1685). In the northwest of the compound are temples dedicated to Subrahmanya (late 13th century), and to its south the 12th-century shrine to Sivakumasundari or Parvati. The ceiling paintings are 17th century. At the southern end of this outer compound is what is said to be the largest shrine to **Ganesh** in India. The next inner compound has been filled with colonnades and passageways. In the innermost shrine are two images of Siva, the Nataraja and the lingam. A later Vishnu shrine to Govindaraja was added by the Vijayanagar kings. The **inner enclosure**, the most sacred, contains four important *Sabhas* (halls), the **deva sabha**, where the temple managers hold their meetings; the **chit sabha** or *chit ambalam* (from which the temple and the town get their names), meaning the hall of wisdom; the **kanakha sabha**, or golden hall; and the **nritta sabha**, or hall of dancing. Siva is worshipped in the *chit ambalam*, a plain wooden building standing on a stone base, in his form as Lord of the Dance, Nataraja. The area immediately over the deity's head is gold plated. Immediately behind the idol is the focus of the temple's power, the Akasa Lingam, representing the invisible element, 'space', and hence is itself invisible. It is known as the Chidambaram secret.

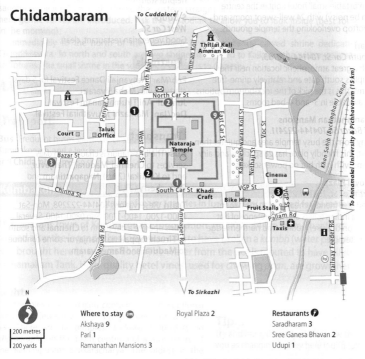

Chidambaram

Where to stay 🛏
Akshaya 9
Pari 1
Ramanathan Mansions 3

Royal Plaza 2

Restaurants 🍴
Saradharam 3
Sree Ganesa Bhavan 2
Udupi 1

$ Raya's

18 Head PO Rd, T0435-242 3170.
Older and dingier than the annexe opposite, but
OK at the price, and the otherwise uninspiring
'garden villas' (**$$**) are family-friendly with
1 double and 1 single bedroom. A/c restaurant
downstairs, exchanges cash.

Restaurants

$$ Sri Venkkatramana Hotel
40 Gandhi Park North St.
Excellent vegetarian restaurant, with pure veg
thali-style meals served in Brahminical cleanliness
in a/c hall, and the usual gamut of South Indian
snacks in the somewhat fly-blown main room.

Shopping

Kumbakonam and its surrounding villages are
renowned centres of bronze sculpture, some
still practicing the traditional '*pancha loha*'
(5 metals – gold, silver, lead copper and iron)
technique reserved for casting temple idols. You
can visit workshops in Kumbakaonam itself, and
in Swamimalai to the west and Nachiyar Koil to
the southeast.

Transport

Bus TN Govt Express buses to **Chennai**, *No 305*,
several daily (7½ hrs); half hourly to **Thanjavur**.
The railway station is 2 km from town centre.
Reasonably frequent trains to **Chennai** (**Egmore**),
6-7 hrs; **Chidambaram** (2 hrs), **Thanjavur**
(50 mins) and **Tiruchirappalli** (2½ hrs).

Car hire Half day for excursions, Rs 400.

★ Thanjavur (Tanjore) *Colour map 7, B5.*

home of the enormous, World Heritage Site of Brihadisvara Temple

The mathematically perfect Brihadisvara Temple is one of the great monuments of
South India and a UNESCO World Heritage Site, its huge Nandi bull washed each
fortnight with water, milk, turmeric and gingelly in front of a rapt audience that packs
out the whole temple compound.

In the heart of the lush, rice-growing delta of the Kaveri, the upper echelons of Tanjore life are
landowners, rather than industrialists, and Thanjavur (population 291,100) itself is mellow in
comparison with Trichy, especially in the old town surrounding the Royal Palace.

Essential Thanjavur

Finding your feet

Most long-distance buses stop at the New
Bus Stand 4 km southwest of the centre, from
where there are frequent buses and autos
(Rs 60) to town. There's a second, more central
bus stand off South Rampart Street, close
to several budget hotels, which has some
direct buses to Chennai. The train station is
at the south end of the town centre, about a
20-minute walk from the Brihadisvara Temple,
with connections to Tiruchirappalli, Chennai
and Bangalore.

Getting around

Most hotels are within a 15-minute walk of the
temple. Auto-rickshaws charge Rs 20-30 for
trips around town. See Transport, page 837.

Sights

Brihadisvara Temple ① *0600-2030, inner
sanctum closed 1230-1600*, known as the Big
Temple, was the achievement of the Chola king
Rajaraja I (ruled AD 985-1012). The magnificent
main temple has a 62-m-high *vimana* (the
tallest in India), topped by a dome carved from
an 80-tonne block of granite, which needed
a 6.5-km-long ramp to raise it to the top. The
attractive gardens, the clean surroundings
and well-lit sanctuaries make a visit doubly
rewarding, especially in the evening.

The entrance is from the east. After crossing
the moat you enter through two *gopurams*, the
second guarded by two *dvarapalas* typical of
the early Chola period, when the *gopurams* on
the outer enclosure walls were dwarfed by the
scale of the *vimana* over the main shrine. An
enormous Nandi, carved out of a single block
of granite 6 m long, guards the entrance to the
sanctuary. According to one of the many myths

that revolve around the image of a wounded Nandi, the Thanjavur Nandi was growing larger and larger, threatening the temple, until a nail was driven into its back.

The temple, built mainly with large granite blocks, has superb inscriptions and sculptures of Siva, Vishnu and Durga on three sides of the massive plinth. Siva appears in three forms, the dancer with 10 arms, the seated figure with a sword and trident, and Siva bearing a spear. The carvings of dancers showing the 81 different Bharat Natyam poses are the first to record classical dance form in this manner.

The main shrine has a large lingam. In the inner courtyard are Chola frescoes on walls prepared with lime plaster, smoothed and polished, then painted while the surface was wet. These were hidden under later Nayaka paintings. Since music and dance were a vital part of temple life and dancing in the temple would accompany the chanting of the holy scriptures which the community attended, Rajaraja also built two housing colonies nearby to accommodate 400 *devadasis* (temple dancers). Subsidiary shrines were added to the main temple at different periods. The Vijayanagara kings built the Amman shrine, the Nayakas the Subrahmanya shrine and the Marathas the Ganesh shrine.

Thanjavur

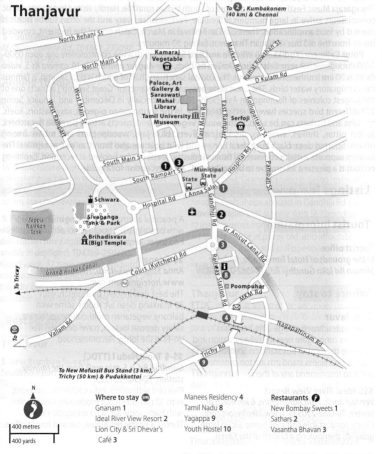

Where to stay 🛏
Gnanam 1
Ideal River View Resort 2
Lion City & Sri Dhevar's Café 3

Manees Residency 4
Tamil Nadu 8
Yagappa 9
Youth Hostel 10

Restaurants 🍴
New Bombay Sweets 1
Sathars 2
Vasantha Bhavan 3

(100 km) for **Point Calimere**, about hourly, 4-4½ hrs. Buses to Kumbakonam, and the odd one to Chennai and Puducherry, also leave from the **State Bus Stand** on South Rampart St.

Taxi Taxis wait at the railway station and along South Rampart St, but drivers quote high rates, eg **Puducherry** Rs 3500, **Madurai** Rs 2500, **Chidambaram** Rs 2000.

Train A handful of daily trains leave for **Chennai Egmore**, 7 hrs. For **Madurai** and points south, it's better to go to Trichy and change; there are several fast passenger trains throughout the day.

Around Thanjavur
Point Calimere (Kodikkarai)

Bus Buses via Vedaranyam, which has services to/from **Thanjavur**, **Tiruchirappalli**, **Nagapattinam**, **Chennai**, etc. From Thanjavur buses leave the **New Bus Stand** for **Vedaranyam** (100 km) hourly (4-4½ hrs); buses and vans from there to **Kodikkarai** (11 km) which take about 30 mins. Taxis from Vedaranyam charge around Rs 600 return to the sanctuary. Avoid being dropped at 'Sri Rama's Feet' on the way, near a shrine that is of no special interest.

Tiruchirappalli (Trichy) and around Colour map 7, B5.
bustling industrial city, home to the island temple of Srirangam

Trichy, at the head of the fertile Kaveri Delta, is an industrial city and transport hub of some significance, with its own international airport connecting southern Tamil Nadu to Singapore and the Gulf. Land prices are high here, and houses, as you'll see if you climb up to its 84-m-high rock fort, are densely packed, outside the elegant doctors' suburbs.

If you are taking public transport you will want to break here to visit the sacred Srirangam temple but if you have your own wheels you may prefer to bypass the city, which has little else to offer by way of easily accessed charms. Allow at least half a day to tour Srirangam, then stay in the more laid-back agricultural centre of Tanjore to the north or the more atmospheric temple madness of Madurai further south.

Sights

Rock Fort (1660), stands on an 84-m-high rock. **Ucchi Pillayar Koil (Vinayaka Temple)** ① *Tue-Sun 0600-1200, 1600-2100, camera Rs 10, video Rs 50*, approached from Chinna Bazar, is worth climbing for the stunning panoramas but don't expect much from the temple. At the top of the first flight of steps lies the main 11th-century defence line and the remains of a thousand-pillared hall,

destroyed in 1772. Further up is a hundred-pillared hall where civic receptions are held. At the end of that flight is the **Tayumanasvami Temple**, dedicated to Siva, which has a golden *vimana* and a lingam carved from the rock itself. There are further seventh-century Pallava cave temples of beautiful carved pillars and panels.

Try to make time to explore the atmospheric old city, particularly **Big Bazar Street** and **Chinna Bazar**. The **Gandhi Market** is a colourful vegetable and fruit market.

Among the dozen or so mosques in the town, the **Nadir Shah Mosque** near the city railway station stands out with its white dome and metal steeple, said to have been built with material taken from a Hindu temple. **St Joseph's College Church** (Church of our Lady of Lourdes), one of several Catholic churches here, was designed as a smaller version of the Basilica at Lourdes in France. It has an unusual

Essential Tiruchirappalli

Finding your feet

Trichy airport, 8 km from the centre, has quietly become a low-rent international air hub, with direct links to Dubai, Colombo, Singapore and Kuala Lumpur; the only domestic service is to Chennai. Taxis charge around Rs 300 to town, or catch a bus from opposite the terminal for around Rs 15. The Junction Railway Station and the two bus stations are in the centre, with many hotels within walking distance.

Getting around

Much of Trichy is quite easy to see on foot, but plenty of autos and local buses run to the Rock Fort and Srirangam. See Transport, page 842.

sandalwood altar but is rather garish inside. The grounds are a peaceful spot. The 18th-century **Christ Church**, the first English church, is north of the Teppakulam, while the early 19th-century **St John's Church** has a memorial plaque to Bishop Heber, one of India's best known missionary bishops, who died in Trichy in 1826.

Tiruchirappalli

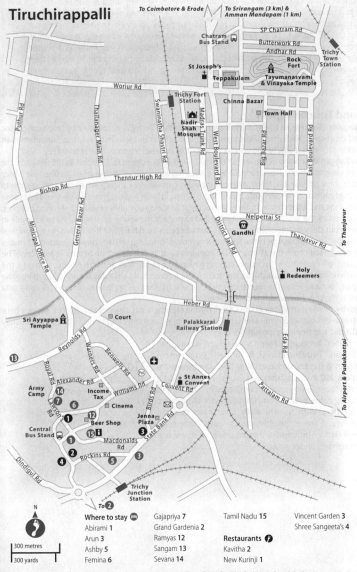

N

300 metres
300 yards

Where to stay
Abirami 1
Arun 3
Ashby 5
Femina 6
Gajapriya 7
Grand Gardenia 2
Ramyas 12
Sangam 13
Sevana 14
Tamil Nadu 15

Vincent Garden 3
Shree Sangeeta's 4

Restaurants
Kavitha 2
New Kurinji 1

Tiruchirappalli

Trichy was mentioned by Ptolemy in the second century BC. A Chola fortification from the second century, it came to prominence under the Nayakas from Madurai who built the fort and the town, capitalizing on its strategic position. In legend its name is traced to a three-headed demon, Trisiras, who terrorized both men and the gods until Siva overpowered him in the place called Tiruchi. Cigar making became important between the two world wars, while the indigenous *bidis* continue to be made, following a tradition started in the 18th century.

Trichy is the country's largest artificial diamond manufacturing centre. Jaffersha Street is known as Diamond Bazar. The town is also noted for its high-quality string instruments, especially veenas and violins.

Around Tiruchirappalli

Srirangam The temple town on the **Kaveri**, just north of Trichy, is surrounded by seven concentric walled courtyards, with magnificent gateways and several shrines. On the way to Srirangam is an interesting river *ghat* where pilgrims take their ritual bath before entering the temple.

Sri Ranganathasvami Temple ① *0700-1300, 1400-1800, camera Rs 50, video Rs 100 (Rs 10 for the rooftop viewing tower), allow about 2 hrs, guides will greet you on arrival (their abilities are highly variable; some tell you that the staircase to the viewpoint will close shortly, which is usually a scam to encourage you to use their services),* is one of the largest in India and dedicated to Vishnu. It has some fine carvings and a good atmosphere. The fact that it faces south, unlike most other Hindu temples, is explained by the legend that Rama intended to present the image of Ranganatha to a temple in Sri Lanka but this was impossible since the deity became fixed here, but it still honours the original destination. The temple, where the Vaishnava reformer Ramanuja settled and worshipped, is famous for its superb sculpture, the 21 impressive *gopurams* and its rich collection of temple jewellery. The 'thousand' pillared hall (904 columns) stands beyond the fourth wall, and fifth enclosure there is the unusual shrine to Tulukka Nachiyar, the god's Muslim consort. Non-Hindus are not allowed into the sanctuary but can enter the fourth courtyard where the famous sculptures of *gopis* (*Radha's* milk maids) in the Venugopala shrine can be seen.

Nearby, on the north bank of the Kaveri, **Amma Mandapam** is a hive of activity. The *ghats*, where devotees wash, bathe, commit cremated ashes and pray, are interesting to visit, although some may find the dirt and smell overpowering.

So named because a legendary elephant worshipped the lingam, **Tiruvanaikkaval** is located 3 km east of Srirangam. It has the architecturally finer **Jambukesvara Temple** ① *200 m east off the main Tiruchi–Chennai road, a short stroll from Srirangam or easily reached by bus, officially 0600-2045, camera Rs 10, non-Hindus are not allowed into the sanctuary,* with its five walls and seven splendid *gopurams* and one of the oldest and largest Siva temples in Tamil Nadu. The unusual lingam under a *jambu* tree always remains under water.

Tip...

The countryside to the west of Sri Ranganathasvami Temple is an excellent place to sample rural Indian life and spend a couple of hours.

Tourist information

Tiruchirappalli

Tourist office
New Central Bus Stand, T0431-241 0136.
There are also counters at the railway station
and the airport.

Where to stay

Tiruchirappalli

$$$-$$ Sangam
Collector's Office Rd, T0431-424 4555,
www.sangamhotels.com.
Very friendly, 90 comfortable a/c rooms,
restaurants (great tandoori), good breakfast
served in the coffee shop, pleasant bar, exchange,
pool and spacious lawns.

$$ Femina
109 Williams Rd, T0431-241 4501,
www.feminahotel.net.
Modern, comfortable 4-storey hotel with
180 clean a/c rooms, a vegetarian restaurant
for great breakfasts, a bar and a pool in the
new block. Good value.

$$ Grand Gardenia
Mannarpuram Junction (1 km south of station),
T0431-404 5000, www.grandgardenia.com.
Excellent newish business hotel with spacious,
sparkling clean rooms and good Chettinadu
restaurant. Currently the best upscale deal in town.

$$ Ramyas
13D/2 Williams Rd, T0431-400 0400,
www.ramyas.com.
117 spotless rooms. Rates include breakfast at
the rooftop restaurant, and there's also a bar.

$$-$ Tamil Nadu (TTDC)
Macdonalds Rd, Cantt, T0431-241 4346.
The typical, almost proverbial state-run hotel,
with a variety of reasonably plush but under
maintained rooms; an OK stay if you can handle
a bit of dust and the odd broken fitting. There's
no restaurant, but plenty of choices are nearby.

$ Abirami
10 Macdonalds Rd, T0431-241 5001.
Old-fashioned hotel, 52 rooms, some a/c with
bath, good, busy a/c restaurant (vegetarian),
and exchange. It's in a noisy location opposite
the bus stand; if you can't get a room at the back,
look elsewhere.

$ Arun
24 State Bank Rd, T0431-241 5021.
35 rooms in a garden setting, with TV. There's
a restaurant and a bar; excellent value.

$ Ashby
17A Junction Rd, T0431-246 0652,
www.ashbyhotel.com.
Set around courtyard, 20 large a/c rooms with
bath, good restaurant, and a bar. The oldest hotel
in town, with plenty of Raj character and a bit
noisy and scruffy, but excellent friendly staff, and
good value.

$ Gajapria
5 Royal Rd, T0431-241 4411,
www.hotelgajapria.com.
Spacious hotel, quieter than most places, with
66 good-value rooms, 28 a/c (no twin beds),
restaurant, bar, library and parking.

$ Sevana
5 Royal Rd, Cantt, T0431-241 5201,
hotelsevana@gmail.com.
Quiet, friendly, 44 rooms, some a/c with bath, a/c
Indian restaurant and a bar.

Restaurants

Tiruchirappalli

Good Indian vegetarian places in Chinna Bazar
are: **$ New Kurinji**, below Hotel Guru Lawson's
Rd, a/c vegetarian; and **$ Ragunath** and
Vasantha Bhawan, *thalis*, good service.

$$ Kavitha
Lawson's Rd.
A/c restaurant serving excellent breakfasts and
generous vegetarian *thalis*.

$$ Sangam's
T0431-246 4480.
Indian and continental.

$ Abirami's
See Where to stay, above, T0431-246 0001.
A/c, Vasantha Bhawan at the back, serves excellent
vegetarian; the front part is a *thali*-type eatery.

$ Shree Sangeetas
2 VOC Rd.
Popular and clean pan-Indian vegetarian place,
close to the bus stand and station.

$ Vincent Garden
Dindigul Rd.
Pleasant garden restaurant and pastry shop, lots of coloured lights but on a busy road.

Festivals

Tiruchirappalli
Mar **Festival of Floats** on the Teppakulam when the temple deities are taken out onto the sacred lake on rafts.

Around Tiruchirappalli
Srirangam
Dec/Jan **Vaikunta Ekadasi** (bus No 1 (C or D) from Trichy or hire a rickshaw), and associated temple car festival, draws thousands of pilgrims who witness the transfer of the image of the deity from the inner sanctum under the golden *vimana* to the *mandapa*.

Tiruvanaikkaval
Special festivals in Jan and the spring.
Aug **Pancha Piraharam** is celebrated and in the month of **Panguni** the images of Siva and his consort Akhilandesvari exchange their dress.

What to do

Tiruchirappalli
Indian Panorama, *5 Anna Av, Srirangam, T0431-422 6122, www.indianpanorama.in.* Tours from Chennai, Bengaluru (Bangalore), Kochi, Madurai and Thiruvananthapuram. Recommended for tours (good cars with drivers), ticketing and general advice.

Transport

Tiruchirappalli
Air The airport, T0431-234 0551, is 8 km from the centre (taxi Rs 250-300). Apart from a couple of daily flights to **Chennai** with **Air India** and **Jet Airways**, most of the traffic here is operated by (mostly low-cost) international carriers, with flights to **Colombo**, **Dubai**, **KL** and **Singapore**.

Bus Local Good city bus service. From airport, Nos 7, 63, 122, 128, take 30 mins. The **Central State Bus Stand** is across from the tourist office (Bus *No 1* passes all the sights); 20 mins to Chatram Bus Stand.
   Long distance The bus stands are 1 km from the railway station and are chaotic; TN Govt Express, T0431-246 0992, Central, T0431-246 0425. Frequent buses to **Chennai** (6 hrs), **Coimbatore** 205 km (5½ hrs), **Kumbakonam** 92 km, **Madurai** 161 km (3 hrs), **Palani** 152 km (3½ hrs), **Thanjavur** (1½ hrs). Also 2 buses to **Kanniyakumari** (9 hrs).

Taxi Taxi companies such as Trichy Call Taxi, T(0)97883-99666, www.trichycalltaxi.com, charge from Rs 600 for a 4-hr/40 km package.

Train Enquiries, T131. Tiruchirappali Junction is the region's most important rail hub. **Bengaluru** (**Bangalore**): 1 daily, 9½ hrs, continues to **Mysore**, a further 3¼ hrs. **Chennai**: at least 20 throughout the day, 5½ hrs; all go via Villupuram (for Puducherry), 3 hrs. **Ernakulam** (**Kochi**): 2 daily, 10-15 hrs. **Madurai**: at least 10 a day, 2¾ hrs.

The Tamil
Hill Stations

The Tamil ghats were once shared between shola forest and tribal peoples. But the British, limp from the heat of the plains, invested in expeditions up the mountains and before long had planted eucalyptus, established elite members' clubs and substituted jackals for foxes in their pursuit of the hunt. Don't expect to find the sheer awe-inspiring grandeur of the Himalaya, but there is a charm to these hills where neatly pleated, green tea plantations run like contour lines about the ghats' girth, bringing the promise of a restorative chill and walking tracks where the air comes cut with the smell of eucalyptus.

★ Udhagamandalam (Ooty) *Colour map 7, B3.*
the Raj's favourite southern hill retreat, now a busy, messy town

Ooty (population 88,400, altitude 2286 m) has been celebrated for rolling hills covered in pine and eucalyptus forests and coffee and tea plantations since the first British planters arrived in 1818. A Government House was built, and the British lifestyle developed with cottages and clubs – tennis, golf, riding – and tea on the lawn.

But the town is no longer the haven it once was; the centre is heavily built up and can be downright unpleasant in the holiday months of April to June, and again around October. It's best to stay either in the grand ruins of colonial quarters on the quiet outskirts where it's still possible to steal some serenity or opt instead for the far smaller tea garden town of Coonoor (see page 848), 19 km down the mountain.

Sights
The **Botanical Gardens** ① *3 km northeast of railway station, 0800-1800, Rs 25, camera, Rs 50, video Rs 500*, house more than 1000 varieties of plant, shrub and tree including orchids, ferns, alpines and medicinal plants, but is most fun for watching giant family groups picnicking and gambolling together among beautiful lawns

Essential Tamil Hill Stations

Finding your feet

The northern Nilgiris or the more southerly Palani Hills offer rival opportunities for high-altitude stopovers on the route between Tamil Nadu, Karnataka and Kerala. The most visited towns of Ooty and Kodai both have their staunch fan bases – Ooty tends to attract nostalgic British and rail enthusiasts, while Kody gets the American vote, thanks in part to its international schools. Both are well connected by road: Kodai is best approached from Madurai; Ooty makes a good bridge to Kerala from Mysore or Tamil Nadu's northern temple towns.

Getting around

The famous narrow-gauge rack-and-pinion Nilgiri Mountain Railway is most dramatic between Coonoor and Mettupalayam, which in turn has trains from Coimbatore and Chennai. The roads worsen dramatically when you cross the Tamil border from Kerala, reflecting the different levels of affluence between the two states. See Transport, page 847.

and glass houses. To the east of the garden in a Toda *mund* is the Wood House made of logs. The **Annual Flower Show** is held in the third week of May. The **Rose Garden** ① *750 m from Charing Cross, 0830-1830*, has over 1500 varieties of roses.

Ooty Lake was built in 1825 as a vast irrigation tank and is now more than half overgrown with water hyacinth, though it is still used enthusiastically for boating and **pedalo hire** ① *0900-1800, Rs 60-110 per hr.*

Kandal Cross ① *3 km west of the railway station*, is a Roman Catholic shrine considered the 'Jerusalem of the East'. During the clearing of the area to make way for a graveyard in 1927, an enormous 4-m-high boulder was found and a cross was erected. Now a relic of the True Cross brought to India by an Apostolic delegate is shown to pilgrims every day. The annual feast is in May.

St Stephen's Church was Ooty's first church, built in the 1820s. Much of the wood is said to be from Tipu Sultan's Lal Bagh Palace in Srirangapatnam. The inside of the church and the graveyard at the rear are worth seeing.

Dodabetta ① *1000-1500, buses from Ooty, autos and taxis (Rs 200 round trip) go to the summit*, is 10 km east of the railway station off the Kotagiri road. Reaching 2638 m, the 'big mountain' is the second highest in the Western Ghats, sheltering Coonoor from the southwest monsoons when Ooty gets heavy rains. The top is often shrouded in mist. There is a viewing platform at the summit. The telescope isn't worth even the nominal Rs 2 fee.

Udhagamandalam (Ooty)

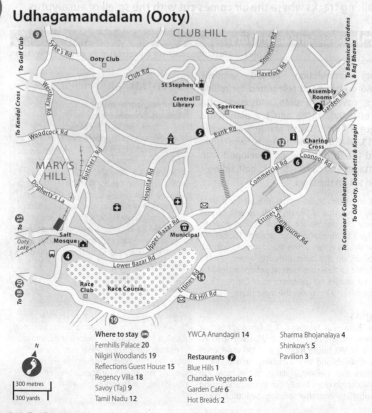

Where to stay 🏠
Fernhills Palace **20**
Nilgiri Woodlands **19**
Reflections Guest House **15**
Regency Villa **18**
Savoy (Taj) **9**
Tamil Nadu **12**

YWCA Anandagiri **14**

Restaurants 🍴
Blue Hills **1**
Chandan Vegetarian **6**
Garden Café **6**
Hot Breads **2**

Sharma Bhojanalaya **4**
Shinkow's **5**
Pavilion **3**

Tamil Nadu culture

The majority of Tamilians are Dravidians with Mediterranean ethnic origins, settled in Tamil Nadu for several thousand years. Tamil is spoken by over 85% of the population, which is 90% Hindu. Five per cent are Christian, a group especially strong in the south where Roman Catholic and Protestant missions have been active for over 500 years. There are small but significant minorities of Muslims, Jains and Parsis.

There are isolated groups of as many as 18 different types of tribal people in the Nilgiri Hills. Some of them are of aboriginal stock although local archaeological discoveries suggest that an extinct race preceded them. The Todas' life and religion revolve around their long-horned buffalo which are a measure of wealth. Their small villages are called munds with around six igloo-like windowless bamboo and dried grass huts. Their chief goddess Tiekirzi, the creator of the indispensable buffalo, and her brother On rule the world of the dead and the living. There are only about 1000 Todas left.

The Badagas are the main tribal group and probably came from Karnataka. They speak a mixture of Kannada and Tamil and their oral tradition is rich in folk tales, poetry, songs and chants. As agriculturalists their villages are mainly in the upper plateau, with rows of three-roomed houses. They worship Siva and observe special tribal festivals. Progressive and adaptable, they are being absorbed into the local community faster than others.

Walks and hikes around Ooty

Hiking or simply walking is excellent in the Nilgiris. It is undisturbed, quiet and interesting. Climbing Dodabetta or Mukurti is hardly a challenge but the longer walks through the *sholas* are best undertaken with a guide. It is possible to see characteristic features of Toda settlements such as *munds* and *boas*.

The **Dodabetta–Snowdon–Ooty walk** starts at Dodabetta Junction directly opposite the 3 km road to the summit. It is a pleasant path that curves gently downhill through a variety of woodland (mainly eucalyptus and conifers) back to Ooty and doesn't take more than a couple of hours. For longer treks, contact **Nilgiris Trekking Association** ① *Kavitha Nilayam, 31-D Bank Rd, or R Seniappan, 137 Upper Bazar, T0423-244 4449, sehi appan@yahoo.com.*

Mukurti Peak ① *buses from Ooty every 30 mins from 0630 or you can take a tour (see page 847), book early as they are popular,* is 36 km away, off the Gudalur road. After 26 km you reach the 6-km-long Mukurti Lake. Mukurti Peak (the name suggests that someone thought it resembled a severed nose), not an easy climb, is to the west. The Todas believe that the souls of the dead and the sacrificed buffaloes leap to the next world from this sacred peak. It is an excellent place to escape for walking, to view the occasional wildlife, to go fishing at the lake or to go boating.

Avalanche ① *24 km from town, bus from Ooty at 1110,* a valley, is a beautiful part of the *shola*, with plenty of rhododendrons, magnolias and orchids and a trout stream running through it, and is excellent for walking. The **Forestry Department Guest House** is clean and has good food. Contact the **Wildlife Warden** ① *1st floor, Mahalingam Building, Ooty, T0423-244098.*

The **River Pykara** ① *19 km from Ooty, several buses 0630-2030, or take a car or bicycle,* has a dam and power plant. There is breathtaking scenery. The **waterfalls**, about 6 km from the bridge on the main road, are best in July though it is very wet then, but they are also worth visiting from August to December.

Tourist information

Tamil Nadu Tourism
Wenlock Rd, T0423-244 3977.
Not very efficient.

Where to stay

Rates quoted are for the high season. Good discounts Jul-Mar except during *puja* and Christmas (add 30% tax in upper categories). Winter nights can be bitterly cold and hotel fireplaces are often inadequate. Avoid the budget accommodation round Commercial Rd and Ettines Rd, particularly if you are a woman travelling alone.

$$$$ Fernhills Royal Palace
Fernhill Post, T0423-244 3910,
www.welcomheritagehotels.in.
After years of stop-start renovation, Wadiyar, the current Mysore maharaja has opened his ancestral palace as a luxury heritage hotel. It offers 19 suites, with teak furniture, wooden panelling, fireplaces and jacuzzis. Spa and gym, plus correspondingly high price tags.

$$$ Savoy (Taj)
77 Sylkes Rd, T0423 222 5500, www.tajhotels.com.
40 well-maintained cottage rooms with huge wooden doors, open fires and separate dressing areas. Even if you're not staying it's worth a tea-time visit for the building's interesting history and lovely gardens, and the wood-panelled dining room serves excellent takes on traditional Tamil food.

$$ Regency Royale Villas
Fernhill Post, T0423-244 2555,
regencyvillas@gmail.com.
The maharaja of Mysore's staff had some of the best sunset views in the Nilgiris from their bungalows. The 6 huge rooms and 13 cottages here are freshly renovated, but the place still retains the somewhat surreal, ramshackle feeling of an ancient English B&B, albeit one with rows of dog-eared photos of men in turbans.

$$ Tamil Nadu (TTDC)
Charing Cross, up the steps by the tourist office, T0423-244 4370.
Pleasant hotel in a tucked away corner of Ooty. Spotless rooms and penthouse with good views, restaurant, bar and exchange. Avoid the food though.

$$-$ The Nilgiri Woodlands
Race Course Rd, T0423-244 2551,
nilgiris_woodlands@yahoo.com.
22 rooms ranging from paint-peeling doubles to spacious cottages. Shared veranda outside racecourse-facing rooms that give onto a garden and the pink/green/blue bungalows of Ooty central. The quiet and spacious rooms tucked round the back (without views) are the best value.

$$-$ YWCA Anandagiri
Ettines Rd, T0423-244 2218,
www.ywcaagooty.com.
Basic and a little institutional, and the hot water can be iffy, but this is the most atmospheric budget accommodation in Ooty, with high-ceilinged 1920s cottages in an extensive garden complex surrounded by tall pines and superb views.

$ Reflections Guest House
North Lake Rd, T0423-244 3834,
www.reflectionsguesthouseooty.com.
Clean, homely, quiet, with good views of the lake, 9 rooms (cheaper dorm beds), pleasant dining and sitting room serving good food, friendly owners. It's Rs 50 for wood for the fire or to use the stove for your own cooking. The plumbing is dodgy, it can get chilly and there's restricted hot water.

Restaurants

There are usually bars in larger hotels. Southern Star is recommended, but pricey.

$$$ Savoy
See Where to stay, above.
Old-world wood-panelled dining hall serving up good food. Also has a bar, café, snooker and table tennis halls.

$$ Chandan Vegetarian
Nahar Nilgiris, Charing Cross, T0423-244 2173. Open 1230-1530, 1900-2230.
Roomy restaurant inside the **Nahar** hotel complex serving up vegetarian North Indian and Chinese food.

$$ The Pavilion
Fortune Hotel, 500 m from town, Sullivan Court, 123 Shelbourne Rd, T0423-244 1415.
In a modern hotel, good multi-cuisine plus a separate bar.

$ Blue Hills
Charing Cross.
Good-value Indian and continental, non-vegetarian dishes.

$ Garden Café
Nahar Nilgiris, Charing Cross. Open 0730-2130.
Lawn-side coffee shop and snack bar with South Indian menu: *iddli, dosa* and *chats* from Rs 30.

$ Hot Breads
Charing Cross.
Tasty hot dogs, pizzas, etc.

$ Hotel Ooty Saravanaa's
302 Commercial Rd. Open 0730-1000, 1130-2230.
The place for super-cheap South Indian breakfast: a large mint green place that does a fast trade in *iddli, dosa* and meals.

$ Sharma Bhojanalaya
12C Lower Bazar Rd.
Gujarati and North Indian food served upstairs in comfortable (padded banquettes) but not an aesthetically pleasing venue. It overlooks the race course, and offers a good vegetarian lunch *thali* (Rs 40).

$ Shinkow's
38/83 Commissioner's Rd (near Collector's Office), T0423-244 2811. Open 1200-1545 and 1830 2145.
Authentic and popular Chinese restaurant, especially busy late evening, with tartan tablecloths and a fish tank. Chicken chilli Rs 120. Highly recommended.

Cafés
Try local institutions **Sugar Daddy** and **King Star** (established in 1942), open 1130-2030, for brilliant home-made chocolates such as fruit'n'nut and fudges.

Festivals

Jan Pongal.
May The **Annual Flower and Dog Shows** in the Botanical Gardens. **Summer Festival** of culture with stars from all over India.

Shopping

Most shops open 0900-1200 and again 1500-2000. The smaller shops keep longer hours.

Higginbotham's, *Commercial Rd, T0423-244 3736. Thu-Mon 0930-1300 and 1550-1930.* Bookseller.
Toda Showroom, *Charing Cross.* Sells silver and tribal shawls.

Variety Hall, *Silver Market.* Old family firm (1890s) for good range of silk, helpful staff. Accepts credit cards.

What to do

Horse riding
Gymkhana Club, *T0423-244 2254. Big bar open 1130-1530 or 1830-2300.* Temporary membership; beautifully situated amidst superbly maintained 18-hole golf course. Riding from Regency Villa: Rs 500 for 2 hrs with 'guide'; good fun but no helmets available.

Tour operators
Tours can be booked through the **TTDC** (at Hotel Tamil Nadu, T0423-244 4370). Ooty and Mudumalai: Ooty Lake, Dodabetta Peak, Botanical Gardens, Mudumalai Wildlife Sanctuary. 0830-2000. Rs 150. Kotagiri and Coonoor: Kotagiri, Kodanad View Point, Lamb's Rock, Dolphin's Nose, Sim's Park. 0830-1830.
Blue Mountain, *Nahar Complex, Charing Cross, T0423-244 3650.* Luxury coach bookings to neighbouring states.
George Hawkes, *52C Nahar Complex, T0423-244 2756.* For tourist taxis.
Sangeetha Travels, *13 Bharathiyar Complex, Charing Cross, T0432-244 4782.* Steam train.
Woodlands Tourism, *Race Course Rd, T0423-244 2551.* Ooty and Coonoor. *Open 0930-1730. Rs 130.* Stunning views.

Yoga
Rajayoga Meditation Centre, *88 Victoria Hall, Ettines Rd, T0423-244 1866.*

Transport

Arrive early for buses to ensure a seat. They often leave early if full. Ghat roads have numerous hairpin bends which can have fairly heavy traffic and very bad surfaces at times. The Gudalur road passes through Mudumalai and Bandipur sanctuaries. You might see an elephant herd and other wildlife, especially at night.

Air The nearest airport is at Coimbatore, 105 km away. Taxis are available.

Bus State government and private buses pull in to the bus stand just south of the railway station, a 10-min walk from the town centre. Frequent buses to **Coimbatore** (every 20 mins, 0530-2000, 3½ hrs), **Coonoor** (every 10 mins, 0530-2045), and **Mettupalayam** (0530-2100, 2 hrs). Daily buses to **Bengaluru** (**Bangalore**) (0630-2000), **Mysore** (0800-1530, 3½-5 hrs),

ON THE ROAD

The Blue Mountain Railway

Ever since 15 June 1899, the narrow-gauge steam *Mountain Railway*, in its blue and cream livery, has chugged from Mettupalayam to Ooty via Coonoor, negotiating 16 tunnels and 31 major bridges and climbing from 326 m to 2193 m. This was the location for the railway scenes of the *Marabar Express* in the film *A Passage to India*.

It's a charming 4½-hour (46-km) journey through tea plantations and forest, but – outside first class – be prepared for an amiable Indian holidaymakers' scrum. There are rest stops at Hillgrove (17 km) and Coonoor (27 km).

For enthusiasts, the pricier and more spacious *Heritage Steam Chariot* runs between Ooty and Runneymede picnic area, 23 km away, at weekends (more often in high season). The drawback is that you can be stranded for hours when the engine breaks down; some decide to scramble to the nearest road to flag down a bus.

Kozhikode (0630-1515), **Chennai** (1630-1830), **Palani** (0800-1800), **Kanniyakumari** (1745), **Kodaikanal** (0630, 9½ hrs via magnificent route through Palani); **Puducherry** (1700); **Salem** (1300). Check timings. Several on the short route (36 km) to **Masinagudi** in Mudumalai, 1½ hrs on a steep and bendy but interesting road.

Train Ooty is the terminus of the Nilgiri Mountain Railway. 4 diesel trains a day run from Ooty to **Coonoor**, 1 hr 10 mins, at 0915, 1215, 1400 and 1800; the 1400 *Ooty-Mettupalayam Passenger 56137* swaps to a steam loco at Coonoor and continues down the wonderfully scenic track to **Mettupalayam**. This train connects with the *Nilgiri Exp* to **Chennai** (for trains to Ooty, see Mettupalayam transport below). Trains sell out so book tickets well in advance.

Coonoor *Colour map 7, B3.*

attractive tea-clad hills at the top of the Nilgiri Mountain Railway

Smaller and much less developed than Ooty, Coonoor (population 45,500, altitude 1800 m) is an ideal starting point for nature walks and rambles through villages. There's no pollution, no noise and very few people. The covered market, as with many towns and cities in South India, is almost medieval and cobblers, jewellers, tailors, pawn brokers and merchants sell everything from jasmine to beetroot. The picturesque hills around the town are covered in coffee and tea plantations.

When you arrive by train or bus (which doesn't always stop at the main bus stand if going on to Ooty), the main town of Lower Coonoor will be to the east, across the river. Upper Coonoor, with the better hotels 2-3 km away, is further east.

The real attraction here is the hiking, though there are a couple of sights in town. The large **Sim's Park** ① *0800-1830, Rs 5*, named after a secretary to the Madras Club, is a well-maintained botanical garden on the slopes of a ravine with over 330 varieties of rose but is only really worth the journey for passionate botanists. Contact the **United Planters' Association of South India (UPASI)** ① *Glenview House, Coonoor, T0423-223 0270, www.upasi.org*, to visit tea and coffee plantations.

The **Wellington Barracks**, 3 km northeast of Lower Coonoor, which are the raison d'être for the town, were built in 1852. They are now the headquarters of the Indian Defence Services Staff College and also of the Madras Regiment, which is over 250 years old, the oldest in the Indian Army.

Lamb's Rock, on a high precipice, 9 km away, has good views over the Coimbatore plains and coffee and tea estates on the slopes. At **Dolphin's Nose** (12 km away, several buses 0700-1615), you can see **Catherine Falls**, a further 10 km away (best in the early morning). **Droog** (13 km away, buses 0900, 1345) has ruins of a 16th-century fort used by Tipu Sultan, and requires a 3-km walk.

Kotagiri ⓘ *29 km from Ooty, frequent services from Coonoor, Mettupalayam Railway Station and Ooty,* has an altitude of 1980 m. It sits on the northeast crest of the plateau overlooking the plains. It has a milder climate than Ooty. The name comes from Kotar–Keri, the street of the *Kotas* who were one of the original hill tribes and who have a village to the west of the town. You can visit some scenic spots from here: **St Catherine Falls** (8 km) and **Elk Falls** (7 km), or one of the peaks, **Kodanad Viewpoint** (16 km) – reached through the tea estates or by taking one of the several buses that run from 0610 onwards – or **Rangaswamy Pillar**, an isolated rock, and the conical Rangaswamy Peak.

Listings Coonoor

Where to stay

Most hotels are 3-5 km from the station and bus stand.

$$$$-$$$ Gateway Hotel
Church Rd, Upper Coonoor, T0423-223 0021, www.tajhotels.com.
32 spacious cottage-style rooms, many with open fires, set in beautiful gardens. Excellent food, though service can be slow, and a wonderful wood-panelled bar. There is also yoga, an Ayurvedic spa and good sports facilities.

$$$ The Tryst
Carolina Tea Estate, T0423-220 7057, www.trystindia.com.
The shelves at this homestay groan under years of hoarding. 5 double rooms with a well-stocked library, snooker table, games galore and gym, plus a huge cottage that sleeps 10. Unexpected and in an outstanding location away from all other accommodation, cradled in the nape of a rolling tea estate. Excellent walking. Book in advance.

$$ 'Wyoming' Holiday Home (YWCA)
Near Hospital, Upper Coonoor (auto from bus stand Rs 25), T0423-245 2008, www.wyoming.co.in.
Set in a house with character and idyllic views, this popular place has 8 large rooms and 2 dorms (8-bedded) and excellent food (no alcohol). There's a garden and friendly, helpful, staff. The manager is qualified in alternative therapies, and runs a clinic and courses. Book ahead.

$ Blue Star
Kotagiri, next to bus station, T04266-274454.
Rooms with a shower and toilet in a modern building.

Restaurants

$ The Only Place
Sim's Park Rd.
Simple, homely, good food.

$ Sri Lakshmi
Next to bus station.
Freshly cooked, quality vegetarian dishes; try paneer butter masala and Kashmiri naan.

What to do

TTDC from Ooty (reserve in Ooty Tourist Office). Coonoor–Kotagiri, 6 hrs; visiting Valley View, Sim's Park, Lamb's Rock, Dolphin's Nose, Kodadu viewpoint.

Transport

Bus Frequent buses to **Ooty** (every 10 mins from 0530) some via Sim's Park and many via Wellington. Also regular services to **Kotagiri** and **Coimbatore** (every 30 mins) through **Mettupalayam**. Direct bus to **Mysore** (or change at Ooty).

Train Coonoor sits at the top of the most scenic section of the Nilgiri Mountain Railway; steam locos from Mettupalayam terminate here, switching to diesel for the run into Ooty. Trains leave to **Ooty** at 0745, 1040, 1235 and 1630 (1½ hrs); and to **Mettupalayam** at 1515 (2½ hrs).

Mettupalayam and the Nilgiri Ghat Road   Colour map 7, B3.

starting point of the Nilgiri Mountain Railway

The journey up to Coonoor from Mettupalayam is one of the most scenic in South India, with superb views over the plains below. Between Mettupalayam and the start of the Ghat road, there are magnificent groves of tall, slender areca nut palms. Mettupalayam has become the centre for the areca nut trade as well as producing synthetic gems. The palms are immensely valuable trees: the nut is used across India wrapped in betel vine leaves – two of the essential ingredients of India's universal after-meal digestive, *paan*.

The town is the starting point of the ghat railway line up to Ooty (see box, page 848). If you take the early morning train you can continue to Mysore by bus from Ooty on the same day, making a very pleasant trip.

Listings Mettupalayam

Where to stay

$ Surya International
345 Ooty Main Rd, T04254-223502.
Quiet, but characterless hotel, often empty, with fairly clean rooms (Rs 150) and a rooftop restaurant.

Restaurants

Karna Hotel in the bus station is good for *dosas*.

Transport

Train The *Nilgiri Express* from Chennai Central arrives in Mettupalayam at 0615, triggering a mad dash for tickets and seats on the tiny 'toy train' of the Nilgiri Mountain Railway, which departs for **Ooty** at 0710 (5 hrs). Only 30 tickets are available for same-day purchase on the toy train, so book as far in advance as possible. Note that the line is subject to landslides and washouts that can close the route for some months; check before travelling. If you're coming from Coimbatore, it is better to arrive in advance at Mettupalayam by bus (quicker and more frequent than local trains). If you have time to spare the engine sheds are interesting to look around. The *Nilgiri Exp 12672*, returns to Chennai at 1945, 10½ hrs; many more options from Coimbatore

Mudumalai Wildlife Sanctuary   Colour map 7, B3.

tigers, leopards and elephant roam at the foot of misty hills

Wildlife

The sanctuary adjoins Bandipur National Park beyond the Moyar River, its hills (at 885-1000 m), ravines, flats and valleys being an extension of the same environment. The park is one of the more popular and is now trying to limit numbers of visitors to reduce disturbance to the elephants.

There are large herds of elephant, gaur, sambar, barking deer, wild dog, Nilgiri langur, bonnet monkey, wild boar, four-horned antelope and the rarer tiger and leopard, as well as smaller mammals and many birds and reptiles. **Elephant Camp** ① *south of Theppakadu, open 0700-0800 and 1600-1700*, tames wild elephants. Some are bred in captivity and trained to work for the timber industry. You can watch the elephants being fed in the late afternoon, learn about each individual elephant's diet and the specially prepared 'cakes' of food.

There are *machans* near waterholes and salt licks and along the Moyar River. With patience you can see a lot, especially rare and beautiful birds. You can spend a day climbing the hill and bathe at the impressive waterfalls. The core area is not open to visitors.

850 · Tamil Nadu The Tamil Hill Stations

Essential Mudumalai Wildlife Sanctuary

Wildlife viewing

You can hire a jeep for about Rs 12 per km but must be accompanied by a guide. The government-run minibus safaris (0600-100, 1400-1800, Rs 135, still camera Rs 25, video Rs 150) are mostly worthless for seeing wildlife aside from deer and peacocks. You're better off going for a drive on the roads around the park after dark; try the roads from the Reception office to Thepakkadu, and from Masinagudi to Bokkapuram. Elephant rides

Tip...

Treks and jeep rides in the remoter parts of the forest with guides can be arranged from some lodges, including **Jungle Retreat** (see Where to stay, below).

from 0700-0800 and 1600-1700 (Rs 215 per person for 30 minutes); check timing and book in advance in Theppakadu or with the **Wildlife Warden** (Mount Stuart Hill, Ooty, T0423-244 4098). They can be fun even though you may not see much wildlife.

The Reception Range Office, Theppakadu (T0423-252 6235, open 0600-1800) is where buses between Mysore and Ooty stop. There is a Ranger Office at Kargudi.

When to go

The best time to visit is September-December and March-May when the undergrowth dies down and it's easier to see animals, especially at dawn when they're on the move. Forest fires can close the park temporarily during February-April.

Listings Mudumalai Wildlife Sanctuary

Where to stay

Advance booking is essential especially during the season and at weekends. Accommodation is better near Masinagudi which also has restaurants and shops but there is some in Bokkapuram, 3 km further south. Ask private lodges for pick-up if arriving by bus at Theppakadu.

$$$$-$$$ Jungle Retreat
Bokkapuram, T0423-252 6469,
www.jungleretreat.com.
The rates have been jacked up radically, but this is still a wonderful, quiet place with spectacular mountain views and a great pool. Wide choice of rooms, including cool stone-walled cottages with private terraces, romantic open-sided treehouses, simple bamboo huts and a well-swept but madly overpriced dorm (Rs 3000 per person, includes all meals). The friendly owners keep high standards and can arrange safaris, good treks with local guides and elephant rides. If you want to eat here, prepare to get slugged for an extra Rs 2000 per day.

$$$ Bamboo Banks Farm Guest House
Masinagudi, T09443-373201,
www.bamboobanks.in.
6 clean rooms, 4 in cottages in a fine setting, with an attractive garden, good food, birdwatching, horse riding and jeep hire.

$$$ Forest Hills Farm
Bokkapuram, T0423-252 6216,
www.foresthillsindia.com.
Friendly place, offering 15 modern rooms with bath, plus a dorm. Recommended.

$$$-$$ Jungle Hut
Near Bokkapuram, T0423-252 6463,
www.junglehut.in.
In a valley, 12 clean, simple rooms with bath in 3 stone cottages plus a few small tents. There's good food ("lovely home cooking"), a pool, jeep hire, game viewing and treks, and a very friendly welcome. Rates include all meals. Recommended.

$$ New Mountania
Masinagudi, T(0)91591 28022,
www.newmountania.com.
Rooms in cottages (prices vary), "nice but a bit overpriced", restaurant, jeep tour to waterfalls, and easy animal spotting (evening is best).

$$-$ Monarch Safari Park
Bokkapuram, on a hillside,
www.mithunhotels.com.
Large grounds, with 16 bungalows and 14 rooms in twin *machan* huts on stilts with bath (rats may enter at night), an open-sided restaurant, bikes, birdwatching, good horse riding (Rs 150 per hr), some sports facilities, and a meditation centre; a "lovely spot". The management are a bit slack but offer friendly, if slow, service.

$ Forest Department Huts
Reserve in advance through Forest Range Officer, Mt Stuart Hill, Ooty, T0423-244 5971, or try your luck at the last minute with the Reception Range Officer, Theppakadu, T0423-252 6235.
Most have caretakers who can arrange food.

Abhayaranyam Rest House
Kargudi.
2 rooms.

Abhayaranyam Annexe
Kargudi.
2 rooms. Recommended.

Log House
Masinagudi.
5 rooms.

Minivet and Morgan
Kargudi.
Dorm, 8 and 12 beds.

Peacock
Kargudi.
50-bed dorm, excellent food.

Rest House and Annexe
Kargudi.
Ask for deluxe rooms.

Rest House
Masinagudi.
3 rooms.

$ Tamil Nadu (TTDC hostel)
Theppakadu, T0423-252 6249.
3 rooms, 24 beds in dorm, restaurant, and a van for viewing.

Transport

Bus Theppakadu is on the main Mysore–Ooty bus route. From **Mysore**, services from 0615 (1½-2 hrs); last bus to Mysore around 2000. From **Ooty** via **Gudalur** on a very winding road (about 2½ hrs); direct 20 km steep road used by buses, under 1 hr. Few buses between Theppakadu and Masinagudi.
   Jeeps are available at bus stands and from lodges.

Coimbatore and the Nilgiri Hills *Colour map 7, B3.*
an important transport junction for several attractive hill areas

Coimbatore
As one of South India's most important industrial cities since the 1930s development of hydroelectricity from the Pykara Falls, Coimbatore (population 1.05 million) holds scant charm to warrant more than a pit stop. It was once the fulcrum of tussles between Tamilian, Mysorean and Keralite coastal rulers (the word *palayam* crops up tellingly often in Coimbatore, its translation being 'encampment') and sadly violence continues today. You are likely to stay here only if fascinated by the cotton trade or stuck for an onward bus or train.

Fact...
Coimbatore's nickname is 'India's Manchester', because it is the subcontinent's capital of cotton weaving; skyscrapers called things such as 'Viscose Towers' aren't uncommon.

Salem
Salem (population 829,300), an important transport junction, is surrounded by hills: the Shevaroy and Nagaramalai Hills to the north and the Jarugumalai Hills to the southeast. It is a busy, rapidly growing industrial town – particularly for textiles and metal-based industries – with modern shopping centres. The old town is on the east bank of the River Manimutheru. Each evening around Bazar Street you can see cotton carpets being made. The **cemetery**, next to the Collector's office, has some interesting tombstones. To the southeast of the town on a ridge of the Jarugumalai Hills is a highly visible *Naman* painted in *chunam* and ochre. On the nearby hill the **temple** (1919) is particularly sacred to the weavers' community. Some 600 steps lead up to excellent views over the town.

Yercaud and the Shevaroy Hills
The beautiful drive up the steep and sharply winding ghat road from Salem quickly brings a sharp freshness to the air as it climbs to over 1500 m. The minor resort of Yercaud (altitude 1515 m) has a small artificial lake, and some attractive though unmarked walks start here; the whole area is

full of botanical interest. There is an orchidarium and a horticultural research station, and a tourist information office in the Tamil Nadu hotel in town.

Just outside town is **Lady's Seat**, overlooking the ghat road, which has wonderful views across the Salem plains. Near the old Norton Bungalow on the Servarayan Temple Road is another well-known local spot, **Bear's Cave**. Formed by two huge boulders, it is occupied by huge colonies of bats.

Listings Coimbatore and the Nilgiri Hills

Where to stay

Coimbatore

$$ Heritage Inn
38 Sivaswamy Rd, T0422-223 1451, www.hotelheritageinn.in.
Standard hotel with good restaurants, internet, excellent service, 63 modern, a/c rooms; good value.

$$ Sabari Nest
739-A Avanashi Rd, 2 km from the railway, T0422-450 5500, www.sabarihotels.com.
38 a/c rooms, some small, restaurant, bar, amazing supermarket downstairs (for Western snacks and last stop for supplies), business facilities, and a roof garden. Recommended.

$$-$ City Tower
Sivaswamy Rd (Just off Dr Nanjappa Rd), Gandhipuram, near the bus stand, T0422-223 0681, www.hotelcitytower.com.
91 excellent redecorated rooms, some a/c, small balconies, 2 restaurants (rooftop tandoori), no alcohol, superb service. Recommended.

$ Channma International
18/109 Big Bazar St, T0422-239 6631.
Oldish art deco-style hotel, with 36 spacious, clean rooms, tiny windows, a restaurant, internet, health club and pool next door.

$ KK Residency
7 Shastri Rd, by Central Bus Stand, Ramnagar, T0422-430 0200.
42 smallish but clean rooms, 6 a/c, good condition, restaurant, friendly service. Recommended.

$ Meena
109 Kalingarayar St, T0422-223 5420.
Small family hotel with 30 clean and pleasant rooms and a vegetarian restaurant.

Salem

Choose a room away from the road if possible.

$$ Salem Castle
A-4 Bharati St, Swarnapuri, 4 km from the railway station, T0427-244 8702, www.hotelsalemcastle.com.
Rather brash, modern hotel with 64 comfortable, spotless a/c rooms. There are restaurants, including a good but expensive Chinese one, and Indian-style ones, a coffee shop, bar, exchange and pool.

$ City View
Omalur Main Rd, T0427-233 4232.
Rooms with bath, some clean, strong a/c, meals and travel agent. **Shree Saravanabhavan** in the same block does good South Indian veg dishes.

$ Ganesh Mahal
323 Omalur Rd, T0427-233 2820.
Modern and comfortable, with 45 pleasant rooms, TV, a good restaurant, and bar.

$ Railway Retiring Rooms
Battered but with olde-worlde feel.

$ Raj Castle
320 Omalur Rd, T0427-233 3532.
21 well-fitted rooms, 4 a/c, some with balcony, TV, hot water in the morning, and a tourist car.

$ Selvam
231 Omalur Rd, T0427-233 4491.
Clean rooms with bath, some a/c
Good restaurant.

Yercaud

Most hotels offer off-season discounts Jan-Mar and Aug-Dec.

$$$-$ Shevaroys
Main (Hospital) Rd, near lake, T04281-222288, www.hotelshevaroys.com.
A wide variety of rooms and cottages, restaurant and bar. Good views.

$$ Sterling Resort
Near Lady's Seat, T04281-222700, www.sterlingholidays.com.
59 rooms, modern, excellent views.

\$\$-\$ Tamil Nadu (TTDC)
Salem-Yercaud Ghat Rd, near the lake,
behind Panchayat Office, T04281-223334.
12 rooms, restaurant and garden.

Restaurants

Coimbatore

\$\$\$ Cloud Nine
City Tower Hotel (see Where to stay, above).
Excellent views from the rooftop of one of
the city's tallest buildings. Good international
food (try asparagus soup) and a buzzing
atmosphere, especially when it's full of families
on Sun evening. Pleasant service but a slightly
puzzling menu.

\$ Peking
556 SS Complex, near Rasi Hospital, DB Rd,
RS Puram, T0422-255 4739.
Dingy looking restaurant, but worth a visit for its
good Chinese food.

\$ Indian Coffee House
Ramar Koil St.
South Indian snacks.

\$ Royal Hindu
Opposite Junction station.
Indian vegetarian dishes.

Festivals

Yercaud
May Summer Festival, focused on the hilltop
cave shrine to Servarayan, is attended by many
tribal people.

What to do

Coimbatore
Aloha, *422 Dr Nanjappa Rd, near Race Course,*
T0422-223 3476, www.aloha-travels.com. Helpful
travel agency.

Transport

Coimbatore
Air Peelamedu Airport, 12 km from the centre,
T0422-2591905, has daily flights to **Bengaluru**
(**Bangalore**), **Chennai**, **Delhi**, **Kochi**, **Kozhikode**
and **Mumbai**. Various city buses run into town;
taxis Rs 250-300; auto-rickshaw Rs 150.

Bus City buses run a good service: several
connect the bus stations in Gandhipuram with
the Junction Railway Station 2 km south. No 20
goes to the airport (Rs 20).

There are 4 long-distance bus stations, off
Dr Nanjappa Rd.

City or '**Town**' **Bus Stand** in Gandhipuram.
Thiruvallur Bus Stand, Cross Cut Rd.
Computerized reservations T0422-226700,
0700-2100, www.tnstc.in/TNSTCOnline. Frequent
Government Express buses to **Madurai** (5 hrs),
Chennai (12 hrs), **Mysore** (6 hrs), **Ooty** (3 hrs),
Tiruchirappalli (5½ hrs).

'**Central**' **Bus Stand** is further south,
on corner of Shastri Rd. State buses to
Bengaluru (**Bangalore**) and **Mysore**; **Ooty** via
Mettupalayam (see below for train connections)
and **Coonoor** every 20 mins, 0400-2400, 5 hrs.

Ukkadam Bus Stand, south of the city, serves
towns within the state (**Pollachi**, **Madurai**) and in
north Kerala (**Pallakad**, **Thrissur**, **Munnar**).

Taxi Tourist taxis and yellow top taxis are
available at the bus stations, railway station and
taxi stands. Rs 2.5 per km; for out-station hill
journeys, Rs 3 per km; minimum Rs 30.

Train Junction station, enquiries, T132,
reservations, T131, 0700-1300, 1400-2030.
Bengaluru (**Bangalore**): *Tilak Exp 11014*,
0800, 7¼ hrs; *Bangalore Exp 12678*, 1245, 7 hrs;
Kanniyakumari: *Kanyakumari Exp 16381*, 0010,
9 hrs. **Chennai**: *West Coast Exp 16628*, 0630,
9 hrs; *Kovai Exp 12676*, 1420, 7½ hrs. **Kochi** (**HT**):
Ernakulam Exp 12677, 1310, 4hrs; *Hyderabad-Kochi*
Exp 17030, 0935, daily, 5½ hrs.

For **Ooty**, it's best to take the bus to
Mettupalayam (see above).

Salem
Bus The **New Bus Stand**, north of the hospital,
off Omalur Rd, T0427-244 6041, buses to all major
towns in Tamil Nadu, Kerala and South Karnataka.

Train Salem is an important junction, with
trains for most destinations in Tamil Nadu, as
well as west to Kerala and north to Bengaluru
and beyond. **Bengaluru**: 10 daily, 4½-6 hrs.
Chennai (**C**): more than 20 a day, 5 hrs.
Ernakulam (Kochi): more than 10 daily, 7-8 hrs.
Madurai: 2 daily, 5 hrs.

Yercaud
Bus There are no local buses but some from
Salem (1 hr) continue to nearby villages.

The climb up the Palanis starts 47 km before Kodaikanal (population 36,500, altitude 2343 m), also known as Kodai, and is one of the most rapid ascents anywhere across the ghats. The views are stunning. In the lower reaches of the climb you look down over the Kambam Valley, the Vaigai Lake and across to the Varushanad Hills beyond, while higher up the scene is dominated by the sawn-off pyramid of Perumal Malai.

Set around a small artificial lake, the town has crisply fresh air, even at the height of summer, and the beautiful scent of pine and eucalyptus make it a popular retreat from the southern plains. Today Kodai is a fast-growing resort, yet it retains a relatively low-key air that many feel gives it an edge over Ooty.

Sights
Star-shaped **Kodaikanal Lake** covers 24 ha and is surrounded by gentle wooded slopes. The walk around the lake takes about one hour; you can also hire pedal boats and go fishing (with permission from the Inspector of Fisheries), although the water is polluted. The International School, established in 1901, has a commanding position on the lakeside, and provides education for children from India and abroad between the ages of five and 18.

The view over the plains from **Coaker's Walk**, built by Lieutenant Coaker in the 1870s, can be magnificent; on a rare clear day you can see as far as Madurai. It is reached from a signposted path just above the bazar, 1 km from the bus stand.

Kurinji Andavar Temple, northeast of the town past Chettiar Park, is dedicated to Murugan and associated with the Neelakurinji flower that carpets the hills in purple flowers once every 12 years (the next mass flowering is due in 2018). There are excellent views of the north and southern plains, including Palani and Vaigai Dams.

The small but interesting **Shenbaganur Museum** ① *5 km down Law's Ghat road, open 1000-1130, 1500-1700*, at the Sacred Heart College seminary, is the local flora and fauna museum, exhibiting 300 orchid species as well as some archaeological remains. It's an attractive walk downhill from the town passing a number of small waterfalls. Some 4 km west of the bus stand at a height of 2347 m, the **Solar Physical Observatory** ① *T04542-240588, open Fri 1000-1230, 1900-2100*, is one of the oldest in the world, established in 1899.

Bear Shola Falls, named because it once attracted bears, is a favourite picnic spot about 2 km from the bus stand. The falls, like most others around Kodai, have been reduced to a trickle outside monsoon season. A pleasant walk or bike/scooter ride leads southwest from the lake along leafy avenues, past the golf course where wild deer and gaur are sometimes seen, to the striking viewpoint at Valley View; a further 3 km away are Pillar Rocks, a trio of impressive granite formations over 120 m high.

Essential Kodaikanal

Finding your feet
Buses make the long climb from Madurai and other cities to the Central Bus Stand, which is within easy walking distance from most hotels. The nearest train station is Kodai Road.

Getting around
Kodai is small enough to walk around, though for some of the sights it is worth getting an unmetered taxi. See Transport, page 859.

BACKGROUND

Kodaikanal

The Palani Hills were first surveyed by British administrators in 1821, but the surveyor's report was not published until 1837, 10 years after Ooty had become the official sanatorium for the British in South India. A proposal to build a sanatorium was made in 1861-1862 by Colonel Hamilton, who noted the extremely healthy climate and the lack of disease, but the sanatorium was never built because the site was so inaccessible. So it was that Kodaikanal became the first hill station in India to be set up not by heat-sick Britons but by American missionaries.

The American Mission in Madurai, established in 1834, had lost six of their early missionaries within a decade. The missionaries had been eyeing a site in the Sirumalai Hills, at around 1300 m, but while these were high enough to offer respite from the heat of the plains they were still prone to malaria. Isolated Kodai, almost 1000 m higher, proved to be the ticket, and the first two bungalows were built by June 1845. Kodai's big transformation came at the turn of the 20th century with the arrival of the car and the bus. In 1905 it was possible to do the whole journey from Kodai Road station to Kodai within the hours of daylight. The present road, up Law's Ghat, was opened to traffic in 1916.

Listings Kodaikanal and the Palani Hills *map p857*

Tourist information

Kodaikanal

Tamil Nadu Tourist Office
Hospital Rd next to the bus stand, T04542-241675. Open 1000-1745 except holidays.
Helpful staff and maps available.

Where to stay

Kodaikanal

Room rates are high in Kody compared to the rest of Tamil Nadu, but so are standards of cleanliness, in every price category. Off-season rates are given here: prices rise by 30-100% Apr-Jun and 12.5% tax is charged everywhere. On Anna Salai cheap basic lodges, mostly with shared bathroom, can charge Rs 800 in season.

$$$ Carlton
Boat Club Rd, T04542-248555,
www.carlton-kodaikanal.com.
Fully modernized but colonial-style hotel with 91 excellent rooms, many with private terraces overlooking the lake. Excellent restaurant, billiards, tennis, golf and boating, often full in season. Recommended.

$$$-$$ Elephant Valley
Ganesh Puram village (20 km from Kodai off Palani road), T0413-265 5751.
This tranquil eco-resort comprises 13 cute rustic stone cottages (some in converted village houses) dotted across a 30-ha organic farm on either side of a rocky river, visited by wild boar, gaur and elephants (best sightings Apr-Jun). The restaurant serves good food based on home-grown veg and herbs, fantastic salads, plus superb coffee which is grown, roasted and ground entirely on site. Highly recommended.

$$$-$$ Villa Retreat
Coaker's Walk, T04542-240940,
www.villaretreat.com.
Rustic, clean place with 8 deluxe rooms in an old house and 3 cottages (with an open fireplace). In a garden setting, with excellent views and good service, but a bit overpriced.

$$ Bala
11/49 Woodville Rd, opposite the bus station (entrance tucked away in private courtyard), T04542-241214, www.balagroups.com.
Friendly and well-kept hotel, with 57 rooms (ask for one on 2nd or 3rd floor as the lower rooms look out on neighbouring walls). Good vegetarian restaurant and friendly staff.

$$ Bison Wells Jungle Lodge

Camp George Observatory, T04542-240566, www.wilderness-explorer.in.

A cottage for the nature purist, with no electricity and space for only 3, a whole mountain range away from the rest of the hill station. Jeep transport from Kody arranged on request at extra cost.

$$ Hilltop Towers

Club Rd, T04542-240413, www.hilltopgroup.in.

26 modern, properly cleaned and comfortable rooms, some noise from passing buses and limited hours for hot water, but the management are very obliging and the complex contains a slew of good restaurants. Recommended.

$$ RR Residency

Boathouse Rd, T04542-244300, www.rrresidency.in.

7 well-furnished, top-quality rooms in a newish hotel, though views are lacking and there's potential olfactory disturbance from adjacent petrol pump. A vegetarian restaurant is next door.

$$-$ Greenlands

St Mary's Rd, Coaker's Walk end, T04542-241099, www.greenlandskodaikanal.com.

Clean, small and friendly budget traveller choice. 15 very basic, clean rooms (jug and bucket of hot water 0700-0900), amazing views. A few newish rooms are less atmospheric but have hot water on tap. Pleasant gardens, and a 62-bed dorm (Rs 300).

Kodaikanal

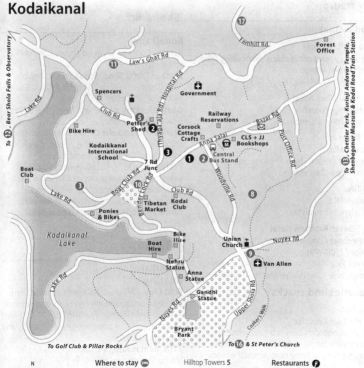

N		
100 metres		
100 yards		

Where to stay 🛏
Bala *2*
Bison Wells *12*
Carlton *3*
Elephant Valley *13*
Greenlands *16*

Hilltop Towers *5*
Kodai Plaza *8*
RR Residency *10*
Vignesh *11*
Villa Retreat *9*
Youth Hostel

Restaurants 🍴
Pastry Corner *1*
Silver Inn *2*
Tava *3*

$ Kodai Plaza
St Anthoia Koil St (walk uphill from the bus stand and turn left down a steep, narrow lane), T04542-240423.
The cheapest choice around the bus stand, rooms are not the cleanest but survivable, and some have good views of distant peaks framed by fluttering prayer flags.

$ Vignesh
Laws Ghat Rd, near the lake, T04542-244348.
Old period-style house, with 6 spacious rooms (can interconnect), good views and in a garden setting. Recommended.

$ Youth Hostel (TTDC)
Fernhill Rd, T04542-241336.
Rooms and dorm beds.

Restaurants

Kodaikanal

$$$ Carlton Hotel
Set in very pleasant grounds overlooking lake and Garden Manor.
Good for tea and snacks.

$$ Royal Tibet Hotel
J's Heritage complex, PT Rd.
Noodle soup and momos.

$$ Silver Inn
Hospital Rd.
Travellers' breakfasts and Indian choices. Popular but slow service.

$$ Tava
Hospital Rd.
Excellent Indian dishes.

$$ Tibetan Brothers Hotel
J's Heritage Complex. Open 1200-2200 (closed 1600-1730).
Serves excellent Tibetan dishes, in a homely atmosphere. Good value. Recommended.

Bakeries and snacks

Eco-Nut
J's Heritage Complex.
Good wholefoods, brown bread, jams, peanut butter, etc (cheese and yoghurts are better and cheaper though in the dairy across the road).

Hot Breads
J's Heritage Complex.
For very good pastries.

Pastry Corner
Anna Salai Bazar.
Brown bread, pastries and chocolate brownies, plus a couple of tables out the front.

Philco's Cold Storage
Opposite Kodai International School.
For home-made chocolate, cakes, frozen foods, delicatessen. Also internet.

Spencer's Supermarket
Club Rd.
Wide range of local and foreign cheeses.

Festivals

Kodaikanal
May Summer Tourist Festival: boat race, flower show, dog show, etc.

Shopping

Kodaikanal
Belgian Convent Shop, *east of town*. Hand-embroidered linen.
Cottage Crafts Shop, *Anna Salai (Council for Social Concerns in Kodai). Mon-Sat 0900-1230 and 1400-1830.* Volunteer-run.
Govt Sales Emporium, *near Township Bus Stand.* Only open in season.
Kashmir Handicrafts Centre, *2 North Shopping Complex, Anna Salai.* Jewellery, brass, shawls, walnut wood crafts and Numdah rugs.
Potter's Shack, *PT Rd.* Lovely earthy cups and vases made by local potters Subramaniam and Prabhu under tutelage of Ray and Deborah Meeker of Puducherry. Visits to the workshop can be arranged, and proceeds go to help disadvantaged children.

What to do

Kodaikanal
Boating
Boat Club, *T04542-241315. Open 0900-1730.* Rents out pedal boats, 6-seater row boats and romantic Kashmir-style *shikaras*, Rs 40-160 per 30 mins plus boatman fees. The boatmen here are friendly and speak good English.
TTDC Boat House, *next door. Open 0900-1730.* Similar services and prices.

Golf
Golf club, *T04542-240323, www.kodaigolf.com.* Kodai's forest-swathed course is one of the most beautiful and (out of season) peaceful

in the world, and the greens and fairways are maintained with minimal watering and no chemical pesticides. A round costs from Rs 500.

Horse riding
Ponies for hire near the Boat House, Rs 300 per hr.

Trekking
A reputable local guide is **Vijay Kumar** (T(0)9994-277373).

Transport

Kodaikanal
Bicycle hire There are several bike hire stands around the lake, charging Rs 10 per hr, Rs 100 per day for good new bikes.

Bus Check timings; reservations are possible. To **Bengaluru** (**Bangalore**), overnight, 12 hrs; **Chennai** (497 km) 12 hrs; **Coimbatore** (171 km) 6 hrs; **Dindigul** (90 km) 3½ hrs, via Kodai Rd; **Madurai** (120 km), 0730-1830, 4 hrs; **Kumily** (for Periyar NP), 5½ hrs, change buses at Vatigundu; **Palani** (65 km) 3 hrs; **Tiruchirappalli** (197 km) 6 hrs. To **Munnar** by bus takes 8 hrs, changing at Palani and Udhamalpet.

Taxi Unmetered taxis available for sightseeing. Tourist taxis from agencies including **Raja's**, near Pastry Corner on Anna Salai, T04542-242422. Taxi transfer to **Munnar** costs around Rs 2600, or Rs 450 for a seat in a shared taxi.

Train Reservations counter off Anna Salai behind **Anjay** hotel, 0800-1200, 1430-1700, Sun 0800-1200. No Foreign Tourist Quota bookings. The nearest station is Kodai Rd, 80 km away, with good connections north towards **Chennai** (9 hrs) and south to **Kanyakumari** (6 hrs) via **Madurai** (1 hr); also overnight trains to **Bengaluru** (10 hrs). Taxi drivers at the station quote Rs 1500-plus to drop you in Kodai, but this price drops if you cross the road and look determined to catch a bus. **Hotel Tamil Nadu**, just south of the station, has rooms if you get stuck.

Around Kodaikanal *Colour map 7, C4.*
pilgrim fervour and leopard-rich mountain sanctuaries

If you're in the mood for an adventure there's a popular semi-official trekking route that links Kodaikanal to Munnar, roughly following the now-overgrown Escape Road built by the British Army in anticipation of a Japanese invasion in 1942. The route follows the Pillar Rocks road, then descends to beautiful Berijam Lake, 21 km southwest of Kodaikanal, where there's an adequate Forest Rest House.

You can visit the lake on a day trip with permission from the **Forestry Department Office** ① *Law's Ghat Rd, Kodaikkanal, T04542-240287; only 10 permits are granted a day so arrive at the office before 1000.* The next day you continue through pine and eucalypt plantations, patches of shola forest and the occasional village to Top Station in Kerala (five to six hours), where there is a Forest Hut and shops and tea stalls selling snacks. From here you can catch a bus or jeep to Munnar, 41 km away. You'll need permission from the Forestry Department in both Kodai and Munnar to complete the trek, and cross-border bureaucratic wrangling can makes this hard to come by. Local guides can help with permits and transport at a charge: try Raja ① *T(0)9842-188893*, or the semi-legendary Kodai Mani ① *T(0)9894-048493*, who knows the trails well and charges accordingly.

If you're in the mood for an adventure there's a popular semi-official two-day trek that links Kodaikanal to Munnar, via beautiful Berijam Lake and Top Station, across the border in Kerala. You'll need permission from the Forestry Department in both Kodai and Munnar; local guides can help with permits and transport. Try Raja ① *T(0)9842-188893*, or the semi-legendary Kodai Mani ① *T(0)9894-048493*, who knows the trails well and charges accordingly.

The ghat road running north from Kodaikanal to **Palani** passes through smallholdings of coffee, oranges and bananas. Inter-planting of crops such as pepper is further increasing the yields from what can be highly productive land, even on steep slopes. The shrine to **Murugan** (Subrahmanya) on top of Palani (or Sivagiri) Hill is an important site of pilgrimage. During the January-February full moon, pilgrims walk from as far afield as Chettinad and Munnar to climb the 659 steps to the shrine. Many carry shoulder poles with

Tip...
Birdwatching is good from Kariam Shola watchtower, 2 km from Topslip.

elaborate bamboo or wooden structures on each end, living out the myth of Idumban, who carried the twin hills of Sivagiri and Shaktigiri from Mount Kailash to their present locations on either end of a bamboo *kavadi*. Around the temple, Palani presents a chaotic but compelling pastiche of pilgrim fervour, religious souvenir shopping and decaying flower garlands.

Anamalai (Indira Gandhi) Wildlife Sanctuary

0600-1800, Rs 15, camera Rs 25, video Rs 150; best time to visit Dec-Jun, closed mid-Feb to mid-Apr, avoid Sun. Reception and Information Centre at Top Slip organizes bus rides, elephant safaris and trekking guides. Day permits from entrance gate at Sethumadai; for overnight stays advance written permission is needed from Wildlife Warden (1176 Meenakalai Salai, Pollachi, 1.5 km out of town on road towards Top Slip, T04259-225356).

This beautiful, unspoilt park covering 960 sq km of grassland, rainforest and mountain shola forest is rarely visited except by Indian day trippers. Wildlife includes Nilgiri langur, lion-tailed macaque, elephant, gaur, tiger, panther, sloth, wild boar, birds – including pied hornbill, drongo, red whiskered bulbul, black-headed oriole – and a large number of crocodiles in the Amaravathi reservoir. There is an elephant camp, claimed to be the largest in Asia, reached by a two- to three-hour minibus ride through the forest (0615, 1130 and 1515, Rs 25), and short elephant rides can be arranged.

There are some **trekking** routes that vary from easy treks to Pandaravara (8 km), Kozhikamuthi (12 km) and Perunkundru peak (32 km), which is demanding. Permits can be obtained from the Range Officer ① *Top Slip, Rs 150-300 per person*. Private guides charge upwards of Rs 100 for a three-hour trek.

The main access town for the park is **Pollachi**, an important trading centre for over 2000 years, as witnessed by the finds of Roman silver coins bearing the heads of the emperors Augustus and Tiberias. Its main appeal nowadays is logistical, with a reasonable choice of places to stay; see below.

Listings Around Kodaikanal

Where to stay

Anamalai (Indira Gandhi) Wildlife Sanctuary

There are several Forest Department rest houses scattered around Top Slip and other parts of the sanctuary including Mt Stuart, Varagaliar, Sethumadai and Amaravathinagar. They may allow only 1 night's stay. Reservations: District Forest Officer, Coimbatore S Div, 176 Meeanakalai Salai, Pollachi, T04259-225356. The friendly canteen in Top Slip serves good *dosa* and *thalis* for lunch.

$ Sakti
144 Coimbatore Main Rd, Pollachi, T04259-223050.
Newish, large place, with smart rooms and a vegetarian restaurant.

Transport

Anamalai (Indira Gandhi) Wildlife Sanctuary

Bus 3 daily buses connect Top Slip with **Pollachi**, which has connections to **Coimbatore** and **Palani**. To **Top Slip**: 0600, 1100, 1500 (but check timings); from Top Slip: 0930, 1300, 1830.

Dindigul, north of Madurai, commands a strategic gap between the Sirumalai Hills to its east and the Palani Hills to the west. The market handles the produce of the Sirumalai Hills, including a renowned local variety of banana. Dindigul is particularly known for its cheroots.

The massive granite rock and **fort** ① *2 km west of the bus stand, 0730-1730, foreigners Rs 100, Indians Rs 5, autos Rs 20*, towers over 90 m above the plain. The Mysore army captured it in 1745 and Haidar Ali was appointed governor in 1755. It was ceded to the British under the Treaty of Seringapatam. There are magnificent views of the town, valley and hills on either side from the top of the rock fort.

Our Lady of Dolours Church, one of several churches in the town, is over 250 years old and was rebuilt in 1970. The Old City is interesting to walk around; you can walk up to the fort from there. The station is 2 km south of the bus stand that has cheap lodges nearby.

Listings Dindigul

Where to stay

$$$ Cardamom House
Athoor village, Kamarajar Lakeside, T(0)93606-91793, www.cardamomhouse.com.
This pretty home of a retired British doctor from Southsea introduces you to Tamil village life in Athoor and is a good bridge for journeys between either Kerala and Tamil Nadu or Trichy and Madurai. Tucked out of the way at the foothills of the Palani hills overlooking the lake, which is rich in birdlife, 7 rooms spread across 3 buildings all with lake views.

$$-$ Maha Jyothi
Spencer Compound, T0451-243 4313, hotelmahajyothi@rediffmail.com.
Range of rooms, a/c, clean, modern, and 24-hr check out.

$ Prakash
9 Thiruvalluvar Salai, T0451-244 1655.
42 clean, spacious rooms. Recommended.

$ Suganya Lodge
93 Thiruvallur Salai (by bus stand), T0451-242 8436.
Small, rather dark a/c rooms, but very clean, friendly staff, good value.

$ Venkateshwar Lodge
Near bus stand, T0451-242 5881.
Very cheap, 50 rooms, no a/c, basic, clean, vegetarian restaurant next door.

Restaurants

Sree Baalaaji Bhavan
Near the bus stand.
Tasty South Indian vegetarian food.

Venu Biryani
Near the bus stand.
A great place to try Dindigul's local take on the biriyani; mutton is the classic, but vegetarian options are available too.

Transport

Bus Good and frequent bus service to **Tiruchirappalli**, **Chennai**, **Salem** and **Coimbatore** and long distance connections.

Train Trains to **Chennai**: more than 10 daily, 6¾ hrs via **Tiruchirappalli,** 1½ hrs. To **Madurai** more than 10 a day, 1¼ hrs.

Madurai
& around

Madurai is a maddening whirl of a temple town: the red-and-white striped sanctuary of the 'fish-eyed goddess' is a towering edifice crested by elaborate gaudy stucco-work *gopurams*, soundtracked by tinny religious songs, peopled by 10,000 devoted pilgrims prostrating themselves at shrines, lighting candles and presenting flower garlands to idols, seeking blessings from the temple elephant or palmistry on the shores of the Golden Lotus Tank. Even the city's town planning reflects the sanctity of the spot: surrounding streets radiate like bicycle spokes from the temple in the mandala architectural style, a sacred form of geometry.

The centre seems all dust and cycle-rickshaws, but Madurai, as the second biggest city in Tamil Nadu, is also a modern industrial place that never sleeps.

Around the city the area of fertile agricultural land is dotted with exotically shaped granite mountain ranges such as Nagamalai (snake hills) and Yanaimalai (elephant hills).

★ Madurai   Colour map 7, C4.

Tamil Nadu's second city, centred on the unmissable Meenakshi temple

There is the usual combination of messy crumbling buildings in Madurai (population 1,017,900) harking back to times of greater architectural aspirations, modern glass-and-chrome palaces, internet cafés, flower sellers, tailors and tinkers and Kashmiri antique and shawl dealers. Further out, in the leafy suburbs to the west and north across the Vaigai River, are museums, lakes and temple tanks. Allow at least two days to explore everything.

Essential Madurai

Finding your feet

The airport is 12 km from town and is linked by buses, taxis and autos to the city centre. The railway station is within easy walking distance of many budget hotels (predatory rickshaw drivers/hotel touts may tell you otherwise). Hire an auto to reach the few north of the river. Most intercity buses arrive at the Mattuthavani Bus Stand 6 km northeast of the centre; those from Kodaikanal and destinations to the northwest

use the Arapalayam Bus Stand, 3 km northwest. Both are linked to the centre by bus and auto. See Transport, page 869.

Getting around

The city centre is compact and the temple is within easy walking distance of most hotels. Prepare for hordes of touts. To visit the sights around the city, buses and taxis are available.

Meenakshi Temple ① *Inner Temple 0500-1230, 1600-2130, foreigners Rs 50, tickets from counters near South Entrance and Thousand-Pillared Hall (valid for multiple entries on same day); art museum 0600-2030, Rs 5. Cameras must be left at storage counter, but phone cameras are permitted. Metal detectors and body searches at entrance gates. Sanctuaries of Meenakshi and Sundareswarar are open only to Hindus. Offers of good viewpoints made by helpful bystanders will invariably turn out to be from the roofs of nearby shops.* This is an outstanding example of Vijayanagar temple architecture and an exact contemporary of the Taj Mahal in Agra. Meenakshi, the 'fish-eyed goddess' and the consort of Siva, has a temple to the south, and Sundareswarar (Siva), a temple to the west. Since she is the presiding deity the daily ceremonies are first performed in her shrine and, unlike the practice at other temples, Sundareswarar plays a secondary role. The temple's nine towering *gopurams* stand out with their colourful stucco images of gods, goddesses and animals which are renewed and painted every 12 years – the most recent touch-up having been completed in February 2009. There are about 4000 granite sculptures on the lower levels. In addition to the Golden Lotus tank and various pillared halls there are five *vimanas* over the sanctuaries.

The temple is a hive of activity, with a colourful temple elephant, flower sellers and **musical performances** ① *1800-1930, 2100-2130.* There is an evening ceremony (arrive by 2100), when an image of Sundareswarar is carried in procession, to a heady accompaniment of whirling pipe and drum music and clouds of incense, from the shrine near the east *gopuram* to Meenakshi, to 'sleep' by her side; he is returned first thing the next morning. The procession around the temple

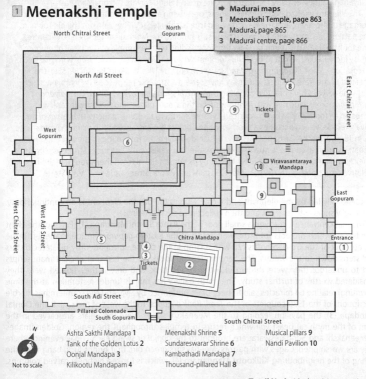

① **Meenakshi Temple**

➜ **Madurai maps**
1 Meenakshi Temple, page 863
2 Madurai, page 865
3 Madurai centre, page 866

North Chitrai Street

North Gopuram

North Adi Street

West Gopuram

West Chitrai Street

West Adi Street

Tickets

Chitra Mandapa

Viravasantaraya Mandapa

East Gopuram

East Chitrai Street

Tickets

South Adi Street

Pillared Colonnade
South Gopuram

South Chitrai Street

Entrance ①

N
Not to scale

Ashta Sakthi Mandapa **1**	Meenakshi Shrine **5**	Musical pillars **9**
Tank of the Golden Lotus **2**	Sundareswarar Shrine **6**	Nandi Pavilion **10**
Oonjal Mandapa **3**	Kambathadi Mandapa **7**	
Kilikootu Mandapam **4**	Thousand-pillared Hall **8**	

BACKGROUND

Madurai

According to legend, drops of nectar fell from Siva's locks on this site, so it was named Madhuram or Madurai, 'the Nectar City'. The city's history goes back to the sixth century BC. Ancient Madurai, which traded with Greece and Rome, was a centre of Tamil culture, famous for its writers and poets during the last period of the three *Sangam* (Tamil 'Academies') nearly 2000 years ago.

By the fourth century, Madurai, Tirunelveli and a part of southern Kerala were under the Pandiyas, a major power from the sixth to the early 10th century. The Pandiyas made Madurai their capital and remained here for 300 years, staying on even during the rule of the Cholas; after Chola power declined in the late 12th century the Pandiyas regained control of Madurai, and they presided over a period of flourishing international trade until Malik Kafur destroyed the city in 1310.

For a period Madurai became a sultanate, but Muslim rule in Tamil Nadu proved as short-lived as it was tenuous. In 1364 the city was recaptured by the Hindu Vijayanagar kings, who remained until 1565, when the defeat of the Vijayanagar Empire by a confederacy of Muslim states forced their leaders to take refuge in Madurai. As the Nayaka kings, they continued to rule well into the 17th century. The Nayakas have been seen essentially as warriors, given an official position by the Vijayanagar rulers, but in Sanskrit the term applied to someone of prominence and leadership. Burton Stein comments, "the history of the Vijayanagara is essentially the history of the great Telugu Nayakas" from Madurai.

The Vijayanagar had been great builders, preserving and enriching the architectural heritage of the town, and the Nayakas held true to their legacy. They laid out the old town in the pattern of a lotus, with narrow streets surrounding the Meenakshi Temple at the centre, and took up the Vijayanagar predilection for building temple complexes with tall *gopurams*. These increased in height to become dominating structures covered profusely with plaster decorations. The tall *gopurams* of Madurai were built by Thirumalai (ruled 1623-1655), the greatest of the Nayaka rulers, and may have served a strategic purpose as they moved away from the earlier Chola practice of giving the central shrine the tallest tower. The *kalyana mandapa* or marriage hall with a 'hundred' or 'thousand' pillars, and the temple tank with steps on all four sides, were introduced in some southern temples, along with the *Nandi* bull, Siva's vehicle, which occupies a prominent position at the entrance to the main Shaivite shrine.

In 1840, after the Carnatic Wars, the British destroyed the fort, filling in the surrounding moat; its original course is now followed by the four Veli streets. The inner streets encircling the central temple are named after the festivals which take place in them and give their relative direction: South 'Chitrai Street, East 'Avani Moola' Street and West 'Masi Street'.

is occasionally led by the elephant and a cow. During the day the elephant is on continual duty, 'blessing' visitors with its trunk and then collecting a small offering.

The main entrance is through a small door of the **Ashta Sakthi Mandapa (1)** (Porch of the Eight Goddesses) which projects from the wall, south of the eastern *gopuram*. Inside to the left is the sacred **Tank of the Golden Lotus (2)**, with a lamp in the centre, surrounded by pillared cloisters and steps down to the waters. The Sangam legend speaks of the test that ancient manuscripts had to undergo: they were thrown into the sacred tank, and only if they floated were they considered worthy of further study. The north gallery has murals (under restoration at the time of writing) relating 64 miracles said to have been performed by Siva, and the southern has marble inscriptions of the 1330 couplets of the *Tamil Book of Ethics*. To the west of the tank is the **Oonjal Mandapa (3)**, the pavilion leading to the Meenakshi shrine. Here the pillars are carved in the form of the mythical beast *yali* which recurs in temples throughout the region. Golden images of Meenakshi and Sundareswarar are brought to the *oonjal* or swing each Friday evening where they are worshipped. Cages with parrots, Meenakshi's green bird that brings luck, hang from the ceiling of the neighbouring **Kilikootu Mandapam (4)**, which is flanked by finely carved columns.

The **Meenakshi shrine (5)** with the principal image of the goddess, stands in its own enclosure with smaller shrines around it.

To the north of the tank is another enclosure with smaller *gopurams* on four sides within which is the **Sundareswarar shrine (6)** guarded by two tall *dwarapalas*. In the northeast corner, the superb sculptures of the divine marriage of Meenakshi and Sundareswarar being blessed by Vishnu and Brahma, and Siva in his 24 forms are in the 19th-century **Kambathadi Mandapa (7)**, around the golden flagstaff.

The **mid-16th century Thousand-pillared Hall (8)** is in the northeast corner of the complex. The 985 exquisitely carved columns include a lady playing the *vina*, a dancing Ganesh, and a gypsy leading a monkey. The art museum here exhibits temple art and architecture, fine brass and stone images, friezes and photos (the labelling could be improved). Just inside the museum to the right is a cluster of five **musical pillars (9)** carved out of a single stone. Each pillar produces a different note which vibrates when tapped. Nayaka musicians could play these as an instrument.

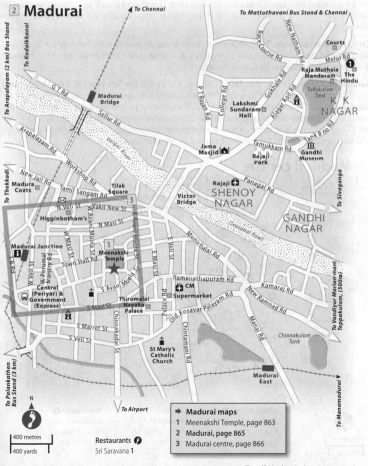

2 Madurai

Madurai maps
1 Meenakshi Temple, page 863
2 Madurai, page 865
3 Madurai centre, page 866

Restaurants
Sri Saravana 1

The **Nandi pavilion (10)** is to the east and is often packed with market stalls peddling flowers, trinkets and coconuts. The long *Pudu Mandapa* (New Mandapa), across the road from the East Tower, is lined with yet more beautiful sculptures of *yalis*, Nayaka rulers and elephants. Beyond lies the base of the unfinished *Raya Gopuram* which was planned to be the tallest in the country.

Northeast of the Meenakshi Temple, off N Avani Moola Street, is the **flower market**, a profusion of colour and activity at its best 0500-0730. It is a two-storey hall with piles of jasmine of all colours, lotuses, and huge jumbles of floral prettiness amid a sea of decomposing mulch of flowers trampled underfoot.

Thirumalai Nayaka Palace ① *0900-1300, 1400-1700, bus 17, 17A, 11, 11A*. Built in 1636 in the Indo-Mughal style, its 15 domes and arches are adorned with stucco work while some of its 240 columns rise to 12 m. Its *Swarga Vilasam* (Celestial Pavilion), an arcaded octagonal structure, is curiously constructed in brick and mortar without any supporting rafters. Special artisans skilled in the use of traditional lime plaster and powdered seashell and quartz have renovated parts. The original complex had a shrine, an armoury, a theatre, royal quarters, a royal bandstand, a harem, a pond and a garden but only about a quarter survives since Thirumalai's grandson removed sections to build another palace in Tiruchirappalli, and the original *Ranga* Vilasam was destroyed by Muslim invaders. It is a bit run down.

Vandiyur Mariammam Teppakulam ① *Buses 4 and 4A take 10 mins from the bus stand and railway station*. To the southeast of town, this has a small shrine in its centre where the annual Float Festival takes place in January/February.

Gandhi Museum ① *1000-1300, 1400-1730, free*. Located in the 300-year-old Rani Mangammal Palace, this is Madurai's best museum: informative, interesting and well laid out. It contains an art gallery, memorabilia (including the *dhoti* Gandhi was wearing when he was shot) and traces the history of the Independence struggle and the Quit India movement. It also has sections for Khadi and Village Industries and some stunning examples of South Indian handicrafts. Yoga classes are held daily (though only in Tamil) at 0630. There's an excellent bookshop.

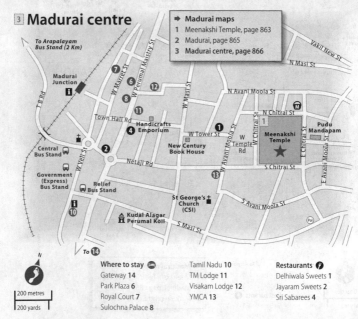

③ **Madurai centre**

➡ Madurai maps
1 Meenakshi Temple, page 863
2 Madurai, page 865
3 Madurai centre, page 866

Where to stay 🛏		Restaurants 🍴
Gateway 14	Tamil Nadu 10	Delhiwala Sweets 1
Park Plaza 6	TM Lodge 11	Jayaram Sweets 2
Royal Court 7	Visakam Lodge 12	Sri Sabarees 4
Sulochna Palace 8	YMCA 13	

Tourist information

Tourist office
W Veli St, T0452-233 4757. Mon-Fri 1000-1745.
Has useful maps, tours (arranged through agents), guides for hire. Also at Madurai Junction Railway Station (Main Hall, open 0630-2030) and the airport counter during flight times.

Where to stay

Tax of up to 20% is added even by modest hotels. Cheap hotels along and around West Peramul Maistry St, 2 blocks east of the railway station, but rooms can be hard to find by late afternoon. Most offer 24-hr checkout. Although there are slick hotels across the Vaigai these are not good value as they lack character and are away from the town's atmosphere. It's best to visit Madurai either from the charming remove of the hilltop Taj, or abandon yourself to the throng and take a room near the temple.

$$$ Gateway (Taj)
Pasumalai Hills, 7 TPK Rd, 5 km southwest of centre on NH7, T0452 663 3000, www.thegatewayhotels.com.
A real oasis, set on top of a hill with great views over surrounding country. The 30 rooms (some in an old colonial house) are set among shady gardens full of peacocks. There's a good bookshop and lovely pool.

$$$ Heritage Madurai
11, Melakkal Main Rd, Kochadai, T0452-238 5455, www.heritagemadurai.com.
A stunning new resort set in the banyan-shaded refuge of the Madurai Club. Standard rooms are big and full of light, while the good value villas come with your own pool and personal chef. A spectacular step-well pool and good restaurants are well worth the 4-km trek to the temple.

$$$-$$ Royal Court
4 West Veli St, T0452-435 6666, www.royalcourtindia.com.
70 extremely clean a/c rooms with bath, satellite TV and great views from rooftop (open 1900-2300). Good value.

$$ Park Plaza
114 W Perumal Maistry St, T0452-301 1111, www.hotelparkplaza.in.
Some of the 56 smart, 60s-print, stylish a/c rooms offer temple views, excellent rooftop restaurant (1700-2300), bar AND all facilities. Free pick-up from airport/railway station. Rates also include breakfast.

$$ Supreme
110 W Perumal Maistry St, T0452-234 3151, www.hotelsupreme.in.
69 slightly tatty but adequately clean rooms with marble and plastic furniture. Good rooftop restaurant with temple views, bar, 24-hr travel desk, exchange and internet booths in the basement. It's a bit noisy and a mite overpriced. Security and service are both wanting.

$ Hotel Tamil Nadu
West Veli St, T0452-233 7471, htn-mdu1@ttdconline.com.
A mint-coloured guesthouse dating from 1968 set around a courtyard attached to the friendly TN tourist office. It badly needs a new lick of paint – it's pretty grubby – but there are TVs, huge rooms and the staff are charming.

$ Sulochna Palace
96 W Perumal Maistry St, T0452-234 1071.
A genuine cheapie, and slightly more salubrious than its bottom-bracket neighbours. Avoid the lower floors where the generator noise is obtrusive.

$ TM Lodge
50 W Perumal Maistry St, T0452-234 1651.
Very clean, 57 rooms with hot water, some a/c, some with TV, and a balcony. They can arrange bookings for rail and bus journeys.

$ Visakam Lodge
9 Kakathope St, T0452-234 1241.
Good-value place with 18 clean rooms. Very popular with Indian tourists.

$ YMCA International Guest House
Main Guard Sq, near the temple, T0452-234 6649, www.ymcamadurai.com.
A great option within spitting distance of the temple. The double rooms here are simple but spacious and clean, the staff are friendly, and profits go to worthwhile projects.

Restaurants

$$ Surya
Supreme (see Where to stay, above).
Open 1600-2400.
7th-floor rooftop restaurant with international as well as Indian menu. Excellent Andhra *thalis*; very busy Sun evenings.

$$ Temple View
Park Plaza (see Where to stay, above).
Excellent rooftop venue.

$ Delhiwala Sweets
W Tower St.
Delicious Indian sweets and snacks.

$ Jayaram Sweets
6-7 Netaji Rd.
Good salty namkeens and fantastic coconut buns.

$ Sri Sabarees
Corner of W Perumal Maistry St and Town Hall Rd.
Serves simple South Indian fare – *thalis* (lunchtime only), *pongal*, *iddli* and *dosai* – but the 2 dining halls are perpetually packed, as is the coffee stall out front.

$ Sri Saravana
7 Melur Rd, opposite Court.
Delicious sweets (try the spectacular milk *peda*) and decent meals, across the river from town. Worth a diversion if you're at the Gandhi Museum.

Entertainment

Folk performances, in the 4 'Chitrai' streets by the temple, every Sat 1700-1800, free.

Meenakshi Temple: 'Bedtime of the God' 2100, is not to be missed (see page 863).
Thirumalai Nayaka Palace: Sound and Light show: English 1845-1930; Rs 5 (take mosquito repellent), sadly, "poor, faded tape". During the day, dance drama and concerts are held in the courtyard.

Festivals

Madurai
Jan Jallikattu Festival (Taming the Bull).
Jan/Feb The annual **Float Festival** marks the birth anniversary of Thirumalai Nayaka. Many temple deities in silks and jewels, including Meenakshi and Sundareswarar, are taken out on a full moon night on floats decorated with hundreds of oil lamps and flowers. The floats carry them to the central shrine to the accompaniment of music and chanting.
Apr/May The 10-day **Chitrai Festival** is the most important at the Meenakshi Temple, celebrating the marriage of Siva and Meenakshi.
Aug/Sep The **Avanimoolam** is the Coronation Festival of Siva when the image of Lord Sundareswarar is taken out to the river bank dressed as a worker.

Shopping

Best buys are textiles, wood and stone carvings, brass images, jewellery and appliqué work for temple chariots. Most shops are on South Avani Moola St (for jewellery), Town Hall Rd, Masi St and around the temple. Kashmiri emporia pay 40-50% commission to the touts who lure you into their shops with spurious promises of views into the temple.

Books
Higginbotham's Book Exchange, *near the temple.*
New Century Book House, 79-80 West Tower St.
Recommended.

Handicrafts
Handicrafts Emporium, *39-41 Town Hall Rd.*
Also try: **Khadi Gramodyog Bhandar** and **Surabhi** on W Veli St.

Textiles and tailors
The market near Pudu Mandapam, next to Meenakshi East Gate, sells fabric and is a brilliant place to get clothes made.
Femina, *10 W Chitrai St.* Similar to the market (you can take photos of the Meenakshi Temple from their rooftop).
Hajee Moosa, *18 E Chitrai St.* Tailoring in 8 hrs.

What to do

Body and soul
Yoga classes at **Gandhi Museum** (T0452-248 1060. Daily at 0630).

Tour operators
Tours can be arranged with **TTDC** (via Hotel Tamil Nadu, West Veli St, T0452-233 7471), or through most hotel desks. **Temple tour** of Madurai and attractive surroundings by a/c coach; half day, 0700-1200, 1500-2000. Rs 125. Recommended for an overview. Apr-Jun: **Courtallam**, Rs 300; **Kodaikanal**, 0700-2100, Rs 300; **Rameswaram**, Rs 275.
Ex-Serviceman Travels, *1 Koodalalagar, Perumal Kovil St, T0452-273 0571.* City tour, half day, 0700,

1500, Rs 140; Kodaikanal or Ramesvaram 0700-1900, Rs 275; overnight to Kanniyakumari, Rs 350.
Indian Panorama (Trichy), *T0431-422 6122, www.indianpanorama.in*. Tours from Madurai (and other towns). The Pandians are very helpful, efficient, South India tours, car with excellent driver. Highly recommended.
Siraj, *28 T P K Rd, opposite Periyar Bus Stand, T097 8859 6388*. Ticketing, good multilingual guides, cars.

Transport

Air Madurai's small airport, T0452-269 0717, is 12 km south of the centre. There are daily direct flights from Chennai, Bengaluru and Hyderabad, with connecting flights from Mumbai and New Delhi; you can also fly cheaply to **Colombo** with Spicejet. The 10A bus runs from the airport to the central Periyar bus stand. Taxis to the centre charge around Rs 375; an auto should cost Rs 150-200.

Airport to the city centre (12 km) by **Pandiyan** coach (calls at the top hotels); taxi (Rs 375) or auto-rickshaw (Rs 150).

Bus Local There is a good network within the city and the suburbs. **Central (Periyar) Bus Stands**, near W Veli St, are now used for buses around town and destinations nearby. Approaching on a bus from the south, to get to the centre, change to a city bus at Tirumangalam (15 km south).

Long distance Most intercity buses use the well-organized **New Central Bus Stand** (Mattuthavani Bus Terminal), 6 km northeast of town (continuation of Alagar Koil Rd),

T0452-421 9938; Rs 100 by rickshaw, or catch city buses 3, 48 or 700. Buses leave from here for **Bengaluru (Bangalore)** (11 hrs), **Ernakulam (Kochi)**, **Chennai** (10 hrs), **Puducherry** (9 hrs), **Thiruvananthapuram** (8 hrs), **Kumbakonum**, **Ramesvaram** (under 4 hrs, every 15 mins), **Thanjavur** (4 hrs), **Tiruchirappalli** (2½ hrs), **Tirunelveli** (4 hrs, Rs 40). Buses for the west and northwest leave from the **Arapalayam Bus Stand**, 3 km northwest of centre (Bus route No 7A, auto-rickshaws Rs 40), T0452-236 1740. Destinations include **Kodaikkanal** (3½ hrs, buses crowded in peak season Apr-Jul), **Coimbatore** (5 hrs, change for Mettupalayam and Ooty), **Periyar/Kumily** (4 hrs), **Salem** (5½ hrs), **Dindigul** (2 hrs).

Rickshaw Auto-rickshaw rates are theoretically Rs 10-15 per km, but drivers quote excessive rates for trips around town. A cycle rickshaw from the station area to temple should cost around Rs 30.

Taxi/car hire Most taxis are unmetered. Local car hire rates begin at 4 hrs/40 km Rs 700, 8 hrs/80 km Rs 1200. **FastTrack** T0452-288 8999.

Train **Madurai Junction** is the main station: enquiries, T131. 0700-1300 and 1330-2000. New Computer Reservation Centre to south of main entrance. Left-luggage facilities. Pre-paid auto-rickshaw kiosk outside. **Bengaluru**: 2 trains daily, 10 hrs, 1 continuing to **Mysore**, 14½ hrs. **Chennai (ME)**: at least 10 a day: *Vaigai Exp 12636*, 0630, 8-9 hrs, via Tiruchirappali, 3 hrs, Villupuram for **Puducherry**, 6 hrs. **Coimbatore**: 3 daily, 6-7 hrs. **Kanniyakumari**: at least 7 daily, 5 hrs. **Ramesvaram**: 3 unreserved passenger trains a day, 4 hrs.

The conch-shaped island of Ramesvaram (population 44,900) is normally lapped by the limpid blue waters of the Gulf of Mannar, but cyclones can whip the sea here into ferocious stormy waves. This is where Rama is believed to have worshipped Siva, making it sacred to both Shaivites and Vaishnavites, and so a pilgrim to Varanasi is expected to visit Ramesvaram next if he is to reach salvation.

The great Ramalingesvara temple, which forms the core of Ramesvaram, is one of India's most memorable, as much for the sight of priests spattering pilgrims with holy water from each of 22 sacred wells as for its cavernous, echoing corridors.

To Ramesvaram and Adam's Bridge

Seen from the air the plains of the Vaigai River form one of the most remarkable landscapes in India, for there are over 5000 tanks, and irrigation has been so developed that barely a drop of water is wasted. The coastal districts of Ramnad have their own highly distinct economy and society. For the Hindus the sandbanks barely concealed in the Palk Strait are like giant stepping stones linking India and Sri Lanka: Adam's Bridge. Both Hindu and Muslim communities have long-established trading links across the Bay of Bengal, to Malaysia and Southeast Asia and to Sri Lanka. Small settlements along the coast like Kilakkarai have long been associated with smuggling. The civil war in Sri Lanka has made it a sensitive region.

Ramesvaram

Non-Hindus are generally turned away, but you might be able to enter if you can tag along with a group of pilgrims doing the holy well circuit (see box, opposite).

The **Ramalingesvara** (or **Ramanathasvami**) **Temple** was founded by the Cholas but most of the temple was built in the Nayaka period (16th-17th centuries). It is a massive structure, enclosed by a huge rectangular wall with *gopurams* in the middle of three sides. Entrances through the east wall are approached through columned *mandapas* and the east *gopuram* is on the wall of the inner enclosure rather than the outer wall. Over 45 m high, it was begun in 1640 but left incomplete until recently. On entering, you see the statue of Hanuman, then the *Nandi* flanked by statues of the Nayaka kings of Madurai, Visvanatha and Krishnama. The north and south *gopurams* were built by Keerana Rayar of the Deccan in about AD 1420; the west *gopuram* is comparatively new.

The most remarkable feature of the temple is its pillared *mandapas*, the longest of which is over 200 m long. The pillars lining the four corridors, nearly 4 m tall, give an impression of almost unending perspective: those on the north and south sides are particularly striking. Tragically, however, the original stone pillars, decorated with scrollwork and lotus motifs, are being progressively phased out in favour of graceless grey concrete facsimiles. You're only likely to see the original versions lying on the ground in piles.

There are two gateways on the east side which give access to the Parvati and Ramalinga shrines at the centre; the masonry shrine is probably the oldest building on the site, going back to 1173.

Essential Ramesvaram

Finding your feet

Ramesvaram is connected to Madurai and other centres by regular bus and train services. The bus stand is 2 km from the centre, the railway station 1 km southwest of the great temple. There are also daily tours from Madurai.

Getting around

Local buses and auto-rickshaws link the bus and train stations to the temple, where there are a few places to stay. See Transport, page 872.

Gandhamadana Parvatam

Gandhamadana Parvatam, 2 km north of Ramesvaram, takes its name from the Sanskrit words *gandha* (fragrance) and *mad* (intoxicate), 'highly fragrant hill'. Dedicated to Rama's feet,

Holy dips

Having bathed in the Ganga at Varanasi, Hindu pilgrims head straight for Ramesvaram, where a bath in the 22 *theertham* (holy wells) dotted within and around the Ramalingesvara temple promise a final release from the chains of *karma*.

The *theertham* circuit is a festive event for the pilgrims, complete with much cheering and song as buckets are emptied over heads, and as a visitor it can offer one of the most atmospheric and memorable temple experiences in Tamil Nadu, especially if you can get yourself adopted by a group of Indian visitors. The locals tend to bring along a change of clothes and submit to a thorough drenching, but if you come overdressed it is possible to request a light sprinkle. It's also traditional, but not obligatory, to taste of the waters; each apparently has a distinct flavour.

Brahmin priests wait at the train and bus stations and along the shoreline east of the temple to greet new arrivals, but the haggling of old has now been replaced by a standard charge of Rs 51 per person, which includes a dunking in each of the wells and access to the inner sanctum. Non-Hindus are traditionally prevented from entering the sanctum, but if you dress appropriately and arrive with a group (day tours from Madurai are an all-but-guaranteed way to join one) there's a good chance the priests will allow you in. If you do the circuit alone, it's best to leave valuables outside the temple: bystanders who offer to watch your bags are not all trustworthy.

this is the spot from which Hanuman is believed to have surveyed the area before taking his leap across the narrow Palk Strait to Sri Lanka. You can get an excellent view from the top of the *mandapa*.

Dhanuskodi

Dhanuskodi ('the end of the bow') is the island's toe-tip where the Bay of Bengal meets the Indian Ocean, so named because Rama, at the request of Vibishana, his friend, destroyed the bridge to Sri Lanka with the end of his bow. Some 20 km to the east of Ramesvaram island, it is considered particularly holy. There is a good beach, on which pilgrims will be making *puja*, and beautiful flat turquoise waters in which they take their holy bath, not to mention excellent views. A trip across the scrappy sand dunes is only recommended for the really hardy – get a local person to go with you. Travel by bus, and then join a pilgrim group on a jeep or lorry for the last desolate few miles (this should cost Rs 50 for a round trip but establish the price up front). Alternatively, take an auto to Adam's Bridge; insist on going as far as the radio mast for beach and fishing shack photos.

Listings Ramesvaram *map p872*

Tourist information

Tourist office
At the bus stand, T04573-221371. Open 1000-1700. Also at the Railway Station (T04573-221373, open (with some breaks) 0700-2030). The Temple Information is on the east side of the temple.

Where to stay

$ Hotel Tamil Nadu (TTDC)
14 East Car St, T04573-221064.
Sea-facing balconies, 53 rooms (2-6 beds), some a/c, clean, grubby restaurant (breakfast from

0700), bar, sea bathing nearby, and exchange. Very popular, so book well in advance.

$ Maharaja
7 Middle St, west of the Temple, T04573-221271.
30 rooms, some a/c with bath; exchange. Temple music is broadcast on loudspeakers, otherwise recommended.

$ Railway Retiring Rooms
T04573-221226.
9 rooms and dorm.

$ Swami Ramanatha Tourist Home
Opposite the museum, T04573-221217.
Good clean rooms with bath, best budget option.

BACKGROUND

Ramesvaram

The *Ramayana* tells how the monkey king Hanuman built the bridges linking Ramnad to Pamban and Danushkodi (a spot where Rama is believed to have bathed) to help Rama rescue Sita from the demon king Ravana. When Rama returned he was told by the *rishis* that he must purify himself after committing the sin of murdering a Brahmin, for *Ravana* was the son of a Brahmin. To do this he was advised to set up a *lingam* and worship Siva. The red image of Hanuman north of the main East Gate illustrates this story.

The original shrine long predates the present great Ramesvaram temple. It is one of India's most sacred shrines and is visited by pilgrims from all over India. The temple benefited from huge donations from the 17th-century *Setupatis* (the so-called guardians of the causeway), who derived their wealth from the right to levy taxes on crossings to the island. The temple stands on slightly higher ground, surrounded by a freshwater lake.

Restaurants

Don't expect anything other than *thalis* here. There are several popular snack stands, with signs only in Tamil, on the road between Mela St and the museum.

Abbirami Hotel
Off East Car St on road towards beach.
Neat place churning out lunchtime meals and tiffin (*dosas*, *vada* and the like) after 1500.

Devasthanam Trust
Has a canteen opposite the east gate of the temple.

Transport

Bicycle hire Bike hire from West Car or East Car St.

Bus Local Marudhu Pandiyan Transport Corporation (MPTC) covers the town and area around. Bus station is 2 km west of town; buses also leave from the train station to the Ramalingesvara Temple, Pamban and Dhanuskodi; and from the temple's east gate to Dhanuskodi roadhead and to Gandhamadana Parvatam.

   Long distance State, MPTC and private bus companies run regular services via **Mandapam** to several towns nearby. **Govt Express Bus Reservations**, North Car St, 0700-2100. Frequent buses to **Madurai**, 173 km (4½ hrs); tourist coaches (hotel-to-hotel) are better.

Taxi A few cars and jeeps are available from the train station and hotels.

Train Ramesvaram Railway Station, enquiries and reservations, T226, open 0800-1300 and

1330-1730. **Chennai**: 2 daily, 12½ hrs, via **Karaikkudi**, 4 hrs, **Tiruchirappalli**, 5½ hrs, and **Villupuram**, 9 hrs. **Madurai**: 3 unreserved passenger trains a day, 4 hrs.

Ramesvaram

500 metres (approx)
500 yards (approx)

Swami Ramanatha
Tourist Home 3
Tamil Nadu 4

Where to stay
Maharaja 1
Railway Retiring Rooms 2

Restaurants
Abbirami 1
Devasthanam Trust 2
Snack Stalls 3

To the south of Madurai is a series of modest towns situated in the lee of the southern ranges of the Western Ghats. From Madurai to Thiruvanathapuram is a comfortable day's drive either via Tirunelveli or over the ghats, but there are several interesting places on the way if you wish to take your time.

Rajapalayam

To Sankaracoil, Rs 12, 30 mins; from there to Kalugumalai, Rs 8, 30 mins, buses to and from Tenkasi, Rs 30, 2 hrs.

The town originated on the dispersal of the Vijayanagar families after 1565. The Sankarankovil temple is worth visiting. The Western Ghats rise to heights of over 1200 m immediately behind the town. Wild elephants still come down through the forests, devastating farmland.

Tenkasi

To Courtallam Falls frequent buses, Rs 8, to Courtallam Bus Stand, then walk through the grey arch to the 'Main Falls'. See Rajapalayam, above, for transport to Tenkasi.

Literally the 'Kashi (Varanasi) of the South', Tenkasi is the nearest town to the Kuttalam (Courtallam) Falls, 6 km away. The impressive 16th-century Visvanatha temple dedicated to Siva has some fine carvings inside. The temple flagstaff is believed to be 400 years old. From Tenkasi the road goes through a low pass into the densely forested hills of Kerala.

Courtallam (Kuttalam)

With average temperatures of 22-23°C, Courtallam is a very popular health resort, especially during the monsoon. The impressive **Main Falls** is in town where the river Chittar cascades over 92 m. The approach is lined with spice, banana chips and knick-knack stalls and at the falls you'll find pilgrims washing themselves and their clothes. The waters, widely believed to have great curative powers, draw big crowds at the **Saral Festival** in July. The **Thirukutralanathar Temple** contains old inscriptions while the small **Chitra Sabha Temple** nearby contains religious murals.

Virudhunagar

The name Virudhupatti (Hamlet of Banners) was changed to Virudhunagar (City of Banners) in 1915, and was upgraded to a full municipality in 1957, reflecting the upwardly mobile social status of the town's dominant local caste, the Nadars. Originally low caste toddy tappers, they have established a wide reputation as a dynamic and enterprising group. The powerful Congress leader, Kamaraj Nadar, was chiefly responsible for Indira Gandhi's selection as prime minister.

Kalugumalai

Some 6 km south of Kovilpatti, Kalugumalai (Kazhugumalai) has a profusion of magnificent fifth-century bas-relief Jain figures on a huge rock which are well worth the detour. The Jain temple is to the north of the rock and is easily missed. There is also an unfinished monolithic cave temple to Siva (c AD 950).

Listings Cardamom Hills

Transport

Virudhunagar
Bus Leave Madurai early morning to catch the Kollam train; get off at police station and go to the end of the road opposite and turn left; the railway station is about 1 km on the right (take a rickshaw if you're carrying heavy luggage).

Train To Kollam and Thiruvananthapuram, Platform 3 across the bridge.

The magnificent palaces of South India's old merchant and banking classes rise from the hot and dusty plains to stand as strong as fortresses and as gaudy as a packet of French Fancies. As the merchants, bankers and money-lenders of the British Empire, the Nattukottai Chettiars raked in enormous riches on their postings to places such as Burma, Sri Lanka, Indochina and South Africa, wealth they ploughed into these glorious architectural pastiches that explode in a profusion of colour in the arid desert-scape.

Now their monumental arches and long processional corridors open onto empty halls, the bats are more at home here than princes and shafts of light break on empty, cob-webbed dining rooms. The Nattukottai Chettiars saw their riches contract with the Second World War and the wanton palaces they built turned into tombstones, the series of south Indian villages they stand in left as virtual ghost towns. Architectural salvage merchants in the main town of Karaikkudi now sell off the portraits and granite pillars this proud caste have been forced to surrender to stave off financial hardship, while Bollywood crews make regular pilgrimages to the old mansions, propping up the owners with *lakhs* of studio rupees in return for the right to daub their chosen colour scheme across the walls.

Karaikkudi is in the heart of Chettinad, and has several typical mansions, particularly along the back lanes leading off busy Sekkalai Road (ask for the Thousand Window House, a well-known landmark). From here you can walk south to the local *santhai* (market), where you can find gold and silversmiths in their workshops, as well as antique and textile shops and several colourful temples.

Devakottai, 18 km south of Karaikkudi, is Chettinad's second largest town and offers similarly rich pickings in the way of old mansions and palaces: look out for the particularly grand Periya Minor's *veedu*.

Kanadukathan, 12 km north of Karaikkudi, has a number of magnificent mansions – some still inhabited by friendly owners (who'll let you have a look around for a Rs 100 donation), others are empty except for bats, monkeys and antique dealers. It has been estimated that the Burma teak and satinwood pillars in a single Chettiar house weighs 300 tonnes, often superbly carved. The plaster on the walls is made from a mixture of lime, egg white, powdered shells and myrobalan fruit (the astringent fruit of the tree *Phyllantles emblica*), mixed into a paste which, when dried, gives a gleaming finish. Most houses have the goddess of wealth, Lakshmi, made of stucco over the main arch.

The **Raja of Chettinad's Palace** ① *0930-1630, free, caretakers provide brief free tours*, is an amazing place overlooking the town's pond and full of sepia, larger-than-life-size portraits of stern family members, the frames garlanded with heavy yellow flowers. Next door is **Visalakshi Ramaswamy's house**, with a museum of local crafts, artefacts and handlooms upstairs. The raja's waiting room at the railway station is also pretty special.

Athangudi, 9 km away, is renowned for its tiles, which grace the floors of most Chettiar mansions; ask locally if you want to visit one of the 30-40 workshops in town. Nearby is Pillaiyarpatti, one of the most important temples in Chettinad, dedicated to Ganesh (known as Pillaiyaru in Tamil Nadu) and with an inner sanctum carved into a natural boulder.

At **Avudayarkoil**, 30 km northeast of Karaikkudi, the **Athmanathar Temple** has one of the most renowned sites in Tamil history. A legend tells that Manickavaskar, a Pandyan prime minister, redirected money intended for the purchase of horses to build the temple. However, his real fame lies as author of the *Thiruvasakam* ('Holy Outpourings'), one of the most revered Tamil poetic texts. Completely off the beaten track, the temple has superb sculptures, and is noted for the absence of any images of Siva or Parvati, the main deities, whose empty pedestals are worshipped. The woodcarvings on the temple car are notable too.

Fact...
Even the roofs of Chettiar buildings are symbols of their owners' wealth; look up to see the wanton use of tiles, layered many times over, on top of each other.

ON THE ROAD

Screen gods

Tamil Nadu's lively temple society also keeps aflame sculpture and the arts, and makes for a people singularly receptive to iconography. Tamil film-making is every bit as prolific and profitable as its closest rival, Hindi-language Bollywood. The state's industry is famous for its dancing and choreography and the super-saturated colour of its film stock. Film stars too, are massive here; worshipped like demigods, their careers often offering them a fast track into politics, where they are singularly well placed to establish personality cults. Two such figures who have hopped from the screen into the state's political driving seat as chief minister are the cherished MGR – MG Ramachandran, the film star and charismatic chief minister during the 1980s – and Jayalalitha, his one-time girlfriend and contentious successor, three times chief minister since 1991 despite being the figure of multiple corruption scandals.

Pudukkottai and around

Pudukkottai, on the northern edge of Chettinad, 50 km south of Trichy, was the capital of the former princely state ruled by the Tondaiman Rajas, founded by Raghunatha Raya Tondaiman in 1686. At one entrance to the town is a ceremonial arch raised by the raja in honour of Queen Victoria's jubilee celebrations. The town's broad streets suggest a planned history; the temple is at the centre, with the old palace and a tank. The new palace is now the District Collector's office.

Thirukokarnam, 5 km north of the railway station, is the site of the rock-cut **Sri Kokarnesvarar Temple** ① *closed 1200-1600*, dates from the Pallava period. The natural rock shelters, caves, stone circles, dolmens and Neolithic burial sites show that there was very early human occupation. The local **museum** ① *Big St, open daily except Fri, 2nd Sat of the month, public holidays, 0930-1700, free, allow 40 mins, recommended*, has a wide range of exhibits including sections on geology, zoology and the economy as well as sculptures and the arts. The archaeology section has some excellent sculptures from nearby temples. There is a notable carving of Siva as *Dakshinamurti* and some fine bronzes from Pudukkottai itself.

Sittannavasal, 13 km away, has a Jain cave temple (eighth century) with sculptures, where monks took shelter when they fled from persecution in North India. In a shrine and veranda there are some fine frescoes in the Ajanta-style and bas-relief carvings. You can also see rock-hewn beds of the monks. The *Brahmi* inscriptions date from the second century BC.

Listings Chettinad

Where to stay

Chettinad

For maximum atmosphere, stay at one of the restored palace hotels. A handful of cheaper options exist in Karaikkudi and other towns, but they do not have the guides on hand to gain access to the old private homes (without whose help the Raja of Chettinad's palace may be the only house you look inside).

$$$ The Bangala
Senjai, T04565-220221, www.thebangala.com.
8 bright and spacious a/c rooms with period colonial furniture, in a restored 1916 bungalow, a heritage guesthouse set amidst orchards and palms. The restaurant serves full-on, totally

authentic Chettinad feasts, which are a fair whack at Rs 800 per meal, but worth it. These meals must be booked in advance. The family here wrote the (coffee table) book on Chettiar architecture and culture.

$$$ Chettinadu Mansion
Behind the raja's palace, Kanadukathan, T04565-273080; bookings T0484-232 1518, www.chettinadumansion.com.
Dating back to 1902, this stunning house takes up half the block, with courtyard after courtyard stretching back from the street. Huge rooms, with a quirky green-brown colour scheme, heavy painted shutters and private rooftop sit-outs, encircle the upper floor. Downstairs is still used for family *pujas* and storing the wedding dowry. Simple Chettinad-

style meals, served in the colonnaded dining room or under stars in the courtyard, cost Rs 450, and the charming Mr Chandramouli, who was born in the house, is often on hand to share stories and business advice.

$$$ Visalam
Kanadukathan, T04565-273302, www.cghearth.com.
Romantic and supremely comfortable high-ceilinged rooms, sparely furnished with Chettiar writing desks and 4-poster beds, in a beautifully restored art deco mansion. The chef serves banana-leaf lunches and does cooking demonstrations, good local guides are available for walking and bike tours, plus there's a huge pool and lawns.

$ Golden Singar
100 Feet Rd, Karaikuddi, T04565-235521.
Remarkably clean and good-value marble-floored rooms (fan-cooled ones are half the price of a/c). It's handy for the bus stand though a bit distant from the market and temples. Clean restaurant downstairs and cheap internet cafés nearby.

$ Hotel Udhayam
A-333 Sekkalai Rd, Karaikuddi, T04565-234068.
Another decent cheap option, similar to the **Golden Singar** but closer to the action.

$ Nivaas
Devakottai, 1st left from bus station coming from the north (no sign in English), T04561-272352.
Basic (no electric sockets), no English spoken.

Festivals

Pudukkottai
Jan/Feb Bullock races (*manju virattu*) are held in the area.

Shopping

Chettinad
Antiques
Muneesvaran Kovil St in Karaikkudi is lined with antiques shops selling old sepia photographs, temple lamps, old advertising posters, scrap book matter, religious paintings and Czech pewter jars.
Old Chettinad Crafters, *Murugen Complex, 37/6 Muneesvaran Kovil St, Karaikkudi, T(0)98428-223060, chettinaduantiques@yahoo.co.in.* One of the best.
VJ Murugesan. Sells old wooden furniture, household articles, wooden pillars, glass.
Venkateswara Furniture and Timber Merchant, *No 8 Keela Oorani West, Karaikkudi, T(0)98424-232112.* If you're in the market for bigger objects and weight is no object, this architectural salvage yard is a good starting point. Bargain hard.

Cotton and fabrics
MM Street and The Weavers' Lane beside the Bangala have Chettinad cotton for sale straight off the loom. Ask locally for the next *sandais*, the colourful local weekly markets.

Transport

Chettinad
Bus Bus routes link **Karaikkudi** with every part of the state. Auto-rickshaws provide slow but relatively cheap transport between towns – Karaikkudi to Kanadukathan should cost around Rs 150.

Train The main station for the area is Karaikkudi, with a couple of daily express trains to Chennai and Rameswaram. Several passenger trains go to Tiruchirappali, stopping at Chettinad station on the edge of Kanadukathan.

Pudukkottai
Bus to **Tiruchirappalli**, **Thanjavur**, **Karaikkudi** via **Kanadukathan** (for Chettinad), **Madurai**, **Ramnad**, **Ramesvaram**, and to **Sittanavasal**.

Train Pudukkottai is 1 hr north of Karaikkudi on the Chennai–Rameswaram line.

Far south

India's southernmost point is a focus of pilgrimage that captures the imagination of millions of Hindus on a daily basis. Kanniyakumari occupies a beautiful headland site where the waters of the Bay of Bengal, the Indian Ocean and the Arabian Sea mingle together and crash upon the rocks. An hour further towards Kerala is Padmanabhapuram Palace, the painstakingly maintained ancient seat of the Travancore rulers. Tirunelveli, one-time capital of the Pandyas, is now a market and educational centre that is often passed over on the trail towards Madurai.

Tirunelveli and Palayamkottai *Colour map 7, C4.*
an attractive town surrounded by a belt of rice fields

On the banks of the Tamraparni, the only perennial river of the south, the rice paddies of Tirunelveli (population 411,300) (*nelveli* means 'paddy-hedge') are irrigated from the river's waters. Rising only 60 km to the east, at an altitude of over 1700 m, the river benefits from both the southwest and southeast monsoons; it tumbles down to the plains where it is bordered by a narrow strip of rich paddy land.

Tirunelveli is now joined with the twin settlement of Palayamkottai. It is a market town and one of the oldest Christian centres in Tamil Nadu. St Francis Xavier settled here to begin his ministry in India in the early 16th century, but it has also been a centre of Protestant missionary activity. In 1896 it became the head of an Anglican diocese, now Church of South India.

Sights
Kanthimathi Nellaiyappar Temple ① *closed 1230-1600, no photography*, is worth visiting; it is a twin temple, with the north dedicated to Siva (Nellaiyappar) and the south to Parvati (Kanthi). Each section has an enclosure over 150 m by 120 m. The temples have sculptures, musical pillars, valuable jewels, a golden lily tank and a 1000-pillared *mandapa*. There is a large white Nandi at the entrance. There is a **car festival** in June/July. The old town area around the temple is well worth a few hours of anyone's time, with the blue-painted houses reminiscent of Jodhpur (but without the tourist crowds). **Palayamkottai** has **St John's Church** (Church Missionary Society) with a spire 35 m high, a landmark for miles around. The town is known for its palm-leaf crafts.

Around Tirunelveli
Tiruchendur, 50 km east of Tirunelveli, has a famous **shore temple** ① *Rs 50 for 'fast darshan', men must remove shirts*, dedicated to Subrahmanya, and considered to be one of his six 'abodes'. It is a hive of activity during festivals. There are caves with rock-cut sculptures along the shore.

Manapad, the predominantly Roman Catholic coastal village 18 km south of Tiruchendur, is where St Francis Xavier is said to have landed and lived in a cave near the headland. The **Holy Cross Church** (1581) close to the sea is believed to house a fragment of the True Cross from Jerusalem.

Where to stay

Tirunelveli

Hotels are often full during the wedding season (Apr-Jun). Book ahead or arrive early. Several budget hotels are clustered near Junction Railway Station, most with a Western toilet and shower.

$$-$ Aryaas
60 Madurai Rd, T0462-233 9001,
www.aryaasgroup.com.
69 rooms, 25 a/c, in a dark bordello-style; the non a/c ones are better value. There are restaurants, including a separate vegetarian one, but it's also a mosquito's heaven, and a bar. Excellent internet café opposite.

$$-$ Bharani
29 Madurai Rd, T0462-233 3234,
www.sribharanihotels.com.
Clean, well-maintained hotel in a large, modern block offering 43 rooms, with hot shower; 10 a/c. There's also a vegetarian restaurant, a lift and ample parking.

$$-$ Janakiram
30 Madurai Rd, near the bus stand, T0462-233 1941, www.srijanakiramhotels.com.
Smart, brightly lit place with 70 clean rooms, with hot shower, some a/c. There's an outstanding vegetarian rooftop restaurant and a lift. Highly recommended.

$ Blue Star
36 Madurai Rd, T0462-421 0501.
Modern hotel offering 50 good-value rooms with cold shower, 10 a/c. Decent veg restaurant, Indian style.

$ Railway Retiring Rooms
Clean, secure rooms and dorm. Excellent value.

Restaurants

Tirunelveli

$ Central Café
Near station.
Good vegetarian dishes.

$ MH Restaurant
Opposite Aryaas.
Modern restaurant serving Western fast food and pizzas.

Transport

Tirunelveli

Bus Good bus connections to **Kanniyakumari**, **Thiruvananthapuram**, and to **Madurai** (it's faster to change buses at Tirumangalam), **Tiruchirappalli** and **Chennai**. For **Courtallam**, go to Tenkasi (1½ hrs) and take bus to Courtallam (20 mins).

Kanniyakumari · Colour map 7, C4.

watch sunset and moonrise over the ocean at India's southern tip

The grubby streets of Kanniyakumari (population 19,700) come alive in the hour before dawn, as thousands throng the shoreline to witness the sunrise over the southern tip of India. This important pilgrimage site is centred on worship of the Goddess Kumari, 'the protector of India's shores'.

The new day is heralded in by the scent of jasmine garlands, the wail of temple music and the whoops and applause of excited children as the sun finally crawls its way over the sea. It's an early-morning party that everyone is invited to join.

The view offshore is dominated by India's answer to the Statue of Liberty: a 133-ft sculpture of the Tamil poet Thiruvalluvar. Just behind is a memorial to the philosopher Swami Vivekananda, a spiritual leader inspired by the Devi. Both can be reached by a quick ferry ride. In April, at full moon, special *chithra pournami* celebrations are held at sunset and the town heaves with crowds who come to see the simultaneous setting and rising of the sun and moon.

Sights

The **Kanniyakumari Temple** ① *0400-1200, 1600-2000, non-Hindus are not allowed into the sanctuary, shoes must be left outside and men must wear a* dhoti *to enter*, overlooks the shoreline. The Devi

Kumari, an incarnation of Parvati, vowed to remain a virgin to her dying day after meddling gods prevented her marriage to Siva. Legend tells that the exceptionally brilliant diamond in the deity's nose ring is visible even from the sea, and the sea-facing temple door is kept closed to prevent ships being misguided by the gem's shimmer.

The **Vivekananda Memorial** ① *0800-1600, Rs 10, ferry Rs 20, 15 mins (see page 881), allow 1 hr for the visit, smoking and eating prohibited, take off shoes before entering*, stands on one of two rocks, about 500 m from the mainland. The Bengali religious leader and philosopher Swami Vivekananda swam out here when a simple monk and devotee of the Devi, to sit in long meditation on this rock in 1892. He left convinced that religion could be a powerful instrument of social regeneration and individual development and was inspired to speak on Hinduism at the Parliament of Religions in Chicago, preaching that "the Lord is one, but the sages describe Him differently". On his return, he founded the Ramakrishna Mission in Chennai, which now has spread across the world. The rock was renamed Vivekananda Rock and a memorial was built in 1970. The design of the *mandapa* incorporates different styles of temple architecture from all over India and houses a statue of Vivekananda. People also come to see Sri Pada Parai, where the 'footprint' of the Devi has been enshrined on the rock.

The massive **Thiruvalluvar Statue** ① *0800-1600, free, ferry Rs 20, 15 mins*, immortalizes the writer of the Tamil classic, *Thirukkural*. The statue is exactly 133 ft (40 m) tall, to correspond with the 133 chapters of his most famous work. Stairs allow visitors to stand at his giant feet.

In 1948 some of Mahatma Gandhi's ashes were brought here for public display before being immersed in the sea. The **Gandhi Mandapam** ① *0700-1900, free*, was built as a memorial to this event. At midday on Gandhi's birthday, 2 October, the sun shines on the spot where his ashes were placed.

The **Wandering Monk Museum** ① *Main Rd, 0830-1200, 1600-2000, Rs 5*, has an informative exhibition on the life and work of Vivekananda. There is also a photo exhibition, in **Vivekanandapuram**, 1 km north, which can be reached by an easy walk along the beach though there is no access from the north side. The **Yoga Kendra** there runs courses from June to December. Further north there is a pleasant sandy beach, 3.5 km along Kovalam Road.

Around Kanniyakumari

Suchindram Temple ① *open to non-Hindus, priests acting as guides may expect donations*, was founded during the Pandiyan period but was expanded under Thirumalai Nayaka in the 17th century. It was also used later as a sanctuary for the rulers of Travancore to the west and so contains treasures from many kingdoms. One of the few temples dedicated to the Hindu Trinity, Brahma, Vishnu and Siva, it is in a rectangular enclosure that you enter through the massive ornate seven-storeyed *gopuram*. North of the

Kanniyakumari

To Trivandrum (NH 47)
& Madurai (NH 7)

Vivekanandapuram

Guganathan
Temple

Main Rd

Church of
Our Lady
of Ransom

N Car St

E Car St

S Car St

Kovalam Rd

Lighthouse

Wandering
Monk
Museum

Jetty

Beach Rd

Toilet

Tamil Nadu
Sales
Emporium

Shops

Vinayaka
Temple

Gandhi
Mandapam

Kanniyakumari
Temple &
Kumari Ghat

Thiruvalluvar
Memorial

Vivekananda
Memorial

N

400 metres

400 yards

Where to stay 🛏
Bharani Guest House 7
Lakshmi 1
Maadhini & Archana
Restaurant 2
Saravana Lodge 6

Seashore 1
Seaview 5
Singaar 9
Sunrock 8
Tamil Nadu & TTDC
Restaurant 10

Restaurants 🍴
Annapoorna 1
Sangam 2
Sravanas 3

Long train leaving

If you're in Kanniyakumari on a Thursday night and stuck for something to do, head up to the station and hop aboard the *Vivek Express*. Chugging out weekly at 2300, this is India's greatest rail-borne endurance test: a four-night, three-day epic that rattles to its conclusion in Dibrugarh, 80-some hours and 4286 km away, in the northeastern corner of Assam.

Apart from a stop in Kochi, the *Vivek* steers clear of big cities, preferring to putter its way through rural Tamil Nadu, Andhra Pradesh and Odisha on its journey to the far northeast. It's not even the quickest way to get to Dibrugarh: you could whittle the journey down by five hours by getting a train to Chennai and changing. Nevertheless, it's an essential fixture on the Indian rail fan circuit.

If you do take the plunge, be warned that the *Vivek Express* typically accumulates around four hours of delays on its marathon journey. As your train idles in rural Assam, three hours behind time and still hours short of your destination, take comfort in the words of Swami Vivekananda, from whom the *Vivek Express* takes its name: "Purity, patience and perseverance overcome all obstacles. All great things must, of necessity, be slow."

temple is a large tank with a small shelter in the middle while round the walls is the typically broad street used for car festivals. Leading to the entrance is a long colonnade with musical pillars and sculptures of Siva, Parvati, Ganesh and Subrahmanya on the front and a huge Hanuman statue inside. The main sanctuary, with a *lingam*, dates from the ninth century but many of the other structures and sculptures date from the 13th century and after. There are special temple ceremonies at sunset on Friday.

Nagercoil, 19 km from Kanniyakumari, is set with a stunning backcloth of the Western Ghats, reflected from place to place in the broad tanks dotted with lotuses. The landscape begins to feel more like Kerala than Tamil Nadu. It is an important railway junction and bus terminal. It is often a bottleneck filled with lorries so be prepared for delays. The old town of **Kottar**, now a suburb, was a centre of art, culture and pilgrimage. The **temple** ① *0630-0900, 1730-2000*, to Nagaraja, after which the town is named, is unique in that although the presiding deity is the serpent god Naga, there are also shrines to Siva and Vishnu as well as images of Jain Tirthankaras, Mahavira and Parsvanatha on the pillars. The temple is alive with snakes during some festivals. Christian missionaries played an important part in the town's development and left their mark in schools, colleges, hospitals and churches of different denominations. There is also a prominent Muslim community in Kottar, reflected in the shops closing on Fridays and remaining open on Sunday.

Listings Kanniyakumari *map p879*

Where to stay

Kanniyakumari

Hotels are in heavy demand; book well ahead. Cheaper places may only offer squat toilets.

$$$-$$ Seashore Hotel
East Car St, T04652-246704,
www.theseashorehotel.com.
Good rooms in a swish new hotel. The rooftop restaurant with ocean views offers Indian and seafood dishes.

$$$-$$ Seaview
East Car St, T04652-247841,
www.hotelseaview.in.
Plush, central hotel with spotlessly clean, a/c rooms. Helpful staff, restaurant and a bar. Recommended.

$$$-$ Hotel Singaar
Main Rd, 2 km from attractions, T04652-247992,
www.hotelsingaarinternational.in.
Smart, popular hotel with comfortable rooms, many with balcony. Good pool and a decent restaurant. Breakfast included.

$$-$ Hotel Tamil Nadu (TTDC)
Beach Rd, T04652-246257, www.ttdconline.com.
Acceptably decrepit rooms in a superb location, with terraces looking out to sea and an attractive garden setting, in a quiet spot away from the busy centre. Popular with Indian families.

$ Bharani
Main Rd, T04652-246260, www.hotelbharani.com.
Best of the cheapies. Quiet and clean rooms all have TV and a balcony. Very friendly management. Recommended.

$ Lakshmi
East Car St, T04652-247203.
Friendly, family-run hotel with clean rooms, some a/c. It can be noisy as guests arrive at 0500 to see the sunrise from the roof. Excellent value.

$ Maadhini
East Car St, T04652-246887,
www.hotelmaadhini.com.
Centrally located hotel with a wide variety of good-value rooms. A/c rooms have balconies with sea views, and there's a restaurant and a bar.

$ Saravana Lodge
Sannathi St, T04652-246007.
Moderately clean, basic rooms. Upstairs rooms open onto wide veranda with a good sea view. Cheerful, helpful staff, but be warned that the temple next door provides a free wake-up call at 0500.

$ Sunrock
Pillyarkoil St, T04652-246167,
hotelsunrock@gmail.com.
Newish hotel tucked away down a back alley. Clean rooms, some a/c, all with terraces, but no views.

Around Kanniyakumari

$ Parvathi Residency
400 PWD Rd, Nagercoil, T04652-402290,
www.hotelparvathiresidency.com.
Clean, good-sized rooms, some with a/c.

$ Rajam
MS Rd, Vadasery, Nagercoil, T04652-276581.
Good-value rooms, restaurant and a roof garden.

Restaurants

Kanniyakumari
You'll find a dozen tiny restaurants serving cheap and tasty snacks of *dosai, vadai, bhaji* and *pakora* on Main Rd between Sth Car St and the **Sangam Hotel**.

$$ Archana
Maadhini (see Where to stay, above).
Good mixed menu of Indian, Chinese and International options.

$ Annapoorna
Sannathi St.
Excellent vegetarian food in clean, bright surroundings. Very popular with families.

$ Sangam
Sangam Hotel, Main Rd.
Good *thalis*.

$ Sravanas
Sannathi St.
Cheap and cheerful vegetarian meals. Recommended.

$ TTDC Restaurant
Hotel Tamil Nadu (see Where to stay, above).
Looks like a barracks, but excellent non-vegetarian Indian meals.

Festivals

Kanniyakumari
Apr **Chithra Pournami** is a special full moon celebration at the temple usually held in the 2nd week of Apr.
Oct Special **Navarathri** celebrations in 1st week of Oct.

Transport

Kanniyakumari
Bus Long-distance buses leave from the station west of town on Kovalam Rd, 15 mins' walk from the centre, T04652-271285. There are frequent services to **Nagercoil** (30 mins) and **Thiruvananthapuram** (2½ hrs, Rs 45). For **Kovalam** and **Varkala** change at **Thiruvananthapuram**. There are 4 daily departures to **Chennai** (16 hrs, Rs 390), via **Madurai** (6 hrs, Rs 145), at 0930, 1345, 1445 and 1630.

Ferry The ferry to **Vivekananda Rock** runs every 30 mins, 0700-1100 and 1400-1700, Rs 20. Expect long queues during festivals.

Train The station is to the north, on Main Rd. Several useful trains arrive and depart from Nagercoil, 15 mins away. To **Chennai**, *Kanyakumari Exp 12634*, 1720, 13½ hrs, via **Madurai** (4½ hrs), **Trichy** (7 hrs) and **Villupuram** (for Puducherry), 11 hrs. **Thiruvananthapuram**:

4 daily, 2 hrs. To **Dibrugarh** in Assam, 80 hrs; see box, page 880.

Around Kanniyakumari

Bus From **Nagercoil** there are frequent buses to **Thiruvananthapuram** (2 hrs); **Kanniyakumari** (30 mins); and **Madurai** (6½ hrs).

Train At **Nagercoil** the railway station is 3 km from the bus station. The daily *Kanniyakumari Mumbai Exp 16382* and *Kanniyakumari Bengaluru Exp 16525* both stop here on their way to and from **Kanniyakumari**. There are frequent bus connections to **Thiruvananthapuram**, **Kanniyakumari** and **Madurai**.

Padmanabhapuram *Colour map 7, C3.*

fascinating architecture and paintings

The restoration methods of Padmanabhapuram, the old palace of the rajas of Travancore, have been criticized. Although decaying somewhat, the Kuthiramalika Palace in Trivandrum – if you are venturing into Kerala – might be better worth looking round. The name Padmanabhapuram (*Padma*, lotus; *nabha*, navel; *puram*, town) refers to the lotus emerging from the navel of Vishnu.

From the ninth century this part of Tamil Nadu and neighbouring Kerala were governed by the Ay Dynasty, patrons both of Jainism and Hinduism. However, the land was always contested by the Cholas, the Pandiyas and the Cheras. By the late 11th century the new Venadu Dynasty emerged from the Chera rulers of Kerala and took control of Kanniyakumari District in AD 1125 under Raja Kodai Kerala Varman. Never a stable kingdom, and with varying degrees of territorial control, Travancore State was governed from Padmanabhapuram between 1590-1790, when the capital was shifted to Thiruvananthapuram. Although the rajas of Travancore were Vaishnavite kings, they did not neglect Siva, as can be seen from various sculptures and paintings in the palace.

The King never officially married and the heir to the throne was his eldest sister's oldest son. This form of matrilineal descent was characteristic of the earlier Chera Empire (who ruled for 200 years from the early 12th century). The palace shows the fine craftsmanship, especially in woodworking, characteristic of Kerala's art and architecture. There are also some superb frescoes and excellent stone-sculpted figures. The outer cyclopean stone wall is fitted together without mortar. It encloses a total area of 75 ha and the palace buildings 2 ha.

Essential Padmanabhapuram

Opening hours

Tuesday-Sunday 0900-1300 and 1400-1630 (last tickets 1600).

Entry fees

Rs 200, child Rs 50 (accredited guide included, but expects a 'donation' after the tour), camera Rs 25, video Rs 1500.

Tip...

It's best to visit at 0900 before the coach parties arrive.

Listings Padmanabhapuram

Transport

Bus Regular buses to **Thiruvananthapuram** and **Kanniyakumari**. Less frequent buses to and from **Kovalam**. From Kovalam, depart approximately 0940 to **Thuckalai**. Return buses from Thuckalai depart 1445, 1530.

Taxi A taxi from Kovalam or Thiruvananthapuram costs Rs 1000.

Background Tamil Nadu

History

Tamil Nadu's cultural identity has been shaped by the Dravidians, who have inhabited the south since at least the fourth millennium BC. Tamil, India's oldest living language, developed from the earlier languages of people who were probably displaced from the north by Aryan-based culture from 2000 BC to 1500 BC.

By the fourth century BC Tamil Nadu was under the rule of three dynasties: the Cholas, the Pandiyas and the Cheras. The Pallavas of Kanchi came to power in the fourth century AD and were dominant between AD 550 and AD 869. Possibly of northern origin, under their control Mahabalipuram (Mamallapuram) became an important port in the seventh century. The Cholas returned to power in AD 850 and were a dominant political force until 1173 before the resumption of Pandiya power for a further century. The defeat of the great Vijayanagar Empire by a confederacy of Muslim states in 1565 forced their leaders south. When Muslim political control finally reached Tamil Nadu it was as brief as it was tenuous.

It was more than 150 years after their founding of Fort St George at Madras in 1639 before the East India Company could claim political supremacy in South India. Haidar Ali, who mounted the throne of Mysore in 1761, and his son Tipu Sultan, allied with the French, won many battles against the English. The Treaty of Paris brought the French empire to a close in 1763. When the Treaty of Versailles brought the French and English together in 1783 Tipu was forced to make peace.

Literature

As the oldest living Indian language, Tamil has a literature stretching back to the early centuries before Christ. A second century AD poets' academy, the Sangamin Madurai, suggests that sages sat at the top of the Tamil social order, followed by peasants, hunters, artisans, soldiers, fishermen and scavengers – in marked contrast to the rest of the subcontinent's caste system. From the beginning of the Christian era Tamil religious thinkers began to transform the image of Krishna from the remote and heroic figure of the epics into the focus of a new and passionate devotional worship –bhakti.

Modern Tamil Nadu

Until 1967 the Assembly was dominated by the Indian National Congress, but after an attempt by the central government to impose Hindi as the national language the Congress Party was routed in 1967 by a regional party, the Dravida Munnetra Kazhagam (DMK). Since then either the DMK, or the splinter party, the All India Anna DMK (AIADMK), has been in power In the state.

The civil war in Sri Lanka caused tremendous stresses in Tamil politics on the mainland, neither the AIADMK nor the DML wanting either to alienate Tamil sentiment, nor wishing to back Sri Lanka's LTTE. Whether the ending of that conflict, and the ousting of President Rajapaksa (whose removal from power in January 2015 was viewed from Chennai as a victory for the Tamil people), brings much needed relief will depend crucially on the political approach adopted by the new Sri Lankan government to the Tamil populations in the island. Tamil leaders in India have been strongly pushing for an investigation into war crimes and human rights abuses allegedly perpetuated by the government leading up to and following the end of the war.

Tamil Nadu's coast bore the brunt of India's casualties of the 2004 tsunami. Along 1000 km of shoreline, at least 8000 people died, and 470,000 were displaced. As well as loved ones, the wave washed away infrastructure: communities, homes, livelihoods, schools, and health clinics.

Kerala

tranquil backwaters, tea plantations and jungle treehouses

Kerala ebbs by at a snail's pace in the slow-flowing networks of lagoons and rivers that make up its backwaters, where canals sit choked with pretty water-lilies and dragonflies bunch over lotus leaves.

In the ramshackle port city of Fort Kochi, it's as if the clocks stopped a few centuries back: wizened traders sift spice, the churches glow lime white, at the harbour's edge lines of cantilevered Chinese fishing nets swoop for their next catch, and medieval streets and antique shops thread the route between the tiny blue-tiled synagogue and grand Dutch wooden palace of Mattancherry.

The southern beaches of Kovalam and Varkala are great places to unwind with Ayurvedic massages, but Malabar, in the north, is the real unsung jewel of the state, an outpost of staunch Hindu religiosity and capital of the Muslim Moplah community. Here, hushed families gather at dawn to watch spectacles of the unique, hypnotic temple dance form Theyyam and, come nightfall, the precision athletes of the swashbuckling martial art Kalarippayattu draw their swords.

Switchback turns bear you from the lush green paddy fields of the plains through rubber plantations and coffee-tree forests up to the tea-shrubs of Thekaddy and Munnar mountain villages, whose nature reserves hide tigers and elephants.

Best for
Ayurveda ■ Backwaters ■ Food ■ Wildlife

Delhi

Kochi

Footprint picks

★ **The Backwaters**, page 903

Cast yourself adrift from life and
watch village life slide by from
a houseboat.

★ **Fort Kochi**, page 916

Quiet lanes huddle beneath vast raintrees in this colonial enclave of Kerala's
biggest city.

★ **Periyar National Park**, page 930

Stride out on foot into tiger and elephant country with former poachers.

★ **Pooram festival, Thrissur**, page 940

Pooram is a week-long festival of pounding drums, gold-bedecked
elephants and non-stop firecrackers.

★ **River Nila**, page 943

This crucible of Keralite culture is the place to witness classical and folk
music and check in for authentic Ayurvedic cleansing.

★ **Wayanad**, page 955

Kerala's most appealing hill station is blanketed in misty jungles and
contoured tea plantations.

Essential Kerala

Finding your feet

Stretching from some of the highest mountains of the Western Ghats to the lush coastal plain, Kerala (population 33.3 million) encapsulates the rich diversity of western India's coastal landscapes. Its narrow coastal fringe has been raised from the sea in the last million years. Inland are rolling hills of laterite, succeeded by the ancient rocks that form the backbone of the Western Ghats.

Getting around

Kerala is famous for its converted rice boat backwaters tours; take the ferry for a more local route around. Bus and car journeys in the backwaters are picturesque too. There are trains from Malabar to Ernakulam and on to Trivantharapuram.

When to go

It's hot all year round. Kerala does not have an extended totally dry season characteristic of the rest of India, but is particularly wet during the monsoon season, from June to September, when many places close. March and April are stiflingly hot. High season is November-March; outside this time prices may drop by up to 50%. Trekking is best December-April. Check www.keralatourism.org/festivalcalendar.php for exact festival dates.

Time required

Two days is enough for a backwaters cruise. Leave a couple of days for Fort Kochi and a few in Varkala. A week will make Malabar a worthwhile detour. Add three days for a wildlife trip into the Ghats, in Periyar or Wayanad.

Food and drink

Kerala's cuisine reflects its diverse religious traditions, its location on the seaboard and the ubiquitous presence of the coconut. Uniquely in India, beef is widely eaten, although seafood is far more common. Fish *moilee* is prepared with coconut milk and spices while for *pollichathu* the fish is baked with chilli paste, curry leaves and spices. Coconut-based dishes such as *thoran*, a dry dish of mixed vegetables chopped very small, herbs and curry leaves, and *avial*, similar to *thoran* but cooked in a sauce, are widely eaten. *Erisseri* is a thick curry of banana or yam and *kichadi* is beetroot or cucumber in coconut-curd paste. You can try these with the soft centred, lacy pancake *appam* or the soft noodle rice cakes *iddiappam*.

Jack fruit, pineapples, custard apples and an endless variety of bananas also play a vital part in many dishes. For dessert, you might get milk *payasam*, made with rice or vermicelli.

Fact...
Malayalam, the state language, is the most recent of the Dravidian languages, developing from the 13th century with its origin in Sanskrit.

Weather Thiruvananthapuram

January	February	March	April	May	June
31°C 22°C 23mm	31°C 23°C 22mm	32°C 24°C 36mm	32°C 25°C 110mm	31°C 25°C 210mm	29°C 24°C 343mm

July	August	September	October	November	December
29°C 23°C 219mm	29°C 24°C 143mm	30°C 24°C 152mm	30°C 24°C 268mm	30°C 23°C 199mm	30°C 23°C 70mm

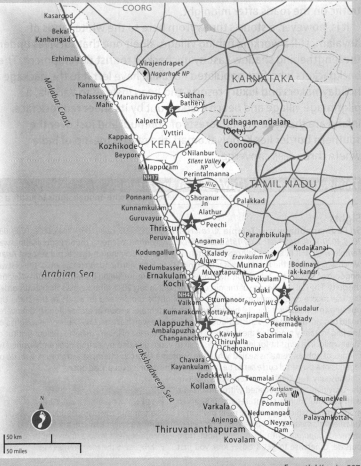

COORG

Kasargod

Bekal
Kanhangad

Ezhimala

Virajendrapet
Nagarhole NP

KARNATAKA

Malabar Coast

Kannur
Thalassery Manandavady
Mahe

Kalpetta

Sulthan
Bathery

Udhagamandalam
(Ooty)

Vyttiri

Coonoor

Kappad
Kozhikode
Beypore

KERALA

Nilanbur
Silent Valley NP
Perintalmanna

Malappuram

NH17

Ponnani

Kunnamkulam

Guruvayur

Thrissur

Peruvanum

Nila

Shoranur
Jn

Alathur

Peechi

Palakkad

TAMIL NADU

Parambikulam

Kodaikanal

Kodungallur

Angamali

Kalady
Aluva

Eravikulam NP

Nedumbassery

Muvattupuzha

Munnar

Bodinay
ak-kanur

Arabian Sea

Ernakulam
Kochi

Vaikom

Devikulam

NH47

Ettumanoor

Periyar WLS

Iduki

Kumarakom

Kottayam

Kanjirapalli

Gudalur

Thekkady

Alappuzha
Ambalapuzha
Changanacherry

Kaviyur
Thiruvalla
Chengannur

Peermade

Sabarimala

Chavara
Kayankulam

Vadckkevla

Tenmalai

*Kuttalam
Falls*

Tirunelveli

Kollam

Ponmudi

Varkala

Anjengo

Nedumangad

Neyyar
Dam

Palayamkottai

Thiruvananthapuram

Kovalam

Lakshadweep Sea

N

50 km
50 miles

Thiruvananthapuram
& the far south

The state capital, a pleasant city built over gently rolling coastal land, is very much a village as soon as you step away from the crowded centre. There's none of the throb, bustle and boom-time of Ernakulam, its opposite city up north, and no one could accuse it of being cosmopolitan; you'll be pushed to find a club, or bar, or even any traffic on the roads after midnight.

It is, however, a stone's throw from here to the white sands of Kovalam, still a working fishing village, albeit one that survives under the lengthening shadow cast by unchecked tourist development. The backpackers who first populated Kovalam have left it to the package holidaymakers and luxury resorts and head instead to Varkala, a pilgrimage village and beach marked out by its sheer red rock face. Inland are the little-visited forests of Ponmudi and just over the southern border lies Kanniyakumari, the sacred toe-tip of India where three seas converge.

Thiruvananthapuram (Trivandrum) and around

gateway to the beaches, but with enough sights to justify a stay

Sights

Sri Padmanabhaswamy Temple ① *East Fort, T0471-245 0233, open 0330-0445, 0630-0700, 0830-1000, 1030-1110, 1145-1200, 1700-1815 and 1845-1920.* According to legend, the Sri Padmanabhaswamy Temple was built in stages to house the statue of Vishnu reclining on the sacred serpent Ananta, which was found in the forest. It was rebuilt in 1733 by Raja Marthanda Varma, king of the erstwhile kingdom of Travancore, who dedicated the whole kingdom, including his rights and possessions, to the deity. The full significance of this gift came to light in July 2011, after Kerala's High Court ordered the Travancore royal family to hand over control of the temple and its assets to the State. Upon opening the six *kallaras* (vaults) hidden beneath the temple, a team of archaeologists discovered a hoard of gold- and jewel-encrusted idols estimated to be worth at least US$22 billion in weight alone. The find instantly propelled the temple to the head of the list of India's richest religious institutions. Meanwhile, in a twist fit for Indiana Jones, a sixth vault, guarded by an iron door emblazoned with images of cobras, remains sealed while the Supreme Court and temple astrologers wrestle over legends of a powerful curse set to be unleashed if the door is ever prised open.

Unusually for Kerala, the temple is built in the Dravidian style associated with Tamil Nadu, with beautiful murals, sculptures and 368 carved granite pillars which support the main pavilion or *kulashekharamandapa*. You can see the seven-storeyed *gopuram* with its sacred pool from outside; otherwise to get a closer look you first

Fact...
The name Thiruvananthapuram is derived from Tiru Ananta Puram, the abode of the sacred serpent Ananta upon whose coils Vishnu lies in the main temple.

Essential Thiruvananthapuram and the far south

Finding your feet

The international airport is 6 km from the centre of Thiruvananthapuram, a 15-minute drive outside rush hour, and half an hour from Kovalam. You can hire a prepaid taxi (Rs 200-300) or auto (about Rs 100) into town or wait for a local bus. At the southern end of Thiruvananthapuram are the central (long-distance) bus station, with services throughout Kerala and into neighbouring Tamil Nadu, and the railway station from where trains run up and down the coast.

Best budget hotels

Manjalikulam Tourist Home, Thiruvananthapuram, page 892
Coco Land, Kovalam, page 897
Hotel Greenland, Kovalam, page 897
Marine Palace, Varkala, page 900
Sea Pearl Chalets, Varkala, page 900

Local buses in Thiruvananthapuram, including those bound for Kovalam, leave from the East Fort City stand opposite the fort entrance, southwest of the station. Buses to Kovalam can drop you at Waller Junction, five minutes' walk from the Samudra Beach hotels. A further 1.5 km on they turn off for the main Kovalam Bus Stand at the Ashok Hotel gate, five minutes from most southern hotels and cafés. Lighthouse Road is steep and narrow, but autos and taxis are able to drive up it. For details, see Transport, page 894.

Best Ayurvedic resorts

Niraamaya, near Kovalam, page 897
Somatheeram Ayurvedic Beach Resort, Chowara Beach, page 897
Dr Franklin's Panchakarma Institute and Research Centre, Chowara, page 898

Getting around

With a population of 1,687,300, Thiruvananthapuram is relatively strung out, though the centre is compact. Autos or taxis are more convenient than the packed buses but bargain hard: businesses have fast acclimatized to the price naivety that goes hand in hand with package tourism. Minimum charges start at Rs 150 for taxis, Rs 20 for autos; thereafter the rate per running kilometre for cars is Rs 12 (non-a/c), Rs 15 (a/c), rickshaws Rs 10. Drivers may be reluctant to accept the going rate. If you're heading for Kovalam, budget on around Rs 250 for a taxi and Rs 175 for an auto.

Useful contacts

Foreigners' Regional Registration Office, City Police Commissioner, Residency Road, Thycaud, T0471-232 0579; allow up to a week for visas, though it can take less. Monday-Saturday 1000-1700.

Tip...

When shopping, bear in mind that prices are relatively high in this region. Traders seldom honour the standard rates for 92.5ct silver, charging by piece not weight.

have to persuade the famously strict Kerala Brahmins to waive the Hindus-only entry restriction. It becomes easier to do so if men have donned a crisp white *dhoti*, women a sari and blouse.

Kuthiramalkia (Puthenmalika) Palace ① *Just next to the temple, Temple Rd, East Fort, T0471-247 3952, Tue-Sun 0830-1330 and 1500-1730, Rs 20, camera Rs 15.* The Travancore king, Maharajah Swathi Thirunal Balarama Varma, was a musician, poet and social reformer, and his palace is a fine reflection of his patronage of the arts. On the upper level a window gives an angle on scores of fine wood-carved horses that look like a huge cavalry charge, and among the portraits painted in the slightly unsettling Indian/European classical hybrid style is one from an artist who trumped his rivals by painting not just eyes that follow you around the room, but also feet. Sadly, it is ill maintained, but a gem nonetheless.

Napier Museum ① *North Park Grounds, city north, T0471-231 8294, Tue-Sun 1000-1645, Wed morning only, closed public holidays.* The museum building is a spectacular landmark. Designed by RF Chisholm in traditional-Kerala-meets-Indo-Saracenic style, it was completed in 1872. Today, it houses a famous collection of eighth to 18th-century South Indian bronzes, mostly from Chola, Vijayanagar and Nayaka periods, a few Jain and Buddhist sculptures and excellent woodcarvings.

Thiruvananthapuram (Trivandrum)

To Kollam (NH 17)

To Ponmadi

Sri Chitra Art Gallery

Zoo

Museum Rd

PMG Circle

LMS Junction

Napier Museum & Open Air Theatre

Crafts Design Centre

University Stadium

Main Central Rd

Swimming Pool

New State Assembly

Christ

Public Library

VELLAYAMBALAM

Police Stadium

St Joseph's Cathedral

Nandavanam Rd

Palayam Junction

Tagore Theatre

M G Rd

KUNNUKUZHI

Town Hall

To 7 11 12, Beach & Airport (6km)

University College

Connemara

VAZHUTAKKAD

Central Survey Office

General Hospital Circle

Spencer Junction

Bakery Junction

Accountant General's Office

Yoga Centre

Statue Rd

Vazhuthacaud Rd

Jaihind Travels

Statue Junction

Secretariat

Foreigners' Registration Office

Kairali Handicrafts

Central Stadium

Panavila Junction

Aries Travel

SMSM Handicrafts

Pulimudu Junction

Press Rd

Housing Board Junction

VANCHIYOOR

THYCAUD

Mahatma Gandhi Rd

Manjalikulam Rd

Residency (KITTS)

Thycaud Hospital Rd

Ayurvedic College

Ayurvedic College Junction

THAMPANOOR

Mettukkada Mukku

Taikkad Junction

Lab Supplies

Chettikulangara Rd

KSRTC Thampanoor Bus Stand

Aristo Junction

Hospital Rd

VALIYASHALA

S S Coil Rd

Aristo Rd

To 6 & Airport

Central Station Rd

Overbridge

Thampanoor Junction

Thakaraparambu Rd

Power House Junction

Power House Rd

N

SRI VENKATESWARAM

Padmavilasam Rd

Fort Bus Station

Verma Travels

200 metres

200 yards

Sri Padmanabhaswamy Temple

EAST FORT

FORT

Kuthiramalika Palace

Buses to Kovalam

To Airport

To Kovalam Beach (16 km)

Thamburu International 9
Thapovan Heritage Home 12
Wild Palms Homestay 10
Youth Hostel 7

Where to stay

Asha 11
Capital 4
Chaithram 1
Greenland 2
Highland 3
Manjikulam Tourist Home 6
Residency Tower 8

Restaurants

Arul Jyoti 2
Indian Coffee House 1
Kalavara 5
Kerala House 7
Mascot 3
Queen's 4
Villa Maya 6

Sri Chitra Art Gallery ① *Just north of the museum, 1000-1645, closed Mon and Wed mornings, Rs 5.* The Sri Chitra gallery has a fine catalogue of Indian art from early to modern schools: works by Raja Ravi Varma, 20th-century pioneer of the radical post-colonial school of painting, sit among paintings from Java, Bali, China and Japan, Mughal and Rajput miniatures. The Tanjore paintings are studded with semi-precious stones.

Zoological park ① *Entrance at southwest corner of park, Tue-Sun 0900-1815, Rs 10, cameras Rs 25.* Set in a hilly woodland of frangipani and jacaranda, the zoological park has a wide collection of animals and a well-labelled botanical garden.

East of Thiruvananthapuram

At the foot of the Western Ghats, 30 km east of Thiruvananthapuram, the **Neyyar Wildlife Sanctuary** ① *free, speedboat for 2 people Rs 250/400, larger boats to view the forests enclosing the lake Rs 25 per person*, occupies a beautiful wooded and hilly landscape, dominated by the peak of Agasthya Malai (1868 m). The vegetation ranges from grassland to tropical, wet evergreen. Wildlife includes gaur, sloth bear, Nilgiri tahr, jungle cat, sambar deer, elephants and Nilgiri langur; the most commonly seen animals are lion-tailed macaques and other monkeys. Tigers and leopards have also been reported. **Neyyar Dam** supports a large population of crocodiles and otters; a crocodile farm was set up in 1977 near the administrative complex.

Immediately to the northeast of the Neyyar Wildlife Sanctuary a section of dense forest, **Agasthya Vanam**, was set aside as a biological park in 1992 to recreate biodiversity on a wide scale. Nearby, the **Sivananda Yoga Vedanta Dhanwantari Ashram** ① *T0471-227 3093, www.sivananda. org/neyyardam, minimum stay 3 days*, runs highly regarded meditation and yoga courses. It is quite an intensive schedule, with classes that start just after dawn and a strict timetable including karma yoga (meditation or devotion to God through physical labour). It is only really suitable for the hardy; others may find it heavy on Hinduism and Indian diet.

Further north sits **Ponmudi** ① *buses from Trivandrum, Thampanoor Bus Stand 0530-1630; return 0615-1905, 2½ hrs,* the nearest hill station to Thiruvananthapuram, 65 km away. In a spectacular and peaceful setting, the tourist complex, though basic, serves as a good base for trekking, birdwatching and visiting the nearby minimalist deer park.

Listings Thiruvananthapuram (Trivandrum) and around *map p890*

Tourist information

Kerala Tourism
Park View, T0471-232 1132, www.kerala tourism.org. Mon-Sat 1000-1700.
Thiruvananthapuram's main tourist office, where you can book half-day tours around the city (Rs 300). There are also offices at Thampanoor Central Bus Station, the railway station and the airport. Tourist offices have plenty of leaflets and information sheets and are very helpful.

Where to stay

$$$ Thapovan Heritage Home
18 km south of town, Nellikunnu, T0471-248 0453, www.thapovan.com.
Rooms in beautiful gardens or overlooking Nellikunu Beach. Ayurvedic treatments, yoga, restaurant.

$$ The Capital, off MG Rd
Near the GPO, Pulimood, T0471-301 2301, www.thecapital.in.
Renovated business hotel, with smallish but clean rooms and some large, excellent value suites. Excellent rooftop restaurant. Friendly.

$$ Residency Tower
Press Rd, T0471-233 1661, www.residencytower.com.
Top-quality a/c rooms in a business hotel, with full facilities. Highly efficient, good restaurants, bar, rooftop pool (non-residents Rs 350). A bit swish.

$$ Wild Palms On Sea
Beach Rd, T0471-275 6781, www.wildpalmsonsea.com.
Modern welcoming guesthouse wih pool right by the beach. Spacious rooms, some a/c. Price includes breakfast.

$$-$ Chaithram (KTDC)
Station Rd, T0471-233 0977, www.ktdc.com.
Very clean decent-sized rooms, all a/c. Next
to railway and bus stand so can be noisy.
Restaurant, bar.

$$-$ Highland
Manjalikulam Rd, T0471-233 2645,
www.highland-hotels.com.
Rs 1100-2300 (plus taxes). Busy hotel with a
wide variety of clean rooms. Budget rooms
are good value.

$$-$ Thamburu International
Aristo Junction, T0471-232 1974,
www.thamburu.com.
Quiet, well-run hotel with wood-panelled walls
and cheesy music in the foyer. Rooms (all with
TV) tend to be on the small side. Some a/c rooms
have balcony.

$ Greenland
Aristo Junction, T0471-232 3485.
Great-value rooms in quiet, immaculate, freshly
renovated hotel, perfectly located within a
couple of mins of both bus and railway stations.
Best budget choice in town.

$ Manjalikulam Tourist Home
Manjalikulam Rd, T0471-233 0776,
www.manjalikulam.com.
Quiet yet central hotel with large, spotlessly
clean 36 rooms. Very friendly staff. Good
value, recommended.

$ Youth Hostel (YHAI)
10 km from the centre, Veli, T0471-250 1230,
youthhostelveli@gmail.com.
Rooms and a dorm surrounded by coconut
groves, with a pretty lagoon and clean beach.
Very cheap vegetarian lunches, boating,
watersports, good views.

East of Thriuvananthapuram

$$$$-$$$ Duke's Forest Lodge
Anappara, near Ponmudi, T0472-285 9273,
www.dukesforestlodge.in. Rs 5500-8500
(plus taxes).
5 luxury villas, each with its own plunge pool,
set on organic estate. Also 4 standard rooms.
Great trekking.

$$-$ Government Guest House
Ponmudi, T0471-289 0211. Rs 600 (plus taxes).
24 rooms and 10 cottages ($$), in attractive
gardens surrounded by wooded hills, spartan
facilities but spacious rooms, restaurant serves

limited but reasonable vegetarian meals, beer
available, also a post office and general store.

Restaurants

$$$ Villa Maya
Airport Rd, Subash Nagar, Injakkal Westfort Rd,
T0471-257 8901, www.villamaya.in.
One of the most beautiful restaurants in Kerala,
set in a restored 18th-century Dutch villa
surrounded by fountains. Dishes span a broad
range of cuisines, from traditional Kerala curries
to Israeli or Moroccan specials. It's pricey and
they don't serve alcohol, but this is a superb
choice for a splurge.

$$ Kalavara
Kalavara Hotel, Press Rd, T0471-272 7034.
Indian, Continental, Chinese, fast food (burgers,
shakes), takeaway. Food average, slow service
but good-value buffets in upstairs thatched
section with a patch of garden. Good ambience,
limited views.

$$ Kerala House
Near Statue Junction, T0471-247 6144.
Kerala cuisine in the basement of shopping
complex. Slow for breakfast but newspapers
available, outside seating in the evening in
roadside car park area is cheaper. Colourful and
fun place to pass some time, even if the food
arrives cold. Try *neem, kappa* and rice (delicious
fish with tapioca), or inexpensive chicken dishes
with coconut; bakery in the complex does
excellent samosas and puffs.

$$ Mascot
Mascot Hotel, Museum Rd, www.mascothotel
thiruvananthapuram.com.
Excellent lunchtime buffet, pleasant, 24-hr coffee
shop for all types of snacks, good value, a cool
haven at midday.

$ Arul Jyoti
MG Rd, opposite Secretariat.
South Indian vegetarian. With a/c family room,
clean, wide choice of good-value dishes, try
jumbo *dosas*. Great Tamil Nadu *thalis*.

$ Indian Coffee House
2 branches on MG Rd, T0471-321 4501,
www.indiancoffeehouse.com, with others
near YWCA, north of the Secretariat, and
near KSRTC Bus Stand (the latter designed
by the English architect Laurie Baker).
Worth seeing, excellent value coffee
and snacks.

Entertainment

Performances of *Kalarippayattu*, Kerala's martial art, can be seen through: **CVN Kalari** (East Fort, T0471-247 4182, 0430-0830); and **Balachandran Nair Kalari Martial Arts Gymnasium** (Parasuvaikal, T0471-223 2686, www.kalari.in).

Festivals

Mar Chandanakuda, at Beemapalli, a shrine on Beach Rd, 5 km southwest of the railway station. 10-day festival when local Muslims go to the mosque, holding incense sticks and pots. Marked by sword play, singing, dancing, elephant procession and fireworks.
Mar-Apr (Meenam) and Oct-Nov (Thulam) **Arattu** is the closing festival of the 10-day celebrations of the Padmanabhaswamy Temple, in which the deity is paraded around the temple inside the fort and then down to the sea.
Sep/Oct Navaratri at the special *mandapa* in Padmanabhaswamy Temple. Several concerts are held which draw famous musicians. **Thiruvonam week** in Sep.
1-10 Oct Soorya Dance Festival.
Nov-Mar A similar **Nishangandhi Dance Festival** is held at weekends when all-important classical Indian dance forms are performed by leading artistes at Nishagandhi open-air auditorium, Kanakakkunnu Palace.

Shopping

Shopping areas include the **Chalai Bazar**, the **Connemara Market** and the main road from Palayam to the East Fort. Usually open 0900-2000 (some take a long lunch break). Although ivory goods have now been banned, inlay on woodcarving and marquetry using other materials (bone, plastic) continue to flourish. *Kathakali* masks and traditional fabrics can be bought at a number of shops.

The shopping centre opposite East Fort Bus Stand has a large a/c shop with a good selection of silks and saris but is not cheap. *Khadi* is recommended from shops on both sides of MG Rd, south of Pulimudu Junction.

Co-optex, *Temple Rd*. Good for fabrics and *lungis*.
Handloom House, *diagonally across from Partha's*. Has an excellent range of fabrics, clothes and export quality dhurries.
Partha's, *towards East Fort*. Recommended.
Raymonds, *KaralKada, East Fort*. Good selection of men's clothing plus pricy tailoring.

Handicrafts

Gift Corner and **Natesan Antique Arts**, *MG Rd*. High-quality goods including old dowry boxes, carved wooden panels from old temple 'cars', miniature paintings and bronzes.
Gram Sree, *MG Rd*. Excellent village crafts.
Kairali, *MG Rd*. Items of banana fibre, coconut, screw pine, mainly utilitarian, also excellent sandal-wood carvings and bell-metal lamps, utensils.
Kalanjali, *Palace Garden, across from the museum*. Recommended.
SMSM Handicrafts Emporium, *behind the Secretariat*. Government-run, heaps of items reasonably priced.

What to do

Body and soul

Institute of Yogic Culture, *Vazhuthacaud*, T0471-304 9349, www.pillaisyogicculture.com. Yoga therapy, Ayurvedic massage.
Sivananda Ashram, *Neyyar Dam*, T(0)9495-630951, www.sivananda.org.in/neyyardam. One of India's most highly regarded yoga teacher training programs.
Vasudeva Vilasam, *Vasudeva Vilasam Rd, East Fort*, T0471-409 1000, www.vasudeva.com. Simple but with experienced professionals.

Swimming

Mascot Hotel, *Cantonment Rd*, www.mascothotel thiruvananthapuram.com. Has a big pool.
Waterworks, *near the museum*, T0471-231 8990. Has a pool.

Tour operators

The following are IATA-approved agencies.
Great India Tour Co, *New Corporation Building, Palayam*, T0471-301 1500, www.gitc.travel. Offers afternoon city tours, among others. Reliable but pricey.
KTDC, *Hotel Chaithram, Station Rd*, T0471-233 0031, www.ktdc.com. Can arrange 2- to 3-day tours to Munnar and Thekkady and also runs the following local tours: **City tour**: daily 0800 and 1330, 5½ hrs including Padmanabhapuram, Puthenmalika Palace, Shangumugham beach and Napier Museum, Rs 300 (Padmanabhapuram is closed on Mon). **Kanniyakumari**: daily 0730-2100, including Kovalam, Padmanabhapuram and Kanniyakumari, Rs 700. Tours can feel quite rushed with little time spent at sights.
TourIndia, *MG Rd*, T0471-233 0437, www.tourindia kerala.com. The pioneers of backwater tourism and Periyar's Tiger Trails trekking program. Highly recommended for innovative and unusual

experiences, eg treehouse holidays or sport fishing off Fort Kochi.

Trekking and birdwatching

Trekking is best Dec-Apr. Obtain permission first from the Chief Conservator of Forests (Wildlife), Forest HQ, Thiruvananthapuram, T0471-232 5385, or the Assistant Wildlife Warden at Neyyar Dam, T0471-227 2182.

Transport

Air The airport, T0471-250 1591, is 6 km west of the centre. There are banks and money exchange facilities including **Thomas Cook**, T0471-250 2470. Transport to town is by local bus no 14, prepaid taxi (Rs 150) or auto (about Rs 100, 20 mins). Prepaid taxis to **Kovalam** cost around Rs 350. Banks at the airport are outside Arrivals. Note that the terminal is closed at night.

Domestic flights to most major Indian cities including: **Bengaluru, Chennai, Delhi, Hyderabad, Kochi, Kolkata, Kozhikode** and **Mumbai**.

International departures include: **Air India Express** to several **Gulf** destinations; **Emirates** to **Dubai**; **Etihad** to **Abu Dhabi**. **Maldivian** to **Malé**; **Silk Air** and **Tiger Airways** to **Singapore**; **Sri Lankan** to **Colombo**.

Bus Local: City Bus Stand, T0471-257 5495. Green buses have limited stops; yellow/red buses continue through town up to museum. Blue/white bus (No 888) to **Kovalam** goes from East Fort Bus Station (30 mins, Rs 9).

Long distance: Buses leave from KSRTC Bus Station, Station Rd, near railway station, T0471-232 3886, www.keralartc.com. Buses to **Kanniyakumari** via **Nagercoil** or direct, 0530, 0930, 1000, 1200, 1500, 1600 and 1830 (2½ hrs) and frequent departures to **Kozhikode** (10 hrs) via **Kollam** (2½ hrs), **Alappuzha** (4 hrs), **Ernakulam/Kochi** (5½ hrs) and **Thrissur** (7 hrs). You can take in a section of the backwaters on the way to Kochi by getting a boat from Kollam. SETC buses leave for destinations in Tamil Nadu, including **Chennai** (12 hrs), **Coimbatore** (8 hrs), **Kanniyakumari** and **Madurai** (7 hrs).

Rickshaw Rickshaws to the **Kovalam** beach area should cost around Rs 150-170. You will need to bargain. Tell auto-rickshaw drivers which beaches you want to get to in advance, otherwise they will charge much more when you get there.

Taxi From town, taxis charge about Rs 12 per km; to **Kovalam**, Rs 290, return Rs 580 (waiting: extra Rs 50 per hr). To **Kanniyakumari** with a stop at **Padmanabhapuram** costs about Rs 1500/2000.

Train Central Station, T132. Reservations in the building adjoining the station; for foreign tourist quota bookings, go to Counter 8 upstairs, open 0700-1300, 1330-1930, Sun 0900-1700; ask to see the Chief Reservations Supervisor. To **Bengaluru**: 2 daily, 18 hrs; **Chennai**: 4 daily, 15 hrs; **Ernakulam** (Kochi): around 20 trains daily, 5¼ hrs, all via **Varkala** (40 mins) and **Kollam** (1 hr); most continue via **Kottayam**, 3 hrs; some via **Alleppey**, 2½ hrs. To **Kanniyakumari**: 4 daily, 2½ hrs. To **Mangalore**: 6 daily, 13 hrs, via **Ernakulam, Thrissur** (5½ hrs), **Kozhikode** (7½ hrs) and **Kannur** (10 hrs).

Kovalam and nearby resorts

Kerala's most developed resort, crammed with hotels, shops and restaurants

Local fishermen's boats still sit on Kovalam's narrow strip of sand right next to sunbathing tourists, but the sleepy Lakshadweep seaside village of old has now been almost completely swallowed up by package tourist infrastructure: Ayurveda parlours, trinkets, tailoring shops and tour operators line every inch of the narrow walkways behind the shore. In peak season it's something of an exotic god's waiting room, popular with pensioners, and it's safe and sedate enough for families. Backpackers tend to return off season.

Beaches

North and south of Kovalam (population 25,400) are four main stretches of beach, about 400 m long, divided by a rocky promontory on which sits the Charles Correa-designed **Leela Hotel**. The area to the north of the promontory, known as **Samudra Beach** and **Pozhikara Beach**, 5 km away offers the most sheltered bathing and the clearest water. The southern beaches, **Lighthouse Beach** and

Kovalam

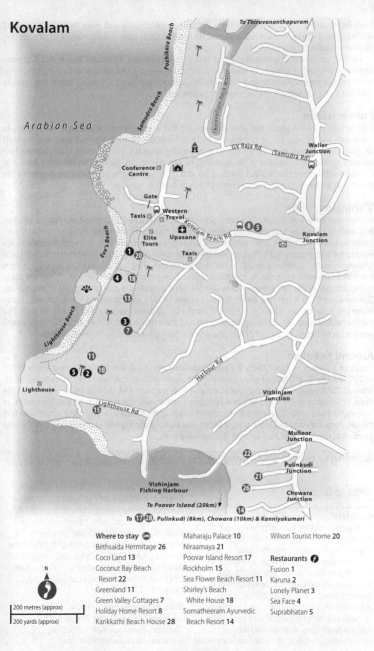

Arabian Sea

To Thiruvananthapuram

Pozhikara Beach

Samudra Beach

Thiruvollam Back Water

GV Raja Rd

Waller Junction

Conference Centre

Gate

Taxis

Western Travel

Samudra Rd

Elite Tours

Upasana

Kovalam Beach Rd

Taxis

Eve's Beach

Kovalam Junction

Lighthouse Beach

Lighthouse

Lighthouse Rd

Harbour Rd

Vizhinjam Junction

Mulloor Junction

Pulinkudi Junction

Chowara Junction

Vizhinjam Fishing Harbour

To Poovar Island (20km)

To Pulinkudi (8km), Chowara (10km) & Kanniyakumari

N

200 metres (approx)

200 yards (approx)

Where to stay
Bethsaida Hermitage 26
Coco Land 13
Coconut Bay Beach
  Resort 22
Greenland 11
Green Valley Cottages 7
Holiday Home Resort 8
Karikkathi Beach House 28

Maharaju Palace 10
Niraamaya 21
Poovar Island Resort 17
Rockholm 15
Sea Flower Beach Resort 11
Shirley's Beach
  White House 18
Somatheeram Ayurvedic
  Beach Resort 14

Wilson Tourist Home 20

Restaurants
Fusion 1
Karuna 2
Lonely Planet 3
Sea Face 4
Suprabhatan 5

Eve's Beach, are more crowded and lively. Lighthouse Beach is far and away the most happening and has a long line of bars screening pirated Hollywood films, cafés selling muesli and pastries and hawkers peddling crafts or drugs.

Further south still is where the classy resorts are clustered. **Pulinkudi Beach** and **Chowara Beach**, respectively 8 km and 10 km to the south, is where to go for hand-and-foot attentiveness, isolation, heritage-style villas and Ayurveda in luxurious surrounds. Chowara Beach has security staff but some sunbathers still feel plagued by hawkers.

Poovar Island
Poovar Island, 20 km south, has several resorts on the landward side of a lagoon, with access to the beach (where you will be bombarded by local fisherkids demanding cash, pens and the shirt off your back) by motorboat. There are now lifeguard patrols but you still need to be careful when swimming. Kovalam's stretch of the Arabian Sea can get rough, particularly between April and October, with strong riptides and swells of up to 6 m. From May the sea level rises, removing the beach completely in places, and swimming becomes very dangerous.

Vizhinjam
Within easy walking distance of Kovalam, sandwiched in between Lighthouse and Poovar beaches but scarcely visited by tourists, is Vizhinjam, a scruffy town with a low-rise string of bangle shops, banana stalls, beauticians and seamstresses sewing jasmine buds onto strings for garlands. It's hard to believe it today but Vizhinjam was once the capital of the Ay rulers who dominated South Travancore in the ninth century AD. In the seventh century they had faced constant pressure from the Pandiyans who kept the Ay chieftains under firm control for long periods. There are rock-cut sculptures in the 18th-century **cave temple** here, including a rough sculpture of Vinandhara Dakshinamurthi in the shrine and unfinished reliefs of Siva and Parvati on the outer wall. Today Vizhinjam is the centre of the fishing industry and is being developed as a major container port. The traditional boats are rapidly being modernized and the catch is sold all over India, but you can still see the keen interest in the sale of fish, and women taking headloads off to local markets.

Around Kovalam
South of Kovalam in Tamil Nadu is **Padmanabhapuram** ① *Tue-Sun 0900-1700 (last tickets 1600), Rs 200, child Rs 50 (accredited guide included, but 'donation' expected after the tour), camera Rs 25, video Rs 1500; best at 0900 before coach parties arrive, see page 899,* the old wooden palace of the Rajas of Travancore. Enclosed within a cyclopean stone wall, the palace served as the capital of Travancore from 1490-1790, and is a beautiful example of the Kerala school of architecture, with fine murals, floral carvings and black granite floors. It makes a great day trip, or a neat stopover if you're heading across the Tamil Nadu border to Kanniyakumari.

Listings Kovalam and nearby resorts *map p895*

Where to stay

Kovalam
Long power cuts are common here, so a/c often doesn't work. Look for rooms with windows on 2 walls to get a good through-breeze. There are numerous budget cottages and rooms to let with a range of rooms from Rs 150-1000. The alleys behind **Lighthouse Beach** tend to have the cheapest accommodation. Scouts greet arrivals at the bus stand but you may pay considerably more if you use their services. You will find rooms to let, behind bars and restaurants, by walking from the **Sea Rock Hotel**

towards the lighthouse, and on the **Samudra Beach** and **GV Raja Rd** (Samudra Rd). Be aware that management of the cheaper hotels often changes hands and hotel names can change from year to year. Rates shown here are for the high season. Prices skyrocket in all hotels for the 3-week peak period (23 Dec-7 Jan), though it still pays to bargain. High season is 1-19 Dec, 11 Jan-28 Feb; in the low season, especially May-Jul, expect 40-75% discounts.

$$$$ Karikkathi Beach House
Near Nagar Bhagavathy Temple at Mulloor Thottam, Pulinkudi, T0471-272 0238, www.karikkathibeachhouse.com.

2 doubles with linked lounge, palm-thatched roof, no a/c or TV, perfect for honeymooners or those used to being kept; the house comes with private beach, chef, waiter and servants. There's a cottage should families or groups need extra beds.

$$$$-$$$ Niraamaya
Pulinkudi, near Kovalam, T0471-226 7333,
www.niraamaya.in.
Sitting high on a rocky bluff between Kovalam and Kannyukamari, this elite resort boasts a world-class spa and offers Ayurveda treatments. There are just 21 traditional Keralite cottages, with 4-posters, big plantation chairs and open-air bathrooms, spread over 9 ha of foresty gardens. Excellent Sivananda yoga on a one-on-one basis at an open-air pavilion overlooking the sea.

$$$$-$$$ Poovar Island Resort
Poovar Island, T0471-221 2068,
www.poovarislandresort.com.
Award-winning boutique hotel with 'floating' cottages where the backwaters meet the sea. Facilities include pool, handicrafts, Ayurveda, watersports.

$$$$-$$$ Somatheeram Ayurvedic Beach Resort
Chowara Beach, south of Kovalam,
T0471-226 8101, www.somatheeram.in.
Kerala's first Ayurvedic resort, and one of its best, with cottages and traditional Keralite houses set in coconut groves dotted over a steep hill above the beach. 20 doctors and 90 therapists work in 5 treatment rooms and 24 massage rooms at the shared Ayurvedic facilities.

$$$$-$$ Bethsaida Hermitage
Pulinkudi, T0471-226 7554,
www.bethsaidahermitage.com.
Eco-friendly stone and bamboo beach *cabanas* surrounded by coconut groves. Profits support a variety of charitable projects. Family-friendly, informal and unpretentious.

$$$$-$$ Coconut Bay Beach Resort
Mulloor, T0471-234 3524, www.coconutbay.com.
Spacious stone villas on beach, good restaurant, friendly. Secluded location in traditional fishing village. Recommended.

$$ Kailasam Yoga and Ayurveda Holidays
Kovalam, T0471-248 4018, book through
Free Spirit Travel, T+44 (0) 1362 683616 (UK),
www.yogaindia.co.uk.
Peaceful oasis set up by a yoga teacher and Ayurvedic physician. Yoga classes held in tiled areas under coconut-leaf roofs, surrounded by trees and open-sided to catch the sea breezes. Price includes all yoga classes.

$$ Maharaju Palace
Lighthouse Beach, T(0)9946-854270,
www.maharajupalace.com.
Beautiful, shady garden setting, quiet and set back from beach. 6 very clean rooms inside and outside cottages complete with chandeliers and frou-frou interiors. Genial staff, very popular.

$$ Rockholm
Lighthouse Rd, T0471-248 0406,
www.rockholm.com.
Very pleasant hotel owned by an Anglo-Indian family with cheerful staff. Good-sized rooms, with balcony, in a wonderful position just above the lighthouse. Direct access to beach. Good terrace restaurant.

$$-$ Coco Land
Between Lighthouse Beach and Eve's Beach,
T0471-248 1341, www.cocolandheritage.com.
Bamboo huts and 'luxury' wood cottages in a little garden set back from the beach. Cottages boast TVs, a/c and hot water. Friendly management. Recommended.

$$-$ Holiday Home Resort
Beach Rd, T0471-248 0497,
www.holidayhomeresort.net.
Cute cottages amid a tree-filled, shady garden with hammocks to laze in. Serene location 10 mins' walk from beach. Excellent, friendly service from the helpful manager, Shar.

$$-$ Hotel Greenland
Lighthouse Beach, T0471-232 3485.
Friendly female manager has a variety of spotlessly clean rooms set amongst her flowery garden. All have porch, fly-screens, 4 have kitchenettes and TV. Cheaper rooms are excellent value. Recommended.

$$-$ Shirley's Beach
Between Lighthouse Beach and Eve's Beach,
T0471-231 7303, www.shirleysbeach.com.
The sea-facing rooms here are a cut above other hotels in this price range. All are breezy and painted a cheerful blue, some with balcony. The owner is a wealth of knowledge. Quiet location, very good value. Recommended.

$ Green Valley Cottages
Between Lighthouse Beach and Eve's Beach,
T0471-248 0636.
Spick and span simple non-a/c rooms with fly-screens and sit-outs. Good value.

$ Sea Flower Beach Resort
Lighthouse Rd, T0471-248 0554,
www.seaflowerkovalam.com.
Great location right on the shore. 5 good-sized
rooms with decent bath and balcony. Helpful
staff, good value, big discounts for long stays.

$ Wilson Tourist Home
Up path behind Neelakanta Hotel,
T0471-248 0052. Rs 600-1200.
Clean, quiet rooms with bath, balcony, fan, some
with a/c. Open-air restaurant, pretty garden,
helpful service. Recommended.

Restaurants

Kovalam
There are hundreds of restaurants here. Service
can be slow, and quality hit-and-miss since
management often changes hands. Below is a
very short list of those that have proved consistent.
The restaurant at the **Taj** is good, if predictable.
The Leela hotel Sun brunch has a giant salad
counter and loud live music. Avoid 'catch of
the day' on Sun – it's unlikely to be fresh. Some
restaurants will screen pirated DVDs, sometimes
to compensate for underwhelming cuisine.

$$ Fusion
Eve's Beach, T0471-248 4153.
Kovalam's take on fusion food doesn't really pull
it off but the cold coffees are exceptional and the
menu has a nice varied mix of international and
Indian food.

$$ Rockholm Hotel
(See Where to stay), Lighthouse Rd.
Very good international food and tandooris
served on a pleasant terrace with beautiful
views, especially early morning.

$$ Sea Face
Eve's Beach, T0471-248 1835, www.seaface.com.
Breezy raised terrace on the beach by a pleasant
pool. Varied choice including versatile fish and
seafood. Friendly and attentive.

$ Karuna
Lighthouse Beach.
Excellent Keralite breakfasts, home-made brown
bread, decent coffee.

$ Lonely Planet
Between Lighthouse Beach and Eve's Beach.
Wholesome, mildly spiced Ayurvedic vegetarian
food. Set around a pond with ducks – and
mosquitoes. Sells recipe books and runs
cookery courses.

$ Suprabhatam
Lighthouse Beach, opposite Hotel Greenland.
South and North Indian vegetarian meals.

Entertainment

Kovalam
Kalakeli Kathakali Troupe, *T0471-248 1818.*
Daily performances at many high-end hotels.

Shopping

Kovalam
Numerous craft shops, including Kashmiri
and Tibetan shops, sell a wide range of goods.
Most are clustered around the bus stand at the
gate of the Ashok with another group to the
south around the lighthouse. Good-quality
paintings, metalwork, woodwork and carpets
at reasonable prices. Gems and jewellery are
widely available but it is notoriously difficult to
be sure of quality. Tailoring is available at short
notice and is very good value with the fabrics
available. Tailors include: **Brother Tailors**, 2nd
Beach Rd; **Raja**, near hotel Surya; and **Suresh**,
next to Garzia restaurant.

Zangsty Gems, *Lighthouse Rd.* Sells jewellery and
silver and has a good reputation for helpfulness
and reliability.

What to do

Kovalam
Body and soul
Ayurvedic treatments are offered by most
upmarket resorts, where a massage will set you
back anything from Rs 700 to more than Rs 2000.
**Dr Franklin's Panchakarma Institute and
Research Centre**, *Chowara, T0471-248 0870,
www.dr-franklin.com.* The good doctor's family
has practised Ayurveda for 4 centuries, and he
himself is the former district medical officer of
the Keralan government. Programmes include
treatment for infertility, sluggishness, paralysis
and obesity. 15-day body purification therapy
(*panchakarma* and *swetakarma*).
Medicus, *Lighthouse Rd, T0471-248 3710, www.
ayurbay.com.* Mrs Babu has a loyal clientele,
many of whom return year after year.
Padma Nair, *Pink Flowers, Lighthouse Beach,
T(0)9895-882915, www.padmakarma.com.* One
of *Kalaripayattu* master Balachandran Nair's
students, Padma Nair offers 1-week yoga holiday
programmes at her village home from US$250.

Fishing

Can readily be arranged through the hotels, as can excursions on traditional catamarans or motor boats. You may be promised corals and beautiful fish just offshore but don't expect to see very much.

Indian martial arts

Guru Balachandran Nair, *is the master of the Indian School of Martial Arts, Parasuvykal, 20 km from Trivandrum, T0471-223 2686, www.kalari.in.* This is a college teaching *Kalaripayattu*, Kerala's traditional martial art, as well as *Kalarichikitsa*, an ancient Indian healing tradition combining Ayurveda with *Marma* therapy, which manipulates the vital pressure points of the body to ease pain. A fighter would have had an intimate knowledge of these points to know what to harm or how to heal. A fascinating place to stay.

Tour operators

There are dozens of tour operators on the roads leading down to the beach and on the beachfront. Nearly all of them offer money exchange, onward travel booking and backwater tours.
Great Indian Travel, *Lighthouse Rd, T0471-248 0173, www.gitstour.com.*
Kerala Tours, *T0858-903 9767, www.keralatours. com.* Wide range of tours, exchange, packages to eco-friendly beach resorts.

Visit India, *Lighthouse Rd, T0471-248 1069.* Friendly and helpful, exchange, short backwater tours from Thiruvallam.

Transport

Kovalam

There are 3 main points of access to Kovalam's beaches. Remember to specify which you want when hiring an auto or taxi.

Bus Local: Frequent buses depart 0540-2100 to East Fort, **Thiruvananthapuram**, from bus stand outside **Ashok Hotel** gate on Kovalam Beach (30 mins, Rs 9). From **East Fort bus station**, walk or catch an auto-rickshaw to town centre (Rs 20).
  Long distance: To **Kanniyakumari**, **Kochi** via **Kollam** (**Quilon**) and **Kottayam**, **Nagercoil**, **Padmanabhapuram**, **Varkala** and **Thodopuzha** via **Kottayam**.

Rickshaw Auto-rickshaw to **Thiruvanantha-puram**, Rs 150-170, but bargain hard.

Taxi From taxi stand or through **Ashok** or **Samudra** hotels. One-way to **Thiruvanantha-puram** or airport, around Rs 300; city sights Rs 1200-1400; **Kanniyakumari**, **Padmanabhapuram**, Rs 2800 (8 hrs); **Kochi**, Rs 4300 (5 hrs); **Kollam**, Rs 2700; **Thekkady**, Rs 2700 (6 hrs). **Note** Fares estimated from http://www.savaari.com.

Varkala

popular but low-key backpacker hangout in a dramatic cliff-top setting

Like Gokarna in Karnataka, Varkala (population 42,300) is a pilgrimage centre for both backpackers and Hindus. The former come for the ruddy beach which lies at the bottom of the dramatic drop of a laterite cliff, the latter for the Vaishnavite Janardhanaswamy Temple and the Sivagiri Mutt of social reformer Sree Narayana Guru.

Sights and beaches

The sea is far from calm (it has lifeguards for good reason), and the main beach, **Papanasam**, accessed by steep steps hacked in the cliffs, is shared between holidaymakers and fishermen. Watch your step around the cliff, particularly at night; carry a torch after dark.
  Along the cliff path, particularly along the **North Cliff**, is the tourist village high street; sizeable concrete hotels, travel agents, internet cafés, tailors stitching out endless pairs of fisherman's trousers and a huge preponderance of Kashmiri and Tibetan salespeople pushing their customary turquoise, silverware and carpets.
  Further north, the tourist shacks bleed into fishing village life around the **Alimood Mosque** (dress modestly).
  The south, bordered by a golden beach, has a lovely village feel, with traditional houses built around the 13th-century temple dedicated to Vishnu. The **Arratu festival** in March-April draws thousands of visitors.
  Opposite is the **Sri Rama Hanuman Temple**, whose large temple tank three-wheeler drivers splash through in the morning, while women thwack their *lungis* clean on its steps. The main 'town' area (including the train station) is a further 2 km inland from Temple Junction.

Golden Island

A two-hour excursion takes you to Golden Island for a glimpse of local backwaters; there's a small temple here but it's the type of visit you'd make for the atmosphere more than anything else. A boat round the island should cost Rs 50 for the hour.

Listings Varkala *map p901*

Where to stay

There are at least 50 guesthouses, plus rooms in private houses. The North Cliff area is compact, so look around until you find what you want: the northernmost area is where the most laid-back, budget options are and has the most character, while the far south side has a few fancier places. None, however, is actually on the beach. Outside the high season of Nov-Mar, prices drop by up to 50%. During the monsoon (Jun-Jul) many close.

$$$ Villa Jacaranda
Temple Rd West, South Cliff, T0470-261 0296, www.villa-jacaranda.biz.
A delightful guesthouse home, with 5 huge rooms elegantly but sparely decorated. Jasmine, birds of paradise and magnolia blossoms are tucked into alcoves, there's a lotus-filled pond and tropical garden and everything is immaculately maintained. Guests have their own keys and entrance. Really special.

$$$-$$ Mektoub
Odayam Beach, T(0)9447-971239.
13 non a/c rooms in a beautiful rustic-mystic hideaway – a place of candles and incense smoke. Charming owner, utterly peaceful, and a minute from uncrowded sand.

$$$-$ Hill View Beach Resort
North Cliff, T0470-260 5744, www.varkalahillview.com.
Self-contained cottages and budget rooms in a smart resort. Internet, airport pick-up, hot water.

$$ Varkala Deshadan
Kurakkanni Cliff, T0470-320 4242, www.deshadancliffbeachresort.com.
Scrupulously clean Chettinadu-style a/c bungalows set around a large pool. Price includes breakfast.

$$-$ Akshay Beach Resort
Beach Rd (about 200 m from beach), T0470-260 2668.
Wide variety of bright, clean rooms. Quiet location away from the cliff. Restaurant, TV lounge, good value.

$$-$ Marine Palace
Papanasam Beach, T0471-260 3204, www.varkalamarine.com.
18 rooms in total with 3 lovely old-style wooden rooms with balconies and a sea view. The honeymoon suite has a truly gigantic bed. Good service and nice tandoori restaurant on the beach. Recommended.

$$-$ Sea Pearl Chalets
Beach Rd, T0470-260 0105, www.seapearlchalets.com.
Circular thatched huts perched scarily near the cliff edge. Great views, breakfast included. Recommended.

$ Government Guest House
Towards The Gateway (see Restaurants), T0470-260 2227, www.dtpcthiruvananthapuram.com.
Immense, high-ceilinged rooms with marble floors and big baths, in the leafy former summer residence of the maharaja. Isolated, idyllic and quiet. Book in advance, recommended.

$ Panchavadi
Beach Rd, T0470-260 0200, www.panchavadi.com.
Excellent location close to beach. 24 Very clean and secure with simple rooms. Budget rooms very good value. Restaurant, helpful staff. Recommended.

$ Sea Splendour
North Cliff end, Odayam Beach, T0470-266 2120, www.seasplendour.com.
Homely choice with simple rooms in retired teacher's guesthouse. Excellent home-cooking (unlimited and spoilt for choice), very peaceful.

$ Sunshine Home/Johnny Cool & Soulfood Café
North Cliff, Varkala Beach, T(0)9341-201295.
Colourful, chilled-out Rasta house set back off the cliff. Bongo drums and Marley posters abound. There's a variety of rooms, some with balcony, plus a little standalone thatched cottage out the back. The café does pastas, noodles, fish and chips – but in its own sweet time.

Restaurants

There are numerous restaurants along North Cliff, most with facsimile menus, slow service and questionable kitchens; take extra care with drinking water here. 'Catch of the day' splayed out for you to inspect, usually costs Rs 100-150 depending upon the type/size of fish, but make sure you don't get 'catch of yesterday' (fresh fish keep their glassy eyes and bright silvery scales). Many restaurants close out of season.

$$$ The Gateway
Gateway Hotel, near Government Guest House.
Every day 1230-1500. Includes pool use. Good-value eat-all-you-want buffet, delicious rich vegetarian cuisine.

$$ Caffé Italiano
North Cliff, T(0)9846-053194.
Good Italian and seafood, but quite pricey.

$$ Sri Padman
Near Hanuman Temple, T0472-260 5422.
Sri Padman's terrace overlooking the temple tank offers the best non-beachfront position in town. Come here for South Indian vegetarian breakfasts served in big stainless steel *thali* trays, and oily *parathas* to sop up spicy curries and coconut chutneys.

$ Clafouti
Clafouti Hotel, North Cliff (see Where to stay).
Fresh pastries and cakes, but standards seem to drop when the French-Keralite owners are away.

Varkala

Where to stay 🛏
Akshay Beach Resort 2
Gateway 20
Govt Guest House 7
Hill View Beach Resort 9
Marine Palace 5
Mektoub 1
Panchavadi 13
Sea Pearl Chalets 18
Sea Splendour 3
Sunshine Home & Johnny Cool Restaurant 6
Varkala Deshadan 8
Villa Jacaranda 16

Restaurants 🍴
Caffé Italiano 1
Clafouti 4
Funky Art cafe 3
Juice Shack 2
Oottupura 5
Sri Padman 8

$ Funky Art Café
North Cliff.
Eclectic multi-cuisine menu. Sometimes hosts local bands playing Varkala versions of Western rock songs, which can be an amusing diversion while waiting for the incredibly slow service.

$ The Juice Shack
Cliffside Varkala, turn off at Tibetan market, T(0)9995-214515.
Shady little spot with healthy juice, good coffee and excellent toasted sandwiches. Brilliant for breakfast – even has Marmite.

$ Oottupura
Cliffside Varkala, near helipad, T0472-260 6994.
A Varkala institution. Excellent 100% vegetarian with 60 curries and everything from Chinese to macaroni cheese. Breakfast can be *iddlies* or toasted sandwiches, all served under a giant pistachio tree covered in fairy lights.

Entertainment

Varkala is a good place to hang out, chill and do yoga but there's no organized nightlife to speak of, only impromptu campfire parties.

Kerala Kathakali Centre, *by the helipad, T0470-2603612.* Holds a daily *Kathakali* demonstration (Rs 150, make-up 1700-1800, performance 1830-2000). The participants are generally students of the art rather than masters.

Shopping

Most of the handicraft shops are run by Kashmiris, who will tell you that everything (including the tie-dye T-shirts) is an antique from Ladakh.

Elegance of India and **Mushtaq**, *Beach Rd.* Sell Kashmiri handicrafts, carpets, jewellery, etc, reported as honest, will safely air-freight carpets and other goods.
Satori, *T(0)9387-653261.* Cliff-top boutique, selling pretty Western clothes made with local fabric and jewelled Rajasthani slippers.
Suresh, *on path south from helipad.* Handicrafts from Karnataka.

What to do

Body and soul
Keraleeyam, *North Cliff.* One of the best of the many yoga/Ayurvedic massage centres.

Lakshmi Herbal Beauty Parlour, *Clafouti Hotel (see Where to stay).* Individual attention, amazing massages plus waxing, henna, etc.
Nature Cure Hospital, *North Cliff.* Opened in 1983, treats patients entirely by diet and natural cures including hydrotherapy, chromotherapy (natural sunbath with different filters) and mud therapy, each treatment normally lasting 30 mins
Naturomission Yoga Ashram, *near the helipad.* Runs 1-, 2- and 7-day courses in yoga, massage, meditation, and healing techniques. Payment by donation.
Scientific School of Yoga, Naturopathy and Massage, *Diana Inn, North Cliff, T0470-320 6294.* 10-day yoga and massage course (2 classes daily) Rs 500, professionally run by English-speaking doctor. Also has a shop selling Ayurvedic oils, soaps, etc.

Tour operators
Most hotels offer tours, air tickets, backwater trips, houseboats, etc, as do the many agents along North Cliff.
JK Tours & Travels, *Temple Junction Varkala, T0802-668 3334. Daily 0900-2100.* Money exchange Lullaby@Varkala, *www.lullabyatvarkala.in.* Runs tours of the local sites, and also introduce tourists to *anganwadis*, childcare centres for underprivileged families. The project helps feed, clothe and educate its beneficiaries.

Transport

Bus To/from **Temple Junction** (not beach) for **Alappuzha** and **Kollam**, but often quicker to go to Paripally on NH47 and catch onward buses from there.

Motorcycle Kovalam Motorcycle Hire, Voyager Travels, Eye's Beach Rd, T0471-248 1993. Next door to **JA Tourist Home**, Temple Junction; and **Mamma Chompo**, Beach Rd.

Rickshaw/taxi Autos and taxis can be found on Beach Rd and near the helipad. Both charge about Rs 50 to train station. Taxi to **Thiruvananthapuram**, Rs 1000 (1¼ hrs).

Train Varkala sits on the Kochi–Trivandrum line, with at least 20 trains a day in each direction. All northbound trains call at **Kollam**, while many of the southbound trains continue to **Kanniyakumari**.

Backwaters

★ Kerala is synonymous with its lyrical backwaters: a watery cat's cradle of endlessly intersecting rivers, streams, lagoons and tanks that flood the alluvial plain between the Indian Ocean and Western Ghats. They run all the way from Kollam via Alappuzha and Kottayam to Kochi to open up a charming slow-tempo window onto Keralite waterfront life: this is the state's lush and fertile Christian belt, Arundhati Roy country, with lakes fringed by bird sanctuaries, idyllic little hamlets, beside huge paddy ponds rustling in the breeze.

The silent daybreak is best, as boats cut through the mist, geese and ducks start to stir along banks, plumes from breakfast fires drift out across the lagoons. As the hamlets and villages wake, Kerala's domestic scene comes to life: clothes are pounded clean, teeth brushed, and smartly turned out primary school children swing their ways to class.

Luxury houseboats are the quintessential way of seeing the waterfront, but they can be shocking polluters, and if your budget or attention span won't stretch that far the state-operated ferries will give you much the same access for a fraction of the fee. Alternatively, borrow a bicycle or move around by car; the roads and canals are interchangeable. Both thread their way through flood plains the size of football pitches, brown lakes with new shoots prodding out and netted fields that protect prawns and fish from snooping white egrets. At dusk young men sit about on bridges or congregate by teashops made of corrugated iron, while others shimmy up coconut palms to tap a fresh supply of sour moonshine toddy, and kids catch fish with poles.

Preserving the backwaters for the future

The backwaters are lagoons fed by a network of perennial rivers with only two permanent outlets to the sea. The salts are flushed out between May and September, but sea waters rush inland by up to 20 km at the end of the monsoon and the waters become increasingly brackish through the dry season. This alternation between fresh and salt water has been essential to the backwaters' aquatic life. However, as land value has rocketed and reclamation for agriculture has reduced the surface water area, the backwaters' fragile ecology has been put at risk. Many of the original swamps have been destroyed and the waters are becoming increasingly saline.

Tourism, too, is taking its toll. Exploring the backwaters in a traditional *kettuvallam* is the ultimate Kerala experience but the popularity of these trips is having an adverse effect on the waterways. However, there are ways to help prevent degeneration.

The trend so far has been for houseboat operators to offer larger, more luxurious boats (some even equipped with plunge pools) to meet the demands of tourists. The powerful outboard motors contribute heavily to pollution levels in the canals. Opting for a smaller boat not only helps ease environmental damage but also allows you to venture into the many narrower and less visited lagoons that the larger boats are unable to access.

Some operators are becoming aware of the damage being caused and are putting responsible travel practices in place. Support these efforts by checking that your houseboat is equipped with a chemical toilet (to prevent your waste being dumped into the canals) and if possible, opting for a solar-powered boat. Alternatively consider hiring a hand-propelled *thoni* or canoe as an entirely carbon neutral way of exploring this unique region.

pink skyscraper sandwiched on the backwaters between the sea and the river, is the ashram of 'Amma' (the hugging 'Mother'). Thousands of people, Western and Indian alike, attend *Darshan* in hope of a hug. The ashram feels a bit lacklustre when Amma is on tour. She has hugged around three million people so far. In the early days, these used to last for minutes; now she averages one hug every 1½ seconds, so she can happily hug 30,000 in a day. The ashram has shops, a bank, library and internet. Smoking, sex and alcohol are forbidden.

Mannarsala Some 32 km before Alappuzha, Mannarsala has a tremendously atmospheric **Nagaraja Temple** buried deep in a dense jungle forest. Traditionally *naga* (serpent) worshippers had temples in serpent groves. Mannarsala is the largest of these in Kerala with '30,000 images of snake gods lined up along the path and among the trees, and many snakes living around the temple. Childless women come for special blessing and also return for a 'thanksgiving' ceremony afterwards when the child born to the couple is placed on special scales and gifts in kind equalling the weight are donated. The temple is unusual for its chief priestess.

Haripad and around The village of **Haripad** has one of Kerala's oldest and most important Subrahmanya temples. The four-armed idol is believed to have been found in a river, and in August the three-day **Snake Boat Race** at **Payipad**, 3 km by bus, commemorates its rescue and subsequent building of the temple. There are boat processions on the first two days followed by competitive races on the third day. There is a guesthouse on **Mankotta Island** on the backwaters; the large comfortable rooms with bath are well kept.

Thottapally Squeezed between the backwaters and the sea, and 12 km from Haripad station, Thottapally makes a good stop on a backwaters trip, two hours from Alappuzha.

Aranmula About 10 km from Chengannur, Aranmula has the **Parthasarathi Temple** and is known for its unique metal mirrors. The **Vallamkali** (or **Utthrittathi**) **festival** on the last day of Onam (August-September) is celebrated with a boat race. The festival celebrates the crossing of the river by Krishna, who is believed to be in all the boats simultaneously, so the challenge is to arrive at the same time, rather than race.

Tourist information

Kollam

District Tourism Promotion Council (DTPC)
Govt Guest House Complex, T0474-275 0170;
also at DTPC bus station, T0474-274 5625, train
station and ferry jetty, www.dtpckollam.com.
Offers cruises, coach tours, and details of
Kathakali performances.

Where to stay

Kollam

$$$$-$$$ Aquasserenne
Paravoor, 15 mins from town by road or boat,
T0474-251 2410.
Splendid backwaters location, well-furnished
chalets (some reassembled Kerala houses) with
TV, restaurant, Ayurvedic massage/treatment,
boat rides.

$$$$-$$$ Fragrant Nature Retreat and Resorts
Paravur, T0474-251 4000,
www.fragrantnature.com.
A 4-star luxury lakeside resort with spa,
swimming pool and jacuzzi. Accommodation
in lakeside rooms or villas.

$$ Nani
Opposite clock tower, Chinnakada, T0474-275
1141, www.hotelnani.com.
Swish business hotel close to the railway station,
with smart if slightly overpriced rooms and
friendly staff.

$ Government Guest House
Ashramam, T0474-274 2838.
Live like the British Raj on a pauper's budget.
12 simply furnished rooms, all with attached
bath, in the sprawling former residence of the
British governor. More expensive rooms have
bathrooms large enough to throw a party in.
High ceilings, shady veranda, huge garden, bags
of character, friendly staff. Some cheaper rooms
are in bland modern building at the back. Meals
on request. Recommended.

$ Tamarind (KTDC)
Ashramam, T0474-274 5538, www.ktdc.com.
Newly renovated rooms in a bland block
building. All rooms with a/c, TV. Nice views of the
waterway. Quiet location, restaurant, boat hire.

Kollam to Alappuzha

$$-$ Coconut Palms
Kumarakodi, T0471-301 8100,
www.coconutpalms.co.in.
Idyllic 200-year-old traditional house in shaded
compound, on backwaters and 100 m from sea.
Yoga, Ayurveda and package deals available.

$ Mata Amritanandamayi Ashram
Vallikkavu, T0476-289 6399, www.amritapuri.org.
Amma's ashram offers spartan but spacious
accommodation in a multi-storey block, with
hugs and South Indian meals included in the
price. Western canteen (at extra cost) serves
American-style meals.

Restaurants

Kollam

$ Eat N Pack
Near Taluk Office, Main St.
Excellent value, clean, good choice of dishes,
friendly. Recommended.

$ Indian Coffee House
Main Rd.
For good coffee and vegetarian and non-
vegetarian South Indian food. Nice waiter service
and good atmosphere.

$ Suprabhatam
Opposite clock tower, Main St.
Adequate vegetarian.

Festivals

Kollam
Jan Kerala Tourism Boat Race.
Apr Colourful 10-day **Vishnu festival** in Asram
Temple with procession and fireworks.
Aug-Sep Avadayattukotta Temple celebrates a
5-day **Ashtami Rohani** festival. **Muharram** too is
observed with processions at the town mosque.

What to do

Kollam
Cruises and boat trips
As well as houseboat trips on traditional
kettuvallams, there are also the much cheaper
options of Kollam–Alappuzha cruises and shorter
canal journeys to Munroe Island. The gentle
pace and tranquil waterways make these tours

very worthwhile, but the heat and humidity may sometimes make overnight stays on houseboats uncomfortable.

DTPC (see Tourist information, above). Offers daily 8-hr backwater cruise from Kollam to Alappuzha; depart 1030 (Rs 300). You can be dropped off halfway at Alumkadavu (Rs 200) or at Vallikkavu for the Ashram (Rs 150). The only stops are for meals; some travellers find the trip a little too long and samey. A good alternative is a canal trip to Munroe Island village; depart 0900, 1300 (6 hrs return, Rs 500).

A more expensive option is to hire a *kettuvallam*. For a 1-bed houseboat prices start at Rs 5000 for overnight, ranging up to Rs 14000 for 2 days and 1 night, inclusive of all meals. There are also cruise packages which combine a day cruise with an overnight stay at a backwater resort (Rs 3500).

Southern Backwaters Tour Operators, *opposite KRSTC Bus Station, Jetty Rd, Kollam, T(0)9495-976037, www.southernbackwaters.com*. Independent operators. A/c deluxe and standard houseboats for 1- to 3-night packages. Also motorboat cruises and Munroe Island tours.

Transport

Kollam

Local auto-rickshaws are plentiful and bikes are available for hire.

Bus Local buses are plentiful. Long-distance buses run from the KSRTC station, T0474-275 2008 Buses every 30 mins from 0600 to **Kochi** (3½ hrs) via **Alappuzha** (2 hrs) and other towns on the coast. Buses run 24 hrs to **Thiruvananthapuram**, leaving every 10 mins in the day and every 30 mins during the night (2 hrs). Change at Thiruvananthapuram for **Kovalam**. It is difficult to get to **Varkala** by bus; take the train.

Car To **Alappuzha**, Rs 2000, from the bus station.

Ferry Public ferries sail to **Ghuhandapuram** at 0730, 1100, 1330, 1545 and 1745 (1 hr, Rs 5) and then return to Kollam. It's an interesting journey with views of village life and Chinese fishing nets on the way. The 1745 departure lets you enjoy sunset over the waterways. See also Backwater cruises under Tour operators, above.

Train Junction railway station, T131, is about 3 km east of the boat jetty and bus station. There are several trains a day south to **Thiruvananthapuram** including the *Island Exp 16526*, 1335 (1¾ hrs), which continues to **Kanniyakumari** (4¼ hrs). All the trains stop at **Varkala** (½ hr).

An equal number of trains head north to **Ernakulam** (**Cochin**) and points beyond, including the *TVC Chennai Exp 12696* (continues to **Chennai**, 15 hrs); and the *Island Exp 16525* (continues to **Bengaluru**, 16 hrs).

Alappuzha (Alleppey) and around

ramshackle town with thousands of houseboats and a vast network of waterways

Alappuzha (pronounced *Alappoorra;* population 177,100) has a large network of canals, choked with the blue flowers of water hyacinth, passing through the town. It's the chief departure point for cruises into the backwaters and the venue for the spectacular snake boat races (see Festivals, page 911). Houseboat trips can be arranged at any of the numerous tour operators in town or directly, by heading to the boat dock just off VCNB Road. Although the town itself doesn't have many tourist sites, it's a pleasant, bustling place to walk around and there's a lovely stretch of undeveloped beach as well.

Mararikulam

On the coast, 15 km north of Alappuzha, Maraikulam is a quiet, secluded beach which, until recently, was only known to the adjoining fishing village. The main village has a thriving cottage industry of coir and jute weaving.

Champakulam and around

Some 16 km southeast of Alappuzha is the hushed backwaters village of **Champakulam** where the only noise pollution is the odd squeak of a bicycle and the slush of a canoe paddle. The Syrian Christian church of St Mary's Forane was built in 1870 on the site of a previous church dating from AD 427. The English-speaking priest is happy to show visitors round. Nearby the St Thomas Statuary makes wooden statues of Christ for export round the world: a 2-m-tall Jesus will set you back US$450. To get there, take the Alappuzha–Changanacherry bus (every 30 minutes) to Moncombu (Rs 4), then an auto-rickshaw to Champakulam (4 km, Rs 12). Alternatively the Alappuzha–Edathna ferry leaves at 0615 and 1715 and stops at Champakulam. In the backwater village of **Edathna**, you can visit the early Syrian St George's Church.

Listings Alappuzha (Alleppey) and around *map below*

Tourist information

ATDC
Komala Rd, Alappuzha, T0477-226 4462, www.atdcalleppey.com.

DTPC
KSRTC bus station near jetty, Alappuzha, T0477-225 3308. Open 0830-2000.
Helpful and offers good backwaters trips.

KTDCI
Motel Araam, Alappuzha, T0477-224 4460.

Where to stay

Book ahead to avoid the scramble off the ferry. Hotels north of Vadai Canal are quieter.

$$$$ Olavipe
Thekanatt Parayil, Olavipe, T0478-252 2255, www.olavipe.com.
Century-old mansion belonging to family of Syrian Christian notables, on a 16-ha organic farm on the lush island of Olavipe. 6 rooms: 4 in the main house and 2 in a cottage.

Alappuzha (Alleppey)

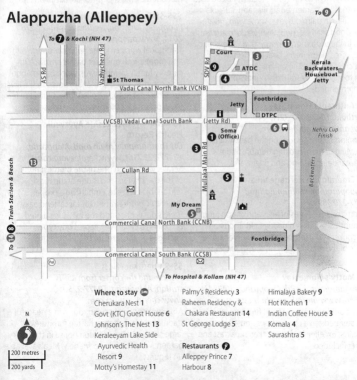

Where to stay 🛏
Cherukara Nest **1**
Govt (KTC) Guest House **6**
Johnson's The Nest **13**
Keraleeyam Lake Side
  Ayurvedic Health
  Resort **9**
Motty's Homestay **11**

Palmy's Residency **3**
Raheem Residency &
  Chakara Restaurant **14**
St George Lodge **5**

Restaurants 🍴
Alleppey Prince **7**
Harbour **8**

Himalaya Bakery **9**
Hot Kitchen **1**
Indian Coffee House **3**
Komala **4**
Saurashtra **5**

$$$$ Purity
Muhamma, Aryakkara (8 km from Alappuzha town), T0484-221 6666, www.malabarhouse.com.
This beautiful Italianate villa, set on an acre of tropical grounds overlooking Lake Vembanad, is the most elegant lodging for miles around, with minimalist decor and a smattering of rare antiques. Huge rooms on the ground floor open out to a grassy lawn, but for the ultimate splurge check in to the huge turquoise-toned suite upstairs, with arched windows hoovering up views of the glassy lake. There's a pool and a discreet spa offering Ayurvedic treatments and yoga classes, and high-class dinners, which the chef can tailor to your wishes, are served around a pond in the courtyard. Superb in every respect and thoroughly recommended.

$$$$-$$$ Marari Beach
Mararikulam, Alappuzha, T0478-286 3801, www.cghearth.com.
Well-furnished, comfortable, local-style cottages (garden villas, garden pool villas and 3 deluxe pool villas) in palm groves – some with private pool. Good seafood, pool, Ayurvedic treatment, yoga in the morning, *pranayama* in the evening, shop, bikes, badminton, beach volleyball, boat cruises (including overnight houseboat), farm tours, friendly staff, discounts Apr-Sep. Recommended.

$$$ Anthraper Home Stay
Cherthala, T0478-281 3211, www.anthrapergardens.com.
Charming country house on the backwaters. Sprawling garden, cooking demonstrations, yoga, canoeing, fishing and river walks.

$$$ Emerald Isle Heritage Villa
Kanjooparambil–Manimalathan, T0477-270 3899.
5 rooms on the shores of an island of lush jungle, surrounded by sunken paddy field. Toddy on tap, cookery courses, boat trips, Ayurveda. The magic of the place begins on the 10-km journey from Alappuzha.

$$$ Motty's Homestay
Kidangamparambu Rd, Alappuzha, T(0)9847-032836, www.mararibeachhomes.com.
Just 2 double rooms, with old furniture and 4-poster beds, in a private house on Alappuzha's outskirts. Excellent home-cooked breakfast and dinner included.

$$$ Raheem Residency
Beach Rd, Alappuzha, T0477-223 9767, www.raheemresidency.com.
Special luxury heritage hotel housed in a beautifully restored colonial 19th-century bungalow, on a pristine piece of Kerala's coast. 10 immaculate rooms, all with a/c and lovely antique furnishings. Palatial living room, jasmine-scented garden, excellent restaurant and a lovely pool under a velvet apple tree. The Irish journalist owner also offers the property as a writers' retreat (contact for prices). Easily the best address in Alappuzha. Recommended.

$$$ Vembanad House Homestay
Puthankayal, Alappuzha, T0478-286 8696, www.vembanadhouse.com.
4 spacious rooms in stately heritage house surrounded by a lake in the pretty Muhamma area. Fresh food from the family farm cooked to Kerala recipes. Traditional architecture with modern bathrooms (no a/c). The house is managed by the delightful Balakrishnan family.

$$$-$$ Pooppally's Heritage Homestay
Pooppally Junction, Nedumudy, T0477-276 2034, www.pooppallys.com.
Traditional wooden cottage (water bungalow) and rooms, with open-air bathrooms, in 19th-century family farmhouse, shaded by a mango tree, set in a garden stretching down to the River Pampa. Great home-cooked food. Catch the ferry to Alappuzha for 90 mins of free houseboat.

$$ Keraleeyam Lakeside Ayurvedic Health Resort
Off Thathampally main road, Alappuzha, T0477-223 7161, www.keraleeyam.com.
Keraleeyam sits on one of the prettiest nubs of the backwaters and is one of the most reasonable places to embark on a proper Ayurvedic programme. Doctors attend daily, there's no alcohol, and the menu is tailored according to your Ayurvedic body type. Cottages on the lake are better than the drab rooms in the main house.

$$-$ Cherukara Nest
Just around the corner from KSRTC bus station, Alappuzha, T0477-225 1509, www.cherukaranest.com.
Airy, cool, spotlessly clean rooms in a peaceful traditional family home. Rattan furniture on large shady porches. Pigeon house in the back garden. Very helpful and friendly. Meals available on request.

$ Johnson's The Nest
Lal Bagh Factory Ward (west of Convent Sq), Alappuzha, T0477-224 5825, www.johnsonskerala.com.
Friendly family-run guesthouse in a quiet street away from the town centre. 6 rooms, each with balcony. Free pick-up from bus station, internet, houseboat facility, popular.

$ Palmy's Residency
North of new Matha footbridge, Alappuzha, T0477-223 5938, www.palmyresidency.com.
Large, clean rooms with fly-screens and fans. Quiet but central location. More expensive rooms have big balconies to lounge in. Local waterway canoe trips (4-5 hrs, Rs 500 per hr). Free bike hire. Recommended.

$ St George Lodge
CCNB Rd, Alappuzha, T0477-225 1620.
Don't let the dilapidated façade put you off – this is an excellent cheapie. 80 very basic but clean rooms, some with attached bath. Friendly staff.

$ Tamarind (KTDC)
Jetty Rd, Alappuzha, T0477-224 4460, www.ktdc.com.
Bright yellow building next door to the KSRTC bus station. More expensive rooms are large but have tired-looking bathrooms. Cheaper bamboo-walled rooms on 3rd floor. Free bike hire, internet.

Restaurants

$$$ Chakara
Raheem Residency, Beach Rd.
Rooftop dining with attentive service and excellent multi-cuisine food. The 4-course set dinner menu (pegged at rupee equivalent to €11) is unbeatable value. Alcohol available.

$$ Alleppey Prince Hotel
AS Rd (NH47), 2 km from town.
International, comfortable a/c restaurant, reasonable food, alcohol in bar only.

$ Harbour
Beach Rd.
Specializes in seafood, also has Indian and European dishes. Excellent value. Alcohol available.

$ Himalaya Bakery
SDV Rd.
Large range of sweet and savoury pastries, and other snacks, to take out or eat in at the tiny seating area.

$ Hot Kitchen
Mullakal Main Rd.
Good for *iddli, dosa, vadai*, etc.

$ Indian Coffee House
Mullakal Main Rd.
Good value, tasty non-vegetarian snacks.

$ Komala
Komala Hotel, Zilla Court Ward.
Excellent South Indian *thalis* and Chinese.

$ SAS
Jetty Rd.
Good South Indian vegetarian and Chinese.

$ Saurashtra
Cullan Rd.
Vegetarian, ample helpings on banana leaf, locally popular.

Festivals

9-12 Jan **Cheruppu** is celebrated in the Mullakkal Devi Temple with a procession of elephants, music and fireworks.
17-19 Jan **Tourism Boat Race**.
Jul/Aug **DTPC Boat Race** (3rd Sat) in the backwaters. **Champakulam Boat Race**, Kerala's oldest, takes place 16-km ferry ride away on 'Moolam' day. The **Nehru Trophy Snake Boat Race**, www.nehrutrophy.com/htm/boat.htm, inaugurated in 1952, is the largest snake boat race in the state. As many as 40 highly decorated 'snake boats' are rowed by several dozen oarsmen before huge crowds. Naval helicopters do mock rescue operations and stunt flying. Entry by ticket; Rs 50-2000 depending on viewing class. There are other snake boat races held throughout the year.

What to do

Houseboat cruises
It's always worth booking in advance during high season, when the theoretical government-set rates (which are printed and displayed in the DTPC booking office at the jetty in Alappuzha) go out the window, and houseboat owners jack the prices up by 50-80%. Houseboats vary widely depending on the number of bedrooms, facilities (some come with a/c, flatscreen TVs and DVD players), quality of food and the crew's level of English. Booking ahead gives you some degree of certainty over the level of luxury you will find; it also allows you to circumvent the persistent dockside touts, whose commissions mean that any discount you can negotiate comes at the

cost of corners cut on the trip. If you're coming outside peak season, and don't mind spending a morning scouting around, making a booking on the spot gives you a chance to inspect a number of boats before agreeing on a price.

The following companies are generally at the top end of the market, but offer reliably good (in some cases superb) service.

CGH Earth, *T0484-301 1711, Kochi, www.cghearth. com*. Runs 'spice boat' cruises in modified *kettuvallams*, which are idyllic if not luxurious: shaded sit-outs, modern facilities including solar panels for electricity, 2 double rooms, limited menu. US$325.

Discovery 1, *Malabar House, Fort Kochi, see page 920*. **Malabar Escapes**' take on the houseboat goes against the grain by being silent, pollutant free, and bright turquoise. Because it's nimble and trips are for a minimum of 3 nights, it's guaranteed to take you far from the wider watery motorways bigger rice boats ply. 1 bedroom, large bathroom and sitting room plus sun deck. Food is to Malabar House's high standard.

DTPC, *Jetty Rd, T0477-225 1796, www.dtpc alappuzha.com*. Runs the same 8-hr backwater cruises as its sister office in Kollam, only in reverse. Departs 1030 from Alappuzha ferry jetty (Rs 300). There is also a shorter round-trip to Kumarakom (4 hrs, Rs 150), and canoe trips through local waterways (Rs 200 per hr).

Lakes and Lagoons Tour Co, *Punnamada, T0477-226 6842, www.lakeslagoons.com*. Solar-powered boats with up to 3 bedrooms. Consistently recommended operator.

Rainbow Cruises, *Mamood Junction opposite jetty, Alappuzha, T0477-223 1110, www.rainbow cruises.in*. Solar powered with high safety standards and emergency speedboat support (houseboats have been known to sink).

Transport

It is only a 5-min walk between the ferry jetty and the KSRTC bus station despite what many local rickshaw drivers will tell you.

Bus From the **KSRTC Bus Station**, T0477-225 2501, there are frequent long-distance buses to **Kochi**, 0630-2330 (1½ hrs); **Thiruvananthapuram**, 0600-2000 (4 hrs) via **Kollam** (2 hrs); **Champakulam**, 0515-2000 (45 mins) and **Kottayam**, 0730-1800 (1½ hrs). There are several buses daily to **Coimbatore**, from 0600 (7 hrs).

Car A car with driver from Alappuzha to **Fort Kochi** (65 km) costs Rs 500-600.

Ferry Public ferries sail from the Boat Jetty T0477-225 2015, swtd.kerala.gov.in, to **Kottayam**, 0730, 0935, 1130, 1430 and 1715 (3 hrs), and **Changanassery**, 1300 and 1645, 3 hrs). Also frequent services to **Nedumudi** (1 hr).

Train The train station, T0477-225 3965, is on the coastal route from **Trivandrum–Varkala–Kollam–Ernakulam**, 3 km from the jetty. Frequent trains in both directions.

Kottayam and Kumarakom

busy town between the backwaters and the mountains

Around Kottayam lies some of the lushest and most beautiful scenery in the state, with hills to its east and backwaters to its west.

Kottayam

Kottayam itself (population 60,700) is the capital of Kerala's Christian community, which belonged to the Orthodox Syrian tradition up till the Portuguese arrival. Two churches of the era survive 2 km north of town, in the 450-year-old **Cheria Palli** ('Small' St Mary's Church), which has beautiful vegetable dye mural paintings over its altar, and the **Valia Palli** ('Big' St Mary's Church), from 1550, with two Nestorian crosses carved on plaques behind two side altars. One has a Pallavi inscription on it, the other a Syriac. The cross on the left of the altar is the original and may be the oldest Christian artefact in India; the one to the right is a copy. By the altar there is an unusual small triptych of an Indian St George slaying a dragon. Note the interesting Visitors' Book (1898-1935); a paper cutting reports that "the church has attracted many European and native gentlemen of high position". Mass at Valia Palli at 0900 on Sunday, and Cheria Palli at 0730 on Sunday and Wednesday. The Malankara Syrian Church has its headquarters at Devalokam.

Ettumanoor

Just north of Kottayam, Ettumanoor has possibly the wealthiest temple in Kerala. The present Mahadeva temple was constructed in 1542, and is famous for its murals depicting scenes from the *Ramayana* and the Krishna legends, both inside and outside the *gopuram*. The typical circular shrine with a copper-covered conical roof encloses a square sanctuary. The **Arattu festival** in March draws thousands of pilgrims when gold elephant statues are displayed. They weigh 13 kg each.

Kumarakom and Vembanad Lake

Tucked among the waterways of Vembanad Lake, in mangrove, paddy and coconut groves with lily-studded shores, is **Kumarakom**, 16 km from Kottayam. Here are stacks of exclusive hotels where you can be buffed and Ayurvedically preened, bent into yoga postures, peacefully sunbathe or take to the water: perfect honeymoon territory.

The tourism department has developed an old rubber plantation set around Vembanad Lake into a **bird sanctuary** ① *1000-1800*. A path goes through the swamp to the main bird nesting area. **Pathiramanal** ('midnight sands') **Island** in the middle of the lake can be reached by boat. The best season for birdlife is June-August; visit in the early morning.

Listings Kottayam and Kumarakom

Tourist information

DTPC
Government Guest House, Nattakom, Kottayam, T0481-256 0479, www.dtpckottayam.com.

Responsible Tourism Travel Desk
T0481-252 4343, Kumarakom.
Books tours to meet local craftsmen.

Where to stay

In Kumarakom 26% taxes are added to bills.

Kottayam

$$$$ Philipkutty's Farm
Pallivathukal, Ambika Market, Vechoor, T0482-927 6530, www.philipkuttysfarm.com.
5 immaculate waterfront villas sharing an island on Vembanad Lake. The delightful working farm boasts coconut, banana, nutmeg, coca and vanilla groves. Delicious home-cooking and personal attention from all the family. No TV. Cooking and painting holidays.

$$ Aida
MC Rd, 2 km from railway, T0481-256 8391, www.hotelaidakerala.com.
Rs 2100 (plus taxes) Clean, pleasant rooms with bath, some with a/c. Front rooms can be noisy. Restaurant, bar, helpful staff.

$$-$ Anjali Park
KK Rd, 4 km from railway, Kottayam, T0481-256 3661.
www.hotelanjalipark.com. Decent rooms with bath and a/c. Good restaurants.

$ Ambassador Hotel
KK Rd (set back), T0481-256 3293.
Friendly Indian-style hotel with good restaurant and bar. Very good value.

$ Kaycee's Residency
Off YMCA Rd, Kottayam, T0481-256 3440.
Good value, clean, decent-sized rooms.

$ PWD Rest House
On a hill 2 km south of Kottayam, T0481-256 8147.
Remarkable late 19th-century building with superb furniture, overlooking vista of paddy fields.

Kumarakom

$$$$ Privacy at Sanctuary Bay
Kannamkara, opposite Kumarakom, T0484-221 6666, www.malabarhouse.com.
Absolute lakeside isolation in a fully staffed but fully self-contained 3-bedroom bungalow. Modern opulent interiors hide behind the old Keralite façade, and there's a stunning veranda looking out across the lake.

$$$$-$$$ Coconut Lagoon (CGH Earth)
Vembanad Lake, T0481-252 5834, www.cghearth.com.
Comfortable heritage *tharavads* (traditional Keralite wooden cottages), heritage mansions and pool villas. Outdoor restaurant facing lagoon, good dinner buffet, pool, yoga, very friendly,

Ayurvedic treatments, attractive waterside location, spectacular approach by boat (10 mins from road). Vechoor cows mow the lawns. Discounts Apr-Sep. Recommended.

$$$-$$ Waterscapes (KTDC)
T0481-252 5861, www.waterscapes kumarakom.com.
Idyllic cottage experience on the backwaters. All chalets have a/c and cable TV. Pool, bar, restaurant.

$$ GK's Riverview Homestay
Valliadu, Aymanam, T0481-259 7527, www.gkhomestay-kumarakom.com.
Set amid paddy fields in the heart of *God of Small Things* country, George and Dai's lovely house offers home comforts in the shape of simple immaculate rooms, hammocks lazily overlooking the river, and superb Kerala cooking. The consummate hosts are always on hand to share secrets of the area, and arrange excellent tours.

Restaurants

Kottayam

$$ Aida
MC Rd.
Large, uninspired menu. Pleasantly cool 'chilled' drinks may arrive slightly warm.

Kumarakom

$$$ Baker's House (Vivanta by Taj)
Kumarakom, T0481-252 5711.
One of Kerala's most atmospheric restaurants, the Baker's House (as featured in *The God of Small Things*) is magic at dusk, when brass lamps twinkle all around the 120-year-old bungalow. Expect to pay for pan-global high-end cuisine, but stick to the Kerala seafood for best results.

Transport

Kottayam

Bus The new **Private Bus Station** is near the railway station. Buses to Alappuzha only leave from the **KSRTC Bus Station**, 2 km away; local buses to **Kumarakom Tourist Village** also run frequently from here. There are fast and frequent long-distance buses to **Alappuzha**, every 45 mins (2 hrs); **Thiruvananthapuram**, every 30 mins (4 hrs); **Kochi**, every 30 mins (1½ hrs) and **Kumily**, every hour (4½ hrs). There are 2 evening departures to **Madurai**, 2045 and 2145 (7 hrs) and 5 buses daily head to **Munnar**, 0600-1600 (5 hrs).

Car Car with driver to **Thekkady**, Rs 1400, 4 hrs.

Ferry Ferries leave from the **Kodimatha Jetty** except during the monsoons, when you should head to the **Town Jetty** 3 km southwest of the train station. Ferries to **Alappuzha**, 0730, 0930, 1130, 1430, 1730 (3 hrs). This is an interesting trip but gets very busy in peak season. Other departures include **Champakulam**, 1530 (4 hrs) and **Mannar**, 1430 (3 hrs).

Train Trains run throughout the day, south to **Thiruvananthapuram** via **Kollam** and **Varkala**, and north to Ernakulam and beyond. No trains to Alappuzha, which is on the parallel coastal line.

Fort Kochi
& Ernakulam

Charming Fort Kochi (Cochin) is a true one-off in modern Kerala: a layer cake of colonial India, where British parade grounds overlay Portuguese forts, where Dutch palaces slowly crumble into the soil alongside synagogues, where every turn takes you down some romantically fossilized narrow winding street. Despite a tourist invasion that's flooded the lanes with antique shops, internet cafés and shops flogging fisherman trousers, parts of the ramshackle island still feel frozen back in the 15th and 16th centuries, and the huge trees here are so old that their parasitic aphids are as tall as trees themselves.

In the southern quarter of Mattancherry, row upon row of wood-fronted doors give glimpses of rice and spice merchants sitting sifting their produce into small 'tasting' bowls. The iconic batwing Chinese fishing nets, first used in the 14th century, stand on the shores of the north fort area, silhouetted against the lapping waters of one of the world's finest natural harbours: a wide bay interrupted by narrow spits of land and coconut-covered islands.

Before arriving in Fort Kochi, however, you have to negotiate the city's modern centre of gravity – grubby, dynamic Ernakulam, a Rs 5 ferry ride and half a world away across the harbour. While Fort Kochi languishes dreamily in the past, its ambitious sibling is expanding outwards and upwards at breakneck pace, propelled by the vast new container terminal on Vallarpadam Island. The first port in India capable of handling the huge container ships that until now have had to berth in Colombo or Singapore, Kochi stands poised to transform India's logistical landscape, and over the next decade this hitherto sleepy southern city will undoubtedly assume a front-and-centre seat in the future of the Indian economy.

Essential Fort Kochi and Ernakulam

Finding your feet

Kochi's mellow little international airport is at Nedumbassery, 36 km northeast of the city centre. The smoothest way into town is to arrange a pick-up from your hotel (Rs 900-1500 depending on type of car and what your hosts feel the market will support). Alternatively, hire a prepaid taxi from the booth after Customs; a transfer to Fort Kochi costs around Rs 800, a little less to downtown Ernakulam. Air-conditioned buses leave the airport for Fort Kochi bus stand, right in the centre next to the Chinese fishing nets, between 0500 and 1900, taking 90 minutes.

Most trains pull into Ernakulam Junction station in the busy city centre. State-run long-distance buses arrive at the Central Bus Stand, 500 m north of Ernakulam Junction, while private buses pull in to the terminal at Kaloor Junction about 2 km further north. Local buses, taxis and auto-rickshaws connect the various transport hubs. A rickshaw from either to the main jetty, for Fort Kochi, costs approximately Rs 25. For details, see Transport, page 926.

Getting around

Fort Kochi has all the sights and a huge number of hotels, and many visitors never leave its cosy bubble. The quiet roads are easy to explore on foot or by bicycle, with an occasional cameo from an auto-rickshaw. If you need to get across to Ernakulam there are two routes: a circuitous trip by bus, taxi or auto-rickshaw (Rs 250-500), or one of the cheap and cheerful ferries that chug across the harbour to Ernakulam's Main Jetty – an enjoyably breezy 30-minute trip that's most atmospheric around sunset (ferries run 0600-2130). From the jetty you can catch a rickshaw to the railway station or bus stand for around Rs 40. Leave plenty of spare time if you need to travel during peak hours. After 2130 public transport begins to grind to a halt and you'll need to take a rickshaw or taxi to get around.

Best Fort Kochi hotels
Malabar House, page 920
Brunton Boatyard, page 920
Old Courtyard, page 920
Caza Maria Hotel, page 921

★ Fort Kochi

attractive historic trading town with Portuguese, British and Dutch influences

Vasco da Gama Square and around

If you land at the Customs Jetty, a plaque in nearby Vasco da Gama Square commemorates the landing of Vasco da Gama in 1500. Next to it is the **Stromberg Bastion**, "one of the seven bastions of Fort Emanuel built in 1767", named after the Portuguese king. Little is left of the 1503 Portuguese fort except ruins. Along the seafront, between the Fort Kochi Bus Stand, the boat jetty and the Dutch cemetery, run the cantilevered Chinese fishing nets. These are not unique to Kochi, but are perhaps uniquely accessible to the short-stay visitor.

St Francis' Church and around

Fort Kochi, Mon-Sat 0930-1730, Sun afternoon, Sun services in English 0800 (except for the 3rd Sun of each month).

Originally dedicated to Santo Antonio, the patron saint of Portugal, St Francis is the first church to reflect the new and European-influenced tradition. The original wooden structure (circa 1510) was replaced by the present stone building (there is no authority for the widely quoted date of 1546). Vasco da Gama died on the site in 1524 and was originally buried in the cemetery. Some 14 years later his body was removed to Portugal. The church was renamed St Francis in 1663, and the Dutch both converted it to a Protestant church and substantially modified it. They retained control until 1795, adding the impressive gable façade at the entrance. In 1804, it became an Anglican church. In 1949 the congregation joined the Church of South India. Note the old string-pulled *punkahs* (fans) and the Dutch and Portuguese gravestones that now line the walls.

Fort Kochi

"If China is where you make your money," declared Italian traveller Nicolas Conti in the Middle Ages, "then Kochi surely is the place to spend it". Kochi has acted as a trading port since at least Roman times, and was a link in the main trade route between Europe and China. From 1795 until India's Independence the long outer sand spit, with its narrow beach leading to the wide bay inland, was under British political control. The inner harbour was in Kochi State, while most of the hinterland was in the separate state of Travancore. The division of political authority delayed development of the harbour facilities until 1920-1923, when the approach channel was dredged so ships that could get through the Suez Canal could dock here, opening the harbour to modern shipping. The current population is around 2.1 million.

Near St Francis' Church, Santa Cruz Cathedral was originally built in 1557 by the Portuguese, and used as a warehouse by the British in the 18th century, was rebuilt in the early 20th century. It has lovely carved wooden panels and pulpit, and an interesting graveyard.

Mattancherry Palace and Parikshith Thampuran Museum
Mattancherry, daily 1000-1700 except Fri and national holidays, Rs 2, photography not allowed.

The palace was first built by the Portuguese around 1557 as a sweetener for the Raja Veera Kerala Varma of Kochi bestowing them trading rights. In 1663, it was largely rebuilt by the new trading power, the Dutch. The layout follows the traditional Kerala pattern known as *nalukettus*, meaning four buildings, which are set around a quadrangle with a temple. There are display cases of the Rajas of Kochi's clothes, palanquins, etc, but these are no match for the amazing murals. The royal bedroom's low wooden walls squeeze the whole narrative of the *Ramayana* into about 45 16th-century panels. Every inch is covered with rich red, yellow, black and white. To the south of the Coronation Hall, the *kovinithilam* (staircase room) has six large 18th-century murals including the coronation of Rama. Vishnu is in a room to the north. Two of the women's bedrooms downstairs have 19th-century murals with greater detail. They relate Kalidasa's *Kumarasambava* and themes from the *Puranas*. If you are of a sensitive disposition avert your eyes from panel 27 and 29, whose deer, birds and other animals are captioned as giving themselves up to 'merry enjoyment', a coy way of describing the furious copulation and multiple penetration in plain view. Krishna, meanwhile, finally works out why he was given so many limbs, much to the evident satisfaction of the gopis who are looking on.

Synagogue
Mattancherry, Sun-Fri 1000-1200, 1500-1700, no video cameras, shoes must be removed.

Dating from 1568 (rebuilt in 1662), the synagogue is near Mattancherry Palace at the heart of what is known as Jew Town, which is a fascinating mixture of shops (some selling antiques), warehouses and spice auction rooms. Stepping inside the synagogue is an extraordinary experience of light and airiness, partly due to the 18th-century blue Cantonese ceramic tiles, hand painted and each one different, covering the floor. There are original glass oil lamps. For several centuries there were two Jewish communities. The earlier group (often referred to as 'black' Jews), according to one source, settled here as early as 587 BC. The earliest evidence of their presence is a copper inscription dated AD 388 by the Prince of Malabar. Those referred to as 'white' Jews came much later, when, with Dutch and then British patronage, they played a major role as trading agents. Speaking fluent Malayalam, they made excellent go-betweens for foreigners seeking to establish contacts. The community has shrunk to six families, with many now settled at Moshav Nevatim in Israel's Negev desert. The second Jewish synagogue (in Ernakulam) is deserted.

① Fort Kochi (Cochin) & Ernakulam

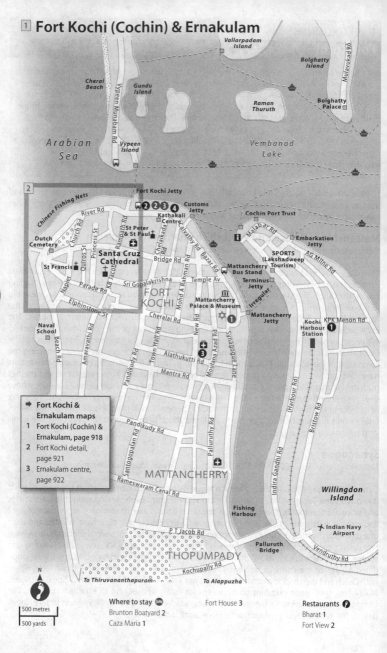

Vallarpadam Island

Bolghatty Island

Cherai Beach

Gundu Island

Raman Thuruth

Bolghatty Palace

Mulavukad Rd

Vypeen Munabam Rd

Arabian Sea

Vypeen Island

Vembanad Lake

Chinese Fishing Nets

Fort Kochi Jetty

Customs Jetty

Cochin Port Trust

River Rd

Kathakali Centre

Malabar Rd

Embarkation Jetty

Dutch Cemetery

St Peter St Paul

Ramoath Rd

Church Rd

Chelakada Rd

Kalvathy Rd

Bazar Rd

SPORTS (Lakshadweep) Tourism

AG Mline Rd

St Francis

Princess St

Quiros St

Jacobs

Santa Cruz Cathedral

Bridge Rd

Mattancherry Bus Stand

Terminus Jetty

Napier

Parade Rd

Sri Gopalakrishna

Mohd A Rahman

Temple Av

Mattancherry Palace & Museum

Irregular

Kochi Harbour Station

KPK Menon Rd

Elphinstone St

FORT KOCHI

Cheralai Rd

New Rd

Synagogue Lane

Mattancherry Jetty

Naval School

Beach Rd

Amaravathi Rd

Pandikudy Rd

Town Hall Rd

Alathukutti Rd

Moulana Azad Rd

Mantra Rd

Harbour Rd

Bristow Rd

Willingdon Island

Pandikudy Rd

Pallaruthy Rd

Indira Gandhi Rd

Sootogopalam Rd

MATTANCHERRY

Rameswaram Canal Rd

Fishing Harbour

→ Fort Kochi & Ernakulam maps
1 Fort Kochi (Cochin) & Ernakulam, page 918
2 Fort Kochi detail, page 921
3 Ernakulam centre, page 922

P T Jacob Rd

Palluruth Bridge

✈ Indian Navy Airport

THOPUMPADY

Kochupally Rd

Vendruthy Rd

To Thiruvananthapuram

To Alappuzha

N

500 metres
500 yards

Where to stay
Brunton Boatyard 2
Caza Maria 1

Fort House 3

Restaurants
Bharat 1
Fort View 2

918 • Kerala Fort Kochi & Ernakulam

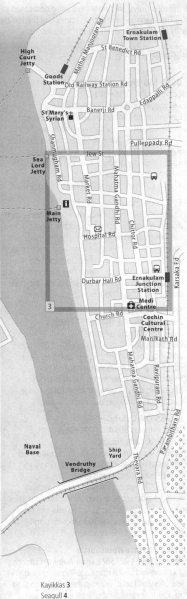

Ernakulam and around

East of Fort Kochi, Ernakulam has the **Museum of Kerala History** ① *1000-1200 and 1400-1600 except Mon and national holidays.* The museum exhibits start with Neolithic man and run through St Thomas and Vasco da Gama. Historical personalities of Kerala are represented with sound and light. Northwest of Ernakulam, **Bolghatty Island** has the 'palace' (circa 1745), set in large gardens and converted into a hotel. It was originally built by the Dutch and then became the home of the British Resident at the court of the Raja of Kochi after 1799. There is still some atmosphere of colonial decay which haunted the old building in its pre-modernized form and gave it much of its charm.

Vypeen Island lies on the northwestern fringe of the harbour. There are quiet beaches here, along with the Portuguese Azhikotta Fort, built around 1503. You can see cannon holes on the walls of the octagonal fort, which was garrisoned by 20 soldiers when it guarded the entrance to the backwaters. Vehicle ferries make the crossing from Fort Kochi.

Our Lady's Convent ① *Palluruthy, Thoppampady, 14 km south, by appointment, T0484-223 0508,* specializes in high-quality needlework lace and embroidery. The sisters are very welcoming and it is an interesting tour with items for sale.

Raksha ① *Yasmin Manzil, VII/370 Darragh-es-Salaam Rd, Kochangadi, T0484-222 7707,* works with children with physical and mental disabilities. Interested volunteers should contact the principal.

Hill Palace Archaeological Museum ① *Thirpunithura, 12 km east of Ernakulam, Tue-Sun 0900-1230, 1400-1700, Rs 11,* has a huge number of historical records and artefacts of the old royal state of Cochin, with portraits, ornaments, porcelain, palm leaf records and ancient musical instruments.

Kalady

Some 45 km northeast of Kochi is the town of Kalady, on the bank of the Periyar River. This popular pilgrimage site was the birthplace of one of India's most influential philosophers, **Sankaracharya**, who lived in the eighth century. He founded the school of *advaita* philosophy, which spread widely across South India. The **Adi Sankara Kirti Stambha Mandapam** ① *0700-1900, small entry fee,* is a nine-storied octagonal tower, 46 m high, and details Sri Sankara's life and works and the Shan Maths, or six ways to worship. Inside the **Shankara Temple** (Hindus only), are two shrines, one dedicated to Sankaracharya and the other to the goddess Sarada. The management of the shrines is in the hands of the Math at Sringeri in Karnataka. Kalady can easily be visited in an afternoon from Kochi.

Listings Fort Kochi and Ernakulam maps p918, p921 and p922

Tourist information

Fort Kochi

Tourist Desk
Tower Rd, T0484-221 6129, www.touristdesk.in.
Open 0900-1800.
This travel agent, with good maps and local information, runs daily backwater tours, has information on more than 2000 temple festivals in Kerala, and runs Costa Malabari guesthouse (see page 954).

Ernakulam

Kerala Tourism Development Corporation (KTDC)
Shanmugham Rd, T0484-235 3234.
Open 0800-1800.

Tourist Desk
Main Boat Jetty, Ernakulam, T0484-237 1761,
see under Fort Kochi, above.

Where to stay

Fort Kochi

Fort Kochi has bags more character than the busy commercial centre of Ernakulam; book well in advance for the Christmas period.

$$$$ Malabar House
1/268 Parade Rd, near St Francis' Church,
T0484-221 6666.
Fort Kochi's original boutique hotel, and still one of its best. Big and beautiful high-ceilinged rooms in a sensitively restored 18th-century mansion, set around a flagstone courtyard with an excellent restaurant and small swimming pool. Helpful staff, reliable airport pick-ups and a funky bar make this a perfect if pricey first place to hang your hat.

$$$$ Old Harbour
Tower Rd, T0484-221 8006,
www.oldharbourhotel.com.
Impeccably restored, 300-year-old Portuguese and Dutch building slap on the harbor front. Rooms have private balconies, some with harbour views. Large garden plus swimming pool, Wi-Fi, Ayurveda, jacuzzi.

$$$$-$$$ Brunton Boatyard
Calvathy Rd, T0484-301 1711,
www.cghearth.com. Discounts Apr-Sep.
Easily the best address in Fort Kochi, adjacent to the Chinese fishing nets on the edge of the Arabian Sea. 18 characterful rooms and 4 deluxe suites, each of which overlooks the harbour in an elegantly restored original boatyard and merchant's house built around a courtyard with a giant rain-tree. Generous swimming pool.

$$$ Koder House
Tower Rd, T0484-221 8485, www.koderhouse.com.
Boutique hotel in a striking heritage town house formerly owned by prominent Jewish family, and sometime home to ambassadors and heads of state. Luxury suites have huge bedrooms, sitting room, bathroom and jacuzzi. Tiny plunge pool in the back courtyard, spa with massage and facials, plus valet, business centre, superb home-cooked food.

$$$-$$ Fort House
2/6A Calvathy Rd, T0484-221 7103,
www.hotelforthouse.com.
Tidy bungalows set in a quiet walled courtyard with its own little jetty. Some rooms charmingly old fashioned, others made from bamboo. Newer, more expensive rooms have modern baths, but they're pretty spartan for the price. Good restaurant overlooking the water.

$$$-$$ Old Courtyard
1/371 Princess St, T0484-221 6302,
www.oldcourtyard.com.
Beautiful, comfortable rooms, superbly styled with old wooden furniture, overlooking large, breezy courtyard of pretty pot plants and sit-outs. The suite is easily the most romantic with a 4-poster bed and white cotton. Attentive liveried staff, breakfast included, average food but excellent cakes and Turkish coffee, and lovely calm atmosphere. Recommended.

$$$-$ Rossitta Wood Castle
Rose St, T0484-221 5671, www.hotelrossitta.com.
300-year-old Dutch mansion. Rooms, with quirky features and lots of wood-panelling, set around an open-air restaurant courtyard. Breakfast included. Art gallery, library internet café, spa, hot water, yoga.

$$ Caza Maria Hotel
6/125 Jew Town Rd, Mattancherry, T(0)9846-050901, cazamaria1@gmail.com.
Just 2 huge and wonderful rooms in beautiful converted house, with tiled floors, wooden furniture and antiques: isolated (the only hotel in Jew Town), romantic and shabbily elegant. Fan only. All meals are included, served at French/Indian restaurant of same name across the street). Highly recommended.

$$ Delight Homestay
Parade Ground, Ridsdale Rd, T0484-221 7658, www.delightfulhomestay.com. Rs 2000-3500.
This lovingly restored Portuguese provides a welcoming peaceful haven. Airy, spotlessly 6 clean rooms open onto a wide terrace, budget rooms are great value. The garden is a riot of colourful blooms. Breakfast is served at the family table. A home away from home. Highly recommended.

$$ Raintree Lodge
Petercelli St, T0484-325 1489, www.fortcochin.com.
Friendly little lodge in quiet location. Large clean rooms all with hot water and a/c. Pretty roof terrace to relax on.

$$-$ Fort Muziris
1/415 Burgar St, T0484-221 5057, www.fortmuziris.com.
Friendly backpacker refuge in the centre of things. The pick of the rooms are the upstairs suites with kitchen and shared terrace.

$ Adam's Old Inn
CC1/430 Burgher St, T0484-221 7595, www.adamsoldinn.com. Rs 750-1000.
Popular budget-traveller haunt in restored old building. Helpful manager.

2 Fort Kochi detail

➡ Fort Kochi & Ernakulam maps
1 Fort Kochi (Cochin) & Ernakulam, page 918
2 Fort Kochi detail, page 921
3 Ernakulam centre, page 922

Where to stay 🛏
Adam's Old Inn 1
Delight Homestay 3
Fort Muziris 2
Koder House 6
Malabar House & Restaurant 7
Old Courtyard 8
Old Harbour 13
Oys Tourist Home 9
Raintree Lodge 12
Rossitta Wood Castle 11
Trinity 5
Vintage Inn 14

Restaurants 🍴
Dal & Roti 1
Kashi 2
Marina 3
Teapot Café 4

200 metres
200 yards

$ Oy's Tourist Home
Burgher St, T(0)9947-594903,
www.oys.co.in. Rs 500-800.
Decent rooms in lovely lamp-lit old building,
with lots of plants. Can be noisy.

$ Vintage Inn
Ridsdale Branch Rd, near Njaliparambu Junction,
T0484-221 5064, www.vintageresorts.in.
Wonderful, homely guesthouse with a cheerful
owner. Airy modern rooms with huge baths
in a quiet corner of town. Excellent value.
Recommended.

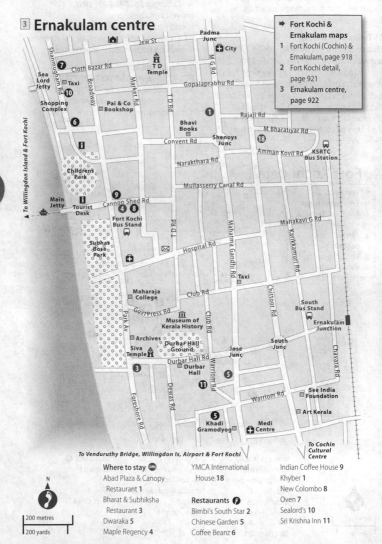

3 Ernakulam centre

> ➡ **Fort Kochi &**
> **Ernakulam maps**
> 1 Fort Kochi (Cochin) &
>   Ernakulam, page 918
> 2 Fort Kochi detail,
>   page 921
> 3 Ernakulam centre,
>   page 922

Where to stay 🛏		
Abad Plaza & Canopy	YMCA International	Indian Coffee House **9**
Restaurant **1**	House **18**	Khyber **1**
Bharat & Subhiksha		New Colombo **8**
Restaurant **3**	**Restaurants 🍴**	Oven **7**
Dwaraka **5**	Bimbi's South Star **2**	Sealord's **10**
Maple Regency **4**	Chinese Garden **5**	Sri Krishna Inn **11**
	Coffee Beanz **6**	

Ernakulam

$$ Abad Plaza
MG Rd, T0484-238 1122, www.abadhotels.com.
Rs 2900 (plus taxes).
A veteran of many monsoons, with large but
slightly moth-eaten rooms all with a/c, fridge
and cable TV. Rooms on street side can be noisy,
quieter rooms on 5th floor. Breakfast included.
Restaurants, gym, Ayurveda clinic, rooftop pool.

$$-$ Bharat
Gandhi Sq, Durbar Hall Rd, T0484-235 3501,
http://bharathotel.com.
Popular business hotel. Clean spacious rooms,
some a/c, best sea-facing. Restaurant with
excellent lunch *thalis* (South and North Indian).
Great service, good value.

$$-$ Dwaraka
MG Rd, T0484-238 3236, www.hoteldwaraka.com.
Centrally located, family-run hotel. Good-sized,
rather noisy rooms with TV, some with balcony,
excellent South Indian restaurant.

$$-$ YMCA International House
Chittoor Rd, 100 m from Central Bus Station,
T0484-238 3789, www.ymcaernakulam.org.
Simple rooms (some a/c), restaurant, welcoming.

Restaurants

Fort Kochi
For a really fresh seafood meal, buy your own fish
from the fishmonger stalls along the shorefront
and take it to one of the nearby 'you buy, we
cook' stalls, such as **Marina** or **Fort View**, where
they'll be grilled or masala-fried with chips.

$$$ Malabar House Residency
See Where to stay.
Excellent seafood platter and chef's salad,
the latter of huge dimensions. Authentic
Mediterranean and local dishes.

$$ Caza Maria
Opposite the hotel, see Where to stay.
Open 1200-2130.
2 large rooms with wooden chairs, frescoes and
old framed prints on the wall. Small menu includes
fish *moilee* and lime rice, *palak paneer* and *chapatti*
and apple pie and ice cream. Great atmosphere.

$ Dal Roti
1/293 Lilly St, T(0)974-6459244.
Firmly established favourite for pukka North
Indian food – delicious *khati* rolls, huge stuffed
parathas – served up by the affable Ramesh and

his family. Don't arrive starving as queues often
stretch out the door.

$ Kashi
Burgher St, Kochi, T0484-221 5769,
www.kashiartgallery.com.
If you've been away a while, **Kashi** is the type of
place you'll fall on in wonder. The first 2 rooms
are the art gallery, the rest is a restaurant where
you can drink coffee fresh from your own
cafetière, or indulge in a perfect cappuccino.
There's a handful of excellently made sweets
and 1-2 dishes they make for breakfast or lunch.

$ Kayikka's
Rahmathulla Hotel, Kayees, New Rd, near
Aanavaadal, Fort Kochi, T0484-222 6080.
Open 1200-1430, 1830-2030.
This family concern is the busiest biryani
restaurant in Kochi and a local institution. Great
mutton and chicken biryanis all week with fish
biryanis on Fri and prawn on Tue. Arrive early to
avoid disappointment.

$ Seagull
Calvathy Rd, T0484-221 7172,
www.thehotelseagull.com.
Good-value seafood, pleasant veranda for drinks
and dining overlooking the harbour.

$ Teapot Café
Peter Celli St, T0484-221 8035.
Bare terracotta roof tiles dangle with teapots
and fans, tables are tea crates and walls are hung
with antique tea-related paraphernalia. Stop
in for a brew of Darjeeling, Assam, Nilgiris or
mint-flavoured teas, an iced coffee, or milkshake.
There's a delicious selection of cakes and
desserts, tasty toasted sandwiches and more
substantial meals like prawn *moilee*, and mustard
fish. With loads of newspapers and magazines
left out for customers to read, it's a lovely place
to while away a couple of hours.

Ernakulam

$$ Bimbi's South Star
Shanmugam Rd.
Generous portions of tasty Indian food.

$$ Khyber
Durbar Hall Rd.
North Indian meals upstairs.

$$ Sealord's
Shanmugam Rd, T0484-238 2472,
www.sealordhotels.com.
Rooftop setting with good fish and Chinese dishes.

$$ Sri Krishna Inn
Warriom Rd, next to Chinmaya Vidya Peeth,
T0484-236 6664, www.sreekrishnainn.in.
One of the best pure-veg places in a city of seafood,
with great North and South Indian options.

$$ Subhiksha
Bharat Hotel, see Where to stay.
Excellent value buffet lunch.

$ Bharat
Willingdon Island.
Very good vegetarian *thalis* and Indian specialities
in clean surroundings.

$ Chinese Garden
Warriom Rd, T0484-236 3710.
Good variety of decent Chinese meals.
Alcohol available.

$ Indian Coffee House
Cannon Shed Rd, T0484-322 3216,
www.indiancoffeehouse.com.
Tasty North and South Indian dishes.

$ New Colombo
Canon Shed Rd.
Good snacks, fruit juices.

Cafés

Coffee Beanz
Shanmugan Rd, www.coffeebeanz.in.
Daily 0900-2300.
Cold coffees, *appam*, *dosa*, popular, poky a/c
coffee bar with just 6 tables.

Oven
Shanmugham Rd.
Good pizzas and snacks (savoury and sweet).

Entertainment

There are daily perfomances of *Kathakali*; see box,
opposite. Arrive early to watch the extraordinary
make-up being applied.

Fort Kochi
ENS Kalari, *Nettoor, T0484-270 0810, www.*
enskalari.org.in. Kalarippayattu performances
daily at 1915 (24 hrs' notice required).
Kerala Kathakali Centre, *River Rd, T0484-221 7552,*
www.kathakalicentre.com. Rustic surroundings but
lively performance, enjoyable; 1830-1930 (make-
up 1700) but check timing, Rs 100.

Ernakulam
Cochin Cultural Centre, *Manikath Rd,*
off Ravipuram Rd, T0484-235 7153,
www.cochinculturalcentre.com. A/c 'theatre',
authentic performance with English explanations;
1830-1930, make-up 1730, Rs 125.
See India Foundation, *Kalathil Parampil Lane*
(enter Chittoor Rd south) near Junction station,
T0484-236 9471. Dr Devan's 'interpreted' taste
of *Kathakali* with esoteric English commentary;
1845-2000 (make-up from 1800), Rs 125.

Festivals

Jan/Feb Ulsavam at the Siva Temple in
Ernakulam for 8 days. Elephant processions
each day, folk dance and music performances.
Aug/Sep Onam.
Nov/Dec Ulsavam at the Tripunithura Temple.

Shopping

Fort Kochi
Fort Kochi coir products (eg mats), carvings on
rosewood and buffalo horn and antiques may
catch your eye here. Several narrow streets in
Jew Town, towards the synagogue, have become
popular for 'antique' hunters in the last 25 years.
All these shops sport a similar range of old (some
faux) and new curios.
Cinnamon, *Stuba Hall, 1/658 Ridsdale Rd, Parade*
Ground, T0484-221 7124, www.cinnamonthestore.
com. Posh clothing, fabrics and interiors shop.
Idiom Books, *branches on VI/183 Synagogue*
Lane, Jew Town and Bastion Rd, T0484-221 7075.
Very good range on India, travel, fiction, religion,
philosophy, etc.
Indian Industries, *Princess St, Fort Kochi, T0484-*
221 6448. One of Fort Kochi's oldest antique
dealers. Lovely family-run store with fixed prices
and no-hassle browsing.

Ernakulam
There are several government emporia on MG Rd,
Ernakulam, including **National Textiles** (another in
Banerji Rd). Other shopping areas are in Broadway,
Super Bazar, Anand Bazar, Prince St and New Rd.

What to do

Fort Kochi
Body and soul
Be Beautiful, *Princess St, T0484-221 5398.*
Open 0900-2030. Good, cheap beauty salon
with massage, hairdressers, pedicure and
manicure in new premises.
Sanathana School of Yoga Studies, *XV/2188-D*
Beach Rd Junction, T0484-229 4155,

ON THE ROAD

Kathakali

The special dance form of Kerala, *Kathakali*, has its origins in the *Theyyam*, a ritual tribal dance of North Kerala, and *Kalaripayattu*, the martial arts practised by the high-caste Nayars, going back 1000 years. In its present form of dance-drama, *Kathakali* has evolved over the last 400 years.

The performance is usually outdoors, the stage bare but for a large bronze oil lamp, with the drummers on one side and the singers with cymbal and gong, who act as narrators, on the other. The art of mime reaches its peak in these highly stylized performances which used to last through the night; now they often take just three to four hours. The costume is comprised of a large billowing skirt, a padded jacket, some heavy ornaments and headgear. The make-up is all-important: *Pacha* (green) characterizing the good and *Kathi* (knife, shape of a painted 'moustache'), the Villain; *Thadi* (bearded), white for superhuman *hanumans*, black for the hunter and red for evil and fierce demons; *Kari* (black) signifying demonesses; *Minukku* (shining) 'simple' make-up representing the gentle and spiritual. The paints are natural pigments while the stiff 'mask' is created with rice paste and lime. The final application of a flower seed in the lower eyelid results in the red eyes you will see on stage.

This classical dance requires lengthy, hard training to make the body supple, the eyes expressive. The 24 *mudras* express the nine emotions of serenity, wonder, kindness, love, valour, fear, contempt, loathing and anger. The gods and mortals play out their roles amid the chaos brought about by human ambition, but the dance ends in peace and harmony restored by the gods.

www.sanathanayoga.com. Daily classes 0730-0930 and 1630-1830, *pranayama* and *asanas* plus 28-day teacher training programmes in a pretty residence in downtown Fort Kochi.

Tour operators
Spice Land Holidays and Entertainments Private Limited, *Suite 2, Saniya Plaza, Rajaji Rd, T91484-237 8022, www.spicelandholidays.com.* Package and customized tours throughout Kerala and the rest of India.

Ernakulam
Tour operators
Hi Tours, *Jomer Arcade, South Junction, Chittoor Rd, T0484-237 7415, www.hi-tours.com.* Efficient and well-connected inbound travel agent, who can hook you up with homestays, authentic Ayurveda retreats and responsible tour operators throughout Kerala. Helpful and highly recommended.
KTDC, *Shanmugham Rd, Ernakulam, T0484-235 3234.* Full- and half-day backwater tours on *kettuvallams*. Full-day tour 0830-1830 (includes lunch); half-day tour 0830-1300 and 1400-1830. Tours include visits to coir factory, spice garden, canoe ride and toddy tapping demonstration. Also daily half-day Kochi sightseeing boat cruises, 0900-1230 and 1400-1730, which cover Bolgatty Island, Chinese fishing nets, St Francis

Church and Mattancherry Palace. Tour departs from Sealord Jetty.
Pioneer Personalized Holidays, *Pioneer House, 5th Cross, Willingdon Island, T0484-266 6148, www.pioneertravels.com.* Fleet of cars with tailor-made tour packages from a well-established and highly competent tour company. Efficient and knowledgeable, with unusual homestay and guesthouse options.
Sundale Vacations, *39/5955 Atlantis Junction, MG Rd, T0484-235 9127, www.sundale.com.* Surface and hotel arrangements in Kerala, specializes in homestays catering to 'foreign independent tourists', promoting insight into Kerala's customs. Programmes from US$467.
Tourist Desk, *Main Boat Jetty, T0484-237 1761, www.touristdesk.in.* One of the best budget tour operators. Daily backwater tours, 0800-1700, Rs 550, using both *kettuvalloms* and canoe. Tour includes visits to see coir making, spice garden, local village and lunch. Also 2- to 3-day tours to Wayanad and Kannur. Highly recommended.
Visit India, *North Janatha Rd, T0484-233 9045, www.visitindiatravel.com.* Half-day backwater tours in a dugout, punted and engineless, through very peaceful shady waterways passing unspoilt villages with toddy tappers, coir making, fishing, etc; led by an excellent guide. Highly recommended. Also offers trips in traditional *kettuvallams*.

Transport

Air

Kochi's airport is at Nedumbassery, 36 km northeast of the city, T0484-261 0012. Hotels charge Rs 900-1500 for airport pick-up, depending on type of car and what the market will support. Prepaid taxis charge around Rs 850 to Fort Kochi, a little less to downtown Ernakulam. A/c buses leave from outside the international terminal for Fort Kochi (Rs 80) via the new intercity bus stand at Vytilla Junction (Rs 60), 3 km west of Ernakulam centre.

Daily domestic flights to: **Bengaluru**, **Chennai**, **Mumbai**, **Delhi** via **Goa**, **Thiruvananthapuram**; and several flights per week to **Coimbatore**, **Hyderabad**, **Kozhikode** and **Tiruchirapalli**.

International flights to: **Abu Dhabi**, **Doha**, **Dubai**, **Kuala Lumpur**, **Kuwait**, **Muscat**, **Sharjah** (UAE) and **Singapore**.

Bus

Local Buses journey between Ernakulam, Willingdon and Fort Kochi frequently during the day. There are no local buses after 2100.

Long distance Buses run from the **KSRTC Bus Station**, Chavara Rd, T0484-237 2033, www. keralartc.com. There are frequent services to **Alappuzha**, every 20 mins (1½ hrs); **Kottayam**, every 30 mins (1½ hrs); **Kozhikode**, every 30 mins (5 hrs) and **Thiruvananthapuram**, every 30 mins (5 hrs). There are 7 departures daily to **Kumily** (6 hrs) or take a bus to Kottayam and change there. There is an 0630 departure to **Munnar** (4 hrs), and departures to **Kannur** at 1445 and 2345 (7 hrs). Interstate services include: 9 daily to **Bengaluru** (14 hrs) via **Kozhikode** (5 hrs) and **Mysore** (10 hrs); **Kanniyakumari**, at 1430 (7½ hrs); and **Chennai** at 1400 (15 hrs) via **Coimbatore** (5 hrs).

Private operators run from **Kalloor** and **Ernakulam Southbus** stands including **Indira Travels**, DH Rd, T0484-236 0693; **SB Travels**, String Dew Building, Tripunithura, T0484-277 7949; and **Princy Tours**, opposite Sealord Hotel, T0484-237 3109, www.princytravels.com. Overnight coaches to **Bengaluru** (12 hrs) and **Mysore** (10 hrs). Departures every 30 mins to **Kottayam** (2 hrs) and **Munnar** (4 hrs). Also to **Chennai** and **Coimbatore**.

Ferry

Regular ferry services connect Ernakulam with Fort Kochi and are the fastest and easiest form of transport. Ferry tickets cost Rs 2.50. Most ferries take bikes and motorbikes. It's also possible to hire a motor boat for up to 20, from Sea Lord jetty in Ernakulam through the **KTDC** office.

Ernakulam **Main Boat Jetty**, Cannon Shed Rd. Ferries depart approximately every 30 mins to Fort Kochi 'Customs' jetty 0555-2130. There are also regular ferries to the Fort Kochi Mattancherry jetty (last departure to Mattancherry is 1845), and to Willingdon Island's 'Embarkation' Jetty from here. Ferries to Bolghatty depart from the High Court Jetty off Shanmugham Rd approximately every 20 mins Mon-Sat 0600-2100.

Fort Kochi Regular departures from Customs jetty 0620-2150. The last ferry leaves for Ernakulam from the Mattencherry jetty at 1930. From the northern Vypeen Jetty there are services every 30 mins to Vypeen Island between 0600-2130.

Willingdon Island There are 2 jetties: 'Embarkation' (north) and 'Terminus' (west). Ferries run every 30 mins to Ernakulam from 'Embarkation' from 0600-2110. From the 'Terminus' jetty there are infrequent services to Mattancherry on Fort Kochi.

Rickshaw

Auto-rickshaw drivers have a reasonably good reputation here. But, if you are likely to arrive late at night, insist on being taken directly to your hotel. A rickshaw between Fort Kochi and Ernakulam should cost around Rs 250. Fares within Fort Kochi or Ernakulam: Rs 30-60.

Taxi

Ernakulam Junction to Fort Kochi, Rs 400. To airport, Rs 700.

Train

Ernakulam/Kochi is on the broad gauge line joining Thiruvananthapuram to Mangalore, Bengaluru and Chennai. Most trains from major cities stop at **Ernakulam Junction** (the main station, booking code: ERS) although a few stop at Ernakulam Town (ERN), T0484-239 0920. Enquiries: Ernakulam Junction, T131 or T0484-237 5131.

Trains to: **Bengaluru**: 3 daily, 11 hrs, via Thrissur (1 hr), Palakkad (2½-4 hrs) and Coimbatore (5 hrs); **Chennai**: 7-10 a day (12 hrs); **Mangalore**: 7-10 a day (10 hrs) via **Thrissur**, **Kozhikode** (4 hrs) and **Kannur** (5-6 hrs); **Thiruvananthapuram**, more than 20 a day, all via **Kollam** and **Varkala**; and **Tiruchirappali**, 1 daily (9 hrs), continues to **Thanjavur** (10 hrs).

Munnar &
Idukki's high ranges

Inland from the plains around Kottayam and Kochi lie the foothills of the Western Ghats, swathed in tropical evergreen forests and an ever-creeping tide of monoculture rubber plantations. As you climb higher these give way to pepper and cardamom, until finally you reach the rolling tea plantations and rarefied air of landlocked Idukki District. To the south sits Thekkady and the unmissable Periyar National Park, home to tiger, wild elephant, and an innovative project that is steadily turning yesterday's poachers into tomorrow's tour guides. Overnight treks into the park's hinterland offer an unmatched opportunity to see big animals up close and on foot, but even on a day visit Periyar can show you some impressive nature: wild boar foraging along the lakeside, butterflies as big as bats bouncing beneath the canopies of prehistoric jack trees, and the thud-thwack-holler as unruly gangs of Nilgiri langur swoop through the high branches of giant figs.

Munnar, meanwhile, five hours uphill from Kochi, is *chai* central: a surreal rippling mosaic of yellow-green tea bushes and red dust roads stretching from valley deep to mountain high, with dark granite peaks pointing like fingers toward the bald grassy dome of South India's highest mountain, Anaimudi. At 1600 m, Munnar is much higher than Thekkady and gets genuinely cold, a fact that made it a favourite summer bolthole for the Raj. Wildlife tourists flock to the nearby Eravikulam National Park for a glimpse of the endangered but semi-tame Nilgiri thar, a variety of ibex, while further to the north are the forests and deeply etched ravines of magnificent, rarely visited Chinnar Wildlife Sanctuary.

Essential Munnar and Idukki's high ranges

Finding your feet

The nearest transport hub for Munnar is Kochi-Ernakulam; Thekkady (Periyar Reserve/Kumily town) is best accessed from Kottayam. There are no train links to the high ranges; buses take a minimum of four hours to climb the hills to both hill stations, and roads linking the two take the same length of time. For details, see Transport, page 938.

Fact...

The first rubber plantation was cultivated in 1902. India is now among the top three rubber producers worldwide, and most of that comes from Kerala. Crops in Kerala are determined by height: tea grows above 1500 m, cardamom, coffee and other spices between 1500 m and 600 m, coconut and rubber below 600 m.

The Midlands (Kottayam to Thekkady)

from the plains to the hills, with excellent views over the ghats

An interesting drive to the hills, this route follows the ghat road, which has superb views down the east side of the ghats onto the Tamil Nadu plains. You may meet herds of Zebu cattle, buffalo and donkeys being driven from Tamil Nadu to market in Kerala. Above 1000 m the air freshens and it can be cold. Be prepared for a rapid change in temperature.

Pala

Lying off the Kottayam–Thekkady road, Pala is a town famous for its learned citizens – graduates of the European-style Gothic university, which was built, along with the Gothic church, by one of its affluent sons. Nehru visited in the 1950s and said that Pala was full of "people of vision". The town was the most literate place in India long before Kerala achieved 100% literacy, and Meenachil Taluka has the highest proportion of educated women in the country. It is also famous for its tamarind and pepper as well as the rubber estates belonging to the Dominic family, who serve hot Syrian-Catholic lunches in their 100-year-old plantation bungalow and 50-year-old estate mansion. Plantation tours to watch latex collection and packing can be arranged through CGH Earth, see page 912.

Erattupetta and Vagamon

Further east lies **Erattupetta**, whose grey St George's Church holds naïve wood-painted doves and disembodied cherubims, and which hosts the **High Range Festival** every April. Carry on for **Vagamon**, a village set on a chain of three hills: Thangal, Murugal and Kurisumala. A dairy farm here is managed by Kurisumala monks.

Peermade

Some 25 km south from Vagamon is Peermade, named after Peer Mohammed, a Sufi saint and crony of the royal family of Travancore. It is surrounded by tea, rubber and cardamom plantations, including **Abraham's Spice Garden**, where a member of the family gives excellent spice tours. Buses between Kottayam and Kumily can drop you here.

Sabarimala

Hidden away in the hills to the south is Sabarimala, the focus of what some say is the world's biggest annual pilgrimage: 55 million Hindu pilgrims a year, almost all men, trek through the forest to the shrine, which is where the god Ayyappan is believed to have meditated after slaying a demoness. Aiyappan is a particularly favoured deity in Kerala and there are growing numbers of devotees. For details of the pilgrimage, see box, opposite. The shrine is only open on specific occasions: **Mandalam**, mid-November to the end of December; **Makaravilakku**, mid-January; **Vishu**, mid-April; **Prathistha** one day in May-June; and during the **Onam** festival in August-September.

A modern mass pilgrimage

Sabarimala pilgrims are readily visible in many parts of South India as they wear black *dhotis* as a symbol of the penance they must undergo for 41 days before they make the pilgrimage. In addition to the black dress, pilgrims must take two baths daily and only eat food at home during this period. The pilgrimage, which begins at Deepavali, is only for males and prepubescent and post-menstrual females, to avoid the defilement believed to be associated with menstruation.

"The pilgrimage in January is deliberately hard", writes Vaidyanathan, because "the pilgrimage to the shrine symbolizes the struggle of the individual soul in its onward journey to the abode of bliss and beatitude. The path of the spiritual aspirant is always long, arduous and hazardous. And so is the pilgrimage to Sabarimala, what with the observance of severe austerities and trekking up forested mountains, risking attacks from wild animals".

Listings The Midlands (Kottayam to Thekkady)

Where to stay

$$$$ Kottukapally Nazarani Tharavad
Palai, T(0)9846-212438,
www.nazaranitharavad.com.
An opportunity to stay with the Kottukapally family (Kerala political royalty). There are grand Byzantine icons, Persian carpets and Travancore brass lamps. The roomy 250-year-old Kerala/Dutch/Spanish-style house of teak, rosewood and Basel tiles has 3 roomy doubles. Book in advance.

$$$$ Serenity Kanam
At Kanam Estate, 25 km east of Kottayam
off Kumily Rd, T0481-245 6353,
www.malabarhouse.com.
This wonderful villa hotel has just 6 huge rooms, decorated with quality art and sculpture, set in a gently restored 1920s bungalow surrounded by rubber plantations and spice gardens. There's a big pool, spa and excellent food, and you can spend a morning exploring the quiet lanes from the back of Lakshmi, the estate elephant. Far from

any sights, but it's worth building in an extra night or 2 just to stay here.

$$$ The Pimenta
Haritha Farms, The Pimenta, Kadalikad Post,
T0485-226 02160, www.thepimenta.in.
An eco-tourism concern in a pepper-growing region. Guest numbers are limited to minimize impact on the village. 4 newly built simple cottages close to the family farmhouse. The family are advocates of the return to traditional methods of agriculture, Haritha grows bio-organic spices, medicinal herbs and tropical fruit and re-plants crops lost to monoculture tea and rubber plantations. All meals included.

$$$ Vanilla County
Mavady Estate, Teekoy, Vagamon,
T(0)9744-183835, www.vanillacounty.in.
At the source of the Meenachil River. A charming, family-friendly place with 3 rooms within 60-year-old estate house that you share with your hosts. Coffee is from the plantation around you and you can swim in nearby natural ponds. Internet access. Price includes all meals.

★ Periyar National Park (Thekkady)

Covering 930 sq km of montane forest and grassland and centred on an attractive lake, the Periyar National Park, 115 km east of Kottayam, may not throw up many tiger sightings nowadays but still attracts more than 300,000 visitors a year for its beautiful setting and unique range of soft adventure activities. Elephants, *gaur* and wild boar, though by no means guaranteed, are regularly spotted from the lake cruise boats, while sloth bear, porcupine and Malabar giant squirrel also haunt the woods.

The sanctuary was established by the old Travancore State government in 1934 and brought under the umbrella of Project Tiger in 1973, but Periyar's finest hour came in 1998 when the Kerala Forest Department, in partnership with the World Bank and the Thekkady Wildlife Society (a local NGO), set up a project to deploy a band of reformed cinnamon poachers from the surrounding villages as tour leaders and forest rangers in remote parts of the park. The camo-clad members of the **Ex-Vayana Bark Collectors Eco Development Committee** now earn a steady income from tourism, not to mention new-found respect within their communities, and their hard-won knowledge of the terrain and sharp instincts for animal behaviour makes them skilled, if not exactly chatty, forest guides. Trekking with them for a day represents your best chance of getting up close with elephants.

The centre of activities in the park is the boat jetty at Thekkady on pretty **Lake Periyar**, 3 km down a beautiful forest road from the tourist village of **Kumily**, which was created in 1895 by a dam that inundated 55 sq km of rich forest. A 180-m-long tunnel now leads the water eastward into the Suruli and Vaigai rivers, irrigating extensive areas of Ramanathapuram and Madurai districts in Tamil Nadu.

Essential Periyar National Park

Finding your feet

With the exception of a couple of government-run hotels down by the lakeside, everything that happens in Periyar happens in the busy little tourist trap of Kumily. The bus stand is at the north end of the main street, a 10-minute walk from most hotels. Buses run down to the lake jetty, or you can hire a bike (a tough ride back up the hill without gears), take an auto-rickshaw, share a jeep, or take the pleasant walk through the woods. For details, see Transport, page 933.

When to go

The best time to visit is December to April, when dry weather brings animals closer to the lake. Dawn and dusk are best for wildlife, so stay overnight (winter nights can get quite cold). Avoid weekends and holidays, and especially the Makaravilakku festival in mid-January, which brings pilgrims by their millions to the Sabarimala shrine (see box, page 929).

Entry fees

Entry to the park costs Rs 300 per day, Rs 105 for children; Indians pay Rs 25/Rs 5.

Exploring the park

The standard way to see Periyar is to take a trip across the lake on a **motor launch** ① *depart 0730, 0930, 1115, 1345 and 1530, Rs 150; tickets on sale 90 mins before departure, no advance reservation required*. You can get good wildlife sightings on the first trip of the morning – elephants, gaur, wild boar, sambar and barking deer are regularly spotted browsing on the banks, and packs of dhole (wild dog) very occasionally seen. However, noisy boats (and their occupants) and the heat soon drive animals away from the shore. Jeeps begin queueing at the park entrance gate from 0500 to get on the first launch of the morning, and there's a mad sprint to the ticket office once you reach the lake's edge.

At the Eco Tourism Office in Kumily you can book a 2½-hour **forest trek** ① *maximum 6 people, depart 0700, 0730, 1000, 1030, 1400, 1430, Rs 200 per person (minimum Rs. 800 per trek), no advance reservations so get to office early to queue; carry water and beware of leeches*. There are good chances of seeing Malabar giant squirrel and Nilgiri langur, but much depends on your guide and not everybody comes face to face with a herd of elephants; some return very disappointed. Guides may also offer to arrange unofficial private walking tours in the park periphery in the afternoon (not the best time for spotting wildlife); try to assess the guide before signing up.

A more rewarding option is to sign up for one of the longer adventures into the park offered by the Ex-Vayana Bark Collectors Eco Development Committee. If you only have a day to spend in the park, spend it on the **bamboo rafting trip** ① *minimum 2 and maximum 10 people Rs 1500 per person (minimum Rs 3000 per trip)*, a full-day odyssey on land and water, trekking through a mosaic of grasslands, dense forest and rocky lakeshore, and navigating a long stretch of the lake on rickety rafts. Bird sightings are fabulous, with great hornbill a real possibility, and the ex-poacher guides have been known to change the route to pursue – in a strictly non-violent sense – herds of elephant. A rifleman accompanies every group to ward off the threat of a charge.

If you've got longer, the **Tiger Trail** covers much the same ground but offers a chance to trek deeper into the forest, camping out for one or two nights (Rs 4000/6000 per person, maximum of six guests). Other activities include the **Jungle Patrol** (a three-hour night trek, where you might spotlight porcupine and nightjars); the full-day **Border Hiking Trail** to a peak overlooking the Kambam Valley; and **bullock cart rides** to a traditional farming village.

Around Thekkady

There are a number of attractions within easy reach of Thekkady. These include the traditional Keralite-style **Mangaladevi Temple**, set amongst dense woodland on the peak of a 1337 m hill, 15 km northeast of Thekkady. Permission to visit the area must be obtained from the Wildlife Warden in Thekkady, though the temple itself is only open during the **Chithra Pounami** holiday. Other picturesque spots around Thekkady include **Pandikuzhi** (5 km) and **Chellarkovil** (15 km).

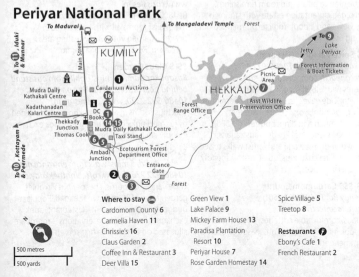

Periyar National Park

Where to stay
Cardomom County 6
Carmelia Haven 11
Chrissie's 16
Claus Garden 2
Coffee Inn & Restaurant 3
Deer Villa 15

Green View 1
Lake Palace 9
Mickey Farm House 13
Paradisa Plantation
Resort 10
Periyar House 7
Rose Garden Homestay 14

Spice Village 5
Treetop 8

Restaurants 🍴
Ebony's Cafe 1
French Restaurant 2

Tourist information

District Tourism Office
Kumily, T0486-922 2620.
Runs plantation tours to Abraham's Spice Garden (4 km) and Vandiperiyar (18 km).

Eco Tourism Office
Ambady Junction, Kumily, T0486-922 4571, www.periyartigerreserve.org.
Has information and books tickets for all treks and tours in the Periyar National Park.

Where to stay

Check www.thekkady.com for information.

$$$$ Lake Palace
Lake Periyar, T0486-922 3887, www.lakepalacethekkady.com.
6 rooms in an interesting building inside the reserve. Idyllic island setting with superb views and wildlife spotting. Access by free ferry (20 mins) from jetty (last trip 1600). Relaxed and informal. Rates include all meals.

$$$$ Paradisa Plantation Retreat
Murinjapuzha, Kottayam–Kumily Rd, T0469-270 1311, www.paradisaretreat.com.
10 traditionally built new cottages with beautiful antique granite pillars and room furnishings, on an organic plantation estate with stunning valley views and a pool. Yoga recommended but booking essential.

$$$$ Spice Village (CGH Earth)
Thekkady–Kumily Rd, T0486-922 4514, www.cghearth.com. Discounts Apr-Sep.
Cottages with elephant grass thatch (cool and dark with wide eaves), spice garden, badminton, tennis, good pool, yoga centre. Excellent restaurant, lunch and dinner buffets (Rs 500), chilled beer. Good cookery demonstrations, great Ayurvedic massage and forest walks to see smaller wildlife. Luxurious, quiet, restful, friendly, with superb service.

$$$$-$$$ Cardamom County
Thekkady Rd, T0486-922 4501, www.raxacollective.com.
Spacious, comfortable cottages, good restaurant, nice pool, friendly (request off-season discount). Recommended.

$$$ Hotel Treetop
Thekkady Rd, T0486-922 3286, www.hoteltreetop.com.
Clean and efficient resort of gabled cottages with all mod cons and private balconies, just on the fringes of the Periyar National Park. Family bungalow has a kitchen and living area. Library, restaurant, Ayurveda massages available.

$$$-$$ Carmelia Haven
Vandanmedu (20 km north on Puliyanmala Rd), T0486-827 0272, www.carmeliahaven.com.
On a tea, spice and coconut plantation, exclusive and private, with a treehouse 6 m above ground, a cave house 3 m below, and a few discreetly spaced cottages in a local style using lots of thatch. An excellent open-air restaurant serves delicious Malabari food. Tours of tea factory, cardamom plantations, treks and boating. Tea and cardamom for sale.

$$ Periyar House (KTDC)
5 mins' walk from the lake, T04869-222026, www.periyarhousethekkady.com.
Pleasant, clean and comfortable rooms. Buffet meals and strong Goan beer available. Good service.

$$-$ Chrissie's
Thekkady Bypass Rd, T0486-922 4155, www.chrissies.in.
Rs 1800-2800 (including taxes). Modern minimalist rooms all with balcony. Lush, peaceful garden with shady seating areas to relax in. Restaurant, yoga studio.

$$-$ Claus Garden
Rosapukandam, 10 mins' uphill from bus stand behind post office, 3rd turning on the right, T0486-922 2320, www.homestay.in.
Spacious rooms in a peaceful house surrounded by jungle. Funky communal area, book exchange, friendly chilled-out vibe.

$$-$ Coffee Inn
Thekkady Rd, 5 mins' walk from entrance gate, T0486-922 2763, www.coffeeinnthekkady.com.
Wide variety of rooms, cheaper huts in quiet garden annex 100 m down the road. Popular budget traveller hang-out. Restaurant, book exchange, friendly. No reservations – rooms are allocated on a first come first served basis.

$ Deer Villa
Thekkady Bypass Rd, T0486-922 3568, www.deervilla.com.
Friendly family home boasting clean, airy rooms with balcony, fan and hot water. Breakfast included. Internet café downstairs.

$ Green View
Hotel Ambadi Junction, Thekkady Bypass Rd, T0486-922 4617, www.sureshgreenview.com.
Suresh and Sulekha run a welcoming 'home away from home' in a rambling house surrounded by mango trees. Hammocks are slung out in the garden. All 16 spotlessly clean rooms have large bathrooms (towels, loo roll and soap provided). Standard and deluxe rooms have cable TV and balcony. Suresh is an ex-tour guide and can provide maps for mountain treks and walks in the area. Meals available on request, cookery classes, breakfast included. Friendly and helpful.

$ Mickey Farm House
Thekkady Bypass Rd, T0486-922 3196, www.mickeyhomestay.com.
Pleasant airy rooms in pretty garden, all with balcony. Cheaper rooms with outside bath. Mickey runs 4- to 7-day treks to Kottayam/Alappuzha (advance notice required). Friendly family, excellent value. Recommended.

$ Rose Garden Homestay
Hotel Ambadi Junction, Thekkady Bypass Rd, T0486-922 3146, www.rosegardenhomestay.com.
Sathi has 6 simply furnished rooms, all with TV, in the back garden of her flowered house. Lots of hanging wicker chairs on porches, Lovely family provides traditional Keralite breakfasts and suppers. Discounts for long stays.

Restaurants

$$$ Spice Village
See Where to stay.
International, excellent food and service, rustic decor, fresh garden vegetables and chef's cooking show nightly.

$$ Coffee Inn
See Where to stay. Open 0700-2200.
International dishes served at tables outside under the palms, bonfire in the evening, relaxed and peaceful. Friendly but very slow service.

$ Ebony's Café
Thekkady Bypass Rd.
Rooftop restaurant with huge range of Indian and international dishes.

$ Edassery's Farm Yard
NH 49 Chattupara Adimali Idukki, T04864-224210. Open 0600-2200.
Makes a good break on the Kottayam–Kumily road with tasty soups and meals, *dosa* and vegetable stews.

$ French Restaurant
Thekkady Rd, T(0)9961-213107.
Good bread, muesli, snacks and coffee.

$ Our Place
Next to Jungle View Homestay, Rosappukandam.
Run by a British/Indian couple, this cosy café serves comfort food from back home alongside excellent Indian vegetarian options.

Entertainment

Kadathanadan Kalari Centre, *Thekkady Rd, Kumily, T(0)9961-740868, www.thekkadytourism.in.* 1-hr demonstration of Kerala's traditional martial art, *Kalarippayattu*. Show time 1800, Rs 200, video charge Rs 250. Also Kathakali shows 1700-1800 and 1900-2000

Mudra Daily Kathakali Centre, *Thekkady Rd, Kumily, T0486-922 2303, www.mudracultural centre.com.* Classical dance theatre show by performers from Kalamandalam school of dance. Kathakali 1700, 1900; Kalari 1800, 1915; Rs 200, video charge Rs 200.

What to do

Tours
Eco Tourism Information Centre, *Hotel Ambadi Junction, Thekkady Bypass Rd, Kumily, T0486-922 2620, www.periyartigerreserve.org.* Organizes a full range of tours within the park: bamboo rafting, tiger trails with 1 or 2 nights' camping, evening jungle patrols, border hiking and treks to tribal settlements.

Transport

Beware of 3-wheelers and guides at the bus station, who are working on commission from guesthouses. Nearly all hotels in Kumily are within a 10-min walk of the bus station.

Bus Local: Minibuses hourly from Kumily go down to **Aranya Nivas** on the lakeside, Rs 2. At Kumily jeep drivers will tell you there is no bus to Thekkady and charge Rs 50 for the trip; autos charge Rs 25 plus.

　　Long distance: From Kumily: frequent services to **Kottayam**, every 20 mins from 0600

(4½ hrs). Regular buses to **Kochi/Ernakulam**, 6 per day, 1st at 0600 (6½ hrs); **Alappuzha**, 6 per day, 1st at 0600 (6 hrs); **Thiruvananthapuram**, 3 per day, 1st at 0830 (8 hrs); **Munnar**, 5 per day, 1st at 0600 (4½ hrs). Daily bus to **Kodaikkanal** (cancelled occasionally), 0630 (5½ hrs), or go to **Vathalakundu** and change. Buses also go from Thekkady itself (behind Aranya Nivas): frequent departures to **Madurai**, every 20 mins, from 0600 (4 hrs).

Munnar

commercial hill station surrounded by emerald green tea estates

A major centre of Kerala's tea industry, Munnar (altitude 1520 m) sits in the lee of Anaimudi, South India's highest peak at 2695 m, and is the nearest Kerala comes to a genuine hill station. The landscape is European Alpine, minus the snow, plus tea bushes – inestimable millions of them. The town is surrounded by about 30 tea estates, among them the highest in the world at Kolukkumalai, yet despite the increasingly commercial use of the hills you can still find forests that are rich in wildlife, including the endangered Nilgiri tahr. The workers on the tea estates are mostly Tamilians who moved here eight or nine generations ago.

The surrounding hills are also home to the rare Neelakurunji orchid (*Strobilanthes*), which covers the hills in colour for a month once every 12 years (next due 2018). During the monsoon, cotton wool swabs of cloud shift and eddy across hillsides, sodden as a sponge with fresh rains, and springs burst their banks and surge across the pathways where villagers, dark-skinned tribals in ski jackets and woollen noddy hats, swing past on Enfields on their way home from a day on the tea plantations.

The road from Kochi

The route from Kochi to Munnar is one of South India's most attractive ghat roads. The one sight of note is the is the 25-sq-km **Salim Ali Bird Sanctuary** ① *Thattekad, 70 km east of Kochi on a side road heading north out of Kothamangalam; contact Assistant Wildlife Warden, Thattekad, T0485-258 8302.* A tropical evergreen and semi-evergreen forest with teak and rosewood plantations, the sanctuary is surrounded by the Periyar River, which remains shallow most of the year. It attracts water birds and the indigenous Malabar grey hornbill, rose and blue-winged parakeet, egret, heron and mynah, while rarer birds like the Ceylon frog-mouth and rose-billed rollers are also sometimes seen here.

Sights

Tata Tea Museum ① *Nullatanni Estate, T04865-230561, www.keralatourism.org, open 0900-1600, Rs 50, closed Mon.* The museum has a heap of artefacts, curios and photographs to help conjure something of the lives of the men who opened up the High Ranges to tea. The crop has grown here for over a century so relics include a rudimentary tea roller from 1905 and a wheel from the Kundale Valley Light Railway that used to transport men and materials between Munnar and Top Station. The museum has descriptions of the fully automated technology of today from the tea factory at Madupatty. The museum can also arrange a visit to this factory, watching tea pickers at work and seeing how the tea is processed.

Essential Munnar

Finding your feet

The easiest access is by bus or taxi from Kochi. There are also daily buses to Kumily and major towns in Kerala and Tamil Nadu. The town is small and pleasant for exploring on foot, although there are autos. It is worth hiring a bike or a jeep for trips out of town. See Transport, page 938.

Christ Church In the centre of Old Munnar, set on a hill immediately above the road in the centre of town, Christ Church was built to serve tea estate managers and workers of the High Ranges. The last English-language service was held in 1981; it is now shared between protestant Tamil and Malayalam worshippers. The exterior is un-prepossessing: rather squat and now blackened by weathering, but inside it

Munnar

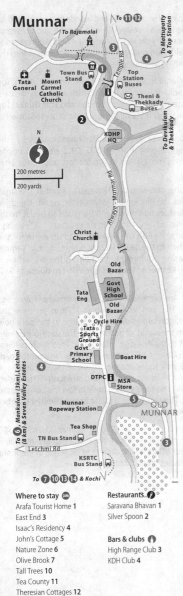

is a charming small church and still contains its original 14 rows of wooden pews. Ask to see the diminutive record of births and deaths of the town's founders, the British planters.

Immediately behind the church a zigzag path up the hill leads to the small pioneer **cemetery** that was established long before the church itself as the chosen burial ground of Mrs Eleanor Knight, General Manager Knight's 24-year-old bride who caught cholera after arriving in the High Range in 1894.

Mount Carmel Roman Catholic Church
The first Catholic church in the High Ranges, Mount Carmel is in Old Munnar on the road up to the Tata General Hospital. The first chapel on the site was founded in 1898 by Friar Alphonse who arrived in Munnar from Spain in 1854. The present church was built by the then Bishop of Vijayapuram in 1938.

High Range Club ① *T04865-230253, www.high rangeclubmunnar.com*. This private members' club is more relaxed than the famously 'Snooty' Ooty Club. A tradition allowed members to hang their hats on the wall of the bar after 30 years of belonging to the club – the last was hung in 1989 to make 51 hats in all. Saturday is strictly jacket and tie only and backpackers will need to scrub up well to get in any day of the week. "We like scholars and researchers, professionals and club people", says the club secretary, "they know how to move in a club". It's a wonderful place with teak floors, squash courts, library and fascinating planters to chat to if you're interested in the planters' social history.

Around Munnar

There are some excellent **cycle rides** around Munnar, not all of them steep. One ride goes up a gentle slope through a beautiful valley 8 km to the **Letchmi Estate**. There is a *chai* stall at the estate and the road continues to the head of the valley for views down to the forest. A second ride (or walk) leaves Munnar by the south road for 3 km, turning left at the Head Works Dam, then takes a right turn past Copper Castle, then left to a tea stall, viewpoint, tea and cardamom plantations, again with superb views. Continue to the next tea pickers' village for a tea stall. A shorter option for this route is to cross the dam and turn left, taking the quiet road north to the **High Range Club** and Munnar.

Mattupetty Lake ① *13 km from Munnar, T04865-230389, visits 0900-1100, 1400-1530, Rs 5.*

At an altitude of 1700 m, Mattupetty Lake is flanked by steep hills and woods. It was created by the small hydroelectricity dam. To its south is the Kerala Livestock Development Board's research and cattle breeding centre, formerly the Indo-Swiss dairy project. In a beautiful semi-Alpine setting surrounded for much of the year by lush green fields, the centre offers interesting insights into the practical realities and achievements of cattle breeding in India today.

Top Station Some 34 km from Munnar on the Tamil Nadu border, at an altitude of 2100 m, Top Station has some of the highest tea estates in India. It is an idyllic spot, with superb views over the Tamil Nadu plains and the edge of the Western Ghats. Stalls serve tea and soft drinks. Top Station took its name from a ropeway that connected it via Middle Station to Lower Station at the valley bottom.

The small town of **Bodinayakkanur**, which can be reached on the Devikulam road, lies in the valley. Buses leave from the shelter north of Munnar post office at 0715, 0915 and 1115 bound for Kovilor, passing Mattupetty Lake and Kundala Dam. Get off at Top Station, return bus after about one hour.

Kolukkumalai Across the valley from Top Station, and around 40 km east of Munnar, the small plantation of Kolukkumalai officially claims to pick the highest tea leaves in the world. The drive to the ridgetop at 2175 m takes two hours (the last section on a plantation road so bad it might be quicker to get out and walk) but the effort is repaid by astonishing views across misty valleys and distant peaks. It's worth being here for sunrise; set off by 0400 and wrap up warm for the journey. A path through the tea bushes leads down to the 1930s factory, where you can sample the local product and watch the antique processing equipment in action. As the plantation is privately owned you need to join a tour to get in; **Kestrel Adventures** (see What to do, page 938) is the main operator.

Eravikulam/Rajamalai National Park ① *21 km northeast of Munnar, www.eravikulam.org, closed Feb-Mar and during the monsoons, Rs 370.* The park was set up in 1978 to preserve the endangered Nilgiri tahr (*Nilgiri ibex*). The conservation programme has resulted in the park now supporting the largest population of the species in the world, of nearly 2000. The sure-footed wild goats live in herds on the steep black rocky slopes of the Anaimudi Mountains. They are brownish, have short, flat horns with the male carrying a thick mane, and can be easily seen around the park entrance. There are also elephants, sambars, gaurs, macaques and the occasional leopard and tiger. The scenery is magnificent, though the walks into the forest are steep and strenuous. There is an easier paved path from the park entrance following the road immediately below the bare granite outcrop of the Naikundi Hill to the Rajamalai Gap. The Forest Department issues a limited number of permits to trek through the park on the **Goldsbury Track**.

Chinnar Wildlife Sanctuary ① *Contact the Forest Information Office in Munnar, T04865-231587.* Adjoining Eravikulam to the north, and spreading down the eastern slope of the ghats into Tamil Nadu, Chinar Wildlife Sanctuary is rarely visited but offers near-guaranteed sightings of elephant and bison. Accommodation is in the form of treehouses and log huts.

Tourist information

DTPC
Old Munnar Bazar, Munnar, T0486-231516,
www.dtpcidukki.com.
The DTPC runs tours of plantations and rents
cycles. Try also the free **Tourist Information
Service** in the Main Bazar opposite the bus
stop, run by Joseph Iype, a veritable mine of
information. For trekking information, Senthil
Kumar of local eco-guiding outfit **Kestrel
Adventures** (see page 938) is hard to beat.

Where to stay

Hotel prices throughout Munnar are high for
what you get, particularly in the summer high
season. Cheaper places can be found around
the bazar and bus stand, where touts will greet
you brandishing the cards of 25-room concrete
block 'cottages'.

The road from Kochi

$$$$-$$$ Plantation Homestay
Mundackal Estate, Pindimana, Kothamangalam
Junction, T0485 257 0717.
4 rooms in a homestay that lies deep inside a
rubber, pepper and coconut plantation. Daisy is
a mean cook and offers lessons (US$20), while
George arranges boat trips to the bird sanctuary.

$$$ Periyar River Lodge
Anakkayam, Kothamanagalam, T(0)9526-
100118, www.periyarriverlodge.com.
2-bedroom cottage in a rubber plantation on
the banks of Periyar River right next to Thattekad
Bird Sanctuary. Bamboo rafting, fishing, forest
treks, jeep safaris to 30-m-high waterfalls for
swimming, boat and bike tours. Lounge, en suite,
river views. Keralite food.

Munnar

$$$$-$$$ Nature Zone
Pullipara, 5 km up dirt track off Letchmi Rd,
west of TN Bus Stand, T(0)9745-433330.
Arriving here is like stepping into Jurassic Park –
you have to get out of the car and unhook the
elephant-repelling electric fence. A leading
outward-bound training centre with stunning
valley views, the drawcards here are the jungly
remoteness and the 2 rustic-chic treehouses, with

branches growing right through the room. The
safari tents down at ground level are okay, but get
pretty musty, and maintenance can leave a bit to
be desired. On-site canteen serves good food.

$$$$-$$$ Tall Trees
Bison Valley Rd, 3 km south of Munnar,
T(0)9447-111726, www.ttr.in.
A drastic price hike means the rather musty
cottages here offer dubious value, but the
location, beneath a canopy of ancient rainforest,
is undeniably magic.

$$$$-$$$ Windermere Estate
Pothamedu, T04865-230512,
www.windermeremunnar.com.
Standalone cottages and an alpine farmhouse
with 5 rooms and an elegant and utterly
comfortable planters' bungalow with 3 rooms.
The whole complex is set around an enormous
granite boulder, that offers sweeping views
of cloud-draped mountains, and there's a
fantastically light and airy reading room done out
with rustic timber furniture and vaulted ceilings.
Pricey but recommended.

$$$ Tea County (KTDC)
1 km north of Munnar, T04865-230460,
www.teacountymunnar.com.
67 immaculately kept rooms set in 3 ha of neat
garden, good facilities, beautiful views, great
walking, own transport essential.

$$$-$$ East End
Temple Rd, Munnar, T04865-230451,
www.eastend.in.
18 pleasant rooms and some cottages (solar
heated water), good but pricey restaurant,
attractively designed, quiet garden location.

$$$-$$ Olive Brook
Bison Valley Rd, Pothamedu,
3 km south of Munnar, T04865-230588,
www.olivebrookmunnar.com.
9 well-appointed but slowly declining double
rooms in beautiful lush location on a cardamom
farm, excellent alfresco barbecues on request.
Price includes meals, trekking and cookery classes.

$$ Isaac's Residency
Top Station Rd, Munnar, T04865-230501.
Excellent quality, 32 lovely rooms with
contemporary furnishings, Executive rooms with
great views, 2 restaurants, bar. Recommended.

$$ John's Cottage
MSA Rd, near Munnar Supply Association, T(0)9447-331831, www.johnscottage homestaymunnar.com.
Small bungalow home in a well-tended lawn running down to the river, with 8 clean rooms. Indian/Chinese food or use of kitchen.

$$-$ Zina Cottages
Near Hill View Hotel in Tata tea plantation, T04865-230349, www.zinacottagesmunnar.com.
Basic and slightly gloomy rooms in a colonial house, but the owners are friendly and the plantation views spectacular. Ask at the **Tourist Information Service** in the bazar (see page 937).

$ Arafa Tourist Home
Upper Bazar, Munnar, T04865-230788.
Riverside lodge with 14 non-a/c rooms with TV and phone. Handy for late-night bus arrivals. Noise travels, but the rooms are clean and good value.

$ Theresian Cottages
North of Munnar before Tea County, T0773-6434405.
3 rooms open off the shared living room of this sweet little 1930s house, and though they're fairly small and dark, each comes with a fireplace, chaise-longue and clean bathroom.

Restaurants

$$ The Greens
East End (see Where to stay).
Pleasant, glassed-in veranda serving good food, or go for the cheap simple meals in the eatery below.

$ Saravana Bhavan
MG Rd.
Clean, cheap and friendly place serving great *dosas* and huge Kerala-style *thalis* on banana leaves.

Bars and clubs

High Range Club
T04865-230253, www.highrangeclub munnar.com.
Charming colonial-style planters' club, members only (or with reciprocal arrangements), visit by asking a planter to introduce you.

KDH Club
On side road opposite DTPC office.
For Tata staff, old-world, visit with permission, excellent pool table.

Shopping

Good for tea, cardamom and pepper.

Munnar Supply Assoc (MSA), *next to tourist information.* Established in 1900, it's a bit of the old world, where you can get everything. Tailors in the bazar can copy your garments in 24 hrs. The newer Main Bazar is to the north.
Uravu, *near Ambady Junction, Idukki, T(0)9387-469369, www.uravu.org.* Fair trade outfit supporting local producers of agrihorticultural products, bamboo products, processed foods, handicrafts, forest honey, spices tea and coffee.

What to do

DTPC, *see Tourist information, page 937.* Runs tours to Tea Valley (0900-1800, Rs 400) and Sandal Valley and Wildlife (1000-1800, Rs 400).
Kestrel Adventures, *PB No 44, Top Station Rd, T(0)9447-031040, www.kestreladventures.com.* Senthil Kumar leads a team of 9 specialist guides, some expert in birds, others in tea growing and history. Highly recommended for camping and trekking, wildlife spotting in Chinnar Wildlife Sanctuary, and the only company in town that can get you into Kolukkumalai for sunrise. Also offers rock climbing, mountain bike tours/hire and jeep safaris.

Transport

Bike hire From the tourist information office, Rs 50 per day. **Kestrel Adventures** (see What to do) has 18-speed mountain bikes.

Bus State buses start and terminate at 2 separate stands south of town, but also call at the **Town Bus Stand** near the market. Enquiries, T04865-230201. Frequent services to **Mattupetty** (30 mins), **Devikulam** (30 mins), **Adimali** (1 hr) and **Top Station** (1 hr). Daily to **Coimbatore** (6 hrs); **Ernakulam/Kochi** (4½ hrs); **Kodaikkanal** 0700 via **Udumalpettai**, change for Palani and Kodai. If the Palani–Kodai Rd is closed a further bus goes to Vatalakundu and then Kodai; **Kottayam** (5 hrs); **Madurai** via **Theni** (5 hrs); **Thekkady** (4½ hrs), leaves from stop next to the post office; **Thiruvananthapuram** (9 hrs), **Thrissur** via **Perumbavoor** (5 hrs).

Jeeps/taxis Shared jeeps and minibus taxis for **Eravikulam** and **Mattupetty Lake** wait around the post office.

Thrissur, Palakkad
& the River Nila

The blue thread of the River Nila, Kerala's equivalent of the Ganges and the crucible of much of the state's rich cultural heritage, stitches together a collection of fascinating sights and experiences in the rarely explored central belt of Kerala between Kochi and Kozhikode. Busy Thrissur, the state's cultural capital, is unmissable in April and May when it holds its annual Pooram festival and millions pack into the city's central square, sardine-style, to watch the elephant procession and fireworks display. Coastal Guruvayur, meanwhile, is among Kerala's most sacred Hindu pilgrimage spots; it is home to one of India's wealthiest temples as well as an elephant yard where huge tuskers and their mahouts relax before they hit the road for the next festival. Inland, the Palakkad Gap cuts a broad trench through the Western Ghats, the only natural break in the mountain chain, providing a ready conduit for roads, railway lines, innumerable waves of historical migrants, and blasts of scorching air from the roasted plains of Tamil Nadu. Palakkad itself is now known as Kerala's granary, and makes a good stopover point on the route to or from Tamil Nadu.

Essential Thrissur, Palakkad and the River Nila

Finding your feet

Trains on the main north–south line stop in Thrissur and Shoranur Junction, a handy jumping-off point for the River Nila. Trains from Kerala to Coimbatore and Chennai call at Palakkad. There are bus connections from these towns to the smaller centres, though to properly explore the cultural and historical riches of the area it's much more efficient to hire a guide and driver. See Transport, page 942.

Thrissur (population 317,500) sits at the west end of the Palakkad Gap, which runs through the low pass between the Nilgiri and the Palani hills. The route through the ghats is not scenic but it has been the most important link to the peninsula interior since Roman times. Thrissur is built round a hill on which stand the Vadakkunnathan Temple and an open green, which form the centre of the earth-shaking festivities. The town's bearings are given in cardinal directions from this raised 'Round'.

Vadakkunnathan Temple
Open 0400-1030, 1700-2030, non-Hindus not permitted inside except during the Pooram festival.

A predominantly Siva temple, is also known as the Rishabhadri or Thenkailasam ('Kailash of the South'). At the shrine to the Jain Tirthankara Vrishabha, worshippers offer a thread from their clothing, symbolically to cover the saint's nakedness. The shrine to Sankara Narayana has superb murals depicting stories from the *Mahabharata*. It is a classic example of the Kerala style of architecture with its special pagoda-like roof richly decorated with fine woodcarving.

The temple plays a pivotal role in the **Pooram** celebrations, held during April and May. This magnificent eight-day cacophony of a festival is marked by colourful processions joined by people of all religious groups irrespective of caste. Platoons of elephants decked out in gold, palm leaves and lamps march to the Vadakkunnathan Temple carrying priests and idols, to the accompaniment of dozens of drums, cymbals and pipes. On the final day temple teams meet on the Tekkinkadu maidan for a showdown of drumming and *Kudumattam* (the name roughly translates as 'umbrella swapping' – one of Kerala's more surreal spectator sports) before a huge fireworks display brings proceedings to a close. In September and October, there are live performances of *Chakyarkothu*, a classical art form. There is a small elephant compound attached to the temple.

Other sights
The **Town Hall** is a striking building housing an art gallery with murals from other parts of the state. In the **Archaeological Museum** ① *Town Hall Rd, Tue-Sun 0900-1500*, ask to see the royal chariot. Next door, the **Art Museum** has woodcarvings, sculptures, an excellent collection of traditional lamps and old jewellery. Nearby, **Thrissur Zoo** ① *Tue-Sun 1000-1700, small fee*, is known for its snake collection. The impressive **Lourdes Church** has an interesting underground shrine.

Guruvayur
As one of the holiest sites in Kerala, Guruvayur, 29 km west of Thrissur, is a heaving pilgrimage centre, filled with stalls and thronged from 0300 to 2200 with people wanting to take *darshan* of Guruvayurappan.

Sri Krishna Temple The 16th-century Sri Krishna Temple is one of the richest in India, and there is a waiting list for the auspicious duty of lighting its oil lamps that stretches to 2025.

On well-augured marriage days there is a scrum in which couples are literally shunted from the podium by new pairs urgently pressing behind them in the queue, and the whole town is geared towards the wedding industry. The temple has an outer enclosure where there is a tall gold-plated flagpost and a pillar of lamps. The sanctum sanctorum is in the two-storeyed srikoil, with the image of the four-armed Krishna garlanded with pearls and marigolds. Photography of the tank is not allowed. Non-Hindus are not allowed inside and are not made to feel welcome.

Guruvayur Devaswom Institute of Mural Painting ① *Mon-Fri 1000-1600*. The temple's inner sanctum is off limits to non-Hindus, but

Tip...
Devotees of the Sri Krishna Temple aren't afraid to put their money where their mouths are: in one month alone the temple can earn as much as Rs 11 million, along with just short of 4 kg of gold and almost 14 kg of silver.

you can visit this tiny educational institute where you can meet and buy finished works from the next generation of mural painters. As with *Kathakali*, the age-old decorative arts of temple culture steadily declined during the 20th century under the weakening structure of feudalism and opposition to the caste system. When the temple lost three walls to a fire in 1970 there were hardly any artists left to carry out renovation, prompting authorities to build the school in 1989. Today the small institute runs a five-year course on a scholarship basis for just 10 students. Paintings sell for Rs 500-15,000 depending on size, canvas, wood, etc.

Punnathur Kotta Elephant Yard ① *0900-1700, bathing 0900-0930, Rs 25, take care as elephants can be dangerous, buses from Thrissur (45 mins).* Situated within a fort 4 km northwest of town, temple elephants (68 at the last count) are looked after here and wild ones are trained. There are some interesting insights into traditional animal training but this is not everyone's cup of tea. Though captive, the elephants are dedicated to Krishna and appear to be well cared for by their attendants. The elephants are donated by pious Hindus but religious virtue doesn't come cheap: the elephants cost Rs 500,000 each.

Kodungallur and around

At one time Kodungallur, 50 km southwest of Trichur on the border of Ernakulam District, was the west coast's major port, and the capital of the Chera king Cheraman Perumal.

Nearby **Kottapuram** is where St Thomas is believed to have landed in AD 52. The commemorative shrine was built in 1952. Kodungallur is also associated by tradition with the arrival of the first Muslims to reach India by sea. Malik-ibn-Dinar is reputed to have built India's first Juma Masjid, 2 km from town. Tiruvanchikulam Temple and the Portuguese fort are worth visiting. The Syrian Orthodox church in **Azikode** blends early Christian architecture in Kerala with surrounding Hindu traditions. Thus the images of Peter and Paul are placed where the *dvarapalas* (doorkeepers) of Hindu temples would be found, and the portico in front of the church is for pilgrims.

Listings Thrissur (Trichur) and around

Tourist information

Thrissur

DTPC Thrissur
Palace Rd, T0487-232 0800, www.dtpcthrissur.com.

Guruvayur

DTPC Guruvayur
Vyjayanti Building, East Nada, Guruvayur, T0487-255 0400.

Where to stay

Thrissur
Reserve ahead for Pooram, when prices rocket.

$$$$-$$$ Kadappuram Beach Resort
Nattika Beach, southwest of Thrissur, T0487-239 4988, www.kadappurambeachresorts.com.
Self-contained complex of bungalows and cottages in traditional Kerala design, but the emphasis here is on the Ayurveda and most come for the 14-day *panchakarma*. The Ayurveda centre is functional and not luxurious, but massage and medical attention are excellent.

After treatments, cross the pretty river to a huge garden of coconut trees and hammocks that separates the hotel from the sea.

$$ Luciya Palace
Marar Rd, T0487-242 4731, www.hotelluciyapalace.com.
35 rooms, 15 a/c, and 2 suites. Large, clean and quiet rooms, TV, garden restaurant, internet next door, good service, very pleasant hotel.

$ Bini Tourist Home
Round North, T0487-233 5703, www.binitouristhome.com.
24 rooms, TV, shower, 10 a/c, basic but clean and spacious rooms, restaurant, bar.

$ Railway Retiring Rooms
Well looked after and very good value.

Guruvayur

$$$-$$ Krishna Inn
East Nada, Guruvayur, T0487-255 0777, www.krishnainn.in.
Glossy hotel with white marble floors and spacious. 24-hr coffee shop, vegetarian, multi-cuisine **Thulasi** restaurant.

$$ Hotel Gokulam Vanamala
South Nada, Guruvayur, T0487-255 5213.
Popular with domestic tourists, very clean rooms
with big beds and TV, telephone and hot water.
A/c, vegetarian restaurant (Keralite food, 0600-
2300), laundry.

$$ Mayura Residency
West Nada, Guruvayur, T0487-255 7174,
www.hotelmayuraguruvayur.com.
65 good-value, well-appointed rooms in high-rise
hotel with excellent views from its rooftop. 24-hr
coffee shop, **Amrutham** vegetarian (continental,
South or North Indian) restaurant.

Restaurants

Most **$** hotels have good restaurants,
particularly Siddhartha Regency's Golden Fork,
on Veliyannur Rd near the station. In general,
though, eating out is still somewhat frowned on
by the traditional Brahmin families of Kerala, so
most eating options are down-at-heel *dhabas*.

Thrissur

$$ City Centre
Next to Priya Tourist Home.
Western snacks, bakery and good supermarket.

$$ Navaratna
Naduvilal, Round West, T0487-242 1994.
Open 1000-2300.
Pure vegetarian North Indian restaurant divided
into booths.

$ Elite Bharat
Chembottil Lane.
Good honest Keralan and South Indian food –
dosas, puttu, thalis – served without ceremony
to huge crowds of locals.

$ Sapphire
Railway Station Rd. Open 0630-2200.
Excellent lime green and stone eatery dishing
up *thalis* and the best chicken biryanis in town.

Festivals

Thrissur
Jan-Feb Several temple festivals involving
elephants are held in the surrounding villages
which can be as rewarding as **Pooram**
(eg **Koorkancherry Thaippoya Mahotsavam**, or
Thaipooya Kavadiyattam, held at Sri Maheswara
Temple, Koorkancherry, 2 km from Thrissur).
Also held at the end of Feb is the **Uthralikavu
Pooram**, at its most colourful at the Sri Ruthura

Mahakalikavu Temple, Parithipra, Vodakancherry,
en route to Shornur Junction.
End Mar 7-day **Arratupuzha Festival** at the
Ayappa Temple, 14 km from Thrissur. On the
5th day the deity parades with 9 decorated
elephants, while on the 6th day **Pooram** is
celebrated on a grand scale with 61 elephants in
the temple grounds.
Apr-May The magnificent 8-day **Pooram**, a
grand festival with elephants, parasols, drums
and fireworks, should not be missed. Several
temples in town participate but particularly the
Thiruvambady and Paramekkavu. It is marked
by very noisy, colourful processions, joined by
people from all religious groups, irrespective of
caste. The festivities are held 1300-1700 and again
at night from around 2000. Elaborately bedecked
elephants (each temple allowed up to 15) specially
decorated with lamps and palm leaves, march to
the Vadakkunnathan Temple carrying priests and
deities to the accompaniment of extraordinary
drumming. On the final day temple teams meet
on the Tekkinkadu *maidan* for the drumming and
Kudumattam competition; the festival terminates
with a huge display of fireworks.
Aug/Sep **Kamdassamkadavu Boat Races** at
Onam. Also performances of **Pulikali**, unique to
Thrissur, when mimers dressed as tigers dance
to drumbeats.

Guruvayur
The following festivals take place at Punnathur
Kotta, 4 km out of town.
Feb/Mar **Utsavam**, 10 days of festivities
start with an elephant race and continue with
colourful elephant processions and performances
of *Krishnanattom* dances. Details from Kerala
tourist offices.
Nov-Dec 5-day **Ekadasi** with performances of
Krishnanattom, a forerunner of *Kathakali* – an
8-day drama cycle.

Transport

Bus There are yellow-top local buses available.
For long distance, there are 3 bus stands.
KSRTC, near railway station, T0487-242 1842,
southwest of 'Round', including several to
Alappuzha (3½ hrs), **Bengaluru** (10 hrs),
Coimbatore (3 hrs), **Guruvayur** (1 hr), **Kochi**
(2 hrs), **Kozhikode**, **Chennai** (13 hrs), **Palakkad**
and **Thiruvananthapuram** (7 hrs). North
(Priyadarshini), just north of 'Round', buses to
Cheruthuruthy, **Ottapalam**, **Palakkad**. Sakthan
Thampuran, 2 km south of 'Round', for frequent
private buses to **Guruvayur**, **Kannur**, **Kozhikode**.

Train Enquiries, T0487-242 3150. All trains connecting Kochi with points north stop in Thrissur. **Ernakulam**: more than 20 trains a day, 1¼ hrs. **Chennai**: *Chennai Mail 12624*, 2040, 10½ hrs. **Bengaluru**: *Bangalore Intercity Exp 12678*, 1020, 9½ hrs. **Mangalore**: *Parasuram Exp 16650*, 1240, 7½ hrs (via **Kozhikode**, 3 hrs).

★ Along the River Nila

verdant cultural region; the place to come for authentic Ayurveda

North of Thrissur the road and railway cut through lush countryside of paddy fields, quiet villages and craggy red hills mantled with coconut and rubber plantations, before crossing the wide sandy bed of the Bharatapuzha River at Shoranur. Known to the people who populate its banks as Nila, this is Kerala's longest river, rising on the eastern side of the Palakkad Gap and winding lazily through 209 km to spill into the Arabian Sea at the bustling fishing port of Ponnani.

Though its flow is severely depleted by irrigation dams and its bed gouged by sand miners, the importance of the river to Kerala's cultural development is hard to overstate: Ayurveda, *Kathakali* (see box, page 925) and the martial art *Kalaripayattu* were all nurtured along the banks of the Nila, not to mention the cacophonous classical music that soundtracks festive blow-outs like the Thrissur Pooram. Folk tradition too is vibrantly represented: elaborately adorned devotees carry colourful effigies to temple festivals, snake worshippers roam house to house performing ancient rituals to seek blessing from the serpent gods, and village musicians sing songs of the paddy field mother goddess, passed down from generation to generation.

Despite all this, the Nila thus far remains refreshingly untouched by Kerala's tourism boom, and few travellers see more of it than the glimpses afforded by the beautiful train ride between Shoranur and Kozhikode. This is in part because there's little tourist infrastructure, few genuine 'sights', and no easy way for a travellers to hook into the cultural scene. Traditional potters and brass-smiths labour in humble workshops behind unmarked houses, while performers (singers and dancers by night, coolies, plumbers and snack sellers by day) only get together for certain events. With your own transport you can search out any number of beautiful riverside temples, but unless you join one of the superb storytelling tours run by local guiding outfit **The Blue Yonder** (see page 944), Kerala Kalamandalam (see below) might be the only direct contact you have with the Nila's rich heritage.

Kerala Kalamandalam

3 km south of river, Cheruthuruthy, south of Shoranur Junction, T04884-262305, www.kalamandalam. org, Mon-Fri 0930-1300, closed public holidays and Apr-May. Frequent private buses from Thrissur's northern bus stand (ask for Vadakkancheri Bus Stand) go straight to Kalamandalam, taking about 1 hr.

This residential school is dedicated to preserving the state's unique forms of performance art. Founded in 1930, after the provincial rulers' patronage for the arts dwindled in line with their plummeting wealth and influence, the Kalamandalam spear-headed a revival of *Kathakali* dancing, along with *ottam thullal* and the all-female drama *mohiniyattam*. The school and the state tourism department run a fascinating three-hour tour of the campus, 'A Day With the Masters' (US$25), with in-depth explanations of the significance and background of the art forms, the academy and its architecture, taking you through the various open air *kalaris* (classrooms) to watch training sessions. There are all-night *Kathakali* performances on 26 January, 15 August, and 9 November. *Koodiyattam*, the oldest surviving form of Sanskrit theatre, is enshrined by UNESCO as an 'oral and intangible heritage of humanity'.

Ponnani

In the bustling port town of Ponnani at the mouth of the Nila, the **Ponnani Juma Masjid** ① *42 km northwest of Thrissur, nearest train station 21 km away at Kuttipuram; admission to non-Muslims not assured, dress conservatively, women should wear a headscarf*, was built in the mid-15th century by the spiritual leader Zainudhin Ibn Ali Ibn Ahmed Ma'bari, who employed a Hindu carpenter to design the exterior. Ignorant of traditional Islamic architecture, the carpenter carved the elaborate teak-wood façade to resemble a Hindu temple incorporating many intricate Hindu designs. The carpenter was killed by a fall from the roof as he finished construction and lies buried inside the mosque. The nearby fishing docks are a hive of activity, but prepare for plenty of attention from local boys.

Listings Along the River Nila

Where to stay

$$$$-$$$ River Retreat
Palace Rd, Cheruthuruthy, T0488-426 2244, www.riverreatreat.in.
Heritage hotel and Ayurvedic resort in the former (and much-extended) home of the maharajas of Kochi. Spacious rooms have a/c, TV and modern baths, great views onto large tree-filled garden that backs onto the Nila. Period furniture adds a nice touch to the airy communal areas. Tours of the local area, restaurant, bar, pool, Wi-Fi.

$$$ Ayurveda Mana
Peringode, via Kootanadu, T0487-256 0228, www.poomullyayurvedamana.com.
Authentic Ayurveda centre set in a fascinating 600-year-old *illam*, with treatments following the traditional methods of Poomully Aram Thampuran, a renowned expert in the discipline. Quiet airy rooms (all with TV) open onto shady veranda and peaceful manicured grounds. Full range of health care treatments available and specialized therapies for arthritis, sports injuries, infertility, etc. All treatments include individually assessed diet, massage and medicine.

$$$ Maranat Mana
Old Ooty–Mysore Rd, Pandikkad (an hour's drive north of Pattambi), T0493-128 6252, www.maranatmana.com.
Special homestay in a traditional *namboodhiri* (Kerala Brahmin) household. Hosts Praveen and Vidya have sensitively converted the 160-year-old guesthouse attached to their ancestral home into 3 cool and airy rooms, all with fans and modern baths. You can visit the sprawling main family residence, one of the last surviving examples of Keralite *pathinaru kettu* ('four courtyards') architecture, which contains a Ganesh shrine to which devotees flock from far and wide. Delicious vegetarian meals included, and local tours, Ayurvedic treatments, yoga classes, cultural activities can be arranged. Fascinating and highly recommended, reservations essential.

$$$ Olappamanna Mana
Vellinezhi, T0466-228 5797, www.olappamannamana.com.
Majestic manor house, in rosewood, teak and jackfruit trees, to the highest Keralite Hindu caste of *namboodris*, parts of which date back 3 centuries. Pure vegetarian cuisine, no alcohol, 6 bedrooms, with bathroom and fan, no a/c.

What to do

If you're in search of Ayurvedic healing at its most authentic and traditional, the River Nila and Palakkad regions, far inland from the pore-clogging salt air coming off the Arabian Sea, are the best places in Kerala to find it. But don't come here expecting 5-star spa masseurs who'll tiptoe around your Western foibles about comfort and bodily privacy. These treatments are administered to you in the almost-raw, on hard wooden beds amid buckets of oil – and when your treatment is over your torturer may accompany you to the shower to make sure you thoroughly degrease.

Body and soul
Arya Vaidya Sala, *Kottakal town, T0483-274 3380, www.aryavaidyasala.com.* One of the biggest and best Ayurvedic centres in India, with a fully equipped hospital offering 4-week *panchkarma* treatments as well as on-site medicine factory and research department.

Tour operators
The Blue Yonder, *T0413-450 2218, www.theblue yonder.com.* Award-winning responsible travel tour operator, focused on conserving local culture and traditions. Tours are carried out in a way that allows travellers to become fully immersed in the region's folk traditions and fables, and travelling here can feel like being in the Arabian Nights. Flexible, individual itineraries can include homestays, cultural performances, monsoon rafting in self-built bamboo-and-inner-tube rafts, backwater cruises, legend and heritage trails. Heartily recommended.

Kerala's rice cellar, prosperous Palakkad (population 130,700) has long been of strategic importance for its gap – the only break in the mountain ranges that otherwise block the state from Tamil Nadu and the rest of India. Whereas once this brought military incursions, today the gap bears tourist buses from Chennai and tractors for the rich agricultural fields here. Few educated modern Keralites care to plough using the old bullock carts (although the tradition is kept alive through *kaalapoottu*, a series of races between yoked oxen held in mud-churned paddy fields every January). The name Palakkad comes from pala, a type of tree, and kadu, which means forest; the area was once thickly covered in forests of this type, but these have long been usurped by paddy fields.

Palakkad Fort
The region is filled with old architecture of *illams* and *tharavadus* belonging to wealthy landowners making a visit worthwhile in itself – but chief among the actual sights is Palakkad Fort, a granite structure in Palakkad town itself, built by Haider Ali in 1766, and taken over by the British in 1790. It now has a Hanuman temple inside. Ask directions locally to the 500-year-old Jain temple of **Jainimedu** in the town's western suburbs, a 10-m-long granite temple with Jain *Thirthankaras* and *Yakshinis* built for the Jain sage Chandranathaswami. Only one Jain family is left in the region, but the area around this temple is one of the only places in Kerala where remnants of the religion have survived.

Kalpathy
Also well worth visiting in the region are the many traditional **Brahmin villages**: Kalpathy, 10 km outside Palakkad, holds the oldest Siva temple in Malabar, dating from AD 1425 and built by Kombi Achan, then Raja of Palakkad. But the village itself, an 800-year-old settlement by a self-contained Tamil community, is full of beautiful houses with wooden shutters and metal grills and is now a World Heritage Site that gives you a glimpse of village life that has been held half-frozen in time for nearly 1000 years. The temple here is called **Kasiyil Pakuthi Kalpathy** meaning Half Banares because its situation on the river is reminiscent of the Banares temple on the Ganges. A 10-day car festival in November centres on this temple and features teak chariots tugged by people and pushed by elephants.

Nelliyampathy
56 km from Palakkad town.

This hill station, with a tiny community of planters, is famous for its oranges, but there are also orchids, bison, elephant and butterflies in abundance. The view across the Keralite plains from Seethakundu is stunning; a third of the district lies spread out under you. The area has good trekking, too.

Megalith trail: Guruvayur to Kunnamkulam
The Palakkad Gap has been one of the few relatively easy routes through the ghats for 3000 years and this area is noted for its megalithic monuments. Megalithic cultures spread from the Tamil Nadu plains down into Kerala, but developed local forms. The small villages of Eyyal, Chovvanur, Kakkad, Porkalam, Kattakampala and Kadamsseri, between Guruvayur and Kunnamkulam, have hoodstones, hatstones, dolmens, burial urns and *menhirs*.

ON THE ROAD

Ramassery Iddli

Another unique feature of Palakkad is the *Ramassery Iddli* made at the Sarswathy tea stall, daily 0500-1830, iddli Rs 1.50, chai Rs 2.50. If you spend any time on the street in South India, your morning meal will inevitably feature many of these tasty steamed fermented rice cakes. Palakkad is home to a peculiar take on the dumpling, one that has been developed to last for days rather than having to be cooked from fresh. The four families in this poky teashop churn out 5000 *iddlis* a day. Originally settlers from somewhere near Coimbatore, in Tamil Nadu, over 100 years ago, they turned to making this variety of *iddli* when there wasn't enough weaving work to sustain their families. They started out selling them door to door, but pretty soon started to get orders for weddings. The *iddlis* are known to have travelled as far afield as Delhi, by plane in a shipment of 300. Manufacturers have started to arrive in order to buy the secret recipe.

Listings Palakkad (Palghat)

Tourist information

Palakkad DTPC
West Fort Rd, Palakkad, T0491-253 8996, www.dtpcpalakkad.com.

Where to stay

$$$$ Kalari Kovilakom
Kollengode, T0492-326 3155, www.kalarikovilakom.com.
The Maharani of Palakkad's 1890 palace has been restored to make this extremely disciplined yet very luxurious Ayurvedic retreat: the indulgence of a palace meets the austerity of an ashram. Treatments include anti-ageing, weight loss, stress management and ailment healing. Lessons include yoga, meditation, Ayurvedic cookery. Strictly no exertion (no sunbathing or swimming). No mod cons (TV, etc), bar, internet. Minimum stay of 14 days.

$$$ Kairali Ayurvedic Health Resort
Kodumbu, T0492-322 2553, www.ayurvedichealingvillage.com.
The 3-day packages at this excellent resort offer an easy entry to Ayurveda. Beautifully landscaped grounds include a dairy and farm, pool and tennis courts.

$$$ Kandath Tharavad
Thenkurussi, T0492-228 4124, www.tharavad.info.
A magical place tucked away in Palakkad's fields, 6 rooms in a 200-year-old mud and teak ancestral home with natural dyed floor tiles of ochre, terracotta and blue. Nadumuttams open out onto the stars and doors are thick wedges of teak and brass. Bagwaldas, your gracious host, will guide you through local customs and culture as engagingly as he steers you through the physical landscape.

$$-$ Fort Palace
West Fort Rd, Palakkad, T0491-253 4621, www.fortpalace.com. Rs 1500-3400 (plus taxes).
19 rooms, groovy old-style hotel some good a/c, restaurant, brash mock turrets. Satellite TV and hot water. Continental/Indian food in restaurant, and bar, both gloomy and packed (lawn service). Nice shared sit-out on 1st floor, spotless, large double beds. Chandeliers, wood panelling.

$$-$ Indraprastha
English Church Rd, Palakkad, T0491-253 4641, www.hotelindraprastha.com. Rs 1700-4000 (plus taxes).
Kitsch and cool: 30 rooms in 1960s block, dark wood, leather banquettes and bronze lettering. Dark bar permanently packed, lawn service, 24-hr vegetarian coffee shop, exchange, internet, bookshop. Multi-cuisine restaurant.

$ Garden House (KTDC)
Malampuzha, T0491-281 5217, www.ktdc.com. Rs 1250-1800 (plus taxes).
17 somewhat chintzy rooms in a 1-star government restaurant on hilltop overlooking the Malampuzha Dam, a popular picnic spot. Mostly non-a/c rooms, pleasant.

Restaurants

Be sure to try an *iddli* from the Sarswarthy tea stall, see box opposite.

$ Ashok Bhavan
GB Rd, Palakkad.
Modest vegetarian South Indian snacks.

$ Hotel Noor Jehan
GB Rd, Palakkad, T0491-252 2717.
Non-vegetarian a/c restaurant that specializes in *moplah biryani* and *pathiri*, rice chappatis.

$ KR Bakes
Palakkad. Open 0900-2300.
Puffs, ice creams, *halva* plus juice bar and savoury meals after 1600.

Transport

Bus KSRTC, buses run from the **Municipal Bus Stand**, T0491-252 7298, www.keralartc.com, to **Coimbatore**, **Kozhikode**, **Mannarghat** (Silent Valley), **Pollachi**.

Train The main **Junction station**, T0491-255 5231, is 5 km northeast of town. Some passenger trains also stop at the more central **Town station**. To **Coimbatore**: frequent trains all day, 1-1½ hrs, some continue to **Chennai** or **Bengaluru**. To **Ernakulam** (Kochi): many trains, 2½ hrs, all go via **Thrissur**, 1-2 hrs. To **Mangalore**:, 9 hrs, via **Kozhikode**, 4 hrs.

Malabar

The Malabar region is the unsung jewel of Kerala: the combination of the state's political administration in the south plus the pious Muslim community and orthodoxy of the Hindu population have made it more resistant to tourist development than the more easy-going Catholic-influenced stretch south from Kochi. Any cohesion between north and south Kerala is political, not cultural: Malabar was under the Madras Presidency before Independence, lumped together with the Travancore south only in 1956. The atmosphere couldn't be more different. The coastal towns of Kozhikode (formerly Calicut), Thalassery and Kannur are strongholds of the Muslim Moplah community, whose long-standing trading links with the Middle East have bred a deep cultural affinity that's reflected in the lime-green houses lining the roads and the increasing number of women seen in purdah. At the same time, Malabar is one of the best places to see Kerala's Hindu religious and cultural traditions in their proper context: *Theyyam* (the ritual temple dance that spawned *Kathakali*) and *Kalaripayattu* (the stunning martial art) are both practised here. Inland from Kozhikode, the glorious hilltop district of Wayanad experiences some of the heaviest rainfall in the world, and its familiar stubble of tea plantations is interspersed with some of the most stunning and accessible rainforest in the state.

Kozhikode (population 436,500) is a major commercial centre for northern Kerala and the centre for Kerala's timber industry; it is also dependent on the petro-dollar, as testified by the scores of direct flights to the Gulf each day. Around 1.2 million Keralites work in the Gulf, generating revenue of about US$12 billion for Kerala. It's also a jumping-off point for Wayanad.

The city itself is engaged in mostly small-scale retail. Off the brash and crowded main boulevard, tiny lanes thread between high laterite walls with everything happening on the street. Remnants of the spice trade remain and the markets are great. Court Road is home to pepper, the black gold that lured Vasco, as well as copra and coconut oil. There are beautiful wooden mosques built like Hindu temples, and in nearby Beypore, where the Chaliyar river meets the Arabian Sea, you still have half a chance of watching the birth of an *uru* – the massive deep-sea hauler-sized wooden boats that have been built by Muslim Khalasi shipbuilders with few technological changes since Cheraman Perumal ordered one for a trip to Arabia in the sixth century.

Kuttichera

The Sunni Muslim quarter of Kuttichera, behind the railway station to the west of town, holds several fascinating multi-tiered **wooden mosques**, set around a huge green pond to which flocks of white-capped elders gather in the late afternoon. Legend has it that a ghost within the pond seizes a human sacrifice each year, releasing the body after three days. The mosques date from the 15th century and bear a puzzlingly close resemblance to Hindu temple structures. **Mishkal Masjid** is one of the oldest, and was named for the wealthy trader who built it, but also look for **Jami Masjid** and **Munchunthi Palli**. The latter has a 13th-century *vattezhuthu* (inscribed slab of stone) that proclaims the donation of the land to the mosque by a Zamorin. Women should cover their head, shoulders and limbs in this area.

Note the size of the houses around here, which are known to accommodate more than 150 family members each. The *puyappala* tradition (literally translates as 'fresh husband') means that each marrying daughter takes the husband back into her parents' home. One house is supposed to have 300 people living under the same roof: each building has an average of three kitchens.

From here you can walk along Beach Road, where crumbling old buildings that were once trading centres are now being busily demolished. The beach itself is more of a town latrine than a place for swimming.

East Hill

The **Pazhassiraja Museum** ① *5 km north of the centre on East Hill, Tue-Sun 0900-1630, Rs 10*, has copies of original murals plus bronzes, old coins and models of the some of the area's megalithic monuments. Next door is the **art gallery**, with an excellent collection of paintings by Indian artists as well as wood and ivory carvings, and the **Krishna Menon Museum** ① *Mon and Wed 1000-1230, 1430-1700, free*, dedicated to the Keralite politician who became a leading left-wing figure in India's post-Independence Congress government.

Around Kozhikode

Kappad, 16 km north, and now the site of a poor, mainly Muslim fishing village, is where Vasco da Gama and his 170 sailors landed on 27th May 1498. There is an old plaque by the approach road to the beach commemorating the event. Although it is a pleasant spot, the sea is unsuitable for swimming since pollution from Kozhikode filters down this far and the beach itself is used as a toilet by the fishermen.

Essential Kozhikode (Calicut)

Finding your feet

Karipur airport, 25 km south, has connections with the Middle East as well as several major Indian cities. The station and main bus stand are on opposite sides of the town centre, both within easy reach of several hotels. Autos are widely available and surprisingly cheap. See Transport, page 951.

Beypore, half an hour south of Calicut, was once a significant port, but is now famous only for its boatyard, where families of Khalasis have used traditional methods to make *urus* (huge wooden vessels) for 1500 years. The wiry Khalasis craft the ships using memorized plans and ancient construction techniques, now mainly for the benefit of wealthy Arab clients who deploy them as luxury yachts or floating restaurants.

Listings Kozhikode (Calicut) *map below*

Tourist information

Kerala Tourism
Railway Station, T0495-270 2606,
www.dtpckozhikode.com.
Has limited information about the town. The branch at the railway station hands out brochures on North Kerala and can help with hotel bookings.

Where to stay

$$$ Harivihar Ayurvedic Heritage Home
Bilathikulam, T0495-276 5865,
www.harivihar.com.
In Calicut's pretty Brahminical suburbs, this immaculate former royal home is surrounded by lawns with giant mango and jackfruit trees and a beautiful green water tank where you can undertake pukka Ayurveda or study Indian

Kozhikode (Calicut)

Where to stay 🛏
Alakapuri Guest House **1**
Arora Tourist Home **2**
Asma Tower **3**

Hyson Heritage **4**
Malabar Palace **5**
Metro Tourist Home **6**

Restaurants 🍴
Dakshin **1**
Sagar **2**
Zain's **3**

philosophy, Sanskrit, vasthu and yoga in a small guesthouse setting run by conventional medics. You can also stay on a B&B basis, in one of 5 doubles and 3 singles. Gentle Sivananda yoga, Ayurveda from Coimbatore Arya Vaidya Pharmacy, no alcohol.

$$$ Tasara
Calicut–Beypore Rd, Beypore, T0495-241 4832, www.tasaraindia.com.
A weaving centre amid a garden of mango and jackfruit trees. Rooms with fan and basic bath. Vasudevan, Balakrishnan and their sisters have been running textile workshops here since 1979, and guests come to take courses in weaving, block-printing, batik, silkscreen and natural dyeing. Price includes all meals, tuition and activities. Good discounts for monthly stays, reservations essential.

$$$-$$ Malabar Palace
GH Rd, Manuelsons' Junction, T0495-272 1511, www.malabarpalacecalicut.com. Rs 3200-4750 (plus taxes).
52 a/c rooms, excellent a/c restaurant, bar, very helpful reception.

$$ Alakapuri
Moulana Mohammed Ali Rd, T0495-272 3451. Bar 1000-2200, dining hall 0700-2200.
40 rooms set around a charming garden brimming with plants and trees and lotus pond. Simple, spacious, with old furniture, phone, tubs and TV. Dates from 1958, and easily Calicut's most characterful mid-range option.

$$ Hotel Asma Tower
Mavoor Rd, T0495-272 3560, www.asmatower.com.
44 a/c and non-a/c rooms in gleaming new tower. Inside, expect 2-tone mint green decor, frosty a/c system, perfumed air, muzak and TV and telephone in every room. Good value.

$$-$ Hyson Heritage
114 Bank Rd, T0495-276 6423, www.hysonheritage.com.
A breezy, efficient and well-maintained business hotel, with 89 spotless, smallish rooms with phone, cable TV, bath, 47 a/c, set around a large courtyard. Ayurvedic treatments available.

$ Arora Tourist Home
Railway Station Rd, T0495-230 6889.
Not as ship-shape as the outside and ground floor suggest, but the huge, cheap rooms here are OK if you just want to dump your bags after a train ride. Street noise dies down overnight, but mosquitoes don't rest.

$ Metro Tourist Home
Mavoor Rd Junction, T0495-276 6582.
42 pleasing rooms, some with TV, a bit noisy, South Indian restaurant. Gloomy with grubby paintwork but clean sheets, big mirrors and good fans.

$ Railway Retiring Rooms
Very spacious, clean, good service.

Restaurants

$$ Malabar Palace
See Where to stay.
International, a/c, excellent food and service.

$ Dakshin
17/43 Mavoor Rd. Open 0630-2230.
Dead cheap place for *dosa*, pizza, cutlet and curd rice (meals from Rs 15).

$ Hotel Sagar
5/3305 Mavoor Rd, T0495-272 5058. Open 0530 onwards.
So popular they've launched their own hotel, and another restaurant (the original is already multistorey). Sagar is famous for its biriyanis, and also does superb breakfasts of *dahl* and *parotta*. Upstairs is for families and a/c rooms; downstairs is the cattle class.

$ Zain's Hotel
Convent Cross Rd.
A simple place run by a Muslim husband and wife. Mussels, biriyanis for Rs 30 and fish curries for Rs 15.

Transport

Air Kozhikode Airport is 30 km south of the city, T0495-271 9491. Domestic flights to **Mumbai**, **Coimbatore**, **Goa**, **Chennai**, and **Tiruchirapalli**. International flights to **Abu Dhabi** (UAE), **Bahrain**, **Doha**, Dubai, **Jeddah**, **Kuwait**, **Muscat**, and **Sharjah** (UAE).

Bus KSRTC, T0495-272 3796, www.keralartc.com, from bus stand on Mavoor Rd (near Bank Rd junction) to **Bengaluru**, **Thiruvananthapuram** (via Thrissur, Ernakulam, Alappuzha, Kollam), 0630-2200 (10 hrs), **Ooty** (see Wayanad, page 955). The **New Bus Stand**, T0495-272 2823, is further east on Mavoor Rd for private buses to the north including **Kannur**. Local buses operate from **Palayam Bus Stand** on Kallai Rd, T0495-272 0397.

Train Enquiries, T0495-270 1234. Trains to **Chennai**, **Coimbatore**, **Ernakulam** (4½ hrs) via **Shoranur** and **Thrissur**, **Goa**, **Mangalore** (5 hrs), **Mumbai**, **Thiruvananthapuram** (9½-10 hrs).

Mahé

The borders of the 9 sq km that make up French Kerala are marked not by baguette bakeries or pavement cafés, but by shops screaming 'Foreign Liquor'. By night, the 35,000 residents of this outpost of Pondicherry disappear to make way for the truckers who rush through to stock up on half-price whiskies and brandies, taking advantage of the colony's special tax status.

By day, however, Mahé is pretty enough: policemen wear French hats and the town is beautifully positioned on a slight hill overlooking the river. It was named after Mahé de Labourdonnais, who captured it for the French in 1725. Many people here still speak French and the very French **Church of St Theresa** celebrates its feast day on 14-15 October. The beaches to the south and north of town are dirty and are not safe for swimming due to undercurrents.

Thalassery (Tellicherry)

Like everywhere along the Malabar's increasingly gold coast, banks here double as pawnbrokers. Despite an obsession with wealth, at the wide, tree-covered street level you'll find a town that's friendly, brilliantly walkable and lined with 19th-century shops complete with original wooden cupboards and cobwebs. It's a town of cricket, cakes and circuses. Author Herman Hesse's mother was born here.

Sights

Fort area and around Thalassery was set up by the British East India Company in 1683 to export pepper and cardamom. In 1708 they obtained permission to build a **fort** which, having survived a siege laid by Haidar Ali, is still standing today on a rocky promontory about 15 m above sea level. Its proud little gateway, raised on a flight of steps, is flanked by colourful mustachioed figures.

There are some attractive old buildings. The Armenian church is rather shabby now but the Catholic church still thrives though the population is largely *Moplah* (Kerala Muslims). The **Odathil Mosque**, believed to be 400 years old, is in the traditional Kerala style with a gabled roof and copper sheeting.

Mambally's Royal Biscuit Factory ① *Near the Old Police Station, T0490-232 1207, 0900-2030.* Established in 1880, claims to be where cake was first baked in Kerala. Nowadays you'll find jam rolls, ketchup, Nestlé milky bars and lime pickle along with the fresh bakes. The downstairs of the double-decker shops is crowded with hessian sacks full of cinnamon from China, cloves from Madagascar, raisins from Afghanistan and star anise from China and Vietnam. Some of the owners are third generation traders.

Fish market ① *0600-1800.* This is one of the liveliest fish markets in Kerala. Men with cleavers stand tall over barracudas and manta, while stacks of clams, mussels, shrimp and mackerel are constantly replenished with new loads. Fish are then sped along the state highway to reach markets in Kochin and Mangalore.

Kalaris and circus training Thalassery is also a centre for training in gymnastics and circus acts, so street performers and acrobats are not uncommon; 90% of India's circus companies originate here. You can see martial arts in local *kalaris*: one of the best being the tricky-to-find *kalari* of **K Viswanathan Gurukkal** ① *MKG Kalari Sangham, Kuzhippangad, PO Chirakkara, T0490-237110, call in advance.*

Muzhapilangad Beach Some 8 km from Thalassery, is nicknamed 'Drive In Beach'. It is an unspoilt, beautifully picturesque 4-km-long stretch of golden sand edged by palm trees at the northern end. Amazingly empty most of the time, it earned its nickname from the local custom of ragging trucks and Ambassadors up and down its firm sands.

Listings Thalassery (Tellicherry)

Where to stay

$$$$ Ayisha Manzil
Court Rd, T(0)9496-189296, www.ayishamanzil.com. Rs16,500 (including all taxes and meals).
A delightful mid-19th-century, colonial-style heritage home overlooking the sea. 6 huge a/c rooms with carved teak and rosewood furniture, massive baths, lots of British and Malabari memorabilia, amazing fresh seafood and cookery courses, temple pond pool, superb panoramic views, excursions.

$$-$ Hotel Pranam
AVK Nair Rd, Narangapuram, T0490-232 0634.
14 cleanish rooms with bath – 4 with a/c, a little grubby. The a/c deluxe room has an extraordinary green carpeted sitting room attached.

$ Paris Presidency
New Paris Complex, Logan's Rd, T0490-234 2666, www.parispresidency.com. Rs 1200-2200 (plus taxes).
24 clean and comfortable rooms with baths, TV, phone, restaurant, wood furniture, bright white walls in busy shopping area. Multi-cuisine restaurant.

Restaurants

$$ Ayisha Manzil
Court Rd, T(0)9496-189296.
Peerless homestay, serving food unlike you'll get anywhere outside a home. Phone for meals in advance.

$ Royal Visitors' Family Restaurant
Pranam Tourist Home, T0490-234 4292. Open 0630-2300.
Grilled mussels, etc.

Kannur (Cannanore)

an agreeable town with good beaches, weaving and Theyyam rituals

Standing on raised ground with cliffs at the sea face, this town boasts a coconut-fringed coastline with some attractive beaches. Weavers' co-operatives and *beedi* factories provide employment but this is also a good place to watch *Theyyam* dances.

Fort area and around

The centre of the Moplah community (a group of Arab descent), Kannur was also the capital of the North Kolathiri Rajas for several hundred years. **Fort St Angelo** ① *0900-1800* was built out of laterite blocks by the Portuguese in 1505 and taken over by the British in 1790 as their most important military base in the south. The picturesque **Moplah town** is round the bay to the south of the fort. The attractive **Payyambalam Beach** is 2 km away.

Kanhirode Weavers' Cooperative Society

Koodali Kannur, T0497-285 7259, 0900-1700, free.

Handloom weavers produce silk and cotton saris, shirts, *lungis* and soft furnishings sold through local cooperatives. Kanhirode Weavers' Cooperative was founded in 1952 on Gandhian principle, has a yearly turnover of Rs 150 million (US$3.7 million) and exports 95% of its pure handloom fabric to the UK for the Futon Bed Company. Spun cotton is shipped in from Coimbatore, and dyed in huge vats after which the cooperative's 450 staff are expected to feed bobbins through the high wooden looms fast enough to make 42 m within 3½ days for women, or three for men. While some weave, others feed the raw heaps of cotton from wire frames onto wheels to make thread – in the silk section they use bicycle wheels. The daily wage is Rs 100 (US$2.45), and apparently the co-op is having trouble recruiting more of the caste, who, as caste rules relax, are going for higher paid jobs elsewhere. A visit here is well worth the journey.

Tourist information

DTPC
*At the railway station, T0497-270 3121,
www.dtpckannur.com.*

Where to stay

$$$-$$ Mascot Beach Resort
*Near Baby Beach, Burnassery, 2 km from the
centre, T0497-270 8445, www.mascotresort.com.*
Good rooms in high-rise business hotel
overlooking the sea, residents-only pool,
located in the quiet cantonment area (Ayurvedic
centre attached).

$$ Costa Malabari
*Near Adykadalaya Temple, 6 km south of town
(by bus, ask to get out at Thazhe Chowwa),
T0484-237 1761, www.touristdesk.in.*
An unpretentious guesthouse converted from
a warehouse with 4 rooms off a main hall. The
owners have authored a book on Kerala's festivals
and have encyclopaedic knowledge of the local
Theyyam scene. Difficult to get to and far from
the centre, but there are 5 idyllic, wholly empty
beaches within walking distance. Meals included.

$$-$ Royal Omars Thavakkara Kannur
*Very close to the railway station and
colourful market area, T0497-276 9091,
http://www.royalomars.com.*
Spanking new, with spacious standard non-
a/c doubles at bargain rates. 60 rooms, TV,
credit cards.

$ Hotel Savoy
Beach Rd, T0497-276 0074.
Bags of character in this super-clean, old-
fashioned complex of bungalow cottages set
around a lawn. A/c cottages are wonderfully
spacious and cool. Bar attached.

Restaurants

$$ Chakara Drive in Restaurant
*Cliff Exotel International, Payyabalam,
T0497-271 2197.*
Specials are sizzlers plus spicy fried *kallumakais*
mussels and Malabar biriyani.

$ Indian Coffee House
Fort Rd.
For snacks.

$ Mascot Beach Resort's Restaurants
*Near Baby Beach, Burnasseri, T0497-270 8445,
www.mascotresort.com.*
Some of the best top-end eating in town.

$ MVK Restaurant
SM Rd, T0497-276 7192. Open 1000-2200.
A local institution which has been packed
from its opening 50 years ago, thanks to its
commitment to fresh, home-ground spice mixes
for its biriyanis, their rice grains steeped in ghee.
Serves beautiful, potent lime tea too.

$ Regency Snacks and Fast Food
Opposite Sangeetha Theatre, SN Park Rd.
Popular café with locals.

$ Your Choice Restaurant
Fort Rd.
Authentic Malabari food.

Entertainment

Theyyam dance
At **Parssinikadavu Temple**, 20 km north of
Kannur, reached by bus. Performances (Dec-Mar)
of ritual dance theatre at dawn (taxi essential) and
often late afternoon to dusk. Pilgrims sometimes
seek blessing from the principal dancer who
may go into a trance after taking on the role of
Mutthapan, a manifestation of Siva as Hunter.

What to do

PVA Ayurvedic Multi Speciality Nursing Home,
*Onden Rd, T0497-276 0609, www.ayurvedaacharya.
com.* The down-at-heel PVA provides training
courses in Ayurveda as well as rejuvenation,
purification packages and direct treatments for
ailments like disc prolapse, psoriasis and obesity.
The 3 doctors here are highly regarded.

Transport

Bus Enquiries: T0497-270 7777. To **Kozhikode**
(2½ hrs), **Mangalore** (4½ hrs), **Mercara** (Coorg)
(6 hrs), **Mysore** (6 hrs).

Train Enquiries: T0497-270 5555. About 15 trains
a day run north to **Mangalore** (2½ hrs) and south
to **Kozhikode** (1½ hrs). Direct trains also run to
Bengaluru (14 hrs), **Chennai** (15 hrs) via **Palakkad**
(5 hrs), **Ernakulam** (6 hrs), **Madgaon** (8 hrs).

low-key towns with a well-preserved fort and unspoiled beaches

Bekal

Bekal, 16 km south of Kasaragod, has an ancient **fort** on the sea, the largest and best preserved in Kerala, which gives superb views of the coastline. Originally built by the Kadamba kings, the fort passed under the control of Vijayanagar and of Tipu Sultan before being brought into the hands of the East India Company. Excavations have exposed some interesting structures. Just outside the fort is the **Sri Mukhyaprana Temple**. North and south of the fort stretch long, largely unspoiled beaches, whose sands the Kerala tourism authorities visualize as a future Kovalam; so far there are just a couple of outlandish and isolated resorts. En route to Bekal the road passes **Ezhimala**, with a beach and a hill famous for its Ayurvedic herbs.

Kasaragod

Kasaragod is the northernmost town in Kerala. From the bus stand, the walk to the sea through a sprawling residential area – mainly Moplah – takes about 30 minutes. The beach is magnificent and deserted. You can walk a long way before scrambling back to the main road, crossing paddy fields, backwaters, and the Konkan railway line. For *Theyyam* and *Yakshagana* performances contact the **Kasaragod DTPC** (see below).

Listings Bekal and Kasaragod

Tourist information

Kasaragod DTPC
*Vidya Nagar, Kasaragod, T04994-256450,
www.dtpckasaragod.com.*

What to do

Bekal Resorts Development Corporation,
Bekal, T0467-227 2007, www.bekal.org. The
tourism-starved north wants a piece of the
houseboat action. Happily it has amazingly
pristine mangroves.

★ Wayanad

South India's most dramatic scenery, with a biosphere reserve

The forest-shrouded shoulders of Chembra Peak stand guard over Wayanad ('land of paddy fields'), a beguiling highland district of spice farms, tea plantations, waterfalls and weird upwellings of volcanic rock, inland from Kozhikode on the picturesque road to Mysore. An easy weekend break from either city, Wayanad so far remains delightfully unspoiled, and its cool misty mornings make a refreshing contrast with the sultry coastal plains.

It's also prime wildlife spotting territory: elephants patrol the woodlands of Muthanga and Tholpetty sanctuaries, while the dense *shola* forests around Vythiri are home to whistling thrushes, leaping frogs and giant squirrels. Many of the plantation bungalows have thrown open their doors as luxurious, atmospheric homestays, and the vogue for building treehouses makes this the best place in India if you want to wake up among the branches of a fig tree looking out over virgin forest.

Essential Wayanad

Finding your feet

The main transport hubs are Kalpetta and Sultan Bathery, with buses from both to Kozhikode and Mysore, and from Sultan Bathery south to Ooty. Local buses connect these towns to the local transfers. However, hiring a car can save a lot of time and hassle.

Kozikode to Muthanga

The road from Kozhikode to Wayanad corkscrews steeply up the Western Ghats, topping out after 65 km at **Vythiri**, a popular but low-key weekend getaway set amid stunning forests, with kayaking and nature walks available at **Pookot Lake**.

At Chundale (5 km from Vythiri) the road divides: the main route continues to busy **Kalpetta**, which offers plenty of hotels and banks but little in the way of charm, while the more appealing Ooty road leads east to **Meppadi**, the starting point for treks up wild and rugged **Chembra Peak** (2100 m) ① *Forest Range Office, Kalpetta Rd, Meppadi, T04936-282001, trekking Rs 1500 per group Plus 150 per person including guide; call ahead to check the track is open*, on whose summit lies a heart-shaped lake. Beyond Meppadi the road continues through the rolling teascapes of Ripon Estate, then through cardamom, coffee, pepper tree and vanilla plantations to reach **Vaduvanchal** (18 km).

Six kilometres south of here, **Meenmutty Falls** ① *Rs 600 per group including guide (ask for Anoop, who speaks English and knows the forest intimately)*, are Wayanad's most spectacular waterfalls, tumbling almost 300 m in three stages. An adventurous forest track leads down to a pool at the base of the second fall; take your swimming things.

Sulthan Bathery (Sultan's Battery), the main town of eastern Wayanad, was formerly known as Ganapathivattom, or 'the fields of Ganapathi'. In the 18th century Tipu Sultan built a fort here, but not much of it remains. Some 12 km southwest of the town are the **Edakkal Caves**, a natural deep crevice set high on a granite hill on which engravings dating back to the Neolithic era have been discovered. Around 30 km to the east is **Muthanga Wildlife Sanctuary** ① *www.wayanad-naturetours.com/place-to-visit.php, 0700-1000 and 1500-1700 (last entry 1600), Rs 110 Indians, RS 300 foreigners, jeep entry Rs 75; jeeps can be hired for Rs 600 per safari*, part of the Nilgiri Biosphere that also includes Karnataka's Bandipur and Tamil Nadu's Mudumalai National Parks. Jeep rides in the sanctuary, noted for its elephants, leave from the entrance gate.

Listings Wayanad

Tourist information

Wayanad DTPC
North Kalpetta, T04936-202134,
www.dtpcwayanad.com.
Run by the efficient and knowledgeable Dinesh, who is a good source of information on trekking and wildlife.

Where to stay

Wayanad is Kerala's treehouse capital, and has superb homestay options, but offers relatively little joy at the budget end. Cheaper places are generally restricted to Kalpetta and Sulthan Bathery.

$$$$ Vythiri Resort
6 km up dirt road east of highway, T04936-255366, www.vythiriresort.com.
Beautiful resort hidden beside a tumbling forest stream, with a choice of cute *paadi* rooms (low beds and secluded courtyards with outdoor shower), high-ceilinged cottages, or a pair of superb new treehouses in the branches of fig trees, one of which involves being hand-winched up and down. Leisure facilities include spa, pool (swimming and 8-ball), badminton and yoga, and

there's a good outdoor restaurant (buffet meals included in price) where you can watch monkeys trying to make away with the leftovers.

$$$ Aranyakam
Valathur (south of Ripon off Meppadi–Vaduvanchal Rd), T04936-280261, T(0)9447-781203, www.aranyakam.com.
Atmospheric homestay in Rajesh and Nima's 70-year-old bungalow, set amid a sea of coffee bushes and avocado trees. Huge rooms in the elegant main house come with raked bare-tile ceilings and balconies, or opt for the valley-facing treehouses where you can look out for deer and sloth bear while watching sunset over Chembra Peak. Nima serves genuine home-style Kerala food in the thatched, open-sided dining room.

$$$ Edakkal Hermitage
On road before Edakkal Caves,
T04936-260123, www.edakkal.com.
A sustainable tourism initiative with 5 comfortable cottages and a sweet, simple treehouse, built in, around and on top of a series of huge boulders. Tree frogs inhabit the bamboo-fringed pond, and the sunset views over paddy fields and mountain ranges are magic. The highlight, though, is dinner, served

in a natural grotto that's lit with hundreds of candles. Price includes meals.

$$-$ Haritagiri
Padmaprabha Rd, T04936-203145, www.hotelharitagiri.com.
Rs 1900-3200 (plus taxes). A modern building in the heart of Kalpetta just off the highway, some a/c rooms, clean and comfortable, restaurant 'reasonable', good value but rather noisy.

$$-$ Regency
On the main road in Sulthan Bathery, T04936-220512, www.issacsregency.com.
Good range of neat and tidy rooms, better value at the cheaper end.

$ PPS Tourist Home
Just off highway at south end of Kalpetta, T04936-203431.
Reasonable rooms, good cheap restaurant.

What to do

The Blue Yonder *see page 944*. Can arrange excellent, forest-savvy guides.

Transport

Bus From **Kalpetta Bus Stand**, T04936-203040, to **Kozhikode**, 3½ hrs, via **Vythiri**; **Mysore** via Sulthan Bathery. From **Sulthan Bathery**, T04936-220217, to **Ambalavayal** (for **Edakkal Caves**), **Vaduvanchal** and **Ooty**.

Lakshadweep

The islands which make up the Lakshadweep ('100,000 islands') group have superb beaches and beautiful lagoons to rival the Maldives, but visiting them requires time and patience, and a willingness to slum it for a few nights. There are, despite the name, only 11 inhabited and 25 uninhabited islands making up the group. Minicoy, the southernmost island, is 183 km from Kalpeni, its nearest neighbour. Geologically they are the northernmost extensions of the chain of coral islands that extends from the far south of the Maldives. The atolls are formed of belts of coral rocks almost surrounding semi-circular lagoons, with none more than 4 m above sea level. They are rich in guano, deposits of centuries of bird droppings. The wealth of coral formations (including black coral) attracts a variety of tropical fish including angel, clown, butterfly, surgeon, sweetlip, snappers and groupers. There are also manta and sting rays, harmless sharks and green and hawksbill turtles. At the right time of the year you may be able to watch turtles laying their eggs. Arriving on the beach at night, each lays 100-200 eggs in holes they make in the sand.

Essential Lakshadweep

Finding your feet

The islands are 225-450 km west of Kerala and have a total land area of 32 sq km. The 11 inhabited islands support a population of 60,600. You can only visit the islands on a package tour. Lakshadweep Tourism's **Society for Promotion of Recreational Tourism and** Sports (SPORTS) and other tour operators organize package tours. Everyone needs a permit, for which you need to provide details of the place and date of birth, passport number, date and place of issue, expiry date and four photos; apply two months ahead. If you plan to dive, get a doctor's certificate. Foreign tourists may only visit Agatti, Kadmat, Kalpeni and the uninhabited islets of Bangaram, Thinnakara, Suheli Par and Cherium; Indians can also visit Kavaratti and Minicoy. Thinakkara and Cheriyam are being developed. For details, see What to do and Transport, page 960.

Tip...

Agatti has a medical centre; emergencies on the islands have helicopter back-up.

Kavaratti and Agatti

Kavaratti, the administrative capital, is in the centre of the archipelago. The Ajjara and Jamath mosques have the best woodcarvings and the former has a particularly good ceiling carved out of driftwood; a well nearby is believed to have medicinal water. The aquarium with tropical fish and corals, the lake nearby and the tombs are the other sights. The woodcarving in the Ajjara is by superb local craftsmen and masons. Kayaks and windsurfers are available for rent, there's a dive centre, plus a bank and a few *dhabas* selling local food.

Some of the other islands in this group are **Andratti**, one of the largest which was first to be converted to Islam, and **Agatti**, which has Lakshadweep's airport, a beautiful lagoon and a palm-shaded resort.

Bangaram, Thinnakara and Kalp

Until recently, uninhabited Bangaram was the best place to stay on the islands, but owing to a dispute with the Lakshadweep administration, the Bangaram Island Resort is closed indefinitely. It's still possible to visit and stay at the very basic SPORTS-managed tented resort.

Across the atoll from Bangaram, tiny Thinnakara has beautiful white sand, views of sunset over the water, and another small tented resort.

Kalpeni and Suheli Par

Kalpeni, with its group of three smaller uninhabited satellite islands, is surrounded by a lagoon rich in corals, which offers excellent snorkelling and diving. The raised coral banks on the southeast and eastern shores are remains of a violent storm in 1847; the Moidin Mosque to the south has walls made of coral. The islands are reputedly free from crime; the women dress in wrap-around *lungis* (sarongs), wearing heavy gold ornaments here without any fear. Villagers entertain tourists with traditional dances, *Kolkali* and *Parichakkali*, illustrating themes drawn from folk and religious legends and accompanied by music and singing.

Suheli Par, 47 km southwest of Kavaratti, consists of a pair of uninhabited islands set on a large atoll. Utterly uninhabited, the atoll forms one of the most important turtle breeding sites in Lakshadweep. The islands' administration plans to build tourist infrastructure in the near future.

Minicoy

Minicoy (Maliku), the southernmost and largest island, is interesting because of its unique Maldivian character, having become a part of the archipelago more recently. Most people speak *Mahl* (similar to *Dhivehi*; the script is written right to left) and follow many of their customs. The ancient seafaring people have been sailing long distances for centuries and the consequential dominance by women may have led Marco Polo to call this a 'female island'. Each of the nine closely knit matrilineal communities lives in an *athir* (village) and is headed by a *Moopan*. The village houses are colourfully furnished with carved wooden furniture. Tuna fishing is a major activity and the island has a cannery and ice storage. The superb lagoon of the palm-fringed crescent-shaped island is enclosed by coral reefs. Good views from the top of the 50-m lighthouse built by the British. You can stay at the **Tourist Huts**.

Amindivi Islands

The Amindivi group consists of the northern islands of **Chetlat**, **Bitra** (the smallest, heavily populated by birds, for a long time a rich source of birds' eggs), **Kiltan** where ships from Aden called en route to Colombo, **Kadmat** and the densely populated **Amini**, rich in coconut palms, which was occupied by the Portuguese. **Kadmat**, an inhabited island 9 km long and only 200 m wide, has a beach and lagoon to the east and west, ideal for swimming and diving. The **Tourist Huts** shaded by palms are away from the local village. The Water Sports Institute has experienced qualified instructors. There are 10 executive and **Tourist Cottages** and a **Youth Hostel** with a dorm for 40.

Where to stay

Kadmat and Agatti islands have basic tourist cottages resembling local huts. Each hut has 1-2 bedrooms, mosquito nets, fans and attached baths; electricity is wind or diesel. Bangaram and Thinnakara are more basic still, with no-frills tents offered at the startling price of Rs 10,000 per night. Meals are served on the beach and are similar to Keralite cuisine, with plenty of coconut. Breakfast might be iddlis or *puris* with vegetables. Lunch and dinner might be rice and vegetable curry, sambhar, meat or fish curry. Vegetarian meals available on request.

What to do

Tourism is still in its infancy and facilities on the islands are limited. Package tours (the only way to visit) are relatively expensive. Tours operate Oct-May; most are late Jan to mid-May. Schedules may change, so allow for extra days when booking onward travel. For a full list of authorized tour operators, see www.lakshadweeptourism. com/agents.html.

SPORTS (Lakshadweep Tourism), *Indira Gandhi Rd, Willingdon Island, Kochi*, T0484-266 8387, T0484-266 6789. Offers a variety of cruise- and island-based packages, starting from Rs 25,000 per person. Also handles bookings for (overpriced) tent resorts on Thinnakara and Bangaram islands.

Watersports

Activities include windsurfing, scuba diving (**Dolphin Dive Centre** on Kavaratti, **Kadmat Diving Centre** and **Diveline**, Agatti), parasailing, waterskiing and snorkelling. Deep-sea fishing (barracuda, sailfish, yellow-fin, trevally) is possible on local boats with crew; serious anglers should bring their own equipment; no diving or deep-sea fishing Apr-Sep.

Transport

Air Agatti has a basic airport. **Indian Airlines** and **Kingfisher** fly to/from **Kochi**, daily except Tue and Sun.

Ferry Ferries connect the islands with **Kochi**, **Mangalore** and **Beypore** (Kozhikode). The crossing takes a minimum of 14 hrs, depending on which island you're heading for. Ship anchors 30-45 mins away from each island; passengers are ferried from there.

Inter-island transfers are by helicopter (when available) during monsoons, 15 May-15 Sep (return US$60), or by pablo boats for 8.

Background Kerala

History

Brahmin myths
The distinctiveness of Kerala's cultural identity is reflected in the Brahmin myths of its origin. As Robin Jeffrey explains, Parasurama, the sixth incarnation of Vishnu, having been banished from India, was given permission by Varuna, the Lord of the Sea, to reclaim all the land within the throw of his axe. When Parasaruma threw the axe it fell from Kanniyakumari to Gokarna, and as the sea withdrew Kerala was formed.

Christianity
Christianity, which is thought to have been brought by St Thomas the Apostle to the coast of Kerala at Kodungallur in AD 52, has its own very long tradition. The equally large Muslim community traces its origins back to the spread of Islam across the Indian Ocean with Arab traders from the seventh century.

The Cheras
The Cheras, who established themselves in the Kuttanad region around Alappuzha as the first Kerala power, developed a wide network of trade links in which both the long-established Christian community and the Jewish community participated fully. However, the neighbouring Cholas launched several successful attacks against Chera power from AD 985. Kerala's matriarchal culture may have originated in the 10th-century conflict with the Cholas. Krishna Chaitanya suggests that as many men were slaughtered there was a surplus of women, encouraging the development of a matrilineal system in which women controlled family property.

The Zamorins and the Portuguese
When Chola power disintegrated at the end of the 11th century, Calicut gradually became dominant under the Zamorin (literally 'Lord of the Sea'), who had well-established contacts with the Arab world. By some accounts the Zamorins were the wealthiest rulers in contemporary India, but were never able to use these advantages to unite Kerala, and during the 16th century the Portuguese exploited the rivalry of the Raja of Kolattiri with the Zamorin of Calicut, being granted permission to trade from Kochi in 1499. Over the following century there was fierce competition and sometimes open warfare between the Portuguese, bent on eliminating Arab trading competition, and the Zamorin, whose prosperity depended on that Arab trade. After a century of hostility, the Dutch arrived on the west coast. The Zamorin seized the opportunity of gaining external support, and on 11 November 1614 concluded a treaty giving the Dutch full trading rights. In 1615 the British East India Company was also given the right to trade by the Zamorin.

The Dutch and the British
By 1633 the Dutch had captured Portuguese forts. The ruler of Kochi rapidly made friends with the Dutch, in exchange for having the new Mattancherry Palace built for him. In the decade after 1740 Raja Marthanda Varma succeeded in uniting a number of petty states around Thiruvananthapuram and led them to a crushing victory over the Dutch in the Battle of Kolachel in 1741. By 1758 the Zamorin of Calicut was forced to withdraw from Kochi, but the Travancore ruler's reign was brief. In 1766 Haidar Ali had led his cavalry troops down onto the western coastal plain, and he and his son Tipu Sultan pushed further and further south with a violence that is still bitterly remembered. In 1789, as Tipu was preparing to launch a final assault on the south of Travancore, the British attacked him from the east. He withdrew his army from Kerala and the Zamorin and other Kerala leaders looked to the British to take control of the forts held by Tipu's officers. Tipu Sultan's first defeat at the hands of Lord Cornwallis led to the Treaty of Seringapatam in 1792, under which Tipu surrendered all his captured territory in northern Kerala, to direct British rule. Travancore and Kochi then became Princely states under ultimate British authority.

Modern Kerala

The majority of the population is Hindu, but as much as a quarter is Christian and there is also a large Muslim population. Religious communities have often lived amicably together. There is no conflict between the varying Hindu sects, and most temples have shrines to each of the major Hindu divinities.

Kerala is the first state in India to claim 100% literacy in some districts and women enjoy a high social status.

Kerala politics have often been unstable – even turbulent – since the first elections were held in March 1957, when Kerala became the first state in the world to democratically elect a Communist government. The debate has always been dominated by the struggle between the Marxist Communist Party, the Congress and various minor parties; and the state government has often been formed by coalitions.

Traditionally Kerala's economy has depended heavily on agriculture, especially tea, rubber, coconut and coconut products.

Recent decades

Recent decades have seen the rise of Kerala as a remittance economy, with large flows of money being repatriated by Malayali workers in the Gulf to invest in land, housing and small-scale industries. Highly educated and increasingly middle class, Keralites have been abandoning old-fashioned and 'menial' industries such as agriculture and where farm fields still exist, they are largely run by Tamils or other migrant workers, who earn more in Kerala than in their home states.

However, the collapse of Dubai's building boom looks set to trigger a reverse exodus, with hundreds of thousands of workers expected to return to Kerala in the next few years. The challenge this poses to the state is enormous, in managing a population whose aspirations have been built around Gulf salaries.

Karnataka

cosmopolitan cities, pristine beaches and hypnotic ruins

The chasm between rural Karnataka and its capital Bengaluru can be shockingly wide. You enter via one of India's most exciting cities. But soon after leaving, you enter a land that seems frozen in time.

Karnataka's interior has been seat to dynasties whose once-great cities now stand largely in dusty ruins. The exquisite Chalukyan and Hoysala temples of Pattadakal and Halebid meet their match in the Islamic palaces of Tipu Sultan in the south, and the onion-dome tombs of his Turkish and Persian antecedents in the northeast. The boulder-strewn ruins of Hampi are utterly hypnotic at sunset.

In the forests of the Western Ghats you'll find some of India's richest wildlife habitat. Visit Nagarhole National Park in the dry season and you'll witness a spectacle, as elephants and deer gather, taking their chances among India's largest population of tiger and leopard.

The stretch of emerald lush Arabian Sea coast is every bit as idyllic as Goa's, and has one of the world's most powerful waterfalls and the town that invented South Indian vegetarian food.

Yet if this dignified corner of India has a signature virtue, it is modesty. Karnataka hardly brags about its treasures. Which means that for now you can still enjoy them as an explorer, minus the crowds.

Best for
Architecture ▪ Beaches ▪ Temples ▪ Wildlife

Footprint picks

★ Bengaluru, page 968

Wander the City Market, soaking up the noise and colour, then jostle your way into one of the city's hip bars.

★ Mysore, page 985

Explore the state's cultural capital, with an impressive royal heritage and interesting palaces and temples.

★ Nagarhole National Park, page 995

One of India's top national parks, home to India's largest and best-protected population of tiger and leopard.

★ Coorg, page 997

Trek through the lush green hills of Coorg, with a cool climate, beautiful scenery and romantic hotels and homestays.

★ Gokarna, page 1014

Hang out with the hippies and Hindus in this fascinating pilgrimage town, with its stunning Om-shaped beach.

★ Hampi, page 1021

Ramble through the sprawling ruins of Hampi, one of India's most important historical sites.

Essential Karnataka

Finding your feet

The Western Ghats, called the Malnad or hill country, in Karnataka (population 52.7 million) have beautiful forests with waterfalls and wildlife parks. To the east stretches the Mysore Plateau. Parts of northern Karnataka are barren, rocky and covered with scrub, but the state in other places is richly fertile (particularly around the 'sugar bowl' region of Mandya) and it has a lush coastline. From Coondapur to Karwar, the estuaries of the short, fast-running rivers flowing west from the ghats still have mangroves, some in uniquely good condition, although commercial exploitation seriously threatens their survival.

Tip...

Since November 2014 many towns and cities in Karnataka have officially adopted authentic Kannadu versions of their names. To help our readers, this guidebook uses the new names in headings but continues to refer to the old, more familiar names in the text. For further information, see box, page 973.

Getting around

Take the Konkan railway, local buses or chartered taxi, especially for the more remote ruins around the Deccan.

When to go

By far the most comfortable time to visit Karnataka is October to March, when the weather is dry and relatively cool. April and

Fact...

The Kannada temple town of Udupi has spawned its own fabled brand of pure vegetarian meal. *Iddli* and *dosa* are traditionally served on a plantain leaf or stainless steel plate; you can taste variations of these dishes all over the state and South India.

May are intensely hot, especially in the central and northern parts, with humidity building up as the monsoon approaches. The southwest monsoon arrives in early June; the heaviest rain comes in July. The whole of the west coast is extremely wet from June to September. A second, lighter monsoon begins in September or October, travelling up the east coast and stretching inland to pour on Bengaluru. The post-monsoon period brings cool air and clear skies and is the best time for mountain views, while winter temperatures can drop close to zero in the higher Western Ghats.

Immediately to the east of the Western Ghats rainfall decreases dramatically. On the plateaux of the south, especially around Bengaluru (Bangalore) and Mysore, temperatures are moderated somewhat by the altitude (generally around 1000 m), and nights are pleasantly cool most of the year.

Time required

Allow for a weekend in Bengaluru, two days in Mysore, a minimum of four days to do Hampi and its environs justice, two to three days for the Western Plateau temples, three days to walk in Coorg, three days for safaris in Nagarhole/Bandipur, and as long as you like in Gokarna.

Weather Bengaluru

January	February	March	April	May	June
☀️ 27°C 15°C 0mm	☀️ 30°C 17°C 0mm	☀️ 33°C 19°C 10mm	🌤️ 34°C 21°C 30mm	⛅ 33°C 21°C 110mm	🌧️ 29°C 20°C 70mm

July	August	September	October	November	December
🌧️ 28°C 19°C 100mm	⛅ 28°C 19°C 130mm	⛅ 28°C 19°C 170mm	⛅ 28°C 19°C 150mm	🌦️ 27°C 17°C 60mm	☀️ 26°C 15°C 10mm

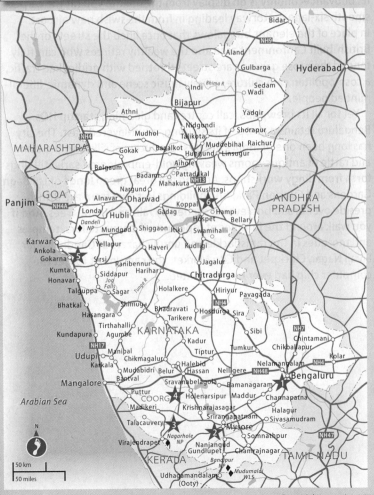

Bidar

NH9

Aland

Gulbarga   Hyderabad

Indi   *Bhima R*

Sedam

Bijapur   Wadi

Athni   Yadgir

Mudhol   Nidgundi

Talikota   Shorapur

MAHARASHTRA   Bagalkot   Muddebihal Raichur

NH4   Gokak   Hungund Linsugur

Belgaum   Badami   Aihole

Nargund   Pattadakal

Mahakuta   NH13

Alnavar   Dharwad   Kushtagi

GOA   Londa   Koppal   6   Hampi

Panjim   NH4A   Gadag   Hospet   Bellary   ANDHRA
PRADESH

Dandeli   Iliti   Swamihalli
NP   Mundgod Shiggaon

Karwar   Yellapur   Haveri   Kudligi

Ankola   Kudligi

Gokarna   5   Sirsi   Ranibennur   Jagalur

Kumta   Siddapur   Hariharn   Chitradurga

Honavar   *Jog*   Sagar
Falls   Holalkere   Hiriyur   Pavagada

Talaguppa   Shimoga   Hosdurga Sira

Bhatkal   Hasangara   Bhadravati   Sibi   NH7

Tirthahalli   Tarikere   Chintamani

Kundapura   Agumbe   KARNATAKA   Chikballapur   Kolar

NH17   Kadur   Tiptur   Tumkur   Nelamanbalam NH4

Udupir   Manipal   Chikmagalur   Nelligere   NH48

Karkala   Belur   Halebid   Hassan   Bengaluru

Mangalore   Mudabidri   Sravanabelagola   Ramanagaram

Bantval   Puttur   Ramanagaram

Arabian Sea   COORG   4   Holenarsipur Maddur   Channapatna

Madikeri   Krishnarajasagar   Halagur   Sivasamudram

Talacauvery   3   Srirangapatnam   NH47

Nagarhole   2   Mysore   Somnathpur
NP

Virajendrapet   Nanjangud   Chamrajnagar

Gundlupet   TAMIL NADU

KERALA   *Bandipur*
NP   *Mudumalai*
WLS

Udhagamandalam
(Ooty)

N

50 km
50 miles

Bengaluru
(Bangalore)

★ Technology capital Bengaluru, the subcontinent's fastest-growing city, is the poster boy of India's economic ascendance. Its buoyant economy is on display from the minute you hit the carpet-smooth six-lane motorway leading in from the swish new airport. In place of the elegant bungalows that once lined the streets of the British-built Cantonment area and the wealthy retirees who carefully tended their rose gardens are streets throttled with gridlocked traffic, a cosmopolitan café culture, a lively music scene and dynamic, liberal-minded people.

Yet for all its brewpubs, call centres and gleaming startup HQs, Bengaluru retains a grasp of its swirling, multi-layered past. The city has long been one of India's greatest producers of silk, and the clang and rattle of antique looms weaving gold-embroidered saris still rings forth from dingy workshops. Around the great green lungs of Lal Bagh Gardens and Cubbon Park, fine buildings left over from the British preside over broad boulevards shaded by rain and flame trees. And if you walk around the jumbles of rope and silk shops, tailors, temples and mosques in the ramshackle and unruly bazars of Gandhi Nagar, Sivaji Nagar, Chickpet and City Market, you can almost forget the computer chip had ever been invented.

Essential Bengaluru

Finding your feet

Bengaluru is served by a glitzy international airport 35 km northeast, three mainline train stations and a long-distance bus station with services throughout central and southern India.

Getting around

Bengaluru is very spread out and you need transport to get around. You also need to allow plenty of time: despite the new Metro and highway flyovers, infrastructure has completely failed to keep pace with the city's population explosion. Road travel at rush hours is best avoided, and even at weekends there is near-gridlock. The Metro, touted as the city's salvation, is at the 'good start' stage: trains currently run along two short and as-yet unconnected stretches, one running east from MG Road, the other running north from Sampige Road (a few hundred metres north of Majestic) via Yesvantpur Station. City buses run a frequent and inexpensive service throughout the city. Taxis and auto-rickshaws are available

Best places to stay
Sri Lakshmi Comforts, page 978
St Mark's Hotel, page 978
Taj West End, page 978
Vellara, page 978
Villa Pottipati, page 979

for trips around town. If you're planning on covering a lot of sights in a day it can work out cheaper to hire a car and driver, but bring a good book to while away the traffic jams. See also Transport, page 983.

Best places to eat
Daddy's Deli, page 980
Karavalli, page 980
MTR, page 979

Orientation

Time has not eroded the distinction in atmosphere between the 'native' city of Kempe Gowda and Tipu Sultan, contained within the crowded narrow lanes east of City Railway Station, and the broad elegant avenues of the Cantonment. In general you'll find the most atmospheric temples and historic sites in the former, while museums and monumental architecture congregate around the magnificent green lung of Cubbon Park further to the northeast.

Fact...

The name Bengaluru is possibly derived from the phrase 'benda kalu', or 'boiling bean' in reference to the meal fed to a lost Prince Hoysala by an old peasant woman who took him in.

Central and South Bengaluru *Colour map 7, A4.*
a vibrant flower market, historic temples and palaces, and botanical gardens

The centre of Kempe Gowda's city lies at the intersection of Avenue Road and Old Taluk Cutchery (OTC) Road, amid the bustling market area of Chickpet. It's worth braving the always-manic traffic to walk through the tangled knot of streets, where shops offering gold jewellery and silk saris jostle for space with peddlers of brass pots and 'fancy stores' selling *mehndi* cones and *bindis*.

City Market

From Chickpet you can walk south to the City Market (officially known as **Krishnarajendra Market**, though most often called **KR Market**), for one of Bengaluru's most compelling visual spectacles. As the wholesale hub of Bengaluru's hyperactive flower industry, the basement of the four-storey building is a whirl of colour and noise from 0400 to 2230. There's a bewildering variety of specializations: you'll find growers coiling up long ropes of marigolds, porters manhandling coracle-sized baskets of jasmine blooms through the crowd, and open-sided stalls where workers

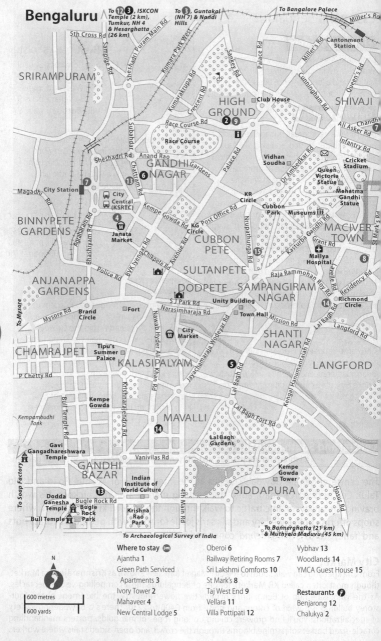

Bengaluru

To 12 3, ISKCON Temple (2 km), Tumkur, NH 4 & Hesarghatta (26 km)
To 3, Guntakal (NH 7) & Nandi Hills
To Bangalore Palace
Miller's Rd

Cantonment Station

5th Cross Rd

SRIRAMPURAM

SHIVAJI

HIGH GROUND

Club House

Race Course Rd

Race Course

GANDHI NAGAR

Anand Rao

Vidhan Soudha

Queen Victoria Statue

Cricket Stadium

Mahatma Gandhi Statue

City Station

City Central (KSRTC)

KR Circle

Cubbon Park

Museums

MACIVER TOWN

BINNYPETE GARDENS

Janata Market

KG Post Office Rd

KG Circle

CUBBON PETE

Mallya Hospital

ANJANAPPA GARDENS

Brand Circle

SULTANPETE

DODPETE

SAMPANGIRAM NAGAR

Fort

Unity Building

To Mysore

Narasimharaja Rd

Town Hall

Richmond Circle

CHAMRAJPET

Tipu's Summer Palace

City Market

SHANTI NAGAR

LANGFORD

P Chetty Rd

KALASIPALYAM

Kempe Gowda

MAVALLI

Lal Bagh Fort Rd

Kempambudhi Tank

Gavi Gangadhareshwara Temple

GANDHI BAZAR

Vanivilas Rd

Indian Institute of World Culture

Lal Bagh Gardens

Kempe Gowda Tower

SIDDAPURA

To Soap Factory

Dodda Ganesha Temple

Bugle Rock Rd

Bugle Rock Park

Bull Temple

Krishna Rao Park

To Archaeological Survey of India

To Bannerghatta (21 km) & Muthyala Maduvu (45 km)

Where to stay 🛏

Ajantha 1
Green Path Serviced Apartments 3
Ivory Tower 2
Mahaveer 4
New Central Lodge 5

Oberoi 6
Railway Retiring Rooms 7
Sri Lakshmi Comforts 10
St Mark's 8
Taj West End 9
Vellara 11
Villa Pottipati 12

Vybhav 13
Woodlands 14
YMCA Guest House 15

Restaurants 🍴

Benjarong 12
Chalukya 2

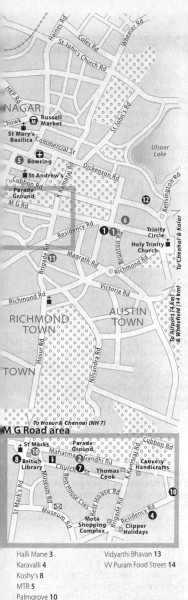

convert those flowers into temple garlands and elaborate designs for weddings and film sets. The upper floors of the market are worth exploring, too, whether or not you're in the market for kitchen hardware or drill bits, and from the first floor there's a great view of the multicoloured scrum down below.

Summer Palace
City Fort, 0800-1730, foreigners Rs 100, Indians Rs 10, video camera Rs 25.

West of the market lies the palace that Tipu Sultan, the perennial thorn in the side of the British, boasted was "the envy of heaven". Tipu's Summer Palace was begun by his father Haidar Ali and was completed by Tipu in 1789. Based on the Daria Daulat Bagh in Srirangapatnam, the understated two-storey structure is largely made of teak with walls and ceilings painted in brilliant colours with beautiful carvings. A room downstairs is given over to documenting Haidar and Tipu's reigns and their struggles against the British.

Lal Bagh
Southeast of the Summer Palace, 0900-1830, Rs 10.

The botanical gardens of Lal Bagh were laid out across 97 ha by Haidar Ali in 1760 and are second only to Kolkata's in size. Tipu introduced a wealth of plants and trees from many countries (there are more than 1800 species of tropical, subtropical and medicinal plants) and the British added a bandstand and spectacular **glass house**, with echoes of London's Crystal Palace and Kew Gardens, home to flower shows in January and August. Sadly, the Indian affection for botanical beauty means that the rose gardens are kept behind bars. At dusk, Lal Bagh is popular with businessmen speed-walking off their paunches, and courting couples and newly-weds who sit on the banks of the lotus pond eating ice cream. The rocky knoll around the **Kempe Gowda tower** has great city views, and is popular at sunset. There are fortnightly Sunday evening performances of Kannada folk theatre, song and dance.

West of Lal Bagh
Just west of Lal Bagh is the Dravida-style **Venkataramana Swamy Temple,** where the Wodeyar Maharaja chose to worship first after his dynasty's rule was reinstated at the end of the 18th century. The area is abuzz in the

Halli Mane 3
Karavalli 4
Koshy's 8
MTR 5
Palmgrove 10
Sukh Sagar 6
Tandoor 1

Vidyarthi Bhavan 13
VV Puram Food Street 14

BACKGROUND
Bengaluru

Human habitation in the Bengaluru region stretches back to at least the Stone Age; megalithic tombs with iron tools dating to 1000 BC have been unearthed within the city limits, and Roman coins from the age of Augustus speak of a commercial centre boasting international connections at the dawn of the millennium.

The modern city of Bengaluru traces its origins to 1537, when the Yelahanka chieftain Kempe Gowda, a feudatory of the Vijayanagar Empire, built a mud fort and four watchtowers, visualizing them as the limits of a great future city. Muslim ruler Haidar Ali strengthened those fortifications, and built many splendid palaces and pleasure gardens, before his death at the hands of the British, leaving his son Tipu Sultan to pick up where he left off. During the Third Mysore War, in 1791, Tipu fought fiercely to hold the city against Earl Cornwallis, who marched down from Calcutta at the head of "the finest, best appointed [army] that ever took the field in India", but his most powerful fortress was taken by a stealthy attack following a siege in March 1791. Cornwallis took control of a large town that was already established as an important manufacturing centre and, after Tipu's death in 1799, he installed the Wodeyar of Mysore as the ruler and the rajas developed Bengaluru into a major city. The Bangalore Cantonment was founded in 1806, and in 1831 the British shifted the capital from Mysore in favour of Bangalore's more congenial climate.

For the next century Bengaluru existed as two cities – the bustling Kannada-speaking "native" City, and the multicultural Cantonment, dominated by the fixtures and fittings of the British military – parade grounds, genteel parks, churches, museums and cinemas – but also populated by immigrants from all over the country.

Bengaluru's great leap forward began in the wake of a devastating outbreak of bubonic plague in 1898, with the government investing in improved sanitation and health facilities in the city. Other innovations followed in a flood: in 1905 India's first electric light bulb fizzed to life in the City Market, and in 1911 the opening of the venerable Indian Institute of Science put the city on the map as a leader in education and research. Under successive Diwans of Mysore, notably M Vishvesvaraya and Sir Mirza Ismail, the city experienced a Golden Age, with high ideas guiding public architecture, urban design and education.

Shortly after Independence, J L Nehru identified Bengaluru as a potential "template of a modern India". The city has since emerged as a pioneering presence in fields ranging from medical science to space exploration, while the rise of home-grown IT companies such as Wipro and Infosys have helped cement the city as India's leading hub for the high-tech industries.

evening as hungry Bengalureans descend on the snack stalls and ice cream vendors of VV Puram's legendary 'food street'.

To the southwest, the hefty Nandi bull at **Bull Temple** ① *Bull Temple Rd, Basavanagudi, 0600-1300, 1600-2100*, was carved at the behest of Kempe Gowda, making it one of the city's oldest temples. The monolithic Nandi was believed to be growing unstoppably until a trident was slammed into his forehead: he now towers nearly 5 m high and is 6 m in length. His huge proportions, draped imperiously in jasmine garlands, are made of grey granite polished with a mixture of groundnut oil and charcoal. Under his hooves you can make out the *veena* or south Indian sitar on which he's resting. Behind him is a yoni-lingam. Just outside the temple are two bodhi trees, with serpent statues draped with sacred strands in offering for children.

To your right as you exit the temple lies **Bugle Rock Park**, a pretty little patch of wood whose trees are packed with fruit bats. It also holds one of Kempe Gowda's four 16th-century

Tip...
For those interested in ancient Indian astrological practices, the **Palm Leaf Library** (No 33, 5th Main Rd, Chamarajpet) is supposed to be the repository for everyone's special leaf, which gives accurate details of character, past, present and future. Locating each leaf is not guaranteed.

ON THE ROAD

Going back to Kannada

On 1 November 2014, Bangalore officially became the latest big Indian city to tread the path taken by Bombay, Madras and Calcutta, trading in the name thrust upon it by tone-deaf British colonists for a brave new life under a more authentic spelling of its indigenous name.

It is joined by 11 other Karnatakan cities and towns: Mysore (now Mysuru), Belgaum (Belagavi), Bellary (Ballari), Bijapur (Vijayapura), Chikamagalur (Chikkamagaluru), Gulbarga (Kalburgi), Hospet (Hosapete), Hubli (Hubballi), Mangalore (Mangaluru), Shimoga (Shivamoga) and Tumkur (Tumakuru).

The campaign to restore the distinctively Kannada 'u' to the end of Bengaluru has been underway for almost a decade, driven by Kannada language scholars and authors, most notably the Booker Prize-nominated UR Ananthamurthy, who died barely three months before his campaign came to fruition.

The plan to reclaim Kannada identity for the state's capital has been carried out with the dignity that seems to be Karnataka's signature civic virtue, free of the chauvinist chest-beating that Maharashtra's political elite deployed in jettisoning Bombay for Mumbai.

Yet the mass renaming isn't without its detractors. Bangalore – a name so synonymous with Indian technical and marketing genius that it became a verb (if you've ever lost your job to invisible lower-paid workers in a developing country, you've been Bangalored) – has serious brand equity, both globally and within the country's own English-speaking elite. Members of the city's highest corporate echelons took to Twitter to declaim against its Bengaluru-ization.

The widespread name changes also present a dilemma for any India guidebook: to embrace the new and sow confusion among readers, or to cling to the familiar like some nostalgic octogenarian colonist. After prolonged meditation and performing the appropriate Vedic rituals, we've decided to hitch our bullock cart to Bengaluru: the name change is too established to ignore. On the other hand, for Mysore-Mysuru et al, the new names are going to take years, even decades, to percolate into everyday usage. Hence, in this edition of the book we've decided to continue using the old names throughout the text, and include the new names in the heading for each section, or wherever most relevant.

watchtowers. Also here is the **Dodda Ganesha Temple** ① *open 0700-1230 and 1730-2030*, named for the towering idol of Ganesh – 18 feet high and 16 feet wide – also carved on the orders of Kempe Gowda.

Northwest of here, the **Sri Gavi Gangadhareshwara Temple** dates back to the ninth-century Chola dynasty. Its most remarkable feature is the 'open window' to the left of the temple, which only once a year (on **Makara Sankrati Day**, 14/15 January) allows a shaft of light to shine between the horns of the stone Nandi bull in the courtyard and to then fall on the Siva lingam in the inner sanctum.

MG Road and around

one of Bengaluru's busiest commercial streets

Traversed by the concrete spans of the new Metro, Mahatma Gandhi (MG) Road is lined with malls, bookshops, silk emporia, restaurants and hotels.

Cubbon Park

At the western end of MG Road lies the 330-acre oasis of Cubbon Park, laid out in 1870 and named after Sir Mark Cubbon, the 19th-century Commissioner of Mysore State. This is one of India's most beautiful urban parks, and a wonderful place to wander at any time of day. Contained within the park's leafy confines are bandstands, fountains and temples, but also wild thickets of bamboo, granite outcrops and lakes where kites and kingfishers swoop for fish.

Standing out in bright red on the northern fringe of the park is the Greco-Colonial **Karnataka High Court**, which served as the seat of government until 1956 when it was replaced by the post-Independence granite of the **Vidhana Soudha**, the state's legislature and secretariat buildings, across the street.

Government Museum
Kasturba Rd, T080-2286 4483, Tue-Sun 1000-1700, Rs 4.

This idiosyncratic and slightly dog-eared museum opened in 1886 and is one of the oldest museums in the country. There are 18 galleries. Downstairs teems with sculptures: a huge-breasted Durga and a 12th-century figure of Ganesh from Halebid sit alongside intricate relief carvings of Rama giving his ring to Hanuman, and there are Buddhas from as far afield as Bihar. An upstairs gallery holds beautiful miniatures in both Mysore and Deccan styles, including a painting of Krishnaraj Wodeyar looking wonderfully surly. There are also Neolithic finds from the Chandravalli excavations, and from the Indus Valley, especially Mohenjo Daro antiquities.

In the same complex, the **K Venkatappa Art Gallery** ① *Kasturba Rd, Cubbon Park, T080-2286 4483, Tue-Sun 1000-1700, Rs 4*, shows a small cross-section of work by the late painter (born 1887). His paintings of the southern hill stations give an insight into the Indian fetishization of all things pastoral, woody and above all cold. There is also the story and blueprints of his truncated design for the Amba Vilas Durbar Hall in Mysore and miniatures by revered painter Abanindranath Tajore (1871-1951), alongside a second portrait of Krishnaraj Wodeyar.

Visvesvaraya Industrial and Technological Museum
Kasturba Rd, next to the Government Museum, Tue-Sun 1000-1800, Rs 15.

This museum will please engineering enthusiasts, especially the basement, which includes a 1917 steam wagon and India's oldest compact aircraft. Others might be left cold by exhibits on the 'hydrostatic paradox' or 'the invention of the hook and eye and zip fastener technology'. Upstairs is a wing devoted to educating the inhabitants of Bengaluru on genetic engineering. You might find the debate a little one-sided: "agricultural biotechnology is a process … for the benefit of mankind," it states in capital letters. A small corner (next to the placard thanking AstraZeneca, Novo Nordisk Education Foundation, Novozymes and Glaxo-SmithKline) is dubbed 'Concerns', but you can see how cloning and genetically strengthened 'golden' rice might seem more attractive when put in the context of the growling Indian belly.

Shivaji Nagar and further east
To the north of here is Shivaji Nagar, an interesting area to explore centred on the 19th-century **Russell Market** and **St Mary's Basilica**, established by French Catholics in 1799 following the defeat of Tipu Sultan. Bengaluru's oldest church, 'Arokya Marie' earned fame during the 1890s for her power to cure plague, and the basilica is still visited by people of all faiths in search of a miracle cure. For a few rupees you can buy a small stamped metal depiction of the part of your body that's suffering, drop it in the box, and await the results.

East of here lies **Ulsoor Lake**, once a favourite swimming hole for British soldiers, now sadly polluted, and beyond, the trendy shopping and bar-hopping district of **Indira Nagar**.

outlandish palaces, British bungalows and Brahmin enclaves

Bangalore Palace
North of Cubbon Park, T080-2336 0818, 1000-1800, foreigners Rs 450, Indians Rs 200, camera Rs 450, video Rs 1000; frequent buses from Majestic/Sivaji Nagar.

This grand, Tudor-style, built by Chamaraja Wodeyar in 1887, is an incongruous pastiche of Windsor Castle complete with battlements and Gothic arches. The entry ticket includes a tour of the Mysore maharajas' collection of art and family portraits.

Cantonment
From the palace you can strike eastward to explore the residential section of the old Cantonment, where suburbs with names like Fraser Town and Cooke Town retain vestiges of old colonial romance. A handful of original bungalows are scattered throughout the area, with their imposing gates, curving driveways and pitched roofs, especially around Dixon Road in Cooke Town.

Karnataka Chitrakala Parishath
Kumara Krupa Rd, www.karnatakachitrakalaparishath.com, Mon-Sat 1000-1730, Rs 50, Indians Rs 10.

West of the palace is this privately owned art school and gallery with an understated but excellent collection of paintings and sculptures, displayed in 12 distinct galleries spanning styles from tribal to international modern art. There's a superb collection of Mysore religious paintings, detailed in gold and gesso, plus a handful of original paintings by Rauschenburg, two rooms dedicated to mystic Himalayan landscapes by Nicholas and Svetislav Roerich, and a strong collection of prints by N Krishna Reddy. The campus hosts frequent markets selling arts and crafts from all over India.

Malleswaram
A few minutes further west, Malleswaram is a bastion of upper-class Bengaluru and has been home to many city notables including the painter Venkatappa. Most of the old bungalows have gone, but it's still worth a visit to see the Shaivite **Kadu Malleshwara Temple**, which predates the settlement by several hundred years and includes a *nagarkatte* (a platform where serpent stones are worshipped). Across the road is the recently unearthed **Nandishwara Temple**, saved from bulldozing thanks to a remarkable Nandi statue that spouts water from an underground channel on to a Shiva lingam.

International Society for Krishna Consciousness Temple (ISKCON)
Hare Krishna Hill, 1R Block, Chord Rd, Rajaji Nagar, 0700-1300, 1615-2030.

This sprawling modern temple complex holds five shrines, a multimedia cinema showing films on the Hare Krishna movement, lofty *gopurams* and the world's tallest *kalash shikara*. Around 9000 visitors make the pilgrimage every day; *bhajans* (religious songs) are sung daily.

Around Bengaluru

silicon suburbs, vineyards and cool mountain retreats

Whitefield
Whitefield, 16 km east of Bengaluru, is the centre of the city's ongoing industrial revolution, and claims to be the fastest growing suburb in Asia. Once best known for the **Sai Baba Ashram** at Brindavan, if you venture out here now it's almost certain to be on business. Whitefield is home to innumerable industrial estates, IT parks and hospitals, not to mention the hotels, international schools and malls which service their employees.

Health tourism

For decades, Western travel to India was synonymous with emaciated hippies, and backpackers' conversations invariably veered towards the scatological as everyone, at some stage, was sure to catch the dread 'Delhi belly'. It's a sign of the times that, although the British National Health Service failed to award India its whole back-up project in 2004, the country has become a very real alternative to private health care, representing huge cost reductions on surgery.

The centrepiece for this emerging industry is arguably Bengaluru, which has the largest number of systems of medicine approved by the World Health Organization in a single city: cardiac, neurology, cancer care and dentistry are just a few of the areas of specialization, and clients include the NHS and America's largest insurance company. Open-heart surgery will set you back US$4500 in Bengaluru, for example, as opposed to US$18,000 abroad. And afterwards, of course, you can recuperate at an Ayurveda resort. Lately Bengaluru has knitted its medical specialists with its IT cred to pioneer virtual medicine too, whereby cardiac experts in the city hold teleconferences with outposts up and down the subcontinent to treat emergencies, examine and monitor patients via phone, text and video, a method specialists at Narayana Hrudayalaya confidently predict will one day become the norm.

Devanahalli

At Devanahalli, 40 km north, stand the monumental walls of the fort where Tipu Sultan was born. Now partially in ruins, the 15th-century fort encircles a mellow village of temples and free-roaming sheep. From here a side road leads towards the Nandi Hills, passing through interesting countryside strewn with temple-topped boulders, and vineyards with grapevines held aloft by great standing stones of hewn grey granite. **Grover** ⓘ *63 Raghunathapura, Devanahalli Rd, Doddaballapur, www.grovervineyards.in,* is one of India's most highly regarded wineries. It offers a three-hour tour, tasting and lunch for Rs 850 on weekdays, Rs 1000 at weekends.

Nandidurg and the Nandi Hills

To get to Nandiburg, take a bus from the Central Bus Stand (ask for the Nandi Hill bus, not Nandidurga); they leave at 0730, 0830, 0930, returning at 1400, 1630, 1830.

Some 57 km north of Bengaluru lies Nandidurg, Tipu's fortified summer retreat in the Nandi Hills, set on top of a granite hill with sheer cliffs on three sides. 'The fort of Nandi', named after Siva's bull, was converted to a pocket-sized hill resort by the British. A drive around the short road encircling the forested hilltop offers great views in all directions, particularly from the 600-m-high cliff, known as 'Tipu's drop'. Within the fort walls is the fascinating **Yoganandeeshwara Temple**, built by the Cholas, whose dark interior is decorated from floor to ceiling with superb carvings.

At the foot of the hill, the ninth-century **Bhoganandeeswara Temple** (the two temples are related, and their locations are symbolic; Bhoga, referring to earthly enjoyment, is located on the plain, while its sister temple is set on high to symbolize the spiritual ascent toward yoga, or union with god) is a good example of the Nolamba style: its walls are quite plain but the stone windows feature carvings of Nataraja and Durga. The 16th century brought typical Vijayanagar period extensions such as the gopuram at the entrance.

Nrityagram

30 km north of Bengaluru, T080-2846 6313, Tue-Sat 1000-1730.

Nrityagram is a dance village where young dancers learn all disciplines of traditional Indian dance. It was founded by the late Odissi dancer Protima Gauri. Guided tours include lunch, dance demonstrations and a short lecture.

Bannerghatta Bio Park

22 km south of the city, T080-2782 8540, Wed-Mon 0900-1300, 1400-1700, Rs 200, Indians Rs 60 including safari; guide Rs 200, video camera Rs 150.

This park covers more than 100 sq km of dry deciduous forest, and is home to wild populations of elephant, bison, boar, deer and the occasional leopard. A portion has been fenced and the Forest Department runs a range of minibus safaris to see tigers, bears and Asiatic lions at close range in almost-natural surroundings (many of the animals here have been rescued from circuses). The park also contains a butterfly garden and an unappealing zoo.

Channapatna and the Ramanagaram Hills

Around 60 km west of the city on the Mysore highway, **Channapatna** is an unassuming town renowned for its handcrafted and highly colourful wooden toys, which are on sale at dozens of roadside shops. The town is surrounded by the extraordinary **Ramanagaram Hills**, which rear out of the surrounding plains in great domes of reddish granite. Popularly known as the 'Sholay Hills' for their starring role in the legendary 1975 Bollywood movie *Sholay*, these hilly outcrops and boulders also provided David Lean and Richard Goodwin the ideal filming location to capture the atmosphere of E M Forster's Barabar Cave for their film of *A Passage to India*; the lower cave sequences were filmed at Savandurga, 40 km north of Channapatna on the way to Magadi; ask at the **Lakshmi** store for directions or a guide. It's a stunning climb up **Kempi Gowda Hill**. There is also a small **forest park** and the upper caves at **Rama Dhavara**, 2 km from Ramanagaram. The caves are visible from the road and easy to find, though only false entrances were made for the film.

Listings Bengaluru (Bangalore) *map p970*

Tourist information

For events, pick up the fortnightly *Time Out* magazine (www.timeoutbengaluru.net), and the bimonthly *City Info* (www.explocity. com). An excellent online resource is www. whatshot.in/bangalore.

India Tourism
KSFC Building, 48 Church St, T080-2558 5417. Mon-Fri 0930-1800, Sat 0900-1300.
Very helpful.

Karnataka State Tourism Development Corporation (KSTDC)
Head office, No 49, Khanija Bhavan, West Entrance, Race Course Rd, T080-2235 2901, www.kstdc.net. Mon-Sat 1000-1730, closed every 2nd Sat.
Booking counters for tours and hotels at Badami House, NR Sq, T080-4334 4334, also has counters at the airport and City Railway Station.

Karnataka Tourism House
8 Papanna Lane, St Mark's Rd, T080-4346 4351.
A one-stop shop for bookings and information.

Where to stay

Cheap hotels share the streets of the ill-named Majestic district, northeast of the bus stand around SC (Subedar Chatram) Rd, with seedy bars and cinemas – a daunting prospect at night. MG Rd offers a more sanitized environment, and has rooms for every budget from backpacker to super-luxury. Top-end hotels can add 25% in taxes.

Central and South Bengaluru

$ Mahaveer
8/9 Tank Bund Rd, opposite the bus station, near City Railway Station, T080-3271 0384.
Basic and decaying place on a noisy road, but just about OK if you want to drop your bags after a long bus ride. The larger deluxe rooms at the back are quieter.

$ New Central Lodge
56 Infantry Rd, at the Central St end, T080-2559 2395.
35 simple, rooms, clean enough, some with bath, hot water (0500-1000).

$ Railway Retiring Rooms
City Railway Station.
23 rooms and cheaper dorm for passengers in transit.

$ Signature Inn
479 OTC Rd, Cottonpet, T080-4090 8204,
www.thesignatureinn.in.
One of the better Majestic area cheapies, with
well-maintained rooms and responsive staff.
24-hr checkout.

$ Vybhav
*60 SC Rd down a passageway opposite
Movieland Talkies, T080-2287 3997.*
As basic as they come, and pretty grimy, but
the rooms are relatively big and airy and some
open onto a shared terrace where pot-bellied
Brahmins hang out and chat. Good value.

MG Road and around

$$$$ Oberoi
39 MG Rd, T080-2558 5858,
www.oberoihotels.com.
160 superb rooms and suites with private
sit-outs, all of which have views across the lush
tropical gardens. Decent-sized swimming pool.
Good restaurants, bar, spa and fitness centre,
beauty salon.

$$$$ Taj West End
23 Race Course Rd, near railway,
T080-6660 5660, www.tajhotels.com.
Charming 1887 colonial property set in beautiful
gardens; much more than a business hotel.
117 immaculately appointed suites and rooms
with balconies and verandas, Wi-Fi, flatscreen
TV. There's also a splendidly restored Heritage
Wing, dating from 1907. **Blue Ginger**, one of
Bengaluru's most romantic garden restaurants,
serves authentic Vietnamese food in low-lit
jungly surroundings.

$$$$-$$$ St Mark's Hotel
4/1 St Mark's Rd, T080-4001 9000,
www.stmarkshotel.com.
This friendly, intimate business hotel is one of the
best high-end deals in the city. Smartly renovated
rooms and excellent value suites come with free
Wi-Fi, and there's an excellent restaurant plus a
rooftop terrace offering great city views. A nearby
spa sends therapists over to give free massages
on Wed night. Price includes breakfast.

$$$ Ivory Tower
12th floor Barton Centre, 84 MG Rd, T080-4178
3333, www.hotelivorytower.com.
22 comfortable, spacious rooms with stunning
views over the city. Huge beds, Wi-Fi, a/c, fridge,
phone. Old fashioned but spotless, good value,
friendly. Good terrace bar and restaurant onsite.

$$$-$ Woodlands Hotel
5 Raja Ram Mohan Roy Rd, Richmond Town,
T080-2222 5111, info@woodlands.in.
Large but charming old-fashioned hotel with
240 rooms (some a/c) and cottages, with
attached baths and fridge, good a/c restaurant,
bar, coffee shop, exchange, safe, good location
but calm, good value. Phone, satellite TV, lockers.

$$ Sri Lakshmi Comforts
117 MG Rd, in alley behind the LIC building,
T080-2555 9388, www.slcomforts.com.
Excellent budget choice right amongst the
MG Rd action, with spartan but clean rooms,
friendly staff and a good *thali* restaurant.

$$-$ Ajantha
22A MG Rd, T080-2558 4321.
62 basic 'deluxe' rooms and much better value
cottages with sitting areas and campbed-
style beds, set in a calm compound filled with
bougainvillea and pot plants. South Indian veg
restaurant, helpful manager.

$$-$ Vellara
126 Brigade Rd, T080-2536 9116,
www.hotelvellara.com.
A grim exterior conceals one of the MG Rd area's
best deals. 36 spacious and well-kept rooms,
which get better the higher up you go. TV and
phone in each room. The value and location are
excellent. Recommended.

$ YMCA Guest House (City)
Nrupathunga Rd, near Cubbon Park,
T080-2221 1848, www.ymcablr.net.
One of the best budget secrets in the city. The
location is wonderfully peaceful, just across the
fence from Cubbon Park, and many of the rooms
open onto an indoor sports hall where you can
sit like Caesar watching badminton or karate
championships. Afternoon cricket matches,
excellent café.

North and West Bengaluru

$$$$ ITC Windsor
Golf Course Rd, T080-2226 9898,
www.itchotels.in.
Elegant and luxurious hotel based around a
Raj-era manor house, with huge suites decked
out in Edwardian finery and spacious rooms in
the adjacent high-rise. The best rooms come
with a private butler. Good pool and health club,
but – unbelievably for a business hotel at this
price – Wi-Fi costs extra.

$$$ Villa Pottipati
142 8th Cross, 4th Main Rd, Mallesaram,
T080-2336 0777, www.neemranahotels.com.
Historic townhouse with 8 rooms, furnished
with rosewood 4-poster neds and sepia Indian
portrait photography. Set in a garden on the
charming quiet tree-lined avenues of Bengaluru's
Brahminical suburbs. A/c and internet facilities,
small plunge pool. Atmospheric, but a bit
lacklustre. Thin mattresses.

$$$-$$ Green Path Serviced Apartments
*32/2 New BEL Rd, Seenappa Layout (north of
centre near Hebbal flyover), T080-4266 4777,
www.thegreenpath.in.*
Comfortable and spacious if slightly anonymous 1-
to 3-bedroom apartments. Built using renewable
materials and run on eco principles including
rainwater harvesting and solar-heated water.
Facilities include Wi-Fi and bicycles to ride to the
local shops. Price includes an organic breakfast.

Around Bengaluru

$$$$ Shreyas Bangalore
*35 km northwest of town in Nelamangala,
T080-2773 7102, www.shreyasretreat.com.*
The place for peace and yoga in 5-star luxury,
with twice-daily classes, silent meditations,
Vedanta consultants and life coaching.
Pampering includes Balinese massage and exotic
fruit body scrubs, and the vegetarian cuisine is
exceptional. Alcohol is forbidden, but there's
a gym, book and DVD library, and in case you
forgot you were in Bangalore, Wi-Fi throughout
the property. 3- to 6-night packages start at
around US$1500.

$$$$ Soukya International Holistic
Health Centre
*Whitefield, 17 km east of Bengaluru,
T080-2810 7000, www.soukya.com.*
This healing centre offers restorative,
personalized programmes: detox, de-stress
and weight loss, or relax with naturopathy
and Ayurveda suited to asthma, diabetes,
hypertension and addictions. Accommodation
is in individual cottages around the lawns,
surrounded by flowers and trees. Programmes
cost US$200-500 a day.

$$$ Alila Bangalore
*100/6, HAL-Varthur Main Rd, Whitefield,
T080-7154 4444, www.alilahotels.com.*
Attractive and efficient upscale hotel with
122 rooms and suites, all dressed up for business
with workstations and free Wi-Fi. The rooftop

infinity pool, organic restaurant and chauffeur
service make this a standout choice for the price
in Whitefield.

$$$ Windflower Prakruthi
*Hegganhalli Village, T080-4901 5777,
www.thewindflower.com.*
This appealing plant-filled resort set among
mango orchards makes a good base for
exploring the Nandi Hills and Devanahalli area.
Spacious, well-equipped cottages come with
huge sunken showers. Activities include ATV
bikes, zorbing and a high-level ropes course.
Packed at weekends, virtually empty midweek.

Restaurants

For excellent, cheap, and fast South Indian
food, head for one of Bengaluru's 5000-odd
darshinis – fast-food style joints where you pay
upfront, take your ticket to the counter, and get
handed a plate of fresh and delicious staples
like *iddli*, *vada* and *dosa*, which you shovel
down standing up around round metal tables.

Shiv Sagar, **Shanthi Sagar**, **Sukh Sagar** and
Kamat are hygienic and efficient restaurant
chains. At the other end of the price scale, the
Sun all you-can-eat brunch at the **Leela** is
popular with expats and the city's business elite.
If you're missing international fast food head for
Brigade and MG Rd and the food court at the
Forum shopping mall. Chains of **Cafe Coffee
Day** are ubiquitous.

Central and South Bengaluru

$ Food Street
VV Puram.
This small lane, leading south off Sajjan Rao
Circle just west of Lal Bagh, is lined with food
carts and cheap hole-in-the-wall snack stands.
It's a hive of activity from 1900-2300. A roving
repast here can have you sampling North Indian
chaats, *iddli*, *ragi roti*, Chinese fast food and
Bengali sweets.

$ MTR (Mavalli Tiffin Rooms)
*11 Lalbagh Rd, T080-222 0022. Tiffin 0600-1100
and 1530-1930, lunch 1230-1430 and 2000-2100.
Closed Mon lunch.*
The quintessential Bengaluru restaurant: a classic
Kannadiga Brahmin vegetarian oozing 1920s
atmosphere, full of Bengaluru elders, at the edge
of Lalbagh gardens. A 14-course lunch lasts
2 hrs, but you'll be lucky to get a table. If you're in
a hurry it does parcels to take away. The simple

vegetarian food is superb, but people watching is half the fun.

$ Vidyarthi Bhavan
32 Gandhi Bazar, T080-2667 7588.
Sat-Thu 0630-1130 and 1400-2000.
Unassuming vegetarian joint in the Basavanagudi district (near Nandi bull and Gandhi Bazar) whose Mysore masala *dosa* is justly famous, served with a side order of butter, coconut chutney and potato and onion curry. Open since 1938.

MG Road and around

$$$ Ebony Restaurant
Ivory Tower (see Where to stay), T080-6134 4880.
Open 1230-1500 and 1930-2300.
Surprisingly good value lunch and dinner buffets (from Rs 395) at this penthouse terrace restaurant, which offers the best views in Bengaluru. Parsi dishes like mutton *dhansak* and curry *chawal*, along with Mughlai, Tandoori and French food. Good veg options.

$$$ Karavalli
At the Taj Gateway, 166 Residency Rd, T080-6660 4519.
The best high-end Indian restaurant in the city, offering upscale Karnataka coastal food.

$$ Benjarong
1/3 Ulsoor Rd, T080-3221 7201.
If you're craving Thai, this is the place. Expect charming service and authentic red curry, dished up with lots of extras.

$$ Coconut Grove
86 Spencer Building, Church St, T080-2559 6149.
Good varied Southern Indian menu, beers, buzzing place with sit-outs under shades.

$$ Daddy's Deli/Red Fork
594 12th Main Rd, off 100 Feet Rd, Indira Nagar, T4115 4372.
Warm and bright café in trendy Indira Nagar, serving first-class Parsi specials alongside brilliant salads and pasta dishes and proper coffee. Highly recommended.

$$ Ente Keralam
12/1 Ulsoor Rd, T3242 1002.
The best place in the city for high-end Keralite cooking – beef curries, fish *thalis* and tender coconut *payasam*.

$$ Koshy's
39 St Mark's Rd, T080-2221 3793.
Open 0900-2330.
This humble, atmospheric restaurant-bar has been an absolute local favourite since the 1950s. Good grills and roasts, Syrian Christian fis curries and Sunday South Indian brunch. Also does Western breakfasts like baked beans on toast, cutlets, eggy bread or eggs any way you like. Stop at the kulfi stand on the kerb outside for a delicious, safe dessert.

$$ Tandoor
MG Rd, T080-2558 4620. Open 1230-1500 and 1900-2330.
Possibly the city's best North Indian restaurant, serving Punjabi, Muglai and Tandoori specialties.

$$ Truffles
22 St Marks Rd, T080-4965 2756.
The place to come if you're craving good Western fast food – proper burgers (beef and veggie versions), garlic mushrooms, sandwiches and cakes. Long queues at weekends, efficient home/hotel delivery service.

$ Chalukya
Race Course Rd, by the Taj West End Hotel.
Excellent vegetarian.

$ Natural Ice Cream
15/16 St Marks Rd.
One of several branches in the city, serving superb ice creams in exotic, totally natural flavours; the *chikku* and *sitaphal* (custard apple) are delicious.

$ Palmgrove
Ballal Residence Hotel, 74/3 III Cross, Residency Rd, T080-2559 7277.
Atmospheric place for Kannada Brahmin food, a/c, serves excellent giant lunch *thalis* for Rs 75.

$ Sweet Chariot Bakery
15/2 Residency Rd and branches all across the city. Open 1030-2030.
Excellent cakes and pastries.

North and West Bengaluru

$ Halli Mane
12 Sampige Rd, Malleswaram.
Fun and buzzing vegetarian canteen decked out like a village house: order at the counter, present your ticket at the relevant counter and elbow yourself a bit of table space. A good place to try Karnataka specials like *ragi roti*.

Bars and clubs

Bengaluru is striving to reclaim its role as India's coolest party town: the pre-midnight curfew that once threw a wet blanket over the hard-rocking bars along Brigade Rd, Residency Rd and Church St is now 0100. Hotel bars are exempt from curfews, and offer a more refined atmosphere: those at the Taj West End have a particular Raj-esque elegance. Note that many better clubs have a hefty cover charge and a couples-only policy to prevent an oversupply of slavering stags.

13th Floor
Hotel Ivory Tower, 84 MG Rd, T080-4178 3355.
The least pretentious bar, with one of the best views of the city.

Church Street Social
46/1, Cobalt Building, Church St.
With a semi-industrial vibe and mismatched vintage furniture, this is a cool and friendly place for a quiet beer in the afternoon. On weekend nights the music reaches fever pitch.

Hard Rock Café
St Mark's Rd, T080-4124 2222.
Brand-phobics beware: this spanking-new venue is one of the hottest tickets in town, with a variety of drinking and dining spaces carved out of a lovely old library building.

Pecos
Rest House Rd, off Brigade Rd.
Connoisseurs of dinge should head directly here for cheap beer and hard-rockin' tunes.

Skyye Lounge
UB City, Vittal Mallya Rd, T080-4965 3219.
Stunning lounge and nightclub, with illuminated glass floor tiles and superb views from the open-air upper deck. The Rs 3000 cover charge ensures a smart but mixed crowd, dancing to hard house, lounge and R&B.

Toit
No 298, 100 Feet Rd, Indira Nagar, T0-1971 3388.
This multi-level brewpub-restaurant serves up excellent house-brewed beers, as accompaniment to good pizzas.

Entertainment

Bengaluru's heady cultural cut-and-thrust has put it at the Indian forefront of scenes from Carnatic classical music to heavy metal, and it's begun to attract big-name international acts. For an exhaustive but ill-edited list of what's going on around the city, check out www.allevents.in; or to find out about upcoming classical music concerts, http://kpjayan.wordpress.com.

Max Mueller Bhavan, *716 Chinmaya Mission Hospital Rd, Indira Nagar, T080-2520 5305, www. goethe.de.* Film screenings, theatre and concerts.
Nadasurabhi, *www.nadasurabhi.org.* Puts on monthly Carnatic classical concerts at a range of venues around the city.
Ranga Shankara, *36/2 8th Cross, II Phase, J P Nagar, www.rangashankara.org.* The city's most active theatre, with shows almost every evening (closed Mon) in English as well as in regional languages.
Ravindra Kalakshetra, *Jayachamaraja Rd, T080-2222 1271.* Kannada theatre and music.

Cultural centres
Alliance Française, *Millers Tank Bund Rd, off Thimmaiah Rd, opposite station, T080-4123 1340.*
British Library, *St Mark's Rd/Church St corner (Koshy's Bldg).* Tue-Sat 1030-1830.
Goethe Institut, *716 CMH RD, Indira Nagar, T080-2520 5305.*

Festivals

Jan/Aug Lal Bagh Flower Show, held on Republic Day (26 Jan) and Independence Day (15 Aug), with floral displays and sculptures.
Apr Karaga. Religious festival dedicated to the goddess Draupadi, in which men of the Thigala community, claimed to descend from the Veerakumars – a mythological army of the Mahabharata – walk on fire, beat themselves with swords, and compete for the honour of bearing an idol of the goddess on their head in a wild, drum-soaked procession through the old city.
Nov/Dec Kadlekai Parishe Centred around the Bull Temple, this 500-year-old harvest festival (literally 'groundnut fair') sees peanut farmers from all over South India offering their crops to Nandi. Sellers line the road with piles of raw, roasted and jiggery-coated peanuts in a riotous village-fair atmosphere.

Shopping

Bengaluru is a byword for shopping in India. **Commercial St**, **MG Rd** and **Brigade Rd** remain favourite hangouts for the city's youth.

Unless you want Western goods, though, the best shopping is in and around the **City Market** (officially known as the KR Market) in Chickpet, where you can get silver, gold and silk saris, and supposedly India's biggest silk wholesale/

retail district. It makes for some seriously fun people-watching when it comes alive at dusk. **Russell Market** in Shivajinagar is stuffed with vegetables, meat and antiques, while Gandhi Bazar in Basavanagudi is a fun place to stroll in the evening, with interesting clothes shops and excellent cheap food.

Shops and markets open early and close late (about 2000) but close 1300-1600.

Books

Blossom Book House, *84/6 Church St*. 4 storeys packed from floor to ceiling with new and second-hand titles.

Gangarams, *48 Church St*. Has a wide-ranging and expanding collection.

Sankar's, *15/2 Madras Bank Rd, T080-2558 6867*. One of the best in the city for new books.

Crafts and gifts

Karnataka is best known for silks, especially saris, and sandalwood products, from oils and incense to intricate carvings. Other local products include Mysore paintings (characterized by gold leaf and bright colours from vegetable and mineral dyes), *dhurries* (carpets incorporating floral and natural motifs, traditionally made from wool though cotton is now more widely used), inlaid woodwork and wooden toys and Channapatna dolls. Bidriware, a form of metalwork whereby silver and gold is inlaid or engraved onto copper and polished with zinc, originates from Bidar in the state's far northeast, but is produced throughout the state.

Watch out for private shops masquerading as branches of the government-owned 'Cottage Industries' chain. While the genuine article will have fixed, reasonably good prices, the (invariably slicker and more salesy) private operators will charge whatever the market will support.

Cauvery Crafts Emporium, *49 MG Rd*. Government-run shop specializing in Karnataka crafts, from cheap and colourful wooden toys to expensive sandalwood carvings.

Central Cottage Industries Emporium, *144 MG Rd*. Another government-owned shop, with fixed prices, carrying crafts from all over India.

Desi, *27 Patalamma St, near South End Circle*.

Kala Madhyam, *45 8th Main, 3rd Cross, Vasanth Nagar, T080-2234 0063, www.kalamadhyam.org*. NGO-run store showcasing artworks, metalwork, pottery, clothing and jewellery made by folk artists and tribal craftspeople throughout India. High quality.

Khadi Gramudyog, *Silver Jubilee Park Rd, near City Market*. For homespun cotton.

Mota Shopping Complex, *Brigade Rd*.

Orange Bicycle, *3353 5th Cross, 12th A Main, Indira Nagar*. Good for Indian kitschy gifts – T-shirts, bags, ornaments.

Raga, *A-13, Devatha Plaza, 131 Residency Rd*. Sells attractive gifts.

UP Handlooms, *8 Mahaveer Shopping Complex, Kempe Gowda Rd*.

Yellow Button Store, *787 12th Main, 1st Cross (Near Sony Center), Indira Nagar*. A careful selection of high-end homewares, decor and jewellery.

Jewellery

Most gold and jewellery is, logically enough, sold on Jewellers St in Shivaji Nagar, but also look along MG Rd, Brigade Rd, Residency Rd and Commercial St.

Silk and saris

Silk is, to many, what shopping in Bengaluru is really all about. There's a vast range available at the following shops.

Deepam, *MG Rd*. Fixed prices, excellent service, 24 hrs from placing an order to making up your designs.

Janardhana, *Unity Building, JC Rd*.

Maa Fabric Galleria, *36/1 Dickenson Rd, T080-4132 0384*. Small, hidden-away shop with a good selection of saris and high-quality silk by the metre. In the back room you can watch craftsmen block-printing designs, and with a few days' notice they'll make customized pieces for you.

Silks Industries, *Jubilee Showroom, 44/45 Leo Complex, MG Rd*. Specializing in traditional Mysore Crepe designs.

Vijayalakshmi, *20/61 Blumoon Complex, Residency Rd*. Will also make shirts.

What to do

Golf

Bangalore Golf Club, *Sankey Rd, T080-2228 7980. Foreign visitors pay US$30*.

KGA Golf Club, *Golf Av, Kodihalli, Airport Rd, T080-4009 0000. Rs 2000*.

Horse racing

Bengaluru is famous for racing and stud farms. **Bangalore Turf Club**, *Race Course Rd, T080-2226 2391, www.bangaloreraces.com. Season May-Jul and Nov-Mar*.

Swimming

The top hotels have become reluctant to let non-residents use their pools. However, there are good municipal pools, in varying states of maintenance, and some private clubs allow casual day visitors.

Builders NGV Club, *National Games Village, KHB, Koramangala, T080-2570 2247, www. buildersngvclub.com.* With swimming pool, badminton, billiards and tennis.

KC Reddy Swim Centre, *Sadhashivanagar near Sankey Tank.* 50-m pool and diving boards, open in 1-hr shifts from 0600-1000, 1230-15.30; ladies only 1530-1630.

Tour operators

Arjun Tours, *8 Bappanna Lane, St Marks Rd, T080-2221 7054, www.arjuntours.com.* Honest and reliable travel agency, good for car hire and hotel bookings, with safe English-speaking drivers. Recommended.

Bluefoot Culture Tours, *www.bluefoot.in.* Kaveri Sinhji's personalized tours offer a behind-the-scenes look at life in Bengaluru. From in-depth explorations of classic city sights like the City Market, to breakfasts at obscure temples and encounters with local social entrepreneurs, the tours are professional and hugely informative. Highly recommended.

Clipper Holidays, *4 Magrath Rd, T080-2559 9032, www.clipperholidays.com.* Tours, treks (everything provided), Kerala backwaters, etc. Very helpful and efficient.

Golden Chariot, *Tourism House, Pappanna Lane, St Marks Rd, T080-4346 4342, www.goldenchariot. org.* A southern counterpart to Rajasthan's famous **Palace on Wheels**, offering luxurious train journeys through Karnataka, Kerala and Tamil Nadu.

Hammock Leisure Holidays, *Indira Nagar, T080-2521 9000, www.hammockholidays.com.* Tailor-made and small group trips around Karnataka and South India, including women-only group journeys.

Karnataka State Tourism Development Corporation (KSTDC), *runs tours from Badami House, opposite Corporation Office, T080-4334 4334, www.karnatakaholidays.net.* **Bangalore city sightseeing**: half-day tours, covering Tipu's Palace, Bull Temple, Lal Bagh, Ulsoor Lake, Vidhan Soudha, Gava Gangadhareshwara Temple and the museums, runs 0730-1400 and 1400-1930; Rs 230, admissions extra, recommended. Full-day tour, to Rajarajeshwari Temple, HAL Museum, Bannerghatta Bio Park, ISKCON temple and more,

0715-2000, Rs 385-485, long and exhausting. Also runs Mysore and Srirangapatnam day tour, 0630-2330, Rs 650-850.

ITDC, *departing from Swiss Complex, No 33 Race Course Rd, T080-2238 6114.* Same schedule as **KSTDC** half-day tour but lasts from 0900-1700 and includes ISKCON, Rs 250. **Mysore** tour, daily 0715-2300, Rs 600-700 including meals.

Walking tours

Bangalore Walks, *T(0)9845-523660, www. bangalorewalks.com.* Excellent guided tours of the city's cultural and historic landmarks, Rs 495 including brunch.

Transport

Air

Bengaluru International Airport (BLR), T080-6678 2251, www.bengaluruairport.com, is the bold new face of Indian airports: it's gleaming, expensive, and the taxi touts in Arrivals greet you in suits. The domestic and international terminals are in the same building, around 35 km northeast of the city by a fast new road. Prepaid taxis in the terminal quote upwards of Rs 1500 to deliver you to the city centre, but perfectly comfortable and reliable metered a/c taxis queue outside Arrivals and work out at roughly half the price – around Rs 900 to MG Rd, or Rs 1100 to Whitefield. Airport buses run every 20-30 mins on 11 fixed routes to and from various parts of the city: Route BIAS-9 to Kempegowda Bus Station (Majestic) and Route BIAS-4 to Jeevan Bhima Nagar (via MG Rd) are the most useful for hotels. **KSRTC**, www.ksrtc.in, also runs twice-daily luxury coaches direct to Mysore at 1030 and 2100.

Bengaluru is becoming an increasingly important international hub, with direct flights to **London**, **Frankfurt** and **Paris**, as well as **Singapore**, **Kuala Lumpur** and many Gulf cities.

Daily domestic flights serve **Chennai**, **Coimbatore**, **Delhi**, **Goa**, **Guwahati**, **Hubli**, **Hyderabad**, **Jaipur**, **Kochi**, **Kolkata**, **Mangalore**, **Mumbai**, **Pune** and **Thiruvananthapuram**.

Bus

City Bus Station (also formally known as **Kempegowda Bus Station**, and informally as simply '**Majestic**'), opposite the City Railway Station, is the very busy but well-organized departure point for services within the city.

Just to the south, the **Central Bus Station** handles long-distance buses run by the governments of **Karnataka (KSRTC)**,

T080-2287 3377; **Andhra Pradesh** (**APSRTC**), T080-2287 3915; **Kerala**, T080-2226 9508; and **Tamil Nadu** (**SETC**), T080-2287 6975. Virtually all long-distance buses, both state-run and private, will leave you at or near the bus stand.

Computerized reservations are available on many services, from the booking counter. There are efficient, frequent and inexpensive services to all major cities in southern and central India. Frequent service to **Mysore** (3 hrs); several to **Hassan** (4 hrs), **Hyderabad**, **Madikeri** (6 hrs), **Madurai** (9 hrs), **Mangalore** (9 hrs), **Ooty** (7 hrs), **Puttaparthi** (4-5 hrs), **Tirupati** (6½ hrs). 'Deluxe' or 'ordinary' coaches run by private operators are usually more comfortable though a bit more expensive. They operate from opposite the Central Bus Station, and from outside Kalasipalyam Bus Station, 3 km to the south.

Car

Firms for city and out-of-town sightseeing include **Classic City Cabs**, T080-2238 6999; **Safe Wheels**, T080-2343 1333; **Angel City Cabs**, T091-6486 7774, driven by women and for female passengers only. Approximate rates are Rs 1000-2000 for 8 hrs or 80 km, then Rs 10-25 per extra kilometre, depending on the type of car. Rates for overnight or extended sightseeing will be higher, with additions for driver overnight charges and hill driving.

Metro

Trains run 0600-2200. For more information, see page 969.

Taxi and autorickshaw

There are prepaid taxi booths at the airport and all 3 railway stations; prices should be clearly marked, and will be a little higher than the meter fare. Minimum charge in a meter taxi is Rs 125, which covers up to 5 km; Rs 10 per extra km. There are several reputable radio taxi companies with clean a/c vehicles and digital meters, including **EasyCabs**, T080-4343 4343, callcenter@ easycabs.com.

Autorickshaws should also operate on a meter system: Rs 25 for the first 2 km, Rs 13 per extra kilometre. In practice it can be hard to persuade drivers to use the meter, especially during rush hour.

Both taxi and rickshaw fares increase by half between 2300 and 0500.

Train

Trains arrive at 1 of 3 main stations: **City**, in Gandhi Nagar next to the main bus stand; **Cantonment**, a few kilometres to the northwest, most convenient for MG Road; and **Yesvantpur** in the inner northern suburbs.

Bangalore City Railway Station (formerly Bangalore Junction), opposite the City Bus Station, is the main departure point; enquiries T131, reservations T139. Computerized advance reservations are in the newer building on left of the entrance; No 14 is the 'Foreigners' Counter'. The Chief Reservations Officer is on the ground floor. Many trains also stop at **Cantonment Station**, T135, and an increasing number of important trains begin at **Yesvantpur Junction**, 10 km north of the city.

Arsikere (for Belur and Halebid temples): more than 10 daily, 2½-4 hrs; **Chennai**: around 10 daily, 5-6 hrs; **Goa** (Londa): 1 daily, plus other weekly/bi-weekly services, 10½ hrs. **Hospet**: overnight *Hampi Exp 16592*, 9 hrs. **Hyderabad**: at least 4 daily, 12 hrs. **Madurai**: 2-3 daily, 10 hrs. **Mangalore**: 2 daily, 12 hrs, 1 continues to **Gokarna Rd**, 17 hrs. **Mumbai** 2-4 daily, 24 hrs. **Mysore**: around 20 daily, 2-3 hrs. **Thiruvananthapuram**: 2 daily, 17 hrs, via **Ernakulam (Kochi)** 12½ hrs.

Mysore &
Southern Maidan

The charming, unruly city of Mysore – the former capital of the princely state – does a brisk trade in shimmering silks, sandalwood and jasmine against a backdrop of the stunning, borderline gaudy, Indo-Saracenic palace. On the outskirts of the city is the empty ruin of Srirangapatnam, the island fortress of Britain's nemesis Tipu Sultan, and the bird-crammed Ranganathittu Sanctuary.

Further east is the Chennakesava Temple of Somnathpur, a spellbinding example of Hoysala architecture. Leopards and tigers stalk the two parklands, Bandipur and Nagarhole, which spill over Karnataka's borders into neighbouring Tamil Nadu and Kerala. Closer to the coast you can climb the ghats to the tiny Kodagu district for forests of wild elephants and coffee plantations nursed by a warrior people. Also in Kodagu lies Sera, the university at the centre of one of India's biggest Tibetan Buddhist refugee settlements.

★ Mysore (Mysuru) *Colour map 7, B3.*

city of palaces – the cultural capital of Karnataka

The centre of Mysore (population 887,000) is a crowded jumble presided over by the gaudy, wondrous kitsch of the Maharaja's Palace, a profusion of turquoise-pink and layered with mirrors. But for some, Mysore's world renown is centred less on the palace, its silk production or sandalwood than on the yoga guru Sri Pattabhi Jois and his Mysore-style ashtanga yoga practice (see box, page 991). This all happens outside the chaotic centre, in the city's beautiful Brahmin suburbs, where wide boulevard-like streets are overhung with bougainvillea.

Maharaja's Palace
Enter by south gate, T0821-243 4425, 1000-1730, Rs 200 includes audio guide, cameras must be left in lockers (free, you take the key), allow 2 hrs if you

Essential Mysore and Southern Maidan

Finding your feet

Mysore is the transport hub for the region with long-distance bus and train connection with most major towns. The railway station is about 1 km to the northwest of the town centre while the three bus stands are all in the centre, within easy reach of the hotels. Despite being Karnataka's second biggest city, it is still comfortably compact enough to walk around, though there are plenty of autos and buses.

Best places to stay...

Green Hotel, Mysore, page 988
Orange County, Coorg, page 996
The Bison, Nagarhole, page 996

wish to see everything, guidebook Rs 10; go early to avoid the crowds; downstairs is fairly accessible for the disabled.

Also known as 'City Palace' (Amba Vilas), the Maharaja's Palace was designed by Henry Irwin and built in 1897 after a fire burnt down the old wooden incarnation. It is in the Indo-Saracenic style in grand proportions, with domes, arches and colonnades of carved pillars and shiny marble floors. The stained glass, wall paintings, ivory inlaid doors and the ornate golden throne (now displayed during **Dasara**) are remarkable. The fabulous collection of jewels is seldom displayed. Try to visit on a Sunday night, public holiday or festival when the palace is lit up with 50,000 fairy lights.

On the ground floor, visitors are led through the 'Car Passage' with cannons and carriages to the *Gombe thotti* (**Dolls' Pavilion**). This originally displayed dolls during **Dasara** and today houses a model of the old palace, European marble statues and the golden *howdah* (the maharaja used the battery-operated red and green bulbs on top of the canopy as stop and go signals to the *mahout*). The last is still used during **Dasara** (see box, opposite) but goddess Chamundeshwari rides on the elephant. The octagonal *Kalyana Mandap* (**Marriage Hall**), or Peacock Pavilion, south of the

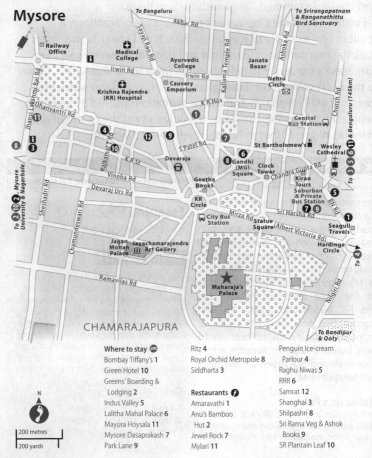

Mysore

Where to stay
Bombay Tiffany's **1**
Green Hotel **10**
Greens' Boarding &
Lodging **2**
Indus Valley **5**
Lalitha Mahal Palace **6**
Mayura Hoysala **11**
Mysore Dasaprakash **7**
Park Lane **9**

Ritz **4**
Royal Orchid Metropole **8**
Siddharta **3**

Restaurants
Amaravathi **1**
Anu's Bamboo
 Hut **2**
Jewel Rock **7**
Mylari **11**

Penguin Ice-cream
Parlour **4**
Raghu Niwas **5**
RRR **6**
Samrat **12**
Shanghai **3**
Shilpashri **8**
Sri Rama Veg & Ashok
 Books **9**
SR Plantain Leaf **10**

Medieval pageantry at Mysore

The brilliantly colourful festival of **Dasara** is celebrated with medieval pageantry for 10 days. Although the Dasara festival can be traced back to the Puranas and is widely observed across India, in the south it achieved its special prominence under the Vijayanagar kings. As the Mahanavami festival, it has been celebrated every year since it was sponsored by Raja Wodeyar in September 1610 at Srirangapatnam. It symbolizes the victory of goddess Chamundeswari (Durga) over the demon Mahishasura. On the last day a bedecked elephant with a golden *howdah* carrying the statue of the goddess processes from the palace through the city to Banni Mantap, about 5 km away, where the Banni tree is worshipped. The temple float festival takes place at a tank at the foot of Chamundi Hill and a car festival on top. In the evening there is a torchlight parade by the mounted guards who demonstrate their keen horsemanship and the night ends with a display of fireworks and all the public buildings are ablaze with fairy lights.

courtyard, has a beautiful stained-glass ceiling and excellent paintings of scenes from **Dasara** and other festivities on 26 canvas panels. Note the exquisite details, especially of No 19. The **Portrait Gallery** and the **Period Furniture Room** lead off this pavilion.

On the first floor, a marble staircase leads to the magnificent **Durbar Hall**, a grand colonnaded hall measuring 47 m by 13 m with lavishly framed paintings by famous Indian artists. The asbestos-lined ceiling has paintings of Vishnu incarnations. A passage takes you past the beautifully ivory-on-wood inlaid door of the **Ganesh Temple**, to the **Amba Vilas** where private audiences (*Diwan-i-Khas*) were held. This exquisitely decorated hall has three doors. The central silver door depicts Vishnu's 10 incarnations and the eight *dikpalas* (directional guardians), with Krishna figures on the reverse (see the tiny Krishna on a leaf, kissing his toes), all done in *repoussé* on teak and rosewood. The room sports art nouveau style, possibly Belgian stained glass, cast iron pillars from Glasgow, carved wood ceiling, chandeliers, etched glass windows and the *pietra dura* on the floors.

The jewel-encrusted **Golden Throne** with its ornate steps, which some like to attribute to ancient Vedic times, was originally made of figwood decorated with ivory before it was padded out with gold, silver and jewels. Others trace its history to 1336 when the Vijayanagar kings 'found' it before passing it on to the Wodeyars who continue to use it during **Dasara**.

Maharaja's Residence ⓘ *1000-1730, Rs 20, no photography*. This is now a slightly underwhelming museum. The ground floor, with a courtyard, displays children's toys, musical instruments, costumes and several portraits. The upper floor has a small weapon collection.

Jayachamarajendra Art Gallery ⓘ *A block west of the palace, 0800-1700, Rs 25, no photography*. Housed in the smaller Jagan Mohan Palace (1861), the gallery holds a priceless collection of artworks from Mysore's erstwhile rulers, including Indian miniature paintings and works by Raja Ravi Varma and Nicholas Roerich. There's also an exhibition of ceramics, stone, ivory, sandalwood, antique furniture and old musical instruments. Sadly, there are no descriptions or guidebooks and many items are randomly displayed.

Other sights
Devaraja Market North of KR Circle, this is one of India's most atmospheric markets: visit at noon when it's injected with fresh pickings of marigolds and jasmines. The bigger flowers are stitched onto a thread and wrapped into rolls which arrived heaped in hessian sacks stacked on the heads of farmers.

Chamundi Hill ⓘ *Immediately to the southeast of town, temple 0600-1400, 1530-1800, 1915-2100; vehicle toll Rs 30, City Bus No 185*. On the hill is a temple to Durga (Chamundeswari), guardian deity to the Wodeyars, celebrating her victory over the buffalo god. There are lovely views, and a giant Nandi, carved in 1659, on the road down. Walk to it along the trail from the top and be picked up by a car later or catch a return bus from the road. If you continue along the trail you will end up having to get a rickshaw back, instead of a bus.

Sandalwood Oil Factory ① *T0821-248 3651, Mon-Sat 0900-1100, 1400-1600 (prior permission required), no photography inside.* This is where the oil is extracted and incense is made. The shop sells soap, incense sticks and other sandalwood items.

Silk Factory ① *Manathavadi Rd, T0821-248 1803, Mon-Sat 0930-1630, no photography.* Here weavers produce Mysore silk saris, often with gold *zari* work. Staff will show you the process from thread winding to jacquard weaving, but they speak little English. The shop sells saris from Rs 3000. Good walks are possible in the Government House if the guard at the gate allows you in.

Sri Mahalingeshwara Temple ① *12 km from Mysore, 1 km off the Bhogadi road (right turn after K Hemmanahalli, beyond Mysore University Campus), taxi or auto-rickshaw.* This 800-year-old Hoysala Temple has been carefully restored by local villagers under the supervision of the Archaeological Survey of India. The structure is an authentic replica of the old temple: here, too, the low ceiling encourages humility by forcing the worshipper to bow before the shrine. The surrounding garden has been planted with herbs and saplings, including some rare medicinal trees, and provides a tranquil spot away from the city.

Listings Mysore *map p986*

Tourist information

Department of Tourism
Old Exhibition Building, Irwin Rd, T0821-242 2096, www.mysore.nic.in. Open 1000-1730. See also www.karnataka.com/tourism/mysore.
There are information counters at the train station and bus stand.

Karnataka State Tourism Development Corporation (KSTDC)
Yatri Nivas, 2 JLB Rd, T0821-242 3652.
Efficient.

Where to stay

May is the most important wedding month and so hotels get booked in advance. In the expensive hotels sales tax on food, luxury tax on rooms and a service charge can increase the bill significantly. The Gandhi Square area has some Indian-style hotels which are clean and good value. Note that JLB Rd is Jhansi Lakshmi Bai Rd, B-N Rd is Bengaluru-Nilgiri Rd.

$$$$-$$$ Lalitha Mahal Palace (ITDC)
Narasipur Rd, Siddartha Nagar T0821-252 6100, www.lalithamahalpalace.in.
54 rooms and suites in the palace built in 1931 for the maharaja's non-vegetarian, foreign guests. In a regal setting near Chamundi Hill, it's an old-fashioned place with some original baths and an extraordinary spraying system. For nostalgia stay in the old wing. There's an attractive pool, but avoid the below par restaurant.

$$$$-$$$ Royal Orchid Metropole
5 JLB Rd, T0821-425 5566, www.royalorchidhotels.com.
After languishing in disrepair for years, the Karnataka government has resuscitated the glorious colonial **Metropole** building. Airy rooms with high ceilings, massage and yoga classes, plus a small pool and excellent restaurant.

$$$$-$$ Green Hotel
Chittaranjan Palace, 2270 Vinoba Rd, Jayalakshmipuram (near Mysore University), T0821-251 2536, www.green hotelindia.com.
The princess's beautiful palace has been lovingly converted with strong sustainable tourism ethos: hot water from solar panels, profits to charity and staff recruited from less advantaged groups. The best of the 31 rooms are in the palace but if you stay in the cheaper, newer block you can still loll about in the huge upper lounges and enjoy the excellent library, chess tables and day beds. Unique, but beyond walking distance from Mysore centre.

$$$-$$ Indus Valley
Near Lalitha Mahal (see above), T0821-247 3437, www.ayurindus.com.
Family-run health resort in a splendid location, halfway up a hill. There are 22 rooms (in the main building or in a cottage), hot showers and Western toilets, TV in lounge, Ayurvedic massage, pleasant walks, vegetarian Ayurvedic restaurant, herbal wines and friendly staff.

$$$-$ Mayura Hoysala (KSTDC)
2 JLB Rd, T0821-242 6160.
20 rooms in this lovely, ochre-painted, ramshackle Raj-style hotel: it's full of chintzy soft furnishings, overspilling with plant pots; en suite bathrooms have both Western and squat loos; tiny white-washed cane stools are propped up on terracing along with mismatched 1970s furniture. Facilities include 3 restaurants, a bar and a tourist desk.

$$$-$ Siddharta
73/1 Guest House Rd, Nazarabad, T0821-428 0999, www.hotelsiddharta.com.
105 rooms, some a/c, huge with baths, good restaurant (Indian vegetarian), exchange, immaculate, well run.

$$-$ Bombay Tiffany's
313 Sayyaji Rao Rd, T0821-243 5255, bombaytiffanys@yahoo.com.
60 clean rooms (12 a/c in the new hotel). The regular rooms are spartan, but the deluxe and a/c ones are very good value. Affable owner.

$$-$ Mysore Dasaprakash
Gandhi Sq, T0821-244 2444, www. mysoredasaprakashgroup.com.
144 rooms in this labyrinthine blue-white complex set around an attractive, large courtyard. Milk coffee-coloured rooms are stocked with wood furniture and scrupulously clean white sheets. Peaceful and quiet despite being slap bang in the centre.

$ Greens' Boarding and Lodging
2722/2 Curzon Park Rd, T0821-242 2415.
Dark hallways give way to green gloss-painted rooms with dark wood furniture. Cool, spacious, central and darn cheap, but bathrooms are not the best.

$ Hotel Ritz
Regency Theatre Complex, Lokaranjan Mahal Rd, T0821-242 9082, www.hotelritzmysore.com.
One of the better cheap deals in town, with big well-kept rooms, free Wi-Fi and a good restaurant serving veg and egg dishes.

$ Park Lane
2720 Sri Harsha Rd, T0821-400 3500, www.parklanemysore.com.
Freshly renovated, with a price hike to match, but the folk-art-rustic rooms are clean and still good value. The noise, including nightly classical Indian performances, from popular downstairs restaurant does travel (open 1030-2330).

Restaurants

$$$ Green Hotel
See Where to stay.
Atmospheric with food served in the palace itself, on a veranda, or under the stars in the hotel's immaculate garden. But not the best food.

$$ Park Lane
See Where to stay.
Red lights hang from the creeper-covered trellis over this courtyard restaurant: turn them on for service. Superb classical music played every evening 1900-2130. Good food, including barbecue nights. Popular, lively and idiosyncratic.

$$ Shanghai
Vinoba Rd. Open 1100-1500, 1830-2300.
Superb Chinese food, despite the shabby interior.

$$ Shilpashri
Gandhi Sq.
Comfortable rooftop restaurant serving reasonably priced tourist-orientated dishes and chilled beers. Friendly but service can be slow.

$ Amaravathi (Roopa's)
Hardinge Circle.
Excellent, spicy hot Andhra meals served on banana leaves.

$ Anu's Bamboo Hut
367 2nd Main, 3rd Stage, Gokulam, T0821-428 9492.
Friendly little rooftop café in the midst of the Western yogi ghetto of Gokulam. The vegetarian buffet (daily except Thu, 1300-1500) is packed with salads and bean dishes, and always sells out quickly; Anu also does good smoothies and lassies from 1700-1900, and offers vegetarian cooking classes. Call ahead.

$ Jewel Rock
Maurya Residency, Sri Harsha Rd.
Dark interior, great chicken tikka, spicy cashew nut chicken, go early to avoid the queues.

$ Mylari
Hotel Mahadeshwara, Nazarbad Main Rd (ask a rickshaw driver). Open in the mornings until 1100.
The best *dosas* in town served on a banana leaf. The surroundings are basic and you may have to queue. The biriyanis are also legendary.

$ Mysore Dasaprakash
See Where to stay.
Good breakfast, huge southern *thali* (Rs 25).

$ Om Shanti
Siddharta (see Where to stay).
Pure vegetarian *thali* place, with a/c and non-a/c sections, thronged with domestic tourists which is a fair reflection of its culinary prowess.

$ RRR
Gandhi Sq.
Part a/c, tasty non-vegetarian food served on plantain leaves, good for lunch.

$ Samrat
Next to Indra Bhavan, Dhanvantri Rd.
Offers a range of tasty North Indian vegetarian dishes.

$ SR Plantain Leaf (Chalukya's)
Rajkamal Talkies Rd.
Decent vegetarian *thalis* served on a banana leaf; also does tandoori chicken.

Cafés and snacks

Bombay Tiffany's
Devraja Market Building.
Try the 'Mysore pak', a ghee-laden sweet.

Indra Café
Sayaji Rd, on the fringes of the market.
Excellent *bhel puri, sev puri* and *channa puri.*

Penguin Ice-cream Parlour
Near KR Hospital, Dhanavantri Rd.
Sofas shared with local teens listening to Hindi pop.

Raghu Niwas
B-N Rd, opposite Ritz.
Does very good breakfasts.

Sri Rama Veg
397 Dhanvantri Rd.
Serves fast food and good juices.

Bars and clubs

The best bars are in hotels (see Where to stay): try the expensive but elegant **Lalitha Mahal Palace** or the funky lounge at the **Adhi Manor**, Chandragupta Rd.

Festivals

Mar-Apr Temple car festival with a 15-day fair, at the picturesque town of Nanjangud, 23 km south (Erode road); **Vairamudi** festival which lasts 6 days when deities are adorned with 3 diamond crowns, at Melkote Temple, 52 km.

11 Aug Feast of St Philomena, 0800-1800, the statue of the saint is taken out in procession through the city streets ending with a service at the Gothic, stained-glass-laden cathedral.
End Sep to early-Oct Dasara, see box, page 987.

Shopping

Books
Ashok, *Dhanvantri Rd, T0821-243 5533.*
Excellent selection.

Clothing
For silks at good prices, try Sayaji Rao Rd but beware those pretending to be government emporia.
Badshah's, *20 Devraj Urs Rd, T0821-242 9799.*
Beautifully finished *salwar kameez*. Mr Yasin speaks good English.
Craft Emporium, *middle part of Vinoba Rd.*
Good selection and quality. Also sells cloth.
Karnataka Silk Industry, *Mananthody Rd, T0821-248 1803. Mon-Sat 1030-1200, 1500-1630.*
Watch machine weaving at the factory shop.

Handicrafts
Superb carved figures, sandalwood and rosewood items, silks, incense sticks, handicrafts. The main shopping area is Sayaji Rao Rd.
Cauvery Arts & Crafts Emporium, *Sayyaji Rao Rd.* For sandalwood and rosewood items, closed Thu (non-receipt of parcel reported by traveller).
Devaraja Market, *North of KR Circle.* Lanes of stalls selling spices, perfumes and much more; including a good 'antique' shop (fixed price) with excellent sandalwood and rosewood items. Worth visiting.
Ganesh, *532 Dhanvantri Rd.*
Shankar, *12 Dhanvantri Rd.*
Sri Lakshmi Fine Arts & Crafts, *opposite the zoo; also has a factory shop at 2226 Sawday Rd, Mandi Mohalla.*

What to do

Body and soul
See box, opposite.
Jois Ashtanga Yoga Research Institute, *www.kpjayi.org.* Not for dilettante yogis at Rs 8000 a month, the minimum period offered.
Sri Patanjali Yogashala, *Parakala Mutt, next to Jaganmohan Palace.* Ashtanga Vinyasa yoga; daily instruction in English from BNS Iyengar, 0600-0900, 1600-1900, US$100 per month: some say the conditions here are slapdash, although teaching is good.

Power yoga

If you know the primary series, speak fluent *ujayyi* breath and know about the *mulla bandha* odds are that you have heard the name of Sri Pattabhi Jois, too. His is the version of yoga that has most percolated contemporary Western practice (it's competitive enough for the type-A modern societies we live in, some argue), and although for most of the years of his teaching he had just a handful of students, things have certainly changed.

Though the Guru left his body in May 2009, a steady flow of international students still make the pilgrimage to his Ashtanga Yoga Nilayam in Mysore, where his daughter Saraswathi and grandson Sharath Rangaswamy continue the lineage.

Saraswathi's classes are deemed suitable for Ashtanga novices, but studying with Sharath is not for dilettante yogis; the Westerners here are extremely ardent about their practice – mostly teachers themselves – and there is a strict pecking order which first-timers could find alienating. Classes start from first light at 0400, and the day's teaching is over by 0700, leaving you free for the rest of the day.

There's no rule that says you must know the series, but it might be better, and cheaper, to dip a toe in somewhere a bit less hardcore and far-flung, such as Purple Valley in Goa (see page 1194).

For details and Sharath's teaching schedule, see www.kpjayi.com.

Swimming

Mysore University, *2 km east of the palace in Saraswathipuram*. Olympic-sized pool, hourly sessions 0630-0830 then 1500-1600, women only 1600-1700.

Southern Star Mysore, *13-14 Vinoba Rd, T0821-242 1689, www.ushalexushotels.com*. More of a pool to relax by and sunbathe.

Tour operators

KSTDC, *Yatri Nivas hotel, 2 JLB Rd, T0821-242 3492*.
Mysore, daily 0715-2030, Rs 155, tours of local sights and Chamundi Hill, Kukkara Halli Lake, Somanathapura, Srirangapatnam and Brindavan Gardens. Tours also run to **Belur**, **Halebid**, and **Sravanabelagola** if there are 10 or more guests: a long and tiring day, but worth it if you are not travelling to Hassan.

Seagull Travels, *8 Hotel Ramanashree Complex, BN Rd, T0821-426 0054*. Good for cars, drivers, flights, wildlife tours, etc, helpful.

Skyway International Travels, *No 370/4, Jansi Laxmibai Rd, T0821-244 4444, www.skywaytour.com*. Excellent travel agency for car hire and accommodation bookings.

TCI, *Gandhi Sq, T0821-526 0294*. Very pleasant and helpful.

Transport

Bus Local City bus station, southeast of KR Circle, T0821-242 5819. To **Silk Weaving Centre**, Nos 1, 2, 4 and 8; **Brindavan Gardens**, No 303; **Chamundi Hill**, No 201;
Srirangapatnam, No 313. **Central Bus Station**, T0821-2529853. **Bandipur**, Platform 9, **Ooty** etc, Platform 11.

Long distance There are 2 bus stations. **Central**, T0821-252 0853, is mainly used by long-distance **SRTC** companies of Karnataka, Tamil Nadu and Kerala, all of which run regular daily services between Mysore and other major cities. The bus station has a list of buses with reserved places. To **Bengaluru**: every 15 mins from non-stop platform. Also frequent services to **Hassan**, 3 hrs; **Mangalore** (7 hrs); and **Ooty** (5 hrs) via **Bandipur** (2 hrs). Daily services to **Coimbatore**; **Gokarna** (12 hrs); **Hospet**: 1930 (10 hrs), very tiring; **Kochi**, 10 hrs; **Kozhikode** via **Wayanad**; **Salem** (7 hrs); **Thiruvananthapuram** (Super deluxe, 14 hrs). Several to **Satyamangalam** (3-4 hrs) where you can connect with buses to Tamil Nadu. The journey is through wilderness and forests with spectacular scenery as the road finally plunges from the plateau down to the plains.

The **Suburban** and **Private bus stands**, T0821-244 3490, serve nearby destinations including **Somnathpur**, around 1 hr direct, or longer via Bannur or via Narasipur. Many private companies near Gandhi Sq operate overnight sleepers and interstate buses which may be faster and marginally less uncomfortable. Book ahead for busy routes.

Car Travel companies and **KSTDC** charge about Rs 700 (4 hrs/40 km) for city sightseeing; Rs 1100 to include Srirangapatnam and Brindavan.

Platform 1. Taxi counter at entrance. To **Hassan**: 10 daily, 2½ hrs. **Bengaluru**: around 20 a day, 2-3 hrs, some via Srirangapatnam. **Chennai**: 2 daily, 7-10½ hrs. **Hospet**: 1 daily, 12½ hrs. **Mangalore**: 2 daily, 8 ½ hrs.

Around Mysore *Colour map 7, B3.*

from ancient palaces and temples to lush forests and wildlife

Srirangapatnam

The island is over 3 km long and 1 km wide so it's best to hire a bicycle from a shop on the main road to get around.

Srirangapatnam (population 21,900), 12 km from Mysore, has played a crucial role in the region since its origins in the 10th century. Occupying an easily fortified island site in the Kaveri River, it has been home to religious reformers and military conquerors. It makes a fascinating day trip from Mysore; Daria Daulat Bagh and the Gumbaz are wonderful.

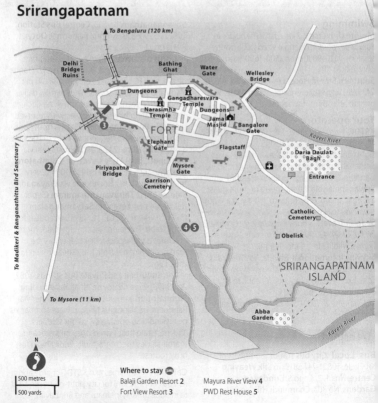

Srirangapatnam

Where to stay 🛏
Balaji Garden Resort **2**
Fort View Resort **3**
Mayura River View **4**
PWD Rest House **5**

The name Srirangapatnam comes from the **Temple of Sri Ranganathaswamy**, which stands aloof at the heart of the fortress, containing a highly humanistic idol of Lord Vishnu reclining on the back of a serpent. Dating from AD 894, it is far older than the fort and town, and was subsequently added to by the Hoysala and Vijayanagar kings. The latter built the fort in 1454, and occupied the site for some 150 years until the last Vijayanagar ruler handed over authority to the Hindu Wodeyars of Mysore, who made it their capital. In the second half of the 18th century it became the capital of Haidar Ali, who defended it against the Marathas in 1759, laying the foundations of his expanding power. He was succeeded by his son Tipu Sultan, who also used the town as his headquarters until Colonel Wellesley, the future Duke of Wellington, established his military reputation by defeating the 'Tiger of Mysore' in battle on 4 May 1799. Tipu died in exceptionally fierce fighting near the north gate of the fort; the place is marked by a simple monument. The fort had triple fortifications, but the British destroyed most of it.

Jama Masjid ① *0800-1300, 1600-2000.* The mosque, which Tipu had built, has delicate minarets, and there are two Hindu **temples**, to Narasimha (17th century) and Gangadharesvara (16th century).

Daria Daulat Bagh (Splendour of the Sea) ① *1 km east of the fort, Sat-Thu 0900-1700, foreigners Rs 100, Indians Rs 5.* Tipu's beautiful summer palace was built in 1784 and is set in a lovely garden. This social historical jewel has colourful frescoes of battle scenes between the French, British and Mysore armies, ornamental arches and gilded paintings on the teak walls and ceilings crammed with interesting detail. The west wall shows Haidar Ali and Tipu Sultan leading their elephant forces at the battle of Polilur (1780), inflicting a massive defeat on the British. As a result of the battle, Colonel Baillie – the defeated British commander – was held prisoner in Srirangapatnam for many years. The murals on the east walls show Tipu offering hospitality to neighbouring princes at various palace durbars. The small museum upstairs has 19th-century European paintings and Tipu's belongings.

To Bengaluru (120 km)

Lokapavini River

Bathing Ghat

GANJAM

Col Baillie's Tomb

Abbé Dubois

Pol

Coracle Hire

Gumbaz Mausoleum

Lal Bagh Palace

Ford

The Gumbaz ① *3 km east, Sat-Thu 0800-1830, donation collected.* This is the family mausoleum, approached through an avenue of cypresses. Built by Tipu in memory of his father, the ornate white dome protects beautiful ivory-on-wood inlay and Tipu's tiger-stripe emblem, some swords and shields. Haider Ali's tomb is in the centre, his wife to the east and Tipu's own to the west.

Ranganathittu Bird Sanctuary
5 km upstream of Srirangapatnam, 0700-1800, foreigners Rs 300, Indians Rs 50, camera Rs 25, video Rs 250. Boats (0830-1330, 1430-1830), foreigners Rs 300, Indians Rs 50. Jun-Oct best. Mysore City Bus 126, or auto-rickshaw from Srirangapatnam. Guided boat trips from the jetty last 15-20 mins.

The riverine site of this sanctuary was established in 1975. Several islands, some bare and rocky, others larger and well wooded, provide excellent habitat for waterbirds, including the black-crowned night heron, Eurasian spoonbill and cormorants. Fourteen species of waterbirds use the sanctuary as a breeding ground from June onwards. There is a large colony of fruit bats in trees on the edge of the river and a number of marsh crocodiles between the small islands.

Somnathpur

This tiny village boasts the only complete Hoysala temple in the Mysore region. The drive east from Srirangapatnam via Bannur is particularly lovely, passing a couple of lakes through beautiful country and pretty, clean villages. The small but exquisite **Kesava Temple** (1268) ⓘ *0900-1700, foreigners Rs 100, Indians Rs 5, allow 1 hr, canteen, buses from Mysore take 1-1½ hrs; via Bannur (25 km, 45 mins) then to Somnathpur (3 km, 15 mins by bus, or lovely walk or bike ride through countryside),* is one of the best preserved of 80 Hoysala temples in this area. Excellent ceilings show the distinctive features of the late Hoysala style, and here the roof is intact where other famous temples have lost theirs. The temple has three sanctuaries with the *trikutachala* (triple roof) and stands in the middle of its rectangular courtyard (70 m long, 55 m wide) with cloisters containing 64 cells around it. From the east gateway is a superb view of the temple with an ambulatory standing on its raised platform, in the form of a 16-pointed star. The pillared hall in the centre with the three shrines to the west give it the form of a cross in plan. Walk around the temple to see the fine bands of sculptured figures. The lowest of the six shows a line of elephants, symbolizing strength and stability, then horsemen for speed, followed by a floral scroll. The next band of beautifully carved figures (at eye level) is the most fascinating and tells stories from the epics. Above is the *yali* frieze, the monsters and foliage possibly depicting the river Ganga and uppermost is a line of *hamsa*, the legendary geese.

Sivasamudram

80 km east of Mysore. Take a bus from Mysore or Bengaluru to Kollegala, then hire a taxi or autorickshaw.

Here, the Kaveri plunges over 100 m into a series of wild and inaccessible gorges. At the top of the falls the river divides around the island of Sivasamudram, the Barachukki channel on the east and the Gaganchukki on the west. The hydroelectricity project was completed in 1902, the first HEP scheme of any size in India. It's best visited during the wet season, when the falls are an impressive sight, as water cascades over a wide area in a series of leaps.

Biligiri Rangaswamy Wildlife Sanctuary

80 km south of Mysore, 0600-0900, 1600-1830, foreigners Rs 2400, Indians Rs 800. From Mysore, access is via Nanjangud (23 km) and Chamarajanagar, where there's a Forest Check Post. For information, contact Deputy Conservator of Forests, Sultan Sheriff Circle, Chamarajanagar, T08226-222059.

A hilly area with moist deciduous and semi-evergreen forests interspersed with grassland, the Biligiri Rangaswamy Hills (altitude 1000-1600 m) represent a biodiversity crossroads between the eastern and western sides of the Ghats. Some of the largest elephant populations east of the divide occur here, along with sloth bear (better sightings here than at other southern sanctuaries), panther, elephant, deer, gaur and the occasional tiger, as well as 270 species of bird. The local Forest Department has recently begun offering treks through the sanctuary, guided by members of the tribal community. The best time for wildlife sighting is November to May. The local Soliga hill tribes pay special respect to an ancient champak tree (*Doddasampige mara*) believed to be 1000 years old and the abode of Vishnu.

Bandipur National Park

96 km southwest of Mysore. 0600-0900, 1530-1830, reception centre 0900-1630; Mysore–Ooty buses stop at the main entrance. Except for jeep safaris run by local lodges, the only access is by the Forest Department's uninspiring 1-hr bus safari: foreigners Rs 100, plus park entry fee of Rs 2400, Indians Rs 800. For information, contact Deputy Conservator of Forests, T08229-236043 (Mysore T0821-248 0901), dcfbandipur@yahoo.co.in.

Bandipur (altitude 780-1455 m, area 874 sq km) was set up by the Mysore maharaja in 1931, and now forms part of the Nilgiri Biosphere Reserve, sharing borders with Mudumalai National Park in

Tamil Nadu and Kerala's Wayanad Wildlife Sanctuary. It has a mixture of subtropical moist and dry deciduous forests (principally teak and anogeissus) and scrubland in the Nilgiri foothills. The wetter areas support rosewood, silk cotton, sandalwood and *jamun*. You may spot gaur, chital (spotted deer), elephant, sambar, flying squirrel and four-horned antelope, but tigers and leopards are rare. There's also a good variety of birdlife including crested hawk, serpent eagles and tiny-eared owls.

★ Nagarhole (Rajiv Gandhi) National Park

50 km west of Mysore, 0600-0900, 1530-1830. Foreigners Rs 2400 per safari (by boat, jeep or bus), Indians Rs 800. Main entrance is at Karapur, on the Mysore–Mananthavady road, close to Kabini River Lodge and several other resorts. Another road enters the park near Hunsur on the northern side, where Deputy Conservator of Forests may grant permission for private jeep safaris and forest treks; enquire in advance on T08222-252064, dcfhunsur@rediffmail.com. Both roads across the park are closed after dusk to allow animal movements.

Nagarhole (meaning 'snake streams') was once the maharajas' reserved forest and became a national park in 1955. Covering gentle hills bordering Kerala, it's now one of India's greatest conservation successes, with predator populations at their maximum possible density and poaching virtually wiped out. The park's habitat range includes swampland, streams, moist deciduous forest, stands of bamboo and valuable timber in teak and rosewood trees. The Kabini River, which is a tributary of the Kaveri, flows through the forest where the upper canopy reaches 30 m. The park is accessible both by road and river. A number of tribesmen, particularly Kurumbas (honey gatherers) who still practise ancient skills, live amongst, and care for, the elephants.

In addition to elephants, the park also has gaur (Indian bison), dhole (Indian wild dogs), wild cats, four-horned antelopes, flying squirrels, sloth bears, monkeys and sambar deer. Tigers and leopards are hard to see except in the pre-monsoon summer, when dry conditions bring prey and predators to the few man-made waterholes. Many varieties of birds include the rare Malabar trogon, great black woodpecker, Indian pitta, pied hornbill, whistling thrush, green imperial pigeon and also waterfowl and reptiles.

The edge of the dam is the best place to view wildlife, particularly during the dry period from March to June, when elephants gather in their hundreds, and other herbivores in even greater numbers, to feast on vegetation left exposed by the receding dam waters.

The Forest Department runs two- to three-hour safaris in the morning and evening – currently the only way to explore the 'tourism' zone of the park, though local operators are campaigning to allow private safaris. Only a limited number of government jeeps are allowed into the park for each session, and to have a chance to get a slot you need to be staying at one of the resorts and lodges around Karapur.

Listings Around Mysore *map p992*

Where to stay

Srirangapatnam

$$ Mayura River View
Mysore Rd, T08236-217454.
Beautifully situated on the croc-filled river with 8 comfortable rooms (2 with a/c), sit-outs and a good vegetarian restaurant (Indian, Chinese). Very quiet and relaxing.

$$-$ Balaji Garden Resort
Mysore Rd (1 km from Piriyapatna Bridge), T08236-217355.
12 good-value cottages and 28 smallish rooms built with some style around a central courtyard. Rooms are well furnished, tiled and comfy; cottages are good value. There's a pool, restaurant.

$$-$ Fort View Resort
On the Bengaluru–Mysore road, T08236-252577.
12 upmarket rooms (4 with corner tub), Rajasthani architecture and huge beds, set in shady landscaped gardens. The restaurant is a little gloomy and overpriced but there's an organic kitchen garden, pool, boating and fishing. Efficient.

$ PWD Rest House
Book ahead at the PWD office near Ranganathaswami Temple, T08236-252051.
Charming former residence of George Harris. Basic rooms, but clean and quiet.

Biligiri Rangaswamy Wildlife Sanctuary

As in most Karnataka wildlife parks, the lodges and forest rest houses here charge foreigners double the rate Indians pay.

$$$ K Gudi Camp
Kyathadevara, book via Jungle Lodges, T080-2559 7025, www.junglelodges.com.
8 twin-bedded quality tents with modern toilets, or 4 rooms with 4 beds at the royal hunting lodge. Simple meals in the open air, elephant rides, birding, trekking. A comfortable experience despite the remoteness.

Bandipur National Park

Reserve rooms in advance; avoid weekends.

$$$ Bandipur Safari Lodge
At Melkamanahalli nearby, T080-4055 4055, www.junglelodges.com.
Simple rooms in cottages and a restaurant under shady trees. Rates include nature walks, park safaris and entry fees.

$$$ Dhole's Den
Kaniyanapura village, T08229-236062, www.dholesden.com.
Lovely small resort, with 2 rooms, a spacious suite and 2 large cottages, done out in modern minimalist style with a minimal-impact ethos: there's no TV or a/c, most electricity comes from wind turbines and solar, and you can pick your own veggies from the organic garden for dinner.

$ Venu Vihar Lodge
20 km from the park reception. Book in advance through the Forest Department, Woodyard, Mysore, T0821-248 0110.
Set in the beautiful Gopalaswamy Hills. Meals are available but take provisions.

Nagarhole National Park

Safari lodges around Nagarhole are, with one notable exception, very expensive, though rates generally include jeep safaris. More affordable rooms are available in homestays around Kutta on the western fringe of the park. A 2-tier pricing structure operates in many lodges and hotels; where applicable, prices quoted are for foreigners.

$$$$ Kabini River Lodge
At Karapur on the reservoir bank, T080-2559 7025, www.junglelodges.com.
Accommodation consists of 14 rooms in a Mysore maharajas' 18th-century hunting lodge and bungalow, 6 newer cabins overlooking the lake or 5 tents, simple but acceptable. Good restaurant and bar, exchange facilities. The package includes meals, sailing, jeep/minibus at Nagarhole, and park tour with a naturalist. Very friendly and well run.

$$$$ Orange County Kabini
Bheeramballi Village, T08228-269100, www.orangecounty.in.
A long slow drive on rutted roads, or a short boat ride across the lake, brings you to this beautiful resort in a tree-shaded compound. Luxurious individual huts, built and furnished in a smart take on tribal style, come with private courtyard pool or spa. 2 restaurants, and a beautiful reading room overlooking the lake, plus guided activities including coracle trips, elephant and bullock cart rides.

$$$ The Bison
1 km from the park gate in Gundathur village, T080-4127 8708, www.thebisonresort.com.
A wildlife camp in the truest sense, this rustic collection of lakeside tents and treehouses come with lashings of Victorian explorer style – hurricane lamps, antique 4-posters, and rickety gangplanks. Lodge owner Shaaz Jung is one of India's best young wildlife photographers, and a passionate and knowledgeable tracker, and a few days spent on safari with him may well represent your best chance in South India of spotting a leopard or tiger. Not luxurious, but superb value and most highly recommended.

$$$ Waterwoods
500 m from Kabini River Lodge, surrounded by the Kabini River, T08228-264421.
Exquisitely furnished ranch-style house, 6 luxury rooms with sit-outs, beautiful gardens on the water's edge, delicious home cooking, solar power, friendly staff, boating, jeep, Ayurvedic massage, gym, swimming and walking. Charming, informal atmosphere, peaceful, secluded.

Transport

Srirangapatnam

Trains and buses between **Bengaluru** and **Mysore** stop here but arrival can be tiresome with hassle from rickshaw drivers, traders and beggars. Buses 313 and 316 from Mysore **City Bus Stand** (half-hourly) take 50 mins.

Bandipur National Park
Bus
Bandipur and the neighbouring Mudumalai NP in Tamil Nadu are both on the Mysore to Ooty bus route, about 2½ hrs south from Mysore and 2½ hrs from Ooty. Buses go to and from **Mysore** (80 km) between 0615-1530.

Nagarhole National Park
Bus From **Mysore**, Mananthavady-bound buses pass through **Karapur** (3 hrs), though you'll need to arrange in advance for your lodge to pick you up. (You can get a cheap look at the Nagarhole forest by catching the bus all the way through to Mananthavady.) **Jungle Lodges**, T080-2559 7021, www.junglelodges.com, buses leave Bengaluru at 0730, stop in Mysore (around 0930), reaching Kabini around 1230; return bus departs 1315.

Train The nearest station is Mysore (96 km).

★ Coorg (Kodagu) *Colour map 7, B3.*

small but perfectly formed forest district

Coorg, once a proud warrior kingdom, then a state, has now shrunk to become the smallest district in Karnataka. It is a beautiful anomaly in South India in that it has, so far, retained its original forests. Ancient rosewoods jut out of the Western Ghat hills to shade the squat coffee shrubs which the British introduced as the region's chief commodity. Like clockwork, 10 days after the rains come, these trees across whole valleys burst as one into white blossom drenching the moist air with their thick perfume, a hybrid of honeysuckle and jasmine.

Although the climate is not as cool as other hill stations, Coorg's proximity by road to the rest of Karnataka makes it a popular weekend bolthole for inhabitants of Bengaluru. The capital of Coorg District, Madikeri, is an attractive small town in a beautiful hilly setting surrounded by the forested slopes of the Western Ghats and has become a popular trekking destination.

Madikeri (Mercara)
The **Omkareshwara Temple in Madikeri** (population: 32,300, altitude 1150 m), dedicated to both Vishnu and Siva, was built in 1820. The tiled roofs are typical of Keralan Hindu architecture, while the domes show Muslim influence. On high ground dominating the town is the **fort** with its three stone gateways, built between 1812-1814 by Lingarajendra Wodeyar II. It has a small **museum** ① *Tue-Sun 0900-1700, closed holidays,* in St Mark's Church as well as the town prison, a temple and a chapel while the palace houses government offices. The **Rajas' Tombs** (*Gaddige*), built in 1820 to the north of the town, are the memorials of Virarajendra and his wife and of Lingarajendra. Although the rajas were Hindu, their commemorative monuments are Muslim in style; Kodagas both bury and cremate their dead. The **Friday Market** near the bus stand is very colourful as all the local tribal people come to town to sell their produce. It is known locally as shandy, a British bastardization of the Coorg word *shante*, meaning market. On Mahadevped Road, which leads to the Rajas' tombs, is a 250-year-old **Siva temple** which has an interesting stone façade. Madikeri also has an attractive nine-hole golf course.

Essential Coorg (Kodagu)

Finding your feet

At present Coorg is only accessible by road, although an airport and railway station are planned. Frequent local and express buses arrive at Madikeri's bus stand from the west coast after a journey through beautiful wooded hills passing small towns and a wildlife sanctuary. From Mysore and Coimbatore an equally pleasant route traverses the Maidan. In winter there is often hill fog at night, making driving after dark dangerous. Madikeri is ideal for walking though you may need to hire an auto on arrival to reach the better hotels.

BACKGROUND

Coorg

Although there were references to the Kodaga people in the Tamil Sangam literature of the second century AD, the earliest Kodaga inscriptions date from the eighth century. After the Vjiayanagar Empire was defeated in 1565, many of their courtiers moved south, establishing regional kingdoms. One of these groups was the Haleri Rajas, members of the Lingayat caste whose leader Virarajendra set up the first Kodaga dynasty at Haleri, 10 km from the present district capital of Madikeri.

The later Kodagu Rajas were noted for some bizarre behaviour. Dodda Vira (1780-1809) was reputed to have put most of his relatives to death, a pattern followed by the last king, Vira Raja, before he was forced to abdicate by the British in 1834. In 1852 the last Lingayat ruler of Kodagu, Chikkavirarajendra Wodeyar, became the first Indian prince to sail to England, and the economic character of the state was quickly transformed. Coffee was introduced, becoming the staple crop of the region.

The forests of Kodagu are still home to wild elephants, which often crash into plantations on jackfruit raids, and other wildlife. The Kodaga, a tall, fair and proud landowning people who flourished under the British, are renowned for their martial prowess; almost every family has one member in the military. They also make incredibly warm and generous hosts – a characteristic you can discover thanks to the number of plantation homestays in inaccessible estates of dramatic beauty pioneered here following the crash in coffee prices. Kodagu also has a highly distinctive cuisine, in which *pandi* curry (pork curry) and *kadumbuttu* (rice dumplings) are particular favourites.

Around Madikeri

Madikeri and the surrounding area makes for beautiful walking but if you want to venture further you'll need to take a guide as paths can soon become indistinct and confusing.

Abbi Falls ① *30-min rickshaw ride (9 km, Rs 150 round-trip).* The journey to the falls is through forests and coffee plantations. It is also an enjoyable walk along a fairly quiet road. The falls themselves are beautiful and well worth the visit. You can do a beautiful short trek down the valley and then up and around above the falls before rejoining the main road. Do not attempt it alone since there are no trails and you must depend on your sense of direction along forest paths. Honey Valley Estate (see page 1000) has a book of walks around the guesthouse.

Bhagamandala ① *36 km southwest, half-hourly service from Madikeri's private bus stand from 0630-2000, Rama Motors tour bus departs 0830, with 30-min stop.* At Bhagmandala the **Triveni bathing ghat** can be visited at the confluence of the three rivers: Kaveri, Kanike and Suiyothi. Among many small shrines the **Bhandeshwara Temple**, standing in a large stone courtyard surrounded by Keralan-style buildings on all four sides, is particularly striking. You can stay at the temple for a very small charge.

Kakkabe ① *35 km south of Madikeri, bus from Madikeri to Kakkabe at 0630, jeep 1 hr.* Kakkabe is a small town, giving access to the highest peak in Coorg, **Thandiandamole** (1800 m). Nearby, **Padi Iggutappa** is the most important temple in Coorg.

Cauvery Nisargadhama ① *0900-1800, Rs 150, still camera Rs 10.* This small island reserve in the Kaveri River is 2 km from Kushalnagar, accessed over a hanging bridge. Virtually untouched by tourism, it consists mostly of bamboo thickets and trees, including sandalwood, and is very good for seeing parakeets, bee eaters, woodpeckers and a variety of butterflies. There is a deer park, pedalo boating, a resident elephant and tall bamboo tree houses for wildlife viewing.

Bylakuppe ① *6 km south of Kushalnagar.* Bylakuppe is home to a large Tibetan settlement, established in 1961. Apart from the cognitive dissonance of seeing Himalayan monks sipping from coconuts in steamy South India, the main point of interest here is the **Namdroling Monastery**, home to a community of 5000 lamas, where the Golden Temple houses beautiful murals and 60-foot high golden statues of the Buddha, Guru Padmasambhava, and Buddha Amitayus. A popular tourist destination on weekends, it's easy enough to visit for a day, but if you wish to stay in Bylakuppe you'll need to apply for an Inner Line Permit; see www.palyul.org.

Dubare Elephant Camp ① *On the road between Kushalnagar and Siddapur, 0830-1200, 1630-1730, Rs 50, Indians Rs 20, plus Rs 200 each for riding, bathing and feeding elephant.* At this government-owned centre on the banks of the Kaveri you can feed and bathe elephants and line up for a short ride. The boat ride across the broad river is an appealing element of the experience in itself.

Listings Coorg

Tourist information

Madikeri

Tourist office
Mysore Rd, south of the Thinmaya statue, T08272-228580.

Coorg Wildlife Society
2 km further out on Mysore Rd, T08272-223505.
Can help with trekking advice and permits for catch-and-release *mahseer* fishing on the Kaveri River.

Where to stay

Madikeri

Power cuts are common so carry a torch and keep candles handy. Book early during holidays.

$$ Capitol Village
5 km southeast of town on Siddapur Rd, T08272-200135.
This traditional Keralan building (tiled roof and wooden beams) is set in a coffee, cardamom and pepper estate with a large pond. There are 13 large, airy rooms and a dorm (Rs 150). It's very quiet with excellent birdlife and outdoor eating under shady trees (Rs 75-150). A rickshaw from the centre costs Rs 100.

$$ Mayura Valley View (KSTDC)
Raja's Seat, T08272-228387, or book at Karnataka Tourism, Bengaluru, T080-2221 2901.
Perched on a cliff-top with stunning views especially at sunset. 25 clean and recently renovated rooms, and a pretty good restaurant. A cut above the usual government-run guesthouse.

$$-$ Chitra
School Rd, near the bus stand, T08272-225372, www.hotelchitra.com.
54 nondescript rooms, simple but clean, with Western toilets and hot showers. North Indian vegetarian restaurant, bar, helpful and knowledgeable English-speaking trekking guide (Mr Muktar).

$$-$ Rajdarshan,116/2 MG Rd
T08272-229142, www.hotelrajdarshan.net.
Modern hotel with 25 well-laid-out clean rooms (in need of renovation) and an excellent restaurant. Staff are friendly and there are views over the town.

$ Cauvery
School Rd, T08272-225492.
26 clean, pleasant but basic rooms with fans, Indian meals, bar, away from the main road. Helpful management, information on trekking (stores luggage).

$ Hilltown
Daswal Rd, T08272-223801, hilltown@rediffmail.com.
38 modern, pleasant and airy rooms with TV in this new hotel with marble floors throughout and a restaurant. Great value. Highly recommended.

$ Popular Residency
Kohinoor Rd, T08272-221644.
New hotel with 10 clean and pleasant rooms, well fitted out, North Indian vegetarian restaurant, good value.

$ Vinayaka Lodge
25 m from the bus stand, T08272-229830.
50 rooms with bath, hot water buckets, friendly staff, clean and quiet (though the bus stand can be noisy in the early morning). Good value.

Around Madikeri

$$$$ Orange County
Karadigodu Post, Siddapur, T08274-258481, www.orangecounty.in.
One of the most beautiful resorts in all of South India, set on a working 300-acre coffee plantation. 63 cottages – some built of traditional red stone and dark timber, others decked out in modern style with high ceilings and big

windows – all but 8 of which come with their own private pool. Warm and friendly staff, several good restaurants, and naturalist-led activities including excellent guided birdwatching and coracle rides on the Kaveri. Highly recommended.

$ Forest Rest House
Cauvery Nisargadhama, contact Forestry Office, Madikeri, T08272-228305, dfo_madikeri@yahoo.com.
11 simple cottages built largely of bamboo and teak, some with balconies on stilts over the water, electricity (no fan), hot water, peaceful (despite nocturnal rats), but poor food.

$ Honey Valley Estate
Yavakapadi, Kakkabe, 3 km up a track only a jeep can manage, T08272-238339, www.honeyvalleyindia.in.
This place has less stunning views than the **Palace Estate** (the house is screened by tall trees) but equally good access by foot to trekking trails. Facilities are mostly better and it can fit over 30 guests. The host family is charming too. Also has a hut 2 km into the forest for those wanting more isolation.

$ Palace Estate
2 km south of Kakkabe (Rs 70 in a rickshaw) along Palace Rd, T08272-238446, www.palaceestate.co.in.
A small, traditional farm growing coffee, pepper, cardamom and bananas lying just above the late 18th-century Nalnad Palace, a summer hunting lodge of the kings of Coorg. The 6 basic rooms with shared veranda have a 180° panorama of forested hills all the way to Madikeri. Isolated and an excellent base for walking; Coorg's highest peak is 6 km from the homestay. Home-cooked local food, English-speaking guide Rs 150.

Restaurants

Madikeri

$ Capitol
Near Private Bus Stand.
Despite its exterior, serves excellent vegetarian fare.

$ Choice
School Rd.
Wide menu, very good food, choice of ground floor or rooftop dining.

$ East End
Gen Thimaya Rd.
Good old-fashioned restaurant, serving excellent *dosas*.

$ Taj
College Rd.
'Cheap and best', clean and friendly.

$ Taste of Coorg
CMC Building, near Town Hall.
The best place for traditional Coorgi delicacies like pork curry with *kadumbuttu* (steamed, ghee-laden rice balls).

$ Udupi Veglands
Opposite the fort.
Lovely, clean, spacious wooden eatery, delicious and cheap vegetarian *thalis*.

What to do

Madikeri
Fishing
Coorg Wildlife Society, *see page 999*. Arranges licences for fishing on the Kaveri River (Rs 500 per day, Rs 1000 weekend). The highlight is the prospect of pulling in a *mahseer*, up to 45 kg in weight; all fish must be returned to the river. Fishing takes place at Trust Land Estate, Valnoor, near Kushalnagar, where there is a lodge; you'll need to bring your own food.

Trekking
Friends' Tours and Travel, *below Bank of India, College Rd, T08272-229974*. Recommended for their knowledge and enthusiasm. Tailor-made treks Rs 275 per person per day including guide, food and accommodation in temples, schools, etc. A base camp is at Thalathmane, 4 km from Madikeri, which people can also stay at even if not trekking. Basic huts and blankets for Rs 50 each, home cooking available nearby at little extra cost.
Hotel Cauvery, *see page 999*. Also arranges treks.

Transport

Madikeri
Auto-rickshaw From Hotel Chitra to **Abbi Falls**, Rs 200 return, including a 1-hr wait at the falls.

Bus From KSRTC Bus Stand, T08272-229134, frequent express buses to **Bengaluru**, Plat 4, from 0615 (6 hrs); **Chikmagalur** (6 hrs); **Hassan** (3½ hrs); **Kannur** (4-5 hrs); **Mangalore**, Plat 2, 0530-2400 (3½ hrs); **Mysore**, Plat 3, half-hourly 0600-2300 (3 hrs) via **Kushalnagar** (for Tibetan settlements), very crowded during the rush hour (4 hrs); and **Thalassery**. Daily to **Coimbatore**, **Madurai**, **Mumbai**, **Ooty**, **Virajpet**.

Private Bus Stand: Kamadenu Travels, above bus stand, T08272-225524, for **Purnima Travels** bus to **Bengaluru**. **Shakti Motor Service** to **Nagarhole** (4½ hrs).

Train The closest stations are Mysore (120 km), Hassan (130 km) and Mangalore (135 km). Computerized reservations office on Main Rd, T08272-225002, Mon-Sat 1000-1700, Sun 1000-1400.

Around Madikeri

The bus from Madikeri to **Nisargadhama** passes park gates 2 km before Kushalnagar. A rickshaw from Kushalnagar costs Rs 40.

Western Plateau

The world's tallest monolith – that of the Jain saint Gommateshwara – has stood majestic, 'skyclad' and lost in meditation high on Sravanabelagola's Indragiri hill since the 10th century. It is a profoundly spiritual spot, encircled by long sweeps of paddy and sugar cane plains, and is one of the most popular pilgrimage points for practitioners of the austere Jain religion. Some male Jain followers of the Digambar or skyclad sect of the faith climb the rock naked to denote their freedom from material bonds. Nearby lie the 11th- and 12th-century capital cities of Halebid and Belur, the apex of Hoysala temple architecture whose walls are cut into friezes of the most intricate soapstone. These villages of the Central Maidan sit in what has been the path of one of the main routes for trade and military movement for centuries.

Western Plateau temples   *Colour map 7, A2.*
ancient capitals with exquisite temple architecture

Sravanabelagola, Belur and Halebid can all be seen in a very long day from Bengaluru, but it's far better to stay overnight near the sights themselves. Hotels in the temple villages tend to be very basic; for more comfortable options look towards the relaxed coffee-growing hill station of Chikmagalur, or Hassan, a pleasant, busy and fast-developing little city.

Hassan

Most visitors do little more than pass through Hassan en route to better things, taking advantage of its good range of hotels and transport connections. The city's main claim to fame is as home to the sinister-sounding Master Control Facility, one of two centres (the other is in Bhopal) responsible for controlling all of India's geostationary satellites.

Belur

Daily 0600-2000, but some temples close 1300-1600; free; carry a torch, ASI-trained guides on-site (often excellent), Rs 200 for 4 visitors, though official rate is higher.

Belur, on the banks of the Yagachi River, was the Hoysala dynasty's first capital and continues to be a significant town that is fascinating to explore. The gloriously elaborate Krishna Chennakesavara Temple

Essential Western Plateau

Finding your feet

Hassan is the main transport hub in the area and a good base for visiting the Western Plateau temples. It has train and direct bus connections with Mysore (three hours) and Bengaluru (4½ hours). There are local buses from Hassan to Halebid, Belur and Sravanabelagola. Alternatively, taxis charge around Rs 1000 for a day tour.

In the Central Maidan, both Chitradurga and Belgaum have bus and train stations with good connections.

Best place to stay...

Hoysala Village Resort, Hassan, page 1005
The Serai, Chikmagalur, page 1006
Taj Gateway, Chikmagalur, page 1006

Temples of Belur and Halebid

The Hoysalas, whose kingdom stretched between the Krishna and Kaveri rivers, encouraged competition among their artisans; their works even bear 12th-century autographs. Steatite (soapstone) meant that sculptors could fashion doily-like detail from solid rock since it is relatively soft when fresh from the quarry but hardens on exposure to air. The temples, built as prayers for victory in battle, are small but superb.

was built over the course of a century from 1116 as a fitting celebration of the victory over the Cholas at Talakad.

Chennakesava Temple At first glance Chennakesava Temple (see also Somnathpur, page 994) appears unimpressive because the super-structure has been lost. However, the walls are covered with exquisite friezes. A line of 644 elephants (each different) surrounds the base, with rows of figures and foliage above. The detail of the 38 female figures is perfect. Look at the young musicians and dancers on either side of the main door and the unusual perforated screens between the columns. Ten have typical bold geometrical patterns while the other 10 depict scenes from the *Puranas* in their tracery. Inside superb carving decorates the hand lathe-turned pillars and the bracket-figures on the ceiling. Each stunning filigree pillar is startlingly different in design, a symptom of the intensely competitive climate the sculptors of the day were working in. The **Narasimha pillar** at the centre of the hall is particularly fine and originally could be rotated. The detail is astounding. The jewellery on the figures is hollow and movable and the droplets of water seem to hang at the ends of the dancer's wet hair on a bracket above you. On the platform in front of the shrine is Santalesvara dancing in homage to Lord Krishna. The shrine holds a 3-m-high black polished deity, occasionally opened for *darshan*. The annual **Car Festival** is held in March-April.

Viranarayana Temple West of **Chennakesava**, Viranarayana Temple has some fine sculpture and smaller shrines around it. The complex is walled with an ambulatory. The entrance is guarded by the winged figure of Garuda, Vishnu's carrier, who faces the temple with joined palms.

Halebid
Daily 0700-1730, free.

The ancient capital of the Hoysala Empire was founded in the early 11th century. It was destroyed by the armies of the Delhi sultanate in 1311 and 1327. The great Hoysalesvara Temple, still incomplete after the best part of a century's toil, survived but the capital lay deserted and came to be called Halebid (ruined village), a name it continues to live up to.

Detour 1 km south to walk around the **Basthalli Garden** filled with remarkably simple 12th-century Jain Bastis. These have lathe-turned and multi-faceted columns, dark interiors and carved ceilings. The smaller **Kedaresvara Temple** with some highly polished columns is on a road going south. There are cycles for hourly hire to visit these quieter sites.

Hoysalesvara Temple The temple set in lawns has two shrines dedicated to Siva with a Nandi bull facing each. The largest of the Hoysala temples, it was started in 1121 but remains unfinished. It is similar in structure to Belur's, but its super-structure was never completed. Belur's real treats are in its interiors, while Halebid's are found on the outside reliefs. Six bands circle the star-shaped temple, elephants, lions, horsemen, a floral scroll and stories from the epics and the *Bhagavata Purana*. This frieze relates incidents from the *Ramayana* and *Mahabharata*; among them Krishna lifting Mount Govardhana and Rama defeating the demon god Ravana. The friezes above show *yalis* and *hamsa* or geese. There are exceptional half life-size deities with minute details at intervals. Of the original 84 female figures (like the ones at Belur) only 14 remain; thieves have made off with 70 down the centuries.

Archaeological Museum ① *Sat-Thu 1000-1700, Rs 5, no photography*. The museum is on the lawn near the south entrance and has a gallery of 12th- to 13th-century sculptures, woodcarvings, idols, coins and inscriptions. Some sculptures are displayed outside. To the west is a small lake.

Sravanabelagola

The ancient Jain statue of Gommateshwara stands on Vindhyagiri Hill (sometimes known as Indrabetta or Indragiri), 150 m above the plain; Chandragiri Hill to the north (also known as Chikka Betta) is just under half that height. The 17-m-high Gommateshwara statue, erected somewhere between AD 980 and AD 983, is of the enlightened prince Bahubali, son of the first Tirthankara (or holy Jain teacher). The prince won a fierce war of succession over his brother, Bharata, only to surrender his rights to the kingdom to take up a life of meditation.

In the town itself is the **Bhandari Basti** (1159, with later additions), about 200 m to the left from the path leading up to the Gommateshwara statue. Inside are 24 images of Tirthankaras in a spacious sanctuary. There are 500 rock-cut steps to the top of the hill that take half an hour to climb. It is safe to leave luggage at the tourist office at the entrance.

Vindhyagiri Hill You'll have to clamber barefoot up over 700 hot steep granite steps that carve up the hill to reach the statue from the village tank (socks, sold on-site, offer protection from the hot stone; take water), or charter a *dhooli* (a cane chair tied between two poles and carried), to let four bearers do the work for you. The small, intricately carved shrines you pass on the way up are the **Odeagal Basti**, the **Brahmadeva Mandapa**, the **Akhanda Bagilu** and the **Siddhara Basti**, all 12th-century except the Brahmadeva Mandapa which is 200 years older.

The carved **statue of Gommateshwara** is nude (possibly as he is a *Digambara* or 'sky-clad' Jain) and captures the tranquillity typical of Buddhist and Jain art. The depth of the saint's meditation and withdrawal from the world is suggested by the spiralling creepers shown growing up his legs and arms, and by the ant hills and snakes at his feet. Although the features are finely carved, the overall proportions are odd: he has huge shoulders and elongated arms but stumpy legs.

The 'magnificent anointment' (or **Mastakabhisheka**) falls every 12th year when Jain pilgrims flock from across India to bid for 1008 *kalashas* (pots) of holy water that are left overnight at the saint's feet. The next morning their contents, followed with ghee, milk, coconut water, turmeric paste, honey, vermilion powder and a dusting of gold, are poured over the saint's head from specially erected scaffolding. Unusually for India, the thousands of devotees watching the event do so in complete silence. The next celebration is in 2017.

Chandragiri Hill There are 14 shrines on Chandragiri Hill and the Mauryan emperor Chandragupta, who is believed by some to have become a Jain and left his empire to fast and meditate, is buried here. The temples are all in the Dravidian style, the **Chamundaraya Basti**, built in AD 982 being one of the most remarkable. There is a good example of a free-standing pillar or *mana-stambha* in front of the **Parsvanathasvami Basti**. These pillars, sometimes as high as 15 m, were placed at the temple entrance. Here, the stepped base with a square cross section transforms to a circular section and the column is then topped by a capital.

Chikmagalur (Chikkamagaluru)

Northeast of Belur, Chikmagalur sits at the centre of one of the country's most important coffee-growing areas. Coffee was first smuggled from Mocha (Yemen) to India in 1670 by the Sufi saint Baba Budan, after whom the surrounding Baba Budangiri Hills are named, and the **Central Coffee Research Institute** was set up here in 1925. Chikmagalur is now a popular weekend destination from Bengaluru, with scores of plantation 'homestays'. There are excellent views from the top of **Mulayanagiri** (1930 m), reached by a motorable road. Chikmagalur town has the Hoysala-style **Kodandarama Temple**, a number of mosques and a moated fort.

Tourist information

Tourist office
Vartha Bhavan, BM Rd, Sravanabelagola,
T08172-268862. Closes 1300-1415.
Very helpful and can look after your bags
while you climb the hill.

Where to stay

Hotels in Belur, Halebid and Sravanabelagola
have only basic facilities, but allow you to see
these rural towns and villages before or after the
tour groups. Due to the climb, Sravanabelagola
particularly benefits from an early start. Hassan
and Chikmagalur are more comfortable.

Hassan

$$$ Hotel Southern Star
BM Rd, T08172-251816, www.ushalexushotels.com.
Large modern hotel with 48 excellent a/c rooms,
hot water, phone, satellite TV, and great views
across the town and countryside. Excellent service.

$$$ Hoysala Village Resort
Belur Rd, 6 km from Hassan, T08172-256764,
www.trailsindia.com.
33 big cottage rooms with hot water, TV, tea and
coffee maker and fan, are spread out across this
landscaped, bird-filled resort. It's rustic, with
small handicraft shops, a good restaurant and
swimming pool and very attentive service.

$$$-$$ The Ashhok Hassan (ITDC)
BM Rd, 500 m from the bus stand, T08172-
268731, www.hassanashok.com.
Dramatic renovation has created 36 lovely rooms
in this immaculate, soundproofed hotel in central
Hassan. Decor is all about clean lines and modern
art, and facilities include all mod cons from a/c to
Wi-Fi. Charming suites have big rattan armchairs;
the Hoysaleshara suite has its own dining room,
bar and steam bath. Excellent service and tidy
garden with pool.

$$-$ Hotel Sri Krishna
BM Rd, T08172-263240.
40 rooms with hot water 0600-1000, TV, some
with a/c, also double-bedded twin suites for 4
and a dorm for 10. There's a busy South Indian
restaurant with plantain leaf service, and car hire.
Good value.

$$-$ Hotel Suvarna Regency
97 BM Rd, 500 m south of the bus stand,
T08172-264006.
70 clean, big a/c rooms, some with bath. It's a bit
musty but the deluxe and suite rooms are nice.
There's a good vegetarian restaurant and car
hire available. Very helpful. Also has 4- to 6-bed
dorms and triples.

Belur

$ Mayura Velapuri (KSTDC)
Temple Rd, T08177-222209.
Reasonably clean and spacious rooms including
6 doubles, 4 triples and 2 dorms sleeping 20
(Rs 75 per person), with hot water and fan. There's
a TV and sitting areas. Friendly staff. Good South
Indian meals served in the restaurant.

$ Vishnu Regency
Main Rd, T08177-223011,
vishnuregency_belur@yahoo.co.in.
20 clean rooms opening onto a courtyard, some
with TV and fan, and hot water in the morning.
It's a welcoming hotel with a shop and good veg
restaurant serving tandoor, curries and *thalis*.

Halebid

$ Mayura Shantala (KSTDC)
T08177-273224.
Inspection Bungalow compound in a nice
garden overlooking the temple. There are
4 twin-bed tiled rooms with fan, nets and bath,
and a kitchen.

Sravanabelagola

The temple Management Committee
(SDJMI), T08176-257258, can help organize
accommodation in basic pilgrim hostels.
Check in the **SP Guest House** by the bus stand.

$ Raghu
Near the base of the steps up to Indragiri,
T08176-257238.
Small and utterly basic but clean rooms above a
decent veg restaurant.

$ Vidyananda Nilaya Dharamshala
Closest to the bus stand, reserve through SDJMI.
Rooms with toilet and fan, bucket baths, blanket
but no sheets, courtyard. Good value.

Chikmagalur

$$$$ The Serai
*7 km from town on the Kadur-Mangalore Rd,
T08262-224903, www.theserai.in.*
Fabulously luxurious new resort owned by the
Coffee Day café chain, with beautiful and very
private villas cascading down the hill among
coffee and pepper bushes. Everything's designed
on clean lines, the villas come with private pools,
and service is discreet and efficient. There's a spa,
billiard room, and daily plantation tours. Popular
with visiting cricketers and movie stars.

$$$ Gateway
*KM Rd, T08262-660660,
www.thegatewayhotels.com.*
29 luxury a/c rooms lined along the pool, superb
staff and food, a good base for visiting Belur and
Halebid (40 km).

Restaurants

Hassan
The veg restaurant and multi-cuisine **Suvarna
Gate** at **Hotel Suvarna Regency** are the best
in town. The restaurant at **Hotel Sri Krisha** is
also popular, while the restaurants attached to
Hassan Ashhok, **Hoysala Village** and **Southern
Star** are best for those worried about hygiene.
See Where to stay, above.

$ GRR
Opposite the bus stand.
For non-veg food and friendly staff.

Belur
This sizeable town has numerous tea shops and
vegetarian stands. **Vishnu Regency Hotel** (see
Where to stay) has the best tourist restaurant.

Transport

Hassan
Bus For local buses, T08172-268418. Long-
distance buses at least hourly to **Belur** from
about 0700 (35 km, 1 hr) and **Halebid** from
about 0800 (31 km, 1 hr); very crowded. Few
direct to **Sravanabelagola** in the morning
(1 hr); alternatively, travel to **Channarayapatna**
and change to bus for Sravanabelagola. Also to
Bengaluru about every 30 mins (4½ hrs), **Goa**
(14 hrs), **Mangalore** (5 hrs), **Mysore** hourly (3 hrs).
If heading for Hampi, you can reserve seats for
the 0730 bus to **Hospet** (9 hrs).

Taxi Taxis charge around Rs 1000 for a day-tour
to **Halebid** and **Belur**, and the same for a trip
to **Sravanabelagola**. Drivers park up along AVK
College Rd near the bus stand.

Train The railway station is 2 km east of centre,
T08172-268222, with connections to **Bengaluru**,
Mysore and **Mangalore**.

Belur
Bus The bus stand is about 1 km from the
temples. Buses run half-hourly to **Hassan** (1 hr;
last at 2030) and **Halebid** (30 mins). Also to
Shimoga, where you can change for **Hampi**
and **Jog Falls** (4 hrs); and to **Mysore** (1½ hrs).

Halebid
Bus The bus stand, where you can get good
meals, is near the temples. KSRTC buses run
half-hourly to **Hassan** (45 mins) and from
there to **Bengaluru**, **Mangalore**, **Mysore**.
Also direct to **Belur** (12 km, 30 mins).

Sravanabelagola
Bus Direct buses to/from **Mysore** and
Bengaluru run in the morning; in the afternoon,
change at **Channarayapatna**. The morning
express buses to/from Mysore serve small villages
travelling over dusty but interesting roads up
to Krishnarajapet, then very few stops between
there and Mysore.

Chitradurga

At the foot of a group of granite hills rising to 1175 m in the south, is Chitradurga, 202 km northwest of Bengaluru. The **Fort of Seven Rounds** ① *2 km from the bus stand, 4 km from the railway station, open sunrise to sunset, closed public holidays, Rs 100, allow 2 hrs*, was built in the 17th century by Nayak Poligars, semi-independent landlords who fled south after the collapse of the Vijayanagar Empire in 1565. They were crushed by Haidar Ali in 1779 who replaced the Nayaka's mud fort with stone and Tipu Sultan built a palace, mosque, granaries and oil pits in it. There are four secret entrances in addition to the 19 gateways and ingenious water tanks which collected rainwater. There are also 14 temples, including a cave temple to the west of the wall. They are placed in an extraordinary jumble of granite outcrops, a similar setting to that of Hampi 300 km to the north. The **Hidimbeshwara Temple** is the oldest temple on the site.

Belgaum (Belagavi)

An important border town, Belgaum (population 399,600) makes an interesting stop on the Mumbai–Bengaluru road or as a trip from Goa. The crowded market in the centre gives a glimpse of India untouched by tourism. With its strategic position in the Deccan Plateau, the town had been ruled by many dynasties including the Chalukyas, Rattas, Vijaynagaras, Bahmanis and the Marathas. Most of the monuments date from the early 13th century. The **fort**, immediately east of the town centre, though originally pre-Muslim, was rebuilt by Yusuf Adil Shah, the Sultan of Bijapur, in 1481. Inside, the **Masjid-i-Sata** (1519), the best of the numerous mosques in Belgaum, was built by a captain in the Bijapur army, Azad Khan. Belgaum is also noted for its Jain architecture and sculpture. The late **Chalukyan Kamala Basti**, with typical beautifully lathe-turned pillars and a black stone Neminatha sculpture, stands within the fort walls. To the south of the fort and about 800 m north of the **Hotel Sanman** on the Mumbai-Bengaluru bypass, is a beautifully sculpted **Jain temple** which, according to an inscription, was built by Malikaryuna.

Listings Central Maidan

Where to stay

Chitradurga

$$-$ Amogha International
Santhe Honda Rd, T08194-220763.
Clean, spacious and modern rooms and some a/c suites. 2 restaurants, good vegetarian, but the service is slow. The best place to stay in town.

$ Mayura Santhe Bagilu
Within the city walls, T08194-224448.
26 acceptable rooms, some with a/c and TV; it can be a bit noisy.

Belgaum

Hotels are mostly on College Rd and PB Rd.

$$-$ Adarsha Palace
College Rd, T0831-243 5777,
www.hoteladarshapalace.com.
Small, modern and personal hotel with some a/c rooms and the excellent **Angaan** vegetarian restaurant (rooftop non-vegetarian). It's good

value and there's a pleasant atmosphere with friendly staff. Recommended.

$$-$ Sanman Deluxe
College St, T0831-243 0777, www.hotelsanman.org.
Similar to **Adarsha Palace**, in a new building (much cheaper in the old **Sanman**), 2 restaurants.

$ Keerthi
On the Pune–Bengaluru Rd, a short walk from the Central Bus Stand, T0831-246 6999.
A large modern hotel with some a/c rooms and a restaurant.

$ Mayura Malaprabha (KSTDC)
Ashok Nagar, T0831-247 0781.
6 simple clean rooms in modern cottages, or a dorm (Rs 40). There's a restaurant, bar and tourist office on site.

$ Milan
Club Rd, 4 km from the train station, T0831-242 5555.
45 rooms with bath (hot shower), some with a/c, vegetarian restaurant, good value.

$ Sheetal
Khade Bazar near bus station, T0831-242 9222.
Noisy Indian-style hotel in a busy and quite
entertaining bazar street. Clean-ish rooms with
bath, vegetarian restaurant.

Restaurants

Belgaum

$ Gangaprabha
Kirloskar Rd.
Recommended for pure-veg food.

$ Zuber Biryaniwala
Kaktives Rd.
For creamy biryanis and good non-veg curries.

Transport

Chitradurga
Bus Buses to/from **Bengaluru**, **Davangere**,
Hospet, **Hubli** and **Mysore**.

Train Train from **Arsikere**, **Bengaluru**,
Guntakal, **Hubli**.

Belgaum
Bus Long-distance buses leave from the **Central
Bus Stand**, T0831-246 7932, to **Panaji** (0600-
1715), **Margao** (0545-1500), **Mapusa** (0715-1715).

Train The train station is near the bus stand, 4 km
south of the centre; autos available. To **Bengaluru**:
2-4 daily, 12 hrs. **Madgaon (Goa)**: 1 daily, 6 hrs.
Mumbai, 1-3 daily, 12 hrs, via Pune, 8 hrs.

Coastal
Karnataka

Despite being sandwiched between the holiday honeypots of Goa and south Kerala, and despite having been given a glittering new name by the tourist board, Karnataka's 'Sapphire Coast' has thus far been slow to attract tourists. Yet the landscapes here are dreamy, riven by broad mangrove-lined creeks and carpeted with neon green paddy fields, and the beaches retain a wild beauty, almost entirely innocent of the joys and perils of banana pancakes, necklace hawkers and satellite TV.

The hilly port town of Mangalore makes a pleasant, relaxing stop between Goa and Kerala, but the jewel in the Sapphire Coast's crown thus far is undoubtedly Gokarna: a hippy stronghold, mass pilgrimage site and tremendously sacred Hindu centre. It's little more than one narrow street lined with traditional wooden houses and temples, but it is packed with pilgrims and has been adopted, along with Hampi, by the Goa overspill: people lured by spirituality and the beautiful, auspiciously shaped Om Beach. The no-frills hammock and beach hut joints of yore have now been joined by the snazzy, eco-conscious CGH Earth's well-regarded boutique yoga hotel, SwaSwara, based on the Bihar school.

Essential Coastal Karnataka

Finding your feet

Mangalore is the main transport hub for the region with an international airport 22 km north, as well as frequent bus and train connections with most towns and cities. Buses ply the Sapphire Coast, with regular connections from Mangalore to Gokarna (five hours). Two train lines serve the region. The Konkan railway carries trains from Mumbai via Goa to Mangalore, while the broad-gauge line goes down the coast to destinations in Kerala, inland Karnataka and Tamil Nadu.

Mangalore is the main service town with several banks and internet cafés. Gokarna is well set up for tourists though facilities are low-key and basic, especially on the beach.

When to go

October to March is best. The Deccan Plateau and the coast are intensely hot in April and May, with humidity building up as the monsoon approaches. The roads between Mangalore and the Deccan Plateau, and some of the coastal roads, are badly affected by the monsoon rains and become very potholed. Jog Falls are at their best from late November to early January.

Best places to stay...
Old Magazine House, page 1017
SwaSwara, page 1017

Set on the banks of the Netravathi and Gurupur rivers, the friendly capital of South Kanara District is rarely explored by Western tourists, but Mangalore (population 328,700) offers some interesting churches and temples and makes a worthy stopping point on your way between beaches. An important shipbuilding centre during Haider Ali's time, it is now a major port exporting coffee, spices and cashew nuts.

Sights

St Aloysius College Chapel ① *Lighthouse Hill, 0830-1300, 1600-2000,* has remarkable 19th-century frescoes painted by the Italian-trained Jesuit priest Moscheni, which cover the walls and ceilings in a profusion of scenes. The town has a sizeable Roman Catholic population (about 20%). The nearby **Old Lighthouse** in Tagore Park was built by Haider Ali.

The tile-roofed low structure of the 10th-century **Mangaladevi Temple** ① *south of the Central train station, bus 27 or 27A, 1600-1200, 1600-2000,* is named after a Malabar Princess, Mangala Devi, who may have given her name to Mangalore.

The 11th-century **Sri Manjunatha Temple** ① *4 km northeast of the centre in the Kadri Hills, 0600-1300, 1600-2000, Rs 30-40 by auto,* has a rough lingam; its central image is a superb bronze Lokeshwara made in AD 968, said to be one of the finest in South India.

Sreemanthi Bai Memorial Museum ① *just north of the KSRTC Bus Station, 0900-1700, free,* has a collection including archaeology, ethnology, porcelain and woodcarvings.

South of the Netravathi River lies **Ullal**, which has a pleasant beach and the *dargah* of **Sayyed Mohammed Shareefulla Madani**, a Sufi saint who sailed here from Medina in the 16th century. The *dargah* itself was built in the 19th century, and is credited with healing powers: You can take a trip out to the sand bar at the river mouth to watch fascinating boat building and river traffic on the Netravathi River.

Around Mangalore

The forested hills of the Western Ghats are home to some wonderful examples of Jain and Hindu sculpture and architecture, easily visited on a long day's excursion from Mangalore or as a break on the journey to Belur and Halebid (see pages 1002 and 1003). The temples are often centres of pilgrimage, such as the **Subrahmanya Temple** at **Sullia** and the Shaivite **Manjunatha Temple** at **Dharmasthala**; the latter, 70 km inland, receives thousands of pilgrims every day. From here you can head north through **Venur**, with a 12-m monolith of Bahubali built in 1605, to **Karkala**, where the Bahubali statue is second in height only to that of Sravanabelagola (see page 1004); the **Mastabhisheka ceremony** is performed here every 12 years (the last one was 2014). Further northeast is the small town of **Sringeri**, near the source of the Tunga River, which is associated with the Hindu philosopher Sankaracharya. South of Karkala lies **Mudabidri**, the 'Jain Varanasi', with a collection of superbly carved *basti*. In Jain tradition, no two columns are alike, and many are elaborately carved with graceful figures and floral and knot patterns.

Listings Mangalore *map p1011*

Tourist information

Main tourist office
City Corporation Building, Lalbagh, just west of the KSRTC Bus Stand, Mangalore, T0824-245 3926. Open 1000-1730.

Where to stay

$$$ Gateway (Taj)
Old Port Rd, T0824-666 0420,
www.tajhotels.com.
87 excellent rooms and 6 spacious suites, some with sea/river view. Good facilities including a restaurant and pool. Friendly service.

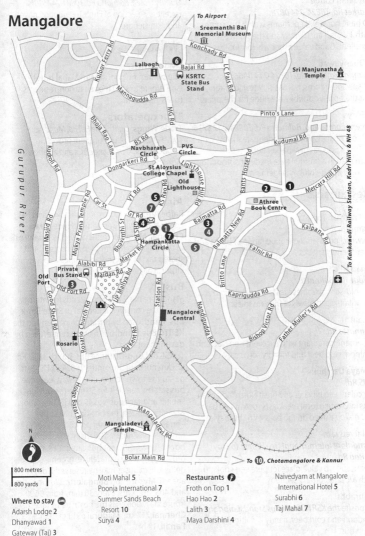

Mangalore

800 metres
800 yards

Where to stay 🛏
Adarsh Lodge **2**
Dhanyawad **1**
Gateway (Taj) **3**

Moti Mahal **5**
Poonja International **7**
Summer Sands Beach
  Resort **10**
Surya **4**

Restaurants 🍴
Froth on Top **1**
Hao Hao **2**
Lalith **3**
Maya Darshini **4**

Naivedyam at Mangalore
  International Hotel **5**
Surabhi **6**
Taj Mahal **7**

$$-$ Poonja International
*KS Rao Rd, T0824-244 0171, www.
hotelpoonjainternational.com.*
154 rooms, central a/c, with a wide range of
facilities including currency exchange. It's
spotlessly clean and the price includes an
excellent buffet breakfast. Great value.

$ Adarsh Lodge
Market Rd, T0824-244 0878.
60 basic but well-kept rooms with bath, some
with TV. Staff are friendly and the service is
excellent. Good value especially for singles.

$ Dhanyawad
Hampankatta Circle, T0824-244 0066.
44 spacious rooms, not the quietest location
but the non-a/c doubles are huge for the price.

$ Surya
Greens Compound, Balmatta Rd, T0824-242 5736.
3 floors of uninspiring but adequate rooms with
bath in a popular backpacker hotel, set back
from road in a tranquil tree-shaded compound.
Friendly and helpful management.

Restaurants

$$ Froth on Top
Balmatta Rd.
Convivial pub, serving a good range of beers and
beer-friendly snacks.

$ Hao Hao
Bridge Rd, Balmatta.
Fun old-school Chinese restaurant dishing out
mountain-sized bowls of fried noodles.

$ Lalith
Balmatta Rd.
Basement restaurant with excellent non-veg and
seafood, cold beer and friendly service.

$ Maya Darshini
GHS Rd.
Succulent veg biryanis and great North Indian fare,
plus interesting local breakfasts such as rice balls
and *goli baje* (fried dough balls with chutney).

$ Naivedyam
*Mangalore International (see Where to stay),
KS Rao Rd.*
Smart, superb value place for pure veg cooking,
with a/c and non-a/c sections.

$ Surabhi
Opposite the KSRTC State Bus Stand, Lalbagh.
Tandoori and cold beer, handy if waiting for a
night bus.

$ Taj Mahal
Hampankatta Circle.
Dingy ancient joint serving superb chilli-laden
upma, crispy *dosa* and good cheap juices.

Shopping

Athree Book Centre, *Sharavasthi Bldg (below
Quality Hotel), Balmatta Rd, T0824-242 5161.*
Excellent selection of English-language novels
and non-fiction.

What to do

Swimming
The swimming pool at **Moti Mahal hotel**
(see Where to stay) is open to non-residents
for Rs 120 per hr.

Tour operators
Trade Wings, *Lighthouse Hill Rd, Mangalore,
T0824-242 6225.* A useful agent providing
good service. Can change TCs and arrange
flight bookings.

Transport

Air
Bajpe Airport is 22 km north of town and has
connections with **Bengaluru**, **Hyderabad**,
Chennai, **Mumbai**, **Delhi**, as well as several cities
in the Gulf. A taxi to/from town costs Rs 400;
shared taxi Rs 100; **Indian Airlines** also runs an
airport coach.

Bus
Mangalore has 2 main bus stands for intercity
buses: the convenient **Central** or **State Bank
Bus Stand**, used by private companies; and the
KSRTC Bus Stand, north of the centre, used by
government buses.

KSRTC Long-Distance Bus Stand, Bajjai Rd,
is 3 km north of the centre, T0824-2211243; to
get to the town centre and railway, leave the
bus station, turn left for 50 m to the private bus
shelter and take bus Nos 19 or 33. The station
is well organized; the booking hall at the
entrance has a computer printout of the
timetable in English. The main indicator
board shows different bus categories: **red** –
ordinary; **blue** – semi-deluxe; **green** – super-
deluxe. (*Exp* buses may be reserved 7 days
ahead). **Mysore** and **Bengaluru**: 296 km, 7 hrs
and 405 km, 9 hrs, every 30 mins from 0600
(route via Madikeri is the best); trains take 20 hrs.
Chennai 717 km; **Madurai** 691 km, 16 hrs.
Panaji, 10 hrs.

Vegetarian victuals

The name of Udupi is associated across South India with authentic Brahmin cooking, which means vegetarian food at its best. But what is authentic Udupi cuisine? Pamela Philipose, writing in the *Indian Express*, suggests that strictly it is food prepared for temple use by Shivali Brahmins at the Krishna temple. It is therefore not only wholly vegetarian, but it also never uses onions or garlic.

Pumpkins and gourds are the essential ingredients, while *sambar*, which must also contain ground coconut and coconut oil, is its base. The spicy pepper water, *rasam*, is compulsory, as are the ingredients jackfruit, heart-shaped colocasia leaves, raw green bananas, mango pickle, red chilli and salt. *Adyes* (dumplings), *ajadinas* (dry curries) and chutneys, including one made of the skin of the ridge gourd, are specialities. Favourite dishes are *kosambiri* with pickle, coconut chutney and *appalam*. At least two vegetables will be served, including runner beans, and rice. Sweets include *payasa* and *holige*.

Buses serve several destinations including **Bengaluru, Bijapur, Goa, Ernakulam, Hampi, Gokarna, Kochi, Mumbai** and **Udupi**.

Rickshaw
Minimum charge Rs 10, though arriving at the **Central** train station or bus stand at night you'll be charged extra. Rs 100 to **Kankanadi Station** from the centre.

Train
Mangalore has 2 train stations. Trains starting and finishing in Mangalore use the **Central** Station; trains on the Mumbai–Kerala line stop at the newer **Mangalore Junction** station at Kankanadi, 10 km east of the city. Trains on the coastal line are prone to long delays. To **Bengaluru**: 1-2 daily, 11 hrs, via **Hassan**, 5½ hrs, and **Mysore**, 8 hrs. **Chennai**: 4 daily, 16-20 hrs, via **Kozhikode, Palakkad, Coimbatore** and **Tiruchirappali**. **Gokarna Rd**: 7-10 daily, 4-5 hrs. **Madgaon**: at least 7 a day, 6 hrs. **Thiruvananthapuram**: 6-10 daily, 12-14 hrs, via **Ernakulam**, 8½ hrs.

Karnataka's Sapphire Coast   *Colour map 7, A2.*
empty beaches, mangrove-fringed estuaries and India's biggest waterfall

Udupi (Udipi)
One of Karnataka's most important pilgrimage sites, Udupi (population 113,000) is the birthplace of the 12th-century saint Madhva, who set up eight sannyasi *maths* (monasteries) in the town. Almost as well known today as the home of a family of Kanarese Brahmins who have established a chain of coffee houses and hotels across South India, it is a pleasant town, rarely visited by foreigners.

According to one legend the statue of Krishna once turned to give a low caste devotee *darshan*. The **Sri Krishna Math**, on Car Street in the heart of the town, is set around a large tank, the *Madhva Sarovar*, into which devotees believe that the Ganga flows every 10 years. There are some attractive *math* buildings with colonnades and arches fronting the temple square, as well as huge wooden temple chariots. This Hindu temple, like many others, is of far greater religious than architectural importance, and receives a succession of highly placed political leaders. Visitors are 'blessed' by the temple elephant. In the biennial **Paraya Mahotsava**, on 17/18 January of even-numbered years, the temple management changes hands (the priest-in-charge heads each of the eight *maths* in turn). The **Seven-Day Festival**, 9-15 January, is marked by an extravagant opening ceremony complete with firecrackers, dancing elephants, brass band and eccentric re-enactments of mythical scenes, while towering wooden temple cars, illuminated by strip lights followed by noisy portable generators, totter around the square, pulled by dozens of pilgrims.

Sri Ananthasana Temple, where Madhva is believed to have dematerialized while teaching his followers, is in the centre of the temple square. The eight important *maths* are around Car Street: Sode, Puthige and Adamar (south); Pejawar and Palamar (west); Krishna and Shirur (north); and Kaniyur (east).

Around Udupi

Some 5 km inland from Udupi, **Manipal** is a university town famous throughout Karnataka as the centre of *Yakshagana* dance drama, which like *Kathakali* in Kerala is an all-night spectacle. **Rashtrakavi Govind Pai Museum** ① *MGM College*, has a collection of sculpture, bronze, inscriptions and coins.

There are good beaches north and south of Udupi, so far with little in the way of accommodation or infrastructure. The closest is at **Malpe**, 5 km west of Udupi, but it's none too appealing: the fishing village at one end of the beach and the fish market on the docks are very smelly, and the beach itself is used as a public toilet in places. If you are prepared for a walk or cycle ride you can reach a deserted sandy beach.

Across the bay is the island of **Darya Bahadurgarh** and 5 km to the southwest is tiny **St Mary's Isle**, which is composed of dramatic hexagonal basalt; Vasco da Gama landed here in 1498 and set up a cross. Boats leave Malpe for the island from 1030; the last one returns at 1700, Rs 70 return.

Bhatkal

One of the many bullock cart tracks that used to be the chief means of access over the Western Ghats started from Bhatkal, a stop on the Konkan Railway. Now only a small town with a mainly Muslim population, in the 16th century it was the main port of the *Vijayanagar* Empire. It also has two interesting small temples. From the north, the 17th-century Jain **Chandranatha Basti** with two buildings linked by a porch, is approached first. The use of stone tiling is a particularly striking reflection of local climatic conditions, and is a feature of the Hindu temple to its south, a 17th-century **Vijayanagar Temple** with typical animal carvings. In the old cemetery of the church is the **tomb of George Wye** (1637), possibly the oldest British memorial in India.

★ Gokarna

Shaivite pilgrims have long been drawn to Gokarna by its temples and the prospect of a holy dip in the Arabian Sea, but it's the latter half of the equation that lures backpackers. The long, broad expanses of beach stretching along the coast, of which the graceful broad curve of **Om Beach** is the most famous, provide an appealing alternative hideaway to Goa, and the busy little town centre plays host to some fascinating cultural inversions: pilgrims wade in the surf in full *salwar kameez* while hippy castaways in bikinis sashay past the temple. And whilst the unspoiled beaches south of town remain the preserve of bodysurfers, *djembe* players and frisbee throwers, the recent rise in incidences of rape (by outsiders, the locals hasten to point out) should serve to remind that travellers would do well to respect local sensitivities.

Gokarna's name, meaning 'cow's ear', possibly comes from the legend in which Siva emerged from the ear of a cow – but also perhaps from the ear-shaped confluence of the two rivers here. Ganesh is believed to have tricked Ravana into putting down the famous Atmalinga on the spot now sanctified in the **Mahabalesvara Temple**. As Ravana was unable to lift the lingam up again, it is called *Mahabala* ('the strong one'). The **Tambraparni Teertha** stream is considered a particularly sacred spot for casting the ashes of the dead.

Beaches around Gokarna

Most travellers head for the beaches to the south. The path from town passing **Kudle Beach** (pronounced *Koodlee*) is easy enough to follow but quite rugged, especially south of **Om Beach** (about 3 km), and should not be attempted with a full backpack during the middle of the day. Stretches of the track are also quite isolated, and even during the day it's advisable for single women to walk with a companion, especially on weekends when large groups of Indian men descend on the beaches with bottles of rum. Both Om and Kudle beaches can get extremely busy in season, when the combination of too many people, a shortage of fresh water and poor hygiene can result in dirty beaches. **Half Moon Beach** and **Paradise Beach**, popular with long-stayers, can be reached by continuing to walk over the headlands and are another 2 km or so apart.

Jog Falls

Inland from Honnavar, just south of Gokarna, these falls, the highest in India, are not the untamed spectacle they once were, but still make a stunning sight if you visit at the end of the wet season; the best times are from late November to early January. Come any earlier and you'll be grappling with leeches and thick mist; any later, and the falls will be more a trickle than a roar, thanks to the 50-km-long **Hirebhasgar Reservoir**, which regulates the flow of the Sharavati River in order to generate hydroelectricity. The **Mysore Power Corporation** releases water to the falls every second Sunday from 1000 to 1800, but even on a low-flow day the scenery and the rugged walk to the base of the falls make a visit worthwhile.

There are four falls. The highest is the **Raja**, with a fall of 250 m and a pool below 40 m deep. Next is the **Roarer**, while a short distance to the south is the **Rocket**, which shoots great gouts of water into the air. Finally comes the **Rani**, which froths elegantly over rocks. A walk to the top (not possible in the monsoons) offers breathtaking views of the cascading river and the valley. Less ambitiously, you can get another excellent view from the Inspection Bungalow on the north side of the river gorge.

Karwar and Anjedive

Karwar, on the banks of the Kalinadi River, is the administrative headquarters of North Kanara District. **Devbagh Beach**, off the coast, has a deep-water naval port protected by five islands. One of these was 'Anjedive' of old, known to seafarers centuries before Vasco da Gama called at the island in 1498, and the Portuguese built a fort there. It was later used as a Goan penal colony. From 1638 to 1752 there was an English settlement here, surviving on the pepper trade. The Portuguese held it for the next 50 years until the old town was destroyed in 1801. Today Karwar, strung out between the port and the estuary, has an unpleasant beach. However, the beaches a little to the south rival those of Goa but are still deserted. Also of interest are the hill fort, an octagonal church, and a 300-year-old temple.

India's Western Naval Command, which controls the 'sword arm' of the subcontinent's powerful Western fleet, has since the 1960s planned to move here from Mumbai – a principally commercial port and one that is worryingly close to Pakistani missiles – but work on the immense **Project Seabird** only began in October 1999. When complete it will become the largest naval base this side of the Suez Canal and will hold 140 plus warships, aircraft and repair dockyards, while the hillsides will

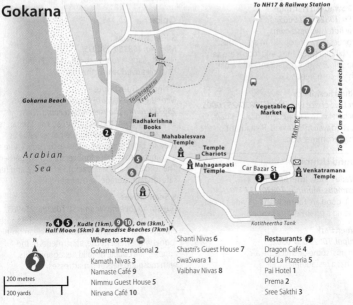

Gokarna

To NH17 & Railway Station

Gokarna Beach

Arabian Sea

Tombranarni Teertha

Sri Radhakrishna Books

Mahabalesvara Temple

Temple Chariots

Mahaganpati Temple

Vegetable Market

Main Rd

Car Bazar St

Venkatramana Temple

To Om & Paradise Beaches

Kotitheertha Tank

To Kudle (1km), Om (3km), Half Moon (5km) & Paradise Beaches (7km)

N

200 metres
200 yards

Where to stay
Gokarna International 2
Kamath Nivas 3
Namaste Café 9
Nimmu Guest House 5
Nirvana Café 10

Shanti Nivas 6
Shastri's Guest House 7
SwaSwara 1
Vaibhav Nivas 8

Restaurants
Dragon Café 4
Old La Pizzeria 5
Pai Hotel 1
Prema 2
Sree Sakthi 3

be put to use concealing submarines. Karwar, crucially, is 900 nautical miles from Karachi versus Mumbai's 580. Since the area is under the control of the Navy it is off-limits to foreigners but driving past it gives a striking portrait of the subcontinent's military might and ambition.

Anshi-Dandeli Tiger Reserve

Enter via Dandeli, 110 km northeast of Karwar, or 74 km east of Hubli. Forest entry fees: Rs 1200, Indian Rs 400. Local forest guides rarely speak English, but staying at the Kali Adventure Camp or Old Magazine House will ensure access to a good naturalist.

Inland from Gokarna on the border with Goa, the conjoined national parks of Anshi and Dandeli protect more than 1000 sq km of endangered Western Ghats forests in the Kali River Basin, and rank as one of Karnataka's richest birding destinations. Some 200 species have been recorded, most notably the four species of hornbills – often seen in flocks numbering into the hundreds, with the rare great hornbill frequently spotted – as well as Sri Lankan frogmouth, orange-headed thrush and blue-headed pitta. The dense forests also provide habitat to a number of black panthers, though these, and the handful of tigers that call the park home, are very rarely seen. Whitewater rafting, jungle walks and jeep safaris are available around Dandeli town.

Listings Karnataka's Sapphire Coast *map p1015*

Where to stay

Udupi

$$-$ Srirama Residency
Opposite the post office, T0820-253 0761.
Top-quality new hotel with 30 excellent rooms, a bar, 2 restaurants and travel desk. Good service.

$$-$ Swadesh Heritage
MV Rd, T0820-252 9605,
www.hotelswadesh.com.
34 spotlessly clean rooms, 14 a/c, in this newish hotel (even the basic rooms are very good value) with 2 restaurants and a bar. Highly recommended.

$ Udupi Residency
Near the Service Bus Stand, T0820-253 0005.
New hotel with 33 excellent rooms, 11 a/c, clean and well maintained. Restaurant on site. Highly recommended.

Around Udupi

$$ Valley View International
On campus, Manipal, T0820-257 1101.
Has 70 good a/c rooms with upmarket facilities including a pool. Recommended.

$ Green Park
Manipal, T0820-257 0562.
38 rooms, some of which are a/c.
Also has a restaurant.

$ Silver Sands
Thottam Beach, 1 km north of Malpe,
T0820-253 7223.
8 pleasant cottages and a restaurant with limited menu. Friendly; recommended.

$ Tourist Home
Halfway to Thotham Beach, Malpe.
4 pleasant, seaside rooms.

Gokarna

$ Kamath Nivas
Main Rd, T08386-256035.
Newish, simple rooms, some with TVs and balconies overlooking the road.

$ Nimmu Guest House
Near the temple, Mani Bhadra Rd, T08386-256730, nimmuhouse@yahoo.com.
Small but decent rooms spread across 2 separate wings; the 5 newest rooms are better value as they are big, bright and catch the breeze. There's also limited roof space for overspill, and a garden. The whole place is laid-back and friendly, and has safe luggage storage. Recommended.

$ Shanti Nivas
Gayatri Rd (behind Nimmu's), T08386-256983.
Set in a coconut grove just inland from the south end of Gokarna Beach. Choose from clean simple rooms in the main house, apartments in the annexe, or a couple of solid hexagonal huts with mosquito nets and mattresses.

$ Shastri's Guest House
Main Rd near the bus stand, T0386-256220.
24 rooms with bath, some have up to 4 beds.
Set back from the road, it's a bit gritty but quiet
and decent value. Luggage storage.

$ Vaibhav Nivas
*Ganjigadde off Main Rd (5 mins' walk from the
bazar), T08386-256714.*
Family-run guesthouse with small rooms, and
an annexe with 10 rooms, some with bath
(Indian and Western WC). Meals and luggage
storage available.

Beaches around Gokarna

The cafés along **Gokarna**, **Kudle**, **Om** and
Paradise beaches let out mud and palm leaf huts
with shared facilities (often just one squat toilet
and a palm-screened shower) for Rs 50-150 a
night during season; many are closed Apr-Oct.
The more expensive huts come with thin
mattresses, fans and mosquito nets, but little in
the way of security. The guesthouses in town
offer to store luggage for a small charge. The
options listed below are secure.

$$$$ SwaSwara
*Om Beach, 15 mins from town, T08386-257131,
www.swaswara.com.*
Elite retreat with 'yoga for the soul' on 12-ha
complex on the curve of gorgeous Om Beach.
Classes taught by Indian *swamis* include:
ashtanga, hasya, kundalini, yoga nidra (psychic
sleep) and meditation. From the hilltop the
thatched Konkan stone villas look like an Ewok
village, with private gardens and a pool; beds are
strewn with flowers in the day and philosophical
quotes in the evening. But despite its size and
expense the resort has virtually no visual impact
on the beach, and fishermen can still shelter
under the mangroves out front. Also offers
Ayurveda, archery, kayaking, trekking, butterfly
and birdwatching, and jungle walks.

$ Gokarna International Resort
Kudle Beach, T08386-257843.
The smartest rooms on Kudle Beach, some with
sea-facing balconies. Ayurvedic massages on site.

$ Namaste Café
Om Beach, T08386-257141. Open all year.
The hub of Om's traveller scene has adequate
en suite rooms, some with beach views,
and a cute but not mosquito-proof bamboo
cottage up in the woods. Travel agent, internet
and food available.

$ Nirvana Café
Om Beach, T08386-329851.
A pleasant complex under some coconut trees,
with a choice of basic huts and solid concrete-
and-tile cottages.

Jog Falls

Hotels are very basic and there are very limited
eating facilities at night. Local families take in
guests. Stalls near the falls serve reasonable
breakfast and meals during the day.

$ Mayura Gerusoppa (KSTDC)
Sagar Taluk, T08186-244732.
This decaying concrete hotel overlooking the falls
has 22 rooms and a 10-bed dorm.

$ PWD Inspection Bungalow
West of the falls, T08186-244333.
Just a handful of neat a/c rooms, preferable to the
various KSTDC options, but a challenge to book.

$ Youth Hostel
Shimoga Rd, T08186-244251.
Utterly basic dorms with mattresses on the floor.

Anshi-Dandeli Tiger Reserve

$$$$ Kali Adventure Camp
*Dandeli, T080-4055 4055,
www.junglelodges.com.*
Professionally run rafting and safari camp, with
comfortable cottages, tents and overpriced
dorms. The best rooms face right onto the river.
Rates include daily jeep safaris and coracle
rides on the Kali to spot crocodiles and birds;
whitewater rafting costs extra.

$$ Old Magazine House
*Ganeshgudi village, T080-4055 4055,
www.junglelodges.com.*
This small encampment of spartan but
comfortable bamboo huts is dedicated to
birdwatchers, with bird baths throughout the
property attracting a huge range of semi-tame
birds. Great for photographers.

Restaurants

Udupi

$ Dwarike
Car St, facing Temple Sq.
Immaculately clean, modern, good service,
comfortable, Western and South Indian food,
excellent snacks, ice creams.

$ Gokul
Opposite Swadesh Heritage (see Where to stay).
Excellent vegetarian, good value.

$ Mitra Samaj
Car St.
Full of pilgrims from the nearby Krishna temple, this humble place churns out endless plates of *iddli*, vada and dozens of variety of *dosa*.

Gokarna
Cheap vegetarian *thalis* are available near the bus stand and along Main St while places towards the town beach serve up the usual array of pancakes, falafel, spaghetti and burgers. Standards are improving on the southern beaches, with Nepali-run kitchens dishing out traveller food, often of excellent quality. If you don't want to add to the mounds of plastic bottles littering the beaches, ask around for cafés that will let you fill your bottle from their cooler – it should cost a little less than the price of a new bottle.

$ Dragon Café
Kudle Beach.
Good *thalis* and *pakora*, excellent pizza and, perhaps, the best mashed potato in Gokarna.

$ Old La Pizzeria
Kudle.
Popular hangout joint. Laundry and internet facilities as well as good Western food.

$ Pai Hotel
Near Venkatramana Temple in Main St.
Good *masala dosa*.

$ Prema
By the car park at Gokarna Beach.
Serves great fruit salads, the best *gudbad* in town and its own delicious soft garlic cheese, but popularity has resulted in slow and surly service.

$ Sree Sakthi
Near Venkatramana Temple.
Superb ice cream and Indian food, comfort snacks (try the home-made oil-free peanut butter on toast). Basic but clean and well run.

Karwar

$$ Fish Restaurant
In the Sidvha Hotel.
Excellent bistro-type place.

Shopping

Gokarna
Sri Radhakrishna Books, *on main road near the beach*. Tiny bookshop with an astonishingly good range of beach reads.

What to do

Gokarna
You can hire canoes from a small office on the northern part of Om Beach for Rs 200 per hr.

Transport

Udupi
Bus Udupi's **State** and **Private** bus stands are next to each other in the central square. From Udupi, frequent service to **Mangalore** (1½ hrs). Mornings and evenings to **Bengaluru** and **Mysore** from 0600; **Hubli** from 0900; **Dharmashala**, from 0600-0945, 1400-1830; **Mumbai** at 1120, 1520, 1700, 1920.

Train The station is 5 km from the town centre; auto, Rs 90. All express and passenger trains between Mangalore and Madgaon in Goa stop here.

Gokarna
Boat Boatmen on Om Beach quote Rs 300-500 for a dropoff to either **Gokarna** or **Paradise Beach**, or Rs 50-100 per person if there's a group. Return trips to Paradise Beach may only give you 30 mins on land.

Bus KSRTC buses provide a good service: **Chaudi** 2 hrs; **Karwar** (via Ankola) frequent (1 hr); **Hospet** 1430 (10 hrs); **Margao**, 0815 (4 hrs); **Mangalore** via **Udupi** 0645 (7 hrs); **Panaji** 0800 (5 hrs). Private sleeper buses to **Bengaluru** and **Hampi** can be booked from agents in the bazar; most depart from Kumta or Ankola.

Taxi Most hotels and lodges offer to organize taxis, but often quote excessive prices; no destination seems to be less than 100 km away. To **Gokarna Rd**, bargain for Rs 120; to **Ankola**, around Rs 550.

Train Gokarna Road Station is 10 km from town, 2 km from the NH17; most trains are met by auto-rickshaws and minibus taxis: Rs 125 to Gokarna Bus Stand, Rs 200 to Om Beach. State buses to/from Kumta pass the end of the station road, a 1-km walk from the station. **Madgaon** (*Margao*): *Matsyagandha Exp 12620*,

1840, 2 hrs; *Mangalore-Madgaon Pass 56640, 1023,* 2¼ hrs. **Mangalore** (**Central**): *Madgaon-Mangalore Pass 56641,* 1528, 5 hrs.

Jog Falls
Bus Daily buses connect Jog Falls with **Honnavar** (2½ hrs) and **Karwar**, both on the Konkan railway line; some Honnavar buses continue to **Kumta** (3 hrs), which has frequent services to **Gokarna**. Direct buses also go daily to **Mangalore** (7hrs), **Bengaluru** (9 hrs), and **Panaji**. Hourly buses to **Shimoga** (4 hrs) for connections to **Belur**, **Hassan** and **Hospet** (7 hrs from Shimoga). For a wider choice of departures get a local bus to **Sagar**, 30 km southeast on NH-206.

Taxi To **Panaji**, Rs 1500 (6 hrs).

Train Jog Falls is 16 km from the railway at **Talguppa**. Trains from **Bengaluru** (**Bangalore**) involve a change in **Shimoga** town.

Karwar
Bus To **Jog Falls**, 0730 and 1500 (6 hrs). Frequent buses to **Palolem**, **Margao** (Madgaon) and **Panaji**, also direct buses to **Colva**. Buses often full; you may have to fight to get on. The road crosses the Kali River (car toll Rs 5) then reaches the Goa border and check post (8 km north).

Northern
Karnataka

Down the centuries, northeast Karnataka has been host to a profusion of Deccani rulers. Hampi, site of the capital city of the Vijayanagar Hindu Empire that rose to conquer the entire south in the 14th century, is the region's most famous, and is an extraordinary site of desolate temples, compounds, stables and pleasure baths, surrounded by a stunning boulder-strewn landscape. The cluster of temple relics in the villages of Aihole, Pattadakal and Badami dates from the sixth century, when the Chalukyans first started experimenting with what went on to become the distinct Indian temple design. Nearby are the Islamic relics of Bijapur and Bidar, sudden plots of calm tomb domes with their Persian inscriptions ghosted into lime, and archways into empty harems; all the more striking for being less visited.

Essential Northern Karnataka

Finding your feet

The closest airport to Hampi is at Hubli (Hubballi), three hours' drive to the west, with flights from Bengaluru, Chennai and Mumbai. Hospet is the area's main transport hub with regular long-distance buses from major towns and cities. It is a 30-minute rickshaw ride to both entrances at Hampi. The Kamalapuram road is better, especially in the rainy season when the slower road to Hampi Bazar is barely passable. Badami is the best base for visiting the Cradle of Hindu architecture temples at Pattadakal, Aihole and Mahakuta, though hiring a car and driver is the most comfortable option. The nearest train station for visiting Hampi is at Hospet, which has regular connections with most major towns. Bijapur, Badami, Gulbarga and Bidar all have train stations with good connections.

When to go

The high season is November to January but accommodation prices can rise by up to 30% during this time. Rooms in Hampi are packed out during the music festival in early November. During the rainy season the road from Hospet to Hampi Bazar is barely passable.

Time required

At least a day to visit Hampi, though you could easily spend several days or weeks here soaking up the atmosphere. The Cradle of Hindu architecture temples can be seen in a day though this might be a push if using public transport.

ancient ruins in a serene riverside setting

Climb any boulder-toppled mountain around the ruins of the Vijayanagar Empire and you can see the dizzying scale of the Hindu conquerors' glory; Hampi was the capital of a kingdom that covered the whole of southern India. Little of the kingdom's riches remain; now the mud huts of gypsies squat under the boulders where noblemen once stood, while the double-decker shopfronts of the old Hampi Bazar, where diamonds were once traded by the kilo, have transformed into a more prosaic marketplace geared to profiting from Western tourists and domestic pilgrims.

Yet away from the hubbub and hassle of the bazar – somewhat reduced since 2012 when the Archaeological Survey of India sent in bulldozers to knock down many of the 'unauthorized' houses and shops – Hampi possesses a romantic, hypnotic desolation that's without parallel in South India. You'll need at least a full day to get a flavour of the place, but for many visitors the chilled-out vibe has a magnetic attraction, and some end up staying for weeks.

Sacred Centre
The road from the west comes over Hemakuta Hill, overlooking the Sacred Centre of **Vijayanagar** (the 'Town of Victory'), with the **Virupaksha Temple** and the Tungabhadra River to its north. On the hill are two large monolithic Ganesh sculptures and some small temples. The road runs down to the village and the once world-famous market place. You can now only see the wide pathway running east from the towering **Virupaksha Temple** (*Pampapati*) with its nine-storey *gopuram*, to where the bazar once hummed with activity. The temple is still in use; note the interesting paintings on the *mandapam* ceiling.

Riverside
You can walk along the river bank (1500 m) to the famous **Vitthala Temple**. The path is easy and passes several interesting ruins including small 'cave' temples – worthwhile with a guide. Alternatively, a road skirts the Royal Enclosure to the south and goes all the way to the Vitthala Temple. On the way back (especially if it's at sunset) it's worth stopping to see **Raghunatha Temple**, on a hilltop, with its Dravidian style, quiet atmosphere and excellent view of the countryside from the rocks above.

   After passing **Achyuta Bazar**, which leads to the **Tiruvengalanatha Temple**, 400 m to the south, the riverside path goes near **Sugriva's Cave**, where it is said that Sita's jewels, dropped as she was abducted by the demon Ravana, were hidden by Sugriva. There are good views of the ancient ruined bridge to the east. Nearby the path continues past the only early period Vaishnavite shrine, the 14th-century **Narasimha Temple**. The **King's Balance** is at the end of the path as it approaches the Vitthala Temple. It is said that the rulers were weighed against gold, jewels and food, which were then distributed to Brahmins.

Vitthala Temple
0830-1700, US$5/Rs 250, allows entry to Lotus Mahal on the same day.

A World Heritage Monument, the Vitthala Temple is dedicated to Vishnu. It stands in a rectangular courtyard enclosed within high walls. Probably built in the mid-15th century, it is one of the oldest and most intricately carved temples, with its *gopurams* and *mandapas*. The *Dolotsava mandapa* has 56 superbly sculpted slender pillars which can be struck to produce different musical notes. It has elephants on the balustrades and horses at the entrance. The

Essential Hampi

Finding your feet

Buses and trains arrive in Hospet, from where it is a 30-minute rickshaw (around Rs 200) or bus ride to Hampi. The site is spread out, so hiring a bicycle is a good idea though some paths are too rough to ride on. You enter the area from the west at Hampi Bazar or from the south at Kamalapuram.

other two ceremonial *mandapas*, though less finely carved, nonetheless depict some interesting scenes, such as Krishna hiding in a tree from the *gopis* and a woman using a serpent twisted around a stick to churn a pot of buttermilk. In the courtyard is a superb chariot carved out of granite, the wheels raised off the ground so that they could be revolved!

Krishnapura

On the road between the Virupaksha Bazar and the Citadel you pass Krishnapura, Hampi's earliest Vaishnava township with a Chariot Street 50 m wide and 600 m long, which is now a cultivated

Hampi-Vijayanagar

To Anegondi & Gangawati

Ruined Bridge

Vitthala Temple

Talarighat   Coracles

King's Balance

Sugriva's Cave

Coracles
Tungabhadra River

Siva Temple   Narasimha Temple

Virupaksha Temple

Kodanda Rama Temple   Achyuta Bazar

HAMPI BAZAR

Tiruvengalanatha Temple

Ganesh
Hemakuta Hill

SACRED CENTRE   Matanga Parvata

To Hospet (12 km)

Krishna Temple
Lakshmi Narasimha Statue

KRISHNAPURA

Dharamsalas

Veerabhadra Temple

Malayavanta

ZENANA ENCLOSURE

Elephant Stables   VIJAYNAGARA

Raghunatha Temple

Nobleman's Palace

Lotus Mahal

To Kampili

Hazara Rama Temple

ROYAL ENCLOSURE

Prasanna Virupaksha Temple

Mahanavami Dibba

To Daroji Bear Sanctuary &

DURBAR ENCLOSURE

Aqueduct

Queen's Bath

Bhima's Gate

Jaina Temple

Archaeological Survey Office

KAMALAPURAM   Dharamsalas

Archaeological Museum

Pattabhi Rama Temple

Nageshwara Temple

N

500 metres
500 yards

To Hospet

Where to stay
Archana 2
Gopi 4
Mayura Bhuvaneswari 1
Mowgli Guest House 5

Padma Guest House 2
Ranjana Guest House 2
Shambhu 3
Shanthi Guest House 6
Sloth Bear Resort 7

Vicky 4

Restaurants
Boomshankar 1
Mango Tree 2

New Shanti 3
Suresh 4

Hampi

Hampi was founded on the banks of the Tungabhadra River in 1336 by two brothers, Harihara and Bukka, and rose to become the seat of the mighty Vijayanagar Empire and a major centre of Hindu rule and civilization for 200 years. The city, which held a monopoly on the trade of spices and cotton, was enormously wealthy – some say greater than Rome – and the now-sorry bazar was packed with diamonds and pearls, the crumbled palaces plated with gold. Although it was well fortified and defended by a large army, the city fell to a coalition of northern Muslim rulers, the Deccan Sultans, at Talikota in 1565. The invading armies didn't crave the city for themselves, and instead sacked it, smiting symbolic blows to Hindu deities and taking huge chunks out of many of the remaining white granite carvings. Today, the craggy 26-sq-km site holds the ghost of a capital complete with aqueducts, elephant stables and baths as big as palaces. The dry arable land is slowly being peeled back by archaeologists to expose more and more of the kingdom's ruins.

The site for the capital was chosen for strategic reasons, but the craftsmen adopted an ingenious style to blend in their architectural masterpieces with the barren and rocky landscape. Most of the site is early 16th century, built during the 20-year reign of Krishna Deva Raya (1509-1529) with the citadel standing on the bank of the river.

field. **Krishna Temple** has a very impressive gateway to the east. Just southwest of the Krishna temple is the colossal monolithic **statue of Lakshmi Narasimha** in the form of a four-armed man-lion with fearsome bulging eyes sheltered under a seven-headed serpent, Ananta. It is over 6 m high but sadly damaged.

The road south, from the Sacred Centre towards the Royal Enclosure, passes the excavated **Prasanna Virupaksha Temple** (misleadingly named 'underground') and interesting watchtowers.

Royal Enclosure

At the heart of the metropolis is the small **Hazara Rama Temple**, the Vaishanava 'chapel royal'. The outer enclosure wall to the north has five rows of carved friezes while the outer walls of the *mandapa* has three. The episodes from the epic *Ramayana* are told in great detail, starting with the bottom row of the north end of the west *mandapa* wall. The two-storey **Lotus Mahal** ① *0600-1800, US$5/Rs250, allows entry to Vitthala Temple on the same day*, is in the **Zenana** or ladies' quarter, screened off by its high walls. The watchtower is in ruins but you can see the domed **stables** for 10 elephants with a pavilion in the centre and the guardhouse. Each stable had a wooden beamed ceiling from which chains were attached to the elephants' backs and necks. In the **Durbar Enclosure** is the specially built decorated platform of the **Mahanavami Dibba**, from which the royal family watched the pageants and tournaments during the nine nights of *navaratri* festivities. The 8-m-high square platform originally had a covering of bricks, timber and metal but what remains still shows superb carvings of hunting and battle scenes, as well as dancers and musicians.

The exceptional skill of water engineering is displayed in the excavated system of aqueducts, tanks, sluices and canals, which could function today. The attractive **Pushkarini** is the 22-sq-m stepped tank at the centre of the enclosure. The road towards Kamalapuram passes the **Queen's Bath**, in the open air, surrounded by a narrow moat, where scented water filled the bath from lotus-shaped fountains. It measures about 15 m by 2 m and has interesting stucco work around it.

Daroji Bear Sanctuary

15 km from Hampi Bazar, daily 0600-1800. Rs 1000, Indians Rs 200.

The relatively new Daroji sanctuary protects 55 sq km of boulder-strewn scrubland, which is home to around 120 sloth bears. The bears have become accustomed to regular treats of honey, courtesy of the park rangers, and a handful of them come regularly to a particular rock to feed. A watchtower placed high above the spot makes this perhaps the best place in India to observe the species in the wild. The sanctuary also has leopard, wolf, jackal, Eurasian horned owl, and good populations of the beautiful painted sandgrouse.

Hospet (Hosapete)

The transport hub for Hampi, Hospet (population 206,200) is famous for its sugar cane; the town exports sugar across India, villagers boil the milk to make *jaggery* and a frothing freshly wrung cup costs you just Rs 4. Other industries include iron ore, biscuit making and the brewing of Royal Standard rum. The main bazar, with its characterful old houses, is interesting to walk around.

Tungabhadra Dam ① *6 km west, Rs 5, local bus takes 15 mins,* is 49 m high and offers panoramic views. One of the largest masonry dams in the country, it was completed in 1953 to provide electricity for irrigation in the surrounding districts.

Muharram, the Muslim festival that marks the death of Mohammed's grandson Imam Hussein, is celebrated with a violent vigour both here and in the surrounding villages and with equal enthusiasm by both the area's significant Muslim population and Hindus. Ten days of fasting is broken with fierce drum pounding, drink and frequent arguments, sometimes accompanied by physical violence. Each village clusters around icons of Hussein, whose decapitation is represented by a golden crown on top of a face covered with long strings of jasmine flowers held aloft on wooden sticks. Come evening, fires are lit. When the embers are dying villagers race through the ashes, a custom that may predate Islam's arrival. The beginnings or ends of livestock migrations to seasonal feeding grounds are marked with huge bonfires. Cattle are driven through the fires to protect them from disease. Some archaeologists suggest that Neolithic ash mounds around Hospet were the result of similar celebrations over 5000 years ago.

Listings Hampi-Vijayanagar and around *map p1022*

Tourist information

Hampi-Vijayanagar

Tourist office
On the approach to Virupaksha Temple, T08394-241339. Open 0800-1230, 1500-1830.
A 4-hr guided tour of the site (without going into the few temples that charge admission) costs around Rs 250.

Where to stay

Hampi-Vijayanagar

Some use Hospet as a base for visiting Hampi; it has plusher accommodation and the nearest railway station. However, it means a 30-min commute to Hampi. Hampi is quieter, more basic and infinitely more atmospheric – though note that the ASI still has notional plans to bulldoze the entire village of Hampi Bazar, so ring in advance. Across the river (by *coracle* or ferry, Rs 15) you can reach the hamlet of Virupapur Gaddi, a beautiful paddy-planted village with budget guesthouses, coco-huts and cottages to stay in. Power cuts are common both sides of the river – a supply of candles and a torch are essential – and mosquitoes can be a real menace. A small selection of the many guesthouses are

listed here. All are similar and mostly in the **$** price category; prices rise 30% at the height of the season, Nov-Jan.

$$$$ Sloth Bear Resort
Near Kannada University, Kamalapur, bookings T080-4055 4055, www.junglelodges.com.
Excellent new nature resort, with tribal-style stone-and-thatch cottages set amid scrub a 20-min drive from Hampi Bazar. Good birding safaris, visits to Daroji Bear Sanctuary and a sunrise trip to Hampi are included. Good food and attentive service.

$$$-$ Mayura Bhuvaneswari
2 km from the site, Kamalapuram, T08394-241574.
Government-run place that feels both weird and worn out; the budget rooms are overpriced, grimy and falling apart, while the newer suites have bizarre ultraviolet tube lights that lend the feel of sleeping in an abandoned nightclub. Decent food and chilled beer, but service is stretched.

$ Archana
Janata Plot, T08394-241547, addihampi@yahoo.com.
The pick of the Hampi Bazar hotels, with 9 clean, quiet rooms (some a/c), good atmosphere and great views from the roof.

$ Gopi
Janata Plot, T08394-241695,
kirangopi2002@yahoo.com.
Clean rooms with hot water, those in the older
wing have Indian toilets.

$ Mowgli Guest House
1.5 km from the ferry in Virupapur Gaddi,
T08533-287033, www.mowglihampi.com.
A wide selection of rooms, from basic cells with
shared bath to cute circular huts and lovely bright
a/c rooms on the 2nd floor with expansive views
over stunningly green paddy fields terracing
down to the river. Hot water a few hours a day,
international restaurant and pool table. Mellow
without being too mellow.

$ Padma Guest House
T08394-241331.
Family guesthouse with 4 double rooms and
currency exchange.

$ Rahul
South of the bus stand.
Quite quiet despite being near the bus stand.
Basic but clean accommodation under nets.
Good simple vegetarian food and views from
the rooftop.

$ Ranjana Guest House
Behind Govt school, T08394-241330.
A friendly guesthouse with 5 rooms, plus hot
water, cheaper rooms have a cooler, rather
than a/c.

$ Shambhu
Janata Plot, T08394-241383,
rameshhampi@yahoo.com.
5 rooms with bath and nets, plenty of plants.
Rooftop restaurants (several egg dishes). Friendly.

$ Shanthi Guest House
Next to Mowgli, Virupapur Gaddi, T08394-
325352, shanthi.hampi@gmail.com.
More chilled-out than its neighbour, with
atmospheric mud huts and a lovely covered
lounge gazing out over the swaying rice and
watching the sunset. Good service, hot water
by the bucket.

$ Vicky
200 m north of the main road (turn off at the
tourist office), T08394-241694, vickyhampi@
yahoo.co.in.
7 rooms (4 with bath) with bucket hot water
and Indian toilets, but there's a good rooftop
restaurant and internet.

Hospet
Station Rd has been renamed Mahatma Gandhi
Rd (MG Rd).

$$$$-$$$ Malligi
6/143 Jambunatha Rd, T08394-228101,
www.malligihotels.com.
188 a/c rooms and large suites. Facilities include
a restaurant, bar by the pool (non-residents pay
Rs 25 per hr), health club, exchange, travel agent
(good Hampi tour). The internet is creakingly
slow and the STD/ISD service overpriced, but it's
generally a pleasant place.

$$-$ Karthik
252 Sardar Patel Rd, T08394-220038.
40 good-sized clean rooms (10 a/c) in a quiet
modern hotel with garden dining. Friendly and
good value.

$$-$ Shanbhag Towers
College Rd, T08394-225910,
shanbhagtowers@yahoo.com.
64 spacious rooms, 32 a/c with tub, TV, fridge, in
this brand new hotel with a breathtaking Hampi
theme. There are restaurants (one rooftop with
great views) and a bar.

$ Nagarjuna Residency
Sardar Patel Rd, opposite Karthik,
T08394-229009.
Spotless, modern, excellent value rooms,
some a/c, extra bed Rs 30-50, very helpful.
Recommended.

$ The Shine
Near the bus stand, Station Rd, T08394-694233,
www.sainakshatra.com.
Sparkly new business hotel, with functional but
pleasant and clean rooms, hot water and lift.
Excellent value.

$ Shivananda
Next to the bus stand, T08394-220700.
23 rooms, 4 a/c, simple but clean, and complete
with resident astrologer.

$ SLV Yatri Nivas
Station Rd, T08394-221525.
15 bright, airy rooms and dormitory in a clean,
well-run hotel. Good vegetarian restaurant
and bar.

$ Viswa
MG Rd, opposite the bus station, away from the
road, T08394-227171.
42 basic rooms (some 4-bed) with bath, adjacent
Shanthi restaurant. No frills but good value.

Restaurants

Hampi-Vijayanagar
All restaurants are vegetarian, eggs are sometimes available.

$ Boomshankar
On the path to the Vittahla Temple.
Well-prepared, fresh river fish.

$ Gopi
See Where to stay.
Good cheap *thalis*.

$ Mango Tree
Janata Plot.
One of the most famous names in town, with a multicultural menu, though its new location lacks the magic that made it a backpacker favourite.

$ Mayura Bhuvaneswari
Kamalapuram.
Cheap adequate meals.

$ New Shanti
Opposite Shanti Guest House, between Virupaksha Temple and the river.
Good carrot/apple/banana/chocolate cakes to order.

$ Suresh
30 m from New Shanti on the path towards the river.
Run by a very friendly family, made to order so takes a while, but worth the wait.

Hospet
The hotels serve chilled beer.

$$ Waves
Malligi.
The multi-cuisine restaurant is next to the pool and serves good food. There's also a bar.

$ Iceland
Station Rd, behind the bus station.
Good South Indian meals.

$ Shanbhag
Near the bus station.
Good South Indian cuisine.

Festivals

Jan-Feb Virupaksha Temple Car festival.
3-5 Nov Hampi Music festival at Vitthala Temple when hotels get packed.

What to do

Hospet
Tour operators
Tours from KSTDC, T08394-221008; **KSRTC**, T08394-228537; and **SRK Tours and Travels** at Malligi Hotel, T08394-224188. All run day-tours to Hampi, some also including Tungabhadra Dam; Rs 100-150 per person. Day trips also go to Aihole, Badami and Pattadakal, 0830-1930, Rs 350 per person, but it's a very long day. Local sightseeing by taxi Rs 800 per day. Bijapur 1-day trip by bus Rs 175, taxi Rs 2100. English-speaking guide but rather rushed.

Transport

Hampi-Vijayanagar
Air The closest airport to Hampi is at Hubli (Hubballi), 3 hrs' drive to the west, with flights from Bengaluru, Chennai and Mumbai.

Bicycle hire Any guesthouse in Hampi Bazar can help you organize bike or scooter hire (bikes Rs 30-40 per day; scooters Rs 200 plus fuel).

Bus Buses to/from Hospet run every 30 mins from the bazar. A few KSRTC long-distance buses also go to **Bengaluru** and **Goa**. Agents in the bazar sell train tickets and seats on overnight sleeper buses to Goa and **Gokarna**, most of which leave from Hospet.

Coracles and ferries Boats take passengers across the river from the jetty west of the Virupaksha Temple, Rs 5 (Rs 10 with luggage). Services stop early in the evening; check the time of the last boat to avoid getting stranded.

Hospet
Bus Frequent buses to **Hampi**'s 2 entry points (Kamalapuram and Hampi Bazar, both taking around 30 mins), from 0530; last return around 2000. The Kamalapuram road is better, especially in the rainy season when the slower road to Hampi Bazar is barely passable.

From the busy bus stand, T08394-228802, express buses run to/from **Bengaluru** (10 hrs) and **Mysore** (10½ hrs). Several daily services to other sites, eg **Badami** (6 hrs), **Bijapur** (6 hrs), **Chitradurga** (3 hrs). More comfortable **Karnataka Tourism** luxury coaches run overnight to various towns. A few buses go direct to **Panaji** (**Goa**) – *Luxury*, 0630 (10½ hrs), State bus, 0830 (reserve a seat in advance); others involve a change in **Hubli** (4½ hrs). **Paulo Travels Luxury**

Sleeper coach from Hotel Priyadarshini, at 1845, Rs 350, daily; **West Coast Sleeper**, from Hotel Shanbhag, 1830, Rs 350; daily (Oct-Mar only); strangers may be expected to share a bunk. It's better to take a train to **Londa** (under 5 hrs) and get a bus to **Madgaon** or **Panaji** (3 hrs).

Rickshaw From the train station to the bus stand should cost about Rs 30. To **Hampi**, Rs 150-200.

Taxi KSTDC, T08394-21008, T08394-28537 or from Malligi Hotel; about Rs 700 per day.

Train Bengaluru: overnight *Hampi Express*, 9 hrs, continues to **Mysore**, 12½ hrs. **Goa**: 4 weekly trains to **Madgaon** (Mon, Wed, Thu, Sat), 7½ hrs; 2 daily to **Londa**, 5½ hrs. **Hyderabad**: 2 a day, 11¾-14 hrs, via **Guntakal** (transfer to mainline Chennai-Mumbai trains). To reach Badami and Bijapur, catch a train to **Gadag** (7-8 daily, 1¼-2 hrs) and change. From Gadag: **Badami**, 7 daily, 1½ hrs; **Bijapur**, 6-8 daily, 4½-5 hrs.

Bijapur (Vijayapura)   Colour map 5, C5.

fascinating Islamic city of mosques, mausoleums, palaces and forts

Mohammed Adil Shah was not a man to be ignored; the tomb he built from the first day of his rule in anticipation of his own death hovers with dark magnificence over Bijapur (population: 326,400) and is so large it can be seen from over 20 km away.

His brooding macabre legacy threw down the gauntlet to his immediate successor. Ali Adil Shah II, who took over from Mohammed in 1656, began his own tomb, which would surely have been double in size and architectural wonder had he not died too soon, 26 years into his reign, with only archways complete. His Bara Kamaan is nearby, while to the north of the city lies Begum's equally thwarted attempt to match Mohammed's strength in death. With its mausoleums, palaces and some of the finest mosques in the Deccan, Bijapur has the air of a northern Muslim city and retains real character. The *chowk* between the bus station and MG Road is quite atmospheric in the evening.

Gol Gumbaz ① *0630-1730, foreigners Rs 100, Indians Rs 5, video camera Rs 25, some choose to just view it from the gate.* Hulking in the background wherever you look in Bijapur is the vast whitewashed tomb of Mohammad Adil Shah, buried here with his wife, daughter and favourite court dancer, underneath the world's second largest dome (unsupported by pillars) – and one of its least attractive. Its extraordinary whispering gallery carries a message across 38 m which is repeated 11 times. However, noisy crowds make hearing a whisper quite impossible; it's quietest in the early morning. Numerous narrow steps in one of the corner towers lead to the 3-m-wide gallery. The plaster here was made out of eggs, cow dung, grass and jaggery. There is an excellent view of the city from the base of the dome. The **Nakkar Khana**, or gatehouse, is now a **museum** ① *1000-1700, Rs 2*, housing an excellent collection of Chinese porcelain, parchments, paintings, armoury, miniatures, stone sculpture and old Bijapur carpets.

Jama Masjid To the south of Gol Gumbaz, this is one of the finest mosques in the Deccan, with a large shallow, onion-shaped dome and arcaded court. Built by Ali Adil Shah I (ruled 1557-1579) during Bijapur's rise to power it displays a classic restraint. The Emperor Aurangzeb added a grand entrance to the mosque and also had a square painted for each of the 2250 worshippers that it can accommodate.

West of here is the **Mehtar Mahal** (1620), whose delicate minarets and carved stone trellises were supposedly built for the palace sweepers.

Citadel Bijapur's Citadel, encircled by its own wall, now has few of its grand buildings intact. One is the Durbar Hall on the ground floor of **Gagan Mahal** ('Sky Palace'), open to the north so that the citizens outside were not excluded. It had royal residential quarters on either side

Essential Bijapur

The railway station is just outside the east wall of the fort less than 1 km from the Gol Gumbaz. Long-distance buses draw in just west of the citadel. Both arrival points are close enough to several hotels. It is easy to walk or cycle round the town. There are also autos and *tongas*; negotiate for the 'eight-sight tour price'.

with screened balconies for the women to remain unseen while they watched the court below. Another worth visiting is the **Jal Manzil**, or the water pavilion, a cool sanctuary. Just to the east is the **Asar Mahal** (circa 1646), once used as a court house with teak pillars and interesting frescoes in the upper floor.

Bara Kaman The Bara Kaman was possibly a 17th-century construction by Adil Shah III. Planned as a huge 12-storey building with the shadow of the uppermost storey designed to fall onto the tomb of the Gol Gumbaz, construction was ended after two storeys with the death of the ruler. An impressive series of arches on a raised platform is all that remains.

Sherza Burj The western gateway to the walled city, Sherza Burj (Lion Gate), has the enormous 55-tonne, 4.3-m-long, 1.5-m-diameter cannon **Malik-i-Maidan** (Ruler of the Plains). Cast in the mid-16th century in Ahmadnagar, it was brought back as a prize of war pulled by "400 bullocks, 10 elephants and hundreds of soldiers". The muzzle, a lion's head with open jaws, has an elephant being crushed to death inside, and the gun's roar was said to be so loud that the gunner used to dive into the tank off the platform to avoid being deafened. Inside the city wall nearby is **Upli Burj**, a 24-m-high watchtower with long guns and water tanks.

Ibrahim Rauza ① *West of the city centre, 0600-1800, Rs 100, Indians Rs 5, video camera Rs 25, visit early morning to avoid crowds.* This palatial 17th-century tomb and mosque was built by Ibrahim Adil Shah during the dynasty's most prosperous period (after the sacking of Vijayanagar) when the arts and culture flourished. The corners of both buildings are decorated with slender minarets and decorative panels carved with lotus, wheel and cross patterns as well as bold Arabic calligraphy,

Bijapur

Where to stay
Godavari 6
Kanishka International 2
Madhuvan International 1
Navaratna International 7
Pearl 8
Railway Retiring Room 5
Samrat 9
Sanman 3
Santosh 4

Restaurants
Kapali 3
Priyadarshini 1
Shrinidhi 2

BACKGROUND

Bijapur

The Chalukyas who ruled over Bijapur were overthrown in the late 12th century. In the early years of the 14th century the Delhi Sultans took it for a time until the Bahmanis, with their capital in Gulbarga, ruled through a governor in Bijapur who declared Independence in 1489 and founded the Adil Shahi Dynasty. Of Turkish origin, they held power until 1686.

The 55-ton cannon was employed against Vijayanagar. Ali Adil Shah I, whose war it was, was somewhat chastened at the destruction his marauding Muslim armies had wreaked on the Hindu empire at Hampi. By way of atonement, and in a show of the inordinate riches that had fallen into his lap by supplanting Vijayanagar, he did his communal civic duty and built the exquisite Jama Masjid. It was his nephew Mohammed, he of the giant Gol Gumbaz, who later commissioned the Quaranic calligraphy that so sumptuously gilds the western wall.

bearing witness to the tolerance of the Adil Shahi Dynasty towards other religions. Near the Rauza is a huge tank, the **Taj Bauri**, built by Ibrahim II in memory of his wife. The approach is through a giant gateway flanked by two octagonal towers.

Listings Bijapur *map p1028*

Tourist information

Tourist office
Opposite the stadium, Bijapur, T08352-250359.
Mon-Sat 1030-1330 and 1415-1730.
Not very useful.

Where to stay

$$ Madhuvan International
Off Station Rd, T08352-255571.
35 rooms, 10 a/c, very pleasant, good vegetarian garden restaurant and rooftop terrace, beer in rooms only, travel desk, but a bit overpriced. Quite noisy till 2330 because of the restaurant.

$$-$ Hotel Kanishka International
Station Rd, T08352-223788,
kanishka_bjp@rediffmail.com.
24 rooms en suite (10 a/c) with decidedly garish decor such as giant mirrors. Facilities include cable TV, telephone, laundry and the excellent **Kamat Restaurant** downstairs.

$ Godavari
Athni Rd, T08352-270828.
48 good rooms, friendly staff, good vegetarian and non-vegetarian food served.

$ Hotel Navaratna International
Station Rd, T08352-222771.
The grand colonnaded drive belies the modest price tag of the 34 rooms here (12 a/c). Communal areas scream with huge modernist paintings

and rooms are done up with colour-coded care. TV, phone and smaller rooms have sit-outs. Very popular non-vegetarian courtyard restaurant, bar and pure vegetarian restaurant. They also have rooms and baths for drivers – a giant leap in the humane direction for an Indian hotel.

$ Hotel Pearl
Opposite Gol Gumbaz, Station Rd,
T08352-256002.
32 rooms (17 a/c) in a modern, 3-storey, scrupulously clean, modest, mint pastel-coloured hotel set round a central courtyard with vegetarian basement restaurant (booze and non-vegetarian food through room service). Telephones, cable TV in all rooms, laundry and parking.

$ Railway Retiring Rooms
Also has a dorm. Very clean; contact the ticket collector on duty.

$ Samrat
Station Rd, T08352-250512.
30 basic rooms, 6 with a/c are passable, but the rest are battered. Good vegetarian garden restaurant but beware of the mosquitoes.

$ Sanman
Opposite Gol Gumbaz, Station Rd,
T08352-251866.
24 clean (6 a/c), pleasant rooms with shower and mosquito nets. Very good value. Separate vegetarian and non-vegetarian restaurants with bar. Recommended.

$ Santosh
T08352-252179.
70 good, clean rooms including some a/c, quieter at the back, convenient, good value.

Restaurants

Most good places to eat are north of Station Rd.

$ Kapali
Opposite bus stand.
Decent South Indian food.

$ Priyadarshini
MG Rd, opposite Gagan Mahal.
Vegetarian snacks.

$ Shrinidhi
Gandhi Chowk.
Quality vegetarian meals.

Festivals

Jan Siddhesvara Temple festival. Music festival accompanied by Craft Mela.

Transport

Bus A service runs between the station and the west end of town. Horse-drawn carriages ply up and down MG Rd; bargain hard.

From the bus stand, T08352-251344, there are frequent services to **Bidar**, **Hubli**, **Belgaum** and **Solapur** (2-2½ hrs). Buses to **Badami**, 3½ hrs. For **Hospet**, travel via Gadag or Ikal. Reservations can be made on the following daily services to **Aurangabad**: 0600, 1830, **Hospet**, **Bengaluru**: 1700, 1800, 1930, 2130 (12 hrs), ultra-fast service at 1900, 2000; **Belgaum**: 0630, **Hubli**: 0900, 1400, 1600, **Hyderabad**: 0600, 1800, deluxe at 2130, **Mumbai** (**CT**): 0800, 1600, 1700, 2030, **Mumbai** (**Kurla**): 1900, 2000, 2100, **Mysore**: 1700, **Panaji**: 1900, and **Vasco de Gama**: 0715. Several private agents also run services to **Bengaluru**, **Mangalore**, **Mumbai** and **Pune** (7 hrs).

Train Computerized Reservation Office opens 0800-2000, Sun 0800-1400. **Solapur** (transfer for main line Mumbai–Hyderabad services): at least 10 daily, 2-3 hrs. **Gadag**: 6 daily, 4 hrs. **Bengaluru**: 2 daily, 15-18 hrs, both continue to **Mysore** (18-21 hrs). Buses are more convenient.

Cradle of Hindu temple architecture *Colour map 5, C5.*
Karnataka's best and most ancient temple architecture

Although Bijapur became an important Muslim regional capital, its surrounding region has several villages which, nearly 1500 years ago, were centres of Chalukyan power and the heart of new traditions in Indian temple building. At a major Indian crossroads, the temples at Aihole represent the first finely worked experiments in what were to become distinct North and South Indian temple styles.

Essential Cradle of Hindu temple architecture

Visiting the temples

Trains from Bijapur to Gadag stop at Badami, which makes a useful hub for visiting other sights. Buses run from Hubli, Hospet and Kolhapur. If you're travelling by bus it's best to visit Badami first, then Pattadakal and Aihole, but since it takes half a day to see Badami, visiting the sites by bus doesn't allow time for Mahakuta. If you want to see all the sights comfortably in a day it is well worth hiring a car in Bijapur, going to Aihole first and ending at Badami.

Aihole
The main temples are now enclosed in a park, open sunrise to sunset, foreigners Rs 100, Indians Rs 5, flash photography prohibited.

Aihole was the first Chalukyan capital, but the site was developed over a period of more than 600 years from the sixth century AD and includes important Rashtrakuta and late Chalukyan temples, some dedicated to Jain divinities. It is regarded as the birthplace of Indian temple architectural styles and the site of the first built temples, as distinct from those carved out of solid rock. Most of the temples were dedicated to Vishnu, though a number were subsequently converted into Shaivite shrines.

There are about 140 temples – half within the fort walls – illustrating a range of developing styles from Hoysala, Dravida, Jain, Buddhist, Nagara and Rekhanagara. There is little else. All the roads entering Aihole pass numerous temple ruins, but the road into the village from Pattadakal and Bagalkot passes the most important group of temples which would be the normal starting point for a visit. Some prefer to wander around the dozens of deserted (free) temples around town instead of joining the crowds in the park.

Durgigudi Temple Named not after the Goddess Durga but because it is close to the *durga* (fort), Durgigudi Temple dates from the late seventh century. It has an early *gopuram* structure and semi-circular apse which imitates early Buddhist *chaitya* halls. There are numerous superb sculptures including a series contained in niches around the ambulatory: walking clockwise they represent Siva and Nandi, Narasimha, Vishnu with Garuda, Varaha, Durga and Harihara.

Lad Khan Temple According to recent research Lad Khan Temple has been dated from around AD 700, not from AD 450 as suggested by the first Archaeological Survey of India reports in 1907. This is indicated by the similarity of some of its sculptures to those of the Jambulinga Temple at Badami, which has been dated precisely at AD 699. Originally an assembly hall and *kalyana mandapa* (marriage hall), it was named after Lad Khan, a pious Muslim who stayed in the temple at the end of the 19th century. A stone ladder through the roof leads to a shrine with damaged images of Surya, Vishnu and Siva carved on its walls. It bears a striking resemblance to the megalithic caves that were still being excavated in this part of the Deccan at the beginning of the period. The roof gives an excellent view of the village.

Gaudar Gudi Temple Close to the Lad Khan Temple, Gaudar Gudi is a small, rectangular Hindu temple, probably dating from the seventh century. It has a rectangular columned *mandapa*, surrounded on three sides by a corridor for circumambulation. Its roof of stone slabs is an excellent example of North Indian architecture.

Chikki Temple Beyond the Gaudar Gudi Temple is a small temple decorated with a frieze of pots, followed by a deep well. There are others in various states of repair. To see the most important of the remaining temples you leave the main park. Excavations are in progress, and the boundaries of the park may sometimes be fenced. Turning right out of the main park, the Bagalkot road leads to the Chikki Temple. Similar in plan to the Gaudar Gudi, this temple has particularly fine carved pillars. The beams which support the platform are also well worth seeing.

Ravan Phadi Cave Temple ① *Reached from the main park entrance on the left, about 300 m from the village.* The cave itself (formerly known as the Brahman) is artificial, and the sixth-century temple has a variety of carvings of Siva both outside and inside. One is in the *Ardhanarisvara* form (half Siva, half Parvati), another depicts Parvati and Ganesh dancing. There is a huge lotus carved in the centre of the hall platform; and two small eighth-century temples at the entrance, the one to the northwest dedicated to Vishnu and that to the south, badly weathered, may have been based on an older Dravidian-style temple.

Buddhist Temple This is a plain two-storey temple on a hill beyond the end of the village on the way to the Meguti Temple. It has a serene smiling Buddha with the Bodhi Tree emerging from his head, on the ceiling of the upper floor. Further uphill is the **Jain temple**, a plain structure lacking the decorations on the plinth, columns and *gopuram* of many Hindu temples. It has a statue of Mahavira in the shrine within. Climb up through the roof for a good view of Aihole.

Meguti Temple Dating to AD 634, the Meguti Temple is reached from the Buddhist Temple down a path leading to a terrace. A left-hand route takes you to the foot of some stairs leading to the top of a hill which overlooks the town. This is the site of what is almost certainly the oldest building in Aihole and one of the oldest dated temples in India. Its date is indicated by an inscription by the court poet to the king Ravikirtti. A Dravidian-style temple, it is richly decorated on the outside, and although it has elements which suggest Shaivite origins, it has an extremely impressive seated Jain figure, possibly Neminath, in the sanctuary which comprises a hall of 16 pillars.

Kunti Group The Kunti Group is a group of four Hindu temples (dating from seventh to ninth centuries). To find them you have to return down to the village. The oldest is in the southeast. The external columns of its *mandapa* are decorated with *mithuna*, or erotic couples. The temple to the northwest has beautifully carved ceiling panels of Siva and Parvati, Vishnu and Brahma. The other two date from the Rashtrakuta period.

Hucchappayya Math Beyond the Kunti Group is the Hucchappayya Math, dating to the seventh century, which has sculptures of amorous couples and their servants, while the beams inside are beautifully decorated. There is a tourist rest house close to the temples should you wish to stay.

Pattadakal

On the banks of the Malaprabha River, Pattadakal – a World Heritage Site – was the second capital of the Chalukyan kings between the seventh and eighth centuries and the city where the kings were crowned. Ptolemy referred to it as 'Petrigal' in the first century AD. Two of their queens imported sculptors from Kanchipuram.

Most of the **temples** ① *sunrise to sunset, foreigners Rs 250, Indians Rs 10*, cluster at the foot of a hill, built out of the pink-tinged gold sandstone, and display a succession of styles of the southern Dravida temple architecture of the Pallavas (even miniature scaled-down models) as well as the North Indian Nagara style, vividly illustrating the region's position at the crossroads of North and South Indian traditions. With one exception the temples are dedicated to Siva. Most of the site is included in the archaeological park. Megalithic monuments dating from the third to fourth centuries BC have also been found in the area.

Jambulinga and Kadasiddheshvara temples Immediately inside the entrance are the small eighth-century Jambulinga and Kadasiddheshvara temples. Now partly ruined, the curved towers survive and the shrine of the Jambulinga Temple houses a figure of the dancing Siva next to Parvati. The gateways are guarded by *dvarapalas*.

Galagnatha Temple Just to the east is the eighth-century Galaganatha Temple, again partly damaged, though its curved tower characteristic of North Indian temples is well preserved, including its *amalaka* on top. A relief of Siva killing the demon Andhaka is on the south wall in one of three original porches.

Sangamesvara Temple Dating from the reign of Vijayaditya (AD 696-733) this is the earliest temple. Although it was never completed it has all the hallmarks of a purely Dravidian style. Beautifully proportioned, the mouldings on the basement and pilasters divide the wall. The main shrine, into which barely any light is allowed to pass, has a corridor for circumambulation and a *lingam* inside. Above the sanctuary is a superbly proportioned tower of several storeys.

Kashi Vishveshvara Temple To the southwest is the late-eighth century North Indian-style Kashi Vishveshvara Temple, readily distinguishable by the *Nandi* in front of the porch. The interior of the pillared hall is richly sculpted, particularly with scenes of Krishna.

Virupaksha and Mallikarjuna temples The largest temples, the Virupaksha (AD 740-744) with its three-storey *vimana* and the Mallikarjuna (AD 745), typify the Dravida style, and were built in celebration of the victory of the Chalukyan king Vikramaditya II over the Pallavas at Kanchipuram by his wife, Queen Trailokyamahadevi. The king's death probably accounted for the fact that the **Mallikarjuna Temple** was unfinished, and you can only mark out some of the sculptures. However, the king's victory over the Pallavas enabled him to express his admiration for Pallava architecture by bringing back to Pattadakal one of the chief Pallava architects. The **Virupaksha**, a Shaivite temple, has a sanctuary surrounded by passageways and houses a black polished stone Siva *lingam*. A further Shaivite symbol is the huge 2.6-m-high chlorite stone *Nandi* at the entrance, contrasting with the pinkish sandstone surrounding it. The three-storey tower rises strikingly above the shrine, the outside walls of which, particularly those on the south side, are richly carved. Many show different forms of Vishnu and Siva, including some particularly striking panels which show Siva appearing out of a *lingam*. Note also the beautifully carved columns inside. They are very delicate, depicting episodes from the *Ramayana*, *Mahabharata* and the *Puranas*, as well as giving an insight into the social life of the Chalukyas. Note the ingenuity of the sculptor in making an elephant appear as a buffalo when viewed from a different side.

Jain temples In the ninth century the Rashtrakutas arrived and built a Jain temple with its two stone elephants a short distance from the centre. The carvings on the temples, particularly on the **Papanatha** near the village which has interesting sculpture on the ceiling and pillars, synthesizes North and South Indian architectural styles.

Badami

Badami (population 25,900) occupies a dramatic site squeezed in a gorge between two high red sandstone hills. Once called Vatapi, after a demon, Badami was the Chalukyan capital from AD 543-757. The ancient city has several Hindu and Jain temples and a Buddhist cave and remains peaceful and charming. The transcendent beauty of the Hindu cave temples in their spectacular setting warrants a visit. The village with its busy bazar and a large lake has whitewashed houses clustered together along narrow winding lanes up the hillside. There are also scattered remains of 18 stone inscriptions (dating from the sixth to the 16th century).

The sites are best visited early in the morning. They are very popular with monkeys, which can be aggressive, especially if they see food. End the day by watching the sun set from the eastern end of the tank. The area is well worth exploring by bicycle.

South Fort ① *Foreigners Rs 100, Indians Rs 5.* The fort is famous for its cave temples, four of which were cut out of the hillside in the second half of the sixth century. There are 40 steps to **Cave 1**, the oldest. There are several sculpted figures, including Harihara, Siva and Parvati, and Siva as Nataraja with 18 arms seen in 81 dancing poses. **Cave 2**, a little higher than Cave 1, is guarded by *dvarapalas* (door keepers). Reliefs of Varaha and Vamana decorate the porch. **Cave 3**, higher still, is dedicated to Vishnu. According to a Kannada inscription (unique in Badami) it was excavated in AD 578. It has

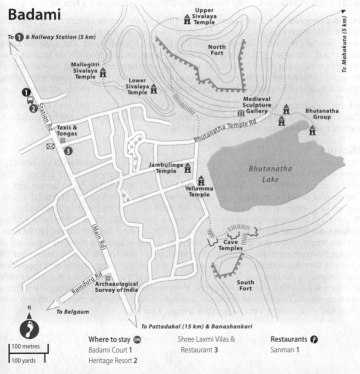

Badami

To ① & Railway Station (5 km)

To Mahakuta (5 km)

Upper
Sivalaya
Temple

North
Fort

Mallegitti
Sivalaya
Temple

Lower
Sivalaya
Temple

Medieval
Sculpture
Gallery

Bhutanatha
Group

Station Rd

Taxis &
Tongas

Bhutanatha Temple Rd

Jambulinga
Temple

Bhutanatha
Lake

Yellamma
Temple

(Main Rd)

Cave
Temples

South
Fort

Ramdurg Rd

Archaeological
Survey of India

To Belgaum

N

100 metres
100 yards

To Pattadakal (15 km) & Banashankari

Where to stay 🛏
Badami Court 1
Heritage Resort 2

Shree Laxmi Vilas &
Restaurant 3

Restaurants 🍴
Sanman 1

numerous sculptures including Narasimha (man-lion), Hari-Hara (Siva-Vishnu), a huge seated Vishnu and interesting friezes. Frescoes executed in the tempera technique are similar to that used in the Ajanta paintings, and so are the carved ceilings and brackets. **Cave 4**, probably about 100 years later than the three earlier caves, is the only Jain cave. It has a statue of the seated Parsvanatha with two *dvarapalas* at the entrance. The fort itself above the caves is closed to the public.

Buddhist Temple and Yellamma Temple The **Buddhist Temple** is in the natural cave close to the ancient artificial Bhutanatha Lake (Agasthya Lake), where the mossy green water is considered to cure illnesses. The **Yellamma Temple** has a female deity, while one of the two Shaivite temples is to Bhutanatha (God of souls); in this form, Siva appears angry in the dark inner sanctuary.

Mallegitti Sivalaya Temple This seventh-century temple is one of the finest examples of the early Southern style. It has a small porch, a *mandapa* (hall) and a narrower *vimana* (shrine), which Harle points out is typical of all early Western Chalukya temples. The slim pilasters on the outer walls are reminders of the period when wooden pillars were essential features of the construction. Statues of Vishnu and Siva decorate the outer walls, while animal friezes appear along the plinth and above the eaves. These are marked by a moulding with a series of ornamental small solid pavilions.

Jambulinga Temple An early temple in the centre of the town near the rickshaw stand. Dating from AD 699 as attested by an inscription and now almost hidden by houses, the visible brick tower is a late addition from the Vijayanagar period. Its three chapels, dedicated to Brahma, Vishnu and Siva, contain some fine carving, although the deities are missing and according to Harle the ceiling decoration already shows signs of deteriorating style. The carvings here, especially that of the Nagaraja in the outside porch, have helped to accurately date the Lad Khan Temple in Aihole (see page 1031). Opposite the Jambulinga Temple is the 10th-century **Virupaksha Temple**.

North Fort temples ① *Rs 2, take water with you.* These mainly seventh-century temples provide an insight into Badami's history. Steep steps, almost 1 m high, take you to 'gun point' at the top of the fort which has the remains of large granaries, a treasury and a watchtower. The **Upper Sivalaya Temple**, though damaged, still has some friezes and sculptures depicting Krishna legends. The North Fort was taken in a day by Colonel Munro in 1918, when he broke in through the east side.

An ancient **dolmen** site can be reached by an easy hike through interesting countryside; allow 3½ hours. A local English-speaking guide, Dilawar Badesha, at Tipu Nagar, charges about Rs 2.

Medieval Sculpture Gallery ① *North of the tank, Sat-Thu 1000-1700, free.* Run by the Archaeological Survey, the gallery contains fine specimens from Badami, Aihole and Pattadakal and a model of the natural bridge at Sidilinapadi, 5 km away.

Mahakuta

Once reached by early pilgrims over rocky hills from Badami, 5 km away, Mahakuta is a beautiful complex of Chalukyan temples dating from the late seventh century and worth a detour. The superstructures reflect influences from both North and South India and one has an Orissan *deul*.

The restored temple complex of two dozen shrines dedicated to Siva is built around a large spring-fed tank within an enclosure wall. The old gateway to the southeast has fasting figures of Bhairava and Chamunda. On entering the complex, you pass the *Nandi* in front of the older **Mahakutesvara Temple** which has fine scrollwork and figures from the epics carved on the base. Larger Siva figures appear in wall niches, including an *Ardhanarisvara*. The temple is significant in tracing the development of the super-structure which began to externally identify the position of the shrine in Dravidian temples. Here the tower is dome-like and octagonal, the tiers supported by tiny 'shrines'. The **Mallikarjuna Temple** on the other side of the tank is similar in structure with fine carvings at the entrance and on the ceiling of the columned *mandapa* inside, depicting Hindu deities and *mithuna* couples. The enclosure has many smaller shrines, some carrying fine wall carvings. Also worth visiting is the **Naganatha Temple**, 2 km away.

Tourist information

Tourist office
Next to Mayura Chalukya, Badami,
T08357-220414.

Where to stay

Badami

There is no formal money exchange but the
Mukambika hotel, opposite the bus stand, may
change small denominations of TCs.

$$$-$$ Badami Court
Station Rd, 2 km from town, T08357-720207.
It's a pleasant stroll to get there or take one of
the frequent buses. 26 clean, modern, though
cramped, rooms with bath (some a/c). There's a
good restaurant, pool (small and only knee-deep;
non-residents Rs 80 per hr), gym and garden. It
has a near monopoly on accommodation and
service; maintenance reflects the absence of
competition. Rates sometimes negotiable, only
accepts rupees.

$$ Heritage Resort
Station Rd, T08357-220250,
www.theheritage.co.in.
Smart and spacious rooms in handsome stone
cottages, each with its own sit-out opening on to
a green lawn. There's a vegetarian restaurant, and
the staff can arrange transport and guides.

$ Shree Laxmi Vilas
Main Rd, T08357-220077.
Simple rooms, 3 with balconies with great views
back to the temples. Right in the thick of it, so it's
interesting but noisy.

Restaurants

Badami

$ Dhabas
Near the Tonga Stand.
Sells snacks.

$ Laxmi Vilas
Near the taxi stand.
Vegetarian meals.

$ Sanman
Near the bus stand.
Non-vegetarian dishes.

Festivals

Pattadakal

Jan **Nrutytsava** draws many famous dancers
and is accompanied by a Craft Mela.
Mar-Apr Temple car festivals at Virupaksha and
Mallikarjuna temples.

Transport

Badami

Bicycle Bike hire from stalls along the main
road, Rs 5 per hr; pleasant to visit Banashankari,
Mahakuta and Pattadakal.

Bus Few daily to **Hospet** (6 hrs), very slow and
crowded but quite a pleasant journey with lots
of stops; **Belgaum** via **Bagalkot** (4 hrs); **Bijapur,**
0645-0930 (4 hrs). Several to **Pattadakal** and
Aihole from 0730. **Aihole** (2 hrs), from there to
Pattadakal (1600). Last return bus from Aihole
1715, via Pattadakal.

Car Hire from Badami with driver for Mahakuta,
Aihole and Pattadakal, about Rs 650.

Train The station is 5 km north on the **Bijapur–**
Gadag line, with 6 trains daily in each direction
(enquire about schedules); frequent buses to town.

The dry and undulating plains from Hospet to Bidar are broken by rocky outcrops providing superb sites for commanding fortresses.

Raichur *Colour map 5, C6.*

The main road from Hospet to Hyderabad passes through the important medieval centre of Raichur (population 205,600), once dominant in the Tungabhadra-Krishna *doab*, now an important but dusty market town, in the middle of a cotton-growing area.

The site of the fort's **citadel** at Raichur gives magnificent views over the vast open spaces of the Deccan plateau nearly 100 m below. Built in the mid-14th century Raichur became the first capital of the Bijapur Kingdom when it broke away from the Bahmani Sultans in 1489. Much of the fort itself is now in ruins, but there are some interesting remains. The **north gate** is flanked by towers, a carved elephant standing about 40 m away. On the inner walls are some carvings, and a tunnel reputedly built to enable soldiers access to barricade the gate in emergency. Near the **west gate** is the old palace. The climb to the citadel begins from near the north gate. In the citadel is a shrine with a row of cells with the **Jami Masjid** in the east. Its eastern gateway has three domes. The top of the citadel is barely 20 sq m.

There are some other interesting buildings in the fort below the hill, including the **Daftar ki Masjid** (Office Mosque), built around 1510 out of masonry removed from Hindu temples. It is one of the earliest mosques in the Deccan to be built in this way, with the bizarre result of producing flat ceilings with pillars carved for Chalukyan temples. The **Ek Minar ki Masjid** ('one-minaret mosque') is in the southeast corner of the courtyard. It has a distinctively Bahmani-style dome.

Gulbarga (Kalburgi)

The fortress at Gulbarga sits in ruins above the town (population 532,000). From 1347 to 1525 Gulbarga served as the first capital of the Bahmanis, but it is also widely known among South Indian Muslims as the home of Saiyid Muhammad Gesu Daraz Chisti (1320-1422) who was instrumental in spreading pious Islamic faith in the Deccan. The annual Urs festival in his memory can attract up to 100,000 people.

The town's sights and hotels are quite spread out so it is worth hiring an auto for half a day. The most striking remains in the town are the fort, with its citadel and mosque, the Jami Masjid, and the great tombs in its eastern quarter.

Fort ① *1 km west of the centre of the present town.* Originally built by Ala-ud-din Bahmani in the 14th century, most of the outer structures and many of the buildings are in ruins. The outer door of the west gate and the *bala hissar* (citadel), a massive structure, however, remain almost intact although the whole place is very overgrown. A flight of ruined steps leads up to the entrance in the north wall; beware of dogs. It's easy to see why the Bahamis were so keen to upgrade their fortress. The fat fort walls at Gulbarga – romantically named as the 'bouquet of lovers' – may sit proud above the more modern artificial lake, and the *bala hissar* itself stands high with its plump rotund columns, but the whole is all too pregnable and modest. And there's no commanding hilltop to provide the impenetrability that the plateaux around Bidar bequeathed the dynasty's subsequent rulers.

All that remains of the palace structures are solitary walls stamped with arches, but the **Jami Masjid**, with its incongruous, uncanny likeness to the mosque at Córdoba in southern Spain, is both active and well maintained (similarities with the mosque at Córdoba have contributed to the legend that it was designed by a North African architect from the Moorish court). Beautiful geometrical angles of archways form as you walk under the 75 small roof domes zigzagging between the four corner domes. The whole area of 3500 sq m is covered by a dome over the *mihrab*, four corner domes and 75 minor domes, making it unique among Indian mosques. It was built by Firoz Shah Bahmani (1397-1432).

Tombs ① *Note that women are not allowed to enter the tombs.* The tombs of the Bahmani sultans are in two groups. One lies 600 m to the west of the fort, the other on the east of the town. The latter have no remaining exterior decoration though the interiors show some evidence of ornamentation.

The Dargah of the Chisti saint, **Hazrat Gesu Nawaz** – also known as Khwaja Bande Nawaz – who came to Gulbarga in 1413 during the reign of Firoz Shah Tughlaq, is open to visitors. The two-storey tomb with a highly decorated painted dome had a mother-of-pearl canopy added over the grave. The **Dargah library**, which has 10,000 books in Urdu, Persian and Arabic, is open to visitors.

The most striking of all the tombs near **Haft Gumbaz**, the eastern group, is that of **Taj-ud-Din Firuz** (1422). Unlike the other tombs it is highly ornate, with geometrical patterns developed in the masonry.

Listings Gulbarga

Where to stay

$ Aditya
Humnabad Rd, T08472-224040.
Reasonable rooms, some a/c with bath, clean vegetarian restaurant, very good value.

$ Pariwar
Humnabad Rd, near the station, T08472-221421, hotelpariwar@yahoo.com.
Some a/c rooms, some cleaner and better value than others. Old but tidy, friendly staff and tasty vegetarian meals (no beer).

$ Santosh
University Rd (east of town), T08472-247991.

Some a/c rooms, good non-vegetarian restaurant (beer). The best in town.

Transport

Bus There are bus connections to Hyderabad (190 km) and **Solapur**.

Train Mumbai (CST): 8 trains daily, 13 hrs. **Bengaluru**: *Udayan Exp 6529*, 1900, 13½ hrs; *Lokmanya Tilak 1013*, 0905, 13 hrs. **Chennai (MC)**: *Chennai Exp 6011* (AC/II), 0130, 15 hrs; *Mumbai Chennai Mail 6009*, 1140, 18 hrs; *Dadar Chennai Exp 1063*, 0605, 14 hrs. **Hyderabad**: *Mumbai-Hyderabad Exp 7031* (AC/II), 0020, 5¾ hrs; *Hussainsagar Exp 7001*, 0740, 5 hrs.

Bidar *Colour map 5, B6.*

Muslim fort and mausoleums

The scruffy bungalow town that is modern-day Bidar (population 172,300) spreads out in a thin layer of buildings both within and outside of the imposing rust-red walls of the 15th-century fort that once played capital to two Deccan-ruling Muslim dynasties. The buildings may be new but there's still a medieval undercurrent to life here.

Islam still grows sturdily: apart from the storehouses of government-subsidized industries to counter 'backwardness', the outskirts are littered with long white prayer walls to mop up the overspill from over-burdened mosques during Id. A few lone tiles, tucked into high corners, still cling to the laterite brick structures that stand in for the succession of immaculately made palaces which must once have glowed incandescent with bright blue, green and yellow designs. Elsewhere you can only see the outline of the designs. The old fort commands grand vistas across the empty cultivated land below. Each successive palace was ruined by invasions then built anew a little further east.

Inner Fort

The Inner Fort, built by Muhammad Shah out of the red laterite and dark trapstone, was later embellished by Ali Barid. The steep hill to the north and east provided natural defence. It was protected to the south and west by a triple moat (now filled in). A series of gates and a drawbridge over the moat to the south formed the main entrance from the town. The second gate, the **Sharaza Darwaza** (1503) has tigers carved in bas relief on either side (Shia symbols of Ali as protector), the tile decorations on the walls and the *Nakkar Khana* (Drum gallery) above. Beyond this is a large fortified area which brings you to

Fact...
Childless couples voluntarily transfer to the nearby Indian Air Force base in the hope that the famous virility-enhancing waters of Bidar will help solve their problem.

the third gate, the huge **Gumbad Darwaza**, probably built by Ahmad Shah Wali in the 1420s, which shows Persian influence. Note the decorated *gumbad* (dome).

You will see the triple moat to the right and after passing through the gateway, to your left are steps leading to the **Rangin Mahal** (Coloured Palace) where Muhammad Shah moved to, after finding the nearby Shah Burj a safe refuge in 1487 when the Abyssinians attacked. This small palace (an indication of the Bahmanis' declining years) was built by him, elaborately decorated with coloured tiles, later enhanced by Ali Barid with mother-of-pearl inlay on polished black granite walls as well as intricate wood carvings. If locked, ask at the museum (see below) for a key.

The old banyan tree and the **Shahi Matbak** (once a palace, but served as the Royal Kitchens) are to the west, with the **Shahi Hammam** (Royal Baths) next to it, which now houses a small **museum**

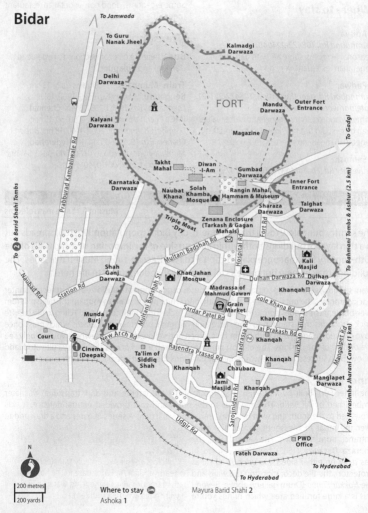

Bidar

To Jamwada

To Guru Nanak Jheel

Kalmadgi Darwaza

Delhi Darwaza

Prabburad Kamballiwale Rd

Kalyani Darwaza

FORT

Mandu Darwaza

Outer Fort Entrance

To Gadgi

Magazine

Karnataka Darwaza

Takht Mahal

Diwan -I-Am

Gumbad Darwaza

Inner Fort Entrance

To 2 & Barid Shahi Tombs

Naubat Khana

Solah Khamba Mosque

Rangin Mahal, Hammam & Museum

Sharaza Darwaza

Talghat Darwaza

To Bahmani Tombs & Ashtur (2.5 km)

Triple Moat -Dry

Zenana Enclosure (Tarkash & Gagan Mahals)

Multani Badshah Rd

Hospital Rd

Fort Rd

Kali Masjid

Shah Ganj Darwaza

Khan Jahan Mosque

Madrassa of Mahmud Gawan

Dulhan Darwaza Rd

Dulhan Darwaza

Khanqah

Station Rd

Naubad Rd

Multani Badshah St

Grain Market

Sardar Patel Rd

Gole Khana Rd

Khanqah

Madrassa Rd

Munda Burj

Jai Prakash Rd

Nutkhan Talim La

Khanqah

Mangalpet Rd

Court

Cinema (Deepak)

New Arch Rd

Rajendra Prasad Rd

Chaubara

Khanqah

To Narasimha Jharani Caves (1 km)

Ta'lim of Siddiq Shah

Khanqah

Jami Masjid

Khanqah

Manglapet Darwaza

Sarojinidevi Rd

Udgir Rd

PWD Office

Fateh Darwaza

To Hyderabad

N

200 metres
200 yards

Where to stay
Ashoka 1

Mayura Barid Shahi 2

BACKGROUND
Bidar

The walled fort town, on a red laterite plateau in North Karnataka, once the capital of the **Bahmanis** and the **Barid Shahis**, remained an important centre until it fell to Aurangzeb in 1656. The Bahmani Empire fragmented into four kingdoms, and the ninth Bahmani ruler, **Ahmad Shah I**, shifted his capital from Gulbarga to Bidar in 1424, rebuilding the old Hindu fort to withstand cannon attacks, and enriching the town with beautiful palaces and gardens. With the decline of the Bahmanis, the Barid Shahi Dynasty founded here ruled from 1487 until Bidar was annexed to Bijapur in 1619. The intermingling of Hindu and Islamic architectural styles in the town has been ascribed to the use of Hindu craftsmen, skilled in temple carving in stone (particularly hornblende), who would have been employed by the succeeding Muslim rulers. They transferred their skill to Muslim monuments, no longer carving human figures, forbidden by Islam, but using the same technique to decorate with geometric patterns, arabesques and calligraphy, wall friezes, niches and borders. The pillars, often of wood, were intricately carved and then painted and burnished with gold to harmonize with the encaustic tiles.

① *0800-1700*. Exhibits include Hindu religious sculptures, Stone Age implements and cannon balls filled with bits of iron.

The **Lal Bagh**, where remains of water channels and a fountain witness to its former glory, and the *zenana*, are opposite the hammam. The **Sola Khamba** (16 columns) or **Zanani Mosque** is to the west (1423). The adjacent **Tarkash Mahal** (possibly refurbished by the Barid Shahis for the harem), to the south of Lal Bagh, is in ruins but still retains some tilework. From behind the mosque you can get to the **Gagan Mahal** (Heavenly Palace) that once carried fine decorations and is believed to have allowed the women to watch animal fights in the moat below from the back of the double hall. There's a good view from the roof. The **Diwan-i-Am** (Hall of Public Audience) is to the northwest of the *Zenana* which once held the *Takht-i-Firoza* (turquoise throne). To the north stands the **Takht Mahal** with royal apartments, audience hall and swimming baths. The steep staircase will take you down to underground chambers.

South of the Royal Apartments is the well that supplied water to the fort palaces through clay pipes. Of the so-called **Hazar** ('thousand') **Kothri** ① *cycling is a good way of exploring the site, free*, you can only see a few underground rooms and passages which enabled a quick escape to the moat when necessary. Further south, the **Naubat Khana** probably housed the fort commander and the musicians. The road west from the Royal Apartments leads to the encircling Fort Wall (about 10 km) with bastions carrying vast cannons, the one to the northwest being the most impressive. You can see the ammunition magazine inside the **Mandu Darwaza** to the east before returning to the main fort entrance.

South of the Inner Fort

As you walk south from the fort you can see the ruins of the **Madrassa of Mahmud Gawan** (1472). It is a fine example of his native Persian architecture and still bears signs of the once-brilliant green, white and yellow tiles which covered the whole façade with swirls of floral patterns and bold calligraphy.

The **Chaubara** is a 23-m circular watchtower at the crossroads, south of the town centre (good views from the top). South of this is the **Jami Masjid** (1430) which bears the Barid Shahis' typical chain and pendant motif. The **Kali Masjid** (1694), south of the Talghat Darwaza, is made of black trapstone. It has fine plaster decorations on the vaulted ceiling. There are also a number of **khanqahs** (monasteries).

Outside the fort

Bahmani tombs ① *The road east from the Dulhan Darwaza, opposite the General Hospital, leads to Ashtur, 0800-1700, free, carry your own torch. These are best seen in the morning when the light is better for viewing the interiors.* The square tombs, with arched arcades all round, have bulbous domes.

The exteriors have stone carvings and superb coloured tile decoration showing strong Persian influence, while the interiors have coloured paintings with gilding.

The **tomb of Ahmad Shah I**, the ninth Bahmani ruler, is impressive with a dome rising to nearly 35 m, and has a particularly fine interior with coloured decorations and calligraphy in the Persian style, highlighted with white borders. To the east and south are minor tombs of his wife and son. The **tomb of Alauddin Shah II** (1458) is possibly the finest. Similar in size to his father's, this has lost its fine painting inside but enough remains of the outer tilework to give an impression of its original magnificence.

On the way back is the **Chaukhandi of Hazrat Khalil-Ullah** which is approached by a flight of steps. Most of the tilework has disappeared but you can see the fine carvings at the entrance and on the granite pillars.

Barid Shahi tombs ① *On the Nanded Rd, west of the old town.* Each tomb once stood in its own garden. That of **Ali Barid** is the most impressive, with the dome rising to over 25 m, with granite carvings, decorative plasterwork and calligraphy and floral patterns on the coloured tiles, which sadly can no longer be seen on the exterior. Here, abandoning the customary *mihrab* on the west wall, Ali Barid chose to have his tomb left open to the elements. It includes a prayer hall, music rooms, a combined tomb for his concubines and a pool fed by an aqueduct are nearby. There are fine carvings on the incomplete tomb to his son **Ibrahim Barid**, to the west. You can also see two sets of granite *ranakhambas* (lit battleposts) which may have been boundary markers. Other tombs show the typical arched niches employed to lighten the heavy walls which have decorative parapets.

The road north from Ali Barid's tomb descends to **Nanak Jhera**, where a *gurdwara* marks the holy place where Sikhs believe a miracle was performed by Guru Nanak and the *jhera* (spring) rose.

Listings Bidar *map p1038*

Where to stay

There are several very basic hotels near Old Bus Station. A roadside Punjabi *dhaba* near the junction of NH9 and the Bidar Rd serves very good meals and is clean (including the toilet at the back).

$ Ashoka
Off Udgir Rd, near Deepak Cinema, T08482-223931.
A bit of a dive, but the best Bidar has to offer, friendly, with 21 clean, good-sized rooms, hot water, some a/c. The 'restaurant' is more of a drinking den.

$ Mayura Barid Shahi (KSTDC)
Opposite the New Bus Stand, T08482-228142.
Small but well-kept rooms, and some larger suites, with a good restaurant downstairs. A good deal for the price.

Shopping

Shops sell excellent *bidriwork*, particularly near the Ta'lim of Siddiq Shah. Craftsmen can be seen in the narrow lanes.

Transport

Auto-rickshaw Easily available, Rs 15 being the going rate for most short hops across town.

Bicycle Cycling is the best way to get around and see the sights. 'Cycle taxis' can be hired for Rs 20 per day from several outlets all over town and near the **New Bus Station**. You may have to ask a few before you find a shop that will rent to you, but persevere. Don't waste time with **Ganesh Cycle Taxi** near the New Bus Station.

Bus There are services from the **New Bus Station**, 1 km west of centre, to most regional destinations, but check timings since the last bus is often quite early. From **Hyderabad** or **Gulbarga** (under 4 hrs), or **Bijapur** (8 hrs). Private buses to **Mumbai**: 1700, 5 hrs, Rs 260. **Pune**: 1530, 3½ hrs, Rs 220. Taxi to **Gulbarga** Rs 800.

Train Bidar is on a branch line from Vikarabad to Parbhani Junction. Too slow to be of much use. There are a couple of daily express trains to **Bengaluru** (13-17 hrs), and slow passenger trains to **Hyderabad**, 6 hrs, plus the occasional express.

Background Karnataka

History

The region between the Tungabhadra and the Krishna rivers was home to some of the earliest settlements in peninsular India, dating back more than 500,000 years. By the Middle Stone Age there was already a regional division appearing between the black cotton soil area of the north and the granite-quartzite plateau of the south. In the north hunters used pebbles of jasper taken from riverbeds while quartz tools were developed to the south. Radiocarbon dating puts the earliest of the first agricultural communities of the peninsula at about 3000 BC in what is now northern Karnataka; millets and gram were already widely grown by the first millennium BC. They have remained staple crops ever since.

Karnataka has borne witness to an alarming array of dynasties, and their ruins. Legend has it that India's first emperor, Chandragupta Maurya, became a Jain and renounced all worldly possessions, retiring to Sravanabelagola to meditate. The Western Gangas, from the third to 11th centuries, and the Banas, from fourth to ninth centuries, controlled large parts of the region. The Chalukyas of central Karnataka took some of the lands between the Tungabhadra and Krishna rivers in the sixth century and built great temples in Badami. They and the Rashtrakutas tried to unite the plateau and the coastal areas while there were Tamil incursions in the south and east. The break-up of the Tamil Chola Empire created a power vacuum in their former fiefdoms. In Karnataka the Hoysalas (11th-14th centuries) seized their chance, and left magnificent temples at their old capitals at Belur, Halebid and Somnathpur, exquisite symbols of their power and their religious authority. Then came the Sangama and Tuluva kings of the Vijayanagar Empire, which reached its peak in the mid-16th century with Hampi as its capital.

Karnataka was repeatedly in the frontline in the power struggle between Hindu and Muslim rulers. Muhammad bin Tughlaq attacked northern Karnataka in the 13th century, and during the Vijayanagar period the Muslim sultanates to the north continued to extend their influence. The Bidar period (1422-1526) of Bahmani rule was marked by wars with Gujarat and Malwa, continued campaigns against Vijayanagar, and expeditions against Orissa. Mahmud Gawan, the Wazir of the Bahmani sultanate, seized Karnataka between 1466 and 1481, and also took Goa, formerly guarded by Vijayanagar kings. By 1530 the kingdom had split into five independent sultanates. At times they came together to defend common interests, and in 1565 they co-operated to oust the Vijayanagar Raja. But two of the sultanates, Bijapur and Golconda, gathered the lion's share of the spoils until the Mughals and British supplanted them.

South Karnataka saw a different succession of powers. While the Mughals were preoccupied fighting off the Marathas, the Hindu Wodeyar rulers of Mysore took Srirangapatnam and then Bengaluru (Bangalore). They lost control to Haidar Aliin 1761, the opportunist commander-in-chief who joined forces with the French to extend his control west to make Srirangapatnam his capital. The fierce Mysore Wars followed and with Haidar Ali's and then his son Tipu Sultan's death, the British restored the Wodeyars' rule in 1799. The Hindu royal family was still administering Mysore up to the reorganization of the states in the 1950s when the maharaja was appointed state governor.

Culture

A fault line runs through mainstream Kannada culture and politics, cleaving society into the northern Karantaka peasant caste, the Lingayats and the Vokkaligas, of the south. Lingayats follow the egalitarian and keen educationalist 12th-century saint Basavanna. The name Vokkaligas comes from 'okkalu', meaning to thresh, and these people are mostly farmers. The Kodavas from the southwest are a culture apart, physically fair and tall, worshippers of the goddess Cauvery and Lord Iguthappa. Karnataka has its share of tribal people. The nomadic Lambanis in the north and west are among several tribal peoples in the hill regions. The Siddis are of African origin, Navayats Arab. The state has a significant Muslim minority of nearly seven million, and Mangalore particularly has a notable Catholic community.

Language

Most people speak the Dravidian language Kannada (Kanarese), although this has fused to form Indo-Aryan dialects in the north. Kannada has the second oldest Dravidian literary tradition. The earliest known classic is the ninth-century Kavirajamarga.

Art and architecture

Karnataka's role as a border territory was illustrated in the magnificent architecture of the Chalukyan Dynasty from AD 450 to 650. Here, notably in Aihole, were the first stirrings of Brahman temple design. Relics show the parallel development of Dravidian and North Indian temple architecture: in Pattadakal alone there are four temples built on North Indian Nagari principles and six built on South Indian Dravidalines. Belur, Halebid and Somnathpur's star-shaped bases, bell-towered shrines and exquisite carvings represent a distinctive combination of both traditions. The Vijayanagara kings advanced temple architecture to blend in with the rocky, boulder-ridden landscape at Hampi. Bijapur has some of the finest Muslim monuments on the Deccan from the austere style of the Turkish rulers to the refinement in some of the pavilions and the world's second largest dome at the Gol Gumbaz.

Dance, drama and music

Open-air folk theatre or Bayalatagrew from religious ritual and is performed in honour of the local deity. Actors improvise their plays on an informal stage. Performances usually start at night and often last into the early hours. The famous Yakshagana or Parijata tends to have just one narrator while other forms have four or five, assisted by a jester. The plots of the Dasarata which enacts several stories and Sannata which elaborates one theme, are drawn from mythology but sometimes highlight real-life incidents. The Doddata is less refined than the Yakshagana but they have much in common, beginning with a prayer to the god Ganesh, using verse, and drawing from the stories of the epics Ramayana and Mahabharata. The costumes are elaborate with fantastic stage effects, loud noises and war cries and vigorous dances.

Modern Karnataka

Karnataka is one of India's most rapidly modernizing states, and an undisputed leader in IT skills, biotech and industrial activity. Based on its early development of aeronautics and high precision machine tools, Bengaluru has become a world centre for the computer industry, receiving a much-quoted seal of approval from Bill Gates. Outside the cities agriculture and forestry remain important. Demand for irrigation is growing rapidly against a backdrop of frequent droughts. The water issue is the cause of escalating tension with neighbouring Tamil Nadu. Karnataka is the origin of 70% of India's raw silk, 70% of its flower exports and is also by far India's largest coffee producer.

Telangana & Andhra Pradesh

The red soil plains of Telangana, carved from the erstwhile state of Andhra Pradesh in 2014, have long been the stage for some of the world's wealthiest men.

The Deccani sultans – whose relish for jewels was sated with the diamonds quarried from rich local seams – left a landscape dotted with their courtly pleasure gardens and palaces, and much of the splendour of its architecture remains, particularly in Hyderabad and its nearby fortress city of Golconda.

And Hyderabad's fortunes have revived along with the success of the software industries who have their headquarters at its glass-and-chrome satellite town of Cyberabad.

Yet away from the capital, Telangana ranks among the nation's most underdeveloped corners, providing a backdrop to a meagre bullock-and-cart pany economy.

The catchments of Andhra Pradesh's great rivers, the Krishna and Godavari, are second in size only to the Ganges and are vital in supporting the lush paddy fields of coastal Andhra Pradesh. Rural Andhra holds the ancient Buddhist centre of Nagarjunakonda and Amaravati, and one of India's most important modern Hindu pilgrimage centres, Tirupati.

Telangana & Andhra Pradesh

thrilling cities, Buddhist ruins and holy haircuts

The red soil plains of Telangana, carved from the erstwhile state of Andhra Pradesh in 2014, have long been the stage for some of the world's wealthiest men.

The Deccani sultans – whose fetish for jewels was sated with the diamonds quarried from rich local seams – left a landscape dotted with their courtly pleasure gardens and palaces and much of the splendour of its architecture remains, particularly in Hyderabad and its nearby fortress city of Golconda.

And Hyderabad's fortunes have revived along with the success of the software industries who have their headquarters at the glass-and-chrome satellite town of 'Cyberabad'.

Yet away from the capital, Telangana ranks among the nation's most underdeveloped corners, providing a backdrop to a meagre bullock-and-cart paddy economy.

The catchments of Andhra Pradesh's great rivers, the Krishna and Godavari, are second in size only to the Ganges and are vital in supporting the lush paddy fields of coastal Andhra Pradesh. Rural Andhra holds the ancient Buddhist centres of Nagarjunakonda and Amaravati and one of India's most important modern Hindu pilgrimage centres, Tirumala.

Best for
Biriyanis ▪ History ▪ Pilgrims ▪ Temples

Footprint picks

★ **Hyderabad's Old City**, page 1048

Wander crowded bazars, visit the huge Mecca Masjid, and try an authentic Hyderabadi biriyani.

★ **Salar Jung Museum, Hyderabad**, page 1049

Check out one of India's greatest private collections of art and antiques.

★ **Golconda Fort**, page 1059

Climb South India's most magnificent fort at sunset.

★ **Warangal**, page 1062

Explore the ruins of the medieval city.

★ **Nagarjunakonda Island**, page 1064

Take a boat ride to Nagarjunakonda Island, one of India's oldest Buddhist sites.

★ **Sri Venkatesvara Temple, Tirupati**, page 1076

Join the pilgrims eager for a precious one-second *darshan* at India's most revered temple.

Essential Telangana and Andhra Pradesh

Finding your feet

The state of Telangana was formed in June 2014, with Hyderabad currently serving as the joint capital of both Telangana and Andhra Pradesh. Andhra Pradesh retains the southern and eastern parts of the region; Telangana comprises the arid central and northwestern areas on the Deccan Plateau. For much of the year the interior of Telangana and Andhra Pradesh (population 75.7 million, area: 275,000 sq km) looks dry and desolate although the great delta of the Krishna and Godavari rivers retains its lush greenness by virtue of their irrigation water. Water is the region's lifeblood, and the great peninsular rivers have a sanctity that reflects their importance. The Godavari, rising less than 200 km north of Mumbai, is the largest of the peninsular rivers. The Krishna rises near Mahabaleshwar at an altitude of 1360 m. After the Ganga these two rivers have the largest watersheds in India.

Getting around

As the sites in Telangana and Andhra Pradesh are spread out, local bus, Ambassador cabs or internal flights are advised. Travel to Tirumalai from Chennai.

When to go

It's either bakingly hot or hit by the northwest monsoon for much of the year; the best time to visit is January to March. The heaviest rainfall is between June and October, but the south gets the benefit of the retreating monsoon between October and December. The interior is in the rain shadow of the Western Ghats and receives less rainfall than much of the coast. Cyclones sweeping across the Bay of Bengal can wreak havoc in the flat coastal districts in November and December. Avoid April and May, when higher temperatures can make travel intolerable. In Hyderabad, aim for a weekend to avoid city congestion.

Time required

Allow three days for Hyderabad. You should also make time to visit the forts and temples.

Food and drink

Andhra food stands out as distinct because of its northern influence and large number of non-vegetarians. The rule of the Muslim Nawabs for centuries is reflected in the rich, spicy local dishes, especially in the area around the capital. Try *haleem* (spiced pounded wheat with mutton), *paya* (soup) or *baghara baigan* (stuffed aubergines). Rice and meat biryani, *nahari*, *kulcha*, egg *paratha*, and *kababs* have a lot in common with northern Mughlai dishes. The abundance of locally grown hot chillies has led to a fiery traditional cuisine, for which 'Andhra-style' is a byword. Also grown locally, good quality grapes (especially *anab-e-shahi*) or *khobani* (puréed apricots) provide a welcome neutralizing effect.

Language

Most of Andhra Pradesh's 78 million people are Dravidians. Over 85% of the population speak Telugu. However, there are important minorities. Tamil is widely spoken in the extreme south, and on the border of Karnataka there are pockets of Kannada speakers. In Hyderabad there are large numbers of Urdu speakers who make up 7% of the state's population.

Weather Hyderabad					
January	**February**	**March**	**April**	**May**	**June**
☀ 29°C 15°C 0mm	☀ 32°C 18°C 10mm	☀ 35°C 21°C 10mm	☀ 38°C 24°C 20mm	⛅ 39°C 26°C 20mm	⛅ 34°C 24°C 100mm
July	**August**	**September**	**October**	**November**	**December**
⛅ 31°C 23°C 170mm	⛅ 30°C 22°C 140mm	⛅ 31°C 22°C 160mm	⛅ 31°C 20°C 80mm	☀ 29°C 17°C 20mm	☀ 28°C 15°C 0mm

Hyderabad
& Telangana

Hyderabad, capital of the newly formed state of Telangana, is one of the poster boys for India's biotech and software boom and has emerged as a great place to soak up the atmosphere of the New India. It's also a city that heaves with history, with its splendid markets, mosques, architecture, museums and pearl bazars. On the outskirts of the city are film-set theme parks, the grand medieval fortress of Golconda and a collection of 17th-century tombs of old rulers lying in gardens of frilly bougainvillea. A day's drive to the southeast lies Nagarjunakonda, where the relocated ruins of one of India's richest Buddhist civilizations rise from the middle of an artificial lake.

Hyderabad and Secunderabad   *Colour map 6, B1.*
shiny tech capital with stunning museums and fascinating ancient core

The twin cities of Hyderabad and Secunderabad (population 6.8 million), founded by the rulers of two separate Muslim dynasties, have long since bled into one conglomerate metropolis.

The southern half, **Hyderabad**, holds the dusty and congested Old City; here you will find the beautiful but faded palaces of Islamic architecture, while the atmospheric lanes around the Char Minar throb with a contemporary Muslim mania. **Secunderabad**, which served as a prominent British army base prior to independence and remains the biggest military cantonment in the country, is separated from Hyderabad by the Hussain Sagar Lake.

N Chandrababu Naidu, Andhra's chief minister from the late 1990s until 2004, had development dreams as lofty as the legendarily eccentric Nizam. The result is a city with town planning unequalled in India, including huge theme resorts where you can stand at minus temperatures (a tribute to the famous heat of Andhra), and Hitech City (brilliantly named 'Cyberabad'; a rival to Silicon Valley and home to Microsoft's first overseas base). The success of these high-tech and biotech industries has spawned a new elite to keep the old pearl peddlers in business since trade from the jewel-draped Nizams dried up.

★ Old City and Char Minar

To celebrate the founding of Hyderabad, Sultan Mohammed Quli Qutb Shah built the lofty archway of **Char Minar** ① *0900-1730, Rs 5*, at the entrance to his palace complex. Capped with four soaring minarets (*char minar* means 'four towers') and holding the city's original mosque on its roof, it has been the showpiece of the city since construction was finished in 1612. Today it stands at the centre of a busy crossroads, surrounded by the Old City's sprawling bazar of pearl, perfume and jewellery shops. The monument is lit up every evening from 1900-2100.

Immediately to the southwest is the vast **Mecca Masjid**, so named because of the red clay bricks from Mecca embedded in its impressive outer walls. The second largest mosque in India and among the seven biggest in the world, construction of the building began in 1614 under the sixth Sultan Abdulla Qutb Shah and was completed by Aurangzeb when he annexed Golconda in 1692. Comprising huge slabs of black granite quarried nearby, the mosque was designed to hold

10,000 people at prayer times. The tombs of the Asaf Jahi rulers, the Nizams of Hyderabad, are in an enclosure with a roof, to the left of the courtyard.

Towards the river is the **Jama Masjid**, the second mosque built in the old city at the end of the 16th century, beyond which on Sadar Patel Road are the four arches of **Charkaman**. The eastern Black Arch was for the drums, the western arch led to the palaces, the northern was the Fish Arch, and the southern arch was for the Char Minar.

Lad Bazar area The heart of the Muslim part of the city, the area around the Mecca Masjid and the Char Minar is a fascinating hive of bazars, made up of beautiful wooden buildings with stone carvings and pink elephant gates, packed with people. You arrive at the **chowk** which has a mosque and a Victorian clock tower.

Southeast of the Lad Bazar is the enormous complex of palaces which were built by the different Nizams, including the grand **Chowmahalla Palace** ① *1000-1700, closed Fri and public holidays, Rs 150, camera Rs 50, video camera Rs 100; T040-2452 2032, www. chowmahalla.com*, a facsimile of the Shah's Palace in Tehran. The stuccoed, domed Durbar Hall, courtyards and gardens have been carefully restored at the behest of Princess Esra, the eighth Nizam's wife. In the Durbar Hall is a platform of pure marble on which the *Takht-e-Nishan* (royal seat) was placed. Nizam Salabhat Jung began the splendid palace complex in 1750, but it was only completed more than a century later by Nizam Afzar-ud-Dawla Bahadur. Refreshed and sparkling after a thorough restoration, the four (*chow*) palaces (*mahal*) of the complex's name – the Afzal Mahal, Mahtab Mahal, Tahniyat Mahal and Aftab Mahal – now play host to a museum packed with artefacts from the Nizam's reign, while the central Khilawat Mubarak (Durbar Hall) has been brought back to its original glory, complete with 19 Belgian crystal chandeliers.

The modern ★ **Salar Jung Museum** ① *Salar Jung Marg, T040-2452 3211, www.salarjung museum.in, Sat-Thu 1000-1700, closed Fri and public holidays, allow 1½ hrs, Rs 150, cameras and bags must be left at counter, tape recorded guides at ticket office*, houses the collection of Sir Yusuf Ali Salar Jung III, the *wazir* (prime minister) to the Nizam between 1899 and 1949. The fact that it is one of only three national museums in India is a telling indication of the extant of the riches he amassed. Originally housed on the edge of the city in one of the palaces, it was rehoused in this purpose-built museum in 1968. Exhibits are described in English, Urdu, Hindi and Telugu. The collection includes Indian textiles, bronzes, paintings and fine ivory art pieces, armoury, Far Eastern porcelain and entertaining curiosities. The Indian miniatures are stunning.

The **High Court**, built on the new roads laid out along the Musi's embankments after the great flood, is a splendid Mughal-style building in the old Qutb Shahi gardens **Amin Bagh**, near Afzal

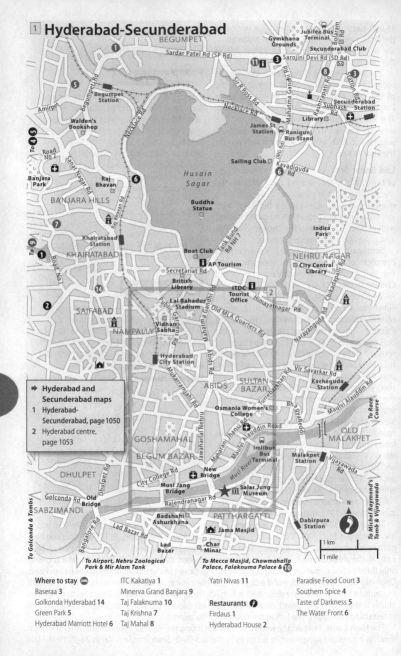

1 Hyderabad-Secunderabad

BEGUMPET

Sardar Patel Rd (SP Rd)

Gymkhana Grounds

Jubilee Bus Terminal

Bolaram

Secunderabad Club

Sarojini Devi Rd (SD Rd)

SIT R Ross Rd

Mahatma Gandhi Rd

Rashtrapati Rd

Secunderabad Station

Begumpet Rd

Begumpet Station

Necklace Rd

James St Station

Library

Subhash Rd

Amirpet

Walden's Bookshop

Necklace Rd

Raniganj Bus Stand

IMG Rd

Kavadiguda Rd

Road No 2

Sailing Club

Santi Nagar Rd

Raj Bhavan

Husain Sagar

Banjara Park

BANJARA HILLS

Bhavan Rd

Buddha Statue

Indira Park

NEHRU NAGAR

Khairatabad Station

KHAIRATABAD

Tank Bund Rd NH 7

City Central Library

Road No 1

Boat Club

Secretariat Rd

AP Tourism

British Library

ITDC Tourist Office

Himayatnagar Rd

2

Narayanguda

Chikadapalli Rd

SAIFABAD

Lal Bahadur Stadium

Old MLA Quarters Rd

Public Gardens

Mahatma Gandhi Rd

Vidhan Sabha

NAMPALLY

Abids Rd

Hyderabad City Station

Vir Savarkar Rd

Kacheguda Station

Mukarramjahi Rd

ABIDS

SULTAN BAZAR

Turrebarkhan Rd

Bhagyanagar Rd

Maulvi Alauddin Rd

GOSHAMAHAL

Maharani Jhansi Rd

Osmania Women's College

OLD MALAKPET

Malakpet Station

Vijayawada Rd

BEGUM BAZAR

Jawaharlal Nehru

Maulvi Alauddin Road

Imlibun Bus Terminal

DHULPET

City College Rd

Dhulpet Rd

New Bridge

Musi River

Bangalore Rd

Musi Jang Bridge

Salar Jung Museum

SABZIMANDI

Golconda Rd

Old Bridge

Rajendranagar Rd

PATTHARGATTI

Dabirpura Station

Badshahi Ashurkhana

Lad Bazar Rd

Jama Masjid

Char Minar

Lad Bazar

N

1 km

1 mile

To Golconda & Tombs

To Airport, Nehru Zoological Park & Mir Alam Tank

To Mecca Masjid, Chowmahalla Palace, Falaknuma Palace & 10

To Michel Raymond's Tomb & Vijayawada

Hyderabad and Secunderabad maps

1 Hyderabad-Secunderabad, page 1050

2 Hyderabad centre, page 1053

Where to stay
Baseraa 3
Golkonda Hyderabad 14
Green Park 5
Hyderabad Marriott Hotel 6

ITC Kakatiya 1
Minerva Grand Banjara 9
Taj Falaknuma 10
Taj Krishna 7
Taj Mahal 8

Yatri Nivas 11

Restaurants
Firdaus 1
Hyderabad House 2

Paradise Food Court 3
Southern Spice 4
Taste of Darkness 5
The Water Front 6

Hyderabad

Hyderabad was the most important centre of Muslim power in Central and South India from the 17th to the 19th centuries. It was founded by the fifth in line of an earlier Muslim dynasty, Mohammad Quli Qutb Shah, in 1591. Through his successors Hyderabad became the capital of a Princely State the size of France, ruled by a succession of Muslim Nizams from 1724 till after India's Independence in 1947. Under their rule many Muslims came to work in the court, from North India and abroad. The Nizam's capital was a highly cosmopolitan centre, drawing extensively on Islamic contacts in North India and in west Asia, notably Persia.

During the 18th century British and French traders spread their influence up the coast. Increasingly they came into conflict and looked for alliances with regional powers. At the end of the 18th century the British reached an agreement with the Nizam of Hyderabad in which he accepted British support in exchange for recognition of British rights to trade and political control of the coastal districts. Thus Hyderabad retained a measure of independence until 1947 while accepting British suzerainty.

There was doubt as to whether the Princely State would accede to India after Partition. The Nizam of Hyderabad would have liked to join fellow Muslims in the newly created Muslim State of Pakistan. However, political disturbances in 1949 gave the Indian Government the pretext to take direct control, and the state was incorporated into the Indian Union.

Ganj Bridge. This was Vincent Esch's most striking work. It was built in 1916 from local pink granite, with red sandstone carved panels and columns, a large archway and domes. These days it is painted pink. A further change is the enclosure of the verandas. The detail is Mughal, but some argue that the structure and internal form are Western.

Next door to the High Court is Esch's **City College** (1917-1920), originally the City High School for boys. Built largely of undressed granite, there are some distinctive Indian decorative features including some marble *jalis*. Esch deliberately incorporated Gothic features, calling his style Perpendicular Mogul Saracenic.

In the opposite direction along the riverbank from the Salar Jung Museum is one of the oldest *imambaras* in the country, the **Badshahi Ashurkhana** (House of Mourning), built in the Qutb Shahi style in the late 16th century. It has excellent tile mosaics and wooden columns in the outer chamber, both later additions.

Over the river is the **Osmania Women's College**, the former British residency built by James Achilles Kirkpatrick – the central character of William Dalrymple's history, *White Mughals* – in 1803. This imposing colonial structure, whose grounds run down to the river bank, was the first symbol of British presence in the city. It was deliberately built to the same proportions as the Char Minar In order to be the only equal to its minarets on the city skyline. After decades of decline, the World Monuments Fund is carrying out structural conservation as well as fundraising for further restoration, while it continues to function as an educational institute for 4000 girl students (whose modesty visitors are urged to respect).

The ornate palace Kirkpatrick built for his Muslim bride was razed in 1861 as a symbol of his perceived immorality. Dalrymple's book was launched from the stately, ochre-painted stately building's Durbar Hall. This is a room of giant chandeliers, French windows, mirrors shipped in from Brighton palaces, tatty fans and glorious floral tracings on its ceiling. The Palladian-villa style central complex, the entrance porch with Corinthian columns, the Durbar Hall, oval offices, billiard rooms and bedrooms were initially independent of the flanking wings, separated by drawbridges, whose pulleys are still in place.

Outlying buildings hold printing presses dating from the 1900s. Turn out of the King's Gate then left down a pathway towards the pigeon rookery to see the model of the Residency that Kirkpatrick had made so his Hyderabadi princess Khairunnissa could see the main house without breaking her *purda*.

Hyderabad Centre: New City

The **Osmania General Hospital** (1918-1921) is the third of Vincent Esch's impressive buildings in Hyderabad. It stands across the river, opposite the High Court. The 200-m-long building was one of the largest and best equipped hospitals in the world when it opened. To its east, also on the river, is the imposing **Asafia State Central Library** (1929-1934) with its priceless collection of Arabic, Persian and Urdu books and manuscripts.

The **Public Gardens** ① *closed public holidays,* in Nampally, north of Hyderabad Station, contain some important buildings including the Archaeological Museum and Art Galleries and the State Legislative Assembly (Vidhan Sabha).

Andhra Pradesh State Museum ① *near the Lal Bahadur Shastri Stadium, 10 mins by car from Banjara Hills area, 1030-1700, closed public holidays, nominal entrance fee, photography Rs 10, guidebook Rs 15,* is a small museum with a crowd-drawing 4000-year-old Egyptian mummy. Behind the museum in Ajanta Pavilion are life-size copies of frescoes from the Ajanta Caves while the Nizam's collection of rare artefacts is housed in the Jubilee Hall.

The **City Railway Station** (1914) was intended by Esch to be pure Mughal in style but built entirely of the most modern material then available: pre-cast, reinforced concrete. It has a wide range of distinctively Indian features including the *chhattris* of royalty, wide *chajjas* (eaves) and onion domes.

Naubat Pahad (Kala Pahad or Neeladri) are two hills situated north of the Public Gardens. The Qutb Shahis are believed to have had their proclamations read from the hill tops accompanied by drums. In 1940 pavilions were built and a hanging garden was laid out on top of one; it's now occupied by the **Birla Planetarium** ① *Fri-Wed at 1130, 1600 and 1800, Rs 20,* and **Science Centre** ① *1030-2000, Rs 20.*

The nearby **Venkatesvara Temple** (Birla Mandir) ① *reached by a stall-lined path opposite Thomas Cook on Secretariat Rd, 0700-1200, 1400-2100, photography of inner sanctum prohibited,* is a modern, stunning white marble temple with an intricately carved ceiling which overlooks Husain Sagar. It was built by the Birlas, the Marwari business family who were responsible for building important new Hindu temples in several major cities, including Laxmi Narayan Temple in New Delhi. Completed in 1976, the images of the deities are South Indian, although the building itself drew craftsmen from the north as well, among them some who claimed to have ancestors who built the Taj Mahal.

The massive State Legislative Assembly building, **Vidhan Sabha**, originally the Town Hall, was built by the Public Works Department (PWD) in 1922. Although Esch had nothing to do with its design, he reportedly admired it for its lightness and coolness, which the building maintained even on the hottest day. **Jubilee Hall** (1936), behind the Vidhan Sabha, is another remarkable PWD building, with clear simple lines.

The deep **Husain Sagar Lake** ① *boat trips organized by APTDC leave from Lumbini Park, near the APTDC office on Secretariat Rd, T040-2345 3315,* was created in the mid-16th century by building the *bund* that links Hyderabad and Secunderabad, and was named to mark the gratitude of Ibrahim Quli Qutb Shah to Hussain Shah Wali, who helped him recover from an illness. The *bund* is a favourite evening promenade for the city dwellers. At the far end of the lake is the **Nizamia Observatory**. The 17.5-m-high, 350-tonne granite **statue of Buddha** was erected in the lake after years of successive disasters and finally inaugurated by the Dalai Lama in 1993. The tank, fed by streams originating from the Musi River, supplies drinking water to Hyderabad. Although it supports a rich birdlife and is used for fish culturing it also receives huge amounts of industrial effluent, agricultural waste and town sewage.

Outside the city centre

Originally a rich nobleman's house, **Falaknuma Palace** (see Where to stay, page 1055) was built in 1873 in a mixture of classical and Mughal styles. Bought by the Nizam in 1897, it has a superb interior (particularly the state reception room) with marble, chandeliers and paintings. The palace houses Eastern and European treasures, including a collection of jade, crystal and precious stones and a superb library. Currently operating as one of India's most luxurious hotels – a high bar to jump – it's particularly atmospheric in the evening, when the lights of Hyderabad twinkle at your feet.

Osmania University ① *T040-2709 6048,* built by the Nizam in 1939, is just outside the city towards the east. Inaugurated in 1917 in temporary buildings, its sprawling campus with its black

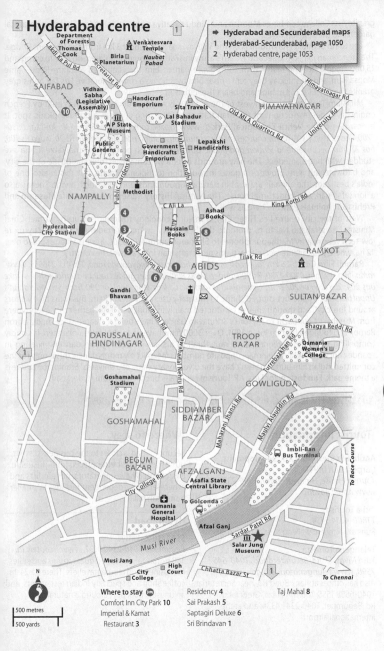

② Hyderabad centre

➡ **Hyderabad and Secunderabad maps**
1 Hyderabad-Secunderabad, page 1050
2 Hyderabad centre, page 1053

Department of Forests
Thomas Cook
Venkatesvara Temple
Birla Planetarium
Naubat Pahad
Lakdi Ka Pul Rd
Secretariat Rd

SAIFABAD

Vidhan Sabha (Legislative Assembly)
Handicraft Emporium
Sita Travels
Lal Bahadur Stadium
HIMAYATNAGAR
Old MLA Quarters Rd
Himayatnagar Rd
University Rd

A P State Museum
Public Gardens
Government Handicrafts Emporium
Lepakshi Handicrafts

Mahatma Gandhi Rd

NAMPALLY

Methodist

C Ali La
Ashad Books
King Kothi Rd

Hussain Books
Hyderabad City Station
Nampally Station Rd
Abid Rd

Tilak Rd
RAMKOT

4
3
5
1
6
8
ABIDS

Gandhi Bhavan
Mukaramjahi Rd

Bank St
SULTAN BAZAR

DARUSSALAM HINDINAGAR

Bhagya Reddi Rd
Osmania Women's College

Jawaharlal Nehru Rd

TROOP BAZAR

GOWLIGUDA

Goshamahal Stadium

Turrebakhan Rd

Mahatma Jhansi Rd
Maulvi Alauddin Rd

GOSHAMAHAL
SIDDIAMBER BAZAR

To Race Course

BEGUM BAZAR
City College Rd
AFZALGANJ

Imbli-Ban Bus Terminal

Asafia State Central Library
To Golconda

Osmania General Hospital

Afzal Ganj
Sardar Patel Rd
Salar Jung Museum ★

Musi River

Musi Jang
City College
High Court
Chhatta Bazar St
To Chennai

N
500 metres
500 yards

Where to stay 🛏
Comfort Inn City Park **10**
Imperial & Kamat Restaurant **3**

Residency **4**
Sai Prakash **5**
Saptagiri Deluxe **6**
Sri Brindavan **1**

Taj Mahal **8**

granite Arts College combines Moorish and Hindu Kakatiya architectural styles. There is a botanical garden and the State Archives.

The **tomb of Michel Raymond** is off the Vijayawada Road, about 3 km from the Oliphant Bridge. The Frenchman joined the second Nizam's army in 1786 as a common soldier and rose to command 15,000 troops. His popularity with the people earned him the combined Muslim-Hindu name Moosa Ram, and even today they remember him by holding a commemorative **Urs fair** at his grey granite tomb, which is 7 m high and bears the initials JR.

Mir Alam Tank, to the southwest of the old city, is a large artificial lake. It was built by French engineers under instructions of the grandfather of Salar Jung III and is a popular picnic spot. It is now part of the **Nehru Zoological Park** ⓘ *www.hydzoo.com, Apr-Jun 0800-1730, Jul-Mar 0830-1700, closed Mon, Rs 30 (extra charges for nocturnal house, safari ride, etc), camera Rs 20, video Rs 100, bus 7Z from Secunderabad Station and Public Garden Rd,* which occupies a remarkable 13-ha site studded with huge boulders. The hilly grounds offer a welcome relief from the bustle of the city, and birdwatching here provides a good introduction to Indian avifauna, but this is also one of India's best zoos (the animals are kept in natural surroundings) and well worth a visit. There's also a lion safari park and a nocturnal house. The **Natural History Museum**, **Ancient Life Museum** and **Prehistoric Animals Park** are here as well.

West of the city centre lies **Hitec City**, a major technology township set up by former Chief Minister Chandrababu Naidu to promote the IT industry in Andhra Pradesh. In a distinctly more low-tech vein, nearby Madhapur is home to **Shilparamam** ⓘ *1100-2300,* a crafts village spread over 12 ha, where you can interact with artisans and craftsman from all over the country.

Ramoji Film City ⓘ *25 km southeast of Hyderabad on the Vijayawada road, T08415-246555, www.ramojifilmcity.com, 0900-1730, Rs 900 (under 12s Rs 800), includes guided tour and various shows, take bus 204, 205, 206 or 207 from Hyderabad (Women's College stop, Koti), or 290 from Secunderabad's Uppal bus stop,* is a sherbet-dipped shrine to the many uses of plaster of Paris. Bus tours take visitors around the 'city', and though they're conducted mainly in Hindi, you'll still gather that everywhere from Mumbai's Chor Bazar to Mysore's Brindavan Gardens have been recreated since media baron Ramoji Rao founded his film lot in 1991. Over 3000 films have been shot here since then. It's oddly compelling to see an audience sit in rapt thrall to a show of aspiring film dancers gyrating in spandex hot pants, while their male opposite numbers inexplicably morris dance; this is only for the committed Indian film buff. It doesn't have the diversionary value of a Universal Studios, but there is a theme park, **Fundustan**, for kids. **AP Tourism** runs daily bus services from Hyderabad.

Listings Hyderabad and Secunderabad *maps p1050 and p1053*

Tourist information

Andhra Pradesh Tourism Development Corporation (APTDC)
Tourism House, Himayatnagar, T040-2326 2151, www.aptdc.gov.in.

India Tourism
T1800-4254 5454.
Runs an excellent walking tour of the old city.

Telangana Tourism
Yatri Nivas, SP Rd, Secunderabad, T040-6457 7598, www.telanganatourism.gov.in.
Also has offices at: Tank Bund Rd, near Secretariat, T040-6558 1555; Tourism Plaza, Greenland Rd, Begumpet, T040-2341 4334; and at the international airport.

Where to stay

Secunderabad is closer to the business district, but Hyderabad is better placed for sightseeing. Larger hotels have generators, but a/c, lifts and other electricity-dependent facilities in smaller hotels can fail.

Hyderabad

$$$$ ITC Kakatiya
Begumpet, T040-2340 0132, www.itchotels.in.
188 exquisitely furnished guest rooms and suites for business and leisure travellers. There's a 24-hr coffee shop and speciality Indian restaurants, and an unusual pool built around a natural rock.

$$$$ Taj Falaknuma
Engine Bowli, Falaknuma, T040-6629 8585,
www.tajhotels.com.
Restored to its original condition the Falaknuma
Palace (see page 1052) now plays host to one
of India's most extraordinary hotels. The pick of
the 60 rooms are the Historical and Royal suites,
fitted out with Edwardian antiques and Italian
marble floors, with sweeping views over the
city or carefully tended lawns. Public areas are
similarly exquisite, with cavernous ballrooms
and dining tables that stretch for miles, and the
overall feeling is akin to being a private guest in
a stately home.

$$$$-$$$ Taj Krishna
Road No 1, Banjara Hills, T040-6666 2323,
www.tajhotels.com.
The flagship luxury Taj hotel in the city's elite
district has Indian and Chinese restaurants,
260 rooms, 24-hr gym, the city's best pool
and nightclub, **Ahala**, beautiful gardens and
immaculate service. The Presidential suite has
its own private pool.

$$$-$$ The Golkonda Hyderabad
Masab Tank, Mahavir Marg, T040-6611 0101,
www.thegolkondahotel.com.
Completely renovated with minimalist decor and
5-star status, the Golkonda has 150 rooms, a/c,
phone, TV, excellent showers. Breakfast included.
Complimentary airport transfers.

$$$-$$ Minerva Grand Banjara
Road No 11, Banjara Hills, T040-6612 7373,
www.minervagrand.com.
A boutique hotel with 44 designer rooms and
suites in the upmarket Banjara Hills, close to
the main commercial, retail and entertainment
centres. Breakfast included.

$$$ Residency (Quality Inn)
Public Garden Rd, T040-3061 6161.
Efficient business hotel, with 95 a/c rooms, polite
service, good vegetarian restaurant and basement
pub, **One Flight Down**. Popular with Indians.

$$ Taj Mahal
4-1-999 Abid Rd, T040-2475 8250,
www.hoteltajmahalindia.com.
75 good-sized simple a/c rooms in 1940s
building. The most characterful of the budget
options, this friendly hotel has good-value rooms,
a busy South Indian vegetarian restaurant and
laundry. Recommended.

$$-$ City Park
Chirag Ali Rd, T040-6610 5510.
Well placed just at the edge of Abid shopping
district. Its 39 bright prefab rooms come with
phone, en suite and writing tables. The rooftop
multi-cuisine restaurant **Degh** has panoramic
views over the city. There's also a car park and
internet, but a stale a/c smell. Breakfast included.

$$-$ Sai Prakash
Nampally Station Rd, T040-2461 1726,
www.hotelsaiprakash.in.
Business hotel with 102 clean, comfortable a/c
rooms and a good restaurant.

$ Imperial
Corner of Nampally Station and Public
Gardens roads (5 mins from Hyderabad station),
T040-6682 7777.
Large hotel with 48 clean rooms, some with bath,
avoid roadside rooms, bucket hot water, helpful
staff and excellent service. It's not recommended
for lone women travellers though.

$ Saptagiri Deluxe
Off Nampally Station Rd, T040-2461 0333.
Peaceful hotel in an interesting area with
36 scrupulously clean rooms. Choice of a/c and
non-a/c. Western toilet, shower. Gets busy so
book in advance.

$ Sri Brindavan
Nampally Station Rd, near the Circle,
T040-2320 3970.
A good budget choice with 70 clean rooms
in a custard-coloured compound set back from
road. Mostly male guests; unsuitable for lone
female travellers. Otherwise decent value, with
good restaurants.

Secunderabad

$$$ Green Park
Begumpet, T040-6651 5151,
www.hotelgreenpark.com.
A sedate and large Indian business and family
hotel with 147 rooms. Rooms come with bath, a/c
and TV. Free Wi-Fi.

$$$ Hyderabad Marriot Hotel
Tank Bund Rd, T040-2752 2999,
www.marriott.com.
Plush business hotel with a charming pool and
spa, set on the shores of Hussain Sagar Lake.
Rates fluctuate according to the city conference
schedule; it's worth phoning ahead. Low
categories exclude breakfast.

$$$ The Manohar
Adjacent to the old airport in Begumpet,
T040-6654 3456, www.themanohar.com.
A full-service business-class hotel with 132 well-appointed rooms and suites, a club lounge overlooking pool and a health club. Check for discounts.

$$$-$$ Hotel Baseraa
1-9 167/168 SD Rd, T040-2770 3200,
www.baseraa.com.
75 tatty but comfortable a/c rooms in busy family hotel with great service and good restaurants.

$$ Yatri Nivas
SP Rd, T040-2346 1855,
www.buttahospitality.com.
Clean, airy, well-kept hotel, with 32 rooms, all a/c, 3 restaurants and a bar.

$ Retiring Rooms
At the railway station.

$ Taj Mahal
88 SD Rd, T040-2781 2106.
Characterful 40-year-old building with 20 faded but good rooms (a/c suite, a/c double, non-a/c double and non-a/c single). Popular veg restaurant.

Restaurants

Hyderabad
To foodies, the city is synonymous with one dish: the Hyderabadi biryani. Succulent mounds of rice, piled high with meat and spices and served with emergency bowls of yoghurt to counter the blistering heat, emerge from the kitchens of grubby and basic cafés along Pathergatti Rd, in the old city near the Char Minar. **Hotel Shaadab** is one of the most famous purveyors. While you're in the area, sample another Hyderabad institution: a cup of extra-sweet and extra-milky Irani chai.

If your tastes run more to the familiar, you'll find many international fast food chains are in the city, as well as the pure vegetarian chain **Kamat**. The shopping malls **Lifestyle** and **Hyderabad Central** have good food courts.

$$$ Taste of Darkness
Inorbit Mall, Hitech City, T040-4201 2428,
www.dialogueinthedarkindia.com/tod.
A unique concept that's part restaurant, part social commentary. Blind waiters lead you through the pitch black dining room, and you 'see' your meal – a simple curry-rice-roti set menu of 1-4 courses – through the eyes of a blind person. A fascinating insight that only heightens your senses of smell and taste.

$$$ The Water Front
Eat St, Necklace Rd, T040-2330 8899.
Open lunch and dinner.
When Hyderabadis need to impress, they go to this open-air restaurant right on Hussain Sagar Lake. The food is coastal Indian and Asian, the bill hefty, and the atmosphere stylish and romantic.

$$$-$$ Firdaus
Taj Krishna hotel (see Where to stay),
T040-6666 2323.
Excellent Mughlai cuisine and one of the only places in the city where you can get the special Hyderabadi treat, *haleem*. Meaning 'patience', this meat, wholewheat and gram dish is slow-cooked and is traditionally made to break the Ramadan fast.

$$ Hyderabad House
Opposite JNTU College, Masab Tank,
T040-2332 7861.
Excellent biryanis and *lukhmis*. Offer parcel service.

$$ Southern Spice
8-2-350/3/2, Road No 3, Banjara Hills, T040-2335
3802. Open for breakfast, lunch and dinner.
Good Andhra, Chettinad, tandoori and Chinese cuisine.

$$-$ Paradise Food Court
38 Sarojini Devi Rd/MG Rd, T040-6631 3721,
www.paradisefoodcourt.com. Open 1100-2400.
Many outlets in the city. Utterly synonymous with biryani, and such an institution that the surrounding area is now named 'Paradise'. You can get parcels from downstairs, eating standing up at the fast food section, or go upmarket at **Persis Gold**.

Bars and clubs

Hyderabad
Mostly in the top-end hotels; nightlife doesn't compare to Bengaluru.
Kismet (at the Park hotel), is the most modish; **One Flight Down** (T040-3061 6161, opposite Hyderabad Railway Station, Public Garden Rd, open 1100-2300) is a modern, British-style pub, with snooker tables and TV. Dark but popular.

Entertainment

Cinema
Some cinemas show English-language films.
Ravindra Bharati, *Public Garden Rd, Saifabad,*
T040-2323 3672. www.ravindrabharathi.org.
Regularly stages dance, theatre and music programmes, a/c.

ON THE ROAD

Craft industries

Andhra's bidriware uses dark matte gunmetal (a zinc and copper alloy) with silver damascening in beautiful flowing floral and arabesque patterns and illustrates the Persian influence on Indian motifs. The articles vary from large vases and boxes, jewellery and plates to tiny buttons and cuff links. The name is derived from Bidar in Karnataka and dates back to the Bahmani rulers.

Miniature wooden figures, animals, fruit, vegetables and birds are common subjects of *Kondapalli* toys which are known for their bright colours. *Nirmal* toys look more natural and are finished with herbal extract which gives them a golden sheen, *Tirupati* toys are in a red wood while *Ethikoppaka* toys are finished in coloured lacquer. Andhra also produces fine figurines of deities in sandalwood.

Hyderabadi jewellers work in gold and precious stones which are often uncut. The craftspeople can often be seen working in the lanes around the Char Minar – shops selling the typical local bangles set with glass lie to the west. Hyderabadi cultured pearls and silver filigree ware from Karimnagar are another speciality.

The state is famous for himru shawls and fabrics produced in cotton/silk mixes with rich woven patterns on a special handloom. Silver or gold threads produce an even richer brocade cloth. A boy often sits with the weavers 'calling out' the intricate pattern.

The All India Handicrafts Board has revived the art of weaving special *ikat* fabrics. Pochampally, a village about 60 km east of Hyderabad, is synonymous for its *ikat* fabric in cotton and silk. The world-famous textile has been awarded IPR (Intellectual Property Rights) protection to safeguard it from imitation and competition. Interestingly, oil is used in the process of dyeing the warp and weft threads before weaving in to produce a pattern, hence the fabric's name *teli rumal* (literally oil kerchief).

Kalahasti, in Andhra's south, and Pedana, in coastal Andhra, produce distinctive Kalamkari cloth paintings (*kalam* refers to the pen used); the dyes come from indigo, turmeric and pomegranate. The blues stand out from the otherwise dullish ochre colours. Designed from mythology tales (*Mahabharata* and *Ramayana*), they make excellent wall hangings.

Sound and light show

Golconda fort, *page 1059*. Spectacularly voiced over by Bollywood legend Amitabh Bhachan.

Shopping

Most shops open 1000-1900. Some close on Fri. Every other shop sells pearls; look for shape, smoothness and shine to determine quality. Size is the last criteria in deciding a pearl's price. Bargain for at least 10% off asking prices. Also look out for *bidri* ware, crochetwork, Kalamkari paintings, *himroo* and silk saris. **Lad Bazar** (around the Char Minar), is great for bangles. For more on Andhra Pradesh's craft tradition, see box, above.

Antiques
Govind Mukandas, *Bank St.*
Humayana, *Taj Banjara hotel.*

Books
Akshara, *8-2-273 Pavani Estates, Road No 2, Banjara Hills, T040-2354 3906.* Excellent collection on all aspects of India in English.

Haziq and Mohi, *Lal Chowk.* Good antiquarian bookshop, especially for Arabic and Persian.

Handicrafts
Government emporia include: **Nirmal Industries** (Raj Bhavan Rd); **Lepakshi**, and **Coircraft** (Mayur Complex), Gun Foundry; and **Co-optex**. There are several others in Abids. Non-government shops may charge a bit more but may have more attractive items.
Bidri Crafts, *Abids.*
Fancy Cloth Store, *21-2-28 Pathergatti, Hyderabad, T040-2452 3983.* For silk. Exports cloth to Selfridges in the UK.
Khadi, *Sultan Bazar and Municipal Complex, Rashtrapati Rd, Secunderabad.*
Kalanjali, *Hill Fort Rd, opposite Public Gardens.* Large selection of regional crafts.
In Secunderabad try: **Baba Handicrafts** (MG Rd); and **Jewelbox** (SD Rd).

Pearls
Mangatrai Pearl and Jewellers, *6-3-883 Punjagutta, T040-2341 1816, www.manga trai.com.*

For quality pearls. Jewellers to Indian nobility, with everything from Basra pearls to black Tahitian pearls.

Cultural centres and libraries
Alliance Française, *near Planetrium, Naubat Pahad, T040-2770 0731*.
Bharatiya Vidya Bhavan, *King Kothi Rd, T040-223 7825*.
British Library, *Secretariat Rd, T040-2323 0774. Tue-Sat 1100-1900*.
Goethe Institute, *Hill Fort Rd, T040-2324 1791*.

Swimming
BV Gurumoorthy Pool, *Sardar Patel Rd*.

Tour operators
APTDC, *T040-2326 2151*. Offers the following tours: **City sightseeing**: full day, 0730-1930, from offices at Yatri Nivas and Secretariat Rd, Rs 250 non a/c and Rs 350 a/c; unsatisfactory as it allows only 1 hr at the fort and includes unimportant sights. **Night tour**: including Golconda sound and light show, Qutb Shahi tombs, boat ride and dinner 1700-2200, Rs 500. **Nagarjunasagar**: Sat and Sun only to Dam, Nagarjunakonda Museum, Right Canal and Ethipothala Falls, 0730-2200, Rs 550 **Ramoji Film City**: 0730-1830, Rs 1100 (entry fee included). Allows 4-5 hrs at the studios, plus Sanghi Temple and shopping time.
TCI, *47 Spurtank Rd. T044-6663 2627, www.tcindia.com*.

Air
Rajiv Gandhi International Airport is 25 km south of the city, T040-6654 6370, www.hyderabad.aero. Transport to town: pre-paid taxis cost Rs 500-600; there are no auto-rickshaws. A/c **Pushpak buses**, T1800-200 4599, www.tsrtcbus.in, run on fixed routes to various parts of the city, including Secunderabad (Rs 250) and Hitech City (Rs 200).

Daily domestic flights to **Ahmedabad**, **Bengaluru**, **Chennai**, **Coimbatore**, **Delhi**, **Goa**, **Jaipur**, **Kochi**, **Kolkata**, **Kozhikode**, **Mumbai**, **Pune**, **Tirupati**, **Vijayawada**, **Visakhapatnam**.

International connections with: **Abu Dhabi**, **Bangkok**, **Doha**, **Dubai**, **Frankfurt**, **Hong Kong**, **Kuala Lumpur**, **London**, **Muscat**, **Sharjah** and **Singapore**.

Bicycle
Hire is readily available (ask for the 'bicycle taxi' shop near Nampally Railway station), Rs 50 per day, but they may ask for a large deposit. Good for visiting Golconda, but the city is only for cyclists who are experienced with heavy, fast-flowing traffic.

Bus
Local City buses are crowded in rush hour. Useful routes: No 119 (Nampally to Golconda); 87 (Nampally to Char Minar); 2/2V (Charminar to Secunderabad Station).

Long distance The vast Imlibun Bus Station (TSRTC, T1800-200-4599, www.tsrtcbus.in) has long-distance state-run buses to all destinations in Telangana/Andhra Pradesh and neighbouring states. Advance reservations available. Private deluxe coaches depart from opposite Hyderabad Railway Station to **Aurangabad**, **Bengaluru** (**Bangalore**), **Mumbai**, **Chennai** and **Tirupati**; reservations from **Royal Lodge**, at the entrance to the station.

Secunderabad has the **Jubilee Bus Station**, T040-2780 2203, with services to major destinations. From Nampally: buses to **Golconda**. **Venus Travel**, opposite Residency Hotel, runs a bus to **Gulbarga**, 0730, 5 hrs.

Car
Ashok Travels, ground floor, Begumpet, T040-2340 3596, www.attindiatourism.com.

Rickshaw and taxis
Auto-rickshaws charge Rs 20 for the first 1.6 km, Rs 11 per km thereafter; they'll use meter after mild insistence. Cycle rickshaws are cheaper. Local taxis charge Rs 40 for the first 2 km, then Rs 21 per km; reliable radio taxi companies include **Easy Cabs**, T040-4343 4343, and **Meru Cabs**, T040-4422 4422.

Train
Trains arrive and depart at 3 main stations: **Hyderabad** Deccan, also known as Nampally; **Secunderabad**; and Kacheguda. Enquiries: T139. Reservations: T134. Buses 20V and 49 link Nampally and Secunderabad stations.

Trains to: **Aurangabad 4-7 daily**, 9½ hrs. **Bengaluru** (Bangalore) 5 daily, 12 hrs. **Chennai** 3-4 daily, 14 hrs. **Delhi** 4-5 daily, 22-26 hrs, via Nagpur (9 hrs) and Bhopal (16 hrs). **Guntakal** (for Hospet and Hampi), 7-15 daily, 6-8 hrs. **Kolkata** (Howrah): 2 daily, **26-30 hrs. Mumbai** (CST), 5 daily, 15-18 hrs. **Tirupati**: 7 daily, 13-15 hrs. **Vijayawada**, over 20 daily, 6 hrs. **Visakhapatnam**, 7 daily, 12-13 hrs.

Golconda *Colour map 1, B6.*

legendary diamond vaults guarded by an imposing medieval fortress

Golconda, one of the most accessible of great medieval fortresses in India, was the capital of the Qutb Shahi kings who ruled over the area from 1507 to 1687. Nizam-ul-Mulk repossessed it in 1724 and restored it to its former glory for a time. Modern day restorations are being carried out by the Archaeological Survey of India.

★ The fort *The numbers in brackets below refer to the map, below.*

T040-2351 2401, 0900-1700, Rs 100, Indians Rs 10. Official guides wait at the entrance (Rs 250), unofficial ones greet you under the Fateh Darwaza. Allow 2-3 hrs. There is an excellent 1-hr son et lumière show in English (Mar-Oct 1900, Nov-Feb 1830; Rs 130/100/70/50); tickets go on sale at Golconda 1 hr before the start. Some people buy their 'sound and light' ticket as soon as the office opens and take a quick tour (45 mins) of the fort before sunset in time for the show.

Originally built of mud in the 12th century by the Hindu Kakatiyas, the fort was reinforced by masonry by the Bahmanis who occupied it from 1363. The massive fort, built on a granite hill, was surrounded by three walls. One encircled the town, another the hill on which the citadel stood and the last joined huge boulders on the high ridge with parts of masonry wall. The citadel's 5-km double wall had 87 bastions with cannons and eight huge gates with outer and inner doors and

Golconda fort

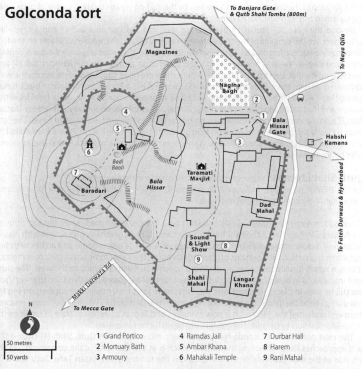

1 Grand Portico	4 Ramdas Jail	7 Durbar Hall
2 Mortuary Bath	5 Ambar Khana	8 Harem
3 Armoury	6 Mahakali Temple	9 Rani Mahal

Essential Golconda

Finding your feet

Golconda is 11 km west of Hyderabad. Buses 119 or 142M from Nampally or 66G from Char Minar take one hour to the fort. Buses 123 and 142S go direct from Char Minar to the Qutb Shahi Tombs, Rs 10. Autos take 30 minutes, Rs 150. Cycling in the early morning is a good option as it's an easy journey.

Tip...

Both the fort and the tombs are popular sites and get crowded and very noisy after 1000; if you arrive early it's worth asking to be allowed in.

guardrooms between. Some of the guns of the Qutb Shahis are still there with fortifications at various levels on the way up.

Another of India's supposed underground tunnels is believed by some to run for about 8 km from a corner of the summit to Gosha Mahal. The fort had an ingenious system of laminated clay pipes and huge Persian Wheels to carry water to cool the palace chambers up to the height of 61 m where there were hanging gardens. The famous diamond vault once held the *Koh-i-noor* and *Hope* diamonds. The fort fell to Emperor Aurangzeb after two attempts, an eight-month siege and the help of a Qutb general-turned-traitor. English traveller Walter Hamilton described it as being almost deserted in 1820: "the dungeons being used by the Nizam of Hyderabad as a prison for his worst enemies, among whom were several of his sons and two of his wives".

The Fateh Darwaza or Victory Gate at the **Grand Portico (1)** entrance, made of teak, with a Hindu deity engraved, is studded with iron spikes as a defence against war elephants. The superb acoustics enabled a drum beat, bugle call or even a clap under the canopy of this gate to be heard by someone at the very top of the palace; it is put to the test by the visiting crowds today. A couple of glass cases display a map and some excavated finds.

Beyond the gate the **Mortuary Bath (2)** on the right has beautiful arches and a crypt-like ceiling; you see the remains of the three-storey **armoury (3)** and the women's palaces on the left. About halfway up is a large water tank or well and to the north is what was once the most densely populated part of the city. Nearby, the domed storehouse turned into the **Ramdas Jail (4)** and has steps inside that lead up to a platform where there are relief sculptures of deities on the wall, dominated by Hanuman. The **Ambar Khana (5)** (granary) has a Persian inscription on black basalt stating that it was built between 1626 and 1672. The steps turn around an enormous boulder with a bastion and lead to the top passing the Hindu **Mahakali Temple (6)** on the way. The breezy **Durbar Hall (7)** is on the summit. It is well worth climbing the stairs to the roof here for good views. The path down is clearly signposted to take you on a circular route through the **harem (8)** and **Rani Mahal (9)**, with its royal baths, back to the main gate. A welcome chilled drink and snack is available at several cafés opposite the gate.

Qutb Shahi tombs *The numbers in brackets below refer to the plan, opposite.*
Sat-Thu 0930-1630, Rs 100, Indians Rs 10, camera Rs 20, Allow 2 hrs, or half a day for a leisurely exploration. Inexpensive guidebook available.

About 800 m north-northwest of Golconda fort on a low plateau (a road leaves the fort through the Banjara Gate) are the Qutb Shahi Tombs. Each tomb of black granite or greenstone with plaster decoration is built on a square or octagonal base with a large onion dome and arches with fine sculptures, inscriptions and remains of glazed decoration. The larger tombs have their own mosque attached which usually comprises an eastward opening hall with a *mihrab* to the west. The sides have inscriptions in beautiful Naksh script, and remnants of the glazed tiles that used to cover them can still be seen in places. The tombs of the rulers were built under their own supervision but fell into disrepair and the gardens ran wild until the end of the 19th century when Sir Salar Jang restored them and replanted the gardens. It is now managed and kept in an excellent state of repair by the Archaeological Survey of India. The gardens are being further improved.

The road north from Golconda fort passes the tomb of **Abdullah Qutb Shah (1)** (1626-1672) as it approaches the entrance to the tombs, which is at the east gate of the compound. On the left side of the road just outside the compound is the tomb of **Abul Hasan Tana Qutb Shahi (2** (ruled 1672-1687). He was the last of the kings to be buried here as the final king in the line of the Qutb Shahi Dynasty, Abul Hasan, died in the fort at Daulatabad in 1704. To the right of the entrance are the tomb of Princess **Hayat Baksh Begum (3)** (died 1677), the daughter of Ibrahim Qutb Shah, and a smaller mosque, while about 100 m directly ahead is the granite tomb of **Muhammad Qutb Shah (4)** (ruled 1612-1626). Tucked away due north of this tomb is that of **Pemamati (5)**, one of the mistresses of Muhammad Qutb Shah, dating from 1663. The path turns south and west around the tomb of Muhammad Qutb Shah. About 100 m to the south is a tank which is still open. The **Badshahi Hammam (11)**, the oldest structure in the compound, is the bath where the body of the king was washed before burial. You can still see the channels for the water and the special platforms for washing the body. The Badshahi kings were Shi'a Muslims, and the 12 small baths in the Hammam stand symbolically for the two *imams* revered by the Shi'a community. Next door, a small **Archaeological Museum** ⓘ *1000-1300, 1400-1630,* has interesting items in glass cases.

To the south of the hammam is a series of major tombs. The most striking lies due south, the 54-m-high mausoleum of **Muhammad Quli Qutb Shah (6)** (ruled 1581-1612), the poet king founder of Baghnagar (Hyderabad). It is appropriate that the man responsible for creating a number of beautiful buildings in Hyderabad should be commemorated by such a remarkable tomb. The underground excavations here have been turned into a Summer House. You can walk right through the tomb and on to the tomb of the fourth king of the dynasty, **Ibrahim Qutb Shah (7)** (ruled 1550-1580), another 100 m to the south. At the west edge of the compound is the octagonal tomb of **Kulsum Begum (8)** (died 1608), granddaughter of Mohammad Quli Qutb Shah. To its east is the tomb of **Jamshid Quli Qutb Shah (9)** (ruled 1543-1550), who was responsible for the murder of his 90-year-old father and founder of the dynasty, **Sultan Quli Qutb Shah (10)** (ruled 1518-1543). This has the appearance of a two-storey building though it is in fact a single-storey structure with no inscription. There are some other small tombs here.

Qutb Shahi tombs

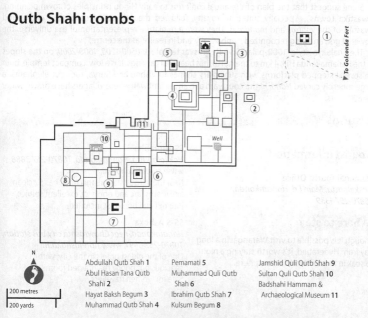

Abdullah Qutb Shah **1**
Abul Hasan Tana Qutb Shahi **2**
Hayat Baksh Begum **3**
Muhammad Qutb Shah **4**

Pemamati **5**
Muhammad Quli Qutb Shah **6**
Ibrahim Qutb Shah **7**
Kulsum Begum **8**

Jamshid Quli Qutb Shah **9**
Sultan Quli Qutb Shah **10**
Badshahi Hammam & Archaeological Museum **11**

The capital of the Kakatiya Empire in the 12th and 13th centuries, the name of Warangal (population 528,600) is derived from the Orugallu (one stone) Hill, a massive boulder with ancient religious significance that stands where the modern town is situated. Warangal is 156 km northeast of Hyderabad and most express trains between Chennai and Delhi stop here.

Sights

At the centre of the '**fort**' ① *0600-1800, US$2*, is a circular area about 1.2 km in diameter. Most of it is now farmland with houses along the road. Near the centre are the ruins of the original Siva temple. Remains include the large beautifully carved stone entrance gateways, replicas of which adorn many of the government offices, hotels and even private residences in the city. The gateways lead to the almost square enclosure, aligned along the cardinal directions and beyond are overturned slabs, smashed columns, brackets and ceiling panels.

Nearby Siva temples are still in use, and to the west is the **Khush Mahal**, a massive royal hall used by the Muslim Shitab Khan in the early 16th century for state functions. It may well have been built on the site of earlier palaces, near its geometric centre, while some structures in the central area may have been granaries.

From the centre, four routes radiate along the cardinal directions, passing through gateways in the three successive rings of fortification. The innermost ring is made of massive granite blocks, and is up to 6 m high with bastions regularly spaced along the wall. The middle wall is of unfaced packed earth, now eroded, while the outermost circuit, up to 5 m high, is also of earth. The four main roads pass through massive gateways in the inner wall, and there are also incomplete gateways in the second ring of fortifications. Some of the original roads that crossed the city have disappeared.

Some suggest that the plan of Warangal conforms to early Hindu principles of town planning. '**Swastika towns**', especially suited to royalty, followed the pattern of concentric circles and swastika of the *yantras* and *mandalas*. They were a miniature representation of the universe, the power of god and king recognized symbolically, and in reality, at the centre.

The Chalukya-style '1000-pillar' **Siva Rudresvar temple** ① *0500-1200, 1600-2000*, on the slopes of the Hanamakonda Hill, 4 km to the north, has beautiful carvings. It is a low, compact temple, built on several stepped platforms with subsidiary shrines to Vishnu and Surya, rock-cut elephants, a large superbly carved *Nandi* in the courtyard and an ancient well where villagers have drawn water for 800 years.

Listings Warangal

Tourist information

Warangal Tourist Office
Nakkalgutta, Main Rd, Hanamkonda,
T0870-257 1339.

Where to stay

Though it is possible to visit Warangal in a long day from Hyderabad, it's worth staying a night to soak in the old-world atmosphere.

$$ Suprabha
Nakkalgutta, Hanamkonda, T0870-257 3888,
www.suprabhahotel.in.
Near the railway station, this hotel has 52 clean airy rooms (a/c and non a/c), excellent service, internet and breakfast included.

$$-$ Ashoka
Hanamkonda, near Chowrashta city bus station,
T0870-257 8491, www.hotelashoka.in.
One of the oldest hotels in the city, with spacious but poorly maintained rooms. Safe for women travellers.

BACKGROUND

Warangal

The city was probably laid out during the reigns of King Ganapatideva (1199-1262) and his daughter Rudrammadevi (until 1294). Warangal was captured by armies from Delhi in 1323, enforcing the payment of tribute. Control of Warangal fluctuated between Hindus and Muslims but between the 14th and 15th centuries it remained in Bahmani hands. Thereafter it repeatedly changed hands, and some argue that although the military fortifications were repeatedly strengthened, the religious buildings were largely destroyed, including the great Siva temple in the middle of the city. Marco Polo was highly impressed by Warangal's riches, and it is still famous for the remains of its temples, its lakes and wildlife, and for its three circuits of fortifications. The modern town itself, however, is not very interesting.

Restaurants

There are lots of 'meals' places around the bus stand.

$ Hotel Surya
Station Rd.
Good-quality food (especially *dum biryani*), if a bit pricey.

Transport

Bus Frequent buses to **Hyderabad** (3½ hrs) and **Vijayawada** (7 hrs).

Train Many Express trains stop here, bound for **Chennai**, **Hyderabad**, **Delhi**, **Mumbai** and **Vijayawada**, among others.

Around Warangal *Colour map 2, B1.*

bird-rich lakes and finely carved temples

Pakhal, Ethurnagaram and Lakhnavaram
Warangal Bus Station to Narsampet. Regular bus service from Narsampet to Pakhal Lake or take a taxi.

The great artificial lakes 40 km northeast of Warangal – from the south, Pakhal, Lakhnavaram, Ramappa and Ghanpur – were created as part of the Kakatiya rulers' water management and irrigation schemes in the 12th and 13th centuries and are still in use. The lakes are fringed with emerging marsh vegetation and surrounded by extensive grasslands, tropical deciduous forests and evergreens. The park was set up in 1952 and has problems of the grazing of domestic livestock and illegal burning.

This is the richest area for wildlife in the state, with tiger, panther, hyena, wild dogs, wild boars, gaur, foxes, spotted deer, jackals, sloth bears and pythons. There are also otters and alligators and a variety of waterbirds and fish in the lakes. Pakhal Lake is especially important as an undisturbed site well within the sanctuary; Laknavaram Lake is 20 km to the north. They are superb for birdwatching (numerous migratory birds in winter) and occasional crocodile spottings. Tigers and panthers live deep in the forest but are rarely seen. Forest rangers might show you plaster casts of tiger pug marks.

Palampet *Colour map 2, B2.*
Palampet lies close to the Ramappa Lake. The **Ramappa Temple**, dedicated to Siva as Rudreswara, was built in 1234 and is one of the finest medieval Deccan temples. The black basalt sculpture is excellent (even richer than that at the 1000-pillar temple) with famous Mandakini figures of female dancers which appear on brackets at the four entrances. The base of the temple has the typical bands of sculpture, the lowest of elephants, the second, a lotus scroll, the third which is the most interesting depicting figures opening a window on the life of the times and finally another floral scroll. There are more fine sculptures inside, some displaying a subtle sense of humour in common with some of the figures outside, and paintings of scenes from the epics on the ceiling. Note that no bottled water is available.

Some 150 km southeast of Hyderabad is one of India's richest Buddhist sites, now almost entirely under the lake created by the Nagarjunasagar Dam, completed in 1960. The remains of a highly cultured Buddhist civilization had remained almost undisturbed for 1600 years until their discovery by AR Saraswati in March 1926. The reconstructed buildings are on a comparatively small scale, in a peaceful setting on top of the hilltop fort, now an island planted with low trees.

Sights

The Ikshvaku's capital was a planned city on the right bank of the Krishna – **Vijayapuri** (city of victory). The citadel had rampart walls on three sides with the river on the fourth. The buildings inside including houses, barracks, baths and wells were probably destroyed by a great fire. The nine **temples** show the earliest developments of Brahmanical temple architecture in South India. The Vishnu temple (AD 278) had two beautifully carved pillars which were recovered from its site. Five temples were dedicated to Siva or Karttikeya. The river bank was dotted with Brahmanical shrines.

Nagarjunakonda excavations also revealed some of India's finest early sculptures and memorial pillars. Over 20 pillars were raised in the memory not just of rulers and nobles but also of artisans and religious leaders. The sculptures represent the final phase of artistic development begun at Amaravati in the second century BC.

The **hill fort** (early 14th-century) has remnants of the Vijayanagar culture though the present layout of the fort probably dates from as recently as 1565. The main entrance was from the northeast, near where the ferry now lands on the island. In places the walls are still over 6 m high, with regular bastions and six gateways. There are two temples in the east, where the museum now stands.

The **museum** ① *Sat-Thu 0900-1600*, has a collection of coins and ornaments, but most importantly sculptures (including a 3-m-high standing Buddha). There are also prehistoric and protohistoric remains and several panels and friezes depicting Buddhist scenes.

Srisailam Wildlife Sanctuary *Colour map 2, C1.*

Information from AP Dept of Forests (see Tourist information, opposite). Cars are not permitted in the reserve 2100-0600. Temperature: 12-42°C. Rainfall: 1500 mm. Best time to visit is Oct-Mar.

The largest of the state's wildlife sanctuaries is at Srisailam (altitude 200-900 m), a popular pilgrimage town on the banks of the Krishna near Nagarjunasagar. The park is India's largest tiger reserve, covering 3560 sq km of the Nallamalai Hills in an area deeply incised by gorges, with deciduous and bamboo forest and semi-desert scrubland. Besides tigers, there are leopards, Indian pangolins, panthers, wild dogs, civets, hyenas, jackals, wolves, giant squirrels, crocodiles, lizards, pythons, vipers, kraits and over 150 species of bird. There is a nature trail signposted 1 km short of Srisailam, or you can walk the access road and explore from there; a guide is available.

Unfortunately the sanctuary is frequently disturbed by Naxalite activity and can be very difficult to get permission to visit. Check the latest position with the Forest Officer.

Srisailam also attracts Shaivite pilgrims, who come for the 14th century **Mallikarjuna Temple**, containing one of India's 12 *jyotirlingas*. Some 300 m long, the outer face has often been attacked and damaged, but is richly decorated with carved scenes from the Hindu epics and a portrait of Krishna Deva Raya, the Vijayanagar Emperor who visited the site in 1514. Non-

Essential Nagarjunakonda

Finding your feet

Buses from Hyderabad arrive at Vijayapuri, which is 7 km from the boat jetty for Nagarjunakonda. Boats leave for the island roughly every hour from 0930; prepare for a chaotic scrum to get on board. The last ferry leaves the island at 1600.

Nagarjunakonda

Rising from the middle of the artificial lake is the Nagarjuna Hill which was once nearly 200 m above the floor of the secluded valley in the northern ranges of the Nallamalais (black hills) which surround the lake on three sides. On the fourth side was the great river Krishna, superimposed on the hills as it flows towards the Bay of Bengal.

Early archaeological work showed the remnants of Buddhist monasteries, many limestone sculptures and other remains. The Archaeological Survey carried out a full excavation of the sites before they were covered by the rising waters of the lake. More than 100 distinct sites ranging from the prehistoric early Stone Age period to the late medieval were discovered. Some of the most important remains have been moved and reconstructed on the hilltop fort. These include nine monuments, rebuilt in their original form, and 14 large replicas of the ruins.

The Ikshvakus made Nagarjunakonda the centre of extraordinary artistic activity from the third century AD. In the mid-fourth century AD the Pallavas pushed north from Tamil Nadu and eclipsed the Ikshvaku Kingdom, reducing Nagarjunakonda to a deserted village. However, during the Chalukya period a Saiva centre was built at Yellaswaram, on the other bank of the Krishna. In the 15th and 16th centuries the hill became a fortress in the contest for supremacy between the Vijayanagar, Bahmani and Gajapati kings. After the fall of the Vijayanagar Empire both the hill and the valley below lost all importance.

Hindus are allowed into the inner sanctuary to witness the daily *puja*. Arrive early to avoid queuing in the middle of the day; the first prayers are at 0545. The **Mahasivaratri festival** draws large crowds. The ancient **Mahakali Temple** on a hill in the Nallamalai forest contains a rare *lingam* attracting large crowds of pilgrims, especially during **Sivaratri**.

Listings Nagarjunakonda

Tourist information

Nagarjunakonda

AP State Tourist Office
Project House, Hill Colony, T08680-277364/277361.
A guide is available through this office; others can be arranged from the APTDC in Hyderabad.

Where to stay

Nagarjunakonda

$$-$ Vijay Vihar (APTDC)
Nagarjuna Sagar, T08680-277362, www.telanganatourism.gov.in.
The most luxurious and picturesque accommodation, with lake-facing rooms and suites (all a/c), bar and restaurant.

$ Nagarjuna Resort
Near the jetty, T08642-242471.
Clean comfortable rooms (a/c and non a/c) and garden, but no views.

Srisailam Wildlife Sanctuary
At the time of writing, the Forest Rest Houses in Srisailam Sanctuary were not accepting bookings. Most accommodation in town (**$$-$**) is managed by the **Temple Management Committee** (T08524-288883, www.srisailamtemple.com).

$ Haritha Hotel (APTDC)
1 km south of Mallikarjuna Temple, T08524-200311, www.aptdc.gov.in/accommodations.html.
Clean a/c and non a/c rooms, garden, veg restaurant.

What to do

Nagarjunakonda
Tour operators
Telangana Tourism. Runs day tours from Hyderabad (Sat and Sun only, 0730-2200, Rs 550). It's a long and tiring day with 4 hrs on a coach each way, but convenient and cheap. From the lakeside village of Nagarjunasagar, boats ferry visitors to the temples and museum on the island (at 0800, 1200, 1500, trip takes 1 hr). If you take

the 2nd boat you still have time to visit the sights and return on the next boat. You can leave your luggage for a few hours at this pier provided someone is on duty.

Transport

Nagarjunakonda
Boat Enquiries T08642-243457. Some ferries are reserved for APTDC tours, which can be organized locally or from Hyderabad. See also What to do and Essential Nagarjunakonda, both above.

Bus Buses from Hyderabad to Macherla stop at **Nagarjuna Sagar** (4 hrs), and buses also go to **Vijayawada**. It's easier, if rushed, to visit on an APTDC day tour (see What to do, above).

Srisailam Wildlife Sanctuary
Srisailam can be reached from Kurnool, 170 km away on the Hyderabad–Bengaluru highway and railway line. From Hyderabad it's a 200-km drive across the wide open Telangana Plateau; buses take about 6 hrs. The nearest train station is Macherla (13 km).

Krishna-Godavari
Delta

The rice-growing delta of the Krishna and Godavari rivers is one of
Andhra Pradesh's most prosperous and densely populated regions,
and the core region of Andhra culture. The flat coastal plains are
fringed with palmyra palms and occasional coconut palms, rice and
tobacco. Inland, barely 40% of the land is cultivated. About 120 km to
the west of the road south to Chennai run the Vellikonda Ranges, only
visible in very clear weather. To the north the ranges of the Eastern
Ghats can often be clearly seen.

Vijayawada and around *Colour map 2, C2.*
inland port surrounded by lush rice-growing country with beaches and backwaters

At the head of the Krishna delta, 70 km from the sea, the city of Vijayawada (population
1,048,000) has been in existence for over 2000 years, and derives its name from the
goddess Kanakdurga or Vijaya, the presiding deity of the city; there is an important
temple to her on a hill beside the river.

The city is surrounded by bare granite hills, which radiate heat during the searing summer:
temperatures of over 45°C are not uncommon in April and May, though in winter they drop to a
positively fresh 20°C.

The Qutb Shahi rulers made Vijayawada an important inland port. It is still a major commercial
town and has capitalized on its position as the link between the interior and the main north–south
route between Chennai and Kolkata. It is also the operational centre of the Krishna delta canal
scheme, one of the earliest major irrigation developments in South India (completed in 1855), which
irrigates nearly one million hectares of land, banishing famine from the delta and converting it into
one of the richest granaries in the country. The **Prakasam Barrage**, over 1 km long, carries the road
and railway lines across the water.

There are several sites with caves and temples with inscriptions from the first century AD.
The **Kanakdurga Temple**, on a hill to the east of town, is the most atmospheric of the temples.
Mogalarajapuram Temple has an Ardhanarisvara statue which is thought to be the earliest in
South India. There are two 1000-year-old Jain temples and the **Hazratbal Mosque**, which has a relic
of the Prophet Mohammed. **Victoria Jubilee Museum** ① *MG Rd, Sat-Thu 1030-1700, free, camera
Rs 5*, has sculpture and paintings.

Amaravati

Located 30 km west of Vijaywada, Amaravati was the capital of the medieval Reddi kings of Andhra,
but some 1500 years before they wielded power Amaravati was a great Mahayana Buddhist centre
(see page 1339). Initially built in the third and second centuries BC, the shrine was dedicated to the
Hinayana sect, but under Nagarjuna was changed into a Mahayana sanctuary where the Buddha
was revered as Amareswara.

Very little remains *in situ*, most of the magnificent sculpted friezes, medallions and railings
having been removed to museums in Chennai, Kolkata and London's British Museum. The onsite
Archaeological Museum ① *Sat-Thu 0900-1700, free, buses via Guntur or by ferry from Krishneveni*

Hotel, contains some exquisitely carved sculptures of the Bodhi Tree alongside a collection of broken panels, *chakras* and caskets holding relics.

Guntur *Colour map 6, C2.*

From Vijayawada the NH5 southwest crosses the barrage (giving magnificent views over the Krishna at sunset) to Guntur, a major town dealing in rice, cotton and tobacco where the ancient charnockite rocks of the peninsula meet the alluvium of the coastal plain. In the 18th century it was capital of the region Northern Circars and was under Muslim rule from 1766 under the Nizam of Hyderabad. The Archaeological Museum in Amaravati exhibits local finds including fourth-century Buddhist stone sculptures. Some 40 km to the south, the unspoiled golden sands of **Suryalanka Beach** see very little tourist traffic; there is a newly built **AP Tourism** resort right on the beach.

Machilipatnam and around

The once-flourishing sea port of Machilipatnam ('fish town'), 60 km southeast of Vijayawada, derived its name from the old city gateways, one of which still stands, decorated with painted fish eyes. A one-time port of the kingdom of Golconda, it was one of the earliest British settlements in India, existent as early as 1611. It is also well known for its Kalamkari painting (see page 1079) widely prevalent in the neighbouring village of Pedana, the art having been fostered by the Qutub Shahis. The beach at Manginapudi, 10 km from Machilipatnam, has black clay sand. This area is battered by frequent cyclones; one in 1864 is said to have taken 30,000 lives.

Rajahmundry and the Konaseema Backwaters *Colour map 2, C3.*

Set on the banks of the Godavari, Rajahmundry was the scene of a bitter 300-year tug-of-war between the Chalukya, Vengi and Orissan kingdoms and the Deccan Muslims, until the French annexed the city in 1753. It is remembered for the poet Nannayya who wrote the first Telugu classic *Andhra Mahabharathamu*, and is also noted for its carpets and sandalwood products. Every 12 years the **Pushkaram** celebration (next in 2015) draws thousands of pilgrims to the river banks.

Rajahmundry makes a convenient base from which to visit both the Eastern Ghats and the coastal districts. Some 80 km northwest of the town, the Godavari cuts through a gorge in the Papi hills, creating a succession of stunningly beautiful lakes, reminiscent of Scottish lochs, where you can take boat trips. Another appealing side trip is to the **Konaseema Delta**, 70 km south of Rajahmundry, a verdant cocktail of coconut groves, mango orchards and paddy fields encircled by the waters of the Godavari and the Bay of Bengal.

AP Tourism operates **houseboat trips** on the Godavari, and a 24-hour trip from Dindi (departs 1000 from the Coconut County resort, bookings T08862-227993, T(0)9848-780524), sailing up past quaint little villages and islands, offers the kind of peace and solitude that have long been missing from the Kerala backwaters. Houseboats have two well-furnished air-conditioned bedrooms; meals and drinks are served on board.

Listings Vijayawada and around

Tourist information

Vijayawada

AP Tourist Office
MG Rd, T0866-257 1393. Open 0600-2000.
Also has counters at the bus stand on Machilipatnam Rd, and the train station.

Where to stay

Vijayawada

There are some **$** hotels on MG Rd near the bus stand and around the railway station.

$$$ Fortune Murali Park
MG Rd, Labbipet, T0866-398 8008,
www.fortunehotels.in.
The smartest rooms in town by a long chalk, plus a host of extra services including babysitting.

$$ Ilapuram
Besant Rd, T0866-257 1282, www.ilapuram.com.
81 large clean rooms, some a/c, restaurants.

$$-$ Berm Park (AP Tourism)
On the banks of Krishna river T0866-241 8057.
30 clean rooms (most a/c), restaurant, tourist office, car hire and boat trips to nearby Bhavani Island.

$ Kandhari International
MG Rd, Labbipet, T0866-249 7797.
Some a/c in the 73 rooms, also restaurants with a/c.

$ Mamata
Eluru Rd, 1 km from centre, T0866-257 1251.
Standard Indian cheapie, with reasonably well-kept rooms (most a/c with bath), good restaurants and friendly staff.

$ Railway Retiring Rooms
Large and well-maintained rooms, an excellent budget option.

$ Santhi
Near Apsara Theatre Governorpet,
T0866-257 7351.
Clean rooms with bath (hot water), and a good vegetarian restaurant.

Guntur

$$-$ Haritha Beach Resort
Suryalanka, Bapatla Mandal, Guntur,
T08643-224616.
13 beach-facing a/c cottages, garden and a multi-cuisine restaurant.

$ Annapurna Lodge
Opposite APSRTC Bus Stand, T0866-222 2979.
A/c and non-a/c rooms, quality meals, and helpful and obliging staff.

$ K & M International
Collectorate Rd, Nagarampalem, T0863-222 2221, www.kandminternationalhotel.com.
The best place in town and often frequented by Telugu cinestars, several of whom hail from Guntur. 42 good rooms, some a/c, and a popular restaurant.

Rajahmundry

$$$-$$ Anand Regency
26-3-7, Jampet, T0883-246 1201,
www.hotelanandregency.com.
Business hotel but with great ambience, good service, 3 restaurants, and arranges sightseeing and boating trips.

$$$-$$ River Bay Hotel
Near Gowthami Ghat, T0883-244 7000,
www.riverbay.co.in.
Decent rooms with excellent river views.
Breakfast included.

$$ Coconut Country Resort
Dindi (the starting point of houseboat cruises),
T0991-287 7055.
32 well-furnished a/c rooms overlooking the river, with a swimming pool and a garden.

Restaurants

Vijayawada
The restaurants in the **Kandhari** and **Mamata** hotel are recommended.

$ Aromas
DV Manor Hotel, MG Rd.
Slick hotel restaurant offering good Punjabi curries.

$ Greenlands
Bhavani Gardens, Labbipet.
Food served in 7 huts on the garden lawns.

Shopping

Vijayawada
Some shops close 1300-1600. Local Kondapalli toys and Machilipatnam Kalamkari paintings are popular.

The emporia are in MG Rd, Eluru Rd, and Governorpet. Recommended are: **Apco** (Besant Rd); **Ashok** (opposite Maris Stella College, T0866-247 6966); **Handicrafts Shop** (Krishnaveni Motel); **Lepakshi** (Gandhi Nagar).

What to do

Vijayawada
KL Rao Vihara Kendram, *Bhavani Island on Prakasham Barrage Lake*. Offers rowing, canoeing, water scooters and pedal boats.

Rajahmundry
Maruthi Tours and Travels, *T0883-242 4577, www.maruthitourism.co.in.* Booking agent for Konaseema backwater cruises, and also conducts daily boat trips to Papi Hills from Rajahmundry, 0730-2100.

Transport

Vijayawada

Bus Good local network in city but buses get very crowded. Long-distance buses to destinations in AP and neighbouring states including **Chennai** (9 hrs) operate from the **New Bus Stand** on MG Rd near the river; enquiries T0866-252 1982.

Car hire From **AP Tourist Office**, see page 1068.

Ferry To **Bhavani Islands**, 0930-1730. Also services between Krishnaveni Hotel and **Amaravati**. Daily 0800. Rs 50 return. Book at hotel or at bus station.

Rickshaw and taxi Very few metered yellow-top taxis. *Tongas*, auto- and cycle-rickshaws are available.

Train Vijayawada is an important junction, with trains to **Chennai** (MC): *Pinakini Exp 12711*, 0600, 7 hrs; *Coromandel Exp 12841* (AC/II), 1045, 6¾ hrs. **Delhi** (HN): *GT Exp 12615*, 0205, 30 hrs; *Link Daksin Exp 12861*, 2130, 31 hrs. **Hyderabad**: *Godavari Exp 12727*, 2355, 7 hrs. **Hospet**: *Amaravati Exp 18047*, 1855, 13 hrs. **Kolkata** (H): *Coromandel Exp 12842* (AC/II), 1525, 22 hrs, via Bhubaneswar, 11½ hrs. **Secunderabad**: *Satavahana Exp 12713*, 0610, 5½ hrs; *Krishna Exp 17405*, 1330, 7 hrs.

Guntur

Bus The APSRTC Bus Stand is well organized and clean. Buses every 30 mins to **Vijayawada** (0600-2300) and **Bapatla** (0600-2000), from where shared auto-rickshaws can get you to **Surylanka**.

Train **Kolkata**: *Falaknuma Exp 12704*, 2035, 21 hrs. **Chennai**: *Hyderabad Chennai Exp 17054*, 2200, 8 hrs. **Hospet**: *Amravati Exp 12604*, 2225, 12 hrs. **Secunderabad**: *Palnadu Exp 12747*, 0545, 5 hrs; *Golconda Exp 17201*, 0530, 8 hrs.

Rajahmundry

Train To **Kolkata** (H): *Coromandel Exp 12842* (AC/II),1830, 19½ hrs. **Vijayawada**: *Coromandel Exp 12841*, 0733, 2¾ hrs; *Chennai Mail 12839*, 1730, 3½ hrs; *Ratnachal Exp12717*, 1530, 3 hrs. **Visakhapatnam**: *Coromandel Exp 12842*, 1830, 3¾ hrs; *Chennai Howrah Mail 12840*, 0909, 4 hrs; *Ratnachal Exp 12718*, 0829, 3½ hrs.

Northeastern
Andhra Pradesh

From Rajahmundry the NH5 travels north over the narrowing coastal plain, the beautiful hills of the Eastern Ghats rising sharply inland. The pattern of life here contrasts sharply with that further south. Higher rainfall and a longer wet season, alongside the greater fertility of the alluvial soils, contribute to an air of prosperity; they also mean you should check weather forecasts before setting out on a journey. Village houses, with their thatched roofed cottages and white painted walls, are quite different and distinctive, as are the bullock carts.

Visakhapatnam *Colour map 2, B4.*

busy port city with good beaches nearby

Set in a bay with rocky promontories, Visakhapatnam (Vizag; population 1,730,320) commands a spectacular position between the thickly wooded Eastern Ghats and the sea. It has become one of the country's most rapidly growing cities.

Already India's fourth largest port, it has developed ship building, oil refining, fertilizer, petrochemical, sugar refinery and jute industries, as well as one of India's newest and largest steel mills. This is also the Navy's Eastern Fleet's home base. On the Dolphin's Nose, a cliff rising 174 m from the sea, is a lighthouse whose beam can be seen 64 km out to sea.

Its twin town of **Waltair** to the north used to be thought of as a health resort with fine beaches, though increasing atmospheric pollution is a problem. **Ramakrishna Beach**, along the 8 km Lawson's Bay and below the 300 m Mount Kailasa, 6 km away, is best. Don't swim at the harbour end of the beach.

Sights

Andhra University was founded in 1926 in the Uplands area of Waltair. The red stone buildings are built like a fortress and sit on a large campus. The country's major **Ship Building Yard** at Gandhigram makes all types of ocean-going vessels: passenger liners, cargo vessels as well as naval ships. The **zoo** to the northeast is large and attempts to avoid cages, keeping its animals in enclosures which are close to their natural habitat.

The **Venkateswara Temple** on the Venkateswa Konda was built in 1866 by the European Captain Blackmoor. The Muslims have a **mausoleum** of the saint Baba Ishaq Madina on the Darga Konda, while the highest Ross Hill has a **Roman Catholic Church**. A Buddhist relic was discovered at Dhanipura nearby.

Simhachalam, 16 km northwest, is noted for its 13th-century Varaha Narasimha Temple, set in the Kailasa Hills, which has some well-known hot springs.

Araku Valley

The Araku Valley, nestling amid the Anantagiri Hills 110 km inland from Vishakhapatnam, lies at the end of one of India's most scenic train rides. The four-hour journey through dense forests is liberally spiced with waterfalls, lush green paddy fields, views of distant blue hills and no less than 48 tunnels, the longest measuring 1.2 km. The valley itself is home to over 17 tribal groups, and in April plays host to the fascinating but strictly non-vegetarian **Itika Pongal**, a hunting festival. The **Tribal Museum** ① *near AP Tourism's Mayuri Resort, 000-1700, Rs 15*, has a small but worthwhile collection of artefacts and exhibits related to tribal life. If you return to Visakhapatnam by road you can stop off at the million-year-old **Borra Caves** and coffee plantations in Ananthagiri; AP Tourism runs this trip as a one- or two-day tour.

Listings Visakhapatnam *map below*

Tourist information

Visakhapatnam

AP Tourism
RTC Complex, T0891-278 8820. Open 1000-1700, closed Sun and 2nd Sat of the month. Also at the railway station (T0891-278 8821).

Where to stay

Visakhapatnam
Late night arrivals are quoted high prices by auto-rickshaws to go to the beach. Stay overnight at a simple hotel near the bus station (walk right from railway station) and move next morning.

Visakhapatnam

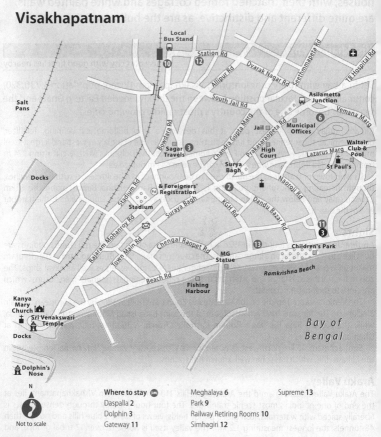

Where to stay 🛏	Meghalaya **6**	Supreme **13**
Daspalla **2**	Park **9**	
Dolphin **3**	Railway Retiring Rooms **10**	
Gateway **11**	Simhagiri **12**	

Not to scale

$$$ Dolphin
Daba Gardens, T0891-256 7000,
www.dolphinhotelsvizag.com.
Family-run hotel with 145 rooms, popular
restaurants, rooftop has good views, live band,
health club, exchange and pool. Excellent service.
Highly recommended but reserve ahead.

$$$ Gateway Hotel
Beach Rd (2 km from centre), T0891-662 3670,
www.thegatewayhotels.com.
93 narrow sea-facing rooms, restaurant (pricey
but generous), best in town, access to an
unremarkable public beach across road.

$$$ Green Park
12-1-17 Waltair Main Rd, T0891-661 5151,
www.hotelgreenpark.com.
Formerly called **Apsara**, this hotel has central a/c,
130 rooms, restaurants, bar, exchange, and very
helpful and friendly staff.

$$$ Park
Beach Rd, T0891-275 4488,
www.theparkhotels.com.
64 rooms, pricey suites, spa with gym, clean
pool, well-kept gardens, slick management,
best for direct beach access (beware of rocks
when swimming), popular with German and
Czech expats.

$$ Rushi Konda Beach Resort (AP Tourism)
*Bhimili Beach Rd, Rushikonda Beach (15 km
north), T0891-278 8826, www.aptdc.gov.in/
haritha_vizag.html.*
Great location, with a superb sea view but poorly
maintained. Ask for rooms in the new block.

$$ Supreme
Beach Rd near Coastal Battery, T0891-278 2472,
www.hotelsupremevizag.com.
54 sea-view rooms (a/c and non a/c) with running
hot and cold water, TV and a multi-cuisine
restaurant. In a great location, and has friendly
staff. Good value.

$ Daspalla
Surya Bagh, T0891-256 4825.
Set back from THE road, this hotel has 102 rooms,
suites (**$$**), central a/c, 2 good restaurants
(continental and *thalis*), exchange and a bar.
No late-night check-in.

$ Meghalaya
*Asilametta Junction (a 5-min walk from the bus,
a short rickshaw ride from station), T0891-275
5141, www.hotelmeghalaya.com.*
Popular with Indian tourists, good value, dull
vegetarian restaurant (non-veg available from
room service), pleasant roof garden, and friendly
and helpful staff.

$ Railway Retiring Rooms
Decent rooms (a/c and non a/c), men's dorm.

$ Simhagiri
*Main Rd 500 m from railway station,
T0891-250 5795.*
A budget traveller favourite, with 35 clean,
spacious rooms (a/c and non a/c).

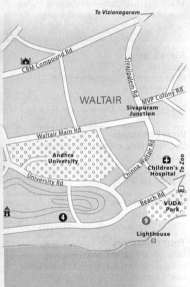

Restaurants 🌔
Infinity **3**
Jaya G Spuds **4**

Northeastern Andhra Pradesh

The area was brought under Muslim rule by the Golconda kings of the Bahmani Dynasty in 1575 and ceded to the French in 1753. In 1765 the Mughal emperor granted the whole area to the East India Company, its first major territorial acquisition in India.

The region is also the most urbanized part of Andhra Pradesh, with a dozen towns of more than 100,000 people. Most are commercial and administrative centres with neither the functions nor the appearance of industrial cities, but they serve as important regional centres for trade, especially in agricultural commodities, and they are the homes of some of Andhra's wealthiest and most powerful families.

Although the building of dams on both the Krishna and the Godavari rivers has eliminated the catastrophic flooding common until the mid-19th century, the totally flat delta, lying virtually at sea level, is still prone to cyclones; in 1864 one claimed over 34,000 lives. The area was completely engulfed by a tidal wave in 1883 when the volcano of Mount Krakatoa blew up 5000 km away, and further catastrophic cyclones in 1977 and 1996, not to mention the 2004 tsunami, caused massive damage and loss of life. You may notice the increasing number of small concrete buildings on raised platforms along the roadside designed to provide temporary shelter to villagers during cyclones.

Araku Valley

$$-$ Mayuri and Valley Resort (AP Tourism)
Next to Tribal Museum, T08936-249201,
www.aptdc.gov.in.
133 rooms and suites, pool, barbecue area, playground, bar and restaurant. Spacious and well maintained. Prior reservation mandatory.

$ Krishnatara Comforts
Padmapuram junction, T08936-249330.
Rooms are good value for money and have great view and friendly staff. Recommended.

$ Rajadhani
Padmapuram junction, T08936-249745.
Clean rooms, and the restaurant serves great Indian and Chinese food.

Restaurants

Visakhapatnam
Most eateries serve alcohol. Apart from hotels, there are restaurants on Station Rd.

$$$ Infinity
Novotel, Beach Rd, T0891-282 2222.
Elegant rooftop place, glass walls with fabulous views of the Bay of Bengal. Come here at sunset for sizzlers and cold beer. Also in the hotel is **Zaffran**, with exquisite Northwest Frontier cuisine.

$ Jaya G Spuds
Beach Rd.
Multi-cuisine restaurant serves good succulent *kababs*.

Festivals

Visakhapatnam
Dec **Navy Mela** and **Navy Day Parade** along Beach Rd.

What to do

Visakhapatnam
Swimming
Waltair Club, www.waltairclub.com. Has a pool.

Tour operators
Various boat operators on the beach at Rushikonda offer boats to go out to sea where there's a good chance of seeing dolphins. Rs 150 per person.
AP Tourism, *RTC Complex, T0891-278 8820.*
Local sightseeing day trip, 0830-1700, Rs 460 a/c and Rs 380 non a/c. Araku Valley rail/road tour, 0600: 1 day Rs 875, 2 days Rs 2150 including accommodation.

Transport

Visakhapatnam

Air Airport is 16 km from city centre; taxi (Rs 650) or auto-rickshaw. Flights to **Hyderabad**, **Bengaluru**, **Bhubaneswar**, **Kolkata**, **Chennai** and Mumbai.

Bus Aseelmetta Junction Bus Station is well organized. APSRTC run services to main towns in the state. Enquiries, T0891-274 6400, reservations 0600-2000. **Araku Valley**, **Guntur** (0930, 1545, 2045), **Hyderabad** (638 km, 1630), **Kakinda**, **Puri** (0700), **Rajahmundry**, **Srikakulam**, **Vijayawada** (1945, 2015), **Vizianagram** (57 km, 0610-2130).

Ferry Operates 0800-1700 between the Harbour and **Yarada Hills**.

Rickshaw Auto-rickshaws are common. Minimum fare Rs 15; night fares exorbitant. Only cycle rickshaws in the centre.

Taxi At airport, train station or from hotels: 5 hrs/50 km, Rs 500; 10 hrs/100 km, Rs 1000.

Train Enquiries, T0891-250 5793. Open 0800-1700. Advance reservations, left of building (facing it). Computer bookings close 2100, Sun 1400. The counter system avoids the crush at the ticket window. City Railway Extension Counter at Turner's Chowltry for Reservations. Taxi from centre, Rs 50.

    Chennai: *Howrah-Chennai Mail 12839*, 1355, 16 hrs. **Kolkata** (H): *Coromandel Exp 12842*, 2210, 15 hrs; *Chennai Howrah Mail 12840*, 1320, 17¼ hrs; **Secunderabad**: *Godavari Exp 12727*, 1725, 13¾ hrs; *VSKP Garib Rath 12739*, 2030, 12 hrs; *East Coast Exp 18645*, 0410, 14 hrs; *Falaknuma Exp 12703*, Tue 2135, 12 hrs. **Tirupati**: *Tirumala Exp 17488*, 1350, 16 hrs. For **Araku Valley**, take *Kirandul Pass 58501*, 0650, 5 hrs. Sit on the right for the best views.

Southern
Andhra Pradesh
& Tamil borders

Southern Andhra plays host to one of India's most astounding religious spectacles, the 10th-century Sri Venkatesvara Temple of Tirupati, to which devotees flock in their tens of thousands for a second's glimpse of the bejewelled deity of Lord Vishnu.

Tirupati and Tirumala   *Colour map 3, A5.*
India's most revered temple, permanently thronged with pilgrims

The Tirumala Hills provide a picture-book setting for the Sri Venkatesvara Temple, possibly the most famous and most revered temple in all India.

So important is the shrine that Bollywood royal Amitabh Bachchan made a special journey here to seek Lord Venkateshwara's blessings prior to his son Abhishek's wedding to Aishwarya Rai. Thankfully for the wedding snaps, but no doubt to the regret of the temple's accountants, Aishwarya didn't actually take part in the ritual for which Tirupati (population 245,500) is renowned: a ceremonial head-shave, with the fallen locks being sold off to the wig-making trade (see box, page 1079).

The main town of Tirupati lies at the bottom of the hill where there are several other temples, some pilgrimage centres in their own right. The seven hills are compared to the seven-headed Serpent God Adisesha who protects the sleeping Vishnu under his hood.

Sights

In Tirupati itself the **Govindarajasvami Temple** (16th to 17th centuries), is the most widely visited. Built by the Nayakas, the successors to the Vijayanagar Empire, the temple has an impressive outer *gopuram*. Of the three *gopurams* the innermost is also the earliest, dating from the 14th to 15th centuries. The main sanctuaries are dedicated to Vishnu and Krishna. Another temple worth seeing is **Kapilesvarasvami**, in a beautiful setting with a sacred waterfall, **Kapila Theertham**.

About 1 km away are strange **rock formations** in a natural arch, resembling a hood of a serpent, a conch and a discus, thought to have been the source of the idol in the temple. There is a sacred waterfall **Akasa Ganga**, 3 km south of the temple. The **Papa Vinasanam Dam** is 5 km north.

★ Sri Venkatesvara Temple

Of all India's temples, this draws the largest number of pilgrims: even on a slow day the grounds swarm with a crowd of 10,000 people, while on festival days the number can be closer to 150,000.

Dating from the 10th century, this temple is believed to have been dedicated by the Vaishnava saint Ramanuja and is known as *Balaji* in the north and *Srinivasa Perumalai* in the south. The town of Tirupati at the base of the hill was established in approximately AD 1131 under the orders of Ramanuja that the temple functionaries who served in the sacred shrines must live nearby.

Although a road runs all the way up the hill to a bus stand at the top, most pilgrims choose to walk up the wooded slope through mango groves and sandalwood forest, chanting *"Om namo*

Essential Sri Venkatesvara Temple

Finding your feet

Flights from Chennai and Hyderabad arrive at the airport 15 km from Tirupati. The railway station in the town centre has several fast trains from Chennai and other southern towns while the main (central) bus stand is 500 m east of it, with frequent express buses to Chennai, Bengaluru (Bangalore) and Hyderabad. Private buses arrive from an incredible array of destinations all across India. To save time and hassle on arrival, try to buy a through Link ticket to Tirumala. See Transport, page 1081.

Getting around

The temple is at Tirumala, 22 km by road from central Tiupati or a tough 4-hr climb on foot. Buses for Tirumala leave from stands near the station every half hour, but there are also share taxis available. Some choose to join pilgrims for the walk uphill, starting before dawn to avoid the heat, though the path is shaded most of the way. Luggage is transported for free from the toll gate at the start of the 15-km path and may be collected from the reception office at Tirumala.

Entry information

No electronic items are allowed in the temple. There are two types of queue: for *darshan*, or viewing. Sarvadarsan is open to all, and it can take between two and five claustrophobic hours to reach the idol (Mondays and Tuesdays tend to be quieter). Those who pay for 'special' *darshan* (Rs 40 and up) enter by a separate entrance and join a shorter queue. The actual *darshan* (0600-1100) itself lasts a precious 1½ seconds, even though the 'day' at the temple may last 21 hours: from *Suprabhatham* (awakening of the deity) at 0330 to *Ekantha seva* at 2330.

The Sudarsanam token system has been introduced to minimize the waiting time for Sarvadarsanam, 'special' *darshan* and other paid *darshan/sevas*; pilgrims can enter the Vaikuntam Queue Complex at Tirumala at the time indicated on the tokens. The tokens are available free of cost at the First Choultry (opposite the Tirupati Railway Station), Second Choultry (behind the Railway Station), Alipiri Bus Stand, Vaikuntam Queue Complex, Pilgrim Amenities Centre (Near CRO) and near the Rambagicha Guest House in Tirumala. TTD has also started the E-Darshan, which makes it possible to book special *darshans* and accommodation at Tirumala in advance through www.ttdonline.com.

Venkatesaya" or "*Govinda, Govinda*" as they walk. Order is maintained by providing 'Q sheds' under which pilgrims assemble.

Theoretically the inner shrines of the Tirumala temple are open only to Hindus. However, foreigners are usually welcome. They are sometimes invited to sign a form to show they sympathize with Hindu beliefs. According to the tourist information leaflet: "The only criterion for admission is faith in God and respect for the temple's conventions and rituals".

The atmosphere inside is unlike any other temple in India. Turnstiles control the never-ending flow of pilgrims into the main **temple complex**, which is through an intricately carved *gopuram* on the east wall. There are three enclosures. The first, where there are portrait sculptures of the Vijayanagar patrons, include Krishnadeva Raya and his queen and a gold-covered pillar. The outer colonnades are in the Vijayanagar style; the gateway leading to the inner enclosure may be of Chola origin. The second enclosure has more shrines, a sacred well, and the temple kitchen, where cooks prepare the holy *prasadam* (consecrated sweet) given to pilgrims after their *darshan*; the kitchen gets through an estimated 4.5 tonnes of ghee a day, supplied direct by pipeline from the dairy.

The main temple and shrine is on the west side of the inner enclosure. The **sanctuary** (ninth to 10th centuries), known as *Ananda Nilayam*, has a domed *vimana* entirely covered with gold plate, and gold covered gates. Inside, dimly lit by oil lamps, stands the image for which people queue for hours to see: a 2-m-high statue of Vishnu (Sri Venkatesvara) carved of black stone, standing on a lotus and richly ornamented with gold and jewels. Two of his four arms carry a conch shell and a *chakra* or discus and he wears a diamond crown which is said to be the most precious single ornament in the world. The idol is flanked by *Sridevi* and *Bhudevi*, Vishnu's consorts.

There is a small **museum** ⓘ *0800-2000*, of temple art in the temple compound, with a collection of stone, metal and wooden images.

Every day is festival day with shops selling holy souvenirs remaining open 24 hours. The image of Sri Venkatesvara is widely seen across South India, in private homes, cars, taxis and in public places, and is instantly recognizable from his black face and covered eyes, shielded so that the deity's piercing gaze may not blind any who look directly at him. In the temple the deity's body is anointed with camphor, saffron and musk.

Around Tirupati

Chandragiri, 11 km southwest, became the capital of the Vijayanagaras in 1600, after their defeat at the battle of Talikota 35 years earlier. The **fort** ⓘ *1930-2015, Rs 30, children Rs 20*, was built on a 180-m-high rock. You can still see the well-preserved defences and some of the palaces and temples, including the Rani Mahal and Raja Mahal with a pretty lily pond and a small museum (closed Friday) containing Chola and Vijayanagar bronzes. A visit to the fort would be incomplete without witnessing the **sound and light show** organized everyday by the APTDC. The Palace of Sri Ranga Raya, built in 1639, witnessed the signing by Sri Ranga Raya of the original land grant entitling the East India Company to build Fort St George, the starting point of modern-day Chennai.

Srikalahasti (Kalahasti) ⓘ *state buses run the 36 km northeast from Tirupati*, is sited on the banks of the Svarnamukhi River at the foot of the Kailasa Hills, the southernmost limit of the Vellikonda Ranges. The town and temple, built in the 16th and 17th centuries, developed largely as a result of the patronage of the Vijayanagar kings and their successors, the Nayakas. The **Kalahastisvara Temple** dominates the town and, like the temple at Tirumala, is built in the Dravida style, set within high walls with a single entrance to the south, with a strong Nayaka influence typified by the columns carved into the shape of rearing animals. The temple is particularly revered for the white stone Siva *lingam* in the western shrine, believed to be worshipped by *sri* (spider), *kala* (king cobra) and *hasti* (elephant). The detached *gopuram* facing the river was built by the Vijayanagar emperor Krishnadeva Raya. The bathing ghats of the Swarnamukhi (golden) River and the temple attract a steady flow of pilgrims.

Tirupati

Where to stay 🛏
Bhimas Deluxe 2
Bhimas Paradise 9
Quality Inn Bliss 10
Mayura 1

Ramee Guestline Days 8
Vasantham Lodge 6
Vishnupriya 7

Restaurants 🍴
Dwarka 1
Laxmi Narayan Bhawan 1

ON THE ROAD

Tirupati haircuts

Sri Venkatesvara Temple, architecturally unremarkable, is probably the wealthiest in India, and the *devasthanam* (or temple trust) now sponsors a huge range of activities, from the Sri Venkatesvara University in Tirupati to hospitals, orphanages and schools. Its wealth comes largely from its pilgrims, numbering on average over 10,000 a day. All pilgrims make gifts, and the *hundi* (offering) box in front of the shrine is stuffed full with notes, gold ornaments and other offerings.

Another important source of income is the hair-cutting service. Many pilgrims come to Tirupati to seek a special favour (eg to seek a suitable wife or husband, to have a child or to recover from illness) and it is regarded as auspicious to grow the hair long and then cut it as a sacrifice. You may see many pilgrims fully shaven at the temple when appearing before the deity. Lines of barbers await the arriving pilgrims. Free numbered ticket and a razor blade can be collected from the public bath hall, which pilgrims take to the barber with the same number to claim a free haircut. The hair is collected, washed and softened before being exported to the American and Japanese markets for wig making.

In addition to its function as a pilgrim centre, the town is known for its *kalamkaris*, colourful **hand-painted textiles** used as temple decoration. You can find pieces for sale in the BP Agraharam area, 1 km west of the temple, but they may come as a disappointment if you've seen the fine examples in Hyderabad's Salar Jung Museum (see page 1049).

South Andhra Coast

Pulicat Lake, on the coast 48 km east of Srikalahasti and 50 km north of Chennai, is the second largest saltwater lagoon in India and one of the most important wetlands for migratory shorebirds on the eastern seaboard of India. The northern area near the islands of Vendadu and Irukkam has large concentrations of greater flamingos. There are also many birds of prey. About 20 km north of Suluru is the **Neelapattu Lake**, which was given protected status in 1976 to conserve a large breeding colony of spotbilled pelicans.

Some 80 km north of Pulicat Lake, the town of **Nellore** derives its name from the sweet-smelling nelli rice, grown in abundance in the area. It is also reputed to produce the best shrimp on the east coast. **Mypadu Beach**, 20 km away, offers golden sands, surf and, outside the weekend rush, a slice of solitude. **AP Tourism** runs a guesthouse on the beach.

Horsley Hills

Popularly known as 'the Ooty of Andhra', this small hill station is located about 114 km west of Tirupati in the Nallamala Range. Nestling at an elevation of 1265 m, the resort is named after WD Horsley, the Collector of Cuddapah District, who chose the spot for his summer residence. It remains more popular with weekending public servants than anybody else, but the hills are thickly forested and home to a wide variety of wildlife, and can make a relaxing break from the roasting Andhra plains. **Madanapalle**, the nearest town 30 km to the south, is the birthplace of the famous 20th-century philosopher J Krishnamurti.

Lepakshi

This tiny village, close to the Karnataka border and 130 km from Bengaluru (Bangalore), houses a massive sculpture of Siva's bull *Nandi*, 5 m high and 8 m long, carved out of a single red granite boulder. Nearby, set on an outcrop of gneiss, is the remarkable **Virabhadra Temple**, built in 1538 under the Vijayanagar emperor Achutyadeva Raya. It has well-preserved sculptures, including a towering 6-m-high *nagalingam* and a life-size Virabhadra, decked with skulls and carrying weapons and apparently bent on revenge, while the roof of the shrine is decorated with what is claimed to be the largest mural in Asia.

Rural Development Trust FVF ① *Bangalore Highway, T08554-31503, fvfatp@hd2.dot. net.in,* an NGO working in over 1500 villages, was started by a former Spanish Jesuit, Vincente Ferrer, more than 30 years ago. The project covers health, education, housing, among other areas. Visitors interested in seeing the work can be accommodated for up to four days.

Puttaparthi *Colour map 3, A4.*

Puttaparthi, a remote village 150 km from Bengaluru, is now famous as the birthplace of **Bhagawan Sri Sathya Sai Baba**, a tremendously popular figure revered by millions as a reincarnation of the Maharashtrian saint Sai Baba of Shirdi. The current Sai Baba's predilection for spectacle (celebrations at his imposing **Prasanthi Nilayam** ashram typically involve stunt shows with massed ranks of motorcycle riders) have led some to dismiss him as a charlatan, and there have been allegations of sexual misconduct by a handful of former devotees. Nevertheless, the ashram provides free schooling and medical care to all comers, and fosters a peaceful atmosphere that attracts people from all around the world.

Listings Tirupati and Tirumala *map p1078*

Tourist information

Tirupati

AP State tourist office
Srinivasam Complex, T0877-228 9219.

APTDC
Sridevi Complex, Tilak Rd, T0877-228 9120.

Karnataka Tourism
Hotel Mayura (see Where to stay).

Tirupati Tirumala Devasthanam (TTD)
TTD Administrative Building, KT Rd, T0877-223 3333, www.tirumala.org.
This is an independent trust that manages the Tirumala Venkateswara Temple. It also has counters at the airport and the railway station,

Where to stay

Tirupati

$$$ Ramee Guestline Days
14-37 Karakambadi Rd, 3 km from town, T0877-228 0800, www.rameehotels.com.
140 rooms, central a/c, restaurants (including non-veg), bar and pool.

$$$-$$ Bliss
Renigunta Rd, T0877-223 7773, www.blisstirupati.com.
72 modern clean a/c rooms, and restaurants.

$$ Bhimas Paradise
33-37 Renigunta Rd, T0877-223 7271, www.hotelbhimas.com.
90 rooms, some a/c, pool, garden, good restaurant.

$$ Mayura
209 TP Area, T0877-222 5925.
65 rooms, half a/c, veg restaurant, exchange. More expensive than others in this price category.

$ Bhimas Deluxe
34-38 Govindaraja Car St, T0877-222 5744, www.hotelbhimas.com.
60 rooms, 40 a/c, restaurant (Indian, a/c) and exchange.

$ Vasantham Lodge
141 G Car St, T0877-222 0460.
Reasonable rooms with bath.

$ Vishnupriya
T0877-225 8667.
134 rooms, some a/c, restaurants, exchange and **Air India** office.

Tirumala

The Temple Trust's *choultries* in Tirumala can accommodate about 20,000 pilgrims. They vary from luxury suites and well-furnished cottages to dorms and unfurnished rooms (some free). Contact T0877-223 3333, www. tirumala.org. Accommodation can also be booked at www.ttdsevaonline.com.

South Andhra Coast

$$ DR Uthama
Near Madras Bus Stand, Nellore, T0861-231 7777.
The best hotel in town, with 51 rooms, pool and health club.

$$-$ Beach Resort
Mypadu, T084988-62255.
21 rooms, right on the beach, restaurant.

Horsley Hills

All accommodation here (except **$$ Forest Rest House** which can be booked from Madanapalle, T08571-279323) is owned by **AP Tourism** (www.aptdc.gov.in).

$$ Haritha Resort
T08571-279324, www.aptdc.gov.in.
Cottages and rooms (a/c and non a/c) on hill top, Governor's Bungalow recommended.

Puttaparthi

Good **$** accommodation in rooms and dorms at the ashram, T08555-287164, www.srisathyasai.org.in. No advance bookings.

Restaurants

Tirupati and Tirumala
Tirupathi-Tirumala Devasthanam Trust (TTD) provides free veg meals at its guesthouses. Outside hotels, veg restaurants include: **Laxmi Narayan Bhawan ($$)** and **Dwarka** (opposite APSRTC Bus Stand); **Indian Coffee House** (TTD Canteen and the APSRTC Bus Stand). **Konark** (Railway Station Rd); **New Triveni** (139 TP Area); **Woodlands** (TP Area). **Tea Board Restaurant** (near the Indian Coffee House). All **$**.

South Andhra Coast
$$ Komala Vilas Hotel
Trunk Rd, Nellore.
Andhra lunch – prawn curry and *chepala pulusu* (murrel fish cooked in tamarind gravy) – eaten with aromatic *nelli* rice. Highly recommended.

Festivals

May/Jun Govind Brahmotsavam.
Sep-Oct Brahmotsavam is the most important festival, especially grand every 3rd year when it is called **Navarathri Brahmotsavam**. On the 3rd day the Temple Car Festival **Rathotsavam** is particularly popular. **Rayalseema Food and Dance** follows later in the month.

Shopping

Copper and brass idols, produced at Perumallapalli village, 8 km away, and wooden toys are sold locally. Try **Poompuhar** (on Gandhi Rd) and **Lepakshi** (in the TP Area).

What to do

Tours
AP Tourism, *Room 15, Srinivasa Choultry, T0877-228 9123, www.aptdc.gov.in/tirupati-tourpackages.html*. Local sightseeing tour starts at the **APSRTC** Central Bus Stand, 0915-1730, covers Kalahasti, Tiruchanur, Kapilateerthamand Srinivasamangapuram, but not the main Venkatesvara temple. Rs 310, from Tirumala Rs 340.

Transport

Air Transport to town by APSRTC coach to **Tirupati** (Rs 50) and **Tirumala** (Rs 80); taxis Rs 450. **Indian Airlines**, **Jet Airways** and **Spicejet** fly to **Hyderabad and Delhi.**

Bus Local The most convenient of many bus stands funnelling pilgrims towards Tirumala are the **Sri Venkatesvara bus stand**, opposite the railway station, and the Sapthagiri bus stand, attached to the main Central/Sri Hari long-distance bus stand. Fleets of buses meet arriving trains, while APSRTC buses run between Tirupati and Tirumala every 3 mins, 0330-2200. Buy a return ticket (valid for 3 days) to avoid queueing on the return journey. In addition, free TTD buses run every 30 mins from the railway station to Alipiri, where the main foot track up Tirumala begins.

   Long distance Most government-run long-distance buses pull into a large cluster of bus stands in the city centre, just east of the railway station. Central/Srihari Bus Stand, T0877-228 9900 for destinations to the east: Chennai (4 hrs), **Kanchipuram** (3 hrs), **Vellore** (2½ hrs), Vijayawada. Srinivasa bus stand, T0877-228 9901, for destinations to the west: **Bengaluru** (6 hrs) and **Hyderabad** (10 hrs). Some buses from Karnataka pick up and drop off at the Alipiri bus stand, T0877-228 9904.

   In Tirumala, buses drop off at the massive Vaikuntam Queue Complex: pick up a return bus from the main bus stand, T0877-228 9905, 500 m southeast of the temple.

Taxi Tourist taxis charge around Rs 1800 for a day trip to Tirumala, including waiting time. **Balaji Travels**, 149 TP Area, T0877-222 4894. **Nithya Caars**, T09394-95 95 95.

Train About half of Tirupati's trains arrive at the main station in the city centre; the rest use nearby Renigunta, 10 km to the east (APSRTC buses meet incoming trains; taxis charge around Rs 500).

Bengaluru, 3-8 daily, 7 hrs; **Chennai**, 6 daily, 3¼ hrs; **Guntakal**, frequent services all day, 6 hrs; **Hyderabad**, 7-10 a day, 13¾ hrs; **Kolkata**, 1 daily, 28 hrs; **Mumbai**, 4 daily, 20-24 hrs; **Vijayawada**, more than 10 a day, 6 hrs.

South Andhra Coast
Train Tirupati–Hyderabad trains stop at Nellore.

Horsley Hills
Bus A direct bus leaves the **Central Bus Station** in Tirupati at 1300. It's easier to go via **Madanapalle**, from where buses for the hills leave every 2 hrs till 1700.

Background Telangana and Andhra Pradesh

History

The first evidence of a people called the Andhras came from Emperor Asoka. The first known Andhra power, the Satavahanas encouraged various religious groups including Buddhists. Their capital at Amaravati shows evidence of the great skill of early Andhra artists and builders. Around AD 150 there was also a fine university at Nagarjunakonda. In 1323 Warangal, to the northeast of the present city of Hyderabad, was captured by the armies of Muhammad bin Tughlaq. Muslim expansion further south was prevented for two centuries by the rise of the Vijayanagar Empire, itself crushed at the Battle of Talikota in 1565 by a short-lived federation of Muslim States; the cultural life it supported had to seek fresh soil. From then on Muslim rulers dominated the politics of central Andhra, Telangana. The Bahmani kingdoms in the region around modern Hyderabad controlled central Telangana in the 16th century. They were even able to keep the Mughals at bay until Aurangzeb finally forced them into submission in the late 17th century.

The Princely State was ruled by Muslim Nizams from the early 18th century, with its capital as Hyderabad. There was doubt as to whether the Princely State would accede to India after Partition. The Nizam of Hyderabad would have liked to join fellow Muslims in the newly created Muslim State of Pakistan. However, political disturbances in 1949 gave the Indian Government the pretext to take direct control, and the state was incorporated into the Indian Union.

Modern Telanga and Andhra Pradesh

Andhra State was created in 1953 from the Telugu-speaking areas of the erstwhile Madras State. This was not enough for those who were demanding statehood for a united Telugu-speaking region – one political leader, Potti Sreeramulu, starved himself to death in protest at the government's refusal to grant the demand – and in 1956 Andhra was merged with Telangana (itself carved from the Telugu parts of the old Hyderabad State) to create the state of Andhra Pradesh. Yet movements to separate the two regions began soon after, spurred by a sense that the interests of dusty, underdeveloped Telangana were being neglected in favour of the fertile coastal districts.

In the 1983 and 1999 elections, a regional party, the Telugu Desam Party (TDP), founded by the film star NT Rama Rao, won a crushing victory, but in 2004, the Congress Party and its ally, the Telangana Rashtra Samiti, reclaimed power. The Congress Chief Minister YS Rajasekhara Reddy (known as YSR) took charge of a state with high debts to the World Bank, where rural poverty was endemic and where suicide had become a major problem among poor farmers. YSR charmed the rural poor with a series of social welfare initiatives, including low-interest loans to women entrepreneurs and free medical treatments for people living below the poverty line. He became one of the most popular leaders in recent Indian history, making serious inroads into Andhra's hitherto intractable Naxalite problem, and he led the Congress Party to a rare absolute majority victory in the May 2009 elections. His death in a helicopter crash over Naxalite-controlled jungle in September 2009 has left a power vacuum in the state that has yet to be convincingly filled.

In June 2014 the Telangana movement finally won its long campaign, for separate statehood. The new state, India's 29th, retains Hyderabad as its capital (the city will also remain capital of Andhra Pradesh for the next decade), but faces severe challenges: outside of the tech hub, it ranks among the most underdeveloped regions of India, and its far-flung rural areas have been a breeding ground for Naxalism. Meanwhile, battle lines have already emerged with the remaining parts of Andhra Pradesh over rights to water and power, with Telangana refusing to release water from the Nagarjunasagar Dam to the heavily irrigated Krishna delta, and Andhra countering with threats to withhold electricity supplies to the new state.

Maharashtra

cave temples, towering forts and India's biggest metropolis

There are some beautiful and fascinating sites in Maharashtra. The earliest of the world-famous frescoes and carvings at Ajanta and Ellora caves date from the second century BC.

Wonderful ruined forts built by the Marathas and the Portuguese are scattered along the 500 km of coastline while others are perched precariously on the hilltops of the Western Ghats. From these fortresses, the 17th-century Marathas, masters in the art of guerrilla warfare, carved out a territory that stretched the width of India.

Today Maharashtra boasts not only India's most vibrant city, Mumbai, and a diverse and rapidly growing industrial economy, but also a rich agricultural hinterland.

Small beaches offer an escape from the busy city while train buffs can enjoy a ride up the scenic narrow-gauge railway to Matheran in the hills.

The thriving modern city of Pune, across the Ghats, attracts the visitors to the lavish Osho Commune, which has drawn large numbers of Westerners in search of an alternative spiritual answer.

Best for
Cave temples ■ City life ■ Forts ■ Wildlife

Footprint
picks

★ **Mumbai**, page 1088

Watch sunset over Marine Drive before diving into the nightlife of
India's most exciting city.

★ **Aurangabad**, page 1117

Climb the stunning fort of Deogiri in the late afternoon.

★ **Kailasanatha Temple, Ellora**, page 1124

Drop to your knees in awe at this exquisitely carved rock temple,
one of India's finest artistic achievements.

★ **Ajanta Caves**, page 1126

Feast your eyes on the rich and well-preserved murals, considered
masterpieces of Buddhist art.

★ **Osho Commune**, page 1140

Check in for a course in meditation or ecstatic dance at the infamous
Zen master's ashram.

★ **Raigad**, page 1147

Scramble up to the crumbling fort of Raigad for an awesome view of
the Western Ghats.

Essential Mahrashtra

Finding your feet

Maharashtra (population 112.4 million) has been described as India's industrial and commercial backbone. The nerve centre of India's stock market, the headquarters of a large number of Indian and multinational companies' operations in India and a major manufacturing state in its own right, Maharashtra has not only India's largest city, Mumbai, but a large number of rapidly industrializing smaller cities. Hills and plateaux give Maharashtra a distinctive topography. In the west the state is guarded by the Sahyadri Range of the Western Ghats, which rise as an abrupt and almost impenetrable wall reaching over 1400 m in places, while the Satpura Range to the north forms a natural border with Madhya Pradesh. The volcanic lavas of the Deccan Trap, which poured out over 65 million years ago as the Indian peninsula broke away from the African coast, gave the plateau that stretches away towards the east both its name and its very distinctive black soils. East of Nagpur the lava gives way to gently rolling granite hills 250-350 m above sea level, an extraordinary landscape of huge open spaces and sweeping views. A number of important rivers rise in the Western Ghats. Most follow the trend of the Godavari and the Krishna, rising within 100 km of the Arabian Sea and then flowing east- wards across the Deccan plateau to the Bay of Bengal. The annual rains also send a number of streams and rivers westward across the undulating Konkan coastal lowlands, which reach their widest near Mumbai, tapering off to a narrow belt towards the border of Goa.

Getting around

Ride the suburban railway network in Mumbai, the narrow gauge up to Matheran and the Konkan railway out of state. In Mumbai cabs and motor rickshaws are plentiful.

When to go

Most of Maharashtra is hot during the daytime throughout the year, the coast being very humid as well. Night-time temperatures fall from November to March. Only the hill stations of the Western Ghats experience much cooler weather, a particular relief in April and May. The southwest monsoon normally breaks on the coast in the second week of June and finishes in September, bringing most of the region's rain in often prolonged and violent storms. The Ghats give rise to a strong rain-shadow effect, which makes the coastal Konkan strip much wetter than the interior upland. Avoid June and July when rainfall is torrential.

Festivals

The majority of Hindu festivals are observed in the state. The highly colourful Ranga Panchami and Holi, marking the beginning of spring, are very popular. Janmashtami (July/August) celebrates the birth of Lord Krishna. Men and boys in local teams form human pyramids to break pots of curds that have been hung from high places. The winners usually take home a 'matka' of money as well. On Ganesh Chaturthi in Mumbai (August/September) massive figures of the ever-popular elephant god Ganesh (the god of overcoming obstacles and the city's

Weather Mumbai

January	February	March	April	May	June
31°C 17°C 15mm	31°C 18°C 0mm	32°C 21°C 0mm	33°C 24°C 0mm	33°C 26°C 21mm	32°C 26°C 504mm

July	August	September	October	November	December
30°C 25°C 819mm	30°C 25°C 547mm	30°C 25°C 325mm	33°C 23°C 81mm	34°C 21°C 113mm	32°C 18°C 4mm

guardian diety) are towed through the streets and immersed in the sea; Pune has special celebrations that last 10 loud days. Dussehra (October), the last day of the nationally celebrated Navratri festival, is significant because it was the day on which the Marathas usually began their military campaigns. The Muslim festival of Mohurram, which commemorates the martyrs of Islam, is often observed by Hindus as well.

Time required

Allow two days for Mumbai and two days for Ajanta and Ellora.

Footprint
picks

1 **Mumbai**, page 1088
2 **Aurangabad**, page 1117
3 **Kailasanatha Temple, Ellora**, page 1124
4 **Ajanta Caves**, page 1126
5 **Osho Commune**, page 1140
6 **Raigad**, page 1147

Food and drink

The main regional dishes reflect Maharashtra's transition position between the wheat-growing regions of the north and the rice-growing coastal lands, while millets are grown in the interior. Lightly spiced vegetables and sweet and sour dishes are popular, with a distinctive emphasis on dried and salted fish such as Bombay duck cooked with lentils. There are also recipes that use sprouted lentils. Konkan cuisine has more in common with the coastal food of Goa and Kerala, revolving around fish and vegetable curries flavoured with coconut. If you're adventurous, try *sol kadhi*, a purple tangy and salty drink made with the sour fruit of the kokum plant mixed in coconut milk and flavoured with spices. Mumbai has the heaviest concentration of Parsis in the country, so try their cuisine here: *dhansak*, a special lentil curry with lamb or chicken cooked with five varieties of spice, or *patrani machli*, fish (often pomfret) stuffed with coconut chutney and coriander, steamed in banana leaves.

Mumbai
(Bombay)

⭐ Maximum City, the City of Dreams, India's economic capital and melting pot. You can throw epithets and superlatives at Mumbai until the cows come home, but it refuses to be understood on a merely intellectual level. Like London and New York, it's a restless human tapestry of cultures, religions, races, ways of surviving and thriving, and one that evokes palpable emotion; whether you love it or hate it, you can't stay unaffected.

From the cluster of fishing villages first linked together by the British East India Company in 1668, Mumbai has swelled to sprawl across seven islands, which now groan under the needs of 21 million stomachs, souls and egos. Its problems – creaking infrastructure, endemic corruption coupled with bureaucratic incompetence, and an ever-expanding population of whom more than two thirds live in slums – are only matched by the enormous drive that makes it the centre of business, fashion and film-making in modern India, and both a magnet and icon for the country's dreams, and nightmares.

The taxi ride from the airport shows you both sides of the city: slum dwellers selling balloons under billboards of fair-skinned models dripping in gold and reclining on the roof of a Mercedes; the septic stench as you cross Mahim Creek, where bikers park on the soaring bridge to shoot the breeze amid fumes that could drop an elephant; the feeling of diesel permeating your bloodstream and the manically reverberating mantra of *Horn OK Please* as you ooze through traffic past Worli's glitzy shopping malls and the fairytale island mosque of Haji Ali. And finally the magic moment as you swing out on to Chowpatty Beach and the city throws off her cloak of chaos to reveal a neon-painted skyscape that makes you feel like you've arrived at the centre of all things.

Essential Mumbai

Best hotels

Taj Mahal Palace, page 1100
Godwin, page 1100
Regency, page 1101
Orchid, page 1101

Finding your feet

Chhatrapati Shivaji International Airport is 30 km from Nariman Point, the business heart of the city. The domestic terminals at Santa Cruz are 5 km closer. Pre-paid taxis to the city centre are good value and take 40-90 minutes; buses are cheaper but significantly slower. If you arrive at night without a hotel booking it is best to stay at one of the hotels near the airports. If you're travelling light (and feeling brave), local trains head into the city from Vile Parle (International) and Santa Cruz (Domestic) stations, but these are daunting at any time (passengers leap off while the train is still moving and will 'help' you if you're in their way) and become impossibly crowded during the morning and evening rush hours.

Getting around

The sights are spread out and you need transport. Taxis are metered and good value. Older taxis carry a rate card to convert the meter reading to the correct fare. You can download the rate card in advance from www.hindustantimes.com/farelist, and various fare conversion apps are available for smartphones. There are frequent buses on major routes, and the two suburban railway lines are useful out of peak hours, but get horrendously crowded. Auto-rickshaws are only allowed in the suburbs north of Mahim Creek.

Best places to eat

Street food and sweets at Kailash Parbat, page 1101
Seafood with a side of Bollywood at Trishna, page 1102
Unlimited Gujarati *thali* at Shree Thaker Bhojanalay, page 1102
Sunday brunch at Olive, page 1102

Useful contacts

Commissioner's Office, Dr DN Road, near Phule Market.
Foreigners' Regional Registration Office, 3rd floor, Special Branch Building, Badruddin Tayabji Lane, behind St Xaviers College, T022-2262 1169.
Passport office, T022-2493 1731.

Gateway of India and Colaba *Colour map 5, B3.*

iconic landmark and the epicentre of Mumbai's tourist scene

Gateway of India

The Indo-Saracenic-style Gateway of India (1927), designed by George Wittet to commemorate the visit of George V and Queen Mary in 1911, is modelled in honey-coloured basalt on 16th-century Gujarati work. The great gateway is an archway with halls on each side capable of seating 600 at important receptions. The arch was the point from which the last British regiment left on 28 February 1948, signalling the end of the empire. The whole area has a huge buzz at weekends. Scores of boats depart from here for **Elephanta Island**, creating a sea-swell which young boys delight in diving into. Hawkers, beggars and the general throng of people all add to the atmosphere. A short distance behind the Gateway is an impressive **statue of Shivaji**.

Taj Mahal Hotel

The red-domed **Taj** was almost completely gutted by fire in the aftermath of the 26/11 terrorist attacks, which saw guests and staff of the hotel taken hostage and several killed, but the hotel swiftly reopened for business. It's worth running the gauntlet of the Taj's airport-strength security to stroll through the corridors of the glorious Old Wing, even more so if you stay for the very Old-Bombay institution of high tea in the Harbour Room. After dark the area around the hotel becomes particularly colourful, with couples and young families taking in the sea air around the Gateway, while a piquant mix of drug dealers, street scammers and pimps rub shoulders with backpackers and the elite of Bollywood in the streets behind the hotel.

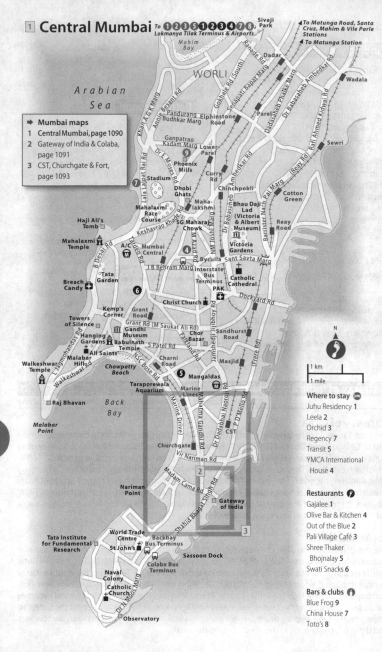

To ① ② ③ ⑤ ① ② ③ ④ ⑦ ⑧ Sivaji
Lokmanya Tilak Terminus & Airports   Park

◀ To Matunga Road, Santa
Cruz, Mahim & Vile Parle
Stations

◀ To Matunga Station

*Arabian
Sea*

*Mahim
Bay*

WORLI

➡ **Mumbai maps**
1 Central Mumbai, page 1090
2 Gateway of India & Colaba,
   page 1091
3 CST, Churchgate & Fort,
   page 1093

Where to stay 🛏
Juhu Residency **1**
Leela **2**
Orchid **3**
Regency **7**
Transit **5**
YMCA International
House **4**

Restaurants 🍴
Gajalee **1**
Olive Bar & Kitchen **4**
Out of the Blue **2**
Pali Village Café **3**
Shree Thaker
Bhojnalay **5**
Swati Snacks **6**

Bars & clubs 🍸
Blue Frog **9**
China House **7**
Toto's **8**

Colaba Causeway

South of the Gateway of India is the crowded southern section of Shahid ('martyr') Bhagat Singh Marg, more popularly known as Colaba Causeway, a brilliantly bawdy bazar; you can buy everything from high-end jeans to cheaply made *kurtas* and knock-off leather wallets at the street stalls, and the colourful cast of characters includes Bollywood casting agents, would-be novelists plotting a

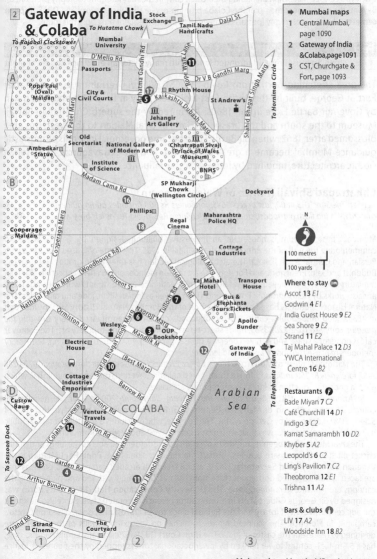

2 Gateway of India & Colaba

To Hutatma Chowk
To Rajabai Clocktower

Stock Exchange
Dalal St
Tamil Nadu Handicrafts
Mumbai University
D'Mello Rd

Bope Walk Lane

A

Passports
Pope Paul (Oval) Maidan
City & Civil Courts
Dr V B Gandhi Marg
Rhythm House
Kaikashru Dubash Marg
St Andrew's
Jehangir Art Gallery

B

Old Secretariat
Ambedkar Statue
National Gallery of Modern Art
Institute of Science
Chhatrapati Sivaji (Prince of Wales) Museum
Madam Cama Rd
SP Mukharji Chowk (Wellington Circle)
BNHS
Dockyard
Phillips
Regal Cinema
Maharashtra Police HQ

Cooperage Maidan

C

Cottage Industries
Convent St
Lansdowne Rd
Taj Mahal Hotel
Transport House
Bus & Elephanta Tours Tickets
Apollo Bunder
Ormiston Rd
Nagroji Marg
Wesley
OUP Bookshop
Mandlik M
Electric House
Gateway of India

D

Cottage Industries Emporium
Cusrow Baug
Venture Travels
Barrow Rd
COLABA
Henry Rd
Walton Rd
Arabian Sea
Mereweather Rd

E

Strand Rd
Strand Cinema
Garden Rd
Arthur Bunder Rd
The Courtyard

1   2   3

→ **Mumbai maps**
1 Central Mumbai, page 1090
2 Gateway of India &Colaba, page 1091
3 CST, Churchgate & Fort, page 1093

N

100 metres
100 yards

Where to stay 🛏
Ascot 13 *E1*
Godwin 4 *E1*
India Guest House 9 *E2*
Sea Shore 9 *E2*
Strand 11 *E2*
Taj Mahal Palace 12 *D3*
YWCA International Centre 16 *B2*

Restaurants 🍴
Bade Miyan 7 *C2*
Café Churchill 14 *D1*
Indigo 3 *C2*
Kamat Samarambh 10 *D2*
Khyber 5 *A2*
Leopold's 6 *C2*
Ling's Pavilion 7 *C2*
Theobroma 12 *E1*
Trishna 11 *A2*

Bars & clubs 🍸
LIV 17 *A2*
Woodside Inn 18 *B2*

successor to *Shantaram* in the **Leopold Café** (another bearer of bullet scars from 26/11), and any number of furtive hash sellers.

Church of St John the Baptist

Early English in style, with a 58-m spire, this church on the northern edge of Colaba was built in 1847-1858 to commemorate the soldiers who died in the First Afghan War. At nearby **Sassoon Dock** you can see fishermen unloading their catch early in the morning (photography prohibited). Beyond the church near the tip of the Colaba promontory lie the **Observatory** and **Old European cemetery** in the naval colony (permission needed to enter). Frequent buses ply this route.

Fort

stunning museums and thronged lanes, with many Victorian buildings floodlit at night

The area stretching north from Colaba to CST (Victoria Terminus) is named after Fort St George, built by the British East India Company in the 1670s and torn down by Governor Bartle Frere in the 1860s. Anchored by the superb Chhatrapati Shivaji Museum to the south and the grassy parkland of Oval Maidan to the west, this area blossomed after 1862, when Sir Bartle Frere became governor. Under his enthusiastic guidance Mumbai became a great civic centre and an extravaganza of Victorian Gothic architecture, modified by Indo-Saracenic influences.

Chhatrapati Shivaji (Prince of Wales) Museum

Oct-Feb Tue-Sun 1015-1800, last tickets 1645; foreigners Rs 300 (includes audio guide), Indians Rs 15, camera Rs 15 (no flash or tripods), students Rs 10, children Rs 5, avoid Tue as it is busy with school visits.

Mumbai's best museum is housed in an impressive building designed by George Wittet to commemorate the visit of the Prince of Wales to India in 1905. The dome of glazed tiles has a very Persian and Central Asian flavour. The archaeological section has three main groups: Brahminical; Buddhist and Jain; Prehistoric and Foreign. The art section includes an excellent collection of Indian miniatures and well displayed *tankhas* along with a section on armour that is worth seeing. There are also works by Gainsborough, Poussin and Titian as well as Indian silver, jade and tapestries. The Natural History section is based on the collection of the Bombay Natural History Society, founded in 1833. Good guidebooks, cards and reproductions on sale. **Jehangir Art Gallery** ① *within the museum complex, T022-2284 3989*, holds short-term exhibitions of contemporary art. The **Samovar** café is good for a snack and a chilled beer in a pleasant, if cramped, garden-side setting. Temporary members may use the library and attend lectures.

The **National Gallery of Modern Art** ① *Sir Cowasji Jehangir Hall, opposite the museum, T022-2285 2457, foreigners Rs 150, Indians Rs 10*, is a three-tiered gallery converted from an old public hall which gives a good introduction to India's contemporary art scene.

St Andrew's Kirk (1819) ① *just behind the museum, daily 1000-1700*, is a simple neoclassical church. At the south end of Mahatma Gandhi (MG) Road is the renaissance-style **Institute of Science** (1911) designed by George Wittet. The Institute, which includes a scientific library, a public hall and examination halls, was built with gifts from the Parsi and Jewish communities.

The **Oval Maidan** has been restored to a pleasant public garden and acts as the lungs and public cricket pitch of the southern business district. On the east side of the **Pope Paul Maidan** is the Venetian Gothic-style **old Secretariat** (1874), with a façade of arcaded verandas and porticos that are faced in buff-coloured porbander stone from Gujarat. Decorated with red and blue basalt, the carvings are in white *hemnagar* stone. The **University Convocation Hall** (1874) to its north was designed by Sir George Gilbert Scott in a 15th-century French decorated style. Scott also designed the adjacent **University Library** and the **Rajabai clock tower** (1870s) next door, based on Giotto's campanile in Florence. The sculpted figures in niches on the exterior walls of the tower were designed to represent the castes of India. The **High Court** (1871-1879), in early English Gothic style, has a 57-m-high central tower flanked by lower octagonal towers topped by the figures of Justice

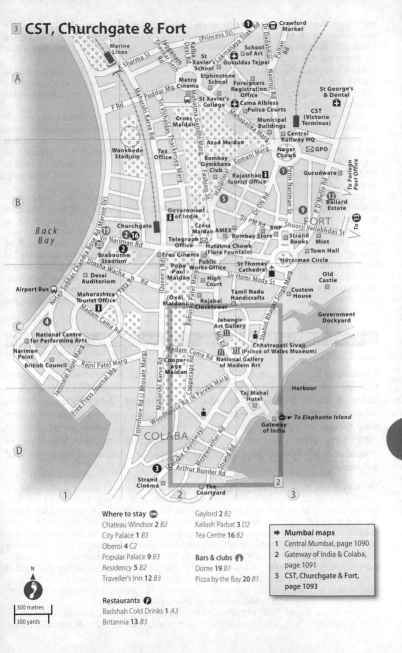

3 CST, Churchgate & Fort

Where to stay 🛏️
Chateau Windsor 2 *B2*
City Palace 1 *B3*
Oberoi 4 *C2*
Popular Palace 9 *B3*
Residency 5 *B2*
Traveller's Inn 12 *B3*

Gaylord 2 *B2*
Kailash Parbat 3 *D2*
Tea Centre 16 *B2*

Bars & clubs 🍸
Dome 19 *B1*
Pizza by the Bay 20 *B1*

Restaurants 🍴
Badshah Cold Drinks 1 *A3*
Britannia 13 *B3*

➡️ **Mumbai maps**
1 Central Mumbai, page 1090
2 Gateway of India & Colaba, page 1091
3 CST, Churchgate & Fort, page 1093

and Mercy. The Venetian Gothic **Public Works Office** (1869-1872) is to its north. Opposite, and with its main façade to Vir Nariman Road, is the gorgeously wrought former **General Post Office** (1869-1872). Now called the Telegraph Office, it stands next to the original Telegraph Office adding romanesque to the extraordinary mixture of European architectural styles.

From here you can walk east and delve into the dense back lanes of the Fort district, crossing the five-way junction of **Hutatma Chowk** ('Martyrs' Corner'), in the centre of which stands the architecturally forgettable but useful landmark of the Flora Fountain (1869). This is an interesting area to explore although there are no particular sights.

Vir Nariman Road cuts through to the elegant tree-shaded oval of **Horniman Circle**, laid out in 1860 and renamed in 1947 after Benjamin Horniman, editor of the pro-independence *Bombay Chronicle* – one of the few English names remaining on the Mumbai map. The park in the middle is used for dance and music performances during the Kala Ghoda Arts Festival, held in January. On the west edge are the Venetian Gothic **Elphinstone Buildings** (1870) in brown sandstone, while to the south is the **Cathedral Church of St Thomas** (1718), which contains a number of monuments amounting to a heroic 'Who's Who of India'.

South of Horniman Circle on Shahid Bhagat Singh Marg, the **Custom House** is one of the oldest buildings in the city, believed to incorporate a Portuguese barrack block from 1665. Over the entrance is the crest of the East India Company. Remnants of the old Portuguese fort's walls can be seen and many Malabar teak 'East Indiamen' ships were built here. Walk north from here and you'll reach the **Town Hall** (1820-1823), widely admired and much photographed as one of the best neoclassical buildings in India. The Corinthian interior houses the **Assembly Rooms** and the **Bombay Asiatic Society**. Immediately north again is the **Mint** (1824-1829)① *visit by prior permission from the Mint Master, T022-2270 3184, www.mumbaimint.org*, built on the Fort rubbish dump, with Ionic columns and a water tank in front of it. The nearby **Ballard Estate** is also worth a poke around while you're in the area, with some good hotels and restaurants, as well as Hamilton Studios, the swanky offices of *Vogue* magazine, and the Mumbai Port Authority.

Around the CST (VT)

Victorian Gothic architecture and bustling markets

Chhatrapati Shivaji Terminus (1878-1887), formerly Victoria Terminus and still known to many elder taxi drivers as 'VT', is far and away the most remarkable example of Victorian Gothic architecture in India. Opened during Queen Victoria's Golden Jubilee year (1887), over three million commuters now swarm through the station daily, though the bustling chaos of old has been reined in somewhat since November 2008's terror attacks, when at least 50 people were shot dead here. Several scenes from *Slumdog Millionaire* were filmed on the suburban platforms at the west end of the station.

The station was built at a time when fierce debate was taking place among British architects working in India as to the most appropriate style to develop to meet the demands of the late 19th-century boom. One view held that the British should restrict themselves to models derived from the best in Western tradition. Others argued that architects should draw on Indian models, trying to bring out the best of Indian tradition and encourage its development. By and large, the former were dominant, but the introduction of Gothic elements allowed a blending of Western traditions with Indian (largely Islamic) motifs, which became known as the Indo-Saracenic style. The station that resulted, designed by FW Stevens, is its crowning glory: a huge, symmetrical, gargoyle-studded frontage capped by a large central dome and a 4-m-high statue of Progress, with arcaded booking halls, stained glass and glazed tiles inspired by St Pancras. The giant caterpillar-like walkway with perspex awnings looks truly incongruous against the huge Gothic structure.

There are many more Victorian buildings in the area around CST, particularly along Mahapalika Marg (Cruickshank Road), which runs northwest of the station past the grand **Municipal Buildings**

BACKGROUND

Mumbai

Hinduism made its mark on Mumbai long before the Portuguese and British transformed it into one of India's great cities. The caves on the island of Elephanta were excavated under the Kalachuris (AD 500-600). Yet, only 350 years ago, the area occupied by this great metropolis comprised seven islands inhabited by Koli fishermen. Britain acquired the marshy and malarial islands in 1661 as part of a dowry paid by the Portuguese when Catherine of Braganza married Charles II and Anglicized the Portuguese name of bom baim to Bombay. Seven years later the East India Company leased the whole area from the Crown for £10 a year, and the company shifted its headquarters to Bombay in 1672.

Isolated by the sharp face of the Western Ghats and the constantly hostile Marathas, Bombay's early fortunes rested on the shipbuilding yards established by progressive Parsis. It thrived entirely on overseas trade and, in the cosmopolitan city this created, Parsis, Sephardic Jews and the British shared common interests and responded to the same incentives.

The modern city began to take shape in the 1780s, when Governor William Hornby began building a causeway to link all of Bombay's islands into a single land mass. Then, with the abolition of the Company's trade monopoly, the doors to rapid expansion were flung open and the city flourished. Trade with England boomed and, under the governorship of Sir Bartle Frere (1862-1869), extravagant Indo-Gothic landmarks sprouted throughout the city. The opening of the Suez Canal in 1870 gave Bombay greater proximity to European markets and a decisive advantage over its eastern rival Kolkata. It has since become the headquarters for many national and international companies, and was a natural choice as home to India's stock exchange (BSE). With the sponsorship of the Tata dynasty, Mumbai has also become the primary home of India's nuclear research programme, with its first plutonium extraction plant at Trombay in 1961 and the establishment of the Tata Institute for Fundamental Research, the most prestigious science research institute in the country.

Renamed Mumbai in 1995 after a long campaign by the right-wing Hindu party Shiv Sena, the city is still growing at a phenomenal pace, and heavy demand for building space means property value is some of the highest on earth. Residential skyscrapers have mushroomed across the city, while the old cotton mills of Lower Parel have been repurposed as shopping and luxury apartment complexes. An even more ambitious attempt to ease pressure on the isthmus is the newly minted city of Navi Mumbai, 90 minutes east of the city, which has malls, apartments and industrial parks, but little of the glamour that makes Mumbai such a magnet.

The latest project is the controversial redevelopment of Dharavi, a 215-ha chunk of prime real estate that houses roughly a million people, mostly in desperately squalid makeshift hovels originally designed to house migrant mill workers. In addition, an uncounted number live precariously in unauthorized, hastily rigged and frequently demolished corrugated iron or bamboo-and-tarpaulin shacks beside railways and roads, while yet more sleep in doorways and on sheets across the pavement.

In recent decades, the pressure of supporting so many people has begun to tell. Communal riots between Hindus and Muslims have flared up a handful of times since the destruction by militant Hindus of the Babri Masjid in 1992. The attacks of November 2008, when Lashkar-e-Taiba terrorists simultaneously attacked the Taj Mahal and Oberoi hotels along with several other tourist destinations, shocked the city and represented a potentially disastrous flashpoint. Yet the citizens chose not to vent their anger on each other, but on the government that had failed to deal effectively with the attacks. Within weeks the front of the Taj had been scrubbed clean and tourists were again packing out the Leopold Café, while CST station emerged from the bullets a cleaner, calmer, less chaotic place. Somehow, whether through economic imperative or a shared mentality of forward thinking, the city always finds a way to bounce back.

(also by Stevens, 1893), and Lokmanya Tilak Marg (Camac Road), which joins Mahapalika Marg at the Metro Cinema traffic circle – a landmark known to every Mumbai cabbie.

Immediately to the north of CST lies **Crawford Market** (1865-1871), now renamed **Mahatma Jyotiba Phule Market** after a Maharashtran social reformer, designed by Emerson in 12th-century French Gothic style, with paving stones imported from Caithness and fountains carved by Lockwood Kipling. The market is divided into bustling sections for fruit, vegetables, fish, mutton and poultry, with a large central hall and clock tower.

Running northwest of Crawford Market towards Mumbai Central Railway Station is **Falkland Road**, the centre of Mumbai's red-light district. Prostitutes stand behind barred windows, giving the area its other name, 'The Cages' – many of the girls are sold or abducted from various parts of India and Nepal. AIDS is very widespread, and a lot of NGOs are at work in the area educating the women about prevention.

North of Crawford Market is **Masjid Station**, the heart of the Muslim quarter, where agate minarets mingle with the pollution-streaked upper storeys of 1960s residential towers. The atmosphere here is totally different from the crumbling colonial architectural glory of the Colaba and Fort area: balconies on faded apartment blocks are bedecked with fairy lights, laundry dries on the window grilles, and at sunset the ramshackle roads hum with taxis, boys wielding wooden carts through traffic and Muslim women at a stroll. One of the city's most interesting markets, the **Chor Bazar** (Thieves' Market) ① *Sat to Thu 1100-1900*, spreads through the streets between the station and Falkland Road. The bazar is a great place to poke around in with tonnes of dealers in old watches, film posters, Belgian- or Indian-made temple lamps, enamel tiles and door knobs. The area around Mutton Street is popular with film prop-buyers and foreign and domestic bric-a-brac hunters.

Marine Drive to Malabar Hill
atmospheric sunset crush of power-walking executives and festive families on the seafront

When the hustle of the city becomes too much, do as the Mumbaikars do and head for the water. The 3-km sweep of Marine Drive (known as the 'Queen's Necklace' for the lines of streetlights that run its length) skirts alongside the grey waters of the Arabian Sea from Nariman Point in the south to exclusive Malabar Hill in the north. This is where you'll see Mumbai at its most egalitarian: servants and *babus* alike take the air on the esplanades in the evening. For an interesting half-day trip, start downtown at Churchgate Station and follow the curving course of the Queen's Necklace to the Walkeshwar Temple out on the end of Malabar Hill; start at lunchtime and you can be strolling back down Marine Drive, ice cream in hand.

Churchgate Station (1894-1896), on Vir Nariman Road at the north end of the Oval Maidan, was the second great railway building designed by FW Stevens. With its domes and gables, Churchgate has an air of Byzantine simplicity that contrasts with CST's full-tilt Gothic overload, but the rush hour spectacle is no less striking: Sebastiao Salgado's famous photograph of commuters pouring out of suburban trains was taken here.

A block to the west is Netaji Subhash Road, better known as **Marine Drive**, which bends northwest past Wankhede cricket stadium, several luxury hotels and the run-down Taraporewala Aquarium. At the north end in the crook of Malabar Hill is **Chowpatty Beach**, a long stretch of grey-white sand that looks attractive from a distance, but is polluted. Swimming here is not recommended but there is a lot of interesting beach activity in the evening. Chowpatty was the scene of a number of important 'Quit India' rallies during the Independence Movement. During important festivals, like **Ganesh Chaturthi** and **Dussehra**, it is thronged with jubilant Hindu devotees.

Mahatma Gandhi Museum (**Mani Bhavan**) ① *west of Grant Rd station at 19 Laburnum Rd, www.gandhi-manibhavan.org, 0930-1800, Rs 10, allow 1 hr*, is north of Chowpatty on the road to Nana Chowk. This private house, where Mahatma Gandhi used to stay on visits to Mumbai, is now a memorial museum and research library with 20,000 volumes. There is a diorama depicting

ON THE ROAD

Dabbawallahs

If you go inside Churchgate station at mid-morning or after lunch, you will see the *dabbawallahs*, members of the Bombay Union of Tiffin Box Carriers. Each morning, the 2500 *dabbawallahs* call on suburban housewives who pack freshly cooked lunch into small circular stainless steel containers – *dabbas*. Three or four are stacked one on the other and held together by a clip with a handle. Typically the *dabbawallah* will collect 30-40 tiffin boxes, range them out on a long pole and cycle to the nearest station. Here he will hand them over to a fellow *dabbawallah* who will transport them into the city for delivery.

Over 100,000 lunches of maybe *sabze* (vegetable curry), chappattis, dahl and pickle make their way daily across town to the breadwinner. The service, which costs a few rupees a day, is a good example of the fine division of labour in India, reliable and efficient, for the *dabbawallahs* pride themselves on never losing a lunch. He makes sure that the carefully prepared *pukka* (proper) food has not in any way been defiled.

important scenes from Gandhi's life, but the display of photos and letters on the first floor is more interesting, and includes letters Gandhi wrote to Hitler in 1939 asking him not to go to war, and those to Roosevelt, Einstein and Tolstoy.

At the end of Chowpatty, Marine Drive becomes Walkeshwar Road and bends southwest to pass the **Jain Temple** (1904), built of marble and dedicated to the first Jain Tirthankar. Much of the colourful decoration depicts the lives of the Tirthankars. Visitors can watch various rituals being performed. Jains play a prominent part in Mumbai's banking and commerce and are one of the city's wealthiest communities. Beyond, on the tip of Malabar Point, is **Raj Bhavan**, now home to the Governor of Maharashtra.

Behind the Jain Temple, Gangadhar Kher Rd (Ridge Road) runs up Malabar Hill to the **Hanging Gardens (Pherozeshah Mehta Gardens)** so named since they are located on top of a series of tanks that supply water to Mumbai. The gardens are well kept with lots of topiary animals and offer an opportunity to hang out with Mumbai's elite, whose penthouse apartments peer down on the park from all sides; there are good views over the city and Marine Drive from the **Kamala Nehru Park** across the road. It's worth a visit after 1700 when it's a bit cooler, but it's reputed to be unsafe after nightfall. Immediately to the north are the Parsi **Towers of Silence**, set in secluded gardens donated by Parsi industrialist Sir Jamshetji Jeejeebhoy. This very private place is not accessible to tourists but it can be glimpsed from the road. Parsis believe that the elements of water, fire and earth must not be polluted by the dead, so they lay their 'vestments of flesh and bone' out on the top of the towers to be picked clean by vultures. The depletion in the number of vultures is a cause for concern, and more and more agiarys now opt for solar panels to speed up the process of decay.

At the end of the headland behind Raj Bhavan stands the **Walkeshwar Temple** ('Lord of Sand'), built about AD 1000 and one of the oldest buildings in Mumbai. In legend this was a resting point for Lord Rama on his journey from Ayodhya to Lanka to free Sita from the demon king Ravana. One day Rama's brother failed to return from Varanasi at the usual time with a *lingam* that he fetched daily for Rama's worship. Rama then made a *lingam* from the beach sand to worship Siva. You'd also do well to visit **Banganga**, a freshwater tank that's part of a 12th-century temple complex. Legend has it that when Rama got thirsty Lakshman raised his bow and shot a *baan* (arrow) into the ground, bringing forth fresh water from the Ganga in this ocean locked island. The site is being renovated and is regularly used as a venue for concerts, festivals and pilgrimages alike.

Other than to catch a train from Mumbai Central Station, relatively few visitors venture into the area north of Marine Drive, yet it contains some great only-in-Mumbai sights which, with judicious use of taxis and the odd suburban train, can easily be combined into a day trip with the coastal sights described above.

On the coast, 1 km north of the Gandhi Museum on Bhulabhai Desai (Warden Road), are the **Mahalakshmi temples**, the oldest in Mumbai, dedicated to three goddesses whose images were found in the sea. Lakshmi, goddess of wealth, is the unofficial presiding deity of the city, and the temple is host to frenzied activity – pressing a coin into the wall of the main shrine is supposed to be a sign of riches to come. Just to the north, **Haji Ali's Mosque** sits on an islet 500 m offshore. The mosque, built in 1431, contains the tomb of Muslim saint Haji Ali, who drowned here while on pilgrimage to Mecca, and as a last request demanded that he be buried neither on land nor at sea. A long causeway, usable only at low tide, links the mosque and tomb to the land, and is lined by Muslim supplicants. The money changers are willing to exchange one-rupee coins into smaller coins, enabling pilgrims to make several individual gifts to beggars rather than one larger one, thereby reputedly increasing the merit of the gift.

From Haji Ali's Tomb go east along Keshavrao Khade Road, passing the **Mahalakshmi Race Course** ① *racing season Nov-Apr, www.rwitc.com*, to SG Maharaj Chowk (**Jacob's Circle**), and turn north to Mahalakshmi Bridge, reachable by local trains from Churchgate. From the bridge there is a view across the astonishing Municipal **dhobi ghats**, where Mumbai's dirty laundry is soaked, smacked in concrete tubs and aired in public by the *dhobis* (washerfolk); vistas unfold in blocks of primary colours, though you may have to fend off junior touts to enjoy them in peace. A short distance further north are the disused Victorian cotton mills of **Lower Parel**. Closed in 1980 after an all-out strike, some remain standing in a state of picturesque ruin (local residents may offer to show you round for Rs 50-100) while others, notably the Phoenix, Mathuradas and Bombay Dyeing mill compounds, have been converted into slick new malls, nightclubs and studio spaces popular with publishers and advertising agencies.

Southeast of Mahalakshmi station in Byculla are the **Veermata Jijibai Bhonsle Udyan** gardens, formerly Victoria Gardens. The attractive 19-ha park is home to Mumbai's **zoo** ① *Thu-Tue 0900-1800, Rs 5*, be warned though, the signboards are missing and while the birds are gorgeous – they have birds of paradise, white peacocks and pink pelicans among others – there's no indication of what you're looking at. The gardens share space with the newly renovated **Bhau Daji Lad Museum** (**Victoria and Albert Museum**) ① *www.bdl museum.org, Thu-Tue, 1000-1730, foreigners Rs 100, Indians Rs 10, children half price*. Inspired by the V&A in London and financed by public subscription, it was built in 1872 in a palladian style and is the second oldest museum in India. The collection covers the history of Mumbai and contains prints, maps and models that show how the seven disjointed islands came to form Mumbai.

Bandra, Juhu Beach and Andheri

trendy northern suburbs, home of beaches and Bollywood stars

If you really want to get under the skin of the city, a jaunt into the suburbs of Bandra, Juhu Beach and Andheri is essential. Close to the airports and relatively relaxed compared to living in the city centre, Bandra and Juhu are popular with Mumbai's upper crust, and most Bollywood A-listers have at least one of their homes here. Bandra is a lively suburb, full of the young and wealthy, with some exciting places to eat and some of the coolest bars, coffee shops, gyms and lounges in the city. Linking Road is home to a long open-air shoe bazar where you can find cheap, colourful sandals and knock-offs of every brand of clothing. Bandra's two seaside promenades, one at Bandra Bandstand by the Taj Lands End Hotel and one at Carter Road, the next bay northwards, feature sea-facing coffee shops with spectacular sunset views.

Juhu Beach, 20 km north of the centre, still retains faint echoes of its past as a relaxed seaside area. Hordes of people still visit every day to walk on the beach, eat *bhel puri* and other spicy street food that delicate stomachs had best avoid, while kids buy balloons and take rides on horse-driven chariots. Beyond the beach Juhu is primarily a residential area, full of spas, luxe apartments and the odd remaining elegant old bungalow. (Bollywood megastar Amitabh Bachchan lives in one a couple of blocks inland on Vailunthlal Mehta Rd, and greets his fans from the balcony every Sunday morning.).

Andheri, spreading north of the airports, is the biggest suburb in Mumbai: it covers 50 sq km, is home to between 1.5 million and four million people depending on who's counting, and has sprung up from villages and mangrove swamps in a mere 30 years. There are few sights of note, but as a city within a city, with its own social subdivisions (mega-trendy residential enclaves and malls to the west, business parks and down-at-heel slums to the east, and a new suburban monorail system), Andheri is set to become Mumbai's second city centre. If you want to explore, the areas to know about are Lokhandwala, New Link Road and Seven Bungalows/Versova; all are in Andheri West.

Listings Mumbai maps p1090, p1091 and p1093

Tourist information

Government of India
123 M Karve Rd, opposite Churchgate, T022-2207 4333. Mon-Sat 0830-1730 (closed 2nd Sat of month from 1230); counters open 24 hrs at both airports; Taj Mahal Hotel, Mon-Sat 0830-1530 (closed 2nd Sat from 1230).

Maharashtra Tourist Development Corporation (MTDC)
CDO Hutments, Madam Cama Rd, T022-2204 4040, www.maharashtratourism.gov.in; Koh-i-Noor Rd, near Pritam Hotel, Dadar T022-2414 3200; Gateway of India, T022-2284 1877. Information and booking counters at international and domestic terminals and online.

Where to stay

Room prices in Mumbai are stratospheric by Indian standards, and there's no such thing as low-season: if possible make reservations in advance or arrive as early in the day as you can. Most hotels are concentrated in the downtown area, between Colaba and Marine Dr, and around the airport in the suburbs of Santa Cruz, Juhu, Bandra and Andheri. There are also several options around Mumbai Central and Dadar stations – handy for a quick getaway or an un-touristy view of the city.

Backpackers usually head for the **Colaba** area, which has some of the cheapest rooms in the city. **Arthur Bunder Rd** is a hotspot, with several places hidden away on upper floors of apartment blocks, usually with shared facilities, cold water and sometimes windowless rooms; arrive early and inspect room first. For a more personal view of the city, consider staying in a private home: there are some good **Airbnb options** (www. airbnb.com), or contact **India Tourism**, 123 M Karve Rd, Churchgate, T022-2203 3144.

Gateway of India and Colaba

$$$$ Taj Mahal Palace
Apollo Bunder, T022-6665 3366,
www.tajhotels.com.
The grand dame of Mumbai lodging, over a
century old. The glorious old wing has been
fully restored and updated after the 2008 terror
attacks, joining the 306 rooms in the **Taj Mahal
Intercontinental** tower. Several top-class
restaurants and bars, plus fitness centre, superb
pool and even a yacht on call.

$$$ Ascot
38 Garden Rd, Colaba, T022-6638 5566,
www.ascothotel.com.
The tan-wood rooms, shoehorned into a graceful
1930s building, veer dangerously close to IKEA
anonymity, but they're generously proportioned
and new, with safe deposit boxes, work desks and
granite shower stalls. Great views from the upper
floors. Breakfast included.

$$$ Godwin
41 Garden Rd, Colaba, T022-2287 2050,
www.hotelgodwin.in.
48 large, clean, renovated, a/c rooms with
superb views from upper floors, mostly helpful
management and a good rooftop restaurant –
full of wealthy Mumbaikars on Fri and Sat night.

$$$ Strand
25 PJ Ramchandani Marg, T022-2288 2222,
strand@vsnl.com.
Tottering old place on the sea front just along
from the Taj. Rooms and the dingy old lifts
have seen better days, but the front-facing
rooms have great sea views, shared by the
popular rooftop restaurant.

$$$ YWCA International Centre
Lane 18, Madame Cama Rd, Colaba,
T022-2202 0598, www.ywcaic.info.
For both sexes, 34 clean and pleasant rooms
with bath, and breakfast and buffet dinner
included in the price. A reliable and sociable
budget option, though the deposit required
to hold your booking is a slight hassle.

$ India Guest House
1/49 Kamal Mansion, near Radio Club,
Arthur Bunder Rd, T022-2283 3769.
20 rooms along long corridor, white partitions
that you could, at a push, jump over. Fan, no toilet
or shower. The corner room has a neat panorama
over the bay. Sound will travel.

$ Sea Shore
*Top floor, 1/49 Kamal Mansion, Arthur Bunder
Rd, T022-2287 4238.*
Kitsch as you like, 15 bright gloss-pink rooms and
purple corridors with plastic flowers, shower in
room but no sink, 7 with window and TV and fan,
8 without. Sea-view room has 4 beds. 2 rooms
come with toilet, TV and hot water.

Fort

$$$ Residency
Corner of DN Rd and Rustom Sidhwa Marg,
T022-6667 0555, www.residencyhotel.com.
Clean and modern rooms in an interesting 19th-
century building halfway between Flora Fountain
and CST. Great location and good value.

$$-$ Popular Palace
104-106 Mint Rd, near GPO, Fort Market,
T022-2269 5506, popularbro@gmail.com.
Small but clean rooms with bath (hot water),
some a/c, helpful staff, good value.

$$-$ Traveller's Inn
26 Adi Murzban Path, Ballard Estate, Fort,
T022-2264 4685, www.hoteltravellersinn.co.
A relatively new addition to Mumbai's backpacker
repertoire, with simple, clean rooms, a 3-bed
dormitory, internet and Wi-Fi, and friendly staff.

Around the CST (VT)

$$ City Palace
121 City Terrace, opposite CST Main Gate,
T022-2261 5515, www.hotelcitypalace.net.
Decrepit guesthouse with tiny but clean rooms
bang opposite the station. An OK place to crash
before catching an early train. Standard rates are
desperately overpriced; try booking via online
agents (see Hotels, page 46).

Marine Drive to Malabar Hill

$$$$ The Oberoi
Nariman Pt, T022-6632 5757,
www.oberoimumbai.com.
Newly renovated and reopened, with beautiful
sea-view rooms, glass-walled bathrooms, and
3 top-class restaurants.

$$$ Chateau Windsor Guest House
86 Vir Nariman Rd, Churchgate, T022-6622 4455,
*www.cwh.in. Friendly and helpful place in a
great location.*
The rooms on the 1st and 3rd floors are the best,
newly renovated with large spotless bathrooms,

marble tiles and balconies. Some of the older rooms are small, poky and dark. Recommended.

$$$ Regency
73 Nepean Sea Rd, T022-66571234, www.regencymumbai.com.
80 modest but immaculate rooms in quiet spot close to the sea at the base of upmarket Malabar Hill. Personable, friendly staff and free breakfast.

Central Mumbai

$$ YMCA International House
18 YMCA Rd, near Mumbai Central, T022-2307 0601.
Decent rooms, some with shared bath, meals included, temp membership Rs 140, deposit Rs 1300, good value, book 3 months ahead.

Bandra, Juhu Beach and Andheri

$$$$ Leela
Near International Terminal, T022-6691 1234, www.theleela.com.
One of the best of the airport hotels, with 460 modern rooms, excellent restaurants, pricey but excellent bar (residents only after 2300), all-night coffee shop, happening nightclub.

$$$ Juhu Residency
148B Juhu Tara Rd, Juhu Beach, T022-6783 4949, www.juhuresidency.com.
Across the road from Juhu Beach, with just 28 attractive refurbished rooms, free Wi-Fi, friendly efficient staff and 2 excellent restaurants. A decent deal by Mumbai standards.

$$$ Orchid
70C Nehru Rd, Vile Parle (east), 5 mins' walk from domestic terminal, T022-2616 4000, www.orchid hotel.com.
Refurbished, attractive rooms, eco-friendly. **Boulevard** restaurant boasts a good midnight buffet and '15-min lightning' buffet. Recommended.

$$ Transit
off Nehru Rd, Vile Parle (east), T022-2612 8882, www.hotel transit.in.
Modern, 54 rooms, reasonable overnight halt for airport, excellent restaurant (draught beer), airport transfer. Special rates for day use (0800-1800).

Restaurants

Gateway of India and Colaba

$$$ Indigo
4 Mandlik Rd, behind Taj Hotel, T022-6636 8999, www.foodindigo.com.
Excellent Mediterranean in smart restaurant, good atmosphere and wine list, additional seating on rooftop.

$$$ Khyber
145 MG Rd, Kala Ghoda, T022-4039 6666.
North Indian. For an enjoyable evening in beautiful surroundings, outstanding food, especially lobster and *reshmi* chicken kebabs, try *paya* soup (goats' trotters).

$$$ Ling's Pavilion
19/21 Mahakavi Bhushan Marg, off Colaba Causeway (behind Taj and Regal Cinema), T022-2285 0023.
Stylish decor, good atmosphere and delightful service, colourful menu, seafood specials, generous helpings. Recommended.

$$ Café Churchill
103-8, East West Court Building, opposite Cusrow Baug, Colaba Causeway, T022-2284 4689. Open 1000-2330.
A tiny café with 7 tables crammed with people basking in a/c, towered over by a cake counter and a Winston Churchill portrait. Great breakfasts, club sandwiches, seafood, fish and chips, lasagne and Irish stew.

$$ Leopold's
Colaba Causeway, T022-2282 8185.
An institution among Colaba backpackers and Mumbai shoppers. The food, predominantly Western with a limited choice of Indian vegetarian, is average and pricey (similar cafés nearby are far better value) but **Leo's** gained cachet from its cameo role in the novel *Shantaram*, and was the first target of the terror attacks in Nov 2008.

$ Bade Miyan
Tullock Rd behind Ling's Pavilion, T022-2202 1447.
Streetside kebab corner, but very clean. Try *baida roti*, *shammi* and *boti* kebabs. The potato *kathi* rolls are excellent veg options.

$ Kailash Parbat
1st Pasta La, Colaba.
Excellent snacks and *chats*, in an old-style eatery also serving Punjabi *thalis*. The milky-sweet *pedas* from the counterare a Mumbai institution.

$ Kamat Samarambh
Opposite Electric House, Colaba Causeway.
Very good and authentic South Indian food,
thalis and snacks. Try the moist, fluffy *uttapam*
and *upma*. Clean drinking water.

Cafés and snacks

Theobroma
24 Cusrow Baug, Colaba Causeway.
Decent coffee and terrific egg breakfasts.
The brownies here are to die for: try the
millionaire brownie or the rum-and-raisin
with coffee. Egg-free cakes available.

Fort

$$$ Trishna
*Sai Baba Marg, Kala Ghoda, next to Commerce
House, T022-2270 3213.*
Good coastal cuisine, seafood, excellent butter
garlic crab. Recommended.

$$ Britannia
*Wakefield House, 11 Sprott Rd, opposite New
Custom House, Ballard Estate, T022-22615264.
Mon-Sat 1200-1600.*
Incredible Parsi/Iranian fare with a delicious berry
pullav made from specially imported Bol berries
(cranberries from Iran). Try the *dhansak* and the
egg curry. Recommended.

Around the CST (VT)

$$ Badshah Cold Drinks & Snacks
*Lokmanya Tilak Marg opposite Crawford
Market, T022-2342 1943.*
Famous for its *kulfi* (hand-churned ice cream)
and fresh fruit juices (drink without ice), it's a
default stop for everyone shopping at Crawford
Market. Good and fast *pav-bhaji* (mixed veg with
buttered rolls).

Marine Drive to Malabar Hill

$$ Gaylord
Vir Nariman Rd, opposite Churchgate.
Charmingly old-school place, superb for North
Indian and European dishes. The attached bakery
does superb pastries.

$$ Shree Thaker Bhojanalay
*31 Dadisheth Agyari Lane, off Kalbadevi Rd,
Marine Lines, T022-2206 9916.*
Hidden up a set of grimy looking stairs in the off-
the-beaten track area of Kalbadevi (inland from

Marine Drive), this decades-old diner serves one
of the city's very best (and priciest) Gujarati *thalis*.
Delicious sweet-spicy dishes keep coming until
you beg for mercy. Definitely worth the cab ride.

$ Tea Centre
78 Vir Nariman Rd, near Churchgate.
A little old-fashioned and colonial, but dozens
of refreshing tea options, and a menu of heavy
Indian food. Good value and a/c.

Central Mumbai

$ Swati Snacks
*Karai Estate, Tardeo Rd, opposite Bhatia
Hospital, T022-6580 8405.*
Gujarati and Parsi snacks along with street foods
made in a hygienic fashion: try *khichdi, sev puri,
pav bhaji, dahi puri* here. Be prepared for a 20-
to 40-min wait, but it's worth it.

Bandra, Juhu Beach and Andheri
Carter Rd in Bandra is lined with snack joints.

$$$ Olive
Union Park, Pali Hill, Bandra, T022-2605 8228.
'Progressive Mediterranean' food, served in an
upscale environment to a cast of Bollywood
celebs. Packed on Thu, when there's live music,
and for brunch on Sun. Also has a branch at
Mahalaxmi racecourse, T022-4085 9595.

$$$ Pali Village Cafe
Ambedkar Rd, Bandra (W), T022-2605 0401.
Super-trendy new restaurant done out in shabby-
chic industrial style, cascading across different
rooms and levels. Good desserts and tapas-style
starters, though the wine list and general vibe
outweigh the quality of food and service.

$$ Gajalee
*Kadambari Complex, Hanuman Rd, Vile Parle
(E), T022-6692 9592, www.gajalee.com; also in
Phoenix Mills.*
Fine coastal cuisine; try fish tikka, stuffed bombay
duck and shellfish with the traditional breads
ghawne and *amboli*.

$$ Out of the Blue
*14 Union Park, off Carter Rd, Khar West,
T022-2600 3000.*
Romantic candlelit restaurant with a Goan
beach-shack vibe. Great sizzlers, and live music
most nights.

Bars and clubs

Gateway of India and Colaba

Wink
Vivanta by Taj President, 90 Cuffe Parade, T022-6665 0975.
Sleek and dark bar serves up first class cocktails, with huge couches for late-night lounging and DJs on Fri and Sat.

Woodside Inn
Opposite Regal Cinema, Colaba.
Cramped pub carved out of stone Gothic building, with decent retro music, good dining upstairs (pizzas and sandwiches are surprisingly decent) and good selection of whiskies. Free Wi-Fi too.

Fort

LIV
Above Khyber Restaurant, MG Rd, Kala Ghoda, T022-6634 6247.
Bollywood dance nights, trippy lights over the dancefloor and a generally cool crowd make this one of SoBo's best nights out.

Marine Drive to Malabar Hill

Dome
Intercontinental Hotel, Marine Dr, T022-3987 9999.
Rooftop restaurant and lounge bar with a stunning view of the Queen's Necklace. Try the grilled prawns with your cocktails.

Pizza by the Bay
143 Marine Dr, T022-2285 1876.
Fun place near Churchgate, with live music, karaoke, good food menu (great starters and desserts), generous portions, wide selection of drinks. Loud and lively.

Central Mumbai

Blue Frog
Mathuradas Mills Compound, NM Joshi Marg, Lower Parel, T022-3015 1765.
Now firmly established as one of Mumbai's best live music and comedy venues, Blue Frog wins for ambience and good food.

Bandra, Juhu Beach and Andheri

China House
Grand Hyatt, off Western Expressway, Santacruz East, T022-6676 1149.
This Chinese restaurant by day transforms after midnight into NoBo's favourite early hours

speakeasy, with crowds pouring in to dance to Bollywood and dodgy Hip Hop and sip expensive drinks.

Toto's
30th Rd, off Pali Naka, Bandra (W).
Retro music, regular clients, and no attitude amid funky automotive decor.

Entertainment

Check *Time Out Mumbai* for upcoming events.

Cinema

Bollywood and international films are screened in dozens of cinemas, most of which are in multi-plexes and malls; timings are listed in local news-papers. Multiplexes in South Mumbai include **INOX** (Nariman Point), **Big Cinemas Metro** (southwest corner of Azad Maidan). Few independent theatres remain: try **Eros** (opposite Churchgate station), **Regal** (Colaba), or **Sterling** (near CST).

Theatre and classical music

Multilingual Mumbai puts on plays in English, Hindi, Marathi and Gujarati, usually beginning at 1815-1900.
National Centre for Performing Arts, *next to Hilton Towers, Nariman Point, T022-6622 3737, www.ncpamumbai.com.* Has regular classical music concerts and an Experimental Theatre, which is predictably hit-and-miss.

Festivals

In addition to the national Hindu and Muslim festivals (see pages 34 and 37) there are the following:
Feb Elephanta Cultural Festival at the caves. Great ambience. Contact **MTDC**, T022-2202 6713, for tickets Rs 150-200 including launch at 1800. **Kala Ghoda Arts Festival**, held in various locations around Colaba and Fort, T022-2284 2520, showcases of all forms of fine arts.
Mar Jamshed Navroz. This is New Year's Day for the Parsi followers of the Fasli calendar. The celebrations, which include offering prayers at temples, exchanging greetings, alms-giving and feasting at home, date back to Jamshed, the legendary King of Persia.
Jul-Aug Janmashtami celebrates the birth of Lord Krishna. Boys and young men form human pyramids and break pots of curd hung up high between buildings.
Aug Coconut Day. The angry monsoon seas are propitiated by devotees throwing coconuts into the ocean.

Aug-Sep Ganesh Chaturthi. Massive figures of Ganesh are towed through the streets to loud techno and storms of coloured powder, before a final *puja* at Chowpatty Beach where they're finally dragged out into the sea. The crowds making their way on foot to the beach cause immense traffic pile ups, and the scene at Chowpatty is chaotic, with priests giving *puja* to Ganesh and roaring crowds of men psyching themselves up for the final push into the ocean. A similar celebration happens shortly after at **Durga Pooja**, when the goddess Durga is worshipped and immersed.

Sep-Oct Dussehra. Group dances by Gujarati women in all the auditoria and residents have their own *garba* and *dandiya* dance nights in the courtyards of their apartment buildings. There are also **Ram leela** celebrations at Chowpatty Beach, where the story of the *Ramayana* is enacted in a dance drama. **Diwali** (The Festival of Lights) is particularly popular in mercantile Mumbai when the business community celebrate their New Year and open new account books. **Eid ul-Fitr**, the celebration when Ramzan with its 40 days of fasting is also observed. Since both the Hindu and Islamic calendar are lunar, there is often overlap between the holidays.

25 Dec Christmas. Christians across Mumbai celebrate the birth of Christ. A pontifical High Mass is held at midnight in the open air at the Cooperage Grounds, Colaba.

Shopping

Most shops are open Mon-Sat 1000-1900, the bazars sometimes staying open as late as 2100. Mumbai prices are often higher than in other Indian cities, and hotel arcades tend to be very pricey but carry good-quality select items. Best buys are textiles, particularly tie-dye from Gujarat, hand-block printed cottons, Aurangabad and 'Patola' silks, gold-bordered saris from Surat and Khambat, handicrafts, jewellery and leather goods. It is illegal to take anything over 100 years old out of the country. CDs of contemporary Indian music in various genres make good souvenirs as well as gifts.

Bazars

Crawford Market (Ambedkar Rd), fun for bargain hunting, and **Mangaldas Market**. Other shopping streets are South Bhagat Singh Marg, M Karve Rd and Linking Rd, Bandra. For a different experience try **Chor (Thieves') Bazar** (on Maulana Shaukat Ali Rd in Central Mumbai), full of finds from Raj leftovers to precious jewellery. Make time to stop at the **Mini Market** (33-31 Mutton St, T022-2347 2425, minimarket@rediffmail.com), nose through the Bollywood posters, lobby cards, and photo-stills. On Fri, 'junk' carts sell less expensive 'antiques' and fakes.

Books

There are lines of second-hand stalls along Churchgate St and near the University. An annual book fair takes place at the Cross Maidan near Churchgate each Dec.
Crossword, *under the flyover at Kemps Corner bridge (east of Malabar Hill)*. Smart, spacious, good selection.
Nalanda, *Taj Mahal Hotel*. Excellent art books, Western newspapers/magazines.
Strand Books, *off Sir PM Rd near HMV, T022-2206 1994*. Excellent selection, best deals, reliable shipping.

Clothes

Benzer, *B Desai Rd, Breach Candy. Daily*. Good saris and Indian garments.
The Courtyard, *41/44 Minoo Desai Marg, Colaba*. Very elite and fashionable mini-mall includes boutiques full of stunning heavy deluxe designs (Swarovski crystal-studded saris, anyone?) by **Rohit Bal** and **Rabani & Rakha** (Rs 17,000 for a sari) but probably most suitable to the Western eye is textile designer **Neeru Kumar's Tulsi**, a cotton textiles designer from Delhi. Beautiful linen/silk stoles and fine *kantha* thread work. There's also a store from top menswear designer **Rajesh Pratap Singh**.
Ensemble, *130-132 South Bhagat Singh Marg, T022-2287 2882*. Superb craftsmanship and service for women's clothes – Indian and 'East meets West'.
Fabindia, *Jeroo Building, 137MG Rd, Kala Ghoda, and 66 Pali Hill, Bandra, www.fabindia.com*. Fair-trade handloom Western and Indian wear including *kurtas*, pants, etc, for men, women and children (also bamboo, earthenware and jute home furnishings, *khadi* and *mulmul* cloth).

Crafts and textiles

Government emporia from many states sell good handicrafts and textiles; several at **World Trade Centre** (Cuffe Parade). In Colaba, a street **Craft Market** is held on Sun (Nov-Jan) in K Dubash Marg.
Anokhi, *4B August Kranti Marg, opposite Kumbala Hill Hospital*. Gifts and handicrafts.
Bombay Electric, *1 Reay House, BEST Marg, Colaba, T022-2287 6276, www.bombayelectric.in*. Pricey, chic, trendsetter art and couture.

ON THE ROAD

Bright lights of Bollywood

Mumbai produces around 860 films a year, making Bollywood the world's second largest film-maker after Hong Kong. The stars live in sumptuous dwellings, many of which are on Malabar Hill, Mumbai's Beverley Hills, and despite the spread of foreign videos, their popularity seems to be undiminished.

It is difficult to get permission to visit a studio during filming but you might try **Film City**, Goregaon East, T022-2840 1533 or **Mehboob Studios**, Hill Road, Bandra West, T022-2642 8045. Alternatively, the staff at the **Salvation Army Hostel** (see Where to stay) may be able to help foreigners get on as 'extras'; Rs 500 per day.

Bombay Store, *Western India House, 1st floor, PM Rd, Fort, www.bombaystore.com. Daily.* Ethnic lifestyle supplies, from home decor and fancy paper to clothing, gifts; best one-stop shop, value for money.

Cottage Industries Emporium, *Apollo Bunder, Colaba.* A nationwide selection, especially Kashmiri embroidery, South Indian handicrafts and Rajasthani textiles. Colaba Causeway, next to BEST, for ethnicware, handicrafts and fabrics.

Curio Cottage, *19 Mahakavi Bhushan Rd, near the Regal Cinema, Colaba, T022-2202 2607.* Silver jewellery and antiques. Natesan in Jehangir Gallery basement; also in Taj Hotel. For fine antiques and copies.

Phillips, *Madame Cama Rd, Colaba.* A pricey Aladdin's cave of bric-a-brac and curios.

Sadak Ali, *behind Taj Hotel, Colaba.* Good range of carpets, but bargain hard.

Jewellery

The **Cottage Industries Emporium**, near Radio Club, Colaba Causeway, has affordable silver and antique jewellery from across India.

Popli Suleman Chambers, *Battery St, Apollo Bunder, Colaba, T022-2285 4757.* Semi-precious stones, gems, garnets and pearls.

Music

Musical instruments on VB Patel Rd, **RS Mayeka** at No 386, **Haribhai Vishwanath** at No 419 and Ram Singh at Bharati Sadan.

Planet M, *opposite CST station; smaller branches in most malls.* Also has book/poetry readings, gigs.

Rhythm House, *next to Jehangir Gallery.* Excellent selection of jazz and classical CDs. Also sells tickets for classical concerts.

Silks and saris

Biba, *next to Crossword, Kemp's Corner, Phoenix Mills, Lower Parel, Bandra (W).* Affordable designer wear for ladies, alterations possible.

Nalli, *Shop No 7, Thirupathi Apartments, Bhulabhai Desai Rd, T022-2353 5577.* Something for every budget.

What to do

Adventure tourism

Maharashtra Tourism, *T022-2204 4040, www. maharashtratourism.gov.in.* Actively encourages adventure tourism (including jungle safaris and water sports) by introducing 'rent-a-tent', hiring out trekking gear and organizing overnight trips; some accommodation included. Prices range from US$35-150 per day/weekend depending on season and activity. It has also set up 27 holiday resorts around the state providing cheap accommodation at hill stations, beaches, archaeological sites and scenic spots. Details from tourist offices.

Odati Adventures, *T(0) 97696 79802, www.odati. com.* Camping, weekend hiking, bike rides, rock climbing and waterfall rappelling around the Mumbai area. If you go rappelling in Malshej Ghat during the monsoon, you'll glimpse thousands of flamingos. Bikes can be hired. Call or book online. Weekend cycle tours are Rs 2000-3000.

Body and soul

Kaivalyadhama, *on Marine Drive next to Taraporewala Aquarium, T022-2281 8417.* Good therapeutic yoga classes.

Iyengar Yogashraya, *Elmac House, 126 Senapati Bapat Marg (off Tulsi Pipe Rd opposite Kamla Mills), Lower Parel, T022-2494 8416, www.bksiyengar.com.* Iyengar drop-in centre. Call before dropping in.

Tour operators

If you wish to sightsee independently with a guide, ask at the tourist office. See page 1099.

Be the Local, *T(0)9930-027370, www.bethelocal toursandtravels.com.* Fascinating walking tours of Dharavi, which take you through some of the cottage industries – from traditional Gujarati pottery to plastic – which sustain Mumbai from within Asia's largest slum. Owned and run by local students, the tours are neither voyeuristic nor intrusive, and photography is prohibited. Rs 400 per person includes transport from Colaba; private tours Rs 3500 for up to 5 people. **Bombay Heritage Walks**, *T022-2369 0992, www. bombayheritagewalks.com*. Informative walking tours specializing in Mumbai's built history, founded by a pair of local architects.

City sightseeing Approved guides from the **India tourist office** (T022-2203 3144). City tour usually includes visits to The Gateway of India, the Chhatrapati Shivaji (Prince of Wales) Museum, Jain temple, Hanging Gardens, Kamla Nehru Park and Mani Bhavan (Gandhi Museum). Suburban tour includes Juhu Beach, Kanheri Caves and Lion Safari Park.

MTDC, *Madam Cama Rd, opposite LIC Building, T022-2284 5678*. City tour Tue-Sun 0900-1300 and 1400-1800, Rs 100. Evening open-top bus tour of Colaba, Marine Drive and Fort, runs Sat and Sun at 1900 and 2015; Rs 150 (lower deck Rs 50). Elephanta tours from Gateway of India. Boat 0900-1415, Rs 130 return; reserve at Apollo Bunder, T022-2284 1877.

Mumbai Magic, *T(0)98677-07414, www.mumbai magic.com*. A vast range of tours covering every inch of the city from Colaba to Bandra and beyond. Highlights include South Indian cuisine tours of Matunga, a walk through the Chor Bazar, and the Mumbai Local tour which hops you around the city by taxi, local train and bus. Personalized itineraries available. Professional and highly recommended.

Transport

Mumbai is one of the 2 main entry points to India, with daily international flights from every continent and frequent domestic connections with every major city in India, and most minor ones.

All flights touch down at **Chhatrapati Shivaji International Airport**, enquiries T022-6685 0222, www.csia.in. The international terminal, freshly redone with some very interesting artworks, is 30 km north of the city. There are exchange counters, ATMs, tourist offices, domestic airline and railway reservation counters, and a cloakroom for left luggage.

The domestic airport, recently renovated with 2 separate terminals – 1A for **Air India** (enquiries T022-6685 1351), 1B for **Jet Airways** and all budget airlines (enquiries T022-2626 1149), is

4 km closer to the city in Santa Cruz and has most of the same facilities. Free shuttle buses link the domestic and international terminals every few mins.

Transport to and from the airport Pre-paid taxis, from counters at the exits, are the simplest way of getting downtown. Give the exact area or hotel and the number of pieces of luggage, and pay at the booth on your way out of the airport. On the receipt will be scribbled the number of your taxi: ask the drivers outside to help you find it, and hand the receipt to the driver at the end of the journey. There is no need to tip, though drivers will certainly drop heavy hints. To **Nariman Point** or **Gateway of India**, about Rs 500, 1-2 hrs depending on traffic. To **Juhu Beach** Rs 300. Metered taxis picked up outside the terminal should be marginally cheaper than a pre-paid, but make sure the driver starts the meter when you get in. The cheaper alternatives – crowded and slow **BEST** buses that connect both terminals with the city, and even more crowded local **trains** – have only economy in their favour. The closest railway stations are **Vile Parle** (for international) and **Santa Cruz** (domestic), both on the Western line to Mumbai Central and Churchgate.

Bus
Local Red **BEST** (Brihanmumbai Electrical Supply Co) buses are available in most parts of Greater Mumbai. There's a handy route finder at www.bestundertaking.com/route.asp; click on the 'Area' tab. Fares are cheap, but finding the correct bus is tricky as the numbers and destinations on the front are only in Marathi; English signs are displayed only beside the back doors. Ask locals to help point out a bus going your way.

Long distance Maharashtra SRTC operates from the Mumbai Central Bus Stand, T022-2307 4272, http://msrtconline.in/timetable.aspx, to most big towns in Maharashtra as well as major destinations in neighbouring states.

Private buses also serve long-distance destinations: most leave from the streets surrounding Mumbai Central, where there are ticket agents, while others leave from Dadar; information and tickets from **Dadar Tourist Centre**, outside Dadar station, T022-2411 3398. Some private buses can be booked in advance on www.redbus.in.

Car
Costs for hiring a car are (for 8 hrs or 80 km): luxury a/c cars Rs 2500; **Indica/Indigo**, a/c

Rs 1700, Companies include: **Auto Hirers**, 7 Commerce Centre, Tardeo, T022-2351 2006 and **Sudarshan Cars, T022**-2431 2700, www.sudarshancars.co.in.

Auto-rickshaw

Not available in Central Mumbai (south of Mahim). Metered; about Rs 11 per km, revised tariff card held by the driver, 25% extra at night (midnight-0500). Some rickshaw drivers show the revised tariff card for taxis!

Taxi

Metered yellow-top cabs and more expensive a/c Cool Cabs are easily available. Meter rates start at around Rs 14 per km. Drivers should carry tariff cards that convert the meter fee into current prices; a new fleet of yellow-top Indica cars have digital meters that show the correct price. Always get a pre-paid taxi at the airport.

A/c radio taxis can be pre-booked. They charge around Rs 20 per km and provide metered receipts at the end of your journey. Tip the driver about 10% if you feel they had to do a lot of waiting. **Megacab**, T022-4242 4242. **Meru Cab**, T022-4422 4422.

Train

Local Suburban electric trains are an economical and fast way to cover long distances in the city and offer an indispensable insight into Mumbai's daily life, but they're desperately overcrowded during peak hours (south-bound 0700-1100, northbound 1700-2000). If you attempt to travel during these times you'll need to stay near the door not to miss your stop, and beware of the local habit of leaping from the train while it's still slowing down into the station (a necessary tactic when there are thousands of people waiting on the platform to push you back in). From South Mumbai, trains start from **Churchgate** for the northern and western suburbs and from **CST (VT)** for the east. There are 'ladies' cars' in the middle and ends. The difference between 1st and 2nd class is not always obvious although 1st class is 10 times more expensive (and usually less crowded). Inspectors fine people for travelling in the wrong class or without a ticket. If you're travelling frequently, invest in a smart card that lets you avoid queues at the ticket counter by printing tickets from a machine.

Long distance Mumbai is the HQ of the **Central and Western Railways**, and is connected by train with every corner of India. Trains pull into several terminals spread all over the city. CST (still widely known as VT; **Indian Railways** booking code CSTM) is the handiest arrival point, close to the main sights and hotels, with trains to/from many popular destinations to the east, north and south. Other trains depart from Mumbai Central (BCT), 4 km north; Dadar (DR/DDR), 10 km north; Bandra (BDTS) in the far northwest; and Lokmanya Tilak Terminus (LTT), in the northern suburb of Kurla. Some long-distance north–south trains (eg Delhi–Kerala) get no closer to the city than Panvel, way out to the northeast; if you end up here, save an expensive taxi ride by jumping on one of the frequent trains coming from Pune. Long-distance trains on popular routes (eg Mumbai–Goa) are invariably heavily booked, especially during holidays; book in advance to be sure of a seat. **Foreign Tourist** counters at Churchgate and CST (opens 0900; arrive early) handle bookings on Indrail Passes and Foreign Tourist Quota; bring your passport and an ATM receipt or currency encashment certificate.

Train timetables change frequently. Check up-to-date departure times on Indiarailinfo.com. **Ahmedabad**, frequent departures, 7-9 hrs. **Agra**: 10 daily, 20-24 hrs. **Aurangabad**: 4 daily, 7 hrs. **Bengaluru**: 1-3 daily, 24 hrs. **Bhopal**: 7 daily, 13-15 hrs. **Chennai**: 3 daily, 24-28 hrs. **Ernakulam (Kochi)**: 2-3 daily, 24-36 hrs. **Guntakal (for Hospet/Hampi)**: 7 daily, 15-17 hrs. **Gwalior**: 3 daily, 21-24 hrs (all via **Jhansi**, 18-21 hrs). **Hyderabad**: 5 daily, 14-17 hrs. **Indore**: 1-3 daily, 14 hrs, via **Ujjain**, 12 hrs. **Jaipur**: 2-4 daily, 18-22 hrs, via **Kota** (for Bundi) and **Sawai Madhopur** (for Ranthambore). **Kolkata**: 4-6 daily, 28-38 hrs. **Lucknow**: 3-5 daily, 24 hrs. **Madgaon** (for Goa): 7 daily, 11-15 hrs. **New Delhi**: at least 10 a day, mostly from BCT, 17-24 hrs. **Pune**: dozens a day, 31/4-4 hrs. **Thiruvananthapuram**: 2-3 daily, 30 hrs. **Udaipur**: 1 train daily except Mon, 17 hrs. **Varanasi**: at least 7 a day, 24-28 hrs.

Around
Mumbai

For a quick getaway from the city it's hard to beat the cool, car-free refuge of Matheran, reached by a beautiful narrow-gauge railway up the Western Ghats. A ferry ride across the bay can take you to the famous Elephanta Caves or to the reasonably good sandy beaches of Chaul and Kihim. To the north stands the old Portuguese fort of Bassein and Buddhist caves in a national park.

Elephanta Caves

heavily forested island with temple caves

Ten kilometres east of the Gateway of India, the Elephanta Island, barely visible in the haze from Mumbai, rises out of the bay like a giant whale. The setting is symbolically significant; the sea is the ocean of life, a world of change (Samsara) in which is set an island of spiritual and physical refuge. The 'caves', excavated over 1000 years ago in the volcanic lava high up the slope of the hill, saw Hindu craftsmen express their view of spiritual truths in massive carvings of extraordinary grace. Sadly, a large proportion have been severely damaged, but enough remains to illustrate something of their skill.

Essential Elephanta Caves

Getting around

Boats to Elephanta Island leave every few minutes from 0900, from the jetty in front of the Gateway of India. The crossing takes about an hour. From the landing place, a 300-m unshaded path along the quayside and then about 110 rough steps lead to the caves at a height of 75 m. The walk along the quay can be avoided when the small train functions (Rs 10 return). The climb can be trying for some, especially if it is hot, though *doolies* (chairs carried by porters) are available for Rs 300 return, Rs 200 one-way. At the start of the climb there are stalls selling refreshments, knick-knacks and curios (including models of the Eiffel Tower), but if you're carrying food watch out for aggressive monkeys.

When to go

Early morning is the best time for light and also for avoiding large groups with guides which arrive from 1000.

Tip...

Maharashtra Tourism normally organizes a festival of classical music and dance on the island in the third week of February.

BACKGROUND

Elephanta Caves

The vast majority of India's 1200 cave sites were created as temples and monasteries between the third century BC and the 10th century AD. Jain, Buddhist and Hindu caves often stand side by side. The temple cave on Elephanta Island, dedicated to Siva, was probably excavated during the eighth century by the Rashtrakuta Dynasty which ruled the Deccan AD 757-973, though the caves may have had earlier Buddhist origins. An earlier name for the island was Garhapuri ('city of forts') but the Portuguese renamed it after the colossal sculpted elephants when they captured Mumbai from the Sultan of Gujarat in 1535, and stationed a battalion there. They reportedly used the main pillared cave as a shooting gallery causing some of the damage you see. Muslim and British rulers were not blameless either.

The site

Tue-Sun, sunrise to sunset; foreigners Rs 250, Indians Rs 10, plus Rs 5 passenger tax. Weekends are very busy. The caves tend to be quite dark so carry a powerful torch.

Entrance Originally there were three entrances and 28 pillars at the site. The entrances on the east and west had subsidiary shrines which may have been excavated and used for different ceremonies. The main entrance is now from the north. At dawn, the rising sun casts its rays on the approach to the *garbagriha* (main shrine), housed in a square structure at the west end of the main hall. On your right is a carving of Siva as Nataraj. On the left he appears as Lakulisa in a much damaged carving. Seated on a lotus, the Buddha-like figure is a symbol of the unconscious mind and enlightenment, found also in Orissan temples where Lakulisa played a prominent role in attempting to attract Buddhists back into Hinduism. From the steps at the entrance you can see the *yoni-lingam*, the symbol of the creative power of the deity.

Main Hall The ribbed columns in the main hall, 5-6 m high and in a cruciform layout, are topped by a capital. At the corner of each pillar is a dwarf signifying *gana* (the earth spirit), and sometimes the figure of Ganesh (Ganapati). To the right, the main **Linga Shrine** has four entrances, each corresponding to a cardinal point guarded by a *dvarpala*. The sanctum is bare, drawing attention to the *yonilingam* which the devotee must walk around clockwise.

Wall panels To the north of the main shrine is **Bhairava killing the demon Andhakasura**. This extraordinarily vivid carving shows Siva at his most fearsome, with a necklace of skulls, crushing the power of Andhaka, the Chief of Darkness. It was held that if he was wounded each drop of his blood would create a new demon. So Siva impaled him with his sword and collected his blood with a cup, which he then offered to his wife Shakti. In winter this panel is best seen in the early afternoon.

Opposite, on the south side of the main shrine is the damaged panel of **Kalyan Sundari**, in which Siva stands with Parvati on his right, just before their wedding (normally a Hindu wife stands on her husband's left). She looks down shyly, but her body is drawn to him. Behind Parvati is her father Himalaya and to his left Chandramas, the moon god carrying a gift – *soma*, the food of the gods. On Siva's left is Vishnu and below him Brahma.

At the extreme west end of the temple are **Nataraja** (left) and **Yogisvara Siva** (right). The former shows a beautiful figure of Ganesh above and Parvati on his left. All the other gods watch him. Above his right shoulder is the four-headed God of Creation, Brahma. Below Brahma is the elephant-headed Ganesh.

On the south wall, opposite the entrance are three panels. **Gangadhara** is on the west. The holy River Ganga (Bhagirathi) flowed only in heaven but was brought to earth by her father King Bhagiratha (kneeling at Siva's right foot). Here, Ganga is shown in the centre, flanked by her two tributaries, Yamuna and Saraswati. These three rivers are believed to meet at Allahabad.

To the left of these is the centre piece of the whole temple, the remarkable **Mahesvara**, the Lord of the Universe. Here Siva is five-headed, for the usual triple-headed figure has one face looking into the rock and another on top of his head. Nearly 6 m high, he unites all the functions of creation, preservation and destruction. Some see the head on the left (your right) as representing Vishnu, the Creator, while others suggest that it shows a more feminine aspect of Siva. To his right is Rudra or Bhairava, with snakes in his hair, a skull to represent ageing from which only Siva is free, and he has a look of anger. The central face is Siva as his true self, Siva Swarupa, balancing out creation and destruction. In this mode he is passive and serene, radiating peace and wisdom like the Buddha. His right hand is held up in a calming gesture and in his left hand is a lotus bud.

The panel to the left has the **Ardhanarisvara**. This depicts Siva as the embodiment of male and female, representing wholeness and the harmony of opposites. The female half is relaxed and gentle, the mirror in the hand symbolizing the woman reflecting the man. Siva has his 'vehicle', Nandi on the right.

To the east, opposite the *garbha-griha*, was probably the original entrance. On the south is Siva and Parvati **Playing chaupar on Mount Kailash**. Siva is the faceless figure. Parvati has lost and is sulking but her playful husband persuades her to return to the game. They are surrounded by Nandi, Siva's bull, celestial figures and an ascetic with his begging bowl.

On the north is **Ravana Shaking Mount Kailash** on which Siva is seated. Siva is calm and unperturbed by Ravana's show of brute strength and reassures the frightened Parvati. He pins down Ravana with his toe, who fails to move the mountain and begs Siva's forgiveness which is granted.

Along the coast *Colour map 5, B3.*

day trips from Mumbai to historic forts and sandy beaches

South of the city
From the New Ferry Wharf at the Gateway of India in Mumbai, it is a 90-min trip to Mandwa (Rs 60-110) then a 6-km bus or auto ride to Kihim; or 30-km bus ride to Chaul.

From the Gateway of India, ferries chug across Mumbai harbour to Mandwa, the jumping off point for a group of Maratha and Portuguese forts and sandy beaches. Though there's nothing much to detain you here if you're bound for Goa and the southern Konkan, they make a pleasant long day trip or weekend away from the city.

Kihim, 10 km south of Mandwa, has clean sand, safe waters and very pleasant surroundings, but the summer sun can be murderously hot.

Another 10 km south is the popular beach town of **Alibag**, where at low tide you can walk across the muddy sand to Kolaba for; it is not worth the Rs 100 entrance fee.

South again is the attractive fort at **Chaul**, build in 1522 by the Portuguese. Similar to Bassein to the north of Mumbai, it never equalled it in importance. The Marathas took it in 1739 and in 1818 it passed into British hands. Little remains of the settlement apart from ruined churches and broken walls. If you look across the creek you will see the hilltop Muslim fort of Korlai.

North Konkan *Colour map 5, B2/3.*
The lowland North Konkan coast forms a narrow strip between the Arabian Sea and the often daunting west facing slopes of the Ghats. Beaches and rice growing valleys are interspersed with poor laterite covered hills.

Bassein (Vasai) ① *Trains go from Mumbai Central to Vasai Rd station, then hire a taxi for 11 km.*
Bassein, at the mouth of the Ulhas River on the mainland, is 60 km north of central Mumbai. Due to silting, the fort on the Bassein Creek is now some distance from the sea. The structure is in ruins, but it is well worth walking round the sea face. Originally built by Bahadur Shah, Sultan of Gujarat, it was one of a chain of forts against the Portuguese. However, the chain was breached, and the Portuguese remodelled the city along their own lines, renaming it **Vasai**. From 1534 to 1739 it became so prosperous as a centre of shipbuilding and the export of Bassein stone that it was called the Court of the North. As a walled city it contained a cathedral, five convents, 13 churches and the splendid houses and palaces of the aristocracy, or Hidalgos, who with members of the religious orders, alone were allowed to live within the walls. The Marathas took Vasai in February 1739 after a long and desperate siege. Almost the whole Portuguese garrison, 800 strong, was killed in the

battle; the Marathas are thought to have lost 5000 men. In 1780 the British evicted the Marathas, only to return it to them three years later under the Treaty of Salbai.

Approached from the north, the fort in the town contains the ruins of St Joseph's Cathedral (1536), St Anthony's, the Jesuit church and the convents, all belonging to Franciscans, Dominicans, Jesuits or Augustinians. **Nalasopara**, 10 km northwest, is the ancient Konkan capital where Buddhist relics have been found.

Sanjay Gandhi National Park
ancient Buddhist caves in a forest setting

Sanjay Gandhi National Park, north of the city at Goregaon, is worth a visit in itself for its dense deciduous and semi-evergreen forest providing a beautiful habitat for several varieties of deer, antelope, butterflies, birds and the occasional leopard. However, the main reason for visiting is for the Kanheri Caves situated in the heart of the park.

Kanheri Caves
The park is also home to hyena and panther, though rarely seen, while three lakes have ducks, herons and crocodiles. Nature trails lead from Film City (reached by bus from Goregaon station). A lion safari leaves from **Hotel Sanjay** near Borivli station.

Some 42 km north of Mumbai, the caves (also known as Mahakali Caves) are on a low hill midway between Borivli and Thane. The hills used to form the central part of Salsette Island, but the surrounding land has long since been extensively built on. Further up the ravine from the caves there are some fine views across the Bassein Fort and out to sea. Still shaded by trees, the entrance is from the south.

There are 109 Buddhist caves, dating from the end of the second to the ninth century AD with flights of steps joining them. The most significant is the **Chaitya Cave** (cave 3) circa sixth century. The last Hinayana chaitya hall to be excavated is entered through a forecourt and veranda. The pillared entrance has well carved illustrations of the donors, and the cave itself comprises a 28 m x 13 m colonnaded hall of 34 pillars. At one end these encircle the 5-m-high *dagoba*. Some of the pillars have carvings of elephants and trees. Some 50 m up the ravine is **Darbar of the Maharajah Cave** (Cave 10). This was a *dharamshala* (rest house) and has two stone benches running down the sides and some cells leading off the left and back walls. Above Cave 10 is **Cave 35** which was a *vihara* (monastery), which has reliefs of a Buddha seated on a lotus and of a disciple spreading his cloak for him to walk on. All the caves have an elaborate drainage and water storage system, fresh rainwater being led into underground storage tanks.

Above the cave complex is **Ashok Van**, a sacred grove of ancient trees, streams and springs. From there, a three-hour trek leads to 'View Point', the highest in Mumbai. There are breathtaking views. Photography is prohibited from the radar station on top of the hill; there are excellent opportunities just below it.

The Ghats represent a historic divide between the outward looking coastal lowlands with the trading centre of Mumbai at their hub, and the much drier interior, a battle ground of successive Indian dynasties. The routes through the Western Ghats from Mumbai climb to nearly 1600 m through the forested slopes, particularly beautiful before the end of the rains in September when wild flowers are everywhere, and rivers and waterfalls are in full flow.

Road travel is often disrupted in the rains, but the railways through the Ghats are spectacular. On the Nashik route alone the line passes through 10 tunnels, over five viaducts and 11 bridges, while the line between Neral and Lonavla passes through stunning countryside of electic green paddy fields and stark rocky ravines.

Matheran *Colour map 5, B3.*
Mumbai's nearest hill station is Matheran (population 6000, altitude 785 m), meaning 'Mother Forest' or 'Wooded Head', which sprawls out along a north–south ridge, offering cool air, pleasant forest walks and splendid views down the almost sheer hillsides to the valleys below. Though very much geared towards the Mumbai weekend crowd, it maintains a unique sense of quiet by banning all forms of motor vehicles within the town. A visit is recommended, but stay for a night as it is too strenuous to do in a day from Mumbai. Check road conditions before planning a trip in the monsoons.
 The best views in town are from Little Chouk, Louisa and Porcupine, also known as **Sunset Point**. Allow one hour to walk and see the stunning sunsets. From the northernmost vantage points you can see the lights of Mumbai on a clear night.
 The most scenic route to Matheran is by the spectacular light railway through the ghats from Neral, which is closed during the monsoon. The steam engines that worked the route for 77 years no longer run, but you can see one proudly displayed at the station. See box, opposite.

Vajreshwari, Akloli and Ganeshpuri
Some 81 km northeast of Mumbai, Vajreshwari is renowned for its temple, built by the Maratha warrior Chamiji Appa after hammering the Portuguese at Bassein, but even more so for the **Akloli hot springs**, which pour into an unattractive collection of concrete tanks beside the river Tansa. There are more springs, quieter than those at Akloli, 2 km away in **Ganeshpuri** – locals claim to be able to boil rice in one of the tanks. The village is full of temples, including one to the 20th-century sage Nityanand, who established the nearby **Shri Gurudev Ashram**, a popular destination for foreign seekers.

Listings The Ghats

Tourist information

Matheran

MTDC Resort
3 km uphill from the centre in Dasturi Naka, T02148-230540.
Offers limited tourist information.

Where to stay

Matheran
Budget hotels near the station can be very noisy. Prices often include meals and rise considerably during holidays (eg Diwali) but most offer good off-season discounts.

$$$$-$$$ The Byke
MG Rd, T02148-230365, www.thebyke.com.
Good pool, 46 comfortable rooms, 5 a/c, great restaurants (pure vegetarian only).

$$$ Lord's Central
MG Rd, T02148-230228, www.matheranhotels.com.
Perched on a ridge with excellent views, 23 colonial-style rooms in 4 bungalows ('Valley' room best), restaurant (meals included), bar, pool, park, riding, friendly. Recommended.

BACKGROUND

India's first railway line

The opening of India's first railway line from Mumbai to Thane in 1853 prepared the route through the Ghats to the Deccan Plateau. Mumbai became the hub of regional and international trade. Victoria Terminus (CST now) was the product of a magnificent era of railway building at the end of the 19th century when the British Raj was striding confidently towards the 20th century.

With the disappearance of the East India Company after the Mutiny, the Government of India took over the responsibility for running the railways. On 16 April 1853 the first train made its run from Mumbai along 32 km of line to Thane. Subsequent advances were rapid but often incredible natural obstacles presented great challenges to the railway builders. The 263-km line to Surat encountered 18 rivers and some of the foundations for the bridges had to be driven 45 m in to the ground to cope with the monsoon floodwaters.

$$$ Usha Ascot
MG Rd, T02148-230360, www.ushaascot.com.
64 rooms, most a/c, as well as a pool, sauna, tennis courts, health club and disco.

$$$-$ Holiday Camp (MTDC)
Dasturi Naka, 30 mins uphill from centre
1 km before Matheran (train stops at camp),
T02148-230540.
39 rooms, cottages for 2-4, and dorm; limited catering.

$$ Girivihar
Shivaji Rd, T02148-230231, www.
giriviharhotelmatheran.com
Quiet, spacious gardens, some rooms with balconies.

$$ Royal Hotel
Kasturba Bhavan, T02148-230247,
www.royalhotelmatheran.com.
Health club, 61 rooms, 5 a/c, restaurant and bar.

$$-$ Hope Hall
MG Marg (opposite Lord's Central), T02148-230253, www.hopehallmatheran.com.
In a pleasant location, this hotel offers good-sized, clean rooms with bath (bucket hot water), and is run by a friendly family.

$ Alexander
Alexander Pt, T02148-230069.
In unspoilt woodland, 24 rooms, 3 a/c, good restaurant.

Restaurants

Matheran

$ Kokan Katta
Bazar Peth, opposite railway station.
High quality Maharashtrian fish and seafood.

$ Kwality Fruit Juice House
MG Rd, south of the train station among many.
Excellent honey and *chikki* (a sweet peanut brittle).

Transport

Matheran
From **Neral**, south of Kalyan, the narrow-gauge train takes 2 hrs to cover the 21 km to Matheran; trains run 5-6 times per day, and advance booking is highly recommended. Try to sit on the right on the way up for the best views; 1st class window seats are Nos 1, 4, 5, 8. To reach Neral from Mumbai CST, take a Pune-bound express train to **Karjat**, and backtrack on one of the regular local trains, or a 'fast' local train direct to Neral. Matheran station is in the town centre. A tax (Rs 25) is charged on arrival (pay before leaving the station). Taxis to Matheran can go no further than the MTDC Resort in **Dasturi Naka**, from where you can walk (porters available for luggage) or take a hand-pulled rickshaw.

Central & northern
Maharashtra

The splendid carved volcanic caves (Hindu, Jain and Buddhist) at Ellora and Ajanta, dating from the sixth and second centuries AD respectively, are among India's finest sights, including monasteries, meditation chambers, cloisters, chapels and colonnaded halls gouged from rock, graced with friezes and shrines. The triumphant Kailasanatha Temple at Ellora represents a staggering feat of vision and craftsmanship. Ajanta's exquisite artistry – Buddha's story etched into a sheer cliff face – was nearly lost to the world, lying hidden under dense jungle from the seventh to the 19th century. Aurangabad, Mughal ruler Aurangzeb's military headquarters during his Deccan campaign, is a spacious town to base yourself en route to the caves. Further afield, in northwest Maharashtra, is the holy city of Nashik.

Nashik (Nasik) and around   Colour map 5, A3.
Kumbh Mela site and capital of India's nascent wine industry

Nashik (population 1.49 million), an unprepossessing mixture of featureless market town, pilgrim centre and sprawling modern industrial estates, nonetheless has an old city area near the ghats with characteristic traditional buildings. It is one of Hinduism's most holy sites, taking its sanctity from its position on the headwaters of the Godavari River and is one of the locations of the 12-yearly Kumbh Mela. But the 'Ganges of the Deccan' also waters a fast-growing city and increasingly successful local vineyards. Caves of ancient Buddhist relics lie just outside town. It commands the strategic route from northwestern India to the southern Deccan.

Sights
Nashik shares the **Kumbh Mela** with Ujjain, Haridwar and Allahabad (see pages 151 and 169) and every 12 years millions of pilgrims converge on the Godavari River (sometimes referred to as the 'Ganga of the Deccan'), to bathe; Nashik hosted the event in 2015. The Godavari, which rises 30 km away at Trimbak, is believed to have a common underground source with the Ganga itself. In the last 10 years Nashik has been one of India's fastest growing cities, but the town itself is undoubtedly ancient, and Ghose suggests that it has an unbroken history of over 2500 years. At Pandu Lena (see below), within a few kilometres of the town centre, palaeolithic settlements have been discovered. Chalcolithic pottery has been found at Gangawadi, 15 km northwest of Nashik. Other finds date from the fifth century BC up to the first century AD and Roman pottery has been found in the third period level. However, none of Nashik's temples are very old. The Vaishnavite **Sundar Narayana Temple** (1756) on the west bank has three black Vishnu images. The **Ramesvara Temple** (18th century) is where Rama is believed to have carried out the funeral rites for his father and to have bathed in the **Rama Kund** nearby. It is a popular place to throw ashes of the dead into the river. The banyan-shaded **Sita Gupha** cave on the east side of town is where Rama's wife hid from Ravana the demon.

Nearby is the **Kala** (black) **Rama Temple** (1782) which has a 25-m-high *shikhara*.

In recent years Nashik has emerged as the centre of India's burgeoning wine industry, with locally produced Shiraz and Sauvignon Blanc from vineyards such as **Chateau Indage** and **Sula** are becoming a fixture on wine lists both in Indian metros and internationally, and the vineyards are attempting to capitalise by promoting Napa-esque wine tourism, with architect-designed tasting rooms, vineyard tours, and ever-more indulgent resorts and restaurants. The pick of the tasting tours is at **Sula** ⓘ *Govardhan Village, off Gangapur-Savargaon road, T0253-223 1663, www.sulawines.com; tours and tasting sessions every hour 1130-1730, Rs 150*, an eco-sensitive vineyard a 40-minute drive west of the city centre.

Pandu Lena

Some 8 km southwest of Nashik there is a group of 24 rock-cut Buddhist monuments on a hillock, the earliest dating from the first century BC. They include over 20 caves. Some have excellent carving, particularly on the exterior doorways. **Cave 3** has 19 monastic cells, a carved Buddha decorates the rear of **Cave 10**, while the exterior of the early **Cave 18**, a *chaitya* (chapel), is finely decorated.

Essential Nashik

Finding your feet

Trains arrive at Nasik Road Station, 7 km south of town. City buses run to town (Rs 5), stopping at Shalimar Circle, three minutes' walk from the Central Bus Stand (CBS) at the town centre; otherwise auto-rickshaws and taxis are around. Buses arrive from Aurangabad at the CBS, close to the budget hotels. Mumbai buses use the Mahamarga Bus Stand, a few kilometres from the centre, where you can get an auto; trains from Mumbai are a faster and better option.

Getting around

Buses to local places of interest use the CBS but a few people speak English in case you need to ask the way. See Transport, page 1116.

Fact...

Near Nashik is Deolali, the town that was host to wartime British transfer camps, and from whose sanatoria we've gained the expression 'doolally'.

Deolali, 7 km southeast, was the transfer camp for British soldiers going home during the two world wars. To go 'Doolally Tap' was to go crazy with boredom waiting there. A mental hospital accommodated these casualties.

Trimbak

The town of Trimbak, 30 km west of Nashik, is centred around the beautiful **Gangasagar Tank**. About 690 steps lead up the hill behind Trimbak to the source of the Godavari itself where you get good views. The town is partly surrounded by a fantastic semi-circle of hills, topped by a near vertical scarp. **Trimbakeshwar Temple**, an 18th-century Siva sanctuary with a *jyotirlinga*, is a pilgrimage site. In February/March a large fair is held; the important **Sinhastha Fair** takes place every 12 years. There is a simple hotel here. **Prayag Tirth**, on the road to Trimbak, has a beautiful stone-lined tank with two temples. Further on near **Anjaneri**, two 300-m-high conical hills are on either side of the road, sweeping round in a broad arc behind the town of Trimbak. Hourly buses from Nashik take about 45 minutes.

Igatpuri

The 'Town of Difficulties' is on top of the plateau at the end of the ghat section of railway. **Kalsubai** (1540 m), the highest mountain in Maharashtra, is visible to the south. About 1 km beyond the town the road passes the end of the beautiful **Beale Lake**. The town is now best known as home to the **Vipassana International Academy** ⓘ *PO Box 6, Dhammagiri, T02553-244076, www.dhamma. org*, which offers austere, deeply challenging but highly regarded 10-day silent meditation retreats.

Jawhar

The former capital of a tribal kingdom, Jawhar is noted for its *warli* paintings. Rice paste or poster colours are used to decorate the hut walls. **Jai Vilas**, the palace (ask locally to visit) and **Bhupatgad**, the fort, still show evidence of the tribal kingdom, while there are attractive waterfalls at Dadar Kopra.

Tourist information

MTDC
T/1 Golf Club, Old Agra Rd, T0253-257 0059.
Sightseeing 0730-1500, Rs 80.

Where to stay

Cheap rooms are hard to come by.

$$$ Beyond
Sula Vineyards, T0253-302 7777,
www.sulawines.com.
Smart and elegant rooms set around a large
pool, with great views across the vines to a lake.
Kayaking and cycling tours available, and buffet
meals are included.

$$$ Gateway (Taj)
P-17 MIDC Ambad, Mumbai-Agra Rd (14 km
from Nasik Rd station, 6 km from city), T0253-
669 2300, www.tajhotels.com.
Well-equipped business hotel in large grounds,
with stylishly light and airy rooms, Wi-Fi and pool.

$$ Panchavati Elite
Trimbak Rd, near Vinod Auto, T0253-257 9031,
www.panchavatihotels.com.
26 rooms, some a/c, restaurants (**Kwality**,
Coffee House) and a cheaper guesthouse.

$$-$ Rama Heritage
Next to Kalika Mandir, Mumbai Naka, T0253-
258 2887, www.hotelramaheritage.com.
Small and efficient business hotel, with plain but
very clean rooms, Wi-Fi and good restaurant.
Good value.

$ Panchavati Yatri
430 Vakil Wadi, Chandak Wadi T0253-257 2291,
www.panchavatihotels.com.
Well run and efficient, 41 rooms, 30 a/c rooms
(cold showers), good Gujarati *thali* restaurant,
bar, coffee shop, Recommended.

$ Pushkaraj
Near Shalimar City Bus Stop, T0253-250 2598.
Restaurant, 30 rooms, helpful.

$ Rajmahal
Opposite the bus stand, T0253-258 0501.
A good bargain, with quiet and well-kept rooms
a few steps from the bus station.

Restaurants

The best restaurants are in hotels, especially
the Taj Residency and Panchavati hotels, for
Indian vegetarian.

$$$ Soma
Sula Vineyards, Govardhan Village,
T0253-302 7777, www.sulawines.com.
Swish winery restaurant serving a variety
of classic Indian dishes, matched with quality
wines grown on the surrounding vines.

$ Dairy Don
MG Rd, 5 & 6 Sathye Baug, MG Rd, and at
Dream Square, near Somani Garden, MG Rd.
Best place in town for natural ice creams and
thick shakes.

$ Nindinee Woodlands
Nashik Pune Rd, near Dwarka).
Recommended for South Indian vegetarian food
and coffee.

$ Shilpa Hotel
430 Ratan Bhuvan, opposite
Deshdoot Newspaper.
Simple yet tasty food. Excellent Gujarati *thalis*.

Transport

Bus/taxi Regular buses to **Mumbai** (Dadar),
6 hrs, from the **Mahamarg Bus Stand** south
of the centre; share taxis are available as far as
Thane, from where local trains run into central
Mumbai. For **Aurangabad** and **Pune**, buses
depart from the **New Central Stand**, 5 hrs.

Train Nasik Rd station is 8 km southeast of
the centre. Local buses and shared taxis for
transfer to town. City booking counter off MG Rd,
Mon-Fri 1000-1700. **Aurangabad**: 4 daily, 3½ hrs.
Mumbai: frequent departures all day, 3½-5 hrs.
New **Delhi**: 3 daily, 24 hrs, via **Bhopal**, 10 hrs, and
Agra, 19 hrs. **Jalgaon** (for Ajanta Caves), frequent
departures, 3 hrs.

Aurangabad (population 1.17 million) is a pleasantly spacious town. The gates are all that is left of the old city walls. There is a university, medical and engineering colleges and an airport to complement the town's industrial and commercial activities.

Originally known as Khadke, the town was founded in 1610 by Malik Ambar, an Abyssinian slave who became the *wazir* (prime minister) to the King of Ahmadnagar. It was later changed to Aurangabad in honour of the last great Mughal, Aurangzeb. His wife is buried in the Bibi ka Maqbara and he is buried in a simple grave at Rauza. It acted as the centre of operations for his Deccan campaign which occupied him for the second half of his 49-year reign.

Sights

The British **cantonment** area is in the southwest quadrant, along the Kham River and can be seen on the way to Ellora. The old Holy Trinity church is in very poor condition. To the northwest is the **Begampura** district in which there is the attractive Pan23 Chakki water mill and the Bibi ka Maqbara, both worth visiting.

Aurangzeb built the 4.5-m-high crenellated city walls in 1682 as defence against the Marathas. **Killa Arrak** (1692), his citadel, lay between the Delhi and Mecca Gates. Little remains, though when it was Aurangzeb's capital over 50 maharajahs and princes attended the court. With Aurangzeb gone, the city's significance faded. At the centre in a grove of trees lies the **Jama Masjid**, a low building with minarets and a broad band carved with Koranic inscriptions running the length of the façade.

Other interesting monuments include: **Kali Masjid** (1600), a six-pillared stone mosque built by Malik Ambar; **Shahganj Masjid** (circa 1720) in the market square with shops on three sides; **Chauk Masjid** (1665), built by Shayista Khan, Aurangzeb's uncle, with five domes; and **Lal Masjid** (1655) in red-painted basalt. The **City Chowk** is worth visiting.

Bibi ka Maqbara ① *sunrise to 2000, foreigners Rs100, Indians Rs 5, floodlit at night*, beyond the Mecca Gate, is the mausoleum of Aurangzeb's wife, Rabia Daurani (1678). The classic lines of a garden tomb give it an impressive setting. However, it is less impressive close up. Modelled on the Taj Mahal, which was completed 25 years earlier, it is about half its size. Far less money was spent (one three hundredth by some estimates) and the comparative poverty of the finish is immediately obvious. It uses marble on the bottom 2 m of the mausoleum and four of the *jali* screens, but plaster elsewhere. The proportions are cramped and the minarets are too heavy in relation to the main mausoleum. Despite its failings it is one of the finest buildings of its period. The brass door carries an inscription which says Ata Ullah was the chief architect and Haibat Rai the maker of the door. On the tomb itself, in place of a marble slab, there is bare earth covered with a decorated cloth, a sign of humility. Light enters through a precisely angled shaft, allowing the early morning sun's rays to light the tomb for three minutes. The second tomb in the corner is said to be that of Rabia Daurani's nurse.

On the same side of the river is the **Pan Chakki** (1696) ① *sunrise to 2000, Rs 5, refreshments*, which has a white marble shrine to Baba Shah Muzaffar, the devout Aurangzeb's spiritual adviser. The pre-Mughal 17th-century water mill for turning large grinding stones was powered by water channelled from a spring some distance away and released through a dam.

Aurangabad Caves ① *3 km north of Aurangabad, sunrise to sunset, foreigners Rs100, Indians Rs 5*. The Aurangabad Caves are very

Essential Aurangabad

Finding your feet

Chikalthana airport is 10 km east of the town with taxis (Rs 250, a/c Rs 350) or hotel transport into the town centre. The railway station is on the southern edge of town, within walking distance of most hotels and the Central Bus Stand just under 2 km north on Dr Ambedkar Road.

Getting around

The city is easy to navigate. There are plenty of autos to see the sights, most of which are too scattered to see on foot. See Transport, page 1120.

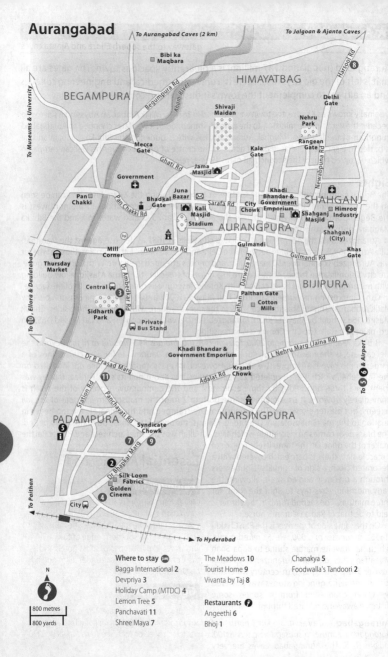

Aurangabad

To Aurangabad Caves (2 km)

To Jalgoan & Ajanta Caves

Bibi ka Maqbara

HIMAYATBAG

To Museums & University

BEGAMPURA

Begumpura Rd

Atun River

Harsol Rd

8

Delhi Gate

Shivaji Maidan

Nehru Park

Rangeen Gate

Mecca Gate

Ghati Rd

Kala Gate

Government

Jama Masjid

Khadi Bhandar & Government Emporium

SHAHGANJ

Pan Chakki

Pan Chakki Rd

Bhadkal Gate

Juna Bazar

Sarafa Rd

City Chowk

Shahganj Masjid

Himroo Industry

Kali Masjid

Shahganj (City)

Stadium

AURANGPURA

Khas Gate

Mill Corner

Aurangpura Rd

Gulmandi

Gulmandi Rd

Thursday Market

To Ellora & Daulatabad

Central

3

Dr Ambedkar Rd

BIJIPURA

Paithan Gate

Sidharth Park

1

Private Bus Stand

Cotton Mills

Darwaza Rd

Paithan

To 5 6 & Airport

2

Khadi Bhandar & Government Emporium

J L Nehru Marg (Jaina Rd)

Dr R Prasad Marg

Adalat Rd

Kranti Chowk

11

NARSINGPURA

Station Rd

Panchayati Rd

PADAMPURA

Syndicate Chowk

5

7

9

Dr Bhapkar Marg

2

Silk Loom Fabrics

Golden Cinema

City

4

To Paithan

To Hyderabad

N

800 metres

800 yards

Where to stay

Bagga International **2**
Devpriya **3**
Holiday Camp (MTDC) **4**
Lemon Tree **5**
Panchavati **11**
Shree Maya **7**

The Meadows **10**
Tourist Home **9**
Vivanta by Taj **8**

Restaurants

Angeethi **6**
Bhoj **1**

Chanakya **5**
Foodwalla's Tandoori **2**

interesting though not a substitute for Ajanta and Ellora. Overlooking the town they fall into two groups of five each, about 1.5 km apart. They date from the Vakataka (fourth and fifth centuries AD) and Kalachuri dynasties (sixth to eighth centuries), though the older Hinayana Cave 4 is believed to be at least first century, if not earlier. Waiting charges for auto-rickshaws can be high – bargain. Or, if it is cool and you are fit, you can walk back to the edge of town and get an auto-rickshaw back.

The **Western Group** are all *viharas* except for the earlier Cave 4 which is a *chaitya*. Cave 1 (incomplete) has finely carved pillars with ornamentation around doorways and walls and figures on brackets. Cave 2 has a shrine and columned hallways, a large Buddha and intricately carved panels. The larger Cave 3 has a plain exterior but superb carvings on 12 pillars of the hallway; the sanctuary has panels illustrating *jataka* stories and a fine large Buddha figure on his throne with attendant devotees illustrating contemporary dress and style. Cave 4, the *chaitya* has a rib-vaulted ceiling with a *stupa* containing relics and a Buddha figure outside. Cave 5 is damaged and retains little of its original carvings.

The **Eastern Group** has more sculptures of women and Bodhisattvas. Cave 6 has a large Buddha supporting Ganesh, indicating a later period when Hinduism was gaining in importance over Buddhism. Note the paintings on the ceiling of the balcony. Cave 7 is regarded as the most interesting of both groups. Columned shrines at each end of the veranda house images of Hariti (right) and six goddesses, including Padmini (left). The central shrine has an ambulatory passage around it and a large preaching Buddha at the back. The wall carvings depict deliverance and numerous female dancers and musicians. The importance of Tara and of Tantric Buddhism is evident here. There is little to see in the unfinished Cave 9; the carvings of pre-Nirvana figures suggest Buddhism was waning. The incomplete Cave 10 illustrates the first stages of cave excavation.

Listings Aurangabad *map p1118*

Tourist information

India Tourism
Krishna Vilas, Station Rd, T0240-236 4999.
Mon-Fri 0830-1830, Sat 0830-1330. An airport
counter is open at flight times.

MTDC
TRC Bldg, Station Rd, T0240-233 4259; also
at railway station, 0430-0830, 1100-1600.
Tue-Sun 0900-1600.

Where to stay

Some hotels offer discounts between Apr and Sep. Most will provide packed lunch for trip to the caves. Most are 24-hr checkout.

$$$$-$$$ Vivanta by Taj
8 N-12 CIDCO, Rauza Bagh, Ajanta Rd, 8 km
from railway station, 9 km from the airport,
T0240-661 3737, www.vivantabytaj.com.
An imposing building set in lovely gardens, on the outskirts of town, with 40 large rooms, quiet swimming, and excellent service.

$$$ Lemon Tree
R 7/2, Chikalthana, Airport Rd, T0240-660 3030,
www.lemontree hotels.com.
Excellent newish hotel with 102 sleek and spacious rooms arranged around a large

pool. Spa and fitness centre, good food and helpful management.

$$$ The Meadows
Gat 135-136, Mitmita village, Ellora Rd, T0240-
267 7412, www.themeadowsresort.com.
A pleasant change from Aurangabad's corporate offerings, with 40 comfortable cottages set among 4.5 ha of bird-filled gardens. Quiet and relaxing.

$$ Bagga International
Opposite Akashwani, Jalna Rd, T0240-235 4000,
www.hotelbagga.com.
Clean and modern if slightly anonymous rooms in a newish business hotel. Good room service, helpful and attentive staff, good value.

$ Devpriya
Balasaheb Powar Chowk near Central Bus Stand,
Dr Ambedkar Rd, T0240-233 2344.
Family hotel, with 62 decent rooms, hot water in morning, restaurant and bar. Good value.

$ Holiday Camp (MTDC)
Station Rd, T0240-233 1513.
Pleasant, busy hotel, offering 48 rooms (22 a/c) with bath and mosquito net, but poor restaurant, bar, and a tourist office. Checkout at 0900. Bedbug problems reported.

$ Panchavati
Off Station Rd, Padampura, T0240-232 8755,
www.hotelpanchavati.com.
Friendly hotel with 25 good value, clean, simple rooms with bath, and a good restaurant.

$ Railway Retiring Rooms
T0240-233 5650.
3 rooms (1 a/c) and a 4-bedded dorm.

$ Shree Maya
Bharuka Complex, behind tourist office,
Padampura Rd, T0240-233 3093.
In a handy location for the railway station, 23 rooms with hot shower, 8 a/c, and restaurant. Bus tickets arranged, and 24-hr checkout. Mixed reports about management.

$ Tourist Home
Station Rd, T0240-233 7212.
Friendly place offering 26 ultra-cheap rooms with bath, and meals.

Restaurants

$$ Angeethi
7 Hill Flyover, Vidya Nagar, CIDCO, Jalna Rd,
T0240-244 1988.
Excellent Marathi specialities. Best chicken dishes in town. Book ahead.

$$ Chanakya
Station Rd, T0240-2352176
North Indian cuisine, served in a restaurant that is partly outdoors. Fashionable, a/c, well-prepared dishes, and a bar.

$$ Foodwalla's Tandoori
500 m from Holiday Camp.
Popular restaurant with a/c, serving tender Indian chicken dishes, good value, bar.

$$ Mastercook
Beed Bypass road, near MIT College.
Popular locally.

$ Bhoj
1st floor, Kamgar Bhavan, CBS Rd.
Excellent Gujarati and Rajasthani *thalis*. Arrive at 1845 to listen to *puja* in the kitchen with chanting and cymbals.

Festivals

Feb/Mar Mahashivratri, large fair at Ghrishneshwara Temple, near Ellora and Ellora Yatra.

Shopping

Shops open Mon-Sat 1000-2000. The city is known for its handwoven Himroo shawls (brocades occasionally with Ajanta motifs), and special textile weaves – *Mashru, Patihani silk* and *Kinkhab* – as well as artificial silk. You can also get good decorative lacquer work, Bidriware and agate articles. The main shopping areas are City Chowk, Gulmandi, Nawabpura, Station Rd, Shahganj, Sarafa, Mondha.

In Shahganj, **Cottage Industries**. On Station Rd, **Silk Loom Fabrics** and **Government Emporium** (opposite Holiday Resort).

Aurangabad Himroo Industry (Zaffar Gate, Mondha Rd). A factory showroom producing beautiful Ajanta patterns in silk. The English speaking owner is very informative. Recommended.

What to do

Swimming
Some top hotels open their pools to non-residents for a fee, eg **Ambassador Ajanta**, Rs 250 (includes other sporting facilities), **Aurangabad Ashok**, Rs 125; **President Park**, Rs 125; and **Vedant** (Quality Inn), Station Rd, T0240-235 0701, Rs 150.

Tours
Ashoka Travels, *Station Rd, T0240-232 0816.* Mr Karolkar arranges hotels, cars and excursions, charges fairly and is reliable.
Classic, *TRC Building, Station Rd, T0240-233 7788, and at Ambassador Ajanta.* Helpful and efficient; car hire, ticketing, hotels, Ajanta/Ellora and city tour, Rs 300/250 per person.
ITDC, *Ashok Tours and Travels counter, near Goldie Cinema, Station Rd, T0240-233 1143.*
MTDC, *see Tourist information, opposite.* Good sightseeing tours to Ajanta, Ellora and the City. The Ajanta tour is highly recommended, but Ellora and City tour visits too many places in too little time. Tours start from **MTDC Holiday Camp** (Station Rd, T0240-233 1513), and pickup from major hotels and the **Central Bus Stand**: Ellora and City Wed-Mon 0930-1800, Rs 200; Ajanta Tue-Sun 0830-1730, Rs 200; book at Window 1 (behind book stall) at bus stand; check times.

Transport

Air The airport is 10 km from the centre and has regular flights to **Delhi**, **Mumbai**, **Jaipur** and **Udaipur**. Transport to town: Taxi, Rs 200 (Rs 300 through travel agents).

Bicycle hire 'Cycle taxi' from shops near railway station north of the bus stand (CBS).

Local bus Services to **Daulatabad**, and **Ellora** (45 mins) from platform 7 of the Central Bus Stand, Ambedkar Rd.

Long distance bus MSRTC operates a/c luxury coaches to **Mumbai Central** (388 km), 10 hrs. Also services to **Ajanta** (3 hrs), **Jalgaon** (4½ hrs), **Nagpur**, **Nashik** and **Pune**. State and private buses run to destinations in other states, including **Ahmedabad**, **Bengaluru** (**Bangalore**), **Bijapur**, **Hubli**, **Hyderabad**, **Indore** and **Udaipur**. Book through agents on Station Rd West, near the bus stand.

Car hire Rs 1800 per day (Rs 1500, a/c) from **Aurangabad Transport Syndicate**, Hotel Rama International, T0240-248 6766.

Rickshaw For auto-rickshaws, insist on using the meter, about Rs 10 per km. Day hire to visit Ellora and Daulatabad, Rs 500-600 from bus station.

Taxi Rates Rs 600 for 4 hrs, 40 km. Rs 1000 for 8 hrs, 80 km.

Train Beware of touts at the station offering package tours to Ellora and Ajanta. Easier by local bus. Aurangabad is well connected to **Mumbai** (4 trains a day, 6,½-8 hrs; **Delhi** (1 daily, 24 hrs, via **Agra**, 20 hrs); and **Hyderabad** (4-6 a day, 10 hrs). Slower local trains run to **Ahmadnagar**, **Jalna**, **Nanded** and **Pune**.

North of Aurangabad

an ancient fort and Aurangzeb's resting place

Daulatabad (Deogiri) *Colour map 5, A4.*

Sunrise to sunset, Rs100 foreigners, Rs 5 Indians, allow 3 hrs. For snacks there are numerous dhabas opposite the entrance. Buses from Aurangabad's Central Bus Stand (platform 8), not all Ellora buses stop here.

Thirteen kilometres from Aurangabad is the fort of Daulatabad or Deogiri, towering above the surrounding countryside. The fort dates from the Yadava period of the 11th-14th centuries although the first fort had probably been built in the ninth century. Before that it had been a Buddhist monastery. It is an extraordinary site, and is particularly attractive in the late afternoon when the crowds have gone. If you are lucky you may get the resident guide who takes visitors through the dark tunnels with a flaming torch.

From Ala-ud-din Khalji's capture of Deogiri in 1296 until Independence in 1947, by which time it was under the control of the Nizam of Hyderabad, the fort remained in Muslim hands. Mohammad bin Tughluq (see page 1302) determined to extend his power south, seized Daulatabad, deciding to make it his capital and populate it with the residents from Delhi. Thousands died as a result of his misconceived experiment. The outermost of the three main ring walls and the bastion gates were probably built by the Muslims.

The Persian style **Chand Minar** (1435) stands at the bottom of the fort, towering as a celebration of victory like the Qutb Minar in Delhi. Its original covering of Persian blue tiles must have made it even more striking. Opposite is the **Jama Masjid** (1318), with 106 pillars taken from a Hindu temple, and a large tank. The 31 m high victory tower built by Ala-ud-din Bahmani to celebrate his capture of the fort has at its base 24 chambers and a small mosque. The path passes bastions, studded gates, a drawbridge and the **Chini Mahal** where Abdul Hasan Tana Shah, the last King of Golconda, was imprisoned in 1687 for 13 years. The 6.6-m long Kila Shikan (Fort Breaker) iron cannon is on the bastion nearby. At the end of the tunnel (see box, above) inside the citadel is a flight of steps leading up to the **Baradari** (Pavilion), said to be the palace of the Yadavi Queen and later Shah Jahan. The **citadel** is reached by climbing 100 more steps and passing through two more gateways. At the top is another cannon with a ram's head on the butt; the Persian inscription around the muzzle reads 'Creator of Storms'.

Khuldabad

Rauza (or Khuldabad) ('Heavenly Abode') is 22 km from Aurangabad and was once an important town around which Aurangzeb built a wall with seven gates. Aurangzeb died at the age of 89 on

Deogiri fortifications

The hillside around Deogiri was made steeper to make scaling the fort extremely difficult. The three concentric walls had strong gates, surrounded by a deep moat and the path climbed through the gates then up the steep slope towards the citadel. Today a new path has been cut to avoid the obstacles that were designed to prevent attackers from gaining entry. There is an L-shaped keep, a long, tortuous tunnel which could be sealed by an iron cover at the top after firing with hot coals, and a chamber which could be filled with noxious fumes. At one point the tunnel divides and meets, to fool attackers to kill each other in the dark. The only genuine access was narrowed so that an invader would have to crawl through the last few metres, making it possible for defenders to kill them on sight. The bodies were disposed of by chutes down into the crocodile infested moat 75 m below. A guide will take you through. Take a torch and allow two hours to get the most out of the extraordinary site.

Friday (the day of his choice), 20 February 1707. His simple tomb is here alongside over 20 other tombs of Muslim rulers of the Deccan. Since Aurangzeb wanted a simple grave as a sign of humility, open to the sky, his grave has no canopy. The marble screen around it was erected later by Lord Curzon and the Nizam of Hyderabad. Close to Aurangzeb's tomb are those of various saints, going back to the 14th century. Some are decorated with silver. There are several relics – hairs of the Prophet's beard said to multiply every year, the Prophet's robe, and the supposed remnants of trees miraculously converted to silver by the saint Saiyed Burhan-ud-Din (died 1344).

Ellora *Colour map 5, A4.*

some of the finest cave temples in India

The Hindu, Jain and Buddhist caves carved in the volcanic rocks at Ellora lie near an important ancient trade route between Ujjain in Madhya Pradesh and the west coast. The caves are thought to be the work of priests and pilgrims who used the route.

Like the caves at Ajanta, Ellora's caves were also abandoned and forgotten. Twelve of the 34 caves are Buddhist (created from circa AD 600-800), 17 Hindu (AD 600-900) and five Jain (AD 800-1100). Most have courtyards in front. They face west and are best seen in the afternoon. To see the caves in chronological order, start at the east end and visit the Buddhist *viharas* first. In this way the magnificent Hindu Kailasnatha temple is seen towards the end.

Buddhist Caves (Nos 1-12)

These belong to the **Vajrayana** sect of the Mahayana (Greater Vehicle) School. The caves include *viharas* (monasteries) and *chaityas* (chapels) where the monks worshipped. It has been suggested that the stone-cut structures were ideally suited to the climate which experienced monsoons, and rapidly became the preferred medium over more flimsy and less durable wood.

Cave 1 A simple *vihara*.

Cave 2 Adjoining is reached by a flight of steps. At the door of the cave are *dwarapala* (guardians) flanked by windows. The interior (14.5 sq m) comprises a hall supported by 12 pillars, some decorated with the pot and foliage motif. In the centre of the back wall is a 3-m-high seated Buddha and two standing Buddhas while along each of the side walls are five Buddhas accompanied by Bodhisattvas and *apsaras* (celestial nymphs).

Cave 3 Similar to Cave 2, having a square central chamber with a Buddha image, this time seated on a lotus. Around the walls are 12 meditation cells.

Cave 4 Two-storeyed and contains a Buddha sitting under the Bo (pipal) tree.

Cave 5 The **Maharwada**, is the largest of the single storeyed caves in this group (17.6 m by 36 m). Two rows of 10 columns each run the length of the cave, as do two raised platforms which were probably tables, suggesting that this cave was a dining hall. There are attractive carvings on the first pillar on the left. The Buddha at the back is guarded on the left by Padmapani, a symbol of purity. On the right is Vajrapani holding a thunderbolt, the symbol of esoteric knowledge and the popular deity of the sect responsible for creating the caves. The Buddha is seated, not cross-legged on the floor as is usual, but on a chair or stool. He demonstrates some of the 32 distinctive marks: three folds in the neck, long ear lobes and the third eye. The *mudra* here signifies the Buddha's first sermon at the Deer Park, see page 1339, and is a teaching pose.

The next four caves can be bypassed as they contain nothing new.

Cave 10 Viswakarma, or 'Carpenter's Cave', is the only *chaitya* (chapel) cave in the group. It used to be a monastery. This is on the ground floor and above are what are presumed to have been the monks' living quarters. In front is a large courtyard approached by a flight of steps. The galleries around it have square-based pillars at the foot of which was a lion facing outwards. At the back of these galleries are two elaborately carved chapels. The exterior decoration gives the impression that instead of stone, wood was the building material, hence 'Viswakarma'. The façade has a trefoil window with *apsara* groups for ornamentation. The main hall is large (26 m by 13 m, 10 m high). The curved fluted 'beams' suggest to some the upturned hull of a ship. The chamber has 28 columns, each with a vase and foliage capital, dividing it up into a nave and aisles. The aisle runs round the decorated *stupa* (*dagoba*) with a colossal 4.5-m 'Preaching Buddha' carved in front of it. The upper gallery, reached by an internal flight of steps, was supposed to have subsidiary shrines at either end but the left hand one was not finished. Decorating the walls are loving couples, indicating how much Buddhism had changed from its early ascetic days. You can get a view of the friezes above the pillars which show Naga queens, symbolic precursors of the monsoon, and dwarfs as entertainers, dancing and playing musical instruments. Sunlight pouring through the circular window at the entrance to the cave gives the cave a truly ethereal quality.

Getting around

The caves at Ellora are 26 km from Aurangabad (45 minutes by road). Hiring a taxi (Rs 650-1050) gives you flexibility to stop at other sites on the way, auto rickshaws cost around Rs 350. Alternatively, join a tour group (Rs 150 per person). Car and driver hired through a travel agent will cost around Rs 1800 return (non a/c). Tour buses usually arrive at the car park, directly in front of the Kailasnatha temple itself. For the elderly and infirm, *dhoolies* (chairs carried by men) are available.

When to go

Wednesday-Monday 0900-1730. The painted caves open at 1000, others at 0900; the light is better in the afternoon.

Entry fees

Kailashnatha entry Rs 250 foreigners (other caves remain free), Rs 10 Indians.

Guides

Guides are available (some European languages and Japanese spoken). There are 'light passes' for groups wishing to see darker caves illuminated (it's best to join a group if you're on your own).

What to take

For visiting Ellora and Ajanta, take lunch and drinks as decent options are limited. Also wear a hat and comfy shoes and take a strong torch. Cameras may be used outside, flash photography and tripods are not allowed inside.

Tip...
Arrive early and see the Kailasnatha first to avoid the very large crowds.

Cave 11 (*Do Thal* – two-storeyed) was found to have a third storey in 1876 when the basement was discovered. The lowest level is a veranda with a shrine and two cells at the back of it. The middle level has eight front pillars and five rear cells of which only the central three are completed and decorated. The upper level has a porch opening into a long colonnaded hall with a Buddha shrine at the rear. Images of Durga and Ganesh suggest that the cave was later used by Hindus. Cave 11 and 12 illustrate the use of the upper levels of these caves as a residence for monks and pilgrim hostels.

Cave 12 (*Tin Thal* – three-storeyed) has cells for sleeping (note the stone benches) on the lower floors but it is the figures of the Buddha which are of particular interest. The rows of seven Buddhas are symbolic of the belief that he appears on earth every 5000 years and has already visited it seven times.

Hindu Caves (Nos 13-29)

These caves lie in the centre of the group and are the most numerous. **Cave 13** is a plain room while **Cave 14** (*Ravana ki khai*, seventh century), is single-storeyed and the last of the collection from the early period. River goddesses and guardians stand at the doorway while inside is a broken image of Durga and figurative panels on the walls of the principle deities, Vishnu, Siva, Lakshmi and Parvati. **Cave 15** (*Das Avatara*, mid-eighth century), reached by a flight of steps, has a large courtyard and is two-storeyed. Beyond the Kailasanatha Temple (Cave 16; see below), **Cave 21** (Ramesvara, late sixth century) has a court with a stone Nandi bull in the middle and side shrines. A linga sanctuary leads off the veranda. This cave is celebrated for its fine sculptures of amorous couples and the gods. **Cave 29** (Dhumar Lena, late sixth century) is very similar to Elephanta (see page 1108) in concept. Access is from three sides, there is a spacious hall with a separate small sanctuary with a lingam at the end. Wall panels depict Siva legends especially as Destroyer.

Ellora caves

Caves 30 - 34 Jain
Indra Sabha
Chhota Kailasa
Dhumar Lena
Ramesvara
Caves 13 - 29 Hindu
Kailasanatha Temple
To Grishneshvara Temple
Viswakarma
Maharwada
Caves 1 - 12 Buddhist
To Daulatabad & Aurangabad

N

Where to stay
Kailas 1

100 metres
100 yards

See text for details

★ Kailasanatha Temple (mid-eighth century onwards)

This is the most magnificent of all the rock-cut structures at Ellora, and is completely open to the elements. It is the only building that was begun from the top. Carved out of 85,000 cu m of rock, the design and execution of the full temple plan is an extraordinary triumph of imagination and craftsmanship. Excavating three deep trenches into the rock, carving started from the top of the cliff and worked down to the base. Enormous blocks were left intact from which the porch, the free standing pillars and other shrines were subsequently carved. The main shrine was carved on what became the upper storey, as the lower floor was cut out below. It is attributed to the Rashtrakuta king Dantidurga (AD 725-755) and must have taken years to complete. **Mount Kailasa** (6700 m), the home of Siva, is a real mountain on the Tibetan plateau beyond the Himalaya. Its distinctive pyramidal shape, its isolation from other mountains, and the appearance to the discerning eye of a swastika etched by snow and ice on its rock face, imbued the mountain with great religious significance to Hindus and Buddhists alike. Kailasa was seen as the centre of the universe, and Siva is Lord of Kailasa, Kailasanatha. To imitate the real snow-covered peaks, the *sikharas* here were once covered with white plaster.

Entrance The temple is 50 m long and 33 m wide and the tower rises 29 m above the level of the court. At the entrance gate, the threshold between the profane and sacred worlds, the goddesses **Ganga** and **Yamuna** form the door jambs. Just inside are two seated sages: **Vyasa**, the legendary author of the *Mahabharata*, and **Valmiki** to whom the *Ramayana* has been ascribed. In the porch four columns carry the North Indian vase and foliage motif, a symbol of fertility and well-being. On each side of the doorway there are images of **Kubera**, the god of wealth, with other symbols of well-being such as the conch shell and the lotus. Two more figures complete the welcoming party. They are **Ganesh** (left), the elephant headed son of Siva, bringer of good fortune, and **Durga** (right), Siva's wife who fought the demons.

In the antechamber opposite is **Lakshmi**, the goddess of wealth. In the courtyard, to your right and left are free-standing elephants. On the left round the corner is a panel depicting **Kama**, the god of desire, carrying his bow and five arrows, one for each of the senses. On the far wall to your left of the entrance, behind the pillars, is the shrine of the **Three River Goddesses** – Ganga (centre), Yamuna (left) and Sarasvati (right). Symbolically they stand for purity, devotion and wisdom respectively. This is a good place to photograph the central shrine. The two carved monolithic pillars are probably stylized flagstaffs indicating royal patronage – a practice that Asoka popularized in the third century BC.

There are two distinct levels taking the worshipper from the courtyard by two staircases flanking the central hall, to the lower level with its processional path and then rising even higher to the upper level of the *mandapa*.

Central Assembly Hall Around the central shrine is a colonnaded hall gouged from the rock, which in places overhangs menacingly. Inside this cloister is a series of panels portraying Siva and Vishnu myths. The whole can be viewed as a sort of instructional picture gallery, a purpose it served for worshippers from ancient times who could not read.

The south facing wall has *Ramayana* stories – **Ravana** offering his heads; Siva and Parvati with Nandi the bull and the lingam (creative power); Siva playing the vina; Siva and Parvati playing dice in a spirit of harmony; the marriage of Siva and Parvati; the origin of the lingam, the symbol of Siva and creative (male) energy; Siva dancing and Siva tricking Parvati. The panel on the south of the mandapa of Ravana shaking Mount Kailasa, attempting to carry it off, disturbing Parvati and her attendants, one of whom is seen frightened and fleeing, and Siva restoring order with the movement of his toe.

Along the north-facing wall are stories from the *Mahabharata* above and Krishna legends below. The panels include **Krishna** stealing buttermilk; Vishnu as **Narasimha**, half man, half lion; Vishnu reclining on **Ananda** the serpent inbetween incarnations; Vishnu the **Preserver**. Finally there is **Annapurna**, Goddess of Plenty.

The inner porch contains two panels, Siva as **Lord of Knowledge** and Siva as **Bhairava** killing the Elephant Demon.

Main Shrine Steps lead to the upper floor which contains a *mandapa* (central hall, 17 m by 16 m) of 16 stout pillars arranged in groups of four, with aisles that correspond to the cardinal points leading to an open central area. At the far end is the *garbhagriha* (shrine) with **Ganga** and **Yamuna** as door guardians. Inside is the *yoni lingam*, symbol of Siva's creative power. Running around the back is a passageway with five small shrine rooms off it, each with a replica of the main temple. The Nataraja painting on the *mandapa* ceiling. There are remnants of paintings on the porch ceilings (particularly to the west) where you will see *apsaras*, dwarfs and animals. The temple rises in a pyramid, heavier and more squat looking than later towers in the north. The shape suggests enormous strength. As you leave, the path to the left leads up and around the temple, giving an interesting bird's-eye view of the magnificent complex.

Jain Caves (Nos 30-34)

These caves are an anticlimax after the Hindu ones, but they have an aura of peace and simplicity. Cave 30 (Chhota Kailasa, early ninth century) was intended as a smaller scale replica of the Kailasanatha Temple but never completed. The columned shrine has 22 *tirthankaras* with *Mahavira* in the sanctuary. Cave 32 (Indra Sabha, early ninth century) is the finest of the Jain series and is dedicated to Mahavir. A simple gateway leads into an open court in the middle of which stands the shrine. The walls have carvings of elephants, lions and *tirthankaras*. The lower of the two is incomplete but the upper has carvings of Ambika and also Mahavir flanked by guardians of earlier *tirthankaras*. The ceiling is richly carved with a massive lotus at the centre and you can see signs of painted figures among clouds.

Listings Ellora *map p1124*

Where to stay

$$ Kailas
Near the bus stand, T02437-244543,
www.hotelkailas.com.

25 decent rooms in a group of 'cottages', best a/c face the caves. There's a dorm in the annexe, a restaurant, very pleasant garden and good service.

★ Ajanta and around *Colour map 5, A5.*

volcanic rock caves daubed with stunning paintings hide in a forested ravine

Older than those at Ellora, the caves date from about 200 BC to AD 650. They are cut from the Deccan Trap in a steep crescent-shaped hillside in the Sahyadri Hills. After the late seventh century, the jungle took over and they lay unnoticed for centuries.

The terrain in which the caves were excavated was a sheer cliff facing a deeply incised river meander. At the height of Ajanta's importance the caves are thought to have housed about 200 monks and numerous craftsmen and labourers. The masterpieces retell the life story of the Buddha and reveal the life and culture of the people of the times, royal court settings, family life, street scenes and superb studies of animals and birds. The *Jatakas* relate the Buddha's previous births – showing the progress of the soul.

Originally the entrance to the caves was along the river bed and most had a flight of stairs leading up to them. The first to be excavated was Cave 10, followed by the first Hinayana caves (in which the Buddha is not depicted in human form), on either side. Later Mahayana caves were discovered, completing the spectrum of Buddhist development in India.

There is a round trip walk, up the side of the valley where all the caves are located then down to the river to cross to the other side. An attractive low level walk through forest brings you back to the roadhead. Caves 1, 2, 10, 16 and 17 have lights. 11, 19 and 26 are also particularly worth visiting.

Mahayana group

Cave 1 (late fifth century) is one of the finest *viharas* (monasteries), remarkable for the number and quality of its murals. A veranda with cells and porches either side has three entrances leading into a pillared hall. Above the veranda are friezes depicting the sick man, old man, corpse and saint encountered by the Buddha, who is shown above the left porch. The hall has 20 ornamented pillars, a feature of the late period caves. Five small monks' cells lead off three sides, and in the centre of the back wall is a large shrine of the Buddha supported by Indra, the rain god. At the entrance are the river goddesses Yamuna and Ganga and two snake-hooded guardians at the base.

The **murals** are among the finest at Ajanta. In the four corners are panels representing groups of foreigners. The Mahajanaka jataka (where the Buddha took the form of an able and just ruler) covers much of the left-hand wall including Renunciation, and the scenes where he is enticed by beautiful dancing girls.

On either side of the entrance to the antechamber of the shrine room are two of the best known murals at Ajanta. On the left is the **Bodhisattva Padmapani** (here holding a blue lotus), in a pose of spiritual detachment, whilst on the right is the **Bodhisattva Avalokitesvara**. Together compassion and knowledge, the basis of Mahayana Buddhism, complement one another. Their size dwarfs the attendants to enhance the godlike stature of the bodhisattva. The Buddha inside the shrine is seated in the teaching position, flanked by the two carved bodhisattvas. Under the throne appears the **Wheel of Life**, with deer representing Sarnath where he preached his first sermon.

Essential Ajanta

Finding your feet

The bus or taxi drive from Aurangabad (106 km) takes 2½ to three hours. All buses and cars stop at the Ajanta T junction, where you transfer to a CNG bus (Rs 20) for the last 4 km to the caves. On arrival, prepare to be swarmed by salesmen, and if you're leaving by bus don't be duped by rickshaw drivers who may try to convince you the closest bus stop is 4 km away. Good tours are available from Aurangabad for Rs 200 per person (a hired non air-conditioned car and driver will cost around Rs 2000-3000). Taxis Rs 1200-1500. Shilod (Silod) is a popular halting place and has a number of restaurants. About 10 km from Ajanta, the road descends from the plateau; there are dramatic views of the Waghora Valley, where the caves are located. Coming from the north, the closest railhead is Jalgaon, with many main line services to Mumbai, Madhya Pradesh and the northeast. See Transport, page 1130.

Fact...

Hiuen-Tsang, recorded in the seventh century (although he did not visit it), a description of the "monastery in a deep defile … large temple with a huge stone image of the Buddha with a tier of seven canopies".

Getting around

The CNG bus drops you near the ticket counter; there's a small canteen here serving average food. The entrance is a short uphill walk along a stepped concrete path. *Dhoolis* are available for hire if you wish to be carried. You can approach the caves from the river bed in the bottom of the valley, where the bus stops; the View Point is worth getting to; if there is water in the stream you have to wade through, but it is much shadier than the path cut out of the cliff.

Entry fees

Tuesday-Sunday 0900-1730, foreigners Rs 250, Indians Rs 10.

Site information

Most caves require you to remove your footware, so wear sandals rather than shoes. No flash photography is allowed. Some caves have electric lights for illuminating the paintings (Rs 5 per group). In the Mahayana caves with paintings there is a restriction on the number of visitors allowed in at any one time. Computer kiosks are planned, designed to show a 'virtual' history of the caves.

One of the sculptural tricks that a guide will display is that when the statue is lit from the left side (as you face it), the facial expression is solemn, suggesting contemplation. Yet from the other side, there is a smile of joy, while from below it suggests tranquillity and peace. Note the paintings on the ceiling, particularly the elephant scattering the lotus as it rushes out of the pond, and the charging bull. Also look for the 'black princess' and the row of the dancer with musicians. On the way out is a pillar that has four deer sculpted skilfully, sharing the same head.

Cave 2 (sixth century) is also a *vihara* hall, 14.6 sq m with 12 pillars, with five cells on each side of the left and right hand walls and two chapels on each side of the ante-chamber and shrine room. The veranda in front has a side chapel at each end. The doorway is richly carved. On the left hand wall is the mural depicting **The Birth of The Buddha**. Next to this is the **'Thousand' Buddhas**, which illustrates the miracle when the Buddha multiplied himself to confuse a heretic. On the right are dancing girls before the king, shown with striking three-dimensional effect.

The cave is remarkable for its painted ceiling, giving the effect of the draped cloth canopy of a tent. The *mandala* (circular diagram of the cosmos) is supported by demon-like figures. The Greek key designs on the border are possibly influenced by Gandharan art, first to third centuries AD. The ceiling decorations portray a number of figures of Persian appearance apparent from the style of beard and whiskers and their clothing.

The **Yaksha** (nature spirits) Shrine in the left chapel is associated with fertility and wealth. The main shrine is that of Buddha in the teaching position, again flanked by the two bodhisattvas, both holding the royal fly whisk. The **Hariti** Shrine on the right is to the ogress who liked eating children!

Tempera techniques in cave painting

To prepare the rock for painting it was chiselled to leave a rough surface. Two layers of mud-plaster containing fibrous material (grain-husk, vegetable fibres and rock grit) was applied, the first coarse, the second fine. Metal mirrors must have been used by the artists, to reflect sunlight into the dark caves. It is thought that the tempera technique was used. On a dry surface, a red cinnabar outline defined the picture, filled in, possibly initially with grey and then numerous colour pigments usually mixed with glue; the completed painting was burnished to give a lustrous finish. The pigments were mainly taken from the land around, the principal ones being red and yellow ochre, white from lime and kaoline, green from glauconite, black from lamp-black and blue from imported lapis lazuli.

The panel on your left as you leave the hall is a *jataka* telling the story of the Bodhisattva's life as the Pandit Vidhura.

Caves 3-7 are late fifth century. **Cave 3** has no veranda and **Cave 4** is the largest *vihara* at Ajanta, planned on an ambitious scale and not completed. The hall is 27 sq m and supported on 28 pillars. Along the walls are cells whilst at the rear is a large shrine. **Cave 5** is unfinished.

Hinayana group

A Hinayana group comes next (**Caves 6-10** and **12**, **13** and **15**) dating from the second century BC. **Cave 6** is on two levels with only seven of the 16 octagonal pillars standing. A shrine contains a seated Buddha. **Cave 7** has no hall. The veranda has two porches each supported by heavy octagonal Elephanta-type columns. These lead to four cells. These and the antechamber are profusely carved. The shrine is that of Buddha, his hand raised in blessing. **Cave 8** (first century BC) is a small vihara. **Cave 9** (circa 100 BC), a *chaitya*, is 14 m long, 14 columns run the length of each side and 11 continue round the *stupa*. The vaulted roof was once wooden ribbed and leads back from a huge arched *chaitya sun* window which throws light on the *stupa* at the rear. Two phases of wall painting have been identified. The earlier ones dating from the construction of the cave can be seen at the far left side and consist of a procession to a *stupa* as well as a thin band above the left colonnade. Above this are later Buddha figures from the Mahayana period when the figures of the Buddha on either side of the entrance were painted.

Cave 10 (circa 150 BC) is much larger. Like the previous cave the roof was once fitted with wooden ribs which subsequently collapsed. The long hall with an apse housing the *stupa* was one of the first excavated and also the first rediscovered by army officers. An inscription above the façade, now destroyed, dated the excavation to the second century BC through a generous donation by the king. The *dagoba* or *stupa* resembles that of Cave 9 and is a double storey drum. There are also paintings dating from the Hinayana and Mahayana periods. The early ones depict figures in costumes resembling those seen at Sanchi, see page 218. Traces of later paintings survive on the pillars and aisle ceilings and later Buddha figures are often superimposed on earlier works. The main subjects of the Hinayana paintings are *jataka* stories. On the rear wall are the King (in a ceremonial headdress) and Queen approaching the Sacred Bodhi Tree, one of the earliest Ajanta paintings.

Cave 11 (originally second century BC, with sixth century alterations), has a veranda and roof painted with birds and flowers, a hall supported by four heavy pillars and a stone bench running along the right side. There are five cells and a shrine of a seated Buddha. **Cave 12** (with glauconite rock wall) and **Cave 13** (second century BC) are small *viharas*. **Cave 14** (fifth century AD) was planned on a grand scale but not completed and can be missed along with **Cave 15** (fifth century) which is a long hall with a Buddha carved out of the rock.

Later Mahayana period

The remaining caves all belong to the Later Mahayana period and date from the fifth century. **Cave 16**, with kneeling elephants at the entrance and the Cobra King, has a 20 m long and 3.5 m deep veranda that carries six plain octagonal pillars. There is a good view of the ravine from here.

Finding and preserving Ajanta

In 1819, a party of British army officers from Madras noticed the top of the façade of Cave 10 while tiger hunting. They investigated and discovered some caves, describing seeing 'figures with curled wigs'. Others made exploratory trips to the fascinating caves. In 1843, James Fergusson, horrified by the ravages of the elements, requested that the East India Company do something to preserve and protect the deteriorating caves.

In 1844 Captain Robert Gill, an artist, was sent to copy the paintings on the cave walls. He spent 27 years living in a small encampment outside, sending each new batch of paintings to Bombay and London. After nearly 20 years his work was almost complete and displayed in the Crystal Palace in London. In December 1866 all but a few of the paintings were destroyed in a fire. Gill soldiered on for another five years before giving up, and died from illness soon afterwards. He is buried in the small European cemetery at Bhusawal, 60 km to the north, 27 km from Jalgaon. The Bombay School of Arts sent out a team to copy the wall paintings under the guidance of the principal John Griffiths in the 1870s. The copies were stored in the Victoria and Albert Museum in London but this also had a fire in 1885, when 87 were destroyed.

In 1918 a team from Kyoto University Oriental Arts Faculty arrived at Ajanta to copy the sculptures. This they did by pressing wet rice paper against the surface to make casts which were then shipped back to Japan. In the early 1920s they were all destroyed by an earthquake.

In 1920 the Ajanta paintings were cleaned by the former Hyderabad Government under whose jurisdiction the caves lay. Two Italian restorers were commissioned and they set about fixing the peeling paintings to the walls of the caves. They first injected case in between the paintings and the plastered wall, then applied shellac as a fixative. The Griffiths team from Bombay had also applied a coat of varnish to bring out the colours of the paintings.

However, these varnishes darkened over the years, rendering the murals less visible. They also cracked, aiding the peeling process and the accumulation of moisture between the wall and the outer membrane. Since 1951 this varnish has been removed by the Archaeological Survey of India, which is now responsible for all restoration at the site. Preservation of the murals still poses enormous challenges.

The magnificent columned hall inside has six cells on each side and a beamed ceiling. The Teaching Buddha is seated on a lion throne. On the left the 'Dying Princess' portrays Nanda's new bride being told that he has been ordained a monk and renounced the world. Her misery is shared by all and everything around her. On the right wall are the remains of a picture of Prince Siddhartha, later the Buddha, using a bow.

Cave 17 (late fifth century) is similar to No 16 in layout and has the greatest number of murals. On the left of the veranda is a painted Wheel of Life. Over the entrance door is a row of seven Past Buddhas and the eighth, the Maitreya or Future Buddha, above a row of amorous Yaksha couples. Sculpted deities are carved on either side.

Murals show scenes from 17 *jatakas*: the worship of the Buddha, the Buddha preaching; Hansa *jataka*, with paintings of geese; Vessantara *jataka*, where the greedy Brahmin is portrayed, grinning; the miraculous 'Subjugation of the rogue elephant', sent to kill the Buddha; and the ogress who turns into a beautiful maiden by day! There are also panels showing royal processions, warriors, an assembled congregation from which you can get an accurate and detailed picture of the times. **Cave 18** (late fifth century) has little of merit and can be missed.

Cave 19 (late fifth century) is a Mahayana *chaitya* hall and was painted throughout. The façade is considered to be one of the most elegant in terms of execution and elaborate ornamentation, and has the arched *chaitya* window set into it. The interior is in the layout seen before, two rows of richly decorated columns leading up to and around the back of the standing Buddha, which here is in front of the slender *stupa*. This tall shrine has a triple stone umbrella above it. Note the seated Nagaraja with attendants.

Cave 20 is comparatively small and has imitation beams carved into the ceiling.

Later caves

The final few caves belong to the seventh century and are a separate and distinct group at the farthest end of the horseshoe near the waterfall. Only one, **Cave 26**, need be visited. **Cave 21** (early seventh century) has a fallen veranda with flanking chapels. **Cave 24** was intended to be the largest *vihara* but was not completed.

Cave 26 is a large *chaitya hall*. A partly damaged columned façade stretches across the front with the customary side chambers at each end. The 3-m-high window is flanked by sculptured Buddha reliefs. Inside, 26 pillars run in an elongated semi-circle around the cylindrical *stupa* which is decorated with Buddhas. The walls are decorated with sculpture, including the temptations by Mara's daughters, but the most striking being a 9-m reclining image of the Parinirvana Buddha about to enter Nirvana, his death mourned by his followers.

The walk back along the promenade connecting the shrines is pleasant enough but the return via the river, waterfall and forest walkway is delightful. Steps lead down from Cave 16 (with the carved elephants). The hilltop opposite the caves offers a fine view of the horseshoe shaped gorge.

Jalgaon

Jalgaon, 64 km from Ajanta on the NH6, is the rail junction for the Ajanta Caves. It was once at the centre of a savannah forest region, the habitat of tigers, leopards and other game. Now it has become an important cotton growing area and is interesting to walk around.

Listings Ajanta and around

Where to stay

Ajanta
Fardapur is 5 km from the caves.

$$ Ajanta T-Junction Holiday Resort
Fardapur, T02438-244033
Small and well-run resort with 6 clean cottages.

$$ Holiday Resort (MTDC)
Fardapur, T02438-244230.
12 basic rooms with bath (a mosquito net is vital and not provided), 16 a/c rooms in gardens are better value dorm (mattress only), restaurant.

$ New KP Park
Fardapur, T02438-202012, www.newkppark.com.
Comfortable budget hotel just 1 km from Fardapur bus stand.

Jalgaon

$$-$ Tourist Resort
Nehru Chowk, Station Rd, T0257-222 5192, www.hoteltouristresort.com.
35 clean spacious rooms with bath, 4 a/c, some have TV, restaurant.

$ Plaza
241 Navi Peth, Station Rd, T0257-222 7354.
Very clean, 10 air-cooled rooms with bath and TV, hot water in bucket, very helpful and friendly manager. Highly recommended.

Restaurants

Jalgaon

$$ Bombay
42 Station Rd, Navi Peth, opposite Anjali.
Excellent food, and a well-stocked bar.

$ Anjali
Opposite the police station.
Great spicy *thalis*.

$ Shreyas
201 Navi Peth.
Inexpensive South Indian vegetarian. Good bakery and ice cream shop on Station Rd.

Transport

Ajanta
Bus Regular buses from Fardapur (5 km from Ajanta Caves) to **Ellora** and **Aurangabad** (3 hrs), and **Jalgaon** (1½ hrs). Some buses also go direct from the caves to Aurangabad.

Taxi Taxis and auto-rickshaws can be hired for the day for visiting the sights. Expect to pay Rs 2000 for round trip from Aurangabad.

Train The caves can also be visited from **Jalgaon**, 59 km, which has the nearest railway station. *Gitanjali Exp* (convenient from Kolkata) does not stop at Jalgaon so best to get off at Bhusaval.

Jalgaon

Bus The **local bus stand** is about 1 km from the railway; auto-rickshaws Rs 10-15 for transfer. Direct buses to **Ajanta** from bus stand, 0815, 1030. Private buses from Station Rd for **Aurangabad**, **Indore**, **Hyderabad**, **Nagpur**, **Pune**, most between 2100-2200. Some via **Fardapur** (1½ hrs), go to Ajanta before going to Aurangabad (first departure 0700, 4 hrs); pleasant, interesting journey.

Train Trains run frequently to **Mumbai** (7¾ hrs), and several times daily to **Delhi** (20 hrs) via **Bhopal** and **Agra** (16 hrs), and **Kolkata** (29 hrs) via **Varanasi** (20 hrs). Also daily trains to **Madgaon** (Goa), 18-22 hrs. **Note** Some useful trains leave from Bhusaval, 27 km east.

Eastern Deccan *Colour map 5, A5, B4 and B5.*

rarely visited region with interesting historical sights

To the east of Aurangabad the road and railway go down the gentle slope of the great basin of the Godavari. Ancient erosion surfaces covered in some of India's richest black lava soils dominate the landscape. Rainfall gradually increases eastwards, and on the lower land the soils are some of the best in the peninsula – rich black soils derived from the lava, though on the higher land the much poorer red soils surface. Given the relative dryness an extraordinarily high percentage is cultivated. Sorghum (*jowar*) and short stapled cotton dominate. In the west, pearl millet.

Jalna

Jalna is the town to which **Abul Fazl**, who wrote the *Ain i Akbari*, was exiled and ultimately murdered by Bir Singh Deo of Orchha, see page 243, at the instigation of Jahangir. The area is dotted with forts. There is a **Dak Bungalow** and a **Rest House** in the town.

Lonar

Lonar, 145 km east of Aurangabad, is famous for its remarkable 2-km-wide **meteor crater**, believed to have formed 50,000 years ago. It contains a pool of green water around which are dotted the ruins of several temples. Wildlife including chinkara and gazelles can be spotted in the woods surrounding the lake, along with peacocks, storks and numerous other species of birds.

Nanded

An important commercial town on the river Godavari, Nanded makes a good place to break the journey between Hyderabad and Aurangabad. Guru Gobind Singh, the 10th Sikh guru, was assassinated here in 1708. There is an important *gurudwara* 1.5 km from the station.

Paithan

One of the oldest cities of the Deccan, Paithan is 55 km south of Aurangabad on the north bank of the Godavari River as it leaves the Nath Sagar reservoir. The **Jayakwadi Project** at Nath Sagar is a large earthen dam and reservoir. The Left Bank scheme is already providing irrigation all the way down the Godavari to Nanded 140 km to the east, and the equivalent Right Bank scheme is in progress.

Paithan is famous for a special kind of silk sari with brocaded gold borders and *pallu* (end-piece). Motifs of geese, parrots, peacocks and stylized leaves, flowers and creepers in dark greens, red and blue are brocaded against the golden background.

Ahmadnagar *Colour map 5, B4.*

Ahmadnagar (population 307,500), an historic Muslim town, has several Islamic monuments to visit. The town was founded in 1490 by Ahmad Nizam Shah Bahri, the son of a Brahmin from Vijayanagar who converted to Islam. His dynasty ruled the territory stretching from Aurangabad to Bassein until 1636. Its Islamic history reflects strong Persian influence, both architecturally in the Persian style Husaini Mosque, and theologically in the presence of Shi'a Muslims from Persia in the court.

Alamgir's Dargah is a small enclosure near the cantonment. Aurangzeb, who had begun his long Deccan campaign 24 years earlier, died here on 3 March 1707. The *dargah* marks his temporary resting place before his body was moved to Aurangabad. To the east is a white marble **Darbar Hall**, well worth visiting for the view from the roof. The fort (1599) is 1 km to the east of the city, 4 km northeast of the railway station. Circular, it has an 18-m-high wall reinforced with 22 bastions. The fort is now occupied by the army, but entry is possible (sign in at gate), to see the 'Leaders' Room' where Nehru and 11 colleagues spent 1942-1945, now a small museum. No photography. Among the numerous **mosques** in the city are the small but attractive Qasim (1500-1508), the Husaini, with its Persian style dome, and the Damadi (1567) with its splendid carved stonework. The Malik-i-Maidan cannon now standing on the Lion Bastion at Bijapur (see page 1028), was cast here. The well-preserved **Tomb of Nizam Shah** is in a large garden on the left bank of the Sina River.

Junnar

The **birthplace of Shivaji** in 1627, Junnar is another rock-cut cave temple site. The hill fort contains a monument commemorating Shivaji and a temple. On the east side of the hill there are more than 50 **Buddhist caves**. Most are *viharas* (monasteries) and date from the second century BC to the third century AD. They comprise the **Tulja Lena Group**, 2 km west of the town, which includes an unusual circular *chaitya* (chapel, Cave 3) with a dome ceiling. The **Bhuta Lena Group** is on the side of Manmodi Hill, 1500 m south of the town. The unfinished *chaitya* hall (Cave 40) has a well preserved façade containing reliefs of Laxmi. The **Ganesh Lena Group** is 4 km south of Junnar on the Lenyadri Hill. Cave 7 is a *vihara* with 19 cells leading off the main congregational hall and a colonnaded veranda. The octagonal columns are repeated in the *chaitya* hall next door (Cave 6).

Shivner Fort rises over 300 m above the plain and is approached from the south by a track that passes over the moat, through four gates, then dog-legs up the final stretch to the plateau. Shivaji's birthplace is to the north and not far from it is a ruined mosque. There are four tanks running down the centre. In the third century the site was a Buddhist *vihara* and on the east face there are about 50 rock cells. Maloji Bhonsla, Shivaji's grandfather, was granted the fort in 1599. Shivaji did not remain in it long as it was captured by the Mughals from the early 1630s. Several attempts to win it back failed.

Bhimashankar

Completely off the beaten track, the pilgrim site of Bhimashankar can be reached by road from Shivner or from the NH50 at Narayangaon. However, even buses are infrequent. The site is important to Hindus for the **Siva temple** built by the Peshwa Nana Phadnavis to house one of Maharashtra's five *jyotirlingas*.

Listings Eastern Deccan

Where to stay

Lonar

$ MTDC Holiday Resort
Near crater, T1800-229930.
Simple self-contained rooms in a clump of new cottages, some with crater views.

Nanded

$ Ashiana Park
Opposite Kala Mandir, off Doctor's Lane, near bus stand, T02462-236412.
Good value and friendly place for an overnight stay, with 21 good rooms and a young enthusiastic manager.

Ahmadnagar

$$-$ Sanket
Tilak Path, Station Rd, T0241-247 0701, www.hotelsanket.com.
30 rooms, some a/c, restaurant.

$ Swastik
Station Rd, 1 km from station, T0241-357575.
Has 25 rooms.

Restaurants

Nanded

$ Gujarati Bhoj Nalya
Sign in Hindi – look for High Class Veg Lunch Home, near bus stand.
Excellent food in an unlikely looking *dhaba*.

Ahmadnagar

$ Panchratna
Shivaji Chowk, T02438-235 9202.
Cheap Indian and continental cuisine.

Transport

Jalna

Bus Regular buses from **Lonar** (2 hrs), **Aurangabad** (2 hrs) and **Nanded** (5 hrs)

Train Several daily local trains to **Aurangabad**. Daily express trains to **Mumbai**, 10 hrs, and **Secunderabad**, 9½ hrs.

Lonar

Bus Buses run from **Jalna** (75 km, 2 hrs), **Jintur** (50 km, 1½ hrs); **Ajanta/Fardapur** (137 km) via **Buldana** and **Mehkar** (total 5 hrs).

Nanded

Bus Connections to many destinations. Several agents by bus stand for private buses.

Train Good connections to **Aurangabad**, 5 hrs; **Bengaluru (Bangalore)** 24½ hrs. **Mumbai**, 12½ hrs. **New Delhi**, 29 hrs (some continue to **Amritsar**, 37 hrs).

Ahmadnagar

Bus Regular buses to **Mumbai**, **Pune** and other towns in the state.

Train Daily to **Bengaluru (Bangalore)**: 19½ hrs; **Bhopal**, 12 hrs; **New Delhi**, 24 hrs; **Pune**, frequent services, 4 hrs, 1 daily continues to **Madgaon (Goa)**, 18¾ hrs.

Southern
Maharashtra

The mushrooming city of Pune is one of India's fastest-growing IT hubs, but pilgrims still flow in for the zen-and-free-love vibes of the Osho ashram. To the northwest lies the touristy hill station of Lonavla while to the southwest stands the hilltop fort of Raigad and, beyond, the more appealing (also touristy) hill station of Mahabaleshwar, whose waterfalls make it a favourite monsoon escape from Mumbai. Further south, Kolhapur and the cotton trade capital of Solapur make for interesting stopovers: the former en route to the stunning beaches of the South Konkan coast, which are every bit as good as Goa's with a fraction of the crowds.

Lonavla and around   *Colour map 5, B3.*

hectic hill town with Buddhist caves nearby

The reputation of Lonavla (population 55,700) as a hill station for Mumbai is scarcely a preparation for the narrow, densely packed street astride the National Highway. The expressway from Mumbai to Bengaluru (Bangalore) now shadows the town. Trinket and knick-knack shops and *chikki* stalls piled high with the famous peanut brittle type sweet, is the strung out reality of the town. Yet it has a reasonable range of hotels and pleasant walks and is a good base for the Karla and Bhaja Caves and the Rajmachi, Lohagaon and Visapur Forts nearby. The railway journey to Kalyan is interesting for rail enthusiasts.

Sights

The town has some lovely walks around and about. **Ryewood Park** is within a few minutes' reach along Ryewood Road. Further along the same road, 1.5 km from the bazar, the scenic **Monsoon Lake** with a small island and its temple has a kilometre long dam which gives a good bird's eye view. A further 2 km along INS Shivaji Road leads to **Bushy Dam** which attracts crowds who come to soak themselves on monsoon weekends. **Old Khandala Road** which joins the highway near Fariyas Hotel was once the main approach to Lonavla. Now it is pleasantly quiet, lined with stately bungalows and is good for an evening stroll. **Tungarli Dam**, a disused water reservoir on a hill, is near **Lion's Den** Hotel and can be reached by taking the left turn from the highway petrol pump near Jewel Resort. Clean public toilets are at the start of Ryewood Road (market end). Pleasant circuits around town start at **Lonavla Bazar**.

Karla Caves

11 km east of Lonavla, north side of the valley, Rs 100 foreigners, Rs 5 Indians.

This is the largest and best preserved Buddhist *chaitya* (chapel) cave in India, dating from the second to first century BC. Here, as at Bhaja, the stone mason imitated the earlier wooden structures; the main *chaitya* shows evidence of stone supporting a wooden gallery. Unlike Ajanta and Ellora it is off the beaten tourist track for foreigners, though it can be crowded with local tourists at weekends.

The approach is across an excavated court. At the massive entrance stands a stone column topped with *sinha stambha* (four lions). The Hindu temple just outside the entrance may have been built over the remains of a second pillar. The façade contains a large horseshoe shaped window above the three doorways (one for the priest and the other two for pilgrims). In front of the side doors were shallow water-filled troughs through which the pilgrims walked to cleanse their feet. The remarkable sun window diffused the light into the hall, falling gently onto the *stupa* at the end. Buddha images (circa fifth century) partly decorate the exterior. There are also panels between the doorways depicting six pairs of donors.

The main chamber (38 m by 14 m), entered through a large outer porch, is supported by 37 pillars. It is 8 m from floor to ceiling which is barrel-vaulted and ribbed with teak beams. There are 15 octagonal columns along either side, each capital having kneeling elephants carrying an embracing couple carved on it. The *stupa* is similar to that in Cave 10 at Ellora but here is topped by a wooden umbrella which is carved with delicate patterns. The other caves to the right of the entrance are of little interest.

Bhaja Caves
11 km east of Lonalva, south side of the valley; 5 km from Karla Caves.

There are 18 caves dating from the second century BC. You will need to climb about 170 steps. **Cave 12** is the best and possibly the first apsidal *chaitya* (a long hall with a semi-circular end) in India. The apse contains a *dagoba*. The vaulted roof of the chapel is supported by 27 columns. The exterior was once covered in a bas-relief, much of this has now been defaced. On either side of the main cave are others which were probably nuns' cells and working quarters. The inner sanctum of the last cave to the south has very fine sculptures, including the 'Dancing Couple'; you will need to tip the caretaker to open the door (surprisingly only the central cell echoes). To the south are 14 *stupas*, five of which are inside the cave.

The ruined **Lohagen Fort** is about 4 km beyond Bhaja and was twice taken and lost by Shivaji. **Visapur Fort**, which stands 600 m from the foot of the hill, is nearby. You can see them from the Bhaja Caves.

Listings Lonavla and around

Tourist information

Lonavla
MTDC
Near Lonavla Railway Station.

Where to stay

Lonavla
With a couple of notable exceptions, accommodation in this grubby town is overpriced.

$$$$-$$$ Duke's Retreat
Mumbai–Pune Rd, 4 km from Lonavla Railway in Khandala, T02114-269201.
62 rooms, restaurant, bar, pool, superb views.

$$$ Adarsh
Near bus stand, T02114-272353.
Efficiently run hotel in a relatively tranquil location, between the bus and train stations but away from the main road, with a good pure vegetarian restaurant.

$$$-$$ Chandralok
Shivaji Rd, opposite the bus stand entrance, T02114-272294.
Large, clean, comfortable airy rooms, some a/c, and excellent unlimited *thalis* (Rs 80-100).

$ DT Shahani Health Home
DT Shahani Rd, behind bus stand, T02114-272784.
Very clean triples in quiet locality, varied menu in canteen.

$ Narayani Dham
Tungarli Rd, near Kaivalyadhama Yoga Centre, T(0)93211 40483.
If you can get one, the bright, clean and modern rooms in this massive gaudy pink temple complex are possibly the best bargain in town. The canteen churns out cheap and delicious Indian meals, and splashing fountains and an on-site cow shed add up to a peaceful and surreal place to spend 1 or 2 nights.

Karla Caves

$$$-$ Holiday Resort (MTDC)
Off the Mumbai–Pune Rd (NH4), T02114-282230.
Vast sylvan surroundings, with 64 clean rooms in cottages for 2-4 (some comfortable a/c), canteen and a bar.

Restaurants

Lonavla

$$ Lonavla Hotel
1st floor, NH-4 near bus stand.
Excellent Indian (try the chicken kebabs), with generous helpings. There's a pleasant ambience bar serving affordable drinks. Very clean, a/c.

$ Shivam Garden Restaurant
Cheaper, but offers equally good and strictly pure vegetarian.

$ Zeus Bakery
MG Rd, near National Chikki.
Burger, sandwiches, snacks, etc, from Rs 25.

Festivals

Lonavla
Feb/Mar Sivaratri is celebrated at Mahadev Temple with great ceremony and a fair.

Shopping

Lonavla
Chikki, the candy mix of jaggery and dried fruit and nuts, is the local favourite, with endless variety in the shops in the market along MG Rd. About Rs 40 per kilo; dried fruit chikki, Rs 200 or more.
Cooper's, *in market near railway station.* Famous for fudge; try coconut or choco walnut.
Shakti, *Shivaji Rd/Flyover junction.* Excellent and unusual concoctions for health seekers; vitamin C-rich Indian gooseberry (*amla*), black sesame (*til*), sugar-free cashew and dried fruit.

What to do

Lonavla
Body and soul
Kaivalyadhama Yogic Health Care Centre, *Valvan Dam approach road, T02114-273039, www.kdham. com.* Founded in 1924 by Swami Kuvalyananda, a pioneer in scientific yoga research and one-time adviser to Gandhi, offers a range of options from 1-week 'nature cure' packages (a holistic approach to curing everything from a bad back

to diabetes, using yoga, massages, diet and very retro hydrotherapy) to a 1-year diploma in yoga and 6-week teacher training courses. There's also an Ayurvedic clinic on site, run under the guidance of respected Pune-based Dr Jagadish Bhutada.
Vedanta Academy, *Malavali Station Rd, T02114-282278, satva@vsnl.com).* A lush haven off the Mumbai Pune Highway offers a free 3-year (or shorter) course for 50 students from around the world. Swami Parthasarathy lectures regularly in London and New York, and insists on a well-integrated mixture of serious study and physical exercise. Phone in advance if you want to visit.

Transport

Lonavla
Bus ST buses to the **caves**: couple of buses to Karla in the morning from 0600, last return about 1900. To **Rajmachi Fort**, buses are unpredictable; **Pune** (62 km) and **Mumbai** (101 km); special a/c every 30 mins, last departure 1630, Rs 81. **Lucky Travels**, Hotel Gulistan, Bombay Pune Rd, near the flyover, T02114-270332, runs fast a/c buses to **Mumbai**, Rs 200.

Rickshaw Auto-rickshaw from Lonavla to the **Karla** and **Bhaja Caves**, Rs 250, more for **Bedsa**. From station to **Kaivalyadhama**, Rs 40.

Taxi JK Travels, T(0)9870-779000, kkuku28@ hotmail.com, friendly and reliable for Mumbai/ Pune airport pickups and local sightseeing.
Karla and **Bhaja** Rs 800. One way to **Mumbai** Rs 1600-2400 (under 3 hrs), **Pune** Rs 900-1100.

Train Enquiries, T02114-272215. Lonavla is on the **Mumbai** (**CST**)–**Pune** line with at least 16 trains daily in each direction. To **Mumbai**, 2½-3 hrs; **Pune**, 1-1½ hrs.

Karla and Bhaja Caves
Tourist taxis from Lonavla charge Rs 800 for 3 hrs, allowing a brief visit to both caves. For Karla Caves: from the Karla/Bhaja crossroads on the NH4 at Karla village, turn left (north). The car park is at the bottom of the ridge with steps up to the caves (20 mins). Buses from Lonavla: a couple from 0600; last return 1900.
For Bhaja Caves: from Karla village on the NH4, a road to the south goes to Bhaja, crossing the railway at Malavli. Vehicles stop at the car park in new Bhaja 'town', from there follow a path and then climb uphill for about 20 mins to the caves. Heavy rain can close part of the Bhaja Rd to vehicles. Local passenger trains stop at Malavli.

After the small towns and seemingly endless spaces of the Deccan Plateau, Pune (population 3.1 million) comes as a vibrant surprise. Touched by the élan of Mumbai, which is within commuting distance, the town comes to life in the early evening with open-air cafés and pavements crowded with young people out to enjoy themselves in a modern, cosmopolitan atmosphere, a place to see and be seen.

It is an important and respected university town and one of the fastest growing IT centres of India, whilst the Osho Meditation Resort continues to attract large numbers of Westerners desperately seeking something.

Sights

The city stands on the right bank of the Mutha River before its confluence with the Mula and was divided up into 19 *peths* (wards). Some were named after the days of their weekly market, others after well-known people.

Near the railway station is the English Gothic-style **Sassoon Hospital** (1867). To the southwest is the **Oleh David Synagogue** (1867), sometimes known locally as the 'Red Mandir', and Sir David Sassoon's Tomb. **St Mary's Church** (1825) to the south was consecrated by Bishop Heber, who toured the country extensively in the 1830s. St Patrick's Cathedral is beyond the Racecourse. Immediately north are the **Empress Gardens**.

Moving back to the west by the river is **Visram Bagh**, an attractive Maratha palace. Now used to house government offices and a post office, the entrance and balcony have beautifully carved woodwork. Opposite is **Raja Kelkar Museum** ⓘ *1378 Shukrawar Peth, closed 26 Jan and 15 Aug, 0930-1830 (last entry 1730), foreigners Rs 200, Indians Rs 15*, which is worth a visit, with a private collection focusing on traditional Indian arts including carved temple doors, musical instruments,

Essential Pune

Finding your feet

The airport, 10 km to the northeast, has flights from major cities. There are airport buses, taxis and rickshaws to the centre. Pune Junction Station is on the main railway line south from Mumbai and has daily direct trains south to Goa, Bengaluru and Kerala, and north towards Delhi and Gujarat. The main station is in the thick of the action: 1 km north of MG Road, the main shopping street, and 2 km west of Koregaon Park and the Osho resort. The other station, Shivaji Nagar, is five minutes further west and handy for the hotels and shops of Deccan Gymkhana. Most buses from the north terminate at the nearby Shivaji Nagar Bus Stand, and those from the south at Swargate, 3 km to the south. The Railway Bus Stand, next to Pune Junction, serves the city and Mumbai.

Getting around

Pune is very spread out so it is best to hire an auto-rickshaw. Shared rickshaws run on popular routes, such as Pune Station to Swargate Bus Stand, and are more frequent but a bit more expensive than the red city buses. See Transport, page 1144.

When to go

The climatic contrast between Pune and the ghats just 70 km away is astonishing. The monsoon winds of June to September drop most of their rain on the ghats, which is over 3500 mm a year compared to Pune's 715 mm.

Useful contacts

Foreigners' Registration Office, ground floor, Main Building, Police Commissioner's Office, Sadhu Waswani Road, T020-2612 8977.

Tip...

The Maratha forts south of Pune are best visited by hiring a car since bus journeys can be slow and tiring.

Pune

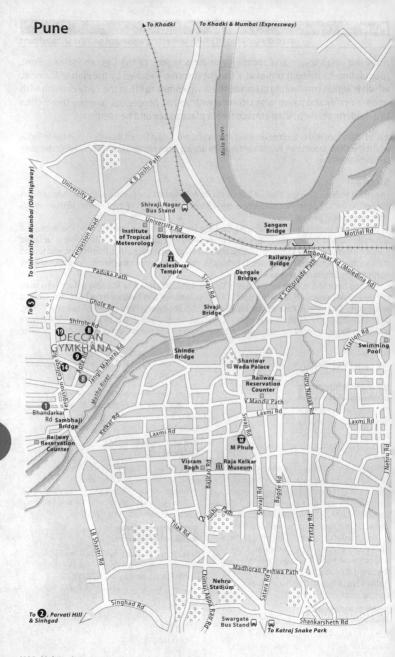

To Khadki

To Khadki & Mumbai (Expressway)

Mula River

K B Josh Path

University Rd

Shivaji Nagar
Bus Stand

University Rd

University Rd

Sangam
Bridge

Motilal Rd

Institute
of Tropical
Meteorology

Observatory

Railway
Bridge

Ambedkar Rd (Moledina Rd)

Pataleshwar
Temple

Dengale
Bridge

Paduka Path

Sivaji Rd

V S Ghorpade Path

Sivaji
Bridge

Ghole Rd

Shirole Rd

DECCAN
GYMKHANA

Jangli Maharaj Rd

Shinde
Bridge

Shaniwar
Wada Palace

Station Rd

Swimming
Pool

Railway
Reservation
Counter

Guru Nanak Rd

Apte Rd

Fergusson College Rd

Mutha River

V Mandir Path

Laxmi Rd

Laxmi Rd

Bhandarkar
Rd

Sambhaji
Bridge

Kelkar Rd

Laxmi Rd

Sivaji Rd

Bagde Rd

Railway
Reservation
Counter

M Phule

Visram
Bagh

Raja Kelkar
Museum

Bajirao Rd

C J Joshi Path

Tilak Rd

Shivaji Rd

Pratap Rd

B Shastri Rd

J Nehru Rd

Madhorao Peshwa Path

Singhad Rd

Nehru
Stadium

Chimaji Appa Rd

Satara Rd

To 2, Parvati Hill
& Sinhad

Swargate
Bus Stand

Shankarsheth Rd

To Katraj Snake Park

Where to stay

Ajit 1
Aurora Towers 3
Blue Diamond 4
Casa Nava 5
Dreamland 6
Homeland 7
Ketan 8
National 9
O 10
Samrat 12
Srimaan 14
Sunderban 15
Surya Villa 16

Restaurants

ABC Farms 1
Abhiruchi 2
Chinese Room 3
Coffee House &
  Landmark Books 4
Garden Court 5
German Bakery 6
Kayani 7
Khyber 8
Latif's 3
Little Italy 10
Malaka Spice 11
Marz-O-Rin 12
Roopali 14
Shiv Kailash 16
Shreya's 9
Terttulia 17
Touche the Sizzler
  & Manney's Books 18
Vaishali 19
Zamu's Place 20

The early home of Shivaji, Pune became the Maratha capital in 1750. After a period under the Nizam of Hyderabad's rule it came under British control in 1817, who then developed it as a summer capital for Mumbai and as a military cantonment. It is now a major growth centre with a booming computer software industry. For all its connections with the Marathas there are few physical reminders of their power. The Campsite has wide streets with a British colonial feel while old Pune still has narrow streets, old shops and brick and mud houses. The town is renowned for its military cantonment and educational and scientific institutions.

pottery, miniature paintings, nutcrackers, brass padlocks and lamps. The vast collection can only be displayed in rotation. **Shaniwar Wada Palace** (1736) ① *0800-1800, foreigners Rs 100, Indians Rs 50; sound and light show in English at 2015, Rs 25*, built by Baji Rao, the last Peshwa's grandfather, was burnt down in 1827. Only the massive outer walls remain. The main entrance is by the iron-spiked Delhi Gate. Elephants were used for crushing people to death in the nearby street. The gardens were irrigated and had the **Hazari Karanje** (thousand jet fountain); in fact there were only 197 jets.

Cross the river by **Shivaji** (Lloyd) **Bridge** into Shivaji Road. Along this are the Pataleshwar Temple and the Military College (1922), a 9-m-high statue of Shivaji (sculpted by VP Karkomar), stands in front. **Sangam** (Wellesley) **Bridge** (1875) is near the confluence of the rivers. **Garden Reach** (1862-1864), 300 m further on, is the family house of the influential Sassoon family. The main road then passes the Institute of Tropical Meteorology and the white-domed observatory.

Raj Bhavan (Government House, 1866) designed by James Trubshawe is in Ganeshkhind. Nearby is the impressive **University of Poona** in a sprawling campus. In Aundha Road, 3 km north, are the **Botanical Gardens**. From here on the way to Holkar's Bridge is **All Saints Church** (1841), containing the regimental colours of the 23rd Bombay Light Infantry. A kilometre southeast is the Roman Catholic **Chapel of St Ignatius**. Cross the river by Holkar's Bridge to the **Tomb of Vithoji Holkar**, trampled by an elephant in 1802, and the Mahadeo Temple built in his memory. Sir Henry St Clair Wilkins designed **Deccan College** (1864).

To the east is the former **Palace of the Aga Khan** (1860) ① *Ahmednagar Rd, 0930-1730, foreigners Rs 100, Indians Rs 5*, who was attracted to Pune by the horse racing. Mahatma Gandhi was placed under house arrest here and his wife Kasturba died here. The small **Gandhi National Memorial** museum with personal memorabilia is worth a visit. Kasturba Gandhi's memorial tomb is on the estate. South of the Bund Garden (Fitzgerald) Bridge are the riverside **Bund Gardens**, a popular place for an evening stroll. Further south towards the railway station is the **Tribal Museum** ① *28 Queens Garden, 1000-1700, free*, an excellent small museum of items relating to the tribal heritage of Maharashtra. Sections include domestic life (utensils, ornaments and instruments), agriculture, weapons and woodcarving.

Koregaon Park, 2 km northeast of the station, is home to the ★ **Osho International Meditation Resort** (the rebranded 'Osho Commune International') ① *T020-6601 9900, www.osho.com, 1-hr tours at 0900 and 1400 (part video, part silent walking tour), Rs 10, buy tickets day before from Visitor Centre, 0900-1200, 1400-1530; visitors who wish to spend longer are screened for HIV; 1st day fee of Rs 1410 (Indians Rs 1060) includes AIDS test and 'welcome morning'; subsequent days Rs 550 (Indians Rs 200); compulsory maroon and white robes cost extra*. The lush landscaped commune, spread over 10 ha, was established in 1974 by the controversial Guru Bhagwan Rajneesh (Osho), and revived in the 1980s after he and his followers were ejected from Oregon amid controversy over the libidinous lifestyle that flourished under Osho's particular brand of Zen. Since his death the ashram's financial base has moved to New York and Zurich, and through the daily meditations and extended courses run at the 'multiversity' attract a hugely diverse community of international visitors, most of whom seem to thoroughly enjoy meeting each other over a spot of Sufi twirling or meditation in the pyramidal auditorium, many feel that the essence of the guru's teachings has been compromised.

Described by the *Wall Street Journal* as the "spiritual Disneyland for disaffected First World yuppies" (there's an Olympic-size pool, frequent parties and a serene guesthouse with rooms from Rs 3500 a night), the ashram has nevertheless done a superb job of greening the suburb of Koregaon Park; the gardens of **Osho Teerth** ① *0600-0900, 1500-1800, free*, a block east of the main ashram entrance, make a beautiful place for a stroll or some meditation.

Parvati Hill, just south of the Mutha Right Bank Canal, has Hindu temples and commands excellent views over the town and surrounding countryside. Pune also has the **National Defence Academy** which trains cadets for the three defence services. There are parks and gardens dotted around the city.

Sinhagarh Fort

Sinhagarh is 24 km southwest of Pune. The 'Lion Fort', situated in the Bhuleshwar range, was a small hill station during the British period. The ruined, roughly triangular **fort** stands in a beautiful setting on a hill 700 m above the land below. The ascent is steep. To the north and south are cliffs topped with 12-m high basalt walls. There were two entrances, the Pune Gate (northeast) and Kalyan Gate (southwest), both protected by three successive gates. On the west side of the hill the wall was continued across a gorge, creating a dam. Mohammad bin Tughluq, see page 1302, captured the fort in 1328, and in 1486 Malik Ahmad, founder of Ahmadnagar took it. Nearly 200 years later the Marathas captured it in what has become a legendary feat of bravery and skill by the commander scaling the cliffs at night and taking the garrison by surprise. To the western end is a small, covered, natural spring (known as 'Dev Taki' or 'God's Tank'), which yields cool, fresh sweet water throughout the year. Sinhagarh is a popular day out for people from Pune. Try the locally produced curd served in black clay pots with jeera seeds, salt and sugar.

On the way to Sinhagarh from Pune you pass the **Khadakwasla reservoir** on the Mutha River. The dam was constructed in 1879, the first large dam in the Deccan.

Around 35 km southeast of Pune at an altitude of 1220 m, the hill fort of **Purandhar** commands a high point on the Western Ghats. It is a double fort, the lower one, **Vajragad** to the east and Purandhar itself. Together they command a narrow passage through the hills. Like other hill forts, Purandhar was defended by curtain walls, in this case 42 km in extent, relieved by three gateways and six bastions. The earliest fortifications date from 1350.

Purandhar Fort

Some 35 km southeast of Pune, at an altitude of 1220 m, this fort commands a high point on the Western Ghats. It is a double fort, the lower one, **Vajragad** to the east and **Purandhar** itself. Together they command a narrow passage through the hills. Like other hill forts, Purandhar was defended by curtain walls, in this case 42 km in extent, relieved by three gateways and six bastions. The earliest fortifications date from 1350.

Listings Pune *map p1138*

Tourist information

MTDC
I-Block, Central Building, at corner of Sassoon and BJ Rds (enter from BJ Rd), T020-2612 6867.
This is only useful if you want to book MTDC accommodation or buy a state map. There are counters at Pune Station, T020-2611 1720, and the airport.

Where to stay

Room rates have soared along with Pune's credentials as a business city, but the recession has bitten and many middle and upper-bracket hotels have been humbled into giving discounts. Genuinely cheap rooms are hard to find; the best bet is to trawl the lanes of Koregaon Park, where auto-rickshaw drivers promise rooms in guesthouses for Rs 300-500. There are also excellent deals in the lower-middle range (Rs1200-3000). Discounts are often available Apr-Sep.

$$$ Blue Diamond (Taj)
11 Koregaon Rd, T020-6602 5555, www.tajhotels.com.
110 rooms, stylish, comfortable and classy, special discounts for business guests with partners.

$$$ O Hotel
North Main Rd, Koregaon Park, T020-4001 1000, www.ohotelsindia.com.

Pune's 1st design hotel, decked out in dark woods and granite, with huge white bathtubs overlapping between bed and bathroom. The 9th-floor spa offers massage and haircuts with a view, and the adjoining resto-bar has Pune's coolest rooftop site, with circular day beds set on granite islands in a shallow pond. Wi-Fi in rooms.

$$$-$$ Sunderban
19 Koregaon Park, next to Osho Resort, T020-2612 4949, www.tghotels.com.
The 58 rooms here vary hugely, from grey and dingy little economy doubles out the back to lovely suites and studios in the art deco main building. Deluxe rooms are good value, with well-worn leather lounges and lots of space. Set around pleasant lawns, and serenaded by Osho meditations from the ashram next door. Wi-Fi available, breakfast included.

$$-$ Casa Nava
Various locations in Koregaon Park, T(0)9823-169507, www.casanava.com.
Superb, individually decorated apartments run by expat interior designer Nava. Some have a boho-chic feel, with colourful day-beds and painted desks overlooking the river, others go for a minimalist white look. Each comes with fully equipped kitchen and internet. Popular with the Osho crowd, and excellent for long stays.

$$ Aurora Towers
9 Moledina Rd, T020-2613 1818, www.hotelauroratowers.com.
68 large rooms with views, good restaurants, friendly service, 24-hr exchange, terraced pool, good value and location near the top of MG Rd. Room reports vary, so ask to see a couple.

$$ Ketan
917/19A Shivajinagar, FC Rd, T020-2565 5081.
28 clean and well-maintained rooms with bath, helpful staff, and a great location opposite Vaishali restaurant.

$$ Samrat
17 Wilson Garden, near Pune Station, T020-2613 7964, thesamrathotel@vsnl.net.
The doubles here represent one of the best deals in town, spotless and modern, set around a soaring lobby, but the suites are bizarre, with 2 TVs placed back to back in the wide open hatch between bedroom and living room. Wi-Fi is extra, buffet breakfast is included.

$$ Srimaan
361/5 Bund Garden Rd, T020-2613 3535.
30 pleasant rooms, clean, Italian restaurant.

$$ Surya Villa
Lane A, behind O Hotel, Koregaon Park, T020-2612 4501, www.hotelsuryavilla.com.
An Osho favourite, with light, clean and spacious rooms, internet downstairs and the popular **Yogi Tree** café serving a pan-global menu from tofu steaks to pasta. The German Bakery is just down the road, too.

$ Ajit
766/3 Deccan Gymkhana, T020-2567 1212.
16 rooms, some a/c, restaurant, small, dark but functional, in a peaceful location.

$ Dreamland
12/2 Connaught Rd, T020-2612 2121.
A typical station hotel, with 43 pretty shabby rooms, some a/c. The location and the excellent Sagar restaurant downstairs are the main reasons to stay.

$ Homeland
18 Wilson Garden, T020-2612 3203, www.hotelhomeland.net.
22 small but reasonably clean rooms in an appealing art deco building. OK for a night.

$ National
14 Sassoon Rd, T020-2612 7780.
Surprisingly quiet for its location opposite the station, this decaying old timber mansion offers decent value en suite doubles and cheaper, grimy cottages with shaded sit-outs in the back yard. The cheapest rooms, gloomy little cells with no windows, share unpleasant toilets. Room service chai and snacks and filtered drinking water available.

Restaurants

Pune has a variety of dining options to rival Mumbai. In Deccan Gymkhana, Jangli Maharaj (JM) Rd claims to have the highest concentration of eateries of any street in India. MG Rd and East St in Camp have juice shops and cafés to keep the shoppers happy, while Koregaon Park and nearby Kalyani Nagar are where expats, ashramites and local cool kids fill up on expensive international fare. Many of the top hotels lay on a Sun brunch; the one at Le Meridien, north side of Pune Station, is among the best.

ABC Farms
North Main Rd, Koregaon Park.
A complex of upscale restaurants and pubs, including Swiss Cheese Garden (for fondues), Shisha Café (Persian food and the best

atmosphere, with hookahs and low-slung day beds), and the popular Curve Bar. No longer the trendiest in town and a bit tired-looking, but still packed on weekends.

$$ Chinese Room
Gen Thimmaya Rd.
One of Pune's oldest Chinese joints. High standards and a loyal fan base. Bar and good ice creams.

$$ Garden Court
76/2 Pashan–NDA Rd, Pashan Hills 5 km west of Gymkhana, T020-2528 4949, www.gardencourtpune.com.
Excellent food and ambience, especially at night when the city lights spread out below. Recommended.

$$ Khyber
1258/2 JM Rd.
Indian with some continental dishes, beer bar and ice creams.

$$ Latif's
Gen Thimmaya Rd.
Good for North Indian, chicken dishes. Recommended.

$$ Little Italy
Srimaan hotel (see Where to stay).
Italian. Recommended for tomato and mozzarella salad, great pizza, pasta, fresh bread, pleasant candlelit atmosphere and.

$$ Malaka Spice
Lane 5, Koregaon Park, T(0)95952 88288.
Indoor-outdoor place surrounded by pot plants, with an interesting menu of pan-Southeast Asian with an Indian twist: the *laksa* is tasty, but not for purists. Wi-Fi.

$$ The Place
Touché the Sizzler, Clover Centre, 7 Moledina Rd, T020-2613 4632.
Open 1130-1530 and 1900-2100. Best sizzlers in town (the sizzler reputedly was invented by the present owner's father). Also chicken platters, super ice creams and spotless toilets. Recommended.

$$ Terttulia
North end of Lane 6, Koregaon Park, T020-2615 2180.
Pune's first effort at a gastro-pub, with specials chalked up on a blackboard (risottos, pizza, etc), and outside tables where the hip young things in wraparound shades and cigarettes glued to their lips enjoy the chilled-out vibe.

$$ Zamu's Place
Dhole Patil Rd.
Western cuisine, with good sizzlers and Parsi dishes.

$ Poona Coffee House
1256/2 Deccan Gymkhana.
A local landmark, good for sandwiches, snacks and sweets.

$ Roopali
FC Rd.
An old favourite for cheap South Indian *thalis* and *dosas*.

$ Shabree
Hotel Parichay, FC Rd.
Unlimited Maharashtrian *thalis*, and traditional vegetarian snacks.

$ Shreya's
1242-B Apte Rd, Deccan Gymkhana.
Friendly waiters dish out superb Maharashtran *thalis* in this clean hotel dining room.

$ Vaishali
FC Rd.
South Indian dishes served in a spotless restaurant. Starts early for breakfast, offering mainly snacks; their special SPDP (Sev Potato Dahi Puri) is a Pune institution, and no one should leave town without trying it. It's also a very popular meeting place and there are queues in the evenings for the lovely rear garden. Highly recommended.

Cafés and snacks

Coffee House
2 Moledina Rd.
Good coffee and South Indian snacks.

Shiv Kailash
Sassoon Rd opposite Pune Station.
The best *lassis* in the city, always crowded.

Bakeries

German Bakery
North Main Rd.
It's business as usual again at this 20-year-old magnet for travellers and Osho ashramites, destroyed by a bomb in Feb 2010, with the same great coffee and pastries.

Kayani
East St.
Irani bakery with a long pedigree, specializing in Mawa cakes and Shrewsbury biscuits.

Marz-O-Rin
MG Rd.
One of the few cafés in Pune to make it onto INTACH's heritage walk, serving good sandwiches, cakes and ice cream since 1965.

Bars and clubs

Check the *Pune Times* supplement in *The Times of India* for listings. FC Rd, MG Rd, Kalyani Nagar and ABC Farms (see Restaurants) are popular student hangouts in the evenings, while the Osho Meditation Resort hosts what devotees claim are the best parties in town. Most clubs open 2130-0200.

1000 Oaks
2417 East St.
Intimate pub with outdoor seating area, live music, family atmosphere, good for a quiet night out.

Club Polaris
At Taj Blue Diamond.
Exclusive feel, reserved for members and hotel guests.

Fire and Ice/Soho's
Next to Bishop's School, Kalyani Nagar.
Literally an old barn, Soho's has pleasant outdoor seating and good food, while Fire and Ice offers a shockingly loud Indian disco.

Scream
Le Meridien hotel.
Huge dancefloor, happening parties.

TDS (10 Downing Street)
Boat Club Rd.
Done out in imitation of an English pub, with a disco upstairs.

Festivals

Aug/Sep Ganesh Chaturthi 11 day MTDC festival with concerts, food fairs, bullock-cart races, folk shows.
Dec/Jan Pune Marathon.

Shopping

The main shopping centres in Pune are in MG Rd (Camp area), Deccan Gymkhana, Karve Rd, Laxmi Rd (for clothing and textiles) and Hanuman Mandir (for silver jewellery and leather *chappals*).

Books and music
Alurkar Music House, *4 Swapna Nagri, Karve Rd*, *T020-2544 0662*. Family-run shop, specialists in Indian classical music.

Crossword Books, *junction of RBM Rd and Connaught Rd, northeast of Pune Station.* Wide range of books, magazines and stationery.
Landmark, *Moledina Rd.* Big new shop on 2 levels, with CDs and DVDs downstairs and a huge selection of books upstairs.
Manney's, *Clover Centre, Moledina Rd.* Comfortable a/c, excellent stock, bargains.
Modern Book Store, *Gen Thimmaya Rd.* Good selection. Recommended.

Crafts and gifts
Either/Or, *same complex as Crossword Books*, *T020-2605 02225, www.eitheror.in.* Funky, ethnic and eco-sensible handmade crafts, textiles, board games, jewellery and homewares. Highly recommended.

Malls
Nirman Shopping Complex, *opposite Shivaji Market, Convent St.* A modern mall.

Markets
Juna Bazar, *in Vir Santaji Ghorpade Rd, near Maldhaka Chowk.* Every Wed and Sun 0900-1500. Excellent flea market, with everything from second-hand saris to antique coins.

Textiles
Look out for Pune saris (cotton-silk weave).
Kalaniketan, *opposite Sancheti Hospital, JM Rd.* For premium silkwear. Wholesale sari market at **Raviwarpeth** ('Sunday Lane').

What to do

Apple Travels, *Amir Hotel Building, Connaught Rd, T020-2665 6883*. Agent for **Indian Airlines**, efficient service.
Pune Municipal Transport (PMT), *T020-2450 3200, www.pmpml.org.* Runs daily 'Pune Darshan' Tours, 0900-1700, Rs 300. Booking at Swargate and Deccan bus depots.

Transport

Air Pune's Lohegaon airport is 10 km northeast of the centre, with daily flights to **Ahmedabad**, **Bengaluru** (**Bangalore**), **Chennai**, **Delhi**, Goa, **Hyderabad**, **Indore**, **Jaipur**, **Kolkata** and **Mumbai** and **Nagpur**; also international flights to **Dubai**. Transport to town: PMPML buses travel to **Deccan Gymkhana**, but they're not very frequent; a taxi will cost around Rs 500. Daily flights to **Ahmedabad**, **Bengaluru** (**Bangalore**), **Chennai**, **Delhi**, **Hyderabad**, **Indore**, **Jaipur**, **Kochi**, **Kolkata**, **Mumbai** and **Nagpur**.

Auto-rickshaw The best mode for getting around town. Drivers should use meter and carry a rate card; Pune Station to Koregaon Park costs Rs 40-50. Swargate to Railway Station Bus Stand Rs 60-70. There are extra charges for out-of-town routes and between 2400-0500. Shared rickshaws meet next to the Town Bus Stand run on key routes, eg to Swargate; drivers call out their destination, Rs 15 per seat.

Local bus Pune Municipal Transport (PMT) buses run throughout the city and suburbs from the **City Bus Stand** next to Pune Station, T020-2444 0417. Routes 2, 3, 4 between Pune Station and **Swargate Bus Stand**; Route 74 Pune Station to Deccan Gymkhana

Long-distance bus MSRTC buses connect Pune with all major towns within the state from three different bus stands.

Pune Railway Station Bus Stand, T020-2612 6218, for Mumbai and the south: **Belgaum**; **Chiplun**; **Ganpatipule**; **Hubli**; **Kolhapur**; **Mumbai**; **Mahabaleshwar**; ASIAD deluxe buses every 15 mins; **Panaji**; **Ratnagiri**; **Solapur**.

Shivaji Nagar Bus Stand, T020-2553 6970, for the east/northeast: **Ahmedabad**; **Alibag**; **Amravati**; **Aurangabad**; **Indore**; **Nagpur**; **Hyderabad**; **Nashik**; **Shirdi**; **Vadodara**.

Swargate Bus Stand, T020-2444 1591, for south/southeast. **Belgaum**; **Kolhapur**; **Solapur**; **Mahabaleshwar**; **Mangalore**; **Ratnagiri**.

Kadamba Transport Corporation, operates the **Panaji** route at 0630, 1800 and 1900, via **Mapusa**; buses poor and often dirty; Booking office open 0900-1200, 1500-1800. *Asiad* and *Express* buses run regular services.

Private companies run more comfortable buses to many of these destinations, and to **Sahar International Airport**, 4 hrs; agents have offices opposite Pune Station.

Car hire About Rs 1300-2200 per day, from **Goodluck Travels**, T(0)7709-202111.

Taxi Ordinary local taxis are not metered, but some companies offer point-to-point billing and time/distance packages, eg **Cel Cabs**, T020-6060 9090. Taxis to/from **Mumbai Airport**, Rs 1700-3200, or shared around Rs 950 per seat; **Share My Route** is one booking service, T(0)95525 23670.

Train The main booking counter is at Pune Junction Station, which has a counter for foreigners on Platform 1. Other booking offices in Deccan Gymkhana (Karve Rd) and Raviwar Peth (NC Kelkar Rd). Enquiries T131, Reservations T132. **Aurangabad**: 1 slow passenger train daily, 11 hrs. **Bengaluru** (Bangalore) via **Guntakal** (for connections to **Hospet/Hampi**): 2-7 daily, 24 hrs. **Mumbai** (**CST**): 17 trains daily, fastest is *Deccan Queen 12124*, 0715, 3½ hrs; all go via **Lonavla**, 1-1½ hrs. **Delhi**: 3 daily, 27¾ hrs. **Hyderabad**: 4-5 daily, 11½ hrs. **Chennai** via **Solapur** and **Guntakal**: 3 daily, 22½ hrs. **Madgaon** (Goa): 1 daily, 14½ hrs.

Mahabaleshwar and around *Colour map 5, B3.*
a popular weekend retreat, with cool weather and forests

Situated in one of the wettest parts of the Western Ghats, Mahabaleshwar (population 13,000, altitude 1370 m) is in a pleasantly wooded setting at the head of the Krishna River. It is the main hill station for Pune, and almost as popular as Matheran among Mumbai weekenders. Cool and relaxed with some good walking trails and excellent views, it's a good place for an overnight stop. The altitude makes the climate pleasant during the dry season. It is, however, becoming increasingly touristy with crowds of Mumbai holidaymakers descending on it, especially during school holidays.

'Discovered' in 1824 by General Lodwick, to whom there is still a monument on the Elephant's Head Point, Mahabaleshwar was declared an official British sanatorium in 1828 and was once the summer capital of the Bombay Presidency. These days there are pleasant walks and waterfalls to visit. **Arthur's Seat** (12 km) looks out over a 600-m precipice to the Konkan. The nine-hole Golf Course is built on a cliff side. **Venna Lake** has boating and fishing. From **Mumbai Point** and the hills around the town you can see the sea on a clear day.

Sights

There are several typical British hill station buildings: **Christchurch** (1842, enlarged 1867); the cemetery; **Frere Hall** (1864) with its mullioned windows and the Club, founded in 1882; **Government House** (1829) on Mount Malcolm; The **Lodwick Monument** (1874) in honour of the town's founder, and the **Beckwith Monument**.

The old town contains three temples (Krishnabai, Ram and Hanuman) which you can walk to from a turn off Elphinstone Road. **Krishnabai** or Panchganga with a self-formed *linga* resembling a piece of volcanic lava, is said to have five streams, including the Krishna, flowing from it. The 13th-century Yadav King Singhan built a small tank at the Krishna's source which starts its 1400-km journey across the Deccan to the sea. This part of the 'Deccan Trap' has underground caverns which hold water and give rise to springs.

Panchgani

Settled as a hill station before Mahabaleshwar, Panchgani is set among casuarinas and silver oak at an altitude of 1334 m, surrounded by the five hills from which it takes its name. It has a compact centre with lovely walks, stunning views and friendly people, which makes it well worth a visit. MTDC can arrange for you to visit some of the old British and Parsi bungalows. The drive to Mahabaleshwar offers beautiful views; sit on the left travelling from Panchgani.

Wai

Wai stands on the left bank of the Krishna River, 14 km east of Panchgani, where the riverside, lined with shady temples, is very attractive, particularly the finely carved *mandapam* in front of the Mahadev temple. Hills rise sharply around the town. On a hilltop **Pandavgad** fort, which according to local tradition was visited by the Pandava brothers of the *Mahabharata*. The town's sanctity is enhanced by its proximity to the source of the Krishna.

Satara

Satara, south of Wai on the NH-4 and 42 km southeast of Mahabaleshwar lies in a hollow near the confluence of the Krishna and Venna rivers. It is considered a place of great sanctity and there are several temples on the banks at **Mahuli**. The cantonment contains Sir Bartle Frere's **Residency** (1820). A 'New Palace' (1838-1844) was built by the engineer responsible for the bridges over the two rivers.

The ruling house of Satara was descended from Sahu, Shivaji's grandson, who was brought up at the Mughal court. Their **mansion**, 200 m from the New Palace, contains a number of Shivaji's weapons. These include the notorious 'tigers' *waghnakh* (claws) with which Shivaji is reputed to have disembowelled Afzal Khan. Other weapons include *Jai Bhavani*, his favourite sword (made in Genoa), and his rhinoceros hide shield. There is a **Historical Museum** (1930) which contains a fine collection of archival material on the Marathas. Satara Road railway station is 6 km from the city and bus stand.

Wasota Fort on the south side of the town can be reached by both road and footpath. Reputedly built by the Raja of Panhala in the 12th century, it's 14-m-high walls (which remain only at the gateway) and buttresses contain the remains of the rajah's palace, a small temple and a bungalow. It passed to the Mughals under Aurangzeb, for a time, after he besieged the fort in 1699, but returned to the Marathas in 1705 with the help of a Brahmin agent who tricked the Mughals.

Pratapgarh

To the west of Mahabaleshwar, the setting for this **Maratha fort** is spectacular. From the summit (1080 m) on which it is sited there is a splendid view down the forested hillside. A road leads to the foot of the hill, then 500 steps run up to the top.

The fort comprises a double wall with corner bastions. The gates are studded with iron spikes. Inside, the Bhavani temple in the lower fort has two *dipmal* (lantern towers); their exteriors are covered with regularly placed projections like giant coat hooks. Presumably lanterns were placed on these or hung from them, the towers then acting as beacons. The upper fort has a Siva temple. Its ramparts can be seen nearly all of the way down the very scenic (but slow) road to Poladpur.

★ Raigad (Raigarh) *Colour map 5, B3.*

63 km northwest of Pratapgarh, foreigners Rs 100, Indians Rs 5, cable car (Rs 150) avoids the 6-km walk up but power failures can cause delays, look for signs for 'Ropeway' leading to a right turn before reaching the end of the paved road and be prepared for a scary ride in a cage.

The views from this three-pronged hilltop fort are magnificent, especially the stunningly beautiful panorama across the lakes to the north. Difficult to reach, the fort is rarely visited by foreigners, though there are plenty of Indian tourists since Shivaji, the greatest hero in Maratha history, once ruled his kingdom from here. Raigad dates from around the 12th century. Known as 'Rairi' it was the seat of a Maratha chief. Later it passed in turn to the Vijayanagaras, the Nizam of Ahmadnagar, the Bijapuri Adil Shahis until Shivaji regained it in 1648 and made it the home of his much-revered mother, Jiji Bai. In 1674 he chose it for his coronation at the hands of Brahmin priests but died here in 1680. Aurangzeb acquired it in 1690 but it soon reverted back to the Marathas who surrendered it to the British in 1818.

The path to the fort climbs 1400 steps from its start at **Wadi**, and makes for a tough hike at any time of year. The flat hilltop is about 2500 m long and 1500 m across at the widest. A bastioned wall encloses it while two outer curtain walls contour round the hillsides. Heavily fortified in each corner of the irregular triangle, in Shivaji's day the fort was one of the strongest in India. The main gate (Maha Darwaza) is flanked by two large bastions, both 21 m high, one concave, the other convex. Inside the fort, the extensive **Palace** and **Queen's Chamber** are placed between two tanks. In the courtyard is a low platform where the throne stood and after the coronation the title Chhatrapati ('Lord of the Umbrella') was bestowed on Shivaji. In the centre of the town was a market which had more than 40 shops in two parallel rows for the 2000 people housed in the fort. To the northeast is Shivaji's **Samadhi** (memorial), as well as a *chhattri* for his dog. If you go up in the evening when the heat has died down, it is extremely atmospheric.

Listings Mahabaleshwar and around

Tourist information

Mahabaleshwar
MTDC Resort
T02168-260318.
Can provide information.

Where to stay

Mahabaleshwar
There are many hotels here; several family-run.

$$$ Brightland Holiday Village
*Nakhinda Village (4 km from the centre),
Kates Pt Rd, T02168-260707,
www.brightlandholiday.com.*
30 rooms, restaurants, bar, pool and gardens.

$$$ Dreamland
*Off MG Rd, behind ST Stand, T02168-260227,
www.hoteldreamland.com.*
105 rooms with view, old cottages and newer a/c suites with cable TV and phone by the pool, restaurant (vegetarian) in large garden.

$$$ Fountain
*Opposite Koyna Valley, T02168-260227,
www.fountainhotel.co.in.*
In Mahabaleshwar's oldest resort, 98 rooms air cooled with TV. The vegetarian restaurant has a good choice.

$$$ Valley View Resort
*Valley View Rd, off James Murray Peth Rd,
T02168-260066, www.valley view-resort.com.*
80 very clean rooms, 40 a/c, real grass to balconies, pure vegetarian restaurant (no beer) and great views from the garden. Recommended.

$$-$ Holiday Resort (MTDC)
2 km from centre (taxi Rs 40), T02168-260318.
Large, popular complex with 100 cottages, rooms and garden suites, dorm (no beds) Rs 100, restaurant, permit room, pleasant setting and atmosphere, tourist office near gate.

$ Grand
Woodlawn Rd, behind Madhusaga, T02168-260228, www.grand-resort.co.in.
Modest and ageing cottages set in a peaceful spot far from the bustle of the main market.

$ Sai Niwas
338 Koli Alley, T02168-261220.
Good value, clean rooms.

Panchgani

$$-$ Amer
188 Chesson Rd, T02168-240211.
Some a/c rooms with bath.

$$-$ Five Hills (MTDC)
Khingar Rd, T02168-240301.
64 doubles and suites, good restaurant.

Restaurants

Mahabaleshwar
The bazar sells local honey which is justly famous, as are jams from locally grown fruit.

$$$-$$ Grapevine Restaurant
Masjid Rd.
Small eclectic restaurant with Thai, Italian and other non-Indian specials. Try lobster, fresh strawberries washed down with Indian 'Chardonnay'. Excellent though pricey.

$ Subraya
Opposite the bus stand.
Friendly place serving excellent *thalis* and milkshakes.

What to do

Mahabaleshwar
MTDC deluxe buses for sightseeing, 1400, Pratapgarh, 0930, 1000, and Panchgani, 1100. Reservations at **Holiday Resort** (www.maharashtratourism.gov.in).

Transport

Mahabaleshwar
Bus For the best views, sit on the right of the bus travelling from Pune to Mahabaleshhwar. Regular services to/from **Pune (Swargate)**, 4 hrs. **MTDC** several deluxe buses daily (except monsoons) to and from **Mumbai** (6½-7 hrs).

Panchgani
Bus Buses run from **Mumbai** (via Mahad) and **Pune** ('Luxury' to Swargate stand only).

Train The nearest railway station is **Satara** (28 km).

Pratapgarh
Bus Buses to **Pratapgarh** from **Mahabaleshwar** (22 km), taking 50 mins.

Raigad
Bus Buses go from **Mumbai** (via Mahad, 210 km) and **Pune** (126 km).

Kolhapur and around   Colour map 5, C4.

interesting and untouristy town with a fascinating temple

Set in the wide open plains of the southern Deccan, Kolhapur (population 485,200), founded under the 10th-century Yadavas, was once one of the most important Maratha states. Shivaji's younger son, inherited the southern regions of his father's kingdom, but after a history of bitter factional dispute it became an important Princely State under the British. Today it has the unlikely distinction of being at the heart of India's small wine producing region, and is also witnessing a flow of foreign investment, making it one of the major industrial centres of Maharashtra. The area has rich bauxite deposits and the damming of the Koyna, a tributary of the Krishna, is providing electricity for aluminium smelting.

Sights

At the core of the old city is the hugely atmospheric **Amba Bai** (Mahalaxmi) **Temple**, dedicated to the mother goddess, which buzzes with devotional activity throughout the day. It has 10th-century foundations, a tall pyramidal tower added in the 18th century and an impressive carved ceiling to the pillared hall. Note Vishnu with the eight *Dikpalas*, see page 693. Immediately to its east, the **Juna Rajwada** (Old Palace), which was badly damaged by fire in 1810, contains a temple to Tuljabhawani, the favourite goddess of Shivaji, and is entered through a traditional drum gallery or *nakkar khana* (music hall). Upstairs in the palace is the Durbar Hall and armoury which contains one of Aurangzeb's swords and other interesting memorabilia.

Much of Kolhapur's architecture can be attributed to the British army engineer Major Charles Mant, whose connection to the city began when he designed a cenotaph for Maharajah Rajaram, who died in Florence in 1871. His **New Palace** (1881), 2 km north of the centre, belongs to the period when all the succession disputes had been resolved and Kolhapur was being governed as a model state. Built out of grey stone around a central courtyard, it's a bizarre blend of Jain temple and Rajasthani palace with a Victorian clock tower perched on top, and is home to the **Shahu Museum** ① *Tue-Sun 1100-1300, 1600-1800*, packed to the ceiling with stuffed animals, jewellery, weapons and other royal paraphenalia collected by the maharaja, who still resides in the palace, and his forefathers.

Among Mant's other buildings in the town are the Town Hall (1873), halfway between the new and old palaces with a small **museum of antiquities** ① *1030-1300, 1330-1730*, the General Library (1875), Albert Edward Hospital (1878) and High School (1879).

The sacred Panchganga River skirts the north of the city, and ghats and temples line its banks. **Brahmapuri Hill**, the Brahmin cremation ground, overlooks the river to the west of town. Nearby is the **Rani's Garden** where the royal family have memorial *chhattris*.

Panhala

Panhala (977 m), 19 km northwest of Kolhapur, is where Rajah Bhoj II, whose territory extended to the Mahadeo Hills north of Satara, had his **fort**. However, it is particularly associated with Shivaji, who often stayed here. The Marathas and Mughals occupied it in turn until the British took it in 1844. The fort is triangular with a 7 km wall with three gates around it, in places rising to 9 m. The Tin Darwaza ('three gates') leads to a central courtyard or 'killing chamber'; the inner gate leads to the Guard Room. The Wagh Gate (partly ruined) adopts similar principles of defence. Inside are vast granaries, the largest of which covers 950 sq m, has 11 m high walls and enabled Shivaji to withstand a five-month siege. By the ruins is a temple to Maruti, the Wind god. To the north is the two-storey palace.

Listings Kolhapur and around

Tourist information

Kolhapur

Goa Tourism
Mohan Travels, 517E Pune–Bangalore Rd, T0231-265 0911.

MTDC
Kedar Complex, Station Rd, T0231-265 2935.

Where to stay

Kolhapur

$$ Woodland
204 E Ward, Tarabai Park (5 mins by rickshaw north of bus stand), T0231-265 0941, www.hotelwoodland.net.
One of the most pleasant in town, bright clean rooms, free in-room broadband hook-up and a great Gujarati *thali* restaurant upstairs, all wrapped in a peaceful garden with burbling fountains.

$ Maharaja
514E Station Rd, opposite bus stand, T0231-265 0829.

Recently renovated budget favourite right by the bus stand, with cheap, decent rooms.

$ Opal
Pune–Bangalore Rd, T0231-253 6767, www.hotelopal.co.in.
Appealing 1960s hotel, with just a handful of a/c and non-a/c rooms, a popular non-veg Maharashtran restaurant, and a ready supply of city maps and info. Undergoing renovation at the time of the update, so prices may rise.

$ Vrindavan Deluxe
Shivaji Park, T0231-266 4343.
A great budget deal, with super-comfortable and clean rooms in a new, airy and attractive hotel a 1-min walk from the bus stand. Veg restaurant.

Panhala

$$$-$$ Valley View Grand
Tabak Baug, Panhala, T02328-235036, www.grandhotelbombay.com.
Set in pretty gardens, this hotel has fabulous views from its rooms and an open-air restaurant serving excellent food.

Restaurants

Kolhapur

The restaurants in the **Opal** and **Woodland** hotels (see Where to stay) are among the best in town.

Transport

Kolhapur

Bus State buses pull into the **Central Bus Stand** on Station Rd. Half-hourly services to **Panhala** (30 mins) and **Pune** (via **Satara**), and several a day to **Belgaum** (2½ hrs), **Bijapur** (4 hrs), **Mahabaleshwar** (4 hrs), **Mumbai Central** (8 hrs), **Panaji** (6 hrs) and **Ratnagiri** (4 hrs). Agents sell tickets for private buses around the bus stand, including several in the Royal Plaza building on Dabholkar Corner. Check departure/arrival points, particularly for Mumbai.

Train Trains to **Kolhapur** arrive via a branch line from Miraj. If booking online, Kolhapur station is known as 'C Shahumharaj Terminus' Enquiries, T131. Direct trains: **Mumbai CST**, twice daily, 13 hrs, via **Pune**, 8 hrs. **Bengaluru,** 17½ hrs, and **Hyderabad**, 21 hrs.

Solapur and east of Pune *Colour map 5, B5.*

prosperous town in Maharashtra's cotton belt

In the heart of the cotton growing area, Solapur (Sholapur) has been a focus of the cotton trade for over a century. Almost entirely an industrial city, it still has an atmospheric area with traditional old buildings along Navee Peth and Rajvadee Chowk.

From Solapur the main road to Pune follows the Bhima River northwest across the vast open fields and scattered settlements of the plateau. It is a region rich in archaeological sites, as it was a major centre of prehistoric settlement.

Pandharpur, on the south bank of the Bhima River, is regarded by many as the spiritual capital of Maharashtra. It has a shrine to Vithoba, an incarnation of Vishnu, dating from 1228. Although some tourist literature puts its origins as early as AD 83 there is no evidence for this early date. There are 12 bathing ghats on the river bank, and during the main pilgrimage times (Ashadhi Ekadashi in July and Kartik Ekadashi in Oct), tens of thousands of pilgrims converge on the town. *Rath Yatra*, or temple car procession, dates back to 1810.

Listings Solapur and east of Pune

Where to stay

Solapur

\$\$ Pratham
560/61 South Sadar Bazar, T0217-231 2580, www.hotelpratham.com.
30 clean, modern, pleasant rooms, half a/c with bath, excellent open-air restaurant, friendly and helpful staff.

\$\$-\$ Srikamal
77 Railway Lines, T0217-2331230, www.hotelsrikamalsolapur.com.
Clean rooms, hot showers, and a good terrace restaurant. Run by a helpful, friendly family.

\$\$-\$ Surya Executive,
Murarji Peth, T0231-272 9880, www.hotelsuryasolapur.com.
Good, clean excellent value, air-cooled rooms, and a restaurant.

\$ Railway Retiring Rooms
Dorm.

Transport

Solapur

Bus Excellent connections to **Mumbai**, **Hyderabad**, **Aurangabad** to the north and **Bijapur** (3 hrs) to the south.

Train Solapur is an important rail junction, and a useful transfer point if you're heading for Hampi and northern Karnataka. To **Bengaluru** (**Bangalore**): 6 daily, 16 hrs. **Bijapur**, 12 daily, 2 hrs. **Hubli**: 5 daily, 9 hrs, via **Bijapur**, **Badami** (5 hrs) and **Gadag** (7 hrs; change here for Hospet/Hampi). **Mumbai**: At least 12 daily, 8½ hrs. **Hyderabad**: 8 daily, 6½ hrs. **Chennai**: 3 daily, 17 hrs.

The 593-km coast route from Mumbai to Goa, now followed by the Konkan Railway and the NH17, runs through the economically backward but scenically attractive South Konkan region. It passes a string of small towns which developed at the heads of estuaries – transshipment points for cargo brought in by sea, then hauled by pack animals over the Ghats.

Although lowland, it is far from flat. Many of the densely wooded slopes have been cleared, leaving bare and unproductive laterites, alternating with patches of intensive rice cultivation and coconut groves. The coastal estuaries support mangrove swamps, while scattered along the beaches are a series of domestic-focused holiday resorts.

Outside holiday weekends this is a quiet, beautiful coast, with serious rewards for explorers who aren't dependent on public transport or a daily dose of banana porridge.

Murud-Janjira

Some 160 km south of Mumbai, the old town of **Murud** contains a number of interesting painted buildings built by the Siddis, a warrior tribe of Abyssinian origin whose descendants still live in the area. An empty palace belonging to the nawab, south of the town centre, is clearly visible from the road to Rajpuri jetty. Signs warn trespassers away, but the caretaker may allow you to look at the ghost of the once opulent lifestyle of the nawabs, Rs 50 tip expected. Some decaying Muslim tombs stand among baobab trees, 1 km south of the jetty.

From here, boats sail to **Janjira Fort** ① *0700-1800, Rs 10, closed Fri 1200-1400*, built by the Siddis and reputedly one of the strongest coastal forts in India: even the fearsome Marathas never captured it. The fort retains a number of remarkable buildings, including mosques, the *topkhana* guarded by canons and a five-storeyed crumbling **palace**. Across the bay is the fort of Padmadurg, built by the Maratha leader Sambhaji to combat the Siddis.

Just north of Murud centre is the temple to the triple-headed **Dattatraya** representing Brahma, Vishnu and Siva. It is worth climbing the 250 steps, not least for the commanding views. **Kashid**, 15 km further north, has an excellent 3-km-long silver-sand beach, which is a popular weekend resort but deserted on weekdays. The sea is polluted and swimming is not advised. A good beach, 2 km away, is suitable for camping and the hills are good for walking.

Chiplun

The NH17 runs south through Khed to Chiplun on the banks of the Vashishti River, fed from the **Koyna Lake**, one of the largest artificial lakes in the Western Ghats. There are spectacular views across the flat valley bottom, criss-crossed by the several courses of the meandering river. After Khed and 10 km before Chiplun, near an attractive small village and temple (difficult to find when travelling north) there is accommodation.

Ratnagiri

Now a rapidly growing and unprepossessing port town with a lot of road works, Ratnagiri ('Jewel hill'), 13 km west off the NH17 at Hathkamba, was the birthplace of two leaders of the Independence Movement, Gangadhar Tilak and GK Gokhale. It was also the internment home for the last king of Burma, King Thibaw, who was held here from 1886 until his death in 1916. His 'palace' is now part of the polytechnic.

Ganpatipule

Revered and much visited by Hindus for its *swayambhu* ('naturally occurring' or 'self-created') Ganesh, Ganpatipule, north of Ratnagiri, has a beautifully white deserted beach which gets busy at weekends. The sea is clean but beware of strong currents. **Jaigad Fort**, 35 km, makes a pleasant excursion.

Vijayadurg (Viziadurg)

A minor road west off the NH17 at Talera leads to the formidable fort guarding the river which was built on an ancient site. The Sultans of Bijapur enlarged it and Sivaji further strengthened it by adding the three outer walls. It has 27 bastions, an inner moat, good water supply and carried 278 guns in 1682. The Maratha pirate Kanhoji Angria made it his base in 1698, plundered European shipping and withstood assaults by the Portuguese and the British.

Malvan and around

A coastal road leads south from Vijayadurg, passing through Devgad, renowned for producing India's sweetest mangoes, to Malvan. The old town runs the length of a crowded little street that leads to a port, from where boats can take you to Sivaji's coastal fort of **Sindhudurg** ① *boatmen charge around Rs 25 per person*, now deserted, which sits atop a low-lying island just off the coast. There are several shrines within the fort – to Maruti, Bhavani, Mahadeo and uniquely to Sivaji. There is an unconventional statue of Sivaji and two well-known temples to Sri Devi Sateri and Rameshwar.

South of Malvan, a narrow road runs down to the peninsula of **Tarkarli**, where casuarina trees straggle along the back of a largely deserted beach. There are a few low-key resorts and guesthouses here, almost exclusively geared towards domestic tourists (signs are in Marathi only). At Karli Creek boatmen offer **dolphin-watching cruises** (best early in the morning), and MTDC runs **houseboat trips** ① *Rs 6050-7100 per room per night, bookings from MTDC offices statewide, www. maharashtratourism.gov.in, or locally on T02362-228785*.

Vengurla

The former trading settlement on an island is now joined to the land. On the NH17, close to the Goa border, the coast here is lined with beautiful white-sand beaches. Salt pans provide an important product for export from the region.

Sawantwadi

Sawantwadi was the capital of the Bhonsle kings of southern Maharashtra who were constantly trying to extend their territory into Goa. Today it is a large and ramshackle but friendly market town, centred around the large Moti Talav ('Pearl Lake') with an out-of-town station on the Konkan Railway. It was once noted for the production of fine hand-painted *ganjifa* (playing cards), which the Sawantwadi royal family is keeping alive by allowing a few artists/craftsmen to work in the once-impressive darbar hall of the **palace** ① *0930-1230, Rs 50*.

The brightly coloured *ganjifa* were originally produced by pasting layers of cloth together, using tamarind seed gum then coating the 'card' with chalk before polishing it with a stone to provide a smooth white base for decorating the face with natural pigments while the back was stiffened with lacquer. The packs of circular cards come in various sizes and suits. The 10 suits of the *Dasavatara* (featuring Vishnu's 10 incarnations), for example, forms a pack of 120 cards while the *Navagraha* (nine planets) has nine suits. The miniature paintings with patterns drawn from mythology, history and nature, often reflect folk traditions. Prices range from Rs 800 to Rs 3000, but the best-decorated cards make their way straight to shops in Mumbai. Local craftsmen also produce painted lacquered furniture, chessmen, board games and candle sticks.

Amboli

From Sawantwadi, a state road goes up the ghats to the minor hill station of Amboli, at an altitude of 690 m. The road continues on to **Belgaum**. Set on the flat-topped heights of the Western Ghats overlooking the coastal plain below, Amboli is a quiet and little-visited resort. There are attractive walks and several waterfalls. **Bauxite mines**, 10 km away, can also be visited.

Redi Beach

Just 3 km north of the Goa border and Tiracol, a turn off from NH17, south of Shiroda, leads to Redi Village and beach. An old **Maratha Fort**, now in ruins but interesting to wander round, dominates the view over a stunning and, for now, rarely visited bay, though plans for wider roads and a large resort are on the table.

Where to stay

Murud-Janjira

$$$ Kashid Beach Resort
500 m from beach across main road, T02144-278501, www.niva link.com/kashid.
25 split-level clean rooms, some with good sea views, bathrooms a bit run down, restaurant (beer appears as 'snacks' on the bill), in large grounds, bike hire.

$$$-$$ Golden Swan Beach Resort
Darbar Rd, T02144-274078,
www.goldenswan.com.
Comfortable rooms in cottages near beach, with an adequate restaurant serving coastal cuisine.

$ Aman Palace
Darbar Rd, T02144-274297.
Simple rooms with bath, and hammocks in the garden.

$ Seashore Resort
South of Golden Swan Resort, T02144-274223, www.seashoreresortmurud.com.
7 rooms with bath, one a/c, run by a friendly family, in a lovely garden on the beach.

Chiplun

There are several very cheap lodges around the town centre and bus stand.

$$$ The Riverview
Dhamandivi, near Parshuram Temple, T02355-259081, www.chiplunhotels.com.
With 37 comfortable rooms, most a/c, an excellent restaurant, pool to indulge in, helipad, in an attractive, peaceful garden setting.

Ganpatipule

$$$-$$ Holiday Resort (MTDC)
T02357-235328.
On the beach among the palm trees is this hotel, with 68 clean, comfortable a/c suites to 4-bed rooms (11 and 12 best) and some musty old tents. There's a poor restaurant which serves beer, poor service and a 0900 checkout, but it's relaxing and is in a great location.

$$ Abhishek
Aare Ware Rd, 500 m down a dirt track opposite Landmark, T022-2437 0801, www.abhishekbeachresortandspa.com.
A typical Indian hotel, which has a restaurant with sea views.

$$ Atithi Parinay
Kolagewadi village, 13 km southeast of Ganpatipule, T(0)90499 81309, www.atithiparinay.com.
Tucked away in the hinterland, this peaceful organic farm-homestay offers a soft introduction to Maharashtran rural life. There's a rustic cottage with a traditional earthen floor, safari tent and a treehouse. Great home-cooked meals, swimming in nearby creek, and visits to boatbuilding workshops.

$$ Landmark
On a hillside going down to the village, T02357-235284, www.hotellandmark.net.
Good rooms, an excellent Chinese/Indian restaurant, and beer.

Malvan

$$$$-$$$ Tarkarli Houseboat
T02365-252390.
The Kerala houseboat experience comes to Maharashtra, with overnight trips on the dolphin-rich waters of Tarkarli Creek.

$$$-$$ MTDC Resort
5 km south of Malvan on Tarkarli Beach, T02365-252390.
Simple self-contained cottages set in a casuarina grove on a quiet stretch of beach. Overpriced for what you get, but the restaurant here has the best variety of food for miles. MTDC also operates a Kerala-style houseboat offering overnight trips (**$$$$**) on the quiet, bird-rich waters of Tarkarli Creek.

$$ Manali Resort
Bandar Rd, 3 km beyond MTDC Resort on Tarkarli Creek, T02365-248550, T(0)9423-304384.
Glass-fronted cabins on top of a dune facing the fishing boats on the beach, and small and super-basic rooms with no views set around the kitchen. Basic fish or veg *thalis* available, or buy supplies in town and the family that runs the place will cook them.

Sawantwadi

$$-$ Mango
Pateshwar Complex, Main Rd, T02363-271041.
Smart business hotel in the heart of the
bazar, with large, sparkling a/c rooms and
a deserted restaurant.

$ Tara
Gandhi Chowk, 5 mins' walk south of bus stand,
T02363-272644, www.tarahotel.in.
Slightly more dog-eared, but the rooms are clean
and bright enough, the staff are friendly, and
there's a dingy little restaurant.

Amboli

$ Green Valley Resort (MTDC/private)
T02363-240239.
A reasonably comfortable base with a choice of
21 rooms including some suites.

$ JRD International
Vengurla–Belgaon Rd, 1 km from bus stand,
T02363-240223, www.hoteljrdinternational.com.
30 pleasant, clean rooms, better in 'cottages',
reasonable Indian restaurant, bar.

Restaurants

Murud-Janjira

$ Nest
Darbar Rd.
Indian including *thalis*.

$ Patil Khanaval
On the seafront.
The best fish in Murud, dusted with turmeric and
tamarind and fried.

Ganpatipule
Cheap *thalis* are served in 2 eateries outside the
Ganesh Temple on the shopping street. Look out
for the local delicacy of *poli* – thin pancakes with
amba poli (dried and crushed mango) or *phanas*
poli (jackfruit).

Malvan

$$ Arun Bhojnalaya
Malvan town.
One of the best places to try Malvan's heavily
sea-focused cuisine: prawns, crabs, and pomfret
in tangy masala.

$ Abhishek
Malvan.
Offers Malvani vegetarian alongside seafood.

Sawantwadi

$ Visava
Gandhi Chowk.
Good South Indian fare and snacks, excellent
thick *lassis*.

Transport

Murud-Janjira
Bus/ferry From **Mumbai Central**, ASIAD
buses cover the 165 km in less than 6 hrs but it's
potentially quicker and certainly more fun to get
a ferry from the **New Ferry Wharf** at the Gateway
of India to **Mandwa**, and from there catch a bus
or taxi to **Murud** (72 km) or **Kashid** via **Alibaug**.
There can be a long wait for buses.

Ganpatipule
Bus Direct State Transport buses run from
Mumbai, **Pune** and **Ratnagiri**.

Malvan
Bus Local buses to **Devgad** up the coast
road, **Kankauli** (on NH-17, for connections
to **Kolhapur**, **Mumbai** and **Pune**), **Kudal** (for
connections to Goa), **Sawantwadi**, **Vengurla**.
Auto-rickshaw to Tarkarli, Rs 80-100.

Sawantwadi
Bus The bus stand is close to the centre.
Buses to **Mapusa** (2 hrs), **Malvan** (2 hrs),
and destinations in southern Maharashtra.

Amboli
Bus/train From the coastal towns of **Ratnagiri**
(210 km) and **Vengurla** (50 km) there are
buses. Or you can get the train to **Kolhapur**
or **Belgaum**, then by local bus.

Vidharba

Maharashtra's winter capital, Nagpur, is the capital of Maharashtrian district Vidharba and is a large political and industrial city. Sevagram, Gandhi's 'village of service' from 1933 to 1942, is now a shrine to the man's principles. The nearby hill station of Chikhaldara, peopled by tribals, marks the southern limits of the Hindi tongue.

Nagpur *Colour map 6, A1.*

an affluent and relaxed city

Nagpur (population 2.4 million), the former capital of the Central Provinces, is one of the older cities of Central India. Today, although it is an important commercial centre attracting new businesses and multinationals, most of the industrial units are thankfully located on the outskirts so Nagpur retains a pleasant feel with friendly inhabitants and signs of fast-growing wealth. Sometimes known as the winter capital of Maharashtra, the area is famous for its oranges, giving it the nickname 'The Orange City'. More recently strawberry farms have grown in importance while the surrounding countryside is a major cotton producing area.

Sights

The city stands on the Nag River and is centred on the **Sitabuldi Fort** ① *only open to the public on 26 Jan and 15 Aug*, which is surrounded by cliffs and a moat. At the highest point there is a memorial to those who fell in the Battle of Sitabuldi between the Marathas and the British. Today the fort is headquarters of the Territorial Army. Among the British buildings scattered around the western half of the city are the red brick Council Hall (1912-1913); the Anglican Cathedral of All Saints (1851), and the High Court (1937-1942), suggestive of Rashtrapati Bhavan in New Delhi.

On the other high hill in the town is the **Raj Bhavan** (Government House). The **Bhonsla Chhattris** are in the Sukrawari area south of the old city. Around town there are also a number of 'tanks' (lakes) and parks; **Maharaj Bagh**, west of the flyover is an attractive park/zoo.

Two kilometres north of the centre on Kamptee Road, the **Narrow Gauge Rail Museum** ① *Tue-Sun 1200-2000, Rs 10*, has an interesting collection of restored steam locos and wagons you can climb on, plus a toy train and park; it's a popular stop for local families in the evening.

Listings Nagpur

Tourist information

MTDC
Sanskruti Bachat Bhavan, opposite Hardeo Hotel, near Lakshmie Theatre, Sitabuldi, T0712-253 3325.
Offers information and **MTDC** accommodation.

Where to stay

$$ hotels don't have all usual facilities of the grade but all have restaurants, bars and free transfer for airport.

$$$-$$ Pride
Wardha Rd, 500 m from airport, T0712-662 2555, www.pridehotel.com.
70 rooms in need of refurbishing, 30 new better ones, a decent restaurant but inefficient reception, and an unappealing pool next to the busy NH7.

$$$-$$ Tuli International
Residency Rd, Sadar, T0712-253 4784, www.tuligroup.com.
Once the best in town, the tired rooms now provide poor value for the price, and service tends

to be chaotic. It's worth considering, however, for its location and the good restaurants.

$$ Darshan Towers
60 Central Av, T0712-661 6845.
Well-furnished rooms, central a/c, hot baths (some tubs), double-glazed so quieter than others, good restaurant/bar, friendly and efficient. Recommended.

$$ Radhika
Panchsheel Sq, Wardha Rd, T0712-252 2011.
60 clean rooms, some larger a/c with hot bath, dark corridors, unreliable TV, restaurant and bar.

$ Blue Moon
Central Av, T0712-272 6061,
micron@bom3.vsnl.net.in.
30 clean rooms, some a/c, TV, room service, with quieter rooms at the rear.

$ Skylark
119 Central Av, T0712-272 4654.
Good value but suffers some noise from the road and nightly disco. 48 rooms in need of a makeover, most a/c, efficient and friendly service. Restaurant does good-value breakfasts.

Restaurants

The hotel restaurants at Darshan Towers and Tuli International are recommended. Several others are along Residency Rd and Wardha Rd near the junction with Central Bazar Rd.

Festivals

Apr/May Ram Naumi, colourful procession in various parts of the city.

Aug/Sep Janmashtami, Krishna's birthday is celebrated with the distinctive tradition of stringing clay pots full of curd high above the streets. Young men try to pull them down by forming human pyramids. **Pola**, the cattle and monsoon harvest festival. **Ganesh Chaturthi**, when idols of Ganesh are immersed in streams and tanks.

Shopping

The main areas are Sitabuldi, Dharampeth, Sadar and Itwari, Mahatma Phule Market. Also try **Gangotri UP Handicrafts** (in Sadar); and **Khadi Gramudyog** (in Mahal).

Transport

Air The airport is 10 km south of the city centre with **flights** to Ahmedabad, Bengaluru, **Delhi, Hyderabad, Jaipur, Kolkata Mumbai**, Pune, Raipur and Srinagar. Taxis charge around Rs 600 to the city.

Bus New Maharashtra ST Bus Stand, Ganesh Peth, southeast of the railway station, T0712-272 6221, to towns in Maharashtra plus **Hyderabad, Allahabad** and **Varanasi**.
  MP Bus Stand, T0712-253 3695, buses to **Bhopal, Indore** and **Raipur**.
  Madhya Pradesh buses use the stand just south of the train station.

Train Nagpur is an important railway junction. The station is in the centre of town. Enquiry T131, Reservations T135. **Chennai**: 5-8 a day, 18 hrs. **New Delhi**: at least 10 a day, 18 hrs. **Hyderabad**: 5-10 a day, 9-12 hrs. **Kolkata**: 5-8 a day, 20½ hrs. **Mumbai**: 8-10 a day, 15 hrs. **Pune**: 3-4 a day, 15 hrs.

Around Nagpur

forts, wildlife and Gandhi's ashram

Ramtek
About 40 km northeast of Nagpur, Ramtek has a **fort** with several Hindu **temples** at its western end, some dating back to the fifth century AD. The fort walls on the well-wooded 'Hill of Rama' were built in 1740 by Raghoji I, the first Bhonsla of Nagpur. The citadel is older and the principal temples are those to Rama and Sita. The fort is approached by a flight of steps from the village of Ambala. The poet Kalidasa wrote his epic *Meghdoot* here. Nearby is **Khindsey Lake**, 8 km, a popular picnic spot with boating facilities. Ramsagar is another lake closer to town. The 15-day **Ramnavami** fair is held in November.

Gandhian ashram
After vowing not to return to Sabarmati Ashram in Ahmedabad until India gained its independence, Mahatma Gandhi established his **Sevagram Ashram** (Gandhian Village of Service) in 1933.
  Jamnalal Bajaj, a dedicated follower of Gandhi, provided the land, 8 km outside of Wardha and 62 km southwest of Nagpur, and the resources to set up the ashram in which Gandhi remained until 1942 and visited regularly until his death in 1948. It is now a national institution where you can visit

the residences **Nivases** and **Kutirs**, see the Mahatma's personal belongings, watch hand-spinning (*khadi* cloth is sold through shops) and attend prayers at the open-air multi-faith Prayer Ground (0430 and 1800). Mahatma Gandhi Research Institute of Medical Sciences and Kasturba Hospital with 325 beds to provide affordable health care for local villagers, is on the bus route. A path from here leads to the Ashram.

The **Magan Sanghralaya** (Centre of Science for Villages) is an alternative technology museum, on the Nagpur Road at **Duttapur**. Visitors are welcome to see papermaking, pottery, latrine making and other crafts. The **Chetna Organic Farm**, nearby, develops sustainable farming techniques. The **Laxmi Narayan Temple** claims to have been the first in India to have allowed Harijans to enter in 1928. The **Viswa Shanti Stupa** (1993), for 'World Peace', with four golden statues of Buddha, is a more recent attraction. Prayers are held each evening in the small prayer hall.

At **Paunar**, 10 km north of Wardha, **Vinoba Bhave**, one of Gandhi's keenest disciples, set up his Ashram. He championed the 'land gift' or **Bhoodan Movement**, seeking with remarkable success to persuade large landowners to give away land to the poor. The self-help concept is kept alive by his followers (mostly women) dressed in blue, unlike other ashramites elsewhere in India who conventionally adopt white or saffron. It is possible to hike across from the Sevagram hospital along a village track for about 45 minutes to get there.

Tadoba National Park
Wed-Mon 0600-1100 (last entry 0930) and 1400-1800 (last entry 1630). Rs 20 per person per safari drive, plus Rs 50-75 for vehicle and Rs 100 for guide; jeep hire with driver Rs1500-2500 per trip. See also What to do.

Approximately 100 km south of Nagpur, the area around Tadoba was once in the possession of the Gond tribals. The compact 120-sq-km park has rich deciduous forest – mainly teak with bamboo, gardenia and satinwood. There are several troops of langur monkeys, palm civets, gaur, jackal, wild boar,

Tip...
Weekends are very busy. The best season to visit is between November and June.

chital, bison, sambar and a few tigers (although you are more likely to see a leopard in the evening). Waterbirds attracted by the perennial circular lake include cattle egrets, purple moorhens and jacanas. It also has quite a number of marsh crocodiles with a breeding farm for the *palustris* species.

There are three zones, of which Moharli and Tadoba offer best wildlife sightings; entry to each zone is limited to 20 vehicles per safari. There are minibuses for viewing, which is best in the evening around lake in the dry season. A road runs around the lake, while other roads radiate to the park perimeter.

Achalpur
Until 1853 this important market town, 194 km west of Nagpur, was the capital of Berar Kingdom, established in 1484 by Imad Shah. The old cantonment, which had been occupied by a regiment of the Hyderabad infantry, was abandoned in 1903.

To the north, and just before reaching Chikhaldara, is the fort of **Gawilgarh** (Gavilgarh). An important fortress of the 15th-century Shahi Dynasty, it was taken over when the kingdom of Ahmednagar expanded in 1574. Arthur Wellesley, subsequently the Duke of Wellington, who had defeated Tipu Sultan of Mysore at Srirangapatnam just four years previously, captured the fort in 1803 during the second Maratha War. The defences were destroyed after the 'Indian Mutiny' in 1858. Today it is a deserted ruin.

Chikhaldara
Known as the only hill station in the Vidharba region and as the northernmost coffee growing region in India, Chikhaldara is high in the Gavilgarh Hills, at an altitude of 1200 m, a branch of the Satpura Mountains. Established as a hill station by the British in 1839, historically the hills marked the southern limits of the core region within which the epics of Hinduism were played out.

It remains a tribal region, peopled largely by the Korkus, an Austric tribal group. The settlement is reputed to have taken its name from Kichaka, a prince who was killed by Bhima, one of the Pandava brothers, for having insulted Draupadi. Today, the Satpura Range in which Chikhaldara lies mark the southern boundary of Hindi speech.

The **Melghat Sanctuary** surrounding Chikaldara was one of the earliest to be designated a Project Tiger reserve. Its altitude makes it pleasantly cool during January-June, the best months to visit. The latest count suggests it has 45 tigers, occasionally seen in the dense and dry deciduous teak forest which also supports panther, gaur, chital, sambar and nilgai.

Listings Around Nagpur

Where to stay

Ramtek

$$-$ Tourist Resort (MTDC/private)
Ramtek, T07114-255620.
Dorm and 10 rooms.

Wardha

$ Ashram Guest House and Yatri Niwas
Sevagram, T07152-284753
Some doubles and dorm, serves cheap vegetarian meals, checkout 0800, friendly, small bookshop of Gandhi's works. Highly recommended (donations welcome), reserve on arrival (or ahead if possible). Alcohol, smoking and non-vegetarian food are prohibited.

$ Yatri Niwas
Paunar.
Similar to the one in Sevagram but more female oriented.

Tadoba National Park

$$ MTDC Rest House
At Moharli Gate, T(0)88792 22057.
One of the better deals around, with acceptably clean rooms and a pleasant lakeside setting. It's often full so book well ahead.

$ Forest Rest Houses
In various areas of the park, can be booked at the Forest Dept, Mul Rd, Chandrapur, T07172-251414, www.mahatadobatiger.com.

Chikhaldara

$$ Convention Complex (MTDC)
T07220-230234.
Simple though adequate, 10 rooms with 4 beds, and dorm with mattresses but no beds (Rs 100), restaurant nearby. Improvements are planned.

$$-$ Green Vallies Resort (MTDC)
Chikhaldara, T07220-230215.
Wide choice, with 20 suites, some a/c.

Restaurants

Wardha

$ Annapurna
Wardha near station, Paunar.
Couple in Saraf Lines.

What to do

Tadoba National Park

It's often easiest to arrange safaris through a hotel or a local naturalist guide; one with a good reputation is Manish Varma, T(0)98606-92422 or T08055920303, manish.varma96@gmail.com.

Transport

Ramtek

Bus Buses from ST Bus Stand, Nagpur, 70 mins. Buses run from Ramtek to **Khindsey Lake**. **Ramsagar** can be reached by auto-rickshaw.

Wardha and around

Bus Several to/from Wardha from **Nagpur**, 77 km, Express 2½ hrs; ask to be dropped off at **Paunar**. Local bus to **Sevagram** (8 km).

Train Share auto-rickshaws from the station to Sevagram (25 mins). **Chennai**: 4-8 a day, 18 hrs. **Kolkata** via **Nagpur** and **Raipur**: 5 daily, 19 hrs. **Mumbai**: 8-10 a day, 14½ hrs. **Nagpur**: Several fast trains daily; slow passenger trains stop at Sevagram, though the bus is quicker and more convenient. **Pune**: 3-4 a day, 18 hrs.

Tadoba National Park

The nearest connections are at **Chandrapur**, 45 km away.

Chikhaldara

Bus State buses from Amaravati, Nagpur, Wardha and Akola. Also, taxis from Amravati (100 km). **Badnera** is on the Mumbai–Kolkata train line, so is a convenient station. Amaravati is on a short spur (10 km) from Badnera.

Background Maharashtra

History

The name Maharashtra was first used in a seventh century AD inscription, but its origins are unclear. One view is that it is derived from the word *rath* (chariot) whose drivers formed an army (*maharathis*). They are thought to have migrated south and settled in the upland area where they mingled with aboriginal tribes.

The dry western margins of the plateau have sites from the earliest prehistoric settlements in India, and Nevasa and Chirki in the Godavari Valley, have Palaeolithic remains. The relatively open lands in the lee of the Ghats were one of the major routes from North to South India but lacked the resources to become the centre of a major political power. In the early period from the eighth to the 14th century there were a number of Hindu kingdoms, followed by the first Muslim dynasty in 1307. The Muslim use of Persian as a court language left its mark on the development of the Marathi language.

The Marathas divided the country into *Swarajya* (homeland – a concept that re-emerged as one of the watchwords of the Independence struggle in the 20th century), and *Mughlai* (territory controlled by foreigners), and set about reclaiming the latter by means of a series of daring raids. The nonpareil hero of this process was Maharashtra's late 17th-century leader Shivaji, whose name still generates a passion enjoyed by very few figures in Indian history. The state's modern political life resonates with the myths of his military abilities, political cunning and Hindu revivalism. Matching the political skills of a Machiavelli to the military ambitions of a Napoleon, within four years of his coronation Shivaji had begun to retake the forts ceded under the treaty with the Mughal Emperor Aurangzeb. By the time of his death from dysentery in 1680 he had re-established a powerful base around Pune and an expanding Maratha Empire.

On Aurangzeb's death in 1707, Shivaji's former kingdom became a confederacy under the charge of a hereditary minister called the Peshwa and four main Maratha chiefs – Holkar, Scindia, Gaekwad and Bhonsla. By 1750 their power reached across India to Orissa, which they occupied, and Bengal, which they attacked. Maratha power was only decisively curbed when they were defeated at Panipat by the Afghan Ahmad Shah Abdali. On the death of the young Peshwa, Madhao Rao I, in 1772, the five Maratha powers became increasingly independent of one another. Weakened and divided, they were unable to resist the advance of British power.

Modern Maharashtra

The present state did not take shape until 1960, when Gujarati areas in the north and Kannada-speaking areas in the south were allocated to Gujarat and Karnataka respectively.

Maharashtra has been described as India's industrial and commercial backbone. The nerve centre of India's stock market, the headquarters of a large number of Indian and multinational companies' operations in India and a major manufacturing state in its own right, Maharashtra has not only India's largest city, Mumbai, but a large number of rapidly industrializing smaller cities. However, agriculture remains important, with cash crops like sugar cane accounting for 30% of the country's total sugar production.

Ethnically, Maharashtra contains a variety of peoples. The Bhil, Warli, Gond, Korku and Gowari tribal groups living in the Satpura and Sahyadri ranges in the north are Australoid aboriginals. The Kunbi Marathas found all over the state are believed to be the descendants of immigrants from the north at the beginning of the Christian era. Parsis first arrived in the region in the eighth century from Persia. Just over 80% of the population is Hindu, with Islam and Buddhism the most numerous minority religions. The Buddhists are recent converts from among formerly outcaste Hindus. Marathi is the main regional language (spoken by 90% of the population), and has undergone a very political revival recently. Both Hindi and English are widely understood, especially in the major cities. Konkani on the west coast and Gondi in the north are important regional languages. Gujarati and its variants are also widely spoken.

Goa

palm-fringed beaches and Portuguese buildings

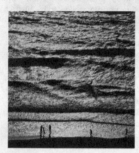

Goa, like San Francisco, Kathmandu and Spain, became a mecca for alternative living in the 1960s. Nowadays, Costa Brava beer bellies intrude among the California tie-dye, but Goa remains, in pockets, unmatched.

In most places you'll find little more than drowsy one-storey guesthouses strung along the beach, with fishermen's boats resting on the sand. Portuguese *fados* drift on the air in colonial villages, while the feral trance crew still hold their own at Shiva Valley.

There is humble everyday beauty elsewhere too. At dawn in the villages, blue mists lie low and hazy across paddy fields and curl at the crumbling fronts of 18th-century Portuguese manors in pink, umber and blue.

Northern beaches around Anjuna and Arambol to Morjim are beautiful and offer a thriving music scene, paragliding and yoga. Central Baga and Calangute appeal to package tourists but have great restaurants and sparkly shops. Southern Goa has special beaches like Agonda, Patnem and Palolem.

Inland Goa is often overlooked, but offers spice plantations, old mansion houses, beautiful waterfalls and sleepy villages.

Best for
Beaches ▪ Shopping ▪ Yoga

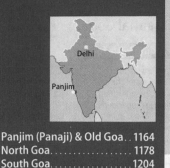

Footprint
picks

★ **Panjim**, page 1167

Explore Panjim's Latin quarters: Altinho and Fontainhas.

★ **Old Goa**, page 1173

Marvel at the imposing cathedrals in the jungle at Old Goa.

★ **Arpora**, page 1189

Browse innovative designs and traditional wares at Arpora Night Market.

★ **Arambol to Morjim**, page 1195

Stroll along the beach at sunset from Arambol to Morjim.

★ **Loutolim and Quepem**, page 1206

Visit the stunning Portuguese mansion houses in the villages of Loutolim and Quepem.

★ **Spice Hills**, page 1225

Travel inland to the spice plantations and western ghats.

Essential Goa

Finding your feet

By Indian standards Goa (population: 1.3 million) is a tiny state. The coastline on which much of its fame depends is only 97 km long. The north and south are separated by the broad estuaries of the Zuari and Mandovi rivers. Joined at high tide to create an island on which Panaji stands, these short rivers emerge from the high ranges of the Western Ghats less than 50 km from the coast.

Getting around

Local buses, chartered minibuses, taxis and motorbike taxis are all the norm. Hiring your own Honda or Enfield is a popular option.

When to go

The warm, dry weather of Goa's tropical winter, from October to March, is the best time to visit. Goa is always warm, but its coastal position means it never becomes unbearably hot. Nonetheless, from early April until the beginning of the monsoon in mid-June, both the temperature and humidity rise sharply, making for steamy hot days and balmy nights. Evenings are chilly in December and January. Avoid the six weeks of monsoon in June and July when

there are torrential storms. Peak season is at Christmas and New Year, when prices sky rocket as the state opens up for the domestic Indian tourist's equivalent of the 'Spring Break'.

Time required

Allow a day for Old Goa and another for Panjim, one day for the palaces of the south, and at least three days' round-trip for Hampi (in Karnataka), because it's a long journey (either overnight or all day) each way and exploring the vast site takes at least a day. Then factor in a bit of beach time; some tire of Goa's beaches after a day or two, some spend a fortnight, some never leave.

Language

Portuguese used to be much more widely spoken in Goa than English was in the rest of India, but local languages remained important. The two most significant were Marathi, the language of the politically dominant majority of the neighbouring state to the north, and Konkani, the language commonly spoken on the coastal districts further south and now the state's official language. English and Hindi are understood in parts visited by travellers.

Weather	Panjim				
January	**February**	**March**	**April**	**May**	**June**
32°C 19°C 2mm	32°C 20°C 0mm	32°C 23°C 0mm	33°C 25°C 8mm	33°C 27°C 59mm	31°C 25°C 825mm
July	**August**	**September**	**October**	**November**	**December**
29°C 24°C 891mm	29°C 24°C 486mm	29°C 24°C 246mm	31°C 24°C 116mm	33°C 22°C 34mm	32°C 21°C 8mm

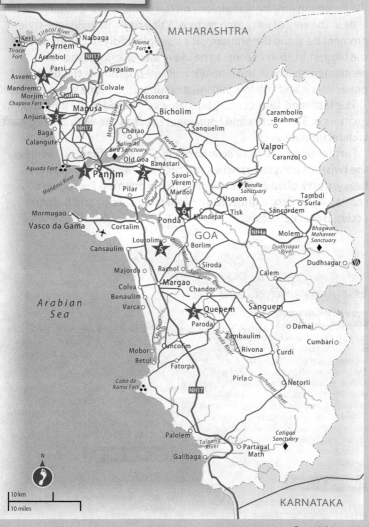

MAHARASHTRA

Tiracol River
Keri
Tiracol Fort
Nalbaga
Alorna Fort
Pernem
Arambol
NH17
Parsi
Dargalim
Asvem
4
Mandrem
Morjim
Chapora Fort
Siolim
Colvale
Assonora
Anjuna
3
Baga
Mapusa
NH17
Bicholim
Carambolin-Brahma
Calangute
Chorao
Sanquelim
Aguada Fort
Salim Ali Bird Sanctuary
Old Goa
Valpoi
Caranzol
Panjim
2
Banastari
Pilar
Savoi-Verem
Mardol
Bondla Sanctuary
Tambdi Surla
Mormugao
Cambarjua Canal
Ponda
6
Usgaon
Sancordem
Vasco da Gama
Cortalim
Khandepar
Tisk
NH4a
Molem
Bhagwan Mahaveer Sanctuary
Cansaulim
Loutolim
5
GOA
Borlim
Dudhsagar River
Dudhsagar
Majorda
Rachol
Siroda
Calem
Colva
Margao
Chandor
Benaulim
Varca
Quepem
5
Sanguem
Damai
Paroda
Zambaulim
Rivona
Curdi
Cumbari
Mobor
Cuncolim
Betul
Fatorpa
Pirla
Kushavati River
Netorli
Cabo de Rama Fort
NH17
Palolem
Talpona River
Cotigao Sanctuary
Partagal Math
Galibaga
KARNATAKA

Arabian Sea

N

10 km
10 miles

Panjim (Panaji)
& Old Goa

Sleepy, dusty Panjim was adopted as the Portuguese capital when the European empire was already on the wane, and the colonizers left little in the way of lofty architecture. A tiny city with a Riviera-style promenade along the Mandovi, it's also splendidly uncommercial: the biggest business seems to be in the sale of *kaju* (cashews), gentlemen-shaves in the *barbieris* and *feni*-quaffing in the booths of pokey bars – and city folk still insist on sloping off for a siesta at lunch.

The 18th- and 19th-century bungalows clustered in the neighbouring quarters of San Thome and Fontainhas stand as the victims of elegant architectural neglect.

Further upriver, a thick swathe of jungle – wide fanning raintrees, the twists of banyan branches and coconut palms – has drawn a heavy, dusty blanket over the relics of the doomed Portuguese capital of Old Goa, a ghost town of splendid rococo and baroque ecclesiastical edifices.

Essential Panjim and Old Goa

Finding your feet

Panjim is the transport hub of Central Goa. Pre-paid taxis or buses run the short distance from Dabolim airport across Mormugao Bay to Panjim. The closest station on the Konkan Railway is at Karmali, 10 km east, with trains from Mumbai to the north and coastal Karnataka and Kerala to the south; taxis and buses run from Karmali to Panjim. The state-run Kadamba buses and private coach terminals are in Patto to the east of town. From there it is a 10-minute walk across the footbridge over the Ourem Creek to reach the city's guesthouses. See Transport, page 1172.

Getting around

Panjim is laid out on a grid and the main roads run parallel with the seafront. The area is very

Best Old World Goa experiences

Fish curry at Viva Panjim, page 1169
Cholta Cholta Walks, page 1172
Houses of Goa Museum, page 1177

easy to negotiate on foot, but autos are readily available. Motorcycle rickshaws are cheaper but slightly more risky. Local buses run along the waterfront from the City Bus Stand past the market and on to Miramar.

Panjim or Panaji?

Panaji is the official spelling of the capital city, replacing the older Portuguese spelling Panjim. It is still most commonly referred to as Panjim, so we have followed usage.

BACKGROUND

Panjim

The Portuguese first settled Panjim as a suburb of Old Goa, the original Indian capital of the sea-faring *conquistadores*, but its position on the left bank of the Mandovi River had already attracted Bijapur's Muslim king Yusuf Adil Shah in 1500, shortly before the Europeans arrived. He built and fortified what the Portuguese later renamed the Idalcao Palace, now the oldest and most impressive of downtown Panjim's official buildings. The palace's service to the sultan was short-lived: Alfonso de Albuquerque seized it, and Old Goa upstream – which the Islamic rulers had been using as both a trading port and their main starting point for pilgrimages to Mecca – in March 1510. Albuquerque, like his Muslim predecessors, built his headquarters in Old Goa, and proceeded to station a garrison at Panjim and made it the customs clearing point for all traffic entering the Mandovi.

The town remained little more than a military outpost and a staging post for incoming and outgoing viceroys on their way to Old Goa. The first Portuguese buildings, after the construction of a church on the site of the present Church of Our Lady of Immaculate Conception in 1541, were noblemen's houses built on the flat land bordering the sea. Panjim had to wait over two centuries – when the Portuguese Viceroy decided to move from Old Goa in 1759 – for settlement to begin in earnest. It then took the best part of a century for enough numbers to relocate from Old Goa to make Panjim the biggest settlement in the colony and to warrant its status as official capital in 1833.

Panjim (Panaji) *Colour map 5a, B1.*

vibrant market and waterfront, baroque church and pretty Portuguese district

The waterfront

The leafy boulevard of Devanand Bandodkar (DB) Marg runs along the Mandovi from near the New Patto Bridge in the east to the Campal to the southwest. When Panjim's transport and communication system depended on boats, this was its busiest highway and it still holds the city's main administrative buildings and its colourful market.

Walking from the east, you first hit **Idalcao Palace** ① *behind the main boat terminal, DB Marg.* Once the castle of the Adil Shahs, the palace was seized by the Portuguese when they first toppled the Muslim kings in 1510 and was rebuilt in 1615 to serve as the Europeans' Viceregal Palace. It was the official residence to Viceroys from 1759 right up until 1918 when the governor-general (the viceroy's 20th-century title) decided to move to the Cabo headland to the southwest – today's Cabo Raj Niwas – leaving the old palace to become government offices. After Independence it became Goa's secretariat building (the seat of the then Union Territory's parliament) until that in turn shifted across the river to Porvorim. It now houses the bureaucracy of the state passport office. Next to it is a striking dark statue of the **Abbé Faria** (1756-1819) looming over the prone figure of a woman. José Custodio de Faria, who went on to become a worldwide authority on hypnotism, was born into a Colvale Brahmin family in Candolim. The character in Dumas' Count of Monte Cristo may have been based on this Abbé.

Further west, on Malacca Road, almost opposite the wharf, are the central library and public rooms of the **Braganza Institute** ① *Mon-Fri 0930-1300, 1400-1745.* It was established as the Instituto Vasco da Gama in 1871 (the anniversary of the date that the Portuguese explorer da Gama sailed round the Cape of Good Hope), to stimulate an interest in culture, science and the arts. It was renamed for Luis Menezes de Braganza (1878-1938), an outstanding figure of social and political reform in early 20th-century Goa. The blue tile frieze in the entrance, hand painted by Jorge Colaco in 1935, is a mythical representation of the Portuguese colonization of Goa. An art gallery upstairs has paintings by European artists of the late 19th and early 20th centuries and Goan artists of the 20th century. The **central library** ① *0930-1300, 1200-1700,* dating from 1832, has a rare collection of religious and other texts.

City centre

The giant whitewashed 16th-century **Church of the Immaculate Conception** ① *Church Sq, Emidio Gracia Rd, Mon-Sat 0900-1230, 1530-1730, Sun 1100-1230, 1530-1700, free, English Mass Mon-Fri 0800, Sun 0830*, looms pristine and large up a broad sweep of steps off the main square, Largo Da Igreja, blue and white flags fluttering at its fringes. Its dimensions were unwarranted for the population of what was at the time of its construction in 1541, in Panjim, little more than a marshy fishing village; its tall, Portuguese baroque twin towers were instead built both to act as a landmark for and to tend to the spiritual needs of arriving Portuguese sailors, for whom the customs post just below the hill at Panjim marked their first step on Indian soil. The church was enlarged in 1600 to reflect its status as parish church of the capital and in 1619 was rebuilt to its present design. Inside is an ornate jewel in Goan Catholicism's trademark blue, white and gold, wood carved into gilt corkscrews, heavy chandeliers and chintz. The classic baroque main altar *reredos* (screens) are sandwiched between altars to Jesus the Crucified and to Our Lady of the Rosary, in turn flanked by marble statues of St Peter and St Paul. The panels in the Chapel of St Francis, in the south transept, came from the chapel in the Idalcao Palace in 1918. Parishioners bought the statue of Our Lady of

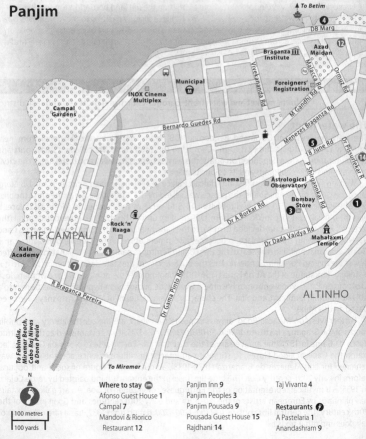

Panjim

To Betim

To Miramar

N

100 metres
100 yards

Where to stay 🛏
Afonso Guest House **1**
Campal **7**
Mandovi & Riorico
Restaurant **12**

Panjim Inn **9**
Panjim Peoples **3**
Panjim Pousada **9**
Pousada Guest House **15**
Rajdhani **14**

Taj Vivanta **4**

Restaurants 🍴
A Pastelaria **1**
Anandashram **9**

Fatima her crown of gold and diamonds in 1950 (candlelight procession every 13 October). The church's feast day is on 8 December.

The Hindu **Mahalaxmi Temple** ① *Dr Dada Vaidya Rd, free,* (originally 1818, but rebuilt and enlarged in 1983) is now hidden behind a newer building. It was the first Hindu place of worship to be allowed in the Old Conquests after the close of the Inquisition. The **Boca de Vaca** ('Cow's Mouth') spring is nearby.

★ Altinho and Fontainhas

On Panjim's eastern promontory, at the foot of the Altinho and on the left bank of the Ourem Creek, sit first the San Thome and then, further south, Fontainhas districts filled with modest 18th- and 19th-century houses. The cumulative prettiness of the well-preserved buildings' colour-washed walls, trimmed with white borders, sloping tiled roofs and decorative wrought-iron balconies make it an ideal area to explore on foot. You can reach the area via any of the narrow lanes that riddle San Thome or take the footbridge across the Ourem Creek from the New Bus Stand and tourist office that feeds you straight into the heart of the district. A narrow road that runs east past the Church of the Immaculate Conception and main town square also ends up here. But probably the best way in

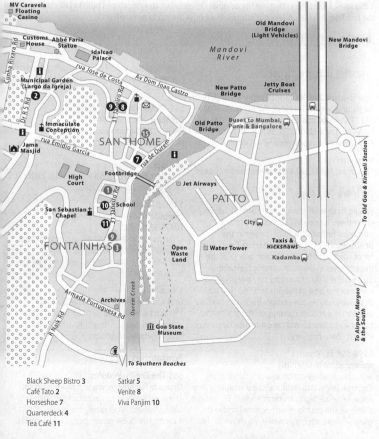

Black Sheep Bistro 3
Café Tato 2
Horseshoe 7
Quarterdeck 4
Tea Café 11

Satkar 5
Venite 8
Viva Panjim 10

is over the Altinho from the Mahalaxmi Temple: this route gives great views over the estuary from the steep eastern flank of the hill, a vantage point that was once used for defensive purposes. A footpath drops down between the Altinho's 19th- and 20th-century buildings just south of San Sebastian Chapel to leave you slap bang in middle of Fontainhas.

The chief landmark here is the small **San Sebastian Chapel** ① *St Sebastian Rd, open only during Mass held in Konkani Mon-Tue, Thu-Sat 0715-0800, Wed 1800-1900, Sun 0645-0730, English Mass Sun 0830-0930, free,* (built 1818, rebuilt 1888) which houses the large wooden crucifix that until 1812 stood in the Palace of the Inquisition in Old Goa where the eyes of Christ watched over the proceedings of the tribunal. Before being moved here, it was in Idalcao Palace's chapel in Panjim for 100 years.

The **Goa State Museum** ① *Patto, 0930-1730, free, head south of Kadamba Bus Stand, across the Ourem Creek footbridge, right across the waste ground and past the State Bank staff training building,* is an impressive building that contains a disappointingly small collection of religious art and antiquities. Most interesting are the original Provedoria lottery machines built in Lisbon that are on the first floor landing. A few old photos show how the machines were used.

Listings Panjim (Panaji) *map p1166*

Tourist information

Goa Tourism Development Corporation (GTDC)
Paryatan Bhavan, 3rd Floor, Patto Plaza, T0832-243 7132, www.goa-tourism.com. Mon-Sat 0900-1130 and 1330-1700, Sun 0930-1400.
Also has an information counter at Dabolim airport.

India Tourism
Church Sq, T0832-222 3412, www.tourism.gov.in.

Where to stay

Panjim has a wide choice of accommodation, while there is none in Old Goa. There are upmarket options south of Panjim in the beach resorts of Miramar and Dona Paula, but for character it's best to book into one of the guesthouses in the atmospheric Fontainhas district. If you don't want to stay overnight you can pack the best of Panjim and Old Goa into a day. Guesthouses have early checkouts to make way for new arrivals coming off the trains and buses and many do not take advance bookings; it's first come first served.

$$$$-$$$ Taj Vivanta
www.vivanta bytaj.com.
A smart upmarket option in a central location. Common areas and restaurants are beautiful (the restaurants are highly recommended). Rooms are a little on the boutique-side, ie small and with glass-walled bathrooms where you have to shut the blinds each time if you are sharing the room. Overall, it has everything you would expect from the Taj group.

$$$-$$ Mandovi
D B Marg, T0832-222 4405, www.hotelmandovigoa.com.
Old building with hints of art deco, relaxing but lacks great character. 66 large a/c rooms (river-facing ones are more expensive); rates include breakfast. **Riorico** restaurant, popular pastry shop, terrace bar and exchange.

$ Hotel Campal
Opposite Kala Academy, Campal, T0832-222 4533.
Clean rooms with TV and a/c possible, hidden in beautiful location in Campal area, near Kala Academy, Inox cinemas and the river. Recommended.

$ Rajdhani
Dr Atmaram Borkar Rd, T0832-222 5362.
Modern business hotel with 35 smallish clean rooms with bath, some a/c (Rs 100 extra). Pure vegetarian restaurant.

Fontainhas

$$$ The Panjim Peoples
Opposite Panjim Inn, www.panjiminn.com.
The latest heritage project from the Sukhija family, this one is genuinely top end with just 4 rooms, antique 4-poster beds and bathtubs,

plus internet access. Changing art exhibitions on the ground floor.

$$ Panjim Inn
E212, 31 Janeiro Rd, T0832-222 6523, www.panjiminn.com.
Goa's first heritage hotel is idiosyncratic, even in the context of the historic Fontainhas district. 14 rooms of varying size all fitted with 4-poster beds, a/c for an extra Rs 250.

$$ Panjim Pousada
Up the road from Panjim Inn.
Slightly cheaper sister hotel to the **Panjim Inn** with double rooms set around a permanent art gallery in a courtyard. It is an evocative, attractive renovation. Best rooms at the back overlook another courtyard. Recommended.

$$-$ Afonso
Near San Sebastian Chapel, Fontainhas, T0832-222 2359.
Atmospheric family-run guesthouse, obliging and friendly, 8 clean rooms with bath, shaded roof terrace for breakfast. It's first come first served, though, as the owners don't take advance bookings. Recommended.

$ A Pousada Guest House
Luis de Menezes Rd, T0832-242 2618.
Pousada's basic rooms are higgledy-piggledy but have a/c, TV and fridge and attached bath. Will take advance bookings.

Restaurants

$$$ Black Sheep Bistro
Swami Vivikenand Rd, next to ICICI Bank, T0832-222 2901.
Their food manifesto is farm, or indeed ocean to table, so sourcing local food as much as possible. Traditional tastes as well as fusion dishes like paella, quesadillas and even a paan cocktail. Recommended.

$$ Horseshoe
Rua de Ourem, T0832-243 1788. Mon-Sat 1200-1430, 1900-1030.
Portuguese/Goan restaurant set in 2 high-ceilinged rooms with exceptionally good service. Most meals excellent value (Rs 60-80) but daily fish specials are far more costly (from Rs 300). The house pudding, a cashew cake, *Bolo San Rival* (Rs 50), trumps all the great main courses.

$$ Quarterdeck
Next to Betim ferry jetty, T0832-243 2905.
Goan, Indian and Chinese cuisine. Their riverside location is the best in Panjim and very pleasant in the evening when brightly lit cruise boats glide gaudily by. Live music.

$$ Venite
31 Janeiro Rd, T0832-222 5537. Mon-Sat 0800-2200, closed in the afternoon.
The most charming of Panjim's eateries has first-floor balconies overlooking the Sao Thome street life and good music. Specializing in fish, this place has a great atmosphere.

$$ Viva Panjim
House No 178, signposted from 31 Janeiro Rd, T0832-242 2405.
This family-run joint in the atmospheric Fontainhas quarter spills out of the restaurant and out into a courtyard, and dishes up Goan specials like *xacuti* and *cafreal* along with seafood, plus takeaway parcels of Indian, Chinese and continental.

$ Anandashram
Opposite Venite, 31 Janeiro Rd.
Serving up platters of fish and veg *thali*, this is a great place to break *pao* (local bread) with the locals. Recommended.

$ Café Tato
Off east side of Church Sq. Closed evenings.
Something of a local institution, tiny little Tato is packed at lunchtime when office workers descend for its limited range of Goan vegetarian food. Expect small platters of chickpea, tomato or mushroom bhaji served with fresh puffed *puris* or soft bread rolls, or vegetarian cutlets and *thalis*. Upstairs is a/c.

$ Satkar
18 June Rd, opposite Bombay Bazar.
Satkar serves up fantastic pure veg food that runs the gamut from South Indian *idlis* and *thalis* to north Indian *sabzi* and tandoor dishes, and the best Punjabi samosas in India. Recommended.

Bakeries, cafés and snacks

$$ A Pastelaria
Dr Dada Vaidya Rd.
Good choice of cakes, pastries and breads. **Mandovi Hotel** has a branch too (side entrance).

$$-$ Tea Cafe
House No 5/218, 31 Janerio Rd.
In the heart of Fontainhas, this is a cosy little café serving up cakes and sandwiches. A nice place to rest before exploring more of Panjim.

Food

The large expat community has brought regional kitchens with them to make for an amazingly cosmopolitan food scene. You can get excellent, authentic Thai spring rolls, Italian wood-baked pizza, German schnitzel, Russian borscht, California wheatgrass shots and everything in between.

Local food is a treat, too, sharing much with the Portuguese palate, and building on the state's bounty in fresh fish and fruit. Unlike wider India, Christianity's heritage means beef is firmly on the menu here, too. Generally, food is hot, making full use of the local bird's-eye chillies. Common ingredients include rice, coconut and cashew nuts.

Spicy calamari or beef *vindalho* marinated in garlic, vinegar and chillies is very popular, quite unlike the vindaloo you'll taste elsewhere. *Chourisso* is Goan sausage of pork pieces stuffed in tripe, boiled or fried with onions and chillies, eaten in bread. *Sorpotel*, a fiery dish of pickled pig's liver and heart seasoned with vinegar and tamarind, is the most famous of Goan meat dishes. *Xacutti* is a hot chicken or meat dish made with coconut, pepper and star anise. For *chicken cafrial*, the meat is marinated in pepper and garlic and braised over a fire. 'Fish curry rice', is the Goan staple (the equivalent of England's fish'n'chips or ham and eggs). Most beach shacks offer a choice of fish depending on the day's catch. *Apa de camarao* is a spicy prawn pie and *reichado* is usually a whole fish, cut in half, and served with a hot masala sauce. *Bangra* is mackerel and pomfret a flat fish; fish *balchao* is a preparation of red masala and onions used as a sauce for prawns or kingfish. *Seet corri* (fish curry) uses coconut. Spicy pickles and chutneys add to the rich variety of flavours. Goan bread is good. *Undo* is a hard-crust round bread. *Kankonn*, hard and crispy and shaped like a bangle, may be dunked in tea. *Pole* is like chapatti, often stuffed with vegetables. The Goan version of the South Indian *iddli* is the *sanaan*.

The favourite dessert is *bebinca*, a layered coconut and jaggery treat of egg yolks and nutmeg. Other sweets include *dodol*, a mix of jaggery and coconut with rice flour and nuts, *doce*, which looks like the North Indian *barfi*, *mangada*, a mango jam, and *bolinhas*, small round semolina cakes. There are also delicious fruits: alfonso mangos in season, the rich jackfruit, papaya, watermelons and cashew nuts.

Drink

Drinks in Goa remain relatively cheap compared to elsewhere in India thanks to the state's low taxes. The fermented juice of cashew apples is distilled for the local brew *caju feni* (fen, froth) which is strong and potent. Coconut or palm *feni* is made from the sap of the coconut palm. *Feni* is an acquired taste; it is often mixed with soda, salt and lime juice.

Bars and clubs

You can't go 20 paces in Panjim without finding a bar: pokey little rooms with a handful of formica tables and chairs and some snacks being fried up in the corner. Many are clustered around Fontainhas. The *feni* (Goa's cashew- or coconut-extracted moonshine) comes delivered in jerry cans, making it cheaper than restaurants.

Entertainment

Read the 'today's events' columns in the local papers for concerts and performances.

Astronomical Observatory, *7th floor, Junta House, 18 June Rd (entrance in Vivekananda Rd)*. 14 Nov-31 May, 1900-2100, in clear weather. Rooftop 6-inch Newtonian reflector telescope and binoculars. Worth a visit on a moonless night, and for views over Panjim at sunset.
Inox, *Campal, near Kala Academy, www.inoxmovies. com*. Fantastic state-of-the-art glass-fronted cinema – like going to the movies in California. You can catch the latest Bolly- and Hollywood blockbusters here, and they try to show the Oscar-nominated best movies every year.
Kala Academy, *D B Marg, Campal, T0832-242 0450, www.kalaacademy.org*. This modern and architecturally impressive centre designed by Charles Correa was set up to preserve and promote the cultural heritage of Goa. There are exhibition galleries, a library and

comfortable indoor and outdoor auditoria. Art exhibitions, theatre and music programmes (from contemporary pop and jazz to Indian classical) are held, mostly during the winter months. There are also music and dance courses.

MV Caravela, *Fisheries dept building, D B Marg, Panjim, www.casinocity.com/in/panjim/caravela*. India's first floating casino is docked on the Mandovi, 66 m of high-rupee-rolling catamaran casino, all plush wall-to-wall carpets, chandeliers and sari-bedecked croupiers. The boat accommodates 300 people, has a sun deck, swimming pool and restaurant and the Rs 1200 entrance includes short eats and dinner and booze from 1730 till the morning.

Festivals

Feb/Mar In addition to the major festivals in Feb, the **Mardi Gras Carnival** (3 days preceding Lent in Feb/Mar) is a Mediterranean-style riot of merrymaking, marked by feasting, colourful processions and floats down streets: it kicks off near the Secretariat at midday. One of the best bits is the red-and-black dance held in the cordoned-off square outside the old world Clube Nacional on the evening of the last day: everyone dresses up (some cross-dressing), almost everyone knows each other, and there's lots of old-fashioned slow-dancing to curiously Country and Western-infused live music. The red and black theme is strictly enforced.

Mar-Apr Shigmotsav is a spring festival held at full moon (celebrated as **Holi** elsewhere in India); colourful float processions through the streets often display mythological scenes accompanied by plenty of music on drums and cymbals.

1st Sun after Easter Feast of Jesus of Nazareth. Procession of All Saints in Goa Velha, on the Mon of Holy Week.

International Film Festival of India, www.iffigoa.org. India's answer to Cannes: a 10-day film mart packed with screenings for the industry and general public alike, with its headquarters based around the Kala Academy and the Inox building on the banks of the Mandovi. Held in Goa since 2004.

Food and Culture Festival at Miramar Beach.

8 Dec Feast of Our Lady of the Immaculate Conception. A big fair is held in the streets around Church Sq and a firework display is put on in front of the church each night of the week before the feast (at 1930). After morning Mass on the Sun, the Virgin is carried in a procession through the town centre.

24 Dec Christmas Eve. This is celebrated with midnight Mass at 140 churches in the state, but some of the best attended are the Church of the Immaculate Conception and Dom Bosco Church in Panjim and the Basilica of Bom Jesus in Old Goa.

Shopping

Books and music

Broadway Books, *next to Rock and Raaga off 18 June Rd, T0832-664 7038*. Largest bookshop in Goa with a good range.

Pedro Fernandes & Co, *Rua Jose de Costa, near Head Post Office, T0832-222 6642*. If you have a hankering to pick up a sitar or learn to play tabla, this small store has a great selection of musical instruments.

Clothes and textiles

Government handicrafts shops are at the tourist hotels and the Interstate Terminus. There are other emporia on RS Rd.

Bombay Store, *Casa Mendes, SV Rd, opposite Old Passport Office*. A new branch of the lifestyle retail store has arrived in Goa close to the main shopping road 18 June Rd, with good selection of fabrics and clothes, as well as cards, stationery and homewares.

Fab India, *Braganza Bungalow, opposite Indoor Stadium, Campal, T0832-246 3096*. This is a particularly lovely branch of the great chain which sells handblock print clothes, textiles, home furnishings and furniture. They have an extensive collection.

Government Emporia, *RS Rd*. Good value for fixed-rate clothes, fabric and handicrafts.

Khadi Showroom, *Municipal (Communidade) Building, Church Sq*. Good value for fixed-rate clothes, fabric and handicrafts. Nehru jackets, plus perishables such as honey and pickles.

Sacha's Shop, *Casa Mendes, next to Bombay Store, T0832-222 2035*. Dubbed a 'curious little space' by the owner, the eponymous Sacha, it is a collection of clothes, flea market finds, designer frocks, organic soaps and textiles.

Velha Goa Galeria, *4/191 Rua De Ourem, Fontainhas, T0832-242 6628*. Hand-painted ceramics, wall hangings and tabletops of tiles.

Wendell Rodricks Design Space, *158 near Luis Gomes Garden, Altinho, T0832-223 8177, www.wendellrodricks.com*. Goa's own fashion designer, brought up in the small village of Colvale, has a beautiful shop in the Altinho district of Panjim. Beautiful fabrics and stylish cuts.

What to do

Cruises

Lots of evening cruises go along the Mandovi River, but as all boats seem to sport loud sound systems it's hardly a peaceful cruise.

Music lessons

Manab Das plays regularly at the **Kala Academy** and the **Kerkar** in Calangute (see page 1179). He and his wife, Dr Rupasree Das, offer sitar and singing lessons to more long-term visitors. To arrange lessons T0832-242 1086 or email manabrupasreegoa@yahoo.in.

Tour operators

Alpha Holidays, *407-409 Dempo Tower, 4th floor, 16 EDC Patto Plaza*, T0832-243 7450, *www.alphagoa.com*.
GTDC *Rua de Ourem*, T0832 243 7132. Goa Tourism offer a range of tours including an eco **Jungle Book Tour** staying a night at Bhagwan Mahaveer Sanctuary.

Walking tours

Cholta Cholta, *T(0)93261 29761*, *www.cholta cholta.com*. Offer insightful themed walking tours around the charming streets of the Latin quarters of Panjim and around Old Goa. Cholta means 'whilst walking' in Konkani.

Transport

Air

The airport is at Dabolim. 29 km via the Zuari Bridge from Panjim. Pre-paid taxis charge Rs 700 to Panjim.

A few international airlines have their offices in Panjim. **Indigo**, **GoAir** and **Spicejet** do the domestic runs.

Auto-rickshaw

Easily available but agree a price beforehand (often Rs 50 minimum); more expensive after dark. Motorcycle taxis and private taxis are a little cheaper.

Bus

Local Crowded **Kadamba (KTC)** buses and private buses operate from the bus stand in Patto to the east of town, across the Ourem Creek, T0832-226 2161. Booking 0800-1100, 1400-1630. The timetable is not strictly observed; buses leave when full. Frequent service to **Calangute** 35 mins; **Mapusa** 15 mins (try to catch a direct one, you will hear someone calling

out what sounds like "durry, durry, durry"!). Via Cortalim (Zuari bridge) to **Margao** 1 hr; **Vasco** 1 hr. To **Old Goa** (every 10 mins) 20 mins, continues to **Ponda** 1 hr. Fares are between Rs 8-20 for these local services.

Long distance: 'Luxury' buses and 'Sleepers' (bunks are shared). Prices double at Diwali, Christmas and New Year, and during the May school holidays. Private operators include **Paulo Travels**, Cardozo Bld, near Kadamba Bus stand, T0832 6637777, www.phmgoa.com, and charge between Rs 450 and 1200 for Panjim to **Mumbai**, for example (15 hrs); similar for Bangalore and Pune.

State buses are run by **Kadamba TC**, **Karnataka RTC**, **Maharashtra RTC**. Check times and book in advance at Kadamba Bus Stand. Unlicensed operators use poorly maintained, overcrowded buses; check before travelling. Fares are cheaper than with private operators, but it's not so easy to book or as comfortable. Expect to pay Rs 350-600 for Panjim to **Mumbai** (15 hrs), similar pricing for **Bangalore** and **Pune**; between Rs 150-400 for **Hampi** (10 hrs).

Car hire

Goa Wheels Unlimited, T0832-402 251, is close by in Calangute, www.goawheelsunlimited.com.

Ferry

Flat-bottomed ferries charge a nominal fee to take passengers (and usually vehicles) when rivers are not bridged. **Panjim-Betim** (the Nehru bridge over the Mandovi supplements the ferry); **Old Goa-Diwar Island**; **Ribandar-Chorao** for Salim Ali Bird Sanctuary.

Taxi

Tourist taxis are white; hire from your hotel or contact **Goa Tourism**, Trionora Apts, T0832-242 4001. Shared-taxis run on certain routes; available near the the ferry wharves, main hotels and market places (up to 5). **Mapusa** from Panjim, around Rs 10 each.

Train

Most trains stop at Thivim and Madgaon, some **Konkan Railway** trains stop at **Karmali**, T0832-228 5798, near Old Goa (20 mins by taxi). **Rail Bookings**, Kadamba Bus Station, 1st floor, 0930-1300 and 1430-1700. **South Central Railway** serves the Vasco-Londa/Belgaum line, and Margao (Madgaon), page 1213.

The white spires of Old Goa's glorious ecclesiastical buildings burst into the Indian sky from the depths of overgrown jungle that has sprawled where admirals and administrators of the Portuguese Empire once tended the oriental interests of their 16th-century King Manuel. The canopies of a hundred raintrees cast their shade across the desolate streets, adding to the romantic melancholy beauty of the deserted capital. Tourists and pilgrims continue to flock to the remains of St Francis Xavier in the giddying baroque Basilica of Bom Jesus, where hawkers thrust spindly votive candles into their hands and compete to slake thirsts with fresh coconut, lime or sugarcane juice.

Basilica of Bom Jesus

The Renaissance façade of Goa's most famous church, the Basilica of Bom (the Good) Jesus, a UNESCO World Heritage Site, reflects the architectural transition to baroque then taking place in Europe. Apart from the elaborate gilded altars, wooden pulpit and the candy-twist Bernini columns, the interior is very simple.

The church has held the treasured remains of **St Francis Xavier**, a former pupil of soldier-turned-saint Ignatius Loyola, the founder of the Order of Jesuits since the 17th century. Francis's canonization was in 1622.

The tomb, which lies to the right of the main chancel (1698), was the gift of one of the last of the Medicis, Cosimo III, Grand Duke of Tuscany, and took the Florentine sculptor Giovanni Batista Foggini 10 years to complete. It is made of three tiers of marble and jasper; the upper tier holds scenes from the saint's life. The casket is silver and has three locks, the keys being held by the Governor, the Archbishop and the Convent Administrator. You can look down on to the tomb from a small window in the art gallery next to the church.

After his canonization, St Francis's body was shown on each anniversary of his death until 1707, when it was restricted to a few special private expositions. In 1752, the cadaver was again paraded to quash rumours that the Jesuits had removed it. The exhibition now happens every 10 years (the last was in January 2015), when the relics are taken to the Sé Cathedral. Feast Day is 3 December.

Sé Cathedral

Across the square sits the Sé Cathedral, dedicated to St Catherine on whose day (25 November) Goa was recaptured by Albuquerque. Certainly the largest church in Old Goa, it could even be the biggest in Asia and was built on the ruins of a mosque by the Dominicans between 1562 and 1623. The building is Tuscan outside and Corinthian inside, with a barrel-vaulted ceiling and east-facing main façade. One of the characteristic twin towers collapsed in 1776 when it was struck by lightning. The remaining tower holds five bells including the Golden Bell (cast in Cuncolim in 1652).

The vast interior, divided into the barrel-vaulted nave with clerestory and two side aisles, has a granite baptismal font. On each side of the

Essential Old Goa

Finding your feet

Old Goa lies on the south bank of the Mandovi on the crest of a low hill 8 km from Panjim. The frequent bus service takes 15-20 minutes. Buses drop you off opposite the Basilica of Bom Jesus; pick up the return bus near the police station. Karmali station on the Konkan Railway, just east of the centre, has taxis for transfers.

Getting around

The major monuments are within easy walking distance of the bus stop.

Admission

All monuments are open daily year round 0830-1730.

Fact...

The Basilica of Bom Jesus is on the World Monuments Fund's list of the world's 100 most endangered sites.

church are four chapels along the aisles; on the right, these are dedicated to St Anthony, St Bernard, the Cross of Miracles and the Holy Spirit, and on the left, starting at the entrance, to Our Lady of Virtues, St Sebastian, the Blessed Sacrament and Our Lady of Life. The clerestory windows are protected by a shield crowned by a balustrade to keep out the sun. The main altar is superbly gilded and painted, with six further altars in the transept. The marble-top table in front of the main altar is where, since 1955, St Francis Xavier's remains have been held during their exposition. The main *reredos* has four panels illustrating the life of St Catherine. There is also an **art gallery** ① *Mon-Thu, Sat 0900-1230, Sun 0900-1030, closed during services, Rs 5.*

Around the cathedral

Southwest of the cathedral's front door are the ruins of the **Palace of the Inquisition**, where over 16,000 cases were heard between 1561 and 1774. The Inquisition was finally suppressed in 1814. Beneath the hall were dungeons. In Old Goa's heyday this was the town centre.

There are two churches and a museum in the same complex as the Cathedral. The **Church and Convent of St Francis of Assisi** is a broad vault of a church with two octagonal towers. The floor is paved with tombstones and on either side of the baroque high altar are paintings on wood depicting scenes from St Francis' life while the walls above have frescoes with floral designs. The original **Holy Spirit Church** in the Portuguese Gothic (manueline) style was begun by Franciscan friars in 1517; everything except the old doorway was replaced by the larger present structure in the 1660s (itself restored 1762-1765). The convent now houses the **Archaeological Museum and Portrait Gallery** ① *T0832-228 6133, Sat-Thu 1000-1230, 1500-1830, Rs 5*, with sculptures pre-dating the Portuguese, many from the 12th-13th centuries when Goa was ruled by the Kadamba Dynasty. There are 'hero stones' commemorating naval battles, and 'sati stones' marking the practice of widow burning.

There is also a rather fine collection of portraits of Portuguese governors upstairs that is revealing both for its charting of the evolution of court dress as well as the physical robustness of the governors inside. Some governors were remarkable for their sickly pallor, others for the sheer brevity of their tenure of office, which must have set the portrait painters something of a challenge.

The ASI booklet on the monuments, *Old Goa*, by S Rajagopalan, is available from the museum, Rs 10.

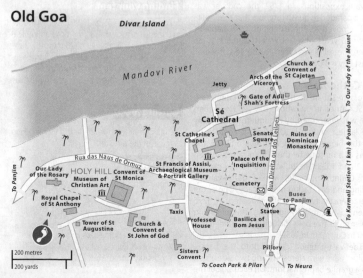

Old Goa

BACKGROUND

Old Goa

Old Goa is to Christians the spiritual heart of the territory. It owes its origin as a Portuguese capital to Afonso de Albuquerque and some of its early ecclesiastical development to St Francis Xavier who was here, albeit for only five months, in the mid-16th century. Before the Portuguese arrived it was the second capital of the Muslim Bijapur Kingdom. Today, all the mosques and fortifications of that period have disappeared and only a fragment of the Sultan's palace walls remain.

Under the Portuguese, Old Goa was grand enough to be dubbed the 'Rome of the East', but it was a flourishing port with an enviable trade even before the Portuguese arrived. The bustling walled city was peopled by merchants of many nationalities who came to buy and sell horses from Arabia and Hormuz, to trade silk, muslin, calico, rice, spices and areca nuts from the interior and other ports along the west coast. It was a centre of shipbuilding and boasted fine residences and public buildings.

After the arrival of the Portuguese, Old Goa swelled still further in size and significance. In the west lay barracks, mint, foundry and arsenal, hospital and prison. The banks of the Mandovi held the shipyards of Ribeira des Gales and next door lay the administrative and commercial centre. Streets and areas of the city were set aside for different activities and merchandise, each with its own character. The most important, Rua Direita ou dos Leiloes (Straight Street), was lined with jewellers, bankers and artisans. It was also the venue for auctions of precious goods, held every morning except Sunday. To the east was the market and the old fortress of Adil Shah, while the true centre of the town was filled with magnificent churches built by the Franciscans, themselves joined by waves of successive religious orders: first the Dominicans in 1548, the Augustinians from 1572, the Carmelites from 1612 and finally the Theatines from 1655.

By the mid-17th century, the city, plagued by cholera and malaria and crippled economically, was abandoned for Panjim.

To the west is **St Catherine's Chapel**. It was built at the gate of the old city on the orders of Albuquerque as an act of gratitude after the Portuguese defeat of the forces of Bijapur in 1510. The original mud and thatch church was soon replaced by a stone chapel which in 1534 became the cathedral (considerably renovated in 1952), remaining so until Sé Cathedral was built.

On the road towards the Mandovi, northeast from the cathedral compound, lies the **Arch of the Viceroys (Ribeira dos Viceroys)**, commemorating the centenary of Vasco da Gama's discovery of the sea route to India. It was built at the end of the 16th century by his great-grandson, Francisco da Gama, Goa's Viceroy from 1597 to 1600. Its laterite block structure is faced with green granite on the side approached from the river. This was the main gateway to the seat of power: on arrival by ship each new Viceroy would be handed the keys and enter through this ceremonial archway before taking office. The statue of Vasco da Gama above the arch was originally surmounted by a gilded statue of St Catherine, the patron saint of the city.

Walking east towards the convent from the arch you pass the **Gate of the Fortress of the Adil Shahs**, probably built by Sabaji, the Maratha ruler of Goa before the Muslim conquest of 1471. The now-ruined palace was home to the Adil Shahi sultans of Bijapur who occupied Goa before the arrival of the Portuguese. It was the Palace of the Viceroys until 1554 after which it served as both the hall of trials for the Inquisition and to house prisoners.

A little further still stands the splendid, domed baroque **Convent and Church of St Cajetan (Caetano)**. Pope Urban III dispatched a band of Italian friars of the Theatine order to spread the Gospel to the Deccani Muslim city of Golconda near Hyderabad but they got a frosty reception so headed back west to settle in Goa. They acquired land around 1661 to build this church, which is shaped like a Greek cross and is partly modelled on St Peter's in Rome. It is the last domed church in Goa.

The crypt below the main altar, where the Italian friars were buried, has some sealed lead caskets that are supposed to contain the embalmed bodies of senior Portuguese officials who never returned home. Next door is the beautiful former convent building which is now a pastoral foundation (closed to the public).

On a hill a good way further east is the modest **Chapel of Our Lady of the Mount**, dating from 1510, which gives you a good idea of how the other churches here must originally have looked. It is a peaceful spot with excellent panoramic views across Old Goa, evocative of the turbulent past when Albuquerque and Adil Shah vied for control of the surrounding area. The altar gilding inside has been beautifully restored. In front of the main altar lies the body of architect Antonio Pereira whose burial slab requests the visitor to say an Ave Maria for his soul.

Holy Hill

Between the domineering central monuments of Old Goa's broad tree-lined centre and Panjim stand the cluster of churches of Holy Hill. The first building you reach (on your left) as you leave the central plaza is the **Church and Convent of St John of God**, built in 1685 and abandoned in 1835. The **Museum of Christian Art** ① *everyday 0930-1700, Rs 5*, is to the right, with 150 items gathered from Goa's churches, convents and Christian homes to give a rich cross section of Indo-Portuguese sacred craft in wood, ivory, silver and gold. There is a little outdoor café too.

Next door sits the **Convent of St Monica** (1607-1627), the first nunnery in India and the largest in Asia. A huge three-storey square building, with the church in the southern part, it was built around a sunken central courtyard containing a formal garden. At one time it was a royal monastery, but in 1964 it became a theological institute, the Mater Dei Institute for Nuns. It was here in 1936 that Bishop Dom Frei Miguel Rangel is believed to have had a vision of the Christ figure on the Miraculous Cross opening his eyes, his stigmata bleeding and his lips quivering as if to speak. The vision was repeated later that year in the presence of the Bishop, the Viceroy Dom Pedro de Silva and a large congregation.

It is well worth the effort of the hike, taking the left fork of the road, to reach the **Royal Chapel of St Anthony** (1543) – dedicated to Portugal's national saint and restored by its government in 1961 – and, opposite, the **Tower of St Augustine**. The Augustinians came to Goa in 1572; the church they immediately began, bar the belfry, now lies in ruins. It once boasted eight chapels, a convent and an excellent library and was enlarged to become one of the finest in the kingdom. It was finally abandoned in 1835 because of religious persecution. The vault collapsed in 1842, burying the image; the façade and main tower followed in 1931 and 1938. Only one of the original four towers survives. The large bell now hangs in Panjim's Church of the Immaculate Conception. The Archaeological Survey of India is spearheading extensive repairs.

Behind is the **Chapel of Our Lady of the Rosary** (1526). Belonging to the earliest period of church building, it is called Manueline after Manuel I, the Portuguese king who oversaw a period of great prosperity that coincided with the country's conquest of Goa. The use of Hindu and Muslim craftsmen in building the chapel led to an architectural style that borrowed from Iberian decoration but also absorbed both local naturalistic motifs and Islamic elements (seen on the marble cenotaph). The church here has a two-storey entrance, a single tower and low flanking turrets. It was from here that Albuquerque directed the battle against the Adil Shahi forces in 1510.

fading Portuguese heritage

Gaspar Dias Fortress

The fortress was finished around 1606. The Panjim–Ribandar causeway, built in 1634, gave it direct land access to the capital at Old Goa and its significance grew accordingly. The walls, likely laterite blocks 1.5 m thick and 5 m high, made space for 16 cannons. These saw repeated action against the Dutch until the middle of the 17th century, but the fortress' importance waned after the Maratha onslaught and it fell into disrepair under 15 years of occupation by a British garrison in the early 19th century. It was made new but the Portuguese army finally abandoned it in 1870 as a result of further damage sustained during the mutiny against the Prefect of 1835. For a while the military still stationed soldiers here to convalesce but by the 20th century it had crumbled beyond recognition. All that is left is one cannon at the Miramar circle that marks the possible site of the fort.

Miramar Beach is a bit grubby but it's a pleasant drive with good views over the sea and, if you've got a little time to kill, it offers the best quick escape from the city.

Cabo Raj Niwas
Closed to the public but you can get passes for Mass on Sun at 0930 on the gate.

The nearby fort Cabo Raj Niwas has fared little better than Gaspar Dias Fortress: six cannons and some bits of wall crumbling in the gardens of Raj Bhavan, or the State Governor's House, are all that remain.

The first small **Our Lady of Cabo shrine** was built in 1541. Documents from 1633 refer to both the chapel and a fort with four guns. A British troop garrison stationed here from 1799 during the Napoleonic Wars explains the overgrown graves in the nearby **British Cemetery**. Around 1844, after the religious orders were abolished, the Archbishop of Goa was given the convent, which he converted into an impressive residence. It was the official address of the governor-general of Goa in 1918. Its grand interior was left intact after the Portuguese left in 1961. The viewing platform near the entrance gives superb views over the sweep of the coastline across the Mandovi estuary to Fort Aguada.

Houses of Goa Museum
www.archgoa.org, Tue-Sun 1000-1900.

A fascinating museum 5 km north of Panjim, in Bardez, created by architect Gerard da Cunha on a traffic island. It's a beautiful building shaped like a ship that follows traditional Goan architecture and style. Inside is a collection of doors, tiles, altars, lamps and rare postcards. It offers a unique insight into Goa's heritage.

North
Goa

While Baga and Calangute, the fishing villages first settled by the 'freaks', now stand as cautionary tales to all that's bad about mass tourism, Anjuna, a place synonymous with psychedelia, drugs and Goa trance parties, has managed to retain a village feel. Despite the existence of its unquestionably shady underbelly, it still has a charming feel – it just gets a little lively at night. The weekly flea market is a brilliant bazar – like Camden or Portobello in London but with sacred cows, sadhus, fakirs and snake charmers – and makes it onto every holidaymaker's itinerary.

But if you stick around you'll find that the little stretch of shoreline from the northern end of Anjuna Beach to the Chapora River is beautifully desolate: rust-coloured rugged cliffs covered with scrub interrupt scrappy bays strewn with laterite boulders. Pretty cliff-backed Vagator stands just south of the romantic ruins of Chapora Fort, with its busy fishing jetty, where trawler landings are met by a welcoming committee of kites, gulls and herons wheeling hungrily on high. Further upstream, around the pretty village of Siolim, young men wade through mangrove swamps to sift the muds for clams, mussels and oysters.

Over the Chapora river lies a strip of beautiful beaches. You can walk the length of the coast from Morjm to Arambol when the tide is out and then even over the cliff to Keri: stunning.

Arambol is a busy hippy backpacker hamlet, with the quieter beach satellites of Mandrem, Asvem and Keri, and the wonderful little Catholic enclave clustered around the ancient Tiracol Fort.

Essential North Goa

Finding your feet

The NH17 acts as the main arterial road between all of Goa's coastal belt. From Panjim, the highway crosses the Mandovi Bridge to the area's main hub, Calangute (16 km from Panjim, 10 km from Mapusa). Buses from Mapusa (20 minutes) and Panjim (35 minutes) arrive at Calangute Bus Stand near the market; a few continue to Baga to the north from the crossroads. You can charter tourist minivans from places such as Panjim and Dabolim. The closest stop on the Konkan Railway route between Mumbai and Mangalore is Thivim near Mapusa. On market days there are boats between Baga and Anjuna. There are buses from Mapusa and Panjim to Calangute, Anjuna, Chapora and Arambol.

Best seafood suppers

Goan fish curry at Britto's, Baga, page 1183
Rawa fried mussels at Anand, Anjuna, page 1192
Pepper-crusted tuna at Sublime, Morjim, page 1200

Getting around

There are 9 km of uninterrupted beach between Fort Aguada and the bridge over Baga river in the north, which takes you to Anjuna. These are split into four beaches, south to north: Sinquerim, Candolim, Calangute and Baga. Each has its own stab at a high street, Calangute's being the most built up. There are taxis, motorcycle taxis, tourist vans and old Ambassador cabs, or cheap but slow public buses. Roads are fairly good for motorbikes and scooters; watch out for speed bumps. Accidents happen with grim regularity, but bikes give you the independence to zip between beaches.

Best places to dance the night away

Clifftop dancefloor at Chronicle, Vagator, page 1193
Good trance stomp at Curlies, Anjuna, page 1193
Live African, gypsy or Indian music at Ash, Arambol, page 1201

Calangute and around *Colour map 5a, A1.*
busy beaches with a few gems

The faultless fawn shoreline of Bardez *taluka*, particularly Calangute, until 40 years ago was a string of fishing villages. Now it acts as sandpit to the bulk of Goa's travel trade. Chock full of accommodation, eateries, travel agents, money changers, beggars and under-dressed, over-sunned charter tourists, the roads snarl up with minivans, buses and bikes, and unchecked development has made for a largely concrete conurbation of breezeblock hotels and mini markets.

For all that, if you squint hard or come in monsoon you can still see what once made it such a hippy magnet: wonderful coconut-fringed sands backed by plump dunes occasionally broken by rocky headlands and coves. The main reason to head this way is for business, banks, or posh food and nightlife. To get out again, you can paddle in the waters of the Arabian Sea all the way between the forts of Aguada and Vagator.

Calangute

More than 25 years of package tourism has guaranteed that there is little left to draw you to Calangute apart from ATMs, some decent restaurants and a quirky hexagonal *barbeiria* (barber's shop) at the northern roundabout. In the 1960s, the village was shorthand for the alternative life, but the main feature of the streets today is their messy Indian take on beach commercialism. Shops peddle everything from cheap ethnic tat to extravagant precious gemstones. The shacks on the beach serve good food and cheap beer and most fly the St George's Cross in tribute to Calangute's charter coin. Between the busy beachfront and the grubby main road, coconut trees give shade to village houses, some of which rent out private rooms.

Away from the town centre, the striking gold and white **Church of St Alex** is a good example of rococo decoration in Goa, while the false dome of the central façade is an 18th-century architectural development. The pulpit and the *reredos* are particularly fine.

Kerkar Art Complex ① *Gaurawaddo, T0832-227 6017, www.subodhkerkar.com*, is a beautiful art space showcasing Subodh Kerkar's paintings and installation work. Inspired by the ocean, nature is both the theme and medium of his work, using shells, light and water to create static waves or, in his recent installations, using fishermen standing on the beach to create the shapes and forms of fishing boats, all captured in stunning black and white photography.

Calangute

To Baga
Casa Goa
COBRAVADDO
Our Lady of Piety
To Mapusa (6 km)
Arabian Sea
Tibetan Market
Football Pitch
St John's
Tibetan Market
Heritage Kathakali Theatre
UMTAVADDO
Menezes Supermarket
CALANGUTE
To Panjim
St Anthony's
GAURAVADDO
Kerkar Art Complex
Day Tripper
Literati
To ❶❻, Acron Arcade, Candolim (1 km), Sinquerim (3 km) & Aguada Fort (4 km)

N

| 200 metres |
| 200 yards |

Villa Goesa 20

Where to stay 🏠
Coco Banana 4
Martin's Guest Rooms 13
The Park 10
Pousada Tauma 17
Saahil 1

Restaurants 🍴
A Reverie 3
Bomras 1
Café Ciocolatti 6
Infanteria 2
Souza Lobo 8
Tibetan Kitchen 5

Baga

Baga is basically Calangute North: there's continuity in congestion, shops, shacks and sun loungers. Here though, there are also paddy marshes, water tanks and salt pans, the beach is still clean, and the river that divides this commercial strip of sand from Anjuna in the north also brings fishermen pulling in their catch at dawn, and casting their nets at dusk. The north bank, or **Baga River**, is all thick woods, mangroves and birdlife; it has quite a different feel, more like a village, with a few classy European restaurants looking out across the river. You can take an hour to wade across the river at low tide, then walk over the crest of the hill and down into Anjuna South, or detour inland to reach the bridge.

Candolim and Sinquerim beaches

The wide unsheltered stretch of beach here, backed by scrub-covered dunes, attracts a fair crowd: more staid than Baga and Calangute to the north, chiefly because its restaurants and hotels are pricier and the average holidaymaker more senior. The road from Calangute to Fort Aguada is lined with shiny glass-fronted shops, while the sands at the foot of the Taj complex offers the full gamut of watersports – jet skis, windsurfers, catamaran and dinghies are all for hire – making it a favourite of India's fun-loving domestic tourists.

Fort Aguada

The Portuguese colonizer's strongest coastal fort was built on this northern tip of the Mandovi estuary in 1612 with one goal: to stay the Dutch navy. Two hundred guns were stationed here along with two magazines, four barracks, several residences for officers and two prisons. It was against the Marathas, though, rather than the Dutch, that Aguada saw repeated action – Goans fleeing the onslaught at Bardez took refuge here – and its ramparts proved time and again impregnable. The main fortifications (laterite walls nearly 5 m high and 1.3 m thick) are still intact, and the buildings at sea level now house Goa's Central Jail, whose 142 male and 25 female inmates are incarcerated in what must be one of the world's prettiest lock-ups.

Bardez

The name Bardez may have come from the term *bara desh* (12 'divisions of land'), which refers to the 12 Brahmin villages that once dominated the region. Another explanation is that it refers to 12 *zagors* celebrated to ward off evil. Or it could be *bahir des*, meaning 'outside land' – ie the land beyond the Mandovi River. It was occupied by the Portuguese as part of their original conquest, and bears the greatest direct imprint of their Christianizing influence.

Reis Magos, the Nerul River and Coco Beach

The position of Reis Magos, across the Mandovi River from Panjim, made it imperative for Albuquerque to station troops on this shoulder of headland from day one of Portuguese rule; today, come for the views to the capital, and for the crumbling **Royal Fort** whose angular 16th-century architecture is now overrun with jungle. Its canons served as the second line of defence against the Dutch after Aguada.

The next door **church** is where the village gets its name – this was where the first Mass on Goan soil was celebrated in 1550, and the Hindu temple was promptly turned over into a church to the three Magi Kings, Gaspar, Melchior and Balthazar, whose stories are told on the inside *reredos*. Fort Aguada and Fort Reis Magos are divided by the Nerul River: stop off at Nerul's **Coco Beach** for lunch and a swim. The temple in the village dates from 1910 and the Church of Our Lady of Remedies from 1569. Coco beach is a lovely quiet spot, but don't tell anyone!

Listings Calangute and around *maps p1180 and p1182*

Where to stay

Calangute

$$$$ The Park
Holiday St Calangute, www.theparkhotels.com.
Boutique number offering up chic white rooms; 2 suites have sea views but to enjoy the beach at its best head to the bar and restaurant. There is a lovely pool as well as cute shop on site. Best doors ever with fantastic photography from Rohit Chawla adorning them.

$$$$ Pousada Tauma
Porbavaddo Calangute, T0832-227 9061, www.pousada-tauma.com.
A shady little complex built of Goa's trademark laterite rock set around a beautiful pool. It's discreet but full of character, with old-fashioned yet understated service. Suites are spacious, but come with shower not bath. Classy without a modern 5-star swagger.

$$$-$$ Villa Goesa
Cobravaddo, off Baga Rd, T0832-227 7535, www.vilagoesa.com.
This quiet, relaxing place, a 300-m walk from the beach, offers 57 clean rooms, some a/c, some

very shaded. Excellent restaurant, lovely gardens, pool and very friendly owners. Recommended.

$$-$ Coco Banana
5/139A Umtavaddo, back from Calangute Beach, T(0)99608 03790, www.cocobananagoa.com.
In a good neighbourhood in the back lanes of Calangute, this is one of the best local guesthouses and has 6 spotless en suite bungalows set in a leafy garden. All rooms come with nets and fridges, some have TV and a/c, and the place is airy, light and comfortable. The Swiss-German owners are caring and helpful. They also rent out 2 apartments in **Casa Leyla**, and have a whole house, **Soledad**, with all mod cons and maid service.

$ Martin's Guest Rooms
Baga Rd, T0832-227 7306, martins@goatelecom.com.
5 rooms in a family house, with attractive verandas and use of a kitchen, but it's on the busy main road and could do with a lick of paint.

$ Saahil
Cobravaddo, Baga Rd, T0832-227 6647.
Lots of big, clean rooms within walking distance of all the action. Good value.

Baga

$$$-$ Cavala
*Sauntavaddo, top end of Baga village,
T0832-227 6090, www.cavala.com.*
Sandwiched between Baga Rd and a big field
stretching towards the mountains, Cavala is
traditional but very well maintained, with friendly
and attentive management, and set in lovely
gardens. The 30 rooms are big, with giant fridges
and huge bathrooms, although only shower.
Some have TV. They have regular music nights
in their popular restaurant and they also have
a new villa for rent in neighbouring Anjuna.
Recommended.

$$-$ Riverside
*Baga River by the bridge, T0832-227 7337,
www.hotelriversidegoa.com.*
In an attractive location overlooking the river,
this place has clean, modern rooms with good
balconies. Some cottages with kitchens available
near the pool. Has a tour group feel about it, but
the lovely location makes up for it.

$ Nani's & Rani's
T0832-227 7014, www.naniranigoa.com.
One of the few local budget options with a
sea view and a relaxing quiet location. There's
an attractive main building, 8 spartan rooms
(shared or own bath), budget meals served
in a pleasant garden, bar, email and STD/ISD.
Renowned healer Dr Patrick hosts sessions and
workshops here on occasion. It's a short walk
across Baga Bridge for nightlife.

Candolim and Sinquerim beaches

$$$$ Vivanta by Taj – Fort Aguada
Sinquerim, T0832-664 5858, www.tajhotels.com.
The self-confessed sprawling Taj complex
spreads over 36 ha. In descending order of cost,
these are 17 hilltop family villas that make up the
Aguada Hermitage, 130 rooms with sea views
at the Fort Aguada Beach Resort, built in the
fort's ruins, and scores of cottages for up to 8
on the beach in the newer and very beautifully
kept Taj Holiday Village, about 2 km away;
there is a shuttle bus between the 2 resorts.
Between the 2 hotels there is a recommended
spa, 2 freshwater pools, 9 restaurants, plus golf,
tennis and a crèche. The Banyan Tree Thai
restaurant is especially recommended.

$$$$-$$$ Aashyana Lakhanpal
*Escrivao Vaddo, Candolim, T0832-248 9225,
www.aashyanalakhanpal.com.*
One of the most stunning places in Goa:
delightful gardens with great swathes of green
lead right down to the beach. If you don't fancy
the beach, there's a lovely pool. And the rooms
and villas are beautifully decorated. This is a great
place to hide away. Recommended.

$$$$-$$$ The Sol
*road opposite Bank of India, Nerul (directly
inland 2 km from Calangute/Sinquerim),
T0832-671 4141, www.thesol.in.*
Designed by fashion designer Tarun Tahiliani this
is a nouveau heritage-style property where they
strive to create an atmosphere that honours Goa
as it once was. Tucked in lush foliage with views
of Sinquerim river, the rooms are big, the beds
are 4-postered.

$$$ Marbella Tourist Home
*left off the road to Taj Fort Aguada Beach Resort,
T0832-247 9551, www.marbellagoa.com.*

Baga

To Anjuna (2 km)
To Anjuna (500m)

St Ann's

Salt Lake

Salt Pans

Baga River

Baga Bridge

Football Pitch

Arabian Sea

BAGA

Lady of Candelaria

Natural Health Centre

Tito's Rd

Bike Hire

To Calangute

N

200 metres
200 yards

Restaurants
Britto's 15
Casa Portuguesa 12
Fiesta 1

Where to stay
Cavala 1
Nani's & Rani's 2
Riverside 3

Bars & clubs
Mambo's 13
Tito's 16

Splendid mock-Portuguese period mansion with 6 lovingly decorated rooms. Its owners have scavenged bona fide antiques and furnishings like mosaic tiles from old villas to create this elegant and unpretentious homestay in a forest at the end of a dirt track. Lovely garden sit-out for meals. All rooms have a/c and cable TV. Recommended.

$ Ludovici Tourist Home
Dando, Sinquerim, T0832-237 9684.
Pretty family home set back off the main road with 4 modest en suite doubles, all with fan. It very much feels that you are one of the family. There's a bar and restaurant and a lovely porch with chairs that gives onto a spacious garden. Sedate and modest guesthouse with traditional charm.

Restaurants

Even Calangute's most ardent detractors will brave a trip for its restaurants, some of which are world class. While costly by Indian standards, a slap-up meal will cost you a fraction of its equivalent at European prices.

Calangute

$$$ A Reverie
Next to The Park, Holiday St, T(0)9823-14927, www.areverie.com.
Award-winning restaurant offering a globally inspired menu in chic surrounds. You can try a Thai vegetable *thali* or opt for Australian John Dory. Although when there is so much local fish available do you need to have Norwegian salmon?

$$$-$$ Souza Lobo
On the beach, T0832-227 6463.
Somewhat of an institution, this place serves up excellent fresh seafood, lobster and sizzlers served on a shaded terrace, well-known restaurant that has managed to retain a good reputation for years.

$ Infanteria
Baga Rd, near beach roundabout.
'The breakfast place' to locals, Rs 125 for a set breakfast, eggs, coffee, juice, toast. Bakery and confectionery. Very atmospheric.

$ The Tibetan Kitchen
At the bottom of a track leading off Calangute Beach Rd.
This airy garden restaurant is part tent, part wicker awning, part open to the skies. Tibet's answer to ravioli – *momos* – are good here, but more adventurous starters such as prawns,

mushrooms and tomatoes on wilting lettuce leaves are exceptional.

Baga

$$$ Casa Portuguesa
Baga Rd.
An institution of a restaurant run by German/Goan couple with live music in the gloriously overgrown jungle of a garden. Strongly recommended.

$$$ Fiesta
Tito's Lane, T0832-227 9894.
Open for dinner Wed-Mon.
Stunning restaurant hidden behind the gaudy Tito's Lane. Beautifully decorated intimate restaurant with fabulous Italian-style food as well as great steaks, fish suppers and cocktails. Recommended.

$$ Britto's Bar and Restaurant
Baga Beach, T0832-227 7331.
Cajie Britto's puddings are an institution and his staff (of 50) boast that in high season you'll be pushed to find an inch of table space from the restaurant's inside right out to the seashore. Fantastic range of traditional Goan dishes such as *vindaloo* and *cafreal*. It's a great spot to watch India on the beach. Highly recommended.

Candolim

$$$ Bomras
Candolim, towards Sinquerim, T(0)97615 91056, bawmra@yahoo.com.
Mouth-watering Burmese and Asian fusion food, such as seared rare tuna, mussel curry and Nobu-esque blackened miso cod. Fantastic vegetarian dishes and curries too, washed down with quite possibly the best cocktail in the world spiced with lemongrass and ginger. Chic setting; amidst the bright lights of Candolim, you could almost blink and miss it. Highly recommended.

$$ Café Ciocolatti
Main road Candolim, T(0)9326-112006.
Fantastic range of all things chocolate. Lovely daytime café. They also do salads to outweigh any potential guilt incurred by eating the orange marmalade brownie.

Bars and clubs

Perennial favourites are Cubana next to the Night Market and Titos, in Baga. The newest additions to the scene are LPK and Sinq in Candolim. For up-to-date event and venue information check out www.whatsupgoa.com.

Calangute

Club WestEnd, *Saligao, 3 km out of Calangute towards Panjim*. This club gets away with hosting 3-day parties by being too remote to disturb anyone and they have an indoor section.

Baga

Cavala, *Sauntavaddo, top end of Baga village*. A genuine bar, with a friendly atmosphere, attentive staff, great cocktails, and occasional live music and 1960s evenings.

Tito's, *Tito's Lane, T0832-227 5028, www.titosgoa. com*. Tito's is an institution in Goa, and has adapted down the decades to reflect the state's changing tourist reality by going from down-at-heel hippie playground in the 1960s to swish international dance club. Now the focus seems to be more on food – are the dancing days of Goa really over? Further along Tito's Lane towards the beach is the Tito's spin-off, **Mambo's**. It's more laid back than the club and free to get in.

Candolim

LPK, *inland from Candolim on Nerul river, www. lpkwaterfronts.com*. Billing itself as India's first super club and "the world's most unique architectural construction", LPK have a little bit of ego and a little bit of media savvy. It certainly is an unusual place to party – dancing in a massive sculpture overlooking the river and Goa jungle, but what's the music like? They appeal to the masses. They are also offering themselves up as the ultimate wedding venue.

Festivals

Calangute

Mar Carnival is best celebrated in villages or in the main district towns but Calangute has brought the party to the tourists.
May (2nd week) The **Youth Fête** attracts Goa's leading musicians and dancers.

Shopping

Calangute

Casa Goa, *Cobravaddo, Baga Rd, T0832-228 1048, cezarpinto@hotmail.com*. Cezar Pinto's shop is a chic lifestyle store: beautifully restored reclining plantation chairs next to plates brought over by the Portuguese from Macau plus modern-day dress from local fashion designer Wendell

Rodricks. Cool modern twists on old Goan shoes by local Edwin Pinto too.
Literati, *off main road, Calangute, parallel to Holiday St, T0832-227 7740, www.literati-goa.com*. Wonderful bookshop in beautiful old house – it's like stumbling into someone's library. The best selection of books, novels, non-fiction and poetry you'll find in Goa. There are sometimes readings here, including an inaugural reading by William Dalrymple.
PlayClan, *Shop No S-3, Ida Maria Resort, next to HDFC bank, Calangute, T(0)9372-280862, www. theplayclan.com*. Fantastic shop selling all manner of clothes, notebooks, lighters and pictures with great colourful cartoon designs created by a collective of animators and designers – giving a more animated view of India's gods, goddesses, gurus and the faces of India **Purple Jungle** in same strip of shops sells similar kitsch India-centric gifts.

Candolim and Sinquerim beaches

Supermarkets like **Delfinos** on Calangute Beach Rd or **Newtons** on Fort Aguada Rd sell staples and lots of imported goods. For silver, head for either of the Tibetan covered handicraft markets where you can buy by weight.
Fabindia, *Sea Shell Arcade, opposite Canara Bank, Candolim*. Branch of this great shop selling textiles, homewares and funky traditional Indian *kurtas* and clothes.
Rust, *409A Fort, Aguada Rd, Candolim, T0832-247 9340*. Everything from wrought-iron furniture to clothes.
Sangolda, *Chogm Rd, opposite Mac de Deus Chapel, Sangolda, T0832-240 9309, sangolda@ sancharnet.in. Mon-Sat 1000-1930*. Lifestyle gallery and café run by the owners of **Nilaya Hermitage** selling handcrafted metalware, glass, ethnic furniture, bed and table linen, lacquerware, wooden objects.
The Private Collection, *1255 Annavado, Candolim Beach Rd, T0832-248 9033*. Ramona Galardi has a good eye and has brought together a great collection of clothes and jewellery from designers based in Goa and also offers some of her own creations. There is also a healing and yoga space.

What to do

Calangute
Body and soul

Ayurvedic Natural Health Centre (**ANHC**), *Baga–Calangute road, Villa 2, Beira Mar Complex,*

www.healthandayurveda.com; also in Saligao.
The **ANHC** is not for the faint-hearted, offering authentic *panchakarma* cleanses; expect almost every cavity to be flushed.

Cyril Yoga, *Naikavaddo, www.cyrilyoga.com.* 4 classes daily – check website for details. All abilities. Inner healing yoga meditation, juice bar, yoga camps and good karma-promoting volunteer activities.

Diving and snorkelling
Goa Aquatics, *Little Italy, Guarravaddo, T(0)98226 85025.* Goa isn't really on the diving map, chiefly because it has only 2 dive sites, both of which have what's known as variable, ie less than great, visibility. However, this outfit offers inexpensive PADI courses. Options range from the half-day Discover Scuba programme (from aged 10 years, Rs 2700) to the 4-day Open Water Diver programme, Rs 14,500. Snorkelling tours also available.

River cruises
Floating Palace, *book through Kennedy's Adventure Tours and Travels, T0832-227 6493, T(0)9823-227 4076, opposite Milky Way in Cobravaddo.* Try a Kerala-style backwater cruise by staying overnight in this 4-cabin bamboo, straw and coir houseboat. You sail from Mandovi in late afternoon, are fed a high tea then a continental dinner as you drift past the Chorao Island bird sanctuary. Much pricier than a similar boat trip in Kerala.

Tour operators
Day Tripper, *Gauravaddo, T0832-227 6726, www.daytrippergoa.com.* Offers tours all over Goa, best deals in the region. Also runs trips to spice plantations, or short tours out of state, for birdwatching or empty beaches in Karnataka. Recommended.

Baga
Boat trips and wildlife
Mikes Marine, *Fortune Travels, Sauntavaddo, by the bus stand at the top end of Baga, T0832-227 6914.* Covered boat, dolphin trips, river cruises and birdwatching.

Rahul Alvares, *all over Goa, based in Parra, T(0)9881-961071, www.rahulalvares.com.* Fancy getting eye-to-eye with a cobra? For an alternative day out in Goa, maybe you want to handle or at least see a wild snake. For the less wild at heart or snakeaphobic, there are also amazing birdwatching trips and jungle camping expeditions. You will be in expert hands with Rahul. He organizes trips all over Goa.

Body and soul
Ayurclinic Goa, *Baga Creek, T(0)96374 73366, www.ayurvedagoa.com.* Under the watchful eye of fantastic Dr Rohit Borkar, you can get a whole host of treatments, massages and *panchakarma* processes here. Has another branch in Mandrem.

Candolim and Sinquerim beaches
Parasailing
Occasionally offered independently on Candolim Beach, Rs 600-850 for a 5-min flight.

Fort Aguada
Taj Sports Complex, **Fort Aguada Beach Resort**. Excellent facilities that are open to non-residents at the **Taj Vivanta**, and a separate access between Aguada Beach Resort and the Holiday Village. There are watersports, like parasailing and wind surfing, as well as yoga and badminton.

Transport

Baga
Bicycle/scooter hire The only place in Baga to hire bikes is 200 m down a small lane past the Hacienda, on the left. Rs 40 per day, a little extra to keep it overnight. Almost every guesthouse owner or hotelier can rustle up a scooter at short notice – expect to pay Rs 200-350 for 1 day, discounts for longer periods. Those recycled water bottles of lurid orange liquid displayed at the side of the road are not Tizer but petrol often mixed with kerosene and therefore not good for the engine. Better to find a proper petrol station, dotted around in Arpora, Vagator and Arambol.

Standing in the nape of one of Goa's east–west ridges lies Bardez's administrative headquarters: a buzzy, unruly market town filled with 1960s low-rise buildings set on former marshland on the banks of the Mapusa River; ('*Maha apsa*' means 'great swamps', a reference to Mapusa's watery past).

Mapusa town won't find its way onto many tourist postcards, but it's friendly, small and messy, is an important transport hub and has an excellent daily **municipal market**, worth journeying inland for, especially on its busiest day, Friday. Open from early morning Monday to Saturday, it peters out 1200-1500, then gathers steam again till night, and has giant rings of *chourica* sausage, tumbles of spices and rows of squatting fruit and vegetable hawkers.

Walk east for the small 16th-century **St Jerome's Church**, or 'Milagres', Our Lady of Miracles (1594), rebuilt first in 1674 then again in 1839 after a candle sparked a devastating fire. In 1961 the roof was badly damaged when the Portuguese blew up a nearby bridge in their struggle with the liberating Indian army. The church has a scrolled gable, balconied windows in the façade, a belfry at the rear and an interesting slatted wood ceiling. The main altar is to Our Lady, and on either side are St John and St Jerome: the *retables* (shelves behind the altar) were brought from Daugim. The church is sacred to Hindus as well as Catholics, not only because it stands near the site of the Shanteri Temple but also because 'Our Lady of Miracles' was one of seven Hindu sisters converted to Christianity. Her lotus pattern gold necklace (kept under lock and key) may also have been taken from a Hindu deity who preceded her.

The **Maruti Temple** ① *west of the market opposite taxi stand*, was built on the site of a firecracker shop where Rama followers in the 1840s would gather in clandestine worship of first a picture, then a silver image, of monkey god Hanuman after the Portuguese destroyed the local Hindu temples.

Moira

Barely 5 km east of Mapusa lies Moira, deep in the belly of a rich agricultural district that was once the scene of Portuguese mass baptisms. The town is ancient – some say it was the site of a sixth or seventh century AD Mauryan settlement – and until the arrival of the Portuguese it must have been a Brahmin village. A total of seven important temples were destroyed during the Inquisition and six idols moved to Mulgaon in Bicholim district (immediately east).

Today the village is dominated by the unusual **Church of Our Lady of the Immaculate Conception**. Originally built of mud and thatch in 1619, it was rebuilt during the 19th century with square towers close to the false dome. The balustrades at the top of the first and second floors run the length of the building and the central doorways of the ground and first floors have Islamic-looking trefoil arches that contrast with the Romanesque flanking arches. There is an interesting exterior pulpit. Inside, the image of the crucifixion is unusual in having its feet nailed apart instead of together. A Siva *lingam* recycled here as the base of the font after its temple was razed is now in the Archaeological Museum at Old Goa.

Moira's famous long red bananas (grown nearby) are not eaten raw but come cooked with sugar and coconuts as the cavity-speeding sweet *figada*.

Listings Mapusa and around

Where to stay

Mapusa

$$$$ Avanilaya
On the island of Corjuem, 9 km east of Mapusa, T0832-2484888, www.avanilaya.com.

Just 4 elegant rooms in this stunning secluded house overlooking the Mapusa River, but potentially by the time of reading there will be more rooms available in neighbouring properties. There's not much to do here except laze in bliss with Ayurvedic massages and facials, and enjoy amazing food and mesmerizing views.

$$$ Wildernest
www.wildernestgoa.com.
Amazing eco resort 1½ hrs from Mapusa. This eco-hotel sprung up as a protest – the land was to be sold to a big mining company but the Wildernest team stepped in and created a hotel and wildlife research centre. For guests there are birdwatching tours and waterfall treks. The luxe log cabins hug the valley with amazing views of the ghats and there is an infinity swimming pool hanging just above the horizon. Working closely with 6 local villages, they offer up delicious home-cooked food. This is an alternative view of Goa. Wholeheartedly recommended.

Restaurants

Mapusa

$ Café on the Corner
In the middle of the market.
A good pit-stop for refuelling during the market.

$ Navtara
On Calangute Rd.
Excellent range of Goan, South and North Indian fare; great *dosas* and yummy mushroom *xacuti* with *puris* for breakfast.

Festivals

Mapusa

Mon of the 3rd week after Easter Feast of Our Lady of Miracles The *Nossa Senhora de Milagres* image is venerated by Christians as well as Hindus who join together to celebrate the feast day of the Saibin. Holy oil is carried from the church to Shanteri temple and a huge fair and a market are held.

Shopping

Mapusa

Municipal Mapusa Bazar, *on the south edge of the fruit and veg market.* Fixed-price basic food supplies like rice, spice, lentils and cereals; useful if you're here long term.
Union Ayurveda, *1st floor, opposite the taxi and bus stand.* Great one-stop shop for all things Ayurvedic, herbal and homeopathic; a phenomenal range of products to keep you travelling healthy.

Transport

Mapusa

Bus To **Calangute** (every 20-30 mins), some continue on to **Aguada** and **Baga**, some go towards **Candolim**; check before boarding or change at Calangute. Non-stop minibuses to **Panjim**; buy tickets from booth at market entrance. Buses also go to **Vagator** and **Chapora** via **Anjuna** and towns near by. Buses to **Tivim** for Konkan Railway and trains to **Mumbai** (allow 25 mins).

Long-distance buses line up opposite the taxi stand and offer near-identical routes and rates. Expect to pay between Rs 450 and 800 for Panjim to **Mumbai** for example (15 hrs); similar for **Bangalore** and **Pune**; between Rs 350 and 600 for **Hampi** with private operators like **Paolo Travels** or **Neeta Volvo**; you can book through any travel agent.

Motorcycle hire Peter & Friends Classic Adventures, Casa Tres Amigos, Socol Vado 425, Parra, Assagao, 5 km east (off the Anjuna Rd), T0832-225 4467, www.classic-bike-india.com. To really get off the beaten track and see India in the raw, go on an enfield bike tour with **Peter & Friends**. Recommended for reliable bikes and tours of Southern India, Himachal and Nepal.

Many families rent out motorbikes and scooters – check the lights etc work before you commit.

Taxis Maximum capacity 4 people. Nearly every restaurant, guest house and family have their own taxi. **Auto-rickshaws** are cheaper. **Motorcycle taxi** (pilots) to **Anjuna** or **Calangute**, also available.

Train Thivim station, on the Konkan Railway, is convenient if you want to head straight to the **northern beaches** (Calangute, Baga, Anjuna and Vagator), avoiding Panjim and Margao. A local bus meets each train and usually runs as far as the Kadamba Bus Stand in Mapusa. From here you either continue on a local bus to the beach or share a tourist taxi (rates above). Enquiries and computerized tickets: T0832-229 8682.

To **Ernakulam** (for Kochi): *Mangalore Exp 12618*, 18 hrs. To **Mumbai** (**CST**): *Mandovi Exp 10104*, 10 hrs; *Konkan Kanya Exp 10112* (evening), 11 hrs. To **Thiruvananthapuram** (**Trivandrum**): *Netravati Exp 16345*, 19 hrs. It is possible to get a local train from Margao (47 km south of Mapusa) to **Canacona** (for **Palolem** and **Agonda**) and **Gokarna**.

When the freaks waded across the Baga River after the squares got hip to Calangute, Anjuna was where they washed up. The village still plays host to a large alternative community: some from that first generation of hippies, but the latest influx of spiritual Westerners has brought both an enterprising spirit and often young families, meaning there's fresh pasta, gnocci, marinated tofu or chocolate brownies to be had, cool threads to buy, great, creative childcare, amazing tattoo artists, alternative therapists and world-class yoga teachers.

For the beautiful life lived cheap Anjuna is still hard to beat; the countryside here is hilly and lush and jungly, the beaches good for swimming and seldom crowded. When you head south along the shore the beach shack soundtracks get progressively more hardcore, until **Curlies**, where you'll still find arm-pumping techno and trance.

The **Flea Market** ① *Dandovaddo, south Anjuna, Oct-Apr Wed 0800 till sunset, water taxis (from Baga) or shared taxis from anywhere in Goa*, is a brilliant hullabaloo with over 2000 stalls hawking everything from Gujarati wooden printing blocks to Bhutanese silver and even Burberry-check pashminas. The trade is so lucrative by the subcontinent's standards that for six months a year

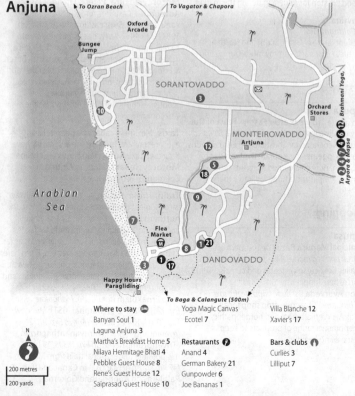

Anjuna

To Ozran Beach
To Vagator & Chapora

Oxford Arcade

Bungee Jump

SORANTOVADDO

Arabian Sea

MONTEIROVADDO
Artjuna

Orchard Stores

To Brahmani Yoga,

To Anjuna & Mapsa

Flea Market

DANDOVADDO

Happy Hours Paragliding

To Baga & Calangute (500m)

N

200 metres
200 yards

Where to stay
Banyan Soul **1**
Laguna Anjuna **3**
Martha's Breakfast Home **5**
Nilaya Hermitage Bhati **4**
Pebbles Guest House **8**
Rene's Guest House **12**
Saiprasad Guest House **10**

Yoga Magic Canvas
Ecotel **7**

Restaurants
Anand **4**
German Bakery **21**
Gunpowder **6**
Joe Bananas **1**

Villa Blanche **12**
Xavier's **17**

Bars & clubs
Curlies **3**
Lilliput **7**

The trance dance experience

The 'freaks' (beatniks with super-nomadic genes, giant drug habits and names like Eight Finger Eddie) first shipped into Goa shortly after the Portuguese left. Some brought guitars on which, after soaking up a bit of Hindu spirituality on the way, they were charged with playing devotional songs at beach campfire parties.

By the end of the 1960s, thousands of freaks were swarming into Goa, often spilling down from Kathmandu, and word got back to proper paid-up acid rock musicians about the scene. Some more substantial entertainment was called for.

The first music to run through the speakers was rock and reggae. Led Zeppelin, The Who and George Harrison rocked up and played live, but the freaks' entertainment was mostly recorded: Santana, Rolling Stones and Bob Marley. Kraftwerk and synth had filtered in by the late 1970s but the shift to electronica only really came in the early 1980s when musicians got bored of the lyrics and blanked out all the words on albums of industrial noise, rock and disco, using the fully lo-fi production method of taping between two cassette decks. Depeche Mode and New Order albums were stripped down for their drum and synth layers. Some of the rock faithful were angry with the change in the soundtrack to their lives; at those early 1980s parties, when the psychedelic-meets-machine-drum sound that still defines Goa trance was first being pumped out, legend has it that the decks had to be flanked by bouncers.

The music, developing in tandem to German nosebleed techno and UK acid house, locked into a worldwide tapestry of druggy drumscapes, but the Goan climate created its own sound. As records would warp in India's high temperatures, music had to be put down on DATS rather than vinyl which in turn meant tracks were played out in full, unmixed. A track had to be interesting enough then, self-contained, so it could be played uninterrupted in full; producers had to pay more attention to intros, middles and outros – in short, the music had to have a story. It also meant there was less art to a set by a trance DJ in Goa than DJs in Manchester, Detroit and Paris, who could splice records together to make their own new hybrid sounds.

Many of the original makers of this music had absorbed a fair whack of psychedelia and had added the inevitable layer of sadhu thinking to this – superficially measured in incense, *oms*, dreads and the swirling dayglo mandalas that unmistakeably mark out a Goa trance party. The music reflected this: sitars noodled alongside sequencer music to make the Goan signature sound.

By the 1990s, though, Ecstasy had arrived in Goa. The whole party scene opened right up, peopled by Spiral Tribe crusties as well as middle-class gap year lovelies and global party scenesters who came looking for an alternative to the more mainstream fare in Ibiza. Paul Oakenfold's Perfecto was a key label in fuelling the sound's popularity but there were more: Dragonfly, The Infinity Project, Return to the Source. Today trance is still a thriving part of the Goa circuit and, although much of it is from European or Japanese studios, there's also the odd home-grown label.

several thousand Rajasthani, Gujaratis, Karnatakans and Tibetans decamp from their home states to tout their wares. The flea had very different origins, and was once an intra-community car boot-style bric-a-brac sale for the freaks. Anjuna's links with trade pre-date the hippies though; the port was an important Arab trading post in the 10th and 12th centuries.

★ **Saturday Night Bazar** ① *Arpora Hill, 1630-2400*, is a more sanitized and less headlong version of the flea. There's no shortage of dazzling stall fronts draped with glittering saris and the beautiful Rajasthani fare, but while there are fewer stalls there's more variety here; expats who've crafted everything from organic yoga clothes and designer mosquito nets to handmade leather goods are more likely to pitch up here than at the Wednesday event. But there's no need to shop at all – the live music and huge range of food stalls make the Night Bazar the weekly social event for tourist and long-stayer alike. You'll find most of North Goa out for the evening, and many businesses shut up shop for the night as a result of the bazar's magnetic appeal. Bring cash and an appetite.

There is another contender on the market scene, with a new Saturday night market setting up in Vagator.

The Anjuna area is also home to two of Goa's best contemporary yoga schools. **Brahmani** ① *www.brahmaniyoga.com*, housed in in the grounds of **Tito's White House**, runs workshops and drop-in classes, from excellent *ashtanga*, Mysore-style, to more free-flowing movement like dance yoga, and *Scaravelli*. Packages with unlimited yoga are offered, but accommodation is not on site or specifically for yoga students. Ten minutes away in the neighbouring village of **Assagao**, the **Purple Valley Yoga Retreat** ① *T0832-226 8364, www.yogagoa.com*, offer retreat packages including yoga and meals (see box, page 1202) and run two-week *Ashtanga* retreats with leading teachers like Sharath Rangaswamy, grandson of Sri K Pattabhi Jois, David Swenson and Nancy Gilgoff, two of the first to introduce *Ashtanga* to the West in the 1970s. Lessons are held in a lovely *shala* in delightful gardens, food is vegetarian and the atmosphere collegiate.

Vagator

Vagator's beaches are possibly Goa's most dramatic: here, muddied sand bays upset by slabs of gray rock, quite different from the bubblings of porous laterite in Anjuna, fall at the bottom of terraced red cliffs planted with coconut trees that lean out towards the crashing waves, some of their trunks painted bright neon from past parties.

Big Vagator Beach is a long sweep of beach to the right of the main access road, behind which stands the profile of the wide outer rim of the ruined **Chapora Fort** against a stunning backdrop of India's western coastline, stretching beyond Goa's northern borders and into Maharashtra. The factory you can just pick out in the distance marks the border.

To your left, running inland, is **Little Vagator Beach**, its terracing lorded over by **Nine Bar**, a giant venue with an unswerving musical loyalty to trance (see box, page 1189). Just out of sight is **Ozran Beach**, christened 'Spaghetti Beach' by English settlers for its Italian community. Though a bit scrappy and dogged by persistent sarong sellers, Spaghetti is more sheltered, more scenic and more remote than the other beaches, ending in tumbled rocks and jungle, with excellent swimming spots. To get straight to Spaghetti from Vagator follow the signposts to Leoney Resorts, then when you reach the headland turn off the tarmac road onto one of the gravel tracks following the sign for Shiva Place shack. There is a new vibey club pulling crowds Chronicle at Vagator.

Chapora Fort

Looming over the north end of Big Vagator Beach, there's little left of Chapora Fort but crumbling blocks of black rock overgrown with tawny grasses and a general air of tranquil ruination. Built by Adil Shah (hence the name, Shah pura), the remaining ramparts lead out to a jutting promontory that affords stunning sunset views across the mouth of the Chapora River, where fishing boats edge slowly out of harbour and seabird flocks settle on the sand spits across from Morjim.

Chapora village itself may be too feral for some tastes. At dusk the smoke from domestic fires spreads a haze through the jungle canopy between which Portuguese houses stand worn and derelict. Down by the river's edge men lean to mend their fuzzy nets while village boys saunter out to bat on threshed fields, and Enfields and Hondas hum along the potholed roads bearing long-stayers and Goan village folk home – many of them toting fresh catch from the buzzing fish market (ignore the stern 'No Entry' signs and ride on in) held every sunset at the harbour. Along the village's main street the shady bars are decked with fairy lights and the internationals (who call Chapora both 'home' and, in an affectionate nod to its less savoury side, 'the Bronx') settle down to nurse their drinks.

The flat arc of the estuary here is perfect for cycling: the rim-side road will take you all the way out to the bridge at **Siolim** where you can loop back to take a look at the **Church of St Anthony**. Built in 1606, it replaced an earlier Franciscan church dating from 1568. Both Goa's Hindu and Catholic communities pray to St Anthony, Portugal's patron saint, in the hope of good fishing catches. The high, flat-ceilinged church has a narrow balustraded gallery and Belgian glass chandeliers, with statues of Jesus and St Anthony in the gabled west end.

Splendid Portuguese houses stand scattered about the village's shadows in varying degrees of disrepair; it's worth walking around to take in some of the façades. You can even stay in one which has been refurbished, the lovely Siolim House, see page 1192. The ferry that once crossed the Chapora River at the northern end of the village no longer runs (there's a bridge instead) but it's worth heading up this way for the little daily fish market and the handful of food stalls selling fresh grilled catch.

Listings Anjuna and around *map p1188*

Where to stay

At the budget end, the best options in Anjuna, Vagator and Chapora tend to be unofficial, privately owned residences.

Anjuna

$$$$ Nilaya Hermitage Bhati
T0832-227 6793, www.nilayahermitage.com.
A luxury retreat in topaz on a hilltop in Arpora overlooking Anjuna. Elite accommodation in 10 unique bungalows and 4 tents in lush gardens set around a beautiful plunge pool. Tennis, badminton, gym, yoga, jogging trail, DVD library and excellent restaurant, highly prized music room, but some have found fault with the warmth of service and food.

$$$ Laguna Anjuna
Sorantovaddo, T(0)9822-227 4131, www.lagunaanjuna.com.
Atmospheric cottages spiralling off behind stunning swimming pool and lush gardens, some with amazing domed ceilings and divan daybeds. Beautiful bathrooms and comfy beds. It's good for a romantic getaway. This is a vibey place serving up great food from the popular restaurant by the frangipani-fringed pool. You can come and use the lovely pool for Rs 150.

$$ The Banyan Soul
Behind German Bakery, off Flea Market Rd, T(0)9820-707283, sumityardi@thebanyansoul.com.
Chic complex of rooms nestled under giant banyan tree. Funky modern rooms with beautiful artistic lighting and all mod cons, sexy showers, TVs and compact verandas. The only drawback is the rooms take up the whole site; there are smart gardens bordering the hotel, but it is a bit boxed in.

$$ Yogamagic Canvas Ecotel
2 km from Anjuna beach, T0832-652 3796, www.yogamagic.net.
With Maharani suites and Rajasthani hunting tents with added bamboo roofs, this is a luxurious campsite surrounded by fields of paddy and palms. Beautifully landscaped, there is a naturally filtered pool, immaculate gardens of bougainvillea, lilies and lotus flowers, yoga and holistic therapies, and everything has been built with a nod towards the environment. The yoga temple is very beautiful.

$$-$ Martha's Breakfast Home
House No 907, Monteiro Vaddo Anjuna, T0832-227 3365, mpd8650@hotmail.com.
Set in the gardens of a house that give onto an orchard. 8 spic-and-span rooms, twin beds, small shower and nice little balconies. Better though are the 2 villas with 2 doubles, little lounges and kitchenettes. Ask for the Sunset Villa, which has incredible views. Basic but perfect.

$ Pebbles
Piqueno Peddem, Flea Market Rd, T(0)880-685 9993, www.anjunapebbles.com.
Well located for market and beach; you could almost get away without getting your own transport which is a rarity for Anjuna. Rooms are basic but great value, and there's a friendly owner. You might want to hide on Wed when the road will be busy outside.

$ Rene's Guest House
Monterio Waddo, opposite Artjuna, T0832-227 3405, renesguesthousegoa@yahoo.co.in.
A gem: 14 rooms around a colourful garden run by a friendly family. Best are the 3 self-contained cottages, with 4-poster beds, good kitchens with gas stove, sinks and big fridges; these are meant for long lets (2 are designed for couples, the other sleeps 3). Individual rooms are decent too.

$ Saiprasad
North beach, T(0)98221 53440, saiprasadguesthouse@gmail.com.
Uninspiring rooms, some with a/c, but in a great location right on the beach, which is unusual for Anjuna. Pretty little gardens and a beachside restaurant.

Vagator

$$$ Living Room
T(0)830-881 1649, www.livingroomhotel.in.
Shiny modern hotel in stark contrast to the rest of the Vagator abodes. Definitely a sign of the changing face of Goa, chic rooms with

all mod cons, nice courtyard pool, Arabian-themed restaurant.

$$$ Ozran Heights Beach Resort
Ozran Beach, T0832-227 4985,
www.ozranheights.com.
"We promise the best view in Goa", proclaims their website and for once they might just be right. This cliffside hangout is a bit pricey, but what a view. The high-end cabins are nicely decorated, and there is also a small pool and on-site restaurant, as well as being neighbours to the immensely popular Greek restaurant, **Thalassa**.

$$ Leoney Resort
10-min walk from beach, T0832-227 3634,
www.leoney resort.com.
13 rooms, 3 cottages, a/c extra Rs 400. Clean, modern, family-run, low-key, quiet, pool.

$ Paradise Huts
Small Vagator, Ozran, T(0)9922-230041.
Good selection of huts on the cliff, some with views, shared bathroom.

$ Santonio, Ozran Beach Rd
Near Holy Cross Chapel, T09769-913217,
www.santonio.in.
Cluster of little garden sheds, sweet though with nice bathrooms.

$ Thalassa Huts
T(0)9850-033537, www.thalassagoa.com.
Tucked behind popular atmospheric Greek restaurant, great huts with attached bathrooms and a couple have their own rooftop chill-out area. It's a short walk down the cliff to the beach. Although staying here might seriously affect your waistline. And there are 2 nice boutiques on site too – be warned.

Chapora Fort and Siolim
Chapora Fort and Siolim cater mainly for long-term budget travellers.

$$$$-$$$ Casa Colvale
Inland on the Chapora river, T0832-241 6737,
www.casacolvale.com.
Beautiful chic rooms and stunning river views make this an exceptional find. It's perfect for getting away from it without actually having to go too far; that's the gift of inland Goa. A lovely pool is on the river and there's another high level infinity pool. There's also lots of fresh seafood and plenty of other dishes on offer.

$$$$-$$$ Riverside Shakti
Guddem Village on the Chapora river,
www.riversideshaktiretreat.com.
Beautiful villa with inspired design, a spiral staircase takes you up to several bedrooms and a rooftop pyramid fit for yoga or chilling. Great river views. This is a perfect space for families or small retreat groups as it sleeps up to 10.

$$$$-$$$ Siolim House
Opposite Vaddy Chapel, Siolim, T0832-227 2138,
www.siolimhouse.com.
Lovingly restored 300-year-old house. This is a stunning property once owned by the governor of Macau. 4-poster beds, epic bathrooms and fantastic large windows. Restored in 1999, it recently had a further facelift in 2009 and the pool is one of the most beautiful places you could find yourself. Great food, and a chilled atmosphere. There is a sister property with just 3 rooms away in another beautifully crafted house – **Little Siolim**. Highly recommended.

Restaurants

Anjuna and around

$$$ Xavier's
Praias de San Miguel (follow signs from behind small chapel near Flea Market site, bring a torch at night), T0832-227 3402.
One of the very first restaurants for foreigners has grown into a smart restaurant, serving excellent fresh seafood, tucked away under palm trees.

$$$-$$ Villa Blanche
Badem Church Rd (better known as International Animal Rescue Rd),
Assagao, T(0)9822-155099.
10 mins' drive from downtown Anjuna, you will find this beautiful daytime retreat. Some of the firm favourites are German meatballs with potato salad, smoked salmon bagels with capers and home-made ice creams. They serve up an infamous Sunday brunch.

$$ Anand
Siolim Rd, Anjuna.
Roadside shack which looks like any other, except for the queue of people waiting for a table. This place has a devoted following from here to Mumbai and serves up the freshest seafood with every type of masala and all the Goan favourites.

$$ Gunpowder
Mapusa road, Assagao, T0832-226 8091,
www.gunpowder.in.
Inland from Anjuna you will find the delicious
Gunpowder restaurant, which offers more
unusual South Indian food and dishes from
Andhra Pradesh. The Delhi institution, **People
Tree**, is on site selling fairtrade clothes and
recycled products.

$$ Joe Bananas
Through the Flea Market behind Curlies.
A family-run place serving amazing fish *thalis* –
the fish is seasoned to perfection or there is a
great array of *bhaji*.

$$-$ German Bakery
*South Anjuna, towards the Flea Market
and Curlies.*
A little fiefdom of bohemian perfection: A huge
garden with a tree canopy above low-slung
booths. Huge salads with every healthy thing
under the sun plus good veggie burgers,
Indian food and extreme juices. This, ladies and
gentlemen, is the original German Bakery, don't
be put off by the copy cats that have taken over
every baking tray around India.

Vagator

$$$ Sakana
*Past petrol pump on Chapora Rd,
T(0)9890-135502.*
Fantastic Japanese food, Sakana is packed out
with the Westerners that call Goa home. They
serve delicious tuna *teriyaki*, beef *yakinuki*, sushi
and wakame salads. Remember to book a table
in advance.

$$$ Thalassa
*On the clifftop overlooking Ozran Beach,
T(0)9850-033537.*
Beautiful restaurant perched on the cliff, amazing
sunset views and great Greek food from *dolmades*
and *souvlaki* and many varieties of lamb dishes
and feta for the vegetarians. Booking essential.
Great boutique on site too.

$$$-$$ Sri
Close to Thalassa, T09822-383795.
Having migrated from Anjuna's Shore Bar to
Vagator, Richard has opened up Sri serving up his
trademark salad platters and delicious Indian and
seafood. There is often live music. Incidentally,
the Shore Bar is a real disappointment.

$$ Bean Me Up
*Near the petrol pump, Vagator, T(0)77690 95356
Closes at 1900 and all day Sat.*
You can choose from salad plates and delicious
tempeh and tofu platters. There's massage
offered on site, a useful noticeboard for mind-
body-spirit stuff, kids' area and a few simple,
clean rooms for rent.

Chapora Fort

$$ La Befa
Chapora Market road.
Some people drive an hour for the roast
beef sandwich here. Or there's Parma ham
or marinated aubergine, all on freshly baked
French bread.

$ Jai Ganesh Juice Bar
The hub of Chapora.
This is the only place to be seen in Chapora for
every juice under the sun.

Bars and clubs

Vagator now boasts the beautiful Chronicle.
For up-to-date event and venue information
check out www.whatsupgoa.com.

Anjuna

Curlies
At the very far south of Anjuna.
A kind of unofficial headquarters of the
scene, playing techno and ambient music,
although **Shiva Valley** next door has taken
over in recent years.

Lilliput
*A few hundred metres north of Curlies,
www.cafelilliput.com.*
Lots of live music and fire-dancing performances
at this beach shack, usually after the flea market
on Wed and sometimes on Fri. Also has an a/c
internet booth.

Vagator

Chronicle
Little Vagator.
With an expansive dancefloor, epic views, cool
cocktails and good DJ line-up, Chronicle is the
new kid on the party scene. Recommended.

Hilltop
Little Vagator Hill, above Vagator.
Although it has suffered from the 2200 curfew, Hilltop just celebrated its 30th birthday fully dressed up for the occasion in fluoro! It has been inventive with day parties Sun 1600-2200. They often host concerts too; in 2013, Talvin Singh played here and Prem Joshua plays each season.

Nine Bar
Ozran Beach.
A booming mud-packed bar with huge gargoyle adornments and a manic neon man carved out of the fountain. Majestic sunset views.

Shopping

Anjuna
Artjuna, *House No 972, Monteiro Vaddo, T0832-321 8468, www.artjuna.com.* Beautiful collection of jewellery, clothes and home decor. Stunning collection of gold jewellery from the owner Moshe, but also cheaper tribal trinkets from Nagaland. They host art shows too. Stays open through the monsoon season. Recommended.
Flea Market, *Wed.* Attracts hordes of tourists from all over Goa. By mid-morning all approach roads are blocked with taxis, so arrive early.
Orchard Stores, *Monteirovaddo.* An amazing selection catering for Western cravings. Olive oil, pasta, fresh cheese, etc, as well as a good range of organic products from all over India and fresh produce from Ambrosia farms in Goa. Locally made soaps and organic supplements too.

What to do

Anjuna
Body and soul
Some excellent yoga teachers teach in Goa during the season, many of whom gravitate towards Anjuna: check the noticeboards at the **German Bakery**, **Thalassa** and **Bean Me Up** (seRestaurants, above). You'll also stumble on practitioners of all sorts of alternative therapies: reiki healers, acupuncturists, chakra and even vortex cleansing.

Goa shopping tips
Do your homework before you buy: prices in tourist shops and Anjuna market are massively inflated, and goods are often worth less than a third of the asking price. 92.5 silver should be sold by weight; check the current value online, but be ready to pay a little more for elaborate workmanship. The bigger Kashmiri shops, particularly, are notorious both for refusing to sell by weight and for their commission tactic whereby rickshaw and taxi drivers get Rs 100 per tourist delivered to shops plus 10% commission on anything sold.

Brahmani Yoga, *at Tito's White House, night market road, Anjuna, www.brahmaniyoga.com.* Drop-in centre for all things yogic – flex your limbs Mysore style, or try *vinyasa* flow, hatha, *pranayama*. There are also 1-day workshops and regular *bhajans*. They also promote beach cleaning Karma Yoga. Deservedly popular.
Healing Here And Now, *The Health Center, St Michael's Vaddo, T0832-227 3487, www.healing hereandnow.com.* If you want an 'ultimate cleanse', sign up for a 5-day detox: fasting, detoxifying drinks and twice-daily enemas. Also offers parasite cleansing, kidney cleanse and wheat grass therapy.
Purple Valley Yoga Retreat (see pages 1190 and 1202). 2-week retreats with celebrities of the *ashtanga vinyasa* yoga circuit. Beautiful backdrop for downward dog poses.
Watsu, *Assagao–Mapusa road, T(0)9326-127020, www.watsugoa.com.* Utterly amazing treatment. Working one-on-one, you are in a heated pool and the practitioner takes you through a range of movements both above and below the water. An underwater massage which takes relaxation to a whole new level. Highly recommended.

Paragliding
Ask at Happy Hours Café, *south Anjuna Beach. Open 1230-1400.* Or visit the hilltop between Anjuna/Baga.

★ Arambol, Keri, Morjim, Asvem and Mandrem   Colour map 5a, A1.

expansive beaches and lingering sunsets

The long bridge that spans the Chapora River joins Bardez to the last – and thus most heavily Hindu – of the new conquests, hilly Pernem *taluka*. This is the gateway to a series of pretty, quieter beaches that hug the coastal road in a nearly unbroken strip up to the Maharashtra border, where a tiny pocket of Catholicism squats in the shadow of the pretty pride of the district, Tiracol Church and Fort.

Haphazard and hippy Arambol has a warm community feel and is rightly popular with open-minded travellers of all ages, who are drawn to its vibey scene, its live music, the dolphins that fin along its beaches and its famous saltwater lake. ★ Sunset takes on the magnitude of a festival in Arambol: people gather to sing, dance, juggle, do *capoeira* or find a silent spot for meditation and contemplation. A great walk at sunset is along the beach from Arambol to Morjim.

To the south, Mandrem and Asvem are more chic and less busy, and will suit those less prepared to compromise on their accommodation. With construction of a new airport near Pernem and a large road bridge over the Tiracol to Maharashtra finally open, Northern Goa is becoming more accessible, and there will be increased development no doubt.

The Bhonsles of Sawantwadi in modern Maharashtra were the last to rule Pernem before being ousted by the Portuguese in 1788, and Maratha influences here remain strong.

Arambol (Harmal)

Arambol, which you reach when the plateau road noses down through paddy fields and cashew trees, is a beautiful long stretch of sand at the bottom of a bumpy dirt track that's fringed with stalls selling brightly coloured, heavily embroidered clothes and pretty *lungis*. This is the creative and holistic hub of Goa; many Western designers, artists, performers, yogis and healers have been inspired to make the area home, and because people have put down roots here, the village is abuzz with industriousness. Flyers advertise *satsang* with smiling Western gurus: drumming circles, yoga teacher training, reiki and belly dancing. Arrive at the right time of year and you might catch the International Juggling Convention in full swing, or stumble across a phenomenal fire-dancing show by performers who work their magic on the stages of Vegas. Arambol is also synonymous with live music, with everything from Indian classical to open mic, Sufi musicians and psychedelic metal bands playing in rotation at the beach bars. Inevitably, though, Arambol's ever-growing popularity means both long and short-term accommodation gets more expensive by the year.

You have to skirt the beach's northern cliff and tiny basalt rocky bays by foot to reach the real lure: a second bay cut off from the roads and a natural 'sweet water' lake that collects at the base of a jungle spring. The lagoon collects just metres from the high tide line where the lush forest crawls down to the water's edge. You can walk up the spring's path to reach a belt of natural mineral clay: an idyllic spot for self-service mud baths. Further into the jungle is the famous banyan tree, its branches straddling 50 m, which has long been a point of Hindu and hippy pilgrimage. Or clamber over the boulders at the north to join the scrappy dirt track over the headland for the half-hour walk it takes to reach the achingly lovely and reliably empty Keri Beach.

> ## Essential Arambol, Keri, Morjim, Asvem and Mandrem
>
> ### Finding your feet
>
> All of Pernem *taluka* is within easy reach of the hotels in Panjim or Calangute, but you'd be doing yourself a disservice to visit what are arguably North Goa's loveliest beaches just on a day trip. Better to set up camp in one and make it your base to explore the rest. If you are crossing the bridge at Siolim on a motorbike turn left off the new main road immediately after the bridge to use the smaller, more scenic coastal roads. There also regular buses to the villages from Mapusa and from Chopdem. Each beach is about 10 minutes apart.

Keri (Querim) and Tiracol Fort

Goa's northernmost beach is uniquely untouched. The drive towards Keri (Querim) along the banks of the Tiracol River from Pernem passes through some stunning rural areas untouched by any tourist development.

Walk across deep dunes to a casuarina thicket and out onto empty sand that stretches all the way from the mouth of the Tiracol river to the highland that splits it from Arambol. **Querim** gets busy on weekends with Indian tourists and occasionally hosts parties, but remains a lovely spot of sand. You can reach the beach from the north on foot from the Tiracol ferry terminal, or from the south by walking round the headland from Arambol. The Tiracol ferry runs every 30 minutes 0600-2130 taking 15 minutes, depending on the tides. The ferry is still charming, but more redundant now the bridge is open.

Tiracol (Terekhol), at the northernmost tip of Goa, is a tiny enclave of just 350 Catholics on the Maharashtra border just 3.5 km across where *feni* production is the biggest business. Its name probably comes from *tir-khol* ('steep river bank') and it's a jungly little patch of land full of cashew trees, banyans, orange blossoms, black-faced monkeys and squirrels.

The small but strategic **fort** ① *0900-1800, cross Tiracol river by ferry (every 30 mins 0600-2130) and walk the remaining 2 km; ferries take cars and motorbikes*, stands above the village on the north side of the Tiracol River estuary on a rugged promontory with amazing views across the water. Its high battlement walls are clearly visible from the Arambol headland. Built by the Maharaja Khem Sawant Bhonsle in the 17th century, it is protected from attacks from the sea, while the walls on the land side rise from a dry moat. It was captured in 1746 by the Portuguese Viceroy Dom Pedro Miguel de Almeida (Marques de Alorna), who renamed it Holy Trinity and had a chapel built inside (now St Anthony's). You can explore the fort's battlements and tiny circular turrets that scarcely seem fit

Arambol Beach

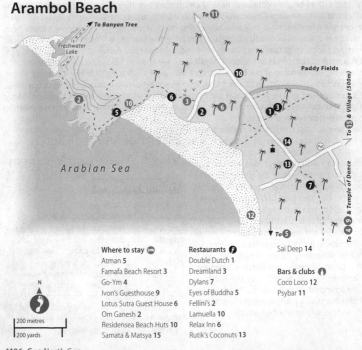

Where to stay 🛏
Atman **5**
Famafa Beach Resort **3**
Go-Ym **4**
Ivon's Guesthouse **9**
Lotus Sutra Guest House **6**
Om Ganesh **2**
Residensea Beach Huts **10**
Samata & Matsya **15**

Restaurants 🍴
Double Dutch **1**
Dreamland **3**
Dylans **7**
Eyes of Buddha **5**
Fellini's **2**
Lamuella **10**
Relax Inn **6**
Rutik's Coconuts **13**

Sai Deep **14**

Bars & clubs 🍸
Coco Loco **12**
Psybar **11**

for slaying the enemy. The views south are magnificent. Steps lead down to a terrace on the south side while the north has an open plateau.

St Anthony's Church① *open on Wed and Sun for Mass at 1730*, inside the tiny fort, was built in the early 1750s soon after the Portuguese takeover. It has a classic Goan façade and is just large enough to cater for the small village. In the small courtyard, paved with laterite blocks, stands a modern statue of Christ. The **Festival of St Anthony** is held here at the beginning of May (usually on the second Tuesday) instead of on the conventional festival day of 13 June.

Morjim (Morji) to Asvem

Morjim, which stands on the opposite side of the estuary from Chapora, has two wide sweeping beaches that both sit at the bottom of separate dead end streets. This inaccessibility means that, development-wise, it has got away relatively unscathed. The southern, protected, turtle beach appears at the end of the narrow track that winds along the north bank of the Chapora river mouth. Loungers, which are mostly empty, are strewn haphazardly north of the official-looking **Turtle Nesting Control Room**.

The wide shoreline with its gentle incline (the water is hip height for about 100 m) is washed by easy rolling breakers, making it one of North Goa's best swimming beaches. The northern beach, or **Little Morjim**, a left turn off the main coast road is, by comparison, an established tourist hamlet with guesthouses and beach huts.

The road from Morjim cuts inland over the low wooded hills running parallel to the coast. After a few kilometres the road drops down to the coast and runs along the edge of northeast tilting **Asvem Beach**. (Morjim faces Chapora to the south and west.) The northern end of this peaceful palm-fringed beach is divided by a small river. It's a great stretch of beach, which, alas, is gaining in popularity, with increasing development.

Mandrem

Mandrem creek forces the road to feed inland where it passes through a small commercial centre with a few shops and a bank. Mandrem village has the **Shri Bhumika Temple** housing an ancient image. In the **Shri Purchevo Ravalnatha Temple** there is a particularly striking medieval image of the half-eagle, half-human Garuda, who acts as the *vahana* (carrier) of Vishnu.

A little further on, a lane off to the left leads down towards the main beach and a secluded hamlet in a beautifully shaded setting. The **beach** is one of the least developed along this stretch of coast; for the moment it is managing to tread that fine line between having enough facilities for comfort and enough isolation to guarantee idyllic peace. Further north there is a lagoon fringed by palm trees and some simple rooms, virtually all with sea view.

Listings Arambol, Keri, Morjim, Asvem and Mandrem *map p1196*

Where to stay

Arambol

$$$-$$ Samata Holistic Retreat Centre
Temple Rd, 10 mins from downtown Arambol,
www.samatagoa.com.
Inspiring retreat centre in a beautiful inland location close to Arambol. Bringing hints of Bali and using reclaimed wood from Indonesia, this exceptional site has accommodation for 40 people with a beautiful pool surrounded by nature and an organic farm. They have 2 great restaurants , **Matsya Freestyle Kitchen** (see Restaurants, below) and **Tamarind**. Samata keeps on inspiring as its profits also go to the **Dunagiri**

Foundation, which works to preserve Himalayan herbs and Ayurvedic plants.

$$-$ Atman
Palm Grove Dando waddo, T(0)869-888 0135,
www.atmangoa.com.
A lovely collection of palm-fringed coco huts with good use of sari drapes and chic decor, all surrounding a pretty restaurant. There is also a yoga space and it's all just steps from the beach. Lots of pretty artwork.

$$-$ Lotus Sutra
Middle of Arambol Beach, T(0)99219 62554, www.lotussutragoa.com.
A gorgeous selection of beach huts, but also a few creature comforts with a/c rooms and hot showers on site. Beautifully done.

$$-$ Residensea Beach Huts
North end of Arambol Beach, close to Arambol Hammocks, T0832-224 2276, www.arambolresidensea.com.
Set in a pretty location with basic bamboo shacks set back from the beach, all huts have fans and secure locker facilities. There are some rooms with attached bathroom, but some huts have shared facilities. A German Shepherd keeps watch.

$ Famafa Beach Resort
Beach Rd, Khalchawada, T0832-224 2516, famafa_in@yahoo.com.
25 rooms in an unimaginative development on the right of the stall-studded road down to the beach. No a/c, but many pitch up for the hot showers.

$ Go-Ym Beach Resort
Dando Waddo, south end of Arambol beach, T(0)89751 54961, www.go-ym.com.
Great little cottages with swathes of coloured fabric and views of the coconut grove. Just moments from the beach, there is also an on-site restaurant.

$ Ivon's Guest House
Girkarwada, T(0)9822-127398.
Popular rooms looking out on to the coconut grove; from the top floor you can just about see the sea. Basic clean rooms with attached bathrooms.

$ Om Ganesh
Cliffside on way to Sweet Lake, T0832-224 2957.
Lots of rooms clustered on the cliffside, with great views and lots of places to hang a hammock. Rooms are basic, but with attached bathroom. Ask at **Om Ganesh** restaurant on cliff or in town at **Om Ganesh General Store**. They now have rooms on the high street above the general store too. Recommended.

Keri and Tiracol Fort
Keri is pretty out of the way and it helps to have your own transport. The beaches around here are dotted with typical budget beach shacks.

$$$$ Fort Tiracol Heritage Hotel
Tiracol, T0236-622 7631, www.heritage resortsingoa.com.
Just 7 exquisite rooms, all with a giant en suite, set in the fort walls that surround the Catholic Church which is still used by the 350 villagers of the wholly Christian Tiracol for their Mass. Goa's most romantic hotel with incredible sea views. Prices include breakfast and delicious dinners. Highly recommended.

$ Dream House
Keri, off main road on way to beach, T(0)9604-800553.
Large rooms with attached bathroom sandwiched between family house and **Coconut Inn** rooftop restaurant.

Morjim to Asvem
This is a beautiful stretch of coastline which is becoming more and more happening and increasingly built up, but there are some special places to stay dotted along the coast.

$$$$ Paros by Amarya
Morjim Beach, www.amaryagroup.com.
White Rajastani tents in a pretty beach setting. Inside these lovely tents, you'll find chic fittings and more Goan colours.

$$$$ Sur La Mer
Above Asvem Beach, T(0)9850-056742, www.surlamergoa.com.
Beautiful rooms with 4-poster beds and super-stylish bathrooms around lovely pool. All have good views of the neighbouring fields and the beach; with special mention going to the stunning penthouse with almost 360-degree views of paradise. The food is also highly praised.

$$$ Yab Yum Eco Resort
Asvem Beach, T0832-651 0392, www.yabyumresorts.com.
10 deluxe 'eco-domes' made of local materials: blue painted lava rocks make up the bases, spread across a huge shady expanse of coconut and banana grove tucked behind a lovely stretch of beach. It's classy, discreet and bohemian. There are also some cottages, a yoga *shala*, swimming pool and a children's teepee crammed with toys. The chic accommodation at their villa, **Artists' House**, is absolutely stunning.

$$$-$$ Leela Cottages
Asvem Beach, T(0)9823-400055,
www.leelacottage.com.
Close to the beach, these are posh wooden huts
with antique doors from a palace in Andhra
Pradesh and decorated with beautiful furniture.
Very stylish. Bear in mind there are a few dance
clubs nearby.

$$ Vayu
Asvem, on the inlet, T(0)9326-130115,
www.vayuadventures.in.
New beautiful construction on many levels with
lovely cottages, huts and tipis, most with sea
views. As well as free yoga, there is access to
many water sports and they host numerous art
exhibitions. Recommended.

$$-$ Palm Grove
Asvem towards Morjim, T(0)9657-063046,
www.palmgroveingoa.com.
Quirky place with cottages and huts named
'Happy Hippie' and 'Rosie Slow', there are comfy
beds and a sweet beach restaurant.

Mandrem

$$$$ Elsewhere's Beach House
T(0)9326-020701, www.aseascape.com.
Elsewhere is 4 lovingly restored 19th-century
houses, just a sigh from the beach. Some are
closer to the sea while others have views of the
saltwater creek. Facilities include maid service,
and a day and nightwatchman, but you pay extra
for a cook. The minimum rental period is 1 week,
at US$2000-4000. There are also the beautiful
Otter Creek Tents with 4-poster beds Rajasthani
style close to the creek.

$$$ Ashiyana
Mandrem River, opposite Villa River Cat by
footbridge, www.ashiyana-yoga-goa.com.
A beautiful place for yoga holidays and detox
retreats. Many rooms have river views and are
stacked with Rajasthani furniture and heaps
of character. It's a peaceful place on large
grounds with several yoga *shalas*, spa and
natural swimming pool. There are a couple of
lovely rooms with domed ceilings as well as the
stunning Lake View and Ashiyana Villas. The
good restaurant serves nourishing healthy food.

$$$ Beach Street
T(0)9423-882600, www.beachstreet.in.
Summer house of the Deshprabhu family built
in the early 1920s, this interesting beachfront
building has had many incarnations including a

prawn hatchery and nightclub. Now the family
have transformed it into a beautiful resort with
a courtyard swimming pool, restaurant and chic
beach cabanas.

$$$-$$ Mandala
Next to Ashiyana, access from Asvem–
Mandrem road, T(0)91582 66093,
www.themandalagoa.com.
The highlights at Mandala are the chic 2-storey
open-plan chalets – downstairs you will find
a swing seat, up the stairs a tented bedroom
with 2 loungers on the front deck. There are also
stylish rooms in the main house and smaller huts
and Maharajah tents. The large pretty gardens
often host live music and an open-air film festival.

$$-$ Villa River Cat
Junasvaddo, T0832-224 7928,
www.villarivercat.com.
13 rooms in a 3-tiered roundhouse overlooking
the river and a wade over deep sand dunes from
the beach. The whole place is ringed with a belt
of shared balconies and comes with big central
courtyards stuffed with swings, sofas, plantation
chairs and daybeds. There's a mosaic spiral staircase
and a cavalier approach to colour: it's downbeat
creative and popular with musicians and actors –
in the best possible way. Cat lovers preferred.

$ Oceanside
Junasvaddo, T(0)9421-40483.
Great little sunny coloured huts and pretty
cottages a short walk from the beach and
with an excellent restaurant on site.

$ O'Saiba
Junasvaddo, T0)8308 415655,
sunnymehara@yahoo.com.
O'Saiba offers a range of coco huts, bungalows
and nicely decorated rooms. It also has a good
restaurant by the beach.

Restaurants

Arambol
There are beach cafés all along the main beach
and around the headland to the north.

$$$ Matsya Freestyle Kitchen
Temple Rd, www.samatagoa.com.
This beautiful restaurant is inspired by the
organic garden of **Samata Retreat** (see Where to
stay, above), the fresh seafood of Goa and fused
with delights from Israeli chef Gome. The menu
changes daily. If you get a chance ask to visit their
organic farm. Highly recommended.

$$ Double Dutch
Beach Rd, T0832-652 5973, doubledutchgoa@ yahoo.co.uk. Open 0700-2300.

Lovely laid-back garden restaurant with lots of leafy foliage and sculptures. Breakfasts are tip top with home-made breads (such as carrot or watermelon seed) and jams – you can also get a full 'English', Goa style. Candlelit in the evening, try Dutch dishes, Indonesian, pastas and the steaks come with the best recommendation. There is a lively Sun morning second-hand market. Recommended.

$$ Fellini's
Beach Rd, T0832-229 2278, arambolfellini95@ yahoo.com. Thu-Tue 1000-2300, Wed 1800-2300.

Fellini's is an institution serving up pizzas and calzone to the hungry masses.

$$ Lamuella
Main Rd, T0832-651 4563.

Atmospheric restaurant in the heart of Arambol. Home-made mushroom or pak choi raviolis, great fish, tagines, salads and huge breakfast platters. This is a great spot to meet and greet. There's also a great shop specializing in clothes crafted by Westerners in Arambol, if you can't face the night market.Recommended.

$ Dreamland Crepes
Main road, near Double Dutch.

Blink-and-you-miss-it 2-tier coffee house serving up fabulous cappuccinos and healthy juices, as well as a wide range of crêpes and sandwiches. And Wi-Fi.

$ Dylans
Coconut grove near El Paso Guesthouse.

If you like your coffee strong, this Manali institution delivers, along with hot melty chocolate cookies. They host a popular open mic night.

$ Eyes Of Buddha
North end of Arambol Beach.

Long on Arambol's catering scene, this place has you well looked after with scrupulously clean avocado salads, a wide range of fish and Indian food, all topped off with a great view of the beach. Highly recommended.

$ Relax Inn
North end of beach.

The only beach shack with a good reputation, this is a firm favourite with the expats. Slow service but worth the wait for *spaghetti alle vongole*, grilled kingfish with ratatouille and a range of fresh pasta dishes. Exceptional, although you cannot book and in season it can be tough to get a table.

$ Sai Deep
Beach Rd.

A family-run *dhaba* offering amazing veg and fish plates at lunchtime, mountainous fruit plates and a good range of Indian and continental food. Great value.

Morjim to Asvem

Join the masses as they descend on La Plage every Sun. Restaurants in Morjim central cater mainly to Russians.

There are plenty of shacks catering to Asvem and Mandrem beaches. Some have free loungers, others charge up to Rs 100.

$$$ La Plage
Asvem, T(0)9822-121712.

Hidden slightly from the beach, you can still feel the breeze in this lovely laid-back restaurant. The food is excellent – you might discover seared rare tuna with *wasabi* mash, calamari risotto, great steaks or even a giant hamburger. Vegetarians well catered for too. Most people daydream about the chocolate *thali* or the *île flottante*. Delicious cocktails, including a fabulous peppery Bloody Mary with mustard seeds and curry leaf. Booking essential.

$$$ Sublime
Morjim Beach, T(0)9822-484051.

Exceptional food is guaranteed at this Goa institution. Chris Saleem Agha Bee offers up a chic spin on the beach shack offering punchy Asiatic beef, delicious rare tuna with anchovy sauce, the renowned mega organic salad and melt-in-the-mouth pesto mozzarella parcels. The cocktails go down very easily and it's a laid-back vibe – the perfect combination for balmy Goan nights. Booking essential. Also check out his new restaurant Elevar in Aswem.

$ Change Your Mind
Asvem Beach.

This typical beach shack serves up great Indian food, tasty fried calamari and monumental fruit plates. You can get refreshing lemon and mint juices and strawberry shakes in season.

$ Pink Orange
Asvem Beach.

Low-level seating overlooking the beach with chilled trance vibe. Menu serves up a great range of salads, tagines, sweet and savoury crêpes, juices, coffees and great chocolate brownies. Recommended.

Mandrem

$$$-$$ Café Nu
Junnaswaddo, Mandrem Beach, T(0)9850-658568.
Another helping from **Sublime** guru Chris
Saleem Agha Bee – great food in laid-back
locale. Mustard-encrusted fish, the non-yogi
burger (Mandrem does cater to a large yogi
clientele), the phenomenal mega organic salad
for the aforementioned yogis and the legendary
chocolate bon-bons. People have been known
to cry when there was a problem with the oven
and the bon-bons were temporarily unavailable.
Good food to linger over. Highly recommended.

$$-$ Sunset
Next to Beach St.
For classic Indian food and tandoori dishes, you
cannot do better than **Sunset**. Their fish and
chicken tikkas are fantastic. They also have the
usual selection of European and Chinese food,
but all done well.

$ Well Garden Pizzeria
Near O'Saiba, off main road.
Sweet garden restaurant with great range of
pizzas, broccoli and pesto pastas and an almost
infamous warm chickoo cake. Service can be a
bit hit or miss though.

Bars and clubs

The new place to be seen is Asvem where
there are several clubs. For up-to-date
event and venue information check out
www.whatsupgoa.com.

Arambol
Live music and performances are the highlight
of being in Arambol. **Ash**, **Surf Club**, **Coco
Loco** and **Psybar** offer up both live music
and DJ nights. **Dylan's** has a great open mic
night. Special mention goes to **Ash**, a stunning
performance space with beautiful artwork
hosting nights as diverse as mesmerizing
bellydancing performances, Siberian shamanic
singing or fantastic fire dancing. At dusk there's
normally drumming, dancing and high spirits
outside **Full Moon** on the beach to celebrate
the sun going down on another day. The sunset
session is becoming a tourist attraction in itself.

Morjim to Asvem
With pricey drinks and sometimes entry fees,
the venues in Morjim and Asvem are mostly
Russian affairs, but **Rock Water** has good
parties and **Marbella** is expensive but popular.

Mandrem
There are frequent concerts and an open-air
cinema festival at **Mandala** and live music and
DJs often at **Beach Street**. There are kirtans
(lively mantra chanting evenings) at **Ashiyana**.
See Where to stay, above, for location details for
these places.

Shopping

Arambol
Arambol Hammocks, *north end of Arambol
Beach, near Eyes of Buddha, www.arambol.com.* The
original and the best place for hammocks and their
famous flying chair designs; these are no ordinary
hammocks and are extremely comfortable. And
now they even have baby hammocks.
Lamuella. Serving up the best of the Western
designers who make Arambol their home, as well
as imported clothes and bikinis from Thailand
and Europe. Stunning jewellery for little magpies
too. Now a new shop in Mandrem too. Highly
recommended.
Vishwa Book Shop, *T(0)992-146 1107. Opens
around noon each day.* Excellent bookshop on
main road with good holiday reads and for all the
yogi types he has a great range of holistic titles
and bestsellers.

Morjim to Asvem
As well as having a great little boutique on site
with lovely clothes and jewellery from Simona
Bassi, **La Plage** has competition on its hands from
Souk, a collection of boutiques in Rajasthani
tents. There is also a cluster of chic beach shack
boutiques including one little black number from
Jade Jagger. But special mention goes to **Dust**
which sells beautifully designed clothes in raw
silk and hand block prints (www.fvmajil.com).

What to do

Arambol
Boat trips and dolphin watching
21 Coconuts Inn, *2nd restaurant on left after
stepping on to the beach.* Morning dolphin-
watching trips.

Body and soul
You can practise every form of yoga here, as
well as learn massage of all styles, have your
chakras balanced, receive Tibetan singing bowl
healing, participate in *satsang*, capoeira on the
beach at sunset, do firewalking and learn all
styles of dance. There is an amazing group of

Sun salutations

It's one of those funny ironies that yoga, now at the zenith of its international popularity, is given a resounding thumbs down by your average metropolitan Indian, who's much more likely to pull on lycra and go jogging or pump iron down the gym than pursue the perfect *trikonasana*. They look with curiosity at the swarms of foreign yogis yearning to pick up extreme postures from the various *guru-jis* scattered about the subcontinent.

There is business to be had in selling enlightenment it turns out. At one place you can pay US$2000 for your course – enlightenment guaranteed and a certificate to prove it. Naturally India has its fair share of spiritual wisdom and compassionate gurus, but there is also a percentage of dodgy dealers and predatory gurus. Be aware of the showmen. Some might baulk at seeking out a Western teacher in India, but often Western teachers have a better understanding of the needs of their students.

India remains one of the best places to study the ancient art, and many people who have embarked on yoga courses purely for its physical benefits also end up reaping some mental and emotional rewards. Yoga done with awareness can give you a taste of the bigger picture. Just keep asking around to find the right teacher.

The large alternative communities settled around Arambol and Anjuna make good starting points if you are looking for some ad hoc teaching, but if you are travelling to India specifically to practice it's worth doing your homework first. Here are some places that are recommended.

Going furthest north first, where there is more yoga than you can shake a yoga mat at. **Samata Holistic Retreat Centre** (www.samatagoa.com) is 10 minutes inland from Arambol proper on a beautiful swathe of land; see also Where to stay, page 1197. Travelling south to Mandrem, you will find **Ashiyana** (www.ashiyana-yoga-goa.com) which has had a recent revamp and offers yoga holidays, yoga drop-in classes, dance and meditation classes, and detox retreats. There is a spa with a range of massage and healing options, and beautiful natural swimming pool. See also Where to stay, page 1199. Inland Mandrem has stunning views and **Himalaya Yoga Valley** on the

internationally trained therapists here, along with lots of practitioners with zero qualifications, so ask around.

Balanced View, *in the rice fields behind Double Dutch, www.balancedview.com*. Arambol has become one of the hubs for Balanced View – guidance to living life in clarity and awareness. Has a great following.

Himalaya Iyengar Yoga Centre, *follow the many signs, T01892-221312, www.hiyogacentre.com*. Established Iyengar centre in town, 5-day courses and teacher training.

Temple of Dance, *off shortcut road towards Ivons, Girka Waddo*. Beautiful location offering dance classes from Bollywood to Gypsy, Balinese to tribal fusion belly dance, as well as fire dancing, hula hooping and *poi*.

Jewellery making and silversmithing

Several places on Arambol high street offer jewellery-making courses; one of the best is with Krishna at **Golden Hand Designs**, on the Kinara junction before Arambol main road.

Paragliding and kitesurfing

Paragliding is synonymous with the hill between Arambol and Keri – ask for Andy at **Arambol Hammocks** on the cliff near **Eyes of Buddha** for tandem flights and the paragliding lowdown. Check boards in **Double Dutch** or **Lamuella** for kitesurfing lessons.

Tour operators

SS Travels, *Main Rd Arambol, near Om Ganesh General Store*. Quality service on tours, tickets and money exchange. Also for **Western Union**. This is the place where all the local ex-pats go. Tried and trusted. There is another branch in Mandrem.

Morjim to Asvem
Body and soul

Raso Vai, *S No 162/2-A, Morjim–Asvem road (towards Mandrem from Morjim), Mardi Wada, Morjim, T(0)9850-973458, www.rasovai.com*. Runs training courses in their signature treatments (Ayuryogic massage and Ayurbalancing), fusion massages encompassing traditional Ayurvedic techniques and yoga stretches as well as offering

hill (www.yogagoaindia.com) with an exceptional yoga teacher training course with a talented team headed up by Lalit Kumar. There is beautiful villa accommodation and a tempting pool, although you have to wash off your yogic sweat before diving in! They run regular trainings throughout the season and then head to Europe and Thailand for the summer months. If you want to take your practice to the next level, this place is inspirational.

In Anjuna, you will find excellent drop-in classes, workshops and their own brand teacher trainings at **Brahmani** (www.brahmaniyoga.com). There is Mysore-style self-practice and excellent ashtanga, as well as a smattering of free-flowing movement yoga classes and and *Scaravelli*. Once a month they have kirtan, or chanting evenings. Close by is **Yogamagic Canvas Ecotel** (www.yogamagic.net) who host a whole range of yoga classes and holidays in their beautiful yoga temple and you can stay like a Maharani in a suite or Rajasthani hunting tents; this is a very special place. Some 10 minutes away in the neighbouring village of Assagao you find the renowned **Purple Valley Yoga Retreat** (www.yogagoa.com) who host the heavyweights of the yoga world like Sharath Rangaswamy, grandson of Sri K Pattabhi Jois, David Swenson and Nancy Gilgoff. Lessons are held in a lovely *shala* in delightful gardens, food is vegetarian and the atmosphere collegiate. Travel a little further into inland Goa to find **Satsanga Retreat** (www.satsangaretreat.com), a beautiful space with two inspiring *shalas*, a lovely pool and great accommodation. This is often where **Brahmani** host their longer trainings.

Skipping to South Goa, **Lotus Yoga Retreats** (www.lotus-yoga-retreat.com) focus on yoga holidays and retreats with guest teachers from Europe, including the fantastic Dynamic Yoga teacher Dina Cohen. They host their events at the beautiful Kaama Ketna.

Seek out different schools in the four corners of India in Pune (BKS Iyengar), Mysore (Pattabhi Jois), Neyyar Dam (Sivananda), Anandapur Sahib (Yogi Bhajan, Kundalini yoga) and Bihar (Paramahamsa Satyananda). There is also the International Yoga Festival in Rishikesh every year in February or March. And now Goa has its very own Yoga Festival. In early January, there is the India Yoga Festival in Aswem Beach.

Good books include: BKS Iyengar's *Light On Yoga*, *Asana*, *Pranayama*, *Mudra*, *Bandha* from the Bihar school and anything by Georg Feuerstein.

more traditional Ayurvedic treatments. Ayurvedic doctor on site. Highly recommended.

Tour operators
Speedy, *near post office, Mazalvaddo, T0832-227 3208. Open 0900-1830.* Very helpful for all your onward travel arrangements; also changes money. Very helpful, comprehensive service.

Watersports
Vayu Adventures, *Aswem, www.vayuadventures.in.* If it involves water and wetsuits, this is the place to come. Surfing, paddle boarding, kayaking and wakeboarding. Highly recommended.

Mandrem
Body and soul
Ashiyana, *see box, above.* Stunning yoga *shalas* in a Balinese-style complex. There is drop-in yoga, meditation and dance here as well as courses and retreats and a range of massage and healing options in their spa.
Himalaya Yoga Valley, *www.yogagoaindia.com.* Exceptional Yoga Teacher Training with talented team headed up by Lalit Kumar. They run regular

trainings throughout the season just outside of Mandrem and then head to Europe and Thailand for the summer months. If you want to take your practice to the next level, this place is inspirational. Highly recommended.

Transport

Arambol
Bus There are regular buses from **Mapusa** and a frequent service from **Chopdem**, 12 km along the main road (1 hr); the attractive coastal detour via **Morjim** being slightly longer. It's a 2-hr walk north through Morjim and Mandrem by the coast.

SS Travels and Tara, in the village, can book train tickets (Rs 100 service charge); and long-distance bus tickets.

Keri and Tiracol Fort
Bus Regular buses from **Mapusa** to Keri.

Mandrem
Bus Regular buses to Mapusa.

South Goa

The prosperous south is poster-paint green: lush coconut thickets that stretch along the coastline blend with broad swathes of iridescent paddy, broken by the piercingly bright white spears of splendid church steeples. Beneath the coastal coconut fronds sit the pretty villages of fishermen and agriculturalists: Salcete *taluka* is where the Portuguese were most deeply entrenched, and in the district's interior lie the beautiful remnants of centuries-old mansion estates built by the Goan colonial elite. Sprawling drawing rooms and ballrooms are stuffed with chandeliers and antiques and paved with splendid marble, every inch the fairytale doll's house.

Margao and coastal Salcete   *Colour map 5a, B2.*

stray inland for amazing mansions

A wide belt of golden sand runs the length Salcete's coast in one glorious long lazy sweep, hemmed on the landward side by a ribbon of low-key beach shacks; tucked inland lie Goa's most imposing and deluxe hotels.

The thrumming nightlife of North Goa is generally absent here, but some beaches, Cavelossim in particular, have been on the receiving end of a building boom kept afloat by Russian package tourists, while Colva has gone all out and built itself a line of Baywatch-style lifeguard shacks, buxom blonde lifesavers not included. Inland, in various states of decline, lie the stately mansions of Goa's landowning classes: worn-out cases of homes once fit for princes.

Essential Margao and coastal Salcete

Finding your feet

The Konkan Railway connects Margao directly with Mumbai, Mangalore and Kerala. Madgaon/Margao station is 1.5 km southeast of the bus stands, municipal gardens and market area (where you'll find most of the hotels and restaurants). Rickshaws charge Rs 15 to transfer or walk the 800 m along the railway line. Interstate buses and those running between here and North Goa use the New Kadamba (State) Bus Stand 2 km north of town. Colva and Benaulim buses leave from the local bus stand east of the gardens. See Transport, page 1213.

Getting around

City buses take you to the town bus stands for destinations south of Margao. There are plenty of auto-rickshaws and eight-seater taxis for hire.

Margao (Madgaon)

Margao is a fetching, bustling market town which, as the capital of the state's historically richest and most fertile *taluka*, Salcete, is a shop window for fans of grand old Portuguese domestic architecture and churches. Sadly, in their haste to get to the nearby beaches, few tourists take the time to explore this charming, busy provincial town.

The impressive baroque **Church of the Holy Spirit** with its classic Goan façade dominates the Old Market square, the Largo de Igreja. Originally built in 1564, it was sacked by Muslims in 1589 and rebuilt in 1675. A remarkable pulpit on the north wall has carvings of the Apostles. There are also some glass cabinets in the north aisle containing statues of St Anthony and of the Blessed Joseph Vaz. Vaz was a home-grown Catholic missionary who smuggled himself to Sri

Lanka dressed as a porter when the Dutch occupation challenged the island's faith. The church's feast day is in June.

The real gem of Margao is the glut of run-down 18th-century houses especially in and around Abade Faria Road, of which **da Silva House** ① *visits arranged via the GTDC*, is a splendid example. Built around 1790 when Inacio da Silva stepped up to become Secretary to the Viceroy, it has a long façade whose roof was once divided into seven separate cropped 'towers', hence its other name, 'Seven Shoulders'; only three of these have survived. The house's grandeur is also evident in its interiors, featuring lavishly carved dark rosewood furniture, gilded mirrors and fine chandeliers. Da Silva's descendants still live in a small wing of the house.

The **municipal market** ① *Mercado de Afonso de Albuquerque*, is a labyrinthine treat of flower garlands, silks and agricultural yield.

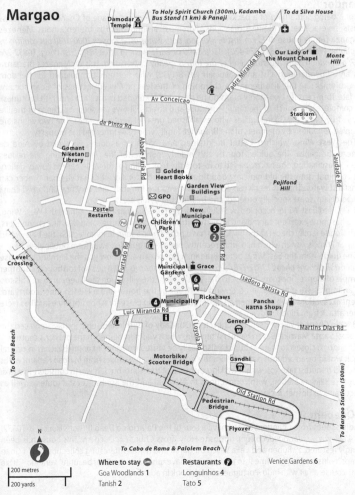

Margao

To Holy Spirit Church (300m), Kadamba Bus Stand (1 km) & Panaji

To da Silva House

Damodar Temple

Our Lady of the Mount Chapel

Monte Hill

Padre Miranda Rd

Av Conceicao

Stadium

de Pinto Rd

Abade Faria Rd

Saudade Rd

Gomant Niketan Library

Golden Heart Books

Garden View Buildings

Pajifond Hill

GPO

Poste Restante

Children's Park

New Municipal

City

V Valaulikar Rd

Isadoro Batista Rd

Level Crossing

M L Furtado Rd

Municipal Gardens

Grace

Rickshaws

Pancha Katna Shops

Martins Dias Rd

Municipality

Luis Miranda Rd

I Loyola Rd

General

To Colva Beach

Motorbike/ Scooter Bridge

Gandhi

Pedestrian Bridge

Old Station Rd

To Margao Station (500m)

Flyover

N

200 metres

200 yards

To Cabo de Rama & Palolem Beach

Where to stay 🛏
Goa Woodlands **1**
Tanish **2**

Restaurants 🍴
Longuinhos **4**
Tato **5**

Venice Gardens **6**

★ Loutolim

By the late 18th century, an educated middle-class elite had emerged in the villages of the Old Conquests. With newly established rights to property, well-to-do Goans began to invest in large homes and very fine living. West of the Zuari River, the villages of Loutolim and Chandor are two of a number that saw the distinct development of estates and houses built on this grand scale. Their houses were stuffed with tokens of their European influence and affluence, mixed with traditions appropriated from their native ancestry, installing personal chapels instead of *devachem kuds*, or Hindu prayer rooms. One beautiful example is the **Figuerda Mansion** (Casa Museu Vicente Joao de Figueiredo) in Loutolim; if you are lucky you will get shown around by the lady of the house who is now in her 80s and has many a story to share about Goa. Ask for directions by the church in Loutolim as there are no signs.

Chandor

Despite being something of a backwater today, the once-grand village of Chandor nonetheless boasts several fine Portuguese mansions. Foremost among them is the enormous **Menezes Braganza family house** ① *13 km east of Margao, both wings usually open 1000-1730 but confirm by telephone; West Wing: T0832-278 4201, 1300-1400 or early evening after 1830; East Wing: T0832-278 4227; a donation of Rs 100 at the end of the tour is greatly appreciated.* Luis de Menezes Braganza was an influential journalist and politician (1878-1938) who not only campaigned for freedom from colonial rule but also became a champion of the less privileged sections of Goan society. The late 16th-century two-storey mansion he inherited (extended in the 18th and 19th centuries), still complete with much of the family furniture and effects, shows the sheer opulence of the life enjoyed by those old Goan families who established great plantation estates. The two wings are occupied separately by members of the Braganza family who have inherited the property.

The **West Wing**, which is better maintained and has finer antiques, is owned by Aida de Menezes Braganza. The guided tour by this elderly member of the family – when she resides here – is fascinating. She has managed to restore the teak ceiling of the 250-year-old library gallery to its original state; the old *mareta* wood floor survived better since this native Goan timber can withstand water. There is much carved and inlaid antique furniture and very fine imported china and porcelain, some specially ordered, and bearing the family crest.

The faded **East Wing**, occupied by Sr Alvaro de Perreira-Braganza, partly mirrors the West Wing. It also has some excellent carved and inlaid furniture and a similar large salon with fine chandeliers. The baroque family chapel at the back now has a prized relic added to its collection, the bejewelled nail of St Francis Xavier, which had, until recently, been kept guarded away from public view.

The guide from the East Wing of the Braganza House can also show you the **Fernandes House** ① *open daily, phone ahead T0832-278 4245, suggested donation Rs 100*, if he's not too busy. It's another example of a once-fine mansion just to the southeast of the village, on the Quepem road. This too has an impressive grand salon occupying the front of the house and a hidden inner courtyard. Recent excavations have unearthed an underground hiding place for when Christian families were under attack from Hindu raiders.

Back in Chandor village itself, the **Church of Our Lady of Bethlehem**, built in 1645, replaced the principal **Sapta Matrika** (Seven Mothers) **temple**, which was demolished in the previous century.

Chandor is closest to Margao but can also easily be visited from Panjim or the beaches in central Goa. It would be an arduous day trip from the northern beaches. Buses from Margao Kadamba Bus Stand (45 minutes) take you within walking distance of the sights but it is worth considering a taxi. Madgaon Railway Station, with connections to Mumbai and the Konkan coastal route as well as direct trains to Hospet, is close by.

★ Quepem

Heading south from Chandor you can have a tour of the **Palacio do Deao** (Priest's House) ① *T0832-266 4029, www.palaciododeao.com*, opposite Holy Cross Church in Quepem. This house has been lovingly restored by Ruben and Celia Vasco da Gama and has an interesting collection of old Goan stamps, coins and books. Time it so that you can have lunch here on their beautiful veranda – it's a multi-course affair with Indo-Portuguese food. Book in advance.

Colva (Colwa)

Although it's just 6 km from Margao and is the tourist hub of the southern beaches, sleepy Colva is a far cry from its overgrown northern equivalent, Calangute. The village itself is a bit scruffy, but the beach ticks all the right boxes: powdery white sand, gently swaying palms, shallow crystalline waters and lines of local fishermen drawing their nets in hand over fist, dumping pounds of mackerel which are left to dry out in glistening silver heaps.

Margao's parasol-twirling elite, in their search for *mudanca* or a change of air, were the first to succumb to Colva's charms. They would commandeer the homes of local fisher-folk, who had decamped to their shacks for months leading up to the monsoon. The shacks have now traded up for gaudy pink and turquoise guesthouses and the odd chi-chi resort, but Colva's holiday scene remains a mostly domestic affair, beloved of Indian fun-seekers who'll willingly shell out the cash to go parasailing for 90 seconds.

Out on the eastern edge of town, the large **Church of Our Lady of Mercy** (Nossa Senhora das Merces), dating from 1630 and rebuilt in the 18th century, has a relatively simple façade and a single tower on the south side that is so short as to be scarcely noticeable, and the strong horizontal lines normally given to Goan churches by three of four full storeys is broken by a narrow band of shallow semi-circular arches above the second floor. But the church is much less famous for its architecture than for the huge fair it hosts, thanks to its association with the miraculous **Menino Jesus**. Jesuit Father Bento Ferreira found the original image in the river Sena, Mozambique, en route to Goa, and brought it to Colva where he took up his position as rector in 1648. The image's miraculous healing powers secured it special veneration.

The **Fama of Menino Jesus festival** (Monday of 12-18 October) sees thousands of frantic devotees flock to kiss the statue in hope of a miracle. Near the church, specially blessed lengths of string are sold, as well as replicas of limbs, offered to the image in thanks for cures.

Betalbatim to Velsao

A short walk from Colva, **Betalbatim** is named after the main Hindu temple to Betall that stood here before the deity was moved to Quela in Ponda for safety. This is a pleasant stretch with a mix of coconut palms and casuarinas on the low dunes. At low tide, when the firm sand is exposed, you can cycle for miles along the beach in either direction.

The broad, flat open beaches to the north – **Velsao**, **Arossim**, **Utorda** and **Majorda** – are the emptiest: the odd fishing village or deluxe resort shelters under coconut thicket canopy.

Bogmalo is a small, palm-fringed and attractive beach that's exceptionally handy for the airport (only 4 km, and a 10-minute drive away). **Hollant Beach**, 2 km further on, is a small rocky cove that is fringed with coconut palms. From Bogmalo village you can get to **Santra Beach**, where fishermen will ferry you to two small islands for about Rs 350 per boat.

The quiet back lanes snaking between these drowsy villages make perfect bicycle terrain and Velsao boasts some particularly grand examples of old mansions.

Verna

The church at Verna (the 'place of fresh air'), inland from the northern Salcete beaches on the NH17, was initially built on the site of the Mahalsa Temple, which had housed the deity now in Mardol (see page 1223) and featured exquisite carvings, but was destroyed and marked by the cross to prevent it being re-used for Hindu worship. As a sanctuary for widows who did not commit *sati*, it was dubbed the Temple of Nuns.

Verna was also picked to house the fifth century BC, 2.5-m-high **Mother Goddess figure** from Curdi in Sanguem, which was under threat of being submerged by the Selaulim Dam project in 1988. Two megalithic sites were found in the area. It is surrounded by seven healing springs. Just north towards Cortalim are the popular medicinal **Kersarval springs**.

Benaulim to Mobor

At Colva Beach's southern end lies tranquil **Benaulim**, which, according to the myth of Parasurama, is 'where the arrow fell' to make Goa. It is now a relaxed village set under palms, where business centres on toddy tapping and fishing. The hub of village activity is Maria Hall crossing, just over 1 km from the beach.

On a hill beyond the village is the diminutive **Church of St John the Baptist**, a fine piece of Goan Christian architecture rebuilt in 1596. Although the gable façade, with twin balustraded towers, is striking, the real treat is inside, in its sumptuous altar *reredos* and wonderful rococo pulpit with its depiction of the Lamb of the Apocalypse from the *Book of Revelation*.

The picturesque lane south from Benaulim runs through small villages and past white-painted churches. Paddy gives way to palm, and tracks empty onto small seaside settlements and deserted beaches. Benaulim has a more alternative vibe to its neighbouring beaches and has the **Goa Chitra Museum** ① www.goachitra.com, which is a beautifully created museum giving insight into the day-to-day living of rice farmers, toddy tappers and fishermen of not-so-yesteryear. They are creating another wing, **Goa Chakra**, focusing on transportation. Benaulim beach runs into **Varca**, and then **Fatrade**, before the main road finally hits the shoreline amid a sprouting of resorts and restaurants at **Cavelossim**. Furthest south, **Mobor**, about 6 km from Cavelossim, lies on the narrow peninsula where the river Sal joins the sea. The Sal is a busy fishing route, but doubles as a lovely spot for boat rides.

Betul

Idyllic Betul, which overlooks Mobor from the opposite bank of the Sal in Quepem *taluka*, is an important fishing and coir village shaded by coconut palms and jackfruit, papaya and banana trees. A sand bar traps the estuary into a wide and protected lagoon and the cool breezes from the sea temper even the hottest Goan high noon. Just after the bridge, which crosses the mouth of a small river, a narrow road off to the right by the shops zigzags through the village along the south side of the Sal.

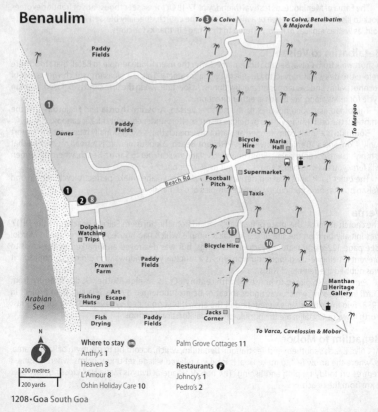

Benaulim

Where to stay 🛏
Anthy's 1
Heaven 3
L'Amour 8
Oshin Holiday Care 10
Palm Grove Cottages 11

Restaurants 🍴
Johncy's 1
Pedro's 2

Roads are now well signposted across Goa and it is easy to drive from Cavelossim to Betul (and indeed onto Agonda ad Palolem) on the scenic routes rather than taking the NH17. Buses from Margao to Betul can be very slow, but there is a fairly regular service stopping in all the settlements along the way (a couple of them continue as far as Cabo de Rama).

Cuncolim

The Jesuits razed Cuncolim's three principal Hindu temples (including the Shantadurga) and built churches and chapels in their stead.

Hindu 'rebels' killed five Jesuits and several converts in reprisal, triggering a manhunt which saw 15 men killed by the captain of Rachol Fort's soldiers. The relics of the Christian 'martyrs of Cuncolim' now lie in the Sé Cathedral in Old Goa (see page 1173). The cathedral's golden bell, Goa's largest, was cast here in 1652.

Listings Margao and coastal Salcete *maps p1205, p1208 and p1210*

Tourist information

Margao

Goa Tourism Development Corporation (GTDC)
Margao Residency, south of the plaza,
T0832-271 5528.

Where to stay

Margao

With Colva and other beaches little over 15 mins away, there is not much point staying in Margao itself.

$$ Goa Woodlands
ML Furtado Rd, opposite City Bus Stand, T0832-271 5522, www.goawoodlandshotel.com.
This swish business hotel has 35 clean, spacious and anonymous rooms. Restaurant, bar, good value although reports have been mixed.

$ Tanish
Reliance Trade Centre, V V Rd, T0832-273 5656.
Newish place with smart, good-value rooms, sharing a business complex with cybercafés and mobile phone dealers. Several good restaurants nearby.

Loutolim

$$$ Casa Susegad
T0832-264 3268, www.casasusegad.com.
This gem of a place tucked away in sleepy Loutolim village has just 5 rooms in a converted 300-year-old Portuguese house. There is a beautiful swimming pool, an enormous games room and delicious food cooked up, sometimes even home-smoked mackerel pâté, or mango pie from the enormous mango trees dotted around the garden. Norman and Carole have done a

remarkable job restoring this place and are very happy to share their little bit of paradise with you.

Chandor

$$$ The Big House
T0832-264 3477, www.ciarans.com.
Ancestral Portuguese/Goan home of John Coutinho, owner of **Ciaran's Camp** in Palolem (see page 1217). 2 bedrooms plus high-beamed ceilings, large sitting room, fully fitted kitchen, hot water, maid service, cable TV, DVD, phone and cooking available. Great for families, couples or groups of friends.

Colva

Most hotels are 6-8 km from Margao Railway Station. Prices rise on 1 Dec. Discounts are possible for stays of a week or more.

$$ C A Guest House
470/2 4th Ward), T0832-278 0047.
Cool and pleasant 2-bed apartments with balconies and basic kitchen in a huge, pastel-pink house.

$ Sea Pearl
476/4 South Ward T0832-278 0176.
Not particularly well maintained, but the big high-ceilinged rooms upstairs with private bath and balcony offer the best cheap deal in town. Good seafood restaurant downstairs.

$ Tourist Nest
2 km from the sea, T0832-278 8624, touristnest@indiatimes.com.
Crumbling old Portuguese house, 12 rooms in secure new block, fan, Rs 200 with bathroom, 2 small self-contained cottages, good restaurant. Old part of house recommended for long stay (Rs 8000 per month for 2 bedrooms), spacious

dining area, large lounge, antique furniture, balcony, bathroom and cooking facilities.

Betalbatim to Velsao

$$$$ Alila Diwa Goa
Adao Waddo, Majorda, T0832-274 6800, www.aliladiwagoa.com.
The latest of the lush hotels to open its doors in the Majorda area, it has already racked up a host of awards. Stunning lobby and beautiful infinity pool – beyond that the rooms are stylish and have lovely balconies. You can even get authentic home cooking; they have enlisted local Goan Edia Cotta to share her family recipes.

Varca to Betul

To Benaulim
To Margao
Varca
Varca Beach
Orlim
To Palolem
Chinchinim
Fatrade Beach
Carmona
Cavelossim
Dona Sylvia
Cavelossim Beach
River Sal
Assolna
To NH17
Betty's Place
Fish Port
Velim
Mobor Beach
Arabian Sea
Betul
Tarrie
To Cabo de Rama

N

1 km
1 mile

Where to stay 😴
Bamboo House 1
Taj Exotica 2

Restaurants 🍴
River View 4

Bars & clubs 🍸
Aqua at Leela Palace Hotel 7

$$$$-$$$ Vivenda Dos Palhacos
Costa Vaddo, Majorda, T0832-322 1119, www.vivendagoa.com.
One of the most charming places you can lay your hat in Goa. Stunning renovation of old Portuguese mansion – all rooms are different; Madras has a beautiful outdoor bathroom so you can shower under the stars, The Chummery is a lovely cottage with its own veranda, there is the Darjeeling with a mezzanine floor and you can stay in a huge luxe tent beyond the pretty swimming pool. Dinners are a fantastic communal affair although obviously you can opt out. Run by the hosts with the most Simon and Charlotte Hayward who come from the lineage of Haywards 5000 and their bar is dedicated to the tipple. Wholeheartedly recommended.

$ Baptista
Beach Rd, Thonvaddo, Betalbatim, T0832-288 0048.
2 simple rooms with fan, 2 self-catering flats with gas stove, use of fridge and utensils (Rs 350), good for long stays with discounts, and a short walk from beach. Friendly family and a friendly dog, once he gets to know you.

$ Manuelina Tourist House
Thonvaddo, behind Ray's, T0832-880 1154.
5 spacious, clean rooms with bath, TV lounge, some food available, pleasant, secure, quiet with a lovely communal veranda next to the banyan tree.

Benaulim to Mobor

$$$$ Taj Exotica
Calvaddo, towards Varca, T0832-658 3333, www.tajhotels.com.
23 ha of greenery and views of virgin beaches from each of its 138 luxurious rooms. Good restaurants, including Mediterranean, nightclub, excellent pool, golf course, floodlit tennis, kids' activities, jacuzzi, watersports, gym, jogging track, library and bike hire. The spa offers treatments such as Balinese massage, acupuncture and aromatherapy.

$$ Bamboo House Goa
Mobor Beach, Behind Leela Kempinski, T(0)976-664 9369, www.bamboohousegoa.com.
This place packs real eco-credentials and works with **Green Goa Works** to reduce their carbon footprint including composting and solar panels. They have also planted 80 varieties of plant around their grounds to prevent soil erosion. Beyond that, it's a pretty little place

with 10 bamboo cottages and swanky bathrooms. Recommended.

$$ Palm Grove Cottages
Vas Vaddo, Benaulim, T0832-277 0059, www.palmgrovegoa.com.
20 clean, spacious but not stylish rooms. The newer blocks at rear with showers and balconies are better. Pleasant palm-shaded garden, good food, Ayurvedic treatments. Not on the beach but plenty of places to hire a bicycle just outside. Welcoming.

$$-$ L'Amour
End of Beach Rd, Benaulim, T0832-277 0404, www.lamourbeachresort goa.com.
Close to the sea, 20 cottage-style rooms amid pleasant gardens, in a well-established hotel run by same team as **Johncy's** beach shack. Good terrace restaurant, handy for exchange and booking rail and bus tickets.

$ Anthy's
Sernabatim Beach (2-min walk south of Furtado's), T(0)9922-854566, www. anthysguesthomes.com.
A tiny collection of simple white cottages with bed, bathroom, mosquito net and not much more, set behind a popular beach café. Simple but nicely done and on a pleasant bit of beach.

$ Heaven
North of Benaulim, Sernabatim Beach, T0832-277 2201, www.heavengoa.in.
Absolutely stunning views of palm trees and green foliage, but it's 500 m from the beach. Great-value rooms and deservedly popular, so book ahead. Also Ayurvedic massage available on site. Recommended.

$ Oshin Holiday Care
House No 126, Vas Vaddo, Benaulim, T0832-277 0069, www.oshins-guesthouse.com.
You'll need a bicycle to get to the beach but the peaceful location overlooking egret and buffalo ponds is well worth it. 14 good large rooms with bath on 3 floors (room 11 is best), breakfast, dinner on request, friendly manager and superb well-kept grounds.

Restaurants

Margao

$$ Longuinhos
Near the Municipality.
Goan, North Indian. Open all day for meals and snacks, bar drinks and baked goodies.

$$ Tato
G-5 Apna Bazar, Complex, V Valaulikar Rd.
Superb vegetarian, a/c upstairs.

$$ Venice Gardens
Near Our Lady of Grace Church, opposite Lohia Maidan, T0832-271 0505.
Little garden oasis in the middle of Margao offering up the usual fare.

Colva

$ Joe Con's
4th Ward.
Excellent fresh fish and Goan dishes, good value.

$ Sagar Kinara
2 mins back from beach overlooking the main road junction.
Rare pure-veg restaurant, offering good-value *thalis* and biryanis on a breezy terrace.

$ Viva Goa
200 m south of roundabout at east end of town.
Local favourite, serving proper Goan food on red-checked tablecloths. Recommended.

Betalbatim to Velsao

It's worth going to Majorda for the food, because there is a range of great restaurants.

$$$ Martin's Corner
Betalbatim (coming from the south, look for sign on left after village), T0832-288 0765.
A huge place in front of an old house, serving great seafood including lobster, tiger prawns and crab. As cricket superstar Sachin Tendulkar has bought a house here, it's become the hangout of choice for holidaying cricket stars and media types.

$$$ Zeebop
Utorda Beach, follow signs to Kenilworth resort, T0832-275 5333, www.zeebopgoa.com.
Lovely beachfront restaurant offering up a delicious range of seafood; try the crab *papads* and great Goan specialities. Recommended.

$$ Roytanzil Garden Pub
Set back from the beach at the end of Majorda beach road past Martin's Corner (no sea views).
Neat grounds, alfresco and small covered area. Seafood and Indian. One of the best restaurants on the south coast.

Benaulim to Mobor

Beach shacks all down the coast offer Goan dishes and seafood at reasonable prices.

$$ La Afra
Tamborim, Fatrade.
Excellent steaks and fresh fish, sensibly priced.
Boatmen ferry holidaymakers to **River Sal**, Betul.

$$ Pedro's
By the car park above the beach, Benaulim.
Good seafood and tandoori. Imaginative
menu, friendly.

$$ River View
Cavelossim.
Tranquil, open-air location, overlooking the
river. Wide choice, international menu and
good ambience, despite being surrounded
by ugly hotels.

$ Johncy's
Benaulim.
Varied menu, good seafood, big portions,
tandoori recommended (after 1830) but service
can be erratic. Pleasant atmosphere though;
backgammon, scrabble.

Bars and clubs

Colva

Boomerang
On the beach a few shacks north of Pasta Hut.
Appealing sea-view drinking hole with pool
table, sociable circular bar, dance floor (although
the music veers wildly from cool to cheesy), and
daytime massages courtesy of Gupta.

Johnny Cool's
Halfway up busy Beach Rd.
Scruffy surroundings but popular for chilled beer
and late-night drinks.

Benaulim to Mobor

Aqua
Leela Palace, Mobor.
A gaming room and cigar lounge which turns
into a late-night disco after 2000.

Art Escape Vaddi beach
South Benaulim, T(0)989-228 6666.
As well as top-notch food, they host live music
from Indian classical and Sufi to rock and folk.

Festivals

Chandor
6 Jan Three Kings Festival Crowds gather
on each year at Epiphany for the Three Kings
Festival, which is similarly celebrated at Reis

Magos, with a big fair, and at Cansaulim (Quelim)
in southern Goa. The 3 villages of Chandor
(Cavorim, Guirdolim and Chandor) come
together to put on a grand show. Boys chosen
from the villages dress up as the 3 kings and
appear on horseback carrying gifts of gold,
frankincense and myrrh. They process through
the village before arriving at the church where
a large congregation gathers.

Colva
12-18 Oct (Mon that falls between these dates)
Fama of Menino Jesus when thousands of
pilgrims flock to see the statue in the Church
of our Lady of Mercy in the hope of witnessing
a miracle.

Benaulim to Mobor
24 Jun Feast of St John the Baptist (Sao Joao)
in Bernaulim gives thanks for the arrival of
the monsoon. Young men wearing crowns of
leaves and fruits tour the area singing for gifts.
They jump into wells (which are usually full) to
commemorate the movement of St John in his
mother's womb when she was visited by Mary,
the mother of Jesus.

Shopping

Margao
The Old Market was rehoused in the 'New'
(Municipal) Market in town. The **covered market**
(Mon-Sat 0800-1300, 1600-2000) is fun to wander
around. It is not at all touristy but holidaymakers
come on their shopping trip to avoid paying
inflated prices in the beach resorts. To catch a
glimpse of the early morning arrivals at the **fish
market** head south from the Municipal Building.

Books and CDs
Golden Heart, *off Abbé Faria Rd, behind the GPO.
Closed 1300-1500.* Bookshop.
Trevor's, *5 Luis Miranda Rd.* Sells CDs.

Clothes
J Vaz, *Martires Dias Rd, near Hari Mandir,
T0832-272 0086.* Good-quality men's tailor.
MS Caro, *Caro Corner.* An extensive range
including 'suiting', and will advise on tailors.

Benaulim to Mobor
Khazana, *Taj Exotica, Benaulim.* A veritable
treasure chest (books, crafts, clothes) culled
from across India. Pricey.
Manthan Heritage Gallery, *main road.*
Quality collection of art items.

What to do

Colva
Tour operators
Meeting Point, *Beach Rd, opposite William Resort, T0832-278 8003. Mon-Sat 0830-1900 (opens later if busy).* Very efficient, reliable flight, bus and train booking service.

Betalbatim to Velsao
Watersports
Goa Diving, *Bogmalo, T(0)83908 62942, www.goadiving.com.* PADI certification from Open Water to Assistant Instructor.

Benaulim to Mobor
Dolphin watching
The trips are scenic and chances of seeing dolphins are high, but it gets very hot (take a hat, water and something comfy to sit on). Groups of dolphins here are usually seen swimming near the surface. Most hotels and cafés offer boat trips, including **Café Dominick** (in Benaulim, signs on the beach). Expect to pay Rs 250-300 per person. **Betty's Place**, *in a road opposite the Holiday Inn in Mobor, T0832-287 1456.* Offers dolphin viewing (0800-1000, Rs 300), birdwatching (1600, Rs 250) and sunset cruises up the river Sal River (1700, Rs 200). Recommended.

Transport

Margao
Bus All state-run local and long-distance buses originate from the **Kadamba Bus Stand** 2 km to the north of town, T0832-271 4699. Those from the south also call at the **local** bus stand west of the municipal gardens, and buses for Colva and Benaulim can be boarded near the Kamat Hotel southeast of the gardens. From the Kadamba stand, city buses and motorcycle taxis (Rs 15) can get you to central Margao.

Frequent services to **Benaulim**, **Colva** and non-stop to **Panjim** (1 hr, buy tickets from booth at Platform 1). Several a day to **Betul**, **Cabo da Rama**, **Canacona** and **Palolem**. Daily to **Gokarna** (1500), but trains are much quicker.

Private buses (eg **Paulo Travels**, Cardozo Building opposite bus stand, T0832-651 1344), to **Bengaluru** (**Bangalore**) (15 hrs); **Mangalore** (8-10 hrs); **Mumbai** (Dadar/CST) (16 hrs); **Pune** (13 hrs).

Rickshaw Most trips in town should cost Rs 30-40; main bus stand to railway Rs 50. The prepaid rickshaw booth outside the station main entrance has high rates but probably better than bartering on the street. Motorcycle taxi drivers hang around quoting cheaper (but still overpriced) fares. Avoid tourist taxis: they can be 5 times the price.

Train Enquiries, T0832-271 2790. The station is on the broad-gauge network is 1 km southwest of central Margao. The reservation office on the 1st floor, T0832-271 2940, is usually quick and efficient, with short queues. Mon-Sat 0800-1400, 1415-2000, Sun 0800-1400. Tickets for **Mumbai**, **Delhi** and **Hospet** (for **Hampi**) should be booked well ahead.

Konkan Kanya Express (night train) and **Mandovi Express** (day train) from **Mumbai** also stop at **Thivim** (for northern beaches; take the local bus into Mapusa and from there catch another bus or take a taxi) and **Karmali** (for Panjim and Dabolim airport) before terminating at **Margao**. Both are very slow and take nearly 12 hrs. From **Mumbai** (**CST**): *Konkan Kanya Exp 10111*, evening train.

To **Delhi** (**Nizamuddin**), the daily service *Mangala Ldweep Exp 12617*, 33 hrs. Going south to **Ernakulam** (**Jn**): *Mangala Lakshaweep Exp 12618*, 16 hrs. **Hospet** (for **Hampi**): *VSG Howrah Express 18048*, Tue, Thu, Fri, Sun, 7 hrs. **Thiruvananthapuram** (**Trivandrum**): *Rajdhani Exp 12432*, Mon, Wed, Thu, 18 hrs (via Mangalore, 5 hrs, and Ernakulam, 13 hrs). *Netravati Exp 16345*, 18 hrs (via Canacona for Palolem beach).

The broad-gauge line between **Vasco da Gama** and **Londa** in Karnataka runs through Margao and Dudhsagar Falls and connects stations on the line with **Belgaum**. There are services to **Bengaluru** (**Bangalore**) *Vasco Chennai Exp 17312*.

Colva
Air From the airport, taxis charge about Rs 800. If arriving by train at Margao, 6 km away, opt for a bus or auto-rickshaw for transfer. Buses pull in at the main crossroads and then proceed down to the beach about 1 km away. Auto-rickshaws claim to have a Rs 30 'minimum charge' around Colva itself.

Bus/taxi Bus tours to **Anjuna**, every Wed for the Flea Market, tickets through travel agents. Also to **Margao**, motorcycle taxi, Rs 80 (bargain hard); auto-rickshaw, Rs 100-120.

Scooter hire Available on every street corner, for Rs 200-250 a day; motorbikes for Rs 300 per day, less for long-term rental, more for Enfields. Bicycles are hard to come by – ask at your hotel.

Betalbatim to Velsao

Bus Buses from Margao (12 km). The **Margao–Vasco** bus service passes through the centre of Cansaulim.

Taxi To/from **airport**, 20 mins (Rs 400); **Margao** 15 mins (Rs 200).

Train Cansaulim station on the **Vasco–Margao** line is handy for **Velsao** and **Arossim** beaches, and **Majorda station** for **Utorda** and **Majorda** beaches. Auto-rickshaws meet trains.
From Cansaulim and Majorda there are 3 trains a day to **Vasco** via **Dabolim** for the airport. Westbound trains head to **Kulem** (for Dudhsagar Falls) via **Margao**.

Benaulim to Mobor

Bicycle/scooter hire Cycle hire from **Rocks**, outside Dona Sylvia in Cavelossim, cycles Rs 10 per hr, Rs 150 a day; scooters Rs 300. In Benaulim, bikes and scooters for hire, Rs 200 and Rs 300 per day.

Bus Buses from all directions arrive at Maria Hall crossing, Benaulim. Taxis and autos from the beach esplanade near Pedro's and at Maria Hall crossing. **Anjuna** Wed Flea Market bus 0930, return 1530, Rs 200; you can take it one-way, but still have to buy a return ticket.
From Margao to **Cavelossim**, the bus is slow (18 km); auto-rickshaws transfer from bus stand to resorts.

Cabo de Rama, Palolem and the far south Colour map 5a, C2.
palm-fringed bays and turtle hideouts

Palolem is the closest Goa gets to a picture-postcard perfect bay: a beautiful arc of palm-fringed golden sand that's topped and tailed with rocky outcrops. Under the canopy of the dense coconut forests lie numerous restaurants and coco-huts. To the north, a freshwater stream and a short swim or wade will get you to the jungle of the tiny Canacona Island.

Palolem's sheer prettiness has made it popular and perhaps less pretty than it once was, prompting some travellers to drift south to the tranquil beaches of neighbouring Colomb, Patnem and Galgibaga (beautiful Rajbag is ring-fenced by a five-star). Patnem, hemmed in by crags and river at either end, doesn't have the same rash of coconut trees that made Palolem so shadily alluring and has mopped up most of the overspill.
Again to the north Agonda is also picking up some of the Palolem overspill, yet it retains its charm as a pretty fishing village strung out along a windswept casuarina-backed bay. There are more dramatic waves here than the calm waters of Palolem and Patnem.
The dramatic ruined fort at Cabo de Rama yields some of Goa's most dramatic views from its ramparts and has empty coves tucked about at its shores.

Cabo de Rama (Cape Rama)

Legend has it that the hero of the Hindu epic *Ramayana* lived in this desolate spot with his wife Sita during their exile from Ayodhya, and the fort predated the arrival of the Portuguese who seized it from its Hindu rulers in 1763. Its western edge, with its sheer drop to the Arabian Sea, gives you a stunning vista onto a secluded stretch of South Goa's coastline.
The main entrance to the **fort** seems far from impregnable, but the outer ramparts are excellently preserved with several cannons still scattered along their length. The gatehouse is only 20 m or so above the sea, and is also the source of the fort's water supply. A huge tank was excavated to a depth of about 10 m, which even today contains water right through the dry season. If a local herdsman is about ask him to direct you to the two springs, one of which gives out water through two spouts at different temperatures.

Agonda

Snake through forests and bright paddy south from Cabo De Rama towards Palolem to uncover artless Agonda, a windswept village backed by mountains of forestry full of acrobatic black-faced monkeys. Local political agitators thwarted plans for a five-star hotel and so have, temporarily at least, arrested the speed of their home's development as a tourist destination. However year on year, more restaurants and coco-huts open up along the length of the beach. There's no house music, little throttling of Enfield engines and you need to be happy to make your own entertainment to stay here for any serious length of time. Less photogenic than Palolem, Agonda Bay has pine-like casuarina trees lining the beach instead of coconuts and palms. The swimming is safe but the sea is livelier than in neighbouring Palolem. The northern end of the beach, close to the school and bus stop, has a small block of shops including the brilliantly beach of original **Fatima stores and restaurant** (Fatima Rodrigues, not one to be a jack of all trades, has limited her menu to just spaghetti and *thali*) and **St Annes bookstore**, a video library.

Hourly buses between Betul and Palolem call at Agonda (and Cabo de Rama). It's also easy to visit for the day by taxi, motorbike or bicycle from Palolem Beach. From Palolem/Chaudi Junction, auto-rickshaws charge Rs 120-150; turn off the road by the **Niki** bar and restaurant.

Palolem

For a short spell, when the police cracked down most severely on parties up north, Palolem looked like it might act as the Anjuna overflow.

Today, **Neptune's Point** has permission to hold parties every Saturday, but so far, Palolem's villagers are resisting the move to make the beach a mini-party destination and authorities are even stumping up the cash to pay for litter pickers. The demographic here is chiefly late 20s and 30-something couples, travellers and students. The large church and high school of **St Tereza of Jesus** (1962) are on the northern edge of town.

Beaches further south

Over the rocky outcrops to the south you come to the sandy cove of **Colomb**. Wholly uncommercial, its trees are pocked with long-stayers' little picket fences and stabs at growing banana plants, their earthy homesteads cheek by jowl with fishermen's huts. The locals are currently holding firm against a controversial development planned by a Russian group, and for now the only sounds here are the rattle of coconut fronds and bird song. Although just a bay away, you could almost be on a different planet to Palolem.

At the end of the track through Colomb, a collection of huts marks the start of the fine sweep of **Patnem Beach**. The 500 villagers here have both put a limit on the number of shacks and stopped outsiders from trading, and as a result the beach has conserved much of its unhurried charm. The deep sandbanks cushion volleyball players' falls and winds whip through kite flyers' sails: but fishing boats far outnumber sun loungers. A hit with old rockers, Israelis and long-stayers, there is no nightlife, no parties and, no coincidence, a healthy relationship between villagers and tourism. Hindu temples in Patnem have music most Fridays and Saturdays, with tabla, cymbals and harmonica.

Further south, wade across a stream (possible before the monsoon) to reach the dune- and casuarina-fringed **Rajbag Beach**, its southern waters a-bob with fishing boats. Although it's virtually unvisited and has perfect swimming, the luxury five-star that opened here in 2004 provoked a storm of protest; allegations against the hotel have included the limited access to the sea, the failure to meet local employment quotas, and the rebuilding of the ancient Shree Vita Rukmayee Temple, which villagers argue was tantamount to the hotel 'swallowing our God'. The isolated **Kindlebaga Beach** is east of Rajbag, 2 km from Canacona.

Galgibaga

Nip across the Talpona River by the ferry to reach a short strip of land jutting out to sea, where well-built houses lie among lucrative casuarina plantations. Like Morjim, **Galgibaga Beach** is a favourite stopover for olive ridley turtles, which travel vast distances to lay their eggs here each November. Shacks are mushrooming, to environmentalists' concern.

Partagali and Cotigao Wildlife Sanctuary

At a left turn-off the NH17, 7 km south of Canacona, to Partagali, a massive concrete gateway marks the way to the temple. If you go a little further, you reach a 2-km-long road that leads to the Cotigao Wildlife Sanctuary. Partagali's **Shri Sausthan Gokarn Partagali Jeevotam Math** is a centre for culture and learning on the banks of the river Kushavati. The *math* (religious establishment) was set up in AD 1475 at Margao when the followers, originally Saivites, were converted and became a Vaishnav sect. During the period of Portuguese Christianization (1560-1568), the foundation was moved south to Bhatkal (in northern Karnataka). The sixth Swami returned the *math* to Partagali, and built its Rama, Lakshman, Sita and Hunuman temple. An ancient *Vatavriksha* (banyan tree) 65 m by 75 m, which represents this Vaishnav spiritual movement, is a sacred meditation site known as *Bramhasthan*. The tree and its *Ishwarlinga* (the *lingam* of the Lord, ie Siva) have drawn pilgrims for more than a millennium. The temple, which also has a typical tall Garuda pillar, celebrates its festival in March/April.

Cotigao Wildlife Sanctuary ① *60 km south of Panjim, www.goaforest.com, year-round 0730-1730 (but may not be worthwhile during the monsoon), Rs 5, 2-wheelers Rs 10, cars Rs 50, camera Rs 25, video Rs 100*, lies in one of the most densely forested areas of the state. The 86-sq-km sanctuary is hilly to the south and east and has the Talpona River flowing through it. There is a nature interpretation centre with a small reference library and map of the park roads at the entrance. The vegetation is mostly moist deciduous with some semi-evergreen and evergreen forest cover. You may be very lucky and spot gazelles, panther, sloth bear, porcupine and hyena, and several reptiles, but only really expect wild boar, the odd deer and gaur and many monkeys. Bird-spotting is more rewarding; rare birds include rufous woodpecker, Malabar crested lark and white-eyed eagle. You need your own vehicle to reach the treetop watchtowers and waterholes that are signposted, 3 km and 7 km off the main metalled road on a variable rough track. There are no guides available, but the forest paths are easy to follow – just make sure you have drinking water and petrol. The chances of seeing much wildlife, apart from monkeys, are slim, since by the opening time of 0730 animal activity has already died down to its daytime minimum.

The first tower by a waterhole is known as **Machan Vhutpal**, 400 m off the road, with great views of the forest canopy. The second tower is sturdier and the best place to spend a night (permission required).

Most visitors come for a day trip, but if you are keen on walking in the forest this is a great place to spend a day or two. You can either stay near the sanctuary office or spend a night in a watchtower deep in the forest. A short way beyond the sanctuary entrance the metalled road passes through a small hamlet where there is a kiosk for the villagers living within the reserve, which sells the usual array of basic provisions. If you are planning to spend a few days in the park it is best to bring your own fresh provisions and then let the staff prepare meals. Rudimentary facilities like snake-proof campsites, with canvas tents available from the forest office. You'll also need written permission to stay in the forest rest house or watchtower from the Deputy Conservator of Forests (third floor, Junta House, Panaji), as far in advance of a visit as possible.

The cheapest way to visit the park is to get a group together from Palolem. If you leave the beach just before 0700 you will be at the park gates when they open. Motorbikes are also allowed in the sanctuary.

Where to stay

Agonda

$$$-$$ Dunhill Beach Resort
Towards south end of the beach, T(0)832-264 7328, www.dunhillbeachresort.in.
Having had a bit of a facelift, Dunhill offers up the most stylish accommodation on the beach with 6 chic wooden cabanas and then cheaper, but large and comfortable rooms at the back. There is a good restaurant serving up all of the usual favourites too.

$$$-$$ Shanti Village
Towards south end of the beach, T(0)9823-962154, www.shantiagonda.com.
With lovely views and chic huts, Shanti has black huts on the beach and an intimate vibe. It's good value and they have another outpost towards the north end of the beach near **Simrose**, where there are cheaper huts, although they're still very nice with tribal masks and textiles to decorate.

$$$-$$ White Sand
North end of the beach, T(0)9823-647 049, www.agonda whitesand.com.
Great-value accommodation, some cabanas have beautiful outside showers and are nicely decorated inside. The menu offers up Euro classics and traditional Goan and Indian fare. They also have **Agonda Villas**: 5 boutique-style Balinese-inspired villas which are more expensive but well worth the money. Recommended.

$$ Blue Lagoon Resort
4 km north of Agonda at Khola beach, T0832-264 7842, www.bluelagooncola.com.
Rajasthani tents set up on this secluded beach north of Agonda – blissful. There are also lovely huts, a restaurant and amazing views. You almost have the beach to yourself for romantic moonlit walks as it is mainly a daytripper beach.

$$-$ Common Home
South end of the beach, T(0)85529 00183.
Innovatively designed a/c rooms with Rajasthani wooden doors, and beach huts with sleek slate bathrooms and cow dung walls – all with interesting furniture and draped fabrics. There are also huts available.

$$-$ Simrose
Towards north end of the beach, T(0)95455 28452, www.simrose-goa.com.
Stylish beach shacks and nice rooms at the back. The pretty restaurant has plenty of little nooks for romantic suppers or shady spots for daytime lounging. Good value. Recommended.

$ Dersy Beach Resort
South end of the beach, T0832-264 7503.
50-year-old family house developed to fit 12 clean rooms with bathrooms. Over the road on the beach are 12 basic bamboo huts with a spotless shared wash block. Good value generally, but in high season the huts are not worth the price.

$ Kaama Kethna
5 km south of Agonda off Palolem Rd, phone reception is patchy so email kaamakethna@ gmail.com, www.kaamakethna.net.
Beautiful bamboo huts with open-air bathrooms perched in the jungle. Part of an enterprising organic farm there are stylish huts, treehouses and a beautiful yoga *shala*. You really feel your only neighbour is the jungle itself with just a mosquito net and swaying sari between you and Nature. The food in the nourishing restaurant comes as much as possible from the farm. You can walk through the jungle to the small Butterfly beach in 40 mins. Recommended.

$ Nana's Nook
Extreme south end of the beach, T(0)9421-244672.
Simple beach huts dotted around a central café with shared bath. The best huts at the front offer ideal views. Recommended.

Palolem
Palolem's popularity has soared inordinately and in high season prices go off the scale.

$$$-$$ Art Resort
South end of beach in Ourem area, T(0)9665-982344, www.art-resort-goa.com.
Colourful seafront cottages with interesting interior design from Riki Hinteregger using khadi natural cotton. Fairly pricey.

$$$-$$ Ciaran's Camp
Beach, T0832-264 3477, www.ciarans.com.
Primo glass-fronted wooden huts are spaced wide apart in palm-covered landscaped gardens; many have their own roof terrace with loungers. They have added more rooms so there is more

chance of getting a super-stylish hut here.
A library, lovely shop, table tennis and great
restaurant plus promises of live jazz all make
it the leader in Palolem cool.

$$ Bhakti Kutir
*Cliffside, south end of the beach, T0832-264
3469, www.bhaktikutir.com.*
This is a hardy perennial of Palolem offering up
eco-friendly chic perched on the hilltop above
Palolem beach. A relaxing place with 2-tier huts
kitted out with antique furniture, compost toilets
and bucket baths. There is a popular super-
healthy restaurant on site offering up a selection
of every grain you can think of.

$$-$ Cozy Nook
At the northern end, T0832-264 3550.
Plastered bamboo huts, fans, nets, shared toilets,
in a good location between the sea and river,
Ayurvedic centre, and art and crafts; friendly staff.
Very popular. Getting a bit pricey.

$ Chattai
*Set back from the beach, behind Bhakti Kutir
and Neptune's Point, T(0)9822-481360,
www.chattai.co.in.*
Fantastic coco huts, most with loungey roof
terraces. Lovely chilled atmosphere. There is
another branch in Agonda.

$ Fernandes
Next to Banyan Tree, T78752 32056.
2 branches of this family-run guesthouse and
restaurant on the beach. Lovely wooden cottages
with attached bathrooms, good value.

$ Green Inn
*On the Agonda road, T(0)9434-053626,
www.palolemgreen inn.com.*
Exceptional location, this 2-storey guesthouse
juts out into the vibrant green rice fields
offering up almost a 360° view of nature. Good
clean rooms with flatscreen TVs and modern
bathrooms; alas no individual balconies, but
amazing views from rooftop restaurant.

$ Papillon
*South end of beach, T(0)9890-495470,
www.papillonpalolem.com.*
Good-value chic beach huts with laid-back vibe,
a cut above the rest.

Beaches further south
The following places are dotted between
Colomb, Patnem and Galjibag. Demand and
room rates rocket over Christmas and New Year.

$$$ Turtle Hil
Patnem, www.turtle-jngle.com.
Stylish huts perched on hill overlooking Patnem
beach – there is also a beautiful riverside villa.

$$$-$$ Cassoi
*Galjibag, T0832 -263 2068,
www.cassoibyciarans.com.*
Eclectic selection of huts, some built in the
round and some like upturned fishing boats –
very special. Run by the same family as **Ciarans**
in Palolem.

$$ April 20
*Next to Home, Patnem, T(0)9960-916989,
www.april20.in.*
Smart 1- and 2-tiered beach bungalows with
nice balconies and great views, formerly called
Goyam & Goyam. Its restaurant is recommended
by the local Westerners who make south Goa
their home.

$$ Hidden Gourmet
*Colomb, T(0)9923-686185,
www.gourmetpatnem.com.*
As the name suggests, this place is off the beaten
track, or at least through the village and tucked
away on the promontory overlooking Patnem
beach. Beautifully decorated stone rooms all
with a stunning ocean view and 2 mango wood
and bamboo huts with stylish open-roofed
bathrooms. Recommended.

$$-$ Papayas
*Patnem, T(0)9923-079447,
www.papayasgoa.com.*
Eco-friendly huts running on solar power with
beautifully kept gardens. Chilled atmosphere
set behind small beachfront restaurant.

$ Namaste
*Patnem, T(0)9850-477189,
www.beachhutbooking.com.*
Variety of wooden huts and bamboo
bungalows which are good value. Good vibe
and lively restaurant. Check out the website for
booking all manner of beach huts in the area.
Recommended.

$ Ordo Sounsar
*Talpona (on the way to Galjibag) T(0)9822-
488769, www.ordosounsar.com.*
Simple beach huts on pretty Talpona beach.
Exceptional restaurant serving up traditional
Goan dishes.

Restaurants

Cabo de Rama

$ Pinto's Bar
Near the fort entrance.
Offers meals and cool drinks on a sandy shaded terrace, may also have rooms available. If there are few visitors about (most likely) order your meal here before exploring the fort to save time waiting later.

Agonda

Most of the places recommended for accommodation also have good food, especially **White Sand** and **Dunhill**.

$$ Blue Planet
Palolem–Agonda road, 5 km before Agonda, T0832-264 7448, www.blueplanet-cafe.com.
This Palolem institution has taken a risk and moved into the countryside just outside Agonda – but it's a beautiful risk to take. The drive is great and there's a lovely view from their new abode. On the menu you will find an array of vegetarian and organic healthy treats.

$$ Space
Palolem–Agonda road, www.thespacegoa.com.
Pretty courtyard restaurant serving up food with a Mediterranean feel. Shop, art gallery and healing space too.

$ Madhu
North end of beach, T(0)9423-813140, www.madhuhuts.com.
Always packed, this beach shack serves up a great range of traditional spicy Goan food as well as a range of Indian, Chinese and continental dishes. Also has good huts available.

Palolem

$$ Café Inn
At the beach road junction.
Best coffee for miles. Funky courtyard café serving up cappuccinos, a huge array of juices, tortilla wraps and unusual pancakes, such as strawberry and meringue.

$$ Dropadi Beach Restaurant and Bar
Routinely packed out. Lobster and lasagne and North Indian food are the specials – the expat community rave about the quality of the fish here.

$$ Ourem 88
Close to Art Resort in Ourem area, T(0)8698-827679.
New player on the Palolem scene offering up exceptional food. With Jodi in the kitchen and Brett out front, there is a relaxed vibe and delicious food with specials like sea bass with rucola mash and great steaks on a menu that changes weekly. And leave room for desserts such as espresso brûlée and an awe-inspiring lemon tart. Booking essential. Highly recommended.

$$ Tavernakki
South end of the beach, Ourem, T(0)8408-090673.
With help from the extremely popular **Thalassa** in northern Goa, Tavernakki offers up big portions of steak and lots of feta as well as souvlaki.

$ Banyan Tree
North end of the beach.
Sitting in the shade of a lovely banyan tree, the menu here focuses on Thai food and mostly gets it just right – good *pad thai* and green curries. Open mic night on Fri.

$ Shiva Sai
Off main road.
Great cheap *thalis*.

Beaches further south

$$ Hidden Gourmet
Colomb, T(0)9923-686185, www.gourmetpatnem.com.
Passionate about their food, the team here serves up a great range of fish and steaks, crisp salads and delicious desserts, all with a stunning view of Patnem beach.

$$ Home
Patnem.
Great range of salads, pastas, and veggie specials like beetroot and vodka risotto – make sure you leave room for their legendary desserts such as chocolate brownie or sharp lemon tart – with a very chilled chic beachfront vibe. They also have accommodation.

$$ Magic View
Colomb, in front of Hidden Gourmet, T(0)9960-917287.
Remarkably popular Italian restaurant delivering fantastic pizzas served up on tree trunks, deliciously decadent pastas such as gorgonzola and fish specials. Choose from 2 views, one overlooking the rocks at Colomb and the other gazing over Patnem.

$$ Ordo Sounsar
Talpona (see Where to stay, above).
Simple menu focusing on Goan food; strangely, a rarity in these parts. Fantastic stuffed mackerel, calamari masala, Goan-style fishcakes, unique papaya curry, fried plantain chips – exceptional stuff. Great jaunt for lunch if you are not staying locally.

$ Mamoos
Set back from beach, Patnem, T0832-264 4261.
Mamoos has served up excellent North Indian food at great prices for years.

Bars and clubs

Palolem

Cuba Beach Cafe
Palolem road, behind Syndicate Bank, T0832-264 3449.
Cool, upbeat bar for a sundowner with regular sunset DJ sessions.

Neptune's Point
T(0)9822-584968.
Wide dancefloor nestled between the rocks for a mellow daily chill-out from 1700-2200 with a proper party on a weekly basis. Hosting headphone parties, although the original Silent Noise parties have moved to a new location (www.silentnoise.com) – an ingenious way to defy the 2200 curfew. Plugged in via wireless 'phones, you can dance your heart out to a choice of 2 DJs and there's no noise pollution. A giant screen plays movies on Wed nights.

Beaches further south

Hare Krishna Hare Ram
Patnem.
Latest place for sunsets and dancing run by old schoolmates, local boys done good.

Festivals

Palolem
Feb Rathasaptami The Shri Malikarjuna Temple 'car' festival attracts large crowds.
Apr Shigmo, also at the Shri Malikarjuna Temple, also very popular.

Shopping

Palolem and Patnem
Chim, *main Palolem Beach road.* Good collection of resort clothes including huge range of bikinis and accessories.
Love India, *Patnem Rd.* Beautiful selection of Indian collectibles as well as owner Julia de Quadros' lovely designs. Clothes and homewares.

What to do

Agonda
Boat hire and cruises
Monsoon, Madhu and **Om Sai** hotels organize trips to the spice plantations and boat trips to Butterfly and Cola beaches. **Aquamer** rents kayaks.

Body and soul
Lotus Yoga Retreats, *www.lotus-yoga-retreat. com.* Run a variety of retreats and yoga experiences at the lovely Kaama Ketna close to Agonda. Recommended.

Palolem
Boat hire and cruises
You can hire boats to spend a night under the stars on the secluded Butterfly or Honeymoon beaches, and many offer dolphin-watching and fishing trips. You can see the dolphins from dry land around Neptune's Point, or ask for rowing boats instead of motorboats if you want to reduce pollution. Mornings 0830-1230 are best. Arrange through **Palolem Beach Resort**, travel agents or a fisherman. Take sunscreen, shirt, hat and water.
Ciaran's Camp, *T0832-264 3477.* Runs 2-hr mountain bike tours or charter a yacht overnight through Ciaran's bar.

Language and cooking courses
Sea Shells Guest House, *on the main road.* Hindi and Indian cookery classes.

Tour operators
Rainbow Travels, *T0832-264 3912.* Efficient flight and train bookings, exchange, Western Union money transfer, safe deposit lockers (Rs 10 per day).

Transport

Agonda

Bus/rickshaw First direct bus for **Margao** leaves between 0600-0630, last at 1000, takes about 1 hr. Alternatively, arrange a lift to the main road and flag down the next bus (last bus for Margao passes by at around 2000, but it is advisable to complete your journey before dark).

Car/scooter hire **Madhu** and **White Sands** in Agonda hire out scooters, motorbikes and cars.

Palolem

Bus Many daily direct buses run between **Margao** and **Canacona** (40 km via Cuncolim), Rs 20, on their way to **Karwar**. From Canacona, taxis and auto-rickshaws charge Rs 50-80 to Palolem beach only 2 km away. From Palolem, direct buses for Margao leave at around 0615, 0730, 0930, 1415, 1515, 1630 and take 1 hr. At other times of the day take a taxi or rickshaw to the main road, and flag down the next private bus. Frequent private services run to Palolem and Margao as well as south into **Karnataka**.

Train From **Canacona Junction station**, 2 km away from Palolem beach. The booking office opens 1 hr before trains depart. Inside the station there is a phone booth and a small chai stall. A few auto-rickshaws and taxis meet all trains. If none is available walk down the approach road and turn left under the railway bridge. At the next corner, known locally as Chaurasta, you will find an auto-rickshaw to take you to Palolem beach (Rs 50) or **Agonda Beach**; expect to pay double for a taxi.

To **Ernakulam Junction**, *Netravati Exp 16345*, 15 hrs, and on to **Thiruvananthapuram** (20 hrs); **Mumbai** (quicker to get train from Madgaon otherwise you go into more obscure station not Mumbai CST).

Beaches further south

Bus/taxi For **Canacona**, buses run to Palolem and Margao and also to Karnataka Direct buses for Margao leave at around 0615, 0730, 0930, 1415, 1515, 1630 and take an hour. Alternatively, take a taxi or rickshaw to the main road and flag down the next private bus. Palolem is 3 km from **Canacona Junction train station**, which is now on the Konkan line.

Ponda &
interior Sanguem

There is enough spirituality and architecture in the neighbouring districts of Ponda and Salcete to reverse even the most cynical notions of Goa as a state rich in beach but weak on culture. Once you've had your fill of basking on the sand you'll find that delving into this geographically small area will open a window on a whole new, and richly rewarding, Goa.

Just over the water lies Salcete and the villages of Goa's most sophisticated and urbane elite, steeped in the very staunchest Catholicism. Here you can see the most eloquent symbols of the graceful living enjoyed by this aristocracy in the shape of palatial private homes, the fruits of their collusion with the colonizers in faith. Ironically, one of the finest – Braganza House in Chandor – is also the ancestral home of one of the state's most vaunted freedom fighters, Luis de Menezes-Braganza.

Ponda and around   *Colour map 5a, B2.*

visit the hidden Hindu heartland of Goa

Ponda, once a centre of culture, music, drama and poetry, is Goa's smallest *taluka*. It is also the richest in Goan Hindu religious architecture. A stone's throw from the Portuguese capital of Old Goa and within 5 km of the district's traffic-snarled and fume-filled town centre are some of Goa's most important temples including the Shri Shantadurga at Queula and the Nagesh Temple near Bandora. Ponda is also a pastoral haven full of spice gardens and wonderfully scenic views from low hills over sweeping rivers. The Bondla Sanctuary in the east of the *taluka*, though small and underwhelming in terms of wildlife, is a vestige of the forest-rich environment that once cloaked the entire foothills of the Western Ghats.

Ponda
Ponda wasn't always the poster-boy for Goa's Hindu identity that it is today. The **Safa Mosque** (Shahouri Masjid), the largest of 26 mosques in Goa, was built by Ibrahim 'Ali' Adil Shah in 1560. It has a simple rectangular chamber on a low plinth, with a pointed pitched roof, very much in the local architectural style, but the arches are distinctly Bijapuri. Because it was built of laterite the lower tier has been quite badly eroded. On the south side is a tank with *meherab* designs for ritual cleansing. The gardens and fountains were destroyed under the Portuguese; today, the mosque's backdrop is set off by low rising forest-covered hills.

Khandepar

Meanwhile, for a picture of Goa's Buddhist history, travel 4 km east from Ponda on the NH4A to Khandepar to visit Goa's best-preserved cave site. Believed to be Buddhist, it dates from the 10th or 11th century. The first three of the four laterite caves have an outer and an inner cell, possibly used as monks' living quarters. Much more refined than others discovered in Goa, they show clear evidence of schist frames for doors to the inner cells, sockets on which wooden doors would have been hung, pegs carved out of the walls for hanging clothing, and niches for storage and for placing lamps. The site is hidden on the edge of a wooded area near a tributary of the Mandovi: turn left off the main road from Ponda, look for the green and red archaeological survey sign, just before the bridge over the river. Turn right after the football pitch then walk down the track off to the right by the electric substation.

Farmagudi

On the left as you approach Farmagudi from Ponda is a **Ganesh temple** built by Goa's first chief minister, Shri D Bandodkar, back in the 1960s. It is an amalgam of ancient and modern styles. Opposite is a statue of Sivaji commemorating the Maratha leader's association with **Ponda's Fort**. The fort was built by the Adil Shahis of Bijapur and destroyed by the Portuguese in 1549. It lay in ruins for over a century before Sivaji conquered the town in 1675 and rebuilt it. The Portuguese viceroy attempted to re-take it in October 1683 but quickly withdrew, afraid to take on the Maratha King Sambhaji, who suddenly appeared with his vast army.

Velinga

Lakshmi-Narasimha Temple ① *just north of Farmagudi at Velinga, from the north take a right immediately after crossing a small river bridge*, is Goa's only temple to Vishnu's fourth avatar. The small half-man, half-lion image at this 18th-century temple was whisked away from the torches of Captain Dioqo Rodrigues in 1567 Salcete. Its tower and dome over the sanctuary are markedly Islamic. Inside there are well-carved wooden pillars In the *mundapa* and elaborate silverwork on the screen and shrine.

Priol

Shri Mangesh Temple ① *Priol, northwest of Ponda on a wooded hill, on the NH4A leading to Old Goa*, is an 18th-century temple to Siva's incarnation as the benevolent Mangesh is one of the most important temples in Goa. Its Mangesh *lingam* originally belonged to an ancient temple in Kushatali (Cortalim) across the river. The complex is typical of Goan Hindu temple architecture and the surrounding estate provides a beautiful setting. Note the attractive tank on the left as you approach, which is one of the oldest parts of the site. The complex, with its *agrashalas* (pilgrims' hostel), administrative offices and other rooms set aside for religious ceremonies, is a good representative of Goan Hindu temple worship: the temple is supported by a large community who serve its various functions. February 25 is **Jatra**.

Mardol

Two kilometres on from Shri Mangesh, the early 16th-century **Mahalsa Narayani Temple** is dedicated to Mahalsa, a Goan form of Vishnu's consort Lakshmi or, according to some, the god himself in female

Essential Ponda

Finding your feet

Ponda town is an important transport intersection where the main road from Margao via Borlim meets the east–west National Highway, NH4A. Buses to Panjim and Bondla via Tisk run along the NH4A, which passes through the centre of town. See Transport, page 1225.

Getting around

The temples are spread out so it's best to have your own transport: take a bike or charter an auto-rickshaw or taxi; you'll find these around the bus stand.

Tourist information

The website for the **Goa Tourism Development Corporation (GTDC)**, www.goatourism.gov.in, is useful for touring this area as they offer several jungle or sanctuary experiences. Another useful resource is the **Deputy Conservator of Forests**, T0832-231 9720.

BACKGROUND

Ponda and around

The Zuari River represented the stormy boundary between the Christianized Old Conquests and the Hindu east for two centuries. St Francis Xavier found a dissolute band of European degenerates in the first settlers when he arrived in the headquarters of Luso-India and recommended the formation of an Inquisition. Founded in 1560 to redress the failings within their own community, the Portuguese panel's remit quickly broadened as they found that their earliest Goan converts were also clinging clandestinely to their former faith. So the inquisitors set about weeding out these 'furtive Hindus', too, seeking to impose a Catholic orthodoxy and holding great show trials every few years with the public executions of infidels. Outside those dates set aside for putting people to death, intimidation was slightly more subtle: shrines were desecrated, temple tanks polluted and landowners threatened with confiscation of their holdings to encourage defection. Those unwilling to switch religion instead had to look for places to flee, carrying their idols in their hands.

When the conquistadors (or *descubridores*) took to sacking shrines and desecrating temples, building churches in their place, the keepers of the Hindu faith fled for the broad river banks and the Cumbarjua creek to its west, to build new homes for their gods.

form *Mohini* (from the story of the battle between the *devas* and *asuras*). The deity was rescued from what was once a fabulous temple in Verna at around the same time as the Mangesh Sivalinga was brought to Priol. The entrance to the temple complex is through the arch under the *nagarkhana* (drum room). There is a seven-storeyed *deepstambha* and a tall brass Garuda pillar which rests on the back of a turtle, acting as an impressive second lamp tower. The half-human half-eagle *Garuda*, Vishnu's vehicle, sits on top. A stone 'cosmic pillar' with rings, next to it, signifies the axis along which the temple is aligned. The new *mandapa* (columned assembly hall) is made of concrete, but is hidden somewhat under the red tiling, finely carved columns and a series of brightly painted carvings of the 10 *avatars*, or incarnations, of Vishnu. The unusual dome above the sanctuary is particularly elegant. A decorative arched gate at the back leads to the peace and cool of the palm-fringed temple tank.

A palanquin procession with the deity marks the February **Mardol Jatra**, **Mahasivaratri** is observed in February/March and **Kojagiri Purnima** celebrated at the August/September full moon.

Bandora

A narrow winding lane dips down to this tiny hamlet and its **temple** ① *head 4 km west from Ponda towards Farmagudi on the NH4A, looking for a fork signposted to Bandora*, to Siva as Nagesh (God of Serpents). The temple's origin is put at 1413 by an inscribed tablet here, though the temple was refurbished in the 18th century. The temple tank, which is well stocked with carp, is enclosed by a white-outlined laterite block wall and surrounded by shady palms. The five-storey lamp tower near the temple has brightly coloured deities painted in niches just above the base, the main *mandapa* (assembly hall) has interesting painted woodcarvings illustrating stories from the epics *Ramayana* and *Mahabharata* below the ceiling line, as well as the *Ashtadikpalas*, the eight Directional Guardians (Indra, Agni, Yama, Nirritti, Varuna, Vayu, Kubera and Ishana). The principal deity has the usual *Nandi* and in addition there are shrines to Ganesh and Lakshmi-Narayan and subsidiary shrines with *lingams*, in the courtyard. The **Nagesh Jatra**, normally in November, is celebrated at full moon to commemorate Siva's victory.

In a valley south of the Nagesh Temple lies the **Mahalakshmi Temple**, thought to be the original form of the deity of the Shakti cult. Mahalakshmi was worshipped by the Silaharas (chieftains of the Rashtrakutas, AD 750-1030) and the early Kadamba kings. The sanctuary has an octagonal tower and dome, while the side entrances have shallow domes. The stone slab with the Marathi inscription dating from 1413 on the front of the Nagesh Temple refers to a temple to Mahalakshmi at Bandora. The *sabhamandap* has an impressive gallery of 18 wooden images of Vishnu. Mahalakshmi is special in that she wears a *lingam* in her headdress and is believed to be a peaceful, 'Satvik', form of Devi; the first temple the Portuguese allowed at Panjim is also dedicated to her.

1224•**Goa** Ponda & interior Sanguem

Queula (Kavale)

Just 3 km southwest from Ponda's Central Bus Stand is one of the largest and most famous of Goa's temples; dedicated to Shantadurga (1738), the wife of Siva as the Goddess of Peace. She earns the Shanti (Sanskrit for peace) prefix here because, at the request of Brahma, she mediated in a great quarrel between her husband and Vishnu, and restored peace in the universe. In the sanctuary here she stands symbolically between the two bickering gods. The temple, which stands in a forest clearing, was built by Shahu, the grandson of the mighty Maratha ruler Sivaji, but the deity was taken from Quelossim well before then, back in the 16th century. It is neoclassical in design: the two-storey octagonal drum, topped by a dome with a lantern, is a classic example of the strong impact church architecture made on Goan temple design. The interior of polished marble is lit by several chandeliers. Steps lead up to the temple complex which has a large tank cut into the hillside and a spacious courtyard surrounded by the usual pilgrim hostels and administration offices.

Shri Sausthan Goud Padacharya Kavale Math, named after the historic seer and exponent of the Advaita system of Vedanta, was founded between Cortalim and Quelossim. This Hindu seminary was destroyed during the Inquisition in the 1560s and was temporarily transferred to Golvan and Chinar outside Goa. After 77 years, in the early 17th century, the Math regrouped here in Queula, the village where the Shantadurga deity (which had also originated in Quelossim) had been reinstalled. There is a temple to Vittala at the Math. The foundation has another Math at Sanquelim.

Listings Ponda and around

Where to stay

Ponda

Ponda is within easy reach of any of Goa's beach resorts and Panjim.

$$-$ Menino
100 m east of bus stand junction, 1st floor,
T0832-664 1585.
20 rooms, some a/c, pleasant, good restaurant serves generous main courses, impressive modern hotel, good value.

Farmagudi

$ Farmagudi Residency (GTDC)
Attractively located though too close to NH4A,
T0832-233 5122.
39 clean rooms, some a/c, dorm (Rs 150), adequate restaurant (eat at **Atish**, above).

Transport

Ponda

Bus Buses to **Panjim** and **Bondla** via Tisk (enquiries, T0832-231 1331), but it is best to have your own transport.

North of Ponda Colour map 5a, B2.

discover the vital health properties of turmeric

★ Spice Hills

There are a number of spice plantations in the foothills around northeast Ponda that have thrown open their gates to offer in-depth tours that detail medicinal and food uses of plants during a walk through these cultivated forests. These are surprisingly informative and fun. Of these, Savoi Spice Plantation is probably the most popular and the guide is excellent.

Savoi Spice Plantation ① *6 km from Savoi, T0832-234 0272, www.savoiplantation.com, 1030-1730, tour Rs 350, 1 hr, awkward to reach by public transport, ask buses from Ponda or Banastari heading for Volvoi for the plantation,* now over 200 years old, covers 40 ha around a large irrigation tank. Half the area is wetland and the other half on a hillside, making it possible for a large variety of plants and trees to grow. The plantation was founded by Mr Shetye and is now in the hands of the fourth generation of his family, who regularly donate funds to local community projects such as the school and temple. All plants are grown according to traditional Goan methods of organic farming. The tour includes drinks and snacks on arrival, and concludes with the chance to buy packets of spices (good gifts to take home) and a tot of *feni* to 'give strength' for the return journey to your resort. You will even be offered several cheap, natural alternatives to Viagra, whether you need them or not.

Pascoal Spice Plantation ① *signposted 1.5 km off the NH4A, near Khandepar between Ponda and Tisk, T0832-234 4268, 0800-1800, tours Rs 300*, is pleasantly located by a river and grows a wide variety of spices and exotic fruit. A guided tour takes you through a beautiful and fascinating setting. Spices can be bought directly from the plantation.

Tropical Spice Plantation ① *Keri, clearly signposted off the NH4A (just south of the Sri Mangesh Temple), T0832-234 0329, tours Rs 300, boats for hire Rs 100*, is a very pleasant plantation situated in a picturesque valley. Guides are well informed and staff are friendly. It specializes in medicinal uses for the spices, the majority of which seem to be good for the skin. At the end of the tour an areca nut picker will demonstrate the art of harvesting by shinning up a tall palm with his feet tied together in a circle of rope. The demonstration ends with the equally impressive art of descent, a rapid slide down the trunk like a fireman. After the tour a delicious lunch is served in the shade overlooking a lake where there are a couple of boats for hire. Visitors arriving in the early morning will find the boats an excellent opportunity for viewing the varied birdlife around the lake.

Bondla Wildlife Sanctuary

20 km northeast of Ponda, mid-Sep to mid-Jun, Fri-Wed 0930-1730. Rs 5, camera Rs 25, video Rs 100, 2-wheelers Rs 10, cars Rs 50. More info at www.goatourism.gov.in. Buses from Ponda via Tisk and Usgaon stop near the sanctuary where you can get taxis and motorcycle taxis. KTC buses sometimes run weekends from Panjim. During the season the Forest Department minibus runs twice daily (except Thu) between Bondla and Tisk: from Bondla, 0815, 1745; from Tisk, 1100 (Sun 1030) and 1900. Check at the tourist office. If you are on a motorbike make sure you fill up with petrol; the nearest pumps are at Ponda and Tisk. Bondla is well signposted from the NH4A east of Ponda (5 km beyond Usgaon, a fork to the right leads to the park up a winding steep road).

Bondla is the most popular of Goa's three sanctuaries because it is relatively easily accessible. The 8-sq-km sanctuary is situated in the foothills of the Western Ghats; sambar, wild boar, gaur (Indian bison) and monkeys live alongside a few migratory elephants that wander in from Karnataka during the summer. The mini-zoo here guarantees sightings of 'Goa's wildlife in natural surroundings', although whether the porcupine and African lion are examples of indigenous species is another matter. Thankfully, the number of animals in the zoo has decreased in recent years and those that remain seem to have adequate space compared to other zoos in India.

The small **Nature Education Centre** has the facility to show wildlife videos, but is rarely used. Five-minute elephant rides are available 1100-1200 and 1600-1700. A deer safari (minimum eight people), 1600-1730, costs Rs 10. The park also has an attractive picnic area in a botanical garden setting and a 2.4-km nature trail with waterholes, lake and treetop observation tower.

Listings North of Ponda

Where to stay

Spice Hills

$$ Savoi Farmhouse
Savoi Plantation, T0832-234 0272, www.savoiplantations.com.
An idyllic traditional Goan-style farmhouse built from mud with 2 adjoining en suite double rooms each with private veranda. Electricity and hot water; rates are for full board and include plantation tour. A night in the forest is memorable, highly recommended. Ideally, stay 2 nights exploring deep into the forested hills, good for birdwatching.

Bondla Wildlife Sanctuary

$ Eco-Cottages
Reserve ahead at Deputy Conservator of Forests, Wildlife Division, 4th floor, Junta House, 18 June Rd, Panjim, T0832-231 9720 (although beds are often available to anyone turning up).
8 basic rooms with attached bath, newer ones better. Also 1 km inside park entrance (which may be better for seeing wildlife at night) are 2 dorms of 12 beds each.

Sanguem, Goa's largest *taluka*, covers the state's eastern hill borderland with the South Indian state of Karnataka. The still-forested hills, populated until recently by tribal peoples practising shifting cultivation, rise to Goa's highest points. Just on the Goan side of the border with Karnataka are the Dudhsagar Falls, some of India's highest waterfalls, where the river, which ultimately flows into the Mandovi, cascades dramatically down the hillside. Both the Bhagwan Mahaveer Sanctuary and the beautiful, small Tambdi Surla Temple can be reached in a day from the coast (about two hours from Panaji).

Bhagwan Mahaveer Sanctuary

29 km east of Pondon on NH4A, T0832-260 0231, or contact Forest Dept in Canacona, T0832-296 5601. Open 0700-1730 except public holidays. Rs 5, 2-wheelers Rs 10, cars Rs 250. Or check Goa Tourism (www.goatourism.gov.in). Entrance to Molem National Park, within the sanctuary, 100 m east of the Tourist Complex, is clearly signposted but the 14 km of tracks in the park are not mapped. Tickets at the Nature Interpretation Centre, 100 m from the police check post in Molem.

Goa's largest wildlife sanctuary holds 240 sq km of lush moist deciduous to evergreen forest types and a herd of gaur (*bos gaurus*, aka Indian bison). The **Molem National Park**, in the central section of the sanctuary, occupies about half the area with the **Dudhsagar Falls** located in its southeast corner; the remote **Tambdi Surla Temple** is hidden in the dense forest at the northern end of the sanctuary. Forest department jeeps are available for viewing within the sanctuary; contact the Range Forest Officer (Wildlife), Molem. Motorbikes, but not scooters, can manage the rough track outside the monsoon period.

In theory it is possible to reach Devil's Canyon and Dudhsagar Falls via the road next to the Nature Interpretation Centre, although the road is very rough and it may require a guide. Make sure you have a full tank of petrol if attempting a long journey into the forest. You can stay overnight.

Sambar, barking deer, monkeys and rich birdlife are occasionally joined by elephants that wander in from neighbouring Karnataka during the summer months, but these are rarely spotted. Birds include the striking golden oriole, emerald dove, paradise flycatcher, malabar hornbill and trogon and crested serpent eagle.

Dudhsagar Falls

Train day trips are organized through Goa Tourism (www.goatourism.gov.in) on Wed and Sun. It's a spectacular journey worth taking in its own right. The railway tracks climb right across the cascades, but trains no longer stop at the falls themselves; to get to the pools at the bottom you can take a road from Kulem, where jeep owners offer 'safaris' through the jungle to the base of the falls. If taking the train simply for the view,

Essential Central and southern interior

Finding your feet

Buses running along the NH4A between Panjim, Ponda or Margao and Belgaum or Bengaluru (Bangalore) in Karnataka stop at Molem, in the north of the *taluka*. Much of the southeastern part of Sanguem remains inaccessible. Trains towards Karnataka stop at Kulem (Colem) and Dudhsagar stations. Jeeps wait at Kulem to transfer tourists to the waterfalls. If you are travelling to Tambdi Surla or the falls from north or central Goa, then the best and most direct route is the NH4A via Ponda. By going to or from the southern beaches of Salcete or Canacona you can travel through an interesting cluster of villages, only really accessible if you have your own transport, to see the sites of rock-cut caves and prehistoric cave art. See Transport, page 1229.

Getting around

There is no direct public transport between Molem and the sites, but the town is the start of hikes and treks in December and January.

it's best to travel through to Belgaum in Karnataka, from where there are good bus and train services back to Goa.

The Dudhsagar Falls on the border between Goa and Karnataka are the highest in India and measure a total drop of about 600 m. The name, meaning 'the sea of milk', is derived from the white foam that the force of the water creates as it drops in stages, forming pools along the way. They are best seen just after the monsoon, between October and December, but right up to April there is enough water to make a visit worthwhile. You need to be fit and athletic to visit the falls.

A rough, steep path takes you down to a viewing area which allows you a better appreciation of the falls' grandeur, and to a beautifully fresh pool which is lovely for a swim (take your costume and towel). There are further pools below but you need to be sure-footed. The final section of the journey is a scramble on foot across stream beds with boulders; it is a difficult task for anyone but the most athletic. For the really fit and adventurous the arduous climb up to the head of the falls with a guide, is well worth the effort. Allow three hours, plus some time to rest at the top.

You can take the train to Kulem, which is about 17 km from the falls, and then pick up a jeep or motorbike to take you to the falls; but it's a rough ride. By road, motorbikes, but not scooters, can get to the start of the trail to the falls from Molem crossroads by taking the road south towards Kulem. There are at least two river crossings, so is not recommended after a long period of heavy rain. The ride through the forest is very attractive and the reward at the end spectacular, even in the dry season. A swim in the pool at the falls is particularly refreshing after a hot and dusty ride. Guides are available but the track is easy to follow even without one. See also Transport, opposite.

Tambdi Surla

A taxi from Panjim takes about 2½ hrs for the 69-km journey. There is no public transport to Tambdi Surla but it is possible to hike from Molem. From the crossroads at Molem on the NH4A, the road north goes through dense forest to Tambdi Surla. 4 km from the crossroads you reach a fork. Take the right fork and after a further 3 km take a right turn at Barabhumi village (there is a sign). The temple is a further 8 km, just after Shanti Nature Resort. Make sure you have enough petrol before leaving Molem. It is also possible to reach the site along minor roads from Valpoi. The entrance to the temple is a short walk from the car park.

This Mahadeva (Siva) Temple is a beautifully preserved miniature example of early Hindu temple architecture from the Kadamba-Yadava period. Tucked into the forested foothills, the place is often deserted, although the compound is well maintained by the Archaeology Department. The temple is the only major remaining example of pre-Portuguese Hindu architecture in Goa; it may well have been saved from destruction by its very remoteness.

Listings Central and southern interior

Where to stay

Bhagwan Mahaveer Sanctuary
Goa Eco Tourism offer the **Jungle Book Tour** where you can stay in tents or cottages inside the sanctuary (www.goatourism.gov.in); take provisions. GTDC accommodation is at the Tourist Complex in Molem, east along the NH4A from the Molem National Park entrance.

$ Molem Forest Rest House
Book via the Conservator's Office, 3rd floor, Junta House, 18 June Rd, Panjim, T0832-231 9720.

Tambdi Surla

$$ Shanti Nature Resort
500 m from temple, T0832-261 0012.
With the emphasis on rest, Ayurvedic treatment and meditation, this resort has 9 large mud huts with palm-thatched roofs, electricity and running water in natural forest setting. There's a restaurant, and spice garden visits, birdwatching, hikes and trips to Dudhsagar, etc, are all arranged (2 nights, US$120). Highly recommended for location and eco-friendly approach.

What to do

Bhagwan Mahaveer Sanctuary
Hiking
Popular hiking routes lead to **Dudhsagar** (17 km), the sanctuary and **Atoll Gad** (12 km), **Matkonda Hill** (10 km) and **Tambdi Surla** (12 km). Contact the **Hiking Association**, 6 Anand Niwas, Swami Vivekananda Rd, Panjim.

Transport

Bhagwan Mahaveer Sanctuary
If coming from the south, travel via Sanguem. The road from Sanvordem to the NH17 passes through mining country and is therefore badly pot-holed and has heavy lorry traffic. From Kulem, jeeps do the rough trip to **Dudhsagar** (Rs 300 per head, Rs 1800 per jeep). The journey is also possible by motorbike (Rs 600 per person).

This is a very tough and tiring journey at the best of times. From Molem, a road to the south off the NH4A leads through the forested hills of Sanguem *taluka* to **Kulem** and **Calem** railway stations and then south to **Sanguem**. From there, a minor road northwest goes to **Sanvordem** and then turns west to **Chandor**.

Bus Buses between **Panjim**, **Ponda** or **Margao**, and **Belgaum/Bengaluru (Bangalore)**, stop at Molem for visiting the Bhagwan Mahaveer Sanctuary and Dudhsagar Falls.

Train From the southern beaches, you can get the *Vasco-Colem Passenger* from Vasco at 0710, or more conveniently Margao (Madgaon) at 0800, arriving at **Kulem (Colem)** at 0930. Return trains at 1640, arriving **Margao** at 1810; leave plenty of time to enjoy the falls. Jeep hire is available from Kulem Station.

Background Goa

History

Some identify Goa in the *Mahabharata* (the Sanskrit epic) as Gomant, where Vishnu, reincarnated as Parasurama, shot an arrow from the Western Ghats into the Arabian Sea and with the help of the god of the sea reclaimed the beautiful land of Gomant. Arab geographers knew Goa as Sindabur. Ruled by the Kadamba Dynasty from the second century AD to 1312 and by Muslim invaders from 1312 to 1367, it was then annexed by the Hindu Kingdom of Vijayanagar and later conquered by the Bahmani Dynasty of Bidar in North Karnataka, who founded Old Goa in 1440.

When the Portuguese arrived, Yusuf Adil Shah, the Muslim King of Bijapur, was the ruler. At this time Goa was an important starting point for Mecca-bound pilgrims, as well as continuing to be a centre importing Arab horses. The Portuguese were intent on setting up a string of coastal stations to the Far East in order to control the lucrative spice trade. Goa was the first Portuguese possession in Asia and was taken by Alfonso de Albuquerque in March 1510. Three months later Yusuf Adil Shah blockaded it with 60,000 men. In November Albuquerque returned with reinforcements, recaptured the city after a bloody struggle, massacred all the Muslims and appointed a Hindu as governor. Mutual hostility towards Muslims encouraged links between Goa and the Hindu kingdom of Vijayanagar.

A Christian-Hindu fault line only appeared when missionary activity in India increased. Franciscans, Dominicans and Jesuits arrived, carrying with them religious zeal and intolerance. The Inquisition was introduced in 1540 and all evidence of earlier Hindu temples and worship was eradicated from the territories of the 'Old Conquests'. Goa became the capital of the Portuguese Empire in the east. It reached its greatest splendour between 1575 and 1600, the age of 'Golden Goa', but when the Dutch began to control trade in the Indian Ocean it declined. The fall of the Vijayanagar Empire in 1565 caused the lucrative trade between Goa and the Hindu state to dry up.

Between 1695 and 1775 the population of Old Goa fell from 20,000 to 1600; by the 1850s only a few priests and nuns remained. When British explorer Richard Burton arrived in Goa in 1850, he described Old Goa, once the oriental capital of Portuguese empire-building ambition and rival to Lisbon in grandeur, as a place of "utter desolation" and its people "as sepulchral-looking as the spectacle around them."

Albuquerque's original conquest was of the island of Tiswadi, where Old Goa is situated, plus the neighbouring areas of Bardez, Ponda, Mormugao and Salcete. These formed the heart of the Portuguese territory, known today as the Old Conquests. The New Conquests cover the remaining areas and which came into Portuguese possession considerably later. By the time they were absorbed, the intolerant force of the Inquisition had passed. As a result, the New Conquests did not suffer as much cultural and spiritual devastation.

The Portuguese came under increasing pressure in 1948-1949 to cede Goa to India. The problem festered until 1961 when the Indian Army, supported by a naval blockade, marched in and brought to an end 450 years of Portuguese rule. Goa became a Union Territory together with the enclaves of Daman and Diu. On 30 May 1987 it became a full state of the Indian Union.

Religion

While in the area of the Old Conquests tens of thousands of people were converted to Christianity, the Zuari River represents a great divide between Christian and predominantly Hindu Goa. Today about 70% of the state's population is Hindu, and there is also a small but significant Muslim minority.

Gujarat

temples, marshes, factories and mangroves in India's Wild West

From the stunning salt plains of the Great Rann of Kachchh in the north to the jungle of Sasan Gir National Park in the south, Gujarat is a fascinating state with picturesque landscapes and some of the world's oldest ports.

The 15th-century scramble for supremacy saw European colonial powers set up trading posts along the coast. Gujarat was the East India Company's first toehold in India but was also key to the British Empire's decline: Mahatma Gandhi led the Salt March in Gujarat that galvanized India's independence movement.

Today, Gujarat has India's fastest-growing economy and is one of its most industrial states. It has a treasure trove of Jain and Hindu buildings, including superb temples at Palitana and Modhera, and Ahmedabad, the former state capital, is a showcase for Gujarat's distinctive regional architecture.

Yet for all its rewards, the state remains off the radar of mainstream tourism and makes a challenging place for independent travel. In particular, the arid peninsula of Kachchh is a barely travelled desert region whose people have a vibrant cultural identity and whose varied landscapes shelter flamingos, pelicans and wild ass.

Best for
Architecture ■ Desert ■ History ■ Wildlife

Footprint
picks

⭐ **Ahmedabad**, page 1236

Explore the city's Islamic and modernist architecture by day and by night.

⭐ **Modhera**, page 1246

Visit the beautiful sun temple at Modhera.

⭐ **Sasan Gir National Park**, page 1272

Hear the roar of a lion at Sasan Gir.

⭐ **Craft villages around Bhuj**, page 1289

See exquisite handicraft Kachchh traditions around Bhuj.

⭐ **Kachchh salt plains**, page 1290

Don't miss travelling across the stunning white salt plains that stretch to the horizon.

Essential Gujarat

Finding your feet

Gujarat (population: 50.6 million, area: 196,000 sq km) has nearly 1600 km of coastline and nowhere is more than 160 km from the sea. Kachchh (Kutch), on the northwest border of the peninsula, rises to heights of around 300 m and is almost desert. To the north is the Great Rann of Kachchh, a 20,700-sq-km salt marsh. To the south is the Little Rann. During the monsoon the Rann floods, virtually making Kachchh an island, while during the hot dry summer months it is a dusty plain.

The Kathiawad Peninsula, also known as Saurashtra, lies to the southeast of the Gulf of Kachchh, bulging southward into the Gulf of Khambhat (Cambay) and rarely rises to more than 180 m.

Northeast Gujarat is a continuation of central Kachchh, with small plains and low hills. The railway line from Mumbai to Delhi runs through these hills that surround Ahmedabad. The Western Ghats extend into southeast Gujarat, the wettest region of the state.

Getting around

Ahmedabad is the hub for the state, with flights from most big cities. There are good train or bus links to all of Gujarat.

A visit to Gujarat can be rewarding but you must be prepared for slow and arduous journeys on public transport and be aware that English is only sporadically spoken outside the larger cities and tourist towns.

A good option is to hire a car with driver or splash out on the **Royal Orient**, Gujarat's answer to the famous 'Palace on Wheels'.

Best hidden treasures

Textiles and embroideries at the Calico Museum, page 1237
Tea at the Mangaldas Ni Haveli, page 1243
Night Heritage Walk, page 1244
Terracotta horses and good luck at Poshina, page 1248
Ruined Hindu and Jain temples in Vijaynagar forest, page 1248

It uses the metre-gauge railway carriages no longer needed in Rajasthan and runs a somewhat whistlestop eight-night tour from Delhi visiting Chittaurgarh, Udaipur, Junagadh, Somnath, Sasan Gir, Diu, Palitana, Ahmedabad and Jaipur. Contact the **Royal Orient**, T011-4305 0608, www.royalorienttrain.com.

Hotels in atmospheric old palaces and converted forts offer the chance to stay off-the-beaten track, but should be booked in advance. Contact a tour operator such as North West Safaris, see page 1244.

When to go

The best time to visit is between October and February. Try and avoid June and July, when even the locals try to escape the crippling heat.

It's dry for most of the year, extremely hot in summer and very cool at night in winter, with some sub-zero temperatures in Ahmedabad. Further south the winter temperatures never fall as far, and the summer temperatures are slightly more moderate. In the far south, around Daman, rainfall is still strongly affected by the southwest

Weather Ahmedabad

January	February	March	April	May	June
29°C 13°C 0mm	31°C 15°C 0mm	36°C 19°C 0mm	40°C 24°C 0mm	41°C 26°C 10mm	39°C 27°C 90mm

July	August	September	October	November	December
34°C 26°C 290mm	35°C 25°C 210mm	34°C 24°C 120mm	36°C 22°C 10mm	33°C 18°C 0mm	30°C 14°C 0mm

monsoon and often exceeds 1500 mm, nearly all between June and October.

However, because Gujarat is marginal to the main rain-bearing winds the total amounts are highly variable, decreasing rapidly northwards. Kachchh, on the borders of the true desert, has recorded less than 25 mm.

Time required

Three to four days for Ahmedabad and nearby sights, and a minimum of one week for Saurashtra, three to four days for Kachchh.

Footprint picks

1 **Ahmedabad**, page 1236
2 **Modhera**, page 1246
3 **Sasan Gir National Park**, page 1272
4 **Craft villages around Bhuj**, page 1289
5 **Kachchh salt plains**, page 1290

Food and drink

Despite an abundance of fish and shellfish, Jain and Hindu orthodoxy has encouraged vegetarianism. The Gujarati diet is chiefly rice, wholemeal *chapati*, a variety of beans and pulses rich in protein, and coconut and pickles; a *thali* would include all these, the meal ending with sweetened yoghurt. The dishes themselves are mild, though somewhat sweeter than those of neighbouring states.

Popular dishes include: *kadhi*, a savoury yoghurt curry with chopped vegetables and a variety of spices; *undhyoo*, a combination of potatoes, sweet potatoes, aubergines (eggplants) and beans cooked in an earthenware pot in the fire; and Surat *paunk*, made with tender kernels of millet, sugar balls, savoury twists and garlic chutney. *Ganthia* or *farsan* (light savoury snacks prepared from chickpea and wheat flour), is a regional speciality. Desserts are very sweet. Surat specializes in *gharis* of butter, dried fruit and thickened milk and rich *halwa*. *Srikhand* is saffron-flavoured yoghurt with fruit and nuts.

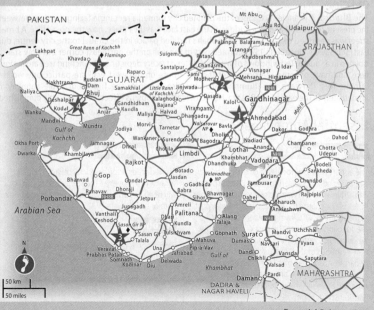

Ahmedabad

★ The congested former capital Ahmedabad spreads out chaotically along both banks of the Sabarmati River. While the modernized west bank holds busy boulevards lined by shopping malls, the Old City remains a maze of narrow winding alleys with carved wooden house fronts and thriving bazars. The outstanding Calico Museum and Mahatma Gandhi's Sabarmati Ashram, as well as the culinary delights, attract visitors to stop for a day or two, though some find the city's noise and pollution off-putting.

Sights   *Colour map 2, C3.*

striking examples of Indian Islamic architecture

In 1411, Ahmad Shah I, the founder of a new dynasty, laid the foundations of the city that was to be his new capital. By 1423 the Jami Masjid, regarded by many as one of the finest mosques in India, was finished. He encouraged others to construct monumental buildings as well. Mahmud I Begarha (ruled 1459-1511) established the third phase of Gujarati provincial architecture, building some of India's most magnificent Islamic monuments.

Old City

The Bhadra The ancient citadel of the planned city formed a rectangle facing the river between the present-day Nehru and Ellis bridges. In the east face was the Palace, now the post office. A broad street was designed to run from Ahmad Shah's fortified palace in the citadel to the city centre, due east. Sidi Sayid's Mosque (c 1570) formed part of the wall on the northeast corner but now stands isolated in a square. Ten windows of wonderful stone tracery depicting a branching tree are famous here, and have become the symbol of the city. Those on the west wall are particularly worthy of note. Teen Darwaza, the triumphal archway (also known as the Tripolia or Triple gateway) is immediately to the east of the Bhadra. Now crowded by shops, its effect is considerably diminished.

Essential Ahmedabad

Finding your feet

The airport is 13 km northeast of town. Regular city buses collect passengers from the airport and arrive at Lal Darwaza, close to many budget hotels. Taxis charge Rs 200-250 from the airport, autos about Rs 100. Train travellers arrive at the Junction Station to the east of the Old City. Rickety old government buses use the Rajpur Gate Terminus to the south, while private buses depart from an array of informal locations around the city. There are plenty of metered taxis and auto-rickshaws to take you to a hotel. See Transport, page 1244.

Getting around

Ahmedabad (population 3.5 million) is far too sprawling to cover all the sights on foot so you will need to struggle with local buses or hire an auto or taxi.

Alcohol

Prohibition is in force. Ask for a liquor permit on arrival in India at the airport tourist counter; getting one in the city is tortuous. Larger hotels may issue 'spot' permits.

Ahmedabad's pols

The old parts of the city are divided into unique, self-contained *pols*, or quarters, fascinating to wander round. Huge wooden doors lead off from narrow lanes into a section of houses with decorative wooden screens and brackets where small communities of people practising a craft or skill once lived. Merchants, weavers, woodworkers, printers and jewellers each had their pol, their houses strung along winding alleys that met in common courtyards and squares. Today, these old quarters are being developed rapidly, with tower blocks rising up from just inside the Old City walls. The guided Heritage Walk (see page 1244) is an excellent way to see some of those that have survived.

Jami Masjid In the Jami Masjid, Ahmedabad has one of the best examples of the second period of Gujarat's provincial architectural development. The essential orientation of the Qibla wall to Mecca meant that the main entrance to the mosque itself had to be in its east wall. The mosque was aligned so that the present Mahatma Gandhi Road passed its north entrance. This is still the point at which you enter by a flight of steps. It is pleasantly quiet and peaceful inside. The vegetable and fruit market near the south entrance is worth visiting for the artistic display of stallholders' wares.

The beauty of the sanctuary is emphasized by the spacious courtyard paved in marble, with a tank in the middle. The façade has a screen of arches flanked by a pillared portico. The two 'shaking minarets', once 26 m high, were destroyed by earthquakes in 1819 and 1957. More than 300 graceful pillars are organized in 15 square bays. The whole rises from a single storey through the two-storey side aisles to the three-storey central aisle. The octagonal lantern, rising through both storeys and covered by a dome, was also strikingly original.

Further east Northeast of the Astodia Gate and a short distance south of the railway station are **Sidi Bashir's Shaking Minarets**, two tall towers connected by a bridge which was once the entrance to the old mosque (now replaced by a modern one). The minarets were believed to shake or vibrate in sympathy as they are cleverly built on a flexible sandstone base to protect against earthquake damage. **Bibi-ki-Masjid** (1454), Gomtipur, southeast of the railway station, also has a shaking minaret.

North of the Bhadra

Around Delhi Gate North of the Old City near Shahpur Gate, the **Mosque of Hasan Muhammad Chishti** (1565) has some of the finest tracery work in Ahmedabad.

There are several Jain temples in the city. The highly decorated white marble **Hathi Singh Temple** (1848) just north of the Delhi Gate, dedicated to Dharamanath, the 15th Jain *Tirthankar*, is maybe the most visited. Along the streets of Ahmedabad, it is common to see Jain *parabdis* (bird sanctuaries).

The early 16th-century **Rani Rupmati Masjid** in Mirzapur district, southwest of Delhi Gate and just south of the **Grand Hotel**, incorporates Hindu and Islamic design. Rupmati was the Sultan's Hindu wife. The carvings in the gallery and the *mihrabs* are particularly attractive. To the southeast is the **Pinjrapol**, or Asylum for Animals.

Calico Museum ① *3 km north of Delhi Gate, www.calicomuseum.com, closed Wed and holidays, free, entry only by somewhat rushed guided tour (minimum group size 15, you may have to wait for others to arrive), tours from 1030-1230 (secular textiles), 1445-1645 (religious textiles, plus superb collection of Chola bronzes), last entry 1515; report at least 15 mins before – only 10 are allowed first come first serve and 15 by organized groups; children under 10 are not permitted, guided tour of the garden is by appointment only.* A part of the Sarabhai Trust, this is one of the finest museums of its kind in the world. It is superbly set in an attractive *haveli* in the botanically interesting Shahi Bagh gardens. Some exhibits date from the 17th century and include rich displays of heavy brocades, fine embroideries, saris, carpets, turbans, maharajahs' costumes and a royal Mughal tent. The religious section exhibits outstanding medieval Jain manuscripts, 14th- to 19th-century Jain icons, *pichhwais*

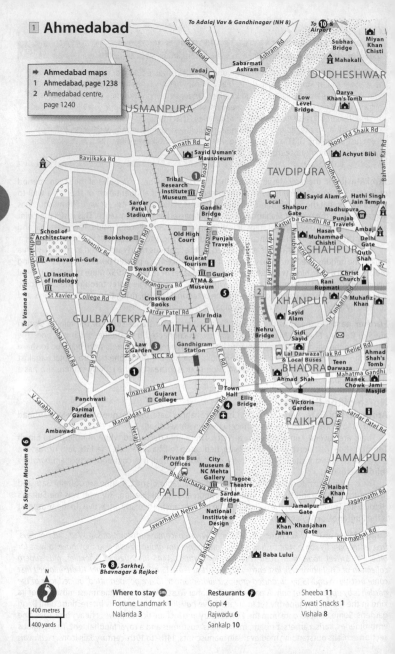

1 Ahmedabad

➡ **Ahmedabad maps**
1 Ahmedabad, page 1238
2 Ahmedabad centre,
   page 1240

To Adalaj Vav & Gandhinagar (NH 8)

To 10 &
Airport

Subhas
Bridge

Miyan
Khan
Chisti

Vadaj Road

Ashram Rd

Mahakali

Vadaj

Sabarmati
Ashram

DUDHESHWAR

USMANPURA

Low
Level
Bridge

Darya
Khan's Tomb

Somnath Rd

Ravjikaka Rd

Noor Md Shaik Rd

Sayid Usman's
Mausoleum

Achyut Bibi

Tribal
Research
Institute
Museum

TAVDIPURA

Sayid Alam

Hathi Singh
Jain Temple

Local

Sardar
Patel
Stadium

Gandhi
Bridge

Shahpur
Gate

Madhupura

Punjab
Travels

Ambaji

Kasturba Gandhi Rd

SHAHPUR

School of
Architecture

Bookshop

Old High
Court

Punjab
Travels

Hasan
Muhammad
Chishti

Delhi
Gate

University Rd

Amdavad-ni-Gufa

Swastik Cross

Gujarat
Tourism

Qutb
Shah

Christ
Church

LD Institute
of Indology

Navarangpura Rd

ATMA &
Museum

Gujarati

Rani
Rupmati

St Xavier's College Rd

Crossword
Books

5

KHANPUR

Muhafiz
Khan

GULBAI TEKRA

Sardar Patel Rd

Air India

Sayid Alam

11

Nehru
Bridge

Sidi
Sayid

Radhakishnan Rd

Law
Garden

3

MITHA KHALI

Gandhigram
Station

Lal Darwaza
& Local Buses

Tilak Rd (Relief Rd)

Ahmad
Shah's
Tomb

NCC Rd

Teen
Darwaza

1

BHADRA

Mahatma Gandhi

Kinariwala Rd

Gujarat
College

Town
Hall

Ahmad Shah

Manek
Chowk

Jami
Masjid

4

Ellis
Bridge

Panchwati

Victoria
Garden

RAIKHAD

Parimal
Garden

Mangaldas Rd

Ambawadi

To Shreyas Museum & 6

Private Bus
Offices

JAMALPUR

City
Museum &
NC Mehta
Gallery

PALDI

Tagore
Theatre

Sardar
Bridge

Haibat
Khan

Jamalpur
Gate

National
Institute of
Design

Jawaharlal Nehru Rd

Khan
Jahan

Khanjahan
Gate

To 8, Sarkhej,
Bhavnagar & Rajkot

Baba Lului

N

400 metres

400 yards

Where to stay 🛏
Fortune Landmark 1
Nalanda 3

Restaurants 🍴
Gopi 4
Rajwadu 6
Sankalp 10

Sheeba 11
Swati Snacks 1
Vishala 8

and *pattachitras*. The secular section contains Indian textiles that featured in trade, historic pieces of tie-dye and embroidery from Gujarat, Punjabi *phulkari* embroideries, *patola* silk saris from Patan, Pashmina shawls from Kashmir, Chamba *rumals* from Himachal and silks from Odisha and South India. It is also open for research. The guides are friendly and charming. Numbers and times are restricted because of lighting considerations and the impact it has on this amazing collection of textiles. **Moti Manor Hotel** is the only place nearby for lunch. Unfortunately you are not allowed to take any bags, including handbags, mobile phones or cameras into the museum and there is only a haphazard system to leave them with security at the gate. Only take essentials.

At **Asarva**, about 1 km northeast of Daryapur Gate, are the *baolis*, which often serve a dual purpose of being a cool, secluded source of water during the summer and a place of religious sanctity.

West of the Sabarmati

Sayid Usman's mausoleum is across the Gandhi bridge, immediately west of Ashram Road. The rauza (circa 1460) is one of the first examples of the Begarha style.

Nearby, the **Tribal Research Institute Museum** ① *Gujarat Vidyapith, Ashram Rd, Mon-Fri 1100-1430 and 1500-1800, Sat 1130-1430*, has recreations of tribal hamlets of Gujarat, as well as weapons, implements, wall art, terracotta figurines and textiles. It makes a good first point of contact for anyone keen to visit tribal areas in the state.

On the west bank of the Sabarmati there is the **Ahmedabad Textile Mill Owners' Association (ATMA)** and museum, both of which were designed by Le Corbusier.

LD Institute of Indology Museum ① *Gujarat University Campus*, contains over 3300 pieces of medieval sculpture, many dating from the 11th to 13th centuries, an outstanding Jain section and archaeological finds. The 'caves' of **Amdavad-ni-Gufa** here were an inspirational venture by the architect Doshi and the artist MF Hussain to display their work. Tribal paintings and other works of art are being added.

Shreyas Museum ① *near Shreyas Railway Crossing, winter Tue-Sun 1030-1730, summer Tue-Sun 0830-1300, closed Diwali, Christmas and school summer holidays, Rs 90 (foreigners)*, has a comprehensive collection of contemporary rural textiles from all over Gujarat: excellent beadwork, embroideries, utensils, religious objects and bullock cart accessories. The children's section upstairs exhibits folk art items, including dance costumes, masks and puppets.

The **City Museum** ① *Tue-Sun 1000-1700, free*, an award-winning design by Le Corbusier with ramps of steps leading up from a pool and its fountains, houses interesting exhibits related to Ahmedabad's history and culture, plus an excellent collection of old and contemporary art, which are superbly exhibited. The **NC Mehta Gallery** here has a vast collection of miniatures from the Rajasthan, Mewar, Mughal, and Kangra schools, among others. The series of 150 paintings on the Gita Govinda theme and a set from the Gujarat Sultanate period are rare exhibits.

Sabarmati Ashram ① *0830-1800, last admission 30 mins before closing, free, Son et Lumière Sun, Wed, Fri (English 2100), closed during monsoons, Rs 5, donations for upkeep gratefully received.* Six kilometres north of the centre is Gandhi's Ashram, Sabarmati Ashram, which was founded in March 1930. It was the starting point for Gandhi's celebrated 385-km Salt March to Dandi in March 1930. He vowed not to return to the ashram until India gained independence. Gandhi and 81 supporters began the march and by the end of it there were 90,000 protesters marching against the unpopular British Salt Tax Laws. Salt manufacture, a government monopoly, was chosen for the protest as it was a commodity every peasant used and could understand. At Dandi beach on 6 April Gandhi went down to the sea and made a small amount of salt, for which he was promptly arrested. In the following months, thousands of Indians followed his example and were arrested by the British. The **Sangrahalaya** includes a library, archives and a picture gallery depicting Gandhi's life in photographs and paintings. Some of the original ashram's work, such as a school for Harijan girls, continues. **Hridaya Kunj**, Gandhi's home for 15 years, containing simple mats, desk, spinning wheel and some personal belongings, overlooks the central prayer corner and the river and remains undisturbed, as does the unfurnished room of his wife, Kasturba.

2 Ahmedabad centre

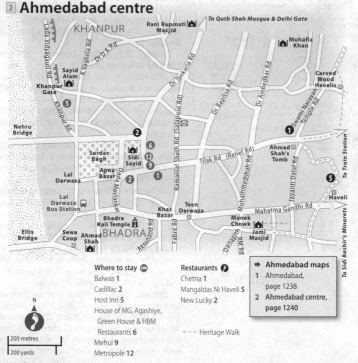

Where to stay 🛏
Balwas **1**
Cadillac **2**
Host Inn **5**
House of MG, Agashiye,
  Green House & HBM
  Restaurants **6**
Mehul **9**
Metropole **12**

Restaurants 🍴
Chetna **1**
Mangaldas Ni Haveli **5**
New Lucky **2**

➡ Ahmedabad maps
1 Ahmedabad,
   page 1238
2 Ahmedabad centre,
   page 1240

- - - Heritage Walk

BACKGROUND
Ahmedabad

Ahmedabad retains a highly distinctive feel born out of a long and continuously evolving social history. It was founded in 1411 by Ahmad Shah I, then king of Gujarat. He made Asaval, an old Hindu town in the south, his seat of power, then expanded it to make it his capital. Almost constantly at war with the neighbouring Rajputs, fortifications were essential. The Bhadra towers and the square bastions of the royal citadel were among the first to be built. The city walls had 12 gates, 139 towers and nearly 6000 battlements.

Although most of the Old City walls have gone, many monuments remain. The provincial Gujarati style flourished from the mid-15th century, and in addition to the religious buildings many of the houses have façades beautifully decorated with woodcarving. The Swami Narayan Temple, Kalipur, Rajani Vaishnav Temple and Harkore Haveli, near Manek Chowk as well as *havelis* on Doshiwadani Pol, illustrate traditional carving skills. Unfortunately, much of the old carving has been dismantled to be sold off to collectors.

The 'new' city, on the west bank, has the site of Mahatma Gandhi's famous Sabarmati Ashram from where he began his historic Salt March in protest against the Salt Law in 1915. Recent developments in urban design have contributed to the city's architectural tradition. Modern Ahmedabad has several showpieces designed by famous architects, among them Le Corbusier, Louis Kahn, Doshi and Correa. The School of Architecture, the National Institute of Design and the Indian Institute of Management (IIM) are national centres of learning.

With a long tradition in craftsmanship under Gujarati Sultans and Mughal Viceroys, Ahmedabad was once one of the most brilliant Indian cities. Its jewellers and goldsmiths are still renowned today; its copper and brassworkers craft very fine screens; and carpenters produce fine *shisham* wood articles. There are skilled stone masons, lacquer artists, ivory and bone carvers, hand-block printers and embroiderers producing exquisite pieces with beads and mirrors.

Trips from Ahmedabad

Vishala, 5 km away from Ahmedabad, is a purpose-built collection of traditional Gujarati village huts serving *thalis* at lunch and dinner, accompanied by music and traditional dancing. It's especially appealing in the evening when it's lit entirely by lanterns.

Indroda Village Deer Park, next to Sarita Udyan by Sabarmati River, has an interesting reptile collection and well-marked nature trails through forests where you may spot nilgai, porcupine, jackal, crested honey buzzard and paradise fly-catcher, among others. There is also a campsite here.

Adalaj is the hamlet where, in a garden setting, one of the finest step wells in India can be found. The Vav (or *baoli*) shows a combination of Hindu, Muslim and Buddhist styles. A flight of steps descends over 30 m to the water. It has four floors, each cooler than the one above. Ornately carved pillars, niches and cross beams create large octagonal landings (now inaccessible) that served as resting places. Remains of the bullock ramp used for drawing water are still visible. Queen Rupabai is believed to have had it built to provide the traveller with a cool and pleasant refuge from the summer heat. A visit is highly recommended. It is 17 km north of Ahmedabad near the Gandhinagar crossroads; autos charge Rs 125-150 return or take the No 85 city bus from Lal Darwaza to the end, then a shared rickshaw to Adalaj, Rs 5, from where the Vav is a 1-km walk.

Tourist information

Gujarat Tourist Office (TCGL)
HK House, opposite Bata, Ashram Rd, T079-2658 9172, www.gujarattourism.com. Mon-Sat, closed Sun and 2nd and 4th Sat each month. Also at the airport and the railway station.

MP Tourist Office
T079-2646 2977.

Rajasthan Tourist Office
Divya Aptmt, near Mithakali Underbridge, off Ashram Rd, T079-2646 9580.

Where to stay

All the chain hotels Radisson Blu, Marriot Courtyard and Hyatt are in Ahmedabad.

$$$$ House of MG
Opposite Sidi Sayid Mosque, Lal Darwaza, T079-2550 6946, www.houseof mg.com.
One of the most atmospheric places you can lay your hat in India. 12 vast, beautifully decorated rooms in a centrally located heritage hotel, surrounded by familial memorabilia, it is like stepping into another time. There's a superb indoor pool, 2 excellent restaurants (see Restaurants, below) and friendly, professional staff. It also offers great audio-based and guided walking tours of the Old City; check out the Night Heritage Walk in particular. A far too-tempting shop is in the lobby. A real gem. Highly recommended.

$$$ Armoise
Besides Havmor, off MG Road, T079-2640 7772, www.amirosehotel.com.
New popular hotel with all mod cons. Good for families and business travellers alike, with a great restaurant too.

$$$ Divans Bungalow
Opposite Gaikwad Haveli, MB Kadri Marg, T079-2535 5428, www.neemranacom.
Great renovation of 19th-century building by Neemrana. Just 8 lovingly restored rooms, hidden garden, fountains and a large veranda. Each room is named after a member of the Kadri family.

$$$ Fortune Landmark
Ashram Rd, T079-3988 4444, www.fortunelandmark.com.
One of the best but on busy main road, this massive hotel has 96 varied rooms; it's worth upgrading to a suite from a standard as you get more for your rupee. Good restaurants (the buffet breakfast sets you up for the day), health club, jacuzzi and pool.

$$$-$$ Nalanda
Mithakhali 6 Rd, T079-2646 8899, www.hotelnalanda.in.
44 clean but run-of-the-mill rooms (standard rooms are pretty small); but in a good location and with an excellent restaurant. Free airport transfer.

$$ Host Inn
Opposite Le Meridien, Khanpur, T079-3022 6555, www.hotelhostinn.com.
Clean a/c rooms in a well-run hotel, unusual deluxe rooms have beds on floor, and hot water can be problematic. Smart restaurant, and there's a friendly and obliging manager, but staff are a little less so.

$ Balwas
6751 Relief Rd, near Electricity House, T079-2550 7135.
After a facelift, this is the best value of the budget places, with 26 clean rooms, 6 small at the rear (with a side entrance), a decent but crowded restaurant attached. In a noisy area, with 24-hr checkout.

$ Cadilac
Opposite Electricity House, Lal Darwaza, T079-2550 7558.
Characterful but dilapidated building with small and basic rooms. Cheap as chapati with and without bath, and a helpful travel desk.

$ Mehul
Hanuman Lane, off Relief Rd opposite Electricity House, T079-2550 6525.
Good value clean rooms (small singles) some a/c, good room service. Quieter than nearby hotels thanks to its alleyway location and slightly better than its older brother hotel **Metropole** next door (T029-2550 7988).

Restaurants

Thalis are around Rs 50; Kathiawadi has more chilli and garlic, while Gujarati is sweetened with sugar and jaggery.

There are some great snacks to be had; check out **Swati Snacks** and **Green House**.

$$$ Agashiye
House of MG (see Where to stay, above).
Attractive Gujarati *thali* restaurant on the terrace of a 1920s heritage building. Unique atmosphere, local music, Gujarati *thalis* topped off with hand-churned ice cream flavoured by the fruits of the season. Beautiful decor and setting, although the street noise does bubble up. Recommended.

$$ Barbecue Nation
Shivalik III, Drive-In Rd.
Chain restaurant popular for kebabs and a 'live grill' at your table. Deservedly popular.

$$ Green House
House of MG, see Where to stay, above.
Even if you don't get to stay at House of MG, both restaurants are exceptional. The downstairs courtyard café serves up a delicious range of traditional Gujarati snacks like patra leaves and potato patties with coconut, or try some spicier *Parsi dhansak*. Their saffron anise *kulfi* is one of the best-selling ice creams on the menu and their house *sharbat* of coconut water and ginger is delicious. Take a minute to browse the lobby for all the memorabilia and photographs before winding up in their beautiful shop. Highly recommended.

$$ Ikobo
Next to Doordarshan Kendra, Drive-in Rd.
Popular with the well-heeled of Ahmedabad and sating their taste for kebabs, Ikobo serves up a wide range of meat and veg sizzlers and *shashlik* dishes.

$$ Mangaldas Ni Haveli
Lakha Patel ni Pol; contact House of MG (see Where to stay, above) for more details.
Stunningly restored wooden *haveli* in the heart of the labyrinthine old city boasts a rooftop café which serves up great breakfasts and afternoon teas, albeit at the top of a pretty rickety staircase. Lots of character. Guided walks start here, including the acclaimed Night Heritage Walk.

$$ Rajwadu
Jivraj Park.
Rural theme restaurant. Rajasthani/Gujarati dinner, delightful open-air garden setting, water courses, folk entertainment, large meals in brass/copper vessels and refills galore. It looks like a Bollywood film set. It's not as authentic as **Vishalla** but it's more comfortable and accessible.

$$ Sheeba
Opposite telephone exchange, Navrangpura.
International, a/c, excellent North Indian (try fish, paneer or chicken *tikkas*), friendly. Continental and Chinese fast-food counter (to avoid excess spices, request when ordering). Highly recommended.

$$ Swati Snacks
Thakorbhai Hall, Law Garden.
Specializing in Gujarati snacks, this slick diner offers up great dishes like *panaki*, a rice pancake cooked between banana leaf and *nariyal kothir tikki* stuffed potato patties. Recommended.

$$ Vishala
5 km southwest of centre.
Village themed restaurant, where you sit cross-legged at low tables (low stools also provided), eat proper Gujarati food off green leaves or metal *thalis*, and drink from clay tumblers. Hospitable, friendly staff, interesting traditional dancing after dinner, touristy in an Indian way and good fun. Meals around Rs 200 with deluxe dinners at Rs 450.

$ Chetna
Krishna Cinema, Relief Rd.
Unlimited Gujarati *thalis* so only if you like your food full power *mirchi* (spicy).

$ La Bella
Behind Preyas High School, Khanpur, Badra.
Serving up delicious Goan specialities so expect fish curry, prawn masala and lots of mutton dishes. Remember Goan food is renowned for its spice levels.

$ New Lucky
Lal Darwaza.
Cheap and cheerful chai and snacks counter, popular for early morning 'bun-butter', with a slightly more elaborate South Indian restaurant attached. The best cheap option in the area.

$ Sankalp
CG Rd.
South Indian, rooftop terrace garden with fountain, good *dosas* and an exceptional range of chutneys. Delicious.

Festivals

14-15 Jan Makar Sankranti marks the end of winter. It is celebrated with kite flying by people of all ages, accompanied by colourful street markets and festivities. Kites come in all colours, shapes and sizes, the best varieties reputedly being available in Manek Chowk and Tankshala, Kalupur. The flying continues after sunset, when the kites are lit with candles.

Sep/Oct Navratri, honouring Goddess Amba (*Shakti*), has special significance here and at Vadodara. 9 days of music and traditional *Garba Ras* dancing. The custom of women balancing clay pots while they dance is still practised.

Shopping

Shops usually open from 0900-1900, most close on Sun. **Manek Chowk** is the main bazar, while **CG Rd** is the centre for malls, brand outlets and upmarket clothing shops. Other centres are **Relief Rd**, **Ashram Rd**, **Lal Darwaza** and **Kapasia Bazar**. Go to the huge **Sunday Market**, on the river bank at Ellis Bridge, in the morning to pick up 'antiques', handicrafts and second-hand books.

Books
Crossword, *B6 Sri Krishna Centre, Mithakhali 6 Rds, T079-2643 0238*. A/c, extensive selection of books, magazines CDs, art supplies and accessories. There is also a branch of **Café Coffee Day** on site.
Mapin, *Darpana Academy, Usmanpura, Ashram Rd*. Specializes in Indian arts. Beautiful selection of greetings cards.

Handicrafts
There's a fantastic shop of art and handicrafts at House of MG (see Where to stay, above). Good bargains at **Satellite Rd** and Law Garden (after 1600), where Kachchhi and Saurashtrian artisans sell embroideries, block prints and handicrafts: appliqué bedspreads, wall hangings, etc, but bargain hard. Gujarat's famous embroideries, *bandhani* and block prints are sold at **Rani-no-Haziro** and **Dalgarwad** near Manek Chowk in the walled city. There are *Khadi Bhandars* and Handloom Houses for textiles on Ashram Rd, between Gandhi Ashram and Natraj Theatre. **Revdi Bazar** and **Sindhi Market** have semi-wholesale textile shops. CG Rd is the upmarket shopping area.
Bhandej, *next to Crossword Bookshop, T079-2642 2181*. Upmarket salon selling stunning fabrics and beautiful locally made clothes.
Bhujodi, *Mithakhali Rd, T079-2640 0967*. Good ethnic-styled clothing and handicrafts.

Garvi and **Gurjari**, *Ashram Rd. Govt. Open 1030-1400, 1500-1900*. Embroidered dresses, block-printed bedspreads, lacquered furniture, etc, well displayed.
Sewa, *above Mirch Masala restaurant, Swastik Crossroads, CG Rd*. A commendable women's co-op producing very fine shadow embroidery and clothes.

What to do

Tour operators
Ahmedabad Municipal Transport Service, *Lal Darwaza, T079-25339 1881*. Offer several routes around the city including key sites like the Sidi Sayid mosque, Gandhi Ashram and ISKCON temple. Rs 125.
Heritage Walking Tours, *0800-1030, Rs 50*. Excellent tour with qualified architects/conservationists; starts at Swaminarayan temple, Relief Rd, Kalupur, of *havelis, pols*, artisans' workshops, etc. Arranged by AMC T079-2539 1811.
House of MG Heritage Walks, *House of MG hotel, www.houseofmg.com*. Fantastic D* Tours audio guided walks around the city armed with an MP3 player. They also run an amazing Night Heritage Walk which is guided by a local and offers fantastic insight into the city. It's like being let into a secret.
North West Safaries, *91/92 Kamdhenu Complex, opposite Sahajanand College, Ambawati, T079-2630 8031, www.northwestsafaries.com*. Experienced local company, highly recommended for hotel booking, car hire and a great insight into Gujarat. They help you explore the wildlife, architecture and handicrafts.

Transport

Air Many international carriers fly into Ahmedabad and you can fly to most key cities within India from here. The following airlines serve the city, but check a third-party website such as www.cleartrip.com or www.makemytrip.com for the latest fares and schedules. **Air India**, T079-2550 5198/99. Other main airlines are **Indigo** T079-2285 8106 and **Jet Airways** T079-3989 3333.

Local bus City service available from main bus station, Lal Darwaza, railway station and all major points in the city.

Long distance bus Central Bus Station, Geeta Mandir, T079-2532 3517; reservations 0700-1900. Advance booking for night services 1500-2300, luxury coach services 1030-1800. Arrive early to find your bus. **ST buses** to

Bhavnagar 4-5 hrs, **Mehsana** (2 hrs on good new road), **Mumbai** (492 km, 11 hrs), **Palitana** 217 km, **Porbandar** 394 km, **Rajkot** 216 km, **Sasan Gir** 385 km, **Surat** 120 km, and **Vadodara** 113 km. **Udaipur** 287 km. Private coaches offering sleeper seating to major towns in Gujarat and Rajasthan leave from around the **ST Bus Stand** and various suburban stands, often leaving at night. Ticket offices and departure points are usually close together. Agencies around ST stand may overcharge for a seat 'booking' then simply flag down the first bus that comes past; cheaper to wait outside stand (ask **Punjab Travels**, from K Gandhi Rd, Delhi Darwaza, and Embassy Market, Ashram Rd, T079-2657 9999). **Shrinath**, Shahibaug Rd, T079-2562 5351, for **Udaipur**.

Rickshaw Drivers readily use meters, which for now give an accurate reading. Station to Khanpur Rd/Sidi Sayid area around Rs 30.

Taxi Cars and 4WDs for hire from **North West Safaries**, see What to do, above, for contact details; **Ahmedabad Taxi Services**, T079-6666 8888.

Train Always confirm from which station train departs. Ahmedabad Junction is on a broad gauge line to Mumbai (Platforms 1-4, near the main entrance) and a metre gauge line to Delhi (Platforms 7-12). Platforms 5 and 6 serve both, according to demand. A small number of trains use Gandhigram station on west bank. Computerized reservations at both stations: 1st class 0800-1530, 2nd class 0800-1430, 1500-2000, T135, enquiry T131. Last-minute berths can also be booked for some trains at a temporary counter on the platform; premium charged. The following leave from Junction unless stated.

Ajmer and Jaipur: *Ahmedabad Haridwar Mail 19105*, 10½ hrs (13 ½ to Jaipur). **Bengaluru (Bangalore)**: *Ahmedabad Bangalore Exp 16501*, 13¾ hrs. **Bhavnagar**: *Bhavnagar Exp 12971*, 5½ hrs. **Chennai**: *Navjivan Exp 12655*, 0630, 22¾ hrs. **Delhi (OD)**: *Ashram Exp 12915*, 16½ hrs. **Kolkata (H)**: *Howrah Exp 12833*, 20 hrs. **Jamnagar**: *Saurashtra Exp 19215*, 7½ hrs. (all stops at **Rajkot**, 2 hrs before Jamnagar). **Jodhpur**: *Ranakpur Exp 14708*, 10 hrs (continues to **Bikaner**, 6 hrs). **Junagadh**: *Veraval Exp 11464*, 8 hrs; **Mumbai Central**: *Shatabdi Exp 12010*, not Sun, 7¼ hrs; *Gujarat Mail 12902*, 8¾ hrs (stops at Vadodra after 2hrs). **Porbandar**: *Mumbai Porbandar Saurashtra Exp 19215*, 10½ hrs. **Udaipur City**: *DSR Express 19944*, 9 hrs.

Around
Ahmedabad

Architecture buffs will find much to occupy them around the capital, from Modhera's ancient Sun Temple and the fabulous step well in Patan to the more modern, esoteric charms of Le Corbusier's Gandhinagar. The hills that rise up toward the Rajasthan border hide a number of wildlife sanctuaries and small palace hotels, while a side trip to the south could take in the Nalsarovar Bird Sanctuary and the desolate remains of Lothal, one of the world's oldest ports.

North of Ahmedabad

a Le Corbusier-designed city and a magnificent ruined Hindu temple

The fertile irrigated land immediately north of Ahmedabad becomes increasingly arid towards Rajasthan. When approaching Mehsana there are signs of the growing economy, including natural gas, fertilizers, milk products and rapeseed oil processing.

Gandhinagar *Colour map 2, C3.*
When Bombay state was divided along linguistic lines into Maharashtra and Gujarat in 1960, a new capital city was planned for Gujarat named after Mahatma Gandhi. As with Chandigarh, Le Corbusier was instrumental in the design of Gandhinagar (population 195,900). The 30 residential sectors around the central government complex are similarly impersonal. Construction began in 1965 and the Secretariat was completed in 1970. Located 23 km north of Ahmedabad, Gandhinagar – with multiplex theatre complexes and parks – has become a popular place for day trippers from Ahmedabad.

Akshardham ① *Sector 20, 0930-1930, closed on Mon, donations, no cameras or electronic devices,* is a temple with a cultural complex and entertainment park and is run by volunteers. Though not on the same scale as its counterpart in Delhi, the pink sandstone main building, floodlit at dusk, exhibits similar architectural influences. It houses a 2-m-high gold leaf idol and some relics of Sri Swaminarayan, who established the headquarters of his 19th-century Vedic revivalist movement in the Gujarati town of Loj. The three exhibition halls feature a variety of informative sound and light presentations relating to Sri Swaminarayan, the *Vedas* and the Hindu epics. Sahajanabad Vun, the garden for meditation, is impressive and has 'singing fountains' and a restaurant. Be respectful with your dress and no bags allowed.

★ Modhera *Colour map 2, C2.*
Sunrise-sunset, foreigners Rs 100, video camera Rs 25. A Classical Dance Festival is held on the 3rd weekend in Jan.

Virtually a deserted hamlet 25 km west of Mehsana, Modhera has the remains of one of the finest Hindu temples in Gujarat. Quite off the beaten track, it retains a great deal of its atmosphere and charm. Visit early in the day as it get busy. The partially ruined **Surya** (Sun) **Temple** (1026), built during the reign of Bhimdev I and consecrated in 1026-1027, two centuries before the Sun Temple at Konark, is a product of the great Solanki period (eighth-13th centuries). Despite the temple's partial destruction by subsequent earthquakes that may have accounted for the collapse of its tower, it remains an outstanding monument, set against the backdrop of a barren landscape. Superb carvings of goddesses, birds, beasts and blossoms decorate the remaining pillars. Over the last 20 years the complex has undergone major restoration by the Archaeological Survey of India that is continuing as funds permit. Unlike the temple at Konark, the main temple stands well above the surrounding land, raised by a high brick terrace faced with stone.

A rectangular *kund* (pool), now dry, over 50 m long and 20 m wide, with flights of steps and subsidiary shrines, faces the front of the temple. A remarkable structure, despite the damage caused by weathering, it is still possible to gain an impression of the excellence of the carving. On the west side of the tank a steep flight of steps leads up to the main entrance of the east *mandapa* through a beautifully carved *torana*, of which only the pillars now remain. The **sabha mandapa**, a pillared hall, is 15 sq m. Note the cusped arches which became such a striking feature of Mughal buildings 600 years later. The corbelled roof of this entry hall, which has been reconstructed, is a low stepped pyramid. Beautiful columns and magnificent carvings decorate the hall. The western part of the oblong temple contains the raised **inner sanctuary**. The upper storeys have been completely destroyed, though it clearly consisted of a low pyramidal roof in front of the tall *sikhara* (tower) over the sanctuary itself. Surya's image in the sanctuary (now missing) was once illuminated by the first rays of the rising sun at each solar equinox (proof of the mathematical and astronomical knowledge of the designers). Images of Surya and Agni are among the more well-preserved carvings on the external walls which also contain some erotic scenes. The interior walls were plain other than for niches to house images of Surya.

Patan

Thirty-five kilometres north of Modhera and little visited, Patan has more than 100 beautifully carved Jain temples and many attractive traditionally carved wooden houses. It remains a centre for fine textiles, particularly silk *patola* saris produced by the characteristic *ikat* technique which involves tie-dyeing

Tip...
To see the beautiful *patola* saris being produced, visit the Salvi brothers' workshop on Patolawala Street, T02766-232274, www.patanpatola.com.

the warp threads before weaving to create designs on the finished fabrics. Only three extended families (at Salvivad and Fatipal Gate) can be seen at work on the highly prized double *ikat* weaving where both the warp and the weft threads are tie-dyed before being set on traditional looms – only to be found in Indonesia and Japan outside India. It takes three to six months to weave a sari, hence each piece sells for at least Rs 120,000; samples are Rs 2000.

The spectacular **Rani ki Vav** (11th century) ⊕ *sunrise-sunset, Rs 100 foreigners; video camera Rs 25, 4 km from Patan Bus Stand*, named after a Solanki queen, is one of the largest step wells in India with superb carvings on seven storeys. Flights of steps lead down to the water, lined by string courses of sculptured voluptuous women, Vishnu avatars and goddesses. The **Sahasralinga Talao**, 4.5 km from Patan Bus Stand, is a cluster of Solanki period (11th-12th century) shrines facing a small lake. Excavations are in progress.

Vadnagar

The town, 40 km northeast of Mehsana, has the finest example of the *torana* arches that characterize North Gujarat. Beautiful sculptures decorate two of the original four 12th-century arched gateways on *kirti stambha* pillars. The Solanki period city gates are beautifully sculpted, the best being near the lake. The impressive 17th-century **Haktesvar temple**, the most important Siva temple in Gujarat, has fine carvings, erotic sculpture and a silver shrine. Tana-Riri, two poetess-singers from Vadnagar, are said to have saved Tansen from the burning effects of the *Deepak Raga* (Song of Fire) by singing the *Maldaar Raga* (Song of Rain). Akbar invited the sisters to sing in his court, but rather than refuse to sing for a Muslim emperor (which was against their custom) they immolated themselves. Their shrine can be seen at Vadnagar.

Taranga

Named after Tara Devi, Taranga, 55 km northeast of Mehsana by bus, has a wonderful complex of well-preserved, if somewhat over-restored, 12th-century Jain temples surrounded by spectacular hills. The large central sandstone temple to Adinatha is beautifully carved with sensual dancing figures, Hindu deities and Jain *Tirthankaras*. Inside is a bejewelled central statue carved out of a single piece of alabaster. There is a scenic trek from the main Adinath temple, passing some dramatic rock formations, to the hilltop Shilp Temple where one of the Jain saints meditated. Panthers have been sighted near the temple complex.

Ambaji

Close to the Rajasthan border, en route to Mount Abu, Ambaji is known for its marble mines. You can see marble artisans at work at this temple town (and at Khedbrahma nearby) where **Bhadra Purnima fair** is held, with processions of flag bearing pilgrims followed by musicians and dancers. A picturesque ropeway goes to Gabbar hill, a holy pilgrimage for Hindus (Rs 40). Ahmedabad-Mount Abu buses stop at Ambaji.

The five 11th- and 12th-century Jain temples just east of Ambaji at **Kumbhariya** ① *0630-1930, Aarti worship 0900-0930 and 1900, tea canteen, very cheap thalis*, are worth visiting for their exquisite marble carvings. Be sure to see the second temple; the main one has been largely rebuilt. Catch a jeep from Ambaji Bus Stand.

Danta

En route from Taranga to Ambaji, the princely state of Danta was known for its cavalry. It is dominated by the medieval **Parmara Rajput fort**. The jungles and rocky hills harbour panther, nilgai and four-horned antelope, and there is extensive birdlife. To explore, bicycles can be hired from in the village.

Poshina

The small 15th-century Poshina fort, 45 km south of Abu Road, stands at the confluence of two holy rivers (Sai and Panhari) with views over the hills. It was the capital of the North Gujarat branch of Vaghela Rajputs. There are ancient Jain and Siva temples nearby as well as tribal villages where you can watch arrow making, potters, basketwork and silversmiths. You will find collections of up to 2000 terracotta horses here – the story goes that you make a wish and then if that wish comes true, you make an offering of one or many horses (depending on the size of the wish) and a *puja*. It's quite magical. The area is home to Bhils, colourful Garasias and Rabaris who herd camels, cattle and goats. The busy and interesting **market** centre is well worth stopping at; the last stretch of the approach road is very poor. Ahmedabad-Ambaji buses stop at Kheroj from where it is possible to get shared jeeps to Poshina (12 km).

Chitra Vichitra Fair is held a fortnight after *Holi* at **Gunbakhari**, 8 km away. It is attended by Bhils, Garasias and Rabaris (some of whom are now abandoning their traditional *dhotis* and turbans). The fair is very colourful with much revelry, dancing and singing, food stalls etc. Matchmaking is often followed by elopements. **Florican Tours** ① *T079-2550 6590*, can arrange visits to the fair. Try staying in a tent (contact **Gujarat Tourism**) during the fair. Delicious flavoured *lassi* is available near the village entrance but ask for it be prepared with your own filtered or mineral water.

Vijaynagar

Stunning ruined Hindu and Jain temples hide away in an enchanting forest in Vijaynagar. Once part of a kingdom ruled by the Rathod Rajputs of Marwar, Vijaynagar is home to beautiful groups of temples. In some places, it feels as if the forest has won as it grows through the

Tip...

Come at sunset for evening prayers at the one active temple dedicated to Shiva inside the forest; it's magical.

temples, but a lot of work has gone into clearing the areas around the temples and there are even paved pathways and signboards. It's incredibly atmospheric, especially late afternoon.

Palanpur and Balaram

The *maqbara* with fine mausolea in the old Nawabi capital of **Palanpur** stands rather neglected. The palace is now the court; look in to see the fabulous ceiling paintings and sandalwood carvings. The 1915 Kirti Stambha has the 700-year-long history of the Nawabs of Palanpur inscribed on it. Nearby **Balaram** has one of the best-kept palace hotels in Gujarat, 3 km off the highway and 14 km north of Palanpur. About 20 km from there, the **Jessore Bear Sanctuary** in the Aravallis has sloth bear (occasionally spotted), panther, nilgai, sambhar, four-horned antelope etc, but these are best seen by climbing Jessore hill.

Where to stay

Gandhinagar

$$$ Fortune Inn Haveli
Sector 11, opposite Sachivalaya, T079-3988 4422, www.fortune hotels.in.
84 below-par rooms, restaurants, exchange, car hire, free airport transfer and Wi-Fi.

$ Youth Hostel
Sector 16, T079-2322 2364.
An excellent place to stay with 2 rooms and 42 beds in 6-bed and 8-bed dorms. No reservations.

Mehsana
Good access to Modhera for the Sun Temple.

$$$-$$ Water World Resort
25 mins' drive out of town, T02762-282351, www.waterworld resort.com.
A/c cottages, modern, Mughal garden with a/c 'royal tents', vegetarian restaurant, wave pool, sports complex, lake.

$ Natraj
1 km from bus stand, T02762-253 301.
12 rooms (dorms to a/c with bath), good veggie restaurant.

Patan

$$-$ Shakar Garden
Opposite sub Station, Tirupati Township, T02766-232 204.
A cheap and cheerful option though not very inspiring; good for a quick visit.

Danta

$$$-$$ Bhavani Villa
On a hilltop, T02749-278705, www.bhavanivilladanta.com.
Very welcoming hotel with 4 modern a/c rooms facing the hills, 1 non-a/c in a colonial period mansion. Delicious Rajput meals and friendly hosts; it's like staying with a family. Great for nature lovers, game drives, horse riding (Rs 400 per hr) and excellent horse safaris (Rs 5000 per person). Ask for a tour of their farm; it's set in lovely scenery. Recommended.

Poshina

$$$ Darbargadh (Heritage Hotel)
Fort complex, reservations through Florican Tours, T079-2550 6590.
Set in a 17th-century wing of the fort with pleasant open courtyards and hill views and old-world charm. It has now been renovated with antiques, Rajasthani miniatures and rare Tanjore paintings. There are 15 comfortable, air-cooled rooms, spicy Indian meals and camel rides. The friendly owner is knowledgeable about local tribes and crafts, and there are good village safaris and folk entertainment. Your host is the Secretary of the Heritage Hotels Association Gujarat. Recommended.

Vijaynagar

$$$-$$ Vijay Villas (Heritage Hotel)
T07926 747690, www.vijayvilasvijaynagar.com.
It's a home away from home in this heritage-style property. Attractive rooms are set around a little courtyard and there's great family food on offer. It's beautifully located near the polo forest. The forest at Vijaynagar is magical.

Balaram

$$ Balaram Palace Resort
Chitrasani, T079-2657 6388 (Ahmedabad), www.balarampalace.com.
This is in a splendid riverside location surrounded by hills but the resort itself is a little bit soulless. Well-restored 1930s palace, with 17 a/c rooms (the interiors may be too modern and characterless for some), 4 colonial rooms with old fireplaces (some windowless) and rooms upstairs with views, Nawab Suite has huge arched windows. There are excellent terrace restaurants, a lovely formal Nawabi garden, a pool fed by a natural cascading spring, good gym and bike hire.

Restaurants

Gandhinagar
Sector 21 has street vendors offering good snacks. Ask for the Bhatiar couple who make *bajra ka rotla* (millet *chapatis*) and chicken curry, meat samosas and dahl in a little shack, not too far from Akshardham. Torana in Sector 28 has good snacks and Punjabi food.

$ **Premawati**
Akshardham Complex.
Gujarati veg food, lime tea, delicious ice cream.

Transport

Gandhinagar
Train and buses to **Ahmedabad** take 1 hr.
ST Bus Station, Sector 11.

Mehsana
Buses from **ST Bus Stand** to **Ahmedabad** on a good new road (2 hrs); **Modhera**, 45 mins, Rs 8,

last return from Modhera 1730; **Patan**, 1¼ hrs. Trains bound for Rajasthan and Delhi from Ahmedabad stop at Mehsana.

Patan
Hourly to **Ahmedabad**, 3 hrs, Rs 60-70, and every 30 mins to **Modhera**, 1 hr, Rs 15.

Palanpur
Ahmedabad and Delhi trains stop here. Direct buses go to **Mount Abu**; **Ambaji** (also share jeeps, Rs 20); **Poshina** through attractive countryside and tribal areas, 1200 (1 hr), Rs 7.

South of Ahmedabad

heritage sites and a notable bird sanctuary

Vautha
The **Vautha Mela**, starting at Kartik Purnima in November, is held at the confluence of the Sabarmati and Vatrak rivers, some 46 km south of Ahmedabad. Less colourful than Pushkar fair it is also far less touristy. About 4000 donkeys, painted in vivid colours, and over 2000 camels are traded. There is a great atmosphere on the river banks early in the morning, with haggling over animals and craft sales. **Gujarat Tourism** provides tents and catering.

Nalsarovar Bird Sanctuary
This sanctuary, 65 km southwest of Ahmedabad, is worth visiting for its waterbirds, which include migratory ducks, flamingos and geese. The lake and the Surendranagar Reservoirs were declared a bird sanctuary in 1969. Uniquely in Saurashtra, Nalsarovar is surrounded by reed beds and marshes though the lake often dries out before the rains. Bharwad and Jat herdsmen and their water buffaloes live on the reed islands; you can get hot buttered millet chapatis and chutney with sweet tea or *lassi* from some shacks. Padhar fisherfolk who live around the lake are good artisans. **Forest Dept Bungalows** have two or three simple rooms and views of lake. The best time to visit is between November and February.

Lothal 'Mound of the dead'
Sat-Thu 1000-1700, Rs 100 for foreigners. There's no shade or proper drinks outlet so carry bottled water.

Southeast of Mohenjo Daro, 720 km as the crow flies, Lothal has some of the most substantial remains of the Harappan culture in India dating from circa 2500-1700 BC. Once a port sandwiched between the Sabarmati River and the Bhogavo River, it is now 10 km inland from the Gulf of Khambhat on a flat, often desolate-looking plain. Thorn scrub and parched soils surround the site and even in February a hot desiccating wind picks up flurries of dust. Lothal's location and function as a port have led most authorities to argue that it was settled by Harappan trading communities who came by sea from the mouths of the Indus. Others suggest that the traders came by an overland route. The site is surrounded by a mud-brick embankment 300 m north–south and 400 m east–west. Unlike the defensive walls at Harappa and Mohenjo Daro, the wall at Lothal enclosed the workers' area as well as the citadel. The presence of a dry dock and a warehouse further distinguish it from other major Harappan sites. Some visitors find that the recent restoration work has made the walls look too modern.

The massive excavated **dry dock** runs along the east wall of the city. A 12-m-wide gap in the north side is believed to have been the entrance by which boats came into the dock, while a spillway over the south wall allowed excess water to overflow. The city wall at this point may have been a wharf for unloading. Excavations of the warehouse suggest that trade was the basis of Lothal's existence. The building at the southwest corner of the wharf had a high platform made of cubical mud-brick blocks, the gaps between them allowing ventilation. Over 65 Indus Valley seals discovered here show pictures of packing material, bamboo or rope, suggestive of trade; one from Bahrain is evidence of overseas trade. Excavations show a **planned city** in a grid pattern, with an underground drainage system, wells and brick houses with baths and fireplaces. The raised brick platform to the southeast may have been a kiln where seals and plaques were baked. Objects found include painted pottery, terracotta toys, ivory, shell, semi-precious stone items, bangles and necklaces made of tiny gold beads. Rice and millet were clearly in use, and there is evidence that horses had been domesticated. The nearby cemetery had large funerary vessels indicating pit burials.

Wadhwan

Northwest of Limbdi, Wadhwan was a princely state of the Jhalas, a Rajput clan. The fortified old township has plenty of interesting architecture including two old step wells with attractive carvings and some fine 11th- to 16th-century temples. It is an ideal place to watch and shop for *bandhani*, wood and stone carving, silverwork and textiles.

The opulent 19th-century **Raj Mahal** (*Bal Vilas*) occupied by the royal family has a grand Durbar hall with chandeliers, frescoes, carved furniture, crystal and velvet curtains, Sheesh Mahal library and billiard room. The vast landscaped gardens contain lily ponds and fountains. Maharajah Chaitanya Dev is a keen restorer of classic cars and has a vintage car collection.

Listings South of Ahmedabad

Where to stay

$$$-$$ Balasinore Garden Palace
45 km from Kheda, T02690-262786.
One of few Nawab-family-run heritage hotels, set in an early 20th-century building with 5 refurbished rooms, delicious Mughlai meals, pleasant orchard garden and tours of the dinosaur site and tribal villages.

Transport

Nalsarovar Bird Sanctuary
Direct bus from **Ahmedabad** (0700, 1500) 2 hrs.

Lothal

Trains from Ahmedabad and Bhavnagar go to Lothal–Burkhi, close to Lothal. Luxury and state buses can drop you at **Gundi** railway crossing; from there *chhakras* (motorbike-rickshaw) charge Rs 5 for the drop to Lothal. Get back on the highway to get a bus to **Ahmedabad** or **Bhavnagar**. It can be a long hard day, with little to see. Taxis (Rs 1000-1200) or motorbikes make it easier: travelling from Ahmedabad, Lothal is 7 km (awful road) from a level crossing on the SH1 near **Bagodra**, at the junction with NH8A. Coming from Bhavnagar, follow the SH1 for 127 km via Vallabhipur and Barwala.

Vadodara
& the old forts

The route south from Ahmedabad crosses the fertile alluvial plains of the Sabarmati and Mahi rivers before entering the Konkan region. The plains gradually give way south to broken hills, while inland parallel ridges reach 500-600 m where strategically placed atmospheric old forts are sited. Rice dominates agriculture further south, but ragi (finger millet) and pulses are also common. A pleasant day trip by car from Vadodara could include the forts of Champaner in the foothills, Pawagadh on a hilltop and Dabhoi Fort.

Vadodara *Colour map 2, C3.*

discover the Gaekwad dynasty

Formerly Baroda, Vadodara (population 1.3 million) was the capital of one of the most powerful princely states. It is now a rapidly expanding industrial town, yet the older part is pleasant and interesting to wander through. The Gaekwad stood high in the order of precedence among rulers, being one of only five to receive a 21-gun salute. He was reputedly so rich that he had a carpet woven of diamonds and pearls, and cannons cast in gold.

Essential Vadodara

Finding your feet

The airport is 9 km away with taxis and auto-rickshaws to town. Better hotels offer free airport transfer. The railway and long-distance bus stations are northwest of town, near hotels. See Transport, page 1255.

Getting around

The local bus station is just opposite the railway station. There are taxis and autos to take you to the town centre and the sights.

Best day trips

Laxmi Vilas Palace, see Sights, right
Pawagadh Fort, page 1255
Sunday market at Chhota Udepur, page 1256

Sights

Many of the city's treasures, which can be seen in the palaces and museums, reflect the wealth of the Gaekwads, a dynasty established by the powerful 18th-century Maratha General, Damaji.

The **Laxmi Vilas Palace** (1880-1890) ① *Rs 100 (no photography)*, was built by RH Chisholm. The magnificent palace is somewhat neglected but the interiors are decorated with Venetian mosaic, Italian marble, porcelain, antique furniture, European stained glass, sculptures, a royal armoury, etc. Nearby is the **Naulakhi Well**, a well-preserved *baoli* which has galleried levels.

Just to the south of the palace, the **Maharajah Fateh Singh Museum** ① *Nehru Rd, Laxmi Vilas Palace, Tue-Sun 1000-1730 (Apr-Jun 1600-1900), Rs 170*, has a good display of the royal state collection of European art (copies of some Murillo, Titian, Raphael, Rubens), a prized collection of paintings by the 19th-century Indian artist Raja Ravi Verma, Chinese and Japanese statuary and European porcelain. Further south, beyond the railway

The oldest narrow gauge

The Vadodara–Dabhoi–Chandod line is the world's oldest surviving narrow-gauge railway. The 19th-century line was commissioned for bullock-drawn locomotives in 1863. Later turned to steam, it is now run by a diesel engine. There are some vintage locomotives including steam engines in the Dabhoi station yard dating back to 1902. Take a ride on this line from Vadodara to Chandod via Dabhoi for the experience.

the **Pratap Vilas** (circa 1910, known as Lalbagh Palace), with a baroque façade, is now the Railway Staff College; permission from the principal is needed to visit the small rail museum. The beautiful **Shiv Mahal Palace**, near the race course, is being renovated as a private residence.

In the town centre, the **Kirti Mandir** (early 20th century), the *samadhi* (memorial ground) of the Gaekwads, has murals by Nandlal Bose and marble busts. The **Kothi Building** (late 19th century) is to the west and now houses the Secretariat. Across the road is the **Nyaya** (Law) **Mandir** (1896), not a temple but the High Court, in Mughal and Gothic styles. The **Jama Masjid** is next door. Further along the road away from the lake are the **Mandvi** (1736), a Muslim pavilion, the dilapidated **Nazar Bagh Palace** (1721), and the **College of Fine Art**, an institute of national renown.

Halfway down Raj Mahal Road are the remarkable buildings of the **Khanderao Market**. One of the old painted *havelis*, the four-storey **Tambekarwada**, residence of the Diwan of Vadodara (1849-1854), acquired by the Archaeological Survey, is well worth visiting. It is between Raopura Road and Dandia Bazar; rickshaw-wallahs appear not to know it so ask near the GPO and walk two minutes.

Sayaji Bagh is an extensive park, popular for evening strolls, with a mildly interesting zoo and a planetarium. The garden also contains the **Maharajah Sayajirao Museum and Art Gallery (Vadodara Museum)** ⓘ *in the Victoria Diamond Jubilee Institute, Sayaji Bagh, 1000-1700, Sat 1000-1645*, designed by RF Chisholm, with sections devoted to archaeology, art, ethnology and ancient Jain sculptures, as well as industrial arts, Mughal miniatures and European paintings. Nearby is the **Archaeology and Ancient History Museum** ⓘ *MS University, Mon-Sat 1400-1700, closed public holidays*. It contains Buddhist antiquities, archaeological finds from North Gujarat and good pre-history exhibits of Gujarat.

Listings Vadodara *map p1254*

Tourist information

Gujarat Tourism
Opposite railway station, T0265-242 7485, www.gujarattourism.com.

Where to stay

There are a range of upmarket chain hotels in Vadodara including Radisson Blu, ITC, Hyatt and Hilton.

$$$$ The Gateway Hotel
Akota Gardens, T0265-661 7676, www.thegatewayhotels.com.
84 luxurious rooms overlooking the palace, with gardens, pool and health club. Recommended.

$$$$-$$$ Surya Palace
Opposite Parsi Agiari, Sayajiganj, T0265-222 6000, www.suryapalace.com.
150 a/c rooms, smart but small rooms, an extensive buffet lunch in an a/c restaurant and business services.

$$$ Express
RC Dutt Rd, T0265-309 5000, www.expresshotelsindia.com.
Central a/c, 65 rooms, restaurants (excellent *thalis* at the beautiful **Mandap** restaurant), cake/sweet shop, helpful staff, unimpressive exterior but pleasant atmosphere.

$$ Apex International
Near Sardar Patel Statue, Sayajigunj, T0265-236 2551, www.hotelapex.com.
This centrally located hotel offers up clean rooms with all the usual mod cons and friendly service. Rates include breakfast.

$$-$ Kaviraj
RC Dutt Rd, T0265-232 3401.
Centrally located hotel with 30 rooms, some a/c, some with hot water, and a restaurant, mostly well known for its wine shop which issues permits till 1830.

$ Neelam
27 Viswas Colony, Alkapuri, T0265-235 6839.
On a quiet side street, the best of the 34 simple rooms have a balcony. Bathrooms are tiny and dark, with bucket hot water, but are clean enough and good value for budget travellers. Many similar $ places on the same street.

Restaurants

$$ Barbeque Nation
RC Dutt Rd, Shreem Shalini Mall.
Popular chain serves up hearty helpings of kebabs, barbecue dishes and a good range of vegetarian options too.

$$ La Quello Mediterranean Kitchen
Race Course Rd, 1 Trivia, Natubhai Circle, www.laquello.com.
Beautiful interiors with lots of greenery and generous portions of vegetarian Italian cuisine.

$$ Mandap
At Express Hotel, see Where to stay, above.
Beautifully ornate restaurant specializing in Gujarati *thalis*. Recommended.

$ Sasuuma
GF 1/2, RC Dutt Rd, Gokulesh complex.
Enormous Gujarati *thalis*; a great place to try local dishes.

Festivals

Mar Navratri is very colourful when local Garba, Dandia and Raas performances are held, and pilgrims head for Pawagadh.
Aug Ganesh Chaturthi is celebrated by the large Maharashtrian population here.

Shopping

Vadodara is a centre for silver jewellery. Shopping areas are Raopura, Mandvi, Teen Darwaza, National Plaza, Leheripura Mandir Bazar and Alkapuri Arcade.
Crossword, *2/1 Arunodaya Society, Alkapuri.*
Wide selection of new books and CDs.
Khadi Bhandar, *Kothi Rd.* For handlooms and local handicrafts.

Vadodara

Where to stay		Surya Palace **7**	La Quello **2**
Apex Intenational **4**			Sasuuma **3**
Express & Mandap **2**	Restaurants		
Neelam **3**	Barbeque Nation **1**		

What to do

Tour operators

Prominent, *7/12 Race Course Circle, T0265-233 5833*. Recommended for ticketing. **Tradewings**, *Sayajiganj, T0265-222 5255*. Changes money (even on Sat).

Transport

Air India, Fatehgunj, T0265-233 0466; airport, T0265-235 4797, www.airindia.com. **Jet Airways**, 11 Panorama Complex, Alkapuri, T0265-3989 3333. Flights to **Mumbai** and **Delhi**.

Local bus From opposite the railway station.

Long distance bus State Transport (ST) stand is a 5-min walk north of the railway station, T0265-276 0600. Reservations 0700-2200. Advance booking 0900-1300, 1330-1700. Buses to **Ahmedabad** every 30 mins, 2 hrs; also to **Diu** via **Bhavnagar**, **Mumbai** (425 km), **Pune**, **Udaipur** and **Mount Abu** and **Ujjain** (403 km), among others.

Taxi Tourist taxis from tourist office and travel agents, also Vadodara Taxi Service on T0800-024 7247

Train Vadodara is on the Western Railways' Delhi–Mumbai broad-gauge line. Enquiries, T139. **Ahmedabad**: any northbound train, including *Gujarat Queen 19109*, 2¼ hrs and *Gujarat Exp 19011*, 2¼ hrs. **Mumbai Central**: *Gujarat Mail 12902*, 6¼ hrs; *Paschim Exp 12926*, 6¼ hrs. **New Delhi**: *Rajdhani Exp 12951*, 2127, 11 hrs. **Porbandar** via Rajkot and Jamnagar: *Saurashtra Exp 19215*, 14 hrs.

Around Vadodara

charming old forts and palaces

Champaner

47 km northeast of Vadodara, open 0900-1800, Rs 250.

Champaner stands at 880 m in the Girnar Hills. Now a UNESCO World Heritage Site, the fortress was the old capital of the local Rajputs, but was lost in 1484 to Mahmud Beghara, who renamed it Muhammadabad and took 23 years to build his new city. In his campaign in Gujarat, the Mughal Emperor Humayun personally led a small team that scaled the walls of the city using iron spikes and then let the rest of the army in through the main gate. With the collapse of the empire, Champaner passed to the Marathas.

In the **old city**, the remains of many 15th- and 16th-century mosques and palaces show a blend of Islamic and Jain traditions, a unique style encouraged by Champaner's relative isolation. The **Jami Masjid** (1523), a large, richly ornamented mosque, is exemplary of the Gujarati style with interesting features such as oriel windows. Few older structures of the Chauhan Rajputs remain: **Patai Rawal palace**, the domed granary **Makai Kota**, the 11th- and 12th-century **Lakulisha Temple** and some old wells.

Some 4 km southwest of Champaner, **Pawagadh Fort** ① *Rs 100* or included in entry price of Champaner, dominates the skyline and is visible for miles around. According to legend, Pavagadh was believed to have been part of the Himalaya carried off by the monkey god Hanuman. Occupying a large area, it rises in three stages: the ruined fort, the palace and middle fort, and finally the upper fort with Jain and Hindu temples, which are important places of pilgrimage. Parts of the massive walls still stand. The ascent is steep and passes several ruins including the Budhia Darwaza (Gate), and the Champavati Mahal, a three-storey summer pavilion. The temple at the summit had its spire replaced by a shrine to the Muslim saint Sadan Shah.

Dabhoi Fort

Dabhoi, 29 km southwest of Vadodara, was fortified by the Solanki Rajputs from 1100 and the fort was built by a King of Patan in the 13th century. Dabhoi is regarded as the birthplace of the Hindu Gujarati architectural style. The fort is a particularly fine example of military architecture with its four gates, a reservoir fed by an aqueduct and farms to provide food at times of siege. The **Vadodara Gate** (northwest) is 9 m high with pilasters on each side and carved with images depicting the reincarnation of Vishnu. The **Nandod Gate** (south) is similarly massive. The **Hira Gate** (east) with carvings, is thought to have the builder buried beneath it. **Mori Gate** (north) lies next to the old palace and on the left of this is the **Ma Kali Temple** (1225), shaped like a cross, with profuse carvings.

Chandod

South of Dabhoi, this is the meeting place of the Narmada's two tributaries with picturesque bathing ghats and several temples. Take a mechanized country-style river boat to visit temples, passing spectacular ravines and water-sculpted rocks.

Chhota Udepur

Around 100 km east of Vadodara, picturesque Chhota Udepur (Chotta Udaipur), centred around a lake, was once the capital of a Chauhan Rajput princely state. The town has palaces and many colonial period buildings. It is the capital of a tribal district where Bhils and Ratwas live in secluded hamlets of a handful of mud huts each. The huts are decorated with wall paintings or *pithoras* (tigers and other animals are favourite subjects) and protected from evil spirits by small terracotta devotional figures. If you stay at Jambugodha Palace (25 km from Chhota Udepur), you can arrange to visit the *pithoras* in a nearby village and get a little insight into village life.

There are colourful weekly *haats* or **markets** in nearby villages which offer an insight into tribal arts, crafts and culture. (The one in town is held by the lake on Saturday – it's quite charming and not touristy at all.) The government-run tribal **museum** in Diwan Bungalow has interesting examples of *pithoras*, folk costumes, artefacts, aboriginal weapons and handicrafts, but the labelling is in Gujarati and the attendant knows little English. There is a better museum 15 km from Chhota Udepur – see below.

Despite its Mughal architectural style, the imposing Rajput **Kusum Vilas** palace, set in 16 ha, has impressive European decorative features inside. The large Mughal-style gardens have fountains, ponds, European marble statuary, a colonnaded art deco pool and tennis courts, while the garages have old cars and interesting carriages.

Dasara Fair here is famous. Other fairs held around **Holi** (March/April) in nearby villages like Kawant, with dancing, music and craft stalls, offer a glimpse of tribal life.

Fifteen kilometres west of Chhota Udepur is the Tribal Academy at **Tejgadh**, which is working to document aboriginal languages and culture in the entire country. There's a great collection of photographs, a good library, mainly covering the local Bhil, Bhilala and Ratwa tribes, and the staff can offer practical advice on visiting local tribes. The canteen offers local food for a nominal fee, and *tadi*, a potent palm liquor, is available in season.

Listings Around Vadodara

Where to stay

Champaner

$$$ Champaner heritage
T079-4007 7333 (Ahmedabad),
www.palacesofindia.com.
Lovely swimming pool and gardens leading up to a grand mansion property with beautiful rooms.

$$ Jambughoda Palace
Jambughoda, 25 km from Champaner and 50 km from Chhota Udepur, T02676-241 258, www.jambughoda.com.
Billed as a 'home for nature lovers', this heritage property is close to the Jambughoda Wildlife Sanctuary and you can also check out *pithora* tribal paintings in nearby villages. Simple rooms

with a charming family. Great home-cooked food with locally grown organic vegetables.

$ Hotel Champaner
On a plateau reached by cable car, run by Gujarati Tourism, T02676-245641.
32 clean rooms and dorm, pleasant garden and lively monkeys.

Chandod

$$-$ Sarita Mandvi Mahal
Juna Mandwa, T011-2568 6868 (Delhi), www.heritagehotelsofindia.com.
10 mins' walk from the river is this 19th-century friendly place with simple rooms, some a/c, dorm beds (Rs 150), library and period furniture. Home-cooked Indian food is served in the courtyard, and there are bullock cart tours of the village and

walking tours in the ravines. A bit shabby but good value.

Chhota Udepur

$$$ Kali Niketan
T(0)9825-556413, http://chhotaudepur.com.
One of the most eccentric palace homestays you will come across, with a ramshackle charm. 1 guestroom has 2 leopards presiding over the bed.

Champaner

Shared jeeps and ST buses from Vadodara and Ahmedabad go to **Machi** where the cable cars start for the ascent to the monuments on the hill; Rs 45 return (only hand baggage of 5 kg allowed), 0900-1300, 1400-1700.

Surat and around *Colour map 5, A3.*

India's diamond and gem centre

Situated on the banks of the Tapti River, Surat (population 2.4 million) was an important trading centre by 1600 but went into decline in the 19th century. Today it is again a rapidly growing industrial and commercial city, but despite its historic significance there is little to attract tourists.

Surat was once the centre of the diamond industry in India and at the height of its production it was estimated that 80% of the world's diamonds were polished here. However, fortunes have recently changed with a downturn in the Chinese market and many diamond workers here lost their jobs in 2015.

Sights

The **museum** ① *Wed-Sat 1045-1345, 1445-1745, Tue, Sun 1445-1745, photography prohibited*, near the castle, has an interesting collection of textiles, furniture, paintings, stamps, coins and ceramics. A strong Muslim influence is evident in several 16th- and 17th-century mosques. There are two Parsi **fire temples** (1823) and the triple-domed **Swami Narayan Temple**. The **Chintamani Jain Temple**, dating from the 15th century, has some fine woodcarvings.

Navsari and around

Navsari, 39 km from Surat, has a historic Parsi fire temple which is one of the most important Zoroastrian pilgrim places in India. You cannot enter the temple but the building and garden are worth seeing from outside. **Dandi**, 13 km from Navsari, is where Gandhiji ended his Salt March from Ahmedabad to the south Gujarat coast, and picked up a handful of salt, see box, page 1241. A monument marks the spot and a photo gallery depicts events in Gandhi's life. **Karadi**, nearby, is where Gandhi was arrested after the Dandi March; his hut is still preserved. There is a small **Gandhi Museum**. You can sleep at the guesthouse, which is very peaceful and friendly; contact '*Om Shanti*', Matwad (English spoken).

Listings Surat and around

Where to stay

$$$$ The Gateway
Athwa Lines, T0261-669 7000,
www.thegatewayhotels.com.
In an attractive location, this modern hotel has 140 rooms, a good restaurant, riverside pool, health club and efficient, polite staff. The smartest in town. Breakfast is included.

$$ Embassy
Sufi Baug, near station, T0261-244 3170,
www.embassyhotelsurat.com.
Modern, pleasant hotel but bare rooms, a/c, and a popular restaurant serving North Indian dishes and Gujarati *thalis*.

$ Vihar
Opposite the railway station, T0261-242 9906.
Basic rooms, but great rooftop views of the city, friendly and safe.

Restaurants

$$ Bhathvari
Vadodara Rd, T(0)9898-011022.
Excellent Kathiawadi and Marwari *thalis* served
on low tables in thatched pavilions in a pleasant
garden environment.

$ Yuvraj
Opposite the Railway Station.
There's a lovely ambience at the rooftop garden
café above Yuvraj Hotel.

Transport

Train **Ahmedabad**: *Shatabdi Exp 2009*, not
Sun, 3½ hrs; *Gujarat Exp 19011*, 4¾ hrs; **Mumbai
Central**: *Kranti Rajdhani 12954*, 3¾ hrs. **New
Delhi**: *Paschim Exp 12925*, 19 hrs. **Rajkot** and
Jamnagar: *Janata Exp 19017*, 10½ hrs (Rajkot),
12½ hrs (Jamnagar).

Saputara   *Colour map 5, A3.*

Gujarat's only hill station

Saputara (altitude 50-1083 m) is a pleasant hill resort created after Independence in
the Sahayadri hills. Set in a tribal region, there is an attractive lake and forests nearby.
It is a relaxing place to enjoy walks, scenic places and folklore but gets very crowded
during weekends and holidays. The resort is ideal for walking. The best time to visit
is November to May.

Sights

The name Saputara is derived from the snake deity, which is worshipped here by the tribal people.
The hub of activity at Saputara is the **lake** which has boating facilities and lake view eating places.
The plateau is rather barren and not particularly appealing but there are some lovely walks around
the hill resort. You could find attractive quartzite rocks, orchids and wild flowers on the trails.

There are good views of the valley from **Sunset Point**, with a 10-minute ropeway service, and
from **Valley View Point**, which involves a strenuous climb of 1.5 km. There are also some old
Maratha hill forts that involve steep climbs and are recommended only for serious trekkers. The
Hatgadh fort offers superb views and a chance to see rock chats, martens and wolf snakes in cracks
on the fort walls. Carry water.

Dangs

The Dangs district comprises more than 300 villages with a population of over 150,000, more than
94% of them belonging to tribal communities. The Bhils, Kunbis, Warlis and Gamits depend on the
forest for their livelihood, obtaining timber, honey and lac. They are known for their traditional
musical instruments and vigorous dances wearing wooden masks. Most villages have a shrine
to Wagha-Deva, the tiger god, sculpted on stone. The **Dangs Cultural and Ecological Museum**,
with a stone serpent at the entrance, offers an insight into the tribal area and the Dangs's natural
history. There are interesting dioramas, folk costumes, tribal weaponry and musical instruments.
The **Artists' Village** holds workshops of bamboo crafts, papier mâché and pottery. **Dangs
Darbar** held at Ahwa, 32 km north, is celebrated with a **tribal fair** around March and April. Tribal chieftains
called Bhil Rajas and Kunbi Rajas, who still receive privy purses from the government, are honoured
during this festival. For **Nag Panchami** tribal huts are decorated with paintings.

Where to stay

$$$ Shilpi Hill Resort
Opposite Govt Shopping Centre, T02631-237231,
www.shilpihillresort.com.
Set back from the main road towards the hills,
this clean and comfortable place has 10 rooms
with attached baths. The restaurant **Vaity** offers
the widest choice of dishes including non-
vegetarian options, and good views and outdoor
seating. Meals are included in rates.

$$$-$ Toran Hill Resort (Gujarat Tourism)
Near the bus stand, T02631-237226.
There is a huge variety of styles and standards
of room, from deluxe a/c cottages and log huts
to dorms. The restaurant serves *thalis* (Rs 25-35).
Book at any tourism office.

$ Anando
Nageshwar Mahadev Rd, T02631-237 202.
Facing the lake with good views, this place offers
23 rooms with bath and a vegetarian restaurant.

Transport

From the NH8, the turn off is at Chikhli to the
west. Petrol is only available at Waghai (51 km
northwest), and at a pump 40 km from Saputara,
on the Nashik road.

Bus State buses run to **Surat** (135 km) and
Nashik (Maharashtra, 80 km).

Train Train from Ahmedabad (400 km) or
Mumbai (255 km) to **Billimora** and then local
bus or taxi; or a narrow-gauge train to **Waghai**.

Daman *Colour map 5, A3.*

memories of Portugal and the trade routes

Daman (population 35,700), set on the coast, retains something of the atmosphere
of its distinctive Portuguese inheritance which linked it both with Mediterranean
Europe and Africa. A few people still use Portuguese in everyday speech, but visitors
expecting a colonial coastal idyll may be disappointed by the scrappy beaches.

Sights

Moti Daman retains something of the
Portuguese atmosphere. The landward (east)
side has a moat and drawbridge. The shaded
main street inside the **fort** wall runs north-south
between attractive arched gateways which have
Portuguese arms carved on them. One shows a
saint carrying a sword but the sculpted giants
on the doorways are modelled on the guardian
dwarpalas at entrances to Hindu temples.

The former **Governor's Palace** and other
administrative buildings are along the main
road while towards the south end is the old
Cathedral Church of Bom Jesus, started in 1559
but consecrated in 1603. Large and airy when
the main south door is open, the chief feature
is its painted and gilt wooden altar reredos and
pulpit. Much of the ornamentation, notably the
gold crowns of the saints, has been stolen. On
the west side of the small square is the old **jail**,
still in use. To the south, against the fort wall, is
the **Rosario Chapel**, formerly the Church of the
Madre Jesus, with a unique feature in Indian
churches of carved and gilded wooden panels

Essential Daman

Finding your feet

The nearest railway station is at Vapi, 13 km
southeast, on the Mumbai–Ahmedabad
line. From there you can get taxis for transfer
(visitors arriving by car pay Rs 20 entry fee) or
walk about 600 m for a bus. Long-distance
buses arrive at the main bus stand in Nani
Daman. See Transport, page 1261.

Orientation

The settlement north of the river, known
as *Nani* (small) Daman, has most of the
accommodation. To the south, *Moti* (large)
Daman has a few colonial remains. Bicycle
hire is available from Nani Daman Bazar.

When to go

Avoid the Indian holiday periods.

illustrating stories from the life of Christ. These include the adoration of the Magi, Jesus teaching in the synagogue as a child, and Mary's ascension. The carved ceiling features charming cherubs.

Jampore Beach, 3 km south of Moti Daman, is planted with casuarina groves and has a sandy beach with safe swimming but is otherwise not very appealing. **Nani Daman**, north of the river, is reached by a bridge across Daman Ganga which gives attractive views of Moti Daman's walls and the country fishing boats on either bank. The smaller **fort** here encloses a church, now used as a school, and a cemetery. Some of the old houses retain beautifully carved wooden doors and lintels. The crowded town is thick with bars trading on Daman's exemption from Gujarati prohibition.

Daman town

To Devka Beach & ❶❹❻❶❷
To Airport

2nd Feb Rd

Main Rd (Devka) Rd

Sea Face Rd

Taxis

BAZAR

Daman Vapi Rd

Nani Daman Rd

❸

Fort of St Jerome

Cemetery

Children's Park

Nani Daman Rd

NANI DAMAN

Fishing Jetty

Daman Ganga River

Gulf of Khambhat

Lighthouse

Government Offices

Ring Rd

Governor's Palace

MOTI DAMAN

FORT

Cathedral Church of Bom Jesus

Jail

Rosario Chapel

To Jampore Beach

N

200 metres
200 yards

Where to stay 🛏
Gold Beach Resort **1**
Miramar **4**
Sandy Resort **6**

Restaurants 🍴
Duke **1**
Ocean Inn **2**
Samrat **3**

Daman Town

The 380-sq-km enclave of Daman, along with Diu and Goa, was a Portuguese possession until taken over by the Indian government in 1961. Its association with Goa ceased when the latter became a state in 1987. It is now a Union Territory with its own Pradesh council. Daman developed at the mouth of the tidal estuary of the Daman Ganga River as a trading centre in 1531. Much of its early commerce was with the Portuguese territories in East Africa. Later (1817-1837), it was a link in the opium trade chain until this was broken by the British.

Listings Daman *map p1260*

Where to stay

There are plenty of cheap places on the seafront.

$$$ Gold Beach Resort
Devka Beach, T0260-2240 5000,
www.goldbeachresort.in.
Large beach resort with a huge swimming pool (with a bar). Good-sized rooms with beach views.

$$ Miramar
Devka Beach, T(0)85111 37601.
One of the oldest in town, this place has rooms with pleasant balconies plus some cottages. There's a pool, and the beachside restaurant plays loud Indian film music till late on weekend nights. They have also opened a new water park resort in the area.

$$-$ Sandy Resort
Devka Beach, T0260-225 4751,
www.sandyresort.com.
Billing itself as a 'class hotel for class people', this is the quietest and most pleasant place in town, across the road from the beach. There are 46 rooms, some with a/c (the best are upstairs), restaurant, disco and pool.

Restaurants

You can get fresh fish lunches and dinners at most hotels, also fish snacks at the bars.

$$ Duke
Devka Beach.
Excellent Parsi and *tandoori* food outdoors in a characterful 1936 building, which is a little crumbly.

$$ Ocean Inn,
20 Devka Moti.
Excellent seafood and fish curries.

$ Samrat
Seaface Rd.
Simple and clean, excellent *thalis*.

Transport

Bus For the bus stand: turn right out of Vapi station, walk 500 m along main road to a T-junction; the stand is nearby, on the left.

Taxi Shared taxis go to Daman but with 8 others can be a squeeze (Rs 20 each); Rs 160 per taxi.

Train Not all trains stop at **Vapi** from Mumbai. *Gujarat Exp 19011*, 3 hrs; From **Ahmedabad**: *Shatabdi Exp 12010*, (except Wed) 4¾ hrs.

Saurashtra

Around the coastal region of the Saurashtra Peninsula are some of India's most remarkable religious sites, from Dwarka in the west to Palitana in the east, while the coastline itself is fringed with some attractive beaches and the former Portuguese territory of Diu. The historic town of Junagadh and wildlife parks also draw visitors. Northern Saurashtra, with Rajkot at its centre, is one of the major groundnut growing regions of India.

Rajkot and around   *Colour map 2, C2.*
bustling commercial city with interesting colonial architecture

Rajkot (population 966,600) has a large number of shopping complexes and heavy traffic, but there are also some fine late 19th-century colonial buildings and institutions since the British Resident for the Western Indian States lived here. There has been rapid industrialization recently, based especially in the processing of agricultural products.

Although there is an early Palaeolithic site at Rajkot, there is very little evidence of the settlement. Rajkot was the capital of the Jadejas, who ruled earlier from a place named Sardhar on the Rajkot–Bhavnagar road, and later set up this new city which became the headquarters of the British representatives in Saurashtra.

Sights

The British impact can be seen in the impressive **Rajkumar College**, a famous public school founded in 1870 set in vast grounds, and the richly endowed **Watson Museum** ① *Jubilee Gardens, Thu-Tue 0900-1230, 1430-1800, closed 2nd and 4th Sat each month, Rs 5, Rs 2 per photo,* with exhibits from the Indus Valley civilization, medieval sculpture, pottery and crafts, and colonial memorabilia. The gardens also contain the **Memorial Institute** and its crumbling Lang Library. **Gandhi Smriti** (Kaba Gandhino Delo), the early home of Mohandas K Gandhi, is in Ghee Kanta Road, between MG Road and Lakahjiraj Road (rickshaw-wallahs know the way).

The **Gandhi Museum** ① *Dharmandra Rd, Mon-Sat 0900-1200, 1500-1800,* in the Gandhi family home (1880), contains photographs and personal effects. Descriptions are mainly in Hindi and Gujarati; guides speak no English. **Rashtriya Shala** is where Mahatma Gandhi went to school and promotes one of his greatest ideals: handloom and handicrafts. Among the textiles being promoted is Patola-style *ikat* silk weaving.

Gondal *Colour map 5, A1.*

The fascinating old town of Gondal, 38 km south of Rajkot, was the capital of one of the most progressive, affluent and efficient princely states of the British period. The exemplary state, ruled by Jadeja Rajputs, had an excellent road network, free compulsory education for all children including girls, sewage systems and accessible irrigation for farmers. The rulers rejected *purdah*, their palaces have no *zenanas*, and imposed no taxes on their subjects, instead earning revenue from rail connections between the port towns of Porbandar and Veraval with Rajkot and cities inland.

The **Naulakha Palace** (1748) ① *0900-1200, 1500-1800, Rs 100,* with a sculpted façade, pretty jharoka windows and carved stone pillars, has an impressive Darbar Hall and a museum of paintings, furniture, brass and silver. Silver items include caskets, models of buildings and scales used for weighing the Maharajah (he was weighed against silver and gold on his 25th and 50th birthday;

the precious metals were then distributed to the poor). A gallery has toys from the 1930s and 1940s. The **Vintage and Classic Car Museum** ① *open same hours, Rs 100,* is one of the finest in the country. Exhibits include 1910 New Engine, 1920s Delage and Daimler, 1935-1955 models, horse-drawn carriages, etc. Boating is possible on **Veri Lake** nearby, which attracts large numbers of rosy pelicans, flamingos, demoiselle and common eastern cranes and many others, particularly in January and February. You can visit the **Bhuvaneshwari Ayurvedic Pharmacy**, founded in 1910, which still prepares herbal medicines according to ancient principles and runs a hospital offering massages and treatment. The early 20th-century **Swaminarayan Temple** has painted interiors on the upper floors.

Wankaner

On a bend of the Machchu River 39 km northeast of Rajkot, Wankaner (*wanka* – curve, *ner* – river), another capital of the Jhala Rajputs, was founded in 1605. The old ruler, Amar Sinhji, was known for his flamboyant lifestyle but also introduced wide-ranging reforms in farmers' co-operatives, education, roads, tramways and internal security. He was also responsible for building the **Ranjitvilas Palace** (1907 extension to the 1880s British Residents' bungalow), visible for miles across the plains. It is built in a strange mix of styles (Venetian façades, a Dutch roof, *jarokha* balconies, a 'Mughal' pavilion, minarets, English clock tower, etc) yet all is very well integrated. The garage has an interesting collection of models from the 1930s and 1940s and a 1921 Silver Ghost, jeeps, wagons and old buggies, while there are Kathiawadi horses in the stables. A part of the palace is now a **museum** brim full of royal memorabilia of a bygone lifestyle. There is an interesting step well with marble balustrade staircases, cool, subterranean chambers and marble statues of Vishnu.

Dhrangadhra

The pretty little village town of Dhrangadhra 84 km northeast of Wankaner is the government Forest Department's headquarters for the **Little Rann of Kachchh Wild Ass Sanctuary** ① *T02754-2325 2666*. It was also the capital of a very progressive princely state, which had English and vernacular schools in 1855 and free education in the early 1900s. Full-day jeep tours of Little Rann, to see wild asses, salt mining communities and a bird sanctuary, is Rs 2000 for two, including a delicious home-cooked lunch. For more information on the **Little Rann of Kachchh**, see page 1293.

Listings Rajkot and around

Where to stay

Rajkot

Like many towns in Saurashtra, Rajkot suffers from critical water shortages; limit water use as much as possible.

$$$ Imperial Palace
Dr Yagnik Rd, T0281-248 0000,
www.theimperialpalace.biz.
The smartest business hotel in town, with an elaborate lobby, in-room internet ports, indoor and outdoor pools, gym, swish restaurant and well-stocked wine shop (alcohol permit required).

$$-$ Galaxy
Jawahar Rd, T0281-222 2905,
www.thegalaxyhotelrajkot.com.
A great value modern hotel with 37 well-furnished, clean rooms, mostly a/c, a pleasant roof garden and exchange (including credit cards). It's well run, with courteous and efficient

staff. There's no restaurant but room service to bring in food. It doesn't look promising from the street, but it's a pleasant surprise once you get upstairs. Access is by lift only. A pick-up and drop off service from the airport is included in the rates.

$ Samrat International
37 Karanpura, T0281-222 2269.
The promising lobby belies adequate but unloved rooms, some a/c. Vegetarian restaurant, genial staff and exchange; the best-kept option near the bus stand.

Muli

There are several lovely heritage properties northeast of Rajkot.

$$$ Ambika Niwas
T(0)79400 77333, www.palacesofindia.com.
Lovely saffron-coloured palace with 15 luxurious rooms. A friendly welcome and good food.

$$$-$$ Bell Guest House
Sayla village, near Muli, T(0)97246 78145.
An atmospheric guesthouse in a beautiful building. Sayla village is charming with many interesting buildings and horse riding can be arranged. Recommended.

Wankaner

$$$ Royal Oasis
T02828-220001, www.heritagehotelsofindia.com.
Stepping back in time, this guesthouse of the Ranjitvilas is set in large fruit orchards with original 1930s art deco features. There is a stunning *vaav* (step well) on site with 3 intricately carved levels, as well as a beautiful art deco pool, although it's empty most of the time. The rooms are a little past their prime. You can eat dinner in the gardens, although mosquitoes can be a problem.

Gondal
Heritage hotels are worth the experience.

$$$$-$$$ Orchard Palace
Palace Rd, near ST Bus Stand, T02825-2245550, www.heritagepalacesgondal.com.
Overlooking mango and lime groves, 6 a/c rooms in one wing of an atmospheric palace, with old-fashioned baths, attractive gardens, 35 vintage cars, pool (but little water to fill it) and excellent dance shows. Mosquitos are a nuisance so burn rings. Good food ("bland European dishes; order Indian in advance" or sometimes a bit of both on the same plate!). Price includes meals. You can also opt to stay in their converted Royal Salon train carriage on site. You can also book through **Northwest Safaries** (www.northwestsafaries.com). Recommended.

$$$ Riverside Palace
By river Gondali, T02825-221950, www.heritagepalacesgondal.com.
A 19th-century palace, with a glassed-in terrace, 11 large, attractive non a/c rooms, 4-poster beds. A similar vibe to Orchard, but a little more lacklustre.

$ Bhuvaneswari Rest House
At Shri Bhuvaneswari Pith Temple, T02825-222 481.
An atmospheric part of town with 2 rest house options. The newer build is good and clean but a bit pricey at Rs 1800 a night. In the older building, it's looking pretty run down and in need of an overhaul. *Thali* meals are available and the temple and Ayurvedic factory close by is fascinating.

Restaurants

Rajkot

$$ Lords Banquet
Sadar.
Renowned for its extensive range of vegetarian food. They excel at Punjabi and South Indian styles, and are deservedly popular.

$ Adingo
Toran, Limda Chowk, Sadar.
Dubbed the Temple of Taste, Adingo specializes in Kathiawada *thalis*, but serve up good Punjabi classics too.

Gondal

$ Dreamland
Kailash Complex, ST Rd.
First-class unlimited Gujarati and Punjabi *thalis*, served in separate rooms, with delightfully cool a/c.

Transport

Rajkot
Air Air India and Jet Airways fly into Rajkot. **Indian**, Angel Chambers, T0281-222 2295, airport T0281-2415 3313, www.airindia.in. **Jet Airways**, T0281-3989 3333, www.jetairways.com, flies to **Mumbai** daily.

Bus The ST bus station is just south of the busy Dhebar Chowk at the centre, with buses to **Junagadh** (2 hrs), **Veraval** (5 hrs), **Jamnagar** (2 hrs), **Dwarka** and **Ahna**. More comfortable private long-distance coaches leave from locations around the city, especially around Shastri Maidan. **Eagle Travels**, T0281-248 0049, www.eaglecorporate.com, runs several luxury buses daily to **Ahmedabad**, as well as to **Mount Abu**, **Mumbai**, **Porbandar**, Udaipur and Vadodara. **Jay Somnath Travels**, Umesh Complex, near Chaudhari High School, T0281-243 3315, have 3-4 buses a day to **Bhuj**.

Train Junction Station **Ahmedabad**: *Rajkot Ahmedabad Exp 19154*, 4¼ hrs; *Sau Janta Exp 19018*, 5¼ hrs (continues to **Vadodara**, 2½ hrs). **Mumbai** (**Central**): *Okha Mumbai Saurashtra Mail 19006*, 14½ hrs; **Vadodara**: same as Mumbai, 7¼-9 hrs.

Bhavnagar (population 511,000) was ruled by progressive rulers from its foundation in 1723. Surrounded by flat and richly cultivated land, it is now a major industrial town and cotton export centre, and is rapidly becoming one of India's most important ship-building ports. However, most of its character is preserved in the bazars of the Old City where you can pick your way through the crowded lanes amongst the old merchants' *havelis*.

Sights

The palace-like **Takhtsinghji Hospital** (1879-1883) was designed by Sir William Emerson. The 18th-century **Darbargadh** (Old Palace, extended 1894-1895), in the town centre, now houses the State Bank but is scarcely visible in the incredibly overcrowded and dirty Darbargadh Bazar. **Barton Museum** (1895) ① *0900-1300, 1400-1800, Rs 5*, in an impressive crescent-shaped building, has a collection of coins, carvings, geological and archaeological finds, farming implements, arms and armour, handicrafts, miniature paintings and excellent bead and silk embroidery. The better known **Gandhi Smriti** ① *0830-1230, 1500-1900, free*, is dedicated to Mahatma Gandhi (he was at university here; his old college is now an Ayurvedic education centre). Photos portray his life and the freedom struggle. There are also letters and mark sheets showing his scores at university. The unremarkable marble **Takhteshwar Temple** on a hillock has good views over the city and the distant coastline.

Victoria Park, 2 km from the centre, is a former royal hunting preserve. Far removed from the image conveyed by its name of a manicured British city park, it has rolling scrub forests and marshes rich in birdlife. Nilgai, hyena, jackal, jungle cat and monitor lizard can all be seen. A pleasant stroll from the Nilambagh Palace, it is a great place for walks. **Gaurishankar Lake**, a popular escape from the city with parks and steps along the embankments, is good for winter birdwatching when cranes, pelicans and ducks arrive. Plovers, terns and other birds nest on the islands.

Velavadar National Park

Some 10 km off the Bhavnagar–Vadodara Highway, 0630-0830 and 1630-1830, closed mid-Jun to mid-Oct, US$5, camera US$5; guide (some don't speak English), US$10 per trip, jeep US$25 per drive. Pay at Forest Range Office at park entrance.

The compact 36 sq km of flat grassland broken by dry open scrubland and patches of thorn forest was set up to protect the Indian blackbuck, of which it has the largest population in the country – about 1000 permanent residents and another 1000 that wander in from the surrounding area. The Bhavnagar royal family came here for cheetah coursing, falconry and hunting and also harvested grass for fodder for their cattle and horses.

The blackbuck is the second largest of the antelopes and the fastest long-distance runner of all animals. It can keep going at a steady 90 kph. The black-and-white dominant males sport spiral horns; the juvenile males are brown and white while the hornless females are brownish, with lighter parts. It is one of the most hunted animals in India, and so is an endangered species. Impressive males clash horns to establish territory and court females. Wolves, their prime predator, have been reduced to only two families, but they can still be seen. The park also contains a few sounders of wild boar in addition to 50-60 nilgai, usually seen near waterholes, jungle cat, which can be seen at dawn and dusk, and jackal. Birdlife is rich with numerous birds of prey including the largest harrier roost in the world; some 1500 to 2000 of these light-bodied hawks gather here at sunset in November and December. During the monsoon the park is the best place in India to spot the lesser florican. In addition to the two rivers that border the park, there are three waterholes and three small pools that attract animals at midday.

Sihor

Midway between Bhavnagar (27 km) and Palitana, the former Gohil Rajput capital has the 17th-century hilltop **Darbargadh Palace** (now government offices). Though rather dilapidated, you can still see some intricate carved wooden balconies and pillars outside and 19th-century wall paintings inside. The Brahm **Kund** (11th-12th century), about 2 km west of Sihor centre and 500 m south of the main road, is a deeply set stepped tank (now empty). It has around 100 sculpted images of deities in small niches, a few of which are still actively worshipped. There are also pillared galleries with rich carvings of musicians. In the village nearby brass utensils are produced as a cottage industry by rolling scrap from the Alang ship breaking yard and beating it into attractive water pots. Villagers are only too happy to show you around their workshops. The **Khodiyar Temple** on the Bhavnagar-Sihor road is in a pretty setting among the hills.

Listings Bhavnagar and around

Where to stay

Bhavnagar

$$$ Nilambag Palace
Ahmedabad Rd, T011-256 8686,
wwwheritagehotelsofindia.com.
A little faded 1850s palace stuffed with the usual array of hunting trophies. The 27 upmarket a/c rooms have long bathrooms with tubs; the main palace is better than the cottage annexe, and twice the price. The lobby has intricate woodcarving, chandeliers and royal portraits, and the grand banquet hall is now a restaurant. There are vast gardens with peacocks and a beautiful stepped pool.

$$$-$$ Narayani Heritage
In grounds of Nilambag Palace, T0278-232 5051.
Plain but spacious rooms in a converted boys' school; rooms open on to a paved courtyard. It shares the facilities of Nilambag Palace. It has an odd atmosphere and definitely feels like an old school.

Velavadar National Park

$$$$ Blackbuck Lodge
Velavadar National Park, T(0)81549 73486,
www.blackbucklodge.com.
A stylish lodge with just 14 luxury villas that fit in beautifully with the natural landscape. Each room has its own spacious veranda and a pool is on the way.

$$ Kaliyar Bhuvan Forest Lodge
Reserve at Forest Office in Bhavnagar,
T0278-242 6425.
Simple but adequate, with 5 small and reasonably furnished rooms. It's prohibitively priced for foreigners. Similarly, food is priced differently for foreigners.

Restaurants

Bhavnagar

Sweet shops around Piramal Chowk and Waghawadi Rd sell melt-in-the mouth *pedas* and *sangam*, a cashew nut candy, as well as savoury snacks like Bhavnagar *ganthias*.

$ Tulsi
Kalanala Chowk.
An attractive little restaurant, with subtle lighting and good mainly North Indian food. Recommended.

Shopping

Bhavnagar

Textiles, locally embroidered cushion covers, shawls, *bandhni* and mock-silver jewellery are good buys. Try **Vora Bazar**, **Radhanpuri Market**, **Amba Chowk**, **Darbargadh Lane** and **Talao** fruit and veg market. Handlooms and handicrafts are best at **Khadi stores** in the Barton Museum building.

Transport

Bhavnagar

Air The airport is 5 km southeast of town and Jet Airways have regular flights; T0278-3989 3333, www.jetairways.com, flies to **Mumbai**.

Bus Frequent rickety buses from the ST stand in the New Town. Routes include: **Palitana** (1¾ hrs); several to **Una for Diu** (6 hrs); **Velavadar** (1 hr). Private operators: **Tanna Travels**, Waghawadi Rd, T0278-242 0477, has luxury coaches (reclining seats) to/from **Ahmedabad**, almost hourly from 0600, 4½ hrs plus short tea break, recommended; to **Vadodara**, 5½ hrs, 3 daily.

Train The station is in the Old City, about 3 km north of the ST Bus Stand. **Ahmedabad**: a slow journey as the line takes a circuitous route to skirt the marshes; buses are generally preferable. *Bandra Exp 12972*, 5½ hrs; continues to **Mumbai** (Bandra). Also several local trains.

Velavadar National Park

A few buses from Bhavnagar; better to hire a car. Alternatively hire a jeep/*chhakra* (motorbike trailer) from Vallabhipur on the Ahmedabad–Bhavnagar highway. A new bridge being built near Bhavnagar port to Adhelai near the park will make access faster and easier.

Palitana and around   Colour map 5, A2.

an important Hindu pilgrimage site and interesting coastal towns

---

Palitana (population 51,900) is renowned for the extraordinary Jain temple complex on Shatrunjaya Hill which attracts domestic pilgrims as well as foreign visitors. No one is allowed to remain on the hill at night, but even during the day there is a peaceful serenity as you listen to the temple bells and pilgrims chanting in the City of the Gods.

Palitana was the capital of a small princely state founded by Shahji, a Gohel Rajput who belonged to the same clan as the Maharajah of Bhavnagar. The river Khari bisects the town. The east bank has hotels, eateries, shopping centres and bus and railway stations, while the west bank has the Willingdon Vegetable Market and some older raj and royal buildings. The last ruler died leaving wives and sisters to fight over the royal palace and mansions that are now decaying but show signs of impressive architecture. The better houses are on Taleti Road.

The busy little town is also known for diamond cutting and horse breeding. South African diamonds are imported from Belgium for cutting and polishing before being re-exported back to Belgium.

Temple complex

Shatrunjaya Hill, 3 km southwest of Palitana, 0700-1900, free, camera Rs 40, visitors should wear clean respectable clothes, leather articles (even watch straps) and food or drink are not allowed in the temple area, but can be left, along with shoes, at the entrance. Take lots of water and a sun hat, arrive by dawn to join the pilgrims, and allow 2 hrs for the climb, 4-5 hrs for the round trip. You can be carried up by a dhooli (string chair – Rs 500 return) but the hassle from aggressive touts in the early stages of the climb can be substantial (rates rise in summer, peaking during fairs and Mahavir Jayanti to Rs 1000).

According to local tradition, Adinatha, the first Tirthankara, visited the hill several times and the first temple was erected by his son. Thereafter, the temple builders could not stop. Jains believe that Pundarika, the chief disciple of Adinatha, attained nirvana here.

Most of the temples are named after their founders and date from the 16th century, although the earliest may date from the 11th. It would appear that many others were destroyed by the Muslims in the 14th and 15th centuries, but later, when Jains obtained religious toleration, they began rebuilding.

The 863 temples are strung along the two ridges of the hill, with further temples in the hollow between, linking them. There are nine enclosures of *tuks* (fortifications) which provided defence. There are lovely views over the flat, cultivated black soils of the coastal plain, and on a clear day after the rains it is sometimes possible to see the Gulf of Khambat away to the east, and the Chamardi peak and the granite range of Sihor to the north.

There are two routes up the 600 m climb. The main route starts in the town of Palitana to the east of the hill, while a shorter and steeper route climbs up from the village of Adpur to the west. Both are excellently made stepped paths. The main pilgrim route starts in Palitana. Over 3500 steps – you will be told more by the *dhoolie* carriers at the bottom – lead up to the temples. There are two long flat stretches, but since some of the path is unshaded, even in winter it can get very hot.

Temples in this southern group include one of **Ramaji Gandharia** (16th century), and the **Bhulavani** (labyrinth, 18th century) which is a series of crypt-like chambers each surmounted with a dome. The **Hathiapol** (Elephant Gate, 19th century) faces southeast. The **Vimalavasi Tuk** occupies the west end of the south ridge. In it is the **Adishvara Temple** (16th century) which dominates the site. It has a double-storey *mandapa* inside which is a large image of Rishabhanatha with crystal eyes and a gold crown of jewels. The **Vallabhai Temple** (19th century) with its finely clustered spires and the large **Motish Temple** (1836) occupy the middle ground between the ridges.

The **Khartaravasi Tuk** is the largest and highest temple complex, stretched out along the northern Ridge and includes the **Adinatha Temple** (16th century). There are quadruple *Tirthankara* images inside the sanctuary.

A comprehensive restoration project is being carried out on some of the temples, with many of the old stone carvings being 'refreshed' using a butterscotch-coloured mortar. It is interesting to watch the craftsmen in action, but some may feel that the new decorations lack the sculptural finesse and timeworn appeal of the originals.

If you wish to take the track down to Adpur turn left out of the complex entrance courtyard where you leave your shoes. Follow the sign to Gheti Pag Gate.

Alang

The beach at Alang has turned into the world's largest scrapyard for redundant ships, the industry yielding rich pickings from the sale of salvaged metal (bronze, copper) and the complete range of ship's fittings from portholes to furniture, diesel engines and lifeboats. Alang village, which is 50 km south of Bhavnagar, has developed this surprising specialization because of the unusual nature of its tides. The twice-monthly high tides are exceptional, reputedly the second highest in the world, lifting ships so that they can be beached well on shore, out of reach of the sea for the next two weeks. During this period the breakers move in unhindered. Labourers' 'huts' line the coast road though many workers commute from Bhavnagar.

Even though entry to Alang port may not be available, the last few kilometres to the port are lined with the yards of dealers specializing in every item of ships' furniture. Valuable items are creamed off before the 'breaking' begins, but if you want 3-cm-thick porthole glass, a spare fridge-freezer or a life jacket, this is the place to browse. However, customs officers always get first choice of valuables as they have to give permission for vessels to be beached, so don't expect too much. Some have found the journey not worth the trouble since they couldn't enter the fenced-off 'lots'.

Alang is only open to tourists with **special permission**, obtained from the **Gujarat Maritime Board** ① *Sector 10A, opposite Air Force Station, Gandhinagar, T079-2323 8346* or in Alang itself. Foreigners report finding it difficult to get permission to enter the beach/port area. Hotels in Bhavnagar may be able to help individuals gain entry but permits for groups are virtually impossible. Photography is not allowed. Strong shoes and modest dress are recommended.

Mahuva and Gopnath

The picturesque town of **Mahuva** (pronounced Mow-va), south of Palitana, was known for its historic port. Beautiful handcrafted furniture with lacquer work and intricate hand painting is made here.

About 30 km northeast of Mahuva, **Gopnath** is where the 16th-century mystic poet Narsinh Mehta is said to have attained enlightenment. Near the lighthouse is the 1940s summer home of late Maharajah Krishna Kumar Singhji of Bhavnagar, part of which is now a hotel. There are pleasant rocky, white-sand beaches – dangerous for swimming but good for walking – and a 700-year-old temple, 1 km away.

Listings Palitana and around

Tourist information

Palitana

Tourist office
Hotel Toran Sumeru, T02848-252327.

Where to stay

Palitana

$$$ Vijay Vilas Palace (Heritage Hotel)
In Adpur, a cattle herders' village ringed by hills, book ahead through North West Safaries, T079-263 08031, www.northwestsafaries.com. Aug-Apr.

There are just 6 rooms in this lovely 1906 lodge, which has an Italian country house feel and is surrounded by greenery. Delicious home-cooked Indian meals are served; non-residents are charged Rs 250 with advance notice. The shorter but steeper route to the Palitana temple complex starts about 200 m away at the temple in Adpur village (follow the milkmaids carrying curd!). It's 7 km from town, tricky to find after dark; rickshaws Rs 75, shared motorbike-rickshaws Rs 6.

$ Sumeru (Gujarat Tourism)
Station Rd, near bus stand, T02848-252327.
This place has a typical Gujarat Tourism vibe: 16 lacklustre rooms, 4 with a/c, 16 dorm beds (Rs 75) with cold water only, restaurant with a limited menu, tourist office and 0900 checkout. But it's good for visiting the temple.

Festivals

Palitana
Mar **Teras Fair** at Gheti (Adpur-Palitana, 4 km from town) 3 days before **Holi**. Thousands of Jain pilgrims attend, joined by villagers who come for free lunches.

Transport

Palitana
Bus ST Bus (0800-1200, 1400-1800) to **Ahmedabad** (often with a change at Dhandhuka), deluxe from Ahmedabad (0700, 0800, 0900); to Bhavnagar (1½ hrs), **Jamnagar**, **Rajkot**, **Surat**, **Una**, **Vadodara** and Veraval (for Sasan Gir). Private de luxe coaches to **Surat** and **Mumbai** via **Vadodara**. Operators: **Paras**, Owen Bridge, T02848-252470. And opposite ST depot: **Khodiar**, T02848-252586 (to Surat).

Taxi For up to 7 passengers, run between **Bhavnagar** (57 km by State Highway) and **Palitana**.

Junagadh *Colour map 5, A1.*
discover evidence of an ancient settlement beneath the urban sprawl

The narrow winding lanes and colourful bazars of the small town of Junagadh (population 168,700), entered by imposing gateways, are evocative of earlier centuries. A large rock with 14 Asokan edicts, dating from 250 BC, stands on the way to the temple-studded Girnar Hill, believed to be a pre-Harappan site. But the modern town is marred by ugly new buildings and dirty slums.

Established by the Mauryans in the fourth century BC, from the second to fourth centuries Junagadh was the capital of Gujarat under the Kshattrapa rulers. It is also associated with the Chudasama Rajputs who ruled from Junagadh from AD 875. The fort was expanded in 1472 by Mahmud Beghada and again in 1683 and 1880. Sher Khan Babi, who took on the title of Nawab Bahadur Khan Babi, declared Junagadh an Independent state in the 1700s. At the time of Partition the Nawab exercised his legal right to accede to Pakistan but his subjects were predominantly Hindu and after Indian intervention and an imposed plebiscite their will prevailed. The Nawab was exiled along with his 100 dogs.

Sights
The old **Uparkot citadel** ① *0700-1900, Rs 5, plus Rs 100 to visit the Buddhist caves*, on a small plateau east of the town, was a stronghold in the Mauryan and Gupta empires. The present walls are said to date from the time of the Chudasama Rajputs (ninth-15th century). The deep moat inside the walls is believed to have once held crocodiles. The Ottoman canons of Suleman Pasha, an ally of the sultans, were moved here after the Muslim forces were unable to save Diu from Portuguese naval forces. The town was repeatedly under attack so there was a huge granary to withstand a long siege. The **Jama Masjid** was built from the remains of a Hindu palace. The 11th-century **Adi Chadi Vav**, a *baoli* with 172 steps and an

Tip...
You can tackle the town on foot allowing plenty of time for Uparkot. However, it's best to get an early start on Girnar Hill with the help of a rickshaw (around Rs 50 return).

impressive spiral staircase, is believed to commemorate two slave girls who were bricked up as sacrifice to ensure the supply of water. The 52-m-deep Naghan Kuva is a huge 11th-century well, which has steps down to the water level through the rocks, with openings to ventilate the path. The **Buddhist cave monastery** in this fort complex dates from Asoka's time. Two of the three levels are open to visitors. The drainage system was very advanced, as shown by the rainwater reservoir. The ventilation cleverly achieved a balance of light and cool breezes. Other Buddhist caves are hewn into the hillsides near the fort.

In the town, the late 19th-century mausolea of the Junagadh rulers, not far from the railway station, are impressive. The **Maqbara** of Baha-ud-din Bhar with its silver doors and intricate, elaborate decoration, has an almost fairground flamboyance. The **Old Mausolea** at Chittakhana Chowk (opposite **Relief Hotel**, which has views of them from the roof), which were once impressive, are now crumbling and overgrown.

The **Durbar Hall Museum** ⓘ *Nawab's Palace, circa 1870, Janta Chowk, Thu-Tue 0900-1215, 1500-1800, Rs 5, plus Rs 2 per photo, small but recommended,* houses royal memorabilia, including portraits, palanquins, gem-studded carpets and costumes.

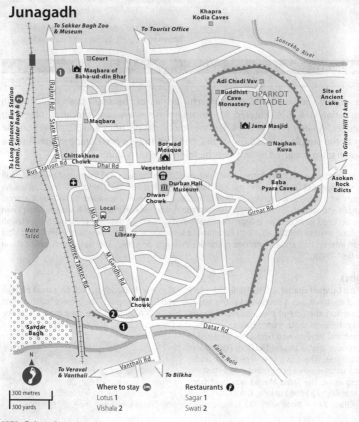

Junagadh

To Sakkar Bagh Zoo & Museum

To Tourist Office

Khapra Kodia Caves

Sonrekha River

To Long Distance Bus Station (300m), Sardar Bagh &

Court

Maqbara of Baha-ud-din Bhar

(Rajkot Rd)

State Highway

Bus Station Rd

Adi Chadi Vav

Buddhist Cave Monastery

UPARKOT CITADEL

Site of Ancient Lake

To Girnar Hill (2 km)

Maqbara

Jama Masjid

Naghan Kuva

Chittakhana Chowk

Dhal Rd

Borwad Mosque

Vegetable

Durbar Hall Museum

Baba Pyara Caves

Asokan Rock Edicts

Diwan Chowk

Girnar Rd

IMG Rd

Jayshree Talkies Rd

Local

Library

Mota Talao

Kalwa Chowk

Datar Rd

Sardar Bagh

Kalwa Nala

N

To Veraval & Vanthali

Vanthali Rd

To Bilkha

300 metres
300 yards

Where to stay 🛏
Lotus 1
Vishala 2

Restaurants 🍴
Sagar 1
Swati 2

Girnar Hill

Girnar Hill, rising 900 m above the surrounding plain, 3 km east of town, has been an important religious centre for the Jains from the third century BC; there are 16 Jain temples on the hill. The climb up this worn volcanic cone by 10,000 stone steps takes at least two hours. You start just beyond Damodar Kund in teak forest; at the foot. **Asokan rock edicts** ① *Thu-Tue 0830-1800, closed holidays, Rs 100*. They are carved in the Brahmi script on a large boulder. The emperor instructed his people to be gentle with women, be kind to animals, to give alms freely and to plant medicinal herbs. The 13 edicts are summed up in the 14th. The climb can be trying in the heat so is best started very early in the morning. You will find tea stalls en route and brazen monkeys. *Dhoolis* are available but are expensive. The charge depends on weight; for example, Rs 1500 for 60 kg to the first group of temples, which are the most interesting. There are good views from the top though the air is often hazy.

Listings Junagadh *map p1270*

Where to stay

Rates double during Diwali (Oct-Nov) when large number of Indians visit Girnar.

$$ The Lotus Hotel
Station Rd, T0285-265 8500,
www.thelotushotel.com.
Almost chic, this very white hotel has a good vibe, Wi-Fi and 24-hr room service.

$ Vishala
3rd floor, Dhara Complex, opposite ST Bus Stand,
T0285-263 1599.
Bright and modern rooms, some veering towards contemporary, some with quite eccentric bamboo decor in a good new hotel. Uncrowded dorm, quite clean, with friendly staff, a good rooftop restaurant and internet. It's high enough above the street to avoid the worst of the traffic noise. Recommended.

Restaurants

Near Kalwa Chowk, try *Dal-Pakwana* (a Sindhi brunch), stuffed parathas, fruit juices (*kesar* mango Apr-Jun). In Azad Chowk, try milk sweets, snacks and curds.

$ Sagar
Jayshree Talkies Rd.
Good Punjabi and Gujarati fare, vegetarian dishes, Indian breakfast (*puri-sabzi*), *iddli* and *lassi*.

$ Swati
Jayshree Talkies Rd.
One of the town's most popular restaurants, clean and comfortable, and with a/c. Serving mainly Punjabi cuisine, with some South Indian and Chinese, all dishes are vegetarian. Good food and *lassi*, and courteous, enthusiastic staff.

Festivals

Feb-Mar **Bhavnath Fair** at **Sivaratri** at Damodar Kund near the Girnar foothills is very spectacular. Attended by *Naga Bawas* (naked sages), who often arrive on decorated elephants to demonstrate strange powers (including the strength of their penis), and colourful tribal people who come to worship and perform *Bhavai* folk theatre.
Nov-Dec A popular 10-day **fair** is held at the Jain temples starting at Kartik Purnima.

Transport

Bus Regular buses to **Ahmedabad**, **Rajkot** (2 hrs), **Veraval**, **Porbandar** and **Sasan Gir** (2½ hrs). One direct bus to **Palitana**, 0500, 6 hrs; otherwise change at **Songadh** (4 hrs).

Train **Ahmedabad**: *Somnath Exp 19222*, 7¼ hrs; *Veraval Ahmedabad Exp 19129*, 7½ hrs; all via **Rajkot**, 2½-3¼ hrs. **Veraval**: *Veraval Exp 11464/11466*, 1¾ hrs.

The sanctuary, 54 km from Junagadh, covers a total area of 1412 sq km, of which 258 sq km at the core is the national park. As a result of over-grazing and agricultural colonization, only about 10% of the park is forest. However, the scrubby look of much of the area represents the original, natural vegetation. The area has rocky hills and deep valleys with numerous rivers and streams, and there are extensive clearings covered with savannah-like fodder grasses.

Essential Sasan Gir National Park

Opening times

Mid-October to mid-February 0700-1200, 1500 to sunset (permits issued 0630-1030 and 1500-1700); mid-February to mid-June 0700-1200, 1600 to sunset (permits 0630-1100, 1600-1730);

Park information

Entry permits can be arranged by some hotels, or applied for in advance or online at www.girlion.in (ie for 0700 safari, apply the previous day at Sinh Sadan Lodge in Sasan village). Permits costing US$40 allow six people in a jeep to enter the park. The new rule is that you have to go in person and show your passport, even if your safari is pre-booked with the hotel. There's an additional charge of Rs 500 if your camera exceeds 7.1 megapixels. Calculate an extra Rs 100 for a guide and tips (some have little English but can make excellent wildlife spotters). Indians pay roughly 10-25% of the foreigner fee. Jeep hire is around Rs 750, but expect all fees, including jeep hire, to increase 25% on Saturdays and Sundays and 50% during Navratri, Diwali and Christmas/New Year. Hotel jeeps cost more but may come with English-speaking drivers. Advance bookings are recommended as a maximum of 35 jeeps are permitted in the sanctuary at one time, distributed over six different routes of 22-50 km. A few jeeps are available on the day (first come, first shove).

When to go

Temperatures vary between 42-7°C. March to May is the best time to visit.

The **Asiatic lion** once had a wide range of natural territory running from North to West India through Persia to Arabia. It is now only found in the Gir forest; the last one seen outside India was in 1942, in Iran. Similar to its African cousin, the tawnier Asian is a little smaller and stockier in build with a skin fold on the belly, a thinner mane and a thicker tuft at the end of its tail. The 1913 census accounted for only 18 in the park. The lions' natural habitat was threatened by the gradual conversion of the forest into agricultural land and cattle herders grazing their livestock here. The conservation programme has been remarkably successful. There are now reckoned to be around 350 animals in the park; too many, some say, for the territory to support. These, and 300-plus **panthers**, make Gir arguably India's best big cat sanctuary, while the existence of a handful of Sudanese villages in the park add to the slightly surreal African-safari feel of the place.

Though there have been attacks on villagers by park lions, these are thought likely to have been provoked as there are few reported man-eaters. Nevertheless, relations between the lions and the human settlements within and around the boundaries are becoming increasingly strained, with several reports of revenge killings of lions (principally for hunting livestock) being reported in the last couple of years. Deaths by poaching are also beginning to occur with disturbing regularity.

Exploring the park

During the course of three to four jeep safaris you have a reasonably good chance of spotting lions. They are more likely to be seen with the help of a good tracker and guide, but the government system for apportioning guides to a different group each session means it is impossible to guarantee the quality of your tracker from one drive to the next; inevitably, some visitors return disappointed. If you don't see one, the Interpretation Zone's safari park has a few lions (see below).

A **watch tower** camouflaged in the tree canopy at Kamleshwar overlooks an artificial reservoir harbouring wild crocodiles but it is poorly located and overcrowded with busloads of noisy visitors at weekends. Other towers are at Janwadla and Gola. For birdwatching, Adhodiya, Valadara, Ratnaghuna and Patyaliyala, are good spots. A walk along Hiran River is also rewarding.

The Tulsishyam **hot springs** in the heart of the forest (Tulsishyam is also a Krishna pilgrimage centre), and Kankai Mata **temple** dedicated to Bhim, the *Mahabharata* hero, and his mother Kunti, add interest.

The **Gir Interpretation Zone** ① *Devaliya, 12 km west of Sasan, foreigners US$20, Indians Rs 75 for 45-min tour by electric minibus; a taxi will charge around Rs 200-300 return including wait*, is 16 sq km of Gir habitat fenced in as a safari park to show a cross section of wildlife; the four or five lions can be easily seen in open scrubland in the area. The lions here are less shy than those in the sanctuary, but you may be frustrated by the briefness of the encounter. Other Gir wildlife includes spotted deer, sambar, nilgai, peafowl. Permits are available at the reception.

The **Crocodile Rearing Centre** ① *near entrance to Sinh Sadan, and road leading to Lion Safari Lodge, 0800-1200, 1500-1800, free*, is full of marsh crocodiles, varying in size from a few centimetres to 1 m, for restocking the population in the sanctuary. Eggs are collected in the park and taken to Junagadh for hatching under controlled conditions. Unfortunately, keepers prod the crocodiles to make them move.

Listings Sasan Gir National Park

Where to stay

$$$$-$$$ Lion Safari Camp
Near Hirenshwar Temple, Chitrod, T02877 296 507, www.campsofindia.com.
Characterful tents with a/c and stylish bathrooms. Good atmosphere.

$$$ Asiatic Lion Lodge
T02877-281 101, www.asiaticlionlodge.com
New lodge with spacious low-rise rooms, a jungleside café and evening campfires.

$$ Gir Birding Lodge
1.5 km north of Sasan down a dirt track, T(0)97239 71843, www.asianadventures.net, or reserve with North West Safaries.
Clean and comfortable cottages and a 2-bedroom suite downstairs in the main lodge, set in a mango orchard over the wall from the national park. Knowledgeable naturalist guides are available. A good buffet breakfast is served on the veranda looking over the wall into the forest. Lots of langurs, leopards are occasionally seen

and lions are often heard! There are beautiful views as you sit on your balcony in the orchard. Highly recommended.

$ Nitin Bhai's Family Rooms Homestay
Near Sasan bus stop, T(0)99790 46700.
Just 5 basic rooms but cleaner than most and a friendly welcome is guaranteed.

Transport

Sasan Gir National Park
Air The nearest convenient airport is Rajkot.

Bus Service to/from **Junagadh** (54 km), 2½ hrs, and **Veraval** (40 km), 2 hrs. The service to **Una** for **Diu** is unpredictable, morning depart 1100. Occasional buses to **Ahmedabad**.

Train From **Junagadh** to Sasan Gir, *352*, 3 hrs, continues to **Delwada** near Diu; return to Junagadh, so it's possible to visit for the day. The route is very attractive. **Talala** is the last major station, 15 km before Sasan, so stock up with fruit, biscuits, liquids there.

Veraval

Veraval is a noisy, unbearably smelly and unattractive town which provides a base for visiting the Hindu pilgrimage site of Somnath at Prabhas Patan. Its importance now is as a fishing port – hence the stench. Seagoing *dhows* and fishing boats are still being built by the sea without the use of any modern instruments, traditional skills being passed down from father to son.

Prabhas Patan (Somnath)

Somnath Temple ① *6 km east of Veraval, puja at 0700, 1200 and 1900*, a major Hindu pilgrimage centre, is said to have been built out of gold by Somraj, the Moon God (and subsequently in silver, wood and stone). In keeping with the legend, the stone façade appears golden at sunset. Mahmud of Ghazni plundered it and removed the gates in 1024. Destroyed by successive Muslim invaders, it was rebuilt on the same spot. The final reconstruction did not take place until 1950 and is still going on. Unfortunately, it lacks character but it has been built to traditional patterns with a soaring 50-m-high tower that rises in clusters. Dedicated to Siva, it has one of the 12 sacred *jyotirlingas*, see page 1283. You cannot take bags of any kind, cameras or mobiles into the temple.

Nearby is the ruined **Rudreshvara Temple**, which dates from the same time as the Somnath Temple and was laid out in a similar fashion. The sculptures on the walls and doorways give an indication of what the original Somnath Temple was like. There is a really old Shiva Linga here – very atmospheric temple.

Krishna was believed to have been hit by an arrow, shot by the Bhil, Jara, when he was mistaken for a deer at Bhalka Teerth, and was cremated at Triveni Ghat, east of Somnath.

Listings South coast

Where to stay

Somnath

$ Shubh Suvidha
Kamal Park, Somnath by-pass, T02876-231695.
Modern block with comfortable a/c and non a/c rooms available. Best value of the slew of identikit hotels in the area.

Transport

Veraval

Somnath Travels, Satta Bazar, T02876-245 185 will obtain tickets for long-distance journeys.

Bicycle Hire from opposite bus station or railway station, some in poor condition (the road between Veraval and Somnath is appalling).

Bus Buses to **Diu**, **Porbandar** (2 hrs), **Bhavnagar** (9 hrs).

Taxi Taxis from Tower Rd and ST bus stands are cheaper than those at the railway station. See **Somnath Travels** above for taxi hire details.

Train Train to **Ahmedabad**: *Somnath Exp 19222*, 11¼ hrs; *Veraval Ahmedabad Exp 19120*, 10¾ hrs.

booze, beaches and Portuguese heritage

The island of Diu (52,000) has a fascinating history and a relaxed atmosphere with little traffic. The north side of the island has salt pans and marshes which attract wading birds, while the south coast has some limestone cliffs and pleasant, sandy beaches. Although often compared to Goa, it is nowhere near as picturesque. The island is still visited by relatively few foreign travellers though its tavernas attract those deprived of alcohol from neighbouring Gujarat and the bars can get noisy especially at the weekend. It can be quite intimidating for women. It's no paradise island, but if you're in the area it offers a welcome break from the rigours of travelling around Gujarat. Most hotels cater for Gujarati families and so can be noisy. Diu town however has a relaxed vibe, crumbling charm and friendly locals.

Diu town

The small town is squeezed between the fort on the east and a large city wall to the west. With its attractively ornamented buildings and its narrow streets and squares, it has more of a Portuguese flavour than Daman. While some visitors find it quite dirty and decaying, and are disappointed by the number of liquor shops, others find Diu an enjoyable little place. The night market is a great place to have a drink and to wander around.

St Paul's Church (1601-1610), on Travessa dos Hospital, the road running from the fort, has a fine baroque façade, impressive wood panelling and an attractive courtyard. At this church, take the left-hand turning on to Rua de Isabel Fernandes for the **Church of St Francis of Assisi** (1593), part of which is a hospital (a doctor is available at 0930 for a free consultation). On Rua de Torres Novas is St Thomas's Church ① *0800-2000*, housing the museum with an interesting local collection. It has been renovated and now houses stone sculptures, woodcarvings and shadow clocks, as well as a café and pleasant rooms to let. These, and the fort, are floodlit at night.

Diu Fort (1535-1541) ① *0700-1800*, considered to be one of Asia's foremost Portuguese forts, was built after the Mughal Emperor Humayun attacked the Sultan of Gujarat with the help of the Portuguese. Until 1960 it garrisoned 350 Portuguese soldiers. Skirted by the sea on three sides and a rock-cut canal on the fourth, it had two moats, one of which was tidal. The lighthouse stands at one end and parts of the central keep are still used as a jail but has few occupants. Despite being damaged, some of the structures – walls, gateways, arches, ramps, bastions – still give us an idea of the formidable nature of the defences. It's worth allowing an hour for a visit.

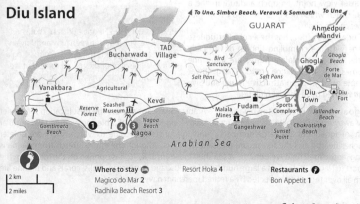

Diu Island

To Una, Simbor Beach, Veraval & Somnath   To Una

GUJARAT

Ahmedpur Mandvi

TAD Village

Bucharwada

Bird Sanctuary

Ghogla

Ghogla Beach

Forte de Mar

Salt Pans

Salt Pans

Diu Town

Diu Fort

Vanakbara

Agricultural

Kevdi

Reserve Forest

Seashell Museum

Malala Mines

Fudam

Sports Complex

Jallandhar Beach

Gomtimata Beach

Nagoa Beach

Nagoa

Gangeshwar

Sunset Point

Chakratirtha Beach

Arabian Sea

N

2 km
2 miles

Where to stay 🛏
Magico do Mar **2**
Radhika Beach Resort **3**

Resort Hoka **4**

Restaurants 🍴
Bon Appetit **1**

BACKGROUND
Diu

Like Daman across the gulf, Diu was a Portuguese colony until 1961. In 1987 its administration was separated from Goa (some 1600 km away), which then became a tate; Diu remains a Union Territory.

From the 14th to 16th centuries the sultans of Oman held the reins of maritime power here. The Portuguese failed to take Diu at their first attempt in 1531 but succeeded three years later. Like Daman, it was once a port for the export of opium from Malwa (Madhya Pradesh) but with the decline of Portugal as a naval power it became little more than a backwater.

About 5000 of the elders here (out of a population of 40,000) still speak fluent Portuguese. There are around 200 Catholic families and the local convent school teaches English, Gujarati, Portuguese and French. The Divechi people remain eligible for Portuguese passports and a few apply daily. Many families have a member working in Lisbon or former Portuguese Africa.

Makata Lane or **Panchwati**, near the Zampa gate, has some impressive old mansions of rich Portuguese and Indian merchants ranging from Venetian Gothic-style bungalows to traditional carved wooden or stone *havelis*.

Around the island

Forte de Mar Forte de Mar (Fortress of Panikot), built in 1535, was strategically important as an easily defended base for controlling the shipping lanes on the northeast part of the Arabian Sea. It has a lighthouse and a chapel to Our Lady of the Sea. It can be approached from Diu jetty when canoes or motor boats are available although landing is not permitted at present. The other fort at the eastern end of the island guarded the mint, while two others once guarded the west at Vanakbara and the bay to the south at Nagoa.

The north The creeks to the north of Diu island have been declared a bird sanctuary. There are watchtowers to spot flocks of shore birds including oyster-catchers, sanderlings and plovers. Lots of herons and ibises, flamingos, pelicans, etc, visit seasonally. Jackals, jungle cats and porcupines are seen in the evening. Bucharwada to the west lacks attractive beaches but has cheap spartan rooms in **Viswas Hotel**.

South and west of Diu Town Several beaches on the south side of Diu Island are easy to get to from Diu town by cycle or auto-rickshaw. **Jallandhar Beach**, to the south, is pleasant and the nearest to Diu. There have been several reports of groups of teenage boys, who not only come to watch and pester tourists but aggressively offer sex. **Chakratirtha Beach**, just southwest, has a sunset view point, an open auditorium and a small beach which has been spoiled by the glut of beachside cabins.

Fudam (or Fofrara) has the air of a Portuguese village with the crumbling Church of Our Lady of the Remedies. **Malala Mines** are limestone quarries off the Nagoa road. **Gangeshwar Temple** nearby has an attractive *Nandi* and Siva *linga* washed by the sea at high tide.

> **Tip...**
> Beaches between Nagoa and Vanakbara are safe all year except between May and July and are often empty, as is the beach along Ghogla. However, beware of the giant thorns that are hazardous to cycle tyres.

Nagoa About 7 km from town, facing the Arabian Sea, **Nagoa** offers the best location for a quiet stay away from Diu town. Its semi-circular palm-fringed beach suitable for swimming is popular with foreigners but also large numbers of Indian tourists who come to watch. There are quieter beaches nearby and the forests are pleasant for walks although the entire stretch from Nagoa is being landscaped for development. A **sea shell museum** ① *Rs 10,* has opened on the road from the airport to Nagoa. It displays a large number of mollusc and crustacean shells, corals and marine life from all over the world, collected by a retired merchant navy captain.

The west Vanakbara, the fishing village on the western tip of the island, has the Church of Our Lady of Mercy. Get to the early-morning fish market and watch the colourful trawlers unload catches of shark, octopus and every kind of fish imaginable. The drying fish on 'washing lines' and waterside activities provide photo opportunities. You can also watch traditional *dhow* building. South of Vanakbara is Gomtimata, a secluded white sand beach where a tourist hostel is expected to open, although there was no evidence of this at the time of writing. There is a ferry service between Gomtimata and the mainland.

Mainland Diu The fishing village of **Ghogla-Ahmedpur Mandvi** on the mainland is also part of Diu. Its name changes to Ahmedpur Mandvi on crossing to the Gujarat side of the border. The beach is good for swimming and it has splendid views of fishing villages and the fort and churches on Diu island. **Jyoti Watersports** and **Magico Do Mar** offer a variety of watersports here including parasailing, speed boating and waterskiing. Beware of the rip tide just a few metres out to sea, which has claimed several lives. Simbor Beach is a pleasant and little-known beach, 27 km from Diu town, off the Una road. It can be reached in 45 minutes from Diu by hiring a moped or scooter. Take food and water.

Listings Diu *maps p1275 and p1278*

Tourist information

Information Assistant
Diu jetty north of Bunder Chowk, T02875-252653, www.diuindia.com.

Tourist Complex
Ghogla. Mon-Fri 0930-1315 and 1400-1745.

Where to stay

Most places are basic. Some have a/c rooms with TV and charge double for these, but offer good discounts in low season. High season is during Diwali, Christmas and New Year and Apr to May.

$$$ Magico do Mar
Ghogla-Ahmedpur Mandvi, T02875-252 567, www.magicodomar.com
Lovely a/c huts with a traditional vibe, Saurashtrian decor and mirrorwork, set around a 1930s mansion of a Junagadh Nawab (best ones are Nos 510-513). Cheaper non-a/c rooms are in an unimpressive bungalow. Fantastic views, good access to beach and some water sports. Recommended.

$$$ Radhika Beach Resort
Nagoa, close to the beach, T02875-275 551, www.radhika resort.com.
24 comfortable a/c rooms in modern villas, with an a/c restaurant, a good pool in a well-tended garden, prompt service and a small provisions store, handy for beach.

$$ The Resort Hoka
100 m from the beach among Hoka palms and trees at Nagoa, T02875-253037, www.resorthoka.com.
10 clean, decent rooms with bath, 3 with shared facilities, set in a pleasant garden. The restaurant serves excellent fresh fish, and there's also a bar, laundry, travel agent and environment-conscious and friendly management. It's not luxurious but it's pleasant and good value. Discounts for long stays.

$$ Sanmaan Palace
Pensao Beira Mar Building, Fort Rd, T02875-253031.
A pleasant colonial house, with a sea-facing balcony, 6 rooms and suites, and a rooftop restaurant. With so many modern places, it's good to see some old-world charm.

$ Heranca Goesa
Behind Diu Museum, T02075 253851.
A very popular and relaxed place run by a local family. They serve leisurely breakfasts and slap-up fish suppers with Goan and Portuguese influences; step in even if you don't get a room here.

Restaurants

Some Catholic homes serve traditional Portuguese food to Western travellers with an hour's notice (ask directions in the Christian locality near St Paul's Church).

$$ Apana
Old Fort Rd.
Large seafood platters (shark, lobster, kingfish and crab), Rs 300, easily shared by 4-6 people. Also some vegetarian dishes. Recommended.

$$ Bon Appetite

Nagoa–Gomti road, 1 km from Nagoa Beach,
T09879593713.

Chilled out place with floor seating, offering up a
range of fresh fish and a small selection of other
fare. Phone to order pizzas from the wood oven.

$$-$ O'Coqueiro

Firangiwada Rd, near Diu Museum,
T09824681565.

Serving up a range of great fish curries or try
the grilled fish and coriander potatoes. There's
a good selection of veg and chicken dishes too,
but seafood is where it's at. Chilled out vibe and
a super-friendly family. Recommended.

$ Ram Vijay

Bundi Chowk, near State Bank of Saurashtra.

Friendly place serving excellent 'home-made' ice
creams: coconut and date 'n' almond are particularly
good. They also sell milk shakes and sodas.

Bars and clubs

The night market, near post office, is very
popular, and people sell beer and tasty snacks
from stalls too. Most bars close around 2130.

Nilesh

Stays open until 2300.

What to do

Cruises

Evening cruises from Bunder Chowk jetty to
Nagoa Beach, with music, Rs 100 per person;
enquire at the tourist office.

Diu Town

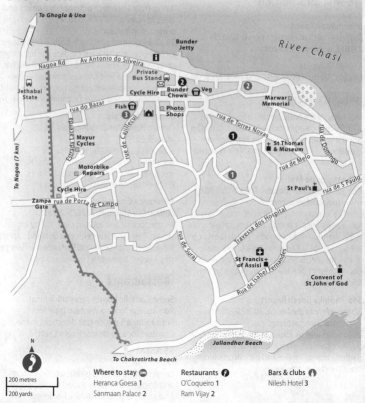

Where to stay	
Heranca Goesa 1	
Sanmaan Palace 2	

Restaurants
O'Coqueiro 1
Ram Vijay 2

Bars & clubs
Nilesh Hotel 3

Tour operators
Oceanic, *Bunder Chowk, T02875-252 1800.*
For ticketing and tours.

Watersports
At Nagoa and Ahmedpur-Mandvi there is parasailing, windsurfing, 8-seater speed boats and jet skiing. A pool/water slide complex is next to Kohinoor on the Diu–Nagoa road.

Transport

Most visitors arrive by long-distance buses either via Una or direct to the island, easiest from Ahmedabad via Bhavnagar. A road bridge connects Diu Town with Ghogla which has more frequent buses.

Forte de Mar

Old Fort Rd

Pedro Bridge

Parade Ground

DIU FORT

Gulf of Khambhat

Air The airport is 6 km west of the town; auto-rickshaws charge around Rs 50 to transfer. **Jet Airways**, at the airport, Nagoa Rd, T02875-3989 3333, www.jetairways.com.

Bicycle Hire about Rs 50 per day. **A to Z**, near Veg Market, Panchwati Rd; **Shilpa**, Bunder Chowk; **Mayur**, past Ankur Hotel (across rough ground, then 20 m along alley to left), excellent bikes; **Daud**, Zampa Gate, well-maintained, new bikes; **Krishna Cycles** at Ghogla.

Local bus Bus stand: to **Nagoa** 3 daily; frequent service to **Bucharwada-Vanakbara** and **Una**.
　Long-distance bus Most long-distance buses operate from the **Jethabai Bus Stand** just south of the bridge to Ghogla. ST services to **Ahmedabad** via Bhavnagar, 0700 (10 hrs); **Bhavnagar**, ask for 1035 'direct bus' as some go through Mahuva and are packed; **Jamnagar** via Junagadh; **Rajkot**, several (7 hrs); **Vadodara**; **Veraval**, several (2½ hrs). Buses often leave 15-20 mins early.
　A wider choice of buses serve Una, 8 km from Diu on the mainland, connected by local buses and auto-rickshaws.
　Private agents in the Main Sq offer buses from the private bus stand to **Mumbai**, **Ahmedabad** and major towns in Gujarat; often more reliable than ST buses. **Goa Travels** serve Bhavnagar, Junagadh (5 hrs) and Palitana.
　Shiv Shakti, **Sahajan and** and **Gayatri Travels** run from the main bus station to **Ahmedabad**, **Bhavnagar**, **Mumbai**, **Vadodara**, etc.
　Vanakbara, at the west end of the island, has buses to **Okha** via **Veraval**, **Porbandar** and **Dwarka**.

Motorbike Hire in the market area; mopeds, scooters and motorbikes cost from about Rs 140-300 a day plus fuel and deposit. **Kismet**, T01875-252971, has good new scooters, friendly service. You can also ask at Radhika Beach Resort

Rickshaw Auto-rickshaw: Rs 30 to **Nagoa**, Rs 25 to **Ghogla**. Demand Rs 100 to **Una** or **Delwada**

Train Delvada, 8 km north between Diu and Una, is the nearest railhead just south of Una; auto-rickshaws demand Rs 100 from Diu to Una or Delwada. The station is a short walk from the centre of town – follow the locals. Slow, crowded trains with hard wooden benches go to **Junagadh** via **Sasan Gir**.

The former capital of the Jethwa Rajput petty princely state, Porbandar (population 133,000) was previously named Sudamapuri, after Krishna's devoted friend, and has a temple dedicated to her. The *dhow*-building tradition that continues on the seashore to the present day reflects a history of maritime trade with North Africa and Arabia. Today, Porbandar is closely associated with Mahatma Gandhi and is also known for its production of gold and silver trinkets, fine-quality silk and cotton manufacture and chemical and cement factories.

Sights

Mahatma Gandhi was born in Porbandar in 1869. Next to the family home with its carved balconies is **Kirti Mandir** ① *sunrise-sunset, but the guide takes a lunch break from 1300-1400,* a small museum that traces his life and contains memorabilia and a library. **Darbargadh**, a short walk from Kirti Mandir, the old palace of the Maharanas of Porbandar, was built in the 1780s but is now deserted. It has some intricate carvings and carved balconies; the rooms inside (if you can get in) have interesting paintings.

Sartanji (or Rana-no) **Choro** (1785), near the ST stand, is the beautiful pleasure pavilion of Maharajah Sartanji, a great poet, writer and music lover. The pavilion has domes, pillars and carved arches and its four sides represent the four seasons.

The Maharana's deserted sprawling **Hazur Palace** is near the seafront. Ask for permission to visit the rooms inside at the office. **Daria Rajmahal**, the splendid turn-of-the-century palace of the Maharana of Porbandar, now a college, has intricate carvings, courtyards, fountains, carved arches and heavily embellished façades. The tower has excellent views of the seashore.

Chaya, 2 km from Chowpatty sea face, is the old capital of the Jetwas. The **Darbargadh Palace** with a beautiful carved balcony, is believed to have secret tunnels and passages to temples and places of safety.

The **Bharat Mandir Hall** in Dayananda Vatika garden is across the Jubilee (Jyubeeli) Bridge. It has a large marble relief map of India on the floor and bas reliefs of heroes from Hindu legends on the pillars. Nearby **Arya Kanya Gurukul** is an experiment in education for girls based on ancient Indian tradition. The dated **planetarium** has shows in Gujarati only. The architecture incorporates different religious styles illustrating Gandhi's open mind.

Jhavar Creek attracts scores of waterbirds. Flamingos, pelicans, storks and heron can be seen from the road in the mangrove marshes. Fisheries have appeared around the creek where the fish put out to dry attract thousands of terns and gulls.

Listings Porbandar

Where to stay

$$-$ Kuber
Bhavsinhji Park, near ST station,
T0286-221 0918.
Most of the 19 rooms have a/c, and suites have fridges. Friendly and helpful manager, free airport transfer. Recommended.

$ Indraprastha
Near ST Station, T0286-224 2681.
Large modern hotel, comfortable, all the usual features, some a/c.

Restaurants

Sudama Chowk near the ST Stand is where locals gather for samosas, *pakodas, bhel, kachori, pau bhaji*, etc, in the evening.

$ Adarsh
MG Rd.
A/c, Indian vegetarian and ice creams.

Swagath
MG Rd.
Pleasant place serving excellent *thalis*. The bazar sells *khajli* (fried dough snack), *thabdi* and *peda* (milk sweets).

Transport

Air Jet Airways, T0286-3989 3333, www. jetairways.com, flies daily to **Mumbai**.

Bus ST buses serve most centres of Gujarat. **Bharat** and **Eagle Travels** run regular private luxury buses to **Ahmedabad**, **Jamnagar**, **Junagadh**, **Rajkot**, etc.

Train Mumbai (Central): *Saurashtra Exp 19216*, 23½ hrs, calls at **Rajkot** and **Ahmedabad**.

Jamnagar and around *Colour map 2, C1.*

seek out the Ayurvedic and yoga university

Jamnagar (population 447,700), now an expanding town, was a 16th-century pearl fishing centre with one of the biggest pearl fisheries in the world until the early 20th century. The famous cricketer Ranjitsinghji was its ruler from 1907 to 1933. The walled city is famous for its embroidery, silverware and *bandhani* (tie-dye) fabrics produced in workshops in the narrow lanes.

Sights

Pirotan Island in the middle of the Ranmal lake in the Old City, reached by a stone bridge, has the **Lakhota Fort** and **Kotha Bastion** ① *Thu-Tue 1030-1300, 1500-1730, closed 2nd and 4th Sun*, with its arsenal. The **fort museum** has a collection of sculpture and pottery found in ruined medieval villages nearby. It is also a pleasant, cool and quiet spot just to relax while

Tip...

Bala Hanuman temple is in the *Guinness Book of Records* for continuous chanting; to date, 13,892 days, over 38 years.

listening to the strains of *Shri Ram, Jai Ram, Jai Jai Ram* wafting across the lake from the **Bala Hanuman Temple**. The temple is worth a visit, especially early evening. The bastion has an old well from which water can be drawn by blowing into a small hole in the floor. The **solarium** uses solar radiation to cure diseases. A group of **Jain temples** in the Old City are profusely decorated with glass, gilding and mirrors.

Northwest of the town centre is the **Ayurvedic University** ① *T0288-266 4866, www. ayurveduniversity.com*, at present the only one in India, which teaches courses to bachelor and postgraduate level in Ayurvedic medicine and yoga. A limited number of places are available for suitably qualified foreign students.

Around Jamnagar

Khijadia Lakes ① *10 km northeast of Jamnagar, US$5, car with up to 6 passengers US$20; camera US$5, professional still camera US$10, video US$500; guide US$5*, are three freshwater lakes surrounded by salt pans and salt marshes. Entirely flooded in the wet season, the lakes remain fresh throughout the dry season, though they occasionally dry out completely. The lakes, a bird sanctuary, are an important staging post for migratory birds, including swallows, martins and wagtails, and many waterfowl.

Marine National Park ① *30 km away, same price as Khijadia Lakes*, offshore from the southern coast of the Gulf of Kachchh, comprises an archipelago of 42 islands noted for their coral reefs and mangroves. It is possible to see dolphins, finless porpoise and sea turtles and a variety of colourful tropical fish. The area also attracts a host of waterbirds. The best island to visit is 1.5-sq-km **Pirotan**. To get there hire motor boats for 15-45 people from Jamnagar jetty (or from Okha) and take a guide. Permits are needed and are available from the Director, Marine National Park, Rajdarshan Ground, Jamnagar. Pirotan is uninhabited except for lighthouse staff.

Where to stay

Jamnagar

$$$-$$ Aram (Heritage Hotel)
Pandit Nehru Rd, 3 km northwest of centre,
T0288-255 1701.
Good a/c rooms in 1940s characterful mansion,
which is a bit on the garish side. Raj memorabilia,
a pleasant vegetarian garden restaurant, and
friendly, good service. At the time of writing, it
was under renovation so maybe prices will go up.

$$-$ Aashiana
New Supermarket, Bedi Gate, 3rd floor, T0288-
255 9110, www.ashiana hotel.com.
Clean a/c rooms with TV, better than the
competition, and a simple restaurant serving
inexpensive Indian vegetarian dishes. Good value.

$ Relax
Opposite Town Hall, T0288-255 6115.
Good clean rooms which are great value.
Excellent mixed dorms, Rs 250.

Transport

Jamnagar
Air Airport, 10 km west. **Indian**, T0288-255 0211,
www.airindia.in, to **Mumbai**.

Bus STC bus services to **Rajkot** (frequent),
Ahmedabad, **Dwarka** and **Porbandar**.

Train Railway station 6 km northwest of town.
Mumbai (**Central**): *Saurashtra Exp 19216*, 20¾ hr
via **Rajkot**, 1¾-2¼ hrs, **Ahmedabad**, 7¼ hrs, and
Vadodara, 10-11½ hrs.

Dwarka and around *Colour map 2, C1.*

a Hindu site popular with pilgrims

A small coastal town on the tip of the Kathiawad Peninsula, Dwarka (population 33,600) is one of the most sacred sites for Vaishnavite Hindus. It has the unique distinction of being one of Hinduism's four 'Holy Abodes' as well as one of its seven 'Holy Places'. Heavily geared up to receive pilgrims, the people are easy going, friendly and welcoming, even to the rarely seen tourist. The beach is good but without any palms for shade.

Archaeological excavations indicate that present-day Dwarka is built on the sites of four former cities. Work in 1990 by the marine archaeologist SR Rao discovered triangular anchors weighing 250 kg similar to those used in Cyprus and Syria during the Bronze Age, suggesting that ships of up to 120 tonnes had used the port around the 14th century BC. Marine research in early 2002 revealed evidence of a substantial city off the coast more than 100 m below current sea level, reviving the debate about the origins of Dwarka's offshore archaeological sites.

The present town mostly dates from the 19th century when Gaekwad princes developed Dwarka as a popular pilgrimage centre. Celebrated as Krishna's capital after his flight from Mathura, thousands come for Krishna's birthday and at Holi and Diwali.

Sights

The 12th-century **Rukmini Temple** has beautifully carved *mandapa* columns and a fine sanctuary doorway, but most of the rest is badly weathered. The mainly 16th-century **Dwarkadisha Temple** ① *0600-1200, 1700-2100,* was supposedly built in one night, and some believe that the inner sanctum is 2500 years old. The sanctuary walls probably date from the 12th century. The exterior is more interesting. The soaring five-storey tower is supported by 60 columns. Non-Hindus may enter after completing a form to show some level of commitment to Hinduism and to Krishna, but no photography is allowed inside and cameras must be left at the entrance. Some visitors are approached for a minimum donation of Rs 100. A **lighthouse** ① *1600-1800 or 1 hr before sunset, whichever is earlier, Rs 1, no photography,* stands to the west of the temples. The good-humoured keepers may treat you to a free private guided tour in exchange for any foreign coin (they all 'collect'). The views are beautiful; it's a very peaceful place to rest a while.

Outside Dwarka, the **Nageshwar Mandir** contains one of the 12 *jyotirlingas* in an underground sanctum. It helps to be agile if you wish to catch a glimpse. **Gopi Talav Teerth** is associated with Krishna (and Arjun) and has several shrines in the complex.

Okha

A small port at the head of the Gulf of Kachchh, Okha is 32 km north of Dwarka. You can visit the Marine National Park by hiring a motor boat from the jetty (see Jamnagar, page 1281). A pilgrimage to Dwarka is not complete without a visit to the island of **Beyt Dwarka** off the coast from Okha. This is where Krishna is believed to have resided while Dwarka was his capital. The 19th-century temple complex contains several shrines and images of Krishna and his 56 consorts. Archaeological excavations have revealed Harappan artefacts which date from the second millennium BC.

Listings Dwarka and around

Where to stay

Dwarka

$$$-$$ Govindhan Greens Resort
Baradiya Village, T(0)90990 79080,
www.govindhangreens.com.
A lovely resort with spacious rooms. There's a nod to the environment as it's a zero plastic zone, focuses on organic farming and has beautiful gardens. Recommended.

$ Toran (Gujarat Tourism)
Near Govt Guest House, T02892-234013.
12 clean, well-maintained rooms with nets, a dorm (Rs 75), courteous service, 0900 checkout, and a "dedicated and friendly manager". Recommended.

Festivals

Dwarka

Aug/Sep Janmashtami. Special worship and fair (Aug).

What to do

Dwarka

Dwarka Darshan. A tour of 4 local pilgrimage sites (Nageshwar Mandir, Gopi Talav Teerth, Beyt Dwarka, Rukmini Temple) by minibus, departs 0800, 1400, 5 hrs (can take 7). Tickets Rs 30; book a day in advance for morning tour. Or visit only Beyt Dwarka for a worthwhile day spent with pilgrims.

Transport

Dwarka

Bus Bus to **Jamnagar**, **Porbandar** and **Somnath**. Private operators run to most major towns.

Train To **Ahmedabad** and **Vadodara**: *Saurashtra Mail 19006*, 10 hrs, and **Mumbai** (**Central**): 20 hrs.

Kachchh (Kutch)

The scenic Maliya Miyana bridge, across salt marshes often filled with birds, gives a beguilingly attractive impression of the gateway to Kachchh. Yet this region is climatically perhaps the least appealing of Gujarat, and it is certainly the most sparsely populated. It is well and truly off the tourist trail.

The various communities such as Rabaris, Ahirs and Meghwals each have a distinct dress that is still an integral part of daily life, and each practise a particular craft, a fact that is being fostered and promoted by a number of co-operatives and NGOs. For the adventurous traveller willing to forego such luxuries as hot showers and reliable bus timetables, Kachchh offers some fascinating opportunities for adventurous, life-affirming travel.

Bhuj *Colour map 2, C1.*

gateway to the salt plains and craft villages of Kachchh

The devastating earthquake in January 2001, which hit 7.7 on the Richter scale and claimed around 20,000 lives, had its epicentre a few kilometres from the old walled town of Bhuj (120,000) with its tightly packed maze of narrow winding streets. Much was destroyed, and most of the town's picturesque heritage buildings suffered extensive damage. Some of the structures described below are being restored by experts, but a number of treasures have been lost permanently. Walking through the old palaces of Rao Lakha and the Aina Mahal can be a haunting experience. The old part of Bhuj still retains its magic though.

Essential Kachchh

Finding your feet

Bhuj airport is served by daily **Jet Airways** flights from Mumbai. Trains from Mumbai and Ahmedabad arrive at the station 2 km north of the centre, with auto-rickshaws for the transfer to town. Buses arrive at the ST stand on the southern edge of the old town. See Transport, page 1288. Permits are required for visits to many communities around Bhuj. Apply with passport and visa plus photocopies to the District Superintendent's Office near Kachchh Museum. Closed on Sunday. There is little official accommodation outside Bhuj, but villagers will readily find you a bed somewhere. The visitor book at the **Annapurna Hotel** (see page 1288) is full of practical tips on travel in this region.

Getting around

Most places of interest in town can be easily reached on foot, with auto-rickshaws and local buses on hand for journeys to surrounding towns. Buses from the ST stand go to the main villages, often just once a day (check time). For more flexibility arrange a taxi or hire a motorbike.

The central peninsula of Kachchh is surrounded by the seasonally flooded Great and Little Ranns. The Gulf of Kachchh to the south, a large inlet of the Arabian Sea, has a marine national park and sanctuary with 42 islands and a whole range of reefs, mudflats, coastal salt marsh and India's largest area of mangrove swamps.

The Kachchh Peninsula is relatively high, covered with sheets of volcanic lava but with often saline soil. Dry and rocky, there is little natural surface water though there are many artificial tanks and reservoirs. Intensive grazing has inhibited the development of the rich vegetation around the tanks characteristic of neighbouring Sindh in Pakistan, and there is only sparse woodland along the often dry river beds. The wetlands are severely over-exploited, but some of the lakes are important seasonal homes for migratory birds including pelicans and cormorants. The Rann of Kachchh in the north runs imperceptibly into the Thar Desert. A hard smooth bed of dried mud in the dry season, some vegetation survives, concentrated on little grassy islands called *bets*, which remain above water level when the monsoons flood the mudflats.

With the arrival of the southwest monsoon in June the saltwater of the Gulf of Kachchh invades the Rann and the Rajasthan rivers pour freshwater into it. It then becomes an inland sea and Kachchh virtually becomes an island. From December to February, the Great Rann is the winter home of migratory flamingos when they arrive near Khavda. There are also sand grouse, imperial grouse, pelicans and avocets.

Local traditional embroidery and weaving is particularly prized. Kachchh is an extraordinary place for tribal peoples and their crafts. When the monsoons flooded vast areas of Kachchh, farming had to be abandoned and handicrafts flourished which not only gave expression to artistic skills but also provided a means of earning a living. Mirrorwork, Kachchh appliqué and embroidery with beads, *bandhani* (tie-dye), embroidery on leather, gold and silver jewellery, gilding and enamelling and colourful wool-felt *namda* rugs are available.

Vast amounts of money and manpower were poured into Bhuj for the recovery effort, and the rapidly transforming town has gained prosperous-looking suburbs, a university and a broad-gauge railway line – perhaps at the cost of some of its cultural uniqueness. Nevertheless, it still forms a hub of trade for scores of tribal villages, and visitors can expect a genuinely warm welcome.

Sights

Among the old buildings in the citadel is the palace of **Rao Lakha** (circa 1752), the fortunate patron of Ramsingh Malam, who after his European adventures became a master clockmaker, architect, glass-blower, tile-maker and much more. A large white mansion with carvings and fretwork, the palace contains a Darbar Hall, State Apartments and the noted **Aina Mahal** (Mirror Palace) ① *0900-1200, 1500-1800, closed Sat, Rs 10, camera Rs 30, video Rs 100.* Some items such as glass paintings have been destroyed, but the exquisite ivory inlaid doors (circa 1708), china floor tiles and marble walls covered with mirrors and gilt decorations could be restored.

The **Fuvara Mahal** (Music Room) ① *next door, included with Aina Mahal ticket, same opening times,* is a curiosity. Surrounded by a narrow walkway, the pleasure hall is a shallow tiled pool with a central platform where the Maharao sat in cool comfort to listen to music, watch dancers or recite his poetry. With its entrance shielded from the hot sun, the candlelit interior with embroidered wall hangings provided a welcome refuge. Ingenious pumps raised water to the tank above to feed the pool with sprinkling fountains. Restoration work is in progress.

Rao Pragmalji's Palace (Prag Mahal; built 1865) ① *daily 0900-1200, 1500-1800, Rs 10,* in red brick, is across the courtyard. The elaborate anachronism was designed by the British engineer Colonel Wilkins (though some guides will say by an Italian architect). It contained a vast Darbar Hall, with verandas, corner towers and zenanas all opulently decorated with carving, gilding, Minton tiles and marble. The upper floors suffered serious damage in the earthquake. There are good views of the surrounding countryside from the tall clock tower connected to the palace by covered galleries. The colourful Swaminarayan Temple is behind the Palace near the lake.

The Italianate **Kachchh Museum** (1877), near Mahadev Gate, is the oldest in Gujarat. It exhibits the largest collection of Kshatrap inscriptions (the earliest, of AD 89), textiles and an anthropological section. Anyone interested in local traditional folk music and instruments may contact Mr UP Jadia here.

Bharatiya Sanskriti Darshan ① *Mandvi Rd, near Collector's Office, Wed-Mon 1100-1700, Rs 50*, is a small, delightful Folk Museum and Reference Library. The collection of 4500 exhibits includes traditional handicrafts, textiles, weaponry and other historic and artistic artefacts, as well as a

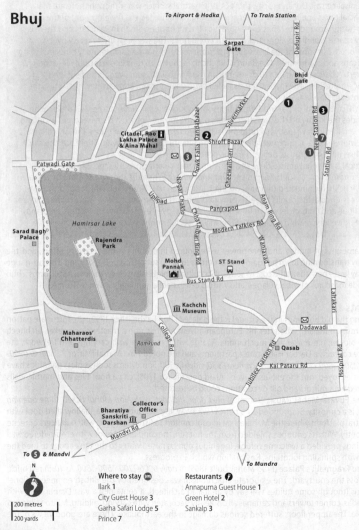

Bhuj

To Airport & Hodka

To Train Station

Sarpat Gate

Dadupir Rd

Bhid Gate

New Station Rd

Station Rd

Silvermarket

Citadel, Rao Lakha Palace & Aina Mahal

Dandabazar

Shroff Bazar

Chowk Falia

Gheewalfserr

Patwadi Gate

Nagar Chaklo

Uplipad

Panjrapod

Chhathari Ring Rd

Modern Talkies Rd

Aham Ring Rd

Wahavad

Hamirsar Lake

Rajendra Park

Sarad Bagh Palace

Mohd Pannah

ST Stand

Bus Stand Rd

Lahtakari

Kachchh Museum

Dadawadi

Maharaos' Chhatterdis

Ramkund

College Rd

Qasab

Kai Pataru Rd

Jubilee Garden Rd

Hospital Rd

Collector's Office

Bharatiya Sanskriti Darshan

Mandvi Rd

To **5** & Mandvi

To Mundra

N

200 metres
200 yards

Where to stay
Ilark 1
City Guest House 3
Garha Safari Lodge 5
Prince 7

Restaurants
Annapurna Guest House 1
Green Hotel 2
Sankalp 3

A melting pot of cultures

Kachchh is a meeting point of Sindhi, Gujarati, Muslim and Rajasthani cultures; the local language is more Sindhi than Gujarati. The arid grasslands to the north, south and west of Bhuj are home to several pastoral tribes: the Bharwad goat herds and shepherds, the Rabari camel and cattle herders, Maldhars who keep buffaloes, Samra and Sindhi Muslim cameleers and others. The communities have Lohan merchants, Langa musicians of the Indian desert and Kanbi Patel agriculturalists among them. They came from near and far; the Sodha Rajputs originated from the area neighbouring Rajasthan now in Pakistan, the Jats from Baluchistan, while the Sindhis claim Abyssinian descent.

recreated village of typical Kachchhi *bhungas* (huts) of different communities. *Kutch – People and their handicrafts*, by PJ Jethi (Rs 100), and postcards are for sale.

Sarad Bagh Palace ① *Sat-Thu 0900-1200, 1500-1800, Rs 10, camera Rs 30, video Rs 100,* west of Hamirsar, the last residence of the Maharao (died 1991) is set in lovely gardens. Exhibits include furniture and exotic ornaments. Further south, the Maharaos' *chhatterdis* (memorial tombs), built of red sandstone, were severely damaged in the 1819 earthquake and again in 2001. Some are beyond repair. Ramkund, nearby, has a stone-lined tank with carvings of Hindu deities.

Qasab ① *11 Nootan Colony, behind Santoshi Mata Mandir, south of town centre,* is an outlet for KMVS (**Kutch Mahila Vikas Sangathan**), a collective of 1200 craftswomen from 130 local villages who are practising and refining their traditional skills to produce high-quality Indian and Western clothes, home furnishings and leather goods. The women market the products themselves, bypassing an intermediary, thus controlling the speed and quality of production and achieving a fairer deal for themselves and their producer group. Their collection and craftsmanship is outstanding. See Shopping, page 1288.

Listings Bhuj *map p1286*

Tourist information

Bhuj Tourist Office
Oppositie Bus Stand, T02892-224 258.

Where to stay

$$$-$$ Garha Safari Lodge
Rudrani Dam, T937-433 5853.
An option for an atmospheric, out-of-town stay, with beautiful views of the lake. 14 whitewashed *bhungas* (local style huts), with tribal furniture and hot water; 7 are air-cooled. There's exchange, a pool and jeep tours. But there have been mixed reports about food, cleanliness and service.

$$$ Hotel Ilark
Station Rd, www.hotelilark.com,
T02832-258 999.
Hotel with all mod cons, smart with attractive traditional textiles. Good food and small branch of Kala Raksha in the lobby.

$$$-$$ Devpura Homestay
T02835-283065, www.devpurahomestay.in.
A charming heritage property which has been beautifully restored. Lovely verandas and sit outs, as well as jewel-coloured rooms, many with arches.

$$$ $$ Prince
Station Rd, T02832-220370,
www.hotelprinceonline.com.
Rooms with bath, not spotless but double glazed against traffic noise, restaurant (varied menu), shops (there is a small Qasab handicrafts outlet in the lobby), free airport transfer and guided tours of local villages Rs 1500 per car. 'Spot' liquor permits available. In a crowded area, credit cards not accepted.

$ City Guest House
Langa St, near Bazar, T02832-221067.
Well-run, excellent value guesthouse, offering 32 clean, quiet rooms, some with their own shower. There's a quiet garden for relaxing, as well as cycle hire and helpful staff. Used by foreign backpackers.

Restaurants

Typical local *dhabelis* (spicy burger of peanuts and potatoes, in a roll) and *bhal* (nuts, gram and vegetables in a spicy sauce) can be sampled on Vaniyawad and Station Rd.

$$ Sankalp
Oasis Hotel, Mews Complex, New Station Rd, behind Hotel Prince.
Branch of this South Indian chain serving up mammoth *dosas* and a mind-boggling array of chutneys.

$$ Toral
Prince Hotel.
Good Gujarati food, vegetarian *thalis*; a bit more expensive than elsewhere, but in a more comfortable setting.

$ Annapurna Guest House
Homely place serving very cheap authentic dishes. They allow you to sample each dish.

Festivals

Feb/Mar 4-day **Rann Utsav (Kachchh Festival)** organized by Gujarat Tourism during **Sivaratri** – tribal crafts, folk dances and music, and tours of nearby sights.
Fairs in many villages (*Nag Panchami*).
Aug-Sep Fairs in the Janmashtami area.

Shopping

Handicrafts

Excellent folk embroidery, leather shoes, appliqué, mirrorwork, block-printed fabrics, painted pottery and local weaving are available. The **market** area stretches from Station Rd to the Darbargadh Palace complex, a maze of alleys specializing in handicrafts. Most shops are closed 1200-1500.

Danda Bazar **Al Md Isha** for outstanding tie-dye; **Khatri Daod** for block-prints, embroideries.

Kansara Bazar For silver jewellery. **Bandhini Ghar**, for tie-dye. **AA Wazir**, opposite General Hospital, near High School, selection of old pieces of embroideries; some for sale.

Qasab, *11 Nootan Colony, T02832-222124, www.kmvs.org.in (also has a small shop in Prince hotel).* A number of NGOs have organized craft cooperatives for the benefit of artisans. Exquisite embroidered goods such as bags, cushion covers, wall hangings, etc, run by informative staff who can explain the process and stories behind the pieces. You can watch as they select and sew. But the real juice of this area is to get out into the villages and visit the craftswomen themselves; for example, at Sumrasar or Ludia.

Shroff Bazar Has craft shops for hassle-free browsing, lots of silver shops, and clothes: **Uday** (T02832-224660), a talented designer (Rs 600 for trousers and top), interesting block prints, excellent tailoring (made-to-measure in a few hours).

What to do

Kutch Ecological and Research Centre, *Tera village, 100 km from Bhuj, T0281-289 305.* Recommended as a contact for birdwatching and wildlife trips; they can help put you in touch with Mohammed Daddu, reported to be a passionate and skilled birding guide. Contact in advance.

Transport

Air Indian Airlines, T02832-244 050, www.airindia.in, and **Jet Airways**, Station Rd, T02832-3989 3333, www.jetairways.com, flies to **Mumbai**. Security is tight.

Bus Frequent service to **Ahmedabad**, 411 km;. **Bhjujodi**; **Mandvi** and **Rapar**; **Rajkot**, 5 hrs. 1-2 daily to **Bhavnagar**; **Jaisalmer**, 8 hrs; **Jamnagar**, **Junagadh**, **Palitana**; **Porbandar**, **Veraval** and **Somnath**. Most long-distance buses are scheduled to arrive at sunrise or sunset, so times change seasonally. 'Luxury buses' with reclining seats, more leg room, comfort stops, etc are strongly recommended. Many private operators cluster around the bus station, and run to major towns in Gujarat.

Train To **Mumbai**: *Bandra Terminus Exp 19116*, 17½ hrs; *Kutch Exp 19032*, 16 hrs. Both via **Ahmedabad**, 7-7½ hrs, and **Vadodara**, 9½-10 hrs. For **Rajasthan**, easiest to go via Ahmedabad.

The vast grasslands of Banni meet the Great Rann in the Khavda region, north of Bhuj. They are home to numerous pastoral nomadic, semi-nomadic and resident people who keep sheep, goats, camels, buffaloes and other livestock. The 40 or so hamlets here are best known for the minute detail of their embroidery. Handicrafts are a living tradition of Kachchh and the girls of these craft villages (population 37,000) make beautifully embroidered garments for their own trousseaus while women produce attractive fabrics for a second income.

More recently, these villages have started focusing on selling handicrafts as their main source of income and there are signs of modernization and commercialization. Some visitors to villages near Bhuj are disappointed to find that the previously nomadic tribes are being housed in whitewashed urban housing in expanded older villages that are losing their traditional architecture. Cement and modern materials are replacing the traditional mud walls and cow dung. However, traditional *bhungas* can still be found. These circular huts with sloping thatched roofs are made from mud plastered with cow dung and are often decorated with hand-painted floral patterns and inlaid with mirrors during festivals. Traditional utensils are still used for cooking, eating and storage in the houses.

★ Craft villages

Dhorodo, 80 km north, is the centre for Mutua embroidery, using chain stitches inset with small mirrors, leather embroidery as well as silver jewellery. **Rudrani Dam** ① *14 km north, 30-min drive from Bhuj on the Sumrasar road,* has the colourful **Rudramata Temple**, originally 17th-century, nearby. The goddess Sati's 'rudra' (frightening) aspect is believed to have fallen on this spot and is hence a place of pilgrimage.

Sumrasar, 25 km northeast, is famous for its Ahir embroidery and Soof embroidery of the Sodhas, done without a plan but by counting the warp and weft of the material. **Kala Raksha** ① *Parkar Vas, Sumrasar Sheikh, near Collector's Office, T02832-277237, www.kala-raksha.org,* is a grassroots organization that maintains a small but fascinating **museum** of heirloom textiles – it's an amazing collection and really interesting to be able to compare the styles of the different tribal embroideries. It works with and trains 180 artisans to create contemporary pieces inspired by their own traditions. It is now run by Judy Frater, the American author of *Threads of Identity*. Tunda Vandh is a good place to see typical *bhungas* of Kachchh. Architecture students come to see, study and photograph the traditional architecture adapted to this hostile climate. The interiors have beautiful Rabari cupboards, chests, inlaid mirrors and paintings.

Loria (**Ludia**), 60 km away, has huts with painted and mirror inlaid walls, and is famed for its wood crafts.

Further north than Ludia, in **Khavda**, you can visit the home of Ibrahim Kaka, where the men make traditional pots and the womenfolk paint them; it is good luck for marriage to have them in your home. There is also a small branch of KMVS (Qasab) here.

Zura, 30 km, produces embroidered footwear and other leather crafts. Copper bells are also made in this village.

Nirona, 40 km northwest, has embroidery, lacquered wood crafts, wood carving and is the only home of highly skilful rogan-painting (fabrics painted using iron rods). Buses from Bhuj take about 1½ hours.

Hodka, 63 km north, is the site of an indigenous tourism project, with a resort comprising tents and *bhungas* built in traditional style, owned and run by the village in cooperation with hospitality professionals and KMVS (see page 1287). Local guides show visitors around the village, providing ample opportunity to interact with the residents, and to buy embroidery direct from the artisans.

Nakhtarana, northwest in the heart of the craft village belt, produces some tie-dye work.

Charri Dund Lake

Charri Dund Lake, a reservoir near Charri village, offers splendid birdwatching opportunities. Flamingos, pelicans, cranes, storks, ducks and other water birds gather in large numbers, especially in winter, while nearby grasslands are filled with passerine and ground dwelling birds. The Banni grasslands are known for their huge eagle and vulture congregations. **The Bombay Natural History Society** ① *www.bnhs.org*, and other organizations monitor bird migrations in the Banni region, and bird-banding camps are set up around Charri Lake. The grasslands are home to wolf, hyena, jackal, Indian and desert foxes and lesser wild cats but are imperilled by the government's decision to convert Banni into pastureland.

Dholavira
250 km northeast of Bhuj, daily 0900-1800.

Dholavira is the site of excavation of a Harappan town (pre-2500 BC) which some estimate to be larger than Mohenjo Daro, in Pakistan. It was only discovered in 1967 and excavation began in 1990. The drive to Khadir beyt, an oasis in the Great Rann, through dazzling salt flats is very scenic. Excavations reveal interesting new finds on a regular basis and show the complex to be on three levels (Citadel, Middle and Lower Towns) with pottery, stone cutting, coppersmithing, drainage systems and town planning at an advanced level. The fortifications with walls, bastions and double ramparts reflect danger from invasions or enemies. An inscribed tablet found here bears 10 letters in the Harappan script, claimed to be the oldest signboard in the world. The bus from Bhuj (via Rapar) takes seven hours. Gujarat Tourism's **Toran Bungalow** provides good accommodation.

★ Salt plains

It is possible to drive further north in this region to experience the start of the salt plains, a desert of salt that stretches into the horizon. When you drive out to the Great Rann of Kachchh it's like driving to the end of the world. You look out onto a white horizon and stand on a bed of salt. Again, it is necessary to get a permit in Bhuj to visit this area as you are getting close to the border.

Listings North of Bhuj

Where to stay

Craft villages

$$$$ Infinity
60 km northwest of Bhuj, T02835-273 433, www.infinityresorts.com.
With a nod to conservation, Infinity is one of 4 beautiful resorts in India (another is in Corbett National Park). Expect luxury tents and a beautiful swimming pool right in the heart of the Kachchh wildlife.

$$$ Rann Visimo
Close to Hodka, T02832-574124, wwwrannvisimo.in.
Similar colourful bunga mud huts to Shaam-e-Sarhad; a good experience of village life.

$$$ Shaam-e-Sarhad
Hodka, 63 km north of Bhuj, T02832-574124, www.hodka.in.
Award-winning, genuine village tourism project, very comfortable and unique accommodation in circular adobe huts or tents, both with attached bath and running water, although a few older women reported a little too much insect life for their liking. Beautifully decorated, amazing food and music under an endless sky – magical. Village visits are free of commercial pressure, and a chance to see local culture. Wholeheartedly recommended.

Craft villages
Buses to Rajkot or Ahmedabad can drop you off at most of the villages.

Bhujodi, 10 km southeast, off the main road and a 10-minute walk from the bus stand, is the centre for pitloom weaving. The weavers have now been organized into a co-operative. They produce colourful *galichas* (carpets), *durries* (rugs), *dhablos* (blankets), and other items from wool, camel and goat hair, cotton and even synthetic fibres. Some embroidery and tie-dye can be seen here as well. Mr Vanka Kana Rabari has reasonably priced local embroidery and other items but not the most select quality. **Shrujan** ① *T02832-240272, www.shrujan.org*, run by the astute Daya Nathani, is another pioneer behind the revival in high-quality Kachchhi handicrafts; the shop sells upmarket embroideries and home furnishings. There is also a nice crafts park near Shrujan at Ashapura if you do not have time to travel into the villages north of Bhuj.

Padhdhar, 22 km southeast of Bhujodi, produces Ahir embroidery using round mirrors with floral and geometrical patterns. **Dhaneti** is also a centre for Ahir and Rabari embroidery. Meet Govindbhai, a local entrepreneur, and his friendly family who will show you the embroidered and mirror inlaid fabrics made for their own use. There are some intricate *pallias* (hero stones) by the village lake.

Dhamanka, 50 km east of Bhuj, is famous for its Ajrakh hand-block printed fabrics, using primarily vegetable dyes – you can watch them boiling up natural indigo and making orange colours from old iron horseshoes and pomegranate skin. Used blocks can be bought here as well as an array of garments and bed linen. You can meet Dr Ismail Khatri who is keeping the tradition alive and supplying big stores like Fab India and Anokhi. He says "True Ajrakh is like stars in the night sky – In Arabic, 'Aj' is the universe and 'Ajrakh' means blue. Clear shining stars show the Ajrakh is good quality." You can also visit Ajrakhpur closer to Bhuj – part of the family relocated here after the earthquake.

Anjar, 22 km southeast, was an early Jadeja Rajput capital of Kachchh, founded 450 years ago. The Jesal-Toral shrine has a romantic tale of the reform of an outlaw prince through the love of a village girl. Anjar is also known for its metalcrafts, especially betel nut crackers and ornaments, *bandhni* and block printing. The 1818 Bungalow of Captain McMurdoch, the first European to settle in Kachchh, now government offices, has some Kamangari paintings on the ground floor.

Mandvi *Colour map 2, C2.*
Mandvi, 54 km southwest of Bhuj, is a pretty little seaside town, with a reservoir in the centre and a river beyond. During the 18th century the town outclassed Bhuj in importance, the sea-faring people dominating the sea trade, taking cotton, rice, spices, etc, to the Persian gulf, Arabia and Zanzibar. The skill of building *dhows* and boats using simple tools is being revived along the river worth having a look.

The town is now a centre for handicrafts like *bandhani* tie-dyed fabrics, jewellery and shell toys. It is a desert town but important agricultural research for the Kachchh region is being carried out here in the Gujarat Agricultural University and the Vivekenand Research Institute, to improve farming in the often hostile environment.

There is an 18th-century **palace** with an Aina Mahal (Mirror Hall) and music rooms which have remains of intricate stone carvings of Dutchmen, tigers and dancing girls and woodcarvings in the courtyard. The magnificent 1940s **Vijay Vilas Palace** ① *Rs 20, camera Rs 20, plus vehicle charge*, with huge domes, combines Indian and European styles. You can see the drawing room with royal memorabilia, and the attractive *jali* windows of the *zenana*. The terrace, reached by a spiral staircase, with excellent sea views, especially at sunset, is ideal for a picnic.

The beaches on the town side are good for swimming and even camel or horse riding. A wind farm next to the beach is working hard to produce an alternative energy source. The Maharao's pleasant **private beach** ① *Rs 30*, is open to visitors and worthwhile for women, to escape hassle from male onlookers. Out of town, you can visit a magnificent new Jain temple.

Towards Gandhidham

On the Mundra Road, 19 km southwest of Anjar, Bhuvad has the ruined 13th-century Bhuvaneshwar Mahadev Temple. The *mandapa* (1289-1290) is supported by 34 unusual pillars (square base, octagonal middle and circular upper section). A local legend describes how the headless body of the chieftain Bhuvad, killed in battle in 1320, fought its way to the village. The *District Gazetteer* records that a shrine with a red headless figure is dedicated to him.

Further east along the coast is the port of **Kandla**, built to replace declining Mandvi. After Independence, Kandla was further developed by the Indian government to service the states in northwest India.

Gandhidham, 27 km north of Kandla, was founded by the Maharaos of Kachchh to accommodate refugees from Sindh in Pakistan after Partition in 1947. The enterprising community made a promising start and now the town is a prosperous business centre, though the old handloom and embroidery co-operatives for refugees still exist. The town has developed with the increasing importance of Kandla as a port having lost Karachi sea port to Pakistan. The Institute of Sindhology is researching on various aspects of Sindhi culture.

Listings South of Bhuj

Where to stay

Mandvi

$$$$ The Beach at Mandvi Palace
On the private beach of Vijay Vilas Palace,
T02834-277 597, www.mandvibeach.com.
A handful of safari-style tents with private bath on an isolated stretch of beach, seafood barbecues on the sand, walks in palace grounds and interesting views of wind farm.

$ Rukmavati Guest House
Near Bridge Gate, T02834-223 558.
Characterful place with clean rooms and kitchen access near the shipbuilding.

Restaurants

Mandvi

Zorba the Buddha (Rajneesh Hotel)
Near Azad Chowk.
Best-value *thalis* in simple dining area. The bazar has fresh coconuts, biscuits and excellent local corn on the cob. In the evening, handcarts emerge with popular snacks.

Transport

Mandvi

Bus Express bus from **Bhuj**, 1 hr; others very slow. From bus station, auto-rickshaws, Rs 50 for return trip to palace (bargain). It's possible to visit **Mundra**, further along the coast from Mandvi, on the same day, and return direct to Bhuj.

Gandhidham

Bus The bus station is a 3-min walk: turn right from the railway station. Frequent buses to **Bhuj**, but very crowded.

Train All trains to and from **Bhuj** stop at Gandhidham. **Mumbai** (**Central**), *Kachchh Exp 19032*, 17 hrs via Ahmedabad and Vadodara.

The 4950-sq-km wild ass sanctuary of the Little Rann of Kachchh (created in 1973) and the 7850-sq-km desert wildlife sanctuary of the Great Rann together would comprise the largest contiguous tract of protected wildlife territory in India were it not divided by a road. The Little Rann is mostly a saline wilderness, broken by *beyts* (islands during the monsoon) covered with grass, bushes, acacia and thorn scrub. The area is under severe threat from the salt works, which clear the vegetation, release toxic effluents into the wetlands and pollute the air. A fast-growing thorn scrub – *Prosopis juliflora* – is destroying most other vegetation.

Wildlife

This is the last home of the **Asiatic wild ass** (locally called *khacchar* or *ghorker*), a handsome pale chestnut brown member of the wild horse family with a dark stripe down the back. Wild asses are usually seen as lone stallions, small groups of mares or harems of a male with mares. Large herds of 40-60 are sometimes seen but they are loosely knit. Males fight viciously, biting and kicking, for their females. Nilgai, antelope and chinkara (Indian gazelle) are other mammals seen, but the chinkara numbers have dwindled due to poaching. Blackbucks have become almost extinct in the Little Rann of Kachchh but are seen in villages nearby. Wolf is the primary predator, though not common. You might spot jackal, desert fox and jungle and desert cat on a drive.

Birdlife is abundant. Houbara bustard, spotted and common Indian sand grouse, nine species of larks, desert warbler, desert wheatear, Indian and cream coloured courser, grey francolin and five species of quails are spotted at the *beyts*. The salt marshes teem with flamingos, pelicans, storks, ducks, herons and wading birds. Thousands of demoiselle and common eastern cranes spend the winter here.

Around Little Rann of Kachchh Sanctuary

The 13th-century **Jhinjwada fort**, on the edge of Little Rann west of Dasada, has majestic gateways. At the southeast corner of the Rann, **Kharaghoda**, southwest of Dasada on the way to Bajana Lake, is particularly interesting. The principal British salt trading post with an old village-pony express, it retains plenty of colonial architecture including Raj bungalows, a cricket pavilion and a bandstand. **Dasada** is a convenient base for visits to the Little Rann. The interesting village has an old fort with wood carvings, 15th-century tombs, potters, a shepherd's colony and nomadic settlements. The Malik Dynasty, who received the 56 km estate in return for military services to the sultan of Ahmedabad, now live in a 1940s mansion, **Fatima Manzil**.

Essential Little Rann of Kachchh Sanctuary

Access

The southern part of the sanctuary is accessible all year, 0600-1800. Entry Rs 1200 (Rs 500 Indians), still camera US$5, at Bajana and Dhrangadhra.

When to go

The best season to visit is late October to mid-March. Temperatures vary from a maximum of 42°C to a minimum of 7°C, while annual rainfall is 1000 mm.

What to take

Wear strong footwear when walking in this area as prosopsis thorns can pierce through thin-soled shoes.

Where to stay

$$$-$$ Camp Zainabad
9 km from Dasada, contact Desert Coursers,
T02757-241 333, www.desertcoursers.net.
A well-located cluster of 16 self-contained *kooba* huts in a eucalyptus grove, Rs 2000 each includes meals and safaris, recreating a local village. Atmospheric but small cots, hard mattresses and sometimes insipid food, a bit shabby around the edges. Enthusiastic owner, from the former ruling family of Zainabad. There are well-organized jeep safaris in the Little Rann, recommended by birders, and also camel/horse/village safaris, and boating at nearby lake.

$$$-$$ Rann Riders
Dasada, T(0)99252 36041, www.rannriders.com.
Beautiful air-cooled rooms in 22 spacious Kachchhi *bhungas* and Kathiawadi *koobas* (huts), all with unique features amid plantation and farms. There are tiled hot showers, a lovely swimming pool, and a great atmosphere at night, often with live music and tribal dancing. Delicious home cooking (especially meat dishes) with home-grown organic vegetables, fresh fish and poultry. Enthusiastic owner and good jeeps for tours. Highly recommended.

$ Guest Houses
Govt, closer to the Rann at Bajana and
Dhrangadhra, where a jeep can be hired for
visiting the Little Rann. Contact the Forest
Department at Dhrangadhra.

What to do

Check with **Rann Riders** (see Where to stay, above) or North West Safaries (see page 1244) for information and guides.

Transport

Bus Dhrangadhra is the main transport base, with ST (Govt) buses from main towns in Gujarat (frequent from **Ahmedabad**, 93 km, 2½ hrs); some continue to **Zainabad**, which has local buses to **Dasada**.

Train Trains between Mumbai/Ahmedabad and Bhuj stop in Dhrangadhra and at **Viramgam**, 33 km southeast of Dasada, but at inconvenient hours of the night. Hotels/resorts can arrange transfer on prior notice, at extra cost.

Background Gujarat

History

Some of India's earliest Stone Age settlements developed in these marginal areas; for example, at Rojadi near Rajkot and Adamgarh near the border with Madhya Pradesh. Other Stone Age settlements have been found around the Sabarmati and Mahi rivers in the south and east of the state.

There are a number of Indus Valley and Harappan centres such as Lothal, Dhoravira, Rangpur, Amri, Lakhabaval and Rozdi. The discovery of a copper ring with a spiral motif, similar to those found in artefacts of ancient Crete, points to the significance of Kuntasi, a Harappan port with a 'factory'.

Rock edicts in the Girnar Hills indicate that Asoka extended his domain into Gujarat. The Sakas (Scythians; AD 130-390) controlled it after the fall of the Mauryan Empire. During the fourth and fifth centuries it formed part of the Gupta Empire. Gujarat attained its greatest territorial extent under the Solanki Dynasty, from the ninth century. The Vaghela Dynasty that followed was defeated by the Muslim Ala-ud-din Khalji, the King of Delhi. There was then a long period of Muslim rule. Ahmad Shah I, the first independent Muslim ruler of Gujarat, founded Ahmadabad in 1411.

The Mughal ruler Akbar took Malwa and Gujarat in a daring military operation in the 1500s; this saw the start of two centuries of Mughal rule, terminated by the Marathas in the mid-18th century.

In the 17th-century scramble for trading bases the Dutch, English, French and Portuguese all established coastal ports here: the British East India Company's first headquarters in India was at Surat, before moving to Bombay. As the British established maritime supremacy all but the Portuguese at Daman and Diu withdrew. The state came under first the control of East India Company in 1818 and, after the 1857 Mutiny (Rebellion), the Crown.

Culture

About 15% of the population is tribal, including the Bhil, Bhangi, Koli, Dhubla, Naikda and Macchi-Kharwa. Mahatma Gandhi was strongly influenced by Jainism, which remains strong in Gujarat today. Gandhi also rejected the deep divisions between high and low caste Hindus, renamed the 'untouchables' as Harijans (God's people), and fought for their rights and dignity. Caste division remains a potent political force in Gujarat today.

Most people speak Gujarati, an Indo-Aryan language of Sanskrit origin but with some Persian, Arabic, Portuguese and English vocabulary deriving from maritime contacts. In the 19th century many Gujaratis went first to East Africa and thence to England, North America and New Zealand.

Within India, Gujaratis are prominent in the business community, and have gained a reputation for philanthropy and spiritual endeavour; even today it is not uncommon for people in the later stages of life to renounce their material possessions and strike out, sometimes with their family in tow, on the ascetic path of the wandering sanyasin.

Background

History

The first village communities in South Asia grew up on the arid western fringes of the Indus Plains 10,000 years ago. Over the following generations successive waves of settlers – sometimes bringing goods for trade, sometimes armies to conquer territory and sometimes nothing more than domesticated animals and families in search of land and peace – moved across the Indus and into India. They left an indelible mark on the landscape and culture of all the countries of modern South Asia.

The first settlers

A site at Mehrgarh, where the Indus Plains meet the dry Baluchistan Hills in modern Pakistan, has revealed evidence of settlement as early as 8500 BC. By 3500 BC agriculture had spread throughout the Indus Plains and in the thousand years following there were independent settled villages well to the east of the Indus. Between 3000 and 2500 BC many new settlements sprang up in the heartland of what became the Indus Valley civilization.

Most cultural, religious and political developments during that period owed more to local development than to external influence, although India had extensive contacts with other regions, notably Mesopotamia. At its height the Indus Valley civilization covered as great an area as Egypt or Mesopotamia. However, the culture that developed was distinctively South Asian. Speculation surrounds the nature of the language, which is still untranslated.

India from 2000 BC to the Mauryas

In about 2000 BC Mohenjo Daro, widely presumed to be the capital of the Indus Valley Civilization, became deserted and within the next 250 years the entire Indus Valley civilization disintegrated. The causes remain uncertain: the violent arrival of new waves of Aryan immigrants (a theory no one now accepts), increasing desertification of the already semi-arid landscape, a shift in the course of the Indus and internal political decay have each been suggested as instrumental in its downfall. Whatever the causes, some features of Indus Valley culture were carried on by succeeding generations.

BC	Northern South Asia	Peninsular India	External events	BC
900,000			Earliest hominids in West Asia	450,000
500,000	Lower Palaeolithic sites from NW to the Peninsula; Pre-Soan stone industries in NW.	Earliest Palaeolithic sites – Narmada Valley; Karnataka; Tamil Nadu and Andhra.	First occupation of North China. Origin of *homo sapiens* in Africa.	150,000
			Homo sapiens in East Asia.	100,000
			First human settlement in Americas (Brazil).	30,000
10,000	Beginning of Mesolithic period.	Continuous occupation of caves and riverside sites.	Earliest known pottery – Kukui, Japan.	10,500
			Ice Age retreats – Hunter gatherers in Europe.	8300
8000	First wheat and barley grown in Indus plains	Mesolithic.	First domesticated wheat, barley in fertile crescent; first burials in North America.	8000
7500	Pottery at Mehrgarh; development of villages	Increase in range of cereals in Rajasthan.	Agriculture begins in New Guinea.	7000
6500	Humped Indian cattle domesticated, farming develops.	Cultivation extends south.	Britain separated from Continental Europe by sea level.	6500

Probably from about 1500 BC northern India entered the Vedic period. Aryan settlers moved southeast towards the Ganga valley. Classes of rulers (*rajas*) and priests (*brahmins*) began to emerge. Conflict was common. In one battle of this period a confederacy of tribes known as the Bharatas defeated another grouping of 10 tribes. They gave their name to the east of the Indus which is the official name for India today – Bharat.

The centre of population and of culture shifted east from the banks of the Indus to the land between the rivers Yamuna and Ganga, the *doab* (pronounced *doe-ahb*, literally 'two waters'). This region became the heart of emerging Aryan culture, which, from 1500 BC onwards, laid the literary and religious foundations of what ultimately became Hinduism, spreading to embrace the whole of India.

The Vedas The first fruit of this development was the Rig Veda, the first of four Vedas, composed, collected and passed on orally by Brahmin priests. While some scholars date the oral origins as early as the beginning of the second millennium BC, the date of 1300 BC to about 1000 BC still seems more probable. In the later Vedic period, from about 1000 BC to 600 BC, the Sama, Yajur and Artha Vedas show that the Indo-Aryans developed a clear sense of the Ganga-Yamuna *doab* as 'their' territory.

From the sixth to the third centuries BC the region from the foothills of the Himalaya across the Ganga plains to the edge of the Peninsula was governed under a variety of kingdoms or Mahajanapadhas – 'great states'. Trade gave rise to the birth of towns in the Ganga plains themselves, many of which have remained occupied to the present. Varanasi (Benaras) is perhaps the most famous example, but a trade route was established that ran from Taxila (20 km from modern Islamabad in Pakistan) to Rajgir 1500 km away in what is now Bihar. It was into these kingdoms of the Himalayan foothills and north plains that both Mahavir, founder of Jainism, and the Buddha were born.

The Mauryas

Within a year of the retreat of Alexander the Great from the Indus in 326 BC, **Chandragupta Maurya** established the first indigenous empire to exercise control over much of the subcontinent. Under his successors, that control was extended to all but the extreme south of peninsular India.

The centre of political power had shifted steadily east into wetter, more densely forested but also more fertile regions. The Mauryans had their base in the region known as Magadh (now Bihar) and

BC	Northern South Asia	Peninsular India	External events	BC
3500	Potter's wheel in use. Long distance trade.		Sumeria, Mesopotamia: first urban civilization.	3500
3000	Incipient urbanization in the Indus plains.	First neolithic settlements in south Deccan (Karnataka). Ash mounds, cattle herding.	First Egyptian state; Egyptian hieroglyphics; walled citadels in Mediterranean Europe.	3100
2500	Indus valley civilization cities of Mohenjo Daro, Harappa and many others.	Chalcolithic ('copper' age) in Rajasthan; Neolithic continues in south.	Great Pyramid of Khufu China: walled settlements; European Bronze Age begins: hybridization of maize in South America.	2530 2500
2000	Occupation of Mohenjo Daro ends.	Chalcolithic in Malwa Plateau, Neolithic ends in south; in Karnataka and Andhra – rock paintings.	Earliest ceramics in Peru. Collapse of Old Kingdom in Egypt. Stonehenge in Britain. Minoan Crete.	2300
1750	Indus Valley civilization ends.	Hill-top sites in south India.	Joseph sold into Egypt – Genesis.	1750

their capital at Pataliputra, near modern Patna. Their power was based on massive military force and a highly efficient, centralized administration.

The greatest of the Mauryan emperors, **Asoka** took power in 272 BC. He inherited a full-blown empire, but extended it by defeating the Kalingans in modern Orissa, before turning his back on war and preaching the virtues of Buddhist pacifism. Asoka's empire stretched from Afghanistan to Assam and from the Himalaya to Mysore.

The state maintained itself by raising revenue from taxation – on everything, from agriculture, to gambling and prostitution. He decreed that 'no waste land should be occupied and not a tree cut down' without permission because all were potential sources of revenue for the state. The *sudras* (lowest of Hindu castes) were used as free labour for clearing forest and cultivating new land.

Asoka (described on the edicts as 'the Beloved of the Gods, of Gracious Countenance') left inscriptions on pillars and rocks across the subcontinent. Over most of India these inscriptions were written in *Prakrit*, using the *Brahmi* script, although in the northwest they were in Greek using the *Kharoshti* script. They were unintelligible for over 2000 years after the decline of the empire until James Prinsep deciphered the Brahmi script in 1837.

Through the edicts Asoka urged all people to follow the code of **dhamma** or dharma – translated by Indian historian Romila Thapar as 'morality, piety, virtue and social order'. He established a special force of *dhamma* officers to try to enforce the code, which encouraged toleration, non-violence, respect for priests and those in authority and for human dignity.

However, Romila Thapar suggests that the failure to develop any sense of national consciousness, coupled with the massive demands of a highly paid bureaucracy and army, proved beyond the abilities of Asoka's successors to sustain. Within 50 years of Asoka's death in 232 BC the Mauryan Empire had disintegrated and with it the whole structure and spirit of its government.

A period of fragmentation: 185 BC to AD 300

Beyond the Mauryan Empire other kingdoms had survived in South India. The Satavahanas dominated the central Deccan for over 300 years from about 50 BC. Further south in what is now Tamil Nadu, the early kingdoms of the Cholas and the Pandiyas gave a glimpse of both power and cultural development that was to flower over 1000 years later. In the centuries following the break up of the Mauryan Empire these kingdoms were in the forefront of developing overseas trade,

BC	Northern South Asia	Peninsular India	External events	BC
1750	Successors to Indus	Copper Age spreads,	Anatolia: Hittite Empire.	1650
1500	Valley. Aryans invade in successive waves. Development of Indo-Aryan language.	Neolithic continues. Gram and millet cultivation. Hill terracing. Cattle, goats and sheep.	New Kingdom in Egypt. First metal working in Peru. First inscriptions in China; Linear B script in Greece, 1650.	1570 1500
1400	Indo-Aryan spread east and south to Ganga – Yamuna doab.	Horses introduced into south. Cave paintings, burials.	Tutankhamun buried in Valley of Kings.	1337
1200	Composition of Rig Veda begins?	Iron age sites at Hallur, Karnataka.	Middle America: first urban civilization in Olmec; collapse of Hittite Empire, 1200.	1200
1000	Earliest Painted Grey Ware in Upper Ganga Valley; Brahmanas begin to be written.	Iron Age becomes more widespread across Peninsula.	Australia: large stone-built villages; David King of Israel, Kingdom of Kush in Africa.	

especially with Greece and Rome. Internal trade also flourished and Indian traders carried goods to China and Southeast Asia.

The classical period – the Gupta Empire: AD 319-467

Although the political power of Chandra Gupta and his successors never approached that of his unrelated namesake nearly 650 years before him, the Gupta Empire which was established with his coronation in AD 319 produced developments in every field of Indian culture. Their influence has been felt profoundly across South Asia to the present.

Geographically the Guptas originated in the same Magadhan region that had given rise to the Mauryan Empire. Extending their power by strategic marriage alliances, Chandra Gupta's empire of Magadh was extended by his son, Samudra Gupta, who took power in AD 335, across North India. He also marched as far south as Kanchipuram in modern Tamil Nadu, but the heartland of the Gupta Empire remained the plains of the Ganga.

Chandra Gupta II reigned for 39 years from AD 376 and was a great patron of the arts. Political power was much less centralized than under the Mauryans and as Thapar points out, collection of land revenue was deputed to officers who were entitled to keep a share of the revenue, rather than to highly paid bureaucrats. Trade with Southeast Asia, Arabia and China all added to royal wealth. That wealth was distributed to the arts on a previously unheard of scale. Some went to religious foundations, such as the Buddhist monastery at Ajanta, which produced some of its finest murals during the Gupta period. But Hindu institutions also benefited and some of the most important features of modern Hinduism date from this time. The sacrifices of Vedic worship were given up in favour of personal devotional worship, known as *bhakti*. Tantrism, both in its Buddhist and Hindu forms, with its emphasis on the female life force and worship of the Mother Goddess, developed. The focus of worship was increasingly towards a personalized and monotheistic deity, in the form of either Siva or Vishnu. The myths of Vishnu's incarnations also arose at this period.

The Brahmins The priestly caste who were in the key position to mediate change, refocused earlier literature to give shape to the emerging religious philosophy. In their hands the *Mahabharata* and the *Ramayana* were transformed from secular epics to religious stories. The excellence of contemporary sculpture both reflected and contributed to an increase in image worship and the growing role of temples as centres of devotion.

BC	Northern South Asia	Peninsular India	External events	BC
800	Mahabharata war – Bhagavad Gita; Aryan invaders reach Bengal. Rise of city states in Ganga plains, based on rice cultivation.		First settlement at Rome. Celtic Iron Age begins in north and east of Alps.	850 800
750		Megalithic grave sites.	Greek city states.	750
700	Upanishads begin to be written; concept of transmigration of souls develops; Panini's Sanskrit grammar.		Iliad composed.	700

Regional kingdoms and cultures

The collapse of Gupta power opened the way for smaller kingdoms to assert themselves. After the brief reign of Harsha in the mid-seventh century, which recaptured something both of the territory and the glory of the Guptas, the Gangetic plains were constantly fought over by rival groups, none of whom were able to establish unchallenged authority. Regional kingdoms developed, often around comparatively small natural regions.

The Deccan The Rashtrakutas controlled much of the central Peninsula between AD 700-950. However, the southern Deccan was dominated by the Chalukyas from the sixth century up to AD 750 and again in the 11th and 12th centuries. To their south the Pandiyas, Cholas and Pallavas controlled the Dravidian lands of what is now Kerala, Tamil Nadu and coastal Andhra Pradesh. The Pallavas, responsible for building the temples at Mamallapuram, just south of modern Madras (Chennai), flourished in the seventh century.

In the eighth century Kerala began to develop its own regional identity with the rise of the Kulashekharas in the Periyar Valley. Caste was a dominating feature of the kingdom's social organization, but with the distinctive twist that the Nayars, the most aristocratic of castes, developed a matrilineal system of descent.

It was the Cholas who came to dominate the south from the eighth century. Overthrowing the Pallavas, they controlled most of Tamil Nadu, south Karnataka and southern Andhra Pradesh from AD 850 to AD 1278. They often held the Kerala kings under their control. Under their kings Rajaraja I (984-1014) and Rajendra (1014-1044) the Cholas also controlled north Sri Lanka, sent naval expeditions to Southeast Asia and successful military campaigns north to the Ganga plains. They lavished endowments on temples and also extended the gifts of land to Brahmins instituted by the Pallavas and Pandiyas. Many thousands of Brahmin priests were brought south to serve in major temples such as those in Chidambaram, and Rajendra wished to be remembered above all as the king who brought water from the holy Ganga all the way to his kingdom.

The Rajputs The political instability and rivalry that resulted from the ending of Gupta power in the north opened the way for waves of immigrants from the northwest and for new groups and clans to seize power. Among these were the Rajputs (meaning 'sons of kings') who claimed descent from a mythical figure who rose out of a pit near Mount Abu. From the seventh century AD Rajputs were always a force to be reckoned with in the northwest, albeit at a comparatively local level. The temples at Khajuraho in Central India, one of contemporary India's most remarkable sites, were built

BC	Northern South Asia	Peninsular India	External events	BC
600	Northern Black Pottery.		First Latin script; first Greek coins.	600
599	Mahavir born – founder of Jainism.		First iron production in China; Zoroastrianism becomes official religion in Persia.	550
563	Gautama Buddha born.			
500	Upanishads finished; Taxila and Charsadda become important towns and trade centres.	Aryans colonize Sri Lanka. Irrigation practised in Sri Lanka.	Wet rice cultivation introduced to Japan.	500
326 321	Alexander at Indus. Chandragupta establishes Mauryan Dynasty.	Megalithic cultures.	Crossbow invented in China.	350

during the Rajput dynasty of the Chandelas (AD 916-1203). However, the Rajputs never succeeded in forging a united front strong enough to establish either effective central government, control internally or protection from external attack.

The spread of Islamic power – the Delhi Sultanate

From about AD 1000 the external attacks which inflicted most damage on Rajput wealth and power came increasingly from the Arabs and Turks. Mahmud of Ghazni raided the Punjab virtually every year between 1000 and 1026, attracted both by the agricultural surpluses and the enormous wealth in cash, golden images and jewellery of North India's temples which drew him back every year. He sacked the wealthy centres of Mathura (UP) in 1017, Thanesar (Haryana) in 1011, Somnath (Gujarat) in 1024 and Kannauj (UP). He died in 1030, to the Hindus just another *mlechchha* ('impure' or sullied one), as had been the Huns and the Sakas before him, soon to be forgotten. Such raids were never taken seriously as a long-term threat by kings further east and as the Rajputs often feuded among themselves the northwest plains became an attractive prey.

Muslim political power was heralded by the raids of Mu'izzu'd Din and his defeat of massive Rajput forces at the Second Battle of Tarain in 1192. Mu'izzu'd Din left his deputy, Qutb u'd Din Aibak, to hold the territorial gains from his base at Indraprastha. Mu'izzu'd Din made further successful raids in the 1190s, inflicting crushing defeats on Hindu opponents from Gwalior to Benaras. The foundations were then laid for the first extended period of such power, which came under the Delhi sultans.

Qutb u'd Din Aibak took Lahore in 1206, although it was his lieutenant Iltutmish who really established control from Delhi in 1211. Qutb u'd Din Aibak consolidated Muslim dominion by an even-handed policy of conciliation and patronage. In Delhi he converted the old Hindu stronghold of Qila Rai Pithora into his Muslim capital and began several magnificent building projects, including the Quwwat-ul-Islam mosque and the Qutb Minar, a victory tower. Iltutmish was a Turkish slave – a *Mamluk* – and the Sultanate continued to look west for its leadership and inspiration. However, the possibility of continuing control from outside India was destroyed by the crushing raids of **Genghis Khan** through Central Asia and from 1222 Iltutmish ruled from Delhi completely independently of outside authority. He annexed Sind in 1228 and all the territory east to Bengal by 1230.

A succession of dynasties followed, drawing on refugees from Genghis Khan's raids and from still further to the west to strengthen the leadership. In 1290 the first dynasty was succeeded by the Khaljis, which in turn gave way to the Tughluqs in 1320. **Mohammad bin Tughluq** (ruled 1324-1351)

BC	Northern South Asia	Peninsular India	External events	BC
300	Sarnath and Sanchi stupas.	First Ajanta caves in original form.	Mayan writing and ceremonial centres established.	300
297	Mauryan power extends to Mysore.			
272-	Asoka's Empire.	Chola Pandiya, Chera	Ptolemy.	285
250	Brahmi script.	kingdoms: earliest	First towns in Southeast Asia.	250
232	Death of Asoka.	Tamil inscriptions.	Rome captures Spain.	206
185	Shunga Dynasty, centred on Ujjain.	Megalithic cultures in hills of south.	Romans destroy Greek states.	146
100	Kharavela King of Kalingans in Orissa. Final composition of Ramayana.	South Indian trade with Indonesia and Rome. Roman pottery and coins in South India.	Indian religions spread to Southeast Asia. Discovery of monsoon winds Introduction of Julian calendar.	100

was described by the Moorish traveller Ibn Batuta as 'a man who above all others is fond of making presents and shedding blood'. This period marked a turning point in Muslim government in India, as Turkish Mamluks gave way to government by Indian Muslims and their Hindu allies. The Delhi sultans were open to local influences and employed Hindus in their administration. In the mid-14th century their capital, Delhi, was one of the leading cities of the contemporary world but in 1398 their control came to an abrupt end with the arrival of the Mongol Timur.

Timur's limp caused him to be called Timur-i-leng (Timur the Lame, known to the west as Tamburlaine). This self-styled 'Scourge of God' was illiterate, a devout Muslim, an outstanding chess player and a patron of the arts. Five years before his arrival in India he had taken Baghdad and three years before that he had ravaged Russia, devastating land and pillaging villages. India had not been in such danger from Mongols since Genghis Khan had arrived on the same stretch of the Indus 200 years before.

After Timur, it took nearly 50 years for the Delhi Kingdom to become more than a local headquarters. Even then the revival was slow and fitful. The last Tughluqs were succeeded by an undistinguished line of Sayyids, who began as Timur's deputies who were essentially Afghan soldier/administrators. They later called themselves sultans and Lodi kings (1451-1526) and moved their capital to Agra. Nominally they controlled an area from Punjab to Bihar but they were, in fact, in the hands of a group of factious nobles.

The Deccan Kingdoms

The Delhi Sultanate never achieved the dominating power of earlier empires or of its successor, the Mughal Empire. It exercised political control through crushing military raids and the exaction of tribute from defeated kings, but there was no real attempt to impose central administration. Power depended on maintaining vital lines of communication and trade routes, keeping fortified strongholds and making regional alliances. In the Peninsula to the south, the Deccan, regional powers contested for survival, power and expansion. The Bahmanis were the forerunners of a succession of Muslim dynasties, who sometimes competed with each other and sometimes collaborated against a joint external enemy.

Across West and South India today are the remains of the only major medieval Hindu empire, the Vijayanagar Empire, to resist effectively the Muslim advance. The ruins at Hampi demonstrate the

BC	North India	Peninsular India	External events	BC
		Satavahanas control much of Peninsula up to 300 AD. Thomas brings Christianity to South India. *Tamil Sangram.*	Rome population of 1 million. Pyramid of the sun at City of Teotihuacan, Mexico.	
78	Kushan rulers in Northwest followed by Scythians.			
		Arikamedu – trade with Rome.		68
			Buddhism reaches China.	
100	Vaishnavism spreads to north and northwest.		Paper introduced in China; first metal work in Southeast Asia.	100
	Lawbook of Manu Gandharan art.	Mahayana Buddhism spreads. Nagarjunakonda major centre in Andhra Pradesh. First cities on Deccan plateau.	Hadrian's wall in Britain.	125
200	Hinayana/Mahayana Buddhist split.			

power of a Hindu coalition that rose to power in the south Deccan in the first half of the 14th century, only to be defeated by its Muslim neighbours in 1565.

For over 200 years Vijayanagar ('*city of victory*') kings fought to establish supremacy. It was an empire that, in the words of one Indian historian, made it 'the nearest approach to a war state ever made by a Hindu kingdom'. At times its power reached from Orissa in the northeast to Sri Lanka. In 1390 King Harihara II claimed to have planted a victory pillar in Sri Lanka. Much of modern Tamil Nadu and Andhra Pradesh were added to the core region of Karnataka in the area under Vijayanagar control.

The Mughal Empire

In North India it is the impact of the Mughal rule that is most evident today. The descendants of conquerors, with the blood of both Tamburlaine and Genghis Khan in their veins, they came to dominate Indian politics from Babur's victory near Delhi in 1526 to Aurangzeb's death in 1707. Their legacy was some of the most magnificent architecture in the world, and a profound impact on the culture, society and future politics of South Asia.

Babur (the tiger) Founder of the Mughal Dynasty, Babur was born in Russian Turkestan on 15 February 1483, the fifth direct descendant on the male side of Timur and 13th on the female side from Genghis Khan. He established the Mughal Empire by leading his cavalry and artillery forces to a victory over the combined armies of Ibrahim Lodi, last ruler of the Delhi Sultanate and the Hindu Raja of Gwalior, at **Panipat**, 80 km north of Delhi, in 1526. When he died four years later, the Empire was far from secured, but he had laid the foundations of political and military power and also begun to establish courtly traditions of poetry, literature and art which became the hallmark of subsequent Mughal rulers. Babur, used to the delights of Persian gardens and the cool of the Afghan hills, was unimpressed by India. In his autobiography he wrote: "Hindustan is a country that has few pleasures to recommend it. The people are not handsome. They have no idea of the charms of friendly society, of frankly mixing together, or of familiar intercourse. They have no genius, no comprehension of mind, no politeness of manner, no kindness or fellow-feeling, no ingenuity or mechanical invention in planning or executing their handicraft works, no skill or knowledge in design or architecture". Babur's depressing catalogue was the view of a disenchanted outsider. Within two generations the Mughals had become fully at home and brought some radical changes. Babur was charismatic. He ruled by keeping the loyalty of his military chiefs, giving them control of large areas of territory.

BC	North India	Peninsular India	External events	BC
300		Rise of Pallavas.	Classic period of	300
319	Chandra Gupta founds		Mayan civilization.	
	Gupta Dynasty (Samudra			
	335, Chandra II 376,		Constantinople founded.	330
	Kumara 415).			
454	Skanda Gupta, the last		End of Roman Empire.	476
	imperial Gupta, takes		Teotihuacan, Mexico,	500
	power. Dies 467.		population 200,000.	
540	Gupta rule ends.		Saint Sophia, Constantinople.	532
550		First Chalukya Dynasty,	Buddhism arrives in Japan.	550
578		Badami cave temple;		
		last Ajanta paintings.		
600	Period of small	Bhakti movement.		
	Indian states.	Chalukyan Dynasty in		
629	Hiuen Tsang travels India.	west and central Deccan.	Death of Mohammad.	632
630		Pallavas in Tamil Nadu.		

Humayun However, their strength posed a problem for Humayun, his successor. Almost immediately after Babur's death Humayun was forced to retreat from Delhi through Sind with his pregnant wife. His son Akbar, who was to become the greatest of the Mughal emperors, was born at Umarkot in Sindh, during this period of exile, on 23 November 1542.

Akbar Akbar was only 13 when he took the throne in 1556. The next 44 years were one of the most remarkable periods of South Asian history, paralleled by the Elizabethan period in England, where Queen Elizabeth I ruled from 1558 to 1603. Although Akbar inherited the throne, it was he who really created the empire and gave it many of its distinguishing features. Through his marriage to a Hindu princess he ensured that Hindus were given honoured positions in government, as well as respect for their religious beliefs and practices. He sustained a passionate interest in art and literature, matched by a determination to create monuments to his empire's political power and he laid the foundations for an artistic and architectural tradition which developed a totally distinctive Indian style. This emerged from the separate elements of Iranian and Indian traditions by a constant process of blending and originality of which he was the chief patron.

But these achievements were only possible because of his political and military gifts. From 1556 until his 18th birthday in 1560, Akbar was served by a prince regent, Bairam Khan. However, already at the age of 15 he had conquered Ajmer and large areas of Central India. Chittor and Ranthambore fell to him in 1567-1568, bringing most of what is now Rajasthan under his control. This opened the door south to Gujarat.

Afghans continued to cause his empire difficulties, including Daud Karrani, who declared independence in East India in 1574. That threat to Mughal power was finally crushed with Karrani's death in 1576. Bengal was far from the last of his conquests. He brought Kabul back under Mughal control in the 1580s and established a presence from Kashmir, Sind and Baluchistan in the north and west, to the Godavari River on the border of modern Andhra Pradesh in the south. Akbar deliberately widened his power base by incorporating Rajput princes into the administrative structure and giving them extensive rights in the revenue from land. He abolished the hated tax on non-Muslims (*jizya*) – ultimately reinstated by his strictly orthodox great grandson Aurangzeb – and ceased levying taxes on Hindus who went on pilgrimage. He also ended the practice of forcible conversion to Islam. Artistic treasures abound from Akbar's court, often bringing together material and skills from across the known world. Akbar's eclecticism had a political purpose; he was trying to build a focus of loyalty beyond that of caste, social group, region or religion. Like

BC	North India	Peninsular India	External events	BC
			Buddhism reaches Tibet.	645
670	Rajputs become powerful force in northwest	Mahabalipuram shore temples.		
712	Arabs arrive in Sind.	Nandivarman II in Tamil Nadu. Pandiyas in Madurai.	Muslim invasions of Spain.	711
757		Rashtrakutas dominate central Peninsula.		
775		Kailasanath Temple, Ellora. Rise of Cholas.	Charlemagne crowned. Settlement of New Zealand. Cyrillic script developed.	800 850 863
950	Khajuraho temples started.	Rajendra Chola.		
			Sung Dynasty in China.	979
984		Rajaraja 1st.		

Roman emperors before him, he deliberately cultivated a new religion in which the emperor attained divinity, hoping to give the empire a legitimacy which would last. While his religion disappeared with his death, the legitimacy of the Mughals survived another 200 years, long after their real power had almost disappeared.

Jahangir Akbar died of a stomach illness in 1605. He was succeeded by his son, Prince Salim, who inherited the throne as Emperor Jahangir ('*world seizer*'). He added little to the territory of the empire, consolidating the Mughals' hold on the Himalayan foothills and parts of central India and restricting his energies to pushing frontiers of art. He commissioned works of art and literature, many of which recorded life in the Mughal court. Hunting scenes conveyed the real dangers of hunting lions or tigers; implements, furniture, tools and weapons were made with lavish care and often exquisite design.

From early youth Jahangir had shown an artistic temperament, but he also became addicted to alcohol and then to opium. In his autobiography, he wrote: "I had not drunk until I was 18 … a gunner said that if I would take a glass of wine it would drive away the feeling of being tired and heavy … After that I took to drinking wine … until wine made from grapes ceased to intoxicate me and I took to drinking arrack (local spirits). By degrees my potions rose to 20 cups of doubly distilled spirits."

Nur Jahan Jahangir's favourite wife, Nur Jahan, brought her own artistic gifts. Born the daughter of an Iranian nobleman, she had been brought to the Mughal court along with her family as a child and moved to Bengal as the wife of Sher Afgan. She made rapid progress after her first husband's accidental death in 1607, which caused her to move from Bengal to be a lady in waiting for one of Akbar's widows.

At the Mughal court in 1611, she met Jahangir. Mutually enraptured, they were married in May. Jahangir gave her the title Nur Mahal (Light of the Palace), soon increased to Nur Jahan (Light of the World). Aged 34, she was strikingly beautiful and had an astonishing reputation for physical skill and intellectual wit. She was a crack shot with a gun, highly artistic, determined yet philanthropic. Throughout her life Jahangir was captivated by her, so much so that he flouted Muslim convention by minting coins bearing her image.

By 1622 Nur Jahan effectively controlled the empire. She commissioned and supervised the building in Agra of one of the Mughal world's most beautiful buildings, the I'timad ud-Daula ('Pillar of government'), as a tomb for her father and mother. Her father, **Ghiyas Beg**, had risen to become

BC	North India	Peninsular India	External events	BC
1001	Mahmud of Ghazni raids Indus plains. Rajput dynasties grow.	Chola kings – navies sent to Southeast Asia: Chola bronzes.	Easter Island stone carvings.	1000
1050	Sufism in North India. Rajput dynasties in northwest.		Norman conquest of England.	1066
1110		Rise of Hoysalas.	First European universities.	1100
1118	Senas in Bengal.			
			Angkor Wat, Cambodia; paper making spreads from Muslim world.	1150
1192	Rajputs defeated by Mu'izzu'd Din.		Srivijaya Kingdom at its height in Java; Angkor Empire at greatest.	1170

A monument to grief?

The grief that Mumtaz's death caused may have been the chief motivating force behind Shah Jahan's determination to build the Taj Mahal, a monument not just to his love for her, but also to the supremacy of Mughal refinement and power. However, that power had to be paid for and the costs were escalating. Shah Jahan himself had inherited an almost bankrupt state from his father. Expenditure on the army had outstripped the revenue collected by tribute from kings and from the chiefs given the rights and responsibility over territories often larger than European countries. Financial deficits forced Shah Jahan onto the offensive in order to guarantee greater and more reliable revenue.

Major reforms helped to reduce the costs of his standing army. However, maintaining the force necessary to control the huge territories owing allegiance to the emperor continued to stretch his resources to the full. By 1648, when he moved his capital to Delhi, the empire was already in financial difficulties and in 1657 the rumour that Shah Jahan was terminally ill immediately caused a series of battles for the succession between his four sons.

Aurangzeb, the second son and sixth child of Shah Jahan and Mumtaz Mahal – tough, intriguing and sometimes cruel, but also a highly intelligent strategist – emerged the winner, to find that Shah Jahan had recovered. Rather than run the risk of being deposed, Aurangzeb kept his father imprisoned in Agra Fort, where he had been taken ill, from June 1658 until his death in February 1666.

one of Jahangir's most trusted advisers and Nur Jahan was determined to ensure that their memory was honoured. She was less successful in her wish to deny the succession after Jahangir's death at the age of 58 to Prince Khurram. Acceding to the throne in 1628, he took the title of Shah Jahan (*Ruler of the World*) and in the next 30 years his reign represented the height of Mughal power.
Shah Jahan The Mughal Empire was under attack in the Deccan and the northwest when Shah Jahan became Emperor. He tried to re-establish and extend Mughal authority in both regions by a combination of military campaigns and skilled diplomacy. Akbar's craftsmen had already carved outstandingly beautiful *jalis* for the tomb of Salim Chishti in Fatehpur Sikri, but Shah Jahan

BC	North India	Peninsular India	External events	BC
1198	First mosque built in Delhi; Qutb Minar Delhi.		Rise of Hausa city states in West Africa.	1200
1206	Delhi Sultanate established.		Mongols begin conquest of Asia under Genghis Khan.	1206
1206	Turkish 'slave dynasty'.	Pandiyas rise.		
			First Thai kingdom.	1220
1222	Iltutmish Sultan of Delhi.			
1230		Konark, Sun Temple, Orissa		
			Marco Polo reaches China.	1275
1290	Khaljis in Delhi; Jalal ud Din Khalji.			
1320-24	Ghiyas ud Din Tughluq.		Black Death spreads from	1348
1324-51	Mohammad bin Tughluq.		Asia to Europe.	

developed the form further. Undoubtedly the finest tribute to these skills is found in the Taj Mahal, the tribute to his beloved wife Mumtaz Mahal, who died giving birth to her 14th child in 1631.

Aurangzeb The need to expand the area under Mughal control was felt even more strongly by Aurangzeb ('The jewel in the throne') than by his predecessors. He had shown his intellectual gifts in his grandfather Jahangir's court when held hostage to guarantee Shah Jahan's good behaviour, learning Arabic, Persian, Turkish and Hindi. When he seized power at the age of 40, he needed all his political and military skills to hold on to an unwieldy empire that was in permanent danger of collapse from its own size. Aurangzeb realized that the resources of the territory he inherited from Shah Jahan were not enough. One response was to push south, while maintaining his hold on the east and north. Initially he maintained his alliances with the Rajputs in the west, which had been a crucial element in Mughal strategy. In 1678 he claimed absolute rights over Jodhpur and went to war with the Rajput clans at the same time embarking on a policy of outright Islamization. However, for the remaining 39 years of his reign he struggled to sustain his power.

The East India Company and the rise of British power
The British were unique among the foreign rulers of India in coming by sea rather than through the northwest and in coming first for trade rather than for military conquest. The ports that they established – Madras, Bombay and Calcutta – became completely new centres of political, economic and social activity. Before them Indian empires had controlled their territories from the land. The British dictated the economy by controlling sea-borne trade. From the middle of the 19th century railways transformed the economic and political structure of South Asia and it was those three centres of British control, along with the late addition of Delhi, which became the foci of economic development and political change.

The East India Company in Madras and Bengal
In its first 90 years of contact with South Asia after the Company set up its first trading post at **Masulipatnam**, on the east coast of India, it had depended almost entirely on trade for its profits. However, in 1701, only 11 years after a British settlement was first established at Calcutta, the Company was given rights to land revenue in Bengal.

The Company was accepted and sometimes welcomed, partly because it offered to bolster the inadequate revenues of the Mughals by exchanging silver bullion for the cloth it bought. However,

BC	North India	Peninsular India	External events	BC
1336		Vijayanagar Empire established, Harihara I.		
1347		Ala-ud-Din sets up		
1351-88	Firoz Shah Tughluq.	Bahmani dynasty, independent of Delhi, in Gulbarga.	Ming dynasty in China established.	1368
			Peking the largest city in the world.	1400
1398	Timur sacks Delhi.		Ming sea-going	1405
1412	End of Tughlaq Dynasty.		expeditions to Africa.	
1414	Sayyid Dynasty.	Bidar/Bahmani Kingdom		1428
1440	Mystic Kabir born in Benaras.	in Deccan.	Aztecs defeat Atzcapatzalco. Incas centralize power.	1438
1451	Afghan Lodi Dynasty established under Bahlul.		Byzantine Empire falls to Ottomans.	1453
1469	Guru Nanak born in Punjab.			
1482		Fall of Bahmanis.	Columbus reaches the Americas; Arabs and Jews expelled from Spain.	1492

in the south the Company moved further towards consolidating its political base. Wars between South India's regional factions gave the Company the chance to extend their influence by making alliances and offering support to some of these factions in their struggles, which were complicated by the extension to Indian soil of the European contest for power between the French and the British.

Robert Clive The British established control over both Bengal and Southeast India in the middle of the 17th century. Robert Clive, in alliance with a collection of disaffected Hindu landowners and Muslim soldiers, defeated the new Nawab of Bengal, the 20-year-old Siraj-ud-Daula, in June 1757 at Plassey (Palashi), about 100 km north of Calcutta.

Hastings and Cornwallis The essential features of British control were mapped out in the next quarter of a century through the work of **Warren Hastings**, Governor-General from 1774 until 1785 and **Lord Cornwallis** who succeeded and remained in charge until 1793. Cornwallis was responsible for putting Europeans in charge of all the higher levels of revenue collection and administration and for introducing government by the rule of law, making even government officers subject to the courts.

The decline of Muslim power

The extension of East India Company power in the Mughal periphery of India's south and east took place against a background of the rising power of Sivaji and his Marathas.

Sivaji and the Marathas Sivaji was the son of a Hindu who had served as a small-scale chief in the Muslim-ruled state of Bijapur. The weakness of Bijapur encouraged Sivaji to extend his father's area of control and he led a rebellion. The Bijapur general Afzal Khan, sent to put it down, agreed to meet Sivaji in private to reach a settlement. In an act which is still remembered by both Muslims and Marathas, Sivaji embraced him with steel claws attached to his fingers and tore him apart. It was the start of a campaign which took Maratha power as far south as Madurai and to the doors of Delhi and Calcutta.

Although Sivaji himself died in 1680, Aurangzeb never fully came to terms with the rising power of the Marathas, though he did end their ambitions to form an empire of their own. While the Maratha confederacy was able to threaten Delhi within 50 years of Aurangzeb's death, by the early 19th century it had dissolved into five independent states, with whom the British ultimately dealt separately.

Nor was Aurangzeb able to create any wide sense of identity with the Mughals as a legitimate popular power. Instead, under the influence of Sunni Muslim theologians, he retreated into

BC	North India	Peninsular India	External events	BC
		Vasco da Gama reaches India.	Inca Empire at its height. Spanish claim Brazil; Safavid Empire founded in Persia.	1498
1500		Vijayanagar dominates		
1506	Sikander Lodi founds Agra.	South India; Krishnadevraya rules 1509-30.		1500
		Albuquerque seizes Goa; Nizamshahis establish		1510
1526	Babur defeats Ibrahim Lodi to establish Mughal power in Delhi.	independent Ahmadnagar sultanate.	Ottomans capture Syria, Egypt and Arabia.	1516
		Dutch, French, Portuguese and Danish traders.	Spaniards overthrow Aztecs in Mexico.	1519
			Potato introduced to Europe from South America.	1525
1540	Sher Shah forces Humayun into exile.			

insistence on Islamic purity. He imposed Islamic law, the *sharia*, promoted only Muslims to positions of authority, tried to replace Hindu administrators and revenue collectors with Muslims, and reimposed the *jizya* tax on all non-Muslims. By his death in 1707 the empire had neither the broadness of spirit nor the physical means to survive.

Bahadur Shah The decline was postponed by the reign of Aurangzeb's son. Sixty-three when he acceded to the throne, Bahadur Shah restored some of its fortunes. He made agreements with the Marathas and the Rajputs and defeated the Sikhs in Punjab before taking the last Sikh guru into his service. Nine emperors succeeded Aurangzeb between his death and the exile of the last Mughal ruler in 1858. It was no accident that it was in that year the British ended the rule of its East India Company and decreed India to be its Indian empire.

Mohammad Shah remained in his capital of Delhi, resigning himself to enjoying what Carey Welch has called "the conventional triad of joys: the wine was excellent, as were the women and for him the song was especially rewarding". The idyll was rudely shattered by the invasion of Nadir Shah in 1739, an Iranian marauder who slaughtered thousands in Delhi and carried off priceless Mughal treasures, including the Peacock Throne.

The East India Company's push for power

Alliances In the century and a half that followed the death of Aurangzeb, the British East India Company extended its economic and political influence into the heart of India. As the Mughal Empire lost its power India fell into many smaller states. The Company undertook to protect the rulers of several of these states from external attack by stationing British troops in their territory. In exchange for this service the rulers paid subsidies to the Company. The British extended their territory through the 18th century as successive regional powers were annexed and brought under direct Company rule.

Progress to direct British control was uneven and often opposed. The Sikhs in Punjab, the Marathas in the west and the Mysore sultans in the south, fiercely contested British advances. Haidar Ali and Tipu Sultan, who had built a wealthy kingdom in the Mysore region, resisted attempts to incorporate them. Tipu was finally killed in 1799 at the battle of Srirangapatnam, an island fort in the Kaveri River just north of Mysore, where Arthur Wellesley, later the Duke of Wellington, began to make his military reputation.

BC	North India	Peninsular India	External events	BC
1542		St Francis Xavier reaches		
1555	Humayun re-conquers Delhi.	Goa.		
1556	Akbar Emperor.			
1565		Vijayanagar defeated.	William Shakespeare born.	1564
		First printing press in Goa.		1566
			Dutch East India Co set up.	1602
1603	Guru Granth Sahib compiled.		Tokugawa Shogunate in Japan.	1603
1605	Jahangir Emperor.		First permanent English	1607
1608		East India Co base at Surat.	settlement in America.	
			Telescope invented in Holland.	1609

The Marathas were not defeated until the 1816-1818 war. Even then the defeat owed as much to internal fighting as to the power of the British-led army. Only the northwest of the subcontinent remained beyond British control until well into the 19th century. Thus in 1799 **Ranjit Singh** was able to set up a Sikh state in Punjab, surviving until the late 1830s despite the extension of British control over much of the rest of India.

In 1818 India's economy was in ruins and its political structures destroyed. Irrigation and road systems had fallen into decay and gangs terrorized the countryside. Thugs and dacoits controlled much of rural areas in Central India and often robbed and murdered even on town outskirts. The stability of the Mughal period had long since passed. From 1818 to 1857 there was a succession of local and uncoordinated revolts in different parts of India. Some were bought off, some put down by military force.

A period of reforms

While existing political systems were collapsing, the first half of the 1800s was also a time of radical social change in territories governed by the East India Company. **Lord William Bentinck** became governor-general at a time when England was undergoing major reform. In 1828 he banned the burning of widows on the funeral pyres of their husbands (**sati**) and then moved to suppress **thuggee** (ritual murder and robbery carried out in the name of the goddess Kali). His most far reaching change was to introduce education in English.

From the late 1830s massive new engineering projects began to be taken up; first canals, then railways. The innovations stimulated change and change contributed to the growing unease with the British presence. The development of the telegraph, railways and new roads, three universities and the extension of massive new canal irrigation projects in North India seemed to threaten traditional society, a risk increased by the annexation of Indian states to bring them under direct British rule. The most important of these was Oudh.

The Rebellion

Out of the growing discontent and widespread economic difficulties came the Rebellion or 'Mutiny' of 1857. On 10 May 1857 troops in Meerut, 70 km northeast of Delhi, mutinied. They reached Delhi the next day, where **Bahadur Shah**, the last Mughal Emperor, took sides with the mutineers. Troops in Lucknow joined the rebellion and for three months Lucknow and other cities in the north were

BC	North India	Peninsular India	External events	BC
1628	Shah Jahan Emperor.		Masjid-i-Shah Mosque in Isfahan.	1616
1632-53	Taj Mahal built.			
		Fort St George, Madras, founded by East India Co.		1639
			Manchus found Ch'ing Dynasty.	1644
			Tasman 'discovers' New Zealand.	1645
1658	Aurangzeb Emperor.		Louis XIV of France – the 'Sun King'.	1653-1715

under siege. Appalling scenes of butchery and reprisals marked the struggle, only put down by troops from outside.

The period of Empire

The 1857 rebellion marked the end not only of the Mughal Empire but also of the East India Company, for the British government in London took overall control in 1858. Yet within 30 years a movement for self government had begun and there were the first signs of a demand among the new Western-educated elite that political rights be awarded to match the sense of Indian national identity.

Indian National Congress Established in 1885, this was the first all-India political institution and was to become the key vehicle of demands for independence. However, the educated Muslim élite of what is now Uttar Pradesh saw a threat to Muslim rights, power and identity in the emergence of democratic institutions which gave Hindus, with their built-in natural majority, significant advantages. Sir Sayyid Ahmad Khan, who had founded a Muslim University at Aligarh in 1877, advised Muslims against joining the Congress, seeing it as a vehicle for Hindu, and especially Bengali, nationalism.

The Muslim League The educated Muslim community of North India remained deeply suspicious of the Congress, making up less than 8% of those attending its conferences between 1900-1920. Muslims from UP created the All-India Muslim League in 1906. However, the demands of the Muslim League were not always opposed to those of the Congress. In 1916 it concluded the Lucknow Pact with the Congress, in which the Congress won Muslim support for self-government, in exchange for the recognition that there would be separate constituencies for Muslims. The nature of the future independent India was still far from clear, however. The British conceded the principle of self-government in 1918, but the reforms already fell far short of heightened Indian expectations.

Mahatma Gandhi Into a tense atmosphere Mohandas Karamchand Gandhi returned to India in 1915 after 20 years practising as a lawyer in South Africa. He arrived as the government of India was being given new powers by the British parliament to try political cases without a jury and to give provincial governments the right to imprison politicians without trial. In opposition to this legislation Gandhi proposed to call a *hartal*, when all activity would cease for a day, a form of protest still in widespread use. Such protests took place across India, often accompanied by riots.

BC	North India	Peninsular India	External events	BC
1677		Shivaji and Marathas.	Pennsylvania founded.	1681
1690	Calcutta founded.			
1699	Guru Gobind Singh forms Sikh Khalsa.	Regional powers dominate through 18th century:	Chinese occupy Outer Mongolia.	1697
1703	Nawabs of Bengal.	Nawabs of Arcot (1707);	Foundation of St Petersburg, capital of Russian Empire.	1703
1707	Death of Aurangzeb; Mughal rulers continue to rule from Delhi until 1858 Nawabs of Avadh.	Maratha Peshwas (1714); Nizams of Hyderabad (1724).		
1739	The Persian Nadir Shah captures Delhi and massacres thousands.			
1757	Battle of Plassey; British power extended from East India.	East India Co strengthens trade and political power through 18th century.	US War of Independence.	1775-8

Mahatma Gandhi

Mohandas Karamchand Gandhi, an English-educated lawyer, had lived outside India from his youth to middle age. He preached the general acceptance of some of the doctrines he had grown to respect in his childhood, notably *ahimsa*, or non-violence. On his return the Bengali Nobel Laureate poet, Rabindranath Tagore, had dubbed him 'Mahatma' – Great Soul. From 1921 he gave up his Western style of dress and adopted the hand spun *dhoti* worn by poor Indian villagers. Yet, he was also fiercely critical of many aspects of traditional Hindu society. He preached against the discrimination of the caste system which still dominated life for the overwhelming majority of Hindus. Often despised by the British in India, his death at the hands of an extreme Hindu chauvinist in January 1948 was a final testimony to the ambiguity of his achievements: successful in contributing so much to achieving India's Independence, yet failing to resolve the bitter communal legacies which he gave his life to overcome.

On 13 April 1919 a huge gathering took place in the enclosed space of Jallianwala Bagh in Amritsar. It had been prohibited by the government and General Dyer ordered troops to fire on the people without warning, killing 379 and injuring at least a further 1200. It marked the turning point in relations with Britain and the rise of Gandhi to the key position of leadership in the struggle for complete independence.

The thrust for Independence Through the 1920s Gandhi developed concepts and political programmes that were to become the hallmark of India's Independence struggle. Ultimately political Independence was to be achieved not by violent rebellion but by *satyagraha* – a 'truth force' which implied a willingness to suffer through non-violent resistance to injustice. In 1930 the Congress declared that 26 January would be Independence Day – still celebrated as Republic Day in India today. Mohammad Iqbal, the Leader of the Muslim League, took the opportunity of his address to the League in the same year to suggest the formation of a Muslim state within an Indian Federation. Also in 1930 a Muslim student in Cambridge, **Chaudhuri Rahmat Ali**, coined a name for the new Muslim state **PAKISTAN**. The letters were to stand 'P' for Punjab, 'A' for Afghania, 'K' for Kashmir, 'S' for Sind with the suffix *'stan'*, Persian for country. The idea still had little real shape however and waited on developments of the late 1930s and 1940s to bear fruit.

By the end of the Second World War the positions of the Muslim League, now under the leadership of **Mohammad Ali Jinnah** and the Congress led by **Jawaharlal Nehru**, were irreconcilable. While major questions of the definition of separate territories for a Muslim and non-Muslim state remained to be answered, it was clear to General Wavell, the British Viceroy through the last years of the war, that there was no alternative but to accept that independence would have to be given on the basis of separate states.

Independence and Partition

One of the main difficulties for the Muslims was that they made up only a fifth of the total population were scattered throughout India. It was therefore impossible to define a simple territorial division which would provide a state to match Jinnah's claim of a *'two-nation theory'*. On 20 February 1947, the British Labour Government announced its decision to replace Lord Wavell as Viceroy with Lord Mountbatten, who was to oversee the transfer of power to new independent governments. It set a deadline of June 1948 for British withdrawal. The announcement of a firm date made the Indian politicians even less willing to compromise and the resulting division satisfied no one.

Independence arrived on 15 August for India and the 14 August for Pakistan because Indian astrologers deemed the 15th to be the most auspicious moment. Several key Princely States had still not decided firmly to which country they would accede. Kashmir was the most important of these, with results that have lasted to the present day.

Modern India

India, with an estimated 1.21 billion people, is the second most populated country in the world after China. That population size reflects the long history of human occupation and the fact that an astonishingly high proportion of India's land is relatively fertile. About 60% of India's surface area is cultivated, compared with 10% in China and 20% in the US. Although the birth rate has fallen steadily over the last 40 years, initially death rates fell faster and the rate of population increase has continued to be nearly 2% – or 18 million – a year.

Politics and institutions

When India became independent on 15 August 1947 it faced three immediate crises. Partition left it with a bitter struggle between Muslims on one side and Hindus and Sikhs on the other which threatened to tear the new country into pieces. An estimated 13 million people migrated between the two new countries of India and Pakistan.

In the years since Independence, striking political achievements have been made. With the two-year exception of 1975-1977, when Mrs Indira Gandhi imposed a state of emergency in which all political activity was banned, India has sustained a democratic system in the face of tremendous pressures. The contest for power has largely become a two-horse race between two free-flowing coalitions, one led by the right-wing Hindu-aligned Bharatiya Janata Party (BJP), the other based around the centre-left United Progressive Alliance (UPA), a coalition of moderate parties formed in 2004 by Sonia Gandhi and dominated by the Congress Party. The general elections in May 2014 saw the BJP surge to power, a hugely effective and personality-driven campaign by the controversial pro-business leader Narendra Modi winning the party the first absolute majority in Indian national elections for three decades.

The constitution

Establishing itself as a sovereign democratic republic, the Indian parliament accepted Nehru's advocacy of a secular constitution. The president is formally vested with all executive powers exercised under the authority of the prime minister.

Parliament has a lower house (*Lok Sabha* – House of the people) and an upper house (*Rajya Sabha* – Council of States). The former is made up of directly elected representatives from the 543 parliamentary constituencies (plus two nominated members from the Anglo-Indian community), the latter of members elected by an electoral college and nominated members.

India's federal constitution devolves certain powers to elected state assemblies. Each state has a governor who acts as its official head. Many states also have two chambers, the upper generally called the Rajya Sabha and the lower (often called the Vidhan Sabha) being of directly elected representatives. In practice many of the state assemblies have had a totally different political complexion from that of the Lok Sabha. Regional parties have played a far more prominent role, though in many states central government has effectively dictated both the leadership and policy of state assemblies.

States and Union Territories Union territories are administered by the president "acting to such an extent as he thinks fit". In practice Union territories have varying forms of self-government. Pondicherry has a legislative Assembly and Council of Ministers. The 69th Amendment to the Constitution in 1991 provided for a legislative assembly and council of ministers for Delhi, elections for which were held in December 1993. The Assemblies of Union Territories have more restricted powers of legislation than full states. Some Union Territories – Dadra and Nagar Haveli, Daman and Diu, all of which separated from Goa in 1987 when Goa achieved full statehood – Andaman and Nicobar Islands and Lakshadweep have elected bodies known as Pradesh Councils.

Secularism One of the key features of India's constitution is its secular principle. Some see the commitment to a secular constitution as having been under challenge from the Hindu nationalism of the BJP.

BACKGROUND

Indian tiger

The economic transformation of India has been one of the greatest business stories of modern times. Now acknowledged as major player in the fields of information technology and pharmaceuticals, in the past five years the economy has been growing at close to 9% a year, largely thanks to an investment boom, and as stifling regulations have been lifted entrepreneurship has flourished. Mukesh Ambani, director of petrochemicals and retail giant Reliance Industries, is currently rated by Forbes as the seventh richest man in the world, and Lakshmi Mittal, head of the world's biggest steel company Arcelor Mittal, is only one place behind him.

So powerful has the economy become that, 60 years after independence, the colonized have turned colonizers. The global ambitions of 'India Inc' have become evident in a series of high-profile buyouts, none more symbolic than the Tata Corporation's US$13.2 billion acquisition of Anglo-Dutch steel giant Corus, a company whose ancestry can be traced to many of the companies that once symbolized Britain's industrial pre-eminence. Chairman Ratan Tata proudly boasted that the takeover was "the first step in showing that Indian industry can step outside its shores into an international market place as a global player". Tata has also snapped up such emblems of Englishness as Jaguar and Tetley Tea and, not content with taking over the world, has set itself to cultivating the ambitions of India's rapidly growingmiddle class. The Nano car, launched in 2009 with a price tag of less than US$1000, together with the Shubh Griha project in suburbanMumbai which sells new apartments for just US$10,000, hasmade the house-and-car lifestyle a realistic aspiration formillions of Indians.

How big a dent the global recession might put in India's plans for growth remains to be seen. The IT industry, dependent on outsourcing dollars from the hard-hit US market, has suffered a profit slowdown and been forced to send workers on yearlong sabbaticals. However, with most of the major banks being publicly owned, the country has been shielded from the worst excesses of the credit crunch, and the relatively low importance of exports – 22% of the economy, compared to China's 37% – puts India in a good position to survive comparatively unscathed.

A bigger issue for India is how to reduce poverty. Arundhati Roy, a notorious fly in the ointment of Indian triumphalism, wrote (in the days before Tata takeovers) that India, having nowhere else to colonize, has made its fortune by colonizing itself. Rich Indians, disconnected from the reality of where their money comes from, pay little regard to the plight of eight-year-old workers hammering fist-sized lumps of rock into powder in Karnataka's iron ore mines, or the villagers whose lands are repossessed so companies can build cars on the cheap. While the media trumpets the nation's new-found power to put men into space, Infosys executives into mansions and millions of rupees into cricketers' pockets, government reports suggest that 75% of people in India survive on less than Rs 20 per day. As much as 40% of the country still exists below the official poverty line, and statistics on child malnourishment (India has the third highest rate in the world, after Timor-L'Este and Yemen), infant mortality (2.1 million children die every year) and corruption (bribes worth Rs 9 billion a year are hoovered up from below-poverty-line households for basic public services such as policing and schooling) show that for all its progress, the economy still has an awful lot of growing up to do.

Judiciary India's Supreme Court has similar but somewhat weaker powers to those of the United States. The judiciary has remained effectively independent of the government except under the Emergency between 1975-1977.

Civil service India continued to use the small but highly professional administrative service inherited from the British period. Renamed the Indian Administrative Service (IAS), it continues to exercise remarkable influence across the country. The administration of many aspects of central and regional government is in the hands of this elite body, who act largely by the constitutional rules which bind them as servants of the state. Many Indians accept the continuing efficiency and high calibre of the top ranking officers in the administration while believing that the bureaucratic system as a whole has been overtaken by widespread corruption.

Police India's police service is divided into a series of groups, numbering nearly one million. While the top ranks of the Indian Police Service are comparable to the IAS, lower levels are extremely poorly trained and very low paid. In addition to the domestic police force there are special groups: the Border Security Force, Central Reserve Police and others. They may be armed with modern weapons and are called in for special duties.

Armed forces Unlike its immediate neighbours Pakistan and Bangladesh, India has never had military rule. It has around one million men in the army, one of the largest armed forces in the world. Although they have remained out of politics the army has been used increasingly frequently to put down civil unrest especially in Kashmir.

Congress Party The Congress won overall majorities in seven of the 10 general elections held before the 1996 election, although in no election did the Congress obtain more than 50% of the popular vote. In 1998 its popular support completely disappeared in some regions and fell below 30% nationally and in the elections of September-October 1999 Sonia Gandhi, Rajiv Gandhi's Italian-born widow, failed to achieve the much vaunted revival in the Party's fortunes. Through 2001 into 2002 a change began with the BJP losing power in state assemblies in the north and becoming increasingly unpopular nationally, and the Congress picking up a wide measure of support, culminating in their victory in the May 2004 general election, when Sonia Gandhi nominated Manmohan Singh as prime minister. However, despite his successes in liberalizing the Indian economy and presiding over breakneck economic growth during 2007, Singh's time at the helm became indelibly associated with a series of scandals involving allocation of national resources to private corporations; the 'Coalgate' scam allegedly cost the nation the equivalent of US$33.4 billion over eight years, during most of which Singh himself held the portfolio of coal minister. In the 2014 elections the Congress won just 44 seats, suffering its worst ever defeat in a general election.

Non-Congress parties Political activity outside the Congress can seem bewilderingly complex. There are no genuinely national parties. The only alternative governments to the Congress have been formed by coalitions of regional and ideologically based parties. Parties of the left – Communist and Socialist – have never broken out of their narrow regional bases. The **Communist Party of India** split into two factions in 1964, with the Communist Party of India Marxist (CPM) ultimately taking power in West Bengal and Kerala. In the 1960s the **Swatantra Party** (a liberal party) made some ground nationally, opposing the economic centralization and state control supported by the Congress.

At the right of the political spectrum, the **Jan Sangh** was seen as a party of right wing Hindu nationalism with a concentrated but significant base in parts of the north, especially among higher castes and merchant communities. The most organized political force outside the Congress, the Jan Sangh merged with the **Janata Party** for the elections of 1977. After the collapse of that government it re-formed itself as the **Bharatiya Janata Party (BJP)**. In 1990-1991 it developed a powerful campaign focusing on reviving Hindu identity against the minorities. In the decade that followed it became the most powerful single party across northern India and established a series of footholds and alliances in the South. Elsewhere a succession of regional parties dominated politics in several key states, including Tamil Nadu and Andhra Pradesh in the south and West Bengal and Bihar in the east.

Recent developments

Relations with Pakistan over possession of Kashmir, and relations between Hindus and Muslims domestically, continue to be dominant issues in Indian politics. Both India and Pakistan sought political advantage from the US-led war on the Taliban in Afghanistan, and when a terrorist attack was launched on the Indian parliament on 13 December 2001 the Indian government pushed massive reinforcements to the entire length of the Pakistan border. Although President Musharraf closed down Lashkar-e-Taiba and Jaish-e-Mohammad, two of the most feared groups operating openly in Pakistan, attacks in Kashmir continued. India's greatest concern is still a collapse of political stability and control in its western neighbour. Talks over Kashmir resumed in February 2011, with then-Prime Minister Manmohan Singh inviting President Asif Ali Zardari to join him for the Cricket World Cup semi-final between India and Pakistan. The two nations entered into closer trade relations thanks to the removal of restrictions on Pakistani investment in India. Encouragingly, there are long-term signs that communal violence between Hindus and Muslims elsewhere in India is on the wane. The Mumbai terror attacks of 26 November 2008 by Pakistan-trained militants did not trigger the anti-Muslim reprisals that many feared, and several commentators credited BJP member Varun Gandhi's hate speeches against Muslims for the party's resounding defeat in the 2009 general election.

However, the change in government in 2014 represents a potentially fundamental turning point. Since coming to power, members of Narendra Modi's right-wing BJP party have indulged in bouts of sabre-rattling, with party elder Subramaniam Swamy touting the prospect of unleashing nuclear weapons on Pakistan. These were ignored by the government, and so far Modi's attempts to balance his party's instinctive antagonism to Pakistan with his own ambitions as a global statesman have resulted in an ambiguous approach to Indo-Pakistan relations. Modi himself is a deeply controversial character. To many Indians he is a cult hero: a powerful orator who promises to restore pride in Indian (or more specifically Hindu) achievements and a stronger national economy, partly by means of aggressively courting large-scale foreign investment. Yet as Chief Minister of Gujarat, he was implicated in the 2002 riots in which around 1000 Muslims were murdered, and there is little dispute that his rise to power has emboldened fundamentalist Hindu voices both in government and in the wider community. At the same time, the Modi government has been quick to squash criticism; books have been banned, environmental and human rights groups have come under surveillance and official harassment. Meanwhile, the government has filed away criticism in the media as "nay-saying" or "jealousy".

Domestically, much attention has been focused on the corruption and illegality that dominates Indian politics. One in five candidates for the 2014 national election was subject to criminal charges ranging from extortion to murder, and the electorate has become justifiably cynical about official corruption, ministerial scandals and the heavy steering hand of business moguls such as Mukesh Ambani. 2011-2012 saw anti-corruption sit-ins and hunger strikes in North India, leading to the formation of the Aam Aadmi (Common Man) Party by Arvind Kejriwal, which campaigned on the promise of a Jan Lokpal – an independent body to root out corruption in politics. The AAP successfully won government in New Delhi, but found its initiatives stifled by the Congress and BJP – vested interests proving more powerful than the common man. After winning a resounding victory in the 2015 Delhi elections, in which it won 67 of 70 seats and offered a glimmer of hope for good governance, the party appears to have begun tearing itself apart amid complaints against Kejriwal's dictatorial style of leadership.

Culture

The graffiti written on the walls of any Indian city bear witness to the number of major languages spoken across the country, many with their own distinct scripts. In all the states of North and West India an Indo-Aryan language – the easternmost group of the Indo-European family – is predominant. Sir William Jones, the great 19th-century scholar, discovered the close links between Sanskrit (the basis of nearly all North Indian languages) German and Greek. He showed that they all must have originated in the common heartland of Central Asia, being carried west, south and east by the nomadic tribes who shaped so much of the following history of both Europe and Asia.

Sanskrit As the pastoralists from Central Asia moved into South Asia from 2000 BC onwards, the Indo-Aryan languages they spoke were modified. Sanskrit developed from this process, emerging as the dominant classical language of India by the sixth century BC, when it was classified in the grammar of **Panini**. It remained the language of the educated until about AD 1000, though it had ceased to be in common use several centuries earlier.

Hindi and Urdu The Muslims brought Persian into South Asia as the language of the rulers, where it became the language of the politically powerful elite. The most striking example of Muslim influence on the earlier Indo-European languages is that of the two most important languages of India and Pakistan, Hindi and Urdu respectively. Most of the other modern North Indian languages were not written until the 16th century or after. Hindi developed into the language of the heartland of Hindu culture, stretching from Punjab to Bihar and from the foothills of the Himalaya to the marchlands of central India.

Bengali At the east end of the Ganga plains Hindi gives way to Bengali (Bangla), the language today of over 50 million people in India, as well as more than 115 million in Bangladesh. Linguistically it is close to both Assamese and Oriya.

Gujarati and Marathi South of the main Hindi and Urdu belt of India and Pakistan is a series of quite different Indo-Aryan languages. Panjabi in both Pakistan and India (on the Indian side of the border written in the Gurumukhi script) and Gujarati and Marathi, all have common features with Urdu or Hindi, but are major languages in their own right.

Dravidian languages The other major language family of South Asia today, Dravidian, has been in India since before the arrival of the Indo-Aryans. Four of South Asia's major living languages belong to this family group – Tamil, Telugu, Kannada and Malayalam, spoken in Tamil Nadu (and northern Sri Lanka), Andhra Pradesh, Karnataka and Kerala respectively.

Each has its own script. All the Dravidian languages were influenced by the prevalence of Sanskrit as the language of the ruling and educated elite. There have been recent attempts to rid Tamil of its Sanskrit elements and to recapture the supposed purity of a literature that stretches back to the early centuries BC. Kannada and Telugu were clearly established by AD 1000, while Malayalam, which started as a dialect of Tamil, did not develop fully until the 13th century. Today the four main Dravidian languages are spoken by 180 million people.

Scripts

It is impossible to spend even a short time in India or the other countries of South Asia without coming across several of the different scripts that are used. The earliest ancestor of scripts in use today was **Brahmi**, in which Asoka's famous inscriptions were written in the third century BC. Written from left to right, a separate symbol represented each different sound.

Devanagari For around 1000 years the major script of northern India has been the Nagari or Devanagari, which means literally the script of the 'city of the gods'. Hindi, Nepali and Marathi join Sanskrit in their use of Devanagari. The Muslim rulers developed a right to left script based on Persian and Arabic.

Dravidian scripts The Dravidian languages were written originally on leaves of the palmyra palm. Cutting the letters on the hard palm leaf made particular demands which had their impact on the forms of the letters adopted. The letters became rounded because they were carved with a stylus. This was held stationary while the leaf was turned. The southern scripts were carried overseas, contributing to the form of the non-Dravidian languages of Thai, Burmese and Cambodian.

Numerals Many of the Indian alphabets have their own notation for numerals. This is not without irony, for what in the Western world are called 'Arabic' numerals are in fact of Indian origin. In some parts of South Asia local numerical symbols are still in use, but you will find that the Arabic number symbols familiar in Europe and the West are common.

Literature

Sanskrit was the first all-India language. Its literature has had a fundamental influence on the region's religious, social and political life. Early literature was memorized and recited. The hymns of the Rig Veda did not reach their final form until about the sixth century BC.

The Vedas

The Rig Veda is a collection of 1028 hymns, not all religious. Its main function was to provide orders of worship for priests responsible for the sacrifices that were central to the religion of Indo-Aryans. Two later texts, the Yajurveda and the Samaveda, served the same purpose. A fourth, the Atharvaveda, is largely a collection of magic spells.

The Brahmanas Central to the Vedic literature was a belief in the importance of sacrifice. At some time after 1000 BC a second category of Vedic literature, the Brahmanas, began to take shape. Story telling developed as a means to interpret the significance of sacrifice. The most famous and the most important of these were the Upanishads, probably written at some time between the seventh and fifth centuries BC.

The Mahabharata The Brahmanas gave their name to the religion emerging between the eighth and sixth centuries BC, Brahmanism, the ancestor of Hinduism. Two of its texts remain the best known and most widely revered epic compositions in South Asia, the *Mahabharata* and the *Ramayana*.

Dating the Mahabharata

Tradition puts the date of the great battle described in the *Mahabharata* at precisely 3102 BC, the start of the present era, and names the author of the poem as a sage, Vyasa. Evidence suggests however that the battle was fought around 800 BC, at Kurukshetra. It was another 400 years before priests began to write the stories down, a process which was not complete until AD 400. The *Mahabharata* was probably an attempt by the warrior class, the Kshatriyas, to merge their brand of popular religion with Brahmanism ideas. The original version was 3000 stanzas long, but it now has over 100,000; eight times as long as Homer's Iliad and the Odyssey put together.

Good and evil The battle was seen as a war of good and evil, the Pandavas being interpreted as gods and the Kauravas as devils. The arguments were elaborated and expanded until the fourth century AD by which time, as Shackle says, "Brahmanism had absorbed and set its own mark on the religious ideas of the epic and Hinduism had come into being". A comparatively late addition to the *Mahabharata*, the *Bhagavad-Gita* is the most widely read and revered text among Hindus in South Asia today.

The Ramayana

Valmiki is thought of in India as the author of the second great Indian epic, the *Ramayana*, though no more is known of his identity than is known of Homer's. Like the *Mahabharata*, it underwent several stages of development before it reached its final version of 48,000 lines.

Sanskrit literature

Sanskrit was the language of the elite. Other languages replaced it in common speech by the third century BC, but it remained in restricted use for over 1000 years after that period. The remarkable Sanskrit grammar of Panini helped to establish grammar as one of the six disciplines essential to understanding the Vedas properly and to conducting Vedic rituals. The other five were phonetics, etymology, meter, ritual practice and astronomy. Sanskrit literature continued to be written in

The story of Rama

Under Brahmin influence, Rama was transformed from the human prince of the early versions into the divine figure of the final story. Rama, the 'jewel of the solar kings', became deified as an incarnation of Vishnu. The story tells how Rama was banished from his father's kingdom. In a journey with his wife, Sita, and helper and friend, Hanuman (the monkey-faced God depicted in many Indian temples, shrines and posters), Rama fought the king Ravana, changed in late versions into a demon. Rama's rescue of Sita was interpreted as the Aryan triumph over the barbarians. The epic is seen as South Asia's first literary poem and is recited in all Hindu communities.

Ravana, demon King of Lanka

the courts until the Muslims replaced it with Persian, long after it had ceased to be a language of spoken communication.

Literally 'stories of ancient times', the Puranas are about Brahma, Vishnu and Siva. They were not compiled until the fifth century AD. The stories are often the only source of information about the period immediately after the early Vedas. Each Purana dealt with five themes: "the creation of the world (*sarga*); its destruction and recreation (*pratisarga*); the genealogy of gods and patriarchs (*vamsa*); the reigns and periods of the Manus (*manvantaras*); and the history of the solar and lunar dynasties".

The Muslim influence

Persian In the first three decades of the 10th century AD Mahmud of Ghazni carried Muslim power into India. For considerable periods until the 18th century, Persian became the language of the courts. Classical Persian was the dominant influence, with Iran as its country of origin and Shiraz its main cultural centre, but India developed its own Persian-based style. Two poets stood out at the end of the 13th century AD, when Muslim rulers had established a sultanate in Delhi, Amir Khusrau, who lived from 1253 to 1325 and the mystic Amir Hasan, who died about AD 1328.

Turki The most notable of the Mughal sponsors of literature, Akbar (1556-1605) was illiterate. Babur left one of the most remarkable political autobiographies of any generation, the Babur-nama, written in Turki and translated into Persian. His grandson Akbar commissioned a biography, the Akbar-nama, which reflected his interest in the world's religions. His son Jahangir left his memoirs, the Tuzuk-i Jahangiri, in Persian. They have been described as intimate and showing an insatiable interest in things, events and people.

The Colonial Period

Persian was already in decline during the reign of the last great Muslim Emperor, **Aurangzeb** and as the British extended their political power so the role of English grew. There is now a very wide Indian literature accessible in English, which has thus become the latest of the languages to be used across the whole of South Asia.

In the 19th century English became a vehicle for developing nationalist ideals. However, notably in the work of **Rabindranath Tagore**, it became a medium for religious and philosophical prose and for a developing poetry. Tagore himself won the Nobel Prize for Literature in 1913 for his translation into English of his own work, Gitanjali. Leading South Asian philosophers and thinkers of the 20th century have written major works in English, including not only MK Gandhi and Jawaharlal

Nehru, the two leading figures in India's Independence movement, but S Radhakrishnan, Aurobindo Ghosh and Sarojini Naidu, who all added to the depth of Indian literature in English.

Several South Asian regional languages have their own long traditions of both religious and secular literature which are discussed in the relevant sections of this book.

Science

Views of the universe Early Indian views of the universe were based on the square and the cube. The earth was seen as a square, one corner pointing south, rising like a pyramid in a series of square terraces with its peak, the mythical Mount Meru. The sun moved round the top of Mount Meru in a square orbit and the square orbits of the planets were at successive planes above the orbit of the sun. These were seen therefore as forming a second pyramid of planetary movement. Mount Meru was central to all early Indian schools of thought, Hindu, Buddhist and Jain.

However, about 200 BC the Jains transformed the view of the universe based on squares by replacing the idea of square orbits with that of the circle. The earth was shown as a circular disc, with Mount Meru rising from its centre and the Pole Star above it.

The science of early India By about 500 BC Indian texts illustrated the calculation of the **calendar**, although the system itself almost certainly goes back to the eighth or ninth century BC. The year was divided into 27 *nakshatras*, or fortnights, years being calculated on a mixture of lunar and solar counting.

Technology The only copy of Kautiliya's treatise on government (which was only discovered in 1909) dates from about 100 BC. It describes the **weapons** technology of catapults, incendiary missiles and the use of elephants, but it is also evident that gunpowder was unknown. Large-scale **irrigation** works were developed, though the earliest examples of large tanks may be those of the Sri Lankan King Panduwasa at Anuradhapura, built in 504 BC. During the Gupta period dramatic progress was made in **metallurgy**, shown in the pure iron pillar which can be seen in the Qutb Minar in Delhi.

Mathematics Conceptions of the universe and the mathematical and geometrical ideas that accompanied them were comparatively advanced in South Asia by the time of the Mauryan Empire and were put to use in the rules developed for building temple altars. Indians were using the concept of zero and decimal points in the Gupta period. Furthermore in AD 499, just after the demise of the Gupta Empire, the astronomer Aryabhatta calculated Pi as 3.1416 and the length of the solar year as 365.358 days. He also postulated that the earth was a sphere rotating on its own axis and revolving around the sun and that the shadow of the earth falling on the moon caused lunar eclipses. The development of science in India was not restricted to the Gupta court. In South India, Tamil kings developed extensive contact with Roman and Greek thinkers during the first four centuries of the Christian era. Babylonian methods used for astronomy in Greece remained current in Tamil Nadu until very recent times. The basic texts of astronomy (the Surya Siddhanta) were completed by AD 400.

Architecture

Over the 4000 years since the Indus Valley civilization flourished, art and architecture have developed with a remarkable continuity through successive regional and religious influences and styles. The Buddhist art and architecture of the third century BC left few remains, but the stylistic influence on early Hindu architecture was profound. From the sixth century AD the first Hindu religious buildings to have survived into the modern period were constructed in South and East India.

Hindu temple buildings

The principles of religious building were laid down by priests in the *Sastras*. Every aspect of Hindu, Jain and Buddhist religious building is identified with conceptions of the structure of the universe. This applies as much to the process of building – the timing of which must be undertaken at astrologically propitious times – as to the formal layout of the buildings. The cardinal directions of north, south, east and west are the basic fix on which buildings are planned. George Michell suggests that in addition to the cardinal directions, number is also critical to the design of the religious building. The key to the ultimate scale of the building is derived from the measurements of the sanctuary at its heart. Indian temples were nearly always built according to philosophical understandings of the universe. This cosmology, of an infinite number of universes, isolated from each other in space, proceeds by imagining various possibilities as to its nature. Its centre is seen as dominated by Mount Meru which keeps earth and heaven apart. The concept of *separation* is crucial to Hindu thought and social practice. Continents, rivers and oceans occupy concentric rings around the mountain, while the stars encircle the mountain in another plane. Humans live on the continent of **Jambudvipa**, characterized by the rose apple tree (*jambu*).

Mandalas The Sastras show plans of this continent, organized in concentric rings and entered at the cardinal points. This type of diagram was known as a **mandala**. Such a geometric scheme could be subdivided into almost limitless small compartments, each of which could be designated as having special properties or be devoted to a particular deity. The centre of the mandala would be the seat of the major god; they provided the ground rules for the building of *stupas* and temples across India and gave the key to the symbolic meaning attached to every aspect of religious buildings.

Temple design The focal point of the temple, its sanctuary, was the home of the presiding deity, the 'womb-chamber' (*garbhagriha*). A series of doorways, in large temples leading through a succession of buildings, allowed the worshipper to move towards the final encounter with the deity to obtain *darshan* – a sight of the god. Both Buddhist and Hindu worship encourage the worshipper to walk clockwise around the shrine, performing *pradakshina*. The elevations are symbolic representations of the home of the gods. Mountain peaks such as Kailasa are common names for the most prominent of the towers. In North and East Indian temples the tallest of these towers rises above the *garbagriha* itself, symbolizing the meeting of earth and heaven in the person of the enshrined deity. In later South Indian temples the gateways to the temple come to overpower the central tower. In both, the basic structure is usually richly embellished with sculpture. When first built this would usually have been plastered and painted and often covered in gems. In contrast to the extraordinary profusion of colour and life on the outside, the interior is dark and cramped but here it is believed, lies the true centre of divine power.

Muslim religious architecture

Although the Muslims adapted many Hindu features, they also brought totally new forms. Their most outstanding contribution, dominating the architecture of many North Indian cities, are the mosques and tomb complexes (*dargah*). The use of brickwork was widespread and they brought with them from Persia the principle of constructing the true arch. Muslim architects succeeded in producing a variety of domed structures, often incorporating distinctively Hindu features such as the surmounting finial. By the end of the great period of Muslim building in 1707, the Muslims had added magnificent forts and palaces to their religious structures, a statement of power as well as of aesthetic taste.

European buildings

Nearly two centuries of architectural stagnation and decline followed the demise of Mughal power. The Portuguese built a series of remarkable churches in Goa that owed everything to Baroque developments in Europe. Not until the end of the Victorian period, when British imperial ambitions were at their height, did the British colonial impact on public rather than domestic architecture begin to be felt. Fierce arguments divided British architects as to the merits of indigenous design. The ultimate plan for New Delhi was carried out by men who had little time for Hindu architecture and believed themselves to be on a civilizing mission. Others at the end of the 19th century wanted to recapture and enhance a tradition for which they had great respect. They have left a series of buildings, both in formerly British ruled territory and in the Princely States, which illustrate this concern with the development of what became known as the Indo-Saracenic style.

In the aftermath of the colonial period, Independent India set about trying to establish a break from the immediately imperial past, but was uncertain how to achieve it. In the event foreign architects were commissioned for major developments, such as Le Corbusier's design for Chandigarh and Louis Kahn's buildings in Dhaka and Ahmedabad. The latter, a centre for training and experiment, contains a number of new buildings such as those of the Indian architect Charles Correa.

Music, dance and film

Music Indian music can trace its origins to the metrical hymns and chants of the Vedas, in which the production of sound according to strict rules was understood to be vital to the continuing order of the Universe. Through more than 3000 years of development and a range of regional schools, India's musical tradition has been handed on almost entirely by ear. The chants of the **Rig Veda** developed into songs in the **Sama Veda** and music found expression in every sphere of life, reflecting the cycle of seasons and the rhythm of work.

Over the centuries the original three notes, which were sung strictly in descending order, were extended to five and then seven and developed to allow freedom to move up and down the scale. The scale increased to 12 with the addition of flats and sharps and finally to 22 with the further subdivision of semitones. Books of musical rules go back at least as far as the third century AD. Classical music was totally intertwined with dance and drama, an interweaving reflected in the term *sangita*.

At some point after the Muslim influence made itself felt in the north, North and South Indian styles diverged, to become Carnatic (Karnatak) music in the south and Hindustani music in the north. However, they still share important common features: *svara* (pitch), *raga* (the melodic structure) and *tala* or *talam* (metre).

Hindustani music probably originated in the Delhi Sultanate during the 13th century, when the most widely known of North Indian musical instruments, the *sitar*, was believed to have been invented. **Amir Khusrau** is also believed to have invented the small drums, the *tabla*. Hindustani music is held to have reached its peak under *Tansen*, a court musician of Akbar. The other important northern instruments are the stringed *sarod*, the reed instrument *shahnai* and the wooden flute. Most Hindustani compositions have devotional texts, though they encompass a great emotional and thematic range. A common classical form of vocal performance is the *dhrupad*, a four-part composition.

The essential structure of a melody is known as a **raga** which usually has five to seven notes and can have as many as nine (or even 12 in mixed ragas). The music is improvised by the performer within certain rules and although theoretically thousands of ragas are possible, only around a 100 are commonly performed. Ragas have become associated with particular moods and specific times of the day. Music festivals often include all night sessions to allow performers a wider choice of repertoire.

Carnatic (Karnatak) music, contemporary South Indian music, is traced back to Tyagaraja (1759-1847), Svami Shastri (1763-1827) and Dikshitar (1775-1835), three musicians who lived and worked in Thanjavur. They are still referred to as the Trinity. Their music placed more emphasis on extended compositions than Hindustani music. Perhaps the best known South Indian instrument is the stringed *vina*, the flute being used for accompaniment with the violin (played rather differently to the European original), an oboe-like instrument called the *nagasvaram* and the drums, *tavil*.

Dance The rules for classical dance were laid down in the Natya shastra in the second century BC, which is still one of the bases for modern dance forms. The most common sources for Indian dance are the epics, but there are three essential aspects of the dance itself, Nritta (pure dance), Nrittya (emotional expression) and Natya (drama). The religious influence in dance was exemplified by the tradition of temple dancers, *devadasis*, girls and women who were dedicated to the deity in major temples. In South and East India there were thousands of *devadasis* associated with temple worship, though the practice fell into widespread disrepute and was banned in independent India. Various dance forms (for example Odissi, Manipuri, Bharat Natyam, Kathakali, Mohinyattam) developed in different parts of the country. India is also rich in folk dance traditions.

Film Filmgoers around the world are taking greater note of Indian cinema, both home-grown and that produced and directed by Indians abroad. Not all fall into the category of a Bollywood '*masala* movie' or 'curry western' churned out by the Mumbai (Bombay) film industry but many offer an insight into what draws millions to watch diverse versions of Indian life on the silver screen. A few titles, both all-time favourites as well as newer releases include: *Pather Panchali, Mother India; Titash Ekti Nadir Naam; Sholay; Bombay; Kuch Kuch Hota Hai; Lagaan; Kabhie Khushi Kabhie Cham; Monsoon Wedding; The Guru; The Warrior; Rang De Basanti; 3 Idiots; Barfi; A Wednesday* and *Kahaani*.

Religion

It is impossible to write briefly about religion in India without oversimplifying. Over 80% of Indians are Hindu, but there are many minorities. Muslims number about 125 million and there are over 23 million Christians, 19 million Sikhs, six million Buddhists and a number of other religious groups. One of the most persistent features of religious and social life is the caste system. This has undergone substantial changes since Independence, especially in towns and cities, but most people in India are still clearly identified as a member of a particular caste group. The government has introduced measures to help the backward, or 'scheduled' castes, though in recent years this has produced a major political backlash.

Hinduism

It has always been easier to define Hinduism by what it is not than by what it is. Indeed, the name 'Hindu' was given by foreigners to the peoples of the subcontinent who did not profess the other major faiths, such as Muslims or Christians. While some aspects of modern Hinduism can be traced back more than 4000 years before that, other features are recent.

Key ideas

According to the Indian philosopher and former president of India, S Radhakrishnan, religion for the Hindu "is not an idea but a power, not an intellectual proposition but a life conviction. Religion is consciousness of ultimate reality, not a theory about God". There is no Hindu organization, like a church, with the authority to define belief or establish official practice. Not all Hindu groups believe in a single supreme God. In view of these characteristics, many authorities argue that it is misleading to think of Hinduism as a religion. Be that as it may, the evidence of the living importance of Hinduism is visible across India. Hindu philosophy and practice has also touched many of those who belong to other religious traditions, particularly in terms of social institutions such as caste, and in post-Independence India religious identity has become an increasingly politicized feature of life.

Darshan One of Hinduism's recurring themes is 'vision', 'sight' or 'view' – **darshan**. Applied to the different philosophical systems themselves, such as *yoga* or *vedanta*, 'darshan' is also used to describe the sight of the deity that worshippers hope to gain when they visit a temple or shrine hoping for the sight of a 'guru' (teacher). Equally it may apply to the religious insight gained through meditation or prayer.

The four human goals Many Hindus also accept that there are four major human goals; material prosperity (*artha*), the satisfaction of desires (*kama*) and performing the duties laid down according to your position in life (*dharma*). Beyond these is the goal of achieving liberation from the endless cycle of rebirths into which everyone is locked (*moksha*). It is to the search for liberation that the major schools of Indian philosophy have devoted most attention. Together with dharma, it is basic to Hindu thought.

The *Mahabharata* lists 10 embodiments of **dharma**: good name, truth, self-control, cleanness of mind and body, simplicity, endurance, resoluteness of character, giving and sharing, austerities and continence. In *dharmic* thinking these are inseparable from five patterns of behaviour: non-violence, an attitude of equality, peace and tranquillity, lack of aggression and cruelty and absence of envy. Dharma, an essentially secular concept, represents the order inherent in human life.

Karma The idea of *karma*, 'the effect of former actions', is central to achieving liberation. As C Rajagopalachari put it: "Every act has its appointed effect, whether the act be thought, word or deed. The cause holds the effect, so to say, in its womb. If we reflect deeply and objectively, the entire world will be found to obey unalterable laws. That is the doctrine of karma". See also box, opposite.

Rebirth The belief in the transmigration of souls (*samsara*) in a neverending cycle of rebirth has been Hinduism's most distinctive and important contribution to Indian culture. The earliest reference is in one of the *Upanishads*, around the seventh century BC, at about the same time as the doctrine of *karma* made its first appearance.

The four stages of life

Popular Hindu belief holds that an ideal life has four stages: the student, the householder, the forest dweller and the wandering dependent/beggar (*sannyasi*). These stages represent the phases through which an individual learns of life's goals and of the means of achieving them.

One of the most striking sights today is that of the saffron-clad *sannyasi* (sadhu) seeking gifts of food and money to support himself in the final stage of his life. There may have been sadhus even before the Aryans arrived. Today, most of these have given up material possessions, carrying only a strip of cloth, a *danda* (staff), a crutch to support the chin during *achal* (meditation), prayer beads, a fan to ward off evil spirits, a water pot, a drinking vessel, which may be a human skull and a begging bowl.

Ahimsa AL Basham pointed out that belief in transmigration must have encouraged a further distinctive doctrine, that of non-violence or non-injury – *ahimsa*. The belief in rebirth meant that all living things and creatures of the spirit possessed the same essential soul. One inscription threatens that anyone who interferes with the rights of Brahmins to land given to them by the king will 'suffer rebirth for 80,000 years as a worm in dung'. Belief in the cycle of rebirth was essential to give such a threat any weight!

Schools of philosophy

It is common now to talk of six major schools of Hindu philosophy. *Nyaya, Vaisheshika, Sankhya, Yoga, Purvamimansa* and *Vedanta*.

Yoga Yoga can be traced back to at least the third century AD. It seeks a synthesis of the spirit, the soul and the flesh and is concerned with systems of meditation and self denial that lead to the realization of the Divine within oneself and can ultimately release one from the cycle of rebirth.

Vedanta These are literally the final parts of the Vedic literature, the *Upanishads*. The basic texts also include the Brahmasutra of Badrayana, written about the first century AD and the most important of all, the *Bhagavad-Gita*, which is a part of the epic *Mahabharata*. There are many interpretations of these basic texts. Three are given here.

Advaita Vedanta holds that there is no division between the cosmic force or principle, *Brahman* and the individual Self, *atman* (also referred to as 'soul'). The fact that we appear to see different and separate individuals is simply a result of ignorance. This is termed *maya* (illusion), but Vedanta philosophy does not suggest that the world in which we live is an illusion. *Jnana* (knowledge) is held as the key to understanding the full and real unity of Self and Brahman. **Shankaracharya**, born at Kalady in modern Kerala, in AD 6, is the best known Advaitin Hindu philosopher. He argued that there was no individual Self or soul separate from the creative force of the universe, or Brahman and that it was impossible to achieve liberation (*moksha*) through meditation and devotional worship, which he saw as signs of remaining on a lower level and of being unprepared for true liberation.

The 11-12th-century philosopher, **Ramanuja**, repudiated ideas of **Vishishtadvaita**. He transformed the idea of God from an impersonal force to a personal God and viewed both the Self and the World as real but only as part of the whole. In contrast to Shankaracharya's view, Ramanuja saw *bhakti* (devotion) as of central importance to achieving liberation and service to the Lord as the highest goal of life. **Dvaita Vedanta** was developed by the 14th-century philosopher, Madhva. He believed that Brahman, the Self and the World are completely distinct. Worship of God is a key means of achieving liberation.

Worship

Puja For most Hindus today, worship ('performing puja') is an integral part of their faith. The great majority of Hindu homes will have a shrine to one of the gods of the Hindu pantheon. Individuals and families will often visit shrines or temples and on special occasions will travel long distances to particularly holy places such as Benaras or Puri. Such sites may have temples dedicated to a major deity but may also have numerous other shrines in the vicinity dedicated to other favourite gods.

BACKGROUND

Karma – an eye to the future

According to the doctrine of karma, every person, animal or god has a being or 'self' which has existed without beginning. Every action, except those that are done without any consideration of the results, leaves an indelible mark on that Self, carried forward into the next life.

The overall character of the imprint on each person's Self determines three features of the next life: the nature of his next birth (animal, human or god), the kind of family he will be born into if human and the length of the next life. Finally, it controls the good or bad experiences that the self will experience. However, it does not imply a fatalistic belief that the nature of action in this life is unimportant. Rather, it suggests that the path followed by the individual in the present life is vital to the nature of its next life and ultimately to the chance of gaining release from this world.

Acts of devotion are often aimed at the granting of favours and the meeting of urgent needs for this life – good health, finding a suitable wife or husband, the birth of a son, prosperity and good fortune. Puja involves making an offering to God and *darshan* (having a view of the deity). Hindu worship is generally, though not always, an act performed by individuals. Thus Hindu temples may be little more than a shrine on a river bank or in the middle of the street, tended by a priest and visited at special times when a darshan of the resident God can be obtained. When it has been consecrated, the image, if exactly made, becomes the channel for the godhead to work.

Holy places Certain rivers and towns are particularly sacred to Hindus. Thus there are seven holy rivers – the Ganga, Yamuna, Indus and mythical Sarasvati in the north and the Narmada, Godavari and Kaveri in the Peninsula. There are also seven holy places – Haridwar, Mathura, Ayodhya and Varanasi, again in the north, Ujjain, Dwarka and Kanchipuram to the south. In addition to these seven holy places there are four holy abodes: Badrinath, Puri and Ramesvaram, with Dwarka in modern Gujarat having the unique distinction of being both a holy abode and a holy place.

Rituals and festivals The temple rituals often follow through the cycle of day and night, as well as yearly lifecycles. The priests may wake the deity from sleep, bathe, clothe and feed it. Worshippers will be invited to share by bringing offerings of clothes and food. Gifts of money will usually be made and in some temples there is a charge levied for taking up positions in front of the deity in order to obtain a darshan at the appropriate times.

Every temple has its special festivals. At festival times you can see villagers walking in small groups, brightly dressed and often high spirited, sometimes as far as 80-100 km.

Hindu deities

Today three Gods are widely seen as all-powerful: Brahma, Vishnu and Siva. While Brahma is regarded as the ultimate source of creation, Siva also has a creative role alongside his function as destroyer. Vishnu in contrast is seen as the preserver or protector of the universe. Vishnu and Siva are widely represented and have come to be seen as the most powerful and important. Their followers are referred to as Vaishnavite and Shaivites respectively and numerically they form the two largest sects in India.

Brahma Popularly Brahma is interpreted as the Creator in a trinity, alongside Vishnu as Preserver and Siva as Destroyer. In the literal sense the name Brahma is the masculine and personalized form of the neuter word Brahman.

In the early Vedic writing, *Brahman* represented the universal and impersonal principle which governed the Universe. Gradually, as Vedic philosophy moved towards a monotheistic interpretation of the universe and its origins, this impersonal power was increasingly personalized. In the *Upanishads*, Brahman was seen as a universal and elemental creative spirit. Brahma, described in early myths as having been born from a golden egg and then to have created the Earth, assumed the identity of the earlier Vedic deity Prajapati and became identified as the creator.

By the fourth and fifth centuries AD, the height of the classical period of Hinduism, Brahma was seen as one of the trinity of Gods – *Trimurti* – in which Vishnu, Siva and Brahma represented

How Sarasvati turned Brahma's head

Masson-Oursel recounts one myth that explains how Brahma came to have five heads. "Brahma first formed woman from his own immaculate substance and she was known as Sarasvati, Savitri, Gayatri or Brahmani. When he saw this lovely girl emerge from his own body Brahma fell in love with her. Sarasvati moved to his right to avoid his gaze, but a head immediately sprang up from the god. And when Sarasvati turned to the left and then behind him, two new heads emerged. She darted towards heaven and a fifth head was formed. Brahma then said to his daughter, 'Let us beget all kinds of living things, men, Suras and Asuras'. Hearing these words Sarasvati returned to earth, Brahma wedded her and they retired to a secret place where they remained together for a hundred (divine) years".

three forms of the unmanifested supreme being. It is from Brahma that Hindu cosmology takes its structure. The basic cycle through which the whole cosmos passes is described as one day in the life of Brahma – the *kalpa*. It equals 4320 million years, with an equally long night. One year of Brahma's life – a cosmic year – lasts 360 days and nights. The universe is expected to last for 100 years of Brahma's life, who is currently believed to be 51 years old.

By the sixth century AD Brahma worship had effectively ceased (before the great period of temple building), which accounts for the fact that there are remarkably few temples dedicated to Brahma. Nonetheless images of Brahma are found in most temples. Characteristically he is shown with four faces, a fifth having been destroyed by the fire from Siva's third eye. In his four arms he usually holds a copy of the Vedas, a sceptre and a water jug or a bow. He is accompanied by the goose, symbolizing knowledge.

Sarasvati Seen by some Hindus as the 'active power' of Brahma, popularly thought of as his consort, Sarasvati has survived into the modern Hindu world as a far more important figure than Brahma himself. In popular worship Sarasvati represents the goddess of education and learning, worshipped in schools and colleges with gifts of fruit, flowers and incense. She represents 'the word' itself, which began to be deified as part of the process of the writing of the Vedas, which ascribed magical power to words. The development of her identity represented the rebirth of the concept of a mother goddess, which had been strong in the Indus Valley Civilization over 1000 years before and may have been continued in popular ideas through the worship of female spirits.

In addition to her role as Brahma's wife, Sarasvati is also variously seen as the wife of Vishnu and Manu or as Daksha's daughter, among other interpretations. Normally white coloured, riding on a swan and carrying a book, she is often shown playing a vina. She may have many arms and heads, representing her role as patron of all the sciences and arts.

Vishnu Vishnu is seen as the God with the human face. From the second century a new and passionate devotional worship of Vishnu's incarnation as Krishna developed in the South. By 1000 AD Vaishnavism had spread across South India and it became closely associated with the devotional form of Hinduism preached by Ramanuja, whose followers spread the worship of Vishnu and his 10 successive incarnations in animal and human form. For Vaishnavites, God took these different forms in order to save the world from impending disaster. AL Basham has summarized the 10 incarnations (see table, page 1328).

Rama and Krishna By far the most influential incarnations of Vishnu are those in which he was believed to take recognizable human form, especially as Rama (twice) and Krishna. As the Prince of Ayodhya, history and myth blend, for Rama was probably a chief who lived in the eighth or seventh century BC. Although Rama is now seen as an earlier incarnation of Vishnu than Krishna, he came to be regarded as divine very late, probably after the Muslim invasions of the 12th century AD. Rama (or Ram, pronounced to rhyme with *calm*) is a powerful figure in contemporary India. His supposed birthplace at Ayodhya became the focus of fierce disputes between Hindus and Muslims in the early 1990s which continue today. Krishna is worshipped extremely widely as perhaps the most human of the gods. His advice on the battlefield of the *Mahabharata* is one of the major sources of guidance for the rules of daily living for many Hindus today.

Vishnu's 10 incarnations

Name	Form	Story
1 *Matsya*	Fish	Vishnu took the form of a fish to rescue Manu (the first man), his family and the Vedas from a flood.
2 *Kurma*	Tortoise	Vishnu became a tortoise to rescue all the treasures lost in the flood, including the divine nectar (Amrita) with which the gods preserved their youth. The gods put Mount Kailasa on the tortoise's back and when he reached the bottom of the ocean they twisted the divine snake round the mountain. They then churned the ocean with the mountain by pulling the snake.
3 *Varaha*	Boar	Vishnu appeared again to raise the earth from the ocean's floor where it had been thrown by a demon, Hiranyaksa. The story probably developed from a non-Aryan cult of a sacred pig.
4 *Narasimha*	Half-man, half lion	Having persuaded Brahma to promise that he could not be killed either by day or night, by god, man or beast, the demon Hiranyakasipu then terrorized everybody. When the gods pleaded for help, Vishnu appeared at sunset, when it was neither day nor night, in the form of a half man and half lion and killed the demon.
5 *Vamana*	A dwarf	Bali, a demon, achieved supernatural power by asceticism. To protect the world Vishnu appeared before him in the form of a dwarf and asked him a favour. Bali granted Vishnu as much land as he could cover in three strides. Vishnu then became a giant, covering the earth in three strides. He left only hell to the demon.
6 *Parasurama*	Rama with the axe	Vishnu was incarnated as the son of a Brahmin, Jamadagni as Parasurama and killed the wicked king for robbing his father. The king's sons then killed Jamadagni and in revenge Parasurama destroyed all male kshatriyas, 21 times in succession.
7 *Rama*	The Prince of Ayodhya	As told in the Ramayana, Vishnu came in the form of Rama to rescue the world from the dark demon, Ravana. His wife Sita is the model of patient faithfulness while Hanuman, is the monkey-faced god and Rama's helper.
8 *Krishna*	Charioteer of Arjuma Many forms	Krishna meets almost every human need, from the mischievous child, the playful boy, the amorous youth to the Divine.
9 The *Buddha*		Probably incorporated into the Hindu pantheon in order to discredit the Buddhists, dominant in some parts of India until the sixth century AD. An early Hindu interpretation suggests that Vishnu took incarnation as Buddha to show compassion for animals and to end sacrifice
10 *Kalki*	Riding on a horse	Vishnu's arrival will accompany the final destruction of this present age, Kaliyuga, judging the wicked and rewarding the good.

Worship of Siva's linga

Worship of Siva's linga – the phallic symbol of fertility, power and creativeness – is universal across India. Its origins lie in the creation myths of the Hindu trinity and in the struggle for supremacy between Hindu sects. Saivite myths illustrate the supreme power of Siva and the variety of ways in which Brahma and Vishnu were compelled to acknowledge his supreme power.

One such story tells how Siva, Vishnu and Brahma emerged from the ocean, whereupon Vishnu and Brahma begged him to perform creation. Siva agreed – but then to their consternation disappeared for 1000 celestial years. They became so worried by the lack of creation that Vishnu told Brahma to create, so he produced everything that could lead to happiness. However, no sooner had Brahma filled the universe with beings than Siva reappeared. Incensed by the usurping of his power by Brahma, Siva decided to destroy everything with a flame from his mouth so that he could create afresh.

As the fire threatened everything, Brahma acknowledged Siva's total power and pleaded with him to spare the creation that Brahma had brought forth. "But what shall I do with all my excess power?" "Send it to the sun", replied Brahma, "for as you are the lord of the sun we may all live together in the sun's energy."

Siva agreed, but said to Brahma "What use is this linga if I cannot use it to create?" So he broke off his linga and threw it to the ground. The linga broke through the earth and went right into the sky. Vishnu looked for the end of it below and Brahma for the top, but neither could find the end. Then a voice from the sky said "If the linga of the god with braided hair is worshipped, it will grant all desires that are longed for in the heart." When Brahma and Vishnu heard this, they and all the divinities worshipped the linga with devotion."

Lakshmi Commonly represented as Vishnu's wife, Lakshmi is widely worshipped as the goddess of wealth. Earlier representations of Vishnu's consorts portrayed her as Sridevi, often shown in statues on Vishnu's right, while Bhudevi, also known as Prithvi, who represented the earth, was on his left. Lakshmi is popularly shown in her own right as standing on a lotus flower, although eight forms of Lakshmi are recognized.

Hanuman The *Ramayana* tells how Hanuman, Rama's faithful servant, went across India and finally into the demon Ravana's forest home of Lanka at the head of his monkey army in search of the abducted Sita. He used his powers to jump the sea separating India from Sri Lanka and managed after a series of heroic and magical feats to find and rescue his master's wife. Whatever form he is shown in, he remains almost instantly recognizable.

Siva Professor Wendy Doniger O'Flaherty argues that the key to the myths through which Siva's character is understood, lies in the explicit ambiguity of Siva as the great ascetic and at the same time as the erotic force of the universe.

Siva is interpreted as both creator and destroyer, the power through whom the universe evolves. He lives on Mount Kailasa with his wife **Parvati** (also known as **Uma**, **Sati**, **Kali** and **Durga**) and two sons, the elephant-headed Ganesh and the six-headed Karttikeya, known in South India as Subrahmanya. In sculptural representations Siva is normally accompanied by his 'vehicle', the bull (*Nandi* or Nandin).

Siva is also represented in Shaivite temples throughout India by the *linga*, literally meaning 'sign' or 'mark', but referring in this context to the sign of gender or phallus and *yoni*. On the one hand a symbol of energy, fertility and potency, as Siva's symbol it also represents the yogic power of sexual abstinence and penance. The *linga* is now the most important symbol of the cult of Siva. O'Flaherty suggests that the worship of the *linga* of Siva can be traced back to the pre-Vedic societies of the Indus Valley civilization (circa 2000 BC), but that it first appears in Hindu iconography in the second century BC. From that time a wide variety of myths appeared to explain the origin of *linga* worship. The myths surrounding the 12 jyotirlinga (*linga* of light) found at centres like Ujjain go back to the second century BC and were developed to explain and justify *linga* worship.

BACKGROUND
Hindu deities

Deity	Association	Relationship
Brahma	Creator	One of Trinity
Sarasvati	Education and culture, "the word"	Wife of Brahma
Siva	Creator/destroyer	One of Trinity
Bhairava	Fierce aspect of Siva	
Parvati (Uma)	Benevolent aspect of female divine power	Consort of Siva, mother of Ganesh
Kali	The energy that destroys evil	Consort of Siva
Durga	In fighting attitude	Consort of Siva
Ganesh/ Ganapati	God of good beginnings, clearer of obstacles	Son of Siva
Skanda	God of War/bringer of disease (Karttikkeya, Murugan, Subrahmanya)	Son of Siva and Ganga
Vishnu	Preserver	One of Trinity
Prithvi/ Bhudevi	Goddess of Earth	Wife of Vishnu
Lakshmi	Goddess of Wealth	Wife of Vishnu
Agni	God of Fire	
Indra	Rain, lightning and thunder	
Ravana	King of the demons	

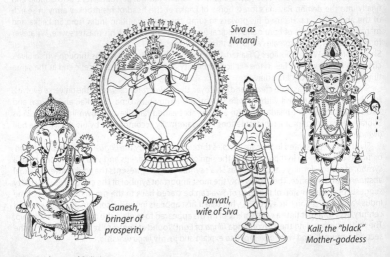

Ganesh, bringer of prosperity

Siva as Nataraj

Parvati, wife of Siva

Kali, the "black" Mother-goddess

Attributes	Vehicle
4 heads, 4 arms, upper left holds water pot and rosary or sacrificial spoon, sacred thread across left shoulder	Hamsa – goose/swan
Two or more arms, vina, lotus, plam leaves, rosary	Hamsa
Linga; Rudra, matted hair, 3 eyes, drum, fire, deer, trident; Nataraja, Lord of the Dance	Nandi – bull
Trident, sword, noose, naked, snakes, garland of skulls, dishevelled hair, carrying destructive weapons	Dog
2 arms when shown with Siva, 4 when on her own, blue lily in right hand, left hand hangs down	Lion
Trident, noose, human skulls, sword, shield, black colour	Lion
4 arms, conch, disc, bow, arrow, bell, sword, shield	Lion or tiger
Goad, noose, broken tusk, fruits	Rat/mouse/ shrew
6 heads, 12 arms, spear, arrow, sword, discus, noose, cock, bow, shield, conch and plough	Peacock
4 arms, high crown, discus and conch in upper arms, club and sword (or lotus) in lower	Garuda – mythical eagle
Right hand in abhaya gesture, left holds pomegranate, left leg on treasure pot	
Seated/standing on red lotus, 4 hands, lotuses, vessel, fruit	Lotus
Sacred thread, axe, wood, bellows, torch, sacrificial spoon	2-headed ram
Bow, thunderbolt, lances	
10 heads, 20 arms, bow and arrow	

Krishna, eighth incarnation of Vishnu

Vishnu, Preserver of the Universe

Durga, Mother-goddess, destroyer of demons

Ardhanarisvara, the male/female form of Siva

Siva's alternative names Although Siva is not seen as having a series of rebirths, like Vishnu, he none the less appears in very many forms representing different aspects of his varied powers. Some of the more common are: **Chandrasekhara** – the moon (*chandra*) symbolizes the powers of creation and destruction. **Mahadeva** – the representation of Siva as the god of supreme power, which came relatively late into Hindu thought, shown as the *linga* in combination with the *yoni*, or female genitalia. **Nataraja** – the Lord of the Cosmic Dance. The story is based on a legend in which Siva and Vishnu went to the forest to overcome 10,000 heretics. In their anger the heretics attacked Siva first by sending a tiger, then a snake and thirdly a fierce black dwarf with a club. Siva killed the tiger, tamed the snake and wore it like a garland and then put his foot on the dwarf and performed a dance of such power that the dwarf and the heretics acknowledged Siva as the Lord. **Rudra** – Siva's early prototype, who may date back to the Indus Valley Civilization. **Virabhadra** – Siva created Virabhadra to avenge himself on his wife Sati's father, Daksha, who had insulted Siva by not inviting him to a special sacrifice. Sati attended the ceremony against Siva's wishes and when she heard her father grossly abusing Siva she committed suicide by jumping into the sacrificial fire. This act gave rise to the term *sati* (*suttee*, a word which simply means a good or virtuous woman). Recorded in the *Vedas*, the self immolation of a woman on her husband's funeral pyre probably did not become accepted practice until the early centuries BC. Even then it was mainly restricted to those of the Kshatriya caste. **Nandi** – Siva's vehicle, the bull, is one of the most widespread of sacred symbols of the ancient world and may represent a link with Rudra, who was sometimes represented as a bull in pre-Hindu India. Strength and virility are key attributes and pilgrims to Siva temples will often touch the Nandi's testicles on their way into the shrine.

Ganesh One of Hinduism's most popular gods, Ganesh is seen as the great clearer of obstacles. Shown at gateways and on door lintels with his elephant head and pot belly, his image is revered across India. Meetings, functions and special family gatherings will often start with prayers to Ganesh and any new venture, from the opening of a building to inaugurating a company, will not be deemed complete without a Ganesh *puja*.

Shakti, the Mother Goddess Shakti is a female divinity often worshipped in the form of Siva's wife Durga or Kali. As Durga she agreed to do battle with Mahish, an *asura* (demon) who threatened to dethrone the gods. Many sculptures and paintings illustrate the story in which, during the terrifying struggle which ensued, the demon changed into a buffalo, an elephant and a giant with 1000 arms. Durga, clutching weapons in each of her 10 hands, eventually emerges victorious. As Kali ('black') the mother goddess takes on her most fearsome form and character. Fighting with the chief of the demons, she was forced to use every weapon in her armoury, but every drop of blood that she drew became 1000 new giants just as strong as he. The only way she could win was by drinking the blood of all her enemies. Having succeeded she was so elated that her dance of triumph threatened the earth. Ignoring the pleas of the gods to stop, she even threw her husband Siva to the ground and trampled over him, until she realized to her shame what she had done. She is always shown with a sword in one hand, the severed head of the giant in another, two corpses for earrings and a necklace of human skulls. She is often shown standing with one foot on the body and the other on the leg of Siva.

The worship of female goddesses developed into the widely practised form of devotional worship called Tantrism. Goddesses such as Kali became the focus of worship which often involved practices that flew in the face of wider Hindu moral and legal codes. Animal and even human sacrifices and ritual sexual intercourse were part of Tantric belief and practice, the evidence for which may still be seen in the art and sculpture of some major temples. Tantric practice affected both Hinduism and Buddhism from the eighth century AD; its influence is shown vividly in the sculptures of Khajuraho and Konark and in the distinctive Hindu and Buddhist practices of the Kathmandu Valley in Nepal.

Skanda The God of War, Skanda (known as Murugan in Tamil Nadu and by other regional names) became known as the son of Siva and Parvati. One legend suggests that he was conceived by the Goddess Ganga from Siva's seed.

Gods of the warrior caste Modern Hinduism has brought into its pantheon over many generations gods who were worshipped by the earlier pre-Hindu Aryan civilizations. The most important is **Indra**, often shown as the god of rain, thunder and lightning. To the early Aryans, Indra destroyed demons in battle, the most important being his victory over Vritra, 'the

BACKGROUND
Auspicious signs

Some of Hinduism's sacred symbols are thought to have originated in the Aryan religion of the Vedic period.

Om The Primordial sound of the universe, 'Om' (or more correctly the three-in-one 'Aum') is the Supreme syllable. It is the opening and sometimes closing, chant for Hindu prayers. Some attribute the three constituents to the Hindu triad of Brahma, Vishnu and Siva. It is believed to be the cosmic sound of Creation which encompasses all states from wakefulness to deep sleep and though it is the essence of all sound, it is outside our hearing.

Svastika Representing the Sun and it's energy, the svastika usually appears on doors or walls of temples, in red, the colour associated with good fortune and luck. The term, derived from the Sanskrit 'svasti', is repeated in Hindu chants. The arms of the symbol point in the cardinal directions which may reflect the ancient practice of lighting fire sticks in the four directions. When the svastika appears to rotate clockwise it symbolizes the positive creative energy of the sun; the anti-clockwise svastika, symbolizing the autumn/winter sun, is considered to be unlucky.

Six-pointed star The intersecting triangles in the 'Star of David' symbol represents Spirit and Matter held in balance. A central dot signifies a particle of Divinity. The star is incorporated as a decorative element in some Muslim buildings such as Humayun's Tomb in Delhi.

Lotus The 'padma' or 'kamal' flower with it's many petals appears not only in art and architecture but also in association with gods and godesses. Some deities are seen holding one, others are portrayed seated or standing on the flower, or as with Padmanabha it appears from Vishnu's navel. The lotus represents purity, peace and beauty, a symbol also shared by Buddhists and Jains and as in nature stands away and above the impure, murky water from which it emerges. In architecture, the lotus motif occurs frequently.

| Om | Svastika | Six-pointed star | Lotus |

Obstructor'. By this victory Indra released waters from the clouds, allowing the earth to become fertile. To the early Vedic writers the clouds of the southwest monsoon were seen as hostile, determined to keep their precious treasure of water to themselves and only releasing it when forced to by a greater power. Indra, carrying a bow in one hand, a thunderbolt in another and lances in the others and riding on his vehicle Airavata, the elephant, is thus the Lord of Heaven. His wife is the relatively insignificant **Indrani**. **Mitra** and **Varuna** have the power both of gods and demons. Their role is to sustain order, Mitra taking responsibility for friendship and Varuna for oaths and as they have to keep watch for 24 hours a day Mitra has become the god of the day and the sun, Varuna the god of the moon. **Agni**, the god of fire, is a god whose origins lie with the priestly caste rather than with the Kshatriyas, or warriors. He was seen in the Vedas as being born from the rubbing together of two pieces of dead wood and as Masson-Oursel writes "the poets marvel at the sight of a being so alive leaping from dry dead wood. His very growth is miraculous". Riding on a ram, wearing a sacred thread, he is often shown with flames leaping from his mouth and he carries an axe, wood, bellows or a fan, a torch and a sacrificial spoon, for he is the god of ritual fire. The juice of the soma plant, the nectar of the gods guaranteeing eternal life, **Soma** is also a deity taking many forms. Born from the churning of the ocean of milk in later stories Soma was identified with the moon. The golden haired and golden skinned god **Savitri** is an intermediary with the great power to forgive sin and as king of heaven he gives the gods their immortality. **Surya**, the god of the sun, fittingly of overpowering splendour is often described as being dark red, sitting on a red lotus or riding a chariot pulled by the seven horses of the dawn (representing the days of the week). **Usha**, sometimes referred to as Surya's wife, is the goddess of the dawn, daughter of Heaven and sister of the night. She rides in a chariot drawn by cows or horses.

Devas and Asuras In Hindu popular mythology the world is also populated by innumerable gods and demons, with a somewhat uncertain dividing line between them. Both have great power and moral character and there are frequent conflicts and battles between them. The **Rakshasas** form another category of semi-divine beings devoted to performing magic. Although they are not themselves evil, they are destined to cause havoc and evil in the real world. The multiple-hooded cobra head often seen in sculptures represents the fabulous snake gods the **Nagas**, though they may often be shown in other forms, even human. In South India it is particularly common to find statues of divine Nagas being worshipped. They are usually placed on uncultivated ground under trees in the hope and belief, as Masson-Oursel puts it, that "if the snakes have their own domain left to them they are more likely to spare human beings". The Nagas and their wives, the **Naginis**, are often the agents of death in mythical stories.

Hindu society

Dharma Dharma is seen as the most important of the objectives of individual and social life. But what were the obligations imposed by dharma? Hindu law givers, such as those who compiled the code of Manu (AD 100-300), laid down rules of family conduct and social obligations related to the institutions of caste and jati which were beginning to take shape at the same time.

Caste Although the word caste was given by the Portuguese in the 15th century AD, the main feature of the system emerged at the end of the Vedic period. Two terms – varna and jati – are used in India itself and have come to be used interchangeably and confusingly with the word caste.

Varna, which literally means colour, had a fourfold division. By 600 BC this had become a standard means of classifying the population. The fair-skinned Aryans distinguished themselves from the darker skinned earlier inhabitants. The priestly varna, the Brahmins, were seen as coming from the mouth of Brahma; the Kshatriyas (or Rajputs as they are commonly called in northwest India) were warriors, coming from Brahma's arms; the Vaishyas, a trading community, came from Brahma's thighs and the Sudras, classified as agriculturalists, from his feet. Relegated beyond civilized Hindu society were the untouchables or outcastes, who were left with the jobs which were regarded as impure, usually associated with dealing with the dead (human or animal) or with excrement.

Many Brahmins and Rajputs are conscious of their varna status, but the great majority of Indians do not put themselves into one of the four varna categories, but into a **jati** group. There are thousands of different jatis across the country. None of the groups regard themselves as equal in status to any other, but all are part of local or regional hierarchies. These are not organized in any institutional sense and traditionally there was no formal record of caste status. While individuals found it impossible to change caste or to move up the social scale, groups would sometimes try to gain recognition as higher caste by adopting practices of the Brahmins such as becoming vegetarians. Many used to be identified with particular activities and occupations used to be hereditary. Caste membership is decided by birth. Although you can be evicted from your caste by your fellow members, usually for disobedience to caste rules such as over marriage, you cannot join another caste and technically you become an outcaste.

Right up until Independence in 1947 such punishment was a drastic penalty for disobeying one's dharmic duty. In many areas all avenues into normal life could be blocked, families would disregard outcaste members and it could even be impossible for the outcaste to continue to work within the locality.

Gandhi spearheaded his campaign for independence from British colonial rule with a powerful campaign to abolish the disabilities imposed by the caste system. Coining the term *Harijan* (meaning 'person of God'), which he gave to all former outcastes, Gandhi demanded that discrimination on the grounds of caste be outlawed. Lists – or 'schedules' – of backward castes were drawn up during the early part of this century in order to provide positive help to such groups. The term itself has now been widely rejected by many former outcastes as paternalistic and as implying an adherence to Hindu beliefs (Hari being a Hindu deity) which some explicitly reject and today the use of the

From liberal reform to a new fundamentalism

The first major reform movement was launched by the Bengali Brahmin, Ram Mohan Roy (1772-1833). He founded the **Brahmo Samaj**, the Society of God, in 1828, "to teach and to practise the worship of the one God". Services were modelled closely on those of the Unitarian Church, but he never broke with orthodox Hinduism. The Brahmo Samaj became very influential, particularly in Bengal, even though it divided and its numbers remained tiny.

In North India reform was carried out under the leadership of what one writer has called "the Luther of modern Hinduism", Dayananda Saraswati (1824-1883). Rejecting idolatry and many of the social evils associated with mid-19th century Hinduism, Dayananda Saraswati established the **Arya Samaj** (the Aryan Society). In the early 19th century the Arya Samaj launched a major attack on the caste system, through recruiting low caste Hindus and investing them with high caste status. At the same time they encouraged a movement for the reconversion of Christians and Muslims (the suddhi movement). By 1931 the Arya Samaj claimed about one million members. With a strongly Hindu nationalist political line, its programme underlay the rise in post-Independence India of the Jana Sangh Party and the present day BJP.

secular term 'dalits' – the 'oppressed' has been adopted in its place. There are several websites devoted to dalit issues, including www.dalits.org.

Marriage, which is still generally arranged by members of all religious communities, continues to be dictated almost entirely by caste and clan rules. Even in cities, where traditional means of arranging marriages have often broken down and where many people resort to advertising for marriage partners in the columns of the Sunday newspapers, caste is frequently stated as a requirement. Marriage is mainly seen as an alliance between two families. Great efforts are made to match caste, social status and economic position, although rules governing eligibility vary from region to region. In some groups marriage between first cousins is common, while among others marriage between any branch of the same clan is strictly prohibited.

Hindu reform movements

In the 19th-century English education and European literature and modern scientific thought, alongside the religious ideas of Christian missionaries, all became powerful influences on the newly emerging Western-educated Hindu opinion. That opinion was challenged to re-examine inherited Hindu beliefs and practice.

Some reform movements have had regional importance. Two of these originated, like the **Brahmo Samaj**, in Bengal. The **Ramakrishna Mission** was named after a temple priest in the Kali temple in Calcutta, Ramakrishna (1834-1886), who was a great mystic, preaching the basic doctrine that 'all religions are true'. He believed that the best religion for any individual was that into which he or she was born. One of his followers, **Vivekananda**, became the founder of the Ramakrishna Mission, which has been an important vehicle of social and religious reform, notably in Bengal.

Aurobindo Ghosh (1872-1950) links the great reformers from the 19th century with the post-Independence period. Educated in English – and for 14 years in England itself – he developed the idea of India as 'the Mother', a concept linked with the pre-Hindu idea of Shakti, or the Mother Goddess. For him 'nationalism was religion'. After imprisonment in 1908 he retired to Pondicherry, where his ashram became a focus of an Indian and international movement, see page 813.

The Hindu calendar While for its secular life India follows the Gregorian calendar, for Hindus, much of religious and personal life follows the Hindu calendar (see also Festivals, page 34). This is based on the lunar cycle of 29 days, but the clever bit comes in the way it is synchronized with the 365-day Gregorian solar calendar of the west by the addition of an 'extra month' (*adhik maas*), every 2½ to three years.

Hindus follow two distinct eras. The *Vikrama Samvat*, which began in 57 BC (and is followed in Goa), and the *Salivahan Saka* which dates from AD 78 and has been the official Indian calendar since 1957. The *Saka* new year starts on 22 March and has the same length as the Gregorian

BACKGROUND

The sacred thread

The highest three *varnas* were classified as 'twice born' and could wear the sacred thread symbolizing their status. The age at which the initiation ceremony (*upanayana*) for the upper caste child was carried out, varied according to class – 8 for a Brahmin, 11 for a Kshatriya and 12 for a Vaishya.

The boy, dressed like an ascetic and holding a staff in his hand, would have the sacred thread (*yajnopavita*) placed over his right shoulder and under his left arm. A cord of three threads, each of nine twisted strands, it was made of cotton for Brahmans, hemp for Kshatriyas or wool for Vaishyas. It was – and is – regarded as a great sin to remove it.

The Brahmin who officiated would whisper a verse from the Rig Veda in the boy's ear, the Gayatri mantra. Addressed to the old solar god Savitr, the holiest of holy passages, the Gayatri can only be spoken by the three higher classes. AL Basham translated it as: "Let us think on the lovely splendour of the god Savitr, that he may inspire our minds".

calendar. In most of South India (except Tamil Nadu) the New Year is celebrated in the first month, *Chaitra* (corresponding to March-April). In North India (and Tamil Nadu) it is celebrated in the second month of *Vaisakh*.

The year itself is divided into two, the first six solar months being when the sun 'moves' north, known as the *Makar Sankranti* (which is marked by special festivals), and the second half when it moves south, the *Karka Sankranti*. The first begins in January and the second in June. The 29-day lunar month with its 'dark' (*Krishna*) and 'bright' (*Shukla*) halves, based on the new (*Amavasya*) and full moons (*Purnima*), are named after the 12 constellations, and total a 354-day year. The day itself is divided into eight *praharas* of three hours each and the year into six seasons: *Vasant* (spring), *Grishha* (summer), *Varsha* (rains), *Sharat* (early autumn), *Hemanta* (late autumn), *Shishir* (winter).

Hindu and corresponding Gregorian calendar months:

Chaitra	March-April	*Ashwin*	September-October
Vaishakh	April-May	*Kartik*	October-November
Jyeshtha	May-June	*Margashirsh*	November-December
Aashadh	June-July	*Poush*	December-January
Shravan	July-August	*Magh*	January-February
Bhadra	August-September	*Phalgun*	February-March

Islam

Even after partition in 1947 over 40 million Muslims remained in India and today there are around 120 million. Islamic contact with India was first made around AD 636 and then by the navies of the Arab Mohammad al Qasim in AD 710-712. These conquerors of Sindh made very few converts, although they did have to develop a legal recognition for the status of non-Muslims in a Muslim-ruled state. From the creation of the Delhi Sultanate in 1206, by Turkish rather than Arab power, Islam became a permanent living religion in India.

The victory of the Turkish ruler of Ghazni over the Rajputs in AD 1192 established a 500-year period of Muslim power in India. By AD 1200 the Turkish sultans had annexed Bihar in the east, in the process wiping out the last traces of Buddhism with the massacre of a Buddhist monastic order, sacked Varanasi and captured Gwalior. Within 30 years Bengal had been added to the Turkish empire and by AD 1311 a new Turkish dynasty, the Khaljis, had extended the power of the Delhi Sultanate to the doors of Madurai.

The early Muslim rulers looked to the Turkish ruling class and to the Arab caliphs for their legitimacy and to the Turkish elite for their cultural authority. From the middle of the 13th century, when the Mongols crushed the Arab caliphate, the Delhi sultans were left on their own to exercise Islamic authority in India. From then onwards the main external influences were from Persia. Small numbers of migrants, mainly the skilled and the educated, continued to flow into the Indian courts.

Islamic patronage

The spread of Islam across India was achieved less by force than by patronage offered by the new rulers to Muslim saints and teachers. These were particularly influential in achieving conversions among the lower Hindu castes.

Islam underwent important modifica- tions in India. From the outset the Muslim invaders had to come to terms with the Hindu majority population. If they had treated them as idolators they would have been forced to give them the choice of conversion or death. The impossibility of governing as a tiny minority on those terms encouraged them to give Indian subjects the status of 'protected peoples'.

Periodically their numbers were augmented by refugees from Mongol repression in the regions to India's northwest as the Delhi Sultanate provided a refuge for craftsmen and artists from the territories the Mongols had conquered from Lahore westwards.

Muslim populations Muslims only became a majority of the South Asian population in the plains of the Indus and west Punjab and in parts of Bengal. Elsewhere they formed important minorities, notably in the towns of the central heartland such as Lucknow. The concentration at the east and west ends of the Ganga valley reflected the policies pursued by successive Muslim rulers of colonizing forested and previously uncultivated land. In the central plains there was already a densely populated, Hindu region, where little attempt was made to achieve converts.

The **Mughals** wanted to expand their territory and their economic base. To pursue this they made enormous grants of land to those who had served the empire and particularly in Bengal, new land was brought into cultivation. At the same time, shrines were established to Sufi saints who attracted peasant farmers. The mosques built in East Bengal were the centres of devotional worship where saints were venerated. By the 18th century many Muslims had joined the **Sunni** sect of Islam. The characteristics of Islamic practice in both these regions continues to reflect this background.

In some areas Muslim society shared many of the characteristic features of the Hindu society from which the majority of them came. Many of the Muslim migrants from Iran or Turkey, the élite **Ashraf** communities, continued to identify with the Islamic elites from which they traced their descent. They held high military and civil posts in imperial service. In sharp contrast, many of the non-Ashraf Muslim communities in the towns and cities were organized in social groups very much like the *jatis* of their neighbouring Hindu communities. While the elites followed Islamic practices close to those based on the Qur'an as interpreted by scholars, the poorer, less literate communities followed devotional and pietistic forms of Islam.

Muslim beliefs The beliefs of Islam (which means 'submission to God') could apparently scarcely be more different from those of Hinduism. Islam, often described as having 'five pillars' of faith (see box, page 1338) has a fundamental creed: 'There is no God but God; and Mohammad is the Prophet of God' (*La Illaha illa 'llah Mohammad Rasulu 'llah*). One book, the *Qur'an*, is the supreme authority on Islamic teaching and faith. Islam preaches the belief in bodily resurrection after death and in the reality of heaven and hell.

The idea of heaven as paradise is pre-Islamic. Alexander the Great is believed to have brought the word into Greek from Persia, where he used it to describe the walled Persian gardens that were found even three centuries before the birth of Christ. For Muslims, Paradise is believed to be filled with sensuous delights and pleasures, while hell is a place of eternal terror and torture, which is the certain fate of all who deny the unity of God.

Islam has no priesthood. The authority of Imams derives from social custom and from their authority to interpret the scriptures, rather than from a defined status within the Islamic community. Islam also prohibits any distinction on the basis of race or colour and most Muslims believe it is wrong to represent the human figure. It is often thought, inaccurately, that this ban stems from the Qur'an itself. In fact it probably has its origins in the belief of Mohammad that images were likely to be turned into idols.

The five pillars of Islam

In addition to the belief that there is one God and that Mohammed is his prophet, there are four requirements imposed on Muslims. Daily prayers are prescribed at daybreak, noon, afternoon, sunset and nightfall. Muslims must give alms to the poor. They must observe a strict fast during Ramadan (no eating or drinking from sunrise to sunset). Lastly, they should attempt the pilgrimage to the Ka'aba in Mecca, known as the Hajj. Those who have done so are entitled to the prefix Hajji before their name.

Islamic rules differ from Hindu practice in several other aspects of daily life. Muslims are strictly forbidden to drink alcohol (though some suggest that this prohibition is restricted to the use of fermented grape juice, that is wine, it is commonly accepted to apply to all alcohol). Eating pork, or any meat from an animal not killed by draining its blood while alive, is also prohibited. Meat prepared in the appropriate way is called *halal*. Finally, usury (charging interest on loans) and games of chance are forbidden.

Muslim sects During the first century after Mohammad's death Islam split in to two sects which were divided on political and religious grounds, the Shi'is and Sunni's. The religious basis for the division lay in the interpretation of verses in the Qur'an and of traditional sayings of Mohammad, the Hadis. Both sects venerate the Qur'an but have different *Hadis*. They also have different views as to Mohammad's successor.

The Sunnis believe that Mohammad did not appoint a successor and that Abu Bak'r, Omar and Othman were the first three caliphs (or vice-regents) after Mohammad's death. Ali, whom the Sunni's count as the fourth caliph, is regarded as the first legitimate caliph by the Shi'is, who consider Abu Bak'r and Omar to be usurpers. While the Sunni's believe in the principle of election of caliphs, Shi'is believe that although Mohammad is the last prophet there is a continuing need for intermediaries between God and man. Such intermediaries are termed Imams and they base both their law and religious practice on the teaching of the Imams.

Akbar, the most eclectic of Mughal emperors, went as far as banning activities like cow slaughter which were offensive to Hindus and celebrated Hindu festivals in court. In contrast, the later Mughal Emperor, Aurangzeb, pursued a far more hostile approach to Hindus and Hinduism, trying to point up the distinctiveness of Islam and denying the validity of Hindu religious beliefs. That attitude generally became stronger in the 20th century, related to the growing sense of the Muslim's minority position within South Asia and the fear of being subjected to Hindu rule.

The Islamic calendar The calendar begins on AD 16 July 622, the date of the Prophet's migration from Mecca to Medina, the Hijra, hence AH (Anno Hejirae). *Murray's Handbook for travellers in India* gave a wonderfully precise method of calculating the current date in the Christian year from the AH date: "To correlate the Hijra year with the Christian year, express the former in years and decimals of a year, multiply by .970225, add 621.54 and the total will correspond exactly with the Christian year." The Muslim year is divided into 12 lunar months, totalling 354 or 355 days, hence Islamic festivals usually move 11 days earlier each year according to the solar (Gregorian) calendar. The first month of the year is *Moharram*, followed by *Safar, Rabi-ul-Awwal, Rabi-ul-Sani, Jumada-ul-Awwal, Jumada-ul-Sani, Rajab, Shaban, Ramadan, Shawwal, Ziquad* and *Zilhaj*.

Buddhism

India was the home of Buddhism, which had its roots in the early Hinduism, or Brahmanism, of its time. Today it is practised only on the margins of the subcontinent, from Ladakh, Nepal and Bhutan in the north to Sri Lanka in the south, where it is the religion of the majority Sinhalese community. Most are very recent converts, the last adherents of the early schools of Buddhism having been killed or converted by the Muslim invaders of the 13th century. However, India's Buddhist significance is now mainly as the home for the extraordinarily beautiful artistic and architectural remnants of what was for several centuries the region's dominant religion.

India has sites of great significance for Buddhists. Some say that the Buddha himself spoke of the four places his followers should visit. **Lumbini**, the Buddha's birthplace, is in the Nepali foothills, near the present border with India. **Bodh Gaya**, where he attained what Buddhists term his 'supreme enlightenment', is about 80 km south of the modern Indian city of Patna; the deer park at **Sarnath**, where he preached his first sermon and set in motion the Wheel of the Law, is just outside Varanasi; and **Kushinagara**, where he died at the age of 80, is 50 km east of Gorakhpur. There were four other sacred places of pilgrimage – **Rajgir**, where he tamed a wild elephant; **Vaishali**, where a monkey offered him honey; **Sravasti**, associated with his great miracle; and **Sankasya**, where he descended from heaven. The eight significant events associated with the holy places are repeatedly represented in Buddhist art.

In addition there are remarkable monuments, sculptures and works of art, from Gandhara in modern Pakistan to Sanchi and Ajanta in central India, where it is still possible to see the vivid evidence of the flowering of Buddhist culture in South Asia. In Sri Lanka, Bhutan and Nepal the traditions remain alive.

The Buddha's Life Siddharta Gautama, who came to be given the title of the Buddha – the Enlightened One – was born a prince into the warrior caste in about 563 BC. He was married at the age of 16 and his wife had a son. When he reached the age of 29 he left home and wandered as a beggar and ascetic. After about six years he spent some time in Bodh Gaya. Sitting under the Bo tree, meditating, he was tempted by the demon Mara, with all the desires of the world. Resisting these temptations, he received enlightenment. These scenes are common motifs of Buddhist art. The next landmark was the preaching of his first sermon on 'The Foundation of Righteousness' in the deer park near Benaras. By the time he died the Buddha had established a small band of monks and nuns known as the *Sangha* and had followers across North India. His body was cremated and the ashes, regarded as precious relics, were divided among the peoples to whom he had preached. Some have been discovered as far west as Peshawar, in Pakistan and at Piprawa, close to his birthplace. From the Buddha's death, or *parinirvana*, to the destruction of Nalanda (the last Buddhist stronghold in India) in AD 1197, Buddhism in India went through three phases. These are often referred to as Hinayana, Mahayana and Vajrayana, though they were not mutually exclusive, being followed simultaneously in different regions.

Hinayana The Hinayana or Lesser Way insists on a monastic way of life as the only path to the personal goal of *nirvana*, see box, opposite, achieved through an austere life. Divided into many schools, the only surviving Hinayana tradition is the **Theravada Buddhism**, which was taken to Sri Lanka by the Emperor Asoka's son Mahinda, where it became the state religion, and spread to southeast Asia as practised in Thailand, Myanmar, Cambodia and Laos today. Suffering, sorrow and dissatisfaction are the nature of ordinary life and can only be eliminated by giving up desire. In turn, desire is a result of the misplaced belief in the reality of individual existence. Theravada Buddhism taught that there is no soul and ultimately no God. *Nirvana* is a state of rest beyond the universe, once found never lost.

Mahayana In contrast to the Hinayana schools, the followers of the Mahayana school (the Great Way) believed in the possibility of salvation for all. They practised a far more devotional form of meditation and new figures came to play a prominent part in their beliefs and their worship – the **Bodhisattvas**, saints who were predestined to reach the state of enlightenment through thousands of rebirths. They aspired to Buddhahood not for their own sake but for the sake of all living things. The Buddha is believed to have passed through numerous existences in preparation for his final mission. Mahayana Buddhism became dominant over most of South Asia and its influence is evidenced in Buddhist art from Gandhara in north Pakistan to Ajanta in Central India and Sigiriya in Sri Lanka.

The Buddha's Four Noble Truths

The Buddha preached Four Noble Truths: that life is painful; that suffering is caused by ignorance and desire; that beyond the suffering of life there is a state which cannot be described but which he termed nirvana; and that nirvana can be reached by following an eightfold path.

The concept of nirvana is often understood in the West in an entirely negative sense – that of 'non-being'. The word has the rough meaning of 'blow out', meaning to blow out the fires of greed, lust and desire. In a more positive sense it has been described by one Buddhist scholar as "the state of absolute illumination, supreme bliss, infinite love and compassion, unshakeable serenity and unrestricted spiritual freedom". The essential elements of the eightfold path are the perfection of wisdom, morality and meditation.

Vajrayana A new branch of Buddhism, Vajrayana, or the Vehicle of the Thunder bold, appeared which began to lay stress on secret magical rituals and cults of female divinities. This new 'Diamond Way' adopted the practice of magic, yoga and meditation. It became associated with secret ceremonies, chanting of mystical 'mantras' and taking part in orgiastic rituals in the cause of spiritual gain in order to help others. The ideal of Vajrayana Buddhists is to be 'so fully in harmony with the cosmos as to be able to manipulate the cosmic forces within and outside himself'. It had developed in the north of India by the seventh century AD, matching the parallel growth of Hindu Tantrism. The magical power associated with Vajrayana requires instruction from a teacher or *lama*, hence the Tibetan form is sometimes referred to as 'Lamaistic'.

Buddhist beliefs Buddhism is based on the Buddha's own preaching. However, when he died none of those teachings had been written down. He developed his beliefs in reaction to the Brahmanism of his time, rejecting several of the doctrines of Vedic religion which were widely held in his lifetime: the Vedic gods, scriptures and priesthood and all social distinctions based on caste. However, he did accept the belief in the cyclical nature of life and that the nature of an individual's existence is determined by a natural process of reward and punishment for deeds in previous lives – the Hindu doctrine of karma, see page 1324 and box, page 1326. In the Buddha's view, though, there is no eternal soul. He denied the identification of the Self with the everchanging Mind-Body (here, some see parallels in the Advaita Vedanta philosophy of Self-*Brahman* in Hinduism). In Buddhism, *Anatta* (no-Self) overcame the egoistical Self, given to attachment and selfishness. Following the Buddha's death a succession of councils was called to try and reach agreement on doctrine. The first three were held within 140 years of the Buddha's death, the fourth being held at Pataliputra (modern Patna) during the reign of the Emperor Asoka (272-232 BC), who had recently been converted to Buddhism. Under his reign Buddhism spread throughout South Asia and opened the routes through Northwest India for Buddhism to travel into China, where it had become a force by the first century AD.

Buddhism's decline The decline of Buddhism in India probably stemmed as much from the growing similarity in the practice of Hinduism and Buddhism as from direct attacks. Mahayana Buddhism, with its reverence for Bodhisattvas and its devotional character, was increasingly difficult to distinguish from the revivalist Hinduism characteristic of several parts of North India from the seventh to the 12th centuries AD. The Muslim conquest dealt the final blow, as it was also accompanied by the large scale slaughter of monks as well as the destruction of monasteries. Without their institutional support Buddhism faded away.

The Jain spiritual journey

The two Jain sects differ chiefly on the nature of proper ascetic practices. The Svetambara monks wear white robes and carry a staff, some wooden pots and a woollen mop for sweeping the path in front of them, wool being the softest material available and the least likely to hurt any living thing swept away. The highest level of Digambara monks will go completely naked, although the lower levels will wear a covering over their genitalia. They carry a waterpot made of a gourd and peacock feathers to sweep the ground before they sit.

Jains believe that the spiritual journey of the soul is divided into 14 stages, moving from bondage and ignorance to the final destruction of all karma and the complete fulfilment of the soul. The object throughout is to prevent the addition of new karma to the soul, which comes mainly through passion and attachment to the world. Bearing the pains of the world cheerfully contributes to the destruction of karma.

Jainism

Like Buddhism, Jainism started as a reform movement of the Brahmanic religious beliefs of the sixth century BC. Its founder was a widely revered saint and ascetic, Vardhamma, who became known as **Mahavir** – 'great hero'. Mahavir was born in the same border region of India and Nepal as the Buddha, just 50 km north of modern Patna, probably in 599 BC. Thus he was about 35 years older than the Buddha. His family, also royal, were followers of an ascetic saint, Parsvanatha, who according to Jain tradition had lived 200 years previously.

Mahavir's life story is embellished with legends, but there is no doubt that he left his royal home for a life of the strict ascetic. He is believed to have received enlightenment after 12 years of rigorous hardship, penance and meditation. Afterwards he travelled and preached for 30 years, stopping only in the rainy season. He died aged 72 in 527 BC. His death was commemorated by a special lamp festival in the region of Bihar, which Jains claim is the basis of the now-common Hindu festival of lights, Diwali.

Unlike Buddhism, Jainism never spread beyond India, but it has survived continuously into modern India, claiming four million adherents. In part this may be because Jain beliefs have much in common with puritanical forms of Hinduism and are greatly respected and admired. Some Jain ideas, such as vegetarianism and reverence for all life, are widely recognized by Hindus as highly commendable, even by those who do not share other Jain beliefs. The value Jains place on non-violence has contributed to their importance in business and commerce, as they regard nearly all occupations except banking and commerce as violent. The 18-m-high free-standing statue of Gommateshvara at Sravana Belgola near Mysore (built about AD 983) is just one outstanding example of the contribution of Jain art to India's heritage.

Jain beliefs Jains (from the word Jina, literally meaning 'descendants of conquerors') believe that there are two fundamental principles, the living (*jiva*) and the non-living (*ajiva*). The essence of Jain belief is that all life is sacred and that every living entity, even the smallest insect, has within it an indestructible and immortal soul. Jains developed the view of ahimsa – often translated as 'non-violence', but better perhaps as 'non-harming'. Ahimsa was the basis for the entire scheme of Jain values and ethics and alternative codes of practice were defined for householders and for ascetics.

The five vows may be taken both by monks and by lay people: not to harm any living beings (Jains must practise strict vegetarianism – and even some vegetables, such as potatoes and onions, are believed to have microscopic souls); to speak the truth; not to steal; to give up sexual relations and practise complete chastity; to give up all possessions – for the *Digambara* sect that includes clothes.

Celibacy is necessary to combat physical desire. Jains also regard the manner of dying as extremely important. Although suicide is deeply opposed, vows of fasting to death voluntarily may be regarded as earning merit in the proper context. Mahavir himself is believed to have died of self-starvation. The essence of all the rules is to avoid intentional injury, which is the worst of all sins. Like Hindus, the Jains believe in *karma*.

Jains have two main **sects**, whose origins can be traced back to the fourth century BC. The more numerous **Svetambaras** – the 'white clad' – concentrated more in eastern and western India, separated from the **Digambaras** – or 'sky-clad'– who often go naked. The Digambaras may well have been forced to move south by drought and famine in the northern region of the Deccan and they are now concentrated in the south of India.

Unlike Buddhists, Jains accept the idea of God, but not as a creator of the universe. They see him in the lives of the 24 **Tirthankaras** (prophets, or 'makers of fords' – a reference to their role in building crossing points for the spiritual journey over the river of life), or leaders of Jainism, whose lives are recounted in the Kalpsutra – the third century BC book of ritual for the Svetambaras. Mahavir is regarded as the last of these great spiritual leaders. Much Jain art details stories from these accounts and the Tirthankaras play a similar role for Jains as the Bodhisattvas do for Mahayana Buddhists. The first and most revered of the Tirthankaras, Adinatha, also known as Rishabnath, is widely represented in Jain temples.

Sikhism

Guru Nanak, the founder of the religion, was born just west of Lahore and grew up in what is now the Pakistani town of Sultanpur. His followers, the Sikhs (derived from the Sanskrit word for 'disciples'), form perhaps one of India's most recognizable groups. Beards and turbans give them a very distinctive presence and although they represent less than 2% of the population they are both politically and economically significant.

Sikh beliefs The first Guru, accepted the ideas of *samsara* – the cycle of rebirths – and *karma*, see pages 1324 and box, page 1326, from Hinduism. However, Sikhism is unequivocal in its belief in the oneness of God, rejecting idolatry and any worship of objects or images. Guru Nanak believed that God is One, formless, eternal and beyond description.

Guru Nanak also fiercely opposed discrimination on the grounds of caste. He saw God as present everywhere, visible to anyone who cared to look and as essentially full of grace and compassion. Some of Guru Nanak's teachings are close to the ideas of the Benaras mystic **Kabir**, who, in common with the Muslim mystic sufis, believed in mystical union with God. Kabir's belief in the nature of God was matched by his view that man was deliberately blind and unwilling to recognize God's nature. He transformed the Hindu concept of *maya* into the belief that the values commonly held by the world were an illusion.

Guru Nanak preached that salvation depended on accepting the nature of God. If people recognized the true harmony of the divine order (*hookam*) they would be saved. Rejecting the prevailing Hindu belief that such harmony could be achieved by ascetic practices, he emphasized three actions: meditating on and repeating God's name (*naam*), 'giving' or charity (*daan*), and bathing (*isnaan*).

Many of the features now associated with Sikhism can be attributed to **Guru Gobind Singh**, who on 15 April 1699, started the new brotherhood called the *Khalsa* (meaning 'the pure', from the Persian word *khales*), an inner core of the faithful, accepted by baptism (*amrit*). The 'five ks' date from this period: *kesh* (uncut hair, the most important, followed by *kangha* (comb, usually of wood), *kirpan* (dagger or short sword), *kara* (steel bangle), and *kachh* (similar to 'boxer' shorts). The dagger and the shorts reflect military influence.

In addition to the compulsory 'five ks', the new code prohibited smoking, eating *halal* meat and sexual intercourse with Muslim women. These date from the 18th century, when the Sikhs were often in conflict with the Muslims. Other strict prohibitions include: idolatry, caste discrimination, hypocrisy and pilgrimage to Hindu sacred places. The Khalsa also explicitly forbade the seclusion of women, one of the common practices of Islam. It was only under the warrior king Ranjit Singh (1799-1838) that the idea of the Guru's presence in meetings of the Sikh community (the *Panth*) gave way to the now universally held belief in the total authority of the **Guru Granth**, the recorded words of the Guru in the scripture.

Sikh worship The meditative worship Guru Nanak commended is a part of the life of every devout Sikh today, who starts each day with private meditation and a recitation of the verses of Guru Nanak himself, the *Japji*. However, from the time of the third Guru, Sikhs have also worshipped as congregations in Gurudwaras ('gateways to the Guru'). The Golden Temple in Amritsar, built at the end of the 16th century, is the holiest site of Sikhism.

Sikhism's Gurus

Guru	Teachings and practice	Developments and events	External powers
1 *Nanak* 1469-1539	The life stories (janam-sakhis) of Guru Nanak, written 50-80 years after his death, recorded wide travels, including Bengal and Mecca, studying different faiths.	Devotional and mystic tradition established by Guru Nanak, similar to that of Kabir.	Delhi sultanates
2 *Angad* 1504-1538	Special ceremonies and festivals began to augment individual devotions.		
3 *Amar Das* 1509-1574	Introduction of worship in Gurudwaras.		Portuguese make contact with India.
4 *Ram Das* 1534-1581	Built first lake temple in Amritsar; the first hereditary guru. Widening of congregational worship.	Tolerance for religious experiment.	Akbar
5 *Arjan Dev*	In 1603-4 collected hymns and sayings of the first 3 Gurus, of Sikh mystics and of his father's and his own in a single volume the Adi Granth (Guru Granth Sahib). Started Amritsar's Golden Temple.	The Adi Granth comprises nearly 6000 hymns, 974 attributed to Guru Nanak. Written in Gurumukhi script, developed from Punjabi by the second Guru.	Akbar and Jahangir. Arjan Dev executed by Jahangir at Lahore
6 *Har Gobind* 1595-1645	Jat caste becomes dominant influence. Sikhs began to take up arms, largely to protect themselves against Mughal attacks. Har Gobind decided to withdraw to the Siwalik Hills.	The next 4 Gurus all spent much of their time outside Punjab in the Siwalik Hills, where they developed new martial traditions.	Jahangir and Shah Jahan
7 *Har Rai* 1630-1661			Shah Jahan
8 *Har Krishna* 1656-1664		Died at Delhi.	Aurangzeb
9 *Tegh Bahadur* 1622-1675		Executed by Aurangzeb.	Aurangzeb
10 *Gobind Singh* 1666-1708	Reformed Sikh government introduced the features now universally associated with Sikhism today. Assassinated at Nanded in Maharashtra.	The Khalsa was open to both men and women, who replaced their caste names with Singh (lion) and Kaur ('lioness' or 'princess') respectively.	Aurangzeb

There are about 23 million Christians in India. Christianity ranks third in terms of religious affiliation after Hinduism and Islam.

The great majority of the Protestant Christians in India are now members of the Church of South India, formed from the major Protestant denominations in 1947, or the Church of North India, which followed suit in 1970. Together they account for approximately half the total number of Christians. Roman Catholics make up the majority of the rest. Many of the church congregations, both in towns and villages, are active centres of Christian worship.

Origins Some of the churches owe their origin either to the modern missionary movement of the late 18th century onwards, or to the colonial presence of the European powers. However, Christians probably arrived in India during the first century after the birth of Christ. There is evidence that one of Christ's Apostles, **Thomas**, reached India in AD 52, only 20 years after Christ was crucified. He settled in Malabar and then expanded his missionary work to China. It is widely believed that he was martyred in Tamil Nadu on his return to India in AD 72 and is buried in Mylapore, in the suburbs of modern Chennai. St Thomas' Mount, a small rocky hill just north of Chennai airport, takes its name from him. Today there is still a church of Thomas Christians in Kerala.

The Syrian church Kerala was linked directly with the Middle East when Syrian Christians embarked on a major missionary movement in the sixth century AD. The Thomas Christians have forms of worship that show very strong influence of the Syrian church and they still retain a Syriac order of service. They remained a close-knit community, who have come to terms with the prevailing caste system by maintaining strict social rules very similar to those of the surrounding upper caste Hindus. They lived in an area restricted to what is now Kerala, where trade with the Middle East, which some centuries later was to bring Muslims to the same region, remained active.

Roman Catholicism The third major development took place with the arrival of the Portuguese. The Jesuit St Francis Xavier landed in Goa in 1542 and in 1557 Goa was made an Archbishopric, see page 1173. Goa today bears testimony to the Portuguese influence on community life and church building. They set up the first printing press in India in 1566 and began to print books by the end of the 16th century.

Northern missions Protestant missions in Bengal from the end of the 18th century had a profound influence on cultural and religious development. On 9 November 1793 the Baptist missionary **William Carey** reached the Hugli River. Although he went to India to preach, he had wide-ranging interests, notably in languages and education and the work of 19th-century missions rapidly widened to cover educational and medical work as well. Converts were made most readily among the backward castes and in the tribal areas. The Christian populations of the tribal hill areas of Nagaland and Assam stem from such late 19th-century and 20th-century movements. But the influence of Christian missions in education and medical work was greater than as a proselytizing force. Education in Christian schools stimulated reformist movements in Hinduism itself and mission hospitals supplemented government-run hospitals, particularly in remote rural areas. Some of these Christian-run hospitals, such as that at Vellore, continue to provide high-class medical care.

Christian beliefs Christian theology had its roots in Judaism, with its belief in one God, the eternal Creator of the universe. Judaism saw the Jewish people as the vehicle for God's salvation, the 'chosen people of God' and pointed to a time when God would send his Saviour, or Messiah. Jesus, whom Christians believe was 'the Christ' or Messiah, was born in the village of Bethlehem, some 20 km south of Jerusalem. Very little is known of his early life except that he was brought up in a devout Jewish family. At the age of 29 or 30 he gathered a small group of followers and began to preach in the region between the Dead Sea and the Sea of Galilee. Two years later he was crucified in Jerusalem by the authorities on the charge of blasphemy – that he claimed to be the son of God.

Christians believe that all people live in a state of sin, in the sense that they are separated from God and fail to do his will. They believe that God is personal, 'like a father'. As God's son, Jesus accepted the cost of that separation and sinfulness himself through his death on the cross. Christians believe that Jesus was raised from the dead on the third day after he was crucified and that he appeared to his closest followers. They believe that his spirit continues to live today and that he makes it possible for people to come back to God.

The New Testament of the Bible, which, alongside the Old Testament, is the text to which Christians refer as the ultimate scriptural authority, consists of four 'Gospels' (meaning 'good news') and a series of letters by several early Christians referring to the nature of the Christian life.

Christian worship Although Christians are encouraged to worship individually as well as together, most forms of Christian worship centre on the gathering of the church congregation. Different denominations place varying emphases on the main elements of worship, but in most church services today the congregation will take part in singing hymns (songs of praise), prayers will be led by the minister, priest or a member of the congregation, readings from the Bible will be given and a sermon preached. For many Christians the most important service is the act of Holy Communion (Protestant) or Mass (Catholic) which celebrates the death and resurrection of Jesus in sharing bread and wine, which are held to represent Christ's body and blood given to save people from their sin.

Zoroastrianism

The first Zoroastrians arrived on the west coast of India in the mid-eighth century AD, forced out from their native Iran by persecution of the invading Islamic Arabs. Until 1477 they lost all contact with Iran and then for nearly 300 years maintained contact with Persian Zoroastrians through a continuous exchange of letters. They became known by their now much more familiar name, the **Parsis** (or Persians).

Although they are a tiny minority (approximately 100,000), even in the cities where they are concentrated, they have been a prominent economic and social influence, especially in West India. Parsis adopted Westernized customs and dress and took to the new economic opportunities that came with colonial industrialization. Families in West India such as the Tatas continue to be among India's leading industrialists, just part of a community that in recent generations has spread to Europe and north America.

Origins Zoroastrians trace their beliefs to the prophet Zarathustra, who lived in Northeast Iran around the seventh or sixth century BC. His place and even date of birth are uncertain, but he almost certainly enjoyed the patronage of the father of Darius the Great. The passage of Alexander the Great through Iran severely weakened support for Zoroastrianism, but between the sixth century BC and the seventh century AD it was the major religion of peoples living from North India to central Turkey. The spread of Islam reduced the number of Zoroastrians dramatically and forced those who did not retreat to the desert to emigrate.

Parsi beliefs The early development of Zoroastrianism marked a movement towards belief in a single God. **Ahura Mazda**, the Good Religion of God, was shown in rejecting evil and in purifying thought, word and action. Fire plays a central and symbolic part in Zoroastrian worship, representing the presence of God. There are eight Atash Bahram – major fire temples – in India; four are in Mumbai, two in Surat and one each in Navsari and Udwada. There are many more minor temples, where the rituals are less complex.

Earth, fire and air are all regarded as sacred, while death is the result of evil. Dead matter pollutes all it touches. Where there is a suitable space therefore, dead bodies are simply placed in the open to be consumed by vultures, as at the Towers of Silence in Mumbai. However, burial and cremation are also common.

Land &
environment

Geography

India falls into three major geological regions. The north is enclosed by the great arc of the Himalaya. Along their southern flank lie the alluvial plains of the Ganga and to the south again is the Peninsula. The island chains of the Lakshadweep and Minicoy off the west coast of India are coral atolls, formed on submarine ridges under the Arabian Sea.

The origins of India's landscapes

Only 100 million years ago the Indian Peninsula was still attached to the great land mass of what geologists call 'Pangaea' alongside South Africa, Australia and Antarctica. Then as the great plates on which the earth's southern continents stood broke up, the Indian Plate started its dramatic shift northwards, eventually colliding with the Asian plate. As the Indian Plate continues to get pushed under the Tibetan Plateau so the Himalaya continue to rise.

The Himalaya The Himalaya dominate the northern borders of India, stretching 2500 km from northwest to southeast. They are unparalleled anywhere in the world. Of the 94 mountains in Asia above 7300 m, all but two are in the Himalaya. Nowhere else in the world are there mountains as high. The Himalaya proper, stretching from the Pamirs in Pakistan to the easternmost bend of the Brahmaputra in Assam, can be divided into three broad zones. On the southern flank are the Shiwaliks, or Outer Ranges. To their immediate north run the parallel Middle Ranges of Pir Panjal and Dhauladhar and to the north again is the third zone, the Inner Himalaya, which has the highest peaks, many of them in Nepal. The central core of the Himalayan ranges did not begin to rise until about 35 million years ago. The latest mountain building period, responsible for the Shiwaliks, began less than five million years ago and is still continuing, raising some of the high peaks by as much as 5 mm a year. Such movement comes at a price and the boundary between the plains and the Himalayan ranges is a zone of continuing violent earthquakes and massive erosion.

The Gangetic Plains As the Himalaya began their dramatic uplift, the trough which formed to the south of the newly emerging mountains was steadily filled with the debris washed down from the hills, creating the Indo-Gangetic plains. Today the alluvium reaches depths of over 3000 m in places (and over 22 km at the mouth of the Ganga in Bangladesh), and contains some of the largest reserves of underground water in the world. These have made possible extensive well irrigation, especially in Northwest India, contributing to the rapid agricultural changes which have taken place. The Indo-Gangetic plains are still being modified. The southern part of Bengal only emerged from the sea during the last 5000 years. The Ganga and the Indus have each been estimated to carry over one million tonnes of silt every year. The silts washed down from the Himalaya have made it possible for intensive rice cultivation to be practised continuously for hundreds of years, though they cause problems for modern irrigation development.

The Peninsula The crystalline rocks of the Peninsula are some of the oldest in the world, the Charnockites – named after the founder of Kolkata, an enthusiastic amateur geologist named Job Charnock, being over 3100 million years old. Over 60 million years ago, when India split from Madagascar, a mass of volcanic lava welled up through cracks in the earth's surface and covered some 500,000 sq km of northern Karnataka, Maharashtra, southern Gujarat and Madhya Pradesh. The fault line which severed India from Africa was marked by a north-south ridge of mountains, known today as the Western Ghats, set back from the sea by a coastal plain which is never more than 80 km wide. In the south, the Nilgiris and Palanis are over 2500 m high. From the crest line of the Western Ghats, the Peninsula slopes generally eastwards, interrupted on its eastern edge by the much more broken groups of hills sometimes referred to as the Eastern Ghats. The east flowing rivers have created flat alluvial deltas which have been the basis of successive peninsular kingdoms.

Climate

India is divided almost exactly by the Tropic of Cancer, stretching from the nearequatorial Kanniyakumari to the Mediterranean latitudes of Kashmir – roughly the same span as from the Amazon to San Francisco, or from Melbourne to Darwin. Not surprisingly, climate varies considerably and high altitudes further modify local climates.

The monsoon The term monsoon refers to the wind reversal which replaces the dry northeasterlies, characteristic of winter and spring, with the very warm and wet southwesterlies of the summer. The arrival of the monsoon is as variable as is the amount of rain which it brings. What makes the Indian monsoon quite exceptional is not its regularity but the depth of moist air which passes over the subcontinent. Over India, the highly unstable moist airflow is over 6000 m thick compared with only 2000 m over Japan, giving rise to the bursts of torrential rain which mark out the wet season.

Winter High pressure builds up over Central Asia. Most of India is protected from the cold northeast monsoon winds by the massive bulk of the Himalaya and daytime temperatures rise sharply in the sun. Right across the Ganga plains night temperatures fall to below 5°C in January and February. To the south the winter temperatures increase having a minimum temperature of around 20°C; however, the winter is a dry season through nearly all of India.

Summer From April onwards much of India becomes almost unbearably hot. Temperatures of over 50°C are not unknown. It is a time of year to get up to the hills. At the end of May very moist southwesterlies sweep across South India and the Bay of Bengal. They then double back northwestwards, bringing tremendously heavy rain first to the eastern Himalaya then gradually spreading northwestwards.

The wet season The monsoon season lasts from between three and five months depending on the region. Many parts of the west coast get a three-month soaking and the Shillong plateau has received as much as 26 m in one year! If you are travelling in the wetter parts of India during the monsoon you need to be prepared for extended periods of torrential rain and major disruption to travel. However, many parts of India receive a total of under 1000 mm a year. Rainfall decreases towards the Northwest, Rajasthan and northern Gujarat merging imperceptibly into desert. Tamil Nadu has an exceptional rainfall pattern, receiving most of its rain during the retreating monsoon, October-December.

Storms Some regions suffer major storms. Cyclones may hit the east coast causing enormous damage and loss of life, the risk being greatest between the end of October and early December.

Humidity The coastal regions have humidity levels above 70% for most of the year which can be very uncomfortable. However, sea breezes often bring some relief on the coast itself. Moving north and inland, between December-May humidity drops sharply, often falling as low as 20% during the daytime.

Vegetation

India's location ensured that 16 different forest types were represented. The most widespread was tropical dry deciduous forest. However, today forest cover has been reduced to about 13% of the surface area, mainly the result of demand for wood as a fuel.

Deciduous forest Two types of deciduous tree remain particularly important, Sal (*Shorea robusta*), now found mainly in eastern Indian and teak (*Tectona grandis*). Most teak today has been planted. Both are resistant to burning, which helped to protect them where people used fire as a means of clearing the forest.

Tropical rainforest In wetter areas, particularly along the Western Ghats, you can still find tropical wet evergreen forest, but even these are now extensively managed. Across the drier areas of the peninsula heavy grazing has reduced the forest cover to thorn scrub.

Mountain forests and grassland At between 1000-2000 m in the eastern hill ranges of India and in Bhutan, for example, wet hill forest includes evergreen oaks and chestnuts. Further west in the foothills of the Himalaya are belts of subtropical pine at roughly the same altitudes. Deodars (*Cedrus deodarus*) form large stands and moist temperate forest, with pines, cedars, firs and spruce, is dominant, giving many of the valleys a beautifully fresh, alpine feel. Between 3000-4000 m alpine forest predominates. Rhododendron are often mixed with other forest types. Birch, juniper, poplars and pine are widespread. There are several varieties of coarse grassland along the southern edge of the Terai and alpine grasses are important for grazing above altitudes of 2000 m. A totally distinctive grassland is the bamboo (*Dendo calamus*) region of the eastern Himalaya.

Trees

Flowering trees Many Indian trees are planted along roadsides to provide shade and they often also produce beautiful flowers. The **silk cotton tree** (*Bombax ceiba*), up to 25 m in height, is one of the most dramatic. The pale greyish bark of this buttressed tree usually bears conical spines. It has wide spreading branches and keeps its leaves for most of the year. The flowers, which appear when the tree is leafless, are cup-shaped, with curling, rather fleshy red petals up to 12 cm long while the fruit produce the fine, silky cotton which gives it its name. Other common trees with red or orange flowers include the dhak (also called 'Flame of the forest' or *Palas*), the gulmohur, the Indian coral tree and the Tulip tree. The smallish (6 m) deciduous **dhak** (*Butea monosperma*) has light grey bark and a gnarled, twisted trunk and thick, leathery leaves. The large, bright orange and sweet pea-shaped flowers appear on leafless branches. The 8- to 9-m-high umbrella-shaped **gulmohur** (*Delonix regia*), a native of Madagascar, is grown as a shade tree in towns. The fiery coloured flowers make a magnificent display after the tree has shed its feathery leaves. The scarlet flowers of the **Indian coral tree** (*Erythrina indica*) appear when its branches with thorny bark are leafless. The tall **tulip tree** (*Spathodea campanulata*) (not to be confused with the North American one) has a straight, darkish brown, slender trunk. It is usually evergreen except in the drier parts of India. The scarlet bell-shaped, tulip-like flowers grow in profusion at the ends of the branches from November to March.

Often seen along roadsides the jacaranda (*Jacaranda mimosaefolia*) has attractive feathery foliage and purple-blue thimble-shaped flowers up to 40 mm long. When not in flower it resembles a Gulmohur, but differs in its general shape. The valuable **tamarind** (*Tamarindus indica*), with a short straight trunk and a spreading crown, often grows along the roadside. An evergreen with feathery leaves, it bears small clusters of yellow and red flowers. The noticeable fruit pods are long, curved and swollen at intervals. In parts of India, the rights to the fruit are auctioned off annually for up to Rs 4000 (US$100) per tree.

Of these trees the silk cotton, the dhak and the Indian coral are native to India. Others were introduced mostly during the last century: the tulip tree from East Africa, the jacaranda from Brazil and the tamarind, possibly from Africa.

Fruit trees The familiar apple, plum, apricot and cherry grow in the cool upland areas of India. In the warmer plains tropical fruits flourish. The large, spreading **mango** (*Mangifera indica*) bears the delicious, distinctively shaped fruit that comes in hundreds of varieties. The evergreen **jackfruit** (*Artocarpus heterophyllus*) has dark green leathery leaves. The huge fruit (up to 90 cm long and 40 cm thick), growing from a short stem directly off the trunk and branches, has a rough, almost prickly skin and is almost sickly sweet. The **banana** plant (*Musa*), actually a gigantic herb (up to 5 m high) arising from an underground stem, has very large leaves which grow directly off the trunk. Each large purplish flower produces bunches of up to 100 bananas. The **papaya** (*Carica papaya*) grows to about 4 m with the large hand-shaped leaves clustered near the top. Only the female tree bears the fruit, which hang down close to the trunk just below the leaves.

Palm trees Coconut palms (*Cocos nucifera*) are common all round the coast of India. It has tall (15-25 m), slender, unbranched trunks, feathery leaves and large green or golden fruit with soft white flesh filled with milky water, so different from the brown fibre-covered inner nut which makes its way to Europe. The 10-15 m high **palmyra palms** (*Borassus flabellifer*), indigenous to South and East India, have distinctive fan-like leaves, as much as 150 cm across. The fruit, which is smaller than a coconut, is round, almost black and very shiny. The **betel nut palm** (*Areca catechu*) resembles the coconut palm, its slender trunk bearing ring marks left by fallen leaf stems. The smooth, round nuts, only about 3 cm across, grow in large hanging bunches. **Wild date palms** (*Phoenix sylvestris*), originally came from North Africa. About 20-25 m tall, the trunks are also marked with the ring bases of the leaves which drop off. The distinctive leaflets which stick out from the central vein give the leaf a spiky appearance. Bunches of dates are only borne by the female tree.

All these palm trees are of considerable **commercial importance**. From the fruit alone the coconut palm produces coir from the outer husk, copra from the fleshy kernel from which coconut oil or coconut butter is extracted, in addition to the desiccated coconut and coconut milk. The sap is fermented to a drink called toddy. A similar drink is produced from the sap of the wild date and the palmyra palms which are also important for sugar production. The fruit of the betel nut palm is wrapped in a special leaf and chewed. The trunks and leaves of all the palms are widely used in building and thatching.

Other trees Of all Indian trees the **banyan** (*Ficus benghalensis*) is probably the best known. It is planted by temples, in villages and along roads. If it grows in the bark of another tree, it sends down roots towards the ground. As it grows, more roots appear from the branches, until the original host tree is surrounded by a 'cage' which eventually strangles it. The famous one in Kolkata's Botanical Gardens is more than 400 m in circumference. Related to the banyan, the **pipal** or peepul (*Ficus religiosa*) also cracks open walls and strangles other trees with its roots. With a smooth grey bark, it too is commonly found near temples and shrines. You can distinguish it from the banyan by the absence of aerial roots and its large, heart-shaped leaf with a point tapering into a pronounced 'tail'. It bears abundant 'figs' of a purplish tinge which are about 1 cm across. The **ashok** or **mast** (*Polyalthia longifolia*) is a tall evergreen which can reach 15 m or more in height. One variety, often seen in avenues, is trimmed and tapers towards the top. The leaves are long, slender and shiny and narrow to a long point. **Acacia** trees with their feathery leaves are fairly common in the drier parts of India. The best known is the **babul** (*Acacia arabica*) with a rough, dark bark. The leaves have long silvery white thorns at the base and consist of many leaflets while the flowers grow in golden balls about 1 cm across. The **eucalyptus** or **gum tree** (*Eucalyptus grandis*), introduced from Australia in the 19th century, is now widespread and is planted near villages to provide both shade and firewood. There are various forms but all may be readily recognized by their height, their characteristic long, thin leaves which have a pleasant fresh smell and the colourful peeling bark. The wispy **casuarina** (*Casuarina*) grows in poor sandy soil, especially on the coast and on village waste land. It has the typical leaves of a pine tree and the cones are small and prickly to walk on. It is said to attract lightning during a thunder storm. **Bamboo** (*Bambusa*) strictly speaking is a grass which can vary in size from small ornamental clumps to the enormous wild plant whose stems are so strong and thick that they are used for construction and for scaffolding and as pipes in rural irrigation schemes.

Flowering plants

Common in the Himalaya is the beautiful flowering shrub or tree, which can be as tall as 12 m, the **rhododendron** which is indigenous to this region. In the wild the commonest colour of the flowers is crimson, but other colours, such as pale purple occur too. From March to May the flowers are very noticeable on the hill sides. Another common wild flowering shrub is **lantana**. This is a fairly small untidy looking bush with rough, toothed oval leaves, which grow in pairs on the square and prickly stem. The flowers grow together in a flattened head, the ones near the middle being usually yellowish, while those at the rim are pink, pale purple or orange. The fruit is a shiny black berry.

Many other flowering plants are cultivated in parks, gardens and roadside verges. The attractive **frangipani** (*Plumeria acutifolia*) has a rather crooked trunk and stubby branches, which if broken give out a white milky juice which can be irritating to the skin. The big, leathery leaves taper to a point at each end and have noticeable parallel veins. The sweetly scented waxy flowers are white, pale yellow or pink. The **bougainvillea** grows as a dense bush or climber with small oval leaves and rather long thorns. The brightly coloured part (which can be pinkish-purple, crimson, orange, yellow, etc) which appears like a flower is not formed of petals, which are quite small and undistinguished, but by large papery bracts.

The trumpet-shaped hibiscus flower, as much as 7 or 8 cm across, has a very long 'tongue' growing out from the centre and varies in colour from scarlet to yellow or white. The leaves are somewhat oval or heart-shaped with jagged edges. In municipal flowerbeds the commonest planted flower is probably the **canna lily**. It has large leaves which are either green or bronzed and lots of large bright red or yellow flowers. The plant can be more than 1 m high. On many ponds and tanks the floating plants of the **lotus** (*Nelumbo nucifera*) and the **water hyacinth** (*Eichornia crassipes*) are seen. Lotus flowers which rise on stalks above the water can be white, pink or a deep red and up to 25 cm across. The very large leaves either float on the surface or rise above the water. Many dwarf varieties are cultivated. The rather fleshy leaves and lilac flowers of the water hyacinth float to form a dense carpet, often clogging the waterways.

Crops

Of India's enormous variety, the single most widespread crop is rice (commonly *Orysa indica*). This forms the most important staple in South and East India, though other cereals and some root crops are also important elsewhere. The rice plant grows in flooded fields called paddies and virtually all planting or harvesting is done by hand. Millets are favoured in drier areas inland, while wheat is the most important crop in the northwest. There are many different sorts of millet, but the ones most often seen are finger millet, pearl millet (bajra) and sorghum (jowar). **Finger millet**, commonly known as ragi (*Eleusine corocana*), is so-called because the ear has several spikes which radiate out, like fingers. Usually less than 1 m high, it is grown extensively in the south. Both **pearl millet** (*Pennisetum typhoideum*), known as *bajra* in the north and *cumbu* in Tamil Nadu) and **sorghum** (*Sorghum vulgare*, known as *jowar* in the north and *cholam* in the south) look similar to the more familiar maize though each can be easily distinguished when the seed heads appear. Pearl millet, mainly grown in the north, has a tall single spike which gives it its other name of bulrush millet. Sorghum bears an open ear at the top of the plant. **Tea** (*Camellia sinensis*) is grown on a commercial scale in tea gardens in areas of high rainfall, often in highland regions. Over 90% comes from Assam and West Bengal in the Northeast and Tamil Nadu and Kerala in the South. Left to itself tea grows into a tree 10 m tall. In the tea gardens it is pruned to waist height for the convenience of the tea pluckers and forms flat topped bushes, with shiny bright green oval leaves. **Coffee** (*Coffea*) is not as widely grown as tea, but high-quality arabica is an important crop in parts of South India. Coffee is also a bush, with fairly long, shiny dark green leaves. The white, sweet smelling flowers, which yield the coffee berry, grow in groups along the stems. The coffee berries start off green and turn red when ripe. **Sugar cane** (*Saccharum*) is another commercially important crop. This looks like a large grass, up to 3 m tall. The crude brown sugar is sold as jaggery and has a flavour of molasses. Of the many spices grown in India, the two climbers pepper and vanilla and the grass-like cardamom are the ones most often seen. The **pepper** vine (*Piper nigrum*) is indigenous to India where it grows in the warm moist regions. As it is a vine it needs support such as a trellis or a tree. It is frequently planted up against the betel nut palm and appears as a leafy vine with almost heart-shaped leaves. The peppercorns cluster along hanging spikes and are red when ripe. Both black and white pepper is produced from the same plant, the difference being in the processing. **Vanilla** (*Vanilla planifolium*), which belongs to the orchid family, also grows up trees for support and attaches itself to the bark by small roots. It is native to South America, but grows well in India in areas of high rainfall. It is a rather fleshy looking plant, with white flowers and long slender pods. **Cardamom** (*Elettaria cardomomum*) is another spice native to India and is planted usually under shade. It grows well in highland areas such as Sikkim and the Western Ghats. It is a herbaceous plant looking rather like a big clump of grass, with long leafy shoots springing out of the ground as much as 2-3 m in height. The white flowers grow on separate shoots which can be upright, but usually sprawl on the ground. It is from these flowers that the seed bearing capsules grow. The **cashew nut** tree (*Anacardium occidentale*) was introduced into India, but now grows wild as well as being cultivated. It is a medium-sized tree with bright green, shiny, rounded leaves. The nut grows on a fleshy fruit called a cashew apple and hangs down below this. **Cotton** (*Gossypium*) is important in parts of the west and south. The cotton bush is a small knee-high bush and the cotton boll appears after the flower has withered. This splits when ripe to show the white cotton lint inside. The **castor oil** plant (*Ricinus communis*) is cultivated as a cash crop and is planted in small holdings among other crops and along roads and paths. It is a handsome plant up to about 2 m in height, with very large leaves which are divided into some 12 'fingers'. The young stems are reddish and shiny. The well-known castor oil is extracted from the bean which is a mottled brown in colour.

Wildlife

India has an extremely rich and varied wildlife, though many species only survive in very restricted environments. Alarmed by the rapid loss of wildlife habitat the Indian government established the first conservation measures in 1972, followed by the setting up of national parks and reserves. Some 25,000 sq km were set aside in 1973 for Project Tiger, but both tiger and leopard populations are sliding to dangerously low levels, largely due to poaching and conflicts with villagers over livestock kills. The same is true of other less well-known species. Their natural habitat has been destroyed both by people and by domesticated animals (there are some 250 million cattle and 50 million sheep and goats). There are now nearly 70 national parks and 330 sanctuaries, as well as programmes of afforestation and coastline preservation. Most sanctuaries and parks are open from October to March.

The animals
The big cats The tiger (*Panthera tigris*), which prefers to live in fairly dense cover, is most likely to be glimpsed as it lies in long grass or in dappled shadow. The **Asiatic lion** (*Panthera leo*) is now found only in the Gir National Park. Less sleek than the African lion, it has a more shaggy coat and a smaller, often black mane. The **leopard**, or **panther** as it is often called in India (*Panthera pardus*), is far more numerous than the tiger, but is even more elusive. The all black form is not uncommon in areas of higher rainfall such as the Western Ghats and Northeast India, though the typical form is seen more often.

Elephant and rhino The **Indian elephant** (*Elephas maximus*) has been domesticated for centuries and today it is still used as a beast of burden. In the wild it inhabits hilly country with forest and bamboo, where it lives in herds which can number as many as 50 or more individuals. They are adaptable animals and can live in all sorts of forest, except in dry areas. Wild elephants are mainly confined to reserves, but occasionally move out into cultivation, where they cause great damage. The **great Indian one-horned rhinoceros** (*Rhinoceros unicornis*) has folds of skin which look like rivet covered armour plating. It stands at up to 170 cm at the shoulder.

Deer, antelope, oxen and their relatives Once widespread, these animals are now largely confined to the reserves. The male deer (stags) carry antlers which are branched, each 'spike' on the antler being called a tine. Antelopes and oxen, on the other hand, have horns which are not branched. There are several deer species in India, mainly confined to very restricted ranges. Three species are quite common. The largest and one of the most widespread is the magnificent **sambar** (*Cervus unicolor*) which can be up to 150 cm at the shoulder. It has a noticeably shaggy coat, which varies in colour from brown with a yellowish or grey tinge through to dark, almost black, in the older stags. The sambar is often found on wooded hillsides and lives in groups of up to 10 or so, though solitary individuals are also seen. The **barasingha** or **swamp deer** (*Cervus duvauceli*), standing about 130 cm at the shoulder, is also quite common. The females are usually lighter and some are spotted, as are the young. The antlers are much more complex than those of the sambar, having as many as 20 tines, but 12 is more usual. Barasingha prefer swampy habitat, but are also seen in grassy areas, often in large herds. The small **chital** or **spotted deer** (*Axis axis*), only about 90 cm tall, are seen in herds of 20 or so, in grassy areas. The bright rufous coat spotted with white is unmistakable; the stags carry antlers with three tines. These animals live in open grasslands, never too far from water. The beautiful **blackbuck** or **Indian antelope** (*Antilope cervicapra*), up to 80 cm at the shoulder, occurs in large herds. The distinctive colouring and the long spiral horns make the stag easy to identify. The coat is chocolate brown above, very sharply demarcated from the white of the underparts. The females do not usually bear horns and like the young, have yellowish brown coats. The larger and heavier **nilgai** or **blue bull** (*Boselaphus tragocamelus*) is about 140 cm at the shoulder and is rather horse-like, with a sloping back. The male has a dark grey coat, while the female is sandy coloured. Both sexes have two white marks on the cheek, white throats and a white ring just above each hoof. The male carries short, forward-curving horns and has a tuft of long black hairs on the front of the neck. They occur in small herds on grassy plains and scrub land.

The very graceful **chinkara** or **Indian gazelle** (*Gazella gazella*) is only 65 cm at the shoulder. The light russet colour of the body has a distinct line along the side where the paler underparts start. Both sexes carry slightly S-shaped horns. Chinkara live in small groups in rather broken hilly countryside. The commonest member of the oxen group is the **Asiatic wild buffalo** or water buffalo (*Bubalus bubalis*). About 170 cm at the shoulder, the wild buffalo, which can be aggressive, occurs in herds on grassy plains and swamps near rivers and lakes. The black coat and wide-spreading curved horns, carried by both sexes, are distinctive. In the high Himalaya, the **yak** (*Bos grunniens*) is domesticated. The wild yak, found on bleak Himalayan hillsides, has a shaggy, blackish brown coat and large horns; the domesticated animals are often piebald and the horns much smaller. The **Indian bison** or **gaur** (*Bos gaurus*) can be up to 200 cm at the shoulder with a heavy muscular ridge across it. Both sexes carry curved horns. The young gaur is a light sandy colour, which darkens with age, the old bulls being nearly black with pale sandy coloured 'socks' and a pale forehead. Basically hill animals, they live in forests and bamboo clumps and emerge from the trees to graze. The **bharal** or **blue sheep** (*Pseudois nayaur*) are found on the open slopes around Ladakh. About 90 cm at the shoulder, it has a grey-blue body and horns that curve backwards over the neck. The rare **Asiatic wild ass** (*Equus hemionus*) is confined to the deserts of the Little Rann of Kachchh. The fawn body has a distinctive dark stripe along the back. The dark mane is short and erect. The **wild boar** (*Sus scrofa*) has a mainly black body and a pig-like head; the hairs thicken down the spine to form a sort of mane. A mature male stands 90 cm at the shoulder and, unlike the female, bears tusks. The young are striped. Quite widespread, they can often cause great destruction among crops. One of the most important scavengers of the open countryside, the **striped hyena** (*Hyena hyena*) usually comes out at night. It is about 90 cm at the shoulder with a large head with a noticeable crest of hairs along its sloping back. The **common giant flying squirrel** (*Petaurista petaurista*) is common in the larger forests of India, except in the northeast. The body can be 45 cm long and the tail another 50 cm. They glide from tree to tree using a membrane stretching from front leg to back leg which acts like a parachute.

In towns and villages The **common langur** (*Presbytis entellus*), 75 cm, is a long-tailed monkey with a distinctive black face, hands and feet. Usually a forest dweller, it is found almost throughout India. The **rhesus macaque** (*Macaca mulatta*), 60 cm, is more solid looking with shorter limbs and a shorter tail. It can be distinguished by the orange-red fur on its rump and flanks. **Palm squirrels** are very common. The **five-striped** (*Funambulus pennanti*) and the **three-striped palm squirrel** (*Funambulus palmarum*) are both about the same size (30 cm long, about half of which is tail). The five-striped is usually seen in towns. The two bats most commonly seen in towns differ enormously in size. The larger so-called **flying fox** (*Pteropus giganteus*) has a wing span of 120 cm. These fruit eating bats, found throughout, except in the driest areas, roost in large noisy colonies where they look like folded umbrellas hanging from the trees. In the evening they can be seen leaving the roost with slow measured wing beats. The much smaller **Indian pipistrelle** (*Pipistrellus coromandra*), with a wing span of about 15 cm, is an insect eater. It comes into houses at dusk, roosting under eaves and has a fast, erratic flight. The **jackal** (*Canis aureus*), a lone scavenger in towns and villages, looks like a cross between a dog and a fox and varies in colour from shades of brown through to black. The bushy tail has a dark tip. The **common mongoose** (*Herpestes edwardsi*) lives in scrub and open jungle. It kills snakes, but will also take rats, mice and chicken. Tawny coloured with a grey grizzled tinge, it is about 90 cm in length, of which half is pale-tipped tail. The **sloth bear** (*Melursus ursinus*), about 75 cm at the shoulder, lives in broken forest, but may be seen on a lead accompanying a street entertainer who makes it 'dance' to music as part of an act. They have a long snout, a pendulous lower lip and a shaggy black coat with a yellowish V-shaped mark on the chest.

Birds

Town and village birds The **white-rumped vultures** that used to hang thick in the air over India's cities have declined at an alarming rate, even after the anti-inflammatory drug Diclofenac (which caused millions of birds to die after feeding on cattle dosed with the drug) was taken off the market. The brown **pariah kite** (*Milvus migrans*, 65 cm) now fills the urban scavenger niche; the more handsome chestnut and white **brahminy kite** (*Haliastur indus*, 48 cm) is largely confined to the waterside. The **house crow** (*Corvus splendens*, 45 cm) on the other hand is a very smart looking bird with a grey body and black tail, wings, face and throat. It occurs in almost every town and village in India. The **jungle crow** (*Corvus macrorhynchos*, 50 cm) originally a bird of the countryside has started to move into populated areas and in the hill stations tends to replace the house crow. Unlike the house crow it is a glossy black all over and has a much deeper, hoarser caw. The **feral pigeon**, or **blue rock dove** (*Columba livia*, 32 cm), found throughout the world, is generally a slate grey in colour. It invariably has two dark bars on the wing and a white rump. The **little brown dove** (*Streptopelia senegalensis*, 25 cm) is bluey grey and brown above, with a pink head and underparts and a speckled pattern on the neck. The **collared dove** (*Streptopelia decaocto*, 30 cm), with a distinct half collar on the back of its neck, is common, especially in the drier parts of India. Bulbuls are common in gardens and parks. The **red-vented bulbul** (*Pycnonotus cafer*, 20 cm), a mainly brown bird, can be identified by the slight crest and a bright red patch under the tail. The **house sparrow** (*Passer domesticus*, 15 cm) can be seen in towns. The ubiquitous **common myna** (*Acridotheres tristis*,

22 cm) feeds on lawns, especially after rain or watering. Look for the white under the tail and the bare yellow skin around the eye, yellow bill and legs and in flight the large white wing patch.

A less common but more striking bird also seen feeding in open spaces is the **hoopoe** (*Upupa epops*, 30 cm), easily identified by its sandy plumage with black and white stripes and long thin curved bill. The marvellous fan-shaped crest is sometimes raised. Finally there is a member of the cuckoo family, the **koel** (*Eudynamys scolopacea*, 42 cm), which is commonly heard during the hot weather – kuoo-kuoo-kuoo, the double note starts off low and flute-like, rises in pitch and intensity, then suddenly stops, only to start all over again. The male is all black with a greenish bill and a red eye; the female streaked and barred.

Water and waterside birds The *jheels* (marshes or swamps) of India form one of the richest bird habitats in the world. Cormorants abound; the commonest, the **little cormorant** (*Phalacrocorax niger*, 50 cm) is found on most inland waters. An almost entirely black bird with just a little white on the throat, it has a long tail and a hooked bill. The **coot** (*Fulica atra*, 40 cm), another common black bird, seen especially in winter has a noticeable white shield on the forehead. The magnificent **sarus crane** (*Grus antigone*, 150 cm) is one of India's tallest birds. It is widespread all year round across northern India, almost invariably in pairs. The bare red head and long red legs combined with its height and grey plumage make it easy to identify. The commonest migrant crane is probably the **common crane** (*Grus grus*, 120 cm), present only in winter, often in large flocks. It has mainly grey plumage with a black head and neck. There is a white streak running down the side of the neck and above the eye is a tuft of red feathers. The **openbill stork** (*Anastomus oscitans*, 80 cm) and the **painted stork** (*Ibis leucocephalus*, 100 cm) are common too and are spotted breeding in large colonies. The former is white with black wing feathers and a curiously shaped bill. The latter, mainly white, has a pinkish tinge on the back and dark marks on the wings and a broken black band on the lower chest. The bare yellow face and yellow down-curved bill are conspicuous. By almost every swamp, ditch or rice paddy up to about 1200 m you will see the **paddy bird** (*Ardeola grayii*, 45 cm). An inconspicuous, buff-coloured bird, it is easily overlooked as it stands hunched up by the waterside. As soon as it takes off, its white wings and rump make it very noticeable. The **bronze-winged jacana** (*Metopidius indicus*, 27 cm) has very long toes which enable it to walk on the floating leaves of water-lilies and there is a noticeable white streak over and above the eye. Village ponds often have their resident bird. The commonest and most widespread of the Indian kingfishers is the jewel-like **common kingfisher** (*Alcedo atthis*, 18 cm). With its brilliant blue upperparts and orange breast it is usually seen perched on a twig or a reed beside the water.

Open grassland, light woodland and cultivated land The **cattle egret** (*Bubulcus ibis*, 50 cm), a small white heron, is usually seen near herds of cattle, frequently perched on the backs of the animals. Equal in height to the sarus crane is the impressive, but ugly **adjutant stork** (*Leptopilos dubius*, 150 cm). This often dishevelled bird is a scavenger and is thus seen near rubbish dumps and carcasses. It has a naked red head and neck, a huge bill and a large fleshy pouch which hangs down the front of the neck. The **rose-ringed parakeet** (*Psittacula krameri*, 40 cm) is found throughout India up to about 1500 m while the **pied myna** (*Sturnus contra*, 23 cm) is restricted to northern and central India. The rose-ringed parakeet often forms huge flocks, an impressive sight coming in to roost. The long tail is noticeable both in flight and when the bird is perched. They can be very destructive to crops, but are attractive birds which are frequently kept as pets. The pied myna, with its smart black and white plumage, is conspicuous, usually in small flocks in grazing land or cultivation. It feeds on the ground and on village rubbish dumps. The all black **drongo** (*Dicrurus adsimilis*, 30 cm) is almost invariably seen perched on telegraph wires or bare branches. Its distinctively forked tail makes it easy to identify. Weaver birds are a family of mainly yellow birds, all remarkable for the intricate nests they build. The most widespread is the **baya weaver** (*Ploceus philippinus*, 15cm) which nest in large colonies, often near villages. The male in the breeding season combines a black face and throat with a contrasting yellow top of the head and the yellow breast band. In the non-breeding season both sexes are brownish sparrow-like birds.

Hill birds Land above about 1500 m supports a distinct range of species, although some birds, such as the ubiquitous **common myna**, are found in the highlands as well as in the lower lying terrain. The highland equivalent of the red-vented bulbul is the **white-cheeked bulbul** (*Pycnonotus leucogenys*, 20 cm) which is found in gardens and woodland in the Himalaya up to about 2500 m and as far south as Mumbai. It has white underparts with a yellow patch under the tail. The black head and white cheek patches are distinctive. The crest varies in length and is most prominent in birds found in Kashmir, where it is very common in gardens. The **red-whiskered bulbul** (*Pycnonotus jocosus*, 20 cm) is widespread in the Himalaya and the hills of South India up to about 2500 m. Its pronounced pointed crest, which is sometimes so long that it flops forward towards the bill, white underparts and red and white 'whiskers' serve to distinguish it. It has a red patch under the tail. In the summer the delightful **verditer flycatcher** (*Muscicapa thalassina*, 15 cm) is a common breeding bird in the Himalaya up to about 3000 m. It is tame and confiding, often builds its nest on verandas and is seen perching on telegraph wires. In winter it is more widely distributed throughout the country. It is an active little bird which flicks its tail up and down in a characteristic manner. The male is all bright blue green with somewhat darker wings and a black patch in front of the eyes. The female is similar, but duller. Another species associated with man is the **white wagtail** (*Motacilla alba*, 21 cm), very common in the Himalayan summer up to about 3000 m. It is found near water, by streams and lakes, on floating vegetation and among the house boats in Kashmir. Its black and white plumage and constantly wagging tail make it easy to identify. Yet another species common in Kashmir and in other Himalayan hill stations is the **red-billed blue magpie** (*Urocissa erythrorhyncha*, 65 cm). With a long tail and pale blue plumage, contrasting with its black head, it is usually seen in small flocks. This is not so much a garden bird, but prefers tea gardens, open woodland and cultivation. The highlands of India, especially the Himalaya, are the home of the ancestors of **domestic hens** and also of numerous beautiful **pheasants**. These are mainly forest dwellers and are not easy to see as they tend to be shy and wary of man. Last but not least, mention must be made of India's national bird, the magnificent and well-known **peafowl** (*Pavo cristatus*, male 210 cm, female 100 cm), which is more commonly known as the peacock. Semi-domesticated birds are commonly seen and heard around towns and villages, especially in the northwest of India. In the wild it favours hilly jungles and dense scrub.

Reptiles and amphibians

India is famous for its reptiles, especially its snakes, which feature in many stories and legends. In reality, snakes keep out of the way of people. One of the most common is the **Indian rock python** (*Python molurus*), a 'constrictor' which kills its prey by suffocation. Usually about 4 m in length, they can be much longer. Their docile nature make them favourites of snake handlers. The other large snakes favoured by street entertainers are cobras. The various species all have a hood which is spread when the snake draws itself up to strike. They are all highly venomous and the snake charmers prudently de-fang them to render them harmless. The best known is probably the **spectacled cobra** (*Naja naja*), which has a mark like a pair of spectacles on the back of its hood. The largest venomous snake in the world is the **king cobra** (*Ophiophagus hannah*) which is 5 m in length. It is usually brown, but can vary from cream to black and lacks the spectacle marks of the other. In their natural state cobras are generally inhabitants of forest regions. Equally venomous, but much smaller, the **common krait** (*Bungarus caeruleus*) is just over 1 m in length. The slender, shiny, blue-black snake has thin white bands which can sometimes be almost indiscernible. They are found all over the country except in the northeast where the cannibalistic **banded krait** with bold yellowish and black bands have virtually eradicated them.

In houses everywhere you cannot fail to see the **gecko** (*Hemidactylus*). This small harmless lizard is active after dark. It lives in houses behind pictures and curtain rails and at night emerges to run across the walls and ceilings to hunt the night flying insects which form its main prey. It is not usually more than about 14 cm long, with a curiously transparent, pale yellowish brown body. At the other end of the scale is the **monitor lizard** (*Varanus*), which can grow to 2 m in length. They can vary from a colourful black and yellow, to plain or speckled brown. They live in different habitats from cultivation and scrub to waterside places and desert. The most widespread crocodile is the freshwater **mugger** or Marsh crocodile (*Crocodilus palustrus*) which grows to 3-4 m in length. The only similar fresh water species is the **gharial** (*Gavialis gangeticus*) which lives in large, fast flowing rivers. Twice the length of the mugger, it is a fish-eating crocodile with a long thin snout and, in the case of the male, an extraordinary bulbous growth on the end of the snout. The enormous, aggressive **estuarine** or **saltwater crocodile** (*Crocodilus porosus*) is now restricted to the brackish waters of the Sundarbans, on the east coast and in the Andaman and Nicobar Islands. It grows to 7 m long and is sleeker looking than the rather docile mugger.

Books

India is a good place to buy English-language books as foreign books are often much cheaper than the published price. There are also cheap Indian editions and occasionally reprints of out-of-print books. There are excellent bookshops in all the major Indian cities.

Art and architecture

Burton, TR *Hindu Art*, British Museum P. Well illustrated; broad view of art and religion.
Cooper, I and Dawson, B *Traditional Buildings of India*, Thames & Hudson.
Michell, G *The Hindu Temple*, Univ of Chicago Press, 1988. An authoritative account of Hindu architectural development.
Ramaswami, NS *Temples of South India*, Chennai, Maps and Agencies, 1996.
KR Srinivasan *Temples of South India*, 3rd ed, New Delhi, National Book Trust, 1985. Good background information.
Sterlin, H *Hindu India*, Köln. Taschen, 1998. Traces the development from early rock-cut shrines, detailing famous examples; clearly written, well illustrated.
Tillotson, G *The Rajput Palaces*, Yale. 1987; *Mughal architecture*, London, Viking, 1990; *The tradition of Indian architecture*, Yale 1989. Superbly clear writing on Indian architecture under Rajputs, Mughals and the British.

Contemporary India

Baru, S *The Accidental Prime Minister*, Viking, 2014. Illuminating insider portrait of the Congress government under Manmohan Singh.
French, P *Liberty or Death*, Harper Collins. Well researched, serious, but very readable.
Guha, R *Patriots and Partisans*, Penguin, 2012. A fine collection of essays on the decline and fall of modern India.
Silver, RB and Epstein, B *India: a mosaic*, New York, NYRB. Distinguished essays on history, politics and literature.
Tully, M *No full stops in India*, Viking, 1991. An often superbly observed but controversially interpreted view of late 20th-century India.

History

Allchin, B and R *Origins of a civilisation*, Viking, Penguin Books, 1997. Authoritative survey of the origins of Indian civilizations.
Basham, AL *The Wonder that was India*, London, Sidgwick & Jackson, 1985. Comprehensive and readable account of the development of India's culture.
Beames, J *Memoirs of a Bengal Civilian*, London, Eland, 1991. A readable insight into the British Raj in the post-Mutiny period.
Dalrymple, W *The Age of Kali*, Penguin 1998.
Danino, M *The Lost River*, 2010. Follows the history of the disappeared, semi-mythical Saraswati River.
Edwardes, M *The Myth of the Mahatma*. Presents Gandhi in a whole new light.
Gandhi, R *The Good Boatman*, Viking/Penguin 1995. An excellent biography by one of Gandhi's noted grandson's.
Gascoigne, B *The Great Moghuls*, London, Cape, 1987.
Giridharadas, A *India Calling*, Harper Collins, 2011. Highly readable account of the rapid changes occurring in Indian society.
Guha, R *India After Gandhi*, Picador 2007. Heavyweight but readable history of the nation.
Keay, J *India: a History*, Harper Collins, 2000. A popular history of the sub continent.
Nehru, J *The discovery of India*, New Delhi, ICCR, 1976.
Robinson, F (ed) *Cambridge Encyclopaedia of India*, Cambridge, 1989. An introduction to many aspects of South Asian society.
Spear, P and Thapar, R *A history of India*, 2 vols, Penguin, 1978.
Wolpert, S *A new history of India*, OUP 1990.

Literature

Adiga, A *White Tiger*, Harper Collins India, 2008. Controversial take on the complexities of modern Indian society.
Ali, A *Twilight in Delhi*, 1940. Poetic portrayal of Delhi at the dawn of British rule.
Boo, K *Behind the Beautiful Forevers*. Compelling collection of tales of life in a Mumbai slum.
Chatterjee, U *English August*, London, Faber, 1988. A wry modern account of an Indian civil servant's year in a rural posting.

Chaudhuri, A *The Immortals*, 2009. Follows the fortunes of an impecunious music teacher in 1970s Bombay.

Chaudhuri, N *The autobiography of an unknown Indian*, Macmillan, London Vivid, witty and often sharply critical accounts of India across the 20th century. Also Thy Hand, Great Anarch!

Kanga, F *Trying to grow*, Bloomsbury, 1989. Mumbai life seen through the experiences of a Parsi family.

Mehta, S *Maximum City*. Various shades of the Mumbai underworld brought vividly to life.

Mistry, R *A fine balance*, Faber, 1995. A tale of the struggle to survive in the modern Indian city.

Naipaul, VS *A million mutinies now*, Penguin, 1992. 'Revisionist' account of India turns away from the despondency of his earlier books (An Area of darkness and India: a wounded civilisation).

Narayan, RK *The Man-eater of Malgudi and Under the Banyan tree and other stories, Grandmother's stories*, London, Penguin, 1985. Gentle and humorous stories of South India.

Ramanuja, AK *The collected essays*, Ed by V Dhawadker. New Delhi, OUP, 1999. Brilliant essays on Indian culture and literature.

Roberts, GD *Shantaram*, Scribe Publications, 2003. A compelling, apparently true and often beautifully written account of an escaped convict's life in the Mumbai underworld. A real page-turner.

Roy, A *The God of Small Things*, Indian Ink/Harper Collins, 1997. Excellent 1st novel about family turmoil in a Syrian Christian household in Kerala.

Rushdie, S *Midnight's children*, London, Picador, 1981. India since Independence, with funny and sharp critiques of South Asian life in the 1980s. *The Moor's Last Sigh*, Viking, 1996, is of particular interest to those travelling to Kochi and Mumbai.

Scott, P *The Raj Quartet*, London, Panther, 1973; Staying on, Longmans, 1985. Outstandingly perceptive novels of the end of the Raj.

Seth, V *A Suitable Boy*, Phoenix House London, 1993. Prize-winning novel of modern Indian life.

Shulman, D *Spring, Heat, Rains*. A fascinating and lyrical travelogue of the landscapes, cultures and poetry of Andhra Pradesh.

Weightman, S (ed) *Travellers Literary Companion: the Indian Sub-continent*. Invaluable introduction to the diversity of Indian writing.

Music and cinema

Menon, RR *Penguin Dictionary of Indian Classical Music*, Penguin New Delhi 1995.

Mohan, L *Bollywood, Popular Indian Cinema*, Joshi (Dakini).

People

Bumiller, E *May you be the mother of one hundred sons*, Penguin, 1991. An American woman journalist's account of coming to understand the issues that face India's women.

Dalrymple, W *Nine Lives*, Bloomsbury 2009.

Holmstrom, L *The Inner Courtyard*. A series of short stories by Indian women, translated into English, Rupa, 1992.

Lewis, N *A goddess in the stones*. An insight into tribal life in Orissa and Bihar.

Varma, PK *Being Indian*, Penguin 2004.

Bijapurkar, R *We are like that only*, Penguin 2007. To understand consumer India.

Karkar, S and K *The Indians*, Viking, 2007. Psychoanalyst and cultural commentator take on the Indian identity.

Lloyd, S *An Indian Attachment*, London, Eland, 1992. A very personal and engaging account of time spent in an Indian village.

Srinivas, MN *The Remembered Village*, 1976. Fascinating, acutely observed study of life, religion and caste relations in a Karnataka village.

Religion

Doniger O'Flaherty, W *Hindu Myths*, London, Penguin, 1974. A sourcebook translated from the Sanskrit. *The Hindus: An Alternative History*, 2009. Scholarly door-stopper infused with wit and humour, pulled from shelves in India after legal action over its frank 'feminist' perspective on Hindu myths.

Eck, DL *India: A Sacred Geography*, 2012. Explores pilgrimage by weaving together the threads of landscape and spirituality.

Fernandes, E *Holy Warriors*, Viking, 2006. An overview of religious extremism in India.

Jain, JP *Religion and Culture of the Jains*, 3rd ed. New Delhi, Bharatiya Jnanapith, 1981.

Rahula, W *What the Buddha Taught*.

Singh, H *The heritage of the Sikhs*, 2nd ed, New Delhi, 1983.

Waterstone, R *India, the cultural companion*, Duncan Baird, 2002. India's spiritual traditions, well illustrated.

Zaehner, RC *Hinduism*, OUP.

Travel

Blank, J *Arrow of the Blue Skinned God*, 2000. Ambitious and perceptive travel tale retracing the journey of Rama in the Ramayana.
Fishlock, T *Cobra Road*, London, John Murray, 1991. Impressions of a news journalist.
Frater, A *Chasing the monsoon*, London, Viking, 1990. Prize-winning account of the human impact of the monsoon's sweep across India.
Keay, J *Into India*, London, John Murray, 1999. Seasoned traveller's introduction to understanding and enjoying India.
Perur, S *If It's Monday It Must Be Madurai*. Turning the genre on its head, Perur reports from a series of guided tours, as much about his Indian fellow tourists as the destinations.
Subramaniam, S *Following Fish*. Quirky, handsomely written travelogue based around the various roles of fish in Indian life.

Wildlife and vegetation

Ali, S *Indian hill birds*, OUP.
Ali, Sand Dillon Ripley, S *Handbook of the birds of India & Pakistan*, (compact ed).
Cowen, DV *Flowering Trees and Shrubs in India*.
Grimmet, R, and Inskipp, C and T *Birds of the Indian Sub-Continent*, 2011.
Ives, R *Of tigers and men*, Doubleday, 1995.
Kazmierczak, K and Singh, R *A birdwatcher's guide to India. Prion*, 2001, Sandy, Beds, UK. Well researched and carrying lots of practical information for all birders.
Menon, V *Field Guide to Indian Mammals*, Helm, 2009.
Polunin, O and Stainton, A *Flowers of the Himalaya*, OUP, 1984. .
Sippy, S and Kapoor, S *The Ultimate Ranthambhore Guide*, 2001. Informative, practical guide stressing conservation.
Thapar and Rathore *Wild tigers of Ranthambhore OUP*, 2000.

Practicalities

Getting there

India is accessible by air from virtually every continent. By far the most common arrival points are Delhi and Mumbai, followed by Chennai, Bengaluru and Kolkata, though excellent connectivity through the Gulf and Southeast Asia makes it just as easy to fly directly into any of India's large cities: Ahmedabad, Amritsar, Hyderabad, Jaipur, Kochi, Pune and Thiruvananthapuram all have international airports, and can make for convenient arrival points if you're willing to endure a few hours in transit. Several carriers permit 'open-jaw' travel, making it easy to arrive in and depart from different cities. In 2015 the cheapest return flights to Mumbai from London started from around £400, but went up to £800-plus as you approached the high seasons of Christmas, New Year and Easter.

Once you're on the ground India's comprehensive internal flight network can get you to destinations throughout the country.

From Europe

Despite the increases to Air Passenger Duty, Britain remains the cheapest place in Europe for flights to India. **British Airways**, **Virgin Atlantic**, **Jet Airways** and **Air India** fly direct from London to Mumbai, while BA also flies direct to Chennai, Bengaluru and Hyderabad. Charter flights run by companies like **Thomas Cook** and **Thomson** operate direct flights from London to Goa.

Air India and **Jet Airways** also serve several airports in mainland Europe, while major European flag carriers including **KLM** and **Lufthansa** fly to Delhi and Mumbai from their respective hub airports.

In most cases the cheapest flights are with Middle Eastern airlines, transiting via airports in the Gulf. Several airlines from the Middle East (eg **Emirates**, **Etihad**, **Gulf Air**, **Kuwait Airways**, **Qatar Airways** and **Oman Air**) offer good discounts to Indian regional capitals from London via their hub cities. This adds a couple of hours to the journey time, but makes it possible to fly to less obvious gateway cities such as Kochi, Thiruvananthapuram and Goa, avoiding the more fraught route via Mumbai (which involves long immigration queues and shuttling from the international to domestic terminal).

TRAVEL TIP
Packing for India

Travel light: it's possible to get most essentials in larger cities and shops in five-star hotels. Here are some items you might find helpful: loose-fitting, light cotton clothes including a sarong. Remember that women should dress modestly at all times; brief shorts and tight vest tops are best avoided, though on the beach modest swimwear is fine. Locally bought inexpensive and cool *kurta pyjama* for men, and *shalwar kameez* for women are excellent options on the plains but it can be cold in the north December to February and everywhere over 1500 m, where heavier clothing is essential. Comfortable sandals or trainers are impotant. Take high-factor sun screen and a sun hat.

Indian pharmacies can be very cheap but aren't always reliable, so take a supply of medicines from home, including inhalers and anti-malarial drugs (Proguanil is not available). Take repellent for protection against mosquitoes. See Health, page 1377.

Photocopies of passport and visa pages, and spare photos are useful when applying for permits or in case of loss or theft.

For budget travellers: nets aren't always provided in cheap hotels so take an impregnated mosquito net. Earplugs are indispensable, and eyeshades can come in handy. Take a good padlock to secure your budget room too, though these can be cheaply bought in India hardware stores. A cotton or silk sheet sleeping bag are useful when you can't be sure of clean linen.

TRAVEL TIP

First impressions

On arrival at any of India's major cities the first impressions can take you aback. The exciting images of an ancient and richly diverse culture which draw many visitors to India can be overwhelmed by the immediate sensations which first greet you. These can be daunting, so even on a short visit to India, give yourself time and space to adjust.

All cities seriously suffer from pollution. Many find India incredibly noisy, both in urban and rural areas, as radios, videos and loudspeakers blare at all times. On stepping out of your hotel or when getting off a bus or train, everybody seems to clamour to sell you their services. Taxi and rickshaw drivers are always there when you don't want them, much less often when you do. There often seems to be no sense of personal space or privacy. Young women are often stared at.

India has a baffling mix of smells, from the richly pungent and unpleasant to the delicately subtle. It is common to see people urinating in public places and defecating in the open countryside, although in recent years this situation has improved slightly with the construction of new public toilets.

Consolidators in the UK can quote some competitive fares, such as: www.skyscanner.net, www.ebookers.com; and North South Travel ① T01245-608291, www.northsouthtravel.co.uk (profits to charity).

From North America

From the east coast, several airlines including **Air India**, **Jet Airways**, **Continental** and **Delta** fly direct from New York to Delhi and Mumbai. **American** flies to both cities from Chicago. Discounted tickets on **British Airways**, **KLM**, **Lufthansa**, **Gulf Air** and **Kuwait Airways** are sold through agents although they will invariably fly via their country's capital cities. From the west coast, **Air India** flies from Los Angeles to Mumbai, and **Jet Airways** from San Francisco to Mumbai via Shanghai. Alternatively, fly via Hong Kong, Singapore or Bangkok using one of those countries' national carriers. **Air Canada** operates between Vancouver and Delhi. **Air Brokers International** ① www.airbrokers.com, is competitive and reputable. **STA Travel** ① www.statravel.com, has offices in many US cities, Toronto and Ontario. Student fares are also available from **Travel Cuts** ① www.travelcuts.com, in Canada.

From Australasia

Qantas, **Singapore Airlines**, **Thai Airways**, **Malaysian Airlines**, **Cathay Pacific** and **Air India** are the principal airlines connecting the continents. **Singapore Airlines** offer the most flexibility, with direct flights to the main Indian cities, as well as to several airports in South India through its subsidiary **Silk Air**. Low-cost carriers including **Air Asia** (via Kuala Lumpur) and **Tiger Airways** (Singapore) also fly to a good choice of destinations in South India, though long layovers and possible missed connections make this a slightly more risky venture than flying with the full-service airlines. **STA** and **Flight Centre** offer discounted tickets from their branches in major cities in Australia and New Zealand. **Abercrombie & Kent** ① www.abercrombiekent.co.uk, **Adventure World** ① www.adventure world.net.au, **Peregrine** ① www.peregrineadventures.com, and **Travel Corporation of India** ① www.tcindia.com, organize tours.

Airport information

The formalities on arrival in India have been increasingly streamlined during the last few years and the facilities at the major international airports greatly improved. However, arrival can still be a slow process. Disembarkation cards, with an attached customs declaration, are handed out to passengers during the inward flight. The immigration form should be handed in at the immigration counter on arrival. The customs slip will be returned, for handing over to the customs on leaving the baggage collection hall. You may well find that there are delays of over an hour at immigration in processing passengers who need help with filling in forms.

BORDER CROSSINGS

India–Bangladesh

Bangaon–Benapol
This crossing is the most reliable if you're travelling to Kolkata from Dhaka and Jessore. On the Bangladesh side rickshaws are available from Benapol, while buses and minibuses go to Bangaon railway station from the border.

Agartala–Akhaura
The border crossing is just 2 km from Agartala, which has flights to Kolkata and is four hours by road to Dhaka. The border post is efficient when open but arrive there before 1500, as formalities often take time. Regulations are subject to change so find out in advance. In London, contact the **Bangladesh High Commission**, T020-7584 0081, www.bhclondon.org.uk.

India–Bhutan

Jaigaon–Phuntsholing
From Bagdogra, the nearest airport in India, it's a three- to four-hour drive to Jaigaon, the rather unkempt Indian border town. The Indian immigration checkpoint is on the main street, about 1 km from the 'Bhutan Gate' at the border town of Phuntsholing, where it is possible to spend a night. Accommodation ranges from the simple **Central Hotel** to the moderate government-run **Druk Hotel**. To enter Bhutan you need an entry permit and a visa from a Bhutanese tour agent.

When departing, note that you'll need to have a printout of your itinerary to get into the airport, and the security guards will only let you into the terminal within three hours of your flight. Many airports require you to scan your bags before checking in, and in rare cases you may also be asked to identify your checked luggage after going through immigration and security checks.

Departure charges
Many Indian airports charge a Passenger Service Fee or User Development Fee to each departing passenger. This is normally incorporated in the ticket price, but in some cases (when fees have increased or been newly introduced) you may need to pay in person before checking in. Keep some spare cash in rupees in case.

Road

Crossings between India and its neighbours are affected by the political relations between them. Get your Indian visa in advance, before arriving at the border. Several road border crossings are open periodically, but permission to cross cannot be guaranteed. Those listed in the Border crossings boxes, above and pages 1362 and 1363, are the main crossings which are usually open all year to tourists.

From Pakistan
Direct 'friendship' buses operate between Lahore and Delhi and between Dhaka and Kolkata, though the Lahore route in particular is subject to suspension or disruption in the event of terror threats. Note also that you are not allowed to take any Indian currency from India into Pakistan. Indian rupees can be changed on a 1:1 basis at the border.

From Europe
The reopening of Iran to travellers of most nationalities has reinstated the Istanbul–Tehran–Quetta route when the political situation in the region is stable.

BORDER CROSSINGS

India–Nepal

Single or multiple-entry 30-day visas cost US$40, to be paid in exact cash (15-day US$25, 90-day US$100). Four crossings are in common use: to Delhi via Banbassa is the shortest direct route between Kathmandu and Delhi, via the Nepali town of Mahendranagar and Banbassa. The other three crossings are described below.

Sonauli–Bhairawa

From Gorakhpur, the usual route to Nepal is to take a bus or shared jeep north to cross the border at Sonauli. At Sonauli, you need to fill in a form and get your exit stamp at the Indian immigration office (near the bus stand). You then proceed to the Nepalese immigration counter to get your entry visa; the counter is open 0530-2100. Payment for Nepalese visa is in cash only. Try to carry US dollars cash (other currencies not accepted), as money changers at the border give terrible exchange rates.

Note that if you leave Gorakhpur after 1400 you will arrive at Sonauli after 1700 and it might be better to stay overnight on the Indian side and walk across or get a rickshaw in the morning to maximize visa days. From the Nepali side you can take a bus/jeep to Bhairawa (6 km) and catch an onward bus to Kathmandu (0630, 0730, 0830, 235 km). Coming from Nepal, the last bus from Sonauli to Gorakhpur leaves at around 2000.

Raxaul–Birganj

From Patna, private buses run daily from Mithapur Bus Stand and state buses go from Gandhi Maidan to Raxaul (six to seven hours), but timings are unreliable and the buses are crowded and uncomfortable. Night buses from Patna reach the border early in the morning; morning buses connect with the night bus to Kathmandu. Either way you have an overnight bus journey, unless you stay overnight at Birganj or Raxaul, which is not recommended. Raxaul has little to offer, but there are a couple of hotels in town if you get stuck.

You need an exit stamp in Raxaul from the Indian immigration office.

You can cross the border to Birganj by rickshaw/*tempo* (15-20 minutes). After crossing the border you need to get an entry stamp from the Nepalese immigration counter (open early morning to late evening). Occasionally an unjustified additional fee is demanded for 'extras', eg registration card, or a 'visa' fee in US dollars. In Birganj the *tempo* stand and bus park are in Adarsh Nagar, to the south of town. In the morning, buses depart from the bus stand east of the clock tower to Tandi Bazar (four hours, for Chitwan), Pokhara (11-12 hours) and Kathmandu (11-12 hours). Even Express buses are slow and packed. Tourist minibuses are the only moderately comfortable option.

Panitanki–Kakarbhitta (Kakarvita)

Kakarbhitta (Kakarvita) is on the Nepalese side of a wide river which forms the border here between India and Nepal. Kakarbhitta has only basic accommodation. A kilometre-long road bridge links it to the Indian town of Panitanki on the east bank. Cycle rickshaws run between the two. A small notice and an Indian flag are all that mark the Indian immigration checkpost which is in a shady grove of trees by the road. The larger Indian town of Bagdogra is 15 km away.

Jeeps go from Siliguri frequently, as well as from Darjeeling.

From the border, buses depart 0300-2400, arriving in Kathmandu (595 km) 16-17 hours later; the journey can be very tiring. It is also possible to fly (seasonally) from Bhadrapur (24 km from Kakarbhitta) to Kathmandu with **Buddha Air** or **Yeti Airlines** (50 minutes). Alternatively, get a taxi to Biratnagar in Nepal (150 km) and fly from there to Kathmandu.

BORDER CROSSINGS

India–Pakistan

The Wagah border, 23 km from Lahore, is the only crossing open. The standard method of crossing is by taking a van from central Lahore which takes you to the border where you walk across through Pakistani and Indian immigration and customs. There are taxis and rickshaws on the Indian side to take you to Wagah/Attari; buses from there go to Amritsar (see page 410). All buses have a police escort. In November 2014 a suicide bomb attack in Wagah killed over 50 people. At the time of writing the UK's FCO does not warn against using the Wagah crossing, but check the latest travel advice before setting out.

The only train crossing is an uncertain one. The Lahore to Amritsar train via the Wagah border post runs twice weekly but it can take five hours to clear customs. It is normally much slower than the bus and is not recommended.

Boat

A few cruise ships stop at some ports like Mumbai, Margao, Kochi and Chennai. Operators include **Swan Hellenic** ① *T0845-246 9700, www.swanhellenic.com.*

From Sri Lanka and the Maldives Rumours of a ferry service to be opened between Sri Lanka's Mannar Island and Rameswaram in Tamil Nadu are, for the moment, still rumours.

Getting around

Air

India has a comprehensive network linking the major cities of the different states. Deregulation of the airline industry has had a transformative effect on travel within India, with a host of low-budget private carriers jockeying to provide the lowest prices or highest frequency on popular routes. On any given day, booking a few days in advance, you can expect to fly from Mumbai to Delhi, Bengaluru or Goa for less than US$100 one way including taxes, while booking a month in advance can reduce the price less than US$50-60.

Competition from the efficiently run private sector has, in general, improved the quality of services provided by the nationalized airlines. The airport authorities too have made efforts to improve handling on the ground; major airports are moving towards allowing paperless entry, but you may still need to convert your e-ticket to a paper ticket at the ticket windows outside the terminal.

The best way to get an idea of the current routes, carriers and fares is to use a third-party booking website such as www.cheapairticketsindia.com (toll-free numbers: UK T0800-101 0928, USA T1-888 825 8680), www.cleartrip.com, www.makemytrip.com, or www.yatra.com. Booking with these is a different matter: some refuse foreign credit cards outright, while others have to be persuaded by phone to give your card special clearance. Tickets booked on these sites are typically issued as an email ticket or an SMS text message – the simplest option if you have an Indian mobile phone. Cleartrip.com and Travelocity.com both accept international credit cards.

Pre-paid taxis to the city are available at all major airports. Some airports have up to three categories, 'limousine', 'luxury' and 'ordinary'. The first two usually have prominent counters and salesmen in suits, while the counter for cheap taxis will have the longest queue; ordinary taxis come in a/c and non-a/c varieties. Insist on being taken to your chosen destination even if the driver claims the city is unsafe or the hotel has closed down. For more details on getting from the airport into the city centre, see the entries for the individual cities.

Air tickets Indian Airlines and Jet Airways offer special seven-, 15- and 21-day unlimited travel deals (some are limited to one sector) from around US$300 to US$800. These deals can be useful if you need to travel extensively (and quickly) in areas beyond the reach of the budget airlines. A 25% discount is given on US dollar fares for travellers aged 12-30 years and 25% discount fares exist on some late-night flights (between 2000 and 0800) between metropolitan cities. Air India has relaunched the companion-free scheme for routes between USA/Canada and UK/Europe.

Delays Be prepared for delays, especially in North India during the winter. Nearly all northern routes originate in Delhi where from early December to February smog is a common morning hazard, sometimes delaying departures by several hours.

Tip...
There is a free telephone service at major airports (occasionally through the tourist office counter) to contact any hotel of your choice.

Rail

India's rail network is a thing of wonder, and train travel in the country is an astonishing bargain: you can spend three nights travelling the length of India by air-conditioned sleeper for slightly less than the cost of a London-Birmingham day return. As well as being the cheapest and most comfortable means of travelling long distances, a train ticket gives you access to railway station Retiring Rooms, basic but usually clean digs within the station which can be a cheap and convenient option for late arrivals or early departures. Above all, you have an ideal opportunity to meet local travellers and catch a glimpse of life on the ground.

High-speed trains
There are several air-conditioned 'high-speed' **Shatabdi** (or 'Century') **Express** for day travel, and **Rajdhani Express** ('Capital City') for overnight journeys. These cover large sections of the network

but due to high demand you need to book them well in advance (up to 90 days). Meals and drinks are usually included.

Luxury trains You can travel like a maharaja on the *Palace on Wheels* (www.palaceonwheels.net), the famous seven-nighter which has been running for many years and gives visitors an opportunity to see some of the 'royal' cities in Rajasthan during the winter months for around US$4200 per person on a twin-share basis (US $3160 per person in September and March). Another train travelling in Rajasthan is the *Royal Rajasthan on Wheels*, which costs US$4375 per person on a twin-share basis for the seven nights. The most luxurious option is the *Maharajah's Express* which has four different itineraries, including one starting in Mumbai and concluding in Delhi which covers Ajanta caves, Udaipur, Jodhpur, Bikaner, Jaipur, Ranthambore and Agra for US$6840 per person on a twin-share basis. It's a wonderful way to travel but time at the destinations is a little compressed for some.

Two other seven-nighters are the *Deccan Odyssey*, a train running in Maharashtra, and the Golden Chariot, a relatively new option running in Karnataka and covering Belur, Halebid, Shravanabelagola and then Hampi and Badami/Aihole/Pattadakal.

Bookings and more information on all these heritage-style trains (including special offers) are available at www.indiarail.co.uk.

Steam trains For rail enthusiasts, the steam-hauled narrow-gauge trains between Kurseong and Darjeeling in North Bengal (a World Heritage Site; see page 577), and between Mettupalayam and Coonoor in the Nilgiri Hills of Tamil Nadu (see page 848) are a special attraction.

Buying tickets

It's best to book your train tickets as far in advance as possible (currently up to 120 days), as trains on popular routes – and all trains during holiday periods – fill up well ahead of departure. You can reserve tickets for virtually any train on the network from one of the 3000-plus computerized reservation centres across India. To reserve a seat at a booking office, note down the train's name, number and departure time and fill in a reservation form before you line up at the ticket window; you can use one form for up to four passengers. At busy stations the wait can take an hour or more.

You can save a lot of time and effort by asking a travel agent to get your tickets for a fee of Rs 50-100. If the class you want is full, ask if tickets are available under any of Indian Rail's special quotas. **Foreign Tourist Quota** (FTQ) reserves a small number of tickets on popular routes for overseas travellers; you need your passport and either an exchange certificate or ATM receipt to book tickets under FTQ. The other useful special quota is **Tatkal**, which releases a last-minute pool of tickets on the day before the train departs: at 1000 for AC classes and 1100 for non-AC. If the quota system can't help you, consider buying a 'wait list' ticket, as seats often become available close to the train's departure time; you can check your wait list status at via SMS or phone the station on the day of departure to check your ticket's status. If you don't have a reservation for a particular train but carry an Indrail Pass, you may get one by arriving three hours early.

Be wary of touts at the station offering tickets, hotels or exchange.

Online train bookings from outside India

If your time is short and you plan to do a lot of train travel on popular routes with limited services (eg Hampi–Goa or Goa–Mumbai) it can be worth trying to reserve your tickets before arriving in India. Be warned, though: online booking is a dazzlingly frustrating process, because IRCTC, the Indian Railways portal that handles all ticket bookings, does not accept foreign credit cards. Nevertheless, with a degree of perseverance it can be done.

You first need to open an account with www.cleartrip.com and begin a dummy train booking, from which point you can register as a user of IRCTC. In this process you'll need to submit an Indian mobile number and postal code – make up any 10-digit number for the former and any six-digit number for the latter.

You should receive an email from IRCTC containing a one-time password (OTP). You'll then need to email care@irctc.co.in, quoting your IRCTC username and attaching a copy of your passport (under 1MB in size), and ask them to email you the separate and all-important SMS OTP. (This may take up to a week, and several chase-up emails.) Once you've got both passwords, you can activate your link with Cleartrip, and, if all goes smoothly, begin booking trains. This process changes often, so before starting it's worth consulting the very active India transport forums at www.indiamike.com.

Classes

A/c First Class, available only on main routes, is the choice of the Indian upper crust, with two- or four-berth carpeted sleeper compartments with washbasin. As with all a/c sleeper accommodation, bedding is included, and the windows are tinted to the point of being almost impossible to see through. **A/c Sleeper**, two and three-tier configurations (known as 2AC and 3AC), are clean and comfortable and popular with middle class families; these are the safest carriages for women travelling alone. **A/c Executive Class**, with wide reclining seats, are available on many Shatabdi trains at double the price of the ordinary **a/c Chair Car** which are equally comfortable.

First Class (non-a/c) is gradually being phased out, and is now restricted to a handful of routes through Tamil Nadu and Kerala, but the run-down old carriages still provide a very enjoyable combination of privacy and windows you can open. **Second Class (non-a/c)** two and three-tier (commonly called **Sleeper**), provides exceptionally cheap and atmospheric travel, with basic padded vinyl seats and open windows that allow the sights and sounds of India (not to mention dust, insects and flecks of spittle expelled by passengers up front) to drift into the carriage. On long journeys Sleeper can be crowded and uncomfortable, and toilet facilities can be unpleasant; it is nearly always better to use the Indian-style squat loos rather than the Western-style ones as they are better maintained.

At the bottom rung is **Unreserved Second Class**, with hard wooden benches. You can travel long distances for a trivial amount of money, but unreserved carriages are often ridiculously crowded, and getting off at your station may involve a battle of will and strength against the hordes trying to shove their way on.

Indrail passes

These allow travel across the network without having to pay extra reservation fees and sleeper charges but you have to spend a high proportion of your time on the train to make it worthwhile. However, the advantages of pre-arranged reservations and automatic access to 'Tourist Quotas' can tip the balance in favour of the pass for some travellers.

Tourists (foreigners and Indians resident abroad) may buy these passes from the tourist sections of principal railway booking offices and pay in foreign currency, major credit cards, traveller's cheques or rupees with encashment certificates. Fares range from US$26 to US$1060 for adults or half that for children.

Indrail passes can also conveniently be bought abroad from special agents. For people contemplating a single long journey soon after arriving in India, the Half- or One-day Pass with a confirmed reservation is worth the peace of mind; two- or four-day passes are also sold.

The UK agent is SDEL ① *103 Wembley Park Drive, Wembley, Middlesex HA9 8HG, T020-8903 3411, www.indiarail.co.uk*. They make all necessary reservations and offer excellent advice. They can advise on Jet Airways and other internal flights.

Indrail pass prices

Period	US$ A/c 2-tier	Period	US$ A/c 2-tier
½ day	26	21 days	198
1 day	43	30 days	248
7 days	135	60 days	400
15 days	185	90 days	530

Cost

Fares for individual journeys are based on distance covered and reflect both the class and the type of train. Higher rates apply on the Mail and Express trains and the air-conditioned Shatabdi and Rajdhani Expresses.

A/c first class costs about double the rate for two-tier shown in the table above, and non a/c second class about half. Children (aged five to 12) travel at half the adult fare. The young (12-30 years) and senior citizens (65 years and over) are allowed a 30% discount on journeys over 500 km (just show your passport).

Rail travel tips Bedding: It can get cold in air-conditioned coaches when travelling at night. Bedding is provided on second class air-conditioned sleepers. On others it can be hired for Rs 30 from the Station Baggage Office for second class.

Berths: It is worth asking for upper berths, especially in second class three-tier sleepers, as they can also be used during the day when the lower berths are used as seats. Once the middle berth is lowered for sleeping the lower berth becomes too cramped to sit on. Passengers with valid tickets but no berth reservations are sometimes permitted to travel overnight, causing great discomfort to travellers occupying lower berths.

Delays: Delays are common on all types of transport, and it's vital to allow plenty of time for making connections. The special **Shatabdi** and **Rajdhani Express** are generally quite reliable. Ordinary Express and Mail trains have priority over local services and occasionally surprise by being punctual, but generally the longer the journey time, the greater the delay. Delays on the rail network are cumulative, so arrivals and departures from mid-stations are often several hours behind schedule. Allow at least two hours for connections, more if the first part of the journey is long distance.

Food and drink: It is best to carry some, though tea, bottled water and snacks are sold on trains and platforms. Carry plenty of small notes and coins on long journeys. On long-distance trains, the restaurant car is often near the upper-class carriages.

Train touts

Many railway stations – and some bus stations and major tourist sites – are heavily populated with touts. Self-styled 'agents' will board trains before they enter the station and seek out tourists, often picking up their luggage and setting off with words such as "Madam!/Sir! Come with me madam/sir! You need top-class hotel …". They will even select porters to take your luggage without giving you any say.

If you have succeeded in getting off the train or even in obtaining a trolley you will find hands eager to push it for you.

For a first-time visitor such touts can be more than a nuisance. You need to keep calm and firm. Decide in advance where you want to stay. If you need a porter on trains, select one yourself and agree a price **before** the porter sets off with your baggage. If travelling with a companion one can stay guarding the luggage while the other gets hold of a taxi and negotiates the price to the hotel. It sounds complicated and sometimes it feels it. The most important thing is to behave as if you know what you are doing!

Internet services Much information is available online via www.railtourismindia.com, www.indianrail.gov.in, www.erail.in and the brilliantly useful www.indiarailinfo.com, where you can check timetables (which change frequently), train numbers, seat availability, the running status of your train, and even forums discussing the cleanliness, average delay, and food quality of each individual train on the network.

Ladies' compartments: A woman travelling alone, overnight, on an unreserved second-class train can ask if there is one of these. Lone female travellers may feel more comfortable in air-conditioned sleeper coaches, which require reservations and are used by Indian families.

Ladies' and seniors' queues: Separate (much shorter) ticket queues may be available for women and senior citizens.

Left luggage: Bags can be left for up to 30 days in station cloakrooms. These are especially useful when there is time to go sightseeing before an evening train. The bags must be lockable and you are advised not to leave any food in them.

Overbooking: Passengers with valid tickets but no berth reservations are sometimes permitted to travel overnight, causing great discomfort to travellers occupying lower berths. Wait-listed passengers should confirm the status of their ticket in advance by calling enquiries at the nearest computerized reservation office. If you have access to www.irctc.in you can also check the waitlist status of your ticket using the PNR number or a travel agent can do this online. At the station, check the reservation charts (usually on the relevant platform) and contact the Station Manager or Ticket Collector.

Porters: These can carry prodigious amounts of luggage. Rates vary from station to station (sometimes listed on a board on the platform) but are usually around Rs 10-25 per item of luggage. Establish the rate first.

Pre-paid taxis: Many main stations have a pre-paid taxi (or auto-rickshaw) service which offers a reliable service at a fair price. If there are no pre-paid taxis ask your hotel for a guide price.

Security: Keep valuables close to you, securely locked, and away from windows. For security, carry a good lock and chain to attach your luggage.

Timetables Regional timetables are available cheaply from station bookstalls; the monthly *Indian Bradshaw* is sold in principal stations. The handy *Trains at a Glance* (Rs 40) lists popular trains likely to be used by most foreign travellers and is available at stalls at Indian railway stations and in the UK from SDEL (see page 1367).

Road

Road travel is sometimes the only choice for reaching many of the places of outstanding interest, particularly national parks or isolated tourist sites. For the uninitiated, travel by road can also be a worrying experience because of the apparent absence of conventional traffic regulations. Vehicles drive on the left – in theory. Routes around the major cities are usually crowded with lorry traffic, especially at night, and the main roads are often poor and slow. There are a few motorway-style expressways, but most main roads are single track. Some district roads are quiet, and although they are not fast they can be a good way of seeing the country and village life if you have the time.

Bus

Buses now reach virtually every part of India, offering a cheap, if often uncomfortable, means of visiting places off the rail network. Very few villages are now more than 2-3 km from a bus stop. Services are run by the State Corporation from the State Bus Stand (and private companies which often have offices nearby). The latter allow advance reservations, including booking printable e-tickets online (check www.redbus.in and www.viaworld.in) and, although tickets prices are a little higher, they have fewer stops and are a bit more comfortable.

Bus categories Though comfortable for sightseeing trips, apart from the very best 'sleeper coaches' even **air-conditioned luxury coaches** can be very uncomfortable for really long journeys. Often the air conditioning is very cold so wrap up. Journeys over 10 hours can be extremely tiring so it is better to go by train if there is a choice. If you must take a sleeper bus (a contradiction in terms), choose a lower berth near the front of the bus. The upper berths tend to be really uncomfortable on bumpy roads. **Express buses** run over long distances (frequently overnight), these are often called 'video coaches' and can be an appalling experience unless you appreciate loud film music blasting through the night. Ear plugs and eye masks may ease the pain. They rarely average more than 45 kph. **Local buses** are often very crowded, quite bumpy, slow and usually poorly maintained. However, over short distances, they can be a very cheap, friendly and easy way of getting about. Even where signboards are not in English someone will usually give you directions. Many larger towns have **minibus** services which charge a little more than the buses and pick up and drop passengers on request. Again very crowded, and with restricted headroom, they are the fastest way of getting about many of the larger towns.

Bus travel tips Some towns have different bus stations for different destinations. Booking on major long-distance routes is now computerized. Book in advance where possible and avoid the back of the bus where it can be very bumpy. If your destination is only served by a local bus you may do better to take the Express bus and 'persuade' the driver, with a tip in advance, to stop where you want to get off. You will have to pay the full fare to the first stop beyond your destination but you will get there faster and more comfortably. When an unreserved bus pulls into a bus station, there is usually an unholy scramble for seats, whilst those arriving have to struggle to get off! In many areas there is an unwritten 'rule of reservation' using handkerchiefs or bags thrust through the windows to reserve seats. Some visitors may feel a more justified right to a seat having fought their way through the crowd, but it is generally best to do as local people do and be prepared with a handkerchief. As soon as it touches the seat, it is yours! Leave it on your seat when getting off to use the toilet at bus stations.

Car

A car provides a chance to travel off the beaten track, and gives unrivalled opportunities for seeing something of India's great variety of villages and small towns. Until recently, the most widely used hire car was the romantic but notoriously unreliable Hindustan Ambassador. You can still find them for hire in many places, but they're gradually giving way to more efficient (and boring) Tata and Toyota models with mod cons such as optional air conditioning – and seat belts. A handful of international agencies offer self-drive car hire (Avis, Sixt), but India's majestically anarchic traffic culture is not for the faint-hearted, and emphatically not a place for those who value such quaint concepts as lane discipline, or indeed driving on your assigned side of the road. It's much more common, and comfortable, to hire not just the car but someone to drive it for you.

The hazards of road travel

On most routes it is impossible to average more than 50-60 kph in a car. Journeys are often very long, and can seem an endless succession of horn blowing, unexpected dangers, and unforeseen delays. Villages are often congested – beware of the concealed spine-breaking speed bumps – and cattle, sheep and goats may wander atwill across the road. Directions can also be difficult to follow. Drivers frequently don't know the way, maps are often hopelessly inaccurate and map reading is an almost entirely unknown skill. Training in driving is negligible and the test often a farce. You will note a characteristic side-saddle posture, one hand constantly on the horn, but there can be real dangers from poor judgement, irresponsible overtaking and a general philosophy of 'might is right'.

Car hire If you fancy the idea of being Lady Penelope and gadding about with your own chauffeur, dream no more. Hiring a car and driver is the most comfortable and efficient way to cover short to medium distances, and although prices have increased sharply in recent years car travel in India is still a bargain by Western standards. Even if you're travelling on a modest budget a day's car hire can help take the sting out of an arduous journey, allowing you to go sightseeing along the way without looking for somewhere to stash your bags.

Local drivers often know their way around an area much better than drivers from other states, so where possible it is a good idea to get a local driver who speaks the state language, in addition to being able to communicate with you. The best way to guarantee a driver who speaks good English is to book in advance with a professional travel agency, either in India or in your home country. Recommended operators with English-speaking drivers are listed in the individual chapters. You can, if you choose, arrange car hire informally by asking around at taxi stands, but don't expect your driver to speak anything more than rudimentary English.

On pre-arranged overnight trips the fee you pay will normally include fuel and inter-state taxes – check before you pay – and a wage for the driver. Drivers are responsible for their expenses, including meals (and the pervasive servant-master culture in India means that most will choose to sit separately from you at meal times). Some tourist hotels provide rooms for drivers, but they often choose to sleep in the car overnight to save money. In some areas drivers also seek to increase their earnings by taking you to hotels and shops where they earn a handsome commission; these are generally hugely overpriced and poor alternatives to the hotels recommended in this book, so don't be afraid to say no and insist on your choice of accommodation. If you feel inclined, a tip at the end of the tour of Rs 100 per day is appropriate.

	Tata Indica non-a/c	Tata Indigo non-a/c	Hyundai Accent a/c	Toyota Innova
8 hrs/80 km	Rs 1200	Rs 1600	Rs 2200	Rs 2500
Extra km	Rs 8	Rs 10	Rs 15	Rs 15
Extra hour	Rs 80	Rs 100	Rs 200	Rs 180
Out of town				
Per km	Rs 8	Rs 10	Rs 15	Rs 15
Night halt	Rs 200	Rs 200	Rs 300	Rs 250

Importing a car Tourists may import their own vehicles into India with a Carnet de Passage (Triptyques) issued by any recognized automobile association or club affiliated to the Alliance Internationale de Tourisme in Geneva. In the UK contact the RAC ① *T0844-891 3111, www.rac.co.uk*.

Self-drive car hire This is still in its infancy and many visitors may find the road conditions difficult and dangerous so take great care. Pedestrians, cattle and a wide range of other animals roam at will. This can be particularly dangerous when driving after dark especially as even other vehicles often have no lights.

Car travel tips When booking emphasize the importance of good tyres and general roadworthiness. On main roads across India **petrol stations** are reasonably frequent, but some areas are poorly served. Some service stations only have diesel pumps though they may have small reserves of petrol. Always carry a spare can. Diesel is widely available and normally much cheaper than petrol. Petrol is rarely above 92 octane. Drivers must have third-party **insurance**. This may have to be with an Indian insurer, or with a foreign insurer who has a national guarantor. You must also be in possession of an International Driving Permit, issued by a recognized driving authority in your home country (eg the AA in the UK, apply at least six weeks before leaving). **Asking the way** can be very frustrating as you are likely to get widely conflicting advice each time you stop to ask (this happens to Indians asking directions too, it's not just a game to play on foreigners!). On the main roads, 'mile' posts periodically appear in English and can help. Elsewhere, it is best to ask directions often and follow the average direction. **Accidents** often produce large and angry crowds very quickly. It is best to leave the scene of the accident and report it to the police as quickly as possible thereafter. Ensure that you have adequate provisions, plenty of food and drink and a basic tool set in the car.

The **Automobile Association (AA)** offers a range of services to members. Chennai: AA of Southern India, AASI Centre, 187 Anna Salai, T044-2852 1162, www.aasindia.in. Mumbai: Western India AA, Lalji Narainji Memorial Building, 76, Vir Nariman Road, Churchgate, T022-2204 1085, www.wiaaindia.com. New Delhi: AA of Upper India, C-8 Qutab Institutional Area, behind Qutab Hotel, T011-2696 5397, www.aaui.org.

Cycling

Cycling is an excellent way of seeing the quiet byways of India. In most small towns you'll find someone to hire a bike from – typically a heavy, fixed-gear Hero, Atlas or BSA with a parcel rack on the back – for about Rs 100 per day. On the flat, these bikes offer a good way of covering reasonably short distances at your own pace.

If you plan to tour more extensively you'll want to buy – or bring – your own cycle. It is possible to cover 50-80 km a day quite comfortably, especially if you ride in early morning and late afternoon and rest during the heat of the day. Night riding, though cooler, can be hazardous because of lack of lighting, poor road surfaces and the high likelihood that you'll end up going headfirst over a dog sleeping on the road.

National highways are manic with potentially lethal levels of traffic hazard, so stick to the country roads, which can be idyllic, especially along the coast, if rather dusty and bumpy. Foreign cyclists are usually greeted with cheers, waves and smiles, and truck drivers are sometimes happy to give lifts to cyclists and their bikes. You can even put your bike on a boat for a backwater trip or on top of a bus. If you want to take your bike on the train, allow plenty of time for booking it in on the brake van at the Parcels office and for filling in forms. Take care not to leave your bike parked anywhere with your belongings.

You can buy a basic second-hand Indian bike for around Rs 1200-1500 with sharp bargaining, and if it's not completely trashed sell it at the end of your trip at not much of a loss. Imported bikes have lighter weight and gears, but are more difficult to get repaired and carry the much greater risk of being stolen or damaged. If you wish to take your own, be sure to take all essential spares including a pump. (It is possible to get Indian spares for 26" wheel cycles.) Bring bungy cords to strap down a backpack and good lights from home. Bike repair shops are universal and charges are nominal; you are usually not far from a 'puncture wallah' who can also make minor repairs cheaply.

For expert advice contact the **Cyclists' Touring Club** ① *T0844-736 8450, www.ctc.org.uk*

Hitchhiking

Hitchhiking is uncommon, partly because public transport is so cheap. If you try, you are likely to spend a very long time on the roadside. However, getting a lift on scooters and on trucks in areas with little public transport can be worthwhile, whilst those riding motorbikes or scooters in Goa can be expected to pick up the occasional hitchhiking policeman. It is not recommended for women on their own.

TRAVEL TIP

On the road on a motorbike

An experienced motorbiker writes: unless you bring your own bike (Carnet de passage, huge deposit) the only acceptable machine is the legendary Enfield Bullet 350 or 500 cc. Humming along the Indian roads or tracks this four stroke classic machine is a must. Also available in diesel version (1.5 litres per 100 km and much cheaper fuel) the 500 cc is much better for travelling with luggage and easier to take home as brakes and 12v lights conform with EC regulations.

Expect a cruising speed of around 50 kph. Riding above 70 kph gets very tiring due to the lack of silent blocks and the nerve-wracking Indian roads. A good average distance is 200 km per day. Riding at night furthers the excitement – practise at home on a death race video first, but bear in mind that accidents can turn into a first-hand lynching experience! If you stop, prepare to settle quickly in cash, but while third party insurance is cheap refunds are less than guaranteed.

Buying   In Delhi, Karol Bagh is the biker's den, where you can have your second-hand bike assembled to order. It's also good for arranging shipping (Rs 13,000 to Europe), and for spares and gear. You can now find good helmets at a fraction of the European price (Studds Rs 300-2000 for a full face type), also goggles, sturdy panniers and extras. A Bullet will cost from Rs 25,000 to Rs 40,000 second hand, or Rs 50,000- Rs 60,000 new. Allow plenty of time to shop around.

Papers   Many Indians and tourists don't bother changing the name on the ownership papers. If you are driving through more than one state this is rash, as it is essential to have the papers in your name, plus the NOC (No Objection Certificate) from the Motor Vehicles Department if you intend to export the vehicle home. Regardless of the dealer's assertions to the contrary, demand the NOC as otherwise you will have to apply for it in the state of origin. You have to allow 15 days.

Spares   Before buying, negotiate the essential extras: mirrors, luggage carriers, better saddle, battery. Spares are cheap and readily available for the 350cc model. Take along a spare throttle and clutch cable, a handful of nuts and bolts, puncture repair kit and pump or emergency canister so you don't have to leave the bike unattended while hitching a lift to the nearest puncture wallah – and of course a full set of tools. Check the oil level daily. Finally, remember that for long distances you can load your bike on a night train (Rs 100 per 100 km). Just turn up at the parcel office with an empty petrol tank at least two hours before departure.

Motorcycling

This is a particularly attractive way of getting around. It is easy to buy new Indian-made motorcycles including the 350cc Enfield Bullet and 100cc Japanese models, including Suzukis and Hondas, made in collaboration with Indian firms. Buying new at a fixed price ensures greater ease and reliability. Buying second hand in rupees takes more time but is quite possible (expect to get a 30-40% discount) and repairs are usually easy to arrange and quite cheap. You can get a broker to help with the paperwork involved (certificate of ownership, insurance, etc) for a fee. They charge about Rs 5000 for a No Objection Certificate (NOC), essential for reselling; it's easier to have the bike in your name. Bring your own helmet and an International Driving Permit. Vespa, Kinetic Honda and other makes of scooters in India are slower than motorbikes but comfortable for short hauls of less than 100 km and have the advantage of a 'dicky' (small, lockable box) for spares, and a spare tyre. See also box, above. Motorbikes and scooters for hire in Goa must have black and yellow number plates. Bikes with other number plates will be cheaper to hire but you will get stopped by the police. Expect to pay between Rs 250 and Rs 500 a day to rent a scooter or bike in Goa.

Peter and Friends Classic Adventures ⓘ *Assagao, Goa, T08322-268467, www.classic-bike-india.com*, organize motorbike tours in Rajasthan and the Himalaya with good back-up. They're well organized, friendly and popular, and also hire Enfield motorbikes in Goa. **Royal Enfield** ⓘ *www.royalenfield.com*, is an Indian website with information on pilgrim tours by motorbike and how to buy a new Bullet.

Taxi

Taxi travel in India is a great bargain, and in most cities you can take a taxi from the airport to the centre for under US$10. Yellow-top taxis in cities and large towns are metered, although tariffs change frequently. These changes are shown on a fare conversion chart which should be read in conjunction with the meter reading. Increased night time rates apply in most cities, and there might be a small charge for luggage. Insist on the taxi meter being flagged in your presence. If the driver refuses, the official advice is to contact the police. When a taxi doesn't have a meter, you will need to fix the fare before starting the journey. Ask at your hotel desk for a guide price. As a foreigner, it is rare to get a taxi in the big cities to use the meter – if they are eager to, watch out as sometimes the meter is rigged and they have a fake rate card. Also, watch out for the David Blaine-style note shuffle: you pay with an Rs 500 note, but they have a Rs 100 note in their hand. This happens frequently at the prepaid booth outside New Delhi train station too, no matter how small the transaction.

Most airports and many major stations have booths where you can book a **prepaid taxi**. For slightly more than the metered fare these allow you to sidestep overcharging and give you the security of knowing that your driver will take you to your destination by the most direct route. You might be able to join up with other travellers at the booth to share a taxi to your hotel or a central point. It's OK to give the driver a small tip at the end of the journey.

At night, always have a clear idea of where you want to go and insist on being taken there. Taxi drivers may try to convince you that the hotel you have chosen 'closed three years ago' or is 'completely full'. Say that you have a reservation.

Rickshaw Auto-rickshaws (autos) are almost universally available in towns across India and are the cheapest and most convenient way of getting about. It is best to walk a short distance away from a hotel gate before picking up an auto to avoid paying an inflated rate. In addition to using them for short journeys it is often possible to hire them by the hour, or for a half or full day's sightseeing. In some areas younger drivers who speak some English and know their local area well may want to show you around. However, rickshaw drivers are often paid a commission by hotels, restaurants and gift shops, and any too-cheap-to-be-true offer of a guided tour will inevitably have you stopping at an endless parade of high-priced pashmina and antique shops. Drivers generally refuse to use a meter, often quote a ridiculous price or may sometimes stop short of your destination. If you have real problems it can help to note down the vehicle licence number and threaten to go to the police. Beware of some rickshaw drivers who show the fare chart for taxis, especially in Mumbai.

Cycle-rickshaws and **horse-drawn tongas** are more common in the more rustic setting of a small town or the outskirts of a large one. You will need to fix a price by bargaining. The animal attached to a tonga usually looks too undernourished to have the strength to pull the driver, let alone passengers.

Maps

For anyone interested in the geography of India, or even simply getting around, trying to buy good maps is a depressing experience. For security reasons it is illegal to sell large-scale maps of areas within 80 km of the coast or national borders.

The 1:1,200,000 road maps published by **Reise Know-How** are the most useful reference points for general travel; there's one each for the Northwest, Northeast and South, and they're printed on waterproof and tear-resistant paper.

State and town plans are published by **TTK Maps**. These are often the best available though they are not wholly reliable. For the larger cities they provide the most compact yet clear map sheets (generally 50 mm by 75 mm format). The **Indian Map Service** publishes road atlases of most states.

The **Survey of India** publishes large scale 1:10,000 town plans of some 70 cities, mostly 20 years or more out of date, as well as topographic maps at the scale of 1:25,000 and 1:50,000 in addition to its 1:250,000 scale coverage. However, maps are regarded as highly sensitive and it is only possible to buy these from main agents of the Survey of India. The export of large-scale maps from India is prohibited.

Local customs

Conduct

Most travellers experience great warmth and hospitality. With it comes an open curiosity about personal matters. You should not be surprised if total strangers ask for details of your job, income and family circumstances or discuss politics and religion.

Respect for the foreign visitor should be reciprocated by a sensitivity towards local customs and culture. How you dress is how people will judge you; cleanliness, modest clothes and a smile go a long way. Scanty, tight clothing draws unwanted attention. Nudity is not permitted on beaches in India and although there are some places where this ban is ignored, it causes much offence. Public displays of intimacy are inappropriate in public. You may at times be frustrated by delays, bureaucracy and inefficiency, but displays of anger and rudeness will not achieve anything positive, and often make things worse. People's concept of time and punctuality is also often rather vague (hence the old joke that IST stands for 'Indian Stretchable Time') so be prepared to be kept waiting.

Courtesy

It takes little effort to learn common gestures of courtesy and they are greatly appreciated. The greeting when meeting or parting, used universally among the Hindus across India, is the palms joined together as in prayer, sometimes accompanied with the word *namaste* (North and West), *namoshkar* (East) or *vanakkam* in Tamil. Muslims use the greeting *assalâm aleikum*, with the response *waleikum assalâm*, meaning 'peace be with you'; 'please' is *mehrbani-se*; 'thank you' is often expressed by a smile, or with the somewhat formal *dhannyabad*, *shukriya* (Urdu), and *nandri* in Tamil.

Hands and eating

Traditionally, Indians use the right hand for giving, receiving, shaking hands and eating, as the left is considered to be unclean since it is associated with washing after using the toilet. In much of rural India cutlery is alien at the table except for serving spoons, and at most humble restaurants you will be offered only small spoons to eat with. If you visit an ashram or are lucky enough to be invited to a temple feast day, you will almost certainly be expected to eat with your hands. Watch and copy others until the technique becomes familiar.

Women *See also page 1393.*

Indian women in urban and rural areas differ in their social interactions with men. To the Westerner, Indian women may seem to remain in the background and appear shy when approached. Yet you will see them working in public, often in jobs traditionally associated with men in the West, in the fields or on construction sites. It is not considered polite for men to photograph women without their consent, so ask before you start snapping.

Women do not usually shake hands with men as physical contact between the sexes is not acceptable. Westernized city women, however, freely offer to shake hands with a foreign visitor. In certain, very traditional rural circles, it is still the custom for men to be offered food first, separately, so don't be surprised if you, as foreign guest (man or woman), are awarded this special status when invited to an Indian home.

Visiting religious sites

Visitors to all religious places should be dressed in clean, modest clothes; shorts and vests are inappropriate. Always remove shoes before entering (and all leather items in Jain temples). Take thick socks for protection when walking on sun-baked stone floors. Menstruating women are considered 'unclean' and should not enter places of worship. It is discourteous to sit with one's back to a temple or shrine. You will be expected to sit cross-legged on the floor – avoid pointing your feet at others when attending prayers at a temple. Walk clockwise around a shrine (keeping it to your right).

Non-Hindus are sometimes excluded from the inner sanctum of **Hindu** temples and occasionally even from the temple itself. Look for signs or ask. In certain temples and on special occasions you may enter only if you wear unstitched clothing such as a *dhoti*.

In **Buddhist** shrines, turn prayer wheels in a clockwise direction. In **Sikh** gurudwaras, everyone should cover their head, even if it is with a handkerchief. Tobacco and cigarettes should not be taken in. In **Muslim** mosques, visitors should only have their face, hands and feet exposed; women should also cover their heads. Mosques may be closed to non-Muslims shortly before formal prayers.

Some temples have a register or a receipt book for **donations** which works like an obligatory entry fee. The money is normally used for the upkeep and services of the temple or monastery. In some pilgrimage centres, priests can become unpleasantly persistent. If you wish to leave a donation, put money in the donation box; priests and Buddhist monks often do not handle money. It is also not customary to shake hands with a priest or monk. *Sanyasis* (holy men) and some pilgrims depend on donations.

Begging and charitable giving

Beggars are often found on busy street corners in large Indian cities, as well as at bus and train stations where they often target foreigners. In the larger cities, beggars are often exploited by syndicates which cream off most of their takings. Yet those seeking alms near religious sites are another matter, and you may see Indian worshippers giving freely to those less fortunate than themselves, since this is tied up with gaining 'merit'. How you deal with begging is a matter of personal choice. Young children sometimes offer to do 'jobs' such as call a taxi, carry shopping or pose for a photo. You may want to give a coin in exchange. While travelling, some visitors prefer to hand out fruit to the many open-palmed children they encounter.

A pledge to donate a part of one's holiday budget to a local charity could be an effective formula for 'giving'. Some visitors like to support self-help cooperatives, orphanages, refugee centres, disabled or disadvantaged groups, or international charities like Oxfam, Save the Children or Christian Aid which work with local partners, by either making a donation or by buying their products. Some of these charities are listed under the appropriate towns. A few (which also welcome volunteers) are listed here.

Akanksha, www.akanksha.org. Mumbai-based charity working with slum kids who have fallen out of formal education.
Concern India Foundation, www.concern indiafoundation.org. An umbrella organization working with local charities.
El Shaddai Charitable Trust, www.child rescue. net, www.scanindia.in. Charity providing food, clothing, shelter and education for orphans and economically deprived children in India.
Oxfam, www.oxfamindia.org.
Salaam Baalak Trust, several centres in Mumbai and Delhi, www.salaambaalaktrust.com. Set up by the team who made the movie *Salaam Bombay* 20 years ago, Salaam Baalak's mission is to give street children the joys of childhood and prepare them for a productive adulthood – they offer food, shelter, education, vocational training.

They hold dramas and dance events to raise awareness about community and health issues.
Save the Children India, www.savethechildren.in.
Share and Care Children's Welfare Society, www.shareand care.org.in. A small but highly regarded organization that runs an orphanage, self-help groups for women, aged care and environmental education programs.
Trek-Aid, www.trek-aid.com. Health, education, etc, through self help schemes for displaced Tibetan refugees.
Urmul Trust, www.urmul.org. Healthcare, education and rural crafts in Rajasthani villages.
Very Special Arts India, www.vsaindia.org. This organization promotes the creative power in people with disabilities and works towards enriching their lives through remedial therapies.

Essentials A-Z

Accident and emergency

Contact the relevant emergency service (police T100, fire T101, ambulance T102) and your embassy. Make sure you obtain police/medical reports required for insurance claims.

Children

Children of all ages are widely welcomed. However, care should be taken when travelling to remote areas where health services are primitive. It's best to visit in the cooler months since you need to protect children from the sun, heat, dehydration and mosquito bites. Cool showers or baths help; avoid being out during the hottest part of the day. Diarrhoea and vomiting are the most common problems, so take the usual precautions. Breastfeeding is best and most convenient for babies. In the big cities you can get safe baby foods and formula milk. It doesn't harm a baby to eat an unvaried and limited diet of familiar food carried in packets for a few weeks if local dishes are not acceptable, but it may be an idea to give vitamin and mineral supplements. Wet wipes and disposable nappies are difficult to find. The biggest hotels provide babysitting. Many European families have permanently relocated to Goa and the facilities here are accordingly good. See also Health, opposite.

Customs and duty free

Duty free

Tourists are allowed to bring in all personal effects 'which may reasonably be required' without charge. The official customs allowance includes 200 cigarettes or 50 cigars, 0.95 litres of alcohol, a camera and a pair of binoculars. Valuable personal items and professional equipment including jewellery, special camera equipment and lenses, laptop computers and sound and video recorders must in theory be declared on a Tourist Baggage Re-Export Form (TBRE) in order for them to be taken out of the country, though in practice it's relatively unlikely that your bags will be inspected beyond a cursory X-ray. Nevertheless, it saves considerable frustration if you know the equipment serial numbers in advance and are ready to show them on the equipment.

In addition to the forms, details of imported equipment may be entered into your passport. Save time by completing the formalities while waiting for your baggage. It is essential to keep these forms for showing to the customs when leaving India, otherwise considerable delays are very likely at the time of departure.

Currency regulations

There are no restrictions on the amount of foreign currency or TCs a tourist may bring into India. If you are carrying more than US$5000 in cash or US$10,000 or its equivalent in cash and TCs you need to fill in a currency declaration form. This could change with a relaxation in the currency regulations.

If you are travelling to Nepal, note that it is illegal to take Indian Rs 500 and Rs 1000 notes into the country. These notes will be confiscated, and offenders are liable to fines or imprisonment.

Prohibited items

The import of live plants, gold coins, gold and silver bullion and silver coins not in current use are either banned or subject to strict regulation. Enquire at consular offices abroad for details.

Export restrictions

Export of antiquities and art objects over 100 years old is restricted. Ivory, musk, skins of all animals, shahtoosh wool and articles made from them are banned, unless you get permission for export. For further information, contact the Indian High Commission or consulate, or check www.cbec.gov.in.

Disabled travellers

India is not geared up for the disabled or wheelchair-bound traveller. Access to buildings, toilets (sometimes squat), pavements, kerbs and public transport can prove frustrating, but it is easy to find people to give a hand to help with lifting and carrying. Provided you are prepared to pay for at least mid-priced accommodation, car hire and taxis, a visit to India should be rewarding.

Some travel companies specialize in exciting holidays, tailor-made for individuals depending on their level of ability. **Global Access**, Disabled Travel Network (www.globalaccessnews.com), is dedicated to providing travel information for

'disabled adventurers' and includes a number of reviews and tips from members of the public.
Accessible Journeys Inc, www.disability travel.com. Runs some packages to India.
Journeys Without Barriers, www.travelanother india.com. An Indian company offering a limited range of wheelchair-accessible journeys.
ResponsibleTravel.com, www.responsibletravel. com. Specializes in eco-friendly holidays and has some tailored to the needs of disabled travellers.

Drugs

Certain areas, such as Goa's beaches, Kovalam, Gokarna and Hampi, have become associated with foreigners who take drugs. These are likely to attract local and foreign drug dealers but be aware that the government takes the misuse of drugs very seriously, and some dealers run a handy sideline as police informants. Anyone charged with the illegal possession of drugs risks facing a fine of Rs 100,000 and up to 20 years' imprisonment. Several foreigners have been imprisoned for drugs-related offences in the last decade.

Electricity

India's supply is 220-240 volts AC, but be aware that there may be pronounced variations in the voltage, and power cuts are common; it may be worth investing in a voltage stabilizer for your laptop. Power back-up by generator or inverter is becoming more widespread, even in humble hotels, though it may not cover a/c. Socket sizes vary so take a universal adaptor; low-quality versions are available locally. Many hotels, even in the higher categories, don't have electric razor sockets.

Embassies and consulates

For information on visas and immigration, see page 1391. For a comprehensive list of embassies (but not all consulates), see http://mea.gov.in/indian-missions-abroad.htm.

Health

Local populations in India are exposed to a range of health risks not encountered in the Western world. Many of the diseases cause major problems for the local poor and destitute and, although the risks to travellers are more remote, they cannot be ignored. Obviously 5-star travel is going to carry less risk than backpacking on a budget.

Health care in the region is varied. There are many excellent private and government clinics/hospitals. As with all medical care, first impressions count. It's worth contacting your embassy or consulate on arrival and asking where the recommended clinics are (ie those used by diplomats). You can also ask about locally recommended medical dos and don'ts. If you do get ill, and you have the opportunity, you should also ask your medical insurer whether they are satisfied that the medical centre/hospital you have been referred to is of a suitable standard.

Before you go

Ideally, you should see your GP or travel clinic at least 6 weeks before your departure for general advice on travel risks, malaria and vaccinations. Make sure you have travel insurance, get a dental check (especially if you are going to be away for more than a month), know your own blood group and if you suffer a long-term condition such as diabetes or epilepsy make sure someone knows or that you have a Medic Alert bracelet/ necklace with this information on it. Remember that it is risky to buy medicinal tablets abroad because the doses may differ and India has a huge trade in counterfeit drugs.

Vaccinations

If you need vaccinations, see your doctor well in advance of your travel. Most courses must be completed by a minimum of 4 weeks before you go. Travel clinics may provide rapid courses of vaccination, but are likely to be more expensive. The following vaccinations are recommended: typhoid, polio, tetanus, infectious hepatitis and diphtheria. For details of malaria prevention, contact your GP or local travel clinic.

The following vaccinations may also be considered: rabies, possibly BCG (since TB is still common in the region) and in some cases meningitis and diphtheria (if you're staying in the country for a long time). Yellow fever is not required in India but you may be asked to show a certificate if you have travelled from Africa or South America. Japanese encephalitis may be required for rural travel at certain times of the year (mainly rainy seasons). An effective oral cholera vaccine (Dukoral) is now available as 2 doses providing 3 months' protection.

A-Z of health risks

Altitude sickness Altitude sickness can creep up on you as just a mild headache with nausea or lethargy during your visit to the Himalaya. The more serious disease is caused by fluid collecting in the brain in the enclosed space of the skull and can lead to coma and death. There is also a lung disease version with breathlessness and fluid infiltration of the lungs. The best cure is to descend as soon as possible. Preventative measures include getting acclimatized and not reaching the highest levels on your first few days of arrival. Try to avoid flying directly into the cities of highest altitude. Climbers like to take treatment drugs as protective measures but this can lead to macho idiocy and death. The peaks are still there and so are the trails, whether it takes you a bit longer than someone else does not matter as long as you come back down alive.

If you receive a venomous **bite or sting** from a snake, spider, scorpion or sea creature, try to identify the creature, without putting yourself in further danger (do not try to catch a live snake). Snake bites in particular are very frightening, but in fact rarely poisonous – even venomous snakes bite without injecting venom. Victims should be taken to a hospital or a doctor without delay. Commercial snake bite and scorpion kits are available, but are usually only useful for the specific types of snake or scorpion. Most serum has to be given intravenously so it is not much good equipping yourself with it unless you are used to making injections into veins. It is best to rely on local practice in these cases, because the particular creatures will be known about locally and appropriate treatment can be given. To prevent bites, do not walk in snake territory in bare feet or sandals – wear proper shoes or boots. For scorpions and spiders, keep beds away from the walls and look inside your shoes and under the toilet seat every morning. Certain tropical sea fish when trodden upon inject venom into bathers' feet. This can be very painful. Wear plastic shoes if such creatures are reported. The pain can be relieved by immersing the foot in hot water (as hot as you can bear) for as long as the pain persists. Citric acid juices in fruits such as lemon are reported as being useful.

Chikungunya This relatively rare mosquito-borne disease has become prevalent in several parts of India, including Kerala, Goa and Gujarat, particularly during the monsoon when flooded areas encourage the carrier mosquitoes to breed. The disease manifests within 12 days of infection and symptoms resemble a severe fever, with headaches, joint pain, arthritis and exhaustion lasting from several days to several weeks; in vulnerable sections of the population it can be fatal. Neither vaccine nor treatment are available, so rest is the best cure.

Dengue fever Unfortunately there is no vaccine against dengue fever and the mosquitoes that carry it bite during the day. Fever, nausea and pain in the head and joints may last for 7-10 days, but symptoms of exhaustion can linger for weeks. Secondary infection with dengue can result in the potentially lethal dengue haemorrhagic fever: early symptoms are irritability, restlessness and abnormal sweatiness, followed by a shock-like state, and bleeding from the pores. Heed all the anti-mosquito measures that you can, and be especially wary in large cities, particularly during rainy periods, when stagnant water is lying around.

Diarrhoea The standard advice for diarrhoea prevention is to be careful with water and ice for drinking. If you have any doubts about where the water came from then boil it or filter and treat it. There are many filter/treatment devices now available on the market. Food can also transmit disease. Be wary of salads (what were they washed in, who handled them), re-heated foods or food that has been left out in the sun having been cooked earlier in the day. There is a simple adage that says wash it, peel it, boil it or forget it. Also be wary of unpasteurized dairy products, these can transmit a range of diseases from brucellosis (fevers and constipation), to listeria (meningitis) and tuberculosis of the gut (constipation, fevers and weight loss).

The key treatment with all diarrhoea is rehydration. Try to keep hydrated by taking the right mixture of salt and water. This is available as Oral Rehydration Salts (ORS) in ready-made sachets or can be made up by adding a teaspoon of sugar and a half teaspoon of salt to a litre of clean water. You can also use flat carbonated drinks. Drink at least 1 large cup of this drink for each loose stool. Drugs such as Imodium and Lomotil are designed to plug up your bowels rather than cure diarrhoea, and are best avoided unless you have an unavoidable long coach/train journey or are on a trek; generally it's better to let the nasties work their way out of your system as nature intended. Antibiotics like Ciproxin (Ciprofloaxcin) – obtained by private prescription in the UK – can be a useful antibiotic for some forms of travellers' diarrhoea. If it persists beyond 2 weeks, with blood or pain, seek medical attention. One good preventative is taking probiotics like Vibact or Bifilac which are available over the counter.

Hepatitis This means inflammation of the liver. The most obvious symptom is a yellowing of your skin or the whites of your eyes. However, prior to this all that you may notice is itching and tiredness. Early on, depending on the type of hepatitis, a vaccine or immunoglobulin may reduce the duration of the illness. There are vaccines for hepatitis A and B; the latter spread through blood and unprotected sexual intercourse, both of these can be avoided. Unfortunately there is no vaccine for hepatitis C or the increasing alphabetical list of other hepatitis viruses.

Leishmaniasis If infected with leishmaniasis, you may notice a raised lump, which leads to a purplish discoloration on white skin and a possible ulcer. The parasite is transmitted by the bite of a sandfly. Sandflies do not fly very far and the greatest risk is at ground levels, so if you can avoid sleeping on the jungle floor do so, under a permethrin-treated net and use insect repellent. Several weeks of treatment is required under specialist supervision.

Leptospirosis Various forms of leptospirosis occur throughout the world, transmitted by a bacterium which is excreted in rodent urine. Fresh water and moist soil harbour the organisms, which enter the body through cuts and scratches. If you suffer from any form of prolonged fever consult a doctor.

Malaria Malaria has some seasonality but it is too unpredictable to not take malaria prophylaxis. Specialist advice should be taken on the best anti-malarials to use.

For **mosquito repellents**, remember that DEET (Di-ethyltoluamide) is the gold standard. Apply the repellent 4-6 hrs but more often if you are sweating heavily. If a non-DEET product is used check who tested it. Validated products (tested at the London School of Hygiene and Tropical Medicine) include Mosiguard, Non-DEET Jungle formula and non-DEET Autan. If you want to use citronella remember that it must be applied very frequently (hourly) to be effective. If you are a target for insect bites or develop lumps quite soon after being bitten, carry an Aspivenin kit.

Prickly heat This a common intensely itchy rash, avoided by frequent washing and by wearing loose clothing. It is cured by allowing skin to dry off through use of powder – and spending a few nights in an a/c hotel.

Remember that **rabies** is endemic throughout certain parts of India, so avoid dogs that are behaving strangely and cover your toes at night from the vampire bats, which also carry the disease. If you are bitten by a domestic or wild animal, do not leave things to chance: scrub the wound with soap and water and/ or disinfectant, try to at least determine the animal's ownership, where possible and seek medical assistance at once. The course of treatment depends on whether you have already been satisfactorily vaccinated against rabies. If you have (and this is worthwhile if you are spending lengths of time in developing countries) then some further doses of vaccine are all that is required. If you are not already vaccinated then anti-rabies serum (immunoglobulin) may be required in addition. It is important to finish the course of treatment.

STDs Unprotected sex can spread HIV, hepatitis B and C, gonorrhoea (green discharge), chlamydia (nothing to see but may cause painful urination and later female infertility), painful recurrent herpes, syphilis and warts, just to name a few. You can cut down the risk by using condoms, a Femidom or avoiding sex altogether.

Sunburn Make sure you protect yourself from the sun with high-factor sun screen and don't forget to wear a hat.

Ticks These usually attach themselves to the lower parts of the body often after walking in areas where cattle have grazed. They swell up as they start to suck blood. The important thing is to remove them gently, so that they do not leave their head parts in your skin, because this can cause a nasty allergic reaction later. Do not use petrol, Vaseline, lighted cigarettes, etc to remove the tick, but, with a pair of tweezers remove the gently by gripping it at the attached (head) end and rock it out in very much the same way that a tooth is extracted.

Tropical flies Certain tropical flies which lay their eggs under the skin of sheep and cattle also occasionally do the same thing to humans with the unpleasant result that a maggot grows under the skin and pops up as a boil or pimple. The best way to remove these is to cover the boil with oil, Vaseline or nail varnish to stop the maggot breathing, then to squeeze it out gently the next day.

If you get ill
Contact your embassy or consulate for a list of doctors and dentists who speak your language, or at least some English. Good-quality healthcare is available in the larger centres but it can be expensive, especially hospitalization; see the list below. Make sure you have adequate insurance.

Ahmedabad
Civil Hospital, Asarwa, T079-2268 3721.
CIMS Hospital, T079-3010 1908, 982-4450 000 (emergency).

Alappuzha (Alleppey) and around
District Hospital, T0477-225 3324.

Almora
District Hospital, Chowk Bazar, T05962-230064 (male)/230426 (female).

Anjuna
St Michael's Pharmacy, Main Rd, Sorranto, T0832-227 4439, open 24 hrs. See Mapusa, below.

Arunachal Pradesh (Itanagar-Naharlagun)
RK Mission Hospital, near Ganga Market, Itanagar-Naharlagun, T0360-221 2263.

Assam (Guwahati)
Down Town Hospital, GS Rd, Dispur, Guwahati, T0361-233 1003, http://downtownhospitals.in. Largest hospital in the Northeast.

Aurangabad
Seth Nandlal Dhoot Hospital, Chikhalthana, T0240-248 9001. Apex, Jalna Rd, T0240-232 6530.

Benaulim
Late-night pharmacy near the main crossroads.

Bhopal
Carewell Hospital, Mahadev Mandir Rd, T0755-254 3983. Mayo Hospital, Shahjahanabad, T0755-645 5541.

Bhubaneswar
Capital Hospital, Unit 6, T0674-239 1983, http://capitalhospital.nic.in, best government hospital in town; Kalinga Hospital, Nandan Kanan Rd, T0674-230 0570, www.kalingahospital.com, private hospital.

Bikaner
PBM Hospital, Hospital Rd, T0151-226331.

Bundi
City Hospital, T941-76060.

Candolim and Sinquerim beaches
Primary Health Centre, Aguada–Siolim Rd, T0832-248 9035. See Mapusa, below.

Chandigarh
General Hospital, T0172-266 301. There are also 24-hr chemists.

Chennai
St John's Ambulance, T044-2819 4630, 24-hr. All-in-One, 34 Nowroji Rd, T044-2641 1911, 0400-2000, 0900-1200 Sun. Chemists: Apollo Pharmacy, many branches including 320 Anna Salai, Teynampet; 52 Usman Rd South, T Nagar. SS Day & Night Chemists, 106D, 1st Main Rd, Anna Nagar. Hospitals: Apollo Hospital, 21 Greams Rd, T044-6060 1066. CSI Rainey, Old Washermanpet, T044-4040 5050, with 24-hr pharmacy. National Hospital, 2nd Line Beach Rd, T044-3303 8493.

Coimbatore
Government Hospital, Trichy Rd.

Coonoor
Lawley Hospital, Mt Rd, T0423-223 1050.

Dehra Dun
Doon Hospital, Amrit Kaur Rd, T0135-265 9355.

Delhi
For hospitals, embassies and high commissions have lists of recommended doctors and dentists. Doctors approved by IAMAT (International Association for Medical Assistance to Travellers) are listed in a directory. Casualty and emergency wards in both private and government hospitals are open 24 hrs. All hospitals listed have 24-hr chemists. Apollo Hospital, Indraprastha, T011-269 5858. Ram Manohar Lohia, Willingdon Crescent, T011-2336 5525, 24-hr A&E. Bara Hindu Rao, Sabzi Mandi, T011-2391 9476. JP Narayan, J Nehru Marg, Delhi Gate, T011-2323 0733. Safdarjang General, Sri Aurobindo Marg, T011-2616 5060. S Kripalani, Shaheed Bhagat Singh Mg, Connaught Pl, T011-2336 3728. Chemists: In Connaught Pl: Nath Brothers, G-2, off Marina Arcade; Chemico, H-45. There are branches of Apollo Pharmacy dotted throughout city.

Dharamshala and McLeodganj
Delek Hospital, T01892-220053/223381, often foreign volunteer doctors, good for dentistry. **Men Tse Khang** (Tibetan Medical Institute) T01892-222484, Gangchen Kyishong, for Tibetan herbal medicine. **Zonal Hospital**, T01892-222133. **Dr Dolma's** and **Dr Dhonden's** clinics, near McLeodganj Bazar for Tibetan treatment.

Diu
Manesh Medical Store is a pharmacy with a doctor in the building.

Fort Kochi and Ernakulam
General Hospital, Hospital Rd, Ernakulam, T0484-238 1768. **Govt Hospital**, Fort Kochi, T0484-283 6544. On MG Rd: **City**, T0484-236 1809, and **Medical Trust Hospital**, T0484-235 8001, have 24-hr pharmacies. **City Dental Clinic**, T0484-236 8164.

Haridwar
District Hospital, Upper Rd, T01334-228470. **RK Mission**, Kankhal, T01334-247 1416. **Chemists**: on Railway and Upper Rd.

Hyderabad-Secunderabad
Continental Hospital, Gachibowli, T040-6700 0000. **Care Hospitals**, Banjara Hills, T040-6725 6666.

Indore
Lifeline Hospital, Meghdoot Gdns, T0731-257 5611. **CHL Apollo Hospital**, Manikbagh Rd, T0731-254 9090. Recommended. **Chemists**: on Maharani Rd.

Jaipur
Hospital, Bhawani Singh Rd, T0141-256 6251. **Jaipur Hospital**, T0141-274 2557. **SMS Hospital**, Sawai Ram Singh Marg, T0141-274 2557.

Jammu
Hospital, T0191-254 7637.

Jodhpur
Jodhpur MG Hospital, T0291-636437.

Kanha National Park
Basic hospitals are **Mandla Civil Hospital** and **Katra Mission Hospital**. Only basic first aid at Mukki, Mocha and Baihar.

Kanniyakumari
General Hospital, off Main Rd, T04652-248505.

Kodaikanal
Van Allan Hospital, T04542-241273, is recommended. Consultations (non-emergency): Mon-Fri 0930-1200, 1530-1630. Sat 1000-1200.

Clean and efficient, good doctors. **Government Hospital**, T04542-241292.

Kolkata
Apollo Gleneagles Hospital, 5B Canel Circular Rd, T033-2320 3040/2122, www.apollogleneagles.in. **Woodlands Hospital**, 8B Alipore Rd, T033-2456 7075-9, www.woodlandshospital.in.

Kollam (Quilon)
District Hospital, T0474-276 8667.

Kota
MBS Hospital, T0744-232 6000.

Kottayam and Kumarakom
District Hospital, T0481-256 3611.

Kovalam and nearby resorts
Emergency assistance either through your hotel or from **Government Hospital** in Thiruvananthapuram. **Upasana Hospital**, near *Le Meridien* gate, T0471-248 0632, has an experienced English-speaking doctor.

Kozhikode (Calicut)
General Hospital, T0495-236 5917.

Leh
SNM Hospital, T01982-252014, open 0900-1700, is well-equipped (also for advice on mountain sickness), after hours, T01982-253629.

Lonavla
Yash Hospital, T02114-324917.

Madurai
Christian Mission Hospital, East Veli St, T0452-232 6458. **Grace Kennet Hospital**, 34 Kennet Rd, T0452-260 1849.

Manali and around
Lady Willingdon Hospital, T01902-252379.

Mandi
Zonal Hospital, T01905-222177.

Manipur (Imphal)
Shija Hospital, T0385-205 5584, www.shija hospitals.com, in Lamphelpat is the best in town.

Mapusa
Ambulance: T0832-226 2372. **Galaxy Hospital**, T0832-226 6666 (emergency). **Vision Hospital**, T0832-225 6788. **Pharmacies**: Including Bardez Bazar; Drogaria, near the Swiss Chapel, open 24 hrs.

Margao
Apollo Victor Hospital, T0832-272 8888; **Holy Spirit Pharmacy**, 24 hrs.

Meghalaya (Shillong)
Nazareth Hospital, Laitumukhrah, T0364-222 4052, www.nazarethshillong.in.

Mizoram (Aizawl)
Presbyterian Hospital, Durtland (7 km), T0389-236 1185.

Mumbai
The larger hotels usually have a house doctor, the others invariably have a doctor on call. Ask hotel staff for prompt action. The telephone directory lists hospitals and GPs. Admission to private hospitals may not be allowed without a large cash advance (eg Rs 50,000). Insurers' guarantees may not be sufficient. **Prince Aly Khan Hospital**, Nesbit Rd near the harbour, T022-2377 7800/900. **Jaslok Hospital**, on Peddar Rd, T022-6657 3333; **Hinduja Hospital**, T022-2445 1515; **Lilavati Hospital**, in Bandra (W), T022-2675 1000 are recommended. Chemists: several open day/night especially opposite Bombay Hospital. **Wordell**, Stadium House, Churchgate; **New Royal Chemist**, New Marine Lines.

Munnar
Excellent **Tata General Hospital**, on the north edge of town on the Rajamalai Rd, T04865-230270.

Mussoorie and Landour
Civil Hospital at Landour, T0135-263 2891. **Community**, South Rd, T0135-263 2053. **St Marys**, Gun Hill Rd, T0135-263 3845.

Nainital
Ambulance: T05942-235022. **BD Pande Govt Hospital**, Mallital, T05942-235012.

Nubra Valley
There is a health centre at Deskit and a dispensary at Panamik.

Palitana
Mansinhji Govt Hospital, Main Rd, T02848-252175.

Panjim
Goa Medical College, close to Panjim at Bambolim, T0832-245 8700, is very busy; **MENEZES Poly Clinic**, Altinho, T0832-222 5918.

Patna
Patna Medical College Hospital, Ashok Raj Path E, T0612-267 0132.

Puducherry
General Hospital, rue Victor Simone, T0413-233 6050; **JIPMER**, T0413-229 6562. **Ashram Dispensary**, Depuis St, near seaside.

Pune
Ruby Hall Clinic, T020-6645 5100. **Sassoon** (Govt), JP Narayan Rd, T020-2612 8000.

Pushkar
Shyama Hospital, Heloj Rd, T94143 14416.

Raipur
Government Medical College Hospital, T0771-251 1101. Private **MMI**, T0771-241 2310.

Rishikesh
AIMS Hospital, Vibhadra Rd, T0135-245 6277. **Nirmal Ashram**, T0135-243 2215.

Shimla
Tara Hospital, The Ridge, T0177-280 3275. **Dr Puri**, Mehghana Complex, The Mall, T0177-280 1936, speaks fluent English, is efficient, and very reasonable.

Sikkim
Central Referral Hospital, 5th Mile, Tandong, Gangtok, T03592-231138.

Thanjavur
Medical College Hospital, T04362-240951.

Thekkady
Kumily Central Hospital, T04869-222045, open 0900-1300 and 1630-2000, 24-hr call out for emergencies.

Thiruvananthapuram
Many chemists, near hospitals; a few near Statue Junction. **General Hospital**, Palayam, T0471-230 3870, **Ramakrishna Ashrama Hospital**, Sasthamangalam, T0471-272 2125, **Cosmopolitan Hospital**, T0471-252 1252.

Thrissur (Trichur)
Amala Institute of Medical Sciences, Amalanagar (9 km, along the Guruvayur Rd), T0487-230 4000. Recommended for medicine, surgery.

Tirunelveli
Hospital in High Ground, Palayamkottai.

Udaipur
Aravali Hospital (private), 332 Ambamata Main Rd, opposite **Charak Hostel**, T0294-243 0222, very clean, professional. Recommended. **Chemist** on Hospital Rd.

Udhagamandalam (Ooty)
Govt Hospital, Hospital Rd, T0423-244 2212.

Vadodara
SSG Hospital, Anadpur, T0265-242 3122.

Varanasi

Heritage Hospital, Lanka (near BHU main entrance), T0542-236 8888, www.heritage hospitals.in. Many hotels have a doctor on call.

Vellore

CMC Hospital, Ida Scudder Rd, T0416-228 2010.

Yercaud

Govt Hospital, 1 km from bus stand; **Providence Hospital**, on road to Lady's Seat, T04281-222505.

Websites

Blood Care Foundation (UK), www.bloodcare. org.uk A Kent-based charity 'dedicated to the provision of screened blood and resuscitation fluids in countries where these are not readily available'. They will dispatch certified non-infected blood of the right type to your hospital/ clinic. The blood is flown in from various centres around the world.

British Travel Health Association (UK), www.btha.org This is the official website of an organization of travel health professionals.

Fit for Travel, www.fitfortravel.scot.nhs.uk This site from Scotland provides a quick A-Z of vaccine and travel health advice requirements for each country.

Foreign and Commonwealth Office (FCO) (UK), www.fco.gov.uk This is a key travel advice site, with useful information on the country, people, climate and lists the UK embassies/consulates. The site also promotes the concept of 'know before you go' and encourages travel insurance and appropriate travel health advice. It has links to Department of Health travel advice site.

The Health Protection Agency, www.hpa. org.uk Up-to-date malaria advice guidelines for travel around the world. It gives specific advice about the right drugs for each location. It also has useful information for those who are pregnant, suffering from epilepsy or planning to travel with children.

Medic Alert (UK), www.medicalalert.com This is the website of the foundation that produces bracelets and necklaces for those with existing medical problems. Once you have ordered your bracelet/necklace you write your key medical details on paper inside it, so that if you collapse, a medic can identify you as having epilepsy or a nut allergy, etc.

Travel Screening Services (UK), www.travel screening.co.uk A private clinic dedicated to integrated travel health. The clinic gives vaccine, travel health advice, email and SMS text vaccine reminders and screens returned travellers for tropical diseases.

World Health Organization, www.who.int The WHO site has links to the *WHO Blue Book* on travel advice. This lists the diseases in different regions of the world. It describes vaccination schedules and makes clear which countries have yellow fever vaccination certificate requirements and malarial risk.

Books

International Travel and Health, World Health Organization Geneva.

Lankester, T, *The Travellers Good Health Guide*.

Warrell, D and Anderson, A (eds), *Expedition Medicine (The Royal Geographic Society)*.

Young Pelton, R, Aral, C and Dulles, W, *The World's Most Dangerous Places*.

Insurance

Insurance is strongly recommended and policies are very reasonable. If you have financial restraints, the most important aspect of any insurance policy is medical care and repatriation. Ideally you want to make sure you are covered for personal items too. Read the small print before heading off so you are aware of what is covered and what is not, what is required to submit a claim and what to do in the event of an emergency. Always buy insurance before setting out as your options will be more limited and generally quite costly once you've departed from your home country.

Internet

Virtually all business-grade hotels and many mid-range and budget places offer a Wi-Fi connection; mostly offered free, though many upmarket places still gouge an extra US$25 a day to turn the signal on. You can also find Wi-Fi at an increasing number of restaurants, bars, coffee shops, traveller hangouts, major airports and certain multinational fast food outlets.

Mobile data in India is cheap by world standards, if you get a local mobile connection, though it's never guaranteed that you'll be able to pick up a strong signal. In some places you may have no option but to fall back on a local internet café. Bear in mind that power cuts and connection failures are a fact of life: compose long emails in Word rather than risk an hour-long missive going up in smoke when the power cuts out.

Language

See also page 1395.
Hindi, spoken as a mother tongue by over 400 million people, is India's official language. The use of English is also enshrined in the Constitution for a wide range of official purposes, notably communication between Hindi and non-Hindi speaking states. The most widely spoken Indo-Aryan languages are: Bengali (8.3%), Marathi (8%), Urdu (5.7%), Gujarati (5.4%), Oriya (3.7%) and Punjabi (3.2%). Among the Dravidian languages Telugu (8.2%), Tamil (7%), Kannada (4.2%) and Malayalam (3.5%) are the most widely used. Most of these languages have their own scripts. In all, there are 15 major and several hundred minor languages and dialects.

English is widely spoken in towns and cities and even in quite remote villages it is usually not difficult to find someone who speaks at least a little English. Outside of major tourist sites, other European languages are almost completely unknown. The accent in which English is spoken is often affected strongly by the mother tongue of the speaker and there have been changes in common grammar which sometimes make it sound unusual. Many of these changes have become standard Indian English usage, as valid as any other varieties of English used around the world. It is possible to study a number of Indian languages at language centres.

LGBT travellers

Apart from a 3-year blip between 2009 and 2012, sex between people of the same gender has been outlawed in India since 1860, and this deeply conservative country is generally not a great place to be out and proud. Even though India has a substantial LGB population (over 2.5 million, a figure widely presumed to mask a vast number who hide their sexuality for fear of violent discrimination), outside the main cities and tourist-friendly areas such as Goa and Kerala, homophobia is endemic. Outright harassment is rare, but overt displays of affection between homosexuals (as indeed between heterosexuals) are likely to cause offence. Although it is common to see young males holding hands in public, this rarely indicates a gay relationship and is usually an expression of friendship. You can connect to local gay communities via websites such as www. gaydelhi.org and www.gaybombay.org. For gay-and lesbian-focused tour operators, try www. rajasthanwithwire.com, www.purpledrag.com, www.indjapink.com and www.pinkvibgyor.com.

Media

International **newspapers** (mainly English language) are sold in the bookshops of top hotels in major cities and occasionally by booksellers elsewhere. India has a large and lively English language press. They all have extensive analysis of contemporary Indian and some international issues. The major papers now have websites, excellent for keeping track of events, news and weather.

The best known are the traditionalist *The Hindu*, www.hinduonline.com. *The Hindustan Times*, www.hindustantimes.com, the slightly more tabloid-establishment *Times of India*, www.timesofindia.com, and *The Statesman*, www.thestatesman.org. *The Economic Times* is good for world coverage. *The Telegraph*, www. telegraphindia.com, has good foreign coverage. *The Indian Express*, www.indianexpress.com, stands out as being consistently critical of the Congress Party and the government. *The Asian Age* is now published in the UK and India simultaneously and gives good coverage of Indian and international affairs. Of the news weeklies, some of the most widely read are current affairs *India Today*, *Frontline* and *The Week*, which are journals in the *Time* or *Newsweek* mould. *Business Today* is of course economy-based, while *Outlook* has a broader remit and has good general interest features. There is also *Outlook Traveller*, probably the best of the domestic travel titles.

India's national **radio** and **television** network, *Doordarshan*, broadcasts in national and regional languages but things have moved on. The advent of cable TV has brought endless replays of ancient cricket matches, Bollywood music videos and vapid soap operas to the most remote corners of the country, and there are over 500 local broadcast television stations – each state has its own local-language current affairs broadcaster plus normally at least one other channel for entertainment. Even modest hotels in small towns now come with a cable connection as standard, making it easy for travellers to keep in touch with world news via *CNN* and *BBC World*, to waste time with Hollywood movies – even to learn yoga (see box, page 169).

Money matters

It can be difficult to use torn or very worn notes. Check notes when you are given them and refuse any that are damaged.

Request some Rs 100 and 50 notes. Rs 500 (can be mistaken for Rs 100) notes reduce 'wallet bulge' but can be difficult to change. A good supply of small denomination notes always comes in handy for bus tickets, cheap meals and tipping. Remember that if offered a large note, the recipient will never have any change.

It can be worth carrying a few clean, new sterling or dollar notes for use where traveller's cheques and credit cards are not accepted. It is likely to be quite a while before euro notes are widely accepted.

Money

US\$1= Rs 66.08, €1=Rs 70.98, £1= Rs 99.37 (Nov 2015). Indian currency is the Indian Rupee (Re/Rs). It is **not** possible to purchase these before you arrive. If you want cash on arrival it is best to get it at the airport bank (either in the UK or once in India), although see if an ATM is available as airport rates are not very generous. Rupee notes are printed in denominations of Rs 1000, 500, 100, 50, 20, 10. The rupee is divided into 100 paise. Coins are minted in denominations of Rs 10, 5, Rs 2, Rs 1 and (the increasingly uncommon) 50 paise. **Note** Carry money in a money belt worn under clothing. Have a small amount in an easily accessible place.

Currency cards

If you don't want to carry lots of cash, prepaid currency cards allow you to preload money from your bank account, fixed at the day's exchange rate. They look like a credit or debit card and are issued by specialist money changing companies, such as **Travelex** and **Caxton FX**. You can top up and check your balance by phone, online and sometimes by text.

Credit cards

Major credit cards are increasingly accepted in the main centres, though in smaller cities and towns it is still rare to be able to pay by credit card. Payment by credit card can sometimes be more expensive than payment by cash, whilst some credit card companies charge a premium on cash withdrawals. **Visa** and **MasterCard** have an ever-growing number of ATMs in major cities and several banks offer withdrawal facilities for Cirrus and Maestro cardholders. It is however easy to obtain a cash advance against a credit card. Railway reservation centres in major cities take payment for train tickets by Visa card which

can be very quick as the queue is short, although they cannot be used for Tourist Quota tickets.

ATMs

By far the most convenient method of accessing money, ATMs are all over India, usually attended by security guards, with most banks offering some services to holders of overseas cards. Banks whose ATMs will issue cash against Cirrus and Maestro cards, as well as Visa and MasterCard, include **Bank of Baroda**, **Citibank**, **HDFC**, **HSBC**, **ICICI**, **IDBI**, **Punjab National Bank**, **State Bank of India (SBI)**, **Standard Chartered** and **UTI**. A withdrawal fee is usually charged by the issuing bank on top of the conversion charges applied by your own bank. There is a Rs 10,000 withdrawal limit. Fraud prevention measures quite often result in travellers having their cards blocked by the bank when unexpected overseas transactions occur; advise your bank of your travel plans before leaving.

Traveller's cheques (TCs)

TCs are almost obsolete, shops and restaurants won't change them, but they do provide peace of mind against theft. Denominations of US\$50 and US\$100 are preferable, with a few of US\$20 to increase your options. American Express or Visa US dollar TCs are recommended. Several banks charge a high fixed commission for changing TCs because they don't really want the bother. Some establishments may ask to see a passport and the customer's record of purchase before accepting. Keep the original purchase slip in a separate place to the TCs and make a photocopy for security. The better hotels will normally change TCs for their guests (often at a poor rate).

Changing money

The **State Bank of India** and several others in major towns are authorized to deal in foreign exchange. Some give cash against Visa/MasterCard (eg **ANZ**). American Express cardholders can use their cards to get either cash or TCs in Mumbai. The larger cities have licensed money changers with offices usually in the commercial sector. Changing money through unauthorized dealers is illegal. Premiums on the currency black market are very small and highly risky. Large hotels change money 24 hrs a day for guests, but banks often give a substantially better rate of exchange. It is best to exchange money on arrival at the airport bank or the Thomas Cook counter. Many international flights arrive during the night and it is generally far easier and less time consuming to change money at the airport than in the city. You should be given a foreign currency encashment certificate when you change money through a bank or authorized dealer; ask for one if it is not automatically given. It allows you to change Indian rupees back to your own currency on departure. It also enables you to use rupees to pay hotel bills or buy air tickets for which payment in foreign exchange may be required. The certificates are only valid for 3 months.

Cost of living

The cost of living in India remains well below that in the West. The average wage per capita is about Rs 68,700 per year (US$1200). Manual, unskilled labourers (women are often paid less than men), farmers and others in rural areas earn considerably less. However, thanks to booming global demand for workers who can provide cheaper IT and technology support functions and many Western firms transferring office functions or call centres to India, salaries in certain sectors have sky rocketed. An IT specialist can earn an average Rs 500,000 per year and upwards – a rate that is rising by around 15% a year.

Cost of travelling

Most food, accommodation and public transport, especially rail and bus, is exceptionally cheap, although the price of basic food items such as rice, lentils, tomatoes and onions have skyrocketed. There is a widening range of moderately priced but clean hotels and restaurants outside the big cities, making it possible to get a great deal for your money.

Budget travellers sharing a room, taking public transport, avoiding souvenir stalls and paid attractions and eating nothing but rice and dhal can get away with a budget of Rs 600-800 (about

US$9-12 or £6-8) a day. This sum leaps up if you drink alcohol (still cheap by European standards at about US$2, £1 or Rs 100 a bottle if you buy from a shop), smoke foreign-brand cigarettes or want to have your own wheels (you can expect to spend between Rs 250 and 400 to hire a scooter per day). Those planning to stay in fairly comfortable hotels and use taxis sightseeing should budget at US$50-80 (£30-50) a day. Then again you could always check into **Ananda Spa** or the **Taj Falaknuma** for Christmas and notch up an impressive US$600 (£350) bill on your B&B alone.

India can be a great place to pick and choose, save a little on basic accommodation and then treat yourself to the type of meal you could only dream of affording back home. Also, be prepared to spend a fair amount more in Mumbai, Hyderabad, Bengaluru (Bangalore) and Chennai, where not only is the cost of living significantly higher but where it's worth coughing up extra for a half-decent room: penny-pinch by the beach when you'll be spending precious little time indoors anyway.

A newspaper costs Rs 5-10 and breakfast for two with coffee can come to as little as Rs 150 in a basic 'hotel', but if you intend to eat banana pancakes or pasta in a backpacker restaurant, you can expect to pay more like Rs 200-400 a plate.

Opening hours

Banks are open Mon-Fri 1030-1430, Sat 1030-1230. **Government offices** open Mon-Fri 0930-1700, Sat 0930-1300 (some open on alternate Sat only). **Post offices** open Mon-Fri 1000-1700, often shutting for lunch, and Sat mornings. **Shops** open Mon-Sat 0930-1800, or often later. Bazars keep longer hours. Top hotels sometimes have a 24-hr money changing service.

Post

Indian post is cheap but unreliable – postcards home are a pure lottery – and delays are common. For the best chance of your letter getting delivered, use a post office where you can hand over mail for franking across the counter, or a top hotel post box. Valuable items should only be sent by registered mail – or by private courier.

Airmail services to Europe, Africa and Australia take at least a week and a little longer for the Americas. Speed post (which takes about 4 days to the UK) is available from major towns. Speed post to the UK costs Rs 955 for the first 250g sent and an additional Rs 105 for each 250g thereafter.

If you're sending a **parcel** home, the only two viable services are Air Mail and the slower and slightly cheaper Surface Air Lifted (SAL). You'll first need to get your parcel stitched into the obligatory cotton packaging – packing services located around major post offices charge around Rs 150-200 per parcel. You address the parcel, obtain stamps from a separate counter, stick stamps and a customs form to the parcel with the provided glue (write 'No commercial value' if returning used clothes, books etc.), then hand it over to the Parcels Counter, obtain a registration slip, and cross your fingers. Costs vary by destination and are normally displayed on a board beside the counter. Delivery can take up to 2 months.

Specialist shippers deal with larger items, normally around US$150 per cubic metre. Courier services (eg **DHL**) are available in the larger towns. Government emporia or shops in the larger hotels will send purchases home if the items are difficult to carry.

Safety

Personal security

In general the threats to personal security for travellers in India are remarkably small. However, incidents of petty theft and violence directed specifically at tourists have been on the increase so care is necessary in some places, and basic common sense needs to be used with respect to looking after valuables. Follow the same precautions you would when at home. There have been much-reported incidents of severe sexual assault in Delhi, Kolkata and some more rural areas in the last few years. Avoid wandering alone outdoors late at night in these places. During daylight hours be careful in remote places, especially when alone. If you are under threat, scream loudly. Be cautious before accepting food or drink from casual acquaintances, as it may be drugged – though note that Indians on a long train journey will invariably try to share their snacks with you, and balance caution with the opportunity to interact.

The left-wing Maoist extremist Naxalites are active in east central India. They have a long history of conflict with state and national authorities, including attacks on police and government officials. The Naxalites have not specifically targeted Westerners, but have attacked symbolic targets including Western companies. As a general rule, travellers are advised to be vigilant in the lead up to and on days of national significance, such as Republic Day (26 Jan) and Independence Day (15 Aug) as militants have in the past used such occasions to mount attacks.

Following a major explosion on the Delhi to Lahore (Pakistan) train in 2007 and the Mumbai attacks in Nov 2008, increased security has been implemented on many trains and stations. Similar measures at airports may cause delays for passengers so factor this into your timing. Also check your airline's website for up-to-date information on luggage restrictions.

That said, in the great majority of places visited by tourists, violent crime and personal attacks are extremely rare.

Travel advice

It is better to seek advice from your consulate than from travel agencies. Before you travel you can contact: **British Foreign & Commonwealth Office Travel Advice Unit**, T0845-850 2829, www.fco.gov.uk. **US State Department's Bureau of Consular Affairs**, USA, T202-647 1488, www.travel.state.gov. **Australian Department of Foreign Affairs Canberra**, Australia, T02-6261 3305, www.smartraveller.gov.au. Canadian official advice is on www.voyage.gc.ca.

Theft

Theft is not uncommon. It is best to keep TCs, passports and valuables with you at all times. Don't regard hotel rooms as being automatically safe; even hotel safes don't guarantee secure storage. Avoid leaving valuables near open windows even when you are in the room. Use your own padlock in a budget hotel when you go out. Pickpockets and other thieves operate in the big cities; crowded areas are particularly high risk. Take special care of your belongings when getting on or off public transport.

When travelling by train, especially overnight, lock your luggage to the metal loops under the seat. Most thefts on trains occur in non-a/c sleeper class carriages – particularly on tourist heavy routes such as Goa–Hampi and Delhi–Varanasi–Kolkata. Travelling bags and cases should be made of tough material, and external pockets (both on bags and on clothing) should never be used for carrying either money or important documents. Strong locks for travelling cases are invaluable, and a leather strap around a case gives extra security. Some travellers prefer to reserve upper berths, which offer some added protection against theft and also the benefit of allowing daytime sleeping. If you put your bags on the upper berth during the day, beware of fellow passengers climbing up for a 'sleep'.

If you have items stolen, they should be reported to the police as soon as possible. Keep a separate record of vital documents, including passport details and numbers of TCs. Larger hotels will be able to assist in contacting and dealing with the police. Dealings with the police can be very difficult and in the worst regions, such as Bihar, even dangerous. The paperwork involved in reporting losses can be time consuming and irritating and your own documentation (eg passport and visas) may be demanded.

In some states the police occasionally demand bribes, though you should not assume that if procedures move slowly you are automatically being expected to offer a bribe. The traffic police are tightening up on traffic offences in some places. They have the right to make on-the-spot fines for speeding and illegal parking. If you face a fine, insist on a receipt. If you have to go to a police station, try to take someone with you.

If you face really serious problems (eg in connection with a driving accident), the official advice is to contact your consular office as quickly as possible. You should ensure you always have your international driving licence and motorbike or car documentation with you.

Confidence tricksters are particularly common where people are on the move, notably around railway stations or places where budget tourists gather. A common plea is some sudden and desperate calamity; sometimes a letter will be produced in English to back up the claim. The demands are likely to increase sharply if sympathy is shown.

Senior travellers

Travellers over 60 can take advantage of several discounts on travel, including 30% on train fares and up to 50% on some air tickets. Ask at the time of booking, since these will not be offered automatically.

Smoking

Several state governments have passed a law banning smoking in all public buildings and transport but exempting open spaces. To avoid fines, check for notices.

Student travellers

Full-time students qualify for an ISIC (International Student Identity Card) which is issued by student travel and specialist agencies (eg Usit, Campus, STA) at home. The card allows certain travel benefits such as reduced prices and concessions into certain sites. For details see www.isic.org or contact **STIC Travels**, www. stictravel.com. Those intending to study in India may get a year's student visa (see page 1392). For details of student travel insurance, see page 1383.

Telephone

The international code for India is +91.

Mobile phones

Practically all business in India is now conducted via mobile phone. Calls and mobile data are incredibly cheap by global standards – local calls cost as little as half a rupee per min – and if you're in the country for more than a couple of weeks and need to keep in touch it can definitely be worth the hassle to get a local SIM card. Arguably the best service is provided by the government carrier **BSNL/MTNL** but connecting to the service is virtually impossible for foreigners. Private companies such as **Airtel**, **Vodafone**, **Idea** and **Tata Indicom** are easier to sign up with, but the deals they offer can be befuddling and are frequently changed. To get the connection you'll need to complete a form, have a local address or receipt showing the address of your hotel, and present photocopies of your passport and visa plus 2 passport photos to an authorized reseller – most phone dealers will be able to help, and can also sell top-up. **Univercell**, www.univercell.in, and **The Mobile Store**, www.themobilestore.in, are widespread and efficient chains selling phones and SIM cards.

India is divided into a number of 'calling circles' or regions, and if you travel outside the region where your connection is based, you will pay higher 'roaming' charges for making and receiving calls, and any problems that may occur – with 'unverified' documents, for example – can be much harder to resolve.

Landlines

You can still find privately run phone booths, usually labelled on yellow boards with the letters 'PCO-STD-ISD'. You dial the call yourself, and the time and cost are displayed on a computer screen. Cheap rate (2100-0600) means long queues may form outside booths. Telephone calls from hotels are usually more expensive (check price before calling), though some will allow local calls free of charge.

A double ring repeated regularly means it is ringing; equal tones with equal pauses means engaged (similar to the UK). If calling a mobile, you're as likely to hear devotional Hindu music or Bollywood hits coming back down the line as a standard ringtone.

One disadvantage of India's tremendous rate of growth is that millions of telephone numbers go out of date every year. Current telephone directories themselves are often out of date and some of the numbers given in this book will have been changed even as we go to press. **Directory enquiries**, T197, can be helpful but works only for the local area code.

Time

India doesn't change its clocks, so from the last Sun in Oct to the last Sun in Mar the time is GMT +5½ hrs, and the rest of the year it's +4½ hrs (USA, EST +10½ hrs and +9½ hrs; Australia, EST -5½ and -4½ hrs).

Tipping

A tip of Rs 10 to a bellboy carrying luggage in a modest hotel (Rs 20 in a higher category) would be appropriate. In upmarket restaurants, a 10% tip is acceptable when service is not already included, while in places serving very cheap meals, round off the bill with small change. Indians don't normally tip taxi drivers but a small extra is welcomed. Porters at airports and railway stations often have a fixed rate displayed but will usually press for more. Ask fellow passengers what a fair rate is.

Tour operators

UK

Ace Cultural Tours, T01223-841055, www.ace culturaltours.co.uk. Expert-led cultural study tours.
Explorations Company, T01367-850566, www.explorationscompany.com. Bespoke holidays, including to the Andaman Islands and Rajasthan.
Colours Of India, T020-8347 4020, www.partnershiptravel.co.uk. Tailor-made cultural, adventure, spa and cooking tours.
Cox & Kings, T020-7873 5000, www.coxandkings.co.uk. Offer high-quality group tours, private journeys and tailor-made holidays to many

of India's regions, from the lavish to the adventurous, planned by experts.
Dragoman, T01728-861133, www.dragoman.com. Overland, adventure, camping.
Exodus, T0845-287 7408, www.exodus.co.uk. Small group overland and trekking tours.
Greaves Tours, T020-7487 9111, www.greaves india.com. Luxury, tailor-made tours using only scheduled flights. Traditional travel such as road and rail preferred to flights between major cities.
Kerala Connections, T01892-722440, www.keralaconnections.co.uk. Excellent tailor-made tours specializing in South India, including Lakshadweep, with great homestays.
MAHout, T01295-758 150, www.mahoutuk.com. Specializes in boutique hotels.
Master Travel, T020-7501 6741, www.master travel.co.uk. Organizes professional study tours in fields including education and healthcare.
Pettitts, T01892-515966, www.pettitts.co.uk. Unusual locations.
Spice Land Holidays Ltd, T0207-183 8963, www.spicelandholidays.com. Package and customized tours.
STA Travel, T0333-321 0099, www.statravel.co.uk. Student and young persons' travel agent.
Steppes Travel, T01285-787557, www.steppes travel.co.uk. Wildlife safaris, tiger study tours and cultural tours with strong conservation ethic.
Trans Indus, T0844 879 3960, www.transindus.com. Upmarket India travel specialists offering tailor-made and group tours and holidays.

Continental Europe
Academische Reizen, Amsterdam, T020-589 2940, www.academische reizen.nl. All-India group culture tours.
Chola Voyages, Paris, T01-4034 5564, www.cholatravels.fr.
La Maison Des Indes, Paris, T01-5681 3838, www.maisondes indes.com. Bespoke or group cultural tours.
Shoestring, Amsterdam, www.shoestring.com. Group and individual tours.

India
Aquaterra Adventures, T011-2921 2641, www.treknraft.com. Trekking, rafting, kayaking, etc, in all Indian Himalayan states.
Banyan Tours and Travels, T0124-456 3800, www.banyantours.com. Pan-Indian operator specializing in bespoke, upmarket travel, with strength in culture, heritage, adventure and wildlife.

The Blue Yonder, T0413-450 2218, www.theblue yonder.com. India's pioneers in responsible travel run wonderful half-day to multi-day trips in Puducherry, Kerala, Sikkim and Rajasthan. Enthusiastic guides and unusual destinations.

Help Tourism, Kolkata/Siliguri/Guwahati, T033-2455 0917, www.helptourism.com. Eco-tours in Assam, Arunachal and North Bengal, involving local communities.

Ibex Expeditions, New Delhi, T011-2646 0244, www.ibexexpeditions.com. Responsible tourism company for tours, safaris and treks. Founding member of the Ecotourism Society of India and award-winner for the most innovative tour operator in India.

Indebo India, New Delhi, T011-4716 5500, www.indebo.com. Customized tours and travel-related services throughout India.

Indiabeat, B-4 Vijay Path, Tilak Nagar, Jaipur, T0141-651 9797, www.indiabeat.co.uk. Specializing in dream trips and once-in-a-lifetime experiences, this British team decamped to Jaipur have great insider knowledge and insight into India.

India Someday, T090-0400 0812. Young agency based in Mumbai, organize general bespoke tours based on up-to-the-minute local knowledge.

Paradise Holidays, New Delhi, T011-4552 0735, www.paradiseholidays.com. Wide range of tailor-made tours, from cultural to wildlife.

Peter and Friends Classic Adventures, T0832-226 8467, www.classic-bike-india.com. An Indo-German company which arranges high-octane tours around South India, Rajasthan and the Himalaya and Nepal on Enfield motorbikes.

Purvi Discovery, T0373-230 1120, www.purvi web.com. Experienced in tours to Arunachal, Assam and other northeast destinations. A quality outfit with quality accommodation.

Royal Expeditions, New Delhi, T011-2623 8545, www.royalexpeditions.com. Specialist staff for customized trips, knowledgeable about options for senior travellers. Owns luxury 4WD vehicles for escorted self-drive adventures in the Himalaya, and offers sightseeing tours in classic cars in Jaipur.

Shanti Travel, T011-4607 7800, www.shanti travel.com. Tailor-made tours throughout India.

North America

Absolute Asia, New York, T1-212-627 1950, www.absolute asia.com. Luxury custom-designed tours: culinary, pilgrimage of the south, honeymoon, 'Jewish India' tour plus Tamil tour combining Tamil Nadu with Sri Lanka.

Alexander and Roberts, T1-800-221-2216, www.alexanderroberts.com. Packages include Kerala spas, houseboats and wildlife, South India and Karnataka, South India and Tamil Nadu, Goa.

Greaves Tours, T1-800-318 7801. See under UK entry, above.

Myths and Mountains, T1-800-670 6984, www.mythsandmountains.com. Culture, crafts and religion.

Original World, T1888-367 6147, www.original world.com. General and spirituality-focused tours, local experts.

Relief Riders International, T1-413-329 5876, www.reliefridersinternational.com. Unique horseback tours through the Thar Desert of Rajasthan, with guests working as support staff to a full-scale aid mission.

Sita World Travel, T1-800-421-5643, www.sita tours. com. Top-end packages like 7-day Ayurveda programmes and Trails of South India tour.

Australia and New Zealand

Adventure World, T1300-295049, www.
adventureworld.com.au. Independent tour
operator with packages from 7 nights in
Kerala. Also in Auckland, T+64-9524 5118,
www.adventureworld.co.nz.

Classic Oriental Tours, T02-9657 2020,
www.classic oriental. com.au. Travel for
groups and independent travellers, all
standards from budget to deluxe.

India Unbound, T1300-889513, www.india
unbound. com.au. Intriguing range of small-
group trips and bespoke private tours.

Intrepid Travel, T1300-797010, www.intrepid
travel.com. Cookery courses to village stays.

Peregrine Adventures, Australia, T1300-
854445, www.peregrineadventures.com.
Small group overland and trekking tours.

Tourist information

There are **Government of India** tourist offices
in the state capitals, as well as state tourist
offices (sometimes **Tourism Development
Corporations**) in some towns and places of
tourist interest. They produce their own tourist
literature, either free or sold at a nominal price,
and some also have lists of city hotels and
paying guest options. The quality of material
is improving though maps are often poor.
Many offer tours of the city, neighbouring
sights and overnight and regional packages.
Some run modest hotels and midway motels
with restaurants and may also arrange car
hire and guides. The staff in the regional and
local offices are usually helpful. Check www.
incredibleindia.org for details of India tourist
offices in your country.

Guide fees

Guides at tourist sites vary considerably in their
knowledge and ability. Government trained and
licensed guides are covered by specified fees.
Local temple and site guides should charge less.
Charges for up to 5 people for half a day are
Rs 1035, for a full day Rs 1300; for 6-15 people
for half a day Rs 1300, for a full day Rs 1700. Add
Rs 450-600 for a language other than English.

Photography

Many monuments and national parks charge
a camera fee ranging from Rs 20 to Rs100 for
still cameras, and as much as Rs 500 for video
cameras (more for professionals). Special permits
are needed from the Archaeological Survey of
India, New Delhi, for using tripods and artificial
lights. When photographing people, it is polite
to first ask; they will usually respond warmly with
smiles. Visitors often promise to send copies of
the photos – don't unless you really mean to do
so. Photography of airports, military installations,
bridges and in tribal and 'sensitive border areas',
is not permitted.

Visas and immigration

For embassies and consulates, see page 1377.
Virtually all foreign nationals, including children,
require a visa to enter India. The rules regarding
visas change frequently, and arrangements for
application and collection also vary from country
to country, so it is essential to check details and
costs with your relevant embassy or consulate.

Visa on arrival

As of 2015 India has brought 113 countries into
its visa-on-arrival scheme, which after several
bizarre false starts is – at time of writing – almost

as simple as it sounds. An e-Visa costs US$60 and is valid for a stay of up to 30 days; the visa cannot be extended, and only permits travel for tourism purposes. Apply at www.indianvisaonline.gov.in, no later than 4 days before your arrival.

How to get a visa

If you want to stay longer or travel for business or study, you'll still need to go through the traditional visa application process. Most consulates have outsourced their visa services: for up-to-date rules, prices and processing times, go to www.vfsglobal.com if you're in Europe or Australia, www.blsindia-canada.com in Canada, or www.in.ckgs.us in the USA.

Consulates remain closed on Indian national holidays. In general, it is easier (though more costly) to apply in advance by post rather than in person, to avoid long waiting times. It's wise to allow a minimum of 15 business days to get your visa – more for journalist and student visas.

Your passport needs at least 1 blank page, and to be valid for 6 months beyond the period of your visit.

If you're applying for your first India visa, there are 2 critical points to note: first, you'll need to source 2 passport photos in a non-standard 2-inch-square size; and second, the helpful checklist is not just for your benefit but an integral part of the application; you need to print and send it with your other forms.

Currently India offers close to 20 different kinds of visa, of which the most likely to be useful are:

Transit For passengers en route to another country (no more than 72 hrs in India).
Tourist Normally valid for 6 months from date of issue (not entry), though some nationalities may be granted visas for up to 10 years. Multiple entry is available, but must be requested on application form.
Business 3-6 months or up to 2 years with multiple entry. A letter from the company giving the nature of business is required.
Medical For treatment in a recognized hospital, for a restricted list of procedures. Valid for up to 1 year, allowing up to 3 entries.
Student Valid up to 1 year from the date of issue. Attach a letter of acceptance from Indian institution and an AIDS test certificate. Allow up to 3 months for approval.

Long stays All foreign visitors who stay in India for more than 180 days need to register with the Foreigners' Registration Office and get an income tax clearance exemption certificate from the Foreign Section of the Income Tax Department in Delhi, Mumbai, Kolkata or Chennai.

Visa extensions Applications should be made to the Foreigners' Regional Registration Offices at New Delhi, Mumbai, Kolkata or Chennai, or an office of the Superintendent of Police in the District Headquarters. After 6 months, you must leave India and apply for a new visa – the Nepal office is known to be difficult. Anyone staying in India for a period of more than 180 days (6 months) must register at a convenient Foreigners' Registration Office.

Permits and restricted and protected areas

Some areas are politically sensitive and subject to restrictions, including the border regions, islands, tribal areas and some Himalayan zones. Special permits are required for foreigners to visit them.

Among the Northeast States, Arunachal Pradesh currently requires foreign nationals to have a Restricted Area Permit (RAP) to enter. Since Jan 2011, special permission is no longer required for foreigns to enter Manipur, Mizoram or Nagaland. For more information, see box, page 620. For the **Andaman Islands**, permits are issued for 30 days on arrival at Port Blair, with a 15-day extension possible, see page 754. Of the **Lakshadweep Islands**, foreigners may visit Bangaram, Agatti and Kadmat only; permits from the Lakshadweep Administration, Wellingdon Island, Harbour Rd, Kochi. For **Sikkim**, permits for 30 days are issued at the border checkpoint to Sikkim and by government tourism offices; see page 598.

Work permits

Foreigners should apply to the Indian representative in their country of origin for the latest information about work permits.

Liquor permits

Periodically some Indian states have tried to enforce prohibition, Kerala being the most recent example. When applying for your visa you can ask for an All India Liquor Permit. Foreigners can also get the permit from any Government of India Tourist Office in Delhi or the state capitals.

Weights and measures

Metric is in universal use in the cities. In remote areas local measures are sometimes used. One lakh is 100,000 and 1 crore is 10 million.

Women travellers

Independent travel is still largely unheard of for Indian women. Although it is relatively safe for women to travel around India, most people find it an advantage to travel with a companion. Even then, privacy is rarely respected and there can be a lot of hassle, pressure and intrusion on your personal space, as well as some outright harassment. Backpackers setting out alone often meet like-minded travelling companions at budget hotels. Cautious women travellers recommend dying blonde hair black and wearing wedding rings, but the most important measure to ensure respect is to dress appropriately, in loose-fitting, non-see-through clothes, covering shoulders, arms and legs (such as a *salwaar kameez*, which can be made to fit in around 24 hrs for around Rs 400-800). Take advantage, too, of the gender segregation on public transport, to avoid hassle and to talk to local women. In mosques women should be covered from head to ankle. **Independent Traveller**, T0870-760 5001, www.independenttraveller.com, runs women-only tours to India.

'Eve teasing', the euphemism for physical harassment, is an unfortunate result of the sexual repression latent in Indian culture, combined with a young male population whose only access to sex education is via the dingy cybercafés. Unaccompanied women are most vulnerable in major cities, crowded bazars, beach resorts and tourist centres where men may follow them and touch them; festival nights are particularly bad for this. Women have reported that they have been molested while being measured for clothing in tailors' shops. If you are harassed, it can be effective to make a scene. Be firm and clear if you don't wish to speak to someone. The best response to staring, whether lascivious or curious, is to avert your eyes down and away. This is not the submissive gesture it might seem, but an effective tool to communicate that you have no interest in any further interaction. Aggressively staring back or confronting the person staring can be construed as a come-on. It is best to be accompanied at night, especially when travelling by rickshaw or taxi in towns. Be prepared to raise an alarm if anything unpleasant threatens.

Most railway booking offices have separate women's ticket queues or ask women to go to the head of the general queue. Some buses have seats reserved for women. See also page 1376.

Working in India

See also Visas and immigration, above. It is best to arrange voluntary work well in advance with organizations in India (addresses are given in some towns, eg Delhi, Darjeeling, Dharamshala, Kolkata and Leh); alternatively, contact an organization abroad.

Students may spend part of their year off helping in a school or teaching English

Voluntary work

Many companies offer tours that include an element of volunteer work. Before signing up, be warned that the 'voluntourism' industry is rife with unnecessary projects conjured up by the agencies themselves and foisted upon destination communities, regardless of whether or not they are needed. Research carefully to find a project that will be right for the community as well as yourself. Charitable organizations in India including **Share and Care** and **Salaam Baalak** (see page 1375) sometimes take volunteers.

In the UK
i to i, www.i-to-i.com.
International Voluntary Service, www.vso.org.uk.
Volunteer Work Information Service, www.workingabroad.com.

In the USA
Amerispan, www.amerispan.com.

In Australia
Australian Volunteers International, www.australianvolunteers.com.

Footnotes

Language

Hindi words and phrases

Pronunciation

a as in *ah*   i as in *bee*
nasalized vowels are shown as an *un*
o as in *oh*   u as *oo* in book

Basics

Hello, good morning, goodbye *namaste*
Thank you/no thank you *dhanyavad* or *shukriya/*
nahin shukriya
Excuse me, sorry *maf kijiye*
Yes/no *ji han/ji nahin*
Never mind/that's all right *koi bat nahin*

Questions

What is your name? *apka nam kya hai?*
My name is ... *mera nam... Hai*
Pardon? *phir bataiye?*
How are you? *kya hal hai?*
I am well, thanks, and you? *main thik hun, aur ap?*
Not very well *main thik nahin hun*
Where is the...? *kahan hai...?*
Who is? *kaun hai?*
What is this? *yeh kya hai?*

Shopping

How much? *Kitna?*
That makes (20) rupees *(bis) rupaye*
That is very expensive! *bahut mahanga hai!*
Make it a bit cheaper! *thora kam kijiye!*

The hotel

What is the room charge? *kiraya kitna hai?*
Please show the room *kamra dikhaiye*
Is there an air-conditioned room? *kya a/c*
kamra hui?
Is there hot water? *garam pani hai?*
... a bathroom/fan/ mosquito net... *bathroom/*
pankha/machhar dani
Is there a large room? *bara kamra hai?*
Please clean it *saf karwa dijiye*
Are there clean sheets/blanket? *saf chadaren/*
kambal hain?
Bill please *bill dijiye*

Travel

Where's the railway station? *railway station*
kahan hai?
How much is the ticket to Agra? *Agra ka ticket*
kitne ka hai?

When does the Agra bus leave? *Agra bus kab jaegi?*
How much? *Kitna?*
Left/right *baien/dahina*
Go straight on *sidha chaliye*
Nearby *nazdik*
Please wait here *yahan thahariye*
Please come at 8 *ath bajai ana*
Quickly *jaldi*
Stop *rukiye*

Restaurants

Please show the menu *menu dikhaiye*
No chillies please *mirch nahin dalna*
...sugar/milk/ice ...*chini/ doodh/baraf*
A bottle of water please *ek botal pani dijiye*
Sweet/savoury *mitha/namkin*
Spoon, fork, knife *chamach, kanta, chhuri*

Time and days

right now	*abhi*
month	*mahinal*
morning	*suba*
year	*sal*
afternoon	*dopahar*
evening	*sham*
night	*rat*
today	*aj*
tomorrow/yesterday	*kal/kal*
day	*din*
week	*hafta*
Sunday	*ravivar*
Monday	*somvar*
Tuesday	*mangalvarl*
Wednesday	*budhvar*
Thursday	*virvar*
Friday	*shukravar*
Saturday	*shanivar*

Numbers

1	*ek*	2	*do*
3	*tin*	4	*char*
5	*panch*	6	*chhai*
7	*sat*	8	*ath*
9	*nau*	10	*das*
11	*gyara*	12	*barah*
13	*terah*	14	*chaudah*
15	*pandrah*	16	*solah*
17	*satrah*	18	*atharah*
19	*unnis*	20	*bis*

100/200	*sau/do sau*
1000/2000	*hazar/do hazar*
100,000	*lakh*

Basic vocabulary

Words such as airport, bank, bathroom, bus, doctor, embassy, ferry, hotel, hospital, juice, police, restaurant, station, stamp, taxi, ticket, train are used locally though often pronounced differently eg *daktarl*, *haspatall*.

and	*aur*
big	*bara*
café/food stall	*dhaba/hotel*
chemist	*dawai ki dukan*
clean	*saf*
closed	*band*
cold	*thanda*
day	*din*
dirty	*ganda*
English	*angrezi*
excellent	*bahut achha*
food/ to eat	*khana*
hot (spicy)	*jhal, masaledar*
hot (temp)	*garam*
luggage	*saman*
medicine	*dawai*
newspaper	*akhbar*
of course, sure	*zaroor*
open	*khula*
police station	*thana*
road	*rasta*
room	*kamra*
shop	*dukan*
sick (ill)	*bimar*
silk	*reshmi/silk*
small	*chhota*
that	*who*
this	*yeh*
town	*shahar*
water	*pani*
what	*kya*
when	*kab*
where	*kahan/kidhar*
which/who	*kaun*
why	*kiun*
with	*ke sathh*

Index

*Entries in **bold** refer to maps*

FOOTPRINT
Features

Advertisers' index

David Stott
Born in the vibrant suburbs of Peterborough, David Stott acquired his taste for India in the womb via the Shah Jehan's butter chicken, but it took 28 years before India (or rather, one insane week in Mumbai) grabbed him in a ferocious cheek pinch and refused to let go. After a decade exploring and writing about South Asia, he's finally decided that the minute you think you get India, you've lost it. David now splits his time between India, Sri Lanka and his home in Australia's Blue Mountains, where he lives with his wife and son.

Vanessa Betts
A freelance writer and editor from England, Vanessa Betts went to India in 1997 as the first stop on a round-the-world ticket, and found that nowhere else could quite compare. She has lived and worked overseas for most of the last 18 years, mainly in Egypt, India and Israel, and is currently based in Singapore. She is the co-author of Footprint *Northeast India* and Footprint *Indian Himalaya*.

Victoria McCulloch
Victoria McCulloch is a nomad currently calling Goa home. Armed with a laptop and a yoga mat, she plies her trade as freelance journalist and Kundalini Yoga teacher. She first ventured to India in 1997, but has been living in 'the motherland' for the last eight years and can now only drink her tea with masala in it. Victoria has also been influenced by the music and chanting in India and is recording her third mantra album.

Acknowledgements

David Stott

After eight years of travelling India on Footprint's behalf, the list of people who've leant a shoulder to the wheel or lent one to cry on has grown beyond recall. Nevertheless, this edition of the *India Handbook* would be a tumbledown palace of broken phone numbers if not for the fastidious eyes of Pune's finest fact checker, Bhushan Sathe. For on-the-road help, thanks especially to Binu Phillip, Ravi at Arjun Tours, leopard-tracker extraordinaire Shaaz Jung, the people at Orange County in Karnataka; The Two Gopis and Moni in Pondicherry, plus the wonderful people at Palais de Mahe and Maison Perumal who nursed me through a vile bout of dengue; Ashish and Rucha Gupta, Sean and Pervin Mahoney, Yatidharmananda, and Tuhin Choudhary. On the home team, a tearful chorus of "Looks Like We Made It" to my India co-conspirators Vanessa Betts and Victoria McCulloch, and an "I'm not worthy" to Felicity, Jo and everyone at Footprint, whose curses at my missed deadlines have somehow remained silent. Finally, thanks beyond words to Helen, for putting up with the risible pay and absurd hours involved in producing these labours of love – and to Ben, for inspiring new directions.

Vanessa Betts

Thank you for your time, help and company to Asit Biswas and Sandip Sammodar in Kolkata; to Bibhuti Borah, Hermanta Das (Network Travels) and Dudu in Assam; to David and Rahul (Travel the Unknown) in the UK; and to Denis P Rayen and his charming family in Meghalaya. In Kashmir, I appreciated the advice of the guys at Himalaya House in Pahalgam and excellent tips from Rouf (Swiss Hotel) and Reshu Boktoo in Srinagar; thanks also to Rimo Travels in Leh. For exploring with me and looking after me, thanks to Lorraine Close, Kevin Eisenstadt, Adil Khan and Niamh Moran. Thanks also to my family, Jane and Mike Betts, Katharine Bowerman and Eran Shaham. Special thanks go to David Stott and Victoria McCulloch for their comradeship and, of course, to Felicity Laughton and Patrick Dawson at Footprint.

Victoria McCulloch

First and foremost thanks to Team India – Vanessa Betts and David Stott – always a pleasure. And to Annie Dare for passing the baton. Huge thanks to Kaushal Desai who gets to wear the King of the Mountain shirt for his in-depth knowledge of the Himalayas. For always looking after me, I'd like to thank Ashwani Bazaz, Satinder Singh and the Pearl Palace team, the Shahi Palace Boys, Anoop Mehrotra and family, Himalaya Yoga Valley, Ilan Dascal, Virasat Experiences and the Aquaterra team. Pranams to those preserving the nature of this land and investing in the environment – Joanna and Tamer and the GaiaMitra Project, Vajra Ben Ashara and the Dunagiri Foundation and the Khem Vilas team. Blessings to Lucie, Ebin and the Masti Home orphanage team. For great insights thanks to Victoria Dyer at Indiabeat, Julia de Quadros, Debbie Mundy, Raj Dylan Nalwa and Surekha Narain. Thanks to David McCulloch for inspiring the wanderlust, and most of all to Adam for keeping me on track with the best masala chai, chauffeuring me round Goa and frequent shoulder massage after long ol' train journeys or hours hunched in front of the computer.

First published in 2016

Om Books International

Corporate & Editorial Office

A-12 Sector 64, Noida – 201 301
Uttar Pradesh, India
Phone +91-120-477 4100
Email: editorial@ombooks.com
Website: www.ombooksinternational.com

Sales Office

107, Ansari Road, Darya Ganj,
New Delhi – 110 002, India
Phone: +91-11-4000 9000, 2326 3363, 2326 5303
Fax: +91-11-2327 8091
Email: sales@ombooks.com
Website www.ombooks.com

Photography credits

Front cover: Curioso/Shutterstock.com. **Back cover Top**: Val Shevchenko/Shutterstock.com **Bottom**: robertharding/SuperStock.com

Colour section Inside front cover: Mint Images/Superstock, David Evison/Shutterstock, saiko3p/Shutterstock, Kishore J/Shutterstock. **Page 1**: anekoho/Shutterstock. **Page 2**: paul prescott/Shutterstock. **Page 4**: dp Photography/Shutterstock. **Page 5**: Kanuman/Shutterstock, filmlandscape/Shutterstock, danm12/Shutterstock. **Page 6**: Elena Anisimova/Shutterstock, Mogens Trolle/Shutterstock, Waj/Shutterstock. **Page 7**: Igor Plotnikov/Shutterstock, Radiokafka/Shutterstock, Pavel Vakhrushev/Shutterstock. **Page 8**: Val Shevchenko/Shutterstock, Aleksandar Todorovic/Shutterstock, age fotostock/superstock. **Page 9**: Jool-yan/Shutterstock, saiko3p/Shutterstock, saiko3p/Shutterstock. **Page 12**: Waj/Shutterstock. **Page 13**: Pisit Rapitpunt/Shutterstock. **Page 14**: Kokhanchikov/Shutterstock. **Page 15**: arindambanerjee/Shutterstock, kosmos111/Shutterstock. **Page 16**: Byelikova Oksana/Shutterstock. **Page 17**: KieuKieu/Shutterstock. **Page 18**: Dchauy/Shutterstock, happystock/Shutterstock. **Page 19**: saiko3p/Shutterstock, f9photos/Shutterstock, Asit Jain/Shutterstock. **Page 20**: Radiokafka/Shutterstock, tusharkoley/Shutterstock, Cornfield/Shutterstock. **Page 21**: Butterfly Hunter/Shutterstock. **Page 22**: AJP/Shutterstock. **Page 24**: saiko3p/Shutterstock, muzato/Shutterstock. **Page 25**: Boonsom/Shutterstock. **Page 26**: Amlan Mathur/Shutterstock, Nisarg Lakhmani/Dreamstime. **Page 27**: Parthkumar Bhatt/Dreamstime. **Page 28**: yakthai/Shutterstock, f9photos/Shutterstock. **Page 29**: Asaf Eliason/Shutterstock, Asaf Eliason/Shutterstock, Mogens Trolle/Shutterstock. **Page 30**: Cornfield/Shutterstock.

Duotones Page 54: Don Mammoser/Shutterstock. **Page 94**: Rawpixel/Shutterstock. **Page 156**: Asaf Eliason/Shutterstock. **Page 204**: Cornfield/Shutterstock. **Page 270**: ijasper/Shutterstock. **Page 394**: Aleksei Sarkisov/Shutterstock. **Page 414**: Kodda/Shutterstock. **Page 480**: OlegD/Shutterstock. **Page 530**: Saikat Paul/Shutterstock. **Page 596**: Tawin Mukdharakosa/Shutterstock. **Page 618**: Daniel J Rao/Shutterstock. **Page 686**: Nila Newsom/Shutterstock. **Page 728**: Pal Teravagimov/Shutterstock. **Page 752**: Soumitra Pendse/Shutterstock. **Page 776**: f9photos/Shutterstock. **Page 884**: Cornfield/Shutterstock. **Page 964**: Waj/Shutterstock. **Page 1044**: Waj/Shutterstock. **Page 1084**: Yongyut Kumsri/Shutterstock. **Page 1160**: Marat Dupri/Shutterstock. **Page 1232**: Shyamal M Majmundar/Shutterstock

Originally published by Footprint Handbooks Ltd, Bath, UK, 2016

Printed in India by Thomson Press Ltd, Faridabad, Haryana

CIP DATA: A catalogue record for this book is available from the British Library

ISBN: 978-93-85609-58-9

Every effort has been made to ensure that the facts in this guidebook are accurate. However, travellers should still obtain advice from consulates, airlines, etc about travel and visa requirements before travelling. The authors and publishers cannot accept responsibility for any loss, injury or inconvenience however caused.

Colour map index

India distance chart

Ahmedabad																
1495 Bengaluru
568 1401 Bhopal
1810 1440 1192 Bhubaneswar
1826 331 1435 1235 Chennai
915 2061 744 1745 2095 Delhi
2423 2932 1855 1483 2718 1959 Guwahati
1208 562 839 1075 688 1499 2370 Hyderabad
657 1985 584 1791 2019 258 1961 1443 Jaipur
595 2094 982 2214 2417 793 2531 1803 570 Jaisalmer
1924 1881 1356 441 1676 1461 1081 1516 1462 2032 Kolkata
1154 1928 678 1265 1962 497 1479 1366 595 1165 980 Lucknow
545 998 779 1507 1329 1407 2746 711 1202 1140 1987 1365 Mumbai
1068 592 1291 1746 923 1912 3020 747 1725 1663 2187 1877 593 Panjim
1258 2403 1086 2099 2437 343 2250 1841 601 1013 1751 840 1742 2254 Shimla
2040 753 2154 1943 708 2814 3426 1315 2697 2635 2384 2681 1543 1001 3156 Thiruvananthapuram
1244 1779 676 965 1813 780 1179 1217 782 1352 680 300 1593 1903 1071 2516 Varanasi

Distances in kilometres   1 kilometre = 0.62 miles

Footprint Mini Atlas
India

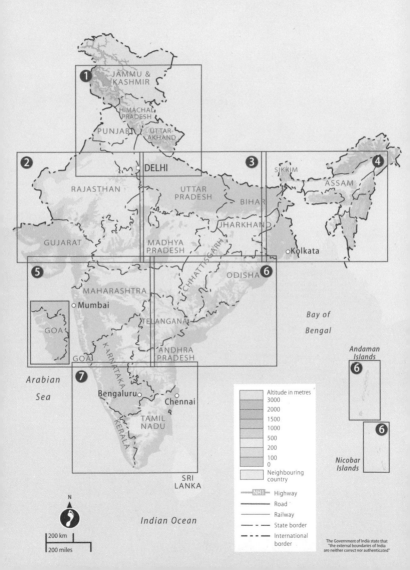

Map 1

Nubra R.

Ladakh Range

Shyok

Tangtse
Lukung
Spangmik

Pangong-Tso

Indus R.

Tashigong

Tso-Moriri

Sarchu
Bara Lacha
Pass

Gardzong

RUPSHU

SPITI

Losar
Batal
Kibber
Kaza
Lalung
Dankar
Tabo
Kungri Gompa
Pin Valley
NP
Sumdo
Gulling
Mudh
Sangam

HIMACHAL

Wangtu
Kalpa
Recong Peo
Sarahan
Sangla
Rampur
Bushahr
Chitkul

PRADESH

Khab
Puh

TIBET
(CHINA)

Yamunotri
Barkot
Gangotri
Meru
Kedarnath

Uttarkashi

Kailash

Badrinath

Hemkund

UTTARAKHAND

Joshimath
Auli

Mussoorie
Tehri
Srinagar

Dehra Dun

Rishikesh
Deoprayag
Byasi
Rudraprayag

Karnaprayag

Nanda Devi

Trisul

Rajaji
NP
Larsno
Haridwar
aharanpur

Gwaldam

Baijnath
Kausani

Roorkee
Kotdwara
Ranikhet
Almora
Pithorgarh

Muzaffarnagar
Nathjabad

Corbett
NP

Khatauli
Nagina
Ramnagar

Bijnor
Kashipur

Nainital
Bhowali
Kathgodam
Haldwani

NEPAL

Meerut

Lalkuan
Banbassa

Mahendranagar

Bilaspur
Kichha

3

Hapur
Sambhal
Moradabad
Chandausi

Rampur

Pilibhit

Dudwa
NP

Bulandshahr
Khurja

Bareilly
Bisalpur

Purampur
Mailani

Nepalganj
Road

Ghaghara R.

Nanpara

UTTAR
PRADESH

Ganga R.

Aligarh
Kasganj

Vrindavan

4

Shahjahanpur

5

Sitapur

Lakhimpur

Bahraich

6

Sravasti
Balrampur

N

50 km
50 miles

The Government of India state that
"the external boundaries of India
are neither correct nor authenticated"

Map 2

PAKISTAN

Ⓐ

Kishangarh
Bhuttewal
Ramgarh
Ghotaru
Jaisalmer
Sam
Thar Desert NP
Khuri

India Gandhi Canal
Gajner NP
Kolayat NH15
Bap
Kakoo
Phalodi Khichan
NH15
Pokaran
Dechhu Osian
Balesar
Jodhpur
Shergarh (Garah)
Cuni
Shiv
Gadra Road (Disused)
Barmer Tilwara
Balotra
Basi
Samdari
Ahor
Jalor Bhenswara Samdan
Daspan
Sheoganj NH14 Bera
Bhinmal Ramsen
Sirohi
Mt Abu Abu Rd

Ⓑ

N

50 km
50 miles

The Government of India state that
"the external boundaries of India
are neither correct nor authenticated"

Dhorimmana

Sanchore

Lakhpat
Great Rann of Kachchh ◆ *Flamingo*
Khavda

GUJARAT

Rapar
Naliya
Nakhtrana Rudrani Dam
Bhuj
Little Rann of Kachchh
Deshalpar
Wanku
Kodai
Anjar Gandhidham
Kandla
Bhadreshwar
Mandvi Mundra
Gulf of Kachchh

Vav
Suigem NH15
Santalpur NH15
Sami
Samakhial NH8A
Kalaghoda
Bajana NH8A
Maliya
Halvad
Dhangadra
Morvi
Jodiya
Dhrol
Jinjwada
Dasada
Patdi
Viramgam

Bhilari
Patan NH14 Kakushi
Chanasma
Modhera
Mehsana
Jinjwada

Deesa Balaram
Palanpur NH8
Taranga Ambaji
Khedbrahma
Visnagar Idar
Himatnagar
NH8
Kalol
Kapadvanj
GANDHINAGAR
Ahmedabad
Kaira Dakor
Nadiad
Anand

Okha Port
Dwarka
Khambaliya
Jamnagar
Dhrol

Nalsarovar NP Bavla
Dholka
Lothal

Tarnetar
Wankaner
Morvi
Surendranagar Bagodra
Dhandhuka
Limbdi NH8A
Lothal
Khambhat
Vadodara

Gop
Bhanwad
①
Porbandar Ranavav
Rajkot
Gondal
Dhoraji
Jetpur
Chotila Ranpur
Hingolgadh
Jasdan
Botad
Babra
Gadhada
②
Dhandhuka
Velavadhar NP ◆
Bhavnagar
Jambusar
Karjan
③
NH8
Bharuch

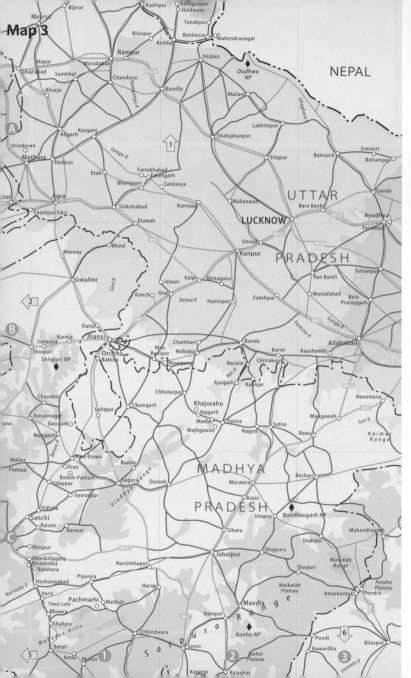

Map 4

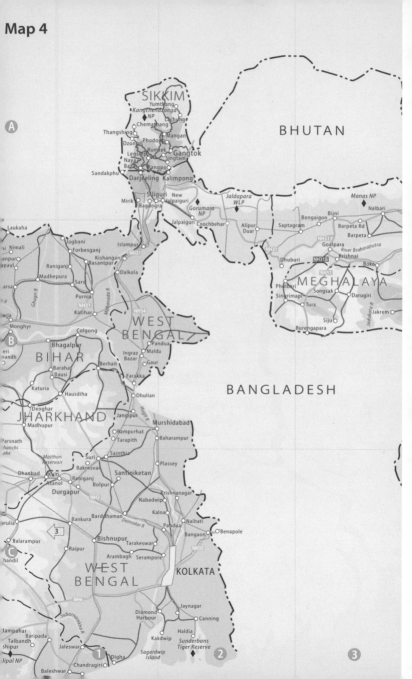

SIKKIM
Yumthang
Kangchendzonga NP
Lachung
Chemashang
Thangshing
Phodong
Mangan
Dzongri
Rumtek
Gangtok
Legship
Singtam
Naya Bazar
Rangpo
Sandakphu
Darjeeling
Kalimpong
Mirik
Siliguri
New Jalpaiguri
Jaldapara WLP
Bagdogra
Gorumara NP
Coochbehar
Jalpaiguri
Alipur Duar
Saptagram

BHUTAN

Manas NP
Nalbari
Bongaigon
Bijni
Barpeta Rd
Goalpara
Barpeta
River Brahmaputra
NH51
Krishnai
Boko
Dhuburi
NH31B
Phulbari
Songsak
MEGHALAYA
Singrimari
Tura
Darugiri
Siju
Jakrem
Burengapara
Jadukata R

Laukaha
Jogbani
Nimali
Forbesganj
anpur
ipaul
Ranianj
Madhepura
Sars
Ghaghi R
arsa
Purnia
NH31
arja
Katihar
Kishanganj
Basantpur
Islampur
Dalkola
NH31
Madepura
Mahananda R
WEST BENGAL
NH34
Monghyr
Colgong
B
Bhagalpur
Panduah
Malda
Ingraz Bazar
BIHAR
Berhait
Gaur
Baraha Bausi
Hausdiha
Farakka
BANGLADESH
Katuria
Dhulian
Deoghar
Jangipur
JHARKHAND
Madhupur
Rampurhat
Murshidabad
Parsnath hanchi ake
Tarapith
Baharampur
Suri
Sainthia
Maithon reservoir
Bakresvar
Plassey
Dhanbad
Kulti
Raniganj
Santiniketan
Asanol
Bolpur
Durgapur
NH2
Krishnanagar
Nabadwip
Bardhaman
Kalna
arulia
Bankura
Damodar R
Pandua
Naihati
3
Bishnupur
Tarakeswar
Bangaon
Benapole
Balarampur
Raipur
Serampore
NH35
handil
Arambagh
WEST BENGAL
KOLKATA
NH6
Subarnarekha R
Jaynagar
ampahar
Baripada
Diamond Harbour
Canning
Talbandh shipur
Jaleswar
Haldia
iipal NP
Digha
Kakdwip
Sunderbans Tiger Reserve
Baleshwar
Chandragiri
Sagardwip Island
1
2
3

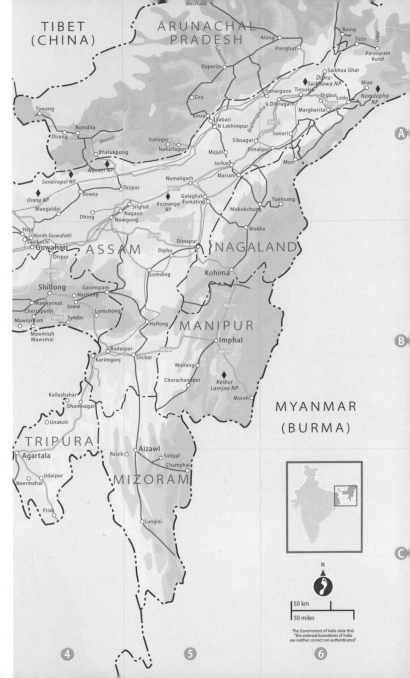

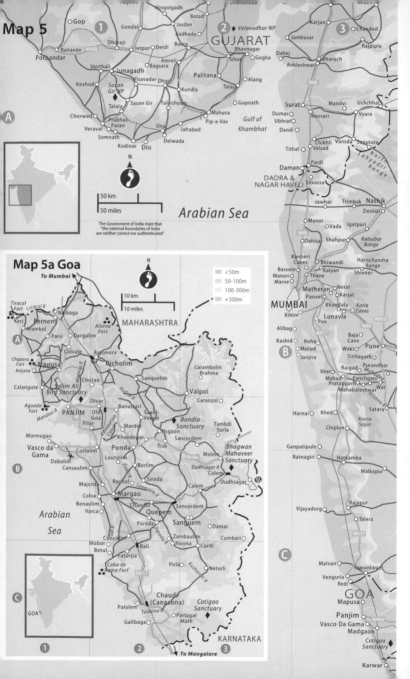

Map 6

MADHYA PRADESH

Shahpur · Chhindwara · Seoni · Pondi · Kawardha · Bilaspur

Satpura

Kanha NP · Phihar Plateau · Maikale Range

Multai · Katangi · Balaghat · Seonath R · Mahanadi R

Tirodi · Bhilai · Raipur · NH6

Ramtek · Bhandara · Gondia · Durg · Rajnandgaon

Nagpur · NH6

Umer · Dhamtari · Nawapura

MAHARASHTRA

Wardha · Nagbhir · Warsa · **CHHATTISGARH**

Sevagram

Hinganghat · Sindewahi · Kanker · Tel R

Warora · *Taroba NP* · Mul

Majri · Tadali · Bastar Hills

Pandharkawada · Ghugus · Chandarapur · Kondagaon

Mahur · Ballarpur · Pappadahandi

Adilabad · Sirpur · *Indravati Plateau*

Nirmal · *Indravati NP* · Jagdalpur · NH43

Godavari R · Satmala Hills · Bijapur · Jeypore

Armur · Manchiraya · *Telangana Plateau* · Baladila Hills

B

illareddi · Ghanpur · Malkangiri

Karimnagar · Palampet · *Laknavaram Lake*

Medak · Siddipett · Warangal · *Pakhal Lake* · Sabari R · Sileru R

greddi · Jangaon · Yellandu · Godavari R

angpalli · Bhongir

cunderabad · Ghatkesar · Kottagudem

Golconda

HYDERABAD · Ibrahimpatnam · Khammam · Rajahmundry · NH5

ad · Tadepallegudem · Samalkot

5 · Eluru · Tanuku · Kakanada

Badeballi · Jaggayyapeta · *Kolleru Lake* · Bhimavaram

Mailepalli · Kondapalli · Narsapur

Devarkonda · Amaravati · Vijayawada

Vijayapuri · Piduguralla · Gudivada

Nagarjunakonda · Macherla · Guntur

Krishna R · Tenali

Alampur · Vinnkonda · Bapatla · *Krishna R*

Atmakur · Srisailam

ANDHRA

Cumbum · Podle · Ongole

Nandyal · Singarayakonda

Giddalur · 7

Ahobilam · Kanigi

Allagadda · **PRADESH**

adpatri · Udayagiri · 1 · Kavali · 2 · 3

N

50 km

50 miles

The Government of India state that "the external boundaries of India are neither correct nor authenticated"

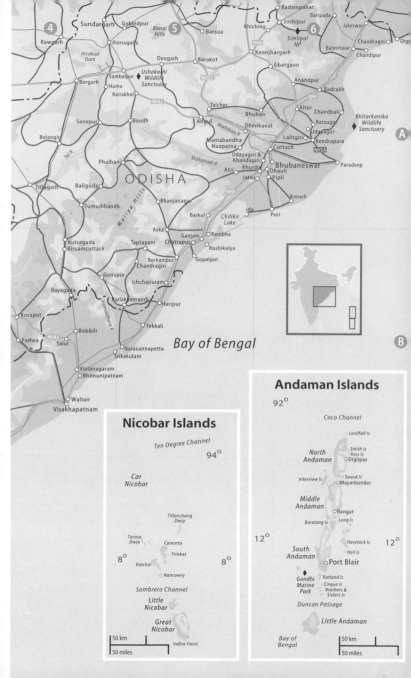

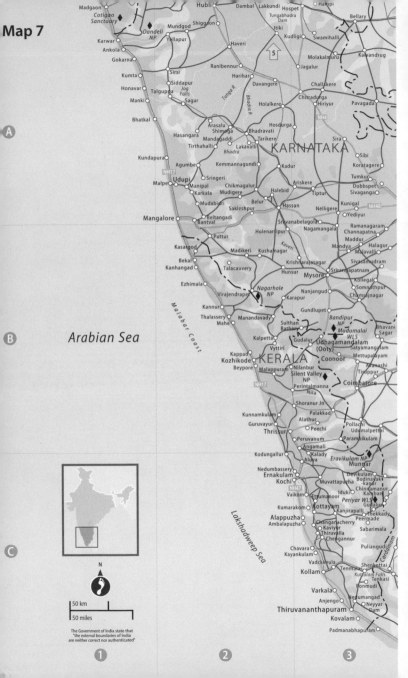

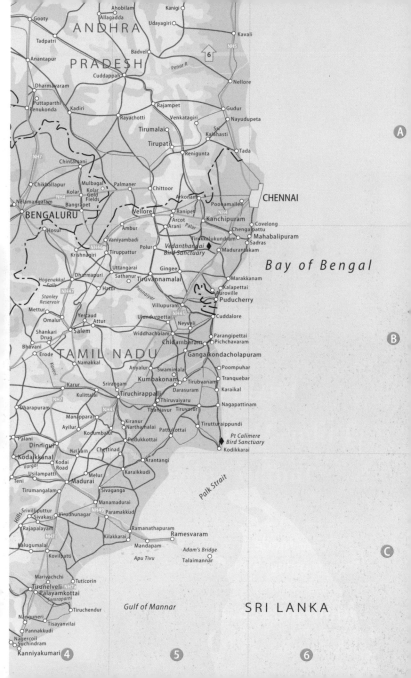